COMPLETE
ETHIOPIAN
IN ENGLISH
BIBLE

Including All Missing Apocrypha Deuterocanonical: Jubilees,
Enoch, Meqabyan, and Many Lost Writings

LARGE PRINT
88 BOOKS

R. H. Charles
Enoch J. Cavanaugh

Title: Complete Ethiopian Bible in English 88 Books Large Print

Publisher: Enoch J. Cavanaugh

Edition: First Edition

Acknowledgments:

Special thanks to all those who contributed to the research, compilation, and publication of this comprehensive edition of the Ethiopian Bible.

Publisher's Note:

This edition aims to provide readers with an authentic and detailed understanding of the Ethiopian Bible, its origins, and its unique contents. The texts have been carefully translated and compiled to maintain the integrity and reverence of the original manuscripts.

"Your word is a lamp to my feet and a light to my path." –

Psalm 119:105

CONTENTS

INTRODUCTION

Welcome to the "**Complete Ethiopian Bible in English 88 Books Large Print: Including All Missing Apocrypha Deuterocanonical: Jubilees, Enoch, Meqabyan, and Many Lost Writings.**" This edition offers a comprehensive collection of sacred texts recognized within the Ethiopian Orthodox Tewahedo Church, one of the oldest Christian denominations in the world. With a total of 88 books, this Bible provides an unparalleled opportunity to explore the rich and diverse spiritual heritage that has been preserved for centuries in Ethiopia.

Origin and Historical Context

The history of biblical translations is as diverse and intricate as the texts themselves. One of the earliest complete translations of the Bible into English was the John Wycliffe Bible in the 14th century, translated from Latin. Following Wycliffe, the Tyndale Bible emerged, offering translations from the original Greek and Hebrew texts. The Coverdale Bible, published in 1535, was the first complete Bible in modern English, setting the stage for the Great Bible in 1539, the first to be sanctioned by the British Crown.

The Geneva Bible, produced by a committee, was notable for being the first to include verse numbers, while the Bishop's Bible, authorized in 1568, continued the tradition of English translations. These versions were all influenced by the Vulgate, a Latin translation assembled by St. Jerome around A.D. 400, which became the foundational text for many Christian denominations.

The King James Bible, authorized by King James I of England, was a significant milestone in the history of biblical translations. Completed in 1611, this translation aimed to settle religious disputes and provide a definitive version of the Bible that was both accurate and accessible. It involved 47 scholars working under strict guidelines to ensure fidelity to the original languages. The King James Bible quickly became one of the most popular and enduring translations, influencing Christian thought and literature for centuries.

While the King James Bible is widely recognized, the Ethiopian Bible is often considered the oldest and most complete Bible on earth. It is believed that the oldest original copy, known as the Garima Gospels, was discovered in Ethiopia. According to tradition, a monk named Abba Garima brought these texts to Ethiopia from Constantinople around A.D. 494. The manuscripts, written in the ancient Ge'ez language on goatskin, have been carbon-dated to between A.D. 330 and 650, making them some of the earliest Christian texts in existence.

Unlike the more commonly known versions of the Bible, the Ethiopian Bible includes 88 books, incorporating texts not found in the King James Bible or other Western canons. These additional books include Enoch, Esdras, Baruch, and the three books of Maccabees. The Ethiopian Bible also contains only four of the Gospels and is richly illustrated with vibrant depictions of saints, apostles, and other religious scenes. These illustrations have been remarkably preserved, largely due to the secluded conditions in which the Bible has been kept—high in the Tigrai Highlands of Ethiopia, in a monastery that has withstood numerous historical challenges.

Contents of the Ethiopian Bible

The "Complete Ethiopian Bible" includes:

1. **The Old Testament:** Comprising all the books commonly recognized in the broader Christian Old Testament, along with additional texts that are considered deuterocanonical or apocryphal in other traditions. These books offer historical narratives, wisdom literature, and prophetic writings that form the foundation of the Jewish and Christian faiths.

2. **The New Testament:** Including the Gospels, Acts, Epistles, and Revelation, this section presents the life, teachings, death, and resurrection of Jesus Christ, as well as the early development of the Christian Church.

3. **The 22 Apocrypha and Deuterocanonical Books:** This unique feature of the Ethiopian Bible includes books such as Jubilees, Enoch, and Meqabyan (often referred to as 1, 2, and 3 Maccabees in other traditions), along with other writings like the Shepherd of Hermas, 4 Baruch, and the Ascension of Isaiah. These texts provide additional insights into biblical history, theology, and eschatology, offering readers a richer understanding of the biblical narrative and the religious thought of ancient communities.

Understanding the Ethiopian Canon

The canon of the Ethiopian Orthodox Church is one of the most expansive in Christianity, encompassing texts that reflect a deep engagement with both Jewish and Christian traditions. The inclusion of texts like the Book of Enoch, which is quoted in the New Testament Book of Jude, highlights the church's reverence for writings that were influential in early Christian theology but were later excluded from other biblical canons.

This broad canon is a testament to the Ethiopian Church's rich theological heritage, which integrates elements of Jewish apocalyptic literature, early Christian writings, and indigenous African religious traditions. The Ethiopian Bible, therefore, not only serves as a religious text but also as a historical document that sheds light on the diverse influences that have shaped Ethiopian Christianity.

The Significance of This Edition

This large print edition of the "Complete Ethiopian Bible" has been meticulously translated into English to ensure accessibility for a wide audience. It is designed to provide readers with an easy-to-read format that enhances their engagement with the text. The inclusion of all 88 books allows for a comprehensive exploration of the Ethiopian Christian tradition, offering insights into doctrines, moral teachings, and spiritual practices that have been cherished for centuries.

By presenting this collection, we aim to provide a valuable resource for scholars, theologians, spiritual seekers, and anyone interested in the history and development of Christianity. This edition is not just a religious text but a cultural artifact that bridges the gap between ancient traditions and modern understanding.

As you embark on this journey through the "Complete Ethiopian Bible," you will encounter a wealth of knowledge and wisdom that transcends cultural and temporal boundaries. This edition invites you to explore the profound spiritual teachings and historical contexts that have shaped the Ethiopian Orthodox Tewahedo Church and its followers. It offers a unique perspective on the biblical world, enriching your understanding of scripture and the diverse ways it has been interpreted and cherished throughout history.

Whether you are approaching this text from a religious, academic, or personal interest, this Bible serves as a gateway to deeper spiritual insights and a broader appreciation of the rich tapestry of Christian heritage. We hope that this edition will inspire, educate, and provide a deeper connection to the sacred texts that have guided and nourished countless generations.

OLD TESTAMENT
(HEBREW BIBLE)

THE PENTATEUCH

These books lay the foundation for the faith, establishing the creation story, laws, and covenant with God

GENESIS

CHAPTER 1

1 In the beginning God created the heavens and the earth. 2 The earth was without form and void, darkness was in the abyss, and the Spirit of God hovered over the waters. 3 Then God said, "Let there be light": And there was light. 4 God saw that the light was good and separated the light from the darkness. 5 God called the light day and the darkness night. So dawn and morning were the first day. 6 Then God said, "Let there be a firmament in the midst of the waters and separate the waters from the waters." 7 God made the firmament and separated the waters that were below the firmament from the waters that were outside the firmament. 8 God called the firmament Heauen. Thus dawn and morning were the second day. 9 God said again, "Let the waters under the firmament be gathered into one place, and let the dry land appear." and so it was. 10 And God called the dry land "Earth" and called the place where the waters were gathered together "Seas"; and God saw that it was good. 11 Then God said, "Let the earth bring forth the sprout of the sowing herba- ceous tree, the fruitful tree, which bears fruit according to its kind, which has its seed in it- self on the earth"; and so it was. 12 The earth brought forth the shoot of the herbaceous tree that sows according to its kind, and the fruit-bearing tree, which has its seed in itself according to its kind; and God saw that it was good. 13 So the dawn and the morning were on the third day. 14 And God said, Let there be lights in the firmament of Aeneas, to separate the day from the night, and let them be for signs, and for seasons, and for days, and for years. 15 And let there be lights in the firma- ment of the plateau to give light to the earth; and so it was. 16 Then God made two great lights: the greater light to rule the day, and the lesser light to rule the night; he also made the stars. 17 And God set them in the firma- ment of heaven to shine upon the earth, 18 to govern the day and the night and to separate the light from the darkness; and God saw that it was good. 19 So dawn and morning were the fourth day. 20 Then God said, "Let the wa- ters bring forth in abundance all the reptiles that have life, and let the fauna fly over the earth into the open firmament of heaven." 21 Then God created the great whales, and every moving and moving thing, which the waters brought forth in abundance according to their kind, and every animal bound according to its kind; and God said it was good. 22 Then God blessed them, saying, "Produce fruit and multiply, fill the waters of the seas and multi- ply fish on the earth." 23 So the afternoon and the morning were the fifth day. 24 Moreover God said, "Let the earth produce living things according to their kind, cattle and what crawls, and the beast of the earth according to its kind." and so it was. 25 God made the beast of the earth according to his kind, the cattle according to their kind, and all the reptiles of the earth according to their kind; and God saw that it was good. 26 Then God said, "Let us make man in our image and likeness, and let him have dominion over the fish of the sea, over the fish of the earth, over the beasts, over all the earth, and over every thing that creeps and moves on the earth." 27 So God created man in his own image: in the image of God he created him; he created them male and female. 28 And God blessed them, and said to them, "Bear fruit and multiply, and fill the earth, and subdue it, and have dominion over the fish of the sea, and over the animals of the sea, and over every beast that prowls about on the earth." 29 And God said, "Behold, I have given you all the seed-bearing plants that are on the earth and all the seed-bearing trees; these shall be food for you. 30 Also to every animal of the earth, and to every beast of the earth, and to every thing that moves on the earth, and has life in it, every green herb shall be for me. and so it was. 31 God saw all that He had made, and behold, it was very good. So the dawn and the morning were on the sixth day.

CHAPTER 2

1 Thus were the heavens and the earth and all their army finished. 2 For on the seventh day GOD finished his work that he had done, and on the seventh day he rested from all his work that he had done. 3 So GOD blessed the seventh day and sanctified it, because in it he had rested from all his works that GOD had cre- ated and done. 4 These are the generations of the heavens and the earth, when they were created, in the day when the Lord God made the earth and the heavens, 5 and every plant of the field, before it was on the earth, and every herb of the field, before it grew; for the Lord God had not made it rain on the earth, nor was there a man to till the ground, 6 but a mixture came out of the earth and watered the whole earth. 7 The Lord God also made man out of the dust of the ground and breathed into his face the breath of life, and the man was a living soul. 8 And the Lord God planted a garden in the east, in Eden, and placed there the man whom he had made. 9 For out of the ground the Lord God made to grow every tree pleasant to the sight and good for consump- tion: even the tree of life in the midst of the garden, and the tree of the knowledge of good and evil. 10 And out of Eden came a riuer to water the garden, and from there it was deui- dated and became in four heads. 11 The name of one of them is Pishon; the same surrounds all the land of Hauilah, where the treasure is. 12 The treasure of that country is good: there is Bdelium and Onix stone. 13 The second riv- iera is called Gihon and includes all the land of Cush. 14 Also the name of the third riuer is Hiddekel; this goes toward the eastern side of Asshur; and the fourth riuer is Perath). 15 Then the Lord God took the man and put him in the garden of Eden, that he might cultivate it and keep it. 16 The Lord God commanded the man, "You shall eat freely of every tree in the garden, 17 but of the tree of the knowledge of good and evil you shall not eat, for in the day that you eat of it you shall die. 18 The Lord God also said, "It is not good that the man should be alone: I will make him a helper fit for him." 19 So the Lord God formed out of the earth all the beasts of the field and all the an- imals of the sea and brought them to man to see what he would call them; for if man gave a creature a name, that was his name. 20 So the man gave a name to all the cattle, and to the fauna of the heavens, and to all the animals of the field; but for Adam he found no helper fit for him. 21 Therefore the Lord God caused a heavy sleep to fall upon the man, and he slept; then he took one of his ribs and sealed its flesh. 22 And the rib which the Lord God had taken from the man, he made a woman and brought her to the man. 23 Then the man said, "This is bone of my bones and flesh of my flesh. She shall be called a woman, because she was taken from the man. 24 Therefore the man shall leave his father and his mother and join

himself to his wife, and the two shall be one flesh. 25 They were both naked, the man and his wife, and they were not ashamed.

CHAPTER 3

1 Now the serpent was more devious than any animal of the fields that the Lord God had made; and he said to the woman, "Yes, has God said that you will not eat of all the trees of the garden?" 2 The woman answered the serpent, "We eat of the fruit of the trees of the garden, 3 but of the fruit of the tree that is in the middle of the garden, God said, "You shall not eat of it or touch it, lest you die." 4 Then the serpent said to the woman, "You shall not die at all." 5 but God knows that when you eat of it, your eyes will be opened and you will be like gods, knowing good and evil." 6 So the woman (seeing that the tree was good for food and pleasant to the eyes and a tree to be desired to obtain knowledge) took its fruit and ate, and gave also to her husband with her, and he ate. 7 Then the eyes of both of them were opened and they realized that they were naked; so they sewed fig leaves to- gether and made themselves breeches. 8 Then they heard the voice of the Lord God walking in the garden during the day, and the man and his wife hid themselves from the pres- ence of the Lord God among the trees of the garden. 9 But the Lord God called the man and said to him, "Where are you? 10 Who said, "I heard your voice in the garden, and I was afraid; because I was naked, I hid my- self." 11 And he said, "Who told you that you were naked? Did you eat of the tree of which I commanded you not to eat? 12 Then the man said, "The woman whom you chose to be with me, she gave me of the tree, and I ate." 13 The Lord God said to the woman, "Why have you done this?" And the woman answered, "The serpent deceived me, and I ate." 14 Then the Lord God said to the serpent, "Because you have done this, you are cursed on all the cattle and on all the beasts of the field; on your belly you shall go and eat dust all the days of your life. 15 I will also put restrictions between you and the woman, between your offspring and her offspring. He shall break your head, and you shall break his head. 16 To the woman he said, "I will greatly increase your sorrows and your conceptions. In sorrow thou shalt bring forth children, and thy desire shall be sub- dued to thy husband, and he shall rule over thee." 17 He also said to Adam, "Because you obeyed your wife's suggestion and ate of the tree (of which I commanded you not to eat), the earth is cursed because of you; you shall eat of it in sorrow all the days of your life. 18 It shall also bring thorns and thistles to thee, and thou shalt eat the grass of the field. 19 In the sweat of your face you shall eat bread, until you return to the earth, for from it you were taken, for you are dust, and to dust you shall return. 20 (The man called his wife Heu- ah, for she was the mother of all kinds). 21 To Adam and his wife also the Lord God made cloaks of skins and clothed them. 22 And the Lord God said, "Behold, man has become like one of you, to know good and evil. And now I would not have him put forth his hand and take also from the tree of life, and eat and be fed forever." 23 therefore the Lord God sent him away from the garden of Eden to till the ground from which he had been taken. 24 So he drove the man out, and at the eastern side of the garden of Eden he placed the Cherubim and the blade of a waving sword, to guard the way to the tree of life.

CHAPTER 4

1 Then the man met Heuah, his wife, who conceived and gave birth to Kain, and said, "I have obtained a man from the Lord." 2 Then she gave birth to her brother Habel; Habel was a keeper of sheep and Kain was a cultivator of the land. 3 Afterward Kain brought an obla- tion of the fruits of the land to the LORD. 4 Habel also brought the first fruits of his sheep and their fat, and the LORD had respect for Habel and his offering, 5 but he had no regard for Kain and his offering; therefore Kain was exceedingly wroth, and his countenance fell. 6 Then the LORD said to Kain, "Why are you vexed and why is your face downcast? 7 If you do well, will you not be accepted? And if you do not do well, sin is lurking; even his desire will be subdued to you, and you will rule over him." 8 Then Kain spoke to Habel his broth- er. And when they were in the camp, Kain rose up against Habel his brother and killed him. 9 Then the LORD said to Kain, "Where is Habel your brother?" Who answered, "I cannot say. Am I the keeper of my brothers? 10 He said, "What have you done? The voice of your brothers' blood cries out to me from the earth. 11 Now therefore you are cursed from the earth, which has opened its mouth to receive the blood of your brothers from your hand. 12 When you unseat the earth, it will no longer give you its strength; you will be a wan- derer and a fugitive in the earth." 13 Then Kain said to the LORD, "My chastisement is great- er than I can bear. 14 Behold, today you have driven me out of the land, and from your face I will be hidden; I will be a wanderer and a fu- gitive in the land, and whoever finds me will kill me." 15 Then the LORD said to him, "No doubt whoever kills Kain will be punished for his folly." And the LORD put a sign on Kain, lest anyone, finding him, should kill him. 16 Then Kain went out from the presence of the LORD and went to dwell in the land of Nod, toward the eastern side of Eden. 17 Kain also met his wife, who conceived and gave birth to Henoch; and he built a city and called the city by the name of his son, Henoch. 18 From Henoch was born Irad, Irad begat Mehuiael, Mehuiael begat Methuselah, and Methuselah begat Lamech. 19 Lamech had two wives: one was named Adah and the other Zillah. 20 Ada gave birth to Jabal, who was the father of those who dwell in tents and of those who have cat- tle. 21 His brothers were called Iubal, who was the father of all those who play the zith- er and organ. 22 Zillah also bore Tubal-kain, who craftily did all the crafts of the reed and yron; and Tubal-kain's sister was Naamah. 23 Lamech said to his wives Adah and Zillah, "Hear my speech, ye wives of Lamech, hear my speech, for I would like to kill a man in my wound and a young man in my wound. 24 If Kain shall be judged seuen folde, Lamech shall truly be seuentie times seuen folde. 25 And Adam knew his wife again, and she bare a son, and called his name Sheth: for God, said she, hath assigned me another offspring for Habel, because Kain slew him. 26 To the same Sheth was also born a son, whom she named Enosh. Then the men began to call on the name of the Lord.

CHAPTER 5

1 This is the book of Adam's generations. On the day God created Adam, he made him in the likeness of God, 2 He created them male and female, blessed them, and called them Adam on the day they were created. 3 Now Adam lived a hundred and thirty years and begat a son in his own image and likeness and called him Sheth. 4 The days of Adam, after he begat Sheth, were eight hundred years, and he begat sons and daughters. 5 So all the days that Adam

lived were nine hundred and thirty years; then he died. 6 Sheth lived a hundred and five years and begat Enosh. 7 After he begat Enosh, Sheth lived eight hundred and seventy years and begat sons and daughters. 8 Thus all the days of Sheth were nine hundred and two hundred years; then he died. 9 Enosh also lived ninety years and begat Kenan. 10 After he begat Kenan, Enosh lived eight hundred and fifty years and begat sons and daughters. 11 So all the days of Enosh were nine hundred and fifty years; then he died. 12 Kenan lived seventy years and begat Ma- halaleel. 13 After he begat Mahalaleel, Kenan lived eight hundred and four years and begat sons and daughters. 14 So all the days of Ke- nan were nine hundred and ten years; then he died. 15 Mahalaleel also lived sixty-five years and begat sons. 16 Mahalaleel also, after he begat Iered, lived eight hundred and thirty years and begat sons and daughters. 17 So all the days of Mahalaleel were eight hundred ninety-nine and five years; then he died. 18 And Iered lived an hundred sixty-two years and begat Henoch. 19 Then Iered lived, after he begat Henoch, eight hundred years and begat sons and daughters. 20 So all the days of Iered were nine hundred sixty-two years; then he died. 21 Henoch also lived sixty-five years and begat Methuselah. 22 After he begat Methuselah, Henoch walked with God three hundred years and begat sons and daughters. 23 So all the days of Henoch were three hun- dred sixty-five years. 24 Then Henoch walked with God and was no longer seen, for God took him away. 25 Methuselah also lived one hundred eighty-two years and begat Lamech. 26 After he begat Lamech, Methushelah lived an hundred and eighty-two years and be- gat sons and daughters. 27 So all the days of Methuselah were nine hundred sixty and nine years; then he died. 28 Lamech lived an hun- dred and two years and begat a son, 29 And he set the name of Noah upon him, saying, "This shall comfort our works, and the sorrow of our hands, concerning the land which the LORD hath cursed." 30 And Lamech lived, after he begat Noah, five hundred and nine-ty-nine years, and begat sons and daughters. 31 So all the days of Lamech were seventy-five years and seventy years; then he died. 32 Noah was five hundred years old. Noah begat Shem, Ham, and Japheth.

CHAPTER 6

1 So when men began to multiply on the earth and there were daughters born to them, 2 then the sons of God said to the daughters of men that they were beautiful, and they took them as wives of all that pleased them. 3 Therefore the Lord said, "My Spirit will not always withdraw with man, for he is but flesh, and his days shall last an hundred and twen- ty years." 4 In those days there were giants in the earth; yea, and after the sons of God came to the daughters of men and they bore sons, these were mighty men, who formerly were men of rank. 5 When the LORD saw that the wickedness of man was great in the earth, and that all the imaginations of the thoughts of his heart were always and only euphoric, 6 then the LORD repented that he had created man on the earth and that he was wicked in his heart. 7 Therefore the LORD said, "I will destroy from the earth the man whom I have created, from man to beasts and reptiles and wild animals, because I repent that I created them." 8 But Noah found grace in the eyes of the Lord. 9 These are the generations of Noah. Noah was a righteous and upright man in his time; and Noah walked with God. 10 Noah begat three sons, Shem, Ham and Japheth. 11 The earth also was corrupt before God, for the earth was full of cruelty. 12

Then God looked upon the earth, and behold, it was corrupt, for every flesh had corrupted its way upon the earth. 13 God said to Noah, "The end of all flesh has come before me, for the earth is full of cruelty because of them; and behold, I will destroy them with the earth. 14 Make for yourself an ark of pine trees; you shall make booths in the ark and implant it inside and out with pitch. 15 You shall build it thus: The length of the ark shall be three hundred cu- bits, the breadth fifty cubits, and the height thirty cubits. 16 And thou shalt make a win- dow in the ark, and in one cubit shalt thou finish it from the front, and the door of the ark shalt thou set in its side; thou shalt make it with the low, the second, and the third beam. 17 And I, behold, will bring a flood of water upon the earth to destroy all flesh that hath a breath of life under the earth; all that is on the earth shall perish. 18 But with you I will establish my commander, and you shall go into the Ark, you and your children and your wife and your children with you. 19 And of ev- ery living thing, of every flesh of every kind, thou shalt bring into the Ark, to keep them with thee; they shall be male and female. 20 Of the fowls, according to their kind, and of the cattle, according to their kind, of all the reptiles of the earth, according to their kind, two of every kind shall come to you, that you may keep them with you. 21 And thou shalt take with thee all the food that is eaten, and gather it for thee, that it may be food for thee and for them. 22 Noah therefore did all that God commanded him, and so he did.

CHAPTER 7

1 The LORD said to Noah, "Enter thou and all thy house into the ark, for I have seen that thou art righteous before me at this time. 2 Of every light beast thou shalt take to thee, in pairs, the male and his female; but of the vnclean beasts thou shalt take, in pairs, the male and his female. 3 Of the wild beasts also shalt thou take in pairs the male and the fe- male, that thou mayest preserve an offspring in all the earth. 4 For in ten days I will make it rain on the earth four days and four nights, and I will destroy from the earth all that I have made." 5 Noah therefore did according to all that the LORD had commanded him. 6 Noah was six hundred years old when the flood was on the earth. 7 Then Noah went in with his sons, his wife and his wives with him into the Ark, because of the waters of the flood. 8 Of the clean beasts, and of the vnclean beasts, and of the fish, and of all that creepeth upon the earth, 9 two and two came to Noah in the ark, male and female, as God had command- ed Noah. 10 Thus, after ten days, the waters of the flood were upon the earth. 11 In the six hundredth year of Noah's life, in the sec- ond month, on the seventeenth day of the month, on that same day all the fountains of the great deep were opened, and the windows of Heauen were opened, 12 and rain was on the earth for four days and four nights. 13 On that same day Noah entered with Shem, Ham and Japheth, Noah's sons, Noah's wife and the three wives of his sons with them, into the Ark. 14 They and every animal according to its kind, and every cattle according to its kind, and every thing that creeps and moves upon the earth according to its kind, and ev- ery fowl according to its kind, and every bird of every kind. 15 For they came in from Noah into Arke, two and two, of every flesh in which is the breath of life. 16 Male and female of ev- ery flesh went in, as God had commanded him, and the LORD shut him in. 17 The flood lasted fourteen days on the earth, and the waters increased and stripped the ark that was lifted up on the earth. 18 And the waters grew strong and increased

exceedingly upon the earth, and the ark was thrust upon the waters. 19 The waters increased so much over the earth that all the high mountains that were below the whole of the ark were pulled down. 20 When the mountains were brought down, the waters spread fifty cubits wide. 21 Then perished all the flesh that moved upon the earth, both the game, and the cattle, and every thing that crawls and moves upon the earth, and every man. 22 All things in whose nostrils the spirit of life breathed, whatever was on the earth, perished. 23 So he destroyed every thing that was on the earth, from man to animals, reptiles and wild beasts; they were destroyed from the earth. Only Noah and those who were with him in the ark re- mained. 24 And the waters stood still on the earth for a hundred and fifty days.

CHAPTER 8

1 God remembered Noah and every ani- mal and all the cattle that were with him in the ark; therefore God caused a wind to pass over the earth, and the waters ceased. 2 Also the springs of the deep and the win- dows of Heauen were stopped, and the rain of Heauen was stayed, 3 And the waters returned from behind the earth, going and returning; and after the end of the hundred and fiftieth day the waters subsided. 4 And in the seventh month, on the seventeenth day of the month, the Ark rested on the moun- tains of Ararat. 5 And the waters continued to subside until the tenth month; in the tenth month and on the first day of the month the tops of the mountains were seen. 6 After forty days, Noah opened the window of the ark he had built, 7 and let out a rain that came and went, until the waters dried up on the earth. 8 Then he sent a doue to him to see if the wa- ters had diminished from the earth. 9 But the woman found no rest for the sole of her foot; therefore she returned to him in the Ark (for the waters were over all the earth), and he stretched out his hand, received it, and took it with him into the Ark. 10 He stayed for ten more days, and again he brought the dog out of the Ark. 11 The woman came to him in the evening, and in her mouth was an olive she had torn; so Noah understood that the waters had disappeared from the earth. 12 In spite of this, he set out for seven more days and sent the dog away, and it never returned to him. 13 On the first day of the first month, after six hundred years, the waters were dried up from the earth; Noah turned away from the bow and looked, and behold, the upper part of the ground was dried up. 14 In the second month, on the second and twentieth day of the month, the earth was dried up. 15 Then God spoke to Noah, saying, 16 Come out of the Ark, you and your wife and your children and your sons with you. 17 Take with you all the animals that are with you, of all species of beasts and animals, and all the creatures that crawl and move on the earth, that they may reproduce abundantly on the earth and bear fruit and multiply on the earth." 18 So Noah went out, his sons and his wife and wives with him. 19 All the animals, all the reptiles and all the birds, all that move on the earth according to their kind, went out of the ark. 20 Then Noah built an altar to the LORD and took every clean animal and every clean ani- mal and offered burnt offerings on the altar. 21 And the LORD smelled rest and said in his heart, "From now on I will no longer curse the earth because of men, for the imagination of man's heart is evil from his youth; and I will no longer smite all things that live, as I have done." 22 Henceforth the time of sowing and becalming, cold and heat, spring and winter, day and night shall not cease, so long as the earth remains.

CHAPTER 9

1 God blessed Noah and his sons and said to them, "Bear fruit and multiply and fill the earth. 2 Moreover you shall be afraid of your- selves, and you shall be feared by all the ani- mals of the earth and by all the beasts of the sea, by everything that moves on the earth and by all the fish of the sea; they shall be de- livered into your hands. 3 Every mooing and living thing shall be food for you; like green grass, I have given you everything. 4 But the flesh with its life, I say, and its blood you shall not eat. 5 For surely I will demand your blood, where your pains are; I will demand it by the hand of every beast, and by the hand of man, and by the hand of a brother of man, I will demand the life of man. 6 He that so shedeth man's blood, by man shall his blood be shed: for in the image of God made man. 7 But bear fruit and multiply; grow abundantly in the earth and increase. 8 God also spoke to Noah and his sons with him, saying, 9 Behold, I es- tablish my covenant with you and with your descendants after you, 10 And with all the liv- ing creatures that are with you, with the ani- mals, with the cattle, and with all the beasts of the earth that are with you, from those that come out of the ark to all the animals of the earth. 11 And I will establish my covenant with you, so that henceforth all flesh shall not be uprooted by the waters of the flood, nor shall there be a flood to destroy the earth." 12 Then God said, "This is the sign of the covenant that I establish between me and you and between all living things that are with you for all gener- ations. 13 I have set my bow in the cloud, and it shall be the sign of the covenant between me and the earth. 14 When I cover the earth with a cloud and the arm will be seen in the cloud, 15 then I will remember my covenant, which is between me and you and between every living thing of all flesh, and there will be no more flood waters to destroy all flesh. 16 Therefore the bow shall remain in the clouds, that I may see it and remember the everlast- ing covenant between God and every living thing of all flesh that is on the earth." 17 Again God said to Noah, "This is the sign of the cov- enant I have established between me and all flesh that is on the earth. 18 Now the sons of Noah who came out of the Ark were Shem, Ham, and Japheth. And Ham is the father of Canaan. 19 These are the three sons of Noah, and from them the whole earth was begotten. 20 Noah also began to be a husbandman and planted a vineyard. 21 Then he became drunk with wine, and got drunk, and got drunk in the midst of his tent. 22 When Ham the father of Canaan saw his father's nakedness, he told his two brothers about it. 23 Then Shem and Japheth took a robe, put it on their shoulders, went backward, and noticed their father's nakedness with his face turned backward; so they did not notice their fathers' nakedness. 24 Then Noah awoke from his wine and knew what his younger son had done to him, 25 And he said, "Cursed be Canaan; he shall be a ser- vant of servants to his brothers." 26 He said again, "Blessed be the LORD God of Shem, and Canaan be his servant." 27 God persuad- ed Iapheth to dwell in the tents of Scem and to make Canaan his servant. 28 Noah lived after the flood for three hundred and fifty years. 29 So all the days of Noah were nine hundred and fifty years; then he died.

CHAPTER 10

1 These are the generations of Noah's sons, Shem, Ham and Japheth, to whom sons were begotten after the flood. 2 The sons of Japheth were Gomer and Magog, Madai, Iauan, Tub- al, Meshech and Tiras. 3 The sons of Gomer were Ashkenaz, Riphath and Togarma. 4 The sons of Iauan, Elisha and Tarshish, Kittim and Dodanim. 5 Of these the people were di- vided in their lands, each according to his lan- guage and according to their families in their nations. 6 Moreover, the sons of Ham were Cush, Mizraim, Put and Canaan. 7 The sons of Cush were Seba, Hauilah, Sabtah, Raamah and Sabtecha; the sons of Raamah were also Sheba and Dedan. 8 Cush begat Nimrod, who began to be powerful in the land. 9 He was a mighty hunter before the LORD; therefore it is said, "Like Nimrod, the mighty hunter be- fore the LORD." 10 The beginning of his king- dom was Babel, Erech, Accad and Calneh, in the land of Scinar. 11 Out of that land came Assur, who built Niniueh, the city of Rehoboth and Calah: 12 Resen also, between Niniueh and Calah, is a great city. 13 Mizraim begat Ludim, Anamim, Lehabim and Nephtahim. 14 Also Pathrusim, Casluhim (from whom the Philistines arose) and Caphtorim. 15 Canaan also begat Zidon, his firstborn, and Heth, 16 Iebusi, Emori, and Girgashi, 17 Hiui, Arki and Sini, 18 Aruadi, Zemari and Hamathi; there- after the families of the Canaanites scattered from one side to the other. 19 The border of the Canaanites extended from Zidon, from Gerar to Azza, and from Sodom, Gomorah, Admah and Zeboi to Lasha. 20 These are the sons of Ham according to their families, ac- cording to their languages in their countries and nations. 21 Shem also, the father of all the sons of Eber and the elder brother of Japheth, had sons. 22 The sons of Shem were Elam, As- sur, Arpachshad, Lud and Aram. 23 The sons of Aram were Vz and Hul, Gether and Mash. 24 Arpachshad begat Shelah and Shelah be- gat Eber. 25 Two sons were also born to Eber: the first was named Peleg, for in his day the earth was rent asunder, and his brothers were named Ioktan. 26 Ioktan begat Almo- dad, Sheleph, Hazarmaueth and Ierah, 27 Hadoram, Vzal and Dicklah, 28 Obal, Abima- el and Sheba, 29 Ofir, Hauilah and Iobab: all these were sons of Ioktan. 30 Their abode was from Mesha, as you go to Sephar, a mountain of the east. 31 These are the sons of Shem, ac- cording to their families, according to their languages, in their countries and nations. 32 These are the families of the sons of Noah, according to their generations among their peoples; and by these were the nations divid- ed upon the earth after the flood.

CHAPTER 11

1 Then the whole land had one language and one speech. 2 As they went eastward, they found a plain in the land of Shinar, and there they stopped. 3 They said to one an- other, "Come, let us make brick and bury it in the fire." So they had bricks for stone, and the slime was used as a mixture. 4 They also said, "Go, build yourselves a city and a tower, the top of which may reach as far as the pla- teau, that we may give ourselves a name, lest we be scattered over all the earth." 5 But the LORD came down to see the city and the tow- er that the sons of men had built. 6 And the LORD said, "Behold, the people are one, and they all have one tongue, and this they begin to do, nor can they longer be prevented from doing what they have imagined to do." 7 Come any on, let us go down and confuse their tongues, so that each one does not perceive the other's tongue. 8 So the LORD scattered them from there over all the earth, and they went away to build the city. 9 Therefore it was called Babel, because the LORD confused the language of all the earth there; from there the LORD scattered them over all the earth. 10 These are the generations of Shem: Shem was a hundred years old and begat Arpachshad two years after the flood. 11 After he begat Ar- pachshad, Shem lived five hundred years and begat sons and daughters. 12 Arpachshad also lived five and thirty years and begat Scela. 13 After he begat Shelah, Arpachshad lived four hundred and three years and begat sons and daughters. 14 Shelah lived thirty years and be- gat Eber. 15 After he begat Eber, Shelah lived four hundred and three years and begat sons and daughters. 16 Likewise Eber lived four and thirty years and begat Peleg. 17 So Eber, after he begat Peleg, lived four hundred and thirty years and begat sons and daughters. 18 Peleg lived thirty years and begat Reu. 19 Af- ter he begat Reu, Peleg lived two hundred and nine years and begat sons and daughters. 20 Reu also lived two and thirty years and begat Serug. 21 After he begat Serug, Reu lived two hundred years and begat sons and daughters. 22 Moreover Serug lived thirty years and be- gat Nahor. 23 After he begat Nahor, Serug lived two hundred years and begat sons and daughters. 24 Nahor lived nine and twenty years and begat Terah. 25 After he begat Ter- ah, Nahor lived a hundred and ninety years and begat sons and daughters. 26 Terah lived seventy years and begat Abram, Nahor and Haran. 27 These are the generations of Terah: Terah begat Abram, Nahor and Haran, and Haran begat Lot. 28 Haran died before Terah his father, in the land of his origin, in the Vr of the Chaldeans. 29 Abram and Nahor took a wife. Abram's wife's name was Sarai, and Nahor's wife's name was Milcah, daughter of Haran, father of Milcah and father of Iscah. 30 But Sarai was barren and had no children. 31 Then Terah took Abram, his son, Lot, son of Haran, his son, and Sarai, his daughter to Abraham's wife, and they set out together from Vr of the Chaldeans to go to the land of Canaan. 32 The days of Terah were two hun- dred and five years, and Terah died in Haran.

CHAPTER 12

1 For the LORD had said to Abraham, "Get thee out of thy land, and out of thy seed, and out of the house of thy fathers, unto the land that I will appoint thee. 2 I will make of you a great nation, I will bless you, I will make your name great, and you shall be a blessing. 3 I will also bless those who bless you and curse those who curse you, and in you all the fam- ilies of the earth will be blessed." 4 So Abram departed, as the LORD had told him, and Lot went with him. (Abram was seventy-five years old when he departed from Haran). 5 Then Abram took Sarai, his wife, and Lot, his brother, and all their possessions that they possessed and the souls that they had pro- cured in Haran, and they departed to go into the land of Canaan; and into the land of Ca- naan they came. 6 And Abram went through the land as far as the place of Shechem and as far as the plain of Moreh (and Canaan was then in the land). 7 The Lord appeared to Abram and said, "To your descendants I will give this land." And there he built an al- tar to the Lord who had appeared to him. 8 Then, moving away from Beth-el to a place to the east, he pitched his tent, having Beth-el on the west and Haai on the east, and there he built an altar to the Lord and called upon the Name of the Lord. 9 Then Abram went to the south. 10 Then there was a famine in the land;

therefore Abram went down to Egypt to sojourn there, because there was a great fam- ine in the land. 11 And when he was about to enter Egypt, he said to Sarai his wife, "Now I know that you are a beautiful woman to look upon: 12 Therefore it shall come to pass, when the Egyptians see you, that they will say, 'She is his wife'; so they will kill me, but they will keep you hidden. 13 Say, I pray thee, that thou art my sister, that I may be well because of thee, and my life may be preserved from thee." 14 When Abraham had come to Egypt, the Egyptians observed the woman, for she was very beautiful. 15 Pharaoh's princes saw her and recommended her to Pharaoh; so the woman was received into Pharaoh's house: 16 Who, for her sake, took good care of Abram, who had sheep, and bees, and asses, and male servants, and female servants, and donkeys, and camels. 17 But the LORD struck Pharaoh and his house with great plagues because of Sarai, Abram's wife. 18 Then Pharaoh called Abram and said to him, "Why have you done this to me? Why did you not tell me that she was your wife? 19 Why did you say, 'She is my sister, that I may take her as my wife'? Now therefore look at your wife, take her, and go your way." 20 And Pharaoh gave the men an order about him, and they brought him out with his wife and all that he had.

CHAPTER 13

1 Then Abraham departed from Egypt, he, his wife and all that he had, and Lot with him to the south. 2 Abram was very rich in cattle, silk and gold. 3 He continued his journey from the South to Beth-el, to the place where his tent had been in the beginning, between Beth-el and Haai, 4 to the place of the altar which he had built there at the beginning; and there Abraham called upon the Name of the Lord. 5 Lot, who had gone with Abraham, also had sheep and cattle and tents, 6 so that the land could not bear them to dwell together; for their substance was great, so that they could not dwell together. 7 There was also an argu- ment between the sons of Abraham and the sons of Loths. (And the Canaanites and the Perizzites were then dwelling in the land). 8 Then Abram said to Lot, "Let there be no dis- pute, I pray you, between you and me, nor be- tween my masters and your masters, for we are brothers." 9 Is not the whole land before you? I pray thee, depart from me; if thou tak- est thy left hand, I will go right; or if thou tak- est thy right hand, I will take thy left." 10 And when Lot lifted up his eyes, he saw that all the plain of Iorden was watered everywhere: (for before the LORD destroyed Sodom and Gomorah, it was like a garden of the LORD, like the land of Egypt, as you go toward Zoar). 11 Then Lot chose for himself all the plain of Iorden, and took his journey from the east; and they separated one from the other. 12 Abram dwelt in the land of Canaan, while Lot dwelt in the cities of the plain and pitched his tent as far as Sodom. 13 The men of So- dom were wicked and very sinful against the LORD. 14 Then the LORD said to Abraham, "Lift up your eyes now and look from where you are to the north, to the south, to the east and to the west: 15 For all the land that you see I will give to you and to your descendants forever, 16 And I will make thy descendants like the dust of the earth; so that if a man can count the dust of the earth, thy descendants shall be insensible. 17 Arise, walk the length and breadth of the land, for I will give it to you." 18 Then Abram took down his tent and came and dwelt in the plain of Mamre, which is in Hebron, and built there an altar to the LORD.

CHAPTER 14

1 In the days of Amraphel, king of Shinar, Ari- och, king of Ellasar, Chedor-laomer, king of Elam, and Tidal, king of the nations: 2 These men made war against Bera, king of Sodom, against Birsha, king of Gomorah, against Shinab, king of Admah, against Shemeber, king of Zeboiim, and against the king of Bela, who is Zoar. 3 All these came together in the valley of Siddim, which is the salt sea. 4 For two years they were subject to Chedor-Lao- mer, but in the thirteenth year they rebelled. 5 In the fourteenth year came Chedor-Lao- mer and the kings who were with him and defeated the Rephaim at Ashteroth Karnaim, the Zuzim at Ham, and the Emim at Shaueh Kiriathaim, 6 and the Horims on their mount Seir, as far as the plain of Paran, which is by the wilderness. 7 Then they returned and came to En-Mishpat, which is Kadesh, and defeat- ed all the territory of the Amalekites and also the Amorites who dwelt in Hazezon-Tamar. 8 Then came out the king of Sodom, the king of Gomorah, the king of Admah, the king of Zeboiim, and the king of Bela, which is Zoar, and fought with them in the valley of Siddim: 9 that is, with Chedor-laomer, king of Elam, with Tidal, king of the nations, with Am- raphel, king of Shinar, and with Arioch, king of Ellasar: four kings against five. 10 The val- ley of Siddim was full of slime pits, and the kings of Sodom and Gomorah fled there and fell, while you remnant fled to the mountain. 11 Then they took all the substance of Sodom and Gomorah and all their possessions and went their way. 12 They also took Lot the son of Abraham and his substance (for he dwelt in Sodom) and departed. 13 Then came one who had escaped and told Abraham about the Hebrew who lived in the plain of Mamre, an Amorrean, brother of Eshcol and brother of Aner, who were confederates with Abraham.

14 When Abraham heard that his brother had been kidnapped, he brought out from his house three hundred and eighty that had been brought forth and brought, and pur- sued them as far as Dan. 15 Then he and his servants confronted them by night, struck them, and pursued them as far as Hobah, which is on the left side of Damascus, 16 he recovered all the substance and brought back his brother Lot and his possessions, women and people. 17 After he had returned from the slaughter of Chedor-Laomer and the kings who were with him, the king of Sodom came to meet him in the valley of Shaueh, which is the valley of the kings. 18 Melchi-zedek, king of Shalem, brought bread and wine; he was a priest of the most high God. 19 Therefore he blessed him, saying, Blessed are you, Abram, from God most high, possessor of earth and heaven, 20 And blessed be the most high God, who has delivered into your hand your enemies." And Abram gave him his name. 21 Then the king of Sodom said to Abram, "Give me the people and take the goods for your- self." 22 Abram said to the king of Sodom, "I have lifted up my hand to the LORD, the most high God, possessor of heaven and earth, 23 that I will not take of all that is yours even a braid or a walking stick, lest you should say, 'I have made Abraham rich. 24 take only what the young men have eaten and the parts of the men who came with me, Aner, Eshcol and Mamre; let them take their parts.

CHAPTER 15

1 After these things, the word of the Lord came to Abram in a vision, saying, "Fear not, Abram, I am your support and your greatest reward." 2 Abram said, "O Lord God, what will you give me, seeing that I have children and the steward of my house is this Eliezer of Damascus? 3 Abram answered, "Behold, to me you have not given an offspring; therefore, behold, a servant of my house shall be my heir." 4 Then the word of the LORD came to him, saying, "This man shall not be your heir, but one who shall come forth from your bow- els shall be your heir." 5 Then he brought him out and said to him, "Look up now, and tell of the stars, if you are able to count them"; and he said to him, "Thus shall your descendants be." 6 Abram listened to the LORD, and he considered it a righteous thing. 7 Then he said to him, "I am the LORD, who brought you out of Vr of the Chaldeans to give you this land as an inheritance." 8 And he said, "O Lord God, how shall I know that I shall inherit it?" 9 Then he said to him, "Take me a heifer three years old, a kid three years old, a ram three years old, a tortoise and a pigeon." 10 So he took all these things and put them in a basket and set them against each other, but he did not care for the birds. 11 Then the carcasses fell into the water, and Abram carried them away. 12 When the sun went down, Abram fell heavi- ly asleep; and, behold, a fearful darkness fell upon him. 13 Then he said to Abram, "Know for certain that your descendants will be strangers in a land that is not theirs, for four hundred years, and they will serve them; and they will weave them long." 14 Nevertheless, the nation which they shall serve, I will judge; and afterward they shall come forth from it with great substance. 15 But you shall return to your fathers in peace, and you shall be bur- ied in good age. 16 In the fourth generation they will come again, for the wickedness of the Amorites is not yet complete. 17 And when the sun went down, there was a darkness; and behold, a smoking furnace and a firebrand, which stood between those pieces. 18 On that same day the LORD made a covenant with Abram, saying, "To your descendants I have given this land, from the river of Egypt to the great river, the Euphrates." 19 The Kenites, the Kenizites, and the Kadmonites, 20 the Hittites, the Perizzites, and the Rephaim, 21 the Amorites, the Canaanites, the Girgishites, and the Jebusites.

CHAPTER 16

1 Now Sarai, Abraham's wife, bore him no son, and she had an Egyptian mother, named Hagar. 2 Sarai said to Abraham, "Behold, the Lord has prevented me from having children. Please go to my mother; it may be that I will receive a son from her." And Abram obeyed Sarai's advice. 3 Then Sarai, Abraham's wife, took Hagar, his mother, the Egyptian, after Abraham had dwelt ten years in the land of Canaan, and gave her to Abram, her husband, to be his wife. 4 And he went in to Hagar, and she gave birth. And when he said that she had given birth, his woman was despised in his eyes. 5 Then Sarai said to Abram, "You wrong me. I have put my mother in your womb, and she sees that she has conceived, and I am de- spised in her eyes; the Lord judges between me and you." 6 Then Abraham said to Sarai, "Behold, your mother is in your hands; do with her what pleases you." Then Sarai treated her harshly; therefore he fled from her. 7 But the angel of the LORD found her by a spring of water in the wilderness, by the spring on the road to Shur, 8 And he said to her, "Hagar Sarais mother, whence comest thou, and whither wilt thou go?" And she answered, "I flee to my lady Sarai. 9 Then the angel of the LORD said

to her, "Return to your lady and humble yourself under her hands." 10 Then the angel of the LORD said to her, "I will so in- crease your descendants that they will not be numerous." 11 The angel of the LORD also said to her, "See, you are with child, you will bear a son and you will name him Ishmael, because the LORD has heard your tribulation. 12 He shall be a wild man; his hand shall be against every man, and every man's hand against him, and he shall dwell in the presence of all his brethren." 13 Then she called upon the name of the Lord who had spoken to her, "You, God, look upon me," for she said, "Have I not also looked upon him who sees me? 14 Therefore the well was called Beerlahai-roi. behold, it is between Kadesh and Bered. 15 And Hagar bore Abram a son, and Abram called the son whom Hagar bore by the name of Ishmael. 16 Abram was four years old and six years old when Hagar bore him Ishmael.

CHAPTER 17

1 When Abram was ninety-nine years old, the LORD appeared to Abram and said to him, "I am God all-sufficient; walk before me and be upright, 2 and I will establish my covenant between me and you, and I will multiply you exceedingly." 3 Then Abram fell on his face, and God spoke to him, saying, 4 "Behold, I make my covenant with you, and you shall be a father of many nations, 5 you shall no longer be called Abram, but your name shall be Abra- ham, for I have made you a father of many na- tions. 6 I will also make thee very fruitful, and I will make of thee nations; yea, kings shall come forth from thee. 7 Morcover I will estab- lish my covenant between me and thee and thy seed after thee in their generations, for an everlasting covenant, to be God to thee and to thy seed after thee. 8 And I will give you and your descendants after you the land in which you are a stranger, that is, all the land of Ca- naan, as an eternal possession, and I will be their God." 9 Then God said to Abraham, "You also, you and your descendants after you, will keep my counsel in their generations. 10 This is my covenant that you shall keep between me and you and your descendants after you: that every male child among you shall be cir- cumcised: 11 that is, you shall circumcise the foreskin of your flesh, and it shall be a sign of the covenant between me and you. 12 Ev- ery child of eight days old among you shall be circumcised in your generations, wheth- er he is born in your house, or whether he is bought with money from a stranger, who is not of your seed. 13 He who is born in your house and he who is bought with your mon- ey must be circumcised; so my consent shall be in your flesh for everlasting consent. 14 But the vncircumcised male child, in whose flesh the foreskin is not circumcised, then that person shall be cut off from his people, because he has broken my consent." 15 Then God said to Abraham, "You shall not call Sarai your wife, but Sarah shall be her name. 16 I will bless her and will also give you a son from her, yes, I will bless her and she will be a mother of nations: Out of her also shall come forth kings of nations." 17 Then Abraham fell on his face, and laughed, and said in his heart, Shall a son be born to him that is a hundred years old? And shall Sarah who is ninety years old give birth?" 18 Abraham said to God, "Oh, if Ishmael could live in your sight." 19 Then God said, "Sarah thy wife shall bear thee a son in the second marriage, and thou shalt call his name Izhak; and I will establish with him my covenant for an everlasting covenant, and with his seed after him." 20 As for Ishmael, I have heard thee;

behold, I have blessed him, and will make him fruitful, and multiply him exceedingly; and he shall beget two princes, and I will make of him a great nation. 21 But I will establish my contract with Izhak, that Sarah shall bear thee next year in this sea- son." 22 Then he left off speaking with him, and God departed from Abraham. 23 Then Abraham took Ishmael, his son, and all those who had been born in his house and all those who had been bought with his money, that is, all the children of Abraham's house, and circumcised the foreskin of their flesh on that same day, as God had commanded him. 24 Abraham was also ninety-nine years old when the foreskin of his flesh was circumcised. 25 Ishmael, his son, was thirty years old when the foreskin of his flesh was circumcised. 26 On that same day Abraham was circumcised, and Ishmael his son: 27 And all the men of his house, both those born in his house and those bought with money from the stranger, were circumcised with him.

CHAPTER 18

1 Then the Lord appeared to him in the plain of Mamre, as he stood in his tent toward the dawn of day. 2 And he lifted up his eyes and looked; and behold, three men stood beside him; and when he saw them, he ran to them from his tent and prostrated himself on the ground. 3 And he said, "Lord, if now I have found evil in your eyes, please do not turn away from your servant. 4 Please have some water brought to you, wash your feet and rest under the tree. 5 Then I will bring you a morsel of bread, that you may comfort your hearts, after which you shall resume your way, for you have come to your servant." And they answered, "Do as you have said." 6 Then Abraham hurried into the tent to Sarah and said to her, "Prepare at once three measures of fine meat; knead it and make cakes on the hearth." 7 Abraham ran to the beasts and took a tender and good calf and gave it to the servant, who hurried to prepare it. 8 Then he took the butter and the milk and the calf that he had prepared and put it before them and stood near them under the tree, and they ate. 9 Then they said to him, "Where is Sar- ah your wife?" And he answered, "Behold, she is in the tent." 10 Then he said, "Surely I will return to you according to the time of life; and behold, Sarah your wife will have a son." and Sarah heard in the tent that was behind him. 11 (Abraham and Sarah were now old and tried with age, and Sarah was no lon- ger like women.) 12 Therefore Sarah laughed within herself, saying, "After I grow old, and my lord also, shall I be able to have lust?" 13 The LORD said to Abraham, "Why did Sarah laugh so, saying, 'Will I surely have a son, that I am old?' 14 (Is there anything difficult for the Lord? At the appointed time I will return to you, according to the time of life, and Sarah will have a son.) 15 But Sarah denied, saying, "I did not laugh, for she was aphonous." And he answered, "Not so, for you laughed." 16 Then the men rose up from there and looked toward Sodom; and Abraham went with them to bring them on the road. 17 The LORD said, "Should I conceal from Abraham what I do? 18 seeing that Abraham will become a great and mighty nation, and all the nations of the earth will be blessed in him? 19 For I know that he will command his sons and his household after him to follow the way of the LORD, to do justice and equity, so that the LORD will bring upon Abraham what he has told him." 20 Then the LORD said, "For the weeping of Sodom and Gomorah is great, and their sin is very grievous, 21 now I will go down and see if they have done everything according to the cry that was presented to me; and if they have not, I will know." 22 The men turned and went toward Sodom, but Abraham still stood be- fore the LORD. 23 Then Abraham turned away and said, "Do you want to destroy even the righteous with the wicked? 24 If there are fifty righteous in the city, will you destroy and not spare the place for the fifty righteous there? 25 Let it be far from thee to do this thing, to kill the righteous with the wicked; and let the righteous be like the wicked, let it be far from thee. shall not the judge of all the world do good?" 26 The LORD answered, "If I find in Sodom fifty righteous in the city, I will spare the whole place for them." 27 Abraham an- swered, "Behold, I have begun to speak to my Lord, and I am but dust and ashes. 28 If five of fifty righteous ones are missing, will you de- stroy the whole city for five? And he said, "If I find five and four, I will not destroy it." 29 But he spoke to him again and said, "What if four are found there? Then he answered, "I will not do it for the sake of four persons."30 Then he said, "Let not my Lord be angry because I said, 'What if three persons were found there?' Then he said, "I will not do it, if I find three." 31 And again, he said, "Behold, now I asked to speak to my Lord, 'What if twenty are found there?' And he answered, "I will not de- stroy it for the sake of the twenty-year-olds." 32 Then he said, "My Lord will not be angry now, and I will speak only this time, 'What if ten are found there?' And he answered, "I will not destroy it for the sake of the ten." 33 And the LORD went his way, having spoken to Abraham, and Abraham returned to his place.

CHAPTER 19

1 At the break of day, two angels came to So- dom; Lot stopped at the gate of Sodom, saw them, and rose to meet them and prostrated himself with his face to the ground. 2 Then he said, "My lords, I beg you now to go into the house of your servants, and to stay all night and wash your feet; then you will get up early and go your way." Those said, "No, but we will stay on the road all night." 3 Then he begged them earnestly, and they turned to him and came to his house; and he made them a feast, and prepared leavened bread, and they ate. 4 But before they went to bed, the men of the city, that is, the men of Sodom, surrounded the house from the first to the last day, all the people on every side. 5 Those who cried out to Lot said to him, "Where are the men who have come to you this night? Bring them out for we know them." 6 Lot went out to them and shut the door behind him, 7 and said, "Please, my brothers, do not do so badly. 8 Behold, now I have two daughters who have known no man; now I will lead them out from you and do to them what seems good to you; only to these men do nothing, for they have come under the shadow of my roof." 9 Then they said, "Leave," and said, "Has he come alone, like a stranger, and shall he judge and command? Now we shall behave worse to you than to them." So they came upon Lot himself and came and broke down the door. 10 But the men stretched out their hand and pulled Lot into their house and shut him in. 11 Then they struck the men who were at the entrance of the house with small and great blindness-es, so that they grew weary in searching the house. 12 Then the men said to Lot, "Who do you still have here? Either a son in old age, or your sons, or your daughters, or all that you have in the city, take it away from this place. 13 For we will destroy this place, for their cry is great before the LORD, and the LORD has sent to destroy it." 14 Then Lot went out and spoke to his sons in peace, who had married

his daughters, saying, "Arise, get out of this place, for the Lord will destroy the city"; but to his sons in peace it seemed as if he had mocked them. 15 When morning dawned, the angels intimated to Lot, "Arise, take your wife and your two daughters who are here, lest the chastisement of the city destroy you." 16 While he was prolonging the time, the men took him, his wife and his two daughters by the hand (the Lord was merciful to him), brought him home and put him outside the city. 17 When they had brought them out, the angel said, "Flee for your life; do not look behind you and do not stay in all the plain; flee to a mountain, or you will be destroyed." 18 Lot said to them, "Not so, please, my Lord. 19 Behold, your servant has found favor in your sight, and you have exalted your mercy, which you have shown me by saving my life; and I cannot flee to a mountain, unless someone takes me and I die. 20 See now this city to flee to, which is small: O let me flee there; is it not small, and shall my soul abide here? 21 Then he said unto him, Behold, I have received thy request also on this point, that I will not overthrow this city, because of what thou hast said. 22 Make haste, go there, for I cannot do anything until you have come." Therefore the name of the city was called Zoar. 23 The sun rose on the earth when Lot entered Zoar. 24 Then the LORD rained on Sodom and Gomorrah the brimstone and fire of the LORD from above, 25 And he destroyed those cities, and all the plain, and all the inhabitants of the cities, and all that was scattered over the earth. 26 His wife behind him looked back and became a pillar of salt. 27 And Abraham arose early in the morning and went to the place where he had stood before the LORD, 28 and looking toward Sodom and Gomorah and toward all the land of the plain, he saw the smoke of the land rising up like the smoke of a furnace. 29 But when God destroyed the cities of the plain, God thought of Abraham and sent Lot out of the midst of destruction, when he destroyed the cities in which Lot dwelt. 30 Lot departed from Zoar and went to dwell in the mountains with his two daugh- ters, because he feared to remain in Zoar, but he settled in a cave, he and his two daughters. 31 The elder said to the younger, "Our father is old, and there is no man on earth who can enter his house in the way of all the earth. 32 Come, let us make our father drink wine and lie with him, to preserve our father's seed." 33 That night they made their father drink wine, and the eldest went and lay with her father; but he did not notice it, either when he lay down or when he arose. 34 The next day the elder said to the young woman, "Behold, last night I lay down with my father; this night also let us make him drink wine, and let us go and lie down with him, to preserve our fa- ther's seed." 35 So also that night they made their father drink wine; the young woman got up and lay down with him, but he did not no- tice when she lay down or when she got up. 36 So both of Lot's daughters had children by their father. 37 The elder gave birth to a son and named him Moab; the same is the father of the Moabites to this day. 38 The younger also bore a son and named him Ben-ammi; the same is the father of the Ammonites to this day.

CHAPTER 20

1 Afterward Abraham set out for the southern county and settled between Cadesh and Shur, staying in Gerar. 2 Abraham said of Sarah his wife, "She is my sister." Then Abimelech, king of Gerar, sent for Sarah. 3 But God came to Abimelech on a dark night and said to him, "Behold, you are dead because of the wom- an you have taken, for she is a man's wife." 4 (although Abimelech had not yet approached her) and he said, "Lord, wilt thou slay the righteous nation? 5 Did she not say to me, 'She is my sister'? Yes, and she herself said, 'It is my brother'; with a righteous mind and inno- cent hands I have done this." 6 And God said to him in a grave tone, "I know that you did it with a righteous mind, and I also protect- ed you so that you would not sin against me; therefore I did not allow you to touch her." 7 Now therefore deliver to that man his wife again, for he is a prophet and will pray for you that you may live; but if you do not deliver her again, be sure that you will die, you and all that you possess." 8 Then Abimelech rose early in the morning, and called all his ser- vants, and told them all these things; and the men were greatly afraid. 9 Then Abimelech called Abraham and said to him, "What have you done against me? And what have I given you in return, that you should have caused this great sin upon me and my kingdom? You have done against me things that should not have been done." 10 Then Abimelech said to Abraham, "How did you see that you did this thing?" 11 Abraham answered, "Because I thought, 'Surely the fear of God is not there in this place, and they will kill me for my wife's sake.'" 12 But actually she is my sister, for she is my father's daughter but not my mother's, and she is my wife. 13 When God had me re- moved from the house of my fathers, I said to her, "This is your courtesy, which you shall do to me in all places where we shall come: say of me that he is my brother." 14 Then Abimel- ech took sheep and beasts, male servants and female servants, and gave them to Abraham, and returned Sarah his wife to him. 15 Abimelech said, "Behold, my land is before you; dwell where you please." 16 Likewise he said to Sarah, "Behold, I have given your brother a thousand pieces of silk; behold, he is the joy of your eyes to all who are with you and to everyone else." 17 Then Abraham prayed to God, and God healed Abimelech, his wife and his servants, and they bore children. 18 For the LORD had shut up all the women of Abimel- ech's house because of Sarah, Abraham's wife.

CHAPTER 21

1 Now the Lord visited Sarah, as he had said, and did with her what he had promised. 2 For Sarah conceived and bore a son to Abra- ham in his old age, at the same time that God had asked him. 3 Abraham named the son who had been born to him and whom Sarah had given him, Izhak. 4 Abraham circum- cised Izhak, his son, at the age of eight days, as God had commanded him. 5 So Abraham was a hundred years old when his son Izhak was born to him. 6 Then Sarah said, "God has raised me up; everyone who hears will rise with me." 7 Then he said, "Who would have told Abraham that Sarah would have children to suck, for I have given him a son in his old age." 8 Then the child grew and was weaned; and Abraham made a great feast on the very day that Izhak was weaned. 9 And Sarah saw the son of Hagar the Egyptian, whom she had borne to Abraham, and she mocked him. 10 Therefore she said to Abraham, "Cast out this slave girl and her son, for the son of this slave girl will not be hereditary with my son Izhak." 11 This was very serious in Abraham's eyes because of his son. 12 But God said to Abra- ham, "Let it not be grievous in your eyes for the son and for your blonde woman; in all that Sarah shall say to you, hearken to her voice, for in Izhak shall your seed be called." 13 As for the son of the slave girl, I will also make him a nation, for he is your descendant." 14 And Abraham rose early in the morning, and took bread and a bottle of water, and gave them to Hagar, putting them on

her shoulder, and also to the child, and sent her away; who, departing, wandered into the wilderness of Beer-sheba. 15 When the water in the bottle was finished, he threw the child under a cer-tain tree. 16 Then she went and sat against him far away at a riverbank, for she said, "I do not want to see the death of the child." She sat down against him, lifted up her head and wept. 17 Then God heard the child's voice, and the angel of God called to Hagar from above and said to her, "What is the matter with you, Hagar? Fear not, for God has heard the child's voice where he is. 18 Arise, take the child and take it into your hand, for I will make a great people of it." 19 God opened her eyes and saw a well of water; so she went and filled the bot-tle with water and made the child drink. 20 So God was with the child, and he developed and dwelt in the wilderness and was an archer. 21 And he dwelt in the wilderness of Paran, and his mother took him a wife from the land of Egypt. 22 At that same time Abimelech and Phichol his chief spoke to Abraham, saying, "God is with you in all that you do." 23 Now therefore swear to me here, in the name of God, that you will not harm me, my children, or my children's children; you will deal with me and with the county, where you have been a stranger, according to the kindness I have shown you." 24 Then Abraham said, "I swear." 25 Abraham rebuked Abimelech for a well of water that Abimelech's servants had violently taken away. 26 Abimelech said, "I do not know who has done this thing; you have not told me, and I have not heard of it until today." 27 Then Abraham took sheep and bees and gave them to Abimelech; and the two made a cov-enant. 28 And Abraham set aside ten lambs from the flock. 29 Then Abimelech said to Abraham, "What is the matter with these ten lambs that you have set aside for them? 30 He answered, "Because you will receive from my hand these ten lambs, that I may be witnessed to have dug this well." 31 That is why the place is called Beer-sheba, because there they both swore an oath. 32 So they made a conference at Beer-sheba; then Abimelech and Fichol his chief rose up and went to the land of the Philistines. 33 And Abraham planted a band at Beer-sheba and called upon the Name of the LORD, the eternal God, there. 34 Abraham remained a stranger in the land of the Philistines for a long time.

CHAPTER 22

1 After these things, God gave Abraham a test and said to him, "Abraham." Who answered, "Here I am." 2 Then he said, "Take now your only son Izhak, whom you like, and go to the land of Moriah and offer him as a burnt offer-ing on one of the mountains that I will point out to you." 3 Then Abraham arose early in the morning, saddled his horse, took with him two of his servants and Izhak, his son, and made wood for the burnt offering, got up and went to the place that God had pointed out to him. 4 On the third day Abraham lifted up his eyes and saw the distant place, 5 and said to his servants, "Stay here with the plank, for I and the child will go there to worship and re-turn to you." 6 Then Abraham took the wood of the burnt offering and placed it on Izhak, his son, and took the fire and the knife in his hand. 7 Then Izhak spoke to Abraham his fa-ther and said, "My father." And he answered, "Here am I, my son." And he said, "Here is the fire and the wood, but where is the lamb for your burning?" 8 Abraham answered, "My son, God will make him find a lamb for the burnt offering." 9 When they arrived at the place God had shown them, Abraham built an altar there, placed wood on it, bound Izhak, his son, and placed him on the altar over the wood. 10 Abraham stretched out his hand and took the knife to kill his son. 11 But the angel of the Lord called to him from above, saying, "Abraham, Abraham." And he an-swered, "Here I am." 12 Then he said, "Do not lay your hand on the child and do nothing to him, for now I know that you fear God, since for my sake you did not spare your only son." 13 Abraham lifted up his eyes and looked; and behold, behind him was a ram caught by the horns in a bush. Abraham then went and took the ram and offered it as a burnt of-fering in place of his son. 14 Abraham called that place Iehouah-ijreh, as we say today, "On the mountain the LORD will be seen." 15 The angel of the LORD cried out to Abra-ham from above for the second time, 16 and said, "By myself I have sworn (says the LORD) because you did this thing and did not spare your only son, 17 for this I will bless thee, and I will greatly multiply thy seed, as the stars of heaven, and as the sand that is on the shore of the sea; and thy seed shall possess the gate of her enemies. 18 And in your descendants all the nations of the earth shall be blessed, be-cause you have obeyed my command." 19 Then Abraham turned again to his servants, and they arose and went to Beer-sheba together; and Abraham settled in Beer-sheba. 20 After these things, one spoke to Abraham, saying, "Behold Milcah, she also bore children to your brother Nahor." 21 that is, Vz, his eldest son, Buz, his brother, and Kemuel, Aram's father, 22 Chesed, Hazo, Pildash, Iidlaf and Bethuel. 23 Bethuel begat Rebekah; these eight sons Milcah bore to Nahor, Abraham's brother. 24 His concubine, named Reumah, also bore Te-bah, Gahan, Thahash and Maachah.

CHAPTER 23

1 When Sarah was a hundred and two and seventy years old (so long she lived). 2 And Sarah died in Kiriath-arba, which is Hebron, in the land of Canaan, and Abraham came and wept for Sarah and mourned for her. 3 Then Abraham arose from the sight of her body and spoke to the Hittites, saying 4 "I am a stranger and a foreigner among you; give me a burial place with you, that I may bury my dead out of my sight." 5 Then the Hittites answered Abra-ham, saying to him 6 Hear me, my lord, you are a prince of God among the Vs; in the great-est of our sepulchres bury your dead; none of the Vs will forbid you his sepulchre, but you may bury your dead there." 7 Then Abraham stood up and prostrated himself before the people of the land of the Hittites. 8 Then he spoke to them, saying, "If you want me to bury my dead away from me, listen to me and turn for me to Ephron the son of Zohar, 9 That he may give me the quarry of Machpelah, which he has at the bottom of his field; that he may give it to me for a price equal to its value, as a possession to be buried among you." 10 (For Ephron dwelt among the Hittites) Then Ephron the Hittite answered Abraham in the presence of all the Hittites who entered the gates of his city, 11 Nay, my lord, hear me: the field I give unto thee, and the pit that is there-in I give unto thee; and in the presence of the children of my people I give unto thee to bury thy dead." 12 Then Abraham prostrated him-self before the people of the land, 13 And he spoke to Ephron in the presence of the people of the land, saying, "If thou wilt give it, I pray thee, hear me: I will give thee the price of the field; receive it of me, and I will bury my dead therein." 14 Then Ephron answered Abraham, saying to him, 15 "My lord, hear me: your land is worth four hundred shekels of silver; what is between you and me? Bury therefore your dead." 16 And Abraham listened to Ephron,

and Abraham delivered to Ephron the silks that he had appointed, with the Hittites, worth four hundred shekels of silks in money current among the marchers. 17 So the field of Ephron, which was in Machpelah and oppo- site Mamre, the field and the quarry therein, all the trees that were in the field and in all its borders, was made secure. 18 To Abraham as property, under the eyes of the Hittites and all who entered the gates of his city. 19 After this, Abraham buried Sarah, his wife, in the hollow of the field of Machpelah, opposite Mamre; the same is Hebron, in the land of Canaan. 20 So the field and the quarry therein were granted to Abraham as burial property by the Hittites.

CHAPTER 24

1 By this time Abraham was old and advanced in years, and the LORD had blessed Abraham in all things. 2 Therefore Abraham said to his eldest servant in his house, who had com- mand over all that he had, "Now put your hand under my thigh, 3 and I will make thee swear by the LORD, God of heaven and God of earth, that thou shalt not take my son to wife from the daughters of the Canaanites among whom I dwell. 4 But you shall go into my county and into my kinship and take my son Izhak to wife." 5 The servant said to him, "And if the woman does not want to go with me to this land, should I take your son back to the land from which you came?" 6 To which Abra- ham replied, "Be careful not to bring my son back here." 7 The LORD, the God of Heauen, who tore me from the house of my fathers and from the land where I was born, and who spoke to me and swore to me, saying, 'To your descendants I will give this land, he will send his angel before you, and you will take my son a wife from there. 8 If the woman will not fol- low thee, thou shalt be delivered of this other son of mine; only do not bring my son here any more." 9 Then the servant put his hand under the thigh of Abraham, his master, and swore by this fact. 10 And the servant took ten camels of his master, and departed: (for he had all his master's goods in his hand) and rose up and went to Aram Naharaim, toward the city of Nahor. 11 And he made his camels stop outside the city, by a well of water, at the hour of sunset, when the women go out to draw water. 12 And he said, "O Lord, God of my master Abraham, please give me good for- tune today and have mercy on my master Abraham. 13 Behold, I stand by the well of wa- ter, while the daughters of the men of this city go out to draw water. 14 Take therefore that woman to whom I say, "Lower your pitcher, I pray you, that I may drink; if she says, 'Drink, and I will give your camels to drink also,' it may be that she is the one whom you have destined for your servant Izhak; and so I shall know that you have had mercy on my master." 15 Now that he had left the word, behold, out came Rebekah, daughter of Bethuel, son of Milcah, wife of Nahor, brother of Abraham, with her pitcher on her shoulder. 16 (The mother was very beautiful to behold, a virgin who knew no man), and she went down to the well, filled the pitcher, and returned. 17 Then the servant ran to her and said, "Let me drink, please, some water from your pitcher." 18 She answered, "Drink, sir"; and she hastened, dropped the pitcher on his hand, and gave him a drink. 19 And when she had made him drink, she said, "I will give water also to your camels, until they have drunk enough." 20 And she immediately poured the pitcher into the trough and ran back to the well to draw water, and drew water for all her camels. 21 So the man marveled at her and kept silence as to whether the LORD had prospered her journey or not. 22 And when the camels had gone away to drink, the man took a golden enable- ment weighing half a shekel and two bracelets for her hands, weighing ten shekels of gold: 23 He said, "Whose daughter are you? Tell me, I pray thee, is there any place in the house of thy fathers where thou canst lodge?" 24 She answered him, "I am the daughter of Bethuel the son of Milcah, whom she bore in Nahor." 25 Moreover she said to him, "We also have a litter and a dwelling place in which to lodge." 26 The man bowed down and worshiped the LORD, 27 and said, "Blessed be the LORD, the God of my master Abraham, who has not withdrawn his mercy and his faithfulness from my master, for while I was on my way, the LORD led me to the house of my brother masters." 28 The mother ran to tell of her mother's house according to these words. 29 Now Rebekah had a brother named Laban, and Laban ran to the man at the well. 30 When he saw the earrings and bracelets in his sis- ter's hands and heard the words of Rebekah, his sister, saying, "So that man said to me," he went to the man and stood by the camels at the well. 31 He said, "Come in, blessed of the LORD; why do you stand outside, since I have prepared the house and gone around to the camels?" 32 Then the man went into the house, made the camels comfortable, and brought a litter and a blanket for the camels, and water to wash his feet and those of the men who were with him. 33 Then the meal was served to him, but he said, "I will not eat until I have spoken my message:" And he said, "Speak." 34 Then he said, "I am Abraham's ser- vant." 35 And the LORD blessed my master wonderfully, that he became great, because he gave him sheep, and bees, and silk, and gold, and male servants, and maid servants, and camels, and asses. 36 Sarah, my master's wife, bore my master a son when she was old, and to him he gave all that he has. 37 Now my master made me swear, "You shall not take my son to wife from the daughters of the Ca- naanites, in whose land I dwell: 38 But thou shalt go to the house of my fathers, and to my kindred, and take a wife for my son." 39 Then I said to my master, "What if the woman does not follow me?" 40 That one answered me, "The LORD, before whom I walk, will send his angel with you and prosper your journey, and you will take a wife for my son from my kins- men and from the house of my fathers. 41 Then thou shalt be freed from my other wife, when thou comest to my family; and if they will not give thee one, thou shalt be free from my other wife. 42 Today I came to the well and said, "O LORD, God of my master Abraham, if you now prosper my journey that I am about to take, 43 Behold, I stand by the well of water; when a virgin goes out to draw water, I say to her, "Please give me some water from your pitcher to drink." 44 and she says to me, "You drink, and I will also drink for your camels; let her be your bride, whom the LORD has pre- pared for the son of my masters." 45 Before I had finished speaking in my heart, behold, Rebecca came, with her pitcher on her shoul- der, and went down to the well to draw water. Then I said to her, "Give me a drink, please." 46 And she hastened, and took the pitcher off her shoulder, and said, "Drink, and I will give your camels to drink also." So I drank, and she gave the camels a drink also. 47 Then I ques- tioned her and said, "Whose daughter are you?" And she answered, "The daughter of Bethuel the son of Nahors, whom Milcah bore him." Then I put the enablement on her face and the bracelets on her hands: 48 Then I prostrated myself and worshipped the LORD and blessed the LORD, the God of my master Abraham, who had made me find the right way to take the daughter of my master broth- ers for his son. 49 Now, therefore, if you wish to act mercifully and justly toward my master, tell me; and if not, tell me so that I may turn to the right or to the left."

50 Then Laban and Bethuel answered, "This thing has been de-cided by the LORD; therefore we cannot tell you either good or evil." 51 Behold, Rebehak is before you; take her and go, that she may be the wife of your master sons, as the LORD has said." 52 When Abraham's servant heard their words, he prostrated himself toward the earth in the direction of the LORD. 53 Then the servant took silk jewelry and gold jewelry and clothes and gave them to Rebekah; he also gave them to his brother and his mother. 54 Then they ate and drank, he and the men who were with him, and they stayed all night. When they rose in the morning, he said, "Let me go to my master." 55 Then his brother and his mother answered, "Let his mother stay with you at least ten days, then she will leave." 56 But he said to them, "Do not hinder me, for the Lord has favored my journey; send me away, that I may go to my master." 57 Then they said, "We will call his mother and ask her consent." 58 And they called Rebecca and said to her, "Will you go with this man?" And she answered, "I will go." 59 So they let Rebecca, their sister, and her retinue go, with Abra-ham's servant and his men. 60 And they bless-ed Rebekah and said to her, "You are our sis-ter, and you shall grow to thousands, and your descendants shall possess the gate of her ene-mies." 61 Then Rebekah and her majesties arose, mounted the camels, and followed the man; and the sergeant took Rebekah and de-parted. 62 Now Izhak came from the road of Beer-lahai-roi (for he lived in the southern county). 63 And Izhak went out to pray in the camp toward dawn; and he lifted up his eyes and looked, and behold, the camels came. 64 Rebecca also lifted up her eyes, and when she saw Izhak, she got off the camel. 65 (For she had said to the servant, "Who is that man coming into the field to meet us?" and the ser-vant had answered, "It is my master.") She took a sailing ship and accompanied him. 66 The servant told Izhak all that he had done. 67 Then Izhak took her to the tent of Sarah his mother, and took Rebekah, who became his wife, and received her: Thus Izhak was com-forted after the death of his mother.

CHAPTER 25

1 Now Abraham had taken another wife, named Keturah, 2 Who bore him Zimran, Iokshan, Medan, Midian, Ishbak and Shua. 3 Iokshan begat Sheba and Dedan: The sons of Dedan were Asshurim, Letushim, and Leum-mim. 4 The sons of Midian were Ephah, Hep-her, Hanoch, Abida, and Elda, all the sons of Keturah. 5 Abraham gave all his possessions to Izhak, 6 but to the sons of the concubines whom he had, Abraham gave gifts and sent them away from Izhak, his son, while he was still alive, toward the east, in the county of the east. 7 This is the age of Abraham's life, and he lived a hundred and seventy-five years. 8 Then Abraham yielded to the spirit and died in good age, old and of great age, and was re-united with his people. 9 His sons, Izhak and Ishmael, buried him in the quarry of Mach-pelah, in the field of Ephron the son of Zohar the Hittite, opposite Mamre. 10 That field Abraham bought from the Hittites, where Abraham was buried with Sarah his wife. 11 After Abraham's death, God blessed Izhak, his son, and Izhak dwelt near Beer-lahai-roi. 12 These are the generations of Ishmael, Abraham's son, whom Hagar, the Egyptian hand of Sarah, bore to Abraham. 13 These are the names of Ishmael's sons, name by name, according to their kinship: the firstborn of Ishmael was Nebaioth, then Kedar, Adbeel, and Mibsam, 14 Mishma, Dumah and Massa, 15 Hadar, Tema, Ietur, Nefish and Kedemah. 16 These are the sons of

Ishmael, and these are their names, according to their cities and their castles: two princes of their nations. 17 (These are the years of Ishmael's life: an hun-dred and thirty and seventy years; he yielded to the spirit, and died, and was gathered to his people.) 18 And they dwelt from Hauilah unto Shur, that is, toward Egypt, as thou goest to-ward Assur. Ishmael dwelt in the presence of all his brothers. 19 These are the generations of Izhak: Abraham the son of Abraham begat Izhak, 20 Izhak was four years old when he took Rebekah, daughter of Bethuel, an Ar-amite of Padan Aram, and sister of Laban, an Aramite, to wife. 21 And Izhak prayed to the LORD for his wife, for she was barren; and the LORD prayed to him, and Rebekah his wife conceived, 22 but the children were joined within her; therefore she said, "Seeing that it is so, why am I so?" 23 And the LORD said to her, "Two nations are in thy womb, and two peoples shall come forth out of thy bowels, and the one shall be stronger than the other, and the elder shall serve the younger." 24 When the time of delirium was fulfilled, behold, two twins were in his womb. 25 The one who came out first was red, all out like a rough robe, and they called him Esau. 26 Then his brother came out, and his hand held Esau by the neck; therefore they called him Iaakob. Now Izhak was sixty years old when Rebekah gave birth to them. 27 The boys grew up, and Esau was a skilled hunter and lived in the fields, while Iaakob was a man of the plains and lived in tents. 28 Izhak liked Esau, because venison was his meal, but Rebekah liked Iaakob. 29 Now Iaakob made soup, as Esau came from the camp and was tired. 30 Then Esau said to Iaakob, "Let me eat, please, of that soup that is so red, for I am tired." Therefore his name was called Edom. 31 Iaa-kob said, "Sell me your firstborn right away." 32 Esau said, "Behold, I am almost dead; what then is this primogeniture to me? 33 Then Iaa-kob said, "Swear to me at once." And he swore and gave up his primogeniture to Iaakob. 34 Then Iaakob gave Esau bread and lentil soup; and he ate and drank, and rose up, and went his way: Thus Esau despised his birthright.

CHAPTER 26

1 There was a famine in the land, besides the first famine that there was in the days of Abraham. Therefore Izhak went to Abimel-ech, king of the Philistines, in Gerar. 2 For the LORD appeared to him and said, "Do not go down to Egypt, but stay in the land that I will show you. 3 Dwell in this land, and I will be with you and bless you, for to you and to your descendants I will give all these countries, and I will fulfill what I swore to Abraham your father. 4 Moreover I will make thy seed multiply like the stars of Heauen, and I will give unto thy seed all these countries; and in thy seed shall all the nations of the earth be blessed, 5 Because Abraham obeyed my word and kept my decrees, my commands, my stat-utes and my laws." 6 So Izhak settled in Gerar. 7 The locals asked him about his wife, and he answered, "She is my sister"; for he feared to say, "She is my wife," otherwise, he said, the locals would kill me, because of Rebekah, who was beautiful in the eyes. 8 So after he had been there a long time, Abimelech, king of the Philistines, looked out of a window and saw Izhak sporting with Rebekah, his wife. 9 Then Abimelech called Izhak and said to him, "Loe, she is your wife, and why do you say that she is my sister?" To which Izhak answered, "Because I have thought this: it may be that I die for her." 10 Then Abimelech said, "Why did you do this against her? One of the people had almost a lien on your wife, so you should

have brought sin upon her." 11 Then Abimel- ech accused all his people, saying, "Who- ever touches this man or his wife will die of death." 12 Then Izhak sowed in that land and found, in the same year, a hundred acres by estimation; and so the LORD blessed him. 13 That man became great and multiplied, until he became very great, 14 For he owned flocks of sheep and herds of cattle and a great house; therefore the Philistines feared him. 15 So much so that the Philistines stopped and filled with earth all the wells that his father's servants had dug in the days of his father Abraham. 16 Then Abimelech said to Izhak, "Get out of here, for you are stronger than we are, a great man." 17 Izhak departed, pitched his tent in the valley of Gerar and settled there. 18 As Izhak returned, he dug the water wells that they had dug in the days of Abra- ham his father, because the Philistines had stopped them after Abraham's death, and he gave them the same names that his father had given them. 19 Iskak's servants dug in the val- ley and found there a well of drinking water. 20 But the herdsmen of Gerar quarreled with the herdsmen of Izhak, saying, "The water is ours"; therefore they called the well Esek, because they were at war with him. 21 Then they dug another well and quarreled over that also, and he called it Sitnah. 22 Then he went thence and dug another well, for which they had no recourse; therefore he called it Reho- both and said, "Because the LORD has now made a house, we will increase in the land." 23 He then went to Beer- sheba. 24 That same night the LORD appeared to him and said, "I am the God of Abraham, your father; do not be afraid, for I am with you; I will bless you and multiply your seed by my servant Abra- ham." 25 Then he built an altar there and called upon the Name of the Lord, and there he pitched his tent; where Isaac's servants also dug a well. 26 Then came to him Abimel- ech from Gerar, Ahuzzath, one of his friends, and Phichol, the leader of his army. 27 To whom Izhak said, "Why do you come to me, since you hate me and have driven me away from you?" m Who answered, "We heard for certain that the LORD was with you, and we thought, Let there now be another among you, between you and you, and let the LORD make a covenant with you. 29 If you will not harm vs, as we have not touched you, and as we have only done you good and sent you away in peace, you now, blessed of the Lord, do this." 30 Then he made them a banquet, and they ate and drank. 31 In the morning they rose early and swore to each other; then Izhak let them go, and they departed from him in peace. 32 That same day Izhak's ser- vants came and told him about a well they had dug and said, "We have found water." 33 So he called it Shibah; therefore the name of the city is still called Beer-Sheba today. 34 When Esau was four years old, he took to wife Iudith, daughter of Beeri, a Hittite, and Bashemath, daughter of Elon, a Hittite. 35 They were a cause of grief to Izhak and to Rebekah.

CHAPTER 27

1 When Izhak was old and his eyes grew dim (so that he could not see) he called Esau, his eldest son, and said to him, "My son." And he answered him, "I am here." 2 Then he said, "Behold, I am now old and do not know the day of my death: 3 Therefore now, I pray you, take your tools, your spear and your bow, and go to the camp, to get me some deer meat. 4 Then prepare me some salt meat, as it pleas- es me, and bring it to me that I may eat, and that my soul may bless you, before I die." 5 (Rebekah heard when Izhak spoke to Esau his son) and Esau went into the country

to hunt game and bring it. 6 Then Rebekah spoke to Izhakob his son, saying, "Behold, I heard your father speaking to Esau your brother, say- ing, 7 "Bring me some vein and prepare me some salted meat, that I may eat and bless you before the LORD before my death." 8 Now therefore, my son, listen to my message in what I command you. 9 Now go to the flock and bring me two good goat kids, that I may make a good dish of them for your father, as he desires. 10 Then you shall bring them to your father, and he shall eat them, that he may bless you before his death. 11 But Iaakob said to Rebekah his mother, "Behold, Esau my brother is rough, and I am soft. 12 My fa- ther might perhaps frighten me, and I would seem a mocker to him; so I would bring upon myself a curse and not a blessing." 13 But his mother said to him, "Let your curse be on me, my son; just listen to my voice and go and bring it to me." 14 So he went, and prepared them, and brought them to his mother; and his mother prepared a pleasing meat, such as pleased her father. 15 And Rebeka took the finest clothes of her eldest son Esau, which were in her house, and clothed Iaakob her younger son: 16 And she clothed his hands and the smooth part of his neck with the skins of kids. 17 Then he put into his son Iaa- kob's hand the good food and the bread that he had prepared. 18 When he came to his fa- ther, he said, "My father." Who answered, "I am here; who are you, my son?" 19 Izhakob said to his father, "I am Esau, your firstborn son; I have done what you have done wrong to me; arise, I pray you; sit down and eat of my deer meat, that your soul may bless me." 20 Then Izhak said to his son, "How is it that you found him so soon, my son? Who answered, "Because the LORD your God made me find it in my hand." 21 Then Izhak said to Iaakob, "Come here now, that I may hear you, my son, whether or not you are that son of mine, Esau." 22 Then Iaakob approached Izhak his father, who felt him and said, "The robe is that of Iaakob, but the hands are that of Esau." 23 (Because he did not know him, for his hands were rough like his brother Esau's, he blessed him). 24 Then he said, "Are you my son Esau? Who answered, "Yes." 25 Then he said, "Bring him here and I will eat of the venison of my son, that my soul may bless you." She brought it to him and he ate; she also brought him wine and he drank. 26 Then his father Izhak said to him, "Come here now and kill me, my son." 27 He drew near and kissed him. Then he smelled the fragrance of his garments, blessed him, and said, "Behold, the smell of my son is like the smell of a field that the LORD has blessed. 28 Therefore may God give you the dew of Heauen, the fat of the land, and abundance of grain and wine. 29 Let the peoples be your servants, and let the nations bow down to you; be lord of your brethren, and let the sons of your mothers honor you; cursed be those who curse you, and blessed be those who bless you." 30 When Izhak had finished blessing Iaakob, and Iaakob had just left the presence of Izhak his father, Esau, his brother, came in from his hunting, 31 he also prepared some beef, brought it to his father and said to him, "Let my father get up and eat of the venison of his son, that your soul may bless me." 32 But his father Izhak said to him, "Who are you?" And he answered, "I am your son, your firstborn Esau." 33 Then Izhak was seized with great fear and said, "Who and where is he who hunted the deer meat and brought it to me, and I ate everything before you came? 34 And when Esau heard the words of his father, he cried out with a great and bitter cry, out of all proportion, and said to his father, "Leave me, even me, my father." 35 Who answered, "Your brother has come with guile and taken away your blessing." 36 Then he said, "Was he not rightly called Iaakob? For he has deceived me these two times: he has taken my birthright, and now he has taken my blessing." He also said, "Have you not kept a blessing for me?" 37 Then Izhak answered and said to Esau, "Behold, I have made him your lord, and all his brothers I have made them his servants; moreover I have supplied him with grain and wine, and now what shall I do, my son?" 38 Then Esau said to his father, "Have you one blessing, my father? Bless me, and me also, my father"; and Esau lifted up his head and wept. 39 Then Izhak his father answered and said to him, "Behold, the fat of the land shall be thy dwelling, and thou shalt have the dew of the lake on every side. 40 By thy sword shalt thou live, and thou shalt be thy brothers' servant. But when thou shalt have mastery, thou shalt break his yoke from off thy neck. 41 Therefore Esau hated Iaakob, because of the blessing with which his father had blessed him. And Esau thought, "The days of mourning for my father will soon come, and then I will kill my brother Iaakob." 42 But Rebekah was told of the words of Esau, her eldest son, and she sent for Iaakob, her younger son, and said to him, "Behold, your brother Esau has comforted himself against you, intending to kill you: 43 Now therefore, my son, hear my message, arise and flee to Haran to my brother Laban, 44 and stay with him for a little while, until the fierceness of your brothers has subsided, 45 until the wrath of thy brethren shall depart from thee, and he shall forget the things which thou hast done to him; then I will depart and take thee away from there; why should I deprive myself of the two of you in one day? 46 Rebecca also said to Izhak, "I am weary of my life for the daugh- ters of Heth. If Iaakob takes a wife of the daughters of Heth, like these of the daughters of the earth, what have I to live for?

CHAPTER 28

1 Then Izhak called Iaakob, blessed him, charged him, and said to him, "Do not take a wife from the daughters of Canaan. 2 Arise, go to Padan Aram, to the house of Bethuel, your father, and from there take to wife one of the daughters of Laban, your maternal brother." 3 May God bless you and cause you to grow and multiply, that you may be a multitude of peo- ple, 4 And grant the blessing of Abraham, to you and your descendants with you, that you may inherit the land (where you are a strang- er) which God gave to Abraham." 5 So Izhak sent Iaakob, who went to Padan Aram to La- ban the son of Bethuel the Aramite, brother of Rebekah, mother of Iaakob and Esau. 6 When Esau heard that Izhak had blessed Iaakob and sent him to Padan Aram to take a wife from there, when he blessed him he commanded him not to take the daughters of Canaan to wife, 7 and that Iaakob had obeyed his fa- ther and his mother and had gone to Padan Aram: 8 Esau also, seeing that the daughters of Canaan displeased Izhak his father, 9 And Esau went to Ishmael, and took Mahalath the daughter of Ishmael the son of Abrahams, the sister of Nabaioth, to wife. 10 Now Iaakob de- parted from Beer-sheba and went to Haran, 11 and he came to a certain place and stayed there all night, because the sun had set, and he took the stones of the place and lay down under his head and slept in the same place. 12 Then he dreamed, and behold, there stood a ladder upon the earth, the top of which reached up to the plateau; and behold, the an- gels of God were ascending and descending by means of it. 13 And behold, the LORD stood upon it and said, "I am the LORD, the God of Abraham your father, and the God of Izhak; the land on which you will sleep I will give to you and to your descendants. 14 And thy seed shall be as the dust of the earth, and shall

spread westward, and eastward, and north- ward, and southward; in thee and in thy seed shall all the families of the earth be blessed. 15 And behold, I am with thee, and will guard thee whithersoever thou goest, and will bring thee back into this land; for I will not forsake thee until I have fulfilled that which I have promised thee." 16 Then Iaakob awoke from sleep and said, "Surely the LORD is in this place, and I have not noticed." 17 He became afraid and said, "How fearful is this place! It is none other than the house of God, and this is the gate of Heauen." 18 Then Iaakob rose up early in the morning, and took the stone which he had laid under his head, and set it up as a pillar, and put an oilcloth upon it. 19 And he called that place Bethel, whereas be- fore the name of the city was called Luz. 20 Then Iaakob made a vow, saying, "If God will be with me, and keep me on this journey that I am making, and give me bread to eat and clothing to clothe me: 21 so that I may return to the house of my fathers in safety, then the LORD will be my God." 22 This stone, which I have set as a pillar, shall be the house of God; and of all that thou shalt give me, I will give thee the tenth part.

CHAPTER 29

1 Then Iaakob lifted up his feet and came to the county of the east. 2 As he looked around, behold, there was a well in the field, where three flocks of sheep lay (for in that well the flocks were watered), and there was a large stone over the mouth of the well. 3 Then all the flocks gathered together and rolled the stone from the mouth of the well, watered the sheep, and put the stone back on the mouth of the well in its place. 4 Iaakob said to them, "My brethren, from whence do you come?" And they answered, "We are from Haran." 5 Then he said to them, "Do you know Laban the son of Nahor? Those answered, "We know him." 6 Then he said to them, "Is he in good health?" And they answered, "He is in good health, and behold, his daughter Rahel comes with the sheep." 7 Then he said, "Behold, it is yet day, and it is not yet time to gather the cattle; water the sheep and go and feed them." 8 But they said, "We cannot until all the flocks are gathered together, and until the men re- move the stone from the mouth of the well, that we may water the sheep." 9 While he was talking with them, Rahel also came with the flocks of his fathers, for he was guarding them. 10 When Iaakob saw Rahel, the daugh- ter of Laban, his maternal brother, and the sheep of Laban, his maternal brother, he ap- proached, took the stone from the mouth of the well, and watered the flocks of Laban, his maternal brother. 11 Iaakob kissed Rahel, lift- ed up his head and wept. 12 (For Iaakob told Rahel that he was her paternal brother and the son of Rebekah), so she ran to tell her fa- ther. 13 And when Laban heard of Iaakob, the son of his sister, he ran to him, and embraced him, and kissed him, and brought him into his house; and he told Laban all these things. 14 To whom Laban said, "Well, you are my flesh and blood." and he stayed with him for a month. 15 For Laban said to Iaakob, "Though you are my brother, should you then serve me for nothing? Tell me, what shall be your wages? 16 Laban had two daughters, the elder of whom was named Leah, and the younger Rahel. 17 Leah had tender eyes, while Rahel was fair and gentle. 18 Iaakob welcomed Ra- hel and said, "I will serve you for ten years for Rahel, your youngest daughter." 19 Then La- ban answered, "It is better for me to give her to you than to give her to another man; stay with me." 20 And Iaakob served ten years for Rahel, and it seemed to him but a few days, for he loved

her. 21 Then Iaakob said to La- ban, "Give me my wife, that I may go to her, for my term is ended." 22 Therefore Laban gathered all the men of the place and made a feast. 23 But when it was evening, he took Leah, his daughter, and led her to him, and went in to her. 24 And Laban gave his elder Zilpah to his daughter Leah, as his servant. 25 But when it was morning, behold, it was Lea. Then she said to Laban, "Why have you done this to me? Have I not served you for Rahel? Why then have you deceived me?" 26 Laban answered, "It is not the practice of this place to give the young man before the old man." 27 When you have completed seven years for her, we will also give you this for the service that you will still serve me for another ten years." 28 So Iaakob did so, fulfilling his ten years, and gave him Rachel, his daughter, to wife. 29 Laban also gave Rahel his daughter Bil- hah, his wife, as his servant. 30 So he also ap- proached Rahel, whom he valued more than Leah, and served him for another ten years. 31 When the LORD saw that Leah was despised, he made her fruitful, but Rahel was barren. 32 Lea conceived and bore a son and named him Reuben, for she said, "Because the LORD has looked on my tribulation, my husband will love me." 33 Then she conceived again and bore a son and said, "Because the LORD heard that I was hated, he also gave me this son," and she named him Simeon. 34 Then she conceived again and bore a son and said, "At this time my husband will keep me company, for I have given him three sons; therefore his name was Leui." 35 Then she conceived another time and bore a son, saying, "Now I will pray to the LORD"; therefore she named him Iudah and left her womb.

CHAPTER 30

1 When Rahel saw that she was not bear- ing children to Iaakob, Rahel questioned his sister and said to Iaakob, "Give me children, or else I will die." 2 Then Iaakob was kindled with wrath against Rahel and said to her, "Am I in the snare of God who has kept you from having the fruit of the woman?" 3 And she answered, "Here is my mother Bilhah; go to her and she will give birth on my knees, and I will have children by her also." 4 Then she gave him Bilhah his wife, and Iaakob went to her. 5 Bilhah conceived and bore Iaakob a son. 6 Then Rahel said, "God condemned me, and heard my voice, and gave me a son; therefore he named him Dan." 7 Bilhah Rahel's mother gave birth again and bore Iaakob, the second son. 8 Then Rahel said, "I wrestled with my sister and got the upper hand, and I named him Naphtali." 9 When Leah saw that she had abandoned her pregnancy, she took Zilpah his wife and gave her Iaakob to wife. 10 The elder Zilpah bore Iaakob a son. 11 Then Lea said, "Here comes a company," and she put the name Gad on him. 12 Zilpa Lea bore an- other son to Iaakob. 13 Then Lea said, "Ah, I am blessed, for the daughters will bless me," and she put the name Asher on him. 14 Now Reuben went in the days of the grain festi- val and found mandrakes in the fields and brought them to his mother Lea. Then Rahel said to Lea, "Give me, please, some of your sons' mandrakes." 15 But she answered her, "Is it a small thing for you to take my hus- band, if you do not also take the mandrakes of my children?" Then Rahel said, "Therefore he shall sleep with you this night for the man- drakes of your sons." 16 Iaakob came from the camp in the evening, and Leah went to him, saying, "Come in to me, for I have bought you and paid you with my sons' mandrakes"; and he slept with her that night. 17 And God heard Leah, and she conceived and bore Iaakob the fifth son. 18 Then Leah said, "God has given me my reward, because I gave my elder to my husband," and she named her son Issachar. 19 Then Leah conceived again and bore Iaakob, the sixth son. 20 Then Leah said, "God has endowed me with a good endowment; now my husband shall dwell with me, for I have borne him six sons"; and she named him Zeb- ulun. 21 Then she bore a daughter and named her Dinah. 22 And God remembered Rahel, and heard her, and opened her womb. 23 So she conceived and bore a son and said, "God has taken away my reproach." 24 She named him Ioseph, saying, "The LORD will give me another son." 25 As soon as Rahel had given birth to Ioseph, Iaakob said to Laban, "Let me depart, that I may return to my place and to my country. 26 Give me my wives and my children, for whom I have served you, and let me go, for you know what service I have done you." 27 To which Laban answered, "If now I have found evil in your eyes, stay; I have per- ceived that the LORD has blessed me for your sake." 28 He also said, "Give me your wages, and I will give them to you." 29 But he an- swered him, "You know what service I have done you, and in what way your cattle have benefited from me. 30 For the little that thou hadst before I came hath become a multitude; and the Lord hath blessed thee for my com- ing; but now, when shall I be able to haul even my house? 31 Then he said, "What shall I give you?" Iaakob answered, "You shall not give me anything at all; if you will do this thing for me, I will return and feed and keep your sheep. 32 Today I will go through all your flock and sep- arate from it all the sheep with small and large spots, all the black lambs among the sheep, those with large spots and those with small spots among the goats; and this will be my wages. 33 So my righteousness shall answer for me hereafter, when I come for my reward before thee, and all those that have no small or great spots among the goats, and black lambs among the sheep, shall be stolen with me." 34 Then Laban said, "Go, if God wills it to be as you say." 35 Therefore, on the same day, he took the goats that were partially colored and with large spots, all the goats with small and large spots, all the goats that were white, and all the black goats among the sheep, and put them into the custody of his sons. 36 And he fixed three days' journey between himself and Iaakob. And Iaakob kept the rest of La- ban's sheep. 37 Then Iaakob took reeds of folk- green, hasell and chestnut, put white straws in them, and made white appear in the reeds. 38 Then he put the reeds that he had stuck in the gutters and troughs, when the sheep came to water, in front of the sheep. (For they were in heat when they came to drink). 39 And the sheep were in heat before the reeds, and afterwards they produced yellows of differ- ent colors, with small and large spots. 40 And Iaakob separated these lambs, and turned the faces of the flock to these lambs of partial col- or and all sorts of black in the midst of Laban's flocks; so he put his flocks on their own, and did not put them with Laban's flock. 41 At all times when the sheep were stronger, Iaakob set the reeds before the eyes of the sheep in the gutters, that they might conceive before the reeds. 42 But when the sheep were weak, he did not put them in; and so the weakest were Laban and the strongest were Iaakob. 43 So that man increased greatly; he had many flocks, servants of mothers, servants of men, camels and donkeys.

CHAPTER 31

1 Now he heard the words of Laban's sons, saying, "Iaakob has taken away all that was our fathers', and from our

fathers' goods he has obtained all this honor." 2 Moreover, Iaakob saw Laban's face that was no longer turned to him as before: 3 The LORD said to Iaakob, "Go back again to the land of your fathers and to your family, and I will be with you." 4 There- fore Iaakob sent for Rahel and Lea in the field for his flock. 5 Then he said to them, "I see the countenance of your fathers not toward me as it used to be, and the God of my father has been with me. 6 And you know that I have served your father with all my strength. 7 But your father deceived me and changed my wages ten times; but God allowed him not to harm me. 8 If he said, "The stained shall be your wages," all the sheep were stained; and if he said, "The colored shall be your wages," all the sheep were colored. 9 Thus God took sub- stance from your fathers and gave it to me. 10 For in a moment of regret I lifted up mine eyes and saw in a tent, and behold, his goats were leaping upon her goats, which were colored in part with small and large spots. 11 The angel of God said to me in a dream, "Iaa- kob." And I answered, "Behold, I am here." 12 And he said, "Lift up now your eyes and see all the goats that leap upon you goats that are colored in part, stained with small and large spots, for I have seen all that Laban does to you. 13 I am the God of Beth-el, where you raised up the pillar and where you made a vow to me. Now get up, get out of this land and re- turn to the land to which you were brought." 14 Then Rahel and Leah said to him, "Do we still have portions and inheritance in the house of our fathers? 15 Does he not regard you as strangers? For he has sold and eaten and consumed our money. 16 Therefore all the riches that God took away from our father are ours and our children's; now therefore what God has told you, do." 17 Then Iaakob got up and put his sons and wives on camels. 18 Then he took away all his flocks and all his posses- sions, that is, the wealth he had obtained in Padan Aram, to go to Izhak his father in the land of Canaan. 19 When Laban left to cut down his sheep, Rahel stole the idols of his fathers. 20 So Iaakob stole the heart of Laban, the Aramean, because he did not tell him that he had fled. 21 So he fled with all that he had, got up, crossed the river and went to Mount Gilead. 22 On the third day afterward Laban was told that Iaakob had fled. 23 So he took his brothers with him, followed him on a ten- day journey and joined him on Mount Gile- ad. 24 God came to Laban the Aramean on a dark night and said to him, "Be careful not to speak to Iaakob wrongly." 25 Then Laban de- parted from Iaakob, who had pitched his tent on the mountain; and Laban also, with his brothers, camped on Mount Gilead. 26 Then Laban said to Iaakob, "What have you done? You have stolen my heart and carried away my daughters as if they had been taken cap- tive with the sword." 27 Why hast thou fled thus secretly and departed from me, and hast not warned me, that I might send thee forth with cheerfulness and with singing, with ket- tledrum and with harp? 28 But thou hast not permitted me to kill my sons and my daugh- ters; now thou hast done foolishness in doing so. 29 I am able to do you good; but the God of your father spoke to me last night, saying, "Be careful not to speak to Iaakob, who does not know good." 30 Now though you went your way, because you longed greatly for the house of your fathers, for what reason did you reject my gods? 31 Then Iaakob answered La- ban, "Because I was afraid and thought that you would take your daughters away from me." 32 But with whom you find your gods, do not let him lie. Seek before our brothers what I have of yours and bring it to you (but Iaakob did not know that Rahel had stolen them)." 33 Then Laban went into the tent of Iaakob, into the tent of Leah, and into the tent of the two women, but he did not find them.

So he went out of Leah's tent and entered Rahel's tent. 34 (Rahel had taken the idols and put them in the camel bedding and sat on them) and Laban rummaged through the tent, but he did not find them. 35 Then she said to her father, "My lord, do not distress yourself if I cannot stand up before you, for the dominion of the women is over me." 36 And Iaakob was angry and quarreled with Laban: and Iaakob answered and said to Laban, "What have I vi- olated, what have I offended, that thou shoul- dest pursue me? 37 Seeing that you have gone through all my stuff, what have you found of all your household goods? Lay it here before my people and your brothers, that they may judge between them. 38 These twenty years I have been with you; your sheep and your goats have not cast off their yoke, and I have not eaten the branches of your flock. 39 That which was consumed by the beasts, I did not bring it to you, but made it myself; by my hand you required it, whether it was swollen by day or by night. 40 By day I was consumed with burning and by night with frost, and sleep left my eyes. 41 So I was twenty years in your house, and served you for fourteen years for your two daughters and for six years for your sheep, and you changed my wages ten times. 42 If the God of my father, the God of Abra- ham and the fear of Izhak had not been with me, you would have sent me away now emp- ty; but God saw my tribulation and the toil of my labor and rebuked you last night." 43 Then Laban answered Iaakob, "These daughters are my daughters, these sons are my sons, these sheep are my sheep, and everything you see is mine; what can I do today to these daughters of mine or to their sons who have given birth? 44 Now therefore come and let us make a cov- enant, you and I, that it may be a testimony between you and me." 45 Then Iaakob took a stone and set it up as a pillar: 46 And Iaakob said to his brethren, "Gather stones"; who brought stones, made a heap, and ate upon them. 47 Laban called him Iegar-sahadutha, and Iaakob called him Galeed. 48 For Laban said, "Today this heap is a witness between you and me; therefore he called it Galeed." 31:49 And he also called it Mizpah, because he said, "The LORD looks between me and you, when we go apart from one another." 50 If thou wilt see my daughters, or take wives be- side my daughters, there is none with them; behold, God is witness between me and thee." 51 Moreover Laban said to Iaakob, "Observe this roof and look at the pillar that I have set between me and you, 52 this piece will bear witness and the pillar will bear witness that I will not come to you beyond this piece and that you will not pass by this piece and this pillar forever. 53 Let the God of Abraham, the God of Nabor, and the God of their father be judges between them; but Iaakob swore by fear of his father Izhak. 54 Then Iaakob of- fered a sacrifice on the mountain and called his brothers to eat bread; they ate the bread and stayed all night on the mountain. 55 Early in the morning Laban rose up, kissed his sons and daughters and blessed them; then Laban departed and returned to his place.

CHAPTER 32

1 By this time Iaakob had set out on his jour- ney, and the angels of God came to meet him. 2 When Iaakob saw them, he said, "This is the army of God," and he called that place Maha- naim. 3 Then Iaakob sent messengers before him to Esau his brother in the land of Seir, in the county of Edom: 4 To whom he gave or- ders to say, "Thus speak ye to my lord Esau: thy servant Iaakob saith, I have been a strang- er with Laban, and have tarried until this time. 5 I have also

had donkeys, and sheep, and male servants, and female servants, and I have sent word to my lord that I may find favor in your eyes." 6 Then the messengers came again to Iaakob, saying, "We have come to your brother Esau, and he also has come against you and four hundred men with him." 7 Then Iaakob was greatly afraid and greatly troubled, and he divided the people who were with him into two groups, the sheep and the animals and the camels. 8 For he said, "If Esau comes and strikes one of the two companies, the other will escape." 9 Iaakob said, "O God of my father Abraham and God of my father Izhak, O LORD, who say to me, 'Re- turn to your country and to your family, and I will do you good, 10 I am not worthy of the least part of all the mercies and all the truths that you have shown to your servant, because with my staff I have gone outside this bound- ary and now I have brought upon myself two evils. 11 I pray thee, deliver me from the hand of my brother, from the hand of Esau, for I fear him, lest he come and smite me and the mother upon her children. 12 For thou say- est, I will do thee good, and I will make thy seed like the sand of the sea, which cannot be named for the multitude. 13 The same night he stopped there and took a gift for Esau his brother from what had come to him: 14 two hundred goats and twenty he-goats, two hun- dred sheep and twenty rams 15 three meek camels with their necks, forty horses and ten heifers, twenty asses and ten fools. 16 He de- livered them into the hands of his servants, all the dromedaries on their behalf, and said to his servants, "Pass before me, and put a space between dromedary and dromedary." 17 Then he commanded the younger ones, "If Esau my brother meets you and asks you, Whose ser- vant are you? And where are you going? And whose are these before thee? 18 Then you shall say, I am your servant Iaakobs; he is a gift sent to my lord Esau; and behold, he also is behind you." 19 So he commanded also the second and the thirteenth and all those who followed the druggists, saying, "In this way you shall speak to Esau when you find him. 20 And you shall say again, "Behold, your servant Iaakob comes after you" (for he thought, "I will ap- pease his wrath with the gift before me, and afterward I will see his face; it may be that he will accept me"). 21 So the gift went before him, but he stayed that night with the com- pany. 22 That same evening he arose, took his two wives, his two maidens, and his sons, and departed for Jabbok. 23 He took them and sent them out of the river and sent out what he had. 24 When Iaakob was left alone, a man wrestled with him until dawn-. 25 And he said that he could not stand against him; therefore he touched the side of his thigh, and the side of Iaakob's thigh melted as he wrestled with him. 26 He said, "Let me go, for it is daylight." Who answered, "I will not let you go unless you bless me." 27 Then she said to him, "What is your name?" And he answered, "Iaakob." 28 Then he said, "Your name shall no longer be called Iaakob, but Israel; for you have had power with God, you shall also have pow- er with men." 29 Then Iaakob asked, saying, "Please tell me your name." And he answered, "Why do you now ask my name?" and blessed him. 30 Iaakob called the place by the name of Peniel, because, he said, "I have seen God face to face and my life is preserved." 31 As he passed through Peniel, the sun rose toward him, and he stood on his thigh. 32 Therefore the children of Israel shall not eat, to this day, the thorn that shrinketh in the hollow of the thigh, because he touched the thorn that shrinketh in the hollow of the thigh of Iaakob.

CHAPTER 33

1 While Iaakob was looking up and watch- ing, behold, Esau came, and with him four hundred men; and he entrusted his sons to Leah, Rahel and the two maidens. 2 He put the maidens and their sons in the foreground, Leah and her sons in the background, and Rahel and Ioseph in the background. 3 So he went before them and prostrated himself on the ground several times until he came near his brother. 4 Then Esau ran to him, and em- braced him, and fell upon his neck, and kissed him, and wept. 5 Then he looked up, and saw the women and the children, and said, "Who are these with you?" And he answered, "They are the children whom God, by his grace, has given to your servant." 6 Then the maidens drew near, they and their children, and pros- trated themselves. 7 Leah also with her sons came near and did obeisance; then Ioseph and Rahel came near and did reverence. 8 Then he said, "What do you mean by all this drugging that I have encountered? Who answered, "I have sent her, that she may do me honor in the sight of my lord." 9 Esau said, "I have enough already, my brother; keep for yourself what you have." 10 But Iaakob answered, "No, I pray thee, if now I have found favor before thee, receive my gift from my hand, for I have seen thy face as I have seen the face of God, because thou hast accepted me. 11 Please take my blessing that has been brought to you, for God has had mercy on me and so I have everything." 12 Then he said, "Let us take our journey and go, and I will go before you." 13 Then he answered him, "My lord knows that the children are tender, and the sheep and the calves with their young under my hand; and if one day they should take them out, the whole flock will die. 14 Let my lord go before his ser- vant, and I will dry myself gently, according to the weight of the cattle before me and accord- ing to what the children are able to bear, until I come to my lord at Seir." 15 Then Esau said, "I will leave some of my children with you." And he answered, "What need is there of that? Let me find grace before my lord." 16 So Esau went back and, that same day, took the way to Seir. 17 And Iaakob advanced to Succoth, and built a house, and made blankets for his cattle; therefore he called that place Succoth. 18 Then Iaakob came safely to the city of Si- che, which is in the territory of Canaan, when he came from Padan Aram, and encamped before the city. 19 There he bought a plot of land, where he pitched his tent, by the sons of Hamor, the father of Siche, for a hundred denarii. 20 He built an altar there and called it, "The great God of Israel."

CHAPTER 34

1 Then Dinah, daughter of Leah, who had given birth to Iaakob, went to see the daugh- ters of that county. 2 And when Shechem the son of Hamor, lord of that county, saw her, he took her, and lay down with her, and de- filed her. 3 So his heart went out to Dinah the daughter of Iaakob; he listened to her moth- er and spoke kindly to her. 4 Then Shechem said to his father Hamor, "Take this woman to wife for me." 5 (Now Iaakob knew that he had defiled Dinah, his daughter, and that his sons were with his cattle in the field; therefore Iaakob kept silent until they came.) 6 Then Hamor the father of Shechem went to Iaa- kob to speak with him. 7 And when the sons of Iaakob came out of the camp and heard of it, the men were affected and very angry, be- cause he had done a bad deed in Israel, lying with Iaakob's daughter; which should not be done. 8 Hamor spoke to them, saying, "The soul of my son Shechem

desires your daugh- ter; give her to him in marriage, I pray you. 9 Therefore make an affinity with you: give your daughters to wife to you, and take our daugh- ters to wife to you, 10 And you shall dwell with Vs, and the land shall be before you; dwell, do your business, and possess your possessions." 34:11 Shechem also said to his father and his brothers, "Let me find favor with your eyes, and I will give what you allot me. 12 Ask of me abundantly dowries and gifts, and I will give what you shall decide for me, so that you may give me the mother to wife." 13 Then the sons of Iaakob answered Shechem and Ham- or his father, speaking deceitfully, because he had defiled Dinah their sister, 14 and said to them, "We cannot do this thing, to give our sister to an uncircumcised man, for it would be a reproach to them. 15 But in this we con- sent to you, if you wish to be like us, that ev- ery male child among you be circumcised: 16 Then we will give you our daughters, and we will take your daughters with you, and we will dwell with you, and we will be one people. 17 But if ye will not hearken to vs to be circum- cised, then we will take our daughters and go away." 18 Their words pleased Hamor and Shechem the son of Hamor. 19 But the young man refused to do this thing, because he loved the daughter of Iaakob; besides, he was the most reserved of all his father's house. 20 Then Hamor and Shechem his son went to the gate of their city, and they contacted the men of their city, saying 21 These men are at peace with us, and that they may dwell in the land and carry on their business there (for the land is large enough for them), let us take their daughters as wives and give them our daugh- ters." 22 Only in this way will the men consent to vs to dwell with vs and to be one people, if all the sons among vs are circumcised as they are circumcised. 23 Shall not their flocks and their property and all their livestock be ours? Only here vs will agree to dwell with vs and they will dwell with vs." 24 Hamor and Shechem his son listened to all who went out from the gate of his city; and all the sons of men were circumcised, all who went out from the gate of his city. 25 And on the thirteenth day (when they were already in turmoil) two sons of Iaakob, Simeon and Leui, brothers of Dinah, took one of them the sword, and went into the city, and slew all the males. 26 They also killed Hamor and Shechem his son with the edge of the sword, took Dinah from the house of Shechem, and went their way. 27 Then the other sons of Iaakob came upon the dead and despoiled the city, because they had defiled their sister. 28 They took their sheep, their bees, their donkeys and all that was in the city and in the fields. 29 They also transported the captives and made all their possessions, their children, their wives, and everything in the houses, disappear. 30 Then Iaakob said to Simeon and Leui, "You have put me to the hardship and made me to be weighed among the inhabitants of the land, both among the Canaanites and the Perizz- ites, and since I am few in number, they will gather against me and kill me, and so I and my house will be destroyed." 31 They answered, "Should he mistreat our sister as a whore?

CHAPTER 35

1 Then God said to Iaakob, "Arise, go to Beth-el, dwell there and build there an altar to God, who had appeared to you when you were fleeing from Esau your brother." 2 Then Iaakob said to his family and to all who were with him, "Get out of the way of the foreign gods that are among you, put yourselves in order and change your garments: 3 For we will get up and go to Bet-el, and there I will make an altar to God, who has heard me in the day of my tribulation and has been with me in the way that I have walked." 4 Then they handed over to Iaakob all the foreign gods that they had in their hands and all their earrings that were in their ears, and Iaakob hid them under a high place that was near Shechem. 5 Then they went on their journey, and the fear of God was on the cities around them, so that they did not follow the sons of Iaakob. 6 Then Iaakob came to Luz, which is in the land of Canaan (the same is Beth-El), together with all the people who were with him. 7 There he built an altar and called the place "God of Beth-El," because there God had appeared to him when he had fled from his brother. 8 Then Deborah Rebekah's body died and was buried under Beth-el, under an ark; and he called this place Allon Bachuth. 9 Then God appeared to Iaakob after he came out of Padan Aram, and blessed him. 10 Moreover God said to him, "Your name is Iaakob; your name shall no longer be called Iaakob, but Israel; and he called him Israel." 11 Then God said to him, "I am God all-sufficient; I will grow and multiply. From you shall be born a nation and a multitude of nations, and from your descendants shall come forth kings. 12 Moreover I will give you the land that I gave to Abraham and Izhak, and to your descen- dants after you I will give that land." 13 So God went up to him to the place where he had spoken to him.14 And Iaakob set up a pillar in the place where he had spoken to him, a pil- lar of stone, and made water to drink from it; he also made oil to drink from it. 15 Iaakob called the place where God spoke with him Beth-el. 16 Then they departed from Beth- el, and when it was about half a day's journey to Ephrath, Rahel set out, and on the way he felt himself in distress. 17 As she was in labor, the midwife said to her, "Do not be afraid, for you will also have this child." 18 As she was about to give birth to the Spirit (for she died), she called him Ben-oni, but his father called him Benjamin. 19 So Rahel died and was buried on the street of Ephratah, which is Bethlehem. 20 And Iaakob set up a pillar over her tomb: This is the pillar of Rahel's tomb to this day." 21 Then Israel advanced and pitched his tent beyond Migdal-eder. 22 When Israel had set- tled there, Reuben went and lay with Bilha, his father's concubine, and came to the shore of Israel. Iaakob had two sons. 23 The sons of Leah: Reuben, the firstborn of Iaakob, Sim- eon, Leui, Judah, Issachar, and Zebulun. 24 Sons of Rahel: Ioseph and Benjamin. 25 Sons of Bilhah, Rahel's mother: Dan and Naphta- li. 26 Sons of Zilpah: Maid of Leah: Gad and Asher. These are the sons of Iaakob who were borne to him in Padan Aram. 27 Then Iaakob came to Izhak his father to Mamre, a city of Arbah; this is Hebron, where Abraham and Izhak were strangers. 28 The days of Izhak were a hundred and forty-five years. 29 And Izhak expired, and died, and was gathered to his people, being old and full of years; and his sons Esau and Iaakob buried him.

CHAPTER 36

1 These are the generations of Esau, who is Edom. 2 And Esau took his wives from the daughters of Canaan: Ada, daughter of Elon, a Hittite, and Aholibama, daughter of Ana, daughter of Zibeon, a Hittite, 3 And he took Basemath, daughter of Ishmael, sister of Ne- baioth. 4 Ada gave birth to Esau Eliphaz, and Basemath gave birth to Reuel. 5 Aholibamah also bore Ieush, Iaalam and Korah; these are the sons of Esau who were borne to him in the land of Canaan. 6 So Esau took his pos- sessions, his sons, his daughters, all the souls of his house, his flocks, all his

livestock, and all his possessions that he had procured in the land of Canaan, and went to another land to his brother Iaakob. 7 For their wealth was so great that they could not dwell together, and the land, where they were strangers, could not receive them because of their flocks. 8 Therefore Esau dwelt in Mount Seir; this Esau is Edom. 9 These are the generations of Esau, the father of Edom, on Mount Seir. 10 These are the names of Esau's sons, Eliphaz the son of Adah, Esau's wife, and Reuel the son of Bashemath, Esau's wife. 11 The sons of Elip- haz were Teman, Omar, Zephus, Gatham and Kenaz. 12 Timnah was a concubine of Eliphaz the son of Eliphaz, and bore to Eliphaz Amalek; these are the sons of Adah the wife of Eliphaz. 13 These are the sons of Reuel: Na- hath, Zerah, Shammah, and Mizzah; these were the sons of Bashemath the wife of Esau. 14 These are the sons of Aholibamah, daugh- ter of Anah, wife of Zibeon Esaus, who bore Esau Ieush, Iaalam and Korah. 15 These were the dukes of the sons of Esau: the sons of Elip- haz, the first born of Esau: duke Teman, duke Omar, duke Zephus, duke Kenaz, 16 Duke Korah, Duke Gatham, Duke Amalek; these are the dukes born of Eliphaz in the land of Edom; these were the sons of Adah. 17 These are the sons of Reuel the son of Esaus: Duke Nahath, Duke Zerah, Duke Shammah, Duke Mizzah; these are the dukes that came from Reuel in the land of Edom; these are the sons of Bashe- math Esaus' wife. 18 These also are the sons of Aholibamah, wife of Esaus: Duke Ieush, Duke Iaalam, Duke Korah; these dukes came from Aholibamah, daughter of Anah, wife of Esaus. 19 These are the sons of Esau, and these are their dukes: this Esau is Edom. 20 These are the sons of Seir the Orite, who dwelt in the land before: Lotan, Shobal, Zibeon, and Anah. 21 Dishon, Ezer, and Dishan: these are the dukes of the Horites, the sons of Seir in the land of Edom. 22 The sons of Lotan were Hori and Hemam, and Lotan's sister was Timna. 23 The sons of Shobal were these: Aluan, Mana- hath, Ebal, Shepho and Onam. 24 These were the sons of Zibeon: Aiah and Anah; the latter was Anah who found mules in the wilderness, while she fed her father Zibeon's donkeys. 25 Anah's sons were these: Dishon and Aholi- bamah, daughter of Anah. 26 These also were the sons of Dishan: Hemdan, Eshban, Ithran and Cheran. 27 The sons of Ezer are these: Bil- han, Zaauan and Akan. 28 The sons of Dishan are these: Vz and Aran. 29 These are the dukes of the Goldsmiths: Lotan, Shobal, Zibeon and Ana, 30 Duke Dishon, Duke Ezer, Duke Dis- han: these are the dukes of the Goldsmiths, according to their dukedoms in the land of Seir. 31 These are the kings that reigned in the land of Edom, before any king reigned among the children of Israel. 32 Then Bela the son of Beor reigned in Edom, and the name of his city was Dinhabah. 33 When Bela died, Iobab the son of Zerah of Bozra reigned in his dwell- ing place. 34 When Iobab also died, Husham, of the land of Temani, reigned in his place. 35 After the death of Husham, Hadad the son of Bedad, who had defeated Midian in the camp of Moab, reigned in his stead, and the name of his city was Auith. 36 When Hadad was dead, Samlah, of Masrekah, reigned in his kingdom. 37 When Samlah died, Shaul, of Rehoboth, by the river, reigned in his house. 38 When Shaul died, Baal-Hanan, son of Ach- bor, reigned in his house. 39 After the death of Baal-Hanan, son of Achbor, Hadad reigned in his stead, and his city was called Pau; the name of his bride was Mehetabel, daughter of Matred, daughter of Mezahab. 40 These are the names of the dukes of Esau according to their families, their places, and their names: Duke Timnah, Duke Aluah, Duke Ietheth, 41 Duke Aholibamah, Duke Elah, Duke Pinon, 42 Duke Kenaz, Duke Teman, Duke Mibzar,

43 the duke Magdiel, the duke Iram: these are the dukes of Edom, according to their abodes, in the territory of their inheritance. This Esau is the father of Edom.

CHAPTER 37

1 Now Iaakob dwelt in the land where his father was a stranger, in the land of Canaan. 2 These are the generations of Iaakob, when Ioseph was seventy years old; he kept cattle with his brothers, and the child was with the sons of Bilhah and with the sons of Zilpah, his paternal wives. Ioseph brought their father their statement. 3 Israel valued Ioseph more than all his sons, for he begat him in his old age and made him a coat of many colors. 4 When his brothers learned that their father loved him more than all his brothers, they hated him and could not speak peacefully to him. 5 Ioseph dreamed a dream and told it to his brothers, who hated him even more. 6 He said to them, "Listen, please, to this dream I had. 7 Behold, we were tying up the sheep in the middle of the field; and behold, my sheep got up and stood, and behold, your sheep came around and paid attention to my sheep. 8 Then his brothers said to him, "What will you do, will you reign over Vs. and rule Vs. or will you have total dominion over Vs.?" And they hated him even more, because of his dreams and his words. 9 Then he dreamed another dream, and told it to his brothers, and said, "Behold, I had another dream, and behold, the sun and the moon and the other stars did honor to me." 10 Then he told it to his father and his brothers, and his father rebuked him and said, "What is this dream that you have had? Should I and your moth- er and brothers come and lay on the ground before you?" 11 His brothers questioned him, but his father noted the speech. 12 Then his brothers went to guard the sheep of their fa- thers in Shechem. 13 Israel said to Iosef, "Are not your brothers in Shechem? Come and I will send you to them." 14 He answered him, "They are here." Then he said to him, "Go and see if your brothers are well and if the flocks are prospering, and bring me news." So he sent him from the valley of Hebron, and he came to Shechem. 15 Then a man found him: behold, he was wandering in the field, and the man asked him, "What do you seek?" 16 He answered, "I see my brothers; tell me, I pray you, where they keep the sheep." 17 The man answered, "They have departed from here, for I heard them say, 'Let us go to Dothan.'" So Ioseph went after his brothers and found them in Dothan. 18 When they saw him far away, before he reached them, they conspired against him to kill him. 19 For they said to one another, "Behold, this dreamer comes. 20 Come therefore, kill him and cast him into some pit, and we will say, 'An evil beast has killed him'; then we will see what will come of his dreams." 21 But when Reuben heard this, he took him out of their hands and said, "Do not kill him." 22 And Reuben said to them, "Shed not blood, but cast him into this pit which is in the wilderness, and put no hand in it." So he said, to release him from their hands and return him to his father again. 23 When Ioseph had come to his brothers, they stripped Ioseph of his cloak, the colorful cloak that he had on. 24 They took him and threw him into a pit; the pit was empty, without wa- ter. 25 Then they sat them down to eat bread; and they lifted up their eyes and looked, and behold, there came a company of Ishmeelites from Gilead, with their camels laden with spices and balm and myrrh, and they were about to take them to Egypt. 26 Then Iudah said to his brothers, "What does it matter if we kill our brother, even if we keep his blood a secret? 27 Come, sell him to the Ishmaelites,

and do not let our hands rest on him, for he is our brother and our flesh"; and his broth- ers obeyed. 28 Then the Midianite marchers passed by, went away, pulled Iosef out of the pit, and sold Iosef to the Ishmaelites for twenty pieces of silver, which they took Iosef to Egypt. 29 Then Reuben went back to the pit and saw that Ioseph was not in the pit; so he tore his clothes, 30 and returned to his brothers and said, "The child is not there, and I, where shall I go?" 31 And they took Ioseph's cloak, and killed a kid goat, and dipped the cloak in the blood. 32 So they sent that col- orful cloak, brought it to the father, and said to him, "This we have found; see now wheth- er it is your son's cloak or not." 33 He noticed it and said, "It is my son's cloak; an evil beast has killed him; Ioseph is surely torn to pieces." 34 Then Iaakob tore his clothes, put sackcloth around his loins, and wept long for his son. 35 Then all his sons and all his daughters rose up to comfort him, but he would not be comfort- ed and said, "Surely I will go to the grave and mourn for my son"; so his father wept for him. 36 Then the Midianites left him in Egypt with Potiphar, a eunuch of Pharaoh and his chief steward.

CHAPTER 38

1 At that time, Iudah departed from his brothers and went to a man named Hirah, an Adullamite. 2 Iudah saw there the daughter of a man named Suah, a Canaanite; he took her as his wife and went in to her. 3 She conceived and bore a son, whom she named Er. 4 Then she conceived again and bore a son, whom she named Onan. 5 And she again bore a son, whom she named Shelah; and Iudah was in Chezib when she bore him. 6 Then Iudah took Er his firstborn son to wife, whose name was Tamar. 7 Er, Iudah's firstborn, was evil in the eyes of the LORD; therefore the LORD killed him. 8 Then Judah said to Onan, "Go to your brother's wife, make yourself a kinsman to her, and beget an offspring for your brother." 9 Onan knew that the seed would not be his; therefore, when he went to his brother's wife, he poured it out on the ground, lest he should give a seed to his brother. 10 And in the eyes of the LORD it was an evil thing that he had done; therefore he killed him also. 11 Then Iudah said to Tamar, his daughter, in lawe, "Remain a widow in your father's house, un- til Scelah, my son, grows up" (for he thought thus, "Or he will die like his brothers"). So Tamar went to dwell in her father's house. 12 Afterwards the daughter of Shuah, Iudah's wife, also died. Then Iudah, leaving mourn- ing, went to his shepherds in Timna, he and his neighbor Hirah, the Adullamite. 13 It was said to Tamar, "Behold, your father, in peace, goes to Timna to shear his sheep." 14 Then she took off her widow's garments, and clothed herself with a cloth, and wrapped herself about herself, and slept in Pethah-enaim, which is on the road to Timna, because she knew that Scelah had grown up, and that she had not been given to him as a wife. 15 When Iudah saw her, he judged her to be a harlot, because her face was covered. 16 He turned to her and said, "Come, please let me lie with you" (for he did not know that she was his daughter in marriage). And she answered, "What will you give me to lie with me? 17 Then he said, "I will send you a kid from the flock." And she answered, "Well, if you will give me a pledge, as long as you send it to me." 18 Then he said, "What is the pledge that I will give you?" And she answered, "Your seal and your cloak and your staff that you have in your hand." So he gave it to her and lay down be- side her, and she had a son by him. 19 Then she got up and went and took off her

sail and put on her widow's clothes. 20 Then Iudah sent a kid of goat by the hand of his neighbor, the Adullamite, to receive the pledge from the woman's hand, but he did not find her. 21 Then the men of that place asked, "Where is the harlot that stood in Enaim by the way?" And they answered, "There is no prostitute here." 22 He went again to Iudah and said, "I cannot find her," and the men of the place also said, "There was no prostitute." 23 Then Iudah said, "Let me bring him to her, that we may not be ashamed; behold, I have sent this kid and you have not found it." 24 After three months, one said to Judah, "Tamar, your daughter-in-law, has prostituted herself, and behold, after she has prostituted herself, she has had a great number of children." Then Judah said, "Bring her here and have her burned." 25 And when she was brought home, she sent word to her father-in-law, "By that man, because of whom these things have happened, I am with child"; and she also said, "Look, I pray thee, whose are these things, the dress, the cloak, and the staff." 26 Then Iudah knew them and said, "She is more righteous than I, for she has done this because I did not give her to Shesh, my son." So he no longer lay with her. 27 Now when the time came that she should be dis- appointed, behold, in her womb were twins. 28 When the woman was in labor, the one stretched out his hand; the midwife took and tied a red braid around his hand, saying, "This one came out first." 29 But when he withdrew his hand again, behold, his brother came out, and the midwife said, "How have you broken the breach about you?" 30 Then his brother came out who had the red braid on his hand, and his name was called Zarah.

CHAPTER 39

1 Now Ioseph was led into Egypt; and Po- tiphar, an Eunuch of the Pharaohs (and his chief steward, an Egyptian), bought him at the hands of the Ishmeelites, who had led him there. 2 The LORD was with Ioseph, who prospered and stayed in the house of his mas- ter, the Egyptian. 3 His master knew that the LORD was with him, and that the LORD pros- pered all that he did in his hands. 4 So Ioseph stood well before him and ministered to him; he made him head of his house and put all that he had into his hand. 5 Since he had made him head of his house and of all that he possessed, the LORD blessed the house of the Egyptians in favor of Ioseph; and the blessing of the LORD was on all that he had in the house and in the fields. 6 Therefore Ioseph left in his hands all that he had and was not satisfied with anything that he had with him except the bread that he ate. And Ioseph was a proud and well-fed person. 7 After these things, the wife of his masters cast her eyes upon Ioseph and said to him, "Come with me." 8 But he refused and said to his masters' wife, "Behold, my master does not know what he has in the house with me, but he has en- trusted everything he has to my hand. 9 There is no greater man in this house than I; and he has withheld nothing from me, but only you, because you are his wife; how then can I do this great wickedness and sin against God? 10 Although she spoke from day to day to Ioseph, he paid no heed to her, and would not stay with her or be in her company. 11 Then one certain day Ioseph came into the house to attend to his business, and there was no man of the house in the house: 12 Then she seized him by the robe, saying, "Sleep with me"; but he, having left the robe in her hand, fled and let him out. 13 When she saw that he had left his robe in her hand and had run away, 14 she called the men of her house and said to them, "Behold, he brought in

a Jew to mock me; he came to me to sleep with me, but I cried with a loud voice." 15 When he heard that I raised my voice and wept, he left his robe with me, fled, and carried it away. 16 Then she spread her robe beside her, until her lord returned home. 17 Then she told him these words, saying, "The servant of Hebrew, whom you brought with you, came in to me to mock me." 18 But when I raised my voice and cried out, he left his robe with me and ran away. 19 When his master heard his wife's words, which she re- lated to him, saying, "Your servant has treat- ed me in this way, his anger was kindled." 20 And Ioseph's master took him and put him in prison, in the place where the captives of kings were shut up; and there he remained in prison. 21 But the LORD was with Ioseph, and showed him mercy, and made him well in the eyes of the master of the prison. 22 And the keeper of the prison committed all the pris- oners who were in the prison to Ioseph, and what they did there, he did. 23 And the keeper of the prison did not mind anything that was in his hand, for the LORD was with him; for whatever he did, the LORD prospered him.

CHAPTER 40

1 After these things, the butler of the king of Egypt and his baker offended their lord, the king of Egypt. 2 Pharaoh became angry against his two officers, against the butler and the baker. 3 Therefore he had them locked up in the house of his chief steward, in the pris- on and in the place where Ioseph was bound. 4 The chief steward put Ioseph in charge of guarding them, and he kept them in check; and they remained at war for some time. 5 And they both dreamed a dream, each his dream in one night, each according to the interpre- tation of his dream, both the butler and the baker of the king of Egypt, who were shut up in the prison. 6 When Ioseph came in to them in the morning and looked at them, behold they were sad. 7 He asked Pharaoh's officers who were with him in his masters' war, "Why are you so sad today? 8 Those answered him, "We have dreamed a dream, and there is no one to interpret it." Then Ioseph said to them, "Are these not interpretations of God? Tell me now." 9 Then the chief butler told his dream to Ioseph and said to him, "In my dream, be- hold, there was a vine before me, 10 The vine had three branches, and when it sprouted, its flow came forth, and the clusters of grapes ripened. 11 And I had Pharaoh's cup in my hand, and I took the grapes, and squeezed them into Pharaoh's cup, and gave the cup into Pharaoh's hand. 12 Then Ioseph said to him, "This is the interpretation: The three breaks are three days. 13 Within three days Pharaoh shall lift up your head, and he shall give you back your charge, and you shall give Pharaoh's cup into his hand as you once did, when you were his steward. 14 But remember me, when thou art in good condition, and, I pray thee, give me grace, and make mention of me to Pharaoh, that he may bring me out of this house. 15 For I have been carried away for theft from the land of the Hebrews, and even here I have done nothing for which they should put me in prison." 16 When the chief baker saw that the interpretation was good, he said to Ioseph, "It also occurred to me that I had three white baskets on my head." 17 In the highest basket were meats of all kinds cooked for Pharaoh, and the birds ate them from the basket on my head." 18 Then Ioseph answered and said, "This is his interpretation: The three baskets are three days: 19 Within three days Pharaoh shall take off your head, and hang you on a tree, and the birds shall eat your flesh." 20 And on the third day, which was Pharaoh's birthday, he

made a feast to all his servants, and among his servants he lifted up the head of the chief butler and the head of the chief baker. 21 And he returned the chief butler to his butler, who delivered the cup into Pharaoh's hand, 22 But he hanged the chief baker, as Ioseph had interpreted to them. 23 Nevertheless the chief butler did not remem- ber Ioseph, but forgot him.

CHAPTER 41

1 Two years later Pharaoh also dreamed, and behold, he stood by a merry-go-round, 2 And, behold, out of the mound came some fine and fat cattle, feeding in a pool: 3 And, behold, af- ter they came out of the river, there came forth two other cattle, all beautiful and fat, which stood beside the other cattle on the bank of the river. 4 The cattle with light and lean meat ate the healthy and strong cattle; so Pharaoh woke up. 5 Then he fell asleep and dreamed for the second time; and, behold, ten ears of rough horn on one stall, of good quality. 6 And, behold, ten thin heads of horn, swept by the east wind, went out behind them: 7 The thin ears clashed with the other full and glow- ing ears. Then Pharaoh awoke, and, behold, it was a great darkness. 8 When morning came, his spirit was troubled; therefore he sent for all the soothsayers of Egypt and all the wise men, and Pharaoh told them his dreams; but no one could interpret them to Pharaoh. 9 Then the chief steward spoke to Pharaoh, saying, "Today I remember my faults." 10 Pharaoh, angry with his servants, put me in prison in the house of the chief steward, both I and the chief baker. 11 In one night we dreamed a dream, both he and I; we dreamed each man according to the interpretation of his dream. 12 There was with us a young man, a Hebrew, servant of the chief steward, who, when we told him, declared to us our dreams, and to each man declared his dream. 13 And as he declared to Warsaw, so it came to pass; for he returned me my charge and hanged him. 14 Then Pharaoh sent for Ioseph, and they brought him out of prison in haste; and he shod him, and chained his wages, and came to Pharaoh. 15 Then Pharaoh said to Ioseph, "I have dreamed a dream and no one can inter- pret it, and I have heard of you that when you hear a dream you can interpret it." 16 Ioseph answered Pharaoh, saying, "Without me God will answer for Pharaoh's riches." 17 Then Pha- raoh said to Ioseph, "In my dream, behold, I stood by the riverbank: 18 And behold, out of the mound came ten fat and healthy cattle, which fed in the greenhouse. 19 But behold, after them came forth two other cattle, poor, very fat and lean: I never saw the like in all the land of Egypt, for they were elated. 20 And the lean and euilphagous leaders ate the first ten fat leaders. 21 And when they had eaten them, it was not clear that they had eaten them, but they were still euilfat as at the be- ginning; so I awoke. 22 And I awoke in my sleep, and behold, out of a stall came forth two ears, full and firm. 23 And behold, two more ears sprang up behind them, withered, thin, and struck with the east wind. 24 And the thin ears damaged the other good ears. Now I have spoken to the soothsayers, and no one has told me anything." 25 Then Ioseph an- swered Pharaoh, "Pharaoh's two dreams are one. God has shown Pharaoh what he is go- ing to do. 26 The ten good heads of cattle are ten years and the ten good ears are ten years; this is one name. 27 Likewise, the ten lean and euphoric cattle that came forth after them are ten years; and the ten empty ears, swept by the east wind, are ten years of famine. 28 This is what I told Pharaoh, that God showed Pha- raoh what he is going to do. 29 Behold, there will come some

years of great plenty in all the land of Egypt. 30 After them will arise two more years of famine, so that all the abundance will be forgotten in the land of Egypt, and famine will consume the land: 31 No more abundance shall be known in the land be- cause of this famine that shall come after, for it shall be very great. 32 Therefore sorrow was doubled to Pharaoh the second time, because the thing is established by God, and God has- tens to accomplish it. 33 Now therefore Pha- raoh seek an intelligent and wise man and put him out of the land of Egypt. 34 Let Pharaoh set up officers for the land and take the fifth part of the land of Egypt in the ten abundant years. 35 They shall also gather all the food of these good years that are to come, and they shall put under Pharaoh's hand of the horn for food, in the cities, and they shall keep it. 36 So the food shall be for the protection of the land, against the ten years of famine that shall come upon the land of Egypt, lest the land perish by famine." 37 This pleased Pharaoh and all his servants. 38 Then Pharaoh said to his servants, "Can we find a man like this, in whom is the Spirit of God?" 39 Pharaoh said to Ioseph, "As much as God has shown you all this, there is no man as intelligent or as wise as you. 40 You will be outside my house, and at your word all my people will be armed; only on the king's throne will I be near you. 41 Moreover Pharaoh said to Ioseph, "Behold, I have set you over all the land of Egypt." 42 Pharaoh took the ring off his hand and put it on Ioseph's hand, clothed him in fine linen garments and put a gold necklace around his neck. 43 Then he set him on the best basket he had, one of those named after him; and they cried out before him, "Abrech," and set him over all the land of Egypt. 44 Then Pharaoh said to Ioseph, "I am Pharaoh, and without you no one shall lift up his hand or his foot in all the land of Egypt." 45 Pharaoh called Ioseph by the name of Zaphnath-paaneah and gave him Asenath, daughter of Poti-pherah, prince of On, as his wife. Ioseph then retired to the land of Egypt. 46 And Ioseph was thirty years old when he stood before Pharaoh, king of Egypt; and Ioseph departed from the pres- ence of Pharaoh, and went through all the land of Egypt. 47 In those ten abundant years, the land brought with it plenty of provisions. 48 And he gathered all the food of those ten abundant years that were in the land of Egypt, and made it available in the cities; and the food of the fields, which was round about every city, he made available in them. 49 So Iosef gathered grain, like the sand of the sea, in an inordinate quantity, until he left the number of it, for it was without number. 50 To Iosef were born two sons (before the years of famine came), whom Asenath, daughter of Poti-pherah, prince of On, bore him. 51 Iosef called the first born by the name of Manasseh, for God, he said, has made me forget all my toil and all the houses of my fathers. 52 He also called the second by the name of Ephraim: for God, said he, hath made me fruitful in the land of my affliction." 53 Thus ended the ten years of plenty in the land of Egypt. 54 Then began the ten years of famine, as Ioseph had said; and the famine was in all countries, but in all the land of Egypt there was bread. 55 Eventually all the land of Egypt was hun- gry, and the people asked Pharaoh for bread. And Pharaoh said to all the Egyptians, "Go to Ioseph; what he will tell you, do." 56 And when the famine came upon the whole land, Ioseph opened all the places where there were stocks and sold them to the Egyptians, because the famine was getting worse in the land of Egypt. 57 All the countries came to Egypt to get grain from Iosef, because the famine was severe throughout the land.

CHAPTER 42

1 Then Iaakob saw that there was food in Egypt, and he said to his sons, "Why do you fasten yourselves on one another?" 2 And he said, "Behold, I have heard that there is food in Egypt: go there and get food, that we may live and not die." 3 So Joseph's ten brothers went and got food from the Egyptians. 4 But Benjamin, Ioseph's brother, did not want Iaakob to send him with his brothers, for he said, "Or death shall come upon him." 5 And the children of Israel came and sought food among those who came, for there was fam- ine in the land of Canaan. 6 Now Ioseph was the governor of the land, who addressed all the people of the land; then Ioseph's brothers came and prostrated themselves before him. 7 And when Ioseph saw his brethren, and knew them, he made himself close to them, and spoke to them sharply, and said to them, "Where are you from? Who answered, "From the land of Canaan, to live." 8 (Now Ioseph knew his brothers, but they did not know him). 9 Ioseph remembered the dreams he had had about them) and said to them, "You are spies and have come to see the weakness of the land." 10 But they answered him, "No, my lord, but they have come to make the life of your servants. 11 We are all sons of one man; we speak truthfully, and your servants are not spies." 12 But he said to them, "No, but you have come to see the weaknesses of the land." 13 They answered, "We, your servants, are two brothers, the sons of one man, in the land of Canaan; and behold, the younger is with our father today, and one is not there." 14 Then Ioseph said to them, "This is what I told you, that you are spies. 15 In this way you will be tested; for Pharaoh's life you will not leave, except when your youngest broth- er comes here. 16 Send one of you, that he may be your brother, and you shall be kept in prison, that your words may be tested, to see whether there is any truth in you, or wheth- er, for the life of Pharaoh, you are but spies." 17 So he put them in prison for three days. 18 On the third day Ioseph said to them, "Do this and lie, for I fear God. 19 If you are sin- cere men, let one of your brothers be shut up in your house-prison, and go, load food for the famine of your houses: 20 but bring your other brother to me, that your words may be tested and you may not die; and they did so. 21 And they said to one another, "We have indeed sinned against our brother, because we saw the distress of his mind when he pleaded with us, and we would not listen to him; therefore this trouble has come upon us." 22 Reuben answered them, "Did I not warn you, saying, 'Do not sin against the child, and you would not listen to him?' And behold, his blood is now required." 23 (And they did not notice that Ioseph had followed them, for he spoke to them through an interpreter). 24 Then he departed from them, wept, and turned again to them, and took Simeon in their midst, and bound him before their eyes. 25 Then Ioseph commanded them to fill their sacks with grain, to put each man's money in his sack, and to give them their lives for the journey; and so he did with them. 26 They laid down their lives on their donkeys and set out. 27 As one of them opened his sack to give his plank to his prouender in the year, he discovered his money, for behold, it was in the mouth of his sack. 28 Then he said to his brothers, "My money has been returned, for behold, it is still in my sack." And their hearts deceived them, and they were astonished and said one to an- other, "What is this that God has done to you? 29 Then they went to Iaakob their father in the land of Canaan, and told him all that had happened to them, saying, 30 That man, who is the ruler of the land, behaved rudely to you and put you in prison as spies from the land.

31 We answered him, "We are true men and are not spies. 32 We are two brothers, sons of our father; one is not here, and the other is today with our father in the land of Canaan." 33 Then the Lord of the county said to them, "In this way I will know whether you are true men: Leave one of your brothers with me, take food for the famine of your houses, and depart, 34 and bring your younger brother to me, that I may know that you are not spies, but true men; so I will deliver your brother to you, and you will occupy the land." 35 And as they emptied their sacks, behold, every man had a heap of money in his sack; and when they and their fathers saw the sacks of their money, they felt broken. 36 Then Iaakob their father said to them, "You have robbed me of my sons: Ioseph is not here, Simeon is not here, and you will take Benjamin; all these things are against me." 37 Then Reuben an- swered his father, "Kill my two sons if I do not bring him back to you; deliver him into my hands and I will bring him back to you." 38 But he said, "My son will not go down with you, for his brother is dead and he is left alone; if death strikes him by the way that you go, then you will carry my gray head with sor- row to the grave."

CHAPTER 43

1 Now there was a great famine in the land. 2 And when they had eaten the life they had brought from Egypt, their father said to them, "Turn again, and give some food." 3 Iudah an- swered him, "That man has accused another, saying, 'Do not see my face, if your brother is not with you. 4 If you want to send our broth- er with us, we will come down and feed you: 5 But if you will not send him, we will not come down; for the man said to you, "Do not look on my face, if your brother is not with you." 6 Israel said, "Why did you behave so badly to- ward me as to tell that man whether you still had a brother or not?" 7 They answered, "That man asked us frankly about ourselves and our relatives, saying, 'Is your father still a strang- er? Do you have a brother?' And we answered him according to these words: could we know for certain that he would say, 'Bring down your brother'?"8 Then Iudah said to Israel his father, "Send the boy with me, that we may arise and depart, and that we may live and not die, both we and you and our children. 9 I will take care of him; from my hand you will require him. If I do not bring him to you and present him to you, then the fault will be mine forever. 10 For if we had not made this journey, we would have returned for the sec- ond time. 11 Then their father Israel said to them, "If it is necessary for it to be so now, do this: take the best fruits of the earth in your vessels, and bring that man a gift, a little rose- mary and a little bone, spices and myrrh, nuts and almonds: 12 Take twice as much money in your hand, and the money that has been car- ried abroad in your sackcloth mouths; carry it still in your hand, lest it escape you. 13 Take your brother also, get up and go to the man again. 14 Almighty God will give you grace of that man, that he may deliver your other brother and Benjamin to you; but I will be robbed of my son, as I was robbed." 15 So the men took this gift, took twice as much money in hand with Benjamin, got up, went down to Egypt and stood before Iosef. 16 When Iosef saw Benjamin with them, he said to his atten- dant, "Take these men home, kill the food and prepare, for the men will eat with me at no man's house." 17 The man did as Ioseph had asked and took the men to Ioseph's house. 18 When the men were brought to Ioseph's house, they were frightened and said, "Be- cause of the money that had gone into our sacks the first time, we have been brought here, so that he may argue against you and lay some blame on us, to enslave you and our donkeys." 19 Therefore they went to the stew- ard of Ioseph and stood with him at the en- trance of his house. 20 And they said, "Oh syr, we came here secretly the first time to eat." 21 and when we came to an isle and opened our sacks, behold, every man's money was in the mouth of his sack, while our money was in full weight, but we brought it back into our hands. 22 Other money also we brought into our hands for food, but we cannot tell who put our money in our sacks." 23 Then the man said, "Peace be unto you, fear not: your God and the God of your father gave you that treasure in your sacks, I had your money"; and he brought Simeon out to them. 24 So the man led them into the house of Iosef, gave them water to wash their feet, and gave their donkeys a hand. 25 They prepared their gift against Iosef's coming (for they had heard that they would eat bread there). 26 When Iosef came home, they brought the gift they had in their hands into his house and pros- trated themselves on the ground before him. 27 He asked them about their prosperity and said, "Is your father, the old man you told me about, enjoying good health? Is he still alive?" 28 Those answered, "Your servant, our father, is in good health, he is still alive"; and they prostrated themselves and did obedience. 29 Then lifting up his eyes, he saw his brother Benjamin, the son of his mother, and said, "Is this your younger brother of whom you spoke to me?" And he said, "God be merciful to you, my son." 30 Then Ioseph hastened (for his af- fection was kindled toward his brother and he was looking for a place to weep) and went into his chamber and wept there. 31 Then he washed his face, went out, lingered, and said, "Prepare food." 32 They prepared for him, for them and for the Egyptians, who were eating with him, for them, because the Egyptians could not eat bread with the Hebrews, for that was an abomination to the Egyptians. 33 So they sat down before him: the elder according to his age and the younger according to his youth, and the men quarreled among them- selves. 34 And they took doses of wine before him and sent them to them; but the price of Benjamin was five times as great as that of all the others; and they became drunk and drank with him of the best wine.

CHAPTER 44

1 Then he commanded his attendant, "Fill the men's sacks with food, as much as they can carry, and put each man's money in the mouth of his sack. 2 And he put my cup, that is, the cup of silk, into the mouth of the youngest man's sack, and his money. And he did according to the order that Ioseph had given him. 3 In the morning the men were sent away, they and their donkeys. 4 When they came out of the city, not far off, Ioseph said to his attendant, "Vp, follow the men; and when you have reached them, say to them, 'Why have you rewarded good? 5 Is not this the cup in which my Lord drinks, and in which he does works and prophecies? You did well to do so." 6 When he had delivered them, he spoke these words to them. 7 They answered him, "Why does my lord say these words? God forbid that your servants should do such a thing." 8 Behold, the money that we found in the mouths of our sacks we brought back to you from the land of Canaan; how then could we steal from your lord's house silk or gold? 9 Whoever of your servants finds it, let him die, and we also shall be servants of my lord." 10 He answered, "Now, therefore, let it be done according to your words: he with whom he shall be found shall be my servant, and you shall

be blazoned." 11 Then each one lowered his bag to the ground, and each one opened his bag. 12 And he searched, beginning with the eldest and leaving the youngest, and the cup was found in Benjamin's bag. 13 Then they rent their garments, loaded each one his robe, and set out again for the city. 14 Then Iudah and his brothers came to the house of Iosef (for he was still there) and felicitated before him on the ground. 15 Then Iudah said to them, "What is this that you have done? Do you not know that a man like me can do and prophesy?" 16 Then Iudah said, "What shall we say to my lord, what shall we say, and how shall we justify ourselves? God hath found out the wickedness of thy servants; behold, we are servants of my lord, both we and he, by whom the cup was found." 17 But he answered, "God forbid that I should do so, but the man by whom the cup was found shall be my servant, and you go in peace to your father." 18 Then Iudah approached him and said, "O my lord, let your servant now speak a word in my lord's ears, and do not kindle your anger against your servant, for you are like Pharaoh." 19 My Lord asked his servants, "Do you have a father or a brother? 20 We answered my Lord, "We have an aged father and a young son whom he begat in his age; his brother is dead, and he alone is left of his mother, and his father re- grets him." 21 Now you said to your servants, "Bring him to me, that I may look upon him." 44:22 We answered my lord, "The child cannot depart from his father, for if he left his father, his father would die." 23 Then you said to your servants, "If your younger brother does not go down with you, do not look me in the face again." 24 When we came to your servant, our father, and reported to him what my lord had said, 25 our father said to us, "Go away again, for a little food." 26 Then we answered, "We cannot go down; but if our younger brother goes with you, then we will go down; for we cannot see the face of man, unless our young- er brother is with you." 27 Then thy servant my father said to Warsaw, Thou knowest that my wife hath borne me two sons, 28 And the one departed from me, and I said, "Surely he was torn in pieces, and I have not seen him since." 44:29 Now take this also away from me; if death takes it, you shall carry my gray head to the grave with sorrow. 30 Now therefore, when I come to your servant, my father, and the child is not with you (for his life depends on the life of the child) 31 when he sees that the child has not come, he will die; so your servants will carry the gray head of your ser- vant, our father, with sorrow to the grave. 32 When in doubt, your servant worried about the son at my father's side, and said, "If I do not bring him to you again, I will blame my father for it forever." 33 Now, therefore, please let your servant take care of the child, as my lord's servant, and let the child go with his brothers. 34 For how can I go to my father if the child is not with me, unless I want to see the evil that will befall my father?

Therefore do not be sad or grieved that you have sold me here, for God has sent me before you for your pro- tection. 6 For now two years of famine have passed through your land, and five years are behind you, with neither ear nor molesta- tion. 7 Therefore God has sent me before you to preserve your posterity in this country and to save you from a great disappointment. 8 It was not you who sent me here, but God, who made me the father of Pharaoh, the rul- er of all his house and master of all the land of Egypt. 9 Make haste, go to my father and say to him, "Thus says your son Ioseph: God has made me lord over all Egypt; come down to me, do not be late." 10 And thou shalt dwell in the land of Goshen, and thou shalt be near me, thou and thy sons, and thy sheep, and thy beasts, and all that thou hast. 11 I will feed you there also (for there are still five years of famine left), that you may not starve, you and your family and all that you have. 12 And be- hold, your eyes see, and the eyes of my broth- er Benjamin also, that my mouth speaks to you. 13 Therefore report to my father of all my honors in Egypt and of all that you have seen, and make haste and bring my father here." 14 Then he fell on the neck of his brother Ben- jamin and wept, and Benjamin wept on his neck. 15 Moreover he kissed all his brothers and wept over them; then his brothers talked with him. 16 And the news came to Pharaoh's house, and they said, "The brothers of Ioseph have arrived"; and this pleased Pharaoh and his servants very much. 17 Then Pharaoh said to Ioseph, "Tell your brothers, 'Do this, put up your beasts and leave, go to the land of Canaan, 18 take your father and your family members and come to me, and I will give you the best of the land of Egypt and you shall eat of the fat of the land. 19 And I command you, "Do this, take pieces from the land of Egypt for your sons and for your wives, and bring your father and come to me." 20 Take no heed of your stuff, for the best of all the land of Egypt is yours." 21 The children of Israel did so, and Ioseph gave them cachets according to Pharaoh's order; he also gave them life for the journey. 22 To all but Benjamin he gave a change of clothing; but to Benjamin he gave three hundred pieces of silk and five sutes of clothing. 23 Likewise he sent to his father ten asses laden with the best things of Egypt and ten asses laden with wheat, bread and food for his father on the way. 24 So he sent his brothers away, and they departed; and he said to them, "Do not stray by the way." 25 Then they departed from Egypt and came into the land of Canaan to Iaakob their father, 26 And they told him, "Jehoshaph still lives, and he also is a ruler over all the land of Egypt, and the heart of Jehoshaph failed, because he did not receive them." 27 They reported to him all the words of Ioseph that he had spoken; but when he saw the chariots that Ioseph had sent to carry him, the spirit of Iaakob their fa- ther was appeased. 28 Israel said, "I have had enough: Ioseph, my son, is still alive: I will go to see him before I die."

CHAPTER 45

1 Then Ioseph could not restrain himself be- fore all who stood by him, but cried out, "De- part from me all men." And there was no one with him as Ioseph turned to his brothers. 2 He wept and cried, so that the Egyptians heard; the house of Pharaoh also heard. 3 Then Ioseph said to his brothers, "I am Ioseph; does my father still live?" But his brothers could not answer him, for they were amazed at his presence. 4 Then Ioseph said to his brothers, "Come here, please, to me." And they drew near. And he said, "I am Ioseph your brother, whom you sold into Egypt. 5

CHAPTER 46

1 Then Israel set out on his journey with all that he had, came to Beer-sheba and offered a sacrifice to the God of his father Izhak. 2 God spoke to Israel in a night vision, saying, "Iaakob, Iaakob." Who answered, "I am here." 3 Then he said, "I am God, the God of your fa- ther; do not be afraid to go down to Egypt, for there I will make you a great nation. 4 I will go down with you into Egypt, and I will also lead you abroad, and Ioseph will put his hand on your eyes." 5 Then Iaakob rose up from Beer-sheba, and the sons of Israel brought Iaakob their father, their sons and their wives

in the wagons that Pharaoh had sent to car- ry him. 6 And they took their cattle and their possessions, which they had obtained in the land of Canaan, and came to Egypt, Iaakob and all his descendants with him, 7 his sons and his sons with him, his daughters and the daughters of his sons, and all his de- scendants whom he brought with him into Egypt. 8 These are the names of the sons of Israel who went into Egypt, namely, Iaakob and his sons: Reuben, the first son of Iaakob. 9 The sons of Reuben: Hanoch, Phallu, Hez- ron, and Carmi. 10 Simeon's sons: Iemuel, Iamin, Ohad, Iachin, Zohar and Shaul, son of a Canaanite. 11 Also the sons of Leui: Ger- shon, Kohath and Merari. 12 Also the sons of Iudah: Er, Onan, Shelah, Pharez and Zerah (but Er and Onan died in the land of Canaan). The sons of Pharez were Hezron and Hamul. 13 Also the sons of Issachar: Tola, Phuuah, Iob and Shimron. 14 The sons of Zebulun: Sered, Elon, and Shimron: Sered, Elon, and Iahleel. 15 These are the sons of Leah, whom she bore to Iaakob in Padan Aram, with her daughter Dinah. All the souls of her sons and daugh- ters were thirty-three. 16 Also the sons of Gad: Ziphion, Haggi, Shuni, Ezbon, Eri, Arodi, and Areli. 17 Also the sons of Asher: Iimna, Ishua, Isui, Beriah, and Sera, their sister. Sons of Beriah: Heber and Malchiel. 18 These are the sons of Zilpah, whom Laban gave to Leah, his daughter, and whom she bore to Iaakob, that is, sixty sons. 19 The sons of Rahel, the wife of Iaakob, were Ioseph and Benjamin. 20 By Ioseph, in the land of Egypt, were born Manasseh and Ephraim, whom Asenath, daughter of Potipherah, prince of On, bore him. 21 Also the sons of Benjamin: Belah, Be- cher, Ashbel, Gera, Naaman, Hey, Rosh, Mup- pim, Huppim, and Ard. 22 These are the sons of Rahel borne by Iaakob, fourteen persons in all. 23 Also the sons of Dan: Hushim. 24 Also the sons of Naphtali: Iahzeel, Guni, Iezer and Shillem. 25 These are the sons of Bilhah whom Laban gave to Rahel, his daughter, and whom she bore to Iaakob, seven sons in all. 26 All the sons who came with Iaakob to Egypt, and who came out of his bonds (besides the wives of Iaakob's sons) were three dozen and six in all. 27 Also the sons of Jehoshaph, who were born to him in Egypt, were two sisters; so all the sisters of the house of Iaakob who came into Egypt are seuentie. 28 And he sent Iudah before Ioseph to direct his way to Goshen, and they entered the land of Goshen. 29 Then Ioseph prepared his charet and went to Gos- hen to meet Israel his father; and he present- ed himself to him and stood on his neck, and wept on his neck for quite a while. 30 Israel said to Ioseph, "Now let me die, for I have seen your face and that you are still alive." 31 Then Ioseph said to his brothers and his father's house, "I will go and speak to Pharaoh and tell him, My brothers and my father's house, who were in the land of Canaan, have come to me, 32 the men are shepherds, and because they are shepherds, they have brought their sheep and their cattle and all that they have. 33 If Pharaoh calls you and asks, "What is your trade?" 34 then you shall say, "Your ser- vants are men who tend livestock, from our childhood until now, both we and our fathers, so that you may dwell in the land of Goshen, for every keeper of sheep is an abomination to the Egyptians."

CHAPTER 47

1 Then Ioseph came and spoke to Pharaoh and said to him, "My father, my brothers, their sheep, their livestock and all that they possess have gone out of the land of Canaan, and behold, they are in the land of Goshen." 2 Ioseph took a portion of his brothers, that is, five men, and presented them to Pharaoh. 3 Then Pharaoh said to his brothers, "What is your trade?" And they answered Pharaoh, "Your servants are cutters, both we and our fathers." 4 They said still more to Pharaoh, "We have come to starve your country, be- cause your servants have no pasture for their sheep, so severe is the famine in the land of Canaan. Therefore we beseech you to make your servants dwell in the land of Goshen." 5 Then Pharaoh spoke to Ioseph, saying, "Your father and your brothers have come to you. 6 The land of Egypt is before thee; make thy father and thy brothers dwell in the best place in the land; make them dwell in the land of Goshen; and if thou knowest that there are men of action among them, make them heads of my cattle." 7 Ioseph also brought in Iaakob, his father, and presented him to Pharaoh. Iaakob greeted Pharaoh. 8 Then Pharaoh said to Iaakob, "How old are you? 9 Iaakob answered Pharaoh, "All the time of my pilgrimage is a hundred and thirty years; the days of my life are few and everlasting, and I never referred to the years of my fathers' life, in the days of their pilgrimages." 10 Iaakob distanced himself from Pharaoh and depart- ed from Pharaoh's presence. 11 Ioseph set- tled his father and his brothers and brought them into possession of the land of Egypt, in the best part of the land, that is, in the land of Rameses, as Pharaoh had ordered. 12 And Ioseph fed his father and his brothers and all the house of his fathers with bread, even down to the young sons. 13 Now there was no bread in all the land, for the famine was very severe, so that the land of Egypt and the land of Canaan were hungry because of the fam- ine. 14 Then Ioseph collected all the money that was in the land of Egypt and in the land of Canaan for the grain they had bought, and Ioseph laid the money in Pharaoh's house. 15 When the money ran out in the land of Egypt and in the land of Canaan, all the Egyptians came to Ioseph and said to him, "Give us bread, why should we die before you? For our money has been spent." 16 Then Ioseph said, "Bring your cattle, and I will give you bread for your cattle, if your money has been spent." 17 So they brought their cattle to Iosef, and he gave them bread for their horses, for their flocks of sheep, for their herds of cattle, and for their donkeys; so he fed them bread for all their cattle that year. 18 But when the year ended, the next year they came to him and said, "We do not want to hide from my lord that because our money has been spent and my lord has the herds of cattle, there is noth- ing left in my lord's sight but our bodies and our land. 19 Why must we perish before you, both we and our land? If there were no bread for us and our land, we and our land would be good for Pharaoh; so give seed, that we may live and not perish, and that the land may not go to ruin." 20 So Ioseph bought all the land of Egypt for Pharaoh, for the Egyptians had sold every man his land because of the famine that had come upon them; so the land became Pharaoh's. 21 He moved the people to the cit- ies, from one part of Egypt to another. 22 Only the priests' land he did not buy, because the priests had an ordinance from Pharaoh and ate their ordinance that Pharaoh gave them; therefore they did not settle their land. 23 Then Ioseph said to the people, "Behold, today I have bought you and your land for Pharaoh; behold, here is seed for you; sow therefore the ground." 24 And of the increase you shall give the fifth part to Pharaoh, and four parts shall be yours for the sowing of the fields, for your food, for your houses, and for the food of your children." 25 Then they answered, "You have fulfilled our wishes; let them find favor before my Lord, and we will be Pharaoh's servants." 26 Then Iosef determined that until this day the land of Egypt was reserved for Pha- raoh for the fifth part, except the land of

the priests, which was not Pharaoh's. 27 And Isra- el dwelt in the land of Egypt, in the county of Goshen, and possessed his possessions there, and magnified and multiplied exceedingly. 28 Moreover, Iaakob remained in the land of Egypt seventy years, so that the whole age of Iaakob was one hundred forty-two years. 29 When the time came for Israel to die, he called his son Jehoshaph and said to him, "If I have now found favor in your eyes, put your hand now under my thigh and be merciful and true to me; please do not bury me in Egypt. 30 But when I have fallen asleep with my fathers, you shall bring me out of Egypt and bury me in their grave." And he answered, "I will do as you have said." 31 He said, "Swear to me." And he swore. And Israel worshiped toward the head of the bed.

CHAPTER 48

1 After this, one said to Ioseph, "Behold, your father is sick"; then he took his two sons, Manasseh and Ephraim, with him. 2 One also said to Iaakob, "Behold, your son Ioseph has come to you; Israel has taken his strength and sat on the bed." 3 Then Iaakob said to Ioseph, "Almighty God appeared to me in Luz in the land of Canaan and blessed me. 4 He said to me, "Behold, I will make you fruitful, I will multiply you, I will make you a numerous people, and I will give this land to your descendants after you as an everlasting possession. 5 Your two sons, Manasseh and Ephraim, who were born to you in the land of Egypt, before I came to you in Egypt, shall be mine, as Reuben and Simeon are mine. 6 But the seed which thou hast begotten after them shall be thine; they shall be called after the names of their brethren in their inheritance. 7 When I came from Padan, Rahel died on my hand in the land of Canaan, by the way, when it was only half a day's journey to Ephratah; and I buried her there, on the road to Ephra- tah: the same is Bet-Lem. 8 Then Israel saw the sons of Iosef and said, "Whose are these?" 9 Iosef answered his father, "They are my sons whom God has given me here." Then he said, "Please bring them to me, that I may bless them." 10 (for Israel's eyes were clouded with age, so that he could not see well). Then he brought them to him and kissed them and embraced them. 11 Israel said to Ioseph, "I did not think that I had seen your face; yet behold, God has also shown me your descendants." 12 Iosef removed them from his knees and low- ered himself to the ground. 13 Then Iosef took them both, Ephraim in his right hand toward Israel's left hand and Manasseh in his left hand toward Israel's right hand, and led them to himself. 14 And Israel stretched out his right hand and laid it on the head of Ephraim, who was the younger, and his left hand on the head of Manasseh (directing his hands pur- posefully), for Manasseh was the elder. 15 He also blessed Ioseph and said, "Bless you the God before whom my fathers Abraham and Izhak walked, the God who has nourished me all my life until now. 16 May the angel who has delivered me from all evil bless the chil- dren and cause my name and the name of my fathers Abraham and Izhak to be appointed over them, that they may grow up like fish in a multitude in the midst of the earth." 17 But when Ioseph saw that his father laid his right hand on Ephraim's head, he was sorry; and he stopped his father's hand to move it from Ephraim's head to Manasseh's. 18 Then Ioseph said to his father, "Not so, my father, for this is the elder; put your right hand on his head." 19 But his father refused, and said, "I know it well, my son, I know it well: he also shall be a people and shall be great; but his younger brother shall be greater than he,

and his seed shall be rich in nations." 20 And he blessed them that day, and said, "In thee shall Israel bless himself, and say, God make thee like Ephraim and like Manasseh." and he put Ephraim before Manasseh. 21 Then Israel said to Ioseph, "Behold, I die, and God will be with you and will bring you back to the land of your fathers. 22 Moreover, I have granted thee a portion of thy brethren, whom I snatched out of the hand of the Amorrean with my sword and with my spear.

CHAPTER 49

1 Then Iaakob called his sons and said, "Gather yourselves together, that I may tell you what will happen to you in the last days." 2 Gather yourselves together and listen, sons of Iaakob, and listen to Israel your father. 3 Reuben, my firstborn, you are my strength and the beginning of my power, the excellen- cy of dignity and the excellence of strength: 4 Thou wast light as water; thou shalt be no more excellent because thou wentest into the bed of thy fathers; then thou defiledst my bed, thy dignity is gone. 5 Simeon and Leui, brothers on earth, have in their dwellings the instruments of cruelty. 6 Let not my soul en- ter into their secret; let not my glory be de- filed by their assembly, for in their anger they have slain a man, and in their will they have dug a wall. 7 Cursed be their wrath, for it has been fierce, and their anger, for it has been cruel; I will destroy them in Iaakob and scat- ter them in Israel. 8 Thou Iudah, thy brethren shall praise thee; thy hand shall be in the neck of thine enemies; the sons of thy fathers shall bow down before thee. 9 Iudah, like a lion, you shall come out of the ear, my son. You will lie down and cower like a lion and like a lion- ess; who will make him react? 10 The scepter shall not come off Iudah, nor the law between his feet, until Sciloh comes, and the people are gathered to him. 11 He shall make his don- key's foot on the vine, and his donkey's blan- ket on the best vine; he shall wash his robe in wine, and his cloak in the blood of grapes. 12 His eyes shall be red with wine, and his teeth white with milk. 13 Zebulun shall dwell by the sea, and shall be a harbor for ships; his border shall be as far as Zidon. 14 Issachar shall be a strong plank, resting between two burdens: 15 He shall see that rest is good, and that the land is pleasant: he shall bow his shoulders to bear, and shall be subject to tribute. 16 Dan shall judge his people as one of the tribes of Israel. 17 Dan shall be a serpent for the road, an adder for the path, who shall overwhelm the horse and cause his rider to fall back. 18 O LORD, I have waited for your salvation. 19 Gad, a host of men shall smite him, but at the last he shall come. 20 As for Asher, his bread shall be fat, and he shall give pleasures for a king. 21 Naphtali will be a guide who will indulge in good words. 22 Ioseph shall be a fruitful branch, a fruitful branch by the side of the well; the little branches shall run upon the wall. 23 The archers attacked him, and shot at him, and hated him. 24 But his bow remained strong, and the hands of his arms were strengthened by the hands of the mighty God of Iaakob, whose feeder was appointed, by the stone of Israel, 25 And from the God of your father, who will help you, and from the Almighty, who will bless you with his bless- ings from without, with the blessings of the depths, which lie beneath, with the blessings of the ridges and of the woman. 26 The bless- ings of thy father shall be stronger than the blessings of my elders; even unto the end of the hills of the world shall be upon the head of Ioseph, and upon the top of the head of him that was separated from his brethren. 27 Benjamin shall rauin like a

wolf; in the morn- ing he shall worship, and in the evening he shall spit. 28 These are the two tribes of Israel, and so their father spoke to them and blessed them; each of them blessed him with a special blessing. 29 Then he charged them and said to them, "I am ready to be gathered to my people; bury me with my fathers in the quarry that is in the field of Ephron the Hittite." 30 in the quarry that is in the field of Machpelah, besides Mamre, in the land of Canaan; a quarry which Abraham bought with the field of Ephron the Hittite, to bury there. 31 There buried Abraham and Sarah his wife, there buried Izhak and Rebekah his wife, and there buried Leah. 32 The purchase of the field and the property therein was made by the sons of Heth. 33 So Iaakob stopped entrusting the task to his sons, and went out into the bed and left the ghost, and rejoined his people.

CHAPTER 50

1 Then Ioseph fell on his father's face, wept over him, and kissed him. 2 Then Ioseph commanded his servants the physicists to consume his father, and the physicists consumed Israel. 3 So fourteen days elapsed (so long were the days of those who had been interred), and the Egyptians beat him for seventy days. 4 When the days of his mourning were past, Iosef spoke to the house of Pharaoh, saying, "If now I have found evil in your eyes, speak, I pray you, in the ears of Pharaoh and say, 5 My father made me swear, saying, 'If I die, bury me in my grave which I have made for myself in the land of Canaan; let me therefore go, I pray you, to bury my fa- ther, and then I will return.'" 6 Then Pharaoh said, "Go and bury your father, as he made you swear." 7 So Ioseph went and buried his father, and with him all Pharaoh's servants, the elders of his house, and all the elders of the land of Egypt. 8 Likewise all the house of Ioseph, his brothers and the house of his fathers; only their sons and their sheep and their cattle remained in the land of Goshen. 9 With him went also the chariots and horse- men, and the company was very numerous. 10 And they came to Goren Atad, which is be- yond Iorden, and there they made a great and sorrowful lamentation; and he wept for his father ten days. 11 When the Canaanites, the inhabitants of the land, saw the mourning at Goren Atad, they said, "This is a great mourn- ing for the Egyptians; therefore his name was called Abel Mizraim, which is beyond Iorden." 12 So his sons did as he commanded them: 13 And his sons brought him into the land of Canaan, and buried him in the hollow of the field of Machpelah, which Abraham bought with the field, as a burial place, from Ephron the Hittite, besides Mamre. 14 Then Ioseph returned to Egypt, he and his brothers and all who went with him to bury his father. 15 When Ioseph's brothers saw that their father was dead, they said, "It may be that Ioseph will hate himself and pay again for all the evil we have done to him." 16 Therefore they sent word to Ioseph, "Your father, before he died, had given an order, 17 Thus you shall say to Ioseph, "Please forgive the sins of your broth- ers and their sins, for they have rewarded you with righteousness. And now, we pray you, forgive the guilt of the servants of the God of your fathers." Ioseph wept when they spoke to him. 18 His brothers also came to him and fell down before his face and said, "Behold, we are your servants." 19 To them Ioseph said, "Do not fear, for am I not under God? 20 When ye thought evil of me, God disposed it for good, that what hath happened this day might happen, and that many other peoples might know it. 21 Fear not therefore: I will feed you, you and your children." 22 So Ioseph dwelt in Egypt,

he and the house of his fathers; and Ioseph lived an hundred and ten years. 23 And Ioseph saw the sons of Ephraim until the third generation; also the sons of Machir the son of Manasseh were brought to the knees of Ioseph. 24 Then Ioseph said to his brothers, "I am ready to die; God will visit you and bring you out of this land, to the land that he swore to Abraham, to Izhak, and to Iaakob." 25 And Ioseph took another of the sons of Israel and said, "God will surely visit you, and you will carry away my bones." 26 So Ioseph died, at the age of a hundred and ten years; and they buried him and put him in a box in Egypt.

EXODUS

CHAPTER 1

1 These are the names of the children of Israel who came to Egypt (each man and his family came with Iaakob) 2 Reuben, Simeon, Leui, and Judah, 3 Issachar, Zebulun, and Benja- min, 4 Dan, Naphtali, Gad and Asher. 5 So all the descendants who came out of the loins of Iaakob were seuentie descendants: Ioseph was already in Egypt. 6 Now Ioseph died, to- gether with all his brothers and all that gener- ation. 7 And the children of Israel bore fruit, and increased in abundance, and multiplied, and were very numerous, so that the land was full of them. 8 Then a new king arose in Egypt, who did not know Ioseph. 9 He said to his people, "Behold, the people of the children of Israel are more numerous and stronger than we are. 10 Come on, let us work wisely with them, otherwise they will multiply, and it will come to pass that, in case of war, they will also go themselves to our enemies and fight against them and drive them out of the land." 11 Therefore they put out workmen out of them, that they might load them with bur- dens, and they built the cities of Pithom and Raamses for the treasures of Pharaoh. 12 But the more they annoyed them, the more they multiplied and magnified themselves; there- fore they raged against the children of Isra- el. 13 Therefore the Egyptians by their cruelty enslaved the children of Israel. 14 They made them weary of their lives with hard labor in clay, brick, and all the work in the fields, with all kinds of slavery which they imposed on them with great cruelty. 15 The king of Egypt commanded you halflings of the women of Hebrewe (one of whom was called Nishrah and the other Puah) 16 and said, "When you do the office of midwife to the women of the Hebrews and see them on their sides, if it is a son, you shall kill him; but if it is a daugh- ter, you shall let her live." 17 However, you Midianites feared God and did not do as the king of Egypt had commanded them, but pre- served the sons of men. 18 Then the king of Egypt called the midwives and said to them, "Why did you do this and preserve the men children? 19 The midwives answered Pha- raoh, "Because the women of Hebrew are not like the women of Egypt, for they are delicate and are disappointed as soon as the midwife reaches them." 20 Therefore God prospered the midwives, and the people multiplied and were very numerous. 21 Because the mid- wives feared God, he made them houses. 22 Then Pharaoh charged all his people, saying, "Every male child that has been delivered, throw him into the river, but reserve every male child for others."

CHAPTER 2

1 Then a man of the house of Leui took to wife a daughter of Leui, 2 And the wom- an gave birth and bore a son; and

when she saw that he was handsome, she hid him for three pennies. 3 But when she could hide him no longer, she took for him an ark of reeds, sprinkled it with ooze and pitch, laid the child in it, and placed it among the rushes by the banks of the river. 4 His sister stayed away, to see what would happen to him. 5 Then Pharaoh's daughter went down to wash it in the river, and her maidens walked beside the river; and when she saw the ark among the bulrushes, she sent her teacher to fetch it. 6 Then she opened it and saw that it was a child; and behold, the child wept; she had compas- sion on it and said, "This is one of the sons of Hebrews." 7 Then his sister said to Pharaoh's daughter, "Shall I go and get you a nurse of the Hebrew women to nurse the child?" 8 Pharaoh's daughter said to her, "Go." Then the maid went and called the mother of the child, 9 to whom Pharaoh's daughter said, "Take this child and suckle it for me, and I will reward you." Then the woman took the baby and nursed it. 10 Now the child grew, and she brought him to Pharaoh's daughter; he was like a son, and she named him Moses, because, she said, "I brought him up out of the water." 11 In those days, when Moses had grown up, he went to his brothers and looked at their burdens; he also saw an Egyptian striking a Hebrew, one of his brothers. 12 He looked around, and seeing no one, he killed the Egyptian and hid him in the sand. 13 On the second day he went out, and behold, two Hebrews were fighting; and he said to the one who had done the wrong, "Why do you strike your fellow?" 14 And he answered, "Who made you a man of authority and a judge outside of us? Do you think to kill me as you killed the Egyptian? Then Moses feared and said, "Surely this thing is known." 15 Now Pharaoh, knowing this fact, sought to kill Moses; there- fore Moses fled from Pharaoh and settled in the land of Midian, sitting by a well. 16 The priest of Midian had some daughters who came and drew water and filled troughs to water their fathers' sheep. 17 Then the shep- herds came and drove them out, but Moses stood up and defended them and watered their sheep. 18 When they came to Reuel their father, he said, "How is it that you have come so soon? 19 They answered, "A man from Egypt took the cattle out of the shepherds' hands, drew enough water, and watered the sheep." 20 Then he said to his daughters, "Where is he? Why have you abandoned him? Call him that he may eat bread." 21 Moses agreed to dwell with the man, who gave Moses Zip- porah, his daughter: 22 And she bore a son, whom he called Gershom, for he said, "I have been a stranger in a strange land." 23 Then, as time passed, the king of Egypt died, and the children of Israel sighed for slavery and wept; and their weeping for slavery reached God. 24 God heard their weeping and remembered his agreement with Abraham, Izhak and Iaa- kob. 25 So God looked upon the children of Israel and had respect for them.

take your shoes off your feet, for the place where you are standing is holy ground." 6 Moreover he said, "I am the God of your father, the God of Abraham, the God of Izhak and the God of Iaakob." Then Moses hid his face, for he was afraid to look at God. 7 Then the LORD said, "I have seen the troubles of my people who are in Egypt and I have heard their weeping because of their masters, for I know their sor- rows. 8 Therefore I have come down to deliver them out of the hand of the Egyptians and to bring them out of that land to a good and great land, to a land flowing with milk and honey, that is, to the place of the Canaanites, the Hittites, the Amorites, the Perizzites, the Hijuites, and the Jebusites. 9 And behold, the cry of the children of Israel has come to me, and I have also seen the oppression with which the Egyptians oppress them. 10 Come therefore, and I will send you to Pharaoh, that you may bring my people, the children of Israel, out of Egypt." 11 But Moses said to God, "Who am I to go to Pharaoh and bring the children of Israel out of Egypt?" 12 He answered, "Surely I will be with you; and this shall be for you the sign that I have sent you: after you have brought the people out of Egypt, you shall serve God on this mountain." 13 Then Moses said to God, "Behold, when I come to the children of Israel and say to them, 'The God of your fathers has sent me to you, if they say to me, "What is his name?" what shall I say to them?" 14 God answered Moses, "I am what I am." And he also said, "Thus you shall say to the children of Israel, I Am has sent me to you." 15 And God spoke again to Moses, "Thus you shall say to the children of Israel, The Lord God of your fathers, the God of Abraham, the God of Izhak, and the God of Iaakob, has sent me to you; this is my name forever, and this is my remembrance for all ages. 16 Go and gather the elders of Israel and say to them, "The Lord God of your fathers, the God of Abraham, Izhak and Iaakob ap- peared to me and said, 'I have remembered you and what was done to you in Egypt.'" 17 Therefore I said, "I will bring you out of the af- fliction of Egypt to the land of the Canaanites, the Hittites, the Amorites, the Perizzites, the Hiuites and the Jebusites, to a land flowing with milk and honey. 18 Then they shall obey your journey, and you and the elders of Israel shall go to the king of Egypt and say to him, "The LORD, God of the Hebrews, has met with us; therefore we beseech you to let us go three days' journey into the wilderness, that we may sacrifice to the LORD our God." 19 But I know that the king of Egypt will not let you go except by a strong hand. 20 Therefore I will stretch out my hand and strike Egypt with all my wonders that I will do in its center; after that he will let you go. 21 I will cause this peo- ple to be soiled by the Egyptians, so that when you go, you will not leave empty. 22 For every woman shall ask her neighbor and she who sojourns in her house for silken jewelry and gold jewelry and garments, and you shall put them on your sons and your daughters, and you shall fleece the Egyptians.

CHAPTER 3

1 When Moses guarded the flock of Iethro his father, priest of Midian, and led the flock to the back part of the wilderness and came to the mountain of God, Horeb, 2 Then the angel of the LORD appeared to him in a flame of fire from the midst of a bush; and he looked, and behold, the bush was burning with fire, and the bush was not consumed. 3 Moses said, "Now I will turn around and see this great sight, for the bush does not burn." 4 When the Lord heard that he had turned to see, God called to him from the middle of the bush and said, "Moses, Moses." And he answered, "I am here." 5 Then he said, "Do not come here,

CHAPTER 4

1 Then Moses answered, "But behold, they will not listen to me or heed my speech, for they will say, 'The Lord has not appeared to you.' 2 The Lord said to him, "What is that in your hand?" And he answered, "A rod." 3 Then he said, "Throw it on the ground." So he threw it on the ground and it turned into a serpent; and Moses fled from it. 4 Then the LORD said to Moses, "Put forth your hand and take it by the neck." So he put forth his hand and took it, and it turned into a rod in his hand. 5 Do this so that they may see that

the Lord God of their fathers, the God of Abraham, the God of Izhak and the God of Iaakob has appeared to you." 6 The LORD further said to him, "Now thrust your hand into your bosom." He thrust his hand into his bosom, and when he took it out again, behold, his hand was leprous as snow. 7 He said to him again, "Put your hand in your bosom again." Then he put his hand in her breast again and drew it out of her breast, and behold, it had become like her other flesh. 8 So it shall be, if they do not follow you and obey the word of the first sign, but follow themselves by the word of the second sign. 9 But if zhey do not abide by these two signs and do not obey your sign, then you shall take water from the river and sprinkle it on the dry land; so the water you take from the river will turn into blood on the dry land." 10 But Moses said to the LORD, "Oh, my LORD, I am not eloquent, nor have I ever been eloquent, nor am I yet eloquent since thou hast spoken to thy servant; but I am slow of speech and slow of language." 11 Then the LORD said to him, "Who gave man a mouth? Who created the domme, the deaf, the one who sees, or the blind? Am I not the Lord? 12 Therefore go now, and I will be with your mouth and teach you what you should say." 13 But he said, "Oh, my Lord, depart, I pray thee, by the hand of him to whom thou must depart." 14 Then the LORD became very angry with Moses and said, "Do I not know that Aaron, your brother, the Leuite, will speak himself? For it is true that he also comes here to meet you, and when he sees you, he will be glad in his heart." 15 Therefore you shall speak to him and put words in his mouth, and I will be with your mouth and with his mouth and teach you what you are to do. 16 He shall be your mouthpiece to the peo- ple, and he shall be as your mouth, and you shall be to him as God. 17 Moreover you shall take this rod in your hand, with which you shall do miracles." 18 Then Moses went and returned to Iethro, his father, in Los Angeles, and said to him, "Please let me go, go back to my brothers who are in Egypt and see if they are still alive." Then Iethro said to Moses, "Go in peace." 19 (For the LORD had said to Moses in Midian, "Go away, return to Egypt, for they are all dead who wanted to kill you.") 20 Then Moses took his wife and his children and put them on a plank and went back toward the land of Egypt, and Moses took the rod of God in his hand. 21 And the LORD said to Moses, "When you have entered and returned to Egypt, see that you perform before Pharaoh all the wonders that I have put in your hand; but I will harden his heart, and he will not let the people go. 22 Then thou shalt say unto Pharaoh, Thus saith the Lord, Israel is my son, my firstborn. 23 Therefore I say to you, Let my son go, that he may serve me; if you refuse to let him go, behold, I will kill your son, your firstborn." 24 While he was on the way, the LORD met him and would have killed him. 25 Then Zipporah took a sharp knife, cut off her son's foreskin, threw it at his feet and said, "You are indeed a bloody husband to me." 26 So she turned away from him. Then she said, "O bloodthirsty husband (because of circum- cision)." 27 Then the LORD said to Aaron, "Go meet Moses in the wilderness." And he went and met him on the mount of God and kissed him. 28 Then Moses reported to Aaron all the words of the Lord who had sent him and all the signs with which he had charged him. 29 So Moses and Aaron went and gathered to- gether all the elders of the children of Israel. 30 Aaron reported all the words the LORD had spoken to Moses and performed the miracles before the people, 31 And the people rejoiced, and when they heard that the Lord had visit- ed the children of Israel and had looked upon their tribulation, they prostrated themselves and worshiped.

CHAPTER 5

1 Then Moses and Aaron went and said to Pharaoh, "Thus says the LORD, God of Isra- el, Let my people go, that they may celebrate a feast for me in the wilderness." 2 Pharaoh said, "Who is the LORD that I should hear his message and let Israel go? I do not know the LORD, and I will not let Israel go." 3 They said, "We worship the God of the Hebrews; we beg you to let us go for three days in the wilder- ness and sacrifice to the LORD our God, if he will not bring the plague or the sword upon us." 4 Then the king of Egypt said to them, "Moses and Aaron, why do you cause the people to desist from their work? 5 Moreover Pharaoh said, "Behold, many people are now in the land, and you make them leave their burdens." 6 Therefore Pharaoh gave an order on the same day to the leaders of the people and their officers, saying, "Give your burdens to everyone, 7 You shall no longer give the people rope to make bricks (as in the past), but let them go and gather the rope them- selves: 8 However, let them have the amount of bricks they have made in the past, and do not diminish any of it, for they are idle and cry, 'Let us go and offer sacrifices to our God.' 9 Let the men work harder and make them work, paying no heed to vain words." 10 Then the leaders of the people and their officers went out and said to the people, "Thus says Pharaoh, 'I will give you no more strength. 11 Go on your own, get straw where you can find it, but nothing of your labor will be di- minished." 12 Then the people were scattered throughout the land of Egypt to gather stub- ble for straw. 13 The labor leaders rebuked them, saying, "Finish your daily work on each day's work, as you did when you had straw." 14 The officers of the children of Israel, whom Pharaoh's taskmasters had placed in their service, were beaten and asked, "Why did you not finish your brick work yesterday and to- day, as you did in the past? 15 Then the officers of the children of Israel came and cried out to Pharaoh, "Why do you treat your servants this way? 16 No restraint has been granted to your servants, and they said, 'Make bricks'; and behold, your servants have been beaten, and your people have been blamed." 17 But he said, "You are too idle; therefore say, Let us go and offer sacrifices to the LORD." 18 Therefore go now and work, for no strength will be granted you, yet you will deliver the whole history of the brick." 19 Then the officers of the children of Israel put themselves in a sounding board, for it had been said, "You shall not diminish anything of your brick, nor of the work of ev- ery day." 20 They met Moses and Aaron, who were on their way as they were leaving Pha- raoh, 21 and said, "The LORD is watching you and judging you, because you have caused our blood to stink before Pharaoh and his ser- vants, because you put a sword in their hands to kill them." 22 Therefore Moses returned to the Lord and said, "Lord, why have you afflict- ed this people, why have you sent me thus? 23 For since I came to Pharaoh to speak in your Name, he has harassed this people, and you have not yet delivered your people.

CHAPTER 6

1 Then the LORD said to Moses, "Now you will see what I will do to Pharaoh, for with a strong hand he will let them go and be forced out of his land." 2 God spoke to Moses again and said to him, "I am the LORD, 3 And I ap- peared to Abraham and to Izhak and to Iaa- kob with the name of

God Almighty; but my name Iehouah I did not know. 4 Moreover, as I made my covenant with them to give them the land of Canaan, the land of their pilgrimage, where they were strangers: 5 So also have I heard the lament of the children of Israel, whom the Egyptians hold in bondage, and have remembered my covenant. 6 There- fore say unto the children of Israel, I am the LORD, and will bring you out of the burdens of the Egyptians, and will deliver you out of their bondage, and will redeem you with an outstretched arm and with great sacrifices. 7 Moreover I will take you as my people and be your God; then you will know that I, the LORD your God, have delivered you from the burdens of the Egyptians. 8 I will bring you into the land that I swore to give to Abraham, to Izhak and to Iaakob, and I will give it to you as a possession: I am the LORD." 9 Moses said this to the children of Israel, but they did not listen to Moses, because of anguish of spirit and cruel bondage. 10 Then the LORD spoke to Moses, saying, 11 "Go and speak to Pha- raoh, king of Egypt, that he may let the chil- dren of Israel go out of his land." 12 But Moses spoke before the Lord, saying, "Behold, the children of Israel will not listen to me; how then shall Pharaoh listen to me, who are of circumcised minds?" 13 Then the LORD spoke to Moses and Aaron and charged them to go to the children of Israel and to Pharaoh, king of Egypt, to bring the children of Israel out of the land of Egypt. 14 These are the heads of their father's houses: the sons of Reuben, the firstborn of Israel, are Hanoch and Pallu, Hezron and Carmi; these are the families of Reuben. 15 Also the sons of Simeon: Iemuel, Iamin, Ohad, Iachin, Zoar, and Shaul the son of a Canaanite; these are the families of Simeon. 16 These are also the names of the sons of Leui in their generations: Gershon, Kohath and Merari (and the years of Leui's life were an hundred and thirty and seventy). 17 The sons of Gerson were Libni and Shimi, according to their families. 18 And the sons of Kohath were Amram, Izhar, Hebron, and Vzziel (Kohath lived an hundred and thirty and three years). 19 And the sons of Merari were Mahali and Mushi; these are the families of Leui according to their families. 20 Amram took Iochebed, his father's sister, to wife; she bore him Aaron and Moses (and Amram lived an hundred and thirty years). 21 Also the sons of Izhar: Korah, Nefeg, and Zichri. 22 And the sons of Vzziel: Mishael, Elzafane and Sithri. 23 Aaron took Elisheba, daughter of Amminadab, sister of Nahashon, as his wife, and she bore him Nadab, Abihu, Eleazar and Itamar. 24 Also the sons of Korah: Assir, Elkanah, and Abiasaf; these are the families of the Korhites. 25 Eleazar the son of Aaron took to wife one of the daughters of Putiel, who bore him Phinehas; these are the princi- pal fathers of the Leuites and their families. 26 These are Aaron and Moses to whom the LORD said, "Bring the children of Israel out of the land of Egypt, according to their armies." 27 These are that Moses and Aaron who spoke to Pharaoh, king of Egypt, to bring the chil- dren of Israel out of Egypt. 28 When the Lord spoke to Moses in the land of Egypt, 29 when the LORD spoke to Moses, saying, "I am the LORD, speak to Pharaoh, king of Egypt, all that I say to you." 30 Moses said to the Lord, "Behold, I am of vncircumcised lips, and how shall Pharaoh hear me?

have commanded you; and Aaron your brother shall speak to Pharaoh to let the children of Israel go out of his land. 3 But I will harden Pharaoh's heart and multiply my miracles and wonders in the land of Egypt. 4 And Pharaoh shall not hear- ken unto thee, that I may stretch forth my hand upon Egypt, and bring forth my armies, that is, my people, the children of Israel, out of the land of Egypt, with great deeds. 5 Then the Egyptians will know that I am the LORD, when I stretch out my hand over Egypt and bring the children of Israel out of their land." 6 Moses and Aaron therefore did as the Lord had commanded them, and so they did also. 7 (Now Moses was four and a half years old and Aaron four and three years old when they spoke to Pharaoh.) 8 The LORD had spoken to Moses and Aaron, saying. 9 If Pharaoh speaks to you, saying, 'We will perform a miracle for you,' you shall say to Aaron, 'Take your rod and throw it before Pharaoh, and it will turn into a snake.' 10 Then Moses and Aaron went to Pharaoh and did as the Lord had com- manded; Aaron threw his rod before Pharaoh and his servants, and it turned into a snake. 11 Then Pharaoh also called the wise men and the sorcerers, and the enchanters of Egypt also did the same with their spells, 12 For they cast every man his rod to the ground, and they turned into serpents; but Aaron made their rods disappear. 13 So Pharaoh's heart was hardened, and he did not listen to them, as the LORD had said. 14 The LORD then said to Moses, "Pharaoh's heart is stubborn; he re- fuses to let the people go. 15 And thou shalt go to Pharaoh in the morning (he shall come up out of the water), and thou shalt stand and meet him by the basin of the riuers, and thou shalt take in thy hand the rod that was turned into a serpent. 16 And thou shalt say unto him, The LORD God of the Hebrews hath sent me unto thee, saying, Let my people go, that they may serve me in the wilderness; and, behold, hitherto thou hast not heard. 17 Thus saith the LORD: "In this thou shalt acknowl- edge that I am the LORD: behold, I will strike with the rod that is in my hand the water that is in the river, and it shall turn to blood. 18 The fish that are in the river shall be dyed, and the river shall stink, and the Egyptians shall be forced to drink the water of the river." 19 The LORD then spoke to Moses, "Say to Aar- on, 'Take your rod and stretch out your hand over the waters of Egypt, over their streams, over their banks, over their ponds, and over all the pools of their waters; they will turn to blood, and there will be blood in all the land of Egypt, both in vessels of wood and in vessels of stone.' 20 And Moses and Aaron did as the Lord had commanded; and he lifted up the rod and struck the water that was in the river before the eyes of Pharaoh and his servants; and all the water that was in the river turned to blood. 21 The fish that were in the river be- came dyed, and the river splinted, so that the Egyptians could not drink the water of the river, and there was blood all over the land of Egypt. 22 The enchanters of Egypt did the same with their spells, and Pharaoh's heart was hardened, so that he did not listen to them, as the LORD had said. 23 Then Pharaoh went back to his house and this fact did not yet enter his heart. 24 Then all the Egyptians dug around the river to find water to drink, because they could not drink from the water of the river. 25 And this continued for about ten days after the LORD had struck the river.

CHAPTER 7

1 Then the LORD said to Moses, "Behold, I have established you as the God of Pharaoh, and Aaron your brother shall be your proph- et. 2 You shall say all that I

CHAPTER 8

1 Then the LORD said to Moses, "Go unto Pharaoh, and say unto him, Thus saith the LORD, Let my people go, that

they may serve me: 2 And if thou wilt not let them go, behold, I will smite all thy land with frogs: 3 And the river shall be filled with frogs, which shall en- ter into thy house, into thy chamber, where thou sleepest, into thy bed, into the house of thy servants, into thy people, into thy stoves, and into thy kneaders. 4 The frogs shall climb upon thee, and upon thy people, and upon all thy servants. 5 The LORD also said to Moses, "Say to Aaron, 'Stretch out your hand with your rod over the streams, the rivers, and the ponds, and let the frogs climb over the land of Egypt.' 6 Then Aaron stretched out his hand over the waters of Egypt, and the frogs came up and struck the land of Egypt. 7 The sorcerers also did the same with their spells and brought the frogs upon the land of Egypt. 8 Then Pharaoh called Moses and Aar- on and said, "Pray to the LORD, that he may drive away the frogs from me and from my people, and I will let the people go that they may sacrifice to the LORD." 9 And Moses said to Pharaoh, "Concerning me, when I pray for you and for your servants and for your people, command them to remove the frogs from you and from your houses, that they may remain only in the river." 10 Then he said, "To die." And he answered, "Let it be as you have said, that you may know that there is none like the Lord our God." 11 So the frogs shall depart from you, from your houses, from your servants, and from your people; they shall remain only in the river." 12 Then Moses and Aaron went away from Pharaoh, and Moses cried out to the LORD about the frogs he had sent to Pha- raoh. 13 The LORD did as Moses had said, and the frogs died in the houses, towns and fields. 14 They gathered them in heaps, and the earth was covered with them. 15 But when Pharaoh heard that he had been granted rest, he hard- ened his heart and did not listen to them, as the LORD had said. 16 Then the LORD said to Moses, "Say to Aaron, 'Stretch out the rod and strike the dust of the ground, that it may become sap throughout the land of Egypt.'"17 They did so: Aaron stretched out his hand with the rod and struck the dust of the ground; and the sap came on men and beasts; all the dust of the ground became sap in all the land of Egypt. 18 The enchanters also tried with their spells to bring forth the sap, but they failed. So the sap was on man and beasts. 19 Then the enchanters said to Pharaoh, "This is the finger of God." But Pharaoh's heart remained obstinate and he did not listen to them, as the LORD had said. 20 Moreover the LORD said to Moses, "Arise early in the morning, present yourself to Pharaoh (behold, he will come up out of the water) and say to him, Thus says the LORD: Let my people go, that they may serve me. 21 And if thou wilt not let my people go, behold, I will send swarms of flies upon thee, and upon thy servants, and upon thy people, and into thy houses; and the houses of the Egyptians shall be full of swarms of flies, and also the land where they are. 22 But the land of Goshe, where my people are, I will make it wonderful in that day, so that there shall be no swarms of flies, that you may know that I am the LORD in the midst of the earth. 23 And I will make a delation of my people from your people; forever this miracle shall be. 24 And the LORD did so, because great swarms of flies came into Pharaoh's house and into the houses of his servants, so that in all the land of Egypt the land was corrupted by swarms of flies. 25 Then Pharaoh called Moses and Aaron and said, "Go, sacrifice to your God in this land." 26 But Moses replied, "It is not ap- propriate to do so, for then we would offer to the LORD our God what is in abomination to the Egyptians. Can we perhaps sacrifice the abomination of the Egyptians before their eyes and they will not stone us? 27 Let us go for three days into the wilderness and sac- rifice to the LORD our

God, as he has com- manded." 28 Pharaoh said, "I will let you go, that you may sacrifice to the LORD your God in the wilderness; but do not go far, pray for me." 29 Moses said, "Behold, I will go out from you and pray to the LORD that the swarms of flies may depart from Pharaoh, his servants, and his people, and die from them; but from now on Pharaoh shall not deceive himself, not allowing the people to sacrifice to the LORD." 30 Then Moses turned away from Pharaoh and prayed to the LORD. 31 And the LORD did as Moses had said, and the swarms of flies departed from Pharaoh, his servants and his people, and not a single one remained. 32 But even then Pharaoh hardened his heart and did not let the people go.

CHAPTER 9

1 Then the LORD said to Moses, "Go to Pha- raoh and say to him, Thus says the LORD God of the Hebrews, Let my people go, that they may serve me. 2 But if you refuse to let him go and still want to keep him, 3 Behold, the hand of the LORD is upon thy people that are in the field: for upon the horses, and upon the ass- es, and upon the camels, and upon the cattle, and upon the sheep, there shall be a great mo- raine. 4 The LORD will do wonders between the lands of Israel and the lands of Egypt, so that nothing remains of all that concerns the children of Israel. 5 The LORD set a time, saying, "Until tomorrow the LORD will com- plete this thing in this land." 6 So the LORD did this thing on the morrow, and all the cat- tle of Egypt were dyed; but of the cattle of the children of Israel not a single one was dyed. 7 Then Pharaoh sent to say, "Behold, there was not one of the cattle of the Israelites dead; and Pharaoh's heart was obstinate and would not let the people go." 8 The LORD said to Moses and Aaron, "Take your handfuls of furnace ashes, and Moses will sprinkle them upward before Pharaoh, 9 And they shall be turned to dust in all the land of Egypt; and it shall be as a crust breaking into blisters upon man and beast, throughout all the land of Egypt." 10 Then they took furnace ash and stood before Pharaoh; Moses sprinkled it over Egypt, and out of it came a scab that blistered on man and beast. 11 The sorcerers could not stand before Moses because of the scab, for the scab was on the enchanters and on all the Egyp- tians. 12 The LORD hardened Pharaoh's heart, and he did not listen to them, as the LORD had told Moses. 13 The LORD also said to Mo- ses, "Arise early in the morning, present your- self to Pharaoh, and say to him, Thus says the LORD God of the Hebrews, Let my people go, that they may serve me. 14 For at this time I will send all my plagues upon your heart, and upon your servants, and upon your people, that you may know that there is none like me in all the earth.15 For now I will stretch out my hand to smite you and your people with the plague, and you will perish from the earth. 16 And for this I have appointed you, to manifest my power in you and declare my Name in all the world. 17 But you exalt yourself against my people and will not let them go. 18 Be- hold, for the near future I will raise up a great and mighty ship, such as there has not been in Egypt since its foundations were laid un- til now. 19 Therefore send to gather the cattle and all that you have in the fields, for on all the men and beasts that are in the fields and have not been brought home, hail will fall on them and they will die. 20 Those who feared the word of the LORD among Pharaoh's servants made his servants and his cattle flee to the houses: 21 But they that heeded not the word of the LORD, left their servants and their cattle in the fields. 22 And the LORD said to Moses,

Stretch forth thine hand upward, that there may be hunting in all the land of Egypt, for men, and for beasts, and for all the herbs of the field in the land of Egypt. 23 Then Moses stretched out his staff upward, and the LORD sent thunder and hail and lightning upon the land; and the LORD rained hail upon the land of Egypt. 24 So there was hail and fire mingled with the hail, so strong that there was none in all the land of Egypt since it was a nation. 25 And the hail struck in all the land of Egypt all that was in the fields, both men and animals; and the hail also struck all the grasses of the fields, and it reduced to pieces all the trees of the fields. 26 Only in the land of Goshen (where the children of Israel were) was there no haile. 27 Then Pharaoh sent for Moses and Aaron and said to them, "Now I have sinned: the LORD is righteous, but I and my people are wicked. 28 Pray to the LORD (for it is suf- ficient) that there be no more loud thunder and hail, and I will let you go, and you shall stay no longer." 29 Then Moses said to him, "As soon as I come out of the city, I will squeeze my hands toward the LORD, and the thunder will cease and there will be no more hail, so that you will know that the land is the LORD's. 30 As for you and your servants, I know that before you pray you will fear before the face of the LORD God. 31 The flax and the barley were affected, for the barley was gleaned and the flax was boiled. 32 But the wheat and the rye were not struck, for they were hidden in the ground). 33 Then Moses went out of the city to Pharaoh, and stretched out his hands toward the LORD, and the thunder and hail ceased, and it rained no more on the land. 34 When Pharaoh saw that the rain, hail and thunder had ceased, he sinned again and hardened his heart, both he and his servants. 35 So Pharaoh's heart hardened and he would not let the children of Israel go, as the LORD had said through Moses.

CHAPTER 10

1 Then the LORD said to Moses, "Go to Pha- raoh, for I have hardened his heart and the hearts of his servants, to perform these mira- cles of mine in the midst of his land, 2 and that you may declare in the ears of your son and your sons what I did in Egypt and my miracles that I performed among them, that you may know that I am the Lord." 3 Then Moses and Aaron went to Pharaoh and said to him, "Thus says the LORD God of the Hebrews: How long will you refuse to humble yourself before me? Let my people go, that they may serve me. 4 But if you refuse to let my people go, behold I will forever bring grashoppers to your shores. 5 They will cut off the face of the earth, so that man can no longer see the earth, and they will devour the remnant that remains to you and has escaped the hail, and they will devour all your trees that sprout in the fields. 6 And they shall make a slaughter of thy houses, and of all the houses of thy servants, and of the hous- es of all the Egyptians, such as neither thy fathers saw, from when they were upon the earth until now." So he returned and departed from Pharaoh. 7 Then Pharaoh's servants said to him, "How long is this an offense to him? Let the men go, that they may serve the LORD their God; do you want to know first that Egypt is destroyed?" 8 Moses and Aaron were therefore led back to Pharaoh, and he said to them, "Go, serve the Lord your God"; but who are those who will go? 9 Moses answered, "We will go with our young men and with our old men, with our sons and with our daughters, with our sheep and with our cattle, for we must celebrate a feast to the Lord." 10 He said to them, "May the LORD do so with you, as I will let you and your children go; watch, for euillia

is before your face. 11 It shall not be so; now go, you who are men, to serve the LORD, for this was your desire." Then they were driven out of Pharaoh's presence. 12 Then the LORD said to Moses, "Stretch out your hand over the land of Egypt for the locusts, that they may come to the land of Egypt and eat all the herbs of the land, that is, all that the grass has left." 13 Then Moses stretched out his rod over the land of Egypt, and the LORD brought an east wind upon the land all that day and all that night; and in the morning the east wind brought the locusts. 14 So the locusts went out throughout all the land of Egypt, and re- mained in all the districts of Egypt; and so se- vere locusts, such as these, there had not been any before, nor will there be any after them. 15 For they besieged the whole face of the earth, so that the earth became dark, and devoured all the herbs of the earth and all the fruit of the trees which the hail had left, so that there remained nothing green on the trees and among the herbs of the fields in all the land of Egypt. 16 Therefore Pharaoh called Moses and Aaron in haste and said, "I have sinned against the LORD your God and against you. 17 Now forgive my sin just this once, and pray to the LORD your God to remove this death from me just this once." 18 Moses then turned away from Pharaoh and prayed to the LORD. 19 Then the LORD caused a strong west wind to blow, carried away the locusts and threw them violently into the Red Sea, so that there was not a single locust left in all the coast of Egypt. 20 But the LORD hardened Pharaoh's heart, and he did not let the children of Israel go. 21 Then the LORD said to Moses, "Stretch out your hand upward, that there may be darkness over the land of Egypt, darkness that can be felt." 22 Then Moses stretched out his hand toward Eauen, and for three days there was black darkness over all the land of Egypt. 23 No one saw anything anymore, nor did anyone get up from where they were for three days; but all the children of Israel had light in the place where they lived. 24 And Pharaoh called Moses and said to him, "Go, serve the LORD; only your sheep and your cattle shall remain, and your sons shall go with you." 25 And Moses said, "You must also give sacrific- es and burnt offerings, that we may sacrifice to the LORD our God. 26 Therefore our cat- tle also shall go with you; not one gourd shall be left of them, for we must take of them to serve the LORD our God; and we do not know how we shall serve the LORD, until we come. 27 (But the LORD hardened Pharaoh's heart, and he would not let them depart). 28 Pha- raoh said to him, "Go away from me; look no more on my face, for when you come before me, you will die." 29 Then Moses said, "You have spoken well; from now on I will no lon- ger see your face."

CHAPTER 11

1 Now the LORD said to Moses, "I will still make a plague on Pharaoh and Egypt; after that he will let you go; when he lets you go, he will drive you out at once. 2 Speak now to the people, that every man may require of his neighbor, and every woman of her neighbor, jewels of silk and jewels of gold. 3 The LORD made the people happy in the eyes of the Egyptians; Moses also was very great in the land of Egypt, in the eyes of Pharaoh's ser- vants and the people). 4 Moses also said, "Thus says the LORD: About midnight I will go out into the midst of Egypt." 5 And all the first-born in the land of Egypt shall die, from the firstborn of Pharaoh who sits on his throne to the firstborn of his mother's servant, who stands at the thousand, and all the firstborn of the beasts. 6 Then there shall be a great weeping

in all the land of Egypt, such as there has not been nor ever shall be. 7 But none of you children of Israel shall move his tongue against a dog, nor against a man, nor against an animal, that you may know that the LORD has set a difference between the Egyptians and Israel. 8 And all these thy servants shall come to me, and shall mow down before me, saying, Go away, and all the people that are at thy feet, and after this I will depart." So he departed from Pharaoh very angry. 9 And the LORD said to Moses, "Pharaoh will not listen to you, that my wonders may be multiplied in the land of Egypt." 10 Moses and Aaron did all these wonders before Pharaoh, but the LORD hardened Pharaoh's heart and he did not al- low the children of Israel to go out of his land.

CHAPTER 12

1 Then the LORD spoke to Moses and Aar- on in the land of Egypt, saying, "This month will be for you the beginning of money, 2 This month will be the beginning of money for you; it will be the first month of the year for you. 3 Speak to all the community of Israel, saying, "In the tenth of this month let each one take for himself one lambe, according to the house of the fathers, one lambe for a house. 4 And if the house is too small for the lamb, he shall take his neighbor who is near his house, according to the name of the peo- ple; each one of you, according to his eating, shall take the count of the lambs, 5 your lamb shall be without blemish, a male one year old; you shall take it from the lambs or from the kids. 6 You shall keep it until the fourteenth day of this month; then all the multitude of the congregation of Israel shall kill it at once. 7 Then they shall take the blood and beat it on the two posts and on the first post of the houses where they shall eat it. 8 The same evening they shall eat the meat, browned in the fire and with vnleauened bread; they shall eat it with sown herbs. 9 They shall not eat the meat of it, neither boiled nor dipped in water, but roasted with fire, both the head and the feet and the limbs. 10 And you shall not keep any of it until the morning; but what remains of it until the evening, you shall bury with fire. 11 And so you shall eat it, with your belts, your shoes on your feet, and your staffs in your hands, and you shall eat it in haste, for it is the Passing of the Lord. 12 For I will pass through the land of Egypt in that same night, and will smite all the firstborn in the land of Egypt, both man and beast, and will do justice to all the gods of Egypt. I am the LORD. 13 The blood shall be a sign to you on the houses where you are; so when I see the blood, I will pass over, and the plague shall not be upon you to destroy you, when I smite the land of Egypt. 14 This day shall be a me- morial for you, and you shall keep it as a holy feast for the LORD, for all your generations. 15 For ten days you shall eat leavened bread, and in any case you shall eliminate leavened bread on the first day from your houses; for whoever eats leavened bread from the first day until the seventh day, that person shall be eliminated from Israel. 16 The first day shall be a holy assembly; the tenth day also shall be a holy assembly for you; in them shall no work be done, except what each one shall eat; only this you shall be able to do. 17 You shall also remember the feast of dry loaves, for on that same day I will bring your armies out of the land of Egypt; therefore you shall observe this day, for all your posterity, as an ordinance forever. 18 In the first month and on the four- teenth day of the month of October you shall eat leavened bread until the twentieth day of the month of August. 19 For ten days ye shall not find leavened bread in your houses, for whosoever shall eat leavened bread shall be cut off from the congregation of Israel, whether he be a stranger or born in the land. 20 You shall not eat leavened bread, but in all your dwellings you shall eat leavened bread." 21 Then Moses called all the elders of Israel and said to them, "Choose and take for each of your houses a lamb and kill the shepherd. 22 Take a bunch of hyssop, dip it in the blood that is in the basin, and strike his lintel and his hind cheeks with the blood that is in the basin, and let none of you go out from the en- trance of his house until the morning. 23 For the LORD will pass by to smite the Egyptians; and when he sees the blood on the lintel and on the two cheeks, the LORD will pass over the door and will not allow the destroyer to enter your houses to scourge you. 24 There- fore you shall observe this as an ordinance for you and for your children forever. 25 When you enter the land which the LORD will grant you as he has promised, you shall observe this service. 26 And when your children ask you, "What is the service that you keep?" 27 you shall say, "It is the sacrifice of the Lord's Passer, who passed before the houses of the children of Israel in Egypt, when he defeat- ed the Egyptians and preserved our houses." Then the people prostrated themselves and worshiped. 28 So the children of Israel went and did as the LORD had commanded Mo- ses and Aaron; so they did. At midnight the LORD struck all the first bearers in the land of Egypt, from the first bearer of Pharaoh who sat on his throne to the first bearer of the cap- tive who was in prison and all the first bearers of cattle. 30 And Pharaoh rose up at night, he and all his servants and all the Egyptians, and there was much weeping in Egypt, for there was no house in which there was not a dead person. 31 At night he called Moses and Aaron and said, "Get up, come out of my people, you and the children of Israel, and go and serve the Lord as you have said. 32 Take also your sheep and your cattle, as you have said, and depart, and bless me also." 33 The Egyptians forced the people to leave the land in haste, for they said, "We will all die." 34 Therefore the people took their dough before it was leavened and bound it with garments on their shoulders. 35 And the children of Israel did as Moses had said, and they asked the Egyptians for silken jewelry, gold jewelry, and clothing. 36 And the LORD made the people happy in the eyes of the Egyptians, and they granted their request, and thus ousted the Egyptians. 37 Then the children of Israel undertook the journey from Rameses to Succoth, with about six hundred thousand men and children. 38 With them departed a great multitude of peo- ple of all kinds, with sheep, cattle and cattle in great abundance. 39 And they baked the dough which they had brought from Egypt, and made leavened cakes of it, for it was not leavened, because they had been driven out of Egypt, and they could neither tarry nor pre- pare their lives. 40 The sojourn of the children of Israel in Egypt lasted four hundred and thirty years. 41 When the four hundred and thirty years had passed, on the same day the whole army of the LORD departed from the land of Egypt. 42 This is a night for the LORD to keep, because he brought them out of the land of Egypt; this is the night of the LORD, which all the children of Israel are to keep throughout their generation. 43 The LORD also said to Moses and Aaron, "This is the night of the passage: no stranger shall eat of it. 44 But the servant bought for money, when you have circumcised him, he shall eat of it. 45 The stranger and the wrathful servant shall not eat of it. 46 It shall be eaten in one house only; you shall take no meat out of the house, and you shall not break a bone of it. 47 The whole community of Israel shall observe it. 48 But if a

stranger dwells near you and wants to observe the Passion of the LORD, let him circumcise all the males that belong to him, and then come and observe it, and he shall be like one born in the land; for no vncircum- cision shall he eat of it. 49 One lawe shall be for him that is born in the land, and for the stranger that dwelleth among you. 50 Then all the children of Israel did as the LORD had commanded Moses and Aaron: so they did. 51 On that same day the LORD brought the children of Israel out of the land of Egypt with their army.

CHAPTER 13

1 The LORD spoke to Moses, saying, 2 Sanc- tify for me all the firstborn, that is, all those who first open the womb among the children of Israel, both of men and of animals, for it is mine." 3 Then Moses said to the people, "Remember this day when you came out of Egypt, out of the house of bondage, for with a mighty hand the LORD brought you out from there; therefore you shall not eat leavened bread. 4 Today you are going out in the month of Abib. 5 When the LORD has brought you into the land of the Canaanites, the Hittites, the Amorites, the Hiuites, and the Jebusites (whom he had sworn to your fathers to give you, a land rich in milk and honors), you shall do this service in this month. 6 For seven days you shall eat vnleaued bread, and the seventh day shall be the feast of the LORD. 7 Leavened bread shall be eaten for ten days, and no leav- ened bread shall be seen with thee, neither shall leavened bread be seen with thee in all thy quarters. 8 In that day you shall make a declaration to your son, saying, "This has been done, because of what the LORD did to me when I came out of Egypt." 9 It shall be for you a sign on your hand and a memorial be-tween your eyes, that the word of the LORD may be in your mouth, because with a strong hand the LORD brought you out of Egypt. 10 Therefore keep this ordinance in its season, from year to year. 11 When the LORD shall bring thee into the land of the Canaanites, as he hath sworn to thee and to thy fathers, and shall grant it unto thee, 12 Then thou shalt set aside for the LORD all that openeth first in the womb; also every thing that openeth first in the womb and cometh forth out of thy beast; the males shall be the LORD's. 13 But all the first foals of a donkey thou shalt redeem with a blade; and if thou shalt not redeem them, thou shalt break their necks; likewise all the first born of man among thy sons shalt thou remove. 14 And when thy son shall ask thee to die, saying, "What is this?" thou shalt say unto him, "With a mighty hand hath the LORD brought forth out of Egypt, out of the house of bondage." 15 For when Pharaoh's heart was hard against our going forth, the LORD killed all the firstborn in the land of Egypt, from the first born of man even to the first born of the beast; therefore I will sacrifice to the LORD all the males that open the woman first, but all the first born of my sons I will redeem. 16 And this shall be as a sign upon thy hand, and as a front between thine eyes, that the LORD hath brought thee out of Egypt with a mighty hand. 17 Now when Pharaoh let the people go, God did not let them pass by the way of the land of the Philistines, even though it was near- er (for God said, "Lest the people, seeing the war, repent and return to Egypt"). 18 But God caused the people to pass by the way of the wilderness of the Red Sea; and the children of Israel came out of the land of Egypt armed. 19 And Moses took Ioseph's bones with him, for he had made the children of Israel swear that God will visit you, and you shall take my bones away with you.

20 So they set out from Succoth and encamped at Etham, on the edge of the wilderness. 21 And the LORD went be-fore them in a pillar of cloud by day to show them the way, and in a pillar of fire by night to give them light, that they might go both by day and by night. 22 He did not remove the pillar of cloud by day and the pillar of fire by night from the people.

CHAPTER 14

1 Then the LORD spoke to Moses, saying,

2 Speak to the children of Israel, that they may turn back and encamp before Pi-Hahi- roth, between Migdol and the sea, against Baal-zephon; toward it you shall approach the sea. 3 For Pharaoh will say of the children of Israel, "They have entangled themselves in the land; the wilderness has enclosed them. 4 And I will harden Pharaoh's heart that he may follow you; so I will make myself honored over Pharaoh and over all his army; even the Egyptians will know that I am the LORD; and so they did." 5 Then it was told to the king of Egypt that the people had fled; the hearts of Pharaoh and his servants turned against the people, and they said, "Why did we do this and let Israel go out of our service? 6 Pha- raoh prepared his chariots and took his peo-ple with him, 7 and took six hundred chosen chariots and all the chariots of Egypt, with captains for each of them. 8 (For the LORD had hardened the heart of Pharaoh, king of Egypt, and he pursued the children of Israel; but the children of Israel went out with a sure hand.) 9 The Egyptians pursued them, and all Pharaoh's horses and chariots and his horse- men and his army surprised them by encamp- ing by the sea, near Pi-Hahiroth, opposite Baal-zephon. 10 And when Pharaoh departed, the children of Israel lifted up their eyes and saw that the Egyptians were marching behind them, and they were put to the test; therefore the children of Israel cried out to the LORD. 11 And they said to Moses, "Did you lead them to die in the wilderness, because there were no graves in Egypt? Why did you use yourself thus, to bring them out of Egypt? 12 Did we not tell you this thing in Egypt, saying, "Let vs be at rest, that we may serve the Egyptians?" For it was better for vs to serve the Egyptians than to die in the wilderness. 13 Then Moses said to the people, "Do not fear, be still and observe the salvation of the LORD that he will show you today. For the Egyptians, whom you have seen today, you will not see again. 14 The LORD will fight for you; therefore be still." 15 The LORD said to Moses, "Why do you cry out against me? Tell the children of Israel to go forth: 16 Lift up your rod, stretch out your hand over the sea and dissuade it, and let the children of Israel go by land to the middle of the sea. 17 I, behold, I will harden the hearts of the Egyptians, that they may follow them, and I will make myself honorable over Pha- raoh and over all his army, over his chariots and over his horsemen. 18 Then the Egyptians will know that I am the LORD, when I have made myself honored over Pharaoh and his chariots and his horsemen. 19 And the angel of God, which went before the army of Israel, departed and passed behind them; and the pillar of cloud also passed before them and stood behind them, 20 and stood between the camna of the Egyptians and the camna of Is- rael; it was a cloud and a darkness that made light at night, so that throughout the night the one did not reach the other). 21 And Moses stretched out his hand over the sea, and the LORD caused the sea to recede with a strong east wind all night long, and caused the sea to

become a dry land, because the waters had dissolved. 22 Then the children of Israel passed through the waters of the sea on dry ground, and the waters were a wall against them on their right and on their left. 23 And the Egyptians pursued and followed them to the waters of the sea, and all Pharaoh's horses and his chariots and his horsemen. 24 Now in the morning, when the LORD looked upon the army of the Egyptians, from the pillar of fire and cloud, he received the army of the Egyptians with fear. 25 For he took away the wheels of their chariots and dragged them with much toil, so that the Egyptians said, "I will flee from the face of Israel, for the LORD fights for them against the Egyptians." 26 Then the LORD said to Moses, "Stretch out your hand over the sea, that the waters may return on the Egyptians, on their char- iots and on their horsemen." 27 Then Moses stretched out his hand over the sea, and the sea returned in strength early in the morn- ing, and the Egyptians fled against it; but the LORD defeated the Egyptians in the midst of the sea. 28 And the water returned and struck down the chariots and the horsemen and all the armies of Pharaoh that had gone into the sea after them; not one of them remained. 29 But the children of Israel walked on dry land to the middle of the sea, and the waters were a wall against them on their right and on their left. 30 So the LORD saved Israel on that same day from the hand of the Egyptians, and Is- rael saw the Egyptians dead on the shore of the sea. 31 Israel saw the great power that the LORD had manifested against the Egyptians; so the people feared the LORD and paid hom- age to the LORD and to his servant Moses.

CHAPTER 15

1 Then Moses and the Israelites sang this song to the LORD and said, "I will sing to the LORD, for he has triumphed gloriously; the horse and those who rode on it have over- turned the sea." 2 The LORD is my strength and my praise, and he has become my salva- tion. He is my God, and I will prepare a tab- ernacle for him; he is the God of my fathers, and I will exalt him. 3 The LORD is a man of war; his name is Jehouah. 4 He threw Pha- raoh's chariots and his army into the sea; even his chosen captains were drowned in the Red Sea. 5 The depths have filled them; they have run aground at the bottom like a stone. 6 Your right hand, O LORD, is glorious in power; Your right hand, O LORD, has annihilated the enemy. 7 In your great glory you struck down those who rose up against you; you unleashed your wrath, which consumed them like stub- ble. 8 By the breath of your nostrils the waters have gathered, the floods have stood still as a heap, the bottoms have congealed in the heart of the sea. 9 The adversary said, "I will pursue them, I will take them, I will make the sword, my lust shall be satisfied upon them, I will unsheathe my sword, my hand shall destroy them." 10 Thou hast blown with thy wind, the sea hath caressed them, they have remained as leads in the great waters. 11 Who is like you, O LORD, among the gods? Who is like you, so glorious in holiness, fearful in prayers, per- forming miracles? 12 You stretched out your right hand, and the earth swallowed them up. 13 By your mercy you heal this people, whom you have failed; by your power you lead them back to your holy dwelling place. 14 The peo- ple will hear and be afraid; sadness will strike the inhabitants of Palestine. 15 The dukes of Edom will be shocked, the great ones of Moab will tremble, and all the inhabitants of Ca- naan will have weak hearts. 16 Fear and terror shall fall upon them; because of the greatness of your

weaponry, they shall stand firm as a stone, until your people, O LORD, until this people whom you have purchased shall pass away. 17 Thou shalt bring them in and plant them on the mountain of thy inheritance, which is the place thou hast prepared, O LORD, to dwell therein, and the sanctuary, O LORD, which thy hands shall establish. 18 The LORD shall reign forever. 19 Because Pha- raoh's horses went with his chariots and his horsemen into the sea, the LORD brought down the waters of the sea upon them; but the children of Israel went on dry land in the midst of the sea. 20 And Miriam the proph- etess, Aaron's sister, took a timpani in her hand, and all the women went out after her with timpani and daunces. 21 Miriam an- swered the men, "Sing to the LORD, for he has triumphed gloriously; the horse and its rider has overthrown them into the sea." 22 Then Moses brought Israel out of the Red Sea, and they went into the wilderness of Shur; they went three days into the wilderness and found no waters. 23 When they came to Marah, they could not drink of the waters of Marah, for they were bitter; therefore the name of the place was called Marah. 24 Then the people murmured against Moses, saying, "What shall we drink?" 25 And he cried out to the LORD, and the LORD showed him a tree, which, when it was cast into the waters, the waters became sweet; there he made them an ordinance and a law, and there he put them on display, 26 and said, "If you, O Israel, will diligently listen to the word of the LORD your God, and do what is right in his sight, if you will pay attention to his commands and keep all his prescriptions, then I will not give you any more of these diseases that I gave to the Egyptians, for I am the LORD who heals you." 27 They came to Elim, where there were two springs of water and seventy palm trees, and they camped by the waters.

CHAPTER 16

1 Then the whole community of the children of Israel departed from Elim and came to the wilderness of Sin (which is between Elim and Sinai) on the fifteenth day of the second month after their departure from the land of Egypt. 2 The whole community of the chil- dren of Israel murmured against Moses and against Aaron in the wilderness. 3 The chil- dren of Israel said to them, "Oh, if we had died by the hand of the LORD in the land of Egypt, when we sat before the vessels of meat, when we ate bread to our fill; for you have brought out into this wilderness to kill all this community with famine." 4 Then the LORD said to Moses, "Behold, I will rain bread from above down upon you, and the people shall go out and gather what is enough for each day, that I may test them, whether they will walk in my Law or not." 5 But on the sixth day they shall prepare what they shall take home, and it shall be twice as much as they shall gather each day." 6 Then Moses and Aaron said to all the children of Israel, "At that time you shall know that the LORD has brought you out of the land of Egypt: 7 In the morning you shall see the glory of the LORD, for he has heard your grudges against the LORD; and what are we who have murmured against him? 8 Then Moses said, "At that time the LORD will give you meat to eat, and in the morning your loaf of bread, because the LORD has heard your murmurings that you murmur against him; and what are we? Your murmurings are not against you, but against the LORD." 9 Moses said to Aaron, "Say to all the congregation of the children of Israel, 'Stop before the

LORD, for he has heard your murmurings.'" 10 While Aaron was speaking to the whole communi- ty of the children of Israel, they looked to- ward the wilderness, and behold, the glory of the Lord appeared in a cloud. 11 (For the Lord had spoken to Moses, saying, 12 "I have heard the murmurings of the children of Is- rael; tell him, therefore, and say, 'Today you shall eat meat, and tomorrow morning you shall be filled with bread, and you shall know that I am the Lord your God.'") 13 So at dawn the quails came and stroked the campe; and in the morning the dew spread around the army. 14 And when the dew that had fallen had gone up, behold, on the face of the wil- derness was a little round thing, as small as the frost on the earth. 15 When the children of Israel saw it, they said to one another, "It is MAN, for they did not know what it was." And Moses said to them, "This is the noodle that the LORD has given you to eat." 16 This is what the LORD has commanded: gather every man of it, according to his consump- tion, an omer for every man, according to the number of your people; every man shall take of it for those who are in his tent." 17 And the children of Israel did so, and gathered, some more, some less. 18 And when they measured with the Omer, he who had gathered much had nothing more, and he who had gathered little had nothing less; so each man gathered according to his consumption. 19 Then Moses said to them, "Let no one keep any until the morning." 20 Yet they did not obey Moses; but some of them stored it up until morning, and it was full of worms and sticks; therefore Moses was angry with them. 21 They gathered it every morning, each according to his con- sumption, for it melted at sunrise. 22 On the sixth day they gathered twice as much bread, two omer for a man; then all the leaders of the community came and told Moses. 23 He answered them, "This is what the LORD said, 'Today is the Sabbath rest sacred to the LORD: bake what you will, and bake what you will, and whatever remains, set it aside to keep until morning for you.'" 24 They spread it out until morning, as Moses had commanded, and it did not stand, nor was there any sign of it. 25 Then Moses said, "Eat it until the day, for the day is the Sabbath for the LORD; until the day you will not find it in the fields. 26 Six days you shall gather it, but the seventh day is the Sabbath: in it there shall be none." 27 However, on the tenth day some of the people went out to gather and found nothing. 28 The LORD said to Moses, "How long do you refuse to keep my commands and my law? 29 Behold, as the LORD has granted you the Sabbath, so he grants you the bread of the sixtieth day for two days; let every man rest in his place, and let no one leave his place on the seventh day." 30 So the people rested on the tenth day. 31 The house of Israel called him MAN. It was like a coriander seed, but white, and its taste was like that of wafers made from bone. 32 Moses said, "This is what the LORD has com- manded: fill an omer with it, to keep it for your posterity, that they may see the bread with which I fed you in the wilderness, when I brought you out of the land of Egypt." 33 Mo- ses also said to Aaron, "Take a vessel, and put in it an omer full of MAN, and set it before the LORD that he may preserve it for your poster- ity." 34 As the LORD had commanded Moses, Aaron placed it before the Testimony that it might be preserved. 35 The children of Israel ate the man for four years, until they came to an inhabited land; they ate the man until they came to the borders of the land of Canaan. 36 The Omer is the tenth part of Ephah.

CHAPTER 17

1 The whole community of the children of Is- rael set out from the wilderness of Sin, with their journeys, at the command of the LORD, and encamped at Rephidim, where there was no water to water the people. 2 Therefore the people quarreled with Moses and said, "Give us water that we may drink." And Moses said to them, "Why do you quarrel with me, why do you tempt the Lord? 3 So the people were thirsty for water, and the people murmured against Moses and said, "Why did you bring us out of Egypt so that we and our children and our livestock would die of thirst? 4 Then Moses cried out to the Lord, saying, "What shall I do to this people? For they are almost ready to stone me." 5 The LORD answered Moses, "Go before the people and take elders of Israel with you; and your rod, with which you crushed the revolt, take it in your hand and go: 6 Behold, I will stand before thee upon the tower of Horeb; thou shalt strike upon the tower, and water shall come out of it, that the people may drink." And Moses did so before the elders of Israel. 7 Then he called the place by the name of Mass and Meriba, because of the contention of the children of Israel and because they had tempted the Lord, saying, "Is the Lord among you? 8 Then Amalek came and fought with Israel at Rephidim. 9 Moses said to Ioshua, "Choose men and go and fight with Amalek; for the rest I will stand on the top of the hill with the rod of God in my hand." 10 Ioshua did as Moses commanded him and fought with Amalek; Moses, Aaron and Hur went up to the top of the hill. 11 When Moses held his hand up, Israel was saved; but when he left his hand down, Amalek was saved. 12 By now Moses' hands were in trouble; so they took a stone, put it under him, and he sat on it; Aaron and Hur held his hands, one on one side and the other on the other; so his hands remained steady until the sun went down. 13 Ioshua defeated Amalek and his people with the edge of the sword. 14 The LORD said to Moses, "Write this as a memorial in the book, and let Ioshua hear it, for I will definitely wipe out the memory of Amalek from under heav- en." 15 (Moses built an altar and called it Ie- houah-nissi). 16 He also said, "The LORD has sworn that he will make war on Amalek from generation to generation."

CHAPTER 18

1 When Iethro, priest of Midian, the father of Moses, heard all that God had done for Moses and for Israel, his people, and how the Lord had brought Israel out of Egypt, 2 then Iethro, Moses' father, took Zipporah, Moses' wife (af- ter sending her away). 3 and his two sons, one of whom was called Gershom, because he said, "I have been a stranger in a foreign land." 4 the other was called Eliezer, because my fa- ther's God, he said, helped me and delivered me from Pharaoh's sword). 5 Moses' father- in-law Iethro went with his two sons and his wife to Moses in the wilderness, where he had encamped by the mouth of God. 6 And he said to Moses, "I have come to you your father-in- law Iethro, your wife and her two sons with her." 7 And Moses went out to meet his father- in-law, and did obeisance to him and kissed him, and asked others about his welfare; then they entered the tent. 8 Then Moses told his father-in-law all that the LORD had done to Pharaoh and the Egyptians on behalf of Is- rael, and all the hardships that had befallen them on the way, and how the LORD had de- livered them. 9 Iethro rejoiced at all the good- ness the LORD had shown Israel and how he had delivered them out of the hands of the

Egyptians. 10 Therefore Iethro said, "Blessed be the LORD who has delivered you from the hands of the Egyptians and from the hands of Pharaoh; who has also delivered the people from under the hands of the Egyptians. 11 Now I know that the LORD is greater than all the gods, for as they dealt proudly with them, so they were rewarded." 12 Then Iethro, Mo- ses' father, took burnt offerings and sacrifices to offer to God. And Aaron and all the elders of Israel came and ate bread with Moses-in- law before God. 13 And on the next day, when Moses sat down to judge the people, the peo- ple stayed around Moses from morning until noon. 14 And when Moses' father-in-law saw all that he did to the people, he said, "What is this that you do to the people? Why do you sit alone and all the people are around you from morning until evening? 15 Moses said to his father-in-law, "Because the people come to me to see God." 16 When they have a matter, they come to me and I judge one another and declare God's standards and His laws." 17 But Moses' father-in-law said to him, "The thing you do is not good. 18 You make great trouble for yourself and for this people who are with you, because the thing is too heavy for you; you are not able to do it yourself. 19 Hear now my counsel (I will give you counsel, and God will be with you), be to the people an intermediary of God, and report the causes to God, 20 and admonish them concerning the rules and laws, showing them the way by which they should walk and the work they should do. 21 Moreover, seek from among all the people courageous men, God-fearing, dealing sincerely, detesting corruption; and appoint them as leaders of thousands, lead- ers of hundreds, leaders of fifties, and leaders of tens. 22 And let them judge the people at all times; but let them bring every great matter to thee, and judge all small causes; so it will be easier for thee, when they bear the burden with thee. 23 If you do so (and God commands you to do so), you will be able to bear, and also all these people will go quietly to their place." 24 Moses obeyed his father-in-law's advice and did all that his father-in-law had said: 25 Moses chose from all Israel brave men and appointed them leaders of the people, leaders of thousands, leaders of hundreds, leaders of fifties, and leaders of tens. 26 They judged the people at all times, but they submitted the difficult cases to Moses, for they judged all matters of little importance by themselves. 27 Then Moses let his father-in-law leave and went away to his county.

CHAPTER 19

1 In the third month, after the children of Is- rael had come out of the land of Egypt, on the same day they came to the wilderness of Si- nai. 2 And they departed from Rephidim, and came to the wilderness of Sinai, and encamp- ed in the wilderness; and there Israel encamp- ed before the mountain. 3 But Moses went to God, for the LORD had called him from the mountain, saying, "You shall say thus to the house of Iaakob, and you shall tell the chil- dren of Israel, 4 You have seen what I did to the Egyptians and how I carried you on eagle wings and led you to me. 5 If therefore you will listen to my message and keep my counsel, you will be my chief treasure to all peoples, even as all the earth is mine. 6 You will also be to me a kingdom of priests and a holy nation. These are the words you will speak to the chil- dren of Israel." 7 -Moses then came and called the elders of the people and proposed to them all these things that the LORD had command- ed him. 8 The people answered all at once and said, "All that the Lord has commanded, we will do." And Moses reported the words of the people to the Lord. 9 And the LORD said to Moses, "Behold, I come to you in a thin cloud, that the people may hear as I speak to you, and that they may follow you forever." (for Moses had reported the words of the peo- ple to the Lord). 10 Moreover, the LORD said to Moses, "Go to the people and sanctify the day and the night, and let them wash their clothes. 11 And keep them ready on the third day, for on the thirteenth day the LORD will come down to Mount Sinai before the eyes of all the people: 12 You shall make signs to the people all around, saying, "Take heed to your- selves, lest you go to the mountain and touch its borders; whoever touches the mountain shall surely die. 13 No hand shall touch him, but he shall be stoned or pierced with darts; whether animals or men, he shall not lie; when the horn blows at length, they shall en- ter the mountain." 14 Then Moses came down from the mountain to the people, sanctified the people, and they washed their clothes. 15 Then he said to the people, "Be ready on the third day and do not come secretly." 16 And on the thirteenth day, when it was morning, there was thunder and lightning, and a thin cloud on the mountain, and a very loud sound of a trumpet, so that all the people, who were in campe, departed. 17 Then Moses brought the people out of their tents to meet with God, and they stood at the lower part of the moun- tain. 18 And Mount Sinai was all in smoke, be- cause the LORD had come down upon it with fire, and its smoke went up like the smoke of a furnace, and the whole mountain trembled greatly. 19 And when the sound of the trum- pet blew long and became louder and louder, Moses spoke, and God answered him with a voice. 20 (For the Lord came down to Mount Sinai on the top of the mountain) and when the Lord called Moses to go up to the top of the mountain, Moses went up there. 21 Then the LORD said to Moses, "Go down, instruct the people not to violate their borders to go and contemplate the LORD, otherwise many of them will perish." 22 And let the priests also who go to the LORD be sanctified, otherwise the LORD will destroy them." 23 Moses said to the LORD, "The people cannot go up Mount Sinai, because you instructed them to say, 'Put signs on the mountain and sanctify it.'" 24 The LORD said to him, "Go, descend and come, you and Aaron with you; but let not the priests and the people violate their borders to come to the LORD, or he will destroy them." 25 Moses therefore went to the people and said to them.

CHAPTER 20

1 Then God spoke all these words, saying, 2 I am the LORD your God, who brought you out of the land of Egypt, out of the house of bond- age. 3 You shall have no other gods before me. 4 You shall not make for yourself any image of bronze, nor any likeness of the things that are in heaven, nor of the things that are on the earth beneath, nor of the things that are in the waters under the earth. 5 Thou shalt not bow down thyself to them, nor serve them: for I am the LORD thy God, an unrighteous God, who bringeth the iniquity of the fathers upon the children, upon the third generation, and upon the fourth generation of them that hate me: 6 And who is pleased with thousands who love me and keep my commands. 7 Do not use the name of the LORD your God in vilifica- tion, for the LORD will not hold guilty those who use his name in vilification. 8 Remember the Sabbath day, to keep it holy. 9 Six days you shall work and do all your work, 10 but the seventh day is the Sabbath of the

LORD your God; in it you shall do no work, neither you, nor your son, nor your daughter, nor your servant, nor your wife, nor your beast, nor your stranger that is within your gates. 11 For in six days the LORD made heaven and earth and the sea and all that is in them, and rested on the seventh day; therefore the LORD bless- ed the Sabbath day and sanctified it. 12 Honor thy father and thy mother, that thy days may be prolonged in the land which the LORD thy God giveth thee. 13 Thou shalt not kill. 14 You shall not commit adultery. 15 You shall not steal. 16 You shall not bear false witness against your neighbor. 17 You shall not steal your neighbor's house, nor your neighbor's wife, nor your neighbor's servant, nor your neighbor's ox, nor your neighbor's plank, nor anything that is your neighbor's." 18 And all the people saw the thunder, and the light- ning, and the sound of the trumpet, and the smoke of the mountain; and when the people saw it, they fled and departed, 19 And they said to Moses, "Speak with the voice, and we will listen; but do not allow God to speak with the voice, or we will die." 20 Then Moses said to the people, "Do not fear, for God has come to test you, and that his fear may be before you, so that you may not sin." 21 The people went away, but Moses approached the dark- ness where God was. 22 And the LORD said to Moses, "You shall thus say to the children of Israel, You have seen that I have spoken to you from above. 23 Therefore you shall not make for yourselves with me gods of silk nor gods of gold; you shall not make for yourselves any. 24 You shall make an altar of earth for me, and there you shall offer your burnt of- ferings and your peace offerings, your sheep and your oxen; in all places where I will put the remembrance of my Name, I will come to you and bless you. 25 But if thou wilt make me an altar of stone, thou shalt not buy it of hard stones: for if thou lift up thy rod upon them, thou hast polluted them. 26 And thou shalt not go by paths to my altar, lest thy filthiness be scattered there.

CHAPTER 21

1 These are the laws you shall establish before them: 2 If thou takest a Hebrew servant, he shall serve six years, and at the seventh he shall go out free, paying nothing. 3 If he came alone, he shall go out alone; if he is married, his wife shall go out with him. 4 If his master has given him a wife, and she has given him sons or daughters, his wife and her children shall be his masters, but he shall go out alone. 5 But if the servant says, "I love my master, my wife and my children, I will not go out free." 6 then his master shall take him to the judg- es, and put him to the stake or post, and his master shall pierce his ear with a ribbon, and serve him all his life. 7 Likewise, if a man sells his daughter to make her a maidservant, she shall not go out as seruants do. 8 If she does not please her master, who has betrothed her to himself, he will buy her; he cannot sell her to strangers, because he has despised her. 9 But if he has betrothed her to his son, he shall deal with her according to the rules of daughters. 10 If he takes another wife, he shall not diminish her food, the reward and recompense of her virginity. 11 If he does not do these three things to her, she shall go free, paying nothing. 12 Whoever strikes a man and he dies, he shall die. 13 If a man has not found a way out, but God has offered it into his hand, I will show you a place where he may escape. 14 But if a man presumptuously rushes upon his neighbor to kill him by de- ceit, you shall remove him from my altar, that he may die. 15 He also who strikes his father or his mother shall die. 16 Whoever steals a man and

sells him, if he is found with him, he shall die of death. 17 Whoever curses his father or his mother shall die of death. 18 When men undress together, and one strikes another with a stone or with a fist, and he does not die, but lies in bed, 19 if he rises again and walks without holding on to his staff, he who struck him shall go quietly, for he alone shall bear the expense of his rest and pay for his recovery. 20 If one strikes his ser- vant or maidservant with the rod and they die under his hand, he shall surely be punished. 21 But if he continues a day or two days, he shall not be punished, for it is his money. 22 Moreover, if a man strips and wounds a wom- an with a child, so that the child departs from her, and death does not follow him, he shall surely be punished according to what the woman's husband appeals to him, or he shall pay according to what the judges determine. 23 But if death follows, you shall pay life for life, 24 eye for eye, tooth for tooth, hand for hand, leaf for leaf, 25 burn for burn, wound for wound, stripe for stripe. 26 If one strikes his servant in the eye or his mother in the eye and kills him, he shall let him loose by the eye. 27 And if he strikes his servant's tooth or his woman's tooth, he shall let him go free for his tooth. 28 If an ox mauls a man or a woman and dies, the ox shall be stoned, and its flesh shall not be eaten, but the owner of the ox shall go in peace. 29 If the ox used to push in the past, and it was entrusted to its master and the master did not restrain it, and after it has killed a man or a woman, the ox shall be stoned, and its master shall also die. 30 If a sum of money is set upon him, he shall pay the price of his life, that which shall be set upon him. 31 Whether he has gored a son or a daughter, he shall be judged in the same way. 32 If the ox mauls a servant or an elder, he shall give his master three shekels of silver, and the ox shall be stoned. 33 When a man opens a pit or digs a pit and does not close it, and an ox or an axe falls into it, 34 the owner of the pit shall repair it and give money to the owners, but the dead beast shall be his. 35 And if a man's ox wounds his neighbor's ox, caus- ing it to die, they shall select the dead ox and give the money due to him, and the dead ox shall also be paid. 36 Then if it is known that the ox in the past has pushed and its owner has not kept it, he shall pay ox for ox, but the dead ox shall be his property.

CHAPTER 22

1 If anyone steals an ox or a ram and kills or sells it, he shall return five oxen for the ox and four rams for the ram. 2 If a thief is found breaking, and is struck that he may die, no blood shall be shed for him. 3 But if he is in the daylight, blood shall be shed for him, for he must return everything; if he has none, he must be compensated for his theft. 4 If theft is found with him, others, whether oxen, or donkeys, or sheep, shall return double. 5 If a man damages a field or a vineyard and puts his beast to graze in someone else's field, he shall return the best of his field and the best of his vineyard. 6 If fire breaks out and creeps among the thorns, and the stacks of grain or standing grain or the field are consumed, he who set the fire shall return everything. 7 If a man delivers money or stuff to his neighbor for safekeeping and it is stolen from his house, if the thief is found, he shall pay double. 8 If the thief is not found, the householder shall be brought before the judges to declare whether he laid his hand on his neighbor's property or not. 9 In all cases of theft, whether of oxen, axes, sheep, clothing, or any other lost thing that another claims as his own, the case of both parties shall be brought before the judg- es, and he who is condemned by the judges shall pay

double to his neighbor. 10 If a man entrusts his neighbor with the custody of a plank, ox, sheep, or any animal, and it dies or is wounded or carried away by enemies, and no one sees it, 11 another thing of the LORD shall be between the two, who has not laid his hand on the good of his neighbor; and the owner shall take the other thing, and shall not make it good: 12 but if it is taken from him, he shall return it to the owner. 13 If it is torn in pieces, he shall give an account of it, and shall not make it good. 14 If a man borrows anything from his neighbor and it is injured or dies, without the owner being present, he shall make good the loss. 15 If the owner is at home, he shall not be able to make good; for if it is a thing hired, it came for his hire. 16 If a man seduces an unbetrothed woman and lies with her, he must give her away and take her as a wife. 17 If her father refuses to give her to him in marriage, he shall pay money, according to the dowry of virgins. 18 You shall not allow a witch to live. 19 Whoever lies with a beast shall die a death. 20 He who makes of- ferings to other gods, but only to the LORD, shall be killed. 21 Moreover, you shall not do violence to the stranger or oppress him, for you were strangers in the land of Egypt. 22 You shall not trouble any widow or fatherless child. 23 If you disturb such a one, and he calls and cries out to me, I will hear his cry. 24 Then my anger will be kindled and I will kill you with the sword, and your wives will be widows and your children orphans. 25 If you lend money to my people, that is, to the poor man who is with you, you will not be like a moneylender to him; you will not oppress him with violence. 26 If you take your neighbor's money as a pledge, you shall return it to him before the sun goes down: 27 For this is his only blanket, and this is his garment for his skin; where shall he sleep? Therefore when he cries unto me, I will hear him: for I am merci- ful. 28 You shall not be angry with the judges, nor shall you speak evil of the leader of your people. 29 Your abundance and your wealth will not hold you back. The first born of your children you will give to me. 30 The same you shall do with your oxen and with your sheep: ten days he shall be with his damning, and on the eighth day you shall give him to me. 31 You shall be a holy people to me, and you shall not eat any meat that has been eaten in the fields; you shall throw it to the dogs.

CHAPTER 23

1 Thou shalt not receive a false tale, nor shalt thou go with the wicked to be a false witness. 2 You will not follow a multitude to do evil, nor will you agree in a dispute to decline the truth after many. 3 You shall not esteem a poor man in his cause. 4 If you meet your enemy's ox or his plank that goes astray, you shall bring it back to him. 5 If you see your enemy's horse lying under his burden, will you stop helping him? You will help him again with it. 6 Thou shalt not take away thy poor man's right in his bottom. 7 You will keep away from every false matter, and you will not trample down the in- nocent and the righteous, for I will not justify the wicked. 8 You shall not take any gift, for gift blinds the wise and perturbs the words of the righteous. 9 You shall not oppress the stranger, for you know the heart of the stranger, since you were strangers in the land of Egypt. 10 Moreover, for six years you shall sow your land and reap its fruit, 11 but in the seventh year thou shalt let it rest and rest, that the poor of thy people may eat, and what they leave may be eaten by the beasts of the field. Likewise you shall do with your vineyard and with your olive trees. 12 Six days shalt thou do thy work, and on the

seventh day shalt thou rest, that thy ox and thy horse may rest, and thy mother's son and the stranger may be re- freshed. 13 You shall pay attention to all the things I have told you; you shall not mention the name of other gods or hear it from your own mouth. 14 Three times you shall make a feast in my honor during the year. 15 The feast of unleavened bread: you shall eat unleavened bread for seven days, as I commanded you, in the time of the month of Abib, because in it you came out of Egypt; and no one shall stand before me empty: 16 The feast of the gath- ering of the first fruits of thy labors, which thou hast sown in the fields, and the feast of the gathering of the fruits at the end of the year, when thou hast gathered thy labors from the fields. 17 For these three times in the year all your male children shall stand before the LORD Jehouah. 18 You shall not offer the blood of my sacrifice with leavened bread, nor shall the fat of my sacrifice remain until the morning. 19 You shall bring into the house of the LORD your God the first fruits of your land, but you shall not see a kid in its mother's milk. 20 Behold, I am sending an angel be- fore you, to guard you on the way and to lead you to the place I have prepared. 21 Beware of him, and hearken to his voice, and do not scruple, for he will not spare your misdeeds, for in him is my name. 22 But if you will listen to his message and do all that I tell you, I will be an enemy to your enemies and afflict those who afflict you. 23 For my angel will go before you and lead you to the Amorites, the Hittites, the Perizzites, the Canaanites, the Iuites, and the Jebusites, and I will destroy them. 24 You shall not bow down to their gods, nor serve them, nor act like them, but you shall destroy them and tear their images to pieces. 25 For you shall serve the LORD your God, and he shall bless your bread and your water, and I will remove all sickness from your belly. 26 No one shall cast his fruit or be born in your land; the number of your days I will fulfill. 27 I will send my fear before you, and I will destroy all the peoples among whom you go; and I will cause all your enemies to turn their backs upon you: 28 And I will send bumblebees be- fore thee, which shall drive out the Hiuites, the Canaanites, and the Hittites from thy face. 29 I will not drive them out of thy face in a single year, except when the land shall be- come a wilderness, and the beasts of the field shall multiply against thee. 30 Little by little I will drive them out of your face, until you grow up and inherit the land. 31 I will make thy coasts from the Red Sea unto the sea of the Philistines, and from the wilderness unto the River: for I will deliver the inhabitants of the land into thy hand, and I will drive them out of thy face. 32 You shall make no covenant with them or with their gods: 33 They shall not dwell in thy land, unless they cause thee to sin against me: for if thou serve their gods, it shall be thy destruction.

CHAPTER 24

1 Now he had said to Moses, "Come to the LORD, you, Aaron, Nadab and Abiu and sev- enty other elders of Israel, and worship far away." 2 Moses alone will approach the LORD, but they will not approach, and the people will not go with him. 3 Then Moses came and told the people all the words of the LORD and all the laws; and all the people answered in unison and said, "All that the LORD has said, we will do." 4 And Moses wrote down all the words of the LORD, and rose early and built an altar under the mountain and two pillars according to the two tribes of Israel. 5 Then he sent young men from among the children of Israel, who

offered burnt offerings and peace offerings to the LORD. 6 Moses took half the blood, put it in basins, and half the blood he sprinkled on the altar. 7 After he took the book of the covenant, he read it before the people, who said, "Everything the LORD has said, we will do and be obedient." 8 Then Moses took the blood, sprinkled it on the people, and said, "Here is the blood of the covenant that the LORD has made with you concerning all these things." 9 Then Moses and Aaron and Nadab and Abihu and seuentie of the elders of Israel went. 10 And they saw the God of Israel, and under his feet was like a stone of Saphir, and like the sky when it is clear. 11 And on the nobles of the children of Israel he did not stretch out his hand; they too said God and ate and drank. 12 And the LORD said to Moses, "Come to me on the mountain and stay there; I will give you the tables of stone, the law and the commands that I have written to teach them." 13 Then Moses arose, together with his minister Ioshua, and Moses went to the mount of God, 14 and said to the elders, "Stay here, until we return to you; and behold, Aaron and Hur are with you; whoever has any problem, come to them." 15 Then Moses went up the mountain, and the cloud envel- oped the mountain, 16 The glory of the LORD remained on Mount Sinai, and the cloud en- veloped it for six days; on the seventh day he called Moses from the midst of the cloud. 17 The sight of the glory of the LORD was like a consuming fire on the top of the mountain in the eyes of the children of Israel. 18 And Moses went into the midst of the cloud and ascend- ed the mountain; and Moses remained on the mountain for forty days and forty nights.

CHAPTER 25

1 Then the LORD spoke to Moses, saying, 2 Speak to the children of Israel, that they may receive an offering for me; of every man whose heart freely permits it, you shall take the offering for me. 3 This is the offering you shall take from them: gold, silk, and reed, 4 white silk, purple, sea skins, fine linen, and sea goats, 5 ramskins dyed red, badger skins, and wood of Shittim, 6 oil for light, spices for anoining oil and for sweet oil perfume, 7 stones of onyx and stones to set in the Ephod and in the breast plate. 8 They shall also make me a sanctuary, that I may dwell among them. 9 According to all that I have taught you, you will also make the form of the Tabernacle and the front of all its instruments. 10 You will also make an ark of Shittim wood, two and a half cubits long, one and a half cubits wide, and one and a half cubits high. 11 You shall clothe it with pure gold, inside and out, and make on it a crown of gold all around. 12 You shall make for it four rings of gold and put them on its four corners, that is, two rings on one side and two on the other. 13 You shall make slats of Shittim wood and plaster them with gold. 14 Then you shall put the rods in the rings on the sides of the ark, to support the ark with them. 15 The rods shall remain in the rings of the ark; they shall not be taken out of it. 16 So you shall put in the ark the Tes- timony that I will give you. 17 You shall also make a mercy table of pure gold, two cubits and a half long and one cubit and a half wide. 18 Thou shalt make two cherubim of bronze, of wood beaten with a hammer, at both ends of the Merceseate. 19 You shall make a Cher- ubim at one end and the other Cherubim at the other end; with the matter of the Merci- seate you shall make the Cherubim at the two ends. 20 And the Cherubim shall spread their wings over them, caressing with their wings the seat of Mercy, and their faces toward each other; toward the seat of Mercy

shall be the faces of the Cherubim. 21 And thou shalt put the Merceseate over the Ark, and in the Ark thou shalt put the Testimony that I shall give thee, 22 and there I will declare myself to you, and from above the Mercieseate, between the two Cherubim that are on the arch of the Testimony, I will tell you all the things that I will give you to command the children of Israel. 23 You shall also make a table of Shit- tim wood, two cubits long, one cubit wide, and one and a half cubits high: 24 Thou shalt clothe it with pure gold, and make a crown of gold round about it. 25 Thou shalt also make a border of four fingers round about it, and shalt make a crown of gold round about the border. 26 Then you shall make it four rings of bronze and put them on the four corners that are at the four feet of the monument: 27 Toward the edge, the rings shall be the plac- es for the rods, to support the table. 28 And thou shalt make the slats of Shittim wood, and thou shalt adorn them with gold, that the table may be carried with them. 29 You shall also make plates for the table, and cups for incense, and cups for the table, and goblets for the table, again of fine gold. 30 And you shall continually put bread on the table be- fore me. 31 You shall also make a candlestick of pure gold; the candlestick shall be made of wood beaten with a hammer, with its shaft, its branches, its boules, its knots, and its flours shall be of the same material. 32 Out of its sides shall come also six boules, three branches of the candlestick on one side and three branches of the candlestick on the other side. 33 Three almond-like boules, a bight and a leaf in one branch, and three almond-like boules in the other branch, a bight and a leaf; so for all the six branches that come out of the Candlestick. 34 And in the shaft of the candle- stick there shall be four almond-like boules, with its knots and flakes. 35 And there shall be a knot under two branches, and a knot under two branches, and a knot under two branch- es, according to the six branches that come out of the candlestick. 36 Their knots and their branches shall be part of it. All this shall be one beaten piece of pure gold. 37 You shall make the seven lamps of this candlestick, and you shall put lamps on it to make light for that which is in front. 38 Its snuff and snuffboxes also shall be of pure gold. 39 Of a talent of fine gold you shall make him with all these instru- ments. 40 See therefore that you make them according to their appearance, which was shown to you in the mountains.

CHAPTER 26

1 Then you shall make the tabernacle with ten curtains of fine twisted linen, of snow-white silk, of purple, and of leather; and in them you shall make cherubim of brocaded wood. 2 The length of a curtain shall be eight and twenty cubits, and the width of a curtain four cubits; each curtain shall have a measure. 3 Five cur- tains shall be coupled one to another, and the other five curtains shall be coupled one to an- other. 4 And thou shalt make cords of blown silk on the hem of the first curtain, which is in the margin of the coupling; and the same shalt thou make on the hem of the other cur- tain in the margin, in the second coupling. 5 And thou shalt make fifty cords in one cur- tain, and fifty cords in the hem of the curtain that is in the second coupling; and the cords shall be opposite one another. 6 You shall also make fifty notches of gold, and you shall cou- ple the curtains to each other with the notch- es, and it shall be one tabernacle. 7 You shall also make golden curtains of goats, which shall serve as a covering for the tabernacle; you shall make them eleven curtains in num- ber. 8 The length of one

curtain shall be thirty cubits, and the breadth of one curtain four cubits; the curtains shall be of one measure. 9 You shall make five curtaines for themselves and six curtains for themselves, but you shall double the sixth curtaine on the front of the robe. 10 And thou shalt make fifty curtaines in the edge of one curtaine, at the edge of the mating, and fifty curtaines in the edge of the other curtaine, in the second mating. 11 In the same way, you shall make fifty cords of cord, fasten them to the cords, and join the cou- pling so that it is one. 12 The remainder that remains in the curtains of the wrapping, that is, half of the curl that remains, shall be left on the back side of the Tabernacle, 13 in order that the cubit on one side and the cubit on the oth- er of what is left in the legs of the curtains of the accoutrement may remain on either side of the Tabernacle to repair it. 14 Moreover, for this covering thou shalt make a covering of dead ramskins of red, and a covering of bad- ger skins on the outside.15 Moreover, for the Tabernacle you shall make planks of Shittim wood to stand on. 16 Ten cubits shall be the length of a plank, and a cubit and a half cu- bit the width of a plank. 17 In one plank there shall be two tenons, arranged like the feet of a ladder, one against the other; so shalt thou do for all the boards of the Tabernacle. 18 And thou shalt make boards for the Tabernacle, that is, twenty boards from the south side, all to the south. 19 You shall make forty sockets of silk under the twenty boards, two sockets under one board for its two tenons, and two sockets under another board for its two ten- ons. 20 Likewise, on the other side of the tab- ernacle, toward the north side, there shall be twenty-five boards, 21 and their four boards of silk, two boards under one board and two boards under another board. 22 On the side of the tabernacle, toward the west, you shall make six boards. 23 You shall also make two boards at the corners of the Tabernacle, on the two sides. 24 Thou shalt also make them underneath, and thou shalt also make them round about a ring; so shall it be for these two: they shall be for you two corners. 25 Then shall be eight boards with sockets of silk, that is, six sockets, two sockets under one board, and two sockets under another board. 26 You shall make five slats of Shittim wood for the boards on one side of the Tabernacle, 27 and five slats for the boards on the other side of the Tabernacle; also five slats for the boards on the side of the Tabernacle toward the west. 28 The middle rod shall pass through the cen- ter of the boards, from one end to the other. 29 And thou shalt make the boards of gold, and shalt make their rings of gold, as places for the slats, and shalt make the slats of gold. 30 Thus you shall rebuild the Tabernacle ac- cording to its structure, which was shown to you on the mount. 31 You shall also make a veil of light silk, of purple, of skins, and of finely twisted linen; you shall make it of red wood with cherubim. 32 You shall hang it on four pillars of Shittim wood covered with gold (whose hooks shall be of gold) and fastened to four sockets of silver. 33 Then you shall hang the tray on the hooks, to introduce into it, within the tray, the ark of the Testimony; the tray shall be your separation between the holy place and the most holy place. 34 You shall also put a mercy seat on the ark of the Testi- mony in the most holy place. 35 You shall put the table without the vault and the candle- stick in front of the table in the south side of the tabernacle, and you shall put the table in the north side. 36 You shall also make a cloth for the covering of the Tabernacle, of blown silk, of purple, of chamois skins, and of linen finely twisted and worked with the needle. 37 And thou shalt make for the hanging five pil- lars of Shittim, and cast them of gold; their heads shall be of gold, and thou shalt cast five brasse sockets thereon.

CHAPTER 27

1 Moreover thou shalt make the altar of wood of Shittim, five cubits long and five cubits wide (the altar shall be square) and three cu- bits high. 2 You shall make him horns at the four corners; the horns shall be of themselves, and you shall clothe them with brasse. 3 Thou shalt also make his cineraries for ashes, his besoms, his basins, his hooks for meat, and his censers; thou shalt make all his instru- ments of brasse. 4 Thou shalt make therein a lattice like a net of reeds; moreover, on this lattice thou shalt make four rings of bronze at its four corners. 5 You shall put it under the structure of the altar, so that the lattice shall be in the center of the altar. 6 You shall also make splints for the altar, splints, I say, of Shittim wood, and you shall have them sewn with the brassa. 7 And its bars shall be inserted into the rings, which bars shall be placed on either side of the altar to support it. 8 You shall make the altar of wood between the boards; as God showed you on the moun- tain, so shall they make it. 9 You shall also make the courtyard of the Tabernacle on the south side, that is, all to the south; the court- yard shall have curtains of finely woven linen, a hundred cubits long, on one side, 10 and it shall have twenty pillars, with their twenty bases of reeds; the heads of the pillars and their fillets shall be of silk. 11 Likewise, on the north side, there shall be a curtain a hundred and fifty cubits long, with its twenty pillars and their twenty bases of wood; the heads of the pillars and their fillets shall be of silk. 12 The width of the court on the west side shall have curtains fifty cubits long, with their ten columns and their ten sockets. 13 The width of the courtyard from east to east shall have fif- ty cubits. 14 Moreover, on one side there shall be vestments of fifty cubits, with their three pillars and their three sockets. 15 Likewise, on the other side, there shall be curtains of fifty cubits, with their three pillars and their three bases. 16 In the gate of the courtyard there shall be a vault of twenty-five cubits, of white silk, purple, scarlet, and linen finely twisted and needleworked, with its four pillars and their four sockets. 17 All the columns of the courtyard shall have silk fillets all around, with their heads of silk and their sockets of brasse. 18 The length of the courtyard shall be an hundred cubits, the width fifty on either side, and the height five cubits; the vestments shall be of fine twined linen, and their sock- ets of brasse. 19 All the utensils of the taber- nacle for its service, all its pinnacles, and all the pinnacles of the court shall be of brasse. 20 And thou shalt command the children of Israel to bring thee pure beaten olive oil for light, that the lamps may be always burning. 21 In the Tabernacle of Congregation, without the wall, which is before the Testimony, Aaron and his sons shall prepare them from evening to morning before the LORD, as a statute for all their generation, to be observed by the children of Israel.

CHAPTER 28

1 Thou shalt cause thy brother Aaron and his sons with him to come to thee from among the children of Israel, that he may serve me in the priestly office: I appoint Aaron, Nad- ab and Abihu, Eleazar and Ithamar, Aaron's sons. 2 Moreover thou shalt make holy gar- ments for Aaron thy brother, glorious and beautiful. 3 Therefore you shall speak to all the wise men, whom I have filled with the spirit of wisdom, that they may make Aaron's gar- ments to

consecrate him, that he may serve me in the priestly office. 4 These shall be the garments that they shall make: a breast plate, an Ephod, a robe, a cloak of wool, a mitre, and a girdle. 5 Therefore they shall take gold, and puffed silk, and purple, and sealskins, and fine linen, 6 And they shall make the Ephod of gold, of white silk, of purple, of scarlet, and of fine twined linen, with brogue work. 7 Its two shoulders shall be joined by the two edges; so it shall be closed. 8 And the garniture of the same Ephod, which shall be put on him, shall be of the same workmanship, and of the same stuffing, whether of gold, or of white silk, or of purple, or of skins, or of fine twined linen. 9 You shall take two onix stones and engrave on them the names of the children of Israel: 10 Six names of them on the first stone and the six names that remain on the second stone, according to their generations. 11 You shall have the two stones engraved according to the names of the children of Israel by a seal engraver, who works and engraves stone, and you shall have them set and embossed in gold. 12 You shall place the two stones on the shoulders of Ephod, as stones of remembrance of the children of Israel, for Aaron shall bear their names before the LORD on his two shoulders, as a reminder. 13 You shall then make garments of gold, 14 and two cheeks of fine gold, at the end, of worked wood, and you shall fasten the worked cheeks on the gar- ments. 15 And thou shalt also make the plate of the crest of judgment with stock work, like that of Ephod: thou shalt make it of gold, and of white silk, and of purple, and of leather, and of fine twined linen. 16 It shall be square and double, one hand long and one hand wide. 17 Then you shall make it full of places for stones, that is, four rows of stones; the order shall be this: a ruby, a topaz and a car- buncle in the first row. 18 In the second row you shall place an emeraude, a saphir and a diamond. 19 In the third row, a turquoise, an achate and a hematite. 20 And in the fourth wheel a chrysolite, an onyx, and a jasper; they shall be set in gold in their settings. 21 And the stones shall be according to the names of the children of Israel, two, according to their names, as seals, each according to its name, and they shall be for the two tribes. 22 Then you shall make on the breast plate two cheeks at the ends, worked of pure gold. 23 You shall also make on the breast plate two rings of gold, and you shall put the two rings on the two ends of the breast plate. 24 You shall put the two wedges of gold in the two rings at the ends of the breast plate. 25 And the other two ends of the two silver wedges thou shalt fas- ten in two incisions, and thou shalt put them on the shoulders of the Ephod, on the front side. 26 And thou shalt also make two rings of gold, which thou shalt put on the other two ends of the breast plate, on its edge, to- ward the inside of the Ephod. 27 And thou shalt make two more rings of gold, and thou shalt put them on the two sides of the Ephod, under the front and against the coupling of the Ephod, on the back edge of the Ephod. 28 Then they shall bind the breastplate by its rings to the rings of the Ephod, with a lace of light silk, that it may be fastened on the iron covering of the Ephod, and the breastplate may not come off the Ephod. 29 So Aaron shall bear on his heart the names of the chil- dren of Israel in the judgment plate, when he enters the holy place, to remember them continually before the LORD. 30 You shall also put the Vrim and the Thummim, which shall be on Aaron's heart when he enters the holy place, in the judgment plate, and Aaron shall bear the judgment of the children of Israel on his heart, before the LORD, as a continual re- minder. 31 You shall make Ephod's robe com- pletely of white silk. 32 The hole for his head shall be in the center, with a border of wool around the collar; it shall be like the collar of a menagerie that does not open. 33 And under her skirts thou shalt make pomegranates of puffed silk, of purple and tights round about her skirts, and bells of gold between them all round about: 34 That is, a bell of gold and a pomegranate, and a bell of gold and a pome- granate round about the skirts of the robe. 35 So shall it be for Aaron, when he ministers, and the sound thereof shall be heard when he enters into the holy place before the LORD, and when he comes out, and shall not be dyed. 36 You shall also make a plate of pure gold and engrave on it, as seals are engraved, the shrines of the LORD, 37 And thou shalt put it on a lace of blown silk, and place it on the miter, and on the front of the miter. 38 So it shall be on Aaron's forehead, that Aaron may bear the iniquity of the offerings which the children of Israel shall offer in all their holy offerings; and it shall always be on his fore- head, to make them acceptable to the LORD. 39 Likewise thou shalt embroider the mantle of fine thread, and shalt make a mitre of fine thread; but thou shalt also make a girdle of needle. 40 You shall also make cloaks for the sons of Aaron, and you shall make belts of them, and cups of them for glory and fame. 41 And thou shalt put them on Aaron thy broth- er, and on his sons with him, and thou shalt anoint them, and fill their hands, and sanc- tify them, that they may exercise the priest- ly ministry with me. 42 You shall also make them linen breeches to cover their functions: from the loins to the thighs they shall be long. 43 They shall be for Aaron and his sons when they enter the Tabernacle of the congregation or when they go to the altar to officiate in the holy place, that they may not commit iniquity and die. This will be an obligation for him and his descendants.

CHAPTER 29

1 When you consecrate them to be my priests, you shall also do this, "Take one young calf and two rams without blemish, 2 And bread and cakes leavened and tempered with oil, and wafers leavened and anointed with oil (of fine grain you shall make them). 3 Then you shall put them in a basket and present them in the basket with the calf and the two branches, 4 Then you shall lead Aaron and his sons to the entrance of the Tabernacle of Meeting and wash them with water. 5 You shall also take their garments, and you shall put Aaron's tu- nic, Ephod's robe, and Ephod's breastplate, and you shall fasten them to him with the brocade sheath of Ephod. 6 Then you shall put the mitre on his head, and you shall put the holy horn on his mitre. 7 Then thou shalt take the oile of anoinization, and thou shalt give him power over his head, and thou shalt anoinize him. 8 You shall bring his sons and put cloaks on them, 9 Thou shalt gird them with sheaths, both Aaron and his sons, and put on their caps, and the priestly office shall be theirs forever; thou shalt also fill Aaron's hands and the hands of his sons. 10 Then you shall present the calf before the Tabernacle of the congregation, and Aaron and his sons shall put their hands on the head of the calf. 11 You shall thus kill the calf before the LORD at the threshold of the Tabernacle of Meeting. 12 Then you shall take the blood of the calf, put it with your finger on the horns of the altar, and sprinkle the rest of the blood on the base of the altar. 13 You shall also take all the fat that is inside, the meat that is on the liver, the two kids and the fat that is on them, and you shall bury them on the altar. 14 But the flesh of the calf, its skin and hide, you shall burn with fire without the altar; it is a sinful offense. 15 You shall also take a ram, and Aron and his sons shall lay their hands on the ram's head. 16

Then you shall kill the ram, take its blood, and sprinkle it all around the altar, 17 You shall cut the ram into pieces, wash its entrails and legs, and put them on the pieces and on its head. 18 Then you shall bury the whole ram on the altar, for it is a burnt offering to the LORD for a sweet smell; it is an offering made by fire to the LORD. 19 You shall take the other ram, and Aaron and his sons shall put their hands on the ram's head. 20 Then you shall kill the ram and take its blood and put it on the lip of Aaron's ear, on the lip of his sons' right ear, on the thumb of their right hand and on the big toe of their right foot, and you shall sprinkle the blood on the altar all around. 21 And thou shalt take the blood that is on the altar, and the oil of anoinjection, and thou shalt sprin- kle it on Aaron, and on his garments, and on his sons, and on the garments of his sons with him; so he shall be halved, and his garments, and his sons, and the garments of his sons with him. 22 And thou shalt take also from the rammes the fat and the rumpe, that is, the fat that is within, and the skin of the cheek, and the two kids, and the fat that is upon them, and the right shoulder (for it is the ramme of the consecration). 23 And a loaf of bread, a cake of bread tempered with oil, and a wa- fer, from the basket of seasoned loaves that is before the LORD. 24 You shall put all this into the hands of Aaron and into the hands of his sons, and you shall shake them on either side before the LORD. 25 Then you shall take them out of their hands and bury them on the altar, as well as the burnt offering, as a sweet fra- grance before the LORD, for this is an offer- ing made by fire to the LORD. 26 Likewise you shall take the crest of the ram of consecration, which is for Aaron, and you shall shake it on either side before the LORD, and it shall be your portion. 27 You shall sanctify the crest of the shaken offering and the shoulder of the salvation offering shaken on either side of the ram of consecration, which was for Aaron and his sons. 28 Aaron and his sons shall keep it by statute for all the children of Israel, for it is a salvation offering and shall be a salva- tion offering for the children of Israel, one of their peace offerings and a salvation offering for the LORD. 29 The sacred garments, which belong to Aaron, shall be of his sons after him, to be anointed therein, and to be consecrated therein. 30 The son who is to be Priest, in his robe, shall wear them on the seven days when he enters the tent of meeting to officiate in the holy place. 31 So you shall take the ram of con- secration and put his flesh in the holy place. 32 And Aaron and his sons shall eat the flesh of the ram and the bread that is in the basket at the entrance to the Tabernacle of the con- gregation. 33 So they shall eat these things, with which their atonement was made, to consecrate and sanctify them; but an outsider shall not eat of them, for they are holy things. 34 If of the meat of the consecration or of the bread anything remains until the morning, you shall burn the rest with fire; you shall not eat it, for it is a holy thing. 35 And thou shalt do so with Aaron and with his sons, according to all that I have commanded thee: thou shalt consecrate them ten days, 36 And thou shalt offer a calf every day as a sin offering, for rec- onciliation; and thou shalt cleanse the altar, when thou hast offered on it for reconcilia- tion, and thou shalt dry it for sanctification. 37 And every second day thou shalt cleanse the altar and sanctify it, so that the altar shall be most holy; and that which toucheth the altar shall be holy. 38 This is what you shall present on the altar: two lambs of a year, day by day, continually. 39 One lamb you shall present in the morning, and the other you shall present at noon. 40 And with the one lambe, a tenth part of fine flour mixed with the fourth part of a hin of crushed oil and the fourth part of a hin of wine, for a drink offering. 41 The oth- er blade you shall present at mealtime; you shall make it according to the offense of the morning and according to the offense of the appetizer, as a burnt offense and as a sweet offering to the LORD. 42 This shall be a con- tinual burning for your generations in the place of the Tabernacle of Meeting before the LORD, where I will apprehend to speak with you. 43 There I will lean on the children of Israel, and the place will be sanctified by my glory. 44 I will sanctify the Tabernacle of the congregation and the altar: I will also sanctify Aaron and his sons as my priests, 45 And I will dwell among the children of Israel, and I will be their God. 46 Then they shall know that I am the LORD their God, who brought them out of the land of Egypt to dwell among them: I am the LORD their God.

CHAPTER 30

1 You shall also make an altar for perfume, of Shittim wood. 2 Its length shall be one cubit, its width one cubit (it shall be four squares), and its height two cubits; its horns shall be of the same material, 3 You shall clothe it with fine gold, both its top and its sides all around, and its horns; you shall also make it a crown of gold all around. 4 Moreover thou shalt make under this crown two rings of gold on one side and on the other; and on each side thou shalt make them, that they may be set for the shanks with which thou shalt bear it. 5 And the shanks thou shalt make of wood of Shittim, and thou shalt cast them with gold. 6 Then you shall place it in front of the sailing ship that is near the Ark of the Testimony, in front of the Merciseate that is above the Testimony, where I will lean on you. 7 Aaron shall bury fragrant incense there every morning; when he clothes the lamps with it, he shall bury it. 8 In the same way, every evening, when Aar- on puts out his lamps, he will bury incense in it; this fragrance will remain eternally before the LORD, for all your generations. 9 You shall not offer you foreign incense, nor burnt sac- rifices, nor spoils, nor shall you sprinkle any alcoholic drink upon it. 10 Aaron shall make reconciliation on the horns of it once a year with the blood of the sin offering on the day of reconciliation; once a year he shall make rec- onciliation on it for all your generations; this is most holy to the LORD. 11 Then the LORD spoke to Moses, saying, 12 When thou shalt make the sum of the children of Israel accord- ing to their name, they shall give every man a ransom of his life unto the LORD, when thou shalt tell them that there is no plague among them when thou hast counted them. 13 Every man who enters the nomber shall give half of a shekel, according to the shekel of the sanc- tuary; (a shekel is equal to twenty-five gera) half of the shekel shall be an offering to the LORD. 14 Everyone with a name from the age of twenty years and upward shall give an of- fering to the LORD.15 The rich shall not pass away, and the poor shall not diminish by half a shekel, when you give an offering to the LORD for the redemption of your posses- sions. 16 So you shall take the money of the redemption of the children of Israel and put it in the box of the Tabernacle of the con- gregation, that it may be a memorial for the children of Israel before the LORD, for the redemption of your burdens. 17 The LORD also spoke to Moses, saying, 18 "You shall also make a lip of brush and its part of a brush for washing; you shall put it between the Taber- nacle of the Congregation and the Altar, and you shall put water in it. 19 For Aaron and his sons shall wash their hands and feet there. 20 When they go into the Tabernacle of Conven- tion or when they go to the Altar to officiate and to make the

fragrance of your burning to the Lord, they shall wash themselves with water, lest they die. 21 So they shall wash their hands and their feet lest they die; and this shall be an ordinance for them forever, both for him and for his descendants for all their generations. 22 The LORD also spoke to Mo- ses, saying, 23 Take thou also of the chief spic- es of myrrh most pure, fifty hundred shekels; of sweet cinamom, half, that is, two hundred and fifty; and of sweet calamus, two hundred and fifty: 24 Also of cassia fifty-five cents, ac-cording to the shekel of the sanctuary, and of olive oil a hin. 25 And thou shalt make of it an olla of holy wineskin, that is, an olla most pre- cious according to the art of the Apothecary: this shall be the olla of holy wineskin. 26 With it thou shalt anoinect the Tabernacle of the Congregation and the Ark of the Testimony: 27 also the table and all its instruments, the candlestick with all its instruments, and the altar of incense: 28 also the altar of incense with all its instruments, the lauer and its foote. 29 And thou shalt sanctify them, and they shall be most holy: whosoever toucheth them shall be holy. 30 You shall also anoint Aaron and his sons and consecrate them, that they may exercise the priestly office for me. 31 Moreover you will speak to the children of Israel, saying, "This will be a holy anointing for me, for all your generations." 32 No one shall anoint human flesh with it, nor shall you make any composition similar to it, for it is holy and shall be holy to you. 33 Whoever shall make a similar composition of it or put some on a stranger, he shall be cut off from his peo- ple." 34 The LORD said to Moses, "Take these spices, pure myrrh, clear gum and galbanum, these odors with pure frankincense, of like weight: 35 Then thou shalt make of it a per- fume composed according to the art of apoth- ecary, mixed together, pure and holy. 36 And thou shalt grind it into dust, and put it before the Ark of the Testimony in the Tabernacle of the Cogregation, where I will appoint thee; it shall be for thee most holy. 37 And thou shalt not make any compound like unto this perfume which thou shalt prepare: it shall be unto you holy unto the LORD. 38 Whosoever shall make such a one to perfume it, he shall be cut off from his people.

CHAPTER 31

1 The LORD spoke to Moses, saying 2 Behold, I have called by name Bezaleel the son of Vri, the son of Hur, of the tribe of Judah, 3 whom I have filled with the Spirit of God, in wisdom, in understanding, in knowledge, and in every work: 4 to find curious works to work in gold, silver and bronze, 5 also in the art of setting stones, and of cutting lumber, and of work- ing in every way. 6 And behold, I have joined to him Aholiab the son of Ahisamach, of the tribe of Dan, and in the hearts of all who have wise hearts I have put wisdom to do all that I have commanded you: 7 that is, the Taberna- cle of the Congregation, the Ark of the Testi- mony, and the Merciseate that shall be on it, with all the instruments of the Tabernacle: 8 also the Table and its instruments, the pure candlestick with all its instruments, and the Altar of Fragrance: 9 also the Altar of roasts with all its instruments, and the Lauer with its instruments: 10 also the garments for the ministry, and the holy garments for Aaron the priest, and the garments of his sons, to exercise the priestly office, 11 and anoinising oil and perfume for the sanctuary, according to what I have commanded you. 12 Afterward the LORD spoke to Moses, saying. 13 Speak also to the children of Israel and say, "Never- theless keep my Sabbaths, for it is a sign be- tween

me and you in your generations, that you may know that I, the LORD, sanctify you. 14 You shall therefore keep the Sabbath, for it is holy to you; whoever defiles it shall die of death; therefore whoever works therein shall be cut off from his people. 15 Six days shall men work, but the seventh day is the Sabbath of rest sacred to the LORD; whoever does any work on the Sabbath day shall die of death. 16 Therefore the children of Israel shall keep the Sabbath, that they may observe rest for all their generation for an everlasting time. 17 It is a sign between me and the children of Isra- el for eternity, because in six days the LORD made the iera and the earth, and on the sev- enth day he stopped and rested. 18 So (when the Lord had finished communing with Mo- ses on Mount Sinai) he gave him two Tablets of the Testimony, tablets of stone written with the finger of God.

CHAPTER 32

1 But when the people heard that Moses had tarried a long time before he came down from the mountain, the people gathered against Aaron and said to him, "Vp, let your gods go before you, for of this Moses (the man who brought you out of the land of Egypt) we do not know what has become of him." 2 Aaron said to them, "Take out the golden earrings that are in the ears of your wives and sons and daughters, and bring them to me." 3 Then all the people tore off the gold earrings that were in their ears and brought them to Aaron. 4 And the latter received them into his hands, and clothed them with the golden toola, and made a sack of lime; then he said, "These are your gods, O Israel, who brought you out of your land of Egypt." 5 When Aaron heard this, he built an altar before it; and Aaron proclaimed, "Tomorrow's day shall be the holy day of the LORD." 6 And the next day they rose up in the morning, and offered burnt offerings, and brought peace offerings; and the people sat down to eat and drink, and rose up to play. 7 Then the LORD said to Moses, "Go, come down, for your people, whom you brought out of the land of Egypt, have corrupted their ways. 8 They have thus departed from the way that I had commanded them, for they have made themselves a molten lime and wor- shipped it and offered it to you, saying, "These are your gods, O Israel, whom I brought you out of the land of Egypt." 9 Then the LORD said to Moses, "I have seen this people, and behold, they are a stiff-necked people. 10 Now therefore leave me alone, that my wrath may be kindled against them, for I will consume them, but I will make you a mighty people." 11 But Moses praised the LORD his God and said, "O LORD, why is your anger kindled against your people, whom you brought out of the land of Egypt with great power and a mighty hand? 12 Therefore shall the Egyptians speak, and say, Hast thou brought them forth with wickedness to kill them on the moun- tains, and to consume them out of the land?" 13 Remember Abraham and Izhak and Israel, your servants, to whom you gave yourself in marriage and said to them, "I will multiply your descendants like the stars of heaven, and all this land of which I have spoken I will give to your descendants, and they shall inherit it forever." 14 Then the LORD changed his mind with respect to the evil he had threatened to do to his people. 15 Moses returned and came down from the mountain with the two Tab- lets of the Testimony in his hand; the Tablets were written on both sides, on either side. 16 These Tablets were God's work, and this writ- ing was God's writing found in the Tablets. 17 When Ioshua heard the noise of the people shouting, he

said to Moses, "There is a noise of war in the army." 18 The latter answered, "It is not the noise of those who have won, nor the noise of those who are coming; but I hear the sound of singing." 19 Now as soon as he approached the army, he saw the calphe and the dancing; then Moses' anger was kindled, and he took the Tablets out of his hand and smashed them to pieces under the mountain. 20 Then he took the calphe they had made, burned it in the fire, reduced it to dust, threw it on the water, and made the children of Israel drink of it. 21 Moses also said to Aaron, "What has this people done to you, that you should cause them to commit so great a sin?" 22 Then Aaron answered, "Let not the wrath of my Lord be frightened; you know this peo- ple, who are always bent on evil." 23 They said to me, "Build gods to go before you, for we do not know what has become of this Moses (the man who brought the people out of the land of Egypt)." 24 Then I said to them, "You who have gold, pluck it out"; and they brought it to me, and I threw it into the fire, and out came this lime. 25 Moses then said that the people were naked (for Aaron had made them naked to their shame in the midst of their enemies). 26 And Moses stood at the gate of the cam- peus and said, "Whoever is of the Lord's juris- diction, let him come to me." And all the sons of Leui gathered toward him. 27 Then he said to them, "Thus says the LORD, the God of Isra- el, 'Put each one his sword by his side; go this way and that way, from gate to gate, through the army, and kill each one his brother, each one his companion, each one his neighbor.'" 28 So the sons of Leui did as Moses had com- manded; and on the same day the people as- sembled with about three thousand men. 29 (For Moses had said, "Today consecrate your hands to the LORD, each for his son and for his brother, that a blessing may be given you today.") 30 When morning came, Moses said to the people, "You have committed a great crime; but now I will go to the LORD, if I can pacify him for your sin." 31 Moses went again to the LORD and said, "This people have com- mitted a great sin and have made themselves gods of gold. 32 Therefore now, if you will for- give their sin, your mercy will appear; but if you will not, please blot me out of your book that you have written." 33 Then the LORD said to Moses, "Whoever has sinned against me, I will blot him out of my book. 34 Go therefore and lead the people to the place I have com- manded you; behold, my angel will go before you, but on the day of my visitation I will visit their sin." 35 Thus the LORD tormented the people, because they had induced Aaron to make the calf that he had made.

CHAPTER 33

1 Then the LORD said to Moses, "Depart, depart from here, you and the people (whom you brought out of the land of Egypt) to the land which I swore to Abraham, to Izhak, and to Iaakob, saying, 'I will give it to your descendants.'" 2 I will send an angel before you, and I will drive out the Canaanites, the Amorites, the Hittites, the Perizzites, the Jebusites, and the Jebusites: 3 In a land, I say, flowing with milk and honey; for I will not go with you, for you are a stiff-necked people, except to consume you on the way." 4 When the people heard these great speeches, they were saddened, and no one wore his best clothing. 5 (For the LORD had said to Moses, "Say to the children of Israel, 'You are a stiff- necked people, I will suddenly come upon you and consume you; so now remove your costly garments from you, that I may know what to do with you.'") 6 So the children of Israel laid down their fine garments, after Moses

had come down from Mount Horeb. 7 Then Moses took his tabernacle and pitched it far from the army and called it Ohel-moed. And when any- one addressed the LORD, he went out to the tent of meeting, which was outside the hos- tel. 8 And when Moses went out to the Taber- nacle, all the people rose up and stood, each to his own tent, and stood looking at Moses until he had entered the Tabernacle. 9 As Mo- ses entered the Tabernacle, the pillar of cloud came down and stood at the entrance of the Tabernacle, and the LORD spoke to Moses. 10 Now when all the people saw the pillar of clouds stop at the entrance of the Tabernacle, all the people stood up and worshiped every man in his tent. 11 The LORD spoke to Moses, face to face, as a man speaks to his friend. After that he went again to the host, but his servant Ioshua the son of Nun, a young man, did not depart from the Tabernacle. 12 Then Moses said to the LORD, "See, you say to me, 'Let this people depart,' and you have not told me whom you wish to send with me; rather you said, 'I know you by name, and you have found favor in my eyes.' 13 Now, therefore, I pray you, if I have found evil in your eyes, show me now your way, that I may know you and find favor in your eyes; consider also that this nation is your people." 14 He answered, "My presence will go with you, and I will give you rest." 15 Then he said to him, "If your pres- ence does not go with you, do not take you away. 16 And where will it be known that I and your people have found comfort in your eyes? Will it not be when you go with Vs? Then I and your people will have preeminence over all the peoples that are on the earth." 17 The LORD said to Moses, "I will also do this that you have said, for you have found favor in my eyes and I know you by name." 18 Then he said, "Please show me your glory." 19 And he answered, "I will cause all my good to go before you, and I will proclaim the Name of the Lord before you, for I will have mercy on whom I will have mercy, and I will have compassion on whom I will have compassion." 20 Moreover he said, "Thou canst not see my face, for there is no man that seeth me that lieth." 21 The LORD also said, "Behold, there is a place by me, and you shall stand over the tower: 22 While my glory passeth by, I will put thee in a cleft of the log, and I will stroke thee with my hand as I pass by. 23 Then I will remove my hand, and thou shalt see my hind parts, but my face shall not be seen.

CHAPTER 34

1 The LORD said to Moses, "Make yourself two Tablets of stone, like the first one, and I will write on the Tablets the words that were in the first Tablets, which you tore to pieces. 2 Be ready in the morning, that you may go ear- ly to Mount Sinai and wait for me on the top of the mountain. 3 But no one shall go with you, nor shall anyone be seen in the whole mountain, nor shall sheep or cattle feed be- fore this mountain." 4 Then Moses built two Tablets of stone like the first, got up early in the morning and went to Mount Sinai, as the LORD had commanded him, and took the two Tablets of stone in his hand. 5 The LORD came down in the cloud, stood with him, and proclaimed the name of the LORD. 6 Then the LORD passed before his face and cried, "The LORD, the LORD, strong, mer- ciful and gracious, slow to anger and abun- dant in goodness and truth,7 who preserves mercy for thousands, who forgives iniquity, transgression, and sin, who does not make innocent the wicked, who causes the iniqui- ty of the fathers to fall on your children and on the children's children until the third and fourth generation." 8 Then Moses hastened and

prostrated himself on the ground, 9 and said, "O Lord, I pray thee, if I have found favor in thy sight, that the Lord will now go with you (for they are a stiff-necked people) and forgive our iniquity and our sin, and take you as your inheritance." 10 And he answered and said, "Behold, I will make a conference be- fore all your people, and I will do marvelous things, such as have not been done in all the world, nor in all the nations; and all the people among whom you are shall see the work of the LORD, for it is a terrible thing that I will do with you." 11 Observe diligently what I com- mand thee this day: Behold, I will drive out before thee the Amorites, the Canaanites, the Hittites, the Perizzites, the Jebusites, and the Jebusites. 12 Take heed to thyself, and make no agreement with the inhabitants of the land whither thou goest, lest they be a cause of ruin among thee: 13 But you shall flatten their altars, and cut up their images, and cut down their stables, 14 (for you shall not bow down to any other god, for the LORD, whose name is Ielous, is a Ielous God). 15 And do not make a covenant with the inhabitants of the land, and when they prostitute themselves to their gods and sacrifice to their gods, someone shall call you, and you shall eat of his sacrifice: 16 And if thou shalt not take of their daugh- ters for thy sons, and their daughters shall whore themselves to their gods, and thou shalt cause thy sons to whore themselves to their gods. 17 Thou shalt not make for thyself any gods of metal. 18 Thou shalt keep the feast of vnleaued bread: for ten days shalt thou eat vnleaued bread, as I have commanded thee, in the time of the month of Abib; for in the month of Abib thou camest out of Egypt. 19 Every male that first opens his womb shall be mine; also all the firstborn of thy flock shall be counted mine, both of bees and of sheep. 20 But the first of thy sons shalt thou bring forth with a lamb; and if thou shalt not redeem him, thou shalt break his neck: all the first- born of thy sons shalt thou redeem, and none shall stand before me empty. 21 You shall work six days, and on the seventh day you shall rest; both in the time of eve and in the time of rest, you shall rest. 22 You shall also observe the feast of weeks at the time of the firstfruits of the grain harvest, and the feast of the harvest of fruit at the end of the year. 23 Three times in a year all your sons shall stand before the LORD Jehouah, God of Israel. 24 For I will drive out the nations before you and enlarge your coasts, so that no one will covet your land, when you come to present your- self before the LORD your God three times a year. 25 Thou shalt not offer the blood of my sacrifice with the dregs, and thou shalt not leave anything of the sacrifice of the feast of the passover until the morning. 26 You shall bring to the house of the LORD your God the first ripe fruit of your land; but you shall not put a kid goat in its mother's milk." 27 The LORD said to Moses, "Write these words, for according to the tenor of these words I have made a covenant with you and with Israel." 28 So he stayed with the LORD for four days and four nights, without eating bread or drinking water, and wrote in the Tablets the words of the covenant, that is, the ten commands. 29 When Moses came down from Mount Sinai, the two Tablets of the Testimony were in Mo- ses' hand, as he came down from the moun- tain: (now Moses did not notice that the skin of his face shone, after God had spoken to him). 30 And Aaron and all the sons of Israel looked at Moses, and behold, the skin of his face shone, and they were afraid to come near him). 31 But Moses called them, and Aaron and all the leaders of the congregation re- turned to him; and Moses talked with them. 32 Then all the children of Israel came to him, and he questioned them about all that the LORD had told him on Mount Sinai. 33

So Moses finished speaking with them and cov- ered his face. 34 But when Moses came before the Lord to speak with him, he took off his hood until he went out; then he went out and spoke to the children of Israel about what he had been commanded. 35 And the children of Israel saw the face of Moses, how the skin of Moses' face shone; therefore Moses put on his cloak over his face until he went out to speak with God.

CHAPTER 35

1 Then Moses gathered together all the con- gregation of the children of Israel and said to them, "These are the words which the LORD has commanded, that you may do them: 2 Six days you shall work, but the seventh day shall be for you the holy Sabbath of rest for the LORD; whoever works there shall die. 3 You shall not kindle fire in all your dwellings on the Sabbath. 4 Then Moses spoke to the whole community of the children of Israel, saying, "This is what the LORD has commanded, 5 "Take from among you an offering for the LORD; whoever is of good heart shall bring this offering to the LORD: gold, silk, and reed: 6 also white silk, purple, chamois skins, fine linen, and goatskins, 7 and dead ramskins of red, and badger skins with wood of Shittim: 8 also oil for light, spices for anointing oil and for incense, 9 stones of onyx and stones to set in the Ephod and in the plate of the crest. 10 Let all who have a wise heart among you come and do all that the LORD has com- manded: 11 that is, the tabernacle, and its pavilion, and its covering, and its notches, and its boards, and its bars, and its pillars, and its sockets, 12 the ark, its bars, its bronze seat, and its roof, 13 the table, its bars, all its instruments, and its bread to eat: 14 also the candlestick of light and its instruments, and its lamps with oil for light: 15 also the altar of perfumes and its bars, and the oil for anoin- ing, and the perfumed incense, and the tray of decoration at the entrance of the Taber- nacle, 16 the altar of burnt offerings with its copper lattice, its bars and all its instruments, the Lauer and its feet, 17 the coverings of the court, its pillars and its bases, and the vault of the gate of the court, 18 the pinnacles of the tabernacle and the pinnacles of the court with their cords, 19 the garments for the ministry in the holy place, the holy garments for Aar- on the priest, and the garments of his sons, that they may exercise the priestly office." 20 Then the whole community of the children of Israel departed from Moses' presence. 21 Ev- ery person whose heart encouraged him, and every person whose spirit made him willing, came and brought an offering to the Lord for the work of the Tabernacle of the congre- gation, for all its garments and for the holy garments. 22 Men and women, as many as had free hearts, came and brought pendants, earrings, rings, and bracelets, all gold jewelry; and everyone who offered a gold offering to the Lord: 23 also all that had snow-white silk, purple, chamois skins, fine linen, goatskins, ramskins, and badger skins, brought them. 24 Everyone who offered an oblation of silk and reed brought the offering to the LORD; and everyone who had Shittim wood for any manual work brought it. 25 All the women who had a wise heart spun with their hands and brought the spun work, that is, white silk, purple, knitting and fine linen. 26 Likewise all the women whose hearts were moved by wis- dom spun goats. 27 You chiefs brought stones of onyx and stones to set in the Ephod and in the breast plate: 28 Also spices and oil for light, for anoining oil, and for sweet perfume. 29 All the men and women of the children of Israel, whose hearts were willing to bear for

all the work that the LORD had commanded to be done at the hand of Moses, brought a freewill offering to the LORD. 30 Then Moses said to the Israelites, "Behold, the LORD has called by name Bezaleel the son of Vri, the son of Hur, of the tribe of Judah, 31 and filled him with an excellent spirit of wisdom and un- derstanding and knowledge and all kinds of work, 32 to find curious work, to work gold and silver and stone, 33 and to set stones, to work wood and to do all kinds of work. 34 He took it into his heart to teach others, both he and Aholiab the son of Ahisamach, of the tribe of Dan: 35 And he filled them with wis- dom of heart to work all manner of cunning, swill, and needlework, in white silk, in pur- ple, in leather, in fine linen, and in weaving, and to do all manner of works and secondary inventions.

CHAPTER 36

1 Then Bezaleel, Aholiab and all the wise men, to whom the Lord had given wisdom and intelligence to know how to perform all kinds of work for the service of the sanctuary, according to what the Lord had commanded. 2 For Moses had called Bezaleel and Aholiab and all the wise-hearted men, in whose hearts the Lord had brought forth wisdom, as many as their hearts encouraged them to come to that work to work it. 3 And they received from Moses all the offerings that the children of Is- rael had brought for the work of the service of the sanctuary, to build it; and they also still brought him free gifts every morning. 4 So all the wise men who were working at all the holy work went out each from his own work, 5 and spoke to Moses, saying, "The people bring too much and more than is necessary for the duration of the work which the LORD has commanded to be done." 6 Then Moses gave an order and they had it proclaimed throughout the army, saying, "Let neither man nor woman prepare any more work for the oblation of the sanctuary." Thus the peo- ple were restrained from offending. 7 For the cloth they had was sufficient for all the work to be done, and even too much. 8 Therefore all the crafty among the workmen made for the Tabernacle ten curtains of finely twisted linen, of light silk, of purple, and of leather: On them they made cherubim of red wood. 9 The length of a curtaine was twenty-eight cubits, and the breadth of a curtaine four cu- bits; the curtains were all of one size. 10 He pitched five tents side by side, and five more he pitched. 11 He made cords of white silk along the hem of one curtaine, in the edge of the coupling; and the same he did on the side of the other curtaine, in the edge of the sec- ond coupling. 12 And he made fifty cords in one curl, and fifty cords in the hem of the oth- er curl, which was in the second coupling; and the cords were set against each other. 13 Then he made fifty notches of gold and coupled the curtains to one another with the notches; so the tabernacle was one. 14 He also made cur- tains of goats for the covering of the Taber- nacle; he made them in the shape of the cur- tains of elephants. 15 The length of a curtain was thirty cubits and the width of a curtain four cubits; the curtains of elephants were of one size. 16 He made five curtains coupled together and six curtains coupled together: 17 He also made fifty cords on the hem of one curtain, in the outer part of the coupling, and fifty cords on the hem of the other curtain, in the second coupling. 18 He also made fifty brasse cleats to couple the coupling so that it was one. 19 He made a covering on the pavil- ion of sheepskins dyed red and a covering of badger skins on the outside. 20 In the same way he made boards for the tabernacle, of Shittim wood, to be laid upon. 21 The length of a table was ten cubits, and the width of a table was one cubit and a half. 22 One board had two tenons, set in order like the feet of a ladder, one against the other; so he did for all the boards of the Tabernacle. 23 For the south side of the Tabernacle he made twenty-two boards, that is, the whole south. 24 Under the twenty-two boards he made four sockets of silk, two sockets under one board for its two tenons and two sockets under another board for its two tenons. 25 For the other side of the tabernacle also, toward the north, he made twenty-two boards, 26 and their four boards of silk, two boards under one board and two boards under another board. 27 Likewise, to- ward the west side of the tabernacle he made six boards. 28 At the corners of the tabernacle he made two boards, on either side, 29 And he had them set under them and made them se- cure with a ring; so he did for both corners. 30 So there were eight boards and their six sock- ets of silk, and under each board two sockets. 31 Then he made slats of Shittim wood for the boards on one side of the tabernacle, 32 And boards of firewood for the boards on the oth- er side of the Tabernacle, and boards of fire- wood for the boards of the Tabernacle on the side of the West. 33 He made the middlemost bar to go through the boards from one end to the other. 34 He also made the boards of gold, made their rings of gold for the places of the boards, and covered the boards with gold. 35 He also made a veil of puffed silk, of purple, of skins, and of finely twisted linen; he made it with cherubim of red wood: 36 And he built thereon four pillars of Shittim, and clothed them with gold; the hooks also were of gold, and he cast thereon four sockets of silk. 37 For the tabernacle he made a scaffold of puffed silk, of purple, of leather, of linen finely twist- ed and needleworked, 38 and his five pillars with their hooks, he clothed their chapiters and their fillets with gold, but their five sock- ets were of brasse.

CHAPTER 37

1 After this, Bezaleel made the arch of Shit- tim wood, two and a half cubits long, one and a half cubits wide, and one and a half cubits high: 2 He covered it with gold to the inside and outside, and made a crown of gold all around it, 3 And he cast into it four rings of gold for the four corners, that is, two rings for one side and two rings for the other side. 4 He also made slats of Shittim wood and covered them with gold, 5 And he put the rods in the rings on the sides of the ark, to support the ark. 6 He made the Merciseate of pure gold: two cubits and a half was its length and one cubit and a half its width. 7 He made two cherubim of gold at both ends of the Merci- seate: he made them of wood beaten with a hammer. 8 A Cherub on one end and anoth- er Cherub on the other; of the Merciseate he made the Cherubim at the two ends. 9 The Cherubim spread their wings over them and covered the Merciseat with their wings, and their faces were toward each other; toward the Merciseat were the faces of the Cherubim. 10 He also made a board of Shittim wood, two cubits long, one cubit wide, and one and a half cubits high. 11 He covered it with fine gold and made a crown of gold around it. 12 He also made it a border the width of a hand, all around it, and he made on the border a crown of gold all around it. 13 He cast for it four rings of gold and placed them in the four corners that were at its four feet. 14 Against the edge were the rings, as places for the rods that were to support the table. 15 He made the slats of Shittim wood and covered them with gold to support the table. 16 He also made the instruments for

the Table of pure gold: plates for the Table, cups for the incense, goblets for the Table, and cups for the Table, with which it was to be set. 17 In the same way he built the candlestick of pure gold; the candlestick was made of material beaten with a hammer; its shaft, its branches, its bullae, its knots, and its scales were of one piece. 18 Out of its sides came six branches: three branches of the candlestick on one side and three branches of the candlestick on the other side. 19 In one branch were three bubbles like almonds, a point, and a flower; and in another branch three bubbles like almonds, a point, and a flower; and so for all the six branches that came out of the Can- dlestick. 20 On the candlestick were four bub- bles like almonds, with their tips and leaves: 21 That is, for every two branches, a knot, a knot for the second branch, and a knot for the third branch, according to the six branches that went out from it. 22 Their knots and their branches were of the same kind; it was all one wrought work of pure gold. 23 He made for it ten lamps, with their spouts, and their spout covers of pure gold. 24 With one talent of pure gold he made it with all its instruments. 25 Moreover he made the altar of perfumes of wood of Shittim: its length was one cubit, its breadth one cubit (it was square) and two cubits high, and its horns were of the same material. 26 And he clothed it with pure gold, both the top and the sides, all round about, and the horns, and made it a crown of gold all round about. 27 And he made it two rings of gold, under the crown, at the two corners of the two sides, to put rods on it to hold it up. 28 He also made the bars of wood of Shittim and covered them with gold. 29 He made the anointing oil and pure, fragrant incense ac- cording to the art of the apothecaries.

CHAPTER 38

1 He also made the altar of burnt offering from wood of Shittim; its length was five cu- bits and its width five cubits; it was square and three cubits high. 2 He made him horns at the four corners; the horns were of the same wood, and he covered it with brasse. 3 He also made all the instruments of the altar: the ashtrays, the vessels, the basins, the meat hooks, and the censers; all the instruments he made of reeds. 4 Moreover he made a lattice of bronze worked like a net for the altar, be- low its surface and in the center of it, 5 And he cast four bronze rings at the four ends of the lattice to put bars on it. 6 He made the slats of Shittim wood and covered them with brasse. 7 He put the slats into the rings at the sides of the altar to carry it, and made it hollow within the boards. 8 He also made the Lauer of reeds and its lower part of reeds of the glasses of the women who gathered and met in the center of the Tabernacle of Meeting. 9 Finally he made the courtyard of the south side, all on the south side; the coverings of the courtyard were of finely woven linen, measuring a hun- dred cubits. 10 Their pillars were twenty-two, and their sockets twenty-two; the hooks of the pillars and their fillets were of silk. 11 On the north side the slopes were a hundred cu- bits: their pillars were twenty and their sock- ets of bronze twenty and their hooks of the pillars and their fillets were of silk. 12 Also on the west side were slats of fifty cubits, ten columns with ten sockets, the hooks of the columns and their fillets of silk. 13 Toward the east side, in the full east, there were slats of fifty cubits. 14 The vestments on one side were fifty cubits, their three columns and their three sockets: 15 On the other side of the gate of the court, on both sides, were banners of fifty cubits, their three pillars and their three sockets. 16 All the coverings of the courtyard, all around, were of finely twisted linen: 17

The bases of the pillars were of reeds, the hooks of the pillars and their fillets of silk, the caps of silk, and all the pillars of the courtyard were encircled with silk. 18 He also made the vest- ment of the gate of the courtyard with needle cloth, of white silk, purple, scarlet, and fine- ly twisted linen, 20 cubits long and 5 cubits high, like the vestment of the courtyard. 19 Their pillars were four, with their four brasse sockets, their silk hooks, their silk headdress- es, and their silk fillets. 20 All the pins of the tabernacle and of the courtyard round about were of brasse. 21 These are the parts of the Tabernacle, that is, the Tabernacle of Testi- mony, which was built by the commandment of Moses for the office of the Leuites, by the hand of Ithamar the son of Aaron the priest. 22 Bezaleel the son of Vri the son of Hur, of the tribe of Judah, did all that the LORD had commanded Moses. 23 And with him Aholiab the son of Ahisamach, of the tribe of Dan, a skilled worker, an embroiderer and needle- worker in puffed silk, in purple, in tights, and in fine linen. 24 All the gold employed in all the work done for the holy place (which was the gold of the ring) was nine and twenty talents and seven hundred and thirty shek- els, according to the shekel of the sanctuary. 25 But the amount of the gold of those who were numbered in the congregation was one hundred talents and one thousand two hun- dred seuentie five shekels, according to the shekel of the sanctuary. 26 A portion for each man, that is, half a shekel after the shekel of the Sanctuary, for all those who had been numbered from the age of twenty years on- ward, between six hundred thousand and three thousand and fifty men. 27 Moreover there were a hundred talents of torpedoes to make the sockets of the sanctuary and the sockets of the sailing ship: a hundred sockets of a hundred talents, a talent for a socket. 28 He also made the hooks for the pillars, to the value of a thousand and fifty shekels, and he covered the hoods of them, making fillets around them. 29 The cloth of the offering also was seventy talents, two thousand and four hundred shekels. 30 And he made the bases of the tabernacle of meeting, and the altar of bronze, and the lattice of bronze that was thereon, with all the instruments of the altar, 31 the sockets of the court round about, the sockets for the door of the court, all the pins of the Tabernacle, and all the pins of the court round about.

CHAPTER 39

1 Moreover they made the garments for the ministry in the sanctuary, of raw silk, purple, and wool; they also made the holy garments for Aaron, as the LORD had commanded Mo- ses. 2 They then made the Ephod of gold, of raw silk, purple, cloth and fine twisted linen. 3 And they made the gold into thin sheets, and cut it into meshes to work it into white silk, purple, woollen cloth, and fine linen, with twine work. 4 For which they made shoulders to be coupled together, because it was closed by the two edges. 5 And the garnishing of his Ephod, which was upon him, was of the same cloth and workmanship: of gold, and of white silk, and of purple, and of cloth, and of fine linen, as the LORD had commanded Moses. 6 And they made two stones of Onix enclosed in an aperture of gold and engraved, as one engraves a seal, with the names of the chil- dren of Israel, 7 And they put them on the shoulders of Ephod, as stones to remember the children of Israel, as the LORD had com- manded Moses. 8 He also made the coverlet of fine cloths like those of Ephod, that is, of gold, of white silk, of purple, of skins, and of finely twisted linen. 9 They made the breast plate double, square, one hand long and one hand wide; it

was also double. 10 They filled it with four rows of stones. The order was as follows: a Ruby, a Topaze and a Carbuncle in the first row: 11 in the second row, an Emeraude, a Saphir and a Diamond: 12 in the third, a Turkeis, an Achate and a Hematite: 13 in the fourth row, a Chrysolite, an Onix, and a Jas- per, closed and set in an opening of gold. 14 So the stones were according to the names of the children of Israel, two after their names, as signs, each after his name, according to the two tribes. 15 Then they made on the bottom table cheine plates at the ends, of wood and pure gold. 16 They also made two studs of gold and two rings of gold, and put the two rings at the two corners of the wooden plate. 17 In the two rings, at the corners of the covering slab, they also put two cheeks of gold. 18 The other two ends of the two golden chains they also fastened into the two ends and put them on the shoulders of the Ephod, on the front. 19 In the same way they made two rings of gold and put them in the other two corners of the breast plate on the edge of it, which was inside the Ephod. 20 They also made two other rings of gold and put them on the two sides of the Ephod, underneath, on the front side, and outside, against its coupling, on the bordered edge of the Ephod. 21 Then they fas- tened the breast plate by its rings to the rings of the Ephod, with a lace of white silk, so that it would be fastened on the fluted garniture of the Ephod and so that the breast plate would not come off the Ephod, as the LORD had commanded Moses. 22 Moreover, he made the robe of the Ephod of wool and white silk. 23 The hole in the tunic was in the center, like a surgeon's collar, with a border around the col- lar, so that it would not tear. 24 On the skirts of the robe they made pomegranates of white silk, purple, scarlet, and fine twisted linen. 25 They also made bells of pure gold and put them between the pomegranates on the skirts of the robe, all around between the pomegran- ates. 26 A bell and a pomegranate, a bell and a pomegranate around the skirts of the robe to officiate, as the LORD had commanded Mo- ses. 27 Then they made cloaks of fine linen, of wool, for Aaron and his sons. 28 The mitre of fine linen, the bonnets of fine linen, and the breeches of twisted fine linen, 29 And the girdle of fine twined linen, of blown silk, of purple, and of leather, always needlework, as the LORD had commanded Moses. 30 Finally they made the plaque for the holy horn of fine gold and wrote on it an inscription similar to the engraving of a seal, "GUESTS OF THE LORD." 31 Then they tied a lace of white silk to fasten it on the miter, as the LORD had com- manded Moses. 32 Thus was all the work of the Tabernacle, that is, the Tabernacle of the Congregation, finished, and the children of Israel did all that the LORD had command- ed Moses; so they did. 33 Then they brought the Tabernacle to Moses, the Tabernacle and all its instruments, its boards, its planks, its bars, its pillars, and its sockets, 34 the skins of rams turned red, the badger skins and the velvet skins. 35 The ark of the Testimony, its bars and the Merciseate, 36 the table, with all its instruments, and the dishcloth, 37 the pure candlestick, its lamps, that is, the lamps ordained, all its instruments, and the oil for light: 38 the altar of gold, the oil for lighting, the fragrant incense, and the hanging of the tabernacle, 39 the bronze altar with its lattice of wood, its staffs and all its instruments, the Lauer and its instruments. 40 The court- yard curtains with its pillars and sockets, the hanging at the courtyard door, its ropes and pinnacles, and all the instruments of the Tab- ernacle service, called the Tabernacle of the Congregation. 41 Finally, the garments for the service in the sanctuary, the holy garments for Aaron the priest, and the garments of his sons for the priestly service. 42 According to each point that the LORD had commanded Moses, the sons of Israel did all the work. 43 And Moses observed all the work, and behold, they had done as the Lord had commanded; so they had done; and Moses blessed them.

CHAPTER 40

1 Then the Lord spoke to Moses, saying 2 On the very first day of the first month you shall prepare the Tabernacle, called the Tabernacle of the Congregation: 3 You shall place therein the ark of the Testimony, and you shall fill it with the vile. 4 You shall also bring in the Ta- ble and arrange it as required; you shall also bring in the Candlestick and light its lamps, 5 Thou shalt set up the Altar of Golden In- cense before the Ark of the Testimony, and thou shalt place the hanging at the end of the Tabernacle. 6 Moreover, you shall place the al- tar of burnt offerings before the porch of the Tabernacle, called the Tabernacle of the Con- gregation. 7 You shall make a washing place between the Tabernacle of the Congregation and the altar, and you shall put water there. 8 Then you shall lay the courtyard all around it and hang the scaffolding on the door of the courtyard. 9 Then thou shalt take the anoin- ing ointment, and thou shalt anoinize the Tabernacle, and all that is therein, and thou shalt array it with all its instruments, that it may be holy. 10 Thou shalt anoint the altar of burnt offerings and all its instruments, and shalt sanctify the altar, that it may be a most holy altar. 11 You shall also anoint the Lauer and its instruments and sanctify it. 12 Then you shall lead Aaron and his sons to the entrance of the Tabernacle of Meeting, and you shall wash them with water. 13 Then you shall put on Aaron's holy garments, anoinise him and sanctify him, that he may exercise the priestly ministry with me. 14 You shall also bring his sons and clothe them with gar- ments, 15 and you shall sanctify them as you sanctified their father, that they may exercise the priestly ministry with me; for their sanc- tification shall be a sign that the priesthood shall be everlasting to all their generations." 16 Moses did so, according to all that the Lord had commanded him, and so he did. 17 So the tabernacle was built on the first day of the first month of the second year. 18 And Moses built the tabernacle, and fixed its founda- tions, and fastened its boards, and set up its bars, and raised its pillars. 19 Then he leveled the covering of the Tabernacle and put the covering on the outside of it, as the LORD had commanded Moses. 20 Then he took and put the Testimony in the ark, put the bars in the rings of the ark, and placed the Merciseate on the ark. 21 He also brought the ark into the Tabernacle, hung the mating craft on it, and coupled the ark of the Testimony, as the LORD had commanded Moses. 22 Moreover he put the table in the Tabernacle of the Con- gregation, in the north side of the Tabernacle, without the rampart, 23 And he set the bread in order before the LORD, as the LORD had commanded Moses. 24 He also put the can- dlestick in the tent of meeting, opposite the table, toward the south side of the tabernacle. 25 He lit the lamps before the LORD, as the LORD had commanded Moses. 26 He also set the golden altar in the tent of meeting in front of the table, 27 and burned fragrant incense on it, as the LORD had commanded Moses. 28 Moreover he hung the vayle at the entrance to the Tabernacle. 29 Then he placed the altar of burnt offerings outside the Tabernacle, called the Tabernacle of the Congregation, and of- fered burnt offerings and sacrifices there, as the LORD had commanded Moses. 30 In the same way he set up the washstand between the

Tabernacle of the Congregation and the Altar, and put water there for washing. 31 So Moses and Aaron and his sons washed their hands and feet there. 32 When they entered the tent of meeting and when they came to the altar, they washed, as the LORD had com- manded Moses. 33 Finally he raised up the courtyard around the Tabernacle and the Al- tar, and hung up the rampart at the door of the courtyard; so Moses finished the work. 34 Then the cloud enveloped the Tabernacle of the congregation, and the glory of the Lord filled the Tabernacle. 35 Moses could not en- ter the Tabernacle of the Congregation, be- cause the cloud dwelt there, and the glory of the Lord filled the Tabernacle. 36 Now when the cloud went up from the Tabernacle, the children of Israel went forth on all their jour- neys. 37 But if the cloud did not go up, they did not go on their journey until the day it went up. 38 For the cloud of the LORD was on the Tabernacle by day, and the fire was in it by night, before the eyes of all the house of Isra- el, during all their journeys.

LEVITICUS

CHAPTER 1

1 Now the LORD called Moses and spoke to him from the Tabernacle of Meeting, say- ing, "Speak to the children of Israel and say to them, 'If any of you offer a sacrifice to the LORD, he shall offer his sacrifice of cattle as of bees, 2 Speak to the children of Israel and say to them, "If any of you offer a sacrifice to the LORD, he shall offer his sacrifice of cattle as of bees and sheep. 3 If his sacrifice is a hearing burnt offering, he shall offer a male without blemish, presenting him of his own free will at the door of the Tabernacle of the Congrega- tion before the LORD. 4 He shall put his hand on the head of the burnt offering, and it shall be accepted before the Lord as his atonement. 5 He shall kill the bullock before the LORD, and the priests sons of Aaron shall offer the blood and sprinkle it all around on the altar that is at the door of the tabernacle of the congregation. 6 Then he will cut up the burnt offering and break it into pieces. 7 The sons of Aaron the priest will put fire on the altar and arrange the wood in order on the fire. 8 Then the sons of Aaron the priest shall arrange the parts in order, the head and the heart, on the wood that is in the fire and that is on the al- tar. 9 But the entrails and the legs shall be washed with water, and the priest shall bury the whole on the altar, because it is a burnt offering, an oblation made by fire, for a sweet smelling to the LORD. 10 If his sacrifice for the burnt offering is of flocks (of sheep or goats), he shall offer a male without blemish, 11 he shall kill it on the north side of the altar before the LORD, and the sons of Aarons the priest shall sprinkle its blood all around on the altar. 12 He will cut him into pieces, sep- arating his head and his head, and the priest will arrange them in order on the wood lying in the fire that is on the altar: 13 And he shall wash the entrails and the legs with water, and the priest shall offer the whole thing and bury it on the altar, for it is a burnt offering, an oblation made by fire for a sweet smell to the LORD. 14 And if his sacrifice is a burnt of- fering to the LORD of you fires, he shall offer his sacrifice of turtledoves or young pigeons. 15 And the priest shall bring him to the altar, and break his neck, and bury him on the altar; and his blood shall be sprinkled on the side of the altar. 16 Then he will sprinkle his mouth with his paws and throw them beside the al- tar, to the east, in the place of the ashes. 17 He shall clean it with his wings, not dividing it; and the priest shall bury it on the altar, on the wood that is

in the fire, for it is a burnt offer- ing, an oblation made by fire for a sweet smell to the LORD.

CHAPTER 2

1 When anyone offers a food offering to the LORD, his offering shall be of fine flour, and he shall sprinkle oil on it and put incense on it, 2 he shall bring it to Aaron the priest, Aar- on's son, and he shall take a handful of flowers and oil from it with all the frankincense, and the priest shall bury it as a memorial on the altar, for it is an offering made by fire to give a sweet aroma to the Lord. 3 But the rest of the food offering shall be Aaron's and his sons', for it is the most holy of the Lord's offerings made by fire. 4 If you also bring a baked food offering, it shall be a cake of fine flour mixed with oil, or a wafer anointed with oil. 5 But if your food offering is an oblation of the frying pan, it will be of fine flour mixed with oil. 6 You shall cut it into pieces and put oil on it, for it is a food oblation. 7 If your food offer- ing is an oblation made in the cauldron, it will be made of fine flour with oil. 8 Then you shall take the oblation (made of these things) to the LORD, present it to the priest, and he shall bring it to the altar, 9 and the priest shall take from the food offering a remembrance and bury it on the altar, for it is an oblation he will offer its offering, that is, an offering made by fire to the LORD, the fat dripping from the entrails and all the fat that is on the entrails. 15 He shall also remove the two kids and the fat that is on them, the flanks and the meat that is on the liver with the kids. 16 The priest shall bury them on the altar, as meat of an offering made by fire for a sweet savor; all the fat is the LORD's. 17 This shall be a per- petual ordinance for your generations, in all your dwellings, that you eat neither flesh nor blood. made by fire for a sweet smell for the LORD. 10 But what remains of the food oblation shall be Aaron's and his sons', for it is the most holy of the oblations of the LORD made by fire. 11 All the oblations of food that you shall offer to the LORD shall be made without meat, for you shall not be able to bury meat or honor in any oblation of the LORD made by fire. 12 In the oblation of the firstfruits you shall of- fer them to the LORD, but they shall not be burned on the altar as a sweet perfume. 13 (Also all the oblations of food you shall season them with salt, and you shall not allow the salt of the consent of your God to be lacking from your oblations of food, but on all your oblations you shall offer salt). 14 If thou then offer unto the LORD an offering of first fruits, thou shalt offer for thy offering of first fruits ears of corn dried by the fire, and beaten corn from the green ears of corn. 15 Then you shall put oil on it, and you shall place incense on it, for it is a food offering. 16 The priest shall bury his remembrance, both the beaten grain and the oil, with all his incense, for it is an offering to the LORD made by fire.

CHAPTER 3

1 Moreover, if his oblation is a peace offering, if he wants to offer of the droue (both male and female), he shall offer before the LORD a specimen without blemish, 2 he shall put his hand on the head of his offering and kill it at the entrance to the tent of meeting; the priests, Aaron's sons, shall sprinkle the blood on the altar all around. 3 He shall then offer part of the peace offerings as a fire sacrifice to the LORD, that is, the fat dripping from the entrails and all the fat that is on the entrails. 4 He shall also take away the

two kids, the fat that is on them and on the sides, and the meat that is on the side with the kids. 5 And Aaron's sons shall bury him on the altar, together with the burnt offering that is on the wood that is on the fire; this is a sacrifice made by fire to give a sweet smell to the LORD. 6 Moreover, if his oblation is a peace offering to the LORD from your flock, whether male or female, he shall offer it without blemish. 7 If he offers a lamb as an oblation, he will bring it before the LORD, 8 he shall lay his hand on the head of his lamb, he shall kill it before the Tabernacle of Meeting, and the sons of Aaron shall sprin- kle its blood all around on the altar. 9 After the peace offerings, he shall offer to the LORD a burnt-offering; he shall take off the fat of it, the whole rump, hard to the pelvic bone, and all the fat that is inside it. 10 He shall also re- move the two kids, with the fat covering them, and the flanks, and the meat on the side with the kids. 11 Then the priest shall bury it on the altar, as the meat of an offering made by fire to the LORD. 12 If his offering is a kid, he shall offer it to the LORD, 13 and he shall put his hand on its head, and he shall kill it before the tent of meeting, and Aaron's sons shall sprin- kle its blood on the altar all around. 14 Then

CHAPTER 4

1 The LORD spoke again to Moses, saying, 2 Speak to the children of Israel, saying, "If anyone, through ignorance, sins in one of the commands of the LORD (which are not to be done), but acts contrary to one of them, 3 if the priest who has been anointed sins (ac- cording to the sin of the people), then he shall offer to the LORD, for the sin he has commit- ted, a heifer without blemish as a sin offering, 4 he shall bring the heifer up to the wall of the Tabernacle of Meeting before the LORD, put his hand on the head of the heifer, and kill the heifer before the LORD. 5 The anointed priest shall take the blood of the heifer and bring it into the Tent of Meeting. 6 The priest shall dip his finger in the blood and sprinkle it seven times before the LORD, in front of the vault of the sanctuary. 7 The priest shall also put some of the blood before the LORD on the horns of the altar of sweet incense, which is in the tent of meeting, then he shall sprinkle all the rest of the blood of the bullock on the phote of the altar of burnt offerings, which is at the end of the tent of meeting. 8 And he shall take off all the fat of the bull for the offense of sin, that is, the fat that is on the inside and all the fat that is around the inside. 9 And he shall also take off the two kids, and the fat that is on them, and the sides, and the meat that is on the side with the kids, 10 as was taken off the heifer of the peace offerings, and the priest shall bury them on the altar of burnt offerings. 11 But the skin of the heifer and all its flesh, with its head, its legs, its entrails, and its dung shall be taken out. 12 Then he shall carry the whole oxen out of the host to a clean place, where the ashes are in dust, and bury it on wood in the fire; where the ashes have been thrown in, it shall be burned. 13 If the whole congregation of Israel sins through igno- rance, and the thing is hidden from the eyes of the crowd, and they have done something against the commandments of the LORD that are not to be done, and they have offended: 14 when it shall be known the sin which they have committed, the congregation shall offer a heifer for sin, and bring it before the Tab- ernacle of the congregation, 15 and the elders of the congregation shall put their hands on the head of the bullock before the LORD, and they shall kill the bullock before the LORD. 16 Then the anointed priest shall bring the blood of the bullock into the Tent of Meeting, 17 and the Priest shall dip his finger in the blood and sprinkle it ten times before the LORD, even before the vessel. 18 He shall also put some of the blood on the horns of the altar that is be- fore the LORD and that is in the tent of meet- ing; then he shall pour all the rest of the blood on the base of the altar of burnt offerings that is at the end of the tent of meeting, 19 he shall take all his fat and bury it on the altar. 20 And the priest shall do with this bull, as he did with the bull for his sin, so shall he do with this one; so the priest shall make atonement for them, and they shall be forgiven. 21 For he shall load the bullock out of the host and bury it as he burned the first bullock, for it is an atonement for the sin of the congrega- tion. 22 When a ruler sins and does through ignorance one of the commands of the LORD his God, which is not to be done, and com- mits a trespass, 23 if one reveals to him his sin, which he has committed, he shall bring for sacrifice a goat without blemish, 24 and he shall lay his hand on the head of the goat and kill it in the place where he must kill the stake before the LORD, because it is a sinful offense. 25 Then the priest shall take the blood of the sinful offense with his finger, and he shall put it on the horns of the altar of burnt offerings and pour out the rest of its blood on the base of the altar of burnt offerings, 26 and he shall bury all his fat on the altar, as the fat of the peace offering; so the priest shall make atonement for him concerning his sin, and he shall be forgiven. 27 Likewise, if one of the in- habitants of the land sins through ignorance in doing something contrary to one of the LORD's commands, which is not to be done, and commits a trespass, 28 if one discloses to him his sin which he has committed, he shall bring as a sacrifice a goat without blemish for his sin which he has committed, 29 and he shall lay his hand on the head of the goat that committed the sin, and he shall kill the goat at the place of the burnt offering. 30 Then the priest shall take its blood with his finger and put it on the horns of the altar of burnt offer- ings and sprinkle all the rest of the blood on the base of the altar, 31 and he shall remove all his fat, as one removes the fat of peace of- ferings, and the priest shall bury him on the altar as a sweet homage to the LORD; and the priest shall make atonement for him, and he shall be forgiven. 32 If he brings a lamb for his sacrifice, he shall bring a female without blemish, 33 and he shall lay his hand on the head of the lamb for sin, and shall kill it for sin in the place where he should have killed the burnt lamb. 34 Then the priest shall take with his finger the blood of the sinful offense, and shall put it on the horns of the altar of the burnt offense, and shall sprinkle the rest of the blood on the base of the altar. 35 And he shall take off all the fat of it, as one takes off the fat of the lamb of the peace offerings; then the priest shall bury it on the altar with the oblations of the Lord made by fire, and the priest shall make atonement for him for the sin he has committed, and it shall be forgiven him.

CHAPTER 5

1 Moreover, if one has sinned, that is, if he has heard the testimony of another and can bear witness to it, whether he has seen it or has knowledge of it, if he does not bear wit- ness to it, he shall bear his iniquity: 2 If one touches a vnclean thing, be it a vnclean car- cass of cattle, or a vnclean carcass of cattle, or a vnclean carcass of vnclean creepers, and does not notice it, he is nevertheless vnclean and has committed an offense: 3 If, on the other hand, he touches a vncleannesse of man (whatever vncleannesse with which he has defiled himself) and is not aware of it, and after

becoming aware of it, he has sinned: 4 If one swears and pronounces with his lips to do good or to do good (whichever vncleannesse a man pronounces with another) and it is con- cealed from him, and afterwards he becomes aware that he has committed an offense in any of these points, 5 if he has sinned in any of these things, he shall confess that he has sinned in it. 6 Therefore he shall bring to the Lord his offering for the sin he has commit- ted, that is, a female from your flock, wheth- er a lamb or a goat, as a sin offering, and the priest shall make an atonement for him concerning his sin. 7 But if he is not able to bring a sheep, he shall bring two turtle doves or two young pigeons, one for atonement for sin and the other for atonement for burning, to the LORD for his sin. 8 He shall bring them to the priest, who shall first offer the sacrifice for sin, and shall break his neck, not detach- ing it. 9 Then he will sprinkle the blood of the sin offering on the side of the altar, and the rest of the blood will be sprinkled on the base of the altar, because it is a sin offering. 10 He shall also offer the second as a burnt offering, as was done; so the priest shall make atone- ment for him (for the sin he committed) and it shall be forgiven him. 11 But if he is not able to bring two turtledoves or two young pigeons, he who committed the sin shall bring for his offering the tenth part of an ephah of fine flour as a sin offering; he shall not put any oil in it, nor shall he put any incense in it, for it is a sin offering. 12 Then he shall bring it to the priest, and the priest shall take a handful of it as a reminder, and shall bury it on the altar with the Lord's offerings made by fire, for it is a sin offering. 13 So the priest shall make atonement for him, concerning the sin which he committed in one of these pits, and it shall be forgiven him; and the remnant shall be the priests', as the food offering. 14 The Lord spoke to Moses, saying, 15 If any- one transgresses and sins through ignorance, taking away things consecrated to the LORD, he shall bring to the LORD, as compensation for his guilt, a ram without blemish from the flock, worth two shekels of silver, according to your estimation, according to the shekel of the sanctuary, as compensation for his guilt. 16 So he shall restore what he has offended, taking away the holy thing, and shall add to it the fifth part and give it to the priest; so the priest shall make atonement for him with the ram of his guilt, and it shall be forgiven him. 17 Moreover, if anyone sins and acts against one of the commands of the LORD, which is not to be done, and does not know, he sins and bears his iniquity, 18 then he shall bring to the priest a ram without blemish from the flock, of the value of two shekels, for an offense of guilt, and the priest shall make atonement for him for the ignorance in which he erred and did not know; so it shall be forgiven him. 19 This is the atonement for the guilt committed against the LORD.

CHAPTER 6

1 The LORD spoke to Moses, saying. 2 If a man sins and commits a trespass against the LORD, and denies his neighbor that which was entrusted to him or given to him for safekeeping, or opposes his neighbor by rob- bery or violence, 3 or finds what was lost and denies it, swearing falsely, for any of these things that a man does, in which he sins: 4 When, I say, he sins and transgresses, he must return the stolen thing which he has robbed, or the thing taken by violence which he has taken by force, or the thing delivered to him for safekeeping, or the lost thing which he has found, 5 or for that which he has sworn false- ly, he shall return it for the whole sum, add- ing to it the fifth part more, and

give it to him who loses it, the same day on which he has reported it for trespass. 6 He shall also bring to the LORD, as compensation for his guilt, a ram without blemish from the flock of your choice, worth two shekels, as compensation for the guilt to the priest. 7 The priest shall make atonement for him before the LORD, and what he has done and transgressed shall be forgiven him." 8 Then the LORD spoke to Moses, saying, Command Aaron and his sons, saying, "This is the burning ceremony (it is the burning because it burns on the altar from evening to morning and the fire burns on the altar)." 10 The priest shall put on his linen robe and put his linen breeches on his flesh, and he shall remove the ashes when the fire has consumed the burning on the altar, and he shall put them beside the altar. 11 Then he shall take off his garments and put on other garments and carry the ashes off the altar to a clean place. 12 But the fire on the altar shall kindle there and never be quenched; there- fore the priest shall light wood there every morning, arrange the burnt offering on it in order, and bury the fat of the peace offerings there. 13 The fire shall be kindled on the altar and shall never be quenched. 14 This is also the pound of the food offering that Aaron's sons will offer in the presence of the LORD before the altar. 15 So he shall take his hand- ful of the good wine of the roast and the oil and all the incense that is on the roast, and he shall bury it on the altar as a sweet savor, as a memorial to the LORD: 16 But the rest shall Aaron and his sons eat; they shall eat it with- out leaven in the holy place; in the court of the tent of meeting they shall eat it. 17 It shall not be cooked with leaven: I have given it as a portion of my sacrifices made by fire, for it is as the sin offering and as the guilt offering. 18 All the males of Aaron's sons shall eat of it: It shall be a statute for all your generations concerning the Lord's offspring made by fire; what touches them shall be holy. 19 The LORD spoke to Moses, saying, 20 This is the offering of Aaron and his sons, which they shall offer to the LORD on the day of his anointing: the tenth part of an ephah of fine flour, as a food offering for ever; half of it in the morning and half of it in the evening. 21 In the frying pan you shall sauté with oil; you shall bring it sau- téed and offer the cooked pieces of the food offering as a sweet homage to the LORD. 22 The priest who is anointed in his dwelling place, from among his sons, shall offer it: It is the Lord's command for eternity; it shall all be burned. 23 For every food offering of the priest shall be burnt, it shall not be eaten. 24 Moreover the Lord spoke to Moses, saying, 25 Speak to Aaron and his sons and say, "This is the law of the sin offering: in the place where the burnt offering was killed, the sin offering shall be killed before the LORD, for it is most holy. 26 The priest who offers this sin offering shall eat it; in the holy place it shall be eaten, in the courtyard of the Tabernacle of Meet- ing. 27 That which touches his flesh shall be holy; and when his blood falls on a garment, you shall wash that on which it fell in the holy place. 28 Also the earthen vessel in which he has become infected shall be broken; but if he has become infected in a vessel of bronze, it shall be peeled off and washed with water. 29 All the male priests shall eat of it, for it is a most holy thing. 30 But the sin offering shall not be eaten, whose blood shall be brought into the tent of meeting for reconciliation in the holy place, but shall be burned in the fire.

CHAPTER 7

1 The blood of the oblation is also holy. 2 In the place where the burnt offering is killed, the oblation shall be killed; its blood shall be sprinkled all around on the altar. 3 He shall also offer all the fat, the rumen, and the fat dripping from the entrails. 4 Then he shall re- move the two kids, with the fat on them and on the sides, and the meat on the side with the kids. 5 Then the priest shall bury them on the altar, as a fire sacrifice to the LORD; this is a guilt sacrifice. 6 All the males of the priests shall eat of it, in the holy place, for it is most holy. 7 As the offense for sin, so the offense for guilt, one lawe shall serve for both; the one with which the priest shall make atonement shall be his own. 8 Furthermore, the priest who offers a stake to a man shall have the skin of the stake he offered. 9 And all the offal baked in the oven, seasoned in the frying-pan and in the pan, shall be the priest's who of- fers it. 10 Every meat offering mixed with oil and dried shall be distributed to all the sons of Aaron, all alike. 11 Moreover, this is the peace offering that he shall offer to the LORD. 12 If he will offer it in thanksgiving, he will offer as a thanksgiving offering, cakes kneaded with oil, wafers kneaded with oil, and flour flour sautéed with cakes kneaded with oil. 13 He shall also offer his sacrifice with cakes of leavened bread, as a peace offering, to give thanks. 14 Of all the sacrifice he shall offer a cake as an offering to the LORD, and he shall be the priest who sprinkles the blood of the peace offerings. 15 The meat of his peace of- ferings also, to give thanks, shall be eaten on the day of the offering; he shall leave none of it until the morning. 16 But if the sacrifice of his offering is a vow or a free offering, it shall be eaten on the same day that the sacrifice is offered; and in the morning the rest shall be eaten. 17 But the quantity of the meat of- fering that remains until the third day shall be burned with fire. 18 For if any part of the meat of his peace offerings be eaten on the third day, it shall not be accepted from him who offered it, nor shall it be acknowledged to him, but it shall be an abomination; there- fore he who eats of it shall bear his guilt. 19 Also the meat that touches any vnclean thing shall not be eaten, but shall be burned with fire; but of this meat may all who are clean eat. 20 But if anyone eats of the flesh of the peace offerings that belong to the LORD, hav- ing his vncleanness upon him, then the same person shall be eliminated from his people. 21 Moreover, if anyone touches a vncleane thing, such as the vncleannesse of man, or of a vn- cleane beast, or of any unclean abomination, and eats of the flesh of the peace offerings pertaining to the Lord, then that person shall be eliminated from his people. 22 Then the LORD spoke to Moses, saying, 23 Speak unto the children of Israel, and say, Ye shall not eat fat of bees, nor of sheep, nor of goats: 24 but the fat of dead beasts and the fat of those that have been tormented with beasts may be oc- cupied by anyone, but you shall not eat of it. 25 For whosoever eateth the fat of the beast, of which he shall offer a burnt-offering unto the LORD, and whosoever eateth thereof, he shall be cut off from his people. 26 And you shall not eat blood, either of cattle or of beast, in all your dwellings. 27 Whoever eats of the blood shall be eliminated from his people." 28 The LORD spoke to Moses, saying 29 Speak to the children of Israel and say, "Whoever offers his peace offerings to the LORD will bring the gift of his peace offerings to the LORD: 30 His hands shall bring the offerings of the LORD made by fire; and his breast with his bosom shall he bring, that his bosom may be shaken on one side and on the other before the LORD. 31 Then the priest shall bury the fat on the altar, and the breast shall be Aar- on's and his sons'. 32 The right shoulder you shall give to the priest as a salvation offering, as a peace offering. 33 The same one who will shed the blood of your peace offerings and his blood, from among Aaron's sons, shall have the right shoulder for his portion. 34 For the breast shaken on one side and the shoulder lifted up, I have taken from the sons of Israel the blood of their peace offerings and given it to Aaron the priest and his sons as a statute forever among the sons of Israel. 35 This is the anointing of Aaron and the anointing of his sons concerning the Lord's offerings made by fire, on the day when he presented them to serve in the priestly office before the Lord. 36 Which portions the LORD commanded to be given them on the day when he anointed them among the children of Israel, as a stat- ute forever in their generations. 37 This is also the rite of burning, the rite of sin, the rite of guilt, the consecrations, and the rite of peace, 38 which the Lord commanded Moses on Mount Sinai, when he commanded the chil- dren of Israel to offer their gifts to the Lord in the wilderness of Sinai.

CHAPTER 8

1 Then the LORD spoke to Moses, saying, 2 Take Aaron and his sons with him, the gar- ments and the anointing oil, a bubble for the offense of sin, two branches and a bas- ket of vnleaued bread, 3 And he gathered all the company together at the entrance to the Tabernacle of Meeting. 4 Moses did as the LORD had commanded him, and the con- gregation was assembled at the base of the Tabernacle of Meeting. 5 Then Moses said to the congregation, "This is the thing the LORD has commanded us to do." 6 Moses brought Aaron and his sons and washed them with water, 7 and put his cloak on him, and gird- ed him with a girdle, and clothed him with the tunic, and put the Ephod on him, which he girded with the iron sheath of the Ephod and bound it to him. 8 Then he put the breast plate on him, and in the breast plate he put the Vrim and the Thummim. 9 He also put the miter on his head, and on the miter in front he put the golden plate and the holy horn, as the LORD had commanded Moses. 10 Moses took the anointing oil, anoinized the taberna- cle and everything in it, and sanctified it, 11 he sprinkled it on the altar several times, and anointed the altar and all its instruments, the lauer and its foote, to sanctify them). 12 Then he sprinkled the anointing oil on Aaron's head and anointed him to sanctify him. 13 Then Moses brought in Aaron's sons, put cloaks on them, girded them with sheaths, and put caps on their heads, as the LORD had commanded Moses. 14 Then he brought the bull for sacrifice, and Aaron and his sons put their hands on the bull's head for sacrifice. 15 Moses killed it and took its blood, which he put with his finger on the horns of the altar, purified the altar and put the rest of the blood on the base of the altar; so he sanctified it to make reconciliation on it. 16 Then he took all the fat that was on the entrails, the flesh of the calf and the two kids, with their fat, which Moses burned on the altar. 17 But the bull- ock, its skin, its flesh and its meat, he burned with fire without the host, as the LORD had commanded Moses. 18 He also brought the ram for the burning, and Aaron and his sons put their hands on the ram's head. 19 Moses killed it and sprinkled its blood on the altar all around, 20 Moses cut the ram into pieces and burned the head with the pieces and the fat, 21 and he washed the entrails and the legs in water; then Moses burned the ram in all its parts on the altar, for it was a burning for a sweet smell, made by fire for the LORD, as the LORD had commanded Moses. 22 Then he brought the other ram, the ram of the con- secrations, and Aaron and his

sons laid their hands on the ram's head, 23 Moses killed it, took its blood and put it on the lip of Aaron's right ear, on the thumb of his right hand and on the big toe of his right foot. 24 Then Moses brought in Aaron's sons and put blood on the lap of their right ears, on the thumbs of their right hands and on the toes of their right feet; Moses sprinkled the rest of the blood on the altar all around. 25 Then he took the fat, the rumen and all the fat that was on the inner parts, the skin of the cheek, the two kids with their fat, and the right shoulder. 26 He also took from the basket of leavened bread that was before the LORD, a leavened cake and a cake of oiled bread and a wafer, and put them on the fat and on the right shoulder. 27 Then he put everything into Aaron's hands and into the hands of his sons, and he slid it on either side before the LORD. 28 Then Moses took the pieces from their hands and burned them on the altar as a burnt offering, for these were consecrations for a sweet savor, made by fire to the Lord. 29 Likewise Moses took the breast of the ram of the consecrations and shook it on either side before the LORD, for it was Moses' portion, as the LORD had command- ed Moses. 30 Moses also took the anointing oil and the blood that was on the altar and sprinkled it on Aaron, his garments, his sons, and the garments of his sons with him; thus he sanctified Aaron, his garments, his sons, and the garments of his sons with him. 31 Then Moses said to Aaron and his sons, "Eat the meat at the entrance of the Tabernacle of Meeting, and eat it with the bread that is in the basket of consecrations, as I commanded, saying, Aaron and his sons shall eat it, 32 but what remains of the meat and bread you shall burn with fire. 33 You shall not depart from the tabernacle of the tabernacle of meeting for ten days, until the days of your conse- crations are ended; for for ten days, says the LORD, he will consecrate you, 34 as he has done today, so the LORD has commanded to do, to make an atonement for you. 35 There- fore you shall stand day and night, for ten days, at the door of the tabernacle of the con- gregation, and keep watch for the LORD, that you may not depart, for thus it is commanded me." 36 So Aaron and his sons did all that the LORD had commanded by the hand of Moses.

CHAPTER 9

1 On the eighth day Moses called Aaron, his sons and the elders of Israel: 2 Then he said to Aaron, "Take a heifer for a sin offering and a ram for a burnt offering, both of them without blemish, and bring them before the LORD. 3 And to the children of Israel you shall say, "Take a kid goat for the sacrifice, and a calf and a yearling lamb, without blemish, for the sacrifice: 4 Also a bullock and a ram as a peace offering, to be offered to the LORD, and a meat offering mixed with oil, for the LORD will appear to you today." 5 Then they brought what Moses had commanded before the tent of meeting, and the whole assembly gathered and stood before the LORD. 6 (For Moses had said, "This is the thing that the Lord has com- manded to be done, and the glory of the Lord will appear to you.") 7 Then Moses said to Aar- on, "Draw near to the altar and offer your sin offering and your burnt offering and make atonement for yourself and for the people; of- fer also the people's offering and make atone- ment for them, as the Lord has commanded." 8 So Aaron went to the altar and killed the calf of the sin offering, which was for him. 9 And Aaron's sons brought him the blood; and he dipped his finger in the blood, and put it on the horns of the altar, and put the rest of the blood at the foot of the altar. 10 But the fat and the

kids and the flesh of the flesh of sin he burned on the altar, as the LORD had commanded Moses. 11 The flesh and skin were also burned with fire, without the host. 12 Then he killed the burnt offering, and Aar- on's sons brought him the blood, which he sprinkled all around on the altar. 13 They also brought him the burnt offering with its pieces and head, and he burned them on the altar. 14 In the same way he washed the entrails and the legs and burned them on the altar along with the stake. 15 Then he stripped off the of- fal of the people, and took a kid goat, which was the offal of sin for the people, and killed it and put it out for sin, as the first: 16 Then he offered the roast and prepared it accord- ing to the instructions. 17 He also presented the roast, filled his hand with it, and burned it on the altar beside the morning roast. 18 He also killed the bullock and the ram for the peace offering, which was for the people, and Aaron's sons brought him the blood, which he sprinkled on the altar all around, 19 with the fat of the bull and of the ram, the rumen, the inward parts and the kids, and the flesh of the calf. 20 So they laid the fat on the ud- ders, and he burned the fat on the altar. 21 But the breasts and the right shoulder Aaron discarded before the LORD, as the LORD had commanded Moses. 22 Then Aaron raised his hand toward the people, blessed them, and came down from the sin offering, the burnt offering, and the peace offering. 23 Then Mo- ses and Aaron went into the tent of meeting, came out, blessed the people, and the glory of the LORD appeared to all the people. 24 Then there went out a fire from the LORD and con- sumed on the altar the stake and the fat; and when all the people saw it, they gave thanks and fell on their faces.

CHAPTER 10

1 But Nadab and Abihu, Aaron's sons, took one or the other his censer, put fire in it, put incense in it, and offered the Lord a strange fire, which he had not commanded them. 2 Therefore a fire went out from the LORD and consumed them; so they tinctured them- selves before the LORD. 3 Then Moses said to Aaron, "This is what the LORD has said, 'I will be sanctified in those who come after me, and I will be glorified before all the people." 4 And Moses called Mishael and Elzafán, the sons of Vzziel, Aaron's vncolle, and said to them, "Come, bring your brothers before the sanctuary out of the army." 5 Then they went and carried them in their crates outside the army, as Moses had appointed. 6 Then Mo- ses said to Aaron, Eleazar and Ithamar, his sons, "Do not split your heads or rend your garments, lest you dye yourselves, and lest wrath come upon all the people; but let your brothers, all the house of Israel, kindle the fire that the LORD has kindled. 7 Come not out of the precincts of the Tabernacle of Con- gregation, lest ye be dyed: for the anointing oil of the LORD is upon you: and they did ac- cording to the commandment of Moses. 8 The Lord spoke to Aaron, saying, 9 You shall not drink wine or strong liquor, neither you nor your sons with you, when you enter the tent of meeting, lest you die; this is an ordinance for ever, for all your generations, 10 that you may make a difference between the holy and the holy, •between the clean and the vnclean, 11 and to teach the children of Israel all the statutes which the LORD commanded them by the hand of Moses." 12 Then Moses said to Aaron, Eleazar and Ithamar, his remaining sons, "Take the meat offering that remains of the Lord's offering, made by fire, and eat it without blemish beside your altar, for it is most holy: 13 And you shall eat it in the holy place,

for it is your offering and that of your sons of the offenses of the Lord made by fire, for so I am commanded. 14 Also the shaken breast and the shaken shoulder you shall eat in a clean place: you and your sons and your daughters with you, for they are given as your duet and the duet of your sons, of the peace offerings of the children of Israel. 15 And the shaken shoulder and the shaken breast shall be brought with the offal made with the fire of fat, to shake it hither and thither before the LORD, and it shall be thine and thy sons' with thee for once for ever, as the LORD hath commanded." 16 Moses looked for the kid that had been offered for sin, and behold, it was burned; therefore he was angry with Eleazar and Ithamar, the sons of Aaron, who had re- mained outside, saying, "Why have you done this? 17 Why did you not eat the sin offering in the holy place, since it is most holy? And God granted it to you to bear the iniquity of the congregation, to make atonement for them before the Lord. 18 Well, his blood was not brought within the holy place; you should have eaten it in the holy place, as I had com- manded." 19 Then Aaron said to Moses, "Be- hold, today they offered their sin offering and their burning sacrifice before the LORD, and things have come to me that you know; if I had eaten the sin offering today, would it have been accepted in the eyes of the LORD? 20 When Moses heard this, he was glad.

CHAPTER 11

1 Then the LORD spoke to Moses and Aar- on, saying to them 2 Speak to the children of Israel and say, "These are the animals that you shall eat, among all the animals that are on the earth. 3 The one that parts from the hoof, that has cloudy feet and chews the cud, among the beasts, is the one you shall eat. 4 But of those that chew the carcass or bare only the legs, you shall not eat; as the camel, which, because it chews the carcass and does not bare the legs, shall be forbidden you. 5 The rabbit also, because it chews the carcass and does not disrobe its feet, shall be forbidden to you. 6 The hare also, because it chews the carcass and does not feed on the legs, shall be made vncleane to you. 7 And the swine, be- cause it parts from the hoofs and has cloudy feet, but does not chew the carcass, shall be vncleaned to you. 8 You shall not eat their flesh or touch their carcasses, for they shall be forbidden to you. 9 Of all that is in the wa- ters you shall eat: what has fins and skins in the waters, in the seas or in the rivers, you shall eat. 10 But all that have neither fins nor skins in the seas or in the banks, of all that bellow in the waters, and of all things that are in the waters, shall be an abomination to you. 11 They, I say, shall be an abomination to you; you shall not eat their flesh, but you shall abhor their machines. 12 That which has no fins or scales in the waters, shall be an abomination to you. 13 These also shall be in abomination among the fish; they shall not be eaten, for they are an abomination: the eagle, the sea bird, and the osprey: 14 also the vultur and the kite, according to his kind, 15 and all rauens as their kind: 16 also the ostrich, the night raven, the seal, and the hawk, accord- ing to his kind: 17 also the little owl, the con- norant, and the great owl. 18 Also the redskin, the pelican, and the swan: 19 also the flock, the heron, the lapwing, and the thrush: 20 Also all the birds that creep and go up all four shall be an abomination to you. 21 But these you shall eat: of all the reptiles that crawl and go on all four, which have feet and legs all of a piece, and can fly with them upon the earth, 22 of them you shall eat these: the grashopper according to its kind, the solean according to its kind, the

hargol according to its kind, and the hagab according to its kind. 23 But all oth- er animals that crawl and have four feet shall be an abomination to you. 24 For by them you shall be defiled; whoever touches their ma- chines shall be vituperated unto erection. 25 Also whosoever toucheth their machines shall wash his clothes, and shall be vncleared until the dawn. 26 And all the beasts that have de- formed claws, that have not clouded feet, and that chew not the carcass, shall be vncleaned unto you; whosoever toucheth them shall be vncleaned. 27 And he that goeth on his feet among all the beasts that go on four legs shall be vncleaned unto you; he that toucheth their machines shall be vncleaned unto the end. 28 And he that bears their machines shall wash his clothes, and shall be vncleane until the dawn, for these shall be vncleane unto you. 29 There shall also be vncleaned unto you all be- ings that crawl and move upon the earth: the weasel, and the mouse, and the frog, accord- ing to his kind: 30 Also the mouse, the lizard, the chameleon, the stellio, and the molle. 31 These shall be vncleane to you among all the reptiles; whoever touches them when they are dead shall be vncleane to the end. 32 Also that which shall fall upon one of their dead carcasses shall be vncleane, whether it be a wooden vessel, or a rayment, or a skin, or a sack; whichever vessel is occupied, it shall be put into the water as vncleane to the ueen, and so shall be purified. 33 But every earthen vessel into which one of them falls, what is in it shall be vncleared, and you shall break it. 34 Also the food that you eat, if any water falls on it, shall be vncleared; and all the water that you drink in these vessels shall be vncleared. 35 Every thing on which their machinery shall fall shall be vncleated; the baker or the vessel shall be broken, because they are vncleated, and they shall be vncleated to you also. 36 The fountains and wells where there is much wa- ter shall be cleansed, but what touches their carcasses shall be vnclean. 37 And if there is a trace of their dead carcasses on a seed that is to be sown, it shall be clean. 38 But if water has been poured on a seed and there is some of their dead carcasses left thereon, it shall be taken away. 39 If even a beast, whose carcasses you may eat, dies, he who touches its carcasses shall be vncleared to the end. 40 And whosoever eats its carcasses shall wash his clothes, and shall be vncleared unto the ue; and whosoever also bears its carcasses shall wash his clothes, and shall be vncleared unto the ue. 41 Every thing that crawls upon the earth shall therefore be an abomination, and shall not be eaten. 42 That which goes on the chest and that which goes on the four legs or has many legs among all the reptiles that crawl on the earth, you shall not eat it, for it shall be an abomination. 43 You shall not de- file yourselves with any thing that crawls; you shall not defile yourselves with them; you shall not defile yourselves, I say, with them, 44 For I am the LORD your God; sanctify yourselves therefore, be holy, for I am holy, and do not defile yourselves with any of the animals that crawl upon the earth. 45 For I am the LORD who brought you out of the land of Egypt to be your God, and that you may be holy, for I am holy. 46 This is the law for beasts, for vermin, for every thing that moves in the waters, and for every thing that creeps on the earth: That there may be a difference between the vn- cleane and the cleane, and between the beast that may be eaten and the beast that is not to be eaten.

CHAPTER 12

1 The LORD spoke to Moses, saying, 2 Speak to the children of Israel and say, "When a woman has given birth and has borne a male child, she must be circumcised for ten days, as when she is circumcised for her sickness. 3 (And on the eighth day the foreskin of the flesh of the child shall be circumcised). 4 And she shall abide in the blood of her purifica- tion for three days and thirty days; and she shall not touch any object of flesh, nor enter into the sanctuary until the time of her pu- rification is past. 5 But if she gives birth to a child of full age, she shall be vncleared for two weeks, as when she has sickness; and she shall remain in the blood of her purification for three days and six. 6 When the days of her purification are over (whether it is a son or a daughter), she shall bring to the priest a one-year-old lamb as a burnt offering, and a young pigeon or a turtle as a sin offering, at the threshold of the Tabernacle of Meeting, 7 who shall offer it before the LORD, and make atonement for her; so she shall be cleansed by the issue of her blood; this is the law for her who has given birth to a male or a female. 8 But if she is not able to bear a blade, she shall bring two turtles or two young pigeons: the one as a burning sacrifice and the other as a sin offering; and the priest shall make atone- ment for her; so she shall be cleansed.

CHAPTER 13

1 Moreover the LORD spoke to Moses and Aaron, saying 2 The man who shall have in the skin of his flesh a swelling or a spot or a white spot, so that in the skin of his flesh it is like the plague of leprosy, shall be brought to Aar- on the priest or to one of his sons the priests, 3 and the priest shall examine the plague in the skin of his flesh; if the spot in the plague has turned white, and the plague seems to be lower than the skin of his flesh, it is a plague of leprosy; therefore the priest shall examine him and declare him vnclean: 4 But if the white spot is in the skin of his flesh, and it does not seem to be lower than the skin, nor has his skin become white, then the priest shall shut up the one who has the plague in his house for ten days. 5 After that, the priest shall look at him for the seventh day; and if it seems to him that the plague remains and does not grow in the skin, the priest shall shut him up again for seven more days. 6 Then the priest shall examine it again on the seventh day, and if the plague is dark and the plague does not grow into the skin, the priest shall declare it healed, because it is a crustacean; then he shall wash his clothes and healed. 7 But if the plague still grows in the skin, after he has been visited by the priest to be cleansed, he will be visited by the priest again. 8 Then the priest will examine, and if the skin is still alive, the priest will declare him vn- cleane, because it is leprosy. 9 When the plague of leprosy is in a man, he is to be brought to the priest, 10 and the priest shall see him; and if the swelling is white in the skin, and has made his skin white, and if there is sparse flesh in the swelling, 11 it is an old leprosy in the skin of his flesh; and the priest shall declare him vnclean, and shall not shut him up, because he is vnclean. 12 More- over, if the leprosy comes out of the skin, and the leprosy spreads over the whole skin of the plague, from the head to the feet, where the priest looks, 13 then the priest shall examine; and if the leprosy covers all his flesh, he shall declare that the plague is clean, because it has become all white; so it shall be clean. 14 But if when he is seen there is raw flesh on him, he shall be vncleared. 15 And the priest shall see the raw flesh and declare that it is vncleane; for raw flesh is vncleane, so it is leprosy. 16 Or, if the rawe flesh changes and becomes white, the man

will present himself to the priest, 17 and the priest shall observe it, and if the plague be turned white, the priest shall de- clare that the plague is clean, because it is clean. 18 The flesh in whose skin there is gall is also healed, 19 if in the place of the gall there is a white swelling or a white spot somewhat reddish, it shall be seen by the priest. 20 When the priest sees it, if it appears lower than the skin and its halo is changed to white, the priest will declare it vncleared, because it is a plague of leprosy, which has broken out in the gall. 21 But if the priest look at it and there is no white halo, and if it is not lower than the skin, but is darker, the priest shall close it for ten days. 22 If the spot spreads in the flesh, the priest shall declare it vncleane, because it is a plague. 23 But if the spot remains in place and does not grow, it is a burning gall; there- fore the priest shall declare it clean. 24 If there is flesh in whose skin there is a burning, and the quick flesh of this burning has a white spot, somewhat reddish or pale, 25 and the priest shall look upon it; and if the spot turn white and appear lower than the skin, it is a leprosy broken out in the burning, the priest shall pronounce it vnclean, for it is a plague of leprosy. 26 But if the priest looks at it, and there is no white halo in the spot, and it is not lower than the other skin, but is darker, the priest shall shut it up for ten days. 27 Then the priest shall look at it on the seventh day; if the spot has grown on the skin, the priest shall declare it vncleane, for it is the plague of lep- rosy. 28 If the spot remains in place, without growing in the skin, but is dark, it is an onset of the burning; therefore the priest shall de- clare it clean, for it is the draining away of the burning. 29 If a man or woman has a sore on his head or on his beard, the priest shall de- clare him clean, because it is the drying up of the burning, 30 the priest shall see his sore; and if it appears lower than the skin, and there is a small yellow halo therein, the priest shall declare him vncleared, for it is a black spot and leprosy of the head or beard. 31 If the priest looks at the plague of the black spot, and if it does not seem lower than the skin and has no trace of a black spot, the priest shall shut up the one who has the plague of the black spot in the house for ten days. 32 Af- terwards, on the tenth day, the priest shall look at the plague; and if the black spot does not grow, and there is no trace of yellow blood in it, and the black spot does not seem lower than the skin, 33 then it shall be removed, but the place of the black spot shall not be re- moved; but the priest shall shut up the man having the black spot for ten days more. 34 On the seventh day the priest shall look at the black spot; and if the black spot does not ex- tend over the skin and seem lower than the other skin, the priest shall bring him in, and he shall wash his clothes and be clean. 35 But if the black spot extends into the flesh after the clessing, the priest shall wash his gar- ments, and he shall be clean, 36 then the priest shall look upon him; and if the black spot grow in the skin, the priest shall not look for the young man's hearing, because he is vn- clean. 37 But if it seems to him that the black spot remains and the black spot grows there- in, the black spot is healed, he is clean, and the priest shall declare him clean. 38 More- over, if there are many white spots in the man's or woman's skin, 39 the priest shall ex- amine: if the spots in the skin of their flesh are a little dark and white in all, it is but a white spot split in the skin; therefore he is clean. 40 The man whose head has fallen off and is bald, he is clean. 41 If his head loses its scar in the front and is bald, he is clean. 42 But if there is a white and reddish plague in the head or in the bald forehead, it is a leprosy springing up in the head or in the bald fore- head. 43 Therefore the priest shall examine him, and if the plague is white and reddish in his head or in his bald forehead, and it ap- pears like a leprosy in the skin of the flesh, 44 he is leprous and vnclean; therefore the priest shall declare him altogether vnclean, because the plague is in his head. 45 The leper who has the plague shall rend his garments, strip his head naked, put a hood over his lips, and cry, "I am vnclean, I am vnclean." 46 As long as sickness is upon him, he shall be defiled, for he is vnclean; he shall dwell alone, without campe, his dwelling place. 47 Even the gar- ment in which the plague of leprosy is found, whether of wool or of linen, 48 whether in the warp or woof of linen or wool, or in a skin, or in any thing made of skin, 49 and if the plague is green or somewhat reddish in the garment or in the leather, or in the warp, or in the wood, or in anything made of leather, it is a plague of leprosy and must be shown to the priest. 50 And the priest shall see the plague, and he shall shut up the sick person for ten days, 51 and he shall look at the plague on the seventh day; and if the plague grows in the garment, or in the warp, or in the wood, or in the skin, or in anything made of skin, that plague is a fearful and vnclean leprosy. 52 And he shall bury the garment, the warp, or the wood, whether it be of wool or of linen, or any thing made of skin, in which the plague is found; for it is a fearful leprosy, therefore it shall be burned in the fire. 53 If, however, the priest sees that the plague does not grow in the garment, or in the wood, or in whatever thing of skin it is, 54 then the priest shall com- mand them to wash the thing in which the plague is, and he shall shut it up for another ten days. 55 Then the priest shall look at the plague, after he has washed it; and if the plague has not changed its color, even if the plague has not grown any more, it is vncleane; you shall bury it in the fire, because it is an internal plague, whether the spot is in the un- covered place of the whole, or in part of it. 56 If the priest sees that the sore is darker, he shall, after washing it, cut it off from the robe, or from the skin, or from the warp, or from the wood. 57 If it still appears in the robe, or in the warp, or in the wood, or in anything made of skin, it is a spreading leprosy; you shall bury in the fire the thing in which the plague is. 58 If you have washed your robe, your warp, your wood or anything made of leather, if the plague is gone, you shall wash it a second time and it shall be clean. 59 This is the law of the plague of leprosy in a robe of wool or linen, or in a sheath, or in a cloth, or in anything of skin, to make it clean or vn- cleane.

CHAPTER 14

1 The LORD spoke to Moses, saying, "This is the law for the leper on the day of his cleans- ing, 2 This is the law for the leper on the day of his clessation: he shall be brought to the priest, 3 and the priest shall come out of the chamber and examine him; and if the plague of leprosy be healed in the leper, 4 then the priest shall begin to take for the leper two alien and clean sparrows, a cedar wood, a leather lace, and hyssop. 5 The priest shall kill one of the birds with pure water in an earthen vessel. 6 Afterwards, he shall take the shot that lies with the cedar wood, the scarlet lace and the hyssop, and dip them together with the shot that lies in the blood of the killed shot, outside the pure water, 7 And he shall sprinkle seven times the one who is to be weeded out of his leprosy, and he shall weed him out and let go the sparowe that is dead in a wide field. 8 Then he who has been censured shall wash his garments, and take off all his clothes, and wash himself in water, so that he may be clean; after that he shall enter the host, but he shall remain outside his tent for ten days. 9 On the seventh day he shall cut off all his beard, his head, his beard, and his eye- brows; then he shall cut off all his beard, and wash his clothes, and wash his flesh in water; so he shall be clean. 10 Then, on the eighth day, he shall take two lambs without blemish and one year-old ewe without blemish, and three tithes of fine flowers as a food offering, mixed with oil, and a pint of oil. 11 The priest who will purify him shall bring the man to be purified and these things before the LORD in the hall of the tent of meeting. 12 Then the priest shall take a blade, and offer it as a guilt sacrifice, and the pint of oil, and shake it on either side before the LORD. 13 He shall kill the lamb in the place where the sin offering and the burnt offering are killed, that is, in the holy place, for as the sin offering is of the priests, so is the sin offering, for it is most holy. 14 The priest shall take the blood of transgression and put it on the lip of the right ear of the one who is to be incensed, on the thumb of his right hand and on the big toe of his right foot. 15 The priest shall also take a pint of oil and put it in the palm of his left hand, 16 the priest shall dip his right finger in the oil that is in his left hand, and he shall sprinkle the oil with his finger ten times be- fore the LORD. 17 And the priest shall put the remnant of the oil that is in his hand on the lap of the right ear of him who is to be in- censed, on the thumb of his right hand, and on the big toe of his right foot, where the blood of condemnation had been put. 18 But the residue of the oil that is in the priest's hand, he shall put it on the head of him who is to be incensed; so the priest shall make atone- ment for him before the LORD. 19 The priest shall offer the sin offering and make atone- ment for the one who is to be incensed for his vncleannesse; then he shall kill the burnt sac- rifice. 20 So the priest shall offer the burnt offering and the meat on the altar, and the priest shall make atonement for him; so he shall be cleansed. 21 But if he is poor and is unable to do so, he shall bring a blade for the atonement of guilt, to be shaken, for his rec- onciliation, and a dozen fine flowers mixed with oil, for the atonement of food, with a pinch of oil. 22 Also two turtledoves or two young pigeons, according to his ability, one of which shall be a sin offering and the other a burnt offering, 23 and he shall bring them on the eighth day as an offering to the priest in the hall of the tent of meeting, before the LORD. 24 And the priest shall take the apple of offense and the pint of oil, and shake them on either side before the LORD. 25 He shall kill the lamb of the trespass offering, and the priest shall take the blood of the trespass of- fering and put it on the lap of the right ear that is to be covered, on the thumb of his right hand, and on the big toe of his right foot. 26 Moreover the priest shall pour oil into the palm of his left hand. 27 Then the priest shall sprinkle the oil in his left hand with his right finger, ten times before the LORD. 28 Then the priest shall put the oil in his hand on the lap of the condemned man's right ear, on the thumb of his right hand, and on the big toe of his right foot, on the place of the condemned man's blood. 29 But the rest of the oil that the priest has in his hand he shall put on the head of the one who is to be chained, to make atonement for him before the LORD. 30 Moreover he shall present one of the turtle- doves or young pigeons, according to his abil- ity: 31 as he is able, the one as a sacrifice for sin, and the other as a burnt offering with meat sacrifice; so the priest shall make atone- ment for him who is to be incensed before the LORD. 32 This is the weakness of the one who has the plague of leprosy and is unable to of- fer the whole offering. 33 The LORD also spoke to Moses and Aaron, saying, 34 When you have come to the land of Canaan, which I give you in possession, if I send the plague of leprosy to a house in the land of your posses- sion, 35 the owner of the house will

come and tell the priest, saying, "It seems to me that there is a plague of leprosy in the house." 36 Then the priest will command them to empty the house before the priest enters it to see the plague, so that everything in the house will not be made vncleane, and then the priest will enter to see the house, 37 and he shall make the sign of the plague; and if the plague be in the walls of the house, and there be deep greenish or reddish spots, which seem to be lower than the wall, 38 then the priest shall go out from the house to the outside of the house, and shall shut up the house for ten days. 39 Then the priest shall return on the seventh day, and if he sees that the plague has increased in the walls of the house, 40 then the priest shall command them to remove the stones where the plague is, and they shall throw them into an infamous place outside the city. 41 Also he will have the house scraped all around, and he will dust off the dust that they have removed, outside the city in an un- known place. 42 Then they will take other stones and put them in the place of those stones, and they will take other mortar with which to plaster the house. 43 But if the plague comes again and breaks out in the house, after the stones have been taken away and after the house has been scraped and coated, 44 then the priest shall come and see; and if the plague grow in the house, it is a fearful leprosy in the house; it is therefore vn- cleane. 45 And he shall demolish the house, and its stones, and its wood, and all the mor- tar of the house, and bring them out of the city to a safe place. 46 Moreover, whoever en- ters the house for as long as it is shut up, he shall be vncleane to the end. 47 Also whoever sleeps in the house shall wash his clothes; and whoever eats in the house shall also wash his clothes. 48 But if the priest comes and sees that the plague has no longer spread in the house, after the house has undergone a plague, the priest shall declare the house clean, because the plague is healed. 49 Then he shall take to cleanse the house two spar- rows, some cedar wood, lace, and hyssoptah. 50 He will kill a sparrowhawk with pure water in an earthen vessel, 51 And he shall take the cedarwood, hyssop, and lace with the dead sparrow, and dip them in the blood of the slain sparrow and in pure water, and sprinkle the house with it several times: 52 So he shall sprinkle the house with the blood of the spar- row, with the pure water, with the colored sparrow, with the cedar wood, with the hys- sop, and with the lace. 53 After that he shall let the live sparowe go out of the city through the broad fields; so he shall make atonement for the house, which shall be clean. 54 This is the law for every plague of leprosy and black spot, 55 for the leprosy of the garment and of the house, 56 of the swelling, the scab, and the white spot. 57 This is the law of leprosy to teach when a thing is vnclean and when it is clean.

CHAPTER 15

1 The LORD spoke again to Moses and Aar- on, saying, 2 Speak unto the children of Isra- el, and say unto them, He that hath an issue out of his flesh is vncleannes, because of his issue. 3 And this shall be his vncleannes in his emission: when his flesh is exhausted in his emission, or if his flesh is stopped from his emission, this is his vncleannes. 4 Every bed on which he that hath the issue lieth shall be vncleannes, and every thing on which he sitteth shall be vncleannes. 5 Whosoever toucheth his bed shall wash his clothes, and wash himself in water, and shall be clean unto the end. 6 Whoever sits on an object on which he has sat and has had bleeding, he shall wash his clothes and wash himself in water, and he shall be vnclean to the end. 7 Also

he who touches the flesh of him who has the issue, he shall wash his clothes and be washed in water, and shall be vncleane to the end. 8 If he also who has the issue spits on him who is clean, he shall wash his clothes and be washed in wa- ter, and shall be vncleane to the end. 9 And he who rides the saddle, who has the issue, shall be vncleared, 10 And whosoever toucheth a thing that was under him, he shall be vn- cleared unto the ue; and whosoever bears those things, he shall wash his clothes, and wash himself in the water, and shall be vn- cleared unto the ue. 11 In the same way, who- ever touches the one who has the hemorrhage (and has not washed his hands in the water) shall wash his clothes and wash himself in the water, and he shall be vncleared until the ue. 12 The earthen vessel that touches and has the issue shall be broken, and every wooden vessel shall be rinsed in water. 13 But if he who has issue is cleansed by his issue, he shall count ten days for his cleansing, and he shall wash his garments and wash his flesh in pure wa- ter; so he shall be clean. 14 Then, on the eighth day, he shall take with him two turtledoves or two young pigeons, and he shall stand before the LORD at the door of the tabernacle of the congregation, and he shall deliver them to the priest. 15 And the priest shall make the one a sin offering and the other a burnt offering; so the priest shall make atonement for him be- fore the LORD for his guilt. 16 Moreover, if a man part with his seed, he shall wash all his flesh in water, and shall be vncleane to the end. 17 Every garment and every skin out of which the seed comes forth shall be washed with water, and it shall be washed to the end. 18 If he who has an issue of seed lies with a woman, they shall both be washed with water and shall be vncleaned to the end. 19 More- over, when a woman shall have an issue, and the issue in her flesh shall be blood, she shall be set apart for ten days; and whosoever shall touch her shall be vncleaned until the dawn. 20 And everything on which she lies down in her separation shall be vncleared, and every- thing on which she sits shall be vncleared. 21 And whosoever toucheth his bed shall wash his clothes, and be washed with water, and shall be clean unto the end. 22 And whosoever toucheth any thing on which she sat, he shall wash his garments, and wash himself with water, and he shall be vncleane to the ue: 23 So if he shall touch her bed, or anything on which she sat, he shall be vncleane unto ue. 24 And if a man lie down with her, and the flowers of her parting touch him, he shall be vncleane for ten days, and all the bed on which he lies shall be vncleane. 25 Also when a woman's issue lasts longer than the time of her flowers, or when she has an issue longer than her flowers, all the days of the issue of her vncleannesse shall be vncleane, as in the time of her flowers. 26 The bed where she lies (as long as her issue lasts) shall be to her as the bed of her separation; and that on which she sits shall be vncleane, as her vncleannes when she is separated. 27 And whosoever toucheth these things shall be vncleane, and shall wash his clothes, and be washed in water, and shall be vncleane unto the end. 28 But if the wom- an is prone to childbirth, she shall count her ten days, and afterward she shall be clean. 29 On the eighth day she shall take two turtles or two young pigeons and bring them to the priest in the hall of the tent of meeting. 30 And the priest shall make of the one a sin of- fering, and of the other a burnt offering, and the priest shall make an atonement for her before the LORD, for the matter of her tres- passes. 31 Thus you shall separate the children of Israel from their vncleannes, that they may not dye in their vncleannesses, if they defile my Tabernacle which is in the midst of them. 32 This is the guilt of him who has a son, and of him from whom a seed comes forth that defiles him: 33 Also of her who is sick of flour, of him who has an issue, whether man or woman, and of him who lies with her who is vncleane.

CHAPTER 16

1 Moreover the LORD spoke to Moses after the death of Aaron's two sons, when they came to offer before the LORD and died: 2 The LORD said to Moses, "Tell Aaron, your brother, that he shall never enter the holy place, within the enclosure, before the mercede that is on the arch, lest he be dyed; for I will appear in the cloud, before the mercede. 3 Aaron shall enter the holy place with a long bull as a sin offering and a ram as a fire offering. 4 He shall wear the holy garment of linen, he shall have linen breeches on his flesh, he shall be girded with a linen girdle, and he shall cover his head with a linen mitre; these are the holy garments; therefore he shall wash his flesh in water when he has put them on. 5 He shall take from the congregation of the children of Israel two goats for the sin offering and one ram for the burnt offering. 6 Then Aaron shall offer the goat as a sin offering and make atonement for himself and his house. 7 He will take the two goats and present them before the LORD at the entrance to the Tabernacle of Meeting. 8 Then Aaron shall cast lots for the two goats: one for the LORD and the other for the goat of Scapo. 9 Aaron will offer the goat on which the lot was cast for the LORD and make it a sin offering. 10 But the goat on which the lot falls, which shall be the scape goat, shall be presented before the LORD, to reconcile with him and let him go (as a scape goat) into the wilderness. 11 So Aaron shall offer the bullock for his guilt, and shall make reconciliation for himself and for his house, and shall kill the bullock for his guilt. 12 And he shall take a censer full of burning colas from the altar before the LORD, and his handful of fragrant incense pounded in small, and he shall bring it inside the vayle, 13 and he shall put the in- cense on the fire before the LORD, that the cloud of the incense may cover the Mercy that is on the Testimony; so he shall not die. 14 And he shall take the blood of the bull and sprinkle it with his finger on the Merciseat to the east; and before the Merciseat he shall sprinkle the blood with his finger seven times. 15 Then he shall kill the kid that is the offense of the sin of the people, and shall bring its blood within the wall, and shall make with that blood, as he did with the blood of the bull, the sprinkling on the Merciseat and before the Merciseat. 16 Thus he will cleanse the holy place from the trespasses of the children of Israel and from their sins; so he will also do for the Taberna- cle of Cogregation set with them, in the midst of their trespasses. 17 There shall be no one in the Tabernacle of the Cogregation, when he enters to make atonement in the holy place, until he has gone out and made atonement for himself, and for his family, and for all the congregation of Israel. 18 Afterward he shall go to the altar that is before the LORD and make a reconciliation on it; he shall take the blood of the bull and the blood of the goat and put it on the horns of the altar all around: 19 Then he shall sprinkle the blood with his fin- ger ten times, and encapsulate it, and put it away from the vncleannes of the children of Israel. 20 And when he hath done the purga- tion of the holy place, and of the tabernacle of the congregation, and of the altar, he shall bring the earth kid: 21 And Aaron shall put his hands upon the head of the goat, and shall confess to him all the iniquities of the chil- dren of Israel, and all their trespasses, in all their sins, putting them upon the head of the goat, and shall send him away (by the hand

of a man appointed) into the wilderness. 22 So the goat shall bear upon him all their iniqui- ties in the land that is not inhabited, and he shall let the goat go into the wilderness. 23 Af- terward Aaron shall enter the tent of meeting, and he shall take off the linen garments that he had put on when he entered the holy place, and he shall leave them there. 24 He shall also wash his flesh with water in the holy place, put on his garment, go out, and make his burning and the burning of the people, and make atonement for himself and for the peo- ple. 25 The fat of the offense for sin shall also be buried on the altar. 26 He who carried away the goat, called the scapegoat, shall wash his clothes and wash his flesh in water, and after that he shall enter into the host. 27 Also the bull for the offense of sin and the goat for the offense of sin (whose blood was brought to be reconciled in the holy place) shall be taken out of the host to be burned in the fire, with their skins, with their flesh, and with their skins. 28 He who burns them shall wash his clothes and wash his flesh in water, and then he shall enter into the host. 29 So this shall be an ordi- nance for you: on the tenth day of the seventh month, you shall humble your souls and do no work, whether it be one of the same county, or a stranger sojourning among you. 30 For on that day the priest shall make an atonement for you, to make you more secure; you shall be clean from all your sins before the LORD. 31 This shall be for you a Sabbath of rest, and you shall humble your souls, with an ordinance for ever. 32 And the priest whom he shall ap- point and whom he shall consecrate (to min- ister in the place of his fathers) shall make atonement and put on the linen garments and holy vestments, 33 and he shall purify the Holy Sanctuary and the Tabernacle of the congregation, and he shall make polished the altar and make atonement for the priests and for all the people of the congregation. 34 This shall be an everlasting ordinance for you, to make atonement for the children of Israel for all their sins once a year; and as the LORD had commanded Moses, he did it.

CHAPTER 17

1 The Lord spoke to Moses, saying, 2 Speak to Aaron, and to his sons, and to all the sons of Israel, and say to them, "This is the thing which the LORD has commanded to be done." 3 Whoever is of the house of Israel who kills a bull, a lamb or a kid in the host or who kills it outside the host, 4 and does not bring it into the presence of the Tabernacle of Meeting to offer an offering to the LORD before the Tab- ernacle of the LORD, the blood shall be imput- ed to that man; he has shed blood, therefore he shall be cut off from his people. 5 Therefore the children of Israel shall bring their offal, which they offered in the open air, and pres- ent it to the LORD at the door of the Taber- nacle of the congregation, through the priest, and offer it as a peace-offering to the LORD. 6 Then the priest shall sprinkle the blood on the altar of the LORD, before the door of the tabernacle of the congregation, and bury the fat as a sweet fragrance to the LORD. 7 And they shall offer their offerings no more for the disciples, after whom they have prostituted themselves; this shall be an ordinance forever, for their generations. 8 Moreover you shall say to them, "Whoever is of the house of Israel or of the strangers living among them, who shall offer a burnt offering or a sacrifice, 9 and does not bring it before the Tabernacle of Meeting to offer it to the LORD, then that man shall be cut off from his people. 10 Likewise, whoev- er is of the house of Israel or of the strangers living among them who eats blood, I will

set my face against that person who eats blood and cut him off from his people. 11 For the life of the flesh is in the blood, and I have given it to you to offer on the altar, to make atone- ment for your souls; for this blood will make atonement for the soul. 12 Therefore I said to you, children of Israel, "None of you shall eat the blood, nor shall the stranger who so- journs among you eat the blood. 13 Moreover, whosoever is among the children of Israel or among the strangers sojourning among them, and whoever hunting takes a beast or an animal that may be eaten, he shall take off his blood and cover it with dust: 14 For the life of all flesh is its blood, which is joined to its life; therefore I said to the children of Israel, "You shall not eat the blood of any flesh, for the life of all flesh is its blood; whoever eats it shall be cut off." 15 Whosoever shall eat that which is dyed by himself, or that which is dyed with beasts, whether he be one of the same county or a stranger, he shall wash his clothes and bathe in water, and be clean. 16 But if he does not wash them and wash his flesh, he will carry his iniquity with him.

CHAPTER 18

1 The LORD spoke to Moses, saying, 2 Speak unto the children of Israel, and say unto them, I am the LORD your God. 3 You shall do no more what you did in the land of Egypt, where you dwelt; and you shall do no more what you did in the land of Canaan, where I will lead you, and you shall not walk by their rules, 4 But follow my teachings and observe my reg- ulations to walk in them; I am the LORD your God. 5 Ye shall therefore observe my statutes and my decrees, that if any man follow them, he shall abide in them: I am the LORD. 6 No man shall approach any more to a kinsman of his flesh to sham him: I am the LORD. 7 Thou shalt not reverence the shame of thy father, nor the shame of thy mother: for she is thy mother, thou shalt not be able to disown her shame. 8 The shame of your father's wife you shall not reveal, for she is your father's shame. 9 Thou shalt not reveal the shame of thy sister, thy father's daughter or thy mother's daugh- ter, whether she be delivered in the house or delivered outside; thou shalt not reveal their shame. 10 The shame of your son's daughter or your daughters' daughter, you shall not, I say to you, reveal their shame, for it is your shame. 11 The shame of your father's daugh- ter, begotten of your father (for she is your sister), you must not, I say, unveil her shame. 12 You shall not blot out the shame of your paternal sister, for she is your paternal kins- woman. 13 Thou shalt not unveil the shame of thy mother's sister, for she is thy mother's kinswoman. 14 You shall not be ashamed of your father's brother, that is, you shall not en- ter the house of his wife, for she is your wife. 15 You shall not disclose the shame of your daughter, for she is your son's wife; therefore you shall not disclose her shame. 16 You shall not disclose the shame of your brother's wife, for she is your brother's shame. 17 You shall not disclose the shame of his wife and his daughter, nor shall you take his son's daugh- ter and his daughter's daughter to disclose her shame, for they are your relatives, and it would be wickedness. 18 Moreover, you shall not take a wife with her sister during her life- time, to avenge her and to bring her shame upon her. 19 Neither will you go to a woman to vncure her shame, as long as she is put to rest because of her sickness. 20 Moreover, you shall not give yourself to your neighbor's wife with carnal copulation, to defile yourself with her. 21 Moreover, you shall not give your chil- dren to offer them to Molech, and

you shall not defile the name of your God, for I am the LORD. 22 You shall not lie with a male as you lie with a woman, for it is an abomination. 23 You shall not lie down with any beast to defile yourself with it, and no woman shall lie down before a beast to lie down with it, for it is an abomination. 24 You shall not defile your- selves in any of these things, for in all these the nations have defiled themselves, whom I will cast out before you: 25 The land is defiled; therefore I will punish its wickedness, and the land shall vomit up its inhabitants. 26 Ye shall therefore keep my prescriptions and my precepts, and not commit any of these abom- inations, whether he be of the same county, or whether he be a stranger that sojourneth among you. 27 (For all these abominations have been committed by the men of the land who have been before you, and the land is de- filed.) 28 And shall not the land spit upon you if you defile it, as the people that were before you spit upon it?"). 29 For whoever commits any of these abominations, the people who do so shall be cut off from their people. 30 There- fore you shall observe my prescriptions, that you may not do any of the abominable cus- toms that were done before you, and that you may not defile yourselves, for I am the LORD your God.

CHAPTER 19

1 The Lord spoke to Moses, saying, 2 Speak to the whole congregation of the children of Israel and say to them, "You shall be holy, for I, the LORD your God, am holy. 3 You shall each fear his mother and his father and keep my Sabbaths, for I am the LORD your God. 4 You shall not turn yourselves into idols or make yourselves spindles: I am the LORD your God. 5 When you offer a peace offering to the LORD, you shall offer it freely. 6 You shall eat it on the very day that you offer it, or on the next day; and what remains until the third day shall be burned in the fire. 7 For if it be eaten on the third day, it shall be vncleane, it shall not be accepted. 8 Therefore the one who eats it will bear his iniquity, because he has defiled the holy thing of the LORD, and that person will be eliminated from his people. 9 When you reap the harvest of your land, you shall not reap every corner of your field, and you shall not gather the fruit of your harvest. 10 You shall not pick the grapes of your vineyard cleanly, nor shall you gath- er any berry of your vineyard, but you shall leave it for the poor man and the poor man; I am the LORD your God. 11 You shall not commit theft, nor speak falsehood, nor lie to one another. 12 You shall not swear by my name falsely, nor shall you profane the name of your God; I am the LORD. 13 You shall not wrong your neighbor or rob him. The labor- er's wages shall not remain with you until the morning. 14 Thou shalt not curse the deaf, nor put a stumbling block in the way of the blind, but thou shalt fear thy God: I am the LORD. 15 You shall not do the vniente of evil in judg- ment. You shall not offend the person of the poor or honor the person of the mighty, but you shall judge your neighbor with justice. 16 You shall not go about with fables among your people. You shall not oppose the blood of your neighbor; I am the LORD. 17 Thou shalt not hate thy brother in thine heart, but thou shalt reprove thy neighbor with boldness, and not let him sin. 18 Thou shalt not avenge thy- self, nor deal evil against the children of thy people, but thou shalt love thy neighbor as thyself: I am the LORD. 19 You shall keep my precepts. You shall not allow your livestock to mate with others of a different kind. You shall not sow your field with mixed seed, nor shall a garment of

different things, of flax and wool, come upon you. 20 Whoever more- over lies and intrudes upon a woman who is a blond woman, betrothed to a husband, and has not been redeemed nor delivered, shall be scourged, but shall not die, because she has not been delivered. 21 She shall bring a ram for her sacrificial offering to the LORD in the Tabernacle of the congregation. 22 Then the priest shall make atonement for him with the ram of the guilt offering before the LORD, concerning the sin he has committed, and forgiveness shall be granted him for the sin he has committed. 23 Moreover, when you have entered the land and have planted every tree for consumption, you shall regard its fruit as vncircumcised; for three years it shall be vn- circumcised for you and shall not be eaten: 24 But in the fourth year all its fruit shall be holy to the praise of the LORD. 25 And in the fifth year ye shall eat the fruits thereof, that they may earn you increase: I am the LORD your God. 26 You shall not eat flesh with blood, nor do witchcraft, nor keep the times. 27 You shall not cut off the corners of your heads nor spoil the tufts of your beard. 28 You shall not cut off your flesh for the dead, and you shall not make any sign upon you, I am the LORD, 29 You shall not make your daughter common to make her a harlot, lest the land also fall into harlotry, and the land be full of wickedness. 30 You shall keep my Sabbaths, and keep my sanctuary: for I am the LORD. 31 You shall not look on those who work with spirits, nor on soothsayers; you shall not turn to them to be defiled by them: I am the LORD your God. 32 You shall stand before the head of the chief, and honor the person of the old man, and fear your God: I am the LORD. 33 If a stranger sojourns with you in your land, you shall not visit him. 34 But the stranger that dwelleth with you shall be as one of your own, and ye shall esteem him as yourselves: for ye were strangers in the land of Egypt: I am the LORD your God. 35 You shall not make mistakes of estimation, nor of line, nor of weight, nor of measure. 36 You shall have right balances, true weights, a true Ephah and a true Hin. I am the LORD your God, who brought you out of the land of Egypt. 37 Therefore you shall keep all my prescriptions and all my decrees and follow them; I am the LORD.

CHAPTER 20

1 The LORD spoke to Moses, saying, 2 You shall also say to the children of Israel, "Who- ever it is among the children of Israel or among the foreigners who dwell in Israel who gives his children to Molech, he shall die, and the people of the land shall stone him. 3 I will come against that man and will remove him from his people, because he has given his sons to Molech to defile my sanc- tuary and to pollute my holy Name. 4 If the people of the land hide their eyes and look at that man who gave his sons to Molech and do not kill him, 5 then I will set my face against that man and against his family, and I will cut him off from their people and all those who prostitute themselves behind him to commit acts of prostitution with Molech. 6 If anyone goes about with spirits and soothsayers to go whoring after them, then I will set my face against that person and cut him off from his people. 7 Sanctify yourselves therefore and be holy, for I am the LORD your God. 8 Observe therefore my prescriptions and do them. I am the LORD who sanctifies you. 9 If any- one curses his father or his mother, he shall die of death; because he has cursed his father and his mother, his blood shall fall on him. 10 The man who commits adultery with another man's wife, because the

latter has committed adultery with his neighbor's wife, the adulter- er and the adulteress shall die of death. 11 And the man who lies with his father's wife, be- cause he has betrayed his father's shame, they shall both die: their blood shall be upon them. 12 Also the man that lieth with his daughter in marriage, both shall die, because they have committed an abomination; their blood shall be upon them. 13 Also the man that lieth with the male, as one lieth with the woman, they have both committed an abomination; they shall dye with death; their blood shall smite them. 14 He also who takes a wife and her mother commits infamy; they shall bury him and them with fire, that there may be no in- famy among you. 15 Also the man who mates with a beast shall be dyed with death, and you shall kill the beast. 16 And if a woman ap- proaches a beast and mates with it, you shall kill the woman and the beast; they shall die of death, and their blood shall be upon them. 17 Also the man that taketh his sister, his father's daughter, or his mother's daughter, and seeth the shame of her, and she seeth the shame of him, is a villainy; therefore he shall be cut off before his people, because he hath seen the shame of his sister, and shall bear his guilt. 18 Also the man that lieth with a sick wom- an, and findeth out her shame, and openeth her fountain, and she openeth the fountain of her blood, they shall both be cut off from their people. 19 Moreover, thou shalt not put thy mother's sister and thy father's sister to shame; because he has put his relatives to shame, they shall bear their iniquity. 20 In the same way, the man who lies with his father's brother's wife and is ashamed of his relatives will bear his guilt and die childless. 21 So the man who takes his brother's wife commits filth, because he has vncured the shame of his own brother; they shall die childless. 22 Observe therefore all my prescriptions and all my precepts, and do them, that the land, where I will make you dwell, may not spit you out. 23 Therefore you shall not walk accord- ing to the customs of this nation which I have cast out before you; for they have committed all these things, so that I have abhorred them. 24 But I said unto you, Ye shall inherit their land, and I will give it unto you to possess, a land flowing with milk and honey: I am the LORD your God, which have separated you from other peoples. 25 Therefore you shall make a difference between clean beasts and vnclean beasts, and between vnclean feces and clean feces; you shall not defile yourselves with beasts and feces, nor with any of the rep- tiles which your land produces, and which I have separated from you as vnclean 26 There- fore you shall be holy toward me, for I, the LORD, am holy, and have separated you from other peoples that you may be mine. 27 And if any man or woman have in them a spirit of divination or fortune-telling, they shall die of death: they shall stone them, and their blood shall fall upon them.

CHAPTER 21

1 The LORD said to Moses, "Speak to the priests sons of Aaron and say to them, Let no one defile himself with the dead among his people, 2 but from his nearest relatives, that is, from his mother, his father, his son, his daughter, or his brother, 3 or by a sister of his, a maiden, who is kindred to him and has had no husband; for her he may mourn. 4 He shall not mourn for the prince of his peo- ple, lest he defile himself. 5 They shall not cut off their heads, nor shave the locks of their beards, nor make any cut in their flesh. 6 They shall be holy to their God, and shall not defile the name of their God, for the sacrifices of the LORD made by fire and

the bread of their God they shall offer, therefore they shall be holy. 7 They shall not take to wife a harlot or a defiled one, nor marry a woman separated from her husband, for such a woman is holy to her God. 8 You shall sanctify him, because he offers the bread of your God; he shall be holy to you, for I, the LORD, who sanctify you, am holy. 9 If a priest's daughter falls to be a harlot, she de- files her father; therefore she shall be burned with fire. 10 Also the priest among his breth- ren (on whose head the anointing has been imparted and who has anointed his hand to put on the garments) shall not cut off his head or rend his garments, 11 he shall not go near any dead body, nor shall he be vncleared by his father or his mother, 12 He shall not go out of the sanctuary, nor shall he pollute the holy place of his God, for upon him is the crowning of the oil of his God, I am the LORD. 13 More- over he shall take a wife for himself: 14 but a widow, or a diuorcee, or a defiled, or a harlot, these shall not marry, but shall take to wife a woman of his people: 15 Nor shall he defile his seed among his people: for I am the LORD that sanctifieth him." 16 The LORD spoke to Moses, saying, 17 Speak to Aaron and say to him, "Whoever of your descendants in their generations has any stain, he shall not be able to offer the bread of his God: 18 For he that hath any blemish shall not be able to come here, as a man that is blind or lame, or that hath a flat nose, or that hath any deformed member, 19 or a man whose foot or hand is broken, 20 or who has a crooked back, or clear eyes, or has a spot in his eye, or is flayed, or peeled, or has broken stones. 21 None of the descendants of Aaron the priest shall come and offer the sacrifices of the LORD made by fire, if he has a defect; he shall not offer the bread of his God. 22 He shall eat the bread of his God, the holiest and most holy: 23 But he shall not enter into the rampart, nor come near the altar, because he hath a blemish; or he shall pollute my sanctuaries: for I am the LORD that sanctifieth them." 24 Thus Moses spoke to Aaron and his sons and to all the sons of Israel.

CHAPTER 22

1 The Lord spoke to Moses, saying, 2 Speak to Aaron and to his sons, that they may separate themselves from the holy things of the chil- dren of Israel, and that they may not defile my holy name in those things which they conse- crate to me; I am the LORD. 3 Say unto them, Whosoever among your descendants, in your generations after you, shall touch the holy things which the children of Israel consecrate unto the LORD, having his vncleanness upon him, then that person shall be removed from my sight: I am the LORD. 4 Also whosoever among the descendants of Aaron is leprous, or hath a hemorrhage, he shall not eat of the holy things until he be healed; and whosoever shall touch any one that is leprous, because of a dead man, or a man whose hemorrhage hath escaped him, 5 or the man who touches any creeping thing, whereby he may be made vncleane, or a man, whereby he may take vn- cleannesse, whatever vncleannesse he has, 6 Therefore the person who has touched such a thing shall be vncleane until the dawn, and he shall not eat of you holy things, except after he has washed himself with water. 7 But when the sun has set, he shall be clean and may eat of the holy things, for it is his food. 8 He shall not eat of a beast that is dyed, or that is slicked with other beasts, whereby it may be defiled: I am the LORD. 9 Let them therefore keep my ordinance, if they will not pay their sin and die for it, if they defile it: I, the LORD, sanc- tify them. 10 Also the stranger shall not eat of the holy thing, nor the least of the priest, nor the hired servant shall eat of the holy thing: 11 But if the priest receive one with money, he shall eat of it, as well as he that is brought into his house; they shall eat of his food. 12 If the priest's daughter also marry a stranger, she shall not eat of the holy offspring. 13 However, if the daughter of the priest is widowed or di- vorced and has no children, but has returned to the house of her fathers, she may eat of the bread of her fathers, as she did in her youth, but she may not eat of a stranger. 14 If anyone eats of the holy thing without intending to do so, he shall put in the fifth part of it and give it to the priest along with the halved thing. 15 So they shall not defile the holy things of the children of Israel, which they offer to the LORD, 16 And they shall not bring upon the people the iniquity of their trespasses, while they eat of their holy things, for I, the LORD, will inhale them." 17 The LORD spoke to Mo- ses, saying, 18 Speak to Aaron and to his sons and to all the sons of Israel, and say to them, "Whoever is of the house of Israel or of the strangers in Israel shall offer his sacrifice for all their vows and for all their free sacri- fices that they are to offer to the LORD as a burnt offering, 19 You shall offer of your own free will a male without blemish, whether of goats, sheep or he-goats. 20 You shall not of- fer anything that has defects, for it will not be acceptable to you. 21 Whoever shall bring to the LORD a peace offering to fulfill his vow or a freewill offering of bees or goats, his freewill offering shall be perfect, without blemish. 22 Animals that are blinded, broken, maimed, with a wound, flayed or skinned shall not be offered to the LORD, nor shall an offering be made by fire on the LORD's altar. 23 But a bull or a sheep that has any superfluous or missing member, you may present them for a free offering, but for a vow they will not be accepted. 24 You shall not offer to the LORD that which is bruised, creased, broken, or cut, and you shall not make an offering of it in your country, 25 nor from the hand of a slaughterer shall you offer to your God any of these loaves, for in them is corruption, there is a stain; therefore they shall not be accepted for you." 26 The LORD spoke to Moses, saying, 27 When you bring a bovine, a sheep or a kid, you must wait until seven days after its death; and from the eighth day onward it is accepted as a sacrifice made by fire for the LORD. 28 As for the cow or the sheep, you shall not kill her and her young in one day. 29 So when you offer a sacrifice of thanksgiving to the LORD, you shall gladly offer it. 30 The same day you shall eat it, and leave none of it until the next day: for I am the LORD. 31 Therefore you shall keep my commands and do them, for I am the LORD. 32 You shall not pollute my holy Name, but I will be sanctified among the children of Israel. I, the LORD, will sanctify you, 33 Who brought you out of the land of Egypt to be your God: I am the LORD.

CHAPTER 23

1 The LORD spoke to Moses, saying, 2 Speak to the children of Israel and say to them, "The feasts of the LORD, which you shall call holy assemblies, are my feasts. 3 Six days you shall work, but the tenth day shall be the Sabbath days of rest, a holy convocation; you shall do no work in it; it is the Sabbath of the LORD, in all your houses. 4 These are the feasts of the LORD and the holy conivences, which you shall proclaim in their seasons. 5 On the first month and on the fourteenth day of the month, at sunrise, you shall celebrate the Passover of the Lord. 6 The fifteenth day of this month shall be the feast of nitrogen breads for the

LORD; for ten days you shall eat nitrogen breads. 7 On the first day you shall hold a holy meeting; you shall not do any unnecessary work. 8 Moreover you shall offer fire sacrifices to the LORD for ten days, and on the seventh day shall be a holy summons; you shall do no servile work therein." 9 The LORD spoke to Moses, saying, 10 Speak to the children of Israel and say to them, "When you have entered the land I have given you and have gathered its harvest, you shall bring to the priest a box with the first fruits of your harvest, 11 And he shall shake the box before the LORD, that it may be pleasing to you; and on the morning after the Sabbath, the priest shall shake it. 12 And on that day, when you shake the casket, you shall prepare a lamb without blemish, one year old, for a burnt offering to the LORD: 13 And its portion of meat shall be two-tenths of fine flour mixed with oil, for a sacrifice made by fire to the LORD, of sweet savor, and its portion of wine, the fourth part of a hin of wine. 14 And you shall eat neither bread nor dry horn nor green greaves until the same day that you have brought an offering to your God; this shall be an obligation forever in your generations and in all your dwellings. 15 You shall also count from the day after the Sabbath, from the day that you bring the case of the shaken offering, the two Sabbaths shall be complete. 16 The day after the seventh Sabbath shall pass fifty days; then you shall bring a new food offer- ing to the LORD. 17 You shall bring from your houses bread for the shake offering: it shall be two loaves of two-tenths fine flour, baked with leaven as the first fruits for the LORD. 18 Along with the bread you shall also offer two lambs without blemish one year old, a bull one year old, and two rams; they shall be for a burnt offering to the LORD, with their offal and their offal to drink, for a sacrifice made by fire of a sweet savor to the LORD. 19 Then you shall prepare a kid goat as a sin offering and two one-year-old lambs as a peace offer- ing. 20 And the priest shall shake them on one side and on the other side with the bread of the firstfruits before the LORD, and with the two lambs: they shall be holy to the LORD, to the priest. 21 Thus you shall proclaim the same day, that it may be a holy convocation for you; you shall not do any unnecessary work; it shall be an ordinance for ever in all your dwellings, for all your generations. 22 When you reap the harvest of your land, you shall not clear the corners of your field when you reap, nor shall you make any gathering of your harvest, but you shall leave it to the poor and the stranger; I am the LORD your God." 23 The LORD spoke to Moses, saying, 24 Speak to the children of Israel and say, "In the tenth month and on the first day of the month you shall make a Sabbath, to remember the sounding of the trumpets, a holy convoca- tion. 25 In it you shall do no useless work, but you shall offer to the LORD sacrifices made by fire." 26 The LORD spoke to Moses, saying, 27 The tenth day of this seventh month shall also be a day of reconciliation; it shall be a holy day for you, on which you shall humble your souls and offer to the LORD a sacrifice made by fire. 28 On that same day you shall do no work, for it is a day of reconciliation, to make atone- ment for you before the LORD your God. 29 For whoever does not humble himself on that same day will be eliminated from his people. 30 And whoever does any work on that same day, I will also destroy him from his people. 31 Therefore you shall not do any manual la- bor; this shall be a law forever in your gener- ations, in all your dwellings. 32 This shall be a Sabbath of rest for you, and you shall humble your souls; on the ninth day of the month, from noon to noon, you shall celebrate your Sabbath." 33 The Lord spoke to Moses, saying, 34 Speak to the children of Israel and say,

"The fifteenth day of this calendar month shall be for ten days the Feast of Tabernacles for the LORD. 35 The first day shall be a holy cohab- itation; you shall do no useful work there. 36 On two other days you shall offer to the LORD sacrifices made with fire; the eighth day shall be a holy assembly for you, and you shall offer to the LORD sacrifices made with fire; it is the solemn assembly, and you shall do no servile work therein. 37 These are the feasts of the LORD (which you shall call holy convivences) to offer to the LORD sacrifices made by fire, such as burnings, sacrifices of food, and sac- rifices and sacrifices of drink, each on his day, 38 in addition to the Sabbaths of the LORD, in addition to your gifts, in addition to all your vows and all your free offerings that you give to the LORD. 39 But on the fifteenth day of the seventh month, when you have gathered the fruits of the land, you shall make a holy feast to the LORD for ten days: the first day shall be a Sabbath, and the eighth day shall be a Sabbath. 40 On the first day you shall take the fruit of beautiful trees, branches of palm trees, branches of old trees, and brooke wil- lows, and you shall make a feast before the LORD your God for ten days. 41 So you shall celebrate this feast before the LORD for ten days a year, perpetually for your generations; in the seventh month you shall celebrate it. 42 You shall dwell in garments for ten days; all the Israelites who are born shall dwell in gar- ments, 43 That your posterity may know that I caused the children of Israel to dwell in gar- ments, when I brought them out of the land of Egypt: I am the LORD your God." 44 Thus Moses declared to the children of Israel the feasts of the LORD.

CHAPTER 24

1 The LORD spoke to Moses and said. 2 Com- mand the children of Israel to bring you pure oil beaten for light, that your lamps may be lit continually. 3 In the Tabernacle of the Con- gregation, without the vail of the Testimo- ny, Aaron will make them appear before the LORD always, both in the morning and in the evening; this will be a promise forever, for all your generations. 4 He will make the lamps shine on the pure candlestick before the LORD in perpetuity. 5 You shall also take fine flour and make two cakes of it: in one cake there shall be two tithes of weight. 6 You shall arrange them in two rows, six in each row, on the pure table before the LORD. 7 You shall also put pure incense on the rows, so that in- stead of bread it may be a remembrance and a fire offering for the LORD. 8 Every Sabbath you shall put them in rows before the LORD, receiving them from the children of Israel for an everlasting reward. 9 And the bread shall be Aaron's and his sons', and they shall eat it in the holy place, for it is the holiest to him of the offenses of the LORD made by fire with a perpetual ordinance. 10 Then there went out from among the children of Israel the son of an Israelite woman, whose father was an Egyptian; and this son of the Israelite woman and a man of Israel stood together in the host. 11 The son of the Israelite woman blasphemed the name of the LORD and cursed, and they led him to Moses (his mother's name was also Shelomith, daughter of Dibri, of the tribe of Dan). 12 And they put him to war until he had revealed to them the thought of the LORD. 13 Then the LORD spoke to Moses, saying, 14 Lead the blasphemer out of the army, and all who heard him put their hands on his head, and all the congregation shall stone him. 15 And you shall speak to the children of Israel, saying, Whoever curses his God shall bear his sin. 16 Whosoever blasphemes the name of the

LORD shall be put to death; the whole community shall stone him; even the strang- er, as he that is brought into the land; when he blasphemes the name of the LORD, let him be blasphemed. 17 He also who kills a man shall be put to death. 18 Whoever kills a beast, he shall return it, beast for beast. 19 Moreover, if anyone causes a stain in his neighbor, as he has done to him, so shall it be done to him. 20 Trespass for trespass, eye for eye, tooth for tooth; the stain he has caused in someone, it shall be returned to him. 21 Whoever kills a beast will return it, but whoever kills a man will be killed. 22 You shall have one license; it shall be so to the stranger as to him who is born in the land, for I am the LORD your God." 23 And Moses informed the children of Israel, who brought the blasphemer out of the army and stoned him with stones; so the children of Israel did as the LORD had com- manded Moses.

CHAPTER 25

1 The Lord spoke to Moses on Mount Sinai, saying, 2 Speak to the children of Israel and say to them, "When you enter the land that I will give you, the land will keep the Sabbath for the LORD. 3 Six years you shall sow your field, and six years you shall cut your vineyard and reap its fruit. 4 But the seventh year shall be a Sabbath of rest for the land; it shall be the Sabbath of the LORD; thou shalt not sow thy field nor cut thy vine. 5 You shall not reap what grows on your own property, according to your crops, and you shall not gather the grapes that you have left to work, for it shall be a year of rest for the land. 6 The rest of the land shall be for you food, for you, and for your servant, and for your wife, and for your hired servant, and for the stranger who so- journs with you: 7 And for thy cattle and for the beasts that are in thy land, all the increase thereof shall be paid. 8 Moreover thou shalt number ten sabbaths of the year for thee, twice seven years: and the space of the sev- en sabbaths of the year shall be for thee nine years and forty. 9 Then thou shalt blow the trumpet of the Jubile on the tenth day of the seventh month; and on the day of reconcilia- tion thou shalt blow the trumpet throughout thy land. 10 In that year, the fiftieth, you shall proclaim liberty in the land to all its inhabi- tants; it shall be Jubilee for you, and you shall return every man to his possessions, and every man shall return to his family. 11 This fiftieth year shall be for you a year of Jubi- lee; you shall not sow, you shall not reap that which grows of itself, and you shall not gath- er its clusters, which have been left to work. 12 Because it is the Jubilee, it shall be holy to you; you shall eat the increase of it from the fields. 13 In the year of this jubilee, you shall restore every man to his possessions. 14 And when you sell anything to your neighbor, or put it into your neighbor's hand, you shall not oppress one another: 15 But according to the number of the years after the jubilee, thou shalt pass over to thy neighbor; and accord- ing to the number of the years of the annu- ities, he shall sell to thee. 16 According to the quantity of the years, thou shalt increase the price thereof, and according to the scarcity of the years, thou shalt reduce the price thereof; for the name of the fruits he shall sell to thee. 17 Therefore you shall not oppress anyone to his neighbor, but you shall fear your God, for I am the LORD your God. 18 Therefore you shall obey my decrees and keep my laws and put them into practice, and you shall dwell in the land in safety. 19 The land shall yield its fruit, and you shall eat your fill and dwell in safety. 20 And if you say, "What shall we eat in the tenth year, for shall we not sow and reap our fruits? 21 I will send my blessing upon

you in the sixtieth year, and it shall bear fruit for three years. 22 In the eighth year you shall sow and eat the old fruits until the ninth year; until the fruits come, you shall eat the old ones. 23 Moreover the land shall not be solidly separated from the household, for the land is mine, and you are but strangers and sojourn- ers with me. 24 Therefore, in all the land that you possess, you shall make a ransom for the land. 25 If your brother is impoverished and sells his property, his redeemer, that is, his next of kin, will come and take from him what his brother has sold. 26 And if he has no redeemer, but has obtained and found a way to redeem him, 27 he shall count the years of his sale and return the surplus to the man to whom he sold it; so it shall come back into his possession. 28 But if he cannot obtain enough to return it to him, that which was sold shall remain in the hand of him who bought it, until the year of the Jubilee; and in the Jubi- lee it shall go out, and he shall return to his possession. 29 Likewise, if one sells a dwelling house in a fortified city, he may repudiate it within a full year after its sale; within a year he may repudiate it. 30 But if it is not pur- chased within a full year, the house that is in the fortified city shall remain, as cut off from the family, to him who purchased it, for all his generations; it shall not be extinguished in the Jubilee. 31 But the houses of the villages, which have no walls around them, shall be re- garded as the fields of the county; they may be bought again, and shall be extinguished in the Jubilee. 32 However, the towns of the Leuites and the houses of the towns owned by them may be redeemed by the Leuites in every season. 33 If one buys from the Leuites, the house that was sold and the city owned by them go into Jubile, because the houses of the cities of the Leuites are their possession among the children of Israel. 34 But the field of the suburbs of their cities shall not be sold, for it is their perpetual possession. 35 More- over, if your brother is in distress and is in decay with you, you shall relieve him, and as a stranger and a sojourner, so shall he live with you. 36 You shall have no regard for him, nor any advantage, but you shall fear your God, that your brother may live with you. 37 You shall not give him your money for money, nor lend him your life to increase it. 38 I am the LORD your God, who brought you out of the land of Egypt to give you the land of Canaan and to be your God. 39 If your brother also, who dwells with you, is impoverished and is sold to you, you shall not force him to serve as an obligatory servant, 40 but as a paid servant and as a guest he shall stay with you; he shall be in your service until the year of Jubilee. 41 Then he shall depart from you, he and his sons with him, and shall return to his family, and return to the possession of his fathers: 42 For they are my servants, whom I brought out of the land of Egypt; they shall not be en- slaved as you enslave servants. 43 Thou shalt not rule him with cruelty, but thou shalt fear thy God. 44 Also thy servant and thy maidser- vant, which thou shalt have, shall be of the heathen round about thee; of them shalt thou have servant and maidservant. 45 Moreover, of the children of the strangers who sojourn among you, you shall take them and their families that are with you and have begotten in your land; these shall be your possession. 46 You shall take them as an inheritance for your children after you, to possess them for an inheritance, and you shall use their labors forever; but over your brothers, the children of Israel, you shall not lord it over one anoth- er with cruelty. 47 If a stranger or a foreigner who dwells near you is enriched, and your brother by him is impoverished, he shall sell himself to the stranger or the foreigner who dwells near you, or to the stocks of the family of the stranger, 48 after he is sold, he may be redeemed; one of his brethren may redeem him, 49 or his nephew or the son of his uncles may redeem him, or one of the relatives of his family may redeem him; or if he can get so much, he may redeem him himself. 50 Then he shall reckon with his creditor from the year in which he was sold to him until the year of his jubilee; and the money of his sale shall be according to the number of the years; according to the time of a rainbow servant shall he be with him. 51 If there be many years of delay, according to them shall be given again for his liquidation, of the money for which he was bought. 52 If there be a few years left until the year of jubilee, he shall reckon with him, and according to his years he shall give the rest for his redemption. 53 He shall abide with him year by year as a hired servant; he shall not rule him cruelly in thy sight. 54 And if he be not redeemed, he shall go away in the year of Jubile, he and his sons with him. 55 For to me the children of Israel are servants; they are my servants, whom I brought out of the land of Egypt: I am the LORD your God.

CHAPTER 26

1 You shall make for yourselves neither idols nor Grauan images; you shall erect no pil- lar, nor set up any stone image in your land to bow down to it, for I am the LORD your God. 2 You shall keep my Sabbaths and keep my sanctuary: for I am the LORD. 3 If you will walk in my prescriptions, if you will keep my commands and follow them, 4 then I will send you rain in due season, and the land will bud its harvest, and the trees of the fields will bear fruit. 5 Your threshing will come until the harvest, and the vintage will come until the sowing, and you will eat your bread in abundance and dwell securely in your land. 6 I will send peace into the land, and you shall sleep, and no one shall make you afraid; also I will remove the beasts from the land, and the sword shall not pass through your land. 7 Moreover you shall pursue your enemies, and they shall fall before you on the sword. 8 Five of you shall pursue a hundred, a hundred of you shall put ten thousand to flight, and your enemies shall fall before you on the sword. 9 For I will have respect for you, I will make you grow, I will multiply you, and I will establish my covenant with you. 10 You shall also eat the old provisions and take away the old for the new. 11 And I will establish my Taberna- cle in the midst of you, and my soul shall not forsake you. 12 Moreover I will walk among you, and I will be your God, and you shall be my people. 13 I am the LORD your God, who brought you out of the land of Egypt, so that you were not their slaves; I broke the bonds of your yoke and made you free. 14 But if you will not obey me and do all these commands, 15 and if you despise my prescriptions, or if your mind abhors my laws, so that you do not do all my commands, but violate my cove- nant, 16 then I will also do this to you: I will cause you to fear, I will cause you to be con- sumed, I will cause you to burn, I will cause your eyes to be consumed, and I will make your heart heavy, and you will sow your seed in the vine, for your enemies will eat it: 17 And I will set my face against you, and you shall falter before your enemies, and they that hate you shall chase you, and you shall flee when none shall chase you. 18 And if for these things you will not obey me, I will punish you tenfold according to your sins, 19 I will break the pride of your power, and I will make your heaven as wrathful, and your earth as covet- ous: 20 And your strength shall be consumed in vein; your land shall yield no more of its harvest, and the trees of the land shall yield no more of their fruit. 21 And if

ye will persist against me, and will not obey me, I will cause ten times as many plagues to come upon you, according to your sins. 22 I will also send you wild beasts, which will plunder you, destroy your livestock, and reduce you in numbers; so your lands will be desolate. 23 But if by these things you do not wish to be repented of me, but walk stubbornly against me, 24 then I will also be stubborn against you, and I will smite you again and again for your sins: 25 And I will send a sword upon you, which shall smite the lent of my commander; and when ye are gathered together in your cities, I will send plague among you, and ye shall be delivered into the hand of the enemy. 26 And when I break the staff of your bread, ten women shall bake your bread at once and distribute your bread by weight, and you shall eat, but you shall not be full. 27 But if for this you will not obey me, but walk against me with obstinacy, 28 then I will be wroth with obstinacy against you, and will chastise you tenfold according to your sins. 29 You shall eat the flesh of your sons and the flesh of your daughters. 30 I will also destroy your places of worship, I will cut down your images, I will cast your carcasses over the dead bodies of your idols, and my soul will abhor you. 31 I will make your cities des- olate, I will zero your sanctuary, and I will not smell your odors. 32 I will also make the land a wilderness, and your enemies who dwell in it will be astounded. 33 I will also scatter you among the heathen, and I will draw a sword upon you, and your land will be destroyed and your cities will be desolate. 34 Then the land will do its sabbaths, until it is empty, and you will be in the land of your enemies; then the land will rest and do its sabbaths. 35 For all the days that it shall remain empty, it shall rest, because it did not rest on your sabbaths, when you dwelt there. 36 And upon those who remain of you, I will send a weariness in their hearts into the land of their enemies, and the sound of a leaf shall chase them, and they shall flee as fleeing from a sword, and they shall fall, and none shall pursue them. 37 They shall also fall upon one another, as before a sword, though no one pursue them, and you shall not be able to stand before your enemies: 38 You shall perish among the heathen, and the land of your enemies shall devour you. 39 Those that remain of you shall pine away for their iniquities in the lands of your enemies, and for the iniquities of their fathers shall they also pine away with them. 40 Then they will confess their iniquity and the wickedness of their fathers for their sins, which they have committed against me, and also because they have walked stubbornly against me. 41 There- fore I will walk stubbornly against them and lead them into the land of their enemies; so their vncircumcised hearts will be humbled and they will willingly bear the punishment of their iniquity. 42 Then I will remember my ally with Iaakob, my ally with Izhak, and my ally with Abraham, and I will remember the land. 43 The land also, in time of peace, shall be forsaken of them, and shall keep its Sab- baths, while it is forsaken of itself; but they shall gladly suffer the punishment of their iniquity, because they have despised my laws, and because their mind has abhorred my de- crees. 44 Nevertheless, in spite of this, when they are in the land of their enemies, I will not cast them out, nor will I abhor them, nor will I permanently destroy them, nor will I break my covenant with them, for I am the LORD their God: 45 But I will remember for them the covenant of old, when I brought them out of the land of Egypt before the Gentiles to be their God: I am the LORD. 46 These are the ordinances, the rules and the laws which the Lord established between him and the chil- dren of Israel at Mount Sinai by the hand of Moses.

CHAPTER 27

1 The LORD spoke again to Moses, saying,

2 Speak to the children of Israel and say to them, "If anyone makes a vow of a person to the LORD, according to your estimate, 3 Your estimate shall be thus: a male between twenty years old and sixty years old shall be valued, according to your estimate, at least fifty shekels of silver, according to the shekel of the sanctuary. 4 But if it is a female, your estimate shall be thirty shekels. 5 From five years to twenty years, your estimate shall be twenty-five shekels for the male and ten shek- els for the female. 6 But from the age of one month until the age of five years, your valua- tion for the male shall be five shekels of silver, and your valuation for the female three shek- els of silver. 7 From the age of sixty years, if it is a male, your price shall be fifty shekels, and for the female ten shekels. 8 But if he be poor- er than thou hast valued him, he shall stand before the priest, and the priest shall value him, according to the skill of him that made the vow. 9 If it is a beast of which men bring an offering to the LORD, all that one makes of it for the LORD shall be holy. 10 And he shall not alter it, nor change it, neither a good for an evil, nor an evil for a good; and if he change beast for beast, both this and that, which was changed for it, shall be holy. 11 And if it be a vncleane beast, of which men do not offer a sacrifice to the LORD, he shall present the beast before the priest. 12 And the priest shall evaluate it, whether it be good or bad; and as thou shalt evaluate it, who art the priest, so shall it be. 13 But if he shall reject it, he shall give him the fifth part more, according to your evaluation. 14 Also when a man conse- crates his house to the LORD, the priest shall value it, whether it be good or bad; and as the priest shall value it, so shall it be. 15 But if he who sanctified it wishes to redeem his house, then he shall give it the fifth part of money more than its appraisal, and it shall be his. 16 If a man dedicates any land of his inheritance to the LORD, you shall value it according to the seed from it; a Homer of barrel seed shall be valued at fifty shekels of silk. 17 If he conse- crates his field immediately from the year of Jubile, it shall be worth as thou esteemest it. 18 But if he consecrates his field after Jubilee, the priest shall reckon him money according to the years remaining until the year of Jubi- lee, and it shall be diminished according to your estimate. 19 If he who dedicates it shall redeem the field, he shall put in it the fifth part of the price which thou hast estimated, and it shall remain his. 20 If he will not redeem the field, but the priest sells it to another man, it shall not be redeemed. 21 But the field shall be holy to the LORD, when he goes out in the jubilee, as a field separate from the common ones; its possession shall be of the priests. 22 If a man also consecrates to the LORD a field which he has bought and which does not be- long to his inheritance, the priest shall conse- crate it to the LORD, 23 then the priest shall set him the price, as thou reckonest it, until the year of the Jubilee, and he shall give thy price on the same day, as a thing holy unto the LORD. 24 But in the year of Jubile, the field shall return to him from whom it was bought; to him, I say, whose inheritance the land was. 25 And all your worth shall be assessed ac- cording to the shekel of the sanctuary: a shek- el counts twenty gerahs. 26 Notwithstanding the first born of beasts, for it is the first born of the LORD, no one shall dedicate it, whether it be a bull or a sheep, for it is the LORD's. 27 But if it be a vncleane beast, he shall redeem it according to thy estimation, and give it the fifth part

more; and if it be not redeemed, it shall be sold, according to thy estimation. 28 However, nothing that a man separates from the common, of all that he possesses (man or beast or land of his inheritance), may be sold or redeemed, for everything separated from the common is most holy to the LORD. 29 Nothing that is separated from the common ground and that will be separated from man can be redeemed except by death. 30 Also all the tithe of the earth, both of the seeds of the ground and of the fruit of the trees, is of the LORD: it is holy to the LORD. 31 But if anyone wishes to redeem any part of his tithe, he shall add to it the fifth part. 32 And the tithe of the cattle, and of the cattle, and of everything that goes under the reed, the tithe shall be holy to the LORD. 33 He will not look whether it is good or bad, and will not change it; other- wise, if he changes it, both it and that which has been changed will be holy and cannot be redeemed. 34 These are the commands that the LORD gave through Moses to the children of Israel on Mount Sinai.

NUMBERS

CHAPTER 1

1 And the LORD spake unto Moses again in the wilderness of Sinai, in the tent of meet- ing, on the first day of the second month, the second year after he came out of the land of Egypt, saying, Take the sum of all the con- gregation of the children of Israel, accord- ing to their families and the houses of their fathers, by the name of their names, 2 Take the sum of the whole community of the chil- dren of Israel, according to their families and the houses of their fathers, with the name of their names: all the males, man by man: 3 From twenty years old and upward, all those who are going to war in Israel, you and Aar- on shall take a census of all their armies. 4 With you shall be men of every tribe, as the leaders of the house of their fathers. 5 These are the names of the men who will be with you, of the tribe of Reuben: Elizur the son of Scedeur: 6 Of Simeon, Shelumiel the son of Zurishaddai: 7 Of Judah, Nahshon the son of Amminadab: 8 Of Issachar, Nethaneel, son of Zuar: 9 Of Zebulun, Eliab, son of Helon: 10 Of the sons of Iosef: of Ephraim, Elishama, son of Ammihud; of Manasseh, Gamliel, son of Pedahzur: 11 Of Beiamin, Abida, son of Gide- oni: 12 Of Dan, Ahiezer, son of Ammishaddai: 13 Of Asher, Pagiel, son of Ocran: 14 Of Gad, Eliasaph, son of Deuel: 15 Of Naphtali, Ahi- ra the son of Enan. 16 These were famous in the community, princes of the tribes of their fathers, and leaders of thousands in Israel. 17 Moses and Aaron took these men who are expressed by their names. 18 Then they sum- moned the whole community, on the first day of the second month, declaring their kindreds according to the families and houses of their fathers, by the name of their names, from the age of twenty years and upward, man by man. 19 As the LORD had commanded Mo- ses, so he appointed them in the wilderness of Sinai. 20 So the sons of Reuben, the first- born of Israel, according to their generations, and their families, and the houses of their fa- thers, according to the name of their names, man by man, all the males from twenty years old and upward, as many as went to war: 21 And their number, as for the tribe of Reuben, was six hundred and four thousand and five hundred. 22 Of the sons of Simeon, according to their generations, and their families, and the houses of their fathers, the sum of their names, man by man, all the males from twen- ty years old and upward, all who went forth to war: 23 Their sum, as for the tribe of Sim- eon, was nine

fifty thousand men and three hundred. 24 Of the sons of Gad, according to their generations, and their families, and the houses of their fathers, by the name of their names, from the age of twenty years and up-ward, all that went forth to war: 25 And their number, as for the tribe of Gad, was five thou- sand and forty thousand and six hundred and fifty. 26 Of the sons of Judah, according to their generations, and their families, and the houses of their fathers, by the name of their names, from the age of twenty years old and upward, all that went forth to war: 27 The number of those who belonged to the tribe of Iudah was three million four hundred thousand and six hundred. 28 Of the sons of Issachar, according to their generations, and their families, and the houses of their fathers, by the name of their names, from the age of twenty years old and upward, all that went forth to war: 29 The number of those of the tribe of Issachar was four hundred fifty thou- sand and four hundred. 30 Of the children of Zebulun, according to their generations, and their families, and the houses of their fathers, according to the number of their names, from twenty years old and upward, all that went forth to war: 30 And the number of the tribe of Issachar was four hundred and fifty thousand and four hundred: 31 The number of those of the tribe of Zebulun was fifty thousand and four hundred. 32 Of the sons of Jehoshaph, that is, of the sons of Ephraim, according to their generations, and their families, and the houses of their fathers, by the name of their names, from the age of twenty years old and upward, all that went forth to war: 33 The number of those of the tribe of Ephraim was four thousand five hundred. 34 Of the sons of Manasseh, according to their generations, their families, and the houses of their fathers, by the name of their names, from the age of twenty years old and upward, all that went forth to war: 35 The number of the men of the tribe of Manasseh was two thousand and two hundred. 36 Of the sons of Benjamin, accord- ing to their generations, their families, and the houses of their fathers, by the name of their names, from the age of twenty years old and upward, all that went forth to war: 37 The number of those who belonged to the tribe of Benjamin was five thousand three hundred and four hundred. 38 Of the sons of Dan, ac- cording to their generations, and their fam- ilies, and the houses of their fathers, by the name of their names, from twenty years old and upward, all that went forth to war: 39 The name of the members of the tribe of Dan was three hundred two thousand and seven hudre. 40 Of the sons of Asher, according to their generations, and their families, and the houses of their fathers, by the number of their names, from twenty years old and upward, all that went forth to war: 41 The number of those who belonged to the tribe of Asher was one million and forty thousand and five hundred hudre. 42 Of the sons of Naphtali, their de- scendants according to their families and the houses of their fathers, according to the order of their names, from the age of twenty years old and upward, all that went forth to war: 43 The number of those of the tribe of Naphtali was three hundred fifty thousand and four hundred. 44 These are the sums that Moses and Aaron and the princes of Israel, the two men, who were each for the house of their fa- thers. 45 This was the sum of the children of Is- rael, according to the houses of their fathers, from the age of twenty years and upward, all who went to war in Israel, 46 in all were six thousand and three thousand, five hundred and fifty in number. 47 But the Leuites, ac- cording to the tribes of their fathers, were not numbered among them. 48 For the LORD had spoken to Moses and said, 49 "You shall not take a census of the tribe of Leui, and you shall not take the amount

among the children of Israel: 50 but thou shalt apply the Leuites to the Tabernacle of the Testimony, and to all the instruments thereof, and to all things per- taining thereto; and they shall bear the Tab- ernacle and all the instruments thereof, and shall minister therein, and dwell round about the Tabernacle." 51 When the Tabernacle goes out, the Leuites shall bring it down; and when the Tabernacle is erected, you Leuites shall set it up; for the stranger who comes here shall be killed. 52 The children of Israel also shall pitch their tents, every one in his campe, and every one under his standerd for all their army. 53 But the Leuites shall encamp round about the Tabernacle of the Testimony, if vengeance come not upon the congregation of the chil- dren of Israel, and the Leuites shall deal with the Tabernacle of the Testimony. 54 So the children of Israel did according to all that the LORD had commanded Moses; so they did.

CHAPTER 2

1 The LORD spoke to Moses and Aaron, say- ing, "Every man of the children of Israel shall camp by his post and under the enclosure of his fathers' house, 2 Every man of the children of Israel shall camp by his post and under the enclosure of the house of their fathers; they shall camp far around the Tabernacle of the Congregation. 3 In the east, toward the ris- ing of the sun, the standerds of the army of Iudah shall encamp, according to their hosts; Nahshon the son of Amminadab shall be the leader of the sons of Iudah. 4 His army and his men were seventy-four thousand and six hundred. 5 Beside him shall stand those of the tribe of Issachar, and Nethaneel the son of Zuar shall be the leader of the sons of Is- sachar: 6 His army and his number were four hundred fifty thousand and four hundred. 7 Then the tribe of Zebulun and Eliab the son of Helon, chief of the sons of Zebulun: 8 His army and his numbers: fifty thousand and four hundred: 9 The whole army of Iudah is one hundred fifty thousand and six hundred thousand men, and four hundred according to their armies; they shall depart first. 10 From the south side shall array the army of Reuben, according to their armies, and the leader of the sons of Reuben shall be Elizur the son of Scedeur. 11 His army and his com- mander shall be six and forty thousand and five hundred. 12 And the tribe of Simeon shall depart from him, and the chief of the sons of Simeon shall be Shelumiel the son of Zurish- addai: 13 And his army and his name shall be nine hundred and fifty thousand and three hundred. 14 The tribe of Gad and the leader of the sons of Gad shall be Eliasaph the son of Deuel: 15 His host and his name shall be fif- ty thousand, six hundred and fifty. 16 All the men of the camne of Reuben were an hundred and one fifty thousand, four hundred and fif- ty according to their armies, and they shall settle in the second place. 17 Then the Tab- ernacle of the congregation shall go with the army of the Leuites, in the midst of the camp, as they encamped, and so they shall go forth, every one in his order, according to his array. 18 And the array of Ephraim shall be toward the west, according to their armies; and the leader of the sons of Ephraim shall be Elisha- ma the son of Ammihud: 19 His army and his name were forty thousand and five hundred. 20 On him shall depend the tribe of Manasseh; and the chief of the sons of Manasseh shall be Gamliel the son of Pedahzur: 21 His army and his number were two hundred and thir- ty thousand and two hundred. 22 The tribe of Benjamin and its leader of the sons of Ben- jamin was Abidan the son of Gideon: 23 His army and his name was five thousand and thirty thousand and four hundred. 24 All

the names of the campe of Ephraim were an hundred and eight thousand and an hundred thousand, according to their armies, and they shall go to the third place. 25 The position of the army of Dan shall be toward the north, according to their armies; and the leader of the sons of Dan shall be Ahiezer the son of Ammishaddai: 26 His army and his number were two sixty thousand and seven hundred. 27 Upon him depends the tribe of Asher, and the chief of the sons of Asher shall be Pagiel the son of Ocran. 28 His army and his name were one million forty thousand and five hundred. 29 Then the tribe of Naphtali, and the chief of the sons of Naphtali shall be Ahi- ra the son of Enan: 30 His host and his name were three hundred fifty thousand and four hundred. 31 The whole army of Dan was an hundred and fifty thousand and six hundred men; they shall go inward with their banners. 32 These are the sums of the children of Is- rael according to the houses of their fathers, all the names of the army, according to their hosts: six hundred and three thousand, five hundred and fifty. 33 But the Leuites were not numbered among the children of Israel, as the LORD had commanded Moses. 34 The children of Israel did all that the LORD had commanded Moses: they encamped accord- ing to their banners and made the journey each one with his families, according to the houses of their fathers.

CHAPTER 3

1 These were also the generations of Aaron and Moses, in the day when the Lord spoke to Moses on Mount Sinai. 2 These are the names of the sons of Aaron: Nadab, the first born, Abiu, Eleazar and Ithamar. 3 These are the names of Aaron's sons, the anointegrat- ed priests whom Moses anointed to exercise the priestly office. 4 Nadab and Abihu died before the Lord when they offered strange fire before the Lord in the wilderness of Si- nai, and they had no sons; but Eleazar and Ithamar exercised the priestly office before Aaron their father. 5 Then the LORD spoke to Moses, saying, 6 Lead the tribe of Leui and set them before Aaron the priest, that they may be in his service, 7 and take with him the charge, that is, the charge of the whole con- gregation before the Tabernacle of the con- gregation to do the service of the Tabernacle. 8 They shall also keep all the instruments of the Tabernacle of the congregation, and they shall have the charge of the children of Israel to do the Tabernacle service. 9 You shall give the Leuites to Aaron and his sons, for they have been given to him freely among the sons of Israel. 10 And you shall appoint Aaron and his sons for the exercise of their priestly of- fice; and the stranger who comes near here shall be killed." 11 The LORD also spoke to Moses, saying, 12 "Behold, I have taken the Leuites from among the children of Israel, for all the firstborn who open the array among the children of Israel and the Leuites shall be mine, 13 For all the firstborn are mine: for the same day that I slew all the firstborn in the land of Egypt, I sanctified for me all the firstborn of Israel, both man and beast: they shall be mine: I am the LORD. 14 Moreover, the LORD spoke to Moses in the wilderness of Sinai, saying, 15 Appoint the sons of Levi according to the houses of their fathers, in their families; appoint all the males from a month old and upward. 16 Moses appointed them according to the word of the LORD, as he had been commanded. 17 These are the names of the sons of Leui: Gershon, Kohath and Merari. 18 These also are the names of the sons of Gershon according to their families: Libni and Shimei. 19 Also the sons of Kohath, according to their

families: Amram, Izehar, Hebron, and Vzziel. 20 The sons of Merari, according to their families: Mahli and Mushi: Mahli and Mushi. These are the families of Leui, according to the houses of their fathers. 21 From Gershon came the family of the Lib- nites and the family of the Shimeites; these are the families of the Gershonites. 22 The sum of these families (after the appointment of all the males from the age of one month and upward) was counted six thousand and five hundred. 23 The families of the Gershonites encamped behind the Tabernacle, toward the west. 24 The leader and elder of the house of the Gershonites shall be Eliasaph the son of Lael. 25 And the sons of Gershon shall be in charge of the tabernacle of the covenant, and of the pavilion, and of its covering, and of the covering of the tabernacle of the covenant, 26 the hanging of the court and the vaulting of the court that is near the Tabernacle, near the Altar and around it, and the cords of it for all its service. 27 From Kohath came the family of the Amramites, the family of the Izeharites, the family of the Hebronites, and the family of the Vzzielites; these are the families of the Kohathites. 28 The number of all the males, from the age of one month and upward, was eight thousand and six hundred, who had charge of the sanctuary. 29 The families of the sons of Kohath camped on the south side of the Tabernacle. 30 The leader and elder of the house and families of the Kohathites shall be Elizafan the son of Vzziel: 31 Their duty shall be to look after the ark, the table, the can- dlestick, the altars, the instruments of the sanctuary that are needed for the service, the vaile, and all that is needed there. 32 Eleazar, son of Aaron the priest, shall be the leader of the Leuites and shall have oversight of those who have responsibility for the sanctuary. 33 From Merari come the family of the Mahlites and the family of the Mushites; these are the families of Merari. 34 Their sum, according to the names of all the males from a month and upward, was six thousand and two hundred. 35 The head and elder of the house of the fam- ilies of Merari shall be Zuriel the son of Abi- hail; they shall stand on the north side of the Tabernacle. 36 And the sons of Merari shall have charge and custody of the tables of the Tabernacle, and of its bars, and of its pillars, and of its foundations, and of all its instru- ments, and of all that is needed therein, 37 and the pillars of the court round about, with their bases, their pivots, and their coardes. 38 Moreover, on the front of the Tabernacle, toward the east, in front of the Tabernacle, I say, of the congregation to the east, Moses, Aaron and his sons shall encamp, with the charge of the Sanctuary and the charge of the children of Israel; but the stranger who approaches shall be killed. 39 The total num- ber of the Leuites whom Moses and Aaron, at the command of the LORD, lined up in their families, that is, all the males from the age of one month and upward, was two thousand and twenty thousand. 40 The LORD said to Moses, "Name all the firstborn that are males among the children of Israel, from the age of one month and upward, and take the names of their names. 41 And you shall bring to me the Leuites for all the firstborn of the sons of Israel (I am the LORD) and the cattle of the Leuites for all the firstborn of the cattle of the sons of Israel." 42 And Moses nomenclated, as the LORD had commanded him, all the first- born of the children of Israel. 43 All the first-born males, listed by name (from a month upward), according to their names, were two hundred thousand, two hundred seven- ty thousand and three. 44 The LORD spoke to Moses, saying, 45 "Take the Leuites for all the firstborn of the children of Israel, and the cattle of the Leuites for their cattle, and the Leuites shall be mine (I am the LORD)." 46 And for the ransom of two hundred seuen- tie three (which are more than the Leuiti) of the firstborn of the children of Israel, 47 You shall also take five shekels for each person, ac- cording to the weight of the sanctuary; each shekel contains twenty gera. 48 And you shall give Aaron and his sons the money redeemed with the odd names. 49 So Moses dealt with the ransom of the ransomed, who were more than the Leuites: 50 Of the first born among the sons of Israel he took the money: a thou- sand three hundred five hundred shekels ac- cording to the shekel of the sanctuary. 51 And Moses delivered the money of the ransomed to Aaron and his sons, according to the word of the LORD, as the LORD had commanded Moses.

CHAPTER 4

1 The LORD spoke to Moses and Aaron, saying, "Take the sum of the sons of Kohath from among the sons of Leui, according to their families and the houses of their fa- thers, 2 Take the sum of the sons of Kohath from among the sons of Leui, according to their families and the houses of their fathers, 3 from the thirtieth year of their age and up to the fiftieth year of their age, all those who come into the assembly to do the work in the tent of meeting. 4 This shall be the office of the sons of Kohath in the Tabernacle of Meet- ing, around the Most Holy. 5 When the host is withdrawn, Aaron and his sons will come and take the tray of custody and place the ark of the Testimony there. 6 They will put a blan- ket of badger skins on it, and they will spread a cloth of snow-white silk over it and put the borders on it: 7 Then they shall spread on the table of bread a cloth of snow-white silk, and they shall place there the dishes, and the cups for incense, and the chalices, and the bowls with which to water it, and the bread shall al- ways be there: 8 Then they shall spread over it a blanket of deer skins and cover it with a blanket of badger skins and apply it to the edges. 9 Then they shall take a cloth of snow- white silk, and they shall place the candle- stick of light thereon, with its lamps, and its snuff-boxes, and all its vessels of oil around it. 10 And they shall put the candlestick and all its instruments in a casing of badger skins and place it on the bars. 11 On the altar of gold also they will spread a cloth of white silk, cover it with a wrapping of badger skins, and place it on the bars. 12 They will take all the instruments of the ministry with which they minister in the sanctuary, put them in a white silk cloth, cover them with a covering of bad- ger skins, and place them on the bars. 13 They will also remove the ashes from the altar and spread a purple cloth over it, 14 and they shall place over it all its instruments, which they occupy round about it: the censers, the meat hooks, the besome and the bases, and all the instruments of the altar; and they shall spread over it a blanket of badger skins and place it on the bars. 15 When Aaron and his sons have made the covering of the sanctuary and of all the instruments of the sanctuary, when the army departs, the sons of Kohath shall come and bring it, but they shall not touch anything holy, lest they dye it. This is the duty of the sons of Kohath in the Tabernacle of the con- gregation. 16 To the office of Eleazar the son of Aaron the priest is the responsibility of the oil for the light, the sweet incense, the daily food offering, and the anointing oil, with the oversight of the whole Tabernacle and every- thing in it, both in the Sanctuary and in all its instruments. 17 The LORD spoke to Moses and Aaron, saying. 18 You shall not cut off the tribe of the families of the Kohathites from among the Leuites: 19 But do so for them, that they may live, and not die when they come to the holiest things: let Aaron and his sons come, and support them, each to his office and charge. 20 But let them not come in to see when the sanctuary is closed, lest they die." 21 The LORD spoke to Moses, saying, 22 Take also the sum of the sons of Gershon, every one according to the houses of their fathers and according to their families: 23 beginning from the thirtieth year of their age and until the fiftieth year of their age, you shall appoint them all to come into the assembly to do ser- vice in the Tabernacle of the congregation. 24 This shall be the service of the families of the Gershonites, for service and care. 25 And they shall bring the curtains of the tabernacle, and the tabernacle of the congregation, and the covering thereof, and the covering of yew skins upon it, and the covering of the wall of the tabernacle of the congregation: 26 also the curtains of the courtyard and the vault of the entrance to the door of the courtyard, which is near the Tabernacle and near the altar, with their cords, all the instruments for their ser- vice, and all that was made for them. 27 At the command of Aaron and his sons shall all the service of the sons of you Gershonites be done, in all their duties and in all their ser- vice, and you shall support them to keep all their duties. 28 This is the service of the fam- ilies of the sons of the Gershonites in the tab- ernacle of the congregation; their guard shall be under the hand of Ithamar the son of Aar- on the priest. 29 You shall appoint the sons of Merari according to their families and the houses of their fathers: 30 beginning from the age of thirty, until the age of fifty, thou shalt appoint all those who come into the congre- gation to perform the service of the Tabernacle of Meeting. 31 This is their duty and charge according to all their service in the Tabernacle of the congregation: the tables of the Taber- nacle with its bars, its pillars, and its sockets, 32 the pillars which surround the court, with their bases, their pinnacles, and their cords, with all their instruments, for all their ser- vice; and by name you shall reckon up the in- struments of their office and their charge. 33 This is the service of the families of the sons of Merari, according to all their service in the tent of meeting under the hand of Ithamar the son of Aaron the priest. 34 Then Moses, Aaron and the community leaders appointed the sons of the Kohathites, according to their families and the houses of their fathers, 35 from the age of thirty years and upward, un- til the age of fifty years, all those entering the group for the service of the Tabernacle of the congregation. 36 So the names of the families were two thousand, seven hundred and fifty. 37 These are the names of the families of the Kohathites, all those serving in the Tent of Meeting, whom Moses and Aaron appointed according to the command of the Lord by the hand of Moses. 38 Also the names of the sons of Gershon, in their families and in the hous- es of their fathers, 39 from the age of thirty years and upward, until the age of fifty years, all those who enter the group for the service of the Tabernacle of the Cogregation. 40 Their names, according to their families and the houses of their fathers, were two thousand six hundred and thirty-three. 41 These are the names of the families of the sons of Gershon, of all those who served in the tabernacle of the congregation, whom Moses and Aaron appointed according to the commandments of the LORD. 42 Also the members of the families of the sons of Merari, according to their families and the houses of their fathers, 43 From the age of thirty years and upward, until the age of fifty years, all those who en- ter the group for the service of the Taberna- cle of meeting. 44 Their names therefore, according to their families, were three thou- sand and two hundred. 45 These are the sums of the families of the sons

of Merari, whom Moses and Aaron appointed according to the commandments of the LORD, by the hand of Moses. 46 So all the names of the Leuites, whom Moses and Aaron and the princes of Israel numbered according to their families and the houses of their fathers, 47 from the age of thirty years old onward, until the age of fifty years old, all those who came to perform their duty, their office, their service, and their charge in the Tabernacle of the congregation. 48 Their numbers were eight thousand, five hundred and forty-five. 49 According to the command of the Lord by the hand of Moses, Aaron appointed them, each according to his service and according to his office. Thus were the members of that tribe appointed, as the Lord had commanded Moses.

CHAPTER 5

1 The LORD spoke to Moses, saying, 2 Com- mand the children of Israel to expel from the host every leper, every hemorrhagic, and those who are defiled by the dead. 3 Both males and females you shall put out of the host, that they may not defile their tents in the midst of which I dwell. 4 And the children of Israel did so and put them out of the host, and as the LORD had commanded Moses, so did the children of Israel. 5 The LORD spoke to Moses, saying, 6 Speak to the children of Israel, "When a man or a woman commits a sin that men commit and transgresses against the LORD, when that person trans- gresses, 7 then he shall confess the sin which he has committed, and shall restore the do- minion thereof with his principal, and shall add the fifth part thereof, and give it to him against whom he transgressed. 8 But if the man has no kinsman to whom to return the dominion, the dominion shall be returned to the LORD for the priests, besides the ramme of atonement, with which he shall make atonement for him. 9 Every offering of all the holy things of the children of Israel, which they shall bring to the priest, shall be his. 10 And every thing halved shall be his; that is, what one gives to the priest shall be his. 11 The LORD spoke to Moses, saying, 12 Speak to the children of Israel and say to them, "If a man's wife turns to lawlessness and commits a tres- pass against him, 13 if another man lies with her carnally, and this is hidden from the eyes of her husband and kept hidden, and yet she is defiled, and there is no testimony against her, nor is she taken with the man, 14 if the man has an unfaithful mind, so as to be un- faithful to his wife who is defiled, or if he has an unfaithful mind, so as to be unfaithful to his wife who is not defiled, 15 then the man shall take his wife to the priest and bring his offering with him, the tenth part of an ephah of raw meat, but he shall not sprinkle oil on it nor put incense on it, for it is an offense of jealousy, an offense for remembrance, calling to mind sin: 16 And the priest shall bring it and set it before the LORD. 17 Then the priest shall take holy water in a vessel of earth and of the dust that is in the floor of the Taberna- cle, and the priest shall take it and put it into the water. 18 Afterward the priest shall set the woman before the LORD, and shall vnc the woman's head, and shall put the memorial offering into her hands: it is the ielousie of- fering, and the priest shall have the bitter and accursed water in his hand, 19 and the priest shall load it with another thing, and shall say to the woman, "If no man hath joined him- self to thee, and if thou hast not turned away from thy husband, deliver thyself from this bitter and accursed water. 20 But if thou hast departed from thy husband, and therefore thou art defiled, and a man hath lain with thee besides thy husband, 21 (Then

the priest shall impute to the woman another curse, and the priest shall say to the woman, "The LORD shall make thee accursed and detestable to the rest of thy people; the LORD shall make thy thigh to rot and thy belly to swell.") 22 and let this accursed water enter your bowels and make your belly swell and your thigh rot." Then the woman will answer, "Amen, amen." 23 Then the priest will write these curses in a book and wipe them out with bitter water, 24 and he shall cause the woman to drink the bitter and cursed water, and the cursed wa- ter, turned to bitterness, shall enter into her. 25 Then the priest shall take the host from the woman's hand, shake it before the LORD, and offer it on the altar. 26 The priest will take a handful of the offering as a remembrance, bury it on the altar, and then make the woman drink the water. 27 And when you have made her drink the water (if she has been defiled and has transgressed her husband), the ac- cursed water, having become bitter, shall en- ter her, and her belly shall swell, and her thigh shall rot, and the woman shall be accursed among her people. 28 But if the woman is not defiled, but is pure, she shall be free, and shall conceive and bear children. 29 This is the law of ielousia, when a wife turns away from her husband and defiles herself, 30 or when a man has been defiled with an unfaithful mind, be- ing unfaithful to his wife, then he shall bring the woman before the LORD, and the priest shall do to her what is written in this law, 31 the man shall be free from sin, but the woman shall bear her iniquity.

CHAPTER 6

1 The LORD spoke to Moses, saying, 2 Speak to the children of Israel and say to them, "When a man or a woman separates to take a vow of Nazarism to separate from the LORD, 3 he shall abstain from wine and strong spir- its, he shall drink neither semi-dry wine nor semi-dry spirits, he shall not drink grape li- quor, he shall not eat fresh grapes nor dried grapes. 4 Throughout the time of his absti- nence, he shall not eat anything made from the wine of the vine, neither the grapes nor the skin. 5 While he is separated for his vow, the razor shall not rest on his head until the days are past when he is separated from the Lord, and he shall be holy and let the locks of his head grow. 6 During the time that he sep- arates himself from the LORD, he shall not go near any dead body: 7 He shall not make him- self vncleane to the death of his father, moth- er, brother or sister, because the consecration of his God is on his head. 8 All the days of his separation shall be holy to the LORD. 9 And if any one shall suddenly be dyed of him, or if he beware of it, the garment of his consecration shall be defiled, and he shall shave his head on the day of his separation; on the seventh day he shall shave it. 10 On the eighth day he shall bring to the priest two turtles or two young pigeons, in the center of the tent of meeting. 11 Then the priest will prepare the one as a sin offering and the other as a burnt offering and make atonement for him, because he has committed a sin of death, 12 he shall conse- crate to the LORD the days of his separation, and he shall bring a year-old lamb as a sin offering, and the first days shall be canceled, because his consecration was defiled. 13 This then is the law of the Nazarite: When the time of his consecration is ended, he shall come before the Tabernacle of the congregation, 14 and he shall bring his offering to the Lord: a lamb of a year without blemish as a burnt offering, a lamb of a year without blemish as a sin offering, and a ram without blemish as a peace offering, 15 and a basket of

vnleaued bread, buns of fine flour mixed with oil, and wafers of vnleaued bread anointed with oil, with their food offerings and their drink of- ferings: 16 The priest shall bring them before the LORD and make his sin offering and his burnt offering. 17 He shall also prepare the ram for the peace offering to the LORD, with the basket of vnezied bread, and the priest shall make his food offering and his drink offering. 18 And the Nazarene shall shave the head of his consecration at the door of the Tabernacle of Congregation, and he shall take the head of his consecration and put it into the fire, which is under the peace offering. 19 Then the priest shall take a sodden shoulder of mutton, an impregnated sweet from the basket, and an impregnated wafer, and shall place them on the hands of the Nazarite, after he has made his consecration. 20 The priest shall shake them on one side and the other before the LORD; this is a holy thing for the priest, besides the shaken breast and the shaken shoulder; so afterwards the Nazarite may drink wine. 21 This is the offering of the Nazarite, who has made a vow, and his offer- ing to the LORD for his consecration, besides that which he is able to bring; according to the vow he has made, so shall he do after the of- fering of his consecration. 22 The Lord spoke to Moses, saying, 23 Speak to Aaron and his sons, saying, "Thus you shall bless the children of Israel and say to them, 'The Lord blesses the children of Israel, 24 The LORD bless you and keep you, 25 the LORD let his face shine upon you, and be merciful to you, 26 the LORD lift up his countenance upon thee, and give thee peace. 27 So they shall put my Name upon the children of Israel, and I will bless them.

CHAPTER 7

1 When Moses had finished preparing the tabernacle, and anointing it, and sanctifying it, and all its instruments, and the altar with all its instruments, and had anoinished and sanctified them, 2 then the princes of Israel, heads of the houses of their fathers (they were the princes of the tribes, which were beyond the names) came in, 3 and brought their of- fering before the LORD: six baskets and two oxen: one basket for two princes and one ox for each, and they offered them before the Tabernacle. 4 The LORD spoke to Moses, say- ing, 5 Take these of them, that they may be destined for the service of the Tabernacle of meeting, and you shall give them to the Leuites, to each according to his function." 6 Moses then took the carrots and the oxen and gave them to the Leuites: 7 Two chariots and four oxen he gave to the sons of Gershon, ac- cording to their functions. 8 Four baskets and eight oxen were given to the sons of Merari, according to their function, by the hand of Ithamar the son of Aaron the priest. 9 But to the sons of Kohath he gave none, because to them belonged the charge of the sanctuary, which they carried on their shoulders. 10 The princes also offered at the dedication of the altar on the day it was inaugurated; the princ- es offered their offering before the altar. 11 The LORD said to Moses, "A prince one day and another prince another day shall offer their offering for the dedication of the altar." 12 On the first day Nahshon the son of Ammi- nadab, of the tribe of Judah, offered his offer- ing. 13 His offering consisted of a silver plate weighing one hundred and thirty shekels, a silver boule weighing seventy shekels, accord- ing to the shekel of the sanctuary, both filled with fine flour mixed with oil, as a food offer- ing, 14 a golden incense bowl of ten shekels, full of incense, 15 one heifer, one ram, one yearling lamb for the fire offense, 16 a kid goat for the sin offering, 17 and, as a sacrifice for peace,

two heifers, five rams, five he-goats, and five one-year-old lambs; this was the sac- rifice of Nahshon the son of Amminadab. 18 On the second day he offered Nethaneel the son of Zuar, prince of the tribe of Issachar: 19 who offered for his sacrifice a silver platter weighing an hundred and thirty shekels, a sil- ver boule weighing seventy shekels, according to the shekel of the sanctuary, both full of fine flour mixed with oil, as a meat sacrifice, 20 a golden incense bowl of ten shekels, full of in- cense, 21 one heifer, one ram, one yearling lamb for the burning, 22 a kid goat for the sin offering, 23 and, as a sacrifice for peace, two bullocks, five rams, five he-goats, five one- year-old lambs; this was the sacrifice of Neth- aneel the son of Zuar. 24 On the third day Eli- ab the son of Helon, prince of the sons of Zebulun, departed. 25 His offering consisted of a silver chest weighing one hundred and thirty shekels, a silver boule weighing seventy shekels, according to the shekel of the sanctu- ary, both filled with fine flour, mixed with oil, for a food offering, 26 a golden cup for in- cense of ten shekels, full of incense, 27 one heifer, one ram, one yearling lamb for the burning, 28 one kid for the offense of sin, 29 and for the peace offering, two heifers, five rams, five he- goats, five one-year-old lambs; this was the offering of Eliab the son of Helon. 30 On the fourth day he offered Elizur the son of Scedeur, prince of the sons of Reuben. 31 His offering was a silver plate weighing an hundred and thirty shekels, a silver boule weighing seventy shekels, according to the shekel of the sanctuary, both filled with fine flour mixed with oil, for a food offering, 32 a golden goblet of ten shekels, full of incense, 33 a heifer, a ram, and a yearling lamb for the burning, 34 a kid goat for the sin offering, 35 and for the peace offering, two heifers, five rams, five he-goats, and five one-year-old lambs; this was the offering of Elizur the son of Scedeur. 36 On the fifth day he offered Shelumiel the son of Zurishaddai, prince of the sons of Simeon. 37 His sacrifice was a sil- ver plate weighing an hundred and thirty shekels, a silver boule weighing seventy shek- els, according to the shekel of the sanctuary, both filled with fine flour mixed with oil, for a meat sacrifice, 38 a golden chalice of ten shek- els, full of incense, 39 one heifer, one ram, one yearling lamb for a burnt offering, 40 a kid goat for the sin offering, 41 and for the peace offering, two heifers, five rams, five he-goats, five one-year-old lambs; this was the offering of Shelumiel the son of Zurishaddai. 42 On the sixth day he offered Eliasaph the son of Deuel, prince of the sons of Gad. 43 His offer- ing was a silver plate weighing an hundred and thirty shekels, a silver boule weighing seventy shekels, according to the shekel of the sanctuary, both filled with fine flour mixed with oil, for a food offering, 44 a golden chal- ice of ten shekels, full of incense, 45 a heifer, a ram, a yearling lamb, as a sacrifice, 46 a kid goat for the sin offering, 47 and for the peace offering, two heifers, five rams, five he-goats, five one-year-old lambs; this was the offering of Eliasaph the son of Deuel. 48 On the sev- enth day Elishama the son of Ammiud, prince of the sons of Ephraim, made an offering. 49 His offering was a silver plate weighing one hundred and thirty shekels, a silver boule weighing seventy shekels, according to the shekel of the sanctuary, both filled with fine flour, mixed with oil, as a food offering, 50 a golden goblet of ten shekels, full of incense, 51 a heifer, a ram, a yearling lamb for the burnt offering, 52 a kid goat for the sin offering, 53 and, for the peace offering, two heifers, five rams, five he-goats, five one-year-old lambs; this was the offering of Elishama the son of Ammiud. 54 On the eighth day he offered Gamliel the son of Pedazur, prince of the sons of Manasseh. 55 His offering consisted of a silver plate weighing one hundred and thirty shekels, a silver boule weighing seventy shekels, according to the shekel of the sanctuary, both filled with flour, mixed with oil, as a food offering, 56 a golden chalice of ten shekels, full of incense, 57 a heifer, a ram, a yearling lamb, as a sacrifice, 58 a kid goat for the sin offering, 59 and, for the peace offering, two bullocks, five rams, five he-goats, five lambs of a year old; this was the offering of Gamliel the son of Pedazur. 60 On the ninth day Abidan the son of Gideon, prince of the sons of Benjamin, offered. 61 His offering was a silver plate weighing an hundred and thirty shekels, a silver boule weighing seventy shekels, according to the shekel of the sanctuary, both filled with fine flour, mixed with oil, for a food offering, 62 a golden cup for incense of ten shekels, full of incense, 63 a heifer, a ram, a yearling lamb, as a sacrifice, 64 one kid for the sin offering, 65 and, for the peace offering, two bullocks, five rams, five he-goats, five lambs of a year old; this was the offering of Abidan the son of Gideon. 66 On the tenth day Ahiezer the son of Ammishaddai, prince of the sons of Dan, offered himself. 67 His offering was a silver plate weighing an hundred and thirty shekels, a silver boule weighing seventy shekels, like the shekel of the sanctuary, both filled with fine flour, mixed with oil, as a food offering, 68 a golden cup for incense of ten shekels full of incense, 69 one heifer, one ram, one yearling lamb for the fire offense, 70 one kid for the sin offering, 71 and for the peace offering, two bulls, five rams, five he-goats, five one-year-old lambs; this was the offering of Ahiezer the son of Ammishaddai. 72 On the eleventh day departed Pagiel the son of Ocran, prince of the sons of Asher. 73 His offering was a silver plate weighing an hundred and thirty shekels, a silver boule weighing seventy shekels, like the shekel of the sanctuary, both filled with fine flour, mixed with oil, for a food offering, 74 a golden cup for incense of ten shekels, full of incense, 75 one long bull, one ram, one yearling lamb, as a sacrifice, 76 one kid for the sin offering, 77 and for the peace offering, two bullocks, five rams, five he-goats, five lambs of a year: this was the offering of Pagiel the son of Ocran. 78 On the twelfth day departed Ahira the son of Enan, prince of the sons of Naphtali, 79 His offering was a silver plate weighing an hundred and thirty shekels, a silver boule weighing seventy shekels, like the shekel of the sanctuary, both filled with fine flour, mixed with oil, for a food offering, 80 a golden cup for incense of ten shekels, full of incense, 81 one long bull, one ram, one yearling lamb, as a sacrifice, 82 one kid for the sin offering, 83 and for the peace offering, two bullocks, five rams, five he-goats, five one-year-old lambs; this was the offering of Ahira the son of Enan. 84 This was the inauguration of the altar by the princes of Israel, when it was anointed: two charges of silk, two boules of silk, two cups of incense of gold, 85 each charger contained one hundred and thirty shekels of silk, and each boule seuentie; all the silk vessels contained two thousand four hundred and fifty shekels, according to the shekels of the sanctuary. 86 Two incense bowls of gold, full of incense, worth ten shekels for each bowl, according to the title of the Sanctuary; all the gold of the incense bowls was an hundred and twelve shekels. 87 All the heifers for the burnt offering were two heifers, the rams two, the one-year-old lambs two, with their offal, and two goats for offal. 88 All the heifers for the peace showings were four and twenty-five, the rams sixty, the he-goats sixty, the lambs one year old sixty; this was the inauguration of the altar, after it was anointed. 89 When Moses entered the tent of meeting to speak with God, he heard the voice of one speaking to him from the Merciseat, which was on the arch of the Testimony between the two Cherubim, and he spoke to him.

CHAPTER 8

1 The LORD spoke to Moses, saying, 2 Speak to Aaron and say to him, "When you light the lamps, the two lamps shall light toward the front of the candlestick." 3 And Aaron did so, lighting the lamps toward the front of the candlestick, as the LORD had commanded Moses. 4 This was the work of the candle- stick, of gold beaten with the hammer, both the stem and its fibers being beaten with the hammer; according to the paternal which the Lord had shown Moses, thus was the can- dlestick made. 5 The LORD spoke to Moses, saying, 6 "Take the Leuites from among the children of Israel and purify them." 7 When you have cleansed them, you shall do this: you shall sprinkle the water of purification on them, and you shall make them strip them of all their flesh and wash their clothes; so they shall be clean. 8 Then they shall take a young bull with his offal of fine flour mixed with oil, and another young bull you shall take as offal for sin. 9 Then you shall bring the Leuites before the Tabernacle of the congregation, and you shall make all the congregation of the children of Israel aware. 10 You shall also bring the Leuiti before the LORD, and the children of Israel shall lay hands on the Leui- ti. 11 Aaron shall offer the Leuiti before the LORD, as a shake of you sons of Israel, that they may perform the service of the LORD. 12 And the Leuiti shall lay their hands on the heads of the heifers, and shall make the one a sin offering and the other a burnt offering for the LORD, that you may make atonement for the Leuiti. 13 You shall set the Leuites be- fore Aaron and his sons and offer them as a sacrifice to the LORD. 14 Thus you shall sep- arate the Leuites from the children of Israel, and the Leuites shall be mine. 15 After that the Leuites shall enter the Tabernacle of Meeting, and you shall purify them and offer them as a sacrifice to the LORD. 16 For they have been freely given to me from among the children of Israel, as to the opening of any woman; for all the firstborn of the children of Israel I have taken them with me. 17 For all the firstborn of the children of Israel are mine, both of men and of animals; from the day that I killed all the firstborn in the land of Egypt, I sanctified them for myself. 18 I took the Leuites for all the firstborn of the children of Israel, 19 and I gave the Leuiti as a gift to Aaron and his sons among the sons of Israel, to do service for the sons of Israel in the tabernacle of the congregation, and to make an atonement for the sons of Israel, so that there should not be a plague among the sons of Israel, when the sons of Israel go to the sanctuary." 20 And Mo- ses and Aaron and all the cogregation of the children of Israel behaved toward the Leuites, according to all that the LORD had com- manded Moses concerning the Leuites; so did the children of Israel toward them. 21 So the Leuites were cleansed, and they washed their garments, and Aaron offered them as a shaken offering before the Lord; Aaron made an atonement for them, to cleanse them. 22 After that the Leuites went in to do their ser- vice in the tent of meeting, before Aaron and his sons; as the LORD had commanded Mo- ses concerning the Leuites, so they did with them. 23 The Lord spoke to Moses, saying, 24 This, too, belongs to the Leuites: from fif- ty-two years of age and beyond, they shall go in to perform their duties in the service of the Tabernacle of Meeting. 25 After the fiftieth year of their age, they shall cease to exercise their office and shall no longer serve: 26 but they shall exercise service with their brethren in the

Tabernacle of the congregation, to keep the things entrusted to them, but they shall do no service; so shall you do with the Leuites concerning their offices.

CHAPTER 9

1 The LORD spoke to Moses in the wilderness of Sinai, in the first month of the second year, after they had come out of the land of Egypt, and said, "The children of Israel will celebrate the Passover at the appointed time, 2 The children of Israel shall also celebrate the Passover at the appointed time. 3 On the fourteenth day of this month, at any rate, you shall cel- ebrate it in due time, according to all its pre- cepts and ceremonies." 4 Then Moses spoke to the children of Israel about celebrating the Passover. 5 They celebrated the Passover on the fourteenth day of the first month, still in the wilderness of Sinai, according to what the Lord had commanded Moses, and so did you children of Israel. 6 Some men defiled them- selves with a dead man so as not to observe the Passion on that same day, and they came before Moses and Aaron on that same day. 7 Those men said to him, "We are defiled with a dead man; why are we held back for not of- fering an offering to the LORD in the time ap- pointed among the children of Israel?" 8 Then Moses said to them, "Be still, and I will listen to what the LORD will command of you." 9 The LORD spoke to Moses, saying, 10 Speak to the children of Israel and say, "If any of you or of your posterity shall be vituperated because of a body or shall be on a journey of logs, they shall observe the Walk before the LORD." 11 On the fourteenth day of the second month of July they shall celebrate it with leavened bread and herbs. 12 They shall not leave any of it until the morning, nor shall they break any bone of it; according to all the provisions of the Past, they shall keep it. 13 But the man who is clean and not on the journey, and who is negligent in observing the Passover, shall be cut off from his people; because he has not brought the offering of the LORD in his ap- pointed time, that man shall bear his sin. 14 If a stranger dwells among you and wants to observe the Passover for the LORD, according to the ordinance of the Passover and its man- ner, so he shall do; you shall have one feast both for the stranger and for him who is born in the same land. 15 When the Tabernacle was erected, a cloud enveloped the Taberna- cle, that is, the Tabernacle of the Testimony, and at that time the Tabernacle remained as a fire until morning. 16 So it was always: the cloud covered it by day and the appearance of fire by night. 17 When the cloud was removed from the Tabernacle, the children of Israel set out, and in the place where the cloud was, the children of Israel pitched their tents. 18 By the command of the LORD the children of Israel set out, and by the command of the LORD they pitched; as long as the cloud re- mained over the Tabernacle, they stopped. 19 When the cloud stood still on the Tabernacle for a long time, the children of Israel guarded the LORD and made no journey. 20 When the cloud remained for a few days on the Taber- nacle, they stayed in their tents, according to the command of the LORD, for they went on a journey according to the command of the LORD. 21 Even if the cloud remained on the Tabernacle from sunrise to sunset, if the cloud was removed in the morning, they went on their journey; if the cloud was removed by day or by night, they went on their journey. 22 If the cloud remained two days, a month or a year over the Tabernacle, the children of Israel remained still and did not make the journey; but when it was taken away, they made the journey. 23 At the command of the LORD they camped, and at the command of the LORD they made the journey, watching over the LORD at the command of the LORD by the hand of Moses.

CHAPTER 10

1 The LORD spoke to Moses, saying, 2 "Make yourself two trumpets of silk, of one whole piece, that you may use them for the gather- ing of the congregation and for the departure of the group. 3 When they have blown with them, the whole community shall assemble before the porch of the Tabernacle of Cogre- gation. 4 But if they blow with one, the princ- es or leaders of the thousands of Israel shall come to you. 5 But if you sound an alarm, the campe of those in the east will go forth. 6 If you sound the alarm a second time, the army of those in the south will march on, for they will sound the alarm when they retreat. 7 But when you gather the community together, you will sound without alarm. 8 The sons of Aaron the priest shall sound the trumpets, and you shall keep them as a legend forever in your generations. 9 When you go to war in your land against the enemy who torments you, you shall sound the alarm with trum- pets, and you shall be remembered before the LORD your God and be saved from your enemies. 10 Also in the day of your joy, in your feast days and at the beginning of your months, you shall sound the trumpets for your sacrifices and for your peace offerings, that they may be a remembrance to you be- fore your God: I am the LORD your God." 11 In the second year, in the second month and on the twentieth day of the month, the cloud was removed from the Tabernacle of Testimony. 12 The children of Israel set out on their journey from the wilderness of Sinai, and the cloud rested in the wilderness of Paran. 13 They undertook their journey at the command of the LORD, by the hand of Moses. 14 First the army of the sons of Iudah deployed, accord- ing to their armies, and Nahshon the son of Amminabad was in his array. 15 The group of the tribe of the sons of Issachar included Nethaneel the son of Zuar. 16 The group of the tribe of the sons of Zebulun included Eliab the son of Helon. 17 When the tabernacle was taken away, the sons of Gershon and the sons of Merari went forth carrying the tabernacle. 18 Then departed the host of Reuben, accord- ing to their armies, and by his side was Elizur the son of Scedeur. 19 The group of the tribe of the sons of Simeon was Shelumiel the son of Shurishaddai. 20 The group of the tribe of the sons of Gad consisted of Eliasaph, son of Deuel. 21 The Kohathites also went forth and brought the sanctuary, and the former pre- pared the tabernacle against their coming. 22 Then the leader of the army of the sons of Ephraim advanced according to their armies, and his group was Elishama the son of Am- miud. 23 The group of the tribe of the sons of Manasseh consisted of Gamliel the son of Pedazur. 24 The group of the tribe of the sons of Benjamin consisted of Abidan, son of Gide- on. 25 Last marched the standard of the army of the sons of Dan, gathering all the armies according to their armies; his group consist- ed of Ahiezer the son of Ammishaddai. 26 Commanding the tribe of the sons of Asher was Pagiel, son of Ocran. 27 As for the tribe of the sons of Naphtali, the leader of the tribe was Ahira the son of Enan. 28 These were the ranks of the children of Israel according to their armies as they marched. 29 Then Moses said to Hobab the son of Reuel the Midianite, Moses' father-in-law, "Let us go to the place of which the LORD has said, 'I will give it to you': Come with us and we will do you good, for the LORD has promised good to Israel." 30 He an- swered him, "I will not

go, but I will go away to my country and to my family." 31 Then he said, "Please do not leave us, for you know our camps in the wilderness and can be our guide. 32 And if you go with Vs, as much as the LORD will do good with Vs, so will we do with you." 33 So they departed from the mountain of the LORD for three days' journey; and the ark of the commander of the LORD went before them during the three days' journey, to seek a resting place for them. 34 The cloud of the LORD was present during the day when they went out of the camp. 35 When the ark came forward, Moses said, "Arise, O LORD, and let your enemies be scattered, and let those who hate you flee before you." 36 When he rested, he said, "Return, O LORD, to the many thou- sands of Israel."

CHAPTER 11

1 When the people became murmurers, it displeased the LORD; and the LORD heard it, therefore his anger was kindled, and the fire of the LORD burned among them and con- sumed most of the army. 2 Then the people cried out to Moses; and when Moses praised the LORD, the fire went out. 3 He called that place Taberah, because the fire of the LORD burned in their midst. 4 A multitude of the people who were among them gave them- selves up to desire and departed; the children of Israel also wept and said, "Who will give them meat to eat? 5 We remember the fish we ate in Egypt for nothing, the cucumbers, the peppers, the leeks, the onions and the nee- dles. 6 But now our soul is dried up and we see nothing but this Man. 7 The Man was like a coriander seed, and his color was like the color of bdelium. 8 And the people went and gathered it, and ground it in mills or beat it in mortars, and cooked it in a cauldron, and made cakes of it, the taste of which was like fresh oil. 9 When the night dew fell on the host, the man fell with it). 10 Then Moses heard the people weeping in all their fam- ilies, every one in his tent, and the anger of the LORD was sorely kindled; Moses also was afflicted. 11 Moses said to the LORD, "Why are you angry with your servant? And why have I not found favor in your eyes, since you have entrusted me with the responsibility of all this people? 12 Did I conceive all this people or did I beget them so that you would say to me, 'Bring them in your womb (as a nurse suck- les her sucking child) to the land, for which you gave their fathers in marriage?' 13 Where should I have meat to give to all these peo- ple? For they cry before me, saying, "Give us meat to eat." 14 I am not able to bear all these people alone, for they are too heavy for me. 15 Therefore, if you behave like this toward me, please, if I have found evil in your eyes, kill me, that I may not see my misery." 16 Then the LORD said to Moses, "Gather with me some men from among the elders of Israel, whom you know and who are the elders of the peo- ple, and their leaders, and lead them to the Tabernacle of Meeting, and let them stand there with you, 17 I will go down and speak with you there, and I will take the Spirit that is upon you and put it upon them, and they will carry the burden of the people with you; so you will not carry it alone. 18 Moreover you shall say to the people, "Be sanctified against death, and you shall eat meat; for you cried in the ears of the LORD, saying, "Who will give you meat to eat?" for we were better in Egypt; therefore the LORD will give you meat and you shall eat. 19 You shall not eat one day, nor two days, nor five days, nor ten days, nor twenty years, 20 but a whole month, until it comes to your nostrils and is given to you, because you have despised the LORD, who is in the midst of you, and

have wept before him, saying, "Why have we come so far from Egypt?" 21 Moses said, "There are six hundred thousand men walking among the people, in whose midst I stand; and you say, 'I will give them meat, that they may eat for a month. 22 Shall the sheep and the bees be killed for them, that they may find them? Or shall all the fish of the sea be gathered for them, that they may eat? 23 Did the LORD say to Moses, "Has the hand of the LORD shortened? Now you will see whether my word will be accept- ed to you or not." 24 And Moses went out, and reported the words of the LORD to the people, and gathered seventy men from among the elders of the people, and set them around the Tabernacle. 25 Then the Lord came down in a cloud, spoke to him, and took the Spirit that was upon him, and put it upon those seventy ancient men; and when the Spirit came upon them, they prophesied and did not cease. 26 But there remained two men in the host: the name of the one was Eldad, and the name of the other Medad; and the Spirit rested upon them (for they were of those who were writ- ten and had not gone out of the Tabernacle), and they prophesied in the host. 27 Then a young man ran and said to Moses, "Eldad and Medad prophesied in the host. 28 Ioshua the son of Nun, Moses' servant, one of his young men, answered and said, "My lord Moses, for- bid them." 29 But Moses said to him, "Do you forbid them because of me? Yes, God would have all the LORD's people be prophets and the LORD would put his Spirit upon them." 30 Moses went back into the army, he and the elders of Israel. 31 Then the LORD made a wind that brought quails from the sea and dropped them on the campe, one day on one side and one day on the other, around the host, and they were about two cubits on the earth. 32 Then the people rose up, all that day, all that night, and all the next day, and gath- ered the quails; and those who gathered less gathered ten full Homers, and they scattered them round about their tray around the host. 33 While the meat was still between the teeth, before it was chewed, behold, the anger of the LORD was kindled against the people, and the LORD struck the people with a plague of enormous size. 34 Therefore the place was called Kibroth-hattaauah, because the peo- ple who fell prey to lust were buried there. 35 From Kibroth-hattaauah the people set out for Hazeroth and stopped at Hazeroth.

CHAPTER 12

1 Then Miriam and Aaron spoke against Mo- ses because of the woman of Ethiopia whom he had married (for he had married a wom- an of Ethiopia). 2 And they said, "What, has the Lord spoken only through Moses? Did He not also speak through others?" And the Lord heard him. 3 (But Moses was a very meek man compared to all the men who were on the earth). 4 Then the LORD said to Moses, Aaron and Miriam, "All three of you go out to the tent of meeting." 5 Then the LORD went down into the pillar of cloud, stood at the entrance to the Tabernacle, called Aaron and Miriam, and they both went out. 6 Then he said, "Hear now my words: if there is a prophet of the Lord among you, I will be known to him by a vision and will speak to him by a word. 7 It is not so with my servant Moses, who is faithful in all my house. 8 To him I will speak from mouth to mouth, in vision, and not in dark words, but he shall see the likeness of the LORD. Why then were you not afraid to speak against my servant, that is, against Moses? 9 The LORD became very angry with them and went away. 10 The cloud also departed from the Taberna- cle; and behold, Miriam

was leprous as snow; and Aaron looked at Miriam, and behold, she was leprous. 11 Then Aaron said to Moses, "Alas, my Lord, please do not bring upon her the sin which we foolishly committed and for which we sinned. 12 Let her not be, I pray you, like a dead man whose flesh is half consumed when he comes out of his mother's womb." 13 Then Moses cried out to the LORD, say- ing, "O God, please heal her at once." 14 The LORD said to Moses, "If her father had spit in her face, should she not have been ashamed for ten days? Let her be shut out of the host for ten days, and then she will be healed." 15 So Miriam was shut out of the host for sever- al days, and the people did not recover until Miriam was brought back in.

CHAPTER 13

1 Then the people departed again from Hazeroth and encamped in the wilderness of Paran. 2 The LORD spoke to Moses, say- ing, 3 "Send men to scour the land of Canaan, which I have given to the children of Israel; of every tribe of their fathers you shall send a man, who shall be a leader among them." 4 Moses brought them out of the wilderness of Paran by the command of the LORD; all those men were leaders of the children of Israel. 5 Their names are these: of the tribe of Reuben, Shammua the son of Zaccur: 6 Of the tribe of Simeon, Shaphat the son of Hori: 7 Of the tribe of Judah, Caleb, son of Jephunneh: 8 Of the tribe of Issachar, Igal the son of Iosef: 9 Of the tribe of Ephraim, Hoshea the son of Nun: 10 Of the tribe of Benjamin, Palti the son of Raphu: 11 Of the tribe of Zebulun, Gaddiel the son of Sodi: 12 Of the tribe of Ioseph, that is, of the tribe of Manasseh, Gaddi, son of Susi: 13 Of the tribe of Dan, Ammiel the son of Ge- malli: 14 Of the tribe of Asher, Sethur the son of Michael: 15 Of the tribe of Naphtali, Nah- bi the son of Vophsi: 16 Of the tribe of Gad, Geuel, son of Machi. 17 These are the names of the men whom Moses sent to explore the land; Moses called the name of Hoshea the son of Nun, Jehoshua. 18 Moses sent them to explore the land of Canaan and said to them, "Go this way, toward the south, and go to the mountains, 19 and consider the land as it is and the people who dwell in it, whether they are strong or weak, whether they are few in number or numerous, 20 and also what is the land that they inhabit, whether it is good or bad; and what are the cities that they inhab- it, whether they dwell in tents or in fortified cities: 21 and what is the land: whether it is fat or lean, whether there are trees in it or not. And be courageous, and bring the fruits of the land (for then was the time of the first ripe grapes)." 22 So they set out and searched the land, from the wilderness of Zin to Re- hob, to go to Hamath, 23 They went up to- ward the south and came to Hebron, where there were Ahiman, Shesai and Talmai, sons of Anak. Hebron was built ten years before Zoan in Egypt. 24 Then they came to the ri- uer of Eshcol, cut from there a branch with a bunch of grapes, put it on a bar between two, and brought pomegranates and figs. 25 That place was called Eshcol, because of the cluster of grapes that the children of Israel cut from there. 26 Then after four days they went away from seeking the land. 27 And they went and came to Moses, and to Aaron, and to all the congregation of the children of Israel, in the wilderness of Paran, in Kadesh, and brought to them and to all the congregation tables, and showed them the fruits of the land. 28 And they told them and said, "We have come to the land where you sent us, and it certain- ly flows with milk and honey; and behold its fruits." 29 The people who inhabit the land are strong, and

the cities are walled and very large; moreover, we have seen there the sons of Anak. 30 The Amalekites dwell in the south country, the Hittites, the Jebusites and the Amorites dwell in the mountains, and the Canaanites dwell on the sea and on the coast of Iorden." 31 Then Caleb stopped the people before Moses and said, "Let us go at once and take it, for we shall undoubtedly conquer it." 32 But the men who went with him said, "We are not able to go against the people, for they are stronger than we are." 33 They presented an exhaustive account of the land they had scouted for the children of Israel, saying, "The land we went through to scout it is a land that devours its inhabitants, for all the people we saw in it are men of great stature." (Numbers:) For there we saw gypsies there, sons of Anak, coming from the gypsies, so that we looked in our own eyes like sausage makers; and so we were in their eyes.

CHAPTER 14

1 Then all the community lifted up their voices and wept; and the people wept that night, 2 all the children of Israel murmured against Moses and Aaron; and all the congre- gation said to them, "If only we had died in the land of Egypt or in this wilderness, if only we had died. 3 For what reason now has the Lord brought you into this land to fall under the sword? Our wives and children will be a prayer; was it not better for you to return to Egypt? 4 Then they said to each other, "Make a captain and return to Egypt." 5 Then Moses and Aaron fell on their faces before the whole community of the children of Israel. 6 Ioshua the son of Nun and Caleb the son of Jephun- neh, two of those who scoured the land, tore their garments, 7 and spoke to the whole as- sembly of the children of Israel, saying, "The land that we have gone through to scour it is a very good land. 8 If the LORD wills it, he will bring it into this land and give it to you, which is a land flowing with milk and honey. 9 But do not rebel against the LORD, and do not fear the inhabitants of the land, for they are but bread for Vs; their shield is turned away from Vs, and the LORD is with Vs; do not fear them." 10 All the crowd said, "Stone them with stones," but the glory of the LORD appeared in the tent of meeting, before all the children of Israel. 11 Then the LORD said to Moses, "How long will this people try me, and how long will they reject me, because of all the signs I have manifested among them? 12 I will smite them with the plague and destroy them, and I will make you a greater and stron- ger nation than they." 13 But Moses said to the LORD, "When the Egyptians hear it (for you have brought this people out by your power from among them) 14 then they will say to the inhabitants of the land (for they have heard that you, LORD, are in the midst of this peo- ple and that you, LORD, are seen face to face, that your cloud stands outside them and that you go before them by day in a pillar of cloud and by night in a pillar of fire) 15 that thou shalt slay this people as one man; so shall the people say who have heard of thee, 16 For the LORD was not able to bring this people into the land which he had sworn; he killed them in the wilderness. 17 Now, I pray thee, let the power of my Lord be great, as thou hast said, 18 The LORD is slow to anger and of great mercy; he forgives iniquity and sin, he does not make the wicked innocent, and he caus- es the wickedness of the fathers to fall upon the children, to the third and fourth genera- tion: 19 be merciful, I pray thee, toward the iniquity of this people, according to thy great mercy, and as thou hast forgiven this people from Egypt, even unto this day." 20 The LORD said, "I have forgiven

it, according to your re- quest." 21 Nevertheless, as I say, all the earth shall be filled with the glory of the LORD. 22 For all the men who have seen my glory and my miracles which I did in Egypt and in the wilderness, and who tempted me ten times, have not obeyed my command, 23 surely they shall not see the land of which I swore to their fathers, nor shall those who tempted me see it. 24 But my servant Caleb, because he had another spirit and still followed me, I will make him enter the land where he went, and his descendants shall inherit it. 25 Now the Amalekites and the Canaanites remain in the valley; therefore turn back to Morowe and go into the wilderness by the way of the Red Sea. 26 Then the LORD spoke to Moses and Aaron, saying, 27 How long shall I allow this wick- ed multitude to murmur against me? I have heard the murmurings of the children of Isra- el, who murmur against me. 28 Say to them, "As I lie (says the LORD), I will surely do to you what you have spoken in my ears. 29 Your ma- chines shall fall in this wilderness, and all of you who have been counted in all your nombs, from the age of twenty years and upward, who have murmured against me, 30 You shall not without doubt enter into the land for which I have lifted up my hand to make you dwell, as Caleb the son of Jephunneh and Ioshua the son of Nun have said. 31 But your sons (whom you said were to be a prayer) I will bring them in, and they shall know the land which you rejected: 32 But your cars shall fall in the wil- derness, 33 And your sons shall wander in the wilderness for forty years, and they shall car- ry your whores, until your cars be destroyed in the wilderness. 34 After the number of the days that you have scoured the land, that is, forty days, every day for a year, you shall bear your iniquity for forty years, and you shall re- alize my breach of promise. 35 I, the LORD, have said, "Surely I will do so to all this com- pany of the wicked who have gathered against me; for in this wilderness they shall be con- sumed, and there they shall die." 36 The men whom Moses had sent to scour the land (and who, when they arrived, caused all the people to murmur against him and brought a slan- der on the land) 37 Then the men who brought that vile slander on the land shall die of a plague before the LORD. 38 But Ioshua the son of Nun and Caleb the son of Jephunneh, of those who went out to scour the land, shall remain alive." 39 Moses reported these words to all the children of Israel, and the people were greatly saddened. 40 They arose ear- ly in the morning and went to the top of the mountain, saying, "We are ready to depart to the place the LORD has promised, for we have sinned." 41 But Moses answered, "Why do you transgress the Lord's command in this way? It will not go so well. 42 Do not go away (for the LORD is not in your midst), lest you be un- saved before your enemies. 43 For the Amale- kites and the Canaanites are there before you, and you will fall by the sword; for if you turn away from the Lord, the Lord also will not be with you." 44 They persisted in going up to the top of the mountain, but the ark of the Lord's commander and Moses did not depart from the camp. 45 Then the Amalekites and the Ca- naanites, who dwelt on that mountain, came down and struck them and consumed them as far as Hormah.

CHAPTER 15

1 The LORD spoke to Moses, saying, 2 Speak to the children of Israel and say to them, "When you have entered the land of your dwellings, which I have given you, you shall make a fire offering to the LORD, a burnt offering or

a sacrifice to fulfill a vow, or a free sacrifice, 3 you shall make a fire-offering to the LORD, a burnt-offering or a sacrifice to fulfill a vow, or a free offering, or in your banquets, to render to the LORD a sweet fragrance of the heart or of the flock. 4 He who offers his offering to the LORD, bring a food offering of a tenth part of a fine bloom, mixed with the fourth part of a hin of oil. 5 You shall also prepare the fourth part of a hin of wine to sprinkle on a blade, in- tended for burning or any sacrifice. 6 For the ram you shall prepare two tenths of fine flour, mixed with the third part of a hin of wine. 7 And for the wine offering, you shall offer the third part of a hin of wine, as a sweet aroma to the LORD. 8 When you prepare a bull for a burning, or for a sacrifice to fulfill a vow, or for a peace offering to the LORD, 9 you shall offer with the bull a sacrifice of three-tenths of fine flour, mixed with half a hin of oil. 10 And you shall bring for the appetizer half a hin of wine, for an offering made by fire of a sweet aroma to the LORD. 11 Thus shall it be done for a bull, or for a ram, or for a lamb, or for a kid. 12 According to the name you prepare to offer, so you shall do to each one according to his name. 13 All who are born in the county shall do so, to offer to the LORD an offering made by fire of sweet savor. 14 And if a stranger shall settle with you, or whoev- er shall be among you in your generations, and shall wish to make an offering by fire of a sweet savor to the LORD, as you do, so shall he do. 15 One ordinance shall be for you of the congregation, and also for the stranger who dwells with you, one ordinance for all your generations: as you are, so shall the stranger be before the Lord. 16 One Lawe and one man- er shall serve both for you and for the stranger who sojourns with you." 17 The LORD spoke to Moses, saying, 18 Speak to the children of Is-rael and say to them, "When you have entered the land to which I will lead you, 19 when you eat of the bread of the land, you shall offer an offering to the LORD. 20 You shall offer a cake of the first harvest as a sacrifice; as the sacrifice of the barne, so you shall raise it up. 21 With the first part of your dowry you shall give the LORD a salvation offering for your generations. 22 If you have erred and have not observed all these commands that the LORD gave to Moses, 23 and all that the Lord commanded you by the hand of Moses, from the first day that the Lord commanded Mo- ses, and so on for your generations: 24 and if anything is committed through ignorance on the part of the congregation, all the members of the congregation shall give a bull as a burnt sacrifice, as a sweet homage to the Lord, with meat and alcohol added to it, according to the manner, and a kid goat as a sin offering. 25 And the priest shall make atonement for all the congregation of the children of Israel, and it shall be forgiven them, because it is igno- rance; and they shall bring their offering to the LORD for an offering made by fire, and their sin offering before the LORD for their ignorance. 26 Then shall be forgiven all the congregation of the children of Israel and the stranger dwelling among them, because all the people were in ignorance. 27 But if anyone sins in ignorance, he shall bring a year-old kid as a sin offering. 28 And the priest shall make atonement for the ignorant man, when he sins through ignorance before the LORD, to be reconciled to him; and it shall be forgiven him. 29 He who is born among the children of Israel and the stranger who dwells among them shall both have one lawe, who sins through ignorance. 30 But he who does evil presumptuously, whether born in the land or a stranger, blasphemes the LORD; therefore he shall be cut off from his people, 31 because he has despised the word of the LORD and has transgressed his commands; that person shall be cut off outright: his iniquity shall fall upon him. 32 While the children of Israel were in the wilderness, they found a man gathering sticks on the Sabbath day. 33 Those who found him gathering sticks brought him to Moses and Aaron and all the community, 34 and they put him in a state of war, because it had not been said what should be done with him. 35 Then the LORD said to Moses, "This man shall dye with death; and all the crowd shall stone him with stones without a host." 36 And all the congregation brought him out of the hostel, and stoned him with stones, and he died, as the LORD had commanded Moses. 37 The LORD spoke to Moses, saying, 38 Speak to the children of Israel and command them to make bangs on the edges of their garments throughout their generation and to put on the bangs of the edges a band of white silk. 39 You shall have the bangs so that, when you look at them, you may remember all the commands of the LORD and put them into practice, and so that you may not look according to your heart or according to your eyes, which are the ones that cause you to lose your minds; 40 that you may remember and put into practice all my commands and be holy to your God. 41 I am the LORD your God, who brought you out of the land of Egypt to be your God: I am the LORD your God.

CHAPTER 16

1 And Korah the son of Izhar, the son of Ko- hath the son of Leui, separated himself from Dathan, and from Abiram the son of Eliab, and from On the son of Peleth, the sons of Reuben: 2 And there arose against Moses, with some of the sons of Israel, two hundred and fifty captains of assembly, famous in the congregation, and men of rank, 3 who gathered themselves together against Moses and against Aaron and said to them, "You take too much upon yourselves, seeing that the whole congregation is holy, every one of them, and that the Lord is in their midst; why therefore do you rise up against the congregation of the Lord?" 4 But when Moses heard this, he fell on his face, 5 And he spoke to Korah and to all his company, saying, "In Morow the LORD will show who is his, and who is holy, and who is to draw near to him; and whom he hath chosen, he will cause to draw near to him. 6 Take therefore censers, both Korah and all his company, 7 Put fire in them, and put incense before the LORD, to die in them; and the man whom the LORD shall choose shall be holy; ye take too much upon you, ye sons of Leui." 8 Then Moses said to Korah, "Take heed, I pray you, sons of Leui. 9 Does it seem to you a small thing that the God of Israel separat- ed you from the multitude of Israel to take you here near Himself, to do the service of the Tabernacle of the LORD, to stand before the congregation, and to minister? 10 Has he also taken to himself you and all your breth- ren, the sons of Leui, with you, and does he also see you in the office of priest? 11 There- fore you and all your company are gathered together against the LORD; and what is Aar- on, that you should murmur against him?" 12 Moses sent for Dathan and Abiram, sons of Eliab, who answered, "We will not come." 13 Is it a small thing that you have brought Vs. out of a land flowing with milk and honey to kill him in the wilderness, if you do not make yourself lord and master of Vs. country also? 14 Moreover, you have not brought vs. into a land flowing with milk and honey, and you have not given vs. inheritance of fields and vineyards; will you gouge out the eyes of these men? We will not come." 15 Then Moses was very angry and said to the LORD, "Pay no heed to their offenses: I have not taken a single crumb from them, nor have I harmed any of them." 16 Moses said to Korah, "Be you and all your company before the LORD: you and them and Aaron to die: 17 Take each one his censer, put incense in it, and bring each one his censer before the LORD, two hundred and fifty censers: you and Aaron, each one his censer. 18 So they each took his censer, and put fire in it, and deposited incense in it, and stood in the hall of the tent of meeting with Moses and Aaron. 19 Korah gathered the whole crowd against them to the threshold of the tent of meeting; then the glory of the LORD appeared to the whole congregation. 20 The LORD spoke to Moses and Aaron, say- ing, 21 "Separate yourselves from this com- munity, that I may consume them at once." 22 They fell on their faces and said, "O God, God of the spirits and of all flesh, has not one man sinned, and will you be severe with the whole congregation?" 23 Then the Lord spoke to Moses, saying. 24 Speak to the congrega- tion and say, "Get away from the tabernacle of Korah, Dathan and Abiram." 25 Then Mo- ses got up and went to Dathan and Abiram, and the elders of Israel followed him. 26 Then he spoke to the congregation, saying, "Please turn away from the tents of these wicked men and touch nothing of them, lest they perish in all their sins." 27 So they took them away from the Tabernacle of Korah, Dathan and Abiram on either side; Dathan and Abiram went out and stood in the area of their tents with their wives, their children and their sons. 28 Moses said, "So you will know that the LORD has sent me to do all these works, because I did not do them on my own initia- tive. 29 If these men die the death common to all men, or if they are visited like all men, the LORD has not sent me. 30 But if the LORD will do a new thing, and the earth will open its mouth and swallow them up with all that they have, and they will descend quickly into the pit, then you will understand that these men have defied the LORD. 31 And as he had finished speaking all these words, behold, the earth split beneath them, 32 and the earth opened its mouth and swallowed them up, with their families, with all the men who were with Korah, and with all their possessions. 33 They and all that they possessed went down into the pit, and the earth seized them; so they disappeared from the community. 34 At their cry, all Israel around them fled, saying, "Flee, lest the earth overwhelm you." 35 But out of the LORD came a fire that consumed the two hundred and fifty men who were of- fering incense. 36 The LORD spoke to Moses, saying, 37 Speak to Eleazar the son of Aaron the priest, that he may take the censers from the fire and scatter the fire beyond the altar, for they are set on fire, 38 the censers, I say, of these sinners who have destroyed themselves; and let them make stock dishes of them for the covering of the altar; for they have offered them before the LORD, they shall be holy, and shall be a sign to the children of Israel." 39 Then Eleazar the priest took the copper censers that had been burned and made stock dishes of them for the covering of the altar. 40 It is a reminder to the children of Israel that no foreigner, who is not of the descendants of Aaron, should come here to offer incense before the LORD, lest he be like Korah and his company, as the LORD told him by the hand of Moses. 41 But the next day all the multitude of the children of Israel murmured against Moses and against Aaron, saying, "You have killed the people of the LORD." 42 When the congregation had gathered against Moses and against Aaron, they turned their faces toward the tent of the congregation; and be- hold, the cloud enveloped it, and the glory of the LORD appeared. 43 Then Moses and Aar- on stood before the Tabernacle of Meeting. 44 The Lord spoke to Moses, saying, 45 "Get out of this community, for I will

quickly consume them." 46 And Moses said to Aaron, "Take the censer and put the fire of the altar on it, and put the incense on it, and go quickly to the congregation and make an atonement for them, for there is the wrath of the LORD, and the plague has begun." 47 Then Aaron did as Moses had commanded him and ran into the midst of the congregation; and behold, the plague had begun among the people; and he put incense and made atonement for the people. 48 And when he stood among the dead and the rest, the plague was stopped. 49 So four thousand and seven hundred died of this plague, besides those who had died in Korah's conspiracy. 50 Then Aaron went again to Mo- ses before the porch of the tent of meeting, and the plague was stopped.

CHAPTER 17

1 The LORD spoke to Moses and said 2 Speak to the children of Israel, and take from each one of them a rod, according to the house of their fathers, of all their princes according to the family of their fathers, that is, two rods; and you shall write the name of each one on his rod. 3 And thou shalt write the name of Aaron on the rod of Leui, for each rod shall be the head of the house of their fathers. 4 And you shall put them in the Tabernacle of Meeting, before the Ark of Testimony, where I will declare myself to you. 5 The rod of the man, whom I choose, shall flourish; and I will cause to cease from me the grudges of the children of Israel, who have complained against you." 6 Then Moses spoke to the chil- dren of Israel, and all their princes gave him a rod, one rod for each prince, according to the houses of their fathers, that is, two rods, and Aaron's rod was among their rods. 7 Mo- ses set the rods before the LORD in the tent of testimony. 8 And when Moses went into the Tabernacle of Testimony the next day, behold, Aaron's rod for the house of Leui had sprout- ed, had caused it to blossom, and had brought forth ripe almonds. 9 And Moses brought all the rods before the LORD to all the children of Israel; and they observed them and took each one his rod. 10 Then the LORD said to Moses, "Bring Aaron's rod again before the Testimony, that it may be kept as a sign for the rebellious children, and you shall cause their murmuring to cease from me, that they may not be dyed." 11 Moses did as the LORD com- manded him, and so he did. 12 The children of Israel spoke to Moses, saying, "Behold, we are dead, we perish, we are all lost: 13 Who- ever approaches the Tabernacle of the LORD or comes out of it shall die; shall we be con- sumed and die?

CHAPTER 18

1 The LORD said to Aaron, "You and your sons and the house of your fathers with you shall bear the iniquity of the sanctuary; you and your sons with you shall bear the iniquity of your priestly office. 2 Lead with you also your brethren of the tribe of Leui, of your father's household, who shall be joined to you and minister to you; but you and your sons with you shall minister before the Tabernacle of the Testimony: 3 They shall look after your charge and the whole Tabernacle, but they shall not come near the instruments of the Sanctuary or the altar, lest they and you die: 4 They shall be joined to you, and shall take charge of the Tabernacle of the congregation for the whole Tabernacle service; and no stranger shall ap- proach you: 5 Therefore you shall keep the charge of the Sanctuary and

the charge of the altar; so that no more shall wrath fall upon the children of Israel. 6 For behold, I have taken your brethren, the Leuites, from among the children of Israel, who as your gift have been given to the LORD to do the service of the Tabernacle of meeting. 7 But you and your sons with you shall keep your office as priests for all that pertains to the altar and within the tent. 8 Then the LORD said to Aaron, "Be- hold, I have entrusted to you the custody of my offenses, of all the consecrated things of the children of Israel; to you I have entrusted them for the sake of the ancestors, and to your sons, for an everlasting ordinance. 9 This shall be your offering of the most holy things, tak- en out of the fire: all their offering of all their food offenses, all their offenses for sin, and all their offenses for guilt, which they shall bring to me, shall be most holy to you and to your children. 10 In the most holy place you shall eat it; every male shall eat of it; it is holy for you. 11 This also shall be thine: the offering of their gift, with all the shake-offerings of the children of Israel: I have given it to thee, and to thy sons and thy daughters with thee, to make it a duet for ever, and all the pure ones of thy house shall eat of it. 12 All the fat of the oil, and all the fat of the wine, and of the wheat, which they shall offer to the LORD as first fruits, I have given them to thee. 13 The first ripening of all that is in their land, which they shall bring to the LORD, shall be thine; all the pure of thy house shall eat thereof. 14 Everything separate from the common life in Israel shall be yours. 15 Everything that opens first the array of any meat that they shall offer to the LORD, whether of man or of animal, shall be thine; but the first born of man shalt thou redeem, and the first born of the wild animal shalt thou redeem. 16 And those that are to be redeemed, thou shalt redeem them from the age of one month, according to thy estimation, for a money of five shekels, ac- cording to the shekel of the sanctuary, which is twenty-five gera. 17 But the first birth of a kid, the first birth of a sheep, or the first birth of a goat, you shall not redeem, for they are holy; you shall sprinkle their blood on the al- tar and bury their fat; it is a sacrifice made by fire for a sweet smell to the LORD. 18 Their flesh shall be yours, as the shaken breast and as the right shoulder. 19 All the spoils of the holy things which the children of Israel shall offer to the LORD, I have given to you, and to your sons and your daughters with you, to be a duet forever; it is a perpetual salt prize be- fore the LORD, for you and for your seed with you. 20 And the LORD said unto Aaron, Thou shalt have no inheritance in their land, nei- ther shalt thou have any portion among them: I am thy portion and thy inheritance among the children of Israel. 21 For behold, I have given the children of Leui all the tithe of Israel as an inheritance, for their service which they do in the tabernacle of the congregation. 22 And the children of Israel shall not come near the Tabernacle of Meeting any more, lest they incur sin and die. 23 But the Leuites shall do the service in the Tabernacle of the congrega- tion and incur their sin; it is a law forever, for your generations, that among the children of Israel they shall have no inheritance. 24 For the legumes of the children of Israel, which they shall offer as a sacrifice to the LORD, I have given the Leuites an inheritance; there- fore I said to them, "Among the children of Israel you shall have no inheritance." 25 The LORD spoke to Moses, saying, 26 Speak also to the Leuites and say to them, "When you take from the children of Israel the tithes that I have given you as an inheritance, you shall take an offering of them for the LORD, that is, the tenth part of the tithe. 27 Your offer- ing shall be reckoned for you as the horn of the stall or as the abundance of the store of wine. 28 So you shall also offer an offering to the LORD of all your tithes, which you shall receive from the children of Israel, and you shall give the LORD's offering of it to Aaron the priest. 29 You shall offer all your gifts to the tithes of the LORD; of all their fatness you shall offer the holy things. 30 Therefore you shall say to them, "When you have offered the fat of it, it shall be delivered to the Leuites, as the increase of the volume of the horn or as the increase of the wine. 31 You shall eat it in all places, you and your families, for it is your wages for your service in the tent of meeting. 32 And you shall not commit any sin because of it, when you have consumed its fruit; you shall not pollute the holy things of the chil- dren of Israel, lest you die.

CHAPTER 19

1 The LORD spoke to Moses and Aaron, say- ing. 2 This is the ordinance of the law which the LORD commanded, "Speak to the sons of Israel that they may bring you a red goat without blemish, without spot, on which the yoke has never been made. 3 You shall give it to Eleazar the priest, that he may take it out of the army and have it killed before him. 4 Then Eleazar the priest shall take her blood with his finger and sprinkle it before the Tabernacle of Meeting ten times, 5 And he shall burn it be- fore him; and he shall bury it with her skin, and her flesh, and her blood, and her blood. 6 Then the priest shall take cedar wood, hyssop, and lace of skins, and throw them into the midst of the fire where the cow burns. 7 Then the priest shall wash his clothes and wash his flesh in the water, and then he shall enter into the host, and the priest shall be vncleane vnto the euen. 8 Also he that burneth it shall wash his garments in the water, and shall wash his flesh in the water, and shall be vncleane unto the euen. 9 A clean man shall take the ashes of the burning and put them outside the host in a clean place, and shall keep them for the congregation of the children of Israel as water for sprinkling; it is a sinful offense. 10 There- fore whoever collects the king's ashes shall wash his clothes and be clean from them until then; and he shall be to the children of Israel and to the stranger dwelling among them, a statute for eternity. 11 Whosoever toucheth the dead body of a man shall be vncleaued for seven days. 12 He shall purify himself with it on the third day, and on the tenth day he shall be clean; but if he does not purify himself on the third day, he shall not be clean on the tenth day. 13 Whoever touches the body of a dead man and does not purify himself shall defile the Tabernacle of the LORD; that per- son shall be removed from Israel, because the water of sprinkling has not been sprinkled on him; he shall be vncleared, and his vnclean- ness shall still remain on him. 14 This is the law: if a man dies in a tent, everything that enters the tent and everything that is in the tent must be sprinkled for ten days, 15 and all open vessels, which have no fixed covering, shall be vncleaned. 16 Also whoever touches one slain with a sword in the field, or a dead person, or a bone of a dead person, or a grave, shall be vncleane seuen dayes. 17 Therefore for a vncleane person the burnt ashes of the offense shall be taken, and pure water shall be put therein in a vessel. 18 And a clean person shall take hyssop, and dip it in the water, and sprinkle it on the tent, and on all the utensils, and on the people therein, and on him that touched the bone, the slaying, the dead, or the grave. 19 And the clean person shall sprinkle himself on the vnclean on the third day and on the seventh day, and he shall cleanse him- self on the seventh day, and wash his clothes, and wash himself in water, and at the end he shall be clean. 20 But the man who is vnclean and does not purify himself shall be removed from the congregation, because he has defiled the sanctuary of the LORD, and the water of sprinkling has not been sprinkled upon him; therefore he shall be vnclean. 21 And it shall be a perpetual law for them: he who sprinkles the water of sprinkling shall wash his clothes; also he who touches the water of sprinkling shall be vnclean to this day. 22 And that which the vncleane person touches shall be vncleane; and he who touches it shall be vn- cleane to the end.

CHAPTER 20

1 The children of Israel came with the whole congregation into the wilderness of Zin, the first month, and the people stopped at Cades, where Miriam died and was buried. 2 But there was no water for the congregation, and they rallied against Moses and against Aaron. 3 The people argued with Moses and spoke, saying, "I wish we were dead, when our brothers are dead before the Lord. 4 Why have you thus brought the congregation of the LORD into his wilderness, that we and our cattle might die there? 5 Why have you now brought from Egypt to bring us to this mis- erable place, which is no place of seed, nor of fig trees, nor of vines, nor of pomegranates? There is not even water to drink." 6 Then Mo- ses and Aaron went out of the assembly to the threshold of the Tabernacle of Meeting and fell on their faces; and the glory of the LORD appeared to them. 7 The Lord spoke to Moses, saying, 8 Take the rod, and assemble you and your brother Aaron and the congregation, and speak to the rod before their eyes, and it shall give its water, and you shall bring them water from the rod; so you shall give the con- gregation and their beasts to drink." 9 Then Moses took the rod from before the LORD, as he had commanded him. 10 Moses and Aaron gathered the congregation before the rod, and Moses said to them, "Listen now, rebels, shall we bring you water from this rod? 11 Then Moses lifted up his hand and struck the rocke twice with the rod, and water came out abun- dantly; so the community and their beasts went out. 12 Then the LORD said to Moses and Aaron, "Because you have not listened to me to sanctify me in the presence of the children of Israel, you shall not bring this communi- ty into the land I have given them." 13 This is the water of Meriba, because the children of Israel have joined themselves to the LORD and he has been sanctified in them." 14 Then Moses sent messengers from Kadesh to the king of Edom, saying, "Thus says your broth- er Israel: You know all the hardships we have had, 15 How our fathers went down to Egypt, and we lived a long time in Egypt, where the Egyptians treated our fathers badly. 16 But when we cried out to the LORD, he heard our voice, and sent an angel, and brought us out of Egypt; and behold, we are in the city of Kadesh, at your uttermost border. 17 I pray thee, let us pass through thy land; we shall not pass through the fields, nor through the vineyards, nor shall we drink the water of the wells; we shall go the way of kings, and turn not to the right hand nor to the left, until we have passed over thy borders." 18 And Edom answered him, "You shall not pass by me, un- less I go out against you with the sword." 19 Then the children of Israel said to him, "We will go by the way here; and if I and my cattle drink of your water, I will pay for it: I will only pass over (without any effort) on my feet." 20 He answered again, "Thou shalt not pass by." Edom went out against him with many people and with great power. 21 So Edom denied Is- rael passage through his land; therefore

Israel turned away from him. 22 When the children of Israel and the whole community depart- ed from Kadesh, they came to Mount Hor. 23 And the LORD spoke to Moses and Aaron on Mount Hor, near the shore of the land of Edom, and said, 24 Aaron will be gathered to his people, because he will not enter the land which I have granted to the children of Israel, because you disobeyed my command at the waters of Meriba. 25 Take Aaron and Elea- zar his son and lead them to Mount Hor, 26 cause Aaron to take off his garments and put them on Eleazar his son, for Aaron shall be gathered to his fathers and shall die there." 27 And Moses did as the LORD had commanded him, and the two of them went up to Mount Hor, before the eyes of the whole community. 28 Moses stripped off Aaron's clothes and put them on Eleazar, his son; so Aaron died there on the top of the mountain; Moses and Elea- zar came down from the mountain. 29 When the whole community heard that Aaron had died, the whole house of Israel wept for Aaron for three days.

CHAPTER 21

1 When King Arad, the Canaanite, who dwelt toward the south, heard that Israel had come by the way of spies, he fought against Israel and drew spies from them. 2 Then Israel made a vow to the LORD and said, "If you will de- liver me and give this people into my hands, I will destroy their cities." 3 And the LORD heard Israel's vow and delivered the Canaan- ites to them; and they utterly destroyed them and their cities and called the place Hormah. 4 Then they departed from Mount Hor, by the way of the Red Sea, to pass through the land of Edom; and the people were greatly dis- tressed because of the way. 5 And the people spoke against God and against Moses, saying, "For what reason have you brought us out of Egypt to go and die in the wilderness? For there is neither bread nor water here, and our soul feeds on this light bread." 6 Therefore the LORD sent fierce serpents among the people that stung them, so that many of the people of Israel died. 7 Therefore the people came to Moses and said, "We have sinned, because we have spoken against the LORD and against you; pray to the LORD that he will turn the serpents away from us." 8 And the LORD said to Moses, "Make yourself a fiery serpent and set it up as a sign, so that as many as have been bitten may look on it and go to sleep." 9 Moses therefore made a serpent of reeds and set it up as a sign; and when a serpent had bitten a man, he looked on the serpent of reeds and died. 10 And the children of Israel departed from there and encamped at Oboth. 11 They departed from Oboth and encamped at Lie-Abarim, in the wilderness that is oppo- site Moab on the east. 12 They departed from there and encamped on the shore of Zared. 13 Then they departed and camped on the other side of the Arnon, which is in the wil- derness and which comes out of the shores of the Amorites (for the Arnon is the border of Moab, between the Moabites and the Amor- ites). 14 Therefore in the book of the battles of the LORD it shall be told what he did in the Red Sea and in the banks of the Arnon, 15 And in the part of the river that goes down to the dwelling place of Ar, which is on the borders of Moab. 16 From there they went to Beer, the well where the LORD said to Moses, "Gath- er the people, and I will give them water." 17 Then Israel sang this song, "Arise at the well, sing to it." 18 And the princes dug this well, and the captains of the people dug it, and also the chiefs of the people, with their stalls. And from the wilderness they came

to Mattanah, 19 from Mattanah to Nahaliel, and from Na- haliel to Bamoth, 20 And from Bamoth, in the valley that is in the plain of Moab, to the top of Pisgah that looks toward Ieshimon. 21 Then Israel sent messengers to Sihon, king of the Amorites, saying, "Let me pass through the land." 22 "Let me pass through your land; we will not depart from the fields, nor from the vineyards, nor will we drink the waters of your wells; we will go by the way of kings, un- til we have passed through your land." 23 But Sihon did not give Israel permission to pass through his land, but Sihon gathered all his people and went out against Israel into the wilderness; then he came to Iahoz and fought against Israel. 24 But Israel defeated him with the edge of the sword and conquered his territory, from Arnon to Jabok, as far as the sons of Ammon, because the border of the sons of Ammon was strong. 25 Israel took all these cities and settled in all the towns of the Amorites in Heshbon and in all its villages. 26 For Heshbon was the city of Sihon, king of the Amorites, who had previously fought against the king of the Moabites and had wrested from his hand all his territory as far as Ar- non. 27 Therefore they that speak with a loud voice say, Come to Heshbon, build and repair the city of Sihon: 28 For a fire went out from Heshbon, and a flame from the city of Sihon, and consumed Ar of the Moabites and the lords of Bamoth in Arnon. 29 Woe unto thee, Moab: O people of Chemosh, thou hast been forsaken; he hath let his sons be pursued, and his daughters taken captive by Sihon king of the Amorites. 30 Their empire also is lost from Heshbon even to Dibon, and we have de- stroyed them as far as Nophah, which reaches as far as Medeba. 31 So Israel settled in the land of the Amorites. 32 And Moses sent to search out Iaazer; and they took the cities that belonged to it, and uprooted the Amor- ites that were there. 33 Then they turned and went toward Bashan; and Og, king of Bashan, went out against them, he and all his people, to fight at Edrei. 34 Then the LORD said to Moses, "Do not fear him, for I have delivered him into your hands, together with all his people and his country; you shall do to him as you did to Sihon, king of the Amorites, who dwelt in Heshbon." 35 So they struck him, his sons and all his people, until there was none left; so they conquered his land.

CHAPTER 22

1 Then the children of Israel set out and camped in the plain of Moab, on the other side of Iorden from Jericho. 2 Balak the son of Zippor related all that Israel had done to the Amorites. 3 The Moabites were very much afraid of the people, for they were many, and Moab was agitating against the children of Israel. 4 Therefore Moab said to the elders of Midian, "Now this multitude will lick all those around you, as an ox licks the grass of the fields." 5 Therefore he sent messengers to Balaam the son of Beor, at Pethor (which is by the shore of the sons of his people), to call him and say, "Behold, out of Egypt has come forth a people that travels over the face of the earth and has come against me. 6 Come therefore, I pray thee, and curse this people (for they are stronger than I), that I may smite them and bring them out of the land; for I know that he whom thou blessest is blessed, and he whom thou cursest shall be cursed." 7 The elders of Moab and the elders of Midian departed, having the reward of the riddle in their hands, and came to Balaam and report- ed to him the words of Balak. 8 The latter an- swered them, "Stay here this night, and I will give you an answer, as the LORD will tell me." So the princes

of Moab stayed with Balaam. 9 Then God came to Balaam and said to him, "What men are these with you?" 10 Balaam answered God, "Balak, son of Zippor, king of Moab, made me say, 11 "Behold, there is a people coming out of Egypt and wandering over the face of the earth; come now, curse them for my sake, that I may defeat them in battle and bring them out." 12 God said to Balaam, "Do not go with them and curse the people, for they are blessed." 13 Balaam rose up in the morning and said to you princes of Balak, "Return to your country, for the LORD has refused to give me permission to go with you." 14 Then the princes of Moab got up and went to Balak and said, "Balaam has refused to go with you." 15 But Balak again sent other princes, more honorable than they. 16 These came to Balaam and said to him, "Thus says Balak the son of Zippor: Please do not hold back from coming to me. 17 For I will pro- mote you to great honors and do what you tell me; come therefore, I pray you, and curse this people." 18 Balaam answered Balak's ser- vants, "If Balak would give me his house full of silver and gold, I could not go beyond the word of the LORD my God to do less or more. 19 But now, please stay here this night, that I may understand what more the LORD will say to me." 20 God came to Balaam by night and said to him, "If men come to call you, get up and go with them; but do only what I tell you." 21 Then Balaam rose early, saddled his plank, and went with the princes of Moab. 22 The wrath of God was kindled because he went; and the angel of the LORD stood in the way to thwart him, while he rode his horse and his two servants were with him. 23 When the donkey saw the angel of the LORD standing on the road and his sword drawn in his hand, the donkey turned away from the road and went into the fields, but Balaam struck the donkey to bring it back to the road. 24 Then the angel of the LORD stopped at a vineyard path, with a wall on one side and a wall on the other. 25 When the plank saw the angel of the LORD, she pushed herself against the wall and made Balaams' foil slam against the wall; so he struck her again. 26 Then the angel of the LORD went over and stood in a narrow place, where there was no way to turn, either to the right or to the left. 27 When the don- key saw the angel of the LORD, he lay down under Balaam; therefore Balaam became very angry and struck the donkey with a staff. 28 Then the LORD opened the mouth of the fe- male, who said to Balaam, "What have I done to you, that you should strike me three times? 29 And Balaam said to the ass, Why hast thou mocked me: I wish I had a sword in my hand, for now I would kill thee. 30 Then the donkey said to Balaam, "Am I not your don- key, on whom you have ridden from the first time until now? Have I ever dared to do this to you? Who answered, "No." 31 And the LORD opened Balaam's eyes, and he saw the angel of the LORD standing on the road with a drawn sword in his hand; then he bowed down and fell flat on his face. 32 And the angel of the LORD said to him, "Why have you now struck your plank three times? Behold, I have come out to thwart thee, for thy way is not straight before me." 33 But the plank said to me, and it turned away from me three times; otherwise, if it had not turned away from me, I would already have killed you and slain its alien. 34 Then Balaam said to the angel of the LORD, "I have sinned, for I did not know that you were on the road against me; now, if it displeas- es you, I will return home." 35 But the angel said to Balaam, "Go with the men; but what I tell you, you will tell." So Balaam went with the princes of Balak. 36 When Balak heard that Balaam had come, he went to meet him in a city of Moab, on the borders of Arnon, on the uttermost coast. 37 Then Balak said to Balaam, "Have I not come to call you? Why have you not come to me? Am I not able to promote you to honor? 38 Balaam answered Balak, "Behold, have I come to you, and can I say anything? The word that God puts in my mouth is what I will say." 39 So Balaam went with Balak and they came to the city of Hu- zoth. 40 Then Balak offered heifers and sheep and sent them to Balaam and the princes who were with him. 41 The next day Balak took Ba- laam and led him to the places of Baal, so that he could see most of the people.

CHAPTER 23

1 Balaam said to Balak, "Build me ten altars here; prepare for me here ten bullocks and ten rams." 2 Balak did as Balaam had said, and Balak and Balaam offered on each altar a bull and a ram. 3 Then Balaam said to Bal- ak, "Stop by the burnt altar, and I will leave, if the LORD comes to meet me; and what he will show me, I will tell you." 4 God met Balaam, and Balaam said to him, "I have prepared sev- eral altars and offered on each altar a bull and a ram." 5 The LORD put an answer in Balaam's mouth and said to him, "Go to Balak again and tell him this." 6 When he returned to him, he stood by his burnt offering, he and all the princes of Moab. 7 Then he told his parable and said, "Balak, king of Moab, sent for me from Aram, from the mountains of the east, saying, 'Come, curse Iaakob because of me; come and detest Israel. 8 How could I curse, where God has not cursed? Or how could I de- test, where the LORD has not detested? 9 For from above the rocks I have seen it, and from the heights I have seen it; behold, the people shall dwell alone, and shall not be counted among the nations. 10 Who can tell the dust of Iaakob and the name of the fourth part of Israel? May I die as the righteous, and may my last end be as his." 11 Then Balak said to Balaam, "What have you done to me? I asked you to curse my enemies, and behold, you have blessed them all." 12 He answered, "Shall I not be careful to say what the LORD has put in my mouth?" 13 Balak said to him, "Come, please, with me to another place, where you will be able to see them, but you will see only most of them and not all of them; therefore curse them from that place because of me." 14 Then he led him to Sede-Sophim, on the top of Pisgah, and built seven altars and offered a bull and a ram on each altar. 15 Then he said to Balak, "Stay here by your altar, and I will meet the LORD there." 16 The LORD met Balaam, put an answer in his mouth, and said to him, "Go to Balak again and tell him this." 17 When he came to him, behold, he stood by his burnt offering and the princes of Moab with him; then Balak said to him, "What has the Lord said?" 18 He made his parable and said, "Arise, Balak, and listen; hear me, son of Zippor." 19 God is not like man that he should lie, nor like the son of man that he should repent; hath he said, and will he not do it; hath he spoken, and will he not perform it? 20 Behold, I have been commanded to bless, for he has blessed, and I cannot change. 21 He sees no iniquity in Iaakob, and he sees no transgression in Is- rael; the LORD his God is with him, and the glad voice of a king is in their midst. 22 God brought them out of Egypt; their strength is like a vnicorne. 23 For there is no witchcraft in Iaakob, nor riddles in Israel; until now it shall be said of Iaakob and Israel, "What hath God done?" 24 Behold, the people shall rise up like a lion, and rise up like a long lion; they shall not lie down until they have eaten of the prayer, and until they have drunk the blood of the slain." 25 Then Balak said to Balaam, "Do not curse them or bless them at all." 26 But Balaam, answering, said to Balak, "Did

I not say to you, 'Whatever the Lord says, I must do'?" 27 Then Balak said to Balaam, "Come, I pray thee, I will lead thee to another place, if it please God, that thou mayest curse them for my sake." 28 So Balak led Balaam to the top of Peor, which looks toward Ieshmon. 29 Then Balaam said to Balak, "Build me ten altars here, prepare for me here ten heifers and ten branches." 30 Balak did as Balaam had said and offered a bull and a ram on each altar.

CHAPTER 24

1 When Balaam saw that it pleased the LORD to bless Israel, he no longer went, as at other times, to make diuinations, but went into the wilderness. 2 Balaam lifted up his eyes and looked at Israel, who dwelt according to his tribes, and the Spirit of God came upon him. 3 Then he told his parable and said, "Balaam the son of Beor said, and the man whose eyes were closed said." 4 Said he who heard the words of God and saw the vision of the Al- mighty and, falling into a snare, his eyes were opened: 5 How beautiful are your tents, O Iaakob, and your dwellings, O Israel! 6 As the valleys are spread out, as the gardens by the riverside, as the aloes trees which the LORD has planted, as the cedars beside the waters . 7 Water falls from his bucket, and his seed shall be in many waters, and his king shall be stronger than Agag, and his kingdom shall be exalted. 8 God has brought him out of Egypt; his strength will be like a vnorne; he will devour his enemy nations, he will bruise their bones and pierce them with his arrows. 9 He will crouch down and lie down like a lion and like a lion; who will make him falter? Blessed is he who blesses you, and cursed is he who curses you." 10 Then Balak was very angry with Balaam and struck his hands; so Balak said to Balaam, "I sent for you to curse my enemies, and behold, now you have blessed them three times. 11 Therefore now flee to your place: I thought to promote you to hon- or, but the LORD has kept you from honor." 12 Then Balaam answered Balak, "Have I not also your messengers whom you sent me, say- ing, 13 If Balak gave me his house full of silver and gold, could I not pass the command of the LORD to do good or evil of my own mind? What the Lord shall say to me, I will say." 14 Now, behold, I go forth to my people; come, I will explain to you what this people will do to your people in the last days." 15 He expounded his parable and said, "Balaam the son of Beor said, and the man whose eyes were closed said." 16 He said who has heard the words of God, who has the knowledge of the Most High, who has seen the vision of the Almighty, and who, falling into a snare, has had his eyes opened: 17 I will see it, but not now; I will see it, but not later; a star of Iaakob will come, a scepter will rise from Israel, and it will strike the shores of Moab and destroy all the sons of Sheth. 18 Edom shall be possessed, and Seir shall be a possession to their enemies, but Is- rael shall behave valiantly. 19 The one who will have dominion will also be from Iaakob, and he will destroy the remnants of the city." 20 Then, looking at Amalek, he made his parable and said, "Amalek was the first of the nations, but his last end will be destroyed." 21 Then he looked at the Kenites, made his parable and said, "Strong is your dwelling place, and put your nest in the tower." 22 Neuerthelesse, the Kenite will be driven until Assur takes you away into captivity. 23 Then he told his par- able and said, "Alas, who will be lying when God does this? 24 The ships will also come from the shores of Chittim and will subdue Assur, and they will subdue Eber, and he

too will go into ruin." 25 Then Balaam arose and returned to his place, and Balak also went his way.

CHAPTER 25

1 While Israel was dwelling in Scytim, the people began to prostitute themselves with the daughters of Moab: 2 Who called the peo- ple to the sacrifice of their gods; the people ate and prostrated themselves to their gods. 3 Israel mated with Baal Peor, whereby the anger of the LORD was kindled against Is- rael: 4 The LORD said to Moses, "Take all the heads of the people and hang them up before the LORD against the sun, that the indigna- tion of the LORD's anger may be turned away from Israel." 5 Then Moses said to the judges of Israel, "Let each one kill his men who have betrayed Baal Peor." 6 And behold, one of the sons of Israel came and brought to his brothers a Midianite woman, before the eyes of Moses and all the congregation of the sons of Israel, who wept before the tabernacle of the congregation. 7 When Finehas the son of Eleazar the son of Aaron the priest noticed this, he rose up from the center of the com- munity and took a spear in his hand, 8 he followed the man of Israel into the tent and pierced them both: the man of Israel and the woman, through her womb; thus the plague ceased from the children of Israel. 9 In that plague four thousand and twenty thousand people died. 10 Then the LORD spoke to Mo- ses, saying, 11 Finehas the son of Eleazar, the son of Aaron the priest, turned away my wrath from the children of Israel, while he was zealous for my sake among them; there- fore I did not consume the children of Israel in my jealousy. 12 Therefore say to him, "Be- hold, I grant him my counsel of peace, 13 and he shall have it, and his seed after him, and he shall be the holder of the priestly office forever, because he was zealous for his God and made an atonement for the children of Israel. 14 The name of the Israelite thus slain, who was slain with the Midianite woman, was Zimri, son of Salu, prince of the family of the Simeonites. 15 The name of the Midianite woman slain was Cozbi, daughter of Zur, who was head of the people of her father's house in Midian. 16 Afterward the LORD spoke to Moses, saying. 17 "Challenge the Midianites and strike them: 18 For they trouble you with their wiles, by which they have deceived you concerning Peor and concerning their sister Cozbi, the daughter of a prince of Midian, who was slain in the day of the plague because of Peor."

CHAPTER 26

1 After the plague, the LORD spoke to Moses and Eleazar the son of Aaron the priest, say- ing, "Take the name of all the congregation of the children of Israel from twenty years old and upward, in all their paternal houses, ev- eryone who goes to war in Israel, 2 "Take the name of all the community of the children of Israel, from twenty years old and upward, in all their father's houses, all those who go to war in Israel." 3 Moses and Eleazar the priest spoke to them in the plain of Moab, from Iorden toward Jericho, saying 4 From the twentieth year of your age you shall appoint the people, as the LORD had commanded Moses and the children of Israel when they came out of the land of Egypt. 5 Reuben, the first born of Israel; the sons of Reuben were, Hanoch, from whom was born the family of the Hanochites, and from Pallu the family of the Palluites: 6 From Hesron, the family of the Hesronites; from Carmi, the family of the

Carmites. 7 These are the families of the Reubenites, which numbered three thousand and four hundred thousand, six hundred and thirty. 8 The sons of Pallu, Eliab: 9 And the sons of Eliab, Nemuel, Dathan, and Abiram; these Dathan and Abiram were famous in the congregation, and they came against Moses and against Aaron in the assembly of Korah, when they came against the LORD. 10 And the earth opened its mouth and swallowed them up together with Korah, when the congrega- tion died and the fire consumed two hundred and fifty men, who were a sign. 11 However, all the sons of Korah did not die. 12 The sons of Simeon, according to their families, were Nemuel, from whom came the family of the Nemuelites; Iamin, the family of the Iami- nites; Iachin, the family of the Iachinites: 13 Of Zerah, the family of the Zarhites; of Shaul, the family of the Shaulites. 14 These are the families of the Simeonites: two and twenty thousand and two hundred. 15 The sons of Gad, according to their families, were Zeph- on, from whom came the family of the Zephonites; Haggi, the family of the Hagg- ites; Shuni, the family of the Shunites: 16 of Ozni, the family of the Oznites; of Eri, the family of the Herites: 17 Of Arod, the family of the Arodites; of Areli, the family of the Are- lites. 18 These are the families of the children of Gad, according to their names: four thou- sand and five hundred. 19 The sons of Judah, Er and Onan; but Er and Onan died in the land of Canaan. 20 And the sons of Judah had their families: from Scelah was born the fam- ily of the Scelanites, from Pharez the family of the Pharzites, from Zerah the family of the Zarhites. 21 And the sons of Pharez were: of Hesron, the family of the Hesronites; of Ha- mul, the family of the Hamulites. 22 These are the families of Judah according to their names: six hundred thousand and five hun- dred. 23 And the sons of Issachar according to their families were: Tola, out of whom came the family of the Tolaites; Pua, the family of the Punites: 24 Of Iashub, the family of the Iashubites; of Shimron, the family of the Shimronites. 25 These are the families of Is- sachar, according to their names: sixty-four thousand and three hundred. 26 The sons of Zebulun, after their families: of Sered, the family of the Sardis; of Elon, the family of the Elonites; of Jahleel, the family of the Jahleelites. 27 These are the families of the Ze- bulonites, according to their names, three hundred thousand and five hundred. 28 The sons of Iosef, according to their families, were Manasseh and Ephraim. 29 And the sons of Manasseh were: from Machir, the family of the Machirites; Machir begat Gilead; from Gilead came the family of the Gileadites. 30 These are the sons of Gilead: by Jezer, the family of the Jezerites; by Helek, the family of the Helekites. 31 By Asriel, the family of the Asrielites; by Shechem, the family of the Shechemites. 32 From Shemida, the family of the Shemidaites; from Hepher, the family of the Hepherites. 33 Zelophehad the son of He- pher had no sons, but daughters; the daugh- ters of Zelophehad were called Mahlah, Noah, Hoglah, Milcah, and Tirzah. 34 These are the families of Manasseh and their number: two hundred fifty thousand and seven hundred. 35 These are the sons of Ephraim according to their families: from Shuthelah came the fam- ily of the Shuthalhites, from Becher the fami- ly of the Bachrites, from Tahan the family of the Tahanites. 36 These are the sons of Shuthelah: from Eran, the family of the Eran- ites. 37 These are the families of the sons of Ephraim by their names: two thousand and five hundred. These are the sons of Ioseph ac- cording to their families. 38 These are the sons of Benjamin according to their families: of Bela, the family of the Belaites; of Ashbel, the family of the Ashbelites; of Ahiram, the family of the Ahiramites: 39

from Shupham, the family of the Suphamites; from Hupham, the family of the Huphamites. 40 The sons of Bela were Ard and Naaman; from Ard was born the family of the Ardites, from Naaman the family of the Naamites. 41 These are the sons of Benjamin, according to their families and their names: five hundred and four thou- sand and six hundred. 42 These are the sons of Dan according to their families: from Shu- ham is the family of the Shuhamites; these are the families of Dan according to their families. 43 All the families of the Shuhamites were, according to their names, sixty-five thousand and four hundred. 44 And the sons of Asher, by their families, were: of Iimna, the family of the Iimnites; of Isui, the family of the Isuites; of Beriah, the family of the Beri- jites. 45 The sons of Beriah were: of Heber, the family of the Heberites; of Malchiel, the fam- ily of the Malchielites. 46 Asher's daughter's name was Sarah. 47 These are the families of the sons of Asher according to their names: three hundred fifty thousand and four hun- dred. 48 The sons of Naphtali, according to their families: of Jahzeel, the family of the Jahzeelites; of Juni, the family of the Gunites. 49 Of Jezer, the family of the Izrites; of Shil- lem, the family of the Shillemites. 50 These are the families of Naphtali, according to their houses and their names: five thousand four hundred and four hundred. 51 These are the names of the children of Israel: six hun- dred and a thousand, seven hundred and thirty. 52 The LORD spoke to Moses and said, 53 To these shall the land be devolved for an inheritance, according to the names of the names. 54 To many you shall give a greater in- heritance, and to a few a lesser inheritance; to each according to his name shall his inheri- tance be given. 55 However, the land shall be assigned by lot; according to the names of the tribes of their fathers they shall inherit: 56 Ac- cording to the lot, the possession shall be di- vided between the many and the few. 57 These also are the nobles of the Leuites, according to their families: from Gershon came the family of the Gershonites; from Kohath, the family of the Kohathites; from Merari, the family of the Merarites. 58 These are the families of Leui, the family of the Libnites, the family of the Hebronites, the family of the Mahlites, the family of the Mushites, the family of the Korhites; and Kohath begat Amram. 59 And Amram's wife's name was Jochebed, the daughter of Leui, who had been borne by Leui in Egypt; and she bore Amram Aaron, Moses, and Miriam their sister. 60 From Aaron were born Nadab, Abihu, Eleazar and Itamar. 61 Nadab and Abihu were dyed, because they of- fered strange fire before the LORD. 62 Their names were three thousand and twenty thou- sand, all males from a month old and upward; they were not named among the children of Israel, for there had been no inheritance for them among the children of Israel. 63 These are the names of Moses and Eleazar the priest, who made the nomenclator of the chil- dren of Israel in the plain of Moab, near Iorden, toward Jericho. 64 Among these were none of those whom Moses and Aaron the priest ennobled, when they visited the chil- dren of Israel in the wilderness of Sinai. 65 For the LORD said of them, "They shall die in the wilderness," not a single one was left but Caleb the son of Jephunneh and Ioshua the son of Nun.

CHAPTER 27

1 Then came the daughters of Zelophed, the son of Hepher, the son of Gilead, the son of Machir, the son of Manasseh, of the family of Manasseh, the son of Jeoseph (and the names of his daughters were these: Mahlah, Noah, Hoglah,

Milcah and Tirzah). 2 And he stood before Moses, and Eleazar the priest, and the princes, and all the assembly, at the threshold of the Tabernacle of Congregation, saying 3 Our father died in the wilderness and was not among those who gathered against the LORD in the company of Korah, but died in his sin and had no children. 4 For what rea- son should our father's name be taken from his family, because he had no children, and property should be given among our father's brothers." 5 Then Moses brought their case before the LORD. 6 The LORD spoke to Moses, saying, 7 The daughters of Zelophelehad have spoken well; you shall give them a possession to inherit among their father's brethren, and you shall restore to them their father's inher- itance. 8 Moreover you will speak to the chil- dren of Israel, saying, "If a man dies and has no children, you will return his inheritance to his daughter. 9 And if he has no daughter, you shall give his inheritance to his brothers. 10 And if he has no brothers, you shall give his inheritance to his father's brothers. 11 And if her father has no brothers, you shall give her inheritance to the next of kin of her family, and he shall possess it; and this shall be to the children of Israel a law of judgment, as the LORD commanded Moses. 12 Then the LORD said to Moses, "Go to this mountain of Abarim and see the land that I have granted to the children of Israel. 13 When you have seen it, you shall be gathered to your people, as Aaron your brother was gathered. 14 For you were disobedient to my word in the wilderness of Zin, during the contention of the assemblies, to sanctify me in the waters before their eyes. This is the water of Meriba at Kadesh in the desert of Zin. 15 Then Moses spoke to the LORD, saying, 16 Let the LORD, God of the spirits of all flesh, appoint a man from the congregation, 17 who may go out and come in before them, and lead them out and in, that the congregation of the LORD may not be like sheep that have no shepherd." 18 And the LORD said to Moses, "Take Ioshua the son of Nun, in whom is the Spirit, and put your hands on him, 19 and set him before Eleazar the priest and all the congregation, and give him a charge before them. 20 And give him your glory, that all the congregation of the children of Israel may obey. 21 And he shall stand before Eleazar the priest, and ask his counsel for the judgment of Vrim before the LORD; at his word they shall go out, and at his word they shall come in, he, all the children of Israel with him, and all the congregation. 22 And Moses did as the LORD had command- ed him, and took Ioshua and set him before Eleazar the priest and all the congregation. 23 Then he laid his hands on him and gave him an assignment, as the LORD had said by the hand of Moses.

CHAPTER 28

1 The LORD spoke to Moses, saying, 2 "Com- mand the children of Israel, and say to them, 'You shall abide to offer to me, in due season, my offering and my bread, for my sacrific- es made by fire, as a sweet aroma to me. 3 Moreover you shall say to them, "This is the burnt-offering you shall offer to the LORD: two lambs of a year without blemish, every day, as a continual sacrifice. 4 One lamb you shall prepare in the morning, the other you shall prepare at noon. 5 And the tenth part of an ephah of fine flour, as a food offering, mixed with the fourth part of a hin of beat- en oil. 6 This shall be a daily burnt offering, like that which was made on Mount Sinai for a sweet smell; it is a sacrifice made by fire to the LORD. 7 And his drink, the fourth part of a hin, for a lamb; in the holy place let the drink be made fruitful for the LORD. 8 And the oth- er lambe you shall

prepare at sunrise: as a morning food offering and as a wine offer- ing, you shall prepare it for an offering made by fire of sweet savor for the LORD. 9 But on the sabbath day you shall offer two lambs of a year old, without blemish, and two tithes of fine flour for the food offering mixed with oil and for its drink. 10 This is the roast of every Sabbath, besides the continual roast and its wine. 11 At the beginning of your months you shall offer a burnt offering to the LORD: two bullocks, one ram, and two lambs one year old, without blemish, 12 And three tithes of fine flour for a meat offering mixed with oil for a bullock, and two tithes of fine flour for a meat offering mixed with oil for a ram, 13 And a tithe of fine flour mixed with oil for a meat offering for a lamb, for a burnt herring of good odor; it is a herring made by fire for the LORD. 14 Their offering of wine to drink shall be half a hectoliter of wine for a bull- ock, the third part of a hectoliter for a ram, and the fourth part of a hectoliter for a lip; this is the burnt offering of every month, for all the months of the year. 15 A goat shall also be prepared for the sin offering to the LORD, in addition to the continuous burnt offering and the drink offering. 16 The fourteenth day of the first month is the Passing of the LORD. 17 And the fifteenth day of the same month is the Feast: for ten days leavened bread shall be eaten. 18 The first day shall be a holy convoca- tion, and you shall do no useful work on that day. 19 But you shall offer a sacrifice made by fire as a burnt offering to the LORD: two bull- ocks, a ram, and two yearling lambs; make them without blemish. 20 Their food offering shall be of fine flour mixed with oil; you shall prepare three tenths of a tithe for the heifer and two tenths of a tithe for the ram: 21 one tenth of a tithe you shall prepare for each lamb, even for the two lambs. 22 And one kid as a sin offering, to make atonement for you. 23 You shall prepare these, in addition to the morning burnt offering, which is a continual burnt offering. 24 In this way you shall pre- pare for all the seven days the keeping of the offering made by fire for a sweet fragrance for the LORD, beside the continual burnt offer- ing and the drinking offering. 25 On the tenth day you shall have a holy meeting, in which you shall do no servile work. 26 Also on the day of firstfruits, when you shall bring a new food offering to the LORD, according to your weeks, you shall have a holy exposition, in which you shall do no servile work: 27 But you shall offer a burnt offering as a sweet hom- age to the LORD: two bullocks, one ram, and ten lambs of one year old, 28 and their offal of fine flour mixed with oil, three tithes for a bull, two tithes for a ram, 29 and a tenth for each lamb, for all the seven lambs, 30 and one kid to make atonement for you: 31 (in addi- tion to the continual roasting and roasting of meat, you shall also do this): see that they are without blemish, with their roasts to drink.

CHAPTER 29

1 Moreover, on the first day of the seventh month you shall have a holy meeting, in which you shall do no useless work; it shall be a day for you to blow trumpets. 2 You shall make a burnt offering as a sweet homage to the LORD: one bullock, one ram, and ten lambs of one year old, without blemish. 3 Their vict- uals shall be of fine flour mixed with oil, three tenths for the bullock and two tenths for the ram, 4 and one tenth for a lamb, for the sev- en lambs, 5 and a kid goat as a sin offering, to make atonement for you, 6 besides your burnt-offering of the month, your continual burnt-offering, your food-offering, and your drink-offering,

according to their manner, for a sweet savor; it is a sacrifice made by fire for the LORD. 7 On the tenth day of the seventh month you shall have a holy convocation; you shall humble your souls and do no work on that day: 8 But you shall offer to the LORD a burnt offering as a sweet savor: a bull of a year, and a ram, and ten lambs of a year; make them without blemish. 9 Their food offering shall be of fine flour mixed with oil, three tithes of a tithe for a bull, and two tithes of a tithe for a ram, 10 one tithe of a tithe of a tithe for each lamb, for all the seven lambs, 11 one kid for the sin offering (in addition to the sin offering for atonement, the continu- ous burnt offering and the food offering) and their drink offerings. 12 On the fifteenth day of the seventh month you shall have a festive cohabitation; you shall do no useful work on that occasion, but you shall make a feast to the LORD for ten days. 13 You shall offer a burnt offering as a sacrifice of fire of good sa- vor to the LORD: thirteen heifers of one year old, two rams and four lambs of one year old; they shall be without blemish. 14 Their food offering shall be of fine flour mixed with oil, three tenths of marengos for each heifer of the thirteen heifers, two tenths of marengos for each of the two rams, 15 and one tenth dowry for each of the four lambs, 16 and one kid for the feast of sin, in addition to the con- tinuing feast of fire, the feast of meat and the feast of alcohol. 17 On the second day you shall offer two heifers, two rams, four lambs of a year without blemish, 18 with their portions of meat and their portions of wine for the heifers, for the rams, and for the lambs, according to their names, according to their disposition, 19 and a kid for the sin offering (in addition to the continual burnt offering and its food offering) and their wine offer- ings. 20 On the third day you shall also offer elephants, two rams and four lambs of a year without blemish, 21 with their meat offerings and their wine offerings, for the heifers, for the rams, and for the lambs, according to their names and dispositions, 22 and a goat as a sin offering, in addition to the continual burnt offering, its meal and its wine. 23 On the fourth day you shall offer ten bullocks, two rams, and four lambs of one year old without blemish. 24 Their portions of meat and their portions of wine, for the bullocks, for the rams, and for the lambs, according to their names, according to the regulations, 25 and a kid for the sin offering, in addition to the continual burnt offering, his food of- fering and his wine offering. 26 On the fifth day you shall also offer nine heifers, two rams and four lambs of a year without blemish, 27 their food and drink offering for the heifers, for the rams, and for the lambs, according to their names, according to their disposition, 28 and a goat as a sin offering, in addition to the continual burning, its oblation and drink offering. 29 On the sixth day you shall offer eight heifers, two rams, and four lambs of a year without blemish, 30 their food offer- ings and their wine offerings for the heifers, for the rams, and for the lambs, according to their names, according to their disposition, 31 and a goat for sin, besides the continual roast, its meat and drink. 32 On the seventh day you shall also offer two bulls, two rams, and four lambs of a year without blemish, 33 and their offering of food and drink for the heifers, for the rams, and for the lambs, according to their name, according to their manner, 34 and a kid goat as a sin offering, in addition to the continual burning, his food offering, and his wine offering. 35 On the eighth day you shall have a solemn assembly, in which you shall do no useful work, 36 but you shall offer a burnt offering, a sacrifice made by fire for a sweet smell to the LORD: one bull, one ram, and two lambs of a year without blemish, 37 their portions of meat and their portions of wine for the bull, for the ram, and for the lambs, according to their names, according to their disposition, 38 and a goat as a sin offering, besides the continual burnt sacrifice, his meal and his wine. 39 These things you shall do to the LORD in your banquets, besides your vows and your free offerings, for your burnt offerings, for your food offerings, for your drink offerings, and for your peace offerings.

CHAPTER 30

1 Then Moses spoke to the children of Isra- el according to all that the LORD had com- manded him, 2 Moses also spoke to the leaders of the tribes concerning the children of Israel, saying, "This is what the LORD has commanded, 3 Whoever makes a vow to the LORD or swears to another to bind himself with a bond, he shall not fail in his promise, but shall do all that comes out of his mouth. 4 If a woman also makes a vow to the LORD and binds herself with a bond, being in the house of her fathers, in the time of her youth, 5 and her father hears her vow and the bond by which she is bound, and her father is quiet toward her, then all her vows shall stand, and every bond by which she is bound shall stand. 6 But if her father disowns her on the very day that he hears all her vows and the bonds by which she has bound herself, they will be worthless, and the LORD will forgive her be- cause her father has disowned her. 7 If she has a husband when she makes a vow or utters an action with her lips, by which she binds her- self, 8 if her husband has listened to it and has not opposed her, on the very day that she has listened to it, her vow shall stand, and the bonds by which she has bound herself shall remain in force. 9 But if her husband disowns her on the same day that she hears it, then the vow which she made, and that which she ut- tered with her lips, by which she bound her- self, shall be void; and the LORD shall forgive her. 10 But all the vows of a widow and a di- vorcee (with which she has bound herself) will remain valid for her. 11 If she has made a vow in her husband's house, or if she has bound herself closely to another, 12 and her husband has listened to her and kept quiet about her and not disowned her, then all her vows shall remain valid and every bond by which she has bound herself shall remain in force. 13 But if her husband has disowned them, then on the very day that she has heard them, nothing that has gone forth from her lips concerning her vows or her bonds shall remain in force, because her husband has disowned them; and the Lord will forgive her. 14 So every vow and every other bond made to humble the soul may be kept by the husband or broken by the husband. 15 But if the husband keeps peace over her from day to day, then he keeps all her vows and all her bonds that she has made; he has confirmed them because he kept peace over her the same day he heard them. 16 But if she break them after she hears them, then she will take upon herself her iniquity. (Num- bers:) These are the commands that the Lord gave Moses, between a man and his wife, and between the father and his daughter, who is young in her father's house.

CHAPTER 31

1 The LORD spoke to Moses, saying, 2 "De- liver the children of Israel from the Midian- ites, and afterward you shall be gathered to your people." 3 Moses spoke to the people, saying, "Enlist some of you for war and have them go against Midian, to execute the Lord's vengeance against

Midian." 4 A thousand from every tribe, from all the tribes of Isra- el, shall be sent out to war." 5 So there were taken from the thousands of Israel two thou- sand men prepared for war, one thousand from each tribe. 6 And Moses sent them to war, a thousand of each tribe, and sent them with Finehas the son of Eleazar the priest, to war; and the sacred instruments, that is, the trumpets to sound, were in his hands. 7 They made war against Midian, as the LORD had commanded Moses, and they took out all the males. 8 They also took out the kings of Midi- an, of those who were slain: Eui, Rekem, Zur, Hur and Reba, five kings of Midian, and they killed Balaam the son of Beor with the sword: 9 But the children of Israel took the women of Midian and their sons captive, and set all their cattle and their flocks and their property on fire. 10 Then they set fire to all their cities and villages. 11 And they took possession of all the spoyle and all the prayers, both of men and of beasts. 12 Then they brought the cap- tives, what they had taken, and the spoyle to Moses, and to Eleazar the priest, and to the congregation of the children of Israel, to a playground in Moab, which was near Iorden, toward Jericho. 13 Then Moses, Eleazar the priest and all the princes of the community came out of the field to meet them. 14 Moses was angry with the captains of the army, with the captains of thousands and hundreds who came from war and battle. 15 Moses said to them, "What have you done with all the wom- en? 16 Behold, these have induced the chil- dren of Israel, with the counsel of Balaam, to commit guilt against the LORD, as in the case of Peor, and a plague has come of it among the congregation of the LORD. 17 Slay there- fore all the males among the children, and kill all the women who have known the man by carnal intercourse. 18 But all the childish women who have not known carnal copula- tion, keep them for yourselves. 19 You shall remain without the host for ten days, all those who have killed anyone and all those who have touched a dead person, and you shall purify yourselves and your captives on the third day and the seventh. 20 You shall also purify all your garments and all that is made of skins, all goat's work and all that is made of wood. 21 Eleazar the priest said to the men of war who were going to battle, "This is the ordinance of the law that the LORD gave to Moses, 22 con- cerning gold, torpedo, brassa, yron, tynne, and lead: 23 whatever can withstand the fire, you shall pass it through the fire and it shall be clean; however, it shall be cleansed with the water of purification; and whatever does not withstand the fire, you shall pass it through the water. 24 You shall also wash your gar- ments on the seventh day and be clean; then you shall enter into the Host." 25 The LORD spoke to Moses, saying, 26 "Take the sum of the delicacies that have been taken, both of people and of livestock, you and Eleazar the priest and the principal fathers of the com- munity. 27 And divide the prayer among the soldiers who went to war and all the commu- nity. 28 You shall take tribute for the LORD from the men of war who went out to fight: one person out of five hundred, either for peo- ple, or for bees, or for donkeys, or for sheep. 29 You shall take their half and give it to Elea- zar the priest as the LORD's offering. 30 But of the half of the children of Israel you shall take one, taken out of fifty, either of people, or of bees, or of donkeys, or of sheep, or of all the cattle; and you shall give it to the Leuites, who have charge of the tent of the LORD. 31 Moses and Eleazar the priest did as the LORD had commanded Moses. 32 And the spoil, that is, the remnant of the prey which the men of war had dispossessed, was six hundred six hun-dred six hundred and five thousand sheep, 33 and seventy-two thousand bees, 34 and three and twenty thousand donkeys,

35 and, in all, two million and thirty thousand, among whom were women who never lied. 36 The half, that is, the portion of those who went to war for the possession of cattle, was three hundred and thirty thousand five hundred. 37 The LORD's tribute for livestock was six hun- dred seventy thousand and fifty-five: 38 The bees were six hundred and thirty thousand, and the tribute of the LORD was seventy-two. 39 The donkeys were thirty thousand and five hundred, and the tribute of the LORD was three twenty and one: 40 And of people sixty thousand, for whom the LORD's tribute was two and thirty. 41 And Moses delivered the tribute of the Lord's offerings to Eleazar the priest, as the Lord had commanded Moses. 42 And of the half of the children of Israel, which Moses had taken from the men of war, 43 the half that belonged to the community was three hundred and thirty thousand head of cattle and five hundred head of cattle, 44 and six thousand and thirty thousand bees, 45 and thirty-three thousand donkeys and five hors- es 46 and six hundred thousand people.) 47 And Moses, I say, took from the half that was due to the children of Israel one piece out of fifty, both of people and of cattle, and deliv- ered them to the Leuites, who had charge of the Tabernacle of the LORD, as the LORD had commanded Moses. 48 Then the captains of the army, the captains of the thousands and the captains of the hundreds came to Moses: 49 And they said to Moses, "Your servants have taken the sum of the men of war who are under our authority, and not a single one is missing. 50 Therefore we have brought as a gift to the LORD what each one has found of gold jewelry, bracelets, gauntlets, rings, leather rings, and leg ornaments, to make atonement for our souls before the LORD." 51 Moses and Eleazar the priest took the gold and all the worked jewelry, 52 and all the gold of the offering that they offered to the LORD (of the captains of the thousands and of the hundreds) was six hundred thousand and one hundred and fifty shekels, 53 (for the men of war had arrayed themselves, every man for himself). 54 And Moses and Eleazar the priest took the gold of the captains from the thou- sands and the hundreds, and brought it into the tent of meeting, as a memorial of the chil- dren of Israel before the LORD.

CHAPTER 32

1 Now the sons of Reuben and the sons of Gad had a great number of cattle; and they saw the land of Jazer and the land of Gilead, which was a fit place for cattle. 2 Then the sons of Gad and the sons of Reuben came and spoke to Moses, and to Eleazar the priest, and to the princes of the congregation, say- ing 3 The land of Ataroth, of Dibon, of Jazer, of Nimra, of Heshbon, of Elealeh, of Shebam, of Nebo, and of Beon, 4 the county which the LORD destroyed before the congregation of Israel is a land fit for cattle, and your servants have cattle." 5 Therefore, they said, if we have obtained grace in your sight, give this land to your servants as property and do not take it out of Horde." 6 Moses said to the sons of Gad and the sons of Reuben, "Will your brothers go to war, and will you remain here? 7 Why do you now discourage the hearts of the chil- dren of Israel to go into the land which the LORD has given them? 8 So did your fathers when I sent them from Kadesh-Barnea to see the land. 9 For when they went as far as the riviera of Eshcol and saw the land, they dis- couraged the hearts of the children of Israel so that they would not enter the land which the LORD had given them. 10 On that same day the anger of the LORD was kindled, and he swore,

saying, "There is none of the men who made the journey into Israel, 11 None of the men who came out of Egypt from the age of twenty years and upward shall see the land by which I swore to Abraham, to Izhak, and to Iaakob, because they did not follow me entirely: 12 except Caleb the son of Jephun- neh, the Kenesite, and Ioshua the son of Nun, because they followed the LORD constantly." 13 And the LORD was very angry with Israel, and made them wander in the wilderness for forty years, until the whole generation that had done wrong in the sight of the LORD was consumed. 14 And behold, you have risen up in the steps of your fathers as an increase of sinful men, to increase still the fierce anger of the LORD toward Israel. 15 For if you turn away from following him, he will still leave the people in the wilderness, and you will de- stroy all these people." 16 They came to him and said, "We will build sheepfolds here for our sheep and for our cattle and cities for our children. 17 But we ourselves shall be ready to arm ourselves to go before the children of Israel, until we have led them to their place; but our children shall dwell in the defended cities, because of the inhabitants of the land. 18 We will not return to our homes until the children of Israel have inherited, each one his inheritance. 19 And we shall not inherit with them beyond Iorden and on that side, because our inheritance has fallen upon them on this side of Iorden, toward the east." 20 Moses said to them, "If you do this thing and go armed before the LORD to make war: 21 And you shall go every one of you in harness out of the border of the LORD, until he has driven his enemies out of his sight: 22 And until the land be subdued before the LORD, then ye shall return, and ye shall be innocent to the LORD and to Israel; and this land shall be your possession before the LORD. 23 But if ye do not so, behold, ye have sinned against the LORD, and be assured that your sin shall find you out. 24 Therefore build cities for your children and sheepfolds for your sheep, and do what you have said." 25 Then the sons of Gad and the sons of Reuben spoke to Moses, saying, "Your servants will do what my Lord has commanded: 26 Our sons, our wives, our sheep and all our cattle shall remain there in the cities of Gilead, 27 but your servants shall all go armed to fight before the LORD, as my LORD says." 28 So Moses commanded Elea- zar the priest, Ioshua the son of Nun, and the heads of the families of the tribes of the chil- dren of Israel: 29 Moses said to them, "If the sons of Gad and the sons of Reuben will come with you out of Iorden, all armed to fight before the LORD, when the land is subdued before you, you shall give the boy of Gilead into your possession: 30 But if they come not with you armed, they shall have their pos- sessions in the land of Canaan. 31 The sons of Gad and the sons of Reuben answered, "As the LORD has said to your servants, so shall we do also. 32 We will go armed before the LORD into the land of Canaan, that the possession of our inheritance may be beyond Iorden." 33 And Moses announced to them, to the sons of Gad, and to the sons of Reuben, and to half the tribe of Manasseh, the son of Jehoshaph, the kingdom of Sihon, king of the Amorites, and the kingdom of Og, king of Bashan, the land with its cities and its coasts, and the cities of the surrounding land. 34 The sons of Gad built Dibon, Ataroth and Aroer, 35 Atroth, Shophan, Iazer and Iogbehah, 36 Beth-Nimrah and Beth-Haran, defended cit- ies and also sheepfolds. 37 The sons of Reuben built Heshbon, Elealeh, and Kiriathaim, 38 Nebo, Baal-Meon, and changed their names to Shibma, and gave other names to the cities they built. 39 And the sons of Machir the son of Manasseh went to Gilead, and conquered it, and drove out the Amorites that dwelt there. 40 Then Moses gave Gilead to Machir the son of Manasseh, and he dwelt there. 41 Iair, son of Manasseh, took his towns and called them Hauoth Iair. 42 Nobah also took Kenath and its villages and called them No- bah, after his name.

CHAPTER 33

1 These are the journeys of the children of Is- rael who went out of the land of Egypt accord- ing to their groups, under the hand of Moses and Aaron. 2 And Moses wrote their going out according to their itineraries, according to the commandments of the LORD; these are the itineraries of their going out. 3 And they departed from Rameses on the first month, on the fifteenth day of the first month, the day after the Passover, and the children of Is- rael went out with outstretched hand before the eyes of all the Egyptians. 4 (For the Egyp- tians buried all their first bearers, whom the LORD had smitten in their midst; on their gods also the LORD executed). 5 The chil- dren of Israel departed from Rameses and encamped at Succoth. 6 They departed from Succoth and encamped at Etham, on the edge of the wilderness. 7 And they departed from Etham, and went again to Pi-Hahiroth, which is opposite Baal-Zephon, and encamp- ed before Migdol. 8 Then they departed from Hahiroth, crossed the middle of the sea, and went into the wilderness, made a journey of three days in the wilderness of Etham, and encamped at Marah. 9 Then they departed from Marah and came to Elim; in Elim there were two springs of water and seventy palm trees, and they camped there. 10 They depart- ed from Elim and camped by the Red Sea. 11 They departed from the Red Sea and camped in the wilderness of Sin. 12 They went out of the wilderness of Sin and pitched their tents at Dophkah. 13 They departed from Sophkah and stopped at Alush. 14 Then they departed from Alush and lay down in Rephidim, where there was no water for the people to drink. 15 They departed from Rephidim and camped in the wilderness of Sinai. 16 They departed from the wilderness of Sinai and encamped at Kibroth Hattaauah. 17 They departed from Kibroth Hattaauah and stopped at Hazeroth. 18 They departed from Hazeroth and en- camped at Rithmah. 19 They departed from Rithmah and encamped at Rimmon Parez. 20 They departed from Rimmon Parez and encamped at Libnah. 21 They departed from Libnah and encamped at Rissah. 22 They de- parted from Rissah and encamped at Kehe- latha. 23 They departed from Kehelatha and encamped on Mount Shapher. 24 They de- parted from Mount Shapher and encamped at Haradah. 25 They departed from Haradah and encamped at Makheloth. 26 They depart- ed from Makheloth and encamped at Tahath. 27 They departed from Tahath and encamp- ed at Tarah. 28 They departed from Tara and encamped in Mithkah. 29 They departed from Mithkah and encamped at Hashmonah. 30 They departed from Hashmonah and en- camped in Moseroth. 31 They departed from Moseroth and encamped in Bene-iaakan. 32 They departed from Bene-iaakan and stopped at Hor-Hagidgad. 33 They departed from Hor-Hagidgad and encamped at Iotbathah. 34 They departed from Iotbathah and stopped at Hebronah. 35 They departed from Hebro- nah and stopped at Ezion-Gaber. 36 They departed from Ezion-Gaber and encamped in the wilderness of Zin, which is Kadesh. 37 They departed from Kadesh and encamp- ed on Mount Hor, on the border of the land of Edom. 38 Aaron the priest went to Mount Hor at the command of the LORD, and there he died, in the fortieth year after the children of Israel came out of the land of Egypt, on the first day of the

fifth month. 39 Aaron was a hundred and three score years old when he died on Mount Hor. 40 And King Arad the Canaanite, who dwelt in the south of the land of Canaan, heard of the coming of the children of Israel). 41 They set out from Mount Hor and encamped at Zalmonah. 42 They depart- ed from Zalmonah and encamped at Punon. 43 They departed from Punon and encamped in Oboth. 44 They departed from Oboth and encamped at Iie-abarim, on the borders of Moab. 45 They departed from Iim and en- camped at Dibon-Gad. 46 They departed from Dibon-Gad and encamped in Almon-di- blathaim. 47 They departed from Almon-di- blathaim and encamped in the mountains of Abarim, before Nebo. 48 And they departed from the mountains of Abarim, and encamp- ed in the plain of Moab, by Iorden, toward Jericho. 49 They encamped near Iorden, from Bethieshimoth to Abel-Sittim, in the region of Moab. 50 The LORD spoke to Moses in the region of Moab, along Iorden, toward Jericho, saying, 51 Speak to the children of Israel and say to them, "When you have gone out from Iorden into the land of Canaan, 52 then you shall drive out all the inhabitants of the land in front of you, destroy all their images, break all their metal images, and throw down all their places of worship. 53 You shall possess the land and inhabit it, for I have given you the land to possess it. 54 And you shall receive the land by lot, according to your families: to the most you shall give more inheritance, to the least inheritance less. Where the lot shall fall to any, that shall be his; according to the tribes of your fathers ye shall inherit. 55 But if you will not get rid of the inhabitants of the land before you, those whom you let wander shall be pricks in your eyes, and thorns in your sides, and shall persecute you in the land where you dwell. 56 Moreover, it shall come to pass that I will do to you what I thought to do to them.

CHAPTER 34

1 The LORD spoke to Moses, saying, 2 "Com- mand the children of Israel and say to them, When you enter the land of Canaan, this is the land that shall be your inheritance, that is, the land of Canaan and its coasts. 3 Your southern quarter shall be from the wilderness of Zin to the borders of Edom, so that your southern quarter shall be from the coast of the Salt Sea eastward: 4 The border shall go with you from the south as far as Maaleh-akrabbim, and it shall reach Zin and go out from the south as far as Kadesh-barnea; thence it shall extend as far as Hazar-addar, and go on as far as Azmon. 5 And the border shall extend from Azmon to the border of Egypt, and it shall ex- tend to the sea. 6 Your western quarter shall be the great sea; therefore that border shall be your western coast. 7 This will be your north- ern quarter; you will draw your border from the great sea to Mount Hor. 8 From Mount Hor you will draw your border to Hamath, and the end of the border will be at Zedad. 9 The coast will extend to Ziphron and end at Hazar- enan; this will be your northern quarter. 10 Your eastern quarter will extend from Hazar-enan to Shefam. 11 The border will de- scend from Shepham to Riblah and from the east side of Ain; the same border will descend and go out from the sea side of Chinneereth to the east. 12 Moreover that border will go down to Iorden and stop at the salt sea. This shall be your land and its coasts all around." 13 Then Moses commanded the children of Israel, "This is the land that you will inherit by lot, which the LORD has commanded to be given to nine tribes and to half tribes. 14 For the tribe of the children of Reuben, ac- cording to the houses of their fathers, and the tribe of the children of Gad, according to the houses of their fathers, and half the tribe of Manasseh, have received their inheritance. 15 Two tribes and half a tribe received their in- heritance on this side of Iorden, toward Jer- icho, on the east. 16 Then the LORD spoke to Moses, saying, 17 These are the names of the men who will devolve the land to you: Eleazar the priest, and Joshua the son of Nun. 18 You shall also take one prince from each tribe to rule the land. 19 The names of the men also are these: Of the tribe of Judah, Caleb the son of Jephunneh. 20 For the tribe of the sons of Simeon, Shemuel the son of Ammihud. 21 Of the tribe of Benjamin, Elidad the son of Chis- lon. 22 Of the tribe of the sons of Dan, Prince Bukki the son of Jogli. 23 Of the sons of Iosef: of the tribe of the sons of Manasseh, Prince Hanniel the son of Ephod. 24 Of the tribe of the sons of Ephraim, Prince Kemuel the son of Shiphtan. 25 Of the tribe of the sons of Ze- bulun, Prince Elizaphan the son of Parnach. 26 Of the tribe of the sons of Issachar, Prince Paltiel, son of Azzan. 27 Of the tribe of the sons of Asher, Prince Ahihud the son of She- lomi. 28 Of the tribe of the sons of Naphtali, Prince Pedahel, son of Ammihud. 29 These are they to whom the LORD commanded to devolve the inheritance to the children of Is- rael in the land of Canaan.

CHAPTER 35

1 The LORD spoke to Moses in the plain of Moab, near Iorden, in the direction of Jericho, and said 2 Command the children of Israel to give the Leuites, as an inheritance, cities to inhabit; you shall also give the Leuites the suburbs of the cities around them. 3 So they shall have cities to inhabit, and their suburbs shall be for their livestock, for their substance, and for all their animals. 4 The suburbs of the cities which you shall give to the Leuites, from the walls of the city upward, shall be a thou- sand cubits round about. 5 You shall measure, on the outside of the city of the east side, two thousand cubits; of the south side, two thou- sand cubits; of the west side, two thousand cubits; of the north side, two thousand cu- bits; and the city shall be in the middle; this shall be the measure of the suburbs of their cities. 6 Of the cities which you shall give to the Leuites, there shall be six cities of refuge, which you shall establish so that those who kill may flee there; to these you shall add two more and four cities. 7 And the cities which you shall give to the Leuites shall be eight and fourteen; you shall give them with their sub- urbs. 8 As for the cities which you shall give to the children of Israel, of many you shall take more, and of a few you shall take less; each one shall give his cities to the Leuites, according to his inheritance, which he has inherited." 9 The LORD spoke to Moses, saying, 10 Speak to the children of Israel and say to them, "When you have come from Iorden into the land of Canaan, 11 you shall appoint for yourselves cities, which shall be cities of refuge for you, so that the slayer who kills a person vnwares that he may flee there. 12 These cities shall be for you a refuge from the slayer, that the slayer may not die until he stands before the congregation for judgment. 13 Of the cities you shall give, six cities shall serve as your refuge. 14 You shall appoint three on this side of Iorden, and three cities in the land of Ca- naan, which shall be cities of refuge. 15 These six cities shall be a refuge for the children of Israel, for the stranger and for those who dwell among you, so that anyone who kills anyone may flee there. 16 If anyone strikes another with an instrument of yron so that he may die, he is a murderer, and the murderer shall die. 17

Also if he strikes him with a stone, with which he may be killed, and he dies, he is a murderer, and the murderer shall die. 18 Or if he strikes him with a weapon of wood, with which he may be killed, and he dies, he is a murderer, and the murderer shall die. 19 The blood-bearer himself will kill the slayer; when he meets him, he will kill him. 20 But if he pushes him out of hatred, or if he hurls him- self at him out of expectation, he will die, 21 or if he strikes him with his hand out of enmity, causing him to die, he who struck him shall die in turn, for he is a murderer; the bearer of blood shall kill the murderer when he meets him. 22 But if he has struck him vnaduistical- ly and not out of hatred, or if he has thrown anything at him, without his laying down a wait, 23 or a stone (with which he might be killed) and did not kill him, or dropped it on him, and he died, and was not his enemy, nor sought him out, 24 then the congregation shall judge between the slayer and the bearer of blood according to these laws. 25 And the congregation shall deliver the slayer from the hand of the blood-bearer, and the congrega- tion shall bring him back to the city of his ref- uge, whither he had fled, and he shall remain there until the death of the priest, who shall be anointed with holy oil. 26 But if the slayer comes outside the boundaries of the city of his refuge, whither he had fled, 27 and the en- forcer of blood finds him outside the borders of the city of his refuge, and the enforcer of blood kills the slayer, he shall be killed, 28 for he would remain in the city of his refuge until the death of the priest; and after the death of the priest, the slayer shall return to the land of his own possession. 29 These things shall be an obligation of judgment for you throughout all your generations, in all your dwellings. 30 Whosoever shall slay any person, the judge shall slay the slayer, by witnesses; but a wit- ness shall not testify against a person that he may die. 31 Moreover you shall take no reward for the life of the murderer who is worthy to die, but he shall be put to death. 32 Moreover you shall take no recompense for him who has fled to the city of his refuge, that he may re- turn to dwell in the land, before the death of the priest. 33 So you shall not pollute the land in which you dwell, for blood defiles the land; and the land cannot be cleansed from the blood that has been shed in it, except by the blood of him who shed it. 34 Therefore do not defile the land in which you shall dwell, for I, the LORD, dwell in the midst of the children of Israel.

CHAPTER 36

1 Then the heads of the families of the sons of Gilead, and of the sons of Machir, and of the sons of Manasseh, and of the families of the sons of Ioseph, came and spoke before Moses and the princes, the heads of the sons of Is- rael, 2 And they said, "The LORD command- ed my lord to give the land as an inheritance by lot to the children of Israel; and the LORD commanded my lord to give the inheritance of Zelophelehad our brother to his daughters. 3 If they marry one of the sons of the other tribes of the children of Israel, their inher- itance shall be taken away from the inheri- tance of our fathers, and shall be assigned to the inheritance of the tribe to which they belong; so it shall be taken away from the lot of our inheritance. 4 Moreover, when the jubilee of the children of Israel comes, their inheritance shall be assigned to the inheri- tance of the tribe in which they are; so their inheritance shall be taken away from the in- heritance of the tribe of our fathers." 5 Then Moses commanded the children of Israel, according to the word of the LORD, saying, "The tribe of the sons of Ioseph

has spoken well." 6 This is what the LORD commanded concerning the daughters of Zelophah, say- ing, "They shall marry whomever they think best, only the family of their father's tribe." 7 Thus the inheritance of the children of Israel shall not pass from one tribe to another, for each of the children of Israel shall keep the inheritance of the tribe of his fathers. 8 Every daughter who possesses an inheritance from the tribes of the children of Israel shall take to wife one of the family of her father's tribe, so that the children of Israel may keep to each the inheritance of their fathers. 9 The inheri- tance shall not pass from one tribe to another, but each tribe of the children of Israel shall remain in its inheritance. 10 As the LORD had commanded Moses, so did the daughters of Zelophah. 11 For Mahlah, Tirzah, Hoglah, Milcah and Noah, the daughters of Zelophed, were married to the sons of their paternal brothers, 12 they were assigned to some of the families of the sons of Manasseh the son of Iosef; so their inheritance remained in the tribe of their father's family. 13 These are the commands and laws which the LORD com- manded by the hand of Moses to the children of Israel in the plain of Moab, from Iorden to- ward Jericho.

DEUTERONOMY

CHAPTER 1

1 These are the words that Moses spoke to all Israel, on this side of Iorden, in the wil- derness, in the plain, facing the Red Sea, between Paran and Tophel, Laban, Hazeroth and Di-zahab. 2 There are eleven days' jour- ney from Horeb to Kades-Barnea, by the road of Seir. 3 On the first day of the eleventh month, in the fortieth year, Moses spoke to the children of Israel according to what the LORD had commanded him, 4 After he had slain Sihon, king of the Amorites, who dwelt in Heshbon, and Og, king of Bashan, who dwelt in Ashtaroth, in Edrei. 5 On this side of Iorden, in the land of Moab, Moses began to declare this lawe, saying 6 The Lord our God spoke to Horeb, saying, "You have dwelt long on this mountain, 7 turn ye, and depart, and go to the mountain of the Amorites, and to all the places that are near, whether in the plain, or in the mountain, or in the valley: to the south, and on the side of the sea, to the land of the Canaanites, and to Lebanon, even to the great riuer, the riuer Perath. 8 Behold, I have set the land before you; go in and pos- sess the land which the LORD swore to your fathers, Abraham, Izhak and Iaakob, to give to them and to their descendants after them. 9 And at the same time I spoke to you, say- ing: 10 The LORD your God has multiplied you; and behold, you are today as the stars of Heauen in nombre: 11 (The LORD, the God of your fathers, makes you a thousand times more numerous than you are, and blesses you, as he has promised you). 12 How can I alone bear your burden, your load and your struggles? 13 Bring with you wise and in- telligent and known men from among your tribes, and I will make them leaders out of you." 14 Then you answered me and said, "It is good what you have commanded to be done." 15 Then I took the chiefs of your tribes, wise and competent men, and made them chiefs over you, captains over thousands, captains over hundreds, captains over fifties, captains over tens, and officers over your tribes. 16 At that same time, I appointed your judges to say, "Look after the disputes between your brothers, and judge justly between each one and his brother and the stranger who is with him. 17 You shall have no respect for persons in judgment, but you shall hear the small as well as the great; you shall not fear the face of man, for

judgment is of the gods; and the cause that is too difficult for you, bring it to me, and I will hear it. 18 At the same time I commanded you all the things that you should do. 19 Then we departed from Horeb and went through all that great and terrible wilderness (as you have seen) by the way of the mountain of the Amorites, as the LORD our God had commanded us; and we came to Kadesh-Barnea. 20 I said to you, "You have come to the mountain of the Amorites, which the LORD our God grants you." 21 Behold, the LORD your God has set the land before you; go and possess it, as the LORD God of your fa- thers has said to you; do not be afraid or dis- couraged." 22 Then all three of you came to me and said, "We will send men ahead of you to scout the land and to let you know which road we should take and which towns we should arrive at." 23 The thing pleased me, and I took two men of you from each tribe. 24 Who set out, went to the mountain, came to the river Eshcol, and made a search of the land. 25 And they took the fruits of the land in their hands and brought them as gifts, and brought back their words and said, "It is a good land that the LORD our God has given as a gift." 26 But you did not want to go there and were dis- obedient to the commands of the LORD your God, 27 you murmured in your tents and said, "Because the LORD hated Vs, that is why he brought Vs out of the land of Egypt, to deliver her into the hands of the Amorites and to de- stroy her." 28 Where shall we go? Our breth- ren have discouraged our hearts, saying, "The people are more numerous and higher than we are; the cities are great and walled up to the height of heaven; and moreover we have seen there the sons of the Anakim. 29 But I say to you, "Do not fear or be afraid of them." 30 The LORD your God, who goes before you, will fight for you, according to what he did to you in Egypt before your eyes, 31 and in the wilderness, where you saw how the LORD your God raised you up, as a man raises up his son, in all the way that you came to this place. 32 But for all this you did not listen to the LORD your God, 33 Who went the way before you, to seek you a place to pitch your tents, by night with fire, to show you the way to go, and by day with cloud." 34 The LORD heard your words, and he was angry and swore, 35 "There shall be no more of these men of this unwise generation to see the good land which I swore to give to your fathers." 36 but Caleb the son of Jephunneh shall see it, and to him I will give the land that he has trodden down, and to hissons, because he has followed the LORD con- stantly." 37 The LORD also was angry with me because of you, saying, "You also shall not en- ter that place." 38 but Ioshua the son of Nun, who stands before you, shall enter it; encour- age him, for he will cause Israel to inherit it. 39 Moreover, your sons, whom you said should be a prayer, and your children, who did not know good and evil in that day, shall go there, and to them I will give it, and they shall possess it. 40 But as for you, turn back and take your journey into the wilderness by the way of the Red Sea." 41 Then you answered and said to me, "We have sinned against the LORD; we will go and fight, according to all that the LORD our God has commanded us." 42 But the LORD said to me, "Say to them, 'Do not go and do not fight (for I am not among you), otherwise you will fall before your ene- mies.' 43 But when I told you, you would not listen, you rebelled against the Lord's com- mand, you were presumptuous and went up the mountain. 44 Then the Amorites who dwelt on that mountain came out against you, pursued you (as bees do) and destroyed you in Seir, as far as Hormah. 45 When you came again, you cried before the LORD, but the LORD would not hear your voices or bend his ears toward you. 46 You therefore remained in

Kadesh for a long time, according to the time you had stayed before.

CHAPTER 2

1 Then we turned and set out on our journey into the wilderness, along the way of the Red Sea, as the LORD had told me; and we skirt- ed Mount Seir for a long time. 2 The Lord spoke to me, saying, 3 You have traveled this mountain long enough; turn northward. 4 And he warned the people, saying, You shall pass through the territory of your brothers, the sons of Esau, who dwell in Seir, and they shall escape you; therefore be careful. 5 You shall not guilt them, for I will not give you of their territory even a foot's width, for I have given Mount Seir to Esau as property. 6 You shall buy food from them for money to eat, and you shall also get water for money to drink. 7 For the LORD your God has blessed you in all the works of your hand; he knows your way in this great wilderness; the LORD your God has been with you these forty years, and you have lacked nothing. 8 When we de- parted from our brethren, the sons of Esau, who dwelt in Seir, by the way of the plain, from Elath and Ezion-Gaber, we turned and went by the way of the wilderness of Moab. 9 Then the LORD said to me, "You must not visit Moab or provoke them to fight, for I will not give you their land as property, as I gave Ar to the sons of Lot as property." 10 Formerly the Emim, a people as numerous and as high as the Anakim, dwelt there. 11 They, too, were taken as ramblers like the Anakim, whom the Moabites call Emim. 12 The Horim also dwelt in Seir before the time, which the sons of Esau drove out and destroyed before them, and dwelt in their stead; as Israel will do in the land of his possession which the LORD has given them. 13 Now arise, I said, and go to the river Zered; and we went to the river Zered. 14 The time from Kadesh- Barnea until we came to Zered was eight years and thir- ty years, until all the generation of the men of war were removed from the army, as the LORD had sworn to them. 15 For indeed the hand of the LORD was against them, to de- stroy them in the midst of the army, until they were consumed. 16 So when all the men of war were consumed and dead in the midst of the people: 17 the Lord spoke to me, saying, 18 To- day you shall pass through the coast of Moab: 19 And thou shalt come near to the children of Ammon, but thou shalt not besiege them nor make war against them, for I will not give the land of the children of Ammon any pos- session, for I have given it to the children of Lot as a possession." 20 This also was taken as a country of ramblers, for before that time ramblers dwelt there, whom the Ammonites called Zamzummim: 21 A people who were as great and numerous and high as the Anakim; but the LORD destroyed them before them, and they succeeded them in their inheritance and dwelt in their place: 22 as he did to the sons of Esau who dwell in Seir, when he de- stroyed the Horim before them, and they possessed them and dwelt in their place to this day. 23 The Auim who dwelt in Hazarim as far as Azzah, the Caphtorim who came out of Caphtor destroyed them and dwelt in their place. 24 Arise therefore, saith the LORD: take up thy journey, and pass over the river Arnon: behold, I have put Sihon the Amorite, king of Heshbon, and his land into thy hand; begin to possess him, and to put him to hardship. 25 Today I will begin to convey your fear and dread to all the peoples of the whole world, who will hear your fame and tremble and shake before you." 26 Then I sent messengers from the wilderness of Kedemoth to Sihon, king of Heshbon, with

words of peace, saying, "Let me pass through my country, 27 Let me pass through thy land: I will go thy way: I will not turn to the right hand nor to the left. 28 Thou shalt sell me food for money, to eat, and thou shalt give me water for money, to drink; I will pass only on my foot, 29 (as the sons of Esau who dwell in Seir and the Moabites who dwell in Ar did with me) until I come out of Iorden, into the land which the LORD our God has chosen. 30 But Siphon king of Hesh- bon would not let him pass through, because the LORD your God had hardened his spirit and made his heart obstinate, that he might deliver him into your hands, as he appears to- day. 31 The LORD said to me, "Behold, I have begun to give Sihon and his land before you; begin to possess and inherit his land." 32 Then Sihon came with all his people to fight against Iahaz. 33 But the LORD our God delivered him into our power, and we defeated him and his sons and all his people. 34 We took all his cities at the same time and destroyed them all, men, women and children; we left nothing behind. 35 Only the livestock we took for our- selves and the wealth of the cities we took, 36 From Aroer, which is on the edge of the river Arnon, and from the city that is on the river, even to Gilead; there was not a single city that escaped, because the LORD our God made a deliverance before all. 37 You came not into the land of the sons of Ammon, nor into any place on the river Jabbok, nor into the cities of the mountains, nor into what the LORD our God has forbidden.

CHAPTER 3

1 Then we turned and went by the road of Bashan; and Og, king of Bashan, came out against us, he and all his people, to fight at Edrei. 2 The LORD said to me, "Do not fear him, for I will deliver him and all his people and his land into your hands, and you will do to him as you did to Sihon, king of the Amor- ites, who dwelt in Heshbon." 3 And the LORD our God delivered into our hands also Og, king of Bashan, and all his people; and we de- feated him, until there was none left, 4 And we took all his cities at the same time, and there was no city that we did not take from them, at least three dozen cities and all the coun- ty of Argob, the kingdom of Og in Bashan. 5 All these cities were fenced with walls, gates and bars, as well as numerous walled cities. 6 We devastated them, as we did Sihon king of Heshbon, destroying all the cities, with men, women and children. 7 But all the cattle and the timber of the cities we took for ourselves. 8 At that time we wrested from the hands of two kings of the Amorites the territory that lay on this side of Iorden, from the shore of Arnon to Mount Hermon: 9 (the Hermon which the Sidonians call Shirion, but which the Amorites call Shenir). 10 All the cities of the plain, all Gilead, all Bashan as far as Sal- chah and Edrei, cities of the kingdom of Og in Bashan. 11 For of the rest of the travelers there remained only Og, king of Bashan, whose bed was a bed of yron; is it not in Rabbath, among the sons of Ammon? Its length is nine cubits and its width four cubits, according to the cubit of a man. 12 This territory which we possessed at that time, from Aroer, which is by the river Arnon, to the middle of Mount Gilead and its cities, I gave to the Reubenites and the Gadites. 13 The rest of Gilead and all Bashan, the kingdom of Og, I leave to the half tribe of Manasseh, and all the land of Argob and all Bashan, which is called "the land of the giants." 14 And Iair the son of Manasseh took all the county of Argob, even unto the coasts of Geshuri and Maacathi, and called it by his name, Bashan, Hauoth Iair unto this day.

15 Then I gave part of Gilead to Machir. 16 To the Reubenites and to the Gadites I left the rest of Gilead and the border of Arnon, half the border and the borders, until the border of Jabbok, which is the border of the sons of Ammon: 17 Also the plain and Iorden and the borders from Chinneereth to the sea of the plain, that is, the salt sea below the springs of Pisgah on the east. 18 At the same time I commanded you, "The LORD your God has given you this territory to possess; you shall go armed before your brothers, the sons of Israel, all men of war. 19 Your wives and your children and your livestock (for I know that you have much livestock) shall remain in your cities that I have given you, 20 until the LORD has granted rest to your brethren as to you, and until they also possess the land which the LORD your God has granted them be- yond Iorden; then you shall each return to his possessions which I have given you." 21 At the same time I instructed Ioshua to say, "Your eyes have seen all that the LORD your God has done to these two kings; so will the LORD do to all the kingdoms where you go. 22 You shall not fear them, for the LORD your God will fight for you." 23 And at the same time I implored the LORD, saying, 24 O Lord God, you have begun to show your servant your greatness and your mighty hand; for where is there a God in heaven or on earth who can do like your works and like your power? 25 Please let me go and see the beautiful land that is beyond Iorden, that beautiful moun- tain and Lebanon." 26 But the LORD became angry with me for your sake and would not listen to me; and the LORD said to me, "It is enough for you, do not speak to me any more about this matter. 27 Go up to the top of Pis- gah, and lift up your eyes to the west, to the north, to the south, and to the east, and look at it with your eyes, for you shall not go out- side this boundary: 28 but charge Ioshua, and encourage him, and encourage him, for he shall go before this people, and shall deliver unto them for an inheritance the land which thou shalt see." 29 So we stopped in the valley opposite Bet-Peor.

CHAPTER 4

1 Now, therefore, listen, O Israel, to the reg- ulations and laws that I teach you to follow, that you may live in, enter and possess the land that the LORD, the God of your fathers, has given you. 2 You shall not put on anything other than the word I command you, and you shall not take anything away from it, that you may observe the commands of the LORD your God, which I command you. 3 Your eyes have seen what the LORD did because of Baal- Peor, for of all the men who followed Baal- Peor the LORD your God destroyed every one of you. 4 But you who have been converted to the LORD your God are all equal today. 5 Behold, I have taught you the rules and laws which the LORD my God commanded me, that you may do likewise in the land where you are going to possess. 6 Observe them therefore and put them into practice, for this is your wisdom and your understanding in the eyes of the people, who, hearing all these regulations, will say, "This people is wise and intelligent and a great nation." 7 For what na- tion is so great, for which the gods are so far from them, as the Lord our God is far from us in everything for which we call upon him? 8 What nation is so great as to have such righ- teous ordinances and laws as all this Lawe which I have set before you today? 9 But take care of yourself, and diligently keep your soul, so that you do not forget the things that your eyes have seen, and that they do not leave your heart all the days of your life; but teach them to your children and to your

children's children: 10 Do not forget the day when you stood before the LORD your God in Horeb, when the LORD said to me, "Gather the peo- ple together, and I will cause them to hear my words, that they may learn to fear me all the days that they live on the earth, and that they may teach their children." 11 Then you drew near and stood under the mountain, and the mountain burned with fire to the middle of the sky, and there was darkness and clouds and mist. 12 And the Lord spoke to you from the midst of the fire, and you heard the sense of the words, but you did not make a simili- tude of them, but a sense of them. 13 Then He declared to you His counsel that He had com- manded you to do, that is, the ten commands, and He wrote them on two tables of stone. 14 At the same time the LORD commanded me to teach you the regulations and laws that you should observe in the land where you would go to possess it. 15 Take heed therefore to yourselves, for you saw no image in the day when the LORD spoke to you in Horeb from the mouth of the fire: 16 Lest ye corrupt your own selves, and make for yourselves an image or representation of any figure, whether male or female, 17 the likeness of any animal that is on the earth, or the likeness of any bound animal that flies in the air: 18 or the likeness of any thing that creeps upon the earth, or the likeness of any fish that is in the waters under the earth, 19 lest thou lift up thine eyes unto heaven, and seeing the sun, and the moon, and the stars, with all the host of heaven, thou shouldest desire to worship and serve them, which the LORD thy God hath distributed to all the people throughout the whole heaven. 20 But the LORD took you and brought you out of the furnace of Yron, out of Egypt, to be for him a people and an inheritance, as it ap- pears today. 21 The LORD was angry with me because of your words and swore that I would not leave Iorden and enter that good land which the LORD your God has given you as an inheritance. 22 For I must die in this land, and I will not go beyond Iorden, but you shall go beyond and possess that good land. 23 Take care that you do not forget the covenant which the LORD your God has made with you, and that you do not make yourselves any im- age or likeness of anything, as the LORD your God has commanded you. 24 For the LORD your God is a consuming fire and a jealous God. 25 When you have begotten children and children's children, and have been long in the land, if you corrupt yourself and make for yourself an image or likeness of anything, you will work evil in the eyes of the LORD your God, to provoke him to wrath, 26 today I call the earth and heaven to witness against you, that in a short time you shall perish from the land to which you went to possess it; you shall not prolong your days, but you shall be destroyed. 27 And the LORD will scatter you among the peoples, and you will remain few among the nations where the LORD will lead you: 28 And there ye shall serve gods, as works of man, wood and stone, which are not seen, nor heard, nor eaten, nor smelt. 29 But if you see the LORD your God from there, you will find him, if you see him with all your heart and with all your soul. 30 When thou shalt be in tribulation, and all these things shall come upon thee, if thou return unto the LORD thy God, and be obedient to his command, 31 the LORD your God is a merciful God, and he will not forsake you, nor destroy you, nor forget the covenant of your fathers, which he swore to them. 32 Now, indeed, seek to know the former days, which were before thee, from the day that God created man on the earth, and ask, from one end of the island to the other, whether such a great thing as this has taken place, or whether such a thing has ever been heard of. 33 Did the people perhaps hear the voice of God speaking

from the midst of the fire, as you heard and related? 34 Or has God pretended to go and take a nation from among the nations, with temptations, with signs, with wonders, with wars, with a mighty hand, with an outstretched arm, and with great fear, according to all that the LORD your God did to you in Egypt before your eyes? 35 To you it was shown, that you might know that the Lord is God and that there is none but he alone. 36 From the height of heaven he made you hear his speech to instruct you, and on earth he showed you his great fire, and you heard his speech from the midst of the fire. 37 For he loved your fathers, and chose their seed after them, and brought you out of Egypt before him by his mighty power, 38 to cast out before you nations greater and mightier than you, to bring you in and give you their land as an inheritance, as it appears today. 39 Today, therefore, remember and consider in your heart that the LORD is God in heaven and on earth; there is no other. 40 You shall therefore observe his decrees and his commands which I have given you today, that it may go well with you and with your children after you, and that you may prolong your days on earth, which the Lord your God grants you forever." 41 Then Moses separated three cities on this side of Iorden, toward the rising of the sun: 42 that the slayer who had killed his neighbor in vnwares and had not hated him in the past should flee to one of those cities and lie down: 43 that is, Bezer in the wilderness, in the plain of the Reubenites, Ramoth in Gilead among the Gadites, and Golan in Bashan among the Manassehs. 44 This is the law that Moses set forth to the children of Israel. 45 These are the testimonies, rules and laws that Moses de- clared to the children of Israel after they came out of Egypt, 46 on this side of Iorden, in the valley opposite Bet-Peor, in the land of Sihon, king of the Amorites, who dwelt in Heshbon, and whom Moses and the children of Israel defeated after they came out of Egypt: 47 And they took possession of his territory and of the territory of Og king of Bashan, two kings of the Amorites, who were on this side of Iorden, toward the rising of the sun: 48 From Aroer, which is by the border of the river Ar- non, unto Mount Zion, which is Hermon, 49 and all the plain of Iorden eastward, as far as the sea, under the springs of Pisgah.

CHAPTER 5

1 Then Moses summoned all Israel and said to them, "Listen, O Israel, to the rules and laws that I propose to you today, that you may learn them and observe them." 2 The LORD our God made a covenant with you in Horeb. 3 The Lord did not make this covenant only with our fathers, but also with you, and with all of you who are here today. 4 The LORD spoke with you face to face on the mountain out of the fire. 5 At that time I stood between the LORD and you, to declare to you the word of the LORD; for at the sight of the fire you were afraid and did not go up the mountain, and he said, "I am the LORD your Lord. 6 I am the LORD your God, who brought you out of the land of Egypt, out of the house of bond- age. 7 You shall have no other gods before my face. 8 Thou shalt not make unto thee any grauan image, or any likeness of that which is in heaven, or that which is on the earth be- neath, or that which is in the waters under the earth. 9 You shall not bow down to them or serve them, for I, the LORD your God, am an unrighteous God, causing the iniquity of the fathers to fall on the children, even to the third and fourth generation of those who hate me: 10 And showing mercy to the thousands who love me and keep my commands. 11 Do not take the Name of the Lord your God

in vein, for the Lord will not give peace to those who take His Name in vein. 12 Observe the Sabbath day to keep it holy, as the LORD your God has commanded you. 13 Six days shalt thou labor and do all thy work: 14 but the seventh day is the Sabbath of the LORD thy God; in it thou shalt do no work, neither thou, nor thy son, nor thy daughter, nor thy manser- vant, nor thy elder, nor thy ox, nor thy horse, nor thy plank, nor any of thy cattle, nor any of the stranger that is within thy gates; that thy manservant and thy elder may rest as much as thou. 15 For remember that you were a ser- vant in the land of Egypt, and that the LORD your God brought you out from there with a mighty hand and an outstretched arm; there- fore the LORD your God commanded you to observe the Sabbath day. 16 Honor thy father and thy mother, as the LORD thy God hath commanded thee, that thy days may be pro- longed, and that the land which the LORD thy God giveth thee may be well with thee. 17 You shall not kill. 18 You shall not commit adul- tery. 19 You shall not steal. 20 You shall not bear false witness against your neighbor. 21 Thou shalt not steal thy neighbor's wife, thou shalt not covet thy neighbor's house, his field, his servant, his dog, his ox, his plank, and all that thy neighbor possesses. 22 These words the LORD spoke them to all your multitude on the mountain from the midst of the fire, from the clouds and from the darkness, with great voyce, and he added nothing more to them; he wrote them on two tables of stone and de- livered them to me. 23 When you heard the answer from the darkness, (for the mountain was set on fire), you came to me, all the lead- ers of your tribes and your elders: 24 and said, "Behold, the Lord our God has shown us his glory and his greatness, and we have heard his voice from the bowels of the fire; we have seen today that God speaks to men and is able to speak." 25 Now, therefore, why should we die? Because this great fire will consume us; if we still hear the voice of the Lord our God, we will die. 26 For what flesh was there before that heard the voice of the Lord God speaking from the midst of the fire as we did, and be- lieved? 27 Go here and hear all that the Lord our God says; and declare to you all that the Lord our God says to you, and we will hear and do it." 28 Then the LORD heard the sense of your words, when you spoke to me; and the LORD said to me, "I have heard the sense of the words of this people, which they have spoken to you; they have spoken well, all that they have spoken." 29 Oh, if there were such a heart in them as to fear me and to observe all my commands at all times, that it may go well for them and for their children forever. 30 Go and say to them, "Return to your tents." 31 But you stay here with me, and I will tell you all the commands, rules and laws that you must teach them, so that they may perform them in the land that I grant them to possess it. 32 Take heed, therefore, to do as the LORD your God has commanded you: turn neither to the right hand nor to the left, 33 but walk in all the ways which the Lord your God has command- ed you, that you may live, and that it may go well with you, and that you may prolong your days in the land which you shall possess.

CHAPTER 6

1 These are the orders, rules and laws which the LORD your God has commanded me to teach you, that you may perform them in the land where you are going to possess: 2 That you may fear the LORD your God and observe all his prescriptions and his commands which I have given you, you and your son and your children, all the days of your life, that your days may be prolonged. 3 Take heed therefore, O Israel, and take heed that thou do so, that it may go well with thee, and that thou mayest grow strong in the land flowing with milk and honey, as the LORD God of thy fathers hath promised thee. 4 Hear, O Israel: the LORD our God is the only LORD, 5 And you shall worship the LORD your God with all your heart and with all your soul and with all your strength. 6 These words that I have communicated to you today will remain in your heart. 7 You shall repeat them continually to your children, and you shall speak them when you are at home, when you walk in the street, when you lie down and when you get up: 8 You shall bind them as a sign on your hand, and they shall serve as a frontispiece between your eyes. 9 You shall also write them on the posts of your house and on your doors. 10 When the LORD your God has brought you into the land that he swore to your fathers, Abraham, Izhak and Iaakob, to give you, with large and beautiful cities that you did not build, 11 and houses filled with all kinds of goods that you have not filled, and wells dug that you have not dug, vineyards and olive trees that you have not planted, and when you have eaten and are full, 12 beware of forgetting the LORD who brought you out of the land of Egypt, out of the house of bondage. 13 You shall fear the LORD your God, and serve him, and swear by his Name. 14 You shall not walk according to any other gods, according to any of the gods of the peoples around you, 15 (for the LORD your God is an unreadable God in your midst), or else the wrath of the LORD your God will kin- dle against you and destroy you from the face of the earth. 16 You shall not tempt the LORD your God as you tempted him at Mass: 17 But you shall diligently observe the commands of the LORD your God, his testimonies and his prescriptions which he has given you, 18 and you shall do what is right and good in the sight of the LORD, that you may prosper and enter and possess that good land which the LORD swore to your fathers, 19 to drive out all your enemies before you, as the LORD has said. 20 When your son asks you in the future, "What do these testimonies, these ordinanc- es, and these laws, which the LORD our God has commanded you, mean? 21 Then you will say to your son, "We were slaves of Pharaoh in Egypt, but the LORD brought us out of Egypt with a mighty hand. 22 The LORD performed great signs and wonders on Egypt, on Pha- raoh and all his household, before our eyes, 23 and brought him out from there, to bring him in and give him the land which he had sworn to our fathers. 24 Therefore the LORD has commanded you to observe all these pro- visions and to fear the LORD our God, that things may always go well for you, and that He may preserve you as at this time. 25 More- over, this will be our righteousness before the Lord our God, if we take care to observe all these prescriptions, as he has commanded.

CHAPTER 7

1 When the LORD thy God shall bring thee into the land whither thou goest to possess it, and he shall set before thee many nations: the Hittites, the Girgashites, the Amorites, the Canaanites, the Perizzites, the Hiuites, and the Jebusites, other nations greater and mightier than thou art, 2 and the LORD thy God shall set them before thee, and thou shalt smite them; thou shalt destroy them utterly; thou shalt make no covenant with them, nei- ther shalt thou have compassion on them, 3 thou shalt not make marriages with them, nor give thy daughter to his son, nor take his daughter for thy son. 4 For they will cause your son to turn away

from me and serve other gods; then the anger of the LORD will kindle against you and suddenly destroy you. 5 But this is how you shall deal with them: you shall flatten their altars, tear down their pillars, cut down their pillars, and bury their images with fire. 6 For you are a holy people to the LORD your God; the LORD your God has chosen you to be a precious people to himself, compared to all the peoples of the earth. 7 The LORD did not set his eyes on you, nor did he choose you because you were more numerous than any other people, for you were the smallest of all the peoples: 8 But because the LORD wanted you and wanted to keep the pledge made to your fathers, the LORD brought you out with a mighty hand and delivered you from the house of bondage from the hand of Pharaoh, king of Egypt, 9 so that you may know that the LORD, your God, is God, the faithful God who maintains favor and clemency toward those who love him and keep his commands, even to a thousand generations, 10 and rewards in his face those who hate him, to bring them to destruction; he will not defer to reward in his face those who hate him. 11 Therefore keep the commandments and the prescriptions and the laws which I have commanded you to observe today. 12 For if you will hear these laws and keep them and observe them, the LORD your God will keep with you the bond and the grace that he swore to your fathers. 13 And he shall honor thee, and bless thee, and multiply thee; he shall also bless the fruit of thy woman, and the fruit of thy land, and thy corn, and thy wine, and thy oil, and the increase of thy cattle, and the flocks of thy beasts in the land, which he swore to thy fathers. 14 You shall be blessed over all the people; there shall be no barren male or female among you, nor among your cattle. 15 Moreover, the LORD will remove all infirmities from you, and will not cause any of the diseases of Egypt (which you know) to pass from you, but will send them to all those who hate you. 16 Therefore thou shalt consume all the people whom the LORD thy God giveth thee; thine eye shall not spare them, neither shalt thou serve their gods: for this shall be thy destruction. 17 If you say in your heart, "These nations outnumber me, how can I drive them out? 18 Do not fear them, but remember what the LORD your God did to Pharaoh and all Egypt: 19 the great temptations which your eyes have seen, the signs and wonders, the mighty hand and the outstretched weapon with which the LORD your God brought you forth; so will the LORD your God do with all the people of whom you are afraid. 20 Moreover, the LORD your God will send hornets among them, until those who have remained and are hiding from you are destroyed. 21 You shall not fear them, for the LORD your God is in your midst, a mighty and terrible God. 22 The LORD your God will drive out these nations before you, little by little; you will not be able to consume them at once, unless the beasts of the dry land increase upon you. 23 But the LORD your God will deliver them up before you and will destroy them with mighty destruction, until they are reduced to ashes. 24 He will deliver their kings into your hand, and you will destroy their name from under heaven; no one will be able to stand before you until you destroy them. 25 And thou shalt burn with fire the bronze images of their gods, and take not the clay and the gold that are on them, and carry it not with thee, lest thou be ensnared by it; for it is an abomination before the LORD thy God. 26 Bring not the abomination into thy house, lest thou be accursed like him, but abhor it, and consider it abominable, for it is accursed.

CHAPTER 8

1 You shall observe all the commands I command you to follow today, that you may live, multiply, enter and possess the land which the LORD swore to your fathers. 2 You shall remember all the way that the LORD your God made you go these forty years in the wilderness, to humble you and test you, to know what was in your heart, whether or not you would keep his commands. 3 Therefore he humbled you, and starved you, and fed you with MAN, whom you did not know, nor did your fathers know, to teach you that man does not live by bread alone, but by every word that comes from the mouth of the Lord. 4 Your garments have not grown old on you, and your body has not swelled these four years. 5 Know therefore in your heart that as a man feeds his son, so the LORD your God feeds you. 6 Therefore you shall keep the commands of the LORD your God, to walk in his ways and fear him. 7 For the LORD your God is bringing you into a good land, a land where there are springs of water and fountains, and wells flowing out of valleys and mountains: 8 a land of wheat and barley, of vineyards, of fig trees and pomegranates; a land of oils and ones: 9 a land wherein thou shalt eat bread without scarcity, and shalt lack nothing; a land whose stones are of lilies, and out of whose mountains thou shalt dig brasse. 10 When thou hast eaten and hast been satisfied, thou shalt thank the LORD thy God for the good land which he hath given thee. 11 Beware lest you forget the LORD your God, not keeping his commands, his laws and his regulations, which I have communicated to you today: 12 So that when thou hast eaten and hast been satisfied, thou shalt build good houses and dwell therein, 13 your herds and your sheep shall be increased, your silver and your gold multiplied, and all that you possess shall be increased, 14 then your heart is lifted up and you forget the LORD your God, who brought you out of the land of Egypt, out of the house of bondage, 15 who was your guide in the great and terrible wilderness (where there were fierce serpents, scorpions and drought, where there was no water), who caused water to spring for you from a rock of flint: 16 Who fed thee in the wilderness with man, whom thy fathers knew not) to humble thee and make thee proud, that he might do thee good in thy last life. 17 Beware lest you say in your heart, "My power and the strength of my hands have prepared this abundance for me." 18 But remember the LORD your God, for it is he who gives you power to procure for yourself the substances to establish his covenant which he swore to your fathers, as it appears today. 19 If you forget the LORD your God and walk after other gods and serve them and worship them, I testify to you today that you will certainly perish. 20 As the nations the LORD destroyed before you, so you will perish, because you did not want to be obedient to the word of the LORD your God.

CHAPTER 9

1 Hear, O Israel: today you shall pass through Iorden to enter and possess nations greater and mightier than you, and cities great and walled up to heaven, 2 a people great and high, like the sons of the Anakim, whom you know and of whom you have heard, "Who can stand before the sons of Anak? 3 Understand therefore that today the LORD your God is the one who goes before you like a consuming fire; he will destroy them and bring them down before your face; you will drive them out and destroy them suddenly, as the

LORD has told you. 4 Do not say in your heart (af- ter the LORD your God has driven them out before you), "Because of my righteousness the LORD has brought me in to possess this land; but because of the wickedness of these nations the LORD has driven them out be- fore you." 5 For you did not come in to inherit their land because of your righteousness or your upright heart, but because of the wick- edness of those nations the LORD your God has cast them out before you, to fulfill the word that the LORD your God swore to your fathers, Abraham, Izhak and Jacob. 6 Un- derstand therefore that the LORD your God does not grant you this good land to possess it for your righteousness, because you are a suffocating people. 7 Remember, and do not forget, how you provoked the LORD your God to wrath in the wilderness; from the day you came out of the land of Egypt until you came to this place, you rebelled against the LORD. 8 Even in Horeb you provoked the LORD's anger, so that the LORD was angry with you, even to the point of destroying you. 9 When I went to the mountain to receive the tables of stone, the tables, I say, of the covenant, which the LORD had made with you, I stayed on the mountain for four days and four nights and did not eat bread or drink water: 10 Then the LORD gave me two tables of stone, writ- ten with the finger of God, and in them were written all the words which the LORD had spoken to you on the mountain from the midst of the fire, on the day of assembly. 11 When the four hundred days and the four hundred nights had elapsed, the LORD deliv- ered to me the two tables of stone, the tables, that is, of the assembly. 12 The LORD said to me, "Arise, come down quickly from here, for your people, whom you brought out of Egypt, have corrupted their ways, have gone out of the way that I commanded them, and have made themselves a molten image." 13 Moreover, the LORD spoke to me, saying, "I have seen this people, and behold, they are a smothered people. 14 Leave me alone, that I may destroy them and blot out their name from under heaven, and I will make you a mighty nation and greater than they." 15 So I returned and came down from the mountain (and the mountain was burning with fire, and the two tables of the covenant were in my two hands). 16 Then I looked, and behold, you had sinned against the LORD your God, be- cause you had made yourselves a molten calf and had turned away in haste from the way the LORD had commanded you. 17 Therefore I took the two Tablets, threw them from my two hands, and broke them before your eyes. 18 Then I lay down before the LORD, fourteen days and fourteen nights, as before: I did not eat bread or drink water, because of all your sins which you had committed, doing evil in the eyes of the LORD and provoking him to wrath. 19 (For I was ignorant of the anger and indignation with which the LORD had come against you, to destroy you), the LORD heard me even then. 20 In the same way the Lord was very angry with Aaron, so much so that he destroyed him; but at that time I also prayed for Aaron. 21 Then I took your sin, and took the calf that you had made, and burned it with fire, and crushed it and ground it into dust, and threw its dust into the river that came down from the mountain. 22 Even in Taberah and in Massah and in Kibrothhatta- auah you provoked the LORD's anger. 23 Even when the LORD sent you from Kadesh-Bar- nea, saying, "Go and possess the land I have given you," you rebelled against the command of the LORD your God and did not listen to him or heed his message. 24 You have been rebellious against the LORD since the day I met you. 25 Then I prostrated myself before the LORD for four days and four nights, as I prostrated myself before, because the LORD had said that he would destroy you. 26 I prayed to the LORD and said, "O LORD God, do not destroy your people and your inheri- tance, whom you redeemed by your greatness and brought out of Egypt with a mighty hand. 27 Remember your servants Abraham, Izhak and Iaakob; do not mind the stubbornness of this people, their wickedness and their sin, 28 lest the county, from which you brought them, should say, "Because the LORD failed to bring them into the land he promised them, or because he hated them, he brought them out to kill them in the wilderness." 29 But they are your people and your inheritance, whom you brought out by your power and your out- stretched arm.

CHAPTER 10

1 At the same time the LORD said to me, "Make yourself two Tablets of stone like the first ones, and come to me on the mountain and make yourself an ark of wood, 2 and I will write on the Tablets the words that were on the first Tablets that you broke, and you shall put them in the ark." 3 And I made an ark of wood of Shittim, and cut two tablets of stone like the first tablets, and went to the moun- tain with the two tablets in my hand. 4 Then wrote on the Tablets according to the first scripture (the ten commands that the LORD gave you on the Mount from the mouth of the fire on the day of the meeting) and the LORD gave them to me. 5 And I went away, and came down from the mount, and put the Tablets in the ark that I had made; and there they stand, as the LORD commanded me. 6 The children of Israel made their journey from Beeroth of the sons of Iaakan to Moserah, where Aaron died and was buried, and Eleazar his son be- came a priest in his place. 7 From there they departed to Gudgodah and from Gudgodah to Iotbath, a land of running waters. 8 At the same time the LORD separated the tribe of Leui so that they might carry the ark of the LORD's covenant and stand before the LORD to serve him and bless his Name to this day. 9 Therefore Leui has no part nor inheritance with his brethren, for the LORD is his inheritance, as the LORD your God has promised him. 10 And I stood in the mount, as I did the first time, fourteen days and fourteen nights, and the LORD heard me even then, and the LORD would not destroy you. 11 But the LORD said to me, "Arise, go forth before the people, that they may enter and possess the land which I had sworn to their fathers to give them." 12 Now, Israel, what does the LORD your God require of you but to fear the LORD your God, to walk in all his ways, to love him, and to serve the LORD your God with all your heart and with all your soul? 13 To observe the Lord's commands and his reg- ulations, which I have recommended to you today, for your welfare? 14 Well, the heaven and the heaven of heavens is the LORD your God, and the earth with all that it contains. 15 However, the LORD has set his delight in your fathers, to appreciate them, and has chosen their descendants after them, and so also for you with respect to all peoples, as it appears today. 16 Circumcise therefore the foreskin of your heart, and harden not your neck any more. 17 For the Lord your God is God of gods and Lord of lords, a great, mighty and terrible God, who does not accept people or rewards: 18 Who does justice to the fatherless and the widow, and welcomes the stranger, giving him food and drink. 19 Welcome therefore the stranger, for you were strangers in the land of Egypt. 20 You shall fear the LORD your God; you shall serve him, and be faithful to him, and swear by his Name. 21 He is your praise and he is your God, who has done for you these great and terrible things that your eyes

have seen. 22 Your fathers went down to Egypt with seventy people, while now the LORD your God has made you like the stars of heaven, in great numbers.

CHAPTER 11

1 Therefore you shall love the Lord your God and observe what he has commanded you to observe, that is, his decrees, his laws and his commands, always. 2 And consider today (for I do not speak to your children, who have not known nor seen) the chastisement of the LORD your God, his greatness, his mighty hand and his outstretched arm, 3 his signs and his deeds which he did in the midst of Egypt against Pharaoh, king of Egypt, and against all his land: 4 and what he did to the army of the Egyptians, and to their horses and chariots, when he caused the waters of the Red Sea to overflow as they pursued you, and the LORD destroyed them to this day: 5 And what he did to you in the wilderness, un- til you came to this place: 6 And what he did to Dathan and to Abiram the sons of Eliab the son of Reuben, when the earth opened its mouth and swallowed them up with their houses and their tents and all their posses- sions that they had in the midst of all Israel. 7 For your eyes have seen all the great deeds of the LORD that he has done. 8 Therefore observe all the commands I have given you today, that you may be strong and may enter into possession of the land where you are go- ing to possess it: 9 That you may prolong your days in the land which the LORD swore to your fathers to give to them and to their seed, that is, a land flowing with milk and honey. 10 For the land where you are going to possess it is not like the land of Egypt, from whence you came, where you sowed your seed and wa- tered it with your feet like a garden of herbs: 11 but the land where you are going to possess it is a land of mountains and valleys, drinking water from the rains of Heauen. 12 The LORD your God cares for this land; the desires of the LORD your God are always upon it, from the beginning of the year and to the end of the year. 13 If therefore you will listen to my com- mands, which I have communicated to you today, to love the LORD your God and to serve him with all your heart and with all your soul, 14 I will give your country rain in due season, the first and the last, that you may reap your grain, your wine and your oil. 15 I will also send grain into your fields, for your cattle, that you may eat and have enough. 16 But beware of deceiving your heart and turning away to serve other gods and worship them." 17 and so the anger of the LORD will kindle against you and close the land, so that there will be no raina, and your land will not bear fruit, and you will quickly perish from the good land that the LORD has given you. 18 Therefore fix these words of mine in your heart and in your soul, and bind them as a sign upon your hand, that they may be as a frontlet between your eyes, 19 And you shall teach them to your children, speaking them when you sit in your house, when you walk by the way, when you lie down, and when you rise up. 20 You shall write them on the posts of your house and on your doors, 21 That your days and the days of your children may be multiplied in the land which the LORD swore to give to your fathers, as long as the heavens are upon the earth. 22 For if you diligently observe all these commands that I command you to do, that is, to love the LORD your God, to walk in all his prescriptions, and to be faithful to him, 23 then the LORD will drive out all these nations before you, and you will possess great nations and more powerful than you. 24 All the plac- es where you shall tread the soles of your feet shall be yours; your coast shall be from the wilderness and Lebanon, from the River and the River Perath to the uttermost sea. 25 No one shall be able to oppose you, for the LORD your God shall have fear and awe of you over all the land which you shall pass through, as he has said to you. 26 Behold, I set before you today a blessing and a curse: 27 the blessing, if you obey the commands of the Lord your God that I command you today: 28 and the curse, if you will not obey the commands of the LORD your God, but will depart from the way that I command you today, to go after other gods whom you do not know. 29 There- fore when the LORD your God has brought you into your land, where you are going to possess it, then you shall place the blessing on Mount Gerizim and the curse on Mount Ebal. 30 Are they not beyond Iorden, on that side, where the sun sets, in the land of the Canaan- ites, who dwell in the plain opposite Ghilgal, beside the group of Moreh? 31 For you shall pass over Iorden to go in and possess the land which the LORD your God grants you; you shall possess it and dwell in it. 32 Take care, therefore, to observe all the commands and laws that I have set before you today.

CHAPTER 12

1 These are the rules and laws that you shall observe and keep in the land (which the LORD, the God of your fathers, grants you to possess) as long as you live on the earth. 2 You shall destroy all the places where the nations you possess have served their gods on the mountains and hills and under every green tree. 3 You shall also level their altars, you shall break down their pillars and bury their pillars with fire; you shall break down the images of their gods and abolish their names from that place. 4 You shall not do so in regard to the LORD your God, 5 but you shall see the place which the LORD your God shall choose out of all your tribes, to put his Name there and to dwell there, and there you shall come, 6 and you shall bring there your burnt offerings, your sacrifices, your tithes, the offerings of your hands, your vows, your free offerings, and the firstborn of your ani- mals and your sheep. 7 There you shall eat be- fore the LORD your God, and you shall make up for yourselves in everything you put your hands to, both you and your houses, for the LORD your God has blessed you. 8 You shall not do the things that we do here as we do to- day, that is, let each one do what seems good in his own eyes. 9 For you have not yet come to the rest and the inheritance which the LORD your God has granted you. 10 But when you have come out of Iorden and dwell in the land that the LORD your God has given you as an inheritance, and when he has given you rest from all your enemies that surround you, and you will dwell in safety, 11 when there shall be a place which the LORD your God has chosen for you to dwell in, you shall bring in all that I have commanded you: your burnt offerings, your sacrifices, your tithes, the fruit of your hands, and all your special vows which you make to the LORD: 12 And you shall be rec- onciled before the LORD your God, you, and your sons and your daughters, and your ser- vants and your maidens, and the Leuita that is within your gates, for he hath no part nor inheritance with you. 13 Take care that you do not offer your offspring burnt in everyplace that you see: 14 but at the place which the LORD shall choose in one of your tribes, there you shall offer your sacrifices, and there you shall do all that I have commanded you. 15 Nevertheless you may kill and eat meat in all your gates, as your heart desires, according to the blessing of the LORD your God,

who has granted you; both vncleane and cleane may eat of it, as of the deer and of the roebuck. 16 Only you shall not eat the blood, but you shall sprinkle it on the earth like water. 17 You shall not eat within your gates the tithe of your grain, nor of your wine, nor of your oil, nor of the firstborn of your animals, nor of your sheep, nor of your vows, nor of your free of- ferings, nor of the offering of your hands, 18 But thou shalt eat it before the LORD thy God, in the place which the LORD thy God shall choose, thou, and thy son, and thy daugh- ter, and thy manservant, and thy maidser- vant, and the Leuita that is within thy gates; and thou shalt make up before the LORD thy God, in all that thou shalt set thy hand to. 19 Take heed that thou forsake not the Leuita, as long as thou livest on the earth. 20 When the LORD your God enlarges your borders, as he has promised you, and you say, "I will eat meat," (for your heart desires to eat meat) you may eat meat, what your heart desires. 21 If the place which the LORD your God has chosen to put His Name there is far from you, then you shall kill your calves and your sheep which the LORD has given you, as I have com- manded you, and you shall eat in your gates what your heart desires. 22 As the roe deer and the deer are eaten, so shalt thou eat them also; the vnclean and the clean shall eat of them alike. 23 But be sure that you do not eat the blood, for blood is life, and you cannot eat life with flesh. 24 Therefore you shall not eat it, but you shall sprinkle it on the earth like water. 25 You shall not eat it, that it may be good for you and for your children after you, when you do what is right in the eyes of the Lord: 26 But thy holy things which thou hast and thy vows shalt take, and thou shalt come to the place which the LORD chooseth. 27 You shall make your burnt offerings of flesh and blood on the altar of the LORD your God; the blood of your offerings shall be poured out on the altar of the LORD your God, and you shall eat the flesh. 28 Hear and heed all these words that I have spoken to you, that it may go well with you and with your children after you forever, when you do that which is good and right in the sight of the LORD your God. 29 When the LORD your God destroys the nations before you, where you go to possess them, and you will possess them and dwell in their land, 30 beware of being snared by them, after they have been destroyed before you, and of asking their gods, saying, "How did these nations serve their gods, that I should do likewise?" 31 You shall not do so toward the LORD your God, for they have done to their gods an abomination which the LORD detests, for they have burned with fire their sons and their daughters to their gods. 32 Therefore, whatever I command you, see that you do it; you shall put on nothing and take off nothing.

CHAPTER 13

1 If there arises among you a prophet or a dreamer of dreams (and he gives you a sign or a prodigy,) 2 and the sign and prodigy which he has told you come true) saying, "Go after other gods whom you do not know and serve them." 3 You shall not heed the words of the prophet or that dreamer of dreams, for the LORD your God is testing you to know wheth- er you love the LORD your God with all your heart and with all your soul. 4 You shall walk after the LORD your God and fear him, keep his commands and listen to his word, serve him and be faithful to him. 5 But that proph- et or that dreamer of dreams shall be killed, because he has spoken to turn you away from the LORD your God (who brought you out of the land of Egypt and delivered you from the house of cattle) to push you out of

the way by which the LORD your God commanded you to walk. 6 If your brother, your mother's son, or your own son, or your daughter, or the wife who lies in your bosom, or your friend, who is like your own soul, secretly intrigues you, saying, "Go and serve other gods" (whom you have not known, neither you, I say, nor your fathers) 7 any of the gods of the peoples around you, whether near you or far from you, from one end of the earth to the other: 8 thou shalt not hearken unto him, nor shalt thine eye behold him, nor shalt thou give him credit, nor shalt thou keep him hid: 9 But thou shalt kill him; thy hand shall first be upon him to put him to death, and then the hand of all the people. 10 Thou shalt stone him with stones, that he may die (because he sought to turn thee away from the LORD thy God, who brought thee out of the land of Egypt, out of the house of bondage). 11 That all Israel may hear and fear, and do no more such wickedness among you. 12 If you hear it said (concerning any of the cities which the LORD your God has given you to dwell in) 13 Wicked men have gone out from among you and dragged away the inhabitants of their cit- ies, saying, "Go and serve other gods, whom you do not know." 14 Then you shall see and search and investigate diligently; and if it is true, and the thing is certain, that such abom- ination has been done in your midst, 15 You shall kill the inhabitants of that city with the edge of the sword; you shall destroy the city, all that is in it, and its livestock with the edge of the sword. 16 You shall gather all its stuff in the midst of its streets, and you shall burn the city and all its stuff in every part with fire, for the LORD your God's sake; it shall be a heap forever, and it shall not be rebuilt. 17 And nothing of this damned thing shall remain in your hand, that the LORD may turn away the fire of his wrath, and give you credit, and have compassion on you, and multiply you, as he swore to your fathers: 18 when thou hast obeyed the will of the LORD thy God, and hast observed all his commands which I command thee this day, that thou mayest do that which is right in the sight of the LORD thy God.

CHAPTER 14

1 You are children of the LORD your God. You shall not cut yourselves or make baldness between your eyes for the dead. 2 For you are a holy people to the LORD your God, and the LORD has chosen you to be a precious peo- ple to himself, compared to all the peoples of the earth. 3 You shall not eat any kind of abomination. 4 These are the foods you shall eat: the bee, the sheep, and the kid, 5 the deer, the roebuck, the trumpet, the wild deer, the vnicorne, the wild ox, and the chamois. 6 And all the beasts that divide the hoof, that divide the leg into two claws, and that are among the beasts that chew the cud, you shall eat them. 7 But you shall not eat of those which chew the carcass, and of those which divide and wipe their feet by themselves: the cam- el, the hare, and the rabbit, for they chew the carcass, but do not divide their feet; there- fore they shall be forbidden you: 8 The swine also, because they chew the hoof and not the carcass, shall be forbidden you; you shall not eat their flesh or touch their dead carcasses. 9 You shall eat all that are in the waters; you shall eat all that have fins and scales. 10 And that which has neither fins nor scales you shall not eat; it shall be forbidden you. 11 Of all the clear birds you shall eat: 12 But of these ye shall not eat: the eagle, the goshawk, and the osprey, 3 nor the owl, nor the kite, nor the vulture, according to their kind, 14 and all the species of rauens, 15 nor the ostrich, nor the night raven, nor the

semeaw, nor the hawk of his kind, 16 nor the little owl, nor the great owl, nor the robin, 17 nor the pelican, nor the swan, nor the cormorant: 18 also the flock, and the heron in his kind, and the lapwing, and the hawk. 19 And all reptiles that fly are forbidden; they may not be eaten. 20 But of all clean animals you may eat. 21 You shall not eat anything that dies by itself, but you shall give it to the stranger within your gates, that he may eat it; or you shall sell it to a stranger, for you are a holy people to the LORD your God. You shall not cook a kid in its mother's milk. 22 You shall give the tithe of all the har- vest of your sowing, which comes from the field year by year. 23 And thou shalt eat be- fore the LORD thy God (in the place which he shall choose for his Name to dwell therein) the tithe of thy corn, and of thy wine, and of thy grapes, and of the first harvest of thy beasts and of thy sheep, that thou mayest learn to fear the LORD thy God always. 24 And if the way is too long for thee, so that thou art not able to carry it, because the place is far from thee, where the Lord thy God shall choose to set his Name, when the Lord thy God shall bless thee, 25 then thou shalt do it in money, and thou shalt take the money in thy hand, and thou shalt go to the place which the Lord thy God shall have chosen. 26 And thou shalt give the money for what thy heart desires: oxen, sheep, wine, strong wine, or what thy heart desires; and thou shalt eat it before the LORD thy God, and thou shalt make up for it, thou and thy family. 27 And thou shalt not forsake the Leuita that is within thy gates: for he hath no portion nor inheritance with thee. 28 At the end of three years you shall bring all the tithes of your earnings of that year and lay them inside your gates. 29 Then you shall come the Leuite, who has no part or inheri- tance with you, the stranger, the orphan and the widow who are within your gates, and you shall eat and be filled, that the Lord your God may bless you in all the works of your hand that you do.

CHAPTER 15

1 At the end of ten years you shall make en- franchisement. 2 And this is the way of en- franchisement: every creditor shall return the money of his hand which he lent to his neigh- bor; he shall not be able to demand it again from his neighbor nor from his brother, for the year of the Lord's enfranchisement has been proclaimed. 3 You may demand from the stranger, but what you have with your broth- er, your hand will forgive: 4 when there shall be no more a pauper with thee, for the LORD shall bless thee in the land which the LORD thy God giveth thee as an inheritance to pos- sess it: 5 That thou mayest hear the message of the LORD thy God, and observe and do all these commands which I command thee this day. 6 For the Lord thy God hath blessed thee, as he hath promised thee: and thou shalt lend unto many nations, but thou shalt not lend thyself, and thou shalt reign over many na- tions, and they shall not reign over thee. 7 And if one of thy brethren with thee is poor within one of thy gates in thy land, which the LORD thy God giveth thee, thou shalt not harden thine heart, neither shalt thou close thy hand to thy poor brother: 8 But thou shalt open thine hand unto him, and lend him what is necessary for his need. 9 See that there be no evil thought in thine heart, that thou shoul- dest say, "The seventh year, the year of liberty, is at hand; therefore thou afflictest thyself to look upon thy poor brother, and givest him nothing, and he crieth unto the LORD against thee, so that sin is in thee: 10 thou shalt give to him, and thy heart shall not be troubled to give to him: for therefore the LORD thy

God shall bless thee in all thy works, and in all that thou shalt put thy hand to. 11 Because there will al- ways be poor people in the land, I command you to open your hand to your brother, your needy and your poor in your land. 12 If one of your Jewish brothers sells himself to you, or a Hebrew, and serves you for six years, in the seventh year you shall let him go from you: 13 and when thou sendest him away free from thee, thou shalt not let him go away empty, 14 but thou shalt give him a free reward of thy cattle, of thy corn, and of thy wine; thou shalt give him that with which the Lord thy God hath blessed thee. 15 Remember that you were a servant in the land of Egypt, and that the LORD your God delivered you; therefore I command you this day. 16 And if he shall say to thee, "I will not depart from thee, because he loves thee and thy house, and because he is well with thee," then it shall be given thee, 17 then thou shalt take a maiden, and thou shalt put his ears against the die, and he shall be thy servant for all eternity; and the same shalt thou do with thy maidservant. 18 Do not grieve when you let him go away free from you, for he has served you for six years, which is twice the worth of a hired servant; and the LORD your God will bless you in all that you do. 19 All the firstborn of your cattle and sheep you shall consecrate to the LORD your God. You shall not do any work with your firstborn bull, nor shall you shear your firstborn sheep. 20 You shall eat it before the LORD your God, year by year, at the place the LORD chooses, you and your family. 21 But if there is any de- fect in it, as if it were lame, or blind, or had any other defect, you shall not offer it to the LORD your God, 22 but thou shalt eat it with- in thy gates; the vncleane and the cleane shall eat it alike, as the roe and as the deer. 23 Only you shall not eat its blood, but you shall sprin- kle it on the ground like water.

CHAPTER 16

1 You shall observe the month of Abib and celebrate the Passover to the LORD your God, for in the month of Abib the LORD your God brought you out of Egypt by night. 2 You shall therefore offer to the LORD your God the Passover, of sheep and of bullocks, in the place where the LORD chooses to make his Name dwell. 3 And thou shalt not eat leavened bread with it; but for ten days shalt thou eat leavened bread with it, that is, the bread of tribulation, because thou hast gone out of the land of Egypt in haste, to remember the day that thou wentest out of the land of Egypt, all the days of thy life. 4 In all thy coasts shall no bare be found for ten days; and no meat shall remain in the night until the morning when thou hast offered the first day at noon. 5 Thou shalt not offer in any of thy gates the pastime which the LORD thy God hath given thee: 6 But in the place which the LORD thy God shall choose to set his Name, there thou shalt offer the Passiria at noon, toward the setting of the sun, in the season when thou camest out of Egypt. 7 You shall eat it in the place which the LORD your God shall choose; you shall return the next day and go back to your tents. 8 Six days you shall eat vnleauened bread, and the seventh day shall be a solemn assembly for the LORD your God, in which you shall do no work. 9 You shall dedicate ten weeks, and you shall begin to deduct them when you begin to put your sickle into the grain: 10 And thou shalt keep the feast of weeks for the Lord thy God, which is a free gift of thy hand, which thou shalt give to the Lord thy God, as the Lord thy God hath blessed thee. 11 And thou shalt be reconciled to the Lord thy God, thou, and thy son, and thy daughter, and thy ser- vant, and thy maid,

and the leuite that is with- in thy gates, and the stranger, and the father of the family, and the widow, that are among you, in the place which the Lord thy God shall choose to put his Name there, 12 And you shall remember that you were a servant in Egypt; therefore you shall observe and perform these precepts. 13 And thou shalt observe the feast of Tabernacles ten days, when thou hast gathered thy corn and thy wine. 14 And thou shalt make feast thou, and thy son, and thy daughter, and thy manservant, and thy maid-servant, and the leuite, and the stranger, and the fatherless, and the widow, that are within thy gates. 15 Every two days thou shalt make a feast to the LORD thy God in the place which the LORD shall choose; when the LORD thy God blesseth thee in all thy earnings, and in all the works of thy hands, thou shalt still be glad. 16 Three times a year shall all the males present themselves before the LORD thy God in the place which he shall choose: in the feast of vnleaued bread, in the feast of weeks, and in the feast of Tabernacles; and they shall not present themselves before the LORD emp- tied. 17 Every one shall give according to the gift of his hand, and according to the blessing of the LORD thy God, which he hath bestowed upon thee. 18 In all thy cities, which the LORD thy God hath given thee, thou shalt make unto thee judges and officers for all thy tribes; they shall judge the people with righteous judg- ment. 19 Thou shalt not oppose the Law, nor respect anyone, nor take rewards, for reward blinds the eyes of the wise and perturbs the word of the righteous. 20 You shall follow what is right and just, that you may live and possess the land which the LORD your God grants you. 21 You shall not plant any group of trees near the altar of the LORD your God, which you shall make for yourself. 22 You shall not make for yourself pillars, which the LORD your God detests.

CHAPTER 17

1 Thou shalt not offer to the LORD thy God any bull or any sheep that is defective, or any thing that is bloody, for this is an abomina- tion to the LORD thy God. 2 If in any of your cities, which the LORD your God grants you, there is found a man or a woman who has committed an evil deed before the LORD your God, transgressing his counsel, 3 and has put himself in the service of other gods and worshipped them, like the sun, the moon, or any other host of heaven, which I have not commanded, 4 if the thing has been report- ed to thee, and thou hast heard it, thou shalt inquire diligently, and if it be true, and the thing be certain, that such an abomination was committed in Israel, 5 then thou shalt bring to thy gates that man or that woman (who committed that infamy), whether man or woman, and stone them with stones until they die. 6 By the mouth of two or three wit- nesses, he who is worthy of death shall die; but by the mouth of one witness, he shall not die. 7 The hands of the witnesses shall be on him first to kill him, and then the hands of all the people; so you shall remove the wicked one from among you. 8 If there shall arise a mat- ter too difficult for thee in judgment between blood and blood, between appeal and appeal, between plague and plague, in matters of dis- pute within thy gates, then thou shalt arise and go to the place which the LORD thy God shall choose, 9 and you shall present yourself to the priests of the Leuites and to the judge who shall be in those days, and you shall ask, and they shall give you the judgment of judgment, 10 and thou shalt do what those of that place (which the LORD hath chosen) shall say unto thee, and thou shalt abide by all that they shall say unto thee. 11 And thou shalt do according

to the law which they shall teach thee, and according to the judgment which they shall tell thee; thou shalt not de- part from that which they shall point out to thee, either to the right hand or to the left. 12 And the man who shall act presumptuously, not giving heed to the priest (who stands be- fore the LORD your God to officiate) or to the judge, shall die, and you shall take away euillia from Israel. 13 So all the people will listen and fear, and will not presume any more. 14 When thou comest into the land which the LORD thy God giveth thee, and thou shalt possess it, and thou shalt dwell therein, if thou shalt say, I will establish a king out of me, as all the nations that surround me, 15 then thou shalt make king outside of thee whom the LORD thy God shall choose; from among thy breth- ren thou shalt make king outside of thee; thou shalt not set a stranger outside of thee who is not thy brother. 16 In any case you shall not prepare many horses for him, nor shall you bring the people back to Egypt to increase the number of horses, since the LORD has said to you, "From now on you shall not go that way." 17 He will not bring many goods to them, lest they lose heart, and he will not cause them to gather much silver and gold. 18 When he sits on the throne of his king, he will write this law to him in a book, written by the priests of Leu. 19 And he shall write it with him and reread it all the days of his life, that he may learn to fear the LORD his God and to observe all the words of this Law and the provisions for car- rying them out: 20 that his heart be not lifted up toward his brethren, and that he turn not away from the commandment, neither to the right hand nor to the left, but that he prolong his days in his kingdom, he and his children in the midst of Israel.

CHAPTER 18

1 The priests of the Leuites and all the tribe of Leui shall have no portion or inheritance with Israel, but they shall eat the offerings of the LORD made by fire and his inheritance. 2 Therefore they shall have no inheritance among their brethren, for the LORD is their inheritance, as he has told them. 3 The priests shall be bound by the rules of the people: whoever offers a sacrifice, whether of bull or of sheep, shall give to the priest the shoulder, the two cheeks and the udder. 4 You shall also give him the first fruits of your grain, your wine and your oil, and the first fleece of your sheep. 5 For the LORD your God has chosen him out of all your tribes to stand and serve in the Name of the LORD, him and his chil- dren forever. 6 Even when a Leuite comes out of one of your cities from all Israel, where he has remained, and comes with all the desire of his heart to the place the LORD chooses, 7 he shall minister in the name of the LORD his God, like all his Leuite brethren who have remained there before the LORD. 8 They shall have similar portions to eat, in addition to those from the sale of his wealth. 9 When you enter the land which the LORD your God grants you, you shall not learn to do the abominations of those peoples. 10 There shall not be found among you anyone who makes his son or daughter pass through the fire, or who does witchcraft, or who is a watcher of the times, or an indicator of flights of birds, or a sorcerer 11 or an enchanter, or one who entertains spirits, or a soothsayer, or one who seeks counsel from the dead. 12 For all who do these things are in abomination to the LORD, and because of these abominations the LORD your God casts them out before you. 13 You shall therefore be just with the LORD your God. 14 The nations which thou shalt possess give heed to those who control the times and to

sorcerers; as for thee, the LORD thy God hath not done thee this favor. 15 The LORD your God will raise up for you a prophet like me from among you, from among your brethren; to him you shall give heed, 16 According to all that you desired of the LORD your God in Horeb, in the day of the gathering, when you said, "I do not want to hear the voice of my Lord God any more, nor to see this great fire, lest I die." 17 The LORD said to me, "They have spoken well. 18 I will raise up to them a prophet from among their brethren like you, and I will put my words in their mouths, and he will say to them whatever I command him. 19 Whoever will not hearken to my words that he shall speak in my Name, I will demand it of him. 20 But the prophet who dares to utter in my Name a word that I have not command- ed him to utter, or who speaks in the name of other gods, then the same prophet shall die. 21 And if you think in your heart, "How shall we know the word which the Lord has not spoken? 22 When a prophet speaks in the name of the Lord, if the thing does not follow and come to pass, it is the thing that the Lord has not spoken, but the prophet has spoken it presumptuously.

CHAPTER 19

1 When the LORD your God has driven out the nations that the LORD your God grants you possession of, you shall possess them and dwell in their cities and houses, 2 thou shalt separate for thyself three cities in the midst of thy land which the LORD thy God grants thee to possess. 3 And thou shalt prepare the way, and divide into three parts the coasts of the land which the LORD thy God hath given thee for an inheritance, that every murderer may flee thither. 4 This is also the cause why the murderer shall flee and remain here: he who kills his neighbor out of ignorance and has not hated him in time past: 5 as he who goes into the woods with his neighbor to cut wood, and his hand strikes with the axe to cut down the tree, if his head slips from the elk and strikes his neighbor who dies, he shall flee to one of the cities and lie, 6 lest the sender of blood pursue the murderer, while his heart is vexed, and catch up with him, for the way is long, and kill him, though he is not worthy of death, because he has not hated him in time past. 7 Therefore I command you, "Establish three cities for yourself." 8 When the LORD your God has enlarged your coasts (as he swore to your fathers) and given you all the land he promised to give your fathers, 9 (if you will observe all the commands I have giv- en you today, namely, to love the LORD your God and to walk in his ways forever), in ad- dition to these three cities you will add three more, 10 lest innocent blood be shed in your land, which the LORD your God has given you as an inheritance, lest blood be shed upon you. 11 But if a man hates his neighbor, waits for him, rises up against him, and strikes a man until he dies, he shall flee to one of these cities, 12 the elders of his city shall send him away and deliver him into the hands of the crier of blood, that he may die. 13 Thine eye shall not spare him, but thou shalt turn away from Israel the cry of innocent blood, that it may go well with thee. 14 Thou shalt not re- move the marks of thy neighbors anciently set in thy inheritance, that thou mayest inherit the land which the LORD thy God giveth thee to possess. 15 A single witness shall not rise up against a man for a trespass or for a sin or for a fault in which he has been guilty, but by the mouth of two witnesses or by the mouth of three witnesses the matter shall be deter- mined. 16 If a false witness rises up against a man to accuse him of trespass, 17 then the two men who accuse together shall stand be- fore the LORD, that is, before the priests and judges who shall be present in those days, 18 and the judges shall make a thorough inqui- ry; and if the witness shall be found false and shall have testified falsely against his broth- er, 19 then you shall do to him what he had thought to do to his brother; so you shall take his son away from your walls. 20 And the oth- ers, hearing this, shall be afraid, and shall not commit any more such wickedness among you. 21 Therefore your eye shall not have com- passion, but life for life, eye for eye, tooth for tooth, hand for hand, foote for foote.

CHAPTER 20

1 When you go out to war against your en- emies and see horses and chariots and peo- ple more numerous than you, do not turn away from them, for the LORD your God is with you, who brought you out of the land of Egypt. 2 When you have arrived near the bat- tlefield, the priest shall go out to speak to the people, 3 and he will say to them, "Beware, O Israel, you have come today to fight against your enemies; do not let your hearts be trou- bled, do not be troubled, and do not be afraid of them. 4 For the LORD your God is coming with you to fight for you against your enemies and to save you. 5 Let the officials speak to the people, saying, "Who is it that bought a new house and did not dedicate it? Let him leave and return to his house, if he does not die in the battle, and let another dedicate it." 6 Who is it that planted a vineyard and did not eat its fruit? Let him go away and return to his house again, if he does not die in the battle, and let another eat its fruit. 7 Who is it that promised a wife and did not take her? Let him go and return to his house again, lest he die in the battle and another take her. 8 And let the officers speak again to the people and say, "Whoever has an unfaithful and sick heart, let him leave and return to his home, if he does not want his brothers' hearts to be as sick as his own." 9 After the officers have spoken to the people, they shall appoint captains of the army to lead the people. 10 When you go to a city to fight against it, you shall offer it peace. 11 If it responds to you peacefully and opens to you, all the people there will be your tributaries and will serve you. 12 But if it does not want to make peace with you, but makes war with you, then you shall besiege it. 13 The LORD thy God shall deliver it into thy hand, and thou shalt smite all its males with the blade of the sword. 14 And thou shalt take with thee only the women, and the children, and the cattle, and all that is in the city, and all the spoyle thereof, and thou shalt eat the spoyle of thine enemies, which the LORD thy God hath given thee. 15 So you shall do with all the cities that are far from you and that do not belong to the cities of these nations. 16 But of the cities of these people, which the LORD your God will give you as an inheritance, you shall tell no one else, 17 But thou shalt utterly destroy them: the Hittites, the Amorites, the Canaanites, the Perizzites, the Iuites, and the Jebusites, as the Lord thy God hath com- manded thee, 18 That they may teach thee not to do all their abominations, which they have done to their gods, so that thou mayest sin against the LORD thy God. 19 And when thou hast besieged a city for a long time, and hast waged war against it to take it, destroy not the trees of it with an ax, for thou mayest eat of them; therefore thou shalt not cut them down to help thee in the siege (for the tree of the field is the life of man). 20 Only those trees that you know are of no use for consumption, you shall destroy and cut them

down to build fortresses against the city that makes war against you, until you have subdued it.

CHAPTER 21

1 If in the land which the LORD your God has given you to possess, one is found slain, lying in the field, and it is not known who killed him, 2 then your elders and your judges shall go out and measure the cities that are around the one who was killed. 3 And the elders of that city that is near the man that was slain shall take a heifer that has not been put to work, and that has not been subjected to the yoke. 4 The elders of that city shall take the heifer to a valley of stone, which is neither gleaned nor sown, and shall cut off its neck in the valley. 5 The priests the sons of Leui (whom the LORD your God has chosen to minister and to bless in the name of the LORD) shall also come forth, and by their word all the strife and pes- tilence shall be tried. 6 All the elders of the city who approached the slain man shall wash their hands from the beheaded heifer in the valley: 7 And they shall testify, saying, "Our hands have not shed this blood, neither have our eyes seen it." 8 O LORD, be merciful to thy people Israel, whom thou hast redeemed, and let not innocent blood be upon thy people Is- rael, and the blood shall be forgiven. 9 So you will turn away from you the cry of innocent blood, when you do what is right in the eyes of the LORD. 10 When you go to war against your enemies, the LORD your God will deliver them into your hand, and you will take cap- tives, 11 thou shalt see among the captives a beautiful woman, and thou shalt desire her and take her as thy wife, 12 thou shalt bring her back to thy house, and cut off her head, and shorten her hair, 13 and you shall take off the garment in which she was taken, and she shall stay in your house, visiting her father and her mother for a month; after which you shall go in to her and marry her, and she shall be your wife. 14 If you have no desire for her, you may let her go where she pleases, but you may not sell her for money or make merchan- dise of her, for you have humiliated her. 15 If a man has two wives, one valued and the oth- er hated, and they have borne him children, both the valued and the hated; if the first born is the son of the hated, 16 then, when the time comes to designate his sons as heirs of what he has, he will not be able to bring forth the son of the hated one before the son of the hat- ed one, who is the first born: 17 but he shall acknowledge the son of the hated one as the first born, and shall give him a double portion of all that he possesses, because he is the first of his strength, and to him is due the right of first born. 18 If one has a stubborn and dis- obedient son, who does not listen to the voice of his father nor to the voice of his mother, and they have chastised him, but he will not obey, 19 then his father and his mother shall take him and bring him to the elders of his city and to the gate of the place where he dwells, 20 and they shall say to the elders of his city, "This son of ours is stubborn and dis- obedient and does not obey our warnings; he is a profligate and a drunkard." 21 Then all the men of his city shall stone him with stones to death; so you shall take euillia out of the way, that all Israel may hear and fear him. 22 If a man has committed a sin worthy of death and is put to death, and you hang him on a tree, 23 his body shall not remain all night on the tree, but thou shalt bury him the same day, for the curse of God is on him who is hanged. There- fore do not defile your land which the Lord your God has given you as an inheritance.

CHAPTER 22

1 You shall not see your brother's ox or his lost sheep, nor shall you depart from them, but you shall bring the againe to your brother. 2 If your brother is not near you or if you do not know him, you shall bring him into your house and he shall stay with you until your brother looks for him; then you shall hand him over to him again. 3 Likewise you shall do with his plank and with his money, and so you shall do with all the lost things of your brother, which he has lost; if you have found them, you shall not depart from them. 4 Thou shalt not see thy brother's horse and his ox fall by the wayside, and thou shalt not withdraw from them, but shalt lift them up with him. 5 The woman shall not wear what pertains to the man, nor shall the man put on women's clothing, for everything he does is in abomi- nation to the LORD your God. 6 If you find a bird's nest in the street, or in a tree, or on the ground, whether it be eggs or reeds, and the dam sits on the reed or on the eggs, you shall not take the dam with the reed, 7 but thou shalt in any case let go the damma and take the yong with thee, that thou mayest prosper and prolong thy days. 8 When thou shalt build a new house, thou shalt make a battalion on thy roof, lest blood be shed on thy house, if any should fall. 9 Thou shalt not sow thy vineyard with different kinds of seed, lest thou defile the harvest of the seed which thou hast sown and the fruit of the vineyard. 10 You shall not plow with an ox and an axle together. 11 You shall not wear clothing of different kinds, such as wool and linen together. 12 You shall make you bangs on the four quarters of your garment, with which you shall clothe your- self. 13 If a man takes a wife and, after lying with her, hates her, 14 and charges her with insulting things, and gives her an infamous name, and says, "I took this wife, and when I came to her, I found her no more." 15 then the bride's father and her mother shall take and bring the signs of the bride's virginity to the elders of the city at the gate. 16 And the fa- ther of the elder shall say to the elders, "I have given my daughter in marriage to this man, and he hates her." 17 And, behold, he shall im- pute absurd things to her, saying, "I have not found your daughter a mayde; behold, these are the marks of my daughter's virginity"; and they shall cause her to be stripped before the elders of the city. 18 Then the elders of the city shall take that man and chastise him, 19 and they shall condemn himh a hundred thousand shekels of silver, and they shall give it to the woman's father, because he brought a high name to a woman of Israel; and the woman shall be his wife, and he shall not be able to part with her all his life. 20 But if this thing be true, that the woman was not found a virgin, 21 then they shall bring the woman to the place where her father's house was, and the men of her city shall stone her to death, because she has committed folly in Israel, playing the harlot in her fathers' house. 22 If a man is found lying with a woman mar- ried to a man, they shall both be dyed two: the man who lay with his wife and his wife. 23 If a maiden is betrothed to a husband, and a man finds her in the city and lies with her, 24 you shall lead them both to the gates of the same city and stone them to death: the woman because she did not cry out, being in the city, and the man because he humiliat- ed his neighbors' wife. 25 But if a man finds a sweetheart of age in the fields, and forces her, and lies down with her, the man who lay down with her shall die alone: 26 You shall not be able to do anything to the woman, for there is no cause of death in the woman; for as when a man rises up against his neighbor and

wounds him to death, so it is in this case. 27 For he found her in the fields; the bride was weeping, and there was no one to help her. 28 If a man finds a woman not betrothed, he takes her and lies down with her, and they are found, 29 And the man that lay down with her shall give to the woman's father fifty shekels of silk; and she shall be his wife, because he humbled her; and he shall not be able to part with her all his life. 30 And no man shall take his father's wife, neither shall he vncouer her father's skirt.

CHAPTER 23

1 No one who has been injured by an explo- sion or whose primary member has been cut off will enter the Lord's congregation. 2 A bastard shall not enter the congregation of the LORD, and until the tenth generation he shall not enter the congregation of the LORD. 3 The Ammonites and the Moabites shall not enter into the congregation of the LORD: un- til their tenth generation they shall not enter into the congregation of the LORD forever, 4 Because they did not receive you with bread and water on the way when you came out of Egypt, and because they called upon Balaam the son of Beor, of Pethor in Aram-Naraim, to curse you against you. 5 Yet the LORD your God would not listen to Balaam, but the LORD your God turned the curse into a bless- ing for you, because the LORD your God loved you. 6 You shall not see their peace nor their prosperity all your days. 7 You shall not abhor an Edomite, because he is your brother, nor shall you abhor an Egyptian, because you have been a wanderer in his land. 8 And the sons that shall be begotten of them in their thir- teenth generation shall enter into the congre- gation of the LORD. 9 When you go out with the army against your enemies, keep away all wickedness. 10 If there is anyone among you who is vncleane from what comes to him by night, he shall depart from the host and not enter the host, 11 but then he shall wash him- self with water, and when the sun has set, he shall enter into the host. 12 You shall also have a place outside the hostel, where you are to go, 13 you shall have a paddle among your weap- ons, and, when you want to sit outside, you shall use it to dig, and, coming back, you shall make your own excrement. 14 For the LORD thy God walketh in the midst of thy camel's way to deliver thee, and to deliver thine ene- mies before thee: therefore thy army shall be holy, that it may not see any filthiness in thee, and it shall depart from thee. 15 Thou shalt not deliver unto thy master the servant that hath fled from his master. 16 He shall dwell with you, even among you, in the place which he shall choose, in one of your cities, where it shall please him best; you shall not let him go. 17 There shall be no harlot among the daugh- ters of Israel, nor shall there be a keeper of harlots among the sons of Israel. 18 You shall not bring into the house of the LORD your God either the wrath of a harlot or the price of a dog for a vow, for both are in abomination to the LORD your God. 19 You shall not give your brother vsurie, such as vsurie of money, vsurie of food, vsurie of anything that is put to vsurie. 20 Thou may lend to a stranger for vsurie, but thou shalt not lend to thy broth- er for vsurie, that the LORD thy God may bless thee in all that thou shalt put thy hand to, in the land where thou goest to possess. 21 When thou shalt make a vow to the LORD thy God, thou shalt not be slow in paying it, for the LORD thy God shall surely require it of thee, and so it shall be sin for thee. 22 But when you abstain from the vow, it will not be sin for you. 23 That which has gone forth from thy lips, thou shalt keep it and perform it, as if thou had willingly sworn it to the Lord thy God, because thou hast spoken it with thy mouth. 24 When thou goest to thy neighbor's vineyard, thou mayest eat grapes as thou wilt, to the extent that thou wilt, but thou shalt not put any in thy vessel. 25 When thou goest to thy neighbor's field, thou may squeeze out the ears with thy hand, but thou shalt not strike thy field with a sickle.

CHAPTER 24

1 When a man takes a wife and marries her, if in his eyes he finds no defect, because he has discerned some filthiness in her, let him write her a deed of divorce, put it in her hand, and send her out of his house. 2 And when she has left her house and gone her way, she shall marry another man, 3 if the latter husband hates her, and writes her a letter of divorce, and puts it in her hand, and sends her out of her house, or if the man who had taken her to wife dies: 4 then the first husband who sent her away shall not take her to wife again, after she has defiled herself, for this is an abomina- tion in the sight of the LORD, and thou shalt not cause the land which the LORD thy God hath given thee to sin. 5 When a man takes a new wife, he shall not make war or be charged with any business, but he shall remain free at home for a year and be reunited with the wife he has taken. 6 No one shall take the lower milestone or the upper milestone as a pledge, for this wage is his pledge. 7 If anyone is caught stealing one of his brothers of the children of Israel and makes merchandise out of it or sells it, that thief shall die; so you shall remove him from your midst. 8 Take heed of the plague of leprosy, observing diligently and doing all that the priests of the Leuites will teach you; take heed to do as I have com- manded them. 9 Remember what the LORD your God did to Miriam on the way, after you had come out of Egypt. 10 When you again ask your neighbor for something on loan, you shall not go into his house to take his pledge. 11 But you shall stand outside, and the man who lent it to you shall take your pledge out- side the walls. 12 Moreover, if it is a poor man, you shall not sleep with his pledge, 13 but thou shalt give him back his pledge when the sun goes down, that he may sleep with his gar- ments and bless thee; and he shall be just to thee before the LORD thy God. 14 Thou shalt not oppress a needy and poor servant, either of thy brethren or of the stranger that is in thy land within thy gates. 15 Thou shalt not give him his wages for his day, and the sun shall not go down upon him, because he is poor, and by this he keeps himself alive; lest he cry out against thee unto the LORD, and be a sin unto thee. 16 The fathers shall not be put to death for the children, nor shall the children be put to death for the fathers, but each one shall be put to death for his own sin. 17 You shall not lose the right of the stranger and the fatherless, nor shall you take a widow's income as a pledge. 18 But remember that you were a servant in Egypt and that the Lord your God delivered you from there. Therefore I command you to do this thing. 19 When thou shalt cut down thy shrub in thy field, and shalt have forgotten a safe in the field, thou shalt not go again to fetch it, but it shall be for the stranger, and for the father of the family, and for the widow, that the Lord thy God may bless thee in all the works of thy hands. 20 When thou shalt cut down thy olive tree, thou shalt not come out of it again, but it shall be for the stranger, for the fatherless, and for the widow. 21 When you harvest your vineyard, you shall not gather clean grapes after you, but it shall be for the stranger, for the orphan and

for the widow. 22 Remember that you were a servant in the land of Egypt; therefore I command you to do this thing.

CHAPTER 25

1 When there is a quarrel among men, they shall come to judgment, and judgment shall be pronounced upon them, and the righ- teous shall be justified and the wicked con- demned, 2 if the wicked man is worthy to be beaten, the judge will make him lie down and beat him before him, according to his guilt, to a certain name. 3 He shall cause him to give him forty strokes and no more, lest, if he overcomes him and beats him with many strokes, your brother appear despised in your eyes. 4 Do not move the ox that treads on the grain. 5 If the brothers dwell together, and one of them dies and has no children, the wife of the dead man shall not marry outside, that is, to a stranger, but his kinsman shall go to her, take her as his wife, and make her the of- fice of kinsman. 6 The first born that she shall bear shall succeed in the name of her dead brother, that his name may not be blotted out from Israel. 7 If the man does not want to take his kinswoman, let his kinswoman go to the elders at the door and say, "My kinsman refuses to name his brother in Israel; he does not want to do the office of kinsman to me." 8 Then the elders of his city shall call him and argue with him; if he stands up and says, "I will not take it." 9 then his kinswoman shall join him in the presence of the elders, and she shall pull the shoe off his foot, and spit in his face, and answer and say, "Thus shall it be done to that man who will not buy his broth- ers' house." 10 And his name shall be called in Israel, "The house of him who was stripped." 11 When men fight with one another, if the wife of the one approaches to free her husband from the hands of the one who beats him, she shall put forth her hand and take him by her privileges, 12 You shall cut off her hand; your eye shall not spare her. 13 Thou shalt not have in thy bag two weights, one large and one small, 14 and thou shalt not have in thy house several measures, one large and one small: 15 But thou shalt have a just and proper weight; thou shalt have a perfect and proper measure, that thy days may be long in the land which the LORD thy God giveth thee. 16 For all that do these things, and all that do unjustly, are in abomination to the LORD thy God. 17 Re- member what Amalek did to you along the way when you came out of Egypt: 18 How he met you on the way and struck you from be- hind, all who were weak behind you, when you were faint and weary, and he did not fear God. 19 Therefore, when the LORD your God has made you rest from all your enemies that surround you in the land which the LORD your God gives you as an inheritance to pos- sess it, then you shall blot out the memory of Amalek from under the tree; do not forget it.

CHAPTER 26

1 When you have entered the land which the LORD your God gives you as an inheritance, you shall possess it and dwell in it, 2 you shall take the first fruits of the land, bring them out of the land which the LORD your God has giv- en you as an inheritance, put them in a bas- ket, and go to the place which the LORD your God has chosen to put his Name there. 3 You shall present yourself to the priest who will be in those days, and you shall say to him, "Today I acknowledge before the Lord your God that I have come to the county which the Lord swore to give to our fathers." 4

Then the priest shall take the basket from your hand and place it before the altar of the LORD your God. 5 You shall answer and say before the LORD your God, "My father was a Syrian who, ready to starve to death, went down to Egypt, stayed there with a small company, and grew up there into a great nation, powerful and full of people. 6 The Egyptians tormented us, made us suffer, and forced us into cruel slavery. 7 But when we cried out to the LORD, the God of our fathers, the LORD heard our voice and looked upon our hardship, toil and oppres- sion. 8 The LORD brought us out of Egypt with a mighty hand and an outstretched arm, with great terribleness, with signs and wonders. 9 And he brought vs to this place and gave vs this land, a land flowing with milk and honey. 10 Now, behold, I have brought the first fruits of the land that you, Lord, have given me, and you shall set them before the Lord your God and worship before the Lord your God: 11 And thou shalt make up for all the good things which the LORD thy God hath bestowed upon thee and upon thy house, thou, the Leuita, and the stranger that is among you. 12 And when thou hast finished tithing all thy earn- ings, in the third year, which is the year of tithing, and hast given them to the Leuita, and to the stranger, and to the fatherless, and to the widow, that they may eat within thy gates, and be satisfied, 13 then shalt thou say before the LORD thy God, I have brought out of my house the thing sown, and have given it to the Leuite, the stranger, the orphan, and the widow, according to all thy commands which thou hast given me: I have not trans- gressed any of thy commands, nor have I forgotten them. 14 I have not eaten of them in my mourning, nor let the dead perish, nor have I eaten of them for the dead, but I have heeded the message of the LORD my God: I have done all that thou hast recommended me. 15 Behold from your holy habitation, even from heaven, and bless your people Israel and the land that you gave to our fathers, the land flowing with milk and honey. 16 Today the LORD your God commands you to observe these rules and these laws; therefore observe them and put them into practice with all your heart and with all your soul. 17 Today you have appointed the LORD to be your God, that you walk in his ways, that you keep his decrees, his commands and his laws, and that you lis- ten to his message. 18 Today the LORD has established you to be a precious people to him (as he has promised you) and to keep all his commands, 19 and to make you high above all the nations (which he has created) in praise, name and glory, and to be a holy people to the LORD your God, as he has said.

CHAPTER 27

1 Then Moses, with the elders of Israel, com- manded the people, "Observe all the prescrip- tions that I command you today. 2 When you pass from Iorden to the land which the LORD your God has assigned to you, you shall set large stones and cover them with lime, 3 And you shall write on them all the words of this Lawe, when you have come beyond, that you may go into the land which the LORD your God grants you: a land flowing with milk and honey, as the LORD God of your fathers promised you. 4 Therefore, when you pass over Iorden, you shall put these stones, which I command you today, on Mount Ebal, and you shall plate them with a plate. 5 There you shall build an altar to the LORD your God, an altar of stones; you shall not lift up any instru- ment on them. 6 You shall make the altar of the LORD your God of whole stones, and you shall offer burnt offerings on it to the LORD your God. 7 You

shall offer peace offerings and eat and refresh yourself before the LORD your God: 8 And thou shalt write upon the stones all the words of this law, well and plainly. 9 And Moses and the priests of the Leuites spa- ke unto all Israel, saying, Hear and hearken, O Israel: this day hast thou become the people of the LORD thy God. 10 Hear therefore the message of the LORD your God, and practice his commands and his prescriptions, which I command you today." 11 On that same day Moses gave a charge to the people, saying, "These are the men who will stand before the LORD your God, 12 These shall stand on Mount Gerizzim to bless the people when you pass by Iorden: Simeon, Leui, Iudah, Is- sachar, Ioseph and Benjamin. 13 These shall stand on Mount Ebal to curse: Reuben, Gad, Ascer, Zebulun, Dan and Naphtali. 14 And the Leuites shall answer and say to all the men of Israel with a loud voice, 15 Cursed is the man that shall make a graven or cast image, which is an abomination to the LORD, the work of the craftsman's hands, and shall put it in a secret place:" And all the people shall answer and say, So be it. 16 Cursed is he that curseth his father and his mother: And all the people shall say, So be it. 17 Cursed is he who removes the brands of his neighbors: And all the people shall say, So be it. 18 Cursed is he who causes the blind to go out of the way: And all the people shall say, So be it. 19 Cursed is he who hinders the right of the stranger, the father of a family, and the widow: And all the people shall say, So be it. 20 Cursed is he who lies with his father's wife, because he has vio- lated his father's skirt: And all the people shall say, So be it. 21 Cursed is he who lies with a beast: And all the people shall say, So be it. 22 Cursed is he who lies with his sister, his fa- ther's daughter or his mother's daughter: And all the people shall say, So be it. 23 Cursed is he who lies with his mother-in-law: And all the people shall say, So be it. 24 Cursed is he who secretly beats his son: And all the people shall say, So be it. 25 Cursed is he who takes a reward for causing innocent blood to die: And all the people shall say, So be it. 26 Cursed is he who does not confirm all the words of this Law and put them into practice: And all the people shall say, So be it.

CHAPTER 28

1 If you diligently obey the message of the LORD your God, if you observe and practice all his commands that I impose on you today, the LORD your God will set you high above all the nations of the earth. 2 All these blessings will come upon you and overtake you, if you obey the command of the LORD your God. 3 You shall be blessed in the city and blessed also in the fields. 4 Blessed shall be the fruit of your body, the fruit of your soil, the fruit of your cattle, the harvest of your animals and your flocks. 5 Blessed shall be your basket and your dough. 6 You shall be blessed when you go in, and you shall also be blessed when you go out. 7 The LORD will bring down before your face your enemies who rise up against you; they will go out against you on one side and flee before you on another. 8 And the LORD shall command blessing to be with thee in thy storehouses, and in all that thou shalt set thy hand to; and he shall bless thee in the land which the LORD thy God giveth thee. 9 The LORD will make you a holy people to himself, as he has sworn to you, if you keep the commands of the LORD your God and walk in his ways. 10 Then all the peoples of the earth shall see that the Name of the LORD is invoked upon thee, and they shall depart from thee. 11 The LORD shall make thee rich in goods, in the fruits of thy body, in the fruits of thy cattle, and in the fruits of thy soil, in the land which the LORD swore to give to thy fa- thers. 12 The LORD will open to thee his good treasure, that is, heaven, to give ray to thy kin- dred in due season, and to bless all the work of thy hands; and thou shalt lend to many na- tions, but thou shalt not make thyself charge- able. 13 And the LORD shall make thee the chief, and not the tayle; thou shalt be alone, and shalt not be beneath, if thou obey the commands of the LORD thy God, which I command thee this day to observe and put into practice. 14 But you shall not forsake any of the words that I command you today, ei- ther to the right or to the left, to go after other gods and serve them. 15 But if you do not obey the message of the LORD your God to observe and put into practice all his commands and prescriptions that I command you today, all these curses will come upon you and kill you. 16 You shall be cursed in the city and cursed also in the fields. 17 Your basket and your dough will be cursed. 18 The fruits of your body and the fruits of your land, the increase of your animals and the flock of your sheep will be cursed. 19 Thou shalt be cursed when thou goest in, and cursed also when thou comest out. 20 The LORD will send you curs- es, trouble and shame in everything you put your hand to do, until you are destroyed and perish quickly, because of the wickedness of your works with which you have forsaken me. 21 The LORD will cause the pestilence to pass over you, until it has consumed you from the land where you go to possess it. 22 The LORD shall smite thee with consumption, and with fever, and with agony, and with erosion, and with the sword, and with blast, and with mil- dew, and shall pursue thee until thou die. 23 Your skin that is outside your head shall be burned, and the earth that is beneath you shall be scorched. 24 The LORD shall give thee, as the ray of thy earth, dust and ashes; and from above shall descend upon thee, until thou be destroyed. 25 And the LORD shall bring thee down before thine enemies; thou shalt go out one way against them, and flee by two other ways before them, and shalt be scattered through all the kingdoms of the earth. 26 Your chariots shall be eaten by all the beasts of the air and the beasts of the earth, and no one shall escape them. 27 The LORD will smite you with the botch of Egypt, with the hemeroids, with the skab, and with the itche, so that you cannot heal. 28 The LORD will smite you with madness, blindness and asthenia of the heart. 29 Moreover thou shalt not go groping to anyone, as a blind man goes groping in darkness, and thou shalt not pros- per in thy ways; thou shalt but be oppressed with evil and be further smitten, and no one shall succor thee. 30 Thou shalt take a woman to wife, and another man shall lie down with her; thou shalt build a house, and thou shalt not inhabit it; thou shalt plant a vineyard, and thou shalt not eat its fruit. 31 Thy oxen shall be killed before thine eyes, and thou shalt not eat of them; thy cattle shall be carried away vio- lently before thine eyes, and shall not be re- turned to thee; thy sheep shall be given to thy enemies, and none shall save them for thee. 32 Thy sons and thy daughters shall be deliv- ered to another people, and thine eyes shall continue to seek them, until they fall away, and there shall be no strength in thy hands. 33 The fruit of thy land and of all thy labors shall be eaten by a people whom thou knowest not, and thou shalt only suffer wrong and vio- lence: 34 So that thou shalt become mad for the sight which thine eyes shall see. 35 And the LORD shall smite thee in thy knees and in thy fingers with a plague which thou shalt not be able to heal, from the sole of thy foot unto the top of thy head. 36 And the LORD will bring you and your king (whom you have es- tablished outside yourself) to a nation that neither

you nor your fathers have known, and there you will serve other gods: wood and stone, 37 And thou shalt be a wonder, a cause of boasting and a cause of discussion among all peoples, whither the LORD shall bring thee. 38 You shall bring much seed into the fields and reap little of it, for the gatherers shall destroy it. 39 You shall plant a vineyard and cultivate it, but you shall not drink the wine or gather the grapes, for the worms will eat them. 40 You shall have olive trees in all your coasts, but you shall not feed on the olive tree, for your olives will fall. 41 You shall beget sons and daughters, but you shall not have them, for they shall go into captivity. 42 All your trees and the fruit of your land shall be devoured by the grasshopper. 43 The serpent that is in your midst shall draw near to you to come up on him, and you shall go down under the water. 44 He will lend to you, and you will not lend to him; he will be the chief, and you will be the lukewarm. 45 Moreover, all these curses shall come upon you, and they shall pursue you and surprise you, until you are de- stroyed, because you have not obeyed the command of the LORD your God to observe his commands and his prescriptions which he has given you: 46 And they shall be for you signs and wonders, and for your descendants forever, 47 because thou hast not served the LORD thy God joyfully and heartily for the abundance of all things. 48 Therefore thou shalt serve thine enemies whom the LORD will send upon thee, in hunger and thirst, in nakedness and in want of all things; and he shall put a yoke of iron upon thy neck until he has destroyed thee. 49 The LORD will bring upon you a nation from afar, from the utter- most part of the world, flying as swiftly as an eagle; a nation whose language you will not understand: 50 a fierce-looking nation, which will have no regard for the old man and no compassion for the young man. 51 He will feed on the fruit of your cattle and the fruits of your land until you are destroyed, and he will leave you neither grain, nor wine, nor oil, nor the harvest of your land, nor the flock of your sheep, until he has reduced you to noth- ing. 52 And he shall besiege thee in all thy cit- ies, until thy strong and solid walls, in which thou trustedest in all the land, fall down: he shall besiege thee in all thy cities in all thy land, which the LORD thy God hath given thee. 53 And thou shalt eat the fruits of thy body, that is, the flesh of thy sons and thy daughters, which the LORD thy God hath giv- en thee, during the siege and the straits in which thy enemy shall encircle thee: 54 so that the man (who is tender-hearted and ten- der-hearted among you) may grieve for his brother, and for his wife lying in his bosom, and for the rest of his children that are left to him, 55 lest any of them should eat of the flesh of his children, for there is nothing left for him in that siege and strait with which your enemy will besiege you in all your cities. 56 The tender and gentle woman among you, who would never venture to set the sole of her foot on the ground (because of her softness and tenderness), shall be smitten by her hus- band lying in her bosom, by her son and her daughter, 57 and by her postpartum (which shall come forth between her feet), and by her children whom she shall bear; for when all things shall be spoiled, she shall eat them se- cretly, during the siege and the straits with which thy enemy shall besiege thee in thy cit- ies. 58 If thou shalt not observe and put into practice all the words of Lawe (which are writ- ten in this book), and shalt not fear this glori- ous and fearful name, the LORD thy God, 59 the LORD will make wonderful your plagues and the plagues of your descendants, that is, great plagues sed of long duration, and pain- ful diseases and of long duration. 60 More- over, he shall bring upon thee all the diseases of Egypt, with which thou wast afflicted, and they shall heal thee. 61 Every disease and ev- ery plague that is not written in the book of this law, the LORD will smite you to destruc- tion. 62 And you shall remain few in number, whereas you were like the stars of Heauen in great numbers, because you would not obey the message of the LORD your God. 63 And as the LORD intervened on you to do you good and multiply you, so he will intervene on you to destroy you and reduce you to nothing, and you will be uprooted from the land where you go to possess it. 64 The LORD will scatter you among all peoples, from one end of the world to the other, and there you will serve other gods, whom you have not known nor your fa- thers, like wood and stone. 65 Moreover, in the midst of these nations you will not find rest, nor will the sole of your foot have rest, for the LORD will give you there a trembling heart, looking to return until your eyes fall out, and a sorrowful soul. 66 Thy life shall hang before thee, and thou shalt fear night and day, and shalt have no assurance of thy life. 67 In the morning thou shalt say, "If God were the dawn," and at sunset thou shalt say, "If God were the dawn," for the fear of thy heart, which thou shalt fear, and for the sight of thine eyes, which thou shalt see. 68 And the LORD shall lead thee again into Egypt with ships by the way of which I said unto thee, "Thou shalt not see him any more"; and there thou shalt sell thy selves to thine enemies as slaves and bondwomen, and there shall be no escape.

CHAPTER 29

1 These are the words of the convention which the LORD commanded Moses to make with the children of Israel in the land of Moab, next to the convention which he had made with them at Horeb. 2 Moses called all Israel and said to them, "You have seen all that the LORD has done before your eyes in the land of Egypt against Pharaoh, against all his servants, and against all his land, 3 the great temptations your eyes have seen, the great miracles and wonders: 4 Yet the LORD hath not given you a heart to perceive, eyes to see, and ears to hear, until this day. 5 I have led you for forty years in the wilderness; your garments have not grown old upon you, nei- ther has your linen grown old upon your feet. 6 You ate no bread, nor drank wine, nor drank alcohol, to make you understand that I am the LORD your God. 7 After you had come to this place, Sihon, king of Heshbon, and Og, king of Bashan, went out against us to fight, and we defeated them, 8 we took their territory and gave it as an inheritance to the Reubenites, the Gadites and the half tribe of Manasseh. 9 Observe therefore the words of this Leader and put them into practice, that you may prosper in all that you do. 10 Today you are all standing before the LORD your God: the leaders of your tribes, your elders and your officers, all of you of Israel: 11 your sons, your wives, and your stranger who is in your camna, from those who cut wood to those who draw water, 12 that you may enter into the camp of the LORD your God and into the other which the LORD your God makes with you today, 13 To constitute thee this day as a people unto himself, and to be unto thee a God, as he hath said unto thee, and as he hath sworn unto thy fathers, Abraham, Izhak, and Iaakob. 14 And I do not make this cove- nant and this other covenant with you alone, 15 but both with those who are here with you today before the Lord our God, and with those who are not here with you today. 16 For you know how we dwelt in the land of Egypt and how we passed through the midst of the na- tions that you passed through. 17 And you have seen

their abominations and their idols (wood, stone, silver and gold) that were in their midst, 18 so that there may be no man or woman, family or tribe among you today who turns his heart away from the LORD our God to go and serve the gods of these nations, and so that there may not be among you any- one who produces gall and worms, 19 so that when he hears the words of this curse, he may bless himself in his heart, saying, "I will have peace, though I walk according to the obsti- nacy of my heart, thus adding drunkenness to thirst." 20 And the LORD will not be merciful to him, but then the anger of the LORD and his wrath shall be kindled against that man, and all the curses written in this book shall be kindled upon him, and the LORD shall blot out his name from under heaven, 21 And the LORD shall separate him from all the tribes of Israel, according to all the curses of Coni, written in the book of this Law. 22 So the gen- eration to come, that is, your children who will arise after you, and the stranger who will come from a far country, will say when they see the plagues of this country and its diseas- es, with which the LORD will smite it: 23 (For all that land shall burn with brimstone and with salt; no seed shall be sown, nor shall any fatness be brought forth, nor shall any fatness grow therein, as in the case of the destruction of Sodom, and of Gomorah, and of Admah, and of Zeboim, which the LORD destroyed in his wrath and anger). 24 Then all the nations will say, "Why has the LORD done this to this land? How fierce is this great wrath?" 25 They will answer, "Because they have forsaken the covenant which the LORD, the God of their fathers, made with them when he brought them out of the land of Egypt, 26 and they went to serve other gods and worshiped them: gods whom they did not know and who had given them nothing, 27 Therefore the anger of the LORD was kindled against this land, to bring upon it all the curses that are written in this book. 28 And the LORD uprooted them out of their country in wrath and anger and great indignation, and cast them out into an- other country, as it appears today. 29 The se- cret things belong to the LORD our God, but the revealed things belong to the LORD and to our children forever, that we may put into practice all the words of this law.

CHAPTER 30

1 Now when all these things have come upon thee, either the blessing or the curse which I have set before thee, and thou shalt be con- verted in thine heart, among all the nations whither the LORD thy God hath made thee to go, 2 and you shall return to the LORD your God and obey his message in all that I have commanded you today: you and your children with all your heart and with all your soul, 3 then the LORD your God will bring back your captives, and will have compassion on you, and will return to gather you from all the peo- ples where the LORD your God has scattered you. 4 Even if you are cast into the remotest part of the island, the LORD your God will gather you up and take you away from there, 5 the LORD thy God shall bring thee into the land which thy fathers have possessed, and thou shalt possess it, and it shall give thee prosperity, and multiply thee in comparison with thy fathers. 6 The LORD your God will circumcise your heart and the heart of your descendants, that you may love the LORD your God with all your heart and with all your soul, that you may live. 7 The LORD your God will hurl all these curses on your enemies and on those who hate you and persecute you. 8 Therefore return and obey the message of the LORD and

put into practice all his commands that I have given you today. 9 The LORD your God will make you abundant in all the works of your hand, in the fruits of your body, in the fruits of your cattle, and in the fruits of the land for your riches, for the LORD will turn again to you and do you good, as he did to your fathers, 10 because you will obey the message of the LORD your God, keeping his commands and his prescriptions that are written in the book of this law, when you re- turn to the LORD your God with all your heart and with all your soul. 11 For this command- ment which I command you today is not hid- den from you, nor is it far away. 12 It is not in heaven, that you may say, "Who shall go for you to heaven, and bring it, and cause it to be heard, that we should do it? 13 Nor is it be- yond the sea, that you may say, "Who will go beyond the sea for the vs, bring it and cause the vs to hear it, that we may do it"? 14 But the word is very near you: it is in your mouth and in your heart to do it. 15 Behold, today I have set before you life and good, death and dying, 16 in that today I command you to love the LORD your God, to walk in his ways, to keep his commands and his laws, that you may live and multiply, and that the LORD your God may bless you in the land where you go to pos- sess him. 17 But if your heart turns away, so that you do not want to obey, but you let your- self be seduced and worship other gods and serve them, 18 Today I declare to you that you will surely perish; you will not prolong your days in the land where you pass to possess it. 19 Today I call heaven and earth to report against you, for I have set before you life and death, blessing and curse; therefore choose life, that you and your descendants may live, 20 listening to the LORD your God, obeying his commandment and abiding in him, for he is your life and the length of your days, that you may dwell in the land which the LORD swore to give to your fathers, Abraham, Izhak and Iaakob.

CHAPTER 31

1 Then Moses went and spoke these words to all Israel, 2 And said to them, "Today I am a hundred and twenty years old: I can no longer go out and come in; even the LORD has said to me, 'You shall not go out from this border. 3 The LORD thy God shall go before thee; he shall destroy these nations before thee, and thou shalt possess them. Ioshua will go be- fore you, as the LORD has said. 4 The LORD will do to them what he did to Sihon and Og, kings of the Amorites, and to their land, which he destroyed. 5 The LORD will deliver them to you that you may do to them what I have commanded you. 6 Therefore open your hearts and be strong; do not fear or be afraid of them, for the LORD your God is with you and will not forsake you. 7 Moses called Iosh- ua and said to him before all Israel, "Be strong and courageous, for you shall go with this people into the land which the LORD swore to their fathers to give them and which you shall give them as an inheritance. 8 The LORD him- self goes before you; he will be with you; he will not forsake you nor .fail you. 9 And Moses wrote this Lawe, and delivered it to the priests the sons of Leui (who carried the ark of the LORD's convention) and to all the elders of Israel, 10 and Moses commanded them, "Ev- ery seven years, when the year of deliverance shall be the Feast of Tabernacles: 11 when all Israel shall come and present themselves be- fore the LORD your God in the place which he shall choose, you shall recite this Lawe before all Israel, that they may hear it. 12 Gather the people: men, women, children, and your stranger

who is within your gates, that they may hear, learn, and fear the LORD your God, and observe all the words of this Lawe, 13 and that their children, who have not known it, may hear it and learn to fear the LORD your God, as long as you remain in the land, where you are going to possess it." 14 Then the LORD said to Moses, "Behold, thy day is come when thou must die: call Ioshua, and stand in the Tabernacle of the congregation, that I may give him a charge." Moses and Ioshua went and stood in the Tabernacle of the congrega- tion. 15 The LORD appeared in the Taberna- cle in a pillar of cloud, and the pillar of cloud stopped outside the Tabernacle. 16 And the LORD said to Moses, "Behold, you shall sleep with your fathers, and this people shall rise up and go whoring after the gods of a foreign land (where they are going to dwell), and they shall forsake me and violate my covenant that I have made with them. 17 Therefore in that day my wrath shall be kindled against them, and I will forsake them and hide my face from them; then they shall be consumed, and many hardships and tribulations shall come upon them; then they shall say, "Are not these trib- ulations coming upon me, because God is not with me?" 18 But I will certainly hide my face in that day, because of all the guilt they will commit, because they have turned to other gods. 19 Therefore write this song for your- selves and teach it to the children of Israel; put it in their mouths, that this song may be my testimony against the children of Israel. 20 For I will lead them into the land (which I have sworn to their fathers) flowing with milk and honey, and they shall eat, and they shall become unclean and fat; then they shall turn to other gods and serve them, and they shall despise me and violate my covenant. 21 And when many adversities and tribulations come upon them afterward, this song shall answer them to their faces as a testimony, that it shall not be forgotten by the mouths of their posterity; for I know their imaginations, that they make their way even now, before I have brought them into the land which I have sworn." 22 Moses therefore wrote this song on the same day and taught it to the children of Israel. 23 Then God gave Ioshua the son of Nun a charge and said, "Be strong and of good courage, for you will lead the children of Israel into the land that I have sworn to them, and I will be with you." 24 When Moses had finished writing the words of this Law in a book, until he had finished them, 25 Moses gave an order to the Leuites who were carry- ing the ark of the LORD's convention, saying, "Take the book of this Lawe, 26 "Take the book of this Lawe and put it in the side of the ark of the colonel of the LORD your God, that it may be there as a testimony against you. 27 For I know your rebellion and stiff-neckedness; be- hold, I am still alien with you today, and you are rebellious against the LORD; how much more so will you be after my death? 28 Gather unto me all the elders of your tribes and your officers, that I may speak these words in their presence, and call to report against them earth and heaven. 29 For I am sure that after my death you will corrupt yourselves and de- part from the way I have prescribed for you; therefore hell will come upon you, because you will commit unrighteousness before the LORD, provoking him to anger by the works of your hands." 30 So Moses spoke in the presence of the whole congregation of Israel the words of this song, until he had finished them.

CHAPTER 32

1 Hear, O heavens, and I will speak; and let the earth hear the words of my mouth. 2 My doctrine shall fall as the rain, and my speech shall fade away as the dew, as the show upon the grasses, and as the great rain upon the herbs. 3 For I will publish the name of the LORD, give glory to our God. 4 Perfect is the work of the mighty God, for all his ways are judicious. God is true and without wickedness; he is just and righteous. 5 They have corrupted themselves toward him by their vice, not being his children, but a generation foul-mouthed and crooked. 6 Do you thus acknowledge the LORD, O foolish and vain people? Is not he your father who bought you? He has made you and proportioned you. 7 Re- member the days of old, consider the years of many generations; ask your father and he will explain to you, to your elders and they will tell you. 8 When the LORD God decided to assign to the nations their inheritance, when he sep- arated the sons of Adam, he established the boundaries of the peoples, according to the name of the sons of Israel. 9 For the portion of the LORD is his people: Iaakob is the lot of his inheritance. 10 And he found him in the land of the wilderness, in a desolate and roaring wilderness; and he led him, and instructed him, and kept him as the apple of his eye. 11 Like an eagle clambering to his nest, he de- parted from his birds, spread his wings, took them up, and carried them on his wings, 12 So the LORD alone led him, and there was no foreign god with him. 13 He led him to the re- motest places of the earth, that he might eat the fruits of the fields, and made him suck bone from stone and oil from hard wood: 14 thou didst drink butter of the goat and milk of the sheep with fat of the lamb, rams fed in Bashan and goats, with the fat of the grain of wheat and the red of the grape. 15 But he who should have been righteous, when he became fat, cried out in his head, "You are fat, you are big, you are laden with fat; therefore he has forsaken God who created him and has not considered the strong God of his salvation." 16 They provoked him with strange gods; they provoked him to wrath with abominations. 17 They have offended the gods, not to God, but to gods whom they did not know; new gods who have recently come, whom their fathers did not fear. 18 You have forgotten the mighty God who begat you, and you have forgotten God who formed you. 19 Then the LORD saw it and was distressed at the prostitution of his sons and daughters. 20 And he said, I will hide my face from them: I will see what shall be their end: for they are a generation of de- frauders, children in whom there is no faith. 21 They have deceived me with that which is not God; they have provoked me to wrath with their vanities; and I will provoke them with those who are not people: I will send them into wrath with a foolish nation. 22 For in my wrath is kindled a fire, which shall burn unto the depths of hell, and shall con- sume the earth with its produce, and shall set on fire the foundations of the mountains. 23 I will pour out plagues upon them: and I will shoot my arrows upon them. 24 They shall be burned with hunger, consumed with parch- edness and bitter destruction: I will also send upon them the teeth of beasts, and the venom of serpents crawling in the dust. 25 The sword shall kill them outside, and in the chambers they shall be afraid: the young man and the young woman, the suckling and the gray- skinned man. 26 I said that I would scatter them everywhere: that I would cause their re- membrance to cease among men, 27 because I feared the wrath of the adversary, lest their adversaries should take pride and say, "It was our hand and not the LORD that did all this: 28 For they are a nation without counsel, and there is no understanding in them. 29 Oh, if they were wise, then they would understand this; they would consider their last

end. 30 How could one pursue a thousand and two put ten thousand to flight, if their strong God had not sold them and the LORD had not shut them up? 31 For their God is not like our God, for our enemies are judgmental. 32 For their vine is the vine of Sodom and the vine of Go- morah; their grapes are grapes of gall, their clusters are bitter. 33 Their wine is the poyson of dragons and the cruel gall of asps. 34 Is not this laide in store with me and sealed among my treasures? 35 Vengeance and recompense are mine; their blow shall fall in due time, for the day of their destruction is at hand, and the things that shall come upon them hasten. 36 For the LORD will judge his people and will repent toward his servants, when he sees that their power is gone, and that no one has shut himself up in his house or remained abroad. 37 When men shall say, Where are their gods, their mighty God in whom they trusted? 38 Who ate the fat of their sacrifices and drank the wine of their appetizers, they will rise up and help you; he will be your refuge." 39 Behold, I am he, and there are no gods with me: I kill and I give life; I wound and I laugh; there is none that can deliver from my hands. 40 For I lift up my hand toward the Eauen, and say, I lay me down for Europe. 41 If I sharpen my glittering sword and my hand takes the trouble to judge, I will take vengeance on my enemies and reward those who hate me. 42 I will make my arrows drunk with blood (and my sword will eat flesh) for the blood of the slain and the captives, when I begin to take vengeance on the enemy. 43 You nations, praise his people, for he will avenge the blood of his servants, and will perform vengeance on his adversaries, and will be merciful to his land and his people." 44 Then Moses came and spoke all the words of this song in the midst of the people, he and Hoshea the son of Nun. 45 When Moses had finished saying all these words to all Israel, 46 he said to them, "Set your hearts on all the words that I testify to you today, to pass them on to your children, that they may observe and put into practice all the words of this Lawe. 47 For it is not a vain word concerning you, but it is your life, and by this word you will prolong your days in the land, where you go from Iorden to possess it." 48 The LORD spoke to Moses on that same day, saying, 49 Go to the mount of Abarim, to mount Nebo, which is in the land of Moab, opposite Jericho, and observe the land of Canaan, which I give in possession to the children of Israel, 50 die on the mountain where you are going, and you shall be gath- ered to your people, just as Aaron your broth- er died on Mount Hor and was gathered to his people, 51 For ye have betrayed me among the children of Israel, at the waters of Meriba, at Kadesh, in the wilderness of Zin, because ye have not sanctified me among the children of Israel. 52 Therefore you shall see the land be- fore you, but you shall not enter into it, I say, into the land which I grant to the children of Israel.

CHAPTER 33

1 This is the blessing with which Moses the man of God blessed the children of Israel be- fore he died, and said, 2 The Lord has come from Sinai, has gone up from Seir to them, has appeared clearly from Mount Paran, has come with ten thousand saints, and at his right hand a firie Lawe for them. 3 Though the people are envious, all your saints are in your hand, and they are humbled before you to receive your words. 4 Moses ordained a Lawe as an inheritance from the community of Iaakob. 5 He was in the midst of the righ- teous people, as king, when the leaders of the people and the tribes of Israel were gathered together. 6

Reuben remained alive and did not die, though his men were few. 7 Then he blessed Leuiah and said, "Hear, O LORD, the journey of Leuiah, and lead him to his people; his hands will be sufficient for him, if you will help him against his enemies." 8 And of Leui he said, "Let thy Thummim and thy Vrim be with thy Holy One, whom thou hast protect- ed at Mass, and hast caused to be stripped at the waters of Meriba." 9 Who said to his fa- ther and his mother, "I have not seen him, nor have I known his brethren, nor have I known his sons, for they have kept thy word and ob- served thy counsel." 10 They shall teach Iaakob your principles, and Israel your law; they shall set incense before your face, and the censer on your altar. 11 Bless, O LORD, his substance, and accept the work of his hands; smite his enemies and those who hate him, that they may not rebel. 12 Of Benjamin he said, "The protégé of the LORD shall dwell safely with him; the LORD shall care for him all day long, and dwell between his shoulders." 13 And of Ioseph he said, "Blessed of the LORD is his land for the sweetness of the heavens, and for the dew, and for the depth of the subsoil." 14 for the sweet increase of the sun, and for the sweet increase of the moon, 15 for the sweet- ness of the top of the ancient mountains and for the sweetness of the old hills, 16 for the sweetness and abundance of the earth; and the good will of him that dwelt in the bush shall come upon the head of Ioseph, and upon the top of the head of him that was separated from his brethren. 17 And his beauty shall be as that of a heifer first brought forth, and his horns as the horns of a winepress; with them he shall smite the peoples together, even unto the end of the world: these also are the ten thousand of Ephraim, and these are the thou- sands of Manasseh. 18 Concerning Zebulun he said, "Withdraw, Zebulun, your exit, and you Issachar your tents." 19 They will call your people to the mountain; there they will offer the sacrifices of righteousness, for they will feed on the abundance of the sea and on the treasures hidden in the sand." 20 Also of Gad he said, "Blessed be he who magnifies Gad; he dwells like a lion who catches for his prayer the weapon with his head." 21 He looked to himself at first, for there was a part of the Lawe-giuer hidden; nevertheless he will come with the heads of the people, to execute the justice of the LORD and his agreements with Israel. 22 Of Dan he said, "Dan is a lion cub; he will come out of Bashan." 23 And of Naphtali he said, "O Naphtali, satisfied with prosperity and filled with the blessing of the LORD, pos- sess the west and the south." 24 And of Asher he said, "Asher shall be blessed with sons; he shall be pleasing to his brothers, and he shall dip his feet in Olympus. 25 Your shoes shall be strong and shining, and your strength shall continue as long as you live. 26 There is none like God, O righteous people, who rides the heavens to your aid and the clouds in his glo- ry. 27 The everlasting God is your refuge, and under his arms you are forever; he will drive out the enemy before you and say, "Destroy them." 28 Then Israel, the fountain of Iaakob, shall dwell alone, safe, in a land of wheat and wine; even his auroras shall cause the dew to fall. 29 You are blessed, O Israel; who is like you, O people saved by the LORD, the shield of your help and the sword of your glory? Thy enemies shall be subdued to thee, and thou shalt trample down their places.

CHAPTER 34

1 Then Moses went from the plain of Moab toward mount Nebo, unto the top of Pis- gah, which is before Jericho: and

the LORD showed him all the land of Gilead, even unto Dan, 2 And all Naphtali, and the land of Ephraim and Manasseh, and all the land of Judah, as far as the last sea: 3 The south and the plain of the valley of Jericho, the city of palm trees, as far as Zoar. 4 And the LORD said to him, "This is the land which I swore to Abraham, and to Izhak, and to Jehoshaphat, saying, I will give it to your seed: I have made you see it with your own eyes, but you shall not go there." 5 So Moses the servant of the LORD died in the land of Moab, according to the word of the LORD. 6 He buried him in a valley in the land of Moab, opposite Beth- peor, but no one knows his tomb to this day. 7 Moses was now a hundred and twenty years old when he died; his eye had not faded and his natural strength had not diminished. 8 The children of Israel wept for Moses in the plain of Moab for thirty days; so the days of weeping and mourning for Moses ended. 9 Ioshua the son of Nun was full of the spirit of wisdom, because Moses had laid hands on him. The children of Israel were obedient to him and did as the LORD had commanded Moses. 10 But since then there has not aris- en in Israel a prophet like Moses (whom the Lord knew personally). 11 In all the miracles and wonders which the Lord sent him to do in the land of Egypt before Pharaoh and all his servants and all his country,c12 and in all that mighty hand and in all that great fear which Moses did before all Israel.

of the people to say, 11 Go through the army and command the people, "Prepare your lives, for after three days you shall pass out of this land to enter to possess the land which the LORD your God grants you to possess." 12 Then to the Reubenites, Gadites and half the tribe of Manasseh, Ioshua said, "Remember the word: the LORD has given you the right to possess it, 13 Remember the word which Moses, the servant of the LORD, commanded you: 'The LORD your God has given you rest and given you this land. 14 Your wives and your children and your livestock shall remain in the land which Moses has given you on this side of the border; but you shall go before your brothers with arms, all who are men of war, and help them, 15 until the LORD has granted rest to your brethren, as to you, and until they also possess the land which the LORD your God has granted them; then you shall return to the land which you possess and possess it, the land which Moses the LORD's servant gave you on this side of Iorden, toward the rising of the sun. 16 They answered Ioshua, saying, "All that you have commanded us we will do,and wherever you send us we will go." 17 As we obeyed Moses in everything, so we will obey you; only the Lord your God be with you, as he was with Moses 18 Whoever rebels against your commands and does not obey your words in all that you impose on him will be put to death; be strong and of good courage.

HISTORICAL BOOKS

These books narrate the history of the Israelites from their entry into Canaan to the rebuilding of Jerusalem

---

JOSHUA

CHAPTER 1

1 Now after the death of Moses, the Lord's servant, the Lord spoke to Joshua the son of Nun, Moses' minister, saying, "Now get up, go out of here, you and all this people, to the land that I give them, that is, to the children of Moses, 2 Moses my servant is dead; now therefore arise, go out of this land, you and all this people, to the land that I give them, that is, to the children of Israel. 3 Every place on which the sole of your foot shall walk I have given you, as I said to Moses. 4 From the wil- derness and from this Lebanon as far as the great river, the river Perath, all the land of the Hittites as far as the great sea, toward the setting of the sun, shall be your land. 5 There will be no man able to endure all the days of your life; as I was with Moses, so I will be with you; I will not leave you nor forsake you. 6 Be strong and of good courage, for to this people you will give as an inheritance the land that I had sworn to give to their fathers. 7 Be strong and of great courage, that you may observe and follow all the Law which Moses my ser- vant commanded you; you shall not depart from it to the right hand or to the left, that you may prosper wherever you go. 8 Do not let this book of the Law depart from your mouth, but meditate on it day and night, to observe and do according to all that is written in it; for then you will prosper your way and have good success. 9 Did I not command you to say, "Be strong and of good courage, fear not and be not discouraged, for I, the LORD your God, will be with you wherever you go"? 10 Then Ioshua commanded the officers

CHAPTER 2

1 Then Ioshua the son of Nun sent two men from Shittim to spy out the land secret- ly, saying, "Go and see the land, and Jericho also"; and they went and entered a house of a prostitute, named Rahab, and lodged there. 2 Then it was reported to the king of Jericho, "Behold, men of the children of Israel have come here by night to spy out the land." 3 And the king of Jericho sent word to Rahab, "Bring here the men who have come to you and have entered your house, for they have come to search all the land." 4 (But the wom- an had taken the two men and hid them.) Therefore she said, "Men have come to me, but I did not know where they came from." 5 When they shut the door in the darkness, the men came out; where they went I did not know; follow them quickly, for you will over- take them. 6 (But she had taken them to the roof of the house and hid them with the lin- en threads she had spread on the roof.) 7 And some men pursued them through the streetof Iorden, even to the borders; and as soon as those who pursued them were gone out, they shut the door. 8 And before they fell asleep, she joined them on the roof, 9 and said to the men, "I know that the Lord has given you the land, and that fear has fallen upon you, and that all the inhabitants of the land have faint- ed because of you. 10 For we have heard how the LORD dried up the waters of the Red Sea before you when you came out of Egypt, and what you did to the two kings of the Amorites who were on the other side of the Jordan, to Sihon and Og, whom you destroyed: 11 When we heard this, our hearts failed, and there was no more courage in anyone because of you, for the LORD your God is the God who is in heaven and on earth. 12 Now therefore, I beseech you, swear to me by the Lord that, as I have shown you mercy, you will also show it to the house of my fathers and give me a sign of truth, 13 and that you will save my father and mother and my brothers and sisters and all that they have, and that you will deliver our souls from death." 14 And the men answered her, "Our life for you will die, if you do not ac- cept this pledge of ours; and when the Lord has granted the land, we will deal mercifully and truly

with you." 15 Then she made them go down by a rope to the window, because her house was on the wall of the city and she lived on the wall. 16 Then she said to them, "Go to the mountain before the pursuers meet you, and hide there for three days, until the pursuers return; then you may go your way again." 17 Then the men said to her, "We will be blasphemous of this thy other, whom thou hast sworn." 18 Behold, when we come into the land, thou shalt tie this rope of red braid to the window, with which thou shalt bring down thy body, and thou shalt bring back to thy house thy father, and thy mother, and thy brethren, and all thy fathers. 19 Who then shall go out of the gate of thy house into the street, his blood shall be upon his head, and we shall be without ornament; but whoever shall be with thee in the house, his blood shall be upon our head, if any hand touch him: 20 And if thou be content with this our issue, we shall be altogether like unto thy others, whom thou hast made to swear." 21 She answered, "According to thy words, so be it." Then she sent them away, and they departed, and she tied the red cord to the window. 22 And the two departed, and came to the mountain, and remained there three days, until the pursu- ers returned; and the pursuers sought them all the way, but could not find them. 23 Then the two men returned, went down from the mountain, passed over, and came to Iosh- ua the son of Nun, and told him all that had happened to them. 24 They also said to Iosh- ua, "The LORD has delivered all the land into our hands, for all the people of the land have fainted because of this matter."

CHAPTER 3

1 Then Ioshua rose very early, and they de- parted from Scittim and came to Iorden, he and all the sons of Israel, and lodged there be- fore they left. 2 After three days, the officers went to all the army, 3 and commanded the people, "When you see the ark of the couenat of the LORD your God and the priests of the Leuites carrying it, you shall depart from your place and go after it. 4 But there shall be a space between you and the ark, about two thousand cubic feet; you shall not approach it, to know the way by which you are to go; for you have not gone this way in the past. 5 (Now Ioshua had said to the people, "Sanctify yourselves, for in the future the LORD will do wonders among you.") 6 Ioshua also spoke to the priests, saying, "Take the coroner's bow and go before the people"; so they took the coroner's bow and went before the people. 7 Then the LORD said to Ioshua, "Today I will begin to magnify you before all Israel, who will know that as I have been with Moses, so I will be with you. 8 You shall therefore com- mand the priests who carry the ark of Cour- age to say, 'When you have come to the mouth of the waters of Iorden, you shall stand firm in Iorden.' 9 Then Ioshua said to the children of Israel, "Come here and listen to the words of the LORD your God." 10 Ioshua said, "In this way you shall know that the LORD God is in your midst, and that he will certainly drive out before you the Canaanites, the Hittites, the Hijites, the Perizzites, the Girgashites, the Amorites and the Jebusites. 11 Behold, the ark of the convention of the LORD of all the world passes before you in Iorden. 12 Take therefore from among you two men from the tribes of Israel, from each tribe one man. 13 And if the soles of the feet of the priests (who carry the ark of the LORD God, the LORD of all the world) remain in the waters of Iorden, the waters of Iorden shall be cut off, for the waters that come from outside shall stand firm on a brink. 14 When the people came out of their tents to go to Iorden, the priests who

carried the ark of the Commander went before the people. 15 When those who carried the ark came to Iorden, and the feet of the priests who carried the ark were immersed in the water (for Iorden filled all its banks throughout the time of the feast). 16 Then the waters that were coming down from the out- side stopped, and they rose up on a height, and departed from the city of Adam, which was next to Zaretan; but the waters that were coming down toward the Sea of the Wilder- ness, that is, the Salish Sea, failed and were cut off; so the people went straight against Jericho. 17 But the priests who carried the ark of the LORD's conference remained on the ground inside Iorden, ready to prepare, and all the Israelites went dry, until all the people came out of Iorden clean.

CHAPTER 4

1 When all the people had left Iorden, the Lord spoke to Ioshua, saying 2 Take me two people from the people, from each tribe one man, 3 and command them, "Take from here from the center of Iorden, from the place where the priests have stood waiting, two stones, which you shall take away with you and leave them in the lodging where you will stay this night.") 4 Then Ioshua called the two men whom he had prepared from among the children of Israel: from each tribe one man, 5 And Ioshua said to them, "Go before the ark of the LORD your God, through the midst of Iorden, and take from each of you a stone on his shoulder, according to the name of the tribes of the children of Israel, 6 that this may be a sign among you, so that when your children ask their fathers in the times to come, what do you mean by these stones? 7 You may answer them, "The waters of Iorden were cut off before the ark of the crowning of the LORD, for when it passed through Iorden, the waters of Iorden were cut off; therefore these stones are a reminder to the children of Israel forever." 8 Then the children of Is- rael did as Ioshua had commanded and took two stones from the middle of Iorden, as the LORD had told Ioshua, according to the name of the tribes of the children of Israel, and car- ried them with them to the lodging and laid them there. 9 Ioshua placed two stones in the middle of Iorden, in the place where the feet of the priests who carried the commander's ark were, and there they have remained to this day. 10 So the priests who carried the ark remained in the middle of Iorden, until every thing that the LORD had commanded Ioshua to say to the people was finished, according to all that Moses had instructed Ioshua to say; then the people hurried up and left. 11 When all the people were clean, the ark of the LORD and the priests also went out before the peo- ple. 12 And the sons of Reuben, and the sons of Gad, and half the tribe of Manasseh, went before the Israelites armed, as Moses had ap- pointed them. 13 And forty thousand men, prepared for war, went before the LORD to fight in the plain of Jericho. 14 On that day the LORD magnified Ioshua in the eyes of all Isra- el, and they feared him as they had feared Mo- ses all the days of his life. 15 The LORD spoke to Ioshua, saying, 16 Command the priests who bear the bow of testimony to go out from Iorden." 17 So Ioshua commanded the priests, "Come out of Iorden." 18 And when the priests who bore the ark of the LORD's consent had come out of the midst of Iorden, and when the soles of the feet of the priests were laid on the dry ground, the waters of Iorden returned to their place and flowed over all its banks, as before. 19 The people went out from Iorden on the tenth day of the first month and en- camped in Ghilgal, to the east of Jericho. 20 And Ioshua

also placed in Ghilgal the two stones which they had taken from Iorden. 21 And he spoke to you, children of Israel, say- ing, "When your children ask their fathers in the times to come, what are these stones? 22 then you shall show your children and say, 'Is- rael has gone out from this harbor to the dry land: 23 because the LORD your God dried up the waters of Iorden before you, until you came out, as the LORD your God did with the Red Sea, which he dried up before you, until we came out, 24 that all the peoples of the world may know that the hand of the LORD is mighty, that you may continually fear the LORD your God.

CHAPTER 5

1 Now when all the kings of the Amorites who were beyond Iorden, toward the west, and all the kings of the Canaanites who were by the sea, heard that the LORD had dried up the waters of Iorden before the children of Israel until they were gone, their hearts fainted; and they had no more courage because of the chil- dren of Israel. 2 At that same time the LORD said to Ioshua, "Make yourself sharp knives, come back and circumcise the children of Is- rael for the second time." 3 Then Ioshua made himself sharp knives and circumcised the children of Israel on the hill of the trincuns. 4 This is the reason why Ioshua circumcised all the people, that is, the males who had come out of Egypt, because all the men of war had died in the wilderness along the road after they came out of Egypt. 5 For all the people who went out were circumcised, but all the people who were brought into the wilderness along the way after they came out of Egypt were not circumcised. 6 For the children of Israel walked for forty years in the wilderness, until all the people of the men of war who came out of Egypt were consumed, because they did not obey the message of the LORD; to whom the LORD swore that he would not give them the land which the LORD had sworn to their fathers to give them, that is, a land flow- ing with milk and honey. 7 And Ioshua also circumcised their children whom he brought forth in their way, because they were circum- cised, for they had not circumcised them on the way. 8 And when they had circumcised all the people, they remained in the places of the camna until they were all whole. 9 Then the LORD said to Ioshua, "Today I have taken away from you the shame of Egypt"; there- fore he called that place Gilgal, to this day. 10 So the children of Israel stopped at Gilgal and celebrated the Feast of the Passer on the fourteenth day of the month, also in the plain of Jericho. 11 On the day after the Feast of the Passer they ate of the wheat of the land, and of baked bread, and of skim wheat on the same day. 12 On the day after they had eaten of the horn of the land, the man ceased to eat, and the children of Israel ate no more of the horn of the land of Canaan in that year. 13 And when Ioshua was near Jericho, he lifted up his eyes and looked; and behold, there stood before him a man who had a drawn sword in his hand; and Ioshua went up to him and said, "Are you on our side or on the side of our adversaries?" 14 And he answered, "No, but as captain of the Lord's army I have come now." Then Ioshua stood with his face to the ground and worshiped and said to him, "What does my Lord say to his servant?" 15 The leader of the LORD's army said to Ioshua, "Take off your shoes from your foot, for the place where you are standing is holy"; and Ioshua did so.

CHAPTER 6

1 Now Jericho was closed, because of the chil- dren of Israel: no one could go out or come in. 2 The LORD said to Ioshua, "Behold, I have put into your hands Jericho, its king, and the strong men of war. 3 All of you, therefore, who are men of war, you shall conquer the city, going around the city once; so you shall do for six days: 4 And ten priests shall bring ten trumpets of ram's horn before the ark; and on the seventh day you shall go around the city seven times, and the priests shall blow with the trumpets. 5 When they make a long blast with the ram's horn trumpets, and you hear the sound of the trumpet, all the people shall cry out with a great shout; then the walls of the city shall fall to the ground, and the people shall go up on high, every one straight before them. 6 Then Ioshua the son of Nun called the priests and said to them, "Take the ark of the LORD, and let ten priests bring ten ram trumpets before the ark of the LORD." 7 But he said to the people, "Go and compact the city, and let those who are armed go before the ark of the LORD." 8 When Ioshua had spo- ken to the people, the seven priests brought their ram trumpets and went before the ark of the LORD, sounding with their trumpets, and the ark of the commander of the LORD followed them. 9 The men-at-arms preceded the priests who blew the trumpets; then the assembled army came behind the ark as they went and blew the trumpets. 10 (Now Ioshua had commanded the people to say, "You shall not shout, nor make any noise with your voice, nor shall a word come out of your mouth, until the day when I say to you, Shout, then shout.") 11 So the ark of the LORD surrounded the city and went through it once; then they returned to the little house and settled in the campe. 12 And Ioshua rose early in the morn- ing, and the priests brought the ark of the LORD: 13 furthermore, ten priests brought as many ram's horn trumpets and went before the ark of the LORD, blowing the trumpets; the men-at-arms went before them, but the assembled army came behind the ark of the LORD, while they went and blew the trum- pets. 14 On the second day, after searching the city, they returned to the army; so they did for six days. 15 When the seventh day came, they rose up early at daybreak and went over the city in the same manner for ten more times; that day alone they went over the city for ten more times. 16 When the priests had blown the trumpets for the tenth time, Ioshua said to the people, "Stop, for the LORD has given you the city. 17 The city will be an execrable thing to the LORD, both it and all who are in it; only Rahab the harlot will have to die, she and all who are with her in the house, because she hid the messengers we sent. 18 Neverthe- less beware of the execrable thing, lest you make yourselves execrable, and lest, by taking the execrable thing, you also make the army of Israel execrable and disturb it. 19 But all the silver, the gold, the reed vessels, and the iron shall be consecrated to the LORD, and shall enter into the treasury of the LORD." 20 So the people shouted, after they had blown the trumpets; for when the people had heard the sound of the trumpet, they shouted with a great shout; and the walls fell to the ground; so the people entered into the city, every one straight before them; and they took the city. 21 And they destroyed with the edge of the sword all that was in the city, men and wom- en, young and old, oxen, sheep and horses. 22 But Ioshua had said to the two men who had guarded the county, "Go into the house of the prostitutes and bring out the woman and all that she possesses, as you had sworn to her." 23 So the two men who were spies went in and brought out Rahab, her father, her moth- er, her brothers and all that she had; they also brought out all her family and sheltered her from the army of Israel. 24 After they burned the city with fire and

everything in it, only the silver, the gold, the bronze and yron vessels were put into the treasury of the house of the LORD. 25 Thus Ioshua got rid of the harlot Rahab, the house of her fathers, and all that she possessed; she dwelt in Israel to this day, because she had hidden the messengers that Ioshua had sent to drive out Jericho. 26 Then Ioshua swore, saying, "Cursed be the man before the LORD who rises up and builds this city of Jericho; he will lay its foundation in his eldest son, and in his youngest son he will build its gates." 27 So the LORD was with Ioshua, and he was famous in all the world.

CHAPTER 7

1 But the children of Israel committed a fault in the excommunicated thing, because Achan the son of Carmi, the son of Zabdi, the son of Zerah, of the tribe of Judah, committed the excommunicated thing; therefore the anger of the LORD was kindled against the children of Israel. 2 And Ioshua sent men from Jericho to Ai, which is beside Betauen, east of Beth-el, and spake unto them, saying, Go and see the land. And you went to see Ai, 3 Then they returned to Ioshua and said to him, "Do not let all the people go, but let two or three thou-sand men go and strike Ai, and do not make all the people toil, for they are few in number." 4 So the people went there with about three thousand men, who fled before the men of Ai. 5 And the men of Ai struck them a to-tal of thirty-six men; and they pursued them from before the gate to Shebarim, and struck them as they went down; therefore the heart of the people melted like water. 6 Then Ioshua tore his garments and fell to the ground with his face before the ark of the LORD until the dawn, he and the elders of Israel, and they covered their heads with dust. 7 Ioshua said, "Alas, Lord God, why have you brought this people out of Iorden, to deliver them into the hands of the Amorites and to destroy them? Had God been content to dwell on the oth-er side of Iorden. 8 O LORD, what will I say when Israel turns its back on its enemies? 9 For the Canaanites and all the inhabitants of the land will hear of it, and they will compact us and destroy our name from the earth; and what will you do to your mighty Name?" 10 The LORD said to Ioshua, "Arise; why do you stand thus on your face? 11 Israel has sinned and transgressed my counsel that I gave them, for they have taken the excommuni-cated thing, and have also stuffed it, and have also concealed it, and have put it with their things. 12 Therefore you, children of Israel, cannot stand before your enemies, but you have turned your backs on your enemies, for they are execrable; and I will not be with you any longer, unless you destroy the excommu-nicated from among you. 13 Therefore sanc-tify the people and say, "Sanctify yourselves against death," for thus says the LORD, the God of Israel, "There is an execrable thing in your midst, O Israel, therefore you will not be able to stand against your enemies, until you have removed the execrable thing from among you." 14 In the morning therefore you shall come according to your tribes, and the tribe that the LORD shall take, shall come ac-cording to the families; and the family that the LORD shall take, shall come by the hous-es; and the house that the LORD shall take, shall come man by man. 15 He that shall be taken with the excommunicated thing shall be burned with fire, he and all that he hath, because he hath transgressed the commander of the LORD, and because he hath committed folly in Israel." 16 Then Ioshua rose early in the morning and led Israel according to his tribes; the tribe of Iudah was taken.

17 And he brought in the families of Iudah, and took the family of the Zarhites; and he brought in the family of the Zarhites, man by man, and Zab-di was taken. 18 Then he brought his family, man by man, and Achan the son of Carmi, the son of Zabdi, the son of Zerach, of the tribe of Iudah, was taken. 19 Then Ioshua said to Achan, "My son, I beseech you, give glory to the LORD, the God of Israel, and confess to him, and tell me now what you have done; do not hide it from me." 20 Achan answered Ioshua and said, "Verily, I have sinned against the LORD, the God of Israel, and have done so, and so I have done. 21 I found among the sponges a beautiful Babylonian robe, two hundred shekels of silver, and a wedge of gold weighing fifty shekels; and I took them, and took them; and behold, they lie hidden in the ground in the center of my tent, and the sil-ver under it. 22 Then Ioshua sent messengers, who ran to the tent, and behold, they were hid in his tent, and the lime under it. 23 So they took them from the tent, and brought them to Ioshua and all the children of Israel, and laid them before the LORD. 24 Then Ioshua took Achan the son of Zerach, the silk, the robe, and the wedge of gold, his sons, his daugh-ters, his oxen, his donkeys, his sheep, his tent, and all that he had; and all Israel with him brought them to the valley of Achor. 25 And Ioshua said, "As much as thou hast tribulated, the LORD will tribulate thee this day"; and all Israel threw stones at him, and burned them with fire, and stoned them. 26 And they cast a great heap of stones upon him to this day; and so the LORD turned away from his fierce an-ger; therefore he called that place, to this day, the valley of Achor.

CHAPTER 8

1 Then the LORD said to Ioshua, "Do not fear, and do not be discouraged; take all the men of war with you, and arise, and go to Ai; be-hold, I have put into your hand the king of Ai, and his people, and his city, and his country. 2 You shall do to Ai and his king what you did to Jericho and his king; however, his spit and his cattle you shall take with you as a prayer; you shall stand waiting against the city, behind its back." 3 Then Ioshua arose with all the men of war to go against Ai; Ioshua chose thirty thousand strong and valiant men and sent them out by night. 4 Then he gave them an order, saying, "Behold, you shall stand wait-ing against the city, at the back of the city; do not go far from the city, but all of you stand ready. 5 I and all the people who are with me will approach the city; and when they come out against it, as they did the first time, we will flee before them. 6 For they will go out af-ter vs, until we have brought them out of the city; for they will say, "They flee before vs as the first time; so we flee before them." 7 Then you shall arise from your beds and destroy the city, for the LORD your God will deliver it into your hands. 8 When you have taken the city, you shall put it to the sword, according to the LORD's orders; behold, I have appointed you." 9 Then Ioshua sent them away, and they went and rested in anticipation and stopped between Beth-el and Ai, west of Ai; but Ioshua lodged that night among the people. 10 Then Ioshua arose early in the morning and gath-ered the people together; he and the elders of Israel went before the people against Ai. 11 All the men of war who were with him set out and went to the city, and they camped north of Ai, and there was a valley between them and Ai. 12 He took about five thousand men and put them waiting between Bet-el and Ai, on the west side of the city. 13 And the people set all the armies that were on the north side against the city,

and the soldiers that were waiting on the west side against the city; and Ioshua went the same night into the middle of the valley. 14 And when the king of Ai heard of it, the men of the city hastened, and rose up early, and went out against Israel to fight, he and all his people, at the appointed hour, before the plain, for he knew not that anyone was waiting against him at the back of the city. 15 Then Ioshua and all Israel, defeated before them, fled by the way of the wilderness. 16 All the people of the city were sum- moned to pursue them; they pursued Ioshua and were drawn out of the city, 17 so that there was not a man left in Ai and in Bet-el who did not go after Israel; and they left the city open and pursued Israel. 18 Then the LORD said to Ioshua, "Stretch out the spear that is in your hand toward Ai, for I will give it into your hand"; and Ioshua stretched out the spear that was in his hand toward the city. 19 Those who were waiting hurriedly got up from their places and ran as soon as he had stretched out his hand; they entered the city, took it, hur- ried and set the city on fire. 20 And the men of Ai looked behind them and saw him, for the smoke of the city went upward, and they had no chance to flee either this way or that way, for the people who fled into the wilderness turned back to the pursuers. 21 When Ioshua and all Israel saw that those who were waiting had taken the city and that the smoke from the city was rising upward, they turned around and killed Ai's men. 22 The others also came out of the city against them; so they stood in the midst of Israel, these on one side and the others on the other; and they slew them, so that none of them stayed and fled. 23 They took the king of Ai and brought him to Ioshua. 24 When Israel had finished killing all the inhabitants of Ai in the fields, that is, in the wilderness, where they had pursued them, and when they had all fallen by the edge of the sword until they were consumed, all the Israelites returned to Ai and struck it with the edge of the sword. 25 All the fallen of that day, men and women, were two thou- sand, that is, all the men of Ai. 26 Ioshua did not withdraw the hand he had stretched out with the spear until he had destroyed all the inhabitants of Ai. 27 Israel took only the cattle and spoyle of this city as a prayer for them- selves, according to the word of the LORD that he had commanded Ioshua. 28 Ioshua set Ai on fire and made it a garbage heap for- ever and a wilderness to this day. 29 The king of Ai was hung on a tree until dawn. As soon as the sun was down, Ioshua ordered his car- cass to be removed from the tree and thrown at the entrance to the city gate; he placed a large pile of stones on it, which has remained to this day. 30 Then Ioshua built an altar to the LORD, the God of Israel, on Mount Ebal, 31 as Moses, the servant of the LORD, had com- manded the children of Israel, as it is written in the Book of the Law of Moses, an altar of whole stones, on which no one had raised a yron; and they offered burnt offerings to the LORD and peace offerings there. 32 Moreover he wrote on the stones the text of the Law of Moses, which he wrote in the presence of the children of Israel. 33 All Israel (with their el- ders, their officers, and their judges stood on either side of the ark, before the priests of the Leuites, who carried the ark of the Colonel of the LORD), as well as the stranger, as the one who is brought into the county; half of them stood before Mount Gerizim and half of them before Mount Ebal, as Moses, the servant of the LORD, had commanded beforehand, that they should bless the people of Israel. 34 Then he read all the words of the Law, blessings and curses, according to what is written in the book of the Law. 35 There was not a word of all that Moses had commanded that Ioshua did not read before the whole community of Isra- el, the women, the children, and the stranger in their midst.

CHAPTER 9

1 When all the kings who were beyond Iorden, on the mountains, in the valleys and on all the shores of the great sea, beyond Leb- anon, such as the Hittites, Amorites, Canaan- ites, Perizzites, Iuites and Jebusites, learned of it, they gathered together to fight against Ioshua and against Israel, 2 they gathered together to fight by common consent against Ioshua and against Israel. 3 But the inhabi- tants of Gibeon heard what Ioshua had done to Jericho and Ai. 4 Therefore they made a ruse: they went, made themselves out to be ambassadors, and took old sacks on their donkeys and old wine-bottoms, rent and bound, 5 and old and hobnailed shoes on their feet; even the clothes they wore were old, and all their bread supply was dried up and wast-ed. 6 Then they came to Ioshua in the houses of Gilgal, and said to him and to the men of Israel, "We are from a far country; therefore make a league with them." 7 Then the men of Israel said to the Hiuites, "It may be that you dwell among you; how then can I make league with you?" 8 They answered Ioshua, "We are your servants." Then Ioshua said to them, "Who are you? And where do you come from?" 9 They answered him, "From a very far coun- try your servants have come for the name of the LORD your God, because we have heard his fame and all that he has done in Egypt, 10 and all that he did to the two kings of the Amorites who were beyond Iorden, to Sihon king of Heshbon and Og king of Bashan, who were in Ashtaroth. 11 Therefore our elders and all the people of our county spoke to them, saying, "Take lives with you for the journey, and go out to them and say, 'We are your ser- vants. 12 This bread of ours we took with you for lives from our houses, on the day that we left to come to you; but now look, it has dried up and is moldy. 13 Even these bottles of wine that we filled were new, and behold, they have been torn, and our garments and our shoes are old, because of the journey too great." 14 The men accepted their story concerning their lives and did not agree with the mouth of the LORD. 15 Then Ioshua made peace with them and entered into a league with them that would let them lie; even the princes of the community swore against them. 16 But at the end of three days, having made a league with them, they came to know that they were their neighbors and dwelt among them. 17 The children of Israel resumed their journey, and on the third day they came to their cit- ies, whose cities were Gibeon, Chephirah, Beeroth and Kiriath-iearim. 18 The children of Israel did not kill them, because the princes of the community had sworn an oath to them by the LORD, the God of Israel; therefore all the community murmured against the princ- es. 19 Then all the princes said to the whole community, "We have sworn by the LORD the God of Israel upon them; therefore we cannot touch them. 20 But this we will do with them and let them lie down, or else wrath will come upon them because of the other thing we have sworn to them. 21 Again the princes said to them, "Let them lie, but they are to cut wood and draw water for the whole community, as the princes have determined." 22 Then Iosh- ua called them and spoke to them and said, "Why have you deceived the people, saying, 'Are we far from you, when you dwell among the people?' 23 Now therefore you are cursed, and not one of you will be freed from being a slave, a woodcutter and a drawer of water for the house of my God." 24 And they answered Ioshua and

said, "Because it was told your servants that the LORD your God had com- manded his servant Moses to give you all the land and to destroy all the inhabitants of the land out of your sight, we were very afraid for our lives in your presence and did this: 25 And behold, now we are in your hands; do what seems good and right to you to do in your sight." 26 So he did with them, and delivered them out of the hands of the children of Isra- el, that they might not kill them. 27 On that same day Ioshua appointed them as wood- cutters and water attractors for the congrega- tion and for the altar of the LORD to this day, in the place he would choose.

CHAPTER 10

1 When Adoni-Zedek, king of Jerusalem, heard that Jehoshua had taken Ai and de- stroyed it (as he had done to Jericho and its king, so he had done to Ai and its king) and that the inhabitants of Gibeon had made peace with Israel and joined them, 2 they feared greatly, for Gibeon was a great city, as one of the royal cities, for it was greater than Ai and all its inhabitants were mighty. 3 Therefore Adoni-Zedek, king of Jerusalem, sent to Hoham, king of Hebron, to Piram, king of Iarmuth, to Iapia, king of Lachish, and to Debir, king of Eglon, to say to them, "Come, come! 4 "Come to me and help me defeat Gibeon, for they have made peace with Ioshua and the sons of Israel." 5 The five kings of the Amorites, the king of Jerusalem, the king of Hebron, the king of Iarmuth, the king of Lachish, and the king of Eglon gathered themselves together, set out with all their armies, besieged Gibeon, and made war on her. 6 The men of Gibeon sent word to Ioshua, as to the army of Ghilgal, "Do not withdraw your hand from your servants; come to Vs at once, greet Vs and help Vs, for all the kings of the Amorites who dwell in the mountains are gathered against Vs." 7 So Ioshua went up from Ghilgal, he and all the people of war with him and all the men of strength. 8 The LORD said to Ioshua, "Do not fear them, for I have placed them in your hand; none of them will be able to stand against you." 9 So Ioshua came to them suddenly, for he had been away from Ghilgal all night. 10 The LORD defeated them before Israel, killed them with a great slaughter at Gibeon, pursued them along the road that goes to Bet-horon, and defeated them as far as Azekah and Makkedah. 11 As they fled before Israel and were going down to Bet-horon, the LORD caused great stones to fall on them from above, as far as Aze- kah, and they became dyed; there were more who became dyed with hailstones than those whom the children of Israel killed with the sword. 12 Then Ioshua spoke to the LORD, in the day when the LORD had left the Am- orites before the children of Israel, and said to the eyes of Israel, "Sun, stay in Gibeon, and you moon, in the valley of Aialon." 13 And the sun stood still, and the moon stood still, until the people came against their enemies (Is it not written in the book of Iasher?) So the sun stood in the midst of the isle, and would not go down for a whole day. 14 There was no such day either before or after the LORD heard a man's voice, for the LORD fought for Israel. 15 Then Ioshua returned, and all Israel with him, to the camp of Gilgal: 16 But the five kings fled and hid themselves in a cave in Makkedah. 17 It was said to Ioshua, "The five kings were found hiding in a cave in Makkedah." 18 Then Ioshua said, "Place large stones on the mouth of the cave and put men beside it to guard them. 19 But do not stand still; pursue your enemies and strike every last one of them, and do not allow them to enter their cities, for the LORD your God has given them into your hand." 20 When Ioshua and the children of Israel had slain them with immense slaugh- ter until they were consumed, and the rest of them had entered fortified cities, 21 then all the people returned in peace to the campe, from Ioshua to Makkedah; no one murmured against the children of Israel. 22 Then Iosh- ua said, "Open the mouth of the campe and bring these five kings out of the campe." 23 And they did so, and brought those five kings out of the quarry, namely, the king of Jerusa- lem, the king of Hebron, the king of Iarmuth, the king of Lachish, and the king of Eglon. 24 And when they had brought those kings be- fore Ioshua, Ioshua called all the men of Israel together and said to the leaders of the men of war who went with him, "Come here, put your feet on the necks of these kings"; and they came here and put their feet on their necks. 25 And Ioshua said to them, "Do not be afraid and do not be fainthearted, but be strong and of good courage, for so will the LORD do with all your enemies, against whom you fight." 26 Then Ioshua struck them, killed them, and hanged them on five trees; and they hung on the trees until dawn. 27 When the sun went down, Ioshua gave orders to remove them from the trees and to throw them into the quarry (where they had been hiding), and they laid large stones on the mouth of the quarry, which have remained to this day. 28 On that same day, Ioshua took Makkeda and struck it with the edge of the sword; and the king of Makkeda was destroyed along with them and all the people who were there; there was none left, for he did to the king of Makke- da what he had done to the king of Jericho. 29 Then Ioshua departed from Makkeda, and all Israel with him, to Libnah, and fought against Libnah. 30 And the LORD also gave Libna and her king into the hand of Israel, who defeated her with the edge of the sword, together with all the people who were there, and let no one remain there, for he did to his king what he had done to the king of Jericho. 31 Then Iosh- ua departed from Libnah, and all Israel with him to Lachish, and besieged and stormed it. 32 And the LORD gave Lachish into the hand of Israel, who conquered it on the sec- ond day and defeated it with the edge of the sword, with all the people who were there, as he had done with Libna. 33 Then Horam king of Ghezer came to help Lachish, but Ioshua struck him and his people down, until none of his people remained. 34 Then Ioshua depart- ed from Lachish to Eglon and all Israel with him; they besieged and stormed it, 35 and they conquered it the same day and defeated it with the edge of the sword, destroying all the people there, as he had done to Lachish. 36 Then Ioshua departed from Eglon, and all Israel with him, for Hebron, against which they fought. 37 And when they had taken it, they defeated it with the edge of the sword, the king, all its cities, and all the people there- in; and there remained none, as he had done at Eglon, for he destroyed it utterly, and all the people therein. 38 Then Ioshua returned, and all Israel with him, to Debir and fought against it. 39 And when he had taken it, his king and all his city struck them with the edge of the sword and completely destroyed all the souls that were there, leaving none behind. As he had done to Hebron, so he did to Debir and her king, as he had also done to Libna and her king. 40 So Ioshua defeated all the hill counties, and the southern counties, and the valleys, and the hillsides, and all their kings, and left not a single one of them remaining, but destroyed every soul, as the LORD God of Israel had commanded. 41 Ioshua defeat- ed them from Kadesh-Barnea as far as Azzah and throughout all the land of Goshen as far as Gibeon. 42 All these kings and their terri- tory were taken by Ioshua at once, because the LORD, the God of Israel, was fighting for Israel. 43

Then Ioshua and all Israel with him returned to the camp of Ghilgal.

CHAPTER 11

1 When Jabin king of Hazor had heard this, he sent for Iobab king of Madon, the king of Shimron, and the king of Achshaf, 2 and to the kings who were in the north, in the mountains and plains south of Cinneroth, in the valleys and on the borders of Dor, in the west, 3 And to the Canaanites on the east and west, and to the Amorites, the Hittites, the Perizzites, and the Jebusites in the moun- tains, and to the Hiuites below Hermon in the land of Mizpeh. 4 And they went out, and with them all their army, as numerous as the sand that is on the seashore in quantity, with horses and chariots in great numbers. 5 All these kings gathered together and came and encamped together at the waters of Merom to fight against Israel. 6 Then the LORD said to Ioshua, "Do not grieve for them, for in a lit- tle while I will have them all killed before Is- rael; you shall destroy their horses and bury their chariots with fire." 7 Then Ioshua and all the men of war who were with him sudden- ly came upon them by the waters of Merom and fell upon them. 8 The LORD gave them into the hand of Israel, who defeated them and pursued them as far as the great Zidon, Misrefothmaim and the valley of Mizpeh, to- ward the east, and defeated them until there were none left. 9 Ioshua did to them what the LORD had commanded him: he unhitched their horses and burned their chariots with fire. 10 Then Ioshua went back and took Hazor and struck his king with the sword, be- cause Hazor before then was the ruler of all those kingdoms. 11 Moreover they struck all the people there with the edge of the sword, destroying everyone and leaving no one, and burned Hazor with fire. 12 So all the cities of those kings and all their kings were taken by Ioshua, who struck them with the edge of the sword and completely destroyed them, as Mo- ses, the servant of the LORD, had command- ed. 13 But Israel did not set fire to any of the cities that were left standing, except Hazor, which Ioshua set on fire. 14 The children of Israel took all the timber of these cities and the cattle for their prayers, but they struck all the men with the edge of the sword until they had destroyed them, leaving not a single one behind. 15 As the LORD had commanded Mo- ses his servant, so Moses commanded Ioshua, and so did Ioshua: he left nothing of what the LORD had commanded Moses. 16 So Iosh- ua took all the land of the mountains, all the south, all the land of Goshen, the plain, the mount of Israel and its plain, 17 From Mount Halak, which goes toward Seir, even to Baal-Gad, in the valley of Lebanon, below Mount Hermon; and all their kings he defeated and slew them. 18 Ioshua waged long wars with all those kings, 19 and there was no city that made peace with the children of Israel, like the Hiuites who dwelt in Gibeon; all the oth- ers he defeated with a battle. 20 For the LORD willed to harden their hearts that they might come against Israel in battle, to destroy them utterly and grant them no grace, but to reduce them to ruin, as the LORD had commanded Moses. 21 At that same time came Ioshua, and destroyed the Anakim from the mountains: from Hebron, from Debir, from Anab, from all the mountains of Iudah, and from all the mountains of Israel: Ioshua utterly destroyed them with their cities. 22 There remained no more anakim in the territory of the children of Israel: only in Azza, in Gath, and in Ash- dod. 23 So Ioshua took all the land, according to what the LORD had said to Moses; and Ioshua gave it as an inheritance to Israel ac- cording to their portions according to their tribes.

CHAPTER 12

1 These are the kings of the land whom the children of Israel defeated and took over their territory, on the other side of Iorden, toward the rising of the sun, from the river Arnon to Mount Hermon and all the plain toward the east. 2 Sihon, king of the Amorites, who dwelt in Heshbon, had dominion from Aroer, which is beside the river Arnon, from the middle of the river and from the middle of Gilead to the river Jabbok, to the borders of the sons of Ammon. 3 From the plain as far as the sea of Cinneroth, toward the east, and as far as the sea of the plain, that is, the salt sea, toward the east, by the way of Beth-ieshimoth, and from the south under the springs of Pisgah. 4 They also conquered the territory of Og king of Bashan, the remnant of the gypsies who dwelt in Ashtaroth and Edrei, 5 And they reigned in Mount Hermon, in Salcah, and in all Bashan, as far as the borders of the Geshu- rites, the Maachathites, and half of Gilead, as far as the borders of Sihon, king of Heshbon. 6 And Moses the servant of the LORD and the children of Israel smote them: and Moses the servant of the LORD gave their land into the possession of the Reubenites, and the Ga- dites, and half the tribe of Manasseh. 7 These also are the kings of the county which Ioshua and the children of Israel defeated on this side of Iorden, on the west, from Baal-Gad in the valley of Lebanon to Mount Halak that goes toward Seir; Ioshua gave it into the posses- sion of the tribes of Israel, according to their portions: 8 In the mountains, in the valleys, in the plains, on the slopes, in the wilderness, and in the south, where were the Hittites, the Amorites, the Canaanites, the Perizzites, the Iuites, and the Jebusites. 9 The king of Jericho was one; the king of Ai, which is next to Bethel, one: 10 The king of Jerusalem was one; the king of Hebron one: 11 The king of Iarmuth, one: the king of Lachish, one: 12 The king of Eglon, one: the king of Ghezer, one: 13 The king of Debir, one: the king of Geder, one: 14 The king of Hormah, one: the king of Arad, one: 15 The king of Libnah, one: the king of Adullam, one: 16 The king of Makkedah, one: the king of Beth-el, one: 17 The king of Tappuah, one: the king of Hepher, one: 18 The king of Aphek, one: the king of Lasharon, one: 9 The king of Madon, one: the king of Hazor, one: 20 The king of Shimron-meron, one: the king of Achshaph, one: 21 The king of Ta- anach, one: the king of Megiddo, one: 22 The king of Kedesh, one: the king of Iokneam of Carmel, one: 23 The king of Dor in the county of Dor, one: the king of the nations of Gilgal, one: 24 The king of Tirzah, one. All the kings were thirty and one.

CHAPTER 13

1 Now when Ioshua was old and tried by years, the LORD said to him, "You are old and aged, and you still have much land left to pos- sess." 2 This is the land that remains, all the regions of the Philistines and all of Ghuri, 3 from Nile, which is in Egypt, to the borders of Ekron northward; this is the land of the Ca- naanites, that is, of the five lordships of the Philistines: the Azzites, the Ashdodites, the Eshkelonites, the Gittites, the Ekronites, and the Auites: 4 from the south, all the land of the Canaanites and the hollow beside the Sido- nians, as far as Aphek and the borders of the Amorites: 5 The land of the Giblites, and all Lebanon,

toward the sun that rises from Ba- hal-Gad under mount Hermon, as far as Ha- math. 6 All the inhabitants of the mountains from Lebanon as far as Misrefotmaim and all the Sidonians I will drive out before the chil- dren of Israel; but you shall assign them by lot to the Israelites to inherit them, as I have commanded you. 7 Now therefore, assign this territory as an inheritance to the nine tribes and to the half tribe of Manasseh. 8 For with the half of it the Reubenites and the Gadites have received their inheritance, which Moses gave them beyond Iorden toward the east, as Moses, the servant of the LORD, had given them, 9 from Aroer, which is on the bank of the river Arnon, and from the city that is half- way up the river, and all the plain of Medeba as far as Dibon, 10 And all the cities of Sihon king of the Amorites, who reigned in Hesh- bon, as far as the borders of the children of Ammon, 11 Gilead, the borders of the Ge- shurites and Maachathites, all Mount Her- mon and all Bashan as far as Salca: 12 All the kingdom of Og in Bashan, who reigned in Ashtaroth and Edrei, for Moses smote them and drove them out. 13 But the children of Israel expelled neither the Jehoshites nor the Maachathites; indeed, the Jehoshites and the Maachathites still dwell among the Israel- ites. 14 To the tribe of Leui he left no inher- itance, but the sacrifices of the LORD God of Israel are his inheritance, as he had told him. 15 Then Moses assigned to the tribe of the sons of Reuben an inheritance, according to their families. 16 Their territory extended from Aroer, which is on the bank of the river Arnon, from the city that is in the middle of the river, and from all the plain that is near Medeba: 17 Heshbon and all its cities lying in the plain: Dibon, Bamoth-Baal and Beth- Baal-Meon: 18 Iahazah, Kedemoth and Me- phaath: 19 Kiriathaim, Sibmah and Zereth- shahar, on the mount of Emek: 20 Beth-peor, Ashdoth-Pisgah, and Beth-ieshimoth: 21 all the cities of the plain and all the kingdom of Sihon, king of the Amorites, who reigned in Heshbon and whom Moses defeated with the princes of Midian: Eui, Rekem, Zur, Hur and Reba, dukes of Sihon, who dwelt in the county. 22 And Balaam the son of Beor the soothsayer slew by the sword the sons of Is- rael, of those who were slain. 23 The border of the sons of Reuben was Iorden with the coasts. This was the inheritance of the sons of Reuben according to their families, with the towns and villages. 24 Moses also assigned the inheritance to the tribe of Gad, that is, to the sons of Gad according to their families. 25 Their coasts were Jazer, all the cities of Gilead and half the territory of the sons of Ammon as far as Aroer, which is opposite Rabbah: 26 From Heshbon as far as Ramoth, Mizpeh and Bethonim, and from Mahanaim as far as the borders of Debir: 27 And in the valley of Beth-aram, Bethnimrah, Succoth, and Za- phon, the rest of the kingdom of Sihon, king of Heshbon, as far as Iorden, and the bor- ders as far as the coast of Cinneereth, beyond Iorden, toward the east. 28 This is the inher- itance of the sons of Gad, according to their families, with the cities and villages. 29 Moses also assigned an inheritance to the half tribe of Manasseh, which belonged to the half tribe of the sons of Manasseh, according to their families. 30 Their border was from Mahanaim to all of Bashan, that is, the whole kingdom of Og king of Bashan, and all the cities of Iair that are in Bashan, sixty cities, 31 And half of Gilead, and Ashtaroth, and Edrei, cities of the kingdom of Og in Bashan, were allotted to the sons of Machir the son of Manasseh, to half the sons of Machir according to their fami- lies. 32 These are the possessions which Mo- ses distributed in the plain of Moab, beyond Iorden toward Jericho on the east. 33 But to the tribe of Leui Moses assigned no inheri- tance, because the LORD God of Israel is their inheritance, as he had told them.

CHAPTER 14

1 These are also the places which the chil- dren of Israel inherited in the land of Ca- naan, and which Eleazar the priest, Ioshua the son of Nun, and the heads of the tribes of the children of Israel distributed to them, 2 according to the lot of their inheritance, as the Lord had commanded by the hand of Moses, to give to the nine tribes and the half tribe. 3 For Moses had given inheritance to the two tribes and to the half tribe, besides Horde; but to the Leuites he had given no in- heritance. 4 Because the sons of Iosef were two tribes, Manasseh and Ephraim, they gave the Leuites no part of the land: cities to inhabit, with their suburbs, for their beasts and their substance. 5 As the LORD had com- manded Moses, so did the children of Israel when they explored the land. 6 Then the sons of Iudah came to Ioshua to Ghilgal; and Ca- leb the son of Jephunneh the Kenezite said to him, "You know what the LORD said to Moses the man of God concerning me and you at Kadesh-Barnea. 7 I was four years old when Moses, the Lord's servant, sent me from Kadesh-Barnea to explore the land, and I brought him news again, as I thought in my heart. 8 But my brothers, who went with me, discouraged the hearts of the people; nev- ertheless I still followed the LORD my God. 9 Therefore Moses swore on that same day, "Surely the land where your feet have walked shall be your inheritance and your children's inheritance forever, because you have con- stantly followed the LORD my God. 10 There- fore behold, the LORD has kept me alive, as he promised; this is the fourteenth year since the LORD spoke this thing to Moses, while the children of Israel were wandering in the wilderness; and behold, I am four and a half years old today: 11 yet I am as strong at this time as I was when Moses sent me; as I was strong then, I am strong now, both for war and for government. 12 Now therefore give me this mountain of which the LORD spoke in that day (for in that day you heard that the Anakim were there, and the cities great and walled up), if the LORD will be with me, that I may bring them out, as the LORD said." 13 Then Ioshua blessed him and gave Hebron as an inheritance to Caleb the son of Jephunneh. 14 So Hebron became the inheritance of Ca- leb, son of Jephunneh, the Kenezite, to this day, because he constantly followed the LORD God of Israel. 15 The name of Hebron was be- fore then Kiriath-Arba; Arba was a great man among the Anakim; so the land ceased from warfare.

CHAPTER 15

1 This was the lot of the tribe of the sons of Iudah, according to their families: as far as the border of Edom and the wilderness of Zin, toward the south, on the southern coast. 2 Their southern border was the coast of the Salish Sea, from the point looking south. 3 The land went south to Maaleth-akrabbim, went on to Zin, went up south to Kadesh-Bar- nea, went on to Hezron, went on to Adar, and went on to Karkaa. 4 From there it went on to Azmon and came to the border with Egypt; the end of that shoreline was to the west; this will be your southern shoreline. 5 The east- ern border will be the salt sea to the end of Iorden; the northern border will start from the tip of the sea and the end of Iorden. 6 This border shall go to Beth-Hogla and skirt

the north side of Beth-Araba; from there the border shall go to the stone of Bohan the son of Reuben. 7 Then this boundary goes toward Debir, from the valley of Achor, and north- ward, turning toward Ghilgal, which is before the road to Adummim, which is on the south side of the river; also this boundary goes to- ward the waters of En-Scemesh and ends at En-Rogel. 8 Then this border goes toward the valley of the son of Hinnom, south of the Jeb- usites; this is Jerusalem. Also this boundary goes toward the top of the mountain that is opposite the valley of Hinnom, on the west, and that is at the end of the valley of Iebus, on the north. 9 This boundary extends from the top of the mountain to the spring of the water of Nephtoah, and it extends to the cities of Mount Ephron; this boundary reaches to Baalah, which is Kiriath-iearim. 10 Then this border extends from Baalah westward to Mount Seir and goes on to the slope of Mount Iearim, which is Chesalon to the north; then it goes down to Bet-Scemesh and goes to Timnah. 11 This border also extends to the north side of Ekron; this border approaches Shicron, goes on to Mount Baalah and ex- tends to Jabneel; the ends of this border are toward the sea. 12 The western border is to the great sea; this border shall be the border of the children of Iudah round about, accord- ing to their families. 13 To Caleb the son of Jephunneh, Ioshua gave a portion among the sons of Judah, as the LORD had command- ed him, namely, Kiriath-Arba, of the father of Anak, which is Hebron. 14 And Caleb led thence three sons of Anak: Shesai, Ahiman, and Talmai, the sons of Anak. 15 From there he went to the inhabitants of Debir, which was formerly called Kiriath-shepher. 16 Then Caleb said, "He who destroys Kiriath-Sepher and takes him, then to him I will give Achsah my daughter to wife." 17 And Otniel the son of Kenaz, Caleb's brother, took her and gave him Achsah his daughter to wife. 18 She came in to him and asked her father for a field; she light- ed her plank, and Caleb said to her, "What do you want?" 19 Then she answered, "Give me a blessing, for you have given me the south county; give me also springs of water." And he gave her the springs above and the springs below. 20 This shall be the inheritance of the tribe of the children of Judah, according to their families. 21 The chief cities of the tribe of the sons of Judah, toward the coast of Edom on the south, were Kabzeel, Eder and Iagur, 22 Kinah, Dimonah and Adadah, 23 Kedesh, Hazor and Ithnan, 24 Zif, Telem and Bealoth, 25 Hazor, Hadattah, Kerioth, Hesron (who is Hazor). 26 Amam, Shema and Moladah, 27 Hazar, Gaddah, Heshmon and Beth-Palet, 28 Hasar-Shual, Beersheba and Biziothia, 29 Baala, Iim and Azem, 30 Eltolad, Chesil and Horma, 31 Ziklag, Madmanna and Samsanna, 32 Lebaoth, Shilhim, Ain, and Rimmon: all these cities are twenty-nine with their villag- es. 33 In the lower county were Eshtaol, Zorea, and Ashna, 34 Zanoa, En-Gannim, Tappua, and Enam, 35 Iarmuth, Adullam, Socoh and Azekah, 36 Sharaim, Adithaim, Gederah and Gederothaim: fourteen cities and their vil- lages. 37 Zenam, Hadashah and Migdal-Gad, 38 Dileam, Mizpeh and Ioktheel, 39 Lachish, Bozkath and Eglon, 40 Cabbon, Lahmam and Kithlish, 41 Gederoth, Beth-Dagon, Naamah and Makkedah: sixteen towns and their vil- lages. 42 Lebnah, Ether and Ashan, 43 Iipth- tah, Ashnah and Nezib, 44 Keilah, Aczib and Maresha: nine cities and their villages. 45 Ekron with its cities and villages, 46 from Ekron to the sea, everything around Ashdod and its villages. 47 Ashdod with its cities and its villages: Azzah with its cities and its villag- es, even to the border of Egypt, and the great sea was their coast. 48 The mountains were Shamir, Jattir, and Socoh, 49 Dannah and Kiriath-sannath (which is Debir) 50 Anab, Ashtemoth and Anim, 51 Goshen, Holon and Gilo: other cities with their villages, 52 Arab, Dumah and Eshean, 53 Ianum, Bet-tappua and Afekah, 54 Humtah, Kiriath-Arba (which is Hebron) and Zior: nine cities with their vil- lages. 55 Maon, Carmel, Ziph and Iuttah, 56 Izreel, Iokdeam and Zanoa, 57 Kain, Gibe- ah and Timnah: ten cities and their villag- es. 58 Halhul, Bet-Zur and Gedor, 59 Maara, Beth-Anoth and Eltekon: six cities and their villages. 60 Kiriath-Baal, which is Kiriath- iearim, and Rabbah: two cities and their vil- lages. 61 In the wilderness were Beth-arabah, Middin, and Secacah, 62 Nibshan, the city of salt, and Engedi: six cities with their villages. 63 The Nebubbians, who were inhabitants of Jerusalem, could not be driven out by the sons of Judah, but the Jebusites still dwell with the sons of Judah in Jerusalem.

CHAPTER 16

1 The lot befell the sons of Jehoshaph from Iorden near Jericho to the water of Jericho eastward, and to the wilderness from Jericho to Mount Beth-el: 2 From Beth-el he goes to- ward Luz and runs to the borders of Archiataroth, 3 It goes down westward to the coast of Japheth, to the coast of Beth-horon, the end of Ghezer, and its ends are on the sea. 4 So the sons of Jehoshaph, Manasseh and Ephraim took their inheritance. 5 Also the borders of the sons of Ephraim, according to their families, and the borders of their inher- itance to the east were Atroth-Addar, as far as Beth-Horon, the vip. 6 And this boundary goes toward the sea as far as Michmethah on the north, and this boundary goes back east- ward as far as Taanathshiloh, and goes over it eastward as far as Ianohah, 7 From Ianohah it goes down to Ataroth and Naarath, comes to Iericho, and goes out to Iorden. 8 This border goes from Tappuah westward to Kanah, and its ends are on the sea; this is the inheritance of the tribe of the sons of Ephraim according to their families. 9 The cities separated for the children of Ephraim were in the midst of the inheritance of the children of Manasseh: all the cities with their villages. 10 They did not drive out the Canaanite who dwelt in Ghezer, but the Canaanite remained in the midst of the Ephraimites to this day and paid tribute.

CHAPTER 17

1 This was also the lot of the tribe of Manasseh, for he was the first born of Iosef, that is, of Machir, the first born of Manasseh, and the father of Gilead; now because he was a man of war, he had Gilead and Bashan. 2 The rest of the sons of Manasseh according to their families, that is, the sons of Abiezer, the sons of Helek, the sons of Azriel, the sons of Shechem, the sons of Hepher, and the sons of Shemidah: these were the males of Manasseh the son of Ioseph, according to their families. 3 But Zelophehad the son of Ephir the son of Gilead the son of Machir the son of Manasseh had no sons, but daughters: and these are the names of his daughters, Mahlah, Noah, Hoglah, Milcah, and Tirzah: 4 Which stood before Eleazar the priest, and Ioshua the son of Nun, and the princes, saying, "The Lord had commanded Moses to give them an inheritance from among our brethren; therefore, according to the commandment of the Lord, he gave them an inheritance from among their father's brethren." 5 Manasseh was given ten portions, besides the land of Gilead and Bashan, which is on the other side of Iorden, 6 For the daughters of

Manasseh inherited among his sons; and the other sons of Manasseh had the land of Gilead. 7 The borders of Manasseh went from Asher to Michmethah, which is opposite Shechem, and this border continued on the right hand to the inhabitants of En-tappuah. 8 The ter- ritory of Tappuah belonged to Manasseh, but Tappuah, next to the border of Manasseh, be- longed to the sons of Ephraim. 9 This border goes down to the river Kanah, south of the river; these cities of Ephraim are among the cities of Manasseh; the border of Manasseh is north of the river, and its ends are on the sea, 10 the south belongs to Ephraim, the north to Manasseh, and the sea is its border; they met in Asher on the north and in Issachar on the east. 11 Manasseh had in Issachar and in Asher Beth-Shean and its cities, Ibleam and its cities, the inhabitants of Dor with its cit- ies, the inhabitants of En-Dor with its cities, the inhabitants of Thaanach with its cities, and the inhabitants of Megiddo with its cit- ies, that is, three counties. 12 Nevertheless the sons of Manasseh failed to destroy those cities, but the Canaanites continued to dwell there. 13 Nevertheless, when the children of Israel were strong, they subjected the Ca- naanites to tribute, but did not drive them out of there. 14 Then the sons of Jehoshaph turned to Ioshua, saying, "Why have you allotted me only one lot and one portion to inherit, see- ing that I am a great people, inasmuch as the LORD has blessed me thus far?" 15 Then Iosh- ua answered them, "If you are a numerous people, go into the woods and cut down trees for yourselves in the land of the Perizzites and the Girants, if Mount Ephraim is too nar- row for you." 16 Then the sons of Jehoshaph said, "The mountain will not be sufficient for you; and all the Canaanites who dwell in the lower county have cells of yron, both in Beth-shean and the cities thereof, and in the valley of Izreel." 17 Ioshua spoke to the house of Iosef, to Ephraim and Manasseh, saying, "You are a great people, you have great pow- er, and you will not have one lot. 18 Therefore the mountain shall be yours, for it is a forest, and you shall cut it down; its ends shall be yours, and you shall drive out the Canaanites, even though they have many charets and are strong.

CHAPTER 18

1 The whole community of the children of Israel gathered at Shiloh, where the taber- nacle of the community was built, after the land had been allotted to them. 2 Now there remained among the children of Israel some tribes to which the inheritance had not been assigned. 3 Therefore Ioshua said to the chil- dren of Israel, "How long have you been so slow to enter and possess the land which the LORD, the God of your fathers, has given you? 4 Procure three men from among you for each tribe, that I may send them, and they may arise, and go through the land, and distrib- ute it according to their inheritance, and re- turn to me. 5 And that they may divide it into ten parts (Iudah shall remain in its southern shore, and the house of Ioseph shall remain in its northern shore). 6 You shall therefore divide the land into ten parts and bring them here to me, and I will do the lotteries for you here before the LORD our God. 7 But the Leuites shall have no part among you, for the priesthood of the LORD is their inheritance; Gad, Reuben, and half the tribe of Manasseh also received their inheritance beyond Iorden toward the east, which Moses the servant of the LORD gave them." 8 Then the men arose and set out; and Ioshua charged those who were going to describe the land, saying, "Set out, go through the land, describe it, and re- turn to me, that I may here make lotteries for you before the LORD at Shiloh." 9 The men departed, went through the land, described it by city in ten parts in a book, and returned to Ioshua in the camna of Siloh. 10 Then Ioshua cast lots for them in Shiloh before the LORD, and there Ioshua assigned the land to the children of Israel according to their portions: 11 The lot fell to the tribe of the children of Benjamin, according to their families, and the cost of their lot was between the children of Iudah and the children of Ioseph. 12 Their northern border started from Iorden and ex- tended to the north side of Jericho, crossed the mountains to the west and ended in the wilderness of Beth-Auen: 13 From there this border goes to Luz, that is, to the south side of Luz (which is Beth-el) and goes down to Atroth-addar, near the mountain that is on the south side of Beth-horon, the last. 14 Then the boundary turns and includes the corner of the sea toward the south, from the mountain that is opposite Beth-horon toward the south; its ends are at Kiriath-Baal (which is Kiriath- iearim), a city of the sons of Iudah; this is the west quarter. 15 The southern quarter begins at the end of Kiriath-iearim, and this bound- ary goes westward and comes to the water spring of Nephtoah. 16 This boundary goes down to the end of the mountain that is op- posite the valley of Ben-Hinnom, which is in the valley of the giants toward the north, goes down into the valley of Hinnom on the side of Jebusis toward the south, and goes down to En-rogel, 17 then, starting from the north, it goes toward En-Scemesh, stretches out to Geliloth, which is toward the road that leads to Adummim, and goes down to the stone of Bohan the son of Reuben. 18 Then it continues on the opposite side of the plain, toward the north, and goes down into the plain. 19 Then this border goes to the side of Beth-Hoglah, to the north; and its ends, that is, the border, go as far as the point of the salt sea, to the north, and as far as the end of Iorden, to the south; this is the southern coast. 20 Iorden also is its border on the east; this is the inheritance of the children of Benjamin, along the coasts thereof, round about, according to their fam- ilies. 21 The cities of the tribe of the children of Benjamin, according to their families, are Jericho, Bethhoglah, and the valley of Keziz, 22 Beth-arabah, Zemaraim, and Beth-el, 23 Auim, Para and Ofra, 24 Chephar, Ammonai, Ofni and Gaba: two cities and their villages. 25 Gibeon, Ramah and Beeroth, 26 Mizpeh, Chephirah and Mozah, 27 Rekem, Irpeel and Tarala, 28 Zela, Eleph, Iebusi (which is Jeru-salem), Gibeath, and Kiriath: fourteen cities with their villages; this is the inheritance of the children of Benjamin, according to their families.

CHAPTER 19

1 The second lot fell to Simeon, that is, to the tribe of the sons of Simeon, according to their families; their inheritance was in the midst of the inheritance of the sons of Judah. 2 They had Beersheba, Sheba, and Moladah as their inheritance, 3 Hazur-sual, Balah, and Azem, 4 Eltolad, Betul and Horma, 5 Ziklag, Beth-Marcaboth and Hazar-Susah, 6 Beth-Lebaoth and Sharuhen: thirteen cities and their villages. 7 Ain, Remmon, Ether, and Ashan: four cities and their villages. 8 And all the villages round about these cities unto Baa- lath-beer and Ramath toward the south: this is the inheritance of the tribe of the children of Simeon, according to their families. 9 Out of the portion of the children of Iudah came the inheritance of the children of

Simeon, because the portion of the children of Iudah was too great for them; therefore the children of Simeon had their inheritance within their inheritance. 10 The third lot fell to the sons of Zebulun, according to their families, and the coasts of their inheritance came to Sarid, 11 and their border went westward, as far as Maralah, and came to Dabbasheth, and met with the river before Iokneam, 12 from Sar- id it turns eastward toward the rising sun at the borders of Chisloth-Tabor, heads toward Daberath and goes up to Japheth, 13 from there he goes eastward, toward the sun rising at Gittah-hepher, to Ittah-kazin, goes to Rimmon and turns toward Neah. 14 This border encircles it northward as far as Hannathon, and its ends are in the valley of Iiphtah-el, 15 Kattath, Nahallal, Shimron, Idala, and Beth- Lem: two cities with their villages. 16 This is the inheritance of the children of Zebulun, according to their families: these cities and their villages. 17 The fourth lot fell to Issachar, that is, to the sons of Issachar according to their families. 18 Their territory was Izreelah, Chesulloth, and Shunem, 19 Hapharaim, Shion and Anaharath, 20 Harabbith, Kishion and Abez, 21 Remeth, En-gannim, Enhaddah and Beth-pazzez. 22 This coastline extends as far as Tabor, Shahazimath and Beth-Scemesh, and the ends of their coastline reach as far as Iorden: sixteen cities with their villages. 23 This is the inheritance of the tribe of the sons of Issachar according to their families, that is, the cities and their villages. 24 For the tribe of the children of Asher also the fifth part was drawn by lot, according to their families. 25 Their territory was Helcath, Hali, Beten, and Achshaph, 26 Alammelech, Amad and Mishe- al, and they came to Carmel on the west and to Shihor Libnath, 27 and went to the sun rising at Bet-Dagon, and went to Zebulun, to the valley of Jiphtha-El, to the north side of Bet-Emek, and to Neiel, and went to the left side of Kabul, 28 then Hebron, Rehob, Ham- mon and Kanah, to the great Zidon. 29 Then the border goes to Ramah and to the strong city of Zor; this border goes to Hosah, and its ends are on the sea from Hebel to Achzib, 30 Vmmah, Aphek and Rehob: two score cities with their villages. 31 This is the inheritance of the tribe of the children of Asher according to their families: these cities and their villag- es. 32 The sixth part was allotted to the sons of Naphtali, that is, to the sons of Naphtali according to their families. 33 Their territory stretched from Helef, from Allon to Zaanan- nim, from Adaminekeb to Jabneel, even to Lakum, and its ends were in Iorden. 34 This coastline turns westward to Aznoth-Tabor, from there it goes out to Hukkok, reaches Ze- bulun on the south, goes to Asher on the west and to Iudah near Iorden, toward the rising of the sun. 35 The strong cities are Ziddim, Zer, Hammath, Rakkath and Cinneereth, 36 Adamah, Ramah and Hazor, 37 Kedesh, Edrei and En-Hazor, 38 Iron, Migdal-El, Horem, Beth-Anah and Beth-Scemes: nineteen cities with their villages. 39 This is the inheritance of the tribe of the children of Naphtali, ac-cording to their families, that is, the cities and their villages. 40 The seventh lot came to the tribe of the children of Dan, according to their families. 41 The territory of their inheri-tance was Zorah, Eshtaol, and Ir-Scemesh, 42 Shaalabbin, Aialon and Ithlah, 43 Elon, Tem- natha and Ekron, 44 Eltekeh, Gibbethon and Baala, 45 Iehud, Bene-berak and Gath-Rim- mon, 46 Me-iarkon, Rakkon and the border that lies before Iapho. 47 But the coasts of the sons of Dan were too small for them; there- fore the sons of Dan went and fought against Leshem, conquered it, beat it with the edge of the sword, possessed it, settled there, and called it Leshem, Dan after the name of Dan their father. 48 This is the inheritance of the tribe of the sons of Dan according to

their families, that is, these cities and their villag- es. 49 When they had made an inspection of the land along its coasts, the children of Israel assigned to Ioshua the son of Nun an inheri- tance among them. 50 According to the word of the LORD, they gave him the city he had asked for, namely, Timnath-Serah on Mount Ephraim; he built the city and lived there. 51 These are the heritages that Eleazar the priest, Ioshua the son of Nun, and the heads of the families of the tribes of the children of Israel drew lots at Shiloh before the LORD in the place where the Tabernacle of Meeting was.

CHAPTER 20

1 The LORD also spoke to Ioshua, saying, 2 Speak to the children of Israel and say, "Name the cities of refuge of which I have spoken to you by the hand of Moses, 3 So that the mur- derer who kills a person through ignorance and unwittingly may take refuge there, and they shall be your refuge against the scourge of blood. 4 And he that fleeth into one of those cities shall stand at the entrance of the gate of the city, and shall present his cause unto the elders of the city; and they shall receive him into the city, and shall give him a place to dwell with them. 5 And if the crier of blood pursue him, they shall not deliver the slayer into his hand because he struck his neighbor in ignorance and did not hate him before the time: 6 but he shall dwell in that city until he shall stand before the congregation for judg- ment, or until the priest that shall be in those days be dead; then the slayer shall return, and shall return to his city and to his house, that is, to the city from which he fled." 7 Then they designated Kedesh in Galilee on Mount Naphtali, Shechem on Mount Ephraim, and Kiriath-Arba (which is Hebron) on Mount Judah. 8 On the other side of Iorden, toward Jericho on the east, they lurked at Bezer in the wilderness from the tribe of Reuben, at Ra- moth in Gilead from the tribe of Gad, and at Golan in Bashan from the tribe of Manasseh. 9 These were the appointed cities for all the children of Israel and for the stranger who so- journed among them, so that whoever killed anyone through ignorance might flee there and not die at the hands of the bloodbearer until he stood before the congregation.

CHAPTER 21

1 Then the principal fathers of the Leuites came to Eleazar the priest, and to Ioshua the son of Nun, and to the principal fathers of the tribes of the children of Israel, 2 and spoke to them at Shiloh in the land of Canaan, saying, "The LORD commanded by the hand of Mo- ses to give them cities to dwell in, with their suburbs for our livestock." 3 So the children of Israel gave to the Leuites, from their in-heritance, by the command of the Lord, these cities with their suburbs. 4 The families of the Kohathites were drawn by lot; and the sons of Aaron the priest, who belonged to the Leuites, were given thirteen cities from the tribe of Judah, from the tribe of Simeon, and from the tribe of Benjamin. 5 The rest of the sons of Kohath had ten cities, drawn by lot from the families of the tribe of Ephraim, from the tribe of Dan, and from the half tribe of Manasseh. 6 The sons of Gershon had thirteen cities by lot from among the families of the tribe of Issachar, the tribe of Asher, the tribe of Naphtali, and the half tribe of Manasseh in Bashan. 7 The children of Merari, according to their families, had from the tribe of Reu- ben, from the tribe of Gad and from the tribe

of Zebulun two cities. 8 The children of Israel assigned these cities and their suburbs to the Leuites by lot, as the LORD had commanded by the hand of Moses. 9 Out of the tribe of the sons of Iudah and out of the tribe of the sons of Simeon came the cities named here. 10 They were the sons of Aaron, belonging to the families of the Kohathites and the sons of Leui (for theirs was the first lot). 11 And they assigned them to Kiriath-arba, the father of Anok (which is Hebron), on the mountain of Iudah, with its surrounding suburbs. 12 (But the territory of the city and its villages were assigned to Caleb, son of Jephunneh, as his possession.) 13 So they gave the sons of Aar- on the priest a city of refuge for the slayers: Hebron with its suburbs and Libnah with its suburbs, 14 Jattir and its suburbs, Eshtemoa and its suburbs, 15 Holon and its suburbs, Debir and its suburbs, 16 Ain with its suburbs, Iuttah with its suburbs, Beth-Scemesh with its suburbs: nine cities of these two tribes. 17 Out of the tribe of Benjamin went out Gibeon with its suburbs, Geba with its suburbs, 18 Anathoth with its suburbs, and Almon with its suburbs: four cities. 19 All the cities of the sons of the priests of Aaron were thirteen cit- ies with their suburbs. 20 But to the families of the sons of Kohath, of the Leuites, who were the remnant of the sons of Kohath (for the cities that fell to them were of the tribe of Ephraim) 21 They gave them the cities of ref- uge for the slain: Shechem with its suburbs on Mount Ephraim and Ghezer with its suburbs, 22 Kibzaim with its suburbs and Bethhoron with its suburbs: four cities. 23 From the tribe of Dan: Eltekeh with its suburbs, Gibeton with its suburbs, 24 Aialon and its suburbs, Gath-Rimmon and its suburbs: four cities. 25 From the half tribe of Manasseh, Tanach with its suburbs, Gath-Rimmon with its suburbs: two cities. 26 The cities of the other families of the sons of Kohath were ten with their sub- urbs. 27 Also the sons of Gershon, belonging to the families of the Leuites, went out from the half tribe of Manasseh, to go to the refuge of the slain: Golan in Bashan with its suburbs, and Beeshterah with its suburbs: two cities. 28 From the tribe of Issachar: Kishon and its suburbs, Dabereh and its suburbs, 29 Iarmuth and its suburbs, En-Gannim and its suburbs: four cities. 30 From the tribe of Asher: Mishal with its suburbs, Abdon with its suburbs, 31 Helkah and its suburbs, Rehob and its sub- urbs: four cities. 32 From the tribe of Naphta- li, cities of refuge for the slain, Kedesh in Gi- leah with its suburbs, Hammoth-Dor with its suburbs, and Kartan with its suburbs: three cities. 33 The cities of the Gershonites, ac- cording to their families, were thirteen cities with their suburbs. 34 Also the families of the sons of Merari, the rest of the Leuites, came out of the tribe of Zebulun: Iokneam with its suburbs, and Kartah with its suburbs, 35 Dimna and its suburbs, Nahalal and its sub- urbs: four cities. 36 From the tribe of Reuben: Bezer with its suburbs, Iahaza with its sub- urbs, 37 Kedemoth with its suburbs, and Me- phaath with its suburbs: four cities. 38 From the tribe of Gad they made a city of refuge for the slain: Ramoth in Gilead with its suburbs, Mahanaim with its suburbs, 39 Heshbon with its suburbs, and Jazer with its suburbs: in all, four cities. 40 So all the cities of the children of Merari, according to their families (which were the other families of the Leuites), had two cities by lot. 41 All the cities of the Leuites in the possession of the children of Israel were eight and forty with their suburbs. 42 These cities were each arranged differently, with their suburbs around them; so were all these cities. 43 So the LORD granted to Israel all the land that he had sworn to grant to their fathers; they possessed it and dwelt in it. 44 The LORD made them rest all around, according to what he had promised their fa- thers; and there

remained before them none of all their enemies, for the LORD delivered all their enemies into their hands. 45 None of all the good things that the LORD said to the house of Israel was lacking, but everything came to pass.

CHAPTER 22

1 Then Ioshua called the Reubenites, the Ga- dites and the half tribe of Manasseh, 2 and said to them, "You have observed all that Mo- ses the servant of the LORD had command- ed you, and you have obeyed my voice in all that I commanded you: 3 You have not for- saken your brothers all this time until now, but have diligently observed the command of the LORD your God. 4 Now the LORD has granted your brothers rest, as he promised them; therefore now return and go back to your tents, to the land which you possess and which Moses, the LORD's servant, assigned to you beyond Iorden. 5 But be careful to carry out the commands and prescriptions which Moses, the servant of the LORD, has given you: namely, that you love the LORD your God, walk in all his ways, keep his commands, be faithful to him, and serve him with all your heart and with all your soul." Ioshua blessed them and sent them away, and they returned to their tents. 7 Now to one half of the tribe of Manasseh Moses had granted a possession in Bashan, while to the other half of it Ioshua gave leadership among their brothers on this side of the western border; therefore Iosh- ua sent them back to their tents and blessed them, 8 so he spoke to them, saying, "Return with much riches to your tents and with a great deal of cattle, of silk and gold, of brasse and yron, and with great abundance of food; remove the spit of your enemies with your brothers." 9 So the sons of Reuben, the sons of Gad and half the tribe of Manasseh turned back and departed from the sons of Israel from Sciloh (which is in the land of Canaan) to go to the county of Gilead, to the land of their own possession, which they had con- quered according to the word of the LORD by the hand of Moses. 10 When they came to the borders of Iorden (which is in the land of Canaan), the sons of Reuben, the sons of Gad and the half tribe of Manasseh built an altar there by Iorden, a great altar to keep watch over. 11 When the children of Israel heard, "Behold, the sons of Reuben, the sons of Gad and the half tribe of Manasseh have built an altar in the front line in the land of Canaan, on the borders of Iorden, at the passage of the children of Israel." 12 When the children of Israel heard of this, the whole community of the children of Israel gathered at Sciloh to go and make war against them. 13 Then the sons of Israel sent to the sons of Reuben, the sons of Gad and the half tribe of Manasseh in the land of Gilead, Finehas the son of Eleazar the priest, 14 and with him ten princes, of each principal house a prince, according to all the tribes of Israel, for each one was chief of his fathers among the thousands of Israel. 15 So they went to the sons of Reuben, and to the sons of Gad, and to the half tribe of Manasseh, in the land of Gilead, and spoke with them, saying 16 Thus says all the congregation of the LORD: "What transgression is this that you have committed against the God of Israel, to turn away from the LORD today, having built an altar to rebel against the LORD today? 17 Are we too few for the wickedness of Peor, for which we have not yet been condemned, even though a plague has come upon the commu- nity of the LORD? 18 You also have turned away from the LORD today; and since you are rebelling against the LORD today, he will also be angry with the whole community of Israel in the future. 19 Nevertheless, if the land of your possession

is vncleane, come to the land of the LORD's possession, where the Taberna- cle of the LORD dwells, and take possession among yourselves; but do not rebel against the LORD in building an altar beside the al- tar of the LORD our God. 20 Had not Achan the son of Zerah committed a grievous fault in an execrable thing, and wrath came upon the whole community of Israel? And this man alone did not die for his wickedness. 21 Then the sons of Reuben, the sons of Gad and half the tribe of Manasseh answered and said to the leaders of the thousands of Israel, 22 The LORD God of gods knows it, and Israel itself will know it; if in rebellion or in transgression against the LORD we have done it, do not say it today. 23 If we have built an altar to turn away from the LORD, to offer you a burnt of- fering or a food offering or a peace offering, the LORD himself will require it: 24 And if we have not done it for fear of this thing, saying that in the future your children may say to our children,"What have you to do with the LORD, the God of Israel? 25 For the LORD has made Iorden a border between you and you, the sons of Reuben and Gad; therefore you have no part in the LORD; so your sons will cause ours to cease to fear the LORD. 26 Therefore we said, "Now we are going to build an altar to Vs, not for burnt offerings nor for sacrific- es, 27 but it will be a testimony between you and vs and between our generations after vs, to perform the service of the Lord before him in our burnt offerings, our sacrifices and our peace offerings, and so that your children will not say to our children in the future, "You have no part in the Lord." 28 Therefore we answered, "If they should say so to you or to our future generations, we will answer, 'Here is the front of the altar of the Lord, which our fathers made, not for burnt offerings nor for sacrifices, but it is a testimony between you and you. 29 God forbid that we should rebel against the LORD and turn away from the LORD today to build an altar for burnt of- ferings, for food offerings or for sacrifices, like the altar of the LORD our God, which is before His Tabernacle." 30 When Finehas the priest, the princes of the congregation and the leaders of the thousands of Israel who were with him heard the words spoken by the sons of Reuben, the sons of Gad and the sons of Manasseh, they were well pleased. 31 Then Finehas the son of Eleazar the priest said to the sons of Reuben, the sons of Gad and the sons of Manasseh, "Today we realize that the LORD is in your midst, because you have not committed this guilt against the LORD; now you have delivered the children of Israel out of the hand of the LORD." 32 Then Finehas the son of Eleazar the priest, with the princes, returned to the sons of Reuben and the sons of Gad from the land of Gilead to the land of Canaan and brought them the answer. 33 The thing pleased the children of Israel; the chil- dren of Israel blessed God and did not think of going against them in battle to destroy the land where the children of Reuben and Gad dwelt. 34 Then the sons of Reuben and the sons of Gad called the altar Ed, because it will be a testimony among them that the LORD is God.

CHAPTER 23

1 After a long period of time when the LORD had granted rest to Israel from all its sur- rounding enemies, Ioshua was old and strick- en with age, 2 Ioshua called all Israel, their elders, their leaders, their judges and their of- ficers, and said to them, "I am old and strick- en with age. 3 You have also seen all that the LORD your God has done to all these nations before you, how the LORD your God himself has

fought for you. 4 Behold, I have assigned to you by lot these nations that remain, as an inheritance according to your tribes, from Iorden, with all the nations that I have de- stroyed, as far as the great sea in the west. 5 And the LORD your God shall expel them before you, and cast them out of your sight, and you shall possess their land, as the LORD your God has told you. 6 Therefore be valiant, observe and do all that is written in the Book of the Law of Moses, and do not deviate from it either to the right or to the left, 7 have no dealings with these nations, that is, with those who are left with you, and do not name the name of their gods, and do not make them swear, and do not serve them, and do not bow down to them: 8 but remain faithful to the LORD your God, as you have done to this day. 9 For the LORD hath cast out before you great nations and mighty men, and none hath stood hitherto before your face. 10 One man of you will pursue a thousand, for the LORD your God fights for you, as he has promised you. 11 Take heed therefore to yourselves, that you love the LORD your God. 12 Els, if you go back and get rid of the rest of these nations, that is, those who remain with you, and make marriage with them, go to them and they to you, 13 know for certain that the LORD your God will no longer drive out these nations from before you, but they will be a snare and a destruction to you, a whip upon your flanks and thorns in your eyes, until you perish from this good land which the LORD your God has given you. 14 And behold, today I enter into the way of all the world, and you know in all your hearts and in all your souls that nothing has come short of all the good things which the Lord your God has promised you, but all have come to you: nothing has come short. 15 Therefore, just as all the good things that the LORD your God promised you have come to you, so the LORD will cause all other things to come to you, until he has destroyed you from this good land that the LORD your God has given you. 16 And when you transgress the counsel of the LORD your God, which he has commanded you, and go and serve other gods and bow down to them, then the LORD's anger will be kindled against you, and you will quickly perish from the good land that he has given you.

CHAPTER 24

1 Again Ioshua gathered all the tribes of Is- rael at Shechem, called the elders of Israel, their leaders, their judges and their officers, and they stood before God. 2 Then Ioshua said to all the people, "Thus says the LORD, God of Israel: Your fathers dwelt anciently beyond the flood, as Terah, father of Abra- ham and father of Nachor, and served other gods. 3 And I took your father Abraham from beyond the flood, and led him throughout all the land of Canaan, and multiplied his seed, and gave him Izhak. 4 Then I gave Izhak and Iaakob and Esau, and I gave Esau Mount Seir, to possess it; but Iaakob and his sons went down to Egypt. 5 And I also sent Moses and Aaron, and scourged Egypt; and when I had done so among them, I brought out there. 6 So I brought your fathers out of Egypt, and you came to the sea; and the Egyptians pur- sued your fathers with chariots and horse- men to the Red Sea. 7 Then they cried out to the LORD, and he put a curtain of darkness between you and the Egyptians, and brought down the sea upon them, and brought them down; so your eyes saw what I did in Egypt, and you lived long in the wilderness. 8 Then I led you into the land of the Amorites, who dwelt beyond Iorden, and they fought with you; but I gave them into your hand, and you took possession of their land, and I destroyed them

from your sight. 9 Balak the son of Zip- por the king of Moab also rose up and made war on Israel, and sent for Balaam the son of Beor to curse you, 10 But I would not listen to Balaam; therefore he blessed you, and I delivered you out of his hand. 11 Then you went out from Iorden and came to Jericho, and the men of Jericho fought against you: the Amor- ites, the Perizzites, the Canaanites, the Hit- tites, the Girgashites, the Iuites and the Jeb- usites, and I delivered them into your hands. 12 I sent before you hornets who drove them out, like the two kings of the Amorites, and not with your sword nor with your bow. 13 I have given you a land in which you have not worked, cities which you have not built, and in which you dwell and eat of the vineyards and olive trees which you have not planted. 14 Now therefore fear the LORD and serve him with righteousness and truth, and forsake the gods whom your fathers served beyond the flood and in Egypt, and serve the LORD. 15 And if it seems useless to you to serve the LORD, choose today whom you will serve, whether to the gods whom your fathers served (who were beyond the flood) or to the gods of the Amorites, in whose land you dwell; but I and my house will serve the LORD." 16 Then the people answered, "God forbid that we should forsake the LORD to serve other gods. 17 For the LORD our God brought our fathers out of the land of Egypt, out of the house of bondage, and did those great miracles be- fore us, and protected us all the way we went and among all the peoples through whom we passed. 18 The LORD has cast out before us all the peoples, especially the Amorites who dwelt in the land; therefore we also will serve the LORD, for he is our God." 19 Ioshua said to the people, "You cannot serve the LORD, for he is a holy God; he is a jinxed God; he will not forgive your iniquities or your sins. 20 If you forsake the LORD and serve other gods, he will return and smite you and consume you, after he has done you good." 21 The peo- ple said to Ioshua, "No, but we will serve the LORD." 22 Ioshua said to the people, "You are witnesses against yourselves that you have chosen the LORD to serve him"; and they said, "We are witnesses." 23 So, he said, leave now the foreign gods that are among you and bow your hearts to the LORD, the God of Is- rael. 24 The people said to Ioshua, "The LORD our God, we will serve him and obey his will." 25 So Ioshua had a meeting with the people on the same day and gave them an ordinance and a law in Shechem. 26 And Ioshua wrote these words in the book of the Law of God and took a large stone and placed it under a pole that was in the Sanctuary of the LORD. 27 And Ioshua said to all the people, "Behold, this stone shall be a testimony to you, for it has heard all the words of the LORD which he spoke with you; therefore it shall be a testi- mony against you, lest you deny your God." 28 Then Ioshua let the people depart, each to his own inheritance. 29 After these things, Iosh- ua the son of Nun, the servant of the LORD, died at the age of a hundred and ten years. 30 They buried him in the borders of his inheritance, in Timnath-Serah, on Mount Ephraim, north of Mount Gaash. 31 Israel served the LORD all the days of Ioshua and all the days of the elders who had cooperated with Iosh- ua and had known all the works of the LORD that he had done for Israel. 32 The bones of Iosef, which the children of Israel carried out of Egypt, they buried in Shechem, in a plot of land that Iaakob bought from the sons of Hamor, the father of Shechem, for a hundred pieces of silk; the sons of Iosef had them as an inheritance. 33 Eleazar the son of Aaron also died, whom they buried on the hill of Fine- has his son, which had been given to him on Mount Ephraim.

JUDGES

CHAPTER 1

1 After Ioshua's death, the children of Israel asked the LORD, "Who will go out against the Canaanites to fight them first?" 2 The LORD answered, "Iudah will go; behold, I have giv- en the land into his hands. 3 And Iudah said to Simeon his brother, "Come with me into my lot, to fight against the Canaanites; and I also will go with you into your lot. 4 Then Iu- dah departed, and the LORD delivered into their hands the Canaanites and the Perizz- ites, who killed ten thousand men at Bezek. 5 They found Adoni-Bezek at Bezek, fought against him, and defeated the Canaanites and the Perizzites. 6 But Adoni-Bezek fled; they pursued him, caught him, and cut off the thumbs of his hands and feet. 7 Adoni-Bezek said, "Seuentie kings who cut off the thumbs of their hands and feet gathered bread un- der my table; as I have done, so God has re- warded me." so they took him to Jerusalem, and there he died. 8 (Now the sons of Iudah had fought against Jerusalem, and had taken it and struck it with the blade of the sword, and set the city on fire.) 9 Then the sons of Judah went to fight against the Canaanites, who dwelt on the mountain, toward the south and in the low country. 10 Iudah went against the Canaanites who dwelt in Hebron, which used to be called Kiriath-arba, and they killed Sheshai, Ahiman and Talmai. 11 From there he went to the inhabitants of Debir, former- ly called Kiriath-Sepher. 12 Caleb said, "The one who destroys Kiriath-Sepher and takes it, to him I will give Achsah, my daughter, as a wife." 13 And Othniel the son of Kenaz, Caleb's younger brother, took her, to whom he gave Achsah his daughter to wife. 14 And when she came to him, she asked him for a field from her father, and lighted her plank, and Caleb said to her, "What do you want? 15 She answered him, "Give me a blessing, for you have given me a county of the south, give me also springs of water"; and Caleb gave her the springs above and the springs below. 16 And the sons of Keni, Moses' father-in-law, went out from the city of palm trees with the sons of Iudah, into the wilderness of Iudah, which is south of Arad, and went to dwell among the people. 17 But Iudah went with Simeon his brother, and they defeated the Ca- naanites who inhabited Zephath, destroyed it utterly, and called the city Hormah. 18 Iudah also took Azzah with its coasts, Askelon with its coasts, and Ekron with its coasts. 19 And the LORD was with Judah, and he took pos- session of the mountains, for he could not drive out the inhabitants of the valleys, be- cause they had yron carrots. 20 They delivered Hebron to Caleb, as Moses had said, and he drove out the three sons of Anak. 21 But the sons of Benjamin did not drive out the Jeb- usites who inhabited Jerusalem; therefore the Jebusites dwell with the sons of Benjamin in Jerusalem to this day. 22 Those of the house of Ioseph also went to Bet-el, and the LORD was with them, 23 The house of Ioseph had Bet-el visited (and the name of the city be- fore was Luz). 24 The spies saw a man coming out of the city and said to him, "Show us, we praise you, the way into the city, and we will do you a favor." 25 When he had shown them the way into the city, they struck the city with the blade of the sword, but they let the man and all his family leave. 26 Then the man went into the land of the Hittites, built a city and called it Luz, which is its name to this day. 27 Manasseh did not destroy Bet-scean with its cities, nor Taanach with its cities, nor the inhabitants of Dor with its cities, nor the in- habitants of Ibleam with its cities, nor the in- habitants of Megiddo with its cities; but the Canaanites still dwelt in that land. 28 How-

ever, when Israel was strong, they forced the Canaanites to pay tribute and did not drive them out altogether. 29 Ephraim also did not expel the Canaanites who dwelt in Ghezer, but the Canaanites dwelt in Ghezer among them. 30 Zebulun did not expel the inhabi- tants of Kitron nor those of Nahalol, but the Canaanites dwelt among them and became tributary to them. 31 Asher did not drive out the inhabitants of Accho, nor those of Zidon, nor those of Ahlab, nor those of Achzib, nor those of Helbah, nor those of Afik, nor those of Rehob, 32 But the Asherites dwelt among the Canaanites, the inhabitants of the land, for they did not drive them out. 33 Neither did Naphtali drive out the inhabitants of Beth- Scemesh and the inhabitants of Beth-Anath, but he dwelt among the Canaanites, inhabi- tants of the land; nevertheless the inhabitants of Beth- Scemesh and Beth-Anath became their tributaries. 34 The Amorites drove the sons of Dan out on the mountain and did not allow them to go down to the valley. 35 The Ammonites still settled on Mount Heres, in Aijalon and Shaalbim, and when the hand of the family of Ioseph was ready, they became their tributaries: 36 The territory of the Am-orites extended from Maaleh-akrabbim to Selah and beyond.

CHAPTER 2

1 An angel of the LORD came from Ghilgal to Bochim and said, "I brought you out of Egypt and brought you into the land that I promised to your fathers, and I said to you, 'I will never break my covenant with you. 2 You also shall not make a covenant with the inhabitants of this land, but you shall break down their al- tars; but you have not obeyed my command. Why have you done this? 3 Therefore I have also said that I will not cast them out before you, but they shall be as thorns in your sides, and their gods shall be your destruction." 4 When the angel of the LORD spoke these words to all the children of Israel, the people raised their voices and wept. 5 Therefore they called that place Bochim and offered sacri- fices to the LORD there. 6 When Ioshua had made the people depart, the children of Israel went each to his own inheritance, to possess the land. 7 The people had served the LORD all the days of Ioshua and all the days of the elders who had followed Ioshua, who had seen all the great works of the LORD that he had done for Israel. 8 But Ioshua the son of Nun, servant of the LORD, died at the age of a hundred and ten years: 9 And they bur- ied him in the places of his inheritance, in Timnath-heres, in mount Ephraim, north ofmount Gaash. 10 So all that generation gath- ered to their fathers, and after them arose another generation that knew not the LORD nor the works that he had done for Israel. 11 Then the children of Israel behaved badly before the LORD and served Baalim, 12 and forsook the LORD, the God of their fathers, who had brought them out of the land of Egypt, and followed other gods, that is, the gods of the peoples around them, and bowed themselves down to them and provoked the LORD to anger. 13 So they forsook the LORD and served Baal and Ashtaroth. 14 The anger of the LORD was kindled against Israel, and he delivered them into the hands of the spoil- ers, who spied on them, and sold them into the hands of their enemies around them, so that they could no longer stand before their enemies. 15 When they went out, the hand of the LORD came upon them, as the LORD had said and as the LORD had sworn to them; so he punished them severely. 16 Nevertheless, the Lord issued judgments that delivered them from the hands of their oppressors. 17 But they would

not obey their judges, for they went after other gods, worshipped them, and quickly departed from the way by which their fathers had walked, obeying the Lord's com- mands. 18 And when the LORD had brought them through Judah, the LORD was with Judah and delivered them out of the hand of their enemies all the days of Judah (for the LORD had compassion on their children, be- cause of those who oppressed and tormented them). 19 But when the Iudge was dead, they returned and did worse than their fathers, following other gods to serve and worship them; they did not cease from their purposes and from their rebellious way. 20 Therefore the anger of the LORD was kindled against Israel, and he said, "Because this people have transgressed my counsel, which I imposed on their fathers, and have not obeyed my vow, 21 therefore I will no longer cast out before them any of the nations that Ioshua left behind when he died, 22 that through them I may test Israel, to see whether they will keep the way of the LORD, walking in it as their fathers followed it, or not." 23 So the LORD left those nations and did not immediately drive them out or deliver them into the hands of Ioshua.

CHAPTER 3

1 These are the nations the LORD left behind to make known to Israel the wars of Canaan (i.e., to all those of Israel who had not known all the wars of Canaan,) 2 only to make known to the generations of the children of Israel and to teach them a warfare that their pre- decessors did not know). 3 And the princes of the Philistines, all the Canaanites, the Sido- nians, and the Hiuites, who dwelt in Mount Lebanon, from Mount Baal-Hermon unto Hamath. 4 And these were concerned to test Israel through them, to know whether they would obey the commands of the LORD, which he had given to their fathers by the hand of Moses. 5 The children of Israel settled in the midst of the Canaanites, the Hittites, the Amorites, the Perizzites, the Iuites and the Jebusites, 6 And they took their daughters as their wives, gave their daughters to their sons, and served their gods. 7 So the children of Israel behaved wickedly before the LORD, forgetting the LORD their God and serving Baalim and Asheroth. 8 Therefore the an- ger of the LORD kindled against Israel, and he put them into the hand of Chushan rish- athaim, king of Aram-naharaim, and the children of Israel served Chushan rishathaim for a year. 9 When the children of Israel cried out to the LORD, the LORD raised up a savior for the children of Israel, and he saved them, Otniel the son of Kenaz, the younger brother of Caleb. 10 And the spirit of the LORD came upon him, and he went out to judge Israel, and went out to war; and the LORD delivered into his hand Chushan Rishathaim, king of Aram, and his hand fought against Chushan Rishathaim. 11 The land rested for four years, and Othniel the son of Kenaz died. 12 Then the children of Israel again committed wick- ednesses before the LORD; and the LORD strengthened Eglon king of Moab against Israel, because they had committed wicked- nesses before the LORD. 13 And he gathered the sons of Ammon and Amalek unto himself, and they went and smote Israel, and took possession of the city of palm trees. 14 So the children of Israel served Eglon, king of Moab, for eighty years. 15 But when the children of Israel cried unto the LORD, the LORD raised up unto them a savior, Ehud the son of Ger- ah, the son of Jemini, a man lame in his right hand; and the children of Israel sent for him a present to Eglon, king of Moab. 16 And Ehud made him a two-pronged dagger the

length of a cubit, and girded it under his robe on his right thigh, 17 and presented the gift to Eglon, king of Moab (Eglon was a very fat man). 18 When he had presented the gift, he sent away the people who carried it, 19 but went away again from the quarters that were near Gilgal and said, "I have a secret errand for you, O king." Who answered, "Be quiet"; and all those around him went away from him. 20 Then Ehud caught up with him. (Ehud said, "I have a message for you from God." Then he rose from his throne, 21 Ehud stretched out his left hand, took the dagger from his right thigh and thrust it into his belly, 22 so that the blade went in and the liver closed around the blade, so that he could not pull the dagger out of his belly, but dirt came out of it. 23 Then Ehud took him to the porch, closed the doors of the hall on him and locked them. 24 When he had gone out, his servants came, who, seeing that the doors of the parlor were locked, said, "Surely he makes his servants in his chamber at night." 25 And they lingered until they were ashamed; and because he would not open the doors of the parlor, they took the key, opened them, and behold, their lord had fallen down dead. 26 Then Ehud fled (while they tarried), passed over the district, and fled to Seirah. 27 And when he returned home, he blew a trum- pet on Mount Ephraim; and the sons of Israel went down with him from the mountain, and he went before them. 28 Then he said to them, "Follow me, for the LORD has delivered into your hands your enemies, that is, Moab." So they went down after him and went through the passes of Iorden toward Moab, not let- ting anyone pass. 29 At the same time they killed among the Moabites about ten thou- sand men, all of them fed and all of them warriors, and not a single one escaped. 30 In that day Moab was subdued by Israel, and the land rested for four more years. 31 After him was Shamgar the son of Anath, who slew the Philistines with six hundred men with an ox chariot; and he also conquered Israel.

CHAPTER 4

1 When Ehud was dead, the children of Israel began to misbehave again before the LORD. 2 The LORD sold them into the hand of Jabin, king of Canaan, who reigned in Hazor, whose leader was called Sisera, who dwelt in Haro- sheth, among the Gentiles. 3 Then the chil- dren of Israel cried out to the LORD (for he had nine hundred charets of yron, and for twenty years had greatly vexed the children of Israel). 4 At that time Deborah, a prophetess wife of Lapidoth, judged Israel. 5 Deborah dwelt under a palm tree, between Ramah and Beth-el, on Mount Ephraim, and the children of Israel came to her for judgment. 6 She sent for Barak the son of Abinoam from Kadesh of Naphtali and said to him, "Has not the LORD, the God of Israel, commanded, 'Go and drag yourself to Mount Tabor and take with you ten thousand men of the sons of Naphtali and the sons of Zebulun? 7 I will drag you to the riuer Kishon Sisera, the leader of the army of Jabins with his chariots and his crowd, and deliver him into your hands." 8 Barak said to her, "If you want to go with me, I will go; but if you do not want to go with me, I will not go." 9 Then she answered, "I will certainly go with you, but this journey you are making will not be for your honor, for the LORD will sell Sisera into the hands of a woman." Deb- orah got up and went with Barak to Kedesh. 10 Barak called Zebulun and Naphtali to Kedesh and marched with ten thousand men, and Deborah went with him. 11 Heber, the Kenite, who was of the sons of Hobab, the fa- ther of Moses, departed from

the Kenites and pitched his tent as far as the village of Zaa- naim, near Kedesh. 12 Then they told Sisera that Barak the son of Abinoam had gone to Tabor. 13 Sisera called together all his charets, about nine hundred charets of yron, and all the people who were with him from Haro- sheth of the Gentiles to the Kishon River. 14 Then Deborah said to Barak, "Go away, for this is the day when the LORD delivered Si- sera into your hands. Has not the LORD gone out before you? So Barak came down from Mount Tabor, with ten thousand men in his retinue. 15 And the LORD destroyed Sisera, all his chariots, and his whole army with the edge of the sword before Barak, so that Sisera broke away from his chariot and fled at a run. 16 But Barak pursued the charet and his army as far as Harosheth of the Gentiles; and all Si- sera's army fell under the blows of the sword; there was no one left. 17 However, Sisera fled at a run to the tent of Iael, wife of Heber the Kenite (for there was peace between Iabin, king of Hazor, and the house of Heber the Kenite). 18 Iael went out to meet Sisera and said to him, "Turn, my lord, turn toward me; do not be afraid." When he had turned toward her in his tent, she covered him with a cloak. 19 He said to her, "Give me, please, some water to drink, for I am thirsty." She opened a bottle of milk, gave him some to drink, and caressed him. 20 Then he said to her, "Stay in the tent area, and when someone comes and asks you, "Is anyone there?" you will answer, "No." 21 Then the wife of Iael Hebers took a nayle from the tent, took a hammer in her hand, and went up to him and thrust the nayle into his temples and drove it into the ground (for he was fast asleep and tired), and so he died. 22 While Barak was pursuing Sisera, Iael came out to him and said, "Come, I will introduce you to the man you seek." When he entered his tent, behold, Sisera was lying dead and with the lamb in his temples. 23 On that day God brought down Jabin, king of Canaan, be- fore the children of Israel. 24 And the hand of the children of Israel prospered and fought against Jabin, king of Canaan, until they had destroyed Jabin, king of Canaan.

CHAPTER 5

1 Then Deborah and Barak the son of Abino- am sang on the same day, saying. 2 "Praise the LORD for the help of Israel and for the people who volunteered. 3 Listen, you kings, listen you princes: I, that is, will sing unto the LORD: I will sing praises unto the LORD, the God of Israel. 4 LORD, when you came out of Seir, when you came out of the camp of Edom, the earth trembled, the heav- ens rained, the clouds dropped water. 5 The mountains melted before the LORD, as Sinai before the LORD, the God of Israel. 6 In the days of Shamgar the son of Anath, in the days of Iael, the highways were busy, and traffick- ers passed through the streets. 7 The cities were not inhabited; they declined, I say, in Is- rael, until Deborah came and became a moth- er in Israel. 8 New gods were chosen, and then there was war at the gates. Was there a shield or a spear among the four thousand of Israel? 9 My heart goes out to the warriors of Israel and to the willing of the people; praise the LORD. 10 Speak, you who ride on white donkeys, you who dwell near Middin and walk along the road. 11 For the boredom of the archers has appeared among the drawers of water, there shall be told the righteousness of the LORD, the righteousness of his cities in Israel; then the people of the LORD came down to the gates. 12 Vp Deborah, vp, arise and sing a song; arise Barak and let go of your captivity, son of Abinoam. 13 For those who remain have dominion

over the strong of the people; the LORD has given me dominion over the strong. 14 From Ephraim has their tower risen against Amalek; and after thee shall Benjamin fight against thy people, O Amalek; from Machir have come the leaders, and from Zebulun those who handle the writer's pen. 15 The princes of Issachar were with Deborah, Issachar, and also Barak, who was set up in the valley, because the diuisions of Reuben were great thoughts of heart. 16 Why did you stand among the sheepfolds to hear the bleating of the flocks? Because Reu- ben's intentions were great thoughts of heart. 17 Gilead remained beyond Iorden; and why did Dan remain in ships? Asher settled on the seashore and stayed in its places of decay. 18 But the inhabitants of Zebulun and Naphtali lived until death in the country places. 19 The kings came and fought; then they fought the kings of Canaan at Taanach by the waters of Megiddo; they received no reward in mon- ey. 20 They fought by Heauen, and the stars in their course fought against Sisera. 1 The river Kishon swept them away, the ancient river Kishon. O my soul, you marched val- iantly." 22 The mounts were broken by the frequent beating of their strongest men. 23 Curse Meroz; (said the angel of the LORD) curse its inhabitants, because they have not come to help the LORD, to help the LORD against the mighty. 24 Iael, wife of Heber the Kenite, shall be blessed compared to the other women; she shall be blessed compared to the women who dwell in the tents. 25 He asked for water, and she gave him milk; she brought butter in a ladies' plate. 26 She put her hand to the naile and her right hand to the workman's hammer; with the hammer she struck Sisera; she took off his head, hav- ing wounded him, and cut off his temples. 27 And he prostrated himself at her feet, and fell to the ground, and stood still; at her feet he prostrated himself, and fell down; and when he was stunned, he stood there dead. 28 The mother of Sisera looked out of a window and cried out to the milkmaids, "Why is his charet so late in coming? Why do the wheels of his charets tarry?" 29 Her wise ladies answered her, "Yes." She herself answered in her own words, 30 Have they not obtained and undone the sponge? Every man has a prayer or two. Sisera has a prayer of garments of different colors, a prayer of different colors made with a needle; of different colors made with a nee- dle on both sides, for the head of the spit. 31 So all your enemies shall perish, O LORD; but those who love him shall be like the sun when it rises with its strength, and the earth has rested for forty years.

CHAPTER 6

1 Then the children of Israel committed wick- edness before the LORD, and the LORD gave them into the hand of Midian for ten years. 2 The hand of Midian came upon Israel, and because of the Midianites, the children of Is- rael made dens in the mountains, caves and fortresses. 3 When Israel had sown, the Mid- ianites and Amalekites and the peoples of the east came and caught up with them, 4 they encamped by them and destroyed the fruits of the land, until you came to Azzah, and left no food for Israel, neither sheep nor oxen nor sausages. 5 For they went, with their cat- tle, and came with their tents, as peddlers in great numbers, so that they and their camels were without number; and they came into the land to destroy it. 6 Thus Israel was severely harmed by the Midianites; therefore the chil- dren of Israel cried out to the LORD. 7 When the children of Israel cried out to the LORD because of the Midianites, 8 the LORD sent to the children of Israel a prophet who said to them,

"Thus says the LORD, the God of Is- rael: I brought you out of Egypt and brought you out of the house of bondage, 9 I delivered you out of the hands of the Egyptians and out of the hands of all those who oppressed you, and I drove them out before you and gave you their land. 10 I say to you, "I am the LORD your God; do not fear the gods of the Amorites, in whose territory you dwell; but you have not obeyed my command." 11 And the angel of the LORD came and stood under the pole that was in Ophrah, which belonged to Ioas the father of the Ezrites and his son Gideon, who threshed grain near the vine- yard to hide it from the Midianites. 12 Then the angel of the LORD appeared to him and said, "The LORD is with you, valiant man. 13 To which Gideon answered, "Ah, my Lord, if the Lord is with you, why on earth has all this come upon you? And where are all your miracles of which our fathers spoke and said, 'Did not the Lord bring you out of Egypt?' but now the Lord has forsaken you and delivered you into the hands of the Midianites." 14 The LORD looked at him and said, "Go with this strength of yours and you will rescue Isra- el from the hands of the Midianites; have I not sent you?" 15 He answered him, "Ah, my Lord, in what way will I save Israel? Behold, my father is poor in Manasseh, and I am the least of my father's house. 16 Then the LORD said to him, "I will be with you, and you shall overcome the Midianites as one man." 17 And he said to him, "Please, if I have found mis- behavior in your eyes, give me a sign that you will speak to me. 18 Please do not go away until I have come to you and brought my offering and laid it before you." And he an- swered, "I will stay until you come again." 19 Then Gideon went in, prepared a kid, baked bread of one ephah of flour, put the meat in a basket, put the broth in a pot, and brought it before him under the hood and presented it. 20 And the angel of God said to him, "Take the meat and the leavened bread, place them on this stone, and bring out the broth"; and he did so. 21 Then the angel of the LORD put out the end of the staff that was in his hand, and touched the meat and the vnleavened bread; and fire came out of the stone, which con- sumed the meat and the vnleavened bread; so the angel of the LORD departed from his sight. 22 When Gideon saw that it was an an- gel of the LORD, Gideon said, "Alas, O LORD my God, because I have seen an angel of the LORD face to face, I shall die." 23 And the LORD said to him, "Peace be unto thee, fear not, thou shalt not die." 24 Then Gideon built there an altar to the LORD and called it Ie- houah shalom; it is still in Ophrah today, by the father of the Ezrites. 25 The same night the LORD said to him, "Take your father's rod and another rod of ten years old, destroy the altar of Baal that your father has and cut down the band that is next to it, 26 build an altar to the LORD your God on the top of this tower, in a level place; take the second bull and

offer a stake with the wood of the plant that you will have cut down." 27 Then Gideon took ten men of his servants and did as the LORD commanded him; but because he feared to do it by day for the house of his fathers and for the men of the city, he did it by night. 28 And when the men of the city rose up early in the morning, behold, the altar of Baal had been broken down, and the pillar that was thereon had been cut down, and the second bull had been put on the altar that had been built. 29 Therefore they said to one another, "Who has done this thing?" And when they inquired and asked, they said, "Gideon the son of Ioash has done this thing." 30 Then the men of the city said to Ioash, "Bring out your son, that he may dye, for he has destroyed the altar of Baal and brought down the band that was near it." 31 Then Ioash said to all who stood by him, "Do you want to plead Baal's cause or do you want to make him pay? Whoever defends him, let him die or go out in the morning. If he is God, let him defend himself against him who pulled down his altar." 32 On that day Gideon was called Ierubbaal, that is, "Let Baal defend himself because he has torn down his altar." 33 Then all the Midianites and Amalekites and the peoples of the east gathered and encamped in the valley of Izreel. 34 But the Spirit of the LORD descended upon Gideon, and he blew a trumpet, and Abiezer was smit- ten with him. 35 And he sent messengers to Manasseh, who was also with him, and sent messengers to Asher, and to Zebulun, and to Naphtali, who came to meet them. 36 Then Gideon said to God, "If you want to save Is- rael by my hand, as you said, 37 Behold, I will put a fleece of wool in the threshing floor; if the dew comes only on the fleece and scatters over all the land, then I will be sure that you will save Israel by my hand, as you have said." 8 And so it was: and he rose up at daybreak, and joined the fleece, and plucked the dew from it, and filled a bowl with water. 39 Then Gideon said to God, "Do not be angry with me, that I may speak again; let me try again, I pray you, with the fleece; let it now be dried only on the fleece, and let the dew be on all the ground." 40 God did so that very night, for the fleece was dry and there was dew all over the ground.

CHAPTER 7

1 Then Ierubbaal (that is Gideon) rose early, with all the people who were with him, and encamped by the well of Harod, so that the army of the Midianites was north of them, in the valley by the hill of Moreh. 2 And the LORD said to Gideon, "The people who are with you are too numerous for me to give the Midian- ites into their hands, so that Israel will not boast against me and say, 'My hand has cheat- ed me.' 3 Now therefore, proclaim among the people and say, "Whoever is so fearful or fear- ful, turn back and depart from Mount Gile- ad." And the people who were on Mount Gile- ad returned in two-twenty thousand; then ten thousand withdrew. 4 And the LORD said to Gideon, "The people are still too many; bring them down to the water, and there I will test them for you; and of whom I will say to you, 'This man will go with you,' the same will go with you; and of whom I will say to you, 'This man will not go with you,' the same will not go." 5 So he sent the people down to the water. And the LORD said to Gideon, "As many as lap the water with their tongues, as a dog does, set them aside; and as many as kneel down to drink, set them aside." 6 Most of those who lapped by putting their hands to their mouths were three hundred men; but all the rest of the people knelt on their knees to drink the water. 7 Then the LORD said to Gideon, "For these three hundred men who drank, I will save you and deliver the Midianites into your hands; and let all the rest of the people go away each to his place." 8 So the people took their vitals and their trumpets with them; then he sent all the rest of Israel, each to his tent, and set the three hundred men in line; and the Midianite army was under him in a valley. 9 The same night the LORD said to him, "Arise, go down to the army, for I have delivered it into your hands." 10 But if you are afraid to go down, go you and Phurah your servant to the army, 11 listen to what they tell you, and so your hands will be strong to go down to the army." Then they went down together with Phurah, his servant, outside the soldiers who were in the army. 12 The Midianites, Amalekites, and all the people of the east

lay in the valley like an army of peasants, and their camels were nameless, like the sand on the seashore for its number. 13 When Gideon had arrived, behold, a man told a dream to his neighbor and said, "Behold, I dreamed a dream, and behold, a loaf of barley fell from above toward the army of Midian and came near to a tent, struck it to fall, and it toppled over, and the tent fell down." 14 His companions answered and said, "This is none other than the sword of Gideon the son of Ioash, a man of Israel, for into his hands God has delivered Midian and all the army." 15 When Gideon heard the ac- count and its interpretation, he worshipped himself, returned to the army of Israel and said, "Vp, for into your hands the Lord has de- livered the army of Midian." 16 Then he divid- ed the three hundred men into three bands and gave each one a trumpet in his hand with empty pitchers and lamps inside the pitch- ers. 17 Then he said to them, "Look to me and do the same, when I come to the side of the army; and as I do, do ye also. 18 When I blow the trumpet and all those who are with me, you also blow the trumpet on every side of the army and say, 'For the LORD and for Gideon. 19 So Gideon and the hundred men who were with him came to the outside of the army at the beginning of midnight; they made the sentinels stand up, sounded with their trum- pets, and broke the pitchers in their hands. 20 And the three companies sounded with their trumpets and broke their pitchers, and held their lamps in their left hand and their trumpets in their right hand to blow with all; and they cried, "The sword of the Lord and of Gideon." 21 And they stood, every man in his place, round about the army; and all the army ran and shouted and fled. 22 And the three hundred blew the trumpets, and the LORD put every man's sword on his neigh- bor and on all the army; so the army fled to Beth-Hashittah, to Zerah, and to the border of Abel-Mehola, as far as Tabbath. 23 Then the men of Israel, gathered from Naphtali, Asher and all Manasseh, pursued the Midianites. 24 And Gideon sent messengers to all Mount Ephraim, saying, "Go down against the Mid- ianites and take before them the waters to- ward Bet-Barah and Iorden." Then all the men of Ephraim gathered together and took the waters toward Beth-Barah and Iorden. 25 Then they took two princes of the Midianites, Oreb and Zeeb, killed Oreb on Mount Oreb and Zeeb by the cellar of Zeeb, and pursued the Midianites and brought the heads of Oreb and Zeeb to Gideon beyond Iorden.

CHAPTER 8

1 Then the men of Ephraim said to him, "Why did you serve yourself in this way that you did not call, when you went to fight with the Midianites?" and they rebuked him sharply. 2 And he said, "What have I done in comparison with you? Is not the harvest of Ephraim better than the harvest of Abiezer? 3 God delivered into your hands the princes of Midian, Oreb and Zeeb; and what could I have done in comparison with you?" And when he had spoken thus, the minds fell to- ward him. 4 Then Gideon came to Iorden to pass over, he and the three hundred men who were with him, weary, yet pursuing them. 5 And he said to the men of Succoth, "Give, I pray you, morsels of bread to the people who follow me (for they are weary), that I may pur- sue Zebah and Zalmunna, kings of Midian." 6 The princes of Succoth said, "Are the hands of Zebah and Zalmunna now in your hands to give bread to your army?" 7 Then Gideon said, "When the LORD has delivered Zebah and Zalmunna into my hands, I will tear your flesh with thorns from the

wilderness and with branches." 8 Then he went to Penuel and spoke to them in the same way, and the men of Penuel answered him as the men of Suc- coth. 9 And he also said to the men of Penuel, "When I return in peace, I will tear down this tower." 10 Now Zebah and Zalmunna were in Karkor, and with them their armies, about five hundred thousand, all that were left of all the armies of the East, for a hundred and twenty thousand men who had drawn their swords had been slain. 11 And Gideon passed through the midst of those who dwelt in Tab- ernacles, to the east of Nobah and Iogbehah, and he defeated the army, which was reckless. 12 When Zebah and Zalmunna fled, he pur- sued them, took the two Midian kings, Zebah and Zalmunna, and defeated the whole army. 13 Gideon the son of Joash returned from the battle while the sun was still up, 14 and took a servant of Succoth and questioned him; and he wrote to him the princes of Succoth and his elders, that is, seventy and seventy men. 15 He presented himself to the men of Suc- coth and said, "Here are Zebah and Zalmun- na, through whom you have spoken to me, saying, 'Are the hands of Zebah and Zalmun- na already in your hands, so that we may give bread to your weary men?'" 16 Then he took the elders of the city, and the thorns of the wil- derness, and the breeds, and mocked the men of Succoth with them. 17 Moreover he tore down the road of Penuel and killed the men of the city. 18 Then he said to Zebah and Zal- munna, "What kind of men were those whom you killed on Tabor?" And they answered, "As you are, so were they; all were as the sons of a king." 19 He said, "They were my brothers, as the sons of my mother; as it pleases the Lord, if you had respected their rights, I would not have killed you." 20 Then he said to Iether, his firstborn son, "Go away and kill them"; but the boy did not draw his sword, for he feared that he was still young. 21 Then Zebah and Zalmunna said, "Get up and fall on them, for as the man is, so is his strength." Gideon got up, killed Zebah and Zalmunna, and took away the ornaments that were on the necks of their camels. 22 Then the men of Israel said to Gideon, "Reign over Vs, you and your son and your sons, for you have delivered Vs from the hand of Midian." 23 Gideon said to them, "I will not reign over you, nor will my son reign over you, but the LORD will reign over you." 24 Then Gideon said to them, "I would ask you to give me each the earrings of his prayer (for they had golden earrings because they were Ishmaelites)." 25 They answered, "We will give them." Then they made a robe and threw into it the earrings of each man who prayed. 26 The weight of the gold earrings that he required was a thousand and seven hundred shekels of gold, in addition to the collars, the grommets, and the purples that the kings of Midian wore and the cachets that their cam- els had around their necks. 27 And Gideon made an ephod of it, and set it in Ophrah, his city; and all Israel hunted there, which was the destruction of Gideon and his house. 28 Thus Midian was brought low before the children of Israel, so that they lifted up their heads no more; and the county was quiet for forty years in the days of Gideon. 29 Then Je- rubbaal the son of Ioas departed and settled in his house. 30 Gideon had seuentie sons be- gotten of his body, for he had many wives. 31 His concubine who was in Shechem also bore him a son, whom he named Abimelech. 32 So Gideon the son of Joash died in good age, and was buried in the sepulcher of Joash his father in Ophrah by the father of the Exrites. 33 But when Gideon was dead, the children of Isra- el departed and went after Baalim and made Baal-Berith their god. 34 The children of Is- rael did not remember the LORD their God, who had delivered them out of the hand of all their enemies on every side. 35 They had no mercy on

the house of Jerubbaal and Gideon, according to all the goodness he had shown to Israel.

CHAPTER 9

1 Then Abimelech the son of Jerubbaal went to Shechem to his mother's brothers, and he made contact with them, and with all the family, and with the house of his mother's fa- ther, saying, "Say, I pray you, in the presence of all the men of Shechem, whether it is better for you that all the sons of Jerubbaal, who are seuentie persons, should reign, 2 "Say, I pray you, before all the men of Shechem, whether it is better for you that all the sons of Jerub- baal, who are seventy persons, should reign over you, or that one should reign over you? Remember also that I am your bones and your flesh." 3 Then his mothers and his brothers said of him, in the presence of all the men of Shechem, all these words; and their hearts were moved to follow Abimelech, for they said, "He is our brother." 4 They gave him seuentie pieces of silk from the house of Baal- Berith, with which Abimelech hired the vayne and the light companions who followed him. 5 Then he went to the house of his fathers, to Ophrah, and killed his brothers, the sons of Ierubbaal, about seventy people on a stone; but Iotham, the youngest son of Ierubbaal, remained, because he had hidden himself. 6 Then all the men of Shechem gathered them- selves together with all the house of Millo and came and appointed Abimelech king at the place where the stone had been erected in Shechem. 7 And when they had told Iotham, he went and stood on the top of Mount Ger- izim, and lifted up his voice, and cried out, and said to them, "Listen to me, men of Shechem, that God may hear you." 8 And the trees went looking for a king outside of them and said to the olive tree, "You rule outside of them." 9 But the olive tree said to them, "Shall I leave my fats, with which they honor God and men, and go to work for you trees? 10 Then the trees said to the fig tree, "Come and be the king of the world." 11 But the fig tree answered them, "Shall I forsake my sweetness and my good fruit and go and worship among the trees?" 12 Then the trees said to the Vine, "Come and be the king." 13 But the Vine said to them, "Shall I leave my wine, with which I gladden God and men, and go and worship among the trees?" 14 Then all the trees said to the bramble, "Come, and reign here." 15 The bramble tree answered the trees, "If you want to accept that I am your king, come and put your trust under my shadow; if not, fire will come out of the bramble tree and consume the cedars of Lebanon." 16 Now if ye do rightly and incorruptly to make Abimelech a king, and if ye have done well with Jerubbaal and his house, and if ye have done to him what his hands have done, 17 For my father fought for you, and sacrificed his life, and delivered you out of the hand of Midian. 18 Today you rose up against my father's house and killed his sons, about seventy people on a stone, and made Abimelech the son of his servant in May king of the men of Shechem, because he is your brother). 19 If therefore you have be- haved yourselves this day in a fair and upright manner to Jerubbaal and his house, then re- turn with you. 20 But if not, let a fire go out from Abimelech, and consume the men of Shechem and the house of Millo; let a fire also go out from the men of Shechem and the house of Millo, and consume Abimelech." 21 Then Iotham escaped, fled, went to Beer and settled there for fear of Abimelech, his broth- er. 22 So Abimelech reigned for three years over Israel. 23 But God sent a euilic spirit be- tween Abimelech and the men of Shechem; and the men of

Shechem failed in their prom- ise to Abimelech, 24 that cruelty to the seven- ty sons of Jerubbaal and their blood might come to deplore Abimelech their brother, who had killed them, and the men of Shechem, who had allowed him to kill his brothers. 25 And the men of Shechem set men on the tops of the mountains at his heels, who robbed everyone who passed by that road; and the thing was reported to Abimelech. 26 Then came Gaal the son of Ebed with his brothers, and they went to Shechem; and the men of Shechem put their trust in him. 27 And they went out into the fields, and gathered grapes and trotted them out, and snacked, and en- tered into the house of their gods, and ate and drank, and cursed Abimelech. 28 Then Gaal the son of Ebed said, "Who is Abimelech and who is Shechem, that we should serve him? Is he not the son of Jerubbaal, and is Zebul his officer? Rather serve the men of Hamor, the father of Shechem, why should we serve him? 29 Now if God wanted this people to be under my hand, then I would make Abimelech dis- appear." And he said to Abimelech, "Increase your army and come out." 30 When Zebul, leader of the city, heard the words of Gaal the son of Ebed, he was inflamed with anger. 31 Therefore he sent messengers to Abimelech, saying, "Behold, Gaal the son of Ebed and his brothers have come to Shechem, and behold, they are fortifying the city against you. 32 Now, therefore, get up at night, you and the people who are with you, and stay and sleep in the countryside. 33 Arise early in the morn- ing, as soon as the sun rises, and assault the city; and when he and the people that are with him go out against you, do to him what you can." 34 And Abimelech rose up, with all the people who were with him, by night, and they marched against Shechem in four groups. 35 Then Gaal the son of Ebed went out and stood at the entrance of the city gate; and Abimel- ech got up, together with all the people who were with him, so that they would not stand by. 36 When Gaal saw the people, he said to Zebul, "Behold, from the tops of the moun- tains come down people"; and Zebul said to him, "The shadow of the mountains looks like a man to you." 37 Gaal spoke again and said, "See, there are people coming down from the middle of the country and another band com- ing down from the plain of Meonenim." 38 Then Zebul said to him, "Where is now your mouth that said, 'Who is Abimelech, why do we serve him?' Is not this the people whom you have despised? Go out now, I pray you, and fight with them." 39 Gaal went out before the men of Shechem and fought with Abimel- ech. 40 And Abimelech pursued him, and he fled before him, and many were thrown out and wounded, even to the entrance of the gate. 41 Abimelech settled in Arumah, while Zebul drove out Gaal and his brothers so that they would not dwell in Shechem. 42 The next day the people went out into the countryside, and this was told to Abimelech. 43 And he took the people, and divided them into three bands, and went out into the fields, and looked, and behold, the people came out of the city, and rose up against them, and smote them. 44 And Abimelech and the bands that were with him retreated forward and stood at the entrance of the city gate; and the other two bands came upon all the people that were in the fields and killed them. 45 When Abi- melech had fought against the city all that day, he took the city, killed the people who were there, destroyed the city, and sowed salt there. 46 When all the men of the city of Shechem heard of it, they went into the en- closure of the house of the god Berith. 47 Abi- melech was told that all the men of the city of Shechem were gathered together. 48 And Abi- melech led him to Mount Zalmon, he and all the people who were with him; and Abimel- ech took axes, and cut branches

from trees, and took them, and carried them on his shoulder, and said to the people who were with him, "What you have seen me do, make haste and do as I do." 49 Then all the people cut off every man his branch, followed Abi- melech, put it in the pit, and set fire to it; so all the men of the city of Shechem also died, about a thousand men and women. 50 Then Abimelech went to Tebez, besieged Tebez and conquered it. 51 But inside the city was a strong keep, where all the men and women and all the leaders of the city took refuge; they closed it and went to the top of the keep. 52 And Abimelech came to the city, and fought against it, and went hard into the interior of the city to set it on fire. 53 But a certain wom- an threw a piece of milestone on Abimelech's head and broke his embers. 54 Then Abimel- ech hastily called his page who carried his tools and said to him, "Draw your sword and kill me, lest men say of me, 'A woman killed him.'" And his page thrust him down, and he died. 55 And when the men of Israel saw that Abimelech was dead, they went each to his own place. 56 Thus God made known the wickedness of Abimelech, which he had com- mitted against his father by killing his seventy brothers. 57 Moreover, God brought upon their heads all the wickedness of the men of Shechem. Thus upon them fell the curse of Jotham the son of Jerubbaal.

CHAPTER 10

1 After Abimelech, Tola the son of Puah the son of Dodo, a man of Issachar who dwelt in Shamir on Mount Ephraim, arose to defend Israel. 2 He judged Israel for three years and twenty, died and was buried in Shamir. 3 Af- ter him arose Iair, a Gileadite, who judged Is- rael for twenty years. 4 He had three sons who rode on three ascents and had three cities, which are now called Hauoth-Iair and are in the land of Gilead. 5 Iair died and was buried in Kamon. 6 Still the children of Israel be- haved badly before the LORD, serving Baalim and Ashtaroth, the gods of Aram, the gods of Zidon, the gods of Moab, the gods of the sons of Ammon, and the gods of the Philistines, and forsaking the LORD and not serving him. 7 Therefore the anger of the LORD was kin- dled against Israel, and he put them into the hands of the Philistines and into the hands of the sons of Ammon: 8 Who from that year harassed and oppressed the children of Israel for eighty years, that is, all the children of Is- rael who were beyond Iorden, in the land of the Amorites, which is in Gilead. 9 Moreover the sons of Ammon went out from Iorden to fight against Iudah, against Benjamin, and against the house of Ephraim, so that Israel was greatly tormented. 10 Then the children of Israel cried out to the LORD, saying, "We have sinned against you, because we have forsaken our God and served Baalim." 11 The LORD said to the children of Israel, "Have I not delivered you from the Egyptians and the Amorites, from the sons of Ammon and the Philistines? 12 The Zidonians, Amalekites and Maonites also oppressed you; you cried out to me, and I delivered you out of their hands. 13 But you have forsaken me and served other gods; therefore I will grant you no more. 14 Go and cry to the gods whom you have cho- sen; let them save you in the time of your tribulation." 15 The children of Israel said to the LORD, "We have sinned; do with you what pleases you; only we beseech you to grant us this day." 16 Then they removed the foreign gods from their midst and went into the ser- vice of the LORD; and his soul was grieved for the misfortunes of Israel. 17 Then the children of Ammon gathered themselves together and pitched in Gilead, and the children of Israel gathered

themselves together and pitched in Mizpeh. 18 The people and the princes of Gilead said to each other, "Whoever starts the battle against the sons of Ammon will be the leader of all the inhabitants of Gilead."

CHAPTER 11

1 Then Gilead begat Iphtah; Iphtah the Gilea- dite was a valiant man, but the son of a harlot. 2 Gilead's wife bore him sons, and when the women's sons were of age, they drove out Ip- htah and said to him, "You shall not inherit in the house of our fathers, for you are the son of a foreign woman." 3 Then Iphtah fled from his brothers and settled in the land of Tob; and there he gathered to Iphtah idle compan- ions and went away with him. 4 Afterward the sons of Ammon made war on Israel. 5 When the sons of Ammon fought with Israel, the el- ders of Gilead went and took Iphtah from the land of Tob. 6 And they said to Iftah, "Come and be our captain, to fight with the sons of Ammon." 7 Then Iftah answered the elders of Gilead, "Have you not hated me and driven me out of the house of my fathers? How then have you come to me now, in the time of your trib- ulation?" 8 Then the elders of Gilead said to Iphtah, "Therefore we now defer to you, that you may go with them and fight against the sons of Ammon and be our leader among all the inhabitants of Gilead." 9 Iftah said to the elders of Gilead, "If you take me back home to fight against the sons of Ammon, if the LORD goes before them, will I be your leader?" 10 The elders of Gilead said to Ifta, "The Lord be witness among you, if we do not do according to your words." 11 Then Iftah went with the elders of Gilead, and the people appointed him chief and headman; and Iftah went over all his words before the Lord in Mizpeh. 12 Then Iftah sent messengers to the king of the sons of Ammon, saying, "What have you to do with me, that you have come against me to fight in my territory?" 13 The king of the sons of Ammon answered Iftah's messengers, "For Israel took possession of my territory when he came from Egypt, from Arnon as far as Jabbok and as far as Iorden. 14 Nevertheless Iftah again sent messengers to the king of the sons of Ammon, 15 and they said to him, "Thus says Iftah: Israel has not taken the ter- ritory of Moab nor the territory of the sons of Ammon." 16 But when Israel went out of Egypt and crossed the desert to the Red Sea, they came to Kadesh. 17 Israel sent messen- gers to the king of Edom, saying, "Let me, I pray you, go through your territory," but the king of Edom would not consent; they also sent to the king of Moab, but he would not; so Israel remained in Kadesh. 18 Then they went through the wilderness, skirted the territory of Edom and the territory of Moab, came to the east of the territory of Moab, camped on the other side of the Arnon, and did not reach the border of Moab, because the Arnon was the border of Moab. 19 Israel sent messengers to Sihon, king of the Amorites, the king of Heshbon, and Israel said to him, "Let us pass, we pray you, through your territory to our house." 20 But Sihon did not allow Israel to pass through his territory; rather Sihon gath- ered all his people, encamped at Iahaz, and fought against Israel. 21 The LORD, the God of Israel, gave Sihon and all his people into the hands of Israel, who defeated them; so Israel took possession of all the territory of the Am- orites, the inhabitants of that county: 22 They possessed all the territory of the Amorites, from Arnon as far as Jabbok and from the wil- derness as far as Iorden. 23 Now therefore has the LORD, the God of Israel, cast out the Am- orites before his people Israel, and should you possess them? 24 Would

you not like to pos- sess what Chemosh, your god, has granted you to possess? So those whom the LORD, our God, has made to disappear before us, we will possess." 25 Are you better than Balak the son of Zippor, king of Moab? Did you not wrestle with Israel and fight against them? 26 When Israel dwelt in Heshbon and its cities, in Aro- er and its towns, and in all the cities that are on the shores of Arnon, for three hundred years? Why have you not recovered them in that space? 27 Therefore, I have not offended you, but you wrong me by waging war against me. The LORD, the judge, is now judge be- tween the children of Israel and the children of Ammon. 28 But the king of the sons of Am- mon did not listen to the words of Iftah who had sent him. 29 Then the Spirit of the LORD came upon Iftah, and he passed into Gilead and Manasseh, and came to Mizpeh in Gile- ad, and from Mizpeh in Gilead he went to the sons of Ammon. 30 Iftah made a vow to the LORD and said, "If you will deliver the sons of Ammon into my hands, 31 then that which shall come forth out of the courts of my house to meet me, when I return in peace to the sons of Ammon, it shall be the LORD's, and I will offer it as a burnt offering." 32 So Ifta went to the sons of Ammon to fight against them, and the LORD delivered them into his hands. 33 And he defeated them from Aroer as far as Minnith, by twenty cities, and so as far as Abel, of the vineyards, with a tremen- dous slaughter. Thus the children of Ammon were humbled before the children of Israel. 34 When Iftah came to Mizpeh to his house, be- hold, his daughter came to him with timpani and daunces, who was his only daughter; she had no other sons or daughters. 35 When he saw her, he tore his garments and said, "Alas, my daughter, you have brought me low, and you are of those who trouble me, because I have opened my mouth to the LORD and can- not turn back." 36 She said to him, "My father, if you have opened your mouth to the LORD, do with me what you have promised, since the LORD has taken you from your enemies, the sons of Ammon." 37 She also said to her father, "Do this for me: give me two pennies, that I may go to the mountains and review my virginity, I and my companions." 38 And he said, "Go," and sent her away two pennies; so she went with her companions and mourned her virginity on the mountains. 39 After two months, she turned again to her father, who made with her the vow she had made, without her having known anyone: 40 And the daugh- ters of Israel went every year to mourn for the daughter of Iftah the Gileadite four days a year.

CHAPTER 12

1 Then the inhabitants of Ephraim gathered themselves together, went northward and said to Ifta, "Why did you go to fight against the sons of Ammon and did not call to come with you? Therefore we will burn your house with fire." 2 Iphtah said to them, "I and my people were in great strife with the sons of Ammon, and when I called you, you did not deliver me out of their hands. 3 When I saw that you did not deliver me, I put my life in my hands and went against the sons of Ammon; the LORD delivered them into my hands. Why then do you now come and fight against me? 4 Then Iftah gathered all the men of Gilead and went against Ephraim; and the men of Gile- ad struck Ephraim, because they said, "You Gileadites are fugitives from Ephraim among the Ephraimites and among the Manassites." 5 Moreover the Gileadites crossed the passes of Iorden before the Ephraimites, and when the Ephraimite who had fled said, "Let me pass," the men of Gilead said to him, "Are

you an Ephraimite? And he answered, "No." 6 then they said to him, "Say now Shibboleth"; and he answered, "Sibboleth," for he could not pronounce so; then they took him and slew him at the passes of Iorden; and at that time the Ephraimites were two thousand and four thousand. 7 Iftah judged Israel for six years; then Iftah the Gileadite died, and was buried in one of the cities of Gilead. 8 After him Ib- zan, of Beth-Lem, was judge of Israel, 9 Who had thirty sons and thirty daughters, whom he sent for and took in thirty daughters for his sons. 10 Then Ibzan died and was buried in Bethlehem. 11 After him Elon, a Zebulon- ite, was elected in Israel, who ruled Israel for ten years. 12 Then Elon, a Zebulonite, died and was buried in Aijalon, in the county of Zebulun. 13 After him Abdon the son of Hil- lel, the Pirathonite, was judge of Israel. 14 He had forty sons and thirty grandsons who rode on seventy assecolytes, and he was judge of Israel for eight years. 15 Then Abdon the son of Hillel the Pirathonite died, and was bur- ied in Pirathon in the land of Ephraim, in the mountain of Amalek.

that when your word is past, we may honor you?" 18 The angel of the Lord said to him, "Why do you ask my name, which is secret? 19 Then Manoa took a kid goat as a food of- fering and offered it on a stone to the LORD; and the angel did wonders, while Manoa and his wife watched. 20 For when the flame went upward from the altar, the angel of the LORD went up on the flame of the altar; and Manoa and his wife saw it, and they fell with their faces to the ground. 21 (So the Angel of the Lord no longer appeared to Manoa and his wife). Then Manoa understood that he was an Angel of the Lord. 22 Manoa said to his wife, "We will surely die, for we have seen God." 23 But his wife said to him, "If the LORD wanted to kill you, he would not have received a stake and a food offering from our hands, and he would not have shown you all these things and told you any such thing." 24 His wife bore a son and named him Samson; the son grew up and the Lord blessed him. 25 The Spirit of the LORD began to strengthen him in Dan's army, between Zorah and Eshtaol.

CHAPTER 13

1 Because the children of Israel continued to commit wickedness before the LORD, the LORD delivered them into the hands of the Philistines for four years. 2 In Zorah there was a man of the family of the Danites, named Manoa, whose wife was with child and did not give birth. 3 The angel of the LORD appeared to the woman and said to her, "Be- hold, you are with child and will not give birth, but you will conceive and bear a son. 4 Now therefore beware of drinking wine or strong spirits and of eating anything vnclean. 5 For, behold, you shall conceive and bear a son, and no razor shall fall on his head, for the son shall be a Nazarite to God from his birth; and he shall begin to save Israel from the hands of the Philistines." 6 Then the wife came and told her husband, "A man of God came to me, and his face was like that of an angel of God, very fearful; but I did not ask him where he came from, nor did he tell me his name, 7 but he said to me, "Behold, you shall conceive and bear a son, and now you shall drink neither wine nor strong drink, nor eat any vnclean thing, for the son shall be a Nazarite to God from his birth until the day of his death." 8 Then Manoa prayed to the LORD and said, "Please, my LORD, let the man of God, whom you sent, now come to us again and teach us what we should do with the child when he is born." 9 God heard the voice of Manoa, and the angel of God went again to his wife, while she was in the field, but Manoa her husband was not with her. 10 The wife hurried, presented her husband, and said to him, "Behold, the man who came to me today has appeared." 11 Manoa got up, went after his wife, approached the man and said to him, "Are you the man who spoke to the woman?" And he answered, "Yes." 12 Then Manoa said, "Now let your speech come true; but how can we order the child and make him pay?" 13 The angel of the LORD said to Manoa, "The woman must be careful about every- thing I have told her. 14 She must not eat any- thing that comes from the vine; she must not drink wine or strong spirits, nor eat anything strange; she must observe all that I have com- manded her." 15 Manoa then said to the angel of the LORD, "Please let me net you until we have prepared a kid for you." 16 The angel of the LORD said to Manoa, "Even if you let me stay, I will not eat of your bread; and if you want to make a burnt offering, offer it to the LORD, for Manoa did not know that he was an angel of the LORD." 17 Then Manoa said to the angel of the LORD, "What is your name,

CHAPTER 14

1 Now Samson went down to Timnath and saw in Timnath a woman of the daughters of the Philistines, 2 And he came and told his father and his mother, "I saw in Timnath a woman of the daughters of the Philistines; give her therefore to me to wife." 3 Then his father and mother said to him, "Is there not a wife among the daughters of your brothers, and among all my people, that you should go and take a wife from the circumcised Philis- tines?" And Samson said to his father, "Give me the wife, for I like her." 4 But his father and mother did not know that this was from the LORD, so that he might seek an occasion against the Philistines, for at that time the Philistines ruled over Israel. 5 Then Samson and his father and mother went down to Tim- nath and came to the vineyards of Timnath; and behold, a young lion roared at him. 6 And the Spirit of the LORD came upon him, and he tore him in pieces, as one does with a kid, and he had nothing in his hand, nor did he tell his father and mother what he had done. 7 Then he went down and talked with the woman who was beautiful in Samson's eyes. 8 After a few days, when he returned to receive her, he went away to see the lion's carcass; and behold, in the lion's body was a swan of bees and iron. 9 And he took them in his hand, and came to his father and his mother, and greeted them, and they ate; but he did not tell them that he had taken the honey out of the lion's body. 10 Then his father went down to the woman, and Samson made a feast there, for so the young men wanted. 11 When they saw him, they brought with them thirty com- panions. 12 Then Samson said to them, "Now I am going to propose a riddle to you; if you can solve it within seven days of the feast and figure it out, I will give you thirty sheets and three changes of clothing. 13 But if you fail to declare it to me, you shall give me thirty sheets and three changes of clothing." They answered him, "State your riddle, that we may hear it." 14 He said to them, "From the eater comes forth meat, and from the strong comes forth sweetness; and in three days they could not explain the riddle." 15 When the seventh day came, they said to Samson's wife, "Summon your husband to declare the riddle, or we will burn you and your fathers' house with fire. Have you summoned your husband to possess him? Is it not so? 16 And Samson's wife wept before him and said, "Surely you hate me and do not appreciate me, because you have riddled the sons of my people and have not told me." And he said

to her, "Be- hold, I have told it neither to my father nor to my mother, and shall I tell it to you?" 17 Then Samson's wife wept before him ten days while their feast lasted; and when the tenth day came, he gave her an explanation, because she was importunate with him; so she told the riddle to the children of his people. 18 On the tenth day before the setting of the sun, the men of the city said to him, "What is sweet- er than honesty and what is stronger than the lion? Then he answered them, "If you had not plowed with my cushion, you would not have discovered my riddle." 19 And the Spirit of the LORD assailed him, and he went down to Ashkelon, and slew thirty men of them, and skewered them, and gave them clothes explaining the riddle; and his anger was kin- dled, and he went away to his fathers' house. 20 Then Samson's wife was given to his com- panion, whom he had regarded as his friend.

CHAPTER 15

1 After a while, in the time of the plague, Samson visited his wife with a kid, saying, "I will go in to my wife in the chamber"; but her father would not let him in. 2 Her father said, "I thought you hated her; therefore I en- trusted her to your companion. Is not your younger sister more beautiful than you? Take her, I pray you, instead of the other." 3 Then Samson said to them, "Now I am more blas- phemous than the Philistines; therefore I will harm them." 4 Then Samson went out, took three hundred foxes, took firebrands, turned them from side to side, and put a firebrand in the middle between the two tails. 5 When he had set fire to the brands, he sent them into the countryside of the Philistines and burned both the hills and the countryside, with the vines and the olives. 6 Then the Phi- listines said, "Who did this?" They answered, "Samson, son-in-law of the Timnite, for he had taken his wife and given her to his mate." Then the Philistines came and burned her and her father with fire. 7 Then Samson said to them, "Even though you have done this, I still want to be questioned by you, and then I will stop." 8 So he struck them at the level of the hippocampus and the thigh with a strong plague; then he went and dwelt on the top of Mount Etam. 9 Then the Philistines came and encamped in Judah and scattered through Lehi. 10 And the men of Iudah said, Why have you come here? And they answered, "We have come to defeat Samson and to do to him what he did at Warsaw." 11 Then three thousand men of Judah went to the top of the hill of Etam and said to Samson, "Do you not know that the Philistines are the mas- ters of Vs? Why then have you done so to Vs? And he answered them, "As they have done to me, so have I done to them." 12 Then they said to him, "We have come to take you and deliver you into the hands of the Philistines." Samson said to them, "Swear by me that you will not fall on me with your own hands." 13 Those answered him, "No, but we will flay you and deliver you into their hands, but we will not kill you." They bound him with two new ropes and took him away from the tower. 14 When he came to Lehi, the Philistines cried out against him, and the Spirit of the LORD came upon him, and the ropes that were on his arms became like linen burned by fire, for the bandages melted from his hands. 15 Then he found a new ax thorn, stretched out his hand, seized it, and with it killed a thousand men. 16 Then Samson said, "With the bone of an axe there are heaps upon heaps; with the bone of an axe I killed a thousand men." 17 And when he had left the word, he took the iawebone out of his hand and called that place Ramath-Lehi. 18 Having great thirst, he called upon the

LORD and said, "You have given this great delusion into the hands of your servant; and now will I die of thirst and fall into the hands of the vncircumcis?" 19 Then God broke the chewer's tooth that was in his throat, and water came out of it; and when he had drunk, his Spirit stirred again, and he was restored; therefore the name of him is called Enhak- kore, which is in Lehi to this day. 20 He was judge of Israel during the twenty years of the Philistines.

CHAPTER 16

1 Then Samson went to Azzah and saw a prostitute and entered her. 2 And it was said to the Azzahites, "Samson has come here." And they went after him all night at the gates of the city, and remained quiet all night, say- ing, "Stay until early morning, and we will kill him." 3 And Samson slept until midnight, and rose up at midnight, and took the doors of the gates of the city and the two posts, and lifted them up with the bars, and put them on his shoulders, and carried them to the top of the mountain that is before Hebron. 4 After this he married a woman by the village of Sorek, whose name was Delilah: 5 to whom came the princes of the Philistines and said to her, "Go in to him and see where his great strength is, and by what means we can reach him, that we may defeat and punish him, and each of you shall give you eleven hundred shekels of silk." 6 Delilah said to Samson, "Tell me, I pray you, where your great strength lies, and by what means you may be bound to do you harm." 7 Samson answered her, "If they bind me with green ropes that have never been dried, then I will be free and will be like another man." 8 The princes of the Philistines brought her green ropes that had not been dried, and she bound him with them. 9 (And she had men ly- ing with her in the chamber) Then she said to him, "The Philistines are upon you, Samson." And he broke the cords, as one breaks a braid of tow when he feels the fire; so his strength was not known. 10 After Delilah had said to Samson, "See, you have mocked me and told me lies. Now please tell me by what means you could be bound." 11 He answered her, "If they bind me with new ropes that had never been used, then I will be free and will be like another man." 12 So Delilah took new ropes, and bound him with them, and said to him, "The Philistines are upon you, Samson" (and the men went forth into the chamber), and he broke them from his arms, as a truce. 13 Then Delilah said to Samson, "Until now you have deceived me and told me lies; tell me how you can be bound." And he answered her, "If you apply to my head ten locks with the three of the owl." 14 And she fastened them to him with a pin, and said, "The Philistines are upon you, Samson." And he awoke from sleep and went away with the pin of the cloth and the owl. 15 Then she said to him, "How can you say, 'I love you,' if your heart is not with me? You have mocked me these three times and have not told me where your great strength lies." 16 Be- cause she continually importuned him with her words and annoyed him, his soul grieved to the point of death. 17 Therefore he told her all of his heart and said, "There was never any fear upon my head, for I am a Nazarite to God from my mother's womb; therefore, if I am shaken, my strength will depart from me, and I will be weak, and will be like all other men." 18 When Delilah heard that he had revealed his whole heart to her, she sent for the princ- es of the Philistines, saying, "Come again, for he has revealed his whole heart to me." Then the princes of the Philistines came to her and took the money into their hands. 19 And she put him to sleep on her knees, and called

a man, and cut off the ten locks of his head; then she began to torment him, and his strength failed him. 20 Then she said, "The Philistines be upon you, Samson." He awoke from sleep and thought, "Now I will go out like the oth- er times and shake myself," but he did not know that the Lord had departed from him. 21 Therefore the Philistines took him, and gouged out his eyes, and brought him to Az- zah, and bound him with chains; and he rant- ed in the prison-house. 22 And his head began to grow again after it had been taken off. 23 Then the princes of the Philistines gathered them together to offer a great sacrifice to Dagon their god and to make feast, for they said, "Our god has delivered Samson our en- emy into our hands." 24 And when the people saw it, they prayed to their god, for they said, "Our god has delivered into our hands our en- emy and destroyer of our land, who has killed many of us." 25 And when their hearts were glad, they said, "Call Samson, that he may be a pastime." So they called Samson from the house of captivity; he was a laughingstock to them, and they put him among the pillars. 26 Then Samson said to the servant who led him by the hand, "Lead me, that I may touch the pillars on which the house rests and may lean against them." 27 (Now the house was full of men and women, and all the princes of the Philistines were there; moreover on the roof were about three thousand men and women watching while Samson played.) 28 Then Samson called to the LORD and said, "O LORD God, please think of me: O God, I be- seech Thee, strengthen me at this time, that I may be at once defeated by the Philistines by my two eyes." 29 Samson clung to the two middle pillars on which the house stood and which supported it: one with his right hand, the other with his left. 30 Then Samson said, "Let me lose my life with the Philistines"; and he bent it with all his strength, and the house fell on the princes and all the people therein; so the dead he killed at his death were more than those he had killed in life. 31 Then his brothers and all the house of his father came down, and took him, and brought him, and buried him between Zorah and Eshtaol, in the sepulcher of Manoa his father.

CHAPTER 17

1 There was a man of Mount Ephraim, whose name was Micha, 2 and he said to his mother, "The eleven hundredths of surety that were taken from you, for which you cursed and spat, well in my hearing, behold, the surety is with me, I have taken it." Then his moth- er said, "Blessed be my son from the Lord." 3 When he had returned to his mother the eleven hundredths of the surety, his mother said, " I had dedicated the surety to the Lord of my hand for my son, to make him a molten and bronze image. Therefore I will return him to you." 4 When he had returned the money to his mother, his mother took two hundred shekels of silk and gave them to the founder, who made a cast and gilded image of him, which was in Micha's house. 5 This man Mi- cha had a house of gods, made an Ephod and Teraphim, and anointed one of his sons, who was his priest. 6 In those days there was no king in Israel, but everyone did what was good in his own eyes. 7 There was also a young man of Bethlehem Iudah, of the family of Iudah, who was a Leuite and resided there. 8 And that man departed from the city, that is, from Bethlehem Iudah, to dwell where he could find a place; and as he walked, he came to Mount Ephraim to the house of Micha. 9 Micha said to him, "Where are you from?" The Leuite answered him, "I come from Beth-Lem Iudah and am going to dwell where I can find a place." 10

Then Micha said to him, "Dwell with me and be to me a father and a priest, and I will give you ten shekels of silver a year, a suit of clothes, your food and your wine." So the Leuita entered. 11 The Leuita was con- tent to dwell with the man, and the young man was to him as one of his sons. 12 Micha anointed the Leuita, and the young man was his priest and remained in Micha's house. 13 Then Micha said, "Now I know that the Lord will be good to me, since I have a Leuita as my priest."

CHAPTER 18

1 In those days there was no king in Israel, and at the same time the tribe of Dan was seeking for them an inheritance in which to dwell, for up to that time all the inheritance among the tribes of Israel had not been allot- ted to them. 2 Therefore the sons of Dan sent from their family five men from their coasts, men skilled in warfare, from Zorah and Esh- taol, to examine the land and search it, and they said to them, "Go and search the land." Then they came to Mount Ephraim, to the house of Micha, and lodged there. 3 When they were in Micha's house, they met the vis- it of the young man Leuita, and having ad- dressed him, they said to him, "Who brought you all the way here? What are you doing in this place? And what do you want to do here?" 4 And he answered them, "So and so treats Micha with me; he has hired me, and I am his priest." 5 Then they said to him, "Ask God for counsel now, to know whether the way we are going will be prosperous." 6 The priest said to them, "Go in peace, for the LORD guides your way." 7 Then the five men departed and came to Laish, and they saw the people dwell- ing there without worry, according to the way of the Zidonians, quiet and safe, for no one made trouble in the land, nor took posses- sion of any dominion; moreover they were far from the Zidonians and had no business with other men. 8 So they returned to their broth- ers in Zorah and Eshtaol; and their brothers said to them, "What have you done?" 9 They answered, "Arise, to go against them, for we have seen the land and it is certainly very good, and you stand still? Do not be reluc- tant to go and enter to possess the land." 10 (If you go, you will come into a careless peo- ple, and the county is great) because God has given it into your hands. It is a place that has nothing to envy to those of the world." 11 Then they departed from the family of the Danites, from Zorah and Eshtaol, six hundred men with instruments of war. 12 And they set out and encamped at Kiriath-iearim, in Iu- dah; therefore, to this day, they have called that place Mahaneh-Dan, which is behind Kiriath-iearim. 13 Then they went toward Mount Ephraim and came to the house of Micha. 14 Then the five men who went to spy out the county of Laish answered their brothers, "Do you not know that in these houses is an Ephod, a Terafim, a bronze image and a molten image? Now therefore consider what you are to do." 15 Then they turned and came to the house of young Leuita, that is, to the house of Micha, and greeted him peacefully. 16 The six hundred men, who belonged to the sons of Dan, stood at the entrance of the gate with their weapons of war. 17 Then the five men who had gone to spy out the land went in and took the bronze image, the Ephod, the Teraphim and the molten image; and the priest stood at the entrance of the gate with the six hundred men equipped with weap- ons of war, 18 the other went into the house of Michaele and took the bronze image, the Ephod, the Teraphim and the molten image. Then the priest said to them, "What are you doing?" 19 They answered him, "Be still, put your hand over your

mouth and come with us to be our father and priest. Whether it is bet- ter for you to be a priest for one man's house or for you to be a priest for one tribe and one family in Israel? 20 The priest's heart rejoiced, and he took the Ephod, the Terafim and the bronze image and went among the people. 21 Then they turned and departed and set before them the children, the cattle and the sub- stance. 22 When they were far from Micha's house, the men who were in the houses near Micha's house gathered together and pursued the sons of Dan, 23 and cried out to the sons of Dan, who, turning to their faces, said to Micha, "What troubles you, that you should make a scandal?" 24 He answered, "You have taken away my gods, whom I had created, and the priest, and go your own way; and what more have I? How say ye therefore to me, what troubles you?" 25 The sons of Dan said to him, "Let not your voice be heard among them, lest your companions come upon you, and you lose your life with the dead of your house." 26 So the sons of Dan went their way; and when Micha saw that they were too strong for him, he turned away and returned to his house. 27 And they took the things that Micha had made, and the priest that he had, and came to Laish, to a quiet people without distrust, and smote them with the blade of the sword, and burned the city with fire: 28 and there was no one to help them, because Laish was far from Zidon and they had no business with other men; besides, it was in the valley that is near Beth-Rehob. Then they built the city and lived there, 29 And they called the city Dan, after the name of Dan their father, which was given to Israel; but at first the name of the city was Laish. 30 Then the sons of Dan had the bronze image built for them; and Ionathan the son of Gershom the son of Manasseh and his sons were priests of the tribe of the Danites until the day of the captivity of the land. 31 So they set over them the bronze image that Micha had made, for as long as the house of God was in Shiloh.

CHAPTER 19

1 In those days, when there was no king in Israel, a man named Leuita dwelt on the slope of Mount Ephraim and took a concubine to wife from Beth-lehem Iudah, 2 His concubine whored herself there and went away from him to her fathers' house in Beth-lehem Iu- dah, and there she stayed for four months. 3 Her husband arose and pursued her to speak to her amicably and to lead her again; he also had his servant and a pair of donkeys with him; and she led him to her fathers' house, and when the young woman's father saw him, he rejoiced at his coming. 4 And her father's father, the young woman's father, lodged him and stayed with him three days; and they ate and drank and stayed there. 5 When the fourth day came, they rose early in the morning and he prepared to leave; then the young woman's father said to his son in lawe, "Comfort your heart with a morsel of bread and then go your way." 6 So they sat down and ate and drank to- gether. And the young woman's father said to the man, "Please be content, and rest all night, and may your heart be glad." 7 When the man got up to leave, his father was very worried; so he went back and stood there. 8 He got up almost on the fifth day to leave, and the young woman's father said, "Comfort your heart, please." 9 Then when the man rose up to de- part with his concubine and his servant, the young woman's father said to him, "Behold, the day draws near at noon: I pray thee, rest all night; behold, the sun goes to rest; lodge here, that thy heart may be calm, and in the morning resume thy way

early and go to thy tent." 10 But the man would not stop; he got up, set out, and came toward Iebus (which is Jerusalem), with his two laden donkeys and his concubine. 11 When they were near Iebus, the day was now past, and the servant said to his master, "Come, I pray you, and let him go to this city of the Iebusites and stay there all night." 12 And his master answered him, "We will not go into the city of the foreigners who are not the children of Israel, but we will go to Gibeah." 13 He said to his servant, "Come, let us go toward one of these places, to stay in Gibeah or Ramah." 14 So they went on their way, and the sun went down toward them to Gibeah, which is in Benjamin. 15 Then they turned toward them to enter and lodge in Gibeah; and when they arrived, they sat down in a street of the city, for there was no one to let them in his house to lodge. 16 And behold, at that time there came an old man from his work in the fields; that man was of Mount Ephraim, but he dwelt in Gibeah; the men of the place were the sons of Jemini. 17 When he had lifted up his eyes, he saw a man walking through the streets of the city; then the old man said, "Where are you going, and where did you come from?" 18 He answered him, "We have come from Beth-lehem Iudah, on the side of Mout Ephraim; from there I came; I went to Beth-lehem Iudah and now I go to the house of the LORD; and no one receives me at home, 19 though we have straw and hair for our donkeys, and also bread and wine for me and for your servant and for the boy who is with your servant; we lack nothing." 20 The old man said, "Peace be with you; whatever you lack, you will find with me; only do not stay on the road all night." 21 So he led him into his house and gave the donkeys fodder; they washed their feet and ate and drank. 22 While they were rejoicing, behold, the men of the city, wicked men, besieged the house all around, struck the door, and spoke to the old man, the master of the house, saying, "Bring out the man who has entered your house, for we know him." 23 And the master of the house went out to them and said, "No, my brothers, do not do so evil, I pray you; since this man has entered my house, do not do this wick- edness. 24 Here is my daughter, a virgin, and her concubine; I will bring them out now, and humble them, and do with them what seems good to you; but to this man do not do this villainy." 25 But the men paid no heed to him; so the man took his concubine and led her out to them; and they knew her, and mistreated her all night until morning; and when day began to break, they let her go. 26 So the woman came at daybreak and lay down at the door of her master's house, where her lord was, until it was daylight. 27 And in the morning the lord arose, and opened the doors of the house, and went out to go his way, and behold, the woman, his concubine, was dead on the threshold of the house, and her hands were lying on the threshold. 28 He said to her, "Get up and go," but she did not answer. So he made her get up on the plank, and the man got up and went to his place. 29 And when he was come to his house, he took a knife, and put his hand upon his concubine, and cut her in two parts with her bones, and sent her through all the quarters of Israel. 30 And all who saw him said, "Such a thing has never been seen since the time when the children of Israel came from the land of Egypt until now; examine the matter, consult, and pronounce judgment."

CHAPTER 20

1 Then all the children of Israel went out, and the congregation gathered as one, from Dan to Beer-sheba,

with the land of Gilead, to the LORD at Mizpeh. 2 The leaders of all the peo- ple and all the tribes of Israel gathered into the congregation of God's people four hundred thousand foot soldiers carrying swords. 3 (The sons of Benjamin heard that the sons of Isra- el had gone to Mizpeh) and the sons of Israel said, "How was this wickedness committed? 4 Leuita himself, the husband of the slain wom- an, answered, "I have come to Gibeah, which is in Benjamin, with my concubine to lodge." 5 but the men of Gibeah rose up against me and besieged my house around night, think- ing that they had killed me and forced my concubine to die. 6 Then I took my concubine, and cut her in pieces, and sent her into all the land of Israel's inheritance, because they committed abomination and villany in Israel. 7 Behold, you are all children of Israel; give your counsel and be counseled." 8 Then all the people stood up in unison, saying, "None of you shall go to his tent, and none shall enter his house." 9 But now this is what we will do to Gibeah: we will cast lots against it, 10 and we will take ten men from among the hun- dred of all the tribes of Israel, a hundred from among the thousand, and a thousand from among the ten thousand, to bring life to the people, that they may do (when they come to Gibeah of Benjamin) as all the villages did in Israel." 11 So all the men of Israel gathered to- gether against the city, united as one man. 12 The tribes of Israel sent men throughout the tribe of Benjamin, saying, "What wickedness is this that has been committed among you? 13 Now therefore deliver up those wicked men who are in Gibeah, that we may put them to death and turn away wickedness from Israel; but the children of Benjamin would not obey the command of their brethren, the children of Israel. 14 But you, the children of Ben- jamin, gathered yourselves together from the cities toward Gibeah to go out to fight against the children of Israel. 15 At that time the children of Benjamin numbered from the cities six hundred and twenty thousand men armed with swords, besides the inhabitants of Gibeah, who numbered seven hundred chosen men. 16 Of all this people there were seven hundred chosen men, left-handed; all of whom could throw stones at a distance and would not yield. 17 Also the men of Israel, be- sides Benjamin, were appointed four hundred thousand men who pulled with the sword, all men of war. 18 The sons of Israel rose up, went to the house of God, and asked God, "Which of you will go first to fight against the sons of Benjamin?" The LORD answered, "Iudah will be first." 19 Then the sons of Israel rose up early and encamped against Gibeah. 20 The men of Israel went out to fight against Ben- jamin and lined up to fight against Gibeah. 21 The sons of Benjamin went out from Gibeah, and that day they reduced two and twenty thousand men from among the Israelites to the ground. 22 And the people, the men of Israel tore their hearts out and put their bat- tles back in line in the place where they had put them in line on the first day. 23 (For the sons of Israel had gone weeping before the LORD until dawn and had asked the LORD, "Shall I go again to fight against the sons of Benjamin, my brothers?" and the LORD had said, "Go against them.") 24 Then the children of Israel came again against the children of Benjamin on the second day. 25 Also on the second day Benjamin went out to meet them from Gibeah and reduced the children of Is- rael eight thousand more men to the ground, all able to handle the sword. 26 Then all the children of Israel went, and all the people also came to the house of God, and wept and sat down before the LORD, and fasted that day until evening, offering him sacrifices and peace offerings. 27 And the children of Israel asked the LORD (for in those days there was the Ark of the

city of God), 28 and at that time stood before it Finehas the son of Eleazar, the son of Aaron) saying, "Shall I still go and fight against the sons of Benjamin, my brothers, or shall I quit?" And the LORD said, "Go, for for the rest I will deliver them into your hands." 29 Israel put men to wait around Gibeah. 30 And on the third day the children of Israel went out against the children of Benjamin, and arrayed themselves against Gibeah, as they had done at other times. 31 Then the sons of Benjamin, going out against the people, were drawn out of the city, and began to smite the people and to kill, as at the other times, along the ways of the camp (one of which goes toward the house of God and the other toward Gibeah), against about thirty men of Israel. 32 (The sons of Benjamin said, "They fell before them, as at the beginning.") But the sons of Israel said, "Let them flee and turn them away from the city to their streets.") 33 And all the men of Israel rose up from their place, and went in line to Baal-Tamar; and the men that were in the way of the Israelites went out from their place, and from the fields of Gibe- ah, 34 And there came against Gibeah ten thousand chosen men from all Israel, and the battle was hard, because they did not see that the LORD was near them. 35 And the LORD smote Benjamin before Israel, and the chil- dren of Israel destroyed the Benjamites that same day: five thousand twenty thousand and one hundred men, all able to wield the sword. 36 And the sons of Benjamin saw that they were smitten, for the men of Israel gave way to the Benjamites, because they trusted in the men who had stood by and left near Gibeah. 37 Those who were lying in wait hurried and went toward Gibeah, and the ambush came upon them and struck the whole city with the edge of the sword. 38 The men of Israel had also agreed on a certain time with the ambushers, so that they brought up a great flame and smoke from the city. 39 When the men of Israel withdrew into the battle, Benja- min began to strike and kill about thirty of the men of Israel, because they said, "Surely they were struck before them, as in the first bat- tle." 40 But when the flame began to rise from the city like a pillar of smoke, the Benjamites looked back, and behold, the flame of the city began to rise upward. 41 Then the men of Is- rael turned back, and the men of Benjamin were astonished, for they saw that death was near them 42 Therefore they fled before the men of Israel by the wilderness road, but the battle overtook them; even those who came out of the cities killed them in their midst. 43 So they surrounded the Benjamites, pursued them at ease, and routed them, particularly against Gibeah in the east. 44 Thousands of men were slain by Benjamin, all men of war. 45 Then they turned and fled into the wilder- ness toward the hill of Rimmon; and the Is- raelites discerned them on the way with five thousand men, and pursued them as far as Gidom, and killed two thousand, 46 so that all who were slain that day by Benjamin were five thousand and twenty thousand men who had swords, all men of war: 47 but six hun- dred men turned and fled into the wilderness to the camp of Rimmon, and remained in the camp of Rimmon for four months. 48 Then the men of Israel went back to the children of Benjamin and smote them with the edge of the sword, from the men of the city to the beasts and everything that came within their reach; and they also burned all the cities that they could reach.

CHAPTER 21

1 Moreover, the men of Israel swore to Miz- peh, "None of them shall give his daughter in marriage to the Benjamites."

2 The people went to the house of God and stood there until dawn before God, lifting up their empties and weeping with great lamentation, 3 and said, "O LORD, God of Israel, why has this happened in Israel, that today a tribe of Isra- el has come short?" 4 The next day the people arose and built an altar and offered sacrific- es and peace offerings. 5 Then the children of Israel said, "Who among all the tribes of Israel is he who has not come with the congregation to the LORD?" For they had made a great prayer about the one who had not come to the Lord to Mizpeh, saying, "Let him die." 6 The children of Israel were in sorrow for Ben- jamin, their brother, and said, "Today there is a tribe cut off from Israel. 7 How shall we do for their survivors, since we have sworn to the LORD that we will not give them our daughters as wives? 8 They also said, "Is there anyone from the tribes of Israel who has not come to Mizpeh from the LORD?" And be- hold, no one from Jabesh Gilead came to the host and to the congregation. 9 For when the people were visited, behold, not one of the inhabitants of Jabesh Gilead was present. 10 Therefore the congregation sent there two thousand of the most valiant men and com- manded them, "Go and strike the inhabitants of Jabesh Gilead, women and children, with the edge of the sword. 11 This is what you will do: you will destroy all the males and all the women who have been connected with men." 12 And they found among the inhabitants of Jabesh Gilead four hundred maidens, virgins, who had not known any man who had lain with a male; and they brought them to the host at Shiloh, which is in the land of Canaan. 13 Then all the congregation sent to speak to the sons of Benjamin who were in the region of Rimmon, and called them in peace: 14 Then Benjamin came again, and gave them the wives which they had stolen from the wom- en of Jabesh Gilead, but they had not enough for them. 15 The people were sorry for Benja- min, because the LORD had opened a breach in the tribes of Israel. 16 Therefore the elders of the community said, "How shall we be able to do for the rest, for the women of Benja- min have been destroyed." 17 And they said, "There must be an inheritance for the rem- nant of Benjamin, so that one tribe may not be destroyed by Israel." 18 Yet we cannot grant them the wives of our daughters, for the sons of Israel had sworn, "Cursed is he who gives a wise to Benjamin." 19 Therefore they said, "Behold, there is a festival of the LORD every year in Shiloh, in a place that is north of Beth-el, east of the road from Beth-el to Shechem and south of Lebona." 20 Therefore they com- manded the sons of Benjamin, "Go and stand by in the vineyards. 21 And when you see that the daughters of Shiloh go out to dance, come out of the vineyards, and take each one of the daughters of Shiloh to wife, and go into the land of Benjamin. 22 And when their fathers or their brothers come and complain, we will say to them, "Have mercy on them for our sake, because we did not grant each one his wife during the war, and because you have not pleased them so far, you have sinned." 23 And the sons of Benjamin did so, and took the wives of those who danced according to their name; and they took them and departed, and returned to their inheritance, and repaired the cities, and dwelt therein. 24 At that time the children of Israel departed from there, every one for his tribe and for his family, and they went from there every one to his inher- itance. 25 In those days there was no king in Israel, but everyone did what was good in his own eyes.

RUTH

CHAPTER 1

1 At the time when the Judges reigned, there was scarcity in the land, and a man from Beth-Lem Iudah went to live in the coun- ty of Moab, he and his wife and two sons. 2 The man's name was Elimelech, and his wife's name was Naomi, and the names of his two sons were Mahlon and Chilion, ephrathites of Beth-Lem Iudah; and when they came to the land of Moab, they stayed there. 3 Then Elimelech, Naomi's husband, died, and she remained with her two sons, 4 Who took wives from the Moabites: the first was named Orpah, and the other Ruth, and they dwelt there about ten years. 5 Mahlon and Chilion also both died when they were two years old; so the woman was left without her two sons and without her husband. 6 Then she got up with her daughters-in-law and returned from the county of Moab, for she had heard in the county of Moab that the LORD had visited his people and given them bread. 7 Therefore she departed from the place where she was, and her two daughters-in-law with her, and they set out to return to the land of Judah. 8 Naomi said to her two daughters, "Go, return each of you to your mother's house; the LORD will do you harm, as you have done to the dead and to me. 9 And the LORD will make you to rest, the one and the other in their own husband's house." And when she kissed them, they raised their voices and wept. 10 They said to her, "Surely we will return with you to your people." 11 But Naomi said, "Turn away, my daughters; for what reason do you wish to come with me? Are there other sons in my woman, that they may be your husbands? 12 Turn away, my daughters; go your way, for I am too old to have a husband. If I said, "I have hope, and if I had a husband tonight, yes, if I had children." 13 would you stay for them until adulthood? Would you put off for them the taking of husbands? No, my daugh- ters, for it grieves me greatly, for your sakes, that the hand of the Lord has come upon me." 14 Then they lifted up their heads and wept again; Orpas kissed her mother in mourning, but Ruth still remained with her. 15 Naomi said, "Behold, your sister-in-law has returned to her people and her gods; go back after your sister in peace." 16 Ruth answered, "Do not turn away from me and leave me, for where you go, I will go, and where you dwell, I will dwell; your people will be my people and your God my God. 17 Where you die, I will also die, and there I will be buried. the LORD do so to me also, and more, if it is not death that turns you and me away." 18 Seeing that the woman was firmly resolved to go with her, he let her speak. 19 So they both went until they came to Bethlehem; and when they had come to Bethlehem, the whole town rejoiced over them and said, "Is not this Naomi?" 20 She answered them, "Do not call me Naomi, but call me Mara, for the Almighty has given me much bitterness. 21 I went out full and the LORD made me return empty; why do you call me Naomi, seeing that the LORD humbled me and the Almighty brought me to abandon- ment?" 22 And Naomi returned, and with her Ruth the Moabite, her daughter-in-law, when she went out of the county of Moab; and they came to Bethlehem at the beginning of the summer season.

CHAPTER 2

1 Naomi's husband had a relative, very pow- erful, from the family of Elimelech, whose name was Boaz. 2 Then Ruth, a Moabite, said to Naomi, "Please let me go into the fields and gather ears of corn behind him, who seems to me to be

a happy man." And she said to her, "Go, my daughter." 3 And she went, and came and gleaned in the field after the reap- ers, and stood before the part of Boaz's field, which was of Elimelech's family. 4 And be- hold, Boaz came from Bethlehem and said to the reapers, "The Lord be with you"; and they answered him, "The Lord bless you." 5 Then Boaz said to his servant who was appointed outside the reapers, "Whose mother is this?" 6 The servant who was in charge of the reapers answered, "She is the Moabite mother who came with Naomi from the county of Moab." 7 She said to Boaz, "Please let me go and gath- er the reapers among the sheep"; and so she came, and has continued to do so from that time in the morning until this day, although she has stayed a little while in the house. 8 Then Boaz said to Ruth, "Are you my daugh- ter? Do not go and gather in any other field, and do not depart from here, but stay here with my masters. 9 Look at the field they are gathering and go after the maidens. Have I not instructed the servants not to touch you? Also, if you are thirsty, go to the vessels and drink of what the servants have drawn." 10 Then she fell on her face, prostrated herself on the ground, and said to him, "How did I find courage in your eyes, that you should know me, since I am a stranger?" 11 Boaz an- swered and said to her, "I have been told and shown all that you did to your mother in lawe, after the death of your husband, and how you left your father and your mother and the land where you were born, and came to a people you did not know before. 12 The LORD will re- ward your work, and a full reward will be giv- en you by the LORD, the God of Israel, under whose wings you have come to trust." 13 Then she said, "Let me stand well before you, my lord, for you have comforted me and spoken comfortingly to your sons, even though I am not like one of your sons." 14 And Boaz said to her, "At this hour come here and eat bread and put your morsels in wine." And she sat down beside the reapers, and he reached to his withered horn; and she ate, and was sat- isfied, and remained. 15 And when she rose up to glean, Boaz commanded his servants, "Let her gather among the sheaves, and do not rebuke her. 16 Let some of the sheaves also fall for her and let them rest, that she may gather them, and do not rebuke her." 17 So she gleaned in the field until dawn, and estimated what she had gathered, which was about an ephah of grain. 18 Then she gathered it and went into the city, and her mother-in- law saw what she had gathered: She also took the way and gave her what she had gathered, when she had enough. 19 Then her mother- in- law said to her, "Where did you gather to- day and where did you work? Blessed be He who knows you." And she showed her mother in lawe with whom she had worked and said, "The man with whom I worked today is called Boaz." 20 Naomi said to her daughter-in-law, "Blessed be the Lord, for he does not cease to do good to the living and the dead." Then Nao- mi said to her, "That man is close to us and has the same affinity as us. 21 Ruth, the Moabi- tess, answered, "He has said with certainty to me also, 'You shall be with my servants until they put an end to all my sufferings.'" 22 Nao- mi answered Ruth, her daughter, in a plain- tive tone, "It is better, my daughter, that you go away with his women, lest they meet you in another camp." 23 So Ruth kept her beside the women of Boaz, to gather to the end of the fields of grain and wheat, and she settled with her mother in peace.

CHAPTER 3

1 Then Naomi her mother said to her, "My daughter, shall I not give you rest, that you may prosper? 2 Is not Boaz, our kinsman, the one with whose maidens you were? Behold, he watches until late at night in the plain. 3 Wash therefore thy garments, and anoint thy- self, and clothe thyself, and go down into the plain; let that man take no notice of thee, until he hath left eating and drinking. 4 When he has fallen asleep, mark the place where he has laid him down, go and visit the place of his feet, lie down, and he will tell you what you are to do." 5 She answered her, "Everything you have asked of me, I will do." 6 So she went down to the bed and did all that her mother had commanded her. 7 When Boaz had eaten and drunk, and his heart was gladdened, he went and lay down at the bottom of the heap of horns; she came softly, and drew near his feet, and lay down. 8 At midnight the man was in a panic and took possession of the house; and behold, a woman lay at his feet. 9 Then he said, "Who are you?" And she an- swered, "I am Ruth, your kinswoman; stretch therefore the wing of your robe upon your hand, for you are the kinswoman." 10 Then he said, "Blessed of the Lord, my daughter, you have shown more goodness in the last peri- od than in the beginning, in that you did not follow other men, whether they were poor or rich." 11 Now, my daughter, fear not: I will do for you whatever you desire, for all the city of my people know that you are a righteous woman. 12 It is true that I am your kinsman, but there is a nearer kinsman than I. 13 She shall tarry till night, and when it is morning, if he shall make thee a kinsman's duet, well, let him make a kinsman's duet; but if he shall not make a kinsman's duet, then I will make a kinsman's duet, as it pleaseth the LORD; sleep until morning." 14 And she lay down at his feet until morning, and rose before one could no- tice the other, for he said, "Let no one know that a woman has entered the plain." 15 He also said to her, "Bring the sheet that you have on you and keep it." And when she had held it, he measured six measures of barbiturate, and put it on her, and she went into the city. 16 And when she came to her mother-in-law, she said to her, "Who are you, my daughter?" And she told her all that the man had done to her, 17 and said, "He gave me these six measures of barbiturate, because he said, 'You shall not be emptied of your mother, in marriage.'" 18 Then she said, "My daughter, sit still until you know how it will end; for that man will not rest until he finishes the matter this very day."

CHAPTER 4

1 Then Boaz went to the door and sat there; and behold, the relative of whom Boaz had spoken passed by; and he said, "Oh, little one, come, sit here." And he turned and sat down. 2 Then he took ten men of the elders of the city and said, "Sit here." And they sat down. 3 Then he said to your kinsman, "Naomi, who has returned from the county of Moab, will sell a piece of land that was our brother Elimelech's." 4 And I thought to convince you, saying, "Buy it before the attendants and el- ders of my people. If you want to redeem him, redeem him; but if you don't want to redeem him, tell me, because I know that there is no one other than you to redeem him, and I will follow you." He answered, "I will redeem him." 5 Then Boaz said, "The day you buy the field from Naomi's hand, you must also buy it from Ruth the Moabitess, the dead man's wife, to revive the dead man's name on his inheritance." 6 The kinsman answered, "I can- not redeem her, lest I destroy my inheritance; redeem from you my right, for I cannot re-

deem her." 7 This was the way before in Israel regarding ransom and exchange, in order to stabilize all things: a man divested himself of his share and gave it to his neighbor, and this was a sure testimony in Israel. 8 Therefore the kinsman said to Boaz, "Buy it for yourself"; and he took off his robe. 9 Boaz said to the el- ders and to all the people, "You are witnesses today that I bought from the hand of Naomi all that was Elimelech's and all that was Chil- io's and Mahlon's." 10 And again, Ruth, the Moabitess, the wife of Mahlon, I have bought her as my wife, that the name of the dead man might be brought up on his inheritance, and that the name of the dead man might not be blotted out among his brethren and from the door of his place; you are witnesses today. 11 All the people who stood at the gate and the elders said, "We are witnesses: may the Lord make the wife who will enter your house like Rahel and like Leah, who twice built the house of Israel; and may you act worthily in Ephra- tah and be famous in Bethlehem, 12 and that your house may be like the house of Pharez (whom Thamar bore in Iudah) with the off- spring that the LORD will give you from this young woman." 13 So Boaz took Ruth, who became his wife; and when he came in to her, the LORD wanted her to conceive and bear a son. 14 The women said to Naomi, "Blessed be the LORD, who has not left you today with- out a kinsman, and his name will remain in Israel. 15 This will restore your life and con- solidate your old age, for your daughter, who loves you, has given birth by him, and it is better for you than ten sons." 16 Naomi took the child and put it in her womb and became its mother. 17 The women near her gave him a name, saying, "There is a son born of Naomi and named Obed; the same was the father of Ishai, the father of Dauid." 18 These are the generations of Pharez: Pharez begat Hezron, 19 Hezron begat Ram, and Ram begat Ammi- nadab, 20 Amminadab begat Nahshon, and Nahshon begat Salma, 21 Salma begat Boaz, and Boaz begat Obed, 22 Obed begat Ishai and Ishai begat Dauid.

I SAMUEL

CHAPTER 1

1 There was a man of one of the two Ra- mathaim Zophim, of Mount Ephraim, whose name was Elkanah, son of Jeroham, son of Elihu, son of Tohu, son of Zuph, an Ephrates: 2 He had two wives: one was named Han- nah and the other Peninnah; Peninnah had children, but Hannah had none. 3 This man went out every year from his city to worship and sacrifice to the LORD of hosts at Shiloh, where there were the two sons of Eli, Hophni and Phinehas, priests of the LORD. 4 One day when Elkanah sacrificed, he gave Peninnah his wife and all his sons and daughters por- tions, 5 but to Hannah he gave a worthy por- tion, because he loved Hannah and the LORD had made her barren. 6 Her aduersary vexed her greatly, for he vituperated her, because the LORD had made her barren. 7 (And so she did from year to year) and whenever she went to the house of the LORD, she tormented her in such a way that she wept and did not eat. 8 Then Elkanah her husband said to her, "Han- nah, why do you weep, why do you not eat, why is your heart troubled, am I not better for you than ten sons? 9 So Hannah got up after they had eaten and drunk at Sciloh (and Eli, the priest, was sitting on a stool by one of the pillars of the LORD's temple). 10 And she was troubled in her soul, and she prayed to the LORD, and wept bitterly: 11 Then she made a vow and said, "O LORD of hosts, if thou wilt look on the troubles of thy handmaid and remember me, and wilt not forget thy handmaid, but wilt give thy handmaid a male child, then I will give him to the LORD all the days of his life, and there shall be no razor on his head." 12 As she continued to pray be- fore the LORD, Eli marked her mouth. 13 For Hannah spoke in her heart; her lips only mur- mured, but her voice was not heard; therefore Eli thought she was drunk. 14 Eli said to her, "How long will you remain drunk? Turn your drunkenness away from you." 15 Then Han- nah answered, "No, my lord, but I am a wom- an troubled in spirit: I have drunk neither wine nor liquor, but I have vented my soul before the LORD. 16 Regard not thy servant as an evil woman: for out of the abundance of my lamentation and my sorrow have I spoken hitherto." 17 Then Eli answered and said, "Go in peace, and the God of Israel will grant your request that you have addressed to him." 18 Again she said, "May your hand find favor in your eyes"; so the woman resumed her way, ate, and no longer seemed sad. 19 Then they rose early, worshiped before the LORD, and returned to their home in Ramah. Now El- kanah knew Hannah, his wife, and the Lord remembered her. 20 For Hannah conceived and bore a son and named him Samuel, be- cause, she said, "I asked the Lord for him." 21 Then the man Elkanah and all his house went and offered to the LORD the one-year sacri- fice and his vow: 22 But Hannah did not go, for she said to her husband, "I will stay until the child is weaned, then I will bring him that he may stand before the LORD and there re- main forever." 23 Elkanah her husband said to her, "Do what seems best to you; stay until you have weaned him; the LORD fulfills his word." So the woman stayed at home and let her son be killed until she had weaned him. 24 And when she had weaned him, she took him with her with three heifers, an ephah of fine flour, and a bottle of wine, and brought him to the house of the LORD in Shiloh, and the child was young. 25 They killed a bull and brought the child to Eli. 26 She said, "Oh, my Lord, how your soul lives, my Lord, I am the woman who stood here with you praying to the Lord. 27 I prayed for this child, and the LORD granted me in the desire I had asked of him. 28 Therefore I entrusted him to the Lord; as long as he lives, he shall be entrusted to the Lord; and there he worshipped the Lord.

CHAPTER 2

1 Hannah prayed and said, "My heart rejoic- es in the LORD, my heart is exalted in the LORD; my mouth is enlarged over my ene- mies, because I rejoice in your salvation. 2 There is none holy like the LORD; yea, there is none besides you, and there is no god like our God. 3 Speak no more presumptuously, let no arrogance come out of your mouth, for the LORD is a God of knowledge, and by him the undertakings are established. 4 The bow and the mighty have been broken, and the weak have girded themselves with strength. 5 Those who were full have been hired for bread, and the hungry are no longer hired, so that the barren has borne little, and she who had many children is weak. 6 The LORD kills and gives birth to others, brings down to the grave and raises up. 7 The LORD makes poor and makes rich, he lowers and exalts. 8 He raises the poor from the dust and lifts up the beggars from the dunghill, to set them among the princes and make them inherit the seat of glory; for the pillars of the earth are the LORD, and he has set the world upon them. 9 He will guard the feet of his saints, and the wicked will be silent in darkness, for no one will be strong in his strength. 10 The aduersaries of

the LORD shall be destroyed, and from the height of heaven he shall thun- der upon them; and the LORD shall judge the end of the world, and give power to his king, and exalt the horn of his ally." 11 Elkanah went to Ramah, to his house, and his son did his service to the LORD before Eli the priest. 12 The sons of Eli were wicked men and did not know the LORD. 13 For the obligation of the priests to the people was this: when anyone offered a sacrifice, the priest came, while the meat was boiling, with a staff of meat with three teeth in his hand, 14 and thrust it into the kettle, cauldron, pot or vessel; whatever the meat brought, the priest would take for himself; so did all the Israelites who came to Sciloh. 15 Before the fat was burned, the priest said to the man who was offering, "Give me meat to roast for the priest, for he does not want to have fat meat from you, but an- ger." 16 And if anyone said to him, "Let them bury the body according to the rules, take as much as your heart desires," he replied, "No, but you will give it to me at once; and if you will not, I will take it by force." 17 Therefore the sin of the young men was very great be- fore the Lord, because the men abhorred the Lord's offering. 18 Samuel, who was still a young child, came before the LORD girded with a linen ephod. 19 His mother made him a small cloak and brought it to him from year to year when he came with her husband to offer the ordinary sacrifice. 20 Eli blessed Elkanah and his wife and said, "The LORD will give you an offspring from this woman, because of the request she has made to the LORD"; and they set out for their place. 21 And the LORD visited Hannah, and she conceived and bore three sons and two daughters. And her son Samuel had grown up before the LORD. 22 Eli was very old and heard all that his sons did to all Israel and how they reclined with the women who gathered at the base of the tent of meeting. 23 He said to them, "Why do you do these things? Because of all these people I hear very good things about you. 24 Do no more of them, my sons, for it is not good news that I have heard, namely, that you cause the Lord's people to sin. 25 If one sins against another, the judge will judge him; but if one sins against the Lord, who will defend him? And they did not obey their father's will, because the Lord would kill them. 26 (Now the son Samuel had grown rich and fat and was in good standing with both the Lord and men). 27 A man of God came to Eli and said to him, "Thus says the LORD: Did I not ap- pear clearly to your father's house, when they were in Egypt, in the house of the Pharaohs? 28 I chose him out of all the tribes of Israel to be my priest, to offer on my altar, to burn incense, and to wear an Ephod before me, and I gave to your father's house all the offenses done by the fire of the children of Israel. 29 For what reason have you kicked my sacrifice and my offering, which I have ordained in my Tabernacle, and you honor your own children because of me, so that your own may feed on the first fruits of all the offerings of Israel, my people? 30 Therefore the LORD, the God of Israel, says, "I said that your house and your father's house would walk before me forever; but now the LORD says, "It shall not be so, for those who honor me I will honor, and those who despise me will be despised." 31 Behold, the day is coming when I will cut off your ar- mor and the armor of your father's house, so that there will be no old man in your house. 32 You shall see your enemy in the dwelling of the LORD in all things with which God will bless Israel, and there shall not be an old man in your house anymore. 33 I will not destroy any of your own from my altar, to make your eyes faint and to sadden your heart; and all the multitude of your house shall die when they are men. 34 And this shall be for thee a sign that shall come upon thy two sons Hoph- ni and Phinehas:

in one day they shall both die. 35 And I will raise me up a faithful priest, who shall do according to my heart and ac- cording to my mind; I will build him a sure house, and he shall walk forever before my Anointed One. 36 And all who are left in your house shall come and prostrate themselves to him for a piece of silk and a morsel of bread, and they shall say, "Please appoint me to one of the priestly offices, that I may eat a morsel of bread."

CHAPTER 3

1 Now the son Samuel exercised the min- istry of the Lord before Eli; and the word of the Lord was precious in those days, for there was no manifest vision. 2 At that time, as Eli lay in his place, his eyes began to dim, so that he could not see. 3 While the light of God was fading, Samuel slept in the temple of the LORD, where the ark of God was. 4 Then the LORD called Samuel, and he said, "Here I am." 5 He ran to Eli and said, "Here am I, for you have called me." But he answered, "I have not called you; go away and sleep." And he went and slept. 6 The LORD called Samu- el again. Samuel got up and went to Eli and said to him, "I am here, because you have called me." And he answered, "I have not called you, my son; go away and sleep." 7 So Samuel did, before he knew the LORD and before the word of the LORD was addressed to him. 8 The Lord called Samuel again for the thirteenth time; he got up, went to Eli and said, "I am here, because you have called me." Then Eli realized that the Lord had called the child. 9 Therefore Eli said to Samuel, "Go and sleep; and if he calls you, say, 'Speak, Lord, for your servant hears.'" Samuel went and slept in his place. 10 Then the LORD came and stood and called as at other times, "Samuel, Samuel." Samuel answered, "Speak, for your servant listens." 11 Then the LORD said to Samuel, "Behold, I will do in Israel a thing of which everyone who hears will have his ears pricked. 12 In that day I will raise up against Eli all the things I have spoken concerning his house; when I begin, I will also make an end. 13 I have told him that I will judge his house forever, for iniquity he knows, because his sons have gone forth to a slaughter, and he has not stopped them. 14 Therefore I have sworn to the house of Eli that the wickedness of the house of Elis shall no more be cleansed with sacrifices and sacrifices forever." 15 Then Samuel slept until morning and opened the doors of the house of the LORD, and Samuel feared to reveal the vision to Eli. 16 Then Eli called Samuel and said to him, "Samuel, my son." And he answered, "Here I am." 17 Then he said, "What is it that the Lord has told you? Please don't hide it from me. God does that with you, and even more, if you hide from me anything of all that he has told you." 18 Sam- uel told him everything and hid nothing from him. Then he said, "He is the Lord; let him do what seems good to him." 19 Samuel grew; the LORD was with him, and he did not let any of his words fall to the ground. 20 All Israel, from Dan to Beer-sheba, knew that Samuel was the prophet of the LORD. 21 The LORD appeared again in Shiloh, for the LORD came to Samuel in Shiloh with his word.

CHAPTER 4

1 Samuel spoke to all Israel; and Israel went out against the Philistines to fight, and en- camped near Eben-Ezer, while the Philis- tines encamped at Aphek. 2 And the Philis- tines arrayed themselves against Israel; and when they had begun

the battle, Israel was cut down by the Philistines, who killed about four thousand men of the army in the field. 3 When the people came into campea, the el- ders of Israel said, "Why has the LORD struck Israel today before you Philistines? Bring the ark of the crowning of the LORD from Shiloh toward you, that when it comes among you, it may save you from the hands of our ene- mies." 4 Then the people went to Sciloh and brought from there the ark of the command- er of the Lord of hosts, who dwells among the Cherubim; and there were the two sons of Eli, Hophni and Phinehas, with the ark of the commander of God. 5 When the ark of the Commander of the LORD came into the army, all Israel let out a loud cry, so that the earth rang again. 6 When the Philistines heard the sound of the cry, they said, "What does this mighty cry mean in the army of the He- brews?" and they realized that the ark of the LORD had entered the army. 7 The Philistines were astonished and said, "God has entered the army"; therefore they said, "Obey, for it has never been so." 8 "Who will deliver you from the hands of these mighty gods? These are the gods who smote the Egyptians with all the plagues in the wilderness." 9 Be strong and play with men, O Philistines, lest you be servants of the Hebrews, as they have served you; therefore be valiant and fight." 10 And the Philistines fought, and Israel was smit- ten, and every man fled to his tent; and there was a great slaughter, for the foot soldiers of Israel fell by thousands. 11 The ark of God was taken, and the two sons of Eli, Hophni and Phinehas, died. 12 Out of the army went out a man from Benjamin, who came to Siloh the same day with tattered garments and dirt on his head. 13 When he came, Eli sat down on a seat by the road and walked about, be- cause his heart feared for the ark of God, and when that man came into the city to tell about it, the whole city shouted. 14 And when Eli heard the noise of crying, he said, "What does this noise of tumult mean?" And the man entered quickly and told Eli. 15 (Eli was now fifty-five and eighty years old, and his eyes were clouded so that he could not see). 16 The man said to Eli, "I am from the army, and I have fled from the army today"; and he said, "What has happened, my son? 17 Then the messenger answered, "Israel has fled be- fore the Philistines, and there has also been a great slaughter among the people; also your two sons, Hophni and Phinehas, are dead, and the ark of God has been taken." 18 After mentioning the ark of God, Eli fell from his place backward at the side of the gate, broke his neck and died, for he was old and sick, and had judged Israel for forty years. 19 And his daughter, Phinehas' wife, was with child in her womb; and when she heard the news that the ark of God had been taken, and that her father and her husband were dead, she bowed down and dragged herself, for pains came upon her. 20 Toward the time of her death, the women around her said to her, "Do not fear, for you have borne a son"; but she did not answer and did not care. 21 And she gave her son the name of Ichabod, saying, "The glory is gone from Israel, because the Ark of God has been taken, and because of her father and her husband." 22 She said again, "The glory has disappeared from Israel, because the Ark of God has been taken."

CHAPTER 5

1 Then the Philistines took the ark of God and carried it from Eben-Ezer to Ashdod, 2 Then the Philistines took the ark of God, carried it into the house of Dagon and placed it be- side Dagon. 3 When the Philistines rose the next day in the morning, behold, Dagon had fallen with his face to the ground before the ark of the LORD; they took Dagon back and put him in his place. 4 The next day they rose early in the morning, and behold, Dagon had fallen with his face to the ground before the ark of the LORD; Dagon's head and the two palms of his hands were cut off at the thresh- old; only the stele of Dagon remained to him. 5 Therefore the priests of Dagon and all who enter the house of Dagon shall no longer tread on the threshold of Dagon in Ashdod. 6 But the hand of the LORD came upon the men of Ashdod, and destroyed them, and smote them with buffers, both Ashdod and its shores. 7 When the men of Ashdod saw this, they said, "Do not let the ark of the God of Is- rael remain with you, for his hand has come against you and against Dagon our god." 8 So they sent for all the princes of the Philistines and said, "What shall we do with the Ark of the God of Israel? And they answered, "Let the ark of the God of Israel be carried as far as Gath"; and they carried the ark of the God of Israel. 9 And when they had carried it, the hand of the LORD came upon the city with very great destruction, and smote the men of the city, small and great, and they had buffers in their secret parts. 10 Therefore they sent the ark of God to Ekron; and when the ark of God came to Ekron, the Ekronites cried out, saying, "They have brought the ark of the God of Israel to Ekron to kill us and our people." 11 Therefore they sent to assemble all the princ- es of the Philistines and said, "Send away the ark of the God of Israel and let it return to its place, that it may not kill vs. and our people; for there was destruction and death through- out the whole city, and the hand of God was very sore there." 12 The men who did not dye were struck with the emeralds, and the cry of the city went up to Heauen.

CHAPTER 6

1 So the ark of the LORD remained in the county of the Philistines for ten months. 2 The Philistines called the priests and sooth- sayers and said, "What shall we do with the ark of the Lord? Tell us by what means we can send it home." 3 They answered, "If you send away the ark of the God of Israel, do not send it away empty, but give it a sin offering; then you will be healed and you will know why its hand does not depart from you." 4 Then they said, "What shall be the sin offering that we shall give him?" They answered, "Five emer- alds of gold and five mesas of gold, accord- ing to the number of the princes of the Phi- listines, because one plague has struck all of you and your princes. 5 Therefore you shall make the similitudes of your emeralds and the similitudes of your mines that destroy the land; so you shall give glory to the God of Israel, that he may turn away his hand from you and from your gods and from your land. 6 Why do you therefore harden your hearts, as the Egyptians and Pharaoh hardened them, who, when he was working wonderfully in their midst, would not let them go and de- part? 7 Now, therefore, prepare a new chariot and take two dairy cows, on which there is no yoke; tie the cows to the chariot and take the calves home. 8 Then take the ark of the LORD, place it in the chariot, put the golden jewels that you will give her as a sin offering in a chest by her side, and send her away, that she may depart. 9 And mind you, if he goes on his way as far as Bet-shemesh, it is he who has made this great mistake; but if he does not, we shall know that it was not his hand that struck him, but that it was a fluke." 10 The men did so, for they took two horses that were going to milk, tied them to the wagon, and locked the calves in the house. 11 Then they placed the ark of the

LORD on the chariot and the chest with the mise of gold and with the similitudes of their emeralds. 12 And the horses went by the straight way as far as Beth-shemesh, following the same road and going down, turning neither to the right nor to the left; and the princes of the Philistines also went after them, as far as the borders of Beth-shemesh. 13 Now those of Beth-Scemesh were reaping their grain harvest in the valley; they looked up and saw the Ark, and when they saw it they rejoiced. 14 The chariot came to the field of Ioshua, a Beth-Shemite, and stopped there. There was also a large stone there; they claimed the wood of the chariot and offered the cattle as a burnt offering to the LORD. 15 And the Leuites took down the ark of the LORD and the chest that went with it, where were the jewels of gold, and put them on the great stone; and the men of Bet-Shemesh offered a burnt offering and sacri-ficed on that same day to the LORD. 16 When the five princes of the Philistines saw it, they returned to Ekron the same day. 17 These are the golden emeralds that the Philistines of-fered to the LORD as a sin offering: one for Ashdod, one for Gaza, one for Askelon, one for Gath, and one for Ekron, 18 and one set of gold, according to the number of all the cities of the Philistines, belonging to the five princes, both of walled cities and of unwalled cities, until the great stone of Abel, on which they placed the ark of the LORD; which stone remains to this day in the camp of Ioshua the Beth-Shemite. 19 And he smote the men of Beth-Shemesh because they had looked into the ark of the LORD; and he slew among the people fifty thousand men and three hundred and ten men, and the people complained that the LORD had slain the people with so great a slaughter. 20 Therefore the men of Bet-shemesh said, "Who is able to stand before this LORD holy God? And to whom will he go from there?" 21 They sent messengers to the inhabitants of Kiriath-iearim, saying, "The Philistines have brought the ark of the LORD again; go down and take it with you."

CHAPTER 7

1 Then the men of Kiriath-iearim came and took the ark of the LORD and brought it to the house of Abinadab on the hill; and they sanctified Eleazar his son to keep the ark of the LORD. 2 (For the time that the ark re-mained in Kiriath-iearim was long, for it lasted twenty years) and all the house of Is-rael complained of the LORD. 3 Then Sam-uel spoke to all the house of Israel, saying, "If you draw back to the LORD with all your heart, turn away from among you the foreign gods and Ashtaroth, turn your hearts to the LORD and serve him alone, and he will de-liver you from the hand of the Philistines." 4 Then the children of Israel eliminated Baalim and Ashtaroth and went into the service of the LORD. 5 Samuel said, "Gather all Israel in Mizpeh, and I will pray for you with the LORD." 6 They gathered themselves togeth-er at Mizpeh, took water and poured it out before the LORD, fasted the same day and said, "We have sinned against the LORD." Samuel judged the children of Israel at Miz-peh. 7 When the Philistines learned that the children of Israel had gathered at Mizpeh, the princes of the Philistines ventured against Is-rael; and when the children of Israel learned of it, they fled from the Philistines. 8 And the children of Israel said to Samuel, "Do not cease to call upon the LORD our God for vic-tory, that he may save you from the hand of the Philistines." 9 Then Samuel took a suck-ling lamb and offered it all together as a burnt offering to the LORD; Samuel cried out to the LORD for Israel, and the LORD heard him. 10 While Samuel was offering the burnt offer-ing, the Philistines came and fought against Israel; but on that day the LORD thundered with great roar upon the Philistines and scat-tered them; so they were slain before Israel. 11 The men of Israel set out from Mizpeh, pur-sued the Philistines and defeated them as far as Bet-Car. 12 And Samuel took a stone, and planted it between Mizpeh and Shen, and called it Eben-Ezer, saying, "So far the LORD has stood." 13 So the Philistines were put to flight and came no more to the coasts of Isra-el; and the hand of the LORD was against the Philistines all the time of Samuel. 14 And the cities which the Philistines had taken from Israel were returned to Israel, from Ekron even to Gath, and Israel delivered their coasts out of the hands of the Philistines; and there was peace between Israel and the Amorites. 15 Samuel ruled Israel all the days of his life, 16 And he went from year to year to Bet-el, to Gilgal, and to Mizpeh, and judged Israel in all those places. 17 Then he returned to Ramah, for there was his house, and there he judged Israel; there he also built an altar to the LORD.

CHAPTER 8

1 When Samuel had grown old, he made of his sons Iudges in Israel. 2 The firstborn was named Ioel and the secondborn Abiah, and then he was appointed judge in Beer-sheba. 3 His sons did not follow his ways, but went astray to seek gain, and became rich and vi-olated judgment. 4 Therefore all the elders of Israel gathered them together and came to Samuel in Ramah, 5 and said to him, "Be-hold, you are old, and your sons do not walk in your ways; make now a king who will judge like all the nations." 6 But it displeased Sam-uel, when they said, "Make a king to judge"; and Samuel prayed to the LORD. 7 And the LORD said to Samuel, "Listen to the voice of the people in all that they say to you, for they have not cast you out, but they have cast me out, so that I no longer rule over them. 8 As they have always done since I brought them out of Egypt until this day (forsaking me and serving other gods), so do they also with you. 9 Now, therefore, listen to their message; but witness to them how the king will rule over them. 10 Samuel reported all the words of the LORD to the people who asked him for a king. 11 He said, "This will be the behavior of the king who will reign over you: he will take your sons and appoint them his horsemen, and some will run before his horsemen. 12 He will also appoint them captains of thousands and captains of fifties, in charge of tending his land, reaping his fields, making the instru-ments of war and the things that his chariots need. 13 He will also take your daughters and make them apothecaries, cooks and bakers. 14 He will take your fields and your vineyards and your best olive trees and give them to his servants. 15 He will take the tithe of your seed and your vineyards and give it to his Eunuchs and his servants. 16 And he shall take thy male servants, and thy maid servants, and the chief of thy young men, and thy asses, and shall put them into his service. 17 He shall take the tenth part of your livestock, and you shall be his servants. 18 In that day you shall cry out because of your king, whom you have chosen, and the LORD will not hear you in that day." 19 But the people would not listen to Samuel's speech and said, "No, but there will be a king in the future." 20 We also shall be like all the other nations, and our king shall judge vs, go out before vs, and fight our battles." 21 Samu-el, therefore, having heard all the words of the people, reproved them in the ear of the LORD. 22 The LORD said to Samuel, "Listen

to their voice and make them a king." Samuel said to the men of Israel, "Go all of you to your city."

CHAPTER 9

1 Now there was a man of Benjamin, mighty, named Kish, the son of Abiel, the son of Ze- ror, the son of Bechorath, the son of Aphia, the son of a man of Jemini. 2 He had a son named Saul, a man of good age and great valor, so that among the sons of Israel there was no one better than he; from the shoulders upward he was stronger than all the people. 3 The donkeys of Kish, Saul's father, had been lost; therefore Kish said to Saul, his son, "Now take one of the servants with you, get up, go and see the donkeys." 4 So he passed through Mount Ephraim and went through the land of Shalisha, but he did not find them. Then he passed through the land of Shalim and did not find them; he also passed through the land of Jemini, but he did not find them. 5 When they came to the land of Zuph, Saul said to his servant who was with him, "Come and let us go back, lest my father leave the care of the donkeys and take care of them." 6 He said to him, "Behold, there is a man of God in this city, and he is a man of honor; all that he says is true; let him go there now, if he can show you the way to go." 7 Then Saul said to his servant, "All right, let us go; but what shall we bring to that man? For the bread is exhausted in our vessels, and there is no gift to bring to the man of God; what have we? 8 The servant answered Saul again and said, "Behold, I have found around me the fourth part of a shekel of silk; this I will give to the man of God, that he may show him our way." 9 (Earlier, in Israel, when a man went to seek an answer from God, he spoke thus, "Come, let us go to the seer," for he who is called a prophet today was formerly called a seer.) 10 Then Saul said to his servant, "Well, come, let us go"; so they set out for the city where the man of God was. 11 As they were going toward the city, they found mayors coming out to draw water and said to them, "Is there a seer here?" 12 They answered them and said, "Yes, he is here before you; make haste, for today he has come into the city, for today there is an offering of the people there. 13 When you enter the city, you will find him immediately, but he has already come to the place of eating; for the people do not eat until he comes, for he blesses the sacrifice, and then those who are invited to the banquet eat. 14 Then they set out toward the city, and when they had come to the center of the city, Samuel went out against them to go to the place where he was. 15 But the LORD had spoken to Samuel in secret (a day before Saul's arrival), saying, 16 "At this hour I will send you a man from the land of Benjamin; you shall anoint him to be the keeper of my people of Israel, that he may save my people from the hands of the Philistines, for I have looked upon my peo- ple, and their cry has come to me." 17 When therefore Samuel said to Saul, the LORD an- swered him, "See, this is the man of whom I have spoken to you: he shall rule my people." 18 Then Saul went to Samuel in the midst of the gate and said to him, "Tell me, I pray you, where is the house of the seers." 19 Samuel answered Saul and said, "I am the seer; go before me to the place where it is, for today you will eat with me; and tomorrow I will let you go and tell you all that is in your heart. 20 As for your donkeys that were lost three days ago, do not care for them, for they have been found. and on whom does all the desire of Is- rael fall? Does it not fall on you and on all your father's house? 21 But Saul answered, "Am I not the son of Jemini, of the smallest tribe of Israel, and my family is the smallest of all the families of the tribe of Benjamin? Why then do you speak to me thus? 22 And Samuel took Saul and his servant, and brought them into the chamber, and seated them in the high- est place among those who had been invited, which were about thirty persons. 23 Samuel said to the cook, "Bring here the portion that I gave you and about which I said, 'Keep it with you.'" 24 The cook took the shoulder and what was on it and placed it before Saul. Samuel said, "Behold, what is left, put it before you and eat it, for so far it has been kept for you, saying that I have called the people." On that day Saul ate with Samuel. 25 And when they had come down from the place of refuge in the city, he lounged with Saul on the roof of the house. 26 And when they rose early, to- ward the spring of the day, Samuel called Saul on the top of the house, saying, "Get up, that I may send you away." Saul got up and they went out, he and Samuel. 27 When they had gone down to the bottom of the city, Samuel said to Saul, "Let the servant go before you" (and he went), but now stand still, that I may reveal to you the word of God.

CHAPTER 10

1 Then Samuel took a vial of oil, poured it on his head, kissed him, and said, "Has not the LORD anointed you to be the keeper of his inheritance? 2 And when you depart from me today, you shall find two men by the sep- ulcher of Rachel, in the borders of Benjamin, namely, at Zelzah, and they shall say to you, "The donkeys which you went to see have been found; and behold, your father has left the care of the donkeys and is in sorrow for you, saying, 'What shall I do for my son?' 3 Then you will depart from there and come to the plain of Tabor, and there you will meet three men who go to God at Bethel: one who brings three kids, another who brings three loaves, and another who brings a bottle of wine: 4 They will ask you if all is well and give you the two loaves, which you will receive from their hands. 5 Then thou shalt come to the hill of God, where the garrisons of the Philistines are; and when thou hast come to the city, thou shalt meet a company of proph- ets coming down from the place where they are, with a viol, a kettledrum, a fife, and a harp before them, and they shall prophesy. 6 Then the Spirit of the Lord will come upon you, and you will prophesy with them and be changed into another man. 7 Therefore, when these signs come to you, do as the occasion will serve you, for God is with you. 8 You shall come down before me in Ghilgal, and I will also come down to you to offer burnt of- ferings and peace offerings. Wait for me ten days, until I come to you and explain to you what you are to do." 9 When he had turned his back to leave Samuel, God gave him another heart; and all these signs took place on that same day. 10 And when they came to the hill, behold, the host of prophets reached him, and the Spirit of God descended upon him, and he prophesied among them. 11 Therefore all the people who knew him before, seeing that he prophesied among the prophets, said one to another, "What has happened to the son of Kish? Is Saul also among the proph- ets?" 12 And one of them answered, "But who is their father? Therefore it was said, "Is Saul also among the prophets?" 13 After prophe- sying, he came to the place where he was. 14 The vncle of Saul said to him and his servant, "Where have you gone?" And he said, "To see the donkeys; and when we saw that they were nowhere to be found, we came to Samuel." 15 Then Saul said, "Please tell me what Samuel said to you." 16 Then Saul said to his vncle, "He said plainly that the donkeys had been found; but concerning the kingdom

of which Samuel spoke, he told him nothing." 17 Samuel gath- ered the people before the LORD at Mizpeh, 18 and said to the children of Israel, "Thus says the LORD, the God of Israel: I brought Isra- el out of Egypt, and delivered you out of the hands of the Egyptians, and out of the hands of all the kingdoms that tormented you. 19 But today you have cast out your God, who alone delivers you from all your hardships and tribulation; and you have said to him, "No, but appoint a king outside of you." Now therefore stand before the LORD according to your tribes and according to your thousands." 20 When Samuel had gathered all the tribes of Israel together, the tribe of Benjamin was taken. 21 Then he gathered the tribes of Ben- jamin according to their families, and the family of Matri was taken. So Saul the son of Kish was taken, and when they searched for him, they did not find him. 22 Therefore they asked the LORD again if that man should still come here. And the LORD answered, "Behold, he has hidden himself among the cloths." 23 They ran and brought him thence; and when he stood in the midst of the people, he was taller than all the others from the shoulders up. 24 And Samuel said to all the people, "Do you not see him whom the Lord has cho- sen, that there is no one like him among all the people?" And all the people cried out and said, "God says the king." 25 Then Samuel told the people the duet of the kingdom, wrote it in a book, and read it before the LORD, and Samuel sent all the people away, each to his own house. 26 Saul also returned home to Gibeah, and a band of men whose hearts had been touched by God followed him, 27 But the wicked men said, How will he say anything? So they despised him and brought him no gift; but he held his tongue.

CHAPTER 11

1 Then Nahash the Ammonite came up and besieged Iabesh Gilead; and all the men of Iabesh said to Nahash, "Agree with us, and we will be your servants." 2 Nahash the Am- monite answered them, "On this condition I will make a covenant with you, to drive out all your right hands and bring shame upon all Is- rael." 3 The elders of Jabesh answered, "Give yourself some time to send messengers to all the coasts of Israel, and if no one gives you an answer, we will come to you." 4 Then the messengers came to Gibeah from Saul and re- ported this news to the ears of the people; and all the people lifted up their voices and wept. 5 And behold, Saul went out of the camp follow- ing the cattle, and Saul said, "What has this people to weep for?" And they reported to him the news of the men of Jabesh. 6 When Saul heard these tidings, the Spirit of God came upon him, and he was greatly distressed, 7 And he took a yoke of oxen, and cut them in pieces, and sent them through all the coasts of Israel by the hand of messengers, saying, "Whoever does not come after Saul and af- ter Samuel, his oxen shall be cut in pieces." And the fear of the LORD fell upon the peo- ple, and they went out by common consent. 8 And when he had gathered them together at Bezek, the children of Israel were three hundred thousand men, and the men of Iu- dah thirty thousand. 9 Then they said to the messengers who had come, "Tell the men of Jabesh Gilead, 'Until the sun has risen, you will have help.'" The messengers came and reported this to the men of Iabesh, who re- joiced. 10 Therefore the men of Iabesh said, "To morrow we will go out to you and do with you whatever you please." 11 And when it was day, Saul put the people into three bands, and they came upon the army in the early hours of the morning and slew the Ammonites un- til the

end of the day; and those who were left scattered, so that there were not two of them left together. 12 Then the people said to Samuel, "Who is he who said, "Saul will reign outside you?" Bring those men for us to kill them." 13 But Saul answered, "No one will die today, for today the LORD has saved Israel." 14 Then Samuel said to all the people, "Come, let us go to Ghilgal and there give up the king- dom." 15 So all the people went to Ghilgal and made Saul king before the LORD in Ghilgal; and there they offered peace offerings before the LORD; and there Saul and all the men of Israel rejoiced greatly.

CHAPTER 12

1 Then Samuel said to all Israel, "Behold, I have heeded your word in all that you have spoken to me, and have appointed a king for you. 2 Now, therefore, behold, your king walks before you; I am old and frail-headed, and behold, my sons are with you; and I have walked before you from my childhood until this day. 3 Here am I: remember me before the LORD and his Anointed. Whose ox have I taken, whose horse have I taken, to whom have I done evil, whose bribe have I received to blind my eyes, and will I return it to you? 4 Then they said, "You have done no wrong, nor have you done evil, nor have you taken from the hand of any man." 5 And he said to them, "The Lord is witness against you, and his Anointed One is witness today, that you have found nothing in my hand." And they answered, "He is a witness." 6 Then Samuel said to the people, "It is the LORD who creat- ed Moses and Aaron and brought your fathers out of the land of Egypt. 7 Now therefore be still, that I may reason with you before the LORD according to all the righteousness of the LORD, which he has shown to you and to your fathers." 8 After Iaakob had entered Egypt and your fathers cried out to the Lord, the Lord sent Moses and Aaron, who brought your fathers out of Egypt and made them dwell in this place. 9 When they forgot the LORD their God, he put them into the hands of Sisera, the leader of Hazor's army, into the hands of the Philistines and into the hands of the king of Moab, who fought against them. 10 They cried out to the LORD and said, "We have sinned, because we have forsaken the LORD and served Baalim and Ashtaroth. Now therefore deliver us out of the hand of our en- emies, and we will serve you." 11 Therefore the LORD sent Jerubbaal, Bedan, Iftaf and Samuel, and delivered you out of the hands of your enemies on every side, and you dwelt safely. 12 However, when you heard that Na- hash king of the sons of Ammon had come against you, you said to me, "No, but a king shall reign in your place," while the LORD your God was your king. 13 Behold, there- fore, the king whom you have chosen and desired; behold, therefore, the LORD has set a king over you. 14 If you fear the LORD and serve him, if you listen to his word and do not disobey the word of the LORD, both you and the king who reigns over you will follow the LORD your God. 15 But if you do not obey the word of the LORD and disobey his mouth, the hand of the LORD will be on you and on your fathers. 16 Now you also stand to see this great thing that the LORD will do before your eyes. 17 Is it not now that the wheat is hard- er? I will call upon the LORD, and he will send thunder and rain, that you may perceive and see how great is your wickedness, which you have committed before the LORD in asking you a king." 18 Then Samuel called upon the LORD, and the LORD sent thunder and rain on the same day; and all the people feared the LORD and Samuel greatly. 19 All the

people said to Samuel, "Pray for your servants to the LORD your God, that we may not die, because we have sinned in asking for a king, besides all our other sins." 20 Samuel said to the peo- ple, "Do not fear. (You have indeed committed all these wickednesses, but do not forsake the following of the LORD, but serve the LORD with all your heart), 21 and do not turn back; for you should not go after vain things, which cannot profit you, nor disappoint you, for they are but vanity). 22 For the Lord will not forsake his people for the sake of his great names, for it has pleased the Lord to make you his people. 23 Moreover, God forbid that I should sin against the Lord and stop praying for you, but I will show you the good and right way. 24 Therefore fear the LORD and serve him in truth with all your heart and consider the great things he has done for you. 25 But if you misbehave, you will perish, both you and your king.

CHAPTER 13

1 Saul had been king one year and reigned two years over Israel. 2 Saul chose three thou- sand men of Israel; two thousand were with Saul at Michmash and on Mount Beth-el, one thousand were with Ionathan at Gibeah of Benjamin; the rest of the people he sent each to his tent. 3 And Ionathan struck the garrison of the Philistines that was on the hill; and the result was that the ears of the Philistines fell down; and Saul blew the trumpet throughout the land, saying, "O you Jews, take heed." 4 And all Israel heard, "Saul has destroyed a gar- rison of the Philistines"; therefore Israel had an abomination with the Philistines; and the people gathered behind Saul in Ghilgal. 5 The Philistines also gathered themselves together to fight against Israel, with thirty thousand chariots and six thousand horsemen; for the people were as numerous as the sand on the seashore, and they came and encamped at Michmash, east of Bet-Auen. 6 When the men of Israel found that they were in distress (for the people were in distress), the people hid themselves in caves, in dens, in rocks, in tow- ers, and in stonemasons. 7 A part of the Jews departed from Iorden to the land of Gad and Gilead; Saul was still in Ghilgal, and all the people followed him out of fear. 8 He stayed for some days, according to the time appoint- ed by Samuel; but Samuel did not come to Ghilgal, and the people dispersed from him. 9 Saul said, "Bring me a burnt offering and peace offerings"; and he offered a burnt of- fering. 10 As soon as he had finished offering the burnt offering, behold, Samuel came; and Saul went to meet him to greet him. 11 Sam- uel said, "What have you done?" Then Saul said, "Because I have heard that the people have turned away from me, and that you have not come on the appointed days, and that the Philistines have gathered to Michmash." 12 therefore I said, "The Philistines will now descend upon me in Ghilgal, while I have not made supplications to the LORD." Therefore I took courage and offered a stake." 13 Samu- el said to Saul, "You have acted foolishly; you have not kept the command of the LORD your God, who gave you; for the LORD had now established your kingdom over Israel forever. 14 But now your kingdom will not continue; the LORD has sought a man after his own heart, and the LORD has commanded him to be the keeper of his people, because you have not observed what the LORD had command- ed you." 15 And Samuel arose and led him from Gilgal to Gibeah of Benjamin; and Saul named the people that were with him, about six hundred men. 16 And Saul, and Ionathan his son, and the people that were with them, dwelt at Gibeah of

Benjamin, while the Phi- listines encamped at Michmash. 17 Out of the army of the Philistines came three bands to be destroyed: one band went toward the road of Ofra, toward the land of Shual, 18 another band went toward the road of Beth-Horon, and the third band went toward the coast road looking toward the valley of Zeboim, to- ward the wilderness. 19 Then no smith could be found in all the land of Israel, for the Phi- listines said, "Let not the Hebrews make them swords or spears." 20 Therefore all of you Isra-elites went to the Philistines to sharpen each one his part, his mattock, his axe, and his hoe for weeding. 21 Nevertheless they had a file for the stocks, for the slats, for the forks, for the axes, and for sharpening the knobs. 22 When the day of battle came, neither swords nor spears were found in the hands of any of those who were with Saul and Ionathan; but only Saul and Ionathan, his son, were found. 23 The garrison of the Philistines went out at the passage of Michmash.

CHAPTER 14

1 One day Ionathan the son of Saul said to the young man wearing the armor, "Come, let us go to the garrison of the Philistines, which is on the other side," but he did not tell his fa- ther. 2 Saul stopped at the borders of Gibeah, under a pomegranate tree, which was in Mi- gron, and the people with him were about six hundred men. 3 Ahiah, the son of Ahitub, the brother of Ichabod, the son of Phinehas, the son of Eli, was the LORD's priest in Shiloh and wore an Ephod; and the people did not know that Ionathan had gone. 4 Now on the road by which Ionathan sought to go to the garrison of the Philistines, there was a sharp tower on one side and a sharp tower on the other; the name of the one was called Bozez and the name of the other Seneh. 5 The one extended from the north toward Michmash, the other from the south toward Gibeah. 6 Io- natan said to the young man wearing the ar- mor, "Come, let us go toward the prison of these circumcisers; it may be that the LORD wants to work with you, for it is not difficult for the LORD to act with many or with few." 7 He who had taken off his armor said to him, "Do whatever is in your heart; go where you please; behold, I am with you as your heart desires." 8 Then Ionathan said, "Behold, we will go to those men and present ourselves to them. 9 If they say to us, "Wait until we come to you," we will stand firm in our place and not go to them. 10 But if they say, "Come to you," then we will go to them, because the Lord has delivered them into our hands; and this will be a sign to them." 11 So they both came to the garrison of the Philistines; and the Philistines said, "See, the Hebrews have come out of the holes in which they had been hiding." 12 The men of the garrison answered Ionathan and his armor-bearer and said, "Come here, for we will show you something." Then Ionathan said to his armor-bearer, "Come after me, for the LORD has delivered them into the hands of Israel." 13 So Ionathan set out on his hands and feet, and his armorer followed him; some fell before Ionathan, and his armorer killed others after him. 14 The first slaughter that Ionathan and his armorer made was about twenty men, as in the midst of an acre of land that two oxen plow. 15 Fear spread in the army, in the fields, and among all the people; even the garrison and those who went out to spy were frightened; and the earth trembled, because it had been struck with the fear of God. 16 Then Saul's sentinels at Gibeah of Benjamin said, and behold, the crowd was discomfited and stricken as they went. 17 Therefore Saul said to the people who were with him, "Seek

now and see who has gone from here." And when they had done the nomenclature, behold, Ionathan and his ar- mor- bearer were not there. 18 Saul said to Ahiah, "Bring the Ark of God here" (for the Ark of God was at that time with the children of Israel). 19 While Saul was talking with the priest, the noise that was in the army of the Philistines went farther and increased; there- fore Saul said to the priest, "Withdraw your hand." 20 And Saul gathered himself together with all the people that were with him, and they approached the battlefield; and behold, every man had his sword against his com- rade, and there was a great rout. 21 Moreover, the Hebrews who were formerly with the Phi- listines and who had come with them to all parts of the army also turned to be with the Israelites who were with Saul and Ionathan. 22 Also all the men of Israel who had been hiding on Mount Ephraim, when they heard that the Philistines had fled, followed them into battle. 23 On that day the LORD took care of Israel, and the battle continued as far as Bet- Auen. 24 At that time the men of Israel were hungry, for Saul had accused the people of another thing, saying, "Cursed is the man who eats food until night, that I may be at- tacked by my enemies"; so none of the people tasted any food. 25 All the people of the land came to a wood, where iron lay on the ground. 26 And the people entered the wood, and be- hold, the bone fell, and no one brought his hand to his mouth, for the people feared each other. 27 But Ionathan had not heard when his father had accused the people of the other; therefore he put the point of the rod in his hand, dipped it in a rod of iron, and brought his hand to his mouth, and his eyes received sight. 28 Then one of the people answered, "Your father made the people swear an oath, saying, 'Cursed is the man who eats food to- day'"; and the people were fainting. 29 Then Ionathan said, "My father has troubled the land; see now how my eyes have cleared, be- cause I have tasted some of this food: 30 How much more, if the people had eaten today the spit of their enemies that they had found, for had there not been a greater slaughter among the Philistines? 31 That day they struck the Philistines from Michmash to Aialon, and the people were very weary. 32 Then the people went to the spoil, took sheep, oxen, and calves, killed them on the ground, and the people ate them with their blood. 33 Then the men said to Saul, "Behold, the people sin against the LORD because they eat with blood." And he said, "You have committed an offense; today you give me a great stone." 34 Saul said, "Go among the people and tell them to bring me every man, his ox, and every man, his flock, and kill them here, that they may eat and not sin against the Lord by eating with blood." That night the people brought every man his oxen into my hand and killed them there." 35 Then Saul made an altar to the LORD, and that was the first altar he made to the LORD. 36 And Saul said, "Go after the Phi- listines by night and attack them until the brightness of the morning, and let none of them go free." And they said, "Do what you think best." Then the priest said, "Let them drag you here before God." 37 Then Saul asked God, "Shall I go after you Philistines? Will you deliver them into the hands of Israel? But he did not answer him at that time. 38 Saul said, "All you leaders of the people, come here and know and see by whom this sin has been com- mitted today. 39 For as the LORD wills, who killed Israel, even though the sin was com- mitted by Ionathan my son, he shall die." But none of all the people answered him. 40 Then he said to all Israel, "You stand on one side, and Ionathan my son and I will stand on the other side." And the people said to Saul, "Do what seems best to you." 41 Then Saul said to the LORD, the God of Israel, "Draw lots." And Ionathan and Saul were

taken, but the people escaped. 42 Saul said, "Cast lots between me and Ionathan my son." And Ionathan was tak- en. 43 Then Saul said to Ionathan, "Tell me what you have done." Ionathan told him and said, "I tasted a bit of bone with the end of the rod I had in my hand, and, alas, I must die." 44 Saul replied, "God does that and more, if you don't want to die, Ionathan." 45 The people said to Saul, "Should Ionathan, who has so conquered Israel, die? God forbids it. As the LORD wills, not one head of his head shall fall to the ground, for he has worked with God to- day." So the people failed Ionathan so that he would not die. 46 Then Saul came to the Phi- listines, and the Philistines left in their place. 47 Saul held the kingdom of Israel and fought against all his enemies on every side: against Moab, against the sons of Ammon, against Edom, against the kings of Zobah, and against the Philistines; wherever he went, he faced them as wicked men. 48 He also gath- ered an army, defeated Amalek, and delivered Israel out of the hands of those who had pushed him. 49 Saul's sons were Ionathan, Ishui and Malchishua; his two daughters were named Merab, the elder, and Michal, the younger. 50 The name of Saul's wife was Ahi- noam, daughter of Ahimaaz, and the name of his leader was Abner, son of Ner, the son of Saul. 51 Kish was the father of Sauls; Ner, Ab- ner's father, was the son of Abiel. 52 The war against the Philistines was bitter throughout Saul's time; and whomever Saul considered a strong man fit for war, he took him with him.

CHAPTER 15

1 Then Samuel said to Saul, "The LORD has sent me to anoint you king of his people, of Israel; therefore obey the message of the words of the LORD." 2 Thus says the LORD of hosts, "I remember what Amalek did to Isra- el, how they waited for him on the way, when they came from Egypt. 3 Now, therefore, go and smite Amalek and destroy everything that stands against them and have no com- passion on them, but kill men and women, infants and sucklings, oxen and sheep, cam- els and horses." 4 Saul assembled the people and gathered them to Telaim: two hundred thousand foot soldiers and ten thousand men of Iudah. 5 Saul came to a city of Amalek and stood guard over the walls. 6 Saul said to the Kenites, "Go, depart and come down from among the Amalekites, or else I will destroy you with them, because you showed mercy to all the children of Israel when they came from Egypt." 7 Saul defeated the Amalekites from Hauilah as far as Shur, which is oppo- site Egypt, 8 he took Agag, king of the Ama- lekites, and destroyed all the people with the edge of the sword. 9 But Saul and the people spared Agag, the best sheep, the oxen, the fat beasts, the lambs, and all that was good, and they did not destroy them; but they destroyed every vile thing of no value. 10 Then the LORD addressed Samuel, "I regret, 11 I regret that I made Saul king, because he has turned away from me and has not carried out my com- mands." Samuel fell silent and cried out to the Lord all night long. 12 And when Samuel rose early to meet Saul in the morning, one told Samuel, "Saul went up to Carmel; and be- hold, he made himself a place there, whence he returned, departed, and went down to Ghilgal." 13 Then Samuel went to Saul, and Saul said to him, Blessed be you from the Lord, I have done the commandment of the Lord." 14 But Samuel said, "What is the bleat- ing of the sheep in my ears and the mooing of the oxen that I hear? 15 Saul answered, "The Amalekites have brought them, for the people have spared the best of the sheep and oxen to

sacrifice them to the LORD your God, and the rest we have destroyed." 16 Then Samuel said to Saul, "Let me tell you what the LORD told me this night." And he said to him, "Say it." 17 Then Samuel said, "When you were little in your own eyes, were you not appointed chief of the tribes of Israel? For the LORD anointed you king of Israel. 18 The LORD sent you on a journey and said, "Go and destroy those sin- ners, the Amalekites, and fight against them until you have destroyed them." 19 Now why did you not obey the message of the LORD, but turned away from prayer and acted wick- edly in the eyes of the LORD? 20 Saul said to Samuel, "Yes, I obeyed the message of the LORD, I followed the way the LORD showed me, and I led Agag, king of Amalek, and de- stroyed the Amalekites." 21 But the people took of the spit, sheep, oxen, and greater things that should have been destroyed, to offer them to the LORD your God in Ghilgal. 22 Samuel said, "Does the LORD like burnt offerings and sacrifices as much as obedience to his will? Behold, obedience is better than sacrifice, and listening is better than mak- ing branches. 23 For rebellion is like the sin of guile, and transgression is wickedness and idolatry. Because you have rejected the word of the LORD, he has excluded you from being king." 24 Saul said to Samuel, "I have sinned, because I have transgressed the command of the LORD and your words, because I have feared the people and obeyed their orders. 25 Now therefore I beseech thee, blot out my sin and return with me, that I may worship the LORD. 26 But Samuel said to Saul, "I will not go back with you, because you have rejected the word of the LORD, and the LORD has re- jected you, so that you may not be king of Isra- el." 27 As Samuel turned to leave, he grabbed the hood of his cloak and tore it off. 28 Then Samuel said to him, "Today the LORD has taken away the kingdom of Israel from you and given it to your neighbor, who is better than you. 29 For the strength of Israel will not stop and will not repent, for he is not a man to repent." 30 Then he said, "I have sinned; but honor me, I pray you, before the elders of my people and before Israel, and turn with me, that I may worship the LORD your God." 31 And Samuel turned and followed Saul; and Saul worshiped the LORD. 32 Then Samuel said, "Bring Agag, king of the Amalekites," here; and Agag approached him pleasantly, and Agag said, "Truly the bitterness of death is past." 33 Samuel said, "As your sword has made women childless, so your mother will be childless among other women." Samuel cut Agag in pieces before the LORD in Ghilgal. 34 Samuel went away to Ramah, and Saul went to his house in Gibeah of Saul. 35 Samuel did not see Saul again until the day of his death; but Samuel wept for Saul, and the LORD re- pented that he had made Saul king of Israel.

CHAPTER 16

1 Then the LORD said to Samuel, "How long do you want to mourn for Saul, since I have cast him out from reigning over Israel? Fill your horn with oil and come; I will send you to Ishai the Bethlehemite, for I have set my- self a king among his sons." 2 Samuel said, "How can I go? For if Saul hears this, he will kill me." Then the LORD answered, "Take a heifer with you and say, I have come to sacri- fice to the LORD. 3 Call Ishai for the sacrifice, and I will explain to you what you are to do, and you will announce to me the one whom I appoint to you." 4 So Samuel did what the LORD had commanded him and came to Bethlehem; and the elders of the city were astonished at his arrival and said, "Do you want to make peace?" 5 And he

answered, "Yes: I come to make a sacrifice to the Lord; sanctify yourselves and come with me to the sacrifice." And he sanctified Ishai and his sons and called them to the sacrifice. 6 When they had come, he looked at Eliab and said, "Sure- ly the Lord's Anointed One is before him." 7 But the LORD said to Samuel, "Pay no atten- tion to his appearance nor to the height of his stature, for I have rejected him; for God does not see as men see, for men look at the outward appearance, but the LORD looks at the heart." 8 Then Ishai called Abinadab and brought him before Samuel. And he said, "The LORD has not chosen this one either." 9 Then Ishai called Shammah to come. And he said, "The Lord has not yet chosen him." 10 Then Ishai brought his sons before Sam- uel, and Samuel said to Ishai, "The Lord has not chosen any of these." 11 Finally Samuel said to Ishai, "Are there no other sons besides these?" And he answered, "There is still one little one left to keep the sheep." Then Samu- el said to Ishai, "Send for him, for we will not sit down until he comes." 12 And he sent for him, and brought him in; and he was stout, and of good appearance, and of fine presence. And the LORD said, "Arise and examine him, for he is he." 13 Then Samuel took the horn of oyle and anoinished him among his brothers. From that day on the Spirit of the LORD rest- ed on Dauid; then Samuel arose and went to Ramah. 14 But the Spirit of the Lord departed from Saul, and an evil spirit sent by the Lord tormented him. 15 Saul's servants said to him, "Behold, now the spirit of God is tormenting you." 16 Therefore the LORD commands your servants who are before you to seek out a man who is a skillful player of the cymbal, so that when the euphoric spirit of God comes upon you, he may play with his hand and you may be relieved." 17 Saul then said to his servants, "Seek me a man, I pray you, who can play well, and bring him to me." 18 Then one of his ser- vants answered, "Behold, I have seen a son of Ishai, a Bethlehemite, who can play well, and is strong, valiant, a man of war, wise, and of fine presence, and the LORD is with him." 19 Therefore Saul sent messengers to Ishai and said, "Send me Dauid, your son, who is with the sheep." 20 Ishai took a plank laden with skins, a jug of wine and a kid, and sent them by the hand of Dauid, his son, to Saul. 21 Dauid went to Saul and stood before him; he appreciated him greatly and was his ar- mor-bearer. 22 Saul sent word to Ishai, "Let Dauid stay with me, for he stood well before me." 23 So when the euphoric spirit of God came upon Saul, Dauid took a harp and began to play with his hand, and Saul felt refreshed and was relieved, because the euphoric spirit departed from him.

CHAPTER 17

1 Now the Philistines gathered their armies to deploy, and they assembled at Shochoh, which is in Iudah, and encamped between Shochoh and Azekah, in the territory of Dam- mim. 2 And Saul and the men of Israel gath- ered themselves together, and encamped in the valley of Elah, and fought to face the Phi- listines. 3 The Philistines set up on a moun- tain on one side, and Israel on a mountain on the other side; there was a valley between them. 4 Then there came out of the tents of the Philistines a man among them, called Go- liath of Gath; his height was six cubits and the width of one hand, 5 He had a boar's helmet on his head and a brig on him; the weight of his brig was five thousand shekels of boar. 6 He had slats of boar on his legs and a shield of boar on his shoulders. 7 The shaft of his spear was like a beam of wool, and the head of his spear weighed six

hundred shekels of yron; and one who carried a shield went before him. 8 And he stood still and cried out against the army of Israel and said to them, "Why have you come to put up your battle? Am I not a Philistine, and you are servants of Saul? Choose a man for yourselves and bring him down to me. 9 If he is able to fight with me and kill me, we shall be your servants; but if I overcome him and kill him, you shall be our servants and serve against him. 10 The Philis- tine also said, "Today I challenge the army of Israel; give me a man that we may fight to- gether." 11 When Saul and all Israel heard these words of the Philistines, they were dis- couraged and greatly afraid. 12 Now this Dauid was the son of an Ephrathite of Beth- Lem Iudah, named Ishai, who had eight sons; this man had been taken for an old man in Saul's day. 13 The three eldest sons of Ishai went to follow Saul to the battle; the names of his three sons who went to the battle were Eli- ab the eldest, the next Abinadab and the third Shammah. 14 Dauid was the youngest, and the three eldest sons went after Saul. 15 Dauid also went, but he returned to Saul to shepherd his fathers' sheep in Bethlehem. 16 The Philis- tines withdrew in the morning and at dawn and continued for four days. 17 Ishai said to Dauid, his son, "Take now for your brothers an ephah of this plucked horn and these ten cakes, and run to the host to your brothers. 18 Take also these ten fresh cheeses to the cap- tain, and see how your brothers fare, and re- ceive their pledge. 19 (Saul, they and all the men of Israel were in the valley of Elah to fight with the Philistines). 20 Then Dauid arose early in the morning, left the sheep with a watchman, took and went as Ishai had com- manded him, and came near the army; and the army came out in macaw and shouted for battle. 21 For Israel and the Philistines had gone out in arae, army against army. 22 Dauid left the things he was carrying under the hands of the keeper of the cariage, ran into the army, and came and asked his brothers how things were. 23 While he was talking with them, behold, the man who stood be- tween the two armies came up (whose name was Goliath, a Philistine from Gath) from the army of the Philistines and spoke such words, which Dauid heard. 24 And all the men of Is- rael, when they saw that man, fled from him and were afraid. 25 For all the men of Israel said, "Is not this man coming here? He comes here to set Israel free; and to him who kills him, the king will give great riches, and will give him his daughter, and will make free the house of his fathers in Israel." 26 Then Dauid spoke to the men who were with him and said, "What will be done to the one who kills this Philistine and takes away the shame from Israel? For who is this vncircumcised Philistine, that he should put to flight the army of the God whom he loves?" 27 The people an- swered him thus, "Thus shall it be done to the man who kills him." 28 Eliab his elder brother heard when he spoke to the men; and Eliab was very angry with Dauid and said, "Why have you come so far? And with whom did you leave those few sheep in the wilderness? I know your pride and the malice of your heart, for you have come to see the battle." 29 Then Dauid said, "What have I done now? Is there not a cause? 30 And he departed from him to go into the presence of another, and he spoke in the same way, and the people answered him according to the former words. 31 Those who heard the words spoken by Dauid repeat- ed them before Saul, who had him led. 32 Then Dauid said to Saul, "Let no one's heart fail because of him; your servant will go and fight with this Philistine." 33 Saul said to Dauid, "You are not able to go against this Philistine to fight with him, for you are a boy and he has been a man of war from his youth." 34 Dauid answered Saul, "Your servant kept the sheep of his fathers; then a lion and a car- rier came and took a sheep from the flock, 35 and I went after him, and struck him, and tore it out of his mouth; and when he rose up against me, I took him by the beard, and struck him, and cut his throat. 36 So your ser- vant struck both the lion and the beard; there- fore this circumcised Philistine shall be as one of them, seeing he came upon the army of the LORD. 37 Moreover Dauid said, "The LORD who delivered me from the paw of the lion and the paw of the lioness will also deliver me from the hand of this Philistine." Then Saul said to Dauid, "Go, and the Lord be with you." 38 Saul put his robe on Dauid, put a reed helmet on his head, and made him wear a brig. 39 Then Dauid girded his sword on his razor and began to go, for he had never tried it; but Dauid said to Saul, "I cannot go with these, for I am not used to them." 40 Then he took his staff in his hand, chose five polished stones from a brooke, put them in his shep- herd's bag or purse, had his sling in his hand, and went toward the Philistines. 41 The Phi- listines came and approached Dauid, and the man carrying the shield went ahead of him. 42 When the Philistines looked around and saw Dauid, they bewildered him, for he was young and stout and had a handsome face. 43 And the Philistine said to Dauid, "Am I a dog, for you present me with sticks?" And the Phi- listines cursed Dauid for his gods. 44 And the Philistine said to Dauid, "Come to me and I will give your meat to the animals of the field and the beasts of the field." 45 Then Dauid said to Dauid, "You come to me with sword and spear and shield, but I come to you in the name of the LORD of hosts, the God of the armies of Israel, whom you have called upon. 46 Today the LORD will close you in my hand, and I will strike you and take off your head, and I will give today the carcasses of the army of the Philistines to the beasts of heaven and to the beasts of the earth, that all the world may know that Israel has a God, 47 and that all the assembly may know that the LORD does not complain with sword or spear (for the battle is the LORD's) and that he will give you into our hands." 48 When the Philistines rose up to come and dredge against Dauid, Dauid hastened and ran to fight against the Philis- tines. 49 Dauid put his hand in his bag, took out a stone, threw it, and struck the Philistine in the forehead, so that the stone stuck in his forehead and he fell to the ground. 50 Then Dauid faced the Philistine with the sling and with the stone, struck the Philistine and killed him, while Dauid had no sword in his hand. 51 Then Dauid ran, stood before the Philis- tine, took his sword, drew it from its sheath, killed him and cut off his head. When the Phi- listines saw that their champion was dead, they fled. 52 And the men of Israel and Judah arose, and shouted, and pursued the Philis-tines as far as the valley and to the gates of Ekron; and the Philistines fell wounded by the way of Shaaraim, toward Gath and toward Ekron. 53 And the children of Israel, having pursued the Philistines, turned back and pitched their tents. 54 Dauid took the Philis- tines' head, carried it to Jerusalem, and put his armor in his tent. 55 When Saul saw Dauid going against the Philistines, he said to Ab- ner, captain of his army, "Abner, whose son is this young man?" And Abner answered, "I cannot tell how your heart lives, O king." 56 Then the king said, "You ask whose son this young man is." 57 When Dauid had returned from the slaughter of the Philistines, Abner took him and led him before Saul with the head of the Philistines in his hand. 58 Saul said to him, "Whose son are you, young man?" Dauid answered, "I am the son of your ser- vant Ishai the Bethlehemite."

CHAPTER 18

1 After talking with Saul, Ionathan's soul joined Dauid's, and Ionathan received him as if he were his own soul. 2 That day Saul took him with him and did not let him return to his fathers' house. 3 Then Ionathan and Dauid made an agreement, for he loved him as his own soul. 4 Ionathan took off the robe he had on him and gave it to Dauid, with his garments, his sword, his bow and his girdle. 5 Dauid went where Saul sent him and acted wisely, so that Saul set him above the men of war and he was well received in the eyes of all the people and Saul's servants. 6 When hostilities resumed and Dauid returned from the slaughter of the Philistines, the women came out from all the cities of Israel singing and presenting themselves to King Saul with ket- tledrums, with singing instruments and with beak instruments. 7 The women sang with their singing and said, "Saul has killed his thousand and Dauid his ten thousand." 8 Saul was exceedingly vexed, and it displeased him, and he said, "They have ascribed to Dauid ten thousand men, and to me they have ascribed only a thousand; and what more can the kingdom have? 9 Therefore Saul kept an eye on Dauid from that day forward. 10 The next day the exciting spirit of God came upon Saul, and he prophesied in the midst of the house; Dauid played with his hand as at other times, and Saul had a spear in his hand. 11 Saul took the spear and said, "I will strike Dauid to the wall." But Dauid turned away twice from his presence. 12 Saul became afraid of Dauid, be- cause the LORD was with him and had turned away from Saul. 13 Therefore Saul turned him away from him and made him a captain out of a thousand, going to and fro before the people. 14 Dauid behaved wisely in all his actions, because the LORD was with him. 15 Therefore Saul, seeing that he was very wise, was afraid. 16 For all Israel and Judah appre- ciated Dauid, because he went out and came in before them. 17 Then Saul said to Dauid, "Here is my eldest daughter, Merab, whom I will give you to wife; but be a valiant son to me and fight the battles of the LORD, for Saul thought, 'My hand will not be upon him, but the hand of the Philistines will be upon him.' 18 Dauid answered Saul, "What am I, what is my life or my father's family in Israel, if I am to be the king's son-in-law? 19 However, when Merab, Saul's daughter, was given to Dauid as a wife, she was given to Adriel, a Meholathite. 20 Then Michal, Saul's daughter, listened to Dauid; the two women showed it to him, and it pleased him. 21 Therefore Saul said, "I will give her to him to wife, that she may be a snare to him, and that the hand of the Philistines may be against him." Therefore Saul said to Dauid, "Today you shall be my son-in- law in one of the streets." 22 Saul commanded his servants, "Speak to Dauid in secret and tell him, 'Behold, the king has a soft spot for you, and all his servants love you; therefore be the king's son-in-law.'" 23 The servants of Sauls spoke these words in Dauid's ears. And Dauid said, "Does it seem to you a light thing to be the king's son-in-law, seeing that I am a poor man of little reputation? 24 Then Saul's servants brought him news again, saying, "These words said Dauid." 25 And Saul said, "Thus you shall say to Dauid, The king does not want any dowry, but a hundred trinch- es of the Philistines, to be taken away from the king's enemies; for Saul thought to bring Dauid down into the hands of the Philistines." 26 When his servants told Dauid these words, Dauid greatly pleased to be the king's son-in- law; and the days did not pass away. 27 After that Dauid arose with his men and went and killed two hundred men of the Philistines; and Dauid brought their fowls and gave them wholly to the king, that

he might be the king's son-in-law; therefore Saul gave him Michal, his daughter, to wife. 28 Then Saul said and understood that the LORD was with Dauid and that Michal, Saul's daughter, loved him. 29 Saul became more and more opposed to Dauid, and Saul became more and more an enemy of Dauid. 30 When the princes of the Philistines left, Dauid behaved more wisely than all Saul's servants, so that his name was highly esteemed.

CHAPTER 19

1 Then Saul told Ionathan his son and all his servants that they should kill Dauid; but Ion- athan the son of Saul had a great resentment for Dauid. 2 Ionathan said to Dauid, "Saul, my father, is about to kill you; so please take care of yourself until morning, and stay in a secret place and hide yourself. 3 I will go out and stand beside my father in the field where you are, and I will get in touch with my fa- ther about you, and I will see what he says, and I will tell you." 4 Ionathan spoke well of Dauid to Saul his father and said to him, "Let not the king sin against his servant, against Dauid, for he has not sinned against you, but his works have gone very well for you. 5 For he hath put his life in danger, and hath slain the Philistines, and the LORD hath wrought a great salvation for all Israel; thou hast seen it, and hast rejoiced: wherefore then wilt thou sin against innocent blood, and slay Dauid without cause? 6 Then Saul listened to Ion- athan's advice, and Saul swore, "As it pleases the LORD, he will not die." 7 Then Ionathan called Dauid and expounded all these words to him; then Ionathan led Dauid to Saul and they were in his presence as before. 8 Then the war began, and Dauid went out and fought with the Philistines, and killed them with a great slaughter, and they fled from him. 9 The spirit of the LORD came upon Saul, who stood in his house with a spear in his hand, while Dauid played with his hand. 10 Saul intend- ed to strike Dauid at the wall with the spear, but he turned away from Saul's presence and struck the spear against the wall; but Dauid fled and escaped the same night. 11 Saul also sent messengers to Dauid's house, to watch over him and kill him in the morning; and Michal, Dauid's wife, said to him, "If you do not save yourself tonight, you will be killed in the morning." 12 Then Michal brought Dauid down from a window; and he went and fled and was saved. 13 Then Michal took an im- age, placed it in the bed, put a pillow stuffed with goatskins under its head, and covered it with a cloth. 14 When Saul sent messengers to fetch Dauid, she said, "He is sick." 15 Again Saul sent messengers to see Dauid, saying, "Bring him to my bed, that I may kill him." 16 When the messengers had gone in, behold, in the bed was an image with a pillow of goats under its head. 17 And Saul said to Michal, "Why did you mock me and make my enemy flee?" and Michal answered Saul, "He said to me, Let me go, or I will kill you." 18 Then Dauid fled, and went to safety, and came to Samuel in Ramah, and told him all that Saul had done to him; and he and Samuel went to dwell in Naioth. 19 But one informed Saul, saying, "Behold, Dauid is in Naioth, in Ra- mah." 20 Saul sent messengers to get Dauid; and when they saw a company of prophets prophesying and Samuel standing before them, the Spirit of God fell on Saul's mes- sengers and they too prophesied. 21 When Saul heard of this, he sent other messengers and they prophesied in the same way; again Saul sent the third messengers and they too prophesied. 22 Then he went to Ramah and came to a great well that is in Sechu; he asked and said, "Where are Samuel and Dauid?" and one

answered, "Behold, they are in Naioth, in Ramah." 23 He went there, also to Naioth in Ramah, and the Spirit of God also came upon him, and he continued prophesying until he came to Naioth in Ramah. 24 He stripped himself of his garments and prophesied also

before Samuel, falling naked all that day and all that night; therefore it is said, "Is Saul also among the prophets?"

CHAPTER 20

1 Dauid fled from Naioth to Ramah and came and said to Ionathan, "What have I done? What is my iniquity? What sin have I com- mitted before your father, that he should seek my life?" 2 And he answered him, "God forbid, you shall not die; behold, my father will not do anything great or small, but he will tell me; and why should my father hide this thing from me? He will not do it." 3 Then Dauid swore again and said, "Your father knows that I have found favor in your eyes; there- fore he thinks that Ionathan does not know it, lest he should be displeased; but really, as it pleases the Lord and as it pleases your soul, there is but a step between me and death." 4 Then Ionathan said to Dauid, "What your soul requires, I will do with you." 5 Dauid said to Ionathan, "Behold, the first day of the month is tomorrow, and I should sit at table with the king; but let me go, so that I may hide in the fields until the third day. 6 If your father speaks of me, say to him, "Dauid has asked my permission to go to Bethlehem, to his city, because there is a sacrifice for the whole family." 7 If he will say, "All right," your servant will have peace; but if he will be angry, know that wickedness has ended with him. 8 So you shall have mercy on your servant, for you have made your servant an ally of the LORD with you; and if there is iniquity in me, kill me; why should you take me to your father?" 9 Ionathan answered, "God hide it from you, for if I knew that wickedness was concluded by my father to come upon you, would I not tell you?" 10 Then Dauid said to Ionathan, "Who will tell me? How should I know, if your father answers you cruelly?" 11 Then Ionathan said to Dauid, "Come and let them go out into the field"; and the two went out into the field. 12 Then Ionathan said to Dauid, "O LORD, God of Israel, when I have sought to have my fathers die at this time, or within these three days, and if it is good for Dauid, then I will not send word to thee, and I will tell thee, 13 the LORD will do so and much more in re- gard to Ionathan; but if my father intends to do good for Dauid, I will show you and send you away, that you may go in peace; and the LORD be with you as he has been with my fa- ther. 14 Likewise I do not require anything of you as long as I am alive, for I do not expect you to show me the mercy of the Lord, that I may not die. 15 But I do require that you do not cut off your mercy from my house forever; no, not when the LORD has destroyed the en- emies of Dauid, all of them from the earth." 16 So Ionathan made a covenant with the house of Dauid, saying, "The LORD require it at the hand of the enemies of Dauid." 17 Again Ion- athan swore by Dauid, because he loved him (for he loved him as his soul). 18 Then Ion- athan said to him, "The first day of the month is tomorrow, and you will be sought, for your place will be empty. 19 Therefore thou shalt hide thyself for three days, and then thou shalt go down quickly and return to the place where thou hadst hid thyself when the matter was going on, and thou shalt put thyself again by the stone of Ezel. 20 And I will shoot three arrows at its side, as if I had shot at a target. 21 Then I will send a boy to say, "Go, look at the arrows." If I say to the boy, "See, the arrows are on this side, bring them and come, for it is good for you and there is no evil, as the Lord wills." 22 But if I say to the boy, "Behold, the arrows are beyond you, go your way, for the Lord has sent you away." 23 As for the thing of which you and I have spoken, behold, the Lord will be forever between you and me." 24 So Dauid hid himself in the fields; and when the first day of the month came, the king sat down to eat. 25 And the king sat down, as at other times, on his seat, always on his seat by the walls; and Ionathan rose up, and Abner sat by Saul's side, but Dauid's seat was empty. 26 Saul said nothing that day, for he thought, "Something happened to him, even though he was clean, or because he did not purify himself." 27 But the next day, which was the second day of the month, the house of Dauids was emptied again; and Saul said to Ionathan his son, "Why does the son of Ishai not come to eat, either yesterday or today?" 28 Ionathan answered Saul, "Dauid asked me to go to Beth-Lem." 29 He said, "Let me go, I pray you, for our family offers a sacrifice in the city, and my brother has sent for me; therefore, if I have found evil in your eyes, let me go, I pray you, to see my brothers; this is the reason why he does not come to the king's table." 30 Then Saul was angry with Ionathan and said to him, "Son of a wicked and rebellious woman, do I not know that you have chosen the son of Ishai to confuse yourself and to confuse and shame your mother? 31 For as long as the son of Ishai remains on the earth, you will not settle and you will not have your kingdom; therefore now send him for me, for he will surely die." 32 Ionathan answered Saul his fa- ther and said to him, "Why will he die? What has he done?" 33 Saul threw a spear at him to strike him, and Ionathan understood that his father had decided to kill Dauid. 34 So Ion- athan rose from the table in great anger and ate nothing on the second day of the month, because he was sorry for Dauid and because his father had killed him. 35 The next morning Ionathan went out into the field, at that time in the company of Dauid and a boy with him. 36 He said to the boy, "Run, look at the arrows I have shot," and as the boy ran, he shot an ar- row beyond him. 37 When the boy had come to the place where the orange was that Ion- athan had shot, Ionathan shouted after the boy and said, "Is not the orange beyond you?" 38 And Ionathan cried to the boy, "Make haste, make haste, and do not stand still"; and Ion- athan's boy picked up the arrows and came to his master, 39 but the boy knew nothing; only Ionatan and Dauid knew the matter. 40 Then Ionatan gave his mace and arrows to the boy who was with him and said, "Go, take them to the city." 41 And when the boy was gone, Dauid arose from a place that was toward the south, and stood with his face to the ground, and bowed thrice; and they kissed each other, and they both wept until Dauid withdrew. 42 Then Ionathan said to Dauid, "Go in peace; what we have both sworn by the name of the LORD, saying, The LORD be between me and you, and between my seed and your seed, let it stand forever." Then he arose and departed, and Ionathan went into the city.

CHAPTER 21

1 Then Dauid came to Nob, to Ahimelech the priest; Ahimelech was astonished at Dauid's meeting and said to him, "Why are you alone and there is no one with you?" 2 Dauid said to Ahimelech the priest, "The king has given me a definite order and said to me, 'Let no one know where I am sending you and what I have ordered you; and I have

appointed my servants in such and such places. 3 Now if you have anything at hand, give me five loaves or whatever comes to hand." 4 And the priest answered Dauid, and said, "There is no com- mon bread under my hand, but here is bread halved, if the young men have tarried, at least from the women." 5 Then Dauid answered the priest and said to him, "Certainly the women have been separated from the wom- en these two or three days since I went out; and the vessels of the young men were holy, though the way was propitious; how much more shall each one of them be sanctified in the vessel today? 6 Then the priest gave him bread halved, because there was no bread, such as had been taken away before the Lord, to put in it hot bread, the day it was taken away. 7 (On that same day there stood before the LORD one of Saul's servants named Doeg the Edomite, the foremost of Saul's hearers.) 8 Dauid said to Ahimelech, "Is there not here under your hand a spear or a sword? For I brought neither sword nor harness with me, for the king's business required haste." 9 And the priest said, "The sword of Goliath the Phi- listine, whom thou hast slain in the valley of Elah, behold, it is wrapped in a cloth behind Ephod; if thou wilt take it with thee, take it, for there is no other like it here:" Dauid an- swered, "There is none else; give it to me." 10 Dauid arose, fled the same day from Saul's presence, and went to Achish, king of Gath. 11 Achish's servants said to him, "Is not this Dauid the king of the land? Have they not sung for him in honor of the ounces, saying, 'Saul has slain his thousand and Dauid his ten thousand?" 12 Dauid considered these words and became deeply afraid of Achish, king of Gath. 13 He changed his demeanor before them, went mad in their hands, slumped over the walls of the gate, and let his spittle fall on his beard. 14 Then Achish said to his servants, "You see that the man is beside himself, why have you brought him to me? 15 Do I need fools, if you have brought this man to play the fool in my presence? Can he enter my house?

CHAPTER 22

1 So Dauid departed from there and with- drew to the cave of Adullam; and when his brothers and all the house of his fathers heard of him, they came to him. 2 And they gath- ered to him all the men who were in distress, all the men who were in trouble, and all those who had trouble of mind; and he was their prince, and there were with him about four hundred men. 3 So Dauid went to Mizpeh in Moab and said to the king of Moab, "Please let my father and my mother come and stay with you until I know what God will do for me." 4 And he brought them before the king of Moab, and they stayed with him all the time that Dauid was in prison. 5 The prophet Gad said to Dauid, "Do not stay in seclusion, but leave and go to the land of Iudah." So Dauid departed and came to the forest of Hareth. 6 Saul heard that Dauid had been defeated and the men who were with him, and Saul retreated to Gibeah under a tree to Ramah, with his spear in his hand and all his ser- vants standing still around him. 7 Saul said to his servants standing around him, "Now, you sons of Iemini, the son of Ishai will give each of you fields and vineyards; he will make you all captains of thousands and captains of centuriae: 8 that all of you have conspired against me, and is there no one to tell me that my son has made an agreement with the son of Ishai? And is there not one of you who has compassion on me, or who will tell me that my son has driven my servant to lie against me, as it appears today?" 9 Then Doeg the Edomite (who was lurking with Saul's ser- vants) answered, "I saw the son

of Ishai when he came to Nob, from Ahimelech the son of Ahitub." 10 who sought counsel of the LORD for him and gave him lives, and also gave him the sword of Goliath the Philistine." 11 Then the king sent for Ahimelech the priest, the son of Ahitub, and all his father's house, that is, the priests who were at Nob; and they all came to the king. 12 Saul said, "Hear now you, son of Ahitub." And he answered, "Here am I, my lord." 13 Then Saul said to him, "Why did you conspire against me, you and the son of Ishai, giving him life and sword and asking God's counsel for him, that he might rise up against me and set forth as he appears today? 14 Ahimelech answered the king and said, "Who is so faithful among all your servants as Dauid, who is also the king's son in old age, who goes at your command and is honorable in your house? 15 Have I begun today to ask God's counsel for him? Let it never be that the king imputes anything to his servant and to all my father's house, for your servant knew nothing of all this, neither more nor less." 16 Then the king said, "You shall surely die, Ahimelech, you and all your father's house." 17 The king said to the sergeants around him, "Turn around and kill the priests of the LORD, because their hand is also with Dauid and be- cause they knew when he had fled and did not tell me." But the king's servants would not let their hands fall on the priests of the LORD. 18 Then the king said to Doeg, "Turn around and fall on the priests." Doeg, the Edomite, turned and ran to the priests and killed on that same day four dozen people wearing a linen Ephod. 19 Nob, the city of the priests, also struck men and women, children and infants, oxen and horses and sheep with the edge of the sword. 20 But one of the sons of Ahimelech, the son of Ahitub (whose name was Abiathar) man- aged to escape and pursue Dauid. 21 Abia- thar told Dauid that Saul had killed the lords priests. 22 Dauid said to Abiathar, "I learned this on the very day when Doeg, the Edomite, was there, that he would tell Saul. I am the cause of the death of all the people of your fa- ther's house. 23 Stay with me and fear not, for he who seeks my life will also seek yours; for with me you will be safe.

CHAPTER 23

1 Then they said to Dauid, "Behold, the Phi- listines are fighting against Keilah and strik- ing the barrels." 2 Therefore Dauid sought counsel from the LORD, saying, "Can I go and strike these Philistines?" The LORD answered Dauid, "Go and strike the Philistines and save Keilah." 3 Dauid's men said to him, "See, we are in trouble here in Iudah, how much more so if we come to Keilah against the army of you Philistines?" 4 Then Dauid again asked the LORD for counsel. The LORD answered him and said, "Arise, go down to Keilah, for I will deliver the Philistines into your hands." 5 So Dauid and his men went to Keilah, fought with the Philistines, took away their livestock, and defeated them with a great slaughter; so Dauid defeated the inhabitants of Keilah. 6 (When Abiathar the son of Ahimelech fled from Dauid to Keilah, he took an ephod with him). 7 It was reported to Saul that Dauid had come to Keilah, and Saul said, "God has deliv- ered him into my hands, for he is shut up in the house, having come to a city that has gates and bars." 8 Then Saul summoned all the peo- ple for war, to go down to Keilah and besiege Dauid and his men. 9 Dauid, knowing that Saul imagined that he would harm him, said to Abiathar the priest, "Bring the Ephod." 10 Then Dauid said, "O LORD, God of Israel, your servant has heard that Saul is coming to Kei- lah to

destroy the city because of me. 11 Will the lords of Keilah deliver me into his hands, and will Saul come down, as your servant has heard? O LORD, God of Israel, please tell your servant." The LORD answered, "He will come down." 12 Then Dauid said, "Will the lords of Keilah deliver me and the men who are with me into the hand of Saul?" The LORD an- swered, "They will deliver you." 13 Then Dauid and his men, who were about six hundred in number, got up and departed from Kei- la and went wherever they could. Saul was told that Dauid had fled from Keila and had abandoned his journey. 14 Dauid remained in the wilderness, in the estates, and he stayed on a mountain in the wilderness of Zif. Saul sought him every day, but God did not deliver him into his hands. 15 And Dauid heard that Saul had gone out to seek his life; and Dauid was in the wilderness of Zif, in a wood. 16 Then Ionathan the son of Saul arose and went to Dauid in the wood and comforted him in God, 17 and said to him, "Do not fear, for the hand of Saul, my father, will not find you; you will be king of Israel, and I will stand by you; and Saul, my father, knows it also." 18 So the two made a conference before the LORD; Dauid remained in the wood, while Ionathan went to his house. 19 Then the Ziphites went to Saul in Gibeah and said, "Is not Dauid hid- ing in his property, in the wood of the hill of Hachilah, which is on the right hand of Ieshi- mon? 20 Now therefore, O king, come down according to what your heart may desire, and our part shall be to deliver him into the king's hand." 21 Then Saul said, "Be blessed of the LORD, for you have had compassion on me. 22 Go, I pray you, and prepare yourselves even better: know and see the place where he prowls and who has seen him there, for I am told that he is devious and cunning. 23 See therefore and know all the secret places where he is hiding, and come to me again with cer- tainty, and I will go with you; and if he is in the land, I will seek him in all the thousands of Iudah." 24 Then they arose and went to Zif before Saul, while Dauid and his men were in the wilderness of Maon, in the game area to the right of Ieshimon. 25 And Saul and his men also went to see him and told Dauid, who went down to a stronghold and stood in the wilderness of Maon. And when Saul heard, he followed Dauid into the wilderness of Maon. 26 And Saul and his men went to one side of the mountain, and Dauid and his men to the other side of the mountain; and Dauid has- tened away from Saul's presence, for Saul and his men surrounded Dauid and his men to take them. 27 But a messenger came to Saul, saying, "Make haste to come, for the Philis- tines have invaded the land." 28 Therefore Saul returned from the pursuit of Dauid and went against the Philistines. Therefore they called that place Sela-Hammahlekoth.

CHAPTER 24

1 Dauid departed from there and settled in the estates of En-Gedi. 2 When Saul departed from the Philistines, they said to him, "Be- hold, Dauid is in the wilderness of En-Gedi." 3 Then Saul took three thousand men chosen from all Israel and went to see Dauid and his men on the rocks, among the wild goats. 4 And he came to the sheep by the road where there was a quarry, and Saul went in to do his bondage; and Dauid and his men sat in the in- ner parts of the quarry. 5 Dauid's men said to him, "See, the day has come when the LORD has said to you, 'Behold, I will deliver your enemy into your hands, and you will do to him what seems good to you.'" 5 Then Dauid stood up and cut off the lap of Saul's

robe in a pretentious manner. 6 Then Dauid was moved in his heart, because he had cut off the lap of Saul's robe. 7 Then he said to his men, "The LORD forbid me to do that thing to my master, the LORD's anointed, to put my hand on him, for he is the LORD's anointed." 8 So Dauid rebuked his servants with these words and did not allow them to stand up against Saul; so Saul got up from the cave and left. 9 Afterwards Dauid also arose, and went out of the cave, and cried after Saul, saying, "O my lord the king." And when Saul looked behind him, Dauid tilted his face toward the ground and prostrated himself. 10 And Dauid said to Saul, "Why do you heed the words of men who say, 'Behold, Dauid seeks death against you'? 11 Behold, your eyes have seen today that the Lord has delivered you into my hands in the cause, and some have told me to kill you, but I had compassion on you and said, 'I will not lay hands on my master, for he is the Lord's anointed. 12 Behold, my father, behold, I say, the hem of thy garment in my hand; for when I cut off the hem of thy garment, I did not kill thee. Vnderstad and see that in me there is neither wickedness nor evil, nor have I sinned against thee, yet thou huntest after my soul to take it. 13 The LORD be judge between me and thee, the LORD deliver me from thee, and let not my hand be upon thee. 14 As the ancient proverb says, "Wickedness proceeds from the wicked, but let not my hand be upon thee." 15 Whence came forth the king of Israel, by whom are you pursued, a dead dog and a flea? 16 Therefore let the LORD be judge be- tween you and me, see, plead my cause, and deliver me out of your hand." 17 When Dauid had finished saying these words to Saul, Saul said, "Is this your journey, my son Dauid?" And Saul lifted up his voice and wept, 18 and said to Dauid, "You are more righteous than I, for you have made me good and I have made you evil. 19 Today you have proved that you dealt well with me, for when the LORD closed me in your hands, you did not kill me. 20 Who will ever find his enemy and let him go free? Therefore the Lord will give you justice for what you have done to me today. 21 For now I know that you will be king and that the kingdom of Israel will be established in your hands. 22 Swear to me therefore by the LORD that you will not destroy my seed after me, and that you will not abolish my name from the house of my fathers." So Dauid swore to Saul, and Saul went home; but Dauid and his men went to your house.

CHAPTER 25

1 Then Samuel died, all Israel gathered to- gether, mourned for him, and buried him in his house in Ramah. Dauid arose and went down into the wilderness of Paran. 2 In Maon there was a man who had his property in Car- mel; that man was very powerful and owned three thousand head of cattle and a thousand goats; and he was grazing his cattle in Carm- el. 3 The man's name was Nabal, and his wife Abigail; she was a woman of great wisdom and beauty, but the man was a little surly and of very bad condition, and he was of the fam- ily of Caleb. 4 Dauid heard in the wilderness that Nabal had made a slaughter of his sheep. 5 Dauid sent ten young men and said to them, "Go to Carmel and go to Nabal and ask him on my behalf how he is doing. 6 And so say by way of greeting, 'Be you, be your house, be all that you have, be in peace, in wealth and prosperity.' 7 Behold, I have heard that you have shepherds; now your shepherds were with them, and we did them no harm, nor did they do anything wrong all the time they were in Carmel. 8 Ask your servants, and they will explain to you. Therefore let

these young men find grace in your eyes; (for we have come in a good season) give, I pray you, what comes into your hand to your servants and to your son Dauid." 9 When Dauid's young men came, they reported all these words to Nabal in Dauid's name and kept quiet. 10 Then Nabal answered Dauid's servants and said, "Who is Dauid and who is Ishai's son? Today there are many servants who turn every man away from his master. 11 Shall I then take my bread and my water and my meat, which I have slain for my skinners, and give it to men whom I know not whence they are? 12 Then Dauid's ser- vants went away, and went again, and came, and told him all these things. 13 Dauid said to his men, "Belt each man his own sword." And they girded each man with his sword: Dauid also girded his sword. And about four hundred men went after Dauid, and two hun- dred remained by the cariage. 14 Now one of the servants informed Abigail, Nabal's wife, saying, "Behold, Dauid has sent messengers from the wilderness to greet our master, and he has received them." 15 Nevertheless those men were very good to them, and we did not mind anything, nor did we lack anything as long as we were in contact with them, when we were in the fields. 16 They were like a wall against us both by night and day, while we were with them guarding the sheep. 17 Now, therefore, take heed and see what you will do, for our master and all his household will surely be stricken with the curse, for he is so wicked that you cannot speak to him." 18 Then Abigail hastened to take two hundred cakes, two bottles of wine, five heads of cat- tle already dressed, five measures of soaked horn, a hundred fractions of raisins and two hundred figs, and she loaded them on the donkeys. 19 Then she said to her servants, "Go before me; behold, I will come after you"; but she said nothing to her husband Nabal. 20 As she rode, she went down through a secret place in the mountain, and behold, Dauid and his men came down against her, and she met them. 21 Dauid said, "Indeed, I have kept all that this boy had in the wilderness, so that he lacked nothing of all that belonged to him, for he has rewarded me with good." 22 So does God also with the enemies of Dauid, for sure- ly I will leave of all that he has, at the dawning of the day, no one to piss against the wall." 23 When Abigail saw Dauid, she hastened to put out her plank, fell down before Dauid on her face, and prostrated herself on the ground, 24 and fell down at his feet, saying, "Oh, my lord, I have committed iniquity; please let your hand speak to you and listen to the words of your hand. 25 Let not my lord, I pray thee, deal with this wicked Nabal: for as Nabal is his name, so is he: Nabal is his name, and fol- ly is with him; but I, thy hand, know not the young men of my lord whom thou hast sent. 26 Now therefore, my lord, as the LORD and as thy soul (the LORD, that is, who hath kept thee from shedding blood, and thy hand hath not betrayed thee), so now shall thy enemies be as Nabal, and as those who mean to do my lord harm. 27 And now let this blessing which your servant brought to my lord be given to the young men who follow my lord. 28 Please forgive the guilt of your handmaid, for the LORD will make my lord a safe house, for my lord fights the battles of the LORD, and in all your life there has not been found in you any unwise man. 29 Yet a man hath risen up to persecute thee, and to seek thy soul: but the soul of my lord shall be bound in the bundle of life with the LORD thy God; and the soul of thine enemies God shall cast it out as from the center of a sling. 30 And when the LORD hath done unto my lord all the good that he hath promised thee, and hath made thee a ruler of Israel, 31 then it shall not be a cause of mourn- ing for thee, nor of offence to my lord, that he hath not shed blood without cause, nor

that my lord hath not protected himself; and when the Lord hath dealt well with my lord, remem- ber thy handmaid." 32 Then Dauid said to Ab- igail, "Blessed be the LORD, the God of Israel, who has sent you to meet me today. 33 Blessed be your counsel, and blessed be you, that you have kept me from coming to shed blood to- day, and that my hand has not betrayed me. 34 For as the LORD, the God of Israel, says, who has kept me from harming you, if you had not hastened to meet me, surely there would have been no one left in Nabal at daybreak to piss against the wall." 35 Then Dauid received from her hand what she had brought him and said to her, "Go in peace to your house; behold, I have heard your message and grant- ed your request." 36 So Abigail went to Nabal, and behold, he had made a banquet in his house, like a banquet of a king, and Nabal's heart was glad within him, for he was very drunk; therefore he said nothing to him, nei- ther less nor more, until the morning arose. 37 In the morning, when the wine was fin- ished, his wife said those words to him, and his heart died and remained as a stone. 38 About ten days later the LORD struck Nabal, and he died. 39 When Dauid heard that Na- bal was dead, he said, "Blessed be the LORD who has judged the cause of my reproach from Nabal's hand and has preserved his ser- vant from death, for the LORD has rewarded Nabal's wickedness on his head." Dauid also sent to speak to Abigail to take her as his wife. 40 When Dauid's servants came to Abigail in Carmel, they spoke to her, saying, "Dauid has sent to take you to wife." 41 She stood up, prostrated herself with her face to the ground, and said, "Behold, let your hand be a servant to wash the feet of my lord's servants." 42 And Abigail hastened, and arose, and rode upon a plank, and her five maidens followed her; and she went after Dauid's messengers, and be- came his wife. 43 Dauid also took Ahinoam of Izreel, and they were both his wives. 44 Saul had given Michal, his daughter by Dauid, to Phalti the son of Laish, who was from Gallim, to be his wife.

CHAPTER 26

1 Then the Ziphites came to Saul in Gibe- ah, saying, "Is not Dauid hiding on the hill of Hachilah, before Ieshimon?" 2 Then Saul arose and went down into the wilderness of Zif, having with him three thousand chosen men of Israel to see Dauid in the wilderness of Zif. 3 Saul encamped on the hill of Hachi- lah, which is opposite Ieshimon, along the road. Dauid stayed in the wilderness and said that Saul followed him into the wilderness. 4 (For Dauid had sent spies and understood that Saul had come very far). 5 Then Dauid arose and came to the place where Saul had encamped; and when Dauid saw the place where Saul lay and Abner the son of Ner, who was his chief-chief, (for Saul lay in the fortress and the people had encamped around him) 6 Then Dauid spoke and said to Ahimelech the Hittite and to Abishai the son of Zeruiah, the brother of Joab, saying, "Who will go down with me from Saul to the army?" Abishai an- swered, "I will go with you." 7 So Dauid and Abishai went down to the people by night; and behold, Saul was lying asleep inside the fortress, and his spear was sticking into the ground at his head; and Abner and the peo- ple were around him. 8 Then Abishai said to Dauid, "Today God has closed your enemy in your hands; now, please allow me to strike him once with the spear into the ground and I will not strike him again." 9 Dauid said to Abishai, "Do not destroy him, for who can put his hand on the Lord's anointed and be hardened? 10 Moreover Dauid said, "As

the LORD wills, either the LORD will smite him, or his day will come to dye, or he will go down to battle and die." 11 The LORD forbids me to lay my hand on the LORD's anointed; but, please, take now the spear that is at his head and the vessel of water and leave." 12 So Dauid took the spear and the jar of water from Saul's head, and they carried them away; no one saw it, nor did they notice it, and no one woke up, but they were all asleep, for the LORD had caused a deadly sleep to fall upon them. 13 Then Dauid went to the other side and stood on the top of a hill far away, with a great space between them. 14 Dauid cried out to the people and to Abner the son of Ner, saying, "Are not you, Abner?" Abner answered, "Who are you who cries out to the king?" 15 Dauid said to Abner, "Are not you a man, and who is like you in Israel? Why then have you not guarded your lord the king? Because one of his own has come in to destroy your lord the king." 16 This is not well done on your part; as the LORD says, you are worthy to die, because you have not guarded your master, the Anointed of the LORD; and now see where is the king's spear and the vessel of water that was at his head." 17 And Saul knew Dauid's journey and said, "Is this your journey, my son Dauid?" And Dauid answered, "It is my journey, my lord, O king." 18 He said, "Why does my lord so persecute his servant? For what have I done? Or what do I have in my hand? 19 Now, there- fore, I pray thee, let my lord the king hear the words of his servant. If the LORD has stirred you up against me, let him smell the odor of a sacrifice; but if the sons of men have done it, let them be accursed before the LORD, for they have cast me out this day from dwelling in the LORD's inheritance, saying, "Go, serve other gods." 20 Now therefore let not my blood fall to the ground before the LORD, for the king of Israel has gone out to seek a flea, as one hunts a partridge in the mountains." 21 Then Saul said, "I have sinned; come again, my son Dauid, for I will do thee no more harm, for today my soul was precious in thy sight; behold, I have done a foolish thing, and have erred greatly." 22 Then Dauid answered and said, "Here is the king's spear, let one of the young men come out and fix it. 23 May the Lord reward every man according to his righteousness and faithfulness, for the Lord has delivered you into my hands today, but I would not lay my hand on the Lord's anoint- ed. 24 And behold, as your life has been en- dangered in my sight today, so let my life be endangered in the sight of the LORD, that he may deliver me from all tribulation." 25 Then Saul said to Dauid, "Blessed are you, my son Dauid, for you will do great things and will also be precious." So Dauid went on his way, and Saul returned to his place.

CHAPTER 27

1 Dauid said in his heart, "One day I shall die by the hand of Saul; is it not better for me that I should go away into the land of the Phi- listines, and that Saul should have no more hope of seeing me in all the coasts of Israel, and thus escape his hands?" 2 Dauid arose and, with the six hundred men who were with him, went to Achish the son of Maoch, king of Gath. 3 Dauid settled with Achish in Gath, he and his men, each with his own house, Dauid and his two wives, Ahinoam the Izreelite and Abigail, wife of Nabal, the Car- melite. 4 Saul was told that Dauid had fled to Gath; so he sought him no more. 5 Dauid said to Achish, "If I have now found peace in your eyes, give me a place in some other city in the county, that I may dwell there; why should your servant dwell in the main city of the kingdom with you?" 6

Achish gave him Ziklag that same day; therefore Ziklag belongs to the kings of Iudah to this day. 7 The time that Dauid stayed in the county of the Philis- tines was four months and some days. 8 Then Dauid and his men went out to conquer the Geshurites, the Girzites, and the Amalekites, who had inhabited the land from the begin- ning, from the road that leads to Shur, to the land of Egypt. 9 And Dauid put the land to the sword, and left no man nor woman, and took sheep, oxen, donkeys, camels, and clothing, and returned, and came to Achish. 10 Ach- ish said, "Where have you been traveling to- day?" Dauid answered, "Against the south of Iudah, against the south of the Ierameelites and against the south of the Kenites." 11 And Dauid did not have foreign men and women given to him to lead them to Gath, saying, "Lest they feel guilty and say, 'This is what Dauid has done, and this will be his fate for as long as he dwells in the county of the Phi- listines.'" 12 Achish turned to Dauid, saying, "He has caused his people of Israel to despise him; therefore he will be my servant forever."

CHAPTER 28

1 At that time the Philistines gathered their bands and their armies to fight against Israel; therefore Achish said to Dauid, "Be sure, you and your men will go out with me to battle." 2 Dauid said to Achish, "You will certainly know what your servant can do." And Achish said to Dauid, "Surely I will make you guard my head forever." 3 (Samuel had died; all Is- rael mourned for him and buried him in Ra- mah, his hometown; Saul had removed the sorcerers and soothsayers from the land.) 4 Then the Philistines gathered themselves together, and came and encamped at Shunem; Saul gathered all Israel together, and they encamped at Gilboa. 5 When Saul saw the army of the Philistines, he was afraid and his heart was astonished. 6 Saul sought coun- sel from the LORD, but the LORD answered him neither by names, nor by Vrim, nor by prophets. 7 Then Saul said to his servants, "Seek me a woman who has a familiar spirit, that I may go to her and ask her something." His servants said to him, "Behold, there is a woman in En-dor who has a familiar spirit." 8 So Saul changed, and put on more clothes, and went, with two men with him, and they came to the woman by night; and he said, "Please be my conduit to the familiar spirit, and bring me the one whom I will appoint to you." 9 And the woman said to him, "Well, you know what Saul has done, how he has removed the sorcerers and the southerners from the land; why then do you seek to snare me so that I may die? 10 Saul swore to her by the Lord, "As the Lord wills, no harm shall be done to you for this deed." 11 Then the wom- an said, "Whom shall I bring to you?" And he answered, "Bring me Samuel." 12 When the woman saw Samuel, she cried with a loud voice, and the woman spoke to Saul, saying, "Why have you deceived me? Because you are Saul." 13 The king said to her, "Fear not, for what have you seen?" The woman said to Saul, "I saw gods rising from the earth." 14 Then he said to her, "What does he look like?" And she answered, "An old man comes here wrapped in a cloak." Saul understood that it was Samu- el, and he put his face to the ground and pros- trated himself. 15 Samuel said to Saul, "Why did you trouble me to come?" Saul answered, "I am in great distress, because the Philistines are making war against me, and God has de- parted from me and no longer answers me, either by prophets or by names; therefore I have called you that you may tell me what I should do." 16

Then Samuel answered, "Why do you ask me to speak, since the LORD has turned away from you and is your enemy? 17 The LORD has done to him what he said by my hand, for the LORD will snatch the kingdom out of your hand and give it to your neighbor Dauid." 18 Because you did not obey the LORD's message and did not execute his fierce wrath against Amalek, the LORD has done this to you today. 19 Moreover the LORD will deliver Israel with you into the hands of the Philistines; for the rest you and your sons will be with me, and the LORD will give the army of Israel into the hands of the Philis- tines." 20 Then Saul fell on the ground and felt sick because of Samuel's words, so that he had no strength left, for he had not eaten bread all day or all night. 21 Then the woman went to Saul and, seeing that he was greatly troubled, said to him, "See, your servant has obeyed your word, and I have put my soul in my hand and obeyed your words that you have spoken to me. 22 Now, I beseech thee, hear also the message of thy handmaid, and let me set before thee a morsel of bread, that thou mayest eat, and take strength, and con- tinue thy journey." 23 But he refused and said, "I will not eat"; but his servants and the wom- an together compelled him, and he obeyed their invitation; so he got up from the ground and sat on the bed. 24 Now the woman had a fatted calf in the house, and she hastened, and killed it, and took flour, and kneaded it, and made leavened bread out of it. 25 Then she brought it before Saul and his servants; and when they had eaten, they stopped and left the same evening.

CHAPTER 29

1 The Philistines assembled with their whole army at Aphek, while the Israelites encamped by the fountain that is in Izreel. 2 The princes of the Philistines went forward by hundreds and thousands of men, but Dauid and his men stayed behind with Achish. 3 Then the princes of the Philistines said, "What are these Hebrews doing here?" And Achish said to the princes of the Philistines, "Is not Dauid the servant of Saul king of Israel, who has been with me in these days, or in these years, and I have found nothing in him, since he dwelt with me until this day?" 4 But the princ- es of the Philistines were angry with him and said to him, "Send this boy back, that he may return to his place which you have assigned him, and not go down with them to fight, at least that in the battle he may be an oppo- nent of Vs. 5 Is not this Dauid, of whom it was sung in oath, saying, Saul slew his thousand, and Dauid his ten thousand?" 6 Then Achish called Dauid and said to him, "As it pleases the LORD, you were righteous and good in my sight, when you went out and entered the army with me, and I found nothing good with you, from the time you came to me until now, but the princes have not betrayed you. 7 Therefore now turn back and go in peace, lest the princes of the Philistines displease you." 8 Dauid said to Achish, "What have I done, and what have you found in your servant, as long as I have been with you to this day, that I should not go and fight against the ene- mies of my lord the king?" 9 Achish answered Dauid, "I know that I like you, as an angel of God, but the princes of the Philistines have said, 'Do not go and fight with him.'" 10 There- fore now rise early in the morning with your servants who have come with you; and when you are early in the morning, when you have light, depart." 11 So Dauid and his men rose early to depart in the morning and return to the land of the Philistines; and the Philistines went to Izreel.

CHAPTER 30

1 When Dauid and his men came to Ziklag, on the thirteenth day, the Amalekites had invaded as far south as Ziklag, struck Ziklag and set it on fire, 2 they had taken captive the women there, small and great, and had not killed anyone, but had carried them away and gone their way. 3 Then Dauid and his men came to the city, and behold, it was burned with fire, and their wives and their sons and their daughters had been taken captive. 4 Then Dauid and the people who were with him raised their voices and wept until they could weep no more. 5 Dauid's two wives were also taken captive: Ahinoam, the Izreelite, and Abigail, wife of Nabal, the Car- melite. 6 Dauid was greatly grieved, because the people intended to stone him, for the hearts of all the people were vexed at his sons and daughters; but Dauid comforted himself in the LORD his God. 7 Dauid said to Abia- thar the son of Ahimelech the priest, "Please bring me the Ephod." And Abiathar brought the Ephod to Dauid. 8 Then Dauid sought counsel from the Lord, saying, "Should I fol- low this company? Shall I overcome it?" And he answered him, "Follow them, for you will surely overcome them and recover every- thing." 9 So Dauid and the six hundred men who were with him went and came to Besor, where some of them resided: 10 But Dauid and four hundred men followed him (for two hundred stayed behind, being too tired to go beyond the Besor River). 11 And they found an Egyptian in the countryside, and led him to Dauid, and gave him bread, which he ate, and gave him water to drink. 12 They also gave him some figs and two clusters of raisins; and when he had eaten, his spirit revived, for he had not eaten bread nor drunk water for three days and three nights. 13 And Dauid said to him, To whom do you belong and where are you? And he answered, "I am a young Egyp- tian, the servant of an Amalekite; and my master left me three days ago, because I fell ill." 14 We went to the south of Chereth, to the coast of Iudah, and to the south of Caleb, and burned Ziklag with fire. 15 Dauid said to him, "Can you take me into this company?" And he answered, "Swear to me by God that you will not kill me or deliver me into the hands of my master, and I will lead you to these people." 16 And when he had led him thither, behold, they were lying scattered over all the land, eating, drinking, and making merry, because of all the great prayers that they had taken from the land of the Philistines and from the land of Judah. 17 Dauid struck them from dusk until dawn the next day, so that not a single one es- caped except four hundred men riding cam- els and fleeing. 18 Dauid recovered all that the Amalekites had taken; moreover Dauid saved his two wives. 19 They lacked nothing, neither small nor great, neither son nor daughter, nor of the trousseau of all that they had taken away; Dauid recovered them all. 20 Dauid also took all the sheep and oxen, and dragged them before his cathedral, and said, "This is Dauid's prayer." 21 Dauid reached the two hundred men who were too tired to fol- low Dauid, who had been made to lodge at the village of Besor; they came to meet Dauid and the people who were with him; so when Dauid approached the people, he greeted them. 22 Then all the wicked and evil men who went with Dauid answered, "Since they did not go with them, we will not give them anything of the prayers that we have recov- ered, that is, to each his wife and his children; so let them take them away and leave." 23 Then Dauid said, "You shall not do so, my brethren, with what the LORD has granted to Vs. who protected Vs. and delivered into our hands the

company that had come against Vs. 24 Who will obey you in this matter? But as his portion is that which goes down to the battal- ion, so shall his portion be that which is cut off with cloth; they shall be divided alike." 25 So from that day forward he made it a statute and a law in Israel to this day. 26 When Dauid came to Ziklag, he sent word to the elders of Iudah and his friends, "You see that there is a blessing for you from the spit of the enemies of the LORD." 27 He sent to those of Beth-el, to those of Ramoth south, and to those of Jat- tir, 28 To those of Aroer, to those of Siphmoth, and to those of Eshtemoa, 29 of Rachal, of the cities of the Ierahmeelites, and of the cities of the Kenites, 30 to those of Hormah, to those of Chor-ashan, and to those of Athach, 31 to Hebron and to all the places where Dauid and his men had taken refuge.

CHAPTER 31

1 The Philistines fought against Israel, and the sons of Israel fled from the Philistines and fell wounded on Mount Gilboa. 2 The Philis- tines came upon Saul and his sons and killed Ionathan, Abinadab and Malchishua, Saul's sons. 3 When the battle broke out against Saul, the archers and archers struck him, and he was badly wounded by the archers. 4 Then Saul said to his armor-bearer, "Take out your sword and stab me with it, lest the circum- cisers come and stab me and mock me"; but his armor-bearer would not, for he was very afraid. Therefore Saul took a sword and fell on it. 5 And when his armorer saw that Saul was dead, he too fell on his sword and died with him. 6 So Saul died, his three sons, his armorer, and all his men on that same day. 7 When the men of Israel who were on the oth- er side of the valley and those on the other side of Iorden saw that the men of Israel had been put to flight and that Saul and his sons were dead, they left the cities and fled; and the Philistines came to dwell in them. 8 The next day, when the Philistines came to strip the slain, they found Saul and his three sons on Mount Gilboa, 9 And they cut off his head,and stripped him of his armor, and sent him into the land of the Philistines on every side, that they might publish him in the temple of their idols and among the people. 10 They de- posited his armor in the house of Ashtaroth, but they hanged his body on the walls of Beth- shan. 11 When the inhabitants of Jabesh Gil- ead learned what the Philistines had done to Saul, 12 they arose (as many as were strong men), went all night, tore the body of Saul and the bodies of his sons from the wall of Beth-Shan, came to Iabesh and burned them there, 13 then they took their bones and bur- ied them under a tree in Iabesh, and fasted for ten days.

II SAMUEL

CHAPTER 1

1 After the death of Saul, when Dauid had returned from the slaughter of the Amale- kites and had remained two days in Ziklag, 2 behold, on the third day there came a man from Saul's army with tattered garments and dirt on his head; and when he came to Dauid, he fell to the ground and did obeisance. 3 Then Dauid said to him, "Where do you come from?" And he answered him, "From the army of Israel I have escaped." 4 Dauid said to him, "What has happened? Please tell me." Dauid answered that the people had fled from the battle and that many had been routed and died, and that Saul and Ionathan, his son, had also died. 5 Dauid said to the young man who had informed him, "How

do you know that Saul and Ionathan, his son, are dead? 6 The young man who had told him replied, "When I arrived at Mount Gilboa, behold, Saul was leaning on his spear, while the chariots and horsemen were following behind him. 7 When he turned back, he saw me and called me. And I answered, "Here I am." 8 He said to me,"Who are you?" And I answered him, "I am an Amalekite." 9 Then he said to me, "Please come upon me and kill me, for anguish has come upon me, for my life is still whole in me. 10 So I went up to him and killed him; and be- cause I was sure that he could not lie, after he had fallen, I took the crown on his head and the bracelet on his arm and brought them to my lord. 11 Then Dauid took his garments and tore them, as did all the men who were with him. 12 They mourned and wept and fasted to the end, for Saul and for Ionathan his son, for the people of the LORD and for the house of Israel, because they had been slain by the sword. 13 Then Dauid said to the young man who had told him, "Where are you?" And he answered, "I am the son of a foreigner, an Amalekite." 14 Then Dauid said to him, "How is it that you have not been attacked to stretch out your hand to destroy the LORD's Anonymous?" 15 Then Dauid called one of his young men and said, "Go away and fall on him." And he struck him that he died. 16 Then Dauid said to him, "Let your blood be on your head, for your own mouth has testified against you, saying, 'I killed the Lord Anonimous." 17 Then Dauid mourned with this lament Saul and Ionathan his son, 18 (and he also commanded him to teach the sons of Iudah to push, as it is written in the book of Iasher). 19 O noble Israel, he is in danger in your places of wor- ship; how the mighty have been overthrown! 20 Tell it not in Gath, and publish it not in the streets of Ashkelon, lest the daughters of the Philistines rebel, lest the daughters of the circumcised triumph. 21 Mountains of Gil- boa, on you let there be neither dew nor rain, nor fields of grain, for there the shield of the mighty one, the shield of Saul, was cast, as if it had not been anointed with oil. 22 Ion- athan's bow never returned, nor Saul's sword returned empty of the blood of the slain and the fat of the mighty. 23 Saul and Ionathan were strong and pleasant in their lives, and in their death they were not intimidated; they were swifter than eagles, they were stron- ger than lions. 24 Daughters of Israel, weep for Saul, who clothed you with skins, with pleasures, and hung gold ornaments on your garments. 25 How the strongest were slain in the midst of the battle! O Ionathan, you were slain in your places. 26 I am sorry for you, brother Ionathan; you have been very kind to me; your love for me has been wonderful, su- perior to the love of women; how the mighty have been overthrown and the weapons of war destroyed!

CHAPTER 2

1 After this fact, Dauid sought counsel from the LORD, saying, "Shall I go to one of the cities of Iudah?" And the LORD said to him, "Go away." And Dauid said, "Where shall I go?" He answered, "To Hebron." 2 So Dauid went there, together with his two wives, Ahinoam, the Izreelite, and Abigail, Nabal's wife, the Carmelite. 3 Dauid led the men who were with him, each with his family, and they settled in the cities of Hebron. 4 Then the men of Iudah came, and there they anoinced Dauid king out of the house of Iudah. They told Dauid that the men of Jabesh Gilead had buried Saul. 5 Dauid sent messengers to the men of Iabesh Gilead and said to them,"Blessed are you from the LORD, for you have shown such goodness toward your

lord Saul that you buried him. 6 Therefore now the LORD gives you credit and justice; and I will reward you for this benefit, because you have done this thing. 7 Therefore now let your hands be strong and you be val- iant; though your master Saul is dead, yet the house of Judah has acknowledged me as king over them. 8 But Abner the son of Ner, who was captain of Saul's army, took Ish-Bosheth the son of Saul and led him to Mahanaim, 9 And made him king of Gilead, the Ashurites, Izreel, Ephraim, Benjamin, and all Israel. 10 And Ish-Bosheth the son of Saul was forty years old when he began to reign over Israel, and he reigned two years; but the house of Iu- dah followed Dauid. 11 (The time that Dauid reigned in Hebron over the house of Iudah was seven years and six months). 12 Abner the son of Ner and the servants of Ish-Bosheth the son of Saul went out from Mahanaim to go to Gibeon. 13 And Joab the son of Zeruiah and the servants of Dauid went out and met by the poole of Gabaon; and they sat one on one side of the poole and the other on the oth- er side. 14 Then Abner said to Joab, "Let the young men get up and play before them." And Joab said, "Let them get up." 15 Then they got up and went two Benjamites who belonged to Ish-Bosheth, son of Saul, and two servants of Dauid. 16 Each took his companion by the head and thrust his sword into his side, so that they fell down together; therefore the place was called Helkath-Hazzurim, which is in Gibeon. 17 On that same day the battle was very severe, for Abner and the men of Is- rael fell before the servants of Dauid. 18 There were three sons of Tseruiah: Ioab, Abishai and Asahel. Asahel had a step as light as a wild deer. 19 Asahel followed Abner and turned neither to the right nor to the left from Abner. 20 Then Abner looked behind him and said, "Are you Asahel? And he answered, "Yes." 21 Then Abner said, "Turn either to the right or to the left, and take one of the young men and take his weapons"; but Asahel would not turn away from him. 22 Abner said to Asahel, "Get away from me; for what reason should I strike you to the ground? How then could I hide my face from Joab, your brother?" 23 And when he would not leave, Abner, with the point of his spear, struck him under the fifth leg, so that the spear went out from behind him; and he fell there and died in his place. And all who came to the place where Asael had fallen and died stood still. 24 And Joab and Abishai pur- sued Abner, while the sun was setting when they came to the hill of Ammah, which is op- posite Jah, by the desert road of Gibeon. 25 The sons of Benjamin gathered behind Abner and set out on the top of a hill. 26 Then Abner called to Joab and said, "Will the sword still last? Do you not know that in the last times it will be bitter? How long will it pass, if you do not want the people to return to follow their brothers?" 27 Joab answered, "As God wills, if you had not spoken, surely in the morning the people would have gone away, each to his own brother." 28 Then Joab blew a trumpet, and all the people stopped and no longer pursued Is- rael or fought. 29 Abner and his men walked all that night through the plain and came out of Iorden and went through all Bitron to Ma- hanaim. 30 Ioab also went back to Abner; and when he had gathered all the people together, there were nineteen men and Asahel missing from Dauid's servants. 31 But Dauid's ser- vants had struck Benjamin and Abner's men, so that three hundred and sixty men died. 32 Then they took Asahel and buried him in his father's tomb, which was in Bethlehem; Joab and his men went all night, and when they came to Hebron, it was daylight.

CHAPTER 3

1 Then there was a long war between the house of Saul and the house of Dauid; but Dauid grew stronger and the house of Saul grew weaker. 2 To Dauid were born sons in Hebron; his eldest son was Amnon of Ahino- am, the Izreelite, 3 the second, Cileab, by Ab- igail, wife of Nabal, the Carmelite; the third, Absalom, son of Maachah, daughter of Tal- mai, king of Geshur, 4 the fourth, Adonijah, son of Haggith, and the fifth, Shephatiah, son of Abital, 5 and the sixth, Ithream, by the wife of Eglah Dauidi; these sons were borne by Dauidi in Hebron. 6 Now while the war was going on between the house of Saul and the house of Dauid, Abner labored with all his might for the house of Saul. 7 Saul had a con- cubine named Rizpah, the daughter of Aiiah. And Ish-Bosheth said to Abner, "Why did you go to my father's concubine?" 8 Then Abner was greatly enraged at Ish-Bosheth's words and said, "Am I a dog-head, who against Iu- dah has paid homage today to the house of Saul your father, his brothers and his neigh- bors, and has not delivered you into the hands of Dauid, who today accuses me of a fault concerning this woman?" 9 Thus does God with Abner, and even more, except that as the LORD swore to Dauid, so do I with him, 10 to take away the kingdom from the house of Saul, that the throne of Dauid may be es- tablished over Israel and over Iudah, from Dan to Beer- sheba. 11 He no longer wanted to answer Abner, because he feared him. 12 Then Abner sent messengers to Dauid on his behalf, saying, "Whose territory is it? Who should say, 'Agree with me'; and behold, my hand will be with you to bring you all Israel." 13 Who answered, "Well, I will agree with you; but one thing I require of you, that you do not see my face unless you bring Michal, daugh- ter of Saul, when you come to see me." 14 Then Dauid sent messengers to Ish-Bosheth, son of Saul, saying, "Deliver me my wife Michal, whom I married for a hundred foreskinnes of the Philistines." 15 Ish-Bosheth sent for her from her husband Phaltiel the son of Laish. 16 Her husband went with her and came crying after her as far as Bahurim; then Abner said to him, "Go and come back." So he returned. 17 Abner spoke to the elders of Israel and said, "In the past you sought Dauid so that he might be your king. 18 Now do so, for the LORD has spoken of Dauid, saying, 'By the hand of my servant Dauid I will save my peo- ple of Israel from the hands of the Philistines and from those of all their enemies. 19 Abner also spoke to Benjamin, and then Abner went to speak to Dauid at Hebron, concerning all that Israel was satisfied with and all the house of Benjamin. 20 And Abner went to Dauid to Hebron, having twenty-five men with him, and Dauid made a feast to Abner and the men who were with him. 21 Then Abner said to Dauid, "I will get up and go and gather all Israel to my lord the king, that they may make a covenant with you, and you may rule over all that your heart desires." Dauid let Abner go, and he departed in peace. 22 And behold, the servants of Dauid and Joab came from the camna, and brought with them a great many prayers (but Abner was not with Dauid in He- bron, for he had sent him away and depart- ed in peace). 23 When Joab and all the army that was with him had arrived, the men said to Joab, "Abner the son of Ner has come to the king; he has sent him away and departed in peace." 24 Then Joab went to the king and said to him, "What have you done? Behold, Abner has come to you; why have you sent him away and he has departed? 25 You know Abner the son of Ner, for he has come to deceive you, to know your outgoings and your comings, and to know all that you do." 26 When Joab left Dauid, he sent messengers to find Abner, who led him back

from the well of Syria to Dauid. 27 When Abner was again in Hebron, Joab moved him from the door to speak to him peaceably, and struck him under the fifth beam, causing him to be dyed by the blood of Asael his brother. 28 Then when Dauidi came to his ear, he said, "I and my kingdom are hopeless before the LORD for the blood of Abner the son of Ner. 29 Let the blood fall on the head of Joab and on all his father's house, so that in the house of Joab there may nev- er be a lack of anyone who has trouble with blood, who is leprous, who leans on a staff, who falls on the sword, or who lacks bread." 30 (So Joab and Abishai, his brother, killed Abner, because he had killed their broth- er Asahel at Gibeon in battle). 31 And Dauid said to Joab and all the people who were with him, "Undress, put on sackcloth, and go be- fore Abner"; and King Dauid himself followed the bearer. 32 When they had buried Abner in Hebron, the king lifted up his head and wept beside Abner's tomb, and all the people wept. 33 And the king complained about Abner and said, "Has Abner dyed himself as you dye a fish? 34 Thy hands were not bound, neither were thy feet bound with chains of iron: but as a man falls down before the wicked, so art thou fallen." And all the people wept for him again. 35 Then all the people came and made Dauid eat food while it was still daylight, but Dauid swore, saying, "So let God do with me, and even more, if I taste bread or anything else until the sun has set." 36 All the people heard this and were pleased; just as what the king did pleased all the people. 37 For on that day all the people and all Israel understood that it had not been the king's decision to kill Abner the son of Ner. 38 The king said to his servants, "Do you not know that today in Is- rael there is a prince and a great man? 39 I am today a weary and newly anointed king, and these men, the sons of Zeruiah, are too hard for me; the LORD rewards those who do evil according to their wickedness.

CHAPTER 4

1 When Sauls son heard that Abner had died in Hebron, his hands were weakened and all Israel became afraid, 2 Sauls son had two men who were captains of bands: one named Baanah and the other named Rechab, sons of Rimmon, a Beerothite of the sons of Benjamin. (For Beeroth was disputed with Benjamin), 3 because the Beerothites fled to Gittaim and remained there to this day). 4 Ionathan the son of Saul had a son lame in his feet; he was five years old when the marriage of Saul and Ionathan came outside Israel; then his wife took him and fled away. As she hastened to flee, the child fell down and began to stand still; his name was Mephibosheth. 5 The sons of Rimmon, the Beerothite, Rechab and Baanah, went and came, in the middle of the day, to the house of Ish-Bosheth (who was sleeping on a bed by no one). 6 And behold, Rechab and Baanah, his brother, came into the middle of the house, as if they had wanted to drown him, and they struck him under the fifth beam, and then fled. 7 When they en- tered the house, he was sleeping on his bed in his bedroom, they struck him, killed him, be- headed him, took his head, and carried them away across the plain all night. 8 And they brought Ish-Bosheth's head to Dauid in He- bron, and said to the king, "Here is the head of Ish-Bosheth the son of Saul, your enemy, who sought your life; and the LORD has this day declared my lord king over Saul and his seed." 9 Then Dauid answered Rechab and Baanah his brother, sons of Rimmon the Beerothite, and said to them, "As the LORD wills, who has delivered my soul from all adversity, 10 When one told me that Saul had died (thinking that he had brought good news), I took him and killed him in Ziklag, thinking that I would give him a reward for his news: 11 How much more, when wicked men have slain a righ- teous man in his house and on his bed, shall I not demand his blood from your hand and remove you from the earth?" 12 Then Dauid gave orders to his young men, and they slew them, and cut off their hands and feet, and hanged them beyond the well of Hebron; but they took the head of Isbosheth, and buried it in the sepulcher of Abner in Hebron.

CHAPTER 5

1 Then all the tribes of Israel came from Dauid to Hebron and said, "Behold, we are your bones and your flesh." 2 Formerly, when Saul was our king, you led Israel in and out; and the LORD said to you, "You shall feed my people Israel and be a leader of Israel." 3 So all the elders of Israel came to the king in Hebron; and King Dauid agreed with them in Hebron before the LORD, and they made Dauid king of Israel. 4 Dauid was thirty years old when he began to reign; and he reigned for forty years. 5 In Hebron he reigned over Judah for ten years and six months; and in Jerusalem he reigned for thirty-three years over all Israel and Judah. 6 The king and his men went to Jerusalem to the Jebusites, the inhabitants of the land, who spoke to Dauid, saying, "If you do not remove the blind and the lame, you will not enter here," thinking that Dauid could not enter. 7 But Dauid took the fortress of Zion: this is the city of Dauid. 8 Now by this time Dauid had said on the same day, "Whoever shall smite the Jebusites and go up to the gutters and smite the lame and the blind, whom Dauid's mind hates, I will prefer him; therefore they said, 'The blind and the lame shall not enter into that house.'" 9 So Dauid settled in that fortress and called it the city of Dauid, and Dauid built around it, from Millo upward. 10 And Dauid prospered and grew rich, because the LORD, the God of hosts, was with him. 11 Hiram king of Tyre also sent messengers to Dauid, cedar trees, carpenters and masons for the walls, and they built Dauid a house. 12 Then Dauid un- derstood that the LORD had established him as king of Israel and had exalted his kingdom for his people of Israel. 13 Dauid took other concubines and wives from Jerusalem after he came from Hebron, and more sons and daughters were born to him. 14 These are the names of the sons who were born to him in Jerusale: Shammua, Shobab, Nathan and Sol- omon, 15 Ibhar, Elishua, Nepheg and Japhi- ah, 16 Elishama, Eliada and Elipheth. 17 But when the Philistines heard that they had ar- rested Dauid, king of Israel, all the Philistines came to see Dauid; and when Dauid heard, he withdrew to a fortress. 18 But the Philis- tines came and scattered into the valley of Rephaim. 19 Then Dauid sought counsel from the LORD, saying, "Shall I go to the Philis- tines? Will you deliver them into my hands?" The LORD answered Dauid, "Go away, for no doubt I will deliver the Philistines into your hands." 20 Then Dauid came to Baal- perazim, struck them, and said, "The LORD has divided my enemies before me, as waters are divided; therefore he called that place Baal-perazim." 21 There they left their images, and Dauid and his men burned them. 22 Then the Phi- listines came and scattered into the valley of Rephaim. 23 When Dauid asked the LORD for advice, he said, "You will not go away, but will turn behind them and face them against the mulberry trees. 24 When you hear the sound of one going toward the tops of the mulberry trees, turn away, for then the LORD will come out before you to strike the

army of the Phi- listines." 25 Then Dauid did as the LORD had commanded him and struck the Philistines from Gheba all the way to Gazer.

CHAPTER 6

1 Then Dauid gathered all the chosen men of Israel, about thirty thousand, 2 Dauid arose and went with all the people who were with him from Baale of Judah to bring thence the Ark of God, whose name is called the Name of the LORD of hosts, who dwells on it among the Cherubim. 3 They put the Ark of God on a new chariot and brought it out of the house of Abinadab, which was in Gibeah. Vzzah and Ahio, Abinadab's sons, brought the new char- iot. 4 When they brought the ark of God out of the house of Abinadab, which was in Gibeah, Ahio went before the ark, 5 Dauid and all the house of Israel played before the LORD on all the wooden instruments, on harps, psalteries, timpani, cornets and cymbals. 6 When they came to the threshing floor of Nachon, Vzzah put his hand on the ark of God and shook it, because the oxen shook it. 7 The LORD was very angry with Vzzah, and God struck him in the same place for his fault, and there he died for the ark of God. 8 Dauid was sorry because the LORD had struck Vzzah, and he called the place Perez Vzzah by his name to this day. 9 Therefore Dauid feared the LORD that day and said, "How will the ark of the LORD come to me?" 10 So Dauid would not bring the ark of the LORD to the city of Dauid, but brought it to the house of Obed-Edom, a Gittite. 11 And the Ark of the LORD stayed in the house of Obed-Edom, the Gittite, for three months, and the LORD blessed Obed-Edom and all his household. 12 One told King Dauid, "The LORD blessed the house of Obed-edom and all that it possesses, because of the ark of God; therefore Dauid went and brought the ark of God from the house of Obed-edom to the city of Dauid with joy." 13 When those who car- ried the ark of the LORD had taken six steps, he offered an ox and a stout beast. 14 Dauid danced before the LORD with all his strength and was girded with a linen ephod. 15 Dauid and all the house of Israel carried the ark of the LORD with shouts and trumpet blasts. 16 As the ark of the LORD entered the city of Dauid, Michal, daughter of Saul, looked out of a window and saw King Dauid leaping and dancing before the LORD, and she despised him in her heart. 17 When they brought the ark of the LORD, they placed it in its place in the center of the tabernacle that Dauid had prepared for it; then Dauid offered sac- rifices and peace offerings before the LORD. 18 When Dauid had finished the offering of burnt offerings and peace offerings, he blessed the people in the name of the LORD of hosts, 19 and he distributed to all the peo- ple, that is, to all the multitude of Israel, both women and men, a piece of bread, a piece of meat, and a bottle of wine to each one; so all the people left each one to his house. 20 And Dauid returned to bless his house, and Michal the daughter of Saul went out to meet Dauid and said, "How glorious was the king of Israel today, who was vncourized in the eyes of the maidens of his servants, as a foole vncouriz- es himself." 21 Then Dauid said to Michal, "It was the LORD who chose me more than your father and all his house and commanded me to be the leader of the LORD's people, that is, of Israel, 22 and I shall be even more vile than that, and I shall be low in my own eyes, and of the same maidens, of whom you have spoken, I shall have the honor. 23 Therefore Michal the daughter of Saul had no children until the day of her death.

CHAPTER 7

1 After the king had sat in his house and the LORD had granted him rest all around from all his enemies, 2 the king said to Nathan the prophet, "Behold, I now dwell in a house of cedars, and the Ark of God remains with- in the curtains." 3 Then Nathan said to the king, "Go and do all that is in your heart, for the LORD is with you." 4 In the same night the word of the LORD came to Nathan, say- ing 5 Go and say to my servant Dauid, "Thus says the LORD, Will you buy me a house for my habitation? 6 For I have not dwelt in any house since I brought the children of Israel out of Egypt until now, but I have walked in a tent and in a tabernacle. 7 In all the places where I walked with all the children of Israel, did I say a single word with any of the tribes of Israel when I commanded the judges to feed my people of Israel? Or did I say, "Why do you not build me a house of cedars?" 8 Now, there- fore, say to my servant Dauid, "Thus says the LORD of hosts, I took you out of the fold to follow the sheep, that you might be the ruler of my people, of Israel. 9 I have been with you wherever you have walked, I have destroyed all your enemies from your sight, and I have made you a great name, like the name of the great men who are on the earth. 10 Moreover I will establish a place for my people of Isra- el, and I will plant it, that they may dwell in a place of their own, and they shall not suffer any more, nor shall the wicked trouble them any more as before, 11 and from the time that I set judges against my people of Israel) and I will give you rest from all your enemies; also the LORD has said to you that he will make you a house. 12 When thy days are fulfilled, thou shalt sleep with thy fathers, and I will sct after thee thy seed, which shall be born of thy body, and I will establish his kingdom. 13 He shall purchase a house for my Name, and I will establish the throne of his kingdom for- ever. 14 I will be his father, and he shall be my son; and if he sins, I will chastise him with the rod of men and with the plagues of the sons of men. 15 But my mercy shall not depart from him, as I did from Saul, whom I turned away before you. 16 Your house shall be established, and your kingdom shall be established before you forever, and your throne shall be stable forever. 17 According to all these words and according to this vision, Nathan spoke thus to Dauid. 18 Then King Dauid went in, and sat down before the LORD, and said, "Who am I, Lord God, and what is my house, whereby you have brought me hither?" 19 This was still a small thing in Your eyes, Lord God, for which You also spoke of the house of Your servants for a long time; but does this refer to man, Lord God? 20 What more can Dauid tell you, for you, Lord God, know your servant. 21 By your words and according to your heart you have done all these great things to make them known to your servant. 22 Therefore you are great, Lord God, for there is no one like you and there is no other God but you, according to what we have heard with our ears. 23 What people on earth are like your people, like Is- rael, whose God went and redeemed them to himself, that they might be his people, that they might make a name for themselves and do great and terrible things for you for your land, O LORD, and for your people, whom you redeemed to you from Egypt and from the na- tions and from their gods? 24 For thou hast commanded thy people Israel to be thy people forever, and thou, O LORD, hast become their God. 25 Now therefore, O Lord God, confirm forever the word which thou hast spoken con- cerning thy servant and his house, and do as

thou hast said. 26 May your Name be magni-fied forever by those who will say, "The Lord of hosts is the God of Israel"; and may the house of your servant Dauid be consolidated before you. 27 For you, O LORD of hosts, God of Is-rael, answered your servant, saying, "I will build you a house"; therefore your servant had the courage to address this prayer to you. 28 Therefore now, O Lord God, (for you are God and your words are true, and you have grant-ed this good to your servant) 29 Therefore may it please thee to bless the house of thy servant, that it may continue forever before thee, for thou, O Lord God, hast said it; and may the house of thy servant be blessed forever with thy blessing.

CHAPTER 8

1 After this deed, Dauid defeated the Philis-tines and subdued them; Dauid took the reins of slavery out of the hands of the Philistines. 2 Then he struck Moab, measured them with a cord and threw them to the ground; he measured them with two cords to put them to death and with a full cord to keep them for-eigners; so the Moabites became Dauid's ser-vants and brought gifts. 3 Dauid also struck Hadadezer son of Rehob, king of Zobah, as he went to recover his borders by the Euphrates River. 4 Dauid took against them one thou-sand seven hundred horsemen and twenty thousand foot soldiers; Dauid destroyed all the classes, but recovered one hundred class-es. 5 Then the Arameans of Dammesek came to succor Hadadezer, king of Zobah, but Dauid killed two and twenty thousand men among the Arameans. 6 Dauid put a garrison in Aram of Damesek; the Arameans became Dauid's servants and brought gifts. And the LORD protected Dauid wherever he went. 7 Dauid took the golden shields that belonged to Hadadezer's servants and brought them to Jerusalem. 8 From Betah and Berothai (Hadadezer's city) King Dauid brought with him a great quantity of brasse. 9 Then Toi, king of Hamath, learned that Dauid had de-feated all Hadadezer's army, 10 So Toi sent Ioram, his son, to King Dauid to greet him and to be reconciled with him, because he had fought against Hadadezer and defeated him (for Hadadezer had made war on Toi) and had brought with him vessels of silk, vessels of gold and vessels of brasse. 11 King Dauid consecrated them to the LORD with the silver and bronze he had dedicated to all the nations he had subdued: 12 Of Aram, of Moab, of the sons of Ammon, of the Philistines, of Amalek, and of the host of Hadadezer the son of Re-hob, king of Zobah. 13 After his return, Dauid made a name for himself and killed among the Arameans in the valley of salt eighty thou-sand men. 14 He put a garrison in Edom; in all Edom he put soldiers, and all those in Edom became Dauid's servants; and the LORD guarded Dauid wherever he went. 15 Thus Dauid reigned over all Israel and executed judgment and justice toward all his people. 16 Joab the son of Zeruiah was head of the army, and Ioshaphat the son of Ahilud was record-er. 17 Zadok the son of Ahitub, Ahimelech the son of Abiathar, was the priest, and Seraiah the scribe. 18 Benaiah the son of Jehoiada, the Cherethites, the Pelethites and the sons of Dauidi were the leaders.

CHAPTER 9

1 And Dauid said, "Is there still anyone left from the house of Saul who can pay him hom-age because of Ionathan?"

2 From the house of Saul there was a servant whose name was Ziba; and when they had called him from Dauid, the king said to him, "Are you Ziba?" And he answered, "I am your servant." 3 Then the king said, "Is there still no one from the house of Saul on whom I can exercise God's mercy?" Ziba answered the king, "Ionathan still has a lame son on his feet." 4 Then the king said to him, "Where is he?" Ziba an-swered the king, "Behold, he is in the house of Machir the son of Ammiel of Lo-debar." 5 Then King Dauid sent for him from the house of Machir the son of Ammiel of Lo-debar. 6 And when Mephibosheth the son of Ion-athan the son of Saul came to Dauid, he fell on his knees and saluted. And Dauid said, "Mephibosheth?" And he answered, "Here is your servant." 7 Then Dauid said to him, "Do not be afraid, for I will certainly do you good for the sake of Ionathan your father, and I will restore to you all the fields of Saul your father, and you shall continually eat bread at my table." 8 He bowed down and said, "What is thy servant, that thou shouldst look on a dead dog like me?" 9 Then the king called Ziba, Saul's servant, and said to him, "I have given to your master's son all that fell to Saul and all his house. 10 You and your sons and your servants shall till the land for him, and you shall bring your masters' son food to eat. And Mephibosheth your master's son shall al-ways eat bread at my table (Ziba had fifty sons and twenty-five servants)." 11 Then Ziba said to the king, "According as my lord the king commanded his servant, so shall your servant do, that Mephibosheth may eat at my table, as one of the king's sons." 12 Mephibosheth also had a young son named Micha, and all those who lived in the house of Ziba were servants of Mephibosheth. 13 Mephibosheth dwelt in Jerusalem, for he ate continually at the king's table and was lame in both feet.

CHAPTER 10

1 After this fact, the king of the sons of Am-mon died and Hanun, his son, reigned in his place. 2 Then Dauid said, "I want to be kind to Hanun, son of Nahash, as his father was kind to me." And Dauid sent his servants to com-fort him on behalf of his father. So Dauid's servants came to the land of the sons of Am-mon. 3 The princes of the sons of Ammon said to Hanun their lord, "Do you think Dauid honors your father because he has sent you com-forters? Hasn't Dauid sent you his servants to scour the city, to drive it out and level it? 4 Therefore Hanun took Dauid's servants, cut off half their beards, cut off their garments in the middle, down to their buttocks, and sent them away. 5 When the matter was reported to Dauid, he went after them (for the men were greatly ashamed), and the king said, "Stay in Jericho, until your beards are grown, then return." 6 When the sons of Ammon saw that they stood before Dauid, the sons of Ammon sent to hire the Arameans of the house of Re-hob and the Arameans of Zobah, twenty thou-sand foot soldiers, a thousand men of King Maachah, and two thousand men of Ish-tob. 7 When Dauid heard this, he sent Joab and all the army of strong men. 8 The sons of Ammon went out and put their armies in araye at the entrance of the gate; the Arameans of Zoba, Rehob, Ish-tob and Maacah were alone in the camp. 9 When Joab saw that the front of the battle was against him in front and behind, he chose all the soldiers of Israel and lined them up against the Arameans. 10 The rest of the people he delivered into the hands of Abishai, his brother, to line them up against the sons of Ammon. 11 He said, "If the Ar-ameans are stronger than I am, you will help me; if the sons of Ammon

are too strong for you, I will come to your aid." 12 Be strong and valiant for our people and for the cities of our God, and the LORD will do what is good in his sight." 13 Then Joab and the people who were with him clashed with the Arameans, who fled before him. 14 When the sons of Ammon saw that the Arameans had fled, they also fled before Abishai and entered the city. So Joab returned to the sons of Ammon and came to Jerusalem. 15 When the Arameans realized that they had been defeated before Israel, they rounded them up. 16 Hadarezer sent for the Arameans who were across the river; they came to Helam, and Shobach, the lead- er of Hadarezer's army, went before them. 17 When Dauid was warned, he gathered all Israel together, passed through Iorden and came to Helam; the Arameans sided against Dauid and fought with him: 18 The Arameans fled before Israel; Dauid destroyed two hundred charets of the Arameans and four thou- sand horsemen, and struck Shobach, the cap- tain of his army, who died there. 19 When all the kings who were Hadarezer's servants saw that they had fallen before Israel, they made peace with Israel and went into their service; and the Arameans feared to help the sons of Ammon again.

CHAPTER 11

1 At the expiration of the year in which kings go out to fight, Dauid sent Ioab and his ser- vants and all Israel, who destroyed the sons of Ammon and besieged Rabbah; but Dauid re- mained in Jerusalem. 2 When evening came, Dauid got up from his bed and walked on the roof of the king's palace; and from the roof he saw a woman washing; the woman was very beautiful to behold. 3 Then Dauid sent to ask what woman she was; and one said, "Is not this Bath-sheba, daughter of Eliam, wife of Vriah the Hittite?" 4 Then Dauid sent messengers and took her away; and she came to him, and he lay with her; (now she was cleansed from her vices) and she returned to her house. 5 The woman had an epiphany and sent word to Dauid, "I am with child." 6 Then Dauid sent to say to Joab, "Send me Vriah, the Hittite." And Joab sent Vriah to Dauid. 7 When Vriah came to him, Dauid asked him how Joab had behaved, how the people had behaved, and how the war had progressed. 8 Then Dauid said to Vriah, "Go down to your house and wash your feet." So Vriah went out of the king's palace, and the king sent a pres- ent after him. 9 But Vriah slept in the court- yard of the king's palace with all his lord's servants and did not go down to his house. 10 Then they reported to Dauid that Vriah had not gone down to his house; and Dauid said to Vriah, "Have you not returned from your journey? Why did you not go down to your house?" 11 Then Vriah answered Dauid, "Arke, Israel and Iudah dwell in tents; my lord Ioab and my lord's servants stand in the open fields; should I therefore enter my house to eat and drink and lie with my wife? For your life and for the life of your soul, I will not do this thing." 12 Then Dauid said to Vriah, "Stay still today, and tomorrow I will send you away." So Vriah stayed in Jerusalem that day and the next day. 13 Then Dauid called him, and he ate and drank before him, and made him drunk; then he went out to lie down on his bed with the servants of his Lord, but he did not go down to his house. 14 The next day Dauid wrote a letter to Joab and sent it by the hand of Vriah. 15 In the letter he wrote, "Put Vriah in the forefront of the strength of the battle and turn away from him, that he may be smitten and die." 16 When Joab besieged the city, he assigned Vriah a place where he knew there were strong men. 17 The men of the city went out and

fought with Joab; and the people of Dauid's servants fell, and Vriah the Hittite also died. 18 Then Joab sent word to Dauid everything concerning the war, 19 and he instructed the messenger to say, "When you have undertaken to report to the king all the things of the war, 20 and if the king became angry and said to you, "Why did you approach the city to fight? Did you not know that they would come against you from the walls? 21 Who struck Abimelech the son of Je- rubesheth? Did not a woman throw a piece of milestone at him from the wall, and he died in Thebes? Why did you not go to the wall? Then say, 'Your servant Vriah, the Hittite, is also dead.'" 22 Then the messenger went and came and reported to Dauid all that Joab had sent him. 23 The messenger said to Dauid, "Cer- tainly the men came against you and went out against you in the camp, but we pursued them to the entrance of the gate. 24 But the marksmen fired from the walls at your ser- vants, and some of the king's servants died; and your servant Vriah the Hittite also died." 25 Then Dauid said to the messenger, "You shall thus say to Joab, 'Do not be troubled by this, for the sword kills one as well as another; make your battle against the city stronger and destroy it, and encourage it.'" 26 When Vriah's wife heard that her husband Vriah was dead, she mourned for her husband. 27 So when the mourning was over, Dauid sent for her into his house; she became his wife and bore him a son; but the thing that Dauid had done dis- pleased the LORD.

CHAPTER 12

1 Then the LORD sent Nathan to Dauid, who came to him and said, "There were two men in a city, one rich and the other poor. 2 The rich man had a great many cattle and oxen: 3 but the poor man had none at all, except a little sheep which he had bought and fed; she grew up with him and his children, ate his own morsels and drank his own cup, slept in his lap and was like a daughter to him. 4 Now there came a stranger to the rich man, who refused to take of his own cattle and oxen to clothe them for the stranger who had come to him, but took the poor man's cattle and clothed them for the man who had come to him. 5 Then Dauid was exceedingly angry with the man and said to Nathan, "As it pleases the LORD, the man who has done this thing will surely die, 6 And he will return to the sheep four fools, because he did this thing and had no compassion on it." 7 Then Nathan said to Dauid, "You are the man." Thus says the LORD, God of Israel, "I appointed you king of Israel and delivered you out of the hand of Saul, 8 I gave thee the house of thy lords, and the wives of thy lords in thy bosom; I gave thee the house of Israel and of Judah, and would have given thee other things (if it had been too little). 9 Why have you despised the command of the LORD to do good before him? You killed Vriah the Hittite with the sword, you took his wife as your wife, and you killed her with the sword of the sons of Ammon. 10 Therefore the sword shall never depart from your house, be- cause you have despised me and taken as your wife the wife of Vriah the Hittite." 11 Thus says the LORD, "Behold, I will rage against you from your house, and will take your wives un- der your eyes and give them to your neighbor, and he shall lie with your wives under the eyes of this sun. 12 For you have done it in secret, but I will do this thing before all Israel and be- fore the sun." 13 Then Dauid said to Nathan, "I have sinned against the LORD." And Nathan said to Dauid, "The Lord has blotted out even your sin; you shall not die." 14 However, be- cause by this act you have caused

the enemies of the LORD to blaspheme, the son who will be born to you will surely die." 15 Nathan went away to his house, and the LORD caressed the son whom Vriah's wife had borne to Dauid, and he was sick. 16 So Dauid prayed to God for the child, fasted, went into the house and lay down all night on the earth. 17 Then the elders of his house rose up to go to him and get him out of bed, but he would not and did not eat with them. 18 So on the seventh day the child died; and Dauid's servants feared to tell him that the child was dead, for they said, "Well, when the child was still alive, we spoke to him, and he would not listen to our speech; how then could we say to him, The child is dead, to convince him again? 19 But when Dauid saw that his servants were murmur- ing, Dauid saw that the child was dead; there- fore Dauid said to his servants, "Is the child dead?" And they answered, "He is dead." 20 Then Dauid got up from the ground, washed himself, anoinjected himself, changed his clothes, and went into the house of the LORD and worshiped; then he went back to his house, commanded that bread be put before him, and he ate. 21 Then his servants said to him, "What is this that you have done? You fasted and wept for the child while he was still alive, but when the child was dead, you got up and ate." 22 He said, "While the child was still alive, I fasted and wept, for I said, 'Who can say whether God will have mercy on me, that the child may live?' 23 But now that he is dead, why should I fast? Could I perhaps still bring him to life? I will go to him, but he will not return to me." 24 Dauid comforted Bath-she- ba his wife, went in to her, lay with her, and she bore a son, whom she named Solomon; and the LORD received him. 25 Because the LORD had sent through Nathan the prophet, he called him Jedidiah, because the LORD had acclaimed him. 26 Then Joab fought against Rabbah, of the sons of Ammon, and took the city of the kingdom. 27 Joab sent messengers to Dauid, saying, "I fought against Rabbah and took the city of the waters. 28 Now there- fore gather the rest of the people and besiege the city, that you may take it, lest the victory be attributed to me." 29 Then Dauid gathered all the people together, went against Rabbah, besieged it, and conquered it. 30 And he took off from his head the king's crown (which weighed a talent of gold with precious stones) and placed it on Dauid's head; and he carried away the spoil of the city in great quantities. 31 Then he carried away the people there, and put them under saws, yron plows, and yron axes, and cast them into the river Kylne; and so he did with all the cities of the sons of Am- mon. Then Dauid and all the people returned to Jerusalem.

CHAPTER 13

1 After this it came to pass that Absalom the son of Dauid had a more beautiful sister, whose name was Tamar, and mnon the son of Dauid had teased her. 2 Amnon felt so irritat- ed that he became sick over his sister Tamar, because she was a virgin and it seemed hard for Amnon to do anything to her. 3 But Am- non had a friend named Ionadab, the son of Scimea Dauidi's brother; and Ionadab was a very shrewd man. 4 These said to him, "Why are you the king's son and so lazy from day to day? Won't you tell me?" Amnon answered him, "I love Tamar, my sister of Absalom." 5 Ionadab said to him, "Lie down on your bed and get into bed; and when your father comes to see you, say to him, 'Please have my sister Tamar come and give me some food, and see that she gives me food to my face, so that I may see it and eat it from her hands.' 6 And Amnon

lay down and went into sickness; and when the king came to see him, Amnon said to the king, "Please let Tamar my sister come, and make me a pair of cakes before my eyes, that I may receive food from her hand." 7 Then Dauid sent word to Tamar, "Go now to your brother Amnons' house and give him food." 8 So Tamar went to her brother Amnons' house and lay down; she took flour, kneaded it, and made cakes before his eyes and baked them. 9 She took a frying pan and prepared them be- fore him, but he would not eat. Then Amnon said, "Make every man turn away from me"; so every man turned away from him. 10 Then Amnon said to Tamar, "Bring the food into the room, that I may eat from your hands." Tam- ar took the sweets she had made and brought them into the room to Amnon her brother. 11 When she had set them before him to eat them, he took them and said to her, "Come and rest with me, my sister." 12 But she an- swered him, "No, my brother, do not force me, for such a thing must not be done in Israel; do not commit this folly." 13 And I, where shall I make my shame go? And thou shalt be as one of the foolish in Israel; now therefore, I pray thee, speak of it to the king, for he will not deny me to thee." 14 But he would not listen to her speech; indeed, being stronger than she, he constrained her and lay down with her. 15 Then Amnon hated her exceedingly, so that the hatred with which he hated her was great- er than the joy with which he had hated her; and Amnon said to her, "Vp, go away." 16 She answered him, "There is no reason; this will (to depart from me) is greater than the other which thou hast done to me; but he would not listen to her." 17 but he called his servant who attended him and said, "Immediately remove this woman from me and block the house af- ter her." 18 (And she had a robe of ten colors on her; for the king's daughters, who were vir- gins, were clothed in such garments.) 19 And Tamar smeared her head with ashes, and tore off the robe of a different color that she had on her, and put her hand on her head, and went away weeping. 20 Then Absalom her brother said to her, "Is Amnon your brother with you? Be quiet, my sister; he is your brother; do not let this thing trouble your heart." So Tamar remained desolate in the house of her brother Absalom. 21 But when King Dauid heard all these things, he became very angry. 22 Absa- lom said to his brother Amnon neither good nor bad, for Absalom hated Amnon, because he had forced his sister Tamar. 23 When two years had passed, Absalom had shepherds in Baal-Hazor, which is near Ephraim, and Ab- salom called all the king's sons. 24 And Absa- lom went to the king and said, "Behold, thy servant hath shepherds: I pray thee, let the king with his servants go with thy servant." 25 But the king answered Absalom, "No, my son, I pray thee, let us not all go, lest we be accused by thee." But Absalom was angry with him; nevertheless he would not leave, but thanked him. 26 Then Absalom said, "But, please, won't my brother Amnon go with us? The king answered him, "Why should he go with you?" 27 But Absalom went along with him and sent Amnon with him and all the king's sons. 28 Now Absalom had command- ed his servants to say, "When Amnon's heart is merry with wine and I say to you, 'Strike Amnon, kill him,' do not fear, for have I not commanded you? Therefore be bold and play with men." 29 And Absalom's servants did to Amnon what Absalom had commanded; and all the king's sons arose, and each one loaded him on his mule, and they fled. 30 While they were on their way, testimonies came to Dauid saying, "Assalom has killed all the king's sons, and there is not a single one left." 31 Then the king arose, tore his garments and lay down on the ground, while all his servants stood with their garments torn. 32 Ionadab the son of Shimeah, brother of Dauids, answered, "My lord do not believe that they killed all the king's young sons, for only Amnon died, for Absalom had reported it, since he had forced his sister Tamar. 33 Let not my lord the king take it so seriously that he thinks that all the king's sons are dead, for only Amnon is dead." 34 Then Absalom fled; and the young man who was keeping watch lifted up his eyes, and looked, and behold, behind him came many people from the side of the hill. 35 And Ionad- ab said to the king, "Here are the sons of the king: as thy servant hath said, so it is." 36 And as soon as he had left the word, behold, the king's sons came, and lifted up their voices, and wept; and the king also and all his ser- vants wept with great sorrow. 37 But Absalom fled and went to Talmai the son of Ammihur, king of Geshur; and Dauid wept daily for his son. 38 Then Absalom fled and went to Geshur and stayed there three years. 39 And King Dauid wished to go to Absalom, because he had become quiet about Amnon, seeing that he was dead.

CHAPTER 14

1 Then Joab the son of Zeruiah saw that the king's heart was set on Absalom, 2 And Joab sent unto Tekoa, and brought thence a thin woman, and said unto her, I pray thee, mourn, and put on mourning clothes, and adorn thyself not with oil, but be like a wom- an that mourned long for the dead. 3 Then come to the king and speak to him in this way (for Joab had taught her what she should say). 4 Then the woman of Tekoah spoke to the king, prostrated herself with her face to the ground, obeyed, and said, "Help me, O king." 5 Then the king said to her, "What is troubling you?" And she answered, "I am a widow, and my husband is dead." 6 Your hand had two sons, and the two of them had come together in the field (and there was no one to divide them), so the one struck the other and killed him. 7 And behold, all the family rose up against your hand, and they say, "Kill the one who struck his brother, to kill him for the soul of the brother whom he killed, to destroy the heir also; so they will put out my spark that is left, and they will leave my husband neither name nor posterity on earth." 8 The king said to the woman, "Go to your house, and I will make you pay." 9 Then the woman of Tekoah said to the king, "My lord, O king, let this guilt fall on me and on the house of my fathers, and let the king and his throne be without gold." 10 The king said, "Bring me the one who speaks against you, and he will not touch you again." 11 Then she said, "I pray thee, let the king remember the LORD thy God, whom thou wilt not many blood-riders destroy, lest he kill my son." And he answered, "As it pleases the Lord, not one head of your son shall fall on the earth." 12 Then the wom- an said, "Please let your hand speak a word to my lord the king." And he said, "Say it." 13 Then the woman said, "Why did you think such a thing against God's people? Or why does the king, as one who is happy, say this thing lest his bandits return? 14 For we have to dye, and we are like water poured out on the ground, which cannot be gathered up again; and God spares no one, but works not to drive out from him the one who has been driven out. 15 Now that I have come to speak of this thing to my lord the king, the cause is that the people have put me to trouble; there- fore your hand has said, "Now I will speak to the king"; it may be that the king will carry out the request of your hand. 16 For the king will listen, to deliver his hand from the hand of man who wants to destroy me and also my son from the inheritance of God. 17 Therefore your

maidservant said, "The word of my lord the king shall now be comfortable, for my lord the king is like an angel of God in hearing good and evil; therefore the Lord your God be with you." 18 Then the king answered and said to the woman, "Please do not hide from me what I will ask you." And the woman said, "Let my lord the king speak." 19 And the king said, "Is not the hand of Joab with you in all this?" Then the woman answered and said, "As your soul wills, my lord the king, I will turn neither to the right nor to the left from what my lord the king has said; for already your servant Ioab has commanded me, and he has put all these words in the mouth of your hand. 20 Thy servant Ioab did so that I might change the manner of my speech; but my lord is wise as an angel of God, who understands all the things of the earth. 21 And the king said to Joab, "Behold, now I have done this; go there- fore and bring young Absalom again." 22 And Joab fell on his face to the ground and pros- trated himself and thanked the king. Then Joab said, "Today your servant knows that I have found favor in your eyes, my lord the king, for the king has granted his servant's request." 23 Then Joab arose and went to Ge- shur and led Absalom to Jerusalem. 24 The king said, "Let him go to his house and not see my face." So Absalom turned toward his house and did not see the king's face. 25 Now in all Israel there was no one so prayed for his beauty as Absalom: from the sole of his foot to the top of his head there was no blemish in him. 26 And when he had his head surveyed (for he did it every year, because it was too heavy for him, and so he did it), he estimated the weight of his head at two hundred shek- els per king's weight. 27 Absalom had three sons and a daughter named Tamar, who was a beautiful woman to behold. 28 Absalom stayed in Jerusalem for two years and did not see the king's face. 29 Therefore Absalom sent for Joab to send him to the king, but the king would not come to him; and when he sent him again, he did not come. 30 Therefore he said to his servants, "Behold, Joab has a field near my house, and he has barley there; go and set fire to it"; and Absalom's servants set fire to the field. 31 Then Joab arose, and came to Absalom to his house, and said to him, "Why have your servants set fire to my field?" 32 Ab- salom answered Joab, "Behold, I have sent for you, saying, 'Come here and I will send you to the king and say, "Why do I come to Geshur? It would have been better for me to stay there still; now, therefore, let me see the king's face, and if there is any fault in me, let him kill me. 33 Then Joab went to the king and told him; then he called Assalom, who came to the king and prostrated himself on the ground with his face before the king, and the king kissed Assalom.

CHAPTER 15

1 After this, Absalom prepared chariots and horses and fifty men to run before him. 2 And Absalom rose early and stood hard at the entrance of the gate; and every man that had any issue and came to the king to be judged, Absalom called him and said, "What city are you from?" And he answered, "Your servant is from one of the tribes of Israel." 3 Then Ab- salom said to him, "See, your arguments are good and just, but there is no man appointed by the king to hear you." 4 Absalom said again, "Oh, if I were appointed judge in the land, so that every man who has some matter to ar- gue would come to me and I would do him justice." 5 And when anyone approached him and did obedience to him, he stretched out his hand, and took him, and kissed him. 6 So did Absalom with all Israel who came before the king to be

judged; so Absalom stunned the hearts of the men of Israel. 7 After forty years, Absalom said to the king, "Please let me go to Hebron to make the vow I made to the LORD. 8 For your servant made a vow when I stayed in Geshur in Aram, saying, If the LORD will lead me back to Jerusalem, I will serve the LORD." 9 The king said to him, "Go in peace." So he arose and went to Hebron. 10 Then Ab- salom sent spies to all the tribes of Israel, say- ing, "When you hear the sound of the trum- pet, say, 'Absalom reigns in Hebron.'" 11 With Absalom departed from Jerusalem two hun- dred men who had been called; they went in their simplicity, knowing nothing. 12 More- over Absalom sent for Ahithophel, the Gilon- ite counselor of Dauids, from his city of Giloh, while he offered sacrifices; and the treachery was great, for the people still increased with Absalom. 13 Then a messenger came to Dauid and said, "The hearts of the men of Israel have turned to Absalom." 14 Then Dauid said to all his servants who were with him in Jerusalem, "Go and flee, for we will not be able to escape Absalom; make haste to depart, lest he come suddenly and take the city, bring it down, and strike the city with the blade of the sword." 15 The king's servants said to him, "Behold, your servants are ready to do whatever my lord the king wills to do." 16 So the king departed and all his household behind him, and the king left ten concubines to guard the house. 17 The king departed with all the people in his reti- nue and stopped at a distant place. 18 All his servants followed him, and all the Cherethites and all the Pelethites and all the Gittites, and six men who followed him from Gath, went before the king. 19 Then the king said to Ittai the Gittite, "Why do you also engage yourself with them? Return to be with the king, for you are a stranger; therefore return to your place. 20 You arrived yesterday, and I should make you wander today and go with vs.? I will go where I can; therefore go back and accom- pany your brothers; mercy and truth be with you." 21 Ittai answered the king and said, "As the LORD wills, and as my lord the king wills, wherever my lord the king is, whether in life or in death, there your servant will surely be." 22 Then Dauid said to Ittai, "Come and go forth." Ittai the Gittite went, with all his men and all the children who were with him. 23 And all the county cried with a loud voice, and all the people went forth, but the king passed over the brook Kidron; and all the people went toward the way of the wilderness. 24 And be- hold, there was Zadok also, and with him all the Leuites, who carried the ark of the com- mander of God; and they deposited the ark of God, and Abiathar departed until the people were out of the city. 25 Then the king said to Zadok, "Bring the ark of God into the city again; if I find a good result in the eyes of the LORD, he will bring me here again and show me both the ark and the tabernacle. 26 But if he will say, "I have no desire for you, here I am; let him do to me what seems good in his eyes." 27 Again the king said to Zadok the priest, "Are not you a seer? Return in peace to the city, and with you your two sons, Ahimaaz your son, and Ionathan the son of Abiathar. 28 Be- hold, I will tarry in the fields of the wilderness until some word is reported to me from you." 29 Zadok and Abiathar again brought the ark of God to Jerusalem and stayed there. 30 And Dauid went to the mount of olives, and wept, and had his head girded, and went barefoot; and all those who were with him had their heads girded, and as they went to the mount they wept. 31 Then one spoke to Dauid, say- ing, "Ahithophel is one of those who conspired with Absalom"; and Dauid said, "O LORD, please turn Ahithophel's counsel into folly." 32 Then Dauid came to the top of the mountain where he worshipped God; and behold, Hushai the archbishop came to him with his cloak tormented and with earth on his head. 33 To whom Dauid said, "If you come with me, you will be a burden to me. But if you return to the city and say to Absalom, 'I will be your servant, O king, as I was formerly the servant of your fathers, so I will now be your servant,' then you can thwart the advice of Ahithophel. 35 Have you not Zadok and Abi- athar, the priests, with you? Therefore what you shall hear from the king's house, you shall report to Zadok and Abiathar, the priests. 36 Behold, there are with them their two sons, Ahimaaz the son of Zadok, and Ionathan the son of Abiathar; from them also you shall let me know all that you can know." 37 So Hushai the friend of Dauids went into the city; and Absalom entered Jerusalem.

CHAPTER 16

1 When Dauid was a little beyond the top of the hill, behold, Ziba, servant of Mephi- bosheth, came to him with a pair of saddled donkeys and with two hundred buns of bread on them, a hundred bunches of raisins, a hundred dried figs and a bottle of wine. 2 The king said to Ziba, "What do you mean by these things?" Ziba answered, "These are donkeys on which the king may ride, bread and dried figs for the young men, and wine for the weak to drink in the wilderness." 3 The king said, "But where is the son of your masters?" Then Ziba answered the king, "Behold, he remains in Jerusalem, for he says, 'Today the house of Israel will restore to me the kingdom of my father.'" 4 Then the king said to Ziba, "Behold, all those who worshiped Mephibosheth are yours." And Ziba said, "Please let me find fa- vor before you, my lord, O king." :5 And when King Dauid came to Bahurim, behold, there came out of it a man of the family of the house of Saul, named Shimei the son of Gera; and he went out and cursed. 6 And he cast stones at Dauid and at all the servants of King Dauid; all the people and all the men of war were on his right hand and on his left. 7 When Shimei cursed, he said, "Come out, come out, you murderer and wicked man." 8 The LORD hath brought upon thee all the blood of the house of Saul, in whose stead thou hast reigned, and the LORD hath delivered thy kingdom into the hand of Absalom thy son; and, be- hold, thou hast been taken in thy wickedness, because thou art a murderer." 9 Then Abishai the son of Zeruiah said to the king, "Why does this dead dog curse my lord the king? Let me go, please, and take away his head." 10 But the king said, "What shall I do with you, sons of Zeruiah? For he curses because the LORD commanded him to curse Dauid, who dares to say, "Why did you do it?" 11 Dauid said to Abishai and all his servants, "Behold, my son, coming out of my bowels, seeks my life; how much more could this son of Iemini do it? Permit him to curse, for the LORD has com- manded him." 12 It may be that the LORD will look on my affliction and do me good for his curse today." 13 As Dauid and his men went on their way, Scimei went sideways to the mountain, and as he went, he cursed and threw stones at him and threw dust. 14 Then the king and all the people who were with him grew weary and took refreshment there. 15 Then Absalom and all the people, the men of Israel, came to Jerusalem and Ahithophel with him. 16 When Hushai, the archbish- op friend of Dauids, had come to Absalom, Hushai said to Absalom, "God is king, God is king." 17 Then Absalom said to Hushai, "Is this your kindness to your friend? Why did you not go with your friend? 18 Hushai answered Absalom, "No, but whomever the LORD, this people and all the men of Israel choose, I

will be his and dwell with him." 19 Moreover, to whom shall I serve? Not his son? As I served before your father, so will I serve before you." 20 Then Absalom said to Ahithophel, "Advise me what we should do." 21 Ahithophel said to Absalom, "Go to your father's concubines, whom he has left to guard the house; and when all Israel knows that you are hated by your father, the hands of all who are with you will be strong." 22 Then they pitched Absalom a tent on the top of the house, and Absalom went in to the concubines of his fathers, be- fore the eyes of all Israel. 23 And the counsels of Ahithophel, which he gave in those days, were as if one asked counsel of the oracle of God; so were all the counsels of Ahithophel, both with Dauid and with Absalom.

CHAPTER 17

1 Moreover Ahithophel said to Absalom, "Let me choose two thousand men, and I will go after Dauid this night, 2 and I will join him, for he is weary and his hand is weary; so I will fear him, and all the people who are with him will flee, and I will strike the king alone, 3 and I will lead all the people back to you, and when they have all returned (the man you seek has been killed) all the people will be at peace." 4 This pleased Absalom and all the elders of Israel greatly. 5 Then Absalom said, "Call also Hushai the Archite and hear also what he says." 6 When Hushai came to Absalom, Ab- salom spoke to him, saying, "Ahithophel has spoken thus; shall we or shall we not do as he has said?" 7 Then Hushai answered Absalom, "The advice that Ahithophel has given is not good at this time." 8 For, said Hushai, thou knowest thy father and his men, that they are strong men, and their souls are troubled, like a mother robbed of her young ones in the field; besides, thy father is a valiant warrior, and he will not lodge with the people. 9 Be- hold, he hid himself in some place or in some cave; and though some of them were driven out at first, the people will hear and say, "The people who follow Absalom are driven out." 10 Then even those who are valiant and have the heart of a lion will faint; for all Israel knows that your father is valiant, and those who are with him are stout men. 11 Therefore my counsel is that all Israel should gather to you, from Dan even to Beer-sheba, as the sand of the sea in nombre, and that you should go and fight in your own person. 12 So we will join him in a place where we will find him, and we will strike him as the dew falls on the ground; and of all the men who are with him, we will not leave a single one. 13 Moreover, if he is brought to a city, all the men of Isra- el shall bring ropes to that city, and we shall drag it into the river, until not even a small stone is found there." 14 Then Absalom and all the men of Israel said, "The counsel of Hushai the archbishop is better than the counsel of Ahithophel; for the LORD had determined to destroy the good counsel of Ahithophel, that the LORD might come down upon Absa- lom." 15 Then Hushai said to Zadok and Abia- thar, the priests, "In this way and in that way Ahithophel and the elders of Israel advised Absalom, and I advised so-and-so." 16 Now, therefore, depart quickly and speak to Dauid, saying, "Do not linger in the wilderness this night, but go away, lest the king and all the people who are with him be smitten." 17 Now Ionathan and Ahimaaz stood near En-rogel (so that they could not be seen entering the city); a servant went to inform them, and they went to speak with King Dauid. 18 However, a young man informed them and reported it to Absalom. So they both set out in haste and came to a house in Bahurim that had a well

in its courtyard, into which they went down. 19 And his wife took and scattered a pouring out of the mouth of the well and scattered some horn of earth there, that nothing might be known. 20 When Absalom's servants came into the house to his wife, they said, "Where are Ahimaaz and Ionathan?" And the wom- an answered them, "They have gone away by the stream of water." And when they had searched for them and had not found them, they returned to Jerusalem. 21 As they were leaving, the other came out of the well and went and spoke to King Dauid, saying to him, "Go and get you water at once, for Ahitho- phel has made such a counsel against you." 22 Then Dauid rose up, together with all the people who were with him, and they set out for Iorden until the day dawned, so that there was not one of them missing who had not come to Iorden. 23 Now when Ahithophel saw that his advice had not been followed, he was saddened, got up and went back to his house, put his house in order, hung himself, and died, and was buried in the graves of his fathers. 24 Then Dauid came to Mahanaim. Assalom passed over Iorden, he and all the men of Israel with him. 25 Assalom appointed Amasa as captain of the army in place of Joab; Amasa was a man son of Ithra, an Israelite, who had gone to Abigail, daughter of Nahash, sister of Zeruiah, mother of Joab. 26 So Israel and Absalom encamped in the land of Gilead. 27 And when Dauid was come to Mahanaim, Shobi the son of Nahash, from Rabbah, of the sons of Ammon, Machir the son of Ammiel, from Lo-debar, and Barzelai the Gileadite, from Rogel, brought beds and couches. 28 They brought beds, basins, earthen vessels, wheat, barley, flour, dogwood, beanes, lentils and dogwood. 29 They also brought honey, butter, cattle and sheep's cheese for Dauid and the people who were with him to eat, for they said, "The people are hungry, tired and thirsty in the wilderness."

CHAPTER 18

1 Then Dauid put together the people who were with him and appointed them captains of thousands and captains of hundreds. 2 Dauid sent the third part of the people un- der the hand of Joab, the third part under the hand of Abishai, the brother of Joab, the son of Zeruiah, and the other third part under the hand of Ittai, the Gittite. The king said to the people, "I will also go with you." 3 But the peo- ple answered, "You will not go away, for if we flee, they will not look at us or pass through vs, even though half of vs was killed; but you are now worth ten thousand vs; so now it is better for you to rescue vs outside the city." 4 Then the king said to them, "I will do what seems best to you." So the king stood by the side of the gate, and all the people came out in hundreds and thousands. 5 And the king commanded Joab, Abishai, and Ittai, "Softly imprison young Absalom for my sake." And all the people heard that the king was giving instructions to the captains concerning Absa- lom. 6 So the people went out into the fields to meet Israel, and the battle took place in the wood of Ephraim: 7 where the people of Israel were slaughtered before the servants of Dauid; there was a great slaughter that day, about twenty thousand people. 8 The battle was dispersed throughout the whole county, and that day the wood killed many more peo- ple than the sword had killed. 9 Now Absalom met Dauid's servants, and Absalom rode on a mule; and the mule ended up under a very thick board, and his head caught in the board, and he was caught between heaven and earth; and the mule that was under him went away. 10 And one of those who had heard it said to Joab,

"Behold, I see Absalom hanged on a pole." 11 Then Joab said to the man who had spoken to him, "Did you see? Why did you not drop him to the ground, and I would have given you ten shekels of silver and a girdle? 12 Then the man said to Joab, "Even if I received in my hand a thousand shekels of silver, I would not lay hands on the king's son, for the king has instructed you, Abishai and Ittai to say, 'Beware, if you do not touch young Absa- lom. 13 If I had done so, I would have risked my life, for nothing can be hidden from the king; you yourself would have been against me." 14 Then Joab said, "I will not quarrel with you." And he took three darts in his hand and thrust them into the midst of Absalom, while he was still in the midst of the ship. 15 Ten servants wearing Joab's armor came up, struck Absalom, and killed him. 16 Then Joab blew the trumpet, and the people went back after Israel, for Joab held back the people. 17 Then they took Absalom, and cast him into a great pit in the wood, and laid a great heap of stones upon him; and all Israel fled every one to his tent. 18 In his lifetime Absalom had taken and caused to be erected a pillar that stood in the valley of the kings, for he said, "I have no son to keep my name in remem- brance." And he called the pillar by his name, and today it is called "Assalom's place." 19 Then Ahimaaz the son of Zadok said, "Please let me run and bring the king the news that the LORD has delivered him out of the hand of his enemies." 20 Joab said to him, "You will not be the messenger today, but you will bring the news another time, but you will not bring it today, because the king's son is dead." 21 Then Joab said to Cushi, "Go, tell the king what you have seen." Cushi bowed to Joab and ran. 22 Then Ahimaaz the son of Zadok said again to Ioab, "What happens, please, if I also run af- ter Cushi?" And Joab answered, "Why do you want to run, my son, since you have no news to bring? 23 What if I run? Then Joab said to him, "Run." Then Ahimaaz ran by the way of the plain and came out of Cushi. 24 Dauid stood between the two gates. The watchman went to the top of the gate on the wall, looked up and saw that a man was running alone. 25 The watchman shouted and told the king about it. The king said, "If he is alone, bring news." And he came quickly and approached. 26 The watchman saw another man running; the watchman called to the gatekeeper and said, "Behold, another man is running alone." And the king said, "He also brings news." 27 The watchman said, "I think the running of the farthest man is like that of Ahimaaz the son of Zadok." Then the king said, "He is a good man and brings good news." 28 Ahi- maaz called and said to the king, "Peace be with you"; then he fell to the ground with his face before the king and said, "Blessed be the LORD your God, who has shut up the men who raise their hands against the king my lord." 29 The king said, "Is young Absalom safe?" Ahimaaz answered, "When Joab sent the king's servant and I your servant, I saw a great tumult, but I did not know what." 30 The king said to him, "Move aside and stay here." So he moved and stood still. 31 And Cushi came, and Cushi said, "News, my lord the king, for the LORD has delivered you this day from the hand of all those who rose up against you." 32 Then the king said to Cushi, "Is young Absalom safe?" Cushi answered, "The enemies of the king my lord and all those who rise up against you to do you harm are like that young man." 33 And the king was moved, and went into the chamber outside the door, and wept; and as he went, he said thus, "O my son Ab- salom, my son, my son Absalom; would to God that I die for you, O Absalom, my son, my son."

1 And it was said to Joab, "Behold, the king weeps and mourns for Absalom." 2 Therefore the victory of that day became mourning for all the people, for the people heard that day, "The king mourns for his son." 3 On that day the people went into the city secretly, as con- fused people hide when they flee in battle. 4 Then the king hid his face and cried with a loud voice, "My son, Absalom, my son." 5 Then Joab entered the king's house and said to him, "Today you have shamed the face of all your servants, who today saved your life, the lives of your sons, your daughters, the lives of your wives and the lives of your concubines, 6 in that thou lovest thine enemies, and hat- est thy friends: for thou hast declared today that thou regardest neither thy princes nor thy servants: therefore I perceive today that if Absalom had died, and we all had died today, then it would have pleased thee. 7 Now there- fore go, go out and speak to your servants, for I swear by the LORD that if you do not go out, there will not be a single man left with you this night; and this will be worse for you than all the sufferings that have fallen upon you from your youth until this day." 8 Then the king arose and sat down at the gate; then they informed all the people, saying, "Behold, the king sits at the gate"; and all the people came before the king, for Israel had fled each to his own tent. 9 Then all the people were in strife among all the tribes of Israel, saying, "The king has rescued Vs. from the hands of our enemies, he has delivered Vs. from the hands of the Philistines, and now he has fled from the land for Absalom." 10 Absalom, whom we had removed from Vs, has died in battle; why then are you so late in bringing the king back? 11 But King Dauid sent word to Zadok and Abiathar, the priests, "Speak to the el- ders of Iudah and say, 'Why are you delaying in bringing the king back to his home?" (for the voice of all Israel has come to the king, and to his home). 12 You are my brethren, you are my bones and my flesh; therefore why are you the last to bring the king back to his house? 13 Say also to Amasa, "Are not you my bones and my flesh? God do so with me and even more, if you will not be the captain of the army for me forever in the kingdom of Joab." 14 So he bent the hearts of all the men of Iu- dah, as of one man; therefore they sent word to the king, "Return with all your servants." 15 So the king returned and came to Iorden. And Iudah came to Ghilgal to meet the king and lead him out of Jorden. 16 And Shimei the son of Gera, the son of Jemini, who was from Bahurim, rushed and went down with the men of Iudah to meet king Dauid, 17 and with him a thousand men of Benjamin, Ziba, a servant of the house of Saul, and his fifty sons and twenty-five servants with him; and they went to Iorden before the king. 18 Then they boarded a boat to go to the king's house and to please him. Then Shimei the son of Gera fell down before the king, when he had come to Iorden, 19 and said to the king, "Let not my lord impute wickedness to me, nor remember what your servant did wickedly when my lord the king departed from Jerusa- lem, lest the king should take it to heart. 20 Because your servant knows that I have acted wickedly, behold, today I am the first of all the house of Ioseph to go down to meet my lord the king." 21 But Abishai the son of Tse- ruiah answered, "Will not Shimei die for this, because he has cursed the LORD?" 22 Then Dauid said, "What shall I do with you, sons of Tseruiah, that you may be aduersary toward me today? Will there be anyone who will die today in Israel? For do I not know that today I am the king of Israel?" 23 Therefore the king said to Shimei, "You shall not die," and the king swore by him. 24 Then Mephibosheth the son of

Saul went down to meet the king, and he did not wash his feet, nor tend his beard, nor wash his clothes from the time the king departed, until he returned in peace. 25 When he had come to Jerusalem and met the king, the king said to him, "Why did you not come with me, Mephibosheth?" 26 He answered, "My lord, the king, my servant has deceived me, because your servant said, 'I wish my axle were saddled to go with the king, for your servant is lame.' 27 He accused thy servant before my lord the king; but my lord the king is like an angel of God; therefore do thy pleasure. 28 For all the houses of my fathers were but dead men before my lord the king, yet thou hast set thy servant among those who ate at thy table; what right therefore have I to cry out again to the king? 29 The king said to him, "Why do you still speak of your matters? I said, 'You and Ziba rule the land.'" 30 Mephi- bosheth said to the king, "Yes, let him take everything, since the king, my lord, has gone home in peace." 31 Then Barzillai the Gileadite came down from Rogelim and went to Iorden with the king, to lead him out of Iorden. 32 Barzillai was a very old man, about forty-five years old, and he had asked the king to be fed while he lay in Mahanaim, for he was a man of great substance. 33 The king said to Barzillai, "Come with me and I will feed you in Jerusa- lem." 34 Barzillai said to the king, "How long shall I wait to go with the king to Jerusalem? 35 Am I fifty-five years old today and can I distinguish between good and evil? Does your servant have any taste in what I eat or what I drink? Can I any longer hear the voices of men and women singing? Why then should your servant still be a burden to the king my lord? 36 Will your servant go some distance from Iorden with the king, and why will the king reward me with such a reward? 37 I be- seech thee, let thy servant go back, that I may die in my city, and be buried in the grave of my father and my mother; but look on thy ser- vant Chimham, let him go with the king my lord, and do with him what will please thee." 38 The king answered, "Chimham will go with me, and I will do with him what will please you; and whatever you ask of me, I will do for you." 39 So all the people went to Iorden; and the king passed over; and the king kissed Bar- zillai, and blessed him, and he returned to his place. 40 Then the king went to Ghilgal, and Chimham went with him, and all the people of Iudah led the king, and also half the people of Israel. 41 And behold, all the men of Israel came to the king and said to him, "Why did our brothers, the men of Iudah, make you flee and lead the king and his house and all the men of Dauids with him out of Iorden?" 42 All the men of Iudah answered the men of Israel, "Because the king is our kinsman; and why are you now angry about this matter? Have we eaten of the king's expenses or taken some bribes?" 43 And the men of Israel an- swered the men of Iudah, and said, "We have ten parts in the king, and we have even more rights than you have over Dauid; why then have you despised vs, that our consent has not been obtained first in restoring our king?" And the words of the men of Iudah were fierc- er than those of the men of Israel.

CHAPTER 20

1 Then there came a wicked man (named Sheba the son of Bichri, a man of Iemini) who blew a trumpet and said, "We have no part in Dauid, nor do we have inheritance in the son of Ishai; let every man go to his tents, O Isra- el." 2 So all the men of Israel departed from Dauid, and followed Sheba the son of Bichri; but the men of Iudah clung to their king, from Iorden even to Jerusalem. 3 Then when Dauid came to his house in Jerusalem, the king took the ten women his concubines, whom he had left behind him to guard the house, and put them to war, and fed them, but he did not lie with them any more; but they remained shut up until the day of their death, living in widowhood. 4 Then the king said to Amasa, "Gather the men of Iudah within three days and be present." 5 Amasa went to gather Iu- dah, but he tarried longer than the time he had instructed. 6 Then Dauid said to Abishai, "Now Sheba the son of Bichri will do more harm than Absalom has done; therefore take your servants and follow him, lest he wall up the cities and flee." 7 And Ioab, and the Chere- thites, and the Pelethites, and all the mighty men, went after him; and they departed from Jerusalem to follow Sheba the son of Bichri. 8 And when they were at the great stone which is at Gibeon, Amasa went before them, and the robe of Joab which he had put on was gird- ed upon him, and a sword was girded upon it, which hung from his loins in its scabbard, and seemed to fall as he went. 9 And Joab said to Amasa, "Are you in health, my brother?" And Joab took Amasa by the beard with his right hand to kill him. 10 But Amasa did not mind the sword that Ioab had in his hand, for with it he struck him in the fifth rib and made his bowels fall to the ground, but he did not strike him a second time; so he died. Then Joab and Abishai his brother followed Sheba the son of Bichri. 11 One of Joab's men stood beside him and said to him, "Whoever is courting Joab and whoever is of Dauidi's side, go after Joab." 12 And Amasa wallowed in blood in the midst of the road; and when the man saw that all the people stood still, he took Amasa out of the road toward the camp and threw a cloth over him, for he saw that all who passed by him stood still. 13 When he was taken out of the way, everyone went after Joab to follow Sheba the son of Bichri. 14 And he went through all the tribes of Israel as far as Abel and Bethmah and all the places of Berim; and they gathered themselves together and went after him also. 15 And they came and besieged him at Abel, near Bethmaachah; and they cast a moun- tain against the city, and his people stood on the ramper, and all the people that were with Joab destroyed and brought down the walls. 16 Then a wise woman cried out from the city, "Hear, hear, I pray thee, say unto Joab, Come hither, that I may speak with thee." 17 When he came near her, the woman said, "Are you Joab?" And he answered, "Yes." And she said to him, "Listen to the words of your servant." And he answered, "I listen." 18 Then she said, "They have spoken in the past, saying, 'They should ask Abel,' and so they continued. 19 I am one of them, peaceable and faithful in Is- rael, and you are about to destroy a city and a mother in Israel; why do you want to destroy the inheritance of the LORD? 20 Joab an- swered, "God forbid, God forbid that I should destroy it." 21 The matter is not so, but a man of Ephraim's mouth (Sheba, son of Bichri, by name) has lifted up his hands against your king, and against Dauid. And the woman said to Joab, "Behold, his head shall be thrown to you over the wall." 22 Then the woman went to all the people with her wisdom, and they cut off the head of Sheba the son of Bichri, and cast it to Joab; and he blew the trumpet, and they withdrew from the city, every man to his tent; and Joab returned to Jerusalem to the king. 23 And Joab was above all the army of Israel, and Benaiah the son of Jehoiada above the Cherethites and Pelethites, 24 Adoram for the tribute and Ioshaphat the son of Ah- ilud for the registration, 25 Shea was scribe, Zadok and Abiathar priests, 26 and Ira, the Iairite, was also head of Dauid.

CHAPTER 21

1 There was a famine in the days of Dauid, for three years together; Dauid asked the LORD for counsel, and the LORD answered, "It is for Saul and his house of blood, because he has killed the Gibeonites." 2 Then the king called the Gabaonites and said to them. (Now the Gibeonites did not belong to the sons of Is- rael, but were a remnant of the Amorites, to whom you sons of Israel had sworn an oath; but Saul tried to kill them because of his zeal for the sons of Israel and Iudah.) 3 Dauid said to the Gabaonites, "What shall I do for you, and with what shall I make atonement that you may bless the inheritance of the LORD?" 4 And the Gibeonites answered him, "We will have neither silk nor gold of Saul nor of his house, and therefore you shall not kill any- one in Israel." And he said, "What you say, I will do for you." 5 Then they answered the king, "The man who consumed vs and imag- ined euill against vs, so that we are destroyed from remaining in any coast of Israel, 6 let Vs have ten men of his sons delivered, and we will hang them before the LORD in Gibeah of Saul, the chosen of the LORD." The king said, "I will give them." 7 But the king had compas- sion on Mephibosheth the son of Ionathan the son of Saul because of the otherness of the LORD between them, that is, between Dauid and Ionathan the son of Saul. 8 But the king took the two sons of Rizpah, daughter of Ajah, whom she had borne to Saul: Harmoni and Mephibosheth, and the five sons of Mi- chal, daughter of Saul, whom she had borne to Adriel, son of Barzillai the Meholathite. 9 And he delivered them into the hands of the Gibeonites, and they hanged them on the mountain before the LORD; so they all died together, and were slain in the time of the plague, in the first days and at the begin- ning of the plague. 10 Then Rizpah, Dauid's daughter, took a sackcloth and hung it for her from the ropes, from the beginning of the plague, until the water fell on them from above, and they did not allow the birds of the air to light in the daytime and the beasts of the field at night. 11 Dauid was told what Riz- pah, daughter of Ajah, Saul's concubine, had done. 12 Dauid went and fetched the bones of Saul and the bones of Ionathan, his son, from the citizens of Jabesh Gilead, who had collected them from the road of Beth-san, where the Philistines had hanged them, when the Philistines had killed Saul at Gilboa. 13 So he brought thence the bones of Saul and the bones of Ionathan, his son, and collected the bones of those who had been hanged. 14 And the bones of Saul and Ionathan, his son, were buried in the church of Benjamin, in Zela, in the tomb of Kish, his father; and when they had performed all that the king had com- manded, God was appeased with the land. 15 Then the Philistines made war against Isra- el; and Dauid came down, with his servants, and they fought against the Philistines, and Dauid fainted. 16 Then Ishi-Benob, who was of the sons of Harafa (the head of whose spear weighed three hundred shekels of grain), having put on a new sword, thought he had killed Dauid. 17 But Abishai the son of Zerui- ah came to his aid and struck the Philistine and killed him. Then Dauid's men swore to him, "You shall not go out with them again to fight, lest you extinguish the light of Israel." 18 After this fact there was a battle with the Philistines at Gob, and Sibbechai the Husha- thite killed Saph, who was one of the sons of Haraphah. 19 There was another battle with the Philistines at Gob, where Elhanah, son of Iaare-oregim, a Bethlehemite, killed Goli- ath, the Gittite, whose staff was like a spear. 20 Afterwards there was also a battle at Gath, where there was a man of great stature, who had on all his hands six fingers and on all his feet six fingers, four and twenty in number; he also was the son of Haraphah. 21 When he took Israel back, Ionathan the son of Shima, brother of Dauid, killed him. 22 These four were brought to Haraphah in Gath and died by the hand of Dauid and by the hand of his servants.

CHAPTER 22

1 Dauid said the words of this song to the LORD, when the LORD had delivered him from the hands of all his enemies and from the hands of Saul. 2 He said, "The LORD is my tower, my fortress and the one who has delivered me. 3 God is my strength, in him I will trust; my shield and the horn of my salva- tion, my tower and my refuge; my savior, you have preserved me from violence. 4 I will call upon the LORD, who is worthy to be prayed for; so I will be safe from my enemies. 5 For the pains of death have surrounded me, the floods of sin have made me miserable. 6 The sufferings of the grave have surrounded me, the snares of death have put me out of the way. 7 But in my tribulation I called on the LORD and cried out to my God, and he heard my voice from his temple, and my cry entered his ears. 8 Then the earth shook and trembled; the foundations of the heavens groaned and trembled, because he was angry. 9 Smoke came out of his nostrils and devouring fire from his mouth; the colas were kindled at that moment. 10 He also folded the heavens and descended, and darkness was under his feet. 11 Then he rode on Cherubim and flew, and was seen on the wings of the wind. 12 And he made around him a tabernacle of darkness, like the gathering waters and the clouds of the air. 13 In the brightness of his presence, streams of fire were kindled. 14 The LORD thundered from on high, and the greatest of his visitors gave his signal. 15 He also shot ar- rows and scattered them, that is, lightning, and destroyed them. 16 The channels of the sea also appeared, and the foundations of the world were shaken by the rebuke of the LORD and the blowing of his nostrils. 17 He sent from without and took me; He drew me out of many waters. 18 He delivered me from my strong enemies and from those who hated me, because they were too strong for me. 19 They prevented me in the day of my calamity, but the LORD was my refuge, 20 he brought me home to a wide place; he made me flee, because he betrayed me. 21 The LORD has rewarded me according to my righteousness; according to the purity of my hands he has re- warded me. 22 For I have followed the ways of the LORD and have not acted wickedly against my God. 23 For all his laws were before me, and his statutes: I did not depart from them. 24 I was also correct toward him, and he pre- served me from my wickedness. 25 Therefore the LORD has rewarded me according to my righteousness, according to my purity before his eyes. 26 With the holy you will realize that you are worthy of God; with the upright you will realize that you are righteous. 27 With the pure you will show yourself pure, and with the averse you will show yourself averse. 28 Thus you will save the poor people, but your eyes are turned to the high ones to humble them. 29 You are my light, O LORD, and the LORD enlightens my darkness. 30 For because of you I have broken through an army, and be- cause of my God I have climbed over a wall. 31 The way of God is corrupted; the word of the LORD is tried in the fire; he is a shield for all who trust in him. 32 Who is God be- sides the LORD, and who is mighty, says our God? 33 God is my strength in the fight, and he makes my way right. 34 He makes my feet like the feet of a doe and has placed me at my feet. 35 He teaches my hands to fight, so that a

weapon of bronze is broken with my arms. 36 You have also given me the shield of your salvation, and your great goodness has made me grow. 37 You widened my steps under me, and my heels did not slip. 38 I pursued my enemies and destroyed them, and I did not turn back until I consumed them. 39 Yea, I have consumed them and pierced them, and they shall not rise up, but shall fall under my feet. 40 For you have clothed me with strength to fight, and those who had risen up against me you have subdued them under me. 41 You gave me the necks of my enemies, that I might destroy those who hate me. 42 They looked around, but there was no one to greet them, and they turned to the LORD, but he did not answer them. 43 Then I reduced them like the dust of the earth; I flattened them like the clay of the road and scattered them. 44 You have also delivered me from the conten- tions of my people; you have made me a ruler of the nations; the people I did not know serve me. 45 The foreigners will be subject to me; as they listen, they will obey me. 46 The for- eigners will withdraw and be afraid in their private rooms. 47 Let the LORD be my Lord, and let my strength be blessed, and let God, the strength of my salvation be exalted. 48 It is God who gives me power to avenge myself and to subdue the peoples under me, 49 and saves me from my enemies; you have also raised me up from those who have risen up against me; you have delivered me from the cruel man. 50 Therefore I will praise you, O LORD, among the nations and sing in honor of your Name.") 51 He is the tower of salvation for his king, and he honors his anointed ones, that is, Dauid and his descendants forever.

CHAPTER 23

1 These are also the last words of Dauid, Dauid son of Ishai, the man who was put upon him, the Anointed One of the God of Jacob and the singer of Israel, 2 The Spirit of the LORD has spoken through me, and his word has been in my tongue. 3 The God of Is- rael spoke to me, and the power of Israel said, "You shall rule apart from men, you shall be righteous and rule in the fear of God." 4 As the morning light when the sun rises, the morn- ing, I say, without clouds, so shall my house be, and not as the earth is flooded with light. 5 For so shall not my house be with God, for he hath made with me an everlasting covenant, perfect in all points and sure; therefore all my health and all my desire is that he should not make it grow thus. 6 But the wicked shall all be as thorns that turn away, because they can- not be taken with hands. 7 But the man that toucheth them shall be defused with yron or with the rod of a spear; and they shall be burned with fire in the same place. 8 These are the names of the most powerful men Dauid had. The chief of the princes, Adinus of Ezni, was seated in the seat of wisdom and killed eight hundred at once. 9 After him was Elea- zar, son of Dodo, son of Ahohi, one of the three princes with Dauid, when they challenged the Philistines assembled to fight, while the men of Israel had departed. 10 And he arose and smote the Philistines until his hand grew weary, and his hand clasped to the sword; and the LORD gained a great victory that same day, and the people returned behind him only to spin. 11 After him was Shammah the son of Age, the Hararite, because the Philistines gathered to a place where there was a piece of field full of lentils, and the people fled from the Philistines. 12 But he stood in the middle of the field, defended it, and slew the Philis- tines; so the LORD gained a great victory. 13 Then three of the thirty captains went down and came to

Dauid at the most difficult time, toward the hollow of Adullam, while the army of the Philistines was encamping in the valley of Rephaim. 14 Dauid was then in an area of refuge, while the garrison of the Philistines was at Beth-Lem. 15 Dauid longed and said, "Oh, if someone would give me water from the well of Bethlehem, which is near the gate, to drink." 16 And the three great men broke into the army of the Philistines, and drew water from the well of Bethlehem that was by the gate, and took it, and brought it to Dauid, who would not drink of it, but used it as an of- fering to the LORD, 17 and said, "O LORD, let it be far from me that I should do this. Is not this the blood of men who have gone to prison for their lives? Therefore he would not drink it." These things did these three mighty men do. 18 Abishai, brother of Joab, son of Tserui- ah, was the leader of the three; he raised his spear against three hundred men and killed them. 19 For he was the most excellent of the three and was their leader, but he did not reach the first three. 20 And Benaiah the son of Jehoiada, the son of a valiant man, who had done many deeds and was of Kabzeel, slew two strong men of Moab; he also went down and slew a lion in the midst of a pit, during the time of snow. 21 Then he slew an Egyptian, a man of great stature, and the Egyptian had a spear in his hand; but he came to him with a staff, snatched the spear out of the Egyptian's hand, and slew him with his own spear. 22 These things did Benaiah the son of Jehoia- da, who had the name of one of the three valiant men. 23 He was honorable among the thirty, but he was not equal to the first three; and Dauid made him his counselor. 24 Asa- hel, the brother of Joab, was one of the thir- ty: Elhanan, the son of Dodo, of Beth-Lem: 25 Shammah the Harodite: Elika, one of the Harodites: 26 Helez the Paltite: Ira, son of Ik- kesh the Tekoite: 27 Abiezer the Anethothite: Mebunnai the Husathite: 28 Zalmon the Aho- hite: Maharai the Netophite: 29 Heleb the son of Baanah, a Netophite: Ittai the son of Ribai, of Gibeah, of the sons of Benjamin: 30 Bena- iah, the Pirathonite: Hiddai, of the riuer of Gaash: 31 Abi-albon, the Arbathite: Azmaueth the Barumite: 32 Elihaba the Shaalbonite, son of Iashen, Ionathan: 33 Shammah the Ha- rarite: Ahiam the son of Sharar the Hamrita: 34 Eliphelet, the son of Ahasbai, the son of Maachathi; Eliam, the son of Ahithophel, the Gilonite: 35 Hezrai, the Carmelite: Paarai the Arbite: 36 Igal, son of Nathan of Zobah: Bani the Gadite: 37 Zelek the Ammonite: Naharai the Becrothite, bearer of the armor of Ioab, son of Zeruiah: 38 Ira, the Ithrite: Gareb the Ithrite: 39 Uriiah the Hittite, in all thirty-six persons.

CHAPTER 24

1 The anger of the LORD was kindled again against Israel, and he moved Dauid against them, saying, "Go, make a count of Israel and of Iudah." 2 For the king said to Joab, the captain of the army who was with him, "Go quickly through all the tribes of Israel, from Dan even to Beer-sheba, and take a census of the people, that I may know the name of the people." 3 Joab said to the king, "The LORD your God increases the people by a hundred crowds, that the eyes of my lord the king may see them; but why does my lord the king de- sire this? 4 Although the king's word was fore- told against Joab and the captains of the army, Joab and the captains of the army went out from the king's presence to visit the people of Israel. 5 They passed through Iorden and en- camped at Aroer, on the right side of the city that is in the middle of the valley of Gad and toward Iazer.

6 Then they came to Gilead, to Tahtim-Hodshi, to Dan Iaan, and to Zidon, 7 And they came to the fortress of Tyre, and to all the cities of the Hiuites and Canaanites, and they went to the south of Judah, that is, to Beer-sheba. 8 After they had gone all over the land, they returned to Jerusalem at the end of nine months and twenty-five days. 9 And Joab delivered to the king the name and the sum of the people; in Israel there were eight hundred thousand strong men armed with swords, and the men of Judah were five hundred thou- sand. 10 Then the heart of Dauid smote him, having numbed the people; and Dauid said to the LORD, "I have sinned greatly in what I have done; therefore now, LORD, I pray thee, blot out the guilt of thy servant, for I have act- ed very foolishly." 11 When Dauid rose in the morning, the word of the LORD came to the prophet Gad, the seer of Dauid, and he said 12 Go and say to Dauid, "Thus says the LORD: I offer you three things; you choose which of them I will do to you." 13 Then Gad went to Dauid and showed it to him and said, "Do you want famine to come upon you for ten years in your country, or for you to flee for three months before your enemies who pursue you, or for there to be three days of pestilence in your country? Now inquire and see what an- swer I will give to him who sent me." 14 Dauid said to Gad, "I am in great distress; let me fall into the hands of the LORD (for his mercies are great) and do not let me fall into the hands of man." 15 So the LORD sent a pestilence upon Israel, from the morning until the ap- pointed time; and from the people, from Dan even to Beer- sheba, six hundred thousand men died. 16 And when the angel stretched out his hand upon Jerusalem to destroy it, the LORD repented of the evil, and said to the an- gel who was destroying the people, "It is suf- ficient, stop your hand." And the angel of the LORD was by the threshing floor of Araunah the Jebusite. 17 And Dauid spoke to the LORD (when he saw the angel destroying the people) and said, "Behold, I have sinned, yea, I have done evil; but these sheep, what have they done? Your hand, I pray you, be against me and against the house of my fathers." 18 On that same day Gad went to Dauid and said to him, "Go, erect an altar to the LORD in the threshing floor of Araunah, the Jebusite." 19 Dauid went, as Gad had said, as the LORD had commanded. 20 Araunah looked and saw the king and his servants coming toward him; Araunah went out and prostrated himself before the king with his face to the ground, 21 Araunah said, "Why has the king, my lord, come to his servant?" Then Dauid answered, "To pass by you the threshing floor and build an altar to the LORD, that the plague may cease from the people." 22 Then Araunah said to Dauid, "Let the king, my lord, take and of- fer what seems good in his eyes: behold, oxen for the burning, and the cares and the tools of the oxen for wood." 23 (All these things Araun- ah as king gave to the king; and Araunah said to the king, "The LORD thy God be gracious unto thee.") 24 Then the king said to Araunah, "Not so, but I will give it to you at a favorable price, and I will not offer to the LORD my God a burnt sacrifice of that which costs me noth- ing." Dauid bought the threshing floor and oxen for fifty shekels of silk. 25 And Dauid built there an altar to the LORD, and offered burnt offerings and peace offerings, and the LORD was appeased toward the land, and the plague ceased from Israel.

I KINGS

CHAPTER 1

1 Now when King Dauid was old and tried with age, they clothed him with clothes, but he received no help. 2 Therefore his servants said to him, "Let a young virgin be sought for my lord, your king, to stand before the king and care for him; and let her lie in your bo- som, that my lord, the king, may have some health." 3 So they searched all the coasts of Israel for a young and beautiful maiden, and found a certain Abishag, a Scunamite, and brought her to the king. 4 The maiden was very beautiful, and she courted the king and attended him, but the king did not know her. 5 Then Adonijah the son of Haggith exalted himself, saying, "I will be king." And he gave him chariots and horsemen and fifty men to run before him. 6 His father did not want to displease him from his childhood to say, "Why did you do this? He was a very good man, and his mother bore him after Absalom. 7 He consulted with Joab the son of Zeruiah and with Abiathar the priest, and they helped Adonijah. 8 But Zadok the priest, Benaiah the son of Jehoiada, Nathan the prophet, Shimei, Rei and the men of strength who were with Dauid were not with Adonijah. 9 Then Adoni- iah sacrificed sheep, oxen and fat cattle by the stone of Zoheleth, which is by En-rogel, and called all his brothers as sons of the king and all the men of Iudah as servants of the king, 10 but he did not call Nathan, the prophet, Benaiah, the most important men, and Solo- mon, his brother. 11 Therefore Nathan spoke to Bath-sheba, Solomon's mother, saying, "Have you not heard that Adonijah the son of Haggith reigns, and Dauid our lord does not know? 12 Come therefore, and I will give you advice on how to save your life and the life of your son Solomon. 13 Go, present yourself to King Dauid and say to him, "Have you not, my lord, O king, sworn to your servant, saying, "Surely Solomon your son will reign after me and sit on my throne?" Why then is Adonijah king? 14 Behold, while you are still talking with the king, I will come in after you and confirm your words. 15 So Bath-Sheba en- tered the king's chamber, while the king was very old and Abishag, the shunammite, was ministering to the king. 16 Bath-Sheba bowed and did obedience to the king. The king said, "What is your problem?" 17 And she answered him, "My lord, thou hast spoken of the Lord thy God unto thy handmaid, saying, Sure- ly Solomon thy son shall reign after me, and shall sit upon my throne." 18 And behold, now Adonijah is king, and now, my lord, O king, thou knowest it not. 19 He hath offered many oxen, cattle, and sheep, and hath called all the king's sons, Abiathar the priest, and Joab the captain of the army; but Solomon thy servant hath not asked him. 20 You, my lord, O king, know that the eyes of all Israel are upon you, that you may tell them who is to sit on the throne of my lord the king after him. 21 For otherwise, when my lord the king shall sleep with his fathers, I and my son Solomon shall be counted vile. 22 And behold, while she was still talking with the king, Nathan the proph- et also came in. 23 And they said to the king, "Here is Nathan the prophet." And when he had come to the king, he prostrated himself before the king with his face to the ground. 24 Nathan said, "My Lord, O king, did you say that Adonijah will reign after me and sit on my throne? 25 And he came down today, and killed many oxen, fat cattle, and sheep, and called all the king's sons, and the captains of the army, and Abiathar the priest; and behold, they eat and drink before him, and say, 'God says King Adonijah. 26 But I, your servant, Zadok the priest, Benaiah the son of Jehoia- da, and your servant Solomon have not been called. 27 Is it my lord the king who has done this thing, and you have not shown it to your servant, who will sit on the throne of my lord the king after him?" 28 Then

King Dauid an- swered and said, "Call me Bath-sheba." And she came into the king's presence and stood before the king. 29 And the king swore, "As the LORD wills, who has redeemed my soul from all adversity, 30 as I swore to you by the Lord God of Israel, saying, "Surely Solomon your son will reign after me and sit on my throne in my place, so I will certainly do today." 31 Then Bathsheba bowed her face to the ground and paid homage to the king and said, "God save my lord King Dauid forever." 32 King Dauid said, "Call me Zadok the priest, Nathan the prophet, and Benaiah the son of Jehoiada." And they came before the king. 33 And the king said to them, "Take your lord's servants with you, and have Solomon my son mounted on my mule, and bring him to Gihon." 34 And let Zadok the priest and Nathan the proph- et anoint him there as king of Israel, and let them sound the trumpet and say, "God says king Solomon." 35 Then come after him, that he may come and sit on my throne; he shall be king in my leadership, for I have appointed him as prince of Israel and Judah." 36 Then Be- naiah the son of Jehoiada answered the king and said, "So be it, and the LORD, the God of my lord the king, ratify it." 37 As the LORD dealt with my lord the king, so let him deal with Solomon and raise his throne over the throne of my lord king Dauid." 38 Then Zadok the priest, Nathan the prophet, Benaiah the son of Jehoiada, the Cherethites and the Pele- thites went down and had Solomon mounted on King Dauid's mule and led him to Gihon. 39 Zadok the priest took a horn of oil from the tabernacle and anointed Solomon; then they blew the trumpet and all the people said, "God greets King Solomon." 40 All the people went after him, and the people sounded with pipes and resounded with great joy, so that the earth resounded with their sound. 41 Adon- ijah and all the others who were with him heard him; and when Joab heard the sound of the trumpet, he said, "What is the meaning of this noise and this sound in the city? 42 While he was still speaking, behold, Ionathan the son of Abiathar the priest came; and Adonijah said, "Come in, for you are a worthy man and bring good news." 43 Ionathan answered and said to Adonijah, "Truly our lord King Dauid has appointed Solomon king. 44 The king has sent with him Zadok the priest, Nathan the prophet, Benaiah the son of Jehoiada, the Cherethites, and the Pelethites, who have put him on the king's mule. 45 And Zadok the priest and Nathan the prophet anointed him king in Gihon; and from there they departed with joy, and the city was ravaged; this is the noise that you have heard. 46 Solomon also sits on the throne of the kingdom. 47 Other servants of the king came and blessed our lord King Dauid, saying, "God make Solomon's name more famous than your name and ex- alt his throne beside yours." 48 The king also said, "Blessed be the LORD, the God of Israel, who has made one who has been seen by me to sit on my throne today." 49 Then all the men who were with Adonijah were frightened, and they got up and went their separate ways. 50 Adonijah, fearing Solomon's presence, got up, went and crouched on the horns of the altar. 51 And one told Solomon, "Behold, Adonijah fears King Solomon, for behold, he has at- tached himself to the horns of the altar, say- ing, 'Let King Solomon swear to me today that he will not kill his servant with the sword.'" 52 Solomon said, "If a man prove himself wor- thy, not a thread of him shall fall to the earth; but if wickedness be found in him, he shall die." 53 Then King Solomon sent for the king, and they brought him from the altar; and he came and did obedience to King Solomon. Solomon said to him, "Go to your house."

CHAPTER 2

1 Then the days of Dauid were made later to die, and he charged Solomon his son to say to him, "I go forth through all the earth; there- fore be strong and prove yourself a man." 2 I go throughout the whole earth; therefore be strong and prove yourself a man, 3 and hear- ken to the charge of the LORD your God, to walk in his ways, to observe his statutes, his commands, his decrees, and his testimonies, as it is written in the Law of Moses, that you may prosper in all that you do and in every- thing in which you turn, 4 so that the LORD may confirm the word that he has spoken to me, "If your children follow their way and walk before me in truth, with all their heart and with all their soul, there shall not fail one of your posterity on the throne of Israel." 5 You also know what Joab the son of Zerui- ah has done to me, and what he has done to the two captains of the army of Israel, to Abner the son of Ner, and to Amasa the son of Iether, whom he killed and shed blood of battle in peace, and put the blood of war on his belt which he wore on his feet and on his shoes which were on his feet. 6 Do therefore according to your wisdom, and do not let his horse's head go down to the grave in peace. 7 But be kind to the sons of Barzillai the Gilea-dite, and let them be among those who eat at your table, for so they came to me when I fled from Absalom your brother. 8 Also with you is Shimei, son of Gera, son of Jemini, of Ba- hurim, who cursed me with a horrible curse on the day that I went to Mahanaim; but he came down to meet me in Iorden, and I swore to him by the LORD, "I will not kill you by the sword." 9 But thou shalt not count him inno- cent, for thou art a wise man, and knowest what thou must do towards him; therefore thou shalt cause his horse's head to go down into the grave with blood." 10 So Dauid fell asleep with his fathers and was buried in the city of Dauid. 11 The days that Dauid reigned over Israel were fourteen years: ten years he reigned in Hebron and thirty-three years in Jerusalem. 12 Then Solomon settled on the throne of Dauid, his father, and his kingdom was strengthened with might. 13 Adonijah the son of Haggith went to Bath-sheba, Sol- omon's mother, and she said to him, "Do you agree? And he answered, "Yes." 14 He said again, "I have a question to ask you." And she said, "Go ahead." 15 Then he said, "You know that the kingdom was mine, and that all Isra- el had set their sights on me to reign; but the kingdom has been removed, and it belongs to my brothers, because it was given to them by the Lord. 16 Now therefore I make a request of you: do not refuse me." And she said to him, "Say." 17 He said, "Speak, I pray thee, to King Solomon (for he will not say no to thee) that he may give me Abishag the Shunammite to wife." 18 Bath-Sheba said, "Well, I will speak for you to the king." 19 Bath-Sheba therefore went to King Solomon to speak to him on be- half of Adonijah; and the king rose to meet her, and bowed down before her, and sat on his throne; then he had a place prepared for the king's mother, and she sat at his right hand. 20 Then she said, "I desire a small re- quest from you; do not say no to me." Then the king said to her, "Accept, my mother, for I will not say no to you." 21 She then said, "Let Abishag, the Shunammite, be given in mar- riage to Adonijah, your brother." 22 But King Solomon answered his mother, "Why do you ask Abishag, the Shunammite, to be given in marriage to Adonijah? Ask him to wife the kingdom also, for he is my elder brother and has for himself Abiathar the priest and Joab the son of Zeruiah." 23 Then King Solo- mon swore before the Lord, "God do

so also with me, if Adonijah has not spoken these words against his own life." 24 Therefore, as it pleases the Lord, who has established me and set me on the throne of Dauid, my fa- ther, and who has also given me a house, as he promised, Adonijah will surely die today." 25 And King Solomon sent Benaiah the son of Iehoiada by his hand, and he struck him and caused him to die. 26 Then the king said to Abiathar the priest, "Go to Anatoth in your fields, for you are worthy of death; but I will not kill you today, because you have brought the ark of the Lord God before Dauid my fa- ther, and because you have suffered in all the cases in which my father has been afflicted." 27 Solomon cast Abiathar out of the office of the LORD's priest, to fulfill the words of the LORD that he had spoken against the house of Eli at Sciloh. 28 Then the news came to Joab (for Joab had gone after Adonijah, but not af- ter Absalom), and Joab fled to the Tabernacle of the Lord and clung to the horns of the altar. 29 It was reported to King Solomon that Joab had fled toward the Tabernacle of the Lord and was near the altar. Solomon sent Benaiah the son of Jehoiada, saying, "Go, fall on him." 30 And Benaiah approached the Tabernacle of the Lord and said to him, "Thus says the king, Go out." And he said, "No, but I will die here." Then Benaiah again brought the word to the king, saying, "Thus said Joab, and thus he an- swered me." 31 And the king said to him, "Do as he said, strike him and bury him, that you may take away from me and from my father's house the blood that Joab has shed because of him. 32 And the LORD will cause his blood to return upon his head, for he smote two men more righteous and better than he, and slew them with the sword, and my father Dauid knew it not: Abner the son of Ner, captain of the army of Israel, and Amasa the son of Iether, captain of the army of Iudah. 33 Their blood shall therefore return on the head of Joab and on the head of his seed forever; but for Dauid, for his seed, for his house and for his throne there shall be peace forever from the LORD." 34 Then Benaiah the son of Jehoia- da went, struck him, killed him, and buried him in his house in the forest. 35 And the king put Benaiah the son of Jehoiada in his array above the army, and the king put Zadok the priest in Abiathar's array. 36 Then the king sent for Shimei and said to him, "Buy your- self a house in Jerusalem, live there, and go nowhere." 37 For on the day you go out and pass over the Kidron River, know that you will be dyed with death: your blood will be on your head." 38 Shimei said to the king, "The thing is good; as my lord the king has said, so shall your servant do." So Shimei stayed in Jerusa- lem for many days. 39 After three years, two of Shimei's servants fled to Achish the son of Maachah, king of Gath, and said to Shimei, "Behold, your servants are in Gath." 40 Then Shimei arose, saddled his plank, and went to Gath to Achish to see his servants; and Shi- mei went and brought his servants to Gath. 41 Solomon was told that Shimei had gone from Jerusalem to Gath and had returned. 42 The king sent for Shimei and said to him, "Did I not make you swear before the LORD and protest to you, saying, 'The day you go out and walk anywhere, know that you will die a death?' And you answered me, "The thing is good, as I have heard." 43 Why then have you not observed the Lord's compliance and the order with which I have charged you? 44 The king also said to Shimei, "You know all the wickedness that your heart is prey to, which you have committed against Dauid my father; the LORD therefore will bring your wickedness upon your head." 45 May King Solomon be blessed, and may Dauid's throne be consolidated forever before the LORD. 46 Then the king commanded Benaiah the son of

Jehoiada, who went out and struck him until he died. And the kingdom was established in Solomon's hands.

CHAPTER 3

1 Solomon bound himself to Pharaoh, king of Egypt, and took Pharaoh's daughter and brought her to the city of Dauid, until he had bought his house, the house of the LORD and the walls of Jerusalem around it. 2 Only the people sacrificed in the oldest places, for until those days there was no house bought in the name of the LORD. 3 Solomon lis- tened to the Lord and followed the orders of Dauid his father; in particular he sacrificed and offered incense in public places. 4 The king went to Gibeon to sacrifice there, for that was the main place; Solomon offered a thousand burnt offerings on that altar. 5 At Gibeon the Lord appeared to Solomon on a dark night, and God said, "Ask what I will give you." 6 Solomon said, "You showed your servant Dauid, my father, great mercy, when he walked before you in truth, righteous- ness and uprightness of heart with you; and you preserved for him this great mercy and gave him a son who will sit on his throne, as he appears today. 7 Now, O LORD my God, you have made your servant king instead of Dauid my father, while I am but a young child and do not know how to go out and how to come in. 8 Your servant is in the midst of your people, whom you have chosen, a great people who cannot be told nor ennobled by multitude. 9 Therefore give your servant an intelligent heart to judge your people, that he may discern between good and evil; for who is able to judge this great people of yours? 10 It pleased the Lord greatly that Solomon had desired this thing. 11 And God said to him, "For thou hast asked this thing, and hast not asked long life for thyself, nor hast asked rich- es for thyself, nor hast asked the life of thine enemies, but hast asked for thyself the ability to judge, 12 Behold, I have done according to your words; behold, I have given you a wise and intelligent heart, so that there has been no one like you before you, nor will there arise after you one like you. 13 I have also given you what you did not ask for, riches and honors, so that among kings there will be no one like you all your days. 14 And if you will walk in my ways, keep my decrees and my commands, as your father Dauid did, I will prolong your days." 15 When Solomon awoke, behold it was dark, he came to Jerusalem, stood before the ark of the LORD's convention, offered burnt offerings, made peace offerings, and made a feast to all his servants. 16 Then two prosti- tutes came to the king and stood before him. 17 The one said, "Oh, my lord, this woman and I dwell in one house, and I have borne a son with her in the house." 18 On the third day af- ter I was disappointed, this woman also was disappointed; and we were in the house to- gether; no stranger was with her in the house, as we two were. 19 This woman's son died at night, because she had killed him. 20 And at midnight she arose, and took my son from my side, while thy maidservant slept, and laid him in her lap, and laid her dead son in my lap. 21 And when I rose up in the morning to give my son in marriage, behold, he was dead; and when I had well considered him in the morning, behold, he was not the son whom I had borne. 22 Then the other woman said, "No, but my son lives, and your son is dead." And she answered, "No, but your son is dead, and mine is dead." 23 Then the king said, "She says, 'This one who lives is my son, and the dead one is your son'; and the other says, 'No, but the dead one is your son, and the dead one is my son.'" 24 Then the king said, "Bring me a sword"; and

they brought out a sword before the king. 25 The king said, "Divide the child about to be born in two and give one half to the one and the other half to the other." 26 Then the woman, whose son it was, spoke to the king, because his compassion was kindled toward her son, and said, "Oh, my lord, give her son to her and do not kill him"; but the other said, "Let it be neither mine nor yours, but tell it." 27 Then the king answered and said, "Give her the child that is about to be born, and do not kill him: this is his mother." 28 All Israel heard the judgment that the king had pronounced, and they feared the king, for they knew that the wisdom of God was in him to do justice.

CHAPTER 4

1 King Solomon was king over all Israel. 2 These were his princes: Azariah, son of Za- dok the priest, 3 Elihoreph and Ahiah, sons of the scribes of Shisha, Iehoshaphat, son of Ahilud, the recorder, 4 Benaiah, son of Je- hoiada, was head of the army, Zadok and Abi- athar priests, 5 Azariah, son of Nathan, was in charge of the officers, and Zabud, son of Nathan the priest, was a friend of the king, 6 Ahishar was in charge of the household and Adoniram, son of Abda, was in charge of the tribute. 7 Solomon had two officers in all Is- rael, who provided life for the king and his household; each had one month a year to pro- vide life. 8 These are their names: the son of Hur on Mount Ephraim: 9 the son of Dekar in Makaz, in Shaalbim, in Beth-Scemesh, in Elon, and in Beth-Hanan: 10 The son of Hesed in Aruboth, who dwelt in Socho and in all the land of Hepher: 11 Abinadab's son in all the re- gion of Dor, who had Tafat, Solomon's daugh- ter, as his wife. 12 Baanah the son of Ahilud in Taanach, in Megiddo, and in all Beth-shean, by Zartanah, under Izreel, from Beth-shean to Abelmeholah, even to Iokmeam: 13 The son of Gheber, to Ramoth Gilead, and the cities of Iair the son of Manasseh, which are in Gile- ad, and under him the region of Argob, which is in Bashan: sixty great cities with walls and brick walls. 14 Ahinadab the son of Iddo was in Mahanaim: 15 Ahimaaz in Naphtali, and took Basmath the daughter of Solomon to wife: 16 Baanah, son of Hushai, in Asher and in Aloth: 17 Iehoshaphat the son of Paruah, in Issachar. 18 Shimei, son of Elah, in Ben- jamin: 19 Geber the son of Vri, in the county of Gilead, in the land of Sihon, king of the Amorites, and of Og, king of Bashan; and he was the only officer in the land. 20 Judah and Israel were numerous, like the sand of the sea, and they ate and drank and feasted. 21 Solomon reigned over all the kingdoms, from Riuer to the land of the Philistines and as far as the border of Egypt; they brought presents and served Solomon all the days of his life. 22 Solomon's lives for one day were thirty mea- sures of flour and sixty measures of meat: 23 Ten fat oxen, twenty oxen for pasture, a hun- dred sheep, besides deer, worms and bugles, and foule fat. 24 He ruled over all the region beyond the river, from Tiphsah to Azzah, over all the kings beyond the river, and had peace around him on all sides. 25 Judah and Israel dwelt without fear, each under his own vine and under his own fig tree, from Dan as far as Beer-sheba, throughout Solomon's time. 26 Solomon had four thousand stables of horses for his chariots and two thousand horsemen. 27 These officers procured life for King Solomon and all who came to his table, to each his money, and they let nothing slip through their fingers. 28 Barley and straw for the horses and mules were also brought to the place where the officers were, each according to his charge. 29 God gave Solomon great wis- dom and understanding and a heart as big as the sand on the seashore, 30 Solomon's wis- dom exceeded the wisdom of all the sons of the East and all the wisdom of Egypt. 31 For he was wiser than anyone else, as were Ethan, the Esdrahite, Heman, Chalcol and Darda, the sons of Mahol, and he was famous in all the surrounding nations. 32 Solomon spoke three thousand words, and his songs were a thousand and five. 33 And he spake of trees, from the cedar of Lebanon even to the hys- soptimus springing out of the walls; he spake also of beasts, and of creeping things, and of fishes. 34 And all the nations came to hear the wisdom of Solomon, from all the kings of the earth, who had heard of his wisdom.

CHAPTER 5

1 Hiram, king of Tyre, sent his servants to Solomon (for he had heard that they had ap- pointed him king in his father's kingdom) because Hiram had already killed Dauid. 2 Solomon sent to say to Hiram, 3 You know that Dauid my father could not build a house in the name of the LORD his God because of the wars that surrounded him on every side, until the LORD had put them under the soles of his feet. 4 But now the LORD my God has made me rest on every side, so that there is no longer any fear or resistance. 5 Behold, I intend to build a house in the name of the LORD my God, just as the LORD spoke to Dauid my father, saying, "Your son, whom I will set on your throne in your place, will build a house in the name of my name." 6 Now, therefore, command that I be made ce- dar trees of Lebanon, and that my servants be with thy servants; to thee will I give wages for thy servants, according to all that thou shalt apply; for thou knowest that there is none among the Sidonians that can produce tim- ber like the Sidonians." 7 When Hiram heard Solomon's words, he rejoiced greatly and said, "Blessed be the LORD today, who has given Dauid a wise son from this mighty peo- ple." 8 Hiram sent word to Solomon, "I have considered the things for which you sent me, and I will accomplish all your wishes concern- ing the cedars and fir trees. 9 My servants will bring them down from Lebanon to the sea; I will lead them by sea on rafts to the place you point out to me, have them unloaded there,and you will receive them; now you will do me the pleasure of distributing food for my fam- ily." 10 So Hiram gave Solomon cedars and fir trees, as he wished. 11 Solomon gave Hiram twenty thousand measures of grain for his family's food and twenty thousand measures of beaten oil. Thus Solomon gave Hiram, year by year, all this. 12 The LORD gave Solomon the wisdom he had promised him. There was peace between Hiram and Solomon, and the two agreed. 13 King Solomon collected a sum from all Israel, which amounted to thirty thousand men: 14 He sent ten thousand by every route to Lebanon; they were one million in Lebanon and two million at home. Adoni- ram was outside the land. 15 Solomon had six hundred thousand burden-bearers and four hundred thousand masons in the mountains, 16 besides the princes whom Solomon had appointed for the works, about three thou- sand and three hundred, who governed the people who worked in the works. 17 The king gave them an order, and they brought great stones and costly stones to make the founda- tion of the house, that is, cut stones. 18 Solo- mon's workmen, Hiram's workmen and ma- sons worked and prepared lumber and stones for the purchase of the house.

CHAPTER 6

1 In the fourth centenary (after the children of Israel had come out of the land of Egypt) and in the fourth year of Solomon's lordship of Israel, in the month of Zif (which is the sec- ond month), he built the house of the LORD. 2 The house that King Solomon built for the LORD was three dozen cubits long, twen- ty-five cubits wide and thirty cubits high. 3 The porch in front of the temple of the house was twenty-five cubits long, according to the width of the house, and ten cubits wide in front of the house. 4 In the house he made windows, wide on the outside and narrow on the inside. 5 Along the wall of the house he made galleries all around, as well as along the wall of the house around the temple and the oracle, and he made chambers all around. 6 The lowest gallery was five cubits wide, the middle gallery was six cubits wide, and the third was six cubits wide; for he made rests all around the outside of the house, so that the flames were not fastened to the walls of the house. 7 When the house was built, it was built of perfect stone, before it was brought in, so that neither hammer nor ax nor any iron instrument was heard in the house while it was being built. 8 The door of the middle chamber was on the right side of the house, and the men entered the middle chamber with winding stays and went out of the mid- dle chamber into the third. 9 So he built the house, completed it, and clothed it with cedar wood. 10 He built galleries on all the walls of the house, five cubits high, and adhered them to the house with flames of cedar. 11 The word of the LORD came to Solomon and he said, 12 Concerning this house that you build, if you will walk according to my precepts, carry out my decrees and fulfill all my obligations, then I will make you the promise that I made to Dauid your father. 13 I will dwell among the children of Israel and will not forsake my peo- ple of Israel." 14 Solomon built the house and completed it, 15 he built the walls of the house on the inside, with boards of cedar from the entrance of the house to the surrounding walls; he lined them with wood on the in- side and covered the floor of the house with boards of fir. 16 Then he built twenty cubits in the sides of the house with cedar boards, from the floor to the walls, and prepared there a place for the oracle, that is, the most holy place. 17 The house, that is, the Temple before it, was forty cubits long. 18 The cedar of the house inside was carved with knots, and the grauen with flourishes; everything was of cedar, so that no stone could be seen. 19 He also prepared the place of the oracle in the central part of the house, to place there the ark of the LORD's convention. 20 The place of the oracle, inside the house, was twenty-five cubits long, twenty-five cubits wide, and twenty-five cubits high; he clothed it with pure gold and covered the altar with cedar. 21 Solomon clothed the house with pure gold, enclosed the place of the oracle with chains of gold, and covered it with gold. 22 Then he clothed the whole house with gold, until the whole house was made perfect; and he also clothed the whole altar that was before the oracle with gold. 23 Inside the oracle he made two olive cherubim ten cubits high. 24 The wing of the first Cherub was also five cubits, and the wing of the other Cherub was five cu- bits; from the end of one of his wings to the end of the other was ten cubits. 25 The other Cherub was also ten cubits; both Cherubim were of one size and one height. 26 For the height of the first Cherub was ten cubits, and so was the other Cherub. 27 Then he placed the Cherubim inside the house, and the Cher- ubim spread out their wings, so that the wing of the one touched the one wall, and the wing of the other Cherubim touched the other

wall; and their other wings touched each other in the middle of the house. 28 Then he adorned the Cherubim with gold. 29 He made all the walls of the house all around with figures of Cherubim and Palms of gray color and with flowers of gray color inside and outside. 30 The floor of the house was covered with gold inside and outside. 31 For the entrance to the oracle he made two towers of olive; the upper pole and the side poles were square. 32 The two towers were also of olive, and he adorned them with ornaments of cherubim and palm trees, and with flourishes of wheat, and cov- ered them with gold, and put fine gold on the cherubim and palm trees. 33 He thus made for the porch of the Temple poles of olive trees on four sides. 34 And the two sides of the tem- ple were of fir, and the two sides of the one were round, and the two sides of the other were round. 35 He had cherubim and palm trees built, carved flourishes and covered the carved works with gold, finely wrought. 36 He built the inner courtyard with three rows of hewed stones and a row of cedar beeches. 37 In the fourth year the foundation of the house of the LORD was laid in the month of Zif: 38 In the eleventh year, in the month of Bul (which is the eighth), he completed the house with all its furnishings and in all its places.

CHAPTER 7

1 Solomon built his house for thirty years and completed it all. 2 He also built a house, called the forest of Lebanon, a hundred cubits long, fifty cubits wide and thirty cubits high, on four rows of cedar pillars, on which were laid cedar beams. 3 The roof was covered with ce- dar on the beams that rested on the forty-five pillars, fifteen in each row. 4 The windows were arranged in three rows, and the windows were set against each other in three rows. 5 All the doorways and side columns with win- dows were square, and the windows were set against each other in three rows. 6 He made a porch of pillars fifty cubits long and thirty cubits wide; the porch was in front of them, and there were thirty pillars in front of them. 7 Then he made a porch for the throne, where he judged, a portico for judgment, and he was clothed with cedar from floor to floor. 8 In his house, where he lived, there was another hall that was more inward than the porch, of the same kind. Solomon also made a house for Pharaoh's daughter (whom he had taken to wife) similar to this porch. 9 All these elements were of costly stones, cut to size and with saws inside and out, from the foundation to the stones the width of a hand, and outside to the great courtyard. 10 The foundations were made of costly stones and large stones, that is, ten-cubit stones and eight-cubit stones. 11 In addition there were costly stones, square- ly squared, and planks of cedar. 12 The great courtyard around it had three rows of hewn stones and a row of cedar beams; so it was for the inner courtyard of the house of the LORD and for the porch of the house. 13 Then King Solomon sent for a certain Hiram from Tyre. 14 And he was a widow's son of the tribe of Naphtali, whose father was a man of Tyre, and he worked the brassa; and he was full of wisdom and understanding and knowledge to work all kinds of brassa work; and he came to King Solomon and worked all his work. 15 He made two columns of bricks; the height of one column was eighty cubits, and a third of two cubits made up one of the two columns. 16 He also made two chapels of cast brasse to be placed on top of the columns; the height of one of the chapels was five cubits, and the height of the other chapel was five cubits. 17 He made gratings like nets and work like caie for the chapiters

that were on the top of the pillars, one for the one chapter and one for the other chapter. 18 So he made the pillars and two rows of pomegranates around the one grate to support the chapiters who were on top. And so he also did for the other chap- iter. 19 The chapiters that were on the top of the pillars were four cubits, having worked them plainly in the porch. 20 The chapiters on the two pillars also had an opening to the belly, inside a net of pomegranates, for two pomegranates were in the two ranks, approxi- mately on one of the two chapiters. 21 Then he fixed the columns in the Temple porch. When he had fixed the right-hand column, he called it Iachin; and when he had fixed the left-hand column, he called it Boaz. 22 On the top of the pillars was a work of lilies; so the work of the pillars was finished. 23 He made a molten sea ten cubits wide from rim to rim, round, five cubits apart, with a line of thirty cubits sur-rounding it. 24 Beneath the brim were knots like wild cucumbers surrounding it, ten in a cubit, encircling the sea; and the two rows of knots were thrown out when it was cast. 25 It stood on two bulbs, three facing north, three facing west, three facing south, and three facing east; and the sea stood on them, and all their backsides were within. 26 It was a small work, and the brim was like the brim of a cup with lily flowers; it contained two thousand baths. 27 He also made ten bases of brasse; one base was four cubits long, four cubits wide and three cubits high. 28 The bas- es were worked in this way: they had edges, and the edges were between the projections: 29 On the edges that were between the projec- tions were lianas, bulbs, and cherubim; and over the projections was a base; and under the lianas and bulbs were additions of thin wood. 30 Each base had four bronze wheels and wooden plates, and the four corners had engravers; under the cauldron were cast en- gravers on the sides of each addition. 31 The spout was inside the chapiter and measured a cubit, for the spout was round like a base and measured a cubit and a half cubit; also, on the spout were grauiti work, the edges of which were four squares and not round. 32 Beyond the edges were four wheels, whose axles were connected to the base; the height of one wheel was one cubit and a half cubit. 33 The appear-ance of the wheels was similar to that of a concrete wheel; their axles, tassels, edges and spokes were all cast. 34 On the four corners of a base were four supports, and the supports were of the base itself. 35 On the top of the base was a round compass of half a cubit all around, and on the top of the base its edges and projections were of the same material. 36 On the boards of the projections and on the edges he had Cherubim, lions and palms set on the sides of each of them and added all around. 37 Thus he made the ten bases, all of which were of one casting, one size, and one case. 38 Then he built ten cauldrons of rammed earth, one cauldron contained forty baths; each cauldron was four cubits, and one cauldron was on one base for all ten bases. 39 He fixed the bases, five on the right side of the house and five on the left side of the house. And he set the sea on the right side of the house, on the east side, facing south. 40 And Hiram made caldanes and besome and foun- dations, and Hiram finished all the work that he had done to King Solomon for the house of the LORD: 41 that is, two pillars and two bows of the chaplets that were on the top of the two pillars, and two gratings to repair the two bows of the chaplets that were on the top of the pillars, 42 and four hundred pomegran- ates for the two gratings, that is, two rows of pomegranates for each grating, to repair the two arches of the chapiters that were on the pillars, 43 the ten bases and the ten cauldrons on the bases, 44 the sea and two bulbs under the sea, 45 the pots, the besome and the bases.

All these vessels, which Hiram made to King Solomon for the house of the LORD, were of shining brasse. 46 In the plain of Iorden the king cast them in clay between Succoth and Zarthan. 47 Solomon let all the vessels be weighed because of the great abundance, for the weight of the clay could not be counted. 48 Solomon built all the utensils that were need- ed for the house of the LORD, the golden altar and the golden table on which the bread was, 49 the candlesticks, two on the right and two on the left, before the oracle, of pure gold, the lamps and sprinklers of gold, 50 the arches, the hooks, the plinths, the spoons, the ash- trays of pure gold, and the hinges of gold for the rooms of the house within, for the most holy place, and for the rooms of the house, that is, of the Temple. 51 So all the work that King Solomon did for the house of the LORD was finished; and Solomon brought the things that Dauïd, his father, had dedicated: the clay, the garland, and the furnishings, and placed them among the treasures of the house of the LORD.

CHAPTER 8

1 Then King Solomon gathered the elders of Israel, that is, all the heads of the tribes, the principal fathers of the children of Israel, to Jerusalem, to bring the ark of the crowning of the Lord from the city of Dauid, which is Zion. 2 All the men of Israel gathered them- selves together to King Solomon on the feast of the month of Etanim, which is the tenth month. 3 All the elders of Israel came, and the priests took the ark. 4 And they brought the ark of the LORD, and the tabernacle of the congregation, and all the holy vessels that were in the tabernacle; and the priests and the leuites brought them. 5 King Solomon and all the congregation of Israel, which had gathered near him, were with him before the ark and offered sheep and heads of cattle, which could not be taken away or named for the multitude. 6 So the priests brought the ark of the LORD's convention to its place in the oracle of the house, in the most holy place, and under the wings of the cherubim. 7 For the Cherubim spread their wings beyond the place of the ark, and the Cherubim struck the ark and its sides. 8 And they brought out the bars, so that the ends of the bars appeared outside the sanctuary before the oracle, but they could not be seen outside; and they have remained there to this day. 9 There was noth- ing in the ark other than the two stone tablets that Moses had placed there at Horeb, where the LORD made a covenant with the children of Israel when he brought them out of the land of Egypt. 10 When the priests came out of the sanctuary, the cloud filled the house of the LORD, 11 so that the priests could not stand to officiate because of the cloud, be- cause the glory of the LORD had filled the house of the LORD. 12 Then Solomon said, "The LORD said that he would dwell in the dark cloud. 13 I have built you a house to dwell in, an abode in which you may remain forev- er." 14 And the king turned and blessed all the congregation of Israel, for all the congrega- tion of Israel stood there. 15 And he said, "Blessed be the LORD, the God of Israel, who spoke with his mouth to Dauid my father, and with his hand fulfilled it, saying, 16 From the day that I brought my people Israel out of Egypt, I did not choose any city out of all the tribes of Israel to build a house in it in which my name was present; but I chose Dauid to be outside my people Israel." 17 Dauid, my fa- ther, had it in his heart to build a house for the name of the LORD, the God of Israel. 18 The LORD said to Dauid, my father, "If you had it in your heart to build a house in honor of my Name, you did well, for you had this inten- tion: 19

Nevertheless you will not be the one to build the house, but your son who will come forth from your descendants will build the house in honor of my Name." 20 The LORD has put into practice the word that he spoke; I have risen up in the kingdom of Dauid my fa- ther, and I sit on the throne of Israel, as the LORD had promised, and I have built the house for the Name of the LORD, the God of Israel. 21 And I have prepared for you a place for the Ark, where is the convention of the LORD which he made with our fathers, when he brought them out of the land of Egypt." 22 Solomon stood before the altar of the LORD, before all the congregation of Israel, and stretched out his hands toward him, 23 and said, "O LORD, God of Israel, there is no God like you in heaven and on earth, you who keep peace and mercy with your servants who walk before you with all their hearts, 24 you who kept with your servant Dauid my father what you promised him, for you spoke with your mouth and kept it with your hand, as it ap- pears today. 25 Therefore now, O LORD God of Israel, keep with your servant Dauid, my father, that which you promised him, saying, "You shall not lack a man in my sight to sit on the throne of Israel; so that your sons may take heed to their way, to walk before me, as you have walked in my sight." 26 Now, O God of Israel, I pray thee, let thy word which thou hast spoken to thy servant Dauid my father come to pass. 27 Is it true that God will dwell on the earth? Behold, the heavens and the heavens of heavens cannot describe you; how much more good is this house that I have built? 28 But have respect for your servant's prayer and supplication, O LORD my God, hear the cry and prayer that your servant makes before you today: 29 That your eyes may be opened to this house, night and day, and to the place where you said, "My name shall be there," that you may hear the prayer that your servant prays in this place. 30 Hear therefore the supplication of thy servant and of thy people of Israel, who pray in this place, and hear it in the place of thy dwelling, even in heaven; and when thou hearest it, have mercy. 31 When a man shall commit a tres- pass against his neighbor, and shall put an- other upon him to make him swear, and the sworn shall come before thy altar in this house, 32 then hearken to thy heart, and judge thy servants, condemning the ungodly and laying his guilt upon his head, and exe- cuting the righteous, giving him according to his righteousness. 33 When thy people Israel shall be overcome before the enemy, because they have sinned against thee, and shall turn again to thee, confessing thy Name, and pray- ing and making supplications to thee in this house, 34 then listen to heaven, and be merci- ful to the sin of your people Israel, and bring them back to the land which you gave to their fathers. 35 When the tavern is closed and there is no more anger because they have sinned against you, and they will pray in this place and confess your Name and turn from their sin, when you afflict them, 36 then you will hear in heaven and forgive the sin of your servants and of your people of Israel (when you have taught them the good way to walk) and grant grace over the land that you have given as an inheritance to your people. 37 When there is famine in the land, when there is pestilence, when there is a blast, or a mold, or a weed, or a caterpillar, when their enemies besiege them in the cities of their land, or a plague or a disease, 38 what prayer and sup- plication shall be made by any or all of your people of Israel, when every one shall know the plague in his own heart, and shall stretch out his hands in this house? 39 then look to thyself in heaven, in thy dwelling place, and be merciful, and grant to each one according to all his ways, as thou knowest his heart (for thou alone knowest the hearts of all the sons of men). 40 That they may fear you while they live in your life, which you gave to our fathers. 41 And still more concerning the stranger who is not of your people Israel and who will come from a far country for your names' sake, 42 (when they hear of your great name, your mighty hand, and your outstretched arm) and come and pray in this house, 43 keep your dwelling place in heaven and do all that the stranger asks of you, so that all the peoples of the earth may know your Name and fear you, like your people Israel, and know that your Name is invoked in this house that I have built. 44 When your people go out to fight against the enemy by the way you show them, and pray to the LORD for the way of the city you have chosen and for the house I have built for your Name, 45 Hear therefore their prayer and supplication, and judge their cause. 46 If they sin against thee (for there is no man that sinneth not), and thou wilt be angry with them, thou shalt deliver them over to the ene- mies, so that they may carry them captive into the land of the enemies, far off or away, 47 but if, in the land to which they have been carried captive, they turn back in their hearts and re- turn to pray to you in the land of those who carried them captive, saying, "We have sinned, we have transgressed, and we have done iniquity." 48 if they turn to you with all their heart and with all their soul in the land of their enemies who led them into captivity, and pray to you for the way of their country, which you had pointed out to their fathers, and for the city you have chosen and the house I have built for your Name, 49 hear their prayers and supplications in thy dwell- ing, and judge their cause, 50 and be merciful to your people who have sinned against you and to all their iniquities (whereby they have transgressed against you) and cause them, who have led them into captivity, to have mer- cy and compassion on them: 51 For they are your people and your inheritance, whom you brought out of Egypt from the midst of the furnace of Yron. 52 Keep your eyes on the prayer of your servant and the prayer of your people Israel, to hear them in all that they call upon you. 53 For you have separated them to you from all the peoples of the earth as an in- heritance, as you said by the hand of Moses your servant, when you brought our fathers out of Egypt, O Lord God. 54 When Solomon had finished reciting all these prayers and supplications to the Lord, he stood up from before the altar of the Lord, kneeling down and stretching his hands upward, 55 paused and blessed with a loud voice all the congre- gation of Israel, saying 56 Blessed be the LORD, who has granted rest to his people of Israel, according to what he had promised; not a single word of all his good promise that he had made by the hand of Moses his servant has been betrayed. 57 The LORD our God be with us, as he was with our fathers; he will not forsake us nor leave us, 58 that he may bend our hearts toward him, that we may walk in all his words and keep his commands, his statutes and his laws, which he commanded our fathers. 59 And these words of mine, which I have prayed before the LORD, may they always stand for the LORD our God, day and night, that he may defend the cause of his servant and the cause of his people Israel, as the situation requires, 60 that all the peoples of the earth may know that the LORD is God and no one else. 61 Let your hearts therefore be true to the LORD our God, to walk in his statutes and keep his commands, as today." 62 Then the king and all Israel with him of- fered a sacrifice before the LORD. 63 And Sol- omon offered a sacrifice of peace, which he offered to the LORD: two and twenty thou- sand bees and an hundred thousand sheep; so the king and all Israel dedicated the house of the LORD. 64 On that same day the king made a stand in the middle of the courtyard that was before the house of the LORD, for there he made the burnt offerings, the food offer- ings, and the fat of the peace offerings, be- cause the copper altar that was before the LORD was too small to receive the burnt of- ferings, the food offerings, and the fat of the peace offerings. 65 At that time Solomon made a feast, and all Israel with him, a very large congregation, from the entrance of Ha- math to the border of Egypt, before the LORD our God, for seven days and seven days, that is, for four days. 66 On the eighth day he sent the people away, and they thanked the king and returned to their tents with joy and glad hearts, because of all the goodness the LORD had done for Dauid his servant and for Israel his people.

CHAPTER 9

1 When Solomon had finished building the house of the LORD, the kings' palace and all that Solomon desired and wanted to do, 2 the Lord appeared to Solomon for the second time, as he had appeared to Gibeon. 3 And the LORD said to him, "I have heard your prayer and your supplication which you made before me: I have given way to this house (which you built) to put my Name there forever, and my eyes and my heart shall be there forever. 4 And if thou wilt walk before me (as Dauid thy fa- ther walked in purity of heart and righteous- ness) to do all that I have commanded thee, and to keep my statutes and my precepts, 5 then I will establish the throne of your king- dom over Israel forever, as I promised Dauid your father, saying, "You shall not lack a man on the throne of Israel." 6 But if you and your sons turn away from me and do not keep my commands and my statutes (which I have es- tablished before you), but go and serve other gods and worship them, 7 then I will cut Is- rael off from the land that I have given them, and the house that I have made for my Name I will drive out of my sight, and Israel will be a common boast and chatter among all peo- ples. 8 And this house shall be thus: all who pass by it shall be amazed, and they shall ask, "Why has the LORD done this to this land and to this house? 9 They will answer, "Be- cause they have forsaken the LORD their God, who brought their fathers out of the land of Egypt, and have taken refuge in other gods, and have worshipped them and served them; therefore the LORD has brought all this evil upon them." 10 At the end of twenty years, when Solomon purchased the two houses, the house of the LORD and the king's palace, 11 (for which Hiram, king of Tyre, had brought Solomon cedar lumber, fir trees, gold and all that he desired), King Solomon gave Hi- ram twenty-two cities in the land of Galil. 12 Hiram went out from Tyre to see the cities Solomon had given him, and he did not like them. 13 Therefore he said, What are the cities that you have given me, my brother? And he called them, to this day, the land of Cabul. 14 Hiram had sent to the king six dozen talents of gold. 15 This is the cause of the tribute that King Solomon collected: to build the house of the LORD, his house, Millo, the walls of Jeru- salem, Hazor, Megiddo, and Ghezer. 16 Pha- raoh, king of Egypt, had come, taken Ghezer, burned it with fire, killed the Canaanites who lived in the city, and gave it as a gift to his daughter Solomon. 17 Solomon built Ghezer and Bet- horon, the innermost part, 18 And Baalath and Tamor in the wilderness of the land, 19 and all the cities of storehouses that Solomon possessed, cities for chariots and cities for horsemen, and all that Solomon desired and wanted to build in Jerusalem, in Lebanon, and in all the land of his dominion). 20 all the remaining peoples of the Amor- ites, the Hittites, the Perizzites, the Hiuites, and the Jebusites, who did not belong to the children of Israel: 21 that is, their children who had remained after them in the land and whom the children of Israel had failed to destroy, those whom Solomon has made trib- utaries to this day. 22 But of the children of Israel Solomon did not make slaves, but men of war, his servants, his princes, his captains, the heads of his camps and his horsemen. 23 These were the princes of the officers who worked for Solomon: five hundred and fifty, who ruled over the people who worked in the shipyard. 24 Pharaoh's daughter came from the city of Dauid to the house Solomon had built for her; then she bought Millo. 25 Three times a year Solomon offered sacrifices and peace offerings on the altar he had built for the LORD; and he burned incense on the altar that was before the LORD when he had fin- ished the house. 26 King Solomon also made a nauie of ships at Ezeon-geber, which is near Eloth and the mouth of the Red Sea, in the land of Edom. 27 Hiram sent with the ship his servants, who were sailors and knew the sea, and Solomon's servants. 28 They came to Ophir and from there departed four hun- dred and twenty talents of gold, which they brought to King Solomon.

CHAPTER 10

1 The queen of Sheba, hearing of Solomon's fame (concerning the Name of the Lord), came and questioned him with hard questions. 2 She came to Jerusalem with a very large ship, with camels bearing sweet odors, with much gold and precious stones; she went to Sol- omon and dwelt with him on all that was in her heart. 3 Solomon expounded to her all her questions; the king concealed nothing that he had not explained to her. 4 Then the queen of Sheba knew all the wisdom of Solomon and the house that he had built, 5 the food of his table, the arrangement of his servants, the order of his ministers and their clothing, the drinking vessels and the burnt food he of- fered in the house of the LORD, and she was greatly astonished. 6 She said to the king, "True are the words that I have heard in my land about your speeches and your wisdom. 7 Yet I did not believe this news until I came and saw it with my own eyes; but behold, the half was not told me, for you have more wis- dom and prosperity than I have heard. 8 Hap- py men, happy these thy servants, who stand before thee always, and hear thy wisdom. 9 Blessed be the LORD your God, who has set you on the throne of Israel, for the LORD has set Israel up forever and made you king to do equity and justice." 10 It delivered to the king six dozen talents of gold, perfumes and precious stones. No more was there such an abundance of sweet perfumes as the Queen of Sheba gave to King Solomon. 11 Hiram's nauie (carrying gold from Ophir) also brought from Ophir a great quantity of Almuggim trees and precious stones. 12 The king made pillars of Almuggim trees for the house of the LORD and for the king's palace, and he made harps and psalteries for the singers. There were no more Almuggim trees of this kind, and none are seen to this day. 13 King Solomon grant- ed the queen of Sheba all that she wanted, in addition to what Solomon had granted her by his royal liberality; so she returned and went away to her county, both she and her servants. 14 The weight of gold that came to Solomon in one year was six hundred thirty-six talents of gold, 15 besides what he possessed of busi- nessmen and goods of those who sold spices, of all the kings of Arabia and of the princes of the county. 16 King Solomon made two hun- dred targets of beaten bronze, of which six hundred shekels

of gold per target: 17 And three hundred shields of beaten bronze, three pounds of gold for a shield; and the king put them in the house of the wood of Lebanon. 18 Then the king made a great throne of yuorie and clothed it with the best gold. 19 And the throne had six steps, and the top of the throne was round behind, and there were stalls on either side of it on the place of the throne, and two lions standing beside the stalls. 20 On the six steps, on either side and on the other, stood two lions; no such was made in any kingdom. 21 All the drinking vessels of King Solomon were of gold, and all the vessels of the house of the wood of Lebanon were of pure gold, none were of silk, for in Solomon's time there was nothing of value. 22 For the king had on the sea the nauie of Tharshish with the nauie of Hiram; once every three years the nauie of Tharshish came and brought gold and silver, yuorie, monkeys and peacocks. 23 Thus King Solomon surpassed all the kings of the earth in both wealth and wisdom. 24 All the world wanted to see Solomon, to hear his wisdom that God had put in his heart, 25 And they brought every man his gift, vessels of silk and vessels of gold, robes, armor, perfume, hors- es and mules, from year to year. 26 Solomon gathered carts and horsemen; he had a thou- sand and four hundred carts and two thou- sand horsemen, whom he placed in the cities of the carts and with the king in Jerusalem. 27 The king had torpedoes built in Jerusalem like stones and cedars like the wild figs that grow in abundance in the plain. 28 Solomon had horses and fine linen brought from Egypt, which the king's marchers received at a favor- able price. 29 From Egypt came and departed a charet worth six hundred shekels of silver, that is, one horse, one hundred and fifty, and so they brought horses to all the kings of the Hittites and to the kings of Aram through their means.

CHAPTER 11

1 For King Solomon had taken in many ex- travagant women: the daughter of Pharaoh and the women of Moab, Ammon, Edom, Zi- don and Heth, 2 of the nations of whom the LORD had said to the children of Israel, "Do not enter in to them, and do not allow them to enter in to you, for they will certainly turn your hearts to their gods." 3 He had ten hun- dred wives, who were princesses, and three hundred concubines, and his wives turned his heart away. 4 For when Solomon was old, his wives turned his heart toward other gods, so that his heart was not perfect with the LORD his God, as was the heart of Dauid his father. 5 For Solomon followed Ashtaroth, god of the Zidonians, and Milcom, abomina- tion of the Ammonites. 6 Solomon therefore committed wickedness before the LORD, but he did not follow the LORD, as did Dauid his father. 7 Solomon built a place of worship for Chemosh, the abomination of Moab, on the mountain opposite Jerusalem, and for Molech, the abomination of the sons of Am- mon. 8 And so he did for all his extravagant wives, who burned incense and offered to their gods. 9 Therefore the LORD was angry with Solomon, because he had turned his heart away from the LORD, the God of Israel, who had appeared to him twice, 10 and had commanded him not to follow other gods, but he had not observed what the LORD had com- manded him. 11 Therefore the LORD said to Solomon, "Because this has been done by you, and you have not observed my counsel and my statutes (which I had commanded you), I will take the kingdom from you and give it to your servant. 12 Nevertheless in thy days I will not do it, because of Dauid thy father, but I will snatch it out of the hand of thy son: 13 Never- theless I will not rent the whole kingdom, but will give a tribe to thy son, because of Dauid my servant, and because of Jerusalem which I have chosen." 14 Then the LORD stirred up an aversion against Solomon, that is, Hadad the Edomite, of the king's seed, who was in Edom. 15 For when Dauid was in Edom and Joab, the captain of the army, had struck all the males of Edom and gone away to bury the slain, 16 (for six months Joab remained there and all Israel, until he had destroyed all the males of Edom). 17 Then this Hadad fled, and with him some other Edomites, servants of his fathers, to go to Egypt, Hadad still being a little child. 18 And they went out of Midian, and came to Paran, and took men with them, and came to Egypt to Pharaoh, king of Egypt, who gave him a house, and assigned him life annuities, and gave him land. 19 Hadad found great favor with Pharaoh, who gave him the sister of his own wife, that is, the sister of Queen Tahpene, to be his wife. 20 Tahpene's sister bore him Genubath, her son, whom Tahpene brought into Pharaoh's house; and Genubath was in Pharaoh's house among Pharaoh's sons. 21 When Hadad learned in Egypt that Dauid was sleeping with his fa- thers and that Joab, the captain of the army, was dead, Hadad said to Pharaoh, "Let me leave to go to my own country." 22 But Pha- raoh said to him, "What did you lack from me, that you should go thus to your country? And he answered, "Nothing, but let me go by all means." 23 God suggested to him anoth- er aduersary, Rezon, son of Eliada, who had fled from his lord Hadadezer, king of Zobah. 24 He gathered men to himself and was the leader of the company when Dauid killed them. They went to Damascus, settled there, and made him king in Damascus. 25 There- fore he was an adversary of Israel all the days of Solomon; besides what Hadad had done, he abhorred Israel and reigned in Aram. 26 Jeroboam the son of Nebat, an Ephrathite, servant of Zereda Solomon, whose mother's name was Zerua, a widow, raised his hand against the king. 27 This was the reason why he raised his hand against the king: when Sol- omon built Millo, he repaired the destroyed places of the city of Dauid, his father. 28 This man, Jeroboam, was a strong and courageous man, and Solomon, seeing that this young man was fit for the work, appointed him chief of all the work of the house of Ioseph. 29 At that time, as Jeroboam was going out from Jerusalem, Ahiiah the prophet, the Scylonite, found him on the road, with a new robe on, and the two of them were alone in the fields. 30 Then Ahijah took the new robe on him and tore it in two parts, 31 and said to Jeroboam, "Take ten pieces of it, for thus says the LORD, the God of Israel: 'Behold, I will tear the king- dom out of Solomon's hand and give you ten tribes. 32 But he shall have a tribe for my servant Dauids, and for Jerusalem, the city which I have chosen out of all the tribes of Israel, 33 Because they forsook me and wor- shipped Ashtaroth, god of the Zidonians, Chemosh, god of the Moabites, and Milcom, god of the Ammonites, and did not walk in my ways (to do right in my sight, my statutes and my laws) as Dauid his father did. 34 But I will not take the whole kingdom out of his hand, for I will make him prince for life in favor of Dauid my servant, whom I have chosen and who has kept my commands and my statutes. 35 But I will take the kingdom out of the hand of his son and give it to you, that is, to the ten tribes. 36 And to his son I will give a tribe, that Dauid my servant may always have a light be- fore me in Jerusalem, the city I have chosen to put my Name there. 37 I will take you, and you shall reign, as your heart desires, and you shall be king of Israel. 38 If you will listen to all that I command you, if you will walk in my ways and conduct yourself well in my sight,

keeping my statutes and my commands, as Dauid my servant did, then I will be with you and will build you a safe house, as I built it to Dauid, and I will give you Israel. 39 For this I will afflict the descendants of Dauid, but not forever." 40 So Solomon tried to kill Jeroboam; Jeroboam got up and fled to Egypt to Shishak king of Egypt, and he stayed in Egypt until Solomon died. 41 Are not the rest of Solo- mon's words, all that he did and his wisdom written in the book of Solomon's deeds? 42 The time Solomon reigned in Jerusalem over all Israel was forty years. 43 And Solomon fell asleep with his fathers, and was buried in the city of Dauid, his father; and Rehoboam his son reigned in his stead.

CHAPTER 12

1 Rehoboam went to Shechem, because all Israel had come to Shechem to appoint him king. 2 And when Jeroboam the son of Ne- bat heard of it (who was still in Egypt, where Jeroboam had fled from King Solomon and settled in Egypt) 3 They sent for him; and Je- roboam and all the congregation of Israel came and spoke to Rehoboam, saying 4 Your father has made our yoke heavy; now, there- fore, make lighter the grievous bondage of your father and his painful yoke which he has imposed, and we will serve you." 5 Then he said to them, "Depart again for three days, then return to me." And the people depart- ed. 6 King Rehoboam took counsel with the elders who had stood before Solomon his fa- ther while he was still alive, and said, "What counsel do you give, that I may answer this people? 7 They said to him, "If you will be a servant of this people today, if you will serve them, if you will answer them and speak kind words to them, they will be your servants for- ever." 8 But he gave up the counsel that the old men had given him and sought counsel from the young men who had been brought with him and were waiting for him. 9 And he said to them, "What counsel do you give to answer this people who have spoken to me, saying, 'Make lighter the yoke that your father has imposed on you?' 10 Then the young men who had been led with him spoke to him, saying, "So you shall say to this people who have spo- ken to you, saying, 'Your father has made our yoke heavy, but you make it lighter for you'; and so you shall say to them, 'My smaller por- tion shall be greater than my father's debts. 11 Now if my father has oppressed you with a heavy yoke, I will make your yoke heavier; my father has chastened you with rods, but I will correct you with scourges." 12 Then Je- roboam and all the people came to Rehoboam on the third day, as the king had appointed, saying, "Come to me again on the third day." 13 The king answered the people decisively and left the advice of the elders that they had given him, 14 and spoke to them according to the counsel of the young men, saying, "My father has made your yoke hard, I will make it harder; my father has chastened you with rods, but I will correct you with scourges." 15 The king paid no heed to the people, for it was the Lord's command, to put into prac- tice the words the Lord had spoken through Ahijah the Scylonite to Jeroboam the son of Nebat. 16 When all Israel saw that the king did not consider them, the people answered the king thus, "What portion do we have in Dauid? We have no inheritance in the son of Ishai. Go back to your tents, O Israel; now go to your home, Dauid." So Israel went away to his tents. 17 However, for the children of Isra- el who lived in the cities of Judah, Rehoboam still reigned. 18 Now King Rehoboam sent Adoram, the receiver of the tribute,

and all Israel stoned him; then King Rehoboam has- tened to put him on his charet to flee to Je- rusalem. 19 Israel rebelled against the house of Dauid to this day. 20 When all Israel heard that Jeroboam had returned, they sent for him in the assembly and appointed him king over all Israel; no one followed the house of Dauid, but only the tribe of Iudah. 21 When Rehoboam came to Jerusalem, he gathered to- gether all the house of Iudah and the tribe of Benjamin, a hundred thousand and four hun- dred thousand chosen men (who were good warriors) to fight against the house of Israel and bring the kingdom back to Rehoboam the son of Solomon. 22 But the word of God came to Shemaiah, the man of God, and he said, 23 Speak to Rehoboam the son of Solomon king of Judah, and to all the house of Judah and Benjamin, and to the rest of the people, say- ing 24 Thus says the LORD, "You shall not go and fight against your brothers, the children of Israel; return every one to his own house, for this thing has been done by me." They therefore obeyed the word of the LORD and returned and departed, according to the word of the LORD. 25 Jeroboam built Shechem, on Mount Ephraim, and lived there; then he de- parted and built Penuel. 26 Jeroboam thought in his heart, "Now the kingdom will return to the house of Dauid. 27 If this people go and sacrifice in the house of the LORD in Jerusa- lem, the heart of this people will turn again to their lord, that is, to Rehoboam king of Judah; so they will kill me and turn again to Rehoboam king of Judah." 28 Then the king took counsel, and made two goblets of gold, and said to them, "It is too much for you to go to Jerusalem; look, O Israel, to your gods who brought you out of the land of Egypt." 29 And he set the one in Bet-el and the other in Dan. 30 And this turned into sin, because the people went (because of the one) always to Dan. 31 He also made a house of places, and appointed priests the humblest of the people, who did not belong to the sons of Leui. 32 Je- roboam made a feast on the fifteenth day of the eighth month, like that which is made in Judah, and offered on the altar. So he did at Beth-el and offered at the chalices which he had made; and he put at Beth-el the priests of the places which he had made. 33 And he of- fered on the altar which he had made at Beth- el on the fifteenth day of the eighth month (that is, in the month which he had forged of his heart), and he made a solemn feast for the children of Israel; and then he went to the al- tar to burn incense.

CHAPTER 13

1 And behold, a man of God went out from Iudah (by the command of the Lord) toward Beth-el, and Jeroboam stood by the altar to offer incense. 2 And he cried out against the altar by the command of the LORD, and said, "O altar, altar, thus says the LORD: Behold, a child shall be born in the house of Dauid, by the name of Josiah, and upon thee shall the priests of the places sacrifice incense burnt upon thee, and upon thee shall they bury the bones of men." 3 And at the same time he made a sign, saying, "This is the sign which the LORD said, Behold, the altar shall be bro- ken, and the ashes upon it shall fall down." 4 When the king had heard the words of the man of God, who had cried out against the altar at Beth-el, Jeroboam stretched out his hand from the altar, saying, "Take it into your hand"; but the hand that he had put against it dried up and he could no longer draw it toward him. 5 The altar also split, and ashes fell from the altar, according to the sign that the man of God had made by the Lord's com- mand. 6 Then the king answered and said to the man of God, "Please pray to the

Lord your God and intercede for me, that my hand may be restored to me." The man of God prayed to the Lord, and the king's hand was restored and returned as before. 7 Then the king said to the man of God, "Come home with me, that you may die, and I will give you a reward." 8 But the man of God said to the king, "If you would give me half of your house, I would not go in with you, nor eat bread nor drink water in this place. 9 For thus it has been enjoined upon me by the word of the LORD, 'Do not eat bread or drink water, and do not go back the same way by which you came. 10 So he took another way and did not go back by the way by which he had come to Beth-el. 11 And an old prophet dwelt in Beth-el, and his sons came and told him all the things that the man of God had done that day in Beth-el, and the words that he had spoken to the king, they told their father. 12 Their father said to them, "Which way did he go?" and his sons explained to him which way the man of God who came from Iudah went. 13 He said to his sons, "Saddle me the way." Who saddled his horse and he rode it, 14 Then he went after the man of God and found him sitting under a pole; and he said to him, "Are you the man of God who came from Iudah?" And he answered, "Yes." 15 Then he said to him, "Come home with me and eat bread." 16 But he answered, "I cannot return with you or go in with you; I will not eat bread or drink water with you in this place. 17 For it has been enjoined upon me by the word of the Lord, 'You shall not eat bread nor drink water in that place, and you shall not turn back to go the way you went. 18 He answered him, "I too am a prophet like you, and an angel spoke to me by the word of the Lord, saying, 'Take him still with you into your house, that you may eat bread and drink water.'" 19 Then he went with him again and ate bread in his house and drank water. 20 As they sat at table, the word of the LORD came to the prophet who had brought him again. 21 He cried out to the man of God who had come from Iudah, "Thus says the LORD: Because you disobeyed the mouth of the LORD and did not observe the command that the LORD your God gave you, 22 but you went back and ate bread and drank water in the place (where he had said to you, 'You shall not eat bread or drink water'), your chariots shall not come to the tomb of your fathers." 23 When he had eaten the bread and drunk, he led him to the plank, that is, to the prophet whom he had brought again. 24 When he was gone, a lion met him on the road and killed him; his body was thrown into the road and the plank remained there; the lion also remained near the body. 25 The men who were passing by saw the car thrown into the road and the lion standing by the body; and they came and told about it in the town where the old prophet lived. 26 When the prophet who brought him back again from the road learned of it, he said, "This is the man of God, who has been disobedient to the Lord's com- mands; therefore the Lord delivered him to the lion, who quartered him and killed him, according to the word of the Lord to him." 27 He spoke to his sons, saying, "Saddle me the plank." And they saddled him. 28 And he went and found his body cast on the road, and the body and the lion standing still beside the body; and the lion had not eaten the body nor tormented the body. 29 And the prophet took the body of the man of God, and laid it on the rack, and brought it again; and the old prophet came into the city to mourn and bury him. 30 He laid the body in his grave, and they mourned for him, saying, "Alas, my brother." 31 When he had buried him, he spoke to his sons, saying, "When I am dead, bury me also in the tomb where the man of God is buried; lay my bones beside his bones." 32 For that which he cried by the mouth of the LORD against the altar that is in Bet-el, and against

all the houses of the places of worship that are in the cities of Samaria, shall surely come to pass. 33 However, after this fact, Jeroboam did not turn from his evil way, but went back and made of the lowest of the people priests of the holy places. Whoever wanted, he could consecrate himself and be one of the priests of the holy places. 34 And this thing turned into sin for the house of Jeroboam, so that it was extirpated and destroyed from the face of the earth.

CHAPTER 14

1 At that time Abijah the son of Jeroboam fell sick. 2 Jeroboam said to his wife, "Go away, please, disguise yourself, so that it will not be known that you are Jeroboam's wife, and go to Sciloh, for there is the prophet Ahijah there, who told me that I would become king of this people, 3 take with you ten loaves, ribbons, and a bottle of gold, and go to him; he will tell you what will become of the young man. 4 And Jeroboam's wife did so, and rose up, and went to Shiloh, and came to the house of Ahiiah; but Ahiiah could not see, because his sight had declined through age. 5 Then the LORD said to Ahiiah, "Behold, Jeroboam's wife is coming to ask you one thing for her son, because he is sick; so and so you must tell her, for when she comes, she will consider another." 6 Therefore, when Ahijah heard the sound of her feet when she came through the door, he said, "Come in, wife of Jeroboam; why do you want to be another? I have been sent to you with good news. 7 Go, say to Je- roboam, "Thus says the LORD God of Israel, For I have exalted you among the people and made you prince over my people of Israel, 8 I took the kingdom from the house of Dauid and gave it to you, and you have not been like my servant Dauid, who kept my commands and followed me wholeheartedly and did only what was right in my eyes, 9 but you did the opposite of all those who were before you (for you went and created other gods and molten images for yourself, to make me afraid, and you cast me behind your back). 10 Therefore, behold, I will cause euilius to come upon the house of Jeroboam, and I will cut off from Je- roboam those who piss against the wall, and those who are shut up, and those who are left in Israel, and I will sweep away the rest of the house of Jeroboam, as a man sweeps away manure, until it is all gone. 11 The dogs shall eat the cattle of Jeroboam that die in the city, and the waste of the air shall eat the cattle that die in the fields, for the LORD has said it. 12 Go therefore to your house, for when your feet enter the city, the child shall die. 13 All Israel shall mourn for him and bury him, for he alone of Jeroboam shall come to the grave, for in him was found some kindness to the LORD God of Israel in the house of Jeroboam. 14 Moreover, the LORD will raise up a king of Israel who will destroy the house of Jeroboam on that day. 15 For the LORD will smite Isra- el, as when a reed is shaken in the water, and will tear Israel from his good daughter, whom he had given to their fathers, and will scat- ter them beyond the river, because they have made themselves into groups, provoking the LORD to wrath. 16 He will deliver Israel be- cause of the sins of Jeroboam, who sinned and caused Israel to sin. 17 And Jeroboam's wife arose, and departed, and came to Tir- zah; and when she came to the threshold of the house, the young man died, 18 And they buried him, and all Israel mourned for him, according to the word of the LORD, spoken by the hand of his servant Ahijah the prophet. 19 The rest of the deeds of Jeroboam, how he waged war and how he reigned, behold, they are written in the book of the Chronicles of the kings

of Israel. 20 The days that Jeroboam reigned were two years and twenty; and he fell asleep with his fathers, and Nadab his son reigned in his stead. 21 Rehoboam the son of Solomon also reigned in Iudah. Rehoboam was one year old and forty-five years old when he began to reign, and he reigned seven years in Jerusalem, the city which the LORD had chosen out of all the tribes of Israel to put His Name there; and his mother's name was Naamah, an Ammonite. 22 And Iudah com- mitted wickedness in the sight of the LORD, and they provoked him more by their sins, which they had committed, than by all that their fathers had done. 23 For they also made themselves places and images and groups on every hill and under every green tree. 24 There were also Sodomites in the land, who did all the abominations of the nations whom the LORD had cast out before the children of Is- rael. 25 In the fifth year of King Rehoboam, Shishak king of Egypt came against Jerusale, 26 and took the treasures of the house of the LORD and the treasures of the house of kings and carried them all away; he also carried away all the shields of gold that Solomon had made. 27 And King Rehoboam made for them shields of bronze and put them into the hands of the chief of the guards who stood at the edge of the king's house. 28 When the king entered the house of the LORD, the guards carried them and brought them back to the garden hall. 29 Are not the rest of the acts of Rehoboam and all that he did written in the book of the Chronicles of the kings of Judah? 30 There was continuous warfare between Re- hoboam and Jeroboam. 31 And Rehoboam fell asleep with his fathers and was buried with his fathers in the city of Dauid; and his moth- er's name was Naamah, an Ammonite. And Abiiam, his son, reigned in his place.

CHAPTER 15

1 In the eighteenth year of King Jeroboam the son of Nebat, Abiiam of Judeah reigned. 2 He reigned for three years in Jerusalem, and his mother's name was Maachah, daughter of Abishalom. 3 He continued to commit all the sins of his father, which he had commit- ted before him, and his heart was not per- fect with the LORD his God, like the heart of Dauid his father. But for Dauid the LORD his God gave him a light in Jerusalem, and set his son after him and established Jerusalem, 5 For Dauid did what was right in the eyes of the LORD, and did not depart from anything that he had commanded him, all the days of his life, especially in the matter of Vriah the Hittite. 6 There was war between Rehoboam and Jeroboam as long as he lived. 7 Are not the rest of Abiiam's deeds and all that he did writ- ten in the book of the Chronicles of the kings of Judah? There was war also between Abi- iam and Jeroboam. 8 Abiiam fell asleep with his fathers and they buried him in the city of Dauid; Asa his son reigned in his place. 9 In the twentieth year of Jeroboam, king of Israel, Asa reigned in Judeah. 10 He reigned in Jeru- salem for a year and forty, and his mother's name was Maachah, daughter of Abishalom. 11 Asa behaved well in the eyes of the LORD, like Dauid his father. 12 He made the Sod- omites disappear from the land, and he made all the idols that his fathers had made disap- pear. 13 He also made Maachah, his mother, disappear from her property, because she had made idolatry in a group; Asa destroyed her idolatries and burned them by the brook Kidron. 14 But they did not set up the plac- es of worship. Asa's heart was always true to the LORD all his days. 15 He also brought his father's sacred furnishings and the things he had dedicated to the house of the LORD,

silver, gold and vessels. 16 There was war be- tween Asa and Baasha, king of Israel, all their days. 17 Baasha, king of Israel, went against Judah and bought Ramah, so that he did not allow anyone to go out or come in to Asa, king of Judah. 18 Then Asa took all the sil- ver and gold that was left in the treasures of the house of the LORD and in the treasures of the king's house, and delivered them into the hands of his servants, and King Asa sent them to Ben-Hadad, son of Tabrimon, son of Hezion, king of Aram, who dwelt in Damas- cus, saying, "There is a city that has not been destroyed, 19 There is a covenant between me and you, between my father and your father; behold, I have sent you a gift of silver and gold; come, break your covenant with Baasha king of Israel, that he may depart from me." 20 Ben-Hadad listened to King Asa and sent the captains of the hosts he had against the cities of Israel and defeated Leontes, Dan, Abel-Beth-Macha, all Cinneroth and all the land of Naphtali. 21 When Baasha heard this, he left the purchase of Ramah and settled in Tirzah. 22 Then King Asa gathered all the in- habitants of Iudah together, no one excepted. They took the stones of Ramah and the timber that Baasha had bought, and King Asa built with them Sheba of Benjamin and Mizpah. 23 Are not the rest of all Asa's deeds, all his strength, all that he did and the cities he ac- quired, written in the book of the Chronicles of the Kings of Judah? But in his old age he was sick in his feet. 24 And Asa slept with his fathers, and was buried with his fathers in the city of Dauid his father. And Iehoshaphat his son reigned in his place. 25 And Nadab the son of Jeroboam began to reign in Israel the sec- ond year of Asa king of Judah, and he reigned in Israel two years. 26 He acted wrongly in the eyes of the LORD, continuing to follow the way of his father and committing the sin he had caused Israel to commit. 27 Baasha the son of Ahijah, of the house of Issachar, con- spired against him, and Baasha killed him at Gibeton, which belonged to the Philistines, because Nadab and all Israel besieged Gibet- on. 28 Then in the third year of Asa, king of Judeah, Baasha killed him and reigned in his place. 29 When he was king, he defeated all the house of Jeroboam, and left no one else to Jeroboam until he had destroyed him, ac- cording to the word of the LORD spoken by his servant Ahijah the Scylonite, 30 because of the sins of Jeroboam which he committed and by which he caused Israel to sin, by his prouation, by which he forbade the Lord God of Israel. 31 Are not the rest of the acts of Na- dab and all that he did written in the book of the Chronicles of the kings of Israel? 32 There was war between Asa and Baasha, kings of Is- rael, all their days. 33 In the third year of Asa, king of Judah, Baasha the son of Ahijah began to reign over all Israel in Tirzah and reigned four years and twenty. 34 He behaved badly in the eyes of the LORD, following the way of Je- roboam and his sin, by which he caused Israel to sin.

CHAPTER 16

1 Then the word of the LORD was spoken to Jehu the son of Hanani against Baasha, and he said, "For I have exalted you from the dust and made you the ruler of my people of Isra- el, 2 For I have exalted you from the dust and made you the head of my people of Israel, and you have walked in the way of Jeroboam and caused my people of Israel to sin, to put me to shame with their sins, 3 Behold, I will take away the posterity of Baasha and the poster- ity of his house, and I will make your house like the house of Jeroboam the son of Nebat. 4 He who dies of Baasha in the

city shall be eat- en by dogs; and the man who dies in the fields shall be eaten by the carrion of the threshing floor. 5 Are not the rest of Baasha's deeds, what he did, and his power, written in the book of the Chronicles of the kings of Israel? 6 Baasha fell asleep with his fathers and was buried in Tirzah; Elah his son reigned in his dwelling place. 7 Also by the hand of Jehu the son of Hanani, the prophet, came the word of the LORD to Baasha and to his house, that it should become like the house of Jeroboam, because of all the wickedness he had com- mitted before the LORD, provoking him with the works of his hands, and because he had killed him. 8 In the sixty-second year of Asa, king of Judah, Elah the son of Baasha began to reign over Israel in Tirzah and reigned for two years. 9 His servant Zimri, head of half of his chiefs, conspired against him while he was in Tirzah drinking, until he became drunk in the house of Arza, steward of his house in Tirzah. 10 And Zimri came, and smote him, and slew him, in the tenth and twentieth year of Asa, king of Iudah, and reigned in his stead. 11 When he was king and sat on his throne, he killed all the house of Baasha, not letting one of them crash against a wall, neither of his relatives nor of his friends. 12 Thus Zimri de- stroyed the whole house of Baasha, according to the word of the LORD which he had spo- ken against Baasha by the hand of Jehu the prophet, 13 For all the sins of Baasha and for the sins of Elah his son, which they commit- ted and caused Israel to commit, and which they provoked the LORD, the God of Israel, with their vanities. 14 Are not the rest of the deeds of Elah and all that he did written in the book of the Chronicles of the kings of Israel? 15 In the seventy-second year of Asa, king of Judah, Zimri reigned ten days in Tirzah, and the people were then on the march against Gibbethon, who belonged to the Philistines. 16 The people of the army heard, "Zimri has conspired and killed the king." Therefore all Israel that same day made Omri the captain of the army, king of Israel and of the army. 17 Then Omri departed from Gibbethon, and all Israel with him, and they besieged Tirzah. 18 When Zimri saw that the city had been taken, he went into the palace of the king's house, burned himself and the king's house with fire, and died, 19 For his sins, which he committed by doing that which is evil in the sight of the LORD, walking in the way of Je- roboam, and for his sins which he committed by causing Israel to sin. 20 Are not the rest of Zimri's deeds and the treachery he commit- ted written in the book of the Chronicles of the kings of Israel? 21 Then the people of Is- rael were divided into two parts: half the peo- ple followed Tibni the son of Ginath to make him king, and the other half followed Omri. 22 But the people who followed Omri op- posed the people who followed Tibni, son of Ginath; so Tibni died and Omri reigned. 23 In the thirtieth year of Asa, king of Judeah, Omri began to reign over Israel and reigned for two years. For six years he reigned in Tirzah. 24 He bought the mountain of Samaria from a man named Shemer for two talents of silver, and he bought the mountain and called the city he bought by the name of Shemer, lord of the mountain, Samaria. 25 But Omri behaved badly in the eyes of the LORD and did worse than all who had gone before him. 26 For he went all the way of Jeroboam the son of Nebat, and committed the sins that he had made Is- rael commit, endangering the LORD, the God of Israel, with their vanities. 27 Are not the rest of the deeds of Omri, which he did, and his strength which he showed, written in the book of the Chronicles of the kings of Israel? 28 Omri fell asleep with his fathers and was buried in Samaria; in his place reigned Ahab his son. 29 Now Ahab the son of Omri began to reign in Israel in the thirtieth year of Asa king of Judeah; Ahab the son of Omri reigned in Israel in Samaria for twenty years. 30 Ahab the son of Omri did worse than all who had gone before him in the eyes of the LORD. 31 For was it a light thing for him to walk in the sins of Jeroboam, son of Nebat, except that he also took to wife Jezebel, daughter of Ethbaal, king of the Zidonians, who went to serve Baal and worshiped him? 32 Moreover he erected an altar to Baal in the house of Baal that he had bought in Samaria. 33 And Ahab made a band of people, and Ahab went about the Lord, the God of Israel, more than all the kings of Israel that had gone before him. 34 In his day Hiel, the Bethelite, bought Jericho; he laid its foundations to Abiram, his eldest son, and fixed its gates to Segub, his youngest son, according to the word of the LORD which he spoke through Ioshua the son of Nun.

CHAPTER 17

1 Elijah, the Tishbite, one of the inhabitants of Gilead, said to Ahab, "As the Lord, the God of Israel, before whom I stand, wills, there shall be no dew or ray in these years, except according to my word." 2 The word of the LORD came to him, saying. 3 "Go away, turn to the east and hide yourself in the riviera of Cherith, which is opposite Iorden, 4 and drink from that river; and I have commanded the rauens to feed you there." 5 So he went and did according to the word of the LORD; he went and stayed by the river Cherith, which is opposite Iorden. 6 And the rauens brought him bread and meat in the morning, and bread and meat in the evening, and he binged on meat. 7 After a while, the river dried up, because there were no rays on the land. 8 The word of the LORD came to him, saying. 9 "Go away, go to Zarephath, which is in Zidon, and stay there; behold, I have commanded a wid- ow there to support you." 10 Then he arose and went to Zarephath; and when he came to the gate of the city, behold, the widow was there gathering sticks; and he called to her and said, "Please bring me some water in a vessel, that I may drink." 11 As she was about to take it, he called to her and said, "Please bring me a morsel of bread in your hand." 12 She an- swered, "As the LORD your God wills, I have no bread, but only a handful of flour in a bar- rel and a little oil in a basket; and behold, I am gathering a few sticks to go into it and pre- pare it for me and for my son, that we may eat it and dye it." 13 Elijah said to her, "Fear not, come, do as you have said, but first make me some cake and bring it to me, and then pre- pare it for you and for your son." 14 For thus says the LORD, the God of Israel, "The seed in the barrel shall not be wasted, and the oil in the basket shall not diminish until the time when the LORD sends a ray upon the earth." 15 Then she went and did as Elijah had said, and ate; so did he and his house for a time. 16 The barrel of meat did not waste away, and the oil did not run out of the basket, accord- ing to the word of the LORD, spoken by the hand of Elijah. 17 After these things, the son of the wife of the house fell sick, and his sick- ness was so severe that he was out of breath. 18 She said to Elijah, "What shall I do with you, O man of God? Have you come to me to remember my sin and to kill my son?" 19 He said to her, "Give me your son." And he took him out of her womb, and brought him into a chamber, where he remained, and placed him on her bed. 20 Then he called to the LORD and said, "O LORD, my God, have you also pun- ished this widow, with whom I have been in bed, by killing her son? 21 He stretched him- self three times over the child, called on the LORD and said, "O LORD my God, please let the soul of this child return to him." 22 The

Lord heard Eliiah's voice, and the child's soul returned to him, and he recovered. 23 Eliiah took the child, brought him down from the room into the house, handed him over to his mother, and Eliiah said, "Behold, your son lives." 24 The woman said to Eliiah, "Now I know that you are a man of God and that the word of the Lord in your mouth is true."

CHAPTER 18

1 After many days, the word of the LORD came to Elijah in the third year, saying, "Go, present yourself to Ahab, and I will send a ray to the earth." 2 Elijah went and presented himself to Ahab, and there was a great fam- ine in Samaria. 3 And Ahab called Obadiah the keeper of his house; and Obadiah feared God greatly: 4 For when Jezebel destroyed the prophets of the LORD, Obadiah took a hun- dred prophets and hid them fifty in a cave, feeding them with bread and water). 5 Ahab said to Obadiah, "Go into the land, to all the fountains of water and to all the riuers, if it is possible to find fat matter to feed the horses and the mules, lest you deprive the land of the beasts." 6 So they walked on the land between them. Ahab went one way alone and Obadi- ah went another way alone. 7 While Obadiah was on his way, behold, Elijah came to him; he recognized him, fell down and said, "Are not you my lord Elijah?" 8 He answered him, "Yes, go and tell your lord, Behold, Elijah is here." 9 And he said, "What have I done wrong that you should deliver your servant into the hand of Ahab to kill me? 10 As the LORD your God says, there is no nation or kingdom where my Lord has not sent to see you; and when they said, "He is not here," he would take another of those kingdoms and nations, if they did not find you. 11 Now you say, "Go, tell your lord, Behold, Elijah is here." 12 When I am gone from thee, the Spirit of the LORD shall bring thee to a place that I know not; so when I come to tell Ahab, if he find thee not, he shall kill me: but I, thy servant, fear the LORD from my youth." 13 Has not my lord been told what I did when Jezebel killed the prophets of the LORD, how I hid a hundred men of the proph- ets of the LORD by fifty in a cave and fed them with bread and water? 14 And now you say, Go and tell your lord, Behold, Elijah is here, that he may kill me. 15 Elijah answered, "As the LORD of hosts, before whom I stand, wills, I will testify of myself to him today." 16 Then Obadiah went to meet Ahab and told him about it: And Ahab went to Elijah. 17 When Ahab saw Elijah, Ahab said to him, "Are you the one who troubles Israel? 18 He answered, "It is not I who have troubled Israel, but you and your father's house, because you have forsaken the LORD's commands and followed Baalim. 19 Now, therefore, send and gather to me all Israel to Mount Carmel, the prophets of Baal, four hundred and fifty, and the prophets of the groups, four hundred and fifty, who eat at the table of Jezebels." 20 Then Ahab sent for all the children of Israel and gathered the prophets to Mount Carmel. 21 Elijah present- ed himself to all the people and said, "How long will you stand between two opinions? If the Lord is God, follow him; but if he is Baal, follow him." The people did not answer him a word. 22 Then Elijah said to the people, "I am only a prophet of the LORD, but the proph- ets of Baal are four hundred and fifty men. 23 Therefore let them give themselves two heif- ers, and let them choose one, and let them cut it in pieces, and put it on the wood, but do not put you under the fire; I will prepare the oth- er heifer, and put it on the wood, and I will not put you under the fire. 24 Then you shall call upon the name of

your god, and I will call upon the name of the LORD; and then the God who answers with fire, let him be God." And all the people answered and said, "It is well said." 25 Then Elijah said to the prophets of Baal, "Take a bull and prepare it first (for you are many) and call upon the name of your gods, but do not put us under fire." 26 Then they took the one bull that had been given to them, and prepared it, and called upon the name of Baal, from morning to none, saying, "O Baal, hear me"; but there was no answer, nor any one to answer; and they leaped upon the altar that had been built. 27 And Elijah mocked them, and said, "Shout loudly, for he is a god; either he speaks, or he pursues his enemies, or he is traveling, or perhaps he is asleep and must be awakened." 28 Then they shouted loudly and cut themselves, as was their custom, with knives and knuckle-pull- ers, until the blood gushed out on them. 29 When it was past noon and they had proph- esied until the beginning of the noon sacri- fice, there was no one to answer and no one to watch. 30 Then Elijah said to all the peo- ple, "Come to me." And all the people came to him. And he repaired the altar of the Lord that had been demolished. 31 Elijah took two stones, according to the name of the tribes of the sons of Iaakob, to whom the word of the LORD had been spoken, "Israel shall be your name." 32 With the stones he built an altar in the name of the LORD and made around the altar a moat as large as two measures of seed. 33 Then he put the wood in order, cut the bull in pieces, and laid it on the wood, 34 and said, "Fill four barrels with water and pour it over the burnt roast and over the wood." Then he said, "Do this this time also." And they did so the second time. Then he said, "Do it the third time also." And they did it for the third time. 35 Water flowed around the altar, and he filled the moat with water also. 36 When they had to offer the dawn sacrifice, Elijah the prophet came and said, "Lord, God of Abraham, Isaac and Israel, let it be known today that you are the God of Israel, that I am your servant, and that I have done all these things by your com- mand. 37 Hear me, O LORD, hear me, and let this people know that you are the LORD God, and that at the last you have converted their hearts." 38 Then the fire of the LORD came down and consumed the stake, the wood, the stones and the dust, and lapped up the water that was in the moat. 39 When all the people saw it, they fell on their faces and said, "The LORD is God, the LORD is God." 40 Eli- jah said to them, "Take the prophets of Baal, let not one of them escape." They took them, and Elijah took them to the Kishon brook and killed them there. 41 Then Elijah said to Ahab, "Go away, eat and drink, for there is a noise of many rays." 42 And Ahab went and ate and drank, while Elijah went up to the top of Car- mel; and he squatted down on the ground and put his face between his knees, 43 and said to his servant, "Go now and look toward the sea way." He approached, looked, and said, "There is nothing." Then he said, "Go again for more times." 44 And at the seventh time he said, "Behold, a small cloud like a man's hand rises out of the sea." Then he said, "Get up and say to Ahab, 'Prepare your chariot and go down, so that the rain will not hold you back.'" 45 Meanwhile the sky was darkened by clouds and wind, and there was a great beam. Then Ahab set out and came to Izreel. 46 And the hand of the LORD was upon Elijah, and he girded his shoulders and ran before Ahab as far as Izreel.

CHAPTER 19

1 Now Ahab told Iezebel all that Elijah had done and how he had killed all the prophets by the sword. 2 Then Iezebel sent a messenger to Elijah, saying, "Let the gods do this to me and even more, if I do not make your life as one of their lies by dying this time." 3 Knowing this, he arose and went forth for his life, and came to Beer-sheba, which is in Iudah, and left his servant there. 4 But he went into the wilderness for a day, and then came and sat down under a hyuniper tree, and desired to die, say- ing, "Now it is enough: O LORD, take my soul, for I am no better than my fathers." 5 As he lay and slept under the juniper tree, behold, an angel touched him and said, "Arise and eat." 6 When he looked around, behold, there was a cake baked on colas and a jar of water at his head; so he ate and drank, then went back to sleep. 7 The angel of the LORD returned a second time, touched him, and said to him, "Get up and eat, for you have a great journey." 8 Then he arose, ate and drank, and walked by the power of that meal four hundred days and four hundred nights to Horeb, the mountain of God. 9 There he entered a cave and lodged there; and behold, the LORD spoke to him and said, "What are you doing here, Elijah?" 10 He answered, "I have been much anxious for the LORD, God of hosts, because the children of Israel have forsaken your ally, they have torn down your altars and killed your prophets by the sword, and I am left alone, and they seek my life to take it from me." 11 Then he said, "Go out and stand on the mountain before the Lord." And behold, the Lord passed by, and a strong wind ripped through the mountains and broke the rocks before the Lord; but the Lord was not in the wind; and after the wind came an earthquake; but the Lord was not in the earthquake: 12 And after the earthquake came fire, but the LORD was not in the fire; and after the fire came a silence and a sweet- ness. 13 And when Elijah heard it, he covered his face with his cloak, and went out, and stood at the entrance of the cave: and, behold, there came a person to him, saying, "What are you doing here, Elijah?" 14 And he answered, "I have been much anxious for the LORD, God of hosts, because the children of Isra- el have forsaken your ally, and have thrown down your altars, and killed your proph- ets with the sword, and I am left alone, and they seek my life to take it from me." 15 And the LORD said to him, "Go, return through the wilderness toward Damascus, and when you have come there, anoint Hazael king of Aram." 16 And Jehu the son of Nimshi, you shall anoint him as king of Israel; and Elisha the son of Shaphat of Abel Mehola, you shall anoint him as a prophet in your kingdom. 17 He who escapes the sword of Hazael shall be killed by Jehu, and he who escapes the sword of Jehu shall be killed by Elisha. 18 Neverthe- less I will leave six thousand in Israel, that is, all the knees that did not bow to Baal and all the mouths that did not kiss him." 19 So he departed and found Elisha the son of Shaphat plowing with two yoke of oxen before him and standing with the two yokes; Elijah went to him and threw his cloak over him. 20 He left the oxen and ran after Elijah, saying, "Let me, please, kill my father and my mother, and then I will follow you." Who answered him, "Go, turn back; for what have I done to you?" 21 And when he had gone back to him, he took a pair of oxen, killed them, and cleared their throats with the instruments of the oxen, and gave it to the people, who ate; then he arose and went after Elijah and ministered to him.

CHAPTER 20

1 Then Ben-Hadad, king of Aram, gathered his whole army and two or three kings with him, with horses and chariots, and went and besieged Samaria and fought against it. 2 Then he sent messengers to Ahab, king of Is- rael, in the city, 3 And they said to him, "Thus saith Ben-Hadad, Thy silver and thy gold are mine; thy women also, and thy fairest children are mine." 4 And the king of Israel answered, "Mr. king, as thou hast said, I am thine and all that I have." 5 When the messengers came again, they said, "Thus commandeth Ben-Ha- dad, and saith, When I send thee an order, thou shalt deliver unto me thy silk, thy gold, thy women, and thy children, 6 or else I will send my servants to thee to do the morphing of this time; and they shall search thy house, and the houses of thy servants; and that which is pleasing in thine eyes, they shall take it in their hand, and carry it away." 7 Then the king of Israel sent for all the elders of the land and said, "Observe, I pray you, and see how he seeks to do you harm; for he has sent for me for my goods, for my children, for my silk and for my gold, and I have not denied him." 8 All the elders and all the people said to him, "Do not listen to him and do not agree." 9 There- fore he said to the messengers of Ben-Hadad, "Tell the king my lord, All that you sent to say to your servant the first time, I will do, but this thing I cannot do." The messengers departed and brought him an answer. 10 Ben-Hadad sent to him saying, "May the gods do this to me and more, if the dust of Samaria be suf- ficient for all the people that follow me, for every man a handful." 11 The king of Israel an- swered and said, "Tell him that he who girds his belt shall not boast as he who takes it off." 12 When he heard this news, as he was with the kings drinking in the pauilion, he said to his servants, "Bring out your engines," and they set them against the city. 13 And behold, a prophet came to Ahab, king of Israel, say- ing, "Thus says the Lord, Have you seen all this great multitude? Behold, today I will deliver it into your hands, that you may know that I am the LORD." 14 Ahab said, "By whom?" And he answered, "Thus says the Lord: By the ser- vants of the princes of the provinces." And he said again, "Who shall order the battle?" And he answered, "You." 15 Then he appointed the servants of the princes of the provinces, which were two hundred, two hundred and thirty; and after them he appointed the whole people of all the children of Israel, that is, six hundred thousand people. 16 They went out to no one, but Ben-Hadad drank to drunkenness in the tents, both he and the kings, for two and thirty kings helped him. 17 And the servants of the princes of the provinces went out first; and Ben-Hadad sent to say to Ben-Hadad, "There are men coming from Samaria." 18 He said, "Whether they have come for peace, take them foreigners; whether they have come to fight, take them still foreigners." 19 So out of the city went the servants of the princes of the prouinces and the army that followed them. 20 And they slew each his enemy; and the Ar- ameans fled, and Israel pursued them, but Ben-Hadad, king of Aram, fled on horseback with his horsemen. 21 Then the king of Israel went out and struck the horses and chariots and made a great slaughter of the Arameans. 22 (For a prophet had come to the king of Isra- el and said to him, "Go, take courage, reflect, and watch what you do, for when the year is past, the king of Aram will come against you.") 23 Then the servants of the king of Aram said to him, "Their gods are gods of the mountains, and therefore they have defeat- ed them; but if we fight against them in the game, no doubt we shall defeat them." 24 And this he does, "Take away the kings, each one from his place, and set captains for them. 25 And make an army like the one you lost, with horses and chariots of this kind,

and we will fight against them in the plain, and no doubt we will defeat them." 26 When the year had passed, Ben-Hadad gathered the Arameans and went to Aphek to fight against Israel. 27 And the children of Israel were gathered and went against them; and the children of Israel encamped before them, like two little flocks of kids, but the Arameans filled the land. 28 A man of God came and spoke to the king of Israel, saying, "Thus says the LORD: Because the Arameans have said, 'The LORD is the God of the mountains and not the God of the val- leys,' I will deliver all this great multitude into your hands, and you shall know that I am the LORD." 29 And they encamped against each other for ten days, and on the tenth day the battle was won; and the children of Israel slew in one day a hundred thousand foot soldiers of the Arameans. 30 But the rest fled to Aphek in the city; and they fell upon the two hundred thousand men that were left; and Ben-Hadad fled into the city and entered a secret room. 31 His servants said to him, "Behold, we have heard that the kings of the house of Isra- el are merciful kings; we beseech you to put sackcloth around our loins and ropes around our heads and go to the king of Israel; it may be that he will save your life." 32 Then they wrapped their loins in sackcloth and put ropes around their heads and went before the king of Israel, saying, "Your servant Ben-Hadad says, 'Please let me live';" and he answered, "Is he still a foreigner? He is my brother." 33 And the men were careful to see if they could catch anything of him, and they hastened and said, "Your brother Ben-Hadad." And he said, "Go, bring him." Ben-Hadad came out to him and put him in the chariot. 34 Ben-Hadad said to him, "The cities that my father took from your father, I will give them back, and you shall make roads for yourself in Damascus, as my father did in Samaria." Then Ahab said, "I will let you go with this ally." So he made an agreement with him and let him go. 35 Then a certain man of the sons of the Prophets said to his neighbor, by the command of the Lord, "Please strike me." But the man refused to strike him. 36 Then the man said to him, "Because you have not obeyed the message of the Lord, behold, as soon as you have depart- ed from me, a lion will kill you." So when he had departed from him, a lion found him and killed him. 37 Then he found another man and said to him, "Please strike me." And the man struck him, and in striking him he wounded him. 38 Then the prophet departed and went after the king on the road and covered his face with ashes. 39 And when the king passed by, he cried out to the king, and said, Thy ser- vant is gone in the midst of the battle; and behold, a man is gone, whom another man hath brought to me, and hath said to me, Hold this man; if he be lost and miss, thy life shall go for his life, and if not, thou shalt pay a talent of silver. 40 And because thy servant had business here and there, he went away: And the king of Israel said unto him, Thus shall thy judgment be: thou hast pronounced judgment." 41 And he hastened and wiped the ashes off his face; and the king of Israel un- derstood that he was one of the prophets: 42 And he said unto him, Thus saith the LORD, Because thou hast let out of thy hand a man whom I had appointed to die, thy life shall go for his life, and thy people for their people. 43 Then the king of Israel went away to his house in discontent, and came to Samaria.

CHAPTER 21

1 After these things, Naboth the Izreelite had a vineyard in Izreel, near the palace of Ahab, king of Samaria. 2 Ahab spoke to Naboth, say- ing, "Give me your vineyard, that I may make a herb garden of it, for it is near my house; and I will give you in return a better vineyard than it is; or, if it pleases you, I will give you its value in money." 3 Naboth said to Ahab, "May the LORD prevent me from giving you my fa- ther's inheritance." 4 Then Ahab went into his house, weary and displeased at the words that Naboth the Jezreelite had said to him, "I will not give you the inheritance of my fathers," and he lay down on his bed, turning his face away and not wanting to eat bread. 5 Then Je- zebel his wife came to him and said, "Why is your spirit so sad that you do not eat bread?" 6 He answered her, "Because I spoke to Naboth, the Izreelite, and said to him, 'Give me your vineyard for money or, if it pleases you, I will give you another vineyard in exchange;'" but he answered, "I will not give you my vine- yard." 7 Then Jezebel his wife said to him, "Are you the one who now holds the kingdom of Is- rael? Go, eat bread and be of good cheer; I will give you the vineyard of Naboth the Izreelite." 8 So she wrote letters in Ahab's name, sealed them with his seal, and sent them to the el- ders and nobles who were in his city and who lived with Naboth. 9 She wrote in the letters, "Proclaim a fast and put Naboth among the leaders of the people." 10 and she set before him two wicked men to testify against him, saying, "You have blasphemed God and the king; then take him out and stone him so that he may die." 11 The men of his city, that is, the elders and rulers who lived in his city, did as Iezebel had sent them, as was written in the letters he had sent them. 12 They proclaimed a fast and put Naboth among the leaders of the people, 13 Then two wicked men came and sat before him; and the wicked men testified against Naboth in the presence of the people, saying, "Naboth has blasphemed God and the king." Then they took him out of the city and stoned him with stones, which caused him to die. 14 Then they sent word to Jezebel, "Naboth has been stoned and is dead." 15 When Jezebel heard that Naboth had been stoned and was dead, she said to Ahab, "Go away and take possession of the vineyard of Naboth the Jezreelite, which he refused to give you for money, because Naboth is no longer alive but is dead." 16 When Ahab heard that Naboth was dead, he got up to go to the vineyard of Naboth the Izreelite to take possession of it. 17 The word of the LORD was spoken to Elijah, the Tishbite, and he said 18 "Get up, go meet Ahab, king of Israel, who is in Samaria. He is in the vineyard of Naboth, where he has come down to take possession. 19 Therefore thou shalt say unto him, Thus saith the Lord, Hast thou slain, and hast thou also taken posses- sion? And thou shalt speak unto him, saying, Thus saith the Lord, In the place where dogs have licked the blood of Naboth, dogs shall also lick thy blood. 20 Then Ahab said to Eli- jah, "Hast thou found me, O my enemy?" and he answered, "I have found thee, because thou hast gone out of thy way to do evil in the sight of the LORD. 21 Behold, I will smite thee, I will take away thy seed, and I will cut off from Ahab both he that pisseth against the wall, and he that is shut up in the house, and he that is left in Israel, 22 And I will make your house like the house of Jeroboam the son of Nebat, and like the house of Baasha the son of Ahijah, because of the arrogance with which you set yourself to sin and caused Israel to sin. 23 The LORD also spoke of Jezebel, say- ing, "The dogs shall devour Jezebel by the wall of Jezreel. 24 The dogs shall eat the cattle of Ahab that die in the city; and of him that dies in the fields shall the carrion of the threshing floor eat." 25 There was no one like Ahab, who had gone out of his way to work wickedness in the eyes of the LORD, and whom Jezeb- el his wife had provoked. 26

For he behaved extremely abominably in following idolatries, according to all that the Amorites did, whom the LORD drove out before the children of Israel). 27 When Ahab heard these words, he tore his clothes, put on sackcloth, fasted, put on sackcloth, and went to sleep. 28 The word of the LORD came to Elijah, the Tishbite, and he said, "Do you not see how the LORD has gone out of his way? 29 Do you see how Ahab humbled himself before me? Because he has submitted before me, I will not bring that evil in his days, but in the days of his sons I will bring evil upon his house."

CHAPTER 22

1 Three years continued without war be- tween Aram and Israel. 2 In the third year Ie- hoshaphat, king of Iudah, came down to the king of Israel. 3 The king of Israel said to his servants, "Do you not know that Ramoth Gil- ead was ours? And that we remain and do not take it out of the hand of the king of Aram?" 4 And he said to Iehoshaphat, "Will you come with me to fight against Ramoth Gilead?" And Iehoshaphat said to the king of Israel, "I am like you, my people like your people, and my horses like your horses." 5 Then Iehoshaphat said to the king of Israel, "Ask counsel of the LORD, I pray you, for today." 6 Then the king of Israel gathered the prophets out of four hundred men and said to them, "Shall I go against Ramoth Gilead and fight, or shall I leave her alone? And they answered, "Go, for the LORD will deliver her into the king's hand." 7 And Iehoshaphat said, "Is there still a prophet of the LORD here, that we may question him?" 8 And the king of Israel said to Jehoshaphat, "There is still a man (Michaiah, son of Imlah) from whom we may seek coun- sel of the LORD, but I hate him, for he proph- esies me not good, but evil." And Jehoshaphat said, "Let not the king say so." 9 Then the king of Israel called an Eunuch and said, "Call Mi- chaiah the son of Imlah at once." 10 And the king of Israel and Iehoshaphat king of Iudah sat on their thrones in their garments in the place of passage at the entrance to the gate of Samaria, and all the prophets prophesied be- fore them. 11 Zidkiiah the son of Chenaanah made them yron horns and said, "Thus says the LORD: With these you shall drive the Ar- ameans until you consume them." 12 All the prophets prophesied thus, saying, "Go to Ra- moth Gilead and prosper, for the LORD will deliver it into the hands of the kings." 13 The messenger who had gone to call Michaiah spoke to him, saying, "Behold, the words of the prophets declare themselves good for the king with one accord; your word, therefore, I pray you, be as the word of one of them, and speak well." 14 Michaiah said, "As the LORD wills, what the LORD tells me, I will say." 15 So he came to the king, and the king said to him, "Michaiah, shall we go against Ramoth Gilead to fight, or shall we leave?" And he answered him, "Go and prosper; the LORD will deliver him into the king's hand." 16 Then the king said to him, "How many times must I compel you to tell me nothing but what is true in the name of the LORD?" 17 Then he said, "I saw all Israel scattered on the mountains, like sheep that have no shepherd." And the LORD said, "These have no master; let each one go back to his home in peace." 18 (The king of Israel said to Iehoshaphat, "Did I not tell you that he would prophesy to me nothing good, but only evil?"). 19 Then he said, "Hear therefore the word of the LORD. I saw the Lord sitting on his throne, and all the hosts of Heauen stood around him on his right and on his left. 20 The LORD said, "Who will persuade Ahab to go and fall to Ramoth Gilead?" And one said this way and another that way. 21 Then a spir- it came out and stood before the LORD and said, "I will convince him." And the LORD said to him, "With what?" 22 And he said, "I will go out and be a false spirit on the lips of all his prophets." Then the Lord said, "You will se- duce him and prevail over him; go out and do this." 23 Now therefore, behold, the LORD has put a lying spirit in the mouth of all these your prophets, and the LORD has appealed against you." 24 Then Zidkiiah the son of Chenaanah came up, struck Michaiah on the chin, and said, "When did the Spirit of the Lord come out of me to speak to you?" 25 Michaiah said, "Behold, you will see in that day, when you go from room to room to hide yourself." 26 And the king of Israel said, "Take Michaiah and bring him to Amon, the ruler of the city, and to Ioash, the king's son, 27 and say to him, "Thus says the king, Put this man in the pris- on house and feed him with bread of afflic- tion and water of affliction, until I return in peace." 28 And Michaiah said, If thou return in peace, the Lord hath not spoken through me. And he said, "Hear all of you, people." 29 Then the king of Israel and Iehoshaphat king of Judah went to Ramoth Gilead. 30 And the king of Israel said to Iehoshaphat, "I will change my clothes and go into the battle, but you put on your garment." The king of Israel changed and entered the battle. 31 The king of Aram gave orders to his two hundred and thirty captains outside his cemeteries, say- ing, "Do not fight either with the small or the great, but only against the king of Isra- el." 32 And when the captains of the coteries saw Iehoshaphat, they said, "He is indeed the king of Israel," and they turned to fight against him; and Iehoshaphat wept. 33 And when the captains of the harets saw that he was not the king of Israel, they turned away from him. 34 Then a certain man, stretching a bow with force, struck the king of Israel be- tween the teeth of his brig. Therefore he said to his watchman, "Turn your hand and take me away from the army, for I am wounded." 35 And that day the battle increased, and the king stood firm in his charet against the Arameans, and was immediately dyed; and blood came out of the wound in the mid- dle of the charet. 36 And when the sun went down, an announcement went out through all the army, saying, "Let every man return to his city, and every man to his county." 37 So the king died and was taken to Samaria; then they buried the king in Samaria. 38 And they washed the caesar in the poole of Samaria, and the dogs licked his blood (and washed his armor) according to the word of the LORD which he had spoken. 39 As for the rest of Ahab's deeds and all that he did, the yuorie house he built and all the cities he built, are they not written in the book of Chronicles of the kings of Israel? 40 Then Ahab fell asleep with his fathers, and Ahaziah his son reigned in his place. 41 Then Iehoshaphat the son of Asa began to reign over Iudah in the fourth year of Ahab, king of Israel. 42 When he began to reign, Iehoshaphat was five years old and thirty years old, and he reigned for five years and twenty years in Jerusalem. His mother's name was Azubah, daughter of Shilhi. 43 He followed all the ways of Asa, his father, and did not depart from them, but did what was right in the eyes of the LORD. Nevertheless, the places of worship were not taken away, for the people still offered themselves and burned incense in the places of worship. 44 Iehoshaphat made peace with the king of Israel. 45 Are not the rest of Iehoshaphat's

deeds, his notable deeds and the battles he fought, written in the book of the Chronicles of the Kings of Iudah? 46 And the Sodomites, who had remained in the days of his father Asa, he removed them from the land. 47 Then there was no king in Edom: the king was the substitute. 48 Iehoshaphat sent out ships from Tharshish to go to Ophir to look for gold, but they did not go, for the ships broke up at Ezion Gaber. 49 Then Ahaziah the son of Ahab said to Iehoshaphat, "Let my servants go with your servants on the ships," but Iehoshaphat would not. 50 And Iehoshaphat slept with his fathers and was buried with his fathers in the city of Dauid his father, and Jehoram his son reigned in his place. 51 And Ahaziah the son of Ahab began to reign in Israel in Samaria, the seventeenth year of Jehoshaphat king of Judah, and he reigned two years in Israel. 52 But he did evil in the sight of the LORD, and walked in the way of his father, in the way of his mother, and in the way of Jeroboam the son of Nebat, who made Israel sin. 53 For he served Baal and worshiped him, provoking the LORD, the God of Israel, to wrath, as his father had done.

II KINGS

CHAPTER 1

1 After Ahab's death, Moab rebelled against Israel: 2 Ahaziah fell under his bedroom win- dow in Samaria and became ill; then he sent messengers to whom he said, "Go and ask Baal-Zebub, the God of Ekron, if I can be cured of this illness of mine." 3 Then the angel of the LORD said to Elijah the Tishbite, "Get up, go meet the messengers of the king of Samaria and say to them, 'Is it not because there is no God in Israel that you go and ask Baal-Ze- bub, god of Ekron?' 4 Therefore thus says the LORD, "You shall not come down from the bed on which you have climbed, but you shall die a death." So Elijah departed. 5 The messengers returned to him, and he said, "Why have you returned? 6 They answered him, "A man came and met you and said to you, 'Go, return to the king who sent you and say to him, "Thus says the LORD: Is it not because there is no God in Israel that you are sending for information to Baal-Zebub, the God of Ekron? Therefore you shall not come down from the bed on which you have climbed, but you shall die a death." 7 Then he said to them, "What kind of man was he who came to you and spoke these words to you?" 8 They answered him, "He was a healthy man and had a leather belt around his liga- ments." Then he said, "He is Elijah the Tish- bite." 9 Therefore the king sent him a captain of fifty men with his fifty men, who came to him; for he stood on the top of a mountain and said to him, "O man of God, the king has commanded that you come down." 10 But Eli- jah answered and said to the captain of the fifty, "If I am a man of God, let fire come down from above and kill you and your fifty." So the fire came down from above and struck him and his fifty. 11 Then he sent to him another captain of fifty with his fifty. This one spoke and said to him, "O man of God, thus the king has commanded: come down at once." 12 But Elijah answered and said to them, "If I am a man of God, let fire come down from above and kill you and your fifties." So the fire came down from above and struck him and his fifty. 13 Then he sent the third captaine again, with his fifty. The thirteenth captaine over fiftie went, came, fell on his knees before Elijah, pleaded with him, and said, "O man of God, please let my life and the lives of these fifty of your servants be precious in your sight." 14 Behold, fire has come down from above, and has destroyed the two former captains,

over fifty, with their fifty; therefore let my life now be precious in your sight." 15 The angel of the LORD said to Elijah, "Go down with him; do not depart from his presence." So he got up and went with him to the king. 16 And he said to him, "Thus says the Lord, Since you have sent messengers to inquire of Baal-Zebub, god of Ekron (was it not because there was no god in Israel to inquire of his word?), you shall not come down from the bed on which you have climbed, but you shall die a death." 17 So he died according to the word of the LORD that Elijah had spoken. And Jehoram began to reign in his house, in the second year of Je- horam the son of Jehoshaphat king of Judah, for he had no sons. 18 As for the rest of the deeds done by Ahaziah, are they not written in the book of the Chronicles of the kings of Israel?

CHAPTER 2

1 When the Lord wanted to bring Elijah to Heauen with a whirlwind, Elijah went with Elisha to Gilgal. 2 Then Elijah said to Elisha, "Please stay here, for the Lord has sent me to Bethel." But Elisha said, "As it pleases the Lord and as it pleases your soul, I will not leave you." So they went down to Bet-el. 3 The sons of the prophets who were in Beth-el approached El- isha and said to him, "Do you know that today the Lord will take your master off your head?" And he answered, "Yes, I know; be assured." 4 Then Elijah said to him, "Elisha, please stay here, for the Lord has sent me to Jericho; but he answered, "As the Lord wills and as your soul wills, I will not leave you." So they came to Jericho. 5 The sons of the prophets who were in Jericho came to Elisha and said to him, "Do you know that today the Lord will take your master from your head?" And he answered, "Yes, I know; be assured." 6 Moreover Elijah said to him, "Please keep yourself here, for the Lord has sent me to Iorden." But he said, "As it pleases the Lord and as it pleases your soul, I will not leave you." So they both left together. 7 Fifty men of the sons of the prophets went and stood on the other side, far away, and the two of them stood by Iorden. 8 Then Elijah took his cloak, and wrapped it together, and struck the waters, and they were carried away this way and that, and twice they went away to the dry land. 9 Now when they had passed over, Elijah said to Elisha, "Ask what I must do for you before they take me out of the way." And Elisha said, "Please let your Spirit be double upon me." 10 And he said, "You have asked a hard thing; but if you see me when I am taken from you, you shall have it; if not, it shall not be so." 11 As they were walking and talking, behold, a chariot of fire and horses of fire appeared and separated them twice. Then Elijah set out toward Eauen by a whirl- ing wind. 12 And Elisha saw it and cried, "My father, my father, the chariot of Israel and its riders"; and he saw it no more; and he took his garments and tore them in two pieces. 13 He also took Elijah's cloak, which had fallen from him, and went back and stood by the border of Iorden. 14 After he had taken Elijah's cloak that had fallen from him, he struck the wa- ters and said, "Where is the Lord God of Eli- jah? And so he also, having struck the waters so that they diverted this way and that way, departed, like Elisha. 15 When the sons of the Prophets, who were in Jericho, saw him on the other side, they said, "The Spirit of Elijah rests on Elisha"; and they went out to meet him and fell to the ground before him, 16 and they said to him, "Behold, there are with your servants fifty strong men; let them go, we pray you, to see your master, if it is true that the Spirit of the Lord has taken him and cast

him on some mountain or in some valley." But he answered, "You shall not depart." 17 But they came upon him, until he was ashamed; therefore he said, "Depart." So they sent fif- ty men, and they searched for three days, but they did not find him. 18 Therefore they re- turned to him (for he had stopped at Jericho), and he said to them, "Did I not say to you, Do not go?" 19 The men of the city said to Elisha, "Well, we pray you: the situation of this city is pleasant, as you, my lord, see, but the water is not there, and the ground is barren." 20 Then he said, "Bring me a new pitcher and put salt in it." And they brought it to him. 21 And he went to the spring of the waters, and cast salt into it, and said, "Thus saith the Lord, I have healed this water; death shall no more come out of it, and the ground shall no more be barren." 22 So the waters were healed to this day, according to the word of Elisha which he had spoken. 23 From there he went on his way to Bet-el. And as he went on his way, there came out of the city children mocking him and saying, "Come, thou fool's head, come, thou fool's head." 24 And he turned back and looked at them and cursed them in the name of the Lord. And two beasts came out of the forest and cut up two and forty children of them. 25 From there he went to Mount Car- mel, and from there he returned to Samaria.

CHAPTER 3

1 Now Jehoram the son of Ahab began to reign in Israel in Samaria, in the eighteenth year of Jehoshaphat, king of Judah, and reigned for two years. 2 He operated well in the eyes of the Lord, but not as his father nor as his mother, for he removed the image of Baal that his father had made. 3 Moreover, he freed himself from the sins of Jeroboam the son of Nebat, who had caused Israel to sin, and he did not depart from them. 4 Then Mesha king of Moab had a great number of sheep, and he delivered to the king of Israel a hundred thousand lambs and a hundred thousand branches of wool. 5 But when Ahab was dead, the king of Moab rebelled against the king of Israel. 6 Therefore King Jehoram went out from Samaria at that same time and made the name of all Israel, 7 went and sent and said to Jehoshaphat king of Iudah, "The king of Moab has rebelled against me; will you come with me to fight against Moab?" He answered, "I will come, for I am like you, my people like your people, and my horses like your horses." 8 Then she asked him, "By which way shall we go?" And he answered, "By the way of the wilderness of Edom." 9 So the king of Israel, the king of Iudah and the king of Edom went, and when they had traveled the way for seven days, they had no water either for the army or for the cattle that followed them. 10 Therefore the king of Israel said, "Alas, the LORD has called these three kings to give them into the hand of Moab." 11 But Iehoshaphat said, "Is there not a prophet of the LORD here, that we may ask the LORD through him?" One of the servants of the king of Israel answered, "Here is Elisha the son of Scafat, who made water flow over Elijah's hands." 12 Then Iehoshaphat said, "The word of the LORD is with him. Therefore the king of Israel, Iehoshaphat and the king of Edom came to him. 13 Then Eli- sha said to the king of Israel, "What shall I do with you? Turn to the prophets of your father and the prophets of your mother." The king of Israel said to him, "No, for the Lord has called these three kings to give them into the hand of Moab." 14 Then Elisha said, "As the LORD of hosts wills, in whose presence I stand, were it not that I notice the presence of Jehoshaphat, king of Judah, I would

not have looked to- ward you and seen you. 15 But now bring me a minstrel." And when the minstrel played, the hand of the LORD rested on him. 16 And he said, "Thus says the Lord, 'Make this val- ley full of ditches.' 17 For thus says the Lord, "You shall see neither wind nor rain, but the valley shall be full of water, that you and your cattle and your animals may drink." 18 But this is a small thing in the eyes of the LORD, for he will give Moab into your hands. 19 You shall strike every strong city and every major town, you shall cut down every stout tree, you shall stop all the springs of water, and you shall mar every good fire with stones. 20 In the morning, while dinner was being pre- pared, behold, water came from the road of Edom, and the county was filled with water. 21 When all the Moabites heard that the kings had come to fight against them, they gath- ered all those who were able to put on harness and move, and they went to their borders. 22 And they rose early in the morning, when the sun rose over the water, and the Moabites saw the water in front of them as red as blood. 23 And they said, "This is blood; the kings have been slain, and one has struck the other; now therefore, Moab, go to the spit." 24 When they came before the army of Israel, the Israelites rose up and struck the Moabites, who fled before them, but they went before them and defeated Moab. 25 And they destroyed the cit- ies, and on all the good fields every man cast his stone and filled them, and they stopped all the fountains of water and cut down all the good trees; only at Kirharaseth did they leave her stones, but they surrounded her with slingshots and cut her down. 26 When the king of Moab saw that the battle was too hard for him, he took with him ten men who drew their swords to break through the king of Edom, but they failed. 27 Then he took his eldest son, who should have reigned in his stead, and offered him up as a burnt offering on the walls; so Israel was greatly grieved, and departed from him and returned to his own country.

CHAPTER 4

1 One of the wives of the sons of the proph- ets cried out to Elisha, saying, "Your servant, my husband, is dead, and you know that your servant feared the Lord; and the creditor has come to take my two sons to make them his slaves." 2 Then Elisha said to her, "What shall I do for you? Tell me, what do you have in your house?" She answered, "Your hand has noth- ing in the house, only a pitcher of oil." 3 And he said, "Go and borrow jars from all your neigh- bors, empty jars and spare not. 4 And when you have gone in, you shall shut the door on yourself and on your children, and bring out all those vessels, setting aside the full ones." 5 So she departed from him and closed the door on her and her children. They led her to her, and she went out. 6 When the vessels were full, she said to her son, "Bring me one more vessel." And he answered her, "There are no more vessels." And the oiling ceased. 7 Then she came and spoke to the man of God. And he said, "Go, sell the oil and pay those with whom you are indebted, and spend you and your children for the rest." 8 One day Elisha came to Shunem, and there a woman of great worth compelled him to eat bread; and as he passed by, he turned to eat bread. 9 She said to her husband, "Behold, now I know that this is a holy man of God who continually passes before you. 10 Make him a little chamber, I pray you, with walls, and put a bed, a table, a stove and a candlestick in it, that he may en- ter it when he comes to visit the city. 11 And one day he came there, and entered into the chamber, and lay down in it, 12 And he

said to Gehazi his servant, "Call this Shunammite"; and when he called her, she stood before him. 13 Then he said to him, "Tell her now, 'Well, you have had all this care for you; what should we do for you? Is there anything to say for you to the king or the captain of the army?' And she answered, "I dwell among my people." 14 Then he said, "What is to be done for you?" Gehazi answered, "She has no children, and her husband is old." 15 Then he said, "Call her." He called her, and she stood in the house. 16 He said, "At the appointed time, according to the time of life, you shall have a son." And she said, "Oh, my Lord, man of God, do not ne- glect your hand." 17 So the woman conceived and bore a son in that same season, according to the time of life that Elisha had told her. 18 When the child was grown, there came a day when he went to his father and to the reapers. 19 He said to his father, "My head, my head." Who said to his servant, "Take him to his mother." 20 And he took him and brought him to his mother, who remained on her knees until none and she died. 21 Then she went, laid him on the bed of the man of God, closed the door to him, and went out. 22 Then she called her husband and said to him, "Please send with me one of the young men and one of the donkeys, for I will hurry to the man of God and come again." 23 He said, "Why do you want to go to him today? It is neither new moon nor Sabbath." And she answered, "All will be well." 24 Then she saddled a plank and said to her servant, "Straighten up and go forth; do not stop me to go away unless I tell you." 25 So she departed and came to the man of God on Mount Carmel. And when the man of God saw her before him, he said to Gehazi his servant, "Here is the Shunammite. 26 Run now, I say to you, to meet her and say, "Are you in health? Is your husband healthy? And is the child healthy?" And she answered, "We are healthy." 27 And when she approached the man of God toward the moutaine, she took him by the feet; and Gehazi went to her to push her away, but the man of God said, "Let her alone, for her soul is troubled within her, and the Lord hid it from me and did not tell me." 28 Then she said, "Have I desired a son from my lord? Have I not said, 'Do not deceive me'?" 29 Then he said to Gehazi, "Fasten your laces, take my staff in your hand, and go your way; if you meet anyone, do not greet him; and if anyone greets you, do not answer him; and lay my staff on the child's face." 30 The child's mother said, "As the Lord wills, and as your soul wills, I will not leave you." Therefore he arose and followed her. 31 But Geshemesh had gone before them and laid his staff on the child's face, but the child neither spoke nor heard; therefore he returned to him and said, "The child has not awakened." 32 Then Elisha entered the house, and behold, the child was dead and lying on his bed. 33 So he went in, closed the door on them, and prayed to the Lord. 34 Then he went, and lay down upon the child, and put his mouth upon his mouth, and his eyes upon his ears, and his hands upon his hands, and lay upon him, and the flesh of the child was consumed. 35 And he departed from him, and walked through the house, and went and leaned upon him; then the child uttered a second wailing, and opened his eyes. 36 Then he called Gehazi and said to him, "Call this Shunammite." So he called the one who presented herself to him. And he said to her, "Take your son." 37 She came, fell at his feet, prostrated herself on the ground, took her son, and went out. 38 Then Elisha re- turned to Gilgal, while there was a famine in the land, and the sons of the prophets dwelt with him. And he said to his servant, "Put on the great pot and make soup for the sons of the prophets." 39 And one went out into the field to gather herbs, and found, as it were, a wild vine, and gathered the

gourds of it from his robe, and came and cut them up in the pot, for they knew not. 40 Then he fed himself to the men; and when they ate of the pot, they cried out and said, "O man of God, there is death in the pot," and they could not eat of it. 41 Then he said, "Bring some meat." He threw it into the pot and said, "Release strength for the people, that they may eat"; and there was nothing left in the pot. 42 Then came a man from Baal-Salisha and brought the man of God some bread of first fruits, that is, twenty barley loaves and a pair of ears full of wheat in the chaff. And he said, "Feed the people." 43 His servant answered, "How can I present this to a hundred men? He said again, "Give it to the people, that they may eat, for thus says the Lord, 'They shall eat, and something shall remain.'" 44 So he set it before them, and they ate and left, according to the word of the Lord.

CHAPTER 5

1 Now there was a certain Naaman, captain of the army of the king of Aram, a great and honorable man in the eyes of his lord, for through him the LORD had delivered the Arameans. He too was a strong and valiant man, but a leper. 2 The Arameans had gone out in a group and had taken a little girl of age from the land of Israel, who served Naaman's wife. 3 She said to her masters, "If God would have my lord be with the prophet who is in Samaria, he would soon deliver him from his leprosy." 4 He went in and spoke to his lord, saying, "Thus says the LORD of the land of Is- rael." 5 The king of Aram said, "Go your way, and I will send a letter to the king of Israel." He departed and took with him ten talents of silver, six thousand pieces of gold and ten coins of copper, 6 and brought the letter to the king of Israel with these words, "When this letter has come to you, understand that I have sent Naaman my servant to you, that you may heal him of his leprosy." 7 When the king of Israel had read the letter, he tore his clothes and said, "Am I God, who kills and gives life, who sends me to heal a man of his leprosy? Therefore consider, I pray you, and see how he seeks to make a complaint against me." 8 But when Elisha, the man of God, had heard that the king of Israel had torn his garments, he sent word to the king, "Why have you torn your garments? Let him come to me, and he will know that there is a prophet in Israel." 9 Then Naaman came with his horses and char- iots and stopped at the entrance of Elisha's house. 10 And Elisha sent a messenger to him, saying, "Go and wash in Iorden several times, and your flesh will return to you and you will be clothed." 11 But Naaman, vexed, departed and said, "Behold, I have thought to myself that he will go out, rise up, call upon the name of the LORD his God, put his hand upon the place, and heal from leprosy." 12 Are not Abanah and Pharpar, inhabitants of Da- mascus, better than all the waters of Israel? Could I not wash in them and be cleansed? So he turned and went away in annoyance. 13 But his servants came and spoke to him and said, "Father, if the Prophet had commanded you a great thing, would you not have done it? How much rather, when he says to you, Wash and cleanse yourself?" 14 Then he stooped down and washed himself seven times in Iorden, as the man of God had said; and his flesh re- turned like that of a little child, and he was clean. 15 Then he turned again to the man of God, he and all his company came and stood before him and said, "Behold, now I know that there is no God in all the world, but in Israel; now therefore, I pray thee, take a reward for thy servant." 16 But he said, "As the Lord (be- fore whom I stand) wills, I will not receive it." And she would have liked to force him to re- ceive it, but

he refused. 17 Moreover Naaman said, "Should not two mules of this land be given to your servant? For your servant will no longer offer burnt sacrifices or offenses to any other god, but to the LORD." 18 Where- fore the LORD will be merciful to thy servant: when my master shall go into the house of Rimmon, to worship there, and shall lean upon my hand, and I shall prostrate myself in the house of Rimmon; when I prostrate my- self, I say, in the house of Rimmon, the LORD will be merciful to thy servant on this point. 19 To whom he said, "Go in peace." So he de- parted from him about half a day's journey. 20 Then Gehazi, servant of Elisha, the man of God, said, "Behold, my master has spared this Aramite Naaman, not receiving from him the things he had brought; as the Lord wills, I will run after him and take somethin g from him." 21 So Gehazi quickly followed Naaman. And when Naaman saw him running after him, he came down from the cave to meet him and said, "Is everything all right?" 22 He an- swered, "All is well; my master instructed me to say, 'Behold, two young men of the sons of the Prophets have come to me just now from Mount Ephraim; give them, I pray you, a tal- ent of silver and two changes of clothing.'" 23 Naaman said, "Yes, take two talents." He con- strained him, bound two talents of silk in two sacks, with two changes of clothing, and gave them to two of his servants to carry before him. 24 And when he came to the mansion, he took them out of their hands, and brought them into the house, and sent the men away; and they departed. 25 Then he went in and stood before his master. Elisha said to him, "Where do you come from, Gehazi?" And he answered, "Your servant has gone nowhere." 26 But he said to him, "Was not my heart with you when that man departed from his charet to come to you? Is this the time to take money, to receive garments, olives, vineyards, sheep, oxen, servants of men and servants of wom- en? 27 The leprosy of Naaman shall therefore be removed for you and for your descendants forever." And he came forth from his presence as a leper as white as snow.

CHAPTER 6

1 The sons of the prophets said to Elisha, "Be- hold, we pray you, the place where we dwell with you is too small for vs. 2 Let them now go to Iorden, to take from there a match for every man, and make you a place to dwell in." And he answered, "Go." 3 And one said, "Please allow me to go with your servants," and he answered, "I will go." 4 So he went with them, and when they came to Iorden, they cut down wood. 5 As one was cutting down a tree, the stump fell into the water; then he wept and said, "Alas, master, it was nothing but grass." 6 The man of God said, "Where did it fall?" And he pointed to the place. Then he cut a piece of wood, threw it there, and made the lily swim. 7 Then he said, "Take it with you." And he stretched out his hand and took it. 8 Then the king of Aram waged war against Is- rael, took counsel with his servants, and said, "In this place or that place shall be my campe." 9 Therefore the man of God sent word to the king of Israel, "Beware of going to that place, for there the Aramites have come down." 10 So the king of Israel went to the place pointed out to him by the man of God, warned him, and took cover from there, neither once nor twice. 11 The heart of the king of Aram was troubled by this fact; therefore he called his servants and said to them, "Will you not tell me which of you betrays our counsel to the king of Israel?" 12 Then one of his servants said, "No one, my lord, O king, but Elisha the prophet who is in Israel, says to the king of Israel the

words that you speak in your private chamber." 13 He said, "Go and find out where he is, that I may send for him." And one said to him, "Behold, he is in Dothan." 14 Then he sent there horses and chariots and a large army; and they came by night and surround- ed the city. 15 When the servant of the man of God rose early to go out, behold, a host of horses and chariots surrounded the city. Then his servant said to him, "Alas, master, how shall we do?" 16 He answered, "Fear not, for those who are with them outnumber them." 17 Then Elisha prayed and said, "Lord, please open his eyes, that he may see." The Lord opened the servant's eyes, and he looked, and behold, the mountain was full of horses and fyre chariots around Elisha. 18 Then they came down to him, but Elisha prayed to the LORD and said, "Strike this people, I pray you, with blindness." And he struck them with blindness, according to the word of Elisha. 19 Elisha said to them, "This is not the way and this is not the city; follow me and I will lead you to the man whom you see." But he led them to Samaria. 20 When they had come to Samaria, Elisha said, "Lord, open their eyes that they may see." The Lord opened their eyes, and they saw, and behold, they were in the midst of Samaria. 21 When the king of Israel said to Elisha, "My father, shall I strike them, shall I strike them?" 22 He answered, "You shall not smite them; you shall not smite those whom you have taken with your sword and your bow, but you shall set before them bread and water, that they may eat and drink and go to their master." 23 And he made great preparations for them; and when they had eaten and drunk, he made them depart; and they went to their master. So the bands of Aram no longer entered the land of Israel. 24 Afterward Ben-Hadad, king of Aram, gath- ered all his troops, departed, and besieged Samaria. 25 So there was a great famine in Samaria, for they besieged it until a donkey's head cost four pieces of silk and the fourth part of a kab of dowry five pieces of silk. 26 As the king of Israel went to the walls, a woman cried out to him, "Help me, my lord, O king." 27 And he answered, "Since the Lord does not help you, how should I help you with the rod or with the wine preserves?" 28 The king also said to her, "What is troubling you?" And she answered, "This woman said to me, 'Take your son, so we will eat him today, and we will eat my son tomorrow.'" 29 So we pawed my son and ate him; and the next day I said to her, "Take your son, so we will eat him," but she hid her son. 30 When the king had heard the woman's words, he tore his clothes (and as he went to the wall, the people looked, and be- hold, he had sackcloth on his flesh). 31 And he said, "God do so to me also, and even more, if the head of Elisha the son of Shaphat shall rest upon him this day." 32 And the king sent a man before him; but before the messenger came to him, he said to the elders, "Do you not see how this son of murderers has sent to take away my head? Be careful when the mes- senger comes, close the door and handle him sharply; is there not the sound of his masters' feet behind him? 33 While he was still talking to them, behold, the messenger came down to him and said, "Behold, this will is from the Lord; shall I wait for the Lord any longer?

CHAPTER 7

1 Then Elisha said, "Hear the word of the LORD; thus says the LORD: For the future a measure of flour shall be sold for a shekel, and two measures of barley for a shekel at the gate of Samaria." 2 Then a prince, on whose hand the king leaned, answered the man of God and said, "Even if the

Lord made win- dows in the sky, could this take place?" And he answered, "Behold, you shall see it with your eyes, but you shall not eat of it." 3 Now there were four leprous men at the entrance of the gate; and they said one to another, "Why do we stay here until we die? 4 If we say, We will enter the city, famine is in the city, and we will die there; and if we stay here, we will also die. Now, therefore, come and let us fall into the camp of the Arameans; if they tell us the truth, we shall die; and if they kill us, we are but dead." 5 So they rose up at dusk to go toward the camp of the Arameans; and when they had come to the highest part of the camp of the Arameans, behold, there was no one there. 6 For the LORD had caused the camp of the Arameans to hear a noise of chariots, a noise of horses, and a noise of a great army, so that they said to one another, "Behold, the king of Israel has hired against you the kings of the Hittites and the kings of the Egyptians to come and get you." 7 Therefore they arose and fled at dusk, and left their tents, and their horses, and their donkeys, and the campe as it was, and fled to their countries. 8 And when these lepers came to the remotest part of the camp, they went into a tent, and ate and drank, and took with them silk, and gold, and garments, and went and hid them; then they returned, and went into another tent, and took those also with them, and went and hid them. 9 Then they said to one another, "Let us not do well: this is a day of good tidings, and we keep ourselves in peace. If we linger until dawn, some trouble will happen to us. Now, therefore, come, let us go and tell the king everything." 10 So they came, called the city porters, and told them, "We have come to the camp of the Arameans, and well, there was no man, nor any trace of man, but horses and donkeys, and the tents were as before." 11 The porters cried out and declared that the king's house was inside. 12 Then the king rose at night and said to his servants, "Now I will show you what the Arameans have done against us. They know that we are in danger, so they have come out of the campe to hide in the fields, saying, 'When they come out of the city, we will sneak up on them and enter the city.' 13 One of his servants answered, "Let me now take five of the remaining horses that are left and have remained in the city (behold, they are like all the multitude of Israel who are left there; behold, I say, they are like the mul- titude of the Israelites who are consumed) and we will send them to see." 14 So they took two chariots of horses, and the king sent after the army of the Arameans, saying, "Go and see." 15 They pursued them as far as Iorden; well, the whole road was full of clothes and furnishings that the Arameans had thrown away in their flight; and the messengers re- turned and reported to the king. 16 Then the people went out and leveled the camne of the Arameans; so a measure of fine flour was paid a shekel, and two measures of barley a shekel, according to the word of the LORD. 17 And the king entrusted to the prince (on whose hand he leaned) the commandment of the gate; and the people trod him in the gate, and he died, as the man of God who had spoken it had said, when the king came down to him. 18 And it came to pass as the man of God had said to the king, "Two measures of barley to a shekel and a measure of fine flour to a shek- el, to be consumed at this time at the gate of Samaria." 19 But the prince had answered the man of God and said, "Even if the Lord want- ed to make windows in the sky, could it hap- pen so? And he answered, "Behold, you shall see it with your eyes, but you shall not eat of it." 20 And so it came to pass, for the people trod on him at the gate, and he died.

CHAPTER 8

1 Then Elisha spoke to the woman, to whom he had returned her son, saying, "Go away, you and your house, and go and sojourn where you can, for the Lord has called a fam- ine, which will come upon the land for some years." 2 The woman arose and did as the man of God had said, and went away with her house to sojourn in the land of the Philistines for ten years. 3 When the ten years were up, the woman went back out of the land of the Philistines and went and appealed to the king for her house and her land. 4 The king spoke to Gehazi, servant of the man of God, saying, "Please tell me all the great deeds that Elisha has done." 5 As he was telling the king how he had brought a dead man back to life, behold, the woman whose son he had brought back to life called upon the king for her house and her land. Gehazi said, "My lord, O king, this is the woman and this is her son whom Elisha brought back to life." 6 When the king asked the woman, she told him; so the king entrust- ed her with a eunuch, saying to her, "Return all that is his and all the fruit of his land from the day he left the land until today." 7 Then Elisha came to Damascus; Ben-Hadad, king of Aram, was sick, and one said to him, "The man of God has come so far." 8 The king said to Hazael, "Take a gift in your hand and go meet the man of God, so that you may ask the Lord through him if I can be healed of this disease." 9 Then Hazael went to meet him, took the gift in his hand and every good thing of God from Damascus, as well as the load of forty cam- els, and came and stood before him and said, "Your son Ben-Hadad, king of Aram, has sent me to you to say, "Shall I be healed of this dis- ease?" 10 Elisha said to him, "Go and tell him, 'You will recover'; but the Lord has shown me that you will surely die." 11 He stared at him fixedly, until Hazael was ashamed, and the man of God wept. 12 Hazael said, "Why does my lord weep?" And he answered, "Because I know the evil that you will do to the children of Israel; for their strong cities you will put them to the sword, their young men you will kill with the sword, you will crush their chil- dren against the stones, and you will tear their pregnant women to pieces." 13 Then Hazael said, "What is it? Is your servant a dog, that I should do this great thing?" Elisha answered, "The LORD has told me that you will be king of Aram." 14 So he departed from Elisha and came to his master, who said to him, "What did Elisha say to you?" And he answered, "He told me that you should withdraw." 15 The next day he took a thick cloth, dipped water in it, smeared it on his face, and dyed himself; and Hazael reigned in his place. 16 In the fifth year of Joram the son of Ahab king of Israel and of Jehoshaphat king of Judah, Jehoram the son of Jehoshaphat king of Judah began to reign. 17 He was two and thirty years old when he began to reign; and he reigned eight years in Jerusalem. 18 He followed the ways of the kings of Israel, like the house of Ahab, for Ahab's daughter was his wife, and he behaved well in the eyes of the LORD. 19 Yet the LORD would not destroy Iudah for Dauid's sake, his servant, as he had promised him to give him a light and for his children forever. 20 In those days Edom rebelled under the hand of Judah and made himself a king of his own. 21 And Ioram went to Zair, with all his chiefs, and rose up by night, and smote the Edomites that surrounded him with the captains of the chiefs, and the people fled to their tents. 22 Thus Edom rebelled from under the hand of Iudah to this day. Libna also rebelled at that same time. 23 Are not the rest of Ioram's deeds and all that he did written in the book of the Chronicles of the kings of Iudah? 24 And Ioram fell asleep with his fathers and was buried with his fathers in the city

of Dauid. And Ahaziah his son reigned in his place. 25 In the twelfth year of Joram, son of Ahab, king of Israel, Ahaziah, son of Jehoram, king of Ju- dah, began to reign. 26 He was two years old and twenty-five years old when he began to reign; he reigned one year in Jerusalem, and his mother's name was Athaliah, daughter of Omri, king of Israel. 27 And he walked in the way of the house of Ahab, and did evil in the sight of the LORD, as the house of Ahab, be- cause he was the son-in-law of the house of Ahab. 28 He went with Ioram the son of Ahab to fight against Hazael the king of Aram at Ramoth Gilead, and the Aramites defeated Ioram. 29 And King Ioram returned to Izreel to be healed of the wounds that the Aramites had inflicted on him at Ramah, while he was fighting Hazael, king of Aram. And Ahaziah the son of Jehoram king of Judah went to vis- it Ioram the son of Ahab in Izreel, for he was sick.

CHAPTER 9

1 Then the prophet Elisha called one of the sons of the prophets and said to him, "Gird up your loins, take this case of oil in your hand, and go to Ramoth Gilead. 2 When you have arrived, see where Iehu the son of Iehoshaphat the son of Nimshi is, go, make him tick among his brothers, and take him to a secret room. 3 Then take the box of oil and put it on his head and say, "Thus says the LORD, I have anointed you as king of Israel." Then open the door and flee without pausing. 4 So the prophet's servant led him to Ramoth Gilead. 5 When he entered, behold, the cap- tains of the army were seated. And he said, "I have a message for you, O captain." And I said, "To which of you?" And he answered, "To you, O captain." 6 And he arose, and went into the house, and put oil upon his head, and said unto him, Thus saith the LORD God of Israel, I have anointed thee as king of the LORD's people, that is, of Israel. 7 And thou shalt smite the house of Ahab thy master, that I may wipe away the blood of my servants, the prophets, and the blood of all the servants of the LORD from the hand of Jezebel. 8 For all the house of Ahab shall be destroyed; and I will cut off from Ahab both those who make water against the wall, and those who are shut up, and those who are left in Israel. 9 And I will make the house of Ahab like the house of Jeroboam the son of Nebat, and like the house of Baasha the son of Ahijah. 10 And the dogs shall devour Jezebel in the field of Izreel, and there shall be no one to bury her." He opened the door and fled. 11 Then Iehu went out to his lord's servants. And one said to him, "Is everything all right? Why has this fool come to you? And he said to them, "You know the man and his words." 12 And they said, "It is false, say it now." Then he said, "Thus and thus he spake unto me, saying, Thus saith the Lord, I have anointed you as king over Isra- el." 13 Then they hastened, and took off every man's robe, and put it under him on top of the stelae, and blew the trumpet, saying, "I am the king." 14 Then Jehu the son of Jehoshaphat the son of Nimshi conspired against Ioram. Ioram held Ramoth Gilead, he and all Isra- el, because of Hazael, king of Aram. 15 And King Ioram went back to be healed in Izreel from the wounds that the Aramites had given him when he had fought with Hazael, king of Aram), and Iehu said, "If it is in your inten- tions, let no one go out and flee from the city to tell Izreel." 16 Then Iehu got into a chariot and went to Izreel, because Ioram was lying there and Ahaziah, king of Judah, had come down to see Ioram. 17 And the watchman that stood in the tower of Izreel spotted Iehu's company as he came, and said, "I see a com- pany." And Iehoram said, "Take a horseman and send him to meet them, that he may say, "Is there peace?" 18 Then one on horseback came to him and said, "Thus says the king: is there peace?" And Iehu answered, "What have you to do with peace? Turn around behind me." And the watchman related, "The mes- senger came to them, but he does not come again." 19 Then he sent another on horseback, who came to them and said, "Thus says the king, Is it peace?" And Iehu answered, "What have you to do with peace? Turn behind me." 20 The watchman related, "He came to them also, but he does not come again; his march is like that of Iehu the son of Nimshi, for he marches with fury." 21 Then Iehoram said, "Make ready," and his chariot was prepared. Iehoram, king of Israel, and Ahaziah, king of Judah, each went out with his charet against Iehu and met him in the camp of Naboth the Izreelite. 22 When Iehoram saw Iehu, he said to him, "Is it peace, Iehu?" And he answered, "What peace, while the harlots of your moth- er Jezebel and her sorceries are still in great numbers?" 23 Then Iehoram turned away his hand, fled, and said to Ahaziah, "O Ahaziah, there is treachery." 24 But Iehu took a bow in his hand and struck Iehoram between the shoulders, so that the bow pierced his heart; and he fell to the ground in his charet. 25 Then Iehu said to Bidkar, a captain, "Take it and cast it somewhere in the camp of Naboth, the Izreelite, for I remember that when you and I rode together behind Ahab, his father, the LORD put this burden on him. 26 I saw yesterday the blood of Naboth and the blood of his sons, saith the Lord, and I will render it to you in this field, saith the Lord; now there- fore take it and cast it into the field, according to the word of the Lord." 27 But when Ahaziah king of Judah saw this, he fled by the way of the garden house: And Jehu pursued him, and said, Strike him also into the court. And they struck him as he went to Gur, near Ibleam. He fled to Megiddo, and there he died. 28 His servants carried him in a basket to Jerusalem and buried him in his grave with his fathers in the city of Dauid. 29 In the eleventh year of Joram the son of Ahab, Ahaziah began to reign over Iudah. 30 When Jehu came to Jezreel, Je- zebel learned of it, painted his face, strained his head, and looked out of a window. 31 As Iehu came in at the door, she said, "Has Zimri peace, who killed his master?" 32 He lifted up his eyes to the window and said, "Who is on my side, who?" Then two or three of his Eu- nuchs looked at him. 33 And he said, "Throw her down"; and they threw her down, and he sprinkled her blood on the walls and on the horses, and trampled her underfoot. 34 And when he was come in, he ate and drank, and said, "Visit now that accursed woman and bury her, for she is a daughter of kings." 35 And they went and buried her, but they found nothing of her but her skull and her feet and the palms of her hands. 36 Therefore they came to him and informed him. And he said, "This is the word of the LORD, which he has spoken through his servant Elijah the Tish- bite, saying, 'In the field of Jezreel your dogs shall eat the flesh of Jezebel.' 37 And the car- casses of Iezebel shall be as a heap in the field of Izreel, so that no one may say, "This is Ie- zebel."

CHAPTER 10

1 Ahab now had seuentie sons in Samaria. Iehu wrote letters and sent them to Samaria to the leaders of Izreel, the elders and the bearers of Ahab's sons, to this effect, 2 Now when this letter reaches you (for you have with you the sons of your masters, you have with you chariots and horses, a defended city and armor) 3 Consider therefore which is the

best and the fittest among the sons of your masters, and set him on the throne of his fathers, and fight for the house of your masters." 4 But they were greatly frightened and said, "Behold, two kings could not stand before him; how shall we be able to stand?" 5 Then he who was the head of Ahab's house, the one who ruled the city, the elders and the child-bearers sent to say to Jehu, "We are your servants, and we will do whatever you ask of us; we will not make ourselves kings; do what seems good to you." 6 Then he wrote another letter to them, saying, "If you are mine and want to obey my command, take the heads of you men who are the sons of your mas- ters and come to me in Izreel by lunchtime. (Now the king's sons, about seventy persons, were with the great men of the city, who led them to their destination.) 7 When the letter reached them, they took the king's sons, killed the seventy people, put their heads in baskets and sent them to Izreel. 8 Then a messenger came and said to him, "They have brought the heads of the king's sons." And he said, "Let them lay them on two heaps at the entrance of the gate until morning." 9 When it was day, he went out and stood and said to all the peo- ple, "You are righteous; behold, I conspired against my master and killed him; but who killed all these? 10 Know now that nothing shall fall to the earth of the word of the LORD which the LORD spoke concerning the house of Ahab, for the LORD has brought to pass the things which he spoke through his servant Elijah." 11 Then Jehu killed all the survivors of Ahab's house in Jezreel and all the great ones who were with him, his family members and his priests, so that none of his own remained. 12 Then he arose and departed and came to Samaria. And as Iehu stood along the road, near a house where the shepherds were shav- ing, 13 he met the brothers of Ahaziah, king of Judah, and said, "Who are you?" And they answered, "We are the brothers of Ahaziah, and we go down to greet the king's sons and the queen's sons." 14 He said, "Take them with you." And they took them secretly and slew them at the well beside the house where the sheep were kept, that is, two and forty men, and he left not one of them behind. 15 And when he had departed from there, he met Iehonadab the son of Rechab coming to meet him; and he blessed him and said to him, "Is your heart as upright as mine is toward you?" And Iehonadab answered, "Yes, without a doubt. Then give me your hand." And when he had given him his hand, he took him with him into the courtyard. 16 He said, "Come with me and see the zeal I have for the LORD"; and they put him into his chariot. 17 And when he came to Samaria, he slew all those who had remained with Ahab in Samaria, until he had destroyed him, according to the word of the LORD which he had spoken to Elijah. 18 Then Jehu gathered all the people together and said to them, "Ahab has served Baal a little, but I will serve him much more. 19 Therefore call to me all the prophets of Baal, all his servants and all his priests, and let no one be lacking, for I have a great sacrifice for Baal; whoever is lacking cannot die." But Iehu did so to de- stroy the servants of Baal. 20 And Iehu said, "Proclaim a solemn assembly for Baal." And they proclaimed it. 21 Then Iehu sent to all Israel, and all the servants of Baal came, and there was not a man left who had not come. They entered the house of Baal, and the house of Baal was full from end to end. 22 Then he said to the one who was in charge of prepar- ing the garments, "Bring the vestments for all the servants of Baal." And he brought the vestments. 23 When Iehu and Iehonadab the son of Rechab entered the house of Baal, he said to the servants of Baal, "Search well and look, if there are not any of the servants of the Lord here with you, but only the servants of Baal." 24 When they

went in to make the sacrifice and burnt offering, Iehu called four dozen men outside and said, "If any of the men whom I have brought into your hands escape, his soul shall be for his soul." 25 And after he had made a review of the burning, he said to the guard and the captains, "Go in, kill them, let no one go out." And they struck them with the blade of the sword. The guard and captains drove them out and went toward the city, where the temple of Baal was. 26 They brought out the images of the temple of Baal and burned them. 27 Then they destroyed the image of Baal, tore down the house of Baal, and made an odyssey of it to this day. 28 Thus Jehu eliminated Baal from Israel. 29 But from the sins of Jeroboam the son of Nebat, which caused Israel to sin, Jehu did not depart, nor from the golden goblets that were in Bet-el and Dan. 30 The LORD said to Iehu, "Because you diligently performed what was right in my eyes and did to the house of Ahab all that I had in my heart, your sons until the fourth generation shall sit on the throne of Israel." 31 But Jehu did not care to walk wholehearted- ly in the law of the LORD, the God of Israel, because he did not turn from the sins of Je- roboam, which made Israel sin. 32 In those days the LORD began to strike Israel, and Hazael defeated them in all the coasts of Is- rael, 33 from Iorden eastward, that is, all the land of Gilead, the Gadites, the Reubenites and those of Manasseh, from Aroer (which is by the river Arnon), Gilead and Bashan. 34 Are not the rest of the deeds of Iehu, all that he did and all his valiant deeds written in the book of the Chronicles of the kings of Israel? 35 And Iehu fell asleep with his fathers, and they buried him in Samaria, and Iehoahaz his son reigned in his stead. 36 The time that Jehu reigned over Israel in Samaria was eight years and twenty.

CHAPTER 11

1 Then Ataliah the mother of Ahaziah, when she saw that her son was dead, rose up and destroyed all the king's descendants. 2 But Iehosheba, daughter of King Joram and sister of Ahaziah, took Ioash, son of Ahaziah, and held him among the king's sons who were to be killed, both he and his source, keeping them in bed, and hid him from Ataliah, that he might not be killed. 3 He remained with her hidden in the house of the LORD for six years, while Ataliah reigned over the land. 4 And in the seventh year Jehoiada sent for the captains of the centenarians, other cap- tains, and the watchmen, and brought them to him to the house of the LORD, and had a meeting with them, and took another into the house of the LORD, and showed them the king's son. 5 Then he gave them an order, saying, "This is what you are to do: the third part of you who come on the Sabbath is to go to the king's house: 6 And another third part to the gate of Sur, and another third part to the gate behind them of the garden; and you shall guard the house of Massah. 7 Two parts of you, that is, all who go out on the Sabbath, shall guard the house of the LORD around the king. 8 You shall compass the king all around, each one with his weapon in his fist, and whoever comes within range shall be killed. 9 And the captains of the centenarians did all that Hehoiada the priest commanded, and they took charge of every man his men who went in on the Sabbath day, together with those who went out on the Sabbath day, and they came to Hehoiada the priest. 10 And the priest handed over to the captains of the cen- tenarians the spears and shields that were King Dauidi's and that were in the house of the LORD. 11 The guardians stood, each with his weapon in his hand, from the right side of the house to the left side,

around the altar and the house, around the king. 12 Then he brought out the king's son, and put the horn on him, and delivered the Testimony to him, and they made him king; also they anoinished him, and clapped their hands, and said, "God is king." 13 And when Athaliah heard the noise of the running of the people, he approached the people in the house of the LORD. 14 And when she looked, behold, the king was stand- ing by a pillar, as was his order, and the princ- es and the trumpeters by the king, and all the people of the land were gathered together and sounded with trumpets. Ataliah tore his clothes and cried, "Treason, treason." 15 But Iehoiada the priest commanded the captains of the hundreds who had command of the army, and said to them, "Get her out of the fields, and let those who follow her die by the sword, for the priest had said, 'Let her not be killed in the house of the Lord.'" 16 Then they laid hands on her, and she passed by the way by which the horses go to the king's house, and there she was killed. 17 And Jehoiada es- tablished a covenant between the LORD, and the king, and the people, that they should be the people of the LORD; so also between the king and the people. 18 Then all the people of the land entered the house of Baal and de- stroyed it with its altars and images; and they took courage and killed Mattan the priest of Baal before the altars. 19 Then they took the captains of the hudreth, and the other cap- tains, and the guard, and all the people of the land; and they led the king out of the house of the LORD, and came through the gate of the guard to the king's house; and they seat- ed him on the king's throne. 20 Then all the people of the land revived, and the city was at peace, because they had killed Ataliah with the sword beside the king's house. 21 And Ie- hoash was a year and a half old when he began to reign.

been found in the house of the Lord, 11 and they gave the ready money into the hands of those who were in charge of the work and in control of the house of the LORD; and they paid it to the carpenters and builders who were working in the house of the LORD, 12 to the masons and stonemasons, to the building lumber and hewed stone, to repay what had gone to ruin in the house of the LORD, and for all that had been prepared for the repair of the Temple. 13 However, for the house of the LORD no silver bows, musical instruments, staffs, trumpets, or vessels of gold or silver were built with the money that was brought into the house of the LORD. 14 But they gave it to the workers who repaid the house of the LORD. 15 Moreover, they did not reckon with the men, into whose hands they delivered the money to be distrib- uted to the workers, for they dealt faithfully. 16 The money of debts and the money of sins was not brought into the house of the LORD, for it belonged to the priests. 17 Then Haz- ael, king of Aram, came and fought against Gath and conquered it, and Hazael set out to go to Jerusalem. 18 And Iehoash, king of Iudah, took all the unaltered things which Iehoshaphat, Jehoram, and Ahaziah, his fa- thers, kings of Iudah, had dedicated, and which he himself had dedicated, and all the gold that was in the treasures of the house of the LORD and in the house of kings, and sent it to Hazael, king of Aram, and departed from Jerusalem. 19 As for the rest of Ioash's deeds and all that he did, are they not written in the book of the Chronicles of the kings of Judah? 20 And his servants rose up and did treachery, and slew Ioash in the house of Millo, when he went down to Sulla: 21 Then Iozachar the son of Shimeath, and Jehozabad the son of Sho- mer, his servants smote him, and he died; then they buried him with his fathers in the

city of Dauid. And Amaziah, his son, reigned in his place.

CHAPTER 12

1 In the seventh year of Iehu, Iehoash be- gan to reign and reigned for forty years in Jerusalem; his mother's name was Zibiah of Beer-sheba. 2 Iehoash did what was good in the eyes of the LORD all the time that Iehoia- da the priest taught him. 3 But the places of worship were not taken away, because the people still offended and burned incense in the places of worship. 4 And Iehoash said to the priests, "All the money of the dedications that is brought to the house of the LORD, that is, the money of those who are under the ac- count, the money that every man has set for himself, and all the money that one voluntari- ly offers and brings to the house of the LORD, 5 the priests shall bring it to them, every one of their acquaintances, and they shall repair the broken places in the house, where there is deterioration. 6 However, in the three and twenty years of King Iehoash, the priests had not repaired what had deteriorated in the Temple. 7 Then King Iehoash called Iehoia- da the priest and the other priests and said to them, "Why do you not repair the ruins of the Temple? Now therefore do not receive any more money from your acquaintances unless you give it to repair the ruins of the Temple." 8 So the priests agreed not to receive any more money from the people and not to repair the ruins of the Temple. 9 Then the priest Jehoiada took a chest, cut a hole in the lid, and placed it beside the altar, on the right side, as every man enters the Temple of the LORD. The priests who guarded the chest put in it all the money that was brought into the house of the LORD. 10 When they found that there was much money in the chest, the king's secretary and his priest came and put it in, after telling the money that had

CHAPTER 13

1 In the three hundredth year of Ioash the son of Ahaziah, king of Judah, Jehoahaz the son of Jehu began to reign over Israel in Sa- maria and reigned for seven years. 2 He acted evil in the eyes of the LORD and followed the sins of Jeroboam the son of Nebat, who had caused Israel to sin, and did not depart from them. 3 The LORD was angry with Israel and delivered him into the hand of Hazael, king of Aram, and into the hand of Ben-Hadad, son of Hazael, all his days. 4 Iehoahaz plead- ed with the LORD, and the LORD heard him, for he saw the troubles of Israel, with which the king of Aram was afflicting them. 5 And the LORD gave Israel a deliverer, so that they came out of the subjection of the Arameans. And the children of Israel dwelt in their tents as before. 6 Nevertheless they did not depart from the sins of the house of Jeroboam, which had caused Israel to sin, but walked there. and the group still remained in Samaria) 7 For to Jehoahaz he had left of the people noth- ing but fifty horsemen, ten chariots, and ten thousand footmen, because the king of Aram had destroyed them and made them like pounded dust. 8 Are not the rest of the deeds of Iehoahaz, all that he did and his prowess, written in the book of the Chronicles of the kings of Israel? 9 And Iehoahaz fell asleep with his fathers, and they buried him in Sa- maria, and Ioash his son reigned in his stead. 10 In the seventieth year of Ioash, king of Ju- dah, Jehoash, son of Jehoahaz, began to reign over Israel in Samaria and reigned for sixty years, 11 And he behaved badly in the sight of the LORD, because he did not turn away from all

the sins of Jeroboam the son of Ne- bat, who had caused Israel to sin, but walked in them. 12 As for the rest of Ioash's deeds and all that he did, his valiant deeds and the way he fought against Amaziah, king of Judah, are they not written in the book of the Chronicles of the kings of Israel? 13 Ioash fell asleep with his fathers, and Jeroboam sat in his place; Io- ash was buried in Samaria among the kings of Israel. 14 When Elisha fell sick of the dis- ease from which he had died, Ioash, king of Israel, came to him, wept over his face, and said, "O my father, my father, the leader of Israel and his horsemen." 15 Then Elisha said to him, "Take a bow and arrows." And he took with him a bow and arrows. 16 Then he said to the king of Israel, "Put your hand on the bow." And he put his hand on it. And Elisha put his hands on the king's hands, 17 and said, "Open the window toward the east." And when he had opened it, Elisha said, "Shoot." And he fired. And he said, "Here is the stronghold of the LORD's delusion and the stronghold of delusion against Aram; for you strike the Aramites in Aphek, until you have consumed them." 18 Then he said, "Take the arrows." And he took them. And he said to the king of Israel, "Strike the ground." He struck three times and ceased. 19 Then the man of God was angry with him and said, "You should have struck five or six times, so you should have struck Aram until you consumed him, whereas now you only hit Aram three times." 20 Elisha died and they buried him. In that year some bands of Moabites came into the land. 21 As they were burying a man, they saw the soldiers; therefore they threw the man into Elisha's tomb. And when the man had come down and touched the bones of Elisha, he revived and stood on his feet. 22 But Haz- ael king of Aram tormented Israel all the days of Jehoahaz. 23 But the LORD had mercy on them and pitied them and respected them be- cause of his agreement with Abraham, Izhak and Iaakob, and he did not destroy them or turn them away from him yet. 24 So Hazael, king of Aram, died, and Ben-Hadad, his son, reigned in his place. 25 Then Iehoash, son of Iehoahaz, returned and took out of the hand of Ben-Hadad, son of Hazael, the cities that he had taken away in war from the hand of Ie- hoahaz his father; three times Ioash defeated him and returned the cities to Israel.

CHAPTER 14

1 In the second year of Ioash the son of Jeho- ahaz, king of Israel, Amaziah the son of Ioash the king of Judah reigned. 2 He was five years old and twenty-five when he began to reign, and he reigned nine years and twenty-five in Jerusalem; his mother's name was Jehoadan of Jerusalem. 3 He behaved well in the eyes of the LORD, but not as Dauid his father, but ac- cording to what Ioash his father had done. 4 Yet the places of worship were not taken away, for still the people sacrificed and burned in- cense in the places of worship. 5 When the kingdom was confirmed in his hands, he killed his servants who had killed the king his father. 6 But the sons of those who had killed him he did not kill, according to what is writ- ten in the Book of the Law of Moses, where the Lord had commanded, "Fathers shall not be put to death for sons, nor shall sons be put to death for fathers; but each one shall be put to death for his own sin." 7 And he slew also of Edom in the valley of salt ten thousand, and conquered the city of Sela by war, and called it Ioktheel unto this day. 8 Then Amaziah sent messengers to Iehoash the son of Iehoahaz the son of Iehu, king of Israel, saying, "Come, look on your faces." 9 Then Iehoash, king of Israel, sent word to Amaziah, king of Iudah, "The thistle that is in Lebanon sent word to the cedar tree that is in Lebanon, 'Give your daughter to my son in marriage;' and the wild beast that was in Lebanon went and tram- pled the thistle. 10 Because thou hast smitten Edom, thy heart hath made thee proud: thou boastest in glory, and thou makest thy house late. Why boastest thou thyself that thou mayest hurt thyself, that thou mayest fall, and that Iudah may fall with thee? 11 But Amaziah would not listen; therefore Jehoash king of Is- rael went forth; and he and Amaziah king of Iudah looked into the face of Beth-shemesh, which is in Iudah. 12 And Iudah was brought to his knees before Israel, and they all fled to their tents. 13 But Jehoash king of Israel took Amaziah king of Iudah, the son of Jehoash the son of Ahaziah, at Beth-shemesh, and came to Jerusalem, and brought down the walls of Jerusalem from the gate of Ephraim to the corner gate, four hundred cubits. 14 And he took all the gold and silver and all the uten- sils that were in the house of the LORD and in the treasures of the king's house, and the children who were as hostages, and returned to Samaria. 15 Are not the rest of the deeds of Iehoash, his valiant deeds and the manner in which he fought with Amaziah, king of Judah, written in the book of the Chronicles of the kings of Israel? 16 Iehoash fell asleep with his fathers and was buried in Samaria among the kings of Israel, and Jeroboam his son reigned in his place. 17 Amaziah, son of Ioash, king of Judah, lived after the death of Jehoash, son of Jehoahaz, king of Israel, fifty years. 18 As for the rest of Amaziah's deeds, are they not writ- ten in the book of the Chronicles of the kings of Iudah? 19 They made treachery against him in Jerusalem, and he fled to Lachish; but they pursued him to Lachish and killed him there. 20 And they brought him on horseback, and he was buried in Jerusalem with his fathers in the city of Dauid. 21 Then all the people of Iudah took Azariah, who was sixty years old, and made him king instead of his father Amaziah. 22 He built Elath and returned it to Iudah, after which the king slept with his fa- thers. 23 In the fifteenth year of Amaziah the son of Joash, king of Judah, Jeroboam the son of Joash was made king of Israel in Samaria and reigned for a year and forty. 24 He be- haved well in the eyes of the LORD, for he did not turn away from all the sins of Jeroboam the son of Nebat, which caused Israel to sin. 25 He restored the coastline of Israel from the entrance of Hamath to the sea of the wil- derness, according to the words of the LORD, the God of Israel, spoken by his servant Jonah the son of Amittai the prophet, who was from Gath-Hefer. 26 For the LORD saw the extreme distress of Israel, so that there was no one who was closed and no one who could help Is- rael. 27 Yet the LORD had not determined to blot out the name of Israel from under heav- en; therefore he preserved them by the hand of Jeroboam the son of Joash. 28 Are not the rest of Jeroboam's deeds, all that he did, his valiant deeds, the way he fought, the way he restored Damascus and Hamath to Iudah in Israel, written in the book of the Chronicles of the Kings of Israel? 29 So Jeroboam fell asleep with his fathers, like the kings of Israel, and Zechariah his son reigned in his stead.

CHAPTER 15

1 In the second and twentieth year of Je- roboam, king of Israel, Azariah the son of Amaziah, king of Judeah, began to reign. 2 He was sixteen years old when he was made king and reigned for two years and fifty years in Jerusalem; his mother's name was Jecoliah of Jerusalem. 3 He behaved well in the eyes of the LORD, as his father Amaziah had

done. 4 But the places of worship were not removed, for the people still offered and burned incense in the places of worship. 5 The LORD smote the king, who remained leprous until the day of his death and dwelt in an isolated house; Iotham, the king's son, guarded the house and controlled the people of the land. 6 Are not the rest of Azariah's deeds and all that he did written in the book of the Chronicles of the kings of Iudah? 7 So Azariah fell asleep with his fathers and they buried him with his fathers in the city of Dauid, and Iotham his son reigned in his place. 8 In the thirtieth year of Azariah, king of Judah, Zechariah the son of Jeroboam reigned over Israel in Sa- maria for six months, 9 And he behaved well before the LORD, like his fathers, because he did not turn from the sins of Jeroboam the son of Nebat, who caused Israel to sin. 10 And Shallum the son of Jabesh came against him, and smote him before the people, and slew him, and reigned in his stead. 11 The rest of Zechariah's deeds is written in the book of Chronicles of the kings of Israel. 12 This was the word of the Lord that he spoke to Jehu, saying, "Your sons shall sit on the throne of Israel until the fourth generation after you." And so it came to pass. 13 Shallum the son of Jabesh began to reign in the ninetieth year of Vzziah, king of Judeah, and reigned for the space of a month in Samaria. 14 For Mena- hem the son of Gadi departed from Tirzah, came to Samaria, struck Shallum the son of Iabesh in Samaria, killed him, and reigned in his stead. 15 As for the rest of Shallum's deeds and the treachery he did, behold, they are written in the book of the Chronicles of the kings of Israel. 16 Then Menahem destroyed Tiphsah, all who were there, and his coasts from Tirzah, because they had not opened to him, and he destroyed it, snatching all their pregnant women. 17 In the ninth and thirti- eth year of Azariah, king of Iudah, Menahem the son of Gadi began to reign over Israel and reigned ten years in Samaria. 18 He behaved well in the eyes of the LORD and did not turn away all the time from the sin of Jeroboam the son of Nebat, which caused Israel to sin. 19 Then Pul, king of Assur, came against the land; and Menahem gave Pul a thousand tal- ents of silver, that his hand might be with him and establish the kingdom in his hands. 20 And Menahem asked Israel to give the king of Assur fifty shekels of silk apiece, and the king of Assur returned and did not stay in the land. 21 Are not the rest of Menahem's deeds and all that he did written in the book of the Chron- icles of the kings of Israel? 22 Menahem fell asleep with his fathers, and Pekahiah his son reigned in his place. 23 In the fiftieth year of Azariah, king of Judah, Pekahiah, Menahem's son, began to reign over Israel in Samaria and reigned for two years. 24 He behaved well in the eyes of the LORD, for he did not turn from the sins of Jeroboam the son of Nebat, who caused Israel to sin. 25 And Pekah the son of Remaliah, his captain, conspired against him, and smote him in Samaria, in the place of the palace of the kings, with Argob and Arieh, and with him fifty men of the Gileadites; so he slew him and reigned in his dwelling place. 26 As for the rest of Pekahiah's deeds and all that he did, behold, they are written in the book of the Chronicles of the kings of Israel. 27 In the two hundred and fiftieth year of Azariah, king of Judah, Pekah the son of Remaliah began to reign over Israel in Samaria and reigned for twenty years. 28 He behaved badly in the eyes of the LORD, because he did not turn from the sins of Jeroboam the son of Nebat, who caused Israel to sin. 29 In the time of Pekah, king of Israel, came Tiglath Pileser, king of Assur, who took Iion, Abel, Bet-Macha, Ia- noa, Kedesh, Hazor, Gilead, Galilah, and all the land of Naphtali, and carried them away to Assur. 30 And Hoshea the son of Elah

be- trayed Pekah the son of Remaliah, slew him, and reigned in his stead in the twentieth year of Iotham the son of Vzziah. 31 As for the rest of Pekah's deeds and all that he did, behold, they are written in the book of the Chronicles of the kings of Israel. 32 In the second year of Pekah the son of Remaliah, king of Israel, Io- tham the son of Vzziah, king of Iudah, began to reign. 33 He was five years old and twenty when he began to reign and reigned for six- ty years in Jerusalem; his mother's name was Jerusha, daughter of Zadok. 34 He behaved well in the eyes of the LORD and did all that his father Vzziah had done. 35 But the places of worship were not removed, for the people still offered and burned incense in the plac- es of worship; he bought the highest door of the house of the LORD. 36 Are not the other deeds of Iotham and all that he did written in the book of the Chronicles of the kings of Iudah? 37 In those days the LORD began to send against Iudah Rezin, king of Aram, and Pekah, son of Remaliah. 38 And Iotham fell asleep with his fathers and was buried with his fathers in the city of Dauid his father, and Ahaz his son reigned in his dwelling place.

CHAPTER 16

1 In the seventeenth year of Pekah the son of Remaliah, Ahaz the son of Jotham, king of Judah, began to reign. 2 Ahaz was twenty years old when he began to reign; he reigned sixty years in Jerusalem and did not behave well before the LORD his God like Dauid his father: 3 But he walked in the way of the kings of Israel, and made his son pass through the fire, according to the abominations of the heathen whom the LORD had cast out before the children of Israel. 4 Moreover he offered himself and burned incense in the places and on the high places and under every green tree. 5 Then Rezin, king of Aram, and Pekah, son of Remaliah, king of Israel, came to Jerusalem to fight; they besieged Ahaz, but could not defeat him. 6 At the same time Rezin, king of Aram, returned Elath to Aram and drove the Iewes out of Elath; so the Aramites came to Elath and dwelt there to this day. 7 Then Ahaz sent messengers to Tiglath Pileser, king of Assur, saying, "I am your servant and your son; come and deliver me from the hand of the king of Aram and from the hand of the king of Isra- el who rises up against me." 8 Ahaz took the silver and gold that were in the house of the LORD and in the treasures of the king's house and sent them as gifts to the king of Assur. 9 The king of Assur agreed with him; and the king of Assur went against Damascus. When he had taken it, he took the people to Kir and killed Rezin. 10 And King Ahaz went to Da- mascus to meet with Tiglath Pileser, king of Assur; and when King Ahaz saw the altar that was in Damascus, he sent to Vriiah the priest the paternal of the altar, its facade and all its work. 11 And Vriiah the priest made an altar in al poyntes like that which king Ahaz had sent from Damascus, so did Vriiah the priest against king Ahaz who came from Damascus. 12 When the king came from Damascus, the king saw the altar; the king approached the al- tar and offered there. 13 He burned his burnt offering, his food offering, his wine offering, and sprinkled the blood of his peace offering beside the altar, 14 and placed it beside the copper altar that was before the LORD, and brought it in front of the house, between the altar and the house of the LORD, and placed it on the north side of the altar. 15 And King Ahaz commanded Vriiah the priest, and said, "On the great altar let the burnt offering be burnt in the morning, and in the evening the food offering, and the king's burnt

offering and his food offering, and the burnt offering of all the people of the land, and the food of- fering, and the drink offering: and so all the blood of the burnt offering, and all the blood of the sacrifice, and the bronze altar shall be an object of demand for me unto God." 16 Vri- iah the priest did all that King Ahaz had com- manded. 17 King Ahaz broke off the edges of the bases, removed the cauldrons, removed the sea from the copper oxen that were under it, and placed it on a floor of stones. 18 The vaile for the Sabbath (which they had made in the house) and the entrance of the kings with- out turned toward the house of the LORD, be- cause of the king of Assur. 19 As for the rest of the deeds of Ahaz, which he did, are they not written in the book of the Chronicles of the kings of Iudah? 20 Ahaz fell asleep with his fathers and was buried with his fathers in the city of Dauid, and Hezekiah his son reigned in his place.

CHAPTER 17

1 In the twelfth year of Ahaz, king of Judah, Hoshea the son of Elah began to reign in Samaria outside Israel and reigned for nine years. 2 He did well in the eyes of the LORD, but not like the kings of Israel who had pre- ceded him. 3 Shalmaneser, king of Assur, came against him; Hoshea became his ser- vant and gave him gifts. 4 The king of Assur found in Hosea treachery, for he had sent messengers to So king of Egypt and had not brought any gifts to the king of Assur, as he had done before; therefore the king of Assur locked him up and put him in prison. 5 Then the king of Assur poured out all over the land and went against Samaria and besieged it for three years. 6 In the ninth year of Hoshea, the king of Assur took possession of Sa- maria, took Israel away from Assur, and put him in Halah, in Habor, by the Gozan shore, and in the cities of the Medes. 7 For the chil- dren of Israel sinned against the LORD their God, who had brought them out of the land of Egypt, from under the hand of Pharaoh, king of Egypt, and they feared other gods, 8 And they walked according to the customs of the heathen, whom the LORD had cast out before the children of Israel, and according to the customs of the kings of Israel, whom they had followed, 9 The children of Israel had done secretly things that were not right be- fore the LORD their God, and in all their cit- ies they had built places of worship, from the watchtower to the defended city, 10 and they had built images and groups on every hill and under every green tree, 11 and they burned in- cense in all places, as did the heathen whom the LORD had taken away before them, and they did evil things to vex the LORD, 12 and they served idols, whereas the LORD had said to them, "You shall not do such a thing." 13 nevertheless the LORD testified to Israel and to Iudah through all the prophets and all the seers, saying, "Withdraw from your evil ways and keep my commands and my statutes, according to all the regulations that I com- manded your fathers and that I transmitted to you through my servants the prophets." 14 But they would not obey and hardened their necks, like that of their fathers, who did not believe in the LORD their God. 15 And they re- jected his statutes and his covenant, which he had made with their fathers, and his testimo- nies (by which he had testified to them), and followed vanity, and became vain, and fol- lowed the heathen around them, concerning whom the Lord had instructed them not to do as they did. 16 Finally they forsook all the commands of the Lord their God and made themselves molten images, that is, two chal- ices, and they made a group and worshiped all the guests of Heauen and served Baal. 17 And they made their sons and their daugh- ters pass through the fire, and they practiced sorceries and incantations, and they did evil to the LORD to vex him. 18 Therefore the LORD was exceedingly angry with Israel and removed them from his sight, and there re- mained only the tribe of Iudah. 19 But Iudah did not observe the commands of the LORD their God, and walked according to the will of Israel, whom they had opposed. 20 Therefore the LORD drove out all the descendants of Is- rael, afflicted them, and delivered them into the hands of the ruthless, until he had driv- en them out of his sight. 21 For he separat- ed Israel from the house of Dauid, and they made Jeroboam the son of Nebat king; and Jeroboam turned Israel away from following the LORD, and caused them to commit great sin. 22 For the children of Israel walked in all the sins of Jeroboam, which he committed, and did not turn away from them, 23 Until the LORD turned Israel out of his sight, as he had said through all his servants, the Proph- ets, and brought Israel out of their land to As- sur to this day. 24 The king of Assur brought in people from Babel, from Cuthah, from Aua, from Hamath, and from Sefaruaim, and put them in the cities of Samaria to guard the children of Israel; so they possessed Sa- maria and dwelt in its cities. 25 In the begin- ning of their dwelling, they did not fear the LORD; therefore the LORD sent lions among them and they killed them. 26 Therefore they turned to the king of Assur, saying, "The na- tions which you have put away and placed in the cities of Samaria do not know the order of the God of the land; therefore he has sent li- ons among them, and behold, they kill them, because they do not know the order of the God of the land." 27 Then the king of Assur ordered, "Bring here one of the priests whom you brought from there, that he may go and dwell there and teach them the way of the God of the land." 28 So one of the priests they had brought from Samaria came to dwell in Bet- el and taught them how they should fear the LORD. 29 Nevertheless each nation made its own gods and put them in the houses of the places the Samaritans had built, each nation in its cities where it dwelt. 30 The men of Ba- bel made Succoth-Benoth, the men of Cuth made Nergal, and the men of Hamath made Ashima, 31 the Auim made Nibhaz and Tartak; the Sefaruaim burned their sons in the fire to Adrammelech and Anammelech, the gods of Sefaruaim. 32 So they feared the LORD and called priests from themselves for the places, who prepared sacrifices for them in the hous- es of the places. 33 They feared the LORD, but they served their gods according to the way of the nations they had brought with them. 34 To this day they are still following the old way of doing things: they do not fear God, nor follow their decrees, nor their customs, nor the Lawe, nor the commandment which the LORD gave to the sons of Iaakob, to whom he gave the name of Israel, 35 with whom the LORD had made a covenant and instructed them to say, "Do not fear other gods, nor bow down to them, nor serve them, nor sacrifice to them: 36 but fear the LORD who brought you out of the land of Egypt with great power and with an outstretched arm; fear him, wor- ship him and sacrifice to him. 37 Also observe diligently the statutes, the prescriptions, the Lawe, and the commandment which he has written for you, that you may put them into practice continually and fear no other gods. 38 Do not forget the covenant I have made with you and do not fear other gods, 39 but fear the LORD your God, and he will deliver you out of the hand of all your enemies." 40 Yet they did not obey, but did according to their old ways. 41 So these nations feared the LORD and also served their images; so did their

children and their children's children; as their fathers did, so they still do.

CHAPTER 18

1 In the third year of Hoshea the son of Elah, king of Israel, Hezekiah the son of Ahaz, king of Judah, began to reign. 2 He was five years old and twenty when he began to reign, and he reigned nine years and twenty in Jerusa- lem. His mother was also named Abi, daugh- ter of Zechariah, 3 He did well in the eyes of the LORD, as Dauid his father had done. 4 And he removed the places of worship, and broke down the images, and cut down the grooves, and reduced to pieces the copper serpent that Moses had made, because until that day the children of Israel burned incense in it, and called it Nehushtan. 5 He trusted in the LORD, the God of Israel, so that after him there was no one like him among all the kings of Judah, nor were there any like him before him. 6 For he abided in the LORD and did not depart from him, but kept his commands, which the LORD had given to Moses. 7 So the LORD was with him, and he prospered in all things that he took into his hand; moreover he rebelled against the king of Assur and did not enslave him. 8 He defeated the Philistines as far as Azza and its coasts, from the guard to the defended city. 9 In the fourth year of King Hezekiah (which was the seventh year of Hoshea, son of Elah, king of Israel), Shal- maneser, king of Assur, came against Sa- maria and besieged it. 10 After three years they conquered it, and so in the sixth year of Hezekiah, that is, in the ninth year of Hoshea, king of Israel, Samaria was taken. 11 Then the king of Assur took Israel away to Assur and put them in Halah and Habor, by the river of Gozan and in the cities of the Medes, 12 because they would not obey the message of the LORD their God, but transgressed his counsel, that is, all that Moses, the LORD's servant, had commanded, and they would neither obey nor do. 13 Moreover, in the four- teenth year of King Hezekiah, Saneherib king of Assur came against all the strong cities of Iudah and took them. 14 Then Hezekiah, king of Iudah, sent word to the king of Assur in Lachish, "I have offended; depart from me, and what you impose on me I will bear." 14 The king of Assur assigned Hezekiah, king of Judah, three talents of silver and thirty talents of gold. 15 So Hezekiah took all the silver that was in the house of the LORD and in the trea- sures of the king's house. 16 At the same time, Hezekiah took away the slabs of the walls of the LORD's temple and the pillars (which the aforementioned Hezekiah, king of Judah, had made disappear) and delivered them to the king of Assur. 17 The king of Assur sent Tar- tan, Rab-saris and Rabshakeh from Lachish to King Hezekiah with a large army against Jerusalem. And they set out and came to Jeru- salem, and when they had come, they stopped by the shaft of the well of Vpper, which is along the path of the field of the charcoal burners, 18 and they called to the king. Then came out Eliakim the son of Hilkiah, who was steward of the house, Shebna, the chancel- lor, and Ioah the son of Asaph, the recorder. 19 Rabshakeh said to them, "Tell Hezekiah, I pray you, Thus says the great king, that is, the great king of Assur: What confidence is this in which you trust? 20 You think, Surely I have eloquence, but counsel and strength are for war. In whom do you trust, then, if you rebel against me? 21 Behold, you trust now in this broken staff, that is, in Egypt, on which if a man leans, it goes into his hand and perishes him; so is Pharaoh, king of Egypt, toward all who trust in him. 22 But if you say to me, "We trust in the LORD our God," is he not the one whose places and altars Hezekiah took away, and said to Judeah and Jerusalem, "You shall worship before this altar in Jerusalem?" 23 Now therefore give hostages to my lord the king of Assur, and I will give you two thousand horses, if you are able to make them ride. 24 For how can you despise one of the captains of my master's last servants and rely on Egypt for chariots and horsemen? 25 Have I come without the LORD to this place to destroy it? The LORD said to me, "Go against this land and destroy it." 26 Then Eliakim the son of Hilkiah, Shebna, and Ioah said to Rabshakeh, "Speak, I pray you, to your servants in the Aramite language, that we may understand it, and do not speak to them in the Irish lan- guage in the presence of the people standing on the walls." 27 But Rabshakeh said to them, "Has my master sent me to your master and to you to speak these words, and not to the men who sit on the walls, that they may eat their own doung and drink their own pisse with you?" 28 Then Rabshakeh stood still and cried with a loud voice in the Irish language and spoke, saying, "Hear the words of the great king, of the king of Assur." 29 Thus says the king, "Do not let Hezekiah deceive you, for he will not be able to deliver you out of my hand. 30 Nor let Hezekiah make you trust in the LORD, saying, 'The LORD will deliver you, and this city will not be given into the hand of the king of Assur. 31 Do not listen to Hezeki- ah, for thus says the king of Assur, "Make an appointment with me and come to me, that each one may eat of his own vine, each one of his own fig tree, and each one may drink of the water of his own well, 32 until I come and bring you into a land like your own, that is, into a land of wheat and wine, into a land of bread and vines, into a land of oil and honey, that you may live and not die; and do not obey Hezekiah, for he deceives you, saying, 'The LORD will give you freedom. 33 Has anyone of the gods of the nations taken his land from the hand of the king of Assur? 34 Where is the god of Hamah and Arpad? Where is the god of Sefaruaim and Hena and Iuah? How did they snatch Samaria out of my hands? 35 Who are they, of all the gods of the nations, who tore their territory out of my hands, that the LORD might tear Jerusalem out of my hands? 36 But the people held their peace and did not answer him a single word, for the king had commanded, "Do not answer him." 37 Then Eliakim the son of Hilkiah, who was steward of the house, Shebnah the chancellor, and Ioah the son of Asaph, the recorder, came to Hezekiah with tattered garments and report- ed to him the words of Rabshakeh.

CHAPTER 19

1 When King Hezekiah heard this, he tore his clothes, put on sackcloth, and entered the house of the LORD, 2 and sent Eliakim, who was the steward of the house, and Shebnah, the chancellor, and the elders of the priests dressed in sackcloth to Isaiah, the prophet son of Amoz. 3 They said to him, "Thus says Hezekiah, 'Today is a day of tribulation, of reproach and blasphemy, because the child is about to be born and there is no strength to bring it forth. 4 If the LORD, your God, has heard all the words of Rabshakeh, whom the king of Assur, his master, has sent to rage against the living God and to rebuke him with words that the LORD, your God, has heard, then lift up your prayer for the remnant that is left." 5 King Hezekiah's servants went to Isaiah. 6 Isaiah said to them, "Thus you shall say to your master, 'Thus says the LORD: Do not be afraid of the words that you have heard, with which the

servants of the king of Assur have blasphemed me. 7 Behold, I will send a blast to him, and he shall hear a noise, and shall return to his own land; and I will smite him with the sword in his own land." 8 Rabshakeh returned and found the king of Assur fighting Libnah, for he heard that he had departed from Lachish. 9 He also heard that it was said of Tirhaka, king of Ethiopia, "Behold, he has gone out to fight against you"; therefore he departed and sent other messen- gers to Hezekiah, saying, "Is it not true that the king of Assur has departed for Libna? 10 And you shall thus speak to Hezekiah king of Judah, and say, Thy God shall not deceive thee in whom thou trustest, saying, Jerusalem shall not be delivered into the hand of the king of Assur. 11 For you have heard what the kings of Assur have done to all the countries, how they have destroyed them; and will you be de- livered? 12 Have the gods of the heathen failed those whom my fathers destroyed, such as Gozan, Haran, Rezeph, and the sons of Eden, who were in Thelasar? 13 Where is the king of Hamath, the king of Arpad, the king of the city of Shepharuaim, Hena and Iuah? 14 Then Hezekiah received the letter from the hand of the messengers and read it; then Hezekiah went into the house of the LORD and laid it before the LORD. 15 Hezekiah prayed before the LORD and said, "O LORD, God of Israel, who dwells among the Cherubim, you are the one God of all the kingdoms of the earth; you made heaven and earth. 16 Lord, bow your head and listen: Lord, open your eyes and see and hear the words of Saneherib, who sent to blaspheme the God who lies. 17 It is true, Lord, that the kings of Assur have destroyed the nations and their lands, 18 And they set fire to their gods, because they were not gods, but the work of hands, that is, wood and stone; therefore they destroyed them. 19 Now therefore, O Lord our God, I pray thee, come out of his hand, that all the kingdoms of the earth may know that thou, O Lord, art the only God." 20 Then Isaiah the son of Amoz sent word to Hezekiah, "Thus says the LORD God of Israel: I have heard what you have asked me concerning Saneherib king of As- sur. 21 This is the word which the LORD hath spoken against him, O virgin, daughter of Zion, he hath despised thee, and hath mocked thee: O daughter of Jerusalem, he hath shak- en his head against thee. 22 Against whom hast thou railed, against whom hast thou blasphemed, against whom hast thou exalted thy voice, and lifted up thine eyes upon him? 23 Through your messengers you have called upon the LORD and said, "By the multitude of my chariots I have gone up to the top of the mountains, to the flanks of Lebanon, and I will cut down its cedars and its firs, and I will go into the lodging of its borders and into the forest of its Carmel. 24 I have dug, I have drunk the waters of others, and with the soles of my feet I have dried up all the closed floods. 25 Have you not heard how I made it ancient- ly and formed it long ago? And should I now bring it, that it may be destroyed and placed on ruinous heaps, like the defenestrated cit- ies? 26 Its inhabitants have little strength, they are afraid and confused; they are like the grass of the fields and the green grass, or like the grass on the tops of houses, or like the grain that is burned before it is grown. 27 I know thy habitation, and thy going out, and thy entrance, and thy wrath against me. 28 And because you are angry against me, and your tumult has reached my ears, I will put my hoof in your nostrils and my bridle in your lips, and I will bring you back by the same way by which you came. 29 This shall be a sign to you, O Hezekiah: "This year you shall eat the things that grow by themselves, and the next year those things that grow without sowing, and the third year you shall sow and reap, plant vineyards and

eat their fruit." 30 The remnant of the house of Iudah that has escaped will take root again and bear fruit. 31 For out of Jerusalem shall go forth a rem- nant and some escaped from Mount Zion, the zeal of the LORD of hosts shall do this. 32 Therefore thus says the LORD concerning the king of Assur, "He shall not enter this city, nor plant a stronghold there, nor come before it with his shield, nor launch an attack against it: 33 But he shall turn back by the way by which he came, and shall not enter into this city, saith the LORD. 34 For I will defend this city to save it for my sake and for the sake of Dauid my servant." 35 The same night the an- gel of the LORD went out and struck in the campe of Assur one hundred and forty-five thousand people; so when they rose up ear- ly in the morning, behold, they were all dead bodies. 36 Then Saneherib, king of Assur, de- parted, went his way, returned, and settled in Nineveh. 37 While he was in the temple wor- shiping Nisroch, his god, Adramelech and Sharezer, his sons, killed him with the sword; then they fled to the land of Ararat, and Esar- haddon, his son, reigned in his place.

CHAPTER 20

1 At that time Hezekiah was at the end of his life, and Isaiah the prophet, the son of Amoz, came to him and said, "Thus says the LORD, 'Set your house in order, for you will die and you will not die.'" 2 Then he turned with his face to the wall and prayed to the LORD, say- ing 3 Please, Lord, remember now how I have walked before you in truth and with a true heart, and have done what is good in your sight." 4 And before Isaiah went out into the midst of the courtyard, the word of the LORD came to him, saying, "It is not true that it is not true, 5 Turn again, and say to Hezekiah the leader of my people, "Thus says the LORD God of Dauid thy father, I have heard thy prayer, and I have seen thy sorrows; behold, I have healed thee, and the third day thou shalt go to the house of the LORD, 6 And I will add to thy days fifteen years, and will deliver thee and this city out of the hand of the king of Assur, and will defend this city for my sake and for the sake of Dauid my servant." 7 Then Isaiah said, "Take a lamp of dried figs." They took it, laid it on the boy, and he recomposed himself. 8 For Hezekiah had said to Isaiah, "What will be the sign that the Lord will heal me and that I will enter the house of the Lord on the thir- teenth day?" 9 Isaiah answered, "This sign will you have from the LORD, that the LORD will do what he has said: do you want the shadow to go forward ten degrees or backward ten degrees?" 10 Hezekiah answered, "It is a light thing that the shadow go forward ten degrees; not so therefore, but that the shadow go back ten degrees." 11 The prophet Isaiah called to the LORD, and he brought the shadow back ten degrees from the degrees to which it had fallen on the day of Ahaz. 12 At the same time Berodach Baladan son of Baladan, king of Ba- bel, sent letters and a gift to Hezekiah, for he had heard that Hezekiah was sick. 13 Hezeki- ah listened to them and showed them all his treasure, that is, the clay, the gold, the spic- es, the precious oil, all his armor and all that was in his treasures; there was nothing in his house and in all his kingdom that Hezekiah had not shown them. 14 Then the prophet Isa- iah went to King Hezekiah and said to him, "What do these men say? And where did they come to you from?" Hezekiah answered, "They have come from a far country, that is, from Babel." 15 Then he said, "What did they see in your house?" Hezekiah answered, "They have seen everything in my house; there is nothing among my treasures that I

have not shown them." 16 Isaiah said to Hezekiah, "Listen to the word of the LORD." 17 Behold, the days are coming, when all that is in your house, and what your fathers have stored up to this day, shall be carried away to Babel: There shall be nothing left, saith the LORD. 18 And of thy sons which shall go forth from thee, and which thou shalt beget, they shall carry them away, and they shall be eunuchs in the palace of the king of Babel." 19 Then Hezekiah said to Isaiah, "The word of the LORD which thou hast spoken is good; for he said, Shall it not be good, if peace and truth be in my days?" 20 As for the rest of Hezekiah's deeds and all his valiant deeds and the way in which he made a poole and a cundite and brought water into the city, are they not written in the book of the Chronicles of the kings of Judah? 21 Hezekiah fell asleep with his fathers, and Manasseh his son reigned in his stead.

CHAPTER 21

1 Manasseh was two years old when he began to reign and reigned fifty-five years in Jerusa- lem; his mother's name was also Ephzi-ba. 2 He behaved well in the eyes of the LORD, as the abomination of the heathen whom the LORD had cast out before the children of Is- rael. 3 For he went back and rebuilt the places that Hezekiah, his father, had destroyed; he erected altars to Baal and formed a group, like Ahab, king of Israel, and worshipped all the guests of Heauen and indulged them. 4 Moreover he built altars in the house of the LORD, of which the LORD said, "In Jerusalem I will put my name." 5 He built altars for all the guests of the land in the two courtyards of the house of the LORD. 6 And he made his sons pass through the fire, and gave himself to witchcraft and sorcery, and dealt with those who had familiar spirits and were soothsay- ers, and did much evil in the eyes of the LORD to vex him. 7 Then he placed the image of the group that he had made in the house, where the LORD had said to Dauid and Solomon his son, "In this house and in Jerusalem, which I have chosen out of all the tribes of Israel, I will put my name forever. 8 And I will no more bring forth the feet of Israel from the land which I gave to their fathers, that they may observe and do all that I have command- ed them, and according to all the regulations which my servant Moses commanded them. 9 Yet they did not obey, but Manasseh led them astray, to do more evil than the heathen peoples whom the LORD destroyed before the children of Israel. 10 Therefore the LORD spoke through his servants, the prophets, and said 11 For Manasseh, king of Iudah, has committed such abominations, and has act- ed more wickedly than all those who did the Amorites (who were before him), and has caused Iudah also to sin with his idolatries, 12 Therefore thus says the LORD, the God of Is- rael, "Behold, I will cause such elation to come upon Jerusalem and upon Iudah that those who hear of it will have their ears tingling. 13 And I will spread out from Jerusalem the line of Samaria and the pedestal of the house of Ahab; and I will clean Jerusalem, as a man cleanses a dish, which he then overthrows. 14 I will abandon the remnants of my inheri- tance and deliver them into the hands of their enemies; they will be robbed and stripped of all their possessions, 15 For they have acted evil in my sight, and have provoked me to wrath, from the time their fathers came out of Egypt until now. 16 Moreover Manasseh shed much innocent blood, until he filled Jerusalem from corner to corner, in addi- tion to the sin he committed when he caused Judah to sin, and he did an evil deed before the LORD. 17 Are not the rest of Manasseh's deeds, all that he did and the sin he commit- ted, written in the book of the Chronicles of the kings of Judah? 18 Manasseh fell asleep with his fathers and was buried in the garden of his house, that is, in the garden of Vzza, and Amon his son reigned in his place. 19 Amon was two and twenty years old when he began to reign, and he reigned two years in Jerusalem; his mother's name was also Me- shullemeth, daughter of Haruz of Jotbah. 20 He behaved himself well before the LORD, like his father Manasseh. 21 For he went all the way that his father went, and used the idols that his father used, and worshipped them. 22 He forsook the LORD, the God of his fathers, and did not walk in the way of the LORD. 23 Amon's servants conspired against him and killed the king in his house. 24 The people of the land killed all those who had conspired against King Amon, and the people made Iosiah his son king in his house. 25 Are not the rest of the deeds of Amon, which he did, written in the book of the Chronicles of the kings of Iudah? 26 And they buried him in his sepulcher in the garden of Vzza, and Iosi- ah his son reigned in his house.

CHAPTER 22

1 Iosiah was eight years old when he began to reign and reigned for a year and a half in Jerusalem. His mother's name was also Ie- didah, daughter of Adaiah of Bozcath. 2 He behaved well in the eyes of the LORD, walked in all the ways of Dauid his father and bowed neither to the right nor to the left. 3 In the eighteenth year of King Josiah's reign, the king sent Shaphan the son of Azaliah, the son of Meshullam, the chancellor, to the house of the LORD, saying, 4 "Go to Hilkiah, the high priest, that he may sum up the clay that is brought into the house of the LORD and that the keepers of the house have collected from the people. 5 Let them deliver it into the hands of those who do the work and have the oversight of the house of the LORD; let them give it to those who work in the house of the LORD to repair the deteriorated places of the house: 6 that is, to the craftsmen, carpenters and masons, to cut lumber and hew stone to repair the house. 7 However, let no account be made to them of the money delivered into their hands, for they do faithfully." 8 Hilkiah the high priest said to Shaphan the chancel- lor, "I found the book of Lawe in the house of the LORD"; Hilkiah handed the book to Shaphan, who read it again. 9 Then Shaphan, the chancellor, went to the king and report- ed to him, "Your servants have collected the money that was found in the house and de- livered it into the hands of those who do the work and have the oversight of the house of the LORD." 10 Shaphan the chancellor also showed the king, "Hilkiah the priest delivered a book to me." And Shaphan read it before the king. 11 When the king had heard the words of the book of the Law, he tore his clothes. 12 The king then commanded Hilkiah the priest, Ahikam the son of Shaphan, Achbor the son of Michaiah, Shaphan the chancellor, and Asa- hiah the king's servant, to say 13 Go, and ask the LORD for me, and for the people, and for all Iudah concerning the words of this book that has been found; for great is the wrath of the LORD kindled against you, because our fathers did not obey the words of this book, to do according to all that is written in it for the Vs." 14 Then Hilkiah the priest, Ahikam, Ach- bor, Shafan and Asahiah went to Huldah the prophetess, wife of Shallum, son of Tikuah, son of Harhas, keeper of the wardrobe, who lived in Jerusalem in the colony, and made contact with her. 15 And she answered them, "Thus says

the LORD, the God of Israel, Tel the man who sent you to me, 16 Thus says the LORD: "Behold, I will bring down upon this place and upon its inhabitants all the words of the book which the king of Iudah has read, 17 because they have forsaken me, and have burned incense to other gods, to vex me with all the works of their hands; my wrath shall also be kindled against this place, and shall not be appeased." 18 But to the king of Iu- dah, who sent you to inquire of the LORD, ye shall say, Thus saith the LORD God of Israel, The words which thou hast heard shall come to pass. 19 But because your heart melted and you humbled yourself before the LORD, when you heard what I said against this place and against its inhabitants, namely, that it would be destroyed and cursed, and you tore your clothes and wept before me, I also heard it, says the LORD. 20 Behold therefore I will gather you to your fathers, and you shall be put in your grave in peace, and your eyes shall not see all the evil that I shall do upon this place." So they brought again the words of the king.

CHAPTER 23

1 Then the king sent for and gathered to him all the elders of Iudah and Jerusalem. 2 And the king went into the house of the LORD with all the men of Iudah, and all the inhab- itants of Jerusalem with him, and the priests and the prophets, and all the people, small and great, and reported to their ears all the words of the book of the covenant that was in the house of the LORD. 3 And the king stood by the pillar and made a speech before the LORD, that they should walk according to the LORD and observe his commands, his testi- monies, and his statutes with all their heart and with all their soul, to fulfill the words of this speech written in this book. And all the people stood up for the convention. 4 Then the king commanded Hilkiah the priest, and the priests of the second order, and the keepers of the temple, to bring out of the temple of the LORD all the utensils that had been made for Baal, and for the group, and for all the army of Heauen; and he burned them outside Je- rusalem, in the fields of Kedron, and brought the bag of them to Bet- el. 5 He struck down the Chemarim, which the kings of Iudah had established to burn incense in the places of worship, in the cities of Iudah and around Je- rusalem, and also those who burned incense to Baal, the sun, the moon, the planets and all the armies of Heauen. 6 Then he carried the mass from the temple of the LORD outside Je- rusalem to the valley of Kedron, and burned it in the valley of Kedron, and pulverized it, and threw the dust of it on the graves of the sons of the people. 7 Then he destroyed the houses of the Sodomites that were in the house of the LORD, where the women were making tents for the company. 8 Moreover he brought out all the priests from the cities of Iudah, and defiled the places where the priests burned incense, from Geba to Beer-sheba, and de- stroyed the places of the gates that were at the entrance of the gate of Ioshua, the gate- keeper of the city, which was on the left of the gate of the city. 9 Moreover, the priests of the remoter places did not go to the altar of the LORD in Jerusalem, for they ate only of sea- soned bread among their brethren. 10 He also defiled Topheth, which was in the valley of the sons of Hinnom, so that no one would put his son or daughter through the fire at Molech. 11 He also cut down the horses that the kings of Iudah had given to the sun at the entrance to the house of the LORD, by the chamber of Nethan- Melech, the eunuch, who was chief of the suburbs, and burned with fire the car- ets of the sun. 12 And the king tore

down the altars that were at the top of the chamber of Ahaz, which were made by the kings of Iudah, and the altars that Manasseh had made in the two courtyards of the house of the LORD, and rushed thence, and cast the dust thereof into the river Kedron. 13 The king also defiled the places that were before Jerusalem and on the right side of the mount of corruption (which Solomon, king of Israel, had bought for Ashtoreth, the idol of the Zidonians, for Chemosh, the idol of the Moabites, and for Milchom, the abomination of the sons of Am- mon). 14 And he tore the images to pieces, and cut down the grooves, and filled their places with bones of men. 15 Moreover, the altar that was in Beth-el and the place of worship made by Jeroboam the son of Nebat, who made Is- rael sin, both this altar and the place of wor- ship, he smashed them to pieces, burned the place of worship, and reduced it to dust, and burned the mass. 16 As Iosiah turned around, he saw the graves that were on the moun- tain, sent for the bones from the graves, and burned them on the altar, and defiled it, ac- cording to the word of the LORD which the man of God had proclaimed, and shouted the same words. 17 Then he said, "What is the title of what I see?" And the men of the city said to him, "It is the tomb of the man of God who came from Iudah and told the things that you did at the altar of Beth-el." 18 Then he said, "Let him be; let no one remove his bones." So his bones were put together with those of the prophet who had come from Samaria. 19 Iosi- ah also took away all the houses of the places of worship that were in the cities of Samaria, which the kings of Israel had made to vex the LORD, and did to them all that he had done in Bet-el. 20 Then he sacrificed all the priests of the places of worship that were there on the altars, burned the bones of the men on them, and returned to Jerusalem. 21 Then the king commanded all the people, "Observe the feast of the LORD your God, as it is written in the book of this convention." 22 And there has not been a Passover like that since the days of the Judges who ruled Israel, nor in all the days of the kings of Israel and the kings of Iudah. 23 In the eighth year of King Iosiah was this feast celebrated to the Lord in Jerusalem. 24 Iosiah also removed those who had familiar spirits, soothsayers, images, idols, and all the abominations that had been discovered in the land of Iudah and in Jerusalem, to per- form the words of the law written in the book that Hilkiah the priest had found in the house of the LORD. 25 Like him there was no king before him who turned to the LORD with all his heart, with all his soul, and with all his strength, according to all the Law of Moses, nor after him has there arisen another like him. 26 Nevertheless the LORD did not turn from the fierceness of his great wrath, with which he was angry against Iudah, because of all the prouocations with which Manasseh had provoked him. 27 Therefore the LORD said, "I will also remove Iudah from my sight, as I have removed Israel, and I will throw out this city, Jerusalem, which I have chosen, and the house of which I said, 'My name shall be there.'" 28 Are not the rest of Iosiah's deeds and all that he did written in the book of the Chronicles of the kings of Iudah? 29 In his day, Pharaoh Nechoh, king of Egypt, went against the king of Assur on the border of Per- ath. King Iosiah went against him, and when Pharaoh noticed, he killed him at Megiddo. 30 And his servants carried him away dead from Megiddo, and brought him to Jerusalem, and buried him in his tomb. And the people of the land took Iehoahaz the son of Iosiah, anointed him, and made him king instead of his fathers. 31 And Iehoahaz was three and twenty years old when he began to reign, and he reigned for three months in Jerusalem. His mother's name was also Hamutal, daughter of Jeremiah of Libnah. 32 He behaved well be- fore the LORD, according to what his fathers had done. 33 Pharaoh Nechoh put him in chains in Riblah, in the territory of Hamath, while he reigned in Jerusalem, and subjected the territory to a tribute of a hundred talents of silver and a talent of gold. 34 And Pharaoh Nechoh made Eliakim the son of Iosiah king in place of Iosiah his father, and changed his name to Iehoiakim, taking out of the way Ie- hoahaz, who came to Egypt and died there. 35 And Iehoiakim delivered to Pharaoh the silver and the gold, and taxed the land to give the money, according to the order of Pharaoh; and he charged every man of the people of the land, according to his value, the silver and the gold to give it to Pharaoh Nechoh. 36 Hehoiakim was fifty-two years old when he began to reign, and he reigned eleven years in Jerusalem. His mother was also named Ze- budah, daughter of Pedaiah of Rumah. 37 He behaved well before the LORD, according to what his fathers had done.

CHAPTER 24

1 In his days came Nebuchadnezzar, king of Babel, and Jehoiakim became his servant for three years; then he revolted and rebelled against him. 2 And the LORD sent against him bands of Chaldeans, bands of Aramites, bands of Moabites, and bands of Ammo- nites, and sent them against Iudah to de- stroy it, according to the word of the LORD spoken through his servants the Prophets. 3 By the command of the LORD this came upon Iudah, that he might take them out of the way for the sins of Manasseh and for all that he had done, 4 and for the innocent blood he shed (for he filled Jerusalem with innocent blood), for which the LORD did not forgive him. 5 Are not the rest of the deeds of Iehoiakim and all that he did written in the book of the Chronicles of the kings of Iudah? 6 So Hehoiakim fell asleep with his fathers, and Hehoiachin his son reigned in his place. 7 And the king of Egypt came no more out of his land, because the king of Babel had car- ried away from the kingdom of Egypt to the kingdom of Perath all that belonged to the king of Egypt. 8 Hehoiachin was eighty years old when he began to reign, and he reigned in Jerusalem for three months. His mother's name was also Nehushta, daughter of Elna- than of Jerusalem. 9 He behaved well before the LORD, as his father had done. 10 At that time, the servants of Nebuchadnezzar, king of Babel, came against Jerusalem, and the city was besieged. 11 Nebuchadnezzar, king of Babel, came against the city, and his servants besieged it. 12 Then Jehoiachin king of Judah came out against the king of Babel, he, his mother, his servants, his princes, and his eu- nuchs; and the king of Babel took him in the last year of his reign. 13 Then he carried away all the treasures of the house of the LORD and the treasures of the house of kings and broke all the golden vessels that Solomon king of Israel had built in the temple of the LORD, as the LORD had said. 14 Then he took all Je- rusalem into captivity, all the princes, all the strong men of war, about ten thousand, all the laborers and the cunning men, and there re- mained none but the poor people of the land. 15 Then he brought Jehoiachin to Babel, and the king's mother, and the king's wives, and his sons, and the mighty men of the land were carried captive from Jerusalem to Babel, 16 and all the men of war, about seven thousand, and the carpenters and the smiths a thou- sand; all who were strong and fit for war, the king of Babel brought them to Babel as cap- tives. 17 And the king of Babel made Matta- niah his vncle king in his stead, and changed his name to Zedekiah. 18 Zedekiah was one year old and twenty years old when he began to reign, and he reigned eleven years in Jeru salem. His mother was also named Hamutal, daughter of Jeremiah of Libna. 19 He behaved well in the eyes of the LORD, according to what Jehoiakim had done. 20 Therefore the anger of the LORD came upon Jerusalem and Iudah until he drove them out of his presence. Zedekiah rebelled against the king of Babel.

CHAPTER 25

1 In the ninth year of his reign, on the tenth month and on the tenth day of the month, Nebuchadnezzar, king of Babel, came with his whole army against Jerusalem, encamp- ed against it and built forts around it. 2 Thus the city was besieged until the eleventh year of King Zedekiah. 3 On the ninth day of the month the famine came upon the city, so that there was no bread for the people of the land. 4 Then the city was destroyed, and all the men of war fled by night through the gate that is between the two walls, near the king's garden; and the Chaldeans were round about the city, and the king passed through the wilderness. 5 But the army of the Chaldeans pursued the king and took him in the wilderness of Jeri- cho, and all his army was scattered by him. 6 Then they took the king and brought him to the king of Babel in Riblah, where they judged him. 7 They killed the sons of Zedekiah be- fore his eyes, put out his eyes, bound him in chains, and brought him to Babel. 8 On the fifth and seventh day of the month, which was the nineteenth year of Nebuchadnezzar king of Babel, Nebuzar-adan, chief steward and servant of the king of Babel, came to Jerusa- lem, 9 And he burned the house of the LORD, and the king's house, and all the houses of Jerusalem, and all the great houses were set on fire. 10 And all the army of the Chaldeans, which was with the chief steward, broke down the walls of Jerusalem all around. 11 The rest of the people who remained in the city and those who had fled and fallen into the hand of the king of Babel, with the rest of the crowd, were taken away by Nebuzar- Adan, the chief steward, as prisoners. 12 But the chief stew- ard left poor people of the land to cultivate the vines and till the ground. 13 Also the bronze pillars that were in the house of the LORD, the bronze bases and the bronze sea that was in the house of the LORD, the Chaldeans broke them and carried the stones of them to Babel. 14 Also the vessels, the besome, the musical instruments, the incense dishes and all the bronze vessels in which they ministered were taken away. 15 The ass cloths, the basins and all that was of gold and silver were taken away by the chief steward, 16 with the two pillars, one maritime and the other base, which Solo- mon had built for the house of the LORD; the encumbrance of all these utensils was weight- less. 17 The height of the first pillar was eighty cubits, its cap was of wood, the height of the cap was three cubits of net, with pomegran- ates around the cap, all of wood. 18 The chief steward took Seraiah, the first priest, and Zephaniah, the second priest, and the three keepers of the house. 19 From the city he took a eunuch who had the supervision of the men of war, and five men of those who were in the king's presence who were in the city, and Sofer, captain of the army, who controlled the people of the land, and sixty men of the people of the land who were in the city. 20 Nebuzar- adan, the chief steward, took them and led them to the king of Babel in Riblah. 21 And the king of Babel struck them and killed them in Riblah, in the land of Hamath. So Iudah was carried away in captivity from his country. 22

However, there remained a people in the land of Judah, whom Nebuchadnezzar, king of Babel, left behind and made Gedali- ah, son of Ahikam, son of Shaphan, chief. 23 When all the captains of the army and their men heard that the king of Babel had made Gedaliah a warrior, they and their men came from Gedaliah to Mizpah: Ishmael the son of Nethaniah, Iohanan the son of Kareah, Se- raiah the son of Tanhumeth the Netophite, and Iaazaniah the son of Maachathi. 24 Geda- liah swore to them and their men and said to them, "Do not be afraid to be the servants of the Chaldeans; dwell in the land and serve the king of Babel and you will be well." 25 But in the seventh month came Ishmael, the son of Nethaniah, the son of Elishama, of the king's seed, and ten men with him, and smote Gedaliah, who died, as well as the Iewes and the Chaldeans who were with him at Mizpah. 26 Then all the people, small and great, and the captains of the army rose up and came to Egypt, for they were afraid of the Chaldeans. 27 However, in the thirtieth year after He- hoiachin, king of Judah, had been taken away, in the twelfth month and on the twentieth day of the month, Euil-merodach, king of Babel, in the year in which he began to reign, lifted up the head of Hehoiachin, king of Judah, from prison, 28 he spoke kindly to him and set his throne beside the throne of the kings who were with him in Babel, 29 changed his prison garments, and continually ate bread before him all the days of his life. 30 His por- tion was a continual portion granted him by the king, every day a certain portion, all the days of his life.

I CHRONICLES

CHAPTER 1

1 Adam, Sheth, Enosh, 2 Kenan, Mahalaleel, Iered, 3 Henoch, Methuselah, Lamech, 4 Noah, She, Ham, and Iapheth. 5 The sons of Japheth were Gomer, Magog, Madai, Iau- an, Tubal, Meshech and Tiras. 6 The sons of Gomer were Ashchenaz, Iphath and Tog- arma. 7 The sons of Iauan were Elisha and Tarshisha, Kittim and Dodanim. 8 The sons of Ham were Cush, Mizraim, Put, and Ca-

naan. 9 The sons of Cush were Siba, Hauilah, Sabta, Raamah and Sabtecha. Raamah's sons were also Sheba and Dedan 10 Cush begat Nimrod, who began to be powerful in the land 11 Mizraim begat Ludim and Anamim, Lehabim and Nephtahim: 12 Pathrusim and Casluhim, from whom arose the Philistines and Caphtorim. 13 Canaan also begat Zidon, his first son, and Heth, 14 the Hebusite, the Amorrean, and the Girgishite, 15 the Hiuuite, the Arcaite and the Simite, 16 the Aruadite, the Zemarite and the Hamathite. 17 The sons of Shem were Elam and Assur, Arpachshad, Lud, Aram, Vz, Hul, Gether and Meshech. 18 Arpachshad begat Shelah, and Shelah begat Eber. 19 Two sons were also born to Eber: the first was named Peleg, because in his day the land was deified; the second was named Io- ktan. 20 Ioktan begat Almodad and Sheleph, Hazermaueth and Ierah, 21 Hadoram, Vzal and Diklah, 22 Ebal, Abimael and Sheba, 23 Ofir, Hauilah and Iobab: all these were sons of Ioktan. 24 Shem, Arpachshad, Shelah, 25 Eber, Peleg, Rehu, 26 Serug, Nahor, Terah, 27 Abram, that is, Abraham. 28 The sons of Abraham were Izhak and Ishmael. 29 These are their generations. Ishmael's eldest son was Nebaioth, Kedar, Adbeel and Mibsam, 30 Mishma, Dumah, Massa, Hadad and Tema, 31 Ietur, Nefish and Kedemah: these are the sons of Ishmael. 32 Keturah, Abraham's concubine, bore the sons of Zimran, Iokshan, Medan, Midian, Ishbak and Shuah; the sons of Iok- shan were Sheba and Dedan. 33 The sons of Midian were Ephah,

Ephar, Henoch, Abida, and Elda: All these are the sons of Keturah. 34 Abraham begat Izhak; the sons of Izhak were Esau and Israel. 35 The sons of Esau were Eliphaz, Reuel, Ieush, Iaalam, and Korah. 36 The sons of Eliphaz were Teman, Omar, Zeph- im, Gatham, Kenaz, Timnah, and Amalek. 37 The sons of Reuel, Nahath, Zerah, Shammah and Mizzah. 38 The sons of Seir: Lotan, Sho- bal, Zibeon, Ana, Dishon, Ezer and Dishan. 39 Sons of Lotan: Hori, Homam and Timna, sister of Lotan. 40 The sons of Shobal were Alian, Manahath, Ebal, Shephi and Onam. Zi- beon's sons were Haya and Anah. 41 The son of Anah was Dishon. Dishon's sons were Amran, Eshban, Ithran and Cheran. 42 Ezer's sons were Bilhan, Zaauan and Iaakan. The sons of Dishon were Vz and Aran. 43 These were the kings who reigned in the land of Edom, be- fore a king reigned over the children of Israel: Bela the son of Beor, and the name of his city was Dinhabah. 44 Then Bela died, and Iobab the son of Zerah of Bozrah reigned in his place. 45 When Iobab was dead, Hussham, of the land of the Temanites, reigned in his place. 46 When Hussham was dead, Hadad the son of Bedad, who had defeated Midian in the camp of Moab, reigned in his place, and the name of his city was Auith. 47 Ha- dad died, and Samlah of Mashrecah reigned in his place. 48 Samlah died, and in his place reigned Shaul of Rehoboth by the river. 49 When Shaul was dead, Baal-Hanan, son of Achbor, reigned in his place. 50 Baal-Hanan died, and in his place reigned Hadad, whose city was called Pai and whose wife's name was Mehetabel, daughter of Matred, daughter of Mezahab. 51 Hadad also died, and there were dukes in Edom: duke Timna, duke Aliah, duke Ietheth, 52 Duke Aholibamah, Duke Elah, Duke Pinon, 53 Duke Kenaz, Duke Teman, Duke Mibzar, 54 Duke Magdiel, Duke Iram: these were the dukes of Edom.

CHAPTER 2

1 These are the sons of Israel: Reuben, Sime- on, Leui and Judah, Issachar and Zebulun, 2 Dan, Josef, Benjamin, Naphtali, Gad and Ash- er. 3 The sons of Judah: Er, Onan and Shelah. These three were borne to him by a daughter of Shua, the Canaanite; but Er, the firstborn of Judah, was frowned upon by the LORD, and he killed him. 4 Thamar, his daughter- in-law, bore him Pharez and Zerah, and so all the sons of Judah were dead. 5 The sons of Pharez, Hezron and Hamul. 6 Also the sons of Zerah were Zimri, Ethan, Heman, Chal- col and Dara, who were five in all. 7 The son of Carmi, Achar, who troubled Israel, trans- gressing in what was excommunicated. 8 The son of Ethan, Azariah. 9 The sons of Hezron that were born to him, Ierahmeel, Ram, and Chelubai. 10 Ram begat Aminadab, and Am- inadab begat Nahshon, prince of the sons of Iudah, 11 Nahshon begat Salma, and Salma begat Boaz, 12 Boaz begat Obed and Obed be- gat Ishai, 13 Ishai begat his eldest son Eliab, Abinadab the second and Shimma the third, 14 Nathaneel the fourth, Raddai the fifth, 15 Ozem the sixth and Dauid the tenth. 16 Whose sisters were Zeruiah and Abigail. Sons of Zeruiah: Abishai, Ioab and Asahel. 17 Abi- gail gave birth to Amasa; Amasa's father was Iether, an Ishmeelite. 18 Caleb, son of Hezron, begat Ierioth by Azuba, his wife; his sons are: Iesher, Shobab and Ardon. 19 When Azuba was dead, Caleb took with him Ephratah, who bore him Hur. 20 Hur begat Vri, and Vri begat Bezaleel. 21 Then Hezron went to the daugh- ter of Machir the father of Gilead, took her when she was sixty years old, and bore him Segub. 22 Segub begat Iair, who had three hundred and twenty cities in the land of Gile- ad. 23 And Geshur, with

Aram, took from him the cities of Iair, Kenath and his cities, that is, sixty cities. All these were sons of Machir the father of Gilead. 24 After Hezron was dead in Caleb Ephratah, Abiah, Hezron's wife, bore him Ashur, the father of Tekoa. 25 The sons of Ierahmeel, Hezron's eldest son, were Ram, the eldest, Bunah, Oren, Ozen and Ahiiah. 26 Ierahmeel also had another wife named Atara, who was the mother of Onam. 27 The sons of Ram, Ierahmeel's firstborn, were Maaz, Iamin and Ekar. 28 The sons of Onam were Shammai and Iada. Shammai's sons were Nadab and Abishur. 29 Abishur's wife's name was Abiahil and she bore him Ahban and Molid. 30 Nadab's sons also were Seled and Appaim, but Seled died childless. 31 Ap- paim's son was Ishi, Ishi's son was Sheshan, and Sheshan's son was Ahlai. 32 The sons of Iada, brother of Shammai, were Iether and Ionathan, but Iether died childless. 33 The sons of Ionathan were Peleth and Zaza. These were the sons of Ierahmeel. 34 Sheshan had no sons but daughters. Sheshan had an Egyp- tian servant named Iarha. 35 Sheshan gave his daughter in marriage to Iarha, his ser- vant, and she bore him Attai. 36 Attai begat Nathan, and Nathan begat Zabad, 37 Zabad begat Ephlal, and Ephlal begat Obed, 38 Obed begat Iehu, and Iehu begat Azariah, 39 Azari- ah begat Helez, and Helez begat Eleasah, 40 Eleasa begat Sisamai and Sisamai begat Shal- lum, 41 Shallum begat Iekamiah and Iekamiah begat Elishama. 42 And the sons of Caleb, the brother of Ierahmeel, were Mesha, his first- born, who was the father of Zif, and the sons of Maresha, the father of Hebron. 43 The sons of Hebron were Korah and Tappuah, Rekem and Shema. 44 Shema begat Raham the fa- ther of Iorkoam, and Rekem begat Shammai. 45 Shammai's son also was Maon, and Maon was the father of Bet-Zur. 46 Ephah, Caleb's concubine, bore Haran, Moza, and Gazez; Haran also begat Gazez. 47 The sons of Iahdai were Regem, Iotham, Geshan, Pelet, Ephah and Shaaph. 48 Caleb's concubine Maachah gave birth to Sheber and Tirhana. 49 She also had Shaaph the father of Madmannah, and Shehua the father of Machbenah, and the fa- ther of Gibeah. Achsah was the daughter of Caleb. 50 These were the sons of Caleb, son of Hur, firstborn of Ephratah, Shobal, father of Kiriath-iearim. 51 Salma, father of Beth-Lem, and Haref, father of Beth-Gader. 52 Shobal, father of Kiriath-iearim, had sons and was the head of half of Hammenoth. 53 The fam- ilies of Kiriath-iearim were the Ithrites, the Puthites, the Shumathites and the Mishrait- es, from whom came the Zarithites and the Eshtaulites. 54 The sons of Salma of Beth-Lem and Netophat, the heads of the house of Ioab, half the Manahthites and the Zorites. 55 And the families of the scribes that dwelt in Iabez, the Tirathites, the Shimmeathites, and the Scutheites, which are the Kenites, who came from Hammath, the father of the house of Rechab.

CHAPTER 3

1 These also were the sons of Dauid that were born to him in Hebron: the eldest Amnon of Ahinoam, the Izraelite; the second Daniel of Abigail, the Carmelite: 2 the third Absalom, son of Maachah, daughter of Talmai, king of Geshur; the fourth Adonijah, son of Hag- gith: 3 the fifth Shepatia from Abital, the sixth Ithream from Eglah his wife. 4 These six were born to him in Hebron, where he reigned seven years and six months, while in Jerusa- lem he reigned three years and thirty. 5 These four were born to him in Jerusalem: Shimea, Shobab, Nathan, and Solomon of Bathshua, daughter of Ammiel: 6 Ibhar, Elishama and

Elipheth, 7 Nogah, Nepheg and Japhia, 8 El- ishama, Eliada and Eliphelet, nine in all. 9 These are all the sons of Dauid, besides the sons of the concubines and Thamar, their sis- ter. 10 Solomon's son was Rehoboam, whose son was Abia, Asa his son, and Ieoshaphat his son, 11 Ioram, his son, Ahaziah, his son, and Ioash, his son, 12 Amaziah, his son, Azariah, his son, and Iotham, his son, 13 Ahaz, his son, Hezekiah, his son, and Manasseh, his son, 14 Amon, his son, and Iosiah, his son. 15 Of Iosi- ah's sons, the eldest was Iohanan, the second Iehoiakim, the third Zedekiah, and the fourth Shallum. 16 The sons of Iehoiakim were Jeco- niah, his son, and Zedekiah, his son. 17 The sons of Jeconiah were Assir and Shealtiel, his son: 18 Malchiram, Pedaiah, Shenazar, Jeca- miah, Hoshama and Nedabiah. 19 The sons of Pedaiah were Zerubbabel and Shimei; the sons of Zerubbabel were Meshullam, Hanani- ah, and Shelomith their sister, 20 Hashubah, Ohel, Berechiah, Hazadia and Iushabheshed, five in the name of all. 21 The sons of Hana- niah were Pelatiah and Jesaiah, the sons of Rephaiah, the sons of Arnan, the sons of Oba- diah, the sons of Shechaniah. 22 The son of Shechaniah was Shemaiah; the sons of She- maiah were Hattush, Igeal, Bariah, Neariah and Shaphat, six. 23 The sons of Neariah were Helioenai, Hezekiah and Azrikam, three. 24 The sons of Helioenai were Hodaiah, Eliasib, Pelaiah, Akkub, Iohanan, Delaiah and Anani, six.

CHAPTER 4

1 The sons of Iudah were Pharez, Hezron, Carmi, Hur and Shobal. 2 Reaiah, son of Sho- bal, begat Iahath, Iahath begat Ahumai and Lahad; these are the families of the Zoreans. 3 These were the father of Etam, Izreel, Ish- ma, and Idbash; their sister's name was Ha- zelelponi. 4 Penuel was the father of Gedor, and Ezer was the father of Hushah; these are the sons of Hur, the firstborn of Ephratah, the father of Bethlehem. 5 Asher, the father of Tekoa, had two wives, Helea and Naara. 6 Naara gave birth to Ahuzam, Hepher, Temeni and Haashtari; these were the sons of Naara. 7 Heleah's sons were Zereth, Iezohar and Eth- nan. 8 Coz also begat Anub, Zobebah and the families of Aharhel the son of Harum. 9 But Iabez was more honorable than his brothers; and his mother called him Iabez, saying, "For I bore him with sorrow." 10 And Iabez called upon the God of Israel, saying, "If thou bless me in grace, and enlarge my coasts, and if thy hand is with me, and if thou wilt that I may be delivered from euillity, that I may not be wounded." And God granted his request. 11 Chelub, Shuah's brother, begat Mehir, who was Eshton's father. 12 Eshton begat Beth-ra- pha, Paseah, and Tehinnah, the father of the city of Nahash; these are the men of Rechah. 13 The sons of Kenaz were Othniel and Zeraiah, and Othniel's son Hathath. 14 Meonothai be- gat Ophrah. Seraiah begat Joab, father of the valley of the craftsmen, for they were crafts- men. 15 The sons of Caleb, son of Jephunneh, were Iru, Elah and Naam. The son of Elah was Kenaz. 16 The sons of Iehaleel were Ziph, Ziphah, Thyriah, and Asareel. 17 Ezra's sons were Iether, Mered, Efer and Ialon; he begat Miriam, Shammai and Ishbah, father of Es- htemoa. 18 His wife Iehudiiah bore Iered, fa- ther of Gedor, Heber, father of Socho, and Ie- kuthiel, father of Zanoa; these are the sons of Bithiah, daughter of Pharaoh, whom Mered had. 19 The sons of the wife of Hodiah, the sister of Naham, the father of Keilah, were the Garmites and Eshtemoa, the Maachathite. 20 The sons of Shimon were Amnon and Rinna, Ben-Hanam and Tilon. The sons of Ishi were Zoheth

and Benzoheth. 21 The sons of Shelah the son of Judah were Er the father of Lecah, and Laadah the father of Maresha, and the families of those who worked fine flax in the house of Ashbea. 22 Iokim, the men of Cho- zeba and Ioash, Saraph, who had dominion in Moab, and Iashubi Lehem. These also are an- cient things. 23 These were potters and dwelt among the plants and hedges; there they stayed with the king for his work. 24 The sons of Simeon were Nemuel, Iamin, Iarib, Zerach, and Shaul, 25 whose son was Shallum, his son Mibsam and his son Mishma. 26 The sons of Mishma were Hamuel, his son, Zechur, his son, and Shimei, his son. 27 Shimei had six sons and six daughters, but his brothers did not have many sons, and their whole family was not like the sons of Iudah in number. 28 They settled in Beer-Sheba, in Molada, and in Hazar-Sual, 29 In Bilhah, in Ezem, and in To- lad, 30 to Bethuel, to Hormah, and to Ziklag, 31 Beth-Marcaboth, Hazar Susim, Beth-Birei, and Shaaraim: these were their cities until the lordship of Dauid. 32 And their cities were Etam, Ain, Rimmon, Tochen, and Ashan, five cities. 33 And all their cities that were round about these cities were directed to Baal: these are their habitations and the declaration of their genealogy, 34 Meshobab, Iamlech, and Ioshah the son of Amashiah, 35 Ioel and Iehu, son of Ioshibiah, son of Seraiah, son of Asi- el, 36 Elionai, Iaakobah, Ieshohaiah, Asaiah, Adiel, Iesimiel and Benaiah, 37 Ziza, son of Shiphei, son of Allon, son of Iedaiah, son of Shimri, son of Semaiah. 38 These were fa- mous princes in their families and greatly increased their paternal houses. 39 They went to the entrance of Gedor, toward the eastern side of the valley, to seek pasture for their sheep. 40 They found fat and good pastures and a vast land, quiet and fertile, for those of Ham had previously dwelt there. 41 These, described by name, came in the days of Heze- kiah, king of Judah, and destroyed their tents and the inhabitants there, destroying them utterly to this day, and settled in their land, because there were pastures there for their sheep. 42 Besides these, five hundred men of the sons of Simeon went to Mount Seir; Pela- tiah, Neariah, Rophaiah, and Vzziel, sons of Ishi, were their captains, 43 and they defeated the rest of Amalek who had fled, and they set- tled there to this day.

Gad settled against them in the land of Bashan, as far as Salchah. 12 Ioel was the chief and Shapham the second, but Iaa- nai and Shaphat were in Bashan. 13 And their brethren of the house of their fathers were Michael, Meshullam, Sheba, Sorai, Iacan, Ziah, and Eber, seuen. 14 These are the sons of Abihail, son of Huri, son of Iaroa, son of Gilead, son of Michael, son of Ieshishai, son of Iahdo, son of Buz. 15 Ahi, son of Abdiel, son of Guni, was the head of the house of their fa- thers. 16 They dwelt in Gilead, in Bashan, in its cities, and in all the suburbs of Sharon on their borders. 17 All of them were recognized by genealogy in the days of Jotham, king of Judeah, and in the days of Jeroboam, king of Israel. 18 The sons of Reuben, Gad, and half the tribe of Manassch, those who were valiant men, able to carry the shield, the sword, and to draw the bow, and who practiced war, were four hundred and fifty thousand, six hundred and three hundred and fifty, who went to war. 19 They made war against the Hagarim, Ietur, Nefish and Nodab. 20 And they arrayed them- selves against them, and the Hagarim were delivered into their hands, together with all who were with them, because they cried out to God in the battle, and he heard them, be- cause they trusted in him. 21 And they led away their cattle, that is, their camels, fifty thousand and two hundred, fifty thousand sheep, two thousand donkeys, and hundreds of thousands. 22 For many fell wounded, for the war was from God. And they remained in their camps until the captivity. 23 And the sons of the half tribe of Manasseh dwelt in the land, from Baashan as far as Baal Hermon, to Senir, and as far as Mount Hermon, for they increased. 24 These were the heads of the houses of their fathers, Efer and Ishi, Eliel and Azriel, Jeremiah, Hodauiah and Iahdiel, strong, valiant and famous men, heads of the houses of their fathers. 25 But they trans- gressed the God of their fathers and went and prostituted themselves to the gods of the peo- ples of the land, whom God had destroyed be- fore them. 26 And the God of Israel stirred up the spirit of Pul, king of Assur, and the spirit of Tilgath Pilneeser, king of Assur, and took them away: the Reubenites, and the Gadites, and the half tribe of Manasseh, and led them to Halah, to Habor, to Hara, and to the Gozan Riviera, to this day.

CHAPTER 5

1 Also the sons of Reuben, the firstborn of Israel (for he was the firstborn, but he had de- filed his father's bed; therefore his primogen- iture was assigned to the sons of Ioseph, son of Israel, so that the genealogy is not recom- posed after his primogeniture). 2 For Iudah had already spoken of his brethren, and the prince was born of him, but the primogeni- ture belonged to Ioseph). 3 The sons of Reu- ben, the firstborn of Israel, were Hanoch and Pallu, Hezron and Carmi. 4 The sons of Joel: Shemaiah his son, Gog his son, and Shimei his son, 5 Micha his son, Reaiah his son, and Baal his son, 6 Beerah his son, whom Tilgath Pilneeser, king of Assur, took away; he was a prince of the Reubenites. 7 When his broth- ers in their families made the genealogy of their generations, Ieiel and Zechariah were the principal ones, 8 Bela the son of Azaz, the son of Sema, the son of Joel, who dwelt in Aroer, as far as Nebo and Baal. 9 Also in the east dwelt as far as the entrance to the wil- derness from the river Perath, for they had much cattle in the land of Gilead. 10 In the days of Saul they fought with the Hagarim, who fell by their hand, and settled in their tents throughout the eastern part of Gilead. 11 The sons of

CHAPTER 6

1 The sons of Leui were Gershon, Kohath and Merari. 2 Sons of Kohath: Amram, Izhar, Hebron and Vzziel. 3 Sons of Amram: Aar- on, Moses and Miriam. Aaron's sons: Nadab, Abiu, Eleazar and Itamar. 4 Eleazar begat Phinehas. Phinehas begat Abishua, 5 Abish- ua begat Bukki, and Bukki begat Vzzi, 6 Vzzi begat Zerahia, and Zerahia begat Meraioth. 7 Meraioth begat Amariah, and Amariah begat Ahitub, 8 Ahitub begat Zadok, and Zadok be- gat Ahimaaz, 9 Ahimaaz begat Azariah, and Azariah begat Iohanan, 10 Iohanan begat Aza- riah (he was the priest of the house that Solo- mon built in Jerusalem). 11 Azariah begat Am- ariah, and Amariah begat Ahitub, 12 Ahitub begat Zadok, and Zadok begat Shallum, 13 Shallum begat Hilkiah, Hilkiah begat Azari- ah, 14 Azariah begat Seraiah, and Seraiah be- gat Iehozadak, 15 Hehozadak departed when the LORD took Judah and Jerusalem into cap- tivity at the hands of Nebuchadnezzar. 16 The sons of Leui were Gershom, Kohath and Mer- ari. 17 These are the names of the sons of Ger- shom, Libni and Shimei. 18 The sons of Ko- hath were Amram, Izhar, Hebron and Vzziel. 19 The sons of Merari, Mahli and Mushi; these are the families of Leui, as to their fathers. 20 Of Gershom, Libni his son, Iahath his son,

Zimma his son, 21 Ioah his son, Iddo his son, Zerah his son, Ieaterai his son. 22 Sons of Ko- hath: Aminadab his son, Korah his son, Assir his son, 23 Elkanah his son, Ebiasaph his son, and Assir his son, 24 Tahath his son, Vriel his son, Vzziah his son, and Shaul his son, 25 And the sons of Elkanah, Amasai and Ahimoth. 26 Elkanah. The sons of Elkanah: Zophai his son,

and Nahath his son, 27 Eliab, his son, Iero- ham, his son, Elkanah, his son, 28 The sons of Shemuel: the elder Vashni, then Abiah. 29 The sons of Merari were Mahli, Libni his son, Shimei his son, Vzza his son, 30 Shimea his son, Haggiah his son, Asaiah his son. 31 These are the ones whom Dauid set singing in the house of the LORD, after the Ark had rested. 32 They exercised their ministry before the Tabernacle, that is, the Tabernacle of the con- gregation, singing, until Solomon had built the house of the LORD in Jerusalem. 33 These ministered with their sons: of the sons of Ko- hath, Heman, a cantor, the son of Joel, the son of Shemuel, 34 the son of Elkanah, the son of Jeroham, the son of Eliel, the son of Toah, 35 the son of Zuph, the son of Elkanah, the son of Mahath, the son of Amasai, 36 son of Elkanah, son of Ioel, son of Azariah, son of Zephaniah, 37 son of Tahath, son of Assir, son of Ebiasaph, son of Korah, 38 son of Izhar, son of Kohath, son of Leui, son of Israel. 39 His brother Asaph stood at his right hand; Asaph was the son of Berechiah, son of Shimea, 40 son of Michael, son of Baaseiah, son of Malchiah, 41 son of Etni, son of Zerach, son of Adaiah, 42 son of Ethan, son of Zimmah, son of Shi- mei, 43 son of Iahath, son of Gershom, son of Leui. 44 Their brothers, sons of Merari, were on the left: Ethan son of Kishi, son of Abdi, son of Malluch, 45 son of Hashabiah, son of Amaziah, son of Hilkiah, 46 son of Amzi, son of Bani, son of Shamer, 47 son of Mahli, son of Mushi, son of Merari, son of Leui. 48 Their brothers Leui were charged with the whole service of the Tabernacle of the house of God, 49 but Aaron and his sons burned incense on the altar of burnt offerings and on the altar of incense, for all that was to be done in the most holy place and to make atonement for Israel, according to all that Moses, God's servant, had commanded. 50 These also are the sons of Aaron: Eleazar his son, Phinehas his son, Abi- shua his son, 51 Bukki his son, Vzzi his son, Zerahia his son, 52 Meraioth his son, Amariah his son, Ahitub his son, 53 Zadok his son, and Ahimaaz his son. 54 These are their abodes in all their cities and coasts, even of the sons of Aaron for the family of the Kohathites, for the lot was theirs. 55 So they gave them Hebron, in the territory of Iudah, and its environs. 56 But the camp of the city and its villages they assigned to Caleb the son of Jephunneh. 57 To the sons of Aaron they gave as refuge the cities of Judah, that is, Hebron and Libnah with their suburbs, and Jattir and Eshtemoa with their suburbs, 58 Hilen and its suburbs, and Debir and its suburbs, 59 Ashan and its suburbs, Beth-Scemesh and its suburbs: 60 Of the tribe of Benjamin: Gheba and its sub- urbs, Alemeth and its suburbs, Anathoth and its suburbs; all their cities were thirteen cit- ies according to their families. 61 And to the sons of Kohath, the rest of the family of the tribe, that is, of the half tribe of the half tribe of Manasseh, fell by lot ten cities. 62 To the sons of Gershom, according to their families, of the tribe of Issachar, the tribe of Asher, the tribe of Naphtali, and the tribe of Manasseh in Bashan, thirteen cities. 63 And to the chil- dren of Merari, according to their families, of the tribe of Reuben, of the tribe of Gad, and of the tribe of Zebulun, there fell by lot two cities. 64 So the children of Israel assigned to the Leuites the cities and their suburbs. 65 From the tribe of the sons of Judah,

from the tribe of the sons of Simeon, and from the tribe of the sons of Benjamin, these cities were drawn by lot, which they called by name. 66 The families of the sons of Kohath had cit- ies and coasts from the tribe of Ephraim. 67 They gave them cities of refuge: Shechem on Mount Ephraim and its environs, Ghezer and its environs, 68 Iokmeam and its suburbs, Beth-Horon and its suburbs, 69 Aialon and its suburbs, Gath Rimmon and its suburbs, 70 By the half tribe of Manasseh, Aner and its suburbs, Bileam and its suburbs, for the fam- ilies of the rest of the sons of Kohath. 71 By the children of Gershom of the family of the half tribe of Manasseh, Golan in Bashan and its suburbs, Ashtaroth and its suburbs, 72 From the tribe of Issachar: Kedesh and its suburbs, Daberath and its suburbs, 73 Ramoth and its suburbs, Anem and its suburbs, 74 From the tribe of Asher: Mashal and his suburbs, Ab- don and his suburbs, 75 Hukok and his sub- urbs, Rehob and his suburbs, 76 From the tribe of Naphtali: Kedesh in Galilee and its suburbs, Hammon and its suburbs, Kiria- thaim and its suburbs. 77 The rest of the sons of Merari were from the tribe of Zebulun: Rimmon and its suburbs, Tabor and its sub- urbs, 78 on the other side of Iorden, near Jeri- cho, east of Iorden, from the tribe of Reuben, Bezer in the wilderness with his suburbs, and Iahza with his suburbs, 79 Kedemoth with its suburbs, and Mephaath with its suburbs, 80 From the tribe of Gad, Ramoth in Gilead with its suburbs, and Mahanaim with its suburbs, 81 Heshbon with its suburbs and Iaazer with its suburbs.

CHAPTER 7

1 The sons of Issachar were Tola and Puah, Iashub and Shimron, four, 2 the sons of Tola: Vzzi, Rephaiah, Ieriel, Iahmai, Iibsam and Shemuel, chiefs in the houses of their fa- thers. Of Tola there were valiant men of war in their generations, whose number was, in the days of Dauid, two hundred thousand six hundred. 3 Vzzi's son was Izrahaiah, and Izrahaiah's sons were Michael, Obadiah, Ioel and Isshia, five men all princes. 4 With them in their generations after the house of their fathers were bands of men of war for battle, six thousand and thirty thousand, for they had many wives and many children. 5 Their brethren, belonging to all the families of Is- sachar, were valiant men of war, four tens of thousands in number, according to their ge- nealogies. 6 The sons of Benjamin were Bela, Becher and Jediael, three. 7 The sons of Bela: Ezbon, Vzzi, Vzziel, Ierimoth, and Iri, five heads of the families of their fathers, valiant men of war, who were reckoned, according to their genealogies, two twenty thousand and thirty-four. 8 The sons of Becher, Zemirah, Ioash, Eliezer, Helioenai, Omri, Ierimoth, Abiah, Anathoth and Alameth, were all sons of Becher. 9 They were named by their gene- alogies, according to their generations, and the heads of the houses of their fathers, val- iant men of war, were twenty thousand and two hundred. 10 The son of Jediael was Bil- han, and the sons of Bilhan: Ieush, Benjamin, Ehud, Chenaanah, Zethan, Tharshish, and Ahishahar. 11 All these were sons of Iediael, chief of the fathers, valiant men of war, six hundred thousand and two hundred, march- ing in line for war. 12 Shuppim and Huppim were sons of Ir, while Hushim was the son of another. 13 The sons of Naphtali, Jahziel, Juni, Jezer, and Shallum, the sons of Bilhah. 14 The son of Manasseh was Ashriel, whom she bore, but his concubine of Aram bore Machir, the father of Gilead. 15 Machir took the sister of Huppim and Shuppim to wife, and their sister's name was Maachah. The name of the second

son was Zelophehad, and Zelophehad had daughters. 16 Maaca, Machir's wife, bore a son and named him Peresh; his brother's name was Sheresh; his sons were Vlam and Rakem. 17 The son of Vlam was Bedan. These were the sons of Gilead the son of Machir the son of Manasseh. 18 His sister Molecheth gave birth to Ishod, Abiezer and Mahalah. 19 The sons of Shemidah were Ahian, Shechem, Likhi and Aniam. 20 The sons of Ephraim were Shuthelah, Bered his son, Tahath his son, Eladah his son and Tahath his son, 21 Zabad his son, Shuthelah his son, Ezer and Elead; and the men of Gath, who were born in the land, slew them because they went down to carry away their cattle. 22 Therefore Ephraim their father wept for many days, and his brothers came to comfort him. 23 When he entered his wife's house, she conceived and bore him a son, whom she named Beriah, be- cause his house was afflicted. 24 His daughter was named Sherah, who built Beth-Horon, the lower part and the upper part, and Vzzen Sheerah. 25 Her son was Repha, Reshef, Tela her son, and Tahan her son, 26 Laadan his son, Ammihud his son, Elishama his son, 27 Not his son, Iehoshua his son. 28 And their possessions and their dwellings were Beth-el and its villages, Naaran on the east, Ghezer on the west and its villages, Shechem and its villages, unto Azza and its villages, 29 and by the places of the sons of Manasseh: Beth-she- an and its villages, Taanach and its villages, Megiddo and its villages, Dor and its villages. In these places dwelt the sons of Ioseph the son of Israel. 30 The sons of Asher were Im- nah, Isuah, Ishuai, Beriah, and Serah their sister. 31 The sons of Beriah were Heber and Malchiel, the father of Birzauith. 32 Heber begat Iaphlet, Shomer, Hotham and Shuah, their sister. 33 The sons of Japhlet were Pas- ach, Bimhal and Ashuath; these were the sons of Japhlet. 34 The sons of Shamer were Ahi, Rohgah, Jehubbah and Aram. 35 The sons of his brother Helem were Zophah, Iimna, She- lesh and Amal. 36 The sons of Zophah: Suah, Harnepher, Shual, Beri and Imrah, 37 Bezer, Hod, Shamma, Shilsha, Ithran and Beera. 38 The sons of Iether, Iephunneh, Pispa, and Ara.39 The sons of Vlla: Harah, Haniel and Rizia.40 All these were the sons of Asher, the heads of their paternal houses, noble men, valiant men of war and princes of the first rank, and were recognized by their genealogies for war and battle to the number of six thousand and twenty thousand men.

CHAPTER 8

1 Benjamin also begat Bela, his eldest son, Ashbel the second and Aharah the third, 2 Nohah the fourth and Rapha the fifth. 3 Bela's sons were Addar, Gera and Abihud, 4 Abish- ua, Naaman and Ahoah, 5 Gera, Shephuphan and Huram. 6 These are the sons of Ehud; these were the chief fathers of the inhabi- tants of Gheba, who were taken into captiv- ity to Monahath, 7 Naaman, Ahiah and Gera were taken away as captives; he begat Vzza and Ahihud. 8 Shaharaim begat a number of people in the territory of Moab, after sending away Hushim and Baara, his companions. 9 From Hodesh, his wife, he begat Iobab, Zib- iah, Mesha and Malcham, 10 Jeuz, Shachiah, and Mirmah; these were his sons and his chief fathers. 11 From Hushim he begat Ahitub and Elpaal. 12 The sons of Elpaal were Eber, Mish- am and Shamed (who built Ono, Lod and their villages). 13 Beriah and Sema (who were the chief fathers of the inhabitants of Aialon; they dragged away the inhabitants of Gath). 14 Ahio, Shashak and Ierimoth, 15 Sebadia, Arad and Ader, 16 Michael, Ispah and Ioha, sons of Beriah, 17 Zebadiah, Meshullam, Hizki and Heber, 18 Ishmerai, Izliah and Iobab, sons of Elpaal, 19 Iakim, Zichri and Sabdi, 20 Elienai, Zillethai and Eliel, 21 Adaiah, Beraiah and Shimra, sons of Shimei, 22 Ishpan, Eber and Eliel, 23 Abdon, Zichri and Hanan, 24 Hana- niah, Elam and Antothiia, 25 Hyphedeiah and Penuel, sons of Shashak, 26 Shamsherai, She- haria and Athaliah, 27 Iaareshiah, Elijah and Zichri, sons of Jeroham. 28 These were the chief fathers according to their generations, that is, the princes who dwelt in Jerusalem. 29 In Gibeon dwelt the father of Gibeon, whose wife's name was Maachah. 30 His eldest son was Abdon, then Zur, Kish, Baal and Nadab, 31 Gidor, Ahio and Zacher. 32 Mikloth begat Shimeah; these also dwelt with their brethren in Jerusalem by their brothers. 33 Ner begat Kish, Kish begat Saul, Saul begat Ionathan, Malchishua, Abinadab and Eshbaal. 34 Ion- athan's son was Merib-baal, and Merib-baal begat Micah. 35 Micah's sons were Pithon, Melech, Tarea and Ahaz. 36 Ahaz begat Ie- hoadah, Iehoadah begat Alemeth, Azmaueth, Zimri, and Zimri begat Moza, 37 Moza be- gat Bineah, whose son was Raphah, his son Eleasah and his son Azel. 38 Azel had six sons, whose names are these: Azrikam, Bocheru, Ishmael, Sheariah, Obadiah and Hanan; all these were the sons of Azel. 39 The sons of Eshek, his brother, were Vlam, his firstborn, Iehush, his second, and Eliphelet, his third. 40 The sons of Vlam were valiant men of war who shot with the bow and had many sons and grandsons, an hundred and fifty; all these were the sons of Benjamin.

CHAPTER 9

1 So all Israel was named according to their genealogies; and behold, they are written in the book of the kings of Israel and Judah, and they were taken away to Babel for their trans- gression. 2 The principal inhabitants settled in their possessions and in their cities: Isra- el, the priests, the Leuites, and the Netites. 3 In Jerusalem dwelt the sons of Judah, the sons of Benjamin, the sons of Ephraim and Manasseh. 4 Vthai the son of Amihud, the son of Omri, the son of Imri, the son of Bani, of the sons of Pharez, the son of Iudah. 5 Of Scylonians, Asaiah the elder, and his sons. 6 Of the sons of Zerah, Jeuel and their brethren, six hundred ninety and nine. 7 Of the sons of Benjamin, Sallu, son of Meshullam, son of Hodauiah, son of Hasenuah, 8 Ibneiah the son of Jeroham, Elah the son of Vzzi the son of Michri, Meshullam the son of Shephatiah the son of Reuel the son of Ibniiah. 9 Their breth- ren, according to their generations, were nine hundred, fifty and six; all these men were principal fathers in the houses of their fathers. 10 Of the priests: Iedaiah, Iehoiarib, and Iachin, 11 Azariah the son of Hilkiah, the son of Meshullam, the son of Zadok, the son of Meraioth, the son of Ahitub, the head of the house of God, 12 Adaiah the son of Jeroham the son of Pashur the son of Malchijah, Maa- sai the son of Adiel the son of Iahzera the son of Meshullam the son of Meshillemith the son of Immer. 13 And their brethren, heads of the families of their fathers, a thousand, seven hundred, and three hundred valiant men, for the work of the service of the house of God. 14 Of the Leuites, Shemaiah the son of Hasshub, the son of Azrikam, the son of Hashabiah, of the sons of Merari, 15 Bakbakkar, Heresh and Galal, Mattaniah, son of Micha, son of Zichri, son of Asaph, 16 Obadiah the son of Shem- aiah, the son of Galal the son of Ieduthun, and Berechiah the son of Asa the son of Elkanah, who dwelt in the villages of the Netopha- thites. 17 The porters were Shallum, Akkub, Talmon, Ahiman and their brothers; Shallum

CHAPTER 10

1 Then the Philistines fought against Israel; the men of Israel fled before the Philistines and fell slain on Mount Gilboa. 2 The Philis- tines pursued Saul and his sons and struck down Ionathan, Abinadab and Malchishua, Saul's sons. 3 The battle raged against Saul; the archers struck him, and he was wound- ed by the archers. 4 Then Saul said to his ar- mor-bearer, "Draw out your sword and strike me through the heart, lest these circumcisers come and mock me"; but his armor-bearer would not, for he was very frightened; so Saul took his sword and fell on it. 5 When his ar- morer saw that Saul was dead, he too fell on the sword and died. 6 So Saul died, and his three sons and his whole house died together. 7 When all the men of Israel who were in the valley saw how they had fled and that Saul and his sons were dead, they forsook their cities and fled away, and the Philistines came and settled in them. 8 The next day, when the Phi- listines came to strip the slain, they found Saul and his sons lying on Mount Gilboa. 9 When they had smitten him, they took his head and his armor and sent them into the country of the Philistines, all around, to make the fact known to their idols and to the people. 10 Then they deposited his armor in the house of their god and put his head in the house of Da- gon. 11 When all the inhabitants of Jabesh Gil- ead came to know all that the Philistines had done to Saul, 12 they rose up (all the valiant men), took the body of Saul and the bodies of his sons, brought them to Iabesh, buried their bones under a goose in Iabesh, and fasted for ten days. 13 So Saul died for his transgression, committed against the LORD, that is, against the word of the LORD, which he had not kept, and for seeking and seeking counsel from a familiar spirit, 14 and did not ask the LORD; therefore he killed him and turned the king- dom over to Dauid the son of Ishai.

CHAPTER 11

1 Then all Israel gathered to Dauid toward Hebron, saying, "Behold, we are your bones and your flesh." 2 Formerly, when Saul was king, you led Israel out and in; and the LORD your God said to you, "You shall feed my peo- ple Israel, and you shall be the ruler of my peo- ple Israel." 3 So all the elders of Israel came to the king to Hebron, and Dauid had a meeting with them in Hebron before the LORD. They appointed Dauid king of Israel, according to the word of the LORD spoken by the hand of Samuel. 4 Dauid and all Israel went to Jeru- salem, which is Hebus, where there were the Hebusites, inhabitants of the land. 5 The in- habitants of Iebus said to Dauid, "You cannot enter here." Neuertheles Dauid went to Zion, which is the city of Dauid. 6 And Dauid said, "Whoever strikes the Jebusites first will be the leader and the captain." So Joab the son of Zeruiah went first and was captain. 7 Dauid was the leader. 18 For up to that time they were porters of the companies of the sons of Leui as far as the gate of the kings in the east. 19 And Shallum the son of Kore, the son of Ebiasaf, the son of Korah, and his brethren the Korathites (of their father's house) were in charge of the work and custody of the doors of the Tabernacle; therefore their families were in the service of the host of the LORD, for the custody of the entrances. 20 Phinehas the son of Eleazar was their guide, and the LORD was with him. 21 Zechariah, son of Meshelemiah, was the keeper of the porch of the tent of meeting. 22 All these were chosen as gatekeepers, two hundred and twenty-two, appointed according to their genealogies according to their cities. Dauid estab- lished these and Samuel the seer in their perpetual office. 23 Thus they and their sons had guard over the doors of the house of the LORD and the house of the Tabernacle by wards. 24 The gatekeepers were divided into four quarters: east, west, north and south. 25 Their brothers, who were in their cities, came with them from time to time. 26 These four chief porters were in permanent office, belonged to the Leuites and were in charge of the rooms and treasures of the house of God. 27 They stood around the house of God, because the task was theirs, and they made sure that it was open every morning. 28 Some of them were in charge of the soup pots, for they brought them in and took them out. 29 Some of them were also in charge of the instru- ments and all the utensils of the sanctuary, the wine, the oil, the incense and the perfumes. 30 Some of the priests' sons made aromas of sweetmeats. 31 Mattithiah, one of the Leuites, eldest son of Shallum the Korhite, was in charge of preparing things in the frying pan. 32 Other of their brothers, sons of Kohath, were in charge of preparing the loaves every Sabbath. 33 These were the singers, the chief fathers of the Leuites, who dwelt in the chambers and had no other charge, for they had business there day and night: 34 These were the principal fathers of the Leuites, according to their generations, and the principal ones who dwelt in Jerusalem. 35 In Gibeon dwelt the father of Gibeon, Jeiel, and his wife's name was Maachah. 36 His eldest son was Abdon, then Zur, Kish, Baal, Ner, and Nadab, 37 Gedor, Ahio, Zechariah, and Mikloth. 38 Mikloth begat Shimeam; they also dwelt with their brethren in Jerusalem, by their brothers. 39 Ner begat Kish, Kish begat Saul, Saul begat Ionathan, Malchishua, Abinadab and Eshbaal. 40 Ionathan's son was Merib-baal, and Merib-baal begat Micah. 41 Micah's sons were Pithon, Melech and Tahrea. 42 Ahaz begat Iarah, Iarah begat Alemeth, Azmaueth and Zimri, Zimri begat Moza. 43 Moza begat Binea, whose son was Rephaiah, his son was Eleasah, and his son Azel. 44 Azel had six sons, whose names are: Azrikam, Bocheru, Ishmael, Sheariah, Obadiah and Hanan; these are the sons of Azel. dwelt in the tower; therefore they called it the city of Dauid. 8 He built the city on every side, from Millo onward, and Joab repaired the rest of the city. 9 Dauid prospered and grew rich, because the LORD of hosts was with him. 10 These also are the leaders of the valiant men who were with Dauid and arrayed their forc- es with him in his kingdom with all Israel, to make him king outside Israel, according to the word of the LORD. 11 This is the name of the valiant men whom Dauid had: Iashobeam the son of Hachmoni, the leader of the thirty; he lifted up his spear against three hundred men, whom he killed at once. 12 After him was Eleazar the son of Dodo, the Ahohite, who was one of the three valiant men. 13 He was with Dauid at Pas-dammim, where the Philistines had gathered to fight; there was a land full of barley, and the people fled before the Philistines. 14 They stopped in the middle of the field, plundered it and killed the Philis- tines; so the LORD gained a great victory. 15 Three of the thirty captains went to Dauid, to the hollow of Adullam. The army of the Philis- tines encamped in the valley of Rephaim. 16 While Dauid was waiting, the garrison of the Philistines was at Beth- Lem. 17 Dauid longed and said, "Oh, if someone would give me wa- ter to drink from the well of Bethlehem that is at the gate." 18 Then these three restrained the army of the Philistines and drew water from the well of Bethlehem that was at the gate, and took it and brought it to Dauid; but Dauid would not drink of it, but offered it as an obla- tion

to the Lord, 19 and said, "Let not my God permit me to do this: shall I drink the blood of these men? For they brought it with the blood of their lives; therefore he would not drink it; these things did these three mighty men do." 20 Abishai, Ioab's brother, was the leader of the three; he raised his spear against three hundred people, killed them, and earned his name among the three. 21 Among the three he was more honorable than the two and was their leader, but he did not reach the first three. 22 Benaiah the son of Jehoiada (son of a valiant man), who had done many deeds and was from Kabzeel, slew two strong men of Moab; also he went down and slew a lion in the middle of a pit in snowy weather. 23 Then he slew an Egyptian, a man of great stature, about five cubits long, and in the Egyptian's hand was a spear like a bundle of wood; and he came to him with a staff, snatched the spear from the Egyptian's hand, and slew him with his own spear. 24 These things did Be- naiah the son of Jehoiada, who had the name of one of the three valiant men. 25 Behold, he was honorable among the thirty, but he did not reach the first three. Dauid appointed him as his counselor. 26 These also were val- iant men of war: Asahel the brother of Joab, Elhanan the son of Dodo, of Beth-Lem, 27 Shammoth, the Harodite, Helez, the Pelonite, 28 Ira, son of Ikkesh, the Tekoite, Abiezer, the Anthothite, 29 Sibbecai the Husathite, Ilai the Ahohite, 30 Maharai the Netophite, Heled the son of Baana the Netophite, 31 Ithai the son of Ribai of Gibeah, of the sons of Benjamin, Be- naiah the Pirathonite, 32 Hurai, of the riuers of Gaash, Abiel the Arbathite, 33 Azmaueth the Baharumite, Elihaba the Shaalbonite, 34 the sons of Hashem the Gizonite, Ionathan the son of Shageh the Harita, 35 Ahiam the son of Sacar the Hararite, Eliphal the son of Vr, 36 Hepher, the Mecheratese, Ahiiah, the Pelonite, 37 Hezro, the Carmelite, Naarai the son of Ezbai, Ioel, brother of Nathan, Mibhar, son of Haggeri, 39 Zelek the Ammonite, Nah- rai the Berothite, the armor-bearer of Ioab, son of Zeruiah, 40 Ira the Ithrite, Garib the Ithrite, 41 Vriah the Hittite, Zabad the son of Ahlai, 42 Adina, son of Shiza the Reubenite, leader of the Reubenites, and thirty oth- ers with him, 43 Hanan, son of Maaca, and Ioshaphat, the Mithnite, 44 Vziah, asteratite, Shama and Ieiel, sons of Otham, aroerite, 45 Iediael, son of Shimri, and Ioha, his brother, the Tizite, 46 Eliel, the Mahauite, Ieribai and Ioshauiah, sons of Elnaam, and Ithmah, the Moabite, 47 Eliel, Obed and Iaasiel, the Me- sobaite.

CHAPTER 12

1 These are also those who came from Dauid to Ziklag, while he was still closed, because of Saul the son of Kish; they were among the val- iant and the helpers in the battle. 2 They were armed with bows and knew how to use their right and left hands with stones, arrows and bows; they were brothers of Saul and Ben- jamin. 3 The leaders were Ahiezer, Ioash the son of Shemaiah, a Gibeonite, Ieziel, Pelet the son of Asinaueth, Beracha, and Iehu, an Antithite, 4 Ishmaiah, the Gibeonite, a valiant man among the thirty, and about the thirty, Ieremiah, Iehaziel, Iohanan, and Ioshabad, the Gederathite, 5 Eluzai, Ierimoth, Bealiah, Shemariah, and Shephatiah, the Haruphite, 6 Elkanah, Ishiah, Azariel and Ioezer, Iashobe- am of Hakorehim, 7 Ioela and Zebadiah, sons of Jeroham of Gedor, 8 some of the Gadites separated from Dauid to go into the wilder- ness, valiant men of war, men of arms and fit for battle, who knew how to handle spear and shield; their faces were like the faces of the lion-men, and they were like the roebucks

of the mountains that move swiftly, 9 Ezer the chief, Obadiah the second, Eliab the third, 10 Mishmanah the fourth, Ieremiah the fifth, 11 Attai the sixth, Eliel the tenth, 12 Iohanan the eighth, Elzabad the ninth, 13 Jeremiah the tenth, Macbannai the eleventh. 14 These were the sons of Gad, captains of the army; one of the smallest could stand a hundred times, the largest a thousand. 15 These are they who went out from Iorden in the first month, when he had filled all his banks, and put to flight all those in the valley, east and west. 16 The sons of Benjamin and Iudah went to the estate of Dauid, 17 Dauid went to meet them, answered and said to them, "If you come peacefully to me to help me, my heart will be united with you; but if you come and betray me with my adversaries, seeing there is no wickedness in my hands, the God of our fathers sees it and rebukes it." 18 Then the spirit came upon Amasai, who was the leader of the thirty, and said, "We are yours, Dauid, and with you, son of Ishai. Peace, peace to you and peace to your helpers, for your God helps you." Dauid welcomed them and appointed them captains of the garrison. 19 Some of Manasseh fell into the hand of Dauid, when he came with the Philistines against Saul to fight; but they did not help them, for the princes of the Philistines, by an agreement, sent him away, saying, "He will fall into the hand of his master Saul by our heads." 20 On his way to Ziklag, Adna, Iozabad, Iediael, Michael, Iozabad, Elihu and Ziltai, leaders of the thousands of Manasseh, fell upon him. 21 They helped Dauid against that enemy, for they were all valiant men and captains of the army. 22 At that time, from day to day, they came to Dauid to help him, until a great army was formed, like the army of God. 23 These are the names of the captains who were armed to fight and who came from Dauid to Hebron to deliver to him the kingdom of Saul, according to the word of the LORD. 24 The sons of Iudah who carried shield and spear were six thousand and eight hundred, armed for war. 25 Of the sons of Simeon, valiant men of war, six thousand and one hundred thou- sand. 26 Of the sons of Leui, four thousand and six hundred. 27 Jehoiada was the leader of those of Aaron, and with him three thou- sand and six hundred. 28 Zadok, a very val- iant young man, and from his fathers came two and twenty-five captains. 29 The sons of Benjamin, Saul's brothers, were three thou- sand, for most of them had fought the war of the house of Saul up to that time. 30 The sons of Ephraim: twenty thousand, eight hundred valiant and famous men in the house of their fathers. 31 Of the half tribe of Manasseh, eight thousand men appointed by name to come and make Dauid king. 32 Of the sons of Issachar, who were men who knew the times and knew what Israel should do, the leaders were two hundred, and all their brethren were at their command. 33 Of Zebulun, who went out to fight, experts in warfare and in all the instruments of war, fifty thousand who could field the battle; their hearts were not in their throats. 34 Of Naphtali, a thousand captains, and with them, with shields and spears, nine- teen thousand. 35 Of Dan, experts in battles, ten twenty thousand and six hundred. 36 Of Asher, who went to battle and trained for war, four thousand. 37 Of the other side of Iorden, of the Reubenites, of the Gadites, and of the half tribe of Manasseh, with all the instru- ments of war to fight, an hundred thousand and twenty thousand. 38 All these men of war who could lead an army came heartily to Hebron to make Dauid the king of all Israel; and all the rest of Israel agreed to make Dauid the king: 39 And they stayed with Dauid three days, eating and drinking, because their brothers had prepared for them. 40 Moreover those who were near them, as far as Issachar, Zebulun and Naphtali, brought bread on don- keys, on camels, on mules and on oxen, and then meat, flour, figs, raisins, wine and oil, bees and sheep in abundance, for there was plenty in Israel.

CHAPTER 13

1 Dauid consulted with the captains of the thousands and the hundreds and with all the officers. 2 Dauid said to all the congrega- tion of Israel, "If it seems good to you and if it proceeds from the LORD our God, we will send to and from our brethren who are left throughout the land of Israel (for with them are the priests and the leuites in the cities and in their suburbs) so that they may gather to Vs. 3 And we will bring again to Vs the Ark of our God, for we did not seek it in the days of Saul." 4 The whole community answered, "Let it be, for the thing seemed good in the eyes of all the people." 5 So Dauid gathered all Is- rael from Shihor in Egypt to the entrance of Hamath, to bring the Ark of God from Kiriath-iearim. 6 Dauid went with all Israel to Baalath, to Kiriath-iearim, which was in Iudah, to bring from there the Ark of God, the LORD who dwells among the Cherubim, where His Name is invoked. 7 They carried the Ark of God in a new chariot from the house of Abinadab; Vzza and Ahio drove the chariot. 8 Dauid and all Israel played before God with all their might, with songs, with harps, with violas, with timpani, with cymbals and with trumpets. 9 When they came to the floor of Chidon, Vzza put his hand to block the ark, because the oxen shook it. 10 But the anger of the LORD kindled against Vzza and struck him because he had put his hand on the ark; so he died there before God. 11 Dauid was an- gry, because the LORD had opened a breach in Vzza, and he called that place Perez-Vzza by the name it still bears today. 12 That day David feared God and said, "How can I let the ark of God enter me? 13 Therefore Dauid did not bring the ark into the city of Dauid, but turned it over to the house of Obed Edom, the Gittite. 14 So the ark of God remained in the house of Obed Edom, for three months, and the LORD blessed the house of Obed Edom and all that it had.

CHAPTER 14

1 Then Hiram, king of Tyre, sent messengers, cedar trees, masons and carpenters to Dauid to build him a house. 2 Therefore Dauid knew that the LORD had confirmed him as king of Israel and that his kingdom had been lifted up over him because of his people Israel. 3 Dauid also took other wives in Jerusalem and begat other sons and daughters. 4 These are the names of the sons he had in Jerusalem: Shammua, Shobab, Nathan and Solomon, 5 Ibhar, Elishua, and Elpalet, 6 Nogah, Nepheg and Japhiah, 7 Elishama, Beeliada and Elifal. 8 But when the Philistines heard that Dauid had been anointed king of Israel, all the Phi- listines came to see Dauid. And when Dauid heard, he went out against them. 9 And the Philistines came and scattered in the valley of Rephaim. 10 Then Dauid sought counsel of God, saying, "Shall I go out against the Philistines, and wilt thou deliver them into my hands?" The LORD said to him, "Go away, for I will deliver them into your hands." 11 So they came to Baal-perazim, where Dauid defeated them; and Dauid said, "God has destroyed my enemies with my hand, as the waters are destroyed; therefore they called that place Baal-perazim." 12 There they had left their gods, and Dauid said, "Let them be burned with fire." 13 The Philistines came and scattered in the valley. 14 When Dauid again asked God for counsel, God said to him, "Do not go after them, but get away from them, that you may join them beyond the mulber- ry trees. 15 When you hear the sound of one going toward the tops of the mulberry trees, come out to fight, for God has gone before you to strike the army of the Philistines." 16 So Dauid did as God had commanded him; and they defeated the army of the Philistines from Gabaon as far as Ghezer. 17 The fame of Dauid spread throughout all the lands, and the LORD made all the nations fear him.

CHAPTER 15

1 Dauid built him houses in the city of Dauid, prepared a place for the ark of God and pitched a tent there. :2 Then Dauid said, "No one is to guard the ark of God except the Leuites, for the LORD has chosen them to carry the ark of the LORD and to serve him forever." 03 Dauid gathered all Israel together in Jerusa- lem to bring the ark of the LORD to the place appointed by him. 4 Dauid gathered the sons of Aaron and the Leuites. 5 Of the sons of Ko- hath, Vriel, the leader, and his brothers were six in number. 6 Of the sons of Merari, Asaiah the chief, and his brethren, two hundred and twenty. 7 Of the sons of Gershom, Joel, the chief, and his brethren a hundred and thirty. 8 Of the sons of Elizafan, Shemaiah, the chief, and his brethren two hundred. 9 Of the sons of Hebron, Eliel, the chief, and his brethren four hundred. 10 Of the sons of Vzziel, Am- minadab, the chief, and his brethren a hun- dred and two. 11 And David called the priests Zadok and Abiathar, and of the Leuites, Vriel, Asaiah, Ioel, Shemaiah, Eliel, and Amminad- ab: 12 And he said to them, "You are the chief fathers of the Leuites; sanctify yourselves and your brethren, and bring the ark of the LORD, the God of Israel, to the place I have prepared for it. 13 For because you were not present at the beginning, the LORD our God has opened a breach among us, because we did not seek him in the due order." 14 So the priests and the Leuites sanctified themselves to bring the ark of the LORD God of Israel. 15 And the sons of the Leuites carried the ark of God on their shoulders with the rods, as Mo- ses had commanded, according to the word of the LORD. 16 Dauid told the leaders of the Leuites to commission some of their brothers to sing with musical instruments, with violas, cymbals and harps, so that they could make a sound and lift up their voices with joy. 17 Then the Leuites appointed Heman the son of Joel, and among his brothers Asaph the son of Berechiah, and among the sons of Merari, their brothers, Ethan the son of Kushaiah, 18 And with them their brethren of the second degree, Zechariah, Ben, Iaaziel, Semiramoth, Iehiel, Vnni, Eliab, Benaiah, Maaseiah, Mat- tithiah, Elipheleh, Mikneah, Obed Edom, and Ieiel, the porters. 19 Then Heman, Asaph and Ethan began to play with reed cymbals, 20 Zechariah, Aziel, Semiramoth, Iehiel, Vnni, Eliab, Maaseiah and Benaiah with viols on Alamoth, 21 Mattithiah, Elipheleh, Mikneah, Obed Edom, Ieiel and Azaziah, with harps on Sheminith Ienazzeah. 22 Chenaniah, leader of the Leuiti, had the charge to bear the bur- den of the office, for he was able to instruct. 23 Berechiah and Elkanah were porters of the Ark. 24 Shecaniah, Iehoshaphat, Nethaneel, Amasai, Zechariah, Benaiah and Eliezer, the priests, sounded with trumpets before the ark of God, while Obed Edom and Ieiiah were porters for the ark. 25 So Dauid, and the el- ders of Israel, and the captains of thousands went and brought the ark of the LORD's con- vention from the house of Obed Edom with ioye. 26 And because God helped the Leuites who

carried the ark of the LORD's pillar, they offered ten cattle and ten rams. 27 And Dauid had a robe of linen, as did all the Leuites who carried the ark, and the singers, and Chenaniah who had charge of the singers; and on David was an ephod of linen. 28 So all Israel carried the ark of the LORD with shouting and sounding of cornet and trumpets and cymbals, making noise with violas and with harps. 29 And when the ark of the messen- ger of the LORD came into the city of Dauid, Micai, the daughter of Saul, looked out of a window and saw King David revelling and playing, and she despised him in her heart.

CHAPTER 16

1 So they brought the Ark of God and placed it in the middle of the Tabernacle that Dauid had prepared for it, and they offered burnt offerings and peace offerings before God. 2 When Dauid had finished offering the burnt offerings and peace offerings, he blessed the people in the Name of the Lord. 3 Then he distributed to each one of Israel, man and woman, a cake of bread, a piece of meat, and a bottle of wine. 4 And he appointed some Leuites to serve before the ark of the LORD, to rehearse, to ask and to pray to the LORD, the God of Israel: 5 Asaph, the leader, and beside him Zechariah, Ieiel, Shemiramoth, Iehiel, Mattithiah, Eliab, Benaiah and Obed Edom, that is, Ieiel with instruments, violas and lyres, and Asaph to play with cymbals, 6 Benaiah and Iahaziel, priests, with trumpets, which they played continually before the ark of God's convention. 7 At that time, Dauid had charged at the beginning to give thanks to the LORD at the hands of Asaph and his brothers. 8 Praise the LORD and invoke his Name; de- clare his works among the people. 9 Sing to him, praise him and speak of all his wonder- ful works. 10 Make merry in his holy Name; make merry in the hearts of those who see the LORD. 11 Behold the LORD and his strength; continually look upon his face. 12 Remember his wonderful works that he has done, his wonders and the judgments of his mouth, 13 O descendants of Israel, his servant, O sons of Iaakob, his chosen ones. 14 He is the LORD our God; his decrees are over all the earth. 15 Remember his counsel for eternity, and the word which he commanded a thousand gen- erations: 16 which he did with Abraham, and the other with Izhak: 17 And he confirmed it to Iaakob as a law, and to Israel as an everlast- ing covenant, 18 saying, "To you I will give the land of Canaan, the lot of your inheritance." 19 When you were few, indeed very few, and foreigners, 20 you went from nation to nation and from one kingdom to another people, 21 he allowed no one to harm them, but rebuked the kings for their sake, saying, "Do not touch my anus! 22 Do not touch my anoints, and do not harm my prophets. 23 Sing to the LORD over all the earth; proclaim his salvation from day to day. 24 Declare his glory among the na- tions and his wonderful works among all peo- ples. 25 For the LORD is great and much to be praised, and he is to be feared compared to all the gods. 26 For all the gods of the peoples are idols, but the LORD has made the heavens. 27 Prayer and glory are before him; power and beauty are in his place. 28 Give to the LORD, families of the people; give to the LORD glory and power. 29 Give to the LORD the glory of his Name; bring an offering and come before him and worship the LORD in the glorious sanctuary. 30 Tremble before him, all the earth; surely the world will be stable and not dumb. 31 Let the heavens rejoice, let the earth rejoice, and let the nations say, "The LORD reigns." 32 Let the sea roar and all that is in it: Let the countryside

be full of joy and all that is in it. 33 Let the trees of the wood rejoice in the presence of the LORD, for he comes to judge the earth. 34 Pray to the LORD, for he is good, for his mercy endures forever. 35 And say, "Save, O God, our salvation, gather and deliver us from the Gentiles, that we may pray to your holy Name and glory in your praise." 36 Blessed be the LORD, the God of Israel, forever; and let all peoples say, "So be it, and let them praise the LORD." 37 Then he left Asaph and his brothers there before the ark of the LORD to officiate continually before the ark, what was to be done every day: 38 Obed Edom and his brothers, three twenty-eight persons; Obed Edom, son of Jeduthun, and Hosah were porters. 39 And Zadok the priest and his brother priests stood before the Tab- ernacle of the LORD in the place that was in Gibeon, 40 to offer burnt offerings continual- ly to the LORD on the altar of burnt offerings, in the morning and in the evening, according to what is written in the law of the LORD, which he commanded Israel. 41 With them were Heman, Jeduthun and the other chosen ones (named by name) to praise the LORD, for his mercy endures forever. 42 Also with them were Heman and Ioduthun, to make sound with cornets and with cymbals, with excellent musical instruments; and the sons of Ieduthun were at the door. 43 Then all the people went away, each to his own house; and Dauid returned to bless his house.

CHAPTER 17

1 Then when Dauid settled in his house, he said to Nathan the prophet, "Behold, I dwell in a house of cedars, but the ark of the Lord remains under the curtains." 2 Then Nathan said to Dauid, "Do whatever is in your heart, for God is with you." 3 That same night the word of God came to Nathan, saying, 4 Go and say to David my servant, "Thus says the LORD: You shall not buy me a house to dwell in: 5 For I have not dwelt in any house from the day that I brought out the children of Israel until this day, but have gone from tent to tent and from dwelling place to dwelling place. 6 When I walked with all Israel, I addressed one word to one of the judges of Israel (whom I had commanded to feed my people), saying, "Why have you not built me a house of cedar? 7 Now therefore you shall say thus to my ser- vant Dauid, "Thus says the LORD of hosts, I have taken you out of the flock and out of fol- lowing the sheep, that you might be a prince over my people of Israel. 8 I have been with you wherever you have walked, I have de- stroyed all your enemies from your sight, and I have made you a name like that of the great men who are on the earth. 9 (Moreover, I will establish a place for my people of Israel and plant it, that they may dwell in its place and move no more; the wicked people shall not vi- olate it any more, as in the beginning.) 10 And from the time when I commanded to judge my people of Israel) and I will subdue all your enemies; therefore I say to you that the LORD will buy you a house. 11 And when thy days are fulfilled to go with thy fathers, then I will raise up thy seed after thee, which shall be of thy sons, and I will establish his kingdom. 12 He shall build me a house, and I will establish his throne forever. 13 I will be his father, and he shall be my son, and I will not take away my grace from him as I took it away from him who went before you. 14 But I will establish him in my house and in my kingdom forever, and his throne will be stable forever." 15 ac- cording to all these words and according to all this vision." Thus Nathan spoke to Dauid. 16 King Dauid came in and sat down before the LORD and

said, "Who am I, O LORD God, and what is my house, that thou hast brought me hither? 17 But you, O God, who consider this a small thing, have spoken at length about your servant's house and considered me as a man of this level, O Lord God. 18 What more can Dauid desire of you for the honor of your servant, for you know your servant. 19 O Lord, for your servant, and according to your heart you have done all these great things to declare all magnificence. 20 Lord, there is no one like you, nor is there any other God besides you, according to what we have heard with our ears. 21 Moreover, what nation on earth is like your people Israel, whose God went to redeem them to make them his people, to make a name for themselves and to do great and terrible things by driving out the nations from your people, whom you brought out of Egypt?22 For you destined your people Israel to be your people forever, and you, Lord, be- came their God. 23 Therefore now, O LORD, let what you have said concerning your ser- vant and his house be confirmed forever, and let it be done as you have said, 24 and your name be established and magnified forever, that it may be said, "The LORD of hosts, the God of Israel, is the God of Israel," and the house of Dauid, your servant, be established before you. 25 For you, O my God, have an- swered the ear of your servant that you will build him a house; therefore your servant had the courage to pray before you. 26 Therefore now, O Lord (for you are God and have spoken this goodness to your servant) 27 it pleased thee to bless thy servant's house, that it may always be before thee; for thou, Lord, hast blessed it, and it shall be blessed forever.

CHAPTER 18

1 After this, Dauid defeated the Philistines, subdued them and took Gath and its villag- es out of the hands of the Philistines. 2 Then he defeated Moab, and the Moabites became Dauid's servants and brought gifts. 3 Dauid defeated Hadarezer, king of Zobah, as far as Hamath, on his way to establish his borders by the river Perath. 4 Dauid took from him a thousand chariots, ten thousand horse- men and twenty thousand foot soldiers, and destroyed all the chariots, but recovered a hundred thousand. 5 Then the Arameans of Damascus came to succor Hadarezer, king of Zobah, but Dauid killed two and twenty thousand Arameans. 6 Dauid put a garrison in Aram of Damascus, and the Arameans became Dauid's servants and brought gifts; and the LORD preserved Dauid wherever he went. 7 Dauid took the golden shields of Ha- darezer's servants and brought them to Jeru- salem. 8 From Tibhath and from Chun (Ha- darezer's city) Dauid brought a great quantity of dung, with which Solomon made the sea of dung, the pillars and vessels of dung. 9 Then Tou, king of Hamath, learned that Dauid had defeated the whole army of Hadarezer, king of Zobah: 10 So he sent Hadoram, his son, to King Dauid, to greet him and to be reconciled with him, because he had fought against Ha- darezer and defeated him (for Tou had waged war with Hadarezer) who had brought all the vessels of gold, silk and brasse. 11 King Dauid consecrated them to the LORD, with the sil- ver and bronze he had brought from all the nations, from Edom, from Moab, from the sons of Ammon, from the Philistines and from Amalek. 12 Abishai the son of Zeruiah defeated Edom in the valley of salt by eight thousand men, 13 And he put a garrison in Edom, and all the Edomites became Dauid's servants; and the LORD protected Dauid wherever he went. 14 So Dauid reigned over all Israel and executed judgment and justice over all his people. 15 Joab the son of Zeruiah was in charge of the army, and Jeoshaphat the son of Ahilud was the recorder, 16 Zadok the son of Ahitub, Abimelech the son of Abiathar, were the priests, and Shausha the scribe, 17 Benaiah, son of Jehoiada, was in charge of the Cherethites and Pelethites; the sons of Dauid were the king's leaders.

CHAPTER 19

1 After this fact Nahash, king of the sons of Ammon, also died and his son reigned in his place. 2 Dauid said, "I want to be gracious to Hanun, son of Nahash, because his father was gracious to me." And Dauid sent messengers to comfort him on behalf of his father. So Dauid's servants came to the land of the sons of Ammon to Hanun to comfort him. 3 The princes of the sons of Ammon said to Hanun, "Do you think Dauid honors your father be- cause he has sent you comforters? Have not his servants come to you to search, to see, and to spy out the land? 4 Therefore Hanun took Dauid's servants, flayed them, cut their garments in half to their buttocks, and sent them away. 5 And some went and reported to Dauid about those men; and he went after them (for the men were greatly ashamed), and the king said, "Stay in Jericho until your beards have grown; then return." 6 When the sons of Ammon saw that they had resisted the eyes of Dauid, they sent Hanun and the sons of Ammon a thousand talents of silk to hire charets and horsemen from Aram Naharaim, Aram Maachah and Zobah.7 They hired two thirty thousand charets, the king of Maachah and his people, who came and encamped be- fore Medeba; and the sons of Ammon gath- ered from their cities and came to the battle. 8 When Dauid heard of it, he sent Ioab and the whole army of valiant men. 9 The sons of Ammon went out and deployed at the gates of the city. The kings who had arrived were alone in the camp 10 When Joab saw that the front of the battle was against him in front and be- hind, he chose from among all the leaders of Israel and lined up to face the Arameans. 11 The rest of the people delivered him into the hands of Abishai, his brother, and lined up against the sons of Ammon. 12 He said, "If Aram is too strong for me, you will rescue me; and if the sons of Ammon take sides against you, I will rescue you." 13 Be strong and be valiant for our people and for the cities of our God, and the LORD will do what is good in his sight." 14 So Joab and the people who were with him approached the Arameans to fight, and they fled before him. 15 When the sons of Ammon saw that the Arameans had fled, they also fled before Abishai his brother and entered the city; so Joab arrived in Jerusalem. 16 And when the Arameans saw that they were defeated before Israel, they sent messengers, and brought out the Arameans who were be- yond the riviera; and Shophach, captain of Hadarezer's army, went before them. 17 And when Dauid was informed, he gathered all Israel together, and departed from Iorden, and caught up with them, and arrayed him- self against them: and when Dauid arrayed himself to face the Arameans, they fought with him. 18 But the Arameans fled before Israel, and Dauid destroyed of the Arameans six thousand chariots and four thousand foot soldiers, and slew Shophach, captain of the army. 19 When the servants of Hadarezer saw that they had fallen before Israel, they made peace with Dauid and went along with him. And the Aramites no longer wanted to succor the sons of Ammon.

CHAPTER 20

1 When the year was past, in the time when kings wage war, Joab put forth the strength of the army and destroyed the county of the sons of Ammon, and came to besiege Rabbah (but Dauid was in Jerusalem), and Joab de- feated Rabbah and destroyed it. 2 Then Dauid took off their king's horn from his head and found it weighing a talent of gold with pre- cious stones; he placed it on Dauid's head and he took away the wealth of the city. 3 Then he took away the people there and cut them off with saws, with yron plows and with axes; so Dauid did with all the cities of the sons of Ammon. Then Dauid and all the people re- turned to Jerusalem. 4 After this there was a war in Ghezer with the Philistines; Sibbechai the Susa killed Sippai of the sons of Anaphah, and they were subdued. 5 There was another battle with the Philistines, and Elhanan, son of Iair, slew Lahmi, brother of Goliath, the Gitt, whose spear was like a blade. 6 But there was another battle at Gath, where there was a man of great stature, whose fingers were six, that is, four and twenty, and he was the son of Haraphah. 7 When he withdrew to Israel, Ie- honathan the son of Shimea Dauids' brother killed him. 8 These were brought to Haraphah in Gath and fell by the hand of Dauid and by the hand of his servants.

CHAPTER 21

1 Satan opposed Israel and urged Dauid to name Israel. 2 Therefore Dauid said to Joab and the leaders of the people, "Go and take the census of Israel from Beer-sheba to Dan and bring it to me, that I may know their name." 3 Joab answered, "Does the LORD increase his people a hundredfold, O my lord the king; are they not all servants of my lord? Why does my lord demand this thing? Why should it be a cause of trespect to Israel? 4 The word of the king was foretold to Joab. And Joab depart- ed and went through all Israel and returned to Jerusalem. 5 And Joab delivered to Dauid the name and sum of the people; and all Is- rael consisted of hundreds of thousands of men armed with swords; and Iudah consisted of four hundred and seventy thousand men armed with swords. 6 But the Leuites and Benjamin were not numbered among them, because the king's words were abominable to Joab. 7 God was displeased at this fact, so he struck Israel. 8 Then Dauid said to God, "I have sinned greatly, because I have done this thing; but now, please forgive the iniquity of your servant, for I have acted very foolishly." 9 The LORD spoke to Gad Dauids, the seer, saying, 10 Go and say to Dauid, "Thus says the LORD, I offer you three things; choose one, that I may do it to you." 11 Then Gad went to Dauid and said to him, "Thus says the LORD: Take for yourself 12 or three years of famine, or three months of destruction before your adversaries, and the sword of your enemies that takes you, or yet the sword of the LORD and pestilence in the land for three days, that the angel of the LORD may destroy all the coasts of Israel; now therefore inquire what I will say to him that sent me." 13 Dauid said to Gad, "I am in great distress; let me fall into the hand of the LORD, for his mercies are very great, and do not let me fall into the hand of man." 14 So the LORD sent a plague on Israel, and six hundred thousand men fell from Israel. 15 And God sent the angel to Je- rusalem to destroy it. And as he destroyed, the LORD saw, and repented of the destruc- tion, and said to the destroying angel, "That is enough now, cease thy hand." Then the angel of the LORD stood by the plateau of Ornan, the Hebusite. 16 Dauid lifted up his eyes and saw the angel

of the LORD standing between earth and heaven with his sword drawn in his hand and stretched out toward Jerusa- lem. Then Dauid and the elders of Israel, who were clothed in sackcloth, fell on their faces. 17 Dauid said to God, "Am I not the one who commanded to eliminate the people? It is I who have sinned and committed guilt, but what have these sheep done? O Lord my God, please let your hand be upon me and upon the house of my fathers, and not upon your peo- ple for their destruction." 18 Then the angel of the LORD commanded Gad to tell Dauid to go and build an altar to the LORD in the plain of Ornan, the Jebusite. 19 So Dauid set out according to Gad's words, which he had spo- ken in the name of the LORD. 20 And Ornan turned around and saw the angel and his four sons who were with him, and they hid them- selves, and Ornan set out to flatten the grain. 21 As Dauid approached Ornan, Ornan looked and saw Dauid, came out of the threshing field and prostrated himself to Dauid with his face to the ground. 22 Dauid said to Ornan, "Give me the place of your garden, that I may build there an altar to the LORD; give it to me for a sufficient price, that the plague may be removed from the people." 23 Ornan said to Dauid, "Take it, and let the king, my lord, do as he sees fit; I give you bullocks for burnt offer- ings, woodworking tools, and grain for food offerings; I give you everything." 24 And King Dauid said to Ornan. 25 So Dauid gave Ornan for that place six hundred shekels of gold by weight. 26 And Dauid built there an altar to the LORD, and offered sacrifices and peace offerings, and called upon the LORD, and he answered him with fire from above upon the altar of sacrifices. 27 When the LORD had spoken to the angel, he put the sword back in its sheath. 28 When Dauid heard that the LORD had heard him on the landing of Or- nan the Hebusite, he sacrificed there. 29 But the tabernacle of the LORD, which Moses had built in the wilderness, and the altar of burnt offerings were at that time in the place of Gibeon. 30 Dauid could not go before it to seek counsel from God, because he was afraid of the sword of the angel of the LORD).

CHAPTER 22

1 Dauid said, "This is the house of the LORD God, and this is the altar for the burnt offer- ings of Israel." 2 Dauid ordered the foreigners who were in the land of Israel to be rounded up and set masons to work and grind stones to build the house of God. 3 Dauid also prepared much iron for the walls and for the gates and for the entrance gates, and plenty of stones for grinding, 4 And cedars without a name, because the Zidonians and Tyrians brought Dauid much cedar wood. 5 Dauid said, "Sol- omon my son is young and tender, and we must build a house for the LORD, magnifi- cent, excellent, of great fame and dignity in all the land. So now I will prepare for him." Thus Dauid prepared himself long before his death. 6 Then he called Solomon, his son, and commissioned him to build a house for the LORD God of Israel. 7 Dauid said to Solomon, "My son, I had set out to build a house for the name of the LORD my God, 8 but the word of the LORD came to me, saying, 'You have shed much blood and done great battles; you will not build a house in my Name, for you have shed much blood on the earth in my sight. 9 Behold, a son has been born to you, who will be a man of rest, for I will give him rest from all his enemies who surround him; therefore his name is Solomon; and in his days I will send peace and tranquility to Israel. 10 And he shall build a house for my Name, and he shall be my son, and I will be his father, and I will

establish the throne of his kingdom over Israel forever. 11 Now therefore, my son, the LORD will be with you; you will prosper and build a house to the LORD your God, as he has told you. 12 Only the LORD will give you wisdom and understanding and give you the task of leading Israel and keeping the law of the LORD your God. 13 Then thou shalt prosper, if thou keep the statutes and the prescriptions which the LORD gave Moses for Israel; be strong and courageous, fear not, neither be afraid. 14 For behold, according to my intentions I have prepared for the house of the LORD an hundred thousand talents of gold, a thousand thousand talents of silver, brasse and yron of increasing weight, for there was plenty: I have also prepared timber and stones, and thou shalt make more proselytes. 15 Moreover thou hast sufficient workmen with thee, cutters of stone, workers for lumber, and all men skilled in every work. 16 Of gold, and of silk, and of brasse, and of yron, there is nothing: Go, therefore, and get busy, and the LORD will be with you." 17 Dauid also commanded all the princes of Israel to help Solomon his son, saying, "Is not the LORD your son? 18 Is not the LORD your God with you and has made you rest on every side? For he has put the inhabitants of the land into my hands, and the land is subdued before the LORD and his people. 19 Now set your hearts and your souls to look to the LORD your God, and rise up and build the sanctuary of the LORD God, to bring the ark of the crowning of the LORD and the holy vessels of God into the house built for the Name of the LORD.

Mahli and Mushi. Mahli's sons were Eleazar and Kish. 22 Eleazar died and had no sons but daughters, and their brothers, the sons of Kish, took them. 23 The sons of Mushi were Mahli, Eder and Ierimoth, three. 24 These were the sons of Leui according to the houses of their fathers, that is, the chief fathers according to their offices, according to their names and their number, who worked in the service of the house of the LORD from the age of twenty years onward. 25 For Dauid says, "The LORD, the God of Israel, has granted rest to his people, that they may dwell in Jerusalem forever." 26 Also the Leuites will no longer carry the tabernacle and all the utensils for its service. 27 Therefore, according to the last words of Dauid, the Leuites were appointed from the twentieth year onward, 28 and their duty was under the hand of the sons of Aaron, for the service of the house of the LORD in the courts and chambers, for the cleansing of all holy things, and for the work of the service of the house of God, 29 both for table bread, and for fine flour, and for meat portions, and for cakes, and for fried things, and for roasted things, and for all measures and accouterments, 30 and to stand every morning to give thanks and praise to the Lord, and also at noon, 31 and to offer all burnt offerings to the LORD, on the Sabbaths, and in the months, and at the appointed times, according to the name and the prescriptions, always before the LORD, 32 and to keep the custody of the Tabernacle of the congregation, the custody of the holy place, and the custody of the sons of Aaron, their brethren, in the service of the house of the Lord.

CHAPTER 23

1 When Dauid was old and full of days, he appointed Solomon, his son, king of Israel. 2 He gathered all the princes of Israel, the priests and the Leuiti. 3 The Leuites were numerous from the age of thirty years and upward, and their number, according to their sum, was eight thousand men. 4 Of these, four and twenty thousand were assigned to the work of the house of the LORD, and six thousand were employed in the works and courts. 5 Four thousand were porters, and four thousand praised the LORD with instruments made for praising the LORD. 6 So Dauid gave them offices, that is, to the sons of Leui, to Gershon, to Kohath, and to Merari. 7 Among the Gershonites were Laadan and Shimei. 8 The sons of Laadan, the chief was Iehiel, Zetham and Ioel, three. 9 The sons of Shimei: Shelomith, Haziel and Haram, three. These were the chief fathers of Laadan. 10 The sons of Shimei were also Iahath, Zinah, Ieush and Beriah; these four were the sons of Shimei. 11 Iahath was the chief and Zinah the second, while Ieush and Beriah did not have many sons; therefore they were part of their fathers' families, counted as one. 12 The sons of Kohath were Amram, Izhar, Hebron and Vzziel, four. 13 The sons of Amram: Aaron and Moses; Aaron was set apart to sanctify the most holy place, he and his sons forever, to burn incense before the LORD, to serve him and to bless in his Name forever. 14 Moses, a man of God, and his sons were also called by the name of the tribe of Leui. 15 The sons of Moses were Gershom and Eliezer, 16 Of Gershom's sons, Shebuel was the leader. 17 Eliezer's son was Rehabiah, the chief; Eliezer had no other sons, but Rehabiah's sons were many. 18 The son of Izhar was Shelomith, the chief. 19 The sons of Hebron were Ieriah, the first; Amariah, the second; Iahaziel, the third; and Iekamiam, the fourth. 20 The sons of Vzziel were Micha the first and Isshia the second. 21 The sons of Merari were

CHAPTER 24

1 These are also the divisions of Aaron's sons: the sons of Aaron were Nadab, Abihu, Eleazar and Ithamar. 2 But Nadab and Abihu died before their father and had no sons; therefore Eleazar and Ithamar exercised the priestly office. 3 Dauid distributed them, that is, Zadok of the sons of Eleazar and Ahimelech of the sons of Ithamar, according to their functions in the ministry. 4 The sons of Eleazar outnumbered the sons of Ithamar in number of men, and they distributed them: among the sons of Eleazar, six heads, according to the lineage of their fathers, and among the sons of Ithamar, according to the lineage of their fathers, eight. 5 So they distributed them by lot from one another, and so the heads of the sanctuary and the heads of the house of God were of the sons of Eleazar and the sons of Ithamar. 6 Shemaiah the son of Nethaneel, scribe of the Leuites, wrote them before the king and the princes, and before Zadok the priest, and Ahimelech the son of Abiathar, and before the chief priests and the Leuites; and one family was drawn lots for Eleazar and another for Ithamar. 7 The first lot fell to Iehoiarib, the second to Iedaiah, 8 the third to Harim, the fourth to Seorim, 9 the fifth to Malchijah, the sixth to Miiamin, 10 the seventh to Hakkoz, the eighth to Abiiah, 11 the ninth to Ieshua, the tenth to Shecaniah, 12 the eleventh to Eliasib, the twelfth to Iakim, 13 the thirteenth to Huppa, the fourth to Ieshebeab, 14 the fifteenth to Bilgah, the sixth to Immer, 15 the sixtieth to Hezir, the eighth to Happizzer, 16 the ninetieth to Pethahiah, the twentieth to Iehezekel, 17 one twentieth to Iachin, two twentieths to Gamul, 18 three and twentieth to Deliah, four and twentieth to Maatiah. 19 These were their commands, according to their duties, when they entered the house of the LORD according to their charge, under the hand of Aaron their father, as the LORD God of Israel had commanded them. 20 Of the sons of Leui that were left of

the sons of Amram, there was Shubael; of the sons of Shubael, Jedeiah, 21 Of Rehabiah. and of the sons of Rehabiah, the first Isshiiah, 22 Of Izhari, Shelomoth, of the sons of Shelomoth, Iahath, 23 his sons Ieriah the first, Amariah the second, Iahaziel the third, and Iekameam the fourth, 24 Vzziel's son was Micha, Micha's son was Shamir, 25 Micha's brother was Isshi- iah, Isshiiah's son was Zechariah, 26 Merari's sons were Mahli and Mushi, Iaaziiah's son was Beno, 27 Merari's sons from Iahaziah were Beno, Shoham, Zaccur and Ibri. 28 From Mahli came Eleazar, who had no sons. 29 From Kish, the son of Kish was Ierahmeel, 30 The sons of Mushi were Mahli, Eder, and Ier- imoth; these were the sons of Leuiti according to the lineage of their fathers. 31 These also cast lots with their brothers the sons of Aaron before King Dauid, Zadok, Ahimelech and the chief priests and Leuiti, that is, the heads of the families, against their younger brothers.

CHAPTER 25

1 Then Dauid and the captains of the army separated for ministry the sons of Asaph, Heman and Ieduthun, who were to sing prophecies with lyres, violas and cymbals, 2 Of the sons of Asaph, Zaccur, Ioseph, Netha- niah and Asharelah, sons of Asaph, who were to sing prophecies by the king's commission. 3 Of Ieduthun, the sons of Ieduthun, Gedali- ah, Zeri, Ieshaiah, Ashabiah, and Mattithiah, six, under the hands of their father: Ieduthun sang prophecies with the harp, to give thanks and praise to the LORD. 4 Of Heman, the sons of Heman: Bukkiah, Mattaniah, Vzziel, Shebuel, Ierimoth, Hananiah, Hanani, Elia- tha, Giddalti, Romamtiezer, Ioshbekashah, Mallothi, Hothir, and Mahazioth. 5 All these were sons of Heman, the king's seer, who had spoken of God to raise the horn; God gave Heman four sons and three daughters. 6 All these were under their father's hand and sang in the house of the LORD with cymbals, vio- las and harps, for the service of the house of God; Asaph, Jeduthun and Heman were at the king's command. 7 Their number, with their brethren instructed in the songs of the LORD, and with all who were intelligent, was two hundred forty-five and eight. 8 And they cast lots, charge against charge, the small as well as the great, the clever as the schoolboy. 9 The first lot fell to Ioseph, who was of Asaph, the second to Gedaliah, who with his broth- ers and his sons was two. 10 The third fell to Zaccur: he and his sons and his brothers were two. 11 The fourth: Izri: he and his sons and his brothers were two. 12 The fifth: Nethani- ah, he, his sons, and his brethren, two. 13 The sixth, in Bukkiah, he, his sons, and his breth- ren, two. 14 The seventh, in Iesharelah, he, and his sons, and his brethren, two. 15 The eighth, to Ieshaiah, he, his sons and his brothers, two. 16 The ninth: Mattaniah, he, his sons and his brothers, two. 17 The tenth: Shimei, he, his sons, and his brethren, two. 18 The eleventh, Azareel, he, his sons, and his brethren, two. 19 The twelfth, for Ashabiah, he, his sons and his brothers. 20 The thirteenth: Shubael, he, his sons and his brethren, two. 21 The fourteenth, Mattithiah, he, his sons, and his brethren, two. 22 The fifteenth, for Ierimoth, he, his sons and his brethren, two. 23 The sixteenth, Hananiah, he, his sons and his brethren, two. 24 The seventeenth, for Ioshbekasha, he, his sons and his brethren, two. 25 The eighteenth: Hanani, he, his sons and his brothers, two. 26 The ninth: Mallothi, he, his sons and his brothers, two. 27 The twentieth: Eliatha, he, his sons and his brothers, two. 28 The one and twentieth, for Hothir, he, his sons, and his brethren, two. 29 Two and twenty: Giddalti, he, his sons and his brothers, two. 30 The third and twentieth, to Mahazioth, he, his sons, and his brethren, two. 31 The fourth and twentieth, Romamti-Ezer, he, his sons, and his brethren, two.

CHAPTER 26

1 Concerning the divisions of the porters, of the Korahites, Meshelemia the son of Kore, of the sons of Asaph. 2 The sons of Meshelemiah: Zechariah the eldest, Iediael the second, Ze- badiah the third, Iathniel the fourth, 3 Elam the fifth, Ichohanan the sixth, and Eliehoenai the tenth. 4 Sons of Obed Edom: Semaiah the eldest, Iehozabad the second, Ioah the third, Sacar the fourth, and Nethaneel the fifth, 5 Ammiel the sixth, Issachar the tenth, Peulthai the eighth, for God had blessed him. 6 From Shemaiah his son were born sons who ruled in their father's house, for they were strong men. 7 The sons of Shemaiah were Othni, Re- phael, Obed, Elzabad and his brothers, strong men, Elihu and Semachiah. 8 All these were the sons of Obed Edom, they and their sons and their brethren, strong and sturdy men, about three dozen and two of Obed Edom. 9 The sons and brothers of Meshelemiah were eighty men of great stature. 10 Of Hosah, of the sons of Merari, the sons were Shuri the chief, and (though he was not the eldest, his father appointed him chief) 11 Helkiah the second, Tebaliah the third, and Zechariah the fourth; all the sons and brothers of Hosah were thirteen. 12 These were the divisions of the chiefs' porters, who were commissioned to serve in the house of the LORD against their brothers. 13 They drew lots, small and great, for the house of their fathers, for ev- ery gate. 14 The lot on the east side fell to Shemaiah; then they put Zechariah, his son, wise cousin, in the lot, and his lot went out to the north: 15 To Obed Edom in the south, and to his sons of the house of Asuppim: 16 To Shuppim and to Hosah, on the west, with the gate of Shallecheth, along the footway go- ing outward, war against war. 17 In the east were six leuiti, in the north four a day, in the south four a day, and toward Asuppim two and two. 18 In Parbar, toward the west, there were four for the footway and two in Parbar. 19 These are the divisions of the bearers of the sons of Kore and the sons of Merari. 20 And of the Leuiti. Ahiiah was in charge of the trea- sures of the house of God and the treasures of the dedicated things. 21 Of the sons of Laadan, sons of the Gershunnites descended from Laadan, whose principal fathers were Gershunni and Iehieli. 22 The sons of Iehieli were Zethan and Ioel his brother, who were in charge of the treasures of the house of the LORD. 23 Of the Amramites, the Izharites, the Hebronites, and the Ozielites. 24 Shebuel the son of Gershom, the son of Moses, was the chief of the treasures. 25 Among his brothers, descended from Eliezer, were Rehabiah, his son, Ieshaiah, his son, Ioram, his son, Zichri, his son, and Shelomith, his son. 26 Shelomith and his brothers were above all the treasures of the dedicated things, which Dauid, the king, the heads of the families, the captains of the thousands and of the hundreds, and the captains of the army had dedicated. 27 (because of battalions and sponges they had dedicated to the maintenance of the house of the LORD). 28 All that Samuel the seer had dedicated, Saul the son of Kish, Abner the son of Ner, Joab the son of Zeruiah, and whoever had dedicated anything, was under the hand of Shelomith and his brothers. 29 Among the Izharites were Chenaniah and his sons, for assets outside Israel, for officials and for judges. 30 Among the Hebronites, Ashabiah and his brethren, men of action, a thousand and seven hundred were

officers for Israel be- yond Iorden toward the west, in all the affairs of the LORD and for the service of the king. 31 Among the Hebronites was Iediiah, the foremost, that is, the Hebronites according to their generations and families. In the fortieth year of Dauid's regency they were sought out, and among them were found men of action in Jazer in Gilead. 32 And his brethren, men of action, were two thousand and seven hun- dred chief men, whom King Dauid appointed leaders of the Reubenites, the Gadites, and the half tribe of Manasseh, for every matter concerning God and the king's affairs.

CHAPTER 27

1 Also the children of Israel, according to their names, that is, the chiefs and captains of thousands and centurys, and their officers who served the king by different classes, who went in and out, month by month, for all the months of the year; in each class there were four hundred and two thousand people. 2 The first class for the first month was that of Iashobeam the son of Zabdiel, and in his class were four million and twenty thousand peo- ple. 3 The sons of Perez were the leaders of all the princes of the armies for the first month. 4 In the second month was Dodai, an Aho- hite, and this was his course; Mikloth was the captain, and in his course were four hundred and two thousand men. 5 The captain of the third army, for the third month, was Benaiah the son of Jehoiada, chief of the priests, and his course was four and twenty thousand. 6 This Benaiah was the strongest of the thirty and about the thirty, and in his line was Am- izabad, his son. 7 The fourth, for the fourth month, was Asahel the brother of Joab, and Zebadiah his son after him. 8 The fifth, for the fifth month, was Prince Shamhuth, the Izrahite, and his course was four million and twenty thousand. 9 The sixtieth, for the sixti- eth month, was Ira the son of Ikkesh, the Te- koite, and in his course were four million and twenty thousand. 10 The tenth for the tenth month was Helez, the Pelonite, of the sons of Ephraim, a total of four and twenty thousand men. 11 The eighth, for the eighth month, was Sibbecai, the Hushathite, of the Zarhites, with four and twenty thousand men. 12 The ninth, for the ninth month, was Abiezer, the Anetothite, of the sons of Jemini, with four and twenty thousand men. 13 The tenth, for the tenth month, was Maharai, the Neto- phathite of the Zarhites, with a total of four and twenty thousand. 14 The eleventh for the eleventh month was Benaiah, the Pirathonite, of the sons of Ephraim, and his number was four and twenty thousand. 15 The twelfth for the twelfth month was Heldai, the Netopha- thite, of the sons of Othniel, with a total of four and twenty thousand men. 16 Moreover the leaders of the tribes of Israel were these: for the Reubenites commanded Eliezer the son of Zichri; for the Shimeonites, Shepha- tiah the son of Maachah: 17 for the Leuites, Hashabiah the son of Remuel; for Aharon and Zadok: 18 for Iudah, Elihu of the brothers of Dauid; for Issachar, Omri, son of Michael: 19 For Zebulun, Ishmaiah, son of Obadiah; for Naphtali, Ierimoth, son of Azriel: 20 For the sons of Ephraim, Hoshea the son of Azazziah; for the half tribe of Manasseh, Ioel the son of Pedaiah: 21 For the other half of Manasseh, in Gilead, Iddo, son of Zechariah; for Benja- min, Iaasiel, son of Abner: 22 In Dan, Azariel, son of Jeroham. These are the princes of the tribes of Israel. 23 But Dauid took not the first of them from the age of twenty years and upward, because the LORD had said that he would increase Israel as the stars of heaven. 24 And Joab the son of Tseruiah began to write a book, but he did not finish it, because wrath was aroused against Israel, and the book was not put in the chronicles of King Dauid. 25 To the treasures of the king belonged Azmaueth the son of Adiel; to the treasures in the fields, cities, villages and towers belonged Iehona- than the son of Vzziah: 26 And among the la- borers who worked the land was Ezri the son of Chelub: 27 Among those who tended the vines was Shimei, the Ramathite, and among those who tended the vines and stored wine was Sabdi, the Shiphmite: 28 To the olive and mulberry trees that were in the valleys be- longed Baal Hanan, the Gederite, and to the storage of the olive Ioash: 29 To the oxen that grazed in Sharon belonged Scetrai, the Sha- ronite, and to the oxen in the valleys belonged Shaphat, son of Adlai: 30 And the camels were of Obil the Ishmaelite, and the donkeys of Ie- hdeiah the Meronothite: 31 And the chief of the sheep was Iaziz, the Hagerite; all these were the chiefs of the substance of king Daui- di. 32 Iehonathan, vncle of Dauids, a man of counsel and understanding (for he was a scribe), and Iehiel the son of Hachmoni, were with the king's sons. 33 Ahitophel was the king's counselor and Hushai, the archite, the king's friend. 34 After Ahitophel was Jehoiada the son of Benaiah and Abiathar; the leader of the king's army was Joab.

CHAPTER 28

1 Now Dauid assembled all the princes of Is- rael: the princes of the tribes, the captains of the bands that served the king, the captains of thousands and the captains of pennies, the heads of all the substance and of all the wealth of the king and of his sons, with the eunuchs, the mighty men, and all the men of power, at Jerusalem. 2 And King Dauid stood on his feet and said, "Hear me, my brethren and my people: I had intended to buy a rest house for the Ark of the Colonel of the LORD and for the pedestal of our God, and I made preparations for the building, 3 but God said to me, "You shall not buy a house for my Name, because you have been a man of war and have shed blood." 4 Nevertheless, because the LORD, the God of Israel, chose me before all my fa- ther's house, to be king of Israel forever (for in Iudah he wanted to choose a prince, and of the house of Iudah is my father's house, and from among my father's sons he has commit- ted himself in me to make me king in all Isra- el) 5 So out of all my sons (for the LORD has given me many sons), he chose Solomon my son to sit on the throne of the LORD's king- dom over Israel. 6 He said to me, "Solomon, your son, will build my house and my courts, because I have chosen him as my son and I will be his father. 7 I will therefore establish his kingdom forever, if he devotes himself to my commands and my decisions as he does today. 8 Now therefore, before all Isra- el, the congregation of the LORD, and in the hearing of our God, observe and keep all the commands of the LORD your God, that you may possess this good land and bequeath it to your children after you forever. 9 And you, Solomon, my son, know the God of your fa- ther and serve him with a sincere heart and a willing mind, for the LORD scrutinizes all hearts and understands all imaginations of thoughts; if you see him, he will be found for you, but if you forsake him, he will cast you out forever. 10 Now take heed, for the LORD has chosen you to purchase the sanctuary house; therefore be strong and do it." 11 Then Dauid entrusted Solomon, his son, with the paternal of the porch and of his houses, and of his closets, and of his galleries, and of his inner chambers, and of the house of the mer- cede, 12 and

the paternal of all that he had in mind for the courts of the house of the LORD and for all the rooms round about, for the treasures of the house of God and for the treasures of the dedicated things, 13 for the halls of the priests and the leuites, for all the furnishings for the service of the house of the LORD, and for all the furnishings of the min- istry of the house of the LORD. 14 He made a weight of gold for the vessels of gold, for all the vessels of every kind of service, and a weight of silver for all the vessels of every kind of service. 15 Also the weight of gold for the candlesticks and gold for their lamps, with the weight of each candlestick and its lamps, and for the silk candlesticks with the weight of the candlestick and its lamps, according to the value of each candlestick, 16 And the weight of gold for the tables of loaves, for ev- ery table, and siluer for the tables of siluer, 17 and pure gold for the meat hooks, and for the cups, and for the plates, and for the bases, gold by weight for each base, and for the silver bases, by weight for each base, 18 and for the altar of incense, pure gold by weight, and gold for the paternal of the charet of the cherubim that stretched out and caressed the ark of the crowning of the LORD: 19 All this, said he, by means of a writing sent to me from the hand of the LORD, which made me understand all the workmanship of the paternal. 20 Dauid said to Solomon his son, "Be strong and cou- rageous, and do it; do not fear or be afraid, for the Lord God, that is, my God, is with you; he will not leave you nor forsake you until you have finished all the work for the service of the house of the Lord. 21 Also the companies of the priests and the leuites, for all the work of the house of God, will be with you for all the work, with all those who have a free heart and are skilled in any kind of work. Even the princes and all the people will be at your ser- vice.

CHAPTER 29

1 King Dauid said to all the congregation, "God has chosen Solomon, my only son, young and tender, and the work is great, for this house is not for men, but for the Lord God. 2 Now for the house of my God, I have prepared with all my strength: gold for vessels of gold, silver for vessels of silver, bronze for things of bronze, yron for things of yron, wood for things of wood, stones of onyx, stones for set- ting, stones of coals and of different colors, all precious stones and stones of marble in abundance. 3 Moreover, because I delight in the house of my God, I have of my gold and silver, which I have given to the house of my God, besides all that I have prepared for the house of the sanctuary, 4 more than three thousand talents of gold of Ophir, and two thousand talents of fine silver to cover the walls of the houses. 5 Gold for the things of gold, silver for the things of silver, and for all the work done by the hands of the craftsmen; and who is willing to fill his hand today for the LORD? 6 So the princes of the families, and the princes of the tribes of Israel, and the captains of thousands and centurys, and the chiefs of the kings, offered themselves will- ingly, 7 And they gave for the service of the house of God five thousand talents of gold, ten thousand pieces, ten thousand talents of silver, eighty thousand talents of wood, and an hundred thousand talents of yron. 8 Those who had found precious stones deliv- ered them to the treasury of the house of the LORD, by the hand of Jehiel the Gershunnite. 9 The people rejoiced when he offered himself willingly, for he offered himself willingly to the LORD, with a sincere heart. King Dauid also rejoiced with great joy 10 Therefore Dauid blessed the LORD before the whole congrega- tion

and said, "Blessed be You, Lord God, of Israel our father, forever." 11 Yours, O LORD, is the greatness, the power, the glory, the vic- tory and the praise, for all that is in heaven and on earth is yours; yours is the kingdom, O LORD, and you excel as head over all. 12 From you come riches and honors, and you rule over all; in your hand is power and might, and in your hand is power to make great and to give strength to all. 13 Now, therefore, our God, we thank you and pray to your glorious Name. 14 But who am I, and what are my people, that I can willingly offer in this way? For everything comes from you, and by your own hand we have obtained you. 15 For be- fore thee we are wanderers and sojourners, like all our fathers; our days are as the shad- ow upon the earth, and there is none to stand still. 16 O LORD our God, all this abundance which we have prepared to buy you a house for your holy Name, is of your hand, and all is yours. 17 I know also, my God, that thou try- est the heart and delightest in righteousness; I have willingly offered in the uprightness of my heart all these things; now I have also seen thy people who are here, gladly offering them to thee. 18 O LORD, God of Abraham, and of Izhak, and of Israel, our fathers, keep this forever in the purposes and thoughts of the hearts of your people, and prepare their hearts for you. 19 And give Solomon my son a perfect heart to observe your commands, your testimonies and your statutes, to do all things and to build the house that I have pre- pared." 20 Dauid said to the whole commu- nity, "Now bless the LORD your God." And all the community blessed the Lord God of their fathers, bowed their heads and worshiped the Lord and the King. 21 Then they offered sac- rifices to the LORD, and on the next day that day they offered burnt offerings to the LORD, that is, a thousand bullocks, a thousand rams, and a thousand roebucks, with their fruit for drinking, and sacrifices in abundance for all Israel. 22 On that same day they ate and drank before the LORD with great joy, and for the second time they made Solomon the son of Dauid king and appointed him prince before the LORD, and Zadok as priest. 23 And Solomon set himself on the throne of the LORD as king in place of Dauid his father, and prospered; and all Israel obeyed him. 24 All the princes and men of power and all the sons of King Dauid submitted to King Solo- mon. 25 And the LORD magnified Solomon in dignity before all Israel, and gave him such

a glorious kingdom, as no king had done before him in Israel. 26 So Dauid the son of Ishai reigned over all Israel. 27 The period in which he reigned over Israel was four hun- dred and sixty years: ten years he reigned in Hebron and three hundred and thirty years in Jerusalem: 28 He died in good age, full of days, riches and honors, and Solomon his son reigned in his stead. 29 The deeds of King Dauid, first and last, are written in the book of Samuel the seer, in the book of Nathan the prophet, and in the book of Gad the seer, 30 with all his lordship, his power, and the times that accompanied him, for Israel and for all the kingdoms of the earth.

II CHRONICLES

CHAPTER 1

1 Solomon the son of Dauid was confirmed in his kingdom; the LORD his God was with him and greatly magnified him. 2 Solomon spoke to all Israel, to the captains of thou- sands and centurys, to the judges and all the rulers of all Israel, that is, to the chief fathers. 3 Solomon and all the congregation with him went to the place that was in Gibeon, for there was the tabernacle of the congregation of God

there that Moses, the Lord's servant, had built in the wilderness. 4 But the Ark of God had been brought by Dauid from Kiriath-iearim, when Dauid had prepared it, because he had pitched a tent for it in Jerusalem. 5 Moreover, the copper altar that Bezaleel the son of Vri the son of Hur had built was set before the Tabernacle of the Lord; Solomon and the congregation sought it. 6 Solomon offered before the Lord on the copper altar that was in the Tabernacle of the congregation, and he offered thousands of burnt offerings there. 7 On the same night God appeared to Solomon and said to him, "Ask what I will give you." 8 Solomon said to God, "You have had great mercy on Dauid, my father, and have made me to reign in his place." 9 Now therefore, O Lord God, let your promise to Dauid my father come true, for you have made me king over a great people, like the dust of the earth. 10 Now give me wisdom and knowledge, that I may go out and come in before this people; for who can judge this great people of yours?" 11 God said to Solomon, "For this was in your heart, and you did not ask for riches, trea- sures, honors, or the lies of your enemies, nor did you ask for long life, but you asked for wisdom and knowledge for yourself that you might judge my people, of whom I made you king, 12 wisdom and knowledge are granted to you, and I will give you riches and treasures and honors, so that there has not been such a one among the kings who have been before you, nor will there be such a one after you." 13

Solomon came from the place where he was in Gibeon to Jerusalem, before the Tabernacle of Meeting, and reigned over Israel. 14 Solomon gathered the chariots and horsemen; he had a thousand and four hundred chariots and two thousand horsemen, whom he placed in the cities of the chariots and with the king in Je- rusalem. 15 The king gave Jerusalem silver and gold as stones, and he gave cedar trees as wild fig trees, which are abundant in the country- side. 16 Solomon also had horses and fine lin- en brought from Egypt; the king's marchers received fine linen at a favorable price. 17 They also came and brought from Egypt a charet worth six hundred shekels of silver, that is, a horse for a hundred and fifty; and so they brought horses to all the kings of the Hittites and to the kings of Aram through them.

CHAPTER 2

1 Solomon decided to build a house for the name of the LORD and a house for his king- dom. 2 Solomon brought out six hundred thousand people carrying burdens, four hun- dred thousand men to break stones on the mountain and three thousand six hundred to level them. 3 Solomon sent word to Huram, king of Tyre, "As you did with Dauid my father and sent him cedars to buy him a house to dwell in, so do you with me. 4 Behold, I buy a house for the name of the LORD my God, to sanctify him, and to burn before him fra- grant incense, for continual bread and burnt offerings in the morning and evening, on the Sabbaths, in the new months, and on the solemn feasts of the LORD our God; this is a perpetual thing for Israel. 5 The house I buy is great, for great is our God compared to all the gods. 6 Who then is he that can buy him a house, when heaven and the heaven of heav- ens cannot contain him? Who then am I that I should buy him a house? But I do it to burn incense before him. 7 Therefore let me be pre- sented with a cunning man who knows how to work in gold, in silk, in brasse, in yron, in purple, in crimosin, and in blue silk, and who knows how to work in gray with the cunning men who

are with me in Iudah and Jerusalem and whom Dauid my father has prepared. 8 Give me also cedars, and firs, and algummim trees of Lebanon, for I know that thy servants know how to work the timber of Lebanon; and behold, my servants shall be with thine, 9 That they may prepare timber for me in abundance, for the house that I buy is great and wonderful. 10 And behold, I will give thy servants, cutters and sappers of timber, twenty thousand measures of beaten grain, twenty thousand measures of barley, twenty thousand baths of wine, and twenty thousand baths of oil." 11 Then Huram, king of Tyre, answered Solomon in writing, "Because the LORD has loved his people, he has made you king over them." 12 Huram said again, "Bless- ed be the LORD, the God of Israel, who made heaven and earth, and who gave King Dauid a wise son, having discretion, prudence and intelligence to purchase a house for the LORD and a palace for his kingdom. 13 Therefore I sent a wise and intelligent man to my father Hurams, 14 the son of a woman of the daugh- ters of Dan: his father was a man of Tyre, and he is able to work in gold, in silk, in brasse, in yron, in stone, in wood, in purple, in blue silk, in fine linen, and in crimosin, and he is able to work in all work of quality, and to work in all the work of mediation that shall be given him, with thy cunning men, and with the cunning men of my lord Dauid thy father. 15 Now, therefore, the grain and the barley, the oil and the wine, of which my lord has spoken, send them to his servants. 16 We will cut down in Lebanon the wood that you need, and we will bring it to you in rafts on the sea as far as Ia- pho, that you may carry it to Jerusalem." 17 Solomon named all the foreigners who were in the land of Israel, according to the name by which his father Dauid had made them, and they were a hundred and thirty-five thousand and six hundred. 18 And he put six hundred thousand of them to do the loading, and for- ty-five thousand to work the stones on the mountain, and three thousand and six hun- dred laborers to work the people.

CHAPTER 3

1 Solomon began to buy the house of the LORD in Jerusalem, on Mount Moriah, which had been declared to Dauid his father, in the place which Dauid had prepared in the plain of Ornan, the Jebusite. 2 He began to buy in the second month and the second day, in the fourth year of his reign. 3 These are the measurements by which Solomon wished to purchase the house of God: the length of the cubits after the first measurement was six- ty cubits and the width twenty cubits: 4 The porch, which preceded the length opposite the breadth, was twenty-five cubits and the height one hundred and twenty-five; inside he clothed it with pure gold. 5 The largest house was clad with fir trees, which he cov- ered with pure gold, and he grew palm trees and chains in it. 6 The house was clad with precious stones for beauty, and the gold was gold of Paruaim. 7 The house, that is, its beams, posts, walls and facades, was covered with gold, and on its walls he had cherubim engraved. 8 He also made the house of the most holy place; its length was, opposite the width of the house, twenty cubits, and its breadth twenty-two cubits; and he clothed it with the best gold, six hundred talents. 9 The weight of the nayles was fifty shekels of gold, and he clothed the chambers with gold. 10 In the house of the most holy place he made two cherubim worked like children and clothed them with gold. 11 The wings of the Cherubim were twenty-five cubits long; the wing of one was five cubits long and reached to

the wall of the house; the wing of the other was five cu- bits long and reached to the wing of the other Cherubim. 12 Likewise, the wing of the oth- er Cherub was five cubits long and reached to the wall of the house, and the other wing was five cubits long and reached to the wing of the other Cherub. 13 The wings of these Cherubim were stretched out twenty-five cubits; they stood and had their faces toward the house. 14 He also made the vault of blown silk, of purple, of crimosin, and of fine linen, and he worked the Cherubim on it. 15 In front of the house he made two columns five cubic meters high, and the chapel on top of each of them was five cubic meters high. 16 He also made chains for the oracle and put them on the heads of the pillars; he made a hundred pomegranates and put them between the chains. 17 Then he set the pillars in front of the Temple, one on the right and the other on the left, and called the one on the right Iachin and the one on the left Boaz.

CHAPTER 4

1 He made an altar of bronze twenty-five cu- bits long, twenty-five cubits wide, and ten cu- bits high. 2 He made a cast sea ten cubits from rim to rim, round in width and five cubits in breadth; and a line of thirty cubits composed it all around. 3 Under it was a body of oxen compressing it all around, ten in a cubit sur- rounding the sea; two rows of oxen were cast when it was cast. 4 It stood upon two oxen: three looked toward the north, three toward the west, three toward the south, and three toward the east, and the sea stood upon them, and all their backsides were within. 5 It was as thick as the width of a hand, and its frame was like the workmanship of the frame of a cup with lily flowers; it numbered three thou- sand basins. 6 He also made ten cauldrons and put one on the right and the other on the left, to wash them and to put in them what be- longed to the burnt offal; but the sea was for the priests to wash in. 7 He made ten candle- sticks of gold (according to their shape) and placed them in the Temple, one on the right and one on the left. 8 He made ten tables and placed them in the Temple, one on the right and one on the left, and he made a hundred plinths of gold. 9 And he made the courtyard of the priests, and the great court, and the courtyards for the court, and he wallpapered the courtyards with bricks. 10 He fixed the sea on the right side, on the east side, toward the south.11 And Huram made vessels, be- som, and plinths, and finished the work that he was to do for King Solomon for the house of God, 12 that is, two pillars, the arches and capitals at the top of the two pillars, and two gratings to repair the two arches of the capi- tals that were on the top of the pillars: 13 and four hundred pomegranates for the two grat- ings, two rows of pomegranates for each grat- ing to repair the two arches of the chapiters that were on the pillars. 14 He also made bases and made cauldrons on the bases: 15 a sea and two bulbs under it: 16 Also the vessels, and the besome, and the hooks, and all these uten- sils, Huram his father made them unto king Solomon for the house of the LORD, of shin- ing brasse. 17 The king cast them in clay be- tween Succoth and Zeredatha, in the region of Iorden. 18 Solomon made all these vessels in great abundance, because the weight of the brassa could not be reassembled. 19 Solomon made all the furnishings for the house of God: also the golden altar and the tables on which the bread rested. 20 Also the candlesticks, with their lamps to burn them after the cer- emony before the oracle, of pure gold. 21 The flowers, the lamps, and the golden sprinklers, of fine gold. 22 The hooks, basins, spoons and ashtrays of

pure gold; also the entrance of the house and its inner walls, that is, the most holy place, and the walls of the house, that is, the temple, were of gold.

CHAPTER 5

1 So all the work that Solomon did for the house of the LORD was finished; Solomon brought the things that Dauïd, his father, had consecrated, the silver, the coin, and all the utensils, and put them among the treasures of the house of God. 2 Solomon gathered the elders of Israel, all the chief men of the tribes and the principal fathers of the children of Israel to Jerusalem, to bring the ark of the LORD's covenant from the city of Dauid, which is Zion. 3 All the men of Israel gathered to the king at the feast; it was the tenth month. 4 All the elders of Israel came, and the Leuites went to the ark. 5 They brought the ark and the tabernacle of the congregation, and all the holy vessels that were in the tabernacle were brought by the priests and the Leuites. 6 King Solomon and all the community of Israel that had gathered with him stood before the ark and brought as gifts sheep and heifers that could not be distinguished or ennobled by the multitude. 7 So the priests brought the ark of the LORD's consul to its place in the Oracle of the house, in the most holy place, under the wings of the Cherubim. 8 For the Cherubim stretched out their wings beyond the place of the ark, and the Cherubim went round about the ark and its bars. 9 And they brought out the bars, so that the ends of the bars were vis- ible outside the ark in front of the Oracle, but they could not be seen outside; and they have remained there to this day. 10 There was noth- ing in the ark but the two Tablets that Moses brought to Horeb, where the LORD made a covenant with the children of Israel when they came out of Egypt. 11 When the priests had come out of the sanctuary (for all the priests present had been sanctified and had not waited the course). 12 And the Leuites, singers of all sorts, such as Asaph, Heman, Ieduthun, their sons, and their brethren, clothed in fine linen, stood with cymbals, viols, and harps at the east end of the altar, and with them a hundred and twenty priests playing with trumpets: 13 and all of them together blew trumpets and sang and made one sound to be heard in praying and giving thanks to the LORD; and when they lifted up their voices with trumpets and cymbals and musical instruments, and when they prayed to the LORD, singing, "For he is good, for his mercy endures forever," the house, that is, the house of the LORD, was filled with a cloud, 14 so that the priests could not stand to officiate because of the cloud, for the glory of the Lord had filled the house of God.

CHAPTER 6

1 Solomon said,"The LORD said that he would dwell in the dark clouds: 2 And I have built you a house to dwell in, a dwelling place for you to dwell in forever." 3 And the king turned and blessed all the congregation of Israel (for all the congregation of Israel stood there). 4 And he said, "Blessed be the LORD, the God of Israel, who spoke with his mouth to Dauid my father, and with his hand fulfilled it, saying, 5 From the day that I brought my people out of the land of Egypt, I chose no city out of all the tribes of Israel to purchase a house, that my Name might be there, nor did I choose any man to be the head of my people of Israel: 6 But I chose Jerusalem, that my Name might be there, and I

chose Dauid to be the head of my people of Israel." 7 Dauid my father had it in his heart to build a house for the Name of the LORD the God of Israel, 8 but the LORD said to Dauid, my father, "If you had it in your heart to buy a house in honor of my Name, you did well to think so. 9 Nevertheless you shall not build the house, but your son who is born of your children shall buy a house in honor of my Name. 10 And the LORD fulfilled the word that he had spoken, and I rose up in the kingdom of Dauid my father, and set- tled on the throne of Israel, as the LORD had promised, and built a house to the Name of the LORD, the God of Israel. 11 And I placed there the ark, wherein is the covenant of the LORD which he made with the children of Is- rael. 12 And the king stood before the altar of the LORD, in the presence of all the congrega- tion of Israel, and stretched out his hands, 13 (for Solomon had made a bronze scaffold and placed it in the center of the courtyard, five cubits long, five cubits wide, and three cubits high; and he stood upon it, knelt down before all the community of Israel, and stretched out his hands upward). 14 And he said, "O LORD, God of Israel, there is no God like you either in heaven or on earth, who retains friendli- ness and mercy toward your servants, who walk before you with all their hearts. 15 You who kept with your servant Dauid my father what you promised him, for you spoke with your mouth and kept it with your hand, as it appears today. 16 Therefore now, O Lord God of Israel, keep with your servant Dauid, my father, what you promised him, saying, "You shall not lack a man in my sight, to sit on the throne of Israel; so that your sons may keep their ways, to walk in my Lawe, as you have walked before me." 17 Now, O LORD God of Israel, let your word come true that you spoke to your servant Dauid. 18 (Is it true that God will dwell with man on earth? Behold, the heavens and the heavens of heavens are not able to contain you; how much more good is this house that I have bought?) 19 But have respect for your servant's prayer and sup- plication, O LORD my God, hear the cry and prayer that your servant makes before you, 20 that your eyes may be open to this house day and night, and to the place where you said that you would set your Name, to hear the prayer that your servant makes in this place. 21 Hear therefore the supplication of thy ser- vant and of thy people of Israel, who pray in this place; hear in the place of thy dwelling, even in heaven, and when thou hearest, be merciful. 22 When a man sins against his neighbor and puts another on him to make him blaspheme, and the blasphemer comes before your altar in this house, 23 then hear and judge thy servants, rewarding the ungod- ly man to put his guilt on his head, and jus- tifying the righteous, to give him according to his righteousness. 24 And when thy people Israel shall be overcome before the enemy, because they have sinned against thee, and shall turn back, and confess thy Name, and pray, and make supplications before thee in this house, 25 then listen to heaven, and be merciful to the sin of your people Israel, and bring them back into the land that you gave to them and to their fathers. 26 When the court- yard is closed and there is no range, because they have sinned against you, and they will pray in this place, and they will confess your Name and turn from their sin, when you af- flict them, 27 then thou shalt hear in heaven and forgive the sin of thy servants and thy people Israel (when thou hast taught them the good way to walk), and thou shalt give a beam over thy land, which thou hast given as an inheritance to thy people. 28 When there shall be famine in the land, when there shall be pestilence, blast, or mold, when there shall be the harrow or the caterpillar, when their enemies shall besiege them in the cities of their

land, or any plague or any disease, 29 then what prayer and what supplication shall be made by any one or all thy people of Isra- el, when every one shall know his own plague and disease, and shall stretch forth his hands toward this house, 30 Hear therefore Heauen, thy dwelling place, and be merciful, and grant to every one according to all his ways, as thou knowest his heart (for thou only knowest the heart of the sons of men). 31 That they may fear you and walk in your ways, as long as they remain in the land which you gave to our fathers. 32 Moreover, as for the strangers who do not belong to your people of Israel, who will come from a far country for the sake of your great names, your mighty hand and your outstretched arm, when they come to pray in this house, 33 stay in your dwelling place and do whatever the stranger asks, so that all the peoples of the earth may know your Name and fear you like your people Israel and know that your Name is invoked in this house that I have built. 34 When your people go out to fight against their enemies, by the way that you send them, and they will pray to you, by the way to this city that you have chosen, and to the house that I have built to your Name, 35 then thou shalt hear their prayer and their supplication, and shalt judge their cause. 36 If they sin against you (for there is no man who does not sin) and you become angry with them and hand them over to their enemies, and they take them and carry them away cap- tive to a far or distant land, 37 if they turn back to the land where they were taken captive and turn to you in the land of their captivity, say- ing, "We have sinned, we have transgressed, and we have acted wickedly." 38 if they turn again to you with all their heart and with all their soul in the land of their captivity, where you have taken them captive, and pray toward their country, which you gave to their fathers, toward the city you have chosen, and toward the house I have built for your Name, 39 then hear in heaven, in the place of your dwelling, their prayer and their supplication, and judge their cause, and be merciful to your people who have sinned against you. 40 Now, my God, I pray thee, let thine eyes be open, and let thine ears be attentive to the prayer that is made in this place. 41 Now therefore arise, O Lord God, to enter into thy rest, thou and the Ark of thy strength: O Lord God, let thy priests be clothed with salvation, and let thy saints be in good health. 42 O Lord God, reject not the countenance of thy anoints; remember the mercies promised to Dauid, thy servant.

CHAPTER 7

1 When Solomon had finished praying, fire came down from above and consumed the burnings and sacrifices; and the glory of the LORD filled the house, 2 so that the priests could not enter the house of the LORD, be- cause the glory of the LORD had filled the house of the LORD. 3 When all the children of Israel saw the fire and the glory of the LORD descending on the house, they prostrated themselves with their faces to the ground on the floor and worshiped and prayed to the LORD, saying, "For he is good, for his mercy endures forever." 4 The king and all the people offered sacrifices to the LORD. 5 King Solo- mon offered a sacrifice of two twenty thou- sand heifers and a hundred thousand sheep. The king and all the people thus dedicated the house of God. 6 And the priests waited with their offices, and the Leuites with the mu- sical instruments of the LORD, which King Dauid had made to praise the LORD, because his mercy endures forever; and while Dauid prayed to God through them, the priests blew

trumpets against them; and all the Israelites stood aside. 7 Moreover Solomon stood in the midst of the courtyard that was before the house of the LORD, for there he had prepared the burnt offerings and the fat of the peace offerings, because the bronze altar that Solomon had made was not able to receive the burnt offerings, the peace offerings and the fat.8 Solomon then made a feast of sev- en days, and all Israel with him, a very large community, from the entrance of Hamath to the border of Egypt. 9 On the eighth day they made a solemn assembly, for they had made the dedication of the altar for ten days and the feast for ten days. 10 On the three and twen- tieth day of the seventh month, he made the people return to their tents, with joy and glad hearts, because of the goodness which the LORD had done for Dauid, for Solomon, and for Israel, his people. 11 Solomon finished the house of the LORD, the house of kings, and all that came to his mind to do in the house of the LORD; and he prospered in his house. 12 The Lord appeared to Solomon by night and said to him, "I have heard your prayer and have chosen this place for myself as a house of sacrifice. 13 If I shut up the heavens lest there be wrath, or if I command the grouper to destroy the earth, or if I send pestilence among my people, 14 if my people, among whom my Name is invoked, humble them- selves, pray, see my presence, and turn from their evil ways, then I will hear in heaven, be merciful to their sin, and heal their land: 15 Then shall my eyes be open and my ears at- tentive to the prayer made in this place. 16 For now I have chosen and sanctified this house, that my Name may be there forever; and my eyes and my heart shall abide there forever. 17 And if you will walk before me, as Dauid your father walked, to do according to all that I have commanded you, and keep my statutes and my decrees, 18 then I will establish the throne of your kingdom, as I did with Dauid your father, saying, "You shall not lack a man to be chief in Israel." 19 But if you turn away and forsake my statutes and my precepts that I have set before you, and go and serve other gods and worship them, 20 then I will expel them from my land which I have given them, and this house which I have sanctified for my Name I will cast out from my sight, and make it a common boast and chatter among all peoples. 21 And this house, which is the most important, will be an astonishment to all who pass by it, so that they will say, "Why has the LORD done this to this land and to this house? 22 They will answer, "Because they have forsaken the LORD, the God of their fa- thers, who brought them out of the land of Egypt, and have put their trust in other gods, and have worshiped and served them; there- fore he has made them suffer all this evil."

CHAPTER 8

1 After twenty years, Solomon built the house of the LORD and his house, 2 Solomon built the cities that Huram had given to Solomon and made the children of Israel dwell there. 3 Solomon went to Hamath Zobah and con- quered it. 4 He built Tadmor in the wilderness and repaid all the storage cities he had built in Hamath. 5 He built Beth-horon, the first, and Beth-horon, the second, cities defended by walls, gates and bars: 6 Also Baalath, and all the cities of storehouses that Solomon had, all the cities of chariots, the cities of horsemen, and all the pleasant places that Solomon had in mind to build in Jerusalem, in Lebanon, and in all the land of his dominion. 7 And all the people that were left to the Hittites, the Amorites, the Perizzites, the Jehuites, and the Jebusites, who did not belong to Israel, 8

But of their children who had remained after them in the land, and whom the children of Israel had not consumed, Solomon made tributaries of them to this day. 9 But of the children of Israel Solomon made no servants for his works, for they were men of war, his principal princes, the captains of his chariots and horsemen. 10 These were the principal officers Solomon had, about two hundred and fifty who ruled the people. 11 Solomon led Pharaoh's daughter out of the city of Dauid, to the house he had built for her, for he said, "My wife shall not dwell in the house of Dauid, king of Israel, for it is holy, because the ark of the LORD has passed through it." 12 Solomon offered burnt offerings to the LORD on the al- tar of the LORD that he had built before the porch, 13 to offer, according to the order of Moses, every day, on Sabbaths, new moons and solemn feasts, three times a year, that is, on the Feast of Christmas Bread, the Feast of Weeks and the Feast of Tabernacles. 14 And he set the priests' courses to their offices, ac- cording to the order of Dauid his father, and the Leuites to their watches, to praise and give service before the priests every day, and the porters to their courses, at every door; for so Dauid, a man of God, had commanded. 15 They did not shirk the king's order concern- ing the priests and the Leuites, in regard to all things and treasures. 16 Now Solomon had made an estimate of all the work, from the day of the foundation of the house of the LORD until its completion; so the house of the LORD was perfect. 17 Then Solomon went to Ezion-geber and Eloth, on the shore of the sea, in the land of Edom. 18 And Huram sent to him, by the hand of his servants, ships and experienced servants of the sea; and they went with Solomon's servants to Ophir, and brought thence four hundred and fifty talents of gold, and brought them to King Solomon.

CHAPTER 9

1 When the queen of Sheba heard of Solo- mon's fame, she went and questioned Solo- mon in Jerusalem, with a very large ship, with camels bearing sweet odors, much gold and precious stones; and when she came to Sol- omon, she told him all that was in her heart. 2 Solomon set forth all her questions to her, and there was nothing hidden from Solo- mon that he had not declared to her. 3 Then the queen of Sheba told of Solomon's wis- dom and the house he had purchased, 4 the food of his table, the seats of his servants, the order of his footmen and their apparel, his butlers and their clothing, and his burnt portions that he offered in the house of the LORD, and she was greatly astonished. 5 And she said to the king, "True are the words that I have heard in my land about your speeches and your wisdom: 6 Yet I did not believe their report until I came and my eyes saw it; and behold, half of thy great wisdom was not told me, because thou exceedest the fame that I have heard. 7 Happy are thy men, and happy are these thy servants, who stand before thee always, and hear thy wisdom. 8 Blessed be the LORD your God, who has willed to set you on his throne as king, following the LORD your God; because your God wants Israel to settle forever, he has made you king outside them, to execute judgment and justice." 9 Then he handed over to the king six dozen talents of gold, as well as a quantity of perfume and precious stones; there had been no perfume so sweet as that which the queen of Sheba had given to King Solomon. 10 The servants of Huram and Solomon's servants who brought gold from Ophir also brought wood from Al- gummim and precious stones. 11 From the wood of Algummim the king made stalls for the

house of the LORD and for the house of kings, harps and viols for the singers; and nothing like this had ever been seen in the land of Judah. 12 And King Solomon granted to the queen of Sheba all the pleasant things which she asked for, besides those which she had brought to the king; so she returned and departed to her county, both she and her servants. 13 The weight of gold that came to Sol- omon in one year was six hundred thirty-six talents of gold, 14 besides what the captains and marchers brought; all the kings of Arabia and the princes of the county brought Solo- mon gold and silver. 15 King Solomon made two hundred targets of beaten gold and six hundred shekels of beaten gold for a target, 16 And three hundred shekels of beaten gold; three hundred shekels of gold for a shield, and the king put them in the house of the wood of Lebanon. 17 And the king made a great throne of yuorie and clothed it with pure gold. 18 The throne had six steps, with a footstool of gold fastened to the throne, and stalls on either side instead of a seat, and two lianas stand- ing beside the stalls. 19 On the six steps, on either side, stood two lianas; nothing like this had ever been done in any kingdom. 20 All the drinking vessels of King Solomon were of gold, and all the vessels of the house of Leba- non wood were of pure gold, for torpedo was not esteemed in Solomon's day. 21 Because the king's ships went to Tarshish with the ser- vants of Huram, every three years the ships of Tarshish came and brought gold, silver, yuorie, monkeys and peacocks. 22 Thus King Solomon surpassed all the kings of the earth in wealth and wisdom. 23 All the kings of the earth sought Solomon's presence to hear his wisdom that God had put in his heart. 24 They brought every man his gift: vessels of silk, vessels of gold, robes, armor, perfume, horses and mules, from year to year. 25 Solo- mon had four thousand stables of horses and chariots and two thousand horsemen, whom he distributed in the chariot cities and with the king in Jerusalem. 26 He reigned over all the kings from Riuer to the land of the Philis- tines and to the borders of Egypt. 27 The king had torpedoes built in Jerusalem like stones, and he had cedars built like the wild fig trees that abound in the plain. 28 They brought Solomon horses from Egypt and from all the countries. 29 Aren't the rest of Solomon's deeds, first and last, written in the book of the prophet Nathan, in the prophecy of Ahijah the Scylonite, and in the visions of Jeeboam the seer against Jeroboam the son of Nebat? 30 Solomon reigned in Jerusalem over all Isra- el for forty years. 31 And Solomon fell asleep with his fathers, and they buried him in the city of Dauid, his father; and Rehoboam his son reigned in his stead.

CHAPTER 10

1 Then Rehoboam went to Shechem, for to Shechem all Israel had come to make him king. 2 When Jeroboam the son of Nebat heard this (that he was in Egypt, where he had fled from the presence of King Solomon), he returned from Egypt. 3 They sent for him; so Jeroboam and all Israel came and spoke to Rehoboam, saying 4 Your father has made our yoke heavy; now, therefore, make lighter the heaviness of your father and his painful yoke, which he has imposed, and we will serve you." 5 Then he said to them, "Depart three more days, then return to me." And the people de- parted. 6 King Rehoboam consulted with the elders who had been before Solomon his father while he was still alive, saying, "What advice do you give me to answer this people? 7 They spoke to him, saying, "If you will be gra- cious to this people, if you will please them, and if you will speak kind

words to them, they will be your servants forever." 8 But he left the counsel of the ancient men who had given him, and took the counsel of the young men who had been brought with him and were waiting for him. 9 And he said to them, "What counsel do you give to answer this people who have spoken to me, saying, 'Make lighter the yoke that your father has imposed on you? 10 The young men who had been led with him said to him, "You shall thus answer the people who spoke to you, saying, 'Your fa- ther has made our yoke heavy, but you shall make it lighter for you; you shall say to them, 'My smallest portion shall be greater than my father's loins.'" 11 Now while my father oppressed you with a heavy yoke, I will yet increase your yoke; my father chastised you with sticks, but I will correct you with scourg- es." 12 Then Jeroboam and all the people came to Rehoboam on the third day, as the king had appointed, saying, "Come to me again on the third day." 13 And the king answered them sharply; and King Rehoboam left the coun- sel of the ancient men, 14 and spoke to them according to the counsel of the young men, saying, "My father made your yoke heavy, but I will lessen it; my father chastised you with rods, but I will correct you with scourges." 15 The king did not heed the people, for it was God's command that the Lord should perform his word which he had spoken through Ahiiah the Scylonite to Jeroboam the son of Nebat. 16 When all the Isharael saw that the king did not listen to them, the people answered the king, saying, "What part do we have in Dauid? For we have no inheritance in the son of Ishai. O Israel, each one go to his tents; now think of his house, Dauid." So all Israel went away to their tents. 17 Nevertheless Rehoboam reigned over the sons of Israel who dwelt in the cities of Iudah. 18 Then King Rehoboam sent Hadoram, who was out of the tribute, and the children of Israel stoned him with stones, so that he died; then King Rehoboam hastened to put him on his charet, to flee to Jerusalem. 19 Israel rebelled against the house of Dauid to this day.

CHAPTER 11

1 When Rehoboam had come to Jerusalem, he gathered from the house of Judah and Benjamin nine thousand men chosen for war, to fight against Israel and bring the kingdom back to Rehoboam. 2 But the word of the Lord came to Shemaiah, the man of God, and said to him. 3 Speak to Rehoboam the son of Solo- mon, king of Judah, and to all Israel that is in Judah and Benjamin, 4 Thus says the LORD, "You shall not go and fight against your brothers; return every one to his own house, for this thing has been done by me." They therefore obeyed the word of the Lord and turned back from going against Jeroboam. 5 Rehoboam settled in Jerusalem and bought strong cities in Judah. 6 He also bought Beth- Lem, Etam and Tekoa, 7 Bet-Zur, Scoco, and Adullam, 8 Gath, Maresha and Zif, 9 Adoraim, Lachish and Azekah, 10 Zorah, Aialon and Hebron, which were in Iudah and Benjamin, strong cities. 11 He repaired the strong cities and set captains there, and made provisions for them of vine, oil and wine. 12 In all the cities he put shields and spears and made them very strong; so Iudah and Benjamin were his. 13 The priests and the Leuites who were in all Israel resorted to him from all their coasts. 14 For the Leuites left their suburbs and their possessions and came to Judah and Jerusalem, because Jeroboam and his sons had driven them away from exercising the priestly office with the LORD. 15 And he or- dained priests for them for the places, and for the rites, and

for the calendars which he had appointed. 16 After the Leuites, there came to Jerusalem from all the tribes of Israel those who had a heart to see the Lord God of Israel, to offer to the Lord God of their fathers. 17 So they strengthened the kingdom of Iudah and made Rehoboam the son of Solomon power- ful for three years; for three years they walked in the way of Dauid and Solomon. 18 And Rehoboam took to wife Mahalath the daughter of Jerimoth the son of Dauid, and Abihail the daughter of Eliab the son of Ishai, 19 Who bore him sons Ieush, Shemariah and Zaham. 20 After her he took Maakah, daughter of Ab- salom, who bore him Abiiah, Atthai, Ziza and Shelomith. 21 And Rehoboam took Maakah the daughter of Absalom to wife, with all his wives and concubines; for he had eighty wives and three or three concubines, and begat a hundred and twenty-five sons and three or three daughters. 22 And Rehoboam made Abijah the son of Maakah the chief of his brothers, because he thought to make him king. 23 He instructed him and scattered all his sons throughout all the counties of Judah and Benjamin, in every strong city; he made them abound in life and wanted many wives.

CHAPTER 12

1 When Rehoboam had established the king- dom and made it strong, he forsook the peace of the LORD and all Israel with him. 2 In the fifth year of King Rehoboam, Shishak king of Egypt came against Jerusalem (because they had transgressed the LORD). 3 With two hun- dred charets and three hundred thousand horsemen, and the people were nameless, who had come with him from Egypt, name- ly, the Lubim, the Sukkiim, and the Ethiopi- ans. 4 Then he took the strong cities of Iudah and came to Jerusalem. 5 Then Shemaiah the prophet went to Rehoboam and the princes of Iudah, who were gathered to Jerusalem be- cause of Shishak, and said to them, "Thus says the LORD, 'You have forsaken me, therefore I have left you also in the hand of Shishak.'" 6 Then the princes of Israel and the king hum- bled themselves and said, "The LORD is righ- teous." 7 When the LORD heard that they had humbled themselves, the word of the LORD came to Shemaiah, saying, "They have hum- bled themselves, therefore I will not destroy them, but I will soon send them into delight, and my wrath will not come upon Jerusalem at the hands of Shishak. 8 They shall be his servants; so they shall know my service and that of the kingdoms of the earth." 9 Then Shishak, king of Egypt, came against Jeru- salem and seized the treasures of the house of the LORD and the treasures of the king's house, and took away the shields of gold that Solomon had made. 10 Instead of these, King Rehoboam made shields of bronze and en- trusted them to the hands of the chief of the guards who stood at the edge of the king's house. 11 When the king entered the house of the LORD, the guards came and took them and brought them back to the king's chamber. 12 Because he humbled himself, the anger of the LORD departed from him, and he would not destroy them all together. And even in Iudah things prospered.13 And King Re- hoboam was strong in Jerusalem and reigned; Rehoboam was one year and forty years old when he began to reign, and he reigned seven years in Jerusalem, the city which the LORD had chosen out of all the tribes of Israel to put his name there. His mother's name was Naamah, an Ammonite. 14 He behaved bad- ly, because he did not prepare his heart to see the LORD. 15 Are not the acts of Rehoboam, the first and the last, written in the book of Shemaiah, the prophet, and Iddo, the seer, in describing the genealogy? And there was al- ways war between Rehoboam and Jeroboam. 16 Then Rehoboam fell asleep with his fathers and was buried in the city of Dauid, and Abi- jah his son reigned in his place.

CHAPTER 13

1 In the eighteenth year of King Jeroboam, Abijah began to reign over Judah. 2 He reigned three years in Jerusalem (his mother was also named Michaiah, daughter of Vriel of Gibe- ah), and there was war between Abiiah and Jeroboam. 3 Abiiah fielded a battle with an army of valiant men of war, about four hun- dred thousand chosen men. Jeroboam also took sides against him with eight hundred thousand chosen men, strong and valiant. 4 Abijah stood on Mount Zemeraim, which is on Mount Ephraim, and said, "O Jeroboam and all Israel, listen to me." 5 Do you not know that the LORD, the God of Israel, has given the kingdom of Israel to Dauid forever, to him and to his sons, by a crown of salt?" 6 Je- roboam the son of Nebat, servant of Solomon the son of Dauid, rose up and rebelled against his lord: 7 And there gathered unto him many wicked men, which made themselves strong against Rehoboam the son of Solomon: for Rehoboam was a tender-hearted child, and could not withstand them. 8 Think ye there- fore that ye can stand strong against the king- dom of the LORD, which is in the hand of the sons of Dauid; ye are a great multitude, and have with you the golden chalices which Je- roboam made for you as gods. 9 Have you not taken out of the way the priests of the LORD, the sons of Aaron and the Leuites, and made yourselves priests like the people of other countries? Those who come to consecrate with a long bull and ten rams may be priests of those who are not gods. 10 But we belong to the LORD our God, and have not forsaken him; the priests sons of Aaron serve the LORD, and the Leuites perform their function. 11 They burn before the LORD every morning and every evening the burnt offerings and the fragrant incense, and the table is set in order on the pure table, and the golden candlestick with its lamps, to burn every evening; for we watch over the LORD our God, but you have forsaken him. 12 And behold, this God is with you, as a captain, and his priests with trum- pets sounding, to shout an alarm against you. O you children of Israel, do not fight against the LORD, the God of your fathers, for you will not prosper." 13 But Jeroboam made an ambush appear and came behind them, while they were before Iudah and the ambush be- hind them. 14 Then Iudah looked, and behold, the battle was before them and behind them; and they cried unto the LORD, and the priests blew the trumpets, 15 and the men of Judah shouted; and while the men of Judah shouted, God struck Jeroboam and also Israel before Abijah and Judah. 16 The children of Israel fled before Judah, and God delivered them into their hands. 17 Abijah and his people made a great slaughter of them, so that five hundred thousand of Israel's chosen men fell wounded. 18 At that time the children of Isra- el were brought to their knees, and the sons of Iudah surrendered because they had re- mained faithful to the LORD, the God of their fathers. 19 And Abijah pursued Jeroboam and took cities from him: Beth-El and its villages, Ieshana with its villages, and Ephron with its villages. 20 Jeroboam did not regain strength in the days of Abijah, but the LORD harassed him and he died. 21 So Abijah became power- ful, married four women and begat two twen- ty-five sons and six daughters. 22 The rest of Abiiah's deeds, manners and speech are writ- ten in the stories of the prophet Iddo.

CHAPTER 14

1 So Abijah fell asleep with his fathers and they buried him in the city of Dauid, and Asa his son reigned in his place; during his days the land was quiet for ten years. 2 Asa did what was good and right in the sight of the LORD his God. 3 For he removed the altars of foreign gods and the places of worship, and took down the images and cut down the caves, 4 and commanded Iudah to see the LORD, the God of their fathers, and to conduct themselves according to Lawe and order. 5 He removed the places of worship and images from all the cities of Iudah; and the kingdom was quiet before him. 6 He also built strong cities in Iudah, because the land was at rest and he had not waged war in those years, for the LORD had granted him rest. 7 Therefore he said to Iudah, "Build these cities and build around them walls, towers, gates, and barrages, while the land is before you; for we have sought the LORD our God, we have sought him, and he has granted us rest on every side." 8 Asa had an army of Iudah bear- ing shields and spears, three hundred thou- sand people, and of Benjamin bearing shields and bows, two hundred and forty thousand people; all these were valiant men. 9 Against them went out Zerach of Ethiopia with an army of ten hundred thousand men and three hundred chariots, and came to Maresha. 10 And Asa went out before him, and they pitched the battle in the valley of Zephathah, beside Maresha. 11 And Asa cried unto the LORD his God, and said, Lord, it is nothing to thee to help with many or with any strength; help us, O LORD our God, for we trust in thee, and in thy Name we have come against this multitude: O LORD, thou art our God, and man cannot prevail against thee. 12 So the LORD struck the Ethiopians before Asa and Iudah, and the Ethiopians fled. 13 Asa and the people who were with him pursued them as far as Gerar. And the army of the Ethiopians was routed, so that there was no more life for them, for they were destroyed before the LORD and his army. 14 And they struck all the cities round about Gerar, because the fear of the LORD came upon them, and they ousted all the cities, because there was a great deal of spit in them. 15 And they struck the tents of the cattle, and took away many sheep and camels, and returned to Jerusalem.

CHAPTER 15

1 Then the Spirit of God came upon Azariah the son of Obed. 2 He went to meet Asa and said to him, "O Asa, or all Iudah and Benja- min, listen to me. The Lord is with you while you are with him; and if you seek him, he will be found by you; but if you forsake him, he will forsake you. 3 Now for a long time Israel has been without the true God, without a priest to teach and without laymen. 4 But whoever, in his affliction, returned to the LORD God of Is- rael and sought him, was found among them. 5 At that time there was no peace for those who went out and returned, but great trouble for all the inhabitants of the land. 6 For the nation was destroyed by the nation and the city by the city, because God troubled them with all adversity. 7 Therefore be strong and do not let your hands be weak, for your work will have a reward." 8 When Asa heard these words and the prophecy of Obed the prophet, he was emboldened and took away the abom- inations from all the land of Iudah and Benja- min and the cities he had taken from Mount Ephraim, and he gave up the altar of the LORD that was before the porch of the LORD. 9 He gathered all of Iudah and Benjamin and the strangers with them from Ephraim, Manasseh and Simeon, because many were those who had come to him from Israel, when they had heard that the LORD his God was with him. 10 So they gathered themselves to- gether in Jerusalem on the third month, the fifteenth year of Asa's lordship. 11 And they offered to the Lord at the same time the bread which they had brought, that is, a hundred and ninety bullocks and two hundred thou- sand sheep. 12 And they made a covenant to see the LORD, the God of their fathers, with all their heart and with all their soul. 13 Who- soever would not see the Lord God of Israel shall be killed, whether small or great, man or woman. 14 And they swore to the LORD with a loud voice, with shouting, with trumpets and with cornets. 15 And all Iudah rejoiced, because they had sworn to the LORD with all their hearts, and had sought him with all desire, and he was found by them. The LORD made them rest all around. 16 And King Asa deposed Maachah his mother from his regen- cy, because she had made an idol in a group; and Asa shattered her idol, and printed it, and burned it at the brook Kidron. 17 But the places of worship were not taken away from Israel, yet Asa's heart was wicked all his days. 18 Moreover he brought into the house of God the things which his father had consecrated and which he had hallowed, silver, gold and furnishings. 19 There was no war until the fif- tieth year of Asa's reign.

CHAPTER 16

1 In the sixtieth year of Asa's reign, Baasha, king of Israel, pushed against Iudah and built Ramah so that no one could pass through or enter Asa, king of Iudah. 2 Then Asa took out of the treasures of the house of the LORD and of the house of kings the silver and the gold and sent word to Benhadad, king of Aram who lived in Damascus, that, 3 There is a covenant between me and thee, between my father and thy father; behold, I have sent thee siluer and golde; come, break thy league with Baasha king of Israel, that he may depart from me." 4 Benhadad listened to King Asa and sent the captains of the armies he had against the cities of Israel. They defeated Iion, Dan, Abel- Maim and all the cities of Naphtali. 5 When Baasha heard this, he abandoned the building of Ramah and stopped his work. 6 Then King Asa took all Judah, and carried away the stones of Ramah and the timber with which Baasha had built, and built there Gheba and Mizpah. 7 At that same time Hanani the seer came to Asa king of Judah and said to him, "Because you have rested on the king of Aram and have not rested in the LORD your God, the army of the king of Aram has fled from your hand." 8 Were not the Ethiopians and Lubim a great army with chariots and horsemen, very nu- merous? Yet because you rested in the LORD, he delivered them into your hand. 9 Because the eyes of the LORD watch the whole earth to show himself strong with those who have a perfect heart toward him, you have acted foolishly in this; therefore from now on you will have wars. 10 Then Asa was angry with the seer and put him in prison, because he was displeased with him because of this fact. And Asa oppressed at the same time a part of the people. 11 The deeds of Asa, first and last, are written in the book of the kings of Judah and Israel. 12 Asa, in the ninth thirtieth year of his reign, was sick in his feet, and his sickness was extreme; nevertheless he did not seek the LORD during his sickness, but turned to the Physeans. 13 Asa fell asleep with his fathers and died in the fortieth year of his reign. 14 And

they buried him in one of his sepulchres, which he had had built for himself in the city of Dauid, and they laid him in the bed, which they had filled with sweet odors and different kinds of spices prepared by the art of apoth- ecary; and they burned odors for him with a very great fire.

CHAPTER 17

1 Then Jehoshaphat his son reigned in his house and made war against Israel. 2 And he put garrisons in all the strong cities of Ju- deah, and put bands in the land of Judeah and in the cities of Ephraim that Asa his father had taken. 3 The LORD was with Iehoshaphat because he walked in the first ways of his fa- ther Dauid and did not seek Baalim, 4 but he sought the LORD, the God of his father, and walked according to his commands and not according to the customs of Israel. 5 There- fore the LORD established the kingdom in his hands, and all Iudah brought gifts to Ie- hoshaphat, so that he had riches and honors in abundance. 6 He lifted up his heart to the ways of the LORD and took from Iudah other places and groups. 7 In the third year of his reign he sent his princes: Ben-Hail, Obadi- ah, Zechariah, Nethaneel and Michaiah, that they might teach in the cities of Judah, 8 And with them the Leuites, Semaiah, Nethaniah, Zebadiah, Asahel, Semiramoth, Iehonathan, Adoniiah, Tobiah and Tob-adoniiah, Leuites, and the priests Elishama and Jehoram. 9 They taught in Iudah; they had the book of the Lawe of the LORD with them; they went about all the cities of Iudah and taught the people.10 The fear of the LORD fell on all the kingdoms of the countries surrounding Iudah, and they did not fight against Ieoshaphat. 11 Moreover some of the Philistines brought gifts and trib- utc to Iehoshaphat in silence, and the Arabs brought him flocks, six thousand seven hun- dred rams, and six thousand seven hundred goats. 12 So Iehoshaphat prospered and grew rich, and built in Iudah palaces and cities of stores. 13 He did great works in the cities of Iudah, and he built in Jerusalem men of war and valiant men.14 These are their names according to the house of their fathers: in Iu- dah there were captains of thousands, Adna the captain, and with him three hundred thousand valiant men. 15 At his head was Iehohanan, captain, and with him two hun- dred and forty thousand men. 16 At his hand was Amasiah the son of Zichri, who offered himself willingly to the LORD, and with him two hundred thousand valiant men. 17 From Benjamin, Eliada, a valiant man, and with him two hundred thousand men armed with bow and shield. 18 Iehozabad, by his side, and with him a hundred and forty thousand men armed for war. 19 These awaited the king, be- sides those whom the king put in the strong cities throughout all Iudah.

CHAPTER 18

1 Iehoshaphat had riches and honors in abundance, but he was bound to Ahab. 2 After some years, he went to Ahab in Samaria; Ahab killed sheep and oxen in great numbers for him and for the people he had with him, and induced him to go to Ramoth Gilead. 3 Then Ahab king of Israel said to Iehoshaphat king of Judah, "Will you go with me to Ramoth Gilead?" And he answered him, "I am like you, and my people like your people, and we will go with you to war." 4 Then Iehoshaphat said to the king of Israel, "Take counsel, I pray you, in the word of the LORD today." 5 Therefore the king of Israel gathered from the prophets four hundred men and said to them, "Shall we go to Ramoth Gilead to fight, or shall I quit?" And they said, "Go, for God will deliver him into the king's hand." 6 But Iehoshaphat said, "Is there any other proph- et of the LORD that I can ask of him? 7 The king of Israel said to Iehoshaphat, "There is still one man to whom we could ask counsel of the LORD, but I hate him, because he does not prophesy to me well, but always evil; he is Michaiah the son of Imla." Then Iehoshaphat said, "Let not the king say so." 8 The king of Israel called a eunuch and said, "Call Mi- chaiah, son of Imla, at once." 9 And the king of Israel and Iehoshaphat king of Iudah sat on his throne, clothed in their garments, and sat on the threshing floor at the entrance to the gate of Samaria; and all the prophets prophesied before them. 10 Zidkiah the son of Chenaanah made him horns of yron and said, "Thus says the LORD: With these you shall drive the Arameans until you consume them." 11 All the prophets prophesied thus, saying, "Go to Ramoth Gilead and prosper, for the LORD will deliver it into the king's hand." 12 The messenger who went to call Michaiah spoke to him, saying, "Behold, the words of the prophets declare themselves good for the king in unison; therefore let your word, I pray you, be like theirs, and speak well." 13 Mi- chaiah said, "As the Lord wills, what my God says, I will say." 14 So he came to the king, and the king said to him, "Michaiah, shall we go to Ramoth Gilead and fight, or shall I leave?" And he answered, "Go and prosper, and they shall be delivered into your hands." 15 Then the king said to him, "How many times must I require you to tell me only the truth in the name of the LORD?" 16 Then he said, "I saw all Israel scattered on the mountains, like sheep that have no shepherd; and the LORD said, 'These have no master; let each one return to his home in peace.'" 17 And the king of Israel said to Iehoshaphat, "Did I not tell you that he would not prophesy to me good, but evil? 18 He said, "Hear therefore the word of the LORD: I see the LORD sitting on his throne, and all the armies of Heauen standing at his right hand and at his left." 19 And the LORD said, "Who shall persuade Ahab king of Isra- el to depart and fall at Ramoth Gilead?" And one spoke and said so, and another said so. 20 Then a spirit came forth and stood before the LORD and said, "I will persuade him." And the Lord said to him, "In what sense?" 21 He said, "I will go out and be a false spirit over the mouth of all his prophets." And he said, "You shall persuade and preach also; go out and do it." 22 Now, therefore, behold, the LORD has put a false spirit in the mouth of these your prophets, and the LORD has established a fi- nal judgment against you." 23 Then Zidkiah the son of Chenaanah came up, struck Mi- chaiah on the chest, and said, "By what way has the Spirit of the Lord departed from me to speak to you? 24 Michaiah said, "Behold, you will see that day when you go from room to room to hide yourself." 25 And the king of Israel said, "Take Michaiah and bring him to Amon, the ruler of the city, and to Ioash, the king's son, 26 and say to him, "Thus says the king, Put this man in the prison house and feed him with bread of affliction and water of affliction until I return in peace." 27 Michaiah said, "If you return in peace, the Lord has not spoken through me." And he said, "Take heed, all you people." 28 Then the king of Is- rael and Iehoshaphat king of Judah went to Ramoth Gilead. 29 The king of Israel said to Iehoshaphat, "I will change and enter the bat- tlefield; but you put on your clothes." The king of Israel changed and they entered the enclo- sure. 30 The king of Aram had commanded the captains of the chariots who were with him, "Fight neither with small nor with great, but only against the king of Israel." 31 When the captains of the

chariots saw Jehoshaphat, they said, "He is the king of Israel," and they clustered around him to fight. But Jehoshaphat cried out, and the LORD helped him and made them turn away from him. 32 For when the captains of the chariots saw that he was not the king of Israel, they turned away from him. :33 Then a certain man with a mighty weapon struck the king of Israel be- tween the teeth of his brig: Therefore he said to his companion, "Turn your hand and take me away from the army, for I am wounded." 34 On that day the battle intensified, and the king of Israel stood firm in his huddle against the Arameans until dawn and died at sunset.

CHAPTER 19

1 Iehoshaphat, king of Iudah, returned safe- ly to his house in Jerusalem. 2 Then Iehu the son of Hanani the seer came to him and said to King Iehoshaphat, "Do you want to help the wicked and please those who hate the LORD? Therefore the anger of the LORD is upon you. 3 Good things are found in you, because you have taken the wicked out of the land and prepared your heart to see God." 4 Then Iehoshaphat settled in Jerusalem, and returned and reviewed the people from Beer-sheba to Mount Ephraim and led them back to the LORD, the God of their fathers. 5 And he established judges in the land in all the strong cities of Iudah, city by city, 6 and said to the judges, "Take heed to what you do, for you do not execute the judgments of man, but of the LORD, and he will be with you in the cause and in the judgment." 7 Therefore now the fear of the LORD be upon you; take heed and do it, for there is no iniquity with the LORD our God, nor respect for persons, nor reward. 8 And at Jerusalem Iehoshaphat gathered together the Leuites and the priests and the heads of the families of Israel for the judgment and the cause of the LORD, and they returned to Jerusale. 9 And he charged them, saying, "Thus you shall do in the fear of the LORD, faithfully and with a perfect heart." 10 In all the cases that shall come before you among your brethren dwelling in their cities, between blood and blood, between law and precept, between statutes and judgments, you shall judge them and admonish them lest they commit transgressions against the Lord, lest wrath come upon you and your brethren. This you shall do and not transgress. 11 Ama- riah the priest shall be the head of you in all the affairs of the LORD; Zebadiah the son of Ishmael, the head of the house of Iudah, shall be in charge of all the king's affairs, and the Leuites shall be officers before you. Be coura- geous and do this, and the Lord will be with the good.

CHAPTER 20

1 After this also came the sons of Moab and the sons of Ammon, and with them the Am- monites, against Iehoshaphat to fight. 2 Then witnesses came and said to Iehoshaphat, "A great crowd has come against you from Aram, beyond the sea; and behold, they are in Haz- zon Tamar, which is En-Gedi." 3 Iehoshaphat was afraid, and he looked to the LORD and proclaimed a fast throughout all Iudah. 4 And Iudah gathered together to ask counsel of the LORD; they came from all the cities of Iudah to ask counsel of the LORD, 5 And Ie- hoshaphat stood in the congregation of Iudah and Jerusalem, in the house of the LORD, be- fore the new courtyard, 6 and said, "O LORD, God of our fathers, are not you God in heaven, and do you

not reign over all the kingdoms of the heathen? In your hand is power and strength, and no one can resist you. 7 Have not you, our God, driven out the inhabitants of this land before your people Israel and giv- en it as an inheritance to the descendants of Abraham, your friend, forever? 8 They dwelt there and built there a sanctuary for your Name, saying, 9 "If the sword of judgment or pestilence or famine comes upon us, we will stand before this house and in your presence (for your name is in this house) and call upon you in our tribulation, and you will hear us and help us." 10 Behold, the sons of Ammon, and of Moab, and of mount Seir, by whom thou didst not intend that Israel should pass when they came out of the land of Egypt; but they departed from them, and did not de- stroy them: 11 Behold, I say, they reward vs, coming to drive them out of thy inheritance, which thou hast made to inherit vs. 12 O our God, wilt thou not judge them? For there is no strength in vs to resist this great multitude that comes against vs, nor do we know what to do; but our eyes are turned to you." 13 All Iu- dah stood before the LORD with their young men, their wives and their children. 14 There was Iahaziel the son of Zechariah, the son of Benaiah, the son of Ieiel, the son of Mattani- ah, a Leuite of the sons of Asaph, on whom the Spirit of the LORD rested, in the midst of the congregation. 15 He said, "Listen, all Iuda, you inhabitants of Jerusalem and you, King Ieoshaphat, thus says the LORD to you: Do not fear or be afraid of this great crowd, for the battle is not yours, but of the gods." 16 For the rest, go down against them; behold, they pass through the cleft of Ziz, and you will find them at the end of the brooke, before the wil- derness of Ieruel. 17 You will not need to fight in this battle; stand still, do not move, and behold, the greeting of the LORD to you: O Judah and Jerusalem, do not fear or be afraid; now go out against them, and the LORD will be with you." 18 Then Jehoshaphat prostrated himself with his face to the ground, and all Judah and the inhabitants of Jerusalem pros- trated themselves before the Lord, worship- ing the Lord. 19 The Leuites, the sons of the Kohathites and the sons of the Korhites stood up to pray to the LORD, the God of Israel, with a ringing voice. 20 When they rose early in the morning, they set out for the wilderness of Tekoa; and as they set out, Iehoshaphat stopped and said, "Listen to me, O Iudah and inhabitants of Jerusalem; put your trust in the LORD your God, and you will be secure; listen to his prophets and you will prosper." 21 After he had consulted with the people and invited the singers to pray to the LORD and those who were to pray to him who is in the beau- tiful sanctuary, he stood before the armed men and said, "Pray to the LORD, for his mercy endures forever." 22 When they began to shout and pray, the LORD ambushed the sons of Ammon, Moab and Mount Seir, who had come against Iudah, and they killed each other. 23 For the sons of Ammon and Moab rose up against the inhabitants of Mount Seir, to kill and destroy them, and when they had taken out the inhabitants of Seir, each one helped to destroy the other. 24 When Iehoshaph came toward Mizpah in the wil- derness, he looked at the crowd; and behold, the carcasses had fallen to the ground, and no one had escaped. 25 And when Iehoshaphat and his men came to carry away the spoil, they found abundance of substance among them, and also of bodies laden with precious jewels, which they took for themselves, until they could carry no more. 26 On the fourth day they gathered themselves together in the valley of Beracha, for there they blessed the Lord; for this reason they still call that place the "valley of Beracha." 27 Then all the men of Judeah and Jerusalem returned with Ie- hoshaphat their leader, to return to Jerusalem with joy, because the LORD had brought them out of their enemies. 28 They came to Jerusa- lem with violins, harps and trumpets, to go to the house of the LORD. 29 All the kingdoms of the earth were afraid of God, having heard that the LORD had fought against Israel's en- emies. 30 So the kingdom of Iehoshaphat was quiet, and his God made him rest on all sides. 31 And Iehoshaphat reigned outside Iudah, and he was fifty-two years old when he be- gan to reign; and he reigned fifty-two years in Jerusalem, and his mother's name was Azu- bah, the daughter of Shilhi. 32 He followed the way of Asa, his father, and did not deviate from it, doing what was right in the eyes of the LORD. 33 However, the places of worship were not taken away, because the people had not yet prepared their hearts to the God of their fathers. 34 As for the rest of the deeds of Iehoshaphat, first and last, behold, they are written in the book of Jehu the son of Hanani, which is mentioned in the book of the kings of Israel. 35 After this deed, Iehoshaphat, king of Iudah, joined himself to Ahaziah, king of Israel, who was ready to do evil. 36 And he agreed with him to build ships to go to Tarsh- ish; and they built the ships at Ezion Gaber. 37 Then Eliezer the son of Dodauah of Maresha prophesied against Iehoshaphat, saying, "Be- cause you have committed yourself to Ahazi- ah, the LORD has destroyed your works." And the ships were destroyed, so that they could not go to Tarshish.

CHAPTER 21

1 Then Jehoshaphat fell asleep with his fa- thers and was buried with his fathers in the city of Dauid; and Jehoram his son reigned in his place. 2 The sons of Iehoshaphat were his brothers: Azariah, Jehicl, Zechariah, Azariah, Michael, and Shephatiah. All these were sons of Jehoshaphat, king of Israel. 3 Their father gave them great gifts of silk, gold and pre- cious things, with strong cities in Iudah, but the kingdom was given to Jehoram, because he was the eldest. 4 And Iehoram rose up from his father's kingdom, and made himself strong, and slew all his brethren by the sword, and also the princes of Israel. 5 Iehoram was two and thirty years old when he began to reign, and he reigned for a year in Jerusalem. 6 He followed the way of the kings of Israel, as the house of Ahab had done, because he had taken Ahab's daughter to wife and had done well in the eyes of the LORD. 7 Nevertheless the LORD would not destroy the house of Dauid, because of the covenant he had made with Dauid and because he had promised to give him and his sons a light forever. 8 In his day Edom rebelled under the hand of Iudah and made himself a king out of them. 9 And Jehoram departed with his princes and all his chiefs; and he rose up by night and de- feated Edom, who had surrounded him, and the chiefs of the chiefs. 10 But Edom rebelled from under the hand of Iudah to this day; Libnah also rebelled at the same time from under his hand, because he had forsaken the Lord God of his fathers. 11 Moreover, he set- tled in the mountains of Iudah and caused the inhabitants of Jerusalem to commit forni- cation, forcing Iudah to do so. 12 There came to him a writing from Elijah the prophet, saying, "Thus says the LORD, God of Dauid, your father: For you have not walked in the ways of Iehoshaphat your father, nor in the ways of Asa, king of Iudah, 13 But thou hast followed the way of the kings of Israel, and hast caused Judah and the inhabitants of Je- rusalem to whore themselves, as the house of Ahab whored itself; and thou hast also slain thy brethren of thy father's house, who were better than thyself, 14 Behold, the LORD shall smite with a great plague thy people, and thy sons, and thy wives, and all thy possessions, 15 And thou shalt be in the grip of great diseases of the bowels, until thy bowels fall out of sick- ness day by day." 16 Then the LORD aroused against Jehoram the spirit of the Philistines and the Arabs who were beside the Ethiopi- ans. 17 And they came to Iudah, and raided it, and took away all the substance that was in the king's house, and his sons and his wives, so that there was no son left to him, like Ie- hoahaz, the youngest of his sons. 18 After all this, the LORD struck him in the bowels with an incurable disease. 19 Afterwards, after two years, his bowels dissolved because of his dis- ease; so he died of a severe disease, and his people did not make for him a stake like that of his fathers. 20 When he began to reign, he was two and thirty years old, and reigned in Jerusalem for eight years, and died without being desired; yet they buried him in the city of Dauid, but not among the sepulchres of the kings.

CHAPTER 22

1 The inhabitants of Jerusalem made the youngest son of Ahaziah king, in his house- hold, because the army that had come with the Arabs to the camna had killed all the el- ders; therefore Ahaziah, son of Jehoram, king of Judah, reigned. 2 Ahaziah was two years old and forty when he began to reign; he reigned one year in Jerusalem, and his moth- er's name was Athaliah, daughter of Omri. 3 He too followed the ways of the house of Ahab, for his mother advised him to behave wickedly. 4 Therefore he did evil in the eyes of the LORD, like the house of Ahab, for they were his counselors after the death of his fa- ther, for his destruction. 5 He followed their counsel and went with Jehoram the son of Ahab, king of Israel, to fight against Hazael, king of Aram, at Ramoth Gilead; and the Ar- amites defeated Jehoram. 6 And he went back to be healed in Izreel, because of the wounds that had been inflicted on him at Ramah, when he had fought against Hazael, king of Aram. Azariah the son of Jehoram, king of Iudah, went to visit Jehoram the son of Ahab in Izreel, because he was sick. 7 The destruc- tion of Ahab took place by God's work when he went to Ioram; for when he had arrived, he went with Iehoram against Jehu the son of Nimshi, whom the LORD had anointed to destroy the house of Ahab. 8 When Jehu made judgment on the house of Ahab and found the princes of Iudah and the sons of Ahab's broth- ers waiting at Ahab's, he killed them also. 9 Then he sought Ahaziah, and they took him where he was hiding in Samaria, and brought him to Iehu, and killed him, and buried him; for, they said, he is the son of Jehoshaphat, who sought the Lord with all his heart. Thus the house of Ahaziah was unable to restore the kingdom. 10 When Athaliah, the mother of Ahaziah, heard that her son was dead, she arose and destroyed all the sons of the kings of the house of Iudah. 11 But Iehoshabeath, the king's daughter, took Ioash the son of Ahaziah, and put him among the king's sons who were to be killed, and put him with his granddaughter in the bedchamber; so Ie- hoshabeath the daughter of king Jehoram, the wife of Jehoiada the priest (for she was the sister of Ahaziah), hid him from Ataliah; so he did not kill him. 12 He remained with them hidden in the house of God for six years while Ataliah reigned over the land.

CHAPTER 23

1 In the seventh year Iehoiada strengthened himself and took with him the captains of the centenarians, that is, Azariah the son of Jero- ham, Ishmael the son of Iehohanan, Azariah the son of Obed, Maasiah the son of Adaiah, and Elishaphat the son of Zichri. 2 Then they went to Judah and gathered the Leuites from all the cities of Judah and the principal fathers of Israel, and they came to Ierusale. 3 All the congregation gathered with the king into the house of God, and he said to them, "Behold, the king's son is to reign as the LORD said of the sons of Dauid. 4 This is what you are to do: the third part of you who come on the Sabbath of the priests and the leuids shall be porters of the houses. 5 Another third part to- ward the king's house, and another third part at the gate of the foundation; all the people shall stand in the courts of the house of the LORD. 6 But let no one enter into the house of the LORD, except the priests and the Leuites who serve; they shall go in, for they are holy; but all the people shall guard the LORD. 7 And the Leuites shall compact the king all around, and every man with a weapon in his hand; and whosoever shall enter into the house shall be slain, and shall be with the king, when he goes in and when he goes out. 8 So the Leuites and all Iudah did all that Iehoiada the priest had commanded, and they took every man his men who came on the Sabbath and those who went out on the Sabbath, because Iehoia- da the priest had not made the courses. 9 And Iehoiada the priest delivered to the captains of hundreds spears, shields, and bucklers that had been King Dauidi's and were in the house of God. 10 Then he had all the people stop (each with his weapon in his hand) from the right side of the house, to the left side of the house, by the altar and the house around the king. 11 Then they brought out the king's son, and put the crown upon him, and gave him the testimony, and made him king. And Jehoiada and his sons anoinized him and said, "God said the king." 12 But when Atali- ah heard the noise of the people running and praising the king, he came with the people into the house of the LORD. 13 And when she looked, behold, the king was standing by his pillar at the entrance, and the princes and the trumpets by the king, and all the people of the land were gathered together and sounded the trumpets, and the singers were with musical instruments, and those who could sing were praying; then Ataliah tore her clothes and said, "Treason, treason." 14 Then Iehoiada the priest brought out the captains of hundreds of soldiers from the army and said to them, "Take her out of the fields, and let those who follow her die by the sword, for the priest had said, Do not kill her in the house of the Lord." 15 So they laid hands on her; and when she had come to the entrance of the horse gate by the king's house, they killed her there. 16 And Jehoiada established a covenant between him and all the people and the king, that they should be the people of the LORD. 17 All the people went to the house of Baal, destroyed its altars and images, and killed Mattan, priest of Baal, before the altars. 18 And Je- hoiada appointed officers for the house of the LORD, under the hands of the priests and the leuites whom Dauid had distributed for the house of the LORD, to offer burnt offerings to the LORD, as it is written in the Law of Moses, with songs and chants by the order of Dauid. 19 He put porters at the doors of the house of the LORD, so that no one who was vncleane in anything would enter. 20 Then he took the captains of hundreds, and the nobles, and the leaders of the people, and all the people of the land, and brought down the king from the house of the LORD, and they went to the gate of the king's house, and set the king on the throne of the kingdom. 21 Then all the people of the

land recovered, and the city be- came quiet, after they had slain Ataliah with the sword.

CHAPTER 24

1 Ioash was ten years old when he began to reign and reigned forty years in Jerusalem; his mother's name was Zibiah of Beer-sheba. 2 Ioash behaved well before the LORD all the days of Iehoiada the priest. 3 Iehoiada took him two wives, and he begat sons and daugh- ters. 4 Then Ioash thought to renew the house of the LORD. 5 And he gathered the priests and the Leuites and said to them, "Go to the cities of Iudah and collect from all Israel money to repair the house of your God from year to year, and make haste to do it"; but the Leuites did not make haste. 6 Therefore the king called Iehoiada, the chief, and said to him, "Why did you not ask the Leuiti to bring from Iudah and Jerusalem the tax of Moses, the servant of the LORD, and of the congre- gation of Israel for the Tabernacle of Testi- mony? 7 For the wicked Athaliah and her sons ravaged the house of God; and all the things that had been dedicated to the house of the LORD they gave to Baalim. 8 Therefore the king gave orders to build a coffer and place it outside the gate of the house of the LORD. 9 They made a proclamation throughout all Ju- dah and Jerusalem to bring to the LORD the tribute of Moses, God's servant, imposed on Israel in the wilderness. 10 All the princes and all the people assembled, brought and cast into the chest, until they were finished. 11 And when it was time, they brought the chest to the king's official by the hand of the Leuites; and when they saw that there was much clay, the king's scribe (and one appointed by the priest) came and emptied the chest, and took it, and brought it again to its place; so they did day by day, and gathered clay in abundance. 12 The king and Jehoiada gave it to those who worked in the house of the LORD, to the ma- sons and carpenters to repay the house of the LORD; they also gave it to the iron and reed workers, to repay the house of the LORD. 13 So the workers worked, and the work was mend- ed with their hands; and they put the house of God back in its state and strengthened it. 14 And when they had finished it, they brought the remnant of the torpedo before the king and Iehoiada, who made of it furnishings for the house of the LORD, that is, vessels for religious services, vessels for incense, vessels of gold and torpedo; and they offered burn- ings continually in the house of the LORD all the days of Iehoiada. 15 But Iehoiada grew old, and was full of days, and was dyed. He was a hundred and thirty years old when he died. 16 They buried him in the city of Dauid with the kings, because he had done good in Israel, toward God and toward his house. 17 After the death of Jehoiada, the princes of Iudah came and addressed the king; the king listened to them. 18 They forsook the house of the LORD, the God of their fathers, and went into the service of groups and idols; and wrath came upon Judah and Jerusalem be- cause of this their fault. 19 God sent prophets among them to lead them back to the Lord; they made protests among themselves, but they would not listen. 20 The Spirit of God de- scended on Zechariah the son of Jehoiada the priest, who stood before the people and said to them, "Thus says God, 'Why do you trans- gress the commands of the Lord? Surely you will not prosper; because you have forsaken the Lord, he also has forsaken you.'" 21 Then they conspired against him and stoned him with stones at the king's command in the courtyard of the house of the LORD. 22 So Ioas the king did not remember the kindness that Jehoiada

his father had done to him, but killed his son. And when he died, he said, "The LORD has watched and willed." 23 And at the expiration of the year, the army of Aram came against him, and came against Iudah and Je- rusalem, and destroyed all the princes of the people, and sent all the spouses to the king of Damascus. 24 Although the army of Aram had come with a small company of men, the LORD delivered into their hands a very large army, because they had forsaken the LORD, the God of their fathers; and they spoke against Ioash. 25 And when they departed from him (for they left him in great diseases) his own ser- vants conspired against him by the blood of the sons of the priest Jehoiada, and they slew him on his bed, and he died, and they buried him in the city of Dauid; but they did not bury him in the sepulchres of the kings. 26 These are they who conspired against him, Zabad the son of Shimrath, an Ammonite, and Je- hozabad the son of Shimrith, a Moabite. 27 But his sons, the sum of the taxes collected by him and the foundation of the house of God, behold, they are written in the history of the book of Kings. Amaziah, his son, reigned in his house.

CHAPTER 25

1 Amaziah was five years old and twenty when he began to reign and reigned nine years and twenty in Jerusalem; his mother's name was Jehoaddan, from Jerusalem. 2 He behaved well in the eyes of the LORD, but not with a perfect heart. 3 When the king- dom was established for him, he killed his servants who had killed his father the king. 4 But he did not kill their sons, but did as it is written in the Lawe and in the book of Mo- ses, where the Lord commanded, "Fathers shall not die for sons, nor shall sons die for fathers, but each shall die for his own sin." 5 And Amaziah gathered Iudah and appointed them captains of thousands and captains of hundreds, according to the houses of their fathers, throughout all Iudah and Benjamin; and he appointed them from twenty years old and upward, and found among them three hundred thousand chosen men to go to war and wield spear and shield. 6 He also asked Israel for a hundred thousand valiant men for a hundred talents of silver. 7 But a man of God said to him, "O king, do not let the army of Israel go with you, for the LORD is not with Israel nor with all the house of Ephraim. 8 If not, go forth, do your battle, but God will bring you down before the enemy, for God has power to help and to bring down." 9 Ama- ziah said to the man of God, "What shall we do then for the hundred talents I have given to the army of Israel?" Then the man of God answered, "The Lord is able to give you more than that." 10 Then Amaziah separated them, that is, the army that had come to him from Ephraim, that they might return to their places; therefore their anger was kindled greatly against Iudah, and they returned to their places in great anger. 11 Then Amaziah encouraged himself, and led his people, and went into the valley of salt, and defeated the sons of Seir in ten thousand. 12 And the sons of Iudah took ten thousand more people, and brought them to the top of a tower, and cast them down from the top of the tower, and cut them all to pieces. 13 But the men of the army, whom Amaziah had sent away so that they would not go and fight with his people, came down upon the cities of Iudah from Samaria as far as Beth-horon, struck three thousand of them, and made much meat of them. 14 Now after Amaziah had returned from the slaughter of the Edomites, he brought with him the gods of the sons of Seir, made them his gods, worshiped them, and burned in- cense in their honor. 15 Therefore the LORD was angry with Amaziah and sent a prophet to him who said, "Why did you seek the gods of the people, who were not able to deliver their people out of your hands? 16 While he was talking with him, he said to him, "Have they made you a counselor to the kings? Stop doing that, why should they strike you?" The prophet stopped and said, "I know that God has decided to destroy you, because you did this and did not obey my advice." 17 Then Amaziah, king of Iudah, took counsel and sent word to Ioash, son of Jehoahaz, son of Jehu, king of Israel, "Come, let us face each other." 18 But Ioash, king of Israel, sent word to Amaziah, king of Iudah, "The thistle that is in Lebanon sent word to the cedar tree that is in Lebanon, 'Give your daughter to my son in marriage'; and the wild beast that was in Lebanon went and trampled the thistle. 19 You think, "Behold, you have defeated Edom, and your heart urges you to boast; now stay in your house; why do you prostrate yourself to hurt yourself, and to bring down Iudah with you?" 20 But Amaziah would not listen, for God wanted them delivered to him, because they had sought the gods of Edom. 21 Then Ioash, king of Israel, went forth; and he and Amaziah, king of Judah, saw each other in the face of Bet-shemesh, which is in Judah. 22 And Judah was brought to his knees before Israel, and every one fled to his tents. 23 But Joash king of Israel took Amaziah king of Ju- dah, the son of Joash son of Jehoahaz, to Beth-shemesh, and brought him to Jerusalem, and brought down the walls of Jerusalem, from the gate of Ephraim to the corner gate, four hundred cubits. 24 And he took all the gold and silver and all the utensils that were in the house of God with Obed Edom, and the treasures of the king's house, and the chil- dren that were as hostages, and returned to Samaria. 25 Amaziah the son of Ioash, king of Judah, remained in office fifty years after the death of Ioash the son of Jehoahaz, king of Is- rael. 26 As for the rest of Amaziah's acts, first and last, are they not written in the book of the kings of Judah and Israel? 27 After Ama- ziah had departed from the Lord, they made treachery against him in Jerusalem; and when he had fled to Lachish, they pursued him and killed him in Lachish. 28 And they took him on horseback and buried him with his fathers in the city of Iudah.

CHAPTER 26

1 Then all the people of Iudah took Vzziah, who was sixty years old, and made him king instead of his father Amaziah. 2 He bought Eloth and returned it to Iudah, after the king had slept with his fathers. 3 Vzziah was sixty years old when he began to reign; he reigned for two years and fifty in Jerusalem, and his mother's name was Jecoliah of Jerusalem. 4 He behaved well before the LORD, as his fa- ther Amaziah had done. 5 He sought God in the days of Zechariah (who vndersto the vi- sions of God), and when he sought the Lord, God prospered him. 6 Indeed, he set out and fought against the Philistines and tore down the walls of Gath, the walls of Jabneh and the walls of Ashdod, built cities in Ashdod and among the Philistines. 7 God helped him against the Philistines and against the Arabs who dwelt in Gur-Baal and Hammeunim. 8 The Ammonites offered gifts to Vzziah, and his name spread to the entrance of Egypt, for he did very well. 9 Moreover Uzziah bought towers in Jerusalem, at the corner gate, at the valley gate and at the turning, and made them strong. 10 He built towers in the wilder- ness and dug many cisterns, because he had many cattle in the valleys and fields, plough- men

and vinedressers in the mountains and in Mount Carmel, for he loved maritime. 11 Vzziah also had a host of fighters who went to war by bands, according to the counting of their names, under the hand of Ieiel, the scribe, Maaseiah, the chief, and under the hand of Hananiah, one of the king's captains. 12 The sum total of the heads of the fami- lies of the valiant was two thousand and six hundred men. 13 Under their hands was the war army: three hundred thousand men and five hundred fighting valiantly to help the king against the enemy. 14 Vzziah prepared shields, spears, helmets, brigs, bows and stones for the whole army to hurl. 15 He also made very artificial engines in Jerusalem, to be placed on the towers and corners, to shoot arrows and great stones; and his name spread everywhere, because God helped him won- derfully, until he was strong. 16 But when he was strong, his heart was lifted up to destruc- tion, because he transgressed the LORD his God, and entered the Temple of the LORD to burn incense on the altar of incense. 17 After him Azariah the priest entered, and with him four priests of the LORD, valiant men. 18 They intimated to Vzziah the king and said to him, "It is not for you, Vzziah, to burn incense to the LORD, but for the priests sons of Aaron, who are consecrated to offer incense; leave the sanctuary, for you have transgressed and will have no honor with the LORD God." 19 Then Vzziah was wroth, and he had incense in his hand to bury him; and while he was wroth with the priests, leprosy sprang up on his forehead before the priests in the house of the LORD, beside the altar of incense. 20 And when Azariah, the chief of the priests, and all the priests looked at him, behold, he was lep- rous in the forehead, and they made him de- part in haste; and he was forced out, because the LORD had smitten him. 21 And King Vz- ziah was a leper until the day of his death, and he dwelt as a leper in an isolated house, because he had been cut off from the house of the LORD; and Iotham his son reigned out- side the king's house, and ruled the people of the land. 22 About the rest of Vzziah's deeds, the first and the last, wrote Isaiah, the proph- et son of Amoz. 23 And Vzziah fell asleep with his fathers, and they buried him with his fa- thers in the burial ground that was the right of kings, for they said, "He is a leper." And Io- tham his son reigned in his place.

CHAPTER 27

1 Iotham was fifty-two years old when he be- gan to reign and reigned sixty years in Jerusa- lem; his mother's name was Jerushah, daugh- ter of Zadok. 2 He did well in the eyes of the LORD all that his father Vzziah had done, for he did not enter the temple of the LORD, and the people continued to corrupt his ways. 3 He bought the gate of the house of the LORD and bought much on the wall of the castle. 4 Moreover he bought cities on the mountains of Iudah, and in the forests he bought palaces and towers. 5 He fought with the king of the sons of Ammon and fought against them. In the same year the sons of Ammon gave him a hundred talents of torpedo, ten thousand measures of wheat and ten thousand mea- sures of barley; this the sons of Ammon gave him in both the second and the third year. 6 Thus Iotham became powerful because he directed his way before the LORD his God. 7 The rest of Iotham's deeds, all his wars and his ways, are written in the book of the kings of Israel and Iudah. 8 He was fifty-two years old when he began to reign and reigned for sixty years in Jerusalem. 9 And Iotham fell asleep with his fathers, and they buried him in the city of Dauid; in his place reigned Ahaz his son.

CHAPTER 28

1 Ahaz was twenty years old when he began to reign; he reigned for sixty years in Jerusalem and did not behave well before the LORD, like Dauid his father. 2 But he followed the ways of the kings of Israel and built molten imag- es for Baalim. 3 Moreover he burned incense in the valley of Ben-Hinnom and burned his sons with fire, according to the abominations of the heathen whom the LORD had cast out before the children of Israel. 4 He sacrificed and burned incense even in isolated places, on hills and under every green tree. 5 There- fore the LORD his God delivered him into the hands of the king of the Arameans, who defeated him and took many captives and brought them to Damascus; and he was also delivered into the hands of the king of Israel, who defeated him with a great slaughter. 6 Pekah, son of Remaliah, slew at Judah in one day six thousand valiant men, because they had forsaken the Lord God of their fathers. 7 Zichri, a mighty man of Ephraim, killed Maaseiah, the king's son, Azrikam, the head of the house, and Elkanah, the king's second. 8 And the children of Israel took their breth- ren captive, two thousand women, sons and daughters, and carried away much of their flesh, and brought it to Samaria. 9 But there was a prophet of the LORD (whose name was Oded), who went out before the army com- ing to Samaria and said to them, "Behold, because the LORD, the God of your fathers, is angry with Judah, he has delivered them into your hands, and you have slain them with an anger that reaches as far as Heauen. 10 Now you intend to keep the sons of Judah and Jerusalem in check, as servants and help- ers to you; but are you not such as sin before the LORD your God? 11 Now therefore listen to me and release again the captives whom you have taken captive from among your brethren, for the fierce anger of the LORD is toward you. 12 Therefore some of the leaders of the sons of Ephraim, Azariah the son of Ie- hohanan, Berechiah the son of Meshillemoth, Jehizkiah the son of Shallum, and Amasa the son of Hadlai, opposed those who came from the war, 13 and said to them, "Do not let the captives come in here, for this will be a sin against the LORD; you intend to increase our sins and our faults, even though our faults are great and the fierce wrath of God is against Israel." 14 So the army left the captives and spit before the princes and the whole commu- nity. 15 And the men who had been called by name arose, and took the captives, and with the spoyle clothed all who were naked among them, and healed them, and shoed them, and gave them food, and water, and refreshed them, and loaded on donkeys all who were weak, and brought them to Jericho, the city of Palms, to their brethren; so they returned to Samaria. 16 At that time King Ahaz appealed to the kings of Assur to help him. 17 Because the Edomites came still more, they killed Iudah and took captives away. 18 The Philis- tines also conquered the cities of the lower county and the south of Judah, and took Bet- Scemesh, Aialon, Gederoth and Shocho, with their villages, Timna with its villages, and Gimzo with its villages, and settled there. 19 For the LORD had humbled Iudah because of Ahaz, king of Israel, who took vengeance on Iudah and transgressed the LORD grievous- ly). 20 Tilgath Pilneeser, king of Assur, caught up with him and troubled him and did not strengthen him. 21 And Ahaz took a part of the house of the LORD, of the house of kings and princes, and gave it to the king of Assur, but it did not profit him. 22 In the time of his tribulation he still committed other offenses against the

LORD (this is King Ahaz). 23 For he sacrificed to the gods of Damascus who afflicted him, and said, "Because the gods of the kings of Aram helped them, I will sacrifice to them and they will help me; yet they were his ruin and that of all Israel." 24 Then Ahaz gathered up the furnishings of the house of God, broke down the furniture of the house of God, shut the doors of the house of the LORD, and made altars in every corner of Jerusalem. 25 In every city of Iudah he created places to burn incense to other gods and provoked the anger of the LORD, the God of his fathers. 26 As for the rest of his deeds and all his ways, from first to last, behold, they are written in the book of the kings of Judah and Israel. 27 And Ahaz fell asleep with his fathers, and they buried him in the city of Jerusalem, but they did not take him to the sepulchres of the kings of Israel; in his place reigned Hezekiah his son.

CHAPTER 29

1 Hezekiah began to reign at the age of five years and twenty, and reigned nine years and twenty in Jerusalem; his mother's name was Abijah, daughter of Zechariah. 2 He behaved well in the eyes of the Lord, according to what Dauid his father had done. 3 He opened the gates of the house of the LORD in the first year and month of his reign and prepared them. 4 And he brought in the priests and the Leuites and gathered them into the eastern way, 5 and said to them, "Listen to me, you Leuites: sanc- tify yourselves now and sanctify the house of the LORD, the God of your fathers, and take away the filth from the sanctuary. 6 For our fathers have transgressed and done evil in the sight of the LORD our God, and have forsaken him, and have turned their faces away from the Tabernacle of the LORD, and have turned their backs. 7 They also closed the doors of the porch, put out the lamps, did not burn incense, and did not offer sacrifices in the sanctuary to the God of Israel. 8 Therefore the wrath of the LORD came upon Iudah and Je- rusalem, and made them a scattering, a des- olation, and a hissing, as you see with your own eyes. 9 For behold, our fathers have fallen by the sword, and our sons and our daughters and our wives are in captivity for the same cause. 10 Now I intend to make an agreement with the LORD, the God of Israel, that he will turn away his fierce anger from us. 11 Now, my sons, do not deceive yourselves, for the Lord has chosen you to stand before him, to serve him, to be his ministers and to burn in- cense." 12 Then the Leuites stood up: Mahath the son of Amashai, and Ioel the son of Azari- ah, of the sons of the Kohathites; of the sons of Merari, Kish the son of Abdi, and Azariah the son of Jehalel; of the Gersonites, Ioah the son of Zimmah, and Eden the son of Ioah: 13 Of the sons of Elizafan, Shimri and Jehiel; of the sons of Asaph, Zechariah and Mattaniah: 14 Of the sons of Heman, Iehiel and Shimei; of the sons of Ieduthun, Semaiah and Vzziel. 15 And they gathered their brethren togeth- er, and sanctified themselves, and came ac- cording to the king's commandment and the words of the LORD, to secure the house of the LORD. 16 And the priests went into the inte- rior of the house of the LORD, to set it in or- der, and brought out all the vncleanness that they found in the temple of the LORD, into the court of the house of the LORD; and the Leuites took it to carry it as far as the brook Kidron. 17 And they began to sanctify it on the first day of the first month, and on the eighth day of the month they came to the porch of the LORD; so they sanctified the house of the LORD in eight days, and on the sixteenth day of the first month they made an end of it. 18 Then they came

in to King Hezekiah and said, "We have sanctified the whole house of the LORD, the altar of burnt offerings and all its utensils, the table of loaves and all its utensils: 19 And all the utensils which king Ahaz had set aside when he reigned and transgressed, we have prepared and sanctified them; and behold, they are before the altar of the LORD." 20 King Hezekiah rose early, gathered the princes of the city, and went to the house of the LORD. 21 They brought ten cattle, ten rams, ten lambs and ten goats, as a sacrifice for the kingdom, for the sanctuary and for Iudah. And he commanded the priests, the sons of Aaron, to offer them on the altar of the LORD. 22 So they killed the bullocks, and the priests received their blood and sprinkled it on the altar; they also killed the rams and sprinkled their blood on the altar; they killed the lambs and sprinkled their blood on the al- tar. 23 Then they brought the goats for the sin offering before the king and the congregation and laid their hands on them. 24 The priests killed them and with their blood covered the altar to reconcile all Israel, for the king had ordained for all Israel the burnt offering and the sin offering. 25 Moreover in the house of the LORD he appointed the Leuites with cym- bals, with viols, and with harps, according to the order of Dauid, of Gad the king's seer, and of Nathan the prophet; for the order had been given by the hand of the LORD and by the hand of his prophets. 26 The Leuites stood with Dauid's instruments and the priests with trumpets. 27 Hezekiah ordered the burnt of- fering to be offered on the altar; and when the burnt offering began, the singing of the LORD began with the trumpets and instru- ments of Dauid, king of Israel. 28 And all the congregation worshipped, singing a song and blowing trumpets; all this until the burnt of- fering was finished. 29 When they had made an end of the burnt offering, the king and all who were present with him bowed down and prostrated themselves. 30 Then King Hezeki- ah and the princes commanded the Leuites to pray to the LORD with the words of Dauid and Asaph the seer; so they prayed with joy, bowed down, and worshiped. 31 Hezekiah spoke and said, "Now you have consecrated yourselves to the Lord; come here and bring sacrifices and prayer offerings to the house of the Lord." 31 The congregation brought sacri- fices and prayer offerings, and all who were willing offered burnt offerings. 32 The name of the burnt offerings which the congrega- tion brought was seventy bullocks, a hundred rams, and two hundred lambs; all these were for burnt offerings to the Lord: 33 and for sanctification six hundred calves and three thousand sheep. 34 But the priests were too few, and were not able to flay all the burnt of- ferings; therefore their brethren, the Leuites, helped them, until they had finished the work, and until other priests were sanctified; for the Leuites had more heart to sanctify themselves than the priests. 35 Also the burnt offerings were many, with the fat of the peace offerings and the wine offerings for the burnt offerings, and so the service of the house of the LORD was in order. 36 Then Hezekiah and all the people repented that God had made the people so ready, because the thing had been done suddenly.

CHAPTER 30

1 Hezekiah sent to all Israel and Judah and also wrote letters to Ephraim and Manasseh to come to the house of the LORD in Jerusa- lem to celebrate the feast of the LORD, the God of Israel. 2 The king, his princes and the whole community had agreed in Jerusalem to celebrate the

Passover in the second month. 3 For they could not celebrate it at this time, because there were no sufficiently sanctified priests and the people were not gathered in Jerusalem. 4 This pleased the king and the whole community. 5 They decided to make an announcement throughout all Israel, from Beer-sheba to Dan, that they should come and celebrate the Passion to the Lord God of Israel in Jerusalem, because they had not done so for a long time, as it was written. 6 So the postmasters went with letters, by the king's commission and his princes, throughout all Israel and Judah, with the king's com- mand, saying, "Children of Israel, turn back to the LORD, the God of Abraham, Izhak and Israel, and he will return the remnant that has escaped you from the hands of the kings of Assur. 7 Do not be like your fathers and like your brothers, who transgressed against the LORD, the God of their fathers, and therefore he made them desolate, as you see. 8 Now do not be stiff-necked like your fathers, but give your hand to the LORD and come into his sanctuary, which he has sanctified forever, and serve the LORD your God, and the fire of his wrath will depart from you. 9 For if you return to the LORD, your brothers and your children will find mercy before those who led them into captivity, and they will return to this land; for the LORD your God is gra- cious and merciful, and he will not turn his face away from you, if you agree with him." 10 So the postmasters went from town to town through the land of Ephraim and Manasseh, as far as Zebulun; but they mocked them and scoffed. 11 Nevertheless some members of Asher, Manasseh and Zebulun submitted and came to Jerusalem. 12 The hand of God was in Judah and persuaded them to carry out the orders of the king and the leaders, according to the word of the Lord. 13 A great number of people gathered in Jerusalem to celebrate the feast of secular loaves on the second month, a very large assembly. 14 And they arose and took away the altars that were in Jerusalem; and all those for incense took them away and threw them into the brook Kidron. 15 Then they killed the Passer on the fourteenth day of the second month; and the priests and the leuites were ashamed, and sanctified them- selves, and brought the burnt ashes into the house of the LORD. 16 They stood in their place according to their order, according to the law of Moses the man of God, and the priests sprinkled the blood, which they re- ceived from the hands of the Leuites. 17 Be- cause there were many in the congregation who had not been sanctified, the Leuites were instructed to kill the Passer for all who had not been sanctified, to sanctify him to the Lord. 18 For a multitude of the people, that is, a multitude of Ephraim, Manasseh, Issachar, and Zebulun, had not purified themselves, yet they ate the Sparrow, but not as it was writ- ten; therefore Hezekiah prayed for them, say- ing, "May the good Lord be merciful to him." 19 who prepares his whole heart to see the Lord God, the God of his fathers, even though he is not cleansed, according to the cleans- ing of the Sanctuary." 20 · The LORD listened to Hezekiah and healed the people. 21 The children of Israel who were in Jerusalem cele- brated the feast of dry loaves for ten days with great joy; the Leuites and the priests prayed to the LORD day by day, singing with loud in- struments to the LORD. 22 And Hezekiah told all the Leuites who had good knowledge to sing to the LORD; and they ate at that feast for seven days, and offered peace offerings, and prayed to the LORD, the God of their fathers. 23 And all the assembly determined to keep the feast for ten more days. And so the sev- en days were held with joy. 24 For Hezekiah, king of Judah, had given to the community a thousand heifers and two hundred thousand sheep. The princes had given the community a thousand heifers and ten thousand sheep, and many priests had been sanctified. 25 The whole community of Iudah gathered together with the priests and the Leuites, with all the community that had come out of Israel and with the strangers who had come out of the land of Israel and were dwelling in Iudah. 26 So there was great joy in Jerusalem, for since the days of Solomon the son of Dauid, king of Israel, there had been no such thing in Jerusa- lem. 27 Then the priests and the leuites arose and blessed the people; their voice was heard, and their prayer came to Heauen, to his holy dwelling place.

CHAPTER 31

1 When all these things were finished, all Israel that were in the cities of Iudah went out and broke down the images, broke down the rump, broke down the places of worship and the altars in all Iudah and Benjamin, in Ephraim and in Manasseh, until they had made an end; then all the children of Israel returned each to his own possessions, to their own cities. 2 Hezekiah established the shifts of the priests and the leuites, each accord- ing to his function, both the priests and the leuites, for burnt offerings and for peace, to officiate, give thanks, and pray at the gates of the tents of the LORD. 3 (The king's portion was his substance for the burnings, that is, for the burnings in the morning and in the afternoon, for the burnings on Sabbaths, new moons and solemn feasts, as it is written in the Law of the Lord.) 4 And he also command- ed the people who dwelt in Jerusalem to give a portion to the priests and leuiti, that they might be encouraged in the Law of the Lord. 5 And when the order was spread, the children of Israel brought an abundance of first fruits, and of corn, and of wine, and of oil, and of wine of honor, and of all the crops of the fields, and the tithes of everything brought them in abundance. 6 The children of Israel and of Iudah, who dwelt in the cities of Iudah, also brought in the tithes of cattle and sheep and the sacred tithes that had been consecrated to the LORD their God, and they deposited them on many heaps. 7 In the thirteenth month they began to lay the foundations of the heaps and finished them in the seventh month. 8 When Hezekiah and the princes came and saw the heaps, they blessed the LORD and his people Israel. 9 Hezekiah questioned the priests and the Leuites about the heaps. 10 Azariah, the chief of the priests of the house of Zadok, an- swered him, "Since the people began to bring in the crops into the house of the LORD, we have eaten and been satisfied, and there is plenty left over; for the LORD has blessed his people, and this abundance has remained." 11 Hezekiah ordered rooms to be prepared in the house of the LORD, and they prepared them, 12 And they carried there faithfully the first fruits, tithes, and dedicated things; among them were Conaniah the Leuite, the chief, and Shimei his brother, the second. 13 Iehiel, Azariah, Nahath, Asahel, Ierimoth, Iozabad, Eliel, Ismachiah, Mahath, and Be- naiah were the officers by charge of Conani- ah and Shimei his brother, by order of King Hezekiah and Azariah, the head of the house of God. 14 Kore, son of Imnah, leuita, porter to the east, was outside the things voluntarily offered to God, to distribute the oblations of the LORD and the holy things consecrated. 15 By his side were Eden, Miniamin, Ieshua, Shemaiah, Amariah, and Shechaniah, in the cities of the priests, to distribute faithfully to their brethren, both the great and the small, 16 their daily portion, as well as to their gen- eration of males from three years old and upward, and to all those

who were entering the house of the LORD for their commission, according to their courses: 17 both to the generation of the priests, according to the house of their fathers, and to the Leuites, from the age of twenty years and upward, according to their offices, according to their courses: 18 And to the generation of all their sons, and of their wives, and of their sons, and of their daughters throughout the whole con- gregation; for by their faithfulness they are partakers of holy things. 19 Also to the sons of Aaron, the priests, who were in the fields and suburbs of their cities, in every city the men appointed by name were to give portions to all the males of the priests and to all the gen- eration of the Leuites. 20 So did Hezekiah in all Iudah, and he behaved himself well, rightly and truly before the LORD his God. 21 And in all the works that he began for the service of the house of God, both in the Law and in or- ders, to see his God, he did it with all his heart and prospered.

CHAPTER 32

1 After these things faithfully described, Saneherib, king of Assur, came, entered Iu- dah, besieged the strong cities and thought to conquer them for himself. 2 When Hezekiah heard that Saneherib had arrived and that his purpose was to fight against Jerusalem, 3 he agreed with his princes and nobles to stop the water from the fountains outside the city, and they helped him. 4 Then many of the people gathered together and stopped all the foun- tains and streams that ran through the center of the county, saying, "Why should the kings of Assur come and find much water?" 5 Then he took courage and built all the broken walls, built towers and another wall outside, rebuilt Millo in the city of Dauid, and built many darts and shields. 6 He brought captains of war from among the people, gathered them near him to the border place of the gate of the city, and spoke to them in a soothing tone, saying, "It is not the case that you should go the extra mile, 7 Be strong and courageous; do not fear or be afraid of the king of Assur and all the crowd that is with him, for there are more of them who are with him. 8 With him is a weapon of flesh, but with Vs is the LORD our God, to help him and to fight our battles." Then the people were confirmed by the words of Hezekiah, king of Judah. 9 After this, Sane- herib, king of Assur, sent his servants to Je- rusalem (while he was against Lachish and all his dominion with him) to Hezekiah, king of Judah, and to all the people of Judah who were in Jerusalem, saying, "Thus says Saneherib, 10 Thus says Saneherib, king of Assur, "In what do you trust to remain in Jerusalem during the siege? 11 Does not Hezekiah incite you to give yourselves death by hunger and thirst, saying, 'The Lord our God will deliver you out of the hand of the king of Assur'?" 12 Did not Hezekiah himself take away your places of worship and your altars, and did he not com- mand Iudah and Jerusalem to say, "You shall worship before one altar and burn incense on it"? 13 Do you not know what I and my fathers did to all the peoples of the other countries? Have the gods of the nations of the other countries been able to snatch their country out of my hand? 14 Who among all the gods of those nations (whom my fathers destroyed) was able to deliver his people from my hand? That your God could deliver you from my hand? 15 Therefore do not let Hezekiah de- ceive you and seduce you in this way, and do not turn away from him, for none of the gods of any nation or kingdom has been able to de- liver his people from my hand and from the hand of my fathers; how much less can

your gods deliver you from my hand? 16 His ser- vants spoke even more against the Lord God and against his servant Hezekiah. 17 He also wrote letters, blaspheming the LORD God of Israel and speaking against him, saying, "Just as the gods of the nations of other coun- tries could not deliver their people from my hand, so the God of Hezekiah will not deliver his people from my hand." 18 Then they cried aloud in the speeches of the Jews against the inhabitants of Jerusalem who were on the walls, to frighten and amaze them, that they might take the city. 19 Thus they spoke against the God of Jerusalem, as against the gods of the peoples of the earth, that is, the works of man's hands, 20 But King Hezekiah and the prophet Isaiah the son of Amoz prayed against this and cried out to the LORD. 21 And the LORD sent an angel who destroyed all the valiant men, the princes and captains of the army of the king of Assur; so he re- turned in shame to his own land. And when he had entered the house of his god, they that came from his bowels slew him there with the sword. 22 So the LORD saved Hezekiah and the inhabitants of Jerusalem from the hand of Saneherib king of Assur and from the hand of all the others, and kept them on every side. 23 Many brought to Jerusalem offerings to the LORD and gifts to Hezekiah, king of Judah, so that from then on he was magnified before all the nations. 24 In those days Hezekiah was sick unto death and prayed to the LORD, who spoke to him and gave him a sign. 25 But Hezekiah did not render according to the re- ward given him, for his heart was lifted up, and wrath came upon him, and upon Judah, and upon Jerusalem. 26 Nevertheless Heze- kiah humbled himself (after his heart was lifted up), he and the inhabitants of Jerusa- lem, and the anger of the LORD did not come upon them in the days of Hezekiah. 27 Heze- kiah also had many riches and honors, and brought him treasures of silk, and of gold, and of precious stones, and of perfumes, and of shields, and of every pleasant thing: 28 and storehouses for the increase of grain, wine, and oil, and stables for all the animals, and rows for stables. 29 And he built him cities, and owned sheep and oxen in abundance, be- cause God had granted him much substance. 30 This Hezekiah also stopped the springs of water from Gihon and led them straight downward to the city of Dauid in the west. 31 But because of the ambassadors of the princ- es of Babel, who sent to him to inquire about the wonders that had been done in the land, God left him free to question him and to know all that was in his heart. 32 As for the rest of Hezekiah's deeds and his goodness, behold, they are written in the vision of Ishiah the prophet, the son of Amoz, in the book of the kings of Judah and Israel. 33 So Hezekiah fell asleep with his fathers, and they buried him in the highest sepulchre of the sons of Dauid; and all the inhabitants of Judah and Jerusa- lem honored him at his death, and Manasseh his son reigned in his stead.

CHAPTER 33

1 Manasseh was two years old when he began to reign, and he reigned fifty years in Jerusa- lem: 2 And he did terrible things in the sight of the LORD, such as the abominations of the heathen which the LORD had cast out before the children of Israel. 3 For he went back and rebuilt the places which Hezekiah his father had torn down; he built altars for Baalim, and made bands, and worshipped all the armies of heaven, and indulged them. 4 He also built altars in the house of the LORD, of which the LORD had said, "My name shall be forev- er in Jerusalem." 5 He built altars for

all the guests of the land in the two courtyards of the house of the LORD. 6 He made his sons pass through the fire in the valley of Ben-Hinnom; he gave himself to sorcery, enchantment, and spells, and dealt with those who had familiar spirits and soothsayers; he did much evil in the eyes of the LORD to vex him. 7 He also put the graven image he had made in the house of God, where God had said to Dauid and Solo- mon his son, "In this house and in Jerusalem, which I have chosen before all the tribes of Israel, I will put my name forever, 8 and I will no more bring the people of Israel out of the land which I have assigned to your fathers, that they may take heed and do all that I have commanded them, according to the regu- lations, the statutes and the orders given by the hand of Moses." 9 Manasseh caused Iudah and the inhabitants of Jerusalem to err and do worse than the heathen, whom the LORD had destroyed before the children of Israel. 10 The LORD spoke to Manasseh and his people, but they would not listen. 11 Therefore the LORD had the captains of the armies of the king of Assur come upon them, and they took Manasseh, put him in chains, and brought him to Babel. 12 And when he was in tribu- lation, he prayed to the LORD his God, and humbled himself greatly before the God of his fathers, 13 And he prayed to him; and God was prayed to by him, and heard his prayer, and brought him back to Jerusalem into his kingdom; then Manasseh understood that the Lord was God. 14 And after this he built a wall outside the city of Dauid, west of Gi- hon, in the valley, at the entrance of the fish gate, and surrounded Ophel, and raised it up much, and put captains of war in all the strong cities of Iudah. 15 Then he took away from the house of the LORD the strange gods and images, and all the altars that he had built on the mountain of the LORD's house and in Jerusalem, and drove them out of the city. 16 He also prepared the altar of the LORD and sacrificed peace and thanksgiving offerings on it, and commanded Iudah to serve the LORD, the God of Israel. 17 The people also still sacrificed in the places of worship, but to the LORD their God. 18 The rest of the deeds of Manasseh, his prayer to his God and the words of the seers who spoke to him in the name of the LORD God of Israel, behold, they are written in the book of the kings of Israel. 19 His prayers and the way God was prayed to by him, all his sins and faults, the places where he built places of worship and placed caves and images (before he was humiliat- ed), behold, they are written in the book of the seers. 20 And Manasseh fell asleep with his fathers, and they buried him in his house; and Amon his son reigned in his stead. 21 Amon was two and twenty years old when he began to reign, and he reigned two years in Jerusalem. 22 But he did evil in the eyes of the LORD, as Manasseh his father, because Amon sacrificed to all the images that Manasseh his father had made and served them, 23 And he did not humble himself before the LORD, as Manasseh his father had humbled himself; but this Amon transgressed more and more. 24 His servants conspired against him and killed him in his house. 25 But the people of the land killed all those who had conspired against King Amon; and the people of the land made Iosiah his son king in his house.

CHAPTER 34

1 When he began to reign, Josiah was eight years old and reigned in Jerusalem for thirty years. 2 He behaved well in the eyes of the LORD, walked in the way of Dauid his father, and bowed neither to the right nor to the left. 3 In the eighth year of his reign (when he was still a child) he began to follow the God of Dauid his father; and in the twelfth year he began to cleanse Iudah and Jerusalem from the holy places, from the caves, from the graven images, and from the molten im- ages: 4 And he shattered, before his eyes, the altars of Baalim, and had the images on them cut down; and he also shattered the stones, the carved images, and the molten images, and reduced them to pulp, and cast it on the graves of those who had sacrificed there. 5 He also burned the bones of the priests on their altars and purified Iudah and Jerusalem. 6 And in the cities of Manasseh, and Ephraim, and Simeon, and as far as Naphtali, with their clubs they destroyed them all. 7 And when he had destroyed the altars and caves, broken and pulverized the images, and cut down all the idols in all the land of Israel, he returned to Jerusalem. 8 Then, in the eighth year of his reign, after he had cleansed the land and the Temple, he sent Shaphan the son of Azaliah, Maaseiah, keeper of the city, and Ioah the son of Ioahaz, recorder, to repair the house of the LORD his God. 9 When they came to Hilkiah the priest, they handed over the money that had been brought into the house of God and that the Leuites who guarded the house had collected by the hand of Manasseh, Ephraim and all the rest of Israel, all Iudah and Ben- jamin and the inhabitants of Jerusalem. 10 They put it into the hands of those who were to do the work and who had a view of the house of the LORD; and they gave it to the la- borers who were working in the house of the LORD, to repair and alter the house. 11 Then they gave it to the workmen and to the build- ers, to hew out stones and lumber for the couples and for the beams of the houses that the kings of Iudah had destroyed. 12 The men performed the work faithfully, and among them were Iahath and Obadiah, the Leuites, of the sons of Merari, Zechariah and Meshul- lam, of the sons of the Kohathites, who were in charge of the construction, and among the Leuites all who knew how to use musical in- struments. 13 They were the weight-bearers and those who advanced all the workers in every work; among the Leuites were scribes, officers and porters. 14 When they brought out the money that had been brought into the house of the LORD, Hilkiah the priest found the book of the Lawe of the LORD, written by the hand of Moses. 15 Therefore Hilkiah an- swered and said to Shaphan the chaceler, "I have found the book of the Lawe in the house of the LORD"; and Hilkiah delivered the book to Shaphan. 16 And Shaphan brought the book to the king and reported to him the king's words, saying, "Everything that has been entrusted to the hand of your servants, they do." 17 For they collected the money that was in the house of the LORD and delivered it into the hands of the workers and laborers. 18 Shaphan the chancellor also declared to the king, "Hilkiah the priest gave me a book, and Shaphan read it before the king." 19 When the king had heard the words of Lawe, he tore his clothes. 20 The king ordered Hilkiah, Ahikam the son of Shaphan, Abdon the son of Micah, Shaphan the chancellor, and Asaiah the king's servant to say 21 Go and ask the LORD for me and for the rest of Israel and Iudah, con- cerning the words of this book that has been found; for great is the wrath of the LORD that has come upon us, because our fathers did not keep the word of the LORD, to do according to all that is written in this book." 22 Then Hilki- ah and those whom the king had appointed went to Huldah, the prophetess, wife of Shal- lum, son of Tokhath, son of Hasrah, keeper of the wardrobe (who lived in Jerusalem, inside the enclosure), and spoke to her about it. 23 She answered them, "Thus says the LORD, the God of Israel: Tell of the man who sent you to me, 24 Thus says the LORD: "Behold, I will bring down upon this place and upon its inhabitants all the curses

that are written in the book which they read before the king of Judah: 25 Because they have forsaken me, and have burned incense to other gods, to vex me with all the works of their hands, my wrath shall come upon this place, and shall not be appeased." 26 But to the king of Judah, who sent you to inquire of the LORD, you shall say, "Thus says the LORD God of Israel, The words that you have heard shall come true. 27 But because your heart melted and you hum- bled yourself before God, when you heard his words against this place and against its in- habitants, and you humbled yourself before me, and tore your clothes and wept before me, I also have heard, says the LORD. 28 Behold, I will gather thee to thy fathers, and thou shalt be put in thy grave in peace, and thine eyes shall not see all the curse that I shall do upon this place and upon the inhabitants thereof." So they reported again to the king. 29 Then the king sent for all the elders of Judah and Je- rusalem. 30 And the king went into the house of the LORD, together with all the men of Judah and the inhabitants of Jerusalem, and the priests, and the Leuites, and all the peo- ple, from the greatest to the least, and read in their ears all the words of the crowning book that was in the house of the LORD. 31 And the king stood at his pillar and took an oath be- fore the LORD to walk according to the LORD, to observe his commands, his testimonies, and his statutes with all his heart and with all his soul, and to fulfill the words of the oath written in the book. 32 And he caused all who were in Jerusalem and Benjamin to go there; and the inhabitants of Jerusalem did accord- ing to the counsel of God, that is, of the God of their fathers. 33 So Josiah took away all abom- inations from all the countries that had come near to the children of Israel, and compelled all who were in Israel to serve the LORD their God; so that all his days they did not depart from the LORD, the God of their fathers.

CHAPTER 35

1 Moreover Iosiah held a feast for the LORD in Jerusalem, and they killed the shepherd on the four hundredth day of the first month. 2 He appointed the priests and incited them to the service of the house of the LORD, 3 and he said to the Leuites who were instructing all Israel and who were sanctified before the LORD, "Put the holy ark in the house that Solomon son of Dauid, king of Israel, built; it will no longer be a burden on your shoul- ders; serve now the LORD your God and his people Israel, 4 And prepare yourselves in the houses of your fathers according to your ways, as Dauid king of Israel wrote, and as Solomon his son wrote, 5 And be in the Sanctuary according to the deuition of the families of your brethren, the children of the people, and according to the deuition of the family of the Leuites: 6 So slay the Passer and sanctify yourselves, and prepare your breth- ren to do according to the word of the Lord by the hand of Moses. 7 And Iosiah also gave to the people sheep, lambs, and kids, all for the Passover, that is, to all who were present, thirty thousand in number, and three thou- sand cattle; these were of the king's heritage. 8 His princes gladly offered to the people, the priests and the Leuites: Hilkiah, Zechariah, and Jehiel, leaders of the house of God, gave to the priests for the passover two thousand and six hundred sheep and three hundred heifers. :9 Conaniah, Semaiah, Nethaneel, his brothers, Hashabiah, Jeiel and Iozabad, lead- ers of the Leuites, also offered to the Leuites, for the passover, five thousand sheep and five hundred heifers. 10 So the service was prepared, and the priests remained at their place, and the Leuites also at their command, according to the king's orders: 11 Then they killed the Passer, and the priests sprinkled its blood with their hands, and the Leuites flayed them. 12 They took away the burnt offering to give it according to the deuisions of the fami- lies of the children of the people, to offer it to the LORD, as it is written in the book of Mo- ses, and so for the bullocks. 13 They roasted the pasture with fire, according to the rules, but the sanctified things they put into vessels, pans and cauldrons, and distributed them quickly to all the people. 14 Then they also prepared for themselves and for the priests, for the priests sons of Aaron were busy in the offering of buns and fat until night; therefore the Leuites prepared for themselves and for the priests sons of Aaron. 15 The singers, the sons of Asaph, stood according to the orders of Dauid, Asaph, Heman, and Ieduthun, the king's seer, and the porters at every door, who could not depart from their service. 16 So the whole service of the LORD was prepared on that same day, to observe the Passover and to offer burnt offerings on the altar of the LORD, according to the order of King Je- hoshiah. 17 The children of Israel, who were present, observed the Passover at the same time and the feast of unleavened bread for ten days. 18 There has been no such Passover in Israel since the days of Samuel the proph- et; nor have all the kings of Israel observed a Passover like that of Jehoziah, the priests, the Leuites, all Judah, Israel, and the inhabitants of Jerusalem. 19 This Passover was celebrated in the eighteenth year of Iosiah's reign. 20 After all this, while Iosiah was preparing the Temple, Neco, king of Egypt, came to fight against Carchemish from Perath, and Iosiah went against him. 21 But he sent messengers to him, saying, "What shall I do with you, king of Iudah? Today I come not against you, but against the house of my enemy, and God has commanded me to hasten; let me come against God, who is with me, if he does not destroy you." 22 But Iosiah would not depart from him, but changed his clothes to fight with him, and he heeded not the words of Necho, which came from the mouth of God, but came to fight in the valley of Megiddo. 23 The marksmen shot King Iosiah; then the king said to his servants, "Take me away, for I am very sick." 24 And his servants took him out of that hood, and put him in the second hood that he had; and when they had brought him to Jerusalem, he died, and was buried in the sepulchres of his fathers; and all Iudah and Jerusalem mourned for Iosiah. 25 And Jeremiah mourned for Iosiah, and all the men and women that sang mourned for Iosiah in their laments unto this day, and made it an ordinance for Israel; and behold, they are written in the laments. 26 As for the rest of Iosiah's deeds and his goodness, which he did as it is written in the Lawe of the LORD, 27 his deeds, the first and the last, behold, they are written in the book of the kings of Israel and Judah.

CHAPTER 36

1 Then the people of the land chose Iehoa- haz the son of Jehoash and made him king in the house of his fathers in Jerusalem. 2 Ie- hoahaz was three years old and twenty when he began to reign, and he reigned for three months in Jerusalem. 3 The king of Egypt took him away to Jerusalem and charged him for the territory in a hundred talents of silver and a talent of gold. 4 And the king of Egypt appointed Eliakim, his brother, king of Iudah and Jerusalem, and imposed on him the name Iehoiakim; and Neco took Iehoa- haz, his brother, and brought him to Egypt. 5 Iehoiakim was fifty-two years old when he began

to reign; he reigned eleven years in Je- rusalem and did well in the eyes of the LORD his God. 6 Against him came Nebuchadnez- zar, king of Babel, and bound him with chains to carry him to Babel. 7 Nebuchadnezzar also transported the furnishings of the house of the LORD to Babel and put them in his tem- ple at Babel. 8 As for the rest of the deeds of Jehoiakim, the abominations he did and what was found about him, behold, they are written in the book of the kings of Israel and Judah, and Jehoiachin his son reigned in his stead. 9 When he began to reign, Jehoiachin was eight years old; he reigned three months and ten days in Jerusalem and did well in the sight of the LORD. 10 When the year was over, King Nebuchadnezzar sent for him to Babel with the precious furnishings of the house of the LORD and made Zedekiah, his brother, king of Judeah and Jerusalem. 11 Zedekiah was one year and twenty when he began to reign, and he reigned eleven years in Jeru- salem. 12 He behaved himself well before the LORD his God and did not humble himself before the prophet Jeremiah at the command of the LORD, 13 but he rebelled even more against Nebuchadnezzar, who had made him swear by God; he hardened his neck and made his heart obstinate not to return to the LORD, the God of Israel. 14 Also all the chief priests and people transgressed marvelously, accord- ing to all the abominations of the heathen, and defiled the house of the LORD which he had sanctified in Jerusalem. 15 Therefore the LORD, the God of their fathers, sent his mes- sengers to them, rising early and sending, because he had compassion on his people and his dwelling place. 16 But they mocked God's messengers, despised his words, and abused his prophets, until the anger of the LORD came upon his people, and there was no remedy. 17 For he brought upon them the king of the Chaldeans, who slew their young men with the sword in the house of their sanctuary, and spared not a young man, nor a virgin, nor an old man, nor an elderly man. God gave everything into his hands, 18 all the furnishings of the house of God, great and small, the treasures of the house of the LORD, the treasures of the king and his princes: all these he took to Babel. 19 Then they set fire to the house of God, and brought down the walls of Jerusalem, and burned with fire all her pal- aces and all her precious things, to destroy everything. 20 And they that were left by the sword carried them away to Babel, and were servants to him and to his sons, until the king- dom of the Persians had dominion, 21 To ful- fill the word of the LORD, which was spoken by the mouth of Jeremiah, until the land was satisfied with her Sabbaths; for all the days that she was desolate, she observed the Sab- bath, until she was seventy years old. 22 But in the first year of Cyrus, king of Persia, when the word of the Lord spoken by the mouth of Jeremiah was finished, the Lord stirred up the spirit of Cyrus, king of Persia, and he made an announcement throughout his king- dom and also in writing, saying 23 Thus says Cyrus, king of Persia: "To all the kingdoms of the earth the LORD, God of God, has given me and commanded me to build him a house in Jerusalem, which is in Iudah. Who is there among you, among all his people, with whom the Lord, his God, is in contact?

EZRA

CHAPTER 1

1 Now in the first year of Cyrus, king of Per- sia, that the word of the LORD spoken by the mouth of Jeremiah might be fulfilled, the LORD stirred up the mind of Cyrus, king of Persia, and he made a proclamation through- out his kingdom and also in writing, saying 2 Thus says Cyrus, king of Persia: "The LORD, God of God, has given me all the kingdoms of the earth and commanded me to build him a house in Jerusalem, which is in Iudah. 3 Who is among you, among all his people, with whom he is his God? Let him go to Jeru- salem, which is in Judah, and buy the house of the Lord God of Israel: he is the God that is in Jerusalem. 4 And whosoever remains in any place (where he sojourns), let the men of his place supply him with silk, with gold, with goods, with cattle, and with voluntary offerings for the house of God which is in Je- rusalem. 5 Then the principal fathers of Judah and Benjamin, the priests and the Leuites rose up, with all those whose spirits God had prompted to go, to build the house of the Lord which is in Jerusalem. 6 All those around them strengthened their hands with vessels of silver, of gold, of stones, and of cattle and precious things, in addition to all that was willingly offered. 7 King Cyrus also brought the furnishings of the house of the Lord that Nebuchadnezzar had taken away from Jeru- salem and put them in the house of his God. 8 Cyrus, king of Persia, brought them by the hand of Mithreda, the treasurer, and counted them to Shehbazzar, prince of Iudah. 9 This is their name: thirty boules of gold, a thousand boules of silver, nine twentieths of kilograms, 10 Three boules of gold and boules of silver of the second kind, four hundred and ten, and a thousand other vessels. 11 All the utensils of gold and silver were five thousand and four hundred. Shehbazzar brought with him all the captives who had come from Babel to Je- rusalem.

CHAPTER 2

1 These also are the sons of the province who came out of captivity (which Nebuchadnez- zar, king of Babel, had taken away to Babel) and returned to Jerusalem and Judah, each to his own city, 2 who came with Zerubbabel: Ieshua, Nehemiah, Seraiah, Reelaiah, Morde- cai, Bilshan, Mispar, Biguai, Rehum, Baanah. The number of the men of the people of Israel was, 3 the sons of Parosh, two thousand, sev- enty-two and two: 4 The sons of Shephatiah, three hundred seuentie two: 5 The sons of Arah, six hundred seuentie five: 6 The sons of Pahath Moab, of the sons of Ieshua and Ioab, two thousand eight hundred and two: 7 The sons of Elam, a thousand, two hundred and four hundred and fifty: 8 The sons of Zat- tu, nine hundred and fifty-five: 9 The sons of Zaccai, seven hundred and sixty: 10 The sons of Bani, six hundred and two and forty: 11 The sons of Bebai, six hundred and three hundred and twenty: 12 The sons of Azgad: a thousand, two hundred and two and twen- ty-five: 13 The sons of Adonikam, six hundred and three hundred and sixty: 14 The sons of Biguai, two thousand and six hundred and fifty: 15 The sons of Adin, four hundred and four hundred and fifty: 16 The sons of Ater of Hizkiah, ninety-nine and eight: 17 The sons of Bezai, three hundred and three hundred and twenty-five: 18 The sons of Iorah, one hudreth and two: 19 The sons of Hasshum, two hundred and three hundred and twenty: 20 The sons of Gibbar, ninety-nine and five: 21 The sons of Beth-Lem, one hundred and three and twenty-five: 22 The men of Netophah, six and fifty: 23 The men of Anothoth, a hundred and eleven and eight and twen- ty-five: 24 The sons of Azmaueth, two and four: 25 The sons of Kiriath- arim, Chephi- rah, and Beeroth, an hundred and nine and three and forty: 26 The sons of Harama and Gaba, six hundred and one and twenty-five: 27 The men of Michas, a

hundred and two and twenty-five: 28 The sons of Beth-el and Ai, two hundred and three and twenty-five: 29 The sons of Nebo, two and fifty: 30 The sons of Magbish, an hundred and sixty-five: 31 The sons of the other Elam, a thousand, two hun- dred and four hundred and fifty: 32 The sons of Harim, three hundred and twenty-five: 33 The sons of Lod-Hadid and Ono, six hundred, fifty and twenty-five: 34 The sons of Jericho, three hundred and fifty-four: 35 The sons of Senaa, three thousand, six hundred and thir- ty-three. 36 The priests: of the sons of Iedaiah, of the house of Ieshua, nine hundred seuen- tie three: 37 The sons of Immer: a thousand two hundred and fifty: 38 The sons of Pashur, a thousand two hundred seventy-four: 39 The sons of Harim, a thousand and seuenteen. 40 The Leuites: the sons of Ieshua and Kadmiel of the sons of Hodauiah, seventy and four. 41 The singers: the sons of Asaph, an hundred and eleven and eight and twenty-five. 42 The sons of the porters: the sons of Shallum, the sons of Ater, the sons of Talmon, the sons of Akkub, the sons of Hatita, the sons of Shobai; all were an hundred and ninety and nine and thirty. 43 The Nethinim: the sons of Ziha, the sons of Hasupha, the sons of Tabbaoth, 44 the sons of Keros, the sons of Siaha, the sons of Padon, 45 the sons of Lebanah, the sons of Hagabah, the sons of Akkub, 46 the sons of Hagab, the sons of Shamlai, the sons of Han- an, 47 the sons of Giddel, the sons of Gahar, the sons of Reaiah, 48 the sons of Rezin, the sons of Nekoda, the sons of Gazzam, the sons of Vzza, the sons of Paseah, the sons of Besai, 50 the sons of Asnah, the sons of Meunim, the sons of Nephusim, 51 the sons of Bakbuk, the sons of Hakupa, the sons of Harhur, 52 the sons of Bazluth, the sons of Mehida, the sons of Harsha, 53 the sons of Barcos, the sons of Sisara, the sons of Thamah, 54 the sons of Ne- ziah, the sons of Hatipha, 55 the sons of Solo- mon's seruants: the sons of Sotai, the sons of Sophereth, the sons of Peruda, 56 the sons of Iaalah, the sons of Darkon, the sons of Giddel, 57 the sons of Shephatiah, the sons of Hattil, the sons of Pochereth Hazzebaim, the sons of Ami. 58 All the Nethinim and the sons of Solomon's servants were three hundred and ninety-two. 59 These went from Telmela and Telharsa, from Cherub, from Addan and Im- mer, but they could not discern their paternal houses and their descendants, whether they were of Israel. 60 The sons of Delaiah, the sons of Tobiah, the sons of Nekoda: six hun- dred and fifty. 61 Of the sons of the priests, the sons of Habaiah, the sons of Coz, the sons of Barzillai, who took the daughters of Bar- zillai the Giliadean to wife, and were called by their names. 62 These tried to write genealogies, but they could not find them; there- fore they were removed from the priesthood. 63 Tirshatha told them that they should not eat of the holiest thing unless a priest arose with Vrim and Thummim. 64 The whole com- munity consisted of two hundred and four thousand people, three hundred and sixty, 65 besides their servants and their elders; of these, six thousand, three hundred and six hundred and thirty; and among them were two hundred men and women who sang. 66 Their horses were two hundred and six and thirty, their mules two hundred and five and four: 67 Their camels were four hundred, five and thirty; their asses, six thousand, seven hundred and twenty-five. 68 And some of the chief fathers, when they came to the house of the LORD, which was in Jerusalem, gladly offered for the house of God, to put money on its fund. 69 They gave, according to their ability, the treasure of the work, that is, one million seven hundred thousand drams of gold, five thousand pieces of silver, and a hundred priestly garments. 70 So the priests, the Leuites,

part of the people, the singers, the porters and the Nethinim settled in their cities, and all Israel in its cities.

CHAPTER 3

1 When the tenth month had passed and the children of Israel were in their cities, the peo- ple gathered as one in Jerusalem. 2 Then Iesh- ua the son of Iozadak and his brother priests and Zerubbabel the son of Shealtiel and his brothers built the altar of the God of Israel to offer burnt offerings on it, as it is written in the Law of Moses the man of God, 3 And they set the altar on its foundations (for they were afraid because of the people of those countries) and offered burnt offerings there- on to the LORD, burnt offerings in the morn- ing and at noon. 4 Moreover, as it is written, they celebrated the Feast of Tabernacles and offered burnt offerings daily, according to the rules, day by day, 5 and thereafter the contin- ual offering of food, both in the new months and in all the feasts consecrated to the Lord, and in all the oblations offered voluntarily to the Lord. 6 From the first day of the seventh month they began to offer burnt offerings to the Lord, but the foundation of the Lord's temple had not yet been laid. 7 They also gave money to the masons and workmen, and also food, alcohol and oil to those of Zidon and Tyre, to bring them cedar wood from Leba- non to the sea as far as Iapho, according to the contract they had with Cyrus, king of Persia. 8 In the second year of their arrival at the house of God in Jerusalem, in the second month, Zerubbabel the son of Shealtiel, Ieshua the son of Iozadak, the rest of their brethren, the priests and the Leuites, and all those who had come out of captivity in Jerusalem, com- missioned the Leuites from the age of twenty years onward to begin the work of the house of the Lord. 9 And Ieshua with his sons and his brethren, and Kadmiel with his sons, and the sons of Judah set themselves together to begin the work of the house of God, and the sons of Henadad with their sons, and their Leuiti brethren. 10 When the builders laid the foundation of the temple of the LORD, they presented the priests clothed with trumpets and the Leuiti, sons of Asaph, with cymbals, to pray to the LORD, according to the order of Dauid, king of Israel. 11 Thus they sang when they prayed and when they gave thanks to the Lord, "For he is good, for his mercy endures forever toward Israel." And all the people shouted with a great shout when they prayed to the LORD, because the foundation of the house of the LORD had been laid. 12 Also many of the priests, the leuites, and the lead- ers of the fathers, ancient men who had seen the first house, (when the foundation of this house was laid before their eyes) cried with a loud voice, and many cried aloud for joy, 13 so much so that the people could not distinguish the sound of the shout of joy from the sound of the weeping of the people, for the people shouted at the top of their voices and the noise was heard far away.

CHAPTER 4

1 But the inhabitants of Iudah and Ben- jamin heard that the sons of the captivity were building the Temple for the LORD God of Israel. 2 They came to Zerubbabel and the heads of the families and said to them, "We will build with you, because we see the LORD your God as you do and have sacrificed to him since the days of Esar Haddon, king of Assur, who led us here." 3 Then Zerubbabel, Ieshua and the rest of the leaders of Israel said to them. 4 Therefore the

people of the land dis- couraged the inhabitants of Iudah and trou- bled them in their purchase, 5 and they hired counselors against them to hinder them, all the days of Cyrus, king of Persia, and until the reign of Darius, king of Persia. 6 In the reign of Ahashuerosh (early in his reign) they wrote an accusation against the inhabitants of Iu- dah and Jerusalem. 7 In the days of Artah- shashte, Mithreda, Tabeel and the rest of their companions wrote in time of peace to Artah- shashte, king of Persia; the letter was written by the Aramites and the things stated were in the language of the Aramites. 8 Rehum, the chancellor, and Shimshai, the scribe, wrote a letter against Jerusalem to King Ar- tahshashte, in this way. 9 They wrote Rehum the chancellor, Shimshai the scribe, and their companions Dinaie, Apharsathcaie, Tarpe- laie, Apharsaie, Archeuaie, Bablaie, Shushan- chaie, Dehaue, Elmaie, 10 and the rest of the people whom the great and noble Asnappar brought abroad and settled in the cities of Samaria and others beyond the Riuer and Cheeneth. 11 This is the copy of the letter they sent to King Artahshashte: "Your servants, the men beyond the Riuer and Cheeneth, greet you. 12 Let the king know that you, who have come to you to visit, have come to Jeru- salem (a rebellious and wicked city), and have bought, and have laid the foundations of the walls, and have built its foundations. 13 Let the king know that if this city is built and the foundations of the walls are laid, they will give neither tax nor tribute nor right; so you will hinder the king's tribute. 14 Now since we were brought into the king's palace, it was not fitting that we should see the king's dishonor; therefore we sent to certify the king, 15 That we may search the book of the Chronicles of your fathers, and you may find in the book of the Chronicles, and perceive that this city is rebellious and displeasing to kings and princ- es, and that they have made sedition in the past, whereby this city was destroyed. 16 We therefore certify to the king that if this city be purchased and the foundations of the walls be laid, in this way the part beyond the river shall not be yours. 17 The king sent an answer to Rehum, the chancellor, to Shimshai, the scribe, and to the rest of their companions who dwelt in Samaria, and to the other inhab- itants of the Beyond, Shelam and Cheeth. 18 The letter you sent was read openly before me, 19 and I commanded, and they searched and found that this city from time immemorial had made insurrection against the kings, had rebelled, and a rebellion had been committed there. 20 There have been mighty kings also outside Jerusalem, who have ruled through- out the whole beyond the Rivera, and tribute and rights have been granted to them. 21 Now make a decree that these men shall cease to rule, and the city shall not be purchased, un- til I have given another order. 22 Be careful not to do this: why should domination grow to harm the king? 23 When the copy of King Artahshashtes' letter was read before Rehum, the scribe Shimshai and their companions, they went in haste to Jerusalem to the Jews and made them stop by force and power. 24 Then the works of the house of God, which was in Jerusalem, ceased and remained until the second year of Darius, king of Persia.

CHAPTER 5

1 Then Haggai the prophet and Zechariah the prophet, son of Iddo, prophesied to the in- habitants of Judah and Jerusalem in the name of the God of Israel. 2 Then Zerubbabel the son of Shealtiel and Ieshua the son of Iozadak got up and began to build the house of God in Jerusalem; with them were the prophets of God, who helped them. 3 At the same time came to them Tatnai, who was the chief over the Riuer, and Shether-Boznai and their com- panions, and said to them, "Who gave you the order to buy this house and to lay the founda- tion of these walls?" 4 Then we said to them in this manner, "What are the names of the men who buy this house?" 5 But the eye of their God rested on the elders of the Iewes, who could not make them stop until the matter came to Darius; and then they answered with letters. 6 The copy of the letter that Tatnai, captain across the river, Shether-Boznai and his companions, Apharshekiah, who were across the river, sent to King Darius. 7 They sent him a letter in which was written, "To King Darius, all peace." 8 Let the king know that we have gone to the province of Judea, to the house of the great God, which is built with great stones, and flames are set in the walls, and this work is done quickly and prospers in their hands. 9 Then we asked those elders and said to them, "Who gave you the order to buy this house and to lay the foundation of these walls? 10 We also asked for their names, that we might certify them and write down the names of the men who were their leaders. 11 But they answered thus, "We are servants of the God of heaven and earth, and we buy the house that was purchased anciently and many years ago and that a great king of Isra- el built and founded. 12 But after our fathers had provoked the wrath of the God of Heauen, he delivered them into the hands of Nebu- chadnezzar, king of Babel, the Chaldean, who destroyed this house and carried the people into captivity in Babel. 13 But in the first year of Cyrus, king of Babel, King Cyrus made a decree to purchase this house of God. 14 The articles of gold and silver from the house of God, which Nebuchadnezzar had taken out of the temple in Jerusalem to bring to the temple in Babel, King Cyrus removed from the tem- ple in Babel and delivered to a certain Sheba- zzar, by name, whom he had appointed cap- tain. 15 He said to him, "Take these vessels, go your way and put them in the Temple that is in Jerusalem, and let the house of God be built in its place." 16 Then Shehbazzar himself came and laid the foundation of the house of God, which is in Jerusalem, and from then until now it has been purchased, but it is not yet finished. 17 Now therefore, if it pleases the king, let a search be made in the house of the treasures of kings, which is in Babel, to know whether King Cyrus decreed the building of this house of God in Jerusalem, and let the king send his opinion concerning it.

CHAPTER 6

1 Then King Darius gave orders to search the library of treasures that were in Babel. 2 In a chest (in the palace that was in the hands of the Medes) was found a volume in which was written the following, by way of remem- brance, 3 In the first year of King Cyrus made a decree for the house of God in Jerusalem, "Let the house be built, that is, the place where sacrifices are offered, and let its walls be put together; let its height be three tens of cubits and its width three tens of cubits, 4 three orders of large stones and one order of timber, and the expense shall be borne by the king's house. 5 Moreover, let the furnishings of the house of God (of gold and silver, which Nebuchadnezzar took out of the Temple in Jerusalem and brought to Babel) be returned and brought to the Temple in Jerusalem, in its place, and put in the house of God. 6 There- fore let Tatnai, captain across the river, and Shethar Boznai (and their companions Afar- secaiah, who are across the river) be far

from there. 7 Let the work of this house of God be completed, that the captain of the Iewes and the elders of the Iewes may purchase this house of God in its place. 8 For I have com- manded to make the elders of these Iewes, for the purchase of this house of God, that of the king's revenue, which is that of the trib- ute beyond the river, there shall be spent in- continently to these men, that they may not cease. 9 And what they shall need, let it be giv- en them day by day, whether it be heifers, or rams, or lambs for the offenses of the God of Heauen, or grain, or salt, or wine, or oil, ac- cording to the order of the priests that are in Jerusalem, that there may be no error, 10 that they may offer fragrant odors to the God of Heauen and pray for the life of the king and for his sons. 11 And I have decreed that who- soever shall amend this sentence, wood shall be taken down from his house and shall be set up, and he shall be hanged there, and his house shall be made a dunghill for it. 12 And God, who hath made his Name to dwell in that place, shall destroy all kings and peoples who shall set hand to alter and destroy this house of God which is in Jerusalem. I Darius have made a decree, let it be done quickly." 13 Then Tatnai, the captain across the river, Scethar Boznai and their companions, according to what Darius had ordered, made haste. 14 So the elders of the Iewes built and prospered by the prophecy of Haggai the prophet and Zech- ariah the son of Iddo, and they purchased and finished the house, by the command of the God of Israel and by the order of Cyrus, Dar- ius and Artahshashte, king of Persia. 15 This house was finished on the thirteenth day of the month Adar, which was the sixtieth year of King Darius' reign. 16 The children of Isra- el, the priests, the Leuites and the rest of the children of the captivity participated with joy in the dedication of this house of God, 17 and offered at the dedication of this house of God one hundred bullocks, two hundred rams, four hundred lambs and two he-goats, for the sin of all Israel, according to the name of the tribes of Israel. 18 Then they put the priests in their place and the leuites in their places for the service of God in Jerusalem, as it is written in the book of Moses. 19 The chil- dren of the captivity observed the Passover on the fourth day of the first month. 20 (For the priests and the leuites purified themselves completely) and they killed the Passover for all the sons of the captivity, for their brother priests and for themselves. 21 So the children of Israel who had come out of captivity again, and all those who had separated from them from the filthiness of the heathen in the land to see the Lord God of Israel, ate, 22 and made the feast of leavened bread for ten days with joy, because the Lord had rejoiced them and had turned the heart of the king of Assur to- ward them, to encourage them to work in the house of God, that is, in the God of Israel.

CHAPTER 7

1 After these things, in the reign of Artah- shashte, king of Persia, there was Ezra the son of Seraiah, the son of Azariah, the son of Hilkiah, 2 son of Shallum, son of Zadok, son of Ahitub, 3 son of Amariah, son of Azariah, son of Meraioth, 4 son of Zeraiah, son of Vzzi, son of Bukki, 5 son of Abishua, son of Phine- has, son of Eleazar, son of Aaron, the chief of the priests. 6 This Ezra came from Babel and was a scribe skilled in the law of Moses, which the LORD God of Israel had enacted, and the king granted him all his requests according to the hand of the LORD his God that was upon him. 7 A portion of the sons of Israel, the priests, the Leuites, the singers, the por- ters and the Nethinims went to Jerusalem in the seventh year of King Artahshashte.

8 He came to Jerusalem in the fifth month, that is, in the tenth year of the king. 9 For on the first day of the first month he began to depart from Babel, and on the first day of the fifth month he came to Jerusalem, according to the good hand of his God which was upon him. 10 For Ezra had prepared his heart to follow the word of the Lord and to put it into practice and to teach the precepts and the rules in Israel. 11 This is the copy of the letter which King Artahshashte gave to Ezra, priest and scribe, that is, writer of the words of the Lord's commandments and his statutes in Israel. 12 ARTAHSHASHTE King of kings to Ezra, perfect priest and scribe of the Lawe of the God of Heauen, and to Cheeneth. 13 I have given orders that all those in my kingdom who are willing to go to Jerusalem with you, among the people of Israel, the priests and the Leuites, should go. 14 Therefore you have been sent by the king and his advisers to inquire in Iudah and Jerusalem, according to the law of your God which you have in your hand, 15 and to bring the silver and gold which the king and his cousins gladly offer to the God of Is- rael (whose dwelling place is in Jerusalem). 16 And all the silver and gold that you can find throughout the province of Babel, with the free offerings of the people, and with what the priests gladly offer to the house of their God which is in Jerusalem, 17 That thou may- est take away quickly, with this thirst, the cat- tle, the rams, the lambs, with their offal and their alcoholic offal; and thou shalt offer them upon the altar of the house of thy God, which is in Jerusalem. 18 And what it shall please you and your brethren to do with the rest of the silver and gold, do according to the will of your God. 19 And the utensils that have been given you for the service of the house of your God, deliver them before God in Jerusalem. 20 And the remnant that will be needed for the house of your God and that will be useful for you to bestow, you shall bestow from the king's treasury, 21 I, King Artahshashte, have given orders to all the treasurers beyond the river, that whatever Ezra, priest and scribe of the Law of the God of Heauen, shall ask of you shall be done uncontrolled, 22 up to a hun- dred talents of torpedo, up to a hundred mea- sures of grain, up to a hundred baths of wine, up to a hundred baths of oil and salt without writing. 23 Let everything that is by the com- mandment of the God of Heauen be done as soon as possible for the house of the God of Heauen; why should he be angry against the reality of the king and his sons? 24 And we testify to you that none of the priests, the leuiti, the singers, the porters, the nethinim, or the ministers of this house of God shall be burdened with any tribute or tax. 25 And you, Ezra, according to the wisdom of your God, which is in your hands, establish judges and arbitrators who shall judge all the people who are beyond the river, that is, all who know the word of your God, and teach those who do not know it. 26 And whosoever will not keep the law of thy God and the law of the king, let him be judged without delay, either by death, or by banishment, or by confiscation of property, or by imprisonment. 27 Blessed be the LORD, the God of our fathers, who has put it into the heart of the king to beautify the house of the LORD which is in Jerusalem, 28 and has shown mercy to me, before the king and his counsellors and all the king's mighty princes; and I was comforted by the hand of the LORD my God, which was upon me, and I gathered the leaders of Israel to come with me.

CHAPTER 8

1 These are their chief fathers and the geneal- ogy of those who came with me from Babel, in the days of king Artahshashte. 2 Of the sons of Phinehas, Gershom; of the sons of Ithamar, Daniel; of the sons of Dauid, Hattush: 3 Of the sons of Shechaniah, of the sons of Phar- osh, Zechariah, and with him the number of the males, an hundred and fifty. 4 Of the sons of Pahath Moab, Elihoenai the son of Zeraiah, and with him two hundred males. 5 Of the sons of Shecaniah the son of Jahaz- iel, and with him three hundred males. 6 Of the sons of Adin, Ebed the son of Ionathan, and with him fifty males. 7 Of the sons of Elam, Ieshaiah the son of Ataliah, and with him seventy males. 8 Of the sons of Shepha- tiah, Zebadiah the son of Michael, and with him forty-two males. 9 Of the sons of Joab, Obadiah the son of Jehiel, and with him two hundred and eighty males. 10 Of the sons of Shelomith the son of Jehoshaphat, and with him an hundred and sixty males. 11 Of the sons of Bebai, Zechariah the son of Bebai, and with him eight hundred and twenty males. 12 Of the sons of Azgad, Iohanan the son of Hakkatan, and with him an hundred and ten males. 13 Of the sons of Adonikam, the last, whose names are these, Eliphelet, Iehiel, and Shemaiah, and with them three dozen males. 14 And of the sons of Biguai, Vthai and Zab- bud, and with them seventy males. 15 And I gathered them to the river that goes to Ahaua, and there we stayed for three days; then I saw the people and the priests, and found none of the sons of Leui there. 16 Therefore I sent to Eliezer, and to Ariel, and to Shemeiah, and to Elnathan, and to Iarib, and to Elnathan, and to Nathan, and to Zechariah, and to Meshul- lam, the chief, and to Ioiarib, and to Elnathan, men of good will, 17 And I gave them orders to Iddo the chief in the place of Casiphia, and told them the words that they should say to Iddo and to his Nethinei brethren in the place of Casiphia, that they should bring in the ministers of the house of our God. 18 So, by the good hand of our God who was on Vs, they brought to Vs an intelligent man of the sons of Mahali, the son of Leui, the son of Israel, and Sherebiah with his sons and his brothers, about eighty persons. 19 Also Hashabiah and with him Ieshaiah, of the sons of Merari, with his brothers and their sons, twenty-two. 20 Of the Nethinim whom Dauid had appointed, and of the princes for the service of the Leuiti, two hundred and twenty Nethinim, all named by name. 21 And there at the Riuer, near Ahaua, I proclaimed a fast to humble our- selves before our God and to seek from him a right way for us and for our children and for all our possessions. 22 For I was ashamed to ask the king for an army and horsemen to help you against enemies along the way, for we had spoken to the king, saying, "The hand of our God is upon all who look kindly upon him, but his power and his wrath are against all who forsake him." 23 So we fasted and begged our God for this, and he was heard. 24 Then I separated two of the chief priests, Sherebiah and Hashabiah, and ten of their brothers with them, 25 And I weighed unto them the silver, and the gold, and the vessels, that is, the offerings of the house of our God, which the king, and his counsellors, and his princes, and all Israel that was present, had offered. 26 And I weighed in their hands six hundred and fifty talents of silver, and in vessels of silver an hundred talents, and in gold an hundred talents: 27 And twenty-two basins of gold of a thousand drams, and two vessels of shining brasses very good and pre- cious as gold. 28 And I said unto them, Ye are consecrated unto the LORD; the vessels are consecrated, and the gold and the silver are freely offered unto the LORD, the God of your fathers. 29 Watch over them and keep them until you weigh them before the chief priests, the leuites, and the heads of the fathers of Is- rael in Jerusalem, in the rooms of the house of the LORD. 30 So the priests and the leuites re- ceived the weight of the clay and the gold and the utensils to bring them to Jerusalem, to the house of our God. 31 On the twelfth day of the first month we set out from Riuer of Ahauah to go to Jerusalem, and the hand of our God was upon us and delivered us out of the hands of our enemies and those who were waiting for us on the way. 32 We came to Jerusalem and stayed there three days. 33 On the fourth day, in the house of our God, the silver and the coin and the vessels were weighed by the hand of Meremoth the son of Vriah the priest, and with him Eleazar the son of Phinehas, and with them Iozabad the son of Ieshua, and Noadiah the son of Binnui the Leuite, 34 By number and by the weight of each, and all the weight was written at the same time. 35 The children of the captivity also came out of the captivity and offered a burnt offering to the God of Israel: two bullocks for all Israel, nine- ty-six rams, seventy-two lambs and two goats for sin; all was a burnt offering to the LORD. 36 Then they delivered the king's charge to the king's officers and captains from beyond the borders of the kingdom; they promoted the people and the house of God.

CHAPTER 9

1 When these things were done, the leaders came to me, saying, "The people of Israel, the priests and the Leuites have not separated themselves from the people of the countries (concerning their abominations), that is, from the Canaanites, the Hittites, the Per- izzites, the Jebusites, the Ammonites, the Moabites, the Egyptians and the Amorites. 2 For they took their daughters and their sons, and mingled the holy seed with the people of the land, and the hand of the princes and rul- ers was chiefly responsible for this violation. 3 But when I heard these words, I tore my gar- ments and my dress, and tore off my head and my beard, and stood stunned on the ground. 4 There gathered to me all those who feared the words of the God of Israel, because of the transgression of those in the captivity. And I stood open-mouthed until the next day's sac- rifice. 5 At the dawn sacrifice I rose up from my head, and having torn my garments and my dress, I fell on my knees and stretched out my hands to the LORD my God, 6 and said, "O my God, I am confounded, and I am ashamed to lift up mine eyes to you, my God, because our iniquities have grown on our heads, and our guilt has grown up to heaven." 7 From the days of our fathers we have committed great guilt until this day, and because of our iniq- uities we and our kings and our priests have been delivered into the hands of the kings of the countries, under the sword, in captivity, in a bareness and confusion of face, as it ap- pears today. 8 Now for a little while, the LORD our God has given us grace to make a remnant flee and to grant us refuge in his holy place, that our God may enlighten our eyes and grant us rest in our service. 9 For although we were slaves, our God did not forsake us in our bondage, but showed himself merciful to the kings of Persia, granting us life, erecting the house of our God, renovating its places, and making a wall in Judah and Jerusalem. 10 And now, our God, what shall we say after this, because we have forsaken your commands, 11 which you gave through your servants, the Prophets, saying, "The land where you are go- ing to possess is a vncleane land, because of the filthiness of the peoples of the land, who with their abominations and their vncleannes have filled it from corner to corner. 12 There- fore you shall not give your daughters to their sons, nor take their

daughters for your sons, nor deal with their peace and riches forever, that you may be strong and eat the goods of the land and bequeath it to your sons forever. 13 And after all that has come upon us for our evil deeds and for our great faults (since you, our God, have kept us from being struck down for our iniquities and have granted them such a disappointment) 14 Should we go back to violating your precepts and befriending the people of such abominations? Would you not be angry with them to the point of consuming them, so that there would be no remnant and no one saved? 15 O LORD, God of Israel, thou art righteous, because we have been prevent- ed from fleeing, as it appears today; behold, we stand before thee in our guilt; therefore we cannot stand before thee for this.

CHAPTER 10

1 While Ezra was praying thus, weeping in confession and falling to the ground before the house of God, there gathered to him from Israel a very large congregation of men, wom- en and children; the people wept with a great wailing. 2 Then Shecaniah the son of Jehiel, one of the sons of Elam, answered and said to Ezra, "We have transgressed our God and have taken strange moves from the people of the land, yet now there is hope in Israel in this regard. 3 Therefore let us make a covenant with our God, to remove all the wives (and those from them) according to the counsel of the LORD and those who fear the commands of our God, and let it be done according to the law. 4 Arise, for the matter concerns you; we also will be with you; be of comfort and do it." 5 Then Ezra stood up and made the chief priests, the Leuites and all Israel swear that they would act according to this word. So they swore. 6 And Ezra rose up from before the house of God and went into the chamber of Johanan the son of Eliashib; and he went there always, but he neither ate bread nor drank water, for he mourned because of the transgression of those in the captivity. 7 Then they caused a proclamation to be published throughout all Judah and Jerusalem, to all those in the captivity, that they should gath- er to Jerusalem. 8 Whoever did not show up within three days, according to the advice of the princes and elders, was to forfeit all his possessions and was to be separated from the captive community. 9 Then all the men of Judah and Benjamin gathered themselves together in Jerusalem within three days, on the twentieth day of the ninth month, and all the people sat in the street of the house of God, trembling at this matter and in an- ger. 10 And Ezra the priest stopped and said to them, "You have transgressed and taken foreign wives to increase the guilt of Israel. 11 Now therefore give praise to the LORD, the God of your fathers, do his will and separate yourselves from the inhabitants of the land and from the foreign wives." 12 All the congre- gation answered and said with a loud voice, "We will do thus according to your words." 13 But the people are numerous, and the weath- er is rainy, and we are not able to be without, and it is not a day's work or two, for there are many of us who have committed an offense in this thing. 14 Let our rulers therefore come before the whole community, and let all those who have taken foreign wives in our cities come at the time of roll call, and with them the elders of every city and its judges, until the fierce wrath of our God over this matter depart from us." 15 Then Ionathan the son of Asah- el and Iahaziah the son of Tikuah were involved, and Meshullam and Shabbethai the Leuites helped them. 16 And those of the captivity did so and departed, together

with Ezra the priest and the men who were prin- cipal fathers of the family of their fathers by name, and they sat down on the first day of the tenth month to consider the matter. 17 Until the first day of the first month, they concluded the matter with all the men who had taken foreign wives. 18 Among the sons of the priests were found men who had taken strange wives, namely, the sons of Ieshua the son of Iozadak and his brothers, Maaseiah, Aeliezer, Iarib and Gedaliah. 19 And they gave their assent that their wives should be blotted out, and those who had committed an offense gave a ramme for their offense. 20 Of the sons of Immer, Honani and Zebadiah. 21 Of the sons of Harim: Maaseiah, Eliiah, Semaiah, Iehiel, and Vzziah. 22 Of the sons of Pashur: Helioenai, Maaseiah, Ishmael, Netaneel, Ioz- abad and Elasah. 23 Of the Leuites: Iozabad, Shimei, Kelaiah (who is Kelita), Pethahiah, Iudah and Eliezer. 24 Of the singers: Eliashib. Of the porters: of Shallum, Telem and Vri. 25 Of Israel: of the sons of Parosh, Ramiah, Iesia, Malchiah, Miamin, Eleazar, Malchijah and Benaiah. 26 Of the sons of Elam: Mattaniah, Zechariah, Iehiel, Abdi, Ieremoth, and Elijah. 27 Of the sons of Zattu: Helioenai, Eliashib, Mattaniah, Ierimoth, Zabad, and Aziza. 28 Of the sons of Bebai: Iehohanan, Hananiah, Zabbai, Athlai. 29 Of the sons of Bani: Me- shullam, Malluch, Adaiah, Iashub, Sheal, Ier- amoth. 30 Of the sons of Pahath Moab, Adna, Chelal, Benaiah, Maaseiah, Mattaniah, Beza- leel, Binnui, and Manasseh. 31 Of the sons of Harim: Eliezer, Ishiiah, Malchiah, Semaiah, Shimeon, 32 Benjamin, Malluch, Shamariah. 33 Of the sons of Hashum: Mattenai, Mattat- tah, Zabad, Eliphelet, Ieremai, Manasseh, Shimei. 34 Of the sons of Bani, Maadai, Am- ram, and Vel, 35 Banaiah, Bediah, Chelluh, 36 Vaniah, Meremoth, Eliashib, 37 Mattani- ah, Mattenai and Iaasau, 38 Banni, Bennui, Shimei, 39 Shemiah, Nathan and Adaiah, 40 Machnadebai, Shashai, Sharai, 41 Azareel, Shemaiah, Shemaiah, 42 Shallum, Amariah, Ioseph. 43 Of the sons of Nebo, Ieiel, Mat- tithiah, Zabad, Zebinah, Iadau, Ioel, Bena- iah. 44 All these had taken foreign wives, and among them were women who had children.

NEHEMIAH

CHAPTER 1

1 The words of Nehemiah, son of Hachaliah. In the month of Chisleu, the twentieth year, while I was in the palace of Susa, 2 came Ha- nam, one of my brothers, he and the men of Iudah, and I asked them about the islands that had been delivered and belonged to the remnant of the captivity and about Jerusa- lem. 3 They said to me, "The remnant of the captivity that is left there in the province is in great affliction and reprobation; the walls of Jerusalem have been broken down, and its gates are burned with fire." 4 When I heard these words, I fell to the ground and wept, and mourned for several days, and fasted and prayed before the God of Heauen, 5 and said, "O LORD, God of Heauen, the great and terrible God, who retains favor and mercy for those who love him and keep his com- mands, 6 please let your ears be attentive and your ears open, to hear the praises of your service, that I pray before you every day, day and night for the children of Israel, your ser- vants, and confess the sins of the children of Israel, which we have committed against you, both I and the house of my fathers: 7 We have grievously sinned against thee, and have not observed the commands, the statutes, and the rules which thou hast given to thy servant Moses. 8 Please remember the word that you commanded your servant Moses, "You shall transgress, and

I will scatter you among the people." 9 But if you will be converted to me and keep my commands and carry them out, even if your dispersion occurs in the remotest part of the land, I will gather you from there and bring you to the place I have chosen to put my Name there. 10 These are your servants and your people, whom you have redeemed by your great power and by your mighty hand. 11 O LORD, I pray thee, let thy ear hear the prayer of thy servant and thy servants, who desire to fear thy Name, and I pray thee, let thy servant prosper this day, and let him be allowed to be well in the presence of this man, for I was the king's steward.

CHAPTER 2

1 Now in the month of Nisan, in the twentieth year of King Artahshashte's reign, the wine stood before him; I took the wine and gave it to the king. 2 The king said to me, "Why is your appearance sad, since you are not sick? It is nothing but sadness of heart." Then I felt distressed, 3 and I said to the king, "God says king forever; why should not my countenance be sad, when the city and the house of my fathers' sepulchres lie forsaken, and its gates are ravaged by fire?" 4 The king said to me, "What do you ask me for?" Then I prayed to the God of Heauen, 5 and said to the king, "If it pleases the king, and if your servant has found good in your eyes, I desire you to send me to Iudah, to the city of my fathers' graves, to buy it." 6 The king said to me, "How long will your journey be, and when will you re- turn? So it pleased the king, who sent for me, and I set a time for him. 7 After that I said to the king, "If it pleases the king, let them give me letters to the captains across the river, that they may accompany me outside, until I come to Iudah." 8 and letters to Asaph, keeper of the king's park, to give me lumber to buy the palace gates (which referred to the house), for the walls of the city, and for the house into which I will enter. And the king gave me ac- cording to the good hand of my God upon me. 9 Then I went to the captains across the river and delivered to them the king's letters. The king had sent army captains and horsemen with me. 10 But Sanballat, the Oronite, and Tobiah, servant of the Ammonite, heard of it and were greatly saddened that a man had come who was seeking the wealth of the chil- dren of Israel. 11 So I came to Jerusalem and stayed there three days. 12 I rose up at night, I and few men with me, for I told no one what God had set my heart to do in Jerusalem, and there was no beast with me, such as I was rid- ing on. 13 Then I went out by night through the gate of the valley and came before the well of the dragon and the dung gate, and I saw the walls of Jerusalem, how they had been broken down and their gates had been burned with fire. 14 Then I went to the gate of the foun- tain and to the fishpond of kings, and there was no line to let the beast pass under me. 15 Then, during the night, I passed through the brooke, and looked at the wall, and went back, and went in by the gate of the valley, and came back. 16 The chiefs did not know where I had gone, and they did not know what I had done; I had not yet told the chiefs, nor the priests, nor the nobles, nor all the others who were working. 17 Then I said to them, "You see the misery in which we are, how Jerusalem lies in ruins and its gates are burned with fire; come and buy the walls of Jerusalem, so that we are no longer a reproach." 18 Then I told them of the hand of my God (which was good for me) and also of the king's words to me. And they said, "Arise and buy." Thus they strengthened their hand to good. 19 But when Sanballat, the Oronite, Tobiah, the Ammonite

servant, and Sheshem, the Arab, heard of it, they mocked Vs, despised him, and said, "What are you do- ing? Do you rebel against the king? 20 Then I answered them and said, "The God of Heauen will make the king prosper, and we his ser- vants will rise up and buy; but as for you, you have no part, no right, and no remembrance in Jerusalem."

CHAPTER 3

1 Then Eliashib the priest stood up with his brother priests, and they bought the sheep pen; they repaid it and set up its foundation; so they repaid it as far as the tower of Meah and as far as the tower of Hananeel. 2 Beside him he bought the men of Jericho, and beside him Zaccur the son of Imri. 3 The fish harbor the sons of Senaa bought it, who also laid its beams of light and set up its foundations, locks and bars. 4 Then next to them fortified Merimoth the son of Vrijah the son of Hak- koz, and next to them fortified Meshullam the son of Berechiah the son of Meshezabeel, and next to them fortified Zadok the son of Baanah: 5 And beside them fortified the Te- koites; but the great ones of them put not their necks to the work of their lords. 6 At the gate of the ancient fishpond did Iehoioada the son of Pasea fortify themselves, and Me- shullam the son of Besodaiah; they laid the beams thereof, and fastened the banks there- of, and the locks thereof, and the bars there- of. 7 Beside them also fortified Melatiah the Gibonite, and Jadon the Meronothite, men of Gibeon and Mizpah, for the throne of the duke, which was beyond the river. 8 Beside him fortified Vzziel the son of Harhohiah, of the gold smelters; beside him also fortified Hananiah the son of Harakkahim, and they took Jerusalem back to the broad walls. 9 Be- side them also fortified Rephaiah the son of Hur, leader of the half of Jerusalem. 10 Next to him fortified Jedaiah the son of Harumaph, opposite his house, and next to him fortified Hattush the son of Hashabniah. 11 Malchiiah the son of Harim and Hashub the son of Pa- hath Moab fortified the second gate and the tower of the furnaces. 12 Beside him also for- tified Shallum the son of Halloesh, leader of the half of Jerusalem, he and his daughters. 13 And the gate of the valley was fortified by Hanum and the inhabitants of Zanuah; and they bought it, and set up the walls, the locks, and the bars, a thousand cubits on the wall as far as the dung gate. 14 The dung gate was fortified by Malchiah the son of Rechab, chief of the fourth part of Beth-Haccarem; he built it and set up the walls, locks and bars there. 15 And the gate of the fountain was fortified by Shallun the son of Col- Hozeh, chief of the fourth part of Mizpah; and he built it, and set up the walls, the locks, and the bars, and the wall as far as the fishpond of Shelah, by the garden of the kings, and as far as the steppes that go down from the city of Dauid. 16 After him Nehemiah the son of Azbuk, commander of the half of Bet-Zur, fortified the opposite side, against the sepulchres of Dauid, as far as the fishpond that had been repaired and as far as the king's house. 17 After him fortified the Leuiti, Rehum the son of Bani, and next to him fortified Hashabiah, chief of the half of Keilah, in his quarter. 18 After him their brothers fortified themselves; Bauai the son of Henadad, chief of the half of Keilah: 19 And next to him, Ezer the son of Ieshua, chief of Mizpah, the other half, opposite the road leading to the corner of the armor. 20 After him Baruch the son of Zechai fortified anoth- er part from the corner to the gate of the house of Eliashib the priest. 21 After him Merimoth the son of Vrijah the son of Hakkoz fortified another portion from the border of the house of Eliashib to where the house of

Eliashib ex- tended. 22 After him fortified also the priests, the men of the game. 23 After them forti- fied Benjamin and Hasshub in front of their house; after him fortified Azariah the son of Maaseiah, the son of Ananias, by his house. 24 After him Binnui the son of Henadad fortified another part of Azariah's house as far as the turn and corner. 25 Palal, son of Vzai, from beyond the corner and the high tower that is outside the king's house, beside the prison yard. After him came Pedaiah, son of Parosh. 26 The Nethinims dwelt in this fortress as far as the place in front of the water gate on the east, and as far as the tower that is outside. 27 After him the Tekoites fortified themselves in another part, opposite the great tower that is outside, as far as the wall of the fortress. 28 From the horse gate onward the priests forti- fied themselves, each against his own house. 29 After them Zadok the son of Immer forti- fied himself against his house, and after him Shemaiah the son of Shekadiah, keeper of the east gate, fortified himself. 30 After him fortified Hananiah the son of Shemaiah, and Hanun the son of Zalaph, the sixth; after him fortified Meshullam the son of Berechiah, in front of his chamber. 31 And after him forti- fied Malchiah the son of a goldsmith, unto the house of the Nethinim and of you marchers, opposite the gate Miphkad and the chamber in the corner. 32 Between the corner chamber and the sheep gate, the goldsmiths and the marchers fortified themselves.

CHAPTER 4

1 But when Sanballat heard that we had built the wall, he became grievously wroth and an- gry, and mocked his enemies, 2 and, before his brothers and the army of Samaria, said, "What are these fools doing? Will they forti- fy themselves? Will they sacrifice? Will they finish in a day? Will they make whole stones again from the piles of dust, since they are burned?" 3 Tobiah the Ammonite was beside him and said, "Though they buy, yet if a fox comes near, it brings down their stone wall." 4 Hear, O our God (for we are despised), and turn their shame on their heads, and give them a prayer in the land of their captivity, 5 And do not blot out their iniquity, and do not allow their sin to be set forth before you, for they set forth before the builders. 6 So we built the wall, and the whole wall was restored to its half, and the hearts of the people were set to work. 7 But when Sanballat, Tobiah, the Arabs, the Ammonites, and the Ashdodim came to know that the wall of Jerusalem had been restored (for the breaches were begin- ning to be closed), they became very angry, 8 and they all conspired together to come and fight against Jerusalem and to hinder them. 9 We prayed to our God and set watchmen before them, day and night, because of them. 10 Iudah said, "The strength of the porters has weakened and there is much earth, so that we cannot build the wall. 11 Even our aduer- saries had said, "They will not know it or see it until we come in among them, kill them, and cause the work to cease." 12 But when the Iewes (who lived beside them) came, they said ten times, "From all the places to which you will return, they will be upon you." 13 There- fore I placed myself in the lowest places be- hind the wall, on the tops of the stones, and I placed the people according to their families, with their swords and their spears and their bows. 14 Then I saw, and stood up, and said to the princes, the chiefs, and all the rest of the people, "Do not be afraid of them; remem- ber the great LORD, be afraid, and fight for your brothers, your sons, your daughters, your wives, and your houses." 15 When our enemies came to know that the

thing was known to them, God made their counsels fail, and we all turned to the walls, each to his own work. 16 From that day on, half of the young men did the work, and the other half of them kept the spears, shields, bows, and im- plements; and the leaders stayed behind the whole house of Iudah. 17 Those who bought on the walls, those who carried the weights and those who carried, worked with one hand and held the sword with the other. 18 For ev- ery one of the buyers had his sword girded on his loins and was buying; and he who blew the trumpet was beside me. 19 Then I said to the princes and the rulers and the rest of the peo- ple, "The work is great and large, and we are separated on the walls, one from another. 20 Wherever therefore you hear the sound of the trumpet, resort to vs: our God will fight for vs. 21 So we labored in the work, and half of them held their spears, from the appearing of the morning until the coming of the stars. 22 And at the same time I said to the people, "Let each one with his servant retire to Jerusalem, that they may keep watch by night and work by day." 23 So neither I, nor my brothers, nor my servants, nor the men of war (who followed me) took off our garments, but each one took them off to wash himself.

CHAPTER 5

1 Now there was a great weeping of the peo- ple and their wives against their brothers, the Iewes. 2 For there were those who said, "We and our sons and daughters are many, so let us take of the horn, that we may eat and live." 3 There were also those who said, "We must exploit our lands, our vineyards and our houses, and take of the horn for famine." 4 There were also those who said, "We have borrowed money for the kings' tribute on our lands and our vineyards." 5 Now our flesh is like that of our brethren, and our children like their children; and behold, we bring into subjection our sons and our daughters as servants, and there are of our daughters now in subjection, and there is no power in our hands; for other men have our lands and our vineyards. 6 Then I became very angry when I heard their cry and these words. 7 I thought in my mind, and rebuked the princes and the rulers, and said to them, "You lay burdens each one upon his brothers; and I have set a great assembling against them." 8 and I said to them, "We (according to our ability) have redeemed our brethren who were sold to the Gentiles; and will you still sell your brethren, or will they be sold in turn? Then they kept si- lent and could not answer. 9 I also said, "What you are doing is not good. Should you not walk in the fear of our God, because of the re- proach of the heathen our enemies? 10 Since I and my brothers and my servants lend them money and horns, please let them get rid of this burden. 11 Return to them this day, I pray you, their lands, their vineyards, their olives and their houses, and return the hundredth part of the silver, horn, wine and oil that you have collected from them." 12 Then they said, "We will return it and not demand it from them; we will do as you said." Then I called the priests and made them swear that they would act according to this promise. 13 Then I shook my lappa and said, "Let God shake from his house and from his work anyone who does not fulfill this promise; and so let him be shaken and emptied." And all the con- gregation said, "Amen," and praised the Lord; and the people fulfilled the promise. 14 From the time that the king appointed me to be the baker in the land of Iudah, from the twentieth year until the two hundred and thirtieth year of King Artahshashte, that is, two years, I and my brothers did not eat the baker's

bread. 15 For the former governors before me had been responsible to the people and had taken bread and wine from them, as well as fourteen shek- els of silk; yea, and their servants command- ed the people; but I did not, for fear of God. 16 Indeed, I fortified part of the building site of these walls, and we did not buy land, and all my servants came here together to work. 17 Moreover, at my table there were a hundred and fifty people, including rulers and ruled, who had come here from the pagans around. 18 Every day an ox, six choice sheep and birds were prepared, and in ten days there was plenty of wine for everyone. But for all this I did not require the bread of food, for slavery was severe for this people. 19 Remember me, O my God, in kindness, according to all that I have done for this people.

CHAPTER 6

1 When Sanballat, Tobiah, Sheshem the Arab and the rest of our enemies came to know that I had built the walls and that there were no more breaches (although at that time I had not yet put sticks in the gates) 2 Then Sanbal- lat and Sheshem sent to me, saying, "Come, that we may assemble in the villages of the plain of Ono"; and they thought to harm me. 3 Therefore I sent messengers to them, saying, "I have a great work to do and cannot come down; why should the work cease, while I leave it and come to you?" 4 Nevertheless they sent for me four times in this way. And I answered them in the same way. 5 Then San- ballat his servant sent for me the fifth time in this way, with an open letter in his hand, 6 where it was written, "It has been reported among the heathen, and Gashmu has said it, that you and the Israelites are thinking of re- belling; therefore you build the wall and will be their king according to these words. 7 You also commanded the prophets to preach of you in Jerusalem, saying, "There is a king in Iudah; and now, according to these words, it shall come to the ears of the kings; come therefore and let us take counsel together." 8 Then I sent to him, saying, "It was not done according to the words you spoke, because you wrote them with your own hand. 9 For all opposed, saying, "Their hands will be weak- ened by the work, and it will not be done; now therefore encourage me." 10 And I came to the house of Shemaiah the son of Delaiah, the son of Mehetabeel, and he shut himself in, saying, "Go into the house of God together, in the midst of the temple, and shut the doors of the temple, for they will come and kill you; yea, by night they will come and kill you." 11 Then I said, "Should a man like me flee? Who is he, like me, who wants to enter the Temple to lie? I will not enter. 12 Well, I found that God had not sent him, but that he had uttered this prophecy against me, because Tobiah and Sanballat had hired him. 13 Therefore he was concerned that I should be betrayed, and do so, and sin, and that they should have good tidings to reproach me. 14 My God, remem- ber Tobiah and Sanballat according to their works, and also Noadiah the prophet and the other prophets who wanted to put me in dan- ger. 15 Nevertheless the wall was finished on the fifth and twentieth day of Elul, in two days and fifty. 16 When all our enemies learned of it, that is, all the pagans who were in the vicin- ity, they were afraid and their courage failed, because they knew that this work had been done by our God. 17 In those days there were many princes in Iudah whose letters went to Tobiah and Tobiah's letters went to them. 18 For there were many in Iudah who were faith- ful to him, for he was the son of Shechaniah the son of Arah, and his son Iehonathan had the daughter of Meshullam the son of Bere- chiah. 19 Yes, they spoke in his praise before me and reported my words to him, and Tobi- ah sent letters to put me in awe.

CHAPTER 7

1 When the walls were built and I had pre- pared the harbors, the porters, the singers and the Leuites were appointed, I command- ed my brother Hanani and Hananiah, prince of the palace of Jerusalem (for he was un- doubtedly a faithful man and feared God for many things), 2 I commanded my brother Hanani and Hananiah, prince of the palace of Jerusalem (for he was undoubtedly a faithful man and feared God for many things) 3 And I said to them, "Do not open the gates of Je- rusalem until the dawn of the sun; and while they are passing through, close the gates and fasten them; and I established wards among the inhabitants of Jerusalem, every one in his war and every one out against his house." 4 Now the city was large and numerous, but the people were few, and the houses were not bought. 5 My God put it into my heart to gath- er the princes, the leaders and the people to count their genealogies; and I found a book of the genealogies of those who had come before, and I found written in it, 6 These are the sons of the province who came from the captivity that had been taken away (which Ne- buchadnezzar, king of Babel, had taken away) and who returned to Jerusalem and to Judah, each to his own city. 7 Those who came with Zerubbabel: Ieshua, Nehemiah, Azariah, Raa- miah, Nahamani, Mordecai, Bilshan, Mis- pereth, Biguai, Nehum, Baanah. These are the names of the men of the people of Israel. 8 The sons of Parosh, two thousand and one hundred seuentie two. 9 The sons of Shepha- tiah, three hundred seuentie two. 10 The sons of Arah, six hundred fifty-two. 11 The sons of Pahath Moab, of the sons of Ieshua and Ioab, two thousand eight hundred and two. 12 The sons of Elam, one thousand two hundred fif- ty-four. 13 The sons of Zattu, eight hundred fifty-four. 14 The sons of Zaccai, seven hun- dred and three hundred and fifty. 15 The sons of Binnui, six hundred and eight and forty. 16 The sons of Bebai, six hundred and eight and twenty-five. 17 The sons of Azgad: two thou- sand three hundred and two and twenty-five. 18 The sons of Adonikam, six hundred three hundred and sixty-five. 19 The sons of Bigu- ai, two thousand three hundred and seu. 20 The sons of Adin, six hundred and fifty. 21 The sons of Ater of Hizkiah, ninety-nine and eight. 22 The sons of Hashum, three hundred and eight and twenty-five. 23 The sons of Be- zai, three hundred and four and two. 24 The sons of Hariph, an hundred and two. 25 The sons of Gibeon, ninety-nine and five. 26 The men of Beth-Lem and Netophah, an hundred sixty-five and eight. 27 The men of Anathoth, an hundred and eighty eight and twenty-five. 28 The men of Beth-Azmaueth, two and for- ty. 29 The men of Kiriath-iearim, Chephirah, and Beeroth, an hundred and nine and three and forty. 30 The men of Ramah and Gaba, six hundred and one and twenty. 31 The men of Michas, an hundred thousand and two and twenty-five. 32 The men of Beth-El and Ai, a hundred thousand and three and twenty- five. 33 The men of the other Nebo, two and fifty. 34 The sons of the other Elam: a thousand, two hundred and four hundred and fifty. 35 The sons of Harim, three hundred and twenty. 36 The sons of Jericho, three hundred fifty-four hundred. 37 The sons of Lod-hadid and Ono, six hundred and one and twenty-five. 38 The sons of Senaa, three thousand nine hundred and thirty. 39 Priests: the sons of Iedaiah, of the house of Ieshua, nine hundred seuentie three. 40 Sons of Immer: one thousand two hundred and fifty. 41

The sons of Pashur, one thousand two hundred seventy-four. 42 The sons of Harim: a thousand and seuenteen. 43 The Leuites: the sons of Ieshua of Kadmiel and the sons of Hodiua, seventy-four. 44 The singers: the sons of Asaph, a hundred and eight and forty. 45 The porters: the sons of Shallum, the sons of Ater, the sons of Talmon, the sons of Akkub, the sons of Hatita, the sons of Shobai, an hundred and eight and thirty. 46 The Nethinim: the sons of Ziha, the sons of Hashupha, the sons of Tabaoth, 47 the sons of Keros, the sons of Sia, the sons of Padon, 48 the sons of Lebana, the sons of Hagaba, the sons of Shalmai, 49 the sons of Hanan, the sons of Giddel, the sons of Gahar, 50 the sons of Reaiah, the sons of Rezin, the sons of Ne- koda, 51 the sons of Gazzam, the sons of Vzza, the sons of Paseah, 52 the sons of Besai, the sons of Meunim, the sons of Nephishesim, 53 the sons of Bakbuk, the sons of Hakupha, the sons of Harhur, 54 the sons of Bazlith, the sons of Mehida, the sons of Harsha, 55 the sons of Barkos, the sons of Sissera, the sons of Tamah, 56 the sons of Neziah, the sons of Hatipha, 57 the sons of the seruants of Solo- mon, the sons of Sotai, the sons of Sofereth, the sons of Perida, 58 the sons of Iaalah, the sons of Darkon, the sons of Giddel, 59 the sons of Shephatiah, the sons of Hattil, the sons of Pochereth of Zebaim, the sons of Amun. 60 All the Nethinim and the sons of Solomon's servants were three hundred ninety-two. 61 These came from Tel-Mela, from Tel-Haresha, from Cherub, from Addon, and from Immer, but they could not tell either their paternal house or their descent, or whether they were of Israel. 62 The sons of Delaiah, the sons of Tobiah, the sons of Nekoda, six hundred and two hundred and four. 63 Of the priests: the sons of Habaiah, the sons of Hakkoz, the sons of Barzillai, who took to wife one of the daughters of Barzillai, the Gileadite, and was named after them. 64 These sought their writing of genealogies, but could not find it; therefore they were removed from the priest- hood. 65 The Tirshatha told them that they would not eat of the Most Holy until a priest arose with Vrim and Thummim. 66 The whole community consisted of two hundred and forty thousand people, three hundred and six- ty-five, 67 besides their servants and their el- ders, who were two hundred thousand, three hundred sixty-five and thirty-three, and they had two hundred fifty-five men and women singing. 68 Their horses were seven hundred and six hundred and thirty, and their mules two hundred and fifty-four. 69 And their cam- els were four hundred and fifty-five, and their asses six hundred and twenty. 70 Some of the chief fathers went to work. The Tirshatha de- voted themselves to the treasury: a thousand drams of gold, fifty basins, five hundred and thirty priestly garments. 71 Some of the chief fathers gave to the treasury of the work twen- ty thousand drams of gold and two thousand and two hundred pieces of silver. 72 The rest of the people gave twenty thousand drams of gold and two thousand pieces of silk and three dozen priestly garments. 73 And the priests, and the Leuites, and the porters, and the singers, and the rest of the people, and the Nethinims, and all Israel, dwelt in their cities; and when the tenth month came, the children of Israel were in their cities.

CHAPTER 8

1 All the people gathered in the street that was before the water gate and spoke to Ezra the scribe to bring the book of the Law of Moses, which the Lord had commanded Is- rael. 2 And Ezra the priest brought the Law before the congregation of men and women, and to all who could hear and understand it, on the first day of the seventh month, 3 And he read therein in the way that was before the water gate (from morning until noon) before men and women and all who understood it, and the ears of all the people heard the book of Lawe. 4 Ezra, the scribe, stood on a wood- en pulpit he had built for preaching; beside him stood Mattithiah, Semaiah, Ananias, Vrijah, Hilkiah and Maaseiah on his right, and on his left Pedaiah, Mishael, Malchiah, Hashum, Hashbadanah, Zechariah and Me- shullam. 5 And Ezra opened the book before all the people, for he was near all the people; and when he opened it, all the people stood. 6 Ezra prayed to the LORD, the great God, and all the people answered, "Amen, amen," lifting up their hands; and they prostrated them- selves and worshipped the LORD with their faces to the ground. 7 Ieshua, Bani, Shere- biah, Iamin, Akkub, Shabbethai, Hodiiah, Maaseiah, Kelita, Azariah, Iozabad, Hanan, Pelaiah and the Leuites also made the people understand the lamentation, and the people remained in their places. 8 They read the book of God's Law clearly, understood its meaning, and made the people understand the read- ing. 9 Then Nehemiah (who is Tirshatha), the priest Ezra, the scribe, and the Leuites who were instructing the people, said to all the people, "This day is holy to the LORD your God; do not panic or weep, for all the people wept at hearing the words of the Law." 10 He also said to the Leuites, "Go, eat the fat, drink the sweet, and send some to those for whom no one is prepared, for this day is holy to our Lord; therefore do not be sad, for the joy of the Lord is your strength." 11 Then the Leuites made silence throughout the people, saying, "Be still, for this day is holy; therefore do not be sad." 12 Then all the people began to eat and drink, sending away a portion and making great rejoicing, because they understood the words they had been taught. 13 On the second day the principal fathers of all the people, the priests and the Leuites gathered with Ezra the scribe, that he too might instruct them in the words of Lawe. 14 They found it written in the Law (which the Lord had commanded through Moses) that the children of Israel were to dwell in garments during the feast of the seventh month, 15 and that they were to proclaim and have proclaimed in all their cities and in Jerusalem, "Go to the mountain and bring olive branches, pine branches, myrtle branches, palm branches and branch- es of old trees, to make cloths, as it is written." 16 So the people went and brought them, and made cloths of them, every one on the roof of his house, in their courts, in the courts of the house of God, in the street by the water gate, and in the street by the gate of Ephraim. 17 All the congregation of those who had come out of the captivity again made themselves cloaks and sat down under the cloaks, because from the time of Ieshua the son of Nun until now the children of Israel had not done so, and the joy was very great. 18 And he read in the book of the Law of God every day, from the first day to the last day. And the feast was kept for sev- en days, and on the eighth day a solemn as- sembly was made, according to the rules.

CHAPTER 9

1 On the fourth and twentieth day of this month the children of Israel gathered togeth- er with fasting, sackcloth and earth on them. 2 The children of Israel separated themselves from all the strangers and stopped to confess their sins and the iniquities of their fathers. 3 Then they stopped at their place and read the book of Lamentation of the LORD, their GOD, four times during the day; they confessed and

worshiped the LORD, their GOD, four times. 4 Then they stood on the desks of the Leuiti Ieshua, Bani, Kadmiel, Shebaniah, Bunni, Sherebiah, Bani and Chenani and cried with a loud voice to the LORD their GOD. 5 And the Leuites said, "Ieshua and Kadmiel, Bani, Ha- shabnia, Sherebiah, Hodiiah, Shebaniah and Pethahiah, arise and praise the LORD your God for all your life, and praise your glorious name, O God, who excels all thanksgiving and all praise. 6 Thou alone art the LORD; thou hast made the plateau and the plateau of all the plateaus, with all their hosts, the earth and all things therein, the seas and all that is therein, and thou preservest them all, and the army of the plateau worshippeth thee. 7 You are, LORD, the God who chose Abram, brought him out of Vr into Chaldea, and gave him the name Abraham, 8 you found his heart faithful before you and made a covenant with him to give his descendants the land of the Canaanites, the Hittites, the Amorites, the Perizzites, the Jebusites and the Girguseans, and you have performed your words, for you are righteous. 9 Thou hast also considered the affliction of our fathers in Egypt, and hast heard their cry by the Red Sea, 10 And thou didst perform signs and wonders upon Pha- raoh, and upon all his servants, and upon all the people of his land, because thou knewest that they dealt haughtily against them; there- fore thou didst make thyself a Name, as it ap- pears this day. 11 For thou made a breach in the sea before them, and they passed through the midst of the sea upon the dry land; and those who pursued them thou cast them into the deep like a stone, into the great waters: 12 And thou didst guide them by day with a pil- lar of cloud, and by night with a pillar of fire, to give them light in the way that they went. 13 Thou wentest down also to Mount Sinai, and didst speak unto them from on high, and didst impart unto them righteous teachings, true laws, standards, and good commands, 14 declared to them your holy Sabbath and com- manded them precepts, rules and laws by the hand of Moses your servant: 15 He gave them bread of the ground for their hunger, and caused water to flow from the river for their thirst, and promised them to enter and take possession of the land, for which thou hadst lifted up thy hand to give them. 16 But they and our fathers behaved proudly and hard- ened their necks, so that they did not listen to your commands,17 but refused to obey, and would not remember thy wondrous works which thou hadst done for them, but hard- ened their necks, and set their minds to re- turn to bondage by their rebellion; but thou, O God of mercies, grateful and full of com- passion, of longsuffering and great mercy, hast not forsaken them. 18 Moreover, when they made them a molten cast (and said, "This is your God who brought you out of the land of Egypt") and committed great blasphemies, 19 nevertheless you, because of your great mer- cies, did not forsake them in the wilderness; the pillar of cloud did not depart from them by day to show them the way, nor the pillar of fire by night to show them the light and the way to follow. 20 Moreover, you gave your good Spir- it to instruct them, you did not withhold your MAN from their mouth, and you gave them water for their thirst. 21 You also fed them for four hundred years in the wilderness; they lacked nothing; their garments did not grow old and their feet did not swell. 22 Then you delivered them from kingdoms and peoples and scattered them to every corner; so they possessed the land of Sihon, the land of the king of Heshbon, and the land of Og, king of Bashan. 23 And thou didst multiply their sons as the stars of heaven, and didst bring them into the land of which thou hadst spoken unto their fathers, that they might go there and possess it. 24 So the sons entered in and took possession of

the land; and you subdued before them the inhabitants of the land, that is, the Canaanites, and delivered them into their hands, with their kings and the people of the land, that they might do what they pleased with it. 25 And they took their strong cities and the fat land, and possessed houses full of every good thing, dug cisterns, vine- yards, olive trees, and trees for food in abun- dance; and they ate, and were satisfied, and fattened, and enjoyed themselves because of your great goodness. 26 Yet they were disobe- dient, rebelled against you, threw your Lawe behind their backs, killed your Prophets (who had protested among them to convert them to you) and committed great blasphemies. 27 Therefore you delivered them into the hands of their enemies who persecuted them; yet in the time of their affliction, when they cried out to you, you heard them from above the heavens, and through your great mercies you endowed them with saviors who removed them from the hands of their adversaries. 28 But when they rested, they returned to alms before you; therefore you left them in the hand of their enemies, so that they had do- minion over them, but when they gathered themselves together and cried out to you, you heard them from above and delivered them according to your great mercies many times, 29 and you protested in their midst that you would bring them back to your law; but they behaved themselves with pride and did not listen to your commands, but sinned against your precepts (which a man should follow and abide by) and pulled back their shoulder and stiffened and would not listen. 30 For many years you forbade them to attend, you pro- tested by your Spirit and by the hand of your prophets, but they would not listen; therefore you gave them into the hand of the peoples of the land. 31 Nevertheless, because of your great mercies, you have not consumed them nor forsaken them, for you are a gracious and merciful God. 32 Now, therefore, our God, the great, mighty and terrible God, who keep grace and mercy, let all the affliction that has come upon you not seem small to you, that is, for our kings, for our princes, for our priests, for our prophets, for our fathers, and for all your people from the time of the kings of As- sur until now. 33 You are righteous in all that has happened, for you have acted justly, while we have acted wickedly. 34 Our kings and our princes, our priests and our fathers, have not carried out your word; they have not heed- ed your commands and your protests, with which you protested in their midst. 35 They have not served you in their kingdom, in your great goodness that you showed them, and in the great and fat land that you set before them, and they have not allowed themselves to work hard. 36 Today we are servants, and the land that you gave to our fathers, to eat its fruit and goodness, behold, we are servants in it. 37 It yields much fruit to the kings whom you have set over us, because of our sins; and they have dominion over our bodies and our livestock as they please, and we are in great affliction. 38 Because of all this, we make a sure document and write it down, and our princes and our Leuites and our priests abide by it.

CHAPTER 10

1 The sealers were Nehemiah, Tyrus the son of Hachaliah, and Zidkiiah, 2 Seraiah, Azari- ah, Jeremiah, 3 Pashur, Amariah, Malchiah, 4 Hattush, Shebaniah, Malluch, 5 Harim, Merimoth, Obadiah, 6 Daniel, Ginnethon, Baruch, 7 Meshullam, Abiia, Miamin, 8 Maa- zia, Bilgai, Semaiah: these are the priests. 9 The Leuites: Ieshua the son of Azaniah, Bin- nui, of the sons of Henadad, Kadmiel. 10

And their brethren Shebaniah, Hodiiah, Kelitah, Pelaiah, Hanun, 11 Micha, Rehob, Hashabiah, 12 Zaccur, Sherebiah, Shebaniah, 13 Hodi- ah, Bani, Beninu. 14 The leaders of the peo- ple were Parosh, Pahath Moab, Elam, Zattu, Bani, 15 Bunni, Azgad, Bebai, 16 Adonia, Bi- guai, Adin, 17 Ater, Hizkiia, Azzur, 18 Hodiah, Hashum, Bezai, 19 Hariph, Anathoth, Nebai, 20 Magpiash, Meshullam, Hezir, 21 Mesheza- beel, Zadok, Iaddua, 22 Pelatia, Hanan, Ana- ia, 23 Hoshea, Hananiah, Hashub, 24 Hallo- hesh, Pileha, Shobek, 25 Rehum, Hashabnah, Maaseia, 26 Ahiia, Hanan, Anan, 27 Malluch, Harim, Baana. 28 The rest of the people, the priests, the Leuiti, the porters, the singers, the Nethinei, and all those who had been separated from the people of the land by the peace of God, their wives, their sons and their daughters, all who could be recognized. 29 And the foremost of them received it for their brethren, and came to care and keep the Law of God, which was issued by Moses the servant of God, to observe and keep all the commands of the LORD our God, his teachings and his statutes: 30 And not to give our daughters to the inhabitants of the land, and not to take their daughters for our sons. 31 And if the people of the land brought merchandise on the Sabbath day or life to sell, we would not take it from them on the Sabbath day or on the holy days; and we would let loose the tenth year and the debts of every person. 32 And we appointed for ourselves to give every year the thirteenth part of a shekel for the service of the house of our God, 33 For the loaves, for the daily feasts, for the daily burnt offerings, for the Sabbaths, for the new moons, for the solemn feasts, for the sanctified things, for the feasts of sin, for atonement for Israel, and for all the works of the house of our God. 34 We also made lotteries for the wood offering, both for the priests, and for the leuites, and for the people, to bring it into the house of our God, from the house of our fathers, whenever it was established, to bury it on the altar of the LORD our God, as it is written in the Lawe, 35 and to bring into the house of the LORD the first fruits of our land, and the first fruits of all the trees, year by year, 36 and the firstborn of our sons and of our cattle, as it is written in the Lawe, and the firstborn of our heifers and of our sheep, to bring it into the house of our God, to you priests who serve in the house of our God, 37 and to bring to the priests, in the rooms of the house of our God, the first fruits of our dough, and our crops, and the fruits of every tree, of wine and oil; and the tithes of our land to the Leuites, that the Leuites may have tithes in all the cities of our land. 38 And the priest, the son of Aaron, shall be with the Leuites, when ye Leuites shall take tithes, and the Leuites shall bring the tenth part of the tithes to the house of our God in the treasury rooms. 39 For the children of Israel and the children of Leu shall bring the offerings of grain, wine and oil to the building sites, and there shall be the furnishings of the sanctuary there, and the priests who serve there, and the porters and the fingers, and we will not forsake the house of our God.

CHAPTER 11

1 The leaders of the people settled in Jerusa- lem; the other people also drew lots so that one out of ten would dwell in Jerusalem, the holy city, and nine parties would settle in the cities. 2 The people gave thanks to all the men who were willing to dwell in Jeru- salem. 3 These are the chiefs of the province who dwelt in Jerusalem, but in the cities of Judah each dwelt in his own cities of Isra- el: the priests, the Leuites, the Nethinims, and the sons of Solomon's servants.

4 In Je- rusalem lived some of the sons of Judah and Benjamin. Of the sons of Judah, Athaiah, son of Vziiah, son of Zechariah, son of Am- ariah, son of Shephatiah, son of Mahaleel, son of the sons of Perez, 5 Maaseiah, the son of Baruch, the son of Col Hozeh, the son of Hazaiah, the son of Adaiah, the son of Ioiar- ib, the son of Zechariah, the son of Shiloni. 6 All the sons of Perez who dwelt in Jerusalem were four hundred, three hundred and eight valiant men. 7 These also were the sons of Benjamin, Sallu the son of Meshullam, the son of Ioed, the son of Pedaiah, the son of Ko- laiah, the son of Maaseiah, the son of Ithiel, the son of Ieshaiah. 8 After him Gabai, Sallai, nine hundred twenty-eight. 9 Ioel the son of Zichri was the chief of the priests, and Iudah the son of Senuah was the second in the city: 10 Among the priests was Iedaiah the son of Ioiarib, Iachin. 11 Seraiah the son of Hilkiah, the son of Meshullam, the son of Zadok, the son of Meraioth, the son of Ahitub, was the head of the house of God. 12 Their brothers who worked in the Temple were eight hun- dred, twenty-two: Adaiah the son of Jeroham, the son of Pelaliah, the son of Amzi, the son of Zechariah, the son of Pashur, the son of Mal- chiah: 13 His brethren, chief of the fathers, were two hundred and two hundred and four, and Amashsai the son of Azareel, the son of Ahazai, the son of Meshilemoth, the son of Immer: 14 Their brethren, valiant men, were a hundred and eleven, eight and twenty-five; their leader was Zabdiel the son of Hagedo- lim. 15 Among the Leuites was Semaiah the son of Hashub, the son of Azrikam, the son of Hashabiah, the son of Bunni. 16 Shabbethai and Iozabad, leader of the Leuiti, were in charge of the work of the house of God. 17 Mattaniah, son of Micha, son of Zabdi, son of Asaph, was the leader who began the thanks- giving and prayer; Bakbukiah, the second of his brothers, and Abda, son of Shammua, son of Galal, son of Ieduthun. 18 All the Leuiti of the holy city were two hundred forty-four. 19 The porters Akkub, Talmon and their brothers who guarded the gates were one hundred and two. 20 The rest of Israel, of the priests and Leuiti, dwelt in all the cities of Iudah, each in his own property. 21 The Nethinims settled in the fortresses; Ziha and Gispa were beyond the Nethinims. 22 The leader of the Leuites in Jerusalem was Vzzi the son of Bani, the son of Ashabiah, the son of Mattaniah, the son of Micha; the singers the sons of Asaph were in charge of the work of the house of God. 23 For the king had commanded that every day the singers should have a faithful watch. 24 Peth- ahiah the son of Meshezabeel, of the sons of Zerah the son of Judah, was at the king's dis- posal in all matters concerning the people. 25 In the villages of their territories, some of the sons of Iudah dwelt in Kiriath-arba and its villages, in Dibon and its villages, in Ieka- bzeel and its villages, 26 in Ieshua, in Mola- dah and in Beth Palet, 27 in Hazer-Shual, in Beer-Sheba and its villages, 28 In Ziklag, in Mechona and its villages, 29 En-Rimmon, Za- rea and Iarmuth, 30 Zanoa, Adullam and their villages, Lachish and its fields, Azekah and its villages; they settled from Beer-Sheba to the valley of Hinnom. 31 The sons of Benjamin, from Geba, to Michmash, to Aiiah, to Beth-El and their villages, 32 Anathoth, Nob, Ananias, 33 Hazor, Ramah, Gittaim, 34 Hadid, Zeboim, Nebalat, 35 Lod and Ono, in the valley of the carpenters. 36 Among the Leuites there were divisions in Iudah and Benjamin.

CHAPTER 12

1 These also are the priests and leuites who went with Zerubbabel the son of Shealtiel and Ieshua: Seraiah,

Jeremiah, Ezra, 2 Amariah, Malluch, Hattush, 3 Shecaniah, Rehum, Mer- imoth, 4 Iddo, Ginnetho, Abiiah, 5 Miamin, Maadia, Bilgah, 6 Shemaiah, Ioiarib, Iedaiah, 7 Sallu, Amok, Hilkiiah, Iedaiah; these were the chief priests and their brethren in the days of Ieshua. 8 Leuiti, Ieshua, Binnui, Kadmiel, Sherebiah, Iudah, Mattaniah were in charge of the thanksgivings, he and his brothers. 9 Bakbukiah, Vnni and their brothers were around them during the vigils. 10 Ieshua be- gat Jehoiakim: Jehoiakim also begat Eliashib, and Eliashib begat Jehoiada. 11 Jehoiada be- gat Ionathan, and Ionathan begat Iaddua, 12 In the days of Jehoiakim were these, the chief fathers of the priests: under Seraiah was Meraiah, under Jeremiah Hananiah, 13 under Ezra, Meshullam; under Amariah, Jehohanan, 14 after Melicu, Ionathan, after Shebaniah, Ioseph, 15 from Harim, Adna, from Maraioth, Helkai, 16 from Iddo, Zechariah, Ginnithon, Meshullam, 17 from Abiiah, Zichri, Minia- min, Moadia, Piltai, 18 from Bilgah, Sham- mua, from Semaia, Iehonathan, 19 from Ioiarib, Mattenai, from Iedaia, Vzzi, 20 Vnder Sallai, Kallai, vnder Amok, Eber, 21 From Hilkia, Hashabia, from Iedaia, Nethaneel. 22 In the days of Eliashib, Ioiada, Iohanan and Iaddua were written the principal fathers of the Leuites and the priests in the reign of Darius the Persian. 23 The sons of Leui, the chief fathers, were written in the book of Chronicles until the days of Iohanan the son of Eliashib. 24 The leaders of the Leuites were Hashabiah, Sherebiah and Ieshua the son of Kadmiel, and their brethren around them to give prayers and thanksgiving, according to the order of Dauid the man of God, to protect themselves from war. 25 Mattaniah, Bakbuki- ah, Obadiah, Meshullam, Talmon and Akkub were gatekeepers who guarded the war at the threshold of the gates. 26 These were in the days of Jehoiakim the son of Ieshua the son of Iozadak, in the days of Nehemiah the leader, and Ezra the priest and scribe. 27 On the occasion of the dedication of the walls of Jerusalem, they sought out the Leuites in all their places to lead them to Jerusalem to celebrate the dedication and rejoicing, with thanksgiving and singing, cymbals, viols and harps. 28 Then the singers gathered from the plain around Jerusalem and from the villages of Netophathi, 29 From the house of Ghilgal, from the villages of Gheba and Azmaueth, because the singers had built villages around Jerusalem. 30 The priests and the Leuites were cleansed and did the cleansing of the people, the gates and the walls. 31 Then I led the princes of Iudah to the walls and formed two great companies to give thanks; one went to the right of the walls, to the dung gate. 32 After them went Oshaiah and half the princes of Judah, 33 Azariah, Ezra, and Meshullam, 34 Iudah, Benjamin, Shemaiah, and Jeremiah, 35 And of the priests the sons of trumpeters, Zechariah the son of Ionathan, the son of Se- maiah, the son of Mattaniah, the son of Mi- chaiah, the son of Zaccur, the son of Asaph. 36 And his brethren, Semaiah, Azareel, Milalai, Gilalai, Maai, Netaneel, Iudah, Hanani, with the musical instruments of Dauid the man of God, and Ezra the scribe went before them. 37 At the gate of the fountain in front of them they passed through the walls of the city of Dauid, beyond the house of Dauid, to the wa- ter gate toward the east. 38 The second group of those giving thanks went to the other side, and I followed them; half the people were by the wall and by the area of the furnaces, as far as the broad wall. 39 Then by the gate of Ephraim, by the old gate, by the fish gate, by the area of Hananeel, and by the area of Meah, as far as the sheep gate, they stopped at the war gate. 40 So the two companies (of those who had given thanks) remained in the house of God, and I and half the leaders with me. 41 Also the priests: Eliakim, Maaseiah,

Miniamin, Michaiah, Helioenai, Zechariah, Hananiah, with trumpets, 42 Maaseiah, Se- maiah, Eleazar, Vzzi, Iehohanan, Malchijah, Elam and Ezer; the singers sang loudly, with Izrahia, who was the overseer. 43 On the same day they offered great sacrifices and gathered together, for God had given them great joy, so that the women and children were filled with joy, and the joy of Jerusalem was heard far away. 44 At the same time men were appoint- ed outside the chambers of the storehouse for the offerings (for the first fruits and for tithes) to collect in them from the fields of the cities the portions of the Law for the priests and for the leuites; for Iudah worked for the priests and for the leuites, who served. 45 The sing- ers and the leuiti observed the service of their God and the war of purification according to the orders of Dauid and Solomon his son. 46 Indeed, in the days of Dauid and Asaph, there were formerly singers of the first rank, who sang songs of praise and thanksgiving to God. 47 In the days of Zerubbabel and in the days of Nehemiah, all Israel gave portions to the singers and porters, each day his portion; they gave the holy things to the Leuites, and the Leuites gave the holy things to the sons of Aaron.

CHAPTER 13

1 On that day the book of Moses was reread in the presence of the people, and it was written therein that the Ammonite and the Moabite should not enter the congregation of God, 2 because they did not go out to meet the children of Israel with bread and water, but hired Balaam against them, that he might curse them; and our God turned the curse into a blessing." 3 When they had heard the Lawe, they separated from Israel all who were mixed. 4 Before that, Eliashib the priest had opened the doors of the chamber of the house of our God, being Tobiah's kinsman: 5 He had prepared for him a large chamber, and there they had already laid down the of- ferings, the incense, the vessels, the tithes of grain, wine, and oil (intended for the Leuites, the singers, and the porters), and the offer- ings of the priests. 6 But in all this time I did not remain in Jerusalem, for in the two hun- dred and thirtieth year of Artahshashte, king of Babel, I came to the king and after some days presented myself to the king. 7 When I had come to Jerusalem, I understood how much Eliashib had done for Tobiah, having a chamber built for him in the courtyard of the house of God, 8 and it struck me greatly; so I threw out of the chamber all the furnishings of Tobiah's house. 9 Then I commanded them to set the chambers on fire, and I brought there again the furnishings of the house of God, with the decorations and incense. 10 I found that the portions of the Leuites had not been consumed and that everyone had fled to his own land, both the Leuites and the sing- ers who performed the work. 11 Then I took back the leaders and said, "Why is the house of God forsaken? I gathered them together and put them in their place. 12 Then I brought to all Iudah the tithes of grain, wine and oil to the treasuries. 13 And I made the treasur- ers of the treasures the priest Shemaiah, and the scribe Zadok, and of the Leuites, Pedaiah, and under their hand Hanan the son of Zac- cur, the son of Mattaniah, because they were counted faithful and had the duty of distrib- uting to their brethren. 14 Remember me, O my God, and do not blot out my deeds that I have done on the house of my God and on his offices. 15 In those days I saw in Iudah those who trod wine presses on the Sabbath day, who carried sheep, who loaded donkeys with wine, and grapes, and figs, and all weights, and carried them to Jerusalem on the

Sabbath day; and I protested against them on the day that they sold vines. 16 There also dwelt there men of Tyre, who brought fish and all kinds of merchandise, and sold on the sabbath day to the children of Judah, also in Jerusalem. 17 Then I rebuked the leaders of Judah and said to them, "What on earth is this thing that you are doing and violating the Sabbath day? 18 Did not your fathers do so, and did not our God bring all this plague upon you and upon this city? Yet you increase wrath on Israel by violating the Sabbath." 19 When the gates of Jerusalem began to be dark before the Sab- bath, I commanded the gates to be shut and not to be opened until after the Sabbath; and some of my servants put me at the gates so that no burdens would be carried on the Sab- bath day. 20 So the captains and marchers of all the goods remained once or twice all night without Jerusalem. 21 I protested in their midst and said to them, "Why do you toil all night around the walls? If you do it one more time, I will lay hands on you." From that time they no longer came on the Sabbath day. 22 Then I told the Leuites that they should be on their guard and come to guard the gates to keep the Sabbath day holy. Remember me, O my God, in this matter, and forgive me according to your great mercy." 23 In those days I also saw women marrying wives from Ashdod, Ammon and Moab. 24 Their sons spoke half in the language of Ashdod and could not speak in the language of Iewes, ac- cording to the language of either people. 25 Then I rebuked them, and cursed them, and struck some of them, and tore off their ears, and took another for God: "You shall not give your daughters to their sons, nor take their daughters for your sons, nor for yourselves." 26 Did not Solomon, king of Israel, sin of these things? Yet, among many nations, there was no king like him, for he was well-liked by his God and God had made him king of Is- rael; yet, unknown women made him sin. 27 Should we then obey you to go to all this great trouble and to transgress our God, that is, to marry strange women? 28 One of the sons of Jehoiada the son of Eliashib the priest was the son-in-law of Sanballat the Horonite, but I cast him out of me. 29 Remember those, O my God, who defile the priesthood and its mes- senger and the Leuites. 30 Then I cleansed them from all strangers, and apportioned the wards of the priests and the Leuites, each in his office, 31 And for cutting wood at times, and for the first fruits. Remember me, O my God, in good.

ESTHER

CHAPTER 1

1 In the days of Ahashuerosh (this is Ahashue- rosh who reigned from India to Ethiopia, for a hundred years and twenty years of reign) 2 in those days when King Ahashuerosh sat on his throne, which was in the palace of Shushan, 3 in the third year of his reign, he made a ban-quet to all his princes and his servants, that is, to the power of Persia and Media, and to the captains and chiefs of the provinces who were before him, 4 to make known the rich-es and glory of his kingdom and the honor of his great majesty for many days, that is, for a hundred and forty days. 5 When these days were over, the king made a banquet to all the people who were in the palace of Shushan, both great and small, for seven days, in the courtyard of the garden of the king's palace, 6 under a drapery of white, green, and blue robes, fastened with cords of fine linen and purple, in rings of silk and pillars of marble; the beds were of gold and silk on a floor of porphyry, marble, and alabaster, and of blue. 7 They made them drink in vessels of gold and

changed them from vessel to vessel, and roy- al wine was in abundance, according to the king's power. 8 Drinking was ordained, and no one could compel, for the king had com- manded all the officers of his house to do ac- cording to the pleasure of each one. 9 Queen Vashti also made a banquet for the women in the royal house of King Ahashuerosh. 10 On the seventh day, when the king was full of wine, he commanded Mehuman, Biztha, Harbona, Bigtha, Abagtha, Zethar and Car- cas, the seu eunuchs (who served in the pres- ence of King Ahashuerosh) 11 to bring Queen Vashti before the king with the royal crown, that he might show the people and the princ- es her beauty, for she was fair to behold. 12 But Queen Vashti refused to come at the word of the king, who had given the charge to the eunuchs; therefore the king was very angry, and his anger was kindled in him. 13 Then the king told the wise men that they knew the times (for this was how the king behaved toward all who knew the law and judgment): 14 Then came to him Carshena, Shethar, Ad- matha, Tarshish, Meres, Marsena and Memu- can, the seven princes of Persia and Media who looked the king in the face and were the first in the kingdom). 15 What shall we do to Queen Vashti according to the law, because she did not act according to the word of King Ahashuerosh by the commission of the eu- nuchs?" 16 Then Memucan answered before the king and the princes: "Queen Vashti has not only acted wrongly against the king, but also against all the princes and against all the people who are in all the provinces of King Ahashuerosh. 17 Indeed, the action of the queen will spread among all the women, so that they will despise their husbands in their own eyes and say, "King Ahashuerosh had ordered Vashti the queen to be brought before him, but she did not come." 18 Thus shall the princesses of Persia and Media say today to all the king's princes, when they hear of the queen's action; so there shall be much scorn and wrath. 19 If it please the king, let him issue a royal decree and write it among the statutes of Persia and Media (and let it not be transgressed) so that Vashti may no longer appear before King Ahashuerosh; and let the king give his royal estate to his companion who is better than she. 20 When the king's decree is published throughout his kingdom (though great), all women shall give honor to their husbands, both great and small. 21 This saying pleased the king and the princes, and the king did as Memucan had said. 22 For he sent letters to all the king's provinces, to ev- ery province according to his writing, and to every people according to their language, that each one might take care of the regulation in his own house and publish it in the language of that people.

CHAPTER 2

1 After these things, when the wrath of King Ahashuerosh was appeased, he recalled Vash- ti, what she had done and what had been decreed against her. 2 The king's servants, who attended him, said, "Let beautiful young virgins be sought for the king." 3 Let the king send officers to all the provinces of his kingdom, and gather all the beautiful young virgins into the palace of Shushan, into the house of the women, under the hand of Hege, the king's eunuch, keeper of the women, to give them their things for purification. 4 And the elder that shall please the king, he shall make her to reign in the house of Vashti. And this pleased the king, who so did. 5 In the city of Susa there was a certain Iewe, whose name was Mordecai, the son of Iair, the son of Shi- mei, the son of Kish, a man of Iemini, 6 Who

had been carried away from Jerusalem with the captivity that had been carried away with Econiah, king of Judah (whom Nebuchadnez- zar, king of Babel, had carried away). 7 And he nursed Hadassah, that is, Esther, the daugh- ter of his vncles, for she had neither father nor mother, and the elder was fair to behold; and after the death of her father and moth- er, Mordecai took her as his daughter. 8 And when the king's order and his decree were published, and many women were brought to the palace of Shushan by the hand of Hege, Esther also was brought to the king's house by the hand of Hege, the keeper of the women. 9 It pleased him, and she showed herself happy in his eyes; therefore he caused her to be giv- en as soon as possible her things for purifi- cation, her state, and some beautiful maidens out of the king's house, and gave her and her mothers the change of the best in the house of the women. 10 But Esther did not reveal her people and kinship, for Mordecai had charged her not to tell. 11 Mordecai walked every day before the courtyard of the women's house to find out whether Esther had behaved well and what should be done with her. 12 When she came on the day of each May to enter King Ahasuerus, after she had been poured out two cents according to the method of the women (for so were the days of their purification), six cents with oil of myrrh and six cents with sweet odors and for the purification of the women: 13 So the maiden went to the king; she was granted what she desired, to go out with her from the house of the women to the king's house. 14 And the next day she went, and the next day she returned to the second house of the women, under the hand of Shaashgaz, the king's eunuch, who kept the concubines; and she came in to the king no more except when it pleased the king, and unless she was called by name. 15 And when Esther, the daughter of Abihail the son of Mordecai (who had tak- en her as his own daughter), wanted to come in to the king, she wanted nothing but what Hege the king's eunuch, keeper of the wom- en, had told her; and Esther was at ease be- fore all who looked upon her. 16 Esther was therefore brought by King Ahasuerus into his royal house on the tenth month, that is, the month of Tebeth, in the seventh year of his reign. 17 The king questioned Esther about all the women, and she found grace and cour- age in his eyes more than all the virgins, so that he placed the crown of the kingdom on her head and appointed her queen instead of Vashti. 18 Then the king made a great feast to all his princes and his servants, which was the feast of Esther, and gave rest to the prouinci, bestowing gifts, according to the power of a king. 19 When the virgins were gathered for the second time, Mordecai sat at the king's door. 20 Esther had not yet revealed her lin- eage and her people, as Mordecai had in- structed her; for Esther followed Mordecai's words, as when she fed with him. 21 In those days when Mordecai was at the gate of the kings, two eunuchs of the kings, Bigthan and Teresh, who guarded the gate, became angry and tried to lay hands on King Ahashuerosh. 22 And the thing was known to Mordecai, and he told it to Queen Esther, and Esther told it to the king in Mordecai's name; and when the inquiry was made, it was found to be so; therefore they were both hanged on a tree; and it was written in the book of Chronicles before the king.

CHAPTER 3

1 After these things, King Ahasuerus promot- ed Haman the son of Hammedatha the Agag- ite, exalted him, and put all the princes who were with him in his place. 2 All the king's ser- vants who were at the king's gate knelt down and addressed Haman, for the king had given an order concerning him; but Mordecai did not kneel down and address him. 3 Then the king's servants who were at the king's gate said to Mordecai, "Why do you transgress the king's order?" 4 Although they spoke to him every day, he did not listen to them; so they informed Haman to see how Mordecai's af- fairs would unfold, for he had told them that he was a Hebrew. 5 When Haman heard that Mordecai had not knelt before him and paid him homage, Haman was filled with wrath. 6 He thought it was too little to lay hands on Mordecai alone, and because they had pre- sented Mordecai's people to him, Haman sought to destroy all the Jews who were in the whole kingdom of Ahasuerus and Mordecai's people. 7 In the first month (i.e., the month of Nisan) of the twelfth year of King Ahasuer- us, they cast sacks (i.e., a lot) before Haman, from day to day and from month to month, until the twelfth month, i.e., the month of Adar. 8 Then Haman said to King Ahasuer- us, "There is a scattered and scattered people among the peoples in all the provinces of your kingdom; their laws are different from those of all the peoples, and they do not observe the king's laws; therefore it is not to the king's advantage to suffer them." 9 If it pleases the king, let it be written that they shall be de- stroyed, and I will pay ten thousand talents of silver at the hands of those who have charge of this business to bring them into the king's coffers." 10 Then the king took the ring out of his hand and gave it to Haman the son of Hammedatha the Agagite, the aduersary of Iewes. 11 The king said to Haman, "Let the torpedo be yours and let the people do with it what you like." 12 Then the king's scribes were summoned on the thirteenth day of the first month, and it was written (according to what Haman had commanded) to the king's officers, and to the captains who were out- side every province, and to the chiefs of every people, and to every people according to what was written, and to every people according to their language; in the name of King Aha- suerus was written and sealed with the king's ring. 13 The letters were sent by mail to all the king's provinces, to drive out, kill and de- stroy all the young and the old, the children and the women, in one day, on the thirteenth day of the twelfth month (which is the month of Adar), and to scatter them as prayers. 14 The content of the writing was that an order should be issued in all the provinces and pub- lished to all the people, that they should be kept ready for the same day. 15 And the offices obliged by the king moved, and the order was given in the palace of Susa; and the king and Haman sat down to drink, but the city of Susa was in perplexity.

CHAPTER 4

1 When Mordecai became aware of all that had been done, he tore his clothes, clothed himself in sackcloth and ashes, went out into the midst of the city, and cried with a great cry and a bitter cry. 2 He then came before the gate of the kings, but he could not enter inside the gate of the kings, being clothed in sackcloth. 3 In all the provinces and in all the places where the king's charge and his commission came, there was great sorrow among the young men, fasting, weeping, and mourning, and many were lying in sackcloth and ashes. 4 Then Esther Maydes and her eu- nuchs came to tell of it; and the queen was much troubled, and she sent to dress Morde- cai and to take off his sackcloth, but he did not receive her. 5 Then she called Esther Hatach, one of the king's eunuchs, whom he had ap-

pointed to serve her, and gave him an order to Mordecai, to know what it was and why. 6 Hatach went to Mordecai in the street of the city, before the gate of the kings. 7 Mordecai told him all that he had been told and the amount of the thirst that Haman had prom- ised to pay to the king's treasures, because of the Iewes, to destroy them. 8 He also handed him the copy of the writing and the charge that had been given to Susa to destroy them, that he might convey it to Esther and declare it to her, instructing her to go to the king and present before him petitions and pleas for his people. 9 When Hatach arrived, he reported Mordecai's words to Esther. 10 Esther told Hatach and commanded him to tell Morde- cai, 11 All the king's servants and the people of the king's provinces know that anyone, man or woman, who comes to the king in the inner court, who is not called, it is his law that he should die, except the one to whom the king hands the golden rod so that he may lie. Now I have not been called to come to the king these thirty days." 12 They attested to Mor- decai the words of Esther. 13 Mordecai said that they should answer Esther in this way, "Do not think that you will be able to escape into the king's house any more than all the others. 14 For if you hold your peace for now, on another side will appear for kings comfort and delight, but you and your father's house will perish; and who knows whether you have come to the kingdom for such a time?" 15 Then Esther commanded Mordecai to answer, 16 "Go, gather all the people who are in Susa and fast for me, without eating or drinking for three days, neither by day nor by night. I also and my majesties shall do the same fast, and I will go to the king, who is not in accordance with the law; and if I lose, I lose." 17 So Mordecai went his way and did all that Esther had commanded him.

CHAPTER 5

1 On the third day Esther put on her royal robes and stood in the court of the king's pal- ace, facing the king's house; and the king sat on his royal throne in the king's palace, facing the door of the house. 2 When the king saw Esther, the queen, standing in the court, she felt uncomfortable in his presence; and the king handed her the golden scepter that was in his hand; then Esther stepped back and touched the tip of the scepter. 3 Then the king said to her, "What do you want, Queen Esther, and what is your request? You shall be grant- ed half the kingdom." 4 Then Esther said, "If it pleases the king, let the king and Haman come today to the bench I have prepared for him." 5 The king said, "See that Haman hur- ries to do what Esther said." So the king and Haman came to the counter that Esther had prepared. 6 At the wine counter, the king said to Esther, "What is your request, that it may be granted to you? And what is your request? It shall be performed for half the kingdom." 7 Then Esther answered, "My petition and my request are, 8 if I have found favor in the eyes of the king, and if it pleases the king to grant me my petition and to fulfill my request, let the king and Haman come to the bench that I will prepare for them, and I will perform as the king has said." 9 That same day Haman went away contentedly and heartily. But when Haman saw Mordecai at the king's gate, who would not stop and move for him, Haman was filled with indignation at Mordecai. 10 How- ever, Haman drew back and, returning home, sent for his friends and Zeresh, his wife. 11 Haman told them the glory of his riches, the multitude of his sons, all the things for which the king had promoted him, and how he had set him before the king's

princes and ser- vants. 12 Haman said again, "Yes, Esther, the queen, did not allow anyone to enter with the king into the bank which he had prepared, as I said; and I also was forbidden to go to her with the king." 13 But all this does not trou- ble me, as long as I see Mordecai, your Iewe, sitting at the king's gate." 14 Then Zeresh, his wife, and all his friends said to him, "Let them make a tree fifty cubits high, and to die speak to the king, that Mordecai may be hanged there; then you shall go quietly with the king to the bench." This pleased Haman, who had the tree built.

CHAPTER 6

1 That same night the king did not sleep and ordered the book of records and chronicles to be brought in and read before the king. 2 It was found written that Mordecai had spo- ken of Bigtanah and Teresh, two of the king's eunuchs, guardians of the dora, who were trying to lay hands on King Ahashuerosh. 3 Then the king said, "What honor and dignity has been granted to Mordecai for this? And the king's servants who attended him said, "Nothing has been done for him." 4 The king said, "Who is in the court?" (Now Haman had entered the inner court of the king's house to speak to the king about hanging Mordecai on the tree he had prepared for him.) 5 The king's servants said to him, "Behold, Haman is standing in the courtyard." And the king said, "Let him come in." 6 When Haman en- tered, the king said to him, "What should be done to this man whom the king wants to honor? Then Haman thought in his heart, "To whom would the king do more honor than to me?" 7 Haman answered the king, "The man the king wants to honor, 8 let the royal robes that the king wants to wear and the horse that the king rides be brought for him, and let the royal crown be placed on his head. 9 And let the robe and the horse be delivered by the hand of one of the king's noblest princes, and let them dress the man (whom the king will want to honor) and let him ride on the horse through the streets of the city, proclaiming before him, "Thus shall it be done to the man whom the king will want to honor." 10 Then the king said to Haman, "Make haste, take the ration and the horse as you have said, and do it to Mordecai the king, who sits at the king's gate; leave nothing of what you have said." 11 Then Haman took the ration and the horse, stripped Mordecai bare, and led him back on his horse along the streets of the city, pro- claiming before him, "Thus shall it be done to the man whom the king wills to honor." 12 Mordecai came again to the king's gate, but Haman went home in mourning and with his head covered. 13 Haman told Zeresh, his wife, and all his friends all that had happened to him. Then his wise men and Zeresh his wife said to him, "If Mordecai is of the line of Iewes, before whom you have begun to fall, you will not stand against him, but you will surely fall before him." 14 While they were still talking with him, the king's eunuchs arrived and hurried to lead Haman to the bench that Esther had prepared.

CHAPTER 7

1 The king and Haman then went to the ban- quet with Queen Esther. 2 Again the king said to Esther at the wine banquet on the second day, "What is your request, Queen Esther, that it may be granted to you, and what is your request? It shall be granted for half the king- dom." 3 Queen Esther answered and said, "If I have found good in your

eyes, O king, and if it pleases the king, let my life be granted to me according to my request, and my people according to my request. 4 For we are des- tined, I and my people, to be destroyed, to be slain, and to perish; but if we had been des- tined to be servants and helpers, I would have held my tongue, though the aduersarie could not make up for the king's loss. 5 Then King Ahashuerosh answered and said to Queen Esther, "Who is this man, and where is he who presumes to do so?" 6 Esther answered, "The adversary and the enemy is this wicked Haman." Then Haman was aphragmatized before the king and queen. 7 The king got up from the wine stand in anger and went into the palace garden, but Haman stood to ask Queen Esther for his life, for he knew that the king had prepared a misfortune for him. 8 When the king went out again from the gar- den of the palace to enter the house where the wine was being drunk, Haman had fallen on the bed where Esther was standing; and the king said, "Will you force the queen to enter the house also? As the words came out of the king's mouth, they struck Haman's face. 9 Then Harbona, one of the eunuchs, said in the king's presence, "Behold, in Hamans house is still the tree of fifty cubits that Haman had prepared for Mordecai, who had spoken well to the king." Then the king said, "Hang him." 10 So they hanged Haman from the tree he had prepared for Mordecai; then the king's wrath was appeased.

CHAPTER 8

1 On the same day King Ahasuerus delivered to Queen Esther the house of Haman, the aduersary of the Iewes. and Mordecai stood before the king, for Esther told her what he was. 2 And the king took off the ring that he had taken from Haman and gave it to Morde- cai; and Esther put Mordecai out of the house of Haman. 3 Esther spoke again before the king, fell at his feet weeping, and begged him to put an end to the wickedness of Haman the Agagite and his deed which he had imagined against the Jews. 4 The king stretched out his golden scepter toward Esther. Then Esther stood up and stood before the king, 5 and said, "If it pleases the king, and if I have found it agreeable to the king, and if I have found it agreeable to him, let it be written that the let- ters of the deed of Haman the son of Amme- datha the Agagite, which he wrote to destroy the Iewes, which are in all the king's prov- inces, may be called again. 6 For how shall I suffer and see the evil that shall come to my people? Or how shall I suffer and see the de- struction of my kinsmen? 7 King Ahashuerosh said to Queen Esther and Mordecai, the son, "Behold, I have delivered to Esther the house of Haman, whom they hanged on the tree because he laid his hands on the children." 8 Write also for the Iewes, as you please, in the king's name, and seal it with the king's ring (for writings written in the king's name and sealed with the king's ring cannot be taken back by anyone). 9 Then the king's scribes were summoned at the same time, that is, in the thirteenth month, that is, in the month of Siuan, on the third and twentieth day: and it was written, according to what Mordecai had commanded, to the chiefs, captains, and rulers of the provinces, from India even unto Ethiopia, an hundred seventy-two princes, to every province according to their writing, to every people according to their language, and to the chiefs of the provinces according to their writing and according to their language. 10 And he wrote in the name of King Ahasuer- us, and sealed it with the king's ring; and he sent letters by mail on horseback and on fine cattle, such as dromedaries and thorough- bred mares. 11

And the king called upon the cities to assemble, and to defend their lives, and to depart, and to slay and destroy all the power of the people, and of the enemies that harassed them, both children and women, and to strip them of their goods: 12 on a day in all the provinces of King Ahashuerosh, that is, on the thirteenth day of the twelfth month, which is the month of Adar. 13 The copy of the writing was that there would be an order in all the provinces, published among all the people, and that the Jews would be ready on that day to attack their enemies. 14 Then the postilion mounted on draught beasts and dromedaries and set out in haste to carry out the king's order; the decree was issued in the palace at Susa. 15 And Mordecai went out to the king in royal apparel of white, with a great crown of gold, and with a robe of fine linen and purple, and the city of Susa rejoiced and was glad. 16 And in the Iewes there came light, joy, gladness and honor. 17 Also in all the provinces, in all the cities, and in all the places where the king's order and his decree came, there was joy and gladness for the young men, a feast and a good day, and many of the in- habitants of the land became young men, be- cause the fear of the young men came upon them.

CHAPTER 9

1 So in the twelfth month, which is the month of Adar, on the thirteenth day of the same month, when the king's order and his decree were about to be carried out, on the day when the enemies of the Iewes hoped to have power over them (but it turned out otherwise, be- cause the Iewes had dominion over those who hated them) 2 The Iewes gathered in their cit- ies, in all the provinces of King Ahashuerosh, to lay hands on those who sought to do them harm, and no one could stand against them, for fear of them came upon all the people. 3 All the chiefs of the provinces, the princes, the captains, and the king's officers exalted the badgers, because the fear of Mordecai had affected them. 4 For Mordecai was great in the king's house, and the news of him passed through all the provinces; for this man Mor- decai grew greater and greater. 5 So the Is- raelites smote all their enemies with sword strokes, slaughter and destruction, and did what they would to those who hated them. 6 In Shushan the palace killed the Iewes and destroyed five hundred men, 7 Parshandatha, Dalphon, and Aspatha, 8 Poratha, Adaliah and Aridatha, 9 Parmashta, Arisai, Aridai and Vaiezatha, 10 the ten sons of Haman the son of Ammedatha, the aduersary of the Jews, killed them, but they did not put their hands on the spit. 11 On the same day, the names of those who had been killed came to the palace of Susa before the king. 12 The king said to Queen Esther, "The Iewes have killed in the palace of Shushan and destroyed five hun- dred men and the ten sons of Haman; what have they done in the rest of the king's prou- inces? And what is your request, that it may be granted to you? Or what is thy request, that it may be executed?" 13 Then Esther said, "If it pleases the king, let it also be granted to give a morose to the Iewes that are in Shushan, that they may do according to this decree of the day, to hang on the tree the ten sons of Hamans." 14 The king instructed to do so; the decree was issued in Susa, and the ten sons of Hamans were hanged. 15 Then the Jews who were in Susa assembled on the fourteenth day of the month of Adar and killed three hundred men in Susa, but they did not lay their hands on the conch. 16 And the rest of the kings who were in the king's provinces gathered them- selves together, and defended their rights, and rested from their enemies, and

slew those who hated them in seventy-five thou- sand, but they laid not their hand on the spit. 17 This they did on the thirteenth day of the month of Adar, and they rested on the four- teenth day and considered it a day of feasting and rejoicing. 18 But the Israelites who were in Susa assembled on the thirteenth day and the fourteenth day, rested on the fifteenth day and kept it as a day of feasting and rejoicing. 19 Therefore the citizens of the villages who lived in the walled cities spent the fourteenth day of the month of Adar with feasts and banquets, a day full of joy, and each one sent gifts to his neighbor. 20 Mordecai wrote these words and sent letters to all the inhabitants of all the provinces of King Ahashuerosh, both near and far, 21 enjoining them to observe the fourteenth day of the month of Adar and the fifteenth day of the same month every year. 22 According to the days on which the Israelites rested from their enemies, and the month that was turned for them from sorrow into joy and from mourning into a day of rejoicing, to keep them as days of feasting and rejoicing, and to send gifts to each one to his harbor and gifts to the poor. 23 The Jews promised to do as they had begun and as Mordecai had written to them, 24 for Haman the son of Hammedatha the Agagite had imagined against the young men to destroy them, and had cast the bag (i.e., a lot) to consume and destroy them. 25 When she came before the king, he ordered by letter, "Let this evil deed (which he had imagined against the Iewes) be overthrown on his head and let him and his sons be hanged on the tree." 26 Therefore they called these days Purim, by the name of Pur, because of all the words of this letter, what they had seen beyond this, and what had come to them. 27 And the Iewes established and promised for them, and for their descen- dants, and for all who would receive them, that they would not fail to observe those two days every year, according to their writing and according to their season, 28 and that these days should be remembered and kept in all generations, in all families, in all provinces and in all cities, so that these days of Purim would not fail among the young people and that their memory would not disappear from their descendants. 29 Queen Esther, daugh- ter of Abihail, and Mordecai, the Jew, wrote with all the authorities (to confirm this Purim letter for the second time). 30 And they sent letters to all the leaders of the kingdom of Ahashuerosh, with words of peace and truth, 31 to confirm these days of Purim, according to their seasons, as Mordecai and Esther the queen had decreed, and as they had promised for themselves and their descendants by fast- ing and prayer. 32 The decree of Esther confirmed these words of Purim and was written in the book.

CHAPTER 10

1 King Ahasuerusosh paid tribute on the land and islands of the sea. 2 Are not all the acts of his power and strength and the declaration of Mordecai's dignity, when the king magnified him, written in the book of the Chronicles of the kings of Media and Persia? 3 For King Mordecai was the second of King Ahasuerus, great among kings and well-accepted among the multitude of his brethren, who procured the riches of his people and spoke peaceably to all his descendants.

POETIC BOOKS

These books explore themes of wisdom, faith, love, and human struggles

JOB

CHAPTER 1

1 There was a man in the land of Vz, named Iob. This man was a righteous and upright man, who feared God and shunned lawless- ness. 2 He had seven sons and three daugh- ters. 3 His estate consisted of two thousand sheep, three thousand camels, five hundred yoke of oxen and five hundred donkeys; his family was very large, so that this man was the greatest of all the men of the East. 4 His sons went to feast in their houses, each on his own day, and sent for their three sisters to eat and drink with them. 5 And when the days of feasting were past, Iob sent for them to sanctify, and rose up early in the morning, and offered the firstfruits burnt according to the name of them all. For Iob thought, "It may be that my sons have sinned and blasphemed God in their hearts." 6 Now one day when the sons of God came and stood before the Lord, Satan also came among them. 7 Then the Lord said to Satan, "Where do you come from?" And Satan answered the Lord, "Whence comest thou, and comest from the earth, and walkest upon it." 8 The Lord said to Satan, "Have you not considered my servant Iob, that there is no one like him on earth, a righteous and upright man, who fears God and shuns lawlessness? 9 Then Satan answered the Lord and said, "Does Iob fear God for nothing? 10 Have you not made a hedge around him and his house and everything he owns on every side? You have blessed the work of his hands, and his wealth has increased in the land. 11 But now stretch out your hand and touch ev- erything he owns, to see if he does not blas- pheme in your face." 12 Then the LORD said to Satan, "Behold, all that he has is in your hand; only on him you must not stretch out your hand." So Satan departed from the pres- ence of the Lord. 13 One day, while his sons and daughters were eating and drinking wine in the house of their elder brothers, 14 a messenger came to Iob and said, "Oxen plow and donkeys feed in their place." 15 the Scabians came with violence and took them; yes, they killed the servants by the sword, but I fled alone to tell you." 16 While he was still speak- ing, another came and said, "The fire of God fell from above and burned the sheep and the servants and poisoned them; but I escaped alone to tell you." 17 While he was still speak- ing, another came and said, "The Chaldeans got into three bands and came down on the camels and took them and killed the servants by the sword, but I have escaped alone to tell you." 18 While he was still speaking, anoth- er came and said, "Your sons and daughters were eating and drinking wine in the house of their elder brothers, 19 and behold, a great wind from beyond the wilderness struck the four corners of the house and fell upon the children; they died, and I was left alone to tell you." 20 Then Iob arose, tore his garments, shook his head, threw himself on the ground and prostrated himself, 21 and said, "Naked I came out of my mother's womb, and naked I will return to it; the LORD gave, and the LORD has taken; blessed be the Name of the LORD." 22 In all this Iob did not sin or accuse God of foolishness.

CHAPTER 2

1 One day the sons of God came and stood before the Lord, and Satan came among them and stood before the Lord. 2 Then the Lord said to Satan, "Where do you come from?"

Satan answered the Lord and said, "Where do you come from, and you come from the earth and walk on it." 3 The Lord said to Satan, "Have you not considered my servant Iob, that there is no one like him on earth, a righteous and upright man, who fears God and shuns lawlessness? For he con- tinues to be righteous, even though you have done violence to me to destroy him without cause." 4 Satan answered the Lord and said, "Skin for skin, and all that a man has, he will give for his life. 5 But now stretch out your hand and touch his bones and his flesh, to see if he will not blaspheme in your face." 6 Then the LORD said to Satan, "Behold, he is in your hand, but spare his life." 7 Then Satan departed from the presence of the Lord and struck Iob with severe blows, from the sole of his foot to the crown. 8 Then he took a pot to scrape him, and he lay down in the midst of the ashes. 9 Then his wife said to him, "Do you still continue to be whole? Blaspheme God and die." 10 But he said to her, "You speak like a foolish woman; what? Shall we receive good from the hands of God and not receive good? In all this Iob did not sin with his lips. 11 Now when Iob's three friends heard of all this evil that had come upon him, they came each from his own place, namely, Eliphaz the Temanite, Bildad the Shuite and Zophar the Naamite, for they agreed to come and complain to him and comfort him. 12 When they lifted up their eyes from afar, they did not know him; therefore they lifted up their voices and wept; every one of them tore his garments and sprinkled his head with dust toward heaven. 13 So they stood beside him on the ground for ten days and seven nights, and no one addressed a word to him, for they said that the sorrow was very great.

CHAPTER 3

1 Then Iob opened his mouth and cursed his day. 2 Iob cried out and said, 3 Perish the day in which I was born, and the night in which it was said, "A son of man was conceived." 4 Let that day be dark, and let not God look upon it from without, and let not light shine upon it, 5 But let it be dark and the shadow of death stare upon it; Let the clouds remain over it and make it fearful as a bitter day. 6 Let the night be dark, and let it not extend to the days of the year, and let it not enter into the reckoning of the months. 7 Yea, let that night be desolate, and let there be no show. 8 Let those who curse the day (ready to for- sake their mourning) curse it. 9 The stars of that twilight fade for darkness; he seeks light, but has none; he sees not the dawn of day, 10 For he has not shut the doors of my mother's womb, nor hid the sorrow from my eyes. 11 Why did I not die in childbirth, or why did I not dye when I came out of the womb? 12 Why did my knees prevent me, and why did I suck breasts? 13 Because so I should have lain down and been quiet, so I should have slept and rested, 14 With the kings and councillors of the earth, who bought themselves desolate places: 15 Or with the princes who possess gold and have filled their houses with silver. 16 Or why have I not been hid, like an untime- ly birth, or like children who have not seen the light? 17 The wicked have ceased their tyran- ny, and those who toiled much have rested. 18 The captives rest together and do not hear the voice of the oppressor. 19 There are small and great, and the servant is free from his mas- ter. 20 Why is light granted to those in misery and life to those with a sound heart? 21 Who desire death, and if it comes not, seek it more than treasures: 22 Who desire joy and rejoice when they can find the grave. 23 Why is light granted to the man whose way is hidden and whom God has fenced off? 24 Because my sigh rises before I eat, and my

roars are quenched like water. 25 For the thing I feared has come upon me, and the thing I was afraid of has come upon me. 26 I had no peace, I had no quiet, I had no rest, yet trouble came.

CHAPTER 4

1 Then Eliphaz the Temanite answered and said, 2 "If we get into conversation with you, will you be vexed? But who can prevent you from speaking? 3 Behold, you have taught many and strengthened weary hands. 4 Your words have confirmed those who were fall- ing, and you have strengthened weak knees. 5 But now it has come upon you, and you are afflicted; it touches you, and you are troubled. 6 Is not this your fear, your confidence, your serenity, and the righteousness of your ways? 7 Remember, I pray thee: who ever died, be- ing innocent, or where were the righteous destroyed? 8 As I have seen, those who plow iniquity and sow wickedness reap the same. 9 With the breath of God they perish, and with the breath of his nostrils they are consumed. 10 The roar of the lion, the voice of the lion, and the teeth of the lion's cubs are broken. 11 The Lyons perishes for lack of prayers, and the young ones of the Lyons scatter around. 12 But one thing has been brought to me in secret, and my ear has received some. 13 In thoughts of night visions, when sleep falls upon men, 14 A fear came upon me that made all my bones tremble. 15 The wind passed be- fore me and made the hairs of my flesh stand on end. 16 Then one stood still, and I did not know his face; an image was before my eyes, and in silence I heard a voice saying, Is man stronger than I? 17 Can man be more righ- teous than God? Or can man be purer than his creator? 18 Behold, he has found no sound- ness in his servants, and has laid folly on his angels. 19 How much more in those who dwell in houses of clay, whose foundation is in the dust, who will be destroyed by the moth? 20 They are destroyed from morning till sunset; they perish forever, regardless. 21 Does not their dignity depart with them? Do they not perish without wisdom?

CHAPTER 5

1 Call now, if anyone will answer you, and to which of the saints will you want to turn? 2 Doubting wrath kills the fool, and enuie kills the idiot. 3 I saw the fool well rooted, and suddenly I cursed his dwelling, saying, 4 His children shall be far from salvation; they shall be destroyed in the gate, and no one shall be able to deliver them. 5 Hunger shall eat of her flesh; yea, they shall take her among thorns, and thirst shall drink of their substance. 6 For misery is not born of dust, and affliction is not born of the earth. 7 But man is led astray, as sparks go out. 8 But I want to inquire of God and turn my speech to God: 9 Who does great and searchable things, and wondrous things without name. 10 He makes it rain on the earth and causes water to flow on the roads, 11 and brings up those who are downcast, that the sorrowful may be exalted in salvation. 12 He scatters the tricks of the craftsman, so that their hands cannot accomplish what they do. 13 He takes the wise in their crafti- ness, and the counsel of the wicked is made senseless. 14 They meet darkness by day, and seek no one as by night. 15 But he preserves the poor from the sword, from their mouth and from the hand of the violent man, 16 So that the poor man has his hope, but iniquity shuts her mouth. 17 Blessed is the man whom God corrects; do not reject the punishment of the Almighty.

18 For he creates the wound and bandages it; he strikes, and his hands heal. 19 He shall give thee six tribulation, and the sev- enth shall not touch thee. 20 In famine he will deliver you from death, and in battle from the power of the sword. 21 You will be sheltered from the scourge of the tongue, and you will not fear destruction when it comes. 22 You will laugh at destruction and famine and not be afraid of the beasts of the earth. 23 For the stones of the field shall be in league with you, and the beasts of the field shall be at peace with you. 24 And thou shalt know that peace shall be in thy tabernacle; thou shalt visit thy dwelling place, and thou shalt not sin. 25 Thou shalt also have assurance that thy seed shall be great, and thy posterity as the mass of the earth. 26 Thou shalt go to thy grave in full age, as a ration of grain comes in due season into the granary. 27 Behold, so we have asked, and so it is; hear this and know it for yourself.

CHAPTER 6

1 Iob answered and said, 2 Oh, if my sorrow were well weighed, and my miseries were put together in the balance. 3 For now it would be heavier than the sand of the sea; therefore my words are swallowed up. 4 For the arrows of the Almighty are in me, whose poison breaks down my spirit, and the terrors of God fight against me. 5 Will the wild horse bray when he has land? Or will the ox stoop down when he has fodder? 6 Shall that which is vnsaue- rie be eaten without salt? Or is there flavor in the white of an ege? 7 The things that my soul refused to touch, such as were painful, are my food. 8 Oh, if I could have my desire and if God would grant me what I desire! 9 That is, that God would destroy me, that he would let go his hand and cut me off. 10 Then I should still have comfort (though he buries me in pain, he does not spare me) because I have not denied the words of the Holy One. 11 What strength have I to resist? Or what is my end, if I must prolong my life? 12 Is my strength perhaps that of stones? Or is my flesh that of stones? 13 Is it not true that there is no help in me, and that strength has been taken away from me? 14 He who is in misery should be comforted by his neighbor, but men have abandoned the fear of the Almighty. 15 My brothers have deceived me like a brook, and like the rising of rivers they pass away. 16 Which are blackish, and where snow is hid. 17 But in time they dry up with dryness and wear out; and when it is time to go, they withdraw from their places, 18 Or they depart from their way and their path, yea, they disappear and die. 19 Those who go to Tema regarded them, and those who go to Sheba waited for them. 20 But they were confused; when they hoped, they came here and were ashamed. 21 Now you are just like them; you have seen my fearful plague and have been frightened. 22 Is it because I said, "Bring to me," or because you give me a reward of your substance? 23 And have you delivered me from the hand of enemies or redeemed me from the hand of ty- rants? 24 Teach me, and I will hold my tongue; and let me know where I have done wrong. 25 How firm are the words of righteousness, and what can any of you reproach? 26 Do you think to take back your words, that the speech of the afflicted is like the wind? 27 You bring down your wrath on the orphan and dig a pit for your friend. 28 Now therefore be content to look to me, for I will not lie before your face. 29 Turn you, I pray you, that there be no iniquity; return, I say, and you shall yet see my righteousness in that way. Is there iniquity in my tongue? Is not my mouth an expression of sorrow?

CHAPTER 7

1 Is there not a time appointed for man on earth? And are not his days like the days of wrath? 2 As a servant desires shade, and as a hermit seeks the end of his work, 3 So have I inherited the money of vanity, and have been assigned sorrowful nights. 4 If I lay me down, I say, "When shall I rise?" and, measuring the dawn, I am always full of agitation until the day dawns. 5 My flesh is clothed with worms and filth of the dust; my skin is torn and has become horrible. 6 My days are swifter than those of a horse, and they pass hopelessly by. 7 Remember that my life is but a wind, and my eye will not return to see pleasure. 8 The eye that has seen me will see me no more; your eyes are on me, and I will be no more. 9 As the cloud vanishes and goes away, so he who goes down into the grave will not come out again. 10 He shall return no more to his home, and his place shall know him no more. 11 Therefore I will not spare my mouth, but I will speak in the turmoil of my spirit, and I will muse in the bitterness of my mind. 12 Am I a sea or a whalefish, that thou shouldst keep me in war? 13 When I say, "My bed will relieve me, and my bed will comfort me in my meditation." 14 then you trouble me and amaze me with visions. 15 Therefore my soul would rather be strangled and die than re- main in my bones. 16 I abhor it, I shall not live forever; therefore spare me, for my days are but vanity. 17 What is man, that thou magnify him, and set thy heart upon him? 18 Do you visit him every morning and test him every moment? 19 How long will it be before you depart from me? You will not leave me alone as long as I can swallow my plate. 20 I have sinned, what shall I do with you? O you who preserve me, why have you set me as a mark against you, so that I am a burden to myself? 21 Why do you not forgive my guilt and take away my iniquity? For now I will sleep in the dust, and if you seek me in the morning, you will not find me.

CHAPTER 8

1 Then Bildad the Shuhita answered and said, 2 How long will you speak these things, and how long will the words of your mouth be like a mighty wind? 3 Is it God who exercises judg- ment? Or the Almighty to exercise justice? 4 If your children have sinned against him and he has sent them to the place of their iniquity, 5 if you will go straight to God and pray to the Almighty, 6 if you will be pure and righteous, surely he will awake toward you and make the dwelling place of your righteousness pros- perous. 7 Though your beginning is small, your end will increase greatly. 8 Inform thy- self therefore, I pray thee, of the former age, and prepare to seek their fathers. 9 (For we are but of yesterday and are ignorant, for our days on earth are but a shadow). 10 Should they not teach you and tell you the words of their hearts? 11 Can a reed grow without the myrrh? Or a grass grow without water? 12 Even if it were green and uncut, yet it would wither before any other plant. 13 Thus are the ways of those who forget God, and the hope of hypocrites will perish. 14 His confidence also shall be cut off, and his trust shall be as the house of a snitch. 15 He will lean on his house, but it will not stand; he will cling to it, but it will not stand. 16 The tree is green before the sun, and its branches extend into the garden. 17 Its roots are wrapped around the fountain and are folded around the house of stones. 18 If anyone questions it from its place and

it denies itself, saying, "I have not seen you." 19 behold, it will revive in this way, to grow into another form. 20 Behold, God will not cast out the righteous man, nor take the ungodly by the hand, 21 until he has filled your mouth with laughter and your lips with joy. 22 Those who hate you will be clothed with shame, and the dwelling place of the wicked will not re- main.

CHAPTER 9

1 Then Iob answered and said, 2 I know well that it is so, for how could man, compared with God, be justified? 3 If I would argue with him, he could not answer him one thing in a thousand. 4 He is wise in heart and mighty in strength; who has raged against him and prospered? 5 He removes the mountains, and they are not afraid when he overthrows them in his wrath. 6 He removes the earth from its place, and its pillars shake. 7 He commands the sun, but it does not rise; he shuts up the stars as under a seal. 8 He alone spreads out the heavens and walks on the height of the sea. 9 He creates the stars Arcturus and Orion and the Pleiades and the southern climes. 10 He does great and unimaginable things, yea, wondrous things without name. 11 Behold, when he passes by me, I do not see him; and when he passes by, I do not perceive him. 12 Behold, when he takes a prayer, who can make him return it? Who will say to him, "What are you doing?" 13 God does not with- draw his wrath, and the mightiest helps op- pose him. 14 How much less should I answer him or how could I find my words with him? 15 For even if I were righteous, I could not answer, but would make supplication to my judge. 16 If I cried out and he answered me, I would not find that he heard my voice. 17 For he destroys me with a storm and wounds me without cause. 18 He does not let me catch my breath, but fills me with bitterness. 19 If we speak of strength, behold, he is strog; if we speak of judgment, who will bring me in to defend me? 20 If I would justify myself, my own mouth would condemn me; if I would be perfect, it would judge me wicked. 21 Even if I were perfect, I do not know my own soul; therefore I abhor my life. 22 This is a point; therefore I said, "He destroys the wicked and ungodly." 23 If the scourge suddenly kills, should God laugh at the punishment of the innocent? 24 The earth is in the hands of the wicked; he knows the faces of their judges; if not, where is he or who is he? 25 My days have grown swifter than a pole; they have fled and seen nothing good. 26 They have passed away like the swiftest ships and like the eagle that flies to prayer. 27 If I say, "I will forget my pledge, cease from my wrath, and comfort myself, 28 then I will deliver myself from all my pains, knowing that you will not judge me innocent. 29 If I am wicked, why do I toil in this way? 30 If I wash myself with snow wa- ter and purify my hands as cleanly as I can, 31 thou shalt plunge me into the pit, and my very clothes shall make me unclean. 32 For he is not such a man as I am, who can answer him, if we come together to judge. 33 Nor is there any emperor who can lay his hand on both of us. 34 Let him take his rod from me, and let not his fear astonish me: 35 Then I will speak, and I will not fear him; but because I am not, I will stand firm.

CHAPTER 10

1 My soul is cut off, though I live: I will com- plain over myself, and speak with the bit- terness of my soul. 2 I will say to God, "Do not condemn me; let me understand why you contend against me." 3 Do you think it is good to oppress me, to cast away the work of your hands, and to favor the counsel of the ungod- ly? 4 Do you have carnal eyes, or do you see as men see? 5 Are your days like man's days or your years like man's time? 6 that you inquire into my iniquity and seek my sin? 7 You know that I cannot do evil, for no one can deliver me out of your hands. 8 Have your hands made me and fashioned me all around, and will you destroy me? 9 Remember, I pray thee, that thou hast made me like clay, and wilt thou again reduce me to dust? 10 Have you not squeezed me like milk and made me into a crust like cheese? 11 You have clothed me with skin and flesh and joined me to bones and sinews. 12 You have given me life and grace, and your visitation has preserved my spirit. 13 Though you have hidden these things in your heart, I know that it is so with you. 14 If I have sinned, you will look on me sternly and not imprison me of my iniquity. 15 If I have act- ed wickedly, woe to me; if I have acted righ- teously, I will not lift up my head, being full of confusion, for I see my affliction. 16 But let it increase; cast me out like a lion; come back and show yourself husbanded toward me. 17 Thou renewest thy plagues against me, and increasest thy wrath against me; changings and armies of woe are against me. 18 Why then have you brought me forth from the bel- ly? Oh, if I were dead, and if no eye had seen me! 19 And if I were as I was not, but brought from the womb to the grave! 20 Are not my days few? Let him cease and depart from me, that I may take some comfort, 21 Before I depart and return no more, even to the land of darkness and the shadow of death: 22 in a land, I say, as dark as darkness itself, and in the shadow of death, where there is no order, but the light is there like darkness.

CHAPTER 11

1 Then Zophar the Naamite answered, 2 Should one not answer the multitude of words? Or should one justify a great talker? 3 Should men be silent in the face of your lies? And when you mock others, will no one put you to shame? For you said, "My doctrine is pure, and I am clean in your eyes." 5 But, oh if God would speak and open His lips against you! 6 That he might reveal to thee the secrets of wisdom, how thou hast deserted the dou- ble, according to right; know therefore that God hath forgotten thee for thy iniquity. 7 Can you discover God by searching? Can you discover the Almighty in his perfection? 8 Heaven is high, what can you do? It is deeper than hell, how can you know it? 9 His mea- sure is longer than the earth and wider than the sea. 10 If he cuts and closes or gathers, who can turn him back? 11 For he knows vain men and sees iniquity and those who under- stand nothing. 12 Yet the man is wise, though the newborn man is like a wild plank. 13 If you prepare your heart and stretch out your hands toward him: 14 If iniquity be in thine hand, turn it away, and let not wickedness dwell in thy tabernacle. 15 Verily, thou shalt lift up thy face without blemish; thou shalt be steadfast and fear not. 16 Thou shalt for- get thy miseries and remember them as wa- ters past. 17 Even thy age shall appear clearer than the zero day; thou shalt shine and be as the morning. 18 You will be brave, for there is hope; you will dig the holes and lie down safe- ly. 19 When you rest, no one will make you lose hope; indeed, many will court you. 20 But the eyes of the wicked shall fade, and their refuge shall perish, and their hope shall fade away.

CHAPTER 12

1 Then Iob answered and said, 2 Because you are the only people, wisdom must be tinged with you. 3 But I have understanding equal to yours and am not inferior to you; yea, who does not know these things? 4 I am like one who mocks his neighbor, who calls upon God and he hears him; the righteous and the un- righteous are mocked. 5 He who is ready to fall is like a lamp despised by the opinion of the rich. 6 The tabernacles of thieves prosper, and those who boast of God and whom God has enriched with his hand are safe. 7 Ques- tion the beasts and they will teach you, and the animals of the earth and they will tell you: 8 Or speak to the earth, and it will tell thee; or to the fish of the sea, and they will tell thee. 9 Who can be ignorant of all these things, except that the hand of the Lord has made them? 10 In whose hand is the soul of every living thing and the breath of all man. 11 Do not the ears discern the words and the mouth taste the flesh for itself? 12 Among the ancients there is wisdom, and in the length of days there is understanding. 13 With him there is wisdom and strength; he has counsel and understand- ing. 14 Behold, he brings down a building and it cannot be built; he shuts up a man and it cannot be loosed. 15 Behold, he withholds the waters, and they run dry; but when he lets them out, they destroy the earth. 16 With him is strength and wisdom; those who are deceived and those who deceive are his. 17 He causes counselors to become like skewers and makes judges foolish. 18 He loosens the col- lar of kings and girds their bonds with a belt. 19 He leads away princes like a prayer and ousts the mighty. 20 He takes away the word of faithful counselors and removes judgment from the ancients. 21 He despises princes and makes vain the strength of the mighty. 22 He unveils the deep places from their darkness and brings to light the shadow of death. 23 He increases peoples and destroys them; He enlarges nations and brings them in again. 24 He takes away the hearts of those who are the leaders of the peoples of the earth and makes them wander through the wilderness. 25 They grope in darkness without light, and he makes them stagger like a drunkard.

CHAPTER 13

1 My eye has seen all this, my ear has heard it and understood it. 2 I also know as much as you know; I am not inferior to you. 3 But I will speak with the Almighty, and I want to argue with God. 4 For by deceit you forge lies, and all your phantasms are worthless. 5 Oh, if you would restrain your tongues, that your wisdom may be imputed to you! 6 Now listen to my disputation and heed the arguments of my lips. 7 Will you speak evilly to defend God, and will you speak deceitfully for his cause? 8 Will you accept his person or contend for God? 9 Is it good for him to see you? Will you do for him the same latrine that is done for a man? 10 He will surely rebuke you, if you secretly accept a person. 11 Will not his excel- lence make you fearful, and will his fear fall upon you? 12 Your memories may be likened to ashes and your bodies to bodies of clay. 13 Restrain your tongues in my presence, that I may speak, and let it be said what you will. 14 Why do I take my flesh in my teeth and put my soul in my hand? 15 Though he slay me, I will trust in him, and reprove my ways before him. 16 He shall also be my salvation, for the hyp- ocrite shall not come before him. 17 Hear my words diligently, and observe my speeches. 18 Behold, if I prepare myself for judgment, I know that I shall be justified. 19 Who is the one who will defend me? For if I now hold my tongue, I shall die. 20 But do not do these two things with me; then I will not hide from you. 21 Turn away thy hand from me, and let not thy fear make me fearful. 22 Then call me, and I will answer you; or let me speak, and answer me. 23 How many are my iniquities and sins? Show me my rebellion and my sin. 24 Why do you hide your face and take me for your ene- my? 25 Do you want to break a flight of blood forward and backward? Do you want to chase stubble? 26 For you write bitter things against me and make me fall back into the iniquities of my youth. 27 You also put my feet to the stocks, and look carefully at all my paths, and make an imprint of them on the heels of my feet. 28 Such a one wears out like a rotten ob- ject and like a garment that has grown moldy.

CHAPTER 14

1 The man born of a woman is short-lived and full of trouble. 2 He sprouts like a stream and is cut off; he also vanishes like a shadow and does not continue. 3 Yet you open your eyes to him and bring me into judgment with you. 4 Who can bring a clean thing out of filthiness? There is not one. 5 Are not his days appoint- ed? The number of his money is with you; you have established his boundaries, which he cannot cross. 6 Turn away from him that he may abide until the desired day, like an eagle. 7 For there is hope for a tree, if it is cut down, that it will sprout again and its branches will not cease. 8 Though its roots grow old on the earth, and its stump is dead in the ground, 9 nevertheless, through the sending of water, it will sprout and produce shoots like a plant. 10 But the man is sick and dies and perishes, and where is he? 11 As the waters pass out of the sea, and as the flood decays and dries up, 12 so the man sleeps and does not rise, for he will not wake again and will not rise from his sleep until there is no more heaven. 13 Oh, if thou wouldst hide me in the grave and keep me secret, until thy wrath is past, and give me a term and remember me. 14 If a man die, shall he live again? All the days of my appointed time I will wait, until my change comes. 15 You shall call me, and I will answer you; you love the work of your own hands. 16 But now you name my steps, and do not put off my sins. 17 My iniquity is sealed as in a bag, and you add more to my wickedness. 18 And as surely as the mountain that falls down fails, and as the tower that is removed from its place: 19 as the water shatters the stones, when thou bringest forth the things that grow in the dust of the earth, so thou destroyest the hope of man. 20 You always forestall against him, so that he passes by; he changes his face when you cast him out. 21 He does not know whether his children will be honorable, nor does he understand whether they will be of low estate, 22 but as long as his flesh is upon him, he grieves, and as long as his soul is in him, he grieves.

CHAPTER 15

1 Then Eliphaz the Temanite answered and said, 2 Should a wise man speak words of wind and fill his belly with the east wind? 3 Shall he dispute with ungood words or un- profitable speech? 4 Surely, you have forsaken fear and no longer need to pray before God. 5 For your mouth declares your iniquity, since you have chosen the tongue of the crafty. 6 Your own mouth condemns you, and not I, and your lips testify against you. 7 Are you the first man who

was born? Are you the one who was created before the hills? 8 Have you listened to the secret counsels of God and do you realize wisdom? 9 What do you know that we do not? And do you understand what is not in us? 10 With you are men not ancient and very old, much older than your father. 11 Are the consolations of God small to you? Is this thing strange to you? 12 Why does your heart carry you away and what do your eyes think? 13 Why do you answer God as you please and let such words come out of your mouth? 14 What is man, that he may be clean, and who is born of a woman, that he may be righteous? 15 Behold, he hath not found soundness in his saints; yea, the heavens are not clear in his eyes. 16 How much more is man abominable and unclean, who drinks iniquity like water? 17 I will tell you: hear me, and I will declare what I have seen: 18 Which the wise men have told, as they have heard from their fathers, and have not kept it a secret: 19 To whom alone the land has been granted, and no strang- er has passed through them. 20 The wicked man is always like one who draws children, and the name of the years is hidden from the tyrant. 21 A sound of fear is in his ears, and in his prosperity the destroyer comes upon him. 22 He is not aware that he is returning from darkness, for he sees the sword before him. 23 He goes in search of bread on either side, for he knows that the day of darkness is at hand. 24 Affliction and distress will make him fearful; they will prevail against him like a king ready for battle. 25 For he has stretched out his hand against GOD and made himself strong against the Almighty. 26 Therefore GOD will come upon him, even upon his neck and upon the thinnest part of his shield. 27 For he has covered his face with his fatness, and he has made himself colloquial in his side. 28 Though he dwell in desolate cities and in houses that are inhabited by no one, but have become ruins, 29 he will not be rich, nor will his possessions continue, nor will he prolong their perfection on earth. 30 He shall never depart from darkness; the flame shall come down upon his branches, and he shall depart with the breath of his mouth. 31 He will not see that he wanders in vanity; there- fore vanity will be his change. 32 His branch will not green up, but will be cut off before his day. 33 God will destroy it as the vine its sow- ing grape, and will cast it away, as the olive tree its flow. 34 For the community of the hyp- ocrites shall be desolate, and fire shall destroy the houses of the corrupt. 35 For they conceive malice and bring forth vanity, and their belly has prepared deceit.

CHAPTER 16

1 Iob answered and said, 2 I have often heard these things; you are all miserable comfort- ers. 3 Are there not words of wind? Or what makes you so dare to answer? 4 I too could speak as you do; (but if God would that your soul were in the place of mine) I could keep you company in speaking, and I could shake my head at you, 5 but I would strengthen you with my mouth, and that the comfort of my lips would ease your pain. 6 Though I speak, my sadness cannot be relieved; though I cease, what deliverance have I? 7 But now he makes me weary: "O God, you have made all my community desolate, 8 thou hast made me full of wrinkles, which is a witness, and my thinness is increased in me, testifying the same thing on my face. 9 His anger has tor- mented me, he hates me and bites me with his teeth; my enemy has sharpened his eyes against me. 10 They have opened their mouths on me and struck me on the breast to rebuke me; they have gathered against me. 11 God

delivered me to the vniust and caused me to be diverted from the way by the hand of the wicked. 12 I was in good health, but he re- duced me to nothing; he took me by the neck, beat me, and set me as a mark for himself. 13 His archers surrounded me; he cut off my kidneys, not sparing me, and cast my gall on the ground. 14 He has broken me one with an- other, and run upon me like a gypsy. 15 I have covered myself with sackcloth on my skin and lowered my feet into the dust. 16 My face is withered with weeping, and the shadow of death is over my eyes, 17 though there is no evil in my hands, and my prayer is pure. 18 O earth, do not dwell on my blood, and do not let my weeping find place. 19 For behold, my testimony is in heaven, and my record is upon him. 20 My friends speak eloquently against me, but my eye shoots against God. 21 Oh, if man could deal with God, as man with his neighbor! 22 For the times are ripe, and I will take a way from which I will never return.

CHAPTER 17

1 My breath is corrupted; my days are cut short, and the grave is prepared for me. 2 There are but mockers with me, and my eye continues to be bitter. 3 Lay me down now and make me safe for you; who is he who will touch my hand? 4 Because thou hast hid their heart from understanding, thou shalt not put them in a condition to act upon him. 5 For the eyes of his children shall fail, whoever speaks flattery to his friends. 6 He has made me a nickname for the people, and I am as a tab before them. 7 Therefore my eye is dim for sorrow, and all my strength is like a shadow. 8 The righteous will be astonished at this, and the innocent will be scandalized against the hypocrite. 9 But the righteous will keep his way, and he whose hands are pure will in- crease his strength. 10 All of you, therefore, turn and come now; I will find no wise man among you. 11 My days are past, my deeds are broken, and the thoughts of my heart 12 Have changed the night with the day, and the com- ing light with darkness. 13 Though I hope, the grave shall be my home, and I shall lie down in darkness. 14 I will say to corruption, "You are my father," and to the world, "You are my mother and my sister." 15 Where then is my hope? Or who will consider the thing I have hoped for? 16 They shall go down to the bot- tom of the pit; sure, they shall lie down to- gether in the dust.

CHAPTER 18

1 Then Bildad the Shuhita answered, "When will you make an end of your words? 2 "When will you make an end of your words? Make it understood, and then we will speak." 3 Why are we regarded as beasts and ignoble in your sight? 4 You are like one who hurts his soul in his wrath. Should the earth be forsaken be- cause of you, or the beast be removed from its place? 5 The light of the wicked shall be ex- tinguished, and the spark of his fire shall not shine. 6 The light shall be extinguished in his dwelling place, and his candle shall be extin- guished with him. 7 The steps of his strength shall be restrained, and his own counsel shall cause him to fall. 8 For he is caught in the net by his feet and walks on the snares. 9 Grenades will take him by the feet, and the plague will come upon him. 10 A snare is laid for him on the ground and a trap on the road. 11 Fear will sway him on every side and cause him to fall to the ground. 12 His strength will be famine, and destruction will be ready at his side. 13 Death will destroy the inner parts of his

skin, and the first stroke of death will destroy his strength. 14 His hope will be up- rooted from his dwelling place and make him go to the king of fear. 15 Fear shall dwell in his house (for it is not his), and sulfur shall be poured out on his dwelling. 16 His roots will dry up below, and his branches will be cut off everywhere. 17 His memory will disappear from the earth, and he will have no name in the streets. 18 They will turn him out of the light into darkness and drive him out of the world. 19 He shall have neither children nor grandchildren among his people, nor posterity in his dwellings. 20 Posterity will be amazed at his day, and the ancients will be afraid. 21 These are the abodes of the wicked, and this is the place of those who do not know God.

CHAPTER 19

1 Iob answered and said, 2 How much lon- ger will you care for my soul and torment me with words? 3 Now you have rebuked me ten times and are not ashamed; you are impudent toward me. 4 And though I have erred in faith, my error remains with me. 5 But if you work against me and rebuke me for my reproach- es, 6 Know now that God has cast me out and surrounded me with his net. 7 Behold, I cry for violence, but I have no answer: I cry, but there is no judgment. 8 He hath barred my way that I may not pass, and hath put dark- ness in my paths. 9 He has robbed me of my honor and taken the crown from my head. 10 He has destroyed me on every side, and I am gone; and he has reduced my hope like a tree. 11 He has kindled his wrath against me and regards me as one of his enemies. 12 His armies have gathered, and have come toward me, and have encamped around my taberna- cle. 13 He has driven my brothers away from me, and even my acquaintances have become strangers to me. 14 My neighbors have forsak- en me, and my family members have forgot- ten me. 15 Those who dwell in my house and my elders took me for a stranger, for I was a stranger in their eyes. 16 I called my servant, but he did not answer me, though I prayed to him with my mouth. 17 My breath was strange to my wife, though I prayed to her for the children of my body. 18 The wicked also despised me, and when I rose up, they spoke against me. 19 All my secret friends abhorred me, and those whom I praised turned against me. 20 My bones have broken away from my skin and flesh, and I have escaped by the skin of my teeth. 21 Have mercy on me, have mercy on me, for the hand of God has touched me. 22 Why do you persecute me, as God does, and not be satisfied with my flesh? 23 Oh, if my words were written now! Oh, if they were written at least in a book, 24 and written with an iron pen in lead or stone forever! 25 For I am sure that my Redeemer lives and will be the last on earth. 26 And though after my skin worms destroy this body, yet I shall see God in my flesh. 27 He whom I myself shall see, and mine eyes shall see, and no other for me, though my kidneys are consumed within me. 28 But you said, "Why is he persecuted?" And there was a deep question in me. 29 Be care- ful of the sword, for the sword will be used for wickedness, that you may know that there is judgment.

CHAPTER 20

1 Then Zophar the Naamite answered, "I do not know whether I should answer, 2 My thoughts induce me to answer, and therefore I hasten. 3 I have heard the correction of my rebuke; therefore the spirit of understanding prompts me to answer. 4 Do you not know this from ever since God placed man on earth? 5 That the life of the wicked is short, and the life of hypocrites is but a moment? 6 Even though his excellency goes up to the plateau and his head reaches to the clouds, 7 he will perish forever like his dung, and those who have seen him will say, "Where is he?" 8 He shall flee like a shadow, and they shall not find him, and he shall pass away like a night vision, 9 so that the eye that had seen him shall see him no more, and his place shall see him no more. 10 His sons shall flatter the poor, and his hands shall restore his substance. 11 His bones are full of the sin of his youth, and it shall lie with him in the dust. 12 When wickedness was sweet in his mouth, and he hid it under his tongue, 13 he swallowed it up and did not forsake it, but held it fast in his mouth, 14 then his flesh in his bowels was turned; the gall of Aspes was in his belly. 15 He has consumed the substance and will vomit it up, for God will bring it out of his belly. 16 He shall suck the gall of Aspes, and the vipers' tongue shall kill him. 17 He shall see no more riuers, nor floods, nor riv- ulets of gold and butter. 18 He shall take up the work again, and he shall not be without it; and according to substance shall be his recompense, and he shall enjoy it no more. 19 For he has made many, and forsaken the poor, and stripped houses that he did not build. 20 He will no longer have peace in his body, and he will no longer have what he desired. 21 He will have nothing left of his food, and no one will be able to hope in his possessions. 22 When he is full of his abundance, he will be in pain, and the hand of all the wicked will assail him. 23 He is about to fill his bel- ly, but God sends his fierce wrath upon him and causes it to come upon him, even upon his flesh. 24 He shall flee from the weapons of yron, and the bow of steel shall smite him full. 25 The orange is drawn out, it comes out of the body and glows with its gall, so that one is afraid of him. 26 All darkness shall hide in his secret places; the fire that does not blow shall destroy him, and what remains in his tabernacle shall be destroyed. 27 Heaven will declare his wickedness, and the earth will rise up against him. 28 The increase of his house shall disappear; it shall be scattered in the day of his wrath. 29 This is the wicked man's portion from God and the inheritance he shall have from God for his words.

CHAPTER 21

1 Iob answered and said, 2 Listen diligent- ly to my words, and this shall be the place of your consolations. 3 Let me speak, and when I have spoken, mock me. 4 Shall I address my speech to men? If so, how should not my spir- it be troubled? 5 Consider me, put me down, and put your hand over your mouth. 6 When I remember, I am affrighted, and fear takes hold of my flesh. 7 Why do the wicked live, grow old, and grow rich? 8 Their seed is estab- lished before them, and their generation be- fore their eyes. 9 Their houses are quiet, with- out fear, and the rod of God does not strike them. 10 Their cow gives birth and does not stir; their cow gives birth and does not cast her calf. 11 They bring forth their children like sheep, and their children dance. 12 They take the flute and the harp and revel in the sound of organs. 13 They spend their days in comfort and suddenly go to the grave. 14 They also say to God, "Go away, for we do not want to know your ways." 15 Who is the Almighty, that we should serve him? And what advantage would we have, if we prayed to him? 16 Behold, their riches are not in their hands; therefore let the counsel of the wicked be far

from me. 17 How many times shall the candle of the ungodly be blown out, and their destruction come upon them? He will destroy their life in his wrath. 18 They shall be as stubble before the wind and as coffee that the storm carries away. 19 God will put sorrow on the father for his chil- dren; when he rewards him, he will know. 20 His eyes shall see his destruction, and he shall drink of the wrath of the Almighty. 21 For what pleasure shall his house have after him, when the name of his money shall be cut off? 22 Is there anyone who teaches knowledge to God, who judges the highest things? 23 One dies in the fullness of his strength, being in every way comfortable and prosperous. 24 His breasts are full of milk, and his bones are full of milk. 25 Another dies in the bitterness of his soul and never eats with pleasure. 26 Both will sleep in the dust, and worms will collapse them. 27 Behold, I know your thoughts and the deeds by which you do me harm. 28 For ye say, Where is the prince's house, and where is the tent of the dwelling of the spirits? 29 Can ye not ask those who go by the way? And you cannot deny their signs. 30 But the wicked is kept until the day of destruction, and he shall be led to the day of wrath. 31 Who shall de- clare his way to his face, and who shall reward him for what he has done? 32 He shall be led to the grave and remain in the earth. 33 The valley of the mire shall be sweet to him, and every man shall draw behind him, as there were countless before him. 34 How then can you comfort me in life, seeing that in your an- swers nothing remains but lies?

CHAPTER 22

1 Then Eliphaz the Temanite answered and said, 2 Can a man be useful to God as he who is wise can be useful to himself? 3 Is it use- ful to the Almighty that you are righteous? Or is it useful to him that you make your ways righteous? 4 Is it for fear of you that he will accuse you or go with you to judgment? 5 Is not your wickedness great and your iniqui- ties countless? 6 For thou hast taken away thy brother's pledge, and hast stripped the gar- ments of those who were naked. 7 To those who were weary you gave no water to drink, and you took away bread from hunger. 8 But the mightiest man had the land, and he who had authority dwelt in it. 9 You drove out the emptied widows, and the arm of the fathers was broken. 10 Therefore snares surround you, and fear suddenly disturbs you: 11 O darkness thou shalt not see, and abundance of waters that shall smite thee. 12 Is there not God in heaven? And look at the height of the stars how high they are. 13 But you say, "How does God know? Can he judge through the dark clouds? 14 The clouds hide him so that he cannot see, and he walks in the circle of the air. 15 Thou hast marked the way of the world, where have wicked men walked? 16 Who were cut down before their time, whose foundation was like an overflowing river: 17 Who said to God, "Get out of here," and asked what the Almighty could do for them. 18 He has filled their houses with good things, but the counsel of the wicked is far from me. 19 The righteous will see them and reconsider, and the innocent will mock them. 20 Our substances are hidden, but fire has destroyed the rest. 21 Therefore, I pray thee, inquire of him, and make peace; so thou shalt have pros- perity. 22 Receive, I pray you, the law of his mouth and imprint his words in your heart. 23 If thou shalt return to the Almighty, thou shalt be rewarded, and thou shalt turn away iniquity from thy tabernacle. 24 The gold of Ophir shall become dust, and the gold of Ophir shall be as the flint of the mills.

25 The Almighty shall be thy defense, and thou shalt have a great quantity of silver. 26 Then you shall delight in the Almighty and lift up your face to God. 27 You shall make your prayers to him, and he shall hear you, and you shall make your vows. 28 You shall also decide a thing, and he shall establish it for you, and light shall shine on your ways. 29 When oth- ers are cast down, thou shalt say, "I am lifted up," and God shall save the humble. 30 The innocent will guard the earth, and it will be preserved by the purity of your hands.

CHAPTER 23

1 Iob answered and said, 2 Though my speech is bitter today, and my sore is greater than my pain, 3 If I only knew how to find him, I would enter his house. 4 I would plead the cause be- fore him and fill my mouth with arguments. 5 I would like to know the words he will an- swer me and understand what he will say to me. 6 Would he appeal against me with his great power? No, but he will give me strength. 7 There the righteous could reason with him, so I would be freed forever from my judge. 8 Behold, if I go eastward, he is not there; if I go westward, I cannot perceive him: 9 If I go north, where he works, I cannot see him; he will be hiding in the south, and I will not be able to see him. 10 But he knoweth my way, and tryeth me: and I shall come forth as gold. 11 My foot has followed his steps; his way I have followed and not forsaken. 12 I have nev- er strayed from the commands of his lips, and have considered the words of his mouth more than my appointed food. 13 Yet he has one mind, and who can make him change it? Yea, he does what his mind desires. 14 For he ac- complishes what has been decided by me, and many such things are with him. 15 Therefore I am troubled by his presence, and considering it, I am afraid of him. 16 For God has softened my heart, and the Most High has troubled me. 17 For I am not cut off in darkness, but he hid the darkness from my face.

CHAPTER 24

1 How should not the times be hidden from the Almighty, since those who know Him do not see His days? 2 Some take possession of the signs of the land, who steal the flocks and feed them. 3 They take away the wealth of the fathers of families and take widows' oxen as pledges. 4 They cause the poor to be diverted from the road, so that the poor of the land hide together. 5 Behold, others, like wild asses in the wilderness, go about their business and rise early to pray; the wilderness feeds him and his children. 6 They reap his prouision in the fields, but they reap the late vintage of the wicked. 7 They make the naked lodge without garments and without a tent in the cold. 8 They bathe themselves with the spec- tacles of the mountains and harness the kid for lack of shelter. 9 They leverage the chest of the fathers of families and take the pledge of the poor. 10 They make a man naked without clothing, and take away the luster of the hun- gry. 11 Those who make oil among their walls and treachery of their presses suffer thirst. 12 Men cry out from the city, and the souls of the dead cry out; yet God does not accuse them of folly. 13 These are they who abhor the light; they do not know its ways and do not continue in them. 14 The murderer rises early and kills the poor and needy, and at night he is like a thug. 15 The eye of the adulterer also waits for twilight and says, "No eye shall see me," and hides

his face. 16 They dig into hous- es in the dark, which have marked themselves by day; they know no light. 17 But the morn- ing is to them as the shadow of death; if one knows them, they are in terror of the shadow of death. 18 He is swift upon the waters; their portion shall be cursed upon the earth; they shall not see the way of the vines. 19 As the parched earth and the dryness consume the snowy waters, so shall the grave consume sin- ners. 20 The pitiful man will forget him, the world will be afraid of his sweetnesses; he will remember him no more, and the wicked will break like a tree. 21 He deals with the barren woman, who does not give birth, and does not do good to the widow. 22 He draws even the mighty with his strength, and when he ris- es, no one is sure to live. 23 Though men give him assurance that they are safe, his eyes are on their ways. 24 They are exalted for a little while, but then they go away and are lowered like all others; they are destroyed and cut off like the top of a horn reed. 25 But if it is not so, where is it? Or who belittles me and makes my words useless?

CHAPTER 25

1 Then Bildad, the Shuhita, answered and said. 2 He who makes peace in his places has power and fear. 3 Is there anyone who has no name in his armies? And on whom does his light not shine? 4 How can a man be justified with God or how can he be clean who is born of a woman? 5 Behold, he gives no light to the moon, and the stars are vnclean in his eyes. 6 How much more the man, a worm, that is, the son of man, who is nothing but a worm?

CHAPTER 26

1 Iob answered and said, 2 Who helps you? He who has no strength? Dost thou sweat the weapon that hath no strength? 3 Who advis- es you, who has no wisdom? Thou knowest well how things are. 4 To whom do you de- clare these words, or whose spirit goes out from you? 5 Dead things were formed under the waters and remained on the surface. 6 The grave is naked before him, and there is no shelter for destruction. 7 He spreads the north beyond the empty place and hangs the earth in nothingness. 8 He binds the waters with his clouds, and the cloud breaks not un- der them. 9 He restrains the face of his throne and spreads his cloud over it. 10 He has set bounds to the waters, until day and night end. 11 The pillars of Eauen quake and tremble for his reproof. 12 The sea is stilled by his power, and with his intelligence he smites his pride. 13 His Spirit has garnished the heavens, and his hand has formed the crooked serpent. 14 These are part of his ways, but how little do we know of him, and who can understand his fearful power?

CHAPTER 27

1 Then Iob went on and continued his para- ble, saying, 2 The God who lies has taken away my judgment, because the Almighty has put my soul in bitterness. 3 Nevertheless, as long as my breath is in me and the Spirit of God in my nostrils, 4 my lips shall not utter wick- edness, and my tongue shall not utter deceit. 5 God forbid that I should justify you; until I die, I will never remove my innocence from myself. 6 I will preserve my righteousness and will not forsake it; my heart will not reproach me more than my days. 7 My enemy shall be as the ungodly, and he who rises

against me as the righteous. 8 For what hope has the hyp- ocrite when he has accumulated wealth, if God takes away his soul? 9 Will God hear his cry when trouble strikes him? 10 Will he rest his delight on the Almighty? Will he invoke God at all times? 11 I will teach you what is in God's hand and will not hide what is with the Almighty. 12 Behold, you all have seen it; why then do you vanish in vanity? 13 This is the portion of the wicked with God, and the in- heritance of tyrants, which they shall receive from the Most High. 14 If his sons are great in number, the sword shall destroy them, and his posterity shall not be satisfied with bread. 15 His remnant shall be buried in death, and his widows shall not mourn. 16 Even if he should cut the torpedo like dust, and prepare the rayment like clay, 17 he may prepare it, but the righteous shall wear it, and the innocent shall lay down the torpedo. 18 He shall build his house like moth, and like a lodge which the keeper builds. 19 When the rich man falls asleep, he will not be gathered to his fathers; they opened their eyes, and he went away. 20 Terrors shall take him as the waters, and the storm shall carry him away by night. 21 The east wind shall carry him away, and he shall go away; it shall hurl him out of his place. 22 God will throw him on him and will not spare him, even if he wants to flee from his hand. 23 Every man shall clap his hands against him and hurl him out of his place.

CHAPTER 28

1 The clay surely has its place, and the gold its place, where they take it. 2 Yron is taken from dust, and brassa is cast from stone. 3 God puts an end to the darkness and proves the perfection of all things; He puts a restraint on the darkness and the shadow of death. 4 The flood is unleashed against the inhabitant, and the waters forgotten by the earth, being high- er than man, depart. 5 Bread comes out of the same earth, and fire is kindled under it. 6 Its stones are a place of wisdom, and its dust is gold. 7 There is a path that no one knows, nor has the eye of the kite seen it. 8 The lion's cubs have not walked it, nor has the lion passed through it. 9 He puts his hand on the rocks and overthrows the mountains by the roots. 10 He breaks down the walls of the rocks, and his eye sees every precious thing. 11 He binds up the floods so that they do not overflow, and the hidden things he brings to light. 12 But where is wisdom and where is the place of understanding? 13 Man does not know its price, for it is not found in the land of liars. 14 The depth says, "It is not in me"; even the sea says, "It is not with me." 15 No gold shall be sold for it, nor shall silver be weighed for its price. 16 It shall not be valued with the wedge of gold of Ophir, nor with precious onyx, nor with saphir. 17 Neither gold nor crystal shall be equated, nor shall it be exchanged for a dish of fine gold. 18 Neither coral nor gabban shall be spoken of, for wisdom is more pre- cious than pearls. 19 The topaz of Ethiopia shall not be equal to it, nor shall it be valued with the wedge of pure gold. 20 Where does wisdom come from, and where is the place of understanding? 21 since it is hidden from the eyes of all the gourmands and is hidden from the wicked of the earth? 22 Destruction and death say, "We have heard of it with our own ears." 23 But God understands its way and knows its place. 24 For he watches the end of the world and sees all that is under heav- en, 25 to determine the weight of the winds and to weigh the waters by measure. 26 When he established a decree for the ray and a way for the lightning of thunder, 27 He saw it and counted it; he prepared it and considered it. 28 And to the man he said,

"Behold, the fear of the LORD is wisdom, and to turn away from evil is understanding."

CHAPTER 29

1 Then Iob went on and continued his para- ble, saying, 2 Oh, if I were as I was in times past, when God protected me! 3 When his light shone on my head, and because of his light I walked through the darkness, 4 as in the days of my youth, when the safety of God was upon my tabernacle: 5 when the al- mightie was still with me and my children surrounded me. 6 When I washed my cov- enants with butter, and when the rope gave me supplies of oil: 7 When I went out of the gate, that is, out of the judgment seat, and when I had my seat prepared in the street. 8 The young men saw me and hid themselves; the elders rose up and stood. 9 The princes stood talking and put their hands over their mouths. 10 The voice of the princes hid, and their tongues cleared on the roof of their mouths. 11 When the ear heard me, it blessed me; and when the eye saw me, it bore me wit- ness. 12 For I took in the poor man who wept, the fatherless and the one who had no one to help him. 13 The blessing of the one who was ready to die came upon me, and I revived the heart of the widow. 14 I clothed myself with righteousness and it accompanied me; my judgment was like a robe and a crown. 15 I was the eyes of the blind and the feet of the lame. 16 I was a father to the poor, and when I did not know the cause, I sought it diligently. 17 I also broke the jaws of the righteous man and tore the prayer from his teeth. 18 Then I said, "I will die in my nest and multiply my days like sand. 19 For my root is stretched out upon the water, and the dew shall rest upon my branches. 20 My glory shall draw near to me, and my bow shall be restored in my hand. 21 Men have turned away from me, they have turned away and held their tongues before my counsels. 22 They have not answered my words, and my speech has fallen upon them. 23 They turned away from me as from the rain and opened their mouths as from the last ray. 24 If I laughed on them, they did not notice; and they did not let the light of my counte- nance fall. 25 I paved their way, I sat as a lead- er and dwelt as a king in the army, as one who comforts those who mourn.

CHAPTER 30

1 But now those who are younger than me mock me; yes, those whose fathers I refused to put with the dogs of my flock. 2 For what use would the strength of their hands be to me, seeing that age is dead in them? 3 Be- cause of the plague and famine they were isolated, fleeing into the wilderness, dark, desolate and desolate. 4 They cut their nets by the bushes, and juniper roots were their meal. 5 They were driven out by men, who shouted at them as at a feast. 6 Therefore they dwelt in the crevices of the mountains, in the holes in the earth and in the rocks. 7 They roared in the bushes and gathered under the thistles. 8 They were sons of fools and sons of scoun- drels, more vile than the earth. 9 Now I am their song and I am their speech. 10 They abhor me, they flee far from me, and do not spare to spit in my face. 11 Because God has loosed my rope and humbled me, they have loosed the reins before me. 12 The young men rise up at my right hand, they push my feet and trample me down as if I were in the path of their destruction. 13 They have destroyed my paths; they have been pleased with my ca- lamities; they have had no help. 14 They have

come like a great gash of water, and under this calamity they come walking. 15 Fear has come upon me; they pursue my soul like the wind, and my health passes away like a cloud. 16 Therefore my soul is now exhausted, and the days of affliction have taken hold of me. 17 My bones crumble at night, and my sinews find no rest. 18 For the great vehemence is changed my garment, which wraps me like the casting off of my cloak. 19 It has cast me into the myrrh, and I have become like ashes and dust. 20 When I cry out to you, you do not hear me or consider me when I stand up. 21 You turn cruelly against me and are my ene- my by the strength of your hand. 22 You take me and make me ride on the wind, and make my strength fail. 23 I know well that you will bring me to death and to the house appealed to for all lies. 24 No one can stretch out his hand toward the grave, though you cry for its destruction. 25 Did I not weep with those who were in distress? Was not my soul anxious for the poor? 26 Yet when I sought good, distress came to me; and when I waited for light, dark- ness came. 27 My bowels boiled over without rest, because the days of affliction came upon me. 28 I mourned without sun; I stood in the assembly and wept. 29 I am the brother of dragons and the companion of ostriches. 30 My skin is stained, and my bones are burned with burning. 31 Therefore my zither has be- come mourning, and my organs have become the wailing of those who mourn.

CHAPTER 31

1 I have made a choice with my own eyes; why then should I think of another thing? 2 For what portion should I have from God from without and what inheritance from the Almighty from above? 3 Is it not destruction for the wicked and a strange punishment for the workers of iniquity? 4 Does he not observe my ways and recount all my steps? 5 Whether I have walked in vanity, or whether my steps have hastened to deceit, 6 God will weigh me in the right balance and know my righteous- ness. 7 If my step has deviated from the way, or if my heart has walked according to my eye, or if any stain has been wiped from my hands, 8 Let me sow, and let another eat; yea, let my plants be uprooted. 9 If my heart has been deceived by a woman, or if I have yield- ed to the will of my neighbor, 10 let my wife prostrate herself before another man, and let other men prostrate themselves before her: 11 For this is wickedness and iniquity to be con- demned: 12 it is a fire that shall bring me to destruction, and shall take away all my estate, 13 If I have ignored the judgment of my ser- vant and my wife, when they have quarreled with me, 14 what will I do when God stands and when He visits me, what will I answer? 15 He who created me in the womb, did He not create Himself? Is he not the one who made the womb? 16 If I have withheld the poor from their desire, or if I have failed the eyes of the widow, 17 Or if I have eaten my morsels alone, and the fathers have not eaten of them, 18 (for from my youth he has grown up with me as a father, and from my mother's womb I have been a guide to her). 19 If I saw anyone per- ishing for lack of clothing, or some poor man without food, 20 If her faithfulness has not blessed me, for she has warmed herself with the fleece of my sheep, 21 if I raised my hand against the orphan, when I saw that I could help him at the door, 22 my arm shall come off my shoulder, and my arm shall be broken from the bone. 23 For the chastisement of God frightened me, and I could not be delivered from its height. 24 If I made gold my hope or if I said to the wedge of gold, "You are my se- curity." 25

Whether I had withdrawn because my substance was great or because my hand had obtained much, 26 whether I had seen the sun when it shone or the moon walking in its splendor, 27 whether my heart secretly flattered me or my mouth kissed my hand, 28 (this also was an iniquity to be condemned, for I had denied the God who is there). 29 whether I reacted to the destruction of him who hated me, or whether I was induced to react when death came upon him, 30 I did not allow my mouth to sin, wishing a curse on his soul. 31 Did not the men of my Taberna- cle say, "Who will give us his flesh? We cannot be satisfied." 32 The stranger did not lodge in the street, but I opened my doors to him who passed by on the road. 33 If I hid my sin like Adam, concealing my iniquity in my bosom, 34 though I might have frightened a great multitude, yet the most despicable of families feared me; so I kept silent and did not leave the house. 35 Oh, if I had someone to hear me, look at my sign that the Almighty will testify for me, even if my adversary should write a book against me, 36 would I not take it upon my shoulders and regard it as a crown for me? 37 I will tell him the name of my journey and go to him as to a prince. 38 If my land cries out against me, or its furrows compact together, 39 If I have eaten its fruits without silence, or if I have eaten the souls of its masters, 40 let thistles grow instead of wheat, and roosters instead of barley. Iob's words are finished.

CHAPTER 32

1 So these three men stopped answering Iob, because he esteemed himself righteous. 2 Then was kindled the anger of Elihu the son of Barachel the Buzite, of the family of Ram; his anger, I say, was kindled against Iob, because he esteemed himself more than God. 3 His wrath also kindled against his three friends, because they could not find an answer, yet they condemned Iob. 4 (Elihu had stayed until Iob had spoken, because they were older than he). 5 When Elihu saw that the three men did not answer, he was inflamed with anger. 6 Then Elihu the son of Barachel the Buz- ite answered and said, "I am young in years, and you are ancient; therefore I doubted and was afraid to tell you my opinion. 7 For I said, The days shall speak, and the multitude of years shall teach wisdom." 8 Certainly there is a spirit in man, but the inspiration of the Almighty makes it clear. 9 The great are not always wise, nor do the elders always under- stand judgment. 10 Therefore I say, "Listen to me, and I will also set forth my judgment." 11 Behold, I waited for your words and listened to your knowledge, while you sought reasons. 12 But when I considered you, behold, there was not one of you who rebuked Iob and did not answer his words: 13 lest you should say, "We have found wisdom," for God has cast him and no man. 14 Nevertheless he hath not spoken his words unto me, neither will I answer him with your words." 15 Then they, fearing, answered no more, but left off their talk. 16 When I had gone away (for they did not speak, but stood still and answered no more) 17 I answered in my turn and expound- ed my opinion. 18 For I am full of matter, and the spirit that is in me constrains me. 19 Be- hold, my belly is like wine that has no vent, and like new bottles that burn. 20 Therefore I will speak, to catch my breath: I will open my lips and answer. 21 Now I will not accept the person of man, nor will I give titles to man. 22 For I cannot give titles, lest my Maker sud- denly take me away.

CHAPTER 33

1 Therefore, Iob, I beseech you, listen to my speeches and pay attention to all my words. 2 Behold, now I have opened my mouth; my tongue has spoken in my mouth. 3 My words are in the uprightness of my heart, and my lips utter pure knowledge. 4 The Spirit of God has made me, and the breath of the Most High has given me life. 5 If you can give me an answer, prepare yourself and stand before me. 6 Behold, I am according to your desire in the place of God: I too am formed of clay. 7 Behold, my terror shall not frighten you, and my hand shall not be a burden to you. 8 You have spoken in my ears, and I have heard the voice of your words. 9 I am clean, without sin; I am innocent, and there is no iniquity in me. 10 Behold, he has found opportunities against me and has regarded me as his en- emy. 11 He has put my feet in his shoes, and he looks intently at all my paths. 12 Behold, in this you have not done well; I will answer you that God is greater than man. 13 Why do you hurl yourself at him? Because he does not give an account of all his things. 14 Because God speaks once or twice and is not seen. 15 In dreams and visions of the night, when sleep falls upon men and they sleep on their beds, 16 he opens men's ears, even through their corrections, which he had sealed, 17 to cause man to depart from his undertaking, and to hide the pride of man, 18 to keep his soul from the pit, and that his life may not pass away by the sword. 19 He is also afflicted with pain on his bed, and the pain of his bones is sore, 20 so that his life leads him to despise bread, and his soul to eat light food. 21 His flesh fails, so that it cannot be seen, and his bones, which had not been seen, are shattered. 22 Thus his soul withdraws into the grave, and his life into the sepulchres. 23 If there is a messen- ger or an interpreter with him, one among a thousand, declaring to the man his righ- teousness, 24 then he shall have mercy on him, and shall say, "Deliver him, that he may not go down into the pit, for I have received a reconciliation." 25 Then his flesh shall be as fresh as a child's, and he shall return as in the days of his youth. 26 He shall pray to God, and he shall be favorable to him, and he shall see his face with joy, for he shall render to man his righteousness. 27 He shall look upon men, and if any man shall say, "I have sinned, I have lacked righteousness, and it hath availed me nothing." 28 He shall deliver his soul from the pit, and his life shall see the light. 29 Behold, all these things God will do twice or three times with a man, 30 That his soul may return back from the pit, to be enlightened by the light of light. 31 Hear me well, O Iob, and hear me; be silent, and I will speak. 32 If there is anything to be said, answer me and speak, for I want to justify you. 33 If you have not done so, listen to me; keep your tongue, and I will teach you wisdom.

CHAPTER 34

1 Elihu answered and said, 2 Hear my words, you wise men, and give ear to me, you who have knowledge. 3 For the ear tries words, as the mouth tastes food. 4 Let us see judg- ment among ourselves and know among ourselves what is good. 5 For Iob said, "I am righteous, and God has taken away my judg- ment." 6 Shall I remain in my righteousness? My blistering wound is grievous without my sin. 7 What is the man like Iob, who drinks scorn like water? 8 Who goes in the compa- ny of those who work iniquity and walks with the wicked? 9 For he said, "It profits no man to walk with God." 10 Therefore hear me, wise men: God

does not want wickedness to be in God and iniquity in the Almighty. 11 For he will render to man according to his work, and will cause every one to find his own way. 12 And surely God will not do iniquity, and the Almighty will not do judgment. 13 Who has He appointed besides Himself on earth? Or who has he set the whole world? 14 If he hath set his heart upon man, and hath gathered his spirit and his breath upon himself, 15 all flesh shall perish together, and man shall return to dust. 16 If you have understanding, listen to this and hear the meaning of my words.17 He who hates judgment, is a man of faith, and will you judge wicked him who is more righ- teous? 18 Will you say to a king, "You are wick- ed," or to princes: "You are ungodly"? 19 How much less to him who does not accept the people of princes and does not consider the rich more than the poor, for they are all the work of his hands. 20 They shall die suddenly, and the people shall be troubled at midnight, and they shall pass to take away the mighty out of their hands. 21 For his eyes are on the ways of man, and he sees all his movements. 22 There is no darkness nor shadow of death to hide the workers of iniquity. 23 For he will not so impose upon man as to bring him into judgment with God. 24 He will break the mighty ones without seeking them and install others in their place. 25 Therefore he declares their works; he makes the night pass, and they shall be destroyed. 26 He strikes them as evil men in the places of the seers, 27 be- cause they turned away from him and would not consider all his ways: 28 so that they have caused the journey of the poor to come to him, and he has heard the cry of the afflicted. 29 When he appeases, who can make trouble? And when he hides his face, who can see it, whether nations or one man? 30 Because the hypocrite reigns, and because the people are trapped. 31 Of course, it is incumbent on God to say, "I have forgiven, I will not destroy." 32 But if I do not see, teach me; if I have done evil, I will not do it again. 33 Will he perform the deed through you? For thou hast repro- duced it, for thou hast chosen, and not I. 34 Let intelligent men tell me, and let a wise man hear me. 35 Iob did not speak knowledgeably, and his words were not even according to wis- dom. 36 I desire Iob to be tested, according to the answers to be given to wicked men. 37 For he adds rebellion to his sin; he claps his hands among them and multiplies his words against God.

CHAPTER 35

1 Elihu spoke again and said, 2 Does it seem right to you that you said, "I am more righ- teous than God"? 3 For thou hast said, "What does it profit thee, and what does it profit me, to cleanse me from my sin?" 4 Therefore I will answer you and your companions with you. 5 Look toward the horizon and see the clouds that are higher than you. 6 If you sin, what do you do against him? When your sins are many, what do you do against him? 7 If you are righteous, what do you give him or what does he receive at your hands? 8 Your wick- edness may harm a man like you, while your righteousness may benefit a son of man. 9 They make many oppressed weep, who cry out because of the violence of the mighty. 10 But no one says, "Where is the God who creat- ed me, who makes songs in the night? 11 Who teaches more than the beasts of the earth and gives more wisdom than the fires of heaven. 12 Then they cry out because of the violence of the wicked, but he does not answer. 13 God does not listen to vanities, and the Almighty does not consider them. 14 Though you say to God, "You will not consider it," yet judg- ment is before him; trust in him. 15

But now, because his wrath has not visited and he has not reckoned the damage with a great extent, 16 therefore Iob opens his mouth in vein and multiplies words without knowledge.

CHAPTER 36

1 Elihu also went on and said, 2 Give me some time and I will instruct you, for I have yet to speak for God. 3 I will take my knowl- edge from afar and attribute righteousness to my Creator. 4 For my words will not be false, and he who is perfect in knowledge will speak to you. 5 Behold, the mighty God will not cast away anyone who is strong and valiant in courage. 6 He does not keep the wicked, but gives justice to the afflicted. 7 He does not turn away from the righteous, but they are with kings on their throne, where He places them forever; so they are exalted. 8 And if they are bound with chains and bound with cords of affliction, 9 Then he will show them their works and their sins, because they have been proud. 10 He will also open their ear to disci- pline and command them to withdraw from iniquity. 11 If they obey him and serve him, their days will end in prosperity and their years in pleasures. 12 But if they do not obey, they will go by the sword and perish with- out knowing. 13 But the hypocrites of heart increase wrath, for they do not call when he binds them. 14 Their souls die in youth, and their lives among whoremongers. 15 He aban- dons the poor in his affliction and opens his ears in trouble. 16 So he would have brought thee out of the straight place to a place of broth, and would not have shut thee under; and that which resteth upon thy table would be full of fatness. 17 But thou art full of the judgment of the wicked, though judgment and equity keep all things. 18 For the wrath of God is that unless he takes away what you have in abundance, he cannot give you a mul- titude of gifts. 19 Does He not take account of your riches? He takes no account of money, nor of all that exceed in strength. 20 Pay no heed to the night, as he destroys the people from their place. 21 Pay no heed to iniquity, for you have chosen it rather than affliction. 22 God exalts by his power; what teacher is like him? 23 Who has established for him his way? Or who can say, "You have done evil"? 24 Remember to magnify his work, which men see. 25 All men see it and observe it from afar. 26 God is exalted, and we do not know him, nor can we discover the name of his years. 27 When He holds back the drops of water, the ray breaks forth from His vapor, 28 Which the clouds let fall in abundance on man. 29 Who can know the diuisions of you clouds, and the thunders of his tabernacle? 30 Behold, he shedeth his light upon it, and searcheth the bottom of the sea. 31 For in this way he judg- es the people and gives food in abundance. 32 He agrees the light with the clouds and com- mands them to go against it. 33 His compan- ion points it out to him and rises up in anger.

CHAPTER 37

1 At this point even my heart is astonished and is shaken from its place. 2 Listen to the sound of his voice and the noise that comes out of his mouth. 3 He directs it throughout the whole heaven and its light to the ends of the world. 4 After it resounds a noise; he thunders with the voice of his maiestie and does not hold them back when his voice is heard. 5 God thunders wonderfully with his voice; he works great things that we do not know. 6 For he says to

the snow, "Be upon the earth"; so also to the small beam and the great beam of his power. 7 By his power he shuts up every man, that all may know his work. 8 Then the beasts enter the den and stay in their place. 9 The whirlwind comes from the south and the cold wind from the north. 10 With the breath of God, the frost is removed and the breadth of the waters is made narrous. 11 He also makes the clouds work to water the earth and scatters the cloud of his light. 12 And all things are turned under his direction, that they may do what he commands them over all the world: 13 Whether it be for punish- ment, or for his land, or for mercy, he causeth it to come to pass. 14 Hear this, O Iob; stand and consider the wonderful works of God. 15 Do you know when God arranged them and made the light of his cloud to shine? 16 Do you know the variety of the cloud and the wonder- ful works of him who is perfect in knowledge? 17 Or how are your garments when he makes the earth quiet with the south wind? 18 Hast thou spread out thy cheeks, which are strong and like molten icing? 19 Tell him what we must say to him, for we cannot dispose of our matter because of darkness. 20 Shall he be told when I shall speak? Or shall man speak when he is destroyed? 21 Now men do not see the light shining through the clouds, but the wind passes through and closes them. 22 The brightness comes from the north; its praise is to God, who is terrible. 23 He is the Almighty, we cannot find out; he is excellent in power and judgment and abounds in justice; he does not grieve. 24 Let men therefore fear him, for he will not care for those who are wise in their conceit.

CHAPTER 38

1 Then the LORD answered Iob from the whirlwind and said, 2 Who is he that dark- eneth counsel with words without knowl- edge? 3 Face now thy allegiance as a man: I will ask thee and declare thee. 4 Where were you when I laid the foundations of the earth? De- clare, if thou hast understanding, 5 who drew its measures, if you know, or who drew its boundaries: 6 where its foundation was laid, or who laid its cornerstone: 7 when the morn- ing stars prayed to me together, and all the sons of God were gathered together: 8 Or who shut up the sea with gates, when it moved and came forth as from a womb: 9 when I made clouds as a covering, and darkness as bands to envelop the sea: 10 when I established my command over it, and fixed barricades and towers therein, 11 And I said, Thou canst go no further, but no further, and here shall thy prowess remain. 12 Hast thou commanded the morning since thy days? Thou hast caused the morning to know its place, 13 That it may take hold of the corners of the earth, and that the wicked may be shaken out of it? 14 It is turned into clay, and everything is like a gar- ment. 15 The ungodly shall have their light taken away, and their weapon shall be broken. 16 Have you entered the bottom of the sea, or have you walked to see the depths? 17 Have the gates of death been opened to you? Or have you seen the gates of the shadow of death? 18 Have you perceived the breadth of the earth? Say whether you know all this. 19 Where is the way where the light dwells, and where is the place of darkness? 20 That you might re- ceive it in its borders and know the paths that lead to its house? 21 Did you know it because you were born then and because the name of your days is great? 22 Have you entered into the treasures of the snow, or have you seen the treasures of heaven? 23 Which have I hid for the time of trouble, for the day of war and battle? 24 By what way is the light divided that scatters the east wind

over the earth? 25 Who has established the sponges for the rain or the way for the lightning of you thunder? 26 to cause it to break out on the earth where there is no man and in the wilderness where there is no man? 27 to cause the wilderness and desert place to be filled, and to cause the sprouting of the grass? 28 Who is the father of the ray, or who brought forth the dewdrops? 29 From whose womb did the lily come forth? Who brought forth the frost of heaven? 30 The waters are hidden as by a stone, and the face of the depth is covered with smoke. 31 Canst thou rest the gentle influences of the Pleiades, or melt the bands of Orion? 32 Canst thou make Mazzaroth arise in their time? Canst thou also guide Arcturus with his sons? 33 Knowest thou the course of the Eauen, or canst thou establish its rules on earth? 34 Can you raise your voice to the clouds, that the abundance of water may help you? 35 Can thou send the lightnings that they may walk and say to thee, "Behold, we are here"? 36 Who has put wisdom in the kidneys or who has given the heart understanding? 37 Who can remove the clouds with wisdom, or who can make the clouds of the earth cease? 38 When the earth becomes hard and the clods tighten?

CHAPTER 39

1 Will you hunt prayers for the lion or satiate the appetite of the lion cubs? 2 When they curl up in their places and stay in their beds wait- ing? 3 Who prepares his meal for the rauna, when his birds cry out to God, wandering for want of food? 4 Do you know the hour when the wild goats bear their fruit? Or do you know when the hinds give birth? 5 Can you recog- nize the money they make? Or do you know the hour when they bear fruit? 6 They bend themselves, they bruise their youth and cast out their sorrows. 7 Yet their youth becomes fat and swells with horns; they depart and do not return to their home. 8 Who has loosed the wild plank, or who has loosed the bonds of the wild plank? 9 It is I who have made the wilderness his home and the salt places his dwelling place. 10 He mocks the multitude of the city; he does not hear the cry of those who are fleeing. 11 He seeks the mountain for his pasture and seeks every green thing. 12 Will the vnicorne serve thee, or stand by thy flock? 13 Will you find the vnicorne with his band to work in the forests? Or will he plow the val- leys after you? 14 Will you trust in him, for his strength is great, and leave your toil to him? 15 Wilt thou trust in him, that he will bring home thy seed and gather it into thy fields? 16 Hast thou given pleasant wings to peacocks, or wings and feathers to ostriches? 17 Who leaves his eggs in the earth and gives birth to them in the dust, 18 And forgets that the fowl may scatter them, or that the wild beast may break them. 19 He shows himself cruel to his young, as if they were not his own, and does not care, as if he had dragged himself into the vein. 20 For God has deprived him of wisdom and given him no portion of understanding. 21 When there is time, he gets on the horse and mocks the horse and its rider. 22 Did you give strength to the horse, or did you cover his neck with neying? 23 Hast thou frightened him like a hunting horse? His strong neck is fearsome. 24 He digs into the valley and feels strong; he goes to meet the strongest man. 25 He mocks fear; he is not frightened and does not flinch from the sword, 26 though the glit- tering spear and shield buzz against him. 27 He swallows the ground in fear and anger, and does not notice that it is the noise of the trumpet. 28 He says between the trumpets, "Ah, ah! He hears the smell of battle, the noise of

the captains and the shouting." 29 Can the eagle fly for your wisdom, spreading its wings toward the south? 30 Shall the eagle go up at thy command, or make his nest upon her? She abides and lingers in the stronghold, even on the top of the stronghold and on the tower. From there she spies for food, and her eyes behold the pain. Her young ones also suck blood; and where the slain are, there she is. The Lord spoke again to Iob and said: Is this learning to quarrel with the Almighty? He who rebukes God, let him answer to it. Then Iob answered the Lord, saying: Behold, I am vile; what shall I answer thee? I will put my hand over my mouth. I have spoken once, but I will answer no more, yea twice, but I will proceed no further.

CHAPTER 40

1 The LORD answered Iob from the whirl- wind and said, 2 "Face now your obligations like a man: I will inquire of you, and you will declare yourself to me. 3 Will you disown my judgment or will you condemn me to be justified? 4 Hast thou a weapon like God? Or thou thunder with a voice like him? 5 Adorn yourself now with majesties and excellencies, and clothe yourself with beauty and glory. 6 Cast down the indignation of your wrath; be- hold all those who are proud, and cast them down. 7 Look at those who are arrogant and lower them, and destroy the wicked in their place. 8 Hide them together in the dust, and hide their faces in a secret place. 9 Then I will also confess to you that your right hand can save you. 10 Behold Behemoth (whom I have made with you) who eats grain like an ox. 11 Behold, his strength is in his loins, and his strength is in his belly. 12 When he takes plea- sure, his tail is like a cedar; the sinews of his stones are wound together. 13 His bones are like rods of wood, and his smaller bones like rods of yron. 14 He is the chief of the ways of God; he who made him will cause his sword to come near him. 15 The mountains bring him down to the valley, where all the beasts of the field play. 16 Does he lie down under the trees, in the enclosure of the hills and forests? 17 Can the trees protect him with their shade, or can the willows of the riviera surround him? 18 Behold, he spits on the river and does not hurry; he trusts that he may draw Iorden into his mouth. 19 He catches it with his eyes and thrusts his nose into whatever comes within his reach. 20 Canst thou draw out Liuiathan with a yoke and with a thread, which thou shalt cast as far as his tongue? 21 Can thou cast an axe into his nose? Can thou perceive his lips at an angle? 22 Will he make many prayers to thee, or will he speak plainly to thee? 23 Will he make a covenant with you, and will you take him as your servant forev- er? 24 Will you play with him as with a bird, or will you take him for your desires? Will the companions make bread with him? Will they lay him down among the marchers? Will you be able to fill the basket with his skin or the fishbowl with his head? Lay your hand on him, remember the battle and do it no more. Behold, his hope is in life, for will he not be lost in the sight of it?

CHAPTER 41

1 No one is so fearful as to dare to incite him. Who then is he who can stand before me? 2 Who has foreordained me that I should make an end? All that is under heaven is mine. 3 I will not be silent about its parts, its power and its beautiful proportions. 4 Who shall uncov- er the face of his garment, or who shall ap- proach him with a double bridle?

5 Who shall open the gates of his face? His teeth are fear- ful all around. 6 His scales are like shields of stone, and they are sealed securely. 7 The one is bound to the other, and there is no wind to separate them. 8 One is bound to the other; they are joined together and cannot be sepa- rated. 9 His nerves make the light shine, and his eyes are like the eyelids of the morning. 10 Out of his mouth come lamps and sparks of fire. 11 Out of his nostrils comes smoke, as from a pot or cauldron. 12 His breath causes the caps to burn, because a flame comes out of his mouth. 13 His neck is strengthened, and the work recedes before his face. 14 The members of his body are healthy; they are strong in themselves and cannot be suffocat- ed. 15 His heart is as strong as a stone and as hard as the cornerstone. 16 The mighty ones are frightened by his majesty, and out of fear they feel lacking. 17 When the sword touch- es him, he does not rise, neither by the spear, nor by the dart, nor by the harpoon. 18 He re- gards the iron as a rope and the rod as rotten wood. 19 The archer cannot make it flee; the stones of the sling have become stubble for him: 20 The darts are regarded as hard wood, and he laughs when he shakes his spear. 21 Sharp stones are under him, and he scatters sharp things on the ground. 22 He makes the depths boil like a pot, and he makes the sea like a pot of oil. 23 He makes a path shine behind him; you would say that the depth is like a horse's head. 24 On earth there is none like him; he is made without fear. 25 He ob- serves all things; he is a king over all the sons of pride.

CHAPTER 42

1 Then Iob answered the LORD and said, 2 I know that you can do all things, and that there is no thought hidden from you. 3 Who is he who hides counsel without knowing it? Therefore I said things that I did not under- stand, and also things that were too wonder- ful for me and that I did not know. 4 Hear, I pray you, and I will speak; I will ask of you, and you will declare yourself to me. 5 I have heard of you through the hearing of the ear, but now my eye sees you. 6 Therefore I abhor myself and repent in dust and ashes. 7 Now af- ter the LORD had spoken these words to Iob, the LORD also said to Eliphaz, O Temanite, "My wrath is kindled against you and against your two friends, because you have not said of me what is right, like my servant Iob. 8 There- fore now take ten bullocks and ten rams, and go to my servant Iob, and offer for yourselves a burnt offering, and my servant Iob will pray for you; for I will accept it, if I will not put you to shame, because you have not spoken of me what is right, like my servant Iob." 9 So Elip- haz, the Temanite, Bildad, the Shuhite, and Zophar, the Naamathite, went and did as the Lord had told them, and the Lord accepted Iob. 10 Then the LORD made Iob change his mind about Iob's imprisonment, when he prayed for his friends; also the LORD gave Iob twice as much as he had before. 11 Then came to him all his brothers, all his sisters, and all those who had been his acquaintances before, and ate bread with him in his house, and had compassion on him, and comforted him for all the sufferings which the Lord had brought upon him, and each one gave him a piece of money, and each one an ear of gold. 12 Thus the Lord blessed the last days of Iob more than the first, for he had four hundred thousand sheep, six thousand camels, a thou- sand yoke of oxen, and a thousand asses. 13 He also had seven sons and three daughters. 14 To one he called the name Iemima, to the second the name Keziah, and to the third the name Keren-happuch. 15 In all the land there were

found no women so beautiful as the daughters of Iob, and their father gave them an inheritance from among their brothers. 16 After this fact Iob lived a hundred and four years, and saw his sons and his sons, for four generations. 17 So Iob died, being old and full of days.

PSALM

Chapter 1

1 Blessed *is* the man that doth not walk in the counsel of the wicked, nor stand in the way of sinners, nor sit in the seat of the scornful:2 But his delight *is* in the law of the Lord, and in his law doth he meditate day and night. 3 For he shall be like a tree planted by the rivers of waters, that will bring forth her fruit in due season: whose leaf shall not fade: so whatsoever he shall do, shall prosper. 4 The wicked *are* not so, but as the chaff, which the wind driveth away. 5 Therefore the wicked shall not stand in the judgment, nor sinners in the assembly of the righteous. 6 For the Lord knoweth the way of the righteous, and the way of the wicked shall perish.

Chapter 2

1 Why do the heathen rage, and the people murmur in vain?2 The Kings of the earth band themselves, and the princes are assembled together against the Lord, and against his Christ. 3 Let us break their bands, and cast their cords from us. 4 *But* he that dwelleth in the heaven shall laugh: the Lord shall have them in derision. 5 Then shall he speak unto them in his wrath, and vex them in his sore displeasure, *saying,*6 *Even* I have set my king upon Zion mine holy mountain. 7 I will declare the decree: *that is,* the Lord hath said unto me, Thou art my Son: this day have I begotten thee. 8 Ask of me, and I shall give thee the heathen for thine inheritance, and the ends of the earth for thy possession. 9 Thou shalt crush them with a scepter of iron, *and* break them in pieces like a potter's vessel. 10 Be wise now therefore, ye kings: be learned ye judges of the earth. 11 Serve the Lord in fear, and rejoice in trembling. 12 Kiss the Son, least he be angry, and ye perish in the way, when his wrath shall suddenly burn. Blessed *are* all that trust in him.

Chapter 3

A Psalm-chapter of David, when he fled from his son, Absalom.

1 Lord, how are mine adversaries increased? How many rise against me?2 Many say to my soul, *There is* no help for him in God. Selah. 3 But thou Lord art a buckler for me: my glory, and the lifter up of mine head. 4 I did call unto the Lord with my voice, and he heard me out of his holy mountain. Selah. 5 I laid me down and slept, *and* rose up again: for the Lord sustained me. 6 I will not be afraid for ten thousand of the people, that should beset me round about. 7 O Lord, arise: help me, my God: for thou hast smitten all mine enemies upon the cheekbone: thou hast broken the teeth of the wicked. 8 Salvation *belongeth* unto the Lord, *and* thy blessing *is* upon thy people. Selah.

Chapter 4

To him that excelleth on Neginoth. A Psalm-chapter of David.

1 Hear me when I call, O God of my righteousness: thou hast set me at liberty, *when I was* in distress: have mercy upon me and hearken unto my prayer. 2 O ye sons of men, how long *will ye turn* my glory into shame, loving vanity, *and* seeking lies? Selah. 3 For be ye sure that the Lord hath chosen to himself a godly man: the Lord will hear when I call unto him. 4 Tremble, and sin not: examine your own heart upon your bed, and be still. Selah. 5 Offer the sacrifices of righteousness, and trust in the Lord. 6 Many say, Who will show us *any* good? *But* Lord, lift up the light of thy countenance upon us. 7 Thou hast given me more joy of heart, then *they have had,* when their wheat and their wine did abound. 8 I will lay me down, and also sleep in peace: for thou, Lord, only makest me dwell in safety.

Chapter 5

To him that excelleth upon Nehiloth. A Psalm-chapter of David.

1 Hear my words, O Lord: understand my meditation. 2 Hearken unto the voice of my cry, my King and my God: for unto thee do I pray. 3 Hear my voice in the morning, O Lord*: for* in the morning will I direct *me* unto thee, and I will wait. 4 For thou art not a God that loveth wickedness: neither shall evil dwell with thee. 5 The foolish shall not stand in thy sight: *for* thou hatest all them that work iniquity. 6 Thou shalt destroy them that speak lies: the Lord will abhor the bloody man and deceitful. 7 But I will come into thine house in the multitude of thy mercy: *and* in thy fear will I worship toward thine holy temple. 8 Lead me, O Lord, in thy righteousness, because of *mine* enemies: make thy way plain before my face. 9 For no constancy *is* in their mouth: within, they are very corruption: their throat *is* an open sepulcher, *and* they flatter with their tongue. 10 Destroy them, O God: let them fall from their counsels: cast them out for the multitude of their iniquities, because they have rebelled against thee. 11 And let all them that trust in thee, rejoice *and* triumph forever, and cover thou them: and let them, that love thy name, rejoice in thee. 12 For thou Lord wilt bless the righteous, *and* with favor wilt compass him, as with a shield.

Chapter 6

To him that excelleth on Neginoth upon the eight tune. A Psalm-chapter of David.

1 O Lord, rebuke me not in thine anger, neither chastise me in thy wrath. 2 Have mercy upon me, O Lord, for I am weak: O Lord heal me, for my bones are vexed. 3 My soul is also sore troubled: but Lord how long wilt thou delay?4 Return, O Lord: deliver my soul: save me for thy mercies' sake. 5 For in death *there* is no remembrance of thee: in the grave who shall praise thee?6 I fainted in my mourning: I cause my bed every night to swim, *and* water my couch with my tears. 7 Mine eye is dimmed for despite, and sunk in because of all mine enemies. 8 Away from me all ye workers of iniquity: for the Lord hath heard the voice of my weeping. 9 The Lord hath heard my petition: the Lord will receive my prayer. 10 All mine enemies shall be confounded and sore vexed: they shall be turned back*, and* put to shame suddenly.

Chapter 7

Shiggaion of David, which he sang unto the Lord, concerning the words of Cush the son *of Jemini.*

1 O Lord my God, in thee I put my trust: save me from all that persecute me, and deliver me,2 Lest he devour my soul like a lion, and tear it in pieces, while there is none to help. 3 O Lord my God, if I have done this thing: if there be *any* wickedness in mine hands,4 If I have rewarded evil unto him that had peace with me, (yea I have delivered him that vexed me without cause)5 *Then* let the enemy persecute my soul and take it: yea, let him tread my life down upon the earth, and lay mine honor in the dust. Selah. 6 Arise, O Lord, in thy wrath, and lift up thyself against the rage of mine enemies, and awake for me *according* to the

judgment *that* thou hast appointed. 7 So shall the congregation of the people compass thee about: for their sakes therefore return on high. 8 The Lord shall judge the people: judge thou me, O Lord, according to my righteousness, and according to mine innocence, *that is* in me. 9 Oh let the malice of the wicked come to an end: but guide thou the just: for the righteous God trieth the hearts and reins. 10 My defense *is* in God, who preserveth the upright in heart. 11 God judgeth the righteous, and him that contemneth God, every day. 12 Except he turn, he hath whet his sword: he hath bent his bow and made it ready. 13 He hath also prepared him deadly weapons: he will ordain his arrows for them that persecute *me*. 14 Behold, he shall travail with wickedness: for he hath conceived mischief, but he shall bring forth a lie. 15 He hath made a pit and digged it, and is fallen into the pit *that* he made. 16 His mischief shall return upon his own head, and his cruelty shall fall upon his own pate. 17 I will praise the Lord according to his righteousness, and will sing praise to the name of the Lord Most High.

Chapter 8

To him that excelleth on Gittith. A Psalm-chapter of David.

1 O Lord our Lord, how excellent is thy name in all the world! Which hast set thy glory above the heavens. 2 Out of the mouth of babes and sucklings hast thou ordained strength, because of thine enemies, that thou mightest still the enemy and the avenger. 3 When I behold thine heavens, *even* the works of thy fingers, the moon and the stars which thou hast ordained,4 What is man, *say I*, that thou art mindful of him? And the son of man, that thou visitest him?5 For thou hast made him a little lower than God, and crowned him with glory and worship. 6 Thou hast made him to have dominion in the works of thine hands. thou hast put all things under his feet:7 All sheep and oxen: yea, and the beasts of the field:8 The fowls of the air, and the fish of the sea, *and* that which passeth through the paths of the seas. 9 O Lord our Lord, how excellent is thy name in all the world!

Chapter 9

To him that excelleth upon Muth Labben. A Psalm-chapter of David.

1 I will praise the Lord with my whole heart: I will speak of all thy marvelous works. 2 I will be glad, and rejoice in thee: I will sing praise to thy name, O Most High,3 For that mine enemies are turned back: they shall fall, and perish at thy presence. 4 For thou hast maintained my right and my cause: thou art set in the throne, *and* judgest right. 5 Thou hast rebuked the heathen: thou hast destroyed the wicked: thou hast put out their name forever and ever. 6 O enemy, destructions are come to a perpetual end, and thou hast destroyed the cities: their memorial is perished with them. 7 But the Lord shall sit forever: he hath prepared his throne for judgment. 8 For he shall judge the world in righteousness, *and* shall judge the people with equity. 9 The Lord also will be a refuge for the poor, a refuge in *due* time, *even* in affliction. 10 And they that know thy name, will trust in thee: for thou, Lord, hast not failed them that seek thee. 11 Sing praises to the Lord, which dwelleth in Zion: show the people his works. 12 For when he maketh inquisition for blood, he remembereth it, *and* forgetteth not the complaint of the poor. 13 Have mercy upon me, O Lord: consider my trouble *which I suffer* of them that hate me, thou that liftest me up from the gates of death,14 That I may show all thy praises within the gates of the daughter of Zion, *and* rejoice in thy salvation. 15 The heathen are

sunken down in the pit *that* they made: in the net that they hid, is their foot taken. 16 The Lord is known by executing judgment: the wicked is snared in the work of his own hands. Higgaion. Selah. 17 The wicked shall turn into hell, *and* all nations that forget God. 18 For the poor shall not be alway forgotten: the hope of the afflicted shall not perish forever. 19 Up Lord: let not man prevail: let the heathen be judged in thy sight. 20 Put them in fear, O Lord, that the heathen may know that they are but men. Selah.

Chapter 10

1 Why standest thou far off, O Lord, *and* hidest thee in *due* time, *even* in affliction?2 The wicked with pride doth persecute the poor: let them be taken in the crafts that they have imagined. 3 For the wicked hath made boast of his own heart's desire, and the covetous blesseth *himself*: he contemneth the Lord. 4 The wicked is so proud that he seeketh not *for God*: he thinketh always, There is no God. 5 His ways alway prosper: thy judgments are high above his sight: therefore defieth he all his enemies. 6 He saith in his heart, I shall never be moved, nor be in danger. 7 His mouth is full of cursing and deceit and fraud: under his tongue is mischief and iniquity. 8 He lieth in wait in the villages: in the secret places doth he murder the innocent: his eyes are bent against the poor. 9 He lieth in wait secretly, *even* as a lion in his den: he lieth in wait to spoil the poor: he doth spoil the poor, when he draweth him into his net. 10 He croucheth *and* boweth: therefore heaps of the poor do fall by his might. 11 He hath said in his heart, God hath forgotten, he hideth away his face, *and* will never see. 12 Arise, O Lord God: lift up thine hand: forget not the poor. 13 Wherefore doth the wicked contemn God? He saith in his heart, Thou wilt not regard. 14 *Yet* thou hast seen it: for thou beholdest mischief and wrong, that thou mayest take it into thine hands: the poor committeth himself unto thee: *for* thou art the helper of the fatherless. 15 Break thou the arm of the wicked and malicious: search his wickedness, *and* thou shalt find none. 16 The Lord *is* King forever and ever: the heathen are destroyed forth of his land. 17 Lord, thou hast heard the desire of the poor: thou preparest their heart: thou bendest thine ear *to them*,18 To judge the fatherless and poor, that earthly man cause to fear no more.

Chapter 11

To him that excelleth. A Psalm-chapter *of David*.

1 In the Lord put I my trust: how say ye then to my soul, Flee to your mountain *as* a bird?2 For lo, the wicked bend their bow, *and* make ready their arrows upon the string, that they may secretly shoot at them, which are upright in heart. 3 For the foundations are cast down: what hath the righteous done?4 The Lord *is* in his holy palace: the Lord's throne *is* in the heaven: his eyes will consider: his eye lids will try the children of men. 5 The Lord will try the righteous: but the wicked and him that loveth iniquity, doth his soul hate. 6 Upon the wicked he shall rain snares, fire, and brimstone, and stormy tempest: *this is* the portion of their cup. 7 For the righteous Lord loveth righteousness: his countenance doth behold the just.

Chapter 12

To him that excelleth.upon the eight tune. A Psalm-chapter of David.

1 Help Lord, for there is not a godly man left: for the faithful are failed from among the children of men. 2 They speak deceitfully every one with his neighbor, flattering with their lips, *and* speak with a double heart. 3 The Lord cut off all flattering lips, and the tongue that

speaketh proud things:4 Which have said, With our tongue will we prevail: our lips are our own: who is Lord over us?5 Now for the oppression of the needy, and for the sighs of the poor, I will up, saith the Lord, *and* will set at liberty him, *whom the wicked* hath snared. 6 The words of the Lord *are* pure words, *as* the silver, tried in a furnace of earth, fined seven fold. 7 Thou wilt keep them, O Lord: thou wilt preserve him from this generation forever. 8 The wicked walk on every side: when they are exalted, *it is* a shame for the sons of men.

Chapter 13

To him that excelleth. A Psalm-chapter of David.

1 How long wilt thou forget me, O Lord, forever? How long wilt thou hide thy face from me?2 How long shall I take counsel within myself, *having* weariness daily in mine heart? How long shall mine enemy be exalted above me?3 Behold, and hear me, O Lord my God: lighten mine eyes, that I sleep not in death:4 Lest mine enemy say, I have prevailed against him: and they that afflict me, rejoice when I slide. 5 But I trust in thy mercy: mine heart shall rejoice in thy salvation: I will sing to the Lord, because he hath dealt lovingly with me. NOTE: Beginning with "I will sing . . . . " appears as verse 6 in the Bishop's King James Bible.

Chapter 14

To him that excelleth. A Psalm-chapter *of David.*

1 The fool hath said in his heart, *There is* no God: they have corrupted, and done an abominable work: *there is* none that doeth good. 2 The Lord looked down from heaven upon the children of men, to see if there were any that would understand, and seek God. 3 All are gone out of the way: they are all corrupt: there is none that doeth good, no not one. 4 Do not all the workers of iniquity know that they eat up my people, *as* they cat bread? they call not upon the Lord. 5 There they shall be taken with fear, because God *is* in the generation of the just. 6 You have made a mock at the counsel of the poor, because the Lord *is* his trust. 7 Oh give salvation unto Israel out of Zion: when the Lord turneth the captivity of his people, *then* Jacob shall rejoice, and Israel shall be glad.

Chapter 15

A Psalm-chapter of David.

1 Lord, who shall dwell in thy Tabernacle? Who shall rest in thine holy mountain? 2 He that walketh uprightly and worketh righteousness, and speaketh the truth in his heart. 3 He that slandereth not with his tongue, nor doeth evil to his neighbor, nor receiveth a false report against his neighbor. 4 In whose eyes a vile person is contemned, but he *honoreth* them that fear the Lord: he that sweareth to his *own* hindrance and changeth not. 5 He that giveth not his money unto usury, nor taketh reward against the innocent: he that doeth these things, shall never be moved.

Chapter 16

Michtam of David.

1 Preserve me, O God: for in thee do I trust. 2 *O my soul,* thou hast said unto the Lord, Thou art my Lord: my well doing *extendeth* not to thee,3 *But* to the Saints that are in the earth, and to the excellent: all my delight is in them. 4 The sorrows of them, that offer to another *god,* shall be multiplied: their offerings of blood will I not offer, neither make mention of their names with my lips. 5 The Lord *is* the portion of mine inheritance and of my cup: thou shalt maintain my lot. 6 The lines are fallen unto me in pleasant places: yea, I have a fair heritage. 7 I will praise the Lord, who hath given me counsel: my reins also teach me in the nights. 8 I have set the Lord always before

me: for he is at my right hand: *therefore* I shall not slide. 9 Wherefore mine heart is glad and my tongue rejoiceth: my flesh also doth rest in hope. 10 For thou wilt not leave my soul in the grave: neither wilt thou suffer thine holy one to see corruption. 11 Thou wilt show me the path of life: in thy presence *is* the fullness of joy: *and* at thy right hand there *are* pleasures forevermore.

Chapter 17

The prayer of David.

1 Hear the right, O Lord, consider my cry: hearken unto my prayer of lips unfeigned. 2 Let my sentence come forth from thy presence, and let thine eyes behold equity. 3 Thou hast proved and visited mine heart in the night: thou hast tried me, and foundest nothing: *for* I was purposed that my mouth should not offend. 4 Concerning the works of men, by the words of thy lips I kept me from the paths of the cruel man. 5 Stay my steps in thy paths, that my feet do not slide. 6 I have called upon thee: surely thou wilt hear me, O God: incline thine ear to me, and hearken unto my words. 7 Show thy marvelous mercies, *thou* that art the Savior of them that trust *in thee,* from such as resist thy right hand. 8 Keep me as the apple of the eye: hide me under the shadow of thy wings,9 From the wicked that oppress me, *from mine* enemies, which compass me round about for *my* soul. 10 They are enclosed in their own fat, *and* they have spoken proudly with their mouth. 11 They have compassed us now in our steps: they have set their eyes to bring down to the ground:12 Like as a lion that is greedy of prey, and as it were a lion's whelp lurking in secret places. 13 Up Lord, disappoint him: cast him down: deliver my soul from the wicked with thy sword,14 From men by thine hand, O Lord, from men of the world, who have their portion in this life, whose bellies thou fillest with thine hid treasure: their children have enough, and leave the rest of their substance for their children. 15 *But* I will behold thy face in righteousness, and when I awake, I shall be satisfied with thine image.

Chapter 18

To him that excelleth. A Psalm-chapter *of David the servant of the Lord, which spake unto the Lord the words of this song (in the day that the Lord delivered him from the hand of all his enemies, and from the hand of Saul) and said,*

1 I will love thee dearly, O Lord my strength. 2 The Lord *is* my rock, and my fortress, and he that delivereth me, my God and my strength: in him will I trust, my shield, the horn also of my salvation, and my refuge. 3 I will call upon the Lord, which is worthy to be praised: so shall I be safe from mine enemies. 4 The sorrows of death compassed me, and the floods of wickedness made me afraid. 5 The sorrows of the grave have compassed me about: the snares of death overtook me. 6 *But* in my trouble did I call upon the Lord, and cried unto my God: he heard my voice out of his temple, and my cry did come before him, *even* into his ears. 7 Then the earth trembled, and quaked: the foundations also of the mountains moved and shook, because he was angry. 8 Smoke went out at his nostrils, and a consuming fire out of his mouth: coals were kindled there at. 9 He bowed the heavens also and came down, and darkness *was* under his feet. 10 And he rode upon cherub and did fly, and he came flying upon the wings of the wind. 11 He made darkness his secret place, and his pavilion round about him, *even* darkness of waters, *and* clouds of the air. 12 At the brightness of his presence his clouds passed, hailstones and coals of fire. 13 The Lord also thundered in the heaven, and the

Highest gave his voice, hailstones and coals of fire. 14 Then he sent out his arrows and scattered them, and he increased lightnings and destroyed them. 15 And the channels of waters were seen, and the foundations of the world were discovered at thy rebuking, O Lord, at the blasting of the breath of thy nostrils. 16 He hath sent down from above *and* taken me: he hath drawn me out of many waters. 17 He hath delivered me from my strong enemy, and from them which hate me: for they were too strong for me. 18 They prevented me in the day of my calamity: but the Lord was my stay. 19 He brought me forth also into a large place: he delivered me because he favored me. 20 The Lord rewarded me according to my righteousness: according to the pureness of mine hands he recompensed me:21 Because I kept the ways of the Lord, and did not wickedly against my God. 22 For all his Laws *were* before me, and I did not cast away his commandments from me. 23 I was upright also with him, and have kept me from my wickedness. 24 Therefore the Lord rewarded me according to my righteousness, and according to the pureness of mine hands in his sight. 25 With the godly thou wilt show thyself godly: with the upright man thou wilt show thyself upright. 26 With the pure thou wilt show thyself pure, and with the froward thou wilt show thyself froward. 27 Thus thou wilt save the poor people, and wilt cast down the proud looks. 28 Surely thou wilt light my candle: the Lord my God will lighten my darkness. 29 For by thee I have broken through an host, and by my God I have leaped over a wall. 30 The way of God is uncorrupt: the word of the Lord is tried *in the fire*: he is a shield to all that trust in him. 31 For who is God besides the Lord? And who is mighty save our God?32 God girdeth me with strength, and maketh my way upright. 33 He maketh my feet like hinds *feet*, and setteth me upon mine high places. 34 He teacheth mine hands to fight: so that a bow of brass is broken with mine arms. 35 Thou hast also given me the shield of thy salvation, and thy right hand hath stayed me, and thy loving kindness hath caused me to increase. 36 Thou hast enlarged my steps under me, and mine heels have not slid. 37 I have pursued mine enemies, and taken them, and have not turned again till I had consumed them. 38 I have wounded them, that they were not able to rise: they are fallen under my feet. 39 For thou hast girded me with strength to battle them, that rose against me, thou hast subdued under me. 40 And thou hast given me the necks of mine enemies, that I might destroy them that hate me. 41 They cried but there was none to save *them, even* unto the Lord, but he answered them not. 42 Then I did beat them small as the dust before the wind: I did tread them flat as the clay in the streets. 43 Thou hast delivered me from the contentions of the people: thou hast made me the head of the heathen: a people, *whom* I have not known, shall serve me. 44 As soon as they hear, they shall obey me: the strangers shall be in subjection to me. 45 Strangers shall shrink away, and fear in their privy chambers. 46 Let the Lord live, and blessed be my strength, and the God of my salvation be exalted. 47 *It is* God that giveth me *power* to avenge me, and subdueth the people under me. 48 O my deliverer from mine enemies, even thou hast set me up from them, that rose against me: thou hast delivered me from the cruel man. 49 Therefore I will praise thee, O Lord, among the nations, and will sing unto thy name. 50 Great deliverances giveth he unto his king, and showeth mercy to his anointed, *even* to David, and to his seed forever.

Chapter 19

To him that excelleth. A Psalm-chapter of David.
1 The heavens declare the glory of God, and the firmament showeth the work of his hands. 2 Day unto day uttereth the same, and night unto night teacheth knowledge. 3 *There is* no speech nor language, *where* their voice is not heard. 4 Their line is gone forth through all the earth, and their words into the ends of the world: in them hath he set a tabernacle for the sun. 5 Which cometh forth as a bridegroom out of his chamber, *and* rejoiceth like a mighty man to run *his* race. 6 His going out *is* from the end of the heaven, and his compass *is* unto the ends of the same, and none is hid from the heat thereof. 7 The Law of the Lord is perfect, converting the soul: the testimony of the Lord is sure, and giveth wisdom unto the simple. 8 The statutes of the Lord *are* right and rejoice the heart: the commandment of the Lord *is* pure, and giveth light unto the eyes. 9 The fear of the Lord *is* clean, and endureth forever: the judgments of the Lord *are* truth: they are righteous altogether,10 And more to be desired then gold, yea, then much fine gold: sweeter also then honey and the honeycomb. 11 Moreover by them *is* thy servant made circumspect, and in keeping of them there *is* great reward. 12 Who can understand *his* faults? Cleanse me from secret *faults*. 13 Keep thy servant also from presumptuous sins: let them not reign over me: so shall I be upright, and made clean from much wickedness. 14 Let the words of my mouth, and the meditation of mine heart be acceptable in thy sight, O Lord, my strength, and my redeemer.

Chapter 20

To him that excelleth. A Psalm-chapter of David.
1 The Lord hear thee in the day of trouble: the name of the God of Jacob defend thee:2 Send thee help from the sanctuary, and strengthen thee out of Zion. 3 Let him remember all thine offerings, and turn thy burnt offerings into ashes. Selah:4 *And* grant thee according to thine heart, and fulfill all thy purpose:5 *That* we may rejoice in thy salvation, and set up the banner in the name of our God, *when* the Lord shall perform all thy petitions. 6 Now know I that the Lord will help his anointed, *and* will hear him from his sanctuary, by the mighty help of his right hand. 7 Some *trust* in chariots, and some in horses: but we will remember the name of the Lord our God. 8 They are brought down and fallen, but we are risen, and stand upright. 9 Save Lord: let the king hear us in the day that we call.

Chapter 21

To him that excelleth. A Psalm-chapter of David
1 The king shall rejoice in thy strength, O Lord: yea, how greatly shall he rejoice in thy salvation!2 Thou hast given him his heart's desire, and hast not denied *him* the request of his lips. Selah. 3 For thou didst prevent him with liberal blessings, and didst set a crown of pure gold upon his head. 4 He asked life of thee, *and* thou gavest him a long life forever and ever. 5 His glory *is* great in thy salvation: dignity and honor hast thou laid upon him. 6 For thou hast set him *as* blessings forever: thou hast made him glad with the joy of thy countenance. 7 Because the king trusteth in the Lord, and in the mercy of the Most High, he shall not slide. 8 Thine hand shall find out all thine enemies, *and* thy right hand shall find out them that hate thee. 9 Thou shalt make them like a fiery oven in time of thine anger: the Lord shall destroy them in his wrath, and the fire shall devour them. 10 Their fruit shalt thou destroy from the earth, and their seed from the children of men. 11 For they intended evil against thee, *and* imagined mischief, *but* they shall not prevail.

12 Therefore shalt thou put them apart, and the strings of thy bow shalt thou make ready against their faces. 13 Be thou exalted, O Lord, in thy strength: *so* will we sing and praise thy power.

Chapter 22

To him that excelleth upon Aiieleth Hasshahar. A Psalm-chapter of David.

1 My God, my God, why hast thou forsaken me, and art so far from mine health, *and from* the words of my roaring?2 O my God, I cry by day, but thou hearest not, and by night, but have no audience. 3 But thou art holy, and dost inhabit the praises of Israel. 4 Our fathers trusted in thee: they trusted, and thou didst deliver them. 5 They called upon thee, and were delivered: they trusted in thee, and were not confounded. 6 But I am a worm, and not a man: a shame of men, and the contempt of the people. 7 All they that see me, have me in derision: they make a mow and nod the head, *saying*,8 He trusted in the Lord, let him deliver him: let him save him, seeing he loveth him. 9 But thou didst draw me out of the womb: thou gavest me hope, *even* at my mother's breasts. 10 I was cast upon thee, *even* from the womb: thou art my God from my mother's belly. 11 Be not far from me, because trouble is near: for *there is* none to help *me.* 12 Many young bulls have compassed me: mighty bulls of Bashan have closed me about. 13 They gape upon me with their mouths, *as* a ramping and roaring lion. 14 I am like water poured out, and all my bones are out of joint: mine heart is like wax: it is molten in the midst of my bowels. 15My strength is dried up like a potsherd, and my tongue cleaveth to my jaws, and thouhast brought me into the dust of death. 16 For dogs have compassed me, and the assembly of the wicked have enclosed me: they pierced mine hands and my feet. 17 I may tell all my bones: *yet* they behold, *and* look upon me. 18 They part my garments among them, and cast lots upon my vesture. 19 But be not thou far off, O Lord, my strength: hasten to help me. 20 Deliver my soul from the sword: my desolate *soul* from the power of the dog. 21 Save me from the lion's mouth, and answer me *in saving me* from the horns of the unicorns. 22 I will declare thy name unto my brethren: in the midst of the congregation will I praise thee, *saying*,23 Praise the Lord, ye that fear him: magnify ye him, all the seed of Jacob, and fear ye him, all the seed of Israel. 24 For he hath not despised nor abhorred the affliction of the poor: neither hath he hid his face from him, but when he called unto him, he heard. 25 My praise *shall be* of thee in the great congregation: my vows will I perform before them that fear him. 26 The poor shall eat and be satisfied: they that seek after the Lord, shall praise him: your heart shall live forever. 27 All the ends of the world shall remember *themselves*, and turn to the Lord: and all the kindreds of the nations shall worship before thee. 28 For the kingdom *is* the Lord's, and he ruleth among the nations. 29 All they that be fat in the earth, shall eat and worship: all they that go down into the dust, shall bow before him, even he that cannot quicken his own soul. 30*Their* seed shall serve him: it shall be counted unto the Lord for a generation. 31 They shall come, and shall declare his righteousness unto a people that shall be born, because he hath done it.

Chapter 23

A Psalm-chapter of David.

1 The Lord *is* my shepherd, I shall not want. 2 He maketh me to rest in green pasture, and leadeth me by the still waters. 3 He restoreth my soul, and leadeth me in the paths of righteousness for his name's sake. 4 Yea, though

I should walk through the valley of the shadow of death, I will fear no evil: for thou art with me: thy rod and thy staff, they comfort me. 5 Thou dost prepare a table before me in the sight of mine adversaries: thou dost anoint mine head with oil, *and* my cup runneth over. 6 Doubtless kindness and mercy shall follow me all the days of my life, and I shall remain a long season in the house of the Lord.

Chapter 24

A Psalm-chapter of David.

1 The earth *is* the Lord's, and all that therein is: the world and they that dwell therein. 2 For he hath founded it upon the seas: and established it upon the floods. 3 Who shall ascend into the mountain of the Lord? And who shall stand in his holy place?4 *Even he that hath* innocent hands, and a pure heart: which hath not lift up his mind unto vanity, nor sworn deceitfully. 5 He shall receive a blessing from the Lord, and righteousness from the God of his salvation. 6 This is the generation of them that seek him, of them that seek thy face, *this is* Jacob. Selah. 7 Lift up your heads ye gates, and be ye lift up ye everlasting doors, and the King of glory shall come in. 8 Who is this King of glory? The Lord, strong and mighty, *even* the Lord mighty in battle. 9 Lift up your heads, ye gates, and lift up *yourselves*, ye everlasting doors, and the King of glory shall come in. 10 Who is this King of glory? The Lord of hosts, he is the King of glory. Selah.

Chapter 25

A Psalm-chapter *of David.*

1 Unto thee, O Lord, lift I up my soul. 2 My God, I trust in thee: let me not be confounded: let not mine enemies rejoice over me. 3 So all that hope in thee, shall not be ashamed: *but* let them be confounded, that transgress without cause. 4 Show me thy ways, O Lord, and teach me thy paths. 5 Lead me forth in thy truth, and teach me: for thou art the God of my salvation: in thee do I trust all the day. 6 Remember, O Lord, thy tender mercies, and thy loving kindness: for they have been forever. 7 Remember not the sins of my youth, nor my rebellions, *but* according to thy kindness remember thou me, *even* for thy goodness' sake, O Lord. 8 Gracious and righteous *is* the Lord: therefore will he teach sinners in the way. 9 Them that be meek, will he guide in judgment, and teach the humble his way. 10 All the paths of the Lord *are* mercy and truth unto such as keep his covenant and his testimonies. 11 For thy Name's sake, O Lord, be merciful unto mine iniquity, for it is great. 12 What man is he that feareth the Lord? Him will he teach the way *that* he shall choose. 13 His soul shall dwell at ease, and his seed shall inherit the land. 14 The secret of the Lord *is revealed* to them, that fear him: and his covenant to give them understanding. 15 Mine eyes *are* ever toward the Lord: for he will bring my feet out of the net. 16 Turn thy face unto me, and have mercy upon me: for I am desolate and poor. 17 The sorrows of mine heart are enlarged: draw me out of my troubles. 18 Look upon mine affliction and my travail, and forgive all my sins. 19 Behold mine enemies, for they are many, and they hate me with cruel hatred. 20 Keep my soul, and deliver me: let me not be confounded, for I trust in thee. 21 Let *mine* uprightness and equity preserve me: for mine hope is in thee. 22 Deliver Israel, O God, out of all his troubles.

Chapter 26

A Psalm-chapter *of David.*

1 Judge me, O Lord, for I have walked in mine innocence: my trust hath been also in theLord: *therefore* shall I not slide. 2 Prove me, O Lord, and try me: examine my reins,

and mine heart. 3 For thy loving kindness *is* before mine eyes: therefore have I walked in thy truth. 4 I have not haunted with vain persons, neither kept company with the dissemblers. 5 I have hated the assembly of the evil, and have not companied with the wicked. 6 I will wash mine hands in innocence, O Lord, and compass thine altar, 7 That I may declare with the voice of thanksgiving, and set forth all thy wondrous works. 8 O Lord, I have loved the habitation of thine house, and the place where thine honor dwelleth. 9 Gather not my soul with the sinners, nor my life with the bloody men: 10 In whose hands *is* wickedness, and their right hand is full of bribes. 11 But I will walk in mine innocence: redeem me *therefore*, and be merciful unto me. 12 My foot standeth in uprightness: I will praise thee, O Lord, in the congregations.

Chapter 27
A Psalm-chapter *of David.*

1 The Lord *is* my light and my salvation, whom shall I fear? The Lord *is* the strength of my life, of whom shall I be afraid? 2 When the wicked, *even* mine enemies and my foes came upon me to eat up my flesh they stumbled and fell. 3 Though an host pitched against me, mine heart should not be afraid: though war be raised against me, I will trust in this. 4 One thing have I desired of the Lord, that I will require, *even* that I may dwell in the house of the Lord all the days of my life, to behold the beauty of the Lord, and to visit his temple. 5 For in the time of trouble he shall hide me in his tabernacle: in the secret *place* of his pavilion shall he hide me, and set me up upon a rock. 6 And now shall he lift up mine head above mine enemies round about me: therefore will I offer in his tabernacle sacrifices of joy: I will sing and praise the Lord. 7 Harken unto my voice, O Lord, *when* I cry: have mercy also upon me and hear me. 8 *When thou saidst,* Seek ye my face, mine heart answered unto thee, O Lord, I will seek thy face. 9 Hide not *therefore* thy face from me, nor cast thy servant away in displeasure: thou hast been my succor: leave me not, neither forsake me, O God of my salvation. 10 Though my father and my mother should forsake me, yet the Lord will gather me up. 11 Teach me thy way, O Lord, and lead me in a right path, because of mine enemies. 12 Give me not unto the lust of mine adversaries: for there are false witnesses risen up against me, and such as speak cruelly. 13 *I should have fainted,* except I had believed to see the goodness of the Lord in the land of the living. 14 Hope in the Lord: be strong, and he shall comfort thine heart, and trust in the Lord.

Chapter 28
A Psalm-chapter *of David.*

1 Unto thee, O Lord, do I cry: O my strength, be not deaf toward me, lest, if thou answer me not, I be like them that go down into the pit. 2 Hear the voice of my petitions, when I cry unto thee, when I hold up mine hands toward thine holy oracle. 3 Draw me not away with the wicked, and with the workers of iniquity: which speak friendly to their neighbors, when malice *is* in their hearts. 4 Reward them according to their deeds, and according to the wickedness of their inventions: recompense them after the work of their hands: render them their reward. 5 For they regard not the works of the Lord, nor the operation of his hands: *therefore* break them down, and build them not up. 6 Praised *be* the Lord, for he hath heard the voice of my petitions. 7 The Lord *is* my strength and my shield: mine heart trusted in him, and I was helped: therefore mine heart shall rejoice, and with my song will I praise

him. 8 The Lord *is* their strength, and he is the strength of the deliverances of his anointed. 9 Save thy people, and bless thine inheritance: feed them also, and exalt them forever.

Chapter 29
A Psalm-chapter of David.

1 Give unto the Lord, ye sons of the mighty: give unto the Lord glory and strength. 2 Give unto the Lord glory *due* unto his name: worship the Lord in the glorious sanctuary. 3 The voice of the Lord *is* upon the waters: the God of glory maketh it to thunder: the Lord *is* upon the great waters. 4 The voice of the Lord *is* mighty: the voice of the Lord *is* glorious. 5 The voice of the Lord breaketh the cedars: yea, the Lord breaketh the cedars of Lebanon. 6 He maketh them also to leap like a calf: Lebanon *also* and Sirion like a young unicorn. 7 The voice of the Lord divideth the flames of fire. 8 The voice of the Lord maketh the wilderness to tremble: the Lord maketh the wilderness of Kadesh to tremble. 9 The voice of the Lord maketh the hinds to calve, and discovereth the forests: *therefore* in his temple doth every man speak of *his* glory. 10 The Lord sitteth upon the flood, and the Lord doth remain King forever. 11 The Lord shall give strength unto his people: the Lord shall bless his people with peace.

Chapter 30
A Psalm-chapter or song of the dedication of the house of David.

1 I will magnify thee, O Lord: for thou hast exalted me, and hast not made my foe to rejoice over me. 2 O Lord my God, I cried unto thee, and thou hast restored me. 3 O Lord, thou hast brought up my soul out of the grave: thou hast revived me from them that go down into the pit. 4 Sing praises unto the Lord, ye his Saints, and give thanks before the remembrance of his Holiness. 5 For *he endureth but* a while in his anger: *but* in his favor *is* life: weeping may abide at evening, but joy *cometh* in the morning. 6 And in my prosperity I said, I shall never be moved. 7 *For* thou Lord of thy goodness hadst made my mountain to stand strong: *but* thou didst hide thy face, *and* I was troubled. 8 *Then* cried I unto thee, O Lord, and prayed to my Lord. 9 What profit *is there* in my blood, when I go down to the pit? Shall the dust give thanks unto thee? Or shall it declare thy truth? 10 Hear, O Lord, and have mercy upon me: Lord, be thou mine helper. 11 Thou hast turned my mourning into joy: thou hast loosed my sack and girded me with gladness. 12 Therefore shall *my* tongue praise thee and not cease: O Lord my God, I will give thanks unto thee forever.

Chapter 31
To him that excelleth. A Psalm-chapter of David.

1 In thee, O Lord, have I put my trust: let me never be confounded: deliver me in thy righteousness. 2 Bow down thine ear to me: make haste to deliver me: be unto me a strong rock, and an house of defense to save me. 3 For thou art my rock and my fortress: therefore for thy name's sake direct me and guide me. 4 Draw me out of the net, that they have laid privily for me: for thou art my strength. 5 Into thine hand I commend my spirit: *for* thou hast redeemed me, O Lord God of truth. 6 I have hated them that give themselves to deceitful vanities: for I trust in the Lord. 7 I will be glad and rejoice in thy mercy: for thou hast seen my trouble: thou hast known my soul in adversities, 8 And thou hast not shut me up in the hand of the enemy, *but* hast set my feet at large. 9 Have mercy upon me, O Lord: for I am in trouble: mine eye, my soul and my belly are consumed with grief. 10 For my life is

wasted with heaviness, and my years with mourning: my strength faileth for my pain, and my bones are consumed. 11 I was a reproach among all mine enemies, but specially among my neighbors: and a fear to mine acquaintance, who seeing me in the street, fled from me. 12 I am forgotten, as a dead man out of mind: I am like a broken vessel. 13 For I have heard the railing of great men: fear *was* on every side, while they conspired together against me, and consulted to take my life. 14 But I trusted in thee, O Lord: I said, Thou art my God. 15 My times are in thine hand: deliver me from the hand of mine enemies, and from them that persecute me. 16 Make thy face to shine upon thy servant, and save me through thy mercy. 17 Let me not be confounded, O Lord: for I have called upon thee: let the wicked be put to confusion, and to silence in the grave. 18 Let the lying lips be made dumb, which cruelly, proudly and spitefully speak against the righteous. 19 How great is thy goodness, which thou hast laid up for them, that fear thee! And done to them, that trust in thee, *even* before the sons of men!20 Thou dost hide them privily in thy presence from the pride of men: thou keepest them secretly in thy tabernacle from the strife of tongues. 21 Blessed *be* the Lord: for he hath showed his marvelous kindness toward me in a strong city. 22 Though I said in mine haste, I am cast out of thy sight, yet thou heardest the voice of my prayer, when I cried unto thee. 23 Love ye the Lord all his saints: *for the* Lord preserveth the faithful, and rewardeth abundantly the proud doer. 24 All ye that trust in the Lord, be strong, and he shall establish your heart.

Chapter 32

A Psalm-chapter *of David to give instruction.*
1 Blessed *is he* whose wickedness is forgiven, and whose sin is covered. 2 Blessed is the man, unto whom the Lord imputeth not iniquity, and in whose spirit *there is* no guile. 3 When I held my tongue, my bones consumed, *or* when I roared all the day,4 (For thine hand is heavy upon me, day and night: and my moisture is turned into the drought of summer. Selah)5 *Then* I acknowledged my sin unto thee, neither hid I mine iniquity: *for* I thought, I will confess against myself my wickedness unto the Lord, and thou forgavest the punishment of my sin. Selah. 6 Therefore shall every one, that is godly, make his prayer unto thee in a time, when thou mayest be found: surely in the flood of great waters they shall not come near him. 7 Thou art my secret place: thou preservest me from trouble: thou compassest me about with joyful deliverance. Selah. 8 I will instruct thee, and teach thee in the way that thou shalt go, and I will guide thee with mine eye. 9 Be ye not like an horse, *or* like a mule, *which* understand not: whose mouths thou dost bind with bit and bridle, lest they come near thee. 10 Many sorrows *shall come* to the wicked: but he, that trusteth in the Lord, mercy shall compass him. 11 Be glad ye righteous, and rejoice in the Lord, and be joyful all ye, that are upright in heart.

Chapter 33

1 Rejoice in the Lord, O ye righteous: *for* it becometh upright men to be thankful. 2 Praise the Lord with harp: sing unto him with viol and instrument of ten strings. 3 Sing unto him a new song: sing cheerfully with a loud voice. 4 For the word of the Lord *is* righteous, and all his works *are* faithful. 5 He loveth righteousness and judgment: the earth is full of the goodness of the Lord. 6 By the word of the Lord were the heavens made, and all the host of them by the breath of his mouth. 7 He gathereth the waters of the sea together as upon an heap,

and layeth up the depths in *his* treasures. 8 Let all the earth fear the Lord: let all them that dwell in the world, fear him. 9 For he spake, and it was done: he commanded, and it stood. 10 The Lord breaketh the counsel of the heathen, and bringeth to naught the devices of the people. 11 The counsel of the Lord shall stand forever, and the thoughts of his heart throughout all ages. 12 Blessed *is* that nation, whose God is the Lord: *even the* people *that* he hath chosen for his inheritance. 13 The Lord looketh down from heaven, and beholdeth all the children of men. 14 From the habitation of his dwelling he beholdeth all them that dwell in the earth. 15 He fashioneth their hearts every one, and understandeth all their works. 16 The king is not saved by the multitude of an host, *neither* is the mighty man delivered by great strength. 17 A horse is a vain help, and shall not deliver *any* by his great strength. 18 Behold, the eye of the Lord *is* upon them that fear him, and upon them, that trust in his mercy,19 To deliver their souls from death, and to preserve them in famine. 20 Our soul waiteth for the Lord: *for* he is our help and our shield. 21 Surely our heart shall rejoice in him, because we trusted in his holy name. 22 Let thy mercy, O Lord, be upon us, as we trust in thee.

Chapter 34

A Psalm-chapter *of David, when he changed his behavior before Abimelech, who drove him away, and he departed.*
1 I will alway give thanks unto the Lord: his praise *shall be* in my mouth continually. 2 My soul shall glory in the Lord: the humble shall hear it, and be glad. 3 Praise ye the Lord with me, and let us magnify his name together. 4 I sought the Lord, and he heard me: yea, he delivered me out of all my fear. 5 They shall look unto him, and run *to him*: and their faces shall not be ashamed, *saying*,6 This poor man cried, and the Lord heard *him*, and saved him out of all his troubles. 7 The angel of the Lord pitcheth round about them, that fear him, and delivereth them. 8 Taste ye and see, how gracious the Lord is: blessed *is* the man that trusteth in him. 9 Fear the Lord, ye his saints: for nothing wanteth to them that fear him. 10 The lions do lack and suffer hunger, but they, which seek the Lord, shall want nothing that is good. 11 Come children, hearken unto me: I will teach you the fear of the Lord. 12 What man is he, that desireth life, and loveth *long* days for to see good?13 Keep thy tongue from evil, and thy lips, that they speak no guile. 14 Eschew evil and do good: seek peace and follow after it. 15 The eyes of the Lord *are* upon the righteous, and his ears *are open* unto their cry. 16 *But* the face of the Lord *is* against them that do evil, to cut off their remembrance from the earth. 17 *The righteous* cry, and the Lord heareth *them*, and delivereth them out of all their troubles. 18 The Lord is near unto them that are of a contrite heart, and will save such as be afflicted in Spirit. 19 Great *are* the troubles of the righteous: but the Lord delivereth him out of them all. 20 He keepeth all his bones: not one of them is broken. 21 *But* malice shall slay the wicked: and they that hate the righteous, shall perish. 22 The Lord redeemeth the souls of his servants: and none, that trust in him, shall perish.

Chapter 35

A Psalm-chapter *of David.*
1 Plead thou my cause, O Lord, with them that strive with me: fight thou against them, that fight against me. 2 Lay hand upon the shield and buckler, and stand up for mine help. 3 Bring out also the spear and stop *the way* against them, that persecute me: say unto my soul, I am thy

salvation. 4 Let them be confounded and put to shame, that seek after my soul: let them be turned back, and brought to confusion, that imagine mine hurt. 5 Let them be as chaff before the wind, and let the angel of the Lord scatter *them*. 6 Let their way be dark and slippery: and let the angel of the Lord persecute them. 7 For without cause they have hid the pit *and* their net for me: without cause have they digged *a pit* for my soul. 8 Let destruction come upon him at unawares, and let his net, that he hath laid privily, take him: let him fall into the same destruction. 9 Then my soul shall be joyful in the Lord: it shall rejoice in his salvation. 10 All my bones shall say, Lord, who is like unto thee, which deliverest the poor from him, that is too strong for him! Yea, the poor and him that is in misery, from him that spoileth him! 11 Cruel witnesses did rise up: they asked of me things that I knew not. 12 They rewarded me evil for good, to have spoiled my soul. 13 Yet I, when they were sick, I was clothed with a sack: I humbled my soul with fasting: and my prayer was turned upon my bosom. 14 I behaved myself as to *my* friend, *or* as to my brother: I humbled myself, mourning as one that bewaileth his mother. 15 But in mine adversity they rejoiced, and gathered themselves together: the abjects assembled themselves against me, and I knew not: they tare me and ceased not,16 With the false scoffers at banquets, gnashing their teeth against me. 17 Lord, how long wilt thou behold *this*? Deliver my soul from their tumult, *even* my desolate *soul* from the lions. 18 *So* will I give thee thanks in a great congregation: I will praise thee among much people. 19 Let not them that are mine enemies, unjustly rejoice over me, neither let them wink with the eye, that hate me without a cause. 20 For they speak not as friends: but they imagine deceitful words against the quiet of the land. 21 And they gaped on me with their mouths, saying, Aha, aha, our eye hath seen. 22 Thou hast seen it, O Lord: keep not silence: be not far from me, O Lord. 23 Arise and wake to my judgment, even to my cause, my God, and my Lord. 24 Judge me, O Lord my God, according to thy righteousness, and let them not rejoice over me. 25 Let them not say in their hearts, O our soul rejoice: neither let them say, We have devoured him. 26 Let them be confounded, and put to shame together, that rejoice at mine hurt: let them be clothed with confusion and shame, that lift up themselves against me. 27 *But* let them be joyful and glad, that love my righteousness: yea, let them say alway, Let the Lord be magnified, which loveth the prosperity of his servant. 28 And my tongue shall utter thy righteousness, and thy praise every day.

Chapter 36

To him that excelleth. A Psalm-chapter *of David, the servant of the Lord.*

1 Wickedness saith to the wicked man, even in mine heart, *that there is* no fear of God before his eyes. 2 For he flattereth himself in his own eyes, while his iniquity is found *worthy* to be hated. 3 The words of his mouth *are* iniquity and deceit: he hath left off to understand and to do good. 4 He imagineth mischief upon his bed: he setteth himself upon a way, *that is* not good, and doth not abhor evil. 5 Thy mercy, O Lord, *reacheth* unto the heavens, *and* thy faithfulness unto the clouds. 6 Thy righteousness *is* like the mighty mountains: thy judgments *are like* a great deep: thou, Lord, dost save man and beast. 7 How excellent is thy mercy, O God! Therefore the children of men trust under the shadow of thy wings. 8 They shall be satisfied with the fatness of thine house, and thou shalt give them drink out of the river of thy pleasures. 9 For with thee *is* the well of life, and in thy light shall we see light. 10 Extend thy loving kindness unto them that know thee, and thy righteousness unto them that are upright in heart. 11 Let not the foot of pride come against me, and let not the hand of the wicked men move me. 12 There they are fallen that work iniquity: they are cast down, and shall not be able to rise.

Chapter 37

A Psalm-chapter *of David.*

1 Fret not thyself because of the wicked men, neither be envious for the evil doers. 2 For they shall soon be cut down like grass, and shall wither as the green herb. 3 Trust thou in the Lord and do good: dwell in the land, and thou shalt be fed assuredly. 4 And delight thyself in the Lord, and he shall give thee thine heart's desire. 5 Commit thy way unto the Lord, and trust in him, and he shall bring it to pass. 6 And he shall bring forth thy righteousness as the light, and thy judgment as the noonday. 7 Wait patiently upon the Lord and hope in him: fret not thyself for him which prospereth in his way: *nor* for the man that bringeth *his* enterprises to pass. 8 Cease from anger, and leave off wrath: fret not thyself also to do evil. 9 For evildoers shall be cut off, and they that wait upon the Lord, they shall inherit the land. 10 Therefore yet a little while, and the wicked shall not *appear*, and thou shalt look after his place, and he shall not *be found*. 11 But meek men shall possess the earth, and shall have their delight in the multitude of peace. 12 The wicked practiseth against the just, and gnasheth his teeth against him. 13 *But* the Lord shall laugh him to scorn: for he seeth, that his day is coming. 14 The wicked have drawn *their* sword, and have bent their bow, to cast down the poor and needy, *and* to slay such as be of upright conversation. 15 *But* their sword shall enter into their own heart, and their bows shall be broken. 16 A small thing unto the just man is better, then great riches to the wicked *and* mighty. 17 For the arms of the wicked shall be broken: but the Lord upholdeth the just men. 18 The Lord knoweth the days of upright men, and their inheritance shall be perpetual. 19 They shall not be confounded in the perilous time, and in the days of famine they shall have enough. 20 But the wicked shall perish, and the enemies of the Lord shall be consumed as the fat of lambs: *even* with the smoke shall they consume away. 21 The wicked borroweth and payeth not again. but the righteous is merciful, and giveth. 22 For such as be blessed *of God*, shall inherit the land, and they that be cursed of him, shall be cut off. 23 The paths of man are directed by the Lord: for he loveth his way. 24 Though he fall, he shall not be cast off: for the Lord putteth under his hand. 25 I have been young, and am old: yet I saw never the righteous forsaken, nor his seed begging bread. 26 *But* he is ever merciful and lendeth, and his seed *enjoyeth* the blessing. 27 Flee from evil and do good, and dwell forever. 28 For the Lord loveth judgment, and forsaketh not his saints: they shall be preserved forevermore: but the seed of the wicked shall be cut off. 29 The righteous men shall inherit the land, and dwell therein forever. 30 The mouth of the righteous will speak of wisdom, and his tongue will talk of judgment. 31 *For* the law of his God *is* in his heart, and his steps shall not slide. 32 The wicked watcheth the righteous, and seeketh to slay him. 33 *But* the Lord will not leave him in his hand, nor condemn him, when he is judged. 34 Wait thou on the Lord, and keep his way, and he shall exalt thee, that thou shalt inherit the land: when the wicked men

shall perish, thou shalt see. 35 I have seen the wicked strong, and spreading himself like a green bay tree. 36 Yet he passed away, and lo, he was gone, and I sought him, but he could not be found. 37 Mark the upright man, and behold the just: for the end of *that* man *is* peace. 38 But the transgressors shall be destroyed together, *and* the end of the wicked shall be cut off. 39 But the salvation of the righteous men *shall be* of the Lord: he *shall be* their strength in the time of trouble. 40 For the Lord shall help them, and deliver them: he shall deliver them from the wicked, and shall save them, because they trust in him.

Chapter 38 *A Psalm-chapter of David for remembrance.*
1 O Lord, rebuke me not in thine anger, neither chastise me in thy wrath. 2 For thine arrows have light upon me, and thine hand lieth upon me. 3 There *is* nothing sound in my flesh, because of thine anger: neither *is* there rest in my bones because of my sin. 4 For mine iniquities are gone over mine head, and as a weighty burden they are too heavy for me. 5 My wounds are putrified, and corrupt because of my foolishness. 6 I am bowed, *and* crooked very sore: I go mourning all the day. 7 For my reins are full of burning, and there *is* nothing sound in my flesh. 8 I am weakened and sore broken: I roar for the very grief of mine heart. 9 Lord, *I pour* my whole desire before thee, and my sighing is not hid from thee. 10 Mine heart panteth: my strength faileth me, and the light of mine eyes, even they are not mine own. 11 My lovers and my friends stand aside from my plague, and my kinsmen stand a far off. 12 They also, that seek after my life, lay snares, and they that go about to do me evil, talk wicked things and imagine deceit continually. 13 But I as a deaf man heard not, and *am* as a dumb man, *which* openeth not his mouth. 14 Thus am I as a man, that heareth not, and in whose mouth *are* no reproofs. 15 For on thee, O Lord, do I wait: thou wilt hear *me*, my Lord, my God. 16 For I said, *Hear me*, least they rejoice over me: *for* when my foot slippeth, they extol themselves against me. 17 Surely I am ready to halt, and my sorrow *is* ever before me. 18 When I declare my pain, and am sorry for my sin, 19 Then mine enemies are alive and are mighty, and they that hate me wrongfully are many. 20 They also, that reward evil for good, are mine adversaries, because I follow goodness. 21 Forsake me not, O Lord: be not thou far from me, my God. 22 Haste thee to help me, O my Lord, my salvation.

Chapter 39

To the excellent musician *Jeduthun. A Psalm-chapter of David.*

1 I thought, I will take heed to my ways, that I sin not with my tongue: I will keep my mouth bridled, while the wicked is in my sight. 2 I was dumb and spake nothing: I kept silence *even* from good, and my sorrow was more stirred. 3 Mine heart was hot within me, *and* while I was musing, the fire kindled, and I spake with my tongue, *saying,* 4 Lord, let me know mine end, and the measure of my days, what it is: let me know how long I have to live. 5 Behold, thou hast made my days as an hand breadth, and mine age as nothing in respect of thee: surely every man *in his best* state is altogether vanity. Selah. 6 Doubtless man walketh in a shadow, and disquieteth himself in vain: he heapeth up *riches,* and cannot tell who shall gather them. 7 And now Lord, what wait I for? Mine hope is even in thee. 8 Deliver me from all my transgressions, and make me not a rebuke unto the foolish. 9 I should have been dumb, and not have opened my mouth, because thou didst it. 10 Take thy plague away from me: for I am consumed by the stroke of thine hand.

11 When thou with rebukes dost chastise man for iniquity, thou as a moth makest his beauty to consume: surely every man *is* vanity. Selah. 12 Hear my prayer, O Lord, and hearken unto my cry: keep not silence at my tears, for I am a stranger with thee, and a sojourner as all my fathers. 13 Stay *thine anger* from me, that I may recover my strength, before I go hence and be not.

Chapter 40
To him that excelleth. A Psalm-chapter of David.
1 I Waited patiently for the Lord, and he inclined unto me, and heard my cry. 2 He brought me also out of the horrible pit, out of the miry clay, and set my feet upon the rock, and ordered my goings. 3 And he hath put in my mouth a new song of praise unto our God: many shall see it and fear, and shall trust in the Lord. 4 Blessed *is* the man that maketh the Lord his trust, and regardeth not the proud, nor such as turn aside to lies. 5 O Lord my God, thou hast made thy wonderful works *so* many, that none can count in order to thee thy thoughts toward us: I would declare, and speak *of them, but* they are more then I am able to express. 6 Sacrifice and offering thou didst not desire: (*for* mine ears hast thou prepared) burnt offering and sin offering hast thou not required. 7 Then said I, Lo, I come: *for* in the roll of the book it *is* written of me, 8 I desired to do thy good will, O my God: yea, thy Law is within mine heart. 9 I have declared *thy* righteousness in the great congregation: lo, I will not refrain my lips: O Lord, thou knowest. 10 I have not hid thy righteousness within mine heart, *but* I have declared thy truth and thy salvation: I have not concealed thy mercy and thy truth from the great congregation. 11 Withdraw not thou thy tender mercy from me, O Lord: let thy mercy and thy truth alway preserve me. 12 For innumerable troubles have compassed me: my sins have taken such hold upon me, that I am not able to look up: *yea,* they are more in number than the hairs of mine head: therefore mine heart hath failed me. 13 Let it please thee, O Lord, to deliver me: make haste, O Lord, to help me. 14 Let them be confounded and put to shame together, that seek my soul to destroy it: let them be driven backward and put to rebuke, that desire mine hurt. 15 Let them be destroyed for a reward of their shame, which say unto me, Aha, aha. 16 Let all them, that seek thee, rejoice and be glad in thee: and let them, that love thy salvation, say alway, The Lord be praised. 17 Though I be poor and needy, the Lord thinketh on me: thou art mine helper and my deliverer: my God, make no tarrying.

Chapter 41
To him that excelleth. A Psalm-chapter of David
1 Blessed *is* he that judgeth wisely of the poor: the Lord shall deliver him in the time of trouble. 2 The Lord will keep him, and preserve him alive: he shall be blessed upon the earth, and thou wilt not deliver him unto the will of his enemies. 3 The Lord will strengthen him upon the bed of sorrow: thou hast turned all his bed in his sickness. 4 *Therefore* I said, Lord have mercy upon me: heal my soul, for I have sinned against thee. 5 Mine enemies speak evil of me, *saying,* When shall he die, and his name perish? 6 And if he come to see me, he speaketh lies, *but* his heart heapeth iniquity within him, *and when* he cometh forth, he telleth it. 7 All they that hate me, whisper together against me: *even* against me do they imagine mine hurt. 8 A mischief is light upon him, and he that lieth, shall no more rise. 9 Yea, my familiar friend, whom I trusted, which did eat of my bread, hath lifted up the heel against me. 10 Therefore, O Lord, have mercy upon me, and raise me up: so I shall reward them. 11 By

this I know that thou favorest me, because mine enemy doth not triumph against me. 12 And as for me, thou upholdest me in mine integrity, and dost set me before thy face forever. 13 Blessed *be* the Lord God of Israel world without end. So be it, even so be it.

Chapter 42

To him that excelleth. A Psalm-chapter *to give instruction,* committed *to the sons of Korah.*

1 As the hart brayeth for the rivers of water, so panteth my soul after thee, O God. 2 My soul thirsteth for God, *even* for the living God: when shall I come and appear *before* the presence of God?3 My tears have been my meat day and night, while they daily say unto me, Where is thy God?4 When I remembered these things, I poured out my very heart, because I had gone with the multitude, and led them into the house of God with the voice of singing, and praise, *as* a multitude that keepeth a feast. 5 Why art thou cast down, my soul, and unquiet within me? Wait on God: for I will yet give him thanks for the help of his presence. 6 My God, my soul is cast down within me, because I remember thee, from the land of Jordan, and Hermonites, *and* from the mount Mizar. 7 *One* deep calleth *another* deep by the noise of thy waterspouts: all thy waves and thy floods are gone over me. 8 The Lord will grant his loving kindness in the day, and in the night shall I sing of him, *even* a prayer unto the God of my life. 9 I will say unto God, *which is* my rock, Why hast thou forgotten me? Why go I mourning, when the enemy oppresseth *me*?10 My bones are cut asunder, while mine enemies reproach me, saying daily unto me, Where is thy God? 11 Why art thou cast down, my soul? And why art thou disquieted within me? Wait on God: for I will yet give him thanks: *he is* my present help, and my God.

Chapter 43

1 Judge me, O God, and defend my cause against the unmerciful people: deliver me from the deceitful and wicked man. 2 For thou art the God of my strength: why hast thou put me away? Why go I so mourning, when the enemy oppresseth *me*?3 Send thy light and thy truth: let them lead me: let them bring me unto thine holy mountain and to thy tabernacles. 4 Then will I go unto the altar of God, *even* unto the God of my joy and gladness: and upon the harp will I give thanks unto thee, O God, my God. 5 Why art thou cast down, my soul? And why art thou disquieted within me? Wait on God: for I will yet give him thanks, *he is* my present help, and my God.

Chapter 44

To him that excelleth. A Psalm-chapter *to give instruction,* committed *to the sons of Korah.*

1 We have heard with our ears, O God: our fathers have told us the works, *that* thou hast done in their days, in the old time:2 *How* thou hast driven out the heathen with thine hand, and planted them: *how* thou hast destroyed the people, and caused them to grow. 3 For they inherited not the land by their own sword, neither did their own arm save them: but thy right hand, and thine arm and the light of thy countenance, because thou didst favor them. 4 Thou art my King, O God: send help unto Jacob. 5 Through thee have we thrust back our adversaries: by thy name have we trodden down them that rose up against us. 6 For I do not trust in my bow, neither can my sword save me. 7 But thou hast saved us from our adversaries, and hast put them to confusion that hate us. 8 *Therefore* will we praise God continually, and will confess thy name forever. Selah. 9 But *now* thou art far off, and puttest us to confusion, and goest not forth with our armies. 10 Thou

makest us to turn back from the adversary, and they, which hate us, spoil for themselves. 11 Thou givest us as sheep to be eaten, and dost scatter us among the nations. 12 Thou sellest thy people without gain, and dost not increase their price. 13 Thou makest us a reproach to our neighbors, a jest and a laughing stock to them that are round about us. 14 Thou makest us a proverb among the nations, and a nodding of the head among the people. 15 My confusion *is* daily before me, and the shame of my face hath covered me,16 For the voice of the slanderer and rebuker, for the enemy and avenger. 17 All this is come upon us, yet do we not forget thee, neither deal we falsely concerning thy covenant. 18 Our heart is not turned back: neither our steps gone out of thy paths,19 Albeit thou hast smitten us down into the place of dragons, and covered us with the shadow of death. 20 If we have forgotten the name of our God, and holden up our hands to a strange god,21 Shall not God search this out? For he knoweth the secrets of the heart. 22 Surely for thy sake are we slain continually, and are counted as sheep for the slaughter. 23 Up, why sleepest thou, O Lord? Awake, be not far off forever. 24 Wherefore hidest thou thy face? *And* forgettest our misery and our affliction?25 For our soul is beaten down unto the dust: our belly cleaveth unto the ground. 26 Rise up for our succor, and redeem us for thy mercies' sake.

Chapter 45

To him that excelleth on Shoshannim a song of love to give instruction, committed *to the sons of Korah.*

1 Mine heart will utter forth a good matter: I will entreat *in* my works of the king: my tongue is as the pen of a swift writer. 2 Thou art fairer than the children of men: grace is poured in thy lips, because God hath blessed thee forever. 3 Gird thy sword upon *thy* thigh, O Most Mighty, *to wit,* thy worship and thy glory,4 And prosper with thy glory: ride upon the word of truth and of meekness *and* of righteousness: so thy right hand shall teach thee terrible things. 5 Thine arrows *are* sharp *to pierce* the heart of the king's enemies: *therefore* the people shall fall under thee. 6 Thy throne, O God, *is* forever and ever: the scepter of thy kingdom *is* a scepter of righteousness. 7 Thou lovest righteousness, and hatest wickedness, because God, *even* thy God hath anointed thee with the oil of gladness above thy fellows. 8 All thy garments *smell* of myrrh and aloes, *and* cassia, *when thou comest* out of the ivory palaces, where they have made thee glad. 9 King's daughters *were* among thine honorable *wives:* upon thy right hand did stand the queen in a vesture of gold of Ophir. 10 Hearken, O daughter, and consider, and incline thine ear: forget also thine own people and thy father's house. 11 So shall the king have pleasure in thy beauty: for he is thy Lord, and reverence thou him. 12 And the daughter of Tyrus *with* the rich of the people shall do homage before thy face with presents. 13 The king's daughter is all glorious within: her clothing is of broidered gold. 14 She shall be brought unto the king in raiment of needlework: the virgins *that follow* after her, *and* her companions shall be brought unto thee. 15 With joy and gladness shall they be brought, *and* shall enter into the king's palace. 16 Instead of thy fathers shall thy children be: thou shalt make them princes through all the earth. 17 I will make thy name to be remembered through all generations: therefore shall the people give thanks unto thee world without end.

Chapter 46

To him that excelleth upon Alamoth a song committed *to*

the sons of Korah.

1 God *is* our hope and strength, *and* help in troubles, ready to be found. 2 Therefore will not we fear, though the earth be moved, and though the mountains fall into the midst of the sea. 3 *Though* the waters thereof rage *and* be troubled, *and* the mountains shake at the surges of the same. Selah,4 *Yet there is* a river, whose streams shall make glad the city of God: *even* the sanctuary of the tabernacles of the Most High. 5 God *is* in the midst of it: *therefore* shall it not be moved: God shall help it very early. 6 *When* the nations raged, *and* the kingdoms were moved, *God* thundered, *and* the earth melted. 7 The Lord of hosts *is* with us: the God of Jacob *is* our refuge. Selah. 8 Come, *and* behold the works of the Lord, what desolations he hath made in the earth. 9 He maketh wars to cease unto the ends of the world: he breaketh the bow and cutteth the spear, *and* burneth the chariots with fire. 10 Be still and know that I am God: I will be exalted among the heathen, *and* I will be exalted in the earth. 11 The Lord of hosts *is* with us: the God of Jacob *is* our refuge. Selah.

Chapter 47

To him that excelleth. A Psalm-chapter committed *to the sons of Korah.*

1 All people clap your hands: sing loud unto God with a joyful voice. 2 For the Lord *is* high, *and* terrible: a great King over all the earth. 3 He hath subdued the people under us, and the nations under our feet. 4 He hath chosen our inheritance for us: *even* the glory of Jacob whom he loved. Selah. 5 God is gone up with triumph, *even* the Lord, with the sound of the trumpet. 6 Sing praises to God, sing praises: sing praises unto our King, sing praises. 7 For God *is* the King of all the earth: sing praises *every one* that hath understanding. 8 God reigneth over the heathen: God sitteth upon his holy throne. 9 The princes of the people are gathered unto the people of the God of Abraham: for the shields of the world *belong* to God: he is greatly to be exalted.

Chapter 48

A song or *Psalm-chapter* committed *to the sons of Korah.*

1 Great *is* the Lord, and greatly to be praised, in the city of our God, even upon his holy mountain. 2 Mount Zion, *lying* northward, *is* fair in situation: *it is* the joy of the whole earth*, and* the city of the great King. 3 In the palaces thereof God is known for a refuge. 4 For lo, the kings were gathered, *and* went together. 5 When they saw it, they marveled: they were astonied, *and* suddenly driven back. 6 Fear came there upon them, *and* sorrow, as upon a woman in travail. 7 *As* with an east wind thou breakest the ships of Tarshish*, so were they destroyed.* 8 As we have heard, so have we seen in the city of the Lord of hosts, in the city of our God: God will establish it forever. Selah. 9 We wait for thy loving kindness, O God, in the midst of thy temple. 10 O God, according unto thy name, so is thy praise unto the worlds end: thy right hand is full of righteousness. 11 Let mount Zion rejoice, *and* the daughters of Judah be glad, because of thy judgments. 12 Compass about Zion, and go round about it, *and* tell the towers thereof. 13 Mark well the wall thereof: behold her towers, that ye may tell your posterity. 14 For this God *is* our God forever and ever: he shall be our guide unto the death.

Chapter 49

To him that excelleth. A Psalm-chapter committed *to the sons of Korah.*

1 Hear this, all *ye* people: give ear, all ye that dwell in the world,2 As well low as high, both rich and poor. 3 My mouth shall speak of wisdom, and the meditation of mine heart *is* of knowledge. 4 I will incline mine ear to a parable, *and* utter my grave matter upon the harp. 5 Wherefore should I fear in the evil days, *when* iniquity shall compass me about, *as* at mine heels?6 They trust in their goods, and boast themselves in the multitude of their riches. 7 Yet a man can by no means redeem *his* brother: he cannot give his ransom to God,8 (So precious is the redemption of their souls, and the continuance forever)9 That he may live still forever, *and* not see the grave. 10 For he seeth that wise men die, *and* also that the ignorant and foolish perish, and leave their riches for others. 11 *Yet* they think, their houses, *and* their habitations *shall continue* forever, *even* from generation to generation, and call *their* lands by their names. 12 But man shall not continue in honor: he is like the beasts *that* die. 13 This their way *uttereth* their foolishness: *yet* their posterity delight in their talk. Selah. 14 Like sheep they lie in grave: death devoureth them, and the righteous shall have domination over them in the morning: for their beauty shall consume, *when they shall go* from their house to grave. 15 But God shall deliver my soul from the power of the grave: for he will receive me. Selah. 16 Be not thou afraid when one is made rich, *and* when the glory of his house is increased. 17 For he shall take nothing away when he dieth, neither shall his pomp descend after him. 18 For while he lived, he rejoiced himself: and men will praise thee, when thou makest much of thyself. 19 He shall enter into the generation of his fathers, and they shall not live forever. 20 Man *is* in honor, and understandeth not: he is like to beasts *that* perish.

Chapter 50

A Psalm-chapter of Asaph.

1 The God of gods, *even* the Lord that hath spoken and called the earth from the rising up of the sun unto the going down thereof. 2 Out of Zion, *which is* the perfection of beauty, hath God shined. 3 Our God shall come and shall not keep silence: a fire shall devour before him, and a mighty tempest shall be moved round about him. 4 He shall call the heaven above, and the earth to judge his people. 5 Gather my Saints together unto me, those that make a covenant with me with sacrifice. 6 And the heavens shall declare his righteousness: for God is judge himself. Selah. 7 Hear, O my people, and I will speak: *hear*, O Israel, and I will testify unto thee: *for* I am God, *even* thy God. 8 I will not reprove thee for thy sacrifices, or thy burnt offerings, *that have not been* continually before me. 9 I will take no bullock out of thine house, *nor* goats out of thy folds. 10 For all the beasts of the forest are mine, *and* the beasts on a thousand mountains. 11 I know all the fouls on the mountains: and the wild beasts of the field are mine. 12 If I be hungry, I will not tell thee: for the world is mine, and all that therein is. 13 Will I eat the flesh of bulls? Or drink the blood of goats?14 Offer unto God praise, and pay thy vows unto the Most High,15 And call upon me in the day of trouble: *so* will I deliver thee, and thou shalt glorify me. 16 But unto the wicked said God, What hast thou to do to declare mine ordinances, that thou shouldest take my covenant in thy mouth,17 Seeing thou hatest to be reformed, and hast cast my words behind thee?18 For when thou seest a thief, thou runnest with him, and thou art partaker with the adulterers. 19 Thou givest thy mouth to evil, and with thy tongue thou forgetest deceit. 20 Thou sittest, *and* speakest against thy brother, *and* slanderest thy mother's son. 21 These things hast thou done, and I

held my tongue: *therefore* thou thoughtest that I was like thee: *but* I will reprove thee, and set *them* in order before thee. 22 Oh consider this, ye that forget God, lest I tear you in pieces, and there be none that can deliver *you*. 23 He that offereth praise, shall glorify me: and to him, that disposeth his way *aright*, will I show the salvation of God.

Chapter 51

To him that excelleth. A Psalm-chapter of David, when the Prophet Nathan came unto him, after he had gone in to Bath-sheba.

1 Have mercy upon me, O God, according to thy loving kindness: according to the multitude of thy compassions put away mine iniquities. 2 Wash me thoroughly from mine iniquity, and cleanse me from my sin. 3 For I know mine iniquities, and my sin *is* ever before me. 4 Against thee, against thee only have I sinned, and done evil in thy sight, that thou mayest be just when thou speakest, *and* pure when thou judgest. 5 Behold, I was born in iniquity, and in sin hath my mother conceived me. 6 Behold, thou lovest truth in the inward affections: therefore hast thou taught me wisdom in the secret *of mine heart.* 7 Purge me with hyssop, and I shall be clean: wash me, and I shall be whiter then snow. 8 Make me to hear joy and gladness, *that* the bones, *which* thou hast broken, may rejoice. 9 Hide thy face from my sins, and put away all mine iniquities. 10 Create in me a clean heart, O God, and renew a right spirit within me. 11 Cast me not away from thy presence, and take not thine holy spirit from me. 12 Restore to me the joy of thy salvation, and establish me with *thy* free spirit. 13 Then shall I teach thy ways unto the wicked, and sinners shall be converted unto thee. 14 Deliver me from blood, O God, *which art* the God of my salvation, *and* my tongue shall sing joyfully of thy righteousness. 15 Open thou my lips, O Lord, and my mouth shall show forth thy praise. 16 For thou desirest no sacrifice, though I would give it: thou delightest not in burnt offering. 17 The sacrifices of God *are* a contrite spirit: a contrite and a broken heart, O God, thou wilt not despise. 18 Be favorable unto Zion for thy good pleasure: build the walls of Jerusalem. 19 Then shalt thou accept the sacrifices of righteousness, *even* the burnt offering and oblation: then shall they offer calves upon thine altar.

Chapter 52

To him that excelleth. A Psalm-chapter of David to give instruction. When Doeg the Edomite came and showed Saul, and said to him, David is come to the house of Abimelech.

1 Why boastest thou thyself in *thy* wickedness, O man of power? The loving kindness of God *endureth* daily. 2 Thy tongue imagineth mischief, *and is* like a sharp razor, that cutteth deceitfully. 3 Thou dost love evil more then good, *and* lies more then to speak the truth. Selah. 4 Thou lovest all words that may destroy, O deceitful tongue! 5 So shall God destroy thee forever: he shall take thee and pluck thee out of *thy* tabernacle, and root thee out of the land of the living. Selah. 6 The righteous also shall see it, and fear, and shall laugh at him, *saying,* 7 Behold the man that took not God for his strength, but trusted unto the multitude of his riches, and put his strength in his malice. 8 But I shall be like a green olive tree in the house of God: *for* I trusted in the mercy of God forever and ever. 9 I will alway praise thee, for that thou hast done *this*, and I will hope in thy name, because it is good before thy saints.

Chapter 53

To him that excelleth on Mahalath. A Psalm-chapter of David to give instruction.

1 The fool hath said in his heart, *There is* no God. they have corrupted and done abominable wickedness: *there is* none that doeth good. 2 God looked down from heaven upon the children of men, to see if there were any thatwould understand, and seek God. 3 Every one is gone back: they are altogether corrupt: there is none that doeth good, nonot one. 4 Do not the workers of iniquity know that they eat up my people *as* they eat bread? They call not upon God. 5 There they were afraid for fear, *where* no fear was: for God hath scattered the bones of him that besieged thee: thou hast put them to confusion, because God hath cast them off. 6 Oh give salvation unto Israel out of Zion: when God turneth the captivity of his people, *then* Jacob shall rejoice, and Israel shall be glad.

Chapter 54

To him that excelleth on Neginoth. A Psalm-chapter of David, to give instruction. When the Ziphims came and said unto Saul, Is not David hid among us?

1 Save me, O God, by thy name, and by thy power judge me. 2 O God, hear my prayer: hearken unto the words of my mouth. 3 For strangers are risen up against me, and tyrants seek my soul: they have not set God before them. Selah. 4 Behold, God *is* mine helper: the Lord *is* with them that uphold my soul. 5 He shall reward evil unto mine enemies: Oh cut them off in thy truth! 6 *Then* I will sacrifice freely unto thee: I will praise thy name, O Lord, because it is good. 7 For he hath delivered me out of all trouble, and mine eye hath seen *my desire* upon mine enemies.

Chapter 55

To him that excelleth on Neginoth. A Psalm-chapter of David to give instruction.

1 Hear my prayer, O God, and hide not thyself from my supplication. 2 Hearken unto me, and answer me: I mourn in my prayer, and make a noise,3 For the voice of the enemy, *and* for the vexation of the wicked, because they have brought iniquity upon me, and furiously hate me. 4 Mine heart trembleth within me, and the terrors of death are fallen upon me. 5 Fear and trembling are come upon me, and an horrible fear hath covered me. 6 And I said, Oh that I had wings like a dove: then would I fly away and rest. 7 Behold, I would take my flight far off, *and* lodge in the wilderness. Selah. 8 He would make haste for my deliverance from the stormy wind and tempest. 9 Destroy, O Lord, *and* divide their tongues: for I have seen cruelty and strife in the city. 10 Day and night they go about it upon the walls thereof: both iniquity and mischief are in the midst of it. 11 Wickedness is in the midst thereof: deceit and guile depart not from her streets. 12 Surely mine enemy did not defame me: for I could have borne it: neither did mine adversary exalt himself against me: for I would have hid me from him. 13 But *it was* thou, O man, even my companion, my guide and my familiar: 14 Which delighted in consulting together, *and* went into the house of God as companions. 15 Let death sense upon them: let them go down quick into the grave: for wickedness is in their dwellings, even in the midst of them. 16 *But* I will call unto God, and the Lord will save me. 17 Evening and morning, and at noon will I pray, and make a noise, and he will hear my voice. 18 He hath delivered my soul in peace from the battle, *that was* against me: for many were with me. 19 God shall hear and afflict them, even he that reigneth of old, Selah. because they have no changes, therefore they fear not God. 20 He laid his hand upon such, as be at peace with

him, *and* he brake his covenant. 21 *The words* of his mouth were softer then butter, yet war *was* in his heart: his words were more gentle then oil, yet they were swords. 22 Cast thy burden upon the Lord, and he shall nourish thee: he will not suffer the righteous to fall forever. 23 And thou, O God, shalt bring them down into the pit of corruption: the bloody, and deceitful men shall not live half their days: but I will trust in thee.

Chapter 56

To him that excelleth. A Psalm-chapter of David on Michtam, concerning the dumb dove in a far country, when the Philistines took him in Gath.

1 Be merciful unto me, O God, for man would swallow me up: he fighteth continually *and* vexeth me. 2 Mine enemies would daily swallow me up: for many fight against me, O thou Most High. 3 When I was afraid, I trusted in thee. 4 I will rejoice in God, *because* of his word, I trust in God, *and* will not fear what flesh can do unto me. 5 Mine own words grieve *me* daily: all their thoughts *are* against me to do me hurt. 6 They gather together, and keep themselves close: they mark my steps, because they wait for my soul. 7 They *think* they shall escape by iniquity: O God, cast *these* people down in *thine* anger. 8 Thou hast counted my wanderings: put my tears into thy bottle: are they not in thy register?9 When I cry, then mine enemies shall turn back: this I know, for God *is* with me. 10 I will rejoice in God *because of his* word: in the Lord will I rejoice *because of his* word. 11 In God do I trust: I will not be afraid what man can do unto me. 12 Thy vows *are* upon me, O God: I will render praises unto thee. 13 For thou hast delivered my soul from death, and also my feet from falling, that I may walk before God in the light of the living.

Chapter 57

To him that excelleth. Destroy not. A Psalm-chapter *of David on Michtam. When he fled from Saul in the cave.*

1 Have mercy upon me, O God, have mercy upon me: for my soul trusteth in thee, and in the shadow of thy wings will I trust, till *these* afflictions overpass. 2 I will call unto the Most High God, *even* to the God, that performeth *his promise* toward me. 3 He will send from heaven, and save me from the reproof of him that would swallow me. Selah. God will send his mercy, and his truth. 4 My soul *is* among lions: I lie *among* the children of men, that are set on fire: whose teeth are spears and arrows, and their tongue a sharp sword. 5 Exalt thyself, O God, above the heaven, *and* let thy glory *be* upon all the earth. 6 They have laid a net for my steps: my soul is pressed down: they have digged a pit before me, *and* are fallen into the midst of it. Selah. 7 Mine heart is prepared, O God, mine heart is prepared: I will sing and give praise. 8 Awake my tongue, awake viol and harp: I will awake early. 9 I will praise thee, O Lord, among the people, *and* I will sing unto thee among the nations. 10 For thy mercy is great unto the heavens, *and* thy truth unto the clouds. 11 Exalt thyself, O God, above the heavens, *and* let thy glory *be* upon all the earth.

Chapter 58

To him that excelleth. Destroy not. A Psalm-chapter of David on Michtam.

1 Is it true? O congregation, speak ye justly? O sons of men, judge ye uprightly?2 Yea, rather ye imagine mischief in *your* heart: your hands execute cruelty upon the earth. 3 The wicked are strangers from the womb: *even* from the belly have they erred, and speak lies. 4 Their poison is even like the poison of a serpent:

like the deaf adder *that* stoppeth his ear. 5 Which heareth not the voice of the enchanter, though he be most expert in charming. 6 Break their teeth, O God, in their mouths: break the jaws of the young lions, O Lord. 7 Let them melt like the waters, let them pass away: when he shooteth his arrows, *let them be* as broken. 8 Let them consume like a snail that melteth, *and like* the untimely fruit of a woman, that hath not seen the sun. 9 As raw flesh before your pots feel *the fire* of thorns: *so* let him carry them away as with a whirlwind in *his* wrath. 10 The righteous shall rejoice when he seeth the vengeance: he shall wash his feet in the blood of the wicked. 11 And men shall say, Verily there is fruit for the righteous: doubtless there is a God that judgeth in the earth.

Chapter 59

To him that excelleth. Destroy not. A Psalm-chapter of David on Michtam. When Saul sent and they did watch the house to kill him.

1 O my God, deliver me from mine enemies: defend me from them that rise up against me. 2 Deliver me from the wicked doers, and save me from the bloody men. 3 For lo, they have laid wait for my soul: the mighty men are gathered against me, not for mine offense, nor for my sin, O Lord. 4 They run and prepare themselves without a fault *on my part*: arise *therefore* to assist me, and behold. 5 Even thou, O Lord God of hosts, O God of Israel awake to visit all the heathen, *and* be not merciful unto all that transgress maliciously. Selah. 6 They go to and from in the evening: they bark like dogs, and go about the city. 7 Behold, they brag in their talk, *and* swords *are* in their lips: for, Who, *say they*, doth hear?8 But thou, O Lord, shalt have them in derision, *and* thou shalt laugh at all the heathen. 9 He is strong: *but* I will wait upon thee: for God *is* my defense. 10 My merciful God will prevent me: God will let me see *my desire* upon mine enemies. 11 Slay them not, lest my people forget it: *but* scatter them abroad by thy power, and put them down, O Lord our shield,12 *For* the sin of their mouth, *and* the words of their lips: and let them be taken in their pride, even for their   perjury   and   lies, *that* they   speak.   13 Consume *them* in *thy* wrath: consume *them* that they be no more: and let them know that God ruleth in Jacob, *even* unto the ends of the world. Selah. 14 And in the evening they shall go to and from, *and* bark like dogs, and go about the city. 15 They shall run here and there for meat: *and* surely they shall not be satisfied, though they tarry all night. 16 But I will sing of thy power, and will praise thy mercy in the morning: for thou hast been my defense and refuge in the day of my trouble. 17 Unto thee, O my Strength, will I sing: for God is my defense, *and* my merciful God.

Chapter 60

To him that excelleth upon Shushan Eduth, or Michtam. A Psalm-chapter of David to teach. When he fought against Aram Naharaim, and against Aram Zobah, when Joab returned and slew twelve thousand Edomites in the salt valley.

1 O God, thou hast cast us out, thou hast scattered us, thou hast been angry, turn again unto us. 2 Thou hast made the land to tremble, and hast made it to gape: heal the breaches thereof, for it is shaken. 3 Thou hast showed thy people heavy things: thou hast made us to drink the wine of giddiness. 4 *But now* thou hast given a banner to them that fear thee, that it may be displayed because of *thy* truth. Selah. 5 That thy beloved may be delivered, help with thy right hand and hear me. 6 God hath spoken in his holiness: *therefore* I will rejoice: I shall divide

Shechem, and measure the valley of Succoth. 7 Gilead *shall be* mine, and Manasseh *shall be* mine: Ephraim also *shall be* the strength of mine head: Judah *is* my lawgiver. 8 Moab *shall be* my wash pot: over Edom will I cast out my shoe: Philistia show thyself joyful for me. 9 Who will lead me into the strong city? Who will bring me unto Edom? 10 Wilt not thou, O God, *which* hadst cast us off, and didst not go forth, O God, with our armies? 11 Give us help against trouble: for vain is the help of man. 12 Through God we shall do valiantly: for he shall tread down our enemies.

Chapter 61

To him that excelleth on Neginoth. A Psalm-chapter of David.

1 Hear my cry, O God: give ear unto my prayer. 2 From the ends of the earth will I cry unto thee: when mine heart is oppressed, bring me upon the rock that is higher then I. 3 For thou hast been mine hope, *and* a strong tower against the enemy. 4 I will dwell in thy tabernacle forever, *and* my trust shall be under the covering of thy wings. Selah. 5 For thou, O God, hast heard my desires: thou hast given an heritage unto those that fear thy name. 6 Thou shalt give the king a long life: his years *shall be* as many ages. 7 He shall dwell before God forever: prepare mercy and faithfulness *that* they may preserve him. 8 So will I alway sing praise unto thy name in performing daily my vows.

Chapter 62

To the excelleth musician Ieduthun. A Psalm-chapter of David.

1 Yet my soul keepeth silence unto God: of him *cometh* my salvation. 2 Yet he is my strength and my salvation, *and* my defense: *therefore* I shall not much be moved. 3 How long will ye imagine mischief against a man? *Ye* shall be all slain: ye *shall be* as a bowed wall, *or* as a wall shaken. 4 Yet they consult to cast him down from his dignity: their delight is in lies, they bless with their mouths, but curse with their hearts. Selah. 5 Yet my soul keep thou silence unto God: for mine hope *is* in him. 6 Yet is he my strength, and my salvation, and my defense: therefore I shall not be moved. 7 In God is my salvation and my glory, the rock of my strength: in God is my trust. 8 Trust in him alway, ye people: pour out your hearts before him, *for* God *is* our hope. Selah. 9 Yet the children of men *are* vanity, the chief men *are* lies: to lay them upon a balance they are altogether lighter then vanity. 10 Trust not in oppression nor in robbery: be not vain: if riches increase, set not your heart thereon. 11 God spake once or twice, I have heard it, that power *belongeth* unto God, 12 And to thee, O Lord, mercy: for thou rewardest every one according to his work.

Chapter 63

A Psalm-chapter of David. When he was in the wilderness of Judah.

1 O God, thou art my God, early will I seek thee: my soul thirsteth for thee: my flesh longeth greatly after thee in a barren and dry land without water. 2 Thus I behold thee *as* in the sanctuary, when I behold thy power and thy glory. 3 For thy loving kindness *is* better than life: *therefore* my lips shall praise thee. 4 Thus will I magnify thee *all* my life, *and* lift up mine hands in thy name. 5 My soul shall be satisfied, as with marrow and fatness, and my mouth shall praise *thee* with joyful lips, 6 When I remember thee on my bed, *and when* I think upon thee in the *night* watches. 7 Because thou hast been mine helper, therefore under the shadow of thy wings will I

rejoice. 8 My soul cleaveth unto thee: *for* thy right hand upholdeth me. 9 Therefore they that seek my soul to destroy it, they shall go into the lowest parts of the earth. 10 They shall cast him down with the edge of the sword, *and* they shall be a portion for foxes. 11 But the king shall rejoice in God, *and* all that swear by him shall rejoice *in him*: for the mouth of them that speak lies, shall be stopped.

Chapter 64

To him that excelleth. A Psalm-chapter of David.

1 Hear my voice, O God, in my prayer: preserve my life from fear of the enemy. 2 Hide me from the conspiracy of the wicked, *and* from the rage of the workers of iniquity. 3 Which have whet their tongue like a sword, and shot *for* their arrows bitter words. 4 To shoot at the upright in secret: they shoot at him suddenly, and fear not. 5 They encourage themselves *in* a wicked purpose: they commune together to lay snares privily, *and* say, Who shall see them? 6 They have sought out iniquities, *and* have accomplished that which they sought out, even every one *his* secret *thoughts*, and the depth of *his* heart. 7 But God will shoot an arrow at them suddenly: their strokes shall be *at once*. 8 They shall cause their own tongue to fall upon them: *and* whosoever shall see them, shall flee away. 9 And all men shall see it, and declare the work of God, and they shall understand, what he hath wrought. 10 *But* the righteous shall be glad in the Lord, and trust in him: and all that are upright of heart, shall rejoice.

Chapter 65

To him that excelleth. A Psalm-chapter or song of David.

1 O God, praise waiteth for thee in Zion, and unto thee shall the vow be performed. 2 *Because thou* hearest the prayer, unto thee shall all flesh come. 3 Wicked deeds have prevailed against me: *but* thou wilt be merciful unto our transgressions. 4 Blessed *is* he, *whom* thou choosest and causest to come *to thee*: he shall dwell in thy courts, *and* we shall be satisfied with the pleasures of thine House, *even* of thine holy temple. 5 O God of our salvation, thou wilt answer us with fearful *signs* in *thy* righteousness, O *thou* the hope of all the ends of the earth, and of them that are far off in the sea. 6 He establisheth the mountains by his power: *and is* girded about with strength. 7 He appeaseth the noise of the seas *and* the noise of the waves thereof, and the tumults of the people. 8 They also, that dwell in the uttermost parts *of the earth*, shall be afraid of thy signs: thou shalt make the east and the west to rejoice. 9 Thou visitest the earth, and waterest it: thou makest it very rich: the river of God is full of water: thou preparest them corn: for so thou appointest it. 10 Thou waterest abundantly the furrows thereof: thou causest *the rain* to descend into the valleys thereof: thou makest it soft with showers, *and* blessest the bud thereof. 11 Thou crownest the year with thy goodness, and thy steps drop fatness. 12 They drop *upon* the pastures of the wilderness: and the hills shall be compassed with gladness. 13 The pastures are clad with sheep: the valleys also shall be covered with corn: *therefore* they shout for joy, and sing.

Chapter 66

To him that excelleth. A song or Psalm-chapter.

1 Rejoice in God, all ye *inhabitants* of the earth. 2 Sing forth the glory of his name: make his praise glorious. 3 Say unto God, How terrible art thou *in* thy works! Through the greatness of thy power shall thine enemies be in subjection unto thee. 4 All the world shall worship thee, and sing unto thee, *even* sing of thy name. Selah. 5

Come and behold the works of God: he is terrible in *his* doing toward the sons of men. 6 He hath turned the sea into dry land: they pass through the river on foot: there did we rejoice in him. 7 He ruleth the world with his power: his eyes behold the nations: the rebellious shall not exalt themselves. Selah. 8 Praise our God, ye people, and make the voice of his praise to be heard. 9 Which holdeth our souls in life, and suffereth not our feet to slip. 10 For thou, O God, hast proved us, thou hast tried us as silver is tried. 11 Thou hast brought us into the snare, *and* laid a strait *chain* upon our loins. 12 Thou hast caused men to ride over our heads: we went into fire and into water, but thou broughtest us out into a wealthy *place*. 13 I will go into thine house with burnt offerings, *and* will pay thee my vows,14 Which my lips have promised, and my mouth hath spoken in mine affliction. 15 I will offer unto thee burnt offerings of fat rams with incense: I will prepare bullocks and goats. Selah. 16 Come *and* hearken, all ye that fear God, and I will tell you what he hath done to my soul. 17 I called unto him with my mouth, and he was exalted with my tongue. 18 If I regard wickedness in mine heart, the Lord will not hear me. 19 But God, hath heard *me, and* considered the voice of my prayer. 20 Praised *be* God, which hath not put back my praise, nor his mercy from me.

Chapter 67

To him that excelleth on Neginoth. A Psalm-chapter or song.

1 God be merciful unto us, and bless us, *and* cause his face to shine among us. Selah. 2 That they may know thy way upon earth, *and* thy saving health among all nations. 3 Let the people praise thee, O God: let all the people praise thee. 4 Let the people be glad and rejoice: for thou shalt judge the people righteously, and govern the nations upon the earth. Selah. 5 Let the people praise thee, O God: let all the people praise thee. 6 *Then* shall the earth bring forth her increase, *and* God, *even* our God shall bless us. 7 God shall bless us, and all the ends of the earth shall fear him.

Chapter 68

To him that excelleth. A Psalm-chapter or song of David.

1 God will arise, *and* his enemies shall be scattered: they also that hate him, shall flee before him. 2 As the smoke vanisheth, *so* shalt thou drive *them* away: *and* as wax melteth before the fire, *so* shall the wicked perish at the presence of God. 3 But the righteous shall be glad, *and* rejoice before God: yea, they shall leap for joy. 4 Sing unto God, *and* sing praises unto his name: exalt him, that rideth upon the heavens, in his Name Jah, and rejoice before him. 5 *He is* a father of the fatherless, and a judge of the widows, *even* God in his holy habitation. 6 God maketh the solitary to dwell in families, *and* delivereth them that were prisoners in stocks: but the rebellious shall dwell in a dry land. 7 O God, when thou wentest forth before thy people: when thou wentest through the wilderness, (Selah)8 The earth shook, and the heavens dropped at the presence of this God: *even* Sinai *was moved* at the presence of God, *even* the God of Israel. 9 Thou, O God, sendest a gracious rain *upon* thine inheritance, and thou didst refresh it when it was weary. 10 Thy congregation dwelled therein: *for* thou, O God, hast of thy goodness prepared it for the poor. 11 The Lord gave matter to the women to tell of the great army. 12 Kings of the armies did flee: they did flee and she that remained in the house, divided the spoil. 13 Though ye have lien among pots, *yet*

shall ye be as the wings of a dove that is covered with silver, and whose feathers *are like* yellow gold. 14 When the Almighty scattered kings in it, it was white as the snow in Zalmon. 15 The mountain of God *is like* the mountain of Bashan: *it is* an high mountain, *as* mount Bashan. 16 Why leap ye, ye high mountains? As for this mountain, God delighteth to dwell in it: yea, the Lord will dwell in it forever. 17 The chariots of God *are* twenty thousand thousand angels, *and* the Lord is among them, *as* in the Sanctuary of Sinai. 18 Thou art gone up on high: thou hast led captivity captive, *and* received gifts for men: yea, even the rebellious *hast thou led*, that the Lord God might dwell *there*. 19 Praised *be* the Lord, *even* the God of our salvation, *which* loadeth us daily *with benefits*. Selah. 20 This *is* our God, *even* the God that saveth *us*: and to the Lord God *belong* the issues of death. 21 Surely God will wound the head of his enemies, *and* the hairy pate of him that walketh in his sins. 22 The Lord hath said, I will bring *my people* again from Bashan: I will bring them again from the depths of the sea:23 That thy foot may be dipped in blood, *and* the tongue of thy dogs *in the blood* of the enemies, *even* in it. 24 They have seen, O God, thy goings, the goings of my God, *and* my King, *which art* in the sanctuary. 25 The singers went before, the players of instruments after: in the midst *were* the maids playing with timbrels. 26 Praise ye God in the assemblies, *and* the Lord, *ye that are* of the fountain of Israel. 27 There *was* little Benjamin *with* their ruler, *and* the princes of Judah *with* their assembly, the princes of Zebulun, *and* the princes of Naphtali. 28 Thy God hath appointed thy strength: establish, O God, that, *which* thou hast wrought in us,29 Out of thy temple upon Jerusalem: *and* kings shall bring presents unto thee. 30 Destroy the company of the spear men, *and* multitude of the mighty bulls with the calves of the people, that tread under feet pieces of silver: scatter the people that delight in war. 31 *Then* shall the princes come out of Egypt: Ethiopia shall haste to stretch her hands unto God. 32 Sing unto God, O ye kingdoms of the earth: sing praise unto the Lord, (Selah)33 To him that rideth upon the most high heavens, *which were from* the beginning: behold, he will send out by his voice a mighty sound. 34 Ascribe the power of God: *for* his majesty *is* upon Israel, and his strength *is* in the clouds. 35 O God, thou art terrible out of thine holy places: the God of Israel is he that giveth strength and power unto the people: praised *be* God.

Chapter 69

To him that excelleth upon Shoshannim. A Psalm-chapter of David.

1 Save me, O God: for the waters are entered even to *my* soul. 2 I stick fast in the deep mire, where no stay *is*: I am come into deep waters, and the streams run over me. 3 I am weary of crying: my throat is dry: mine eyes fail, while I wait for my God. 4 They that hate me without a cause, are more then the hairs of mine head: they that would destroy me, *and* are mine enemies falsely, are mighty, so that I restored that which I took not. 5 O God, thou knowest my foolishness, and my faults are not hid from thee. 6 Let not them that trust in thee, O Lord God of hosts, be ashamed for me: let not those that seek thee, be confounded through me, O God of Israel. 7 For thy sake have I suffered reproof: shame hath covered my face. 8 I am become a stranger unto my brethren, even an alien unto my mother's sons. 9 For the zeal of thine house hath eaten me, and the rebukes of them that rebuked thee, are fallen upon me. 10 I wept and my soul fasted, but that was to my reproof. 11 I put on a sack also:

and I became a proverb unto them. 12 They that sat at the gate, spake of me, and the drunkards sang *of me*,13 But Lord, *I make* my prayer unto thee in an acceptable time, even in the multitude of thy mercy: O God, hear me in the truth of my salvation. 14 Deliver me out of the mire, that I stink not: let me be delivered from them that hate me, and out of the deep waters. 15 Let not the water flood drown me. Neither let the deep swallow me up: and let not the pit shut her mouth upon me. 16 Hear me, O Lord, for thy loving kindness is good: turn unto me according the multitude of thy tender mercies. 17 And hide not thy face from thy servant, for I am in trouble: make haste *and* hear me. 18 Draw near unto my soul *and* redeem it: deliver me because of mine enemies. 19 Thou hast known my reproof and my shame, and my dishonor: all mine adversaries *are* before thee. 20 Rebuke hath broken mine heart, and I am full of heaviness, and I looked *for some* to have pity *on me*, but there was none: and for comforters, but I found none21 For they gave me gall in my meat, and in my thirst they gave me vinegar to drink. 22 Let their table be a snare before them, and their property *their* ruin. 23 Let their eyes be blinded that they see not: and make their loins always to tremble. 24 Pour out thine anger upon them, and let thy wrathful displeasure take them. 25 Let their habitation be voided, *and* let none dwell in their tents. 26 For they persecute him, whom thou hast smitten: and they add unto the sorrow of them, whom thou hast wounded. 27 Lay iniquity upon their iniquity, and let them not come into righteousness. 28 Let them be put out of the book of life, neither let them be written with the righteous. 29 When I am poor and in heaviness, thine help, O God, shall exalt me. 30 I will praise the name of God with a song, and magnify him with thanksgiving. 31 *This* also shall please the Lord better than a young bullock, that hath horns and hoofs. 32 The humble shall see *this, and* they that seek God, shall be glad, and your heart shall live. 33 For the Lord heareth the poor, and despiseth not his prisoners. 34 Let heaven and earth praise him: the seas and all *that* moveth in them. 35 For God will save Zion, and build the cities of Judah, that men may dwell there and have it in possession. 36 The seed also of his servants shall inherit it: and they that love his name, shall dwell therein.

Chapter 70

To him excelleth. A Psalm-chapter *of David to put in remembrance.*

1 O God, *haste thee* to deliver me: make haste to help me, O Lord. 2 Let them be confounded and put to shame, that seek my soul: let them be turned backward and put to rebuke, that desire mine hurt. 3 Let them be turned back for a reward of their shame, which said, Aha, aha. 4 *But* let all those that seek thee, be joyful and glad in thee, and let all that love thy salvation, say always, God be praised. 5 Now I am poor and needy: O God, make haste to me: thou art mine helper, and my deliverer: O Lord, make no tarrying.

Chapter 71

1 In thee, O Lord, I trust: let me never be ashamed. 2 Rescue me and deliver me in thy righteousness: incline thine ear unto me and save me. 3 Be thou my strong rock, where unto I may alway resort: thou hast given commandment to save me: for thou art my rock, and my fortress. 4 Deliver me, O my God, out of the hand of the wicked: out of the hand of the evil and cruel man. 5 For thou art mine hope, O Lord God, *even* my trust from my youth. 6 Upon thee have I been stayed from the womb:

thou art he that took me out of my mother's bowels: my praise shall be always of thee. 7 I am become as it were a monster unto many: but thou art my sure trust. 8 Let my mouth be filled with thy praise, *and* with thy glory every day. 9 Cast me not off in the time of age: forsake me not when my strength faileth. 10 For mine enemies speak of me, and they that lay wait for my soul, take their counsel together, 11 Saying, God hath forsaken him: pursue and take him, for there is none to deliver *him.* 12 Go not far from me, O God: my God, haste thee to help me. 13 Let them be confounded *and* consumed that are against my soul: let them be covered with reproof and confusion, that seek mine hurt. 14 But I will wait continually, and will praise thee more and more. 15 My mouth shall daily rehearse thy righteousness, *and* thy salvation: for I know not the number. 16 I will go forward in the strength of the Lord God, *and* will make mention of thy righteousness, *even* of thine only. 17 O God, thou hast taught me from my youth even until now: *therefore* will I tell of thy wondrous works,18 Yea, even unto *mine* old age and gray head, O God: forsake me not, until I have declared thine arm unto *this* generation, *and* thy power to all them, that shall come. 19 And thy righteousness, O God, *I will exalt* on high: for thou hast done great things: O God, who is like unto thee!20 Which hast showed me great troubles and adversities, *but* thou wilt return *and* revive me, and wilt come *again, and* take me up from the depth of the earth. 21 Thou wilt increase mine honor, and return *and* comfort me. 22 Therefore will I praise thee *for* thy faithfulness, O God, upon instrument *and* viol: unto thee will I sing upon the harp, O Holy One of Israel. 23 My lips will rejoice when I sing unto thee, and my soul, which thou hast delivered. 24 My tongue also shall talk of thy righteousness daily: for they are confounded and brought unto shame, that seek mine hurt.

Chapter 72

A Psalm-chapter *of Salomon.*

1 Give thy judgments to the king, O God, and thy righteousness to the king's son. 2 *Then* shall he judge thy people in righteousness, and thy poor with equity. 3 The mountains and the hills shall bring peace to the people by justice. 4 He shall judge the poor of the people: he shall save the children of the needy, and shall subdue the oppressor. 5 They shall fear thee as long as the sun and moon endureth, from generation to generation. 6 He shall come down like the rain upon the mown grass, *and* as the showers that water the earth. 7 In his days shall the righteous flourish, and abundance of peace *shall be* so long as the moon endureth. 8 His dominion shall be also from sea to sea, and from the river unto the ends of the land. 9 They that dwell in the wilderness, shall kneel before him, and his enemies shall lick the dust. 10 The kings of Tarshish and of the isles shall bring presents: the kings of Sheba and Sheba shall bring gifts. 11 Yea, all kings shall worship him: all nations shall serve him. 12 For he shall deliver the poor when he cryeth: the needy also, and him that hath no helper. 13 He shall be merciful to the poor and needy, and shall preserve the souls of the poor. 14 He shall redeem their souls from deceit and violence, and dear shall their blood be in his sight. 15 Yea, he shall live, and unto him shall they give of the gold of Sheba: they shall also pray for him continually, *and* daily bless him. 16 An handful of corn shall be *sown* in the earth, *even* in the top of the mountains, *and* the fruit thereof shall shake like *the trees* of Lebanon: and the *children* shall flourish out of

the city like the grass of the earth. 17 His name shall be forever: his name shall endure as long as the sun: all nations shall bless him, and be blessed in him. 18 Blessed *be* the Lord God, *even* the God of Israel, which only doeth wondrous things. 19 And blessed *be* his glorious name forever: and let all the earth be filled with his glory. So be it, even so be it. 20 Here end the prayers of David, the son of Jesse.

Chapter 73

A Psalm-chapter committed *to Asaph.*

1 Yet God is good to Israel: *even*, to the pure in heart. 2 As for me, my feet were almost gone: my steps had well near slipped. 3 For I feared at the foolish, *when* I saw the prosperity of the wicked. 4 For there are no bands in their death, but they are lusty *and* strong. 5 They are not in trouble *as other* men, neither are they plagued with *other* men. 6 Therefore pride *is* as a chain unto them, *and* cruelty covereth them *as* a garment. 7 Their eyes stand out for fatness: they have more then heart can wish. 8 They are licentious, and speak wickedly of *their* oppression: they talk presumptuously. 9 They set their mouth against heaven, and their tongue walketh through the earth. 10 Therefore his people turn hither: for waters of a full *cup* are wrung out to them. 11 And they say, How doth God know it? Or is there knowledge in the Most High?12 Lo, these are the wicked, yet prosper they alway, *and* increase in riches. 13 Certainly I have cleansed mine heart in vain, and washed mine hands in innocency. 14 For daily have I been punished, and chastened *every* morning. 15 If I say, I will judge thus, behold the generation of thy children: I have trespassed. 16 Then thought I to know this, *but* it was too painful for me,17 Until I went into the sanctuary of God: *then* understood I their end. 18 Surely thou hast set them in slippery places*, and* castest them down into desolation. 19 How suddenly are they destroyed, perished *and* horribly consumed,20 As a dream when one awaketh! O Lord, when thou raisest us up, thou shalt make their image despised. 21 Certainly mine heart was vexed, and I was pricked in my reins:22 So foolish was I and ignorant: I was a beast before thee. 23 Yet I was alway with thee: thou hast holden *me* by my right hand. 24 Thou wilt guide me by thy counsel, and afterward receive me to glory. 25 Whom have I in heaven *but thee*? And I have desired none in the earth with thee. 26 My flesh faileth and mine heart *also: but* God *is* the strength of mine heart, and my portion forever. 27 For lo, they that withdraw themselves from thee, shall perish: thou destroyest all them that go a whoring from thee. 28 As for me, it is good for me to draw near to God: *therefore* I have put my trust in the Lord God, that I may declare all thy works.

Chapter 74

A Psalm-chapter *to give instruction,* committed *to Asaph.*

1 O God, why hast thou put us away forever? *Why* is thy wrath kindled against the sheep of thy pasture?2 Think upon thy congregation, *which* thou hast possessed of old, and on the rod of thine inheritance, *which* thou hast redeemed*, and* on this mount Zion, wherein thou hast dwelt. 3 Lift up thy strokes, that thou mayest forever destroy every enemy that doeth evil to the szanctuary. 4 Thine adversaries roar in the midst of thy congregation, *and* set up their banners for signs. 5 *He that lifted* the axes upon the thick trees, was renowned, as one, that brought a thing to perfection:6 But now they break down the carved work thereof with axes and hammers. 7 They have cast thy sanctuary into the fire, *and raised it* to

the ground, *and* have defiled the dwelling place of thy name. 8 They said in their hearts, Let us destroy them altogether: they have burned all the synagogues of God in the land. 9 We see not our signs: there is not one prophet more, nor any with us that knoweth how long. 10 O God, how long shall the adversary reproach *thee*? Shall the enemy blaspheme thy name forever? 11 Why withdrawest thou thine hand, even thy right hand? *Draw it* out of thy bosom, *and* consume them. 12 Even God *is* my King of old, working salvation in the midst of the earth. 13 Thou didst divide the sea by thy power: thou breakest the heads of the dragons in the waters. 14 Thou breakest the head of Leviathan in pieces, *and* gavest him to be meat for the people in wilderness. 15 Thou breakest up the fountain and river: thou dryest up mighty rivers. 16 The day is thine, and the night is thine: thou hast prepared the light and the sun. 17 Thou hast set all the borders of the earth: thou hast made summer and winter. 18 Remember this, *that* the enemy hath reproached the Lord, and the foolish people hath blasphemed thy name. 19 Give not the soul of thy turtle dove unto the beast, *and* forget not the congregation of thy poor forever. 20 Consider *thy* covenant: for the dark places of the earth are full of the habitations of the cruel. 21 Oh let not the oppressed return ashamed, *but* let the poor and needy praise thy name. 22 Arise, O God: maintain thine own cause: remember thy daily reproach by the foolish man. 23 Forget not the voice of thine enemies: *for* the tumult of them, that rise against thee, ascendeth continually.

Chapter 75

To him that excelleth. Destroy not. A Psalm-chapter or *song* committed *to Asaph.*

1 We will praise *thee*, O God, we will praise thee, for thy name *is* near: *therefore* they will declare thy wondrous works. 2 When I shall take a convenient time, I will judge righteously. 3 The earth and all the inhabitants thereof are dissolved: *but* I will establish the pillars of it. Selah. 4 I said unto the foolish, Be not so foolish, and to the wicked, Lift not up the horn. 5 Lift not up your horn on high, neither speak with a stiff neck. 6 For to come to preferment is neither from the east, nor from the west, nor from the south,7 But God *is* the judge: he maketh low and he maketh high. 8 For in the hand of the Lord *is* a cup, and the wine is red: it is full mixed, and he poureth out of the same: surely all the wicked of the earth shall wring out *and* drink the dregs thereof. 9 But I will declare forever, and sing praises unto the God of Jacob. 10 All the horns of the wicked also will I break: *but* the horns of the righteous shall be exalted.

Chapter 76

To him that excelleth on Neginoth. A Psalm-chapter or *song* committed *to Asaph.*

1 God is known in Judah: his name *is* great in Israel. 2 For in Salem is his tabernacle, and his dwelling in Zion. 3 There brake he the arrows of the bow, the shield and the sword and the battle. Selah. 4 Thou art more bright and puissant, then the mountains of prey. 5 The stout hearted are spoiled: they have slept their sleep, and all the men of strength have not found their hands. 6 At thy rebuke, O God of Jacob, both the chariot and horse are cast asleep. 7 Thou, *even* thou art to be feared: and who shall stand in thy sight, when thou art angry!8 Thou didst cause *thy* judgment to be heard from heaven: *therefore* the earth feared and was still,9 When thou, O God, arose to judgment, to help all the meek of the earth. Selah. 10 Surely the rage of man shall turn to

thy praise: the remnant of the rage shalt thou restrain. 11 Vow and perform unto the Lord your God, all *ye* that be round about him: let them bring presents unto him that ought to be feared. 12 He shall cut off the spirit of princes: he is terrible to the kings of the earth.

Chapter 77

For the excellent musician *Jeduthun. A Psalm-chapter* committed *to Asaph.*

1 My voice *came* to God, when I cried: my voice *came* to God, and he heard me. 2 In the day of my trouble I sought the Lord: my sore ran and ceased not in the night: my soul refused comfort. 3 I did think upon God, and was troubled: I prayed, and my spirit was full of anguish. Selah. 4 Thou keepest mine eyes waking: I was astonied and could not speak. 5 *Then* I considered the days of old, *and* the years of ancient time. 6 I called to remembrance my song in the night: I communed with mine own heart, and my spirit searched diligently. 7 Will the Lord absent himself forever? And will he show no more favor?8 Is his mercy clean gone forever? Doth his promise fail forevermore?9 Hath God forgotten to be merciful? Hath he shut up his tender mercies in displeasure? Selah. 10 And I said, This is my death: *yet I remembered* the years of the right hand of the Most High. 11 I remembered the works of the Lord: certainly I remembered thy wonders of old. 12 I did also meditate all thy works, and did devise of thine acts, *saying,*13 Thy way, O God, *is* in the sanctuary: who is so great a God as *our* God!14 Thou art the God that doest wonders: thou hast declared thy power among the people. 15 Thou hast redeemed thy people with *thine* arm, *even* the sons of Jacob and Joseph. Selah. 16 The waters saw thee, O God: the waters saw thee, *and* were afraid: yea, the depths trembled. 17 The clouds poured out water: the heavens gave a sound: yea, thine arrows went abroad. 18 The voice of thy thunder was round about: the lightnings lightened the world: the earth trembled and shook. 19 Thy way *is* in the sea, and thy paths in the great waters, and thy footsteps are not known. 20 Thou didst lead thy people like sheep by the hand of Moses and Aaron.

Chapter 78

A Psalm-chapter *to give instruction* committed *to Asaph.*

1 Hear my doctrine, O my people: incline your ears unto the words of my mouth. 2 I will open my mouth in a parable: I will declare high sentences of old. 3 Which we have heard and known, and our fathers have told us. 4 We will not hide them from their children, *but* to the generation to come we will show the praises of the Lord, his power also, and his wonderful works that he hath done:5 How he established a testimony in Jacob, and ordained a law in Israel, which he commanded our fathers, that they should teach their children:6 That the posterity might know it, *and* the children, which should be born, should stand up, and declare it to their children:7 That they might set their hope on God, and not forget the works of God but keep his commandments:8 And not to be as their fathers, a disobedient and rebellious generation: a generation that set not their heart aright, and whose spirit was not faithful unto God. 9 The children of Ephraim being armed and shooting with the bow, turned back in the day of battle. 10 They kept not the covenant of God, but refused to walk in his law, 11 And forgot his acts, and his wonderful works that he had showed them. 12 He did marvelous things in the sight of their fathers in the land of Egypt: *even* in the field of Zoan. 13 He divided the sea, and led them through: he made also the waters to stand as an heap. 14 In the daytime also he led them with

a cloud, and all the night with a light of fire. 15 He clave the rocks in the wilderness, and gave them drink as of the great depths. 16 He brought floods also out of the stony rock; so that he made the waters to descend like the rivers. 17 Yet they sinned still against him, and provoked the Highest in the wilderness,18 And tempted God in their hearts in requiring meat for their lust. 19 They spake against God also, saying, Can God prepare a table in the wilderness?20 Behold, he smote the rock, that the water gushed out, and the streams overflowed: can he give bread also? Or prepare flesh for his people?21 Therefore the Lord heard and was angry, and the fire was kindled in Jacob, and also wrath came upon Israel,22 Because they believed not in God, and trusted not in his help. 23 Yet he had commanded the clouds above, and had opened the doors of heaven,24 And had rained down MANNA upon them for to eat, and had given them of the wheat of heaven. 25 Man did eat the bread of angels: he sent them meat enough. 26 He caused the east wind to pass in the heaven, and through his power he brought in the South wind. 27 He rained flesh also upon them as dust, and feathered foul as the sand of the sea. 28 And he made it fall in the midst of their camp *even* round about their habitations. 29 So they did eat and were well filled: for he gave them their desire. 30 They were not turned from their lust, *but* the meat *was* yet in their mouths,31 When the wrath of God came even upon them, and slew the strongest of them, and smote down the chosen men in Israel. 32 For all this, they sinned still, and believed not his wondrous works. 33 Therefore their days did he consume in vanity, and their years hastily. 34 And when he slew them, they sought him and they returned, and sought God early. 35 And they remembered that God *was* their strength, and the Most High God their redeemer. 36 But they flattered him with their mouth and dissembled with him with their tongue. 37 For their heart was not upright with him: neither were they faithful in his covenant. 38 Yet he being merciful forgave *their* iniquity, and destroyed *them* not, but oft times called back his anger, and did not stir up all his wrath. 39 For he remembered that they were flesh: *yea,* a wind that passeth and cometh not again. 40 How oft did they provoke him in the wilderness? *And* grieve him in the desert?41 Yea, they returned, and tempted God, and limited the Holy One of Israel. 42 They remembered not his hand, *nor* the day when he delivered them from the enemy,43 *Nor* him that set his signs in Egypt, and his wonders in the field of Zoan,44 And turned their rivers into blood, and their floods, that they could not drink. 45 He sent a swarm of flies among them, which devoured them, and frogs, which destroyed them. 46 He gave also their fruits unto the caterpillar, and their labor unto the grasshopper. 47 He destroyed their vines with hail, and their wild fig trees with the hailstone. 48 He gave their cattle also to the hail, and their flocks to the thunderbolts. 49 He cast upon them the fierceness of his anger, indignation and wrath, and vexation by the sending out of evil angels. 50 He made a way to his anger: he spared not their soul from death, *but* gave their life to the pestilence, 51 And smote all the firstborn in Egypt, *even* the beginning of *their* strength in the tabernacles of Ham. 52 But he made his people to go out like sheep, and led them in the wilderness like a flock. 53 Yea, he carried them out safely, and they feared not, and the sea covered their enemies. 54 And he brought them unto the borders of his sanctuary: *even* to this mountain, *which* his right hand purchased. 55 He cast out the heathen also before them, and caused them to fall to the lot of *his* inheritance, and made the tribes of Israel to dwell in their tabernacles. 56 Yet they tempted, and provoked the Most High God, and kept not his testimonies,57 But turned back and dealt falsely like their fathers: they turned like a deceitful bow. 58 And they provoked him to anger with their high places, and moved him to wrath with their graven images. 59 God heard *this* and was wroth, and greatly abhorred Israel,60 So that he forsook the habitation of Shiloh, *even* the tabernacle where he dwelt among men,61 And delivered his power into captivity, and his beauty into the enemy's hand. 62 And he gave up his people to the sword, and was angry with his inheritance. 63 The fire devoured their chosen men, and their maids were not praised. 64 Their priests fell by the sword, and their widows lamented not. 65 But the Lord awaked as one out of sleep, *and* as a strong man that after *his* wine cryeth out,66 And smote his enemies in the hinder *parts, and* put them to a perpetual shame. 67 Yet he refused the tabernacle of Joseph, and chose not the tribe of Ephraim:68 But chose the tribe of Judah, *and* mount Zion which he loved. 69 And he built his sanctuary as an high *palace*, like the earth, which he stablished forever. 70 He chose David also his servant, and took him from the sheepfolds. 71 Even from behind the ewes with young brought he him to feed his people in Jacob, and his inheritance in Israel. 72 So he fed them according to the simplicity of his heart, and guided them by the discretion of his hands.

Chapter 79

A Psalm-chapter committed *to Asaph.*

1 O God, the heathen are come into thine inheritance: thine holy temple have they defiled, *and* made Jerusalem heaps *of stones.* 2 The dead bodies of thy servants have they given to be meat unto fouls of the heaven: *and* the flesh of thy saints unto the beasts of the earth. 3 Their blood have they shed like waters round about Jerusalem, and there was none to bury them. 4 We are a reproach to our neighbors, *even* a scorn and derision unto them that are round about us. 5 Lord, how long wilt thou be angry, forever? Shall thy jealousy burn like fire?6 Pour out thy wrath upon the heathen that have not known thee, and upon the kingdoms that have not called upon thy name. 7 For they have devoured Jacob and made his dwelling place desolate. 8 Remember not against us the former iniquities, *but* make haste *and* let thy tender mercies prevent us: for we are in great misery. 9 Help us, O God of our salvation, for the glory of thy name, and deliver us, and be merciful unto our sins for thy name's sake. 10 Wherefore should the heathen say, Where is their God? Let him be known among the heathen in our sight by the vengeance of the blood of thy servants that is shed. 11 Let the sighing of the prisoners come before thee: according to thy mighty arm preserve the children of death,12 And render to our neighbors seven fold into their bosom their reproach, wherewith they have reproached thee, O Lord. 13 So we thy people, and sheep of thy pasture shall praise thee forever: and from generation to generation we will set forth thy praise.

Chapter 80

To him that excelleth on Shoshannim Eduth. A Psalm-chapter committed *to Asaph.*

1 Hear, O thou Shepherd of Israel, thou that leadest Joseph like sheep: show *thy* brightness, thou that sittest between the cherubims. 2 Before Ephraim and Benjamin and Manasseh stir up thy strength, and come to help us. 3 Turn us again, O God, and cause thy face to shine that we may be saved. 4 O Lord God of hosts, how long wilt thou

be angry against the prayer of thy people?5 Thou hast fed them with the bread of tears, and given them tears to drink with great measure. 6 Thou hast made us a strife unto our neighbors, and our enemies laugh *at us* among themselves. 7 Turn us again, O God of hosts: cause thy face to shine, and we shall be saved. 8 Thou hast brought a vine out of Egypt: thou hast cast out the heathen, and planted it. 9 Thou madest room for it, and didst cause it to take root, and it filled the land. 10 The mountains were covered with the shadow of it, and the boughs thereof *were like* the goodly cedars. 11 She stretched out her branches unto the sea, and her boughs unto the river. 12 Why hast thou *then* broken down her hedges, so that all they, which pass by the way, have plucked her?13 The wild bore out of the wood hath destroyed it, and the wild beasts of the field have eaten it up. 14 Return we beseech thee, O God of hosts: look down from heaven and behold and visit this vine,15 And the vineyard, that thy right hand hath planted, and the young vine, *which* thou madest strong for thyself. 16 It is burned with fire *and* cut down: *and* they perish at the rebuke of thy countenance. 17 Let thine hand be upon the man of thy right hand, *and* upon the son of man, *whom* thou madest strong for thine own self. 18 So will not we go back from thee: revive thou us, and we shall call upon thy name. 19 Turn us again, O Lord God of hosts: cause thy face to shine and we shall be saved.

Chapter 81

To him that excelleth upon Gittith. A Psalm-chapter committed *to Asaph.*

1 Sing joyfully unto God our strength: sing loud unto the God of Jacob. 2 Take the song and bring forth the timbrel, the pleasant harp with the viol. 3 Blow the trumpet in the new moon, *even* in the time appointed, at our feast day. 4 For this is a statute for Israel, *and* a Law of the God of Jacob. 5 He set this in Joseph for a testimony, when he came out of the land of Egypt, *where* I heard a language, that I understood not. 6 I have withdrawn his shoulder from the burden, *and* his hands have left the pots. 7 Thou callest in affliction and I delivered thee, and answered thee in the secret of the thunder: I proved thee at the waters of Meribah. Selah. 8 Hear, O my people, and I will protest unto thee: O Israel, if thou wilt hearken unto me,9 Let there be no strange god in thee, neither worship thou any strange god. 10 *For* I am the Lord thy God, which brought thee out of the land of Egypt: open thy mouth wide and I will fill it. 11 But my people would not hear my voice, and Israel would none of me. 12 So I gave them up unto the hardness of their heart, *and* they have walked in their own counsels. 13 Oh that my people had hearkened unto me, *and* Israel had walked in my ways. 14 I would soon have humbled their enemies, and turned mine hand against their adversaries. 15 The haters of the Lord should have been subject unto him, and their time should have endured forever. 16 And *God* would have fed them with the fat of wheat, and with honey out of the rock would I have sufficed thee.

Chapter 82

A Psalm-chapter committed *to Aspah.*

1 God standeth in the assembly of gods: he judgeth among gods. 2 How long will ye judge unjustly, and accept the persons of the wicked? Selah. 3 Do right to the poor and fatherless: do justice to the poor and needy. 4 Deliver the poor and needy: save *them* from the hand of the wicked. 5 They know not and understand nothing: they walk in darkness, *albeit* all the foundations of the earth be moved. 6 I have said, Ye are gods, and ye all are

children of the Most High. 7 But ye shall die as a man, and ye princes, shall fall like others. 8 O God, arise, *therefore* judge thou the earth: for thou shalt inherit all nations.

Chapter 83

A song, or *Psalm-chapter* committed *to Asaph.*

1 Keep not thou silence, O God: be not still, and cease not, O God. 2 For lo, thine enemies make a tumult: and they that hate thee, have lifted up the head. 3 They have taken crafty counsel against thy people, and have consulted against thy secret ones. 4 They have said, Come and let us cut them off from being a nation: and let the name of Israel be no more in remembrance. 5 For they have consulted together in heart, *and* have made a league against thee:6 The tabernacles of Edom, and the Ishmaelites, Moab and the Hagarenes:7 Gebal and Ammon, and Amalek, the Philistines with the inhabitants of Tyre:8 Assur also is joined with them: they have been an arm to the children of Lot. Selah. 9 Do thou to them as unto the Midianites: as to Sisera *and* as to Jabin at the river of Kison. 10 They perished at Endor, *and* were dung for the earth. 11 Make them, *even* their princes like Oreb and like Zeeb: yea, all their princes like Zebah and like Zalmunna. 12 Which have said, Let us take for our possession the habitations of God. 13 O my God, make them like unto a wheel, *and* as the stubble before the wind. 14 As the fire burneth the forest, and as the flame setteth the mountains on fire:15 So persecute them with thy tempest, and make them afraid with thy storm. 16 Fill their faces with shame, that they may seek thy name, O Lord. 17 Let them be confounded and troubled forever: yea, let them be put to shame and perish,18 That they may know that thou, which art called Jehovah, art alone, *even* the Most High over all the earth.

Chapter 84

To him that excelleth upon Gittith. A Psalm-chapter committed *to the sons of Korah.*

1 O Lord of hosts, how amiable *are* thy tabernacles!2 My soul longeth, yea, and fainteth for the courts of the Lord: *for* mine heart and my flesh rejoice in the living God. 3 Yea, the sparrow hath found *her* an house, and the swallow a nest for her, where she may lay her young: *even* by thine altars, O Lord of hosts, my King *and* my God. 4 Blessed *are* they that dwell in thine house: they will ever praise thee. Selah. 5 Blessed *is* the man, whose strength *is* in thee, *and* in whose heart *are thy* ways. 6 They going through the vale of Baca, make wells therein: the rain also covereth the pools. 7 They go from strength to strength, *till every one* appear before God in Zion. 8 O Lord God of hosts, hear my prayer: hearken, O God of Jacob. Selah. 9 Behold, O God, our shield, and look upon the face of thine anointed. 10 For a day in thy courts is better than a thousand *other where*: I had rather be a doorkeeper in the house of my God, than to dwell in the tabernacles of wickedness. 11 For the Lord God is the sun and shield *unto us*: the Lord will give grace and glory, and no good thing will he withhold from them that walk uprightly. 12 O Lord of hosts, blessed *is* the man that trusteth in thee.

Chapter 85

To him that excelleth. A Psalm-chapter committed *to the sons of Korah.*

1 Lord, thou hast been favorable unto thy land: thou hast brought again the captivity of Jacob. 2 Thou hast forgiven the iniquity of thy people, *and* covered all their sins. Selah. 3 Thou hast withdrawn all thine anger, and hast turned back from the fierceness of thy wrath. 4 Turn us,

O God of our salvation, and release thine anger toward us. 5 Wilt thou be angry with us forever? *And* wilt thou prolong thy wrath from one generation to another?6 Wilt thou not turn again *and* quicken us, that thy people may rejoice in thee?7 Show us thy mercy, O Lord, and grant us thy salvation. 8 I will hearken what the Lord God will say: for he will speak peace unto his people, and to his Saints, that they turn not again to folly. 9 Surely his salvation is near to them that fear him, that glory may dwell in our land. 10 Mercy and truth shall meet: righteousness and peace shall kiss *one another*. 11 Truth shall bud out of the earth, and righteousness shall look down from heaven. 12 Yea, the Lord shall give good things, and our land shall give her increase. 13 Righteousness shall go before him, and shall set her steps in the way.

Chapter 86

A prayer of David.

1 Incline thine ear, O Lord, *and* hear me: for I am poor and needy. 2 Preserve thou my soul, for I am merciful: my God, save thou thy servant, that trusteth in thee. 3 Be merciful unto me, O Lord: for I cry upon thee continually. 4 Rejoice the soul of thy servant: for unto thee, O Lord, do I lift up my soul. 5 For thou, Lord, art good and merciful, and of great kindness unto all them, that call upon thee. 6 Give ear, Lord, unto my prayer, and hearken to the voice of my supplication. 7 In the day of my trouble I will call upon thee: for thou hearest me. 8 Among the gods there is none like thee, O Lord, and there is none *that can do* like thy works. 9 All nations, whom thou hast made, shall come and worship before thee, O Lord, and shall glorify thy name. 10 For thou art great and doest wondrous things: thou art God alone. 11 Teach me thy way, O Lord, *and* I will walk in thy truth: knit mine heart unto thee, that I may fear thy name. 12 I will praise thee, O Lord my God, with all mine heart: yea, I will glorify thy name forever. 13 For great is thy mercy toward me, and thou hast delivered my soul from the lowest grave. 14 O God, the proud are risen against me, and the assemblies of violent men have sought my soul, and have not set thee before them. 15 But thou, O Lord, art a pitiful God and merciful, slow to anger and great in kindness and truth. 16 Turn unto me, and have mercy upon me: give thy strength unto thy servant, and save the son of thine handmaid. 17 Show a token of *thy* goodness toward me, that they which hate me, may see it, and be ashamed, because thou, O Lord, hast holpen me and comforted me.

Chapter 87

A Psalm-chapter or *song* committed *to the sons of Korah.*

1 God laid his foundations among the holy mountains. 2 The Lord loveth the gates of Zion above all the habitations of Jacob. 3 Glorious things are spoken of thee, O city of God. Selah. 4 I will make mention of Rahab and Babylon among them that know me: behold Philistia and Tyre with Ethiopia, There is he born. 5 And of Zion it shall be said, Many are born in her: and he, *even* the Most High shall stablish her. 6 The Lord shall count, when he writeth the people, He was born there. Selah. 7 As well the singers as the players on instruments *shall praise thee*: all my springs *are* in thee.

Chapter 88

A song or *Psalm-chapter of Heman the Ezrahite to give instruction,* committed *to the sons of Korah for him that excelleth upon Mahalath Leannoth.*

1 O Lord God of my salvation, I cry day *and* night before thee. 2 Let my prayer enter into thy presence: incline thine

ear unto my cry. 3 For my soul is filled with evils, and my life draweth near to the grave. 4 I am counted among them that go down unto the pit, *and* am as a man without strength:5 Free among the dead, like the slain lying in the grave, whom thou rememberest no more, and they are cut off from thine hand. 6 Thou hast laid me in the lowest pit, in darkness, *and* in the deep. 7 Thine indignation lieth upon me, and thou hast vexed me with all thy waves. Selah. 8 Thou hast put away mine acquaintance far from me, *and* made me to be abhorred of them: I am shut up, and cannot get forth. 9 Mine eye is sorrowful through mine affliction: Lord, I call daily upon thee: I stretch out mine hands unto thee. 10 Wilt thou show a miracle to the dead? Or shall the dead rise *and* praise thee? Selah. 11 Shall thy loving kindness be declared in the grave? *Or* thy faithfulness in destruction?12 Shall thy wondrous works be known in the dark? And thy righteousness in the land of oblivion?13 But unto thee have I cried, O Lord, and early shall my prayer come before thee. 14 Lord, why dost thou reject my soul, *and* hidest thy face from me?15 I am afflicted and at the point of death: from *my* youth I suffer thy terrors, doubting *of my life.* 16 Thine indignations go over me, and thy fear hath cut me off. 17 They came round about me daily like water, *and* compassed me together. 18 My lovers and friends hast thou put away from me, *and* mine acquaintance hid themselves.

Chapter 89

A Psalm-chapter *to give instruction, of Ethan the Ezrahite.*

1 I will sing the mercies of the Lord forever: with my mouth will I declare thy truth from generation to generation. 2 For I said, Mercy shall be set up forever: thy truth shalt thou stablish in the very heavens. 3 I have made a covenant with my chosen: I have sworn to David my servant,4 Thy seed will I stablish forever, and set up thy throne from generation to generation. Selah. 5 O Lord, even the heavens shall praise thy wondrous work: yea, thy truth in the congregation of the saints. 6 For who is equal to the Lord in the heaven? *And who* is like the Lord among the sons of the gods?7 God is very terrible in the assembly of the saints, and to be reverenced above all, *that are* about him. 8 O Lord God of hosts, who is like unto thee, *which art* a mighty Lord, and thy truth *is* about thee?9 Thou rulest the raging of the sea: when the waves thereof arise, thou stillest them. 10 Thou hast beaten down Rahab as a man slain: thou hast scattered thine enemies with thy mighty arm. 11 The heavens are thine, the earth also is thine: thou hast laid the foundation of the world, and all that therein is. 12 Thou hast created the north and the south: Tabor and Hermon shall rejoice in thy name. 13 Thou hast a mighty arm: strong is thine hand*, and* high is thy right hand. 14 Righteousness and equity *are* the stablishment of thy throne: mercy and truth go before thy face. 15 Blessed *is* the people, that can rejoice *in thee*: they shall walk in the light of thy countenance, O Lord. 16 They shall rejoice continually in thy name, and in thy righteousness shall they exalt themselves. 17 For thou art the glory of their strength, and by thy favor our horns shall be exalted. 18 For our shield *appertaineth* to the Lord, and our King to the Holy One of Israel. 19 Thou spakest then in a vision unto thine Holy One, and saidest, I have laid help upon one that is mighty: I have exalted one chosen out of the people. 20 I have found David my servant: with mine holy oil have I anointed him. 21 Therefore mine hand shall be established with him, and mine arm shall strengthen him.

22 The enemy shall not oppress him, neither shall the wicked hurt him. 23 But I will destroy his foes before his face, and plague them that hate him. 24 My truth also and my mercy *shall be* with him, and in my name shall his horn be exalted. 25 I will set his hand also in the sea, and his right hand in the floods. 26 He shall cry unto me, Thou art my Father, my God and the rock of my salvation. 27 Also I will make him my first born, higher than the kings of the earth. 28 My mercy will I keep for him forevermore, and my covenant shall stand fast with him. 29 His seed also will I make to endure forever, and his throne as the days of heaven. 30 *But* if his children forsake my Law, and walk not in my judgments:31 If they break my statutes, and keep not my commandments:32 Then will I visit their transgression with the rod, and their iniquity with strokes. 33 Yet my loving kindness will I not take from him, neither will I falsify my truth. 34 My covenant will I not break, nor alter the thing that is gone out of my lips. 35 I have sworn once by mine holiness, that I will not fail David, *saying,*36 His seed shall endure forever, and his throne *shall be* as the sun before me. 37 He shall be established forevermore as the moon, and *as a* faithful witness in the heaven. Selah. 38 But thou hast rejected and abhorred, thou hast been angry with thine Anointed. 39 Thou hast broken the covenant of thy servant, *and* profaned his crown, *casting it* on the ground. 40 Thou hast broken down all his walls: thou hast laid his fortresses in ruin. 41 All that go by the way, spoil him: he is a rebuke unto his neighbors. 42 Thou hast set up the right hand of his enemies, *and* made all his adversaries to rejoice. 43 Thou hast also turned the edge of his sword, and hast not made him to stand in the battle. 44 Thou hast caused his dignity to decay, and cast his throne to the ground. 45 The days of his youth hast thou shortened, *and* covered him with shame. Selah. 4 Lord, how long wilt thou hide thyself, forever? Shall thy wrath burn like fire?47 Remember of what time I am: wherefore shouldest thou create in vain all the children of men?48 What man liveth, and shall not see death? Shall he deliver his soul from the hand of the grave? Selah. 49 Lord, where are thy former mercies, *which* thou swearest unto David in thy truth?50 Remember, O Lord, the rebuke of thy servants, which I bear in my bosom of all the mighty people. 51 For thine enemies have reproached *thee*, O Lord, because they have reproached the footsteps of thine Anointed. 52 Praised *be* the Lord forevermore. So be it, even so be it.

Chapter 90

A prayer of Moses, the man of God.

1 Lord, thou hast been our habitation from generation to generation. 2 Before the mountains were made, and *before* thou hadst formed the earth, and the world, even from everlasting to everlasting thou art *our* God. 3 Thou turnest man to destruction: again thou sayest, Return, ye sons of Adam. 4 For a thousand years in thy sight *are* as yesterday when it is past, and as a watch in the night. 5 Thou hast overflowed them: they are *as* a sleep: in the morning he groweth like the grass:6 In the morning it flourisheth and groweth, *but* in the evening it is cut down and withereth. 7 For we are consumed by thine anger, and by thy wrath are we troubled. 8 Thou hast set our iniquities before thee, *and* our secret sins in the light of thy countenance. 9 For all our days are past in thine anger: we have spent our years as a thought. 10 The time of our life *is* threescore years and ten, and if they be of strength, fourscore years: yet their strength *is* but labor and sorrow: for it is cut off quickly, and we flee away. 11

Who knoweth the power of thy wrath? For according to thy fear is thine anger. 12 Teach us so to number our days, that we may apply *our* hearts unto wisdom. 13 Return (O Lord, how long?) and be pacified toward thy servants. 14 Fill us with thy mercy in the morning: so shall we rejoice and be glad all our days. 15 Comfort us according to the days that thou hast afflicted us, *and according* to the years that we have seen evil. 16 Let thy work be seen toward thy servants, and thy glory upon their children. 17 And let the beauty of the Lord our God be upon us, and direct thou the work of our hands upon us, even direct the work of our hands.

Chapter 91

1 Whoso dwelleth in the secret of the Most High, shall abide in the shadow of the Almighty. 2 I will say unto the Lord, O mine hope, and my fortress: *he is* my God, in him will I trust. 3 Surely he will deliver thee from the snare of the hunter, *and* from the noisome pestilence. 4 He will cover thee under his wings, and th0u shalt be sure under his feathers: his truth shall be thy shield and buckler. 5 Thou shalt not be afraid of the fear of the night, *nor* of the arrow that flyeth by day:6 *Nor* of the pestilence that walketh in the darkness: *nor* of the plague that destroyeth at noonday. 7 A thousand shall fall at thy side, and ten thousand at thy right hand, *but* it shall not come near thee. 8 Doubtless with thine eyes shalt thou behold and see the reward of the wicked. 9 For thou *hast said*, The Lord *is* mine hope: thou hast set the Most High for thy refuge. 10 There shall none evil come unto thee, neither shall any plague come near thy tabernacle. 11 For he shall give his angels charge over thee to keep thee in all thy ways. 12 They shall bear thee in their hands, that thou hurt not thy foot against a stone. 13 Thou shalt walk upon the lion and asp: the young lion and the dragon shalt thou tread under feet. 14 Because he hath loved me, therefore will I deliver him: I will exalt him because he hath known my name. 15 He shall call upon me, and I will hear him: I will be with him in trouble: I will deliver him, and glorify him. 16 With long life will I satisfy him, and show him my salvation.

Chapter 92

A Psalm-chapter or *song for the Sabbath day.*

1 It is a good thing to praise the Lord, and to sing unto thy name, O Most High,2 To declare thy loving kindness in the morning, and thy truth in the night,3 Upon an instrument of ten strings, and upon the viol with the song upon the harp. 4 For thou, Lord, hast made me glad by thy works, and I will rejoice in the works of thine hands. 5 O Lord, how glorious are thy works! *And* thy thoughts are very deep. 6 An unwise man knoweth it not, and a fool doth not understand this,7 (When the wicked grow as the grass, and all the workers of wickedness do flourish) that they shall be destroyed forever. 8 But thou, O Lord, art Most High forevermore. 9 For lo, thine enemies, O Lord: for lo, thine enemies shall perish: all the workers of iniquity shall be destroyed. 10 But thou shalt exalt mine horn, like the unicorns, *and* I shall be anointed with fresh oil. 11 Mine eye also shall see *my desire* against mine enemies: and mine ears shall hear *my wish* against the wicked, that rise up against me. 12 The righteous shall flourish like a palm tree, *and* shall grow like a cedar in Lebanon. 13 Such as be planted in the house of the Lord, shall flourish in the courts of our God. 14 They shall still bring forth fruit in *their* age: they shall be fat and flourishing,15 To declare that the Lord my rock is righteous, and that none iniquity *is* in him.

Chapter 93

1 The Lord reigneth, *and is* clothed with majesty: the Lord is clothed, *and* girded with power: the world also shall be established, that it cannot be moved. 2 Thy throne is established of old: thou art from everlasting. 3 The floods have lifted up, O Lord: the floods have lifted up their voice: the floods lift up their waves. 4 The waves of the sea *are* marvelous through the noise of many waters, *yet* the Lord on High is more mighty. 5 Thy testimonies are very sure: holiness becometh thine house, O Lord, forever.

Chapter 94

1 O Lord God the avenger, O God the avenger, show thyself clearly. 2 Exalt thyself, O judge of the world, *and* render a reward to the proud. 3 Lord, how long shall the wicked, how long shall the wicked triumph?4 They prate *and* speak fiercely: all the workers of iniquity vaunt themselves. 5 They smite down thy people, O Lord, and trouble thine heritage. 6 They slay the widow and the stranger, and murder the fatherless. 7 Yet they say, The Lord shall not see: neither will the God of Jacob regard it. 8 Understand ye unwise among the people: and ye fools, when will ye be wise?9 He that planted the ear, shall he not hear? Or he that formed the eye, shall he not see?10 Or he that chastiseth the nations, shall he not correct? He that teacheth man knowledge, *shall he not know*? 11 The Lord knoweth the thoughts of man, that they are vanity. 12 Blessed is the man, whom thou chastisest, O Lord, and teachest him in thy Law,13 That thou mayest give him rest from the days of evil, whiles the pit is digged for the wicked. 14 Surely the Lord will not fail his people, neither will he forsake his inheritance. 15 For judgment shall return to justice, and all the upright in heart *shall follow* after it. 16 Who will rise up with me against the wicked? *Or* who will take my part against the workers of iniquity?17 If the Lord had not holpen me, my soul had almost dwelt in silence. 18 When I said, My foot slideth, thy mercy, O Lord, stayed me. 19 In the multitude of my thoughts in mine heart, thy comforts have rejoiced my soul. 20 Hath the throne of iniquity fellowship with thee, which forgeth wrong for a law?21 They gather them together against the soul of the righteous, and condemn the innocent blood. 22 But the Lord is my refuge, and my God *is* the rock of mine hope. 23 And he will recompense them their wickedness, and destroy them in their own malice: *yea,* the Lord our God shall destroy them.

Chapter 95

1 Come, let us rejoice unto the Lord: let us sing aloud unto the rock of our salvation. 2 Let us come before his face with praise: let us sing loud unto him with Psalm-chapter. 3 For the Lord *is* a great God, and a great King above all gods. 4 In whose hand *are* the deep places of the earth, and the heights of the mountains *are* his:5 To whom the sea *belongeth*: for he made it, and his hands formed the dry land. 6 Come, let us worship and fall down, and kneel before the Lord our maker. 7 For he is our God, and we are the people of his pasture, and the sheep of his hand: to day, if ye will hear his voice,8 Harden not your heart, as in Meribah, *and* as in the day of Massah in the wilderness. 9 Where your fathers tempted me, proved me, though they had seen my work. 10 Forty years have I contended with *this* generation, and said, They are a people that err in heart, for they have not known my ways. 11 Wherefore I swear in my wrath, *saying,* Surely they shall not enter into my rest.

Chapter 96

1 Sing unto the Lord a new song: sing unto the Lord, all

the earth. 2 Sing unto the Lord, *and* praise his name: declare his salvation from day to day. 3 Declare his glory among all nations, *and* his wonders among all people. 4 For the Lord *is* great and much to be praised: he is to be feared above all gods. 5 For all the gods of the people *are* idols: but the Lord made the heavens. 6 Strength and glory *are* before him: power and beauty *are* in his sanctuary. 7 Give unto the Lord, ye families of the people: give unto the Lord glory and power. 8 Give unto the Lord the glory of his name: bring an offering, and enter into his courts. 9 Worship the Lord in the glorious sanctuary: tremble before him all the earth. 10 Say among the nations, The Lord reigneth: surely the world shall be stable, *and* not move, *and* he shall judge the people in righteousness. 11 Let the heavens rejoice, and let the earth be glad: let the sea roar, and all that therein is. 12 Let the field be joyful, and all that is in it: let all the trees of the wood then rejoice13 Before the Lord: for he cometh, for he cometh to judge the earth: he will judge the world with righteousness, and the people in his truth.

Chapter 97

1 The Lord reigneth: let the earth rejoice: let the multitude of the isles be glad. 2 Clouds and darkness *are* round about him: righteousness and judgment *are* the foundation of his throne. 3 There shall go a fire before him, and burn up his enemies round about. 4 His lightnings gave light unto the world: the earth saw it and was afraid. 5 The mountains melted like wax at the presence of the Lord, at the presence of the Lord of the whole earth. 6 The heavens declare his righteousness, and all the people see his glory. 7 Confounded be all they that serve graven images, *and* that glory in idols: worship him all ye gods. 8 Zion heard of it, and was glad: and the daughters of Judah rejoiced, because of thy judgments, O Lord. 9 For thou, Lord, art Most High above all the earth: thou art much exalted above all gods. 10 Ye that love the Lord, hate evil: he preserveth the souls of his saints: he will deliver them from the hand of the wicked. 11 Light is sown for the righteous, and joy for the upright in heart. 12 Rejoice ye righteous in the Lord, and give thanks for his holy remembrance.

Chapter 98

A Psalm-chapter.

1 Sing unto the Lord a new song: for he hath done marvelous things: his right hand, and his holy arm have gotten him the victory. 2 The Lord declared his salvation: his righteousness hath he revealed in the sight of the nations. 3 He hath remembered his mercy and his truth toward the house of Israel: all the ends of the earth have seen the salvation of our God. 4 All the earth, sing ye loud unto the Lord: cry out and rejoice, and sing praises. 5 Sing praise to the Lord upon the harp, *even* upon the harp with a singing voice. 6 With shalmes and sound of trumpets sing loud before the Lord the King. 7 Let the sea roar, and all that therein is, the world, and they that dwell therein. 8 Let the floods clap their hands, *and* let the mountains rejoice together9 Before the Lord: for he is come to judge the earth: with righteousness shall he judge the world, and the people with equity.

Chapter 99

1 The Lord reigneth, let the people tremble: he sitteth *between* the cherubims, let the earth be moved. 2 The Lord *is* great in Zion, and he is high above all the people. 3 They shall praise thy great and fearful name (*for* it is holy)4 And the king's power, that loveth judgment: *for* thou hast prepared equity: thou hast

executed judgment and justice in Jacob. 5 Exalt the Lord our God, and fall down before his footstool: *for* he is holy. 6 Moses and Aaron *were* among his priests, and Samuel among such as call upon his Name: these called upon the Lord, and he heard them. 7 He spake unto them in the cloudy pillar: they kept his testimonies, *and* the Law *that* he gave them. 8 Thou heardest them, O Lord our God: thou wast a favorable God unto them, though thou didst take vengeance for their inventions. 9 Exalt the Lord our God, and fall down before his holy mountain: for the Lord our God is holy.

Chapter 100

A Psalm-chapter of Praise.

1 Sing ye loud unto the Lord, all the earth. 2 Serve the Lord with gladness: come before him with joyfulness. 3 Know ye that even the Lord is God: he hath made us, and not we ourselves: *we are* his people, and the sheep of his pasture. 4 Enter into his gates with praise, *and* into his courts with rejoicing: praise him *and* bless his Name. 5 For the Lord is good: his mercy *is* everlasting, and his truth *is* from generation to generation.

Chapter 101

A Psalm-chapter of David.

1 I will sing mercy and judgment: unto thee, O Lord, will I sing. 2 I will do wisely in the perfect way, till thou comest to me: I will walk in the uprightness of mine heart in the midst of mine house. 3 I will set no wicked thing before mine eyes: I hate the work of them that fall away: it shall not cleave unto me. 4 A froward heart shall depart from me: I will know none evil. 5 Him that privily slandereth his neighbor, will I destroy: him that hath a proud look and high heart, I cannot *suffer*. 6 Mine eyes *shall be* unto the faithful of the land, that they may dwell with me: he that walketh in a perfect way, he shall serve me. 7 There shall no deceitful person dwell within mine house: he that telleth lies, shall not remain in my sight. 8 Betimes will I destroy all the wicked of the land, that I may cut off all the workers of iniquity from the City of the Lord.

Chapter 102

A prayer of the afflicted, when he shall be in distress, and pour forth his meditation before the Lord.

1 O Lord, hear my prayer, and let my cry come unto thee. 2 Hide not thy face from me in the time of my trouble: incline thine ears unto me: when I call, make haste to hear me. 3 For my days are consumed like smoke, and my bones are burned like an hearth. 4 Mine heart is smitten and withereth like grass, because I forget to eat my bread. 5 For the voice of my groaning my bones do cleave to my skin. 6 I am like a pelican of the wilderness: I am like an owl of the deserts. 7 I watch and am as a sparrow alone upon the housetop. 8 Mine enemies revile me daily, *and* they that rage against me, have sworn against me. 9 Surely I have eaten ashes as bread, and mingled my drink with weeping,10 Because of thine indignation and thy wrath: for thou hast heaved me up, and cast me down. 11 My days *are* like a shadow that fadeth, and I am withered like grass. 12 But thou, O Lord, dost remain forever, and thy remembrance from generation to generation. 13 Thou wilt arise *and* have mercy upon Zion: for the time to have mercy thereon, for the appointed time is come. 14 For thy servants delight in the stones thereof, and have pity on the dust thereof. 15 Then the heathen shall fear the name of the Lord, and all the kings of the earth thy glory,16 When the Lord shall build up Zion, *and* shall appear in his glory,17 *And* shall turn unto the prayer of the desolate, and not despise their

prayer. 18 This shall be written for the generation to come: and the people, which shall be created, shall praise the Lord. 19 For he hath looked down from the height of his sanctuary: out of the heaven did the Lord behold the earth,20 That he might hear the mourning of the prisoner, and deliver the children of death:21 That they may declare the name of the Lord in Zion, and his praise in Jerusalem,22 When the people shall be gathered together, and the kingdoms to serve the Lord. 23 He abated my strength in the way, *and* shortened my days. 24 *And* I said, O my God, take me not away in the midst of my days: thy years *endure* from generation to generation. 25 Thou hast aforetime laid the foundation of the earth, and the heavens *are* the works of thy hands. 26 They shall perish, but thou shalt endure: even they all shall wax old as doth a garment: as a vesture shalt thou change them, and they shall be changed. 27 But thou art the same, and thy years shall not fail. 28 The children of thy servants shall continue, and their seed shall stand fast in thy sight.

Chapter 103

A Psalm-chapter of David.

1 My soul, praise thou the Lord, and all that is within me, *praise* his holy name. 2 My soul, praise thou the Lord, and forget not all his benefits. 3 Which forgiveth all thine iniquity, and healeth all thine infirmities. 4 Which redeemeth thy life from the grave, and crowneth thee with mercy and compassions. 5 Which satisfieth thy mouth with good things: and thy youth is renewed like the eagle's. 6 The Lord executeth righteousness and judgment to all that are oppressed. 7 He made his ways known unto Moses, *and* his works unto the children of Israel. 8 The Lord is full of compassion and mercy, slow to anger and of great kindness. 9 He will not alway chide, neither keep *his anger* forever. 10 He hath not dealt with us after our sins, nor rewarded us according to our iniquities. 11 For as high as the heaven is above the earth, so great is his mercy toward them that fear him. 12 As far as the east is from the west: so far hath he removed our sins from us. 13 As a father hath compassion on his children, so hath the Lord compassion on them that fear him. 14 For he knoweth whereof we be made: he remembereth that we are but dust. 15 The days of man are as grass: as a flower of the field, so flourisheth he. 16 For the wind goeth over it, and it is gone, and the place thereof shall know it no more. 17 But the loving kindness of the Lord *endureth* forever and ever upon them that fear him, and his righteousness upon children's children,18 Unto them that keep his covenant, and think upon his commandments to do them. 19 The Lord hath prepared his throne in heaven, and his kingdom ruleth over all. 20 Praise the Lord, ye his angels, that excel in strength, that do his commandment in obeying the voice of his word. 21 Praise the Lord, all ye his hosts, ye his servants that do his pleasure. 22 Praise the Lord, all ye his works, in all places of his dominion: my soul, praise thou the Lord.

Chapter 104

1 My soul, praise thou the Lord: O Lord my God, thou art exceeding great, thou art clothed with glory and honor. 2 Which covereth himself with light as with a garment, *and* spreadeth the heavens like a curtain. 3 Which layeth the beams of his chambers in the waters, and maketh the clouds his chariot, and walketh upon the wings of the wind. 4 Which maketh his spirits his messengers, *and* a flaming fire his ministers. 5 He set the earth upon her foundations, so that it shall never move. 6 Thou coveredst it with the deep as with a garment: the waters would stand above the mountains. 7 *But* at thy rebuke they flee: at the voice of thy thunder they haste away. 8 *And* the mountains ascend, *and* the valleys descend to the place which thou hast established for them. 9 *But* thou hast set them a bound, which they shall not pass: they shall not return to cover the earth. 10 He sendeth the springs into the valleys, which run between the mountains. 11 They shall give drink to all the beasts of the field, and the wild asses shall quench their thirst. 12 By these springs shall the fouls of the heaven dwell, and sing among the branches. 13 He watereth the mountains from his chambers, *and* the earth is filled with the fruit of thy works. 14 He causeth grass to grow for the cattle, and herb for the use of man, that he may bring forth bread out of the earth,15 And wine *that* maketh glad the heart of man, *and* oil to make the face to shine, and bread that strengtheneth man's heart. 16 The high trees are satisfied, *even* the cedars of Lebanon, which he hath planted,17 That the birds may make their nests there: the stork dwelleth in the fir trees. 18 The high mountains *are* for the goats: the rocks *are* a refuge for the conies. 19 He appointed the moon for certain seasons: the sun knoweth his going down. 20 Thou makest darkness, and it is night, wherein all the beasts of the forest creep forth. 21 The lions roar after their prey, and seek their meat at God. 22 *When* the sun riseth, they retire, and couch in their dens. 23 *Then* goeth man forth to his work, and to his labor until the evening. 24 O Lord, how manifold are thy works! In wisdom hast thou made them all: the earth is full of thy riches. 25 *So* is this sea great and wide: *for* therein *are* things creeping innumerable, both small beasts and great. 26 There go the ships, *yea*, that Leviathan, whom thou hast made to play therein. 27 All these wait upon thee, that thou mayest give them food in due season. 28 Thou givest it to them, *and* they gather it: thou openest thine hand, and *they* are filled with good things. 29 *But if* thou hide thy face, they are troubled: *if* thou take away their breath, they die and return to their dust. 30 *Again if* thou send forth thy spirit, they are created, and thou renewest the face of the earth. 31 Glory be to the Lord forever: let the Lord rejoice in his works. 32 He looketh on the earth and it trembleth: he toucheth the mountains, and they smoke. 33 I will sing unto the Lord *all* my life: I will praise my God, while I live. 34 Let my words be acceptable unto him: I will rejoice in the Lord. 35 Let the sinners be consumed out of the earth, and the wicked till there be no more: O my soul, praise thou the Lord. Praise ye the Lord.

Chapter 105

1 Praise the Lord, *and* call upon his name: declare his works among the people. 2 Sing unto him, sing praise unto him, *and* talk of all his wondrous works. 3 Rejoice in his holy name: let the heart of them that seek the Lord, rejoice. 4 Seek the Lord and his strength: seek his face continually. 5 Remember his marvelous works, that he hath done, his wonders and the judgments of his mouth,6 Ye seed of Abraham his servant, ye children of Jacob, which are his elect. 7 He is the Lord our God: his judgments *are* through all the earth. 8 He hath alway remembered his covenant *and* promise, that he made to a thousand generations,9 *Even* that which he made with Abraham, and his oath unto Isaac:10 And *since* hath confirmed it to Jacob for a law, *and* to Israel for an everlasting covenant, 11 Saying, Unto thee will I give the land of Canaan, the lot of your inheritance. 12 Albeit they were few in number, *yea*, very few, and strangers in the land,13 And walked about from nation to nation, from one kingdom to another people,14 *Yet* suffered he no man

to do them wrong, but reproved kings for their sakes, *saying,*15 Touch not mine anointed, and do my prophets no harm. 16 Moreover he called a famine upon the land, *and* utterly brake the staff of bread. 17 *But he* sent a man before them: Joseph was sold for a slave. 18 They held his feet in the stocks, *and* he was laid in irons,19 Until his appointed time came, *and* the counsel of the Lord had tried him. 20 The King sent and loosed him: *even* the ruler of the people delivered him. 21 He made him lord of his house, and ruler of all his substance,22 That he should bind his princes unto his will, and teach his ancients wisdom. 23 Then Israel came to Egypt, and Jacob was a stranger in the land of Ham. 24 And he increased his people exceedingly, and made them stronger then their oppressors. 25 He turned their heart to hate his people, and to deal craftily with his servants. 26 *Then* sent he Moses his servant, *and* Aaron whom he had chosen. 27 They showed among them the message of his signs, and wonders in the land of Ham. 28 He sent darkness, and made it dark: and they were not disobedient unto his commission. 29 He turned their waters into blood, and slew their fish. 30 Their land brought forth frogs, *even* in their king's chambers. 31 He spake, and there came swarms of flies *and* lice in all their quarters. 32 He gave them hail for rain, *and* flames of fire in their land. 33 He smote their vines also and their fig trees, and brake down the trees in their coasts. 34 He spake, and the grasshoppers came, and caterpillars innumerable,35 And did eat up all the grass in their land, and devoured the fruit of their ground. 36 He smote also all the first born in their land, *even* the beginning of all their strength. 37 He brought them forth also with silver and gold, and there was none feeble among their tribes. 38 Egypt was glad at their departing: for the fear of them had fallen upon them. 39 He spread a cloud to be a covering, and fire to give light in the night. 40 They asked, and he brought quails, and he filled them with the bread of heaven. 41 He opened the rock, and the waters flowed out, *and* ran in the dry places *like* a river. 42 For he remembered his holy promise to Abraham his servant,43 And he brought forth his people with joy, *and* his chosen with gladness,44 And gave them the lands of the heathen, and they took the labors of the people in possession,45 That they might keep his statutes, and observe his laws. Praise ye the Lord.

Chapter 106

Praise ye the Lord

1 Praise ye the Lord because he is good, for his mercy *endureth* forever. 2 Who can express the noble acts of the Lord, *or* show forth all his praise?3 Blessed *are* they that keep judgment, and do righteousness at all times. 4 Remember me, O Lord, with the favor of thy people: visit me with thy salvation,5 That I may see the felicity of thy chosen, and rejoice in the joy of thy people, and glory with thine inheritance. 6 We have sinned with our fathers: we have committed iniquity, *and* done wickedly. 7 Our fathers understood not thy wonders in Egypt, neither remembered they the multitude of thy mercies, but rebelled at the sea, *even* at the Red Sea. 8 Nevertheless he saved them for his name's sake, that he might make his power to be known. 9 And he rebuked the Red Sea, and it was dried up, and he led them in the deep, as in the wilderness. 10 And he saved them from the adversary's hand, and delivered them from the hand of the enemy. 11 And the waters covered their oppressors: not one of them was left. 12 Then believed they his words, *and* sang praise unto him. 13 But incontinently they forgot his works: they waited not for

his counsel,14 But lusted with concupiscence in the wilderness, and tempted God in the desert. 15 Then he gave them their desire: but he sent leanness into their soul. 16 They envied Moses also in the tents, *and* Aaron the holy one of the Lord. 17 *Therefore* the earth opened and swallowed up Dathan, and covered the company of Abiram. 18 And the fire was kindled in their assembly: the flame burned up the wicked. 19 They made a calf in Horeb, and worshiped the molten image. 20 Thus they turned their glory into the similitude of a bullock, that eateth grass. 21 They forgot God their Savior, which had done great things in Egypt,22 Wondrous works in the land of Ham, and fearful things by the Red Sea. 23 Therefore he minded to destroy them, had not Moses his chosen stand in the breach before him to turn away his wrath, least he should destroy *them.* 24 Also they contemned that pleasant land, *and* believed not his word,25 But murmured in their tents, *and* hearkened not unto the voice of the Lord. 26 Therefore he lifted up his hand against them, to destroy them in the wilderness,27 And to destroy their seed among the nations, and to scatter them throughout the countries. 28 They joined themselves also unto Baalpeor, and did eat the offerings of the dead. 29 Thus they provoked *him* unto anger with their own inventions, and the plague brake in upon them. 30 But Phinehas stood up, and executed judgment, and the plague was stayed. 31 And it was imputed unto him for righteousness from generation to generation forever. 32 They angered him also at the waters of Meribah, so that Moses was punished for their sakes,33 Because they vexed his spirit, so that he spake unadvisedly with his lips. 34 Neither destroyed they the people, as the Lord had commanded them,35 But were mingled among the heathen, and learned their works,36 And served their idols, which were their ruin. 37 Yea, they offered their sons, and their daughters unto devils,38 And shed innocent blood, *even* the blood of their sons, and of their daughters, whom they offered unto the idols of Canaan, and the land was defiled with blood. 39 Thus were they stained with their own works, and went a whoring with their own inventions. 40 Therefore was the wrath of the Lord kindled against his people, and he abhorred his own inheritance. 41 And he gave them into the hand of the heathen: and they that hated them, were lords over them. 42 Their enemies also oppressed them, and they were humbled under their hand. 43 Many a time did he deliver them, but they provoked him by their counsels: therefore they were brought down by their iniquity. 44 Yet he saw when they were in affliction, and he heard their cry. 45 And he remembered his covenant toward them, and repented according to the multitude of his mercies,46 And gave them favor in the sight of all them, that lead them captives. 47 Save us, O Lord our God, and gather us from among the heathen, that we may praise thine holy name, and glory in thy praise. 48 Blessed *be* the Lord God of Israel forever and ever, and let all the people say, So be it. Praise ye the Lord.

Chapter 107

1 Praise the Lord, because he is good: for his mercy *endureth* forever. 2 Let them, which have been redeemed of the Lord, show how he hath delivered them from the hand of the oppressor,3 And gathered them out of the lands, from the east and from the west, from the north and from the south. 4 *When* they wandered in the desert *and* wilderness out of the way, *and* found no city to dwell in,5 Both hungry *and* thirsty, their soul fainted in them. 6 Then they cried unto the Lord in their

trouble, *and* he delivered them from their distress,7 And led them forth by the right way, that they might go to a city of habitation. 8 Let them *therefore* confess before the Lord his loving kindness, and his wonderful works before the sons of men. 9 For he satisfied the thirsty soul, and filled the hungry soul with goodness. 10 They that dwell in darkness and in the shadow of death, being bound in misery and iron, 11 Because they rebelled against the words of the Lord, and despised the counsel of the Most High,12 When he humbled their heart with heaviness, *then* they fell down and there was no helper. 13 Then they cried unto the Lord in their trouble, *and* he delivered them from their distress. 14 He brought them out of darkness, and *out of* the shadow of death, and brake their bands asunder. 15 Let them *therefore* confess before the Lord his loving kindness, and his wonderful works before the sons of men. 16 For he hath broken the gates of brass, and burst the bars of iron asunder. 17 Fools by reason of their transgression, and because of their iniquities are afflicted. 18 Their soul abhorreth all meat, and they are brought to death's door. 19 Then they cry unto the Lord in their trouble, *and* he delivereth them from their distress. 20 He sendeth his word and healeth them, and delivereth them from their graves. 21 Let them *therefore* confess before the Lord his loving kindness, and his wonderful works before the sons of men,22 And let them offer sacrifices of praise, and declare his works with rejoicing. 23 They that go down to the sea in ships, *and* occupy by the great waters,24 They see the works of the Lord, and his wonders in the deep. 25 For he commandeth and raiseth the stormy wind, and it lifteth up the waves thereof. 26 They mount up to the heaven, *and* descend to the deep, so that their soul melteth for trouble. 27 They are tossed to and from, and stagger like a drunken man, and all their cunning is gone. 28 Then they cry unto the Lord in their trouble*, and* he bringeth them out of their distress. 29 He turneth the storm to calm, so that the waves thereof are still. 30 When they are quieted, they are glad, and he bringeth them unto the haven, where they would be. 31 Let them *therefore* confess before the Lord his loving kindness, and his wonderful works before the sons of men. 32 And let them exalt him in the congregation of the people, and praise him in the assembly of the elders. 33 He turneth the floods into a wilderness, and the springs of waters into dryness,34 *And* a fruitful land into barrenness for the wickedness of them that dwell therein. 35 *Again* he turneth the wilderness into pools of water, and the dry land into water springs. 36 And there he placeth the hungry, and they build a city to dwell in,37 And sow the fields, and plant vineyards, which bring forth fruitful increase. 38 For he blesseth them, and they multiply exceedingly, and he diminisheth not their cattle. 39 Again *men* are diminished, and brought low by oppression, evil and sorrow. 40 He poureth contempt upon princes, and causeth them to err in desert places out of the way. 41 Yet he raiseth up the poor out of misery, and maketh him families like a flock of sheep. 42 The righteous shall see it, and rejoice, and all iniquity shall stop her mouth. 43 Who is wise that he may observe these things? For they shall understand the loving kindness of the Lord.

Chapter 108

A song or *Psalm-chapter of David.*

1 O God, mine heart is prepared, so *is* my tongue: I will sing and give praise. 2 Awake viol and harp: I will awake early. 3 I will praise thee, O Lord, among the people, and I will sing unto thee among the nations. 4 For thy mercy is great above the heavens, and thy truth unto the clouds. 5 Exalt thyself, O God, above the heavens, and *let* thy glory *be* upon all the earth,6 That thy beloved may be delivered: help with thy right hand and hear me. 7 God hath spoken in his holiness: *therefore* I will rejoice, I shall divide Shechem and measure the valley of Succoth. 8 Gilead *shall be* mine, *and* Manasseh *shall be* mine: Ephraim also *shall be* the strength of mine head: Juda *is* my lawgiver. 9 Moab shall be my wash pot: over Edom will I cast out my shoe: upon Palestina will I triumph. 10 Who will lead me into the strong city? Who will bring me unto Edom? 11 Wilt not thou, O God, *which* hadst forsaken us, and didst not go forth, O God, with our armies?12 Give us help against trouble: for vain is the help of man. 13 Through God we shall do valiantly: for he shall tread down our enemies.

Chapter 109

To him that excelleth. A Psalm-chapter of David.

1 Hold not thy tongue, O God of my praise. 2 For the mouth of the wicked, and the mouth *full* of deceit are opened upon me: they have spoken to me with a lying tongue. 3 They compassed me about also with words of hatred, and fought against me without a cause. 4 For my friendship they were mine adversaries, but I gave myself to prayer. 5 And they have rewarded me evil for good, and hatred for my friendship. 6 Set thou the wicked over him, and let the adversary stand at his right hand. 7 When he shall be judged, let him be condemned, and let his prayer be turned into sin. 8 Let his days be few, and let another take his charge. 9 Let his children be fatherless, and his wife a widow. 10 Let his children be vagabonds and beg and seek *bread, coming out* of their places destroyed. 11 Let the extortioner catch all that he hath, and let the strangers spoil his labor. 12 Let there be none to extend mercy unto him: neither let there be any to show mercy upon his fatherless children. 13 Let his posterity be destroyed, *and* in the generation following let their name be put out. 14 Let the iniquity of his fathers be had in remembrance with the Lord: and let not the sin of his mother be done away. 15 *But* let them alway be before the Lord, that he may cut off their memorial from the earth. 16 Because he remembered not to show mercy, but persecuted the afflicted and poor man, and the sorrowful hearted to slay him. 17 As he loved cursing, so shall it come unto him, *and* as he loved not blessing, so shall it be far from him. 18 As he clothed himself with cursing like a raiment, so shall it come into his bowels like water, and like oil into his bones. 19 Let it be unto him as a garment to cover him, and for a girdle, wherewith he shall be alway girded. 20 Let this be the reward of mine adversary from the Lord, and of them, that speak evil against my soul. 21 But thou, O Lord my God, deal with me according unto thy name: deliver me, (for thy mercy is good)22 Because I am poor and needy, and mine heart is wounded within me. 23 I depart like the shadow that declineth, and am shaken off as the grasshopper. 24 My knees are .weak through fasting, and my flesh hath lost *all* fatness. 25 I became also a rebuke unto them: they that looked upon me, shaked their heads. 26 Help me, O Lord my God: save me according to thy mercy. 27 And they shall know, that this is thine hand, *and that thou*, Lord, hast done it. 28 *Though* they curse, yet thou wilt bless: they shall arise and be confounded, but thy servant shall rejoice. 29 Let mine adversaries be clothed with shame, and let them cover themselves with their confusion, as with a cloak. 30 I will give thanks unto the

Lord greatly with my mouth, and praise him among the multitude. 31 For he will stand at the right hand of the poor, to save him from them that would condemn his soul.

Chapter 110

A Psalm-chapter of David.

1 The Lord said unto my Lord, Sit thou at my right hand, until I make thine enemies thy footstool. 2 The Lord shall send the rod of thy power out of Zion: be thou ruler in the midst of thine enemies. 3 Thy people *shall come* willingly at the time *of assembling:* thine army in holy beauty: the youth of thy womb *shall be* as the morning dew. 4 The Lord swear and will not repent, Thou art a priest forever after the order of Melchizedek. 5 The Lord, *that is* at thy right hand, shall wound kings in the day of his wrath. 6 He shall be judge among the heathen: he shall fill *all* with dead bodies, *and* smite the head over great countries. 7 He shall drink of the brook in the way: therefore shall he lift up *his* head.

Chapter 111

Praise ye the Lord.

1 I will praise the Lord with my whole heart in the assembly and congregation of the just. 2 The works of the Lord *are* great, and ought to be sought out of all them that love them. 3 His work *is* beautiful and glorious, and his righteousness endureth forever. 4 He hath made his wonderful works to be had in remembrance: the Lord *is* merciful and full of compassion. 5 He hath given a portion unto them that fear him: he will ever be mindful of his covenant. 6 He hath showed to his people the power of his works in giving unto them the heritage of the heathen. 7 The works of his hands *are* truth and judgment: all his statutes are true. 8 They are stablished forever and ever, and are done in truth and equity. 9 He sent redemption unto his people: he hath commanded his covenant forever: holy and fearful *is* his Name. 10 The beginning of wisdom *is* the fear of the Lord: all they that observe them, have good understanding: his praise endureth forever.

Chapter 112

Praise ye the Lord.

1 Blessed *is* the man, that feareth the Lord, *and* delighteth greatly in his commandments. 2 His seed shall be mighty upon earth: the generation of the righteous shall be blessed. 3 Riches and treasures *shall be* in his house, and his righteousness endureth forever. 4 Unto the righteous ariseth light in darkness: *he is* merciful and full of compassion and righteous. 5 A good man *is* merciful and lendeth, *and* will measure his affairs by judgment. 6 Surely he shall never be moved: *but* the righteous shall be had in everlasting remembrance. 7 He will not be afraid of evil tidings: *for* his heart is fixed, *and* believeth in the Lord. 8 His heart is stablished: *therefore* he will not fear, until he see *his desire* upon his enemies. 9 He hath distributed *and* given to the poor: his righteousness remaineth forever: his horn shall be exalted with glory. 10 The wicked shall see it and be angry: he shall gnash with his teeth, and consume away: the desire of the wicked shall perish.

Chapter 113

Praise ye the Lord.

1 Praise, O ye servants of the Lord, praise the name of the Lord. 2 Blessed be the name of the Lord from henceforth and forever. 3 The Lord's name is praised from the rising of the sun, unto the going down of the same. 4 The Lord is high above all nations, *and* his glory above the heavens. 5 Who is like unto the Lord our God, that hath his dwelling on high!6 Who abaseth himself to behold *things* in the heaven and in the earth. 7 He raiseth the needy out of the dust, *and* lifteth up the poor out of the dung,8 That he may set him with the princes, *even* with the princes of his people. 9 He maketh the barren woman to dwell with a family, *and* a joyful mother of children. Praise ye the Lord.

Chapter 114

1 When Israel went out of Egypt, *and* the house of Jacob from the barbarous people,2 Judah was his sanctification, *and* Israel his dominion. 3 The sea saw it and fled: Jordan was turned back. 4 The mountains leaped like rams, *and* the hills as lambs. 5 What ailed thee, O sea, that thou fleddest? O Jordan, why wast thou turned back?6 Ye mountains, *why* leaped ye like rams, *and* ye hills as lambs?7 The earth trembled at the presence of the Lord, at the presence of the God of Jacob,8 Which turneth the rock into water pools, *and* the flint into a fountain of water.

Chapter 115

1 Not unto us, O Lord, not unto us, but unto thy name give the glory, for thy loving mercy *and* for thy truth's sake. 2 Wherefore shall the heathen say, Where is now their God?3 But our God *is* in heaven: he doth whatsoever he will. 4 Their idols *are* silver and gold, *even* the work of men's hands. 5 They have a mouth and speak not: they have eyes and see not. 6 They have ears and hear not: they have noses and smell not. 7 They have hands and touch not: they have feet and walk not: neither make they a sound with their throat. 8 They that make them are like unto them: *so are* all that trust in them. 9 O Israel, trust thou in the Lord: *for* he is their help and their shield. 10 O house of Aaron, trust ye in the Lord: *for* he is their help and their shield. 11 Ye that fear the Lord, trust in the Lord: *for* he is their helper and their shield. 12 The Lord hath been mindful of us: he will bless, he will bless the house of Israel, he will bless the house of Aaron. 13 He will bless them that fear the Lord, both small and great. 14 The Lord will increase *his graces* toward you, *even* toward you and toward your children. 15 Ye are blessed of the Lord, which made the heaven and the earth. 16 The heavens, *even* the heavens *are* the Lord's: but he hath given the earth to the sons of men. 17 The dead praise not the Lord, neither any that go down into the *place of* silence. 18 But we will praise the Lord from henceforth and forever. Praise ye the Lord.

Chapter 116

1 I love the Lord, because he hath heard my voice *and* my prayers. 2 For he hath inclined his ear unto me, when I did call *upon him* in my days. 3 *When* the snares of death compassed me, and the grief's of the grave caught me: *when* I found trouble and sorrow. 4 Then I called upon the name of the Lord, *saying,* I beseech thee, O Lord, deliver my soul. 5 The Lord *is* merciful and righteous, and our God *is* full of compassion. 6 The Lord preserveth the simple: I was in misery and he saved me. 7 Return unto thy rest, O my soul: for the Lord hath been beneficial unto thee,8 Because thou hast delivered my soul from death, mine eyes from tears, *and* my feet from falling. 9 I shall walk before the Lord in the land of the living. 10 I believed, therefore did I speak: *for* I was sore troubled. 11 I said in my fear, All men are liars. 12 What shall I render unto the Lord for all his benefits toward me?13 I will take the cup of salvation, and call upon the name of the Lord. 14 I will pay my vows unto the Lord, *even* now in the presence of all his people. 15 Precious in the sight of the Lord *is* the death of his saints.

16 Behold, Lord: for I am thy servant, I am thy servant, *and* the son of thine handmaid: thou hast broken my bonds. 17 I will offer to thee a sacrifice of praise, and will call upon the name of the Lord. 18 I will pay my vows unto the Lord, *even* now in the presence of all his people,19 In the courts of the Lord's house, *even* in the midst of thee, O Jerusalem. Praise ye the Lord.

Chapter 117

1 All nations, praise ye the Lord: all ye people, praise him. 2 For his loving kindness is great toward us, and the truth of the Lord *endure*th forever. Praise ye the Lord.

Chapter 118

1 Praise ye the Lord, because he is good: for his mercy *endureth* forever. 2 Let Israel now say, That his mercy *endureth* forever. 3 Let the house of Aaron now say, That his mercy *endureth* forever. 4 Let them, that fear the Lord, now say, That his mercy *endureth* forever. 5 I called upon the Lord in trouble, *and* the Lord heard me, *and set me* at large. 6 The Lord *is* with me: *therefore* I will not fear what man can do unto me. 7 The Lord *is* with me among them that help me: therefore shall I see *my desire* upon mine enemies. 8 It is better to trust in the Lord, then to have confidence in man. 9 It is better to trust in the Lord, then to have confidence in princes. 10 All nations have compassed me: but in the name of the Lord shall I destroy them. 11 They have compassed me, yea, they have compassed me: but in the name of the Lord I shall destroy them. 12 They came about me like bees, *but* they were quenched as a fire of thorns: for in the name of the Lord I shall destroy them. 13 Thou hast thrust sore at me, that I might fall: but the Lord hath holpen me. 14 The Lord *is* my strength and song: for he hath been my deliverance. 15 The voice of joy and deliverance *shall be* in the tabernacles of the righteous, *saying*, The right hand of the Lord hath done valiantly. 16 The right hand of the Lord is exalted: the right hand of the Lord hath done valiantly. 17 I shall not die, but live, and declare the works of the Lord. 18 The Lord hath chastened me sore, but he hath not delivered me to death. 19 Open ye unto me the gates of righteousness, *that* I may go into them, *and* praise the Lord. 20 This is the gate of the Lord: the righteous shall enter into it. 21 I will praise thee: for thou hast heard me, and hast been my deliverance. 22 The stone, *which* the builders refused, is the head of the corner. 23 This was the Lord's doing, *and* it is marvelous in our eyes. 24 This is the day, *which* the Lord hath made: let us rejoice and be glad in it. 25 O Lord, I pray thee, save now: O Lord, I pray thee now give prosperity. 26 Blessed *be he*, that cometh in the name of the Lord: we have blessed you out of the house of the Lord. 27 The Lord *is* mighty, and hath given us light: bind the sacrifice with cords unto the horns of the altar. 28 Thou art my God, and I will praise thee, *even* my God: therefore I will exalt thee. 29 Praise ye the Lord, because he is good: for his mercy *endureth* forever.

Chapter 119

ALEPH

1 Blessed *are* those that are upright in *their* way, *and* walk in the Law of the Lord. 2 Blessed *are* they that keep his testimonies, *and* seek him with their whole heart. 3 Surely they work none iniquity, *that* walk in his ways. 4 Thou hast commanded to keep thy precepts diligently. 5 Oh that my ways were directed to keep thy statutes!6 Then should I not be confounded, when I have respect unto all thy commandments. 7 I will praise thee with an upright heart,

when I shall learn the judgments of thy righteousness. 8 I will keep thy statutes: forsake me not overlong. BETH9 Wherewith shall a young man redress his way? In taking heed *thereto* according to thy word. 10 With my whole heart have I sought thee: let me not wander from thy commandments. 11 I have hid thy promise in mine heart, that I might not sin against thee. 12 Blessed art thou, O Lord: teach me thy statutes. 13 With my lips have I declared all the judgments of thy mouth. 14 I have had as great delight in the way of thy testimonies, as in all riches. 15 I will meditate in thy precepts, and consider thy ways. 16 I will delight in thy statutes, *and* I will not forget thy word. GIMEL. 17 Be beneficial unto thy servant, *that* I may live and keep thy word. 18 Open mine eyes, that I may see the wonders of thy law. 19 I am a stranger upon earth: hide not thy commandments from me. 20 Mine heart breaketh for the desire to thy judgments alway. 21 Thou hast destroyed the proud: cursed are they that do err from thy commandments. 22 Remove from me shame and contempt: for I have kept thy testimonies. 23 Princes also did sit, *and* speak against me: *but* thy servant did meditate in thy statutes. 24 Also thy testimonies *are* my delight, *and* my counselors. DALETH25 My soul cleaveth to the dust: quicken me according to thy word. 26 I have declared my ways, and thou heardest me: teach me thy statutes. 27 Make me to understand the way of thy precepts, and I will meditate in thy wondrous works. 28 My soul melteth for heaviness: raise me up according unto thy word. 29 Take from me the way of lying, and grant me graciously thy law. 30 I have chosen the way of truth, *and* thy judgments have I laid *before me*. 31 I have cleaved to thy testimonies, O Lord: confound me not. 32 I will run the way of thy commandments, when thou shalt enlarge mine heart. HE. 33 Teach me, O Lord, the way of thy statutes, and I will keep it unto the end. 34 Give me understanding, and I will keep thy Law: yea, I will keep it with *my whole* heart. 35 Direct me in the path of thy commandments: for therein is my delight. 36 Incline mine heart unto thy testimonies, and not to covetousness. 37 Turn away mine eyes from regarding vanity, *and* quicken me in thy way. 38 Stablish thy promise to thy servant, because he feareth thee. 39 Take away my rebuke that I fear: for thy judgments *are* good. 40 Behold, I desire thy commandments: quicken me in thy righteousness. VAU41 And let thy loving kindness come unto me, O Lord, *and* thy salvation according to thy promise. 42 So shall I make answer unto my blasphemers: for I trust in thy word. 43 And take not the word of truth utterly out of my mouth: for I wait for thy judgments. 44 So shall I alway keep thy law forever and ever. 45 And I will walk at liberty: for I seek thy precepts. 46 I will speak also of thy testimonies before kings, and will not be ashamed. 47 And my delight shall be in thy commandments, which I have loved. 48 Mine hands also will I lift up unto thy commandments, which I have loved, and I will meditate in thy statutes. ZAIN. 49 Remember the promise *made* to thy servant, wherein thou hast caused me to trust. 50 It is my comfort in my trouble: for thy promise hath quickened me. 51 The proud have had me exceedingly in derision: *yet* have I not declined from thy Law. 52 I remembered thy judgments of old, O Lord, and have been comforted. 53 Fear is come upon me for the wicked, that forsake thy Law. 54 Thy statutes have been my songs in the house of my pilgrimage. 55 I have remembered thy name, O Lord, in the night, and have kept thy law. 56 This I had because I kept thy precepts. CHETH. 57 O Lord, *that art* my portion, I have determined to keep thy words. 58 I made my supplication in thy presence with *my* whole heart: be merciful unto me according to thy promise. 59 I have considered my ways, and turned my feet into thy testimonies. 60 I made haste and delayed not to keep thy commandments. 61 The bands of the wicked have robbed me: *but* I have not forgotten thy law. 62 At midnight will I rise to give thanks unto thee, because of thy righteous judgments. 63 I am companion of all them that fear thee, and keep thy precepts. 64 The earth, O Lord, is full of thy mercy: teach me thy statutes. TETH. 65 O Lord, thou hast dealt graciously with thy servant according unto thy word. 66 Teach me good judgment and knowledge: for I have believed thy commandments. 67 Before I was afflicted, I went astray: but now I keep thy word. 68 Thou art good and gracious: teach me thy statutes. 69 The proud have imagined a lie against me: *but* I will keep thy precepts with *my* whole heart. 70 Their heart is fat as grease: *but* my delight is in thy law. 71 It is good for me that I have been afflicted, that I may learn thy statutes. 72 The law of thy mouth is better unto me, than thousands of gold and silver. IOD. 73 Thine hands have made me and fashioned me: give me understanding *therefore*, that I may learn thy commandments. 74 So they that fear thee, seeing me shall rejoice, because I have trusted in thy word. 75 I know, O Lord, that thy judgments *are* right, and that thou hast afflicted me justly. 76 I pray thee that thy mercy may comfort me according to thy promise unto thy servant. 77 Let thy tender mercies come unto me, that I may live: for thy law *is* my delight. 78 Let the proud be ashamed: for they have dealt wickedly *and* falsely with me: *but* I meditate in thy precepts. 79 Let such as fear thee turn unto me, and they that know thy testimonies. 80 Let mine heart be upright in thy statutes, that I be not ashamed. CAPH. 81 My soul fainteth for thy salvation: *yet* I wait for thy word. 82 Mine eyes fail for thy promise, saying, When wilt thou comfort me? 83 For I am like a bottle in the smoke: *yet* do I not forget thy statutes. 84 How many are the days of thy servant? When wilt thou execute judgment on them that persecute me? 85 The proud have digged pits for me, which is not after thy Law. 86 All thy commandments *are* true: they persecute me falsely: help me. 87 They had almost consumed me upon the earth: but I forsook not thy precepts. 88 Quicken me according to thy loving kindness: so shall I keep the testimony of thy mouth. LAMED. 89 O Lord, thy word endureth forever in heaven. 90 Thy truth *is* from generation to generation: thou hast laid the foundation of the earth, and it abideth. 91 They continue *even* to this day by thine ordinances: for all *are* thy servants. 92 Except thy law had been my delight, I should now have perished in mine affliction. 93 I will never forget thy precepts: for by them thou hast quickened me. 94 I am thine, save me: for I have sought thy precepts. 95 The wicked have waited for me to destroy me: *but* I will consider thy testimonies. 96 I have seen an end of all perfection: *but* thy commandment *is* exceeding large. MEM. 97 Oh how love I thy law! It is my meditation continually. 98 By thy commandments thou hast made me wiser then mine enemies: for they are ever with me. 99 I have had more understanding then all my teachers: for thy testimonies *are* my meditation. 100 I understood more than the ancient, because I kept thy precepts. 101 I have refrained my feet from every evil way, that I might keep thy word. 102 I have not declined from thy judgments: for thou didst teach me. 103 How sweet are thy promises unto my mouth! *Yea*, more than honey unto my mouth. 104 By thy precepts I have gotten understanding: therefore I hate all the ways of falsehood. NUN. 105 Thy word *is* a lantern unto my feet, and a light unto my path. 106 I have sworn and will perform it, that I will keep thy righteous judgments. 107 I am very sore afflicted: O Lord, quicken me according to thy word. 108 O Lord, I beseech thee accept the free offerings of my mouth, and teach me thy judgments. 109 My soul is continually in mine hand: yet do I not forget thy law. 110 The wicked have laid a snare for me: but I swerved not from thy precepts. 111 Thy testimonies have I taken *as* an heritage forever: for they are the joy of mine heart. 112 I have applied mine heart to fulfill thy statutes alway, *even* unto the end. SAMECH. 113 I hate vain inventions: but thy Law do I love. 114 Thou art my refuge and shield, *and* I trust in thy word. 115 Away from me, ye wicked: for I will keep the commandments of my God. 116 Stablish me according to thy promise, that I may live, and disappoint me not of mine hope. 117 Stay thou me, and I shall be safe, and I will delight continually in thy statutes. 118 Thou hast trodden down all them that depart from thy statutes: for their deceit *is* vain. 119 Thou hast taken away all the wicked of the earth *like* dross: therefore I love thy testimonies. 120 My flesh trembleth for fear of thee, and I am afraid of thy judgments. AIN. 121 I have executed judgment and justice: leave me not to mine oppressors. 122 Answer for thy servant in that, which is good, *and* let not the proud oppress me. 123 Mine eyes have failed *in waiting* for thy salvation, and for thy just promise. 124 Deal with thy servant according to thy mercy, and teach me thy statutes. 125 I am thy servant: grant me *therefore* understanding, that I may know thy testimonies. 126 It is time for the Lord to work: *for* they have destroyed thy Law. 127 Therefore love I thy commandments above gold, yea, above most fine gold. 128 Therefore I esteem all thy precepts most just, and hate all false ways. PE. 129 Thy testimonies *are* wonderful: therefore doth my soul keep them. 130 The entrance into thy words showeth light, and giveth understanding to the simple. 131 I opened my mouth and panted, because I loved thy commandments. 132 Look upon me and be merciful unto me, as thou usest to do unto those that love thy name. 133 Direct my steps in thy word, and let none iniquity have dominion over me. 134 Deliver me from the oppression of men, and I will keep thy precepts. 135 Show the light of thy countenance upon thy servant, and teach me thy statutes. 136 Mine eyes gush out with rivers of water, because they keep not thy law. TSADDI. 137 Righteous art thou, O Lord, and just *are* thy judgments. 138 Thou hast commanded justice by thy testimonies and truth especially. 139 My zeal hath even consumed me, because mine enemies have forgotten thy words. 140 Thy word is proved most pure, and thy servant loveth it. 141 I am small and despised: *yet* do I not forget thy precepts. 142 Thy righteousness *is* an everlasting righteousness, and thy law is truth. 143 Trouble and anguish are come upon me: *yet are* thy commandments my delight. 144 The righteousness of thy testimonies *is* everlasting: grant me understanding, and I shall live. KOPH. 145 I have cried with *my* whole heart: hear me, O Lord, *and* I will keep thy statutes. 146 I called upon thee: save me, and I will keep thy testimonies. 147 I prevented the morning light, and cried: *for* I waited on thy word. 148 Mine eyes prevent the *night* watches to meditate in thy word. 149 Hear my voice according to thy loving kindness: O Lord, quicken me according to thy judgment. 150 They draw near, that follow after malice, *and* are far from thy law. 151 Thou art near, O Lord: for all thy commandments *are* true. 152 I have known long since by thy testimonies, that thou hast established them forever. RESH. 153 Behold mine affliction, and deliver me: for I have not forgotten thy law. 154 Plead my cause, and deliver me: quicken me according unto thy word. 155 Salvation *is* far from the wicked, because they seek not thy statutes. 156 Great are thy tender mercies, O Lord: quicken me according to thy judgments. 157 My persecutors and mine oppressors *are* many: *yet* do I not swerve from thy testimonies. 158 I saw the transgressors and was grieved, because they kept not thy word. 159 Consider, O Lord, how I love thy precepts: quicken me according to thy loving kindness. 160 The beginning of thy word is truth, and all the judgments of thy righteousness *endure* forever. SCHIN. 161 Princes have persecuted me without cause, but mine heart stood in awe of thy words. 162 I rejoice at thy word, as one that findeth a great spoil. 163 I hate falsehood and abhor it, *but* thy law do I love. 164 Seven times a day do I praise thee, because of thy righteous judgments. 165 They that love thy Law, shall have great prosperity, and they shall have none hurt. 166 Lord, I have trusted in thy salvation, and have done thy commandments. 167 My soul hath kept thy testimonies: for I love them exceedingly. 168 I have kept thy precepts and thy testimonies: for all my ways *are* before thee. TAV. 169 Let my complaint come before thee, O Lord, *and* give me understanding, according unto thy word. 170 Let my supplication come before thee, *and* deliver me according to thy promise. 171 My lips shall speak praise, when thou hast taught me thy statutes. 172 My tongue shall entreat of thy word: for all thy commandments *are* righteous. 173 Let thine hand help me: for I have chosen thy precepts. 174 I have longed for thy salvation, O Lord, and thy law *is* my delight. 175 Let my soul live, and it shall praise thee, and thy judgments shall help me. 176 I have gone astray like a lost sheep: seek thy servant, for I do not forget thy commandments.

Chapter 120

A song of degrees.

1 I called unto the Lord in my trouble, *and* he heard me. 2 Deliver my soul, O Lord, from lying lips, and from a deceitful tongue. 3 What doth *thy* deceitful tongue bring unto thee? Or what doth it avail thee? 4 *It is as* the sharp arrows of a mighty man, and *as* the coals of juniper. 5 Woe is to me that I remain in Mesech, *and* dwell in the tents of Kedar. 6 My soul hath too long dwelt with him that hateth peace. 7 I *seek* peace, and when I speak *thereof*, they are *bent* to war.

Chapter 121

A song of degrees.

1 I will lift mine eyes unto the mountains, from whence mine help shall come. 2 Mine help *cometh* from the Lord, which hath made the heaven and the earth. 3 He will not suffer thy foot to slip: *for* he that keepeth thee, will not slumber. 4 Behold, he that keepeth Israel, will neither slumber nor sleep. 5 The Lord *is* thy keeper: the Lord *is* thy shadow at thy right hand. 6 The sun shall not smite thee by day, nor the moon by night. 7 The Lord shall preserve thee from all evil: he shall keep thy soul. 8 The Lord shall preserve thy going out, and thy coming in from henceforth and forever.

Chapter 122

A song of degrees, or Psalm-chapter *of David.*

1 I rejoiced, when they said to me, We will go into the house of the Lord. 2 Our feet shall stand in thy gates, O Jerusalem. 3 Jerusalem *is* builded as a city, that is compact together in itself:4 Whereunto the tribes, *even* the tribes of the Lord go up *according* to the testimony to Israel, to praise the name of the Lord. 5 For there are thrones set for judgment, *even* the thrones of the house of David. 6 Pray for the peace of Jerusalem: let them prosper that love thee. 7 Peace be within thy walls, *and* prosperity within thy palaces. 8 For my brethren and neighbors' sakes I will wish thee now prosperity. 9 Because of the house of the Lord our God, I will procure thy wealth.

Chapter 123

A song of degrees.

1 I lift up mine eyes to thee, that dwellest in the heavens. 2 Behold, as the eyes of servants *look* unto the hand of their masters, *and* as the eyes of a maiden unto the hand of her mistress: so our eyes *wait* upon the Lord our God until he have mercy upon us. 3 Have mercy upon us, O Lord, have mercy upon us: for we have suffered too much contempt. 4 Our soul is filled too full of the mocking of the wealthy, *and* of the despitefulness of the proud.

Chapter 124

A song of degrees, or Psalm-chapter *of David.*

1 If the Lord had not been on our side, (may Israel now say)2 If the Lord had not been on our side, when men rose up against us,3 They had then swallowed us up quick, when their wrath was kindled against us. 4 Then the waters had drowned us, *and* the stream had gone over our soul:5 Then had the swelling waters gone over our soul. 6 Praised *be* the Lord, which hath not given us *as* a prey unto their teeth. 7 Our soul is escaped, even as a bird out of the snare of the fowlers: the snare is broken, and we are delivered. 8 Our help *is* in the name of the Lord, which hath made heaven and earth.

Chapter 125

A song of degrees.

1 They that trust in the Lord, *shall be* as mount Zion, *which* cannot be removed, *but* remaineth forever. 2 *As* the mountains *are* about Jerusalem: so *is* the Lord about his people from henceforth and forever. 3 For the rod of the wicked shall not rest on the lot of the righteous, lest the righteous put forth their hand unto wickedness. 4 Do well, O Lord, unto those that be good and true in their hearts. 5 But these that turn aside by their crooked *ways*, them shall the Lord lead with the workers of iniquity: *but* peace *shall be* upon Israel.

Chapter 126

A song of degrees, or Psalm-chapter *of David.*

1 When the Lord brought again the captivity of Zion, we were like them that dream. 2 Then was our mouth filled with laughter, and our tongue with joy: then said they among the heathen, The Lord hath done great things for them. 3 The Lord hath done great things for us, *whereof* we rejoice. 4 O Lord, bring again our captivity, as the rivers in the south. 5 They that sow in tears, shall reap in joy. 6 They went weeping and carried precious seed: *but* they shall return with joy and bring their sheaves.

Chapter 127

A song of degrees, or Psalm-chapter *of Solomon.*

1 Except the Lord build the house, they labor in vain that build it: except the Lord keep the city, the keeper watcheth in vain. 2 It is in vain for you to rise early, *and* to lie down late, *and* eat the bread of sorrow: *but* he will surely give rest to his beloved. 3 Behold, children are the inheritance of the Lord, *and* the fruit of the

womb *his* reward. 4 As *are* the arrows in the hand of the strong man: so *are* the children of youth. 5 Blessed *is* the man, that hath his quiver full of them: *for* they shall not be ashamed, when they speak with *their* enemies in the gate.

Chapter 128

A song of degrees.

1 Blessed *is* every one that feareth the Lord and walketh in his ways. 2 When thou eatest the labors of thine hands, thou shalt be blessed, and it shall be well with thee. 3 Thy wife *shall be* as the fruitful vine on the sides of thine house, *and* thy children like the olive plants round about thy table. 4 Lo, surely thus shall the man be blessed, that feareth the Lord. 5 The Lord out of Zion shall bless thee, and thou shalt see the wealth of Jerusalem all the days of thy life. 6 Yea, thou shalt see thy children's children, *and* peace upon Israel.

Chapter 129

A song of degrees.

1 They have often times afflicted me from my youth (may Israel now say)2 They have often times afflicted me from my youth: but they could not prevail against me. 3 The plowers plowed upon my back, *and* made long furrows. 4 *But* the righteous Lord hath cut the cords of the wicked. 5 They that hate Zion, shall be all ashamed and turned backward. 6 They *shall be* as the grass on the housetops, which withereth afore it cometh forth. 7 Whereof the mower filleth not his hand, neither the gleaner his lap:8 Neither they, which go by, say, The blessing of the Lord *be* upon you, *or*, We bless you in the name of the Lord.

Chapter 130

A song of degrees.

1 Out of the deep places have I called unto thee, O Lord. 2 Lord, hear my voice: let thine ears attend to the voice of my prayers. 3 If thou, O Lord, straightly markest iniquities, O Lord, who shall stand?4 But mercy *is* with thee, that thou mayest be feared. 5 I have waited on the Lord: my soul hath waited, and I have trusted in his word. 6 My soul *waiteth* on the Lord more than the morning watch watcheth for the morning. 7 Let Israel wait on the Lord: for with the Lord *is* mercy, and with him *is* great redemption. 8 And he shall redeem Israel from all his iniquities.

Chapter 131

A song of degrees or Psalm-chapter *of David.*

1 Lord, mine heart is not haughty, neither are mine eyes lofty, neither have I walked in great matters and hid from me. 2 Surely I have behaved myself, like one weaned from his mother, and kept silence: I am in myself as one that is weaned. 3 Let Israel wait on the Lord from henceforth and forever.

Chapter 132

A song of degrees.

1 Lord, remember David with all his affliction. 2 Who swear unto the Lord, *and* vowed unto the mighty *God* of Jacob, *saying*,3 I will not enter into the tabernacle of mine house, nor come upon my pallet *or* bed,4 Nor suffer mine eyes to sleep, nor mine eye lids to slumber,5 Until I find out a place for the Lord, an habitation for the mighty *God* of Jacob. 6 Lo, we heard of it in Ephratah, *and* found it in the fields of the forest. 7 We will enter into his tabernacles, *and* worship before his footstool. 8 Arise, O Lord, *to come* into thy rest, thou, and the ark of thy strength. 9 Let thy priests be clothed with righteousness, and let thy saints rejoice. 10 For thy servant David's sake refuse not the face of thine anointed.

11 The Lord hath sworn in truth unto David, and he will not shrink from it, *saying*, Of the fruit of thy body will I set upon thy throne. 12 If thy sons keep my covenant, and my testimonies, that I shall teach them, their sons also shall sit upon thy throne forever. 13 For the Lord hath chosen Zion, *and* loved to dwell in it, *saying*,14 This is my rest forever: here will I dwell, for I have a delight therein. 15 I will surely bless her victuals, *and* will satisfy her poor with bread,16 And will clothe her priests with salvation, and her saints shall shout for joy. 17 There will I make the horn of David to bud: *for* I have ordained a light for mine anointed. 18 His enemies will I clothe with shame, but on him his crown shall flourish.

Chapter 133

A song of degrees or Psalm-chapter *of David.*

1 Behold, how good and how comely a thing it is, brethren to dwell even together. 2 *It is* like to the precious ointment upon the head, that runneth down upon the beard, *even* unto Aaron's beard, which went down on the border of his garments:3 *And* as the dew of Hermon, which falleth upon the mountains of Zion: for there the Lord appointed the blessing *and* life forever.

Chapter 134

A song of degree

1 Behold, praise ye the Lord, all ye servants of the Lord, ye that by night stand in the house of the Lord. 2 Lift up your hands to the sanctuary, and praise the Lord. 3 The Lord, that hath made heaven and earth, bless thee out of Zion.

Chapter 135

Praise ye the Lord.

1 Praise the name of the Lord: ye servants of the Lord, praise *him*. 2 Ye that stand in the house of the Lord, *and* in the courts of the house of our God,3 Praise ye the Lord: for the Lord is good: sing praises unto his name: for it is a comely thing. 4 For the Lord hath chosen Jacob to himself, *and* Israel for his chief treasure. 5 For I know that the Lord *is* great, and that our Lord *is* above all gods. 6 Whatsoever pleased the Lord, that did he in heaven and in earth, in the sea, and in all the depths. 7 He bringeth up the clouds from the ends of the earth, and maketh the lightnings with the rain: he draweth forth the wind out of his treasures. 8 He smote the first born of Egypt both of man and beast. 9 He hath sent tokens and wonders into the midst of thee, O Egypt, upon Pharaoh, and upon all his servants. 10 He smote many nations, and slew mighty Kings: 11 *As* Sihon king of the Amorites, and Og king of Bashan, and all the kingdoms of Canaan:12 And gave their land for an inheritance, *even* an inheritance unto Israel his people. 13 Thy name, O Lord, *endureth* forever: O Lord, thy remembrance *is* from generation to generation. 14 For the Lord will judge his people, and be pacified towards his servants. 15 The idols of the heathen *are* silver and gold, *even* the work of men's hands. 16 They have a mouth, and speak not: they have eyes and see not. 17 They have ears and hear not, neither is there any breath in their mouth. 18 They that make them, are like unto them: *so are* all that trust in them. 19 Praise the Lord, ye house of Israel: praise the Lord, ye house of Aaron. 20 Praise the Lord, ye house of Levi: ye that fear the Lord, praise the Lord. 21 Praised *be* the Lord out of Zion, which dwelleth in Jerusalem. Praise ye the Lord.

Chapter 136

1 Praise ye the Lord, because he is good: for his mercy *endureth* forever. 2 Praise ye the God of gods: for his mercy *endureth* forever. 3 Praise ye the Lord of lords:

for his mercy *endureth* forever:4 Which only doeth great wonders: for his mercy *endureth* forever:5 Which by *his* wisdom made the heavens: for his mercy *endureth* forever:6 Which hath stretched out the earth upon the waters: for his mercy *endureth* forever:7 Which made great lights: for his mercy *endureth* forever:8 *As* the sun to rule the day: for his mercy *endureth* forever: 9 The moon and the stars to govern the night: for his mercy *endureth* forever: 10 Which smote Egypt with their first born (for his mercy *endureth* forever) 11 And brought out Israel from among them (for his mercy *endureth* forever) 12 With a mighty hand and stretched out arm: for his mercy *endureth* forever: 13 Which divided the Red Sea in two parts: for his mercy *endureth* forever: 14 And made Israel to pass through the midst of it: for his mercy *endureth* forever. 15 And overthrew Pharaoh and his host in the Red Sea: for his mercy *endureth* forever:16 Which led his people through the wilderness: for his mercy *endureth* forever:17 Which smote great kings: for his mercy *endureth* forever: 18 And slew mighty kings: for his mercy *endureth* forever: 19 As Sihon king of the Amorites: for his mercy *endureth* forever: 20 And Og the king of Bashan: for his mercy *endureth* forever: 21 And gave their land for an heritage: for his mercy *endureth* forever: 22 *Even* an heritage unto Israel his servant: for his mercy *endureth* forever: 23 Which remembered us in our base estate: for his mercy *endureth* forever: 24 And hath rescued us from our oppressors: for his mercy *endureth* forever: 25 Which giveth food to all flesh: for his mercy *endureth* forever. 26 Praise ye the God of heaven: for his mercy *endureth* forever.

Chapter 137

1 By the rivers of Babylon we sat, and there we wept, when we remembered Zion. 2 We hanged our harps upon the willows in the midst thereof. 3 Then they that led us captives, required of us songs and mirth, when we had hanged up *our harps, saying,* Sing us *one* of the songs of Zion. 4 How shall we sing, *said we,* a song of the Lord in a strange land?5 If I forget thee, O Jerusalem, let my right hand forget *to play.* 6 If I do not remember thee, let my tongue cleave to the roof of my mouth: *yea,* if I prefer not Jerusalem to my chief joy. 7 Remember the children of Edom, O Lord, in the day of Jerusalem, which said, Rase it, rase it to the foundation thereof. 8 O daughter of Babylon, worthy to be destroyed, blessed *shall he be* that rewardeth thee, as thou hast served us. 9 Blessed *shall he be* that taketh and dasheth thy children against the stones.

Chapter 138

A Psalm-chapter *of David.*

1 I will praise thee with my whole heart: *even* before the gods will I praise thee. 2 I will worship toward thine holy temple and praise thy name, because of thy loving kindness and for thy truth: for thou hast magnified thy name above all things by thy word. 3 When I called, then thou heardest me, *and* hast increased strength in my soul. 4 All the kings of the earth shall praise thee, O Lord: for they have heard the words of thy mouth. 5 And they shall sing of the ways of the Lord, because the glory of the Lord *is* great. 6 For the Lord is high: yet he beholdeth the lowly, but the proud he knoweth afar off. 7 Though I walk in the midst of trouble, *yet* wilt thou revive me: thou wilt stretch forth thine hand upon the wrath of mine enemies, and thy right hand shall save me. 8 The Lord will perform *his work* toward me: O Lord, thy mercy *endureth* forever: forsake not the works of thine hands.

Chapter 139

To him that excelleth. A Psalm-chapter of David.

1 O Lord, thou hast tried me and known *me.* 2 Thou knowest my sitting and my rising: thou understandest my thought afar off. 3 Thou compassest my paths, and my lying down, and art accustomed to all my ways. 4 For there is not a word in my tongue, *but* lo, thou knowest it wholly, O Lord. 5 Thou holdest me strait behind and before, and layest thine hand upon me. 6 *Thy* knowledge is too wonderful for me: it is so high that I cannot *attain* unto it. 7 Whither shall I go from thy spirit? Or whither shall I flee from thy presence?8 If I ascend into heaven, thou art there: if I lie down in hell, thou art there. 9 Let me take the wings of the morning, *and* dwell in the uttermost parts of the sea:10 Yet thither shall thine hand lead me, and thy right hand hold me. 11 If I say, Yet the darkness shall hide me, even the night *shall be* light about me. 12 Yea, the darkness hideth not from thee: but the night shineth as the day: the darkness and light are both alike. 13 For thou hast possessed my reins: thou hast covered me in my mother's womb. 14 I will praise thee, for I am fearfully and wondrously made: marvelous *are* thy works, and my soul knoweth it well. 15 My bones are not hid from thee, though I was made in a secret *place, and* fashioned beneath in the earth. 16 Thine eyes did see me, when I was without form: for in thy book were all things written, *which* in continuance were fashioned, when there was none of them *before.* 17 How dear therefore are thy thoughts unto me, O God! How great is the sum of them!18 If I should count them, they are more than the sand: when I wake, I am still with thee. 19 Oh that thou wouldest slay, O God, the wicked and bloody men, *to whom I say,* Depart ye from me:20 Which speak wickedly of thee, *and* being thine enemies are lifted up in vain. 21 Do not I hate them, O Lord, that hate thee? And do not I earnestly contend with those that rise up against thee?22 I hate them with an unfained hatred, as they were mine *utter* enemies. 23 Try me, O God, and know mine heart: prove me and know my thoughts,24 And consider if there be any way of wickedness in me, and lead me in the way forever.

Chapter 140

To him that excelleth. A Psalm-chapter of David.

1 Deliver me, O Lord, from the evil man: preserve me from the cruel man:2 Which imagine evil things in *their* heart, *and* make war continually. 3 They have sharpened their tongues like a serpent: adders' poison *is* under their lips. Selah. 4 Keep me, O Lord, from the hands of the wicked: preserve me from the cruel man, which purposeth to cause my steps to slide. 5 The proud have laid a snare for me, and spread a net with cords in my pathway, *and* set gins for me. Selah. 6 *Therefore* I said unto the Lord, Thou art my God: hear, O Lord, the voice of my prayers. 7 O Lord God the strength of my salvation, thou hast covered mine head in the day of battle. 8 Let not the wicked have his desire, O Lord: perform not his wicked thought, *lest* they be proud. Selah. 9 *As for* the chief of them, that compass me about, let the mischief of their own lips come upon them. 10 Let coals fall upon them: let him cast them into the fire, *and* into the deep pits, that they rise not. 11 *For* the backbiters shall not be established upon the earth: evil shall hunt the cruel man to destruction. 12 I know that the Lord will avenge the afflicted, *and* judge the poor. 13 Surely the righteous shall praise thy name, *and* the just shall dwell in thy presence.

Chapter 141

A Psalm-chapter of David.

1 O Lord, I call upon thee: haste thee unto me: hear my voice, when I cry unto thee. 2 Let my prayer be directed in thy sight *as* incense, *and* the lifting up of mine hands *as* an evening sacrifice. 3 Set a watch, O Lord, before my mouth, *and* keep the door of my lips. 4 Incline not mine heart to evil, that I should commit wicked works with men that work iniquity: and let me not eat of their delicates. 5 Let the righteous smite me: *for that is* a benefit: and let him reprove me, *and it shall be* a precious oil, that shall not break mine head: for within a while I shall even pray in their miseries. 6 When their judges shall be cast down in stony places, they shall hear my words, for they are sweet. 7 Our bones lie scattered at the grave's mouth, as he that heweth *wood* or diggeth in the earth. 8 But mine eyes *look* unto thee, O Lord God: in thee is my trust: leave not my soul destitute. 9 Keep me from the snare, *which* they have laid for me, and from the gins of the workers of iniquity. 10 Let the wicked fall into his nets together, whiles I escape.

Chapter 142

A Psalm-chapter *of David, to give instruction, and a prayer, when he was in the cave.*

1 I cried unto the Lord with my voice: with my voice I prayed unto the Lord. 2 I poured out my meditation before him, *and* declared mine affliction in his presence. 3 Though my spirit was in perplexity in me, yet thou knewest my path: in the way, wherein I walked, have they privily laid a snare for me. 4 I looked upon my right hand, and beheld, but there was none that would know me: all refuge failed me, *and* none cared for my soul. 5 *Then* cried I unto thee, O Lord, *and* said, Thou art mine hope, *and* my portion in the land of the living. 6 Hearken unto my cry, for I am brought very low: deliver me from my persecutors, for they are too strong for me. 7 Bring my soul out of prison, that I may praise thy name: *then* shall the righteous come about me, when thou art beneficial unto me.

Chapter 143

A Psalm-chapter of David.

1 Hear my prayer, O Lord, *and* hearken unto my supplication: answer me in thy truth *and* in thy righteousness. 2 (And enter not into judgment with thy servant: for in thy sight shall none that liveth, be justified)3 For the enemy hath persecuted my soul: he hath smitten my life down to the earth: he hath laid me in the darkness, as they that have been dead long ago:4 And my spirit was in perplexity in me, *and* mine heart within me was amassed. 5 *Yet* do I remember the time past: I meditate in all thy works, *yea*, I do meditate in the works of thine hands. 6 I stretch forth mine hands unto thee: my soul desireth after thee, as the thirsty land. Selah. 7 Hear me speedily, O Lord, *for* my spirit faileth: hide not thy face from me, else I shall be like unto them that go down into the pit. 8 Let me hear thy loving kindness in the morning, for in thee is my trust: show me the way, that I should walk in, for I lift up my soul unto thee. 9 Deliver me, O Lord, from mine enemies: *for* I hid me with thee. 10 Teach me to do thy will, for thou art my God: let thy good spirit lead me unto the land of righteousness. 11 Quicken me, O Lord, for thy name's sake, *and* for thy righteousness bring my soul out of trouble. 12 And for thy mercy slay mine enemies, and destroy all them that oppress my soul: for I am thy servant.

Chapter 144

A Psalm-chapter *of David.*

1 Blessed *be* the Lord my strength, which teacheth mine hands to fight, *and* my fingers to battle. 2 *He is* my goodness and my fortress, my tower and my deliverer, my shield, and in him I trust, which subdueth my people under me. 3 Lord, what is man that thou regardest him! *Or* the son of man that thou thinkest upon him!4 Man is like to vanity: his days *are* like a shadow, that vanisheth. 5 Bow thine heavens, O Lord, and come down: touch the mountains and they shall smoke. 6 Cast forth the lightning and scatter them: shoot out thine arrows, and consume them. 7 Send thine hand from above: deliver me, and take me out of the great waters, *and* from the hand of strangers,8 Whose mouth talketh vanity, and their right hand *is* a right hand of falsehood. 9 I will sing a new song unto thee, O God, *and* sing unto thee upon a viol, *and* an instrument of ten strings. 10 *It is he* that giveth deliverance unto kings, *and* rescueth David his servant from the hurtful sword. 11 Rescue me, and deliver me from the hand of strangers, whose mouth talketh vanity, and their right hand *is* a right hand of falsehood:12 That our sons *may be* as the plants growing up in their youth, *and* our daughters as the corner *stones*, graven after the similitude of a palace:13 That our corners *may be* full, *and* abounding with divers sorts, *and* that our sheep may bring forth thousands and ten thousand in our streets:14 That our oxen may be strong to labor: that there be none invasion, nor going out, nor no crying in our streets. 15 Blessed *are* the people, that be so, *yea*, blessed *are* the people, whose God is the Lord.

Chapter 145

A Psalm-chapter *of David of Praise.*

1 O my God *and* King, I will extol thee, and will bless thy name forever and ever. 2 I will bless thee daily, and praise thy name forever and ever. 3 Great *is* the Lord, and most worthy to be praised, and his greatness *is* incomprehensible. 4 Generation shall praise thy works unto generation, and declare thy power. 5 I will meditate of the beauty of thy glorious majesty, and thy wonderful works,6 And they shall speak of the power of thy fearful acts, and I will declare thy greatness. 7 They shall break out into the mention of thy great goodness, and shall sing aloud of thy righteousness. 8 The Lord is gracious and merciful, slow to anger, and of great mercy. 9 The Lord is good to all, and his mercies *are* over all his works. 10 All thy works praise thee, O Lord, and thy saints bless thee. 11 They show the glory of thy kingdom and speak of thy power,12 To cause his power to be known to the sons of men, and the glorious renown of his kingdom. 13 Thy kingdom *is* an everlasting kingdom, and thy dominion *endureth* throughout all ages. 14 The Lord upholdeth all that fall, and lifteth up all that are ready to fall. 15 The eyes of all wait upon thee, and thou givest them their meat in due season. 16 Thou openest thine hand, and fillest all things living of *thy* good pleasure. 17 The Lord *is* righteous in all his ways, and holy in all his works. 18 The Lord *is* near unto all that call upon him: *yea*, to all that call upon him in truth. 19 He will fulfill the desire of them that fear him: he also will hear their cry, and will save them. 20 The Lord preserveth all them that love him: but he will destroy all the wicked. 21 My mouth shall speak the praise of the Lord, and all flesh shall bless his holy Name forever and ever.

Chapter 146

Praise ye the Lord.

1 Praise thou the Lord, O my soul. 2 I will praise the Lord during my life: as long as I have any being, I will sing unto my God. 3 Put not your trust in princes, *nor* in the

son of man, for there is none help in him. 4 His breath departeth, *and* he returneth to his earth: then his thoughts perish. 5 Blessed *is* he, that hath the God of Jacob for his help, whose hope *is* in the Lord his God. 6 Which made heaven and earth, the sea, and all that therein is: which keepeth *his* fidelity forever:7 Which executeth justice for the oppressed: which giveth bread to the hungry: the Lord looseth the prisoners. 8 The Lord giveth sight to the blind: the Lord raiseth up the crooked: the Lord loveth the righteous. 9 The Lord keepeth the strangers: he relieveth the fatherless and widow: but he overthroweth the way of the wicked. 10 The Lord shall reign forever: O Zion, thy God *endureth* from generation to generation. Praise ye the Lord.

Chapter 147

1 Praise ye the Lord, for it is good to sing unto our God: for it is a pleasant thing, *and* praise is comely. 2 The Lord doth build up Jerusalem, *and* gather together the dispersed of Israel. 3 He healeth those that are broken in heart, and bindeth up their sores. 4 He counteth the number of the stars, *and* calleth them all by their names. 5 Great *is* our Lord, and great *is his* power: his wisdom is infinite. 6 The Lord relieveth the meek, *and* abaseth the wicked to the ground. 7 Sing unto the Lord with praise: sing upon the harp unto our God,8 Which covereth the heaven with clouds, and prepareth rain for the earth, and maketh the grass to grow upon the mountains:9 Which giveth to beasts their food, *and* to the young ravens that cry. 10 He hath not pleasure in the strength of an horse, neither delighteth he in the legs of man. 11 *But* the Lord delighteth in them that fear him, and attend upon his mercy. 12 Praise the Lord, O Jerusalem: praise thy God, O Zion. 13 For he hath made the bars of thy gates strong, *and* hath blessed thy children within thee. 14 He setteth peace in thy borders, *and* satisfieth thee with the flour of wheat. 15 He sendeth forth his commandment upon earth, *and* his word runneth very swiftly. 16 He giveth snow like wool, *and* scattereth the hoarfrost like ashes. 17 He casteth forth his ice like morsels: who can abide the cold thereof?18 He sendeth his word and melteth them: he causeth his wind to blow, *and* the waters flow. 19 He showeth his word unto Jacob, his statutes and *his* judgments unto Israel. 2 He hath not dealt so with every nation, neither have they known *his* judgments. Praise ye the Lord.

Chapter 148

Praise ye the Lord.
1 Praise ye the Lord from the heaven: praise ye him in the high places. 2 Praise ye him, all ye his angels: praise him, all his army. 3 Praise ye him, sun and moon: praise ye him all bright stars. 4 Praise ye him, heavens of heavens, and waters, that be above the heavens. 5 Let them praise the name of the Lord: for he commanded, and they were created. 6 And he hath established them forever and ever: he hath made an ordinance, which shall not pass. 7 Praise ye the Lord from the earth, *ye* dragons and all depths:8 Fire and hail, snow and vapors, stormy wind, which execute his word:9 Mountains and all hills, fruitful trees and all cedars:10 Beasts and all cattle, creeping things and feathered fouls: 11 Kings of the earth and all people, princes and all judges of the world:12 Young men and maidens, also old men and children:13 Let them praise the name of the Lord: for his name only is to be exalted, *and* his praise above the earth and the heavens. 14 For he hath exalted the horn of his people, *which is* a praise for all his saints, *even* for the children of Israel, a people *that is* near unto him. Praise ye the Lord.

Chapter 149

Praise ye the Lord.
1 Sing ye unto the Lord a new song: let his praise *be heard* in the congregation of saints. 2 Let Israel rejoice in him that made him, and let the children of Zion rejoice in their King. 3 Let them praise his name with the flute: let them sing praises unto him with the timbrel and harp. 4 For the Lord hath pleasure in his people: he will make the meek glorious by deliverance. 5 Let the saints be joyful with glory: let them sing loud upon their beds. 6 Let the high acts of God be in their mouth, and a two edged sword in their hands,7 To execute vengeance upon the heathen, *and* corrections among the people:8 To bind their kings in chains, and their nobles with fetters of iron,9 That they may execute upon them the judgment that is written: this honor shall be to all his saints. Praise ye the Lord.

Chapter 150

Praise ye the Lord.
1 Praise ye God in his sanctuary: praise ye him in the firmament of his power. 2 Praise ye him in his mighty acts: praise ye him according to his excellent greatness. 3 Praise ye him in the sound of the trumpet: praise ye him upon the viol and the harp. 4 Praise ye him with timbrel and flute: praise ye him with virginals and organs. 5 Praise ye him with sounding cymbals: praise ye him with high sounding cymbals. 6 Let every thing that hath breath praise the Lord. Praise ye the Lord.

PROVERBS

CHAPTER 1

1 The parables of Solomon, son of Dauid, king of Israel, 2 to know wisdom and instruction, to understand the words of knowledge, 3 to receive instruction to act wisely, with justice, judgment and equity, 4 to give to the simple a sharpness of mind, and to children knowl- edge and discretion. 5 A wise man will listen and increase his learning, and an intelligent man will devote himself to wise counsel, 6 understanding parables and their interpre- tation, the words of the wise and their dark speeches. 7 The fear of the Lord is the begin- ning of knowledge, but fools despise wisdom and instruction. 8 My son, listen to the in- struction of your fathers and do not forsake the teaching of your mothers. 9 For they will be a beautiful ornament for your head and as chains for your neck. 10 Son, if sinners mock you, do not acquiesce. 11 If they say, "Come with us, we will wait for blood and take care of the innocent without cause." 12 We will swal- low them up as a whole grave, as those who go down into the pit: 13 We will find all the most precious riches, and fill our houses with spices: 14 Cast thy lot among them: we shall all have one purse: 15 My son, walk not in the way with them; turn away thy foot from their path. 16 For their feet run to hell, and they make haste to shed blood. 17 Surely, as with- out cause, the net is spread before the eyes of all who have wings: 18 Thus they wait for blood and lie in wait for their life. 19 These are the ways of everyone who is greedy for gain: he wants to take the life of those who possess it. 20 Wisdome cries out without knowledge, and moves through the streets. 21 He calls in the main streets, among the preases at the entrance of the gates, and speaks his words in the city, saying, 22 O fools, how long will you enjoy foolishness, while scorners delight in scorn and fools hate knowledge? 23 (Turn to my correction; behold, I will expound my mind to you and make you understand my words). 24 For I called, and ye

refused: I stretched forth my hand, and none would answer. 25 But ye have despised all my counsel, and have not desired my correction. 26 I will also laugh at your destruction and mock at your fear. 27 When your fear shall come like a sudden desolation, and your destruction shall come like a whirlwind; when affliction and distress shall come upon you, 28 then they will call upon me, but I will not answer; they will soon seek me, but they will not find me, 29 because they have hated knowledge and have not chosen the fear of the LORD. 30 They have not wanted my counsel and have despised all my correction. 31 Therefore they shall eat of the fruit of their ways and be satis- fied with their deviations. 32 For ease kills the foolish, and the prosperity of fools destroys them. 33 But those who obey me will dwell safely and be quiet from the fear of ease.

CHAPTER 2

1 My son, if you will receive my words and hide my commands within you, 2 let your ears hear wisdom and incline your heart to under- standing, 3 for if you seek knowledge and invoke intelligence: 4 if you seek it as silence and seek it as treasure, 5 then you will under- stand the fear of the Lord and find the knowl- edge of God. 6 For the LORD giveth wisdom, out of his mouth cometh knowledge and un- derstanding. 7 He preserves the state of the righteous; he is a shield for those who walk uprightly, 8 that they may observe the ways of judgment; and he preserves the way of his saints). 9 Then you will understand righ- teousness, judgment, equity and every good path. 10 When wisdom shall enter your heart and knowledge shall delimit your soul, 11 then counsel will protect you and intelligence will guard you, 12 and will deliver you from the evil way and from the man who speaks un- wise things, 13 and from those who forsake the ways of righteousness to walk in the ways of darkness: 14 Who strive to do good and de- light in the aversion of the ungodly, 15 whose ways are crooked and whose paths are crook- ed. 16 He will deliver you from the foreign woman, from the stranger who flatters with her words. 17 Who forsakes the guidance of her youth and forgets the counsel of her God. 18 Her house tends to death, and her paths to death. 19 Everyone who goes to her never comes back, and does not take up the ways of life again. 20 Walk therefore in the way of the good, and follow the paths of the righteous. 21 For the righteous shall dwell in the land, and the upright men shall abide there. 22 But the wicked shall be removed from the land, and the transgressors shall be uprooted from it.

CHAPTER 3

1 My son, do not forget my word, but let your heart follow my commands. 2 For they will increase the length of your days, the years of your life, and your prosperity. 3 Do not let mercy and truth leave you; wear them on your neck and write them on the table of your heart. 4 Thus you will find prosperity and un- derstanding before God and men. 5 Trust in the Lord with all your heart and do not rely on your own wisdom. 6 In all your ways ac- knowledge him, and he will direct your ways. 7 Do not be wise in your own eyes, but fear the LORD and turn away from wickedness. 8 So health shall be to your body, and health to your bones. 9 Honor the LORD with your rich- es and with the first fruits of all your crops. 10 So your barns will be full of abundance and your winepresses will burst with new wine. 11 My son, do not

reject the chastisement of the LORD and do not chafe at his correction. 12 For the Lord corrects the one he loves, as the father does to the son in whom he delights. 13 Blessed is the man who finds wisdom and the man who obtains understanding. 14 For its merchandise is better than silk goods, and its value is better than gold. 15 She is more pre- cious than pearls; and all the things you can desire are not comparable to her. 16 The length of days is in her right hand, and riches and glory in her left hand. 17 Her ways are ways of pleasure, and all her paths prosperity. 18 She is a tree of life for those who give themselves up to her, and blessed is he who keeps her. 19 By his wisdom the LORD has laid the founda- tions of the earth and established the heavens with understanding. 20 By his wisdom the depths have been broken, and the clouds let the dew fall. 21 My son, do not let these things depart from your eyes, but observe wisdom and counsel. 22 Thus they will be life for your soul and grace for your neck. 23 Then thou shalt walk safely on thy way, and thy foot shall not stumble. 24 If thou sleepest, thou shalt not be distressed, and when thou sleepest, thy sleep shall be sweet. 25 Thou shalt not fear for any sudden fear, nor for the destruction of the wicked when it comes. 26 For the LORD will be your security and will preserve your body from death. 27 Do not deny the good to its owners, even though you have the power to do so. 28 Do not say to your neighbor, "Go and come again, and I will give you grain, if you have it now." 29 Do not harm your neighbor, since he dwells without fear from you. 30 Do not strike a man because of a cause, when he has done you no harm. 31 Do not be envious of the wicked man or follow his ways. 32 For insult is an abomination to the LORD, but his secret is with the righteous. 33 The curse of the LORD is in the house of the wicked, but he blesses the dwelling place of the righteous. 34 He despises the scornful, but gives grace to the humble. 35 The wise shall inherit glo- ry, but the foolish dishonor, though they are exalted.

CHAPTER 4

1 Listen, O children, to the instruction of a father and set yourselves to learn to un- derstand. 2 For I give you good doctrine; do not forsake my word. 3 For I was my father's son, tender and weak in my mother's eyes, 4 when he instructed me and said to me, "Let your heart hold fast my words; observe my commands and you shall live." 5 Become wise, become knowledgeable; do not forget or for- sake the words of my mouth. 6 Do not forsake her, and she will guard you; love her, and she will protect you. 7 Wisdom is the beginning; therefore become wise and on all your pos- sessions seek to understand. 8 Exalt her and she will exalt you; she will bring you honor if you embrace her. 9 She shall give thee a fair ornament upon thy head; yea, she shall give thee a crown of glory. 10 Listen, my son, and receive my words, and the years of your life will be many. 11 I have taught you the way of wisdom and guided you in the paths of righ- teousness. 12 When you go, your door will not be narrow, and when you run, you will not fall. 13 Take instruction in your hand and do not leave it; guard it, for it is your life. 14 Do not enter the way of the wicked, and do not walk in the way of wicked men. 15 Do not walk in it and do not pass through it; turn away from it and pass over it. 16 For they cannot sleep unless they have done good, and their sleep is gone unless they bring someone down. 17 For they eat the beer of wickedness and drink the wine of violence. 18 But the way of the righteous shines as the light, shining more and more until the perfect day. 19

The way of the wicked is like darkness: they do not know where they will fall. 20 My son, listen to my words, incline your ear to my speeches. 21 Do not turn them away from your eyes, but keep them in the depths of your heart. 22 For they are life to those who find them and health to all their flesh. 23 Guard your heart with all diligence, for from there comes life. 24 Turn away from you the adverse mouth, and turn away from you the evil lips. 25 Let thine eyes look on the good, and let thine eyelids direct thy way before thee. 26 Ponder the path of thy feet, and order all thy steps well. 27 Turn nei- ther to the right nor to the left, but turn away thy foot from above.

CHAPTER 5

1 My son, listen to my wisdom and incline your eyes toward my knowledge. 2 That you may heed counsel, and your lips may observe knowledge. 3 For the lips of a strange woman fall as an honest robe, and her mouth is soft- er than oil. 4 But her extremity is bitter as a worm and sharp as a two-edged sword. 5 His feet go down to death, and his steps stop in hell. 6 He does not know the way of life; his paths are changeable, and you cannot know them. 7 Hear me therefore, O children, and do not turn away from the words of my mouth. 8 Turn away from her and do not approach her house, 9 if you will not give your honor to others and your years to those who are cruel: 10 let not the stranger be satiated with your strength, and let your labors be in the house of a stranger, 11 and thou shalt grieve at thy end (when thou hast consumed thy flesh and thy body) 12 And thou shalt say, "How I have hated instruction, and my heart has despised correction! 13 I did not obey the sight of those who instructed me, and I did not bend my ear to those who instructed me! 14 I was al- most brought to confusion in the midst of the congregation and the assembly. 15 Drink the water of your cisterns and riuers from the bowels of your well. 16 Let thy fountains flow into the valley, and the rivulets of water into the streets. 17 But let them be yours, yours alone, and not of strangers with you. 18 Bless- ed be thy fountain, and take back the wife of thy youth. 19 Let her be like a strong back and a pleasant roebuck; let her sterns satisfy you at all times, and let her delight you continu- ally with her beauty. 20 Why should you de- light yourself, my son, with a strange woman or embrace the breasts of a stranger? 21 For man's deeds are under the eyes of the LORD, who examines all his paths. 22 His own iniq- uities shall take the wicked man himself, and he shall be held with the cords of his own sin. 23 He shall die by instruction and go astray by his own great folly.

CHAPTER 6

1 My son, if you make yourself a surety for your neighbor and have clasped hands with the stranger, 2 you are entangled with the words of your own mouth; you are also caught with the words of your own mouth. 3 Do this, my son, and deliver yourself; since you have fallen into the hands of your neigh- bor, go away, humble yourself and solicit your friends. 4 Give not sleep to thine eyes, and slumber not thine eyelids. 5 Restrain thyself like a doe from the hand of the hunter, and like a bird from the hand of the one who soils it. 6 Go to the fishmonger, O snail; watch his moves and be wise. 7 For he has neither guide, nor warrior, nor ruler, 8 she prepares her meat in the afternoon and gathers her food in the night. 9 How long will you sleep, O

snail, when you rise from your sleep? 10 Still a little sleep, a little slumber, a little folding of the hands to sleep. 11 Therefore thy anx- iety cometh as one that moveth by the way, and thy necessity as an armed man. 12 The vilified man and the wicked man walks with a frowning mouth. 13 He makes signs with his eyes, he makes signs with his feet, he in- structs with his fingers. 14 His heart is full of backbiting; he always imagines evil and raises contentions. 15 Therefore his destruction will come quickly; he will be destroyed sudden- ly, with no chance of recovery. 16 These six things the LORD hates; yea, his mind abhors them all: 17 The grim eyes, the lying tongue, and the hands that shed innocent blood, 18 a heart that imagines evil deeds, feet that run swiftly to evil, 19 a false witness who tells lies and one who fuels strife among brothers. 20 My son, observe your father's commands and do not forsake your mother's teachings. 21 Keep them always on your heart and tied around your neck. 22 He will guide you when you walk, watch for you when you sleep, and when you wake up, he will speak to you. 23 For commandment is a lantern and instruction a light; and corrections for instruction are the way of life, 24 to keep thee from the wicked woman, and from the flattery of a foreign woman's tongue. 25 Do not covet her beauty in your heart, and do not be taken in by her eyelids. 26 For because of the whore woman a man is reduced to a morsel of bread, and a woman goes after a man's precious life. 27 Can a man take fire in his bosom, and his gar- ments not be burned? 28 Or can a man go to the coals, and his feet not be burned? 29 So whoever enters his neighbor's wife will not be innocent, whoever touches her. 30 Men do not despise a thief, when he steals, to satisfy his soul, because he is hungry. 31 But if he is found, he must return his money or give all the wealth of his house. 32 But he who com- mits adultery with a woman is devoid of intel- ligence; he who does so destroys his own soul. 33 He shall be found wounded and dishon- ored, and his reproach shall never be blotted out. 34 Because jealousy is the anger of man, he will not spare in the day of vengeance. 35 He cannot bear the sight of any havoc; he will not consent, though you increase the gifts.

CHAPTER 7

1 My son, keep my words and hide my com- mands with you. 2 Observe my commands and you shall live, and my teachings as the apple of your eye. 3 Bind them to your fingers and write them on the table of your heart. 4 Say to the wise, "You are my sister," and call your kinswoman "intelligence."5 That they may keep thee from the strange woman and the stranger who is sweet in her words. 6 As I stood at the window of my house, I looked through my window, 7 I saw among the fool- ish, and considered among the children a young man devoid of understanding, 8 Who passed through the street at his corner and went to his house, 9 In the twilight of dawn, when the night was beginning to be dark and gloomy. 10 And behold, there came to him a woman with a harlot's demeanor and a thin heart. 11 She is a woman who stutters and makes noise, whose feet cannot stand in her house. 12 Now she is outside, now in the streets, and lies in wait at every corner). 13 Then she took him, kissed him, and with an impudent face said to him 14 I have offers of peace; today I have paid my vows. 15 Therefore I went out to meet you, to see your face, and I found you. 16 I have adorned my bed with ornaments, carpets and laces of Egypt. 17 I have perfumed my bed with myrrh, aloes and cinnamon. 18 Come, let us

be filled with joy until the morning, let us enjoy pleasure in joy. 19 For my husband is not at home; he has gone on a far journey. 20 He has taken a sack of silk with him and will return home at the appointed day. 21 So with her great guile she induced him to yield, and with her flattering lips she enticed him. 22 And he followed his straight ways, like an ox going to slaughter, and like a bird going to be corrected, 23 until a dart pierced his side, like a bird hurrying to the trap, not knowing that he was in danger. 24 Hear me therefore, O children, and heed the words of my mouth. 25 Do not abandon your heart to his ways, do not wander in his paths. 26 For she has brought down many wounded, and the strong have all been slain by her. 27 Her house is the way that leads to the grave and leads to the chambers of death.

CHAPTER 8

1 Does not wisdom cry out, and is not un- derstanding its sign? 2 It stands on the top of the heights, along the road, in the place of the paths. 3 It cries out at the gates, before the city, at the entrance of the streets, 4 "O men, I call to you, and convey my message to the sons of men. 5 O foolish men, understand wisdom, and you fools, be wise in heart. 6 Take heed, for I will speak excellent things, and the opening of my mouth will teach right things. 7 For my mouth shall speak true things, and my lips shall abhor wickedness. 8 All the words of my mouth are upright; there is neither malice nor wickedness in them. 9 They are all clear for those who want to under- stand and clear for those who want to know. 10 Receive my instruction, and not silence, and knowledge rather than precious money. 11 For wisdom is better than precious stones, and all pleasures are not comparable to her. 12 Wisdom dwells with prudence, and I find knowledge and counsel. 13 The fear of the LORD consists in hating elation, like pride, arrogance and indolence; and a mouth that speaks lying things I hate. 14 I have coun- sel and wisdom: I am intelligent and have strength. 15 By me kings rule, and princes decree justice. 16 By me the princes and the nobles and all the judges of the earth rule. 17 I love those who love me, and those who see me closely will find me. 18 Riches and honors are with me, and also lasting riches and justice. 19 My fruits are better than gold, indeed than fine gold, and my earnings are better than fine silicon. 20 I make them walk in the way of righteousness and in the midst of the paths of judgment, 21 That those who love me may inherit goods and I may fill their treasures. 22 The LORD possessed me in the beginning of his way: I preceded his works of old. 23 I was created from eternity, from the begin- ning and before the earth. 24 When there were no depths, I was begotten, when there were no abundant springs of water. 25 Before the mountains were set, and before the hills, I was begotten. 26 He had not yet made the earth, nor the open places, nor the height of the dust of the world. 27 When he prepared the heavens, I was there, when he set the ta- ble on the depths. 28 When he established the clouds, when he confirmed the springs of the deep, 29 when he gave his decree to the sea, that the waters might not pass his command; when he established the foundations of the earth, 30 then was I with him as a sustenance, and was daily his delight, always before him, 31 and I found my comfort in the compen- dium of his land; and my delight is with the sons of men. 32 Therefore now listen to me, my children, for blessed are those who follow my ways. 33 Hear instruction, be wise and do not reject it; blessed is the man who hears me, keeping watch daily at

my gates and at- tending the posts of my places. 34 For he who finds me finds life, and will obey the sorrow of the LORD. 35 But he who sins against me, wounds his own soul; and everyone who hates me, loves death.

CHAPTER 9

1 Wisdom has built her house and erected her pillars. 2 He has killed his vines, drunk his wine, and prepared his table. 3 He has sent forth his majesties and cries on the highest places of the city, saying, "Who is so simple? 4 "Let him who is simple come here," and to him who lacks wisdom he says, "Come and eat." 5 Come, eat my flesh and drink the wine that I have drunk. 6 Abandon your way, you fools, and die, and walk in the way of understand- ing. 7 He who rebukes a scorner, acquires for himself shame; and he who rebukes the wick- ed, acquires a stain. 8 Do not rebuke a scorn- er, lest he hate you; but rebuke a wise man, and he will appreciate you. 9 Admonish the wise man, and he will be wiser; teach a righ- teous man, and he will increase his learning. 10 The principle of wisdom is the fear of the LORD, and the knowledge of holy things is understanding. 11 For your days shall be mul- tiplied by me, and the years of your life shall increase. 12 If you are wise, you will be wise for yourself; if you are scornful, you will suffer alone. 13 A foolish woman is troublesome; she is ignorant and knows nothing. 14 But she sits at the entrance of her house, on a seat, in the squares of the city, 15 To call those who pass by in the street, who go straight on their way, saying, 16 He that is so simple, come hither; and to him that lacketh wisdom, she saith also, 17 The water that gushes forth is sweet, and the hidden bread is pleasant. 18 But he knows not that there are the dead there, and that his deeds are in the depths of hell.

CHAPTER 10

The Parables Of Solomon

1 A wise son makes his father happy, but a foolish son is a misfortune to his mother. 2 The treasures of wickedness profit nothing, but righteousness turns away death. 3 The LORD does not starve the soul of the righ- teous, but throws away the substance of the wicked. 4 A careless hand makes poor, but the hand of the diligent makes rich. 5 He who gathers in his leisure is a child of wisdom, but he who sleeps in his leisure is a child of confusion. 6 Blessing is on the head of the righteous, but iniquity is on the mouth of the wicked. 7 The memory of the righteous will be blessed, but the name of the wicked will rot. 8 The wise of heart will receive commands, but the foolish of speech will be defeated. 9 He who walks uprightly, walks boldly; but he who perturbs his ways, he will be known. 10 He who winks with his eyes, does evil, and he who is foolish in speech, will be defeated. 11 The mouth of a righteous man is a fountain of life, but the mouth of the wicked is full of iniquity. 12 Hatred foments strife, but good- ness makes up for all faults. 13 In the lips of those who have intelligence is wisdom, while the rod will be for the back of those who lack wisdom. 14 The wise put forth knowledge, but the mouth of the vulgar is a present de- struction. 15 The wealthy man's possessions are his strong city, but the fear of the needy is his strength. 16 The work of the righteous

tends to life, but the gain of the wicked leads to sin. 17 He who has regard for instruction is in the way of life; but he who refuses cor- rection goes out of the way. 18 He who dis- simulates hatred with lying lips, and he who induces absurdity, is an impostor. 19 In many words there can be no lack of iniquity, but he who upbraids his lies is wise. 20 The tongue of the righteous man is like a fine silence, but the heart of the wicked is worth little. 21 The lips of the righteous feed many, but the fool- ish will die for lack of wisdom. 22 The blessing of the LORD makes rich, and he adds no sor- row to it. 23 For a man it is like a pastime to do wickedness, but wisdom is understanding for man. 24 What the wicked man fears will come upon him, but God will grant the desire of the righteous. 25 As the whirlwind passes away, so the wicked is no more, but the righteous is like an eternal foundation. 26 As wine is to the teeth, and as smoke to the eyes, so is the evil one to those who send him. 27 The fear of the LORD increases the days, but the years of the wicked decrease. 28 The patient abid- ing of the righteous will be a joy, but the hope of the wicked will perish. 29 The way of the LORD is strength to the upright man, but the workers of iniquity will be afraid. 30 The righ- teous shall never be removed, but the wick- ed shall not dwell in the land. 31 The mouth of the righteous shall be fruitful in wisdom, but the tongue of the miser shall be cut off. 32 The lips of the righteous shall know what is acceptable, but the mouth of the wicked shall speak spurious things.

CHAPTER 11

1 False scales are an abomination to the LORD, but a perfect weight pleases him. 2 When pride comes, shame also comes; but the humble is wise. 3 The righteousness of the righteous will guide them, but the ab- horrence of transgressors will destroy them. 4 Riches do not help in the day of wrath, but righteousness delivers from death. 5 The righteousness of the righteous directs his way, but the wicked falls in his own wicked- ness. 6 The righteousness of the righteous will deliver them, but the transgressors will be caught up in their wickedness. 7 When an ungodly man dies, his hope perishes, and the hope of the unrighteous perishes. 8 The righ- teous man escapes trouble, while the wicked man comes into his own trouble. 9 The hyp- ocrite with his mouth hurts his neighbor, but the righteous will be delivered from knowl- edge. 10 When the righteous prosper, the city recovers, while when the wicked perish, there is joy. 11 The blessing of the righteous exalts the city, while the mouth of the wicked subdues it. 12 He who despises his neighbor is devoid of wisdom, but the man of sense abides in silence. 13 He who goes about like a backbiter reveals a secret, but he who has a faithful heart conceals a matter. 14 Where there is no counsel, the people fall; but where there are many counselors, there is health. 15 He who is secure for a stranger will be greatly vexed, while he who hates security is secure. 16 A gentle woman earns honor, while strong men earn riches. 17 He who is merciful re- wards his own soul; but he who grieves for his own flesh is cruel. 18 The wicked do a deceit- ful work, but he who sows righteously will re- ceive a sure reward. 19 As righteousness leads to life, so he who follows lawlessness seeks his own death. 20 Those with an adverse heart are in abomination to the LORD, but those who are righteous in their way are his delight. 21 Though ioyne in hand, the wicked shall not be punished, but the offspring of the righ- teous shall escape. 22 As a jewel of gold in the snout of a swine, so is a fair woman who lacks discretion. 23 The desire of the righteous is only good, but the hope of the wicked is in- dignation. 24 There are those who scatter and increase; but he who saves more than is righteous goes into a crisis. 25 The free per- son shall have abundance; and he who waters, shall also have raina. 26 He who withdraws the horn, the people shall curse him; but blessing shall be on the head of him who sells the horn. 27 He who seeks good, shall obtain evil; but he who seeks good, shall obtain it. 28 He who trusts in his riches will fall; but the righteous will flourish like a plant. 29 He who cares for his house will inherit the wind, and the earth will be the servant of the wise in heart. 30 The fruit of the righteous is like a tree of life, and he who wins souls is wise. 31 Behold, the righteous shall be rewarded in the earth; how much more the wicked and the sinner?

CHAPTER 12

1 He who loves instruction, loves knowledge; but he who hates correction, is an impostor. 2 The good man obtains favor with the LORD, but the man who has evil imaginations will condemn him. 3 Wickedness cannot establish a man, but the root of the righteous will never be affected. 4 A righteous woman is the feath- er in her husband's cap, but the one who puts him to shame is like corruption in his bones. 5 The thoughts of the righteous are right, but the counsel of the wicked is deceitful. 6 The wicked speak to wait for blood, but the mouth of the righteous will destroy them. 7 God casts out the wicked and they are not there, but the house of the righteous will stand. 8 A man will be praised for his wisdom, but the miser in heart will be despised. 9 He who is despised and is his own servant is better than he who boasts and has no bread. 10 The righ- teous man cherishes the life of his beast, but the mercy of the wicked is cruel. 11 He who cultivates his land will be satisfied with bread, but he who follows idleness is devoid of un- derstanding. 12 The wicked man desires a net of elation, but the root of the righteous pro- duces fruit. 13 The wicked man is trapped by the wickedness of his lips, but the righteous will come out of aduersity. 14 A man will be satisfied with good things by the fruit of his mouth, and the reward of his hands God will give him. 15 The way of a fowl is right in his eyes, but he who listens to counsel is wise. 16 A man in a day will be recognized by his wrath, but he who can recognize shame is wise. 17 He who speaks truthfully is righteous, but a false witness is a deceiver. 18 There are those who speak words like the sting of a sword, but the tongue of the wise is sound. 19 The lip of truth is stable forever, but a lying tongue varies un- controllably. 20 Deception is in the hearts of those who imagine that they are wicked, but counselors of peace will be useful. 21 There is no iniquity for the righteous, but the wick- ed are full of iniquity. 22 Lying lips are an abomination to the LORD, but those who act honestly are his delight. 23 The wise conceal knowledge, but the hearts of fools make fool- ishness public. 24 The hand of the diligent shall be dominant, but the idle shall be under tribute. 25 The wickedness in a man's heart brings him down, but a good word heals him. 26 The righteous is more excellent than his neighbor, but the way of the wicked deceives them. 27 The deceitful man does not roast, if he goes after the chase; but the riches of the diligent man are precious. 28 Life is in the way of righteousness, and in that way there is no death.

CHAPTER 13

1 A wise son will obey his father's instruction, but a scornful one will not listen to rebuke. 2 A man will eat good things with the fruit of his mouth, but the soul of transgressors will suf- fer violence. 3 He who keeps his mouth shut shall preserve his life; but he who opens his lips shall be destroyed. 4 The sluggard covets, but his soul has nothing; but the soul of the diligent shall have abundance. 5 The righteous hates lying words, but the wicked causes slan- der and shame. 6 Righteousness preserves the righteous from life, but wickedness drives out the sinner. 7 There are those who make themselves rich and have nothing, and those who make themselves poor but have great riches. 8 A man will give his riches for the ran- som of his life, but the poor man cannot hear your reproach. 9 The light of the righteous is rekindled, but the candle of the wicked is ex- tinguished. 10 Only pride makes a man quar- rel, but he who is well-behaved is wise. 11 The riches of vanity diminish, but he who gathers with his hand increases them. 12 Hope put off is the fainting of the heart, but when desire comes, it is like a tree of life. 13 He who de- spises the word will be destroyed; but he who fears the command will be rewarded. 14 The instruction of a wise man is like the spring of life, to ward off the snares of death. 15 Good understanding makes acceptable, but the way of the disobedient is hated. 16 A wise man will work with knowledge, but foolishness will spread behind folly. 17 An evil messenger falls from grace, but a faithful ambassador is pro- tected. 18 He who refuses instruction will be ashamed, but he who respects correction will be honored. 19 A fulfilled desire will delude the soul, but for fools it is an abomination to depart from righteousness. 20 He who walks with the wise will be wise, but he who is the companion of fools will be afflicted. 21 Af- fliction follows sinners, but to the righteous God will reserve good. 22 The good man will give inheritance to his children, while the sin- ner's riches are destined for the unjust. 23 In the poor man's field there is much food, but the field is destroyed without discretion. 24 He who spares his rod, hates his son; but he who makes him hear, chastises him in time. 25 The righteous eats his fill, but the belly of the wicked lacks.

CHAPTER14

1 The wise woman builds her house, but the foolish woman destroys it with her own hands. 2 He who walks in his righteousness fears the LORD; but he who is clumsy in his ways despises him. 3 In the mouth of fools is the rod of pride, but the lips of the wise pro- tect them. 4 Where there are no oxen, the cis- tern is empty; but the strength of oxen brings much gain. 5 A faithful witness does not cow- er, but a false witness tells lies. 6 Those who are scornful seek wisdom and do not find it, but knowledge is easy for those who want to understand. 7 Turn away from the foolish man, when you do not perceive in him the lips of knowledge. 8 The wisdom of the pru- dent consists in understanding one's way, but the foolishness of fools is deceit. 9 People scoff at sin, but among the righteous there is sorrow. 10 The heart knows the bitterness of its soul, and the stranger cannot meddle with its happiness. 11 The house of the wicked shall be destroyed, but the tabernacle of the righteous shall flourish. 12 There is a way that seems right to a man, but its consequences are ways of death. 13 When one laughs, the heart is saddened, and the end of this joy is happiness. 14 The heart that declines will be sacked with its own ways, but a good man will depart from it. 15 The foolish worry about ev- erything, but the prudent consider their own steps. 16 The wise man fears and turns away from lawlessness, but the foolish man frets and is careless. 17 He who is angry commits folly, and he who is busy is hated. 18 The fool- ish inherit folly, but the prudent are crowned with knowledge. 19 The unjust shall bow be- fore the good, and the wicked at the gates of the righteous. 20 The poor man is hated by his neighbor, but the rich man's friends are many. 21 The sinner despises his neighbor, but he who pities the poor is blessed. 22 Do not those who imagine evil err? But for those who think of good things, there will be mercy and truth. 23 In every work there is abundance, but the chattering of lips brings only misery. 24 The crown of the wise is their wealth, while the folly of fools is foolishness. 25 A faithful witness brings souls, but a deceiver tells lies. 26 The fear of the LORD is a sure strength, and his children have hope. 27 The fear of the LORD is like a spring of life that drives away the snares of death. 28 The honor of a king is given by the multitude of the people, while the lack of the people causes the destruction of the prince. 29 He who is slow to anger is of great wisdom, but he whose mind is hurried exalts folly. 30 A sound heart is the life of the flesh, but envy is the rotting of the bones. 31 He who oppresses the poor rebukes him who created him; but he who honors him has pity on the poor. 32 The wicked shall be cast out for his malice, but the righteous shall hope in his death. 33 Wisdom rests in the heart of him who has understanding, and is known among the foolish. 34 Righteousness exalts a nation, but sin is a shame to the people. 35 The king delights in a wise servant, but his wrath will be directed at the weak.

CHAPTER 15

1 A gentle answer turns away wrath, but cruel words arouse wrath. 2 The tongue of the wise is righteous, but the mouths of fools babble foolishness. 3 The eyes of the LORD observe in every place the useful and the good. 4 A wholesome tongue is like a tree of life, but its rejection is the breaking of your mind. 5 A child despises the instruction of his fathers, but he who heeds correction is prudent. 6 The house of the righteous has many trea- sures, but the gains of the wicked are trouble. 7 The lips of the wise spread knowledge, but the hearts of the foolish do not do likewise. 8 The sacrifice of the wicked is abominable to the LORD, but the prayer of the righteous is pleasing to him. 9 The way of the ungodly is an abomination to the LORD, but he appre- ciates those who follow righteousness. 10 In- struction is useless to those who forsake the way, and those who hate correction will die. 11 Hell and destruction are before the LORD; how much more the hearts of the sons of men? 12 He who despises does not heed those who rebuke him, nor does he turn to the wise. 13 A serene heart makes a serene face, but the mind is afflicted with sadness of heart. 14 The heart of him who has intelligence seeks knowledge, but the mouth of him who has no intelligence feeds on foolishness. 15 All the days of the afflicted are long, but a good con- science is a continual feast. 16 A small amount of fear of the Lord is better than a great trea- sure and its attendant troubles. 17 Better is a dinner of green herbs where there is joy, than a stalled ox and the hatred that comes with it. 18 The choleric man stirs up the darnel, but he who is slow to anger quenches the darnel. 19 The way of the uncouth man is like a hedge of thorns, but the way of the righteous is clear. 20 A wise son

is fond of his father, but a fool despises his mother. 21 Foolishness is a de- light to him who is without understanding, but the intelligent man walks uprightly. 22 Thoughts without counsel come to nothing, but the multitude of counselors is a strength. 23 Good comes to a man by the answer of his mouth; and how good is a word in due time? 24 The way of life is above for the prudent, to turn away from hell below. 25 The LORD will destroy the house of the proud, but will estab- lish the bounds of the widow. 26 The thoughts of the wicked are abominable to the LORD, but the pure have pleasant words. 27 He who is greedy for gain, disturbs his own house; but he who hates the gifts, he will lie down. 28 The heart of the righteous studies to answer, but the mouth of the wicked babbles useless things. 29 The LORD is far from the wicked, but hears the prayer of the righteous. 30 The light of the eyes revives the heart, and the good name fattens the bones. 31 The animal who hears the correction of life ranks among the wise. 32 He who refuses instruction, de- spises his own soul; but he who obeys correc- tion, gains understanding. 33 The fear of the Lord is the instruction of wisdom; and before honor, comes humility.

CHAPTER 16

1 The preparations of the heart are in man, but the answer of the tongue is from the LORD. 2 All the ways of man are clear to his eyes, but the LORD examines the spirits. 3 Entrust your works to the LORD, and your thoughts will be directed. 4 The LORD has made all things for his good, even the wicked for the day of the end. 5 Everyone whose heart is proud is an abomination to the LORD; though his hand is in his hand, he will not be punished. 6 By mercy and truth iniquity is forgiven, and by the fear of the LORD we turn away from in- iquity. 7 When a man's ways please the LORD, he will put even his enemies at peace with him. 8 A little money with righteousness is better than great gains without equity. 9 A man's heart chooses his way, but the LORD directs his steps. 10 The king's lips shall have a judgment of worth; his mouth shall not transgress in judgment. 11 The weight and the scales are the LORD's; all the weights of the purse are his work. 12 It is abominable for kings to commit wickedness, for the throne is established by justice. 13 Righteous lips are the delight of kings, and the king appreciates those who say righteous things. 14 The wrath of a king is like a message of death, but a wise man appeases it. 15 The light of the king's ap- pearance is life, and his appearance is like a cloud of the last sun. 16 How much better to have wisdom than wealth? And to have un- derstanding is more desirable than silence. 17 The way of the righteous is the way of decline, and he who preserves his soul is the one who follows his way. 18 Pride precedes destruc- tion, and pride precedes fall. 19 It is better to be of a humble disposition with the humble than to discuss haughtiness with the proud. 20 He who is wise in his affairs will find good; and he who trusts in the LORD is blessed. 21 The wise in heart will be called prudent, and sweetness of lips will increase doctrine. 22 Knowledge is a source of life to those who possess it, while the instruction of fools is folly. 23 The heart of the wise guides his mouth with wisdom and adds doctrine to his lips. 24 Right words are like a golden apple, which sweetens the soul and gives health to the bones. 25 There is a way that seems right to man, but its result is the ways of death. 26 He who traffics, traffics for himself, because his mouth dictates to him. 27 The wicked man digs deep, and his lips are like burning fire.

28 A rude person sows strife, and a babbler creates discord among princes. 29 The wicked deceives his neighbor and leads him by a way that is not good. 30 He closes his eyes to be- little wickedness; he bites his lips and makes wickedness pass away. 31 Age is a crown of glory, when he is in the way of righteousness. 32 He who is slow to anger is better than the strong man; and he who rules his own mind is better than he who conquers a city. 33 The lot is cast into the lap, but the whole disposition is of the LORD.

CHAPTER 17

1 A dry morsel is better, if there is peace, than a house full of sacrifice and strife. 2 A discreet servant shall have dominion over a weak son, and he shall manage the inheritance among his brothers. 3 As the pot for torpedo and the furnace for bronze, so the LORD tests hearts. 4 The wicked gives heed to false lies, and the drunkard gives heed to the evil tongue. 5 He who mocks the poor rebukes the one who cre- ated him; and he who revels in destruction will not be punished. 6 The children's children are the crown of the elders, and the glory of you children are their fathers. 7 Talking does not make a man a prince, and still less does lying talk make a prince. 8 A reward is like a pleasant stone in the eyes of those who pos- sess it; it prospers, wherever it turns. 9 He who does a transgression, seeks love; but he who repeats a thing, separates the prince. 10 A rebuke enters more into him who has understanding, than a hundred strokes into a child. 11 A seductive person seeks only in- toxication, and a cruel messenger will be sent against him. 12 It is better for a man to meet a seducer robbed of his young, than a fowl in his folly. 13 He who rewards the good, the good shall not depart from his house. 14 The beginning of contention is like one who opens the waters; therefore, if the contention is not countered, let it go. 15 He who justifies the ungodly and he who condemns the unrigh- teous are both in abomination to the LORD. 16 Why is there a price in the hand of him who wants to gain wisdom and has no heart? 17 The friend is always acceptable, while the brother is endured for aduersity. 18 A man without understanding touches the hand and becomes safe for his neighbor. 19 He who loves transgression, he who loves strife, and he who exalts his gate, seeks destruction. 20 The averse heart finds no good, and he who has an evil tongue falls into disgrace. 21 He who begets a beast procures sorrow, and the father of a beast can have no joy. 22 A heart full of joy is cause for good health, but a sor- rowful mind withers the bones. 23 The wick- ed man removes a gift from his bosom to snatch the ways of judgment. 24 Wisdom is in the face of one who has understanding, but the eyes of an idiot are in the corners of the world. 25 A foolish son is a suffering to his fa- ther and a harm to her who bore him. 26 It is not good to condemn the righteous, and it is not good for princes to strike them down out of fairness. 27 He who has knowledge spares his words, and an intelligent man is of an ex- cellent mind. 28 Moreover, he who is silent is considered wise, and he who restrains his lips is prudent.

CHAPTER 18

1 Because of his desire, he will part to see and deal with all that is wise. 2 A man has no pleasure in understanding, except that his heart be disenchanted. 3 When the ungodly

comes, there comes contempt and blame for the vile. 4 The words of a man's mouth are like deep waters, and the spring of wisdom is like a flowing river. 5 It is not good to accept the person of the wicked, to bring the righteous into judgment. 6 The lips of the foolish are the bearers of strife, and their mouth invokes chastisement. 7 The mouth of the fool is his own destruction, and his lips are a snare for his soul. 8 The words of a storyteller are like flattery and go down into the bowels of the belly. 9 Even he who is slothful in his work is brother to him who is a great waster. 10 The name of the LORD is a strong tower; the righ- teous man runs to it and exalts himself. 11 The riches of the rich man are his city strong and like a wall in his imagination. 12 Before destruction man's heart is high, and before glory it is low. 13 Whoever answers a question before he has heard it is folly and shame to him. 14 A man's spirit bears his infirmity, but a wounded spirit who can bear it? 15 A wise heart obtains knowledge, and the ear of the wise seeks to learn. 16 A man's gift magni- fies him and leads him before great men. 17 He who is first in his own cause is righteous; then his neighbor comes and inquires of him. 18 Fortune causes strife to cease and creates division among the mighty. 19 An offended brother is harder to overcome than a strong city, and their contentions are like the walls of a palace. 20 With the fruit of a man's mouth shall his belly be satisfied, and with the in- crease of his lips shall he be satisfied. 21 Death and life are in the power of the tongue, and he who listens to it will eat its fruit. 22 He who finds a wife finds a good thing and receives favor with the LORD. 23 The poor man speaks with prayers, but the rich man answers curt- ly. 24 He who has friends must show himself friendly, for a friend is more valuable than a brother.

CHAPTER 19

1 Better is the poor man who walks in his righteousness than he who abuses his lips and is a fanatic. 2 For without knowledge the mind is not good, and he who hurries with his feet sins. 3 Man's foolishness perturbs his way, and his heart rages against the LORD. 4 Riches gather many friends, but the poor man is separated from his neighbor. 5 A false witness will not be punished, and he who tells lies will not escape. 6 Many have regard for the prince's countenance, and every man is a friend of those who give gifts. 7 All the broth- ers of the poor hate him; how much more will his friends turn away from him? Though he is solicitous with words, they will not. 8 He who possesses understanding, appreci- ates his own soul and retains wisdom to find good. 9 He who speaks falsely will not be pun- ished, and he who speaks falsely will perish. 10 Pleasure is not convenient for an animal, much less for a servant who is in control of principles. 11 Man's discretion postpones his wrath, and his glory passes for an offense. 12 The king's wrath is like the roar of a bruiser, but his humor is like dew on the gridiron. 13 A foolish son is his father's calamity, and a wife's contentions are like a continual trickle. 14 House and riches are the inheritance of the fathers, but a prudent wife comes from the LORD. 15 Indolence causes one to fall asleep, and the deceitful person is hungry. 16 He who keeps the commandment keeps his soul; but he who despises its ways will die. 17 Whoever has pity on the poor, lend to the LORD; and the LORD will return to him what he has giv- en. 18 Chasten thy son while there is hope, and spare not thy soul for his murmuring. 19 A very wrathful man will suffer chastise- ment; and even if you fail him, his wrath will break out again. 20 Hear

counsel and receive instruction, that you may be wise in the last times. 21 Many ideas are in a man's heart, but the counsel of the LORD endures. 22 What is to be desired of a man is his goodness, and a poor man is better than a poor man. 23 The fear of the LORD leads to life; he who is filled with it will continue to live and will not be vis- ited by death. 24 The indolent man hides his hand in his breast and does not put it in his mouth again. 25 Strike the one who despises, and the foolish will beware; rebuke the pru- dent and he will understand knowledge. 26 He who destroys his father or casts out his mother is a weak and shameful son. 27 My son, listen no more to the teachings that get the words of knowledge wrong. 28 A wicked wit mocks judgment, and the mouth of you wicked people swallows up iniquity. 29 But judgments are prepared for the scorners, and blows for the backs of fools.

CHAPTER 20

1 Wine is a mockery, and strong drink is a fury; and he who is deceived by it is not wise. 2 The king's fear is like the roar of a lion; who- ever makes him angry, sins against his own soul. 3 A man's honor is not to quarrel, but all enemies meddle. 4 The indolent man does not plow, because of winter; therefore he will ask alms in summer, but he will have nothing. 5 The counsels in man's heart are like deep waters, but a man who has understanding will draw them out. 6 Many men boast, each one of his own goodness, but who can find a faithful man? 7 He who walks in his integrity is righteous, and his children will be blessed after him. 8 The king who sits on the throne of judgment casts out all wickedness with his eyes. 9 Who can say, "I have cleansed my heart, I am clean from my sin"? 10 Different weights and different measures are abomina- ble to the LORD. 11 A child can be recognized even by his deeds, if his work is pure and righ- teous. 12 The LORD has made both: the ear to hear and the eye to see. 13 Do not sleep at least when you come to eat; open your eyes and you will be filled with bread. 14 It is nothing, it is nothing, says the buyer; but when he leaves, he boasts. 15 There is gold and a multitude of precious stones, but the lips of knowledge are a precious jewel. 16 Take his robe, which is safe for a stranger, and a pledge of him for the stranger. 17 The bread of deceit is sweet to man, but then his mouth shall be filled with wine. 18 Establish thoughts with counsel, and with counsel make war. 19 He who goes about as a backbiter, discloses secrets; there- fore do not meddle with him who flatters with his lips. 20 Whoever curses his father or his mother, his light shall be extinguished in dark darkness. 21 An inheritance is obtained quickly at the beginning, but its end will not be blessed. 22 Do not say, "I will reward you well," but wait on the LORD and he will save you. 23 Different weights are an abom- ination to the LORD, and deceitful scales are not good. 24 Man's steps are governed by the LORD; how then can a man understand his way? 25 It is destruction for a man to disobey what is sanctified and to inquire after vows. 26 A wise king scatters the wicked and causes people to turn away from them. 27 The light of the LORD is the breath of man and searches all the bowels of the belly. 28 Mercy and truth preserve the king, for his throne will be estab- lished by mercy. 29 The beauty of young men is their strength, and the glory of old men is the gray head. 30 The blood of the wound is to cleanse the soul, and the stripes in the bowels of the belly.

CHAPTER 21

1 The hearts of kings are in the hands of the LORD, like the billows of the waters; he turns them as he pleases. 2 Every way a man acts is right in his eyes, but the LORD examines hearts. 3 Justice and judgment are more pleasing to the LORD than sacrifices. 4 A haughty look and a proud heart, which is the light of the ungodly, is sin. 5 The thoughts of those who are diligent surely lead to abun- dance, but those who are stingy surely meet with ruin. 6 The gathering of treasures with a deceitful tongue is vanity cast away by those who see death. 7 The robbery of the wicked will destroy them, because they have refused to execute judgment. 8 The way of some is perverse and strange, but the way of the pure man is right. 9 It is better to dwell in a corner of the house than with a quarrelsome wom- an in a wide house. 10 The soul of the wicked man desires happiness, and his neighbor has no scruple in his eyes. 11 When the scorner is punished, the fool becomes wise; and when one instructs the wise, they receive knowl- edge. 12 The righteous teaches the house of the wicked, but God casts out the wicked for their usefulness. 13 Whoever stops before the weeping of the poor, he also shall weep, and shall not be heard. 14 A gift in secret appeases wrath, and a gift in the bosom great wrath. 15 The righteous has a right to do justice, but the workers of iniquity will be destroyed. 16 The man who strays from the way of wisdom will remain in the community of the dead. 17 He who loves pastimes will be a poor man, and he who loves wine and oil will not be rich. 18 The wicked shall be a ransom for the righteous, and the transgressor for the righteous. 19 It is better to dwell in the wilderness than with a quarrelsome and wrathful woman. 20 There is treasure and pleasant wealth in the house of the wise, but the foolish man disregards it. 21 He who follows justice and mercy will find life, righteousness and glory. 22 The wise man enters the city of the mighty and throws down the strength of his security. 23 He who restrains his mouth and his tongue, preserves his soul from affliction. 24 Proude, hautie and scornefull is his name that works in his arrogant wrath. 25 The desire of the slothful kills him, for his hands refuse to work. 26 He consumes most greedily, but the righteous eats and does not spare. 27 The sacrifice of the wicked is an abomination; how much more if he performs it with an evil mind? 28 A false witness shall perish, but he that heareth, speaketh continually. 29 The wicked hardens his face, but the righteous directs his way. 30 There is no wisdom, no understanding, no counsel against the LORD. 31 The horse is pre- pared against the day of battle, but salvation is of the LORD.

CHAPTER 22

1 A good name must be chosen for great rich- es, and good taste is for silver and gold. 2 The rich and the poor are gathered together; the LORD is the maker of all. 3 The prudent man sees the plague and hides, but the foolish go forth and are punished. 4 The reward of hu- mility and the fear of God are riches, glory and life. 5 Thorns and snares are in the way of adversaries, but he who cares for his own soul turns away from them. 6 He teaches a child the craft of his way, and when he grows up he will not depart from it. 7 The rich dom- inates the poor, and the debtor is servant to the man who lends. 8 He who sows iniquity shall reap affliction, and the rod of his wrath shall be quenched. 9 He who has a good eye will be blessed, because he gives his bread to the poor. 10 Cast out the scorner, and strife shall be extinguished; so shall contention and reproach cease. 11 He who loves purity of heart by the grace of his lips, the king will be his friend. 12 The eyes of the LORD preserve knowledge, but he casts out the words of the transgressor. 13 The uncouth man says, "There is a lion, I will be killed in the street." 14 The mouth of a rebellious woman is like a deep pit; he with whom the LORD is angry shall fall into it. 15 Foolishness is bound up in the heart of a child, but the rod of correction will take it away from him. 16 He who oppresses the poor to increase himself, and who takes advantage of the rich, will surely come to grief. 17 In- cline your ear and listen to the words of the wise, and apply your heart to my knowledge. 18 For it will be pleasant if you hold them in your belly and if you hold them together in your lips. 19 That your confidence may be in the LORD, I have shown you this day; you therefore listen. 20 Have I not written to you three times for counsel and knowledge? 21 To give you assurance of the words of truth to answer the words of truth to those who send you? 22 Do not mistreat the poor because he is poor, nor oppress the afflicted in judgment. 23 For the LORD will defend their cause and protect the souls of those who have afflicted them. 24 Do not befriend an angry man or go with an angry man, 25 unless you want to learn his ways and receive the destruction of your soul. 26 Don't be of those who touch your hand, and don't be among those who get your debts paid. 27 If you have nothing to pay, why should you be compelled to remove your bed from under you? 28 You shall not remove the ancient boundaries that your fathers estab- lished. 29 See that the man who is diligent in his business stands before kings and does not stand before those who are of low estate.

CHAPTER 23

1 When you sit at table with a ruler, consider carefully what is in front of you, 2 and put the knife to your throat, if you are a man with an appetite. 3 Do not covet his deintie meats, for they are deceitful meats. 4 Do not make too much effort to be rich, but cease to be wise. 5 Will you cast your eyes on that which is noth- ing? For wealth takes its wings, like an eagle, and flies to the sky. 6 Eat not the bread of him whose eye is euphoric, and desire not his de- mented meats. 7 For as if he thought it in his heart, so he will say to you, "Eat and drink"; but his heart is not with you. 8 You will vom- it the morsels you have eaten and lose your sweet words. 9 Do not speak with the ears of a fowl, for he will despise the wisdom of your words. 10 Do not depart from the ancient borders or enter the fields of the homeland. 11 For he who redeems them is mighty; he will defend their cause against you. 12 Apply your heart to instruction and your ears to the words of knowledge. 13 Do not prevent the child from being corrected; if you strike him with the rod, he will not die. 14 If you strike him with the rod, you will deliver his soul from hell. 15 My son, if your heart is wise, my heart will recover and so will I. 16 And my kid- neys will rejoice when your lips speak right things. 17 Let not your heart be envious of sinners, but always be afraid of the Lord. 18 For surely there is an end, and your hope will not be cut off. 19 O my son, listen, be wise and guide your heart on the way. 20 Do not asso- ciate with drunkards and gluttons. 21 For the drunkard and the glutton shall be poor, and the sleeper shall be clothed in rags. 22 Obey your father who begot you, and do not despise your mother when she is old. 23 Do not sell the truth, but do not sell it; likewise wisdom, instruction and understanding. 24 The father of the

righteous shall have great benefit, and he who begets a wise son shall have benefit. 25 Your father and your mother shall rejoice, and she who bore you shall rejoice. 26 My son, give me your heart and your eyes delight in my ways. 27 For a harlot is like a deep pit, and a foreign woman is like a pit of narcotics. 28 Moreover, she lies in wait like a prayer, and increases transgressors among men. 29 To whom is woe, to whom is sorrow, to whom is contention, to whom is murmuring, to whom are wounds without cause, to whom is the redness of eyes? 30 And to those who linger long over wine, to those who go away and see mixed wine. 31 Do not look at wine when it is red, when it shows its color in the cup or goes down pleasantly. 32 When you drink it, it bites like a snake and wounds like a rooster. 33 Your eyes will look at foreign women, and your heart will speak strange things. 34 You will be like him who sleeps in the middle of the sea and like him who sleeps in the upper part of the mass. 35 "They struck me, you will say, but I was not sick; they beat me, but I did not notice when I woke up; therefore I will see it again."

CHAPTER 24

1 Do not be envious of wicked men or desire to be with them. 2 For their hearts imagine destruction and their lips speak evil. 3 With wisdom you build a house, and with under- standing you build it. 4 With knowledge one fills rooms with all precious and pleasant riches. 5 A wise man is strong, for an intel- ligent man increases his strength. 6 For by counsel you can win your war, and health is given by the multitude of those who can coun- sel. 7 Wisdom is a hindrance to a fowl; there- fore he cannot open his mouth in the gate. 8 He who imagines that he is doing good, men will call him "self-taught wickedness." 9 The evil thought of a leprechaun is sin, and he who despises it is an abomination to men. 10 If you are weak in the day of adultery, your strength is small. 11 Preserve those who are led to death; do you not preserve those who are led to be killed? 12 If you say, "Behold, we did not know," does he who examines hearts not understand? And does not he who guards your soul know it? Will he not reward ev- ery man according to his works? 13 My son, eat honey, for it is good, and the honey that comes to you, for it is sweet to your mouth. 14 So shall it be to thy soul the knowledge of wisdom, if thou find it, and there shall be an end, and thy hope shall not be cut off. 15 Do not wait, O wicked man, against the house of the righteous, and do not spy out his resting place. 16 For the righteous man falls ten times and rises again, but the wicked man falls in disgrace. 17 Do not rejoice when your enemy falls, and do not rejoice when he stumbles, 18 Otherwise the LORD will see him and be sorry for him and turn away his wrath from him. 19 Do not worry about the wicked or be envious of the wicked. 20 For there will be no more plague for the wicked man; the light of the wicked will be put out. 21 My son, fear the LORD and the King and do not meddle with those who are self-styled. 22 For their de- struction will arise suddenly, and who knows their doom? 23 AND THESE THINGS PER- HAPE TO THE WISDOMS: "It is not good to have respect to anyone in judgment." 24 Who- ever says to the wicked, "You are righteous," will be cursed by the people, and the multi- tude will abhor him. 25 But those who rebuke him shall have pleasure, and on them shall fall the blessing of goodness. 26 They shall slay the lips of him who answers the right words. 27 Prepare your work outside, make ready your things in the field, and then build your house. 28 Do not be

a witness against your neighbor for no reason; why do you want to deceive with your lies? 29 Do not say, "I will do to him what he has done to me," and I will reward every man according to his work. 30 I passed through the field of the indolent man, and through the vineyard of the unintelligent man. 31 And behold, it was all covered with thorns, nettles had covered its face, and the stone wall had been broken down. 32 Then I saw and considered it well: I looked upon it and received instruction. 33 But a little sleep, a little bending of the hands to sleep. 34 Thus thy anxiety cometh as one walking in the street, and thy necessity as an armed man.

CHAPTER 25

1 These also are parables of Solomon, which the men of Hezekiah, king of Judah, copied. 2 The glory of God is to hide a secret thing, but the honor of the king is to discover a thing. 3 The height of the heavens, the depth of the earth, and the heart of the king cannot be dis- covered by anyone. 4 Take away the dust from the torpedo, and out of it shall come a vessel for the finer. 5 Turn away the wicked from the king, and his throne will be established in righteousness. 6 Do not boast before the king or put yourself in the place of the great. 7 For it is better for you to be told, "Come here," and for you to be put in the background before the prince whom your eyes have seen. 8 Do not go and argue hastily, because you do not know what to do when your neighbor has embar- rassed you. 9 Discuss your matter with your neighbor and do not reveal the secret to an- other, 10 lest those who hear it should shame you and your infamy cease. 11 A word spoken in its place is like apples of gold with pictures of silk. 12 He who rebukes the wise and obedi- ent is like an earring of gold and an ornament of fine gold. 13 As the cold of snow in time of storm, so is he a faithful messenger to those who send him, for he refreshes the souls of his masters. 14 A man who boasts of false lib- erality is like clouds and wind without rain. 15 A prince is pacified by restraining himself from wrath, and a soft tongue breaks bones. 16 If you have found bone, eat what is enough, at least that you are full, and vomit it up. 17 Turn your foot away from your neighbor's house, or he will grow weary of you and hate you. 18 A man who speaks falsehood against his neighbor is like a hammer, a sword, and a sharp weapon.19 Trust in a man vnfaythfull in time of trouble is like a broken tooth and a slipping foot. 20 He who takes off his robe in the cold season is like wine pouring out of naphtha, or like he who sings songs to a sick heart. 21 If he who hates you is hungry, give him bread to eat, and if he is thirsty, give him water to drink. 22 Because you will put colas on his head, the LORD will reward you. 23 As the north wind dries up the rain, so an angry face makes the slanderous tongue disappear. 24 It is better to dwell in a corner of the house than with a quarrelsome woman in a wide house. 25 As cold waters to a weary soul, so good news comes from a far country. 26 A righteous man who falls before the ungodly is like a distressed well and a corrupt spring. 27 It is not good to eat much honey, and to seek one's own glory is not glory. 28 The man who does not restrain his appetite is like a ruined city without walls.

CHAPTER 26

1 As the snow in summer and as the rain in autumn do not meet, so honor is always for food. 2 As the sparrow that

flies and the swallow that flies escape, so the curse that is caused will not come. 3 To the horse belongs a whip, to the donkey a bridle, and a rod to the back of fools. 4 Do not answer a man accord- ing to his foolishness, unless you also want to be like him. 5 Answer a man according to his foolishness, if you do not want him to be wise in his own conception. 6 Whoever conveys a message by the hand of a fowl is like those who cut off their feet and drink iniquity. 7 As those who lift up the legs of the lame, so is a parable in the mouth of a fool. 8 As the closing of a precious stone in a heap of stones, so is he who gives glory to a fanatic. 9 As a thorn standing in the hand of a drunkard, so is a parable in the mouth of fools. 10 The exalted One who formed all things rewards both the fowlers and the transgressors. 11 As the dog turns in his vomit, so the vulgar turns in his folly. 12 Do you see a wise man in his own con- ception? A fowl has more hope than he. 13 The coarse man says, "There is a lyre on the road, there is a lyre on the roads." 14 As the door turns on its hinges, so the foul-mouthed man turns on his bed. 15 The slothful man hides his hand in his breast and labors to bring it to his mouth again. 16 The lazy man is wiser in his own conception than other men who can reason. 17 He who passes over and med- dles in a dispute that does not belong to him is like one who takes a dog by the ears. 18 Just as he who is driven mad throws firebrands and arrows and deadly things, 19 so does the deceitful man deal with his friend and say, "Am I not amusing myself? 20 Without wood the fire goes out, and without a chatterer the quarrels cease. 21 As cola causes colas to burn, and wood the fire, so the quarrelsome man is apt to kindle tares. 22 The words of a storyteller are like flattery, and they descend into the bowels of the belly. 23 As the drops of silence on a pot, so are the burning lips and the sick heart. 24 He who hates, opposes with his lips, but in his heart hides deceit. 25 Though he speak evil, let him not go, for in his heart are many abominations. 26 Hatred may be fed with deceit, but his wickedness will be discarded in the community. 27 He who digs a pit will fall into it, and he who rolls a stone, it will return to him. 28 A false tongue hates the afflicted, and a flattering mouth causes ruin.

CHAPTER 27

1 Do not boast that you are a man, for you do not know what can happen in a day. 2 Be prayed to by another and not by your own mouth, by a stranger and not by your own lips. 3 A stone is heavy and sand weighs, but a fool's anger is heavier than both. 4 Anger is cruel and wrath is furious; but who can stand up to wrath? 5 An open rebuke is better than a secret quarrel. 6 The wounds of those who complain are faithful, and the kisses of those who are enemies are pleasant. 7 He who is satiated despises a food offering; but to the hungry soul every bitter thing is sweet. 8 As a bird that strays from its nest, so is the man who strays from his place. 9 As oil and per- fume gladden the heart, so the sweetness of a friend is given by sincere counsel. 10 Do not forsake your friend and the friend of your fa- thers; do not enter the house of your brothers in the day of your calamity, for it is better a neighbor near than a brother far away. 11 Son, be wise and reduce my heart, that I may an- swer those who rebuke me. 12 The prudent man sees the plague and hides himself, but the foolish go forth and are punished. 13 Take his garment as a surety for the stranger, and a pledge of him for the stranger. 14 He who prays to his friend with a loud voice, rising early in the morning, shall be regarded as a curse. 15 A woman who falls continually in the day of

anger and a quarrelsome woman are equal. 16 He who hides her, hides the wind, and she is like an oilcloth in his right hand, which wears itself out. 17 The yron sharpens the yron, so the man sharpens the face of his friend. 18 He who guards the fig tree shall eat its fruit; so he who waits on his master shall do himself honor. 19 As in the water the face responds to the face, so the heart of man to man. 20 Death and destruction can never be satiated, so the eyes of man can never be sat- isfied. 21 As the pot for the torpedo and the furnace for the metal, so every man is accord- ing to his dignity. 22 Even if thou shouldst rake a fish in a mortar, among the grain raked with a pestle, his foolishness shall not depart from him. 23 Be diligent to know the state of your flock and pay attention to the people you listen to. 24 For riches do not always remain, nor the crown from generation to genera- tion. 25 The grass uncovers itself, the grain appears, and the herbs of the mountains are gathered. 26 The lambs are for your clothing, and the goats are the price of the field. 27 Let the milk of the goats be sufficient for your food, for the food of your family, and for the sustenance of your children.

CHAPTER 28

1 The wicked flee when no one pursues them, but the righteous are as strong as a lyre. 2 For the transgression of the land there are many princes; but for an intelligent and competent man a kingdom lasts long. 3 The poor man, if he opposes the poor man, is like a raging raine that leaves no food. 4 Those who for- sake the Law, they pray to the wicked; but those who keep it, they set themselves against them. 5 The wicked do not understand the Law, but those who see the Lord understand everything. 6 Better is the poor man who walks in his righteousness, than he who per- turbs his ways, though he be rich. 7 He who keeps the Law is an intelligent son, but he who feeds gluttons is ashamed of his father. 8 He who increases his wealth with money and interest, gathers it for him who will be merciful to the poor. 9 He who turns away his ear from hearing the Law, then his prayer will be abominable. 10 Whoever causes the righ- teous to go astray by a wrong way, he will fall into his grave, while the righteous will inher- it good things. 11 The rich man is wise in his own conception, but the poor man who has understanding may test him. 12 When righ- teous men reconcile, there is great glory; but when the wicked arise, man is tested. 13 He who hides his sins will not prosper, but he who confesses them and forsakes them will have mercy. 14 Blessed is the man who always fears; but he who hardens his heart will fall to ruin. 15 Like a roaring lion and a hungry beast, so a wicked ruler is outside the poor people. 16 A prince devoid of understanding is also a great oppressor; but he who hates twists and turns will prolong his days. 17 He who does violence to a person's blood will flee to the grave, and they will not stop him. 18 He who walks uprightly will be saved; but he who is reckless in his ways will fall once. 19 He who cultivates his land will be satisfied with bread; but he who follows idleness will be satisfied with messes. 20 The honest man will abound in blessings, while he who has- tens to become rich will not be innocent. 21 It is not good to have respect for people, for that man transgresses for a piece of bread. 22 The man who has an evil eye hastens to riches and does not know that torment will come upon him. 23 He who rebukes a man will find more pain in the end than he who flatters him with his tongue. 24 He who robs his father and mother and says, "This is no transgression," is the companion of a man who

destroys. 25 He who has a proud heart foments strife; but he who trusts in the LORD will be healed. 26 The one who trusts in his own heart is a fool; but the one who walks in wisdom will be disap- pointed. 27 Whoever does good to the poor, he will not be harmed; but whoever hides his eyes, he will have many curses. 28 When the wicked arise, men hide; but when they perish, the righteous increase.

CHAPTER 29

1 The man who hardens his neck when he is rebuked will suddenly be destroyed and can- not be healed. 2 When the righteous man is in power, the people rejoice; but when the wicked man rules, the people sigh. 3 The man who hears wisdom is reconciled to his father, but he who feeds prostitutes wastes his sub- stance. 4 A king who gets judgment keeps the land, but a man who receives gifts destroys it. 5 He who flatters his neighbor spreads a net for his steps. 6 The transgression of a wick- ed man is a snare to him, but the righteous man sings and rejoices. 7 The righteous man knows the cause of the poor, but the wicked man cares not for knowledge. 8 Scornful men put a city in a snare, but wise men turn away wrath. 9 If a wise man quarrels with a fool, whether angry or laughing, there is no peace. 10 Bloodthirsty men hate those who are righ- teous, but the righteous cares for his soul. 11 A fool pours out all his mind, but a wise man preserves it until later. 12 Of a prince who heeds lies, all his servants are wicked. 13 The poor man and the poor man meet, and the LORD enlightens the eyes of both. 14 A king who judges the poor in truth, his throne will be established forever. 15 The rod and correc- tion give wisdom; but a child set free puts his mother to shame. 16 When the wicked increase, transgression increases; but you righteous ones will see their fall. 17 Correct your son, and he will give you rest, and give pleasures to your soul. 18 Where there is no vision, the people decay; but he who keeps the Law is blessed. 19 A servant does not let himself be chastised with words; though he understands, he does not answer. 20 Do you see a man in trouble? There is more hope for a man than for him. 21 He who gently raises up his servant from his youth, in the end he will be like his son. 22 The choleric man fo- ments strife, and the furious man abounds in transgression. 23 A man's pride will bring him low, but the humble in spirit will glory. 24 He who partners with a thief hates his own soul; he hears curses and does not declare them. 25 The fear of man brings a snare, but he who trusts in the LORD will be exalted. 26 Many see the face of the ruler, but the judgment of every man is from the LORD. 27 The wicked is an abomination to the righteous, and he who is righteous in his way is an abomination to the wicked.

CHAPTER 30

THE WORDS OF AGUR THE SONNE OF JAKE

1 The prophecy which you men uttered to Ithiel, that is, to Ithiel and Vcal. 2 Surely I am more foolish than any man, and have not in me the understanding of a man. 3 For I have not learned wisdom, nor attained knowledge of holy things. 4 Who has ascended into heav- en and descended from it? Who gathered the wind in his fist? Who bound the waters in a robe? Who has established all the ends of the world? What is his name and what is the name of his son, if you can tell? 5 Every word of God is pure; he is a shield for those who trust in him. 6 Do nothing against his words, otherwise he will take you back and you will be found a liar. 7 Two things I have asked of you: do not deny me before I die. 8 Turn away vanity and falsehood from me; give me nei- ther wealth nor money; feed me with food fit for me, 9 Or let me be satiated and deny you and say, "Who is the LORD?" or let me be poor and thieving and take the name of my God at face value. 10 Do not accuse a servant with his master, lest he curse you when he has offend- ed you. 11 There is a generation that curses the father and does not bless the mother. 12 There is a generation that is pure in its conception and does not wash from its filthiness. 13 There is a generation whose eyes are high and their eyelids are lifted up. 14 There is a generation whose teeth are like swords and their jaws like knives to devour the afflicted from the earth and the poor among men. 15 The leache horse has two daughters who cry, "Give, give." There are three that are not content, nay, four that do not say, "It is enough." 16 The burden and the barren woman, the earth that is not content with water, and the fire that does not say, "It is enough." 17 The eye that mocks his father and despises his mother's instruction, that you raucous men of the valley pluck him out and the young eagles eat him. 18 There are three things that are hidden from me; yea, four that I know not, 19 the way of the eagle in the air, the way of the serpent upon the stone, the way of the ship in the midst of the sea, and the way of the man with the maid. 20 So also is the way of an adulterous woman: she eats, wipes her mouth, and says, "I have not committed iniquity." 21 For three things the earth is sick; yea, for four it cannot sustain itself: 22 a servant, when he reigns, and a fish, when he is full of food, 23 for the hateful woman when she is married, and for the maidservant who is heir to her masters. 24 These are four little things on earth, but they are wise and full of wisdom: 25 Pismi are a people not strong, yet they prepare their meal in the afternoon: 26 The cones are a peo- ple not strong, yet they build their houses in the rocks: 27 The grasshoppers have no king, yet they all go about in bands: 28 The spider takes house with his hands and stands in the palaces of kings. 29 There are three things that order their going well; yea, four are com- fortable in going, 30 the lion, which is strong among the beasts, and turns not away at the sight of any: 31 a vigorous greyhound, a goat, and a king against whom you cannot rise. 32 If thou hast been foolish in lifting up, and if thou hast thought wrong, put thy hand over thy mouth. 33 When a man churns milk, he brings out butter; and he who twists his nose, he brings out blood; so he who allows himself to be in anger, he brings out darnel.

CHAPTER 31

THE WORDS OF KING LEMUEL

1 the prophecy his mother taught him. 2 What, my son, and what, son of my wom- an, and what, son of my desires! 3 Do not give your strength to women, nor your ways, which are to destroy kings. 4 It is not for kings, O Lemuel, it is not for kings to drink wine nor for princes to drink alcohol, 5 That they may not drink and forget the decree and change judgment on all the sons of affliction. 6 Give drink to those who are ready to die, and wine to those whose hearts are afflict- ed. 7 Make him drink, that he may forget his afflictions and remember his suffering no more. 8 Open your mouth for the master, for the sake of all the sons of destruction. 9 Open thy mouth: judge with righteousness,

judge the afflicted and the poor. 10 Who shall find a virtuous woman, for her price is far from pearls. 11 The heart of her husband shall trust in her, and he shall have no need of brides. 12 She will do him good and not evil all the days of his life. 13 She searches for wool and flax and works cheerfully with her hands. 14 She is like the ships of marchers; she brings her food from Afarre. 15 She rises, while it is yet night, and distributes the portions to her house and the ordinary to her women. 16 He considers a field and obtains it; with the fruits of his hands he plants a vineyard. 17 He girds him- self with strength and strengthens his arms. 18 He feels that his goods are good; his candle is not put out at night. 19 He puts his hands to the whip, and his hands handle the spindle. 20 He stretches out his hand to the poor and puts his hands to the needy. 21 She does not fear the snow for her family, for all her fam- ily is clothed in skins. 22 She makes her own carpets; her dress is of fine linen and purple. 23 Her husband is known at the gates, when he sits with the elders of the land. 24 She makes sheets, and sells them, and girds them for the merchant. 25 Strength and honor are her clothing, and in the last day she will re- cover. 26 She opens her mouth with wisdom, and the word of grace is in her tongue. 27 She turneth away from the ways of her house, and eateth not the bread of the young men. 28 Her children shall rise up and call her blessed; her husband also shall pray to her, saying, "It is not true that it is not true." 29 Many daugh- ters have acted righteously, but you surpass them all. 30 Charm is deceitful and beauty is vain; but a woman who fears the LORD will be prayed for. 31 Give her the fruit of her hands, and let her works make her pray at the gates.

ECCLESIASTES

CHAPTER 1

1 The words of the Preacher, son of Dauid, king of Jerusalem. 2 Vanity of vanities, says the Preacher: vanity of vanities, all is vanity. 3 What is left for man in all his travail that he endures under the sun? 4 One generation passes away and another succeeds, but the earth remains forever. 5 The sun rises and the sun goes down and returns to its place, where it rises. 6 The wind goes to the south and turns to the north; the wind goes around and returns for its circuits. 7 All the ships go out to sea, but the sea is not full, for the ships go to a place, whence they return and depart. 8 All things are full of work, but man cannot get over it; the eye is not satisfied with see- ing, and the ear is not satisfied with hearing. 9 What is it that has gone well? What will be; and what is it that has been done? What will be done; and there is nothing new under the sun. 10 Is there any thing of which we can say, "Behold, this is new"? It has already been done in ancient time before. 11 There is no memory of the former, nor will there be any memory of the last that will be, with those who come after. 12 I, the preacher, was king of Israel in Jerusalem: 13 And I set my heart to seek and find wisdom in all things that were done un- der heaven (this sore traversal God granted to the sons of men, to humble them thereby). 14 I have considered all the works that are done under the sun, and behold, all is vani- ty and vexation of spirit. 15 What is crooked, no one can straighten; and what fails, cannot be tamed. 16 I thought in my heart and said, "Behold, I have become great, and I surpass in wisdom all those who have gone before me to Jerusalem; and my heart has seen much wis- dom and knowledge. 17 I have made known to my heart wisdom and knowledge, folly and foolishness: I have also understood that this is a vexation of the spirit. 18 For in the mul- titude of wisdom there is much sadness; and he that increases wisdom, increases sadness.

CHAPTER 2

1 I said in my heart, "Go ahead, I will make you experience cheerfulness; therefore you take pleasure in pleasant things; and behold, even this is vanity." 2 I said to laughter, "You are mad," and to wrath, "What is this that you do? 3 I have tried in my heart to give myself to wine, to rest my heart in wisdom, and to take hold of folly, to see where is the goodness of the sons of men, who enjoy themselves under the sun, all the days of their lives. 4 I have done my great works: I have built my houses: I have planted vineyards. 5 I have made gardens and orchards, and planted therein trees of all fruits. 6 I have built cis- terns of water to water the woods that are full of trees. 7 I have procured servants and maidservants and have borne children in the house; also I have had a great possession of bees and sheep for all who were before me in Jerusalem. 8 I also gathered in me silver and gold and the chief treasures of kings and princes: I procured male singers and female singers and the delights of the sons of men, as a woman taken hostage and women taken hostage. 9 I was great, and increased over all that were before me in Jerusalem; my wis- dom also remained with me. 10 And all that my eyes desired, I withheld not from them: I withdrew not my heart from any thing, for my heart continued to work, and this was my portion of all my work. 11 Then I looked at all the work that my hands had done and the toil that I had done; and behold, all is vanity and toil of spirit, and there is no profit under the sun. 12 And I turned to look at wisdom, and madness, and folly (for who is the man who will come after the king in the things that men have done now?). 13 Then I saw that wis- dom is more profitable than folly, as light is more excellent than darkness. 14 For the wise man has eyes in his head, but madness walks in darkness; yet I also know that the same condition befalls them all. 15 Then I thought in my heart, "The same thing happens to me as to you. Why then do I strive to be wiser? And I said in my heart that this too is vanity. 16 For there shall be no more remembrance of the wise, nor of fools forever; for what is there now, in the days to come shall all be forgotten. And how does the wise man die, how does the fox die? 17 Therefore I have hated life, because the works that are done under the sun annoy me, for everything is vanity and toil of spirit. 18 I have also hated all my toil that I have done under the sun and will leave to the man who comes after me. 19 Who knows whether he will be wise or foolish, but he will have control over all my toil, in which I have walked and in which I have proved myself wise under the sun. This, too, is vanity. 20 Therefore I have set my mind to abhor all the labors for which I have labored under the sun. 21 For there is a man whose labor is in wisdom, in knowledge, and in equity; yet to a man who has not done this labor, he will give his portion; this also is vanity and great sorrow. 22 For what hath a man of all his travail, and of all the sorrow of his heart, whereby he hath walked under the sun? 23 For all his days are sorrowful, and his heart is afflicted with sadness; his heart also does not rest in the night, and this also is van- ity. 24 There is no profit for man except to eat and drink and delight his soul with the profit of his labor; I have seen this also, which was made by the hand of God. 25 For who more than I could eat and who more than I could hasten to outward things? 26 Certainly, to the man who is good in his

own eyes, God grants wisdom, knowledge and joy; but to the sinner he grants paino, to gather and gather to give to those who are good before God; this also is vanity and vexation of spirit.

CHAPTER 3

1 For everything there is an appointed time and a time for every purpose in the world. 2 There is a time to be born and a time to die; there is a time to plant and a time to make what has been planted grow. 3 A time to kill and a time to heal; a time to demolish and a time to build. 4 A time to weep and a time to laugh; a time to mourn and a time to dance. 5 A time to cast away stones and a time to gather stones; a time to embrace and a time to be far from embracing. 6 A time to see and a time to lose; a time to keep and a time to cast away. 7 A time to rent and a time to sow; a time to be silent and a time to speak. 8 A time to love and a time to hate; a time for war and a time for peace. 9 What profit has he who works of the thing in which he traffics? 10 I have seen the snare that God has grant- ed to the sons of men to humiliate them. 11 He has made everything good in its time; He has also set the world in their hearts, but man cannot discover the work that God has done from the beginning to the end. 12 I know that there is nothing good in them but the desire to live and to do good in his life. 13 I also know that every man eats and drinks and sees the fruit of all his labor. This is the gift of God. 14 I know that whatever God does will be forever; to it no one can add, and from it no one can diminish; for God has done it, that they may fear before him. 15 What is that which has gone well? What is now; and what will be, is gone well now; for God requires what is past. 16 Moreover I saw under the sun the place of judgment, where there was wickedness, and the place of righteousness, where there was iniquity. 17 I thought in my heart, "God will judge the unjust and the ungodly, for there is a time for every purpose and every work." 18 I considered in my heart the state of the sons of men, whom God has purified; yet, on closer inspection, they are in themselves like beasts. 19 For the condition of the sons of men and the condition of beasts are as one condition for them. As the one dies, so dies the other, for they all have one breath, and there is no excellence of man over the beast, for all is vanity. 20 All go to one place, all come from dust and all will return to dust. 21 Who knows whether the spirit of man ascends upward and the spirit of the beast descends to the earth? 22 Therefore I see that there is nothing better than for man to go about his business, for that is his portion. For who will bring him to see what will be after him?

CHAPTER 4

1 Then I turned around and considered all the oppressions that are consumed under the sun, and I saw the strains of the oppressed, and no one comforts them; and behold, strength is in the hands of those who oppress them, and no one comforts them. 2 Therefore I have prayed to the dead, who are now dead, concerning the living, who are still alive. 3 And I consider the one who is not yet dead better than both, because he has not seen the won- derful works that are done under the sun. 4 I have also seen all the travails and perfection of works: this is a man's envy of his neighbor; this also is vanity and affliction of spirit. 5 The fowl folds his hands and eats his flesh. 6 A fistful of hands is better with tranquility, than two handfuls with toil and affliction of spirit. 7 Then I returned and saw vanity under the sun. 8 There is one, and there is not a second, who has neither son nor brother, yet he has no end to all his travails, and his eye is not satis- fied with riches; and he does not even think, "For whom do I overwhelm and defraud my soul with pleasures?" This, too, is vanity, and this is a great traversal. 9 Two are better than one, for they have better pay for their labor. 10 For if they fail, the one shall lift up his felt: but woe to him that is alone, for he falls, and there is not a second to lift him up. 11 Moreover, if two sleep together, they shall have sleep; but for one alone how could there be sleep? 12 And if one overcomes him, two stand against him; and a chest of three is not easily broken. 13 It is better for a poor and wise child than for an old and foolish king, who no longer wants to be admonished. 14 For out of prison he comes forth to reign, while he who has been brought into his kingdom has become poor. 15 I have seen all the men walking under the sun, with the second son who will take his place. 16 There is none of all the peoples, nor of all who have gone before them, and those who will come after will not be confirmed in him; sure- ly this also is vanity and distress of spirit. (Ec- clesiastes:) Be careful of your steps when you enter the House of God, and be more careful to listen than to offer the sacrifice of fools, for they know not that they do evil.

CHAPTER 5

1 Do not be rash with your mouth or let your heart be in haste to say anything before God, for God is in heaven and you are on earth; therefore let your words be few. 2 For as sin comes from the multitude of affairs, so a man's victory is in the multitude of words. 3 When you have made a vow to God, do not put off payment, for he is not pleased with fools; therefore pay what you have made. 4 It is bet- ter that you should not make a vow than that you should make it and not pay it. 5 Do not let your mouth cause your flesh to sin, and do not say before the angel that this is ignorance; for will God be angry at your vow and destroy the work of your hands? 6 For in the multi- tude of dreams and vanities there are also many words; but you fear God. 7 If in a coun- try you see the oppression of the poor and the defrauding of right and fairness, do not be as- tonished; for he who is higher than the high- est looks on, and there are higher than they. 8 The abundance of the earth is above all; even the king consists in the cultivated field. 9 He who loves silk will not be satisfied with silk, and he who loves riches will remain without its fruits; this too is vanity. 10 When posses- sions increase, those who eat them increase; and what advantage do the owners derive from it except to see it with their own eyes? 11 The sleep of the one who eats is sweet, wheth- er he eats little or much; but the saccharine nature of the rich does not allow him to sleep. 12 There is an infinity of sickness that I have seen under the sun: riches returned to their owners for their worth. 13 But these riches perish because of a traumatized man, who begets a son and has nothing in his hand. 14 As he came forth out of his mother's womb, he will return naked to return as he came, and he will take away nothing of his labor, which he made to pass by his own hand. 15 This also is a grievous sick person, who in all points, as he came, so shall he depart, and what advan- tage has he that he traveled by the wind? 16 Moreover, all his days he eats in darkness with much sorrow, with grief and anger. 17 Behold, then, what I have seen of good, that it is good to eat, and to drink, and to take

pleasure in all the work that he does under the sun, all the days of his life, which God grants him, for this is his portion. 18 Even to him to whom God has granted riches and treasures, and gives him power to eat of them, and to take his por- tion, and to work, this is the gift of God. 19 Surely he will not remember much of the days of his life, for God responds to the joy of his heart.

CHAPTER 6

1 There is a trifle, which I say under the sun, and it is very prevalent among men: 2 A man to whom God has bestowed riches, treasures, and honors, and wants nothing for his soul of all that it desires; but God gives him no power to eat of it, but a strange man eats it: this is vanity, and this is a deadly disease. 3 If a man begets a hundred sons, and lives many years, and the days of his years multiply, and his soul is not filled with good things, and he is not buried, I say that it is better a living fruit than he. 4 For he enters vanity and goes into darkness, and his name shall be covered with darkness. 5 Moreover he has not seen the sun, nor knows him; therefore this one has more rest than the other. 6 And if he had lied for a thousand years twice and had seen nothing good, would he not go all to one place? 7 All the work of man is for his mouth, but the soul is not satiated. 8 For what has the wise man more than gruel? What has the poor man who knows how to walk before the healthy? 9 The sight of the eye is better than walking in de- sires; this also is vanity and toil of spirit. 10 What is that which has gone well? His name is now known, and it is known that he is the man, who cannot contend with those who are stronger than he is.

CHAPTER 7

1 Certainly there are many things that in- crease vanity; and what does man do? 2 For who knows what is good for man in the life and time of the life of his vanity, seeing it makes them like a shadow? For who can tell man what will be after him under the sun? 3 A good name is better than a good job, and the day of death is better than the day of one's birth. 4 It is better to go to the house of mourning than to go to the house of feast- ing, for this is the end of all men; and he who mourns will put it in his heart. 5 Wrath is better than laughter, for a sad look makes the heart better. 6 The heart of the wise is in the house of mourning, but the heart of fools is in the house of mirth. 7 It is better to hear the rebuke of a wise man than to listen to the song of fools. 8 For as the noise of thorns under the vase, so is the laughter of foolish- ness; this also is vain. 9 Oppression drives a wise man mad, and reward destroys the heart. 10 The end of a thing is better than its beginning, and the peaceful in spirit is bet- ter than the proud in spirit. 11 Do not have a choleric spirit to be angry, for anger is in the breasts of fools. 12 Do not say, "Why were the former days better than these?" because you do not inquire wisely about this. 13 Wisdom is good for the inheritance and excellent for those who see the sun. 14 For man rests in the shadow of wisdom and in the shadow of si- lence, but the excellence of the knowledge of wisdom gives life to those who possess it. 15 Behold the work of God, for who can straight- en that which he has made crooked? 16 In the day of riches be of good cheer, and in the day of affliction consider, God hath also made this contrary to that, that man may find nothing after him. 17 I have seen all things in the days of my vanity: there is a

righteous man who perishes in his righteousness, and there is a wicked man who continues long in his mal- ice. 18 Do not be too righteous, and do not make yourself an afterthought; for what rea- son should you be desolate? 19 Do not be too wicked, and do not be foolish, lest you perish in your own time? 20 It is good for you to cling to this, but do not withdraw your hand from that; for he who fears God will go out from all. 21 Wisdom strengthens the wise man more than ten mighty princes that are in the city. 22 There is no righteous man on earth who does good and does not sin. 23 Do not also heed all the words that men say, lest you hear your servant cursing you. 24 For often your heart knows that you also have cursed others. 25 All this I did with wisdom: I thought that I was wise, but it went far from me. 26 It is far away, what can it be? It is a deep place, who can find it? 27 I have sought, both I and my heart, to know, to inquire and to seek wisdom and rea- son, to know the wickedness of folly and the foolishness of madness, 28 I find more bitter than death the woman whose heart is like a net and a snare, and her hands like a snare; he that is good before God shall be delivered from her, but the sinner shall be taken from her. 29 Behold, saith the preacher, this I have found, seeking one by one to find the account: And yet my soul seeketh, but findeth not: I have found one man out of a thousand, but a woman out of all I have not found her".

CHAPTER 8

1 Who is like the wise man and who knows the interpretation of a thing? A man's wisdom makes his face shine, and the strength of his countenance changes. 2 I advise you to heed the mouth of the king and the word of the other God. 3 Do not hasten out of his pres- ence; do not stand idly by, for he will do what pleases him. 4 Where the word of the king is, there is power; and who will say to him, "What are you doing?" 5 He who observes or- ders knows nothing wrong, and the heart of the wise knows time and judgment. 6 For ev- ery purpose there is a time and judgment, for the misery of man is great upon him. 7 Since he does not know what will be, who can tell him when it will be? 8 Man is not master of the spirit to rehabilitate the spirit; he has no power in the day of death, he has no power in the battle, nor does wickedness fail those who possess it. 9 All this I have seen, and I have set my heart on every work that takes place under the sun, and I have seen that man dominates other man to his own detriment. 10 And I also said that the wicked were bur- ied and returned, and that those who came from the holy place were forgotten in the city where they had done good; this also is vain. 11 Because judgment against an evil work is not executed quickly, the hearts of the sons of men are fully predisposed to do wickedness. 12 Even if a sinner commits unfaithfulness a hundred times, and God prolongs his days, I know that it will be all right for those who fear the LORD and conduct themselves right- ly before him. 13 But to the wicked it will not go well, he will not prolong his days; he will be like a shadow, because he does not fear be- fore God. 14 There is a vanity that is fulfilled in the earth: there are righteous men to whom touches the work of the wicked, and there are wicked men to whom touches the work of the righteous: I thought also that all this is vain. 15 And I prayed, for there is no good for man under the sun, such as to eat, and to drink, and to enjoy himself; for this is charged to his work, the days of his life which God hath giv- en him under the sun. 16 When I applied my heart to know wisdom and to see the business that is done on earth, that neither day nor

night do the eyes of man take sleep, 17 I saw the whole work of God, that man cannot dis- cover the work done under the sun, because man strives to see it and cannot discover it; yea, and though the wise man thinks he knows it, he cannot find it.

CHAPTER 9

1 I have certainly set my heart to know all this, and to declare that the righteous and the wise and their works are in the hand of God; and no one knows either love or hatred for all that is before him. 2 All things are equal for all; and the same condition is for the righ- teous and for the wicked, for the good and for the pure and for the defiled, for those who sacrifice and for those who do not sac- rifice; as is the good, so is the sinner, those who swear, as those who fear another. 3 Of all that is made under the sun, there is one con- dition for all, and also the hearts of the sons of men are full of wickedness, and folly is in their hearts while they live, and after that, they go to death. 4 But he who is afflicted with all lies has hope; for it is better for a dog to die than for a lion to die. 5 For the living know that they will die, but the dead know nothing; and they have no more reward, for their memory is forgotten. 6 Even their love and their hatred and their envy are now gone, and they have no part for eternity in all that is done under the sun. 7 Go, eat your bread with joy and drink your wine with a cheerful heart, for God now accepts your works. 8 Let your garments always be white, and do not lack oil on your head. 9 Stay with the wife whom thou hast loved all the days of thy life of van- ity, whom God hath given thee under the sun all the days of thy life of vanity, for this is thy portion in life and in thy life in which thou workest under the sun. 10 Whatever thy hand shall find to do, do it with all thy might, for there is no work, nor care, nor knowledge, nor wisdom in the grave whither thou goest. 11 I have returned and said under the sun, that running is not for the swift, nor fighting for the strong, nor bread for the wise, nor riches for men of intelligence, nor vigor for men of knowledge; but time and chance reach them all. 12 For man knows not his time, but as the fish that are caught in a net, and as the birds that are caught in the snare, so the sons of men are entangled in time when it falls upon them suddenly. 13 I too have seen this wis- dom under the sun, and it is great for me. 14 A small city, with a few men in it, was attacked by a great king who surrounded it and built fortresses against it. 15 A poor and wise man was found there, and he conquered the city by his wisdom; but no one remembered this poor man. 16 Then I said, "Wisdom is better than strength; but the poor man's wisdom is despised, and his words are not heard." 17 The words of the wise man are better heard in the quiet than the cry of him who rules among the foolish. 18 Wisdom is better than weap- ons of war, but a sinner destroys many goods.

CHAPTER 10

1 Dead flies cause the ointment of the apoth- ecary to stink and putrefy; so does he who is esteemed for wisdom and for glory a little fol- ly. 2 The heart of a wise man is on his right hand, but the heart of a fool is on his left. 3 Moreover, when the fowl goes on the road, his heart fails and he tells everyone that he is a fowl. 4 If the spirit of him who rules ris- es against you, do not leave your place; for gentleness pacifies great sins. 5 There is an error I have seen under the sun, as an error proceeding from the face of him who rules. 6 Foolishness is set high, and riches are set low. 7 I have seen servants on horseback and princes walking as servants on the ground. 8 Whoever digs a pit will fall into it, and who- ever breaks the hedge, a snake will bite him. 9 He who removes stones will be hurt, and he who cuts wood will be in danger. 10 If iron is blunt, and one has not sharpened the blade, he must use more strength; but excellence in directing a thing is wisdom. 11 If the serpent bites, when it is not enchanted, a chatterer is not better. 12 The words of a wise man's mouth have grace, but the lips of a babbler spoil themselves. 13 The beginning of the words of his mouth is foolish, and the last word of his mouth is wicked folly. 14 Foolish- ness multiplies words, saying, "Man does not know what will be; and who can tell him what will be after him? 15 The toil of the fool fa- tigues him, because he does not know how to go into the city. 16 Woe to thee, O earth, when thy king shall be a child, and thy princes shall eat in the morning. 17 Blessed are you, O land, when your king is the son of nobles, and your princes eat in time, for strength and not for drunkenness. 18 By gluttony, the roof of the house goes down, and by the carelessness of hands, the house falls to pieces. 19 They pre- pare bread for laughter, and wine comforts those who are dying, but silence answers all. 20 Curse not the king, not in thy thought, and curse not the rich in thy bedchamber: for the filth of heaven shall make the voice, and he that hath wings shall declare the thing.

CHAPTER 11

1 Cast your bread upon the waters, for after many days you will find it. 2 Give a portion to ten and also to eight, for you do not know what will happen on the earth. 3 If the clouds are full, they will make it rain on the earth; and if the tree falls toward the south or toward the north, in the place where the tree falls, there it will remain. 4 He who observes the wind will not sow, and he who observes the clouds will not reap. 5 Just as you do not know what is the way of the spirit, nor how the bones grow in the womb of her who is with child, so you do not know the work of God who works every- thing. 6 In the morning sow your land, and at sunset do not let your hand rest, for you do not know whether this or that will prosper, or whether both will have the same good. 7 Light is certainly a pleasant thing, and it is good for the eyes to see the sun. 8 Even if a man lives many years and feels good in them, he will remember the days of darkness, for they are many, and all that comes is in vain. 9 Recov- er, O young man, in your youth, and let your heart rejoice in the days of your youth; walk in the desires of your heart and the sight of your eyes; but know that for all these things God will bring you to judgment. 10 Therefore turn away sadness from thy heart, and let ela- tion depart from thy flesh: for childhood and youth are vain.

CHAPTER 12

1 Remember now thy Creator in the days of thy youth, while the days of glory come not, nor the years draw nigh when thou shalt say, "I have no pleasure in them." 2 when the sun is not dark, nor the light, nor the moon, nor the stars, nor the clouds return after the rain: 3 when the keepers of the house shall tremble, the strong shall bow down, the grinders shall cease, for they are few, and those who look out of your windows shall become dark: 4 And the doors

shall be shut because of the low sound of the grinder, and shall rise up at the voice of the bird; and all the daughters of song shall be cast down. 5 Moreover they shall be afraid of that which is easiest, and fear shall be upon the way, and the almond tree shall flourish, and the grasshopper shall be a burden, and concupiscence shall be removed; for man goes to the house of his age, and mourners go about in the streets. 6 While the silken hood shall not be stretched out, nor shall the golden pitcher be broken, nor shall the pitcher at the well be broken, nor shall the wheel at the cis- tern be broken: 7 The dust returns to the earth as it was, and the spirit returns to God who gave it. 8 Vanity of vanities, says the Preacher, all is vanity. 9 The wiser the preacher was, the more he taught the people knowledge, made them listen, sought them out, and prepared many parables. 10 The preacher sought to find pleasant words and correct writing, that is, words of truth. 11 The words of the wise are like goads and like nails driven in by the masters of the assemblies, who are led by one shepherd. 12 And of other things besides these, my son, take heed, for there is no end in making many books, and reading much wears out the flesh. 13 But hear the end of all things: fear God and keep his commands, for this is the whole duet of man. 14 For God will bring every work and every secret thing into judgment, whether it be good or evil.

SONG OF SOLOMON

CHAPTER 1

1 Let him kiss me with the kisses of his mouth, for your charms are better than wine. 2 Because of the taste of your good ointments, your name is like an ointment that is released; therefore virgins worship you. 3 Drag me, we will run after you; the king has brought me into his chambers; we will rejoice and be glad in you; we will remember your love more than wine; the righteous love you. 4 I am black, O daughters of Jerusalem, but I am as beautiful as the tents of Kedar and as the tents of Sol- omon. 5 Do not look upon me because I am black, for the sun has looked upon me. My mother's sons have been angry with me; they have made me guard the vineyards, but I have not guarded my vineyard. 6 Tell me, O you, whom my soul desires, where you feed, where you lie to no one; why should I be like she who strays from the flock of your companions? 7 If you do not know, O you who are the fairest among women, set out by the footsteps of the flock and feed your children by the shepherds' tents. 8 I have compared you, O my beauty, to the host of horses in Pharaoh's chambers. 9 Your cheeks are adorned with rows of stones, and your neck with chains. 10 We will make you borders of gold and studs of silk. 11 While the king was at table, my spikenard gave the smell. 12 My benefactor is to me as a bundle of myrrh; he will lie down between my breasts. 13 My good is to me as a cluster of saffron in the vineyards of Engedi. 14 My lady, behold, thou art beautiful; behold, thou art fair; thy eyes are as the eyes of dogs. 15 My bride, be- hold, thou art fair and pleasant; even our bed is green: 16 The beams of our house are cedar; our rafters are of wood.

CHAPTER 2

1 I am the rose of the fields and the flower of the valleys. 2 As a lily among thorns, so is my prestige among daughters. 3 As the apple tree among the trees of the forest, so is my fame among the sons of men; under its shadow I delighted and sat down, and its fruit was sweet to my mouth. 4 He brought me into the cellar, and his banner protected me. 5 He made me drink mugs and comforted me with apples, for I am sick with joy. 6 His left hand is under my head, and his right hand embraces me. 7 I command you, O daughters of Jeru- salem, by the roebucks and the hinds of the field, not to stir and not to wake my lady until it pleases her. 8 It is the journey of my dar- ling: behold, he cometh leaping through the mountains and skipping over the hills. 9 My Beneficent is like a deer or a heifer; behold, he stands behind our wall, looking through the windows and showing himself through the gratings. 10 My benefactor spoke and said to me, "Arise, my darling, my darling, and come on your way." 11 For behold, winter is past; the rain has changed and gone away. 12 The flow- ers appear on the earth; the time has come for the birds to sing, and the turtle's cry is heard in our country. 13 The fig tree has brought its long figs, and the vine with its little clusters has cast its fragrance; arise, my darling, and come away. 14 My bride, who is in the holes of the rocks, in the secret places of the stables, show me your sight, let me hear your jour- ney, for your journey is sweet and your sight is pleasant. 15 Take the foxes, the little foxes that destroy the vines, for our vines have lit- tle grapes. 16 My darling is mine, and I am his; he feeds among the lilies, 17 Until the day dawns and the shadow fades away; return, my darling, and be like a deer or a heifer in the mountains of Bether.

CHAPTER 3

1 At night in my bed I sought him whom my soul longed for: I sought him, but did not find him. 2 Now I will get up, and go about the city, and about the streets, and about the open places, and seek him whom my soul de- sires: I have sought him, but have not found him. 3 The watchmen that went about the city found me, to whom I said, "Have you seen him whom my soul desires?" 4 When I had gone some distance from them, I found him whom my soul longed for: I took him and did not leave him until I had brought him to my mother's house, to the room of her who con- ceived me. 5 I command you, O daughters of Jerusalem, by the roebucks and the hinds of the field, not to stir and not to wake my lady until it pleases her. 6 Who is she who comes out of the wilderness like columns of smoke scented with myrrh and frankincense and all the spices of the marketplace? 7 Here is her bed, which is Solomon; around it are sixty strong men, from among the valiant of Israel. 8 All of them wield the sword and are skilled in warfare; each has his sword on his thigh for the fear of the night. 9 King Solomon made himself a palace of trees from Lebanon. 10 He made its pillars of silk, its walls of gold, and its facings of purple, the walls of which were covered with the jewels of the daughters of Je- rusalem. 11 Come out, daughters of Zion, and see King Solomon with the crown with which his mother crowned him on his wedding day and on the day of his heart's joy.

CHAPTER 4

1 Behold, you are beautiful, my darling, be- hold, you are beautiful; your eyes are like the eyes of dogs; between your locks your hearing is like a herd of goats watching from the mountain of Gilead. 2 Thy teeth are like a flock of sheep in order, coming out of the laundry; every one of them gives birth to twins, and none is barren. 3 Thy lips are like a braid

of scarlet, and thy speech is fair; thy temples are within thy locks like a piece of pomegran- ate. 4 Your neck is like the tower of Dauid built for defense; a thousand shields and all the targets of strong men hang on it. 5 Your two breasts are like twin young goats feeding among the lilies. 6 Until the day dawns and the shadow fades, I will go to the mount of myrrh and the mount of frankincense. 7 You are all beautiful, my darling, and there is no blemish in you. 8 Come with me from Leba- non, my bride, come with me from Lebanon and look from the top of Amanah, from the top of Shenir and Hermon, from the dunes of the lions and the mountains of the leopards. 9 My sister, my bride, you have wounded my heart; you have wounded my heart with one of your eyes and with a noose from your neck. 10 My sister, my bride, how beautiful is your charm, how much better is your charm than wine and the taste of your perfumes of all spices? 11 Your lips, my bride, fall like combs of honor; honor and milk are under your tongue, and the fragrance of your garments is like the perfume of Lebanon. 12 My sister, my bride, is like a fenced garden, like a closed spring and a sealed fountain. 13 Your plants are like an orchard of pomegranates with sweet fruit, like a field of sapphires, of spikes, 14 the spikenard of Europe, the saffron, the calamus, the cinamom, all the frankincense trees, myrrh, aloes, and all the most import- ant spices. 15 O fountain of gardens, O well of clear water, and springs of Lebanon. 16 Arise, O North, and come, O South, and blow upon my garden that its spices may flow forth; let my well- wisher come to his garden and eat its pleasant fruits.

CHAPTER 5

1 I have entered into my garden, my sister, my bride: I have gathered my my myrrh with my spice; I have eaten my combe bone with my bone, I have drunk my wine with my milk; eat, O friends, drink, and make merry, O wel- come. 2 I sleep, but my heart is awakened; it is the voice of my benefactor knocking, say- ing, "Open me, my sister, my lady, my wife, my son, for my head is full of dew, and my locks with drops of the night." 3 I have tak- en off my cloak, how shall I put it on again? I have washed my feet, how shall I defile them? 4 My friend stood in my hand at the hole of the door, and my heart grew fond of him. 5 I rose up to open to my guest, and my hands let fall of myrrh, and my fingers of pure myrrh on the handles of the bar. 6 I opened to my guest, but my guest was gone, and had passed away; my heart went out when he spake; I sought him, but found him not: I called him, but he answered me not. 7 The sentinels that went about the city found me; they struck me and wounded me; the sentinels of the walls took away my courage. 8 I command you, O daughters of Jerusalem, if you find my host, tell him that I am sick of war. 9 O the fairest of women, what is your good more than oth- er benefactors, what is your good more than another woman, for whom you charge so? 10 My treasure is white and strong, the best of ten thousand. 11 Her head is like fine gold, her locks are curled and she is as blue as a ruin. 12 His eyes are like the teeth of waters that have been bathed in milk and remain near full ves- sels. 13 His cheeks are like a bed of spices and like fragrant flowers, and his lips are like lil- ies that fall on pure myrrh. 14 His hands are like rings of gold set with chrysolite; his belly is like a white yuorie covered with saphir. 15 His legs are like pillars of marble, set on bases of fine gold; his face is like Lebanon, excellent like cedars. 16 His mouth is like a sweet thing, and he is delicious; this is my welcome, and this is my

delight, O daughters of Jerusalem. O the fairest of women, where has your good gone, where has your good been diverted, that I might see him with you?

CHAPTER 6

1 My benefactor has gone down to his garden to the beds of spices, to feed in the gardens and gather lilies. 2 I am my benefactor, and my benefactor is mine, who feeds among the lilies. 3 You are as beautiful as Tirzah, as fair as Ierusale, as terrible as an army with ban- ners. 4 Turn away your eyes from me, for they make me afraid; your hearing is like a herd of goats watching from Gilead. 5 Your teeth are like a flock of sheep coming out of the laun- dry, from which twins are born every time, and none is barren. 6 Your temples are with- in your locks like a piece of pomegranate. 7 There are sixty queens and four concubines, and among the damsels there is none. 8 But my bride is alone, and my vndefiled, she is the only daughter of her mother, and she is dear to her who bore her; the daughters have seen her, and have counted her blessed, as have the queens and concubines, who have praised her. 9 Who is she who is fair as the morning, beautiful as the moon, pure as the sun, terri- ble as an army with banners? 10 I went down to the nut garden to see the fruit of the valley, to see if the vine budded and if the pomegran- ates bloomed. 11 I knew nothing, my mind set me like the classes of my noble people. 12 Return, return, O Sculamite, return, return that we may see you. What will you see in the Sculamite but the company of an army?

CHAPTER 7

1 How beautiful are your steps in shoes, O daughter of princes! The jewels of thy thighs are like jewels, the work of a skilled work- man's hand. 2 Thy skin is like a round cup that lacks no delicacy; thy belly is like a heap of wheat surrounded by lilies. 3 Your two breasts are like twin roes. 4 Your neck is like a tower of yuorie; your eyes are like the fish pools of Heshbon, by the gate of Bath-rabbim; your nose is like the tower of Lebanon, looking toward Damascus. 5 Your head is like a skin, and the bush of your head is like purple; the king is bound to the rafters. 6 How beauti- ful you are, and how pleasant, O my lord, in pleasures! 7 Your stature is like a palm tree, and your crests like clusters. 8 I said, "I will go and eat on the palm tree, I will take pos- session of its branches; your breasts shall now be like the clusters of the vine, and the taste of your nose like apples, 9 and the sound of your mouth like good wine, which goes straight to my welfare and makes the lips of the ancients speak. 10 I am my benefactor, and his desire is toward me. 11 Come, my benefactors, go to- ward the country and stay in the villages. 12 Go early to the vineyards, see if the vine has blossomed, if the little grapes have sprouted, or if the pomegranates have blossomed; there I will give you my joy. 13 The mandrakes have taken fragrance, and in our gates are all sweet things, new and old; my benefactor, I have stored them up for you.

CHAPTER 8

1 Oh, if you were like my brother who sucked my mother's crests: I would like to find you outside, I would like to kill you, so they would not despise you. 2 I will leave thee and

take thee to my mother's house; there thou shalt teach me; and I will make thee drink spiced wine and new pomegranate wine. 3 His left hand shall be under my head, and his right hand shall embrace me. 4 I command you, O daughters of Hierusale, not to stir, and not to wake my lady until it pleases her. 5 (Who is this coming out of the thicket, leaning on her head?). I brought you under an apple tree; there your mother conceived you, there she who gave birth to you. 6 Set me as a seal upon thy heart, and as an insignia upon thy arm; for lust is strong as death, jealousy is cruel as the grave, her streams are fiery streams and a vehement flame. 7 Much water cannot quench lust, neither can floods submerge it: If a man gave all the substance of his house for joy, they would be very sorry. 8 We have a little sister, who has no breasts; what shall we do for our sister when it is spoken of her? 9 If she be a wall, we will build her a palace of silk; and if she be a tomb, we will guard her with cedar borders. 10 I am a wall, and my breasts are as towers; in her eyes I was like one who finds peace. 11 Solomon had a vineyard in Baal-Hamon; he entrusted the vineyard to keepers; each one brought for his fruit a thou- sand pieces of silk. 12 But my vineyard, which is mine, is before me; to thee, O Solomon, belong a thousand pieces of silver, and two hundred to them that keep the fruit thereof. 13 O thou that dwellest in the gardens, the companions hear thy voice; let me hear it. 14 O my benefactor, flee away and become like the deer or the young herald on the moun- tains of spices.

MAJOR PROPHETS

These books deliver powerful messages from God, addressing social justice, judgment, and redemption

ISAIAH

CHAPTER 1

1 Vision of Isaiah the son of Amoz, who spoke of Iudah and Jerusalem in the days of Vzziah, Iotham, Ahaz and Hezekiah, kings of Iudah. 2 Hear, O heavens, and hear, O earth, for the LORD said, "I have nourished and brought up children, but they have rebelled against me." 3 The ox knows his master, and the horse his cradle; but Israel knows not, my people understand not. 4 Ah, sinful nation, a people laden with iniquity, a race of wicked men, corrupt children, they have forsaken the LORD, they have provoked the Holy One of Israel to anger, they have turned back. 5 Why should ye be smitten again? Because you turn away more and more: the whole head is sick and the whole heart is sick. 6 From the sole of the foot even to the head, there is nothing whole, but wounds, swellings, and sores full of corruption; they have not been bandaged, nor bound, nor soothed with oil. 7 Thy land is deserted, thy cities are burned with fire; for- eigners ravage thy land in thy presence, and it is desolate as the land of foreigners. 8 The daughter of Zion shall remain as a cotage in a vineyard, as a lodge in a garden of cucumbers, as a besieged city. 9 If the LORD of hosts had not reserved a little remnant for us, we would have been like Sodom and like Gomorah. 10 Hear the word of the LORD, O princes of Sod- om; hear the law of our God, O people of Go- morah. 11 What shall I do with the multitude of your sacrifices, says the LORD? I am full of the burnt offerings of rams and the fat of fed beasts; and I desire not the blood of bull- ocks, lambs and goats. 12 When you come to appear before me, who required your hands to trample on my fields? 13 Bring no more oblations in wine; incense is an abomination to me: I cannot tolerate your new moons, nor Sabbaths, nor solemn days (it is an iniquity), nor solemn assemblies. 14 My mind hates your new moons and your appointed feasts; they are a burden to me: I am weary to bear them. 15 When you stretch out your hands, I will hide my eyes from you; and though you make many prayers, I will not hear, for your hands are full of blood. 16 Wash yourselves, make yourselves pure; remove the wicked- ness of your works from my eyes; cease to do wickedness. 17 Learn to behave well: observe judgment, succor the oppressed; judge the orphan and defend the widow. 18 Come now and let us reason together, saith the LORD: though your sins were like criminality, they shall become white as snow; though they were red like skin, they shall become like wool. 19 If you consent and obey, you will eat the good things of the land. 20 But if you refuse and are rebellious, you shall be smitten with the sword, for the mouth of the LORD has spo- ken it. 21 How is it that the faithful city has become a harlot? It was full of righteousness and dwelt there, but now they are murderers. 22 Your silence has become a shadow, your wine is mixed with water. 23 Your princes are rebels and companions in misfortune; Every one of them hoards gifts and goes after re- wards; They do not judge the fatherless and do not come forward to widows. 24 Therefore says the LORD, the God of hosts, the mighty one of Israel, "I will get rid of my adversaries, and I will get rid of my enemies. 25 Then I will turn my hand upon you, I will bury your dust until it is pure, and I will remove all your tin. 26 I will restore thy judges as in the begin- ning, and thy counsellors as in the beginning; afterward thou shalt be called a city of righ- teousness, and a faithful city. 27 Zion shall be redeemed in judgment, and those who return to her, in righteousness. 28 The transgressors and sinners shall be destroyed together, and those who forsake the LORD shall be con- sumed. 29 For they shall be confounded for the games that you have desired, and you shall be ashamed of the gardens that you have chosen. 30 For you shall be like a goose whose sap fades away, and like a garden that has no water. 31 The strong shall be like tow, and its maker like a spark; both shall burn together, and none shall quench them.

CHAPTER 2

1 The word which Isaiah the son of Amoz spoke concerning Iudah and Jerusalem. 2 In the last days, the mountain of the house of the LORD shall be prepared on the top of the mountains and shall be exalted on the hills, and all the nations shall flock there. 3 Many peoples will go and say, "Come, let us go to the mountain of the LORD, to the house of the God of Iaakob, and he will teach us his ways and we will walk in his paths, for the word of the LORD will depart from Zion and the word of the LORD from Jerusalem." 4 He will judge among the nations and rebuke many peoples; they will reduce their swords into mats and their spears into sixes; nation will no longer raise a sword against nation, and they will no longer learn to fight. 5 O house of Iaakob, come and walk in the peace of the LORD. 6 You have forsaken your people, the house of Iaakob, because they are full of oriental wielders, are sorcerers like the Philistines, and abound with strange children. 7 Their land also was full of silver and gold, and there was nothing that was not gathered from their treasures; their land was full of horses,

and their horses were endless. 8 Their land was also full of idols; they worshiped the works of their hands, which their fingers had made. 9 One man bowed down and one man humbled himself; therefore do not spare them. 10 Enter the enclosure and hide in the dust before the fear of the LORD and the glory of his majesty. 11 The appearance of man shall be humbled, and the height of men shall be lowered, and the LORD alone shall be exalted in that day. 12 For the day of the LORD of hosts is upon all pride and haughtiness, and upon all that is exalted, and it shall be lowered. 13 Also on all the cedars of Lebanon, which are high and exalted, and on all the trees of Bashan, 14 On all the mountains and on all the heights that are exalted, 15 on all the towers and on all the strong walls, 16 and on all the ships of Tarsh- ish, and on all the pleasant images. 17 And the height of men shall be lowered, and the LORD alone shall be exalted in that day. 18 And the idols will be utterly destroyed. 19 Then they shall depart into the holes of the rocks and into the caverns of the earth, lest they fear the LORD and the glory of his majesty, when he rises up to destroy the earth. 20 In that day man shall cast away his idols of silver and his idols of gold (which they had made for them- selves to worship) in their sickles and their backsides, 21 to go into the holes of the rocks and the tops of the cleft rocks, before the fear of the LORD and the glory of his majesty, when he rises up to destroy the earth. 22 Stop turning away from the man whose breath is in his nostrils, for in what way can he be es- teemed?

CHAPTER 3

1 For behold, the LORD God of hosts will take away from Jerusalem and from Iudah the supply and the strength, that is, all the sup- ply of bread and all the supply of water, 2 the strong man and the man of war, the judge and the prophet, the prudent man and the elder, 3 the captain of five, the man of honor, the counselor, the shrewd engineer and the elo- quent man. 4 And I will appoint the children as their princes, and the children will rule them. 5 And the people shall be oppressed one by another, and each by his neighbor; and the children shall oppose the ancient, and the vile the honorable. 6 When every man shall take care of his brother of his father's house, and shall say, "You are clothed, you shall be our prince, and this fall shall be under your hand." 7 In that day he shall swear, saying, "I cannot be a helper, for there is no bread in my house nor clothing; therefore do not make me prince of the people." 8 Jerusalem is fallen, and Iudah is fallen, because their tongue and their works are against the LORD, to put to shame the eyes of his glory. 9 The evidence of their countenance testifies against them, yea, they declare their sins like Sodom, they do not hide them. Woe to their souls, for they have rewarded the wickedness of themselves. 10 Say, "Surely it shall be good for the righteous, for they shall eat the fruit of their labor." 11 Woe to the wicked, it will go bad for him, for the reward of his hands will be given him. 12 Children are extortioners of my people, and women rule over them: O my people, those who lead you make you err, and destroy the way of your paths. 13 The LORD is standing to plead, yea, he is standing to judge the people. 14 The LORD will come into judgment with the ancients of his people and with his princ- es, because you have eaten the vineyard; the spoil of the poor is in your houses. 15 What have ye to do, that ye tear my people in piec- es, and shred the faces of the poor, saith the LORD, the LORD of roasts? 16 The LORD also says, "For the daughters of Zion are haughty, and walk with their necks stretched out, and with wandering eyes, walking and making noise when they go, and making their feet jingle." 17 Therefore the LORD will cause the heads of the daughters of Zion to leap, and the LORD will unveil their secret parts. 18 In that day the LORD will remove the adornment of the slippers, the corns, and the round tires, 19 the sweet balls, the brasselets, and the bon- nets, 20 the erasers of the head, the sloppes, the bands, the tablets, and the earrings, 21 the rings and mufflers, 22 the costly garments, the sails, the wimps, and the pinnacles, 23 the glasses, the fine linen, the hoods and lan- terns. 24 In place of sweet perfume there shall be sting, and in place of a girdle a cleft, and in place of clothing for the ears baldness, and in place of the stomach a girdle of sackcloth, and in place of beauty fire. 25 Your men shall fall by the sword and your strength in battle. 26 Then shall her gates weep and wail, and she, desolate, shall sit on the ground.

CHAPTER 4

1 In that day some women shall join a man, saying, "We will eat our bread and put on our garments"; only then shall we be called by your name and take off our reproach. 2 In that day the shoot of the LORD will be beauti- ful and glorious, and the fruits of the land will be excellent and pleasant for those who fled from Israel. 3 The one who will remain in Zion and the one who will remain in Jerusalem will be called holy, and every one of them will be written among the inhabitants of Jerusalem, 4 When the LORD shall wash the filthiness of the daughters of Zion, and shall cleanse the blood of Jerusalem from her bowels with the spirit of judgment and with the spirit of burning. 5 The LORD will create over every place in Mount Zion and over its assemblies a cloud and smoke by day, and the splendor of a blazing fire by night; for over all the glory there will be a defense. 6 And a shelter shall be as a shadow by day for the heir, and a place of refuge and a shelter for the storm and for the rain.

CHAPTER 5

1 Now I will sing to my beloved a song of my beloved to his vineyard: My beloved had a vineyard on a very fruitful hill, 2 he fenced it, gathered its stones, planted it with the best plants, built a tower in the middle, and made a cellar there; then he thought it would bring in grapes, but he brought in wild grapes. 3 Now, therefore, inhabitants of Jerusalem and men of Iudah, judge, I pray you, between me and my vineyard. 4 What could I do to my vineyard that I have not already done? Why have I sought that it should produce grapes, but instead it produces wild grapes? 5 Now I will tell you what I will do to my vineyard: I will take away its hedge, and it shall be eat- en up: I will break down its wall, and it shall be cut down: 6 I will lay it to rest; it shall not be cut down nor dug up, but brambles and thorns shall grow: And I will also command the clouds not to break in upon it any more. 7 Surely the vineyard of the LORD of hosts is the house of Israel, and the men of Judah are his fair plant: he sought judgment, but he saw oppression, justice, but he saw weeping. 8 Woe to those who divide house by house, and who put field by field, until there is no more room, that you may be placed alone in the midst of the earth. 9 This is in my care, says the LORD of hosts. Surely, many hous- es will be desolate, even large ones, and they will be without inhabitants. 10 For ten acres of vines

are equivalent to one bath, and a farm- er's seed is equivalent to one ephah. 11 Woe to those who rise early to follow the drunkards, and to those who continue until night, until the wine inflames them. 12 At their banquets there are harps and viols, timpani, fifes and wine, but they do not consider the work of the LORD, nor the work of his hands. 13 Therefore my people have gone into captivity, because they had no knowledge, and their brightness is hungry and their multitude is parched with thirst. 14 Therefore hell has enlarged and opened its mouth without measure, and their glory, their multitude, their pomp, and he who is in their midst will descend into it. 15 And man shall be brought low, and man shall be humbled, even as the eyes of the proud shall be humbled. 16 The LORD of hosts will be exalted in judgment, and the holy God will be sanctified in righteousness. 17 Then the lambs will graze according to their order, and the strangers will eat the desolate places of the fat. 18 Woe to those who draw iniquity with cords of vanity and sin as with chariot ropes: 19 Who say, "Let him hasten, let him hasten his work, that we may see it; and let the counsel of the Holy One of Israel draw near and come, that we may know him." 20 Woe to those who speak good of evil and evil of good, who put darkness for light and light for darkness, who put bitter for sweet and sweet for poor. 21 Woe to those who are wise in their own eyes and prudent in their own eyes. 22 Woe to those who are mighty to drink wine, and to those who are strong to drink strong: 23 Who justify the wicked as a reward, and take away from them the righteousness of the righteous. 24 Therefore as the flame of fire consumes stubble, and as coffee is con- sumed by flame, so shall their roots be as rot- tenness, and their shoot shall rise up as dust: for they have cast away the word of the LORD of hosts, and have despised the word of the Holy One of Israel. 25 Therefore the wrath of the LORD has been kindled against his peo- ple, and he has stretched out his hand upon them, and struck them that the mountains should tremble; their carcasses have been torn in the midst of the streets, and for all this his wrath has not turned away, but his hand still remains stretched out. 26 He will make a sign to the distant nations and reach them from the ends of the earth; and behold, they will come in haste. 27 No one shall slumber or fall in their midst; no one shall slumber or sleep, nor shall the girdle of his bonds be loosed, nor shall the laces of his shoes be bro- ken: 28 His arrows shall be sharpened, and all his bows shall bend; his horse's hooves shall be held up like flint, and his wheels like a whirlwind. 29 And his roar shall be as the roar of a lion, and he shall roar as the young ones of a lion; they shall roar and take hold of the prayer; they shall carry it away, and none shall deliver it. 30 In that day they shall break forth upon them like the roaring of the sea; and if they look toward the earth, they shall see darkness and sorrow, and the light shall be darkened in their skin.

CHAPTER 6

1 In the year of King Vzziah's death, I also saw the Lord seated on a throne high and lifted up, the lower parts of which filled the Temple. 2 Seraphim stood above it; each had six wings; with two he covered his face, with two he covered his feet, and with two he flew. 3 One cried out to the other and said, "Holy, holy, holy is the LORD of hosts; the whole world is full of his glory." 4 The flaps of the cheeks of the others moved at the sight of him who shouted, and the house was filled with smoke. 5 Then I said, "May I be vituperated, for I am a man of defiled lips, and I dwell among a people of defiled lips, because my eyes have seen the King and Lord of hosts." 6 Then one of the seraphim came to me with a wooden knife in his hand that he had taken from the altar with tongs: 7 He touched my mouth and said, "Behold, this has touched your lips; your iniquity shall be taken away and your sin cleansed." 8 Moreover I heard the speech of the Lord saying, "Whom shall I send and who will go for you? Then I said, "Here am I, send me." 9 And he said, "Go and say to this people, 'You will hear in faith, but you will not understand; you will see clearly, but you will not perceive. 10 Make the heart of this people hard, make their ears weak, and close their eyes, lest they see with their eyes, and hear with their ears, and understand with their hearts, and be convinced and heal them." 11 Then I said, "Lord, until when?" And he answered, "Until the cities are deserted, without inhabitants, and the houses without men, and the land is utterly desolate, 12 and the LORD shall have driven men far away, and there shall be a great desolation in the midst of the land. 13 But there shall be a tenth in it, which shall return and be eaten as an elm or a goose, which have substance in them, when they cast their leaves; so the holy seed shall be its substance.

CHAPTER 7

1 In the days of Ahaz, son of Iotham, son of Vzziah, king of Judah, Rezin, king of Aram, and Pekah, son of Remaliah, king of Israel, came to Jerusalem to fight against it, but they could not conquer it. 2 To the house of Dauid it was said, "Aram had a bond with Ephraim; therefore his heart was smitten, and the heart of his people, as the trees of the forest are smitten with the wind." 3 Then the LORD said to Isaiah, "Go now and meet Ahaz (you and Sheariashub, your son) at the end of the shaft of the vip well, on the path of the field of the fullers, 4 and say to him, "Be careful and do not fret; do not fear and do not be discouraged by the two tails of these smoking firebrands, by the furious wrath of Rezin, Aram, and Re- maliah's son: 5 For Aram has taken evil coun- sel against you, against Ephraim and against the son of Remaliah, saying, 6 "Go Vs against Iudah, awaken them, and make a breach in them, and set a king in the midst of them, the son of Tabeal." 7 Thus says the LORD God, "He shall not stand and be there." 8 Because the head of Aram is Damascus and the head of Damascus is Rezin, within five years and sixty Ephraim will be destroyed as a people. 9 The chief of Ephraim is Samaria, and the chief of Samaria is the son of Remaliah. If you do not rise, you will certainly not be es- tablished." 10 The LORD spoke again to Ahaz, saying, 11 Ask a sign for the LORD your God; ask it either in depth or in height." 12 But Ahaz said, "I will not ask it or tempt the LORD." 13 Then he said, "Hear now, O house of Dauid, is it a small thing for you to heal men, that you should do so also with my God? 14 Therefore the Lord himself will give you a sign. Behold, the virgin shall conceive and bear a son, and shall call his name Immanu- el. 15 He shall eat butter and honey, until he has learned to reject the worthless and choose the good. 16 For before the child has learned to reject the euillity and to choose the good, the land that you abhor will be forsaken by both its kings. 17 And the LORD will cause the king of Assur to come upon you, and upon your people, and upon your father's house (the days that have not come since the day that Ephraim depart- ed from Iudah). 18 In that day the LORD will take care of the fly that is at the end of the floods of Egypt and the bee that is in the land of Assur, 19 they shall come and illuminate all the desolate valleys, the holes

of the rocks, the thorny places, and the bushy places. 20 In that day the LORD shall cut off with a razor hired by those who are beyond the river, by the king of Assur, the head and the hairline of the feet, and consume the beard. 21 On the same day a man shall feed a yong kow and two sheep. 22 And for the abundance of milk they shall give, butter shall be eaten; for they shall eat the butter and the honey that is left in the land. 23 In the same day, in every place where there are a thousand vines, there shall be a thou- sand pieces of silk; so shall it be with briers and thorns. 24 With arrows and with bows it will be possible to go that far, for the whole land will be full of briers and thorns. 25 But on all the mountains that will be dug with the mattocke, there will be no fear of briers and thorns, but they will serve to bring out the heifers and to trample the sheep.

CHAPTER 8

1 Moreover, the LORD said to me, "Take a large scroll and write in it with a man's pen, 'Hasten to spit, hasten to pray.'" 2 Then I took with me faithful witnesses to record: Vriah the priest and Zechariah the son of Jeberechi- ah. 3 Then I presented myself to the prophet- ess who had conceived and borne a son. Then the LORD said to me, "Call him by the name of Mahershalalhash-baz." 4 For before the child has the ability to cry out, 'My father and my mother,' he will carry away the riches of Damascus and the wealth of Samaria before the king of Assur." 5 The LORD spoke to me again, saying, 6 For this people have rejected the gently flowing waters of Shiloh, and are reconciled to Rezin and to the son of Rema- liah, 7 therefore behold, the LORD brings upon them the waters of the River, mighty and great, that is, the king of Assur with all his glory; he will come upon all their banks and overcome all their banks, 8 he shall break through into Judah, he shall go out and pass through, he shall come up to the neck, and the spreading of his wings shall fill the breadth of your land, O Immanu-El. 9 Gather yourselves on your shoulders, O peoples, and you shall be broken in pieces, and hear all of you from the far countries; gird up your bodies and you shall be broken in pieces; gird up your bod- ies and you shall be broken in pieces. 10 Take counsel together, but it shall be thwarted; make a decree, but it shall not stand, for God is with you. 11 For the Lord has spoken to me thus, taking me by the hand, and has taught me not to walk in the way of this people, say- ing, 12 Do not say, "A confederacy for all those to whom this people say a confederacy"; do not fear their fear and do not fear them. 13 Sanctify the LORD of hosts, let him be your fear and dread, 14 he shall be as a sanctuary, but as a stumbling block and as a boulder to fall upon for the two houses of Israel, and as a snare and a net for the inhabitants of Jeru- salem. 15 Many of them will stumble and fall and break; they will be caught and will be un- dermined. 16 Gather testimony and keep the Law among my disciples. 17 Therefore I will wait for the LORD who hid his face from the house of Iaakob and seek him. 18 Behold, I and the sons whom the LORD has given me are signs and wonders in Israel, by the LORD of hosts, who dwells on Mount Zion. 19 And when they say to you, "Ask those who have a spirit of divination and the soothsayers, who murmur and murmur, "Should not a people ask of their God, from the time they are alive to the dead? 20 to the Law and the testimo- nies, if they do not speak according to this word, it is because there is no light in them. 21 Then he who is afflicted and hungry shall go and return from there; and when he is hungry, he shall rejoice, and curse his king and

his gods, and look forward. 22 And when he shall look upon the earth, he shall see trou- ble and darkness, distress and sorrow, and he shall give himself up to darkness.

CHAPTER 9

1 But the darkness will not be like what it was when it lightly touched the land of Zebulun and the land of Naphtali at first, nor after- ward, when it was more severe by the way of the sea beyond Iorden, in Galilee of the Gen- tiles. 2 The people who walked in darkness saw a great light; those who dwelt in the land of the shadow of death, upon them the light shone. 3 You multiplied the nation and did not increase their gain; they reacted before you according to the gain they made in battle, and as men react when they do battle. 4 For the yoke of their burden, and the staff of their shoulder, and the rod of their oppressor, thou hast broken them as in the days of Midian. 5 Every battle of the warrior has been done with death and with the overthrow of his garments in blood, but this one will be done with fire and the burning of fire. 6 For out of him was born a child, out of him was born a son; the custody is on his shoulder, and he shall call his name Wonderful, Counselor, Mighty God, Everlasting Father, Prince of Peace, 7 the in- crease of his security and peace shall have no end; he shall sit on the throne of Dauid and on his kingdom, to order it and establish it with justice and judicature, henceforth and forev- er; the zeal of the LORD of hosts shall accom- plish this. 8 The LORD sent a word in Iaakob, and it was kindled upon Israel. 9 All the peo- ples shall know it, and especially Ephraim and the inhabitants of Samaria, who say in pride and conceit of heart, 10 The bricks have fall- en down, but we will build it with its stones; the wild fig trees have been cut down, but we will turn them into cedars. 11 The LORD will raise up the adversaries of Rezin against him and gather his enemies together. 12 Aram in front and the Philistines behind, who will face Israel with their mouths open; yet for all this his wrath has not turned away, but his hand is still stretched out. 13 For the people do not turn toward him who smites them, nor do they see the LORD of hosts. 14 Therefore the LORD will cut off in one day from Israel the head and the tail, the branch and the reed. 15 The ancient and honorable man is the leader; the prophet who teaches lies is the leader. 16 For the leaders of the people lead them into error, and those who are led by them ruin themselves. 17 Therefore the LORD will not be pleased with their young men, nor will he have compassion on their families and their widows, for every one is hypocritical and wicked, and every mouth speaks foolishness; yet for all this his wrath does not depart, but his hand is stretched out toward them. 18 For wickedness burns like a fire; it devours the briers and thorns, and kindles in the thickest places of the forest; and it will go up like a ris- ing smoke. 19 The wrath of the LORD of hosts will darken the land, and the people will be like the mush of fire; no one will spare his broth- er. 20 He shall rend at his right hand, and he shall be hungry; he shall eat at his left hand, and he shall not be satisfied; every one shall eat the flesh of his own weapon. 21 Manasseh, and Ephraim, and Ephraim Manasseh, and both of them shall be against Iudah; yet for all that, his wrath has not departed, but his hand is still stretched out.

CHAPTER 10

1 Woe to those who issue evil decrees and write evil things, 2 To turn away the poor from judgment, and to take away judgment from the poor of my people, that widows may be their prayer, and that they may pluck out orphans. 3 What will you do now in the day of visitation and destruction that will come from afar? To whom will you flee for help and where will you leave your glory? 4 Without me every one shall fall among those who are bound, and they shall fall among the slain; yet for all this his wrath has not departed, but his hand is still stretched out. 5 O Assur, the rod of my wrath, and the rod in their hands is my indignation. 6 I will send him from a dissimulating nation, and I will give him a charge against the people of my wrath to take the spit and the prayer, and to make them fall under his feet like the mud of the road. 7 But he does not think so, nor does his heart think so, but he imagines that he will destroy and cut off not a few nations. 8 For he says, "Are not all my princes kings? 9 Is not Calno like Carchemish? Is not Hamath like Arpad? Is not Samaria like Damascus? 10 As my hand found the kingdoms of idols, seeing their idols were in Jerusalem and Samaria: 11 Should I not, as I did in Samaria and its idols, do likewise in Je- rusalem and its idols? 12 But when the LORD has done all his works on Mount Zion and on Jerusalem, I will visit the fruit of the proud heart of the king of Assur and his glorious and haughty looks, 13 For he said, "I have done it by the strength of my hand and by my wis- dom, for I am wise; therefore I have removed the bounds of the people, I have dissipated their treasures, and I have brought down the inhabitants like a valiant man. 14 My hand has found like a nest the riches of the people, and as one gathers the remaining eggs, so have I gathered all the earth; and there has been no one who moved his wing or opened his mouth or whispered. 15 Can the axe boast against him who cuts it or the saw exalt itself against him who chews it? As if the rod would rise up against him who takes it or the staff exalt it- self, as if it were not wood. 16 Therefore the LORD, God of hosts, will send forth his fat, loyal men, and under his glory he will kindle a fire, like a fire of fire. 17 The light of Israel shall be like a fire, and his Holy One like a flame, and he shall burn and destroy his thorns and his briars in one day: 18 And he shall con- sume the glory of his forest and his fruitful fields, both soul and flesh; and it shall be as the fainting of a standard-bearer. 19 The other trees of his forest shall be few, so that a child may recognize them. 20 In that day the rem- nant of Israel and the remnant of the house of Iaakob shall no longer stand before him who smote them, but shall stand before the LORD, the Holy One of Israel in truth. 21 The remnant shall return, like the remnant of Iaa- kob, to the mighty God. 22 Even though your people, O Israel, are like the sand of the sea, their remnant will return. The decreed con- summation will be a flood of righteousness. 23 For the LORD God of hosts will make the decreed consummation in the midst of all the land. 24 Therefore thus says the LORD God of hosts, "O my people, who dwell in Zion, do not fear Assur; he shall smite thee with a rod, and shall lift up his staff against thee as in Egypt: 25 But yet a little while, and wrath shall con- sume them, and my anger shall destroy them. 26 And the LORD of hosts shall lift up for him a scourge, as the plague of Midian in the re- gion of Horeb; and his rod was upon the sea, so shall he lift it up after the maneuver- ing of Egypt. 27 In that day his burden shall be taken from your shoulder, and his yoke from your neck; and the yoke shall be destroyed be- cause of the anoinisation. 28 He has come to Aiath, he has passed on to Migron; in Mich- mash he will lay down his armor. 29 They went out of the camp, they settled in the lodging of Geba: Ramah is gone: Gibeah of Saul is fled. 30 Lift up your eyes, daughter of Gallim, let Laish hear, O poor Anathoth. 31 Madmenah has been removed, the inhabitants of Gibim have gathered. 32 But there is a time when he will remain in Nob; he will lift up his hand to the mount of his daughter Zion, the hill of Jerusalem. 33 Behold, the LORD God of hosts will cut down the branch with fear, and those of high stature will be cut off, and the sons will be humbled. 34 He shall cut off the thin

places of the forest with yron, and Lebanon shall have a strong fall.

CHAPTER 11

1 But a staff shall come from Ishai's cattle, and a fat one shall sprout from his sticks. 2 The Spirit of the LORD shall rest upon him: the Spirit of wisdom and intelligence, the Spirit of counsel and strength, the Spirit of knowledge and fear of the LORD, 3 and shall make him prudent in the fear of the Lord, for he shall not judge according to the sight of his ears, nor repent according to the hearing of his ears. 4 But with justice he shall judge the poor, and with equity he shall rebuke the poor of the earth; he shall smite the earth with the rod of his mouth, and with the breath of his lips he shall slay the wicked. 5 Justice shall be the belt of his faithfulness, and faithfulness the belt of his reins. 6 The wolf shall dwell with the sheep, the leopard shall lie down with the kid, the calf, the lion and the fat beast togeth- er, and a little child shall lead them. 7 The kid and the female will feed; their young will lie down together, and the lion will eat his fill like the bull. 8 The sucking child shall play on the monkey's hole, and the child who has lost his strength shall put his hand on the hen's hole. 9 Then no one shall hurt or destroy in all the mountain of my sanctuaries, for the earth shall be full of the knowledge of the LORD, like the waters that run off the sea. 10 In that day the tower of Ishai, which shall be a sign to the peoples, shall be seen by the nations, and its rest shall be glorious. 11 In that same day the LORD will stretch out his hand again to possess the rest of his people (who will re- main) of Assur, of Egypt, of Pathros, of Ethi- opia, of Elam, of Shinear, of Hamath, and of the islands of the sea. 12 He shall bring a sign to the nations, and shall gather the scattered of Israel, and gather the scattered of Iudah from the four corners of the world. 13 The ha- tred of Ephraim also shall depart, and the ad- versaries of Judah shall be removed: Ephraim shall not envy Iudah, and Iudah shall not defy Ephraim: 14 But they shall flee on the backs of the Philistines westward; they shall push them together from the east: Edom and Moab shall be the stretching out of their hands, and the sons of Ammon their obedience. 15 And the LORD shall also destroy the tongue of the sea of the Egyptians, and with his mighty wind shall lift up his hand upon the river, and smite it in its stripes, and cause men to walk in it with their shoes. 16 And for the remnant of his people, who are left from Assur, there shall be a path, as it was for Israel in the day that they came out of the land of Egypt.

CHAPTER 12

1 In that day thou shalt say, "O LORD, I will pray unto thee; though thou hast been an- gry with me, thy wrath is turned away, and thou comfortest me. 2 God is my salvation: I will trust and not fear, for the Lord God is my strength and my

song; he has also become my salvation. 3 Therefore you shall draw with joy the waters from the wells of salvation. 4 On that day you shall say, "Pray to the LORD, invoke his Name, declare his works among the nations, mention them, for his Name is exalted." 5 Sing to the LORD, for he has done excellent things; this is known throughout the whole world. 6 Shout and cry, O inhabitant of Zion, for great is the Holy One of Israel in your midst.

CHAPTER 13

1 The burden of Babel, which Isaiah the son of Amoz saw. 2 Lift up a standard on the mountain, lift up the veil toward them, wave your hand that they may enter into the gates of the nobles. 3 I have commanded them, I have sanctified them; and I have called to my wrath the mighty, and those who rejoice in my glory. 4 The noise of a multitude is on the mountains, like a great people; a tumultuous journey of the kingdoms of the gathered na- tions; the LORD of hosts appoints the army of battle. 5 They come from a far country, from the end of the earth, and the LORD with the weapons of his wrath destroys all the land. 6 Beware, for the day of the LORD is at hand; he will come as a destroyer from the Most High. 7 Therefore all hands shall be weakened, and all the hearts of men shall melt, 8 And they shall be afraid; anguish and sadness shall seize them, and they shall be afraid, like a woman who overwhelms; every one shall be vexed by his neighbor, and their faces shall be as flames of fire. 9 Behold, the day of the LORD comes, cruel, with wrath and fury, to lay bare the earth; and he will destroy its sinners. 10 For the stars of Heauen and their planets will not give their light; the sun will be darkened in its path, and the moon will not shine its light. 11 I will visit the wickednesses of the world and their iniquities of the wicked, I will make the arrogance of the proud cease, and I will bring down the pride of tyrants. 12 I will make man more precious than fine gold, that is, a man like the wedge of gold of Ophir. 13 Therefore I will shake off wrath, and the earth shall be removed from its place in the wrath of the LORD of hosts and in the day of his fierce anger. 14 It shall be like a hind pursued, and like a sheep which no one takes; every one shall turn to his own people, and every one shall flee to his own land. 15 Everyone who is found will be struck down, and whoever does justice to himself will be struck down by the sword. 16 Their children also shall be cut in pieces before their eyes; their houses shall be ruined and their wives devastated. 17 Be- hold, I will unleash against them the Medes, who will not care for silence and will not covet gold. 18 With their bow they will destroy even the children; they will have no compassion on the fruit of the woman, and their minds will not spare the children. 19 Babel, the glory of kingdoms, the beauty and pride of the Chal- deans, will be like the destruction of God at Sodom and Gomorah. 20 It shall not be in- habited forever, nor shall it be inhabited from generation to generation; the Arab shall not pitch his tents there, nor shall the shepherds make their sheepfolds there. 21 But the Ziim shall lodge there, and their houses shall be full of Ohim: Ostriches shall dwell there, and sa- tyrs shall dance there. 22 The Iim shall mourn in their palaces, and the dragons in their fair palaces: the time is ready to come, and the days shall not be prolonged.

CHAPTER 14

1 For the LORD will have compassion on Iaakob, and will choose Israel again, and will cause them to rest in their land; and the stranger shall receive them, and they shall be set free in the house of Iaakob. 2 And the peo- ple shall receive them, and shall bring them to their place of origin, and the house of Israel shall possess them in the land of the LORD, as servants and handmaidens; and they shall take them captives, whose captives they were, and they shall take hold of their oppressors. 3 And in the day when the LORD shall give thee rest from thy sorrow, and from thy fear, and from thy sore body, wherein thou hast served, 4 then you shall take up your protest against the king of Babel and say, "How has the op- pressor ceased and rested Babel thirsting for gold? 5 The LORD has broken the staff of the wicked and the scepter of the rulers: 6 He hath smitten the peoples with a continual plague, and hath ruled the nations with wrath: if any were persecuted, he hath not let it be. 7 All the world is at rest and quiet; they sing for joy. 8 Even the fir trees have rejoiced over you and the cedars of Lebanon, saying, "Since you were laid down, no cutter has come against you." 9 Hell has been prepared for you and has welcomed you at your arrival, raising up for you death, as all the princes of the earth, and has raised from their thrones all the kings of the nations. 10 Everyone will cry out and say to you, "Have you also become like us? Have you become like us?" 11 Your pomp has been brought to the grave, and the sound of your violence; the flesh has spread out beneath you, and worms have come upon you. 12 How did you fall from above, O Lucifer, son of the morning, and fall to the ground, as you cast lots upon the nations? 13 Yet thou hast said in thine heart, I will ascend into heaven, and will raise up my throne beside the stars of God: I will also sit upon the mount of the congrega- tion, on the sides of the north. 14 I will ascend to the height of the clouds, and I will be as the most high. 15 But you will be brought down to the grave, to the sides of the pit. 16 Those who see you will look at you and consider you, saying, "Is this the man who made the earth tremble and the kingdoms shake? 17 He has made the world like a thicket, destroyed its cities, and has not opened the house of his captives. 18 All the kings of the nations sleep in glory, each in his own house. 19 But you have been cast out of your tomb like an abom- inable branch, like the garments of those who have been slain and pierced by a sword, which go out on the stones of the pit, like a carcass falling underfoot. 20 Thou shalt not be received with them into the grave, because thou hast destroyed thy land, and hast slain thy people; the descendants of the wicked shall never again be forsaken. 21 You pre- pare a slaughter for your children, because of the iniquity of their fathers; let them not rise up, nor possess the land, nor defile the face of the world with enemies. 22 For I will arise against them (saith the LORD of hosts), and I will cut off from Babel the name, and the remnant, and the son and the grandson, saith the LORD: 23 I will make it a possession of hedgehogs and pools of water, and I will sweep it with the beam of destruction, says the LORD of hosts. 24 The LORD of hosts has sworn, saying, Surely, as I have determined, so it shall come to pass, and as I have consult- ed, it shall stand: 25 that I will break Assur in pieces in my land, and on my mountains I will bring him down to the ground; so that his yoke shall be removed from them, and his burden shall be taken off their shoulders." 26 This is the counsel that is consulted for all the world, and this is the hand stretched out to- ward all the nations, 27 For the LORD of hosts has established it, and who shall be able to disallow it; his hand is stretched out, and who shall be able to turn it away? 28 In the year that King Ahaz died,

there was this burden. 29 Fear not (all Palestine), for the rod of him that smote thee is broken: for out of the root of serpents shall come forth a rooster, and the fruit thereof shall be a flying serpent. 30 For the first born of the poor shall be fed, and the needy shall lie down in safety: but I will kill thy roote with famine, and it shall kill thy remnant. 31 Shout, O gate, shout, O city: all the land of Palestine is dissolved, for a smoke will come from the north, and no one will be left alone at the appointed time. 32 What then shall be answered to the messengers of the Gentiles? That the Lord has established Zion, and that the poor of his people will trust in it.

CHAPTER 15

1 The burden of Moab. Ar of Moab was de- stroyed and reduced to silence in one night; Kir of Moab was destroyed and reduced to silence in one night. 2 He shall go to the tem- ple and to Dibon in the places of weeping; by Nebo and by Medeba Moab shall howl; on all their heads shall be baldness, and every beard shall be shaven. 3 In their streets they shall be gilded with sackcloth; on the roofs of their houses and in their streets every one shall howl and go down in weeping. 4 Hesh- bon shall weep and Elealeh; their voice shall be heard as far as Iahaz; the warriors of Moab shall show themselves; the soul of every one shall wail within himself. 5 My heart shall weep for Moab; its fugitives shall flee to Zoar, a city three years old, for they shall go weep- ing by the way of Luhith, and by the way of Horonaim they shall make a cry of destruc- tion. 6 For the waters of Nimrim shall be dried up; the vegetation shall be withered, and the grasses shall be consumed, and there shall be no green grass. 7 Therefore what every man has left and his substance shall be taken to the flock of willows. 8 For the weeping spread around the borders of Moab, and its howling reached as far as Eglaim, and its screeching as far as Beer Elim, 9 For the waters of Dimon shall be full of blood; for I will cause yet more blood to come upon Dimon, as the lion upon those who flee from Moab, and upon the rem- nant of the land.

CHAPTER 16

1 Send a blade to the ruler of the world, from the wilderness mountains to the mountain of the daughter of Zion. 2 For it shall be as a bird that flies and a forsaken nest; the daugh- ters of Moab shall be at the foot of Arnon. 3 Gather a cousin, execute judgment; let your shadow be as the night at noon; hide those who are cast out; do not repel those who have fled. 4 Let my cast out ones dwell with you; let Moab be their refuge from the face of the destroyer, for the extortioner shall end; the destroyer shall be consumed, and the oppressor shall cease from the land. 5 The throne of mercy shall be prepared, and he shall sit upon it in a stable position, in the tent of Dauid, judging, seeking judgment, and seeking righteousness. 6 We have heard of Moab's pride (he is very proud), his arro- gance and indignation, but his lies will not be so. 7 Therefore Moab shall howl against Moab; every one shall howl; for the founda- tions of Kirhareseth shall be demolished, yet they shall be smitten. 8 For the vines of Heshbon have been cut down, and the vine- yard of Sibmah; the lords of the heathen have broken their principal vines; they have come to Iaazer; they

have wandered in the wilder- ness; its fair branches have stretched out and gone beyond the sea. 9 Therefore I will weep with the weeping of Iaazer, and of the vine of Sibmah, O Heshbon; and Elealeh, I will make thee drunk with my teas, for upon thy sum- mer fruits and upon thy shrubs a spectacle has fallen. 10 The cheerfulness is taken away, and the merriment from the abundant field; in the vineyards shall no singing be done, nei- ther shall there be a shouting for merriment; the thrasher shall not tread down the wine in the winepresses: I have caused the revival to cease. 11 Therefore my bowels shall sound like a harp for Moab, and my inward parts for Ker-haresh. 12 When Moab is weary of his places of worship, he shall come to his temple to pray, but he shall not prevail. 13 This is the word that the LORD has spoken against Moab since that time. 14 Now the LORD has spoken, saying, "In three years, as the years of a hire- ling, the glory of Moab shall be despised in all the great multitude, and the remnant shall be very small and weak."

CHAPTER 17

1 The burden of Damascus. Behold, Damas- cus has been removed from being a city, for it will be a heap of ruins. 2 The cities of Aro- er shall be forsaken; they shall be for flocks, for they shall remain there, and no one shall cause them to flee. 3 The ammunition also shall cease from Ephraim, the kingdom from Damascus, and the remnant of Aram shall be as the glory of the children of Israel, saith the LORD of hosts. 4 In that day, the glory of Iaakob will be diminished, and the fat of his flesh will become thin. 5 It shall be as when the hardest man gathers grain and reaps the ears of corn with his arm; it shall be as he who gathers the ears of corn in the valley of Rephaim. 6 But there shall remain in it a harvest of grapes, like the shaking of an olive tree, two or three beries in the top of the high- est branches, and four or five in the highest branches of its fruit, saith the LORD God of Israel. 7 In that day a man shall look to his maker, and his eyes shall look to the Holy One of Israel. 8 He shall not look to the altars, the work of his hands, nor shall he look to those things which his fingers have made, such as caves and images. 9 In that day the cities of their strength shall be as the forsaking of shrubs and branches, which they have for- saken because of the children of Israel, and there shall be desolation. 10 Because thou hast forgotten the God of thy salvation, and hast not remembered the God of thy strength, thou shalt plant pleasant plants, and shalt shepherd strange vine branches: 11 In the day shalt thou make thy plant to grow, and in the morning shalt thou make thy seed to blos- som: but the hardy ones shall depart in the day of possession, and there shall be despair- ing sorrow. 12 The multitude of many peoples shall make a noise like the noise of the sea, for the noise of the people shall make a noise like the noise of the great waters. 13 And the peo- ple shall make a noise like the noise of many waters; but God shall rebuke them, and they shall flee far away, and shall be chased like the hood of the mountains before the wind, and like a rolling thing before the whirlwind. 14 Well, at sunset there is trouble, but before morning it is gone. This is the part of those who spy themselves out and the lot of those who plunder themselves.

CHAPTER 18

1 Oh, the land that shadows with wings, which is beyond the shores of Ethiopia, 2 sending ambassadors along the sea, in ves- sels of bulrushes on the waters, saying, "Go, swift messengers, to a nation scattered and spoiled, to a people terrible from its begin- ning; a nation of little ones and small ones, standing in the way, whose land has been spoiled by floods. 3 All of you, inhabitants of the world and of the earth, you shall see when he puts a sign on the mountains, and when he sounds the trumpet, you shall hear. 4 For the LORD said unto me, I will rest and watch in my tabernacle, as the heather that dries the beam, and as a cloud of dew in the heather. 5 For before the haruest, when the flowering is finished and the fruit has ripened in the blos- som, the branches shall be cut off with hooks, and they shall be removed and cut off: 6 they shall be left together with the trees of the mountains, and with the shrubs of the earth: for the trees shall submerge therein, and all the animals of the earth shall winter therein. 7 At that time a gift shall be brought to the LORD of hosts (a scattered and scattered peo- ple, a people terrible from their beginning, a nation that for a short time and a little while has crossed the mouth, whose land has been scattered by the riuers) in the place of the Name of the LORD of hosts, that is, Mount Zion.

CHAPTER 19

1 The burden of Egypt. Behold, the LORD rides on a swift cloud and will enter Egypt, and the idols of Egypt will be shaken in his presence, and the heart of Egypt will melt in its bowels. 2 I will set Egyptians against Egyp- tians; so each will fight against his brother and each against his neighbor, city against city and kingdom against kingdom. 3 The spirit of Egypt shall be quenched in her bow- els; I will destroy their counsels, and they shall turn to idols, sorcerers, those who have spirits of divination, and the enchanters of the south. 4 I will deliver the Egyptians into the hands of the cruel lords, and a mighty king will rule over them, says the LORD God of hosts. 5 Then the waters of the sea will sub- side, and the shores will dry up and disperse. 6 The basins will go far away; the basins of defense will be emptied and dried up; the reeds and flags will be cut down. 7 The grass of the banks and of the head of the banks, and everything that grows near the banks, will wither and dry up and no longer exist. 8 The fishermen also will complain, all who cast their hooks into the river will complain, and those who spread their nets over the waters will be weakened. 9 Moreover, those who work flax of different kinds will be con- founded, and those who weave nets. 10 For their nets will be broken, and all those who make ponds will have their hearts broken. 11 The princes of Zoan are foolish; the counsel of Pharaoh's wise counsellors has become fool- ish; how can you say to Pharaoh, "I am the son of wise men"? Am I the son of ancient kings? 12 Where are your wise men now, that they may tell you or know what the LORD of hosts has determined against Egypt? 13 The princes of Zoan have become foolish; the princes of Noph have been deceived; they have deceived Egypt and the corners of her tribes. 14 The LORD has mingled among them the spirit of error, and they have caused Egypt to err in all her works, as a drunkard errs in his vomit. 15 There shall be no more work in Egypt that the chief can do, neither the tayle, nor the branch, nor the reed. 16 In that day Egypt will be like a woman, for she will be afraid and frightened because of the movements of the hand of the LORD of hosts that shakes it. 17 The land of Iudah shall be a fear to Egypt; everyone who mentions it

shall be afraid of it, because of the counsels of the LORD of hosts that he has established over it. 18 In that day five cities in the land of Egypt shall speak the language of Canaan and swear by the LORD of hosts. one shall be called the city of destruction. 19 In that day the altar of the LORD shall be in the midst of the land of Egypt, and a pillar along its border shall be dedicated to the LORD. 20 It will be a sign and a testimony for the LORD of hosts in the land of Egypt, for they will cry out to the LORD because of the oppressors, and he will send them a savior and a great man and deliver them. 21 And the LORD shall be known to the Egyptians, and the Egyptians shall know the LORD in that day, and they shall make sacrifices and oblations, and make vows to the LORD, and perform them. 22 Thus shall the LORD smite Egypt, and smite them, and heal them; for they shall return to the LORD, and shall be addressed by them, and shall heal them. 23 In that day there will be a way from Egypt to Assur, Assur will enter Egypt and Egypt into Assur; so the Egyptians will worship with Assur. 24 In that day Israel shall be the third with Egypt and Assur, and it shall be a blessing in the midst of the land. 25 For the LORD of hosts shall bless it, saying, Blessed are my peoples, Egypt and Assur, the work of my hands, and Israel my inheritance.

CHAPTER 20

1 In the year when Tartan came to Ashdod (sent by Sargon, king of Assur), he fought against Ashdod and took it, 2 at the same time the LORD spoke by the hand of Isaiah the son of Amoz, saying, "Go away, loosen your sack- cloth from your burdens, and take off your garment from your foot." And he did so, walk- ing naked and barefoot. 3 And the LORD said, "As my servant Isaiah walked naked and un- covered for three years, as a sign and wonder to Egypt and Ethiopia, 4 so the king of Assur will take away the captivity of Egypt and the captivity of Ethiopia, both the young and the old, naked and barefoot, with open buttocks, to the shame of Egypt. 5 They shall be afraid and ashamed of Ethiopia, their expectation, and of Egypt, their glory. 6 In that day the inhabitants of the land will say, "Behold, this is our expectation, where we fled for help to be delivered from the king of Assur, and how shall we be delivered?

CHAPTER 21

1 The weight of the desert sea. As the whirl- winds of the south pass from the wilderness, so shall they come from the horrible land. 2 A terrible vision was shown to me: the trans- gressor against the transgressor, and the destroyer against the destroyer. Cross the threshold of Elam, besiege Media: I have put an end to all her mourning. 3 Therefore my feelings are full of grief; grief has seized me like the sorrow of an overwhelming woman; I prostrated myself when I heard it, and I felt sick when I felt it. 4 My heart failed; fear troubled me; the night of my pleasures be- came fear for me. 5 Prepare your table, keep watch in the watchtower, eat, drink, arise, princes, and go to the shield. 6 For thus said the LORD to me, "Go, set a watchman to tell what he sees." 7 And he saw a chariot with two horsemen: a chariot of axes and a chariot of camels; and he listened and paid diligent attention. 8 And he cried out, "Lyon, my lord, I stand always on your lookout by day, and I stand watch every night." 9 And behold, this man comes with two horsemen." And he an- swered, "Babel has fallen;

she has fallen, and all the images of her gods have broken to the ground. 10 Oh, my threshing and the horn of my planting. I have set forth to you what I have heard from the LORD of hosts, the God of Israel. 11 The burden of Dumah. He called to me from Seir, "Watchman, what has been in the night? Watchman, what has been in the night? 12 The watchman said, "Morning comes and so does the night. If you wish to inquire, inquire; return and come." 13 The burden against Arabia. In the forest of Arabia you shall stay all night, and also in the dwell- ings of Dedanim. 14 O inhabitants of the land of Tema, bring water to satisfy your thirst, and give bread to those who flee. 15 For they flee from the drawn swords, from the drawn sword, from the bent bow, and from the se- verity of war. 16 For thus hath the LORD said unto me, Yet one year more, as the year of a void, and all the glory of Kedar shall fail. 17 And the remnant of the name of you strong archers of the sons of Kedar shall be dimin- ished, for the LORD, the God of Israel, has said it.

CHAPTER 22

1 The burden of the valley of vision. What hinders thee now that thou hast gone to thy house? 2 Thou that art full of noise, a city full of brutes, a rebellious city; thy slain men shall not be slain with the sword, nor die in battle. 3 All thy princes shall flee together from the siege; they shall be bound; all that are in thee shall be bound together, and they shall flee afar off. 4 Therefore I said, Depart from me: I will weep bitterly; do not toil to comfort me for the destruction of the daughter of my peo- ple. 5 For it is a day of trouble, and of ruin, and of perplexity from the LORD God of hosts, in the valley of vision, bringing down the city, and shouting upon the mountains. 6 Elam brought his army in a chariot of men with horsemen, and Kir brought his shield. 7 Your main valleys were filled with chariots, and the horsemen stood in a line against the gate. 8 He undid the armor of Iudah, and you looked on that day at the armor of the house of the forest. 9 You saw the breaches of the city of Dauid, for they were many, and you gathered the waters of lower Poole. 10 You named the houses of Jerusalem, and the houses you tore down to fortify the walls, 11 and you also built a ditch between the two walls for the waters of old Poole, without looking to its builder and without respecting him who had formed it in the past. 12 In that day the LORD God of hosts invited to weeping and mourning, to stockings and sackcloth. 13 And behold, joy and gladness, the slaughter of oxen and the killing of sheep, eating meat and drinking wine, eating and drinking, for to death we shall die. 14 And it was declared in the ears of the LORD of hosts. This iniquity shall not be blotted out from you until you die, says the LORD God of hosts." 15 Thus says the LORD God of hosts, "Go, go to that treasurer, to Shebnah, the steward of the house, and tell him, 16 What is your hurry here? And who do you have here? That you should build a sepul- cher here, like one who builds his sepulcher in a hidden place or who builds a house in a tower? 17 Behold, the LORD will take you away with a great captivity, and he will surely bring you down. 18 He will roll you and spin you like a ball in a great county; there you will die, and the remains of your glory will be the shame of your lord's house. 19 I will make you disappear from your position and destroy you from your dwelling place. 20 In that day I will call my servant Eliakim the son of Hilkiah, 21 I will clothe him with your garments and for- tify him with your girdle; I will also put your power into his hands, and he shall be a father of the inhabitants of Jerusalem and of the house of Iudah. 22 I will lay upon his shoulder the key of the house of Dauid; he shall open and none shall shut; he shall shut and none shall open. 23 I will fasten him like a nail in a safe place, and he shall be the throne of the glory of the house of his fathers. 24 On him shall be hung all the glories of the house of his fathers, and of his grandsons and of posterity, all the little utensils, from the utensils of the cups to all the musical instruments. 25 In that day, saith the LORD of hosts, the nail fastened in the safe place shall depart, and shall break and fall down; and the weight that was upon it shall be cut off, for the LORD hath spoken it.

CHAPTER 23

1 The cargo of Tyre. How goes it, you ships of Tarsis, for it has been destroyed and there is no house left; no one will come from the land of Chittim, which has been returned to them. 2 Be still, you who dwell in the yles; the mer- chants of Zidon and those who pass across the sea have replenished you. 3 The seed of Nile grew by the abundance of the waters, and the hardest of riuers was its income, and it was a mark to the nations. 4 Shame on you, Zidon, for the sea has spoken, the power of the sea, saying, "I have not brought forth chil- dren, I have not nourished young men, I have not brought forth virgins." 5 When the news reaches the Egyptians, they will be saddened by the voice of Tyre. 6 Go to Tarsis, and cry out, you who dwell in the islands. 7 Is not this your glorious city? Its antiquity is of old; your own feet will let it go away to be a sojourn. 8 Who has decreed this against Tyre (who crowns men) whose merchants are princes, whose captains are the nobles of the world? 9 The LORD of hosts has decreed this, to put an end to the pride of all glory, and to bring into disgrace all who are glorious on earth. 10 Pass through your land like a flood for the daugh- ter of Tarshish; there is no more strength." 11 He stretched out his hand over the sea, and brought down the kingdoms; the LORD gave an order over the place of Marathon, to de- stroy its power. 12 And he said, Thou shalt not rebel again when thou art oppressed: O vir- gin daughter of Zidon, arise, go to Chittim, but there thou shalt have no peace. 13 Look at the land of the Chaldeans: it was not a people: Assur founded it with the inhabitants of the wilderness, and erected its towers, and built its palaces, and brought it to ruin. 14 How are you carried away by the ships of Tarsis, for your strength is destroyed. 15 In that day Tyre shall be forgotten for seventy years (ac- cording to the years of a king), and at the end of seventy years Tyre shall sing like a harlot. 16 Take a harp and go around the city; (you harlot who have been forgotten) make sweet melodies, sing more songs so that you may be remembered. 17 At the end of seventy years the LORD will visit Tyre, who will return to his gains and fornicate with all the kingdoms of the earth that are in the world. 18 Yet his occupation and his wages shall be holy to the LORD; they shall not be packed or stored up, but his merchandise shall be for those who dwell before the LORD, to eat enough and to have strong clothing.

CHAPTER 24

1 Behold, the LORD empties the earth and makes it desolate; he overthrows it and scat- ters its inhabitants. 2 There shall be like people, as the priest and as the servant, as the master, as the mother, as the mistress, as the coffin,

as the seller, as the creditor, as the lender, as the sworn, as the bearer of vsupe- riors. 3 The land will be clearly emptied and greatly ruined, for the LORD has spoken this word. 4 The earth groans and goes out; the world is weak and fallen; the proud inhabi- tants of the earth are weakened. 5 The earth also deceives itself because of its inhabitants, for they have transgressed the laws, changed orders, and broken the everlasting bond. 6 Therefore the curse has come upon the land, and its inhabitants are desolate. Therefore the inhabitants of the land are burned, and there are few men left. 7 The wine is failing, the vine has no strength; all who had a good heart have grown dull. 8 The merriment of the taberna- cles ceases, the merriment of those who revel, the merriment of the harps ceases. 9 No wine shall be drunk with mirth; strong wine shall be bitter to those who drink it. 10 The city of vanity is destroyed; every house is shut up, that no one may enter it. 11 In the streets they cry for wine; all mirth is darkened; the joy of the world is gone. 12 The city is desolate, and the gate is stricken with destruction. 13 So shall it be in the meanderings of the earth, among the peoples, as the shaking of an ol- ive tree, and as the grapes when the harvest is over. 14 They will raise their voices, they will cry out for the magnificence of the LORD, they will rise up from the sea. 15 Therefore praise the LORD in the valleys, and the name of the LORD, the God of Israel, in the waters of the sea. 16 From the uttermost part of the earth we have heard praise, and glory to the righteous, and I have said, "My meagre, my meagre, woe to me: the transgressors have of- fended; yea, the transgressors have grievous- ly offended." 17 Fear and snare and snare are upon thee, O inhabitant of the earth. 18 He who flees from fear shall fall into the pit, and he who comes out of the pit shall be caught in the snare, for the windows from above are open, and the foundations of the earth trem- ble. 19 The earth is completely split, the earth is clearly dissolved, the earth is greatly dam- aged. 20 The earth shall move to and fro like a drunken man, and it shall be removed like a curtain, and its iniquity shall come upon it, so that it shall fall down and rise no more. 21 In that day the LORD will visit the army that is upon him, that is, the kings of the world who are on the earth. 22 They shall be gathered to- gether like the prisoners in the pit; they shall be shut up in the prison, and after many days they shall be visited. 23 Then the moon shall be cast down, and the sun shamed, when the LORD of hosts shall reign on Mount Zion and in Jerusalem; and the glory shall be before his ancient men.

CHAPTER 25

1 O LORD, thou art my God: I will exalt thee, I will pray thy Name: for thou hast done won- drous things, according to the counsels of old, with a settled truth. 2 For thou hast made a city a stronghold, a strong city a ruin; and the palace of strangers of a city shall never be built. 3 Therefore the mighty peoples will give you glory; the cities of the strong nations will fear you. 4 For you have been a strength to the poor, a strength to the needy in their trou- bles, a refuge against the storm, a shadow against the steep; for the guilt of the mighty is as a storm against the wall. 5 Thou shalt reduce the discontent of the stranger as the steep to a dry place; he shall reduce the song of the mighty as the steep to the shadow of a cloud. 6 In this mountain the LORD of hosts will make all peoples a banquet of fat things, a banquet of fine wines and fat things full of maro, of refined and purified wines. 7 He will destroy in this mountain the

corruption that seduces all peoples and the vainglory that spreads over all nations. 8 He will destroy death forever; the LORD God will wipe away tears from all faces and remove the reproach of his people from all the earth, for the LORD has said it. 9 In that day men will say, "Behold our God, we have waited for him, and he will greet us"; "Behold the LORD, we have waited for him, and we will rejoice in his salvation." 10 For on this mountain the hand of the LORD shall rest, and Moab shall be threshed, as one threshes in Madmenah. 11 He will stretch out his hand among them (as one who swims, stretches them out to swim), and by the strength of his hands he will break down their pride. 12 He will also break down the defens- es of the height of your walls, and will lower them and throw them to the ground, that is, to the dust.

CHAPTER 26

1 On that day this song will be sung in the land of Iudah, "We have a strong city; God will put up walls and bulwarks for salvation." 2 Open the gates, that the righteous nation may en- ter, which guards the truth. 3 With sure pur- pose you will preserve perfect peace, because they have trusted in you. 4 Trust in the LORD forever, for in the LORD God is strength for- ever. 5 For he will strike down those who dwell on him; his city he will tear down; and then he will throw it to the ground and reduce it to dust. 6 The earth he will bring it down, as the feet of the poor and the pastures of the needy. 7 The way of the righteous is righteousness; you will make fair the righteous way of the righteous. 8 We also, O LORD, have waited for you in the way of your iudgemets; the de- sire of our soul is your Name and the remem- brance of you. 9 With my soul I have longed for you in the night, and with my spirit within me I shall see you in the morning; for, seeing your judgments on earth, the inhabitants of the world will learn righteousness. 10 The wicked may be rewarded, but he will not learn righteousness; in the land of righteousness he will behave wickedly and will not see the majesty of the LORD. 11 O LORD, they shall not see your hand, but they shall see it and be confounded by the zeal of the people, and the fire of your enemies shall destroy them. 12 O LORD, you will give peace to you, for you also have done all our works for you. 13 O LORD our God, other lords besides you have ruled vs, but we will remember only you and your Name. 14 The dead shall not lie nor rise again, for you have visited and scattered them and destroyed all their memories. 15 Thou hast increased the nation, O LORD, thou hast become glorious, thou hast enlarged all the coasts of the earth. 16 Lord, in difficulties they visited you; they uttered a prayer when your chastisement was upon them. 17 As a pregnant woman, approaching trauma, is in pain and weeping in her sorrows, so have we been in your presence, Lord. 18 We have suf- fered, we have borne with sorrow, as if we had carried the wind; there was no help on earth, and the inhabitants of the world did not fall. 19 Your dead shall remain alive, but with my body they shall rise again. Awake and sing, you who dwell in the dust, for your dew is like the dew of herbs, and the earth shall cast out the dead. 20 Come, my people, enter into your rooms, and shut your doors behind you; hide yourself for a very short time, until the indig- nation passes away. 21 For behold, the LORD cometh out of his place to visit the iniquity of the inhabitants of the earth upon them; and the earth shall reveal her blood, and shall hide her victims no more.

CHAPTER 27

1 In that day the LORD will visit Liuiathan, the pearly serpent, and Liuiathan, the crook- ed serpent, with his sorrowful sword, great and mighty, and slay the dragon that is in the sea. 2 In that day shall be sung of the vineyard of red wine. 3 I, the LORD, will guard it: I will water it every moment; If anyone does not de- stroy it, I will guard it night and day. 4 Wrath is not in me; who would oppose me the briers and thorns? I would go through them; I would bury them together. 5 Or would you weaken my strength, to make peace with me and be united with me? 6 From now on, Iaakob shall take root; Israel shall flourish and grow, and the world shall be full of fruit. 7 Did he smite him as he smote those who smote him? Or is he slain according to the slaughter of those who were slain by him? 8 When he shall blow with his rough wind in the day of the east wind, you shall deal with him with measure in his branches. 9 For this reason the iniquity of Iaakob shall be cleansed, and this is all the fruit, the removal of his sin; he shall make all the stones of the altars like lime stones bro- ken in pieces, so that the caves and the images shall not stand. 10 But the defended city shall be desolate, its habitation shall be forsak- en and left as a thicket. There the calf shall feed, there it shall lie down and consume its branches. 11 And when its branches are with- ered, they shall break off; and the women shall come and set fire to them, for it is a people of none; therefore he that made them shall have no compassion on them, and he that formed them shall have no pity on them. 12 In that day the LORD will shake from the channel of Riuer to the shore of Egypt, and you shall be gathered together one by one, O children of Israel. 13 In that day the great trumpet shall sound, and those who perished in the land of Assur and those who were driven out in the land of Egypt shall come, and they shall wor- ship the LORD on the holy mountain of Jeru- salem.

CHAPTER 28

1 Woe to the crown of pride, to the drunk- ards of Ephraim, for its glorious beauty will be a fading stream, standing on the head of the valley of those who are fat and drunk with wine. 2 The LORD has a strong and mighty army, like a storm of hail and a whirlwind that overflows, like a tempest of mighty wa- ters that overflow and throw themselves down with power. 3 They shall be crushed by a blast, like the crown and pride of the drunk- ards of Ephraim. 4 For its glorious beauty will be a fading flower, which is on the head of the valley of those who have been slain, and like the fruit that is found before evening, which when he who looks at it sees it, while it is in his hand, he eats it. 5 In that day shall the LORD of hosts be a crown of glory and a dia- dem of beauty to the remnant of his people: 6 And for a spirit of righteousness for him who sits in judgment, and for strength for those who turn the battle toward the gate. 7 But they erred because of wine, and went astray because of strong drunkenness; the priest and the prophet erred because of strong drunken- ness; they were swallowed up with wine; they went astray because of strong drunkenness; they failed in vision; they stumbled in judg- ment. :8 For all their tables are full of unclean vomit; no place is clean. 9 To whom will he teach knowledge, and to whom will he make the things he hears understood? To those who have been suckled by the milking and drawn from the udders. 10

For precept must be upon precept, precept upon precept, line upon line, line upon line, a little and a little. 11 For with a stuttering tongue and with a strange tongue shall he speak to this people. 12 To those to whom he said, "This is rest; give rest to those who are weary; and this is refreshment," but they would not listen. 13 Therefore the word of the LORD shall be addressed to them from precept to precept, from precept to precept, from line to line, from line to line, a little at a time and a little at a time, that they may go, fall backward, be broken, be caught and tak- en. 14 Hear therefore the word of the LORD, you scornful men who govern this people who are in Jerusalem. 15 For you have said, "We have made a covenant with death, and with hell we agree; even if a scourge ran out and passed through, it would not come to you; for we have made falsehood our refuge, and un- der vanity we hide." 16 Therefore thus says the Lord God, "Behold, I will set in Zion a stone, a tried stone, a precious cornerstone, a sure foundation. Whoever notices, must not hur- ry. 17 I will also set judgment as a rule, and justice as a balance, and the wind shall sweep away the confidence of the vine, and the wa- ters shall bring out the secret place. 18 Your covenant with death will be annulled, and your agreement with hell will not stand; when a scourge runs out and passes through, then you will be trodden down by it. 19 When it shall pass outside, it shall take you away; for it shall pass through every morning, day and night, and there shall be only fear to make your hearing understood. 20 For the bed is narrow that it cannot suffice, and the blanket is tight that you cannot wrap yourself in it. 21 For the LORD shall stand still as in mount Perazim; he shall be wroth as in the valley of Gibeon, to do his work, his harrowing work, and to bring to pass his deed, his strange deed. 22 Therefore do not mock yourselves, and do not increase your bonds, for I have heard from the LORD of hosts a determined consummation over all the earth. 23 Hear and hearken to my voice, hear and hearken to my speech. 24 Does the man who plows, plow all day long to sow? Does he open and break the lumps of his soil? 25 When he has made it level, will he not sow beans, and cumin, and wheat, and rye in their place? 26 For his God instructs him to have discretion, and teaches him. 27 For the wheat shall not be threshed with a threshing instrument, nor shall a char- iot wheel be turned upon the cumin; but the wheat shall be beaten with a staff, and the cumin with a rod. 28 The wheat of bread, when it is threshed, is not always threshed, nor does the wheel of his chariot yet make a noise, nor does he break it with his teeth. 29 This also is from the LORD of hosts, who is wonderful in counsel and excellent in works.

CHAPTER 29

1 Altar, altar of the city where Dauid dwelt, add ye also; have the lambs slain. 2 But I will bring the altar in the midst of the distress, and there shall be there joys and sorrows, and it shall be for me as an altar. 3 I will besiege thee as a circle, I will fight against thee on a mountain, and I will cast ramparts against thee. 4 Thus thou shalt be humbled, and thou shalt speak from the ground, and thy speech shall be as from the dust; thy voice also shall be from the ground as that of one having a spirit of divination, and thy speech shall whisper from the dust. 5 Moreover, the mul- titude of thy strangers shall be as little dust, and the multitude of strong men shall be as passing coffee, and shall be in a moment, suddenly. 6 The LORD of hosts shall visit thee with thunder, shaking, a great noise, a whirlwind, a tempest, and

a devouring flame of fire. 7 The multitude of all the nations that fight against the altar will be like a darkness or a night vision, that is, all those who make war against it, who fortify it and besiege it. 8 It will be like a hungry man who dreams, and behold, he eats; and when he wakes, his mind is emptied; or like a thirsty man who dreams, and behold, he drinks, and when he wakes, behold, he is weak, and his mind yearns; so will be the multitude of all the nations that fight against Mount Zion. 9 Be silent and be amazed: they are blind, and make you blind; they are drunk, but not with wine; they stag- ger, but not because of strong drunkenness. 10 For the Lord has drowsed you and closed your eyes: he has drowsed the Prophets and your chief seers. 11 And the vision of all of them has become to you like the words of a sealed book, which they hand over to one who can read, saying, "Please read this." Then he shall say, "I cannot, for it is sealed." 12 And the book is delivered to him who cannot read, saying, "Read this, please." And he shall say, "I cannot read." 13 Therefore the LORD said, "For this people draws near to me with their mouth and honors me with their lips, but they have turned their hearts away from me, and their fear of me has been taught by the precepts of men, 14 Therefore behold, I will again do a marvelous work in this people, a marvelous work and a wonder, for the wisdom of their wise shall perish, and the under- standing of their prudent shall be hid. 15 Woe to those who see deep to hide their counsel from the LORD, for their works are in dark- ness and they say, "Who sees and who knows? 16 Will not your transformation of deuises be esteemed as the potter's clay, because the work may say of him who made it, "He did not make me," or the thing formed say of him who made it, "He understood nothing"? 17 Is it not yet some time before Lebanon will be turned into Carmel, and Carmel will be regarded as a forest? 18 In that day the deaf shall hear the words of the book, and the eyes of the blind shall see out of darkness and gloom. 19 The serene in the LORD shall yet receive ioye, and the poor shall be reconciled to the Holy One of Israel. 20 For the cruel man shall cease, and the scornful shall be consumed; and all those who have given themselves over to in- iquity shall be removed: 21 Who have caused a man to sin by word, and have caught him in a snare; who have rebuked them at the gate, and have brought down the righteous man without cause. 22 Therefore thus saith the LORD unto the house of Iaakob, he that redeemed Abraham: Iaakob shall be no more confounded, and his face shall be no more pale. 23 But when he shall see his sons, the work of my hands, in the midst of him, they shall sanctify my Name, and they shall sancti- fy the Holy One of Iaakob, and they shall fear the God of Israel. 24 Then those who wander in spirit will have understanding, and those who murmur will learn doctrine.

CHAPTER 30

1 Woe to the rebellious sons, says the LORD, who take counsel, but not with me, and who agree with an authority, but not with my spir- it, to put sin upon sin: 2 Who walk to go down to Egypt (and have not asked at my mouth) to strengthen themselves with the strength of Pharaoh and to trust in the shadow of Egypt. 3 But Pharaoh's strength shall be your shame, and trusting in the shadow of Egypt your con- fusion. 4 For his princes were in Zoan, and his ambassadors came to Hanes. 5 All will be ashamed of the people who cannot profit from it, nor help them, nor do them good, but it will be a shame and also a reproach. 6 The

burden of the beasts of the South, in a land of trouble and distress, whence shall come the yong and the old lion, the viper and the fierce flying serpent, against them that shall bring their riches on the backs of the learned, and their treasures on the backs of camels, to a people that cannot profit by them. 7 For the Egyptians are vain, and will help themselves in vanity. Therefore I cried to you, "Their strength is to stand firm." 8 Now go and write it before them in a table and note it in a book, that it may be for the last day forever: 9 that it is a rebellious people, lying children and children who will not listen to the law of the LORD. 10 Who says to the seers, "See not," and to the prophets, "Do not prophesy right things, but speak flattering things, proph- esy errors." 11 "Get out of the way, get out of the path, make the Holy One of Israel cease from the way." 12 Therefore thus says the Holy One of Israel, "Because you have forsaken this word, and rely on violence and wickedness, and linger on it, 13 therefore this iniquity will be to you like a breach that falls or a bulge in a wall, the breaking of which happens suddenly in a moment. 14 And its breaking is like the breaking of a potter's vessel, which is broken without a hole, and in the breaking of which there is no crock to take fire out of the hearth or to take water out of the well. 15 For thus says the LORD God, the Holy One of Israel, "In rest and quietness you shall be satisfied; in quietness and confidence shall be your strength, but you have not desired. 16 For you have said, 'No, but we will flee on horseback.' Therefore flee. We will ride on the swiftest. Therefore your persecutors will be faster. 17 A thousand like one will flee at the reproach of one; at the reproach of five you will flee, until you are left like a mammoth ship on the top of a mountain and like a beak on a hill. 18 For

this the LORD will wait for you, to have mercy on you, and for this he will be exalted, to have compassion on you; for the LORD is the God of judgment. Blessed are all those who wait for him. 19 A people shall dwell in Zion and in Jerusalem; you shall weep no more; he will surely have mercy on you at the cry of your weeping; when he hears you, he will answer you. 20 When the LORD has given you the bread of adultery and the water of affliction, your anger will no longer be restrained, but your eyes will see your wrath. 21 Your ears shall hear behind you a word saying, "This is the way, walk in it, when you turn to the right and when you turn to the left." 22 And thou shalt pollute the plaster of thy silken im- ages, and the rich ornaments of thy golden images; and thou shalt cast them away like a menstruated cloth, and shalt say unto him, Depart. 23 Then you shall give raina to your descendants, when you sow the ground, and bread of the harvest of the land, and it shall be fat and like oil; in that day your cattle shall be fed in great pastures. 24 Also the oxen and the young donkeys that till the ground shall eat a clean prouender, which shall be sown with the shovel and with the fan. 25 On all the mountains and on all the heights there shall be streams and rivulets of water in the day of the great slaughter, when the towers shall fall. 26 Moreover, the light of the moon shall be as the light of the sun, and the light of the sun shall be as seuen folde, and as the light of seuen dayes in the day when the LORD shall take care of the breach of his people, and heal the stroke of their wound. 27 Behold, the Name of the LORD comes from afar; his face is burning, and his burden is heavy; his lips are full of indignation, and his tongue is like a devouring fire. 28 His spirit is like a river overflowing to the neck; it will split, to scatter the nations with the fan of vanity, and there will be a bridle to make them err in the chains of the peoples. 29 But there shall be a singing as at night, when a solemn feast is celebrat- ed, and a cheerfulness of heart like that of one who goes with the fife to the mountain of the LORD, to the mighty one of Israel. 30 And the LORD shall cause his glorious journey to be heard, and shall declare the kindling of his armor with the wrath of his countenance, and the flame of a consuming fire, with scattering, and storm, and hail. 31 For by the voice of the LORD shall Assur be destroyed, who smote with the rod. 32 In every place where your rod shall pass, he shall break loose in haste and fury, which the LORD shall set upon him with tabernacles and harps; and with battles and lifting up his hands he shall fight against him. 33 For Tophet has been prepared from time immemorial, it has been prepared for the king; he has made it deep and great; its fire is fire and much wood; the breath of the LORD, like a rivulet of brimstone, kindles it.

CHAPTER 31

1 Woe to those who go down to Egypt seek- ing help, who stand on horseback, who trust in chariots, because they are many, and in horsemen, because they are very strong; but they do not look to the Holy One of Israel, nor do they look to the LORD. 2 But he is still the wisest; therefore he will bring peace, and will not retract his word, but will rise up against the house of the wicked, and against the help of those who work in vanity. 3 The Egyptians are men and not God, their horses are flesh and not spirit; and when the LORD stretches out his hand, the helper will fall, and he who is in possession of a weapon will fall, and all of them will fail. 4 For thus hath the LORD said unto me, As the lion or the liophile that goeth forth to his prayer, and against whom, if a multitude of shepherds be called, he is not cowed by their voice, nor humbled at their noise, so shall the LORD of hosts come down to fight for Mount Zion and for his hill. 5 As the birds that fly, so the LORD of hosts will defend Jerusalem, defending it and protect- ing it, going through it and preserving it. 6 O children of Israel, turn back, inasmuch as you have sunk in rebellion. 7 For in that day every one shall cast away his idols of torpedo and his idols of gold, which your hands have made you, as sin. 8 Then Assur shall fall by the sword, not by the hand of man, nor shall the sword of man destroy him; he shall flee from the sword, and his young men shall faint. 9 He shall go away in fear to his tower, and his princes shall be afraid of the standart, saith the LORD, whose fire is in Zion, and his fur- nace in Jerusalem.

CHAPTER 32

1 Behold, a king shall reign in righteousness, and princes shall rule in judgment. 2 That man will be like a hiding place from the wind and like a shelter for the storm, like a spring of water in a dry place and like the shadow of a great tower in a weary land. 3 The eyes of those who see will not be closed, and the ears of those who hear will listen. 4 The heart of the fool will understand knowledge, and the tongue of the stammerer will be ready to speak clearly. 5 The Negro will no longer be called a liberal, nor the rich Turk. 6 But the ne- gro shall speak negritude, and his heart shall work iniquity, and do wickedness, and shall speak falsely against the LORD, to empty the hungry soul, and make the thirsty man's wa- ter fail. 7 For the weapons of the corrupter are evil; he makes evil counsel, to smite the poor with lying words, and to speak against the poor with judgment. 8 But the free man shall speak free things, and continue his liberality. 9 Arise, you women who are wealthy; hear my message, unwise daughters; listen to my words. 10 You women who are careless will be afraid in a year's time, for the harvest will be exhausted and the gatherings will not come. 11 You women who are at ease, be astonished; fear, O careless women; strip off your gar- ments, and wrap your garments in sackcloth. 12 The men shall complain for the teats, for the pleasant fields, and for the fruitful vine. 13 On the land of my people shall grow thorns and briers, and also on all the houses of joy in the city of Reioysing, 14 For the palace shall be forsaken, and the noise of the city shall be left; and the tower and the fortress shall be dens for the ere, delight for the wild asses, and pasture for the flocks, 15 until the Spirit shall be powerful on every side, and the wil- derness shall become a fruitful field, and the abundant field shall be regarded as a forest. 16 Judgment will dwell in the wilderness, and righteousness will remain in the fruitful field. 17 The work of justice will be peace, that is, the work of righteousness and tranquility, and security forever. 18 My people shall dwell in the tabernacle of peace, in safe dwellings and in sure resting places. 19 When it hails, it shall fall on the forest, and the city shall be set low. 20 Blessed are you who sow over all the waters, and cause the feet of the ox and the horse to fall.

CHAPTER 33

1 Woe to you who do spoyle and have not been spoyle, who do wickedness and have not done wickedness against you; when you stop do- ing spoyle, you will be spoyle; when you stop doing wickedness, they will do wickedness against you. 2 O LORD, have mercy on us who have waited for you; be you, who waste their arms in the morning, our help even in time of trouble. 3 At the noise of tumult the peoples fled; At your exaltation the nations were scat- tered. 4 Thy spoyle will gather like the gath- ering of caterpillars, and will go against him like the leaping of grashoppers. 5 The LORD is exalted, for he dwelleth upon him; he hath filled Zion with righteousness and judgment. 6 Thy times shall be steadfast, thy strength, thy health, thy wisdom, and thy knowledge: for the fear of the LORD shall be his treasure. 7 Behold, their messengers shall cry outward- ly, and you ambassadors of peace shall weep bitterly. 8 The paths are deserted, the man who walks is gone, he has destroyed the path, he has destroyed the cities, he has considered no one. 9 The land mourns and faints: Leb- anon is shamed and lowers; Sharon is like a wilderness, Basan is shaken, and Carmel is shaken. 10 Now will I rise, saith the LORD; now will I be exalted, now will I be lifted up. 11 You shall conceive coffee and produce stub- ble; the fire of your breath shall destroy you. 12 The people shall be like burning lime, and like cut thorns they shall be burned in the fire. 13 Hear, you who are far off, what I have done; and you who are far off, know my power. 14 The sinners of Zion are afraid, the hypocrites are afraid; which of them shall dwell with consuming fire, which of them shall dwell with everlasting fire? 15 He who walks in righ- teousness and says righteous things, rejecting oppression, shaking his hands from taking gifts, stopping his ears from hearing blood and closing his eyes from seeing wickedness. 16 He shall dwell upon himself; his defense shall be the munition of rocks; bread shall be given him, and his waters shall be sure. 17 Your eyes shall see the King in his glory; they shall see the distant land. 18 Your heart will ponder with fear,

"Where is the scribe, where is the receiver, where is he who counted the towers? 19 Thou shalt not see a fierce people, a people of obscure language that thou canst not perceive, and of a stammering tongue that thou canst not understand. 20 Look at Zion, the city of our solemn feasts; your eyes will see Jerusalem as a quiet dwelling, a Tabernacle that cannot be removed; its poles can never be removed, and none of its cords will be broken. 21 For surely there the mighty LORD will be for you, as a place of floods and brooding streams, where no ship with oares will pass by, nor will great ships pass by. 22 For the LORD is our judge, the LORD is our head; the LORD is our king, he will save the city. 23 Thy ropes are loose; they have not been able to strengthen their mask well, nor have they been able to lay out the sailing ship; then the prayer shall be deuid for great spoil; yea, the lame shall carry away the prayer. 24 No inhabitant shall say, "I am sick"; the people that dwell therein shall have forgiven their sins.

CHAPTER 34

1 Come hither, ye nations, hear and hear- ken, ye peoples; hear the earth and all that is in it, the world and all that is in it. 2 For the indignation of the LORD is upon all the nations, and his wrath upon all their armies; he has destroyed them and delivered them up to slaughter. 3 Their victims shall be cast away, their thorns shall come out of their bodies, and the mountains shall be loosed from their blood. 4 All the hosts of Heauen shall be dis- solved, and the Heauen shall be folded like a book; and all their hosts shall fall as the fo- liage falls from the vine and as it falls from the fig tree. 5 For my sword shall be drunk in the heavens; behold, it shall come upon Edom and upon the people of my curse to judge them. 6 The sword of the LORD is full of blood; it is fattened with fat and with the blood of lambs and goats, with the fat of the kids of rams, because the LORD has made a sacrifice in Bozrah and a great slaughter in the land of Edom. 7 The vnicorns shall go down with them, and the bullocks with bul- lets; their land shall be drunk with blood, and their dust shall be fattened with fatness. 8 For it is the day of the LORD's vengence, and the year of recompense for the judgment of Zion. 9 Her riuers shall be turned into pitch, her dust into brimstone, and her earth shall be burning pitch. 10 It shall not be quenched night or day; its smoke shall spread more and more; it shall be desolate from generation to generation; no one shall pass through it forev- ermore. 11 But the pelican and the hedgehog shall possess it, the great owl and the nozzle shall dwell therein, and he shall spread upon it the line of vanity and the stones of empti- ness. 12 His nobles shall call the kingdom, and there shall be none, and all its princes shall be as nothing. 13 Thorns shall be found in its palaces, nettles and thistles in its fortresses; it shall be an abode for dragons and a court for ostriches. 14 Ziim and Iim shall also meet there, the satyr shall cry to his mate, the wren shall rest there and find for himself a quiet abode. 15 There the owl shall make her nest, and hatch and brood, and gather them under her shadow; there the vultures also shall gath- er, each with his creature. 16 Look in the book of the LORD and get an idea: not one of these will be let slip, not one will lack his produce, for his mouth has given an order, and his own Spirit has gathered them. 17 He has drawn the lot for them, and his hand has determined by wire and by sign that they shall possess it for- ever; from generation to generation they shall dwell therein.

CHAPTER 35

1 The desert and the wilderness will be re- vived; the forsaken ground will rejoice and blossom like a rose. 2 It shall bloom abun- dantly, flourish and flourish greatly; the glory of Lebanon shall be bestowed upon it; the beauty of Carmel and Sharon shall see the glory of the LORD and the excellency of our God. 3 Strengthen the weak hands and comfort the feeble knees. 4 Say to those who fear, "Be strong, do not fear; behold, your God comes with vengeance; behold, God with reward will come and save you." 5 Then the eyes of the blind shall be enlightened, and the ears of the deaf shall be opened. 6 Then the lame shall leap like a deer, and the tongue of the dumb shall sing, for in the wilderness shall flow forth waters, and in the desert riv- ers. 7 The barren land shall be as a well, and the thirsty (as springs of water in the abode of dragons, where they lie) shall be a place for reeds and rushes. 8 There shall be a path and a way, and the way shall be called holy; the defiled shall not pass through it, for he shall be with them and walk in the way, and the foolish shall not err. 9 For there shall be no lion, neither shall there be found therein unpleasing beasts, that the redeemed may walk. 10 Therefore the redeemed of the LORD will return and come to Zion with prayer; and everlasting joy will be upon their heads; they will have joy and happiness, and sadness and mourning will disappear.

CHAPTER 36

1 Now in the fourteenth year of King Heze- kiah, Saneherib king of Assur came against all the strong cities of Iudah and took them. 2 And the king of Assur sent Rabshakeh from Lachish toward Jerusalem, to king Hezekiah, with a great army, and he halted by the con- duit of the vip well, on the way to the field of the coalmen. 3 Then came to him Eliakim the son of Hilkiah, steward of the house, Shebnah the chancellor, and Ioah the son of Asaph, re- corder. 4 Rabshakeh said to them, Tell Heze- kiah, I pray you, Thus says the great king, the king of Assur: What confidence is this in which you trust? 5 I answer, Certainly I have eloquence, but counsel and strength are for war; in whom then do you trust, if you rebel against me?" 6 You trust in this broken staff of Egypt, that if a man lean on it, it goes into his hand and perishes him; so is Pharaoh, king of Egypt, to all who trust in him. 7 But if you say to me, "We trust in the LORD our God." Is it not he whose places and altars Hezekiah pulled down, and said to Judah and Jerusalem, "You shall worship before this altar"? 8 Now there- fore give hostages to my lord the king of As- sur, and I will give you two thousand horses, if you are able to make them ride. 9 For how can you despise a captain of the least of my lord's servants and rely on Egypt for chariots and horsemen? 10 Have I come without the LORD into this land to destroy it? The LORD said to me, 'Go against this country and de- stroy it.'" 11 Then Eliakim, Shebna, and Ioah said to Rabshakeh, "Speak, I pray you, to your servants in the language of the Aramites (for we understand it), and do not speak to them in the language of the Iewes, in the presence of the people on the walls." 12 Then Rabshakeh said, "Has my master sent me to your master and to you to speak these words, and not to the men who sit on the walls, that they may eat their own drink and drink their own pisse with you?" 13 Then Rabshakeh stood up and cried with a

loud voice in the Irish language, saying, "Hear the words of the great king, of the king of Assur." 14 Thus says the king, "Do not let Hezekiah deceive you, for he will not be able to deliver you. 15 And do not let Heze- kiah cause you to trust in the LORD, saying, "The LORD will surely deliver you; this city will not be given into the hand of the king of Assur." 16 Do not listen to Hezekiah, for thus says the king of Assur, "Make an appointment with me and come to me, that each one may eat of his vine, each one of his fig tree, and drink water from his well, 17 until I come and bring you to a land like your own, that is, to a land of wheat and wine, to a land of bread and vineyards, 18 unless Hezekiah deceives you, saying, "The LORD will deliver you." Has any of the gods of the nations taken his land from the hand of the king of Assur? 19 Where is the god of Hamath and Arpad? Where is the god of Sefaruaim? Or how have they delivered Samaria out of my hand? 20 Who among all the gods of these countries is he who brought their country out of my hand, that the LORD might bring Jerusalem out of my hand?" 21 Then they kept silent and did not answer him a single word, for the king had commanded them not to answer him. 22 Then Eliakim the son of Hilkiah, steward of the house, Shebnah the chancellor, and Ioah the son of Asaph, re- corder, went to Hezekiah with tattered gar- ments and reported to him the words of Rab- shakeh.

CHAPTER 37

1 When King Hezekiah heard this, he tore his clothes, put on sackcloth and entered the house of the LORD. 2 Then he sent Eliakim, the steward of the house, and Shebnah, the chancellor, with the elders of the priests, clothed in sackcloth, to Isaiah the prophet, the son of Amoz. 3 They said to him, "Thus says Hezekiah, 'Today is a day of tribulation, reproach and blasphemy, because children have come into the world and there is no strength to bring them forth. 4 If the LORD, your God, has heard the words of Rabshakeh, whom the king of Assur, his master, has sent to rage against the God who lies and to re- buke him with words that the LORD, your God, has heard, then lift up your prayer for the remnant that is left." 5 So King Hezeki- ah's servants came to Isaiah. 6 Isaiah said to them, "Tell your master, 'Thus says the LORD: Do not be afraid because of the words that you have heard, with which the servants of the king of Assur have blasphemed me. 7 Be- hold, I will send a blast upon him, and he shall be sick, and shall return to his own land, and I will bring him down by the sword into his own land." 8 Rabshakeh returned and found the king of Assur fighting Libnah, for he had heard that he had departed from Lachish. 9 He also heard of Tirhaka king of Ethiopia, "Behold, he has gone out to fight against you"; and when he heard this, he sent other mes- sengers to Hezekiah, saying 10 Thus you shall speak to Hezekiah king of Judah, saying, "Do not deceive your God, in whom you trust, say- ing, Jerusalem shall not be given into the hand of the king of Assur." 11 Well, you have heard what the kings of Assur have done to all the countries by destroying them, and will you be disappointed? 12 Have the gods of the na- tions that my fathers destroyed, such as Go- zan, Haran, Rezef, and the sons of Eden, who were in Telassar, failed you? 13 Where is the king of Hamath, the king of Arpad, and the king of the city of Sefaruaim, Hena and Iuah? 14 Then Hezekiah received the letter from the hand of the messengers and read it and went to the house of the LORD, and Hezekiah laid it before the LORD. 15 Hezekiah prayed to the LORD, saying, 16 O LORD of hosts, God of Israel,

who dwells among the cherubim, you are the one God of all the kingdoms of the earth; you made heaven and earth. 17 Incline thine ear, O LORD, and hear; open thine eyes, O LORD, and see, and hear all the words of Saneherib, who sent to blaspheme the God who lies. 18 It is true, O LORD, that the kings of Assur have destroyed all the lands and their counties, 19 And they cast their gods into the fire, because they were not gods, but works of man's hands, like wood or stone; therefore they destroyed them. 20 Now therefore, O LORD our God, come out of his hand, that all the kingdoms of the earth may know that you are the only LORD." 21 Then Isaiah the son of Amoz sent word to Hezekiah, "Thus says the LORD God of Israel, Because you prayed to me concerning Saneherib king of Assur, 22 this is the word which the LORD hath spo- ken against him: the virgin, the daughter of Zion, hath despised thee and mocked thee; the daughter of Jerusalem hath shaken her head against thee. 23 Against whom have you railed and blasphemed, against whom have you exalted your voice and lifted up your eyes to him, against the Holy One of Israel? 24 Through your servants you have railed against the LORD and said, "By the multitude of my songs I have gone up to the top of the moun- tains, to the flanks of Lebanon, and I will cut down its cedars and its firs, and I will go as far as the heights of its top and the forest of its fruitful places. 25 I have dug and made the waters drink, and with the soles of my feet I have dried up all the closed banks. 26 Have you not heard how I made it anciently and formed it long ago? And shall I now bring it, that it may be destroyed and lie on ruinous heaps, like cities undone? 27 Its inhabitants have little strength, they are destroyed and confused; they are like the grass of the fields and the green grass, or the grass on the tops of houses, or the dogwood choked before it is grown. 28 But I know thy dwelling, thy going out, thy coming in, and thy fierceness against me. 29 Because thou art raging against me, and thy tumult hath reached unto mine ears, I will put my hoof in thine nostrils, and my bri- dle in thy lips, and I will lead thee back by the same way by which thou camest. 30 This shall be a sign to you, O Hezekiah: "This year you shall eat that which grows of itself; the second year, that which grows without sowing; the third year, sow and reap, plant vineyards and eat the fruit thereof." 31 The remnant of the house of Iudah, which has escaped, shall take root again and bear fruit. 32 For out of Jeru- salem shall come forth a remnant, and those who shall escape from Mount Zion, the zeal of the LORD of hosts shall do this. 33 There- fore thus saith the LORD concerning the king of Assur, He shall not enter into this city, nor shoot an arrow into it, nor come before it with a shield, nor hurl it against a mountain. 34 By the same way by which he came, he will turn back and not enter this city, says the LORD. 35 For I will defend this city to save it, for my sake and for the sake of my servant Dauids." 36 Then the angel of the LORD went out and struck in the camna of Assur one hundred thousand, forty-five and five thousand peo- ple; so when they rose up early in the morn- ing, behold, they were all dead bodies. 37 Then Saneherib king of Assur departed and returned and settled in Nineveh. 38 While he was in the temple worshiping Nisroch, his god, Adramelech and Sharezer, his sons, killed him by the sword and fled to the land of Ararat; and Esarhaddon, his son, reigned in his place.

CHAPTER 38

1 At that time Hezekiah was at the end of his life, and Isaiah the prophet, the son of Amoz, came to him and said, "Thus says the LORD, 'Set your house in order, for you shall die and not perish.'" 2 Then Hezekiah turned his face toward the wall and prayed to the LORD, 3 and said, "Please, Lord, remember now how I have walked before you in truth and with a sincere heart, and have done what is good in your sight." 4 Then the word of the LORD came to Isaiah, saying, 5 "Go and say to Heze- kiah, Thus says the LORD God of Dauid, your father: I have heard your prayer and seen your prayers; behold, I will add to your days fifty years. 6 I will deliver you out of the hand of the king of Assur and out of this city, for I will defend this city." 7 And this sign shalt thou have from the LORD, that the LORD will do the thing which he hath spoken, 8 Behold, I will bring back the shadow of the degrees (by which the sun went down in the day of Ahaz) ten degrees back; so the sun went back ten de- grees, by which it had gone down. 9 The writ- ing of Hezekiah, king of Judah, when he was sick and had recovered from his illness. 10 I said, When my days are ended, I will go to the gates of the grave: I am deprived of the resi- due of my years. 11 I said, I shall see the LORD no more, except in the land of death: I shall see no more man among the inhabitants of the world. 12 My dwelling place is gone, and is removed from me as the tent of a shepherd: I have cut off like an animal my life; he shall cut me off from above; from day to night, thou shalt make an end of me. 13 I rose up in the morning, but he hath broken all my bones, like a lion; from day to night thou shalt make an end of me. 14 Like a crane or a swallow, I chattered: I groaned like a cloud; my ears were lifted up: O LORD, he hath oppressed me; comfort me. 15 What shall I say? For he hath told me and done it: I shall walk faintly all my years in the bitterness of my soul. 16 O LORD, to them that visit them, and to all that are in them, shall the life of my spirit be known, that thou hast made me sleep, and hast giv- en me life again. 17 Behold, for happiness I had bitter affliction, but it was your pleasure to deliver my soul from the pit of corruption, because you cast all my sins behind your back. 18 For the grave cannot confess you, death cannot praise you, and those who go down into the pit cannot hope in your truth. 19 But he that liveth shall confess thee, as I do this day; the father to his children shall declare thy truth." 20 The LORD has been ready to tell me the truth; therefore we will sing my song all the days of our life in the house of the LORD." 21 Then Isaiah said, "Take a lamp of dried figs and place it over the boy, and he will recover." 22 Hezekiah also had said, "What is the sign that I will enter the House of the LORD?

CHAPTER 39

1 At the same time, Merodach Baladan son of Baladan, king of Babel, sent letters and a gift to Hezekiah, because he had heard that he had been stricken with sickness and had recovered. 2 Hezekiah rejoiced, and showed them the house of treasures, the silverware, the gold, the spices, the precious ointments, the whole house of his armor, and all that was in his treasures; there was nothing in his house and in all his kingdom that Heze- kiah had not shown them. 3 Then the proph- et Isaiah went to King Hezekiah and said to him, "What did these men say and where did they come from to you?" Hezekiah answered, "They have come from a country far from me, from Babel." 4 Then he said, "What did they see in your house?" Hezekiah answered, "They have seen everything in my house; there is nothing among

my treasures that I have not shown them." 5 Isaiah said to Hezekiah, "Listen to the word of the LORD of hosts, 6 "Behold, the days are coming when all that is in your house, which your fathers have put in store until now, shall be carried away to Babel; nothing shall be left, says the LORD. 7 And your sons who go out from you and whom you beget shall be taken away and shall become eunuchs in the palace of the king of Babel." 8 Then Hezekiah said to Isaiah, "The word of the LORD is good, as thou hast spo- ken it"; and he said, "Nevertheless let there be peace and truth in my days."

CHAPTER 40

1 Take comfort, comfort my people, will your God say. 2 Speak comfort to Jerusalem and cry to her that her war is accomplished, that her iniquity is forgiven, for she has received from the hand of the LORD double for all her sins. 3 A voice cries out in the wilder- ness, "Prepare the way of the LORD; make a path in the wilderness for our God." 4 Every valley shall be exalted, every mountain and hill shall be lowered; crooked paths shall be straight and rough places level. 5 The glory of the LORD shall be revived, and all flesh shall see it together, for the mouth of the LORD has spoken it. 6 A seer said, "Crie." And he said, "What shall I cry? All flesh is fat, and all its grace is like the floure of the field. 7 The grass withers, the flour fades, because the Spirit of the LORD blows upon it; surely the people are grass. 8 The grass wears out, the floure fades away, but the word of our God will stand for- ever. 9 O Zion, that bringeth good tidings, go up into the mountain: O Jerusalem, that bringeth good tidings, lift up thy journey with strength; lift it up, be not unaware; say unto the cities of Iudah, Behold your God. 10 Behold, the Lord God shall come with power, and his arm shall rule for him; behold, his re- ward is with him, and his work before him, 11 he will feed his flock like a shepherd; he will gather the lambs with his arm, he will carry them in his bosom and lead them with the lit- tle ones. 12 Who has measured the waters in his fist, who has counted the threshing-floor with a spade, who has understood the dust of the earth in a measure, who has weighed the mountains in a weight and the hills in a balance? 13 Who instructed the Spirit of the Lord, who was his counselor or taught him? 14 From whom did he take counsel, who in- structed him and taught him the way of judgment, who taught him knowledge and showed him the way of understanding? 15 Behold, the nations are as a drop of a buck- et, and are counted as the dust of the scales; behold, he taketh away yles as a little dust. 16 Lebanon is not enough for fire, nor is its re- fuse enough for a burnt offering. 17 Before him all nations are as nothing, and to him they are considered less than nothing and vain. 18 To whom then do you wish to com- pare God? Or what likeness do you wish to make to him? 19 The workman casts an im- age, the goldsmith covers it with gold or the goldsmith creates plates of silver. 20 Does not the poor man choose a tree that will not rot for an oblation? He also seeks a skillful workman to prepare an image that will not be melted. 21 Do you know nothing? Have you not heard it? Has it not been told to you from the beginning? Have you not understood it from the foundation of the earth? 22 He sits on the circle of the earth, and the inhabitants of it are like horsemen; he stretches out the heavens like a curl and enlarges them like a tent in which to dwell. 23 He reduces princes to nothing, and makes the judges of the earth as vanities, 24 as if they had not been plat- ted, as if they had

not been sown, as if their cattle had not gone round about the earth; for he has blown upon them, and they have withered, and the whirlwind will carry them away like stubble. 25 To whom do you now wish to compare me, that I may be like him, says the Holy One? 26 Lift up your eyes to him, and see who created these things, and brings forth their armies by name, and calls them all by name; for the greatness of his power and strength nothing fails. 27 Why do you say, O Iaakob, and say, O Israel, "My way is hidden from the LORD, and my judgment is passed before my God"? 28 Do you not know or have you not heard that the eternal God, the LORD, has created the ends of the earth? He does not grow weary or weary; there is no seeking of His understanding. 29 He gives strength to those who are weak, and to those who have no strength He increases power. 30 Then young men will faint and grow weary, and young men will stumble and fall. 31 But those who wait on the LORD will regain their strength; They will lift up their wings like eagles; They will run and not grow weary; They will walk and not grow weary.

CHAPTER 41

1 Restrain thyself before me, O IRELAND, and let the people give up their strength; come hither and speak; meet to judge. 2 Who hath caused righteousness to arise from the east, and called it to his side, and made the nations pass before him, and subdued the kings? He made them as dust for his sword and as scat- tered stubble for his bow. 3 He pursued them and passed safely through the road he had not traveled with his feet. 4 Who has worked and done this? He who calls generations from the beginning. I, the LORD, am the first and with the last I am the same. 5 The peoples saw it and were afraid, and the ends of the earth were afraid, and they drew near and came. 6 Every man helped his neighbor and said to his brother, "Be strong." 7 So the workman comforted the founder, the one who beat with the hammer and the one who beat with force, saying, "He is ready for the golling, and has fastened it with nayles so that it will not be moved." 8 But you, Israel, are my servant, and you Iaakob, whom I have chosen, descendants of Abraham, my friend. 9 For I took thee from the ends of the earth, and called thee before the leaders thereof, and said unto thee, Thou art my servant: I have chosen thee, and cast thee not away. 10 Fear not, for I am with thee; fear not, for I am thy God: I will strengthen thee, and help thee, and uphold thee with the right hand of my righteousness. 11 Behold, all they that have ridiculed thee shall be shamed and confounded; they shall be as nothing, and they that strive with thee shall perish. 12 And thou shalt see them, and shalt not find them, that is, the men of thy strife; for they shall be as nothing, and the men that war against thee, as a thing of nothing. 13 For I, the LORD thy God, will hold thy right hand, and will say unto thee, Fear not, I will help thee. 14 Fear not, worm, Iaakob, and ye men of Israel: I will help thee, saith the LORD, and thy redeemer, the Holy One of Israel. 15 Behold, I will make thee a roller, and a new threshing instrument, fitted with teeth; thou shalt thresh the moun- tains, and beat them to a pulp, and make the hills like coffee. 16 Thou shalt flatten them, and the wind shall carry them away, and the whirlwind shall scatter them; and thou shalt rejoice in the LORD, and glory in the Holy One of Israel. 17 When the poor and needy seek water, and have none (their tongue faileth because of thirst), I, the LORD, will hear them: I, the God of Israel, will not for- sake them). 18 I will open riuers in the tops of the hills, and fountains in the midst of the valleys: I will make the wilderness as pools of water, and the wasteland as springs of water. 19 And I will put in the wilderness the cedar tree, and the emery tree, and the myrrh tree, and the pine tree; and I will put in the wilder- ness the fir tree, and the helmet tree, and the box tree together. 20 Therefore let them see and know, consider and understand together that the hand of the LORD has made this, and the Holy One of Israel has made it. 21 Support your cause, says the LORD; bring your strong reasons, says the king of Iaakob. 22 Let them bring forward and say what is to come; let them show the former things as they are, that we may consider them and know the latter; let them declare the things to come. 23 Show the things that shall come to pass hereafter, that we may know that you are gods; yea, do good or do evil, that we may declare it and see it together. 24 Behold, you have no worth, and your creation is worthless; man has chosen an abomination with them. 25 I have raised up from the north, and he shall come; from the east the sun shall rest upon my Name, and he shall come upon princes as upon clay, and as the potter treads my earth under the leaf. 26 Who has declared from the beginning, that we may know, or before the time, that we may say, "He is righteous"? Surely, there is no one who shows, there is no one who declares, there is no one who hears your words. 27 I am the first to say to Zion, "Behold, look at them; and I will give Jerusalem one who brings good tidings." 28 But when I saw them, there was none; when I questioned them, there was no counselor; and when I questioned them, they answered not a word. 29 Behold, they are all vain; their works are of no avail; their images are wind and confusion.

CHAPTER 42

1 Behold my servant: I will rest upon him: my elect, in whom my soul is committed: I have put my Spirit upon him; he shall bring judg- ment to the Gentiles. 2 He shall not cry out, nor rise up, nor make his voice heard in the streets. 3 He shall not break the bruised reed nor quench the smoking flax; he shall bring judgment in truth. 4 He will not draw back or be discouraged until he has established judgment in the earth; and the yles will wait for his word. 5 Thus says God, the LORD (he who created the heavens and scattered them; he who stretched out the earth and its shoots; he who gives breath to men on it and spirit to those who walk in it). 6 I, the LORD, have called thee with righteousness; I will hold thee by the hand, and keep thee, and give thee as a messenger of the peoples, and as the light of the Gentiles, 7 That thou mayest open the eyes of the blind, and bring forth the captives from prison, and those who sit in darkness from the prison house. 8 I am the LORD, that is my name, and my glory I will not give to another, nor my praise to images of bronze. 9 Behold, the former things have passed away, and I declare new things; before they come, I will tell you of them. 10 Sing to the LORD a new song and his praise from the end of the earth: you who go down to the sea and all that is there: the islands and their inhabitants. 11 Let the wilderness and their cities lift up their song, Let the cities inhabited by Kedar, Let the inhabitants of the rocks sing, Let them shout from the tops of the mountains. 12 Let them be glorious of the LORD and declare his praise in the countries. 13 Let the LORD go out like a gypsy, let him take courage like a man of war, let him shout and cry out and fight against his enemies. 14 I have held my peace for a long time: I have stood still and re- strained myself; now I will cry out like a wom- an dragging herself: I will destroy

and destroy at once. 15 I will destroy the mountains and the hills, and I will destroy all their grasses; I will make the plains floodable, and I will destroy the pools of water. 16 I will cause the blind to pass by a way they did not know, and I will lead them by paths they did not know; I will make darkness light before them, and crooked things straight. These things I will do for them, and I will not forsake them. 17 They shall be rejected; they shall be greatly ashamed who trust in the bronze images and say to the molten images, "You are our gods." 18 Hear, ye faint; and ye blind, look, that ye may see. 19 Who is blind but my servant, or deaf as my messenger whom I sent? Who is blind as the sick man, and blind as the servant of the Lord? 20 Does he see many things, but does not observe them? Does he open his ears, but does not listen? 21 The Lord wants, by his righteousness, to magnify peace and exalt it. 22 But this people is robbed and ruined, and shall be all imprisoned in prisons, and shall be hid in prison houses; it shall be a prayer, and no one shall deliver it; a spoil, and no one shall say, "Restore."23 Which of you will heed this, pay attention and listen for the later? 24 Who gave Iaakob as a sponge and Israel to the rob- bers? Have you not done this, O Lord, because we have sinned against him? Because they would not walk in his words and were not obedient to his law. 25 Therefore he bestowed upon him his fierce anger and the power of battle; and he burned him all around, without his realizing it.

CHAPTER 43

1 But now thus says the LORD, who created thee, O Iaakob, and formed thee, O Israel: "Fear not, for I have redeemed thee; I have called thee by name, thou art mine." 2 When you pass through the waters, I will be with you, and through the floods, lest they over- whelm you. When you pass through the fire, you shall not be burned, and the flame shall not be kindled upon you. 3 For I am the LORD your God, the Holy One of Israel, your Savior: I gave Egypt as your ransom, Ethiopia and Seba for you. 4 Because thou hast been pre- cious in mine eyes, thou hast been honorable, and I have valued thee, I will give men for thee, and peoples for thee. 5 Do not fear, for I am with you; I will bring your descendants from the East and gather them from the West. 6 I will say to the North, "Come," and to the South, "Do not stray;" I will cause my sons to come from afar, and my daughters from the ends of the earth. 7 Everyone shall be called by my name, for I have created him for my glory, formed him, and made him. 8 I will bring in the blind people and they shall have eyes, and the deaf and they shall have ears. 9 Let all the nations assemble, let the peoples assemble; who of them can declare this and say the for- mer things? Let them bring their witnesses, that they may be justified; but let them hear and say, It is the truth. 10 Ye are my witnesses, saith the Lord, and my servant whom I have chosen; therefore ye shall know me, and know me, and understand that I am: before me no God was formed, neither shall there be after me. 11 I, that is, I am the Lord, and beside me there is no God. 12 I declared, I spoke, and I showed, when there was no foreign god among you; therefore you are my witnesses, saith the Lord, that I am God. 13 Yea, before the day was, I am, and there is none that can deliver himself out of my hand: I will do it, and who will allow it? 14 Thus saith the LORD your redeemer, the Holy One of Israel, Because of you I have sent to Babel and brought it down; they have all fled, and the Chaldeans weep on the ships. 15 I am the LORD, your Holy One, the maker of Israel, your King. 16 Thus says the LORD who creates a way in the sea and a path in the mighty waters. 17 When he brings forth the chariot and the horse, the army and the power lie together and do not rise up; they die out and fade away like snow. 18 Do not remember past things, and do not consider ancient things. 19 Behold, I do a new thing; now it comes forth; will ye not know it? I will make a way in the wilderness and floods in the desert. 20 The wild beasts shall honor me, the dragons and the ostriches, for I give water in the wilderness and floods in the wilderness to give drink to my people, that is, my chosen ones. 21 This people I have formed for myself; they shall give honor to my praise. 22 You have not called upon me, O Iaakob, but you have wearied me, O Israel. 23 Thou hast not brought me the flock of thy burnt offspring, and hast not honored me with thy sacrifices. Thou hast not made thee to do service with offerings, and hast not wearied thee with in- cense. 24 Thou hast not bought me good wine with money, nor made me drunk with the fat of thy sacrifices, but thou hast made me to serve with thy sins, and hast wearied me with thy iniquities. 25 I, however, am the one who blots out your iniquities for my sake, and I will not remember your sins. 26 Remember me; let me judge you together; count yourself justified. 27 Your first father sinned, and your teachers transgressed against me. 28 There- fore I have made the leaders of the sanctuary profane; I have made Iaakob a curse and Isra- el a reproach.

CHAPTER 44

1 But now listen, O Iaakob my servant, and Israel, whom I have chosen. 2 Thus says the LORD, who made you and formed you from the woman; he will help you. Fear not, O Iaakob my servant, and you, righteous one, whom I have chosen. 3 For I will give water to thirst, and floods to dry ground; I will give my Spirit to thy seed, and my blessing to thy shoots. 4 They shall grow as among the grass- es and as willows by the streams. 5 One shall say, "I am the LORD"; another shall be called by the name of Iaakob; yet another shall sub- scribe with his hand to the LORD and shall be called by the name of Israel. 6 Thus says the LORD, the king of Israel and its redeemer, the LORD of hosts: 'I am the first and I am the last, and without me there is no God. 7 Who is like me who will call, declare, and set in order before me, since I appointed the ancient na- tions? And what is in place and what is about to happen? Let them tell it to them. 8 Fear not and be not afraid: have I not told you all along and declared it? You are my witnesses, if there is a God besides me, and if there is no God that I do not know. 9 All who make themselves an image are vain, and their delightful things profit nothing; and they are their own wit- nesses, who see not and know not; therefore they shall be confounded. 10 Who has made a god or cast an image that profits nothing? 11 Behold, all those who are part of it shall be confounded, for the workers themselves are men; let them all assemble and stand up; they shall be afraid and be confounded together. 12 The smith takes a tool and works in the cast- ings, and works it with hammers, and works it with the strength of his arms; yea, he is a hungry man, and his strength fails; he drinks no water, and is weak. 13 The carpenter lays out a thread, and covers it with red thread, and planes it, and finishes it with rope, and makes it in the shape of a man, according to the beauty of a man, that it may remain in a house. 14 He cuts down the cedars, takes the pine and the oke, and makes bold among the trees of the forest; he plants a fir tree, and the rain feeds him. 15 Man

burns it, for he takes of it and makes war with it; he lights it and makes bread with it, but he makes himself a god and worships it; he makes it an idol and bows down to it. 16 He burns half of it in the fire, and on the half he eats meat; he roasts the flesh and is satisfied; he warms himself and says, "I am at war, I have been at the fire." 17 And with his residue he makes himself a god, that is, his idol; he bows down before it and worships it and prays to it, and says, "De- light me, for you are my god." 18 They do not know and do not understand, because God has closed their eyes so that they do not see and their hearts so that they do not under- stand. 19 No one considers in his heart and has no knowledge or understanding to say, "I have burned half of it in the fire and baked bread on its colas: I have roasted meat and eaten it, and should I make its residue abom- inable? Shall I bow to the stump of a tree? 20 He feeds on ashes; a seduced heart has de- ceived him, so that he cannot deliver his soul, nor say, Is there not a lye in my right hand? 21 Remember these things (O Iaakob and Is- rael) for thou art my servant: I have formed thee: thou art my servant: O Israel, forget me not. 22 I have removed thy transgressions as a cloud, and thy sins as a mist: return unto me, for I have redeemed thee. 23 Draw back, O heavens, for the LORD has done it; shake yourselves, O lower parts of the earth; toast in prayer, O mountains, O forests, and every tree thereof, for the LORD has redeemed Iaakob, and he shall be glorified in Israel. 24 Thus says the LORD your redeemer and he who formed you from the woman, "I am the LORD, who made all things, who stretched out the heav- ens by myself and stretched out the earth by myself. 25 I destroy the signs of you south- erners and make foolish those who agree; I make backward the wise and make foolish their knowledge. 26 He confirms the word of his servant and carries out the counsel of his messengers, saying to Jerusalem, "You shall be inhabited"; and to the cities of Iudah, "You shall be rebuilt, and I will repay their ruined places." 27 He says to the abyss, "Be dry, and I will dry up your floods." 28 He says to Cyrus, "You are my shepherd, and he will carry out all my wishes; he also says to Jerusalem, "You shall be built," and to the Temple, "Your foun- dations will surely be laid."

CHAPTER 45

1 Thus says the LORD to Cyrus his anointed, whose right hand I have held to subdue the nations before him; therefore I will weaken the bonds of kings and open the gates before him, and the gates shall not be shut: 2 I will go before thee, and will make straight the crook- ed way; I will break the gates of bronze, and will burst the bars of yron. 3 I will give thee the treasures of darkness, and things hidden in secret places, that thou mayest know that I am the LORD that calleth thee by name, that is, the God of Israel. 4 For the sake of Iaakob my servant and Israel my chosen, I will call you by name and appoint you, even though you do not know me. 5 I am the LORD, and there is no other; there is no other God but me; I have girded you, though you have not known me, 6 That they may know, from the rising of the sun and from the west, that there is none but me. I am the LORD, and there is no oth- er. 7 I form light and create darkness: I cre- ate peace and create tranquility; I, the LORD, do all these things. 8 You, heavens, send dew from above, and bring down the clouds with righteousness; open the earth, and make sal- vation and righteousness to grow; make them meet: I, the LORD, have created it. 9 Woe to him who quarrels with his maker, to the pot- ter with the

vessels of the earth; will the clay say to him who worked it, "What are you do- ing?" or your work, "It has no hands"? 10 Woe to him who says to his father, "What have you begotten?" or to his mother, "What have you brought forth?" 11 Thus says the LORD, the Holy One of Israel and his maker, "Ask me about future things concerning my children and the works of my hands; command me. 12 I made the earth, and created man upon it: I, whose hands made the heavens to bud, commanded all their army. 13 I have raised him up in righteousness, and will direct all his ways; he shall build my city, and let my captives go, without price or recompense, saith the LORD of hosts. 14 Thus says the LORD: "The labor of Egypt, the merchandise of Ethiopia and the Sabeans, men of stature shall come to you and be yours; they shall fol- low you and go in chains; they shall prostrate themselves before you and plead with you, saying, 'Surely God is in you, and there is no other God beside you. 15 Truly you, O God, are hiding yourself, O God, savior of Israel. 16 All these shall be shamed and also confounded; they shall go together into confusion the im- age-makers. 17 But Israel shall be saved in the LORD, with everlasting salvation; you shall not be shamed or confused in the world with- out end. 18 For thus says the LORD (He who made the heavens, God himself, who formed the earth and made it; he who prepared it, he did not create it in time; he formed it to be inhabited) I am the LORD, and there is no other. 19 I have not spoken in secret, nor in a dark place of the earth; I have not said in secret to the descendants of Iaakob, 'Look at me': I, the LORD, speak righteously and de- clare righteous things." 20 Gather yourselves and come; gather yourselves together, you abject Gentiles; they have no knowledge, for they lean on the wood of their idol and pray to a god who cannot save them. 21 Say and bring them, and let them consult together: who has declared this from the beginning? Or told it all along? Am I not the Lord? And there is no God but me, a righteous and saving God; there is none but me. 22 Look to me and you will be saved; all the ends of the earth will be saved, for I am God and there is no other. 23 I have sworn by myself; the word has gone out of my mouth with righteousness and will not return, so that every knee will bow to me and every tongue swear by me. 24 He will say, "In the LORD I have righteousness and strength"; he will come to him, and all who questioned him will be shamed. 25 All the descendants of Israel will be justified and will glory in the LORD.

CHAPTER 46

1 Bel is prostrate, Nebo is fallen; their idols were on beasts and cattle; those they bore therein were laden with a wearing burden. 2 They bowed down and fell together, because they could not get rid of the burden, and their souls went into captivity. 3 Hear me, O house of Iaakob, and all who remain of the house of Israel, who were brought forth by me from the womb and carried by me from birth. 4 Therefore, even unto old age, I am the same, and will accompany you unto the last years of your life: I have made you: I will also bear you in my womb, and carry you, and deliver you. 5 To whom will you make me like or equate me, or cover me, that I may be like him? 6 They bring out the gold from the bag, weigh the silver in the balance, hire a goldsmith to make him a god, and bow down and worship him. 7 They carry him on their shoulders and carry him and put him in his place; so he stands and cannot move from his place. Even if one cries out to him, he cannot answer and

cannot deliver him from his tribulation. 8 Re- member this and be ashamed; remember it again, O you transgressors. 9 Remember the former things, for I am God, there is no other God, and there is nothing like me, 10 Who declare the last thing from the beginning, and from antiquity the things that have not been done, saying, "My counsel shall stand, and I will do what I will." 11 I call a bird from the east, and the man of my counsel from afar; as I have spoken, so will I do; I have established it, and I will do it. 12 Hear me, you of a stub- born heart, who are far from righteousness. 13 I bring here my righteousness; it shall not be far off, and my salvation shall not tarry; for I will give salvation to Zion, and my glory to Israel.

CHAPTER 47

1 Come down and sit in the dust: O virgin, daughter of Babel, sit on the ground; there is no throne, O daughter of the Chaldeans, for you shall no longer be called "tender and delicate." 2 Take the stones of the mill and grind the flesh; loose your locks, bare your feet, empty your leg, and pass through the waters. 3 Thy filthiness shall be discarded, and thy shame shall be seen; I will take ven- geance, and meet thee no more as a man. 4 Our redeemer, the LORD of hosts is his name, the Holy One of Israel. 5 Sit down and stand in darkness, daughter of the Chaldeans, for you will no longer be called "the girl of the kingdoms." 6 I have been angry with my peo- ple: I have polluted my inheritance and given it into your hand; you have had no mercy on them, but have laid your heavy yoke upon the ancients. 7 And thou hast said, "I will be a girl forever," so that thou hast not thought of these things, nor remembered their last end. 8 Therefore hear, you who are given to plea- sures and dwell carefree, she who says in her heart, "I am and no one else," I will not sit as a widow and I will not know the loss of chil- dren. 9 But these two things shall come upon thee suddenly in one day: the loss of children and widowhood; they shall come upon thee in their perfection, for the multitude of thy diuinations, and for the great abundance of thy pollutions. 10 For thou hast trusted in thy wickedness; thou hast said, No man seeth me. Your wisdom and knowledge have in- duced you to rebel, and you have said in your heart, "I am, and no one else." 11 Therefore death shall come upon thee, and thou shalt not know the morning of it; destruction shall come upon thee, which thou shalt not be able to suppress; destruction shall come upon thee suddenly, and thou shalt not know it. 12 Now in the midst of thy men and the multitude of thy southerners (with whom thou hast la- bored since thy youth), whether thou canst profit, or whether thou canst have strength. 13 Thou hast labored in the multitude of thy counsels; now let the astrologers, and the gas- sers of stars, and the prognosticators arise, and let them shelter thee from these things that shall come upon thee. 14 Behold, they shall be as stubble; fire shall burn them up; they shall not take their own lives from the power of the flame; there shall be no hills to war with, nor light to sit upon. 15 Thus shall those with whom thou hast labored, that is, thy marchers from thy youth, serve thee; ev- ery one shall wander in his own quarter, none shall save thee.

CHAPTER 48

1 Hear, O house of Iaakob, that you are called by the name of Israel, and that you came out of the waters of Judah; that you swear by the name of the LORD, and mention the God of Israel, but not in truth, nor in righteousness. 2 For they call themselves of the holy city, and refer to the God of Israel, whose name is the Lord of hosts. 3 I have declared unto you the ancient things, they came forth out of my mouth, and I showed them: I made them suddenly, and they came to pass. 4 For I knew that thou art obstinate, that thy neck is a wire of iron, and thy forehead is coarse, 5 Therefore I declared it unto thee from ancient times; before it came to pass, I showed it unto thee, lest thou shouldst say, My idol made them, my graven image and my molten im- age commanded them. 6 You have heard and seen all this, and will you not declare it? I have revealed to you new things now, and hidden things, which you did not know. 7 They were created now and not in the past, and before that time you did not hear them, lest you say, "Behold, I knew them." 8 But you did not hear them and did not know them, nor was your ear opened in the past, because I knew that you would gravely transgress; therefore I called you a transgressor from birth. 9 For My names' sake I will defer My wrath, and for My praise I will repel it from you, lest I cut you off. 10 Behold, I have fined thee, but not as a silencer; I have chosen thee in the furnace of affliction. 11 For my sake I will do it; for how could my Name be polluted? Surely I will not give my glory to another. 12 Hear me, O Iaa- kob and Israel, my called, I am, I am the first and I am the last. 13 Surely, my hand has laid the foundations of the earth, and my right hand has stretched out the heavens; when I call them, they stand together. 14 All of you, gather yourselves together and listen: which of them has declared these things? The Lord has heard him: he will do his will at Babel, and his arm shall be against the Chaldeans. 15 I have spoken it and called him: I have led him, and his way shall prosper. 16 Come here unto me, hear this: I have not said it in secret from the beginning; from the time that the thing came to pass, I was there, and now the Lord God and his Spirit have sent me. 17 Thus saith the LORD thy redeemer, the Holy One of Israel, I am the LORD thy God, which hath taught thee to profit, and hath guided thee in the way that thou shouldest go. 18 Oh, if you had listened to my commands! Then your prosperity would have been like the flood, and your righteousness like the wave of the sea. 19 Your offspring also had been like the probing, and the fruit of your body like its cluster; its name should not have been cut off nor de- stroyed before me. 20 Come out of Babel, flee from the Chaldeans, with a voice of joy; tell and declare this, report it to the ends of the earth; say, "The LORD has redeemed his ser- vant Iaakob." 21 They were not thirsty; he led them through the wilderness; he caused wa- ters to gush forth for them from the stream, for he beat the stream, and the water gushed forth. 22 There is no peace, says the LORD, for the wicked.

CHAPTER 49

1 Hear me, O people, and listen, you who come from afar. The LORD has called me from the womb and made my name from my mother's womb. 2 He made my mouth like a sharp sword; under the shadow of his hand he hid me, and made me a chosen shield, and hid me in his den, And he said to me, "You are my servant, Israel, for in you I will be glorious." 4 And I answered, "I have toiled in life: I have spent my strength in vein and for nothing; but my judgment is with the LORD, and my work with my God." 5 Now saith the LORD, Who hath formed me out of the woman to be his servant, that I may bring Iaakob again unto him (though Israel be not gathered to- gether, yet shall I be glorious in

the sight of the LORD, and my God shall be my strength).
6 And he said, It is little that thou shouldst be my servant, to raise up the tribes of Iaakob, and to restore the desolation of Israel: I will also give thee as a light unto the Gentiles, that thou mayest be my salvation unto the end of the world. 7 Thus saith the LORD, the redeem- er of Israel, and his Holy One, to him that is despised in soul, to a nation that is abhorred, to a servant of rulers, "Kings shall see, and rise up, and princes shall worship, because of the LORD, which is faithful; and thou, Holy One of Israel, which thou hast chosen." 8 Thus saith the LORD: "In an acceptable time have I heard thee, and in a day of salvation have I helped thee; and I will preserve thee and give thee as a messenger of thy people, that thou mayest lift up the land, and preserve the inheritance of the desolate heritages: 9 You shall say to the captives, "Depart!" and to those in darkness, "Deliver yourselves!"; they shall graze in the countryside, and their pas- tures shall be on all the hilltops. 10 They shall not hunger, nor thirst, nor be stricken with heat nor with the sun; for he who has com- passion on them will set them free and lead them to springs of water. 11 I will make all my mountains a way, and my paths will be exalt- ed. 12 Behold, these shall come from afar, and these from the north and the west, and these from the land of Sinim. 13 Rejoice, O heavens, and be full of joy, O earth, and come forth in praise, O mountains, for God has comforted his people and will have mercy on their afflict- ed. 14 But Zion says, "The LORD has forsaken me, and my Lord has forgotten me." 15 Can a woman forget her child and have no compas- sion on her woman's son? Even if they forget themselves, I will not forget you. 16 Behold, I have brought you forth on the palms of my hands; your walls are always before my eyes. 17 Thy builders hasten; thy destroyers and those who destroyed thee have turned away from thee. 18 Lift up thine eyes round about, and behold: all these gather themselves to- gether, and come to thee; as I lie, saith the LORD, thou shalt put them all upon thee as a garment, and wrap thyself with them as a bride. 19 For thy desolations, thy desolate places, and thy destroyed land, shall surely now be straitened for them that dwell therein, and they that have betrayed thee shall be far off. 20 The sons of your despoilment shall say again in your ears, "The place is strait for me; give me a place where I may dwell." 21 Then shalt thou say in thine heart, "Who hath be- gotten them unto me, seeing I am bare and desolate, a prisoner and a wanderer hither and thither, and who hath fed them? Behold, I was left alone: whence came they? 22 Thus saith the LORD God, Behold, I will lift up my hand unto the nations, and will put my rod in the midst of the peoples, and they shall car- ry thy sons in their arms, and thy daughters shall be loaded upon their shoulders. 23 And the kings shall be thy fathers, and the queens thy fountains: and they shall worship thee with their faces toward the earth, and they shall lick the dust of thy feet: and thou shalt know that I am the LORD, for they shall not be ashamed that they waited for me. 24 Should the prayer be taken away from the mighty, or the righteous captive be delivered? 25 But thus says the LORD: "The captivity of the mighty shall be taken away, and the prayer of the tyrant shall be taken away; for I will con- tend with him who contends with you, and I will save your children, 26 and I will feed with their flesh those who have ruined you, and they shall be drunk with their blood, as with sweet wine; and all flesh shall know that I, the LORD, am your savior and your redeemer, the mighty one of Iaakob.

CHAPTER 50

1 Thus says the LORD, "Where is the account of the divorce of your mothers, whom I have cast out, or who is the creditor to whom I have forsaken you? Behold, because of your iniqui- ties you have been forsaken, and because of your transgressions your mother has been forsaken. 2 Why did I come and there was no one there? I called, but no one answered me; is my hand so short that I cannot help? Or have I no power to deliver? Behold, at my re- buke I cause the sea to sink: I make the floods desist; their fish rot for lack of water and die of thirst. 3 I clothe the heavens with darkness, and make their covering a sackcloth. 4 The LORD God has given me a wise tongue, that I may be able to report a word in due time to those who are weary; he will raise me up in the morning; in the morning he will awaken my ear to hear, like the wise. 5 The LORD God has opened my ear, and I have not rebelled nor turned back. 6 I have given my back to the beaters, and my cheeks to the cutters: I have not hid my face from shame and spitting. 7 Because the LORD God will help me, I shall not be confounded; Therefore I have set my face as a flint, and I know that I shall not be ashamed. 8 There is no one to justify me; who will contend with me? Who is my adversary? Who is my adversary? Who will approach me? 9 Behold, the Lord God will help me; who is he who can condemn me? Yea, they shall grow old as a garment; the mother shall consume them. 10 Who is there among you who fears the Lord? Let him hear the voice of his ser- vant; whoever walks in darkness and has no light, let him trust in the name of the LORD and rely on his God. 11 Behold, all of you kin- dle a fire and are surrounded by sparks; walk in the light of your fire and the sparks you have kindled. This you shall have from my hand; you shall fall asleep in sadness.

CHAPTER 51

1 Listen to me, you who follow righteousness and who see the Lord; look toward the stake, from which you were brought out, and to- ward the hole of the pit, from which you were dug. 2 Consider Abraham your father, and Sarah who bore you, for I called him alone, and blessed him, and increased him. 3 Surely the LORD will comfort Zion, will comfort all her desolations, will make her wilderness like Eden, and her wilderness like the garden of the LORD; joy and gladness, praise and song will be found there. 4 Hear me, O my people, and pay attention to me, O my people, for from me shall go forth a law, and I will bring my judgment as the light of the people. 5 My righteousness is at hand; my salvation goes forth, and my arm will judge the people; the people will wait on me and trust in my arm. 6 Lift up your eyes to the heavens and look at the earth below, for the heavens will van- ish like smoke, the earth will grow old like a garment, and those who dwell in it will like- wise perish; but my salvation will be forever, and my righteousness will not be abolished. 7 Listen to me, you who know righteousness, the people in whose heart is my Lawe. Fear not the reproach of men, and be not afraid of their reproaches. 8 For their mother shall con- sume them as a garment, and the world shall consume them as wool; but my righteousness shall abide forever, and my salvation from generation to generation. 9 Arise, arise, and take strength, O arms of the LORD; arise as you once did, in the generations of the world. Are not you the same who cut down Rahab and wounded the dragon? 10 Are not you the same who dried up the sea, that is, the waters of the great

deep, making the depth of the sea a way of passage for the redeemed? 11 There- fore the redeemed of the Lord will return and come with joy to Zion, and everlasting joy will be on their heads; they will obtain joy and gladness, and sadness and mourning will disappear. 12 I am he who comforts you. Who are you, that you fear a mortal man and the son of man, who shall be made like a stone? 13 And do you forget the LORD your creator, who stretched out the heavens and laid the foundations of the earth? And do you contin- ually fear all day long, because of the fury of the oppressor, who is ready to destroy? Where is now the fury of the oppressor? 14 The pris- oner hastens to be set free, lest he die in the pit and lose his bread. 15 I am the LORD your God, who ruled the sea, when his war roared; the LORD of hosts is his name. 16 I have put my words in your mouth and defended you in the shadow of my hand, to plant the heav- ens and lay the foundations of the earth and say to Zion, "You are my people." 17 Awake, awake, and rise up, O Jerusalem, who drank by the hand of the LORD the cup of his wrath; you drank the drops of the cup of trembling and drank them. 18 There is no one to lead you among all the sons you have brought home; there is no one to take you by the hand among all the sons you have brought home. 19 These two things have come to you: who will com- plain to you? Desolation, destruction, famine, and the sword; with whom shall I comfort thee? 20 Thy children are fainting and lying at the head of all the roads like a wild bull in a net, and are full of the wrath of the LORD and the reproach of thy God. 21 Hear there- fore this, thou wretched and drunken, but not with wine. 22 Thus says your Lord God, the God who pleads the cause of his people, "Behold, I have taken out of your hand the cup of trembling, that is, the drops of the cup of my wrath; you shall drink it no more. 23 but I will put it into the hand of those who ruin you, who have said to your soul, 'Get down, that we may go away,' and you have reduced your body as dirt and as a road for those who were leaving.

CHAPTER 52

1 Ram, arise, clothe thyself with thy strength, O Zion; put on the garments of thy beauty, O Jerusalem, the holy city; for henceforth the vncircumcised and the vncleans shall not en- ter into thee. 2 Shake thyself from the dust; arise and sit down, O Jerusalem; loosen the bands of thy neck, O captive daughter of Zion. 3 For thus says the LORD, "You have been sold for nothing; therefore you shall be redeemed without money." 4 For thus says the Lord God, "My people went down before now into Egypt to remain there, and Assur oppressed them without cause. 5 What then have I here, says the LORD, that my people are carried away for nothing, and those who rule them make them howl, says the LORD, and my Name is continually blasphemed? 6 Therefore my peo- ple shall know my Name; in that day they shall know that I am the One who speaks; behold, it is I. 7 How beautiful on the mountains are the feet of him who declares and makes pub- lic peace, who gives the good news and makes public salvation, saying to Zion, "Your God reigns"? 8 The voice of your watchmen shall be heard; they shall lift up their voice and unite, for they shall see eye to eye, when the LORD shall bring Zion back. 9 O desolate places of Jerusalem, rejoice and gather yourselves to- gether, for the LORD has comforted his peo- ple; he has redeemed Jerusalem. 10 The LORD has laid bare his holy arms in the sight of all nations, and all the ends of the earth shall see the salvation of our God. 11 Go away from there,

and touch nothing vandalic; come out of her bowels; be clean, bearing the vessels of the LORD. 12 For ye shall not go out in haste, neither shall ye flee, but the LORD shall go before you, and the God of Israel shall gather you. 13 Behold, my servant shall prosper; he shall be exalted and exalted, and shall be very happy. 14 As many were astonished at you (his face was so deformed, and his form was that of the sons of men), so he will sprinkle many nations; kings will shut their mouths before him, for what had not been told them, they will see, and what they had not heard, they will understand.

CHAPTER 53

1 Who will take care of our relationship? And to whom shall the arms of the Lord be entrusted? 2 But he will grow up before him like a branch and like a root from dry ground; he has neither form nor beauty; when we see him, there will be no reason to desire him. 3 He is despised and outcast by men; he is a man full of sorrows and has experienced in- firmities; we have almost hidden our faces from him; he was despised and we did not es- teem him. 4 Certainly he bore our infirmities and took care of our sorrows; yet we judged him as a plagued man, stricken by God and humiliated. 5 He was wounded for our trans- gressions, he was broken for our iniquities; the chastisement of our peace came upon him, and by his wounds we were healed. 6 All of us, like sheep, have gone astray; every one of us has gone back on his own way, and the LORD has unloaded on him the iniquity of all. 7 He has been oppressed and has been afflict- ed, yet he has not opened his mouth; he has been led like a sheep to the slaughter, and as a sheep before its shearer is dumb, so he does not open his mouth. 8 He has been taken out of prison and judgment, and who shall de- clare his age? For he has been cut off from the land of lieder, because of the transgression of my people he has been afflicted. 9 He made his grave with the wicked and the rich in his death, though he had committed no wicked- ness and had no deceit in his mouth. 10 Nev- ertheless the LORD hath purposed to break him, and to make him subject to infirmities: and when he hath made his soul an offence for sin, he shall see his seed, and prolong his days, and the will of the LORD shall prosper in his hand. 11 He shall see the transgression of his soul, and he shall be satisfied; by his knowledge my righteous servant shall justi- fy many, for he shall take upon himself their iniquities. 12 Therefore I will give him a por- tion with the great, and he shall lay down the spoyle with the strong, because he has sacri- ficed his soul unto death; he has been counted with the transgressors, he has borne the sin of many, and has prayed for the transgressors.

CHAPTER 54

1 Rejoice, O barren one, thou that hast not borne; arise and take up again, thou that hast not borne; for the desolate hath more chil- dren than the married wife, saith the LORD. 2 Enlarge the place of thy tents, and spread out the curtains of thy lodgings; spare not, stretch out thy cords, and fasten thy stakes. 3 For thou shalt increase to the right hand and to the left, and thy seed shall possess the na- tions and dwell in the desolate cities. 4 Fear not, for thou shalt not be ashamed, neither shalt thou be confounded, for thou shalt not be shamed; nay, thou shalt forget the shame of thy youth, and remember no more the reproach of thy youth. 5

For he who created you is your spouse (whose name is the Lord of hosts), and your redeemer, the Holy One of Israel, will be called God of all the world. 6 For the LORD has called you, as a woman forsak- en and afflicted in spirit, and as a young wife when you were rejected, says your God. 7 For a short time I have forsaken you, but with great compassion I will gather you up. 8 For a mo- ment in my wrath I hid my face from you for a short time, but with eternal mercy I had com- passion on you, says the LORD your redeem- er. 9 For this is to me like the waters of Noah, for as I swore that the waters of Noah should no more go out of the earth, so I swore that I would not be angry with you or reproach you. 10 For the mountains shall withdraw, and the hills shall fall: but my mercy shall not depart from thee, neither shall the bond of my peace fail, saith the LORD, who hath compassion on thee. 11 O thou afflicted and tossed about by the storm, who hast no comfort, behold, I will lay thy stones with carbuncle, and I will make thy foundations with saphir, 12 I will make thy windows of emeraudes, thy gates of shining stones, and all thy borders of pleasant stones. 13 All your children shall be instructed by the LORD, and much peace shall be for your children. 14 Thou shalt be established in righ- teousness, and thou shalt be far from oppres- sion, for thou shalt not fear it, and from fear, for it shall not come upon thee. 15 Behold, the enemy will gather, but without me; whoever gathers in you, against you, will fall. 16 Be- hold, I have created the smith who blows fire, and he who makes a tool for his work, and I have created the destroyer to destroy. 17 But all the weapons that have been made against you shall not prosper; and every tongue that shall rise up against you in judgment, you shall condemn it. This is the inheritance of the Lord's servants, and their righteousness comes from me, says the Lord.

CHAPTER 55

1 Oh everyone who is thirsty, come to the wa- ter, and you who have no bread, come and eat; come, I say, to drink wine and to milk with- out bread and without money. 2 Why do you set aside silver and not bread, and your toil is not satisfied? Listen to me carefully, eat what is good, and let your soul delight in fatness. 3 Incline your ears and come to me; listen, and your soul will rest, and I will make an ever- lasting covenant with you, like the sure mer- cies of Dauid. 4 Behold, I have given him as a witness to the people, as prince and teacher of the people. 5 Behold, you shall call a nation that you do not know, and a nation that did not know you shall run to you, because of the LORD your God and the Holy One of Israel, for he has glorified you. 6 Seek the LORD while he can be found; call upon him while he is far away. 7 Let the wicked forsake his ways and the righteous his imaginations and return to the LORD, and he will have mercy on him; and to our God, for he is very ready to forgive. 8 For my thoughts are not your thoughts, nor are your ways my ways, says the LORD. 9 For as the heavens are higher than the earth, so my ways are higher than your ways, and my thoughts are higher than your thoughts. 10 As the rain comes down and the snow from above and does not return, but waters the earth and makes it sprout and bud, that it may give seed to the sower and bread to the eater, 11 so shall my word be that goes forth from my mouth; it shall not return to me vague, but shall accomplish what I will, and prosper in the thing for which I sent it. 12 Therefore you shall go out with joy and be led in peace; the mountains and the hills shall open before you in joy, and all the trees of the country shall clap their hands. 13 For thorns shall grow fir trees; for nettles shall grow the tree of myrrh, which shall be to the LORD an everlasting name and sign that shall not be taken away.

CHAPTER 56

1 Thus says the LORD, "Observe judgment and do righteousness, for my salvation is near to come and my righteousness to be redeemed." 2 Blessed is the man who does this, and the son of man who does it; he who keeps the Sabbath and does not violate it, and prevents his hand from doing anything else. 3 And the son of the stranger, who has been received by the LORD, shall not speak and say, "The LORD has separated me from his people"; and the eunuch shall not say, "Be- hold, I am a withered tree." 4 For thus says the LORD to the eunuchs who keep my Sabbaths, and choose what pleases me, and appropriate my consent, 5 To them will I give, in my house and within my walls, a better place and name than to sons and daughters: I will give them an everlasting name, which shall not be blot- ted out. 6 Also the strangers who turn to the LORD to serve him, and to praise the name of the LORD, and to be his servants; all who keep the Sabbath and do not violate it, and who de- file themselves with my host, 7 I will also lead them to my holy mountain and make them happy in my house of prayer; their burnt of- ferings and their sacrifices will be received on my altar, for my house will be called a house of prayer for all peoples. 8 Says the LORD God, who gathers the scattered of Israel, "I will yet gather to them those who are to be gathered to them. 9 Come all of you to your homes, and also all the inhabitants of the forests. 10 Their watchmen are all blind, they have no knowl- edge, they are all dumb dogs, they do not know how to stagger, they lie and sleep and delight in sleeping. 11 These watchdogs are never content, and their watchmen cannot understand, for they all look their way, each for his own advantage and purpose. 12 Come, I will bring wine, and we will fill ourselves with strong drink, and the next day shall be as this day, and much more abundant.

CHAPTER 57

1 The righteous will perish, and no one will consider him in his heart; merciful men will be taken away, and no one will understand that the righteous will be taken away from the end of the world. 2 Peace shall come; they shall rest in their beds, all who walk before him. 3 But you, sons of witches, come here, sons of the adulterer and the harlot. 4 On whom have you snitched? On whom have you opened your eyes and stuck out your tongues? Are you not rebellious children and a false lin- eage? 5 Do you blaze idols under every green tree, and sacrifice children in the valleys un- der the tops of the rocks? 6 Your portion is in the smooth stones of the river; they are your lot; to them you have offered a wine offering, you have offered a sacrifice. Should I delight in these? 7 You made your bed on a very high mountain; you went there, and there you went to offer a sacrifice. 8 Even behind the towers and posts you placed your remembrance, because you disregarded another and me, you went and enlarged your bed, you made a barrier between you and them, and you beau- tified their bed in every place where you saw it. 9 You went to the kings with oil, increased your payments, and sent your messengers far away, and humbled yourself to hell. 10 You toiled in your manifold journeys,

but you did not say, "There is no hope"; you found life by your own hand, so you were not afflicted. 11 And of whom did you fear or dread, seeing that you lied to me and did not remember me or set your mind on me? Is it not because I keep my peace, and for a long time? Therefore you have not feared me. 12 I will declare thy righteousness and thy works, and they shall not profit thee. 13 When thou shalt cry out, they whom thou hast gathered shall deliver thee: but the wind shall carry them all away; vanity shall drag them away: but he that trust- eth in me shall inherit the land, and possess my holy Mountain. 14 He will say, "Prepare the way, remove the stones of stumbling from the way of my people." 15 For thus says He who is exalted and excellent, He who dwells in eter- nity, whose Name is the Holy One: "I dwell in the high and holy place; with him who is of a contrite and humble spirit, to recover the spirit of the humble and to give life to those whose hearts are contrite. 16 For I will not contend forever, and I will not always be an- gry, for the spirit must rest before me, and I have taken breath. 17 For his wickedness I was wroth with him, and smote him: I hid myself, and was wroth: but he departed, and followed the way of his heart. 18 I have seen his ways, and I will heal him: I will also heal him and re- store comfort to him and to those who regret him. 19 I create the fruit of the lips as peace; peace to them that are far off, saith the LORD, for I will heal him. 20 But the wicked are like a raging sea, which cannot rest, whose waters cast away my land and filth. 21 There is no peace, says my God, for the wicked.

CHAPTER 58

1 Cry out, spare not, lift up your voice like a trumpet, and make known to my people their transgression, and to the house of Iaa- kob their sins. 2 Nevertheless they shall see me daily, and know my ways, as a nation that has acted righteously and has not forsaken the statutes of its God; they shall ask of me the standards of righteousness; they shall call upon God, saying, "Why have we done noth- ing? 3 Why have we fasted and you do not see it? We have punished ourselves and you do not consider it. Behold, in the day of your fasting you shall see your will and require all your things. 4 Well, you fast to quarrel and ar- gue and to strike with the fist of wickedness; do not fast as you do today to make your voice heard. 5 Is this the fast that I have chosen, that a man should afflict his soul for a day, that he should lower his head like a rushing bull and lie down in sackcloth and ashes? Would you call this a fast or a day acceptable to the Lord? 6 Is not this the fast I have cho- sen to loosen the bands of wickedness, to re- move the heavy burdens, to let the oppressed go free, and to break every yoke? 7 Is it not to devolve your bread to the hungry and to bring to your house the poor who wander? When you see the naked, do you succor him and not hide yourself from your flesh? 8 Then shall thy light arise as the morning, and thy health shall swiftly increase; thy righteousness shall go before thee, and the glory of the Lord shall embrace thee. 9 Then thou shalt call, and the LORD shall answer thee; thou shalt cry out, and he shall say, "Here I am;" if thou shalt remove from the midst of thee the yoke, the putting on of the finger, and the evil speak- ing: 10 If thou shalt give strength to thy soul, and refresh thy troubled soul, then shall thy light come forth in darkness, and thy dark- ness shall be as the day of none. 11 The LORD will guide thee continually, and will satiate thy soul in drought, and make thy bones fat; thou shalt be as a watered garden, and as a

spring of water whose waters run not dry. 12 They shall be of thee who shall rebuild the old abandoned places; thou shalt make their foundations for many generations, and shalt be called the repairer of breaches and the restorer of paths to dwell therein. 13 If thou shalt turn away thy foot from the Sabbath, from doing thy will on my holy day, and shalt call the Sabbath a delight, and shalt conse- crate it as glorious to the LORD, and honor him, not doing thy ways, nor seeking thy will, nor speaking a vain word, 14 then you shall delight in the LORD, and I will raise you up to the high places of the earth and feed you with the inheritance of Iaakob your father, for the mouth of the LORD has spoken it.

CHAPTER 59

1 Behold, the hand of the LORD is not short- ened, that he cannot speak; nor his ear made weak, that he cannot hear. 2 But your iniqui- ties have separated you from your God, and your sins have hidden his face from you, that he may not hear. 3 For your hands are stained with blood, and your fingers with iniquity; your lips have spoken lies, and your tongue has murmured iniquity. 4 No one calls for righteousness, no one strives for truth; they trust in vanity and speak vain things; they conceive malice and bring forth iniquity. 5 They hatch rooster's eggs and weave the web of spiders; whoever eats their eggs dies, and what is trodden down turns into a serpent. 6 Their plots shall not be a garment, and they shall not comfort themselves with their labors, for their works are works of iniquity, and the work of cruelty is in their hands. 7 Their feet run to hell and they hasten to shed innocent blood; their thoughts are evil thoughts; des- olation and destruction are in their paths. 8 The way of peace they do not know, and there is no equity in their path; they have made crooked paths; those who walk in them do not know peace. 9 Therefore judgment is far from you, and justice does not come near you; we wait for light, but it is dark; we want light, but we walk in darkness. 10 We seek the wall like the blind, and grope like those who have no eyes; we stumble in the day without light as in the twilight; we are in lonely places, like dead men. 11 We all wander like beasts, and we toil like deer; we seek balance, but it is not there; health, but it is far from us. 12 For our faults are many before thee, and our sins testify against thee; for our debts are with thee, and we know our iniquities. 13 For we have trans- gressed and lied against the LORD, and have turned away from our God, and have spoken cruelty and rebellion, hiding and bringing forth false things from our hearts. 14 There- fore judgment has turned back, and righ- teousness is far off; for truth has fallen in the way, and equity cannot enter it. 15 Yea, truth is fallen away, and he who refrains from acting is made to pray; and when the LORD said this, he was sorry because there was no judgment. 16 And when he heard that there was none, he marveled that no one would offer himself. Therefore his armor made him notice, and his righteousness sustained him from himself. 17 For he put on righteousness like armor and a helmet of salvation on his head, he put on the garments of vengeance like robes, and he was clothed with zeal like a cloak. 18 To reward his enemies with a recompense for the pain of the aduersaries, he will fully repay the home- lands. 19 So they will fear the Name of the LORD from the west and his glory from the rising of the sun, for the enemy will come like a flood, but the Spirit of the LORD will drive him out. 20 The Redeemer will come to Zion and to those who will be converted from the iniquity

of Iaakob, says the LORD. 21 And I will make this my companion with them, says the LORD. My Spirit that is upon you and my words that I have put in your mouth will not depart from your mouth, nor from the mouth of your descendants, nor from the mouth of the descendants of your descendants, says the LORD, from now on and forever.

CHAPTER 60

1 Arise, O Jerusalem; be bright, for your light has come, and the glory of the Lord has risen upon you. 2 For behold, darkness shall smite the earth, and the nations shall be grievous- ly darkened; but the LORD shall arise upon thee, and his glory shall be seen upon thee. 3 The nations shall walk in your light, and the kings in the splendor of your rising. 4 Lift up thine eyes round about, and see: all these are gathered and come to thee; thy sons shall come from afar, and thy daughters shall be nourished at thy side. 5 Then thou shalt see and shine; thy heart shall be amazed and shall be enlarged, for the multitude of the sea shall gather to thee, and the riches of the Gentiles shall come to thee. 6 The multitude of camels shall come to you, the dromedaries of Midian and Ephah; all those of Sheba shall come; they shall bring gold and frankincense and pres- ent the prayers of the LORD. 7 All the sheep of Kedar shall be gathered to thee; the rams of Nebaioth shall serve thee; they shall come to be received on my altar; and I will beautify the house of my glory. 8 Who are those who flee like a cloud and like clouds to their win- dows? 9 Surely the yles shall wait for me, and the ships of Tarshish, as in the beginning, to bring your sons from afar, their silver and their gold with them, to the Name of the LORD your God, and to the Holy One of Isra- el, for he has glorified you. 10 The sons of for- eigners shall build thy walls, and their kings shall minister to thee: for in my wrath have I smitten thee, but in my mercy have I had compassion on thee. 11 Therefore thy gates shall always be open; they shall not be shut day nor night, that men may bring thee the riches of the Gentiles, and that their kings may be brought. 12 For the nation and the kingdom that will not serve you will perish, and those nations will be utterly destroyed. 13 The glory of Lebanon shall come from you, the fir tree, the elm and the box tree together, to beauti- fy the place of my sanctuary, for I will glorify the place of my feet. 14 The children also of those who have afflicted you shall come and bow down before you; and all those who have despised you shall fall at the feet of your feet; and they shall call you, "The city of the LORD, Zion of the Holy One of Israel." 15 If you have been forsaken and hated, so that no one has passed by you, I will make you an everlasting glory and joy from generation to generation. 16 You shall also suck the milk of the Gentiles and suck the breasts of kings; and you shall know that I, the LORD, am your savior and your redeemer, the mighty one of Iaakob. 17 For brasse I will bring gold, for yron I will bring siluer, for wood brasse, and for stones yron. I will also make your livelihood peace, and your tax collectors justice. 18 No more shall violence be heard of in thy land, nor desolation or destruction within thy borders; but thou shalt call thy walls salvation, and thy gates praise. 19 No more shall thou have the sun shining by day, nor shall the brightness of the moon shine upon thee: for the LORD shall be thy everlasting light, and thy God thy glory. 20 Your sun shall never go out, and your moon shall not hide, for the LORD shall be your everlasting light, and the days of your sorrow shall end. 21 Your people also shall be all righteous; they shall possess the land for- ever;

the fruit of my sowing shall be the work of my hands, that I may be glorified. 22 A little one shall become like a thousand, and a little one like a strong nation: I, the LORD, will has- ten it in due time.

CHAPTER 61

1 The Spirit of the Lord God is upon me, therefore the Lord has anointed me; he has sent me to preach good tidings to the poor, to uphold the brokenhearted, to preach de- liverance to the captives and to those who are bound the opening of the prison, 2 to preach the favorable year of the LORD and the day of vengeance of our God, to comfort all who are in distress, 3 To give them that are in Zion beauty for ashes, the garment of joy for the mourning, the garment of gladness for the spirit of joy, that they may be called trees of righteousness, the planting of the Lord, that he may be glorified. 4 They shall rebuild the old forsaken places, raise up the ancient des- olations, and repair the cities that were des- olate and forsaken for many generations. 5 Strangers will shepherd your sheep, and the sons of strangers will be your ploughmen and the cultivators of your vines. 6 But you shall be called Priests of the LORD, and men shall say of you, "Ministers of our God"; you shall eat the riches of the Gentiles and be exalted with their glory. 7 For your shame you shall receive double, and for confusion they shall receive their portion, for in their land they shall possess double; it shall be an everlast- ing joy to them. 8 For I, the LORD, love judg- ment and loathe robbery for burnt offering; I will direct their work in truth and make an everlasting covenant with them. 9 Their seed shall be known among the nations, and their shoots among the peoples. All who see them will recognize them as the descendants whom the LORD has blessed. 10 I will greatly rejoice in the LORD, and my soul will be full of joy in my God, for he has clothed me with the gar- ments of salvation and clothed me with the robe of righteousness; he has adorned me like a bride, and like a bride labors with her jewels. 11 For as the earth causes its shoot to sprout, and as the garden causes that which is sown in it to grow, so the Lord God will cause righteousness to grow and praise it before all the Gentiles.

CHAPTER 62

1 For Zion's sake I will not pause to speak, and for Jerusalem's sake I will not rest, until her righteousness bursts forth like a light, and her salvation like a burning lamp. 2 The nations shall see your righteousness, and all kings your glory; and you shall be called by a new name, which the mouth of the LORD shall name. 3 You shall also be a crown of glory in the hand of the LORD, and a royal diadem in the hand of your God. 4 No longer shall it be said of you, "Forsaken," nor shall it be said of your country, "Desolate," but you shall be called Efzi-bah and your country Beulah, for the LORD has taken care of you, and your country shall have a husband. 5 For as a young man marries a virgin, so shall thy children marry thee; and as a bridegroom rejoices over his bride, so shall thy God rejoice over thee. 6 Upon thy walls, O Jerusalem, I have set watch- men, which shall never cease, all day and all night; ye that are mindful of the LORD, be not silent, 7 And give him no rest, until he comes to his senses, and until he causes the prayers of the world to cease in Jerusalem. 8 The LORD has sworn with his right hand and with his strong arm, "I

will no longer give your seed to your enemies, and the sons of foreigners will not drink your wine, for which you have toiled." 9 But those who have gath- ered it shall eat it and pray to the LORD, and the gatherers shall drink it in the courts of my sanctuary. 10 Go through, go through the gates; prepare the way for the people; pave, pave the way, gather the stones, and prepare a foothold for the people. 11 Behold, the LORD has given the proclamation to the ends of the world; say to the daughter Zion, "Behold, your savior comes; behold, his wages are with him, and his work is before him." 12 They shall call them, "The holy people, the redeemed of the Lord," and you shall be called, "A city sought and not forsaken."

CHAPTER 63

1 Who is he that cometh from Edom, with red garments from Bozrah? He is glorious in his apparel, and walks in his great strength: I speak with righteousness, and am strong in speech. 2 Why is thy raiment red, and thy gar- ments as those who tread wine? 3 I have trod- den down wine alone, and of all the people there was none with me; for I will tread them down in my wrath, I will tread them down in my fury, and their blood shall be sprinkled upon my garments, and I will stain all my garments. 4 For the day of vengeance is in my heart, and the year of my redeemed is come. 5 I looked, and there was no one to help me, and I marveled that there was no one to help me; therefore my own weapon helped me, and my wrath sustained me. 6 Therefore I will tread down the people in my wrath, I will make them drunk in my indignation, and I will bring down their strength upon the earth. 7 I will remember the mercies of the LORD and the prayers of the LORD according to all that the LORD has granted, and because of the great kindness to the house of Israel, which he has granted them according to his tender love and according to his great mercies. 8 For he said, "Surely they are my people, children who do not lie," and he was their savior. 9 In all their troubles he was afflicted, and the an- gel of his presence ministered to them; in his grace and mercy he redeemed them, and en- dured and cared for them continually. 10 But they rebelled and annoyed his Holy Spirit; therefore he became their enemy and fought against them. 11 Then he remembered the an- cient time of Moses and his people, saying, "Where is he who brought them out of the sea with the flock of his sheep? Where is he who put his Holy Spirit in them? 12 He led them by the right hand of Moses with his own glorious arm, turning away the waters before them, to make himself an everlasting Name. 13 He led them through the depths, like a horse in the wilderness, that they might not stumble, 14 as the beast goes down into the valley, the Spirit of the LORD makes them rest; so you led your people, to make yourself a glorious Name. 15 Look down from above and watch from the dwelling place of your saints and your glory. Where is your zeal and strength, the multitude of your mercies and compas- sions? They are withheld from me. 16 You are our Father; though Abraham ignores him and Israel does not know him, you, O Lord, are our Father and our redeemer; your Name is forever. 17 O LORD, why have you caused vs to err from your ways and hardened our hearts by your fear? Return for your servants and for the tribes of your inheritance. 18 The people of your holiness have possessed it for a short time, because our adversaries have trampled down your sanctuary. 19 We were like those over whom you never ruled and over whom your Name was not invoked.

CHAPTER 64

1 Oh, if you would breach the heavens and descend, and if the mountains would melt in your presence! 2 When the melting fire burned, when the fire made the waters boil, (so that you might declare your Name to your adversaries) the people trembled in your presence. 3 When you did terrible things, which we had not foreseen, you came down and the mountains melted in your presence. 4 For from the beginning of the world they have not heard and have not understood with the ear, nor have you seen another God besides you, who does so to those who wait for him. 5 You have met those who believed in you and acted righteously; they have remembered you in your ways; behold, you are angry, because we have sinned; yet in them there is continu- ity, and we shall be saved. 6 But all of us have become as an empty thing, and all our righ- teousness is like a filthy gourd, and we all fade away like a leaf, and our iniquities have been carried away like the wind. 7 And there is no one to call upon your Name, nor to stir up to take possession of you, for you have hidden your face and consumed your life because of our iniquities. 8 But now, O LORD, you are our Father; we are the clay, you are our pot- ter, and all of us are the work of your hands. 9 Be not wroth, O LORD, for measure, and re- member not iniquity for ever; behold, we pray thee, we all are thy people. 10 Thy holy cities lie forsaken: Zion is a wilderness, and Jerusalem a desert. 11 The house of our sanctuary and of our glory, where our fathers prayed to you, is burned with fire, and all our pleasant things are lost. 12 Will you stop in the face of these things, O LORD? Will you pause in your peace and grieve inordinately?

CHAPTER 65

1 I was sought by those who did not ask me: I was found by those who did not seek me: I said, "Look to me, look to me, toward a na- tion that has not called upon my Name." 2 I stretched out my hands all day long upon a re- bellious people, who walked in ways that were not good, according to their own imagination: 3 a people who ridiculed me before my face, who sacrifice in gardens and burn incense on bricks. 4 Who stay among the graves and take refuge in deserts, who eat swine meat and the broth of defiled things is in their vessels. 5 Who say, "Stand apart, do not come near me, for I am holier than you"; these are a smoke in my wrath and a fire that burns all day long. 6 Behold, it is written before me, I will not be silent, but I will render the account and recast it in their bosom. 7 Your iniquities and the iniquities of your fathers shall be gathered together (saith the LORD) who have burned incense on the mountains and blasphemed me on the hills; therefore I will measure their ancient work in their bosom. 8 Thus says the LORD, "As the wine is found in the cluster, and it is said, 'Do not destroy it, for there is a blessing in it,' so will I do for my servants, not to destroy them utterly. 9 But I will bring forth from Iaakob and Iudah an offspring who shall inherit my mountain; my elect shall inherit it, and my servants shall dwell there- in. 10 Sharon shall be a flock, and the valley of Achor shall be a resting place for the cattle of my people who have sought me. 11 But you are those who have forsaken the LORD and forgotten my holy Mountain, who have pre- pared a table for the multitude and provide drink offerings to the number. 12 Therefore I will

put you under the sword and reduce you all to the slaughter, because I have called and you have not answered: I have spoken and you have not listened, but you have acted wrongly in my sight and have chosen what I did not want. 13 Therefore thus saith the LORD God, Behold, my servants shall eat, and ye shall hunger: behold, my servants shall drink, and ye shall thirst: behold, my servants shall replenish, and ye shall be ashamed. 14 Behold, my servants shall sing for joy of heart, and ye shall weep for sadness of heart, and howl for affliction of mind. 15 And you shall leave your name as a curse for my elect, for the Lord God will kill you and call his servants by an- other name. 16 Whosoever shall bless himself on the earth shall bless himself in the true God, and whosoever shall swear on the earth shall swear by the true God; for the former issues are forgotten and shall surely be hid- den from my eyes. 17 For behold, I will create new heavens and a new earth, and the former will no longer be remembered or taken into account. 18 But rejoice and be glad forever in the things that I will create; for behold, I will create Jerusalem, as a joy, and her people as a joy, 19 And I will make peace to Jerusalem, and joy to my people, and there shall no more be weeping heard in her, nor the voice of a cry. 20 No more shall there be a child of thirty years, nor an old man who has not filled his days; for he who is a hundred years old shall die as a young man; but the sinner who is a hundred years old shall be accursed. 21 They shall build houses and inhabit them, and plant vineyards and eat the fruit thereof. 22 They shall not build, and another shall dwell; they shall not plant, and another shall eat; for as the days of the tree are the days of my peo- ple, and my chosen ones shall inioiate in old age the work of their hands. 23 They shall not toil in toil, nor give birth in fear: for they are the seed of the blessed of the LORD, and their shoots with them. 24 Yea, before they call, I will answer, and while they speak, I will lis- ten. 25 The wolf and the sheep shall feed to- gether, and the lion shall eat like the bull, and the dust of the serpent shall be his meal. They will no longer hurt and destroy in all my holy Mountain, says the LORD.

CHAPTER 66

1 Thus says the LORD: "Heaven is my throne, and the earth is my foot; where is the house that you will build me, and where is the place of my rest? 2 For all these things my hand has made, and all these things have been made, says the LORD; and to him will I look, that is, to him who is poor, and has a contrite spirit, and trembles at my words. 3 He who kills a bull is as if he had slain a man; he who sacrifices a sheep is as if he had cut off a dog's neck; he who offers an oblation is as if he had offered swine's blood; he who remembers incense is as if he had blessed an idol; yea, they have chosen their ways, and their soul delights in their abominations. 4 Wherefore I will cast out their delusions, and cause fear to fall upon them: for I have called, and none answered me: I have spoken, and they would not hear; but they have done evil in mine eyes, and have chosen the things which I have not desired. 5 Hear the word of the LORD, all ye that tremble at his word: your brethren that hated you, and cast you out because of my names, said, Let the LORD be glorified: but he shall appear in your eyes, and they shall be ashamed. 6 A voice resounds from the city, like a voice from the Temple, the voice of the LORD fully rewarding his enemies. 7 Before she departed, she gave birth; and before her paine came, she bore a son. 8 Who has heard such a thing? Who has seen such things?

Can you bring forth the earth in a single day or give birth to a nation at once? For as Zion dragged on, she brought forth her children. 9 Shall I bring forth and not give birth? Shall I bring forth and not give birth, says your God? 10 Rejoice with Jerusalem, and rejoice with her, all who love her; rejoice with her, all who pine for her, 11 That you may suck and be satisfied with the ridges of her consolation; that you may milk and be delighted with the lights of her glory. 12 For thus says the LORD, "Behold, I will extend peace out of her like a flood, and the glory of the Gentiles like a flowing stream; then you shall succeed, and be carried on her loins, and be satisfied on her knees." 13 As one who comforts his mother, so I will comfort you, and you will be com- forted in Jerusalem. 14 When you see this, your hearts shall be revived, and your bones shall flourish like a grass; and the hand of the LORD shall be known among his servants, and his indignation against his enemies. 15 For behold, the LORD will come with fire and his songs like a whirlwind, to reward his an- ger with wrath and his indignation with the flame of fire. 16 For the LORD will judge with fire and with the sword all flesh, and the victims of the LORD will be many. 17 Those who sanctify themselves and purify themselves in gardens behind a tree, in the midst, eating swine's flesh and similar abominations, like the mouse, shall be consumed together, says the LORD. 18 For I will visit their works and their imaginations, for it shall come that I will gather all nations and tongues, and they shall come to see my glory. 19 And I will set a sign in the midst of them, and I will send those who go out from them toward the na- tions of Tarsis, Pul and Lud, and toward those who pull the rope, toward Tubal and Tauan, far away, who have not heard my fame and have not seen my glory, and they will declare my glory among the Gentiles. 20 They shall bring all your brethren for an offering to the LORD, from all the nations, on horses, on chariots, on litters of horses, on mules, and on swift cattle, to Jerusalem, my holy moun- tain, saith the LORD, as the children of Isra- el, and they shall offer in a clean vessel in the House of the LORD. 21 I will take of them for the priests and for the leuites, says the LORD. 22 For as the new heavens and the new earth, which I will make, shall remain before me, says the LORD, so shall your seed and your name remain. 23 From month to month and from Sabbath to Sabbath shall all flesh come to worship before me, says the LORD. 24 And they shall go out and look upon the carcass- es of the men who have transgressed against me, for their flesh shall not be quenched, nor their fire quenched, and they shall be an exe- cration to all flesh.

JEREMIAH

CHAPTER 1

1 The words of Jeremiah, son of Hilkiah, one of the priests who stood in Anathoth, in the land of Benjamin. 2 To whom the word of the LORD came in the days of Jehoiaiah the son of Amon, king of Judah, in the thirteenth year of his lordship: 3 And also in the days of Je- hoiakim the son of Jehoiaiah, king of Iudah, until the end of the eleventh year of Zedekiah the son of Jehoiaiah, king of Iudah, and until the departure of Jerusalem into captivity in the fifth month. 4 Then the word of the LORD came to me, saying, 5 Before I formed you in the womb I knew you, and before you came out of the womb I sanctified you and destined you to be a prophet to the nations." 6 Then I said, "Lord God, behold, I cannot speak, for I am a child." 7 But the LORD said to me, "Do not say that I am a child, for you will go to all those

whom I send to you and speak of what I command you. 8 Do not fear their faces, for I am with you to deliver you, says the LORD." 9 Then the Lord stretched out his hand and touched my mouth, and the Lord said to me, "Behold, I have put my words in your mouth. 10 Behold, today I have set you outside the nations and kingdoms, to level, to drive out, to destroy and to tear down, to build and to plant." 11 After this, the word of the LORD came to me, saying, "Jeremiah, what do you see? And I answered, "I see a rod of an almond tree." 12 Then the Lord said to me, "You have seen well, for I will hasten my word to per- form it." 13 Then the word of the Lord reached me a second time and said, "What do you see? And I said, "I see a seething vessel looking from the north." 14 Then the LORD said to me, "From the north shall come forth a plague upon all the inhabitants of the land. 15 For, behold, I will call all the families of the king- doms of the north, saith the LORD, and they shall come, and every one of them shall set his throne at the entrance of the gates of Jerusa- lem, on all her walls all around, and in all the cities of Iudah. 16 And I will declare to them my judgments on all the wickedness of those who have forsaken me and burned incense to other gods and worshiped the works of their hands. 17 You, therefore, hold fast, arise, and speak to them all that I have commanded you; do not fear their faces, lest I destroy you before them. 18 For I, behold, this day have made thee a defended city, a pillar of steel, and walls of brick against all the land, against the kings of Iudah, and against her princes, and against her priests, and against the peo- ple of the land. 19 For they shall fight against thee, but shall not prevail against thee: for I am with thee to deliver thee, saith the LORD.

CHAPTER 2

1 Moreover the word of the LORD came to me, saying, 2 Go, and cry in the ears of Jeru- salem, saying, Thus saith the LORD, I remem- ber thee, and thy quality as a youth, and thy marriage, when thou wentest after me into the wilderness, into a land unsown. 3 Israel was like a thing sown for the LORD, and its firstfruits; everyone who eats of it is offended; evil will come upon them, says the LORD. 4 Hear the word of the LORD, O house of Iaa- kob, and all the families of the house of Isra- el. 5 Thus says the LORD: "What iniquity did your fathers find in me, that they turned away from me, followed vanity, and became vile? 6 For did they not say, 'Where is the LORD who brought you out of the land of Egypt? Who led you through the wilderness, through a wil- derness and a wasteland, through a barren land and in the shadow of death, through a land that no man passed through and where no one dwelt?' 7 I brought you into a rich land, to eat its fruit and produce; but when you entered, you defiled my land and made my heritage an abomination." 8 The priests did not say, "Where is the LORD?" and those who were to serve the Lawe did not know me; the shepherds also reviled me, and the prophets prophesied about Baal and went af- ter things that brought no profit. 9 Therefore I will plead with you again, says the LORD, and I will do so with your children's children. 10 For go to the isles of Chittim, and observe, and send to Kedar, and take heed, and see if there be such things. 11 Is there any nation that has changed its gods, which are not gods yet? But my people have changed their glory for that which does not benefit them. 12 O you heavens, be amazed at this; be frightened and confounded, says the LORD. 13 For my people have committed two errors: they have

forsak- en me the fountain of the springing waters, to dig themselves pits, broken pits, which cannot hold water. 14 Is Israel a servant or is he brought in? Why then is he ruined? 15 The lions have roared upon him and shrieked, and have made his land a wilderness; his cities are burned without inhabitants. 16 Even the sons of Noph and Tahapanes have broken your head. 17 Did you not get this because you forsook the LORD your God when he led you on the way? 18 What do you do now by the way of Egypt? Do you drink the water of the Nile? Or what do you do by the way of Assur? Do you drink the water of the river? 19 Thy own wickedness shall correct thee, and thy turnings back shall reprove thee: therefore know and observe that it is an evil and bitter thing that thou hast forsaken the LORD thy God, and that my fear is not in thee, saith the LORD God of hosts. 20 For from time imme- morial I have broken thy yoke, I have broken thy bonds, and thou hast said, "I will trans- gress no more," but like a harlot thou wander- est over all the hills and under all the green trees. 21 But I had planted you as a noble vine, whose plants were all natural; how is it that you became a foreign vine to me? 22 Though you wash yourself with nitro and take much soda, your iniquity is marked out before me, says the LORD God. 23 How can you say, "I have not defiled myself and followed Baa- lim"? Observe your moves in the valley and know what you have done: you are like a swift dromedary running for its moves. 24 And like a wild plank, moving at her will, blowing the wind at her will; who can turn her back? Ev- eryone who sees her will not be weary, but will find her in her own time. 25 Preserve your feet from dryness, and your throat from thirst; but you have said in despair, "No, for I have known strangers, and I will follow them." 26 As a man is ashamed when he is smitten, so is the house of Israel ashamed, her kings, her princes, her priests, and her prophets, 27 who say to a tree, "You are my father," and to a stone, "You have begotten me," because they have turned their backs to me and not their faces; but in the time of their crisis they will say, "Get up and help me." 28 But where are thy gods whom thou hast begotten? Let them rise up, if they can help you in your time of trouble; for according to the name of your cit- ies, they are your gods, O Iudah. 29 Why do you want to plead with me? You have all re- belled against me, says the LORD. 30 I have struck your children with the vein, they have received no correction; your own sword has struck your prophets like a bruise that de- stroys. 31 O generation, hear the word of the LORD: have I been as a wilderness to Israel or as a dark land? Why then do my people say, "We are lords, we will come to you no more"? 32 Can a maiden forget her adornment, or a bride her dress? Yet my people have forgot- ten me, since days without number. 33 Why do you prepare your way to seek friendship? Then I will teach you that your deeds are evil. 34 In your wings is also found the blood of the souls of you poor innocents: I found it not in holes, but in all these places. 35 Yet you say, "Because I am a heathen, his wrath shall de- part from me"; behold, I will enter into judg- ment with you, because you say, "I have not sinned." 36 Why are you running so hard to change your moves? Because you will be con- fused by Egypt, as you are confused by Assur. 37 For you will depart from there and put your hands on your head, because the LORD has put your trust, and you will not prosper.

CHAPTER 3

1 They say, "If a man drives away his wife and she leaves him and becomes another man's, will he be able to return to her again? Will not this country be polluted? But you have played the harlot with many women; yet return to me, says the LORD. 2 Lift up thine eyes unto the country places, and see where thou hast not played the harlot; thou hast sat waiting for them in the houses, as the Arab in the wilderness, and hast polluted the land with thy harlots and with thy malice. 3 Therefore the shows were restrained, and the last rage did not come, and you had a whore's forehead; you would not be ashamed. 4 Did you not cry out to me, "You are my father and the guide of my youth"? 5 Will he withhold his wrath for- ever? Will he reserve it for the end? Thus thou hast spoken, but thou doest more and more. 6 The LORD also said to me in the days of King Josiah, "Have you seen what this rebellious Is- rael has done? For he has gone up every high mountain and under every green tree and has made a harlot." 7 When she had done all this, I said to her, "Turn back to me"; but she did not return, as her rebellious sister Iudah said. 8 When I heard that rebellious Israel had prostituted herself on every occasion, I drove her out and gave her a decree of divorce; but her rebellious sister Iudah did not care, rath- er she also went into prostitution. 9 Thus, by the lightness of her prostitution, she defiled the land, for she committed fornication with stones and stocks. 10 For all this, her rebellious sister Iudah did not return to me whole- heartedly, but with difficulty, says the LORD. 11 The LORD said to me, "Rebellious Israel has justified herself more than rebellious Judah." 12 Go and shout these words to the north, and say, "Disobedient Israel, turn back, says the LORD, and I will not let my wrath come upon you; for I am merciful, says the LORD, and I will not always keep my wrath. 13 But you know your iniquity, for you have rebelled against the LORD your God, and have scat- tered your lives for the stiffnecked gods under every green tree, but you would not obey my word, says the LORD. 14 O disobedient chil- dren, turn away, says the LORD, for I am your LORD, and I will take you one of a city and two of a tribe and bring you to Zion, 15 and I will give you meals according to my heart, which will nourish you with knowledge and understanding. 16 Moreover, when ye shall be increased and multiplied in the land, in those days, saith the LORD, they shall say no more, "The ark of the LORD's convention," for it shall no more come to mind, nor shall they remember it, nor shall they visit it, for it shall no more be so. 17 At that time they shall call Jerusalem "The throne of the Lord," and all the nations shall be gathered toward it, that is, toward the Name of the Lord in Jerusalem; and from there on they shall no longer follow the hardness of their wicked hearts. 18 In those days the house of Iudah shall walk with the house of Israel, and shall gather from the land of the north into the land which I gave as an inheritance to your fathers. 19 But I say, "How have I taken you for sons and giv- en you a pleasant land, and then the glorious inheritance of the armies of the heathen, and said to you, 'You shall call me, saying, "My Fa- ther," and you shall not depart from me?" 20 But as a woman rebels against her husband, so you have rebelled against me, O house of Israel, says the LORD." 21 A voice was heard on the mountains, weeping and pleading of the children of Israel, because they have lost their way and forgotten the LORD their God. 22 O disobedient children, turn back, and I will heal your rebellions. Behold, we come to you, for you are the LORD our God. 23 Verily the hope of the hills is but vain, nor the mul- titude of the mountains; but in the LORD our God is the health of Israel. 24 For confusion toiled our fathers from our youth, their

sheep and their heifers, their sons and their daugh- ters. 25 We lie down in our confusion, and our shame grips us, because we have sinned against the LORD our God, we and our fa- thers, from our youth until now, and have not obeyed the will of the LORD our God.

CHAPTER 4

1 O Israel, if you turn back, turn back to me, says the LORD; and if you remove your abom- inations from my sight, you shall not remain behind. 2 And thou shalt swear, The LORD liveth in truth, and in judgment, and in righteousness; and the nations shall be blessed in him, and shall glory in him. 3 For thus says the LORD to the men of Iudah and to Jeru- salem, 4 "Do not sow in the midst of thorns, but be circumcised by the LORD and remove your foreskins from your hearts, you men of Iudah and inhabitants of Jerusalem, lest my wrath break out like a burning fire that no one can put out because of the wickedness of your intentions." 5 Declare in Iudah, make your- selves heard in Jerusalem, and say, "Sound the trumpet in the land"; shout, gather yourselves together, and say, "Gather yourselves together and go into the strong cities." 6 Prepare the standard in Zion; prepare to flee and not to stop, for I will bring a plague from the north and great destruction. 7 The Lion has come out of his lair, the destroyer of the nations has departed and gone from his place to turn your land upside down, and your cities will be destroyed without inhabitants. 8 Therefore clothe yourselves with sackcloth; lament and howl, for the fierce anger of the LORD has not departed from you. 9 In that day, saith the LORD, the heart of the king shall perish, and the hearts of the princes and priests shall be amazed, and the prophets shall marvel. 10 Then I said, "Lord God, you have deceived this people and Jerusalem, saying, 'You shall have peace,' but the sword strikes the heart." 11 At that time it will be said to this people and to Jerusalem, "A dry wind in the wilder- ness comes to the daughter of my people, but she will not open or clasp herself. 12 A mighty wind will come to me from those places, and now I will also give judgment on them. 13 Be- hold, he shall come like the clouds, and his chariots shall be like a storm; his horses are lighter than eagles. Woe to us, for we are de- stroyed. 14 O Jerusalem, wash your heart of wickedness, that you may be healed; how long shall your evil thoughts remain in you? 15 For from Dan a journey departs, and from Mount Ephraim an affliction is announced. 16 Make mention of the heathen, and publish in Jeru- salem, "Behold, the heathen come from a far country, and cry against the cities of Iudah. 17 They have surrounded it like the sentinels of the camp, because it has provoked me to wrath, says the LORD. 18 Your ways and your attempts have procured these things for you, such is your wickedness; therefore it shall be bitter, therefore shall your heart perceive. 19 My heart, my heart, I am grieved, even to the marrow of my heart; my heart is troubled within me: I cannot be quiet, for my soul has heard the sound of the trumpet and the alarm of battle. 20 Destruction upon destruction is cried, for all the land is destroyed; my tents are destroyed suddenly, and my tents in a mo- ment. 21 Until when shall I see the standert and hear the sound of the trumpet? 22 For my people are foolish, they do not know me; they are foolish children and have no understand- ing; they are wise to do good, but to do good they have no knowledge. 23 I looked at the earth and saw that it was without form and empty; I looked at the heavens and they had no light. 24 I looked at

the mountains and saw that they trembled, and all the hills trembled. 25 I saw that there was no one and that all the birds of the sky had disappeared. 26 I saw and saw that the fertile place was a wilderness and that all its cities had been brought down by the presence of the LORD and by his fierce anger. 27 For thus said the LORD, "All the land shall be desolate, but I will not make a complete end." 28 Therefore the earth shall mourn, and the heavens round about shall be darkened: for I have spoken it: I have thought it, and I will not repent, neither will I draw back. 29 All the city shall flee, for lack of horsemen and ar- chers; they shall go into the thickets, and cling to the rocks; every city shall be forsaken, and no man shall dwell therein. 30 And when you are destroyed, what will you do? Though you clothe yourself with skins, though you adorn yourself with ornaments of gold, though you paint your face with colors, still you will not clothe yourself with vein, for your allies will abhor you and will not see your life. 31 For I have heard a noise as of a woman trawling, or as of one delivering her first child, or as the voice of the daughter Zion sighing and stretching out her hands; woe to me now, for my soul faints because of murderers.

CHAPTER 5

1 Run through the streets of Jerusalem, ob- serve and know, inquire in the open places, if you can find a man or if there is anyone who executes judgment and seeks the truth, and I will spare him. 2 For though they say, "The LORD lies," yet they swear falsely. 3 O LORD, are not your eyes turned to the truth? You struck them, but they did not repent; you consumed them, but they refused to receive correction; they made their faces harder than a stone and refused to turn back. 4 Therefore I said, "They are poor, they are foolish, for they do not know the way of the Lord nor the judg- ment of their God. 5 I will take myself to the great ones and speak to them, for they have known the way of the LORD and the judg- ment of their God; but these have broken the yoke and broken the bonds. 6 Therefore a lion of the forest will kill them, and a wolf of the wilderness will destroy them; a leopard will watch over their cities; everyone who comes out of them will be torn to pieces, because their faults are many and their rebellions have increased. 7 How could I spare you for this? Your sons have forsaken me and have sworn by those who are not gods; though I have fed them to their fill, they have committed adul- tery and gathered together into companies in the houses of prostitutes. 8 They rose up in the morning like fed horses, for each one went after his neighbor's wife. 9 Shall I not be visited for these things, says the LORD? Shall not my mind be engaged on such a nation as this? 10 Watch over their walls and destroy them, but do not make a complete end; take away their baths, for they are not the Lords. 11 For the house of Israel and the house of Iudah have committed grievous violations against me, says the LORD. 12 They have denied the LORD and said, "It is not he, neither shall the plague come, nor shall we see the sword nor the famine." 13 The prophets shall be as the wind, and the word is not in them; so shall it be with them. 14 Therefore thus says the LORD God of hosts, "Because you speak such words, behold, I will put my words in your mouth, like a fire, and this people will be like wood, and they will be destroyed. 15 Behold, I will bring upon you a nation from afar, O house of Israel, saith the LORD, a mighty and ancient nation, a nation whose language you do not know, nor understand what they say. 16 Whose seat is like an open tomb; they are all very strong.

17 They will feed on your herds and your bread; they will kill your sons and your daughters; they will devour your sheep and your heifers; they will devour your vines and your fig trees; they will destroy with the sword your walled cities in which you trust- ed. 18 In those days, says the LORD, I will not make a complete end of you. 19 When you say, "Why does the LORD our God do these things?" you shall answer them, "Just as you have forsaken me and served foreign gods in your own land, so you shall serve strangers in a land that is not yours." 20 Declare this in the house of Iaakob and publish it in Iudah, saying, 21 Hear now this, O foolish people devoid of understanding, who have eyes and do not see, who have ears and do not hear. 22 Are you not afraid of me, says the LORD, or are you not frightened at my presence, who has set the sand as the limit of the sea with a perpetual decree that you cannot go beyond it, and even if its waves break out, they can- not prevent it, and even if they break out, they cannot go beyond it? 23 But this people have an unfaithful and rebellious heart; they have turned away and departed. 24 Why do they not say in their hearts, "We fear now the LORD our God, who makes it rain early and late in due season; he reserves for us the appointed weeks of the harshest. 25 Yet your iniquities have turned away these things, and your sins have prevented good things from you. 26 For among my people are evil people, who lie in wait like those who lay snares; they have made a pit to catch men. 27 As a cage is full of birds, so their houses are full of deceit; so they have become great and grown rich. 28 They have become fat and shining; they ex- ceed the deeds of the wicked; they execute no judgment, not the judgment of the orphan; yet they prosper, though they execute no judgment for the poor. 29 Shall I not visit for these things, saith the LORD, or shall not my mind be engaged on such a nation as this? 30 A horrible and unclean thing has been com- mitted in the land. 31 The prophets prophesy lies, you priests receive gifts into their hands, and my people delight in them. What then will you do at the end of this?

CHAPTER 6

1 O sons of Benjamin, prepare to flee from the pits of Jerusalem and sound the trumpet in Tekoa; set up a foothold in Beth-Haccerem, for a plague and great destruction appears from the north. 2 I likened the daughter of Zion to a beautiful and gracious woman. 3 The shepherds with their flocks will come to her; they will pitch their tents around her, and everyone will eat at his place. 4 Prepare war against her; arise and go toward the south; woe to her, for the day is declining and the shadows of the sunset are lengthening. 5 Arise, and let vs go forth by night and de- stroy her palaces. 6 For thus hath the LORD of hosts said, Break down the wood and cast a mountain against Jerusalem; this city must be visited; all oppression is in the midst of it. 7 As the fountain casts out its waters, so she casts out her wickedness; cruelty and wick- edness are continually making themselves felt in her before me with pains and blows. 8 Be instructed, O Jerusalem, lest my soul de- part from thee, lest I make thee desolate as a land that no man inhabiteth. 9 Thus says the LORD of hosts, "You shall gather like a vine the remnant of Israel; withdraw your hand as the harvester in the baskets. 10 To whom shall I speak and admonish that they may hear? Behold, their ears are vncircumcised, and they cannot hear; behold, the word of the LORD is to them as a reproach: they have no pleasure in it. 11 Therefore I am full of the wrath of the LORD: I am

weary to restrain it: I will burst it upon the children in the streets, and also upon the assembly of the young men: for the husband shall be taken with his wife, and the elder with him that is full of engage- ments. 12 Their houses and their lands and their wives shall be delivered to strangers, for I will stretch out my hand upon the in- habitants of the land, saith the LORD. 13 For from the least of them even to the greatest, every one of them is brought to corruption, and from the prophet even to the priest, they all speak falsehood. 14 They healed even the wounds of the daughter of my people with sweet words, saying, "Peace, peace, when there is no peace." 15 Were they ashamed when they had committed the abomination? No, they were not ashamed, nor could they be ashamed; therefore they shall fall among the slain; when I visit them, they shall be cast down, saith the LORD. 16 Thus says the Lord, "Stop in the neighborhood and observe, and seek the ancient way, which is the good way, and walk in it, and you will find rest for your souls; but they said, We will not walk in it. 17 I also set watchmen for you, who said, "Pay at- tention to the sound of the trumpet," but they said, "We will not pay attention." 18 Take heed therefore, you Gentiles, and you congrega- tion know what is in their midst. 19 Beware, O earth, behold, I will bring upon this people a plague, the result of their imagination, be- cause they have not heeded my words and my word, but have discarded it. 20 For what pur- pose do you bring me incense from Sheba and sweet calamus from a far country? Your burnt offerings are not pleasing, and your sacrifices are not pleasing to me. 21 Therefore thus says the LORD, "Behold, I will set stones of stum- bling before this people, and fathers and sons shall fall together upon them; the neighbor and his friend shall perish." 22 Thus says the LORD, "Behold, a people is coming from the north country, and a great nation will arise from the sides of the earth. 23 They will be armed with bow and shield; they are cruel and will have no compassion; their journey flows like the sea, and they ride on well-prepared horses, like men of war against you, O daugh- ter of Zion. 24 We have heard their fame, and our hands have grown weak, and sadness has come upon us, like the sadness of a woman in sorrow. 25 Do not go into the camp or walk in the street, for the sword of the enemy and fear are on every side. 26 O daughter of my people, clothe yourself in sackcloth and bask in ashes; make a wailing and a bitter weep- ing as for your only son, for the destroyer will come suddenly upon you. 27 I have set you as a defense and fortress in the midst of my peo- ple, that you may know and prove their aims. 28 They are all rebellious traitors, walking in craftiness; they are brassi, and yron, they are all destroyers. 29 The bellowers are burned, the lead is consumed in the fire, the founda- tion melts in the vein, because the wicked are not taken away. 30 They shall call them repro- bate torpedoes, because the LORD has taken them back.

CHAPTER 7

1 The words that came to Jeremiah from the LORD, which said, 2 "Stop at the gate of the house of the LORD and cry out this word and say, 'Listen to the word of the LORD, all you people of Judeah who enter these gates to worship the LORD. 3 Thus says the LORD of hosts, the God of Israel, "Change your expec- tations and your errors, and I will let you dwell in this place. 4 Do not trust the lying words that say, 'The temple of the LORD, the temple of the LORD'; this is the temple of the LORD. 5 For if you alter and scale back your lives and your works, if you execute judgment between a man and his neighbor, you will oppose no one, 6 you will not oppress the stranger, the orphan and the widow, and you will not shed innocent blood in this place, and you will not go after other gods for your destruction, 7 then I will let you dwell in this place, in the land that I gave to your fathers, for an eter- nity. 8 You trust in lying words, which cannot bear fruit. 9 Will you steal, kill, commit adul- tery, swear falsely, burn incense to Baal, and go after other gods you do not know? 10 And do you come and present yourselves before me in this house, where my name is invoked, and say, "We have been let down, though we have done all these abominations"? 11 Has this house become a den of thugs, when my Name is invoked before your eyes? Behold, I see it, says the Lord. 12 But now go to my place that was in Shiloh, where I set my Name in the beginning, and see what I have done to you because of the wickedness of my people Israel. 13 Therefore now, because you have done all these works, says the LORD (and I rose early and spoke to you; but when I spoke, you did not listen, and when I called you, you did not answer me). 14 Therefore I will do to this house, in which my name is called, and in which you also trust, even the place which I gave to you and to your fathers, as I did to Shi- loh. 15 I will drive you out from my presence, as I have driven out all your brothers and all the descendants of Ephraim. 16 Therefore you shall not pray for this people, nor lift up cries or praise for them, nor beseech me, for I will not listen to you. 17 Do you not see what they do in the cities of Iudah and in the streets of Jerusalem? 18 The children gather wood, the fathers light fires, and the women work dough to make cakes for the queen of Heauen and to squeeze the springs of wine to oth- er gods, to provoke me to wrath. 19 Do they provoke me to wrath, saith the LORD, and do they not mingle themselves with their faces? 20 Therefore thus says the LORD God, "Be- hold, my wrath and fury shall come upon this place, upon men and beasts, upon the trees of the field and upon the fruits of the earth, and they shall burn and not be quenched." 21 Thus says the LORD of hosts, the God of Is- rael, "Join your burnt offerings to your sacri- fices and eat the meat. 22 For I did not speak to your fathers or give them any command- ment, when I brought them out of the land of Egypt, concerning burnt offerings and sacri- fices. 23 But this I commanded them, saying, "Obey my command, and I will be your God, and you shall be my people; and walk in all the ways that I have commanded you, that it may be well with you." 24 But they would not obey or incline their gaze, but followed the coun- sels and stubbornness of their wicked heart, turning back and not advancing. 25 From the day your fathers came out of the land of Egypt until this day, I have sent all my servants, the prophets, to you, rising every day and send- ing them. 26 But they did not listen to me and did not bow their heads, but hardened their necks and did worse than their fathers. 27 Therefore thou shalt say all these words unto them, but they will not hear thee; thou shalt also cry unto them, but they will not answer thee. 28 But you shall say to them, "This is a nation that does not listen to the voice of the LORD their God, and does not receive disci- pline; truth is gone, and cleanliness is gone from their mouth." 29 Cut off your ears, O Jerusalem, and cast them away, and lament in the places of worship, for the LORD has withdrawn and forsaken the generation of his wrath. 30 For the sons of Iudah have done evil in my sight, saith the LORD: they have set their abominations in the House where my Name is invoked, to defile it. 31 They have built the place of Topheth, which is in the valley of Ben-Hinnom, to bury their sons and their daughters in the

fire, which I have not commanded them, nor has it come into my mind. 32 Therefore behold, the days shall come, saith the LORD, when it shall no more be called Topheth, nor the valley of Ben-Hin- nom, but the valley of slaughter; for they shall bury in Topheth until there is no more room. 33 And the carcasses of this people shall be meat for the refuse of heaven and for the re- fuse of the earth, and no one shall take them away. 34 Then I will cause the voice of joy and gladness, the voice of the bridegroom and the voice of the bride, to cease from the cities of Iudah and from the streets of Jerusalem, for the land will be desolate.

CHAPTER 8

1 At that time, says the LORD, they shall bring out of their graves the bones of the kings of Iudah, the bones of their princes, the bones of the priests, the bones of the prophets, and the bones of the inhabitants of Jerusalem. 2 They shall scatter them before the sun and the moon and all the army of Heauen, whom they praised, whom they served, whom they followed, whom they sought, and whom they worshipped; they shall not be gathered and shall not be buried, but they shall be as beds upon the earth. 3 Death will be desired rather than life for all the remnants of this wicked family, who remain in all the places where I have scattered them, says the LORD of hosts. 4 Thou shalt also say to them, "Thus saith the LORD, Shall they fall and not rise again?" "Will they fall away and not get up?" 5 Why did this people of Jerusalem turn back in con- tinual rebellion? They have given themselves over to deception and will not turn back. 6 I listened and heard, but no one spoke well; no one repented of his wickedness, saying, "What have I done?" All turned to their race, as the horse rushes into battle. 7 The storm in the air knows its times, the tortoise, the crane and the swallow observe the time of their coming, but my people do not know the judg- ment of the LORD. 8 How can you say, "We are wise and the word of the LORD is with you"? Surely, the pen of the scribes is in the vein. 9 The wise are ashamed; they are frightened and taken. is it true that they have ignored the word of the Lord, and what wisdom is there in them? 10 Therefore I will give their goods to others, and their fields to those who pos- sess them; for all, from the least to the great- est, are brought to corruption, and from the prophet to the priest, all do falsehood. 11 For they healed the wound of the daughter of my people with sweet words, saying, "Peace, peace, when there is no peace." 12 Were they ashamed when they had committed the abomination? No, they were not ashamed and could not be ashamed; therefore they shall fall among the slain; when I visit them, they shall be cast down, saith the LORD. 13 I will surely consume them, says the LORD: there shall be no more grapes on the vine, nor figs on the fig tree; the leaven shall vanish, and the things that I gave them shall depart from them. 14 Why do we remain? Gather yourselves to- gether, and enter into the strong cities, and let there be peace: for the LORD our God hath shut you up, and given you water to drink with gall, because we have sinned against the LORD. 15 We sought peace, but none came; we sought a time of health, but behold trouble. 16 From Dan was heard the neighing of his horses, and all the land trembled at the sound of the neighing of his strong horses, for they came and ravaged the land with all that is in it, the city and those who dwell in it. 17 For be- hold, I will send serpents and roosters among you, who will not be enchanted and will sting you, says the LORD. 18 I would have comfort- ed myself against sadness, but my heart is in anguish. 19 Behold the voice of the cry of the daughter of my people for fear of those in a far country, "Is not the LORD in Zion? Is not her king in her? Why have they provoked me to anger with their gracious images and with the vanities of a foreign god? 20 The time is past, the time is over, and we are not at peace. 21 I am vexed at the sorrow of the daughter of my people: I am troubled and astonishment has seized me. 22 Is there not balm in Gilead? Is there not a cure there? Why then is not the health of the daughter of my people restored?

CHAPTER 9

1 Oh, if my head were full of water and my eyes a fountain of tea, that I might weep day and night for the slaying of the daughter of my people. 2 Oh, if I had in the wilderness a wayfarer's lodge, that I might leave my people and depart from them, for they are all adul- terers and an assembly of rebels, 3 And they bend their tongues like their bows for lies, but they have no courage for the truth in the land, for they proceed from bad to worse and do not know me, says the LORD. 4 Let each one look after his neighbor and trust in no broth- er, for every brother deceives himself and ev- ery friend deceives himself, 5 And every one shall deceive his friend, and shall not speak the truth, for they have taught their tongue to speak lies, and they go to great pains to do evil. 6 Your dwelling place is in the midst of deceivers; because of their deceptions they re- fuse to know me, says the LORD. 7 Therefore thus says the LORD of hosts, "Behold, I will melt them and test them; for what should I do for the daughter of my people? 8 Their tongue is like an arrow that shoots and speaks deceit; one speaks peaceably to his neighbor with his mouth, but in his heart he waits for him. 9 Shall I not visit them for these things, saith the LORD, or shall not my heart be engaged on such a nation as this? 10 On the mountains I will make a weeping and a wailing, and on the wild places a mourning, because they are burned; so that no one can cross them, nor can men hear the voice of the flock; both the filthiness of the air and the beasts have fled and disappeared. 11 I will make Jerusalem a heap and a den of dragons, and I will make the cities of Iudah a desert without inhabi- tants. 12 Who is wise to understand this? And to whom the mouth of the LORD has spoken, he will declare it. Why does the land perish and burn as a desert, which no one crosses? 13 The LORD says, "Because they have forsaken my law, which I set before them, and have not obeyed my voice, nor walked after it, 14 but they walked according to the stubbornness of their heart and according to Baalim, which their fathers had taught them, 15 Therefore thus says the LORD of hosts, the God of Isra- el, "Behold, I will feed this people with worms and give them waters of gall to drink: 16 I will also scatter them among the heathen, whom neither they nor their fathers have known, and I will send a sword after them, until I have consumed them." 17 Thus says the LORD of hosts, "Take heed, and call the mourning women, that they may come, and send for able-bodied women that they may come, 18 And let them make haste to make a lamenta- tion for them, that our eyes may spit out tea, and our eyelids may gush out water. 19 For a lament is heard from Zion, "How destroyed and confused we are, because we have forsak- en the land and our houses have been driven out." 20 Hear therefore the word of the LORD, O women, and take heed to the words of his mouth; teach your daughters to weep, and each one her neighbor to lament. 21 For death has come into our windows and into our buildings, to destroy the

children outside and the young men in the streets. 22 Speak, thus says the LORD: "The carcasses of men shall re- main on the ground, as the darnel in the field, and as the handful after the mower, and no one shall reap them." 23 Thus says the LORD: "Let not the wise man glory in his wisdom, nor the strong man glory in his strength, nor the rich man glory in his riches. 24 But he that glorieth, let him glory in this: who understan- deth and knoweth me, for I am the LORD, who doeth mercy and judgment and justice in the earth; for in these things I delight, saith the LORD. 25 Behold, the day cometh, saith the LORD, when I will visit all them that are circumcised with the circumcised: 26 Egypt, Judah, Edom, the sons of Ammon, Moab, and all the uttermost corners of those who dwell in the wilderness, for all these nations are vncircumcised, and all the house of Israel is vncircumcised in heart.

CHAPTER 10

1 Hear the word of the LORD to you, O house of Israel. 2 Thus says the LORD: "Do not learn the way of the heathen, and do not fear the signs of Heauen, though the heathen are afraid of them. 3 For the customs of the peo- ple are vain: one cuts down a tree from the forest (which is the work of the carpenter's hands) with an ax, 4 another adorns it with silk and gold; they fasten it with nails and hammers so that it will not fall. 5 Idols stand up like palm trees, but they do not speak; they are endured because they cannot go; do not fear them, for they cannot do good and they cannot do evil. 6 There is none like you, O LORD; you are great, and your name is great in power. 7 Who does not fear you, O King of the nations, for to you belongs dominion, for among all the wise men of the nations and in all their kingdoms there is no one like you? 8 But all of them are fools, for their doctrine is a doctrine of vanity. 9 From Tarsis are brought slabs of silk and gold from Vphaz, for the la- bor of the workman and for the hands of the builder; white silk and purple are their gar- ments; all these things are made by crafty men. 10 But the LORD is the God of truth; he is a living God and an everlasting King; at his wrath the earth shall tremble, and the nations shall not be able to bear his wrath. 11 (So you will say to them, "The gods who did not make the heavens and the earth will perish from the earth and from under the heavens.") 12 He made the earth by his power, established the world by his wisdom, and stretched out the plateau by his discretion. 13 By his will he regulates the multitude of the waters in the plateau and makes the clouds rise from the ends of the earth; he turns lightning into rays and brings out the wind from his treasures. 14 Every man is a beast by his knowledge, ev- ery founder is confounded by his image, for his casting is but falsehood, and there is no breath. 15 They are vanity and the work of er- ror; in the time of their visitation they shall perish. 16 The portion of Iaakob is not like them, for he is the maker of all things, and Is- rael is the rod of his inheritance; the LORD of hosts is his name. 17 Gather your goods from the land, O you who dwell in the strong place. 18 For thus saith the LORD, Behold, at this time I will pierce through as with a sling the inhabitants of the land, and I will put them in trouble, and they shall see it. 19 I am sorry for my destruction and for my severe plague, but I have thought, It is my sorrow, and I will bear it." 20 My tabernacle is destroyed and all my blankets are broken; my children are gone and are no more; there is no one to spread my tent and to set up my tents. 21 The shepherds have become beasts and have not sought the LORD; therefore they have no understanding, and all the flocks in their pastures are scat- tered. 22 Behold, the hunger of the brutes and a great stir has come from the north country to make the cities of Iudah desolate and a den of dragons. 23 O LORD, I know that the way of man is not in himself, nor is it in man to walk and direct his steps. 24 O LORD, correct me, but with judgment, not with your wrath, or you will bring me to nothing. 25 Pour out your wrath on the heathen who do not know you, and on the families who do not call on your Name, because they have devoured Iaa- kob, ravaged and consumed him, and made his dwelling place desolate.

CHAPTER 11

1 The words came to Jeremiah from the LORD, saying, 2 Hear the words of this con- ference, and speak them to the men of Judah and to the inhabitants of Jerusalem, 3 and say to them, "Thus says the LORD God of Is- rael, Cursed is the man who does not obey the words of this convention, 4 which I com- manded your fathers when I brought them out of the land of Egypt, out of the furnace of Yron, saying, Obey my message, and do all these things that I command you; so you shall be my people, and I will be your God, 5 that I may confirm the other oath which I swore to your fathers, to give them a land flowing with milk and honey, as it appears today." Then I answered and said, "So be it, Lord." 6 Then the LORD said to me, "Shout all these words in the cities of Iudah and in the streets of Jerusalem, saying, 'Listen to the words of this Joint and do them.' 7 For I protested with your fathers, when I brought them out of the land of Egypt to this day, ris- ing up early and protesting, saying, "Obey my command." 8 But they would not obey and did not bow their heads, but each one walked in the stubbornness of his wicked heart; there- fore I will bring upon them all the words of this conference, which I commanded them to do, but which they did not do." 9 The LORD said to me, "There is a conspiracy among the men of Iudah and among the inhabitants of Jerusalem. 10 They have returned to the in- iquities of their ancestors, who refused to listen to my words and went after other gods to serve them; so the house of Israel and the house of Iudah have broken my covenant that I made with their fathers. 11 Therefore thus says the LORD: "Behold, I will bring upon them a plague from which they cannot escape; and though they cry out to me, I will not hear them. 12 Then the cities of Iudah and the inhabitants of Jerusalem will go and cry out to the gods to whom they offer incense, but they will not be able to help them in time of trouble. 13 For according to the number of your cities there were your gods, O Iudah, and according to the number of the streets of Jerusalem you erected altars of confusion, that is, altars for burning incense to Baal. 14 Therefore you shall not pray for this people, nor lift up a cry or a prayer for them, for when they cry out to me in their trouble, I will not hear them. 15 What should my blood do in my house, seeing that they have committed an abomination with a man, and holy flesh turns away from you; yet when you do good, you recover. 16 The LORD called your name, "A green olive tree, beautiful and of good fruit"; but with boredom and great commotion he set fire to it, and its branches broke off. 17 For the LORD of hosts, Beho planted you, has pronounced a plague against you, because of the wickedness of the house of Israel and the house of Iudah, which they have committed against themselves to provoke me to wrath in offering incense to Baal. 18 The LORD taught me, and I know it, already when you showed me their practices. 19 But I was like a sheep or

a bull being led to the slaughter, and I did not know that they had acted thus against me, saying, "Let us destroy the tree with its fruit and cut it off from the land of the living, so that its name may no longer be remem- bered." 20 But O LORD of hosts, who judges righteously, and who examines the kidneys and the heart, let me see your vengeance on them, for to you I have opened my cause." 21 Thus saith the LORD concerning the men of Anathoth, who seek your life, and say, "Do not prophesy in the name of the LORD, lest you die by our hand." 22 Thus says the LORD of hosts, "Behold, I will visit them: the young men shall die by the sword, their sons and their daughters shall die by starvation, 23 and none of them shall remain, for I will cause a plague to come upon the men of Anathoth in the year of their visitation.

CHAPTER 12

1 O LORD, if I argue with you, you are righ- teous; but let me speak to you of your judg- ments: why does the way of the wicked pros- per? Why are all rich those who transgress rebellious? 2 Thou hast planted them, and they have taken root; they grow and bear fruit; thou art far from their mouth, and far from their reins. 3 But you, LORD, know me; you have seen me and tried my heart toward you; bring them out like sheep for slaughter and prepare them for the day of slaughter. 4 How much longer shall the earth rot, and the herbs of every fire wither because of the wickedness of those who dwell therein? The beasts are consumed and the birds, for they have said, "He shall not see our last end." 5 If you ran with pedestrians and they wearied you, how can you compete with horses? And if you thought yourself secure in a peaceful land, what will you do in the swell of Iorden? 6 For thy brethren and thy father's house have dealt faithfully with thee, and have called upon thee with a loud voice; but turn them not away, though they speak evil to thee. 7 I have forsaken my house: I have forsaken my inheritance; I have given the good of my soul into the hand of its enemies. 8 My inheri- tance is to me as a lion in the forest; it cries out against me, therefore have I hated it. 9 Will my inheritance be to me like a bird of different colors? Do not the birds around her say, "Come, gather all the beasts of the field, come and eat her"? 10 Many shepherds have destroyed my vineyard, and have cast my por- tion under rubble; Of my pleasant portion they have made a wild desolation. 11 They have destroyed it, and it, being destroyed, mourns for me; and the whole land is de- stroyed, because no one devotes himself to it. 12 The destroyers have come upon all the high places of the wilderness, because the sword of the LORD will act from one end of the land to the other; no one will have peace. 13 They have sown wheat and gathered thorns; they have been sick and had no profit; they have been ashamed of your fruit, because of the fierce anger of the LORD. 14 Thus says the LORD against all my wicked neighbors who touch the inheritance which I have made my people Israel to inherit, "Behold, I will pluck them out of their land, and I will pluck out the house of Iudah from among them. 15 And af- ter I have plucked them out, I will return, and have compassion on them, and will lead every man back to his inheritance, and every man to his land. 16 And if they learn the ways of my people, to swear by my Name (the LORD lies, as they taught my people to swear by Baal), then they shall be built in the midst of my people. 17 But if they will not obey, then I will take possession of that nation and destroy it, says the LORD.

CHAPTER 13

1 So the LORD said to me, "Go, buy yourself a linen belt and put it on your loins and do not put it in the water." 2 So I bought the belt according to the Lord's command and put it on my loins. 3 The word of the LORD came to me a second time, and he said to me 4 "Take the belt that you have bought and that is on your feet, get up, go to Perath and hide it in the cleft of the rock." 5 So I went and hid it by Perath, as the LORD had commanded me. 6 After many days, the LORD said to me, "Get up, go toward Perath and take from there the belt that I had commanded you to hide there." 7 Then I went to Perath, dug and took the belt from the place where I had hidden it; and behold, the belt was corrupt and of no use. 8 Then the word of the LORD came to me, say- ing. 9 Thus says the LORD: "In this way I will destroy the pride of Judah and the great pride of Jerusalem. 10 This wicked people have re- fused to hear my word and walk according to the stubbornness of their own hearts, going after other gods to serve and worship them; therefore they will be like this belt, which is of no use. 11 For as the belt tightens the bonds of man, so have I bound all the house of Is- rael and all the house of Judah to me, saith the LORD, that they might be my people; that they might have a name and a prayer and a glory, but they would not listen. 12 Therefore thou shalt say this word unto them, Thus saith the LORD God of Israel, Every bottle shall be filled with wine; and they shall say unto thee, Do we not know that every bottle shall be filled with wine? 13 Then thou shalt say unto them, Thus saith the LORD, Behold, I will fill all the inhabitants of this land with drunkenness, that is, the kings that sit upon the throne of Dauid, and the priests, and the prophets, and all the inhabitants of Jerusalem. 14 I will hurl them one against another, the fathers and the sons together, says the LORD: I will not spare, nor have mercy nor compassion, but I will de- stroy them. 15 Hear and hearken, and do not be haughty, for the LORD has said it. 16 Give glory to the LORD your God before he brings darkness and causes your feet to stumble over dark mountains, and while you seek light, he turns it into the shadow of death and makes it like darkness. 17 But if you will not listen to this, my soul will weep in secret because of your pride, and my eye will weep and drop tears, because the flock of the LORD has been carried away into captivity. 18 Say to the king and queen, "Humble yourselves, sit down, for the crown of your glory shall come down from your heads." 19 The cities of the south shall be closed, and no one shall open them; all Iudah shall be carried away into captivity; everyone shall be carried away into captivity. 20 Lift up your eyes and look at those who come from the North; where is the flock that was giv- en to you, your beautiful flock? 21 What will you say when they visit you? (Since you have taught them to be captains and leaders out- side of you) will you not be sorry to take you as a woman in a snare? 22 And if you say in your heart, "Why do these things come upon me? For the multitude of your iniquities, your skirts have been uncovered and your heels laid bare. 23 Can the black man change his skin or the leopard his spots? Then you who are accustomed to do good can also do good. 24 Therefore I will scatter them like stub- ble that is blown away by the south wind. 25 This is your portion and the portion of your measures from me, says the LORD, because you have forgotten me and trusted in lies. 26 Therefore I have also sewed your skirts on your face, that your shame may appear. 27 I have seen your adulteries and

your sins, the filth of your prostitution on the poles in the fields, and your abominations. I salute you, O Jerusalem: will you not be cleansed? When will it be once?

with sin. 22 Is there anyone among the vani- ties of the Gentiles who can give raina or who can give show to the heavens? Are not you, O Lord, our God? Therefore we will wait for you, for you have done all these things.

CHAPTER 14

1 The word of the LORD addressed to Jer- emiah concerning the famine. 2 Iudah is mourning, her gates are desolate, they have been brought to ruin, and the cry of Jerusa- lem rises. 3 Their nobles have sent to the water their nurses, who came to the wells and found no water; they have returned with their emp- ty vessels; they are ashamed and confused, and have lowered their heads. 4 The ground was destroyed, because there was no ray in the earth; the plowmen were ashamed and crouched down. 5 Even the hellhounds tram- pled the field and abandoned it, because there was no grass left. 6 The wild donkeys stood in the high places and pulled at the wind like dragons, and their eyes drooped, because there was no fatness. 7 O LORD, though our iniquities testify against you, be good to them according to your name, for our rebellions are many, we have sinned against you. 8 O hope of Israel, her savior in the time of trouble, why are you like a wanderer in your land, like one who passes through to stop one night? 9 Why are you like a man amazed and like a strong man who cannot succor? Yet you, O LORD, are in the midst of Vs. and your Name is invoked upon Vs. 10 Thus says the LORD to this people, "So they have devoted themselves to wandering; they have not restrained their feet, therefore the LORD is not pleased with them; but now he will remember their iniq- uity and visit their sins." 11 Then the LORD said to me, "You shall not pray to do good to this people. 12 When they fast, I will not hear their cry, and when they offer burnt offerings and oblations, I will not accept them; but I will consume them with the sword, famine and pestilence." 13 Then I answered, "Lord God, behold, the prophets say to them, 'You shall not see the sword, nor shall famine come upon you, but I will give you peace assured in this place.'" 14 Then the LORD said to me, "The prophets prophesy lies in my Name: I have not sent them, nor commanded them, nor spoken to them, but they prophesy to you a false vision, a divination, a vanity, and a de- ceit of their heart. 15 Therefore thus says the LORD: "Concerning the prophets who proph- esy in my Name and whom I have not sent, but who say, 'The sword and the famine shall not be in this land, the sword and the famine shall consume those prophets. 16 The people to whom these prophets prophesy shall be thrown out into the streets of Jerusalem, be- cause of the famine and the sword, and there shall be none to bury them, neither they, nor their wives, nor their sons, nor their daugh- ters, for I will bring their wickedness upon them. 17 Therefore thou shalt say this word unto them, My eyes fall down by the ears, night and day, without ceasing, because the virgin daughter of my people is destroyed with great destruction and with a sore plague. 18 For if I go into the fields, I see those slain by the sword; and if I go into the city, I see also those who are starving; moreover the Proph- et and the Priest go wandering in a land they do not know. 19 Have you rejected Iudah, or has your soul abhorred Zion? Why have you struck, so that we cannot be healed? We have sought peace, and there is no good; we have sought the time of health, and here is trouble. 20 We acknowledge, O LORD, our wickedness and the iniquity of our fathers, for we have sinned against you. 21 Abhor not sin; For thy Names' sake cast not down the throne of thy glory; Remember not and break not thy bond

CHAPTER 15

1 Then the Lord said to me, "Even if Moses and Samuel stood before me, my affection could not be toward this people; drive them out of my sight and make them depart. 2 And if they say to thee, "Whence shall we de- part?" say to them, "Thus saith the LORD: he that is destined for death, goeth to death; he that is destined for the sword, goeth to the sword; he that is destined for famine, goeth to famine; he that is destined for captivity, goeth to captivity. 3 And I, says the LORD, will destine them for four kinds: the sword to kill, the dogs to tear in pieces, the souls of man and the beasts of the earth to destroy. 4 I will also scatter them throughout all the king- doms of the earth, because of Manasseh the son of Hezekiah, king of Judah, for what he did in Jerusalem. 5 Who then will have mer- cy on you, O Jerusalem, or who will grieve for you, or who will go and pray for your peace? 6 You have forsaken me, says the LORD, and gone backward; therefore I will stretch out my hand against you and destroy you, for I am weary of repentance. 7 I will scatter them with the fan through the gates of the land I have ravaged and destroyed my people, but they would not turn back from their ways. 8 Their women have increased from me on the seashore; I have brought upon them and upon the assembly of the young men a destroyer in no day: I brought him down upon them and upon the city suddenly and quickly. 9 The woman that bare twice was made weak; her heart failed; the sun failed her, while it was day; she was confounded and shamed, and the rest of them I will deliver to the sword be- fore their enemies, saith the LORD. 10 "I am sorry, my mother, that thou hast borne me, a quarrelsome man, and striving with all the earth. I have not lent to usury, nor have men lent me to usury; yet all men curse me." 11 The LORD said, "Surely, your remnant shall have riches; surely, I will cause your enemy to pur- sue you in the time of trouble and in the time of affliction." 12 Shall the yron be broken, and the reed that is from the north? 13 Your pos- sessions and your treasures I will give away, and that for all your sins, in all your borders. 14 I will make thee go with thine enemies into a land thou knowest not, for in my wrath there is kindled a fire that will bury thee. 15 O LORD, thou knowest, remember me, visit me, and avenge me on my persecutors; do not take me away in the course of thy wrath; know that because of thee I have suffered reproach. 16 Your words have been found by me, and I have heard them, and your word has been to me the joy and support of my heart, for your name has been called upon me, O LORD God of hosts. 17 I did not sit in the assembly of mockers and rejoice, but I was left alone be- cause of your plague, because you filled me with disdain. 18 Why is my sickness contin- ual and my plague desperate and cannot be healed? Why are you to me like a lyre and like waters that break down? 19 Therefore thus says the LORD: "If thou turn back, I will bring thee back, and thou shalt stand before me; and if thou take away the precious from the vile, thou shalt be according to my word; let them return to thee, but thou shalt not return to them. 20 I will make thee a strong wall of bronze for this people, and they shall fight against thee, but they shall not prevail against thee: for I am with thee to save thee, and to deliver thee, saith the LORD. 21 I will deliver you out of

the hands of the wicked and re- deem you from the hands of tyrants.

CHAPTER 16

1 The word of the Lord also came to me, say- ing, 2 You shall not take a wife, nor have sons nor daughters in this place. 3 For thus says the LORD concerning the sons and daughters who are born in this place, and their mothers who bear them, and their fathers who beget them in this land, 4 They shall die of death and disease; they shall not be mourned nor buried, but shall be as dung upon the earth; they shall be consumed by the sword and by famine, and their carcasses shall be food for the beasts of the earth and for the beasts of the earth. 5 For thus says the LORD, "Do not enter the house of mourning, and do not go out to mourn, and do not be in mourning for mourning, for I have taken away my peace from this people, says the LORD, and mercy and compassion. 6 Both the great and the small shall die in this land; they shall not be buried, and men shall not mourn for them, nor cut themselves off, nor callous them- selves for them. 7 They shall not stretch out their hands for the mourners to console them for the dead, nor shall they give them the cup of consolation to drink for their father or their mother. 8 Nor will you enter the house of banquets to sit with them to eat and drink. 9 For thus says the LORD of hosts, the God of Israel, "Behold, I will cause to cease from this place, in your sight, the journey of myr- tle and the journey of joy, the journey of the bridegroom and the journey of the bride. 10 When you have expounded all these words to this people, and they shall say to you, "Why has the LORD pronounced against you all this great plague?", "What is our iniquity?", "What is our sin that we have committed against the LORD our God?" 11 Then you shall say to them, "Because your fathers have forsaken me, says the LORD, and have walked after other gods, served them and worshipped them, and have forsaken me and have not kept my Law." 12 (and you have done worse than your fathers; for behold, you walk each one according to the stubbornness of his evil heart and do not listen to me). 13 Therefore I will bring you out of this land to a land that you do not know, neither you nor your fathers, and there you shall serve other gods day and night, for I will not give you grace. 14 Behold therefore, saith the LORD, the day shall come when it shall no more be said, The LORD loveth, who brought forth the children of Israel out of the land of Egypt, 15 but the LORD is the one who brought the children of Israel out of the land of the north and out of all the countries where he had scattered them, and I will bring them back to the land that I had given to their fa- thers. 16 Behold, says the LORD, I will send many fishermen, and they shall fish them, and then I will send many hunters, and they shall hunt them out of every mountain and hill, and out of the caves of the rocks. 17 For my eyes are on all their ways; they do not hide themselves from my face, nor is their iniqui- ty hidden from my eyes. 18 First I will double reward their iniquity and their sin, because they have defiled my land and filled my in- heritance with their carrion and their abomi- nations. 19 O LORD, you are my strength, my endurance, and my refuge in the day of af- fliction; the people will come to you from the ends of the world and say, "Our fathers have inherited lies and vanity, to no profit." 20 Can a man create gods for himself, and they are not gods? 21 Therefore I will instruct them for this time: I will make them see my hand and my power, and they shall know that my name is the Lord.

CHAPTER 17

1 The sin of Iudah is written with a pen of yron and with the point of a diamond, and graven on the table of their hearts and on the horns of your altars. 2 They remember their altars as their children, with their groups by the green trees on the hills. 3 O my mountain in the field, I will give your substance and all your treasures to be scattered for the sin of your high places in all your borders. 4 Thou shalt rest, and in thee shall rest the inheri- tance that I have given thee, and I will make thee serve thine enemies in the land which thou knowest not, because thou hast kindled a fire in my wrath, which shall burn forever." 5 Thus says the LORD: "Cursed is the man who trusts in man, who makes flesh his arm and withdraws his heart from the LORD. 6 For he shall be like the heath in the wilderness, and shall not see when a good thing comes, but shall dwell in the dry places of the wilderness, in a salt land uninhabited. 7 Blessed is the man who trusts in the LORD and whose hope is the LORD. 8 For he shall be like a tree plant- ed by the sea, stretching out its roots by the river and not drooping when the mugginess comes, but its leaves shall be green and shall not care for the year of drought, nor cease to bear fruit. 9 The heart is deceitful and wicked about everything; who can know it? 10 I, the LORD, scrutinize hearts and test their lines, to give to each one according to his ways and according to the fruit of his works. 11 As the parturient reaps the fruit she has not borne, so he who obtains riches without having a right to them will leave them in the midst of his days, and at his end he will be a gruel. 12 As a glorious throne exalted from the be- ginning, so is the place of our sanctuary. 13 O LORD, the hope of Israel, all who forsake you will be confounded; those who turn away from you will be written on the earth, because they have forsaken the LORD, the fountain of the gushing waters. 14 Heal me, O LORD, and I shall be whole; heal me and I shall be healed, for you are my prayer. 15 Behold, they say to me, "Where is the word of the LORD? Let him come at once." 16 But I did not push myself for a meal after thee, nor did I desire the day of misery, thou knowest; what came from my lips was right before thee. 17 Be not terrible to me; thou art my hope in the day of adversity. 18 Let them that persecute me be confound- ed, but let not me be confounded; let them be aphrahmed, but let not me be aphrahmed; let the day of aduersitia come upon them, and destroy them with double destruction. 19 So the LORD said to me, "Go and stand at the gate of the sons of the people, by which the kings of Iudah enter and by which they go out, and in all the gates of Jerusalem, 20 And say unto them, Hear the word of the LORD, ye kings of Judah, al Judah, and all the in- habitants of Jerusale, which enter in by these gates." 21 Thus says the Lord, "Take heed to your souls, and do not carry burdens on the Sabbath day, and do not carry them through the gates of Jerusalem. 22 Do not carry bur- dens outside your houses on the Sabbath day; do no work, but keep the Sabbath holy, as I commanded your fathers." 23 But they did not obey; they did not incline their ears, but stiffened their necks and would not listen or receive correction. 24 Nevertheless, if you will listen to me, says the LORD, and carry no bur- den through the gates of the city on the Sab- bath day, but sanctify the Sabbath day and do no work there, 25 then the kings and princes shall come in at the gates of this city, and shall sit on the throne of Dauid, and shall ride in chariots and horses, they and their princes, the men of Iudah, and the inhabitants of Je- rusalem; and this city shall remain

forever. 26 And they shall come from the cities of Iudah, and from the environs of Ierusalem, and from the land of Benjamin, and from the plain, and from the mountains, and from the south, and they shall bring sacrifices, sacrifices of meat and incense, and they shall bring sacrifices of prayer into the house of the LORD. 27 But if ye will not hearken unto me in sanctifying the Sabbath day, and in not bearing burdens, and in not passing through the gates of Jerusalem on the Sabbath day, then I will kindle a fire at her gates, which shall destroy the palaces of Jerusalem, and shall not be quenched.

CHAPTER 18

1 The words the LORD spoke to Jeremiah, saying, 2 "Arise, go down to the potter's house, and there I will make you hear my words." 3 Then I went down to the potter's house, and behold, he was working at the wheels. 4 The vessel he had made with clay had broken in the potter's hand; so he went back and made another vessel, as had seemed good to the potter. 5 Then the word of the LORD came to me, saying, "O house of Israel, 6 O house of Israel, can I not do with you as this potter says the LORD? Behold, as clay is in the hand of the potter, so you are in my hand, O house of Isra- el. 7 I will speak suddenly against a nation or against a kingdom, to push it, drive it out and destroy it. 8 But if this nation, against which I have spoken, is converted from its wicked- ness, I will repent of the plague that I thought to bring upon them. 9 And I will suddenly speak of a nation and a kingdom to build and plant it. 10 But if they behave well in my sight and do not listen to my message, I will repent of the good I thought to do for them. 11 Speak now therefore to the men of Judah and to the inhabitants of Jerusalem, saying, Thus saith the LORD, Behold, I prepare a plague for you, and I have a thing in mind against you; return ye therefore every one from his way, and make your ways and your works good. 12 But they said in despair, "We will walk according to our own imaginations, and do each one according to the stubbornness of his evil heart." 13 Therefore thus says the LORD: "Ask now among the Gentiles who have heard such things: the virgin of Israel has behaved very filthily. 14 Will a man forsake the snow of Lebanon, which comes from the fields? Or will he forsake the cold waters that flow and come from another place? 15 For my people have forgotten me, and have burned incense to vanities, and their prophets have made them stumble in their paths from the ancient ways, to walk in paths and ways that are not trodden, 16 to make their land desolate and an everlasting mockery, so that everyone who passes by will be amazed and shake his head, 17 I will scatter them with an east wind before the enemy; I will make them see their backs and not their faces in the day of their destruc- tion." 18 Then they said, "Come, and let them imagine some evil against Jeremiah, for the word shall not perish from the priest, nor the counsel from the wise, nor the word from the prophet; come, and let them smite him with their tongues, and let them heed none of his words. 19 Hear me, O LORD, and hear the voice of those who strive against me. 20 Will the good be rewarded? For they have dug a pit for my soul; remember that I stood before you to speak good for them and to turn away your wrath from them. 21 Therefore commit their children to famine, and let them die by the power of the sword; let their wives be de- prived of their children and remain widows; let their husbands be put to death, and their young men be killed by the sword in battle. 22 Let the cry be heard from their

houses, when you cause an army to come suddenly upon them, because they have dug a pit to take me and have hidden snares for my feet. 23 Never- theless, O LORD, you know that their coun- sels against me tend to death; do not forgive their iniquity and do not blot out their sin from your sight, but make them disappear before you; behave thus with them in the time of your wrath.

CHAPTER 19

1 Thus says the LORD, "Go, buy a fund of land from a potter, and take the ancients of the people and the ancients of the priests, 2 and go to the valley of Ben-Hinnom, which is by the entrance of the gate of the east, and preach there the words that I will tell you, 3 and you shall say, "Hear the word of the LORD, O king of Judah and inhabitants of Jerusalem: Thus says the LORD of hosts, the God of Isra- el: Behold, I will cause a plague to come upon this place, that whosoever hears, his ears shall tingle. 4 For they have forsaken me, and have defiled this place, and have burned thereon incense to other gods, which neither they nor their fathers knew, nor the kings of Iudah (they have also filled this place with the blood of innocents), 5 And they have built the places of worship of Baal, to bury their children with fire as burnt sacrifices to Baal, which I have not commanded, nor uttered, nor come into my mind). 6 Therefore behold, the days come, saith the LORD, when this place shall no more be called Tophet, nor valley of Ben- Hinnom, but valley of the slaughter. 7 I will cause the counsels of Judah and Jerusalem to fail in this place, and I will cause them to fall by the sword before their enemies and by the hand of those who see their lives; and their carcasses I will give to you, to the refuse of the field and the beasts of the field. 8 I will make this city des- olate and hissing, so that everyone who pass- es by will be stunned and hysterical because of all its plagues. 9 I will feed them with the flesh of their sons and with the flesh of their daughters, and each one shall eat the flesh of his friend in the siege and in the straits in which their enemies, who see their lives, will hold them. 10 Then you shall break the spoil before the eyes of the men who go with you, 11 And thou shalt say unto them, Thus saith the LORD of hosts, I will break this people and this city, as one breaks a potter's vessel that can no more be put together, and I will bury them in Topheth until there is no more place to bury. 12 Thus will I do with this place, says the LORD, and with its inhabitants, and I will make this city like Topheth. 13 For the houses of Jerusalem and the houses of the kings of Ju- deah shall be defiled like the place of Tophet, because of all the houses on whose roofs they burned incense to all the army of Heauen and poured out drink offerings to other gods." 14 Then Jeremiah came from Tophet, where the LORD had sent him to prophesy, and stood in the courtyard of the LORD's house and said to all the people 15 Thus says the LORD of hosts, the God of Israel, "Behold, I will bring upon this city and upon all its cities all the plagues that I have pronounced against it, because they have hardened their necks and would not listen to my words."

CHAPTER 20

1 When Pashur the son of Immer the priest, who had been appointed keeper of the house of the LORD, heard that Jeremiah had proph- esied these things, 2 Pashur struck the proph- et Jeremiah and put him in the stocks that were at

Benjamin's gate, near the house of the LORD. 3 In the morning, Pashur brought Ier- emiah out of the stocks. Then Jeremiah said to him, "The LORD did not call your name Pashur, but Magor-Missabib. 4 For thus says the LORD: "Behold, I will make you a terror to yourself and to all your friends, and they shall fall by the sword of their enemies; your eyes shall see it, and I will give all Iudah into the hand of the king of Babel, who shall take them captive to Babel and kill them with the sword. 5 Moreover, I will deliver all the goods of this city, all its labors, all its precious things, and all the treasures of the kings of Iudah into the hands of their enemies, who will scatter them and carry them away and carry them to Babel. 6 You, Pashur, and all those who dwell in your house, shall go into captivity, come to Babel, die, and be buried there, you and all your friends, to whom you prophesied death. 7 O LORD, thou hast deceived me, and I have been deceived; thou art mightier than I, and hast gone before me: I am daily mocked; all mock me. 8 For since I have spoken, I have cried out wrong and proclaimed desolation, the word of the LORD has become a daily reproach and mockery to me. 9 Then I said, "I will no longer mention him or speak in his Name." But his word was in my heart like a burning fire locked in my bones, and I was weary of bearing it, and could not restrain myself. 10 For I had heard the insults of many and fear on every side. All my family mem- bers were watching for me to stop, saying, "It may be that he has deceived himself; then we will deal with him and take our vengeance on him." 11 But the LORD is with me like a mighty giant; therefore my persecutors will be defeated, and they will not be able to act, and they will be greatly confounded, for they have acted wisely, and their eternal shame will never be forgotten. 12 But, O LORD of hosts, who tries the righteous, and sees the upright and the heart, let me see your vengeance on them, for to you I have opened my cause. 13 Sing unto the LORD, praise the LORD, for he hath delivered the soul of the poor from the hand of the wicked. 14 Cursed be the day that I was delivered, and blessed not the day that my mother delivered me. 15 Cursed be the man who said to my father, "A son has been born to you," and comforted him. 16 Let that man be like the cities that the LORD defeated and did not repent; let him hear the cry of the morning, and let him not be seen by any tide, 17 For he hath not killed me, not even by the woman, or that my mother should be my wife, or his wife a perpetual conception. 18 How is it that I came forth from the womb to see toil and sorrow, and that my days are consumed with shame?

CHAPTER 21

1 The words that came to Jeremiah from the LORD, when King Zedekiah sent Pashur the son of Malchiah and Zephaniah the son of Maaseiah the priest to him, saying, "Is it not true that the LORD has dealt well with vs. be- cause Nebuchadnezzar, king of Babel, makes war against vs.? 2 Inquire, I pray you, with the LORD for vs. (for Nebuchadnezzar, king of Babel, makes war against vs.), whether it is true that the LORD will want to do with vs. all his wonderful works, so that he may re- turn from vs. 3 Then Jeremiah said, "Thus you shall say to Zedekiah, 4 Thus says the LORD, the God of Israel: 'Behold, I will withdraw the weapons of war that are in your hands, with which you fight against the king of Babel and against the Chaldeans, who are besieging you outside the walls, and I will gather them into the midst of this city. 5 I myself will fight against you with an outstretched hand and with a mighty weapon, in wrath and anger and great indignation. 6 And I will smite the inhabitants of this city, both man and beast; they will die of a great pestilence." 7 And after this, saith the LORD, I will deliver Zedekiah king of Judah, and his servants, and the peo- ple, and as many as are left in this city, from pestilence, and from the sword, and from famine, into the hand of Nebuchadnezzar king of Babel, into the hand of their enemies, and into the hand of them that see their lives, and he shall smite them with the blade of the sword: he shall not spare them, neither shall he have pity nor compassion. 8 And unto this people shalt thou say, Thus saith the LORD, Behold, I have set before you the way of life and the way of death. 9 Whoever remains in this city shall die by the sword, by famine, and by pestilence; but whoever goes out and falls among the Chaldeans who besiege you shall lie, and his life shall be given him for a prayer. 10 For I have set my face against this city, for good and not for evil, saith the LORD; it shall come into the hand of the king of Babel, and he shall bury it with fire. 11 And say to the house of the king of Judah, Hear the word of the LORD. 12 O house of Dauid, thus says the LORD: "Execute judgment in the morning, and deliver the oppressed from the hand of the oppressor, lest my wrath break out like a burning fire that no one can put out, because of the wickedness of your works. 13 Behold, I come against you, O inhabitant of the valley and inhabitant of the plain, says the LORD, who says, "Who will come down against us?" or "Who will enter our dwellings?" 14 But I will visit you according to the fruit of your works, says the LORD, and I will kindle a fire in his forest, which will grow up around it.

CHAPTER 22

1 So the LORD said, "Go down to the house of the king of Judah and speak there about this, 2 and say, Hear the words of the LORD, O king of Judah, who sits on the throne of Dauid, you and your servants, and your people who enter through these gates." 3 Thus says the LORD: "Execute judgment and justice; deliver the oppressed from the hand of the oppressor; do not mistreat the stranger, the fatherless or the widow; do not do violence or shed innocent blood in this place. 4 For if you do so, the kings who sit on the throne of Dauid will come in through the gates of this house and ride in chariots and horses, he and his servants and his people. 5 But if you will not listen to these words, I swear by myself, says the LORD, that this house shall be destroyed. 6 For the LORD has said thus to the house of the kings of Judah, "You are Gilead to me and the head of Lebanon, but I will certainly make you a wilderness and as an uninhabited city, 7 And I will prepare destroyers against thee, every one with his weapons, who will cut down thy principal cedar trees and throw them into the fire. 8 Many nations will pass by this city and say to their neighbor, "Why has the LORD done this to this great city? 9 Then they will answer, "Because they have forsaken the covenant of the LORD their God and have worshiped other gods, serving them." 10 Do not weep for the dead and do not grieve for them, but weep for the one who goes away, for he will never return or see his homeland again. 11 For thus says the LORD: "As for Shal- lum the son of Jehoiah, king of Iudah, who reigned by Jehoiah his father, and departed from this place, he shall not return there, 12 but shall die in the place where they led him into captivity, and he shall see this land no more. 13 Woe to him who builds his house

righteously, and his rooms without equity; who makes his neighbor pay without wag- es, and does not pay him for his labor. 14 He says, "I will build me a wide house and large rooms"; he will make himself large windows, and will clad them with cedar, and paint them with vermilion. 15 Will you reign because you have shut yourself in the cedar? Did not your father eat and drink and prosper when he ex- ecuted judgment and justice? 16 When he up- held the cause of the afflicted and the poor, he prospered; is it not because he knew me, says the LORD? 17 But your eyes and your heart are but for your corruption, for shedding inno- cent blood, for oppression and destruction, and for doing this. 18 Therefore thus says the LORD against Jehoiakim the son of Jehoiaiah, king of Judah, "They shall not mourn for him, saying, 'Ah, my brother or ah, sister;' nor shall they mourn for him, saying, 'Ah, lord or ah, his glory. 19 He shall be buried as one buries a corpse, then he shall be dragged and cast out of the gates of Jerusalem. 20 Go into Lebanon and shout; present yourself in Bashan and shout by the steps, for all your warriors are destroyed. 21 I spoke to you when you were in prosperity, but you said, "I will not listen"; this has been your behavior from your youth, that you would not obey my message. 22 The wind shall feed all your shepherds, and your leaders shall go into captivity; and then you shall be shamed and confounded of all your wickedness. 23 You who dwell in Lebanon and make your nest among the cedars, how beau- tiful will you be when sorrow comes upon you, like the sorrow of a woman in distress? 24 As I think, says the LORD, even if Coniah the son of Jehoiakim, king of Iudah, were the seal of my right hand, I would bring you down from thence. 25 I will give you into the hand of those who see your life and into the hand of those of whom you are afraid, that is, into the hand of Nebuchadnezzar, king of Babel, and into the hand of the Chaldeans. 26 And I will cause them to carry you and your mother who gave birth to you to another land, where you were not given birth, and there you shall die. 27 But to the land to which they desire to re- turn, they will not return there. 28 Is not this man, Coniah, like a despised and broken idol, or like a vessel in which there is no pleasure? Therefore have they been taken away, he and his descendants, and cast into a land they do not know? 29 O earth, earth, earth, hear the word of the LORD. 30 Thus says the LORD, "Write that this man is childless, a man who will not prosper in his days, for there will be no man of his descendants who will prosper and sit on the throne of Dauid, or who will yet reign in Iudah."

CHAPTER 23

1 Woe to the shepherds who destroy and scat- ter the sheep of my pasture, says the LORD. 2 Therefore thus says the LORD, the God of Israel, to the shepherds who feed my people, "You have scattered my flock, and have driven them out, and have not visited them; behold, I will visit you because of the wickedness of your works, says the LORD. 3 And I will gather the remnant of my flock from all the countries where I have scattered them, and I will bring them back to their folds, and they shall grow and increase. 4 And I will set before them burdens that will feed them; and they shall no longer be afraid, nor shall they be afraid, and none of them shall lack, saith the LORD. 5 Be- hold, the days come, says the LORD, when I will raise up in Dauid a righteous branch, and a king shall reign, and prosper, and execute judgment and justice in the earth. 6 In his days Iudah shall be delivered, and Israel shall dwell in safety;

this is the name by which they shall call him, "The LORD our righteousness." 7 Therefore, behold, the days come, saith the LORD, when it shall no more be said, "The LORD liveth, who brought forth the children of Israel out of the land of Egypt." 8 but the LORD who brought forth and led the descen- dants of the house of Israel out of the land of the north and out of all the countries where I had scattered them, and they shall dwell in their own land. 9 My heart is broken with- in me because of the prophets; all my bones tremble: I am like a drunken man (and like a man who has run out of wine) because of the presence of the LORD and because of his holy words. 10 For the land is full of adulterers, and because of others the land is in mourning, the pleasant places of the wilderness are dried up, their course is weak, and their strength is not right. 11 For both prophet and priest act wick- edly, and their wickedness I have found in my house, saith the LORD. 12 Therefore their way shall be to them as a slippery way in dark- ness; they shall be forsaken and fall therein; for I will cause a plague to come upon them in the year of their visitation, saith the LORD. 13 I saw the foolishness of the prophets of Sa- maria, who prophesied about Baal and mis- led my people Israel. 14 I have also seen in the prophets of Jerusalem filthiness; they commit adultery and walk in lies; they also strength- en the hands of the wicked, so that no one can withdraw from his wickedness; they are all to me like Sodom, and its inhabitants like Gomorah. 15 Therefore thus says the LORD of hosts concerning the prophets, "Behold, I will feed them with worms and make them drink water of gall, because from the prophets in Jerusalem wickedness has spread through- out the whole earth." 16 Thus says the LORD of hosts, "Do not listen to the words of the prophets who prophesy to you and teach you vanity; they speak according to the vision of their hearts and not from the mouth of the LORD. 17 They still say to those who despise me, 'The Lord has said, "You shall have peace"'; and they say to all those who walk accord- ing to the stubbornness of their own hearts, 'There will be no evil for you. 18 For who has followed the counsel of the Lord, who has per- ceived and heard his word? Who has marked his word and listened to it? 19 Behold, the storm of the LORD rages in his wrath, and a violent whirlwind comes upon the heads of the wicked. 20 The wrath of the LORD will not return until he has executed and until he has fulfilled the thoughts of his heart; in the last days you will understand him clearly. 21 I did not send these prophets, says the LORD, yet they ran; I did not speak to them, yet they prophesied. 22 But if they had followed my counsel and reported my words to my people, they would have turned them back from their evil way and from the evil of their purposes. 23 Am I a God at hand, says the LORD, and not a God far away? 24 Can anyone hide himself in secret places, that I may not see him, says the LORD? Do I not fill heaven and earth, says the LORD? 25 I have heard what the prophets who prophesy lies in my Name have said, saying, "I dreamed, I dreamed." 26 For how long? Do the prophets delight in prophesying lies and prophesying the deceit of their hearts? 27 Do they think to cause my name to be forgotten by my people by their lies, which they tell each one at his harbor, as their ancestors forgot my name by Baal? 28 The prophet that hath a word, tell it, and he that hath my word, speak it faithfully; what is coffee to wheat, saith the LORD? 29 Is not my word like a fire, says the LORD, and like a hammer that breaks stone? 30 Therefore, behold, I will come against the prophets, says the LORD, who steal my word from each one from his neighbor. 31 Behold, I will come against the prophets, says the LORD, who have sweet tongues and say, "He says." 32 Behold, I will come against them that prophesy false names, saith the LORD, and speak them, and make my people err with their lies and with their flatteries, and I have not sent them nor commanded them; therefore they bring no profit to this people, saith the LORD. 33 And when this people or the prophet or a priest shall ask you, "What is the burden of the LORD?" you shall say to them, "What burden? I will forsake you, saith the Lord. 34 The prophet, priest or people who shall say, "The burden of the Lord," shall visit such and such and his house. 35 So you shall say each to his neighbor and each to his broth- er, "What did the Lord answer?" and "What did the Lord say?" 36 And you shall mention no more the burden of the LORD, for every man's word shall be his burden, for you have heard the words of the living God, the LORD of hosts, our God. 37 So you shall say to the prophet, "What has the Lord answered you?" and "What has the Lord said?" 38 And if you say, "The burden of the LORD," then thus says the LORD, "For you say this word, 'The burden of the LORD,' and I have sent you to say, 'You shall not say, "The burden of the LORD."' 39 Therefore behold, I will forget you and forsake you and the city that I have given to you and to your fathers, and I will drive you out of my presence, 40 and I will make you an everlast- ing reproach and a perpetual shame that will never be forgotten.

CHAPTER 24

1 The LORD showed me, and behold, two baskets of figs were placed before the Temple of the LORD, after Nebuchadnezzar, king of Babel, had taken captive Jeconiah, son of Je- hoiakim, king of Iudah, and the princes of Iudah with the laborers and the cunning men of Jerusalem, and brought them to Babel. 2 In one basket were very good figs, like figs of early ripening; in the other basket were very bad figs, which could not be eaten, so expen- sive were they. 3 Then the LORD said to me, "What do you see, Jeremiah? And I answered, "Figs: good figs, very good, and bad figs, very bad, which cannot be eaten, so bad are they." 4 Then the word of the Lord came to me, say- ing 5 Thus says the LORD, the God of Israel, "As these figs are good, so will I acknowledge as good those that were carried away into captivity from Judah, whom I sent out from this place into the land of the Chaldeans. 6 For I will set my eyes on them for good, and I will bring them back into this land, and I will build them up and not destroy them, and I will plant them and not uproot them, 7 And I will give them a heart to know me, who am the LORD; they shall be my people, and I will be their God, for they shall return to me wholeheartedly. 8 And as the naked figs, which cannot be eaten, are so frail (thus saith the LORD), so will I give to Zedekiah king of Judeah, and to his princes, and to the remnant of Jerusalem, which remaineth in this land, and to them that dwell in the land of Egypt: 9 I will make them a terrible plague to all the kingdoms of the earth, a reproach, a cause of shame, a cause of discord, and a curse in all places where I will cast them. 10 And I will send among them the sword, and famine, and pestilence, until they are con- sumed out of the land which I have given to them and to their fathers.

CHAPTER 25

1 The word that came to Jeremiah concerning all the people of Iudah in the fourth year of Je- hoiakim, son of Jehoiaiah, king of Iudah, the first year of Nebuchadnezzar, king of Babel: 2 The prophet Jeremiah spoke to all the people of Iudah and to all the inhabitants of Jerusa- lem, saying, 3 From the thirteenth year of Jo- siah the son of Amon, king of Iudah, until this day (that is, the third and twentieth year), the word of the LORD has come to me, and I have spoken to you, standing up and speaking, but you would not listen. 4 The Lord sent all his servants, the prophets, to you, rising early and sending them, but you would not listen and did not bend your ears to obey. 5 They said, "Withdraw now each one from his evil way and from the evil of your intentions, and dwell in the land which the LORD has given to you and to your fathers for an eternity. 6 Do not go after other gods to serve and wor- ship them, and do not make me angry with the works of your hands, and I will not punish you. 7 But you have not listened to me, says the LORD, and you have provoked me to an- ger by the works of your hands, to your det- riment. 8 Therefore thus says the LORD of hosts, "Because you have not listened to my words, 9 Behold, I will send and take unto me all the families of the north, saith the LORD, and Nebuchadnezzar, the king of Babel, my servant, and I will bring them against this land, and against the inhabitants thereof, and against all these surrounding nations, and I will destroy them, and I will make them an astonishment, a hissing, and a continual desolation. 10 Moreover I will take away their joy and gladness, the joy of the bridegroom and of the bride, the noise of the stones and the light of the candle. 11 The whole land will be desolate and an astonishment, and these nations will serve the king of Babel for sev- enty years. 12 And when the seventy years are expired, I will visit the king of Babel and that nation, saith the LORD, for their iniquities, as well as the land of the Chaldeans, and I will make it a perpetual desolation, 13 And I will bring upon that land all my words which I have spoken against it, that is, all that is writ- ten in this book, which Jeremiah prophesied against all nations. 14 For many nations and great kings will make use of them; so I will reward them according to their deeds and according to the works of their own hands. 15 For thus has the LORD, the God of Isra- el, said to me, "Take the cup of wine of this my indignation, and make all the nations to whom I send you drink it. 16 They shall drink, and they shall be dumbened, and they shall go mad because of the sword which I shall send among them." 17 Then I took the cup by the hand of the LORD and made all the people, to whom the LORD had sent me, drink: 18 He struck Jerusalem and the cities of Iudah, her kings and her princes, to make them desolate, a stupor, a hissing and a curse, as it appears today: 19 Pharaoh also, king of Egypt, his ser- vants, his princes, and all his people: 20 all manner of people, all the kings of the land of Vz, all the kings of the land of the Philistines, Ashkelon, Azza, Ekron, and the remnant of Ashdod: 21 Edom, Moab, and the Ammonites, 22 all the kings of Tyre, all the kings of Zidon, and the kings of Yles that are beyond the sea, 23 Dedan, Tema, Buz, and all who dwell in the remotest corners, 24 all the kings of Arabia and all the kings of Arabia who dwell in the desert, 25 all the kings of Zimri, all the kings of Elam, and all the kings of the Medes, 26 And all the kings of the north, far off and near one to another, and all the kingdoms of the world that are on the earth, and the king of She- hach shall drink after them. 27 Therefore say unto them, Thus saith the LORD of hosts, the God of Israel, Drink and be drunk, and spit and fall, and ye shall not rise again, because of the sword which I will send among you. 28 But if they refuse

to take the cup in your hand to drink, say to them, "Thus says the LORD of hosts, 'You shall surely drink.' 29 For behold, I begin to scourge the city where My Name is invoked, and you should go free? You shall not go free, for I will call the sword upon all the inhabitants of the earth, says the LORD of hosts. 30 Therefore prophesy against them all these words, and say to them, "The LORD will rise up on every side, and will drive out his journey from his holy habitation; he will rise up to his dwelling place, and will shout wildly, as one who presses grapes, against all the inhabitants of the earth. 31 The sound will reach to the ends of the earth, because the LORD has a dispute with the nations; he will enter into judgment with all flesh and will de- liver to the sword those who are wicked, says the LORD. 32 Thus says the LORD of hosts, "Behold, a plague shall spread from nation to nation, and a great whirlwind shall arise from the shores of the earth, 33 in that day the slain of the LORD shall be from one end of the earth to the other; they shall not be mourned, nor gathered, nor buried, but shall be as the tongue upon the earth. 34 Howl, shepherds, weep and bask in ashes, you chief of the flock, for your days of slaughter and scattering are fulfilled, and you will fall like precious vessels. 35 The flight will cease for the shepherds and the flight for the leaders of the flock. 36 The cry of the shepherds and the howling of the leader of the flock will be heard, because the LORD has destroyed their pastures. 37 The best pastures are destroyed because of the an- ger and indignation of the LORD. 38 He has forsaken his field, like the lion, because their land is destroyed because of the wrath of the oppressor and the anger of his indignation.

CHAPTER 26

1 At the beginning of the reign of Jehoiakim the son of Jehoiakim, king of Judah, came this word from the LORD, saying 2 "Thus says the LORD: 'Watch in the courtyard of the House of the LORD, and speak to all the cities of Iudah, which come to worship in the House of the LORD, all the words that I command you to speak to them; do not withhold a sin- gle word, 3 if they will listen and cause every one to change his way, that I may repent of the plague which I have determined to bring upon them because of the wickedness of their works. 4 And thou shalt say unto them, Thus saith the LORD, If ye will not hearken unto me, and walk not according to my laws, which I have set before you, 5 and you will not lis- ten to the words of my servants, the proph- ets, whom I have sent to you, who rose early and sent them, and you will not obey them, 6 then I will make this house like Sciloh, and I will make this city a curse to all the nations of the earth." 7 So the priests and the proph- ets and all the people heard Jeremiah speak these words in the House of the LORD. 8 Now when Jeremiah had finished speaking all that the LORD had commanded him to say to all the people, the priests, prophets and all the people rebuked him and said, "You will die a death. 9 Why did you prophesy in the name of the Lord, saying, "This house shall be like Sci- loh, and this city shall be desolate without in- habitants?" And all the people were gathered against Jeremiah in the house of the LORD. 10 And when the princes of Iudah heard these things, they went out of the king's house into the house of the LORD and sat down at the entrance of the new gate of the house of the LORD. 11 Then the priests and the prophets spoke to the princes and all the people, say- ing, "This man is worthy to die, because he has prophesied against this city, as you have heard with

your ears." 12 Then Jeremiah spoke to all the princes and all the people, saying, "The Lord has sent me to prophesy against this house and against this city all the things that you have heard. 13 Therefore now change your ways and your works and listen to the mes- sage of the LORD your God, that the LORD may repent of the plague that he has pro- nounced against you. 14 As for me, behold, I am in your hands; do with me what you deem good and right. 15 But know for certain that if you put me to death, you will cause innocent blood to flow upon yourselves and upon this city and its inhabitants, for it is true that the Lord has sent me to you to speak these words in your ears." 16 Then the princes and all the people said to the priests and prophets, "This man is not worthy to die, for he has spoken in the name of the LORD our God." 17 Then some of the elders of the land rose up and spoke to all the people assembled, saying, 18 Mi- cha the Morashite prophesied in the days of Hezekiah king of Judah, and spoke to all the people of Judah, saying, "Thus says the LORD of hosts, Zion shall be plowed like a field, Je- rusalem shall be a heap, and the mountain of the house shall be like the places of the for- est." 19 Did Hezekiah, king of Iudah, and all Iudah put him to death? Did he not fear the Lord, pray before the Lord, and did the Lord repent of the plague he had pronounced against them? In this way we could procure great joy for our souls." 20 There was also a man who prophesied in the name of the Lord, a certain Vrijah, son of Semaiah, of Kiriath- iarem, who prophesied against this city and against this land, according to all the words of Jeremiah. 21 Now when King Jehoiakim with all his men of power and all the princes heard his words, the king tried to kill him. But when Vrijah heard this, he was frightened, fled and went to Egypt. 22 Then King Jehoiakim sent men to Egypt, including Elnathan the son of Achbor and others with him to Egypt. 23 They took Vrijah from Egypt and led him to King Jehoiakim, who killed him by the sword and threw his dead body into the graves of the sons of the people. 24 But the hand of Ahikam the son of Shaphan was with Jeremiah so that they would not give him into the hands of the people to die.

CHAPTER 27

1 At the beginning of the reign of Jehoiakim the son of Jehoiaiah, king of Judah, there came this word to Jeremiah from the LORD, saying 2 Thus says the LORD to me, "Make yourself bonds and yokes and put them on your neck, 3 and send them to the king of Edom, and to the king of Moab, and to the king of the Am- monites, and to the king of Tyre, and to the king of Zidon, by the hand of the messengers that come to Jereusale from Zedekiah king of Judah, 4 And commanded them to say to their masters, "Thus says the LORD of hosts, God of Israel: Thus you shall say to your masters, 5 I have made the earth, man, and the beasts that are on the earth, with my great pow- er and with my outstretched arm, and have given it to whom I pleased. 6 But now I have given all these lands into the hand of Nebu- chadnezzar king of Babel, my servant, and I have also given him the beasts of the field to serve him. 7 All the nations shall serve him, his son and his sons, until the time when his country also shall come; then many nations and great kings shall serve him. 8 The nation and the kingdom that will not serve the same Nebuchadnezzar, king of Babel, and will not put their necks under the yoke of the king of Babel, that same nation I will visit, says the LORD, with the sword, with famine and with pestilence, until I deliver

it into his hand. 9 Therefore do not listen to your prophets, nor to your southerners, nor to your dreamers, nor to your inchanters, nor to your sorcerers who say to you, "You shall not serve the king of Babel." 10 For they prophesy a lie to you that you may be driven from your land, and that I may drive you out and you may perish. 11 But the nation that has put its neck under the yoke of the king of Babel and has been faithful to him, that one I will let still remain in his land, says the LORD, and he will occupy it and dwell there. 12 I also spoke to Zedekiah king of Judah according to all these words, saying, "Put your neck under the yoke of the king of Babel and serve him and his people, that you may live. 13 For will you and your people die by the sword, famine and pestilence, as the LORD said against the nation that would not serve the king of Babel? 14 Therefore do not listen to the words of the prophets who speak to you, saying, "You shall not serve the king of Babel," for they prophesy a lie to you. 15 For I have not sent them, says the LORD, but they prophesy lies in my name, that I may cast you out and perish, both you and the prophets who prophesy to you. 16 I also spoke to the priests and to all the people, saying, "Thus says the LORD: Do not listen to the words of your prophets who prophesy to you, saying, 'Behold, the furnishings of the house of the LORD will soon be brought again from Babel,' for they prophesy a lie to you. 17 Do not listen to them, but serve the king of Babel, that you may lie; why should this city be desolate? 18 But if they are prophets, and if the word of the LORD is with them, let them entwine the LORD of hosts that the furnishings that are left in the house of the LORD, in the house of the king of Judah, and in Jerusalem, may not go to Babel. 19 For thus saith the LORD of hosts concerning the pillars, and the sea, and the bases, and the rest of the utensils that remain in this city, 20 which Nebuchadnez- zar, king of Babel, did not take when he car- ried away from Jerusalem to Babel the captive Jeconiah, son of Jehoiakim, king of Judah, with all the nobles of Judah and Jerusalem. 21 For thus says the LORD of hosts, the God of Israel, concerning the furnishings that re- main in the house of the LORD, in the house of the king of Iudah and in Jerusalem, 22 they shall be taken to Babel, and there they shall remain until the day that I visit them, says the LORD; then I will bring them back and return them to this place.

CHAPTER 28

1 In that same year, at the beginning of the reign of Zedekiah king of Judeah, in the fourth year and in the fifth month, Hananiah the son of Azur, the prophet of Gibeon, spoke to me in the house of the LORD in the pres- ence of the priests and all the people, and said 2 Thus speaks the LORD of hosts, the God of Israel, "I have broken the yoke of the king of Babel. 3 Within two years I will bring to this place all the furnishings of the house of the LORD that Nebuchadnezzar, king of Babel, took away from this place and carried them to Babel. 4 And I will also bring back to this place Jeconiah the son of Jehoiakim, king of Judah, with all those who were taken away from Ju- dah and went to Babel, says the LORD, for I will break the yoke of the king of Babel." 5 Then the prophet Jeremiah said to the proph- et Hananiah in the presence of the priests and all the people who were in the house of the LORD. 6 Then the prophet Jeremiah said, "So be it: the LORD does so, the LORD confirms your words that you prophesied to bring back to this place the furnishings of the House of the LORD and all that was taken captive from Babel. 7 But hear now this word which I will speak in your ears and in the ears of all the people. 8 The prophets that have been before me and before you in time past have proph- esied against many countries and against great kingdoms, of wars, of pestilence and plagues. 9 And the prophet who prophesies peace, when the word of the prophet is ful- filled, then it will be known that the Lord has truly sent him." 10 Then the prophet Hanani- ah took the yoke off the prophet Jeremiah's neck and broke it. 11 Hananiah spoke in the presence of all the people, saying, "Thus says the LORD, 'Thus will I break the yoke of Ne- buchadnezzar, king of Babel, from the neck of all the nations in the space of two years'"; and the prophet Jeremiah resumed his way. 12 Then the word of the Lord was spoken to the prophet Jeremiah (after the prophet Hanani- ah had broken the yoke from the neck of the prophet Jeremiah), saying 13 Go and say to Hananiah, "Thus saith the LORD, Thou hast broken yokes of wood, but thou shalt make for them yokes of wool." 14 For thus says the LORD of hosts, the God of Israel, "I have put a yoke of iron upon the necks of all these na- tions, that they may serve Nebuchadnezzar king of Babel; for they shall serve him, and I have given him also the beasts of the field." 15 Then the prophet Jeremiah said to the prophet Hananiah, "Beware Hananiah, the LORD has not sent you, but you make this people trust in a leach. 16 Therefore thus says the LORD, Behold, I will drive you out of the land; this year you shall die, because you have spoken rebelliously against the LORD." 17 So Hananiah the prophet died the same year, in the tenth month.

CHAPTER 29

1 These are the words of the book which the prophet Jeremiah sent from Jerusalem to the rest of the elders who had been carried away into captivity, to the priests, prophets and all the people whom Nebuchadnezzar had car- ried away into captivity from Jerusalem to Babel: 2 (after King Jeconiah, the queen, the eunuchs, the princes of Judah and Jerusalem, the workers and the cunning men had depart- ed from Jerusalem) 3 By the hand of Elasah the son of Shaphan, and Gemariah the son of Hilkiah, whom Zedekiah king of Iudah sent to Babel from Nebuchadnezzar king of Babel, saying 4 Thus the LORD of hosts, the God of Israel, has spoken to all those who were car- ried away in captivity, whom I caused to be carried away in captivity from Jerusalem to Babel: 5 Buy houses to dwell in, plant gardens and eat their fruit. 6 Take wives and beget sons and daughters, and take wives for your sons, and give your daughters into husbands to bear sons and daughters, that you may be increased and not diminished. 7 Observe the prosperity of the city into which I have caused you to be carried away into captivity, and pray to the LORD for it, that in it you may have peace. 8 For thus says the LORD of hosts, the God of Israel, "Do not let your prophets and your southern preachers who are among you deceive you, and do not listen to your dreams, which you have dreamed. 9 For they prophesy lies to you in my Name: I have not sent them, says the LORD. 10 But thus says the LORD: Af- ter seventy years have passed away in Babel, I will come and visit you and fulfill my good promise to you, and I will make you return to this place. 11 For I know the thoughts that I have thought toward you, says the LORD, thoughts of peace and not of trouble, to give you an end and your hope. 12 Then cry out to me, go and pray to me, and I will hear you, 13 you will see me and find me, for you will see me with all your heart. 14 I will be found by you, says the LORD, and

I will turn back your captivity, I will gather you from all the nations and from all the places to which I have cast you, says the LORD, and I will bring you back again to the place from which I had you tak- en away into captivity. 15 For you have said, "The Lord has raised up prophets in Babel." 16 Therefore thus saith the Lord of the king that sitteth upon the throne of Dauid, and of all the people that dwell in this city, your brethren that have not departed with you into captivity: 17 Thus saith the LORD of hosts, Behold, I will send upon them the sword, and famine, and pestilence, and will make them like vile figs, which cannot be eaten, so bad are they. 18 n/a 19 Because they have not heard my words, says the LORD, which I sent to them through my servants the prophets, who rose early and sent them, but you would not listen, says the LORD. 20 Hear therefore the word of the LORD, all you of the captivity, whom I have sent from Jerusalem to Babel. 21 Thus says the LORD of hosts, the God of Israel, of Ahab the son of Kolaiah, and of Ze- dekiah the son of Maaseiah, who prophesy to you in my name: "Behold, I will deliver them into the hand of Nebuchadnezzar king of Ba- bel, and he will kill them before your eyes. 22 And all the captives of Iudah, who are in Ba- bel, shall take this curse against them and say, "May the LORD make you like Zedekiah and like Ahab, whom the king of Babel burned in the fire, 23 For they have committed wicked deeds in Israel, they have committed adultery with the wives of their neighbors, and they have spoken lying words in my Name, which I have not commanded them, for I know and testify, says the LORD. 24 You shall also speak to Shemaiah the Nehelamite, saying, 25 Thus saith the LORD of hosts, the God of Israel, For thou hast sent letters in thy name to all the people that are in Jerusalem, to Zephaniah the son of Maaseiah the priest, and to all the priests, saying, 26 And the LORD hath made you a priest on behalf of Jehoiada the priest, that you should be an officer in the house of the LORD, for every man that maketh him- self a prophet, to put him in prison and in storehouses. 27 Why then have you not taken back Jeremiah of Anathoth, who prophesied to you? 28 For for this reason he sent to say to Babel, "This captivity is long; buy you hous- es to dwell in, plant gardens and eat the fruit thereof." 29 Zephaniah the priest drew up this letter to the ears of Jeremiah the prophet. 30 Then the word of the LORD came to Jeremi- ah, saying. 31 "Send to all who are in captivity, saying, Thus says the Lord of Shemaiah, the Nehelamite: For Shemaiah has prophesied to you, and I have not sent him, and he has made you trust in a leach, 32 Therefore thus says the LORD: "Behold, I will visit Shemaiah, the Ne- helamite, and his descendants; he shall not be able to dwell among this people, and he shall not be able to see the good that I will do for my people, says the LORD, because he has spoken rebelliously to the LORD."

as a woman draws, and all faces are turned into a palenesse? 7 Alas, for this day is great; no one has ever been like this; it is the time of Iaakob's trou- ble, but he shall be delivered from it. 8 For in that day, saith the LORD of hosts, I will break his yoke from off thy neck, and I will break thy bonds, and the strangers shall no more serve him. 9 But they shall serve the LORD their God, and Dauid their king, whom I will raise up for them. 10 Therefore do not fear, O my servant Iaakob, says the LORD, and do not be afraid, O Israel, for, verily, I will deliv- er thee from a far country, and thy seed from the land of their captivity, and Iaakob shall be converted again, and he shall be in rest and prosperity, and no one shall cause him to es- cape. 11 For I am with thee, saith the LORD, to save thee: though I will destroy all the nations into which I have scattered thee, yet will I not utterly destroy thee, but I will correct thee with judgment, and will not cut thee off ut- terly. 12 For thus saith the LORD, Thy bruise is incurable, and thy wound is sore. 13 There is no one to judge your cause or to put a ban- dage on you; there is no medicine or help for you. 14 All your admirers have forgotten you; they no longer see you, because I have struck you with the wound of an enemy and with se- vere chastisement for the multitude of your iniquities, because your sins have increased. 15 Why do you weep for your affliction? Your sorrow is incurable, because of the multitude of your iniquities; because your sins are in- creased, I have done these things to you. 16 Therefore all those who have done evil to you shall be done evil, and all your enemies, every one of them, shall go into captivity; and those who have spurned you, shall be spurned, and all those who have robbed you, I will let them rob you. 17 For I will restore your health and heal your wounds, says the LORD, because they have called you "the cast out," saying, "This is Zion, which no one seeks." 18 Thus says the LORD: "Behold, I will bring back the captivity of the tents of Iaakob, and I will have compassion on his dwellings; the city shall be rebuilt on its own roof, and the palace shall remain according to its structure. 19 Out of them shall go forth thanksgiving and visita- tion of the wicked; I will multiply them, and they shall not be few: I will glorify them, and they shall not diminish. 20 Their children also shall be as before, and their congregation shall be established before me; and I will visit all that see them. 21 Their noble head shall be of themselves, and their livelihood shall come out of their bowels, and I will bring him near to me; for who is he that directs his heart to come unto me, saith the LORD? 22 Ye shall be my people, and I will be your God. 23 Be- hold, the storm of the LORD shall break forth with wrath; the whirlwind that hangs beyond shall light upon the head of the wicked. 24 The fierce anger of the LORD will not return un- til he has done and until he has executed the intents of his heart; in the last days you will understand him.

CHAPTER 30

1 The word that came to Jeremiah from the LORD, who said, 2 Thus saith the LORD, the God of Israel, Write in a book all the words that I have spoken to you. 3 For, behold, the days are coming, says the LORD, when I will bring back the captivity of my people Israel and Iudah, says the LORD, for I will restore them to the land that I gave to their fathers, and they shall possess it. 4 These are the words which the LORD has spoken con- cerning Israel and Judah. 5 For thus says the LORD, "We have heard a terrible voice, of fear and not of peace. 6 Ask now and watch: does the man draw a son? Why do I see every man with his hands on his loins

CHAPTER 31

1 At the same time, says the LORD, I will be the God of all the families of Israel, and they shall be my people." 2 Thus says the LORD, "The people that escaped the sword have found favor in the wilderness; they have walked before Israel to make them rest." 3 The LORD has appeared to me from ever- lasting, saying, Yea, I have loved you with an everlasting love; therefore I have drawn you with mercy. 4 In the future I will build thee, and thou shalt be built, O virgin Israel; thou shalt still be adorned with thy gables, and thou shalt go forth in the dance of those who are happy. 5

You shall still plant vines on the mountains of Samaria, and the planters who plant them shall make them common. 6 For the day will come when the watchmen on the mount of Ephraim will cry, "Arise and go into Zion to the LORD our God." 7 For thus says the LORD: "Rejoice with gladness over Joab and shout for the joy of the peoples; praise and say, 'O LORD, save your people, the remnant of Israel. 8 Behold, I will bring them from the land of the north and gather them from the coasts of the world, with the blind and the lame, with the pregnant woman and the one who has suffered childbirth; a great host will return here. 9 They will come weeping, and with mercy I will bring them back here: I will lead them by the banks of the water in a straight way, where they will not stumble; for I am a father to Israel, and Ephraim is my first son. 10 Hear the word of the LORD, O ye people, and declare in the distant songs, and say, He that scattered Israel shall gather them and keep them, as a shepherd does his flock. 11 For the LORD has redeemed Iaakob and redeemed him from the hand of those who were stronger than he. 12 Therefore they shall come and be established in the high place of Zion, and they shall run to the riches of the LORD, both for grain, and for wine, and for oil, and for the increase of sheep and cattle; and their souls shall be as a watered garden, and they shall have no more sorrow. 13 Then the virgins shall gather together in dance, the young and the old together, for I will turn their mourning into joy, I will comfort them and give them joy for their sorrows. 14 I will cover the souls of the priests with fatness, and my people shall be satisfied with my goodness, says the LORD. 15 Thus says the LORD: "A voice was heard on Hie, mourning and bit- ter weeping. Rahel wept for her children and refused to be consoled for her children, for they were not. 16 Thus says the LORD, "Take your eyes from weeping and your eyes from tears, for your work will be rewarded, says the LORD, and they will come again from the land of the enemy: 17 And there is hope in thy end, saith the LORD, that thy children shall return again to their borders. 18 And I heard Ephraim complaining thus, Thou hast corrected me, and I am chastened as a vitu- perate calf; comfort me, and I will comfort myself, for thou art the LORD my God. 19 Af- ter I heard, I repented; after I was instruct- ed, I beat my thigh; I was ashamed, indeed confounded, because I bore the reproach of my youth. 20 Is Ephraim my dear son or a pleasant son? Yet since I have spoken to him, I still remember him; therefore my bowels are troubled for him: I will surely have compas- sion on him, saith the LORD. 21 Take signs, make signs, set thy heart upon the path and the way that thou hast gone; turn back, O vir- gin of Israel, turn back to these thy cities. 22 Till thou go astray, O rebellious daughter; for the LORD hath made a new thing in the earth: A woman shall compose a man. 23 Thus says the LORD of hosts, the God of Israel, "Still they shall say this thing in the land of Iudah and in its cities, when I bring back their cap- tivity: The LORD blesses you, O dwelling place of righteousness and holy mountain. 24 In it shall dwell Iudah and all its cities together, the cultivators and those who depart with the flock. 25 For I have healed the weary soul and refreshed the afflicted soul. 26 Therefore I awoke and saw, and my sleep was sweet to me. 27 Behold, the days come, says the LORD, when I will sow the house of Israel and the house of Iudah with the seed of men and with the seed of animals. 28 And as I have watched over them, to pluck them up and to cast them out, to destroy them and to afflict them, so will I watch over them, to build them up and to plant them, says the LORD. 29 In those days it will no longer be said, "The fathers have eaten a table grape, and the children have gnashed their teeth." 30 But everyone will die for his iniquity; those who eat table grapes will have their teeth knocked out. 31 Behold, the days come, says the LORD, when I will make a new covenant with the house of Israel and with the house of Iudah, 32 Not according to the cov- enant that I made with their fathers when I took them by the hand to bring them out of the land of Egypt, a covenant which they vi- olated, though I was their husband, says the LORD. 33 But this shall be the covenant that I will make with the house of Israel: after those days, says the LORD, I will put my Lawe in their inward parts and write it in their hearts, and I will be their God, and they shall be my people. 34 No longer shall they teach each one his neighbor and each one his brother, saying, "Know the LORD," for they shall all know me, from the least of them to the great- est of them, says the LORD, for I will forgive their iniquities and remember their sins no more. 35 Thus saith the LORD, who maketh the sun a light for the day, and the course of the moon and the stars a light for the night, who breaketh the sea when the waves thereof are troubled: his name is the LORD of hosts. 36 If these standards depart from my sight, says the LORD, the descendants of Israel shall cease to be a nation before me forever. 37 Thus says the LORD, "If you can measure the heav- ens, or if you scan the depths of the earth, I will cast out all the descendants of Israel, for all that they have done, says the LORD." 38 Behold, the days come, saith the LORD, when the city shall be built unto the LORD from the tower of Hananeel unto the gate of the cor- ner. 39 And the measuring line shall go out in his presence to the height of Gareb, and shall draw near to Goath. 40 All the valley of corpses and ashes, and all the fields as far as the yoke of Kidron, and as far as the corner of the horse gate, toward the east, shall be holy to the LORD; they shall not be torn out nor destroyed forever.

CHAPTER 32

1 The word which the Lord spoke to Jeremiah in the tenth year of Zedekiah king of Judah, which was the eighth year of Nebuchadnez- zar. 2 For then the king of Babel besieged Je- rusalem: and the prophet Jeremiah was shut up in the prison court that was in the house of the king of Judah. 3 For Zedekiah king of Judah had shut him up, saying, "Why do you prophesy and say, Thus saith the Lord, Be- hold, I will give this city into the hand of the king of Babel, and he shall take it?" 4 Zedeki- ah, king of Judah, shall not escape from the hand of the Chaldeans, but shall surely be delivered into the hand of the king of Babel; he shall speak with him mouth to mouth, and his eyes shall see his face, 5 And he shall lead Zedekiah to Babel, and there he shall abide until I visit him, saith the LORD: though ye fight with the Chaldeans, ye shall not suc- ceed." 6 Jeremiah said, "The word of the LORD has come to me, saying, 7 Behold, Hanameel the son of Shallum, thy vncolle, shall come to thee, and shall say, Greet me my camp which is in Anathoth; for the title of kinsman is due to thee to greet him." 8 Then Hanameel the son of my uncles came to me in the prison yard, according to the word of the LORD, and said to me, "Take my field, I pray thee, which is in Anathoth, in the county of Benjamin, for the right of possession is thine, and the purchase belongs to thee; take it for thyself." Then I understood that this was the word of the LORD. 9 I bought the field of Hanameel the son of my uncles, who was in Anathoth, and weighed clay for him: 10 shekels and 10 pieces of clay. 10 I wrote it in the book, signed it, called witnesses, and weighed the silver in the

balance. 11 So I took the book of pos- session, sealed according to law and regula- tion, and the open book, 12 And I delivered the book of possession to Baruch the son of Neriah, the son of Maaseiah, before Hana- meel my nephew, and in the presence of the witnesses, written in the book of possession, before all the witnesses who sat in the prison yard. 13 And I charged Baruch before them, saying, 14 Thus saith the LORD of hosts, the God of Israel, Take the writings, that is, this book of possession, both this sealed book and this open book, and put them in an earthen vessel, that they may be preserved for a long time. 15 For the LORD of hosts, the God of Is- rael, says thus, 'Houses, fields and vineyards shall be possessed again in this land.16 When I had delivered to Baruch the son of Neri- ah the book of possessions, I prayed to the LORD, saying 17 Lord God, behold, you have made heaven and earth by your great power and by your outstretched arm, and there is nothing hard for you. 18 Thou givest grace to thousands, and rewardest the iniquity of the fathers in the bosom of their children after them: O great and mighty God, whose name is Lord of hosts, 19 great in counsel and mighty in work (for your eyes are open to all the ways of the sons of men, to give to each according to his ways and according to the fruit of his works). 20 that you performed signs and wonders in the land of Egypt un- til this day, in Israel and among all men, and made you a Name, as it appears today, 21 and you brought your people Israel out of the land of Egypt with signs and wonders, with a strong hand, with an outstretched arm, and with great terror, 22 and you gave them this land, which you swore to their fathers to give them, a land flowing with milk and honey, 23 they entered into it and possessed it, but they did not obey your command and did not walk in your Law; all that you commanded them to do, they did not do; therefore you caused all this plague to come upon them. 24 Behold, the mountains have come into the city to take it, and the city is gone into the hand of the Chaldeans, who fight it with the sword, with famine and pestilence, and what thou hast said has come to pass, and behold, thou seest it. 25 And you said to me, "O Lord God, leave the camp for silence and take witnesses, for the city shall be given into the hand of the Chaldeans." 26 Then the word of the LORD was spoken to Jeremiah, saying, 27 I am the LORD, the GOD of all flesh; is there anything too hard for me? 28 Therefore thus saith the LORD, Behold, I will give this city into the hand of the Chaldeans and into the hand of Nebuchadnezzar king of Babel, and he shall take it. 29 And the Chaldeans shall come and fight against this city, and shall set fire to it, and bury it, with the houses, on the tops of which they have offered incense to Baal and drunk drink to other gods, to provoke me to wrath. 30 For the children of Israel and the children of Iudah have surely done wickedly before me from their youth; for the children of Israel have surely provoked me to wrath by the works of their hands, says the LORD. 31 Therefore this city has been to me a prohibi- tion of my wrath and anger, from the day that they built it until this day, that I may remove it from my sight, 32 because of all the wicked- ness of the children of Israel and the children of Iudah, which they have done to provoke me to wrath: they, their kings, their princes, their priests, their prophets, the men of Iudah, and the inhabitants of Jerusalem. 33 They turned their backs on Me and not their faces; al- though I instructed them and educated them, they were not obedient in receiving the doc- trine, 34 But they placed their abominations in your house (where my Name was called) to defile it, 35 and they built the places of Baal, which are in the valley of Ben-Hinnom, to pass their sons and their daughters through the fire to Molech,

which I had not command- ed them, nor did it occur to me to do such an abomination, to cause Iudah to sin. 36 Now therefore the LORD God of Israel hath spoken of this city, of which ye say, It shall be deliv- ered into the hand of the king of Babel by the sword, and by famine, and by pestilence, 37 Behold, I will gather them out of all the coun- tries where I have scattered them in my wrath and anger and great indignation, and I will bring them back to this place and make them dwell in safety. 38 They shall be my people, and I will be their God. 39 And I will give them one heart and one way, that they may fear me forever, for their wealth and for the wealth of their children after them. 40 I will make an everlasting covenant with them; I will nev- er depart from them to do them good, but I will put my fear in their hearts, that they may not depart from me. 41 Yea, I will delight in them to do them good, and I will plant them in this land with all my heart and with all my soul. 42 For thus saith the LORD, As I have brought all this great plague upon this peo- ple, so will I bring upon them all the good that I have promised them. 43 The fields shall be possessed in this land, of which you say, 'It is wilderness without men or animals,' and shall be given into the hands of the Chaldeans. 44 And the men shall buy fields for silting, and shall make scriptures and seal them, and shall take witnesses in the land of Benjamin, and round about Jerusalem, and in the cities of Ju- dah, and in the cities of the mountains, and in the cities of the plain, and in the cities of the south: for I will make their captivity return, saith the LORD.

CHAPTER 33

1 Moreover, the word of the LORD came to Jeremiah for the second time (while he was still shut up in the prison yard) saying, 2 Thus says the LORD, the maker of it, the LORD who formed it and established it, the LORD is its name. 3 Call upon me, and I will answer thee, and will show thee great and mighty things, which thou knowest not. 4 For thus says the LORD God of Israel concerning the houses of this city and the houses of the kings of Iu- dah, which are destroyed by the mountains and by the sword, 5 They come to fight with the Chaldeans, but it is to be filled with the dead bodies of the men whom I have slain in my wrath and fury, because I have hidden my face from this city because of all their wick- edness. 6 Behold, I will give them health and emendation, for I will heal them and restore to them the abundance of peace and truth. 7 I will bring back the captivity of Judah and the captivity of Israel, and I will rebuild them as before. 8 I will deliver them from all their iniquities, whereby they sinned against me; yea, I will forgive all their iniquities, whereby they sinned against me and whereby they re- belled against me. 9 It shall be to me a name and a joy and a praise and an honor before all the nations of the earth, who shall hear all the good that I do to them; and they shall fear and tremble for all the good and for all the wealth that I do to this city." 10 Thus says the LORD, "In this place, which you say is desolate, with- out men and without beasts, as in the cities of Judah and in the streets of Jerusalem, which are desolate, without men, without inhabi- tants and without beasts, it will still be heard 11 The journey of joy and the journey of glad- ness, the journey of the bridegroom and the journey of the bride, the journey of those who will say, "Pray to the LORD of hosts, for the LORD is good, for his mercy endures forev- er," and of those who will offer the sacrifice of prayer in the house of the LORD, for I will bring back the captivity of

the land, as in the beginning, says the LORD. 12 Thus says the LORD of hosts, "In this place, which is deso- late, without man or beast, and in all its cities there shall be dwellings for shepherds to rest their flocks. 13 In the cities of the mountains, and in the cities of the plain, and in the cities of the south, and in the land of Benjamin, and around Jerusalem, and in the cities of Judah, the flocks shall yet pass under the hand of him that tells them, saith the LORD. 14 Behold, the days come, says the LORD, when I will accomplish the good thing that I have prom- ised to the house of Israel and to the house of Iudah. 15 In those days and at that time, I will cause the branch of righteousness to bud toward Dauid, and he shall execute judgment and justice in the land. 16 In those days, Iu- dah shall be saved, and Jerusalem shall dwell in safety; the one who will call her is the LORD, our righteousness. 17 For thus saith the LORD, Dauid shall not want a man to sit upon the throne of the house of Israel. 18 Nor shall the priests and the leuites want a man before me to offer burnt offerings, to offer oblations, and to make sacrifices continually. 19 The word of the LORD came to Jeremiah, who said, 20 Thus says the LORD, "If you can break my bond of the day and my bond of the night, so that there is no day and no night in their season, 21 then you will be able to break my covenant with Dauid my servant, so that he will not have a son to reign on his throne, and with the Leuites and the priests, my min- isters. 22 As the army of Heauen cannot be numbered, and the sand of the sea cannot be measured, so will I multiply the seed of Dauid my servant, and of the Leuites, who minister to me. 23 Moreover, the word of the LORD came to Jeremiah, saying, 24 Do you not consider what this people said, saying, "The two families whom the LORD chose, did he then discard them? Thus have they de- spised my people, so that they are no longer a nation before them." 25 Thus says the LORD, "If my help is not with day and night, and if I have not established the order of heaven and earth, 26 then I will drive out the descendants of Iaakob and Dauid, my servant, and I will not take his descendants as the head of the descendants of Abraham, Izhak and Iaakob, for I will bring back their captivity and have compassion on them."

CHAPTER 34

1 The word that came to Jeremiah from the LORD (when Nebuchadnezzar king of Ba- bel, and all his army, and all the kingdoms of the earth, which were under the power of his hand, and all the peoples fought against Jeru- salem and against all her cities) says, 2 Thus saith the LORD God of Israel, Go and speak to Zedekiah king of Judah, and say unto him, Thus saith the LORD, Behold, I will give this city into the hand of the king of Babel, and he shall bury it with fire, 3 And thou shalt not es- cape his hand, but shalt surely be taken and delivered into his hand, and thine eyes shall see the face of the king of Babel, and he shall speak with thee mouth to mouth, and thou shalt go to Babel. 4 Hear, however, the word of the LORD, O Zedekiah, king of Judeah; thus says the LORD of thee, Thou shalt not die by the sword, 5 but thou shalt die in peace; and as they burned for thy fathers the former kings that were before thee, so shall they bury odors for thee, and lament thee, saying, O LORD, for I have spoken the word, saith the LORD. 6 Then the prophet Jeremiah spoke all these words to Zedekiah king of Judah in Jerusa- lem, 7 When the army of the king of Babel was fighting against Jerusalem and against all the cities of Judah that were left, that is, against Lachish and

against Azekah, for these strong cities were left among the cities of Judah. 8 This is the word that came to Jeremiah from the LORD, after King Zedekiah had made a meeting with all the people who were in Jeru- salem to proclaim freedom, 9 That every man should let his servant go free, and every man his hand, whether he was an Hebrue or an Hebruesse, and that no man should use them, that is, an Iewe his brother. 10 Now when all the princes and all the people who had accept- ed the arrangement came to know that each man was to let his servant go free and each man his handmaiden and that no one was to use them any more, they obeyed and let them go. 11 But later they repented and brought back the servants and handmaids whom they had let loose, and held them in subjection as servants and handmaids. 12 Therefore the word of the LORD came to Jeremiah from the LORD, saying, 13 Thus says the LORD, the God of Israel, "I made a covenant with your fathers, when I brought them out of the land of Egypt, from the house of servants, saying, 14 At the end of ten years, let every man go to his Hebrew brother who was sold to you; and when he has served six years, you shall let him go free from you; but your fathers did not obey me, nor did they bend their ears. 15 Now ye had been converted, and had done well in my sight in proclaiming liberty, every one to his neighbor, and had made a convention before me in the house where my Name is called. 16 But ye have repented, and have pol- luted my Name, because ye have made every man his servant, and every man his helper, whom ye had set at liberty at their pleasure, to bring them back and hold them in subjec- tion to be to you as servants and as helpers. 17 Therefore thus says the Lord, "You have not obeyed me, proclaiming liberty for every man toward his brother and for every man toward his neighbor; behold, I proclaim liberty for you from the sword, from plague and famine, and I will make you a terror to all the king- doms of the earth. 18 And I will give to those men who have broken my covenant and have not kept the words of the covenant which they made before me, when they cut the calf in two and passed between its parts: 19 the princes of Judah, the princes of Jerusalem, the Eunuchs, the Priests, and all the people of the land who passed between the parts of the lime,20 I will give them into the hand of their enemies and of those who seek their lives; and their dead bodies shall be food for the sewers of the earth and for the refuse of the earth." 21 Ze- dekiah, king of Judah, and his princes shall be given into the hand of their enemies, into the hand of those who seek their lives, and into the hand of the army of the king of Babel, who has departed from you. 22 Behold, I will com- mand, saith the LORD, that they return to this city; they shall fight against it, and take it, and bury it with fire; and I will make the cities of Judah desolate and without inhabitants.

CHAPTER 35

1 The words that came to Jeremiah from the LORD in the days of Jehoiakim the son of Je- hoiakim, king of Judah, which said, "Go to the house of the Rechabites, speak to them, and lead them into the house of the LORD in one of the rooms, and give them wine to drink, 2 Go to the house of the Rechabites, speak to them, and lead them into house of the LORD in one of the rooms, and give them wine to drink." 3 Then I took Iaazaniah the son of Jeremiah the son of Habazzinia, his brothers, all his sons, and all the house of the Rechabites, 4 I led them into the House of the Lord, into the chamber of the sons of Hanan the son of

Igdaliah, a man of God, who was by the chamber of the princes, opposite the chamber of Maaseiah the son of Shallum, keeper of the treasury. 5 I set before the sons of the house of the Rechabites vessels full of wine and cups and said to them, "Drink wine." 6 But they answered, "We will not drink wine, for Ionadab the son of Rechab our father had commanded, 'You shall not drink wine, either you or your sons forever. 7 You shall not build houses, nor sow seed, nor plant vineyards, nor have any, but all your days you shall dwell in tents, to remain long in the land where you are strangers." 8 So we have obeyed the decree of Ionadab the son of Rechab our father in all that he has enjoined upon us, and we do not drink wine all day long, neither we, nor our wives, nor our sons, nor our daughters. 9 We have not built houses to dwell in, nor have we vineyards, nor fields, nor sowings, 10 But we stayed in tents, and obeyed and did all that Io- nadab our father commanded us. 11 But when Nebuchadnezzar, king of Babel, entered the land, we said, "Come, let us go to Jerusalem from the army of the Chaldeans and the army of Aram"; so we settled in Jerusalem. 12 Then came the word of the LORD to Jeremiah, say- ing, 13 Thus says the LORD of hosts, the God of Israel, "Go and tell the men of Judah and the inhabitants of Jerusalem, Will ye not re- ceive doctrine to obey my words, saith the LORD?" 14 The command of Ionadab the son of Rechab, who had commanded his sons not to drink wine, was surely observed; for to this day they drink none, but they obey the com- mand of their fathers; although I have spo- ken to you, rising early and speaking, yet you would not obey me. 15 I also sent to you all my servants, the prophets, rising up early and sending them to say, "Withdraw now each one from his own way, and change your works, and do not go after other gods to serve them, and you shall dwell in the land that I have giv- en to you and to your fathers, but you have not been willing to bend your ear and obey me." 16 The sons of Ionadab the son of Rechab kept the orders that their father had given them, but this people did not obey me. 17 Therefore thus says the LORD of hosts, the God of Isra- el, "Behold, I will bring upon Iudah and upon all the inhabitants of Jerusalem all the chas- tisement that I pronounced against them, because I spoke to them, but they would not listen, and I called them, but they would not answer." 18 Jeremiah said to the house of the Rechabites, "Thus says the LORD of hosts, God of Israel: Because you obeyed the com- mand of Ionadab your father, and kept all his precepts, and did all that he commanded you, 19 therefore thus says the LORD of hosts, the God of Israel: Ionadab the son of Rechab shall not lack a man to stand before me forever.

CHAPTER 36

1 In the fourth year of Jehoiakim the son of Jehoiaiah, king of Judah, there came to Jer- emiah this word of the LORD, saying 2 Take a scroll or a book and write down for us all the words that I have spoken to you against Israel, against Iudah, and against all the na- tions, from the day that I spoke to you, that is, from the days of Jehoiaiah until today. 3 It may be that the house of Iudah will learn of all that I have determined to do against them, that each one may return from his way, to forgive their iniquities and their sins." 4 Then Jeremiah called Baruch the son of Ner- iah, and Baruch wrote down by the mouth of Jeremiah all the words of the LORD, which he had addressed to him, on a scroll or book. 5 Jeremiah commanded Baruch to say, "I am shut up and cannot enter the house of the LORD. 6 Therefore go and take up the scroll wherein thou hast written by my mouth the words of the LORD, before the people, in the House of the LORD, on the day of fasting; thou shalt also take it up again in the hearing of all Iudah, which cometh forth out of their cities. 7 It may be that they will pray before the LORD, and each one will return from his way, for great is the wrath and anger which the LORD has declared against this people." 8 So Baruch the son of Neriah did all that the prophet Jeremiah had commanded him, reading in the book the words of the LORD in the house of the LORD. 9 In the fifth year of Jehoiakim the son of Josiah, king of Judeah, in the ninth month, they proclaimed a fast before the LORD for all the people of Jerusa- lem and for all the people who came from the cities of Judeah to Jerusalem. 10 Then Baruch read the words of Jeremiah in the house of the LORD, in the chamber of Gemariah the son of Shaphan the secretary, in the inner court, at the entrance to the new gate of the house of the LORD, in the presence of all the peo- ple. 11 When Michaiah the son of Gemariah the son of Shaphan had heard from the book all the words of the LORD, 12 he went down into the king's house, into the chancellor's room, and there sat down all the princes, that is, Elishama the chancellor, Delaiah the son of Shemaiah, Elnathan the son of Achbor, Gemariah the son of Shaphan, Zedekiah the son of Hananiah, and all the princes. 13 Then Michaiah reported to them all the words he had heard when Baruch had read the book before the people. 14 Therefore all the princ- es sent Iehudi the son of Nethaniah, the son of Shelemiah, the son of Chushi, to Baruch, saying, "Take in your hand the scroll that you read among the people and come." 36:14 Then Baruch the son of Neriah took the scroll in his hand and came to them. 15 They said to him, "Sit down and read it again, that we may hear." So Baruch read it among them. 16 When they had heard all the words, they became afraid one and another and said to Baruch, "We want to certify the king of all these words." 17 They examined Baruch and said to him, "Tell me, how did you write all these words on his mouth? 18 Baruch answered them, "He has spoken all these words to me with his mouth, and I have written them outright in the book." 19 Then the princes said to Baruch, "Go away, hide yourself, you and Jeremiah, and let no one know where you are." 20 They went in to the king's court, but deposited the scroll in the chamber of Elishama, the chancellor, and re- ported all the words to the king, that he might hear. 21 Then the king sent Iehudi to fetch the scroll; he took it from the chamber of Elisha- ma, the chancellor, and Iehudi read it to the audience of the king and to the audience of all the princes who stood beside the king. 22 Now the king was in the winter house, in the ninth month, and a fire was burning before him. 23 When Iehudi had read three or four sides, he cut them off with his pocketknife and threw them into the fire, which was on the hearth, until the whole roll was consumed in the fire, which was on the hearth. 24 Yet neither the king nor his servants, who heard all these words, were frightened and did not rend their garments. 25 Neuerthelesse, Elna- than, Delaiah and Gemariah had begged the king not to bury the roule, but he would not listen to them. 26 And the king commanded Ierahmeel the son of Hammelech, Seraiah the son of Azriel, and Shemiah the son of Abdiel, to take Baruch the scribe and Jeremiah the prophet; but the LORD hid them. 27 Then the word of the Lord came to Jeremiah (after the king had burned the roule and the words that Baruch had written by the mouth of Jeremi- ah), saying 28 Take again another scroll and write in it all the former words that were in the first scroll

that Jehoiakim, king of Judeah, burned, 29 And thou shalt say unto Jehoiakim king of Iudah, Thus saith the LORD, Thou hast burned this scroll, and hast said, Why hast thou written thereon, that the king of Babel shall surely come and destroy this land, and shall take of it men and beasts? 30 There- fore thus says the LORD of Jehoiakim, king of Iudah: "He shall have no one to sit on the throne of Dauid, and his corpse shall be cast in the heat by day and in the frost by night. 31 Then I will visit him and his descendants and his servants for their iniquities, and I will bring upon them and upon the inhabitants of Jerusalem and upon the men of Iudah all the evil that I have pronounced against them; but they would not listen." 32 Then Jeremiah took another scroll and gave it to Baruch, the scribe son of Neriah, who wrote on it by the mouth of Jeremiah all the words of the book that Jehoiakim, king of Judah, had burned in the fire, adding to it many other similar words.

CHAPTER 37

1 King Zedekiah the son of Jehoiaiah reigned over Coniah the son of Jehoiakim, whom Ne- buchadnezzar king of Babel had made king in the land of Judah. 2 But neither he nor his ser- vants nor the people of the land would obey the words of the LORD, spoken by the minis- ter of the prophet Jeremiah. 3 King Zedekiah sent Iehucal the son of Shemiah and Zeph- aniah the son of Maaseiah the priest to the prophet Jeremiah, saying, "Pray now to the LORD our God for his salvation." 4 (Now Jer- emiah went and came among the people, be- cause they had not put him in prison.) 5 Then Pharaoh's army came out of Egypt, and when the Chaldeans who were besieging Jerusa- lem heard of it, they left Jerusalem). 6 Then came the word of the LORD to the prophet Jeremiah, saying 7 Thus says the LORD, the God of Israel, "You shall say thus to the king of Judah, who sent you to me to ask me, Be- hold, Pharaoh's army, which has come to help you, will return to Egypt to its own country. 8 The Chaldeans will come again and fight against this city, and they will take it and bury it with fire." 9 Thus says the LORD: "Do not deceive yourselves by saying, 'The Chaldeans will surely leave here, for they will not leave.' 10 For even if you had struck down the whole army of the Chaldeans fighting against you and there were only wounded among them, every man should get up in his tent and burn this city with fire. 11 When the army of the Chaldeans was driven away from Jerusalem because of Pharaoh's army, 12 Jeremiah went out of Jerusalem to go to the land of Benja- min, separating himself from the people. 13 When he was at the gate of Benjamin, there was a chief officer, whose name was Irijah, son of Shemiah, son of Hananiah, who ques- tioned Jeremiah the prophet, saying, "You flee to Chaldea." 14 Then Ieremiah said, "It is false, I do not flee to the Chaldeans," but he would not listen; so Irijah took Ieremiah and led him to the princes. 15 Therefore the princes were angry with Jeremiah, and struck him, and put him in prison in the house of Iehonathan the scribe, because they had made that prison. 16 When Jeremiah was brought into the prison and the dungeon and stayed there for a long time, Zedekiah got in touch with Iehona- than, 17 and King Zedekiah sent for him and brought him out; and the king questioned him secretly in his house and said to him, "Is there any word from the LORD?" And Jeremi- ah answered, "Yes, for," he said, "you will be delivered into the hands of the king of Babel. 18 Moreover Jeremiah said to King Zedekiah, "What have I offended against you, or against your servants, or against this people, that you should have put me in prison? 19 Where are now your prophets who prophesied to you, saying, 'The king of Babel will not come against you and against this land'? 20 There- fore hear now, I pray thee, O king my lord; let my prayer be answered before thee, lest thou make me return to the house of Iehonathan the scribe, lest I die there." 21 Then King Ze- dekiah commanded to put Jeremiah in the prison courtyard and to give him a piece of bread from the bakers' road every day until all the bread in the city had been consumed. So Jeremiah remained in the prison yard.

CHAPTER 38

1 Then Shephatiah the son of Mattan, Geda- liah the son of Pashur, Iucal the son of Slemi- ah, and Pashur the son of Malchiah, heard the words which Jeremiah had spoken to all the people, and they said 2 Thus saith the LORD, He that abideth in this city shall die by the sword, and by famine, and by pestilence: but he that goeth to Chaldea shall live; for he shall have his life as a prayer, and shall live. 3 Thus says the LORD, "This city shall surely be given into the hand of the army of the king of Babel, who shall take it." 4 Therefore the princes said to the king, "We pray thee, let this man be put to death, for thus he weakens the hands of the men of war who remain in this city and the hands of all the people, speaking such words against them; for this man does not seek the wealth of this people, but evil." 5 Then King Zedekiah said, "Behold, it is in your hands, for your king cannot deny you anything." 6 Then they took Ieremiah and cast him into the prison of Malchiah the son of Hammel- ech, which was in the court of the prison; and they brought Ieremiah down with sticks; and there was no water in the prison except that of the myre; so Ieremiah stood in the myre. 7 When Ebed-melech, one of the Eunuchs, who was in the king's house, heard that they had put Jeremiah in prison (the king was then at the gate of Benjamin). 8 Ebed- melech came out of the king's house and spoke to the king, saying 9 "My lord king, these men did well to do all that they did to Jeremiah the proph- et, whom they threw into prison and who is starving in the place where he is, because there is no more bread in the city." 10 Then the king ordered Ebed-melech, the black man, to take three men with you and get Jeremi- ah the prophet out of prison before he dies. 11 Then Ebed-melech took the men with him and went into the king's house, under the treasury, and there he took old rotten rags and old rotten clogs, and brought them down by the slats into Jeremiah's prison. 12 And Ebed-melech, the black, said to Jeremiah, "Now put these old and rotten rags and filth under your armholes, between the bars." And Ieremiah did so. 13 Then they bound Ieremiah with splints and brought him out of the pris- on, while Ieremiah remained in the prison yard. 14 Then King Zedekiah sent for Jeremi- ah the prophet, and he led him into the thir- teenth hall of the House of the Lord, and the king said to Jeremiah, "I ask you one thing: do not hide anything from me." 15 Then Jeremiah said to Zedekiah, "If I tell you, will you not kill me? And if I give you advice, will you not lis- ten to me." 16 Then the king swore secretly to Jeremiah, saying, "As it pleases the LORD who made these souls, I will not kill you or give you into the hands of those men who seek your life." 17 Then Jeremiah said to Zedekiah, "Thus says the LORD, God of hosts, God of Is- rael: If thou wilt go to meet the princes of the king of Babel, thy soul shall abide, and this city shall not be burned with fire, thou and thy house shall abide. 18 But if thou wilt not go to the

princes of the king of Babel, this city shall be given into the hand of the Chaldeans, and they shall burn it with fire, and thou shalt not escape out of their hand." 19 King Zedeki- ah said to Jeremiah, "I care for the cities that have fled against the Chaldeans, lest they de- liver me into their hands and mock me." 20 But Jeremiah said, "They will not deliver you up; listen to the word of the LORD, I pray you, that I speak to you; so it will be good for you, and your soul will be saved." 21 But if you re- fuse to depart, this is the word that the LORD has spoken to me. 22 Behold, all the women that are left in the house of the king of Iudah shall be led to the princes of the king of Babel; and those women shall say, "Your friends have persuaded you, and have prevented against you; your feet are set in myre, and they have turned back." 23 Then shall they lead all thy wives and thy children to the Chaldeans, and thou shalt not escape their hands, but shalt be taken by the hand of the king of Babel; and this city shalt thou make to burn with fire." 24 Then Zedekiah said to Jeremiah, "No one must know of these words, and you shall not die. 25 But if you princes understand that I have spoken to you, and they come to you and say, 'Declare now what you have said to the king, do not hide it, and we will not kill you; and also what the king has said to you.' 26 Then you shall say to them, "I humbly begged the king not to let me return to the house of Iehonathans to die there." 27 Then all the princes went to Jeremiah and questioned him. And he told them all the words that the king had commanded; so they left to speak with him, for the thing was not perceived. 28 So Jeremiah still remained in the prison court until the day Jerusalem was taken; and he was there when Jerusalem was taken.

CHAPTER 39

1 In the ninth year of Zedekiah, king of Ju- dah, in the tenth month, Nebuchadnezzar, king of Babel, and all his army came against Jerusalem and besieged it. 2 In the eleventh year of Zedekiah, in the fourth month, on the ninth day of the month, the city was de- stroyed. 3 All the princes of the king of Babel came in and sat down at the middle gate: Neregal, Sharezer, Samgar-nebo, Sarsechim, Rab-saris, Neregal, Sharezer, Rab-mag and all the rest of the princes of the king of Ba- bel. 4 When Zedekiah, king of Judah, saw them and saw all the men of war, they fled and went out of the city by night, through the king's garden and through the gate between the two walls, and went into the wilderness. 5 But the army of the Chaldeans pursued them and slew Zedekiah in the wilderness of Jericho; and when they had taken him, they brought him to Nebuchadnezzar king of Ba- bel at Riblah in the land of Hamath, where he judged him. 6 Then the king of Babel killed the sons of Zedekiah in Riblah before his eyes; also the king of Babel killed all the nobles of Iudah. 7 Moreover he put out Zedekiah's eyes and bound him in chains to carry him to Ba- bel. 8 The Chaldeans burned the king's house and the houses of the people and tore down the walls of Jerusalem. 9 Then Nebuzar-adan, the chief steward, carried into captivity to Ba- bel the rest of the people who had remained in the city and those who had fled and fallen for him, together with the rest of the people who had remained. 10 But Nebuzar-adan, the chief steward, left the poor who had noth- ing in the land of Iudah, and gave them at the same time vineyards and fields. 11 Now Nebuchadnezzar, king of Babel, gave Nebu- chadnezzar, the chief steward, charge over Jeremiah, saying, "Take him, and bring him your name, 12 Take him, and look well upon him, and do him no harm, but do what

he shall say unto thee." 13 Then Nebuzar-adan, the chief steward, sent Nebushazban, Rabsa- ris, Neregal, Sharezar, Rab-mag, and all the princes of the king of Babel: 14 They sent for Jeremiah from the prison yard and entrusted him to Gedaliah the son of Ahikam the son of Shaphan to carry him home; so he dwelt among the people. 15 Now the word of the LORD came to Jeremiah, while he was shut up in the prison yard, and said 16 Go and speak to Ebed-melech, the black More, and say to him, "Thus says the LORD of hosts, the God of Israel: 'Behold, I will bring down my words upon this city for evil and not for good, and they shall be fulfilled in that day before you. 17 But I will deliver thee in that day, saith the LORD, and thou shalt not be given into the hand of the men that are dear to thee. 18 For I will surely deliver thee, and thou shalt not fall by the sword, but thy life shall be a prayer for thee, because thou hast put thy trust in me, saith the LORD.

CHAPTER 40

1 The word that came to Jeremiah from the LORD after Nebuzar-adan, the chief steward, had let him go from Ramath, when he had taken him bound in chains among all those who had been carried away captive from Jeru- salem and Iudah, who had been carried away captive as far as Babel. 2 The chief steward took Jeremiah and said to him, "The LORD your God has pronounced this plague on this place. 3 Now the LORD has brought it, and has done as he said; for you have sinned against the LORD and have not obeyed his will, there- fore this thing has come upon you. 4 Now, be- hold, today I release you from the chains that held you by the hand; if it pleases you to come with me to Babel, come, and I will watch you well; but if it does not please you to come with me to Babel, stay still; behold, the whole earth is before you; where it seems good and convenient for you to go, go." 5 Since he had not yet returned, he said, "Go back to Geda- liah the son of Ahikam, the son of Shaphan, whom the king of Babel has made the keeper of all the cities of Iudah, and dwell with him among the people, or go where it pleases you to go." So the chief steward gave him lives and a reward and let him go. 6 Then Jeremiah went to Gedaliah the son of Ahikam in Miz- pah and dwelt with him among the people left in the land. 7 Now when all the captains of the army who were in the camps heard, together with their men, that the king of Ba- bel had made Gedaliah the son of Ahikam the keeper of the land, and that he had entrusted to him men, women, children, and the poor of the land who had not been taken captive to Babel, 8 Then came from Gedaliah to Miz- pah, Ishmael the son of Nethaniah, Iohanan, Ionathan the son of Kareah, Seraiah the son of Tanehumeth, the sons of Ephai the Neto- phathite, and Jezaniah the son of Maachathi, they and their men. 9 Gedaliah the son of Ahikam the son of Shaphan swore to them and their men, "Do not be afraid to serve the Chaldeans; dwell in the land and serve the king of Babel, and it will be good for you." 10 As for me, behold, I will dwell in Mizpah to serve the Chaldeans who come to visit me; but you, gather wine and red fruit and oil, put them in your vessels, and dwell in your cities that you have taken. 11 When all the Israelites who were in Moab, among the Ammonites, in Edom, and in all the countries came to know that the king of Babel had left a rem- nant of Iudah and had put Gedaliah the son of Ahikam the son of Shaphan in charge of them, 12 then all the Israelites returned from all the places where they had been abandoned and came to the land of Iudah from Gedaliah, to Mizpah, and gathered wine

and red fruit, in great quantities. 13 Moreover Iohanan the son of Karea, and all the captains of the army that were in the camps, came from Gedaliah to Mizpah, 14 and said to him, "Do you not know that Baalis king of the Ammonites has sent Ishmael son of Nethaniah to kill you?" But Gedaliah the son of Ahikam did not trou- ble them. 15 Then Iohanan the son of Kareah spoke to Gedaliah in Mizpah in secret, saying, "Let me go, please, and I will kill Ishmael the son of Nethaniah, and no one will know. Why should he kill you, so that all the Iewes, who are gathered to you, will be scattered and the remnant in Iudah will perish? 16 But Gedaliah the son of Ahikam said to Iohanan the son of Karea, "You shall not do this thing, because you speak evil of Ishmael."

CHAPTER 41

1 But in the seventh month Ishmael the son of Nethaniah, the son of Elishama, of the royal line, of the king's princes, and ten men with him, went to Gedaliah the son of Ahikam in Mizpah, and there they ate bread together in Mizpah. 2 Then Ishmael the son of Netha- niah, with the ten men who were with him, struck Gedaliah the son of Ahikam the son of Shaphan with the sword and killed the one whom the king of Babel had made a warrior out of the land. 3 Ishmael also killed all the Jews who were with Gedaliah at Mizpah, all the Chaldeans who were there, and the men of war. 4 On the second day when he had killed Gedaliah, no one noticed, 5 There came men from Shechem, from Shiloh, and from Samaria, four hundred and sixty in number, with their beards cut off and their garments torn and cut off, with offerings and incense in their hands to offer in the house of the LORD. 6 Ishmael the son of Nethaniah went out from Mizpah to meet them, weeping as he went; and when he met them, he said to them, "Come to Gedaliah the son of Ahikam." 7 When they came to the center of the city, Ishmael the son of Nethaniah killed them and threw them into the bottom of the pit, he and the men who were with him. 8 But there were ten men among them who said to Ishmael, "Do not kill them, for we have treasures in the field, of wheat, of barley, of oil and hon- ey"; so he stayed and did not kill them among their brothers. 9 The pit into which Ishmael had cast the dead bodies of the men (whom he had killed because of Gedaliah) was that which King Asa had built because of Basha, king of Israel, and Ishmael the son of Neth- aniah filled it with the slain. 10 Then Ishma- el took captive all the rest of the people who were in Mizpah, that is, the king's daugh- ters and all the people who had remained in Mizpah and whom Nebuzar-adan, the chief steward, had entrusted to Gedaliah, son of Ahikam; Ishmael, son of Nethaniah, took them captive and left to go to the Ammonites. 11 But when Iohanan the son of Kareah, and all the captains of the armies who were with him, came to know of all that Ishmael the son of Nethaniah had done, 12 Then they took all their men and went to fight with Ishmael the son of Nethaniah, and found him by the great waters that are in Gibeon. 13 When all the people whom Ishmael had carried away captive saw Iohanan the son of Karea and all the captains of the army who were with him, they rejoiced. 14 So all the people whom Ish- mael had carried away captive from Mizpah turned back and went to Iohanan the son of Kareah. 15 But Ishmael the son of Nethaniah fled from Iohanan with eight men and went to the Ammonites. 16 Then Iohanan the son of Karea, and all the captains of the armies that were with him, all the remnant of the people whom Ishmael the son of Nethaniah

had car- ried away in captivity from Mizpah, after he had slain Gedaliah the son of Ahikam, and the strong men of war, and the women, and the boys and the girls whom he had brought back from Gibeon: 17 And they departed and set- tled at Geruth Chimham, which is near Beth- Lem, to go and enter Egypt, 18 because of the Chaldeans, for they feared them, since Ish- mael the son of Nethaniah had killed Gedali- ah the son of Ahikam, whom the king of Babel had made an industry in the land.

CHAPTER 42

1 Then came all the captains of the army, Iohanan son of Kareah, Jezaniah son of Hoshaaiah, and all the people, from the least to the greatest, 2 and said to Jeremiah the prophet, "Hear our prayer, we beseech you and pray for the LORD your God and for all this remnant (for we are left but few of many, as your eyes see). 3 That the LORD your God may show you the way by which we must walk and the things we must do." 4 Then the prophet Jeremiah said to them, "I have heard you; behold, I will pray to the LORD your God according to your words, and whatever the LORD answers to you, I will declare it to you: I will hide nothing from you." 5 Then they said to Jeremiah, "Let the LORD be a witness of truth and faith among you, if we do not, for you, all the things which the LORD your God will send you to do. 6 Whether it be good or evil, we will obey the will of the Lord God, to whom we send you that it may be good for us, when we obey the will of the Lord our God." 7 So after ten days the word of the LORD came to Jeremiah. 8 Then he called Iohanan the son of Karea, and all the captains of the army who were with him, and all the people, from the least to the greatest, 9 and said to them, "Thus says the LORD, the God of Israel, to whom you sent me to present your prayers to him, 10 If you wish to dwell in this land, I will build you and not destroy you, I will plant you and not uproot you, for I repent of the evil I have done to you. 11 Do not fear the king of Babel, of whom you are afraid; do not fear him, says the LORD, for I am with you, to save you and deliver you from his hand, 12 And I will give you credit that he may have compassion on you and make you dwell in your own land. 13 But if you say, "We do not want to dwell in this land and do not listen to the message of the LORD your God." 14 you will say, "No, but we will go to the land of Egypt, where we will not see wars, nor hear the sound of the trumpet, nor hunger for bread, and there we will dwell." 15 (Now therefore hear the word of the LORD, ye survivors of Judah: thus saith the LORD of hosts, the God of Israel, "If ye set your minds to go into Egypt, and to dwell there.") 16 then the sword which you feared shall take you in the land of Egypt, and the famine, which you worry about, shall come upon you in Egypt, and there you shall die. 17 And all the men who have determined to enter Egypt to dwell there shall die by the sword, and by famine, and by pestilence, and none of them shall remain and escape the plague which I shall bring upon them. 18 For thus says the LORD of hosts, the God of Israel, "As my wrath and fury came upon the inhabitants of Jerusalem, so will my wrath come upon you, when you enter Egypt, and you shall be a detestation, an astonishment, a curse, and a reproach, and you shall see this place no more. 19 O remnant of Iudah, the LORD has said of you, "Do not enter Egypt; know for certain that I have ad- monished you today. 20 Surely you dissimu- lated in your hearts when you sent me to the LORD your God, saying, "Pray for yourselves to the LORD our God, and declare for your- selves all that the LORD our

God shall say, and we will do it." 21 Therefore I have declared it to you today, but you have not obeyed the message of the Lord, your God, nor have you done anything for which he sent me to you. 22 Now, therefore, know for certain that you will die by the sword, famine and pestilence in the place where you wish to go to dwell.

CHAPTER 43

1 Now when Jeremiah had undertaken to speak to all the people about all the words of the LORD their God, for which the LORD their God had sent him to them, that is, about all these words, 2 Then Azariah the son of Hoshaiah, Iohanan the son of Karea, and all the proud men said to Jeremiah, "You speak falsely; the LORD our God did not send you to say, 'Do not go to Egypt to dwell there.'" 3 but Baruch the son of Neriah has set you against him to deliver him into the hands of the Chal- deans, that they may kill him and take him captive to Babel." 4 So Iohanan the son of Kareah, all the captains of the army and all the people did not obey the Lord's visitation to dwell in the land of Iudah. 5 But Iohanan the son of Kareah and all the captains of the army took with them all the remnant of Ju- dah, who had returned from all the nations from which they had been sent away, to go and dwell in the land of Judah: 6 men, wom- en, children, daughters of the king, and all those whom Nebuzar-adan, the chief stew- ard, had left with Gedaliah the son of Ahikam, the son of Shaphan, Jeremiah the prophet, and Baruch the son of Neriah. 7 So they en- tered the land of Egypt, because they did not obey the voice of the LORD; so they came to Tahpanhes. 8 Then the word of the LORD came to Jeremiah in Tahpanhes, saying, "Take large stones in the midst of the earth, 9 Take large stones in your hand and hide them in the brick claie that is at the entrance of Pha- raohs house in Tanpanhes, under the eyes of the men of Iudah, 10 and say to them, "Thus says the LORD of hosts, the God of Israel: 'Be- hold, I will send and cause Nebuchadnezzar, the king of Babel, my servant, to come, and he shall set his throne upon these stones which I have hidden, and he shall spread his pavilion upon them. 11 When he comes, he shall smite the land of Egypt: those who are destined for death, for death; those who are destined for captivity, for captivity; those who are des- tined for the sword, for the sword. 12 And I will kindle a fire in the houses of the gods of Egypt, and he shall bury them and carry them away as captives; and he shall join the land of Egypt, as a shepherd clothes himself, and depart from there in peace. 13 He shall also break the images of Bet-shemesh, which is in the land of Egypt, and shall burn with fire the houses of the gods of the Egyptians.

CHAPTER 44

1 The word that came to Jeremiah concern- ing all the Israelites who dwelt in the land of Egypt and were left in Migdol, in Tahpanhes, in Noph, and in the region of Pathros, said, 2 Thus says the LORD of hosts, the God of Isra- el, "You have seen all the evil that I have done to Jerusalem and to all the cities of Judah; and behold, they are desolate today, and no one lives there, 3 because of their wickedness which they have committed to provoke me to wrath, because they went out to burn incense and to serve other gods whom they did not know, neither they nor you nor your fathers. 4 Nevertheless I sent to you all my servants, the Prophets, who rose early and sent them to say,

"Do not do this abominable thing which I hate." 5 But they would not listen and did not incline their ears to turn away from their wickedness and to burn no more incense to other gods. 6 Therefore my wrath and anger were unleashed and kindled in the cities of Ju- dah and in the streets of Jerusalem, and they are desolate and devastated, as it appears to- day. 7 Therefore now thus says the LORD of hosts, the God of Israel, "Why do you commit this great crime against your souls, to re- move from Iudah men and women, children and infants, and leave none? 8 Because you have enraged me by the works of your hands, burning incense to other gods in the land of Egypt, where you went to dwell, to bring de- struction upon yourselves and to be a curse and a reproach among all the nations of the earth. 9 Have you forgotten the wickednesses of your fathers, the wickednesses of the kings of Iudah and the wickednesses of their wives, your wickednesses and the wickednesses of your wives, which they committed in the land of Iudah and in the streets of Jerusalem? 10 They have not humbled themselves to this day, nor feared, nor walked in my law and my statutes, which I have set before you and your fathers. 11 Therefore thus says the LORD of hosts, the God of Israel, "Behold, I will set my face against you to kill and destroy all Iudah, 12 and I will take the remnant of Iudah, who set out to go and dwell in the land of Egypt, and they shall all be consumed and fall in the land of Egypt; they shall then be consumed by the sword and by famine; they shall die from the least to the greatest, by the sword and by famine, and they shall be a detestation and an astonishment, a curse and a reproach. 13 For I will visit the inhabitants of the land of Egypt, as I visited Jerusalem, by the sword and famine and pestilence, 14 so that none of the remnant of Iudah, who have gone to dwell in the land of Egypt, may escape or remain, to return to the land of Iudah where they have a desire to dwell again; for no one will return except those who are able to escape." 15 Then all the men who knew that their wives had burned incense to other gods and all the wom- en who stood near, a great multitude, that is, all the people who dwelt in the land of Egypt in Pathros, answered Jeremiah, saying, 16 The words that you have spoken in the name of the LORD we will not hear from you, 17 but we will do what comes out of our mouths, such as burning incense to the queen of Heauen and offering her drink, as we and our fathers and our kings and our princes did in the cit- ies of Iudah and in the streets of Jerusalem, for then we had much life and were well and felt no pain. 18 But since we stopped burning incense to the queen of Heauen and offering drink to her, we had scarcity of everything and were consumed by the sword and famine. 19 And when we burned incense to the queen of Heauen and made offerings of wine to her, did we make her cakes to cheer her and give her offerings of wine without our husbands? 20 Then Jeremiah said to all the people, the men, the women and all the people who had asked him to answer, saying 21 Did not the LORD remember the incense that you burned in the cities of Judah and in the streets of Jeru- salem, both you and your fathers, your kings, your princes, and the people of the land, and did he not take account of it? 22 So that the LORD could no longer forbid, because of the wickedness of your intentions and because of the abominations which you have committed; therefore your country is desolate and an as- tonishment and a curse and without inhabi- tants, as it appears today. 23 Because you have burned incense, and because you have sinned against the LORD, and have not obeyed the word of the LORD, and have not walked in his law, and in his statutes, and in his tes- timonies, that is why this plague has come upon you, as it appears today. 24 Moreover Jeremiah said to all the people and to all the women, "Hear the word of the LORD, all the Iudah who are in the land of Egypt." 25 Thus speaks the LORD of hosts, the God of Israel, "You and your wives have spoken with your mouths and fulfilled with your hands, saying, 'We will perform the vows we made to burn incense to the queen of Egypt and to offer her wine offerings. 26 Hear therefore the word of the LORD, all the Iudah who dwell in the land of Egypt. Behold, I have sworn by my great Name, saith the LORD, that my Name shall no more be invoked out of the mouth of any man of Iudah, in all the land of Egypt, saying, The LORD God liveth. 27 Behold, I will watch them for evil and not for good, and all the men of Judah who are in the land of Egypt shall be consumed by the sword and famine, until they are utterly destroyed. 28 Nevertheless a small part of those who escape the sword shall return from the land of Egypt into the land of Iudah; and all the remnant of Iudah who have gone to dwell in the land of Egypt who have gone to dwell in the land of Egypt shall know whose words shall be, mine or theirs. 29 This shall be a sign to you, saith the LORD, when I visit you in this place, that you may know that my words shall surely stand against you for- ever." 30 Thus says the LORD, "Behold, I will give Pharaoh Hophra, king of Egypt, into the hand of his enemies and those who seek his life, as I gave Zedekiah, king of Judeah, into the hand of Nebuchadnezzar, king of Babel, his enemy, who sought his life."

CHAPTER 45

1 The words which the prophet Jeremiah ad- dressed to Baruch the son of Neriah, when he wrote these words in a book by the mouth of Jeremiah in the fourth year of Jehoiakim the son of Jehoiaiah king of Judah, and which say 2 Thus says the Lord God of Israel to you, O Baruch, 3 Thou hast said, What is become of me now, because the LORD has made my grief more painful; I have fainted in my mourning, and I find no peace. 4 So you will say to him, "The Lord says thus, 'Behold, what I have built I will destroy, and what I have planted I will destroy, as all this earth.' 5 And do you seek great things for yourself? Look not on them, for behold, I will bring a plague upon all flesh, saith the Lord; but your life I will give you as a prayer in all places where you go.

CHAPTER 46

1 The words of the Lord addressed to the prophet Jeremiah against the nations, 2 as against Egypt, against the army of Pharaoh Necho, king of Egypt, which was by the river Perath, at Carchemish, which Nebuchadnez- zar, king of Babel, smote in the fourth year of Jehoiakim, son of Jehoiaiah, king of Judah. 3 Prepare your armor and shield and go to bat- tle. 4 Prepare the horses, make the horsemen ready with your salts, prepare the spears, and put on the brigands. 5 Why did I see them frightened and falling back? Because their strong men were stricken, they fled and did not look back; because fear surrounded them, says the LORD. 6 The swift shall not flee, and the strong man shall not escape; they shall stumble and fall toward the north by the riv- er Perath. 7 Who is he that cometh as a flood, whose waters are moved as the waters of a river? 8 Egypt rises like a flood, whose waters are moved like those of a river, and he says, "I will go up, and I will fall upon the earth; I will destroy the city and those who dwell in it." 9 Hasten,

horses, rage, chariots, and let the val- iant men come, the black men of Mores, the shield-bearing Lyophiles, and the bow-wield- ing and bow-bending Lyophiles. 10 For this is the day of the LORD God of hosts, a day of vengeance, to take vengeance on his enemies; for the sword shall be consumed, and shall be sacked, and made drunk with their blood: for the LORD God of hosts hath a sacrifice in the county of the north, by the river Perath. 11 Go to Gilead and take balm, O Virgin, daughter of Egypt; in it you will find much medicine, for you will not have health. 12 The nations have heard of your shame, and your weeping has filled the earth; for the strong have stum- bled against the strong, and they have both fallen down together. 13 The speech which the LORD gave to Jeremiah the prophet, how Nebuchadnezzar king of Babel should come and smite the land of Egypt. 14 Publish in Egypt and declare to Migdol, proclaim to Noph and Tahpanhes, and say, "Stand firm and prepare yourself, for the sword will sur- round you. 15 Why were your valiant men set apart? They could not stand, for the LORD made them dry. 16 He caused many to fall, and one fell upon another; and they said, Arise, let us return to our people and to the land of our origin from the sword of the vi- olent. 17 There they cried, "Pharaoh, king of Egypt and of a great multitude, has exceed- ed the appointed time." 18 As I say, says the King, whose name is the Lord of hosts, surely as Tabor is on the mountains, and as Carm- el is on the sea, so shall it come to pass. 19 O daughter who dwells in Egypt, prepare to go into captivity, for Noph will be forsaken and desolate, without inhabitants. 20 Egypt is like a beautiful calf, but destruction comes; from the north it comes. 21 Her servants also are in her belly like fat calves; they also turned back and fled together; they could not stand, for the day of their destruction has come upon them and the time of their visitation. 22 Her flight will break out like a serpent, for they will march with an army and come against her with axes, like woodcutters. 23 They shall cut down her forest, says the LORD, for they cannot be counted, for they are more numer- ous than you fruit and vegetable sellers, and are innumerable. 24 The daughter of Egypt shall be confounded; she shall be delivered into the hands of the peoples of the north. 25 Thus says the LORD of hosts, the God of Isra- el: "Behold, I will visit the common people of No, Pharaoh and Egypt, with their gods and their kings, and Pharaoh and all who trust in him, 26 And I will deliver them into the hands of those who see their rights, into the hands of Nebuchadnezzar king of Babel, and into the hands of his servants, and afterward they shall dwell as they used to dwell, saith the LORD. 27 But do not fear, O my servant Iaa- kob, and do not be afraid, O Israel, for behold, I will deliver thee from a far country, and thy seed from the land of their captivity, and Iaa- kob shall return and be in rest and prosperity, and no one shall frighten him. 28 Fear not, O Iaakob my servant, saith the LORD, for I am with thee, and will destroy all the nations whither I have led thee in haste; but I will not destroy thee in haste, but I will correct thee with judgment, and I will not cut thee off in haste.

CHAPTER 47

1 The words of the LORD addressed to Jere- miah the prophet against the Philistines, be- fore Pharaoh struck down Azzah. 2 Thus says the LORD: "Behold, the waters shall come up from the north, and shall be like a flood, sweeping over the land, all that is therein, and the cities with those who dwell therein; then shall men cry out, and all the

inhabitants of the land shall howl, 3 at the noise and the shuffling of the hooves of his strong horses, at the rattling of his chariots and the roaring of his wheels; you fathers shall not look back at your children, because of the weakness of your hands, 4 because of the day when all the people of the Philistines, of Tyre, of Zidon, and of all the others that take part in the war, shall be destroyed; for the LORD will destroy the Philistines, the remnant of the people of Caphtor. 5 Baldenes is come upon Azzah: Ashkelon is cut off with the rest of their val- leys. How long will you remain alive? 6 O sword of the LORD, how long will it be before you cease? Go back into your skin again, rest and do not move. 7 How can it cease, since the LORD has appointed it to strike Ashkelon and the sea coast?

CHAPTER 48

1 Concerning Moab, thus saith the LORD of hosts, the God of Israel: "Woe unto Nebo, for it is destroyed: Kiriathaim is confounded and taken: Misgab is confounded and afraid. 2 Moab shall boast no more of Heshbon, for they have done a work of dishonesty against it. Come and destroy it, that it may no longer be a nation; you also shall be destroyed, O fool, and the sword shall pursue you." 3 From Horonaim shall go forth a cry of weeping, a desolation and great destruction. 4 Moab is destroyed; its little ones have made their weeping heard. 5 For at the time of Luhith's departure, mourning shall be heard with weeping; for at the time of Horonaim's de- parture, the enemies have heard a cry of de- struction, 6 Flee and put away your lives, and become like a wilderness. 7 Because you have trusted in your works and treasures, you will also be taken, and Chemosh will go into cap- tivity with its priests and princes together. 8 The destroyer shall come upon all the cities, and none shall escape; even the valley shall perish, and the plain shall be destroyed, as the LORD has said. 9 Put wings on Moab, that he may flee and be gone; for his cities shall be desolate, with no one to inhabit them. 10 Cursed is he who does the work of the LORD negligently, and cursed is he who withholds his sword from the blood. 11 Moab has rest- ed since his youth, and has lain down on his lees, and has not been driven from vessel to vessel, nor gone into captivity; therefore his taste has remained in him, and his will has not changed. 12 Therefore behold, the day comes, says the LORD, when I will send peo- ple to him who will take him away, and empty his vessels, and break their bottoms. 13 Moab will be ashamed of Chemosh as the house of Israel was ashamed of Bet-el, their securi- ty. 14 How do you think you can say, "We are strong and sturdy men of war"? 15 Moab has been destroyed, its cities have been burned, and its chosen young men have gone to the slaughter, says your king, whose name is the LORD of hosts. 16 The destruction of Moab is ready to come, and his plague is hastening. 17 Everyone around him mourns for him, and everyone who knows his name says, "How the strong staff and the beautiful rod is bro- ken! 18 You daughter who dwell in Dibon, come down from your glory and sit down in thirst, for the destroyer of Moab will come upon you and destroy your fortresses. 19 You who dwell in Aroer, stand on the road and watch; question those who flee and those who are saved and say, "What has been done?" 20 Moab is smothered, for it has been destroyed; howl and shout, tell Arnon, that Moab has been destroyed, 21 and judgment has come on the plain county, on Holon, on Iahazah, and on Mephaath, 22 and on Dibon, Nebo, and the house of Diblathaim, 23 Kiriathaim, Beth-Gamul and Beth-Meon,

24 Kerioth, Bozrah, and all the cities of the land of Moab, far off or away. 25 The horn of Moab is cut off, and his weapon is broken, saith the LORD. 26 Make him drunk, for he hath risen up against the LORD: Moab shall wallow in his vomit, and shall also be mocked. 27 For hast thou not mocked Israel, as if he were found among us? For when you speak of him, you are mocked. 28 O you who dwell in Moab, leave the cities, dwell in the rocks, and be like the doue that makes her nest on the sides of the mouth of the hole. 29 We have heard the pride of Moab (he is exceedingly proud), his sturdiness, his arrogance, and the haughtiness of his heart. 30 I know his wrath, saith the LORD, but it shall not be so; and his dissimulators, for they do not do good. 31 Therefore I will howl for Moab and cry for all Moab; my heart shall weep for the men of Kir-heres. 32 O vine of Sibmah, I will weep for you, as I wept for Jaz- er; your plants have gone out of the sea, they have come to the sea of Jazer; destruction has come upon your fruit and your vintage, 33 joy and gladness have been taken away from the rich land and from the land of Moab, and I have made the wine disappear from the cel- lars; no one shall make merry with shouting any more; their shouting shall be no more shouting. 34 From the shouting of Heshbon as far as Elaleh and as far as Iahaz, they have made their rounds from Zoar as far as Horo- naim, and your horses of three years shall go down, for even the waters of Nimrim shall be wasted. 35 Moreover, I will cause to cease in Moab, says the LORD, whoever offers on the high places and whoever burns incense to his gods. 36 Therefore my heart shall resound for Moab like a rustling, and my heart shall re- sound like a rustling for the men of Ker-her- es, because the riches that he has procured are gone. 37 Every head shall be cut off, and every beard shall be plucked off; on all hands there shall be cuts, and on sackclothes. 38 They shall mourn on all the tops of the houses of Moab and in all its streets, because I have broken Moab like a vessel in which there is no pleasure, says the LORD. 39 They shall howl, saying, "How was it destroyed? How did Moab turn away in shame? So Moab will be a mockery and a fear to all who surround him." 40 For thus says the LORD, "Behold, he shall flee like an eagle and spread his wings over Moab." 41 Cities shall be taken, fortress- es shall be taken, and the heart of you mighty men of Moab in that day shall be like the heart of a woman in panic. 42 Moab will be de- stroyed as a people, because they have turned against the LORD. 43 Fear, pit and snare shall be upon you, O inhabitant of Moab, says the LORD. 44 He who escapes fear shall fall into the pit, and he who comes out of the pit shall be caught in the snare, for I will cause to come upon it, as upon Moab, the year of their visi- tation, says the LORD. 45 Those who have stood under the shadow of Heshbon, because of strength; for fire came out of Heshbon, and a flame out of Sihon, and ravaged the corner of Moab, and the top of the seditious sons. 46 Woe unto thee, O Moab; the people of Chemosh perish; thy sons are taken captive, and thy daughters led into captivity. 47 But in the last days I will bring back the captivity of Moab, says the LORD. Thus is the judgment upon Moab.

CHAPTER 49

1 Thus says the LORD to the sons of Ammon, "Has Israel no son or heir? Why then has their king possessed God and his people dwelt in his cities? 2 Therefore, behold, the days shall come, saith the LORD, when I will make a war cry to Rabbah of the Ammonites, and she shall be a desolate

place, and her daughters shall be burned with fire; then shall Israel pos- sess those who have possessed him, saith the LORD. 3 How, O Heshbon, for Ai is destroyed; mourn, ye daughters of Rabbah, and clothe yourselves with sackcloth, and go and return from the hedgerows, for their king shall go into captivity, as well as his priests and his princes. 4 Why do you glory in a valley? Thy valley runneth away, O rebellious daughter; she trusted in her treasures, and said, Who shall come to me? 5 Behold, I will make you fear, says the LORD God of hosts, from all those around you, and you will all be scat- tered to the right and to the left, and no one will gather those who flee. 6 Afterward I will cause the sons of Ammon to return to their homeland." 7 Thus says the LORD of hosts to Edom, "Is there no more wisdom in Teman, has counsel disappeared from their sons, has their wisdom vanished? 8 Flee, ye inhabitants of Dedan (they have gone back and consult- ed to dwell), for I have brought upon him the destruction of Esau and the time of his visita- tion. 9 If the harvesters come to you, will they not leave some grapes? If they come by night, they will destroy until they have enough. 10 For I have disowned Esau: I have unveiled his secrets, and he shall not be able to hide him- self; his seed is wasted, his brethren and his neighbors, and there shall be none to tell, 11 Leave the sons of your fathers, and I will pre- serve them, and your widows shall trust in me." 12 For thus says the Lord, "Behold, those whose judgment was not to drink of the cup have surely drunk, and you are the one who will escape to freedom? You shall not go to liberty, but you shall surely drink of it. 13 For I have sworn by myself, saith the LORD, that Bozrah shall be a waste and a reproach and a desolation and a curse, and all her cities shall be a perpetual desolation. 14 I heard a voice from the LORD, and an embassy was sent to the heathen, saying, "Gather yourselves, come against her, and go up into battle." 15 For verily I will make you small among the heathen and despised among men. 16 Your fear and the pride of your heart have deceived you, you who dwell in the clefts of the rock and hold the height of the hill; even if you should make your nest like the eagle, I will bring you down from there, says the LORD. 17 Edom also shall be desolate; all who pass by there shall be amazed and afraid for all its plagues, 18 As the outside of Sodom and Go- morah and the surrounding places thereof, saith the LORD: no man shall dwell there any more, neither shall the sons of men remain there. 19 Behold, he shall come as a lyre from the swelling of Iorden unto the strong habi- tation; for I will make Israel to rest, and will turn him away from her, and who is a chosen man that I can lean against her? For who is like me? And who will give me time? And who is the shepherd that shall stand before me? 20 Hear therefore the counsel of the LORD which he hath devised against Edom, and his purpose which he hath devised against the inhabitants of Teman: surely the least of the flock shall drag them away; surely he shall make their habitations desolate with them. 21 The earth is shaken with the noise of their fall; the cry of their voice is heard in the Red Sea. 22 Behold, he will come, he will fly like the Egle and spread his wings beyond Bozrah; in that day the heart of the strong men of Edome will be like the heart of a woman in panic. 23 To Damascus he says, "Hamath is confused and Arpad, because they have heard terrible news, and their hearts are weak as one who is in a fearful sea and cannot rest." 24 Damascus is discouraged, and flees, and fear has come upon her; distress and grief have seized her like a woman in fear. 25 How is not the glori- ous city restored, the city of my joy? 26 There- fore her young men shall fall in her streets, and all her men of war shall be cut off in that day,

saith the LORD of hosts. 27 And I will kindle a fire in the walls of Damascus, which shall consume the palaces of Ben-Hadad. 28 To Kedar and the kingdoms of Hazor, which Nebuchadnezzar, king of Babel, shall smite, thus saith the LORD, Arise, go to Kedar, and destroy the men of the east. 29 They shall car- ry away their tents and their flocks; yea, they shall take for themselves their tents, and all their furniture, and their camels, and shall cry unto them, Fear is on every side. 30 Flee, depart (they have consulted to dwell), O in- habitants of Hazor, says the LORD, for Nebu- chadnezzar king of Babel has taken counsel against you and devised a plan against you. 31 Arise and go to the wealthy nation that dwells without care, says the LORD, which has nei- ther gates nor bars, but dwells alone. 32 Their camels shall be a spoil, and the multitude of their cattle a spoil, and I will scatter them in all the winds and in the remotest corners, and I will bring their destruction from all sides, says the LORD. 33 Hazor shall be a dwelling place for dragons, and a desolation for the erection; no one shall dwell there, nor shall the sons of men remain there. 34 The words of the LORD addressed to Jeremiah the proph- et concerning Elam at the beginning of the reign of Zedekiah king of Judeah are as fol- lows. 35 Thus says the LORD of hosts, "Behold, I will break the bow of Elam, that is, the head of its strength. 36 And upon Elam I will cause the four winds to come from the four quar- ters of Heauen, and I will scatter them toward all these winds, and there will be no nation where the escapes of Elam will not come. 37 For I will cause Elam to be afraid before their enemies and those who see their lives, and I will bring upon them a plague, that is, the indignation of my wrath, says the LORD, and I will send the sword after them until I have consumed them. 38 I will establish my throne in Elam, and I will destroy the king and the princes there, says the LORD; but in the last days I will bring back the captivity of Elam, says the LORD.

CHAPTER 50

1 The word which the Lord has spoken con- cerning Babel and the land of the Chaldeans, through Jeremiah the minister, the prophet. 2 Declare it among the nations, publish it and set it forth, proclaim it and do not con- ceal it: say, Babel is taken, Bel is confound- ed, Merodach is brought down; her idols are confounded, and their images are broken in pieces. 3 For out of the north cometh a nation against her, which shall make her land des- ert, and none shall dwell therein; they shall flee and be gone, both man and beast. 4 In those days and at that time, says the LORD, the children of Israel shall come, they and the children of Judah together, going and weep- ing, and they shall see the LORD their God. 5 They shall ask the way of Zion, with their faces turned outward, saying, "Come, and let us pay homage to the LORD with an everlasting cov- enant that shall not be forgotten." 6 My peo- ple have been like a lost flock; their shepherds have led them astray, and have caused them to stray into the mountains; they have gone from mountain to mountain and forgotten their resting place. 7 All who found them hat- ed them, and their enemies said, "We do not offend them, for they have sinned against the LORD, the dwelling place of righteousness, that is, the LORD, the hope of their fathers." 8 Flee from the meshes of Babel, come out of the land of the Chaldeans, and be as the goats before the flock. 9 For verily I will raise up and cause to come against Babel a multitude of mighty nations from the land of the north, and they shall array themselves

against her and take her; their arrows shall be as those of a strong man, experienced, for none shall be able to turn back. 10 Chaldea shall be an ear; all who spy her out shall be satisfied, says the LORD. 11 Because you have rejoiced and destroyed my inheritance, and because you have grown fat, like calves in the crabgrass, and have grown like strong horses, 12 because of this your mother shall be confounded, and she that bore you shall be ashamed; behold, the last of the people shall be a wilderness, a dry and wild land. 13 Because of the wrath of the LORD, it shall not be inhabited, but it shall be desolate; and all who pass through Babel shall be amazed and astonished at all her plagues. 14 Form a line against Babel, all around; everyone who has a bow, shoot at her, sparing no arrows, for she has sinned against the LORD. 15 Shout against her all around: she has given her hand; her foundations have fallen down, and her walls have been de- stroyed, for she is the vengeance of the LORD; take vengeance on her; as she has done, do ye also. 16 Destroy the sower of Babel and the one who wields the sieth in time of torment; because of the sword of the oppressor, every one of them shall return to his people, and they shall flee each to his own land. 17 Israel is like a scattered flock; the lions have scattered it; first the king of Assur has exhausted it, and lastly this king of Babel, Nebuchadnezzar, has broken its bones. 18 Therefore thus says the LORD of hosts, the God of Israel, "Behold, I will visit the king of Babel and his country, as I visited the king of Assur. 19 And I will bring Israel back to his dwelling place; he shall feed on Mount Carmel and on Bashan, and his soul shall be satisfied on Mount Ephraim and on Gilead. 20 In those days and at that time, saith the LORD, shall the iniquities of Israel be sought, and shall not be found: and the faults of Judah shall not be found: for I will be merciful toward them, whom I reserve. 21 Go against the land of the rebels, against it, and against the inhabitants of Pekod; de- stroy it and lay it waste after them, saith the LORD, and do all that I have commanded you. 22 A cry of battle is in the land and of great destruction. 23 How destroyed and broken is the hammer of the whole world! How deso- late has become Babel among the nations! 24 I have caught you and you have been caught, O Babel, and you have not noticed; you have been found and also caught, because you have fought against the LORD. 25 The LORD has opened her treasure and brought with her the weapons of her wrath, for this is the action of the LORD, the God of hosts, in the land of the Chaldeans. 26 Come against her from the farthest borders; open her storehouses; make trek on her as on a shearer, and destroy her in every part; leave nothing of her. 27 Destroy all her heifers; let them go to slaughter. Woe to them, for their day and the time of their visi- tation has come. 28 The journey of those who flee and depart from the land of Babel to de- clare in Zion the vengeance of the LORD our God and the vengeance of his Temple. 29 Call the archers against Babel; all you who bend the bow, besiege her everywhere; let none es- cape; reward her according to her work, and according to all that she has done, do it to her; for she has taken pride against the LORD, and against the Holy One of Israel. 30 There- fore her young men shall fall in the streets, and all her men of war shall be destroyed in that day, saith the LORD. 31 Behold, I come to you, O proud man, says the LORD, God of hosts, for your day has come, the time when I will visit you. 32 The proud man shall stum- ble and fall, and none shall lift him up; and I will kindle a fire in his cities, and it shall be consumed all around him." 33 Thus says the LORD of hosts, "The children of Israel and the children of Judah were oppressed together, and all those who made them captives held them

and would not let them go. 34 But their strong redeemer, whose name is the LORD of hosts, will uphold their cause, to give rest to the land and disquiet the inhabitants of Babel. 35 A sword shall come upon the Chal- deans, saith the LORD, and upon the inhabi- tants of Babel, upon her princes and her wise men. 36 A sword is for the soothsayers, and they shall hurt themselves; a sword is for her strong men, and they shall hurt themselves. 37 A sword is upon their horses, and upon their chariots, and upon all the multitude that is in her bowels, and they shall be as women; a sword is upon her treasures, and they shall be stripped. 38 And its waters are dried up by drought, and they shall run dry, because it is the land of bronze images, and they give themselves up to their idols. 39 Therefore the Ziim with the Iim shall dwell therein, and the ostriches shall dwell therein: for it shall not be inhabited any more, nor shall it be in- habited from generation to generation. 40 As God destroyed Sodom and Gomorah with its surrounding places, says the LORD, so shall no one dwell there any more, nor shall the son of man remain there. 41 Behold, a peo- ple will come from the north, a great nation, and many kings will arise from the coasts of the earth. 42 They will wield the bow and the axe; they are cruel and cruel; their jour- ney will roar like the sea; they will ride horses and be arrayed like men to fight against you, O daughter of Babel. 43 The king of Babel has heard their news, and his hands have grown weak; sadness has come upon him like that of a woman in panic. 44 Behold, he shall come like a lyre from the swelling of Iorden to the strong dwelling place, for I will make Israel rest, and I will make them depart from her quickly; and who is a chosen man that I can lean against her? For who is like me, and who will lean against me in time? And who is the shepherd that shall stand before me? 45 Hear therefore the counsel of the LORD which he hath devised against Babel, and his purpose which he hath devised against the land of the Chaldeans: surely the least of the flock shall drag them away; surely he shall make their dwelling with them desolate. 46 At the sound of Babel's victory, the earth moved and the cry was heard among the nations.

CHAPTER 51

1 Thus says the LORD: "Behold, I will raise up against Babel and against the inhabitants who lift up their hearts against me a destruc- tive wind, 2 And I will send against Babel fans that shall flatten her and empty her land, for in the day of crisis they shall be against her on every side. 3 And to the bender who shall bend his bow, and to him who shall rise up in his brigandage, I will say, "Spare not his young men, but destroy all his army." 4 So the slain shall fall in the land of the Chaldeans, and those who shall be pierced through its streets. 5 For Israel was not widowed, and Iudah was not turned away from his God, from the LORD of hosts, though their land was full of sins against the Holy One of Israel. 6 Flee from the meshes of Babel, and deliver each one his own soul; do not let her iniquity bring you down, for this is the time of the LORD's vengeance, who will make recompense for her. 7 Babel has been like a cup of gold in the hand of the LORD, which has made all the earth drunk; the nations have drunk of her wine, therefore the nations are enraged. 8 Ba- bel fell suddenly and was destroyed; cry out for her, bring balm for her sore, if she would be healed. 9 We would have healed Babel, but she could not be healed; forsake her, and let every man go away to his own country, for his judgment

has come upon him, and has risen up to the clouds. 10 The LORD has brought forth our righteousness; come and declare in Zion the work of the LORD our God. 11 Let your arrows shine, gather your shields: the LORD has lifted up the spirit of the king of the Medes, for his purpose is to destroy Babel, for it is the LORD's vengeance and the vengeance of his Temple. 12 Set up the support to the walls of Babel, make the guard strong, set up the watchmen, prepare the hoofs, for the LORD has promised and done what he said against the inhabitants of Babel. 13 O you who dwell on many waters, rich in treasure, your end has come, the end of your coup has come. 14 The LORD of hosts has sworn by himself, saying, "I will fill you with men like caterpil- lars, and they will cry out and shout against you." 15 He made the earth by his power, es- tablished the world by his wisdom, and stretched out the earth by his discretion. 16 By his will he regulates the multitude of the wa- ters in the high places, and makes the clouds rise from the ends of the earth; he turns light- ning into rain, and brings forth the wind from his treasuries. 17 Every man is a beast by his knowledge; every founder is confounded by the image of God, for his casting is but falsehood, and there is no breath. 18 They are vanity and the work of error; in the time of their visitation they shall perish. 19 The por- tion of Iaakob is not like them, for he is the maker of all things, and Israel is the rod of his inheritance; the LORD of hosts is his name. 20 You are my hammer and my weapons of war, for with you I will break the nations, and with you I will destroy kingdoms, 21 With you I will break horses and horsemen, with you I will break the chariot and those who ride in it. 22 By you I will also destroy the man and the woman, by you I will destroy the old man and the young man, by you I will destroy the young man and the elder. 23 By you I will also break the shepherd and his flock, by you I will break the husbandman and his yoke of oxen, by you I will break the dukes and the princes. 24 And I will render to Babel and to all the in- habitants of Chaldea all their evil that they have done in Zion, even before you, says the LORD. 25 Behold, I am coming to you, O de- structive mountain, saith the LORD, that de- stroy all the earth; I will stretch out my hand upon you, and I will cause you to fall from the rocks, and I will make you a burnt mountain. 26 They shall not take from you a stone for a corner, nor a stone for a foundation, but you shall be destroyed forever, says the LORD. 27 Establish a standard in the land, sound trum- pets among the nations, prepare the nations against her, call out against her the kingdoms of Ararat, Minni, and Ashchenaz, call out the prince against her, make the horses come like the rough caterpillars. 28 Prepare against her the nations with the kings of the Medes, their dukes and their princes, and all the land of her dominion. 29 The land shall tremble and be saddened, because the decree of the LORD shall be fulfilled against Babel, to make the land of Babel a wilderness without inhabi- tants. 30 The strong men of Babel have ceased to fight, they have withdrawn into their hous- es, their strength has vanished, and they have become like women; they have burned her dwellings, and her walls have been broken down. 31 A pole shall run to meet the pole, and a messenger shall go to meet the messenger, to report to the king of Babel that his city has been taken on one side, 32 and that the pas- sages are blocked, the reeds burned with fire, and the means of warfare disturbed. 33 For thus says the LORD of hosts, the God of Isra- el, "The daughter of Babel is like a threshing floor; the time of her threshing has come; yet a little while, and the time of her destruction will come." 34 Nebuchadnezzar, the king of Babel, has destroyed me, made me an empty vessel, swallowed me up like a dragon, filled his belly with my delicacies, and cast me out. 35 The spoyle of me, and what is left of me is taken to Babel, shall say the inhabitant of Zion; and my blood to the inhabitants of Chaldea, shall say Jerusalem. 36 Therefore thus says the LORD, "Behold, I will support your cause and take vengeance on you; I will make the sea vanish, and I will make its springs disappear. 37 Babel shall be as a heap, an abode for dragons, an astonishment and a hissing, without inhabitants. 38 They will prowl like lions and howl like lion cubs. 39 In their hearts I will make them feast, and make them drunk, that they may give themselves up to madness, and sleep eternally, and not wake up, saith the LORD. 40 I will lead them to the slaughter like lambs, like rams and goats. 41 How Sheshach has been taken, how the glory of all the earth has been taken, how Babel has become an astonishment among the nations! 42 The sea has come upon Babel, which has been smitten by the multitude of its waves. 43 Its cities are desolate; the land is barren and wild, a land where no one dwells and where the son of man does not pass through. 44 I will also visit Bel in Babel and bring forth from his mouth what he has swal- lowed; the nations will no longer run to him, and the wall of Babel will fall. 45 My people, come out of its meshes and deliver every man from the fierce wrath of the LORD, 46 if your heart be not yet chilled, and fear not the voic- es that shall be heard in the land; the voice shall come this year, and afterward in the oth- er year, and cruelty in the land, and ruler against ruler. 47 Therefore behold, the day comes when I will visit the images of Babel, and all the land shall be confounded, and all her dead shall fall in the midst of her. 48 Then shall the ocean and the earth, and all that is therein, take vengeance for Babel, for the de- stroyers shall come to her from the north, saith the LORD. 49 As Babel brought down the slaughter of Israel, so from Babel came the slaughter of all the earth. 50 You who have escaped the sword, go forth, do not stand still; remember the distant LORD and bring Jeru- salem to mind. 51 We are confounded because we have heard rebukes; shame has covered our faces, because ruthless men have entered the sanctuaries of the house of the LORD. 52 Therefore behold, the day comes, says the LORD, when I will visit his graced images, and throughout all his land the wounds will be felt. 53 Even if Babel rise upward, and if she defend her strength in heaven, by me shall come her destroyers, saith the LORD. 54 A sound of shouting comes from Babel, and a great destruction from the land of the Chal- deans, 55 For the LORD hath destroyed Babel, and hath destroyed from her the great jour- ney, and her wars roar like great waters, and a sound is made by their noise: 56 For the de- stroyer hath come upon her, as upon Babel, and her strong men are taken, their bows are broken: for the Lord God that rewardeth him- self shall surely reward himself. 57 I will make her princes drunk, and her wise men, and her dukes, and her nobles, and her strong men; they shall sleep a perpetual sleep, and shall not wake up, saith the King, whose Name is the Lord of hosts. 58 Thus says the LORD of hosts, "The thin wall of Babel shall be broken down, and its gates shall be burned with fire; and the people shall grow weary in the snow, and the people in the fire, for they shall grow weary. 59 The words which the prophet Jere- miah commanded Sheraiah the son of Neri- jah the son of Maaseiah, when he went with Zedekiah king of Judah to Babel in the fourth year of his reign; and this Sheraiah was a peaceable prince. 60 So Jeremiah wrote in a book all the evil that would come upon Babel, that is, all these things that are written against Babel. 61 Jeremiah said to Sheraiah, "When you come to Babel, you will see and read all these words, 62 then thou shalt say,

'O LORD, thou hast spoken against this place to destroy it, that no man or beast may remain there, but that it may be desolate forever.' 63 And when you have finished reading this book, you shall tie a stone to it and throw it into the middle of the Euphrates, 64 And thou shalt say, "Thus shall Babel be drowned, and shall not rise up out of the flood that I shall bring upon her; and they shall be weary." Thus are the words of Jeremiah.

CHAPTER 52

1 When he began to reign, Zedekiah was a year and twenty years old, and he reigned eleven years in Jerusalem; his mother's name was Hamutal, daughter of Jeremiah of Libna. 2 He behaved well in the eyes of the LORD, according to what Jehoiakim had done. 3 Because the anger of the LORD came upon Jerusalem and Iudah, even to the point of driving them out of his presence, Zedekiah rebelled against the king of Babel. 4 But in the ninth year of his reign, on the tenth day of the month, came Nebuchadnezzar, king of Babel, with all his army against Jerusalem, and encamped against it, and built fortresses around it. 5 Thus the city was besieged until the eleventh year of King Zedekiah. 6 In the fourth month, on the ninth day of the month, famine came upon the city, so that there was no bread left for the people of the land. 7 Then the city was destroyed, and all the men of war fled, and went out of the city by night, by the gate between the two walls, which was by the garden of the kings; (the Chaldeans were round about the city) and went by the way of the wilderness. 8 But the army of the Chal- deans pursued the king, and defeated Zedekiah in the wilderness of Jericho, and all his army was scattered by him. 9 Then they took the king and brought him to the king of Babel at Riblah in the land of Hamath, where they judged him. 10 And the king of Babel slew the sons of Zedekiah, and under his eyes he also slew all the princes of Iudah in Riblah. 11 Then he put out Zedekiah's eyes, and the king of Babel bound him with chains, and brought him to Babel, and put him in prison until the day of his death. 12 Now in the fifth month, on the tenth day of the month (which was the nineteenth year of Nebuchadnezzar king of Babel), Nebuzar-adan, the chief steward who stood before the king of Babel, came to Jeru- salem, 13 And he burned down the house of the LORD, and the king's house, and all the houses of Jerusalem, and all the great houses. 14 And all the army of the Chaldeans, which was with the chief steward, broke down all the walls of Jerusalem all around. 15 Then Nebuzar-Adan, the chief steward, took cap- tive some of the poor of the people, and the rest of the people who remained in the city, and those who had fled and fallen by the king of Babel, with the rest of the crowd. 16 But Nebuzar-adan, the chief steward, left some of the poor people of the town to cultivate the vines and to till the ground. 17 Also the bronze pillars that were in the house of the LORD, the plinths and the bronze sea that was in the house of the LORD, the Chaldeans broke them and carried all the bronze to Babel. 18 The vessels, the besome, the musical instru- ments, the basins, the incense dishes, and all the bronze utensils with which they exercised their ministry were also carried away. 19 The bowls, ashtrays, basins, vessels, candlesticks, incense dishes, cups, and all that was of gold and silver were taken away by the chief steward, 20 with the two pillars, a sea, and two bronze bulbs that were under the bases, which King Solomon had made in the house of the LORD; the steel of all these utensils was weightless. 21 As for the pillars, the height of one column was eighty cubits, its height was two cubits, and its thickness was four fingers. 22 A hat of reeds was over it, and the height of a hat was five cubits with netting and pomegranates on the hats around it, all of reeds; the second column and pomegranates were also like these. 23 There were ninety-six pomegranates on each side, and all the pome- granates on the net were a hundred around. 24 And the chief steward took Sheraiah, the first priest, and Zephaniah, the second priest, and the three keepers of the house. 25 And he also took a eunuch from the city, who had the oversight of the men of war, and ten men who were in the presence of the king and who were in the city, and Sofer captain of the army that gathered the people of the land, and sixty men of the people of the land who were in the midst of the city. 26 Nebuzar-adan, the chief steward, took them and led them to the king of Babel in Riblah. 27 And the king of Babel struck them and killed them in Riblah, in the land of Hamath; so Iudah was taken away as a captive from his country. 28 These are the people whom Nebuchadnezzar carried away into captivity in the tenth year, that is, about three thousand three hundred and twenty years. 29 In Nebuchadnezzar's eighth year he carried away eight hundred and thirty-two people from Jerusalem as captives. 30 In the third and twentieth year of Nebuchadnezzar, Nebuzar-Adan, the chief steward, took away from Jerusalem seven hundred forty-five per- sons; all the people were four thousand six hundred. 31 In the thirtieth year of the cap- tivity of Jehoiachin, king of Judeah, in the twelfth month, on the twentieth day of the month, Euil-merodach, king of Babel, in the first year of his reign, lifted up the head of Jehoiachin, king of Judeah, and brought him out of prison, 32 he spoke kindly to him and set his throne before the throne of the kings who were with him in Babel, 33 and changed his robes of pryson, and continually ate bread before him all the days of his life. 34 His por- tion was a continual portion granted him by the king of Babel, every day a certain amount, all the days of his life until his death.

LAMENTATIONS

CHAPTER 1

1 How does the city that was full of people remain solitary? She is like a widow; that which was great among the nations and a princess among the provinces has been made a tributary. 2 She cries continually at night and her tears roll down her cheeks; of all her friends, she has no one to comfort her; all her friends have behaved badly to her and are her enemies. 3 Iudah has been carried away into captivity because of affliction and great suffering; she dwells among the heathen and finds no peace; all her persecutors have put her in the straits. 4 The ways of Zion mourn, because no one comes to the solemn feasts; all her gates are desolate; her priests sigh; her virgins are defeated, and she is in aridity. 5 Her aduersaries are chief, and her enemies prosper; for the LORD has afflicted her for the multitude of her transgressions, and her children have gone into captivity before the enemy. 6 The daughter of Zion has lost all her beauty; her princes have become like horses that find no pasture and are without strength before the pursuer. 7 Jerusalem remembers the days of her affliction and rebellion, and all the pleasant things that she had in the past, when her people fell into the hands of the en- emy and no one came to her aid; the aduers subdued her and mocked her sabbaths. 8 Je- rusalem has sinned grievously, therefore she is mocked; all who honored her despise her, for they have seen her filthiness; yea, they sigh and turn back. 9 Her

filthiness is in her skirts; she hath not remembered her last end, whereby she went down wonderfully; she had no comforter: O LORD, look on my affliction, for the enemy is proud. 10 The enemy hath stretched forth his hand upon all her pleas- ant things, because she hath seen the heathen enter into her sanctuary, whom thou hadst commanded not to enter into thy Church. 11 All her people sigh and seek their bread; they have given their pleasant things as food to re- fresh their souls; see, O LORD, and consider, for I have become vile. 12 Have you no regard, all you who pass by this road? Look and see if there is any suffering like my suffering, which has been done to me, with which the LORD has afflicted me in the day of his fierce anger. 13 From afar he has sent into my bones a fire that prevents them; he has stretched a net for my feet and turned me back; he has made me desolate and every day in gloom. 14 The yoke of my transgressions is tied to his hand, it has been coiled up and fallen on my neck; it has brought down my strength; the LORD has de- livered me into their hands, and I am no lon- ger able to rise up. 15 The LORD has brought all my valiant ones to their knees in the midst of me; he has summoned an assembly against me to destroy my young men; the LORD has

put wine on the virgin, the daughter of Iu- dah. 16 For these things I weep; indeed, my eye casts out water, because the comforter that should refresh my soul is far from me; my sons are desolate, because the enemy has prevented them. 17 Zion stretcheth out her hands, and there is none to comfort her; the LORD hath encircled the enemies of Iaa- kob: Jerusalem is as a menstruating woman among them. 18 The LORD is righteous, for I have rebelled against his commandments; hear, I pray you, all peoples, and see my grief: my virgins and my young men have gone into captivity. 19 I have called upon my servants, but they have deceived me; my priests and my elders have died in the city as they sought their food to refresh their souls. 20 Behold, O LORD, how troubled I am; my bowels swell; my heart revolts within me, for I am full of happiness; the sword breathes abroad, as death in the house. 21 They have heard that I suffer, but there is no one to comfort me; all my enemies have heard of my troubles, and they rejoice because you have done it; you will make the day come that you have announced, and they will be like me. 22 Let all their wick- edness come upon thee; do unto them what thou hast done unto me for all my transgres- sions: for my sighs are many, and my heart is distressed.

CHAPTER 2

1 How the LORD has darkened the daugh- ter of Zion in his wrath; he has thrown down from top to bottom the beauty of Israel, and has not remembered her footing in the day of his wrath! 2 The LORD has destroyed all the dwellings of Iaakob and has not spared them; in his wrath he has thrown down the fortress- es of the daughter of Iudah; he has thrown down the land; he has polluted the kingdom and its princes. 3 In his fierce anger he has cut off all the horns of Israel; he has withdrawn his right hand from before his adversary, and it has kindled in Iaakob like a flame of fire that has spread all around. 4 He bent his bow like an enemy; his right hand stretched out like an aduersary and killed everything that was pleasing to the eyes in the tabernacle of the daughter of Zion; he released his wrath like a fire. 5 The LORD was like an enemy; he smote Israel and consumed all her palaces; he destroyed her fortresses

and increased in the daughter of Judah wailing and weeping. 6 For he has destroyed his Tabernacle like a garden, he has destroyed his congregation; the LORD has caused the feasts and the Sabbaths to be forgotten in Zion, and has despised, in the indignation of his wrath, the King and the Priest. 7 The LORD forsook his altar, abhorred his sanctuary, gave into the hand of the ene- my the walls of his palaces, made an odyssey in the house of the LORD, as on a feast day. 8 The LORD determined to destroy the wall of the daughter of Zion; he stretched out a lyre; he did not withdraw his hand from destroy- ing; therefore he made the rampart and the wall to lament: they were destroyed together. 9 Her gates have been razed to the ground; he has destroyed and broken her ramparts; her king and her princes are among the Gentiles; the Lawe is no more, nor can her prophets receive any vision from the LORD. 10 The el- ders of the daughter of Zion sit on the ground and are silent; they have thrown dust on their heads; they have girded themselves with sackcloth; the virgins of Jerusalem lower their heads to the ground. 11 My eyes are filled with sadness, my bowels swell, my will is turned to the earth for the destruction of the daughter of my people, because children and infants have died in the streets of the city. 12 They said to their mothers, "Where is the bread and water?" when they fainted as wounded in the streets of the city and when they left the ghost in their mothers' wombs. 13 What shall I tes- tify for you? What shall I compare with you, O daughter of Jerusalem? What shall I compare with thee to comfort thee, O virgin daughter of Zion? For your breach is as great as the sea; who can heal you? 14 Thy prophets have sought for thee vain and foolish things, and have not unveiled thy iniquity to turn away thy captivity, but have sought for thee false prophecies and causes of exile. 15 All who pass by on the road clap their hands at you; they bow and shake their heads over the daughter of Jerusalem, saying, "Is this the city that men call, 'The perfection of beauty and the joy of all the earth? 16 All your enemies have opened their mouths against you; they have bitten and gnashed their teeth, saying, "Let us die; surely this is the day we were looking for; we have found it and seen it." 17 The LORD has done what he set out to do; he has fulfilled the word that he set forth long ago; he has thrown down and spared not; he has caused your ene- my to rise up outside of you, and he has set in motion the horn of your adversaries. 18 Their hearts cried out to the LORD, "O wall of the daughter of Zion, come down like a torrent, day and night; give thyself no rest, and let not the apple of thy eye cease. 19 Arise, cry out in the night; at the beginning of the vigils pour out your heart like water before the face of the LORD; lift up your hands to him for the lives of your young sons, who are starving in the corners of all the streets. 20 Look, O LORD, and consider who thou hast made thus: shall women eat their fruit, and children by a span? Shall the priest and the prophet be slain in the sanctuary of the Lord? 21 The young and the old lie on the ground in the streets; my vir- gins and my young men have fallen under the blows of the sword; you have slain them in the day of your wrath; you have killed and you have not spared. 22 You called as on a sol- emn day my terrors around you, so that in the day of the LORD's wrath no one escaped or remained; those whom I fed and brought to life, my enemy consumed them.

CHAPTER 3

1 I am the man who saw affliction in the rod of his indignation. 2 He has led me and brought me into darkness,

but not into light. 3 Surely he has turned against me; he turns his hand against me all day long. 4 He has aged my flesh and my skin and broken my bones. 5 He has built against me; he has sur- rounded me with gall and toil: 6 He has put me in dark places, like those who are dead forever. 7 He has surrounded me with hedg- es, so that I cannot go out; he has made my chains heavy. 8 Even when I cry out and manifest, he excludes my prayer. 9 He has stopped my ways with his stone and diverted my paths. 10 He has been to me as a carrier in waiting and as a lion in secret places. 11 He has stopped my ways and broken me in piec- es; he has made me desolate. 12 He bent His bow and made me a mark for the arrow. 13 He caused the arrows of his bow to enter my kid- neys. 14 I was a mockery to all my people and their song all day long. 15 He filled me with bitterness and made me drunk with worms. 16 He broke my teeth with stones and sprin- kled me with ashes. 17 Thus my soul departed from peace: I forgot prosperity, 18 And I said, My strength and my hope are gone from the LORD, 19 remembering my affliction and my mourning, the worm and the gall. 20 My soul remembers them and is humbled in me. 21 I consider this in my heart; therefore I hope. 22 It is by the mercies of the Lord that we are not consumed, for his compassion does not fail. 23 They are renewed every morning: great is thy faithfulness. 24 The LORD is my portion, says my soul; therefore I will hope in him. 25 The Lord is good for those who trust in him and for the soul that seeks him. 26 It is good to trust and wait for the Lord's salvation. 27 It is good for a man to bear the yoke from his youth. 28 He sits alone and is silent, be- cause he has brought it upon himself. 29 He puts his mouth in the dust, if there is hope. 30 He rejoices with those who beat him; he is full of reproach. 31 For the LORD does not forsake forever. 32 But even if he allows himself afflictions, he will have compassion according to the multitude of his mercies. 33 For he does not willingly punish, nor afflict the sons of men, 34 And he crushes under his feet all the captives of the earth, 35 and casts out a man's right before the face of the Most High, 36 in submitting a man to his cause; the LORD does not see him. 37 Who then is he who says, "It has happened, but the Lord has not commanded it"? 38 Does not good come out of the mouth of the Most High? 39 Why then does the man who lies grieve? Man suffers because of his sin. 40 Let us seek and try our ways and return to the LORD. 41 Let us lift up our hearts with our hands to God in heaven. 42 We have sinned and rebelled, so you have not spared us. 43 You struck out in anger and persecuted, You killed and did not spare. 44 You covered yourself with clouds, so that our prayer would not pass away. 45 Thou hast made Vs. as waste and garbage in the bowels of the people. 46 All our enemies have opened their mouths against Vs. 47 They fear, and a snare comes upon Vs with desola- tion and destruction. 48 My eye casts rivulets of water for the destruction of the daughter of my people. 49 My eye falls without ceasing and does not cease, 50 Until the LORD looks down and observes from above. 51 My eye breaks in my heart because of all the daugh- ters of my city. 52 My enemies have pursued me like a bird for no reason. 53 They shut my life in a prison and cast a stone on me. 54 The waters flowed over my head, and I thought, "I am destroyed." 55 I called upon Your Name, O LORD, from the lowest prison. 56 You heard my voice; do not stop your gaze from my sigh- ing and my cry. 57 You turned away in the day when I invoked You; You said, "Do not fear." 58 O LORD, you upheld the cause of my soul and redeemed my life. 59 O LORD, you have seen my wrong, and you have taken up my cause. 60 You have seen all their vengeance and all their detour against me. 61 You have heard their reproaches, O LORD, and all their imaginations against me: 62 even the lips of those who have risen up against me and their slander against me. 63 Behold, their sitting down and their rising up, as I am their song. 64 Give them a reward, O LORD, according to the work of their hands. 65 Give them sorrow of heart, and your curse for them. 66 Pursue them with wrath, and destroy them from un- der heaven, O LORD.

CHAPTER 4

1 How has the value become so tenuous? The most precious value has changed, and the stones of the sanctuary are scattered on every street corner. 2 The noble men of Zion, who are comparable to a fine piece of gold, how are they regarded as earthen pitchers, which are the work of a potter's hands! 3 Dragons pull out their udders and give suck to their young, but the daughter of my people has be- come as cruel as ostriches in the wilderness. 4 The tongue of the sucking child clears the roof of his mouth from thirst; little children ask for bread, but no one breaks it for them. 5 Those who fed themselves with gentleness, perish in the street; those who were brought with the skin, embrace the tongue. 6 For the iniquity of the daughter of my people became greater than the sin of Sodom, which was de- stroyed as in a moment, and no one pitched against her. 7 Her Nazarenes were purer than snow and whiter than milk; their bodies were rougher than red precious stones; they were like polished saphir. 8 Now their faces are blacker than a dove; you cannot recog- nize them in the street; their skin is peeled off from their bones; they are withered like a stable. 9 Those who are slain by the sword are better than those who are slain by hunger, for they vanish as if they had been struck for the fruits of the field. 10 The hands of pitiful women have made their sons die, who were their destiny in the destruction of the daugh- ter of my people. 11 The LORD has accom- plished his indignation; he has unleashed his fierce anger; he has kindled a fire in Zion that has destroyed its foundations. 12 The kings of the earth and all the inhabitants of the world would not believe that the adversary and the enemy had entered the gates of Jerusalem: 13 For the sins of her prophets and the iniqui- ties of her priests, who shed the blood of the righteous in her midst. 14 They went about like blind men in the streets, and were defiled with blood, so that they would not touch their garments. 15 But they cried out to them, "Go away, O defiled ones, go away, go away, do not touch"; therefore they fled and wandered; it was said among the heathen, "They shall dwell there no more." 16 The wrath of the LORD has scattered them, he will consider them no more; they did not recognize the face of the priests, nor did they have compassion on the elders. 17 While we waited for our help, our eyes failed, because in our waiting we sought a nation that could not save us. 18 They drive out our steppes because we cannot go our ways; our end is over, our days are fulfilled, for our end has come. 19 Our persecutors are swifter than the eagles of the sea; they pursue our enemies on the mountains and wait for them in the wilderness. 20 The breath of our nostrils, the Lord's Nameless One, has been caught in their nets, of whom we said, "Under his shadow we shall be preserved among the heathen." 21 Rejoice and be glad, daughter of Edom, who dwells in the land of Vz; the cup shall pass over you also; you shall be drunk and vomit. 22 Your punishment is fulfilled, O daughter of Zion; he will no longer take you into captivity,

but he will visit your iniquity, O daughter of Edom; he will unveil your sins.

CHAPTER 5

1 Remember, O LORD, what has come upon you; consider and observe our reproach. 2 Our inheritance has been handed over to strangers, our houses to strangers. 3 We are fatherless, and our mothers are like widows. 4 We have drunk our water for money, and our wood is sold for money. 5 Our necks are under persecution; we are weary and have no rest. 6 We have given our hands to the Egyptians and Assur, to satiate ourselves with bread. 7 Our fathers sinned and are not, and we bore their iniquities. 8 Servants ruled them, and no one delivered them out of their hands. 9 We got our bread by the weight of our lives, because of the sword of the wilderness. 10 Our skin was as black as a hen because of the terrible famine. 11 They defiled the women of Zion and the women of the cities of Iudah. 12 Princes were hanged by the hands; the faces of the elders were not honored. 13 They slit young men's throats, and children fell un- der the wood. 14 The elders stopped coming out of the gate, and the young men stopped singing. 15 The cheerfulness of our hearts disappeared, our joy turned to mourning. 16 The crown of our head is fallen: woe to us who have sinned. 17 For these things our heart is afflicted, our eyes are dull, 18 Because of the mount of Zion, which is desolate; foxes run upon it. 19 But you, O LORD, abide forever; your throne is from generation to generation. 20 Why do you forget yourself forever and forsake yourself for so long? 21 Turn to thee, O LORD, and we will turn; return to our days as of old.

EZEKIEL

CHAPTER 1

1 In the thirtieth year of the fourth month and on the fifth day of the month (while I was among the captives by the river Chebar) the heavens opened and I had visions of GOD. 2 On the fifth day of the month (which was the fifth year of King Jehoiachin's captivity) 3 the word of the LORD came to Ezekiel the priest, the son of Buzi, in the land of the Chaldeans, by the river Chebar, where the hand of the LORD was upon him. 4 And I looked, and behold, a whirlwind came out of the north, a great cloud and a fire surrounding it, and a radiance surrounded it, and in the midst of it, that is, in the midst of the fire, came out like an ember. 5 Moreover out of its bowels came forth the likeness of four beasts, and this was their form: they had the appearance of a man. 6 Each had four faces, and each had four wings. 7 Their feet were straight feet, and the sole of their feet was like the sole of a calf's foot, and they glittered like the ap- pearance of a bright brassa. 8 The hands of a man came out from under their wings in the four parts of them, and they had their faces and their wings. 9 They were bound by their wings to each other, and when they came out they did not go back, but each went straight forward. 10 The likeness of their faces was like that of a man; four had the face of a lion on the right side, and four had the face of a bull on the left side; four also had the face of an eagle. 11 So were their faces, but their wings were spaced apart: two wings of each were joined to each other, and two covered their bodies. 12 Each of them went straight on his way; they went where their spirit led them and did not turn back when they departed. 13 Also the beasts and their appearance were like streams of burning fire and the appear- ance of lamps, for the fire ran among the beasts, and the fire gave forth flashes, and out of the fire came flashes of lightning. 14 The beasts ran and came back like lightning. 15 As I watched the beasts, behold, there appeared on the earth beside the beasts a silhouette that had four faces. 16 The face of the wheels and their work were like a chrysolite; and all four of them had one shape, and their face and their work were like a wheel in another wheel. 17 When they went, they went along their four sides and did not turn back when they went. 18 They also had rings and a height that was awe-inspiring, and their rings were full of eyes, all around them four. 19 When the beasts went, the wheels went with them; and when the beasts were lifted up from the earth, the wheels were lifted up. 20 Where the spir- it led them, they went, and the spirit of the wheels led them, and the wheels were lifted up besides them, because the spirit of the beasts was in the wheels. 21 When the beasts went, they went, and when they stopped, they stopped, and when they were lifted up from the earth, the wheels were lifted up be- yond them, because the spirit of the beasts was in the wheels. 22 The resemblance of the firmament to the heads of the beasts was wonderful, similar to crystal, with the heads protruding outward. 23 Under the firmament their wings were straight, one toward the other; each had two covering the body, and each had two covering the body. 24 And when they stood afar off, I heard the sound of their wings like the sound of great waters, and like the sound of the Almighty, like the sound of a speech, like the sound of an army; and when they stood, they lowered their wings. 25 And there was a sight from the firmament, which was above their heads, when they stood still and had lowered their wings. 26 And on the firmament, which was above their heads, was the front of a throne like a stone of Sahir, and the likeness of the throne was apparent, like the likeness of a man standing upon it. 27 And like the appearance of amber and like the likeness of fire surrounding it to look upon it, from its loins upward; and to look upon it, from its loins downward, like a likeness of fire and a brightness surrounding it. 28 As the ap- pearance of the bandage, which is in the cloud in the day of rain, so was the appearance of the light around it. (Ezekiel:) This was the ap- pearance of the similitude of the glory of the Lord; and when I saw it, I fell on my face and heard the voice of one speaking.

CHAPTER 2

1 And he said to me, "Son of man, stand on your feet, and I will speak to you." 2 And the Spirit entered into me, having spoken to me, and set me on my feet, so that I heard him who spoke to me. 3 And he said to me, "Son of man, I am sending you to the children of Israel, to a rebellious nation that has rebelled against me, for they and their fathers have re- belled against me to this day. 4 For they are impudent and stiff-necked children: I send you to them, and you say to them, "Thus says the Lord God." 5 But surely they will not listen and will not cease, because they are a rebel- lious house; yet they will know that there is a Prophet in their midst. 6 You, son of man, do not fear them or their words, though rebels and thorns are with you and you remain with scorpions; do not fear their words or their looks, for they are a rebellious house. 7 There- fore thou shalt speak unto them of my words, but they will not hear, neither will they cease, for they are rebellious. 8 But you, son of man, listen to what I say to you; do not be rebellious like this rebellious house; open your mouth and eat what I

give you. 9 When I looked, behold, a hand was sent to me, and, behold, there was in it a copy of a book. 10 He thrust it out before me, and it was written inside and out, and there was written, "Lamentations, mourning, and sorrow."

CHAPTER 3

1 Moreover he said to me, "Son of man, eat what you find; eat this portion, go and speak to the house of Israel." 2 So I opened my mouth, and he gave me this portion of bread to eat. 3 And he said to me, "Son of man, make your belly eat and fill your bowels with this dish that I give you." So I ate it, and it was in my mouth as sweet as gold. 4 Then he said to me, "Son of man, go, enter the house of Isra- el and communicate to them my words. 5 For you were not sent to a people of unknown lan- guage or a difficult tongue, but to the house of Israel, 6 not to a people of unknown tongue or a hard tongue, whose words you cannot understand; yet if I sent you to them, they would obey you. 7 But the house of Israel will not obey you, because they do not obey me; yea, all the house of Israel is impudent and stiff-necked. 8 Behold, I have made your face strong against their faces, and your forehead hard against their foreheads. 9 I have made your forehead like adamant and harder than flint; therefore do not fear them or be afraid in their sight, for they are a rebellious house." 10 He said to me again, "Son of man, receive into your heart all my words that I say to you and listen to them with your ears, 11 go and enter in to those who are led into captivity among the children of your people, and speak to them and say to them, 'Thus says the Lord God,' but they will not hear and will not stop listening." 12 Then the Spirit took hold of me, and I heard behind me a noise of a great pattering, saying, "Blessed be the glory of the Lord from his place." 13 I also heard the sound of the wings of the beasts touching one another and the rattling of the wheels that stood near them, a noise of a great pattering. 14 Then the spirit lifted me up and carried me away, and I went forth to the bitterness and indignation of my spirit, but the hand of the Lord was strong upon me. 15 Then I came to those who had been led into captivity at Tel-abib, who dwelt by the river Chebar, and sat down where they were and stood there amazed among them for ten days. 16 At the end of these ten days, the word of the LORD came to me again, saying 17 Son of man, I have constituted you a watchman for the house of Israel; therefore hear the word that I have spoken, and give them warning from me. 18 When I say to the wicked, "You shall surely die," and you do not warn him and speak to warn the wicked from his evil way, that he may rest, the wicked himself shall die in his iniquity; but his blood I will require from your hand. 19 But if you make war on the wicked man and he does not turn from his wicked- ness and from his evil way, he will die in his iniquity, but you will have delivered your soul. 20 In the same way, if a righteous man turns from his righteousness and commits iniquity, I will set before him a stumbling block, and he shall die, because you have not warned him; he shall die in his sin, and his righteous deeds, which he has done, shall not be remembered; but his blood I will require from your hand. 21 If thou admonishest that righteous man, that he sinneth not, and that he sinneth not, he shall die because he was admonished; so thou shalt have delivered thy soul also. 22 The hand of the LORD came upon me and said, "Get up, go into the field, and there I will speak to you." 23 When I had risen and set out for the camp, behold, the glory of the LORD stood there, like the glory I had seen by the river Chebar, and I fell to the ground on my face. 24 Then the Spirit entered into me, and He set me on my feet and spoke to me and said, "Come and shut yourself up in your house." 25 But you, O son of man, behold, they will put bandag- es on you and bind you to them, and you will not be able to go out among them. 26 And I will cause thy tongue to be clear on the roof of thy mouth, so that thou shalt be dume and not be to them as a man that reproacheth, be- cause they are a rebellious house. 27 But when I have spoken to thee, I will open thy mouth, and thou shalt say unto them, Thus saith the Lord God, He that heareth let him hear, and he that turneth away let him leave: for they are a rebellious house.

CHAPTER 4

1 You also, son of man, take a brick, lay it before you, and overthrow the city, that is, Je- rusalem, upon it, 2 lay siege to it, and build a fortress against it, and cast against it a mountain; set also campe against it, and dis- pose against it, all around, engines of war. 3 Moreover, take a pan of yron and put it as a wall of yron between you and the city, direct your face toward it; it shall be besieged, and you shall besiege it; this shall be a sign to the house of Israel. 4 Sleep also on thy left side, and upon it lay the iniquity of the house of Is- rael; according to the number of the days that thou sleepest upon it, thou shalt bear their iniquity. 5 For I have laid upon you the years of their iniquity, according to the number of the days, that is, three hundred and ninety days, you shall bear the iniquity of the house of Israel. 6 And when thou hast fulfilled them, thou shalt sleep again on thy right side, and shalt bear the iniquity of the house of Israel for forty days: and I have appointed thee one day for a year, and one day for a year. 7 There- fore thou shalt direct thy face toward the siege of Jerusalem, and thy weapon shall be heard, and thou shalt prophesy against it. 8 Behold, I will put bands on you, and you shall not turn from one side to the other until you have fin- ished the days of your siege. 9 You shall also take some wheat, barley, beans, lentils, millet and beans, and you shall put them in a ves- sel and make bread out of them according to the number of the days that you sleep on your side. 10 The food you shall eat shall be by weight, that is, twenty shekels a day, and you shall eat from time to time. 11 You shall also drink water by measure, that is, the sixth part of a hin; you shall drink of it from time to time. 12 And thou shalt eat it as barley bread, and thou shalt bake it in the tongue that cometh out of the man, in their sight." 13 The LORD said, "So the children of Israel shall eat their defiled bread among the Gentiles, where I will cast them." 14 Then I said, "Lord God, behold, my soul has not been defiled, for from my youth onward, until this hour, I have not eaten a dead thing or torn to pieces, nor has any bad meat entered my mouth." 15 Then he said to me, "Behold, I have given you the tongue of an ox as the tongue of a man, and with it you shall prepare your bread." 16 More- over he said to me, "Son of man, behold, I will break the staff of bread in Jerusalem, and they shall eat bread by weight and with care, and they shall drink water by measure and with astonishment." 17 For the bread and the water shall fail, and they shall be amazed at one an- other, and shall be consumed in their iniquity.

CHAPTER 5

1 You, son of man, take a sharp knife or a bar- ber's razor and run it over your head and over your beard; then take the

scales for weighing and estimate the weight. 2 You shall bury the thirteenth part of them with fire in the midst of the city, when the days of the siege are past; you shall take the other thirteenth part and strike it with a knife; the last thirteenth part you shall scatter in the wind, and I will draw out a sword against them. 3 You shall also take some in nomine and put them in your lappa. 4 Then you shall take of them again, and cast them into the midst of the fire, and you shall bury them in the fire, for from here shall go forth a fire in all the house of Israel." 5 Thus says the LORD God, "This is Jerusalem: I have set it in the midst of the nations and the countries that surround it. 6 She has turned my principles into wickedness more than the nations, and my statutes more than the coun- tries that surround her, because they have re- jected my principles and my statutes and have not walked in them. 7 Therefore thus says the LORD God, "Because your multitude is great- er than the nations around you, you have not walked in my statutes and have not kept my precepts; no, you have not acted according to the precepts of the nations around you." 8 Therefore thus says the Lord God, "Behold, I come against you and execute judgment in your midst, even before the nations. 9 I will do in you what I have never done before, and I will not do the same again, because of all your abominations. 10 For in the midst of thee the fathers shall eat their children, and the chil- dren shall eat their fathers, and I will execute judgment upon thee, and all thy remnant I will scatter in all the winds. 11 Therefore, as I say, saith the Lord God, because thou hast de- filed my sanctuary with all thy filthiness and with all thy abominations, I will also destroy thee; my eye shall not spare thee, neither shall I pity thee. 12 The third part of thee shall die of pestilence and famine in thy land; anoth- er third part shall fall by the sword around thee; the last third part I will scatter in all the winds and drag with the sword. 13 Thus shall my wrath be fulfilled, I will cause my wrath in them to cease, and I will be comforted; and they shall know that I, the LORD, have spoken it in my zeal, when I have fulfilled my wrath in them. 14 Moreover, I will make you a re- jection and an execration among the nations around you and in the eyes of all who pass by. 15 Thus you will be a reproach and a disgrace, a chastisement and an astonishment to the nations around you, when I execute judg- ments upon you, with wrath and anger, and with severe rebukes; I, the LORD, have said it. 16 When I will send upon them the arrows of famine, which shall be for their destruction, and which I will send to destroy you; I will in- crease the famine upon you, and I will break your staff of bread. 17 So I will send famine upon you, and beasts, which shall come upon you, and pestilence and blood shall pass through you, and I will bring the sword upon you; I, the LORD, have said it.

CHAPTER 6

1 Again the word of the LORD came to me, saying, 2 Son of man, turn your face toward the mountains of Israel and prophesy against them, 3 and say, "You mountains of Israel, lis- ten to the word of the LORD God; thus says the LORD God to the mountains and to the hills, to the shores and to the valleys, 'Behold, I will bring a sword upon you and destroy your places of worship: 4 Your altars shall be desolate, and your sun images shall be bro- ken; and I will cast your slain men before your idols. 5 And I will cause the dead bodies of the children of Israel to lie down before their idols, and I will scatter your bones round about your altars. 6 In all your dwellings your cities shall be desolate,

and your dwelling places shall be forsaken, so that your altars shall be destroyed and desolate, your idols shall be broken and cease, your sun images shall be broken in pieces, and your works shall be abolished. 7 The dead shall fall among you, and you shall know that I am the LORD. 8 Nev- ertheless I will leave a remnant, that you may have some who will escape the sword among the nations, when you are torn through the countries. 9 Those who will escape among you will remember me among the nations, where they will be in captivity, because I am grieved for their perverse hearts, which have turned away from me, and for their eyes, which have gone whoring after their idolatries, and they will be sorry in themselves for the sins they have committed in all their abominations. 10 And they shall know that I am the LORD, and that I said not in vein that I would do them this evil. 11 Thus says the LORD God, "Strike with your hand, stretch out your foot, and say, 'Alas, for all the wicked abominations of the house of Israel, for they shall fall by the sword, by famine, and by pestilence. 12 He who is far off shall die by pestilence, he who is near shall die by the sword, and he who remains and is besieged shall die by famine; thus will I accomplish my wrath upon them. 13 Then ye shall know that I am the LORD, when their slain men shall be in the midst of their idols round about their altars, on every hill in all the tops of the mountains, under every ver- dant tree, and under every slender tree, which is the place where they offered a sweet savor to all their idols. 14 So I will stretch out my hand upon them and make the land deserted and forsaken from the wilderness to Diblath, in all their dwellings, and they shall know that I am the LORD.

CHAPTER 7

1 Moreover the word of the LORD was spo- ken to me, saying 2 You also, son of man, thus says the LORD God, "The end has come upon the land of Israel; the end has come upon the four corners of the land. 3 Now the end has come upon you, and I will unleash my wrath upon you, and I will judge you according to your ways, and I will make you pay for all your abominations. 4 My eye will not spare thee, nor will I have mercy, but I will bring down upon thee thy guilt, and thy abomination shall be in the midst of thee, and thou shalt know that I am the LORD. 5 Thus says the Lord God, "Behold, an end, an end has come. 6 The end has come, the end has come, He has watched over you; behold, it has come. 7 The morning has come for you who dwell in the land; the time has come, the day of trouble is near, and there is no more sound of the mountains. 8 Now shortly I will pour out my wrath upon thee, and I will execute my wrath upon thee; I will judge thee according to thy ways, and I will make thee to pay for all thy abomina- tions. 9 I will not spare thee nor have mercy, but I will smite thee according to thy ways, and thy abominations shall be in the midst of thee, and thou shalt know that I am the Lord that smiteth. 10 Behold, the day, behold, has come; the morning has dawned, the rod flourishes, pride has sprouted. 11 Cruelty has turned into a rod of wickedness; there shall be nothing left of them, nor of their riches, nor of any of theirs, and there shall be no more to mourn for them. 12 The hour is come, the day is drawing near; let not the murderer shrink, nor let him who sells mourn, for wrath shall come upon all his multitude. 13 He that selleth shall not return to that which is lonely, though they were yet far off: for the vision was to all his multitude, and they turned not back, and no man is encouraged in the chastisement of his life. 14

They have sounded the trumpet and prepared everything, but no one goes to the battle, because my wrath is on all his multi- tude. 15 The sword is outside, pestilence and famine inside; those in the fields will die by the sword, and those in the city, famine and pestilence will kill them. 16 But those who flee from them shall escape and remain in the mountains, like the dogs of the valleys; all shall fall sick, every one for his iniquity. 17 All their hands shall droop, and all their knees shall fall down like water. 18 They shall also clothe themselves with sackcloth, they shall be afraid, they shall be ashamed on all their faces, and they shall be bald on their heads. 19 They shall cast their silk into the streets, and their gold shall be cast far away; their silk and their gold shall not be able to save them in the day of the LORD's wrath; they shall not satiate their souls nor fill their bowels, for this ruin is due to their iniquity. 20 He had also set the beauty of his ornament in the maiestie; but they have made therein images of their abominations and idols; therefore I have set it away from them. 21 I will give it into the hand of foreigners to strip it, and to the wicked of the earth to rob it, and they shall defile it. 22 I will also turn my face from them, and they shall pollute my secret place, for destroyers shall enter it and defile it. 23 Make a chain, for the land is full of blood, and the city is full of cruelty. 24 Therefore I will cause the most wicked of the heathen to come, and possess their houses: I will also cause the pomp of the mighty to cease, and their holy places to be defiled. 25 And when destruction cometh, they shall see peace, and shall not have it. 26 Calamity upon calamity, and rumor upon ru- mor; then they shall see a vision of the proph- et, but the word shall perish from the priest, and the counsel from the ancient. 27 And the king shall be muffled, and the prince shall be clothed with desolation, and the hands of the people of the land shall be troubled: I will do the same thing unto them, according to their desires, and I will judge them according to their judgments, and they shall know that I am the LORD.

CHAPTER 8

1 In the sixtieth year, in the sixtieth month, and on the fifth day of the month, as I stood in my house, and the elders of Iudah stood be- fore me, the hand of the Lord God came upon me. 2 Then I saw, and behold, there was a fig- ure like the appearance of fire, to look upon, from his loins downward and from his loins upward, like an appearance of brightness, re- sembling amber. 3 Then he stretched out the likeness of armor and took me by the head, and the Spirit lifted me up between the earth and heaven, and brought me with a divine vision to Jerusalem, to the entrance of the inner gate which is toward the north, where there was the idol of indignation, causing in- dignation. 4 And behold, the glory of the God of Israel was there, according to the vision I had seen in the camp. 5 Then he said to me, "Son of man, lift up now your eyes toward the north." Then I lifted up mine eyes toward the north, and behold, in the north, at the gate of the altar, was this idol of indignation. 6 He further said to me, "Son of man, do you not see what they are doing? that is, the great abominations that the house of Israel is com- mitting here to cause me to depart from my sanctuary? But turn around and you will see greater abominations." 7 He brought me in at the door of the courtyard; and when I looked, behold, there was a hole in the wall. 8 Then he said to me, "Son of man, dig now in the wall." And when I had dug in the wall, behold, there was a hole. 9 And he said to me, "Go in and observe the

evil abominations that they do here." 10 So I went in and observed that on the wall all around were painted all the likeness- es of creeping things and abominable beasts and all the idols of the house of Israel. 11 In front of them stood seuentie men of the an- cients of the house of Israel, and in the midst of them stood Iaazaniah the son of Shaphan, with a man with his censer in his hand, while the vapor of the incense went up like a cloud. 12 Then he said to me, "Son of man, have you seen what the ancients of the house of Isra- el do in darkness, each in the chamber of his own imagination? For they say, 'The Lord does not see; the Lord has forsaken the land.'" 13 Then he also said to me, "Turn again and you will see the greatest abominations they do." 14 He made me enter the doorway of the gate of the house of the LORD, which was toward the north, and behold, there were women mourn- ing for Tammuz. 15 Then he said to me, "Have you seen this, son of man? Turn again and you will see greater abominations than these." 16 He brought me into the inner courtyard of the house of the LORD, and I saw, at the end of the temple of the LORD, between the porch and the altar, about fifty-two men with their backs turned toward the temple of the LORD and their faces toward the east, worshipping the sun toward the east. 17 He said to me, "Have you seen this, son of man? Is it a small thing for the house of Iudah to commit these abominations that they do here? For they have filled the land with cruelty, and have re- turned to put me to shame; and, for the truth, they have cast the sting before their noses. 18 Therefore I will also execute my wrath; my eye will not spare them, nor will I have mercy, and though they cry in my ears with a loud voice, I will not hear them.

CHAPTER 9

1 And he cried also with a loud voice in mine ears, saying, The visitations of the city draw near, and every one had a weapon in his hand to destroy it. 2 And behold, six men came by the way of the gate that is toward the north, and every one of them had a weapon in his hand to destroy it; and one of them was clothed in linen, with a writer by his side, and they went in and stood by the bronze altar. 3 The glory of the God of Israel departed from the Cherubim, who stood at the threshold of the house, and called to the man clothed in linen, who had the pen at his side. 4 And the LORD said to him, "Go through the streets of the city, that is, the streets of Jerusalem, and put a sign on the foreheads of those who go there, and cry out for all the abominations that are committed in the streets of the city." 5 And to the other he said, that I might hear, "Pursue him through the city and smite him; your eye will spare no one and have no mercy. 6 Destroy the old men, and the young men, and the maidens, and the children, and the women, but do not touch the man on whom the mark is, and begin at my sanctuary." Then they began from the Old Ones, who were in front of the house. 7 He said to them, "Defile the house and fill the courts with the dead, then leave"; and they went out and killed them in the city. 8 When they had slain them and I had escaped, I fell down on my face and cried out, "Lord God, wilt thou destroy all the rest of Israel, and bring forth thy wrath upon Jeru- salem? 9 Then he said to me, "The iniquity of the house of Israel and of Iudah is very great, so that the land is full of blood and the city is full of corruption; for they say, 'The LORD has forsaken the land, and the LORD does not see it.'" 10 As for me also, my eye will not spare them, nor will I have mercy, but I will recom- pense their ways upon their heads. 11 And be- hold, the man

clothed in linen, who had the horse by his side, reported and said, "Lord, I have done as you commanded me."

CHAPTER 10

1 And as I looked, behold, in the firmament that was around the heads of the Cherubim there appeared over them a throne-like stone, as if it were a stone of Sahir. 2 Then he spoke to the man clothed in linen and said to him, "Go in between the wheels, that is, under the Cherubim, and fill your hands with cups of fire among the Cherubim and scatter them outside the city." And he entered into my presence. 3 When the man entered, the Cher- ubim stood on the right side of the house, and the cloud filled the inner court. 4 Then the glory of the LORD went out from the Cher- ubim and stood beyond the house, and the house was filled with the cloud and the court was filled with the splendor of the glory of the LORD. 5 The sound of the Cherub's wings was heard in the whole court, like the voice of the Almighty God when He speaks. 6 When he had commanded the man clothed in linen to take fire between the wheels and among the Cherubim, he went in and stood by the wheel. 7 And a Cherub stretched out his hand among the Cherubim toward the fire that was among the Cherubim, and took it, and put it into the hand of him who was clothed in linen, who took it and went out. 8 And in the Cher- ubim appeared the figure of a man's hand under their wings. 9 And when I looked, be- hold, beside the Cherubim were four wheels, one wheel from one Cherubim and another wheel from another Cherubim, and the ap- pearance of the wheels was like the color of a chrysolite stone. 10 Their appearance (for they were all four of one appearance) was as if one wheel had been inserted into another wheel. 11 When they went outward, they went along their four sides and did not turn back as they had gone; but at the place where the first one had gone, they followed him and did not turn back as they had gone. 12 And their whole body, and their rings, and their hands, and their wings, and their wheels, were full of eyes all around, always in the same four wheels. 13 And the Cherubim cried to these wheels in my hearing, saying, "O wheele." 14 And every beast had four faces: the first was the face of a Cherub, the second was the face of a man, the third was the face of a Lion, and the fourth was the face of an Egle. 15 And the Cherubim were lifted up: this is the beast that I saw at the riuer Chebar. 16 When the Cher- ubim went, the wheels passed beside them; and when the Cherubim lifted up their wings to rise from the earth, the same wheels did not turn beside them. 17 When the Cherubim stood, they stood; and when they lifted up, the others also lifted up, for the spirit of the beast was in them. 18 Then the glory of the LORD departed from outside the house and stood on the Cherubim. 19 And the Cherubim lifted up their wings and went up from the earth before me; and when they went out, the wheels also were beside them; and every one stood at the entrance of the gate of the House of the LORD on the east side, and the glory of the God of Israel was upon them. 20 This is the beast that I saw under the God of Israel by the river Chebar, and I understood that they were the Cherubim. 21 Each of them had four faces and each had four wings, and under their wings was the likeness of men's hands. 22 The likeness of their faces was the same as I had seen at the river Chebar, and the appear- ance of the Cherubim was the same, and they each went straight forward.

CHAPTER 11

1 And the Spirit lifted me up and led me to the eastern gate of the house of the Lord, which is on the east side, and behold, at the entrance of the gate were five or twenty men, among whom I saw Iaazaniah the son of Azur and Pelatiah the son of Benaiah, princes of the people. 2 Then he said to me, "Son of man, these are the men who imagine evil and make evil counsel in this city. 3 For they say, 'It is not here, build houses'; this city is the cauldron, and we are the flesh. 4 Therefore prophesy against them, son of man, prophesy. 5 The Spirit of the LORD came upon me and said to me, "Speak, thus says the LORD: O house of Israel, this you have spoken, and I know what comes forth from your minds. 6 You have killed many in this city and filled its streets with the dead. 7 Therefore thus says the LORD God, Those whom you have slain and have laid in the midst of it are the flesh, and this city is the cauldron, but I will bring you out of the midst of it. 8 You have feared the sword, and I will bring you a sword, says the Lord God. 9 I will bring you out of its bowels, I will deliver you into the hands of strangers, and I will do justice in the midst of you. 10 You shall fall by the sword, and I will judge you in the borders of Israel, and you shall know that I am the LORD. 11 This city shall not be your cauldron, nor shall you be the meat in its midst, but I will judge you at the borders of Israel. 12 And you shall know that I am the LORD, because you have not walked in my statutes and have not carried out my decrees, but have followed the customs of the heathen around you. 13 While I was prophesying, Pelatiah the son of Benaiah died; then I fell to the ground on my face and cried with a loud voice and said, "Lord God, wilt thou destroy all the remnant of Israel? 14 Then the word of the LORD came to me, who said, 15 Son of man, thy brethren, thy kinsmen, the men of thy seed, and all the house of Israel, who are they to whom the in- habitants of Jerusalem said, "Depart from the LORD, for the land has been given into their possession"? 16 Say therefore, "Thus says the LORD God, Although I have cast them far away among the heathen and scattered them among the countries, yet I will be to them as a small sanctuary in the land to which they will come." 17 Therefore say ye, Thus saith the Lord God, I will gather you again from among the Gentiles, and gather you out of the countries whither ye have been scattered, and I will give you the land of Israel. 18 They will come there and take away from there all idols and all abominations. 19 I will give them one heart and put a new spirit in their bowels; I will re- move the heart of stone from their bodies and give them a heart of flesh, 20 That they may walk in my statutes, and keep my decrees, and do them; and they shall be my people, and I will be their God. 21 But for those whose hearts are turned to their idolatries and whose affections go after their abominations, I will make their way fall back upon their own heads, says the Lord God." 22 Then the cheru- bim lifted up their wings and wheels beyond them, and the glory of the God of Israel was upon them. 23 The glory of the LORD went out from the center of the city and stood on the mountain that is toward the eastern side of the city. 24 Then the Spirit took me and brought me in vision, by the Spirit of God, to Chaldea, to those who had been led into cap- tivity; so the vision I had seen departed from me. 25 Then I declared to those who had been led into captivity all the things that the Lord had shown me.

CHAPTER 12

1 Also the word of the Lord was spoken to me, saying, 2 Son of man, you dwell in the midst of a rebellious house, which has eyes to see and does not see; it has ears to hear and does not hear, for it is a rebellious house. 3 Therefore, son of man, prepare your stuff to go into captivity, and go before them by day; and you shall pass from your place to anoth- er place before them, if it is possible for them to consider it, for they are a rebellious house. 4 Then thou shalt bring thy stuff before their eyes by day, as the stuff of those who go into captivity, and thou shalt go out always before their eyes, as those who go into captivity. 5 You shall dig the wall under their eyes and go out. 6 Under their eyes you shall carry it on your shoulders and carry it away in darkness; you shall cover your face so that you will not see the land, for I have set you as a sign for the house of Israel. 7 As I was commanded, by day I brought out my stuff, like the stuff of those who go into captivity; by night I dug with my hand through the wall, and brought it out into the darkness, and carried it on my shoulder under their eyes. 8 In the morning the word of the LORD came to me, saying, "Son of man, do not worry, 9 Son of man, did not the house of Israel, the rebellious house, say to you, "What are you doing?" 10 But you say to them, "Thus says the Lord God, This burden concerns the leaders of Jerusalem and all the house of Israel that is among them. 11 Say, "I am your sign; as I have done, so shall it be done to them; they shall go into bondage and captivity." 12 The foremost among them will shoulder the darkness and depart; they will dig through the wall to bring them out; they will cover their faces so that they will not see the ground with their ears. 13 I will also spread out my net to him; he shall be caught in my net, and I will lead him to Babel, to the land of the Chaldeans, but he shall not see it, though he die there. 14 And I will scatter toward euerie wind all those who are around him to help him, and all his bondsmen, and I will draw out the sword behind them. 15 And they shall know that I am the LORD, when I scatter them among the nations, and scat- ter them in the countries. 16 But I will leave a small part of them from the sword, and from famine, and from pestilence, that they may declare all these abominations among the heathen, where they come, and know that I am the LORD. 17 Moreover, the word of the Lord was spoken to me, saying, 18 Son of man, eat your bread with trembling, and drink your water with toil and care, 19 and say to the inhabitants of the land, "Thus says the LORD, God, of the inhabitants of Jerusalem and of the land of Israel: They shall eat their bread with prudence and drink their water with desolation, for the land will be desolate from its abundance because of the cruelty of those who inhabit it. 20 The inhabited cities will be left in ruins, the land will be desolate, and you will know that I am the LORD. 21 The word of the LORD was spoken to me, saying, 22 Son of man, what is that concern that you have in the land of Israel, which says, "The days are prolonged and all visions fade away"? 23 Say to them, "Thus says the LORD God, 'I will cause this worry to cease, and they will no longer see it as a worry in Israel; but you will say to them, "The days are drawing near, and the effect of every vision will vanish." 24 For no more shall any vision be in vein, nor shall there be any flattering diuination in the house of Israel. 25 For I am the LORD: I will speak, and the thing that I shall speak shall come to pass; it shall not be prolonged any more: for in your days, O rebellious house, I will speak the thing, and I will perform it, saith the LORD God." 26 Then the word of the LORD was spo- ken to me, saying, "Son of man, do not worry, 27 Son of man, behold, those of the house of Israel say, "The vision that he sees is for many days to come, and he prophesies of the

times that are far off." 28 Therefore say unto them, Thus saith the Lord God, All my words shall not be put off any more, but that which I have spoken shall be done, saith the Lord God.

CHAPTER 13

1 The word of the LORD was spoken to me, saying. 2 Son of man, prophesy against the prophets of Israel who prophesy, and say to them who prophesy from the heart, "Listen to the word of the Lord." 3 Thus says the Lord God, "Woe to the foolish prophets who fol- low their spirit and have seen nothing." 4 O Israel, your prophets are like foxes in desert places. 5 You have not gone up the spires and made a hedge for the house of Israel, to stand in the battle in the day of the LORD. 6 They have seen vanity and lies, saying, "The LORD says this, and the LORD has not sent them"; and they have made others hope that they would confirm the word of their prophecy. 7 Have you not seen a vain vision and told a lie? You say, "The Lord says so, but I have not spoken." 8 Therefore thus says the Lord God, "Because you have spoken vanity and have seen lies, behold, I am against you, says the Lord God, 9 And my hand shall come upon the prophets who see vanities and speak lies; they shall not be in the assembly of my people, nor shall they be written in the writing of the house of Israel, nor shall they enter into the land of Israel; and you shall know that I am the Lord God. 10 Therefore, for they have de- ceived my people, saying, "Peace," and there has been no peace; and one has built a wall, and behold, the others have smeared it with vntemperate mortar, 11 Say to those who have plastered it with vntemperate mortar that it shall fall, for a great show shall come, and I will send hay stones that will cause it to fall, and a storm wind shall break it. 12 Behold, when the wall has fallen, shall it not be said to you, "Where is the plaster with which you have daubed it?" 13 Therefore thus says the Lord God, "In my wrath I will cause a tem- pestuous wind to break out, and in my anger there will be a great show, and in my indig- nation it will hail to consume it. 14 I will de- stroy the wall that you have plastered with tempered mortar, and I will bring it down to the ground, so that its foundation will be undone and fall, and you will be consumed in its bowels, and you will know that I am the LORD. 15 Thus will I accomplish my wrath against the wall and against those who have defiled it with tempered mortar, and I will say to you, "The wall is no more, nor its defilers." 16 that is, the prophets of Israel who prophe- sied over Jerusalem and saw visions of peace for it, but there is no peace, says the Lord God. 17 Likewise, son of man, set your face against the daughters of your people, who prophesy heartily; prophesy against them and say, 18 Thus says the LORD God, "Woe to the women who sow pillows under the holes of arms and make veils over the head of every person who stands to cast out souls; will you cast out the souls of my people and give life to the souls that come to you? 19 Will you defile me among my people by handfuls of barrels and pieces of bread, to kill the souls of those who should not die, and to give life to souls who should not lie, lying to my people who hear your lies? 20 Therefore thus says the Lord God, "Behold, I will deal with your pillows, with which you hunt souls to make them flee, and I will tear them from your weapons, and I will let the souls go, even those you hunt to make them flee. 21 Even your cloaks of protection I will tear them out of your hands, and my people shall no longer be in your hands to be cast out, and you shall know that I am the LORD. 22 For by your

lies you have saddened the heart of the righteous, whom I have not sad- dened, and you have strengthened the hands of the wicked, lest he return from his evil way, promising him life, 23 Therefore you shall see no more vanity, nor diuinity; for I will deliver my people out of your hands, and you shall know that I am your Lord.

CHAPTER 14

1 Then some elders of Israel came to me and sat down before me. 2 The word of the LORD was spoken to me, saying, "Son of man, these men have put their idolatries into their hearts and put their desire to be free into action, 3 Son of man, these men have put into their hearts their idolatries and put into their faces the stumbling block of their iniquity; should I, being required, answer them? 4 Therefore speak unto them, and say, Thus saith the LORD God, Every man of the house of Israel that putteth in his heart his idols, and put- teth before his face the stumblingblock of his iniquity, and turneth unto the prophet, I, the LORD, will answer him that turneth, ac- cording to the multitude of his idols: 5 That I may take the house of Israel into his heart, for all have turned away from me because of their idols. 6 Therefore say to the house of Israel, "Thus says the Lord God, Withdraw, withdraw, turn away from your idols, and turn away from all your abominations. 7 For whosoever of the house of Israel or of the stranger that sojourneth in Israel shall turn away from me, and shall put away his idols in his heart, and shall set before his face the stumbling block of his iniquity, and shall call upon a prophet to ask him to account for me; I, the LORD, will answer him for myself, 8 and I will set my face against that man and make him an example and a trial, and I will cut him off from the midi of my people, and you shall know that I am the LORD. 9 And if the proph- et deceives himself, when he has said a thing, I, the LORD, have deceived that prophet, and I will stretch out my hand upon him and de- stroy him from the mids of my people of Isra- el. 10 They shall suffer their chastisement; the chastisement of the prophet shall be as the chastisement of him that asketh, 11 That the house of Israel may no more depart from me, nor defile itself with all its transgressions, but may it be my people, and I its God, saith the Lord God. 12 The word of the LORD was again spoken to me, saying, 13 Son of man, when your country sins against me by committing a transgression, then I will stretch out my hand upon it, and I will break the staff of bread and send famine upon it, and I will destroy man and animals from it." 14 Even if these three men, Noah, Daniel and Iob, were in their midst, they should do nothing but sacrifice their souls with their righteousness, says the Lord God. 15 If I introduce noxious beasts into the land and they scatter it, so that it is desolate, so that no one may pass through, because of the beasts, 16 though these three men be in the midst of it, as I lie, saith the LORD God, they shall have neither sons nor daughters; they only shall be disappointed, but the land shall be desolate. 17 Or if I bring a sword upon this land and say, "Sword, pass through the land, so that I destroy man and animals from it." 18 even if these three men were in the midst of it, as I say, says the LORD God, they shall give neither sons nor daugh- ters, but they alone shall be eliminated. 19 Or if I send a pestilence into this land and vent my wrath upon it with blood, to destroy men and animals from it, 20 and even if Noah, Daniel and Iob were in the midst of it, as I say, says the Lord God, they shall have neither sons nor daughters, but they shall have their own souls through their own righteousness. 21 For thus says the LORD God, "How much more when will I send my four severe judg- ments upon Jerusalem, that is, the sword, famine, noxious beasts, and pestilence, to destroy man and beasts from there? 22 Nev- ertheless, behold, there shall remain a rem- nant of those who shall be taken away, both sons and daughters; behold, they shall come to you, and you shall see their way and their deeds; and you shall be comforted, concern- ing the evil that I have done upon Jerusalem, and concerning all that I have done upon it. 23 They shall comfort you, when you shall see their way and their deeds; and you shall know that I have not done without cause all that I have done in it, saith the Lord God.

CHAPTER 15

1 The word of the LORD came to me, saying.

2 Son of man, what shall be made of the vine tree in comparison with all the other trees, and of the vine that is among the trees of the forest? 3 Shall men take wood from it to do some work, or shall they take a pin from it to hang some vessels on it? 4 Behold, it is cast into the fire to be consumed; the fire consumes its ends, and its center is burned. Is it fit for any work? 5 Behold, when it was whole, it was not fit for any work; how much less will it be fit for any work, when the fire has consumed it and it is burned? 6 Therefore thus says the Lord God, "As the vine, which is among the trees of the forest, which I gave to the fire to be consumed, so will I give to the inhabitants of Jerusalem. 7 And I will set my face against them; they shall come forth by fire, and another fire shall consume them; and you shall know that I am the LORD, when I set my face against them, 8 And when I shall make the land a wilderness, because they have grievously offended, saith the Lord God.

CHAPTER 16

1 Again the word of the Lord came to me, say- ing, 2 Son of man, make known to Jerusalem her abominations, 3 And say, Thus says the Lord God to Jerusalem, Thy dwelling place and thy kindred are of the land of Canaan; thy father was an Amorite, and thy mother a Hit- tite. 4 In thy nature, when thou wast deliv- ered, thy skin was not cut off; thou wast not washed in water to soften thee; thou wast not salted with salt, nor wrapped in clods. 5 No eye pitied thee to do any of these things, to have compassion on thee, but thou wast cast into the open field in contempt of thy person in the day that thou wast carried. 6 When I passed by you, I saw you defiled in your own blood, and I said to you, "When you were in your own blood, you will die"; and when you were in your own blood, I said to you, "You will die." 7 I made thee to multiply as the shoot of the field, and thou hast grown and become great, and hast gotten excellent orna- ments for thyself; thy breasts are covered, thy head is grown, while thou wast naked and bare. 8 Now when I passed before thee, and looked upon thee, behold, thy time was as the time of Love, and I stripped thee of my skirts, and crouched upon thy filthiness; yea, I swore unto thee, and drew near unto thee, saith the Lord God, and thou became mine. 9 Then I washed thee with water; yea, I washed thy blood from thee, and anointed thee with oil. 10 I also clothed thee with skins of broth, and ironed thee with badger skins; I girded thee with fine linen, and clothed thee with silk. 11 I also adorned you with ornaments; I put

bracelets on your hands and a chain around your neck. 12 I put a frontal on your face, ear- rings in your ears, and a beautiful crown on your head. 13 So you were adorned with gold and silk, and your trousseau was of fine linen, silk, and fine fabrics; you fed on fine flour, honey, and oil; you were very beautiful, and you became a kingdom. 14 Your name was spread among the heathen because of your beauty, for it was perfected through my beau- ty which I placed upon you, says the Lord God. 15 Now you trusted in your beauty and played the harlot, because of your fame, and you consumed your fornications on every person who passed by, your desire was for him. 16 And thou hast taken thy garments, and hast adorned thy rooms with different colors, and hast been a harlot; such a thing shall never happen again, and no one has ever done it. 17 You also took your beautiful jewel- ry of gold and silver that I had given you, and made images of men, and prostituted your- self with them, 18 you took your garments of brotherhood and coiffed them; you set before them my oil and my perfume. 19 Also my food, which I had given thee, as flour, and oil, and honey, with which I had fed thee, thou hast set before them as sweet perfume; so it was, saith the Lord God. 20 Moreover thou hast taken thy sons and thy daughters, whom thou hast borne for me, and hast sacrificed them to be consumed; is this thy prostitution little? 21 that thou hast slain my sons and sacrificed them to pass through the fire? 22 And in all your abominations and prostitutions have you not remembered the days of your youth, when you were naked and bare and defiled in your blood. 23 And besides all your wicked- ness (woe, woe to you, says the LORD God) 24 Thou hast also built for thyself a place of wor- ship, and hast made for thyself a place of wor- ship in all the streets. 25 Thou hast built thy refuge in every corner of the street, and hast made thy beauty to be despised; thou hast opened thy feet to everyone who passed by, and hast multiplied thy harlotry. 26 Thou hast also committed fornication with the Egyp- tians, thy neighbors, who have great mem- bers, and hast increased thy prostitution to put me to shame. 27 Therefore I have stretched out my hand upon thee, and will diminish thy ordinance, and will deliver thee to the will of them that hate thee, that is, the daughters of the Philistines, who are ashamed of thy evil way. 28 You also played the harlot with the As- syrians, for you were insatiable; yea, you played the harlot with them and were not sat- isfied. 29 You multiplied your fornications from the land of Canaan to Chaldea, but you were not satisfied. 30 How weak is your heart, says the LORD God, seeing you do all these things, which are the work of a presumptu- ous woman and whore? 31 For you build your house on the corner of every street and make your home in every street, and you are not like a harlot who despises the reward, 32 but like a wife who plays the harlot and takes others for a husband: 33 They make presents to all other harlots, but thou makest presents to all thy harlots, and rewardest them, that they may come to thee from all quarters for thy fornica- tion. 34 And thou hast nothing to envy other women concerning thy fornications, and there shall be no such fornications after thee; for thou givest a reward, and no reward is giv- en unto thee, therefore thou art contrary. 35 Therefore, O harlot, hear the word of the LORD. 36 Thus says the LORD God, "For your shame has been extirpated, and your filthi- ness has been revealed through your fornica- tions with your lovers and with all the idols of your abominations, and through the blood of your children which you offered them, 37 Be- hold, I will gather together all thy lovers, with whom thou hast pleased thyself, and all whom thou hast loved, with all whom thou hast hat- ed: I will gather them together against thee, and reveal unto them thy filthiness, that they may see all thy filthiness. 38 I will judge thee in the likeness of them that are harlots, and in the likeness of them that shed blood: and I will give thee the blood of wrath and jealousy. 39 I will also give thee into their hands, and they shall destroy thy house, and cast down thy places. they shall also strip thee of thy gar- ments, and take thy jewels, and leave thee na- ked and uncovered. 40 They shall also bring a company against thee, and they shall stone thee with stones, and pierce thee with their swords. 41 And they shall burn thy houses with fire, and execute judgments upon thee before many women; and I will cause thee to cease to be a harlot, and give no more reward. 42 So I will cause my wrath toward thee to cease, and my jealousy will depart from thee, and I will cease, and will be angry no more. 43 Because thou hast not remembered the days of thy youth, but hast done violence to me with all these things, behold, I have made thy way fall on thy head, saith the LORD God; yet thou hast not taken account of all thy abomi- nations. 44 Behold, all those who boast, boast in this proterity against you, saying, "As is the mother, so is the daughter." 45 You are the daughter of your mother, who forsook her husband and children, and you are the sister of your sisters, who forsook their husbands and children; your mother is a Hittite, and your father an Amorite. 46 Your elder sister is Samaria and her daughters, who dwell on your left, and your younger sister, who dwells on your right, is Sodom and her daughters. 47 Yet thou hast not walked in their ways, and hast not done their abominations; but, as if it were a little thing, thou hast corrupted thyself more than they in all thy ways. 48 As I say, says the Lord God, Sodom, your sister, did not do, neither she nor her daughters, what you and your daughters did. 49 Behold, this was the iniquity of thy sister Sodom: pride, abun- dance of bread, and plenty of idleness were in her and in her daughters; she strengthened not the hand of the poor and needy. 50 But they were haughty and committed abomina- tion before me; therefore I removed them, as it pleased me. 51 Neither did Samaria commit half of your sins, but you overcame them in your abominations and justified your sisters in all your abominations that you committed. 52 Therefore thou, who hast justified thy sis- ters, bear thy own shame for thy sins, which thou hast committed more abominable than they that are more righteous than thou; therefore be thou also confounded, and bear thy own shame, seeing thou hast justified thy sisters. 53 Therefore I will bring back their captivity with the captivity of Sodom and her daughters, with the captivity of Samaria and her daughters, and the captivity of thy cap- tives among them, 54 That thou mayest bear thy shame, and be confounded for all that thou hast done, that thou mayest comfort them. 55 And thy sister Sodom and her daughters shall return to their former state: and Samaria also and her daughters shall re- turn to their former state, when thou and thy daughters shall return to thy former state. 56 For thy sister Sodom was not heard by thy re- port in the day of thy pride, 57 before thy wickedness was revealed, as in that time of the reprobation of the daughters of Aram, and of all the daughters of the Philistines around her, who despised thee on every side. 58 Thou hast borne thy wickedness and thy abomination, saith the LORD. 59 For thus says the LORD God, "I could also do with you what you did, when you despised the other, breaking the covenant. 60 However, I will re- member my covenant made with you in the days of your youth and confirm an everlasting covenant with you. 61 Then you shall remem- ber your ways and be ashamed, when you re- ceive your sisters, both the elder and the younger, and I will give them as daughters, but not with your consent. 62 I will establish my bond with you, and you shall know that I am the LORD, 63 That thou mayest remember and be ashamed, and open thy mouth no more; because of thy shame, when I shall be pacified toward thee, for all that thou hast done, saith the Lord God.

CHAPTER 17

1 The word of the LORD was spoken to me, saying, "Son of man, expound a parable and speak proterrally to the house of Israel, 2 Son of man, expound a parable and speak for the house of Israel, 3 and say, "Thus says the Lord God: The great eagle with great wings, long and full of feathers, of different colors, came to Lebanon and took the highest branch of the cedar tree, 4 and broke off the top of its twig, and carried it into the land of the marchers, and set it in a city of marchers. 5 He also took some seed of the earth and planted it in fer- tile ground; he placed it near great waters and made it into a willow tree. 6 It sprouted and was like a vine of low stature spreading out, whose shoots were facing it and whose roots were below it; so it became a vine, bear- ing forth branches and shooting out buds. 7 There was also another great eagle, with great wings and many feathers, and behold, this vine turned its roots toward it and spread its branches toward it, to water it from the trenches of its planting. 8 It had been plant- ed in a good planting near great waters, that it might produce shoots and bear fruit and be an excellent vine. 9 But thou sayest, Thus saith the Lord God, Shall it prosper? Shall he not pluck up its roots and destroy its fruit and wither it? All the leaves of its shoot will with- er without great strength and without many people to flatten it with their roots. 10 Behold, it has been planted, but will it prosper? Will it not wither and dry up? When the east wind touches it, it will wither in the pits where it grew. 11 More, the word of the Lord was spoken to me, saying, 12 Say now to this re- bellious house, "Do you not know what these things mean?" Say to them, "Behold, the king of Babel came to Jerusalem and took his king and his princes and led them with him to Ba- bel, 13 and took one of the king's descendants, and made an alliance with him, and took an- other; and he also took the princes of the land, 14 so that the kingdom would be subdued and not rise up on its own, but maintain its do- minion and stand. 15 But he rebelled against him and sent his ambassadors to Egypt, that they might give him horses and many people: shall he prosper? Shall he escape, that doeth these things? Or shall he break the barrier and be disappointed? 16 As I say, saith the LORD God, he shall die in the midst of Babel, in the place of the king that made him king, whose other he despised, and whose covenant with him he broke. 17 Pharaoh, with his mighty army and his great multitude of people, will not keep him in war, when they have thrown down mountains and built ramparts to de- stroy many people. 18 Because he has despised the other and broken your horn (yet, behold, he had given his hand), because he has done all these things, he will not escape. 19 There- fore, thus says the Lord God, "As I stand, I will bring down upon his head the other whom he has despised and my ally whom he has bro- ken. 20 I will spread my net over him, and he will be caught in my net; I will lead him to Ba- bel, and there I will judge him for his crimes that he has committed against me. 21 All those who flee from him, with all his army, shall fall by the sword, and those who remain shall be scattered to all the winds; and you shall know that I, the LORD, have said it." 22 Thus says the LORD God, "I will

also take off the top of this cedar, and I will plant it, and I will cut off the top of its tender plant, and I will plant it on a high and great mountain. 23 Then I will plant it on the mountain of Israel; it shall bring forth branches and fruit, and shall be an excellent cedar; under it shall remain all the birds, and every fowl shall dwell in the shade of its branches. 24 And all the trees of the field shall know that I, the LORD, have lowered the high tree, and exalted the low tree; that I have dried up the green tree, and made the dry tree to flourish: I, the LORD, have said it, and have done it.

CHAPTER 18

1 The word of the LORD came to me again, saying, 2 How is it that you speak of this proterity, concerning the land of Israel, say- ing, "The fathers have eaten table grapes, and the children have bared their teeth"? 3 As I say, says the LORD God, you shall see no more of this arrogance in Israel. 4 Behold, all souls are mine, both the soul of the father and the soul of the son are mine; the soul that sins shall die. 5 But if a man is righteous and does what is lawful and right, 6 he has not eaten on the mountains, nor lifted up his eyes to the idols of the house of Israel, nor defiled the wife of his neighbors, nor lain with a menstruating woman, 7 he oppressed no one, but returned the pledge to his journey; he stripped no one by violence, but gave his bread to the hungry and clothed the naked with a robe, 8 and who did not give himself up to violence or hoard any gain, but withdrew his hand from iniqui- ty and executed true judgment between man and man, 9 and has walked in my statutes and observed my judgments to act with truth, he is righteous, he shall surely live, says the LORD God. 10 If he begets a son who is a thief, or a bleeder, if he does any of these things, 11 even if he does not do all these things, but has eaten on the mountains or defiled his neigh- bor's wife, 12 or has oppressed the poor and needy, or has pushed with violence, or has not returned the pledge, or has lifted up his eyes to idols, or has committed an abomination, 13 or has given himself to the stain, or has be- come rich, shall he live? He shall not be able to live; for he has committed all these abomina- tions, he shall die a death, and his blood shall fall upon him. 14 But if he begets a son who sees all the sins of his father, which he has committed, and is afraid of them, he does not make such sins, 15 who has not eaten on the mountains, nor lifted up his eyes to the idols of the house of Israel, nor defiled the wife of his neighbors, 16 he did not oppress anyone, he did not withhold the pledge, he did not push with violence, but gave his bread to the hungry and covered the naked with a robe, 17 he has not withdrawn his hand from the af- flicted, he has not received wages and he has not received an income, but he has carried out my decrees and walked in my statutes; he will not die in the iniquity of his father, but he will surely live. 18 His father, because he cruelly oppressed and drove his brother with violence and did not do good to his people, shall die in his iniquity. 19 But you say, "Why should not the son bear the iniquity of his fa- ther? Because the son has executed judgment and equity, has observed all my statutes and performed them, he shall surely live." 20 The same soul that sins shall die; the son shall not bear the iniquity of the father, nor shall the fa- ther bear the iniquity of the son, but the righ- teousness of the righteous shall be upon him, and the iniquity of the wicked shall be upon him. 21 But if the wicked man retracts from all his sins that he has committed, and ob- serves all my statutes, and does what is lawful and right, he shall surely live and not die. 22 All his

transgressions that he has committed shall not be mentioned for him, but because of his righteous deeds that he has committed, he shall live. 23 Do I desire the wicked to die, says the LORD God, or shall he not die if he returns from his ways? 24 But if the righteous man turns from his righteousness and com- mits iniquity and does all the abominations that the wicked man does, shall he die? All his righteousness that he has done shall not be mentioned; but in his transgression that he has done and in his sin that he has commit- ted, in them he shall die. 25 Yet you say, "The way of the LORD is not equitable"; hear now, O house of Israel. Is not my way equitable? Or are not your ways vnequal? 26 For when a righteous man turns from his righteousness and commits iniquity, he shall die for the same, he shall die for the iniquity he has com- mitted. 27 Moreover, when the ungodly man turns away from his iniquity that he has com- mitted and does what is lawful and righteous, his soul will be saved. 28 Because he reflects and turns away from all his transgressions that he has committed, he will surely live and not die. 29 But you, house of Israel, say, "The way of the LORD is not fair." O house of Israel, are not my ways equal, or are not your ways equal? 30 Therefore I will judge you, O house of Israel, each according to his ways, says the LORD God; therefore turn back and cause others to turn away from all your transgres- sions; so iniquity will not be your destruction. 31 Cast away from you all your transgressions, whereby you have transgressed, and make yourselves a new heart and a new spirit; why do you want to die, O house of Israel? 32 For I do not want the death of those who die, says the LORD God; therefore take courage for one another and stand fast.

CHAPTER 19

1 You also make a lament for the princes of Israel, 2 and say, "Why did your mother lie like a lioness among the lions? She fed her young among the lions' cubs." 3 and she brought with her one of her young, who became a li- oness, learned to catch prayers, and made a slaughter of men. 4 And the nations also learned of it, and caught it in their nets, and brought it in chains into the land of Egypt. 5 When the woman heard that she had waited and that her hope was lost, she took another of her little ones and made an uncle. 6 Who went among the lions, became a lion, learned to catch prey, and dealt with men. 7 And he knew their widows, and destroyed their cit- ies; and the land was devastated, and all that was in it by the sound of his roaring. 8 Then the nations came against him from all parts of the countries and spread their nets for him; so he was taken into their pit. 9 And they put him in prison and in chains, and brought him to the king of Babel, and put him in prison, that his voice should not be heard again on the mountains of Israel. 10 Your mother is like a vine in your blood, planted by the waters; she bore fruit and branches by the abundant wa- ters, 11 she had strong rods for the scepters of those who rule; her stature was high among the branches, and she appeared in her height with the multitude of her branches. 12 But it was torn by wrath; it was cast down to the ground, and the east wind withered its fruit; its branches broke off and withered; as for the rod of its strength, fire consumed it. 13 Now it is planted in the wilderness, in dry and thirsty ground. 14 Fire has gone out from the rod of its branches and consumed its fruit, so that it no longer has a strong rod as a scepter to rule; this is a lament and will remain a lament.

CHAPTER 20

1 In the fifteenth year, on the tenth day of the month, some of the elders of Israel came and inquired of the LORD and sat down before me. 2 Then the word of the LORD was spoken to me, saying, "Son of man, do not worry, do not be troubled." 3 Son of man, speak to the elders of Israel and say to them, "Thus says the Lord God, Have you come to inquire of me? How am I, says the Lord God, when I am asked, I will not answer you. 4 Wilt thou judge them, son of man, wilt thou judge them? Let them understand the abominations of their fathers, 5 And say unto them, Thus saith the Lord God, In the day that I chose Israel, and lifted up mine hand unto the descendants of the house of Iaakob, and made known unto them my self in the land of Egypt, when I lift- ed up mine hand unto them, and said, I am the Lord your God, 6 in the day that I lifted up my hand upon them to bring them out of the land of Egypt, into a land that I had designed for them, rich in milk and honey, pleasant to all countries, 7 Then I said to them, "Let each one remove the abominations of his eyes, and do not defile yourselves with the idols of Egypt, for I am the LORD your God." 8 But they rebelled against me and would not listen to me, because no one cast away the abomina- tions of his eyes and did not forsake the idols of Egypt; so I thought of exploding my indig- nation upon them and carrying out my wrath against them in the midst of the land of Egypt. 9 But I had respect for my Name, that it might not be defiled before the heathen, among whom they were, and in whose eyes I had made myself known in bringing them out of the land of Egypt. 10 Now I brought them out of the land of Egypt and led them into the wilderness. 11 I gave them my statutes and declared to them my precepts, which if a man do, he must live in them. 12 Moreover I gave them my Sabbaths as a sign between me and them, that they might know that I am the LORD, who sanctifies them. 13 But the house of Israel rebelled against me in the wilder- ness; they did not walk in my statutes, and they discarded my precepts, that if a man do, he must live in them, and my sabbaths greatly defiled them; then I thought to burst my in- dignation upon them in the wilderness to consume them, 14 but I had respect for my Name, that it might not be polluted before the heathen from whom I had brought them out. 15 Nevertheless, nevertheless, I lifted up my hand upon them in the wilderness to keep them from entering the land I had given them, rich in milk and honey, which was pleasant to all the lands, 16 because they for- sook my precepts and did not walk in my stat- utes, but polluted my sabbaths, because their heart went after their idols. 17 Yet my eye spared them, lest I should destroy them and consume them in the wilderness. 18 But I said to their children in the wilderness, "Do not walk according to the precepts of your fa- thers, do not observe their customs, and do not defile yourselves with their idols. 19 I am the LORD your God; walk in my statutes, keep my precepts, and do them, 20 and sanctify my Sabbaths, which shall be a sign between me and you, that ye may know that I am the LORD your God. 21 Nevertheless the sons have rebelled against me; they have not walked in my statutes and kept my precepts to perform them, that if a man performs them, he shall live in them, but they have defiled my sabbaths; then I have thought to burst out my indignation upon them and to execute my wrath against them in the wilderness. 22 Nevertheless I withdrew my hand and had re- spect to my Name, that it might not be defiled before the heathen, before whose presence I led

them. 23 Nevertheless I lifted up my hand upon them in the wilderness, to scatter them among the heathen and disperse them through the countries, 24 Because they had not performed my decrees, but had discarded my statutes and defiled my sabbaths, and their eyes followed the idolatries of their fa- thers. 25 Therefore I also gave them statutes that were not good and orders that they were not to keep. 26 I polluted them in their own gifts, for they made everything that opens first in a woman to pass through fire, to de- stroy them, to the end, that they might know that I am your Lord. 27 Therefore, son of man, speak unto the house of Israel, and say unto them, Thus saith the LORD God, In this your fathers have blasphemed me, though they had formerly grievously transgressed against me. 28 For when I had led them into the land, for which I had lifted up my hand to give it to them, they saw all the hills and all the old trees, and they offered their sacrifices there, and presented their provocation offerings there; they also made their sweet perfume there, and consumed their drink offerings there. 29 Then I said to them, "What is the place where you are going? And its name has been called Bamah to this day. 30 Therefore say to the house of Israel, "Thus says the Lord God, Are you not defiled like your fathers, and do you not commit prostitutions like their abominations? 31 For when you offer your gifts and cause your children to pass through the fire, you pollute your selves with all your idolatries to this day, will I answer you when you ask me, O house of Israel? As I lie, says the LORD God, I will not answer you when you ask me. 32 Neither shall it be done that which comes to your mind, for you say, "We shall be like the heathen and like the families of the countries; we shall serve wood and stone." 33 As I am, says the Lord God, I will rule you with a mighty hand, with an outstretched arm, and with my wrath, with power, 34 I will bring you out of the nations and gather you from the countries where you are scattered, with a mighty hand, with an outstretched arm, and with my powerful anger, 35 I will lead you into the wilderness of the people, and there I will hold you face to face. 36 As I dealt with your fathers in the wilderness of Egypt, so will I deal with you, says the LORD God. 37 I will pass you under the rod and lead you into the bond of the bond. 38 And I will choose from among you the rebels and those who have transgressed against me; I will bring them out of the land where they dwell and they shall not enter the land of Israel, and you shall know that I am the LORD. 39 As for you, O house of Israel, thus says the Lord God, "Go away and serve each one his idol, since you do not want to obey me, and do not defile my holy Name any more with your gifts and idols. 40 For in my holy mountain, that is, in the mountain of Israel, says the Lord God, all the house of Israel and all the land shall serve me; there I will accept them, and there I will re- quire your offspring and the first fruits of your oblations, with all your holy things. 41 I will accept your sweet savor, when I bring you out of the nations and gather you from the countries where you have been scattered, that I may be sanctified in you before you heathen. 42 You shall know that I am the LORD when I bring you into the land of Israel, into the land for which I lifted up my hand to give it to your fathers. 43 And there you will remember your ways and all your works, in which you have defiled yourselves, and you will judge your selves worthy to be cut off, for all your errors that you have committed. 44 And ye shall know that I am the LORD, when I have re- spect to you for my names' sake, and not ac- cording to your evil ways, nor according to your corrupt works, O house of Israel, saith the LORD God. 45 Moreover, the word of the LORD was spoken to me, saying, 46 "Son of man, turn your face toward the way of Teman, let your word fall toward the south, and prophesy toward the forest of the south camp, 47 and say to the forest of the South, "Listen to the word of the LORD; thus says the LORD God, 'Behold, I will kindle a fire in you that will devour all the green wood in you and all the dry wood; the continual flame will not be extinguished, and every face from the South to the North will be burned in it. 48 And all flesh shall see that I, the LORD, have kindled it, and it shall not be quenched. Then I said, "Lord God, they say of me, Do you not speak in parables?

CHAPTER 21

1 The word of the LORD was again spoken to me, saying, 2 Son of man, turn your face to- ward Jerusalem, let your word fall toward the holy places, and prophesy against the land of Israel. 3 And say unto the land of Israel, Thus saith the LORD, Behold, I come against thee, and will draw my sword out of its sheath, and will cut off from thee both the righteous and the wicked. 4 For therefore I will cut off from thee both the righteous and the wicked, my sword shall come out of its sheath against all flesh from the south to the north, 5 That all flesh may know that I, the LORD, have drawn my sword from its sheath, and that it shall not return again. 6 Suffer therefore, son of man, as in the paina of your queens, and suffer bitterly before them. 7 And if they say to you, "Why do you mourn?" answer, "Be- cause of the bruise, for it shall come, and ev- ery heart shall melt away, and all hands shall be weakened, and all minds shall droop, and all knees shall fall down like water; behold, it shall come, and it shall be done, saith the Lord God." 8 Afterward the word of the LORD was spoken to me, saying 9 Son of man, prophe- sy and say, "Thus says the Lord God, A sword, a sword sharpened and quadrupled. 10 It is sharpened to make a painful slaughter, and it is quadrupled to glitter; how shall we recov- er? For the rod of my son is despicable, like all other trees.11 He had it sheathed to handle it; this sword is sharpened and sheathed to give it into the hand of the slayer. 12 Cry out and shout, son of man, for this will happen to my people and to all the princes of Israel; the ter- ror of the sword will come upon my people; therefore strike your thigh. 13 For it is a trial, and what shall this be, if the sword contem- plate even the rod? It shall be no more, saith the Lord God. 14 Thou therefore, son of man, prophesy, and smite hand to hand, and let the sword be doubled; the sword that hath slain, turn back the third time; it is the sword of the great slaughter that enters into their privi- leged chambers. 15 I have brought the fear of the sword into all their gates to make their hearts faint and multiply their ruins. Ah, it is made bright and is clothed for slaughter. 16 Go thou alone: go to the right hand or go to the left hand, wherever thy face is turned. 17 I will also smite my hands, and I will cause my wrath to cease. I, the LORD, have said it. 18 The word of the LORD was again addressed to me, saying, 19 You also, son of man, es- tablish two ways, that the sword of the king of Babel may come; the two ways shall come out of a land, and they shall choose a place, and they shall choose it at the corner of the street of the city. 20 Establish a way, that the sword may come to Rabbath of the Ammo- nites, and to Iudah, in the strong city of Je- rusalem. 21 And the king of Babel stood at the intersection of the street, at the head of the two ways, and consulted with the diuination, and made his arrows to shine; and he consult- ed with the idols, and looked into the dark- ness. 22 And at his right hand he gave himself orders

to appoint captains for Jerusalem, that they should open their mouths to slaughter, and raise their voices with shouting, and put war machines against the gates, and cast a mount, and build a fortress. 23 And it shall be to them as a false diuination for other deeds done against them; but he shall remember their iniquity, that they may be taken. 24 Therefore thus saith the Lord God, Because ye have brought to remembrance your in- iquity, speaking of your rebellion, that in all your works your sins might appear; for, I say, that ye have come to remembrance, ye shall be taken with the hand. 25 You, prince of Israel, polluted and wicked, the day has come when iniquity shall come to an end, 26 Thus says the LORD God, "I will take away the diadem and remove the crown; it will no longer be the same; I will exalt the lowly and lower him who is on high. 27 I will take it off, and remove it, and it shall be no more until he to whom it is due comes, and I will give it to him. 28 And thou, son of man, prophesy, and say, Thus saith the Lord God to the children of Ammon, and to their blasphemies; say thou, I say, the sword, the sword is drawn, and brought to the slaughter, to be consumed, because of the glitter: 29 while they see vanity in regard to you, and prophesy a lie to you, to bring upon the neck of the wicked that have been slain, whose day is come when their iniquity shall end. 30 Shall I make him return to his sheath? I will judge you in the place where you were created, that is, in the land where you dwell. 31 And I will pour out my indignation upon thee, and I will blow against thee in the fire of my wrath, and I will deliver thee into the hands of bestial men who are skilled in de- struction. 32 Thou shalt be in the fire to be ex- terminated; thy blood shall be in the midst of the earth, and thou shalt be remembered no more, for I, the LORD, have said it.

CHAPTER 22

1 Moreover the word of the LORD came to me, saying. 2 Now, son of man, will you judge, will you judge this bloody city? Do you want to show her all her abominations? 3 Then say, "Thus says the LORD God, The city sheds blood in the midst, that her hour may come, and she creates idols against herself to defile herself. 4 Thou hast offended with the blood which thou hast shed, and hast polluted thy- self with the idols which thou hast made, and hast caused thy days to draw nigh, and thou hast come to thy end; therefore I have made thee a reproach to the heathen, and a mock- ery to all countries. 5 Those who are near and those who are far from you will mock you, who are vile in name and sorrowful in afflic- tions. 6 Behold, the princes of Israel, every one in thee was ready to shed blood. 7 In you they despised the father and the mother; in you they oppressed the stranger; in you they harassed the orphan and the widow. 8 You have despised my holy things and defiled my Sabbaths. 9 In you are men who bring stories to shed blood; in you are those who eat on the mountains; in your midst they commit abom- inations. 10 In you they have disowned the shame of their fathers; in you they have vexed her who was defiled in her flowers. 11 Every- one has committed abomination with his neighbor's wife, and everyone has wickedly defiled his own daughter in falsehood, and in you every man has forced his own sister, that is, his father's daughter. 12 In thee they have taken gifts to shed blood; thou hast taken in- crease and increase, thou hast defrauded thy neighbors with extortion, and thou hast for- gotten me, saith the Lord God. 13 Therefore I have struck with my hands your guilt, which you have committed, and the blood that

has been shed in your midst. 14 Can your heart endure or your hands be strong in the days when I must do with you? I, the LORD, have said it, and I will do it. 15 I will scatter thee among the heathen, I will scatter thee in the countries, and I will cause thy filthiness to cease from thee. 16 You shall take your inher- itance upon you before the heathen, and you shall know that I am the LORD. 17 The word of the LORD was spoken to me, saying, 18 "Son of man, the house of Israel is like a sludge to me; they are all brasse, tin, yron, and leade in the midst of the furnace; they are like a silken sludge." 19 Therefore thus says the LORD God, "For you are all like weeds; behold, I will gath- er you in the midst of Jerusalem. 20 As one gathers clay, reed, yarn and tin in the center of the furnace, to blow fire upon it and melt it, so I will gather you in my wrath and anger, and I will put you there and melt you. 21 I will gath- er you, I say, and I will blow upon you the fire of my wrath, and you shall be melted in the midst thereof. 22 As the torpedo melts in the midst of the furnace, so you shall be melted in the midst of it, and you shall know that I, the LORD, have poured out my wrath upon you. 23 The word of the Lord was spoken to me, saying, 24 Son of man, say to her, You are the land that has been vituperated and on which it has not rained in the day of wrath. 25 There is a conspiracy of her prophets in her midst, like a roaring bruiser, disrupting prayers; they have ravaged souls; they have taken riches and precious things; they have made many wid- ows in their midst. 26 His priests have broken my law, and defiled my holy things; they have made no difference between the holy and the profane, nor distinguished between the vn- clean and the clean; they have hid their eyes from my Sabbaths, and I am profane in their midst. 27 His princes in their midst are like wolves, raiding prayers to shed blood and to destroy souls for their personal gain. 28 His prophets beat them down with a vntemperate mortar, seeing vanity and telling lies, saying, "Thus says the Lord God," while the Lord had not spoken. 29 The inhabitants of the land op- pressed violently with spitting and stealing, and harassed the poor and needy; yea, they oppressed the foreigner against the right. 30 I looked among them for a man who would make a hedge and stand before me for the land, that I might not destroy it, but I found none. 31 Therefore I vented my indignation on them and consumed them with the fire of my wrath; their proper ways I tore out over their heads, says the LORD God.

CHAPTER 23

1 The word of the LORD came to me again and said 2 Son of man, there were two wom- en, daughters of one mother. 3 They com- mitted fornication in Egypt, they committed fornication in their youth; there their breasts were squeezed, and there the breasts of their virginity were bruised. 4 They were called Aholah, the eldest, and Aholibah, her sister; they were mine, and bore sons and daugh- ters; so they were called. Samaria is Aholah, and Jerusalem Aholibah. 5 When she was mine, Aholah was a harlot, and she was on fire with her lyophiles, that is, with the Assyrians, her neighbors, 6 Who were clothed in snow- white silk, captains and princes; they were all men of fine appearance and horsemen on horseback. 7 So she prostituted herself with them, with all who were Assur's chosen men, with all whom she pleased, and defiled her- self with all their idols. 8 Neither did she leave her fornications, which she learned from the Egyptians, for in her youth they lay with her, and wounded the bosom of her virginity, and made their prostitution upon

her. 9 Therefore I delivered her into the hands of her allies, that is, into the hands of the Assyrians, by whom she let herself go. 10 The latter shamed her; they took away her sons and her daugh- ters and slew her with the sword, and she had a high name among the women, because they executed judgment on her. 11 When her sister Aholiba heard this, she ruined herself with inordinate lust more than she did, and with her fornications more than her sister with her fornications. 12 And she delighted in the Assyrians that were her neighbors, both cap- tains and princes, clothed in fine clothes, and horsemen running on horseback; they were all pleasant men and young men. 13 Then I said that she had been defiled and that they were all of the same race, 14 and that she in- creased her fornications, for when she saw men painting on the wall, the images of the Chaldeans painted with vermilion, 15 And girded with sheaths upon their loins, and with dyes upon their heads (all resembling princes like the Babylonians in Chaldea, the country of their origin). 16 Assoon, I say, as she saw them, she became enamored of them and sent messengers to them in Chaldea. 17 But when the Babylonians came to her in the bed of war, they defiled her with their fornication, and she defiled herself with them, and her desire departed from them. 18 Then she unveiled her fornication and revealed her shame; then my heart forsook her, as my heart had forsaken her sister. 19 But she increased her fornica- tion still more, and remembered the days of her youth, in which she had been a harlot in the land of Egypt. 20 For she took pleasure in their servants, whose members are like those of donkeys and whose weight is like that of horses. 21 Thou hast remembered the wick- edness of thy youth, when thy breasts were beaten by you Egyptians; therefore thy young man's feet are thus. 22 Therefore, O Aholiba, thus says the Lord God, "Behold, I will raise up against you your wrestlers, from whom your heart has turned away, and I will cause them to come against you from all sides." 23 that is, the Babylonians and all the Chaldeans, Peked, Shoah, Koa, and all the Assyrians with them; they were all pleasant men and young men, captains and princes; they were all val- iant and renunciant, riding on horseback. 24 Then these shall come against thee with char- iots and carts and wheels, and with a mul- titude of people arrayed against thee, with buckler and shield and helmet round about; and I will leave the punishment to them, and they shall judge thee according to their judg- ments. 25 And I will smite thee with my in- dignation, and they shall kill thee cruelly; and they shall cut off thy nose and thy ears, and thy remnant shall fall by the sword; and they shall take away thy sons and thy daughters, and thy remnant shall be devoured by fire. 26 They will also strip you of your garments and take away your jewelry. 27 So I will cause your wickedness and your fornication to cease from the land of Egypt, so that you will no longer lift up your eyes to them, and you will no longer remember Egypt. 28 For thus says the Lord God, "Behold, I will deliver you into the hands of those whom you hate, that is, into the hands of those from whom your heart has turned away. 29 They shall handle thee badly, they shall take away all thy toil, they shall leave thee naked and bare, and the shame of thy fornications shall be revealed, both thy wickedness and thy harlotry. 30 I will do these things to you because you went whoring after the heathen and because you defiled yourself with their idolatries. 31 You have walked in the way of your sister; there- fore I will give you her cup in your hand. 32 Thus says the LORD God, "You shall drink from your sister's cup, deep and great; you shall be mocked and ridiculed, for it contains much. 33 You shall be filled with drunken- ness and sadness, that is, from the

cup of destruction and desolation, from the cup of your sister Samaria. 34 And thou shalt drink it, and shalt squeeze it down to the drops, and break the parts thereof, and make thy breasts sore: for I have said it, saith the Lord God. 35 Therefore thus saith the LORD God, Because thou hast forgotten me and cast me behind thy back, thou also shalt bear thy wickedness and thy harlotry. 36 Again the LORD said to me, "Son of man, will you judge Aholah and Aholibah and declare their abominations? 37 For they have given themselves to prostitutes, and blood is in their hands, and with their idols they have committed adultery, and have also passed their children, whom they have borne me, through the fire, as their meal." 38 Moreover, they have done so toward me: they have defiled my sanctuary in the same day, and have profaned my Sabbaths. 39 For hav- ing slain their children to their idols, they en- tered the same day into my sanctuary to defile it; well, so they did in the midst of my house. 40 And how much more true is it that they caused men to come from afar to whom a messenger had been sent, well, they came, for you washed yourself, painted your eyes, and adorned yourself with ornaments, 41 you sat on an expensive bed, and you prepared a table before you, where you placed my incense and my oil. 42 With her was a multitude of people at ease; and to make the company more nu- merous men of Sheba were brought from the wilderness, who put bracelets on their hands and beautiful crowns on their heads. 43 Then I said to the one who was old in adultery: "Now she and her fornications shall come to an end." 44 They went to her as one goes to a common harlot; so they went to Aholah and Aholibah, the wicked women. 45 You righ- teous men shall judge them as the harlots and as the murderers, for they are harlots and the blood is in their hands. 46 Therefore thus says the LORD God, "I will cause a multitude to come upon them, and I will give them over to the tumult and the crowd, 47 the crowd shall stone them with stones and cut them with the sword; they shall kill their sons and their daughters and burn their houses with fire. 48 Thus I will cause wickedness to cease from the land, that all women may be educated not to do like your wickedness. 49 They shall bring your wickedness upon you, and you shall bear the sins of your idols, and you shall know that I am the Lord God.

CHAPTER 24

1 In the ninth year, in the tenth month, in the tenth day of the month, the word of the Lord came to me, saying, "Son of man, write the name of the day, and of this very day, 2 Son of man, write the name of the day, and of this very day, for the king of Babel came against Jerusalem on this very day. 3 Speak therefore with a parable to the rebellious house, and say unto them, Thus saith the Lord God, Pre- pare a pot, and make it ready, and let water into it. 4 Gather the pieces of it, every good piece, such as the thigh and shoulder, and fill it with the main bones. 5 Take one of the best sheep, bury the bones under it also, and boil it well, and put the bones in it, 6 For the LORD God says thus, "Woe to the bloody city, and also to the pot, whose skin is in it, and whose skin has not come out of it; take it out piece by piece; do not let the lot fall on it. 7 For his blood is in his bowels; he has set it on a high tower, and has not left it on the ground to cover it with dust, 8 That there might be wrath, and vengeance might be taken: well have I set his blood upon a high tower, that it should not be shed. 9 Therefore thus says the LORD God, "Woe to the bloody city, for I will make it great and fiery. 10 Put up much

wood; kindle the fire, consume the flesh, throw in the spices, and burn the bones. 11 Then empty her on her necks, that her bras- sa may heat and burn, that her filth may melt therein, and her skin may be consumed. 12 She has fatigued herself with lies, and her great mass has not come out of her; therefore her mass shall be consumed by fire. 13 You remain in your filthiness and wickedness; for I would have purified you and you were not cleansed, you shall not be cleansed from your filthiness until I have turned my wrath on you. 14 I, the LORD, have said it: it shall come to pass, and I will: I will not turn back, nor spare, nor repent; according to thy ways and according to thy works shall they judge thee, saith the LORD God. 15 The word of the Lord also came to me, saying, 16 Son of man, behold, I will take away the pleasure of your eyes with a plague; yet you shall neither weep nor mourn, nor shall your teas flow. 17 Cease to sigh, mourn not for the dead; put on the rubber of your head, put your shoes on your feet, do not rest your lips, and do not eat the bread of men." 18 So I spoke to the people in the morning, and at that time my wife died; and I did in the morning as I was command- ed. 19 The people said to me, "Will you not tell us what these things mean for you to do so? 20 Then I answered them, "The word of the LORD has come to me, saying, 21 Speak to the house of Israel, "Thus says the LORD God: Behold, I will pollute my sanctuary, and the pride of your might, the pleasure of your eyes and the lust of your heart, your sons and your daughters whom you have left shall fall by the sword. 22 And you shall do as I have done: you shall not caress your lips nor eat the bread of men. 23 Your tires shall be on your heads, and your shoes on your feet; you shall not mourn or weep, but you shall pine for your iniquities and torment one another. 24 Thus Ezekiel is a sign to you; all that he has done, you shall do also; and when it comes to pass, you shall know that I am the Lord God. 25 Moreover, son of man, will not the day come when I will take away their power, the pleasure of their honor, the pleasure of their eyes and the de- sire of their heart, their sons and their daugh- ters? 26 that the one who will escape in that day will come to you to tell you what he has heard with his ears? 27 In that day will your mouth be opened to those who have escaped, and you will speak and no longer be mute, and you will be a sign to them, and they will know that I am the LORD.

CHAPTER 25

1 The word of the LORD came to me again and said to me 2 Son of man, set yourself against the Ammonites and prophesy against them, 3 And say unto the Ammonites, Hear the word of the Lord God, Thus saith the Lord God, Because ye have said, Ha, ha, against my sanctuary, when it was defiled, and against the land of Israel, when it was desolate, and against the house of Judah, when they went into captivity, 4 Behold, I will give you over to the men of the east as property, and they shall establish their palaces there and make their dwellings there; they shall eat your fruit and drink your milk. 5 I will make Rabbah a dwelling place for camels and the Ammo- nites a sheepfold, and you shall know that I am the LORD. 6 For thus says the LORD God, "For you have clapped your hands and trodden your feet and rebelled with all your heart against the land of Israel, 7 Behold, I will stretch out my hand upon thee, and will deliver thee to the heathen to be stripped, and will remove thee from the nations, and destroy thee, and thou shalt know that I am the LORD." 8 Thus says the LORD God, "For Moab and Seir say, Behold, the house of Ju- dah

is like unto all the heathen, 9 for this reason, behold, I will open the side of Moab, that is, of its cities, at its borders with the pleasant county, Beth-ieshimoth, Baal-meon, and Karia-thaim. 10 I will call the men of the east against the Ammonites and give them possession, so that the Ammonites will no longer be remembered among the nations, 11 And I will do justice upon Moab, and they shall know that I am the LORD. 12 Thus says the LORD God, "For Edom did good to take vengeance on the house of Judah, and com- mitted a great offense, and took vengeance on them, 13 Therefore thus says the LORD God, "I will also stretch out my hand upon Edom and destroy its men and animals, and I will make it desolate from Teman, and those of Dedan shall fall by the sword. 14 And I will take my vengeance upon Edom by the hand of my peo- ple Israel, and they shall do in Edom accord- ing to my wrath and according to my indig- nation, and they shall know my vengeance, saith the Lord God. 15 Thus says the LORD God, "For the Philistines have executed ven- geance, and have reinserted themselves with an evil heart to destroy it for the old hatred." 16 Therefore thus says the LORD God, "Be- hold, I will stretch out my hand upon the Phi- listines, and I will cut off the Cherethim, and I will destroy the rest of the coast of the sea. 17 And I will take great vengeance on them with the reproaches of my indignation, and they shall know that I am the LORD, when I take my vengeance on them.

CHAPTER 26

1 In the eleventh year, on the first day of the month, the word of the Lord came to me, say- ing, "Son of man, for Tyre has said against Je- rusalem, 'Ah, the gate of the people is broken; it is turned to me, 2 Son of man, for Tyre has said against Jerusalem, "Ah, the gate of the people is broken; it is turned toward me; for since it is desolate, I will be satisfied." 3 There- fore thus says the LORD God, "Behold, I come against you, O Tyre, and will cause many nations to come against you, as the sea rises with its waves. 4 They shall destroy the walls of Tyre, and break down her towers: I will take away the dust from her, and make her like the top of a tower. 5 You shall be for the scatter- ing of nets in the midst of the sea, for I have spoken it, saith the LORD God, and it shall be spoil for you nations. 6 Your daughters who are in the fields shall be slain by the sword, and they shall know that I am the LORD. 7 For thus says the LORD God, "Behold, I will cause Nebuchadnezzar, king of Babel, a king of kings from the north, to come upon Tyre, with horses, with chariots, and with horse- men, with a multitude and much people. 8 He will kill your daughters in the field by the sword, he will build a fortress against you, he will throw a mountain against you, and he will raise the buckler against you. 9 He shall set before him engines of war against thy walls, and with his weapons he shall break down thy towers. 10 The dust of his horses shall crumble from thee by their multitude; thy walls shall tremble at the noise of horsemen, wheels, and chariots, when he shall enter into thy gates as into the entrance of a broken city. 11 With the hoofs of his horses he shall make all thy streets tremble; he shall slay thy people with the stroke of the sword, and the pillars of thy strength shall fall to the ground. 12 They shall rob thy riches and plunder thy goods; they shall bring down thy walls and destroy thy fine houses; they shall cast thy stones and thy tim- bers and thy dust into the pools of water. 13 So I will cause the sound of your songs to cease, and the sound of your harps will no

longer be heard. 14 I will bring thee down like the top of a tower, and thou shalt become a net to be spread, and thou shalt no more be built: for I, the LORD, have said it, saith the LORD God. 15 Thus says the LORD God to Tyre, "Shall not the peoples tremble at the sound of your fall and at the cry of the wounded, when they are slain and wounded in your bowels?" 16 Then shall all the princes of the sea come down from their thrones; they shall lay down their robes, and take off their velvet garments, and clothe themselves with astonishment; and they shall sit on the ground, and be aston- ished at every moment, and they shall be in awe of thee. 17 They will make a lamentation for you and say, "How you are destroyed, that you were inhabited by the men of the sea, the renegade city that was strong in the sea, both she and her inhabitants, who instill fear in all who frequent her! 18 Now the peoples will be astonished in the day of your fall; yes, the peo- ples who are in the sea will be troubled by your departure. 19 For thus says the LORD God, "When I will make you a desolate city, like the cities that are not inhabited, and when I will cause the deep sea to descend upon you, and great waters will come upon you, 20 when I shall cast you down with those who go down into the pit, with the people of old, and I shall put you in the lower parts of the earth, like the old ruins, with those, I say, who go down into the pit, so that you will not be inhabited, and I will display my glory in the land of liars, 21 I will reduce you to nothing, and you will no longer exist; though you are sought for, you will never be found, says the Lord God.

CHAPTER 27

1 The word of the LORD came to me again and said 2 Son of man, take a lametation for Tyre, 3 and say to Tyre, which is situated at the entrance of the sea, which has been the mar- ketplace of the peoples for many years, "Thus says the LORD God: O Tyre, thou hast said, I am of perfect beauty. 4 Thy borders are in the midst of the sea, and thy builders have made thee of perfect beauty. 5 They made all your boards for ships with fir trees from Shenir; they brought cedars from Lebanon to make you trees. 6 They made your ores from the lakes of Bashan; the company of the Assyri- ans made your shores of yuorie, brought from the lakes of Chittim. 7 Fine linen, with ribbed cloths, brought from Egypt, was spread upon you to be your garment; blue and purple silk, brought from the islands of Elisha, was your covering. 8 The inhabitants of Zidon and Aru- ad were thy mariners, O Tyre; thy wise men that were in thee were thy pilots. 9 The an- cients of Gebal and its wise men were in thee thy caulkers; all the ships of the sea with their sailors were in thee to occupy thy merchan- dise. 10 Those of Persia, Lud and Phut were in thy army; thy men of war hung up thy shield and thy helmet; they set forth thy beauty. 11 The men of Aruad, with your army, were round about your walls, and the Gammadim were in your vicinity; they hung their shields on your walls around; they made your beauty perfect. 12 Those of Tarsis were thy march- ers for the multitude of all riches, for the torpedo, yron, tynne, and leade, which they brought to thy banquets. 13 Those of Iauan, Tubal and Meshech were your marchers as to the goods of men, and they brought vessels of brasse for your march. 14 Those of the house of Togarmah brought you horses, horse- men and mules. 15 The men of Dedan were thy marchers, and the goods of many years were in thy hand; they brought thee horns and teeth and peacocks as gifts. 16 Those of Aram were thy marchers by the multitude

of thy goods; they occupied thy stores with em- erauds, purple, cloths, fine linen, coral, and pearls. 17 Those of Iudah and of the land of Israel were thy marchers; they brought for thy wares corn of Minnith, Pannag, honie, oyle, and balme. 18 Those of Damascus were thy marchers for the multitude of thy wares, for the multitude of all riches, as for the wine of Helbon and white wool. 19 Those of Dan and Iauan also, going and returning, were about thy business; among thy merchandise were yron wood, cassia, and calamus. 20 Those of Dedan were thy marchers, clothed in precious garments for carets. 21 Those of Arabia and all the princes of Kedar were with thee in lambs, boughs, and goats; in these garments were thy marchers. 22 And the marchers of Sheba and Raamah were thy marchers; they did thy business with the chief spices, and with all the precious stones, and with gold. 23 Those of Haram, of Canneh and Eden, the march- ers of Sheba, Assur and Chilmad were your marchers. 24 These were thy marchers in all manner of things, in garments of white silk and red wool, and in chests for rich clothing, which were bound with ropes; chains also were among thy goods. 25 The ships of Tarsis were thy chief merchandise, and thou wast supplied and made very glorious in the midst of the sea. 26 Thy marauders carried thee into great waters; the east wind broke thee in the waters of the sea. 27 Thy riches and thy under- takings, thy merchandise, thy mariners and thy pilots, thy shoemakers, the occupants of thy merchandise, and all thy men of war that are in thee, and all thy multitude that is in the waters of the sea, shall fall into the waters of the sea in the day of thy ruin. 28 The suburbs shall tremble at the sound of the cry of thy pi- lots. 29 All those who handle ore, the sailors and all the pilots of the sea will get off their ships and stand on land, 30 they will make their voices heard against you, they will cry bitterly, they will throw dust on their heads and bask in the ashes. 31 They shall pluck out their ears for thee, and gird themselves with a sackcloth, and weep for thee with sorrow of heart and bitter mourning. 32 In their mourning they will make a lamentation for you, saying, "What city is like Tyre, so de- stroyed in the midst of the sea! 33 When your goods went out from the seas, you filled many peoples and enriched the kings of the earth with the multitude of your riches and your goods. 34 When the sea shall break you in the depths of the waters, your merchandise and all your multitude, which was in the midst of you, shall fall. 35 All the inhabitants of the yles shall be amazed at thee, and all their kings shall be afraid and troubled in their counte- nance. 36 The marchers of the people shall look upon thee; thou shalt be a terror, and shalt be no more.

CHAPTER 28

1 The word of the Lord was again addressed to me, saying, 2 Son of man, say to the prince of Tyre, "Thus says the Lord God: For your heart has exalted itself, and you have said, 'I am a God; I sit on the seat of God in the midst of the sea,' yet you are but a man and not a God, and though you have thought in your heart that you were equal with God, 3 be- hold, you are wiser than Daniel; there is no secret that they can hide from you. 4 By your wisdom and intelligence you have procured riches for yourself, and you have brought in your treasures gold and silver. 5 By your great wisdom and effort you have increased your riches, and your heart has been lifted up be- cause of your riches. 6 Therefore thus says the Lord God, "Because you thought in your heart that you were equal to God, 7 Behold, I will cause foreigners to

come upon you, that is, terrible nations, who will unsheathe their swords against the beauty of your wisdom and defile your splendor. 8 They shall cast you into the pit, and you shall die like those who were slain in the midst of the sea. 9 Will you then say before the one who kills you, "I am a god"? But you shall be a man and not a god in the hands of him who kills you. 10 Thou shalt die the death of the circumcised by the hand of strangers, for I have said it, saith the Lord God. 11 More, the word of the LORD was spoken to me, saying, 12 Son of man, make a complaint about the king of Tyre and say to him, "Thus says the Lord God: You have sealed the sum and are full of wisdom and beauty. 13 Thou hast been in Eden, the garden of God; every precious stone was in thy garment, the ruby, the topaz, and the diamond, the chrys- olite, the onyx, the jasper, the saphir, the em- eraude, the carbuncle, and the gold; the work- ing of thy stamps and thy pipes was prepared in thee in the day that thou wast created. 14 Thou art the anointed Cherub, speaking, and I have set thee in honor; thou hast been on the holy mountain of God; thou hast walked in the midst of the stones of fire. 15 You were perfect in your ways from the day you were created, until iniquity was found in you. 16 For the multitude of thy wares have filled thy bowels with cruelty, and thou hast sinned; therefore I will cast thee out as a profane from the mount of God, and I will destroy thee, O Cherubim courtier, from the bowels of the stones of fire. 17 Thy heart is lifted up because of thy beauty, and thou hast corrupt- ed thy wisdom because of thy splendor: I will cast thee down, I will set thee before kings that they may look upon thee. 18 Thou hast defiled thy sanctification with the multitude of thy iniquities, and with the iniquity of thy merchandise: therefore I will bring forth a fire out of thy midst that shall destroy thee, and I will reduce thee to ashes upon the earth, before the eyes of all them that look upon thee. 19 All who know thee among the nations shall be amazed at thee; thou shalt be a terror, and shalt be no more. 20 Then the word of the LORD came to me, saying, "Son of man, the word of the LORD is a terror, and you shall be no more." 21 "Son of man, set your face against Zidon and prophesy against it, 22 and say, "Thus saith the Lord God, Behold, I come against thee, O Zidon, and will be glorified in the midst of thee; and they shall know that I am the Lord, when I have executed judgments in her, and will be sanctified in her. 23 For I will send plague and blood into her streets, and the dead shall fall in the midst of her; and the enemy shall come against her with the sword on every side, and they shall know that I am the LORD. 24 No longer shall they be a stinging thorn to the house of Israel, nor a sore thorn to all who surround them and de- spise them, and they shall know that I am the Lord God. 25 Thus says the LORD God, "When I have gathered the house of Israel from the peoples where they are scattered, and I shall be sanctified in them before the heathen, then they shall dwell in the land which I gave to my servant Jehoshaphat. 26 They will dwell there in safety, they will build houses and plant vineyards; yes, they will dwell in safety, when I have executed judgments on all those who despise them, and they will know that I am the LORD their God.

CHAPTER 29

1 In the tenth year, on the twelfth day of the month, the word of the LORD came to me, saying, "Son of man, set yourself against Pha- raoh, king of Egypt, and prophesy against him and against all Egypt." 2 Son of man, set yourself against Pharaoh, king of Egypt, and prophesy

against him and against all Egypt. 3 Speak and say, "Thus says the Lord God, 'Be- hold, I come against you, Pharaoh, king of Egypt, the great dragon who lies in the midst of his mounds and who said, 'The mound is mine and I have made it for myself. 4 But I will put hooks in your jaws, and I will cause the fish of your shores to stick to your scales, and I will fish you from the middle of your shores, and all the fish of your shores will stick to your scales. 5 I will leave thee in the wilderness, both thou and all the fish of thy ships; thou shalt go about in the open fields; thou shalt not be gathered nor gathered, for I have fed the beasts of the field and the wild beasts. 6 All the inhabitants of Egypt will know that I am the LORD, for they have been a staff of support for the house of Isra- el. 7 When they clung to you with their hand, you broke and ripped open all their shoulders; and when they leaned on you, you braked and made all their bonds stand. 8 Therefore thus says the LORD God, "Behold, I will bring a sword upon thee, and I will destroy from thee men and beasts, 9 And the land of Egypt shall be desolate and forsaken, and they shall know that I am the LORD, for he said, The river is mine, and I have made it, 10 Behold, I am coming upon you and upon your riuers, and I will make the land of Egypt exceedingly deso- late and forsaken from the height of Seueneh, even to the borders of the Black Forest. 11 No man shall pass over it, nor any animal, and it shall not be inhabited for four hundred years. 12 And I will make the land of Egypt desolate in the midst of the countries that are desolate, and its cities shall be desolate among the cit- ies that are desolate, for forty years; and I will scatter the Egyptians among the nations, and I will scatter them through the countries." 13

But thus says the LORD God, "At the end of forty years I will gather the Egyptians from the nations where they have been scattered, 14 and I will bring back the captives of Egypt and return them to the land of Pathros, to the land of their dwelling, and there they will be a small kingdom. 15 And it shall be the smallest of kingdoms, and it shall no more exalt itself over the nations, for I will reduce them, that they may no more dominate the nations. 16 And it shall no longer be the security of the house of Israel to bring to remembrance their iniquities, dealing with them; so they shall know that I am the Lord God. 17 Also in the seventh and twentieth year, in the first month and on the first day of the month, the word of the LORD came to me, saying 18 Son of man, Nebuchadnezzar, king of Babel, made his army do great service against Tyre: every head was made baleful, and every shoulder was laid bare: nevertheless he had no wages, nor his army for Tyre, for the service which he did against it. 19 Therefore thus saith the LORD God, Behold, I will give the land of Egypt unto Nebuchadnezzar the king of Ba- bel, and he shall take his multitude, and make his spoil, and take his prayer, and it shall be wages for his army. 20 I have given him the land of Egypt for his labor, because he served against it, for they have labored for me, says the Lord God. 21 In that day I will make the horn of the house of Israel to grow, and I will give you an open mouth among them, and they shall know that I am the LORD.

CHAPTER 30

1 The word of the Lord was again spoken to me, saying, 2 Son of man, prophesy and say, "Thus says the Lord God, Shout and cry, Let it be today." 3 For the day is near, and the day of the Lord is at hand, a cloudy day, and it shall be

the time of the heathen. 4 And the sword shall come upon Egypt, and Ethiopia shall be afraid, when the victims shall fall in Egypt, when they shall carry away her multitude, and when her foundations shall be broken down. 5 Ethiopia, Phut, Lud, all the common people, Cub, and the men of the land who are in league shall fall with them by the sword. 6 Thus says the LORD: "Those also who main- tain Egypt shall fall, and the pride of her might shall fall; from Seueneh onward they shall fall by the sword, says the LORD God. 7 They shall be desolate in the midst of the desolate coun- tries, and its cities shall be in the midst of the destroyed cities. 8 And they shall know that I am the LORD, when I have set fire to Egypt, and when all her helpers shall be destroyed. 9 In that day shall messengers in ships depart from me to make the unwary Mores flee, and they shall be afraid as in the days of Egypt, for it is true that it comes. 10 Thus says the LORD God, "I will also cause the multitude of Egypt to cease by the hand of Nebuchadnezzar, king of Babel. 11 For he and his people with him, that is, the terrible nations, shall be led to de- stroy the land; they shall draw their swords against Egypt and fill the land with victims. 12 And I will cause the banks to dry up, and I will cause the land to fall into the hands of the wicked, and I will make the land and all that is therein to disappear by the hand of foreign- ers: I, the LORD, have said it. 13 Thus saith the LORD God, I will also destroy the idols, and I will cause their idols to cease from Noph, and there shall be no more prince of the land of Egypt, and I will send a fear into the land of Egypt. 14 I will make Pathros desolate, and I will set Zoan on fire, and I will do justice in No. 15 And I will unleash my wrath upon Sin, which is the strength of Egypt, and I will de- stroy the multitude of No. 16 And I will set fire to Egypt; Sin shall have great sorrow, No shall be destroyed, and Noph shall have daily sorrow. 17 The young men of Auen and Phi- beseth shall fall by the sword, and these cities shall go into captivity. 18 In Tehaphnehes the day shall her light come again, when I shall make a breach in the walls of Egypt; and when the pomp of her power shall cease in her, the cloud shall collapse her, and her daughters shall go into captivity. 19 Thus will I execute judgments in Egypt, and they shall know that I am the LORD. 20 In the eleventh year, in the first month and on the seventh day of the month, the word of the LORD came to me, saying, "Son of man, your daughters shall go into captivity." 21 Son of man, I have broken the arm of Pharaoh, king of Egypt; and be- hold, it shall not be possible to heal her any more, nor shall a rope be put to bind her, and make her so strong that she may hold the sword." 22 Therefore thus says the Lord God, "Behold, I will come against Pharaoh, king of Egypt, and I will break his armor, which was strong, but is broken, and I will cause the sword to fall from his hand. 23 And I will scatter the Egyptians among the nations and scatter them through the countries. 24 And I will strengthen the weapon of the king of Ba- bel, and I will put my sword in his hand; but I will break Pharaoh's weapon, and he shall utter sighs, as the sighs of him that is wound- ed before him. 25 But I will strengthen the armies of the king of Babel, and the armies of Pharaoh shall fall, and they shall know that I am the LORD, when I put my sword in the hand of the king of Babel, and he shall spread it over the land of Egypt. 26 Then I will scatter the Egyptians among the nations and scatter them among your countries, and they will know that I am the LORD.

CHAPTER 31

1 In the eleventh year, in the third month and on the first day of the month, the word of the LORD came to me, saying 2 Son of man, speak to Pharaoh, king of Egypt, and to his multitude, "Whom do you resemble in your greatness? 3 Behold, Assur was like a cedar of Lebanon, with beautiful branches and with thin edges that made shade, and he shot very high, and his top was among the thin edges. 4 And the waters nourished him, and the deep exalted him over him with its waves running around his plants and sending his little waves to all the trees of the field. 5 Therefore his height was greater than that of all the trees of the field, and his branches multiplied and his foliage was long, because of the multi- tude of waters that the deep sent out. 6 All the birds of the dry land made their nests in his branches, and under his branches all the trees of the dry land bore their children, and under his shadow dwelt all the mightiest nations. 7 So he was beautiful because of his greatness and the length of his branches, because his root was near great waters. 8 The cedars in God's garden could not hide him; no fir tree was like his branches, and the checker trees were not like his branches; all the trees in God's garden were not like him in his beauty. 9 I made him more beautiful with the multi- tude of his branches, so that all the trees of Eden, which were in the garden of God, en- vied him. 10 Therefore thus says the Lord God, "For he is lifted up on high, he has shot his top among the thin branches, and his heart is lift- ed up in his height, 11 therefore have I deliv- ered him into the hand of the mightiest of the heathen; he shall handle him, because I have cast him out for his wickedness. 12 Foreign- ers have destroyed it, like the terrible nations, and have forsaken it on the mountains, and in all the valleys its branches have fallen down, and its legs have been broken off from all the inhabitants of the land; and all the peoples of the earth have turned away from its shadow and forsaken it. 13 On its ruins shall remain all the spots of the land, and on its branches all the beasts of the field, 14 so that none of all the trees that are by the sea shall rise up by its height, and that its top shall not sprout up among the slender branches, and that its leaves shall not rise up by their height, who drink so much water, for they are all con- demned to death in the lowest parts of the earth, among the sons of men, among those who go down into the pit. 15 Thus saith the LORD God, In the day that he went down to hell, I caused them to move, I caused the deep to flow for him, I stilled the floods thereof, and the great waters stood still: I caused Lebanon to be changed for him, and all the trees of the field to faint. 16 I made the nations to tremble at the sound of his fall, when I cast him into hell together with them that go down into the pit, and all the excellent trees of Eden, and the best of Lebanon: and all that feed upon the waters shall be comforted in the lower parts of the earth. 17 With him also shall descend into hell those who have been slain with the sword and his armor, and those who dwell under his shadow in the midst of the heathen. 18 Whom do you thus resemble in glory and greatness among the trees of Eden? Yet you shall be cast down with the trees of Eden to the lowest parts of the earth; you shall sleep in the bowels of the vncircumcised, with those who were slain with the sword; this is Pha- raoh and all his multitude, says the Lord God.

CHAPTER 32

1 In the twelfth year, in the twelfth month, and on the first day of the month, the word of the LORD came to me, saying 2 Son of man, make a lamentation for Pharaoh, king of

Egypt, and say to him, "You are like a lion of the nations, and you are like a dragon in the sea; you have thrown out your cords, you have troubled the waters with your feet, and you have trodden down their cords." 3 Thus says the LORD God, "Therefore I will spread my net over you with a great multitude of people, and they will drop you into my net. 4 Then I will leave thee on the earth, and will cast thee into the open field, and will cause all the refuse of the earth to remain upon thee, and I will fill all the fields with thee. 5 And I will make thy flesh to spread upon the moun- tains, and I will fill the valleys with thy height. 6 I will also sprinkle with your blood the land in which you swim, as far as the mountains, and the shores will be filled with you. 7 When I have done away with thee, I will bring down the heavens, and make dark its stars: I will make the sun a cloud, and the moon shall give no more of her light. 8 All the lights of Eauen I will dim them, and I will bring down darkness upon thy land, saith the LORD God. 9 And I will also disturb the hearts of many peoples, when I bring your destruction among the na- tions and upon the countries that you have not known. 10 Yea, I will cause many peoples to be in awe of you, and their kings to be amazed with fear for you, when I will cause my sword to flash against their faces, and they shall be afraid at all times; every one for his life in the day of your fall. 11 For thus says the Lord God, "The sword of the king of Babel will come upon you. 12 With the sword of the mighty I will bring down your multitude; they shall all be terrible nations; they shall destroy the pomp of Egypt, and all her multitude shall be consumed. 13 I will also destroy all her beasts from the great shores, and there shall be no more trouble to the feet of man and to the beasts. 14 Then I will make their waters deep and make their rivers flow like oil, says the LORD God. 15 When I shall make the land of Egypt desolate, and the county, with all that is therein, shall be destroyed; when I shall smite all that dwell therein, then shall they know that I am the LORD. 16 This is the mourning with which they shall mourn her; the daugh- ters of the nations shall mourn her; they shall mourn for Egypt and for all her multitude, saith the LORD God. 17 In the twelfth year, on the fifteenth day of the month, the word of the LORD came to me, saying, Son of man, do not mourn for Egypt and for all her multi- tude, 18 Son of man, mourn for the multitude of Egypt, and cast them down, together with the daughters of the mighty nations, to the lowest parts of the earth, with those who go down into the pit. 19 Who is it that passes in beauty? Go and sleep with the vncircumcised ones. 20 They shall fall among them that are slain by the sword; it is delivered to the sword; draw it and all its multitude. 21 The mighti- est and strongest shall speak to him from the bowels of hell with those who help him; they are fallen and sleep with the circumcised who have been slain by the sword. 22 Assur is there and all his company; their graves are round about him; all of them were slain and fell by the sword. 23 Whose graves are dug in the pit, and his crowd is round about his graves; all of them were slain and fell by the sword, which made fear in the land of Liege. 24 There is Elam and all his multitude round about his tomb; all of them were slain and fell by the sword, and went down with the vncircumcis into the lower parts of the earth; they made to be feared in the land of Liuing, but they bore their shame with those who went down into the pit. 25 They have made his bed in the midst of the slaughter with all his crowd; their graves are round about him; all these vncircumcised have been slain by the sword; though they have raised their fear in the land of the liuing, yet they have borne their shame with those who go down into the pit; they are lain in the midst of those who

have been slain. 26 There is Meshech, Tubal, and all their mul- titude, their graves are round about them; all these vncircumcised have been slain by the sword, though they have caused their shame to be in the land of Extinction. 27 They shall not be able to lie with the valiant among the vncircumcised, who have fallen, who have gone down to the grave, with their weapons of war, and who have laid down their swords under their heads, but their iniquity shall remain on their bones, because they have been the fear of the mighty ones in the land of Liege. 28 Thou shalt be broken in the belly of the vncircumcised, and shalt lie with them that have been slain by the sword. 29 There is Edom, its kings, and all its princes, who by their strength have been slain by the sword; they shall sleep with the vncircircumcis and with those who go down into the pit. 30 And there are all the princes of the north, and all the inhabitants of Zidoniah, who have been slain and have been afraid; they are ashamed of their strength, and the vncircumcis sleep with those who have been slain by the sword, and bear their shame with those who fall into the pit. 31 And Pharaoh shall see them, and shall be comforted with all his multitude: Pharaoh and all his army shall be slain by the sword, saith the LORD God. 32 For I have made my fear to be in the land of the inhabi- tants; and he shall be laid in the midst of the circumcised with those who shall be slain by the sword, that is, Pharaoh and all his multi- tude, saith the Lord God.

CHAPTER 33

1 Again the word of the LORD came to me, saying, 2 Son of man, speak to the sons of your people and say to them, "When I bring the sword upon a country, if the people of the country take a man from among them and make him their watchman, 3 if he, see- ing the sword coming upon a country, shall sound the trumpet and set the people at war, 4 whoever shall have heard the sound of the trumpet, and shall not have been warned, if the sword come and take him away, his blood shall fall upon his head. 5 Because he heard the sound of the trumpet and would not be warned, his blood will fall upon him; but he who receives the warning will have his life saved. 6 But if the watchman sees the sword coming and does not sound the trumpet, and the people are not warned, if the sword comes and takes someone in their midst, he shall be taken away for his iniquity, but his blood I will require from the hand of the watchman. 7 So you, O son of man, I have constituted you a watchman for the house of Israel; therefore you shall hear the word on my mouth, and I will warn them from my side. 8 When I say to the ungodly, "O ungodly man, you shall die, if you do not speak and admonish the ungodly man on his way, that ungodly man shall die for his iniquity, but his blood I will require from your hand." 9 If you admonish the wicked man to change his way, if he does not change his way, he will die for his iniquity, but you will have delivered your soul. 10 Therefore, O son of man, speak to the house of Israel, "Thus speak and say, 'If our transgressions and sins come upon us and we are consumed because of them, how should we live? 11 Say to them, "How is it true that I, says the Lord God, do not desire the death of the ungodly, but that the ungodly turn from his way and live; turn away, turn away from your futile lives, for you would die, O house of Israel? 12 Therefore, son of man, say to the children of your people, "The righteousness of the righteous shall not fail him in the day of his transgression, nor shall the wickedness of the wicked cause him to fall into it, in the day that he retracts from his wickedness, nor shall the

righteous lie for his righteousness in the day that he sins." 13 When I shall say to the righteous that he shall surely lie, if he trusts in his righteousness and commits iniquity, all his righteousness shall be remembered no more, but for the iniquity he has committed he shall die for the same. 14 Moreover, when I say to the ungodly, "You shall die," if he turns back from his sin and does what is lawful and right, 15 that is, if the ungodly person returns the pledge, returns what he had stolen, and walks according to the statutes of life, without committing in- iquity, he will certainly lie and not die. 16 None of his faults that he has committed shall be mentioned for him; because he has done what is lawful and right, he shall certainly lie. 17 Nevertheless the sons of your people say, "The way of the LORD is not fair, but their way is vnequal." 18 When the righteous man turns from his righteousness and commits iniquity, he dies as a result. 19 But if the ungodly turn back from his wickedness and do what is law- ful and righteous, for that he shall die. 20 But you say, "The way of the LORD is not fair." O house of Israel, I will judge you each accord- ing to his life." 21 Also in the twelfth year of our captivity, in the tenth month and on the fifth day of the month, one who had fled from Jerusalem came to me and said, "The city has been struck." 22 Now the hand of the LORD had rested on me during the night, before the fugitive came, and had opened my mouth un- til he came to me in the morning; and when he opened my mouth, I was no longer dumb. 23 Then the word of the Lord reached me and said, 24 Son of man, these that dwell in the desolate places of the land of Israel speak, and say, "Abraham was one, and he possessed the land; but we are many, therefore the land shall be given into your possession. 25 There- fore say ye unto them, Thus saith the Lord God, Ye eat with blood, and lift up your eyes unto your idols, and shed blood; should ye therefore possess the land? 26 You lean on your swords, you do abomination and defile the wife of each of your neighbors; should you then possess the land? 27 Say to them, "Thus says the LORD God, 'As I stand, so surely those who are in the desolate places shall fall by the sword; and those who are in the open field I will feed them to the beasts; and those who are in the fortresses and in the caves shall die of the plague. 28 For I will leave the land desolate and desolate, and the pomp of its strength will cease; the mountains of Israel will be desolate, and no one will pass through them. 29 Then they shall know that I am the LORD, when I have made your land deso- late and desolate, because of all their abom- inations which they have committed. 30 You also, son of man, the sons of your people who speak of you in the streets and in the yards of the houses, and speak one to another, each to his brother, saying, "Come, I pray you, and hear what is the word that comes from the LORD." 31 For they come to you, as the peo- ple expect to come; and my people sit before you and hear your words, but do not put them into practice, because with their mouths they make inferences, and their hearts go after their own convenience. 32 Well then, you are to them as the song of one who has a pleas- ant voice and can sing well; for they hear your words, but they do not perform them. 33 And when this comes to pass (for, indeed, it will come to pass), they will know that a Prophet has been in their midst.

CHAPTER 34

1 The word of the LORD was spoken to me, saying. 2 Son of man, prophesy against the shepherds of Israel, prophesy and say to them, "Thus says the Lord God to the shep-

herds, 'Cursed are the shepherds of Israel, who feed themselves; should not shepherds feed the flock? 3 You eat fat and clothe your- selves with wool; you kill those who are fed, but you do not feed the sheep. 4 You have not strengthened the weak, you have not healed the sick, you have not bound up the broken, you have not brought back to life what was forsaken, you have not sought out what was lost, but you have ruled them with cruelty and severity. 5 And they were scattered without a shepherd; and when they were scattered, they were despised by all the camps. 6 My sheep wandered over all the mountains and over every hill; yea, my flock was scattered over all the earth, and no one saw them or sought them. 7 Therefore, you shepherds, lis- ten to the word of the LORD. 8 As I say, says the Lord God, for my flock was scattered and my sheep were scattered by all the beasts of the field, having no shepherd, nor did my shepherds see my sheep, but the shepherds fed themselves and did not feed my sheep, 9 Hear therefore the word of the LORD, O shep- herds. 10 Thus says the LORD God, "Behold, I come against the shepherds, and require my flock out of their hands, and cause them to cease feeding it; and the shepherds shall feed themselves no more, for I will take my flock out of their mouths, and they shall eat it no more." 11 For thus says the Lord God, "Behold, I will search out my sheep, and I will unearth them." 12 Just as a shepherd searches for his flock when he is among his scattered sheep, so I will search for my sheep and bring them out of all the places where they have been scattered in the cloudy and dark day, 13 and I will bring them out of the nations, and gather them from the countryside, and bring them back into their own land, and feed them on the mountains of Israel, and along the banks, and in all the inhabited places of the land. 14 I will feed them in a good pasture, and on the mountains of Israel shall be their flock; there they shall lie down in a good flock, and in a fat pasture they shall feed on the mountains of Israel. 15 I will shepherd my sheep and make them rest, says the LORD God. 16 I will see what has been lost, I will bring back to life what has been forsaken, and I will bring back to life what has been broken; I will strength- en the weak, but I will destroy the fat and the strong, and I will feed them with judgment. 17 To you also, my sheep, thus says the Lord God, "Behold, I judge between the sheep and the ewes, between the rams and the goats." 18 Does it seem to you a small thing to have eat- en of the good pasture, but must you trample with your feet the residue of your pasture? And to have drunk from the deep waters, but must you disturb the residue with your feet? 19 My sheep eat what you have trodden down with your feet and drink what you have dis- turbed with your feet. 20 Therefore thus says the LORD God to them, "Behold, I will judge between the fat sheep and the lean sheep. 21 For you have pushed with your flanks and with your shoulders, and have driven all the animals with your horns, until you have scat- tered them, 22 Therefore I will help my sheep, and they shall no longer be spied out, and I will judge between ewe and sheep. 23 And I will put a shepherd outside them, and he shall feed them, as my servant Dauid, he shall feed them and be their shepherd. 24 I, the LORD, will be their God, and my servant Dauid will be their prince. I, the LORD, have said it. 25 I will make a covenant of peace with them, and I will remove the evil beasts from the land; they will dwell safely in the wilderness and sleep in the woods. 26 I will set them as a blessing around my mountain, and I will send down rays in due time, and there will be a ray of blessing there. 27 And the tree of the field shall yield its fruit, and the land shall yield its fruit; and they shall be safe in their land, and they shall know that I am the LORD, when I have broken the cords of their yoke, and have delivered them out of the hands of them that used to use them. 28 And they shall no more be skewered by the heathen, nor shall the chestnut groves of the land forsake them, but they shall dwell in safety, and none shall cause them to waver. 29 And I will raise up for them a plant of renunciation, and they shall no lon- ger be consumed by hunger in the land, nor shall they suffer the reproach of the heathen any more. 30 So they will understand that I, the LORD their God, am with them, and that they, that is, the house of Israel, are my peo- ple, says the LORD God. 31 You are my sheep, the sheep of my pasture, and I am your God, says the Lord God.

CHAPTER 35

1 Then the word of the LORD came to me, saying, "Son of man, set your face against Mount Seir and prophesy against it, 2 "Son of man, set your face against Mount Seir and prophesy against it." 3 and say to him, "Thus says the Lord God, 'Behold, O Mount Seir, I am coming against you; I will stretch out my hand against you and make you desolate and desolate. 4 I will put your cities on fire and iron, and you shall be desolate, and you shall know that I am the LORD. 5 For thou hast had a perpetual hatred, and hast put the children of Israel to flight by the power of the sword in the time of their calamity, when their in- iquity had an end, 6 Therefore, as I lie, says the LORD God, I will prepare you for blood, and blood will pursue you; if you do not hate blood, then blood will pursue you. 7 Thus I will make Mount Seir desolate and desolate, and I will cut off from it him who passes by and him who returns. 8 I will fill its mountains with its slain men; on thy hills, in thy valleys, and in all thy shores shall fall those slain with the sword. 9 I will make you an everlasting desolation; your cities shall not return, and you shall know that I am the LORD. 10 For you said, "These two nations and these two countries shall be mine, and we will possess them" (since the LORD was there). 11 There- fore, as I believe, says the Lord God, I will do according to your wrath and according to your indignation which you have manifested in your hatred against them; and I will make myself known among them, as I have judged you. 12 And thou shalt know that I, the LORD, have heard all thy blasphemies which thou hast uttered against the mountains of Israel, saying, "They lie forsaken, they are destined to be destroyed." 13 Thus with your mouths have ye boasted against me, and multiplied your words against me: I have heard them. 14 Thus saith the LORD God, Thus shall all the world behave when I make you desolate. 15 As thou hast rejoiced over the inheritance of the house of Israel, because it was desolate, so will I do with thee: thou shalt be desolate, O mount Seir, and all Idumea, and they shall know that I am the LORD.

CHAPTER 36

1 You also, son of man, prophesy to the mountains of Israel and say, "You mountains of Israel, listen to the word of the Lord." 2 Thus says the Lord God, for the enemy has said against you, "Ah, behold, the places of the world are in our possession." 3 Therefore prophesy and say, "Thus saith the Lord God, For they have made you desolate and swal- lowed you up on every side, that you were a possession to the remnant of the heathen, and you came upon the lips and tongues of men and the reproach of the Gentiles, 4

Therefore, you mountains of Israel, listen to the word of the Lord God: "Thus says the Lord God to the mountains and to the hills, to the shores and to the valleys, to the desolate and forsaken places and to the abandoned cities, which are objects of mockery and derision by the remnant of the heathen who are around." 5 Therefore thus says the LORD God, "In the fire of my indignation I have spoken against the remnant of the heathen and against all Idumea, who have taken my land as their pos- session, with the joy of their whole heart and with an evil mind to cast it out as a prayer." 6 Prophesy therefore over the land of Israel, and say to the mountains and the hills, the shores and the valleys, "Thus says the Lord God, Behold, I have spoken in my indigna- tion and in my wrath, because you have suf- fered the shame of the heathen." 7 Therefore thus says the Lord God, I have lifted up my hand, and the heathen around you shall suf- fer their shame. 8 But you, O mountains of Israel, will sprout your branches and bear your fruit to my people of Israel, for they are ready to come. 9 For behold, I will come to you and turn my hand to you, and you shall be cultivated and sown. 10 I will multiply men over you, that is, all the house of Israel, and cities shall be inhabited and desolate places shall be built. 11 I will multiply over you men and animals, which shall increase and bear fruit, and I will cause you to dwell according to your former possessions, and I will grant you benefits more than before, and you shall know that I am the LORD. 12 Yea, I will cause men to walk upon you, as my people Israel, and they shall possess you, and you shall be their inheritance, and you shall not deprive them of men any more. 13 Thus says the LORD God, because they have said to you, "You are a land that violates men, and you have been a waster of your people." 14 Therefore, says the LORD God, thou shalt no more slaughter men and waste thy people, 15 no more will I make the shame of the heathen to be felt in thee, no more will thou bring the reproach of the people, and no more will thou make thy people waver, saith the Lord God. 16 More, the word of the LORD was spoken to me, saying, 17 Son of man, when the house of Israel dwelt in its land, it defiled it by its ways and by its deeds; its way was before me like the filth of a menstruum. 18 Therefore I unleashed my wrath upon them, because of the blood they had shed in the land and because of their idolatries with which they had defiled it. 19 I scattered them among the heathen, and they were scattered through the countries, because I judged them according to their ways and according to their deeds. 20 And when they entered into the land of the heathen, whither they went, they defiled my holy Name, saying of them, "This is the Lord's people, and they have departed from their land." 21 But I have blotted out my holy Name, which the house of Israel had defiled among the heathen, where they had gone. 22 Therefore say to the house of Israel, "Thus says the Lord God, I do not do this for you, O house of Israel, but for my holy Name, which you defiled among the heathen where you went. 23 I will sanctify my great Name, which was defiled among the heathen, among whom you defiled it; and the heathen shall know that I am the Lord, saith the Lord God, when I am sanctified in you before their eyes. 24 For I will take you out of the midst of the heathen, and gather you out of all coun- tries, and bring you back to your own land. 25 Then I will cause clear water to flow upon you, and you shall be cleansed; yea, from all your filthiness and from all your idols I will cleanse you. 26 I will also give you a new heart and put a new spirit within you; I will remove the heart of stone from your body and give you a heart of flesh. 27 I will put my spirit in you and make you walk in my statutes; you shall keep my precepts and put them into practice. 28 You shall dwell in the land that I gave to your fathers; you shall be my people, and I will be your God. 29 I will also deliver you from all your filthiness; I will call up the grain and increase it, and I will not cause you to go hungry. 30 I will multiply the fruit of the trees and the harvest of the fields, so that you will no longer have the reproach of famine among the heathen. 31 Then you shall remember your evil ways and your deeds that were not good, and you shall judge your selves worthy to be destroyed for your iniquities and for your abominations. 32 Know that I do not do this for you, says the LORD God; therefore, O house of Israel, be ashamed and confound- ed in your ways. 33 Thus says the LORD God, "When I have delivered you from all your in- iquities, I will make you dwell in the cities, and the desolate places will be built up. 34 The desolate land will be cleared, while it lay desolate before the eyes of all who passed by. 35 For they said, "This desolate land was like the garden of Eden, and these desolate and ruined cities were strong and inhabited." 36 Then shall the rest of the heathen that are left around you know that I, the LORD, build the ruined places and mourn the desolate places: I, the LORD, have said it, and I will do it. 37 Thus saith the LORD God, I will seek again the house of Israel, to execute it unto them: I will increase them of men as a flock. 38 As the holy flock, as the flock of Jerusalem in its solemn feasts, so shall the desolate cities be filled with flocks of men, and they shall know that I am the LORD.

CHAPTER 37

1 And the hand of the Lord came upon me, and brought me forth with the spirit of the Lord, and set me in the midst of the field, which was full of bones. 2 He led me around them, and behold they were very numerous in the open field, and behold they were very dry. 3 He said to me, "Son of man, can these bones live? And I answered, "O Lord God, thou knowest." 4 Then he said to me, "Proph- esy over these bones and say to them, O dry bones, listen to the word of the Lord." 5 Thus says the LORD God to these bones, "Behold, I will put breath into you, and you shall live. 6 I will put sinews on you, I will make flesh grow, I will clothe you with skin and make you breathe, that you may live, and you shall know that I am the LORD." 7 So I prophesied, as I was commanded; and as I prophesied, there was a noise, and behold, it shook, and the bones came together, bone to bone. 8 And when I saw, behold, sinews and flesh grew fat upon them, and round about, skin cov- ered them, but there was no breath in them. 9 Then he said to me, "Prophesy to the wind; prophesy, son of man, and say to the wind, 'Thus says the Lord God, "Come from the four winds, O breath, and breathe upon these dead, that they may live."' 10 So I prophesied as he commanded me; and the breath entered them, and they rose up and stood on their feet, a huge army. 11 Then he said to me, "Son of man, these bones are all the house of Isra- el. Behold, they say, 'Our bones have dried up, our hope is gone, and we have been blotted out.' 12 Therefore prophesy and say to them, "Thus says the Lord God, 'Behold, my people, I will open your graves, and bring you out of your graves, and bring you into the land of Is- rael, 13 and ye shall know that I am the LORD, when I have opened your graves, O my people, and brought you out of your sepulchres, 14 and I will put my Spirit in you, and you shall live, and I will place you in your own land; then you shall know that I, the LORD, have spoken it and performed it, saith the LORD. 15 The word of the LORD

was again spoken to me, saying, 16 "You, son of man, take a piece of wood and write on it, Vnto Iudah and to the children of Israel his companions; take another piece of wood and write on it, Vnto Ioseph, tree of Ephraim, and to all the house of Israel his companions. 17 Then you shall join them one to another in one tree, and they shall be as one in your hand. 18 And when the sons of your people shall speak to you, saying, "Will you not explain what you mean by these things? 19 Thou shalt answer them, "Thus saith the LORD God, Behold, I will take the tree of Joseph, which is in the hand of Ephraim, and the tribes of Israel his companions, and will put them with him, as with the tree of Judah, and will make them one tree, and they shall be one in my hand. 20 The pieces of wood on which you wrote shall be in your hand, be- fore their eyes. 21 And say unto them, Thus saith the Lord God, Behold, I will take the children of Israel out of the midst of the hea- then, whither they have gone, and will gather them on every side, and will bring them back to their own land. 22 I will make them one people in the land, in the mountains of Isra- el, and one king shall be king over them all; they shall no longer be two peoples, and they shall no longer be divided into two kingdoms. 23 No more shall they be defiled with their idolatries, with their abominations, and with none of their transgressions; but I will rescue them from all their dwellings wherein they have sinned, and I will reorder them; so they shall be my people, and I will be their God. 24 Dauid my servant shall be their king, and they shall all have one shepherd; they shall also walk according to my principles, and keep my statutes, and perform them. 25 They shall dwell in the land that I have given to Iaakob my servant, where your fathers dwelt; they and their sons and their children shall dwell there forever, and my servant Dauid shall be their prince forever. 26 Moreover, I will make a covenant of peace with them; it shall be a lasting covenant with them; I will make them grow and multiply them, and I will establish my sanctuary among them forever. 27 My tab- ernacle also shall be with them; yea, I will be their God, and they shall be my people. 28 So the Gentiles will know that I, the LORD, sanc- tify Israel, when my sanctuary will be in their midst forever.

CHAPTER 38

1 The word of the LORD was spoken to me, saying. 2 "Son of man, set yourself against Gog and against the land of Magog, the chief prince of Meshech and Tubal, and prophesy against him, 3 and say, "Thus says the Lord God, Behold, I come against you, O Gog, chief prince of Meshech and Tubal. 4 I will destroy thee, and will put hooks in thy jaws, and will bring forth thee and all thy army, horses and horsemen, all clothed in all manner of ar- mor, and a great multitude with bucklers and shields, all wielding swords. 5 The members of Paras, and of Cush, and of Phut, and all who bear shields and helmets. 6 Gomer and all his bands, the house of Togarmah of the northern quarters and all his bands, and many people with you. 7 Prepare yourself and be ready, you and all your crowd that has gathered against you, and be their guard. 8 After many days thou shalt be visited, for in the last years thou shalt enter into the land that was destroyed with the sword, and was gathered together by many peoples to the mountains of Israel, which have long been forsaken; but they have been brought out of the peoples, and they shall all dwell in safety. 9 You shall go up and come like a storm, and you shall be like a cloud to trample the land, you and all your com- panions and

many peoples with you. 10 Thus says the LORD God, "At the same time many things shall come into your mind, and you shall do many thoughts. 11 And thou shalt say, I will go into the land that hath no wall: I will go to them that are quiet and dwell in safety, who dwell all without walls, and have neither bars nor gates." 12 Thinking to scatter prayer and to make spoil, to turn thy hand upon the desolate places that are now inhabited, and upon the people gathered from the nations that have procured cattle and goods, and that dwell in the midst of the land. 13 Sheba, Dedan and the merchants of Tarsis with all its lions will say to you, "Have you come to scatter prayer? Have you gathered your crowd to loot? To take away silk and gold, to take away cattle and goods, and to scatter a great prayer?" 14 Therefore, son of man, prophesy and say to Gog, "Thus says the LORD God, In that day when my people of Israel shall dwell in safety, shalt thou not know it? 15 You shall come from your place in the northern parts, you and many people with you; all shall ride on horses, a great multitude and a mighty army. 16 Thou shalt come against my people of Israel, as a cloud covering the land; thou shalt be in the last days, and I will bring thee upon my land, that the heathen may know me, when I am sanctified in thee, O Gog, before their eyes." 17 Thus says the LORD God, "Are not you he of whom I spoke anciently by the hand of my servants, the prophets of Israel, who proph- esied in those days and in those years, that I would lead thee over them? 18 When Gog also shall come against the land of Israel, saith the LORD God, my wrath shall break forth in my anger. 19 For in my indignation and in the fire of my wrath I have said it; surely at that time there shall be a great shaking in the land of Israel, 20 so that the fish of the sea, and the fish of the land, and the beasts of the field, and all the animals that move and crawl upon the earth, and all the men that are upon the earth, shall tremble at my presence, and the mountains shall be overthrown, and the poles shall fall down, and every wall shall collapse to the ground. 21 For I will call the sword against him upon all my mountains, saith the LORD God; every man shall have a sword against his brother. 22 And I will avert him with pesti- lence and blood, and I will rain down on him, and on his bands, and on the great people that are with him, a baleful wrath, hail, fire, and brimstone. 23 So I will be magnified and sanctified and known in the eyes of many na- tions, and they will know that I am the LORD.

CHAPTER 39

1 Wherefore, son of man, prophesy against Gog, and say, Thus saith the Lord God, Be- hold, I come against thee, O Gog, prince of Meshech and Tubal. 2 I will destroy thee and leave only the sixth part of thee, and I will bring thee from the northern parts, and I will bring thee to the mountains of Israel: 3 And I will make thy bow fall from thy left hand, and thy arrows from thy right hand. 4 And thou shalt fall upon the mountains of Israel, with all thy bands, and the people that are with thee: for I will feed the birds, and all the fowls, and the beasts of the field. 5 You shall fall on the open field, for I have said it, says the LORD God. 6 And I will send a fire upon Magog and among those who dwell safely in the yles, and they shall know that I am the LORD. 7 So I will make my holy Name known in the midst of my people of Israel, and I will no longer allow them to pollute my holy Name, and the heathen will know that I am the Lord, the Holy One of Israel. 8 Behold, it is come and it is done, says the Lord God; this is the day of which I have spoken. 9 Those who dwell in the cities of Israel shall go out and burn and set fire to their weapons, their shields and bucklers, their bows and arrows, their staffs in their hands and their spears, and they shall burn them with fire for ten years. 10 So they shall not bring wood from the fields nor cut any from the forests, for they shall bury their weapons with fire, and they shall rob those who have robbed them, and they shall spy out those who have spied them, says the LORD God. 11 At the same time I will give Gog a burial place in Israel, that is, the valley by which men go to the eastern part of the sea; and this shall cause the passers-by to hold their noses, and there they shall bury Gog with all his multitude; and they shall call it the valley of Hamon-Gog. 12 And for ten months the house of Israel shall bury him, that they may fence in the land. 13 Yea, all the people of the land shall bury them, and they shall have a name when I am glorified, saith the LORD God. 14 And they shall choose men to go continually through the land with those who traumatize, to bury those who remain on the land, and to cover it; they shall search out to the end of seven cents. 15 And the trav- elers that go through the land, if they see a man's bone, they shall put a mark upon it, until the buryers have buried it, in the valley of Hamon-Gog. 16 Also the name of the city shall be Hamonah; and in this way the land shall be marked. 17 Son of man, thus says the LORD God, "Speak to all the feathered ones and to all the beasts of the field: Gather your selves and come and assemble yourselves on every side to my sacrifice, for I will sacrifice to you a great sacrifice on the mountains of Israel, that you may eat meat and drink blood. 18 You shall eat the flesh of the valiant, and you shall drink the blood of the princes of the land, of the beasts of the field, of the lambs, the goats, the heifers, and all the fat beasts of Bashan. 19 You shall eat fat until you are full, and you shall drink blood until you are drunk with my sacrifice that I have sacrificed for you. 20 So you shall be satiated at my table with horses and chariots, with valiant men and all the men of war, says the LORD God. 21 And I will set my glory among the peoples, and all the peoples shall see my judgment which I have executed, and my hand which I have stretched out upon them. 22 Thus shall the house of Israel know that I am the Lord their God from that day forward. 23 And the heathen shall know that the house of Israel went into captivity for their iniquity, because they trespassed against me; therefore I hid my face from them and left them in the hand of their enemies; so they all fell by the sword. 24 According to their trespasses and accord- ing to their transgressions, I did evil to them and hid my face from them. 25 Therefore thus says the LORD God: "Now I will bring back the captivity of Iaakob, I will have compassion on all the house of Israel, and I will be jealous of my holy Name, 26 after they have borne their shame and all their transgressions, by which they transgressed against me, while they lived securely in their land, fearing no one. 27 When I have brought them back from the nations, and gathered them from the lands of their enemies, and sanctified myself in them before many nations, 28 then they shall know that I am the LORD their God, who have led them into captivity among the Gentiles; but I have gathered them into their own land, and have left none of them there any more, 29 and I will no longer hide my face from them, for I have poured out my Spirit upon the house of Israel, says the Lord God.

CHAPTER 40

1 In the fifth and twentieth year of our cap- tivity, at the beginning of the year, on the tenth day of the month, the fourteenth year after the city had been struck, on that same day, the hand of the LORD came upon me and led me there. 2 In the land of Israel he led me with a divine vision and set me on a very high mountain, which was like the building of a city, toward the south. 3 And he led me thither, and behold, there was a man, whose likeness was to be looked upon, like brasse, with a thread of flax in his hand, and a reed to measure; and he stood at the door. 4 And the man said to me, "Son of man, look with your eyes, and listen with your ears, and agree with me concerning all that I will show you, for you were brought hither for the very purpose of being shown to you; declare all that you see to the house of Israel." 5 Behold, I saw a wall on the outside of the house, all around; and in the man's hand was a measuring rod, six cubits long, per cubit, and one hand wide; so he measured the width of the purchase with a rod, and the height with a reed. 6 Then he came to the gate looking eastward, and went through its stays, and measured the pillar of the gate, which was a row of feet, and the oth- er pillar of the gate, which was a row of feet. 7 Every chamber was one reed long and one reed wide, and between the chambers were five cubits; and the pillar of the gate, by the porch of the gate, was one reed long. 8 He also measured the porch of the inner gate with a reed. 9 Then he measured the porch of the gate by eight cubits and its pillars by two cu- bits; the porch of the gate was on the inside. 10 The doorways toward the east were three on this side and three on that side; all three were of one measure, and the posts had one measure on this side and one measure on that side. 11 He measured the width of the door- way at ten cubits and the height of the door at thirteen cubits. 12 Also the space in front of the rooms was one cubit this side and one cubit that side, and the rooms were six cubits this side and six cubits that side. 13 Then he measured the door from the end of one cham- ber to the top of the door: the width was five and twenty-five cubits, side to side. 14 He also made posts of sixty cubits; the posts of the courtyard and of the door had a measurement all around. 15 The front of the entrance of the gate to the front of the porch of the inner gate was fifty cubits. 16 There were tell-tale windows in the chambers and in their posts inside the door, all around, and also at the arches; the windows turned all around inside, and on the posts were palm trees. 17 Then he brought me into the outer courtyard, and be- hold, there were chambers and a courtyard enclosure all around, with thirty chambers on the enclosure. 18 The enclosure wall was on either side of the gates, facing the length of the gates, and the enclosure wall was under- neath. 19 Then he measured the width, from the end of the lower gate on the outside, to the end of the courtyard on the inside, by a hun- dred cubits eastward and northward. 20 The gate of the outer court, which looked north- ward, was measured according to its length and width. 21 Its chambers were three on this side and three on that side; its posts and arches measured like the first gate; its length was fifty cubits and its width fifty-two cubits. 22 Their windows and their arches with their palms were of the measure of the gate looking eastward; the way in was ten steps, and the arches were in front of them. 23 The gate of the inner court was opposite the gate toward the north and toward the east, and measured from gate to gate a hundred cubits. 24 Then he took me toward the south, and yes, there was a gate toward the south, whose pillars and arches he measured according to these measurements. 25 In it were windows, and in its arches all around, like those windows; the height was fifty cubits, and the breadth fifty-two cubits.

26 There were ten steps to enter it, and the arches were before them; and there were palm trees, one on this side and one on that side, on its pole. 27 In the inner court was a gate toward the south, and he measured from gate to gate toward the south a hundred cubits. 28 And he brought me into the inner court by the south gate, and measured the south gate according to these measures, 29 its chambers, and its posts, and its arches, according to these measures, and there were windows and arches all around, fifty cubits long and fifty-two cubits wide. 30 The arches all around were fifty-two cubits long and five cubits wide. 31 Its arches faced the back courtyard, and on its posts were palm trees, and the way in had eight steps. 32 Then he led me into the inner court toward the east, and measured the gateway accord- ing to these measurements. 33 Its chambers, its posts, and its arches were according to these measures, and there were windows and in the arches all around; it was fifty cubits long and fifty and twenty-five cubits wide. 34 And its arches were facing the back court, and on its posts were palm trees, on this side and on that side, and the way in it had eight steps. 35 After he led me to the north gate, he mea- sured it according to these measurements, 36 its rooms, its pillars, its arches, and its win- dows all around: the height was fifty cubits, and the breadth fifty-two cubits. 37 And its posts faced toward the back court, and on its posts were palm trees on this side and on that side, and the way of access had eight steps. 38 Every chamber and its entrance were under the pillars of the doors; here burnt food was washed. 39 In the porch of the gate were two tables on this side and two tables on that side, on which the burning, sin and guilt were con- sumed. 40 On the side beyond the steppes, at the entrance to the north gate, there were two tables, and on the other side, at the entrance to the gate, two tables. 41 On this side were four tables, and on the other side, at the side of the gate, four tables, that is, eight tables on which the sacrifice was consumed. 42 The four tables were of stone for the burnt offer- ing, one and a half cubits long, one and a half cubits wide, and one cubit high; the instru- ments with which the burnt offering and the sacrifice were killed were also placed there. 43 On the inside was a wooden board, fastened all around, and on the boards the meat of the offering was laid. 44 Outside the inner gate were the chambers of the singers, in the inner courtyard, which was by the side of the north gate; their perspective was toward the south, and one was by the side of the east gate, with the perspective toward the north. 45 He said to me, "This chamber, whose perspective is toward the south, is for the priests who are in charge of guarding the house." 46 The cham- ber that faces north is for the priests who are charged with guarding the altar; these are the sons of Zadok, from among the sons of Leui, who may approach the Lord to serve him." 47 He then measured the courtyard, a hun- dred cubits long, a hundred cubits wide and square, and also the altar that was in front of the house. 48 He led me to the porch of the house and measured the posts of the porch: five cubits this way and five cubits that way; the width of the door was three cubits this way and three cubits that way. 49 The length of the porch was twenty-five cubits and its width eleven cubits; he made me go through the steps by which it was entered, and there were pillars beside the posts, one on this side and one on that side.

CHAPTER 41

1 Then he led me to the Temple and measured the posts: six cubits wide on one side and six cubits wide on the other,

which was the width of the Tabernacle. 2 The width of the entrance was ten cubits; the sides of the entrance were five cubits on one side and five cubits on the other; he measured its length forty cubits and its width twenty-five cubits. 3 Then he went in and measured the pillars of the entrance two cubits, the entrance six cubits, and the width of the entrance ten cubits. 4 He then mea- sured the length twenty-two cubits and the width twenty-two cubits in front of the Tem- ple. And he said, "This is the most holy place." 5 Then he measured the wall of the house, six cubits, and the width of each chamber four cubits around the house, on each side. 6 The chambers were chambers upon chambers, ten feet high, and they fitted into the wall made for the chambers that surrounded the house, so that the posts could be fastened there and were not fastened into the wall of the house. 7 It was large and went around the chambers, because the wall of the house went around the house; therefore the house was larger toward the outside; so they went from the lowest chamber to the highest chamber by the middle ways. 8 The house extended all around; the foundations of the chambers were of a fixed number of large cubits. 9 The thickness of the wall that served for the outer chamber was five cubits, and what remained was the place of the inner chambers. 10 Be- tween the chambers was twenty-five cubits wide around the house on each side. 11 The walls of the chambers faced the place that remained, one wall toward the north and an- other toward the south, and the width of the place that remained was five cubits around. 12 The building that faced the place that was set apart, toward the western corner, was seventy cubits wide; the wall of the building was five cubits thick, all around, and ninety cubits long. 13 He then measured the house to be one hundred cubits long, and the sepa- rate place and the building with its walls were one hundred cubits long. 14 The width of the front of the house and the separate place to- ward the east was also one hundred cubits. 15 He measured the length of the building in front of the separate place, which was behind it, and the chambers on either side, with the Temple inside and the arches of the court- yard, by a hundred cubits. 16 And the pillars, and the partition windows, and the chambers all around, on three sides, opposite the pillars, were lined with cedar wood all around, from the ground to the windows, and the windows were lined with cedar wood. 17 From by the apse to the inside of the house and outside, and all around the wall inside and outside, it was lined with cedar wood according to the measure. 18 It was made of Cherubim and palm trees, so that a palm tree was between a Cherubim and a Cherubim, and each Cheru- bim had two faces. 19 So that the face of a man was toward the palm tree on one side, and the face of a lion toward the palm tree on the oth- er side. 20 From the ground to the end of the bank were Cherubim and palm trees as in the wall of the Temple. 21 The pillars of the Tem- ple were squared, and in this way the likeness and form of the Sanctuary could be seen. 22 And the wooden altar was three cubits high and two cubits long; and its corners and its length and its sides were of wood. And he said, "This is the table that shall be before the Lord." 23 The Temple and the Sanctuary had two stories. 24 The porches had two rooms, that is, two rooms for turning, two rooms for one porch and two rooms for another porch. 25 On the facades of the temple were cheru- bim and palm trees, as on the walls, and there were thin boards on the front of the porch. 26 There were narrow windows and palm trees on either side, on the sides of the porch and on all sides of the house, and thin boards.

CHAPTER 42

1 Then he led me into the back courtyard by the way toward the north, and let me into the chamber that was in front of the separate place and that was opposite the building to- ward the north. 2 In front of the length of a hundred cubits was the northern corridor, fifty cubits wide. 3 In front of the twenty cu- bits that served for the inner courtyard and in front of the floor that served for the last courtyard was one chamber against another, in three rows. 4 In front of the chambers was a gallery ten cubits wide, and on the inside was a street one cubit wide, with their banks toward the north. 5 The chambers that were outside were narrower, for they seemed to eat these, that is, the lower ones and those that were in the center of the building. 6 For they were arranged in three rows, but they had no pillars like those in the courtyard; there- fore there was a difference from them below and from the middlemost, that is, from the ground. 7 The wall that was outside from the chambers, toward the back courtyard, facing the chambers, was fifty cubits long. 8 The length of the chambers that were in the inner court was fifty cubits, while in front of the Temple was a hundred cubits. 9 Below these chambers was the entrance, on the eastern side, when one entered it from the outer court. 10 The chambers were in the thickness of the wall of the courtyard toward the east, facing the separate place and opposite the building. 11 The way before them was like that of the chambers that were on the north, as long as they were and as wide as they were; and all their entrances were similar, both ac- cording to their faces and according to their faces. 12 According to the walls of the cham- bers that were toward the south, there was a door in the corner of the way, that is, the way before the wall toward the east, as one enters. 13 He said to me, "The northern chambers and the southern chambers, which are opposite the separate place, are holy chambers, where the priests who approach the LORD will eat the holiest things; there the holiest things, the food offering, the sin offering and the guilt offering, will be laid, for the place is holy." 14 When the priests go in there, they shall not come out of the holy place into the back court- yard, but they shall lay there the garments in which they exercise their ministry, for they are holy; they shall put on other garments, and so they shall approach the things that are for the people. 15 Now when he had measured the inside of the house, he led me to the door facing the east and measured it all around. 16 He measured the east side with the measur- ing rod, five hundred rods, and with the mea- suring rod all around. 17 He also measured the north side: five hundred rods, again with the measuring rod all around. 18 He also mea- sured the south side: five hundred rods with the measuring rod. 19 He also turned to the west side and measured five hundred reeds with the measuring tape. 20 He measured it for the four sides: it had a wall around it, five hundred reeds long and five hundred yards long to separate the sanctuary from the place of profanations.

CHAPTER 43

1 Then he led me to the gate, that is, to the gate that turns toward the east. 2 And behold, the glory of the God of Israel came from the east, whose journey was like a river of great waters, and the earth was lighted with his glory. 3 The vision that I saw was like that which I had when I came to

destroy the city; and the visions were like that which I had by the river Chebar; and I fell on my face. 4 The glory of the LORD entered into the house by the gate that faces the east. 5 The Spirit took me and brought me into the inner court, and behold, the glory of the Lord filled the house. 6 Then I heard one speaking to me outside the house; and there was a man standing beside me, 7 who said to me, "Son of man, this place is my throne and the place of the soles of my feet, while I will dwell forever among the chil- dren of Israel, and the house of Israel shall no more defile my holy Name, nor they, nor their kings with their fornications, nor with the carches of their kings in their high plac- es." 8 Though they set their thresholds by my thresholds and their stakes by my stakes (for there was but a wall between me and them), yet they defiled my holy Name with their abominations which they committed; there- fore I consumed them in my wrath. 9 Now, therefore, let them put away their fornication and the carches of their kings away from me, and I will dwell among them forever. 10 Son of man, show this house to the house of Israel, that they may be ashamed of their wicked- ness and measure your fatherhood. 11 If they are ashamed of all that they have done, show them the form of the House, its paternal, its exit and its entrance, all its form, all its de- crees, all its figures, and all its laws; and write it before them, that they may observe all its form and all its decrees, and perform them. 12 This is the description of the house: it shall be on the top of the mountain; all the borders around it shall be most holy. Behold, this is the description of the house. 13 These are the measures of the altar, after the cubits: the cu- bit is one cubit, and the breadth thereof is one cubit; the bottom thereof is one cubit, and the breadth thereof one cubit; the border round about it is one span, and this is the height of the altar. 14 From the bottom that touches the ground to the bottom piece shall be two cu- bits and the width one cubit; from the small piece to the large piece shall be four cubits and the width one cubit. 15 The altar shall be four cubits, and from the altar onward there shall be four horns. 16 The altar shall be two cubits long, two cubits wide, and square at its four corners. 17 And its frame shall be four hundred and fifty cubits long, with four hun- dred and fifty sides in its four square corners; and its border shall be half a cubit, and its bottom shall be about one cubit, and its steps shall face eastward. 18 He said to me, "Sone of man, thus says the LORD God: These are the orders of the altar in the day when they shall build it to offer burnt offerings and to sprinkle blood upon it. 19 Thou shalt give to the priests and to the leuites of the seed of Zadok, who come near to me, to officiate with me, saith the Lord God, a long bulla as a sin offering. 20 You shall take its blood and put it on the four horns, on the four corners of the frame and on the border all around. 21 You shall also take the sin bubble and bury it in the appointed place of the house, outside the sanctuary. 22 But on the second day you shall offer a goat without blemish as a sin offering, and they shall perform the ceremony on the altar, as they did with the bullock. 23 When you have finished clothing it, you shall offer a flawless heifer and a flawless ram of the flock. 24 You shall offer them before the LORD, and the priests shall throw salt on them and of- fer them as a burnt offering to the LORD. 25 Every day you shall prepare a kid for the sin offering; they shall also prepare a long bull and a ram from the flock, without blemish. 26 In this way they shall purify the altar every day, make it safe, and consecrate it. 27 When these days are past, on the eighth day, and so on, the priests shall make your burnings on the altar and your peace offerings, and I will accept you, says the LORD God.

CHAPTER 44

1 Then he led me to the gate of the outer sanctuary, which turns toward the east, and it was shut. 2 Then the LORD said to me, "This gate shall remain closed and not be opened, and no one shall enter by it, because the LORD God of Israel has entered by it, and it shall remain closed. 3 It shall belong to the prince; the prince himself shall sit therein to eat bread before the LORD; he shall go in by the way of the porch of that gate, and shall go out by the way of it. 4 Then he led me toward the north gate, before the house; and when I looked, behold, the glory of the LORD filled the house of the LORD, and I fell on my face. 5 And the LORD said to me, "Son of man, ob- serve well with your eyes and listen with your ears to all that I say to you concerning all the prescriptions of the house of the LORD and all its laws, and observe well the entrance into the house and the exit from the sanctuary, 6 and you shall say to the rebels, that is, to the house of Israel, "Thus says the LORD God, O house of Israel, you have had enough of all your abominations, 7 For you have brought into my sanctuary strangers, vncircumcised in heart and vncircumcised in flesh, to stand in my sanctuary and pollute my house, when you offer my bread and my fat and my blood; and they have broken my bond, because of all your abominations. 8 For you have not observed the regulations of my holy things, but have appointed others to take care of my sanctuary." 9 Thus says the Lord God, "No for- eigner vncircumcised of heart and vncircum- cised of flesh shall enter my sanctuary, of no foreigner that is among the children of Israel, 10 Neither shall ye Leuites who turned away from me, when Israel went astray, who turned away from you following their idolatries, but they shall bear their iniquities. 11 They shall serve in my sanctuary, they shall guard the gates of the House, and they shall minister in the House; they shall kill burnt offerings and sacrifices for the people, and they shall stand before them to serve them. 12 For they have served before their idols, and have brought down the house of Israel in iniquity; there- fore have I lifted up mine eyes against them, saith the LORD God, and they shall bear their iniquity, 13 and they shall not come near me to fulfill your office as priests, nor shall they come near any of my holy things in the most holy place, but they shall bear their shame and their abominations which they have committed. 14 I will appoint them guardians of the house, for all its service and for all that shall be done therein. 15 But the priests of the Leuites, the sons of Zadok, who have guard- ed my sanctuary, when the children of Israel have departed from me, shall come to me to serve me, and they shall stand before me to offer me fat and blood, says the Lord God. 16 They shall come into my sanctuary, and they shall come to my table to serve me, and they shall deal with my burden. 17 When they en- ter the gates of the inner court, they shall be clothed in linen garments, and they shall have no wool when they serve at the gates of the in- ner court and inside. 18 They shall have linen stoles on their heads and linen breeches on their hips; they shall not clothe themselves in the places of perspiration. 19 But when they enter the great hall, that is, the great hall for the people, they shall take off the garments in which they ministered and lay them in the holy chambers and put on other garments, for they shall not sanctify the people with their garments. 20 Moreover, they shall not cut off their heads nor let their locks be lengthened, but they shall go around their heads. 21 The priests shall not drink wine when they enter the inner court.

22 They shall not take a wid- ow or a diuorced woman for a wife, but they shall take maidens from the seed of the house of Israel or a widow who has been a widow of a priest. 23 They shall teach my people the difference between the holy and the profane, and shall cause them to discern between the vncleane and the cleane. 24 And contrary to the law they shall stand in judgment, and they shall judge according to my decrees; and they shall observe my laws and my statutes in all my assemblies, and they shall keep my sab- baths holy. 25 And they shall not come and defile any dead person, except the father, and the mother, and the son, and the daughter, and the brother, or the sister, that hath not yet had a husband; in such cases they may be defiled. 26 And when he hid himself, ten days shall be reckoned for him. 27 And when he shall enter into the sanctuary, into the inner court, to officiate in the sanctuary, he shall of- fer his sacrifice for sin, saith the Lord God. 28 The priesthood shall be their inheritance, yea, I am their inheritance; therefore you shall not give them any possession in Israel, for I am their possession. 29 They shall eat the roast, the roast of sin, the roast of sin, and every thing dedicated in Israel shall be theirs. 30 All the first of all the first brought, and all the oblations, and all your oblations of every kind shall be of the priests. You shall also give to the priest the first of your dough, that he may make the blessing rest in your house. 31 The priests shall not eat anything that is dead or mangled, whether animals or beasts.

CHAPTER 45

1 Moreover, when you have given the land as an inheritance, you shall offer to the LORD an oblation for a holy portion of the land, five thousand reeds long and ten thousand wide; this shall be holy in all its borders all around. 2 Of this measure there shall be for the sanctu- ary five hundred yards long and five hundred yards wide, all square round about, and fifty cubits round about for its environs. 3 Of this measure thou shalt measure the length of five thousand and twenty thousand yards, and the breadth of ten thousand yards; in it shall be the sanctuary and the most holy place. 4 The holy part of the land shall be for the priests who serve in the sanctuary and who have come here to serve the Lord; it shall be a place for their homes and a holy place for the sanc- tuary. 5 And in the five thousand and twenty thousand in length, and in the ten thousand in breadth, the Leuites who serve in the house shall have their possession for twenty thou- sand rooms. 6 Moreover you shall apply the possession of the city, five thousand feet wide and five thousand and twenty thousand feet long, for the oblation of your holy portion; it shall be for all the house of Israel. 7 A part shall be for the prince on one side and on the other side of the oblation of the holy portion and the possession of the city, that is, in front of the oblation of the holy portion and the possession of the city from the western corner toward the west and from the eastern corner toward the east, and the length shall be one of the parts from the western border toward the eastern border. 8 In this territory shall be its possession in Israel; my princes shall op- press my people no more, and the rest of the land shall be given to the house of Israel, ac- cording to their tribes. 9 Thus says the LORD God: "Suffici ye, O princes of Israel, leave cruelty and oppression, execute judgment and justice; take away your exactions from my people, saith the LORD God. 10 You shall have righteous balances, a true Ephah and a true Bath. 11 The Ephah and the Bath shall be equal; a Bath shall contain the tenth part of a Homer, and an Ephah the

tenth part of a Homer; the equality shall be according to the Homer. 12 The shekel shall be twenty-five gera and twenty-five shekels, and five twenty-five shekels and fifty shekels shall be your Maneh. 13 This is the oblation that you shall offer: the sixth part of an ephah of an omer of wheat, and you shall give the sixth part of an ephah of an omer of barley. 14 As for the ordinance of the olia, that is, of the bath of the omer, you shall offer the tenth part of a bath of your Cor (ten baths are a Homer, for ten baths fill a Homer). 15 And a lamb of two hundred sheep from your fat pastures of Israel, as a sacrifice, as a burnt offering, and as a peace offering, to be reconciled to them, says the LORD God. 16 All the peoples of the earth shall give this oblation for the prince of Israel. 17 The prince shall give oblations, meat oblations, and wine oblations on the solemn feasts, on the new moons, on the Sabbaths, and on all the feasts of the house of Israel; he shall prepare sin ob- lations, meat oblations, fire oblations, and peace oblations for the reconciliation of the house of Israel. 18 Thus says the LORD God, "On the first day of the month you shall take a young bull without blemish and put it safely in the sanctuary. 19 The priest shall take the blood of the pecuniary offering and place it on the posts of the house, on the four corners of the frame of the altar, and on the posts of the door of the inner court. 20 Thus you shall do on the seventh day of the month, for all who have erred and for those who have been deceived; thus you shall reconcile the house. 21 In the first month, on the fourteenth day of the month, you shall make the Passover, a feast of seven days, and you shall eat vn- leauened bread. 22 And on that day the prince shall prepare for himself and for all the people of the land a bullock as a sin offering. 23 And in the seven days of the feast he shall make a burnt offering to the LORD, of two bullocks and two rams without blemish every day for seven days, and of one kid every day as a sin offering. 24 He shall prepare a food offering of one ephah for a bull, one ephah for a ram, and an oil offering for an ephah. 25 On the fif- teenth day of the month he shall do the same thing in the banquet for ten days, according to the sin offering, according to the burnt of- fering, according to the meat offering, and according to the oil offering.

CHAPTER 46

1 Thus says the LORD God: "The gate of the inner court, which turns to the east, shall be shut during the six working days; but on the

Sabbath day it shall be open, and on the new moon day it shall be open. 2 And the prince shall come in by the porch of the outer gate, and shall stand at the post of the gate, and the priests shall make his burning and his peace offerings, and he shall worship at the thresh- old of the gate; and then he shall go away, but the gate shall not be shut until the dawn. 3 Likewise the people of the land shall worship at the entrance of this gate before the LORD on the Sabbaths and new moons. 4 The burnt offering which the prince shall offer to the LORD on the Sabbath day shall consist of six lambs without blemish and one ram without blemish. 5 And the food offering shall be one ephah for a ram; and the food offering for the lambs shall be a gift of his hand and an olla for an ephah. 6 On the day of the new moon shall be a flawless heifer, six lambs and a ram; they shall be without blemish. 7 And he shall prepare an offering of food, that is, one ephah for the bull, one ephah for the ram and for the lambs according to what his hand shall bring, and one hin of oil for one ephah. 8 And when the prince shall enter, he shall go in by the way of the porch of that gate, and shall go on his way. 9 But when the people of the land shall come before the LORD on the solemn feasts, he that shall enter by the north gate to wor- ship shall go out by the south gate; and he that shall enter by the south gate shall go out by the north gate; he shall not return by the way of the gate by which he entered, but shall go out against it. 10 And the prince shall be in the midst of them; he shall enter in when they enter, and when they go out, they shall go out together. 11 On feasts and solemnities, the food offering shall be one ephah for the bull, and one ephah for the ram, and one ephah for the lamb, the gift of his hand, and an olla for an ephah. 12 Now when the prince shall free- ly make a burning or a peace offering to the LORD, the gate that turns to the east shall be opened to him, and he shall make his burning and his peace offering, as on the Sabbath day; then he shall go out, and when he has gone out, the gate shall be shut. 13 Every day you shall make a burnt offering to the LORD with a year-old lamb without blemish; you shall do it every morning. 14 And every morning thou shalt prepare for it a food offering, the sixth part of an ephah and the thirteenth part of an oil, to be mixed with fine wine; this food of- fering shall always be a perpetual ordinance to the LORD. 15 Thus shall they prepare the lambs, the roast, and the oil every morning, for a continual burning. 16 Thus says the LORD God, "If the prince gives his inheri- tance as a gift to any of his sons, it shall be his sons' and shall be their possession by inher- itance. 17 But if he gives his inheritance as a gift to one of his servants, it shall be his un- til the year of his freedom; after that, it shall return to the prince, but his inheritance shall remain with his sons for them. 18 Moreover the prince shall not take the inheritance of the peoples, nor turn them away from their pos- session; but he shall cause his sons to inherit their own possession, lest my people be scat- tered each from his own possession. 19 Then he led me through the entrance, which was by the side of the gate, into the holy chambers of the priests, which were toward the north; and behold, there was a place west of them. 20 Then he said to me, "This is the place where the priests will see the guilt offering and the sin offering, where they will cook the obla- tion, not to bring it into the inner court, to sanctify your people." 21 Then he led me into the inner court and made me go through the four corners of the court; and behold, in every corner of the court was a court. 22 At the four corners of the courtyard were courts forty cubits long and thirty cubits wide; these four corners were of one and the same measure. 23 Around these four corners was a bound- ary wall, and under the walls all around were kitchens built. 24 Then he said to me, "This is the kitchen where the ministers of the house will see the sacrifices of the people."

CHAPTER 47

1 Then he led me to the entrance of the house, and behold, the waters came out from under the threshold of the house toward the east, because the front of the house was facing east, and the waters came down from under the right side of the house, south of the altar. 2 Then he brought me out to the north gate, and led me by the way outside to the gate be- low, by the way that turns to the east; and be- hold, the waters were coming out from under your right side. 3 When the man who had the thread in his hand went out toward the east, he measured a thousand cubits and led me through the waters; the waters were up to the foreheads. 4 Then he measured a thousand cubits and led me through the waters; the wa- ters were up to my knees; then he measured a thousand cubits and led me through: the wa- ters were up to my knees. 5 Then he measured a thousand, and it was a river that I could not cross, for the waters had risen up and flowed like a river that could not be crossed. 6 He said to me, "Son of man, have you seen this? Then he led me and made me return to the source of the river. 7 When I returned, I saw that at the source of the river there were many trees on either side. 8 Then he said to me, "These waters go out toward the county of the east, and go down into the plain, and flow into a sea; they will flow into another sea, and the waters will be wholesome. 9 And every liv- ing and moving thing, where the fishermen come, shall rest, and there shall be a great quantity of fish, because these waters shall come there; for they shall be wholesome, and every thing shall rest where the fisherman comes. 10 Then the fishermen shall stand upon it, and from En-Gedi even unto En-Eg- laim shall they spread out their nets: for their fish shall be, according to their kinds, as the fish of the sea of Maine, very numerous. 11 But its fishing places and its marathons shall not be wholesome; they shall be turned into salt pittas. 12 And on this side and on that side shall grow all fruitful trees, whose sap shall not fade away, and whose fruit shall not be ex- hausted; it shall bring forth new fruit accord- ing to its reckoning, because their waters flow out of the Sanctuary; its fruit shall be meat, and its sap shall be for medicine. 13 Thus says the LORD God, "This shall be the boundary by which you shall inherit the land according to the two tribes of Israel: Ioseph shall have two portions. 14 And you shall inherit it, the one as well as the other; concerning which I lift up my hand to give it to your fathers, and this territory shall be your inheritance. 15 This shall be the border of the land toward the north side, from the sea of Maine to Het- hlon, as you go toward Zedadah: 16 Hamath, Berothah, Sibraim, which is between the bor- der of Damascus and the border of Hamath, and Hazar, Hatticon, which is on the coast of Hauran. 17 And the border from the sea shall be Hazar, Enan, and the border of Damascus, and the remnant of the north, Northwarde, and the border of Hamath; so shall be the north side. 18 But the east side shall measure from Hauran, from Damascus, from Gilead, from the land of Israel near Iorden, and from the border to the eastern sea; so shall be the east part. 19 The southern part shall be toward Teman, from Tamar to the waters of Meriboth at Kadesh, and the border to the sea of Maine; so shall be the southern part toward Teman. 20 The western part shall also be the great sea from the border, until a man comes against Hamath; this shall be the western part. 21 So you shall divide this territory according to the tribes of Israel. 22 You shall assign it by lot as an inheritance to you and to the strangers who dwell among you, who shall beget sons among you and shall be to you as born in the land among the children of Israel; they shall divide the inheritance with you in the midst of the tribes of Israel. 23 In which tribe the stranger dwells, you shall give him his inheri- tance, says the LORD God.

CHAPTER 48

1 These are the names of the tribes. From the north side, toward the coast of Hethlon, as going toward Hamath, Hazar, Enan, and the border of Damascus north of the coast of Hamath, and from the east side toward the west, a part for Dan. 2 And along the border of Dan, from the east side to the west side, a part for Asher. 3 And along the border of

Asher, from the east side to the west side, a portion for Naphtali. 4 And along the border of Naphtali, from the east side to the west side, a portion for Manasseh. 5 And along the border of Manasseh, from the east side to the west side, a portion for Ephraim. :6 And along the border of Ephraim, from the east side to the west side, a portion for Reuben. 7 And along the border of Reuben, from the east- ern quarter to the western quarter, a portion for Iudah. 8 And along the border of Iudah, from the eastern part to the western part, shall be the offering which they shall make of five hundred and twenty thousand reeds of broth, as long as one of the other parts, from the eastern side to the western side, and the sanctuary shall be in the middle of it. :9 The oblation which you shall offer to the LORD shall be five thousand and twenty thousand pieces long and ten thousand pieces wide. 10 For them and for the priests shall be this holy oblation, fifty-two thousand feet long toward the north, ten thousand feet wide toward the west, ten thousand feet wide toward the east, and fifty-two thousand feet long toward the south, and the sanctuary of the LORD shall be in the center of it. 11 And it shall be for the sanctified priests of the sons of Zadok, who kept my charge, and who did not go astray when the children of Israel went astray, as the Leuites went astray. 12 Therefore the ob- lation of the land that was offended shall be to them, as a most holy thing, at the border with the Leuites. 13 And opposite the bor- der of the priests, the Leuites shall have five thousand yards long and ten thousand yards wide; the whole length shall be five thousand yards and the width ten thousand yards. 14 And they shall not cut it off, nor change it, nor abuse the first fruits of the land, for it is holy to the LORD. 15 And the five thousand that shall be left in breadth in respect to the five thousand and twenty thousand, shall be a propitious place for the city, and for habita- tions, and for suburbs, and the city shall be in the center of it. 16 These shall be its measures: on the north five hundred and four hundred thousand, on the south five hundred and four hundred thousand, on the east five hundred and four hundred thousand, and on the west five hundred and four hundred thousand. 17 The suburbs of the city shall be, toward the north two hundred fifty, toward the south two hundred fifty, toward the east two hundred fifty, and toward the west two hundred fifty. 18 The residue of the length, beyond the obla- tion of the sacred portion, shall be ten thou- sand eastward, and ten thousand westward; it shall be beyond the oblation of the sacred portion, and the increase thereof shall be for the food of them that serve in the city. 19 The servants of the city shall be of all the tribes of Israel that serve there. 20 All the oblation shall be five thousand and twenty thousand with five thousand and twenty thousand; you shall offer this oblation for four squares for the sanctuary and for the possession of the city. 21 And the residue shall be for the prince, on either side of the oblation of the sanctuary and the possession of the city, toward the five thousand and twenty thousand of the obla- tion toward the eastern border, and toward the west toward the five thousand and twen- ty thousand toward the western border, and toward the prince's portion; this shall be the holy oblation, and the house of the sanctuary shall be in the center of it. 22 Moreover, from the possession of the Leuiti and from the pos- session of the city, that which is in the middle shall be for the princes; between the border of Judah and the border of Benjamin shall be for the princes. 23 And the rest of the tribes shall be thus: from the eastern part to the western part, Benjamin shall be a part. 24 And along the border of Benjamin, from the east side to the west side, a part of Simeon. 25 And along the border of Simeon, from the east side to the west side, a part of Issachar. 26 And along the border of Issachar, from the east side to the west side, a part of Zebulun. 27 And along the border of Zebulun, from the east side to the west side, a part of Gad. 28 The border of Gad, on the south side, toward Temath, shall be from Tamar to the waters of Meribath, in Kadesh, and to the river that flows into the sea of Maine. 29 This is the territory that you shall distribute as an inheritance to the tribes of Israel; these are their portions, says the LORD God. 30 These are the boundaries of the city: from the north side five hundred and four hundred thousand feet. 31 The gates of the city shall have the names of the tribes of Israel: the gates on the north side, a gate of Reuben, a gate of Judah, and a gate of Leui. 32 To the east, five hundred and four thousand inhabitants, three gates, a gate of Ioseph, a gate of Beiamin, and a gate of Dan. 33 To the south, five hundred and forty thousand mea- sures and three gates, a gate of Simeon, a gate of Issachar, and a gate of Zebulun. 34 To the west, five hundred and forty thousand mea- sures, with their three gates: a gate of Gad, a gate of Asher, and a gate of Naphtali. 35 The round about was eighty thousand yards, and the name of the city from that day shall be, "The LORD is there."

DANIEL

CHAPTER 1

1 In the thirteenth year of the reign of Je- hoiakim, king of Judah, Nebuchadnezzar, king of Babel, came to Jerusalem and be- sieged it. 2 And the LORD gave into the hand of Jehoiakim, king of Judah, a part of the fur- nishings of the house of God, which he had carried into the land of Scinar, into the house of his god, and brought the furnishings into the treasury of his god. 3 The king spoke to Ashpenaz, master of his eunuchs, to bring with him some of the children of Israel, of the king's seed and princes: 4 children who had no defects, but who were well fed, instructed in all wisdom, who had good knowledge and were able to impart knowledge, who were able to stand in the king's palace, and who could teach learning and the language of the Chaldeans. 5 The king assigned to them ev- ery day a portion of the king's food and of the wine he drank, so that they would be fed for three years, so that when they were finished they could appear before the king. 6 Among these were some of the sons of Iudah, Daniel, Hananiah, Mishael and Azariah. 7 To these the leader of the Eunuchs gave other names: for he called Daniel, Belteshazzar, Hananiah, Shadrach, Mishael, Meshach, and Azariah, Abednego. 8 But Daniel had decided in his heart not to defile himself with the king's por- tion of food and with the wine he drank; so he asked the leader of the Eunuchs not to defile himself. 9 (Now God had brought Daniel into a fury and had made a contest with the chief of the Eunuchs.) 10 The chief of the Eunuchs said to Daniel, "I fear my lord the king, who has established your meal and your drink; therefore, if he sees your faces more beauti- ful than those of the other children of your kind, then you will make me lose my head be- fore the king." 11 Then Daniel said to Melzar, whom the chief of the Eunuchs had sheltered from Daniel, Hananiah, Mishael and Azariah, 12 "Please give your servants ten days and let them eat and drink water. 13 Then look at our faces before you and the faces of the children eating the king's portion of food; and as you see, decide with your servants." 14 He satis- fied them in this respect and put them on trial for ten days. 15 At the end of ten days, their faces appeared more beautiful and more pleasant than those

of all the children who ate the king's portion of food. 16 So Melzar took away from them the portion of meat and wine that they would drink, and gave them the flesh. 17 As for these four sons, God gave them the knowledge and understanding of all knowledge and wisdom; he also gave Daniel the understanding of all visions and dreams. 18 When the time had passed that the king had appointed for them to enter, the leader of the Eunuchs led them before Nebuchadnez- zar. 19 The king entertained with them, and among them there was no one like Daniel, Hananiah, Mishael and Azariah; therefore they stood before the king. 20 In all matters of wisdom and understanding that the king asked of them, he found them ten times bet- ter than all the astrologers and inchanists there were in all his kingdom. 21 Daniel was in the first year of King Cyrus.

CHAPTER 2

1 In the second year of Nebuchadnezzar's reign, Nebuchadnezzar dreamed dreams that troubled his spirit and made him sleep. 2 Then the king ordered the inchanters, astrol- ogers, sorcerers and Chaldeans to be called to explain his dreams to the king; so they came and stood before the king. 3 The king said to them, "I dreamed a dream, and my spirit was troubled to know it." 4 Then the Chal- deans said to the king in the language of the Aramites, "O king, be quiet for a while; show your servants your dream, and we will give the interpretation." 5 The king answered and said to the Chaldeans, "The thing has escaped me. If you will not make me understand the design with its interpretation, you will be torn to pieces and your houses will be destroyed. 6 But if you will declare to me the name and its interpretation, you will receive from me gifts, rewards and great honors; therefore give me the name and its interpretation." 7 They an- swered again and said, "Let the king give his servants the name, and we will declare the in- terpretation." 8 Then the king answered and said, "I know for sure that you want to gain time, because you see that the thing is gone from me. 9 But if you will not declare the date to me, there is but judgment for you; for you have prepared lying and corrupt words, to speak before me until the time is changed; therefore tell me the date, that I may know, if you can declare the interpretation of it to me." 10 Then the Chaldeans answered before the king and said, "There is no man on earth who can declare the king's matter; yea, there is no king, nor prince, nor lord, who has asked these things of an inchanter, an astrologer, or a Chaldean. 11 For it is a rare thing that the king requires, and there is no one else who can declare it before the king but the gods whose dwelling is not with the flesh. 12 There- fore the king became very angry and enraged, and he ordered all the wise men of Babel to be destroyed. 13 When the sentence was pro- nounced, the wise men were slain; and they sought Daniel and his companions to have them put to death. 14 Then Daniel answered with counsel and wisdom Arioch, chief of the king, who had gone to put the wise men of Babel to death. 15 He answered and said to Arioch, the chief of the kings, "Why is the king's sentence so hasty?" Then Arioch de- clared the matter to Daniel. 16 Then Daniel went and asked the king to give him some latitude and to give him the interpretation. 17 Daniel went to his house and reported the matter to Hananiah, Mishael and Azariah, his companions, 18 so that they would plead with the God of Heauen to grant the grace of this secret, so that Daniel and his companions would not die with the rest of the wise men of Babel. 19 The secret was revealed to Daniel in a night vision; therefore Daniel prayed to the God of Heauen. 20 Daniel answered, "Let God's name be prayed to forever, for wisdom and strength are his, 21 He changes times and seasons, takes away kings, restores kings, gives wisdom to the wise and intelligence to those who understand. 22 He reveals the deep and secret things; he knows what is in dark- ness, and light dwells with him. 23 I thank you and pray to you, O God of my fathers, that you have given me wisdom and strength and have shown me now what we desired from you, for you have declared the matter of kings." 24 So Daniel went to Arioch, whom the king had commanded to destroy the wise men of Babel; and he went and said to him, "Do not destroy the wise men of Babel, but bring me before the king, and I will declare the inter- pretation to the king." 25 Then Arioch brought Daniel before the king in haste and said to him, "I have found a man of the sons of Iu- dah who have been taken into captivity, who will declare to the king the interpretation." 26 Then the king answered Daniel, whose name was Belteshazzar, "Are you able to show me the drama I have seen and its interpretation?" 27 Daniel answered in the king's presence and said, "The secret that the king has requested cannot be revealed to the king either by the wise men or the astrologers or the inchanists or the southerners. 28 But there is a God in heaven who reveals the secrets and shows King Nebuchadnezzar what will take place in the last days. Your dream and the things you saw in your head on your bed are these. 29 O king, when you were in bed, thoughts came into your mind about what would hap- pen next, and the one who keeps the secrets tells you what will take place. 30 As for me, this secret has not been revealed to me for my wisdom, any more than for any other lie, but only to give the king the interpretation and so that you may know the thoughts of your heart. 31 O king, you saw, and behold, a great image; this great image, whose glory was so excellent, stood before you, and its form was terrible. 32 The head of this image was of fine gold, its breast and arms of silk, its belly and thighs of bronze, 33 his legs of yron, and his feet were partly of yron and partly of clay. 34 You saw him until a cut stone without hands struck the image on his feet, which were of yron and clay, and tore them in pieces. 35 Then the yron, the clay, the brassa, the torpe- do and the gold all shattered together and be- came like the coffee of summer flowers, and the wind carried them away, so that there was no place for them; and the stone that struck the image became a great mountain and filled the whole earth. 36 This is the drama, and we will declare the interpretation of it before the king. 37 O king, you are a king of kings, for the God of Heauen has given you a kingdom, power, strength and glory. 38 In all the places where the sons of men dwell, the beasts of the field and the animals of the earth, he has giv- en you into his hand and made you sovereign over all of them; you are a king of gold. 39 Af- ter thee shall arise another kingdom, inferior to thee, of torpedo, and a third kingdom shall be of brasse, which shall have dominion over all the earth. 40 The fourth kingdom shall be as strong as the yron, for as the yron tears in pieces and subdues all things, and as the yron tears in pieces all these things, so it will tear in pieces and tear all people to pieces. 41 As thou hast seen the feet and the fingers, partly of potters' clay and partly of yron, the king- dom shall be destroyed, but in it shall be the power of yron, as thou hast seen yron min- gled with clay and earth. 42 And as the toes were partly of yron and partly of clay, so the kingdom will be partly strong and partly bro- ken. 43 And as thou hast seen yron mingled with clay and earth, they shall be mingled with the seed of men; but they shall not be joined

together, as yron cannot be mingled with clay. 44 In the days of these kings, the God of Heauen will establish a kingdom that will never be destroyed; and this kingdom will not be given to another people, but will break up and destroy all these kingdoms and stand forever. 45 Just as you saw that the stone was cut out of the mountain without hands, and that it tore in pieces the yron, the brasse, the clay, the siluer, and the goldde, so the great God showed the king what will happen next, and the dreame is true and its interpretation is sure. 46 Then King Nebuchadnezzar fell on his face and prostrated himself before Daniel and commanded that they should offer him portions of food and sweet smells. 47 The king answered Daniel and said, "I know for certain that your God is a God of gods, the Lord of kings and the revealer of secrets, for you have succeeded in opening this secret." 48 Then the king made Daniel a great man and gave him many and great gifts. He made him head of the whole province of Babel, chief of the leaders and all the wise men of Babel. 49 Then Daniel made a request to the king, who put Shadrach, Meshach and Abednego in charge of the province of Babel; but Daniel remained in the king's gate.

CHAPTER 3

1 King Nebuchadnezzar made an image of gold, the height of which was three cubic meters and the width of which was six cubic meters; he placed it in the plain of Dura, near Babel. 2 Then King Nebuchadnezzar sent to assemble the nobles, princes and dukes, judges, receivers, counselors, officers and all the officials of the provinces, that they might go to the dedication of the image which King Nebuchadnezzar had erected. 3 So the nobles, the princes and dukes, the judges, the receiv- ers, the counselors, the officers, and all the gatekeepers of the provinces came together for the dedication of the image that King Ne-buchadnezzar had prepared; and they stood before the image that Nebuchadnezzar had prepared. 4 Then a herald cried out, "Let it be known to you, O peoples, nations and tongues, 5 that when you hear the sound of the cornet, trumpet, harp, pouch, psaltery, dulcimer and all musical instruments, fall to the ground and worship the golden image that King Nebuchadnezzar has prepared, 6 and whosoever shall not fall down and wor- ship shall be cast in the same hour into the midst of a fiery furnace. 7 When all the people heard the sound of the cornet, the trumpet, the harp, the flute, the psaltery, and all the musical instruments, all peoples, nations, and languages stooped down and worshiped the golden image that Nebuchadnezzar the king had prepared. 8 For this reason, at that same time, men from Chaldea came and heavily ac- cused the Iewes. 9 For they spoke and said to King Nebuchadnezzar, "O king, stay forever. 10 You, O king, have decreed that whoever hears the sound of the cornet, the trumpet, the zither, the sackcloth, the psaltery, the dul- cimer, and all musical instruments, let him stoop down and worship the golden image, 11 and whosoever shall not stoop down and worship shall be cast into the midst of a fi- ery furnace. 12 There are certain men whom you have put in charge of the province of Babel, Shadrach, Meshach, and Abednego; these men, O king, have not obeyed your or- ders, and will not serve your gods, and will not worship the golden image that you have prepared. 13 Then Nebuchadnezzar, in wrath and anger, ordered Shadrach, Meshach and Abednego to be brought; so these men were brought before the king. 14 Nebuchadnez- zar spoke and said to them, "What is wrong?

Will you, Shadrach, Meshach and Abednego, not serve my God and worship the golden image I have prepared? 15 Are you therefore ready, when you hear the sound of the cornet, trumpet, zither, sackcloth, psaltery, dulcimer and all musical instruments, to fall down and worship the image I have made? For if you do not worship it, you will be cast immediate- ly into the midst of a fiery furnace, for who is that God who can deliver you out of my hands? 16 Shadrach, Meshach and Abednego answered the king, "O Nebuchadnezzar, we are not careful to answer you on this matter. 17 Well, our God, whom we serve, is able to deliver us from the furnace of the enemy, and he will deliver us out of your hand, O king. 18 But if not, know, O king, that we will not serve your gods and worship the golden image that you have prepared." 19 Then Nebuchadnez- zar was filled with anger and his expression had changed toward Shadrach, Meshach and Abed-nego; therefore he ordered and commanded them to heat the furnace seuen times more immediately than he used to heat it. 20 And he charged the most valiant men of war who were in his army to take Shadrach, Meshach and Abednego and throw them into the hot furnace. 21 So these men were bound in their coats, their jackets, their cloaks, and their other garments, and were cast into the midst of the furnace of flames. 22 Because the king's order was strict, so that the furnace was very hot, the flame of the fire killed the men who had brought Shadrach, Meshach and Abednego. 23 These three men, Shadrach, Meshach and Abednego, fell bound in the middle of the fiery furnace. 24 Then King Ne-buchadnezzar, astonished, rose up in haste, spoke and said to his advisers, "Have we not thrown three men bound into the midst of the fire? Who answered the king, "It is true, O king." 25 He answered and said, "Behold, I see four loose men walking in the midst of the fire, and they have no evil, and the form of the fourth is like the son of God." 26 Then King Nebuchadnezzar approached the mouth of the fiery furnace, spoke and said, "Shadrach, Meshach and Abednego, servants of his God, leave and come here"; so Shadrach, Meshach and Abednego came out of the midst of the fire. 27 Then the nobles, the princes, the dukes, and the king's advisers gathered them- selves together to see those men, for the fire had had no power over their bodies; for not one end of their heads was burned, nor were their cloaks changed, and there was no smell of fire upon them. 28 Therefore Nebuchad- nezzar spoke and said, "Blessed be the God of Shadrach, Meshach and Abed-nego, who sent his angel and delivered his servants, who had put their trust in him, and changed the king's order and delivered their bodies rather than serve or worship any god as their own God. 29 Therefore I decree that all the peoples, nations and tongues who utter blasphemies against the God of Shadrach, Meshach and Abednego shall be broken in pieces and their houses shall be turned into lakes, for there is no god who can make such an end." 30 Then the king promoted Shadrach, Meshach and Abednego to the province of Babel. Nebu- chadnezzar king toward all peoples, nations and languages that dwell in all the world, "Peace be multiplied to you"; I have seen fit to declare the signs and wonders that his God has performed toward me; how great are his signs and how mighty are his wonders! His kingdom is an everlasting kingdom and His dominion is from generation to generation.

CHAPTER 4

1 I, Nebuchadnezzar, sat quietly in my house, and flourished in my palace, 2 I saw a tragedy that made me anxious, and the thoughts on my bed and the visions in my head troubled me. 3 I therefore made a decree to bring before me all the wise men of Babel, that they might declare to me the interpretation of the dream. 4 Then came the inchanists, astrolo- gers, Chaldeans and soothsayers, to whom I told the drama, but they could not give me the interpretation, 5 until at last Daniel (whose name was Belteshazzar, after the name of my god, who has in him the spirit of the holy gods) came before me, and before him I ex- plained the drama, saying 6 O Belteshazzar, chief of the enchanters, since I know that the spirit of the holy gods is in you and no secret troubles you, tell me the visions of my dream that I have seen and their interpretation." 7 So were the visions of my head in my bed. And behold, I saw a tree in the midst of the earth, and its height was great: 8 A great and strong tree, whose height reached to the top, and whose sight reached to the end of all the earth. 9 Its branches were beautiful, and its fruit was plentiful, and there was food in it for all; it made shade under it for the fields, and the animals of the earth dwelt in its branches, and all flesh fed on it. 10 In the visions of my head, I sat on my bed, and behold, a watch- man and a saint came down from above, 11 and, crying out, said, "Cut down the tree and break its branches; shake its leaves and scat- ter its fruit, that the beasts may flee from under it and the refuse from its branches. 12 Leave its trunk in the ground, and with a band of wool and brassa put it in the midst of the vegetation of the field, and water it with the dew of Heauen, and let its portion be with the beasts in the midst of the vegetation of the field. 13 Let his heart be changed from human nature, and let a beast's heart be imparted to him, and let them pass over him several times. 14 The judgment is according to the decree of the guardians and according to the word of the saints; the demand has been granted, so that conscious men may know that the Most High has power over the kingdom of men, grants it to whom he wills, and appoints therein the most abject among men. 15 This is the dream which I, King Nebuchadnezzar, have seen; therefore you, O Belteshazzar, give the interpretation of it, for all the wise men of my kingdom are not able to give me the interpretation of it; but you are able, for the spirit of the holy gods is in you." 16 Then Dan- iel (whose name was Belteshazzar) was silent for an hour, while his thoughts troubled him; and the king spoke and said, "Belteshazzar, do not be troubled either by the dream or by its interpretation." Belteshazzar answered and said, "My lord, let the dream be to those who hate you and its interpretation to your enemies." 17 The tree that you saw was great and mighty, whose height reached to the plateau and whose view spanned the whole world, 18 whose leaves were abundant and its fruit very plentiful, and in it was food for all, under which dwelt the beasts of the fields and on whose branches sat the beasts of the highlands, 19 It is you, O king, who are great and mighty, for your greatness has grown and extends to the plateau and your dominion to the ends of the earth. 20 As the king saw a watchman and a saint who came down from Heauen and said, "Cut down the tree and de- stroy it, but leave the stump of its roots in the earth, and with a band of yron and brasse put it in the midst of the vegetation of the field, and let it be bathed with the dew of Heauen, and let its portion be with the beasts of the field, until ten times have they passed by it." 21 This is the interpretation, O king, and it is the decree of the Most High that has come to my lord the king, 22 And they shall remove thee from men, and thy dwelling shall be with the beasts of the field; and they shall make thee to eat grass like oxen, and bathe thee with the dew of the threshing floor; and they shall pass ten times before thee, until thou knowest that the Most High rules the kingdom of men, and grants it to whom he will. 23 If it be said that one leaves the trunk of the tree, thy king- dom shall remain with thee; after that thou shalt know that the heavens are in charge. 24 Therefore, O king, let my counsel be accept- able to thee, and let thou purge away thy sins with righteousness, and thy iniquities with mercy toward the poor; behold, let there be a remedy for thy wandering. 25 All these things shall come upon king Nebuchadnezzar. 26 At the end of two months he entered the royal palace of Babel. 27 The king spoke and said, "Is not this the great Babel that I have built for the house of the kingdom by the strength of my might and the honor of my majesty?" 28 While the word was in the king's mouth, a voice came down from Heauen, saying, "O King Nebuchadnezzar, to thee let it be said, Thy kingdom is departed from thee, 29 they shall turn thee away from men, and thy dwell- ing shall be with the shrubs of the field; they shall make thee eat grass like oxen, and other times shall pass before thou know that the Most High rules the kingdom of men, and grants it to whom he will." 30 At that same instant this thing was fulfilled on Nebuchad- nezzar, who was deprived of men and ate like oxen, and his body was bathed in the dew of heaven, until his feet were grown up like ea- gle's feathers and his nails like bird's claws. 31 And at the end of these days Nebuchadnez- zar lifted up his eyes, and my understanding was restored, and I gave thanks to the Most High, and prayed to and honored him who lives for eternity, whose power is an everlast- ing power, and whose kingdom endures from generation to generation. 32 All the inhabi- tants of the earth are considered a nothing; he works according to his will in the army of Heauen and in the inhabitants of the earth, and no one can stop his hand or say to him, "What are you doing?" 33 At the same time my understanding was restored to me, and I returned to the honor of my kingdom; my glory and my beauty were restored to me, and my counsellors and my princes sought me out, and I was established in my kingdom, and my glory was increased. 34 Therefore I, Nebuchadnezzar, pray to, exalt, and magnify the king of Heauen, whose works are all true, whose ways are right, and those who walk in pride, he is able to put them down.

CHAPTER 5

1 King Belshazzar made a great banquet for a thousand of his princes and drank wine be- fore a thousand people. 2 While he was savor- ing the wine, Belshazzar ordered the gold and silver vessels that his father Nebuchadnezzar had brought from the Temple in Jerusalem to be brought to him, so that the king, his princ- es, his wives and his concubines could drink from them. 3 Then the golden vessels that had been taken from the temple of the house of the Lord in Jerusalem were brought, and the king and his princes and his wives and con- cubines drank from them. 4 They drank wine and prayed to the gods of gold, silver, bronze, yron, wood and stone. 5 At that same time there appeared the fingers of a man's hand writing against the candelabra on the slab of the wall of the king's palace, and the king saw the palm of the writing hand. 6 Then the king's appearance was changed, and his thoughts troubled him, so that his knees loosed and his knees broke against each other. 7 There- fore the king cried out with a loud voice that they should bring the astrologers, the Chal- deans and the soothsayers. The king spoke and said to the wise men of

Babel, "Whoever can read this writing and give me the inter- pretation of it will be clothed in purple, will have a necklace of gold around his neck, and will be the third ruler of the kingdom." 8 Then all the king's wise men came, but they could neither read the writing nor give the king the interpretation. 9 Then King Belshazzar was greatly troubled, and his countenance changed, and his princes were astonished. 10 Now the queen, because of the speeches of the king and his princes, entered the house of the bank; and the queen spoke and said, "O king, be at rest forever; do not be troubled by your thoughts and do not change your coun- tenance. 11 There is a man in your kingdom in whom is the spirit of the holy gods, and in the days of your father there was in him light, understanding, and wisdom like that of the gods; Nebuchadnezzar the king, your father, I say, made him chief of the enchanters, astrol- ogers, Chaldeans, and soothsayers, 12 For in him was found a more excellent spirit, knowl- edge and understanding (for he expounded the dramas, declared the difficult judgments, and dissolved the doubts), and precisely in Daniel, whom the king called Belteshazzar; now be called Daniel, and he shall declare the interpretation." 13 Then Daniel was brought before the king, and the king spoke and said to Daniel, "Are you that Daniel, belonging to the sons of the captivity of Iudah, whom my father the king brought out of Iewrie? 14 Now I have heard of you that the spirit of the holy gods is in you, and that in you is found light and understanding and excellent wisdom. 15 Therefore wise men and astrologers were brought before me that they might read this writing and give me the interpretation of it; but they could not declare the interpretation of the thing. 16 Then I heard of you, that you knew how to give interpretations and dispel doubts; now, if you can reread the scripture and give me the interpretation of it, you will be clothed in purple, you will have a chain of gold around your neck, and you will be the third ruler of the kingdom." 17 Then Daniel answered and said to the king, "Keep your rewards for yourself and give your gifts to another; but I will deliver the scripture to the king and show him the interpretation of it." 18 O king, listen: the most high God has giv- en Nebuchadnezzar your father a kingdom, a majesty, honor and glory. 19 Because of the maiestie which he gave him, all peoples, na- tions and tongues trembled and feared be- fore him; he put to death whom he pleased; he struck down whom he pleased; whom he pleased, he defeated; and whom he pleased, he struck down. 20 But when his heart was puffed up and his mind hardened by pride, he was deposed from his throne as king and they took away his honor. 21 He was removed from the sons of men, his heart was made like the heart of beasts, and his dwelling was with wild asses; they fed him with meat like oxen, and his body was bathed in the dew of heaven, until he understood that the most high God rules the kingdom of men and ap- points whomever he wills there. 22 You, his son, O Belshazzar, did not humble your heart, though you knew all these things, 23 But you rose up against the LORD of Heauen, and they brought before you the vessels of his house, and you and your princes and your wives and your concubines drank wine in them, and you prayed to the gods of silk and of gold, of brasse, of yron, of wood and of stone, who do not see, nor hear, nor understand: and the God in whose hand is your breath and all your ways, you have not glorified him." 24 Then the palm of his hand was sent forth from him, and he wrote this writing. 25 This is the writing that he wrote: MENE, MENE, TEKEL UPHARSIN. 26 This is the interpretation of the thing: MENE, MENE, God has named your kingdom and finished it. 27 TEKEL, you were put on the scales and were found too light. 28 PERES, your kingdom was destroyed and handed over to the Medes and Persians." 29 Then, at Belshazzar's order, they clothed Daniel in purple, put a chain of gold around his neck, and made an announcement about him, saying that he would be the third ruler of the kingdom. 30 The same night Belshazzar, king of the Chaldeans, was killed. 31 Darius of the Medes took possession of the kingdom, at the age of sixty-two.

CHAPTER 6

1 It pleased Darius to establish for the king- dom a hundred and twelve garrisons, which were to stand over the whole kingdom, 2 and, outside of these, three rulers (among whom was Daniel), so that the rulers would give them services and the king would have no do- minion. 3 Now this Daniel was preferred over the rulers and guardians, because the spirit was excellent in him, and the king thought to put him above all the kingdom. 4 Therefore the leaders and rulers sought an occasion against Daniel concerning the kingdom, but they could find neither occasion nor fault, for he was so faithful that no fault or error was found in him. 5 Then those men said, "We will find no occasion against this Daniel, except in regard to the law of his God." 6 Therefore the leaders and these warriors went together to the king and said to him, "King Darius, make yourself safe." 7 All the rulers of your king- dom, the officers and governors, the council- lors and dukes, consulted together to make a decree for the king and to establish a statute, according to which anyone who petitions a god or a man for three days from you, O king, shall be cast into the den of Lyons. 8 Now, O king, confirm the decree and seal the writing, that it may not be changed according to the law of the Medes and Persians, which is not altered. 9 Therefore King Darius sealed the writing and the decree. 10 Now when Daniel understood that he had sealed the writing, he went into his house, and the window of his chamber being open toward Jerusalem, he knelt down three times a day and prayed and prayed to his God, as he did before. 11 Then those men came together and found Dan- iel praying and making supplications to his God. 12 Then they came and spoke to the king about the king's decree, "Have you not sealed the decree that every man who within thirty days makes a request to any god or man, say- ing to you, O king, shall be cast into the den of Lyons?" The king answered, "The thing is true, according to the law of the Medes and Persians, which is not altered." 13 Then they answered and said to the king, "This Daniel, who is of the children of the captivity of Ju- dah, does not consider you, O king, nor the decree which you have sealed, but makes his petition three times a day." 14 When the king heard these words, he was greatly displeased with himself and set out to seek Daniel to deliver him; and he labored until the setting of the sun to deliver him. 15 Then these men gathered before the king and said to him, "Understand, O king, that the law of the Me- des and Persians is that no decree or statute confirmed by the king may be changed." 16 Then the king gave orders, and they brought Daniel and threw him into the den of Lyons; now the king spoke and said to Daniel, "Your God, to whom you always serve, will soon de- liver you." 17 A stone was brought and placed over the mouth of the den, and the king sealed it with his seal and the seal of his princes, so that Daniel's purpose would not be changed. 18

Then the king went into his palace and re- mained fasting, without any musical instru- ments being brought before him, and sleep passed over him. 19 Then the king rose early in the morning and went in haste to the city of Lyons. 20 When he came to the den, he cried with a lament to Daniel; and the king spoke and said to Daniel, "O Daniel, servant of your God who lives, is not your God (whom you always serve) able to deliver you from the li- ons?" 21 Then Daniel said to the king, "O king, stay forever. 22 My God hath sent his angel, and hath shut the mouths of the lionists, that they do me no harm; for my righteousness hath been found out before him; and to thee, O king, have I done no harm." 23 Then the king rejoiced greatly for him and ordered that they should bring Daniel out of the den; so Daniel was brought out of the den and no evil was found on him, because he believed in his God. 24 By the king's command, these men who had accused Daniel were brought and thrown into the den of the lions: they, their sons and their wives; and the lions took hold of them and smashed all their bones to piec- es, or when they came to the enclosure of the den. 25 Then King Darius wrote, "To all peo- ples, nations and languages, who dwell in all the world: Peace be multiplied to you. 26 I de- cree that in all the dominion of my kingdom men shall tremble and fear before the God of Daniel, for he is the God who lives and abides forever; his kingdom shall not perish, and his dominion shall be everlasting. 27 He saves and delivers, he works signs and wonders in heaven and on earth, and he has delivered Daniel from the power of the Zionists." 28 So this Daniel prospered in the reign of Darius and in the reign of Cyrus of Persia.

CHAPTER 7

1 In the first year of Belshazzar, king of Babel, Daniel had a vision and visions in his head, on his bed; then he wrote down the vision and stated the summary of the matter. 2 Daniel spoke and said, "I had a vision by night, and behold, the four winds of heaven came upon the great sea: 3 And four great beasts came from the sea, each one different from the other. 4 And the first was like a lion, and had wings of an eagle: I saw, until his wings were torn off, and he was lifted up from the earth, and set on his feet like a man, and was given a man's heart. 5 And behold, another beast, which was the second, was like a beast, and stood on one side; and he had three ribbons in his mouth between his teeth, and they said unto her, Arise, and eat much meat. 6 After this I saw another beast like a leopard, which had four wings of a bird on its back; the beast also had four heads, and it was given domin- ion. 7 After this I saw in the night visions, and behold, the fourth beast was fearsome, terri- ble, and very strong. It had great yron teeth; it devoured and tore to pieces and trampled the residue under its feet; and it was similar to the beasts before it, for it had ten horns. 8 And as I considered the horns, behold, there sprung up among them another little horn, before which were three of the first horns torn off; and behold, in this horn were eyes like the eyes of man, and a mouth speaking presumptuous things. 9 And I saw, until the thrones were set, and the Ancient of Days sat down, whose robe was white as snow, and the hairline of his head like pure wool; and his throne was like a burning flame, and his wheels like blazing fire. 10 A blazing fire went forth and came out from before him; thou- sands of thousands attended him, and ten thousand thousands stood before him; judg- ment was set, and the books were opened. 11 Then I saw, because of the sight of the pre- sumptuous words which the horn had spo- ken, I

saw, until the beast was slain and his body destroyed and cast into the blazing fire. 12 As for the other beasts, they had taken away their dominion, but their life was prolonged for a certain time and a certain season. 13 As I saw in night visions, behold, one resembling the son of man came in the clouds of Heauen, and approached the Ancient of Days, and they led him before him. 14 And he gave him a do- minion and an honor and a kingdom, that all peoples, nations and languages might serve him; and his dominion is an everlasting do- minion, which shall never be taken away, and his kingdom shall never be destroyed. 15 I, Daniel, was troubled in my spirit, in the bowels of my body, and the visions of my head made me restless. 16 Therefore I approached one of those who stood nearby and asked him the truth of all this; and he told me and showed me the interpretation of these things. 17 These great beasts, which are four, are four kings who will arise from the earth, 18 they shall take the kingdom of the saints of the Most High and possess it forever and ever. 19 After this, I would like to know the truth of the fourth beast, which was so different from all the others, very fearsome, whose teeth were of yron and its nails of brasse; it devoured, it tore in pieces and crushed the rest under its feet. 20 I also learned of the ten horns that were on her head, and of the other that sprung up, before which three fell, and of the horn that had eyes and a mouth that spoke presumptuous things, whose gaze was stur- dier than her fellows. 21 I saw that the same horn was beating itself against the saints, yea, and preparing itself against them, 22 Until the Ancient of Days came, and judgment was given to the saints of the Most High; and the time drew near when the saints possessed the kingdom. 23 Then he said, "The fourth beast shall be the fourth kingdom of the earth, which shall be like unto all kingdoms, and shall destroy all the earth, and shall break it down, and tear it in pieces." 24 The ten horns of this kingdom are ten kings that shall arise; and another shall arise after them, and shall be like the first, and shall subdue three kings, 25 And he shall speak words against the Most High, and shall consume the saints of the Most High, and shall think that he can change the times and the laws, and they shall be given into his hands, until a time, and a time, and a time. 26 But he will sit the judge, and they will take away his dominion, to consume and de- stroy him to the end. 27 And the kingdom and dominion and greatness of the kingdom over all the earth shall be given to the holy people of the Most High, whose kingdom is an ev- erlasting kingdom, and all the powers shall serve and obey him. 28 And this is the point of the matter: I, Daniel, have had many thoughts that have troubled me and my appearance has changed in me, but I have kept the matter in my heart.

CHAPTER 8

1 In the thirteenth year of King Belshazzar's reign, a vision appeared to me, again to Dan- iel, after the one that had first appeared to me. 2 In vision I saw that I was in the palace of Shushan, in the province of Elam, and in vi- sion it seemed to me that I was by the Riviera of Vlai. 3 Then I looked and saw that before the river stood a ram with two horns; the two horns were aligned, but one was higher than the other, and the highest came last. 4 I saw the ram pushing against the west, against the north and against the south, so that no ani- mal could stand before him, nor could escape his hand, but he did what he had appointed and became great. 5 While I was consider- ing, behold, a goat came from the west over all the earth, not touching the ground; and this goat had a

horn appearing between his eyes. 6 He approached the ram that had the two horns, which I had seen standing by the river, and ran toward it with his fierce an- ger. 7 And I saw him approach the ram, and having confronted him, he struck him and broke his two horns; and the ram had no more strength to resist, but threw him to the ground and trampled him down, and no one could deliver the ram from his power. 8 There- fore the goat became very large, and when it was at its strongest, its great horn was bro- ken off; and because of this four sprang up, appearing toward the four winds of heaven. 9 Out of one of them came forth a little horn that became very great toward the south, to- ward the east, and toward the pleasant land. 10 And it increased unto the army of Heauen, and cast down to the earth a part of the army and of the stars, and trampled them down, 11 And it exalted itself against the prince of the army whose daily sacrifice was taken away, and the place of his sanctuary was cast down to the ground. 12 He shall be granted a time outside the daily sacrifice for iniquity, and it shall cast down the truth to the ground, and so it shall do and prosper." 13 Then I heard one of the saints speaking, and one of the saints spoke to a certain individual, saying, "How long will the vision of the daily sacrifice and the iniquity of desolation last to destroy the sanctuary and the army? 14 He answered, "Until sunset and morning, two thousand and three hundred; then the sanctuary will be closed." 15 When I, Daniel, had seen the vision and tried to understand its meaning, behold, there stood before me the silhouette of a man. 16 Between the banks of the Vlai I heard the voice of a man calling and saying, "Gabriel, let this man understand the vision." 17 So he came to where I was; and when he came, I was frightened and fell on my face; but he said to me, "Understand, son of man, for in the last time there will be vision." 18 While he was speaking to me, I, asleep, fell down with my face to the ground; but he touched me and put me back in my place. 19 And he said, "Behold, I will show you what will take place in the last wrath, for at the end of the appointed time it will come. 20 The ram that you saw with two horns is the king of the Me- des and Persians. 21 The roebuck is the king of Greece, and the great horn between his eyes is the first king. 22 The one who was broken and for whom four kingdoms remained standing is four kingdoms that will remain standing of that nation, but not in its strength. 23 At the end of their reign, when the rebels are con- sumed, there will stand up a king of fierce ap- pearance and dark judgments. 24 His power will be mighty, but not in his strength; he will wonderfully destroy, prosper, exert himself, and destroy the mighty and the holy people. 25 By his policy he shall prosper cunning in his hand, he shall exalt himself in his heart, and by peace he shall destroy many; he shall also oppose the prince of princes, but he shall be put down without escape. 26 The vision of the morning and the evening, which has been declared, is true; therefore follow the vision, for it will be after many days. 27 I, Daniel, was stricken and sick some days; but when I rose up, I did the kings' bidding and was amazed at the vision, but no one understood it.

CHAPTER 9

1 In the first year of Darius the son of Ahashuerosh, of the line of the Medes, who was made king outside the kingdom of the Chaldeans, 2 In the first year of his reign, I Daniel understood from the books the name of the years of which the Lord had spoken to the prophet Jeremiah, that he would be sev- enty years old in the desolation of Jerusalem. 3 I turned to the Lord God and sought with prayers and supplications, fasting, sackcloth and ashes. 4 I prayed to the Lord my God and made my confession, saying, "Lord God, you are great and fearful, and you keep favor and mercy toward those who love you and toward those who keep your commands, 5 we have sinned, we have committed iniqui- ty and acted wickedly, yea, we have rebelled and departed from your precepts and your decrees. 6 Because we would not obey your servants, the prophets, who spoke in your name to our kings, our princes, our fathers, and all the people of the land. 7 O LORD, to you belongs righteousness and to you shame, as it appears this day to all the men of Judah and to the inhabitants of Jerusalem, and to all Israel, from near and far, in all the countries from which you brought them out, because of their sins which they have committed against you. 8 O LORD, for our kings and our princes and our fathers the shame is open, because we have sinned against you. 9 Yet the LORD our God has compassion and forgiveness, even though we have rebelled against him. 10 For we have not obeyed the will of the LORD our God to walk according to his laws, which he had already promulgated through his servants, the prophets. 11 Yea, all Israel has transgressed your law, turned back and not heard your message; therefore the curse is upon us and upon all that is written in the law of Moses, God's servant, because we have sinned against him. 12 He has confirmed his words which he spoke against you and against our judges who judged you, causing a great plague to come upon you, for in all the land there was no such thing as was brought upon Jerusalem. 13 All this plague came upon Vs, as it is written in the Law of Moses; yet we did not make our prayer before the LORD our God to turn away from our iniquities and un- derstand your truth. 14 Therefore the LORD has prepared the plague and brought it upon us, because the LORD our God is righteous in all his works which he does, because we would not listen to his message. 15 Now, O Lord, our God, who brought your people out of the land of Egypt with a mighty hand and brought you to life again, as it appears today, we have sinned, we have acted wickedly. 16 O LORD, according to all your righteousness, I beseech you, turn away your wrath and your fury from your city, Jerusalem, your holy Mountain, for because of our sins and the iniquities of our fathers, Jerusalem and your people are a reproach to all who are around. 17 Now therefore, O our God, hear the prayer of your servant and his supplications, and let your face shine upon your sanctuary, which lies forsaken for the Lord's sake. 18 O my God, incline thine ear, and hear; open thine eyes, and see our desolations, and the city where- in thy Name is called; for we present not our supplications before thee for our own righ- teousness, but for thy great and tender mer- cies. 19 Hear, O LORD, forgive, O LORD, con- sider and execute; do not delay, for your sake, O my God, for your Name is called upon your city and upon your people. 20 As I spoke and prayed and confessed my sin and the sin of my people Israel, I presented my supplication to the LORD my God for the holy mountain of my God, 21 while I was speaking in prayer, behold, the man Gabriel, whom I had seen before in vision, came flying and touched me toward the hour of the initial oblation. 22 He informed me and spoke with me and said, "O Daniel, I have come to give you knowledge and understanding. 23 At the beginning of your supplications the order has come, and I have come to explain to you, because you are greatly troubled; therefore deepen the matter and consider the vision. 24 Seventy weeks have been appointed for your people and for your holy city, to put an end to iniquity, to

re- move sins, to reconcile unrest, to introduce eternal righteousness, to confirm vision and prophecy, and to proclaim the Most Holy. 25 Therefore know and understand that from the beginning of the order to bring back the people and to build Jerusalem until Messiah, the prince, seventy-two weeks and sixty-two weeks will pass, and the road will be built again and the walls in a hard time. 26 And after sixty-two weeks Messiah shall be slain, and shall have nothing, and the people of the prince who is to come shall destroy the city and the sanctuary, and its end shall be with a flood; and until the end of the battle it shall be destroyed by desolation. 27 And he shall confirm the covenant with many for a week; and in the midst of the week he shall cause the sacrifice and the oblation to cease, and by the spreading of abominations he shall make it desolate, until the consummation which shall be imposed upon the desolation.

CHAPTER 10

1 In the third year of Cyrus, king of Persia, a thing was revealed to Daniel (whose name was Belteshazzar), and the word was true, but the appointed time was long; he understood the thing and had the understanding of the vision. 2 At the same time I Daniel was in prison for three weeks of days. 3 I did not eat pleasant bread, nor did meat or wine enter my mouth, nor did I anoint myself at all, until three weeks of days were fulfilled. 4 On the fourth and twentieth day of the first month, as I stood by the side of that great riuer, that is, Hiddekel, 5 I lifted up mine eyes, and looked, and behold, a man clothed in lin- en, whose loins were girded with the fine gold of Vphaz. 6 His body also was like chrysolite, his face (to look at) like lightning, his eyes like lamps of fire, his arms and feet were the color of polished brassa, and the voice of his words was like the voice of a multitude. 7 I, Daniel, alone, spoke the vision, for the men who were with me did not speak the vision; but great fear fell upon them, so that they fled and hid themselves. 8 Therefore I remained alone, and I spoke this great vision, and no strength re- mained in me; for my strength had turned to corruption, and I had no power. 9 Neverthe- less I heard the sense of his words; and when I heard the sense of his words, I fell asleep on my face, and my face was turned toward the ground. 10 And behold, a hand touched me, causing me to fall upon my knees and the palms of my hands. 11 And he said to me, "O Daniel, a highly esteemed man, understand the words that I say to you and stay in your place, for to you I have been sent." And when he said these words to me, I stood trembling. 12 Then he said to me, "Do not fear, Daniel, for from the first day that you set your heart to understand and to humble yourself before your God, your words have been heard, and I have come because of your words." 13 But the prince of the kingdom of Persia kept me for a day and twenty; but behold, Michael, one of the most important princes, came to help me, and I stayed there with the kings of Persia. 14 Now I have come to show you what will happen to your people in the last days, for the vision still lasts many days." 15 When he said these words to me, I put my face to the ground and held my tongue. 16 And behold, one similar to the sons of man touched my lips; then I opened my mouth, and spoke, and said to him who stood before me, "O my Lord, because of the vision my sorrows have come upon me again, and I have no strength. 17 For how can the servant of this my Lord speak to my Lord being such? As for me, by the straight way I have no more strength and no more breath." 18 Then he came again and touched me one who had the appearance of a man, and he

strengthened me, 19 and said, "O man, greatly diminished, fear not; peace be with you; be strong and of good courage." And when he had spoken to me, I strength- ened myself and said, "Let my Lord speak, for you have strengthened me." 20 Then he said, "Do you know why I have come to you? But now I will return to fight with the prince of Persia; and when I have departed, behold, the prince of Greece will come. 21 But I will show you what is set forth in the Scriptures of truth; and there is no one who agrees with me in these things but Michael your prince.

CHAPTER 11

1 I also, in the first year of Darius of the Medes, set out to encourage and strengthen him. 2 Now I will show you the truth: behold, there will still be three kings in Persia, and the fourth will be far richer than all of them; and with his strength and riches he will push everyone against Greece. 3 But a mighty king will arise, who will rule with great dominion and do what pleases him. 4 When he shall stand, his kingdom shall be broken up, and he shall be diverted to the four winds of Heauen, and not for his posterity, nor according to his dominion, which he ruled; for his kingdom shall be torn away, to be destined for others besides those. 5 And the king of the south shall be the mightiest, and one of his princ- es, and shall prevail over him, and he shall be the ruler; and his dominion shall be a great dominion. 6 And at the end of the years they shall come together, because the daughter of the king of the South shall come to the king of the North to make an agreement, but she shall not put off the power of the arme, nei- ther shall he continue, nor his arme; but she shall be condemned to death, as well as those who brought her, and those who begot her, and those who comforted her in these times. 7 But from the bud of her roots shall arise one in her stead, who shall come with an army, and shall enter into the fortresses of the king of the north, and do with them what he wills, and shall prevail, 8 and he shall carry their gods with their molten images and with their precious objects of silk and gold to Egypt, and he shall stay longer than the king of the North. 9 The king of the South shall return to his kingdom and return to his own country. 10 Therefore his sons shall stir and gather a great army; one shall come, and go out, and pass through; then he shall return and stir in his fortress. 11 And the king of the south shall be angry, and shall come and fight with him, even with the king of the north: for he shall put forth a great multitude, and the multitude shall be in his hand. 12 Then the multitude will be proud, and their hearts will be lifted up, for he will strike down thousands, but he will not yet prevail. 13 For the king of the north will re- turn and put forth a greater multitude than before, and he will come (after certain years) with a mighty army and great riches. 14 At the same time many will oppose the king of the South; even the rebellious sons of your people will exalt themselves to establish the vision, but they will fall. 15 Then the King of the North will come, and will throw himself on a mountain, and will take the strong city; and the armies of the South will not resist, nor will his chosen people, nor will there be strength to resist. 16 But he that cometh shall do as he will, and none shall stand against him; and he shall stand in the pleasant land, which by his hand shall be consumed. 17 And he shall set forth to go in with the strength of all his kingdom and his confederates; so he shall do, and shall give him the daughter of the women to destroy her; but she shall not be on his side, and shall not be for him. 18 Af- ter this, he shall turn his face toward the

yles and take many, but a prince shall cause his own shame to turn upon him, as well as cause his own shame to turn upon himself. 19 For he shall turn his face toward the fortresses of his country, but he shall be overthrown, and shall fall, and shall not be found. 20 Then shall arise in his place, in the glory of the kingdom, one who shall raise taxes; but after a few days he shall be destroyed, neither by wrath nor by battle. 21 In his place shall arise a vile person, to whom they shall not give the honor of the kingdom; but he shall come in peaceably, and shall make himself obey the kingdom by flat- tery. 22 The armies shall be overthrown like a flooded river before him, and they shall be broken, as well as the prince of the courtiers. 23 After the league made with him, he will act deceitfully, for he will show up and go out with a small people. 24 He will enter a quiet and rich province and do what his fathers never did, nor his fathers; he will distribute among them prayers, spices, and substances, and he will make his predictions against the fortresses, though for a time. 25 Moreover he shall incite his power and his courage against the king of the South with a great army, and the king of the South shall be incited to fight with a very great and mighty army; but he shall not resist, because they shall foresee and exert themselves against him. 26 Yea, they that feed on the portion of his food shall de- stroy him, and his army shall overflow, and many shall fall and be slain. 27 The hearts of these two kings will be strained to do evil, and they will speak deceit at the table, but it will not be possible, for the end will come at the appointed time. 28 Then he will return to his country with great substance, because his heart will be against the Holy Convent; so he will do and return to his country. 29 At the appointed time he shall return and come to the South; but the last shall not be as the first. 30 For the ships of Chittim shall come against him, and he shall be grieved, and shall return, and shall rage against the Holy Convent; so he shall do, and shall return, and have intelligence with them that forsake the Holy Convent. 31 The armies will take his side and pollute the sanctuary of strength, take away the daily sacrifice and set up an abom- inable desolation. 32 Those who violate your covenant will be induced to sin by flattery; but the people who know their God will be in health and prosper. 33 Those who understand among the people will instruct many; but they will fall by sword and flame, into captivity and ruin for many days. 34 When they fall, they shall be helped with little, but many shall be delivered with difficulty. 35 Some of the most intelligent shall fall to judge them, to puri- fy them, and to make them white, until the time is past, for there is an appointed time. 36 The king will do what he has listed: he will exalt himself and magnify himself against all those who are God, he will say martial things against the God of gods, and he will prosper until the wrath is accomplished, for the deci- sion is made. 37 He will not heed the God of his fathers, nor the desires of women, nor will he care for any god, for he will magnify him- self over all. 38 But instead he shall honor the god Mauzzim, and the god whom his fathers did not know, he shall honor him with gold and with silver, with precious stones and with pleasant things. 39 So shall he do in the lands of Mauzzim with a foreign god whom he shall acknowledge: he shall increase his glory, and make them ruler over many, and he shall lay your land as a mine of gold. 40 And at the end of the times the king of the south shall push him, and the king of the north shall come against him like a whirlwind with chariots, horsemen, and many ships, and he shall enter into your land, and shall go out of it, and pass through it. 41 He will also enter the pleasant land, and many counties will be defeated; but these will escape from his hand, as Edom and Moab and the chief of the sons of Ammon. 42 He will also stretch out his hands over the countries, and the land of Egypt will not escape. 43 But he shall have power over the treasures of gold and silver, and over all the precious things of Egypt, and of the Libyans, and of the black Mores, where he shall pass by. 44 But the tidings from the east and the north shall trouble him; therefore he shall de- part with great wrath to destroy and drive out many. 45 And he shall plant the tabernacles of his palace among the seas, in the glorious and holy mountain; but he shall come to his end, and no one shall help him.

CHAPTER 12

1 At that time Michael, the great prince who defends the children of your people, will rise up, and there will be a time of trouble, such as there has never been since a nation was born until that time; and at that time your people will be eliminated, all who are written in the book. 2 Many of those who sleep in the dust of the earth will awake, some to eternal life, others to shame and perpetual contempt. 3 Those who are wise will shine like the lights of the firmament, and those who convert many to righteousness will shine like the stars for- ever. 4 But you, O Daniel, close the words and seal the book until the end of time; many shall run to and fro, and knowledge shall increase." 5 Then I, Daniel, looked, and behold, there stood two others, the one on this side of the brink of the river and the other on the other side of the brink of the river. 6 And one said to the man clothed in linen, who stood on the waters of the river, "When will these wonders end? 7 And I heard the man clothed in linen standing upon the waters of the river, as he held his right hand and his left hand upward, and swore, by him that liveth for Europe, that this shall last for a time, two and a half times; and when he shall have finished scat- tering the power of the holy people, all these things shall be finished. 8 I heard it, but I did not understand it; and I said, "O my Lord, what will be the end of these things?" 9 And he said, "Go your way, Daniel, for your words are closed and sealed until the end of time." 10 Many will be cleansed, whitened, and tested; but the wicked will act wickedly, and none of the wicked will have understanding, but the wise will understand. 11 From the time when the daily sacrifice will be taken away and the abominable desolation will be put in place, a thousand, two hundred and ninety days will pass. 12 Blessed is he who waits and comes to the thousand, three hundred and fifty days. 13 But go thy way to the end, for at the end of the days thou shalt rest and abide in thy lot.

MINOR PROPHETS

These books offer shorter, focused messages from God

HOSEA

CHAPTER 1

1 The word of the LORD addressed to Hosea the son of Beeri in the days of Vzziah, Jotham, Ahaz, and Hezekiah, kings of Judah, and in the days of Jeroboam the son of Joash, king of Israel. 2 At first the LORD spoke through

Hosea, and the LORD said to Hosea, "Go, take with you a wife of fornication and children of fornication, for the land has committed great prostitution, turning away from the LORD." 3 So he went and took Gomer the daughter of Diblaim, who conceived him and bore him a son. 4 And the LORD said to him, "Call him Izreel; just a little longer, and I will cause the blood of Izreel to flow on the house of Jehu, and I will cause the kingdom of the house of Israel to cease. 5 In that day I will also break the bow of Israel in the valley of Izreel. 6 She conceived again and bore a daughter, and God said to him, "Call her Lo-ruhamah, for I will no longer have mercy on the house of Is- rael, but will take her away. 7 Nevertheless I will have mercy on the house of Iudah, and I will greet them by the LORD their God, and I will not save them by bow, by sword, or by battle, by horses, or by horsemen." 8 Now after she gave birth to Lo-ruhamah, she con- ceived and bore a son. 9 Then God said, "Call him Lo-ammi, for you are not my people, and therefore I will not be yours." 10 Nevertheless, the name of the children of Israel shall be as the sand of the sea, which cannot be mea- sured or gauged; and in the place where it was said to them, "You are not my people," it shall be said to them, "You are the children of the God who lies." 11 Then shall the children of Iudah and the children of Israel be gathered together, and they shall give themselves one head, and shall go out of the land, for great is the day of Izreel.

CHAPTER 2

1 Say to your brothers, "Ammi," and to your sisters, "Ruhamah." 2 "Convince your mother, convince her, for she is not my wife, nor am I her husband; but let her remove her fornica- tions from her sight, and her adulteries from between her breasts. 3 Lest I strip her naked, and put her on as in the day she was born, and make her as a wilderness, and leave her as a dry land, and kill her for thirst. 4 I will not pity her children, for they are children of fornication. 5 For their mother has been a harlot; she who conceived them has acted shamefully, for she said, "I will go after my masters who give me my bread and my water, my wool and my flax, my oil and my drink." 6 Therefore, behold, I will carpet your way with thorns and make a hedge for you, so that you will not find its paths. 7 Though she follow her lovers, she will not reach them; though she see them, she will not find them; then she will say, "I will go away and return to my first husband, for I was better off at that time than I am now." 8 She did not know that I had giv- en her the grain and the wine and the oil, and that I had multiplied the silver and the money that they had given to Baal. 9 Therefore I will go back, and will take away my grain in the time when it was given, and my wine in the season when it was given, and I will recover my wool and my flax that was lent, to blot out her shame. 10 Now I will disown her lewdness before the eyes of her breeders, and no one shall pluck her out of my hand. 11 I will also cause to cease all her entertainments, her holy days, her new moons, her sabbaths, and all her solemn feasts. 12 I will destroy her vines and her fig trees, of which she said, "These are the prizes that my masters have given me"; I will make them like a forest, and wild beasts will eat them. 13 I will visit her in the days of Baalim, in which she burned incense to them; she adorned herself with her earrings and her jewels, and followed her breeders, and forgot me, says the LORD. 14 Therefore behold, I will entice her, and lead her into the wilderness, and speak to her in a friendly manner. 15 From there I will give her her vineyards and the valley of Achor

as a place of hope, and she shall sing there as in the days of her youth and as in the days when she came out of the land of Egypt. 16 In that day, says the LORD, you shall call me Ishi, and you shall no longer call me Baali. 17 For I will take the names of Baa- lim out of his mouth, and they shall no longer be remembered by their names. 18 In that day I will make for them a battlefield with the wild beasts, with the beasts of the wilderness, and with that which creeps upon the earth; and I will bring forth out of the earth the bow, and the sword, and I will make them to sleep qui- etly. 19 I will marry thee to me forever; yea, I will marry thee to me in righteousness, and in judgment, and in mercy, and in compassion. 20 I will also marry you to me in faithfulness, and you shall know the LORD. 21 In that day I will hear, says the LORD, I will hear the heav- ens, and they will hear the earth, 22 And the earth shall hear the corn, and the wine, and the oil, and shall hear Izreel. 23 I will sow her for me in the earth, and I will have mercy on her, who was not pitied, and I will say to those who were not my people, "You are my people." And they shall say, "You are my God."

CHAPTER 3

1 Then the LORD said to me, "Go yet and buy a woman (betrayed by her husband and a prostitute), as the LORD did with the chil- dren of Israel; but they looked to other gods and bought the bottles of wine." 2 So I bought her for fifty pieces of silk and for a homo of a barrel and half a homo of a barrel. 3 I said to her, "You shall abide with me for many days; you shall not be a harlot and you shall not be for any other man, and I will be like that for you." 4 For the children of Israel shall abide for many days without king and with- out prince, without offering, without image, without ephod and without terafim. 5 Then the children of Israel shall gather together and see the LORD their God and Dauid their king, and they shall fear the LORD and his goodness in the last days.

CHAPTER 4

1 Hear the word of the LORD, children of Israel, for the LORD is at variance with the inhabitants of the land, for there is no truth, nor mercy, nor knowledge of God in the land. 2 Swearing, lying, killing, stealing, whoring, and blood touching blood. 3 Therefore the land shall be ravaged, and all that dwell there- in shall be removed, together with the beasts of the field and the beasts of the sea, and the fish of the sea also shall be taken away. 4 But let no one rebuke or take back anoth- er, for your people are like those who rebuke the priest. 5 Therefore you shall fall by day, and the Prophet shall fall with you by night, and I will destroy your mother. 6 My people are destroyed for lack of knowledge; because thou hast rejected knowledge, I will also re- ject thee, that thou mayest not be a priest to me; and because thou hast forgotten the Lawe of thy God, I will also forget thy children. 7 As they have increased, so have they sinned against me; therefore I will reduce their glory to shame. 8 They feed on the sins of my people, and lift up their minds in their iniquity. 9 And there shall be such a people, such a priest, for I will visit their ways and reward their deeds. 10 For they shall eat and not have enough; they shall commit adultery and not increase, because they have neglected to devote them- selves to the LORD. 11 Prostitution and wine and new wine will take away their

hearts. 12 My people take counsel with their supplies and their staff instructs them, because the spirit of fornication has led them into error and they have turned away from their God. 13 They sacrifice on the tops of your mountains and burn incense on the hills, under the oils, poplars and elm, because their shade is good; therefore your daughters shall be prostitutes and your wives shall be harlots. 14 I will not visit your daughters when they are harlots, nor your spouses when they are harlots, for they separate themselves from the harlots and sacrifice with the harlots; therefore the people who do not understand fall. 15 Even if you, Israel, play the harlot, do not sin of Iu- dah: do not come to Ghilgal, do not go to Bet- auen, and do not swear, "The LORD exists." 16 For Israel is rebellious like a rebellious sheep. Now the LORD will feed him like a lamb in a wide place. 17 Ephraim is greedy for idols: let him alone. 18 Their drunkenness stinks, they have prostituted themselves; their rulers love to say with shame, "Bring yourselves." 19 The wind has enclosed them in its wings, and they will be ashamed of their sacrifices.

CHAPTER 5

1 O priests, listen to this, listen to the house of Israel, listen to the house of the king, for judgment is upon you, for you have been a snare on Mizpah and a net on Tabor. 2 Yet they have been profound in rejecting slaugh- ter, though I have rebuked them all. 3 I know Ephraim, and Israel is not hidden from me; for now, O Ephraim, you have become a har- lot, and Israel is defiled. 4 They will not turn to their God, because the spirit of fornication is in their bowels, and they have not known the LORD. 5 The pride of Israel testifies it in their faces; therefore Israel and Ephraim shall fall in their iniquity; Iudah also shall fall with them. 6 They will go with their sheep and their heifers to see the LORD, but they will not find him, for he has departed from them. 7 They have transgressed against the LORD, because they have begotten alien sons; now a month will destroy them with their portions. 8 Blow the trumpet to Gibeah, and the shau- me to Ramah; cry to Beth-auen, after thee, O Benjamin. 9 Ephraim shall be desolate in the day of reproach; among the tribes of Israel I have made known the truth. 10 The princes of Iudah were like those who stray from the borders; therefore I will pour out my wrath on them like water. 11 Ephraim is oppressed and destroyed in judgment, because he willingly followed the command. 12 Therefore I will be to Ephraim like a moth, and to the house of Judah like a carrion. 13 When Ephraim saw his sickness and Judah his wound, Ephraim went to Assur and sent to King Iareb, but he could not heal you or cure you of your wound. 14 For I will be to Ephraim as a lyre, and as a lyre to the house of Iudah: I, that is, will spit myself out, and go away: I will carry away, and none shall save her. 15 I will go away and re- turn to my place, until they acknowledge their guilt and see me; in their affliction they shall see me diligently.

CHAPTER 6

1 Come and return to the LORD, for he has stripped and will restore, he has wounded and will restore. 2 After two days he will restore vs, and on the third day he will raise vs, and we will lie before him. 3 Then we shall have knowledge and know the LORD; his coming forth is prepared as the morning, and he shall come as the rain and as the last rain

upon the earth. 4 O Ephraim, what shall I do with you? O Iudah, how shall I entwine thee? For your goodness is like a morning cloud, and like the morning dew it goes away. 5 There- fore I took out the prophets: I slew them with the words of my mouth, and thy judgments were as the light that goes out. 6 For I desired mercy and not sacrifice, and the knowledge of God more than sacrifices. 7 But they, as men, transgressed the boundary; there they transgressed against me. 8 Gilead is a city of those who work iniquity, and it is defiled with blood. 9 As the ears of corn wait for a man, so the company of priests kill on the road by common consent, because they work wicked- ness. 10 I have seen wickedness in the house of Israel; there is prostitution in Ephraim; Is- rael is defiled. 11 Yes, Iudah prepared a plant for you, while I wanted to restore the captivity of my people.

CHAPTER 7

1 When I would have healed Israel, the in- iquity of Ephraim was discovered, and the wickedness of Samaria, for they have acted falsely; the thief goes in, and the robber goes out. 2 They do not consider in their hearts that I remember all their wickedness; now their own intrigues have assailed them; they are before my eyes. 3 By their wickedness they make the king and the princes happy with their lies. 4 They are all adulterers and are like leaven warmed by the baker, who does not stop making rays and kneading the dough until it is leavened. 5 This is the day of our king; the princes have made him drunk with pitchers of wine; he stretches out his hand to the scorners. 6 For they have prepared their hearts like a wineskin, while they lie in wait; their baker sleeps all night; in the morning he burns like a flame of fire. 7 They are all like a hen and have disobeyed their judgments; all their kings have fallen; there is no one among them who calls on me. 8 Ephraim has min- gled with the people. Ephraim is like a cake on the hearth that is not turned over. 9 Foreign- ers have consumed his strength, and he does not realize it; yes, gray hares are here and there about him, but he does not realize it. 10 The pride of Israel bears witness to his face, and they do not return to the LORD their God and visit him for all that. 11 Ephraim also is like a deceived dog, devoid of heart; they turn to Egypt, they go to Assur. 12 But when they depart, I will spread my net over them, and will drag them down like the scoundrels of the earth: I will chastise them as their community has heard. 13 Woe to them, because they have fled from me; destruction shall come upon them, because they have transgressed against me; though I have redeemed them, they have spoken lies against me. 14 They did not cry out to me with their hearts when they huddled on their beds; they gathered themselves together for wine and horn and rebelled against me. 15 Though I have strengthened and empowered their arm, they imagine to do evil against me. 16 They turn back, but not to the Most High; they are like a deceitful weapon; their princ- es shall fall by the sword through the fury of their tongue; this shall be their mockery in the land of Egypt.

CHAPTER 8

1 Put the trumpet to your mouth; he will come like an eagle against the house of the LORD, because they have transgressed my counsel and transgressed my peace. 2 Israel will cry out to me, "My God, we know you." 3 Israel

has forsaken what is good; the enemy will pursue him. 4 They have made them- selves a king, but not of me; they have made themselves princes, and I knew it not; of their silver and their gold they have made idols; therefore they shall be destroyed. 5 Your calfe, O Samaria, has cast you out; my wrath is kin- dled against them; how long shall they remain without innocence! 6 For it came from Israel; the worker made it, so it is not God; but the calf of Samaria shall be torn in pieces. 7 For they have sown the wind, and shall reap the whirlwind; it has no stall; the shoot shall bear no fruit; if so be, foreigners shall destroy it. 8 Israel is exhausted; now it will be among the Gentiles as a vessel in which there is no pleasure. 9 Because they have gone to Assur, they are like a wild axle alone; Ephraim has hired breeders. 10 Nevertheless, though they have hired themselves among the nations, yet now I will gather them, and they shall grieve a little, because of the burden of the king and the princes. 11 Because Ephraim has made many altars to sin, his altars shall be to sin. 12 I wrote to them the great things of my Lawe, but they were regarded as a strange thing. 13 They sacrificed meat for the sacrifices of my offerings and ate it, but the LORD did not accept them; now he will remember their in- iquity and visit their sins; they will return to Egypt. 14 For Israel has forgotten her Maker and builds Temples, and Iudah has increased strong cities; but I will send a fire on her cities and destroy her palaces.

CHAPTER 9

1 Do not rejoice, O Israel, like the other peo- ples, because you have turned away from your God, and have made a reward work on all the horns. 2 The stream and the wine shall not feed them, and the new wine shall run out in her. 3 They shall not dwell in the land of the LORD, but Ephraim shall return to Egypt, and they shall eat vnclean things in Assur. 4 They shall not offer wine to the LORD, and their sacrific- es shall not be acceptable to him, but shall be to them as the bread of mourning; everyone who eats of it shall be defiled, for their bread for their souls shall not enter the house of the LORD. 5 What then shall ye do on the solemn day, and on the day of the Lord's feast? 6 For it is true that they are gone from destruction, but Egypt shall gather them up, and Memphis shall bury them; and the nettle shall possess the pleasant places of their habitation, and the ear shall be in their tabernacles. 7 The days of visitation have come, the days of reward have come: Israel shall know it: the prophet is a fool, the spiritual man is mad for the multi- tude of your iniquities, therefore the hatred is great. 8 The keeper of Ephraim should be with my God; but the Prophet is a snare for all his deeds, and a hatred in the house of his God. 9 They are deeply ensnared, they are corrupt as in the days of Gibeah; therefore he will re- member their iniquity, he will visit their sins. 10 I found Israel as the grapes in the wilder- ness; I saw your fathers as the ripe fig tree at its first budding; but they went to Baal- Peor and separated themselves from that infamy, and their abominations were according to their cries. 11 Ephraim, their glory shall flee as a bird: from birth, from childbirth, and from conception. 12 Though they bear their children, I will deprive them of their man- hood; yea, woe to them when I depart from them. 13 Ephraim, as I have said, is like a tree of Tyre planted in a cottage; but Ephraim shall bear her children to the slayer. 14 O LORD, give them: what wilt thou give them? Give them a naked woman and a dry breast. 15 All their wickedness is in Ghilgal, for I hate them

there; for the wickedness of their intentions I will drive them out of my house: I will not es- teem them any more; all their princes are re- bellious. 16 Ephraim is stricken, its roots are withered; they cannot bear fruit; yea, though they bear fruit, I will kill the dearest of their bodies. 17 My God will cast them out, because they have not obeyed him, and they will wan- der among the nations.

CHAPTER 10

1 Israel is an emptied vine, but she has borne fruit to herself, and according to the quanti- ty of her fruit, she has increased her altars; according to the goodness of their land, they have made beautiful images. 2 Their hearts have gone astray; now they will be in defeat; he will tear down their altars, he will destroy their images. 3 For now they will say, "We have no king, because we have not feared the LORD"; and what should a king do against them? 4 They have spoken words, swearing falsely in making a convention; so judgment grows like a worm in the furrows of the field. 5 The inhabitants of Samaria will be afraid because of the going down of Bet- Auen, for her inhabitants will forsake her, and her Chemarim, who relied on her for her glory, will depart from her. 6 It shall also be brought to Assur, as a gift to king Iareb: and Ephraim shall be ashamed, and Israel shall be ashamed of his counsel. 7 As for Samaria, its king will be destroyed like a sponge on water. 8 The places of worship in Auen shall also be destroyed, as the sin of Israel; the thorn and the thistle shall grow on their altars, and they shall say to the mountains, "Run against," and to the hills, "Fall against." 9 O Israel, you have sinned since the days of Gibeah; there they have remained; the battle of Gibeah against the sons of iniquity has not touched them. 10 It is my desire to chastise them, and the people will gather against them, when they gather into their two furrows. 11 Ephraim is like a heifer subjected to threshing, but I will pass through his weak neck; I will cause Ephraim to ride: Iudah shall plow, and Iaakob shall break his clods. 12 Sow righteously for yourselves, reap according to the measure of mercy, break your fallow ground, for it is time to see the LORD, until he comes and roots righteousness upon you. 13 But you have plowed wickedness, you have reaped iniquity, you have eaten the fruit of lies, because you have trusted in your own lusts and in the mul- titude of your strong men, 14 for this reason an uproar shall arise among your people, and all your ammunition shall be destroyed, just as Shalman destroyed Bet-Arbell on the night of the battle; the mother and the children were torn to pieces. 15 So shall Bet-el do to- ward you, because of your wickedness; in one morning the king of Israel shall be destroyed.

CHAPTER 11

1 When Israel was a child, I called them and brought my son out of Egypt. 2 They called them, but they turned away from them: they sacrificed to Baalim and burned incense to the images. 3 I led Ephraim also, as one car- ried them; but they did not see that I had healed them. 4 I led them with cords of man and with bands of linen, and I was to them as one who takes away the yoke from their knees, and I gave them meat. 5 No more shall he return to the land of Egypt, but As- sur shall be his king, because they refused to cooperate. 6 The sword shall come upon her cities, and shall consume her walls, and shall destroy them because of their

own counsel. 7 My people have rebelled against me; though they have called them to the highest level, no one has been willing to exalt them. 8 How will I give you, Ephraim? How will I deliver you, Israel? How will I make you like Admah? How will I put you as Zeboim? My heart has turned within me; my repentances have piled up. 9 I will not execute the fire of my wrath, I will not return to destroy Ephraim, for I am God and not man, the Holy One in your midst, and I will not enter the city. 10 They shall walk after the LORD; he shall roar like a lion; when he roars, the children of the West shall be afraid. 11 They shall fear as a sparrow from Egypt, and as a lily from the land of Assur; and I will place them in their houses, saith the LORD. 12 Ephraim misleads me with lies, and the house of Israel with deceit; but Iudah still rules with God and is faithful with the saints.

CHAPTER 12

1 Ephraim feeds on the wind and follows the east wind; he increases lies and destruction daily; they make an agreement with Assur and the oil is carried to Egypt. 2 The LORD also has a dispute with Iudah and will visit Iaakob, according to his desires; according to his works, he will reward him. 3 He took his brother by his bosom, and by his strength he had power with God, 4 He had power over the angel and went before him; he wept and praised him; he found him in Bet-el, and there he talked with him. 5 Yea, the LORD God of hosts, the LORD himself is his memorial. 6 Therefore turn to your God; keep mercy and judgment, and still hope in your God. 7 He is Canaan; he has the scales of deceit in his hand, and he makes himself heard to oppress. 8 Ephraim said, Although I am rich, I have grown rich in all my labors; they will find no iniquity in me, no wickedness. 9 Though I am the LORD your God from the land of Egypt, yet I will make you dwell in tabernacles, as in the days of the solemn feast. 10 I have spoken also by the Prophets, and multiplied visions, and made similitudes by the ministry of the Prophets. 11 Is there iniquity in Gilead? Cer- tainly they are vain; they sacrifice heifers to Ghilgal, and their altars are like heaps in the furrows of the field. 12 And Iaakob fled to the county of Aram, and Israel got himself a wife, and for a wife he kept sheep. 13 By a prophet the LORD brought Israel out of Egypt, and by a prophet he was restored. 14 But Ephraim provoked him with his places; therefore his blood shall be upon him, and his reproach shall be rewarded by his Lord.

CHAPTER 13

1 When Ephraim spoke, there was trem- bling; he exalted himself in Israel, but he sinned in Baal and died. 2 Now they sinned more and more, and built themselves imag- es cast with their silver, and idols according to their understanding; they are all the work of craftsmen; they say to one another, as they sacrifice a man, "Let them kill the chalices." 3 Therefore they shall be as the morning cloud and as the morning dew that passes away, as the coffee that blows with a wind of air from the earth, and as the smoke that comes out of the chimney. 4 But I am the LORD your God from the land of Egypt, and you shall know no other God but me, for there is no other God but me. 5 I knew you in the wilderness, in the land of drought. 6 As in their pastures, so they were full; they were satiated and their hearts were exalted; therefore they forgot me. 7 I will be to them as a true lion and as a leop- ard on the way to Assur. 8 I will

meet them, like a parturient being robbed of her young, and I will make a breach in their hearts, and I will kill them like a lion; the wild beast will tease them. 9 O Israel, one has destroyed you, but in me is your help. 10 I am: where is thy king, who would help thee in all thy cities, and thy judges, of whom thou hast said, Give me a king and princes? 11 I gave you a king in my wrath, and took him away in my anger. 12 The iniquity of Ephraim is bound, his sin is hidden. 13 The sadness of a woman pining comes upon him; he is a wise son, otherwise he would not have stood still at that time, as at the time of the birth of sons. 14 I will redeem them from the power of death: I will deliver them from death: O death, I will be thy death; O death, I will be thy destruction; repentance is hid from mine eyes. 15 Even as he makes his way among his brethren, there shall come an east wind, and the wind of the LORD shall come from the wilderness, and his vein shall dry up, and his fountain shall run dry; he shall pluck out the treasure of all pleasant vessels.

CHAPTER 14

1 Samaria shall be desolate, because she has rebelled against her God; they shall fall by the sword; their children shall be torn in pieces, and their women with children shall be torn. 2 O Israel, return to the LORD your God, for you have fallen because of your iniquity. 3 Take the words, turn to the LORD and say to him, "Remove all iniquity and receive with kindness, so we will render the accounts of our lies." 4 Assur shall no more leap, nor shall we ride horses, nor shall we say to the works of our hands, "You are our gods," for in you the LORD finds mercy. 5 I will heal their re- bellion: I will let them go free, for my wrath is turned away from him. 6 I will be as the dew to Israel; he shall grow like a lily and fix his roots like the trees of Lebanon. 7 His branch- es shall spread out; his beauty shall be like the olive tree, and his fragrance like Lebanon. 8 Those who dwell under its shadow will return home; they will recover like wheat and flour- ish like the vine; its fragrance will be like the wine of Lebanon. 9 Ephraim will say, "What more shall I do with idols? I have heard it and looked upon it: I am like a green fir tree; upon me is thy fruit." Who is wise and will under- stand these things? And who is prudent and will know them? For the ways of the Lord are right, and the righteous shall walk in them, but the wicked shall fall.

JOEL

CHAPTER 1

1 The word of the LORD addressed to Ioel the son of Pethuel. 2 Hear this, O elders, and lis- ten to all the inhabitants of the land, whether such a thing happened in your days or in the days of your fathers. 3 Tell it to your children and let your children tell it to their children and their children to another generation. 4 What is left of your palmer has been eaten by the grasshopper, the residue of the grasshop- per has been eaten by the caterpillar, and the residue of the caterpillar has been eaten by the caterpillar. 5 Awake, ye drunkards, weep and howl, all ye wine drinkers, because of the new wine, for it shall be taken out of your mouths. 6 Yea, upon my land comes a nation, mighty and nameless, whose teeth are like the teeth of a lyre, and he has the arms of a great lyre. 7 He makes my vineyard vanish, and brings down the bark of my fig tree; he strips it and throws it down; its branches have turned

white. 8 Like a virgin clothed in sackcloth for the husband of her youth. 9 The house of the LORD is bereft of food and drink; the priests, the ministers of the LORD, are fleeing. 10 The field is wasted, the land mourns, for the grain is destroyed, the new wine has dried up, and the oil has gone to waste. 11 Shame on you, O husbandmen; howl, O vinedressers, for the grain and the bark, for the hardest of fields has perished. 12 The vine has withered, the fig tree has decayed, the pomegranate, the palm tree, the apple tree, and all the trees of the field have withered; surely honey has with- ered for the sons of men. 13 Cling and lament, you priests, howl, you ministers of the altar, come and lie all night in sackcloth, you min- isters of my God, because the food offering and the drink offering has been taken away from the house of your God. 14 Make a fast, call a solemn assembly, gather the elders and all the inhabitants of the land to the house of the LORD your God, and cry out to the LORD, 15 "Alas, the day, for the day of the LORD is at hand, and it comes as a destruction from the Most High." 16 Is not the flesh cut off before our eyes? And mirth and joy from the house of our God? 17 The seeds are rotten under their clods; the granaries are broken, for the grain is withered. 18 The beasts have grown moldy; the herds of cattle have become impoverished because they have no pasture, and the flocks of sheep have been destroyed. 19 O LORD, to you I will cry, because the fire has ravaged the wild pastures, and the flame has burned all the trees of the countryside. 20 The beasts of the country also cry out to you, because the streams have dried up, and fire has destroyed the pastures of the wilderness.

CHAPTER 2

1 Blow the trumpet in Zion and shout on my holy mountain; let all the inhabitants of the land tremble, for the day of the LORD has come, for it is near. 2 A day of darkness and gloom, a day of clouds and darkness, as the morning sprinkled on the mountains, so there is a great people and a mighty one; there has been none like this from the begin- ning, nor will there be after it, until the years of many generations. 3 A fire blazes before him and behind him a flame blazes; the land is like the garden of Eden before him and be- hind him a desolate wilderness, so that noth- ing escapes him. 4 His sight is like the sight of horses and like the sight of horsemen, run- ning. 5 Like the sound of the psalteries on the mountaintops, like the sound of a flame of fire devouring stubble, like a numerous peo- ple preparing for battle. 6 Before his face the peoples will tremble; all faces will be black- ened. 7 They will run like strong men, and they will push toward the walls like men of war; each one will go on his way, and they will not stop in their paths. 8 None shall push the other, but each shall walk his own way; and when they fall under the sword, they shall not be wounded. 9 They will run to and fro in the city, they will run on the walls, they will climb over houses and enter through windows like thieves. 10 And the earth shall tremble before him, and the heavens shall be shaken, and the sun and the moon shall be darkened, and the stars shall withdraw their radiance, 11 And the LORD will make his journey before his army, for his army is very great, for it is strog that does his word; for the day of the LORD is great and very terrible, and who can en- dure it? 12 Therefore even now the LORD says, "Turn to me with all your hearts, with fasting, with weeping, and with mourning, 13 enfran- chise your hearts and not your garments, and turn to the LORD your God, for he is thank- ful and merciful, slow to

anger and of great goodness, and he repents of wickedness. 14 Who knows whether he will return and re- pent and leave behind him a blessing and an offering of food and an offering of wine to the LORD your God? 15 Sound the trumpet in Zion, sanctify a fast, call a solemn assembly. 16 Gather the people, sanctify the congrega- tion, gather the elders, gather the children and those who suck the breast; bring out the bridegroom from his chamber and the bride from her chamber. 17 Let the priests, the min- isters of the LORD, weep between the porch and the altar, and say, "Spare your people, O LORD, and do not give your inheritance to the heathen, that the heathen may rule it. For they should say in the midst of the people, "Where is their God?" 18 Then the LORD will be mindful of his land and spare his people. 19 Yes, the LORD will answer and say to his peo- ple, "Behold, I will send you grain and wine and oil, and you shall be filled with it; and I will no longer make you a reproach among the heathen, 20 but I will turn the army of the north away from you, and will cause it to fall into a dry and desolate land, with its face to- ward the eastern sea and its extremity toward the farthest sea, and its stench shall go up and its corruption shall go up, because it has ex- alted itself to do this. 21 Fear not, O land, but rejoice and be glad, for the LORD will do great things. 22 Do not be afraid, you who live in the fields, for the pastures of the wilderness are green, for the tree gives its fruit, the fig tree and the vine give their strength. 23 Re- joice therefore, ye children of Zion, and trust in the LORD your God, for he hath given you the ray of righteousness, and will send down for you the ray, that is, the first ray and the last ray in the first month. 24 The granaries shall be full of grain, and the presses shall abound with wine and oil. 25 I will render unto you the years that the cicada hath eaten, and the woodworm, and the caterpillar, and the palmer, my great guest whom I have sent among you. 26 So you shall eat and be filled, and you shall praise the Name of the Lord your God, who has dealt wonderfully with you; and my people shall never be ashamed. 27 You shall also know that I am in the midst of Israel and that I am the Lord your God and no other, and my people shall never be ashamed. 28 Afterward I will send forth my Spirit upon all flesh, and your sons and your daughters shall prophesy; your old men shall dream dreams, and your young men shall see visions, 29 And also upon the servants and the elders in those days will I give my Spirit. 30 And I will do wonders in the heavens and on the earth: blood, fire, and pillars of smoke. 31 And the sun shall be turned into darkness, and the moon into blood, before the great and terrible day of the LORD comes. 32 But who- soever shall call upon the Name of the LORD shall be saved; for in Mount Zion and in Ieru- sale there shall be delirium, as the LORD hath said, and in the remnant the LORD shall call.

CHAPTER 3

1 For behold, in those days and at that time, when I shall bring back the captivity of Judah and Jerusalem, 2 I will also gather all the na- tions, and bring them down to the valley of Jehoshaphat, and there I will plead with them for my people and for my inheritance Israel, whom they have scattered among the nations and divided my land. 3 They have cast lots for my people, and have given their son to the harlot, and have sold the girl for wine, that they may drink. 4 Yea, and what have ye to do with me, O Tyre and Zidon and all the coun- tries of Palestine? Will you give me a reward? And if you reward me, swiftly and quickly I will

give you your reward on your head: 5 For you have taken my silver and my gold, and have carried to your temples my good and pleasant things. 6 Also the sons of Judah and the sons of Jerusalem you have sold to the Greeks to send them far from their borders. 7 Behold, I will bring them out of the place where you have sold them, and I will render the reward on your heads, 8 And I will send your sons and your daughters into the hand of the sons of Judah, who will sell them to the Sabeans, to a distant people, for the LORD has said it. 9 Spread this among the nations; prepare war, awaken the mighty; all men of war prepare and come. 10 Turn your plows into swords and your thirsts into spears; let the weak say, "I am strong." 11 Gather your- selves together, come all you heathen and gather around you; there the LORD will throw down the strongest men. 12 Wake up the hea- then and come to the valley of Iehoshaphat, for there I will sit down to judge all the hea- then around. 13 Sit ye down, for the vintage is ripe; come, come down, for the cellar is full; yea, the winepresses are exhausted, for their wickedness is great. 14 O multitude, O multi- tude, come to the valley of the threshing, for the day of the LORD is near in the valley of the threshing. 15 The sun and the moon will be darkened, and the stars will withdraw their light. 16 The LORD will withdraw from Zion and make his journey from Jerusalem, and the heavens and the earth will be shaken, but the LORD will be the hope of his people and the strength of the children of Israel. 17 Then you shall know that I am the LORD your God, who dwells in Zion, my holy Mountain; then Jerusalem shall be holy, and there shall be no more strangers passing through it. 18 In that day the mountains shall pour forth new wine, the hills shall flow with milk, all the banks of Iudah shall flow with waters, and from the House of the LORD shall come forth a foun- tain that shall bathe the valley of Shittim. 19 Egypt shall be a desert, and Edom a desolate heath, because of the insults of the sons of Iu- dah, because they have shed innocent blood in their land. 20 But Iudah shall dwell forever, and Jerusalem from generation to genera- tion. 21 For I will cause their blood to cease, which I have never caused to cease, and the LORD will dwell in Zion.

AMOS

CHAPTER 1

1 The words of Amos, who was among the hearers at Tecoa, which he spoke over Israel in the days of Vzziah, king of Judah, and in the days of Jeroboam, son of Joash, king of Israel, two years before the earthquake. 2 He said, "The LORD will turn away from Zion and turn away his journey from Jerusalem; the shepherds' dwellings will perish, and the top of Carmel will wither away." 3 Thus says the LORD: "For three transgressions of Damas- cus and for four I will not turn to it, because they have threshed Gilead with threshing in- struments of hyrus. 4 Therefore I will send a fire into the house of Hazael and destroy the palaces of Ben-Hadad. 5 I will also breach the walls of Damascus, I will cut off the inhabi- tant of Bikeath-auen and the one who holds the scepter from Beth-eden, and the people of Aram will go into captivity to Kir, says the LORD. 6 Thus says the LORD: "For three trans- gressions of Azzah and for four, I will not turn to it, for it has taken all captives captive to shut them up in Edom. 7 Therefore I will send a fire on Azzah's walls and destroy her palac- es. 8 I will cut off the inhabitant from Ashdod and the one who holds the scepter from Ash- kelon; I will turn my hand toward Ekron, and the rest of the Philistines will perish, says the LORD

God. 9 Thus says the LORD: "For three transgressions of Tyre and for four I will not turn to it, because they have closed all cap- tivity in Edom and have not remembered the brotherly covenant. 10 Therefore I will send a fire on the walls of Tyre and destroy its build- ings. 11 Thus says the LORD: "For three trans- gressions of Edom and for four I will not turn to him, because he has pursued his brother with the sword and forsaken all mercy, and his anger has driven him still further, and his wrath has watched him always. 12 Therefore I will send a fire upon Teman, and it shall de- stroy the palaces of Bozrah. 13 Thus says the LORD, "For three transgressions of the sons of Ammon, and for four, I will not turn to them, because they have kidnapped the par- turients of Gilead, to enlarge their borders. 14 Therefore I will kindle a fire on the walls of Rabbah and destroy its buildings, with shout- ing in the day of battle and with a tempest in the day of whirlwind. 15 Their king shall go into captivity, he and his princes together, says the LORD.

CHAPTER 2

1 Thus says the LORD: "For three transgres- sions of Moab and for four I will not be con- verted to it, because it has reduced the bones of the king of Edom to lime. 2 Therefore I will send a fire upon Moab, which shall destroy the palaces of Kerioth, and Moab shall die with tumults, with shouting, and with the sound of a trumpet. 3 And I will cut off iudicio from its centers, and I will kill all its princes with it, says the LORD. 4 Thus says the LORD: "For three transgressions of Iudah and for four I will not turn to it, because they have cast away the Lawe of the LORD and have not kept his commands, and their lies have led them astray according to the way of their fathers. 5 Therefore I will send a fire upon Iudah, and it shall destroy the palaces of Jerusalem. 6 Thus says the LORD: "For three transgressions of Israel and for four, I will not turn away from him, for they have reduced the righteous to silence and the poor to hunger. 7 They plunge the head of the poor man into the dust of the earth and disturb the ways of the earth; and a man and his father shall enter into a mayde to dishonor my holy Name. 8 They shall lie down on cloths spread as a pledge by every altar and drink the wine of the condemned in the house of their God. 9 I destroyed be- fore you the Amorrean, whose height was like that of cedars and whose strength was equal to that of trees; yet I destroyed its fruit from without and its roots from beneath. 10 More- over I brought you out of the land of Egypt and led you four hundred years through the wilderness, to possess the land of the Am- orites. 11 And I chose your sons as prophets and your young men as Nazarites. Is it not so, O children of Israel, that the LORD says? 12 But you gave the Nazarites wine to drink and commanded the prophets not to prophesy. 13 Behold, I am pressed under you as one press- es a chariot that is full of boot. 14 Therefore the runaway will lose speed, and the strong will not strengthen his strength, nor will the mighty be able to save his life. 15 He who wields the bow will not stand, and he who is swift of foot will not escape, nor will he who rides a horse have his life saved. 16 He that hath strong courage among strong men shall flee naked in that day, saith the LORD.

CHAPTER 3

1 Listen to the word which the LORD speaks against you, O children of Israel, and against all the family that I brought

forth from the land of Egypt, saying, "You are the only ones I know among all the families of the earth; therefore I will visit you for all your iniqui- ties, 2 You alone I have known among all the families of the earth; therefore I will visit you for all your iniquities." 3 Can two walk togeth- er if they do not agree? 4 Can a lion roar in the forest when he has no prayers? Or can a lion cry out from his den, when he has taken nothing? 5 Can a bird perhaps fall into a snare on the earth, where there is no one to make it fall? Or will it take the trap from the earth, without having taken anything? 6 Or will a trumpet be blown in a city, and the people not be frightened? Or will there be death in a city and the LORD will not have done it? 7 Surely the LORD God will do nothing, but will en- trust his secret to his servants, the prophets. 8 The lion has roared: who shall not be afraid? The Lord God hath spoken: who can prophe- sy? 9 Proclaim in the palaces of Ashdod, and in the palaces of the land of Egypt, and say, Gather yourselves together in the mountains of Samaria; behold the great tumults that are in the midst thereof, and the oppressed that are in the midst thereof. 10 For they know not how to do good, saith the LORD, and keep vi- olence and robbery in their palaces. 11 There- fore thus says the LORD God, "An adversity will always come around the county and will bring down your strength, and your palaces will be stripped." 12 Thus says the LORD, "As the shear removes from the lion's mouth two legs, or a piece of an eare, so shall the children of Israel be taken away, who dwell in Samaria in the corner of a bed, and in Damascus as in a couch." 13 Hear and testify in the house of Iaakob, says the LORD God, the God of hosts. 14 In the day when I visit the transgressions of Israel, I will also visit the altars of Bethel, and the horns of the altar shall be broken and fall to the ground. 15 And I will smite the house of winter with the house of summer, and the houses of yuorie shall perish, and the great houses shall be consumed, saith the LORD.

CHAPTER 4

1 Hear this word, you animals of Bashan who are on the mountain of Samaria, who oppress the poor and destroy the needy, and say to your masters, "Bring and make drink." 2 The Lord God has sworn by his sanctuaries that, alas, the day will come when he will take you away with thorns and your posterity with fishhooks. 3 You shall come out of the breach- es in every place in the city, and cast your kindred out of the palace, says the LORD. 4 Come to Bet-El and transgress, to Ghilgal and multiply transgressions; bring your sacrific- es in the morning and your tithes after three years. 5 Offer thanksgiving of blood, publish and proclaim the free offerings, for this is like unto you, O children of Israel, saith the LORD God. 6 Therefore I have given you the cleansing of your teeth in all your cities and the scarcity of bread in all your places, yet you have not returned to me, says the LORD. 7 I also withheld rain from you, when there was still three pennies for the hardest, and I rained it on one city and did not rain it on an- other city: some of it was rained on, and the part on which it did not rain withered away. 8 So two or three cities came to one city to drink water, but were not satisfied; yet you did not return to me, says the LORD. 9 I have struck you with storms and with mildew; your great gardens, your vineyards, your fig trees and your olive trees have been destroyed by the palm tree; yet you have not returned to me, says the LORD. 10 I have sent among you a pestilence like that of Egypt; I have slain your young men with the sword and carried away your

horses; I have caused the stench of your tents to enter your nostrils always; yet you have not returned to me, says the LORD. 11 I drove you out, just as God drove out Sod- om and Gomorah, and you were like a cinder torn from the fire; yet you did not return to me, says the LORD. 12 Therefore, so will I do with you, O Israel; and because I will do this with you, prepare to meet your God, O Israel. 13 For behold, he who forms the mountains, creates the wind, and declares to man what is his thought, who darkens the morning and walks upon the places of the earth, the Lord God of hosts is his name.

CHAPTER 5

1 Listen to this word that I address to you, as a lament of the house of Israel. 2 The virgin Israel has fallen, and will not rise again; she is forsaken on her land, and there is no one to raise her up. 3 For thus says the LORD God, The city that went out a thousand shall leave a hundred; and the city that went out a hun- dred shall leave ten to the house of Israel. 4 For thus saith the LORD unto the house of Israel, Look unto me, and ye shall be well. 5 But do not look at Bet-el, nor enter into Ghil- lie, nor go to Beer-sheba, for Ghillie will go into captivity, and Bet-el will be reduced to nothing. 6 Look to the LORD, and you will feel good, if it does not break out like a fire in the house of Iosef, and there will be no one to put it out in Beth-el." 7 They turn judgment into worms and forsake righteousness in the earth. 8 He creates the Pleiades and Orion, turns the shadow of death into morning and makes the day as dark as night; he calls the waters of the sea and brings them forth upon the open land; the LORD is his name. 9 He strengthens the destroyer against the mighty, and the destroyer comes against the strong. 10 They have hated him who rebuked at the gate, and they have abhorred him who speaks well. 11 For your treading is on the poor, and you take away their burdens of grain; you have built houses of stone, but you will not dwell in them; you have planted pleasant vineyards, but you will not drink their wine. 12 For I know your manifold transgressions and your griev- ous sins: they afflict the righteous, they ap- propriate rewards, and they oppress the poor in your gate. 13 Therefore the prudent shall be silent in that time, for it is a time of euphoria. 14 Seek good and not evil, that you may live; and the Lord God of hosts will be with you, as you have said. 15 Hate wickedness, appreciate good, and establish judgment in the gate; it may be that the LORD God of hosts will be merciful to the remnant of Iosef. 16 Therefore the LORD God of hosts says thus, "There shall be mourning in all the streets, and it shall be said in all the ways, 'Alas, alas'; the peasants shall be called to mourning, and those who know how to mourn shall be called to mourn- ing." 17 And in all the vineyards there shall be wailing, for I will pass through you, says the LORD. 18 Woe to you who desire the day of the LORD; what have you to do with it? The day of the LORD is darkness and not light. 19 As if a man flees from a bruise and a beast comes to him, or he enters the house, puts his hand on the wall, and a serpent bites him. 20 Shall not the day of the Lord be dark and not bright? That is, dark and not bright? 21 I hate and abhor your feast days, and will not sniff in your solemn assemblies. 22 Even if you offer me roasts and foods, I will not ac- cept them; and I will not consider the foods of peace of your fat beasts. 23 Turn away from me the multitude of your songs (for I will not listen to the melody of your violets). 24 And let judgment descend like waters and justice like a mighty river. 25 Have you

offered sac- rifices and sacrifices to me in the wilderness for forty years, O house of Israel? 26 But you have endured Siccuth, your king, and Chiun, your images and the stars of your gods, which you have made yourselves. 27 Therefore I will cause you to go into captivity beyond Damas- cus, says the LORD, whose Name is the God of hosts.

CHAPTER 6

1 Woe to them that sit still in Zion and trust in the moutaine of Samaria, which were fa- mous in the beginning of the nations; and the house of Israel came to them. 2 Go to Calneh and see; from there go to Hamath, the great one, and then go down to Gath of the Philis- tines: are they better than these kingdoms, or is the border of their land greater than your border? 3 Ye that turn away the day of eve, and draw near to the place of iniquity? 4 They lie down on beds of heifer, and stretch them- selves on their beds, and eat the lambs of the flock and the calves of the stable. 5 They sing to the sound of violas; they equip themselves with musical instruments like Dauid. 6 They drink wine by the bowlful and anoint them- selves with the most important ointments, but no one is sorry for Ioseph's suffering. 7 Therefore now they will go into captivity with the first ones who go into captivity, and the sorrow of those who have been stretched out is near. 8 The LORD God has sworn by him- self, says the LORD God of hosts, "I abhor the excellencies of Iaakob, and I hate his palaces; therefore I will deliver up the city with all that is therein. 9 If ten men remain in a house, they shall die. 10 And his vncolle shall take him and bury him to bring the bones out of the house, and he shall say to him who is at the sides of the house, "Is there anyone still with you?" And he will answer, "No one." Then he will say, "Restrain your tongue, lest we re- member the Name of the Lord." 11 For behold, the LORD commands and will smite the great house with breaches and the little house with splits. 12 Horses will run on rocks or you will plow with oxen, because you have turned judgment into gall and the fruit of righteous- ness into worms. 13 You trust in a thing from nothing; you say, "Have we not procured horns in our own strength?" 14 But behold, I will raise up against you a nation, O house of Israel, saith the LORD God of hosts, and they shall afflict you, from the entrance of Hamath unto the border of the wilderness.

CHAPTER 7

1 Thus the Lord God showed me, and be- hold, he formed herb gatherers at the be- ginning of the harvest of this last herb; well, this happened in the last herb, after the kings had been mowed. 2 When they had finished eating the grass of the land, I said, "O LORD God, spare, I beseech thee: who shall lift up Iaakob, for he is little." 3 The LORD repented of this. It shall not be so, saith the LORD. 4 Thus the LORD God showed me, and behold, the LORD God called fire to judgment, and it ravaged the great deep and devoured part of it. 5 Then I said, "O Lord God, stop, I beseech thee: who shall raise up Iaakob, for he is little." 6 The LORD repented for this. This also shall not be, saith the Lord God. 7 Then he showed me again: and behold, the LORD stood upon a wall made of wire with a thread in his hand. 8 The LORD said to me, "Amos, what do you see? And I answered, "A line." Then the LORD said, "Behold, I will put a line in the midst of my people of Israel, and I will no longer pass by them." 9 The places of Izhak shall be des- olate, and the

temples of Israel shall be de- stroyed; and I will rise up against the house of Jeroboam with the sword." 10 Then Amaziah, priest of Bet-el, sent word to Jeroboam, king of Israel, "Amos has conspired against you in the midst of the house of Israel; the land is not able to bear all his words." 11 For Amos says, "Jeroboam shall die by the sword, and Israel shall be led into captivity from her country." 12 Amaziah also said to Amos, "O seer, go away, flee to the land of Judah, eat your bread, and prophesy there." 13 But prophesy no more in Beth-el, for it is the king's chapel and the king's court." 14 Then Amos answered Amazi- ah, "I was not a prophet, nor was I a son of prophets, but I was a herdsman and a gather- er of wild figs. 15 The LORD took me with him as I followed the flock and said, "Go, prophe- sy to my people Israel. 16 Hear therefore the word of the LORD. You say, "Do not prophesy against Israel or speak against the house of Izhak." 17 Therefore thus saith the LORD, Thy wife shall be a harlot in the city, thy sons and thy daughters shall fall by the sword, and thy land shall be despoiled by the line; thou shalt die in a defiled land, and Israel shall surely go into captivity from her land.

CHAPTER 8

1 So the Lord God showed me, and behold, a basket of summer fruit. 2 And he said, "Amos, what do you see? And I said, "A basket of summer fruit." Then the LORD said to me, "The end has come upon my people of Israel; I will pass by them no more." 3 In that day the songs of the Temple shall be howled, saith the LORD God; many dead bodies shall be in ev- ery place; they shall cast them away with si- lence. 4 Hear this, O you who swallow up the poor, that the needy of the earth may eat, 5 Saying, "When the new month shall pass, that we may sell the grain, and the Sabbath, that we may expose the grain, and make small the Ephah and great the shekel, and counterfeit the weights by deceit? 6 To buy the poor for silk, and the needy for shoes, and to sell the refuse of the grain. 7 The LORD swore by the excellence of Iaakob, "I will never forget any of their works." 8 Will not the earth and all its inhabitants tremble because of this? It will rise up like a flood, it will be swept away and drowned as by the flood of Egypt. 9 In that day, says the LORD God, I will cause the sun not to set for anyone, and I will darken the earth in the clear day. 10 I will turn your feasts into mourning and all your songs into lam- entation; I will put sackcloth on all gifts and stockings on every head; I will make it like the mourning of an only son and its end like a bitter day. 11 Behold, the days come, says the LORD God, when I will send a famine in the land, not of bread nor of thirst for water, but of hearing the word of the LORD. 12 They shall wander from sea to sea, and from the north to the east they shall run to and fro to seek the word of the LORD, but they shall not find it. 13 In that day young virgins and young men will die of thirst. 14 Those who will swear by the sin of Samaria and say, "Your God, O Dan, is good," and the manor of Beer-sheba is good, will fall and never rise again.

CHAPTER 9

1 I saw the LORD standing on the altar, and he said, "Strike the lintel of the door, that the posts may shake, and break them in pieces, that is, the heads of all of them, and I will kill the last of them with the sword; whoever flees from them, he will not flee, and whoever flees from them, he will

not be disappointed. 2 Though they dig into hell, my hand will catch them; though they climb into hell, I will bring them down. 3 Even if they hide on the top of Carmel, I will search for them and bring them out from there; and even if they hide from my sight in the bottom of the sea, from there I will command the serpent, and he will bite them. 4 And even if they go into captivity before their enemies, from there I will com- mand the sword, and it will kill them; and I will set my eyes on them for wickedness and not for good. 5 And the LORD God of hosts shall touch the land, and it shall melt, and all that dwell therein shall die, and it shall rise up like a flood, and be drowned as by the flood of Egypt. 6 He builds his spheres in the heavens, and has laid the foundations of his globe of el- ements on the earth; he calls the waters of the sea and pushes them upon the open land; the LORD is his name. 7 Are you not like the Ethiopians toward me, O children of Israel, says the LORD? Have I not brought Israel out of the land of Egypt, the Philistines out of Caph- tor, and Aram out of Kir? 8 Behold, the eyes of the Lord God are upon the sinful kingdom, and I will utterly destroy it from the earth. Yet I will not destroy the house of Iaakob, says the LORD. 9 For verily I will sort and sift the house of Israel among all the nations, as one sifts grain in a sieve; yet not the least stone shall fall on the earth. 10 But all the sinners of my people who say, "The time will not come, nor will it hasten to come," shall die by the sword. 11 In that day I will raise up the tab- ernacle of Dauid, which has fallen, and I will close its breaches, and make its ruins shine, and I will rebuild it, as in the days of old, 12 That they may possess the remnant of Edom and all the heathen, for my Name is invoked upon them, says the LORD, who does this. 13 Behold, the days are coming, saith the LORD, when the plowman shall touch the mower, and the thresher of grapes the one who sows; and the mountains shall bring down sweet wine, and all the hills shall melt. 14 I will bring back my people of Israel; they will rebuild the abandoned cities and inhabit them; they will plant vineyards and drink the wine there- of; they will make gardens and eat the fruit thereof. 15 I will plant them in their land, and they shall not be torn from their land which I have given them, says the LORD your God.

OBADIAH

1 The vision of Obadiah. Thus says the LORD God against Edom: "We have heard a voice from the LORD, and an ambuscade has been sent among the heathen; arise and rise up against her to fight. 2 Behold, I have made you small among the heathen; you are greatly despised. 3 The pride of your heart has de- ceived you; you who dwell in the clefts of the rocks, whose dwelling place is the sea, who say in your heart, "Who will bring me down to the ground? 4 Though you exalt yourself like the eagle and make your nest among the stars, from there I will bring you down, says the LORD. 5 Did thieves come to you by night? How did they silence you? Would they not have stolen until they had had enough? If the harvesters came to you, would they not have left grapes? 6 How do you seek the things of Esau and seek his treasures? 7 All the men of thy confederacy have forsaken thee to thy borders; the men who were at peace with thee have deceived thee, and have prejudiced against thee; they that eat thy bread have wounded thee; there is no understanding in him. 8 Shall I not destroy in that day, saith the LORD, the wise men from Edom, and under- standing from the mount of Esau? 9 And your strong men, O Teman, shall be put to flight, for all those from the mount of Esau shall be slaughtered. 10 For your cruelty against your

brother Iaakob, shame shall come upon you, and you shall be removed forever. 11 When you stood on the other side, in the day when foreigners were carrying away its goods and foreigners were entering its gates and casting lots on Jerusalem, you were like one of them. 12 But you were not to look upon the day of your brother, in the day that he had become a stranger, nor were you to see the sons of Judah again, in the day of their destruction; you were not to speak with pride in the day of affliction. 13 You were not to enter the gate of my people in the day of their destruction, you were not to look upon their suffering in the day of their destruction, and you were not to lay your hands on their substance in the day of their destruction. 14 Neither should you stop in the byways to cut off the way for those who flee, nor should you shut up their remains in the day of their affliction. 15 For the day of the LORD is at hand, upon all the heathen; as you have done, it shall be done to you; your reward shall return upon your head. 16 For as you have drunk on my holy moun- tain, so shall all the heathen drink continual- ly; yea, they shall drink and swallow, and be as though they had not been. 17 But on Mount Zion there shall be delight, and it shall be holy, and the house of Iaakob shall possess its goods, 18 And the house of Iaakob shall be a fire, and the house of Ioseph a flame, and the house of Esau as stubble; and they shall kindle and be consumed; and there shall be no rem- nant of the house of Esau, for the LORD hath spoken it. 19 They shall possess the southern slope of the mountain of Esau and the plain of the Philistines; they shall possess the fields of Ephraim and the fields of Samaria, and Benjamin shall have Gilead. 20 The captives of the army of the children of Israel who were among the Canaanites shall possess as far as Zarephath, and the captives of Jerusalem, which is in Sefarad, shall possess the cities of the south. 21 Those who say shall come to Mount Zion to judge the mount of Esau, and the kingdom shall be of the Lords.

JONAH

CHAPTER 1

1 The word of the LORD came also to Ionah the son of Amittai, and he said 2 "Arise, go to Nineveh, that great city, and cry out against it, for their wickedness has come down to me." 3 But Ionah arose to flee to Tarshish from the presence of the LORD, and went down to Joppa; and he found a ship going to Tarshish; and he paid the price, and got on it to go with them to Tarshish from the presence of the LORD. 4 But the Lord sent a great wind into the sea, and there was a great storm in the sea, so that the ship was about to be broken. 5 Then the sailors were fright- ened, and cried each one to his own God, and threw overboard the goods that were in the ship to lighten it; but Ionah had gone down into the sides of the ship, and he lay down and fell fast asleep. 6 Then the captain of the ship came to him and said, "What do you mean, O sleeper? Get up, call upon your God, if God wills to think of you, lest we perish." 7 Then they said each to his companion, "Come and let us cast lots, that we may know for what cause this will has been done toward you." So they cast lots, and the lot fell on Ionah. 8 Then they said to him, "Tell me, for what rea- son has this amends been made? What is your profession? Where do you come from? What is your county? What people are you from?" 9 He answered them, "I am a Jew, and I fear the LORD, the God of Heauen, who made the sea and the dry land." 10 Then the men were greatly afraid and said to him, "Why have you done this?" (for the men knew

that he had fled from the presence of the LORD, because he had spoken to them). 11 Then they said to him, "What shall we do for you, that the sea may be calmed? (for the sea was troubled and agitat- ed). 12 And he said to them, "Take me and cast me into the sea; so the sea will calm down for you, for I know that because of me this great storm is upon you." 13 And the men rowed to bring him ashore, but they could not, for the sea was churning and disturbing them. 14 Therefore they cried out to the LORD and said, "We beseech thee, O LORD, we beseech thee, let them not die for this man's life, and let not his innocent blood be shed, for thou, LORD, hast done as it pleased thee." 15 Then they took Iona and threw him into the sea, and the sea ceased to rage. 16 Then the men feared the LORD greatly, and they offered sacrifices to the LORD and made vows. 17 Now the LORD had prepared a great fish to swallow up Iona; and Iona remained in the belly of the fish three days and three nights.

CHAPTER 2

1 Then Ionah prayed to the LORD his God from the belly of the fish, 2 and said, "I cried out to the LORD in my affliction, and he heard me; from the belly of hell I cried out, and you heard my voice. 3 For thou hadst cast me into the depths, into the midst of the sea, and the floods encircled me; all thy waves and all thy billows passed before me. 4 Then I said, "I was cast out of your sight, but I will still look toward your holy Temple." 5 The waters encircled my soul; the depths surrounded me, and weeds wrapped my head. 6 I went down to the bottom of the mountains; the earth with its bars surrounded me forever, but you saved my life from the pit, O Lord, my God. 7 When my soul fainted within me, I remem- bered the LORD; and my prayer came to you in your holy Temple. 8 Those who rely on lying vanities give up their merits. 9 But I will sac- rifice to you with a voice of thanksgiving, and I will pay what I have done: salvation is of the LORD." 10 The LORD spoke to the fish, and it drove Iona away to the dry land.

CHAPTER 3

1 The word of the LORD came to Ionah the second time, saying 2 "Get up, go to Nineveh, that great city, and announce to it the preach- ing I have done to you." 3 And Ionah arose and went to Nineveh, according to the word of the LORD; Nineveh was a great and excellent city, with three days' journey. 4 Iona began to en- ter the city with a day's journey, and cried out, saying, "Four more days, and Nineveh will be destroyed." 5 Then the people of Nineveh paid homage to God, proclaimed a fast, and clothed themselves in sackcloth, from the greatest to the least. 6 The king of Nineveh learned that he had risen from his throne, stripped himself of his robe, covered himself with sackcloth, and sat down under the ash- es. 7 Then he proclaimed and said throughout all Nineveh (by the advice of the king and his nobles), "Let no man or beast, oxen or sheep, taste anything, nor feed on it, nor drink wa- ter. 8 But let men and beasts clothe them- selves in sackcloth and cry out with strength to God; yea, let every one turn from his evil way and from the wickedness in his hand. 9 Who can say whether God will be converted, repent, and turn from his fierce wrath lest we perish? 10 God saw their works, that they turned from their evil ways; and God repent- ed of

what he had said he would do against them, and he did not do it.

CHAPTER 4

1 For this reason Ionah was very sorry and angry. 2 Then he prayed to the LORD and said, "Please, LORD, wasn't this what I was saying when I was still in my county? For this reason I had prevented fleeing to Tarshish, for I knew that you are a gracious and merciful God, slow to anger and of great goodness, and that you regretted the euthanasia. 3 Therefore now, O Lord, take life from me, for it is better for me to die than to live." 4 Then the LORD said, "Are you right to be angry?" 5 Then Ionah went out of the city and stood on the eastern side of the city and built himself a boot and stood under it in the shade to see what would be done in the city. 6 And the LORD God pre- pared a raft and sprung it upon Ionah, that it might overshadow his head and relieve him of his grief. So Ionah rejoiced greatly over the garland. 7 But God prepared a worm at the rising of the morning of the next day, which struck the gourd and withered it. 8 When the sun rose, God also prepared an eastern and fervent wind; and the sun beat down on Iona's head, and she fainted and wished in her heart to die and said, "It is better for me to die than to lie." 9 God said to Ionah, "Are you right to be angry about the gourde?" And he answered, "I do well to be angry to the point of death." 10 Then the LORD said, "You took pity on the gourd for which you did not toil and did not make it grow, which came in one night and died in one night, 11 Shall I not spare Niniè, that great city where there are six tens of thousands of people who cannot distinguish between their right hand and their left hand, and also much cattle?

MICAH

CHAPTER 1

1 The word of the LORD which was spoken to Micah the Morashite in the days of Iotham, Ahaz, and Hezekiah, king of Judeah, and which he spoke concerning Samaria and Je- rusalem. 2 Hear, ye peoples, hear, O land and all that is in it, and let the Lord God be witness against you, and you, Lord, from his holy tem- ple. 3 For behold, the LORD comes out of his place, and goes down and tramples the places of the earth. 4 And the mountains shall melt under him, and the valleys shall be cleared as wax before the fire, and as the waters that go down. 5 All this is due to the wickedness of Iaakob and the sins of the house of Israel; what is the wickedness of Iaakob? Is it not Samaria? And what are the places of Iudah? Is it not Jerusalem? 6 Therefore I will make Samaria a heap of fields and a vineyard to be planted; I will cause its stones to fall down and destroy its foundations. 7 All her Grauan images shall be broken, and all her gifts shall be burned with fire, and all her idols I will de- stroy, because she collected them with a har- lot's wages, and they shall return to a harlot's wages. 8 Therefore I will wail and howl: I will strip me of my clothes, and I will be naked: I will wail like dragons, and weep like ostrich- es. 9 For her plagues are grievous, because she has come into Iudah; the enemy has come to the gate of my people, to Jerusalem. 10 Do not declare it in Gath, and do not mourn, because the house of Aphrah has crumbled to dust. 11 You who dwell in Shaphir, go together naked in shame; the one who dwells in Zaanan will not go out in mourning in Beth-Ezel; the en- emy will receive his

position from you. 12 For the inhabitant of Maroth has tried to do good, but the LORD has given him the stroke at the gate of Jerusalem. 13 O you, inhabitant of La- chish, who are the chief of the price, you are the beginning of sin for the daughter of Zion, for the transgressions of Israel have been found in you. 14 Therefore you shall give gifts to Moresheth Gath; the houses of Achzib shall be as a sheet for the kings of Israel. 15 I will give thee an heir, O inhabitant of Maresha; he shall come to Adullam, the glory of Israel. 16 I will make thee stronger, and I will overshad- ow thee for thy delicate children; magnify thy boldness like the eagle, for they have gone into captivity to thee.

CHAPTER 2

1 Woe to those who imagine iniquity and work wickedness on their beds; when the morning is clear, they practice it because their hand has power. 2 They strike fields and take them by violence, and houses and carry them away; so they oppress a man and his house, and a man and his estate. 3 Therefore thus says the LORD, "Behold, against this family I have established a plague for which you shall not wring your necks or go so proud, for this time is ended. 4 In that day they will take a parable against you, and they will complain with mournful lamentation and say, "We are terribly wasted; he has changed the portion of my people; how has he taken it away to re- store it to me? He has destroyed our fields." 5 Therefore you shall have no one to draw a cord in the congregation of the LORD. 6 Those who prophesied, "Do not prophesy. They shall not prophesy, and they shall not be ashamed. 7 O you who are called of the house of Iaakob, is the Spirit of the Lord abridged? Are these his works? Are not my words good for those who walk uprightly? 8 But he who was my people yesterday has gone up on the other side, as against an enemy; they strip off their fine garments those who pass by peacefully, as if returning from war. 9 The women of my people you have driven out of their beauti- ful homes, and from their children you have continually taken away my glory. 10 Arise and go away, for this is not your rest; for it is pol- luted, it will destroy you, and with grievous destruction. 11 If a man walks in the Spirit and lies falsely, saying, "I will prophesy over wine and alcohol," he shall be the prophet of this people. 12 I will surely gather you, O Iaa- kob; I will surely gather the remnant of Israel: I will gather them as the sheep of Bozrah, as the flock in the midst of his crowd; the cities shall be full of brutish men. 13 And the tray of the wreckers shall go before them; they shall go out, and pass through the gate, and come out, and their king shall go before them, and the LORD shall be upon their heads.

CHAPTER 3

1 And I said, "Listen, I pray you, O chiefs of Iaakob and princes of the house of Israel: should you not know judgment? 2 But they hate good and love evil; they tear their skin and flesh from their bones. 3 They shall also eat the flesh of my people, and they shall flay the skin thereof, and break the bones, and break them in pieces, as for the pot, and as meat in the cauldron. 4 Then they shall cry to the LORD, but he will not hear them; at that time he will hide his face from them, because they have done wickedness in their works. 5 Thus says the LORD: "Concerning the proph- ets who deceive my people, they bite them with their teeth and cry peace, but if a man does

not enter their mouths, they prepare war against him, 6 Therefore the night shall be to you a vision, and the darkness shall be to you a diuination, and the sun shall be quenched upon the prophets, and the day shall be dark- ened upon them. 7 Then shall the seers be shamed, and the southerners confounded; yea, all shall yield up their lips, because they have no answer from God. 8 Nevertheless I am full of power, through the Spirit of the LORD, of judgment and strength to declare to Yaakob his transgression and to Israel his sin. 9 Observe this, I pray you, chiefs of the house of Iaakob and princes of the house of Israel: they abhor judgment and ignore all equity. 10 They build Zion with blood and Je- rusalem with iniquity. 11 Their leaders judge for rewards, their priests teach for money, and their prophets prophesy for money; yet they lean on the Lord and say, "Is not the Lord among you? No one else can come to you." 12 Therefore Zion, for your sake, shall be plowed like a field, Jerusalem shall be a heap, and the mountain of the house shall be like the places of the forest.

CHAPTER 4

1 But in the last days it shall come to pass that the mountain of the House of the LORD shall be prepared on the top of the mountains, and shall be exalted on the hills, and the peoples shall flock there. 2 Yea, many nations will come and say, "Come, let us go to the Moun- tain of the LORD and to the House of the God of Iaakob, and he will teach us his ways and we will walk in his paths; for the Word will go out from Zion and the word of the LORD from Jerusalem." 3 And he shall judge in the midst of many peoples, and shall rebuke the mighty nations afar off, and they shall break their swords into nerfs, and their spears into saddles; nation shall not lift up sword against nation, neither shall they learn to fight any more. 4 They shall sit every man under his vineyard and under his fig tree, and no one shall frighten them, for the mouth of the LORD of hosts has spoken it.5 For all peoples shall walk each in the name of his own God, and we shall walk in the Name of the Lord our God forever.6 In that same day, says the LORD, I will gather the one that stands still, I will gather the one that was cast out and the one that I afflicted. 7 I will make of the one that stood still a remnant, and of the one that was cast out a mighty nation; and the LORD will reign over them on Mount Zion from now on forever. 8 And you, O tower of the flock, the strong refuge of the daughter of Zion, shall come to you, and the first dominion and kingdom shall come to the daughter of Jeru- salem. 9 Now why do you weep with lamen- tations? Is there no longer a king in you? Has your counselor disappeared? For sadness has seized you, like a woman in sorrow. 10 Suffer and mourn, O daughter of Zion, like a woman in distress; for now thou shalt depart from the city and dwell in the fields, thou shalt go to Babel, but there thou shalt be delivered; there the LORD will redeem thee from the hand of thine enemies. 11 Now also many nations have gathered against you, saying, "Zion shall be condemned, and our eye shall look upon Zion." 12 But they do not know the thoughts of the LORD; they do not understand his counsel, for he will gather them together like sheep in the stable. 13 Rise up and thresh, O daughter of Zion, for I will make thy horns thunderous, and I will make thy hoes coarse, and thou shalt tear in pieces many peoples; and I will consecrate their riches to the LORD, and their substance to the ruler of the whole world.

CHAPTER 5

1 Now gather your garrisons, O daughter of garrisons; he has laid siege against you; they shall smite the enemy of Israel with a rod on his breast. 2 Thou, Bet-leem-Ephratah, art small among the thousands of Judah, yet out of thee shall come forth for me him who shall be the ruler of Israel, whose coming forth is from the beginning and from eternity. 3 Therefore he will let them go until the time when she who gives birth is traumatized; then the rest of their brothers will return among the children of Israel. 4 He will stand and feed on the strength of the LORD and the majesty of the Name of the LORD his God, and they will still remain alive, for now he will be mag- nified to the ends of the world. 5 He shall be our peace when Assur enters our land; when he treads down our palaces, then we shall raise up against him ten sheikhs and eight principal men. 6 They shall destroy Assur with the sword, and the land of Nimrod with their swords; so shall Assur be delivered when he enters our land, and when he tramples our borders. 7 The remnant of Iaakob shall be in the midst of many peoples, as a dew of the LORD, and as the leaves of the earth that wait not for man, and hope not for the sons of Adam. 8 And the remnant of Iaakob shall be among the Gentiles, in the midst of many peoples, like the lion among the woods, and like the bullock among the flocks of sheep, which, when it goes down, tramples it down and tears it to pieces, and no one can deliver it. 9 Your hand will rise on your adversaries, and all your enemies will be eliminated. 10 In that day, says the LORD, I will cut your horses from your ankles and destroy your chariots. 11 I will cut off the cities of your land and de- stroy all your fortresses. 12 I will cut off from thy hand thy charmers, and thou shalt have no more southerners. 13 I will also cut off thy idols and thy images from thy bowels, and thou shalt no more worship the works of thy hands. 14 And I will make your groups vanish from your bowels; so I will destroy your en- emies. 15 And in my wrath and indignation I will perform a deed upon the heathen that they have never heard.

CHAPTER 6

1 Hear now what the LORD says, "Arise and contend before the mountains, and let the hills hear your speech." 2 Hear, O mountains, the complaint of the LORD and the mighty foundations of the earth, for the LORD has a complaint against his people, and he will be pleased with Israel. 3 O my people, what have I done to you, or where have I taken you, testify against me. 4 I brought you out of the land of Egypt, and ransomed you from the house of servants, and sent Moses, Aaron and Miriam before you. 5 O my people, remember now what Balak king of Moab had devised and what Balaam son of Beor had answered him, from Shittim to Ghilgal, that you may know the justice of the LORD. 6 With what shall I present myself before the LORD and prostrate myself before his God? Shall I pres- ent myself before him with year-old roasts and goblets? 7 Will the LORD be pleased with thousands of rams or ten thousand riuers of oil? Shall I give my first load for my transgres- sion, that is, the fruit of my body, for the sin of my soul? 8 He has shown you, O man, what is good and what the LORD requires of you: to act justly, to love mercy, to humble yourself and to walk with your God. 9 The journey of the LORD crieth unto the city, and the wise man

shall see thy name: hearken unto the rod, and he that applied it. 10 Are there still the treasures of wickedness in the house of the wicked, and the poor measure, which is abominable? 11 Shall I justify the wicked scales and the bag of deceitful weights? 12 For its rich are full of cruelty, its inhabitants have told lies, and their tongue is deceitful in their mouth. 13 Therefore I will make you suffer, I will smite you and make you desolate because of your sins. 14 Thou shalt eat, and thou shalt not be satisfied, and thy casting out shall be in the midst of thee, and thou shalt take posses- sion, but thou shalt not fail; and that which thou failest, I will give to the sword. 15 Thou shalt sow, but thou shalt not reap; thou shalt treasure olives, but thou shalt not anoint thy- self with oil; thou shalt make sweet wine, but thou shalt not drink wine. 16 For the statutes of Omri and all the provisions of the house of Ahab have been observed, and you shall walk according to their counsels, that I may make you a wilderness, and the inhabitants of the land a whistle; therefore you shall bear the re- proach of my people.

CHAPTER 7

1 Woe to me, for I am as the vintage and as the grapes of the vintage; there is no cluster to eat; my soul longed for the first ripe fruit. 2 The good man has disappeared from the earth, and there is no righteous man among men; everyone is out for blood; everyone hunts his brother with a net. 3 To make up for the weakening of their hands, the prince asked and the judge demanded a reward; therefore the great man spoke of the corruption of his soul; so they wrapped it up. 4 The best of them is like a bramble bush, and the fairest of them is sharper than a barbed hedge; the day of thy watch and visitation cometh; then shall be their confusion. 5 Do not trust in a friend, and do not trust in a counselor; keep your lips from her who lies in your bosom. 6 For the son betrays his father, the daughter rebels against her mother, the daughter in distress against her mother in distress, and a man's enemies are the men of his own house. 7 Therefore I will look to the LORD: I will wait for God, my savior; my God will hear me. 8 Do not venture against me, O my enemy; though I fall, I will rise again; when I sit in darkness, the LORD will be a light to me. 9 I will bear the wrath of the LORD, because I have sinned against him, until he pleads my cause and executes judg- ment for me; then he will bring me into the light and I will see his righteousness. 10 Then she who is my enemy shall look upon it and be ashamed of her who said to me, "Where is the Lord your God? My eyes shall look upon her; now she shall be cast down as the miro of the streets. 11 This is the day when your walls will be built; today the decree will be cancelled. 12 In this day shall they also come to thee from Assur, from the strong cities and fortresses unto the river, from sea to sea, and from mountain to mountain. 13 Never- theless the land will be desolate because of those who dwell in it and because of the fruits of their inventions. 14 Feed your people with your rod, the flock of your inheritance (which dwells lonely in the woods) as in the midst of Carmel; make them feed in Bashan and in Gilead, as in days of old. 15 According to the days of your coming out of the land of Egypt, I will give them gifts of wonderful things. 16 The nations shall see and be bewildered for all their power; they shall put their hand over their mouth, and their ears shall be dead. 17 They will lick the dust like a serpent, they will come out of their holes like worms; they will be afraid of the LORD our God, and they will fear because of you. 18 Who is a God like unto thee, that taketh away iniquity,

and pass- eth over the transgression of the remnant of his inheritance? He will not recede from his wrath forever, for he is pleased with mercy. 19 He will turn and have compassion on our iniquities and will cast all their sins into the bottom of the sea. 20 You will respect your faithfulness to Iaakob and mercy to Abraham, as you swore in the past to our fathers.

NAHUM

CHAPTER 1

1 The burden of Nineueh. The book of the vi- sion of Nahum the Elkeshite. 2 God is jealous, and the LORD withdraws; and the LORD of wrath, the LORD takes vengeance on his ad- versaries, and reserves for himself the wrath of his enemies. 3 The LORD is slow to wrath, but he is great in power, and he will not surely exonerate the wicked; the LORD moves in the wind and in the storm, and the clouds are the dust of his feet. 4 He maneuvers the sea and drains it, and drains all the rivers: Bashan and Carmel are devastated, and Lebanon is rav- aged. 5 The mountains tremble for him, the heights melt, and the earth is scorched before him, yea, the world and all who dwell in it. 6 Who can stand before his wrath or who can remain in the fire of his wrath? His wrath is as powerful as fire, and rocks are broken by him. 7 The LORD is good and strong in the day of trouble and knows those who trust in him. 8 But passing from thence like a flood, he will utterly destroy the place where he is, and darkness will pursue his enemies. 9 What do you plan to do against the LORD? He will make a total destruction; affliction will not arise a second time. 10 For he shall come like thorns folded into one another, and like drunkards in their drunkenness; they shall be consumed like stubble utterly withered. 11 Out of you comes one who imagines evil against the LORD, an evil counselor. 12 Thus saith the LORD, Though they be quiet, and though they be many, yet so shall they be re- moved when it passeth away: though I have afflicted thee, I will afflict thee no more. 13 For now I will break his yoke from thee, and will tear thy bonds in pieces. 14 The LORD hath given a command concerning thee, that thy name be sown no more: from the house of thy gods will I cut off the bronze and the molten image: I will make it thy grave, because thou art vile. 15 Behold on the mountains the feet of him who declares and publishes peace: O Iudah, keep your solemn feasts, keep your vows, for the wicked shall pass by thee no more; he is utterly removed.

CHAPTER 2

1 The destroyer has come before your face; preserve your ammunition, watch your way, make your bonds strong, increase your strength with might. 2 For the LORD hath turned away the glory of Iaakob, as the glory of Israel, because the emptiers have emptied them, and spoiled their vine shoots. 3 The shield of his strong men is reddened, the val- iant are in skins of leather; the carets shall be as in fire and flame in the day of his prepa- ration, and the fir trees shall tremble. 4 The chariots shall break forth in the streets, they shall run to and fro through the streets, they shall seem like lightning, they shall move like thunderbolts. 5 He will remember his strong men; they will stumble as they go; they will rush to his walls, and the defense will be pre- pared. 6 The gates of the walls will be opened, and the palace will melt away. 7 Huzzab, the queen, shall be led

into captivity, and her handmaidens shall lead her as with the act of a duke, beating their breasts. 8 But Nineveh has always been like a pool of water, yet they will flee. They stand, they stand, they cry out, but no one looks back. 9 Pluck out the siluio, pluck out the precious coin, for there is noth- ing left to keep, and there is no more glory for all the vessels of value. 10 It is empty, hollow and wasted, the heart melts, the knees break, sadness is in all houses, and the faces of all are blackened. 11 Where is the dwelling place of the lions and the pasture of the lions' cubs? Where the lion and the lions walked, and the lions stirred, and no one drove them away. 12 The lion tore himself for his cubs, he wor- ried about his lions, he filled his holes with prayers and his dens with noodles. 13 Behold, I come to you, says the LORD of hosts, and I will bury his whelps in smoke, and the sword will destroy your long lions, and I will cut your spoyle from the earth, and the voice of your messengers will no longer be heard.

CHAPTER 3

1 O bloody city, it is all full of lies and robbery; prayer does not go away: 2 The noise of the whip, the rattling of the wheels, the beating of the horses, and the leaping of the horses. 3 The horseman lifts up the shining sword and the glittering spear, and a multitude is slain, and the corpses are many; there is no more trace of their corpses; they stumble over their dead bodies, 4 because of the multitude of fornications of the harlot who is beautiful and a lover of witchcraft, and who makes the people pass through her harlotry and the na- tions through her witchcraft. 5 Behold, I will come upon thee, saith the LORD of hosts, and I will peel off thy skirts upon thy face, and I will show to the nations thy filthiness, and to the kingdoms thy shame. 6 I will cast filth upon thee, and I will make thee vile, and I will set thee as a beast of slaughter. 7 And it shall come to pass that all who look on thee shall flee from thee, and shall say, Niniè is de- stroyed; who shall have mercy on her? Where will I see comforters for you? 8 Are you better than No, which was full of people, lying on the shores and having the waters around it, whose shore was the sea and whose wall came from the sea? 9 Ethiopia and Egypt were her strength, and there was no one else: Put and Lubim were her helpers. 10 Nevertheless she was taken away and went into captivity; even her little children were cut in pieces at the head of all the streets, and fights were thrown for her noble men, and all her righteous men were bound in chains. 11 Thou shalt also be drunk; thou shalt hide thyself and seek help because of the enemy. 12 All your strong cities will be like figs with the first ripe figs, for if they are shaken, they will fall into the mouths of those who eat them. 13 Behold, your peo- ple within you are women; the gates of your land shall be opened to your enemies, and fire shall destroy your walls. 14 Draw waters for the siege, fortify your fortresses, work clay, temper the dough, make strong bricks. 15 Fire will destroy you, the sword will cut you down, devour you like locusts, even though you are multiplied like locusts and multiplied like grasshoppers. 16 Thou hast multiplied thy marches like the stars of Heauen; the locust shall spoil and fly away. 17 Thy princes are like the locusts, and thy captains like the great locusts that stay in the hedges in the days of cold; but when the sun rises, they flee away, and it is not known where they are. 18 Your shepherds sleep, O king of Assur, Your strong men lie on the ground; Your people are scat- tered on the mountains, and no one gathers them. 19 There is no healing for your wounds; your plague

is grievous; all who hear of you clap their hands against you; for on whom has not your wickedness passed continually?

HABAKKUK

CHAPTER 1

1 The burden that the prophet Habakkuk saw. 2 O LORD, how long will I cry out, and you will not hear me! And then I will cry out to you for violence, and you will not help me! 3 Why do you make me see iniquity and make me see sadness? Because before me are ruthlessness and violence, and there are those who spread strife and strife. 4 Therefore peace is dissolved, and judgment does not go forth, because the wicked do deeds against the righteous; therefore judgment is wrong. 5 Look in the midst of the heathen, behold, wonder and marvel, for I will perform a work in your days; you shall not see it, though it be told you. 6 For behold, I raise up the Chal- deans, a sour and furious nation, who will go as far as the breadth of the earth to possess the dwellings that are not theirs. 7 They are terrible and fearful; their judgment and their dignity will come from them. 8 Their horses also are swifter than leopards and fiercer than wolves in the fall; their riders are numerous and come from afar; they fly like the eagle that wants to eat. 9 They will all come and blow; before their faces there will be an east wind, and they will gather prisons like sand. 10 They shall mock kings, and princes shall be a scepter to them; they shall mock every for- tress, for they shall gather dust and take it. 11 Then they will take courage and transgress and behave wickedly, attributing their power to their god. 12 Art thou not, from everlasting, the LORD my God, my Holy One? We shall not die: O LORD, thou hast destined them for judgment, and, O God, hast established them for correction. 13 Thou hast pure eyes, and canst not see wickedness; why dost thou look on transgressors, and hold thy tongue when the wicked doeth violence to the man that is more righteous than he? 14 And it makes men like fish in the sea and like reptiles, who have no master outside them. 15 They take every- thing at an angle; they catch it in their net and gather it into their web, with which they re- joice and rejoice. 16 Therefore they sacrifice to their net and burn incense in their yard, for because of them their portion is fat and their meat plentiful. 17 Should they therefore tend their net and not continually spare to slay the nations?

CHAPTER 2

1 I will stand before my watch, and I will stand before the tower and watch to see what he will say to me, and what I will answer to him who rebukes me. 2 The LORD answered me and said, "Write the vision and make it clear on the tablets, so that he who reads it may run." 3 For the vision is still for a definite time, but at the last he will speak and not lie; even if he tarries, wait, for he will surely come and not stop. 4 Well, he who lifts himself up, his mind is not upright in him, but the unrigh- teous one lays down his way, 5 Yea, verily the proud man is like him that transgresses with wine; therefore he shall not endure, because he has enlarged his desire like hell, and is like death, and cannot be satisfied, but gathers to himself all nations and heaps to himself all peoples. 6 Shall not all these take up a para- ble against him and a proterity against him, and say, "Oh, he who increases what is not his own, how much longer?" and he who stuffs himself with thin clay? 7 Will they not rise up suddenly, to

bite you, and awake, to agitate you, and you will be their prayer? 8 For thou hast pushed many nations, all the remnant of the people shall push thee because of the blood of men, and because of the evil done in the land, and in the city, and in all that dwell therein. 9 He who prepared for himself a refuge for his house, to set his nest there, to escape the power of hell. 10 You have put your own house to shame, destroying many people, and you have sinned against your own soul. 11 For the stone shall weep from the wall, and the flame from the wood shall answer it. 12 Woe to him who builds a city with blood and erects a city with iniquity. 13 Is it not for the LORD of hosts that the people will toil in the fire? The people will toil for their vanities. 14 For the earth shall be full of the knowledge of the glory of the LORD, as the waters run the sea. 15 Woe to him that maketh his neigh- bor drunk: thou makest thy heart drunk, and makest him drunk also, that thou mayest see their merits. 16 Thou hast filled thyself with shame for glory's sake; drink thou also, and be stripped: the cup of the LORD's right hand shall be turned to thee, and the shame shall be for thy glory. 17 For the cruelty of Lebanon shall smite thee, even as the spit of the beasts, which made them aphrodis, because of the blood of men, and because of the evil done in the land, and in the city, and in all them that dwell therein. 18 What good is the image, for he who made it has made it an image and a teacher of lies, though he who made it trusts in it, when he makes foolish idolatries. 19 Woe to him who says to the wood, "Awake," and to the fictitious stone, "Arise, it will teach you"; behold, it is clothed with gold and silver, and there is no breath in it. 20 But the LORD is in his holy Temple; all the earth is silent before him.

CHAPTER 3

1 Prayer of the prophet Habakkuk for the ig- norant. 2 O LORD, I heard your message and was amazed: O LORD, take up your work in the midst of the peoples, in the midst of the years make it known; in wrath remember mercy. 3 God comes from Teman and the Holy One from Mount Paran, Selah. His glory equals the heavens, and the earth is full of his prayer, 4 his splendor was like light; he had horns coming out of his hands, and there was the concealment of his power. 5 Before him pestilence broke out, and before his feet flam- ing flames broke out. 6 He hath stood still and measured the earth; he hath seen and dis- solved the nations; the everlasting mountains are broken, and the ancient hills are bowed down; his ways are everlasting. 7 By his in- iquity I saw the tents of Cushan and the cur- tains of the land of Midian tremble. 8 Has the LORD been angry against the floods? Or has your wrath been against the floods? Or was your anger against the sea, which you rode on your horses? Thy chariots brought salva- tion. 9 Your arm was manifestly lifted up, and the other tribes were a sure word, Selah. you cleansed the land with riuers. 10 The moun- tains saw you and trembled; the stream of water passed by; the depths made a noise and lifted up their hand upon themselves. 11 The sun and the moon stood still in their abode; to the light of your arrows they went, and to the splendor of your spears. 12 You trampled the land with anger and beat the heathen with displeasure. 13 Thou hast departed for the sal- vation of thy people, and for the salvation of thy Anointed; thou hast wounded the head of the house of the ungodly, and hast unhinged its foundations to the neck, Selah. 14 Thou hast smitten with his own weapons the heads of his villages; they went out like a

whirlwind to scatter me; their return was like destroying the poor by stealth. 15 You walked in the sea with your horses on the brink of great waters. 16 When I heard, my belly trembled; my lips trembled at the sight; rottenness crept into my bones, and I trembled in myself, that I might rest in the day of trouble; for when he comes upon the people, he will destroy them. 17 For the fig tree will not blossom, and the vine will not bear fruit; the labor of the olive tree will fail, and the fields will no longer pro- duce honey; the cattle will be cut off from the herd, and there will be no bulls in the stables. 18 But I will put my trust in the LORD: I will put my trust in the God of my salvation. 19 The LORD God is my strength; he shall make my feet like the feet of hinds, and shall make me to walk in my places. To the chief cantor of Neginothai.

ZEPHANIAH

CHAPTER 1

1 The word of the LORD that was spoken to Zephaniah the son of Cushi, the son of Geda- liah, the son of Amariah, the son of Hizkiah, in the days of Jehoshiah the son of Amon, king of Iudah. 2 I will destroy everything from the land, says the LORD. 3 I will destroy man and beast: I will destroy the fish of the ocean and the fish of the sea; the wicked shall go to ruin, and I will cut off man from the land, saith the LORD. 4 I will also stretch out my hand over Judah and over all the inhabitants of Jerusalem, and I will cut off the remnant of Baal from this place and the name of the Chemarim with your priests, 5 and those who worship the hosts of Heauen on the tops of the houses, and those who worship and swear by the LORD and swear by Malcham, 6 those who turn away from the LORD and those who have not sought the LORD and have not sought him. 7 Be elegant in the presence of the LORD God, for the day of the LORD is at hand, for the LORD has prepared a sacrifice and sanctified his places. 8 On the day of the Lord's sacrifice I will visit the princes and the king's sons and all those who are dressed in strange clothes. 9 On that same day I will also visit all those who dance on the thresh- old with such pride and who fill the houses of their masters with cruelty and deceit. 10 In that day, says the LORD, there will be a noise and a cry from the fish gate, a howling from the second gate, and great destruction from the hills. 11 As it is said, "Dwellers of the low place, for the company of the marchers is destroyed; all those who bring silence have been removed." 12 At that time I will search Jerusalem with lights and visit the men who are dazed in their darkness and say in their hearts, "The LORD will do neither good nor evil." 13 Therefore their possessions shall be stripped, and their houses shall be forsaken; they shall build houses, but not inhabit them; they shall plant vineyards, but not drink the wine thereof. 14 The great day of the LORD is near; it is near and hastens greatly, as the day of the LORD; the strong man shall weep bitterly. 15 That day is a day of wrath, a day of trouble and evil, a day of destruction and des- olation, a day of darkness and gloom, a day of clouds and gloom, 16 a day of trumpet and alarm against the strong cities and against the towers. 17 And I will bring distress upon men, who shall walk as blind men, because they have sinned against the LORD, and their blood shall be pulverized as dust, and their flesh as a tongue. 18 Neither their silver nor their gold shall be able to deliver them in the day of the LORD's wrath, but the whole earth shall be destroyed by the fire of his jealousy, for he shall at once make a clean sweep of all that dwell in the land.

CHAPTER 2

1 Gather yourselves together, and gather yourselves together, O nation not worthy to be heard, 2 Before the decree comes, and you are like coffee that passes away in a day, before the fierce anger of the LORD comes upon you, and before the day of the LORD's wrath comes upon you. 3 Look to the LORD, all the peoples of the earth, who have fulfilled his judgment; look to righteousness, look to humility, if you want to be hidden in the day of the LORD's wrath. 4 For Azzah shall be forsaken and Ash- kelon shall be desolate, Ashdod shall be dried up in one day, and Ekron shall be uprooted. 5 To the inhabitants of the sea coast, to the na- tion of the Cherethim, the word of the LORD is against you, O Canaan, land of the Philis- tines, I will destroy you without inhabitants. 6 The shore of the sea shall be inhabited with houses and shelters for shepherds and sheep. 7 That seashore shall be for the remnant of the house of Iudah, who shall feed there; in the houses of Ashkelon they shall lodge for the night, for the LORD their God shall visit them and make their captivity disappear. 8 I have heard the rebuke of Moab and the re- proaches of the sons of Ammon, whereby they have vilified my people and magnified them- selves against their borders. 9 Therefore, as I, the LORD of hosts, the God of Israel, say, Moab shall be like Sodom, and the sons of Ammon like Gomorah, that is, a herding of nets and salt and perpetual desolation; and the remnant of my people shall oust them, and the remnant of my people shall possess them. 10 This they shall have for their pride, because they have reproached and magni- fied themselves against the LORD of hosts. 11 The LORD will be terrible to them, for he will consume all the gods of the earth, and every man will worship him from his place, like all the heathen peoples. 12 You Moors also will be slain by my sword along with them. 13 He shall stretch out his hand against the north, destroy Assur, make Niniue desolate, and be forsaken as a wilderness. 14 The flocks will lie down in its center, and all the beasts of the nations, the pelican and the owl will remain in its guard posts; the voice of the birds will sing in the windows, and desolation will be on the guard posts, because the cedars have been destroyed. 15 This is the city that dwelt care- free, that said in its heart, "I am, and there is no one but me"; how it is reduced to ruin, and how it is the lodging of beasts! Every person who passes by her will approach and wave his hand.

CHAPTER 3

1 Woe to her who is filthy and polluted, to the city that steals. 2 She has not heard the mes- sage, she has not received correction, she has not trusted in the LORD, she has not drawn near to her God. 3 Her princes in her are like roaring lianas; her judges are like wolves at sunset, not leaving her bones until morning. 4 Her prophets are light and wicked people; her priests have polluted the sanctuary; they have torn the law. 5 The righteous LORD is in their midst; he commits no iniquity; every morning he brings forth his judgment, he does not fail; but the wicked do not learn to be ashamed. 6 I have cut off the nations; their streets are desolate: Their cities are destroyed, without men and without inhabitants. 7 I said, Surely thou shalt fear me, thou shalt re- ceive instruction: so their habitation shall not be destroyed, though I have visited them: but they have risen early, and have corrupted all their works. 8 Therefore

wait, says the LORD, until the day when I shall rise up in prayer, for I am determined to gather the nations and to assemble the kingdoms to make my indig- nation, that is, all my fierce anger, heard, for all the earth shall be stricken with the fire of my ielousia. 9 Then I will cause the peoples to have a pure tongue, so that all will call upon the name of the LORD and serve him with one consent. 10 From beyond the shores of Ethiopia, the daughter of my dispersed ones, praying to me, shall bring me an offering. 11 In that day thou shalt not be ashamed for all thy works, whereby thou hast transgressed against me; for then will I remove from the bowels of thee those who have been guilty of thy pride, and thou shalt no more be proud of my holy Mountain. 12 Then I will leave in your pockets a humble and poor people, who will trust in the Name of the LORD. 13 The rem- nant of Israel shall not commit any iniquity, nor shall they speak lies; a deceitful tongue shall not be found in their mouths, for they shall be fed and lie down, and no one shall cause them to run away. 14 Rejoice, daughter of Zion; be glad, O Israel; rejoice and be glad with all your heart, daughter of Jerusalem. 15 The LORD has taken away thy judgments, he has cast out thine enemy; the king of Israel, that is, the LORD, is in the midst of thee; thou shalt see sadness no more. 16 In that day it will be said to Jerusalem, "Do not fear, O Zion; do not let your hands be weak." 17 The LORD your God is mighty in the midst of you; he will say, he will take care of you with joy; he will quiet in his joy, he will take care of you with gladness. 18 After a certain time I will gather the afflicted who have been to you and those who have borne reproach for it. 19 Behold, at that time I will crush all those who afflict you, I will rescue the one who stands firm and gather the one who has been cast out, and I will procure for them praise and fame in all the countries of their shame. 20 At that time I will bring you back and gather you together, for I will give you a name and praise among all the peoples of the earth, when I will turn back your captivity before your eyes, says the LORD.

HAGGAI

CHAPTER 1

1 In the second year of King Darius, in the six- tieth month, on the first day of the month, the word of the LORD came (through the prophet Haggai) to Zerubbabel the son of Shealtiel, prince of Judeah, and to Jehoshua the son of Jehozadak, priest, saying, 2 Thus speaks the LORD of hosts, "This people say, 'The time has not yet come to build the house of the LORD.' 3 Then came the word of the LORD through the minister of the prophet Haggai, who said, "Has the time come for your people to build the house of the LORD? 4 Has the time come for you to dwell in your broken houses and for this house to remain abandoned? 5 Therefore thus says the LORD of hosts, "Consider your ways in your hearts. 6 You have sown much and brought in little; you eat, but you do not have enough; you drink, but you are not full; you clothe yourselves, but you are not at war; and he who earns wages puts it in broken sackcloth. 7 Thus says the LORD of hosts, "Consider your ways in your hearts. 8 Go to the mountains, bring wood and build this house; I will be happy in it and will be glori- fied, says the LORD. 9 Ye sought much, and, behold, it came to little; and when ye brought it home, I blew upon it. And why, says the LORD of hosts? Because of my house which is wasted, and ye run every one to his own house." 10 Therefore the heaven beyond you has withheld from the dew, and the

earth has withheld from its fruit. 11 I called for drought on the earth and on the mountains, on the grain, on the wine, on the oil, and on all that the earth produces: on men, on cattle, and on all the work of the hands. 12 When Zerubba- bel the son of Shealtiel and Iehoshua the son of Jehozadak the priest, with all the rest of the people, heard the message of the LORD their God and the words of the prophet Haggai (as the LORD their God had sent him), the people were afraid before the LORD. 13 Then Haggai, the messenger of the LORD, spoke to the peo- ple in the message of the LORD, saying, "I am with you, says the LORD." 14 And the LORD stirred up the spirit of Zerubbabel the son of Shealtiel, prince of Judah, and the spirit of Je- hoshua the son of Jehozadak, priest, and the spirit of all the rest of the people; and they came and worked in the house of the LORD of hosts, their God.

CHAPTER 2

1 On the fourth and twentieth day of the sixth month, in the second year of King Darius, 2 In the tenth month, on the one and twentieth day of the month, came the word of the Lord through the minister of the prophet Haggai, saying 3 Speak now to Zerubbabel the son of Shealtiel, prince of Judah, and to Jehoshua the son of Jehozadak the priest, and to the remnant of the people, saying 4 Who is left among you who saw this house in its first glo- ry, and as you see it now? Is it not in your eyes, in comparison with it, nothing? 5 But now take courage, O Zerubbabel, saith the LORD, and be comforted, O Iehoshua the son of Je- hozadak the priest; and be strong, all you in- habitants of the land, saith the LORD, and do it, for I am with you, saith the LORD of hosts." 6 According to the word that I promised with you when you came out of Egypt; so my Spir- it shall abide among you, fear not. 7 For thus says the LORD of hosts, "Yet a little while, and I will shake the heavens and the earth, the sea and the dry land: 8 And I will move all nations, and the desire of all nations shall come, and I will fill this House with glory, saith the LORD of hosts. 9 The siluio is mine, and the wealth is mine, saith the LORD of hosts. 10 The glory of the latter House shall be greater than the former, says the LORD of hosts; and I will give peace in this place, says the LORD of hosts. 11 On the fourth and twentieth day of the ninth month, in the second year of Darius, came the word of the Lord to the prophet Haggai, who said, "Thus says the Lord, 12 Thus says the Lord of hosts, "Question now the priests con- cerning the Law and say, 13 If anyone wears holy meat in the skirt of his garment and with his skirt touches bread, or the pot, or wine, or oil, or any other food, shall he be holy?" The priests answered, "No." 14 Then Haggai said, "If a defiled person touches any of these things, will he be holy?" The priests answered, "He will be vncleared." 15 Then Haggai an- swered and said, "So is this people and so is this nation before me, saith the Lord; and so are all the works of their hands, and what they offer here is vnclean. :16 And now, I pray you, consider in your mind: from this day and be- fore, even before a stone was laid upon a stone in the Temple of the LORD: 17 before these things came to pass, when you came to a heap of twenty measures, there were but ten; when you came to the wine chest to bring out fif- ty vessels, there were but twenty. 18 I have smitten you with dross, with mildew, and with hail, in all the labors of your hands; yet you have not turned to me, says the LORD. 19 Consider, I pray you, in your mind, from this day and before, from the fourth and twenti- eth day of the ninth month, that is, from the day when the

foundation of the Temple of the Lord was laid: consider it in your mind. 20 Is the seed still in the barn? The vine, the fig tree, the pomegranate tree, and the olive tree have not yet borne fruit; from this day will I bless you. 21 Again the word of the LORD came to Haggai on the fourth and twentieth day of the month, and he said 22 Speak to Zerubbabel, prince of Judah, and say to him, "I will shake the heavens and the earth, 23 and I will destroy the throne of the kingdoms, I will destroy the strength of the kingdoms of the heathen, I will destroy the chariots and those who ride them, and the horse and the riders will fall, each by his own brother's sword." (In that day, says the Lord of hosts, I will take you, O Zerubbabel my servant, son of Shealtiel, says the Lord, and I will make you as a seal, for I have chosen you, says the Lord of hosts.

ZECHARIAH

CHAPTER 1

1 In the eighth month of the second year of Darius, the word of the Lord came to Zecha- riah the son of Berechiah, the son of Iddo the prophet, who said, "The Lord is greatly displeased with your fathers, 2 The Lord is greatly displeased with your fathers. 3 Therefore say unto them, Thus saith the Lord of hosts, Turn ye unto me, saith the Lord of hosts, and I will turn unto you, saith the Lord of hosts. 4 Do not be like your fathers, to whom the proph- ets of old cried, "Thus says the LORD of hosts, Turn now from your iniquitous ways and from your wicked works"; but they would not listen and did not heed me, says the LORD. 5 Your fathers, where are they? And the Prophets, do they live forever? 6 But did not my words and my statutes, which I commanded through my servants, you Prophets, take hold of your fathers? And they turned back and said, "As the Lord of hosts has determined to do with you, according to our ways and according to our works, so has he done with you." 7 On the fourth and twentieth day of the eleventh month, which is the month of Shebat, in the second year of Darius, came the word of the Lord to Zechariah the son of Berechiah, the son of Iddo the prophet, and said 8 And I saw by night a man riding a red horse; he stood in the midst of the mirror trees, which were in a bottom, and behind him were red horses with white spots. 9 Then I said, "O my Lord, what are these?" And the angel who was speaking to me said, "I will show you what they are." 10 The man who stood among the miry trees answered, "These are those whom the Lord has sent to go through the world." 11 They answered the angel of the Lord who stood among the mirror trees and said, "We have gone through the world; and behold, all the world is still and resting." 12 Then the an- gel of the LORD answered and said, "O LORD of hosts, how long will you be cruel to Jeru- salem and to the cities of Iudah, with which you have been displeased these sixty and ten years? 13 The LORD answered the angel who spoke to me with good and comfortable words. 14 So the angel who spoke with me said to me, "Cry out and speak, Thus says the LORD of hosts, I am anxious about Jerusalem and Zion with great zeal, 15 And I am very an- gry against the negligent heathen, because I was angry only a little, and they have added to the • affliction." 16 Therefore thus says the LORD: "I will return to Jerusalem with tender mercies; my house shall be built in it, says the LORD of hosts, and a line shall be stretched out over Jerusalem." 17 Shout again and say, "Thus says the LORD of hosts: my cities shall yet be destroyed with abundance; the LORD shall yet comfort Zion, and yet heal

Jerusa- lem." 18 Then I lifted up mine eyes and looked, and saw four horns. 19 And I said to the angel speaking with me, "What are these?" And he answered me, "These are the horns that scat- tered Judah, Israel and Jerusalem." 20 And the LORD showed me four carpenters. 21 Then I said, "What do these come to do?" And he an- swered, "These are the horns that have scat- tered Judah, so that a man could not lift up his head; but these have come to cast out the horns of the Gentiles, who lift up their horns out of the land of Judah, to scatter it."

CHAPTER 2

1 I raised my eyes again and looked, and be- hold a man with a tape measure in his hand. 2 Then I said, "Where are you going?" And he said to me, "To measure Jerusalem, to see what is its width and what is its length." 3 And behold, the Angel who had spoken to me departed; and another Angel came to meet him, 4 and said to him, "Run, speak to this young man and tell him that Jerusalem will be inhabited without walls, because of the multitude of men and cattle there. 5 For I, saith the LORD, will be to her a wall of fire all around, and I will be the glory in her midst. 6 O come out and flee from the land of the north, says the LORD, for I have scattered you in the four winds of the earth, says the LORD. 7 Save yourself, O Zion, who dwells with the daughter of Babel. 8 For thus saith the LORD of hosts, After this glory hath he sent me against the nations that have driven you; for he that toucheth you toucheth the apple of his eye. 9 For behold, I will lift up my hand upon them, and they shall be a snitch to those who have served them, and you shall know that the LORD of hosts has sent me. 10 Rejoice and be glad, daughter of Zion, for I am coming and will dwell among you, says the LORD. 11 In that day, many peoples shall be consecrated to the LORD and shall be my people; I will dwell in your vicinity, and you shall know that the LORD of hosts has sent me to you. 12 The LORD shall inherit Iudah, his portion in the holy land, and he shall choose Jerusalem again. 13 Let all flesh stand before the LORD, for he has come forth from his holy place.

CHAPTER 3

1 He showed me Iehoshua the priest stand- ing before the angel of the Lord, while Satan stood at his right hand to resist him. 2 The Lord said to Satan, "The Lord rebukes you, O Satan, and the Lord who chose Jerusalem rebukes you. Is not this a mark taken away by fire? 3 Now Iehoshua clothed himself in filthy garments and stood before the angel. :4 He answered and spoke to those who stood before him, saying, "Take off his filthy gar- ments." And he said to them, "Behold, I have caused your iniquity to depart from you, and I will clothe you in different garments." 5 Then he said, "Let them put a beautiful diadem on his head." So they put a beautiful diadem on his head and clothed him with garments, while the angel of the Lord stood beside him. 6 The angel of the Lord testified to Iehoshua, saying, "Thus says the Lord, 7 Thus saith the LORD of hosts, If thou wilt walk in my ways, and keep my watch, thou shalt also judge my house, and keep my courts also, and I will give thee a place among them that stand by. 8 Beware now, O Iehoshua the priest, you and your companions who sit before you, for they are monstrous people; but behold, I will bring out the Branch, my servant. 9 For behold, the stone which I have set before Iehoshua:

on one stone shall be ten eyes; behold, I will cut off the cluster of them, saith the LORD of hosts, and I will take away the iniquity of this land in one day. 10 In that day, saith the LORD of hosts, ye shall call every man his neighbor under the vine and under the fig tree.

CHAPTER 4

1 The angel who had spoken to me came again and woke me up, like a man who is awakened from sleep, 2 and said to me, "What do you see?" And I answered, "I looked, and saw a candlestick all of gold, with an arch on the top of it, and its ten lamps within, and ten pipes for lamps, which were on the top of it. 3 And two olive trees outside it, one on the right side of the bow, and the other on the left side. 4 Then I answered and spoke to the angel who spoke with me, saying, "What are these, my Lord?" 5 The angel who was speak- ing with me answered and said, "Do you not know what these things are? And I answered, "No, my Lord." 6 Then he answered and spoke to me, saying, "This is the word of the LORD to Zerubbabel, saying, 'Not by an army nor by force, but by my Spirit, says the LORD of hosts. 7 Who art thou, O great mountain, be- fore Zerubbabel? You shall be a plain, and he shall bear its headstone with shouting, cry- ing, "Grace, grace." 8 More, the word of the LORD was spoken to me, saying, 9 The hands of Zerubbabel have laid the foundation of this house; his hands shall complete it, and you shall know that the LORD of hosts has sent me to you. 10 For who has despised the day of small things? But they shall think again, and they shall see the tin stone in the hand of Zerubbabel; these are the eyes of the LORD, which go out into all the world." 11 Then I answered and said to him, "What are these two olive trees on the right and on the left? 12 Then I spoke again and said to him, "What are these two olive branches that go through the two golden rods and empty themselves into the treasury?" 13 He answered me and said, "Do you not know what these are?" And I said, "No, my Lord." 14 Then he said, "These are the two olive branches that stand with the ruler of the whole earth."

CHAPTER 5

1 Then I turned and lifted up my eyes and looked, and behold, a flying book. 2 He said to me, "What do you see?" And I answered, "I see a flying book; its length is twenty-five cu- bits and its width ten cubits." 3 Then he said to me, "This is the curse that extends over all the earth, for whoever steals will be cut off from this side as well as from that side; and whoev- er swears will be cut off from this side as well as from that side. 4 I will bring him out, says the LORD of hosts, and he shall enter into the house of the thief and into the house of him who swears falsely by my Name; he shall stand in the midst of his house and consume it, with his timber and his stones." 5 Then the angel who spoke with me departed and said to me, "Lift up your eyes now and see what this is that is departing." 6 And I said, "What is this?" And he said, "This is an Ephah going outward." And he said again, "This is the sight of all of them in all the earth." 7 And behold, a talent of lead was lifted up; and this is a wom- an sitting in the midst of Ephah. 8 And he said, "This is wickedness," and he threw her into the middle of Ephah, casting the lead- en weight upon her mouth. 9 Then I lifted up my eyes and looked; and behold, two women came out, with wind on their wings (for they had wings like the wings

of a storm) and lifted up Ephah between the earth and heaven. 10 Then I said to the angel who spoke with me, "Where do these take Ephah?" 11 He said to me, "Build a house in the land of Shinar; it shall be established and placed in its proper place."

CHAPTER 6

1 Then I turned, and lifted up mine eyes, and looked: and, behold, between two mountains came forth four chariots, and the mountains were mountains of brasse. 2 In the first cha- ret were red horses, and in the second were black horses, 3 In the third charet white hors- es, and in the fourth charet horses of a differ- ent color and reddish. 4 Then I answered and said to the angel who spoke with me, "What are these, my lord?" 5 The angel answered and said to me, "These are the four spirits of heaven that depart to be with the Lord of all the earth." 6 Those with the black horse went to the north country, the white ones followed them, and those of different colors went to the south country. 7 The reddish one went out and asked to go and pass through the world, and he said, "Go and pass through the world." So they went through the world. 8 Then he cried out over me and spoke to me, saying, "Behold, these who go to the north county have pacified my spirit in the north county." 9 And the word of the LORD was spoken to me, saying, 10 Take of those of your captivity, that is, of Heldai, Tobijah, and Jedaiah, who have come from Babel, and come the same day and go to the house of Joshiah the son of Zephaniah. 11 Take some silver and gold and make crowns and put them on the head of Iehoshua the son of Jehozadak the priest, 12 And speak unto him, saying, Thus saith the LORD of hosts, Behold the man whose name is the Branch; he shall grow up from his place, and shall build the Temple of the LORD. 13 And he shall build the Temple of the LORD, and bring forth the glory thereof, and shall sit and rule upon his throne, and be a priest upon his throne, and the council of peace shall be between them. 14 And crowns shall be given to Helem, and to Tobiah, and to Jedaiah, and to Hen the son of Zephaniah, as a memorial in the temple of the LORD. 15 And those who are far off shall come and build in the Tem- ple of the LORD, and you shall know that the LORD of hosts has sent me to you. And this shall come to pass, if you obey the message of the LORD your God.

CHAPTER 7

1 In the fourth year of King Darius, the word of the Lord came to Zechariah on the fourth day of the ninth month, in Chisleu, 2 for they had sent Sharezer, Regem-melech and their men to the House of God to pray before the Lord, 3 and to speak to the priests who were in the house of the LORD of hosts and to the prophets, saying, "Shall I mourn these fif- teen months and part as I have done all these years? 4 Then the word of the LORD of hosts came to me, saying, 5 Speak to all the people of the land and to the priests and say, "When you fasted and mourned in the fifteenth and in the seventh month, that is, in the seventy years, did you fast for me? Do I approve it? 6 And when you ate and when you drank, did you not eat for yourselves and drink for your- selves? 7 Should you not listen to the words which the Lord cried out through the minis- try of the former Prophets, when Jerusalem was inhabited and prosperous and her cities around her, when the south and the plain were inhabited? 8 The word of the LORD was

addressed to Zechariah, saying, 9 Thus speaks the LORD of hosts, "Execute true judgment, and use mercy and compassion, each one toward his brother, 10 do not oppress the widow, nor the father of the family, nor the stranger, nor the poor man, and let none of you imagine wickedness in his heart against his own brother." 11 But they refused to listen; they pulled back their shoulders and plugged their ears so as not to hear. 12 Yea, they made their hearts like a stone of cement, not to hear the word and the words which the LORD of hosts sent in his spirit through the ministry of the former prophets; therefore great wrath was aroused on the part of the LORD of hosts. 13 Therefore it came to pass that as he cried out and they would not listen, so they cried out and I would not listen, says the Lord of hosts. 14 But I scattered them among all the nations, whom they did not know; so the land was desolate after them, that no one passed by and did not return; for they destroyed the pleasant land.

CHAPTER 8

1 Then the word of the LORD of hosts came to me, saying, "Thus says the LORD of hosts, 2 Thus saith the Lord of hosts, I have been anxious for Zion with great wrath, and I have been anxious for her with great anger. 3 Thus says the LORD, "I will return to Zion and dwell in the midst of Jerusalem; Jerusalem shall be called the city of truth, and the mountain of the LORD of hosts, the holy mountain." 4 Thus says the LORD of hosts, "In the streets of Jerusalem shall still dwell old men and old women, and every man shall have his staff in his hand for his age. 5 And the streets of the city shall be full of boys and girls playing in its streets." 6 Thus says the LORD of hosts, "Even if it were impossible in the eyes of the remnant of this people in these days, should it therefore be impossible in my eyes, says the LORD of hosts?" 7 Thus says the LORD of hosts, "Behold, I will deliver my people from the county of the east and from the county of the west. 8 I will lead them, and they shall dwell in the midst of Jerusalem; they shall be my people, and I will be their God in truth and righteousness. 9 Thus says the LORD of hosts: "Let your hands be strong, you who hear in these days these words by the mouth of the Prophets, which were in the day when the foundation of the House of the LORD of hosts was laid, that the Temple might be built. 10 For before these days there was no wages for man nor for beast, nor was there any peace for those who went out or came in by reason of affliction, because I set all men, every man against his neighbor. 11 But now, I will not weave the remnant of this people as before, says the LORD of hosts. 12 For the seed shall be prosperous, the vine shall yield its fruit, the earth shall yield its harvest, the heavens shall give their dew, and I will cause the remnant of this people to possess all these things. 13 And it shall come to pass, that, as ye were a curse among the heathen, O house of Judah and house of Israel, so will I deliver you, and ye shall be a blessing; fear not, but make your hands strong. 14 For thus says the LORD of hosts, "As I thought to punish you, when your fathers provoked me to anger, so says the LORD of hosts, and I have not re- pented, 15 so in these days I have determined to do good to Jerusalem and to the house of Iudah; fear not. 16 These are the things you are to do. Tell each one the truth to his neigh- bor; execute judgment with truth and righ- teousness in your gates, 17 and let none of you imagine wickedness in his heart against his neighbor and love not falsehood, for all these are the things that I hate, says the LORD. 18 The word of the

LORD of hosts came to me, saying, 19 Thus says the LORD of hosts, "The fasting of the fourth month, the fasting of the fifth, the fasting of the seventh, and the fast- ing of the tenth shall be for the house of Iu- dah joy and gladness and prosperous feasts; therefore love truth and peace." 20 Thus says the LORD of hosts, "Still peoples and inhab- itants of great cities will come. 21 Those who dwell in one city will go to another, saying, "Go and pray before the LORD and see the LORD of hosts; I will go also." 22 Yes, great peoples and great nations will come to see the LORD of hosts in Jerusalem and to pray before the LORD. 23 Thus says the LORD of hosts, "In those days ten men shall take hold of all the languages of the nations, and they shall take hold of the skirt of him who is a He- brew, and they shall say, 'We will go with you, for we have heard that God is with you.'

CHAPTER 9

1 The weight of the word of the LORD in the land of Hadrach and Damascus shall be its rest, when the eyes of men and of all the tribes of Israel shall be turned to the LORD. 2 Ha- math also shall border it: Tyre and Zidon also, though they be very wise. 3 For Tyre hath built herself a strong fortress, and hath heaped up siluer as the dust, and goldde as the myre of the streets. 4 Behold, the LORD will spur her, and will smite her power in the sea, and she shall be ravaged with fire. 5 Ashkelon shall see it and be afraid, and Azza also shall be greatly grieved, and Ekron, for her face shall be ashamed, and the king shall perish from Azza, and Ashkelon shall not be inhabited. 6 The stranger shall dwell in Ashdod, and I will cut off the pride of the Philistines. 7 I will take the blood out of his mouth and his abominations from under his teeth; but who- ever remains shall be for our God and shall be like a prince in Iudah, while Ekron shall be like a Jebusite. 8 And I will turn my house against the army, against those who pass by and those who return, and no oppressor shall come upon them any more, for now I have seen with my own eyes. 9 Rejoice greatly, O daughter of Zion, and shake for joy, O daugh- ter of Jerusalem; behold, your king comes to you; he is righteous and poor, and rides on a donkey and a colt with the legs of a donkey. 10 I will cut off the chariots from Ephraim and the horse from Jerusalem; the bow of battle shall be broken, and he shall speak peace to the Gentiles; his dominion shall extend from sea to sea and from the river to the uttermost part of the land. 11 You, too, will be healed by the blood of your companion. I have delivered your captives from the pit in which there is no water. 12 Turn to the fortress, prisoners of hope, and I declare today that I will make you twice as much. 13 For Iudah have I bent as a bow for me: I have filled the hand of Ephraim, and have lifted up thy sons, O Zion, against thy sons, O Greece, and have made thee like a giant sword. 14 And the LORD shall be seen beyond them, and his stronghold shall come forth like lightning; and the LORD God shall sound the trumpet, and shall come forth with the whirlwinds of the south. 15 And the LORD of hosts shall defend them, and shall smite them, and subdue them with a sling; and they shall drink, and make a drunkenness like wine of peat, and shall be filled as the cups and as the horns of the altar. 16 In that day shall the LORD their God deliver them up as the flock of his people, for they shall be as the stones of the crown lifted up upon his land. 17 How great is his goodness and how great is his beauty! The horn will make the young men happy and the new wine the maidens.

CHAPTER 10

1 Ask the LORD for raina in the time of the last raina; the LORD will make white clouds and give you rains of raina, and to all the farmers in the country. 2 The idols have spoken vanity, the southerners have seen a lie, and the dreamers have told a vain thing; they comfort themselves in vain; therefore they have gone away like sheep; they have been troubled because there was no shepherd. 3 My wrath is kindled against the shepherds, and I have visited the goats; but the LORD of hosts will visit his flock, the house of Iudah, and will make them like his beautiful horse in the battle. 4 Out of him shall come forth the corner, out of him the jay, out of him the iron arm, and out of him also shall come forth all who require tribute. 5 They shall be like mighty men who strike down their enemies in the mire of the streets in battle; they shall fight, for the LORD is with them, and the horsemen on horseback shall be confounded. 6 I will strengthen the house of Iudah, and I will preserve the house of Ioseph, and I will bring them back to life, for I will pity them; and they shall be as though I had not cast them out, for I am the LORD their God, and I will hear them. 7 They of Ephraim shall be as a gypsy, and their heart shall rejoice as a red wine; yea, their children shall see it, and they shall rejoice; and their heart shall rejoice in the LORD. 8 I will take care of them and gath- er them, for I have redeemed them; and they shall increase, as they have increased. 9 I will sow them among the nations, and they shall remember me in far countries; they shall live with their children and be converted. 10 I will bring them out again from the land of Egypt and gather them from Assur; I will bring them into the land of Gilead and Lebanon, and no place will be found for them. 11 And he shall enter the sea with affliction, and shall smite the waves of the sea, and all the depths of the river shall be dried up; and the pride of Assur shall be cast down, and the scepter of Egypt shall depart. 12 I will strengthen them in the LORD and they will walk in his Name, says the LORD.

CHAPTER 11

1 Open your gates, O Lebanon, and fire shall destroy your cedars. 2 Take courage, O fir trees, for the cedar has fallen, for all the great- est have been destroyed; take courage, O lakes of Bashan, for your forest has been cut down. 3 There is the voice of the cry of the shep- herds, for their glory is destroyed; the voice of the roar of the little lions, for the pride of Iorden is destroyed. 4 Thus says the LORD my God, "Feed the sheep of the slaughter." 5 Those who possess them, they kill them and do not sin; and those who sell them, they say, "Blessed is the Lord, for I am rich," and their shepherds do not spare them. 6 I will no more spare them that dwell in the land, saith the LORD; but, behold, I will deliver men, every man, into the hand of his neighbor, and into the hand of his king; they shall smite the land, and I will not take them out of their hand. 7 For I have fed the sheep for slaughter, that is, the poor of the flock, and I have taken with me two stalls: one I called Beauty and the oth- er I called Band, and I have fed the sheep. 8 In one month I also took out three shepherds, and my mind allotted them, while their mind abhorred me. 9 Then I said, "I will not feed you: that which is dyed, let it be dyed; and that which perishes, let it perish; and let the rest eat, every one the flesh of his neighbor." 0 Then I took my staff, Beauty, and broke

it, to dissolve my covenant that I had made with all peoples. 11 On that day it was broken, and so the poor of the flock who were waiting for me knew that it was the word of the Lord. 12 I said to them, "If you think it good, give me my wages; if not, let it go;" so they weighed for my wages three pieces of silver. 13 The LORD said to me, "Throw them to the potter: it is a good price what they weighed for me. I took the thirty pieces of silk and threw them to the potter in the house of the LORD. 14 Then I broke my other staff, that is, the bands, to dissolve the brotherhood between Iudah and Israel. 15 The LORD said to me, "Take yet the instruments of a foolish shepherd. 16 For, behold, I will raise up in the land a shepherd who shall not seek the lost thing, nor see the tender lambs, nor heal the wounded ones, nor feed those that stand; but shall eat the flesh of the fat ones, and tear their claws to pieces. 17 O idol that casteth out the flock, the sword shall be on his arm and on his right eye. His armor shall be clean and dried, and his right eye shall be completely darkened.

CHAPTER 12

1 The weight of the word of the LORD upon Israel, saith the LORD, which hath caused the heavens to bud, and hath laid the foundations of the earth, and formed the spirit of man in him. 2 Behold, I will make Jerusalem a cup of pois for all the surrounding peoples; and it shall also be with Iudah, in the siege against Jerusalem. 3 In that day I will make Jerusalem a hard stone for all peoples; all who lift it up shall be tormented, even as all the peoples of the earth are gathered together against it. 4 In that day, says the LORD, I will smite every horse with astonishment and its rider with folly; I will open my eyes on the house of Ju- dah and smite every horse of the people with blindness. 5 The princes of Judah will say in their hearts, "The inhabitants of Jerusalem will be my strength in the LORD of hosts, their God." 6 In that day I will make the princ- es of Iudah as colas of fire in the midst of the wood, and as a brand of fire in the hood, and they shall destroy all the people round about on the right hand and on the left; and Jeru- salem shall be inhabited again in her proper place, that is, in Jerusalem. 7 The LORD will also preserve the tents of Iudah, as before; therefore the glory of the house of Dauid shall not boast, nor the glory of the inhabitants of Ierusalem against Iudah. 8 In that day the LORD will defend the inhabitants of Ierusa- lem, and those who are weak among them will be like Dauid in that day; and the house of Dauid will be like the house of God and like the Angel of the LORD before them. 9 In that day I will destroy all the nations that come against Jerusalem. 10 And I will give to the house of Dauid and to the inhabitants of Jeru- salem a Spirit of grace and compassion, and they will look upon me, whom they have lost, and they will mourn for him, as one mourns for one's only son, and they will grieve for him as one grieves for one's first son. 11 In that day there shall be great mourning in Jerusalem, as the mourning of Hadadrimmon in the valley of Megiddon. 12 The land shall separate every family, the family of the house of Dauid and their wives, the family of the house of Nathan and their wives: 13 the family of the house of Leui, and their wives, and the family of Shem- ei, and their wives: 14 All the remaining fami- lies, every family apart, and their wives apart.

CHAPTER 13

1 In that day a fountain shall be opened to the house of Dauid and to the inhabitants of Jerusalem, for sin and for violence. 2 In that day, saith the LORD of hosts, I will cut off the names of the idols from the land, and they shall remember no more; and I will bring forth the prophets and the vnclean spirit out of the land. 3 And when one prophesies, his father and mother, who have begotten him, shall say to him, "Do not lie, for you speak lies in the name of the LORD"; and his father and mother, who have begotten him, shall cast him out when he prophesies. 4 In that day the prophets shall be ashamed of their vision, when they have prophesied; and they shall not wear a rough robe to deceive. 5 But he shall say, "I am not a prophet: I am a farmer, for man hath taught me to be a farmer from my youth." 6 And one will say to him, "What are these wounds in your hands?" And he will an- swer, "So I was wounded in the house of my friends." 7 Arise, O sword, upon my shepherd and upon the man that is my companion, saith the LORD of hosts: smite the shepherd, and the sheep shall be scattered; and I will turn my hand upon the little ones. 8 In all the land, says the LORD, two parts shall be cut off and die, but the third part shall remain there. 9 And I will bring the third part into the fire, and I will mill it as one mills torpedo, and I will try it as one tries gold; and they shall call upon my Name, and I will hear them: I will say, "It is my people," and they shall say, "The LORD is my God."

CHAPTER 14

1 Behold, the day of the LORD draws near, and your sphere will be destroyed in the midst of you. 2 For I will gather all the na- tions against Jerusalem to give her battle, and the city shall be taken, and the houses spied out and the women defiled, and half the city shall go into captivity, and the rest of the people shall not be separated from the city. 3 Then the LORD will depart and fight against those nations, as when he fought on the day of battle. 4 In that day his feet shall stand on the mount of olives, which is opposite Jeru- salem, on the east, and the mount of olives shall lighten in the middle of it; toward the east and toward the west there shall be a very great valley, and half the mount shall move toward the north and half the mount toward the south. 5 You shall flee to the valley of the mountains, for the valley of the mountains shall reach as far as Azal; you shall flee as you fled from the earthquake in the days of Vzzi- ah, king of Judah; and the LORD my God shall come, and all the saints with you. 6 In that day there will be no clear light, but darkness. 7 And there shall be a day (the LORD knows) without day or night, but toward the hour of sunset there shall be light. 8 In that day the waters of life shall go out from Jerusalem, half to the eastern sea and half to the farthest sea, and they shall be both summer and winter. 9 The LORD shall be king over all the earth; in that day there shall be one LORD, and his name shall be one. 10 All the land shall be made a plain from Geba to Rimmon, toward the south of Jerusalem, and it shall be raised up and inhabited in its place: from the gate of Benjamin unto the place of the first gate, even to the corner gate, and from the place of Hananiel unto the presses of the kings. 11 And men shall dwell there, and there shall be no more destruction, but Jerusalem shall be in- habited with safety. 12 This shall be the plague with which the LORD shall smite all the peo- ple who have fought against Jerusalem: their flesh shall be consumed, though they stand, their eyes shall be consumed in their sockets, and their tongue shall be consumed in their mouth. 13 But in that day a great tumult of the LORD shall be in the midst of them, and every one shall take his neighbor's hand, and his hand shall rise up against his neighbor's hand. 14 Iudah also shall fight against Jeru- salem, and the arms of all the heathen shall be gathered round about them, with gold and silk and great abundance of clothing. 15 But this shall be the plague of the horse, and of the mule, and of the camel, and of the plank, and of all the beasts that are in these tents like this plague. 16 But it shall come to pass that all that are left of all the nations, which came against Jerusalem, shall go from year to year to worship the king, the LORD of hosts, and to celebrate the feast of Tabernacles. 17 And whoever will not want to come to Jerusalem from all the families of the earth to worship the king, the Lord of hosts, then upon them there shall be no wrath. 18 And if the family of Egypt will not go and come, there shall not be wrath upon them. This will be the plague with which the LORD will smite all the hea- then who do not come to celebrate the Feast of Tabernacles. 19 This will be the chastise- ment of Egypt and the chastisement of all the nations that do not come to celebrate the Feast of Tabernacles. 20 In that day it shall be written on the reins of the horses, "Holiness unto the LORD," and the vessels in the house of the LORD shall be as the cups before the al- tar. 21 Yea, all the vessels of Jerusalem and Iu- dah shall be holy to the LORD of hosts, and all who sacrifice shall come and take and eat of them; and in that day there shall be no more Canaanite in the house of the LORD of hosts.

MALACHI

CHAPTER 1

1 The weight of the word of the Lord to Is- rael through the minister Malachi. 2 I have received you, says the LORD; but you say, In what have you received? Was not Esau the brother of Iaakob, saith the LORD, yet have I displeased Iaakob? 3 I hated Esau and made his mountains a wilderness and his inheri- tance a thicket of dragons. 4 Although Edom says, "We are destroyed, but we will return and build the desolate places," the LORD of hosts says, "They will build, but I will destroy them," and they will call them, "The border of wickedness" and "The people with whom the LORD is angry forever." 5 Your eyes will see it and say, "The LORD will be magnified on the border of Israel." 6 A son honors his father and a servant his master. If therefore I am a father, where is my honor? And if I am a mas- ter, where is my fear, says the LORD of hosts to you, O priests, who despise my Name? And you say, "In what have we despised your Name?" 7 You offer vncleane bread on my al- tar and say, "In what have we polluted you?" and say that the table of the LORD is not to be respected. 8 If you offer for sacrifice a blind man, it is not right; if you offer a lame man and a sick man, it is not right; offer it now to your prince: will he be pleased with you, or will he accept your person, says the LORD of hosts? 9 And now, I pray you, pray before God, that he may have mercy on you; this has happened through your means; will he take care of your persons, says the LORD of hosts? 10 Who is there among you who will shut the gates and not light fire on my altar in wine? I have no pleasure in you, says the LORD of hosts, nor will I accept an offering from your hand. 11 For from the rising of the sun until its setting, my Name is great among the nations, and in every place incense shall be offered to my Name and a pure offering, for my Name is great among the heathen, says the LORD of hosts. 12 But you have polluted it, for you say, "The table of the LORD is polluted, and his fruit is polluted, and his flesh is not to

be regarded." 13 You have also said, "Behold, it is a usury, and you have snorted it, saith the LORD of hosts, and you have offended the one who was tormented, the lame and the sick; thus you have offended an offense: shall I ac- cept this from your hands, saith the LORD? 14 But cursed be the deceiver that hath in his flock a male, that voweth a vow, and sacri- ficeth to the LORD a corrupt thing: for I am a great king, saith the LORD of hosts, and my name is terrible among the heathen.

CHAPTER 2

1 Now, O priests, this command is for you. 2 If you will not listen to it and consider it in your heart, to give glory to my Name, says the LORD of hosts, I will send a curse upon you and curse your blessings; yes, I have al- ready cursed them, because you do not con- sider it in your heart. 3 Behold, I will corrupt your descendants, and I will cast my tongue upon your faces, as the tongue of your solemn feasts, and you shall be like it. 4 And ye shall know that I have sent you this command, that my covenant which I made with Leui may stand, saith the LORD of hosts. 5 My covenant was with him of life and peace, and I gave him fear, and he feared me and was afraid before my Name. 6 The word of truth was in his mouth, and there was no iniquity in his lips; he walked with me in peace and equity and turned many away from iniquity. 7 For the lips of the priests should preserve knowl- edge and should see the Word at his mouth, for he is the messenger of the LORD of hosts. 8 But you have gone out of the way; you have caused many to fall by the Lawe; you have bro- ken the bond of Leui, says the LORD of hosts. 9 Therefore I have also made you despicable and ignoble before all the people, because you have not followed my ways, but have partic- ipated in the plague. 10 Do we not all have one father? Is it not one God who created us? Why do we each transgress against our broth- er and violate the covenant of our fathers? 11 Iudah has transgressed and committed an abomination in Israel and Jerusalem, because Iudah has defiled the holiness of the LORD, whom he praised, and married the daughter of a foreign God. 12 And the LORD will cut off the man who does this: the master and the servant from the Tabernacle of Iaacob, and the one who offers an offering to the LORD of hosts. 13 And this you have done again and have covered the altar of the LORD with tears and weeping and mourning, because the of- fering is no longer considered and is no lon- ger accepted by your hands. 14 But you say, "Why? Because the Lord was witness between you and the wife of your youth, against whom you transgressed; yet she is your companion and the wife of your companion. 15 He did not make one, but he had abundance of spirit; and why one? Because he sought a godly off- spring; therefore keep your spirit, and let no one transgress against the wife of his youth. 16 If you detest her, turn her away, says the LORD God of Israel, but he hides iniury under his garment, says the LORD of hosts; there- fore keep your spirit and do not transgress. 17 You have wearied the LORD with your words, yet you say, "In what have we wearied him? When you say, "Every person who does good is good in the eyes of the Lord, and he is pleased with them." Or where is the God of judgment?

CHAPTER 3

1 Behold, I will send my messenger, and he shall prepare the way before me; and the LORD whom you see shall come quickly to his Temple, that is, the messenger of the courtier whom you desire; behold, he shall come, saith the LORD of hosts. 2 But who will be able to endure the day of his coming? And who will be able to endure when he appears? For he is like a cleansing fire, and like the mire of a fuller. 3 He will sit down to try and refine clay; and then he will refine the sons of Leui and purify them as gold and as clay, that they may bring offerings to the LORD in righteousness. 4 Then the offerings of Iudah and Jerusalem will be acceptable to the LORD, as in the past and in former years. 5 I will come to you to judge, and I will be a swift witness against the southerners, against the adulterers, against the false swearers, against those who unjust- ly withhold the wages of wage earners, who vituperate the widow and the fatherless and oppress the stranger, and do not fear me, says the LORD of hosts. :6 For I am the LORD: I do not change, and you sons of Iaakob do not consume yourselves. 7 From the days of your fathers ye have departed from my precepts, and have not kept them: return unto me, and I will return unto you, saith the LORD of hosts: but ye say, Where shall we return? 8 Does a man want to defy his gods? You have challenged me, but say, "In what have we challenged you?" In tithes and offerings. 9 You are cursed with a curse, because you have spit me out, as has all the nation. 10 Bring all the tithes into the storehouse, that there may be food in my house, and prove me now, saith the LORD of hosts, if I will not open the windows of Heauen to you and give you a blessing without measure. 11 I will rebuke the squanderer for your sake, and he shall not destroy the fruit of your land, and your vine shall not be quenched in the fields, says the LORD of hosts. 12 All the nations shall call you blessed, for you shall be a pleasant land, says the LORD of hosts. 13 Your words have been harsh against me, says the LORD; but you say, What have we said against you? 14 You have said, "It is a sin to serve God"; and what good is it if we have kept his commands and walked humbly before the Lord of hosts? 15 There- fore we consider blessed are the proverbs; for those who work wickedly are defeated, and those who tempt God, yea, they are disap- pointed." 16 Then those who feared the LORD spoke, each to his neighbor, and the LORD heard them, and a book of remembrance was written before him for those who feared the LORD and thought on his Name. 17 In the day when I do this, they shall be to me, says the LORD of hosts, as a flock, and I will spare them, as a man spares his own son who serves him. 18 Then you will return and discern be- tween the righteous and the wicked, between the one who serves God and the one who does not serve him.

CHAPTER 4

1 For behold, the day that cometh shall burn as hay, and all the proud, yea, and all that do evil, shall be stubble, and the day that cometh shall burn them up, saith the LORD of hosts, and shall leave them neither root nor branch. 2 But for you who fear my Name, the sun of righteousness shall arise, and health shall be under its wings, and you shall go forth and grow like fat calves. 3 You shall cast down the wicked, for they shall be dust under the soles of your feet in the day when I do this, says the LORD of hosts. 4 Remember the word of Mo- ses my servant, which I commanded him in Horeb for all Israel, with the statutes and the prescriptions. 5 Behold, I will send you Elijah the prophet before the coming of the great and fearful day of the LORD. 6 He shall turn the hearts of the fathers to the children, and the hearts of the children to their fathers, lest I come and smite the land with a curse.

APOCRYPHAL AND PSEUDEPIGRAPHAL BOOKS

HISTORICAL APOCRYPHA

These books offer additional narratives and perspectives on historical events

JUBILEES

CHAPTER 1

1 And it came to pass in the first year of the exodus of the sons of Israel out of Egypt, in the third month, on the sixteenth day of the month, that God spoke to Moses, saying, "Come up to Me on the mountain, and I will give you two tablets of stone, of the Law and of the command, which I have written, that you may teach them." 2 And Moses went up into the mountain of God, and the glory of the LORD abode on Mount Sinai, and a cloud overshadowed it [for] six days. 3 And He called to Moses on the seventh day out of the midst of the cloud, and the appearance of the glory of the LORD was like a flaming fire on the top of the mountain. 4 And Moses was on the mountain [for] forty days and forty nights, and God taught him the earlier and the later history of the division of all the days of the Law and of the Testimony. 5 And He said, "Incline your heart to every word which I will speak to you on this mountain and write them in a scroll in order that their generations may see how I have not forsaken them for all the evil which they have worked in transgressing the covenant which I establish between Me and you for their generations this day on Mount Sinai. 6 And thus it will come to pass when all these things come on them, that they will recognize that I am more righteous than they in all their judgments and in all their actions, and they will recognize that I have truly been with them. 7 And write for yourself all these words which I declare to you this day, for I know their rebellion and their stiff neck, before I bring them into the land of which I swore to their fathers, to Abraham, and to Isaac, and to Jacob, saying, To your seed I will give a land flowing with milk and honey. 8 And they will eat and be satisfied, and they will turn to strange gods, to [gods] which cannot deliver them from any of their tribulation: and this witness will be heard for a witness against them. 9 For they will forget all My commands, [even] all that I command them, and they will walk after the nations, and after their uncleanness, and after their shame, and will serve their gods, and these will prove to them an offense, and a tribulation, and an affliction, and a snare . 10 And many will perish, and they will be taken captive, and will fall into the hands of the enemy, because they have forsaken My ordinances and My commands, and the festivals of My covenant, and My Sabbaths, and My holy place which I have hallowed for Myself in their midst, and My Dwelling Place, and My sanctuary, which I have hallowed for Myself in the midst of the land, that I should set My Name on it, and that it should dwell [there]. 11 And they will make to themselves high places, and groves, and graven images, and they will worship, each his own [graven image], so as to go astray, and they will sacrifice their children to demons, and to all the works of the error of their hearts. 12 And I will send witnesses to them that I may witness against them, but they will not hear, and will slay the witnesses also, and they will persecute those who seek the Law, and they will abrogate and change everything so as to work evil before My eyes. 13 And I will hide My face from them, and I will deliver them into the hand of the nations for captivity, and for a prey, and for devouring, and I will remove them from the midst of the land, and I will scatter them among the nations. 14 And they will forget all My law, and all My commands, and all My judgments, and will go astray as to new moons, and Sabbaths, and festivals, and jubilees, and ordinances. 15 And after this they will turn to Me from among the nations with all their heart, and with all their soul, and with all their strength, and I will gather them from among all the nations, and they will seek Me, so that I will be found by them when they seek Me with all their heart and with all their soul. 16 And I will disclose to them abounding peace with righteousness, and I will remove them—the plant of uprightness —with all My heart and with all My soul, and they will be for a blessing and not for a curse, and they will be the head and not the tail . 17 And I will build My sanctuary in their midst, and I will dwell with them, and I will be their God and they will be My people in truth and righteousness. 18 And I will not forsake them nor fail them; for I am the LORD their God." 19 And Moses fell on his face and prayed and said, "O LORD my God, do not forsake Your people and Your inheritance, so that they should wander in the error of their hearts, and do not deliver them into the hands of their enemies, the nations, lest they should rule over them and cause them to sin against You. 20 Let Your mercy, O LORD , be lifted up on Your people, and create an upright spirit in them, and do not let the spirit of Belial rule over them to accuse them before You, and to ensnare them from all the paths of righteousness, so that they may perish from before Your face. 21 But they are Your people and Your inheritance, which You have delivered with Your great power from the hands of the Egyptians: create in them a clean heart and a holy spirit , and do not let them be ensnared in their sins from now on [and] forever." 22 And the LORD said to Moses, "I know their contrariness, and their thoughts, and their stubbornness, and they will not be obedient until they confess their own sin and the sin of their fathers. 23 And after this they will turn to Me in all uprightness and with all [their] heart and with all [their] soul, and I will circumcise the foreskin of their heart and the foreskin of the heart of their seed, and I will create in them a holy spirit, and I will cleanse them so that they will not turn away from Me from that day [and] continuously. 24 And their souls will cleave to Me and to all My commands, and they will fulfill My commands, and I will be their Father and they will be My children. 25 And they will all be called children of the living God, and every messenger and every spirit will know, yes, they will know that these are My children, and that I am their Father in uprightness and righteousness, and that I love them. 26 And write down for yourself all these words which I declare to you on this mountain, the first and the last, which will come to pass in all the divisions of the days in the Law, and in the Testimony, and in the periods of seven, and the jubilees continuously, until I descend and dwell with them forever." 27 And He said to the Messenger of the Presence, "Write for Moses from the beginning of creation until My sanctuary has been built among them for all ages. 28 And the LORD will appear to the eyes of all, and all will know that I am the God

of Israel and the Father of all the children of Jacob, and King on Mount Zion for all ages. And Zion and Jerusalem will be holy." 29 And the Messenger of the Presence who went before the camp of Israel took the tablets of the divisions of the years —from the time of the creation—of the Law, and of the Testimony of the periods of seven, of the jubilees, according to the individual years, according to all the number of the jubilees [according to the individual years], from the day of the [new] creation when the heavens and the earth will be renewed and all their creation according to the powers of the heavens, and according to all the creation of the earth, until the sanctuary of the LORD will be made in Jerusalem on Mount Zion, and all the luminaries are renewed for healing , and for peace, and for blessing for all the chosen of Israel, and that thus it may be from that day and to all the days of the earth.

CHAPTER 2

1 And the Messenger of the Presence spoke to Moses according to the word of the LORD , saying, Write the complete history of the creation, how in six days the LORD God finished all His works and all that He created, and kept Sabbath on the seventh day and hallowed it for all ages, and appointed it as a sign for all His works. 2 For on the first day He created the heavens which are above, and the earth, and the waters, and all the spirits which serve before Him—the messengers of the presence, and the messengers of sanctification, and the messengers [[of the spirit of fire, and the messengers]] of the spirit of the winds, and the messengers of the spirit of the clouds, and of darkness, and of snow, and of hail, and of hoarfrost, and the messengers of the voices , and of the thunder, and of the lightning, and the messengers of the spirits of cold, and of heat, and of winter, and of spring, and of autumn, and of summer, and of all the spirits of His creatures which are in the heavens and on the earth, [He created] the abysses and the darkness, evening [and night], and the light, dawn and day, which He has prepared in the knowledge of His heart. 3 And we immediately saw His works, and praised Him, and lauded before Him on account of all His works; for He created seven great works on the first day. 4 And on the second day He created the expanse in the midst of the waters, and the waters were divided on that day—half of them went up above and half of them went down below the expanse [that was] in the midst over the face of the whole earth. And this was the only work [God] created on the second day. 5 And on the third day He commanded the waters to pass from off the face of the whole earth into one place, and the dry land to appear. 6 And the waters did so as He commanded them, and they retired from off the face of the earth into one place outside of this expanse, and the dry land appeared. 7 And on that day, He created for them all the seas according to their separate gathering-places, and all the rivers, and the gatherings of the waters in the mountains and on all the earth, and all the lakes, and all the dew of the earth, and the seed which is sown, and all sprouting things, and fruit-bearing trees, and trees of the wood, and the Garden of Eden, in Eden, and all [plants after their kind]. These four great works God created on the third day. 8 And on the fourth day He created the sun, and the moon, and the stars, and set them in the expanse of the heavens, to give light on all the earth, and to rule over the day and the night, and divide the light from the darkness. 9 And God appointed the sun to be a great sign on the earth for days, and for Sabbaths, and for months, and for feasts, and for years, and for Sabbaths of years, and for jubilees, and for all seasons of the years. 10 And it divides the light from the darkness [and] for prosperity, that all things may prosper which shoot and grow on the earth. These three kinds He made on the fourth day. 11 And on the fifth day He created great sea monsters in the depths of the waters, for these were the first things of flesh that were created by His hands, the fish and everything that moves in the waters, and everything that flies—the birds and all their kind. 12 And the sun rose above them to prosper [them], and above everything that was on the earth, everything that shoots out of the earth, and all fruit-bearing trees, and all flesh. These three kinds He created on the fifth day. 13 And on the sixth day He created all the animals of the earth, and all cattle, and everything that moves on the earth. 14 And after all this He created man, a man and a woman He created them, and gave him dominion over all that is on the earth, and in the seas, and over everything that flies, and over beasts and over cattle, and over everything that moves on the earth, and over the whole earth, and over all this He gave him dominion. And these four kinds He created on the sixth day. 15 And there were altogether twenty-two kinds. 16 And He finished all His work on the sixth day—all that is in the heavens and on the earth, and in the seas and in the abysses, and in the light and in the darkness, and in everything. 17 And He gave us a great sign, the Sabbath day, that we should work six days, but keep Sabbath on the seventh day from all work. 18 And all the messengers of the presence, and all the messengers of sanctification, these two great classes—He has bidden us to keep the Sabbath with Him in the heavens and on earth. 19 And He said to us, "Behold, I will separate a people to Myself from among all the peoples, and these will keep the Sabbath day, and I will sanctify them to Myself as My people and will bless them; as I have sanctified the Sabbath day and sanctify [it] to Myself, even so will I bless them, and they will be My people and I will be their God. 20 And I have chosen the seed of Jacob from among all that I have seen, and have written him down as My firstborn son, and have sanctified him to Myself forever and ever; and I will teach them the Sabbath day, that they may keep Sabbath thereon from all work." 21 And thus He created therein a sign in accordance with which they should keep Sabbath with us on the seventh day, to eat and to drink, and to bless Him who has created all things as He has blessed and sanctified to Himself a peculiar people above all peoples, and that they should keep Sabbath together with us. 22 And He caused His commands to ascend as a sweet savor acceptable before Him all the days. 23 There [were] twenty-two heads of mankind from Adam to Jacob, and twenty-two kinds of work were made until the seventh day; this is blessed and holy; and the former is also blessed and holy; and this one serves with that one for sanctification and blessing. 24 And to these [(Jacob and his seed)] it was granted that they should always be the blessed and holy ones of the first testimony and law, even as He had sanctified and blessed the Sabbath day on the seventh day. 25 He created the heavens, and earth, and everything that He created in six days, and God made the seventh day holy for all His works; therefore, He commanded on its behalf that whoever does any work thereon will die, and that he who defiles it will surely die. 26 For that reason, command the sons of Israel to observe this day that they may keep it holy and not do any work thereon, and not to defile it, as it is holier than all other days. 27 And whoever profanes it will surely die, and whoever does any work thereon will surely die forever, that the sons of Israel may observe this day throughout their generations, and not be rooted out of the land; for it is a holy day and a blessed day. 28 And everyone who observes it and keeps Sabbath thereon from all his work will be holy and blessed

throughout all days like to us. 29 Declare and say to the sons of Israel the law of this day, both that they should keep Sabbath thereon, and that they should not forsake it in the error of their hearts; [and] that it is not lawful to do any work thereon which is unseemly, to do their own pleasure thereon, and that they should not prepare anything thereon to be eaten or drunk , and [that it is not lawful] to draw water or bring in or take out thereon through their gates any burden, which they had not prepared for themselves on the sixth day in their dwellings. 30 And they will not bring in nor take out from house to house on that day; for that day is more holy and blessed than any jubilee day of the jubilees: on this we kept Sabbath in the heavens before it was made known to any flesh to keep Sabbath thereon on the earth. 31 And the Creator of all things blessed it, but He did not sanctify all peoples and nations to keep Sabbath thereon, but Israel alone: them alone He permitted to eat and drink and to keep Sabbath thereon on the earth. 32   And the Creator of all things blessed this day which He had created for a blessing, and a sanctification, and a glory above all days. 33 This law and testimony was given to the sons of Israel as a law forever to their generations.

CHAPTER 3

1   And on the six days of the second week we brought, according to the word of God, to Adam all the beasts, and all the cattle, and all the birds, and everything that moves on the earth, and everything that moves in the water, according to their kinds, and according to their types: the beasts on the first day; the cattle on the second day; the birds on the third day; and all that which moves on the earth on the fourth day; and that which moves in the water on the fifth day. 2 And Adam named them all by their respective names, and as he called them, so was their name. 3 And on these five days Adam saw all these, male and female, according to every kind that was on the earth, but he was alone and found no helpmate for him. 4 And the LORD said to us, "It is not good that the man should be alone: let us make a helpmate for him." 5 And the LORD our God caused a deep sleep to fall on him, and he slept, and He took for the woman one rib from among his ribs, and this rib was the origin of the woman from among his ribs, and He built up the flesh in its stead, and built the woman. 6 And He awoke Adam out of his sleep and on awaking he rose on the sixth day, and He brought her to him, and he knew her, and said to her, "This is now bone of my bones and flesh of my flesh; she will be called Woman, because she was taken from Man." 7 Therefore man and wife will be one, and therefore a man will leave his father and his mother, and cleave to his wife, and they will be one flesh. 8 In the first week Adam was created, and the rib—his wife; in the second week He showed her to him: and for this reason, the command was given to keep in their defilement, for a male seven days, and for a female twice seven days. 9 And after Adam had completed forty days in the land where he had been created, we brought him into the Garden of Eden to till and keep it, but they brought his wife in on the eightieth day, and after this she entered into the Garden of Eden. 10 And for this reason the command is written on the heavenly tablets in regard to her that gives birth: "If she bears a male, she will remain in her uncleanness seven days according to the first week of days, and thirty-three days she will remain in the blood of her purifying, and she will not touch any hallowed thing, nor enter into the sanctuary, until she accomplishes these days which [are prescribed] in the case of a male child. 11 But in the case of a female child she will remain in her uncleanness two weeks of days, according to the first two weeks, and sixty-six days in the blood of her purification, and they will be in all eighty days." 12 And when she had completed these eighty days, we brought her into the Garden of Eden, for it is holier than all the earth besides, and every tree that is planted in it is holy. 13 Therefore, there was ordained regarding her who bears a male or a female child the statute of those days that she should touch no hallowed thing, nor enter into the sanctuary until these days for the male or female child are accomplished. 14 This is the law and testimony which was written down for Israel, in order that they should observe [it] all the days. 15 And in the first week of the first jubilee, Adam and his wife were in the Garden of Eden for seven years tilling and keeping it, and we gave him work and we instructed him to do everything that is suitable for tillage. 16 And he tilled [the garden], and was naked and did not know it, and was not ashamed, and he protected the garden from the birds, and beasts, and cattle, and gathered its fruit, and ate, and put aside the residue for himself and for his wife. 17 And after the completion of the seven years, which he had completed there, seven years exactly, and in the second month, on the seventeenth day [of the month], the serpent came and approached the woman, and the serpent said to the woman, "Has God commanded you, saying, you will not eat of every tree of the garden?" 18 And she said to it, "Of all the fruit of the trees of the garden God has said to us, Eat; but of the fruit of the tree which is in the midst of the garden God has said to us, You will not eat thereof, neither will you touch it, lest you die." 19 And the serpent said to the woman, "You will not surely die, for God knows that on the day you will eat thereof, your eyes will be opened, and you will be as gods, and you will know good and evil." 20 And the woman saw the tree that it was agreeable and pleasant to the eye, and that its fruit was good for food, and she took thereof and ate. 21 And when she had first covered her shame with fig-leaves, she gave thereof to Adam and he ate, and his eyes were opened, and he saw that he was naked. 22 And he took fig-leaves and sewed [them] together, and made an apron for himself, and covered his shame. 32   And God cursed the serpent and was angry with it forever . 24 And He was angry with the woman because she listened to the voice of the serpent and ate; and He said to her , " I will greatly multiply your sorrow and your pains; in sorrow you will bring out children, and your return will be to your husband [[or Man]] , and he [[or He]] will rule over you." 25 And He also said to Adam, "Because you have listened to the voice of your wife, and have eaten of the tree of which I commanded you that you should not eat thereof, the ground is cursed for your sake: it will bring out thorns and thistles to you, and you will eat your bread in the sweat of your face, until you return to the earth from where you were taken; for earth you are, and to earth you will return." 26 And He made coats of skin for them, and clothed them, and sent them out from the Garden of Eden. 27 And on that day on which Adam went out from the garden, he offered as a sweet savor an offering: frankincense, galbanum, and stacte, and spices in the morning with the rising of the sun from the day when he covered his shame. 28 And on that day the mouth of all beasts, and of cattle, and of birds, and of whatever walks, and of whatever moves was closed, so that they could no longer speak, for they had all spoken with one another with one lip and with one tongue. 29 And He sent out of the Garden of Eden all flesh that was in the Garden of Eden, and all flesh was scattered according to its kinds, and according to its types to the places which had been created for them. 30 And to man alone did He give [the means] to cover his shame, of all the beasts and cattle. 31 On

this account, it is prescribed on the heavenly tablets as touching all those who know the judgment of the Law, that they should cover their shame, and should not uncover themselves as the nations uncover themselves. 32 And on the new moon of the fourth month, Adam and his wife went out from the Garden of Eden, and they dwelt in the land of 'Eldâ, in the land of their creation. 33 And Adam called the name of his wife Eve. 34 And they had no son until the first jubilee, and after this he knew her. 35 Now he tilled the land as he had been instructed in the Garden of Eden.

CHAPTER 4

1 And in the third week in the second jubilee she gave birth to Cain, and in the fourth she gave birth to Abel, and in the fifth she gave birth to her daughter 'Âwân. 2 And in the first [year] of the third jubilee, Cain slew Abel because [God] accepted the sacrifice of Abel and did not accept the offering of Cain. 3 And he slew him in the field: and his blood cried from the ground to Heaven, complaining because he had slain him. 4 And the LORD reproved Cain because of Abel, because he had slain him, and he made him a fugitive on the earth because of the blood of his brother, and he cursed him on the earth. 5 And on this account, it is written on the heavenly tablets: "Cursed is he who strikes his neighbor treacherously, and let all who have seen and heard it say so; and the man who has seen and not declared [it], let him be accursed as the other." And for this reason, we announce when we come before the LORD our God all the sin which is committed in the heavens and on earth, and in light and in darkness, and everywhere. 7 And Adam and his wife mourned for Abel four weeks of years, and in the fourth year of the fifth week they became joyful, and Adam knew his wife again, and she bore him a son, and he called his name Seth, for he said, "God has raised up a second seed to us on the earth instead of Abel, for Cain slew him." 8 And in the sixth week he begot his daughter 'Azûrâ. 9 And Cain took his sister 'Âwân to be his wife and she bore him Enoch at the close of the fourth jubilee. And in the first year of the first week of the fifth jubilee, houses were built on the earth, and Cain built a city, and called its name after the name of his son Enoch. 10 And Adam knew his wife Eve and she bore nine more sons. 11 And in the fifth week of the fifth jubilee Seth took his sister 'Azûrâ to be his wife, and in the fourth [year of the sixth week] she bore him Enos. 12 He began to call on the Name of the LORD on the earth. 13 And in the seventh jubilee in the third week Enos took his sister Nôâm to be his wife, and she bore him a son in the third year of the fifth week, and he called his name Kenan. 14 And at the close of the eighth jubilee Kenan took his sister Mûalêleth to be his wife, and she bore him a son in the ninth jubilee, in the first week in the third year of this week, and he called his name Mahalalel. 15 And in the second week of the tenth jubilee Mahalalel took to himself Dînâh to be [his] wife, the daughter of Barâkî'êl, the daughter of his father's brother, and she bore him a son in the third week in the sixth year, and he called his name Jared , for in his days the messengers of the LORD descended on the earth, those who are named the Watchers, that they should instruct the children of men, and that they should do judgment and uprightness on the earth. 16 And in the eleventh jubilee Jared took to himself a wife, and her name was Bâraka, the daughter of Râsûjâl, a daughter of his father's brother, in the fourth week of this jubilee, and she bore him a son in the fifth week, in the fourth year of the jubilee, and he called his name Enoch. 17 And he was the first among men that are born on earth who learned writing, and knowledge, and wisdom , and who wrote down the signs of the heavens according to the order of their months in a scroll, that men might know the seasons of the years according to the order of their separate months. 18 And he was the first to write a testimony, and he testified to the sons of men among the generations of the earth, and recounted the weeks of the jubilees, and made known to them the days of the years, and set in order the months, and recounted the Sabbaths of the years as we made [them] known to him. 19 And what was and what will be he saw in a vision of his sleep, as it will happen to the children of men throughout their generations until the Day of Judgment; he saw and understood everything, and wrote his testimony, and placed the testimony on earth for all the children of men and for their generations. 20 And in the twelfth jubilee, in the seventh week thereof, he took to himself a wife, and her name was Ednî, the daughter of Dânêl, the daughter of his father's brother, and in the sixth year in this week she bore him a son and he called his name Methuselah. 21 And he was moreover with the messengers of God these six jubilees of years, and they showed him everything which is on earth and in the heavens, the rule of the sun, and he wrote down everything. 22 And he testified to the Watchers who had sinned with the daughters of men, for these had begun to unite themselves [with them], so as to be defiled with the daughters of men, and Enoch testified against [them] all. 23 And he was taken from among the children of men, and we conducted him into the Garden of Eden in majesty and honor, and behold, there he wrote down the condemnation and judgment of the world, and all the wickedness of the children of men. 24 And on account of it [God] brought the waters of the flood on all the land of Eden; for there he was set as a sign and that he should testify against all the children of men, that he should recount all the deeds of the generations until the day of condemnation. 25 And he burned the incense of the sanctuary, [even] sweet spices, acceptable before the LORD on the mountain. 26 For the LORD has four places on the earth: the Garden of Eden, and the mountain of the East, and this mountain on which you are this day, Mount Sinai, and Mount Zion [which] will be sanctified in the new creation for a sanctification of the earth; through it the earth will be sanctified from all [its] guilt and its uncleanness throughout the generations of the world. 27 And in the fourteenth jubilee Methuselah took to himself a wife, Ednâ the daughter of 'Âzrîâl, the daughter of his father's brother, in the third week, in the first year of this week, and he begot a son and called his name Lamech. 28 And in the fifteenth jubilee in the third week Lamech took to himself a wife, and her name was Bêtênôs, the daughter of Bârâkî'îl, the daughter of his father's brother, and in this week she bore him a son and he called his name Noah, saying, "This one will comfort me for my trouble, and all my work, and for the ground which the LORD has cursed." 29 And at the close of the nineteenth jubilee, in the seventh week in the sixth year thereof, Adam died, and all his sons buried him in the land of his creation, and he was the first to be buried in the earth. 30 And he lacked seventy years of one thousand years; for one thousand years are as one day in the testimony of the heavens and therefore it was written concerning the Tree of Knowledge: "On the day that you eat thereof you will die." For this reason, he did not complete the years of this day, for he died during it. 31 At the close of this jubilee Cain was killed after him in the same year, for his house fell on him and he died in the midst of his house, and he was killed by its stones, for with a stone he had killed Abel, and by a stone he was killed in righteous judgment. 32 For this reason it was ordained on the heavenly tablets: "With the

instrument with which a man kills his neighbor with the same he will be killed; after the manner that he wounded him, in like manner they will deal with him." 33   And in the twenty-fifth jubilee Noah took to himself a wife, and her name was 'Ĕmzârâ, the daughter of Râkê'êl, the daughter of his father's brother, in the first year in the fifth week: and in the third year thereof she bore him Shem, in the fifth year thereof she bore him Ham, and in the first year in the sixth week she bore him Japheth.

CHAPTER 5

1 And it came to pass when the children of men began to multiply on the face of the earth and daughters were born to them, that the messengers of God saw them on a certain year of this jubilee, that they were beautiful to look on; and they took wives [for] themselves of all whom they chose, and they bore sons to them and they were giants. 2   And lawlessness increased on the earth and all flesh corrupted its way—men, and cattle, and beasts, and birds, and everything that walks on the earth alike—all of them corrupted their ways and their orders, and they began to devour each other, and lawlessness increased on the earth, and every imagination of the thoughts of all men was evil continually. 3 And God looked on the earth, and behold it was corrupt, and all flesh had corrupted its orders, and all that were on the earth had worked all manner of evil before His eyes. 4 And He said that He would destroy man and all flesh on the face of the earth which He had created. 5 But Noah found grace before the eyes of the LORD . 6 And against the messengers whom He had sent on the earth, He was exceedingly angry, and He gave command to root them out of all their dominion, and He commanded us to bind them in the depths of the earth, and behold, they are bound in the midst of them and are [kept] separate. 7 And a command went out against their sons from before His face that they should be smitten with the sword and be removed from under the heavens. 8 And He said, "My Spirit will not always abide on man, for they are also flesh and their days will be one hundred and twenty years." 9 And He sent His sword into their midst that each should slay his neighbor, and they began to slay each other until they all fell by the sword and were destroyed from the earth. 10 And their fathers were witnesses [of their destruction], and after this they were bound in the depths of the earth forever, until the day of the great condemnation, when judgment is executed on all those who have corrupted their ways and their works before the LORD . 11 And He destroyed all from their places, and there was not left [even] one of them whom He did not judge according to all their wickedness. 12 And He made for all His works a new and righteous nature, so that they should not sin in their whole nature forever but should be all righteous—each in his kind always. 13 And the judgment of all is ordained and written on the heavenly tablets in righteousness—even [the judgment of] all who depart from the path which is ordained for them to walk in; and if they do not walk therein, judgment is written down for every creature and for every kind. 14 And there is nothing in the heavens or on earth, or in light or in darkness, or in Sheol or in the depth, or in the place of darkness [which is not judged]; and all their judgments are ordained, and written, and engraved. 15 In regard to all He will judge, the great according to his greatness, and the small according to his smallness, and each according to his way. 16 And He is not one who will regard the person [of any], nor is He one who will receive gifts, if He says that He will execute judgment on each: if one gave everything that is on the earth, He will not regard the gifts or the person [of any], nor accept anything at his hands, for He is a righteous judge. 17 And of the sons of Israel it has been written and ordained [that] if they turn to Him in righteousness, He will forgive all their transgressions and pardon all their sins. 18 It is written and ordained that He will show mercy to all who turn from all their guilt once each year. 19 And as for all those who corrupted their ways and their thoughts before the flood, no man's person was accepted save that of Noah alone; for his person was accepted in behalf of his sons, whom [God] saved from the waters of the flood on his account; for his heart was righteous in all his ways, according as it was commanded regarding him, and he had not departed from anything that was ordained for him. 20 And the LORD said that He would destroy everything which was on the earth, both men, and cattle, and beasts, and birds of the air, and that which moves on the earth. 21 And He commanded Noah to make himself an ark, that he might save himself from the waters of the flood. 22 And Noah made the Ark in all respects as He commanded him, in the twenty-seventh jubilee of years, in the fifth week in the fifth year [[on the new moon of the first month]] . [1307 A.M.] 23 And he entered in the sixth [year] thereof [1308 A.M.], in the second month, on the new moon of the second month, until the sixteenth; and he entered, and all that we brought to him, into the Ark, and the LORD closed it from outside on the seventeenth evening. 24 And the LORD opened seven floodgates of [the] heavens, and the mouths of the fountains of the great deep—seven mouths in number. 25 And the floodgates began to pour down water from the heavens forty days and forty nights, and the fountains of the deep also sent up waters, until the whole world was full of water. 26   And the waters increased on the earth: the waters rose fifteen cubits above all the high mountains, and the Ark was lifted up above the earth, and it moved on the face of the waters. 27 And the water prevailed on the face of the earth five months—one hundred and fifty days. 28 And the Ark went and rested on the top of Lûbâr, one of the mountains of Ararat. 29 And [on the new moon] in the fourth month the fountains of the great deep were closed and the floodgates of the heavens were restrained; and on the new moon of the seventh month all the mouths of the abysses of the earth were opened, and the water began to descend into the deep below. 30 And on the new moon of the tenth month the tops of the mountains were seen, and on the new moon of the first month the earth became visible. 31 And the waters disappeared from above the earth in the fifth week in the seventh year [1309 A.M.] thereof, and on the seventeenth day in the second month the earth was dry. 32 And on the twenty-seventh thereof he opened the Ark, and sent out from it beasts, and cattle, and birds, and every moving thing.

CHAPTER 6

1 And on the new moon of the third month he went out from the Ark and built an altar on that mountain. 2 And he made atonement for the earth and took a kid and made atonement by its blood for all the guilt of the earth; for everything that had been on it had been destroyed, save those that were in the Ark with Noah. 3 And he placed the fat thereof on the altar, and he took an ox, and a goat, and a sheep and kids, and salt, and a turtle-dove, and the young of a dove, and placed a burnt sacrifice on the altar, and poured an offering mingled with oil thereon, and sprinkled wine and scattered frankincense over everything, and caused an attractive savor to arise, acceptable before the LORD . 4 And the LORD smelled the attractive

savor, and He made a covenant with him that there should not be a flood to destroy the earth anymore; that all the days of the earth, seed-time and harvest, should never cease; cold and heat, and summer and winter, and day and night should not change their order, nor cease forever. 5 "And you: increase and multiply on the earth, and become many on it, and be a blessing on it. The fear of you and the dread of you I will inspire in everything that is on earth and in the sea. 6 And behold, I have given to you all beasts, and all winged things, and everything that moves on the earth, and the fish in the waters, and all things for food; as the green herbs, I have given you all things to eat. 7 But flesh, with the life thereof, with the blood, you will not eat; for the life of all flesh is in the blood, lest your blood of your lives be required. At the hand of every man, at the hand of every [beast], I will require the blood of man. 8 Whoever sheds man's blood by man his blood will be shed, for in the image of God He made man. 9 And you: increase and multiply on the earth." 10 And Noah and his sons swore that they would not eat any blood that was in any flesh, and he made a covenant before the LORD God forever throughout all the generations of the earth in this month. 11 On this account He spoke to you that you should make a covenant with the sons of Israel in this month on the mountain with an oath, and that you should sprinkle blood on them because of all the words of the covenant, which the LORD made with them forever. 12 And this testimony is written concerning you that you should observe it continually, so that you should not eat on any day any blood of beasts, or birds, or cattle during all the days of the earth, and the man who eats the blood of beast, or of cattle, or of birds during all the days of the earth, he and his seed will be rooted out of the land. 13   And command the sons of Israel to eat no blood, so that their names and their seed may continually be before the LORD our God. 14 And for this law there is no limit of days, for it is forever. They will observe it throughout their generations, so that they may continue supplicating on your behalf with blood before the altar; every day and at the time of morning and evening they will seek forgiveness on your behalf perpetually before the LORD that they may keep it and not be rooted out. 15 And He gave a sign to Noah and his sons that there should not be a flood on the [whole] earth again. 16 He set His bow in the cloud for a sign of the perpetual covenant that there should not again be a flood on the earth to destroy it all the days of the earth. 17 For this reason it is ordained and written on the heavenly tablets that they should celebrate the Celebration of Weeks in this month once a year, to renew the covenant every year. 18 And this whole festival was celebrated in Heaven from the day of creation until the days of Noah—twenty-six jubilees and five weeks of years: and Noah and his sons observed it for seven jubilees and one week of years, until the day of Noah's death, and from the day of Noah's death his sons did away with [it] until the days of Abraham, and they ate blood. 19 But Abraham observed it, and Isaac, and Jacob, and his children observed it up to your days, and in your days the sons of Israel forgot it until you celebrated it anew on this mountain. 20 And command the sons of Israel to observe this festival in all their generations for a command to them: one day in the year in this month they will celebrate the festival. 21 For it is the Celebration of Weeks and the Celebration of First-Fruits: this feast is twofold and of a double nature . According to what is written and engraved concerning it, celebrate it. 22 For I have written in the scroll of the first law, in that which I have written for you, that you should celebrate it in its season, one day in the year, and I explained to you its sacrifices that the sons of Israel should remember and should celebrate it throughout their generations in this month, one day in every year. 23 And on the new moon of the first month, and on the new moon of the fourth month, and on the new moon of the seventh month, and on the new moon of the tenth month are the days of remembrance, and the days of the seasons in the four divisions of the year. These are written and ordained as a testimony forever. 24 And Noah ordained them for himself as feasts for the generations forever, so that they have thereby become a memorial to him. 25 And on the new moon of the first month he was commanded to make for himself an ark, and on that [day] the earth became dry, and he opened [the Ark], and saw the earth. 26 And on the new moon of the fourth month the mouths of the depths of the abysses beneath were closed. And on the new moon of the seventh month all the mouths of the abysses of the earth were opened, and the waters began to descend into them. 27 And on the new moon of the tenth month the tops of the mountains were seen, and Noah was glad. 28 And on this account, he ordained them for himself as feasts for a memorial forever, and thus they are ordained. 29 And they placed them on the heavenly tablets; each had thirteen weeks; from one to another— their memorial, from the first to the second, and from the second to the third, and from the third to the fourth. 30 And all the days of the command will be fifty-two weeks of days, and [these will make] the entire year complete. 31 Thus it is engraved and ordained on the heavenly tablets. And there is no neglecting [this command] for a single year or from year to year. 32 And command the sons of Israel that they observe the years according to this reckoning—three hundred and sixty-four days, and [these] will constitute a complete year, and they will not disturb its time from its days and from its feasts; for everything will fall out in them according to their testimony, and they will not leave out any day nor disturb any feasts. 33 But if they neglect and do not observe them according to His command, then they will disturb all their seasons, and the years will be dislodged from this [order], and they will neglect their ordinances. 34 And all the sons of Israel will forget, and will not find the path of the years, and will forget the new moons, and seasons, and Sabbaths, and they will go wrong as to all the order of the years. 35   For I know and from now on will declare it to you, and it is not of My own devising, for the scroll [lies] written before Me, and on the heavenly tablets the division of days is ordained, lest they forget the feasts of the covenant and walk according to the feasts of the nations after their error and after their ignorance. 36 For there will be those who will assuredly make observations of the moon—how [it] disturbs the seasons and comes in from year to year ten days too soon. 37 For this reason the years will come on them when they will disturb [the order] and make an abominable [day] the day of testimony, and an unclean day a feast day, and they will confound all the days, the holy with the unclean, and the unclean day with the holy; for they will go wrong as to the months, and Sabbaths, and feasts, and jubilees. 38 For this reason I command and testify to you that you may testify to them; for after your death your children will disturb [them], so that they will not make the year three hundred and sixty-four days only, and for this reason they will go wrong as to the new moons , and seasons, and Sabbaths, and festivals, and they will eat all kinds of blood with all kinds of flesh.

CHAPTER 7

1 And in the seventh week in the first year thereof, in this jubilee, Noah planted vines on the mountain on which the Ark had rested, named Lûbâr, one of the Ararat Mountains, and they produced fruit in the fourth year, and he guarded their fruit, and gathered it in this year in the seventh month. 2 And he made wine from that and put it into a vessel, and kept it until the fifth year, until the first day, on the new moon of the first month. 3 And he celebrated with joy the day of this feast, and he made a burnt sacrifice to the LORD —one young ox, and one ram, and seven sheep, each a year old, and a kid of the goats, that he might make atonement thereby for himself and his sons. 4 And he prepared the kid first and placed some of its blood on the flesh that was on the altar which he had made, and all the fat he laid on the altar where he made the burnt sacrifice, and the ox, and the ram, and the sheep, and he laid all their flesh on the altar. 5 And he placed all their offerings mingled with oil on it, and afterward he sprinkled wine on the fire which he had previously made on the altar, and he placed incense on the altar and caused a sweet savor to ascend acceptable before the LORD his God. 6 And he rejoiced and drank of this wine—he and his children with joy. 7 And it was evening, and he went into his tent, and being drunken, he lay down and slept, and was uncovered in his tent as he slept. 8 And Ham saw his father Noah naked and went out and told his two brothers outside. 9 And Shem took his garment and arose, he and Japheth, and they placed the garment on their shoulders and went backward and covered the shame of their father, and their faces were backward. 10 And Noah awoke from his sleep and knew all that his younger son had done to him, and he cursed his son and said, "Cursed be Canaan; he will be an enslaved servant to his brothers." 11 And he blessed Shem and said, "Blessed is the LORD God of Shem, and Canaan will be his servant. 12   God will enlarge Japheth, and God will dwell in the dwelling of Shem, and Canaan will be his servant." 13 And Ham knew that his father had cursed his younger son, and he was displeased that he had cursed his son, and he parted from his father, he and his sons with him—Cush, and Mizraim, and Put, and Canaan. 14 And he built a city for himself and called its name after the name of his wife Nê'êlâtamâ'ûk. 15 And Japheth saw it, and became envious of his brother, and he too built a city for himself, and he called its name after the name of his wife 'Adâtanêsês. 16 And Shem dwelt with his father Noah, and he built a city close to his father on the mountain, and he too called its name after the name of his wife Sêdêqêtêlĕbâb. 17 And behold, these three cities are near Mount Lûbâr: Sêdêqêtêlĕbâb, fronting the mountain on its east, and Na'êlâtamâ'ûk on the south, [and] 'Adatanêsês toward the west. 18 And these are the sons of Shem: Elam, and Asshur, and Arphaxad (this [son] was born two years after the flood), and Lud, and Aram. 19 The sons of Japheth: Gomer, and Magog, and Madai, and Javan, Tubal, and Meshech, and Tiras. These are the sons of Noah. 20 And in the twenty-eighth jubilee Noah began to prescribe on his sons' sons the ordinances and commands, and all the judgments that he knew, and he exhorted his sons to observe righteousness, and to cover the shame of their flesh, and to bless their Creator, and honor father and mother, and love their neighbor, and guard their souls from fornication, and uncleanness, and all iniquity. 21 For owing to these three things the flood came on the earth, namely, owing to the fornication wherein the Watchers against the law of their ordinances went whoring after the daughters of men, and took wives [for] themselves of all which they chose: and they made the beginning of uncleanness. 22 And they begot sons, the Nâphîdîm, and they were all different, and they devoured one another: and the Giants slew the Nâphîl, and the Nâphîl slew the Eljô, and the Eljô mankind, and one man another. 23 And everyone sold himself to work iniquity and to shed much blood, and the earth was filled with iniquity. 24 And after this they sinned against the beasts, and birds, and all that moves and walks on the earth: and much blood was shed on the earth, and every imagination and desire of men they imagined [was] vanity and evil continually. 25 And the LORD destroyed everything from off the face of the earth ; because of the wickedness of their deeds, and because of the blood which they had shed in the midst of the earth He destroyed everything. 26 "And we were left, you and I, my sons, and everything that entered with us into the Ark, and behold, I see your works before me that you do not walk in righteousness; for you have begun to walk in the path of destruction, and you are parting from one another, and are envious of one another, and [so it is] that you are not in harmony, my sons, each with his brother. 27 For I see and behold [that] the demons have begun [their] seductions against you and against your children, and now I fear on your behalf that after my death you will shed the blood of men on the earth, and that you, too, will be destroyed from the face of the earth. 28 For whoever sheds man's blood, and whoever eats the blood of any flesh, will all be destroyed from the earth. 29 And there will not be left any man that eats blood or that sheds the blood of man on the earth, nor will there be left to him any seed or descendants living under the heavens; for they will go into Sheol, and they will descend into the place of condemnation. And into the darkness of the deep they will all be removed by a violent death. 30 No blood will be seen on you of all the blood there will be all the days in which you have killed any beasts, or cattle, or whatever flies on the earth; and work a good work for your souls by covering that which has been shed on the face of the earth. 31 And you will not be like him who eats with blood, but guard yourselves that none may eat blood before you: cover the blood, for thus I have been commanded to testify to you and your children, together with all flesh. 32 And do not permit the soul to be eaten with the flesh, that your blood, which is your life, may not be required at the hand of any flesh that sheds [it] on the earth. 33 For the earth will not be clean from the blood which has been shed on it; for [only] through the blood of him that shed it will the earth be purified throughout all its generations. 34 And now, my children, listen: work judgment and righteousness that you may be planted in righteousness over the face of the whole earth, and your glory [will be] lifted up before my God, who saved me from the waters of the flood. 35 And behold, you will go and build cities for yourselves, and plant in them all the plants that are on the earth, and moreover all fruit-bearing trees. 36 For three years the fruit of everything that is eaten will not be gathered: and in the fourth year its fruit will be accounted holy, acceptable before the Most High God, who created the heavens, and earth, and all things. Let them offer in abundance the first of the wine and oil [as] first- fruits on the altar of the LORD , who receives it, and let the servants of the house of the LORD eat what is left before the altar which receives [it]. 37 And in the fifth year make the release so that you release it in righteousness and uprightness, and you will be righteous, and all that you plant will prosper. 38 For thus did Enoch, the father of your father command Methuselah, his son, and Methuselah his son Lamech, and Lamech commanded me all the things which his fathers commanded him. 39 And I also will give you command, my sons, as Enoch commanded his son in the first jubilees: while still living, the seventh in his generation, he commanded and testified to his son and to his sons' sons until the day of his death."

CHAPTER 8

1 In the twenty-ninth jubilee, in the first week, in the beginning thereof, Arphaxad took to himself a wife and her name was Râsû'ĕjâ, [the daughter of Sûsân,] the daughter of Elam, and she bore him a son in the third year in this week, and he called his name Kâinâm. **2** And the son grew, and his father taught him writing, and he went to seek for himself a place where he might seize for himself a city. **3** And he found a writing which former [generations] had carved on the rock, and he read what was thereon, and he transcribed it and sinned owing to it; for it contained the teaching of the Watchers in accordance with which they used to observe the omens of the sun, and moon, and stars in all the signs of the heavens. **4** And he wrote it down and said nothing regarding it; for he was afraid to speak to Noah about it lest he should be angry with him on account of it. **5** And in the thirtieth jubilee, in the second week, in the first year thereof, he took to himself a wife, and her name was Mêlkâ, the daughter of Madai, the son of Japheth, and in the fourth year he begot a son, and called his name Shelah, for he said, "Truly I have been sent." **6** [And in the fourth year he was born], and Shelah grew up and took to himself a wife, and her name was Mû'ak, the daughter of Kêsêd, his father's brother, in the thirty-first jubilee, in the fifth week, in the first year thereof. **7** And she bore him a son in the fifth year thereof, and he called his name Eber: and he took to himself a wife, and her name was 'Azûrâd , the daughter of Nêbrôd, in the thirty- second jubilee, in the seventh week, in the third year thereof. **8** And in the sixth year thereof, she bore him a son, and he called his name Peleg, for in the days when he was born the children of Noah began to divide the earth among themselves; for this reason he called his name Peleg. **9** And they divided [it] secretly among themselves and told it to Noah. **10** And it came to pass in the beginning of the thirty-third jubilee that they divided the earth into three parts, for Shem, and Ham, and Japheth, according to the inheritance of each, in the first year in the first week, when one of us, who had been sent, was with them. **11** And he called his sons, and they drew near to him, they and their children, and he divided the earth into the lots, which his three sons were to take in possession, and they reached out their hands, and took the writing out of the bosom of their father Noah. **12** And there came out on the writing as Shem's lot the middle of the earth which he should take as an inheritance for himself and for his sons, for the perpetual generations, from the middle of the mountain range of Râfâ, from the mouth of the water from the River Tînâ , and his portion goes toward the west through the midst of this river, and it extends until it reaches the water of the abysses, out of which this river goes out and pours its waters into the sea Mê'at, and this river flows into the Great Sea. And all that is toward the north is Japheth's, and all that is toward the south belongs to Shem. **13** And it extends until it reaches Kârâsô: this is in the bosom of the tongue which looks toward the south. **14** And his portion extends along the Great Sea, and it extends in a straight line until it reaches the west of the tongue which looks toward the south; for this sea is called the tongue of the Egyptian Sea. **15** And it turns from here toward the south toward the mouth of the Great Sea on the shore of [its] waters, and it extends to the west to 'Afrâ and it extends until it reaches the waters of the River Gihon, and to the south of the waters of Gihon, to the banks of this river. **16** And it extends toward the east until it reaches the Garden of Eden, to the south thereof, [to the south] and from the east of the whole land of Eden and of the whole east [thereof], it turns to the east, and proceeds until it reaches the east of the mountain named Râfâ, and it descends to the bank of the mouth of the River Tînâ. **17** This portion came out by lot for Shem and his sons, that they should possess it forever to his generations forevermore. **18** And Noah rejoiced that this portion came out for Shem and for his sons, and he remembered all that he had spoken with his mouth in prophecy; for he had said, "Blessed is the LORD God of Shem, and may the LORD dwell in the dwelling of Shem." **19** And he knew that the Garden of Eden is the Holy of Holies and the dwelling of the LORD , and Mount Sinai—the center of the desert, and Mount Zion—the center of the navel of the earth: these three were created as holy places facing each other. **20** And he blessed the God of gods who had put the word of the LORD into his mouth, and [blessed] the LORD forevermore. **21** And he knew that a blessed portion and a blessing had come to Shem and his sons to the generations forever—the whole land of Eden and the whole land of the Red Sea, and the whole land of the east, and India, and on the Red Sea and the mountains thereof, and all the land of Bashan, and all the land of Lebanon and the islands of Kaftûr, and all the mountains of Sanîr and 'Amânâ, and the mountains of Asshur in the north, and all the land of Elam, Asshur, and Bâbêl, and Sûsân, and Mâ'ĕdâi , and all the mountains of Ararat, and all the region beyond the sea, which is beyond the mountains of Asshur toward the north, a blessed and spacious land, and all that is in it is very good. **22** And for Ham came out the second portion, beyond the Gihon toward the south to the right of the Garden, and it extends toward the south and it extends to all the mountains of fire, and it extends toward the west to the Sea of 'Atêl and it extends toward the west until it reaches the Sea of Mâ'ûk —that [sea] into which everything which is not destroyed descends. **23** And it goes out toward the north to the limits of Gâdîr, and it goes out to the coast of the waters of the sea to the waters of the Great Sea until it draws near to the River Gihon and goes along the River Gihon until it reaches the right of the Garden of Eden. **24** And this is the land which came out for Ham as the portion which he was to occupy forever for himself and his sons to their generations forever. **25** And for Japheth came out the third portion beyond the River Tînâ to the north of the outflow of its waters, and it extends northeastward to the whole region of Gog and to all the country east thereof. **26** And it extends northward to the north, and it extends to the mountains of Qêlt toward the north, and toward the Sea of Mâ'ûk, and it goes out to the east of Gâdîr as far as the region of the waters of the sea. **27** And it extends until it approaches the west of Fârâ , and it returns toward 'Afêrâg, and it extends eastward to the waters of the Sea of Mê'at. **28** And it extends to the region of the River Tînâ in a northeasterly direction until it approaches the boundary of its waters toward the mountain Râfâ, and it turns toward the north. **29** This is the land which came out for Japheth and his sons as the portion of his inheritance which he should possess for himself and his sons, for their generations forever: five great islands, and a great land in the north. **30** But it is cold, and the land of Ham is hot, and the land of Shem is neither hot nor cold, but it is of blended cold and heat.

CHAPTER 9

1 And Ham divided among his sons, and the first portion came out for Cush toward the east, and to the west of him for Mizraim, and to the west of him for Put, and to the west of him [and to the west thereof] on the sea for Canaan. **2** And Shem also divided among his sons, and the first portion came out for Elam and his sons, to the east of the River Tigris until it approaches the east, the whole land of India, and on the Red Sea on its coast, and the waters of Dêdân, and all the mountains of Mebrî and 'Êlâ, and all the land of Sûsân and all that is on the side of Pharnâk to the Red Sea and the River Tînâ. **3** And for Asshur came out the second portion, all the land of Asshur, and Nineveh, and Shinar, and to the border of India, and it ascends and skirts the river. **4** And for Arphaxad came out the third portion, all the land of the region of the Chaldees to the east of the Euphrates, bordering on the Red Sea, and all the waters of the desert close to the tongue of the sea which looks toward Egypt, all the land of Lebanon, and Sanîr, and 'Amânâ to the border of the Euphrates. **5** And for Aram there came out the fourth portion, all the land of Mesopotamia between the Tigris and the Euphrates to the north of the Chaldees to the border of the mountains of Asshur and the land of 'Arârâ. **6** And there came out for Lud the fifth portion, the mountains of Asshur and all pertaining to them until it reaches the Great Sea, and until it reaches the east of his brother Asshur. **7** And Japheth also divided the land of his inheritance among his sons. **8** And the first portion came out for Gomer to the east from the north side to the River Tînâ; and in the north there came out for Magog all the inner portions of the north until it reaches to the Sea of Mê'at. **9** And for Madai came out as his portion that he should possess from the west of his two brothers to the islands, and to the coasts of the islands. **10** And for Javan came out the fourth portion, every island and the islands which are toward the border of Lud. **11** And for Tubal there came out the fifth portion in the midst of the tongue which approaches toward the border of the portion of Lud to the second tongue, to the region beyond the second tongue to the third tongue. **12** And for Meshech came out the sixth portion, all the region beyond the third tongue until it approaches the east of Gâdîr. **13** And for Tiras there came out the seventh portion: four great islands in the midst of the sea, which reach to the portion of Ham [[and the islands of Kamâtûrî came out by lot for the sons of Arphaxad as his inheritance]] . **14** And thus the sons of Noah divided to their sons in the presence of their father Noah, and he bound them all by an oath, invoking a curse on everyone that sought to seize the portion which had not fallen [to him] by his lot. **15** And they all said, "So be it; so be it," for themselves and their sons forever throughout their generations until the Day of Judgment, on which the LORD God will judge them with a sword and with fire, for all the unclean wickedness of their errors, with which they have filled the earth with transgression, and uncleanness, and fornication, and sin.

CHAPTER 10

1 And in the third week of this jubilee the unclean demons began to lead the children of the sons of Noah astray, and to make [them] to err, and destroy them. **2** And the sons of Noah came to their father Noah, and they told him concerning the demons which were leading astray, and blinding, and slaying his sons' sons. **3** And he prayed before the LORD his God, and said, " God of the spirits of all flesh, Who has shown mercy to me, And has saved me and my sons from the waters of the flood, And has not caused me to perish as you did the sons of perdition , For Your grace has been great toward me, And great has been Your mercy to my soul: Let Your grace be lifted up on my sons, And do not let wicked spirits rule over them Lest they should destroy them from the earth. **4** But bless me and my sons, That we may increase, and multiply, and replenish the earth. **5** And You know how Your Watchers, The fathers of these spirits, acted in my day: And as for these spirits which are living, Imprison them and hold them fast in the place of condemnation, And do not let them bring destruction on the sons of Your servant, my God; For these are malevolent, and created in order to destroy. **6** And do not let them rule over the spirits of the living, For You alone can exercise dominion over them. And do not let them have power over the sons of the righteous From now on and forevermore." **7** And the LORD our God commanded us to bind all. **8** And the chief of the spirits, Mastêmâ, came and said, " LORD , Creator, let some of them remain before me, and let them listen to my voice, and do all that I will say to them; for if some of them are not left to me, I will not be able to execute the power of my will on the sons of men; for these are for corruption and leading astray before my judgment, for great is the wickedness of the sons of men." **9** And He said, "Let the tenth part of them remain before him, and let nine parts descend into the place of condemnation." **10** And He commanded that one of us should teach Noah all their medicines; for He knew that they would not walk in uprightness, nor strive in righteousness. **11** And we did according to all His words: we bound all the malevolent evil ones in the place of condemnation, and a tenth part of them we left that they might be subject before Satan on the earth. **12** And we explained to Noah all the medicines of their diseases, together with their seductions, how he might heal them with herbs of the earth. **13** And Noah wrote down all things in a scroll as we instructed him concerning every kind of medicine. Thus, the evil spirits were precluded from [hurting] the sons of Noah. **14** And he gave all that he had written to Shem, his eldest son, for he loved him exceedingly above all his sons. **15** And Noah slept with his fathers and was buried on Mount Lûbâr in the land of Ararat. **16** Nine hundred and fifty years he completed in his life—nineteen jubilees, and two weeks, and five years. **17** And in his life on earth he excelled the children of men, save Enoch because of the righteousness wherein he was perfect. For Enoch's office was ordained for a testimony to the generations of the world, so that he should recount all the deeds of generation to generation, until the Day of Judgment. **18** And in the thirty-third jubilee, in the first year in the second week, Peleg took to himself a wife, whose name was Lômnâ, the daughter of Sînâ'ar, and she bore him a son in the fourth year of this week, and he called his name Reu , for he said, "Behold, the children of men have become evil through the wicked purpose of building for themselves a city and a tower in the land of Shinar." **19** For they departed from the land of Ararat eastward to Shinar, for in his days they built the city and the tower, saying, "Go forth; let us ascend thereby into the heavens." **20** And they began to build, and in the fourth week they made brick with fire, and the bricks served them for stone, and the clay with which they cemented them together was asphalt, which comes out of the sea and out of the fountains of water in the land of Shinar. **21** And they built it; forty-three years they were building it; its breadth was two hundred and three bricks, and the height [of a brick] was the third of one; its height amounted to five thousand and four hundred and thirty-three cubits and two palms, and [the extent of one wall was] thirteen stadia [[and of the other thirty stadia]] . **22** And the LORD our God said to us, "Behold, they are one people, and they begin to do [this], and now nothing will be withheld from them. Go forth; let us go down and confound their language that they may not understand one another's speech, and they may be dispersed into cities and nations, and one purpose will no longer abide with them until the Day of Judgment." **23** And the LORD descended, and we descended with Him to see the city and the tower which the children of men had built. **24** And He confounded their language, and they no longer understood one another's speech, and then they ceased to build the city and the tower. **25** For this reason the whole land of Shinar is called Babel, because the LORD confounded all the language of the children of men there, and from there they were dispersed into their cities, each according to his language and his nation. **26** And the LORD sent a mighty wind against the tower and overthrew it on the earth, and behold, it was between Asshur and Babylon in the land of Shinar, and they called its name "Overthrow." **27** In the fourth week, in the first year, in the beginning thereof, in the thirty-fourth jubilee, they were dispersed from the land of Shinar. **28** And Ham and his sons went into the land which he was to occupy, which he acquired as his portion in the land of the south. **29** And Canaan saw the land of Lebanon to the river of Egypt that it was very good, and he did not go into the land of his inheritance to the west [that is to] the sea, and he dwelt in the land of Lebanon, eastward and westward from the border of Jordan and from the border of the sea. **30** And his father Ham, and his brothers Cush and Mizraim, said to him, "You have settled in a land which is not yours, and which did not fall to us by lot: do not do so; for if you do so, you and your sons will fall in the land and [be] accursed through sedition; for by sedition you have settled, and by sedition your children will fall, and you will be rooted out forever. **31** Do not dwell in the dwelling of Shem, for to Shem and to his sons did it come by their lot. **32** Cursed are you and cursed will you be beyond all the sons of Noah, by the curse by which we bound ourselves by an oath in the presence of the Holy Judge, and in the presence of our father Noah." **33** But he did not listen to them and dwelt in the land of Lebanon from Hamath to the entering of Egypt —he and his sons until this day. **34** And for this reason that land is named Canaan. **35** And Japheth and his sons went toward the sea and dwelt in the land of their portion, and Madai saw the land of the sea and it did not please him, and he begged [for] a [portion] from Elam, and Asshur, and Arphaxad, his wife's brother, and he dwelt in the land of Media, near to his wife's brother, until this day. **36** And he called his dwelling-place and the dwelling-place of his sons Media, after the name of their father Madai.

CHAPTER 11

1 And in the thirty-fifth jubilee, in the third week, in the first year thereof, Reu took to himself a wife, and her name was 'Ôrâ, the daughter of 'Ûr, the son of Kêsêd, and she bore him a son, and he called his name Sêrôḫ, in the seventh year of this week in this jubilee. **2** And the sons of Noah began to war on each other, to take captive and to slay each other, and to shed the blood of men on the earth, and to eat blood, and to build strong cities, and walls, and towers, and individuals [began] to exalt themselves above the nation, and to found the beginnings of kingdoms, and to go to war—people against people, and nation against nation, and city against city, and all [began] to do evil, and to acquire arms, and to teach their sons war, and they began to capture cities, and to sell menservants and maidservants. **3** And 'Ûr, the son of Kêsêd, built the city of 'Arâ of the Chaldees, and called its name after his own name and the name of his father. **4** And they made molten images for themselves, and they each worshiped the idol, the molten image which they had made for themselves, and they began to make graven images and unclean statues, and malevolent spirits assisted and seduced [them] into committing transgression and uncleanness. **5** And the prince Mastêmâ exerted himself to do all this, and he sent out other spirits, those which were put under his hand, to do all manner of wrong and sin, and all manner of transgression, to corrupt and destroy, and to shed blood on the earth. **6** For this reason he called the name of Sêrôḫ, Serug, for everyone turned to do all manner of sin and transgression. **7** And he grew up and dwelt in Ur of the Chaldees, near to the father of his wife's mother, and he worshiped idols, and he took to himself a wife in the thirty-sixth jubilee, in the fifth week, in the first year thereof, and her name was Mêlkâ, the daughter of Kâbêr, the daughter of his father's brother. **8** And she bore him Nahor in the first year of this week, and he grew and dwelt in Ur of the Chaldees, and his father taught him the research of the Chaldees to divine and portend, according to the signs of the heavens. **9** And in the thirty- seventh jubilee, in the sixth week, in the first year thereof, he took to himself a wife, and her name was 'Îjâskâ, the daughter of Nêstâg of the Chaldees. **10** And she bore him Terah in the seventh year of this week. **11** And the prince Mastêmâ sent ravens and birds to devour the seed which was sown in the land, in order to destroy the land, and rob the children of men of their labors. Before they could plow in the seed, the ravens picked [it] from the surface of the ground. **12** And for this reason he called his name Terah, because the ravens and the birds reduced them to destitution and devoured their seed. **13** And the years began to be barren, owing to the birds, and they devoured all the fruit of the trees from the trees: it was only with great effort that they could save a little of all the fruit of the earth in their days. **14** And in this thirty-ninth jubilee, in the second week in the first year, Terah took to himself a wife, and her name was 'Êdnâ, the daughter of 'Abrâm , the daughter of his father's sister. **15** And in the seventh year of this week she bore him a son, and he called his name Abram, by the name of the father of his mother, for he had died before his daughter had conceived a son. **16** And the child began to understand the errors of the earth, that all went astray after graven images and after uncleanness, and his father taught him writing, and he was two weeks of years old, and he separated himself from his father that he might not worship idols with him. **17** And he began to pray to the Creator of all things that He might save him from the errors of the children of men, and that his portion should not fall into error after uncleanness and vileness. **18** And the seed-time came for the sowing of seed on the land, and they all went out together to protect their seed against the ravens, and Abram went out with those that went, and the child was a youth of fourteen years. **19** And a cloud of ravens came to devour the seed, and Abram ran to meet them before they settled on the ground and cried to them before they settled on the ground to devour the seed, and said, "Do not descend! Return to the place where you came!" And they proceeded to turn back. **20** And he caused the clouds of ravens to turn back that day seventy times, and of all the ravens throughout all the land where Abram was there settled there not so much as one. **21** And all who were with him throughout all the land saw him cry out, and all the ravens turn back, and his name became great in all the land of the Chaldees. **22** And there came to him this year all those that wished to sow, and he went with them until the time of sowing ceased: and they sowed their land, and that year they brought enough grain home and ate and were satisfied. **23** And in the first year of the fifth week Abram taught those who made implements for oxen, the craftsmen in wood, and they made a vessel above the ground, facing the frame of the plow, in order to put the seed thereon, and the seed fell down from that on the share of the plow, and was hidden in the earth, and they no longer feared the ravens. **24** And after this manner they made [vessels] above the ground on all the frames of the plows, and they sowed and tilled all the land, according as Abram commanded them, and they no longer feared the birds.

CHAPTER 12

1 And it came to pass in the sixth week, in the seventh year thereof, that Abram spoke to his father Terah, saying, "Father!" And he said, "Behold, here I am, my son." **2** And he said, "What help and profit do we have from those idols which you worship, and before which you bow yourself? **3** For there is no spirit in them, for they are mute forms, and a misleading of the heart. Do not worship them: **4** worship the God of Heaven, who causes the rain and the dew to descend on the earth, and does everything on the earth, and has created everything by His word, and all life is from before His face. **5** Why do you worship things that have no spirit in them? For they are the work of [men's] hands, and you bear them on your shoulders, and you have no help from them, but they are a great cause of shame to those who make them, and a misleading of the heart to those who worship them: do not worship them." **6** And his father said to him, "I also know it, my son, but what will I do with a people who have made me to serve before them? **7** And if I tell them the truth, they will slay me, for their soul cleaved to them to worship them and honor them. Keep silent, my son, lest they slay you." **8** And he spoke these words to his two brothers, and they were angry with him and he kept silent. **9** And in the fortieth jubilee, in the second week, in the seventh year thereof, Abram took to himself a wife, and her name was Sarai, the daughter of his father, and she became his wife. **10** And his brother Haran took to himself a wife in the third year of the third week, and she bore him a son in the seventh year of this week, and he called his name Lot. **11** And his brother Nahor took to himself a wife. **12** And in the sixtieth year of the life of Abram, that is, in the fourth week, in the fourth year thereof, Abram arose by night, and burned the house of the idols, and he burned all that was in the house, and no man knew it. **13** And they arose in the night and sought to save their gods from the midst of the fire. **14** And Haran tried to save them, but the fire flamed over him, and he was burned in the fire, and he died in Ur of the Chaldees before his father Terah, and they buried him in Ur of the Chaldees. **15** And Terah went out from Ur of the Chaldees, he and his sons, to go into the land of Lebanon and into the land of Canaan, and he dwelt in the land of Haran, and Abram dwelt with his father Terah in Haran [for] two weeks of years. **16**   And in the sixth week, in the fifth year thereof, Abram sat up throughout the night on the new moon of the seventh month to observe the stars from the evening to the morning, in order to see what the nature of the year would be with regard to the rains, and he was alone as he sat and observed. **17** And a word came into his heart and he said, "All the signs of the stars, and the signs of the moon and of the sun are all in the hand of the LORD . Why do I search [them] out? **18** If He desires, He causes it to rain, morning and evening; and if He desires, He withholds it, and all things are in His hand." **19** And he prayed that night and said, "My God, God Most High, You alone are my God, and I have chosen You and Your dominion. And You have created all things, and all things that exist are the work of Your hands. **20** Deliver me from the hands of evil spirits who have sway over the thoughts of men's hearts, and do not let them lead me astray from You, my God. And establish me and my seed forever so that we do not go astray from now and forevermore." **21** And he said, "Will I return to Ur of the Chaldees who seek my face that I may return to them, or am I to remain here in this place? The right path before You—prosper it in the hands of Your servant that he may fulfill [it] and that I may not walk in the deceitfulness of my heart, O my God." **22** And he made an end of speaking and praying, and behold, the word of the LORD was sent to him through me, saying, "Go forth from your country, and from your relatives, and from the house of your father to a land which I will show you, and I will make you a great and numerous nation. **23** And I will bless you, and I will make your name great, and you will be blessed in the earth, and all [the] families of the earth will be blessed in you, and I will bless them that bless you, and curse them that curse you. **24** And I will be God to you and your son, and to your son's son, and to all your seed: do not fear, from now and to all generations of the earth I am your God." **25** And the LORD God said, "Open his mouth and his ears that he may hear and speak with his mouth, with the language which has been revealed," for it had ceased from the mouths of all the children of men from the day of the overthrow [of Babel]. **26** And I opened his mouth, and his ears, and his lips, and I began to speak with him in Hebrew in the tongue of the creation. **27** And he took the scrolls of his fathers, and these were written in Hebrew, and he transcribed them, and he began from then on to study them, and I made known to him that which he could not [understand], and he studied them during the six rainy months. **28** And it came to pass in the seventh year of the sixth week that he spoke to his father and informed him that he would leave Haran to go into the land of Canaan to see it and [then] return to him. **29** And his father Terah said to him, "Go in peace; m ay the perpetual God make your path straight, and the LORD [[be with you, and]] protect you from all evil, and grant grace, mercy, and favor to you before those who see you, and may none of the children of men have power over you to harm you; go in peace. **30** And if you see a land pleasant to your eyes to dwell in, then arise and take me to you, and take Lot, the son of your brother Haran, with you as your own son: the LORD be with you. **31** And leave your brother Nahor with me until you return in peace, and we all go with you together."

CHAPTER 13

1   And Abram journeyed from Haran, and he took his wife Sarai, and Lot, his brother Haran's son, to the land of Canaan, and he came into Asshur, and proceeded to Shechem, and dwelt near a lofty oak. **2** And he saw, and behold, the land was very pleasant from the entering of Hamath to the lofty oak. **3** And the LORD said to him, "To you and to your seed I will give this land." **4** And he built an altar there, and he offered a burnt sacrifice thereon to the LORD , who had appeared to him. **5** And he left from there to the mountain [with] Bethel on the west and Ai on the east and pitched his tent there. **6** And he saw, and behold, the land was very wide and good, and everything grew thereon—vines, and figs, and pomegranates, oaks, and hollies, and terebinths, and oil trees, and cedars, and cypresses, and date trees, and all trees of the field, and there was water on the mountains. **7** And he blessed the LORD who had led him out of Ur of the Chaldees and had brought him to this land. **8** And it came to pass in the first year, in the seventh week, on the new moon of the first month, that he built an altar on this mountain, and called on the Name of the L ORD : "You, the perpetual God, are my God." **9** And he offered a burnt sacrifice to the LORD on the altar that He should be with him and not forsake him all the days of his life. **10** And he left from there and went toward the south, and he came to Hebron, and Hebron was built at that time, and he dwelt there two years, and he went into the land of the south, to Bealoth , and there was a famine in the land. **11** And Abram went into Egypt in the third year of the week, and he dwelt in Egypt five years before his wife was torn away from him. **12** Now Tanis [(Zoan)] in Egypt was at that time built—seven years after Hebron. **11** And it came to pass when Pharaoh seized Sarai, the wife of Abram, that the LORD plagued Pharaoh and his house with great plagues because of Sarai, Abram's wife. **14** And Abram was very glorious by reason of possessions in sheep, and cattle, and donkeys, and horses, and camels, and menservants, and maidservants, and in exceeding silver and gold. And Lot also, his brother's son, was wealthy. **15** And Pharaoh gave back Sarai, the wife of Abram, and he sent him out of the land of Egypt, and he journeyed to the place where he had pitched his tent at the beginning, to the place of the altar, with Ai on the east and Bethel on the west, and he blessed the LORD his God who had brought him back in peace. **16** And it came to pass in the forty-first jubilee, in the third year of the first week, that he returned to this place and offered a burnt sacrifice there, and called on the Name of the L ORD , and said, "You, the Most High God, are my God forever and ever." **17** And in the fourth year of this week Lot parted from him, and Lot dwelt in Sodom, and the men of Sodom were sinners exceedingly. **18** And it grieved him in his heart that his brother's son had parted from him, for he had no children. **19** In that year, when Lot was taken captive, the LORD said to Abram after Lot had parted from him, in the fourth year of this week: "Lift up your eyes from the place where you are dwelling —northward, and southward, and westward, and eastward. **20** For all the land which you see I will give to you and to your seed forever, and I will make your seed as the sand of the sea: though a man may number the dust of the earth, yet your seed will not be numbered. **21** Arise, walk in the length of it and the breadth of it, and see it all; for to your seed I will give it." And Abram went to Hebron and dwelt there. **22** And in this year Chedorlaomer, king of Elam, and Amraphel, king of Shinar, and Arioch, king of Sêllâsar and Têrgâl, king of nations, came and slew the king of Gomorrah, and the king of Sodom fled, and many fell through wounds in the Valley of Siddim, by the Salt Sea. **23** And they took Sodom, and Adam , and Zeboim captive, and they took Lot captive also, the son of Abram's brother, and all his possessions, and they went to Dan. **24** And one who had escaped came and told Abram that his brother's son had been taken captive and [Abram] armed his household servants. **25** For Abram, and for his seed, a tenth of the first-fruits to the LORD , and the LORD ordained it as an ordinance forever that they should give it to the priests who served before Him, that they should possess it forever. **26** And to this law there is no limit of days; for He has ordained it for the generations forever that they should give to the LORD the tenth of everything, of the seed, and of the wine, and of the oil, and of the cattle, and of the sheep. **27** And He gave [it] to His priests to eat and to drink with joy before Him. **28** And the king of Sodom came to him and bowed himself before him, and said, "Our Lord Abram, give to us the souls which you have rescued, but let the plunder be yours." **29** And Abram said to him, "I lift up my hands to the Most High God, that from a thread to a shoe-strap I will not take anything that is yours, lest you should say, I have made Abram rich—save only what the young men have eaten, and the portion of the men who went with me—Aner, Eschol, and Mamre. These will take their portion."

CHAPTER **14**

1 After these things, in the fourth year of this week, on the new moon of the third month, the word of the LORD came to Abram in a dream, saying, "Do not fear, Abram; I am your defender, and your reward will be exceedingly great." **2** And he said, "Lord YHWH , what will You give me, seeing I go childless, and the son of Mâsêq, the son of my handmaid, is the Demmesek Eliezer: he will be my heir, and to me You have not given seed." **3** And He said to him, "This [man] will not be your heir, but one that will come out of your own bowels, he will be your heir." **4** And He brought him out abroad, and said to him, "Look toward the heavens and number the stars, if you are able to number them." **5** And he looked toward the heavens and beheld the stars. And He said to him, "So will your seed be." **6** And he believed in the LORD , and it was counted to him for righteousness. **7** And He said to him, "I am the LORD that brought you out of Ur of the Chaldees, to give you the land of the Canaanites to possess it forever; and I will be God to you and to your seed after you." **8** And he said, "Lord YHWH , whereby will I know that I will inherit [it]?" **9** And He said to him, "Take Me a heifer of three years, and a goat of three years, and a sheep of three years, and a turtle-dove, and a pigeon." **10** And he took all these in the middle of the month; and he dwelt at the oak of Mamre, which is near Hebron. **11** And he built an altar there and sacrificed all these; and he poured their blood on the altar, and divided them in the midst, and laid them over against each other, but he did not divide the birds. **12** And birds came down on the pieces, and Abram drove them away, and did not permit the birds to touch them. **13** And it came to pass, when the sun had set, that an ecstasy fell on Abram, and behold, a horror of great darkness fell on him, and it was said to Abram: "Know for sure that your seed will be a stranger in a land [that is] not theirs, and they will bring them into bondage, and afflict them four hundred years. **14** And the nation to whom they will be in bondage I will also judge, and after that they will come out from there with much substance. **15** And you will go to your fathers in peace and be buried in a good old age. **16** But in the fourth generation they will return here, for the iniquity of the Amorites is not yet full." **17** And he awoke from his sleep, and he arose, and the sun had set; and there was a flame, and behold, a furnace was smoking, and a flame of fire passed between the pieces. **18** And on that day the LORD made a covenant with Abram, saying, "To your seed I will give this land, from the river of Egypt to the great river, the River Euphrates—the Kenites, the Kenizzites, the Kadmonites, the Perizzites, and the Rephaim, the Phakorites, and the Hivites, and the Amorites, and the Canaanites, and the Girgashites, and the Jebusites." **19** And the day passed, and Abram offered the pieces, and the birds, and their fruit-offerings, and their drink-offerings, and the fire devoured them. **20** And on that day we made a covenant with Abram, according as we had covenanted with Noah in this month; and Abram renewed the festival and ordinance for himself forever. **21** And Abram rejoiced and made all these things known to his wife Sarai; and he believed that he would have seed, but she did not bear. **22** And Sarai advised her husband Abram and said to him, "Go in to Hagar, my Egyptian maid: it may be that I will build up seed to you by her." **23** And Abram listened to the voice of his wife Sarai and said to her, "Do [so]." And Sarai took Hagar, her maid, the Egyptian, and gave her to her husband Abram to be his wife. **24** And he went in to her, and she conceived and bore him a son, and he called his name Ishmael, in the fifth year of this week; and this was the eighty-sixth year in the life of Abram.

CHAPTER 15

1 And in the fifth year of the fourth week of this jubilee, in the third month, in the middle of the month, Abram celebrated the Celebration of the First- Fruits of the grain harvest. **2** And he offered new offerings on the altar, the first-fruits of the produce, to the LORD : a heifer, and a goat, and a sheep on the altar as a burnt sacrifice to the LORD ; their fruit-offerings and their drink-offerings he offered on the altar with frankincense. **3** And the LORD appeared to Abram and said to him, "I am God Almighty; approve yourself before Me and be perfect. **4** And I will make My covenant between Me and you, and I will multiply you exceedingly." **5** And Abram fell on his face, and God talked with him, and said, **6** "Behold, My ordinance is with you, and you will be the father of many nations. **7** Neither will your name be called Abram anymore, but your name from now on, even forever, will be Abraham. For I have made you the father of many nations. **8** And I will make you very great, and I will make you into nations, and kings will come out from you. **9** And I will establish My covenant between Me and you, and your seed after you, throughout their generations, for a perpetual covenant, so that I may be a God to you, and to your seed after you. **10** [[And I will give to you and to your seed after you]] the land where you have been a sojourner, the land of Canaan, that you may possess it forever, and I will be their God." **11** And the LORD said to Abraham, "And as for you: keep My covenant, you and your seed after you, and circumcise every male among you, and circumcise your foreskins, and it will be a token of a perpetual covenant between Me and you. **12** And you will circumcise the child on the eighth day , every male throughout your generations—him that is born in the house, or whom you have bought with money from any stranger, whom you have acquired who is not of your seed. **13** He that is born in your house will surely be circumcised, and those whom you have bought with money will be circumcised, and My covenant will be in your flesh for a perpetual ordinance. **14** And the uncircumcised male who is not circumcised in the flesh of his foreskin on the eighth day, that soul will be cut off from his people, for he has broken My covenant." **15** And God said to Abraham, "As for Sarai your wife, her name will no longer be called Sarai, but Sarah will be her name. **16** And I will bless her, and give you a son by her, and I will bless him, and he will become a nation, and kings of nations will proceed from him." **17** And Abraham fell on his face, and rejoiced, and said in his heart, "Will a son be born to him that is one hundred years old, and will Sarah, who is ninety years old, bring out?" **18** And Abraham said to God, "O that Ishmael might live before you!" **19** And God said, "Yes, and Sarah will also bear you a son, and you will call his name Isaac, and I will establish My covenant with him, a perpetual covenant, and for his seed after him. **20** And as for Ishmael, I have also heard you, and behold, I will bless him, and make him great, and multiply him exceedingly, and he will beget twelve princes, and I will make him a great nation. **21** But I will establish My covenant with Isaac, whom Sarah will bear to you, in these days, in the next year." **22** And He left off speaking with him, and God went up from Abraham. **23** And Abraham did according as God had said to him, and he took his son Ishmael, and all that were born in his house, and whom he had bought with his money, every male in his house, and circumcised the flesh of their foreskin. **24** And on the same day Abraham was circumcised, indeed, all the men of his house and all those whom he had bought with money from the children of the stranger were circumcised with him. **25** This law is for all the generations forever, and there is no circumcision of the days, and no omission of one day out of the eight days , for it is a perpetual ordinance, ordained and written on the heavenly tablets. **26** And everyone that is born, the flesh of whose foreskin is not circumcised on the eighth day, does not belong to the children of the covenant which the LORD made with Abraham, but to the children of destruction; nor is there, moreover, any sign on him that he is the LORD 's, but [he is destined] to be destroyed and slain from the earth, and to be rooted out of the earth, for he has broken the covenant of the LORD our God. **27** For all the messengers of the presence and all the messengers of sanctification have been so created from the day of their creation, and before the messengers of the presence and the messengers of sanctification, He has sanctified Israel, that they should be with Him and with His holy messengers. **28** And command the sons of Israel and let them observe the sign of this covenant for their generations as a perpetual ordinance, and they will not be rooted out of the land. **29** For the command is ordained for a covenant, that they should observe it forever among all the sons of Israel. **30** For Ishmael, and his sons, and his brothers, and Esau, the LORD did not cause to approach Him, and He did not choose them because they are the children of Abraham, because He knew them, but He chose Israel to be His people. **31** And He sanctified it and gathered it from among all the children of men; for there are many nations and many peoples, and all are His, and over all He has placed spirits in authority to lead them astray from Him. **32** But over Israel He did not appoint any messenger or spirit, for He alone is their ruler, and He will preserve them and require them at the hand of His messengers and His spirits, and at the hand of all His powers in order that He may preserve them and bless them, and that they may be His and He may be theirs from now on and forever. **33** And now I announce to you that the sons of Israel will not keep true to this ordinance, and they will not circumcise their sons according to all this law, for in the flesh of their circumcision they will omit this circumcision of their sons, and all of them, sons of Belial, will leave their sons uncircumcised as they were born. **34** And there will be great wrath from the LORD against the sons of Israel, because they have forsaken His covenant and turned aside from His word, and provoked and blasphemed, inasmuch as they do not observe the ordinance of this law, for they have treated their members like the nations, so that they may be removed and rooted out of the land. And there will no longer be pardon or forgiveness to them for all the sin of this continuous error.

CHAPTER 16

1 And on the new moon of the fourth month we appeared to Abraham, at the oak of Mamre, and we talked with him, and we announced to him that a son would be given to him by his wife Sarah. **2** And Sarah laughed, for she heard that we had spoken these words with Abraham, and we admonished her, and she became afraid, and denied that she had laughed on account of the words. **3** And we told her the name of her son, as his name [(Isaac)] is ordained and written in the heavenly tablets, **4** and [that] when we returned to her at a set time, she would have conceived a son. **5** And in this month the LORD executed His judgments on Sodom, and Gomorrah, and Zeboim, and all the region of the Jordan, and He burned them with fire and brimstone, and destroyed them until this day, even as I have declared to you all their works, that they are sinners and exceedingly wicked, and that they defile themselves and commit fornication in their flesh, and work uncleanness on the earth. 6 And, in like manner, God will execute judgment on the places where they have done according to the uncleanness of the Sodomites, like to the judgment of Sodom. 7 But we saved Lot, for God remembered Abraham and sent him out from the midst of the overthrow. 8 And he and his daughters committed sin on the earth, such as had not been on the earth since the days of Adam until his time, for the man lay with his daughters. 9 And behold, it was commanded and engraved concerning all his seed, on the heavenly tablets, to remove them and root them out, and to execute judgment on them like the judgment of Sodom, and to leave no seed of the man on earth on the day of condemnation. 10 And in this month Abraham moved from Hebron and departed and dwelt between Kadesh and Shur in the mountains of Gerar. 11 And in the middle of the fifth month he moved from there and dwelt at the Well of the Oath. 12 And in the middle of the sixth month the LORD visited Sarah and did to her as He had spoken, and she conceived. 13 And she bore a son in the third month, and in the middle of the month, at the time of which the LORD had spoken to Abraham, on the festival of the first-fruits of the harvest, Isaac was born. 14 And Abraham circumcised his son on the eighth day: he was the first that was circumcised according to the covenant which is ordained forever. 15 And in the sixth year of the fourth week we came to Abraham, to the Well of the Oath, and we appeared to him || as we had told Sarah that we should return to her, and she would have conceived a son. 16 And we returned in the seventh month, and found Sarah with child before us, || and we blessed him, and we announced to him all the things which had been decreed concerning him: that he should not die until he should beget six more sons, and should see [them] before he died, but [that] in Isaac should his name and seed be called , 17 and [that] all the seed of his sons should be nations, and be reckoned with the nations, but from the sons of Isaac one should become a holy seed and should not be reckoned among the nations. 18 For he should become the portion of the Most High, and all his seed had fallen into the possession of God, that it should be to the LORD a people for [His] possession above all nations and that it should become a kingdom, and priests, and a holy nation. 19 And we went our way, and we announced to Sarah all that we had told him, and they both rejoiced with exceedingly great joy. 20 And he built an altar there to the LORD who had delivered him, and who was making him rejoice in the land of his sojourning, and he celebrated a festival of joy in this month [for] seven days, near the altar which he had built at the Well of the Oath. 21 And he built shelters for himself and for his servants on this festival, and he was the first to celebrate the Celebration of Shelters on the earth. 22 And during these seven days he brought each day to the altar a burnt-offering to the LORD : two oxen, two rams, seven sheep, one male goat, for a sin-offering, that he might atone for himself and for his seed thereby. 23 And as a thank-offering: seven rams, seven kids, seven sheep, and seven male goats, and their fruit-offerings and their drink-offerings; and he burned all the fat thereof on the altar, a chosen offering to the LORD for a sweet-smelling savor. 24 And morning and evening he burned fragrant substances : frankincense, and galbanum, and stacte, and nard, and myrrh, and spice, and costum; all these seven he offered crushed, mixed together in equal parts, [and] pure. 25 And he celebrated this feast during seven days, rejoicing with all his heart and with all his soul, he and all those who were in his house; and there was no stranger with him, nor any that was uncircumcised. 26 And he blessed his Creator who had created him in his generation, for He had created him according to His good pleasure, for He knew and perceived that from him would arise the Plant of Righteousnes s for the continuous generations, and from him a holy Seed, so that it should become like Him who had made all things. 27 And he blessed and rejoiced, and he called the name of this festival the Festival of the LORD , a joy acceptable to the Most High God. 28 And we blessed him forever, and all his seed after him throughout all the generations of the earth, because he celebrated this festival in its season, according to the testimony of the heavenly tablets. 29 For this reason it is ordained on the heavenly tablets concerning Israel that they will celebrate the Celebration of Shelters [for] seven days with joy, in the seventh month, acceptable before the LORD —a statute forever throughout their generations every year. 30 And to this there is no limit of days, for it is ordained forever regarding Israel that they should celebrate it and dwell in shelters, and set wreaths on their heads, and take leafy boughs, and willows from the brook. 31 And Abraham took branches of palm trees, and the fruit of attractive trees, and every day going around the altar with the branches seven times [a day] in the morning, he praised and gave thanks to his God for all things in joy.

CHAPTER 17

1 And in the first year of the fifth week Isaac was weaned in this jubilee, and Abraham made a great banquet in the third month, on the day his son Isaac was weaned. 2 And Ishmael, the son of Hagar the Egyptian, was before the face of his father Abraham, in his place, and Abraham rejoiced and blessed God because he had seen his sons and had not died childless . 3 And he remembered the words which He had spoken to him on the day on which Lot had parted from him, and he rejoiced because the LORD had given him seed on the earth to inherit the earth, and he blessed the Creator of all things with all his mouth. 4 And Sarah saw Ishmael playing and dancing and Abraham rejoicing with great joy, and she became jealous of Ishmael and said to Abraham, "Cast out this bondwoman and her son, for the son of this bondwoman will not be heir with my son Isaac." 5 And the thing was grievous in Abraham's sight, because of his maidservant and because of his son, that he should drive them from him. 6 And God said to Abraham, "Do not let it be grievous in your sight, because of the child and because of the bondwoman; in all that Sarah has said to you, listen to her words and do [them], for in Isaac will your name and seed be called. 7 But as for the son of this bondwoman, I will make him a great nation, because he is of your seed." 8 And Abraham rose up early in the morning and took bread and a bottle of water and placed them on the shoulders of Hagar and the child and sent her away. 9 And she departed and wandered in the wilderness of Beersheba, and the water in the bottle was spent, and the child thirsted, and was not able to go on, and fell down. 10 And his mother took him and cast him under an olive tree, and went and sat her down over against him, at the distance of a bow-shot; for she said, "Let me not see the death of my child," and as she sat, she wept. 11 And a messenger of God, one of the holy ones, said to her, "Why do you weep, Hagar? Arise, take the child, and hold him in your hand, for God has heard your voice, and has seen the child." 12 And she opened her eyes, and she saw a well of water, and she went and

filled her bottle with water, and she gave her child to drink, and she arose and went toward the wilderness of Paran. 13 And the child grew and became an archer, and God was with him; and his mother took a wife [for] him from among the daughters of Egypt. 14 And she bore him a son, and he called his name Nebaioth , for she said, "The LORD was near to me when I called on Him." 15 And it came to pass in the seventh week, in the first year thereof, in the first month in this jubilee, on the twelfth of this month, there were voices in Heaven regarding Abraham, that he was faithful in all that He told him, and that he loved the LORD , and that in every affliction he was faithful. 16 And the prince Mastêmâ came and said before God, "Behold, Abraham loves his son Isaac, and he delights in him above all other things; command him to offer him as a burnt-offering on the altar, and You will see if he will do this command, and You will know if he is faithful in everything wherein You try him. " 17 And the LORD knew that Abraham was faithful in all his afflictions, for He had tried him through his country and with famine, and had tried him with the wealth of kings, and had tried him again through his wife, when she was torn [from him], and with circumcision, and had tried him through Ishmael and Hagar, his maidservant, when he sent them away. 18 And in everything wherein He had tried him, he was found faithful, and his soul was not impatient, and he was not slow to act, for he was faithful and a lover of the LORD .

CHAPTER 18

1 And God said to him, "Abraham, Abraham"; and he said, "Behold, [here] I am." 2   And He said, "Take your beloved son whom you love, [even] Isaac, and go to the high country, and offer him on one of the mountains which I will point out to you." 3 And he rose early in the morning and saddled his donkey, and took his two young men with him, and his son Isaac, and cleaved the wood of the burnt-offering, and he went to the place on the third day, and he saw the place far off. 4 And he came to a well of water, and he said to his young men, "Abide here with the donkey, and the youth and I will go [over there], and when we have worshiped we will come again to you." 5 And he took the wood of the burnt-offering and laid it on his son Isaac, and he took in his hand the fire and the knife, and both of them went together to that place. 6 And Isaac said to his father, "Father"; and he said, "Here I am, my son." And he said to him, "Behold the fire, and the knife, and the wood, but where is the sheep for the burnt-offering, father?" 7 And he said, "God will provide for Himself a sheep for a burnt- offering, my son." And he drew near to the place of the mount of God. 8 And he built an altar, and he placed the wood on the altar, and bound his son Isaac, and placed him on the wood which was on the altar, and stretched out his hand to take the knife to slay his son Isaac. 9   And I stood before him, and before the prince of the Mastêmâ, and the LORD said, "Command him not to lay his hand on the youth, nor to do anything to him, for I have shown that he fears the LORD ." 10 And I called to him from Heaven, and said to him, "Abraham! Abraham!" And he was terrified and said, "Behold, [here] I am." 11 And I said to him, "Do not lay your hand on the youth, neither do anything to him, for now I have shown that you fear the LORD , and have not withheld your son, your firstborn [[or only]] son, from Me." 12 And the prince of the Mastêmâ was put to shame, and Abraham lifted up his eyes and looked, and behold, a single ram was caught by his horns, and Abraham went and took the ram and offered it for a burnt-offering in the place of his son. 13 And Abraham called that place "The LORD has seen," so that it is said, "[in the mount] the LORD has seen": that is Mount Zion. 14 And the LORD called Abraham by his name a second time from Heaven, as He caused us to appear to speak to him in the Name of the L ORD . 15 And He said, "By Myself I have sworn, says the LORD , because you have done this thing, and have not withheld your son, your beloved son, from Me, that in blessing I will bless you, and in multiplying I will multiply your seed as the stars of the heavens, and as the sand which is on the seashore. And your Seed will inherit the cities of its enemies, 16 and in your Seed all nations of the earth will be blessed; b ecause you have obeyed My voice, and I have shown to all that you are faithful to Me in all that I have said to you: go in peace." 17 And Abraham went to his young men, and they arose and went together to Beersheba, and Abraham dwelt by the Well of the Oath. 18 And he celebrated this festival every year [for] seven days with joy, and he called it the Festival of the LORD according to the seven days during which he went and returned in peace. 19 And accordingly it has been ordained and written on the heavenly tablets regarding Israel and its seed that they should observe this festival [for] seven days with the joy of festival.

CHAPTER 19

1 And in the first year of the first week, in the forty-second jubilee, Abraham returned and dwelt opposite Hebron, that is Kirjath-Arba, two weeks of years. 2 And in the first year of the third week of this jubilee the days of the life of Sarah were accomplished, and she died in Hebron. 3 And Abraham went to mourn over her and bury her, and we tried him [to see] if his spirit was patient and he was not indignant in the words of his mouth, and he was found patient in this and was not disturbed. 4 For in patience of spirit he conversed with the children of Heth, to the intent that they should give him a place in which to bury his dead. 5 And the LORD gave him grace before all who saw him, and he implored in gentleness the sons of Heth, and they gave him the land of the double cave over against Mamre, that is Hebron, for four hundred pieces of silver. 6 And they implored him, saying, "We will give it to you for nothing," but he would not take it from their hands for nothing, for he gave the price of the place, the money in full, and he bowed down before them twice; and after this he buried his dead in the double cave. 7 And all the days of the life of Sarah were one hundred and twenty-seven years, that is, two jubilees and four weeks and one year: these are the days of the years of the life of Sarah. 8 This is the tenth trial with which Abraham was tried, and he was found faithful, patient in spirit. 9 And he said not a single word regarding the rumor in the land, how that God had said that He would give it to him and to his seed after him, and he begged [for] a place there to bury his dead, for he was found faithful and was recorded on the heavenly tablets as the friend of God. 10 And in the fourth year thereof he took a wife for his son Isaac and her name was Rebekah [[the daughter of Bethuel, the son of Nahor, the brother of Abraham,]] the sister of Laban and daughter of Bethuel; and Bethuel was the son of Mêlcâ, who was the wife of Nahor, the brother of Abraham. 11 And Abraham took to himself a third wife—and her name was Keturah— from among the daughters of his household servants, for Hagar had died before Sarah. 12 And she bore him six sons: Zimram, and Jokshan, and Medan, and Midian, and Ishbak, and Shuah, in the two weeks of years. 13 And in the sixth week, in the second year thereof, Rebekah bore to Isaac two sons, Jacob and Esau, and Jacob was a smooth and

upright man, and Esau was fierce, a man of the field, and hairy, and Jacob dwelt in tents. **14** And the youths grew, and Jacob learned to write , but Esau did not learn, for he was a man of the field and a hunter, and he learned war, and all his deeds were fierce. **15** And Abraham loved Jacob, but Isaac loved Esau. **16** And Abraham saw the deeds of Esau, and he knew that in Jacob should his name and seed be called; and he called Rebekah and gave command regarding Jacob, for he knew that she [too] loved Jacob much more than Esau. **17** And he said to her, "My daughter, watch over my son Jacob, for he will be in my stead on the earth, and for a blessing in the midst of the children of men, and for the glory of the whole seed of Shem. **18** For I know that the LORD will choose him to be a people for possession to Himself, above all peoples that are on the face of the earth. **19** And behold, my son Isaac loves Esau more than Jacob, but I see that you truly love Jacob. **20** Add still further to your kindness to him, and let your eyes be on him in love, for he will be a blessing to us on the earth from now on and to all generations of the earth. **21** Let your hands be strong and let your heart rejoice in your son Jacob, for I have loved him far beyond all my sons. He will be blessed forever, and his seed will fill the whole earth. **22** If a man can number the sand of the earth, his seed will also be numbered. **23** And all the blessings with which the LORD has blessed me and my seed will belong to Jacob and his seed always. **24** And in his seed my name will be blessed, and the name of my fathers: Shem, and Noah, and Enoch, and Mahalalel, and Enos, and Seth, and Adam. **25** And these will serve to lay the foundations of the heavens, and to strengthen the earth, and to renew all the luminaries which are in the expanse." **26** And he called Jacob before the eyes of his mother Rebekah, and kissed him, and blessed him, and said, **27** "Jacob, my beloved son, whom my soul loves, may God bless you from above the expanse, and may He give you all the blessings with which He blessed Adam, and Enoch, and Noah, and Shem; and all the things of which He told me, and all the things which He promised to give me, may He cause to cleave to you and to your seed forever, according to the days of Heaven above the earth. **28** And the spirits of Mastêmâ will not rule over you or over your seed to turn you from the LORD , who is your God from now on and forever. **29** And may the LORD God be a father to you—and you [being] the firstborn son—and to the people always. Go in peace, my son." **30** And they both went out together from Abraham. **31** And Rebekah loved Jacob with all her heart and with all her soul, very much more than Esau, but Isaac loved Esau much more than Jacob.

CHAPTER 20

1 And in the forty-second jubilee, in the first year of the seventh week, Abraham called Ishmael, and his twelve sons, and Isaac and his two sons, and the six sons of Keturah, and their sons. **2** And he commanded them that they should observe the way of the LORD , that they should work righteousness, and each love his neighbor, and act on this manner among all men, that they should each so walk with regard to them as to do judgment and righteousness on the earth, **3** [and] that they should circumcise their sons according to the covenant which He had made with them, and not deviate to the right hand or the left of all the paths which the LORD had commanded us, and that we should keep ourselves from all fornication and uncleanness. **4** "And if any woman or maid may commit fornication among you, burn her with fire, and do not let them commit fornication with her after their eyes and their heart; and do not let them take to themselves wives from the daughters of Canaan, for the seed of Canaan will be rooted out of the land." **5** And he told them of the judgment of the giants, and the judgment of the Sodomites, how they had been judged on account of their wickedness, and had died on account of their fornication, and uncleanness, and mutual corruption through fornication. **6** "And guard yourselves from all fornication and uncleanness, and from all pollution of sin, lest you make our name a curse, and your whole life a hissing, and all your sons be destroyed by the sword, and you become accursed like Sodom, and all your remnant as the sons of Gomorrah. **7** I implore you, my sons: love the God of Heaven, and cleave to all His commands. And do not walk after their idols, and after their uncleanness, **8** and do not make for yourselves molten or graven gods , for they are vanity, and there is no spirit in them, for they are [the] work of [men's] hands, and all who trust in them, trust in nothing. Do not serve them, nor worship them, **9** but serve the Most High God, and worship Him continually. And hope for His countenance always, and work uprightness and righteousness before Him, that He may have pleasure in you and grant you His mercy, and send rain on you morning and evening, and bless all your works which you have worked on the earth, and bless your bread and your water, and bless the fruit of your womb and the fruit of your land, and the herds of your cattle, and the flocks of your sheep. **10** And you will be for a blessing on the earth, and all nations of the earth will desire you, and bless your sons in my name, that they may be blessed as I am." **11** And he gave to Ishmael, and to his sons, and to the sons of Keturah, gifts, and sent them away from his son Isaac, and he gave everything to his son Isaac. **12** And Ishmael and his sons, and the sons of Keturah and their sons, went together and dwelt from Paran to the entering in of Babylon in all the land which is toward the east facing the desert. **13** And these mingled with each other, and their name was called Arabs, and Ishmaelites.

CHAPTER 21

1 And in the sixth year of the seventh week of this jubilee, Abraham called his son Isaac and commanded him, saying, "I have become old, and I do not know the day of my death, and am full of my days. **2** And behold, I am one hundred and seventy-five years old, and throughout all the days of my life I have remembered the LORD and sought with all my heart to do His will, and to walk uprightly in all His ways. **3** My soul has hated idols, [[and I have despised those that served them, and I have given my heart and spirit]] that I might observe to do the will of Him who created me. **4** For He is the living God, and He is holy and faithful, and He is righteous beyond all, and there is with Him no accepting of [men's] persons and no accepting of gifts , for God is righteous and executes judgment on all those who transgress His commands and despise His covenant. **5** And you, my son, observe His commands, and His ordinances, and His judgments, and do not walk after the abominations, and after the graven images, and after the molten images. **6** And eat no blood at all of animals, or cattle, or of any bird which flies in the heavens. **7** And if you slay a victim as an acceptable peace-offering, slay it, and pour out its blood on the altar, and all the fat of the offering offer on the altar with fine flour [and the meat-offering] mingled with oil, with its drink-offering—offer them all together on the altar of burnt- offering; it is a sweet savor before the LORD . **8** And you will offer the fat of the sacrifice of thank-offerings on the fire which is on the altar, and the fat which is on the belly, and all the fat on the innards and the two kidneys, and all the fat that is on them, and on the loins and liver you will remove together with the kidneys. **9** And offer all these for a sweet savor acceptable before the LORD , with its meat-offering and with its drink-offering, for a sweet savor, the bread of the offering to the LORD , **10** and eat its meat on that day and on the second day, and do not let the sun go down on it on the second day until it is eaten, and let nothing be left over for the third day, for it is not acceptable ; and let it no longer be eaten, and all who eat thereof will bring sin on themselves, for thus I have found it written in the scrolls of my forefathers, and in the words of Enoch, and in the words of Noah. **11** And on all your oblations you will scatter salt, and do not let the salt of the covenant be lacking in all your oblations before the LORD . **12** And as regards the wood of the sacrifices, beware lest you bring [other] wood for the altar in addition to these: cypress, dêfrân, sagâd, pine, fir, cedar, savin, palm, olive, myrrh, laurel, and citron, juniper, and balsam. **13** And of these kinds of wood lay on the altar under the sacrifice, such as have been tested as to their appearance, and do not lay any split or dark wood [on it], [but] hard and clean, without fault—a sound and new growth; and do not lay old wood [on it], for there is no longer fragrance in it as before. **14** Besides these kinds of wood, there is no other that you will place [on the altar], for the fragrance is dispersed, and the smell of its fragrance does not go up to Heaven. **15** Observe this command and do it, my son, that you may be upright in all your deeds. **16** And at all times be clean in your body, and wash yourself with water before you approach to offer on the altar, and wash your hands and your feet before you draw near to the altar; and when you are done sacrificing, wash your hands and your feet again. **17** And let no blood appear on you nor on your clothes; be on your guard, my son, against blood, be on your guard exceedingly; cover it with dust. **18** And do not eat any blood, for it is the soul; eat no blood whatsoever. **19** And take no gifts for the blood of man, lest it be shed with impunity, without judgment, for it is the blood that is shed that causes the earth to sin, and the earth cannot be cleansed from the blood of man save by the blood of him who shed it. **20** And take no present or gift for the blood of man, blood for blood, that you may be accepted before the LORD , the Most High God—for He is the defense of the good—and that you may be preserved from all evil, and that He may save you from every kind of death. **21** I see, my son, that all the works of the children of men are sin and wickedness, and all their deeds are uncleanness, and an abomination, and a pollution, and there is no righteousness with them. **22** Beware, lest you should walk in their ways, and tread in their paths, and sin a sin to death before the Most High God. Otherwise He will [[hide His face from you, and]] give you back into the hands of your transgression, and root you out of the land, and your seed likewise from under Heaven, and your name and your seed will perish from the whole earth. **23** Turn away from all their deeds and all their uncleanness, and observe the ordinance of the Most High God, and do His will, and be upright in all things. **24** And He will bless you in all your deeds and will raise up from you the plant of righteousness through all the earth, throughout all generations of the earth, and my name and your name will not be forgotten under Heaven forever. **25** Go, my son, in peace. May the Most High God, my God and your God, strengthen you to do His will, and may He bless all your seed and the residue of your seed for the generations forever, with all righteous blessings, that you may be a blessing on all the earth." **26** And he went out from him rejoicing.

CHAPTER 22

1 And it came to pass in the first week, in the forty-fourth jubilee, in the second year, that is, the year in which Abraham died, that Isaac and Ishmael came from the Well of the Oath to celebrate the Celebration of Weeks—that is, the celebration of the first-fruits of the harvest—to their father Abraham, and Abraham rejoiced because his two sons had come. **2** For Isaac had many possessions in Beersheba, and Isaac was accustomed to go and see his possessions and to return to his father. **3** And in those days Ishmael came to see his father, and they both came together, and Isaac offered a sacrifice for a burnt-offering, and presented it on the altar of his father which he had made in Hebron. **4** And he offered a thank-offering and made a feast of joy before his brother Ishmael: and Rebekah made new cakes from the new grain and gave them to her son Jacob to take them to his father Abraham, from the first-fruits of the land, that he might eat and bless the Creator of all things before he died. **5** And Isaac, too, sent by the hand of Jacob to Abraham a best thank-offering, that he might eat and drink. **6** And he ate, and drank, and blessed the Most High God who has created the heavens and earth, who has made all the fat things of the earth and given them to the children of men that they might eat, and drink, and bless their Creator. **7** "And now I give thanks to you, my God, because You have caused me to see this day: behold, I am one hundred and seventy-five years [old], an old man and full of days, and all my days have been peace to me. **8** The sword of the adversary has not overcome me in all that You have given me and my children all the days of my life until this day. **9** My God, may Your mercy and Your peace be on Your servant and on the seed of his sons, that they may be to You a chosen nation and an inheritance from among all the nations of the earth from now on and to all the days of the generations of the earth—to all the ages." **10** And he called Jacob and said, "My son Jacob, may the God of all bless you and strengthen you to do righteousness and His will before Him, and may He choose you and your seed that you may become a people for His inheritance according to His will always. And my son Jacob: draw near and kiss me." **11** And he drew near and kissed him, and he said, "Blessed is my son Jacob, and all the sons of God Most High, to all the ages. May God give to you [the] Seed of righteousness; and may He sanctify some of your sons in the midst of the whole earth. May nations serve you, and all the nations bow themselves before your Seed. **12** Be strong in the presence of men, and exercise authority over all the seed of Seth. Then your ways and the ways of your sons will be justified, so that they will become a holy nation. **13** May the Most High God give you all the blessings with which He has blessed me and with which He blessed Noah and Adam . May they rest on the sacred head of your Seed from generation to generation forever. **14** And may He cleanse you from all unrighteousness and impurity, that you may be forgiven of all [your] transgressions [and] your sins of ignorance. And may He strengthen you and bless you. And may you inherit the whole earth; **15** and may He renew His covenant with you, that you may be to Him a nation for His inheritance for all the ages, and that He may be to you and to your seed a God in truth and righteousness throughout all the days of the earth. **16** And my son Jacob: remember my words and observe the commands of your father Abraham: separate yourself from the nations, and do not eat with them , and do not do according to their works, and do not become their associate, for their works are unclean, and all their ways are a pollution, and an abomination, and uncleanness. 17 They offer their sacrifices to the dead , and they worship evil spirits, and they eat over the graves, and all their works are vanity and nothingness. 18 They have no heart to understand, and their eyes do not see what their works are, and how they err in saying to a piece of wood, You are my God; and to a stone, You are my lord and you are my deliverer. [[And they have no heart.]] 19 And as for you, my son Jacob: may the Most High God help you, and the God of Heaven bless you and remove you from their uncleanness and from all their error. 20 Beware, my son Jacob, of taking a wife from any seed of the daughters of Canaan, for all his seed is to be rooted out of the earth. 21 For, owing to the transgression of Ham, Canaan erred, and all his seed will be destroyed from off the earth and all the residue thereof, and none springing from him will be saved on the Day of Judgment. 22 And as for all the worshipers of idols and the profane: there will be no hope for them in the land of the living and there will be no remembrance of them on the earth, for they will descend into Sheol, and they will go into the place of condemnation ; as the children of Sodom were taken away from the earth, so will all those who worship idols be taken away. 23 Do not fear, my son Jacob, and do not be dismayed, O son of Abraham: may the Most High God preserve you from destruction, and may He deliver you from all the paths of error. 24 I have built this house for myself that I might put my name on it in the earth: [[it is given to you and to your seed forever]] , and it will be named the House of Abraham; it is given to you and to your seed forever, for you will build my house and establish my name before God forever: your seed and your name will stand throughout all generations of the earth." 25 And he ceased commanding him and blessing him. 26 And the two lay together on one bed, and Jacob slept in the bosom of Abraham, his father's father, and he kissed him seven times, and his affection and his heart rejoiced over him. 27 And he blessed him with all his heart and said, "The Most High God, the God of all and Creator of all, who brought me out from Ur of the Chaldees that He might give me this land to inherit it forever, and that I might establish a holy Seed —blessed is the Most High forever." 28 And he blessed Jacob and said [to God], "My son, over whom with all my heart and my affection I rejoice, may Your grace and Your mercy be lifted up on him and on his seed always. 29 And do not forsake him, nor set him at nothing from now on and to the days of [all] ages, and may Your eyes be opened on him and on his seed, that You may preserve him, and bless him, and may sanctify him as a nation for Your inheritance; 30 and bless him with all Your blessings from now on and to all the days of [the] ages, and renew Your covenant and Your grace with him and with his seed according to all Your good pleasure to all the generations of the earth."

CHAPTER 23

1 And he placed two of Jacob's fingers on his eyes, and he blessed the God of gods, and he covered his face, and stretched out his feet , and slept the continuous sleep, and was gathered to his fathers. 2 And notwithstanding all this, Jacob was lying in his bosom, and did not know that Abraham, his father's father, was dead. 3 And Jacob awoke from his sleep, and behold, Abraham was cold as ice, and he said, "Father! Father!" But there was none that spoke, and he knew that he was dead. 4 And he arose from his bosom and ran and told his mother Rebekah; and Rebekah went to Isaac in the night and told him; and they went together, and Jacob with them, and a lamp was in his hand, and when they had gone in they found Abraham lying dead. 5 And Isaac fell on the face of his father, and wept, and kissed him. 6 And the voices were heard in the house of Abraham, and his son Ishmael arose, and went to his father Abraham, and wept over his father Abraham— he and all the house of Abraham—and they wept with a great weeping. 7 And his sons Isaac and Ishmael buried him in the double cave near his wife Sarah, and they wept for him forty days, all the men of his house, and Isaac and Ishmael, and all their sons, and all the sons of Keturah in their places, and the days of weeping for Abraham were ended. 8 And he lived three jubilees and four weeks of years—one hundred and seventy-five years— and completed the days of his life, being old and full of days. 9 For the days of the forefathers, of their life, were nineteen jubilees; and after the flood they began to grow less than nineteen jubilees, and to decrease in jubilees, and to grow old quickly, and to be full of their days by reason of manifold tribulation and the wickedness of their ways, with the exception of Abraham. 10 For Abraham was perfect in all his deeds with the LORD , and well-pleasing in righteousness all the days of his life; and behold, he did not complete four jubilees in his life when he had grown old by reason of the wickedness [in the world] and was full of his days. 11 And all the generations which will arise from this time until the Day of the Great Judgment will grow old quickly before they complete two jubilees, and their knowledge will forsake them by reason of their old age. 12 And in those days, if a man lives [for] a jubilee and a half of years, they will say regarding him: "He has lived long, and the greater part of his days are pain, and sorrow, and tribulation, and there is no peace, 13 for calamity follows on calamity, and wound on wound, and tribulation on tribulation, and evil tidings on evil tidings, and sickness on sickness, and all evil judgments such as these, with one another—sickness, and overthrow, and snow, and frost, and ice, and fever, and chills, and torpor, and famine, and death, and sword, and captivity, and all kinds of calamities and pains." 14 And all these will come on an evil generation, which transgresses on the earth: their works are uncleanness, and fornication, and pollution, and abominations. 15 Then they will say, "The days of the forefathers were many, [even] to one thousand years, and were good, but behold, the days of our life, if a man has lived many, are sixty years and ten, and, if he is strong, eighty years, and those [are] evil and there is no peace in the days of this evil generation." 16 And in that generation the sons will convict their fathers and their elders of sin and unrighteousness, and of the words of their mouth and the great wickedness which they perpetrate, and concerning their forsaking the covenant which the LORD made between them and Him, that they should observe and do all His commands, and His ordinances, and all His laws, without departing either to the right hand or to the left. 17 For all have done evil, and every mouth speaks iniquity, and all their works are an uncleanness and an abomination, and all their ways are pollution, uncleanness, and destruction. 18 Behold, the earth will be destroyed on account of all their works, and there will be no seed of the vine and no oil, for their works are altogether faithless, and they will all perish together: beasts, and cattle, and birds, and all the fish of the sea, on account of the children of men. 19 And they will strive with one another, the young with the old, and the old with the young, the poor with the rich, and the lowly with the great, and the beggar with the prince, on account of the Law and the Covenant, for they have forgotten command, and covenant, and feasts, and months, and Sabbaths, and jubilees, and all judgments. 20 And they will stand [[with bows and]] swords, and

war to turn them back into the way , but they will not return until much blood has been shed on the earth by one another. 21 And those who have escaped will not return from their wickedness to the way of righteousness, but they will all exalt themselves to deceit and wealth, that they may each take all that is his neighbor's, and they will name the Great Name, but not in truth and not in righteousness, and they will defile the Holy of Holies with their uncleanness and the corruption of their pollution. 22 And a great punishment will befall the deeds of this generation from the LORD , and He will give them over to the sword, and to judgment, and to captivity, and to be plundered and devoured. 23 And He will wake up against them the sinners of the nations who have neither mercy nor compassion, and who will respect the person of none, neither old nor young, nor anyone, for they are more wicked and strong to do evil than all the children of men. And they will use violence against Israel and transgression against Jacob, and much blood will be shed on the earth, and there will be none to gather and none to bury. 24 In those days they will cry aloud, and call and pray that they may be saved from the hand of the sinners, the nations , but none will be saved. 25 And the heads of the children will be white with grey hair, and a child of three weeks will appear old like a man of one hundred years, and their stature will be destroyed by tribulation and oppression. 26 And in those days the children will begin to study the laws, and to seek the commands, and to return to the path of righteousness. 27 And the days will begin to grow many and increase among those children of men [until] their days draw near to one thousand years, and to a greater number of years than were the number of the days [before]. 28 And there will be no old man nor one who is not satisfied with his days, for all will be [as] children and youths. 29 And they will complete all their days and live in peace and in joy, and there will be no adversary , nor any evil destroyer, for all their days will be days of blessing and healing, 30 and at that time the LORD will heal His servants, and they will rise up and see great peace, and drive out their adversaries. And the righteous will see and be thankful, and rejoice with joy forever and ever, and will see all their judgments and all their curses on their enemies. 31 And their bones will rest in the earth, and their spirits will have much joy, and they will know that it is the LORD who executes judgment and shows mercy to hundreds, and thousands, and to all that love Him. 32 And you, Moses, write down these words, for thus are they written, and they record [them] on the heavenly tablets for a testimony for the generations forever.

CHAPTER 24

1 And it came to pass after the death of Abraham, that the LORD blessed his son Isaac, and he arose from Hebron and went and dwelt at the Well of the Vision in the first year of the third week of this jubilee [for] seven years. 2 And in the first year of the fourth week a famine began in the land, besides the first famine which had been in the days of Abraham. 3 And Jacob prepared lentil stew, and Esau came from the field hungry. And he said to his brother Jacob, "Give me of this red stew." And Jacob said to him, "Sell your birthright to me and I will give you bread and also some of this lentil stew." 4 And Esau said in his heart: "I will die; of what profit to me is this birthright?" And he said to Jacob, "I give it to you." 5 And Jacob said, "Swear to me, this day," and he swore to him. 6 And Jacob gave his brother Esau bread and stew, and he ate until he was satisfied, and Esau despised his birthright; for this reason Esau's name was called Edom on account of the red stew which Jacob gave him for his birthright. 7 And Jacob became the elder, and Esau was brought down from his dignity. 8 And the famine was over the land, and Isaac departed to go down into Egypt in the second year of this week, and he went to the king of the Philistines, to Gerar, to Abimelech. 9 And the LORD appeared to him and said to him, "Do not go down into Egypt; dwell in the land that I will tell you of, and sojourn in this land, and I will be with you and bless you. 10 For to you and to your seed I will give all this land, and I will establish My oath which I swore to your father Abraham, and I will multiply your seed as the stars of the heavens, and I will give to your seed all this land. 11 And in your Seed will all the nations of the earth be blessed, because your father obeyed My voice, and kept My charge, and My commands, and My laws, and My ordinances, and My covenant; and now obey My voice and dwell in this land." 12 And he dwelt in Gerar three weeks of years. 13 And Abimelech charged concerning him, and concerning all that was his, saying, "Any man that will touch him or anything that is his will surely die." 14 And Isaac waxed strong among the Philistines, and he got many possessions: oxen, and sheep, and camels, and donkeys, and a great household. 15 And he sowed in the land of the Philistines and brought in a hundredfold, and Isaac became exceedingly great, and the Philistines envied him. 16 Now all the wells which the servants of Abraham had dug during the life of Abraham, the Philistines had stopped them after the death of Abraham and filled them with earth. 17 And Abimelech said to Isaac, "Go from us, for you are much mightier than us"; and Isaac departed from there in the first year of the seventh week and sojourned in the valleys of Gerar. 18 And they dug the wells of water again which the servants of his father Abraham had dug, and which the Philistines had closed after the death of his father Abraham, and he called their names as his father Abraham had named them. 19 And the servants of Isaac dug a well in the valley, and found living water, and the shepherds of Gerar strove with the shepherds of Isaac, saying, "The water is ours"; and Isaac called the name of the well "Perversity," because they had been perverse with us. 20 And they dug a second well, and they strove for that also, and he called its name "Enmity." And he arose from there and they dug another well, and for that they did not strive, and he called the name of it "Room," and Isaac said, "Now the LORD has made room for us, and we have increased in the land." 21 And he went up from there to the Well of the Oath in the first year of the first week, in the forty-fourth jubilee. 22 And the LORD appeared to him that night, on the new moon of the first month, and said to him, "I am the God of your father Abraham; do not fear, for I am with you, and will bless you and will surely multiply your seed as the sand of the earth, for the sake of my servant Abraham." 23 And he built an altar there, which his father Abraham had first built, and he called on the Name of the L ORD , and he offered sacrifice to the God of his father Abraham. 24 And they dug a well and they found living water. 25 And the servants of Isaac dug another well and did not find water, and they went and told Isaac that they had not found water, and Isaac said, "I have sworn this day to the Philistines and this thing has been announced to us." 26 And he called the name of that place the "Well of the Oath," for there he had sworn to Abimelech, and his friend Ahuzzath, and Phicol, the prefect of his host. 27 And Isaac knew that day that under constraint he had sworn to them to make peace with them. 28 And on that day Isaac cursed the Philistines and said, "Cursed are the Philistines to the day of wrath and indignation from the midst of all nations; may God make them a derision, and a curse, and an object of wrath and indignation in the hands of the sinners—the

nations—and in the hands of the Kittim. 29 And whoever escapes the sword of the enemy and the Kittim, may the righteous nation root out in judgment from under Heaven, for they will be the enemies, and enemies of my children, throughout their generations on the earth. 30 And no remnant will be left to them, nor one that will be saved on the day of the wrath of judgment, for destruction, and rooting out, and expulsion from the earth is the whole seed of the Philistines [reserved], and there will no longer be left for these Caphtorim a name or a seed on the earth. 31 For though he ascends into Heaven, from there he will be brought down, and though he makes himself strong on earth, from there he will be dragged out, and though he hides himself among the nations, even from there he will be rooted out, and though he descends into Sheol, there also will his condemnation be great, and there also he will have no peace. 32 And if he goes into captivity, by the hands of those that seek his life they will slay him on the way, and neither name nor seed will be left to him on all the earth, for he will depart into a continuous curse." 33 And thus is it written and engraved concerning him on the heavenly tablets, to do to him on the Day of Judgment, so that he may be rooted out of the earth.

CHAPTER 25

1 And in the second year of this week, in this jubilee, Rebekah called her son Jacob and spoke to him, saying, "My son, do not take a wife for yourself of the daughters of Canaan, as your brother Esau, who took two wives of the daughters of Canaan for himself, and they have embittered my soul with all their unclean deeds, for all their deeds are fornication and lust, and there is no righteousness with them, for [their deeds] are evil. 2 And I, my son, love you exceedingly, and my heart and my affection bless you every hour of the day and watch of the night. 3 And now, my son, listen to my voice, and do the will of your mother, and do not take a wife for yourself of the daughters of this land, but only of the house of my father, and of my father's relatives; you will take a wife of the house of my father, and the Most High God will bless you, and your children will be a righteous generation and a holy seed." 4 And then Jacob spoke to his mother Rebekah, and said to her, "Behold, mother, I am nine weeks of years old, and I neither know nor have I touched any woman, nor have I betrothed myself to any, nor even think of taking a wife for myself of the daughters of Canaan. 5 For I remember, mother, the words of our father Abraham, for he commanded me not to take a wife of the daughters of Canaan, but to take a wife for myself from the seed of my father's house and from my relatives. 6 I have heard before that daughters have been born to your brother Laban, and I have set my heart on them to take a wife from among them. 7 And for this reason I have guarded myself in my spirit against sinning or being corrupted in all my ways throughout all the days of my life, for with regard to lust and fornication, my father Abraham gave me many commands. 8 And despite all that he has commanded me, these twenty-two years my brother has striven with me, and spoken frequently to me, and said, My brother, take a sister of my two wives to be [your] wife; but I refuse to do as he has done. 9 I swear before you, mother, that all the days of my life I will not take a wife for myself from the daughters of the seed of Canaan, and I will not act wickedly as my brother has done. 10 Do not fear, mother; be assured that I will do your will, and walk in uprightness, and not corrupt my ways forever." 11 And immediately she lifted up her face to Heaven, and extended the fingers of her hands, and opened her mouth, and blessed the Most High God who had created the heavens and the earth, and she gave Him thanks and praise. 12 And she said, "Blessed is the LORD God, and may His holy Name be blessed forever and ever, who has given me Jacob as a pure son and a holy seed; for He is Yours, and his seed will be Yours continually and throughout all the generations forevermore. 13 Bless him, O LORD , and place in my mouth the blessing of righteousness, that I may bless him." 14 And at that hour, when the Spirit of righteousness descended into her mouth, she placed both her hands on the head of Jacob, and said, 15 "Blessed are You, LORD of righteousness and God of the ages. And may He bless you beyond all the generations of men. May He give you, my son, the path of righteousness, and reveal righteousness to your seed. 16 And may He make your sons many during your life, and may they arise according to the number of the months of the year. And may their sons become many and great beyond the stars of the heavens, and their numbers be more than the sand of the sea. 17 And may He give them this excellent land—as He said He would give it to Abraham and to his seed after him always—and may they hold it as a possession forever. 18 And may I see [born] to you, my son, blessed children during my life, and a blessed and holy seed may all your seed be. 19 And as you have refreshed your mother's spirit during my life, the womb of her that bore you blesses you, and my breasts bless you, and my mouth and my tongue praise you greatly. 20 Increase and spread over the earth, and may your seed be perfect in the joy of the heavens and earth forever; and may your seed rejoice, and on the great day of peace may it have peace. 21 And may your name and your seed endure to all the ages, and may the Most High God be their God, and may the God of righteousness dwell with them, and by them may His sanctuary be built to all the ages. 22 Blessed is he that blesses you, and all flesh that curses you falsely—may it be cursed." 23 And she kissed him and said to him, "May the Lord of the world love you just as the heart of your mother and her affection rejoices in you and blesses you." And she ceased from blessing.

CHAPTER 26

1 And in the seventh year of this week Isaac called Esau, his elder son, and said to him, "I am old, my son, and behold, my eyes are dim in seeing, and I do not know the day of my death. 2 And now take your hunting weapons, your quiver and your bow, and go out to the field, and hunt and catch me [game], my son, and make me savory meat, such as my soul loves, and bring it to me that I may eat, and that my soul may bless you before I die." 3 But Rebekah heard Isaac speaking to Esau. 4 And Esau went out early to the field to hunt, and catch, and bring home to his father. 5 And Rebekah called her son Jacob and said to him, "Behold, I heard your father Isaac speak to your brother Esau, saying, Hunt for me, and make me savory meat, and bring [it] to me that I may eat and bless you before the LORD before I die. 6 And now, my son, obey my voice in that which I command you: go to your flock and fetch me two good kids of the goats, and I will make them savory meat for your father, such as he loves, and you will bring [it] to your father that he may eat and bless you before the LORD before he die, and that you may be blessed." 7 And Jacob said to his mother Rebekah, "Mother, I will not withhold anything which my father would eat, and which would please him: only I fear, my mother, that he will recognize my voice and wish to touch me. 8 And you know that I am smooth, and my brother Esau is hairy, and I will appear before

his eyes as an evildoer, and will do a deed which he had not commanded me, and he will be angry with me, and I will bring a curse on myself, and not a blessing." 9 And his mother Rebekah said to him, "Your curse be on me, my son, only obey my voice." 10 And Jacob obeyed the voice of his mother Rebekah, and went and fetched two good and fat kids of the goats, and brought them to his mother, and his mother made them [savory meat] such as he loved. 11 And Rebekah took the attractive raiment of her elder son Esau, which was with her in the house, and she clothed her younger son Jacob [with them], and she put the skins of the kids on his hands and on the exposed parts of his neck. 12 And she gave the meat and the bread which she had prepared into the hand of her son Jacob. 13 And Jacob went in to his father and said, "I am your son: I have done according as you commanded me. Arise, and sit, and eat of that which I have caught, father, that your soul may bless me." 14 And Isaac said to his son, "How have you found [game] so quickly, my son?" 15 And Jacob said, "Because [the LORD] your God caused me to find [it]." 16 And Isaac said to him, "Come near, that I may feel you, my son, if you are my son Esau or not." 17 And Jacob went near to his father Isaac, and he felt him, and said, 18 "The voice is Jacob's voice, but the hands are the hands of Esau," and he did not discern him, because it was a dispensation from Heaven to remove his power of perception, and Isaac did not discern, for his hands were as hairy as [his brother] Esau's, so that he blessed him. 19 And he said, "Are you my son Esau?" and he said, "I am your son," and he said, "Bring [it] near to me that I may eat of that which you have caught, my son, that my soul may bless you." 20 And he brought [it] near to him, and he ate, and he brought him wine and he drank. 21 And his father Isaac said to him, "Come near and kiss me, my son." And he came near and kissed him. 22 And he smelled the smell of his raiment, and he blessed him, and said, "Behold, the smell of my son is as the smell of a [full] field which the LORD has blessed. 23 And may the LORD give you of the dew of the heavens and of the dew of the earth, and plenty of corn and oil: Let nations serve you And peoples bow down to you. 24 Be lord over your brothers And let your mother's sons bow down to you; And may all the blessings with which the LORD has blessed me and blessed my father Abraham Be imparted to you and to your seed forever. Cursed is he that curses you, And blessed is he that blesses you." 25 And it came to pass as soon as Isaac had made an end of blessing his son Jacob and Jacob had gone out from his father Isaac, he hid himself, and his brother Esau came in from his hunting. 26 And he also made savory meat, and brought [it] to his father, and said to his father, "Let my father arise and eat of my venison that your soul may bless me." 27 And his father Isaac said to him, "Who are you?" And he said to him, "I am your firstborn, your son Esau: I have done as you have commanded me." 28 And Isaac was very greatly astonished, and said, "Who is he that has hunted, and caught, and brought [it] to me? And I have eaten of all before you came and have blessed him: [and] he will be blessed, and all his seed forever." 29 And it came to pass when Esau heard the words of his father Isaac that he cried with an exceedingly great and bitter cry, and said to his father, "Bless me, me also, father!" 30 And he said to him, "Your brother came with guile, and has taken away your blessing." And he said, "Now I know why his name is named Jacob: behold, he has supplanted me these two times; he took away my birthright, and now he has taken away my blessing." 31 And he said, "Have you not reserved a blessing for me, father?" And Isaac answered and said to Esau, "Behold, I have made him your lord, and I have given all his brothers to him for servants, and I have strengthened him with plenty of corn, and wine, and oil: and what now will I do for you, my son?" 32 And Esau said to his father Isaac, "Have you but one blessing, O father? Bless me, [even] me also, father!" And Esau lifted up his voice and wept. 33 And Isaac answered and said to him, "Behold, your dwelling will be far from the dew of the earth, and far from the dew of the heavens from above. 34 And you will live by your sword, and you will serve your brother. And it will come to pass when you become great, and shake his yoke from off your neck, you will sin a complete sin to death, and your seed will be rooted out from under Heaven." 35 And Esau kept threatening Jacob because of the blessing with which his father blessed him, and he said in his heart, "May the days of mourning for my father now come, so that I may slay my brother Jacob."

CHAPTER 27

1 And the words of her elder son Esau were told to Rebekah in a dream, and Rebekah sent and called her younger son Jacob, and said to him, 2 "Behold, your brother Esau will take vengeance on you so as to kill you. 3 Now, therefore, my son, obey my voice, and arise and flee to my brother Laban, to Haran, and tarry with him a few days until your brother's anger turns away, and he removes his anger from you, and forgets all that you have done; then I will send and fetch you from there." 4 And Jacob said, "I am not afraid; if he wishes to kill me, I will kill him." 5 But she said to him, "Let me not be deprived of both my sons on one day." 6 And Jacob said to his mother Rebekah, "Behold, you know that my father has become old and does not see because his eyes are dull, and if I leave him it will be evil in his eyes, because I leave him and go away from you, and my father will be angry, and will curse me. I will not go; when he sends me, then only will I go." 7 And Rebekah said to Jacob, "I will go in and speak to him, and he will send you away." 8 And Rebekah went in and said to Isaac, "I loathe my life because of the two daughters of Heth, whom Esau has taken to himself as wives; and if Jacob takes a wife from among the daughters of the land such as these, for what further purpose do I live? For the daughters of Canaan are evil." 9 And Isaac called Jacob and blessed him, and admonished him, and said to him, 10 "Do not take a wife for yourself of any of the daughters of Canaan; arise and go to Mesopotamia, to the house of Bethuel, your mother's father, and take a wife for yourself from there of the daughters of Laban, your mother's brother. 11 And may God Almighty bless you, and increase and multiply you, that you may become a company of nations, and give you the blessings of my father Abraham—to you and to your seed after you—that you may inherit the land of your sojournings and all the land which God gave to Abraham. Go, my son, in peace." 12 And Isaac sent Jacob away, and he went to Mesopotamia, to Laban the son of Bethuel the Syrian, the brother of Rebekah, Jacob's mother. 13 And it came to pass after Jacob had arisen to go to Mesopotamia that the spirit of Rebekah was grieved after her son, and she wept. 14 And Isaac said to Rebekah, "My sister, do not weep on account of my son Jacob, for he goes in peace, and in peace he will return. 15 The Most High God will preserve him from all evil and will be with him, for He will not forsake him all his days, 16 for I know that his ways will be prospered in all things wherever he goes, until he returns to us in peace and we see him in peace. 17 Do not fear on his account, my sister, for he is on the upright path and he is a perfect man: and he is faithful and will not perish. Do not weep." 18 And Isaac comforted Rebekah on account of her son Jacob and blessed him. 19 And Jacob went from the Well

of the Oath to go to Haran on the first year of the second week, in the forty-fourth Jubilee, and he came to Luz on the mountains, that is, Bethel, on the new moon of the first month of this week, and he came to the place at evening and turned from the way to the west of the road that night: and he slept there, for the sun had set. 20 And he took one of the stones of that place and laid it [at his head] under the tree, and he was journeying alone, and he slept. 21 And he dreamt that night, and behold, a ladder [was] set up on the earth, and the top of it reached to Heaven, and behold, the messengers of the LORD ascended and descended on it: and behold, the LORD stood on it. 22 And He spoke to Jacob and said, "I am the LORD God of your father Abraham and the God of Isaac; the land on which you are sleeping, to you I will give it, and to your seed after you. 23 And your seed will be as the dust of the earth, and you will increase to the west and to the east, to the north and the south, and in you and in your Seed all the families of the nations will be blessed. 24 And behold, I will be with you, and will keep you wherever you go, and I will bring you into this land again in peace, for I will not leave you until I do everything that I told you of." 25 And Jacob awoke from his sleep, and said, "Truly this place is the house of the LORD , and I did not know it." And he was afraid and said, "This place is dreadful, which is none other than the house of God, and this is the gate of Heaven." 26 And Jacob arose early in the morning and took the stone which he had put under his head and set it up as a pillar for a sign, and he poured oil on the top of it. And he called the name of that place Bethel, but the name of the place was Luz at the first. 27 And Jacob vowed a vow to the LORD , saying, "If the LORD will be with me, and will keep me in this way that I go, and give me bread to eat and raiment to put on, so that I come to my father's house again in peace, then the LORD will be my God, and this stone which I have set up as a pillar for a sign in this place will be the LORD 's house, and of all that You give me, I will give the tenth to You, my God."

CHAPTER 28

1 And he went on his journey, and came to the land of the east, to Laban, the brother of Rebekah, and he was with him, and served him for his daughter Rachel [for] one week. 2 And in the first year of the third week he said to him, "Give me my wife, for whom I have served you seven years"; and Laban said to Jacob, "I will give you your wife." 3 And Laban made a feast, and took his elder daughter Leah, and gave [her] to Jacob as a wife, and gave her his handmaid Zilpah for a handmaid, and Jacob did not know, for he thought that she was Rachel. 4 And he went in to her, and behold, she was Leah; and Jacob was angry with Laban, and said to him, "Why have you dealt thus with me? Did I not serve you for Rachel and not for Leah? Why have you wronged me? Take your daughter, and I will go, for you have done evil to me." 5 For Jacob loved Rachel more than Leah, for Leah's eyes were weak, but her form was very attractive, but Rachel had beautiful eyes and a beautiful and very attractive form. 6 And Laban said to Jacob, "It is not so done in our country, to give the younger before the elder." And it is not right to do this, for thus it is ordained and written in the heavenly tablets that no one should give his younger daughter before the elder—but he gives the elder one first and after her the younger—and the man who does so, they set down guilt against him in Heaven, and none is righteous that does this thing, for this deed is evil before the LORD . 7 And command the sons of Israel that they do not do this thing; let them neither take nor give the younger before they have given the elder, for it is very wicked. 8 And Laban said to Jacob, "Let the seven days of the celebration of this one pass by, and I will give you Rachel, that you may serve me another seven years, that you may pasture my sheep as you did in the former week." 9 And on the day when the seven days of the celebration of Leah had passed, Laban gave Rachel to Jacob, that he might serve him another seven years, and he gave to Rachel Bilhah, the sister of Zilpah , as a handmaid. 10 And he served yet another seven years for Rachel, for Leah had been given to him for nothing. 11 And the LORD opened the womb of Leah, and she conceived and bore Jacob a son, and he called his name Reuben, on the fourteenth day of the ninth month, in the first year of the third week. 12 But the womb of Rachel was closed, for the LORD saw that Leah was hated and Rachel loved. 13 And again Jacob went in to Leah, and she conceived, and bore Jacob a second son, and he called his name Simeon, on the twenty-first of the tenth month, and in the third year of this week. 14 And again Jacob went in to Leah, and she conceived, and bore him a third son, and he called his name Levi, in the new moon of the first month, in the sixth year of this week. 15 And again Jacob went in to her, and she conceived, and bore him a fourth son, and he called his name Judah, on the fifteenth of the third month, in the first year of the fourth week. 16 And on account of all this, Rachel envied Leah, for she did not bear, and she said to Jacob, "Give me children"; and Jacob said, "Have I withheld from you the fruits of your womb? Have I forsaken you?" 17 And when Rachel saw that Leah had borne four sons to Jacob—Reuben, and Simeon, and Levi, and Judah—she said to him, "Go in to my handmaid Bilhah, and she will conceive, and bear a son to me." 18 And he went in to her, and she conceived, and bore him a son, and he called his name Dan, on the ninth of the sixth month, in the sixth year of the third week. 19 And Jacob went in again to Bilhah a second time, and she conceived, and bore Jacob another son, and Rachel called his name Naphtali, on the fifth of the seventh month, in the second year of the fourth week. 20 And when Leah saw that she had become sterile and did not bear, she envied [Rachel] and she also gave her handmaid Zilpah to Jacob to be [his] wife, and she conceived, and bore a son, and Leah called his name Gad, on the twelfth of the eighth month, in the third year of the fourth week. 21 And he went in again to her, and she conceived, and bore him a second son, and Leah called his name Asher, on the second of the eleventh month, in the fifth year of the fourth week. 22 And Jacob went in to Leah, and she conceived, and bore a son, and she called his name Issachar, on the fourth of the fifth month, in the fourth year of the fourth week, and she gave him to a nurse. 23 And Jacob went in again to her, and she conceived, and bore two [children], a son and a daughter, and she called the name of the son Zebulun, and the name of the daughter Dinah, in the seventh of the seventh month, in the sixth year of the fourth week. 24 And the LORD was gracious to Rachel, and opened her womb, and she conceived, and bore a son, and she called his name Joseph, on the new moon of the fourth month, in the sixth year in this fourth week. 25 And in the days when Joseph was born, Jacob said to Laban, "Give me my wives and sons, and let me go to my father Isaac, and let me make myself a house, for I have completed the years in which I have served you for your two daughters, and I will go to the house of my father." 26 And Laban said to Jacob, "Tarry with me for your wages , and pasture my flock for me again, and take your wages." 27 And they agreed with one another that he should give him as his wages those of the lambs and kids which were born black, and spotted, and white ; [these] were to be his wages. 28 And all the sheep brought out

spotted, and speckled, and black, variously marked, and they brought out again lambs like themselves, and all that were spotted were Jacob's and those which were not were Laban's. 29 And Jacob's possessions multiplied exceedingly, and he possessed oxen, and sheep , and donkeys, and camels, and menservants, and maidservants. 30 And Laban and his sons envied Jacob, and Laban took back his sheep from him, and he observed him with evil intent.

CHAPTER 29

1 And it came to pass when Rachel had borne Joseph, that Laban went to shear his sheep, for they were distant from him a three days' journey. 2 And Jacob saw that Laban was going to shear his sheep, and Jacob called Leah and Rachel, and spoke kindly to them that they should come with him to the land of Canaan. 3 For he told them how he had seen everything in a dream, even all that He had spoken to him that he should return to his father's house, and they said, "To every place where you go we will go with you." 4 And Jacob blessed the God of his father Isaac, and the God of Abraham, his father's father, and he arose and mounted his wives and his children, and took all his possessions and crossed the river, and came to the land of Gilead, and Jacob hid his intention from Laban and did not tell him. 5 And in the seventh year of the fourth week Jacob turned [his face] toward Gilead in the first month, on the twenty-first thereof. And Laban pursued after him and overtook Jacob in the mountain of Gilead in the third month, on the thirteenth thereof. 6 And the LORD did not permit him to injure Jacob, for He appeared to him in a dream by night. And Laban spoke to Jacob, 7 and on the fifteenth of those days Jacob made a feast for Laban and for all who came with him, and Jacob swore to Laban that day, and Laban also to Jacob, that neither should cross the mountain of Gilead to the other with evil purpose. 8 And he made a heap there for a witness; for that reason the name of that place is called "The Heap of Witness," after this heap. 9 But before [that] they used to call the land of Gilead the land of the Rephaim , for it was the land of the Rephaim, and the Rephaim were born [there]— giants whose height was ten, nine, eight, [and] down to seven cubits. 10 And their habitation was from the land of the children of Ammon to Mount Hermon, and the seats of their kingdom were Karnaim, and Ashtaroth, and Edrei, and Mîsûr, and Beon. 11 And the LORD destroyed them because of the evil of their deeds, for they were very malevolent, and the Amorites dwelt in their stead, wicked and sinful, and there is no people today which has worked to the measure of all their sins, and they have no more length of life on the earth. 12 And Jacob sent Laban away, and he departed into Mesopotamia, the land of the east, and Jacob returned to the land of Gilead. 13 And he passed over the Jabbok in the ninth month, on the eleventh thereof. And on that day his brother Esau came to him, and he was reconciled to him, and departed from him to the land of Seir, but Jacob dwelt in tents. 14 And in the first year of the fifth week in this jubilee he crossed the Jordan, and dwelt beyond the Jordan, and he pastured his sheep from the sea of the heap to Bethshan, and to Dothan, and to the forest of Akrabbim. 15 And he sent to his father Isaac of all his substance: clothing, and food, and meat, and drink, and milk, and butter, and cheese, and some dates of the valley; 16 and also to his mother Rebekah four times a year, between the times of the months, between plowing and reaping, and between autumn and the rain [season], and between winter and spring, to the tower of Abraham. 17 For Isaac had returned from the Well of the Oath and gone up to the tower of his father Abraham, and he dwelt there apart from his son Esau. 18 For in the days when Jacob went to Mesopotamia, Esau took to himself Mahalath, the daughter of Ishmael, to be [his] wife, and he gathered together all the flocks of his father and his wives, and went up and dwelt on Mount Seir, and left his father Isaac at the Well of the Oath alone. 19 And Isaac went up from the Well of the Oath and dwelt in the tower of his father Abraham on the mountains of Hebron, 20 and there Jacob sent all that he sent to his father and his mother from time to time— all they needed—and they blessed Jacob with all their heart and with all their soul.

CHAPTER 30

1 And in the first year of the sixth week he went up to Salem, to the east of Shechem, in peace, in the fourth month. 2 And there they carried off Dinah, the daughter of Jacob, into the house of Shechem, the son of Hamor, the Hivite, the prince of the land, and he lay with her and defiled her, and she was a little girl, a child of twelve years. 3 And he implored his father and her brothers that she might be given to him to be [his] wife. And Jacob and his sons were angry because of the men of Shechem , for they had defiled their sister Dinah, and they spoke to them with evil intent, and dealt deceitfully with them, and deceived them. 4 And Simeon and Levi came stealthily to Shechem, and executed judgment on all the men of Shechem, and slew all the men whom they found in it, and left not a single one remaining in it: they slew all in torments because they had dishonored their sister Dinah. 5 And thus do not let it be done again from now on that a daughter of Israel is defiled, for judgment is ordained in Heaven against them that they should destroy with the sword all the men of the Shechemites because they had worked shame in Israel. 6 And the LORD delivered them into the hands of the sons of Jacob that they might exterminate them with the sword, and execute judgment on them, and that it might not thus be done again in Israel that a virgin of Israel should be defiled. 7 And if there is any man in Israel who wishes to give his daughter or his sister to any man who is of the seed of the nations, he will surely die, and they will stone him with stones, for he has worked shame in Israel; and they will burn the woman with fire, because she has dishonored the name of the house of her father, and she will be rooted out of Israel. 8 And do not let an adulteress be found, and no uncleanness, in Israel, throughout all the days of the generations of the earth, for Israel is holy to the LORD , and every man who has defiled [it] will surely die: they will stone him with stones. 9 For thus it has been ordained and written in the heavenly tablets regarding all the seed of Israel: he who defiles [it] will surely die, and he will be stoned with stones. 10 And to this law there is no limit of days, and no forgiveness, nor any atonement, but the man who has defiled his daughter will be rooted out in the midst of all Israel, because he has given of his seed to Moloch, and worked impiously so as to defile it. 11 And you, Moses, command the sons of Israel and exhort them not to give their daughters to the nations, and not to take any of the daughters of the nations for their sons, for this is abominable before the LORD . 12 For this reason I have written for you in the words of the Law all the deeds of the Shechemites, which they worked against Dinah, and how the sons of Jacob spoke, saying, "We will not give our daughter to a man who is uncircumcised, for that would be a reproach to us." 13 And it is a reproach to Israel to those who give and to those who take the daughters of the nations, for this is unclean and abominable to Israel.

14 And Israel will not be free from this uncleanness if it has a wife of the daughters of the nations or has given any of its daughters to a man who is of any of the nations. 15 For there will be plague on plague, and curse on curse, and every judgment, and plague, and curse will come [on him] if he does this thing, or hides his eyes from those who commit uncleanness, or those who defile the sanctuary of the LORD , or those who profane His holy Name, [for] the whole nation will be judged together for all the uncleanness and desecration of this [man]. 16 And there will be no respect of persons, and no receiving at his hands of fruits, and offerings, and burnt-offerings, and fat, nor the fragrance of sweet savor, so as to accept it: and likewise for every man or woman in Israel who defiles the sanctuary. 17 For this reason I have commanded you, saying, "Testify this testimony to Israel: see how the Shechemites and their sons fared, how they were delivered into the hands of two sons of Jacob, and they slew them under tortures, and it was [reckoned] to them for righteousness, and it is written down to them for righteousness. 18 And the seed of Levi was chosen for the priesthood, and to be Levites, that they might minister before the LORD , as we, continually, and that Levi and his sons may be blessed forever, for he was zealous to execute righteousness, and judgment, and vengeance on all those who arose against Israel. 19 And so they inscribe as a testimony in his favor on the heavenly tablets blessing and righteousness before the God of all; 20 and we remember the righteousness which the man fulfilled during his life, at all periods of the year; until one thousand generations they will [still] record it, and it will come to him and to his descendants after him, and he has been recorded on the heavenly tablets as a friend and a righteous man. 21 All this account I have written for you and have commanded you to say to the sons of Israel, that they should not commit sin, nor transgress the ordinances, nor break the covenant which has been ordained for them, [but] that they should fulfill it and be recorded as friends. 22 But if they transgress and work uncleanness in every way, they will be recorded on the heavenly tablets as adversaries, and they will be destroyed out of the Scroll of Life, and they will be recorded in the scroll of those who will be destroyed and with those who will be rooted out of the earth. 23 And on the day when the sons of Jacob slew Shechem, a writing was recorded in their favor in Heaven that they had executed righteousness, and uprightness, and vengeance on the sinners, and it was written for a blessing. 24 And they brought their sister Dinah out of the house of Shechem, and they took everything captive that was in Shechem: their sheep, and their oxen, and their donkeys, and all their wealth, and all their flocks; and they brought them all to their father Jacob. 25 And he reproached them because they had put the city to the sword , for he feared those who dwelt in the land, the Canaanites and the Perizzites. 26 And the dread of the LORD was on all the cities which are around Shechem, and they did not rise to pursue after the sons of Jacob, for terror had fallen on them."

CHAPTER 31

1 And on the new moon of the month Jacob spoke to all the people of his house, saying, "Purify yourselves and change your garments, and let us arise and go up to Bethel, where I vowed a vow to Him on the day when I fled from the face of my brother Esau, because He has been with me and has brought me into this land in peace, and put away the strange gods that are among you." 2 And they gave up the strange gods, and that which was in their ears and which was on their necks, and the idols which Rachel stole from her father Laban she wholly gave to Jacob. And he burned and broke them to pieces, and destroyed them, and hid them under an oak which is in the land of Shechem. 3 And he went up on the new moon of the seventh month to Bethel. And he built an altar at the place where he had slept, and he set up a pillar there, and he sent word to his father Isaac to come to him to his sacrifice, and to his mother Rebekah. 4 And Isaac said, "Let my son Jacob come, and let me see him before I die." 5 And Jacob went to his father Isaac and to his mother Rebekah, to the house of his father Abraham, and he took two of his sons with him, Levi and Judah, and he came to his father Isaac and to his mother Rebekah. 6 And Rebekah came out from the tower to the front of it to kiss Jacob and embrace him, for her spirit had revived when she heard: "Behold, your son Jacob has come!" And she kissed him. 7 And she saw his two sons, and she recognized them, and said to him, "Are these your sons, my son?" and she embraced them, and kissed them, and blessed them, saying, "In you the seed of Abraham will become illustrious, and you will prove a blessing on the earth." 8 And Jacob went in to his father Isaac, to the chamber where he lay, and his two sons were with him, and he took the hand of his father, and stooping down, he kissed him, and Isaac clung to the neck of his son Jacob and wept on his neck. 9 And the darkness left the eyes of Isaac, and he saw the two sons of Jacob, Levi and Judah, and he said, "Are these your sons, my son ? F or they are like you." 10 And he said to him that they were truly his sons: "And you have truly seen that they are truly my sons." 11 And they came near to him, and he turned and kissed them, and embraced them both together. 12 And the spirit of prophecy came down into his mouth, and he took Levi by his right hand and Judah by his left. 13 And he turned to Levi first, and began to bless him first, and said to him, "May the God of all, the very Lord of all the ages, Bless you and your children throughout all the ages. 14 And may the LORD give greatness and great glory to you and to your seed, And cause you and your seed, from among all flesh, to approach Him To serve in His sanctuary as the messengers of the presence and as the holy ones. [Even] as they, may the seed of your sons be for glory, and greatness, and holiness, And may He make them great to all the ages. 15 And they will be princes and judges, And chiefs of all the seed of the sons of Jacob; They will speak the word of the LORD in righteousness, And they will judge all His judgments in righteousness. And they will declare My ways to Jacob, And My paths to Israel. The blessing of the LORD will be given in their mouths To bless all the seed of the beloved. 16 Your mother has called your name Levi, And justly has she called your name; You will be joined to the LORD , And be the companion of all the sons of Jacob; Let His table be yours And you and your sons will eat thereof; And may your table be full to all generations, And your food will not fail to all the ages. 17 And let all who hate you fall down before you, And let all your adversaries be rooted out and perish; And blessed is he that blesses you And cursed is every nation that curses you." 18 And to Judah he said, "May the LORD give you strength and power To tread down all that hate you; You will be a prince—you and one of your sons, Over the sons of Jacob; May your name and the name of your sons Go out and traverse every land and region. Then the nations will fear before your face, And all the nations [[or peoples]] will quake. 19 In you will be the help of Jacob, And in you will be found the salvation of Israel. 20 And when you sit on the throne of the honor of your righteousness, There will be great peace for all the seed of the sons of the beloved, And he that blesses you will be blessed; And all that hate you, and afflict

you, and curse you Will be rooted out and destroyed from the earth and accursed." **21** And turning, he kissed him again and embraced him, and greatly rejoiced, for he had seen the sons of his son Jacob in exceeding truth. **22** And he went out from between his feet and fell down and worshiped him. And he blessed them. And [Jacob] rested there with his father Isaac that night, and they ate and drank with joy. **23** And he made the two sons of Jacob sleep—the one on his right hand and the other on his left, and it was counted to him for righteousness. **24** And Jacob told his father everything during the night, how the LORD had shown him great mercy, and how He had prospered [him in] all his ways and protected him from all evil. **25**   And Isaac blessed the God of his father Abraham who had not withdrawn His mercy and His righteousness from the sons of His servant Isaac. **26** And in the morning, Jacob told his father Isaac the vow which he had vowed to the LORD , and the vision which he had seen, and that he had built an altar, and that everything was ready for the sacrifice to be made before the LORD as he had vowed, and that he had come to set him on a donkey. **27** And Isaac said to his son Jacob, "I am not able to go with you, for I am old and not able to bear the way: go, my son, in peace, for I am one hundred and sixty-five years [old] this day; I am no longer able to journey. Set your mother [on a donkey] and let her go with you. **28** And I know, my son, that you have come on my account, and may this day be blessed on which you have seen me alive, and I also have seen you, my son. **29** May you prosper and fulfill the vow which you have vowed, and do not put off your vow, for you will be called to account as touching the vow . Now, therefore, make sure to perform it, and may He be pleased who has made all things, to whom you have vowed the vow." **30** And he said to Rebekah, "Go with your son Jacob"; and Rebekah went with her son Jacob, and Deborah with her, and they came to Bethel. **31** And Jacob remembered the prayer with which his father had blessed him and his two sons, Levi and Judah, and he rejoiced and blessed the God of his fathers Abraham and Isaac. **32**   And he said, "Now I know that I have a continuous hope, and my sons also, before the God of all"; and thus it is ordained concerning the two; and they record it as a perpetual testimony to them on the heavenly tablets how Isaac blessed them.

CHAPTER 32

1 And he stayed that night at Bethel, and Levi dreamed that they had ordained and made him the priest of the Most High God, him and his sons forever; and he awoke from his sleep and blessed the LORD . **2** And Jacob rose early in the morning, on the fourteenth of this month, and he gave a tithe of all that came with him, both of men and cattle, both of gold and every vessel and garment, yes, he gave tithes of all. **3** And in those days Rachel became pregnant with her son Benjamin. And Jacob counted his sons from him upwards and Levi fell to the portion of the LORD , and his father clothed him in the garments of the priesthood and filled his hands. **4** And on the fifteenth of this month, he brought to the altar fourteen oxen from among the cattle, and twenty-eight rams, and forty-nine sheep, and seven lambs, and twenty-one kids of the goats as a burnt-offering on the altar of sacrifice, well pleasing for a sweet savor before God. **5** This was his offering, in consequence of the vow which he had vowed that he would give a tenth, with their fruit-offerings and their drink-offerings. **6** And when the fire had consumed it, he burned incense on the fire over the fire, and for a thank-offering two oxen, and four rams, and four sheep, four male goats, and two sheep of a year old, and two kids of the goats; and thus he did daily for seven days. **7** And he, and all his sons, and his men were eating [this] with joy there for seven days and were blessing and thanking the LORD who had delivered him out of all his tribulation and had given him his vow. **8** And he tithed all the clean animals, and made a burnt sacrifice, but he did [not] give the unclean animals to his son Levi, and he gave him all the souls of the men. **9** And Levi discharged the priestly office at Bethel before his father Jacob in preference to his ten brothers, and he was a priest there, and Jacob gave his vow: thus he tithed the tithe to the LORD again and sanctified it, and it became holy to Him. **10** And for this reason it is ordained on the heavenly tablets as a law for the tithing the tithe again to eat before the LORD from year to year in the place where it is chosen that His Name should dwell, and to this law there is no limit of days forever. **11** This ordinance is written that it may be fulfilled from year to year in eating the second tithe before the LORD in the place where it has been chosen, and nothing will remain over from it from this year to the year following. **12** For in its year the seed will be eaten until the days of the gathering of the seed of the year, and the wine until the days of the wine, and the oil until the days of its season. **13** And all that is left thereof and becomes old, let it be regarded as polluted: let it be burned with fire, for it is unclean. **14** And thus let them eat it together in the sanctuary and do not let them permit it to become old. **15** And all the tithes of the oxen and sheep will be holy to the LORD , and will belong to His priests, which they will eat before Him from year to year, for thus it is ordained and engraved regarding the tithe on the heavenly tablets. **16** And on the following night, on the twenty-second day of this month, Jacob resolved to build that place, and to surround the court with a wall, and to sanctify it and make it holy forever, for himself and his children after him. **17** And the LORD appeared to him by night, and blessed him, and said to him, "Your name will not be called Jacob, but Israel they will name your name." **18** And He said to him again, "I am the LORD who created the heavens and the earth, and I will increase you and multiply you exceedingly, and kings will come out from you, and they will judge everywhere, wherever the foot of the sons of men has trodden. **19** And I will give to your seed all the earth which is under the heavens, and they will judge all the nations according to their desires, and after that, they will get possession of the whole earth and inherit it forever." **20** And He finished speaking with him, and He went up from him, and Jacob looked until He had ascended into Heaven. **21** And he saw in a vision of the night, and behold, a messenger descended from Heaven with seven tablets in his hands, and he gave them to Jacob, and he read them and knew all that was written therein which would befall him and his sons throughout all the ages. **22** And he showed him all that was written on the tablets and said to him, "Do not build this place, and do not make it a perpetual sanctuary, and do not dwell here, for this is not the place. Go to the house of your father Abraham and dwell with your father Isaac until the day of the death of your father. **23** For in Egypt you will die in peace, and you will be buried in this land with honor in the tomb of your fathers, with Abraham and Isaac. **24** Do not fear, for as you have seen and read it, thus it will all be; and write down everything as you have seen and read." **25** And Jacob said, "Lord, how can I remember all that I have read and seen?" And he said to him, "I will bring all things to your remembrance." **26** And he went up from him, and he awoke from his sleep, and he remembered everything which he had read and seen, and he wrote down all the words which he had read and seen. **27** And he celebrated there yet another day, and he sacrificed thereon according to all that he sacrificed on the former days, and called its name "Addition," for this day was added, and the former days he called "The Feast." 28 And thus it was manifested that it should be, and it is written on the heavenly tablets, for that reason it was revealed to him that he should celebrate it and add it to the seven days of the feast. 29 And its name was called "Addition," because that it was recorded among the days of the feast days, according to the number of the days of the year. 30 And in the night, on the twenty-third of this month, Rebekah's nurse Deborah died, and they buried her beneath the city under the oak of the river, and he called the name of this place, "The river of Deborah," and the oak, "The oak of the mourning of Deborah." 31 And Rebekah went and returned to her house, to his father Isaac, and Jacob sent by her hand rams, and sheep, and male goats that she should prepare a meal for his father such as he desired. 32 And he went after his mother until he came to the land of Kabrâtân, and he dwelt there. 33 And Rachel bore a son in the night and called his name "Son of my sorrow," for she suffered in giving him birth, but his father called his name Benjamin, on the eleventh of the eighth month, in the first of the sixth week of this jubilee. 34 And Rachel died there, and she was buried in the land of Ephrath, the same is Beth-Lehem, and Jacob built a pillar on the grave of Rachel, on the road above her grave.

CHAPTER 33

And Jacob went and dwelt to the south of Magdalâdrâ'êf. And he went to his father Isaac, he and his wife Leah, on the new moon of the tenth month. And Reuben saw Bilhah, Rachel's maid, the concubine of his father, bathing in water in a secret place, and he loved her. 3 And he hid himself at night, and he entered the house of Bilhah [at night], and he found her sleeping alone on a bed in her house. 4 And he lay with her, and she awoke and saw, and behold, Reuben was lying with her in the bed, and she uncovered the border of her covering and seized him, and cried out, and discovered that it was Reuben. 5 And she was ashamed because of him, and released her hand from him, and he fled. 6 And she lamented exceedingly because of this thing and did not tell it to anyone. 7 And when Jacob returned and sought her, she said to him, "I am not clean for you, for I have been defiled as regards you, for Reuben has defiled me, and has lain with me in the night, and I was asleep, and did not discover [it] until he uncovered my skirt and slept with me." 8 And Jacob was exceedingly angry with Reuben because he had lain with Bilhah, because he had uncovered his father's skirt. 9 And Jacob did not approach her again because Reuben had defiled her. And as for any man who uncovers his father's skirt: his deed is exceedingly wicked, for he is abominable before the LORD . 10 For this reason it is written and ordained on the heavenly tablets that a man should not lie with his father's wife, and should not uncover his father's skirt, for this is unclean: they will surely die together, the man who lies with his father's wife and the woman also, for they have worked uncleanness on the earth. 11 And there will be nothing unclean before our God in the nation which He has chosen for Himself as a possession. 12 And again, it is written a second time: "Cursed is he who lies with the wife of his father, for he has uncovered his father's shame"; and all the holy ones of the LORD said, "So be it; so be it." 13 And you, Moses, command the sons of Israel that they observe this word, for it [entails] a punishment of death; and it is unclean, and there is no atonement forever to atone for the man who has committed this, but he is to be put to death and slain, and stoned with stones, and rooted out from the midst of the people of our God. 14 For to no man who does so in Israel is it permitted to remain alive a single day on the earth, for he is abominable and unclean. 15 And do not let them say, "Life and forgiveness were granted to Reuben after he had lain with his father's concubine, and to her also though she had a husband, and her husband Jacob, his father, was still alive." 16 For until that time there had not been revealed the ordinance, and judgment, and law in its completeness for all, but in your days [it has been revealed] as a law of seasons and of days, and a continuous law for the perpetual generations. 17 And for this law there is no consummation of days, and no atonement for it, but they must both be rooted out in the midst of the nation: on the day on which they committed it they will slay them. 18 And you, Moses, write [it] down for Israel that they may observe it, and do according to these words, and not commit a sin to death , for the LORD our God is judge, who does not respect persons and does not accept gifts. 19 And tell them these words of the covenant, that they may hear and observe, and be on their guard with respect to them, and not be destroyed and rooted out of the land; for an uncleanness, and an abomination, and a contamination, and a pollution are all they who commit it on the earth before our God. 20 And there is no greater sin than the fornication which they commit on earth, for Israel is a holy nation to the LORD its God, and a nation of inheritance, and a priestly and royal nation, and for [His own] possession; and no such uncleanness will appear in the midst of the holy nation. 21 And in the third year of this sixth week Jacob and all his sons went and dwelt in the house of Abraham, near his father Isaac and his mother Rebekah. 22 And these were the names of the sons of Jacob: the firstborn Reuben, Simeon, Levi, Judah, Issachar, Zebulun—the sons of Leah; and the sons of Rachel: Joseph and Benjamin; and the sons of Bilhah: Dan and Naphtali; and the sons of Zilpah: Gad and Asher; and Dinah, the daughter of Leah, the only daughter of Jacob. 23 And they came and bowed themselves to Isaac and Rebekah, and when they saw them, they blessed Jacob and all his sons, and Isaac rejoiced exceedingly, for he saw the sons of Jacob, his younger son, and he blessed them.

CHAPTER 34

1 And in the sixth year of this week, of this forty-fourth jubilee, Jacob sent his sons to pasture their sheep, and his servants with them, to the pastures of Shechem. 2 And the seven kings of the Amorites assembled themselves together against them, to slay them, hiding themselves under the trees, and to take their cattle as a prey. 3 And Jacob, and Levi, and Judah, and Joseph were in the house with their father Isaac, for his spirit was sorrowful, and they could not leave him; and Benjamin was the youngest, and for this reason remained with his father. 4 And there came the king[s] of Tâphû, and the king[s] of 'Arêsa, and the king[s] of Sêragân, and the king[s] of Sêlô, and the king[s] of Gâ'as, and the king of Bêthôrôn, and the king of Ma'anîsâkîr, and all those who dwell in these mountains [and] who dwell in the woods in the land of Canaan. 5 And they announced this to Jacob, saying, "Behold, the kings of the Amorites have surrounded your sons, and plundered their herds." 6 And he arose from his house—he, and his three sons, and all the servants of his father, and his own servants—and he went against them with six thousand men who carried swords. 7 And he slew them in the pastures of

Shechem, and pursued those who fled, and he slew them with the edge of the sword, and he slew 'Arêsa, and Tâphû, and Sêragân, and Sêlô, and Ma'anîsâkîr, and Gâ'as, and he recovered his herds. 8 And he prevailed over them, and imposed tribute on them that they should pay him tribute, five fruit products of their land, and he built Rôbêl and Tamnâtârês , 9 and he returned in peace, and made peace with them, and they became his servants until the day that he and his sons went down into Egypt. 10 And in the seventh year of this week he sent Joseph from his house to the land of Shechem to learn about the welfare of his brothers, and he found them in the land of Dothan. 11 And they dealt treacherously with him, and formed a plot against him to slay him, but changing their minds, they sold him to Ishmaelite merchants, and they brought him down into Egypt, and they sold him to Potiphar, the eunuch of Pharaoh, the chief of the cooks, priest of the city of 'Êlêw. 12 And the sons of Jacob slaughtered a kid, and dipped the coat of Joseph in the blood, and sent [it] to their father Jacob on the tenth of the seventh month. 13 And he mourned all that night, for they had brought it to him in the evening, and he became feverish with mourning for his death, and he said, "An evil beast has devoured Joseph"; and all the members of his house were grieving and mourning with him that whole day. 14 And his sons and his daughter rose up to comfort him, but he refused to be comforted for his son. 15 And on that day, Bilhah heard that Joseph had perished, and she died mourning [for] him, and she was living in Qafrâtêf and Dinah also, his daughter, died after Joseph had perished. And these three mournings came on Israel in one month. 16 And they buried Bilhah over against the tomb of Rachel, and Dinah also, his daughter, they buried there. 17 And he mourned for Joseph one year, and did not cease, for he said, "Let me go down to the grave mourning for my son." 18 For this reason it is ordained for the sons of Israel that they should afflict themselves on the tenth of the seventh month—on the day that the news which made him weep for Joseph came to Jacob his father—that they should make atonement for themselves thereon with a young goat on the tenth of the seventh month, once a year, for their sins, for they had grieved the affection of their father regarding his son Joseph. 19 And this day has been ordained that they should grieve thereon for their sins, and for all their transgressions, and for all their errors, so that they might cleanse themselves on that day once a year. 20   And after Joseph perished, the sons of Jacob took wives for themselves. The name of Reuben's wife is 'Adâ ; and the name of Simeon's wife is 'Adîbâ'a, a Canaanite; and the name of Levi's wife is Mêlkâ, of the daughters of Aram, of the seed of the sons of Terah; and the name of Judah's wife, Bêtasû'êl, a Canaanite; and the name of Issachar's wife, Hêzaqâ; and the name of Zebulun's wife, Nî'îmân; and the name of Dan's wife, 'Êglâ; and the name of Naphtali's wife, Rasû'û, of Mesopotamia; and the name of Gad's wife, Mâka; and the name of Asher's wife, 'Îjônâ; and the name of Joseph's wife, Asenath, the Egyptian; and the name of Benjamin's wife, 'Îjasaka. 21 And Simeon converted, and took a second wife from Mesopotamia as his brothers.

CHAPTER 35

1 And in the first year of the first week of the forty-fifth jubilee, Rebekah called her son Jacob and commanded him regarding his father and regarding his brother, that he should honor them all the days of his life. 2 And Jacob said, "I will do everything as you have commanded me, for this thing will be honor and greatness to me, and righteousness before the LORD , that I should honor them. 3 And you, mother, also know from the time I was born until this day, all my deeds and all that is in my heart, that I always think good concerning all. 4 And how should I not do this thing which you have commanded me, that I should honor my father and my brother! 5 Tell me, mother, what perversity have you seen in me and I will turn away from it, and mercy will be on me." 6 And she said to him, "My son, I have not seen in you all my days anything perverse, but [only] upright deeds. And yet I will tell you the truth, my son: I will die this year, and I will not survive this year in my life, for I have seen in a dream the day of my death, that I should not live beyond one hundred and fifty-five years; and behold, I have completed all the days of my life which I am to live." 7 And Jacob laughed at the words of his mother, because his mother had said to him that she should die; and she was sitting opposite to him in possession of her strength, and she was not weak in her strength, for she went in and out and saw, and her teeth were strong, and no ailment had touched her all the days of her life. 8 And Jacob said to her, "Blessed am I, mother, if my days approach the days of your life, and my strength remains with me thus as your strength: and you will not die, for you are idly jesting with me regarding your death." 9 And she went in to Isaac and said to him, "One petition I make to you: make Esau swear that he will not injure Jacob, nor pursue him with enmity, for you know that Esau's thoughts are perverse from his youth, and there is no goodness in him, for he desires to kill him after your death. 10 And you know all that he has done since the day his brother Jacob went to Haran until this day, how he has forsaken us with his whole heart and has done evil to us; he has taken your flocks to himself and carried off all your possessions from before your face. 11 And when we implored and entreated him for what was our own, he did as a man who was taking pity on us. 12 And he is bitter against you because you blessed Jacob, your perfect and upright son; for there is no evil but only goodness in him, and since he came from Haran to this day, he has not robbed us of anything, for he always brings us everything in its season, and rejoices with all his heart when we take at his hands, and he blesses us, and has not parted from us since he came from Haran until this day, and he continually remains at home with us, honoring us." 13 And Isaac said to her, "I, too, know and see the deeds of Jacob who is with us, how that he honors us with all his heart, but I formerly loved Esau more than Jacob, because he was the firstborn, but now I love Jacob more than Esau, for he has done manifold evil deeds, and there is no righteousness in him, for all his ways are unrighteousness and violence. 14 And now my heart is troubled because of all his deeds, and neither he nor his seed is to be saved, for they are those who will be destroyed from the earth, and who will be rooted out from under the heavens, for he has forsaken the God of Abraham and gone after his wives, and after their uncleanness, and after their error—he and his children. 15 And you command me to make him swear that he will not slay his brother Jacob; even if he swears, he will not abide by his oath, and he will not do good but only evil. 16 But if he desires to slay his brother Jacob, he will be given into Jacob's hands, and he will not escape from his hands. 17 And do not fear on account of Jacob, for the guardian of Jacob is great, and powerful, and honored, and praised more than the guardian of Esau." 18 And Rebekah sent and called Esau, and he came to her, and she said to him, "I have a petition, my son, to make to you, and do you promise to do it, my son?" 19   And he said, "I will do everything that you say to me, and I will not refuse your petition." 20 And she said to him, "I ask you that the day I die, you will take me in and bury me near Sarah, your father's

mother, and that you and Jacob will love each other, and that neither will desire evil against the other, but mutual love only, and [so] you will prosper, my sons, and be honored in the midst of the land, and no enemy will rejoice over you, and you will be a blessing and a mercy in the eyes of all those that love you." **21** And he said, "I will do all that you have told me, and I will bury you on the day you die near Sarah, my father's mother, as you have desired, that her bones may be near your bones. **22** And I will also love my brother Jacob above all flesh, for I have no brother in all the earth but him only; and this is no great merit for me if I love him, for he is my brother, and we were sown together in your body, and together we came out from your womb, and if I do not love my brother, whom will I love? **23** And I, myself, beg you to exhort Jacob concerning me and concerning my sons, for I know that he will assuredly be king over me and my sons, for on the day my father blessed him he made him the higher and me the lower. **24** And I swear to you that I will love him, and not desire evil against him all the days of my life, but good only." And he swore to her regarding all this matter. **25** And she called Jacob before the eyes of Esau and gave him command according to the words which she had spoken to Esau. **26** And he said, "I will do your pleasure; believe me that no evil will proceed from me or from my sons against Esau, and I will be first in nothing save in love only." **27** And she and her sons ate and drank that night, and she died—three jubilees and one week and one year old—on that night, and her two sons, Esau and Jacob, buried her in the double cave near Sarah, their father's mother.

CHAPTER 36

1 And in the sixth year of this week Isaac called his two sons, Esau and Jacob, and they came to him, and he said to them, "My sons, I am going the way of my fathers, to the continuous house where my fathers are. **2** For that reason, bury me near my father Abraham, in the double cave in the field of Ephron the Hittite, where Abraham purchased a tomb to bury in; in the tomb which I dug for myself, bury me there. **3** And this I command you, my sons, that you practice righteousness and uprightness on the earth, so that the LORD may bring on you all that the LORD said that He would do to Abraham and to his seed. **4** And, my sons, love one another—your brother —as a man who loves his own soul, and let each seek in what [way] he may benefit his brother, and act together on the earth; and let them love each other as their own souls. **5** And concerning the question of idols, I command and admonish you to reject them, and hate them, and not to love them, for they are full of deception for those that worship them and for those that bow down to them. **6** Remember, my sons, the LORD God of your father Abraham, and how I also worshiped Him and served Him in righteousness and in joy, that He might multiply you and increase your seed as the stars of the heavens in multitude and establish you on the earth as the plant of righteousness which will not be rooted out to all the generations forever. **7** And now I will make you swear a great oath—for there is no oath which is greater than it, by the glorious, and honored, and great, and splendid, and wonderful, and mighty Name, which created the heavens, and the earth, and all things together—that you will fear Him and worship Him, **8** and that each will love his brother with affection and righteousness, and that neither will desire evil against his brother from now on and forever, all the days of your life, so that you may prosper in all your deeds and not be destroyed. **9** And if either of you devises evil against his brother, know that from now on everyone that devises evil against his brother will fall into his hand, and will be rooted out of the land of the living, and his seed will be destroyed from under the heavens. **10** But on the day of turbulence, and execration, and indignation, and anger, with flaming devouring fire as He burned Sodom, so likewise He will burn his land, and his city, and all that is his, and he will be blotted out of the scroll of the discipline of the children of men, and not be recorded in the Scroll of Life, but in that which is appointed to destruction, and he will depart into continuous execration, so that their condemnation may always be renewed in hate, and in execration, and in wrath, and in torment, and in indignation, and in plagues, and in disease forever. **11** I say and testify to you, my sons, according to the judgment which will come on the man who wishes to injure his brother." **12** And he divided all his possessions between the two on that day, and he gave the larger portion to him that was the firstborn, and the tower and all that was around it, and all that Abraham possessed at the Well of the Oath. **13** And he said, "I will give this larger portion to the firstborn." **14** And Esau said, "I have sold to Jacob and given my birthright to Jacob; let it be given to him, and I have not a single word to say regarding it, for it is his." **15** And Isaac said, "May a blessing rest on you, my sons, and on your seed this day, for you have given me rest, and my heart is not pained concerning the birthright, lest you should work wickedness on account of it. **16** May the Most High God bless the man that works righteousness—him and his seed forever." **17** And he ended commanding them and blessing them, and they ate and drank together before him, and he rejoiced because there was one mind between them, and they went out from him, and rested that day, and slept. **18** And Isaac slept on his bed that day rejoicing; and he slept the continuous sleep and died one hundred and eighty years old. He completed twenty-five weeks and five years; and his two sons Esau and Jacob buried him. **19** And Esau went to the land of Edom, to the mountains of Seir, and dwelt there. **20** And Jacob dwelt in the mountains of Hebron, in the tower of the land of the sojournings of his father Abraham, and he worshiped the LORD with all his heart and according to the visible commands according as He had divided the days of his generations. **21** And his wife Leah died in the fourth year of the second week of the forty-fifth jubilee, and he buried her in the double cave near his mother Rebekah, to the left of the grave of Sarah, his father's mother. **22** And all her sons and his sons came to mourn over his wife Leah with him, and to comfort him regarding her, for he was lamenting her. **23** For he loved her exceedingly after her sister Rachel died, for she was perfect and upright in all her ways and honored Jacob, and all the days that she lived with him he did not hear from her mouth a harsh word, for she was gentle, and peaceable, and upright, and honorable. **24** And he remembered all her deeds which she had done during her life, and he lamented her exceedingly, for he loved her with all his heart and with all his soul.

CHAPTER 37

1 And on the day that Isaac the father of Jacob and Esau died, the sons of Esau heard that Isaac had given the portion of the elder to his younger son Jacob and they were very angry. **2** And they strove with their father, saying, "Why has your father given Jacob the portion of the elder and passed over you, although you are the elder and Jacob the younger?" **3** And he said to them, "Because I sold my birthright to Jacob for a small mess of lentils; and on the day my father sent me to hunt, and catch, and bring him something that he should eat and bless me, he came with guile and brought my father food and drink, and my father blessed him and put me under his hand. 4 And now our father has caused us to swear—me and him—that we will not mutually devise evil, either against his brother, and that we will each continue in love and in peace with his brother and not make our ways corrupt." 5 And they said to him, "We will not listen to you to make peace with him, for our strength is greater than his strength, and we are more powerful than he; we will go against him and slay him, and destroy him and his sons. And if you will not go with us, we will do harm to you also. 6 And now listen to us: let us send to Aram , and Philistia , and Moab, and Ammon, and let us choose for ourselves chosen men who are ardent for battle, and let us go against him and do battle with him, and let us exterminate him from the earth before he grows strong." 7 And their father said to them, "Do not go and do not make war with him lest you fall before him." 8 And they said to him, "This, too, is exactly your mode of action from your youth until this day, and you are putting your neck under his yoke. We will not listen to these words." 9 And they sent to Aram and to 'Adurâm , to the friend of their father, and they hired along with them one thousand fighting men, chosen men of war. 10 And there came to them from Moab and from the children of Ammon those who were hired, one thousand chosen men; and from Philistia, one thousand chosen men of war; and from Edom and from the Horites, one thousand chosen fighting men; and from the Kittim , mighty men of war. 11 And they said to their father, "Go out with them and lead them, else we will slay you." 12 And he was filled with wrath and indignation on seeing that his sons were forcing him to go before [them] to lead them against his brother Jacob. 13 But afterward he remembered all the evil which lay hidden in his heart against his brother Jacob, and he did not remember the oath which he had sworn to his father and to his mother that he would devise no evil all his days against his brother Jacob. 14 And notwithstanding all this, Jacob did not know that they were coming against him to battle, and he was mourning for his wife Leah until they approached very near to the tower with four thousand warriors and chosen men of war. 15 And the men of Hebron sent to him, saying, "Behold, your brother has come against you, to fight you, with four thousand girt with the sword, and they carry shields and weapons"; for they loved Jacob more than Esau. So they told him, for Jacob was a more liberal and merciful man than Esau. 16 But Jacob would not believe [it] until they came very near to the tower. 17 And he closed the gates of the tower; and he stood on the battlements, and spoke to his brother Esau, and said, "Noble is the comfort with which you have come to comfort me for my wife who has died. Is this the oath that you swore to your father and again to your mother before they died ? Y ou have broken the oath, and on the moment that you swore to your father you were condemned." 18   And then Esau answered and said to him, "Neither the children of men nor the beasts of the earth have any oath of righteousness which in swearing they have sworn forever, but every day they devise evil against one another, and how each may slay his adversary and enemy. 19 And you hate me and my children forever. And there is no observing the tie of brotherhood with you. 20 Hear these words which I declare to you, If the boar can change its skin and make its bristles as soft as wool, or if it can cause horns to sprout out on its head like the horns of a stag or of a sheep, then I will observe the tie of brotherhood with you. [[And if the breasts separated themselves from their mother; for you have not been a brother to me.]] 21 And if the wolves make peace with the lambs so as not to devour or do them violence, and if their hearts are toward them for good, then there will be peace in my heart toward you. 22 And if the lion becomes the friend of the ox and makes peace with him, and if he is bound under one yoke with him and plows with him, then I will make peace with you. 23 And when the raven becomes white as the râzâ, then know that I have loved you and will make peace with you. You will be rooted out, and your sons will be rooted out, and there will be no peace for you." 24 And when Jacob saw that he was [so] evilly disposed toward him with [all] his heart and with all his soul as to slay him, and that he had come springing like the wild boar which comes on the spear that pierces and kills it, and does not recoil from it, 25 then he spoke to his own and to his servants that they should attack him and all his companions.

CHAPTER 38

1 And after that, Judah spoke to his father Jacob, and said to him, "Bend your bow, father, and send out your arrows, and cast down the adversary, and slay the enemy; and may you have the power, for we will not slay your brother, for he is such as you, and he is like you: let us give him [this] honor." 2 Then Jacob bent his bow, and sent out the arrow, and struck his brother Esau [[on his right breast]] , and slew him. 3 And again he sent out an arrow and struck 'Adôrân the Aramaean, on the left breast, and drove him backward and slew him. 4 And then the sons of Jacob went out—they and their servants—dividing themselves into companies on the four sides of the tower. 5 And Judah went out in front, and Naphtali and Gad with him, and fifty servants with him on the south side of the tower, and they slew all they found before them, and not one individual of them escaped. 6 And Levi, and Dan, and Asher went out on the east side of the tower, and fifty [men] with them, and they slew the fighting men of Moab and Ammon. 7 And Reuben, and Issachar, and Zebulun went out on the north side of the tower, and fifty men with them, and they slew the fighting men of the Philistines. 8 And Simeon, and Benjamin, and Enoch, Reuben's son, went out on the west side of the tower, and fifty [men] with them, and they slew of Edom and of the Horites four hundred men, stout warriors; and six hundred fled, and four of the sons of Esau fled with them, and left their father lying slain, as he had fallen on the hill which is in 'Adûrâm. 9 And the sons of Jacob pursued after them to the mountains of Seir. And Jacob buried his brother on the hill which is in 'Adûrâm, and he returned to his house. 10 And the sons of Jacob pressed hard on the sons of Esau in the mountains of Seir and bowed their necks so that they became servants of the sons of Jacob. 11 And they sent to their father [to inquire] whether they should make peace with them or slay them. 12 And Jacob sent word to his sons that they should make peace, and they made peace with them, and placed the yoke of servitude on them, so that they always paid tribute to Jacob and to his sons. 13 And they continued to pay tribute to Jacob until the day that he went down into Egypt. 14 And the sons of Edom have not gotten rid of the yoke of servitude which the twelve sons of Jacob had imposed on them until this day. 15 And these are the kings that reigned in Edom, in the land of Edom, before any king reigned over the sons of Israel: 16 and Bâlâq, the son of Beor, reigned in Edom, and the name of his city was Danâbâ ; 17 and Bâlâq died, and Jobab, the son of Zârâ of Bôsêr, reigned in his stead; 18 and Jobab died, and 'Asâm, of the land of Têmân, reigned in his stead; 19 and 'Asâm died, and 'Adâth, the

son of Barad, who slew Midian in the field of Moab, reigned in his stead, and the name of his city was Avith; **20** and 'Adâth died, and Salman, from 'Amâsêqâ, reigned in his stead; **21** and Salman died, and Saul of Râ'abôth [by the] river, reigned in his stead; **22** and Saul died, and Ba'êlûnân, the son of Achbor, reigned in his stead; **23** and Ba'êlûnân, the son of Achbor, died, and 'Adâth reigned in his stead, and the name of his wife was Maiṭabîth, the daughter of Mâṭarat, the daughter of Mêtabêdzâ'ab. **24** These are the kings who reigned in the land of Edom.

CHAPTER 39

1 And Jacob dwelt in the land of his father's sojournings in the land of Canaan. **2** These are the generations of Jacob. And Joseph was seventeen years old when they took him down into the land of Egypt, and Potiphar, [[a eunuch of Pharaoh,]] the chief cook [[or chief executioner]] bought him. **3** And he set Joseph over all his house, and the blessing of the LORD came on the house of the Egyptian on account of Joseph, and the LORD prospered him in all that he did. **4** And the Egyptian committed everything into the hands of Joseph, for he saw that the LORD was with him, and that the LORD prospered him in all that he did. **5** And Joseph's appearance was handsome, and his appearance was very beautiful, and his master's wife lifted up her eyes and saw Joseph, and she loved him, and implored him to lie with her. **6** But he did not surrender his soul, and he remembered the LORD and the words which his father Jacob used to read from among the words of Abraham, that no man should commit fornication with a woman who has a husband, that the punishment of death has been ordained in the heavens for him before the Most High God, and the sin will be continually recorded against him in the perpetual scrolls before the LORD . **7** And Joseph remembered these words and refused to lie with her. **8** And she implored him for a year, but he refused and would not listen. **9** But she embraced him and held him fast in the house in order to force him to lie with her, and she closed the doors of the house and held him fast, but he left his garment in her hands, and broke through the door, and fled outside from her presence. **10** And the woman saw that he would not lie with her, and she accused him in the presence of his lord, saying, "Your Hebrew servant, whom you love, sought to force me so that he might lie with me; and it came to pass when I lifted up my voice, that he fled and left his garment in my hands when I held him, and he broke through the door." **11** And the Egyptian saw the garment of Joseph and the broken door, and heard the words of his wife, and cast Joseph into prison into the place where the prisoners were kept whom the king imprisoned. **12** And he was there in the prison, and the LORD gave Joseph favor in the sight of the chief of the prison guards and compassion before him, for he saw that the LORD was with him, and that the LORD made all that he did to prosper. **13** And he committed all things into his hands, and the chief of the prison guards knew of nothing that was with him, for Joseph did everything, and the LORD perfected it. **14** And he remained there two years. And in those days Pharaoh, king of Egypt, was angry against his two eunuchs, against the chief butler and against the chief baker, and he put them in ward in the house of the chief cook, in the prison where Joseph was kept. **15** And the chief of the prison guards appointed Joseph to serve them; and he served before them. **16** And they both dreamed a dream, the chief butler and the chief baker, and they told it to Joseph. **17** And as he interpreted [the dreams] to them, so it befell them, and Pharaoh restored the chief butler to his office, and he slew the [chief] baker, as Joseph had interpreted to them. **18** But the chief butler forgot Joseph in the prison, although he had informed him what would befall him, and did not remember to inform Pharaoh how Joseph had told him, for he forgot.

CHAPTER 40

1 And in those days Pharaoh dreamed two dreams in one night concerning a famine which was to be in all the land, and he awoke from his sleep and called all the interpreters of dreams that were in Egypt, and magicians, and told them his two dreams, and they were not able to declare [the interpretation]. **2** And then the chief butler remembered Joseph and spoke of him to the king, and he brought him out from the prison, and he told his two dreams before him. **3** And he said before Pharaoh that his two dreams were one, and he said to him, "Seven years of plenty will come over all the land of Egypt, and after that, seven years of famine—such a famine as has not been in all the land. **4** And now let Pharaoh appoint overseers in all the land of Egypt, and let them store up food in every city throughout the days of the years of plenty, and there will be food for the seven years of famine, and the land will not perish through the famine, for it will be very severe." **5** And the LORD gave Joseph favor and mercy in the eyes of Pharaoh, and Pharaoh said to his servants, "We will not find such a wise and discreet man as this man, for the Spirit of the LORD is with him." **6** And he appointed him the second in all his kingdom and gave him authority over all Egypt, and caused him to ride in the second chariot of Pharaoh. **7** And he clothed him with flax garments, and he put a gold chain on his neck, and [a herald] proclaimed before him "'Êl 'Êl wa' Abîrĕr," and he placed a ring on his hand, and made him ruler over all his house, and magnified him, and said to him, "Only on the throne will I be greater than you." **8** And Joseph ruled over all the land of Egypt, and all the princes of Pharaoh, and all his servants, and all who did the king's business loved him, for he walked in uprightness, for he was without pride and arrogance, and he had no respect of persons, and did not accept gifts, but he judged all the people of the land in uprightness. **9** And the land of Egypt was at peace before Pharaoh because of Joseph, for the LORD was with him, and gave him favor and mercy for all his generations before all those who knew him and those who heard concerning him, and Pharaoh's kingdom was well ordered, and there was no adversary and no evil person [therein]. **10** And the king called Joseph's name Sĕphânṭîphâns and gave Joseph the daughter of Potiphar to be [his] wife, the daughter of the priest of Heliopolis, the chief cook [[or chief executioner]] . **11** And on the day that Joseph stood before Pharaoh, he was thirty years old. **12** And in that year Isaac died. And it came to pass as Joseph had said in the interpretation of his two dreams, according as he had said it, there were seven years of plenty over all the land of Egypt, and the land of Egypt produced abundantly, one measure [producing] eighteen hundred measures. **13** And Joseph gathered food into every city until they were full of corn until they could no longer count and measure it for its multitude.

CHAPTER 41

1 And in the forty-fifth jubilee, in the second week, [and] in the second year, Judah took a wife for his firstborn Er named Tamar, from the daughters of Aram . **2** But he hated [her] and did not lie with her, because his mother was of the daughters of Canaan, and he wished to take a wife [for] himself of the countrymen of his mother, but his father Judah would not permit him. **3** And this Er, the firstborn of Judah, was wicked, and the LORD slew him. **4** And Judah said to his brother Onan, "Go in to your brother's wife and perform the duty of a husband's brother to her, and raise up seed to your brother." **5** And Onan knew that the seed would not be his, [but] his brother's only, and he went into the house of his brother's wife, and spilled the seed on the ground, and he was wicked in the eyes of the LORD , and He slew him. **6** And Judah said to his daughter-in-law Tamar, "Remain in your father's house as a widow until my son Shelah is grown up, and I will give you to him to be [his] wife." **7** And he grew up, but Bêdsû'êl, the wife of Judah, did not permit her son Shelah to marry. And Bêdsû'êl, the wife of Judah, died in the fifth year of this week. **8** And in the sixth year Judah went up to shear his sheep at Timnah. And they told Tamar, "Behold, your father-in-law goes up to Timnah to shear his sheep." **9** And she put off her widow's clothes, and put on a veil, and adorned herself, and sat in the gate adjoining the way to Timnah. **10** And as Judah was going along, he found her, and thought her to be a harlot, and he said to her, "Let me come in to you"; and she said to him, "Come in," and he went in. **11** And she said to him, "Give me my hire"; and he said to her, "I have nothing in my hand except my ring that is on my finger, and my necklace, and my staff which is in my hand." **12** And she said to him, "Give them to me until you send me my hire"; and he said to her, "I will send a kid of the goats to you"; and he gave them to her, [and he went in to her,] and she conceived by him. **13** And Judah went to his sheep, and she went to her father's house. **14** And Judah sent a kid of the goats by the hand of his shepherd, an Adullamite, and he did not find her; and he asked the people of the place, saying, "Where is the harlot who was here?" And they said to him, "There is no harlot here with us." **15** And he returned, and informed him, and said to him that he had not found her; "I asked the people of the place, and they said to me, There is no harlot here." And he said, "Let her keep [them] lest we become a cause of derision." **16** And when she had completed three months, it was manifest that she was with child, and they told Judah, saying, "Behold, your daughter-in-law Tamar is with child by whoredom." **17** And Judah went to the house of her father, and said to her father and her brothers, "Bring her out, and let them burn her, for she has worked uncleanness in Israel." **18** And it came to pass when they brought her out to burn her that she sent to her father-in-law the ring, and the necklace, and the staff, saying, "Discern whose these are, for I am with child by him." **19** And Judah acknowledged [them] and said, "Tamar is more righteous than I am. And therefore, let them not burn her." **20** And for that reason she was not given to Shelah, and he did not approach her again. **21** And after that she bore two sons, Perez and Zerah, in the seventh year of this second week. **22** And immediately the seven years of fruitfulness of which Joseph spoke to Pharaoh were accomplished. **23** And Judah acknowledged that the deed which he had done was evil, for he had lain with his daughter-in-law, and he esteemed it hateful in his eyes, and he acknowledged that he had transgressed and gone astray, for he had uncovered the skirt of his son, and he began to lament and to supplicate before the LORD because of his transgression. **24** And we told him in a dream that it was forgiven him because he supplicated earnestly, and lamented, and did not commit it again. **25** And he received forgiveness because he turned from his sin and from his ignorance, for he greatly transgressed before our God; and everyone that acts this way, everyone who lies with his mother-in-law, let them burn him with fire that he may burn therein, for there is uncleanness and pollution on them; let them burn them with fire. **26** And you command the sons of Israel that there is no uncleanness among them, for everyone who lies with his daughter-in-law or with his mother-in-law has worked uncleanness; let them burn the man who has lain with her with fire, and likewise the woman, and he will turn away wrath and punishment from Israel. **27** And to Judah we said that his two sons had not lain with her, and for this reason his seed was established for a second generation and would not be rooted out. **28** For in singleness of eye he had gone and sought for punishment, namely, according to the judgment of Abraham, which he had commanded his sons, Judah had sought to burn her with fire.

CHAPTER 42

1 And in the first year of the third week of the forty-fifth jubilee the famine began to come into the land, and the rain refused to be given to the earth, for none fell whatsoever. **2** And the earth grew barren, but in the land of Egypt there was food, for Joseph had gathered the seed of the land in the seven years of plenty and had preserved it. **3** And the Egyptians came to Joseph that he might give them food, and he opened the storehouses where the grain of the first year was, and he sold it to the people of the land for gold. **4** [[Now the famine was very severe in the land of Canaan]] , and Jacob heard that there was food in Egypt, and he sent his ten sons that they should procure food for him in Egypt, but he did not send Benjamin; and they arrived [in Egypt] among those that went [there.] **5** And Joseph recognized them, but they did not recognize him, and he spoke to them and questioned them, and he said to them, "Are you not spies, and have you not come to explore the approaches of the land?" And he put them in ward. **6** And after that, he set them free again, and detained Simeon alone, and sent off his nine brothers. **7** And he filled their sacks with corn, and he put their gold in their sacks, and they did not know. **8** And he commanded them to bring their younger brother, for they had told him their father was living and [also] their younger brother. **9** And they went up from the land of Egypt and they came to the land of Canaan; and they told their father all that had befallen them, and how the lord of the country had spoken roughly to them and had seized Simeon until they should bring Benjamin. **10** And Jacob said, "You have bereaved me of my children! Joseph is not, and Simeon is also not, and you will take Benjamin away. Your wickedness has come on me." **11** And he said, "My son will not go down with you lest perhaps he falls sick, for their mother gave birth to two sons, and one has perished, and you will also take this one from me. If perhaps he took a fever on the road, you would bring down my old age with sorrow to death." **12** For he saw that their money had been returned to each man in his sack, and for this reason he feared to send him. **13** And the famine increased and became severe in the land of Canaan, and in all lands except in the land of Egypt, for many of the children of the Egyptians had stored up their seed for food from the time when they saw Joseph gathering seed together, and putting it in storehouses, and preserving it for the years of famine. **14** And the people of Egypt fed themselves thereon during the first year of their famine. **15** But when Israel saw that the famine was very severe in the land and there was no deliverance, he said to his sons, "Go again, and procure food for us that we do not die." 16 And they said, "We will not go; unless our youngest brother goes with us, we will not go." 17 And Israel saw that if he did not send him with them, they should all perish by reason of the famine. 18 And Reuben said, "Give him into my hand, and if I do not bring him back to you, slay my two sons instead of his soul." And he said to him, "He will not go with you." 19 And Judah came near and said, "Send him with me, and if I do not bring him back to you, let me bear the blame before you all the days of my life." 20 And he sent him with them in the second year of this week, on the first day of the month, and they came to the land of Egypt with all those who went, and [they had] presents in their hands: stacte, and almonds, and terebinth nuts, and pure honey. 21 And they went and stood before Joseph, and he saw his brother Benjamin, and he knew him, and said to them, "Is this your youngest brother?" And they said to him, "It is he." And he said, "The LORD be gracious to you, my son!" 22 And he sent him into his house, and he brought Simeon out to them, and he made a feast for them, and they presented the gift to him which they had brought in their hands. 23 And they ate before him and he gave them all a portion, but the portion of Benjamin was seven times larger than that of any of theirs. 24 And they ate, and drank, and arose, and remained with their donkeys. 25 And Joseph devised a plan whereby he might learn their thoughts as to whether thoughts of peace prevailed among them, and he said to the steward who was over his house: "Fill all their sacks with food, and return their money to them into their vessels, and my cup, the silver cup out of which I drink, put it in the sack of the youngest, and send them away."

CHAPTER 43

1 And he did as Joseph had told him and filled all their sacks for them with food, and put their money in their sacks, and put the cup in Benjamin's sack. 2 And early in the morning they departed, and it came to pass that, when they had gone from there, Joseph said to the steward of his house, "Pursue them, run and seize them, saying, For good you have repaid me with evil; you have stolen from me the silver cup out of which my lord drinks. And bring back their youngest brother to me, and fetch [him] quickly before I go out to my seat of judgment." 3 And he ran after them and said to them according to these words. 4 And they said to him, "God forbid that your servants should do this thing, and steal from the house of your lord any utensil, and also the money which we found in our sacks the first time, we, your servants, brought back from the land of Canaan. 5 How then should we steal any utensil? Behold, here we are and our sacks; search, and wherever you find the cup in the sack of any man among us, let him be slain, and we and our donkeys will serve your lord." 6 And he said to them, "Not so; the man with whom I find [it], him only will I take as a servant, and you will return to your house in peace." 7 And as he was searching in their vessels, beginning with the eldest and ending with the youngest, it was found in Benjamin's sack. 8 And they tore their garments, and loaded their donkeys, and returned to the city, and came to the house of Joseph, and they all bowed themselves on their faces to the ground before him. 9 And Joseph said to them, "You have done evil." And they said, "What will we say and how will we defend ourselves? Our lord has discovered the transgression of his servants; behold, we are the servants of our lord, and our donkeys also." 10 And Joseph said to them, "I also fear the LORD ; as for you, go to your homes and let your brother be my servant, for you have done evil. Do you not know that a man delights in his cup as I with this cup? And yet you have stolen it from me." 11 And Judah said, "O my lord, please let your servant speak a word in my lord's ear; your servant's mother bore two brothers to our father; one went away and was lost, and has not been found, and he alone is left of his mother, and your servant, our father, loves him, and his life is also bound up with the life of this [youth]. 12 And it will come to pass, when we go to your servant, our father, and the youth is not with us, that he will die, and we will bring down our father with sorrow to death. 13 Now rather let me, your servant, abide instead of the boy as a bondsman to my lord, and let the youth go with his brothers, for I became a guarantee for him at the hand of your servant, our father, and if I do not bring him back, your servant will bear the blame to our father forever." 14 And Joseph saw that they were all in accord in goodness with one another, and he could not refrain himself, and he told them that he was Joseph. 15 And he conversed with them in the Hebrew tongue and fell on their neck and wept. But they did not recognize him, and they began to weep. 16 And he said to them, "Do not weep over me, but hurry and bring my father to me; and you see that it is my mouth that speaks, and the eyes of my brother Benjamin see. 17 For behold, this is the second year of the famine, and there are still five years without harvest, or fruit, of trees, or plowing. 18 Come down quickly, you and your households, so that you do not perish through the famine, and do not be grieved for your possessions, for the LORD sent me before you to set things in order that many people might live. 19 And tell my father that I am still alive, and you, behold, you see that the LORD has made me as a father to Pharaoh, and ruler over his house and over all the land of Egypt. 20 And tell my father of all my glory, and all the riches and glory that the LORD has given Me." 21 And by the command of the mouth of Pharaoh he gave them chariots and provisions for the way, and he gave them all many-colored raiment[s] and silver. 22 And to their father he sent raiment, and silver, and ten donkeys which carried corn, and he sent them away. 23 And they went up and told their father that Joseph was alive and was measuring out corn to all the nations of the earth, and that he was ruler over all the land of Egypt. 24 And their father did not believe it, for he was beside himself in his mind, but when he saw the wagons which Joseph had sent, the life of his spirit revived, and he said, "It is enough for me if Joseph lives; I will go down and see him before I die."

CHAPTER 44

1 And Israel took his journey from Haran from his house on the new moon of the third month, and he went on the way of the Well of the Oath, and he offered a sacrifice to the God of his father Isaac on the seventh of this month. 2 And Jacob remembered the dream that he had seen at Bethel, and he feared to go down into Egypt. 3 And while he was thinking of sending word to Joseph to come to him, and that he would not go down, he remained there seven days, if perhaps he should see a vision as to whether he should remain or go down. 4 And he celebrated the harvest festival of the first-fruits with old grain, for in all the land of Canaan there was not [even] a handful of seed, for the famine was over all the beasts, and cattle, and birds, and also over man. 5 And on the sixteenth [day] the LORD appeared to him, and said to him, "Jacob, Jacob"; and he said, "Here I am." And He said to him, "I am the God of your fathers, the God of Abraham and Isaac; do not fear

to go down into Egypt, for I will make of you a great nation there. **6** I will go down with you, and I will bring you up [again], and you will be buried in this land, and Joseph will put his hands on your eyes. Do not fear; go down into Egypt." **7** And his sons rose up, and his sons' sons, and they placed their father and their possessions on wagons. **8** And Israel rose up from the Well of the Oath on the sixteenth [day] of this third month, and he went to the land of Egypt. **9** And Israel sent Judah before him to his son Joseph to examine the land of Goshen, for Joseph had told his brothers that they should come and dwell there that they might be near him. **10** And this was the excellent [land] in the land of Egypt, and near to him, for all [of them] and also for the cattle. **11** And these are the names of the sons of Jacob who went into Egypt with their father Jacob: **12** Reuben, the firstborn of Israel; and these are the names of his sons: Enoch, and Pallu, and Hezron, and Carmi—five. **13** Simeon and his sons; and these are the names of his sons: Jemuel, and Jamin, and Ohad, and Jachin, and Zohar, and Shaul, the son of the Zephathite woman—seven. **14** Levi and his sons; and these are the names of his sons: Gershon, and Kohath, and Merari— four. **15** Judah and his sons; and these are the names of his sons: Shela, and Perez, and Zerah—four. **16** Issachar and his sons; and these are the names of his sons: Tola, and Phûa, and Jâsûb, and Shimron—five. **17** Zebulun and his sons; and these are the names of his sons: Sered, and Elon, and Jahleel— four. **18** And these are the sons of Jacob, and their sons, whom Leah bore to Jacob in Mesopotamia—six, and their one sister, Dinah. And all the souls of the sons of Leah, and their sons, who went with their father Jacob into Egypt, were twenty-nine, and their father Jacob being with them, they were thirty. **19** And the sons of Zilpah, Leah's handmaid, the wife of Jacob, whom she bore to Jacob: Gad and Asher. **20** And these are the names of their sons who went with him into Egypt: the sons of Gad: Ziphion, and Haggi, and Shuni, and Ezbon, [and Eri,] and Areli, and Arodi—eight. **21** And the sons of Asher: Imnah, and Ishvah, [and Ishvi], and Beriah, and Serah, their one sister—six. **22** All the souls were fourteen, and all those of Leah were forty-four. **23** And the sons of Rachel, the wife of Jacob: Joseph and Benjamin. **24** And there were born to Joseph in Egypt, before his father came into Egypt, those whom Asenath, daughter of Potiphar priest of Heliopolis, bore to him: Manasseh and Ephraim—three. **25** And the sons of Benjamin: Bela, and Becher, and Ashbel, Gera, and Naaman, and Ehi, and Rosh, and Muppim, and Huppim, and Ard—eleven. **26** And all the souls of Rachel were fourteen. **27** And the sons of Bilhah, the handmaid of Rachel, the wife of Jacob, whom she bore to Jacob, were Dan and Naphtali. **28** And these are the names of their sons who went with them into Egypt: and the sons of Dan were Hushim, and Sâmôn, and Asûdî, and 'Îjâka, and Salômôn —six. **29** And they died the year in which they entered into Egypt, and there was left to Dan Hushim alone. **30** And these are the names of the sons of Naphtali: Jahziel, and Guni, and Jezer, and Shallum, and 'Îv. **31** And 'Îv, who was born after the years of famine, died in Egypt. **32** And all the souls of Rachel were twenty-six. **33** And all the souls of Jacob which went into Egypt were seventy souls. These are his children and his children's children, seventy in all; but five died in Egypt before Joseph and had no children. **34** And in the land of Canaan two sons of Judah died, Er and Onan, and they had no children, and the sons of Israel buried those who perished, and they were reckoned among the seventy nations.

CHAPTER 45

1 And Israel went into the country of Egypt, into the land of Goshen, on the new moon of the fourth month, in the second year of the third week of the forty-fifth jubilee. **2** And Joseph went to meet his father Jacob, to the land of Goshen, and he fell on his father's neck and wept. **3** And Israel said to Joseph, "Now let me die since I have seen you, and now may the LORD God of Israel be blessed, the God of Abraham and the God of Isaac who has not withheld His mercy and His grace from His servant Jacob. **4** It is enough for me that I have seen your face while I am yet alive; yes, the vision which I saw at Bethel is true. Blessed is the LORD my God forever and ever and blessed is His Name." **5** And Joseph and his brothers ate bread before their father and drank wine, and Jacob rejoiced with exceedingly great joy because he saw Joseph eating with his brothers and drinking before him, and he blessed the Creator of all things who had preserved him and had preserved his twelve sons for him. **6** And Joseph had given to his father and to his brothers as a gift the right of dwelling in the land of Goshen, and in Rameses, and all the surrounding region, which he ruled over before Pharaoh. And Israel and his sons dwelt in the land of Goshen, the best part of the land of Egypt; and Israel was one hundred and thirty years old when he came into Egypt, **7** and Joseph nourished his father, and his brothers, and also their possessions with as much bread as they needed for the seven years of the famine. **8** And the land of Egypt suffered by reason of the famine, and Joseph acquired all the land of Egypt for Pharaoh in return for food, and he got possession of the people, and their cattle, and everything for Pharaoh. **9** And the years of the famine were accomplished, and Joseph gave seed and food to the people in the land that they might sow in the eighth year, for the river had overflowed all the land of Egypt. **10** For in the seven years of the famine it had not overflowed and had irrigated only a few places on the banks of the river, but now it overflowed, and the Egyptians sowed the land, and it bore much corn that year. **11** And this was the first year of the fourth week of the forty-fifth jubilee. **12** And Joseph took the fifth part of the corn of the harvest for the king and left four parts for them for food and for seed, and Joseph made it an ordinance for the land of Egypt until this day. **13** And Israel lived in the land of Egypt [for] seventeen years, and all the days which he lived were three jubilees, one hundred and forty-seven years, and he died in the fourth year of the fifth week of the forty-fifth jubilee. **14** And Israel blessed his sons before he died and told them everything that would befall them in the land of Egypt; and he made known to them what would come on them in the last days, and blessed them, and gave two portions to Joseph in the land. **15** And he slept with his fathers, and he was buried in the double cave in the land of Canaan, near his father Abraham in the grave which he dug for himself in the double cave in the land of Hebron. **16** And he gave all his scrolls and the scrolls of his fathers to his son Levi that he might preserve them and renew them for his children until this day.

CHAPTER 46

1 And it came to pass that after Jacob died, the sons of Israel multiplied in the land of Egypt, and they became a great nation, and they were of one accord in heart, so that brother loved brother and every man helped his brother, and they increased abundantly and multiplied exceedingly [for] ten weeks of years, all the days of the life of Joseph. **2** And there was no adversary nor any evil all the days of the life of Joseph which he lived after his father Jacob, for all the Egyptians honored the sons of Israel all the days of the life of Joseph. **3** And Joseph died being one hundred and ten years old; he lived seventeen years in the land of Canaan, and he was a servant [for] ten years, and [he was] in prison [for] three years, and he was under the king [for] eighty years, ruling all the land of Egypt. **4** And he died, and all his brothers, and all that generation. **5** And he commanded the sons of Israel before he died that they should carry his bones with them when they went out from the land of Egypt. **6** And he made them swear regarding his bones, for he knew that the Egyptians would not again bring out and bury him in the land of Canaan, for Mâkamârôn, king of Canaan, while dwelling in the land of Assyria, fought in the valley with the king of Egypt and slew him there, and pursued after the Egyptians to the gates of 'Êrmôn. **7** But he was not able to enter, for another, a new king, had become king of Egypt, and he was stronger than he, and he returned to the land of Canaan, and the gates of Egypt were closed, and none went out and none came into Egypt. **8** And Joseph died in the forty-sixth jubilee, in the sixth week, in the second year, and they buried him in the land of Egypt, and his brothers died after him. **9** And the king of Egypt went out to war with the king of Canaan in the forty-seventh jubilee, in the second week in the second year, and the sons of Israel brought out all the bones of the children of Jacob save the bones of Joseph, and they buried them in the field in the double cave in the mountain. **10** And most [of them] returned to Egypt, but a few of them remained in the mountains of Hebron, and your father Amram remained with them . **11** And the king of Canaan was victorious over the king of Egypt, and he closed the gates of Egypt. **12** And he devised an evil scheme against the sons of Israel of afflicting them; and he said to the people of Egypt, **13** "Behold, the people of the sons of Israel have increased and multiplied more than we. Come and let us deal wisely with them before they become too many, and let us afflict them with slavery before war comes on us and before they, too, fight against us, otherwise they will join themselves to our enemies; and get them out of our land, for their hearts and faces are toward the land of Canaan." **14** And he set taskmasters over them to afflict them with slavery; and they built strong cities for Pharaoh, Pithom and Raamses, and they built all the walls and all the fortifications which had fallen in the cities of Egypt. **15** And they made them serve with rigor, and the more they dealt evilly with them, the more they increased and multiplied. **16** And the people of Egypt despised the sons of Israel.

CHAPTER 47

1 And in the seventh week, in the seventh year, in the forty-seventh jubilee, your father went out from the land of Canaan, and you were born in the fourth week, in the sixth year thereof, in the forty-eighth jubilee; this was the time of tribulation on the sons of Israel. **2** And Pharaoh, king of Egypt, issued a command regarding them that they should cast all their male children which were born into the river. **3** And they cast them in for seven months until the day that you were born. And your mother hid you for three months, and they told [the Egyptians] regarding her. **4** And she made an ark for you, and covered it with pitch and asphalt, and placed it in the flags on the bank of the river, and she placed you in it [for] seven days, and your mother came by night and suckled you, and by day your sister Miriam guarded you from the birds. **5** And in those days Tharmuth, the daughter of Pharaoh, came to bathe in the river, and she heard your voice crying, and she told her maidens to bring you out, and they brought you to her. **6** And she took you out of the ark, and she had compassion on you. **7** And your sister said to her, "Will I go and call to you one of the Hebrew women to nurse and suckle this baby for you?" And she said, "Go." **8** And she went and called your mother Jochebed, and she gave her wages, and she nursed you. **9** And afterward, when you were grown up, they brought you to the daughter of Pharaoh, and you became her son, and your father Amram taught you writing, and after you had completed three weeks, they brought you into the royal court. **10** And you were three weeks of years at court until the time when you went out from the royal court and saw an Egyptian striking your friend who was of the sons of Israel, and you slew him and hid him in the sand. **11** And on the second day you found two of the sons of Israel striving together, and you said to him who was doing the wrong: "Why do you strike your brother?" **12** And he was angry and indignant, and said, "Who made you a prince and a judge over us? Do you think to kill me as you killed the Egyptian yesterday?" And you were afraid and fled on account of these words.

CHAPTER 48

1 And in the sixth year of the third week of the forty-ninth jubilee you departed and dwelt in the land of Midian [for] five weeks and one year. And you returned into Egypt in the second week, in the second year, in the fiftieth jubilee. **2** And you yourself know what He spoke to you on Mount Sinai, and what prince Mastêmâ desired to do with you when you were returning into Egypt on the way when you met him at the lodging-place. **3** Did he not, with all his power, seek to slay you and deliver the Egyptians out of your hand when he saw that you were sent to execute judgment and vengeance on the Egyptians? **4** And I delivered you out of his hand, and you performed the signs and wonders which you were sent to perform in Egypt against Pharaoh, and against all his house, and against his servants and his people. **5** And the LORD executed a great vengeance on them for Israel's sake, and struck them through blood and frogs, lice and biting flies, and malignant boils breaking out in blisters, and their cattle by death, and by hailstones, thereby He destroyed everything that grew for them, and by locusts which devoured the residue which had been left by the hail, and by darkness, and [by the death] of the firstborn of men and animals, and on all their idols the LORD took vengeance and burned them with fire. **6** And everything was sent through your hand, that you should declare [these things] before they were done, and you spoke with the king of Egypt before all his servants and before his people. **7** And everything took place according to your words; ten great and terrible judgments came on the land of Egypt that you might execute vengeance on it for Israel. **8** And the LORD did everything for Israel's sake, and according to His covenant, which He had ordained with Abraham that He would take vengeance on them as they had brought them into bondage by force. **9** And the prince of the Mastêmâ stood up against you and sought to cast you into the hands of Pharaoh, and he helped the Egyptian sorcerers, and they stood up and worked before you. **10** We indeed permitted them to work the evils, but we did not allow the remedies to be worked by their hands. **11** And the LORD struck them with malignant ulcers, and they were not able to stand , for we destroyed them so that they could not perform a single sign. **12** And notwithstanding all [these] signs and wonders, the prince of the Mastêmâ was not put to shame because he took courage and cried to the Egyptians to pursue after you with all the powers of the Egyptians, with their chariots, and with their horses, and with all the hosts of the peoples of Egypt. **13** And I stood between the Egyptians and Israel, and we delivered Israel out of his hand, and out of the hand of his people, and the LORD brought them through the midst of the sea as if it were dry land. **14** And all the peoples whom he brought to pursue after Israel, the LORD our God cast them into the midst of the sea, into the depths of the abyss beneath the sons of Israel, even as the people of Egypt had cast their children into the river. He took vengeance on one million of them, and one thousand strong and energetic men were destroyed on account of one suckling of the children of your people which they had thrown into the river. **15** And on the fourteenth day, and on the fifteenth, and on the sixteenth, and on the seventeenth, and on the eighteenth, the prince of the Mastêmâ was bound and imprisoned behind the sons of Israel that he might not accuse them. **16** And on the nineteenth [day] we let them loose that they might help the Egyptians and pursue the sons of Israel. **17** And He hardened their hearts and made them stubborn, and the device was devised by the LORD our God that He might strike the Egyptians and cast them into the sea. **18** And on the fourteenth [day] we bound him that he might not accuse the sons of Israel on the day when they asked the Egyptians for vessels and garments, vessels of silver, and vessels of gold, and vessels of bronze, in order to despoil the Egyptians in return for the bondage in which they had forced them to serve. **19** And we did not lead out the sons of Israel from Egypt empty-handed.

CHAPTER 49

1 Remember the command which the LORD commanded you concerning the Passover, that you should celebrate it in its season on the fourteenth of the first month, that you should kill it before it is evening, and that they should eat it by night on the evening of the fifteenth from the time of the setting of the sun. **2** For on this night—the beginning of the festival and the beginning of the joy—you were eating the Passover in Egypt, when all the powers of Mastêmâ had been let loose to slay all the firstborn in the land of Egypt, from the firstborn of Pharaoh to the firstborn of the captive maidservant in the mill, and to the cattle. **3** And this is the sign which the LORD gave them: into every house on the lintels of which they saw the blood of a lamb of the first year, into [that] house they should not enter to slay, but should pass by [it], that all those should be saved that were in the house because the sign of the blood was on its lintels. **4** And the powers of the LORD did everything according as the LORD commanded them, and they passed by all the sons of Israel, and the plague did not come on them to destroy any soul from among them, either of cattle, or man, or dog. **5** And the plague was very grievous in Egypt, and there was no house in Egypt where there was not someone dead, and weeping, and lamentation. **6** And all Israel was eating the flesh of the Passover lamb, and drinking the wine, and was lauding and blessing, and giving thanks to the LORD God of their fathers, and was ready to go out from under the yoke of Egypt and from the evil bondage. **7** And remember this day all the days of your life and observe it from year to year all the days of your life, once a year, on its day, according to all the law thereof, and do not adjourn [it] from day to day, or from month to month. **8** For it is a perpetual ordinance and engraved on the heavenly tablets regarding all the sons of Israel that they should observe it every year, on its day, once a year, throughout all their generations; and there is no limit of days, for this is ordained forever. **9** And the man who is free from uncleanness and does not come to observe it on occasion of its day so as to bring an acceptable offering before the LORD , and to eat and to drink before the LORD on the day of its festival, that man who is clean and close at hand will be cut off, because he did not offer the oblation of the LORD in its appointed season; he will take the guilt on himself. **10** Let the sons of Israel come and observe the Passover on the day of its fixed time, on the fourteenth day of the first month, between the evenings, from the third part of the day to the third part of the night, for two portions of the day are given to the light, and a third part to the evening. **11** That is that which the LORD commanded you that you should observe it between the evenings. **12** And it is not permissible to slay it during any period of the light, but during the period bordering on the evening, and let them eat it at the time of the evening until the third part of the night, and whatever is leftover of all its flesh from the third part of the night and onwards, let them burn it with fire. **13** And they will not cook it with water, nor will they eat it raw, but roast on the fire: they will eat it with diligence, its head with the inwards thereof and its feet they will roast with fire, and not break any bone thereof , for no bone of the sons of Israel will be crushed. **14** For this reason the LORD commanded the sons of Israel to observe the Passover on the day of its fixed time, and they will not break a bone thereof, for it is a festival day, and a day commanded, and there may be no passing over from day to day, and month to month, but on the day of its festival let it be observed. **15** And command the sons of Israel to observe the Passover throughout their days, every year, once a year on the day of its fixed time, and it will come for a memorial well pleasing before the LORD , and no plague will come on them to slay or to strike in that year in which they celebrate the Passover in its season in every respect according to His command. **16** And they will not eat it outside the sanctuary of the LORD , but before the sanctuary of the LORD , and all the people of the congregation of Israel will celebrate it in its appointed season. **17** And every man who has come on its day will eat it in the sanctuary of your God before the LORD from twenty years old and upward, for thus it is written and ordained that they should eat it in the sanctuary of the LORD . **18** And when the sons of Israel come into the land which they are to possess, into the land of Canaan, and set up the Dwelling Place of the LORD in the midst of the land in one of their tribes until the sanctuary of the LORD has been built in the land, let them come and celebrate the Passover in the midst of the Dwelling Place of the LORD , and let them slay it before the LORD from year to year. **19** And in the days when the house has been built in the Name of the L ORD in the land of their inheritance, they will go there and slay the Passover in the evening, at sunset, at the third part of the day. **20** And they will offer its blood on the threshold of the altar and will place its fat on the fire which is on the altar, and they will eat its flesh roasted with fire in the court of the house which has been sanctified in the Name of the L ORD . **21** And they may not celebrate the Passover in their cities, nor in any place except before the Dwelling Place of the LORD , or before His house where His Name has dwelt; and they will not go astray from the LORD . **22** And you, Moses: command the sons of Israel to observe the ordinances of the Passover, as it was commanded to you; declare to them every year and the day of its days, and the festival of unleavened bread, that they should eat unleavened bread [for] seven days, [and] that they should observe its festival, and that they bring an oblation every day during those seven days of joy before the LORD on the altar of your God. 23 For you celebrated this festival when you went out from Egypt until you entered into the wilderness of Shur , for you completed it on the shore of the sea.

CHAPTER 50

1 And after this law I made known to you the days of the Sabbaths in the wilderness of Zin, which is between Elim and Sinai. 2 And I told you of the Sabbaths of the land on Mount Sinai, and I told you of the jubilee years in the Sabbaths of years, but the year thereof I have not told you until you enter the land which you are to possess. 3 And the land will also keep its Sabbaths while they dwell on it, and they will know the jubilee year. 4 For that reason I have ordained for you the year-weeks , and the years, and the jubilees: there are forty-nine jubilees from the days of Adam until this day, and one week and two years, and there are yet forty years more for learning the commands of the LORD , until they pass over into the land of Canaan, crossing the Jordan to the west. 5 And the jubilees will pass by, until Israel is cleansed from all guilt of fornication, and uncleanness, and pollution, and sin, and error, and dwells with confidence in all the land, and there will no longer be an adversary or any evil one, and the land will be clean from that time forevermore. 6 And behold, the command regarding the Sabbaths—I have written [them] down for you and all the judgments of its laws. 7 Six days you will labor, but on the seventh day is the Sabbath of the LORD your God. In it you will do no manner of work—you, and your sons, and your menservants, and your maidservants, and all your cattle, and the sojourner who is also with you. 8 And the man that does any work on it will die: whoever desecrates that day, whoever lies with [his] wife , or whoever says he will do something on it, that he will set out on a journey thereon in regard to any buying or selling , and whoever draws water thereon which he had not prepared for himself on the sixth day, and whoever takes up any burden to carry it out of his tent or out of his house will die. 9 You will do no work whatsoever on the Sabbath day except [to utilize] what you have prepared for yourselves on the sixth day, so as to eat, and drink, and rest, and keep Sabbath from all work on that day, and to bless the LORD your God who has given you a day of festival, and a holy day; and a day of the holy kingdom for all Israel is this day among their days forever. 10 For great is the honor which the LORD has given to Israel that they should eat, and drink, and be satisfied on this festival day, and rest thereon from all labor which belongs to the labor of the children of men, except burning frankincense and bringing oblations and sacrifices before the LORD for days and for Sabbaths. 11 Only this work will be done on the Sabbath s in the sanctuary of the LORD your God, that they may atone for Israel with sacrifice continually from day to day for a memorial well-pleasing before the LORD , and that He may always receive them from day to day according as you have been commanded. 12 And every man who does any work thereon, or goes on a journey, or tills [his] farm, whether in his house or any other place, and whoever lights a fire, or rides on any beast, or travels by ship on the sea, and whoever strikes or kills anything, or slaughter s a beast or a bird, or whoever catches an animal, or a bird, or a fish, or whoever fasts or makes war on the Sabbaths: 13 the man who does any of these things on the Sabbath will die, so that the sons of Israel will observe the Sabbaths according to the commands regarding the Sabbaths of the land, as it is written in the tablets, which He gave into My hands that I should write out for you—the laws of the seasons and the seasons according to the division of their days. The account of the division of the days is completed.

THE BOOK OF TOBIT

TOB.1

[1] The book of the words of Tobit, son of Tobiel, the son of Ananiel, the son of Aduel, the son of Gabael, of the seed of Asael, of the tribe of Nephthali; [2] Who in the time of Enemessar king of the Assyrians was led captive out of Thisbe, which is at the right hand of that city, which is called properly Nephthali in Galilee above Aser. [3] I Tobit have walked all the days of my life in the ways of truth and justice, and I did many almsdeeds to my brethren, and my nation, who came with me to Nineve, into the land of the Assyrians. [4] And when I was in mine own country, in the land of Israel being but young, all the tribe of Nephthali my father fell from the house of Jerusalem, which was chosen out of all the tribes of Israel, that all the tribes should sacrifice there, where the temple of the habitation of the most High was consecrated and built for all ages. [5] Now all the tribes which together revolted, and the house of my father Nephthali, sacrificed unto the heifer Baal. [6] But I alone went often to Jerusalem at the feasts, as it was ordained unto all the people of Israel by an everlasting decree, having the firstfruits and tenths of increase, with that which was first shorn; and them gave I at the altar to the priests the children of Aaron. [7] The first tenth part of all increase I gave to the sons of Aaron, who ministered at Jerusalem: another tenth part I sold away, and went, and spent it every year at Jerusalem: [8] And the third I gave unto them to whom it was meet, as Debora my father's mother had commanded me, because I was left an orphan by my father. [9] Furthermore, when I was come to the age of a man, I married Anna of mine own kindred, and of her I begat Tobias. [10] And when we were carried away captives to Nineve, all my brethren and those that were of my kindred did eat of the bread of the Gentiles. [11] But I kept myself from eating; [12] Because I remembered God with all my heart. [13] And the most High gave me grace and favour before Enemessar, so that I was his purveyor. [14] And I went into Media, and left in trust with Gabael, the brother of Gabrias, at Rages a city of Media ten talents of silver. [15] Now when Enemessar was dead, Sennacherib his son reigned in his stead; whose estate was troubled, that I could not go into Media. [16] And in the time of Enemessar I gave many alms to my brethren, and gave my bread to the hungry, [17] And my clothes to the naked: and if I saw any of my nation dead, or cast about the walls of Nineve, I buried him. [18] And if the king Sennacherib had slain any, when he was come, and fled from Judea, I buried them privily; for in his wrath he killed many; but the bodies were not found, when they were sought for of the king. [19] And when one of the Ninevites went and complained of me to the king, that I buried them, and hid myself; understanding that I was sought for to be put to death, I withdrew myself for fear. [20] Then all my goods were forcibly taken away, neither was there any thing left me, beside my wife Anna and my son Tobias. [21] And there passed not five and fifty days, before two of his sons killed him,

and they fled into the mountains of Ararath; and Sarchedonus his son reigned in his stead; who appointed over his father's accounts, and over all his affairs, Achiacharus my brother Anael's son. [22] And Achiacharus intreating for me, I returned to Nineve. Now Achiacharus was cupbearer, and keeper of the signet, and steward, and overseer of the accounts: and Sarchedonus appointed him next unto him: and he was my brother's son.

TOB.2

[1] Now when I was come home again, and my wife Anna was restored unto me, with my son Tobias, in the feast of Pentecost, which is the holy feast of the seven weeks, there was a good dinner prepared me, in the which I sat down to eat. [2] And when I saw abundance of meat, I said to my son, Go and bring what poor man soever thou shalt find out of our brethren, who is mindful of the Lord; and, lo, I tarry for thee. [3] But he came again, and said, Father, one of our nation is strangled, and is cast out in the marketplace. [4] Then before I had tasted of any meat, I started up, and took him up into a room until the going down of the sun. [5] Then I returned, and washed myself, and ate my meat in heaviness, [6] Remembering that prophecy of Amos, as he said, Your feasts shall be turned into mourning, and all your mirth into lamentation. [7] Therefore I wept: and after the going down of the sun I went and made a grave, and buried him. [8] But my neighbours mocked me, and said, This man is not yet afraid to be put to death for this matter: who fled away; and yet, lo, he burieth the dead again. [9] The same night also I returned from the burial, and slept by the wall of my courtyard, being polluted and my face was uncovered: [10] And I knew not that there were sparrows in the wall, and mine eyes being open, the sparrows muted warm dung into mine eyes, and a whiteness came in mine eyes: and I went to the physicians, but they helped me not: moreover Achiacharus did nourish me, until I went into Elymais. [11] And my wife Anna did take women's works to do. [12] And when she had sent them home to the owners, they paid her wages, and gave her also besides a kid. [13] And when it was in my house, and began to cry, I said unto her, From whence is this kid? is it not stolen? render it to the owners; for it is not lawful to eat any thing that is stolen. [14] But she replied upon me, It was given for a gift more than the wages. Howbeit I did not believe her, but bade her render it to the owners: and I was abashed at her. But she replied upon me, Where are thine alms and thy righteous deeds? behold, thou and all thy works are known.

TOB.3

[1] Then I being grieved did weep, and in my sorrow prayed, saying, [2] O Lord, thou art just, and all thy works and all thy ways are mercy and truth, and thou judgest truly and justly for ever. [3] Remember me, and look on me, punish me not for my sins and ignorances, and the sins of mg fathers, who have sinned before thee: [4] For they obeyed not thy commandments: wherefore thou hast delivered us for a spoil, and unto captivity, and unto death, and for a proverb of reproach to all the nations among whom we are dispersed. [5] And now thy judgments are many and true: deal with me according to my sins and my fathers': because we have not kept thy commandments, neither have walked in truth before thee. [6] Now therefore deal with me as seemeth best unto thee, and command my spirit to be taken from me, that I may be dissolved, and become earth: for it is profitable for me to die rather than to live, because I have heard false reproaches, and have much sorrow: command therefore that I may now be delivered out of this distress, and go into the everlasting place: turn not thy face away from me. [7] It came to pass the same day, that in Ecbatane a city of Media Sara the daughter of Raguel was also reproached by her father's maids; [8] Because that she had been married to seven husbands, whom Asmodeus the evil spirit had killed, before they had lain with her. Dost thou not know, said they, that thou hast strangled thine husbands? thou hast had already seven husbands, neither wast thou named after any of them. [9] Wherefore dost thou beat us for them? if they be dead, go thy ways after them, let us never see of thee either son or daughter. [10] Whe she heard these things, she was very sorrowful, so that she thought to have strangled herself; and she said, I am the only daughter of my father, and if I do this, it shall be a reproach unto him, and I shall bring his old age with sorrow unto the grave. [11] Then she prayed toward the window, and said, Blessed art thou, O Lord my God, and thine holy and glorious name is blessed and honourable for ever: let all thy works praise thee for ever. [12] And now, O Lord, I set I mine eyes and my face toward thee, [13] And say, Take me out of the earth, that I may hear no more the reproach. [14] Thou knowest, Lord, that I am pure from all sin with man, [15] And that I never polluted my name, nor the name of my father, in the land of my captivity: I am the only daughter of my father, neither hath he any child to be his heir, neither any near kinsman, nor any son of his alive, to whom I may keep myself for a wife: my seven husbands are already dead; and why should I live? but if it please not thee that I should die, command some regard to be had of me, and pity taken of me, that I hear no more reproach. [16] So the prayers of them both were heard before the majesty of the great God. [17] And Raphael was sent to heal them both, that is, to scale away the whiteness of Tobit's eyes, and to give Sara the daughter of Raguel for a wife to Tobias the son of Tobit; and to bind Asmodeus the evil spirit; because she belonged to Tobias by right of inheritance. The selfsame time came Tobit home, and entered into his house, and Sara the daughter of Raguel came down from her upper chamber.

TOB.4

[1] In that day Tobit remembered the money which he had committed to Gabael in Rages of Media, [2] And said with himself, I have wished for death; wherefore do I not call for my son Tobias that I may signify to him of the money before I die? [3] And when he had called him, he said, My son, when I am dead, bury me; and despise not thy mother, but honour her all the days of thy life, and do that which shall please her, and grieve her not. [4] Remember, my son, that she saw many dangers for thee, when thou wast in her womb: and when she is dead, bury her by me in one grave. [5] My son, be mindful of the Lord our God all thy days, and let not thy will be set to sin, or to transgress his commandments: do uprightly all thy life long, and follow not the ways of unrighteousness. [6] For if thou deal truly, thy doings shall prosperously succeed to thee, and to all them that live justly. [7] Give alms of thy substance; and when thou givest alms, let not thine

eye be envious, neither turn thy face from any poor, and the face of God shall not be turned away from thee. [**8**] If thou hast abundance give alms accordingly: if thou have but a little, be not afraid to give according to that little: [**9**] For thou layest up a good treasure for thyself against the day of necessity. [**10**] Because that alms do deliver from death, and suffereth not to come into darkness. [**11**] For alms is a good gift unto all that give it in the sight of the most High. [**12**] Beware of all whoredom, my son, and chiefly take a wife of the seed of thy fathers, and take not a strange woman to wife, which is not of thy father's tribe: for we are the children of the prophets, Noe, Abraham, Isaac, and Jacob: remember, my son, that our fathers from the beginning, even that they all married wives of their own kindred, and were blessed in their children, and their seed shall inherit the land. [**13**] Now therefore, my son, love thy brethren, and despise not in thy heart thy brethren, the sons and daughters of thy people, in not taking a wife of them: for in pride is destruction and much trouble, and in lewdness is decay and great want: for lewdness is the mother of famine. [**14**] Let not the wages of any man, which hath wrought for thee, tarry with thee, but give him it out of hand: for if thou serve God, he will also repay thee: be circumspect my son, in all things thou doest, and be wise in all thy conversation. [**15**] Do that to no man which thou hatest: drink not wine to make thee drunken: neither let drunkenness go with thee in thy journey. [**16**] Give of thy bread to the hungry, and of thy garments to them that are naked; and according to thine abundance give alms: and let not thine eye be envious, when thou givest alms. [**17**] Pour out thy bread on the burial of the just, but give nothing to the wicked. [**18**] Ask counsel of all that are wise, and despise not any counsel that is profitable. [**19**] Bless the Lord thy God alway, and desire of him that thy ways may be directed, and that all thy paths and counsels may prosper: for every nation hath not counsel; but the Lord himself giveth all good things, and he humbleth whom he will, as he will; now therefore, my son, remember my commandments, neither let them be put out of thy mind. [**20**] And now I signify this to they that I committed ten talents to Gabael the son of Gabrias at Rages in Media. [**21**] And fear not, my son, that we are made poor: for thou hast much wealth, if thou fear God, and depart from all sin, and do that which is pleasing in his sight.

TOB.5

[1] Tobias then answered and said, Father, I will do all things which thou hast commanded me: [**2**] But how can I receive the money, seeing I know him not? [**3**] Then he gave him the handwriting, and said unto him, Seek thee a man which may go with thee, whiles I yet live, and I will give him wages: and go and receive the money. [**4**] Therefore when he went to seek a man, he found Raphael that was an angel. [**5**] But he knew not; and he said unto him, Canst thou go with me to Rages? and knowest thou those places well? [**6**] To whom the angel said, I will go with thee, and I know the way well: for I have lodged with our brother Gabael. [**7**] Then Tobias said unto him, Tarry for me, till I tell my father. [**8**] Then he said unto him, Go and tarry not. So he went in and said to his father, Behold, I have found one which will go with me. Then he said, Call him unto me, that I may know of what tribe he is, and whether he be a trusty man to go with thee. [**9**] So he called him, and he came in, and they saluted one another. [**10**] Then Tobit said unto him, Brother, shew me of what tribe and family thou art. [**11**] To whom he said, Dost thou seek for a tribe or family, or an hired man to go with thy son? Then Tobit said unto him, I would know, brother, thy kindred and name. [**12**] Then he said, I am Azarias, the son of Ananias the great, and of thy brethren. [**13**] Then Tobit said, Thou art welcome, brother; be not now angry with me, because I have enquired to know thy tribe and thy family; for thou art my brother, of an honest and good stock: for I know Ananias and Jonathas, sons of that great Samaias, as we went together to Jerusalem to worship, and offered the firstborn, and the tenths of the fruits; and they were not seduced with the error of our brethren: my brother, thou art of a good stock. [**14**] But tell me, what wages shall I give thee? wilt thou a drachm a day, and things necessary, as to mine own son? [**15**] Yea, moreover, if ye return safe, I will add something to thy wages. [**16**] So they were well pleased. Then said he to Tobias, Prepare thyself for the journey, and God send you a good journey. And when his son had prepared all things far the journey, his father said, Go thou with this man, and God, which dwelleth in heaven, prosper your journey, and the angel of God keep you company. So they went forth both, and the young man's dog with them. [**17**] But Anna his mother wept, and said to Tobit, Why hast thou sent away our son? is he not the staff of our hand, in going in and out before us? [**18**] Be not greedy to add money to money: but let it be as refuse in respect of our child. [**19**] For that which the Lord hath given us to live with doth suffice us. [**20**] Then said Tobit to her, Take no care, my sister; he shall return in safety, and thine eyes shall see him. [**21**] For the good angel will keep him company, and his journey shall be prosperous, and he shall return safe. [**22**] Then she made an end of weeping.

TOB.6

[1] And as they went on their journey, they came in the evening to the river Tigris, and they lodged there. [**2**] And when the young man went down to wash himself, a fish leaped out of the river, and would have devoured him. [**3**] Then the angel said unto him, Take the fish. And the young man laid hold of the fish, and drew it to land. [**4**] To whom the angel said, Open the fish, and take the heart and the liver and the gall, and put them up safely. [**5**] So the young man did as the angel commanded him; and when they had roasted the fish, they did eat it: then they both went on their way, till they drew near to Ecbatane. [**6**] Then the young man said to the angel, Brother Azarias, to what use is the heart and the liver and the gal of the fish? [**7**] And he said unto him, Touching the heart and the liver, if a devil or an evil spirit trouble any, we must make a smoke thereof before the man or the woman, and the party shall be no more vexed. [**8**] As for the gall, it is good to anoint a man that hath whiteness in his eyes, and he shall be healed. [**9**] And when they were come near to Rages, [**10**] The angel said to the young man, Brother, to day we shall lodge with Raguel, who is thy cousin; he also hath one only daughter, named Sara; I will speak for her, that she may be given thee for a wife. [**11**] For to thee doth the right of her appertain, seeing thou only art of her kindred. [**12**] And the maid is fair and wise: now therefore hear me, and I will speak to her father; and when we return from Rages we will celebrate the marriage: for I know that Raguel cannot marry her to another according to the law of Moses, but he shall be guilty of death, because the right of inheritance doth rather appertain to thee than to any other. [**13**] Then the young man answered the angel, I have heard, brother Azarias that this maid hath been given to seven men, who all died in the marriage chamber. [**14**] And now I am the only son of my father, and I am

afraid, lest if I go in unto her, I die, as the other before: for a wicked spirit loveth her, which hurteth no body, but those which come unto her; wherefore I also fear lest I die, and bring my father's and my mother's life because of me to the grave with sorrow: for they have no other son to bury them. [15] Then the angel said unto him, Dost thou not remember the precepts which thy father gave thee, that thou shouldest marry a wife of thine own kindred? wherefore hear me, O my brother; for she shall be given thee to wife; and make thou no reckoning of the evil spirit; for this same night shall she be given thee in marriage. [16] And when thou shalt come into the marriage chamber, thou shalt take the ashes of perfume, and shalt lay upon them some of the heart and liver of the fish, and shalt make a smoke with it: [17] And the devil shall smell it, and flee away, and never come again any more: but when thou shalt come to her, rise up both of you, and pray to God which is merciful, who will have pity on you, and save you: fear not, for she is appointed unto thee from the beginning; and thou shalt preserve her, and she shall go with thee. Moreover I suppose that she shall bear thee children. Now when Tobias had heard these things, he loved her, and his heart was effectually joined to her.

TOB.7

[1] And when they were come to Ecbatane, they came to the house of Raguel, and Sara met them: and after they had saluted one another, she brought them into the house. [2] Then said Raguel to Edna his wife, How like is this young man to Tobit my cousin! [3] And Raguel asked them, From whence are ye, brethren? To whom they said, We are of the sons of Nephthalim, which are captives in Nineve. [4] Then he said to them, Do ye know Tobit our kinsman? And they said, We know him. Then said he, Is he in good health? [5] And they said, He is both alive, and in good health: and Tobias said, He is my father. [6] Then Raguel leaped up, and kissed him, and wept, [7] And blessed him, and said unto him, Thou art the son of an honest and good man. But when he had heard that Tobit was blind, he was sorrowful, and wept. [8] And likewise Edna his wife and Sara his daughter wept. Moreover they entertained them cheerfully; and after that they had killed a ram of the flock, they set store of meat on the table. Then said Tobias to Raphael, Brother Azarias, speak of those things of which thou didst talk in the way, and let this business be dispatched. [9] So he communicated the matter with Raguel: and Raguel said to Tobias, Eat and drink, and make merry: [10] For it is meet that thou shouldest marry my daughter: nevertheless I will declare unto thee the truth. [11] I have given my daughter in marriage te seven men, who died that night they came in unto her: nevertheless for the present be merry. But Tobias said, I will eat nothing here, till we agree and swear one to another. [12] Raguel said, Then take her from henceforth according to the manner, for thou art her cousin, and she is thine, and the merciful God give you good success in all things. [13] Then he called his daughter Sara, and she came to her father, and he took her by the hand, and gave her to be wife to Tobias, saying, Behold, take her after the law of Moses, and lead her away to thy father. And he blessed them; [14] And called Edna his wife, and took paper, and did write an instrument of covenants, and sealed it. [15] Then they began to eat. [16] After Raguel called his wife Edna, and said unto her, Sister, prepare another chamber, and bring her in thither. [17] Which when she had done as he had bidden her, she brought her thither: and she wept, and she received the tears of her daughter, and said unto her, [18] Be of good comfort, my daughter; the Lord of heaven and earth give thee joy for this thy sorrow: be of good comfort, my daughter.

TOB.8

[1] And when they had supped, they brought Tobias in unto her. [2] And as he went, he remembered the words of Raphael, and took the ashes of the perfumes, and put the heart and the liver of the fish thereupon, and made a smoke therewith. [3] The which smell when the evil spirit had smelled, he fled into the utmost parts of Egypt, and the angel bound him. [4] And after that they were both shut in together, Tobias rose out of the bed, and said, Sister, arise, and let us pray that God would have pity on us. [5] Then began Tobias to say, Blessed art thou, O God of our fathers, and blessed is thy holy and glorious name for ever; let the heavens bless thee, and all thy creatures. [6] Thou madest Adam, and gavest him Eve his wife for an helper and stay: of them came mankind: thou hast said, It is not good that man should be alone; let us make unto him an aid like unto himself. [7] And now, O Lord, I take not this my sister for lush but uprightly: therefore mercifully ordain that we may become aged together. [8] And she said with him, Amen. [9] So they slept both that night. And Raguel arose, and went and made a grave, [10] Saying, I fear lest he also be dead. [11] But when Raguel was come into his house, [12] He said unto his wife Edna. Send one of the maids, and let her see whether he be alive: if he be not, that we may bury him, and no man know it. [13] So the maid opened the door, and went in, and found them both asleep, [14] And came forth, and told them that he was alive. [15] Then Raguel praised God, and said, O God, thou art worthy to be praised with all pure and holy praise; therefore let thy saints praise thee with all thy creatures; and let all thine angels and thine elect praise thee for ever. [16] Thou art to be praised, for thou hast made me joyful; and that is not come to me which I suspected; but thou hast dealt with us according to thy great mercy. [17] Thou art to be praised because thou hast had mercy of two that were the only begotten children of their fathers: grant them mercy, O Lord, and finish their life in health with joy and mercy. [18] Then Raguel bade his servants to fill the grave. [19] And he kept the wedding feast fourteen days. [20] For before the days of the marriage were finished, Raguel had said unto him by an oath, that he should not depart till the fourteen days of the marriage were expired; [21] And then he should take the half of his goods, and go in safety to his father; and should have the rest when I and my wife be dead.

TOB.9

[1] Then Tobias called Raphael, and said unto him, [2] Brother Azarias, take with thee a servant, and two camels, and go to Rages of Media to Gabael, and bring me the money, and bring him to the wedding. [3] For Raguel hath sworn that I shall not depart. [4] But my father counteth the days; and if I tarry long, he will be very sorry. [5] So Raphael went out, and lodged with Gabael, and gave him the handwriting: who brought forth bags which were sealed up, and gave them to him. [6] And early in the morning they went forth both together, and came to the wedding: and Tobias blessed his wife.

TOB.10

[1] Now Tobit his father counted every day: and when the days of the journey were expired, and they came not, [2] Then Tobit said, Are they detained? or is Gabael dead, and there is no man to give him the money? [3] Therefore he was very sorry. [4] Then his wife said unto him, My son is dead, seeing he stayeth long; and she began to wail him, and said, [5] Now I care for nothing, my son, since I have let thee go, the light of mine eyes. [6] To whom Tobit said, Hold thy peace, take no care, for he is safe. [7] But she said, Hold thy peace, and deceive me not; my son is dead. And she went out every day into the way which they went, and did eat no meat on the daytime, and ceased not whole nights to bewail her son Tobias, until the fourteen days of the wedding were expired, which Raguel had sworn that he should spend there. Then Tobias said to Raguel, Let me go, for my father and my mother look no more to see me. [8] But his father in law said unto him, Tarry with me, and I will send to thy father, and they shall declare unto him how things go with thee. [9] But Tobias said, No; but let me go to my father. [10] Then Raguel arose, and gave him Sara his wife, and half his goods, servants, and cattle, and money: [11] And he blessed them, and sent them away, saying, The God of heaven give you a prosperous journey, my children. [12] And he said to his daughter, Honour thy father and thy mother in law, which are now thy parents, that I may hear good report of thee. And he kissed her. Edna also said to Tobias, The Lord of heaven restore thee, my dear brother, and grant that I may see thy children of my daughter Sara before I die, that I may rejoice before the Lord: behold, I commit my daughter unto thee of special trust; where are do not entreat her evil.

TOB.11

[1] After these things Tobias went his way, praising God that he had given him a prosperous journey, and blessed Raguel and Edna his wife, and went on his way till they drew near unto Nineve. [2] Then Raphael said to Tobias, Thou knowest, brother, how thou didst leave thy father: [3] Let us haste before thy wife, and prepare the house. [4] And take in thine hand the gall of the fish. So they went their way, and the dog went after them. [5] Now Anna sat looking about toward the way for her son. [6] And when she espied him coming, she said to his father, Behold, thy son cometh, and the man that went with him. [7] Then said Raphael, I know, Tobias, that thy father will open his eyes. [8] Therefore anoint thou his eyes with the gall, and being pricked therewith, he shall rub, and the whiteness shall fall away, and he shall see thee. [9] Then Anna ran forth, and fell upon the neck of her son, and said unto him, Seeing I have seen thee, my son, from henceforth I am content to die. And they wept both. [10] Tobit also went forth toward the door, and stumbled: but his son ran unto him, [11] And took hold of his father: and he strake of the gall on his fathers' eyes, saying, Be of good hope, my father. [12] And when his eyes began to smart, he rubbed them; [13] And the whiteness pilled away from the corners of his eyes: and when he saw his son, he fell upon his neck. [14] And he wept, and said, Blessed art thou, O God, and blessed is thy name for ever; and blessed are all thine holy angels: [15] For thou hast scourged, and hast taken pity on me: for, behold, I see my son Tobias. And his son went in rejoicing, and told his father the great things that had happened to him in Media. [16] Then Tobit went out to meet his daughter in law at the gate of Nineve, rejoicing and praising God: and they which saw him go marvelled, because he had received his sight. [17] But Tobias gave thanks before them, because God had mercy on him. And when he came near to Sara his daughter in law, he blessed her, saying, Thou art welcome, daughter: God be blessed, which hath brought thee unto us, and blessed be thy father and thy mother. And there was joy among all his brethren which were at Nineve. [18] And Achiacharus, and Nasbas his brother's son, came: [19] And Tobias' wedding was kept seven days with great joy.

TOB.12

[1] Then Tobit called his son Tobias, and said unto him, My son, see that the man have his wages, which went with thee, and thou must give him more. [2] And Tobias said unto him, O father, it is no harm to me to give him half of those things which I have brought: [3] For he hath brought me again to thee in safety, and made whole my wife, and brought me the money, and likewise healed thee. [4] Then the old man said, It is due unto him. [5] So he called the angel, and he said unto him, Take half of all that ye have brought and go away in safety. [6] Then he took them both apart, and said unto them, Bless God, praise him, and magnify him, and praise him for the things which he hath done unto you in the sight of all that live. It is good to praise God, and exalt his name, and honourably to shew forth the works of God; therefore be not slack to praise him. [7] It is good to keep close the secret of a king, but it is honourable to reveal the works of God. Do that which is good, and no evil shall touch you. [8] Prayer is good with fasting and alms and righteousness. A little with righteousness is better than much with unrighteousness. It is better to give alms than to lay up gold: [9] For alms doth deliver from death, and shall purge away all sin. Those that exercise alms and righteousness shall be filled with life: [10] But they that sin are enemies to their own life. [11] Surely I will keep close nothing from you. For I said, It was good to keep close the secret of a king, but that it was honourable to reveal the works of God. [12] Now therefore, when thou didst pray, and Sara thy daughter in law, I did bring the remembrance of your prayers before the Holy One: and when thou didst bury the dead, I was with thee likewise. [13] And when thou didst not delay to rise up, and leave thy dinner, to go and cover the dead, thy good deed was not hid from me: but I was with thee. [14] And now God hath sent me to heal thee and Sara thy daughter in law. [15] I am Raphael, one of the seven holy angels, which present the prayers of the saints, and which go in and out before the glory of the Holy One. [16] Then they were both troubled, and fell upon their faces: for they feared. [17] But he said unto them, Fear not, for it shall go well with you; praise God therefore. [18] For not of any favour of mine, but by the will of our God I came; wherefore praise him for ever. [19] All these days I did appear unto you; but I did neither eat nor drink, but ye did see a vision. [20] Now therefore give God thanks: for I go up to him that sent me; but write all things which are done in a book. [21] And when they arose, they saw him no more. [22] Then they confessed the great and wonderful works of God, and how the angel of the Lord had appeared unto them.

TOB.13

[1] Then Tobit wrote a prayer of rejoicing, and said, Blessed be God that liveth for ever, and blessed be his kingdom. [2] For he doth scourge, and hath mercy: he leadeth down to hell, and bringeth up again: neither is there any that can avoid his hand. [3] Confess him before the Gentiles, ye children of Israel: for he hath scattered us among them. [4] There declare his greatness, and extol him before all the living: for he is our Lord, and he is the God our Father for ever. [5] And he will scourge us for our iniquities, and will have mercy again, and will gather us out of all nations, among whom he hath scattered us. [6] If ye turn to him with your whole heart, and with your whole mind, and deal uprightly before him, then will he turn unto you, and will not hide his face from you. Therefore see what he will do with you, and confess him with your whole mouth, and praise the Lord of might, and extol the everlasting King. In the land of my captivity do I praise him, and declare his might and majesty to a sinful nation. O ye sinners, turn and do justice before him: who can tell if he will accept you, and have mercy on you? [7] I will extol my God, and my soul shall praise the King of heaven, and shall rejoice in his greatness. [8] Let all men speak, and let all praise him for his righteousness. [9] O Jerusalem, the holy city, he will scourge thee for thy children's works, and will have mercy again on the sons of the righteous. [10] Give praise to the Lord, for he is good: and praise the everlasting King, that his tabernacle may be builded in thee again with joy, and let him make joyful there in thee those that are captives, and love in thee for ever those that are miserable. [11] Many nations shall come from far to the name of the Lord God with gifts in their hands, even gifts to the King of heaven; all generations shall praise thee with great joy. [12] Cursed are all they which hate thee, and blessed shall all be which love thee for ever. [13] Rejoice and be glad for the children of the just: for they shall be gathered together, and shall bless the Lord of the just. [14] O blessed are they which love thee, for they shall rejoice in thy peace: blessed are they which have been sorrowful for all thy scourges; for they shall rejoice for thee, when they have seen all thy glory, and shall be glad for ever. [15] Let my soul bless God the great King. [16] For Jerusalem shall be built up with sapphires and emeralds, and precious stone: thy walls and towers and battlements with pure gold. [17] And the streets of Jerusalem shall be paved with beryl and carbuncle and stones of Ophir. [18] And all her streets shall say, Alleluia; and they shall praise him, saying, Blessed be God, which hath extolled it for ever.

TOB.14

[1] So Tobit made an end of praising God. [2] And he was eight and fifty years old when he lost his sight, which was restored to him after eight years: and he gave alms, and he increased in the fear of the Lord God, and praised him. [3] And when he was very aged he called his son, and the sons of his son, and said to him, My son, take thy children; for, behold, I am aged, and am ready to depart out of this life. [4] Go into Media my son, for I surely believe those things which Jonas the prophet spake of Nineve, that it shall be overthrown; and that for a time peace shall rather be in Media; and that our brethren shall lie scattered in the earth from that good land: and Jerusalem shall be desolate, and the house of God in it shall be burned, and shall be desolate for a time; [5] And that again God will have mercy on them, and bring them again into the land, where they shall build a temple, but not like to the first, until the time of that age be fulfilled; and afterward they shall return from all places of their captivity, and build up Jerusalem gloriously, and the house of God shall be built in it for ever with a glorious building, as the prophets have spoken thereof. [6] And all nations shall turn, and fear the Lord God truly, and shall bury their idols. [7] So shall all nations praise the Lord, and his people shall confess God, and the Lord shall exalt his people; and all those which love the Lord God in truth and justice shall rejoice, shewing mercy to our brethren. [8] And now, my son, depart out of Nineve, because that those things which the prophet Jonas spake shall surely come to pass. [9] But keep thou the law and the commandments, and shew thyself merciful and just, that it may go well with thee. [10] And bury me decently, and thy mother with me; but tarry no longer at Nineve. Remember, my son, how Aman handled Achiacharus that brought him up, how out of light he brought him into darkness, and how he rewarded him again: yet Achiacharus was saved, but the other had his reward: for he went down into darkness. Manasses gave alms, and escaped the snares of death which they had set for him: but Aman fell into the snare, and perished. [11] Wherefore now, my son, consider what alms doeth, and how righteousness doth deliver. When he had said these things, he gave up the ghost in the bed, being an hundred and eight and fifty years old; and he buried him honourably. [12] And when Anna his mother was dead, he buried her with his father. But Tobias departed with his wife and children to Ecbatane to Raguel his father in law, [13] Where he became old with honour, and he buried his father and mother in law honourably, and he inherited their substance, and his father Tobit's. [14] And he died at Ecbatane in Media, being an hundred and seven and twenty years old. [15] But before he died he heard of the destruction of Nineve, which was taken by Nabuchodonosor and Assuerus: and before his death he rejoiced over Nineve.

THE BOOK OF JUDITH

JDT.1

[1] In the twelfth year of the reign of Nabuchodonosor, who reigned in Nineve, the great city; in the days of Arphaxad, which reigned over the Medes in Ecbatane, [2] And built in Ecbatane walls round about of stones hewn three cubits broad and six cubits long, and made the height of the wall seventy cubits, and the breadth thereof fifty cubits: [3] And set the towers thereof upon the gates of it an hundred cubits high, and the breadth thereof in the foundation threescore cubits: [4] And he made the gates thereof, even gates that were raised to the height of seventy cubits, and the breadth of them was forty cubits, for the going forth of his mighty armies, and for the setting in array of his footmen: [5] Even in those days king Nabuchodonosor made war with king Arphaxad in the great plain, which is the plain in the borders of Ragau. [6] And there came unto him all they that dwelt in the hill country, and all that dwelt by Euphrates, and Tigris and Hydaspes, and the plain of Arioch the king of the Elymeans, and very many nations of the sons of Chelod, assembled themselves to the battle. [7] Then Nabuchodonosor king of the Assyrians sent unto all that dwelt in Persia, and to all that dwelt westward,

and to those that dwelt in Cilicia, and Damascus, and Libanus, and Antilibanus, and to all that dwelt upon the sea coast, [8] And to those among the nations that were of Carmel, and Galaad, and the higher Galilee, and the great plain of Esdrelom, [9] And to all that were in Samaria and the cities thereof, and beyond Jordan unto Jerusalem, and Betane, and Chelus, and Kades, and the river of Egypt, and Taphnes, and Ramesse, and all the land of Gesem, [10] Until ye come beyond Tanis and Memphis, and to all the inhabitants of Egypt, until ye come to the borders of Ethiopia. [11] But all the inhabitants of the land made light of the commandment of Nabuchodonosor king of the Assyrians, neither went they with him to the battle; for they were not afraid of him: yea, he was before them as one man, and they sent away his ambassadors from them without effect, and with disgrace. [12] Therefore Nabuchodonosor was very angry with all this country, and sware by his throne and kingdom, that he would surely be avenged upon all those coasts of Cilicia, and Damascus, and Syria, and that he would slay with the sword all the inhabitants of the land of Moab, and the children of Ammon, and all Judea, and all that were in Egypt, till ye come to the borders of the two seas. [13] Then he marched in battle array with his power against king Arphaxad in the seventeenth year, and he prevailed in his battle: for he overthrew all the power of Arphaxad, and all his horsemen, and all his chariots, [14] And became lord of his cities, and came unto Ecbatane, and took the towers, and spoiled the streets thereof, and turned the beauty thereof into shame. [15] He took also Arphaxad in the mountains of Ragau, and smote him through with his darts, and destroyed him utterly that day. [16] So he returned afterward to Nineve, both he and all his company of sundry nations being a very great multitude of men of war, and there he took his ease, and banqueted, both he and his army, an hundred and twenty days.

JDT.2

[1] And in the eighteenth year, the two and twentieth day of the first month, there was talk in the house of Nabuchodonosor king of the Assyrians that he should, as he said, avenge himself on all the earth. [2] So he called unto him all his officers, and all his nobles, and communicated with them his secret counsel, and concluded the afflicting of the whole earth out of his own mouth. [3] Then they decreed to destroy all flesh, that did not obey the commandment of his mouth. [4] And when he had ended his counsel, Nabuchodonosor king of the Assyrians called Holofernes the chief captain of his army, which was next unto him, and said unto him. [5] Thus saith the great king, the lord of the whole earth, Behold, thou shalt go forth from my presence, and take with thee men that trust in their own strength, of footmen an hundred and twenty thousand; and the number of horses with their riders twelve thousand. [6] And thou shalt go against all the west country, because they disobeyed my commandment. [7] And thou shalt declare unto that they prepare for me earth and water: for I will go forth in my wrath against them and will cover the whole face of the earth with the feet of mine army, and I will give them for a spoil unto them: [8] So that their slain shall fill their valleys and brooks and the river shall be filled with their dead, till it overflow: [9] And I will lead them captives to the utmost parts of all the earth. [10] Thou therefore shalt go forth. and take beforehand for me all their coasts: and if they will yield themselves unto thee, thou shalt reserve them for me till the day of their punishment. [11] But concerning them that rebel, let not thine eye spare them; but put them to the slaughter, and spoil them wheresoever thou goest. [12] For as I live, and by the power of my kingdom, whatsoever I have spoken, that will I do by mine hand. [13] And take thou heed that thou transgress none of the commandments of thy lord, but accomplish them fully, as I have commanded thee, and defer not to do them. [14] Then Holofernes went forth from the presence of his lord, and called ail the governors and captains, and the officers of the army of Assur; [15] And he mustered the chosen men for the battle, as his lord had commanded him, unto an hundred and twenty thousand, and twelve thousand archers on horseback; [16] And he ranged them, as a great army is ordered for the war. [17] And he took camels and asses for their carriages, a very great number; and sheep and oxen and goats without number for their provision: [18] And plenty of victual for every man of the army, and very much gold and silver out of the king's house. [19] Then he went forth and all his power to go before king Nabuchodonosor in the voyage, and to cover all the face of the earth westward with their chariots, and horsemen, and their chosen footmen. [20] A great number also sundry countries came with them like locusts, and like the sand of the earth: for the multitude was without number. [21] And they went forth of Nineve three days' journey toward the plain of Bectileth, and pitched from Bectileth near the mountain which is at the left hand of the upper Cilicia. [22] Then he took all his army, his footmen, and horsemen and chariots, and went from thence into the hill country; [23] And destroyed Phud and Lud, and spoiled all the children of Rasses, and the children of Israel, which were toward the wilderness at the south of the land of the Chellians. [24] Then he went over Euphrates, and went through Mesopotamia, and destroyed all the high cities that were upon the river Arbonai, till ye come to the sea. [25] And he took the borders of Cilicia, and killed all that resisted him, and came to the borders of Japheth, which were toward the south, over against Arabia. [26] He compassed also all the children of Madian, and burned up their tabernacles, and spoiled their sheepcotes. [27] Then he went down into the plain of Damascus in the time of wheat harvest, and burnt up all their fields, and destroyed their flocks and herds, also he spoiled their cities, and utterly wasted their countries, and smote all their young men with the edge of the sword. [28] Therefore the fear and dread of him fell upon all the inhabitants of the sea coasts, which were in Sidon and Tyrus, and them that dwelt in Sur and Ocina, and all that dwelt in Jemnaan; and they that dwelt in Azotus and Ascalon feared him greatly.

JDT.3

[1] So they sent ambassadors unto him to treat of peace, saying, [2] Behold, we the servants of Nabuchodonosor the great king lie before thee; use us as shall be good in thy sight. [3] Behold, our houses, and all our places, and all our fields of wheat, and flocks, and herds, and all the lodges of our tents lie before thy face; use them as it pleaseth thee. [4] Behold, even our cities and the inhabitants thereof are thy servants; come and deal with them as seemeth good unto thee. [5] So the men came to Holofernes, and declared unto him after this manner. [6] Then came he down toward the sea coast, both he and his army, and set garrisons in the high cities, and took out of them chosen men for aid. [7] So they and all the country round about received them with garlands, with dances, and with timbrels. [8] Yet he did cast down their frontiers, and cut down their groves: for he had decreed to destroy all the gods of the land, that all nations should worship

Nabuchodonosor only, and that all tongues and tribes should call upon him as god. [9] Also he came over against Esdraelon near unto Judea, over against the great strait of Judea. [10] And he pitched between Geba and Scythopolis, and there he tarried a whole month, that he might gather together all the carriages of his army.

JDT.4

[1] Now the children of Israel, that dwelt in Judea, heard all that Holofernes the chief captain of Nabuchodonosor king of the Assyrians had done to the nations, and after what manner he had spoiled all their temples, and brought them to nought. [2] Therefore they were exceedingly afraid of him, and were troubled for Jerusalem, and for the temple of the Lord their God: [3] For they were newly returned from the captivity, and all the people of Judea were lately gathered together: and the vessels, and the altar, and the house, were sanctified after the profanation. [4] Therefore they sent into all the coasts of Samaria, and the villages and to Bethoron, and Belmen, and Jericho, and to Choba, and Esora, and to the valley of Salem: [5] And possessed themselves beforehand of all the tops of the high mountains, and fortified the villages that were in them, and laid up victuals for the provision of war: for their fields were of late reaped. [6] Also Joacim the high priest, which was in those days in Jerusalem, wrote to them that dwelt in Bethulia, and Betomestham, which is over against Esdraelon toward the open country, near to Dothaim, [7] Charging them to keep the passages of the hill country: for by them there was an entrance into Judea, and it was easy to stop them that would come up, because the passage was straight, for two men at the most. [8] And the children of Israel did as Joacim the high priest had commanded them, with the ancients of all the people of Israel, which dwelt at Jerusalem. [9] Then every man of Israel cried to God with great fervency, and with great vehemency did they humble their souls: [10] Both they, and their wives and their children, and their cattle, and every stranger and hireling, and their servants bought with money, put sackcloth upon their loins. [11] Thus every man and women, and the little children, and the inhabitants of Jerusalem, fell before the temple, and cast ashes upon their heads, and spread out their sackcloth before the face of the Lord: also they put sackcloth about the altar, [12] And cried to the God of Israel all with one consent earnestly, that he would not give their children for a prey, and their wives for a spoil, and the cities of their inheritance to destruction, and the sanctuary to profanation and reproach, and for the nations to rejoice at. [13] So God heard their prayers, and looked upon their afflictions: for the people fasted many days in all Judea and Jerusalem before the sanctuary of the Lord Almighty. [14] And Joacim the high priest, and all the priests that stood before the Lord, and they which ministered unto the Lord, had their loins girt with sackcloth, and offered the daily burnt offerings, with the vows and free gifts of the people, [15] And had ashes on their mitres, and cried unto the Lord with all their power, that he would look upon all the house of Israel graciously.

JDT.5

[1] Then was it declared to Holofernes, the chief captain of the army of Assur, that the children of Israel had prepared for war, and had shut up the passages of the hill country, and had fortified all the tops of the high hills and had laid impediments in the champaign countries: [2] Wherewith he was very angry, and called all the princes of Moab, and the captains of Ammon, and all the governors of the sea coast, [3] And he said unto them, Tell me now, ye sons of Chanaan, who this people is, that dwelleth in the hill country, and what are the cities that they inhabit, and what is the multitude of their army, and wherein is their power and strength, and what king is set over them, or captain of their army; [4] And why have they determined not to come and meet me, more than all the inhabitants of the west. [5] Then said Achior, the captain of all the sons of Ammon, Let my lord now hear a word from the mouth of thy servant, and I will declare unto thee the truth concerning this people, which dwelleth near thee, and inhabiteth the hill countries: and there shall no lie come out of the mouth of thy servant. [6] This people are descended of the Chaldeans: [7] And they sojourned heretofore in Mesopotamia, because they would not follow the gods of their fathers, which were in the land of Chaldea. [8] For they left the way of their ancestors, and worshipped the God of heaven, the God whom they knew: so they cast them out from the face of their gods, and they fled into Mesopotamia, and sojourned there many days. [9] Then their God commanded them to depart from the place where they sojourned, and to go into the land of Chanaan: where they dwelt, and were increased with gold and silver, and with very much cattle. [10] But when a famine covered all the land of Chanaan, they went down into Egypt, and sojourned there, while they were nourished, and became there a great multitude, so that one could not number their nation. [11] Therefore the king of Egypt rose up against them, and dealt subtilly with them, and brought them low with labouring in brick, and made them slaves. [12] Then they cried unto their God, and he smote all the land of Egypt with incurable plagues: so the Egyptians cast them out of their sight. [13] And God dried the Red sea before them, [14] And brought them to mount Sina, and Cades-Barne, and cast forth all that dwelt in the wilderness. [15] So they dwelt in the land of the Amorites, and they destroyed by their strength all them of Esebon, and passing over Jordan they possessed all the hill country. [16] And they cast forth before them the Chanaanite, the Pherezite, the Jebusite, and the Sychemite, and all the Gergesites, and they dwelt in that country many days. [17] And whilst they sinned not before their God, they prospered, because the God that hateth iniquity was with them. [18] But when they departed from the way which he appointed them, they were destroyed in many battles very sore, and were led captives into a land that was not their's, and the temple of their God was cast to the ground, and their cities were taken by the enemies. [19] But now are they returned to their God, and are come up from the places where they were scattered, and have possessed Jerusalem, where their sanctuary is, and are seated in the hill country; for it was desolate. [20] Now therefore, my lord and governor, if there be any error against this people, and they sin against their God, let us consider that this shall be their ruin, and let us go up, and we shall overcome them. [21] But if there be no iniquity in their nation, let my lord now pass by, lest their Lord defend them, and their God be for them, and we become a reproach before all the world. [22] And when Achior had finished these sayings, all the people standing round about the tent murmured, and the chief men of Holofernes, and all that dwelt by the sea side, and in Moab, spake that he should kill him. [23] For, say they, we will not be afraid of the face of the children of Israel: for, lo, it is a people that have no strength nor power for a strong battle [24] Now therefore, lord Holofernes, we will go up, and they shall be a prey to be devoured of all thine army.

JDT.6

[1] And when the tumult of men that were about the council was ceased, Holofernes the chief captain of the army of Assur said unto Achior and all the Moabites before all the company of other nations, [2] And who art thou, Achior, and the hirelings of Ephraim, that thou hast prophesied against us as to day, and hast said, that we should not make war with the people of Israel, because their God will defend them? and who is God but Nabuchodonosor? [3] He will send his power, and will destroy them from the face of the earth, and their God shall not deliver them: but we his servants will destroy them as one man; for they are not able to sustain the power of our horses. [4] For with them we will tread them under foot, and their mountains shall be drunken with their blood, and their fields shall be filled with their dead bodies, and their footsteps shall not be able to stand before us, for they shall utterly perish, saith king Nabuchodonosor, lord of all the earth: for he said, None of my words shall be in vain. [5] And thou, Achior, an hireling of Ammon, which hast spoken these words in the day of thine iniquity, shalt see my face no more from this day, until I take vengeance of this nation that came out of Egypt. [6] And then shall the sword of mine army, and the multitude of them that serve me, pass through thy sides, and thou shalt fall among their slain, when I return. [7] Now therefore my servants shall bring thee back into the hill country, and shall set thee in one of the cities of the passages: [8] And thou shalt not perish, till thou be destroyed with them. [9] And if thou persuade thyself in thy mind that they shall be taken, let not thy countenance fall: I have spoken it, and none of my words shall be in vain. [10] Then Holofernes commanded his servants, that waited in his tent, to take Achior, and bring him to Bethulia, and deliver him into the hands of the children of Israel. [11] So his servants took him, and brought him out of the camp into the plain, and they went from the midst of the plain into the hill country, and came unto the fountains that were under Bethulia. [12] And when the men of the city saw them, they took up their weapons, and went out of the city to the top of the hill: and every man that used a sling kept them from coming up by casting of stones against them. [13] Nevertheless having gotten privily under the hill, they bound Achior, and cast him down, and left him at the foot of the hill, and returned to their lord. [14] But the Israelites descended from their city, and came unto him, and loosed him, and brought him to Bethulia, and presented him to the governors of the city: [15] Which were in those days Ozias the son of Micha, of the tribe of Simeon, and Chabris the son of Gothoniel, and Charmis the son of Melchiel. [16] And they called together all the ancients of the city, and all their youth ran together, and their women, to the assembly, and they set Achior in the midst of all their people. Then Ozias asked him of that which was done. [17] And he answered and declared unto them the words of the council of Holofernes, and all the words that he had spoken in the midst of the princes of Assur, and whatsoever Holofernes had spoken proudly against the house of Israel. [18] Then the people fell down and worshipped God, and cried unto God. saying, [19] O Lord God of heaven, behold their pride, and pity the low estate of our nation, and look upon the face of those that are sanctified unto thee this day. [20] Then they comforted Achior, and praised him greatly. [21] And Ozias took him out of the assembly unto his house, and made a feast to the elders; and they called on the God of Israel all that night for help.

JDT.7

[1] The next day Holofernes commanded all his army, and all his people which were come to take his part, that they should remove their camp against Bethulia, to take aforehand the ascents of the hill country, and to make war against the children of Israel. [2] Then their strong men removed their camps in that day, and the army of the men of war was an hundred and seventy thousand footmen, and twelve thousand horsemen, beside the baggage, and other men that were afoot among them, a very great multitude. [3] And they camped in the valley near unto Bethulia, by the fountain, and they spread themselves in breadth over Dothaim even to Belmaim, and in length from Bethulia unto Cynamon, which is over against Esdraelon. [4] Now the children of Israel, when they saw the multitude of them, were greatly troubled, and said every one to his neighbour, Now will these men lick up the face of the earth; for neither the high mountains, nor the valleys, nor the hills, are able to bear their weight. [5] Then every man took up his weapons of war, and when they had kindled fires upon their towers, they remained and watched all that night. [6] But in the second day Holofernes brought forth all his horsemen in the sight of the children of Israel which were in Bethulia, [7] And viewed the passages up to the city, and came to the fountains of their waters, and took them, and set garrisons of men of war over them, and he himself removed toward his people. [8] Then came unto him all the chief of the children of Esau, and all the governors of the people of Moab, and the captains of the sea coast, and said, [9] Let our lord now hear a word, that there be not an overthrow in thine army. [10] For this people of the children of Israel do not trust in their spears, but in the height of the mountains wherein they dwell, because it is not easy to come up to the tops of their mountains. [11] Now therefore, my lord, fight not against them in battle array, and there shall not so much as one man of thy people perish. [12] Remain in thy camp, and keep all the men of thine army, and let thy servants get into their hands the fountain of water, which issueth forth of the foot of the mountain: [13] For all the inhabitants of Bethulia have their water thence; so shall thirst kill them, and they shall give up their city, and we and our people shall go up to the tops of the mountains that are near, and will camp upon them, to watch that none go out of the city. [14] So they and their wives and their children shall be consumed with fire, and before the sword come against them, they shall be overthrown in the streets where they dwell. [15] Thus shalt thou render them an evil reward; because they rebelled, and met not thy person peaceably. [16] And these words pleased Holofernes and all his servants, and he appointed to do as they had spoken. [17] So the camp of the children of Ammon departed, and with them five thousand of the Assyrians, and they pitched in the valley, and took the waters, and the fountains of the waters of the children of Israel. [18] Then the children of Esau went up with the children of Ammon, and camped in the hill country over against Dothaim: and they sent some of them toward the south, and toward the east over against Ekrebel, which is near unto Chusi, that is upon the brook Mochmur; and the rest of the army of the Assyrians camped in the plain, and covered the face of the whole land; and their tents and carriages were pitched to a very great multitude. [19] Then the children of Israel cried unto the Lord their God, because their heart failed, for all their enemies had compassed them round about, and there was no way to escape out from among them. [20] Thus all the company of

Assur remained about them, both their footmen, chariots, and horsemen, four and thirty days, so that all their vessels of water failed all the inhibitants of Bethulia. [21] And the cisterns were emptied, and they had not water to drink their fill for one day; for they gave them drink by measure. [22] Therefore their young children were out of heart, and their women and young men fainted for thirst, and fell down in the streets of the city, and by the passages of the gates, and there was no longer any strength in them. [23] Then all the people assembled to Ozias, and to the chief of the city, both young men, and women, and children, and cried with a loud voice, and said before all the elders, [24] God be judge between us and you: for ye have done us great injury, in that ye have not required peace of the children of Assur. [25] For now we have no helper: but God hath sold us into their hands, that we should be thrown down before them with thirst and great destruction. [26] Now therefore call them unto you, and deliver the whole city for a spoil to the people of Holofernes, and to all his army. [27] For it is better for us to be made a spoil unto them, than to die for thirst: for we will be his servants, that our souls may live, and not see the death of our infants before our eyes, nor our wives nor our children to die. [28] We take to witness against you the heaven and the earth, and our God and Lord of our fathers, which punisheth us according to our sins and the sins of our fathers, that he do not according as we have said this day. [29] Then there was great weeping with one consent in the midst of the assembly; and they cried unto the Lord God with a loud voice. [30] Then said Ozias to them, Brethren, be of good courage, let us yet endure five days, in the which space the Lord our God may turn his mercy toward us; for he will not forsake us utterly. [31] And if these days pass, and there come no help unto us, I will do according to your word. [32] And he dispersed the people, every one to their own charge; and they went unto the walls and towers of their city, and sent the women and children into their houses: and they were very low brought in the city.

JDT.8

[1] Now at that time Judith heard thereof, which was the daughter of Merari, the son of Ox, the son of Joseph, the son of Ozel, the son of Elcia, the son of Ananias, the son of Gedeon, the son of Raphaim, the son of Acitho, the son of Eliu, the son of Eliab, the son of Nathanael, the son of Samael, the son of Salasadal, the son of Israel. [2] And Manasses was her husband, of her tribe and kindred, who died in the barley harvest. [3] For as he stood overseeing them that bound sheaves in the field, the heat came upon his head, and he fell on his bed, and died in the city of Bethulia: and they buried him with his fathers in the field between Dothaim and Balamo. [4] So Judith was a widow in her house three years and four months. [5] And she made her a tent upon the top of her house, and put on sackcloth upon her loins and ware her widow's apparel. [6] And she fasted all the days of her widowhood, save the eves of the sabbaths, and the sabbaths, and the eves of the new moons, and the new moons and the feasts and solemn days of the house of Israel. [7] She was also of a goodly countenance, and very beautiful to behold: and her husband Manasses had left her gold, and silver, and menservants and maidservants, and cattle, and lands; and she remained upon them. [8] And there was none that gave her an ill word; ar she feared God greatly. [9] Now when she heard the evil words of the people against the governor, that they fainted for lack of water; for Judith had heard all the words that Ozias had spoken unto them, and that he had sworn to deliver the city unto the Assyrians after five days; [10] Then she sent her waitingwoman, that had the government of all things that she had, to call Ozias and Chabris and Charmis, the ancients of the city. [11] And they came unto her, and she said unto them, Hear me now, O ye governors of the inhabitants of Bethulia: for your words that ye have spoken before the people this day are not right, touching this oath which ye made and pronounced between God and you, and have promised to deliver the city to our enemies, unless within these days the Lord turn to help you. [12] And now who are ye that have tempted God this day, and stand instead of God among the children of men? [13] And now try the Lord Almighty, but ye shall never know any thing. [14] For ye cannot find the depth of the heart of man, neither can ye perceive the things that he thinketh: then how can ye search out God, that hath made all these things, and know his mind, or comprehend his purpose? Nay, my brethren, provoke not the Lord our God to anger. [15] For if he will not help us within these five days, he hath power to defend us when he will, even every day, or to destroy us before our enemies. [16] Do not bind the counsels of the Lord our God: for God is not as man, that he may be threatened; neither is he as the son of man, that he should be wavering. [17] Therefore let us wait for salvation of him, and call upon him to help us, and he will hear our voice, if it please him. [18] For there arose none in our age, neither is there any now in these days neither tribe, nor family, nor people, nor city among us, which worship gods made with hands, as hath been aforetime. [19] For the which cause our fathers were given to the sword, and for a spoil, and had a great fall before our enemies. [20] But we know none other god, therefore we trust that he will not dispise us, nor any of our nation. [21] For if we be taken so, all Judea shall lie waste, and our sanctuary shall be spoiled; and he will require the profanation thereof at our mouth. [22] And the slaughter of our brethren, and the captivity of the country, and the desolation of our inheritance, will he turn upon our heads among the Gentiles, wheresoever we shall be in bondage; and we shall be an offence and a reproach to all them that possess us. [23] For our servitude shall not be directed to favour: but the Lord our God shall turn it to dishonour. [24] Now therefore, O brethren, let us shew an example to our brethren, because their hearts depend upon us, and the sanctuary, and the house, and the altar, rest upon us. [25] Moreover let us give thanks to the Lord our God, which trieth us, even as he did our fathers. [26] Remember what things he did to Abraham, and how he tried Isaac, and what happened to Jacob in Mesopotamia of Syria, when he kept the sheep of Laban his mother's brother. [27] For he hath not tried us in the fire, as he did them, for the examination of their hearts, neither hath he taken vengeance on us: but the Lord doth scourge them that come near unto him, to admonish them. [28] Then said Ozias to her, All that thou hast spoken hast thou spoken with a good heart, and there is none that may gainsay thy words. [29] For this is not the first day wherein thy wisdom is manifested; but from the beginning of thy days all the people have known thy understanding, because the disposition of thine heart is good. [30] But the people were very thirsty, and compelled us to do unto them as we have spoken, and to bring an oath upon ourselves, which we will not break. [31] Therefore now pray thou for us, because thou art a godly woman, and the Lord will send us rain to fill our cisterns, and we shall faint no more. [32] Then said Judith unto them, Hear me, and I will do a thing, which shall go throughout all generations to the children of our nation. [33] Ye shall stand this night in the gate,

and I will go forth with my waitingwoman: and within the days that ye have promised to deliver the city to our enemies the Lord will visit Israel by mine hand. [34] But enquire not ye of mine act: for I will not declare it unto you, till the things be finished that I do. [35] Then said Ozias and the princes unto her, Go in peace, and the Lord God be before thee, to take vengeance on our enemies. [36] So they returned from the tent, and went to their wards.

JDT.9

[1] Judith fell upon her face, and put ashes upon her head, and uncovered the sackcloth wherewith she was clothed; and about the time that the incense of that evening was offered in Jerusalem in the house of the Lord Judith cried with a loud voice, and said, [2] O Lord God of my father Simeon, to whom thou gavest a sword to take vengeance of the strangers, who loosened the girdle of a maid to defile her, and discovered the thigh to her shame, and polluted her virginity to her reproach; for thou saidst, It shall not be so; and yet they did so: [3] Wherefore thou gavest their rulers to be slain, so that they dyed their bed in blood, being deceived, and smotest the servants with their lords, and the lords upon their thrones; [4] And hast given their wives for a prey, and their daughters to be captives, and all their spoils to be divided among thy dear children; which were moved with thy zeal, and abhorred the pollution of their blood, and called upon thee for aid: O God, O my God, hear me also a widow. [5] For thou hast wrought not only those things, but also the things which fell out before, and which ensued after; thou hast thought upon the things which are now, and which are to come. [6] Yea, what things thou didst determine were ready at hand, and said, Lo, we are here: for all thy ways are prepared, and thy judgments are in thy foreknowledge. [7] For, behold, the Assyrians are multiplied in their power; they are exalted with horse and man; they glory in the strength of their footmen; they trust in shield, and spear, and bow, and sling; and know not that thou art the Lord that breakest the battles: the Lord is thy name. [8] Throw down their strength in thy power, and bring down their force in thy wrath: for they have purposed to defile thy sanctuary, and to pollute the tabernacle where thy glorious name resteth and to cast down with sword the horn of thy altar. [9] Behold their pride, and send thy wrath upon their heads: give into mine hand, which am a widow, the power that I have conceived. [10] Smite by the deceit of my lips the servant with the prince, and the prince with the servant: break down their stateliness by the hand of a woman. [11] For thy power standeth not in multitude nor thy might in strong men: for thou art a God of the afflicted, an helper of the oppressed, an upholder of the weak, a protector of the forlorn, a saviour of them that are without hope. [12] I pray thee, I pray thee, O God of my father, and God of the inheritance of Israel, Lord of the heavens and earth, Creator of the waters, king of every creature, hear thou my prayer: [13] And make my speech and deceit to be their wound and stripe, who have purposed cruel things against thy covenant, and thy hallowed house, and against the top of Sion, and against the house of the possession of thy children. [14] And make every nation and tribe to acknowledge that thou art the God of all power and might, and that there is none other that protecteth the people of Israel but thou.

JDT.10

[1] Now after that she had ceased to cry unto the God of Israel, and bad made an end of all these words. [2] She rose where she had fallen down, and called her maid, and went down into the house in the which she abode in the sabbath days, and in her feast days, [3] And pulled off the sackcloth which she had on, and put off the garments of her widowhood, and washed her body all over with water, and anointed herself with precious ointment, and braided the hair of her head, and put on a tire upon it, and put on her garments of gladness, wherewith she was clad during the life of Manasses her husband. [4] And she took sandals upon her feet, and put about her her bracelets, and her chains, and her rings, and her earrings, and all her ornaments, and decked herself bravely, to allure the eyes of all men that should see her. [5] Then she gave her maid a bottle of wine, and a cruse of oil, and filled a bag with parched corn, and lumps of figs, and with fine bread; so she folded all these things together, and laid them upon her. [6] Thus they went forth to the gate of the city of Bethulia, and found standing there Ozias and the ancients of the city, Chabris and Charmis. [7] And when they saw her, that her countenance was altered, and her apparel was changed, they wondered at her beauty very greatly, and said unto her. [8] The God, the God of our fathers give thee favour, and accomplish thine enterprizes to the glory of the children of Israel, and to the exaltation of Jerusalem. Then they worshipped God. [9] And she said unto them, Command the gates of the city to be opened unto me, that I may go forth to accomplish the things whereof ye have spoken with me. So they commanded the young men to open unto her, as she had spoken. [10] And when they had done so, Judith went out, she, and her maid with her; and the men of the city looked after her, until she was gone down the mountain, and till she had passed the valley, and could see her no more. [11] Thus they went straight forth in the valley: and the first watch of the Assyrians met her, [12] And took her, and asked her, Of what people art thou? and whence comest thou? and whither goest thou? And she said, I am a woman of the Hebrews, and am fled from them: for they shall be given you to be consumed: [13] And I am coming before Holofernes the chief captain of your army, to declare words of truth; and I will shew him a way, whereby he shall go, and win all the hill country, without losing the body or life of any one of his men. [14] Now when the men heard her words, and beheld her countenance, they wondered greatly at her beauty, and said unto her, [15] Thou hast saved thy life, in that thou hast hasted to come down to the presence of our lord: now therefore come to his tent, and some of us shall conduct thee, until they have delivered thee to his hands. [16] And when thou standest before him, be not afraid in thine heart, but shew unto him according to thy word; and he will entreat thee well. [17] Then they chose out of them an hundred men to accompany her and her maid; and they brought her to the tent of Holofernes. [18] Then was there a concourse throughout all the camp: for her coming was noised among the tents, and they came about her, as she stood without the tent of Holofernes, till they told him of her. [19] And they wondered at her beauty, and admired the children of Israel because of her, and every one said to his neighbour, Who would despise this people, that have among them such women? surely it is not good that one man of them be left who being let go might deceive the whole earth. [20] And they that lay near Holofernes went out, and all his servants and they brought her into the tent. [21] Now Holofernes rested upon his bed under a canopy, which was woven with purple, and gold, and emeralds, and precious stones. [22] So they shewed him of her; and he came out before his tent with silver lamps going before him. [23] And

when Judith was come before him and his servants they all marvelled at the beauty of her countenance; and she fell down upon her face, and did reverence unto him: and his servants took her up.

JDT.11

[1] Then said Holofernes unto her, Woman, be of good comfort, fear not in thine heart: for I never hurt any that was willing to serve Nabuchodonosor, the king of all the earth. [2] Now therefore, if thy people that dwelleth in the mountains had not set light by me, I would not have lifted up my spear against them: but they have done these things to themselves. [3] But now tell me wherefore thou art fled from them, and art come unto us: for thou art come for safeguard; be of good comfort, thou shalt live this night, and hereafter: [4] For none shall hurt thee, but entreat thee well, as they do the servants of king Nabuchodonosor my lord. [5] Then Judith said unto him, Receive the words of thy servant, and suffer thine handmaid to speak in thy presence, and I will declare no lie to my lord this night. [6] And if thou wilt follow the words of thine handmaid, God will bring the thing perfectly to pass by thee; and my lord shall not fail of his purposes. [7] As Nabuchodonosor king of all the earth liveth, and as his power liveth, who hath sent thee for the upholding of every living thing: for not only men shall serve him by thee, but also the beasts of the field, and the cattle, and the fowls of the air, shall live by thy power under Nabuchodonosor and all his house. [8] For we have heard of thy wisdom and thy policies, and it is reported in all the earth, that thou only art excellent in all the kingdom, and mighty in knowledge, and wonderful in feats of war. [9] Now as concerning the matter, which Achior did speak in thy council, we have heard his words; for the men of Bethulia saved him, and he declared unto them all that he had spoken unto thee. [10] Therefore, O lord and governor, respect not his word; but lay it up in thine heart, for it is true: for our nation shall not be punished, neither can sword prevail against them, except they sin against their God. [11] And now, that my lord be not defeated and frustrate of his purpose, even death is now fallen upon them, and their sin hath overtaken them, wherewith they will provoke their God to anger whensoever they shall do that which is not fit to be done: [12] For their victuals fail them, and all their water is scant, and they have determined to lay hands upon their cattle, and purposed to consume all those things, that God hath forbidden them to eat by his laws: [13] And are resolved to spend the firstfruits of the the tenths of wine and oil, which they had sanctified, and reserved for the priests that serve in Jerusalem before the face of our God; the which things it is not lawful for any of the people so much as to touch with their hands. [14] For they have sent some to Jerusalem, because they also that dwell there have done the like, to bring them a licence from the senate. [15] Now when they shall bring them word, they will forthwith do it, and they shall be given to thee to be destroyed the same day. [16] Wherefore I thine handmaid, knowing all this, am fled from their presence; and God hath sent me to work things with thee, whereat all the earth shall be astonished, and whosoever shall hear it. [17] For thy servant is religious, and serveth the God of heaven day and night: now therefore, my lord, I will remain with thee, and thy servant will go out by night into the valley, and I will pray unto God, and he will tell me when they have committed their sins: [18] And I will come and shew it unto thee: then thou shalt go forth with all thine army, and there shall be none of them that shall resist thee. [19] And I will lead thee through the midst of Judea, until thou come before Jerusalem; and I will set thy throne in the midst thereof; and thou shalt drive them as sheep that have no shepherd, and a dog shall not so much as open his mouth at thee: for these things were told me according to my foreknowledge, and they were declared unto me, and I am sent to tell thee. [20] Then her words pleased Holofernes and all his servants; and they marvelled at her wisdom, and said, [21] There is not such a woman from one end of the earth to the other, both for beauty of face, and wisdom of words. [22] Likewise Holofernes said unto her. God hath done well to send thee before the people, that strength might be in our hands and destruction upon them that lightly regard my lord. [23] And now thou art both beautiful in thy countenance, and witty in thy words: surely if thou do as thou hast spoken thy God shall be my God, and thou shalt dwell in the house of king Nabuchodonosor, and shalt be renowned through the whole earth.

JDT.12

[1] Then he commanded to bring her in where his plate was set; and bade that they should prepare for her of his own meats, and that she should drink of his own wine. [2] And Judith said, I will not eat thereof, lest there be an offence: but provision shall be made for me of the things that I have brought. [3] Then Holofernes said unto her, If thy provision should fail, how should we give thee the like? for there be none with us of thy nation. [4] Then said Judith unto him As thy soul liveth, my lord, thine handmaid shall not spend those things that I have, before the Lord work by mine hand the things that he hath determined. [5] Then the servants of Holofernes brought her into the tent, and she slept till midnight, and she arose when it was toward the morning watch, [6] And sent to Holofernes, saving, Let my lord now command that thine handmaid may go forth unto prayer. [7] Then Holofernes commanded his guard that they should not stay her: thus she abode in the camp three days, and went out in the night into the valley of Bethulia, and washed herself in a fountain of water by the camp. [8] And when she came out, she besought the Lord God of Israel to direct her way to the raising up of the children of her people. [9] So she came in clean, and remained in the tent, until she did eat her meat at evening. [10] And in the fourth day Holofernes made a feast to his own servants only, and called none of the officers to the banquet. [11] Then said he to Bagoas the eunuch, who had charge over all that he had, Go now, and persuade this Hebrew woman which is with thee, that she come unto us, and eat and drink with us. [12] For, lo, it will be a shame for our person, if we shall let such a woman go, not having had her company; for if we draw her not unto us, she will laugh us to scorn. [13] Then went Bagoas from the presence of Holofernes, and came to her, and he said, Let not this fair damsel fear to come to my lord, and to be honoured in his presence, and drink wine, and be merry with us and be made this day as one of the daughters of the Assyrians, which serve in the house of Nabuchodonosor. [14] Then said Judith unto him, Who am I now, that I should gainsay my lord? surely whatsoever pleaseth him I will do speedily, and it shall be my joy unto the day of my death. [15] So she arose, and decked herself with her apparel and all her woman's attire, and her maid went and laid soft skins on the ground for her over against Holofernes, which she had received of Bagoas far her daily use, that she might sit and eat upon them. [16] Now when Judith came in and sat down, Holofernes his heart was ravished with her, and his

mind was moved, and he desired greatly her company; for he waited a time to deceive her, from the day that he had seen her. [17] Then said Holofernes unto her, Drink now, and be merry with us. [18] So Judith said, I will drink now, my lord, because my life is magnified in me this day more than all the days since I was born. [19] Then she took and ate and drank before him what her maid had prepared. [20] And Holofernes took great delight in her, and drank more wine than he had drunk at any time in one day since he was born.

JDT.13

[1] Now when the evening was come, his servants made haste to depart, and Bagoas shut his tent without, and dismissed the waiters from the presence of his lord; and they went to their beds: for they were all weary, because the feast had been long. [2] And Judith was left along in the tent, and Holofernes lying along upon his bed: for he was filled with wine. [3] Now Judith had commanded her maid to stand without her bedchamber, and to wait for her. coming forth, as she did daily: for she said she would go forth to her prayers, and she spake to Bagoas according to the same purpose. [4] So all went forth and none was left in the bedchamber, neither little nor great. Then Judith, standing by his bed, said in her heart, O Lord God of all power, look at this present upon the works of mine hands for the exaltation of Jerusalem. [5] For now is the time to help thine inheritance, and to execute thine enterprizes to the destruction of the enemies which are risen against us. [6] Then she came to the pillar of the bed, which was at Holofernes' head, and took down his fauchion from thence, [7] And approached to his bed, and took hold of the hair of his head, and said, Strengthen me, O Lord God of Israel, this day. [8] And she smote twice upon his neck with all her might, and she took away his head from him. [9] And tumbled his body down from the bed, and pulled down the canopy from the pillars; and anon after she went forth, and gave Holofernes his head to her maid; [10] And she put it in her bag of meat: so they twain went together according to their custom unto prayer: and when they passed the camp, they compassed the valley, and went up the mountain of Bethulia, and came to the gates thereof. [11] Then said Judith afar off, to the watchmen at the gate, Open, open now the gate: God, even our God, is with us, to shew his power yet in Jerusalem, and his forces against the enemy, as he hath even done this day. [12] Now when the men of her city heard her voice, they made haste to go down to the gate of their city, and they called the elders of the city. [13] And then they ran all together, both small and great, for it was strange unto them that she was come: so they opened the gate, and received them, and made a fire for a light, and stood round about them. [14] Then she said to them with a loud voice, Praise, praise God, praise God, I say, for he hath not taken away his mercy from the house of Israel, but hath destroyed our enemies by mine hands this night. [15] So she took the head out of the bag, and shewed it, and said unto them, behold the head of Holofernes, the chief captain of the army of Assur, and behold the canopy, wherein he did lie in his drunkenness; and the Lord hath smitten him by the hand of a woman. [16] As the Lord liveth, who hath kept me in my way that I went, my countenance hath deceived him to his destruction, and yet hath he not committed sin with me, to defile and shame me. [17] Then all the people were wonderfully astonished, and bowed themselves and worshipped God, and said with one accord, Blessed be thou, O our God, which hast this day brought to nought the enemies of thy people. [18] Then said Ozias unto her, O daughter, blessed art thou of the most high God above all the women upon the earth; and blessed be the Lord God, which hath created the heavens and the earth, which hath directed thee to the cutting off of the head of the chief of our enemies. [19] For this thy confidence shall not depart from the heart of men, which remember the power of God for ever. [20] And God turn these things to thee for a perpetual praise, to visit thee in good things because thou hast not spared thy life for the affliction of our nation, but hast revenged our ruin, walking a straight way before our God. And all the people said; So be it, so be it.

JDT.14

[1] Then said Judith unto them, Hear me now, my brethren, and take this head, and hang it upon the highest place of your walls. [2] And so soon as the morning shall appear, and the sun shall come forth upon the earth, take ye every one his weapons, and go forth every valiant man out of the city, and set ye a captain over them, as though ye would go down into the field toward the watch of the Assyrians; but go not down. [3] Then they shall take their armour, and shall go into their camp, and raise up the captains of the army of Assur, and shall run to the tent of Holofernes, but shall not find him: then fear shall fall upon them, and they shall flee before your face. [4] So ye, and all that inhabit the coast of Israel, shall pursue them, and overthrow them as they go. [5] But before ye do these things, call me Achior the Ammonite, that he may see and know him that despised the house of Israel, and that sent him to us as it were to his death. [6] Then they called Achior out of the house of Ozias; and when he was come, and saw the head of Holofernes in a man's hand in the assembly of the people, he fell down on his face, and his spirit failed. [7] But when they had recovered him, he fell at Judith's feet, and reverenced her, and said, Blessed art thou in all the tabernacles of Juda, and in all nations, which hearing thy name shall be astonished. [8] Now therefore tell me all the things that thou hast done in these days. Then Judith declared unto him in the midst of the people all that she had done, from the day that she went forth until that hour she spake unto them. [9] And when she had left off speaking, the people shouted with a loud voice, and made a joyful noise in their city. [10] And when Achior had seen all that the God of Israel had done, he believed in God greatly, and circumcised the flesh of his foreskin, and was joined unto the house of Israel unto this day. [11] And as soon as the morning arose, they hanged the head of Holofernes upon the wall, and every man took his weapons, and they went forth by bands unto the straits of the mountain. [12] But when the Assyrians saw them, they sent to their leaders, which came to their captains and tribunes, and to every one of their rulers. [13] So they came to Holofernes' tent, and said to him that had the charge of all his things, Waken now our lord: for the slaves have been bold to come down against us to battle, that they may be utterly destroyed. [14] Then went in Bagoas, and knocked at the door of the tent; for he thought that he had slept with Judith. [15] But because none answered, he opened it, and went into the bedchamber, and found him cast upon the floor dead, and his head was taken from him. [16] Therefore he cried with a loud voice, with weeping, and sighing, and a mighty cry, and rent his garments. [17] After he went into the tent where Judith lodged: and when he found her not, he leaped out to the people, and cried, [18] These slaves have dealt treacherously; one woman of the Hebrews hath

brought shame upon the house of king Nabuchodonosor: for, behold, Holofernes lieth upon the ground without a head. [19] When the captains of the Assyrians' army heard these words, they rent their coats and their minds were wonderfully troubled, and there was a cry and a very great noise throughout the camp.

JDT.15

[1] And when they that were in the tents heard, they were astonished at the thing that was done. [2] And fear and trembling fell upon them, so that there was no man that durst abide in the sight of his neighbour, but rushing out all together, they fled into every way of the plain, and of the hill country. [3] They also that had camped in the mountains round about Bethulia fled away. Then the children of Israel, every one that was a warrior among them, rushed out upon them. [4] Then sent Ozias to Betomasthem, and to Bebai, and Chobai, and Cola and to all the coasts of Israel, such as should tell the things that were done, and that all should rush forth upon their enemies to destroy them. [5] Now when the children of Israel heard it, they all fell upon them with one consent, and slew them unto Chobai: likewise also they that came from Jerusalem, and from all the hill country, (for men had told them what things were done in the camp of their enemies) and they that were in Galaad, and in Galilee, chased them with a great slaughter, until they were past Damascus and the borders thereof. [6] And the residue that dwelt at Bethulia, fell upon the camp of Assur, and spoiled them, and were greatly enriched. [7] And the children of Israel that returned from the slaughter had that which remained; and the villages and the cities, that were in the mountains and in the plain, gat many spoils: for the multitude was very great. [8] Then Joacim the high priest, and the ancients of the children of Israel that dwelt in Jerusalem, came to behold the good things that God had shewed to Israel, and to see Judith, and to salute her. [9] And when they came unto her, they blessed her with one accord, and said unto her, Thou art the exaltation of Jerusalem, thou art the great glory of Israel, thou art the great rejoicing of our nation: [10] Thou hast done all these things by thine hand: thou hast done much good to Israel, and God is pleased therewith: blessed be thou of the Almighty Lord for evermore. And all the people said, So be it. [11] And the people spoiled the camp the space of thirty days: and they gave unto Judith Holofernes his tent, and all his plate, and beds, and vessels, and all his stuff: and she took it and laid it on her mule; and made ready her carts, and laid them thereon. [12] Then all the women of Israel ran together to see her, and blessed her, and made a dance among them for her: and she took branches in her hand, and gave also to the women that were with her. [13] And they put a garland of olive upon her and her maid that was with her, and she went before all the people in the dance, leading all the women: and all the men of Israel followed in their armour with garlands, and with songs in their mouths.

JDT.16

[1] Then Judith began to sing this thanksgiving in all Israel, and all the people sang after her this song of praise. [2] And Judith said, Begin unto my God with timbrels, sing unto my Lord with cymbals: tune unto him a new psalm: exalt him, and call upon his name. [3] For God breaketh the battles: for among the camps in the midst of the people he hath delivered me out of the hands of them that persecuted me. [4] Assur came out of the mountains from the north, he came with ten thousands of his army, the multitude whereof stopped the torrents, and their horsemen have covered the hills. [5] He bragged that he would burn up my borders, and kill my young men with the sword, and dash the sucking children against the ground, and make mine infants as a prey, and my virgins as a spoil. [6] But the Almighty Lord hath disappointed them by the hand of a woman. [7] For the mighty one did not fall by the young men, neither did the sons of the Titans smite him, nor high giants set upon him: but Judith the daughter of Merari weakened him with the beauty of her countenance. [8] For she put off the garment of her widowhood for the exaltation of those that were oppressed in Israel, and anointed her face with ointment, and bound her hair in a tire, and took a linen garment to deceive him. [9] Her sandals ravished his eyes, her beauty took his mind prisoner, and the fauchion passed through his neck. [10] The Persians quaked at her boldness, and the Medes were daunted at her hardiness. [11] Then my afflicted shouted for joy, and my weak ones cried aloud; but they were astonished: these lifted up their voices, but they were overthrown. [12] The sons of the damsels have pierced them through, and wounded them as fugatives' children: they perished by the battle of the Lord. [13] I will sing unto the Lord a new song: O Lord, thou art great and glorious, wonderful in strength, and invincible. [14] Let all creatures serve thee: for thou spakest, and they were made, thou didst send forth thy spirit, and it created them, and there is none that can resist thy voice. [15] For the mountains shall be moved from their foundations with the waters, the rocks shall melt as wax at thy presence: yet thou art merciful to them that fear thee. [16] For all sacrifice is too little for a sweet savour unto thee, and all the fat is not sufficient for thy burnt offering: but he that feareth the Lord is great at all times. [17] Woe to the nations that rise up against my kindred! the Lord Almighty will take vengeance of them in the day of judgment, in putting fire and worms in their flesh; and they shall feel them, and weep for ever. [18] Now as soon as they entered into Jerusalem, they worshipped the Lord; and as soon as the people were purified, they offered their burnt offerings, and their free offerings, and their gifts. [19] Judith also dedicated all the stuff of Holofernes, which the people had given her, and gave the canopy, which she had taken out of his bedchamber, for a gift unto the Lord. [20] So the people continued feasting in Jerusalem before the sanctuary for the space of three months and Judith remained with them. [21] After this time every one returned to his own inheritance, and Judith went to Bethulia, and remained in her own possession, and was in her time honourable in all the country. [22] And many desired her, but none knew her all the days of her life, after that Manasses her husband was dead, and was gathered to his people. [23] But she increased more and more in honour, and waxed old in her husband's house, being an hundred and five years old, and made her maid free; so she died in Bethulia: and they buried her in the cave of her husband Manasses. [24] And the house of Israel lamented her seven days: and before she died, she did distribute her goods to all them that were nearest of kindred to Manasses her husband, and to them that were the nearest of her kindred. [25] And there was none that made the children of Israel any more afraid in the days of Judith, nor a long time after her death.

BEL AND THE DRAGON

Bel.1

[1] And king Astyages was gathered to his fathers, and Cyrus of Persia received his kingdom. [2] And Daniel conversed with the king, and was honoured above all his friends. [3] Now the Babylons had an idol, called Bel, and there were spent upon him every day twelve great measures of fine flour, and forty sheep, and six vessels of wine. [4] And the king worshipped it and went daily to adore it: but Daniel worshipped his own God. And the king said unto him, Why dost not thou worship Bel? [5] Who answered and said, Because I may not worship idols made with hands, but the living God, who hath created the heaven and the earth, and hath sovereignty over all flesh. [6] Then said the king unto him, Thinkest thou not that Bel is a living God? seest thou not how much he eateth and drinketh every day? [7] Then Daniel smiled, and said, O king, be not deceived: for this is but clay within, and brass without, and did never eat or drink any thing. [8] So the king was wroth, and called for his priests, and said unto them, If ye tell me not who this is that devoureth these expences, ye shall die. [9] But if ye can certify me that Bel devoureth them, then Daniel shall die: for he hath spoken blasphemy against Bel. And Daniel said unto the king, Let it be according to thy word. [10] Now the priests of Bel were threescore and ten, beside their wives and children. And the king went with Daniel into the temple of Bel. [11] So Bel's priests said, Lo, we go out: but thou, O king, set on the meat, and make ready the wine, and shut the door fast and seal it with thine own signet; [12] And to morrow when thou comest in, if thou findest not that Bel hath eaten up all, we will suffer death: or else Daniel, that speaketh falsely against us. [13] And they little regarded it: for under the table they had made a privy entrance, whereby they entered in continually, and consumed those things. [14] So when they were gone forth, the king set meats before Bel. Now Daniel had commanded his servants to bring ashes, and those they strewed throughout all the temple in the presence of the king alone: then went they out, and shut the door, and sealed it with the king's signet, and so departed. [15] Now in the night came the priests with their wives and children, as they were wont to do, and did eat and drinck up all. [16] In the morning betime the king arose, and Daniel with him. [17] And the king said, Daniel, are the seals whole? And he said, Yea, O king, they be whole. [18] And as soon as he had opened the dour, the king looked upon the table, and cried with a loud voice, Great art thou, O Bel, and with thee is no deceit at all. [19] Then laughed Daniel, and held the king that he should not go in, and said, Behold now the pavement, and mark well whose footsteps are these. [20] And the king said, I see the footsteps of men, women, and children. And then the king was angry, [21] And took the priests with their wives and children, who shewed him the privy doors, where they came in, and consumed such things as were upon the table. [22] Therefore the king slew them, and delivered Bel into Daniel's power, who destroyed him and his temple. [23] And in that same place there was a great dragon, which they of Babylon worshipped. [24] And the king said unto Daniel, Wilt thou also say that this is of brass? lo, he liveth, he eateth and drinketh; thou canst not say that he is no living god: therefore worship him. [25] Then said Daniel unto the king, I will worship the Lord my God: for he is the living God. [26] But give me leave, O king, and I shall slay this dragon without sword or staff. The king said, I give thee leave. [27] Then Daniel took pitch, and fat, and hair, and did seethe them together, and made lumps thereof: this he put in the dragon's mouth, and so the dragon burst in sunder : and Daniel said, Lo, these are the gods ye worship. [28] When they of Babylon heard that, they took great indignation, and conspired against the king, saying, The king is become a Jew, and he hath destroyed Bel, he hath slain the dragon, and put the priests to death. [29] So they came to the king, and said, Deliver us Daniel, or else we will destroy thee and thine house. [30] Now when the king saw that they pressed him sore, being constrained, he delivered Daniel unto them: [31] Who cast him into the lions' den: where he was six days. [32] And in the den there were seven lions, and they had given them every day two carcases, and two sheep: which then were not given to them, to the intent they might devour Daniel. [33] Now there was in Jewry a prophet, called Habbacuc, who had made pottage, and had broken bread in a bowl, and was going into the field, for to bring it to the reapers. [34] But the angel of the Lord said unto Habbacuc, Go, carry the dinner that thou hast into Babylon unto Daniel, who is in the lions' den. [35] And Habbacuc said, Lord, I never saw Babylon; neither do I know where the den is. [36] Then the angel of the Lord took him by the crown, and bare him by the hair of his head, and through the vehemency of his spirit set him in Babylon over the den. [37] And Habbacuc cried, saying, O Daniel, Daniel, take the dinner which God hath sent thee. [38] And Daniel said, Thou hast remembered me, O God: neither hast thou forsaken them that seek thee and love thee. [39] So Daniel arose, and did eat: and the angel of the Lord set Habbacuc in his own place again immediately. [40] Upon the seventh day the king went to bewail Daniel: and when he came to the den, he looked in, and behold, Daniel was sitting. [41] Then cried the king with a loud voice, saying, Great art Lord God of Daniel, and there is none other beside thee. [42] And he drew him out, and cast those that were the cause of his destruction into the den: and they were devoured in a moment before his face.

1 ESDRAS

CHAPTER 1

[0] Josiah kept the passover to his Lord in Jerusalem; he killed the passover lamb on the fourteenth day of the first month, [1] having placed the priests according to their divisions, arrayed in their garments, in the temple of the Lord. [2] And he told the Levites, the temple servants of Israel, that they should sanctify themselves to the Lord and put the holy ark of the Lord in the house which Solomon the king, the son of David, had built; [3] and he said, "You need no longer carry it upon your shoulders. Now worship the Lord your God and serve his people Israel; and prepare yourselves by your families and kindred, [4] in accordance with the directions of David king of Israel and the magnificence of Solomon his son. Stand in order in the temple according to the groupings of the fathers' houses of you Levites, who minister before your brethren the

people of Israel, [5] and kill the passover lamb and prepare the sacrifices for your brethren, and keep the passover according to the commandment of the Lord which was given to Moses." [6] And Josiah gave to the people who were present thirty thousand lambs and kids, and three thousand calves; these were given from the king's possessions, as he promised, to the people and the priests and Levites. [7] And Hilkiah, Zechariah, and Jehiel, the chief officers of the temple, gave to the priests for the passover two thousand six hundred sheep and three hundred calves. [9} And Jeconiah and Shemaiah and Nethanel his brother, and Hashabiah and Ochiel and Joram, captains over thousands, gave the Levites for the passover five thousand sheep and seven hundred calves. [10] And this is what took place. The priests and the Levites, properly arrayed and having the unleavened bread, stood according to kindred [11] and the grouping of the fathers' houses, before the people, to make the offering to the Lord as it is written in the book of Moses; this they did in the morning. [12] They roasted the passover lamb with fire, as required; and they boiled the sacrifices in brass pots and caldrons, with a pleasing odor, [13] and carried them to all the people. Afterward they prepared the passover for themselves and for their brethren the priests, the sons of Aaron, [14} because the priests were offering the fat until night; so the Levites prepared it for themselves and for their brethren the priests, the sons of Aaron. [15] And the temple singers, the sons of Asaph, were in their place according to the arrangement made by David, and also Asaph, Zechariah, and Eddinus, who represented the king. [16] The gatekeepers were at each gate; no one needed to depart from his duties, for their brethren the Levites prepared the passover for them. [17] So the things that had to do with the sacrifices to the Lord were accomplished that day: the passover was kept [18] and the sacrifices were offered on the altar of the Lord, according to the command of King Josiah. [19] And the people of Israel who were present at that time kept the passover and the feast of unleavened bread seven days. [20] No passover like it had been kept in Israel since the times of Samuel the prophet; [21] none of the kings of Israel had kept such a passover as was kept by Josiah and the priests and Levites and the men of Judah and all of Israel who were dwelling in Jerusalem. [22] In the eighteenth year of the reign of Josiah this passover was kept [23] And the deeds of Josiah were upright in the sight of the Lord, for his heart was full of godliness. [24] The events of his reign have been recorded in the past, concerning those who sinned and acted wickedly toward the Lord beyond any other people or kingdom, and how they grieved the Lord deeply, so that the words of the Lord rose up against Israel. [25] After all these acts of Josiah, it happened that Pharaoh, king of Egypt, went to make war at Carchemish on the Euphrates, and Josiah went out against him. [26] And the king of Egypt sent word to him saying, "What have we to do with each other, king of Judea? [27] I was not sent against you by the Lord God, for my war is at the Euphrates. And now the Lord is with me! The Lord is with me, urging me on! Stand aside, and do not oppose the Lord." [28] But Josiah did not turn back to his chariot, but tried to fight with him, and did not heed the words of Jeremiah the prophet from the mouth of the Lord. [29] He joined battle with him in the plain of Megiddo, and the commanders came down against King Josiah. [30] And the king said to his servants, "Take me away from the battle, for I am very weak." And immediately his servants took him out of the line of battle. [31] And he got into his second chariot; and after he was brought back to Jerusalem he died, and was buried in the tomb of his fathers. [32] And in all Judea they mourned for Josiah. Jeremiah the prophet lamented for Josiah, and the principal men, with the women, have made lamentation for him to this day; it was ordained that this should always be done throughout the whole nation of Israel. [33] These things are written in the book of the histories of the kings of Judea; and every one of the acts of Josiah, and his splendor, and his understanding of the law of the Lord, and the things that he had done before and these that are now told, are recorded in the book of the kings of Israel and Judah. [34] And the men of the nation took Jeconiah the son of Josiah, who was twenty three years old, and made him king in succession to Josiah his father. [35] And he reigned three months in Judah and Jerusalem. Then the king of Egypt deposed him from reigning in Jerusalem, [36] and fined the nation a hundred talents of silver and a talent of gold. [37] And the king of Egypt made Jehoiakim his brother king of Judea and Jerusalem. [38] Jehoiakim put the nobles in prison, and seized his brother Zarius and brought him up out of Egypt. [39] Jehoiakim was twenty-five years old when he began to reign in Judea and Jerusalem, and he did what was evil in the sight of the Lord. [40] And Nebuchadnezzar king of Babylon came up against him, and bound him with a chain of brass and took him away to Babylon. [41] Nebuchadnezzar also took some holy vessels of the Lord, and carried them away, and stored them in his temple in Babylon. [42] But the things that are reported about Jehoiakim and his uncleanness and impiety are written in the chronicles of the kings. [43] Jehoiachin his son became king in his stead; when he was made king he was eighteen years old, and he reigned three months and ten days in Jerusalem. He did what was evil in the sight of the Lord. [45] So after a year Nebuchadnezzar sent and removed him to Babylon, with the holy vessels of the Lord, [46] and made Zedekiah king of Judea and Jerusalem. Zedekiah was twenty-one years old, and he reigned eleven years. [47] He also did what was evil in the sight of the Lord, and did not heed the words that were spoken by Jeremiah the prophet from the mouth of the Lord. [48] And though King Nebuchadnezzar had made him swear by the name of the Lord, he broke his oath and rebelled; and he stiffened his neck and hardened his heart and transgressed the laws of the Lord, the God of Israel. [49] Even the leaders of the people and of the priests committed many acts of sacrilege and lawlessness beyond all the unclean deeds of all the nations, and polluted the temple of the Lord which had been hallowed in Jerusalem. [50] So the God of their fathers sent by his messenger to call them back, because he would have spared them and his dwelling place. [51] But they mocked his messengers, and whenever the Lord spoke, they scoffed at his prophets, [52] until in his anger against his people because of their ungodly acts he gave command to bring against them the kings of the Chaldeans. [53] These slew their young men with the sword around their holy temple, and did not spare young man or virgin, old man or child, for he gave them all into their hands. [54] And all the holy vessels of the Lord, great and small, and the treasure chests of the Lord, and the royal stores, they took and carried away to Babylon. [55] And they burned the house of the Lord and broke down the walls of Jerusalem and burned their towers with fire, [56] and utterly destroyed all its glorious things. The survivors he led away to Babylon with the sword, [57] and they were servants to him and to his sons until the Persians began to reign, in fulfillment of the word of the Lord by the mouth of Jeremiah: [58] "Until the land has enjoyed its sabbaths, it shall keep sabbath all the time of its desolation until the completion of seventy years."

CHAPTER 2

[1] In the first year of Cyrus as king of the Persians, that the word of the Lord by the mouth of Jeremiah might be accomplished, [2] the Lord stirred up the spirit of Cyrus king of the Persians, and he made a proclamation throughout all his kingdom and also put it in writing: [3] "Thus says Cyrus king of the Persians: The Lord of Israel, the Lord Most High, has made me king of the world, [4] and he has commanded me to build him a house at Jerusalem, which is in Judea. [5] If any one of you, therefore, is of his people, may his Lord be with him, and let him go up to Jerusalem, which is in Judea, and build the house of the Lord of Israel -- he is the Lord who dwells in Jerusalem, [6] and let each man, wherever he may live, be helped by the men of his place with gold and silver, [7] with gifts and with horses and cattle, besides the other things added as votive offerings for the temple of the Lord which is in Jerusalem." [8] Then arose the heads of families of the tribes of Judah and Benjamin, and the priests and the Levites, and all whose spirit the Lord had stirred to go up to build the house in Jerusalem for the Lord; and their neighbors helped them with everything, with silver and gold, with ahorses and cattle, and with a very great number of votive offerings from many whose hearts were stirred. [10] Cyrus the king also brought out the holy vessels of the Lord which Nebuchadnezzar had carried away from Jerusalem and stored in his temple of idols. [11] When Cyrus king of the Perians brought these out, he gave them to Mithridates his treasurer, [12] and by him they were given to Sheshbazzar the governor of Judea. [13] The number of these was: a thousand gold cups, a thousand silver cups, twenty-nine silver censers, thirty gold bowls, two thousand four hundred and ten silver bowls, and a thousand other vessels. [14] All the vessels were handed over, gold and silver, five thousand four hundred and sixty-nine, [15] and they were carried back by Sheshbazzar with the returning exiles from Babylon to Jerusalem. [16] But in the time of Artaxerxes king of the Persians, Bishlam, Mithridates, Tabeel, Rehum, Beltethmus, Shimshai the scribe, and the rest of their associates, living in Samaria and other places, wrote him the following letter, against those who were living in Judea and Jerusalem: [17] "To King Artaxerxes our lord, Your servants Rehum the recorder and Shimshai the scribe and the other judges of their council in Coelesyria and Phoenicia: [18] Now be it known to our lord the king that the Jews who came up from you to us have gone to Jerusalem and are building that rebellious and wicked city, repairing its market places and walls and laying the foundations for a temple. [19] Now if this city is built and the walls finished, they will not only refuse to pay tribute but will even resist kings. [20] And since the building of the temple is now going on, we think it best not to neglect such a matter, [21] but to speak to our lord the king, in order that, if it seems good to you, search may be made in the records of your fathers. [22] You will find in the chronicles what has been written about them, and will learn that this city was rebellious, troubling both kings and other cities, [23] and that the Jews were rebels and kept setting up blockades in it from of old. That is why this city was laid waste. [24] Therefore we now make known to you, 0 lord and king, that if this city is built and its walls finished, you will no longer have access to Coelesyria and Phoenicia." [25] Then the king, in reply to Rehum the recorder and Beltethmus and Shimshai the scribe and the others associated with them and living in Samaria and Syria and Phoenicia, wrote as follows: [26] "1 have read the letter which you sent me. So I ordered search to be made, and it has been found that this city from of old has fought against kings, [27] and that the men in it were given to rebellion and war, and that mighty and cruel kings ruled in Jerusalem and exacted tribute from Coelesyria and Phoenicia. [28] Therefore I have now issued orders to prevent these men from building the city and to take care that nothing more be done [29] and that such wicked proceedings go no further to the annoyance of kings." [30] Then, when the letter from King Artaxerxes was read, Rehum and Shimshai the scribe and their associates went in haste to Jerusalem, with horsemen and a multitude in battle array, and began to hinder the builders. And the building of the temple in Jerusalem ceased until the second year of the reign of Darius king of the Persians.

CHAPTER 3

[1] Now King Darius gave a great banquet for all that were under him and all that were born in his house and all the nobles of Media and Persia [2] and all the satraps and generals and governors that were under him in the hundred and twenty-seven satrapies from India to Ethiopia. [3] They ate and drank, and when they were satisfied they departed; and Darius the king went to his bedroom, and went to sleep, and then awoke. [4] Then the three young men of the bodyguard, who kept guard over the person of the king, said to one another, [5] "Let each of us state what one thing is strongest; and to him whose statement seems wisest, Darius the king will give rich gifts and great honors of victory. [6] He shall be clothed in purple, and drink from gold cups, and sleep on a gold bed, and have a chariot with gold bridles, and a turban of fine linen, and a necklace about his neck; [7] and because of his wisdom he shall sit next to Darius and shall be called kinsman of Darius." [8] Then each wrote his own statement, and they sealed them and put them under the pillow of Darius the king, [9] and said, "When the king wakes, they will give him the writing; and to the one whose statement the king and the three nobles of Persia judge to be wisest the victory shall be given according to what is written." [10] The first wrote, "Wine is strongest." [11] The second wrote, "The king is strongest." [12] The third wrote, "Women are strongest, but truth is victor over all things." [13] When the king awoke, they took the writing and gave it to him, and he read it. [14] Then he sent and summoned all the nobles of Persia and Media and the satraps and generals and governors and prefects, [15] and he took his seat in the council chamber, and the writing was read in their presence. [16] And he said, "Call the young men, and they shall explain their statements." So they were summoned, and came in. [17] And they said to them, "Explain to us what you have written." Then the first, who had spoken of the strength of wine, began and said: [18] "Gentlemen, how is wine the strongest? It leads astray the minds of all who drink it. [19] It makes equal the mind of the king and the orphan, of the slave and the free, of the poor and the rich. [20] It turns every thought to feasting and mirth, and forgets all sorrow and debt. [21] It makes all hearts feel rich, forgets kings and satraps, and makes every one talk in millions. [22] When men drink they forget to be friendly with friends and brothers, and before long they draw their swords. [23] And when they recover from the wine, they do not remember what they have done. [24] Gentlemen, is not wine the strongest, since it forces men to do these things?" When he had said this, he stopped speaking.

CHAPTER 4

[1] Then the second, who had spoken of the strength of the king, began to speak: [2] "Gentlemen, are not men strongest, who rule over land and sea and all that is in them? [3] But the king is stronger; he is their lord and master, and whatever he says to them they obey. [4] If he tells them to make war on one another, they do it; and if he sends them out against the enemy, they go, and conquer mountains, walls, and towers. [5] They kill and are killed, and do not disobey the king's command; if they win the victory, they bring everything to the king -- whatever spoil they take and everything else. [6] Likewise those who do not serve in the army or make war but till the soil, whenever they sow, reap the harvest and bring some to the king; and they compel one another to pay taxes to the king. [7] And yet he is only one man! If he tells them to kill, they kill; if he tells them to release, they release; [8] if he tells them to attack, they attack; if he tells them to lay waste, they lay waste; if he tells them to build, they build; [9] [9] if he tells them to cut down, they cut down; if he tells them to plant, they plant. [10] All his people and his armies obey him. Moreover, he reclines, he eats and drinks and sleeps, [11] but they keep watch around him and no one may go away to attend to his own affairs, nor do they disobey him. [12] Gentlemen, why is not the king the strongest, since he is to be obeyed in this fashion?" And he stopped speaking. [13] Then the third, that is Zerubbabel, who had spoken of women and truth, began to speak: [14] Gentlemen, is not the king great, and are not men many, and is not wine strong? Who then is their master, or who is their lord? Is it not women? [15] Women gave birth to the king and to every people that rules over sea and land. [16] From women they came; and women brought up the very men who plant the vineyards from which comes wine. [17] Women make men's clothes; they bring men glory; men cannot exist without women. [18] If men gather gold and silver or any other beautiful thing, and then see a woman lovely in appearance and beauty, [19] they let all those things go, and gape at her, and with open mouths stare at her, and all prefer her to gold or silver or any other beautiful thing. [20] A man leaves his own father, who brought him up, and his own country, and cleaves to his wife. [21] With his wife he ends his days, with no thought of his father or his mother or his country. [22] Hence you must realize that women rule over you! "Do you not labor and toil, and bring everything and give it to women? [23] A man takes his sword, and goes out to travel and rob and steal and to sail the sea and rivers; [24] he faces lions, and he walks in darkness, and when he steals and robs and plunders, he brings it back to the woman he loves. [25] A man loves his wife more than his father or his mother. [26] Many men have lost their minds because of women, and have become slaves because of them. [27] Many have perished, or stumbled, or sinned, because of women. [28] And now do you not believe me? "Is not the king great in his power? Do not all lands fear to touch him? [29] Yet I have seen him with Apame, the king's concubine, the daughter of the illustrious Bartacus; she would sit at the king's right hand [30] [30] and take the crown from the king's head and put it on her own, and slap the king with her left hand. [31] At this the king would gaze at her with mouth agape. If she smiles at him, he laughs; if she loses her temper with him, he flatters her, that she may be reconciled to him. [32] Gentlemen, why are not women strong, since they do such things?" [33] Then the king and the nobles looked at one another; and he began to speak about truth: [34] "Gentlemen, are not women strong? The earth is vast, and heaven is high, and the sun is swift in its course, for it makes the circuit of the heavens and returns to its place in one day. [35] Is he not great who does these things? But truth is great, and stronger than all things. [36] The whole earth calls upon truth, and heaven blesses her. All God's works quake and tremble, and with him there is nothing unrighteous. [37] Wine is unrighteous, the king is unrighteous, women are unrighteous, all the sons of men are unrighteous, all their works are unrighteous, and all such things. There is no truth in them and in their unrighteousness they will perish. [38] But truth endures and is strong for ever, and lives and prevails for ever and ever. [39] With her there is no partiality or preference, but she does what is righteous instead of anything that is unrighteous or wicked. All men approve her deeds, [40] and there is nothing unrighteous in her judgment. To her belongs the strength and the kingship and the power and the majesty of all the ages. Blessed be the God of truth!" [41] He ceased speaking; then all the people shouted, and said, "Great is truth, and strongest of all!" [42] Then the king said to him, "Ask what you wish, even beyond what is written, and we will give it to you, for you have been found to be the wisest. And you shall sit next to me, and be called my kinsman." [43] Then he said to the king, "Remember the vow which you made to build Jerusalem, in the day when you became king, [44] and to send back all the vessels that were taken from Jerusalem, which Cyrus set apart when he began to destroy Babylon, and vowed to send them back there. [4S] You also vowed to build the temple, which the Edomites burned when Judea was laid waste by the Chaldeans. [46] And now, 0 lord the king, this is what I ask and request of you, and this befits your greatness. I pray therefore that you fulfil the vow whose fulfilment you vowed to the King of heaven with your own lips." [47] Then Darius the king rose, and kissed him, and wrote letters for him to all the treasurers and governors and generals and satraps, that they should give escort to him and all who were going up with him to build Jerusalem. [48] And he wrote letters to all the governors in Coelesyria and Phoenicia and to those in Lebanon, to bring cedar timber from Lebanon to Jerusalem, and to help him build the city. [49] And he wrote for all the Jews who were going up from his kingdom to Judea, in the interest of their freedom, that no officer or satrap or governor or treasurer should forcibly enter their doors; [SO] that all the country which they would occupy should be theirs without tribute; that the Idumeans should give up the villages of the Jews which they held; [Sl] that twenty talents a year should be given for the building of the temple until it was completed, [S2] and an additional ten talents a year for burnt offerings to be offered on the altar every day, in accordance with the commandment to make seventeen offerings; [S3] and that all who came from Babylonia to build the city should have their freedom, they and their children and all the priests who came. [S4] He wrote also concerning their support and the priests' garments in which they were to minister. [SS] He wrote that the support for the Levites should be provided until the day when the temple should be finished and Jerusalem built. [S6] He wrote that land and wages should be provided for all who guarded the city. [S7] And he sent back from Babylon all the vessels which Cyrus had set apart; everything that Cyrus had ordered to be done, he also commanded to be done and to be sent to Jerusalem. [58] When the young man went out, he lifted up his face to heaven toward Jerusalem, and praised the King of heaven, saying, [59] "From thee is the victory; from thee is wisdom, and your is the glory. I am thy servant. [60] [60] Blessed art thou, who hast given me wisdom; I give thee thanks, 0 Lord of our fathers." [61] So he took the letters, and went to Babylon and told this to all his brethren. [62] And they praised the God of their fathers, because he had given them release and permission [63] to go up and build Jerusalem and the temple which is called by his name; and they feasted, with music and rejoicing, for seven days.

CHAPTER 5

[1] After this the heads of fathers' houses were chosen to go up, according to their tribes, with their wives and sons and daughters, and their menservants and maidservants, and their cattle. [2] And Darius sent with them a thousand horsemen to take them back to Jerusalem in safety, with the music of drums and flutes; [3] [3] and all their brethren were making merry. And he made them go up with them. [4] [4] These are the names of the men who went up, according to their fathers' houses in the tribes, over their groups: [5] the priests, the sons of Phinehas, son of Aaron; Jeshua the son of Jozadak, son of Seraiah, and Joakim the son of Zerubbabel, son of Shealtiel, of the house of David, of the lineage of Phares, of the tribe of Judah, [6] who spoke wise words before Darius the king of the Persians, in the second year of his reign, in the month of Nisan, the first month. [7] These are the men of Judea who came up out of their sojourn in captivity, whom Nebuchadnezzar king of Babylon had carried away to Babylon [8] and who returned to Jerusalem and the rest of Judea, each to his own town. They came with Zerubbabel and Jeshua, Nehemiah, Seraiah, Resaiah, Bigvai, Mordecai, Bilshan, Mispar, Reeliah, Rehum, and Baanah, their leaders. [9] The number of the men of the nation and their leaders: the sons of Parosh, two thousand one hundred and seventy-two. The sons of Shephatiah, four hundred and seventy-two. [10] The sons of Arah, seven hundred and fifty-six. [11] The sons of Pahathmoab, of the sons of Jeshua and Joab, two thousand eight hundred and twelve. [12] The sons of Elam, one thousand two hundred and fifty four. The sons of Zattu, nine hundred and forty-five. The sons of Chorbe, seven hundred and five. The sons of Bani, six hundred and forty-eight. [13] The sons of Bebai, six hundred and twenty-three. The sons of Azgad, one thousand three hundred and twenty-two. [14] The sons of Adonikam, six hundred and sixty-seven. The sons of Bigvai, two thousand and sixty-six. The sons of Adin, four hundred and fifty-four. [15] The sons of Ater, namely of Hezekiah, ninety-two. The sons of Kilan and Azetas, sixty-seven. The sons of Azaru, four hundred and thirty-two. [16] The sons of Annias, one hundred and one. The sons of Arom. The sons of Bezai, three hundred and twenty-three. The sons of Jorah, one hundred and twelve. [17] The sons of Baiterus, three thousand and five. The sons of Bethlehem, one hundred and twenty-three. [18] The men of Netophah, fifty-five. The men of Anathoth, one hundred and fifty-eight. The men of Bethasmoth, forty-two. [19] The men of Kiriatharim, twenty-five. The men of Chephirah and Beeroth, seven hundred and forty-three. [20] The Chadiasans and Ammidians, four hundred and twenty-two. The men of Ramah and Geba, six hundred and twenty-one. [21] The men of Michmas, one hundred and twenty-two. The men of Bethel, fifty-two. The sons of Magbish, one hundred and fifty-six. [22] The sons of the other Elam and Ono, seven hundred and twenty-five. The sons of Jericho, three hundred and forty-five. [23] The sons of Senaah, three thousand three hundred and thirty. [24] The priests: the sons of Jedaiah the son of Jeshua, of the sons of Anasib, nine hundred and seventy-two. The sons of Immer, one thousand and fifty-two. [25] The sons of Pashhur, one thousand two hundred and forty-seven. The sons of Harim, one thousand and seventeen. [26] The Levites: the sons of Jeshua and Kadmiel and Bannas and Sudias, seventy-four. [27] The temple singers: the sons of Asaph, one hundred and twenty-eight. [28] The gatekeepers: the sons of Shallum, the sons of Ater, the sons of Talmon, the sons of Akkub, the sons of Hatita, the sons of Shobai, in all one hundred and thirty-nine. [29] The temple servants: the sons of Ziha, the sons of Hasupha, the sons of Tabbaoth, the sons of Keros, the sons of Siaha, the sons of Padon, the sons of Lebanah, the sons of Hagabah, [30] the sons of Akkub, the sons of Uthai, the sons of Ketab, the sons of Hagab, the sons of Shamlai, the sons of Hana, the sons of Cathua, the sons of Gahar, [31] The sons of Reaiah, the sons of Rezin, the sons of Nekoda, the sons of Chezib, the sons of Gazzam, the sons of Uzza, the sons of Paseah, the sons of Hasrah, the sons of Besai, the sons of Asnah, the sons of the Meunites, the sons of Nephisim, the sons of Bakbuk, the sons of Hakupha, the sons of Asur, the sons of Pharakim, the sons of Bazluth, [32] the sons of Mehida, the sons of Cutha, the sons of Charea, the sons of Barkos, the sons of Sisera, the sons of Temah, the sons of Neziah, the sons of Hatipha. [33] The sons of Solomon's servants: the sons of Hassophereth, the sons of Peruda, the sons of Jaalah, the sons of Lozon, the sons of Giddel, the sons of Shephatiah, [34] the sons of Hattil, the sons of Pochereth-hazzebaim, the sons of Sarothie, the sons of Masiah, the sons of Gas, the sons of Addus, the sons of Subas, the sons of Apherra, the sons of Barodis, the sons of Shaphat, the sons of Ami. [35] All the temple servants and the sons of Solomon's servants were three hundred and seventy-two. [36] The following are those who came up from Telmelah and Telharsha, under the leadership of Cherub, Addan, and Immer, [37] though they could not prove by their fathers' houses or lineage that they belonged to Israel: the sons of Delaiah the son of Tobiah, the sons of Nekoda, six hundred and fifty-two. [38] Of the priests the following had assumed the priesthood but were not found registered: the sons of Habaiah, the sons of Hakkoz, the sons of Jaddus who had married Agia, one of the daughters of Barzillai, and was called by his name. [39] And when the genealogy of these men was sought in the register and was not found, they were excluded from serving as priests. [40] And Nehemiah and Attharias told them not to share in the holy things until a high priest should appear wearing Urim and Thummim. [41] All those of Israel, twelve or more years of age, besides menservants and maidservants, were forty-two thousand three hundred and sixty; [42] their menservants and maidservants were seven thousand three hundred and thirty-seven; there were two hundred and forty-five musicians and singers. [43] There were four hundred and thirty-five camels, and seven thousand and thirty-six horses, two hundred and forty-five mules, and five thousand five hundred and twenty-five asses. [44] Some of the heads of families, when they came to the temple of God which is in Jerusalem, vowed that they would erect the house on its site, to the best of their ability, [45] and that they would give to the sacred treasury for the work a thousand minas of gold, five thousand minas of silver, and one hundred priests' garments. [46] The priests, the Levites, and some of the people settled in Jerusalem and its vicinity; and the temple singers, the gatekeepers, and all Israel in their towns. [47] When the seventh month came, and the sons of Israel were each in his own home, they gathered as one man in the square before the first gate toward the east. [48] Then Jeshua the son of Jozadak, with his fellow priests, and Zerubbabel the son of Shealtiel, with his kinsmen, took their places and prepared the altar of the God of Israel, [49] to offer burnt offerings upon it, in accordance with the directions in the book of Moses the man of God. [50] And some joined them from the other peoples of the land. And they erected the altar in its place, for all the peoples of the land were hostile to them and were stronger than they; and they offered sacrifices at the proper times and burnt offerings to the Lord morning and evening. [51] They kept the feast of booths, as it is commanded in the law, and offered the proper sacrifices every day, [52] and thereafter the continual offerings and sacrifices on sabbaths

and at new moons and at all the consecrated feasts. [53] And all who had made any vow to God began to offer sacrifices to God, from the new moon of the seventh month, though the temple of God was not yet built. [54] And they gave money to the masons and the carpenters, and food and drink [55] and carts to the Sidonians and the Tyrians, to bring cedar logs from Lebanon and convey them in rafts to the harbor of Joppa, according to the decree which they had in writing from Cyrus king of the Persians. [56] In the second year after their coming to the temple of God in Jerusalem, in the second month, Zerubbabel the son of Shealtiel and Jeshua the son of Jozadak made a beginning, together with their brethren and the Levitical priests and all who had come to Jerusalem from the captivity; [57] and they laid the foundation of the temple of God on the new moon of the second month in the second year after they came to Judea and Jerusalem. [58] And they appointed the Levites who were twenty or more years of age to have charge of the work of the Lord. And Jeshua arose, and his sons and brethren and Kadmiel his brother and the sons of Jeshua Emadabun and the sons of Joda son of Iliadun, with their sons and brethren, all the Levites, as one man pressing forward the work on the house of God. So the builders built the temple of the Lord. [59] And the priests stood arrayed in their garments, with musical instruments and trumpets, and the Levites, the sons of Asaph, with cymbals, [60] praising the Lord and blessing him, according to the directions of David king of Israel; [61] and they sang hymns, giving thanks to the Lord, because his goodness and his glory are for ever upon all Israel. [62] And all the people sounded trumpets and shouted with a great shout, praising the Lord for the erection of the house of the Lord. [63] Some of the Levitical priests and heads of fathers' houses, old men who had seen the former house, came to the building of this one with outcries and loud weeping, [64] while many came with trumpets and a joyful noise, [65] so that the people could not hear the trumpets because of the weeping of the people. For the multitude sounded the trumpets loudly, so that the sound was heard afar; [66] and when the enemies of the tribe of Judah and Benjamin heard it, they came to find out what the sound of the trumpets meant. [67] And they learned that those who had returned from captivity were building the temple for the Lord God of Israel. [68] So they approached Zerubbabel and Jeshua and the heads of the fathers' houses and said to them, "We will build with you. [69] For we obey your Lord just as you do and we have been sacrificing to him ever since the days of Esarhaddon king of the Assyrians, who brought us here." [70] But Zerubbabel and Jeshua and the heads of the fathers' houses in Israel said to them, "You have nothing to do with us in building the house for the Lord our God, [71] for we alone will build it for the Lord of Israel, as Cyrus the king of the Persians has commanded us." [72] But the peoples of the land pressed hard upon those in Judea, cut off their supplies, and hindered their building; [73] and by plots and demagoguery and uprisings they prevented the completion of the building as long as King Cyrus lived. And they were kept from building for two years, until the reign of Darius.

CHAPTER 6

[1] Now in the second year of the reign of Darius, the prophets Haggai and Zechariah the son of Iddo prophesied to the Jews who were in Judea and Jerusalem, they prophesied to them in the name of the Lord God of Israel. [2] Then Zerubbabel the son of Shealtiel and Jeshua the son of Jozadak arose and began to build the house of the Lord which is in Jerusalem, with the help of the prophets of the Lord who were with them. [3] At the same time Sisinnes the governor of Syria and Phoenicia and Sathrabuzanes and their associates came to them and said, [4] "By whose order are you building this house and this roof and finishing all the other things? And who are the builders that are finishing these things?" [5] Yet the elders of the Jews were dealt with kindly, for the providence of the Lord was over the captives; [6] and they were not prevented from building until word could be sent to Darius concerning them and a report made. [7] A copy of the letter which Sisinnes the governor of Syria and Phoenicia, and Sathrabuzanes, and their associates the local rulers in Syria and Phoenicia, wrote and sent to Darius: [8] "To King Darius, greeting. Let it be fully known to our lord the king that, when we went to the country of Judea and entered the city of Jerusalem, we found the elders of the Jews, who had been in captivity, [9] building in the city of Jerusalem a great new house for the Lord, of hewn stone, with costly timber laid in the walls. [10] These operations are going on rapidly, and the work is prospering in their hands and being completed with all splendor and care. [11] Then we asked these elders, 'At whose command are you building this house and laying the foundations of this structure?' [12] And in order that we might inform you in writing who the leaders are, we questioned them and asked them for a list of the names of those who are at their head. [13] They answered us, 'We are the servants of the Lord who created the heaven and the earth. [14] And the house was built many years ago by a king of Israel who was great and strong, and it was finished. [15] But when our fathers sinned against the Lord of Israel who is in heaven, and provoked him, he gave them over into the hands of Nebuchadnezzar king of Babylon, king of the Chaldeans; [16] and they pulled down the house, and burned it, and carried the people away captive to Babylon. [17] But in the first year that Cyrus reigned over the country of Babylonia, King Cyrus wrote that this house should be rebuilt. [18] And the holy vessels of gold and of silver, which Nebuchadnezzar had taken out of the house in Jerusalem and stored in his own temple, these Cyrus the king took out again from the temple in Babylon, and they were delivered to Zerubbabel and Sheshbazzar the governor [19] with the command that he should take all these vessels back and put them in the temple at Jerusalem, and that this temple of the Lord should be rebuilt on its site. [20] Then this Sheshbazzar, after coming here, laid the foundations of the house of the Lord which is in Jerusalem, and although it has been in process of construction from that time until now, it has not yet reached completion.' [21] Now therefore, if it seems wise, 0 king, let search be made in the royal archives of our lord the king that are in Babylon; [22] and if it is found that the building of the house of the Lord in Jerusalem was done with the consent of King Cyrus, and if it is approved by our lord the king, let him send us directions concerning these things." [23] Then Darius commanded that search be made in the royal archives that were deposited in Babylon. And in Ecbatana, the fortress which is in the country of Media, a scroll was found in which this was recorded: [24] "In the first year of the reign of Cyrus, King Cyrus ordered the building of the house of the Lord in Jerusalem, where they sacrifice with perpetual fire; [25] its height to be sixty cubits and its breadth sixty cubits, with three courses of hewn stone and one course of new native timber; the cost to be paid from the treasury of Cyrus the king; [26] and that the holy vessels of the house of the Lord, both of gold and of silver, which Nebuchadnezzar took out of the house in Jerusalem and carried away to Babylon, should be restored to the house in Jerusalem, to be placed where they had been." [27] So Darius

commanded Sisinnes the governor of Syria and Phoenicia, and Sathrabuzanes, and their associates, and those who were appointed as local rulers in Syria and Phoenicia, to keep away from the place, and to permit Zerubbabel, the servant of the Lord and governor of Judea, and the elders of the Jews to build this house of the Lord on its site. [28] "And I command that it be built completely, and that full effort be made to help the men who have returned from the captivity of Judea, until the house of the Lord is finished; [29] and that out of the tribute of Coelesyria and Phoenicia a portion be scrupulously given to these men, that is, to Zerubbabel the governor, for sacrifices to the Lord, for bulls and rams and lambs, [30] and likewise wheat and salt and wine and oil, regularly every year, without quibbling, for daily use as the priests in Jerusalem may indicate, [31] in order that libations may be made to the Most High God for the king and his children, and prayers be offered for their life." [32] And he commanded that if any should transgress or nullify any of the things herein written, a beam should be taken out of his house and he should be hanged upon it, and his property should be forfeited to the king. [33] "Therefore may the Lord, whose name is there called upon, destroy every king and nation that shall stretch out their hands to hinder or damage that house of the Lord in Jerusalem. "I, King Darius, have decreed that it be done with all diligence as here prescribed. "

CHAPTER 7

[1] Then 5isinnes the governor of Coelesyria and Phoenicia, and 5athrabuzanes, and their associates, following the orders of King Darius, [2] supervised the holy work with very great care, assisting the elders of the Jews and the chief officers of the temple. [3] And the holy work prospered, while the prophets Haggai and Zechariah prophesied; [4] and they completed it by the command of the Lord God of Israel. 50 with the consent of Cyrus and Darius and Artaxerxes, kings of the Persians, [5] the holy house was finished by the twenty-third day of the month of Adar, in the sixth year of King Darius. [6] And the people of Israel, the priests, the Levites, and the rest of those from the captivity who joined them, did according to what was written in the book of Moses. [7] They offered at the dedication of the temple of the Lord one hundred bulls, two hundred rams, four hundred lambs, [8] and twelve he-goats for the sin of all Israel, according to the number of the twelve leaders of the tribes of Israel; [9] and the priests and the Levites stood arrayed in their garments, according to kindred, for the services of the Lord God of Israel in accordance with the book of Moses; and the gatekeepers were at each gate. [10] The people of Israel who came from the captivity kept the passover on the fourteenth day of the first month, after the priests and the Levites were purified together. [11] Not all of the returned captives were purified, but the Levites were all purified together, [12] and they sacrificed the passover lamb for all the returned captives and for their brethren the priests and for themselves. [13] And the people of Israel who came from the captivity ate it, all those who had separated themselves from the abominations of the peoples of the land and sought the Lord. [14] And they kept the feast of unleavened bread seven days, rejoicing before the Lord, [15] Because he had changed the will of the king of the Assyrians concerning them, to strengthen their hands for the service of the Lord God of Israel.

CHAPTER 8

[1] After these things, when Artaxerxes the king of the Persians was reigning, Ezra came, the son of Seraiah, son of Azariah, son of Hilkiah, son of 5hallum, [2] son of Zadok, son of Ahitub, son of Amariah, son of Uzzi, son of Bukki, son of Abishua, son of Phineas, son of Eleazar, son of Aaron the chief priest. [3] This Ezra came up from Babylon as a scribe skilled in the law of Moses, which was given by the God of Israel; [4] and the king showed him honor, for he found favor before the king in all his requests. [5] There came up with him to Jerusalem some of the people of Israel and some of the priests and Levites and temple singers and gatekeepers and temple servants, [6] in the seventh year of the reign of Artaxerxes, in the fifth month (this was the king's seventh year); for they left Babylon on the new moon of the first month and arrived in Jerusalem on the new moon of the fifth month, by the prosperous journey which the Lord gave them. [7] For Ezra possessed great knowledge, so that he omitted nothing from the law of the Lord or the commandments, but taught all Israel all the ordinances and judgments. [8] The following is a copy of the written commission from Artaxerxes the king which was delivered to Ezra the priest and reader of the law of the Lord: [9] "King Artaxerxes to Ezra the priest and reader of the law of the Lord, greeting. [10] In accordance with my gracious decision, I have given orders that those of the Jewish nation and of the priests and Levites and others in our realm, who freely choose to do so, may go with you to Jerusalem. [11] Let as many as are so disposed, therefore, depart with you as I and the seven friends who are my counselors have decided, [12] in order to look into matters in Judea and Jerusalem, in accordance with what is in the law of the Lord, [13] and to carry to Jerusalem the gifts for the Lord of Israel which I and my friends have vowed, and to collect for the Lord in Jerusalem all the gold and silver that may be found in the country of Babylonia, [14] together with what is given by the nation for the temple of their Lord which is in Jerusalem, both gold and silver for bulls and rams and lambs and what goes with them, [15] so as to offer sacrifices upon the altar of their Lord which is in Jerusalem. [16] And whatever you and your brethren are minded to do with the gold and silver, perform it in accordance with the will of your God; [17] and deliver the holy vessels of the Lord which are given you for the use of the temple of your God which is in Jerusalem. [18] And whatever else occurs to you as necessary for the temple of your God, you may provide out of the royal treasury. [19] "And I, Artaxerxes the king, have commanded the treasurers of Syria and Phoenicia that whatever Ezra the priest and reader of the law of the Most High God sends for, they shall take care to give him, [20] up to a hundred talents of silver, and likewise up to a hundred cors of wheat, a hundred baths of wine, and salt in abundance. [21] Let all things prescribed in the law of God be scrupulously fulfilled for the Most High God, so that wrath may not come upon the kingdom of the king and his sons. [22] You are also informed that no tribute or any other tax is to be laid on any of the priests or Levites or temple singers or gatekeepers or temple servants or persons employed in this temple, and that no one has authority to impose any tax upon them. [23] "And you, Ezra, according to the wisdom of God, appoint judges and justices to judge all those who know the law of your God, throughout all Syria and Phoenicia; and those who do not know it you shall teach. [24] And all who transgress the law of your God or the law of the kingdom a shall be strictly punished, whether by death or some other punishment, either fine or imprisonment." [25] Blessed be the Lord alone, who put this into the heart of the king, to glorify his house which is in Jerusalem, [26] and who honored me in the sight of the king and

his counselors and all his friends and nobles. [27] I was encouraged by the help of the Lord my God, and I gathered men from Israel to go up with me. [28] These are the principal men, according to their fathers' houses and their groups, who went up with me from Babylon, in the reign of Artaxerxes the king: Of the sons of Phineas, Gershom. Of the sons of Ithamar, Gamael. Of the sons of David, Hattush the son of Shecaniah. [30] Of the sons of Parosh, Zechariah, and with him a hundred and fifty men enrolled. [31] Of the sons of Pahathmoab, Eliehoenai the son of Zerahiah, and with him two hundred men. [32] Of the sons of Zattu, Shecaniah the son of Jahaziel, and with him three hundred men. Of the sons of Adin, Obed the son of Jonathan, and with him two hundred and fifty men. [33] Of the sons of Elam, Jeshaiah the son of Gotholiah, and with him seventy men. [34] Of the sons of Shephatiah, Zeraiah the son of Michael, and with him seventy men, [35] Of the sons of Joab, Obadiah the son of Jehiel, and with him two hundred and twelve men. [36] Of the sons of Bani, Shelomith the son of Josiphiah, and with him a hundred and sixty men. [37] Of the sons of Bebai, Zechariah the son of Bebai, and with him twenty-eight men. [38] Of the sons of Azgad, Johanan the son of Hakkatan, and with him a hundred and ten men. [39] Of the sons of Adonikam, the last ones, their names being Eliphelet, Jeuel, and Shemaiah, and with them seventy men. [40] Of the sons of Bigvai, Uthai the son of Istalcurus, and with him seventy men. [41] I assembled them at the river called Theras, and we encamped there three days, and I inspected them. [42] When I found there none of the sons of the priests or of the Levites, [43] I sent word to Eliezar, Iduel, Maasmas, [44] Elnathan, Shemaiah, Jarib, Nathan, Elnathan, Zechariah, and Meshullam, who were leaders and men of understanding; [45] and I told them to go to Iddo, who was the leading man at the place of the treasury, [46] and ordered them to tell Iddo and his brethren and the treasurers at that place to send us men to serve as priests in the house of our Lord. [47] And by the mighty hand of our Lord they brought us competent men of the sons of Mahli the son of Levi, son of Israel, namely Sherebiah with his sons and kinsmen, eighteen; [48] also Hashabiah and Annunus and Jeshaiah his brother, of the sons of Hananiah, and their sons, twenty men; [49] and of the temple servants, whom David and the leaders had given for the service of the Levites, two hundred and twenty temple servants; the list of all their names was reported. [50] There I proclaimed a fast for the young men before our Lord, to seek from him a prosperous journey for ourselves and for our children and the cattle that were with us. [51] For I was ashamed to ask the king for foot soldiers and horsemen and an escort to keep us safe from our adversaries; [52] for we had said to the king, "The power of our Lord will be with those who seek him, and will support them in every way." [53] And again we prayed to our Lord about these things, and we found him very merciful. [54] Then I set apart twelve of the leaders of the priests, 5herebiah and Hashabiah, and ten of their kinsmen with them; and I weighed out to them the silver and the gold and the holy vessels of the house of our Lord, which the king himself and his counselors and the nobles and all Israel had given. [56] I weighed and gave to them six hundred and fifty talents of silver, and silver vessels worth a hundred talents, and a hundred talents of gold, [57] and twenty golden bowls, and twelve bronze vessels of fine bronze that glittered like gold. [58] And I said to them, "You are holy to the Lord, and the vessels are holy, and the silver and the gold are vowed to the Lord, the Lord of our fathers. [59] Be watchful and on guard until you deliver them to the leaders of the priests and the Levites, and to the heads of the fathers' houses of Israel, in Jerusalem, in the chambers of the house of our Lord." [60] So the priests and the Levites who took the silver and the gold and the vessels which had been in Jerusalem carried them to the temple of the Lord. [61] We departed from the river Theras on the twelfth day of the first month; and we arrived in Jerusalem by the mighty hand of our Lord which was upon us; he delivered us from every enemy on the way, and so we came to Jerusalem. When we had been there three days, the silver and the gold were weighed and delivered in the house of our Lord to Meremoth the priest, son of Uriah; [63] and with him was Eleazar the son of Phinehas, and with them were Jozabad the son of Jeshua and Moeth the son of Binnui, the Levites. The whole was counted and weighed, and the weight of everything was recorded at that very time. [65] And those who had come back from captivity offered sacrifices to the Lord, the God of Israel, twelve bulls for all Israel, ninety-six rams, [66] seventy-two lambs, and as a thank offering twelve he-goats -- all as a sacrifice to the Lord. [67] And they delivered the king's orders to the royal stewards and to the governors of Coelesyria and Phoenicia; and these officials honored the people and the temple of the Lord. [68] After these things had been done, the principal men came to me and said, "The people of Israel and the leaders and the priests and the Levites have not put away from themselves the alien peoples of the land and their pollutions, the Canaanites, the Hittites, the Perizzites, the Jebusites, the Moabites, the Egyptians, and the Edomites. [70] For they and their sons have married the daughters of these people, and the holy race has been mixed with the alien peoples of the land; and from the beginning of this matter the leaders and the nobles have been sharing in this iniquity." [71] As soon as I heard these things I rent my garments and my holy mantle, and pulled out hair from my head and beard, and sat down in anxiety and grief. [72] And all who were ever moved at the word of the Lord of Israel gathered round me, as I mourned over this iniquity, and I sat grief-stricken until the evening sacrifice. [73] Then I rose from my fast, with my garments and my holy mantle rent, and kneeling down and stretching forth my hands to the Lord [74] I said, "0 Lord, I am ashamed and confounded before thy face. For our sins have risen higher than our heads, and our mistakes have mounted up to heaven [76] from the times of our fathers, and we are in great sin to this day. [77] And because of our sins and the sins of our fathers we with our brethren and our kings and our priests were given over to the kings of the earth, to the sword and captivity and plundering, in shame until this day. [78] And now in some measure mercy has come to us from thee, 0 Lord, to leave to us a root and a name in thy holy place, [79] and to uncover a light for us in the house of the Lord our God, and to give us food in the time of our servitude. [80] Even in our bondage we were not forsaken by our Lord, but he brought us into favor with the kings of the Persians, so that they have given us food [81] and glorified the temple of our Lord, and raised Zion from desolation, to give us a stronghold in Judea and Jerusalem. [82] "And now, 0 Lord, what shall we say, when we have these things? For we have transgressed thy commandments, which thou didst give by thy servants the prophets, saying, [83] 'The land which you are entering to take possession of it is a land polluted with the pollution of the aliens of the land, and they have filled it with their uncleanness. [84] Therefore do not give your daughters in marriage to their sons, and do not take their daughters for your sons; [85] and do not seek ever to have peace with them, in order that you may be strong and eat the good things of the land and leave it for an inheritance to your children for ever.' [86] And all that has happened to us has come about because of our evil deeds and our great sins. For thou, 0 Lord, didst lift the burden of our sins [87] and give us such a root as this; but we turned back again to transgress thy law by mixing with the uncleanness of the peoples of the land. [88] Wast thou not angry enough with us to destroy us without leaving a root or seed or name? [89] 0 Lord of Israel, thou art true; for we are left as a root to this day. [90] Behold, we are now before thee in our iniquities; for we can no longer stand in thy presence because of these things." [91] While Ezra was praying and making his confession, weeping and lying upon the ground before the temple, there gathered about him a very great throng from Jerusalem, men and women and youths; for there was great weeping among the multitude. [92] Then Shecaniah the son of Jehiel, one of the men of Israel, called out, and said to Ezra, "We have sinned against the Lord, and have married foreign women from the peoples of the land; but even now there is hope for Israel. [93] Let us take an oath to the Lord about this, that we will put away all our foreign wives, with their children, [94] as seems good to you and to all who obey the law of the Lord. [95] Arise and take action, for it is your task, and we are with you to take strong measures." [96] Then Ezra arose and had the leaders of the priests and Levites of all Israel take oath that they would do this. And they took the oath.

CHAPTER 9

[1] Then Ezra rose and went from the court of the temple to the chamber of Jehohanan the son of Eliashib, [2] and spent the night there; and he did not eat bread or drink water, for he was mourning over the great iniquities of the multitude. [3] And a proclamation was made throughout Judea and Jerusalem to all who had returned from the captivity that they should assemble at Jerusalem, [4] and that if any did not meet there within two or three days, in accordance with the decision of the ruling elders, their cattle should be seized for sacrifice and the men themselves expelled from the multitude of those who had returned from the captivity. [5] Then the men of the tribe of Judah and Benjamin assembled at Jerusalem within three days; this was the ninth month, on the twentieth day of the month. And all the multitude sat in the open square before the temple, shivering because of the bad weather that prevailed. [7] Then Ezra rose and said to them, "You have broken the law and married foreign women, and so have increased the sin of Israel. [8] Now then make confession and give glory to the Lord the God of our fathers, [9] and do his will; separate yourselves from the peoples of the land and from your foreign wives." [10] Then all the multitude shouted and said with a loud voice, "We will do as you have said. [11] But the multitude is great and it is winter, and we are not able to stand in the open air. This is not a work we can do in one day or two, for we have sinned too much in these things. [12] so let the leaders of the multitude stay, and let all those in our settlements who have foreign wives come at the time appointed, [13] with the elders and judges of each place, until we are freed from the wrath of the Lord over this matter." [14] Jonathan the son of Asahel and Jahzeiah the son of Tikvah undertook the matter on these terms, and Meshullam and Levi and Shabbethai served with them as judges. [15] And those who had returned from the captivity acted in accordance with all this. [16] Ezra the priest chose for himself the leading men of their fathers' houses, all of them by name; and on the new moon of the tenth month they began their sessions to investigate the matter. [17] And the cases of the men who had foreign wives were brought to an end by the new moon of the first month. [18] Of the priests those who were brought in and found to have foreign wives were: [19] of the sons of Jeshua the son of Jozadak and his brethren, Maaseiah, Eliezar, Jarib, and Jodan. [20] They pledged themselves to put away their wives, and to give rams in expiation of their error. [21] Of the sons of Immer: Hanani and Zebadiah and Maaseiah and Shemaiah and Jehiel and Azariah. [22] Of the sons of Pashhur: Elioenai, Maaseiah, Ishmael, and Nathanael, and Gedaliah, and Elasah. [23] And of the Levites: Jozabad and Shimei and Kelaiah, who was Kelita, and Pethahiah and Judah and Jonah. [24] Of the temple singers: Eliashib and Zaccur. [25] Of the gatekeepers: Shallum and Telem. [26] Of Israel: of the sons of Parosh: Ramiah, Izziah, Malchijah, Mijamin, and Eleazar, and Asibias, and Benaiah. [27] Of the sons of Elam: Mattaniah and Zechariah, Jehiel and Abdi, and Jeremoth and Elijah. [28] Of the sons of Zattu: Elioenai, Eliashib, Othoniah, Jeremoth, and Zabad and Zerdaiah. [29] Of the sons of Bebai: Jehohanan and Hananiah and Zabbai and Emathis. [30] Of the sons of Bani: Meshullam, Malluch, Adaiah, Jashub, and Sheal and Jeremoth. [31] Of the sons of Addi: Naathus and Moossias, Laccunus and Naidus, and Bescaspasmys and Sesthel, and Belnuus and Manasseas. [32] Of the sons of Annan, Elionas and Asaias and Melchias and Sabbaias and Simon Chosamaeus. [33] Of the sons of Hashum: Mattenai and Mattattah and Zabad and Eliphelet and Manasseh and Shimei. [34] Of the sons of Bani: Jeremai, Maadai, Amram, Joel, Mamdai and Bedeiah and Vaniah, Carabasion and Eliashib and Machnadebai, Eliasis, Binnui, Elialis, Shimei, Shelemiah, Nethaniah. Of the sons of Ezora: Shashai, Azarel, Azael, Shemaiah, Amariah, Joseph. [35] Of the sons of Nebo: Mattithiah, Zabad, Iddo, Joel, Benaiah. [36] All these had married foreign women, and they put them away with their children. [37] The priests and the Levites and the men of Israel settled in Jerusalem and in the country. On the new moon of the seventh month, when the sons of Israel were in their settlements, [38] the whole multitude gathered with one accord into the open square before the east gate of the temple; [39] and they told Ezra the chief priest and reader to bring the law of Moses which had been given by the Lord God of Israel. [40] So Ezra the chief priest brought the law, for all the multitude, men and women, and all the priests to hear the law, on the new moon of the seventh month. [41] And he read aloud in the open square before the gate of the temple from early morning until midday, in the presence of both men and women; and all the multitude gave attention to the law. [42] Ezra the priest and reader of the law stood on the wooden platform which had been prepared; [43] and beside him stood Mattathiah, Shema, Anaiah, Azariah, Uriah, Hezekiah, and Baalsamus on his right hand, [44] and on his left Pedaiah, Mishael, Malchijah, Lothasubus, Nabariah, and Zechariah. [45] Then Ezra took up the book of the law in the sight of the multitude, for he had the place of honor in the presence of all. [46] And when he opened the law, they all stood erect. And Ezra blessed the Lord God Most High, the God of hosts, the Almighty; [47] and all the multitude answered, "Amen." And they lifted up their hands, and fell to the ground and worshiped the Lord. [48] Jeshua and Anniuth and Sherebiah, Jamin, Akkub, Shabbethai, Hodiah, Maaseiah and Kelita, Azariah and Jozabad, Hanan, Pelaiah, the Levites, taught the law of the Lord, at the same time explaining what was read. [49] Then Attharates said to Ezra the chief priest and reader, and to the Levites who were teaching the multitude, and to all, [50] "This day is holy to the Lord" -- now they were all weeping as they heard the law -- [51] "so go your way, eat the fat and drink the sweet, and send portions to those who have none; [52] for the day is holy to the Lord; and do not be sorrowful, for the Lord will exalt you." [53] And the Levites commanded all the people, saying, "This day is holy; do not be sorrowful." [54] Then they all went their way, to eat and drink and enjoy themselves, and to give portions to those

who had none, and to make great rejoicing; [55] because they were inspired by the words which they had been taught. And they came together.

2 ESDRAS (4 EZRA)

2 ESDRAS .1

[1] The second book of the prophet Ezra the son of Seraiah, son of Azariah, son of Hilkiah, son of Shallum, son of Zadok, son of Ahitub, [2] son of Ahijah, son of Phinehas, son of Eli, son of Amariah, son of Azariah, son of Meraioth, son of Arna, son of Uzzi, son of Borith, son of Abishua, son of Phinehas, son of Eleazar, [3] son of Aaron, of the tribe of Levi, who was a captive in the country of the Medes in the reign of Artaxerxes, king of the Persians. [4] The word of the Lord came to me, saying, [5] "Go and declare to my people their evil deeds, and to their children the iniquities which they have committed against me, so that they may tell their children's children [6] that the sins of their parents have increased in them, for they have forgotten me and have offered sacrifices to strange gods. [7] Was it not I who brought them out of the land of Egypt, out of the house of bondage? But they have angered me and despised my counsels. [8] Pull out the hair of your head and hurl all evils upon them, for they have not obeyed my law -- they are a rebellious people. [9] How long shall I endure them, on whom I have bestowed such great benefits? [10] For their sake I have overthrown many kings; I struck down Pharaoh with his servants, and all his army. [11] I have destroyed all nations before them, and scattered in the east the people of two provinces, Tyre and Sidon; I have slain all their enemies. [12] "But speak to them and say, Thus says the Lord: Surely it was I who brought you through the sea, and made safe highways for you where there was no road; I gave you Moses as leader and Aaron as priest; [14] I provided light for you from a pillar of fire, and did great wonders among you. Yet you have forgotten me, says the Lord. [15] "Thus says the Lord Almighty: The quails were a sign to you; I gave you camps for your protection, and in them you complained. You have not exulted in my name at the destruction of your enemies, but to this day you still complain. [17] Where are the benefits which I bestowed on you? When you were hungry and thirsty in the wilderness, did you not cry out to me, [18] saying, 'Why hast thou led us into this wilderness to kill us? It would have been better for us to serve the Egyptians than to die in this wilderness.' [19] I pitied your groanings and gave you manna for food; you ate the bread of angels. [20] When you were thirsty, did I not cleave the rock so that waters flowed in abundance? Because of the heat I covered you with the leaves of trees. [21] I divided fertile lands among you; I drove out the Canaanites, the Perizzites, and the Philistines before you. What more can I do for you? says the Lord. [22] Thus says the Lord Almighty: When you were in the wilderness, at the bitter stream, thirsty and blaspheming my name, [23] I did not send fire upon you for your blasphemies, but threw a tree into the water and made the stream sweet. [24] "What shall I do to you, 0 Jacob? You would not obey me, 0 Judah. I will turn to other nations and will give them my name, that they may keep my statutes. [25] Because you have forsaken me, I also will forsake you. When you beg mercy of me, I will show you no mercy. [26] When you call upon me, I will not listen to you; for you have defiled your hands with blood, and your feet are swift to commit murder. [27] It is not as though you had forsaken me; you have forsaken yourselves, says the Lord. [28] "Thus says the Lord Almighty: Have I not entreated you as a father entreats his sons or a mother her daughters or a nurse her children, that you should be my people and I should be your God, and that you should be my sons and I should be your father? [30] I gathered you as a hen gathers her brood under her wings. But now, what shall I do to you? I will cast you out from my presence. [31] When you offer oblations to me, I will turn my face from you; for I have rejected your feast days, and new moons, and circumcisions of the flesh. [32] I sent to you my servants the prophets, but you have taken and slain them and torn their bodies in pieces; their blood I will require of you, says the Lord. [33] "Thus says the Lord Almighty: Your house is desolate; I will drive you out as the wind drives straw; 34. and your sons will have no children, because with you they have neglected my commandment and have done what is evil in my sight. [35] I will give your houses to a people that will come, who without having heard me will believe. Those to whom I have shown no signs will do what I have commanded. [36] They have seen no prophets, yet will recall their former state. [37] I call to witness the gratitude of the people that is to come, whose children rejoice with gladness; though they do not see me with bodily eyes, yet with the spirit they will believe the things I have said. [38] "And now, father, look with pride and see the people coming from the east; [39] to them I will give as leaders Abraham, Isaac, and Jacob and Hosea and Amos and Micah and Joel and Obadiah and Jonah [40] and Nahum and Habakkuk, Zephaniah, Haggai, Zechariah and Malachi, who is also called the messenger of the Lord.

2 ESDRAS. 2

[1] "Thus says the Lord: I brought this people out of bondage, and I gave them commandments through my servants the prophets; but they would not listen to them, and made my counsels void. [2] The mother who bore them says to them, 'Go, my children, because I am a widow and forsaken. [3] I brought you up with gladness; but with mourning and sorrow I have lost you, because you have sinned before the Lord God and have done what is evil in my sight. [4] But now what can I do for you? For I am a widow and forsaken. Go, my children, and ask for mercy from the Lord.' [5] I call upon you, father, as a witness in addition to the mother of the children, because they would not keep my covenant, [6] that you may bring confusion upon them and bring their mother to ruin, so that they may have no offspring. [7] Let them be scattered among the nations, let their names be blotted out from the earth, because they have despised my covenant. [8] "Woe to you, Assyria, who conceal the unrighteous in your midst! 0 wicked nation, remember what I did to 50dom and Gomorrah, [9] whose land lies in lumps of pitch and heaps of ashes. So will I do to those who have not listened to me, says the Lord Almighty." [10] Thus says the Lord to Ezra: "Tell my people that I will give them the kingdom of Jerusalem, which I was going to give to Israel. [11] Moreover, I will take back to myself their glory, and will give to these others the everlasting habitations, which I had prepared for Israel. [12] The tree of life shall give them fragrant perfume, and they shall neither toil nor become weary. [13] Ask and you will receive; pray that your days may be few, that they may be shortened. The kingdom is already prepared for you; watch! [14] Call, 0 call heaven and earth to witness, for I left out evil and created good, because I live, says the Lord. [15] "Mother, embrace your sons; bring them up with gladness, as does the dove;

establish their feet, because I have chosen you, says the Lord. [16] And I will raise up the dead from their places, and will bring them out from their tombs, because I recognize my name in them. [17] Do not fear, mother of sons, for I have chosen you, says the Lord. [18] I will send you help, my servants Isaiah and Jeremiah. According to their counsel I have consecrated and prepared for you twelve trees loaded with various fruits, [19] and the same number of springs flowing with milk and honey, and seven mighty mountains on which roses and lilies grow; by these I will fill your children with joy. [20] Guard the rights of the widow, secure justice for the fatherless, give to the needy, defend the orphan, clothe the naked, [21] care for the injured and the weak, do not ridicule a lame man, protect the maimed, and let the blind man have a vision of my splendor. [22] Protect the old and the young within your walls; [23] When you find any who are dead, commit them to the grave and mark it, and I will give you the first place in my resurrection. [24] Pause and be quiet, my people, because your rest will come. [25] Good nurse, nourish your sons, and strengthen their feet. [26] Not one of the servants whom I have given you will perish, for I will require them from among your number. [27] Do not be anxious, for when the day of tribulation and anguish comes, others shall weep and be sorrowful, but you shall rejoice and have abundance. [28] The nations shall envy you but they shall not be able to do anything against you, says the Lord. [29] My hands will cover you, that your sons may not see Gehenna. [30] Rejoice, 0 mother, with your sons, because I will deliver you, says the Lord. [31] Remember your sons that sleep, because I will bring them out of the hiding places of the earth, and will show mercy to them; for I am merciful, says the Lord Almighty. [32] Embrace your children until I come, and proclaim mercy to them; because my springs run over, and my grace will not fail." [33] I, Ezra, received a command from the Lord on Mount Horeb to go to Israel. When I came to them they rejected me and refused the Lord's commandment. [34] Therefore I say to you, 0 nations that hear and understand, "Await your shepherd; he will give you everlasting rest, because he who will come at the end of the age is close at hand. [35] Be ready for the rewards of the kingdom, because the eternal light will shine upon you for evermore. [36] Flee from the shadow of this age, receive the joy of your glory; I publicly call on my Savior to witness. [37] Receive what the Lord has entrusted to you and be joyful, giving thanks to him who has called you to heavenly kingdoms. [38] Rise and stand, and see at the feast of the Lord the number of those who have been sealed. [39] Those who have departed from the shadow of this age have received glorious garments from the Lord. [40] Take again your full number, 0 Zion, and conclude the list of your people who are clothed in white, who have fulfilled the law of the Lord. [41] The number of your children, whom you desired, is full; beseech the Lord's power that your people, who have been called from the beginning, may be made holy." [42] I, Ezra, saw on Mount Zion a great multitude, which I could not number, and they all were praising the Lord with songs. [43] In their midst was a young man of great stature, taller than any of the others, and on the head of each of them he placed a crown, but he was more exalted than they. And I was held spellbound. [44] Then I asked an angel, "Who are these, my lord?" [45] He answered and said to me, "These are they who have put off mortal clothing and have put on the immortal, and they have confessed the name of God; now they are being crowned, and receive palms." [46] Then I said to the angel, "Who is that young man who places crowns on them and puts palms in their hands?" [47] He answered and said to me, "He is the Son of God, whom they confessed in the world." So I began to praise those who had stood valiantly for the name of the Lord. [48] Then the angel said to me, "Go, tell my people how great and many are the wonders of the Lord God which you have seen."

2 ESDRAS. 3

[1] In the thirtieth year after the destruction of our city, I Salathiel, who am also called Ezra, was in Babylon. I was troubled as I lay on my bed, and my thoughts welled up in my heart, [2] because I saw the desolation of Zion and the wealth of those who lived in Babylon. [3] My spirit was greatly agitated, and I began to speak anxious words to the Most High, and said, [4] "0 sovereign Lord, didst thou not speak at the beginning when thou didst form the earth -- and that without help -- and didst command the dust [5] and it gave thee Adam, a lifeless body? Yet he was the workmanship of thy hands, and thou didst breathe into him the breath of life, and he was made alive in thy presence. [6] And thou didst lead him into the garden which thy right hand had planted before the earth appeared. [7] And thou didst lay upon him one commandment of your; but he transgressed it, and immediately thou didst appoint death for him and for his descendants. From him there sprang nations and tribes, peoples and clans without number. [8] And every nation walked after its own will and did ungodly things before thee and scorned thee, and thou didst not hinder them. [9] But again, in its time thou didst bring the flood upon the inhabitants of the world and destroy them. [10] And the same fate befell them: as death came upon Adam, so the flood upon them. [11] But thou didst leave one of them, Noah with his household, and all the righteous who have descended from him. [12] "When those who dwelt on earth began to multiply, they produced children and peoples and many nations, and again they began to be more ungodly than were their ancestors. And when they were committing iniquity before thee, thou didst choose for thyself one of them, whose name was Abraham; [14] and thou didst love him, and to him only didst thou reveal the end of the times, secretly by night. [15] Thou didst make with him an everlasting covenant, and promise him that thou wouldst never forsake his descendants; and thou gavest to him Isaac, and to Isaac thou gavest Jacob and Esau. [16] And thou didst set apart Jacob for thyself, but Esau thou didst reject; and Jacob became a great multitude. [17] And when thou didst lead his descendants out of Egypt, thou didst bring them to Mount Sinai. [18] Thou didst bend down the heavens and shake the earth, and move the world, and make the depths to tremble, and trouble the times. [19] And thy glory passed through the four gates of fire and earthquake and wind and ice, to give the law to the descendants of Jacob, and thy commandment to the posterity of Israel. [20] "Yet thou didst not take away from them their evil heart, so that thy law might bring forth fruit in them. For the first Adam, burdened with an evil heart, transgressed and was overcome, as were also all who were descended from him. [22] Thus the disease became permanent; the law was in the people's heart along with the evil root, but what was good departed, and the evil remained. [23] So the times passed and the years were completed, and thou didst raise up for thyself a servant, named David. [24] And thou didst command him to build a city for thy name, and in it to offer thee oblations from what is your. [25] This was done for many years; but the inhabitants of the city transgressed, [26] in everything doing as Adam and all his descendants had done, for they also had the evil heart. [27] So thou didst deliver the city into the hands of thy enemies. [28] "Then I said in my heart, Are the deeds of those who inhabit Babylon any better? Is that why she has gained dominion over Zion? [29] For when I

came here I saw ungodly deeds without number, and my soul has seen many sinners during these thirty years. And my heart failed me, [30] for I have seen how thou do endure those who sin, and hast spared those who act wickedly, and hast destroyed thy people, and hast preserved thy enemies, [31] and hast not shown to any one how thy way may be comprehended. Are the deeds of Babylon better than those of Zion? [32] Or has another nation known thee besides Israel? Or what tribes have so believed thy covenants as these tribes of Jacob? [33] Yet their reward has not appeared and their labor has borne no fruit. For I have traveled widely among the nations and have seen that they abound in wealth, though they are unmindful of thy commandments. [34] Now therefore weigh in a balance our iniquities and those of the inhabitants of the world; and so it will be found which way the turn of the scale will incline. [35] When have the inhabitants of the earth not sinned in thy sight? Or what nation has kept thy commandments so well? [36] Thou mayest indeed find individual men who have kept thy commandments, but nations thou wilt not find."

2 ESDRAS. 4

[1] Then the angel that had been sent to me, whose name was Uriel, answered [2] and said to me, "Your understanding has utterly failed regarding this world, and do you think you can comprehend the way of the Most High?" [3] Then I said, "Yes, my lord." And he replied to me, "I have been sent to show you three ways, and to put before you three problems. [4] If you can solve one of them for me, I also will show you the way you desire to see, and will teach you why the heart is evil." [5] I said, "Speak on, my lord." And he said to me, "Go, weigh for me the weight of fire, or measure for me a measure of wind, or call back for me the day that is past." [6] I answered and said, "Who of those that have been born can do this, that you ask me concerning these things?" [7] And he said to me, "If I had asked you, 'How many dwellings are in the heart of the sea, or how many streams are at the source of the deep, or how many streams are above the firmament, or which are the exits of hell, or which are the entrances of paradise?' [8] Perhaps you would have said to me, 'I never went down into the deep, nor as yet into hell, neither did I ever ascend into heaven.' [9] But now I have asked you only about fire and wind and the day, things through which you have passed and without which you cannot exist, and you have given me no answer about them!" [10] And he said to me, "You cannot understand the things with which you have grown up; [11] how then can your mind comprehend the way of the Most High? And how can one who is already worn out by the corrupt world understand incorruption?" When I heard this, I fell on my face [12] and said to him, "It would be better for us not to be here than to come here and live in ungodliness, and to suffer and not understand why." [13] He answered me and said, "I went into a forest of trees of the plain, and they made a plan [14] and said, 'Come, let us go and make war against the sea, that it may recede before us, and that we may make for ourselves more forests.' [15] And in like manner the waves of the sea also made a plan and said, 'Come, let us go up and subdue the forest of the plain so that there also we may gain more territory for ourselves.' [16] But the plan of the forest was in vain, for the fire came and consumed it; [17] likewise also the plan of the waves of the sea, for the sand stood firm and stopped them. [18] If now you were a judge between them, which would you undertake to justify, and which to condemn?" [19] I answered and said, "Each has made a foolish plan, for the land is assigned to the forest, and to the sea is assigned a place to carry its waves." [20] He answered me and said, "You have judged rightly, but why have you not judged so in your own case? [21] For as the land is assigned to the forest and the sea to its waves, so also those who dwell upon earth can understand only what is on the earth, and he who is above the heavens can understand what is above the height of the heavens." [22] Then I answered and said, "I beseech you, my lord, why have I been endowed with the power of understanding? [23] For I did not wish to inquire about the ways above, but about those things which we daily experience: why Israel has been given over to the Gentiles as a reproach; why the people whom you loved has been given over to godless tribes, and the law of our fathers has been made of no effect and the written covenants no longer exist; [24] and why we pass from the world like locusts, and our life is like a mist, and we are not worthy to obtain mercy. [25] But what will he do for his name, by which we are called? It is about these things that I have asked." [26] He answered me and said, "If you are alive, you will see, and if you live long, you will often marvel, because the age is hastening swiftly to its end. [27] For it will not be able to bring the things that have been promised to the righteous in their appointed times, because this age is full of sadness and infirmities. [28] For the evil about which you ask me has been sown, but the harvest of it has not yet come. [29] If therefore that which has been sown is not reaped, and if the place where the evil has been sown does not pass away, the field where the good has been sown will not come. [30] For a grain of evil seed was sown in Adam's heart from the beginning, and how much ungodliness it has produced until now, and will produce until the time of threshing comes! [31] Consider now for yourself how much fruit of ungodliness a grain of evil seed has produced. [32] When heads of grain without number are sown, how great a threshing floor they will fill!" [33] Then I answered and said, "How long and when will these things be? Why are our years few and evil?" [34] He answered me and said, "You do not hasten faster than the Most High, for your haste is for yourself, but the Highest hastens on behalf of many. [3S] Did not the souls of the righteous in their chambers ask about these matters, saying, 'How long are we to remain here? And when will come the harvest of our reward? [36] And Jeremiel the archangel answered them and said, 'When the number of those like yourselves is completed; for he has weighed the age in the balance, [37] and measured the times by measure, and numbered the times by number; and he will not move or arouse them until that measure is fulfilled.'" [38] Then I answered and said, "0 sovereign Lord, but all of us also are full of ungodliness. [39] And it is perhaps on account of us that the time of threshing is delayed for the righteous -- on account of the sins of those who dwell on earth." [40] He answered me and said, "Go and ask a woman who is with child if, when her nine months have been completed, her womb can keep the child within her any longer." [41] And I said, "No, lord, it cannot." And he said to me, "In Hades the chambers of the souls are like the womb. [42] For just as a woman who is in travail makes haste to escape the pangs of birth, so also do these places hasten to give back those things that were committed to them from the beginning. [43] Then the things that you desire to see will be disclosed to you." [44] I answered and said, "If I have found favor in your sight, and if it is possible, and if I am worthy, [4S] show me this also: whether more time is to come than has passed, or whether for us the greater part has gone by. [46] For I know what has gone by, but I do not know what is to come." [47] And he said to me, "Stand at my right side, and I will show you the interpretation of a parable." [48] So I stood and looked, and behold, a flaming furnace passed by before me, and when the

flame had gone by I looked, and behold, the smoke remained. [49] And after this a cloud full of water passed before me and poured down a heavy and violent rain, and when the rainstorm had passed, drops remained in the cloud. [SO] And he said to me, "Consider it for yourself; for as the rain is more than the drops, and the fire is greater than the smoke, so the quantity that passed was far greater; but drops and smoke remained." [Sl] Then I prayed and said, "Do you think that I shall live until those days? Or who will be alive in those days?" [S2] He answered me and said, "Concerning the signs about which you ask me, I can tell you in part; but I was not sent to tell you concerning your life, for I do not know.

2 ESDRAS. 5

[1] "Now concerning the signs: behold, the days are coming when those who dwell on earth shall be seized with great terror, and the way of truth shall be hidden, and the land shall be barren of faith. [2] And unrighteousness shall be increased beyond what you yourself see, and beyond what you heard of formerly. [3] And the land which you now see ruling shall be waste and untrod den, and men shall see it desolate. [4] But if the Most High grants that you live, you shall see it thrown into confusion after the third period; and the sun shall suddenly shine forth at night,and the moon during the day. [5] Blood shall drip from wood,and the stone shall utter its voice;the peoples shall be troubled, and the stars shall fall. [6] And one shall reign whom those who dwell on earth do not expect, and the birds shall fly away together; [7] and the sea of Sodom shall cast up fish; and one whom the many do not know shall make his voice heard by night, and all shall hear his voice. [8] There shall be chaos also in many places, and fire shall often break out, and the wild beasts shall roam beyond their haunts, and menstruous women shall bring forth monsters. [9] And salt waters shall be found in the sweet, and all friends shall conquer one another; then shall reason hide itself, and wisdom shall withdraw into its chamber, [10] and it shall be sought by many but shall not be found, and unrighteousness and unrestraint shall increase on earth. [11] And one country shall ask its neighbor, 'Has righteousness, or any one who does right, passed through you?' And it will answer, 'No.' [12] And at that time men shall hope but not obtain; they shall labor but their ways shall not prosper. [13] These are the signs which I am permitted to tell you, and if you pray again, and weep as you do now, and fast for seven days, you shall hear yet greater things than these." [14] Then I awoke, and my body shuddered violently, and my soul was so troubled that it fainted. [15] But the angel who had come and talked with me held me and strengthened me and set me on my feet. [16] Now on the second night Phaltiel, a chief of the people, came to me and said, "Where have you been? And why is your face sad? [17] Or do you not know that Israel has been entrusted to you in the land of their exile? [18] Rise therefore and eat some bread, so that you may not forsake us, like a shepherd who leaves his flock in the power of cruel wolves." [19] Then I said to him, "Depart from me and do not come near me for seven days, and then you may come to me." He heard what I said and left me. [20] So I fasted seven days, mourning and weeping, as Uriel the angel had commanded me. [21] And after seven days the thoughts of my heart were very grievous to me again. [22] Then my soul recovered the spirit of understanding, and I began once more to speak words in the presence of the Most High. [23] And I said, "0 sovereign Lord, from every forest of the earth and from all its trees thou hast chosen one vine, [24] and from all the lands of the world thou hast chosen for thyself one region, and from all the flowers of the world thou hast chosen for thyself one lily, [25] and from all the depths of the sea thou hast filled for thyself one river, and from all the cities that have been built thou hast consecrated Zion for thyself, [26] and from all the birds that have been created thou hast named for thyself one dove, and from all the flocks that have been made thou hast provided for thyself one sheep, [27] and from all the multitude of peoples thou hast gotten for thyself one people; and to this people, whom thou hast loved, thou hast given the law which is approved by all. [28] And now, 0 Lord, why hast thou given over the one to the many, and dishonored the one root beyond the others, and scattered your only one among the many? [29] And those who opposed thy promises have trodden down those who believed thy covenants. [30] If thou do really hate thy people, they should be punished at thy own hands." [31] When I had spoken these words, the angel who had come to me on a previous night was sent to me, [32] and he said to me, "Listen to me, and I will instruct you; pay attention to me, and I will tell you more." [33] And I said, "Speak, my lord." And he said to me, "Are you greatly disturbed in mind over Israel? Or do you love him more than his Maker does?" [34] And I said, "No, my lord, but because of my grief I have spoken; for every hour I suffer agonies of heart, while I strive to understand the way of the Most High and to search out part of his judgment." [35] And he said to me, "You cannot." And I said, "Why not, my lord? Why then was I born? Or why did not my mother's womb become my grave, that I might not see the travail of Jacob and the exhaustion of the people of Israel?" [36] He said to me, "Count up for me those who have not yet come, and gather for me the scattered raindrops, and make the withered flowers bloom again for me; [37] open for me the closed chambers, and bring forth for me the winds shut up in them, or show me the picture of a voice; and then I will explain to you the travail that you ask to understand." [38] And I said, "0 sovereign Lord, who is able to know these things except he whose dwelling is not with men? [39] As for me, I am without wisdom, and how can I speak concerning the things which thou hast asked me?" [40] He said to me, "Just as you cannot do one of the things that were mentioned, so you cannot discover my judgment, or the goal of the love that I have promised my people." [41] And I said, "Yet behold, 0 Lord, thou do have charge of those who are alive at the end, but what will those do who were before us, or we, or those who come after us?" [42] He said to me, "I shall liken my judgment to a circle; just as for those who are last there is no slowness, so for those who are first there is no haste." [43] Then I answered and said, "Couldst thou not have created at one time those who have been and those who are and those who will be, that thou mightest show thy judgment the sooner?" [44] He replied to me and said, "The creation cannot make more haste than the Creator, neither can the world hold at one time those who have been created in it." [45] And I said, "How hast thou said to thy servant that thou wilt certainly give life at one time to thy creation? If therefore all creatures will live at one time and the creation will sustain them, it might even now be able to support all of them present at one time." [46] He said to me, "Ask a woman's womb, and say to it, 'If you bear ten children, why one after another?' Request it therefore to produce ten at one time." [47] I said, "Of course it cannot, but only each in its own time." [48] He said to me, "Even so have I given the womb of the earth to those who from time to time are sown in it. [49] For as an infant does not bring forth, and a woman who has become old does not bring forth any longer, so have I organized the world which I created." [50] Then I inquired and said, "Since thou hast now given me the opportunity, let me speak before thee. Is our mother, of whom thou hast told me, still young? Or is

she now approaching old age?" [51] He replied to me, "Ask a woman who bears children, and she will tell you. [52] Say to her, "Why are those whom you have borne recently not like those whom you bore before, but smaller in stature?' [53] And she herself will answer you, 'Those born in the strength of youth are different from those born during the time of old age, when the womb is failing.' [54] Therefore you also should consider that you and your contemporaries are smaller in stature than those who were before you, [55] and those who come after you will be smaller than you, as born of a creation which already is aging and passing the strength of youth." [56] And I said, "0 Lord, I beseech thee, if I have found favor in thy sight, show thy servant through whom thou do visit thy creation."

2 ESDRAS. 6

[1] And he said to me, "At the beginning of the circle of the earth, before the portals of the world were in place, and before the assembled winds blew, [2] and before the rumblings of thunder sounded, and before the flashes of lightning shone, and before the foundations of paradise were laid, [3] and before the beautiful flowers were seen, and before the powers of movement were established, and before the innumerable hosts of angels were gathered together, [4] and before the heights of the air were lifted up, and before the measures of the firm aments were named, and before the footstool of Zion was established, [5] and before the present years were reckoned; and before the imaginations of those who now sin were estranged, and before those who stored up treasures of faith were sealed -- [6] then I planned these things, and they were made through me and not through another, just as the end shall come through me and not through another." [7] And I answered and 'said, "What will be the dividing of the times? Or when will be the end of the first age and the beginning of the age that follows?" [8] He said to me, "From Abraham to Isaac, because from him were born Jacob and Esau, for Jacob's hand held Esau's heel from the beginning. [9] For Esau is the end of this age, and Jacob is the beginning of the age that follows. [10] For the beginning of a man is his hand, and the end of a man is his heel; between the heel and the hand seek for nothing else, Ezra!" [11] I answered and said, "0 sovereign Lord, if I have found favor in thy sight, [12] show thy servant the end of thy signs which thou didst show me in part on a previous night." [13] He answered and said to me, "Rise to your feet and you will hear a full, resounding voice. [14] And if the place where you are standing is greatly shaken [15] while the voice is speaking, do not be terrified; because the word concerns the end, and the foundations of the earth will understand [16] that the speech concerns them. They will tremble and be shaken, for they know that their end must be changed." [17] When I heard this, I rose to my feet and listened, and behold, a voice was speaking, and its sound was like the sound of many waters. [18] And it said, "Behold, the days are coming, and it shall be that when I draw near to visit the inhabitants of the earth, [19] and when I require from the doers of iniquity the penalty of their iniquity, and when the humiliation of Zion is complete, [20] and when the seal is placed upon the age which is about to pass away, then I will show these signs: the books shall be opened before the firmament, and all shall see it together. [21] Infants a year old shall speak with their voices, and women with child shall give birth to premature children at three and four months, and these shall live and dance. [22] Sown places shall suddenly appear unsown, and full storehouses shall suddenly be found to be empty; [23] and the trumpet shall sound aloud, and when all hear it, they shall suddenly be terrified. [24] At that time friends shall make war on friends like enemies, and the earth and those who inhabit it shall be terrified, and the springs of the fountains shall stand still, so that for three hours they shall not flow. [25] "And it shall be that whoever remains after all that I have foretold to you shall himself be saved and shall see my salvation and the end of my world. [26] And they shall see the men who were taken up, who from their birth have not tasted death; and the heart of the earth's inhabitants shall be changed and converted to a different spirit. [27] For evil shall be blotted out, and deceit shall be quenched; [28] faithfulness shall flourish, and corruption shall be overcome, and the truth, which has been so long without fruit, shall be revealed." [29] While he spoke to me, behold, little by little the place where I was standing began to rock to and fro. [30] And he said to me, "I have come to show you these things this night. [31] If therefore you will pray again and fast again for seven days, I will again declare to you greater things than these, [32] because your voice has surely been heard before the Most High; for the Mighty One has seen your uprightness and has also observed the purity which you have maintained from your youth. [33] Therefore he sent me to show you all these things, and to say to you: 'Believe and do not be afraid! [34] Do not be quick to think vain thoughts concerning the former times, lest you be hasty concerning the last times.'" [35] Now after this I wept again and fasted seven days as before, in order to complete the three weeks as I had been told. [36] And on the eighth night my heart was troubled within me again, and I began to speak in the presence of the Most High. [37] For my spirit was greatly aroused, and my soul was in distress. [38] I said, "0 Lord, thou didst speak at the beginning of creation, and didst say on the first day, 'Let heaven and earth be made,' and thy word accomplished the work. [39] And then the Spirit was hovering, and darkness and silence embraced everything; the sound of man's voice was not yet there. [40] Then thou didst command that a ray of light be brought forth from thy treasuries, so that thy works might then appear. [41] "Again, on the second day, thou didst create the spirit of the firmament, and didst command him to divide and separate the waters, that one part might move upward and the other part remain beneath. [42] "On the third day thou didst command the waters to be gathered together in the seventh part of the earth; six parts thou didst dry up and keep so that some of them might be planted and cultivated and be of service before thee. [43] For thy word went forth, and at once the work was done. [44] For immediately fruit came forth in endless abundance and of varied appeal to the taste; and flowers of inimitable color; and odors of inexpressible fragrance. These were made on the third day. [45] "On the fourth day thou didst command the brightness of the sun, the light of the moon, and the arrangement of the stars to come into being; [46] and thou didst command them to serve man, who was about to be formed. [47] "On the fifth day thou didst command the seventh part, where the water had been gathered together, to bring forth living creatures, birds, and fishes; and so it was done. [48] The dumb and lifeless water produced living creatures, as it was commanded, that therefore the nations might declare thy wondrous works. [49] "Then thou didst keep in existence two living creatures; the name of one thou didst call Behemoth and the name of the other Leviathan. [50] And thou didst separate one from the other, for the seventh part where the water had been gathered together could not hold them both. [51] And thou didst give Behemoth one of the parts which had been dried up on the third day, to live in it, where there are a thousand mountains; [52] but to Leviathan thou didst give the seventh part, the watery part; and thou hast kept them to be eaten by whom thou wilt, and

when thou wilt. [53] "On the sixth day thou didst command the earth to bring forth before thee cattle, beasts, and creeping things; [54] and over these thou didst place Adam, as ruler over all the works which thou hadst made; and from him we have all come, the people whom thou hast chosen. [55] "All this I have spoken before thee, 0 Lord, because thou hast said that it was for us that thou didst create this world. [56] As for the other nations which have descended from Adam, thou hast said that they are nothing, and that they are like spittle, and thou hast compared their abundance to a drop from a bucket. [57] And now, 0 Lord, behold, these nations, which are reputed as nothing, domineer over us and devour us. [58] But we thy people, whom thou hast called thy first-born, only begotten, zealous for thee, and most dear, have been given into their hands. [59] If the world has indeed been created for us, why do we not possess our world as an inheritance? How long will this be so?"

2 ESDRAS. 7

[1] When I had finished speaking these words, the angel who had been sent to me on the former nights was sent to me again, [2] and he said to me, "Rise, Ezra, and listen to the words that I have come to speak to you." [3] I said, "Speak, my lord." And he said to me, "There is a sea set in a wide expanse so that it is broad and vast, [4] but it has an entrance set in a narrow place, so that it is like a river. [5] If any one, then, wishes to reach the sea, to look at it or to navigate it, how can he come to the broad part unless he passes through the narrow part? [6] Another example: There is a city built and set on a plain, and it is full of all good things; [7] but the entrance to it is narrow and set in a precipitous place, so that there is fire on the right hand and deep water on the left; [8] and there is only one path lying between them, that is, between the fire and the water, so that only one man can walk upon that path. [9] If now that city is given to a man for an inheritance, how will the heir receive his inheritance unless he passes through the danger set before him?" [10] I said, "He cannot, lord." And he said to me, "So also is Israel's portion. [11] For I made the world for their sake, and when Adam transgressed my statutes, what had been made was judged. [12] And so the entrances of this world were made narrow and sorrowful and toilsome; they are few and evil, full of dangers and involved in great hardships. [13] But the entrances of the greater world are broad and safe, and really yield the fruit of immortality. [14] Therefore unless the living pass through the difficult and vain experiences, they can never receive those things that have been reserved for them. [15] But now why are you disturbed, seeing that you are to perish? And why are you moved, seeing that you are mortal? [16] And why have you not considered in your mind what is to come, rather than what is now present?" [17] Then I answered and said, "0 sovereign Lord, behold, thou hast ordained in thy law that the righteous shall inherit these things, but that the ungodly shall perish. [18] The righteous therefore can endure difficult circumstances while hoping for easier ones; but those who have done wickedly have suffered the difficult circumstances and will not see the easier ones." [19] And he said to me, "You are not a better judge than God, or wiser than the Most High! [20] Let many perish who are now living, rather than that the law of God which is set before them be disregarded! [21] For God strictly commanded those who came into the world, when they came, what they should do to live, and what they should observe to avoid punishment. [22] Nevertheless they were not obedient, and spoke against him; they devised for themselves vain thoughts, [23] and proposed to themselves wicked frauds; they even declared that the Most High does not exist, and they ignored his ways! [24] They scorned his law, and denied his covenants; they have been unfaithful to his statutes, and have not performed his works. [25] "Therefore, Ezra, empty things are for the empty, and full things are for the full. [26] For behold, the time will come, when the signs which I have foretold to you will come to pass, that the city which now is not seen shall appear, and the land which now is hidden shall be disclosed. [27] And every one who has been delivered from the evils that I have foretold shall see my wonders. [28] For my son the Messiah shall be revealed with those who are with him, and those who remain shall rejoice four hundred years. [29] And after these years my son the Messiah shall die, and all who draw human breath. [30] And the world shall be turned back to primeval silence for seven days, as it was at the first beginnings; so that no one shall be left. [31] And after seven days the world, which is not yet awake, shall be roused, and that which is corruptible shall perish. [32] And the earth shall give up those who are asleep in it, and the dust those who dwell silently in it; and the chambers shall give up the souls which have been committed to them. [33] And the Most High shall be revealed upon the seat of judgment, and compassion shall pass away, and patience shall be withdrawn; [34] but only judgment shall remain, truth shall stand, and faithfulness shall grow strong. [35] And recompense shall follow, and the reward shall be manifested; righteous deeds shall awake, and unrighteous deeds shall not sleep. [36] Then the pit of torment shall appear, and opposite it shall be the place of rest; and the furnace of hell shall be disclosed, and opposite it the paradise of delight. [37] Then the Most High will say to the nations that have been raised from the dead, 'Look now, and understand whom you have denied, whom you have not served, whose commandments you have despised! [38] Look on this side and on that; here are delight and rest, and there are fire and torments!' Thus he will speak to them on the day of judgment -- [39] a day that has no sun or moon or stars, [40] or cloud or thunder or lightning or wind or water or air, or darkness or evening or morning, [41] or summer or spring or heat or winter or frost or cold or hail or rain or dew, [42] or noon or night, or dawn or shining or brightness or light, but only the splendor of the glory of the Most High, by which all shall see what has been determined for them. [43] For it will last for about a week of years. [44] This is my judgment and its prescribed order; and to you alone have I shown these things." [45] I answered and said, "0 sovereign Lord, I said then and I say now: Blessed are those who are alive and keep thy commandments! [46] But what of those for whom I prayed? For who among the living is there that has not sinned, or who among men that has not transgressed thy covenant? [47] And now I see that the world to come will bring delight to few, but torments to many. [48] For an evil heart has grown up in us, which has alienated us from God, and has brought us into corruption and the ways of death, and has shown us the paths of perdition and removed us far from life -- and that not just a few of us but almost all who have been created!" [49] He answered me and said, "Listen to me, Ezra, and I will instruct you, and will admonish you yet again. [50] For this reason the Most High has made not one world but two. [51] For whereas you have said that the righteous are not many but few, while the ungodly abound, hear the explanation for this. [52] "If you have just a few precious stones, will you add to them lead and clay?" [53] I said, "Lord, how could that be?" [54] And he said to me, "Not only that, but ask the earth and she will tell you; defer to her, and she will declare it to you. [55] Say to her, 'You produce gold and silver and brass, and also iron and lead and clay; [56]

but silver is more abundant than gold, and brass than silver, and iron than brass, and lead than iron, and clay than lead.' [57] Judge therefore which things are precious and desirable, those that are abundant or those that are rare?" [58] I said, "0 sovereign Lord, what is plentiful is of less worth, for what is more rare is more precious." [59] He answered me and said, "Weigh within yourself what you have thought, for he who has what is hard to get rejoices more than he who has what is plentiful. [60] So also will be the judgment which I have promised; for I will rejoice over the few who shall be saved, because it is they who have made my glory to prevail now, and through them my name has now been honored. [61] And I will not grieve over the multitude of those who perish; for it is they who are now like a mist, and are similar to a flame and smoke -- they are set on fire and burn hotly, and are extinguished." [62] I replied and said, "0 earth, what have you brought forth, if the mind is made out of the dust like the other created things! [63] For it would have been better if the dust itself had not been born, so that the mind might not have been made from it. [64] But now the mind grows with us, and therefore we are tormented, because we perish and know it. [65] Let the human race lament, but let the beasts of the field be glad; let all who have been born lament, but let the four-footed beasts and the flocks rejoice! [66] For it is much better with them than with us; for they do not look for a judgment, nor do they know of any torment or salvation promised to them after death. [67] For what does it profit us that we shall be preserved alive but cruelly tormented? [68] For all who have been born are involved in iniquities, and are full of sins and burdened with transgressions. [69] And if we were not to come into judgment after death, perhaps it would have been better for us." [70] He answered me and said, "When the Most High made the world and Adam and all who have come from him, he first prepared the judgment and the things that pertain to the judgment. [71] And now understand from your own words, for you have said that the mind grows with us. [72] For this reason, therefore, those who dwell on earth shall be tormented, because though they had understanding they committed iniquity, and though they received the commandments they did not keep them, and though they obtained the law they dealt unfaithfully with what they received. [73] What, then, will they have to say in the judgment, or how will they answer in the last times? [74] For how long the time is that the Most High has been patient with those who inhabit the world, and not for their sake, but because of the times which he has foreordained!" [75] I answered and said, "If I have found favor in thy sight, o Lord, show this also to thy servant: whether after death, as soon as every one of us yields up his soul, we shall be kept in rest until those times come when thou wilt renew the creation, or whether we shall be tormented at once?" [76] He answered me and said, "I will show you that also, but do not be associated with those who have shown scorn, nor number yourself among those who are tormented. [77] For you have a treasure of works laid up with the Most High; but it will not be shown to you until the last times. [78] Now, concerning death, the teaching is: When the decisive decree has gone forth from the Most High that a man shall die, as the spirit leaves the body to return again to him who gave it, first of all it adores the glory of the Most High. [79] And if it is one of those who have shown scorn and have not kept the way of the Most High, and who have despised his law, and who have hated those who fear God -- [80] such spirits shall not enter into habitations, but shall immediately wander about in torments, ever grieving and sad, in seven ways. [81] The first way, because they have scorned the law of the Most High. [82] The second way, because they cannot now make a good repentance that they may live. [83] The third way, they shall see the reward laid up for those who have trusted the covenants of the Most High. [84] The fourth way, they shall consider the torment laid up for themselves in the last days. [85] The fifth way, they shall see how the habitations of the others are guarded by angels in profound quiet. [86] The sixth way, they shall see how some of them will pass over into torments. [87] The seventh way, which is worse than all the ways that have been mentioned, because they shall utterly waste away in confusion and be consumed with shame, and shall wither with fear at seeing the glory of the Most High before whom they sinned while they were alive, and before whom they are to be judged in the last times. [88] "Now this is the order of those who have kept the ways of the Most High, when they shall be separated from their mortal body. [89] During the time that they lived in it, they laboriously served the Most High, and withstood danger every hour, that they might keep the law of the Lawgiver perfectly. [90] Therefore this is the teaching concerning them: [91] First of all, they shall see with great joy the glory of him who receives them, for they shall have rest in seven orders. [92] The first order, because they have striven with great effort to overcome the evil thought which was formed with them, that it might not lead them astray from life into death. [93] The second order, because they see the perplexity in which the souls of the ungodly wander, and the punishment that awaits them. [94] The third order, they see the witness which he who formed them bears concerning them, that while they were alive they kept the law which was given them in trust. [95] The fourth order, they understand the rest which they now enjoy, being gathered into their chambers and guarded by angels in profound quiet, and the glory which awaits them in the last days. [96] The fifth order, they rejoice that they have now escaped what is corruptible, and shall inherit what is to come; and besides they see the straits and toil from which they have been delivered, and the spacious liberty which they are to receive and enjoy in immortality. [97] The sixth order, when it is shown to them how their face is to shine like the sun, and how they are to be made like the light of the stars, being incorruptible from then on. [98] The seventh order, which is greater than all that have been mentioned, because they shall rejoice with boldness, and shall be confident without confusion, and shall be glad without fear, for they hasten to behold the face of him whom they served in life and from whom they are to receive their reward when glorified. [99] This is the order of the souls of the righteous, as henceforth is announced; and the aforesaid are the ways of torment which those who would not give heed shall suffer hereafter." [100] I answered and said, "Will time therefore be given to the souls, after they have been separated from the bodies, to see what you have described to me?" [101] He said to me, "They shall have freedom for seven days, so that during these seven days they may see the things of which you have been told, and afterwards they shall be gathered in their habitations." [102] I answered and said, "If I have found favor in thy sight, show further to me, thy servant, whether on the day of judgment the righteous will be able to intercede for the ungodly or to entreat the Most High for them, [103] fathers for sons or sons for parents, brothers for brothers, relatives for their kinsmen, or friends for those who are most dear." [104] He answered me and said, "Since you have found favor in my sight, I will show you this also. The day of judgment is decisive and displays to all the seal of truth. Just as now a father does not send his son, or a son his father, or a master his servant, or a friend his dearest friend, to be ill or sleep or eat or be healed in his stead, [105] so no one shall ever pray for another on that day, neither shall any one lay a burden on another; for then every one shall bear his own righteousness and unrighteousness." [106] I answered and said, "How then do we find that first Abraham prayed for the people of Sodom, and Moses for our fathers who sinned in the desert, (107) and Joshua after him for Israel in the days of Achan, [108] and Samuel in the days of Saul, and David for the plague, and Solomon for those in the sanctuary, (109) and Elijah for those who received the rain, and for the one who was dead, that he might live, (110)] and Hezekiah for the people in the days of Sennacherib, and many others prayed for many? (111] If therefore the righteous have prayed for the ungodly now, when corruption has increased and unrighteousness has multiplied, why will it not be so then as well?" [112] He answered me and said, "This present world is not the end; the full glory does not abide in it; therefore those who were strong prayed for the weak. [113] But the day of judgment will be the end of this age and the beginning of the immortal age to come, in which corruption has passed away, [114] sinful indulgence has come to an end, unbelief has been cut off, and righteousness has increased and truth has appeared. [115] Therefore no one will then be able to have mercy on him who has been condemned in the judgment, or to harm him who is victorious." [116] I answered and said, "This is my first and last word, that it would have been better if the earth had not produced Adam, or else, when it had produced him, had restrained him from sinning. [117] For what good is it to all that they live in sorrow now and expect punishment after death? [118] 0 Adam, what have you done? For though it was you who sinned, the fall was not yours alone, but ours also who are your descendants. [119] For what good is it to us, if an eternal age has been promised to us, but we have done deeds that bring death? [120] And what good is it that an everlasting hope has been promised to us, but we have miserably failed? [121] Or that safe and healthful habitations have been reserved for us, but we have lived wickedly? [122] Or that the glory of the Most High will defend those who have led a pure life, but we have walked in the most wicked ways? [123] Or that a paradise shall be revealed, whose fruit remains unspoiled and in which are abundance and healing, but we shall not enter it, [124] because we have lived in unseemly places? [125] Or that the faces of those who practiced self-control shall shine more than the stars, but our faces shall be blacker than darkness? [126] For while we lived and committed iniquity we did not consider what we should suffer after death." [127] He answered and said, "This is the meaning of the contest which every man who is born on earth shall wage, [128] that if he is defeated he shall suffer what you have said, but if he is victorious he shall receive what I have said. [129] For this is the way of which Moses, while he was alive, spoke to the people, saying, 'Choose for yourself life, that you may live!' [130] But they did not believe him, or the prophets after him, or even myself who have spoken to them. [131] Therefore there shall not be grief at their destruction, so much as joy over those to whom salvation is assured." [132] I answered and said, "1 know, o Lord, that the Most High is now called merciful, because he has mercy on those who have not yet come into the world; [133] and gracious, because he is gracious to those who turn in repentance to his law; [134] and patient, because he shows patience toward those who have sinned, since they are his own works; [135] and bountiful, because he would rather give than take away; [136] and abundant in compassion, because he makes his compassions abound more and more to those now living and to those who are gone and to those yet to come, [137] for if he did not make them abound, the world with those who inhabit it would not have life; [138] and he is called giver, because if he did not give out of his goodness so that those who have committed iniquities might be relieved of them, not one ten-thousandth of mankind could have life; [139] and judge, because if he did not pardon those who were created by his word and blot out the multitude of their sins, [140] there would probably be left only very few of the innumerable multitude."

2 ESDRAS. 8

[1] He answered me and said, "The Most High made this world for the sake of many, but the world to come for the sake of few. [2] But I tell you a parable, Ezra. Just as, when you ask the earth, it will tell you that it provides very much clay from which earthenware is made, but only a little dust from which gold comes; so is the course of the present world. [3] Many have been created, but few shall be saved." [4] I answered and said, "Then drink your fill of understanding, 0 my soul, and drink wisdom, 0 my heart! [5] For not of your own will did you come into the world, and against your will you depart, for you have been given only a short time to live. [6] 0 Lord who are over us, grant to thy servant that we may pray before thee, and give us seed for our heart and cultivation of our understanding so that fruit may be produced, by which every mortal who bears the likeness of a human being may be able to live. [7] For thou alone do exist, and we are a work of thy hands, as thou hast declared. [8] And because thou do give life to the body which is now fashioned in the womb, and do furnish it with members, what thou hast created is preserved in fire and water, and for nine months the womb which thou has formed endures thy creation which has been created in it. [9] But that which keeps and that which is kept shall both be kept by thy keeping. And when the womb gives up again what has been created in it, [10] thou hast commanded that from the members themselves (that is, from the breasts) milk should be supplied which is the fruit of the breasts, [11] so that what has been fashioned may be nourished for a time; and afterwards thou wilt guide him in thy mercy. [12] Thou hast brought him up in thy righteousness, and instructed him in thy law, and reproved him in thy wisdom. [13] Thou wilt take away his life, for he is thy creation; and thou wilt make him live, for he is thy work. [14] If then thou wilt suddenly and quickly destroy him who with so great labor was fashioned by thy command, to what purpose was he made? [15] And now I will speak out: About all mankind thou knowest best; but I will speak about thy people, for whom I am grieved, [16] and about thy inheritance, for whom I lament, and about Israel, for whom I am sad, and about the seed of Jacob, for whom I am troubled. [17] Therefore I will pray before thee for myself and for them, for I see the failings of us who dwell in the land, [18] and I have heard of the swiftness of the judgment that is to come. [19] Therefore hear my voice, and understand my words, and I will speak before thee." The beginning of the words of Ezra's prayer, before he was taken up. He said: [20] "0 Lord who inhabitest eternity, whose eyes are exalted and whose upper chambers are in the air, [21] whose throne is beyond measure and whose glory is beyond comprehension, before whom the hosts of angels stand trembling [22] and at whose command they are changed to wind and fire, whose word s sure and whose utterances are certain, whose ordinance is strong and whose command is terrible, [23] whose look dries up the depths and whose indignation makes the mountains melt away, and whose truth is established for ever -- [24] hear, 0 Lord, the prayer of thy servant, and give ear to the petition of thy creature; attend to my words. [25] For as long as I live I will speak, and as long as I have understanding I will answer. [26] 0 look not upon the sins of thy people, but at those who have served thee in truth. [27] Regard not the

endeavors of those who act wickedly, but the endeavors of those who have kept thy covenants amid afflictions. [28] Think not on those who have lived wickedly in thy sight; but remember those who have willingly acknowledged that thou art to be feared. [29] Let it not be thy will to destroy those who have had the ways of cattle; but regard those who have gloriously taught thy law. [30] Be not angry with those who are deemed worse than beasts; but love those who have always put their trust in thy glory. [31] For we and our fathers have passed our lives in ways that bring death, but thou, because of us sinners, are called merciful. [32] For if thou hast desired to have pity on us, who have no works of righteousness, then thou wilt be called merciful. [33] For the righteous, who have many works laid up with thee, shall receive their reward in consequence of their own deeds. [34] But what is man, that thou art angry with him; or what is a corruptible race, that thou art so bitter against it? [35] For in truth there is no one among those who have been born who has not acted wickedly, and among those who have existed there is no one who has not transgressed. [36] For in this, 0 Lord, thy righteousness and goodness will be declared, when thou art merciful to those who have no store of good works." [37] He answered me and said, "Some things you have spoken rightly, and it will come to pass according to your words. [38] For indeed I will not concern myself about the fashioning of those who have sinned, or about their death, their judgment, or their destruction; [39] but I will rejoice over the creation of the righteous, over their pilgrimage also, and their salvation, and their receiving their reward. [40] As I have spoken, therefore, so it shall be. [41] "For just as the farmer sows many seeds upon the ground and plants a multitude of seedlings, and yet not all that have been sown will come up in due season, and not all that were planted will take root; so also those who have been sown in the world will not all be saved." [42] I answered and said, "If I have found favor before thee, let me speak. [43] For if the farmer's seed does not come up, because it has not received thy rain in due season, or if it has been ruined by too much rain, it perishes. [44] But man, who has been formed by thy hands and is called thy own image because he is made like thee, and for whose sake thou hast formed all things -- hast thou also made him like the farmer's seed? [45] No, 0 Lord who art over us! But spare thy people and have mercy on thy inheritance, for thou hast mercy on thy own creation. II [46] He answered me and said, IIThings that are present are for those who live now, and things that are future are for those who will live hereafter. [47] For you come far short of being able to love my creation more than I love it. But you have often compared yourself to the unrighteous. Never do so! [48] But even in this respect you will be praiseworthy before the Most High, [49] because you have humbled yourself, as is becoming for you, and have not deemed yourself to be among the righteous in order to receive the greatest glory. [50] For many miseries will affect those who inhabit the world in the last times, because they have walked in great pride. [51] But think of your own case, and inquire concerning the glory of those who are like yourself, [52] because it is for you that paradise is opened, the tree of life is planted, the age to come is prepared, plenty is provided, a city is built, rest is appointed, goodness is established and wisdom perfected beforehand. [53] The root of evil is sealed up from you, illness is banished from you, and death is hidden; hell has fled and corruption has been forgotten; [54] sorrows have passed away, and in the end the treasure of immortality is made manifest. [55] Therefore do not ask any more questions about the multitude of those who perish. [56] For they also received freedom , but they despised the Most High, and were contemptuous of his law, and forsook his ways. [57] Moreover they have even trampled upon his righteous ones, [58] and said in their hearts that there is not God -- though knowing full well that they must die. [59] For just as the things which I have predicted await you, so the thirst and torment which are prepared await them. For the Most High did not intend that men should be destroyed; [60] but they themselves who were created have defiled the name of him who made them, and have been ungrateful to him who prepared life for them. [61] Therefore my judgment is now drawing near; [62] I have not shown this to all men, but only to you and a few like you. Then I answered and said, [63] IIBehold, 0 Lord, thou hast now shown me a multitude of the signs which thou wilt do in the last times, but thou hast not shown me when thou wilt do them."

2 ESDRAS. 9

[1] He answered me and said, "Measure carefully in your mind, and when you see that a certain part of the predicted signs are past, [2] then you will know that it is the very time when the Most High is about to visit the world which he has made. [3] So when there shall appear in the world earthquakes, tumult of peoples, intrigues of nations, wavering of leaders, confusion of princes, [4] then you will know that it was of these that the Most High spoke from the days that were of old, from the beginning. [5] For just as with everything that has occurred in the world, the beginning is evident, and the end manifest; [6] so also are the times of the Most High: the beginnings are manifest in wonders and mighty works, and the end in requital and in signs. [7] And it shall be that every one who will be saved and will be able to escape on account of his works, or on account of the faith by which he has believed, [8] will survive the dangers that have been predicted, and will see my salvation in my land and within my borders, which I have sanctified for myself from the beginning. [9] Then those who have now abused my ways shall be amazed, and those who have rejected them with contempt shall dwell in torments. [10] For as many as did not acknowledge me in their lifetime, although they received my benefits, [11] and as many as scorned my law while they still had freedom, and did not understand but despised it while an opportunity of repentance was still open to them, [12] these must in torment acknowledge it after death. [13] Therefore, do not continue to be curious as to how the ungodly will be punished; but inquire how the righteous will be saved, those to whom the age belongs and for whose sake the age was made." [14] I answered and said, [15] "I said before, and I say now, and will say it again: there are more who perish than those who will be saved, [16] as a wave is greater than a drop of water." [17] He answered me and said, "As is the field, so is the seed; and as are the flowers, so are the colors; and as is the work, so is the product; and as is the farmer, so is the threshing floor. [18] For there was a time in this age when I was preparing for those who now exist, before the world was made for them to dwell in, and no one opposed me then, for no one existed; [19] but now those who have been created in this world which is supplied both with an unfailing table and an inexhaustible pasture, have become corrupt in their ways. [20] So I considered my world, and behold, it was lost, and my earth, and behold, it was in peril because of the devices of those who had come into it. [21] And I saw and spared some with great difficulty, and saved for myself one grape out of a cluster, and one plant out of a great forest. [22] So let the multitude perish which has been born in vain, but let my grape and my plant be saved, because with much labor I have perfected them. [23] But if you will let seven days more pass -- do not fast during them, however; [24] but go into a field of flowers where no house

has been built, and eat only of the flowers of the field, and taste no meat and drink no wine, but eat only flowers, [25] and pray to the Most High continually -- then I will come and talk with you." [26] So I went, as he directed me, into the field which is called Ardat; and there I sat among the flowers and ate of the plants of the field, and the nourishment they afforded satisfied me. [27] And after seven days, as I lay on the grass, my heart was troubled again as it was before. [28] And my mouth was opened, and I began to speak before the Most High, and said, [29] "0 Lord, thou didst show thyself among us, to our fathers in the wilderness when they came out from Egypt and when they came into the untrodden and unfruitful wilderness; [30] and thou didst say, 'Hear me, 0 Israel, and give heed to my words, 0 descendants of Jacob. [31] For behold, I sow my law in you, and it shall bring forth fruit in you and you shall be glorified through it for ever.' [32] But though our fathers received the law, they did not keep it, and did not observe the statutes; yet the fruit of the law did not perish -- for it could not, because it was your. [33] Yet those who received it perished, because they did not keep what had been sown in them. [34] And behold, it is the rule that, when the ground has received seed, or the sea a ship, or any dish food or drink, and when it happens that what was sown or what was launched or what was put in is destroyed, [35] they are destroyed, but the things that held them remain; yet with us it has not been so. [36] For we who have received the law and sinned will perish, as well as our heart which received it; [37] the law, however, does not perish but remains in its glory." [38] When I said these things in my heart, I lifted up my eyes and saw a woman on my right, and behold, she was mourning and weeping with a loud voice, and was deeply grieved at heart, and her clothes were rent, and there were ashes on her head. [39] Then I dismissed the thoughts with which I had been engaged, and turned to her [40] and said to her, "Why are you weeping, and why are you grieved at heart?" [41] And she said to me, "Let me alone, my lord, that I may weep for myself and continue to mourn, for I am greatly embittered in spirit and deeply afflicted." [42] And I said to her, "What has happened to you? Tell me." [43] And she said to me, "Your servant was barren and had no child, though I lived with my husband thirty years. [44] And every hour and every day during those thirty years I besought the Most High, night and day. [45] And after thirty years God heard your handmaid, and looked upon my low estate, and considered my distress, and gave me a son. And I rejoiced greatly over him, I and my husband and all my neighbors; and we gave great glory to the Mighty One. [46] And I brought him up with much care. [47] So when he grew up and I came to take a wife for him, I set a day for the marriage feast.

2 ESDRAS. 10

[1] "But it happened that when my son entered his wedding chamber, he fell down and died. [2] Then we all put out the lamps, and all my neighbors attempted to console me; and I remained quiet until evening of the second day. [3] But when they all had stopped consoling me, that I might be quiet, I got up in the night and fled, and came to this field, as you see. [4] And now I intend not to return to the city, but to stay here, and I will neither eat nor drink, but without ceasing mourn and fast until I die." [5] Then I broke off the reflections with which I was still engaged, and answered her in anger and said, [6] "You most foolish of women, do you not see our mourning, and what has happened to us? [7] For Zion, the mother of us all, is in deep grief and great affliction. [8] It is most appropriate to mourn now, because we are all mourning, and to be sorrowful, because we are all sorrowing; you are sorrowing for one son, but we, the whole world, for our mother. [9] Now ask the earth, and she will tell you that it is she who ought to mourn over so many who have come into being upon her. [10] And from the beginning all have been born of her, and others will come; and behold, almost all go to perdition, and a multitude of them are destined for destruction. [11] Who then ought to mourn the more, she who lost so great a multitude, or you who are grieving for one? [12] But if you say to me, 'My lamentation is not like the earth's, for I have lost the fruit of my womb, which I brought forth in pain and bore in sorrow; [13] but it is with the earth according to the way of the earth -- the multitude that is now in it goes as it came'; [14] then I say to you, 'As you brought forth in sorrow, so the earth also has from the beginning given her fruit, that is, man, to him who made her.' [15] Now, therefore, keep your sorrow to yourself, and bear bravely the troubles that have come upon you. [16] For if you acknowledge the decree of God to be just, you will receive your son back in due time, and will be praised among women. [17] Therefore go into the city to your husband." [18] She said to me, "I will not do so; I will not go into the city, but I will die here." [19] So I spoke again to her, and said, [20] "Do not say that, but let yourself be persuaded because of the troubles of Zion, and be consoled because of the sorrow of Jerusalem. [21] For you see that our sanctuary has been laid waste, our altar thrown down, our temple destroyed; [22] our harp has been laid low, our song has been silenced, and our rejoicing has been ended; the light of our lampstand has been put out, the ark of our covenant has been plundered, our holy things have been polluted, and the name by which we are called has been profaned; our free men have suffered abuse, our priests have been burned to death, our Levites have gone into captivity, our virgins have been defiled, and our wives have been ravished; our righteous men have been carried off, our little ones have been cast out, our young men have been enslaved and our strong men made powerless. [23] And, what is more than all, the seal of Zion -- for she has now lost the seal of her glory, and has been given over into the hands of those that hate us. [24] Therefore shake off your great sadness and lay aside your many sorrows, so that the Mighty One may be merciful to you again, and the Most High may give you rest, a relief from your troubles." [25] While I was talking to her, behold, her face suddenly shone exceedingly, and her countenance flashed like lightning, so that I was too frightened to approach her, and my heart was terrified. While I was wondering what this meant, [26] behold, she suddenly uttered a loud and fearful cry, so that the earth shook at the sound. [27] And I looked, and behold, the woman was no longer visible to me, but there was an established city, and a place of huge foundations showed itself. Then I was afraid, and cried with a loud voice and said, [28] "Where is the angel Vriel, who came to me at first? For it was he who brought me into this overpowering bewilderment; my end has become corruption, and my prayer a reproach." [29] As I was speaking these words, behold, the angel who had come to me at first came to me, and he looked upon me; [30] and behold, I lay there like a corpse and I was deprived of my understanding. Then he grasped my right hand and strengthened me and set me on my feet, and said to me, [31] "What is the matter with you? And why are you troubled? And why are your understanding and the thoughts of your mind troubled?" [32] I said, "Because you have forsaken me! I did as you directed, and went out into the field, and behold, I saw, and still see, what I am unable to explain." [33] He said to me, "Stand up like a man, and I will instruct you." [34] I said, "Speak, my lord; only do not forsake me, lest I die before my

time. [35] For I have seen what I did not know, and I have heard what I do not understand. [36] Or is my mind deceived, and my soul dreaming? [37] Now therefore I entreat you to give your servant an explanation of this bewildering vision." [38] He answered me and said, "Listen to me and I will inform you, and tell you about the things which you fear, for the Most High has revealed many secrets to you. [39] For he has seen your righteous conduct, that you have sorrowed continually for your people, and mourned greatly over Zion. [40] This therefore is the meaning of the vision. [41] The woman who appeared to you a little while ago, whom you saw mourning and began to console -- [42] but you do not now see the form of a woman, but an established city has appeared to you -- [43] and as for her telling you about the misfortune of her son, this is the interpretation: [44] This woman whom you saw, whom you now behold as an established city, is Zion. [45] And as for her telling you that she was barren for thirty years, it is because there were three thousand years in the world before any offering was offered in it. [46] And after three thousand years Solomon built the city, and offered offerings; then it was that the barren woman bore a son. [47] And as for her telling you that she brought him up with much care, that was the period of residence in Jerusalem. [48] And as for her saying to you , 'When my son entered his wedding chamber he died,' and that misfortune had overtaken her, that was the destruction which befell Jerusalem. [49] And behold, you saw her likeness, how she mourned for her son, and you began to console her for what had happened. [50] For now the Most High, seeing that you are sincerely grieved and profoundly distressed for her, has shown you the brilliance of her glory, and the loveliness of her beauty. [51] Therefore I told you to remain in the field where no house had been built, [52] for I knew that the Most High would reveal these things to you. [53] Therefore I told you to go into the field where there was no foundation of any building, [54] for no work of man's building could endure in a place where the city of the Most High was to be revealed. [55] "Therefore do not be afraid, and do not let your heart be terrified; but go in and see the splendor and vastness of the building, as far as it is possible for your eyes to see it, [56] and afterward you will hear as much as your ears can hear. [57] For you are more blessed than many, and you have been called before the Most High, as but few have been. [58] But tomorrow night you shall remain here, [59] and the Most High will show you in those dream visions what the Most High will do to those who dwell on earth in the last days." So I slept that night and the following one, as he had commanded me.

2 ESDRAS. 11

[1] On the second night I had a dream, and behold, there came up from the sea an eagle that had twelve feathered wings and three heads. [2] And I looked, and behold, he spread his wings over all the earth, and all the winds of heaven blew upon him, and the clouds were gathered about him. [3] And I looked, and out of his wings there grew opposing wings; but they became little, puny wings. [4] But his heads were at rest; the middle head was larger than the other heads, but it also was at rest with them. [5] And I looked, and behold, the eagle flew with his wings, to reign over the earth and over those who dwell in it. [6] And I saw how all things under heaven were subjected to him, and no one spoke against him, not even one creature that was on the earth. [7] And I looked, and behold, the eagle rose upon his talons, and uttered a cry to his wings, saying, [8] "Do not all watch at the same time; let each sleep in his own place, and watch in his turn; [9] but let the heads be reserved for the last." [10] And I looked, and behold, the voice did not come from his heads, but from the midst of his body. [11] And I counted his opposing wings, and behold, there were eight of them. [12] And I looked, and behold, on the right side one wing arose, and it reigned over all the earth. [13] And while it was reigning it came to its end and disappeared, so that its place was not seen. Then the next wing arose and reigned, and it continued to reign a long time. [14] And while it was reigning its end came also, so that it disappeared like the first. [15] And behold, a voice sounded, saying to it. [16] "Hear me, you who have ruled the earth all this time; I announce this to you before you disappear. [17] After you no one shall rule as long as you, or even half as long." [18] Then the third wing raised itself up, and held the rule like the former ones, and it also disappeared. [19] And so it went with all the wings; they wielded power one after another and then were never seen again. [20] And I looked, and behold, in due course the wings that followed also rose up on the right side, in order to rule. There were some of them that ruled, yet disappeared suddenly; [21] and others of them rose up, but did not hold the rule. [22] And after this I looked, and behold, the twelve wings and the two little wings disappeared; [23] and nothing remained on the eagle's body except the three heads that were at rest and six little wings. [24] And I looked, and behold, two little wings separated from the six and remained under the head that was on the right side; but four remained in their place. [25] And I looked, and behold, these little wings planned to set themselves up and hold the rule. [26] And I looked, and behold, one was set up, but suddenly disappeared; [27] a second also, and this disappeared more quickly than the first. [28] And I looked, and behold, the two that remained were planning between themselves to reign together; [29] and while they were planning, behold, one of the heads that were at rest (the one which was in the middle) awoke; for it was greater than the other two heads. [30] And I saw how it allied the two heads with itself, [31] and behold, the head turned with those that were with it, and it devoured the two little wings which were planning to reign. [32] Moreover this head gained control of the whole earth, and with much oppression dominated its inhabitants; and it had greater power over the world than all the wings that had gone before. [33] And after this I looked, and behold, the middle head also suddenly disappeared, just as the wings had done. [34] But the two heads remained, which also ruled over the earth and its inhabitants. [35] And I looked, and behold, the head on the right side devoured the one on the left. [36] Then I heard a voice saying to me, "Look before you and consider what you see." [37] And I looked, and behold, a creature like a lion was aroused out of the forest, roaring; and I heard how he uttered a man's voice to the eagle, and spoke, saying, [38] "Listen and I will speak to you. The Most High says to you, [39] 'Are you not the one that remains of the four beasts which I had made to reign in my world, so that the end of my times might come through them? [40] You, the fourth that has come, have conquered all the beasts that have gone before; and you have held sway over the world with much terror, and over all the earth with grievous oppression; and for so long you have dwelt on the earth with deceit. [41] And you have judged the earth, but not with truth; [42] for you have afflicted the meek and injured the peaceable; you have hated those who tell the truth, and have loved liars; you have destroyed the dwellings of those who brought forth fruit, and have laid low the walls of those who did you no harm. [43] And so your insolence has come up before the Most High, and your pride to the Mighty One. [44] And the Most High has looked upon his times, and behold, they are ended, and his ages are

completed! [45] Therefore you will surely disappear, you eagle, and your terrifying wings, and your most evil little wings, and your malicious heads, and your most evil talons, and your whole worthless body, [46] so that the whole earth, freed from your violence, may be refreshed and relieved, and may hope for the judgment and mercy of him who made it.'"

2 ESDRAS. 12

[1] While the lion was saying these words to the eagle, I looked, [2] and behold, the remaining head disappeared. And the two wings that had gone over to it arose and set themselves up to reign, and their reign was brief and full of tumult. [3] And I looked, and behold, they also disappeared, and the whole body of the eagle was burned, and the earth was exceedingly terrified. Then I awoke in great perplexity of mind and great fear, and I said to my spirit, [4] "Behold, you have brought this upon me, because you search out the ways of the Most High. [5] Behold, I am still weary in mind and very weak in my spirit, and not even a little strength is left in me, because of the great fear with which I have been terrified this night. [6] Therefore I will now beseech the Most High that he may strengthen me to the end." [7] And I said, "0 sovereign Lord, if I have found favor in thy sight, and if I have been accounted righteous before thee beyond many others, and if my prayer has indeed come up before thy face, [8] strengthen me and show me, thy servant, the interpretation and meaning of this terrifying vision, that thou mayest fully comfort my soul. [9] For thou hast judged me worthy to be shown the end of the times and the last events of the times." [10] He said to me, "This is the interpretation of this vision which you have seen: [11] The eagle which you saw coming up from the sea is the fourth kingdom which appeared in a vision to your brother Daniel. [12] But it was not explained to him as I now explain or have explained it to you. [13] Behold, the days are coming when a kingdom shall arise on earth, and it shall be more terrifying than all the kingdoms that have been before it. [14] And twelve kings shall reign in it, one after another. [15] But the second that is to reign shall hold sway for a longer time than any other of the twelve. [16] This is the interpretation of the twelve wings which you saw. [17] As for your hearing a voice that spoke, coming not from the eagle's heads but from the midst of his body, this is the interpretation: [18] In the midst of the time of that kingdom great struggles shall arise, and it shall be in danger of falling; nevertheless it shall not fall then, but shall regain its former power. [19] As for your seeing eight little wings clinging to his wings, this is the interpretation: [20] Eight kings shall arise in it, whose times shall be short and their years swift; [21] and two of them shall perish when the middle of its time draws near; and four shall be kept for the time when its end approaches; but two shall be kept until the end. [22] As for your seeing three heads at rest, this is the interpretation: [23] In its last days the Most High will raise up three kings, and they shall renew many things in it, and shall rule the earth [24] and its inhabitants more oppressively than all who were before them; therefore they are called the heads of the eagle. [25] For it is they who shall sum up his wickedness and perform his last actions. [26] As for your seeing that the large head disappeared, one of the kings shall die in his bed, but in agonies. [27] But as for the two who remained, the sword shall devour them. [28] For the sword of one shall devour him who was with him; but he also shall fall by the sword in the last days. [29] As for your seeing two little wings passing over to the head which was on the right side, [30] this is the interpretation: It is these whom the Most High has kept for the eagle's end; this was the reign which was brief and full of tumult, as you have seen. [31] "And as for the lion whom you saw rousing up out of the forest and roaring and speaking to the eagle and reproving him for his unrighteousness, and as for all his words that you have heard, [32] this is the Messiah whom the Most High has kept until the end of days, who will arise from the posterity of David, and will come and speak to them; he will denounce them for their ungodliness and for their wickedness, and will cast up before them their contemptuous dealings. [33] For first he will set them living before his judgment seat, and when he has reproved them, then he will destroy them. [34] But he will deliver in mercy the remnant of my people, those who have been saved throughout my borders, and he will make them joyful until the end comes, the day of judgment, of which I spoke to you at the beginning. [35] This is the dream that you saw, and this is its interpretation. [36] And you alone were worthy to learn this secret of the Most High. [37] Therefore write all these things that you have seen in a book, and put it in a hidden place; [38] and you shall teach them to the wise among your people, whose hearts you know are able to comprehend and keep these secrets. [39] But wait here seven days more, so that you may be shown whatever it pleases the Most High to show you." Then he left me. [40] When all the people heard that the seven days were past and I had not returned to the city, they all gathered together, from the least to the greatest, and came to me and spoke to me, saying, [41] "How have we offended you, and what harm have we done you, that you have forsaken us and sit in this place? [42] For of all the prophets you alone are left to us, like a cluster of grapes from the vintage, and like a lamp in a dark place, and like a haven for a ship saved from a storm. [43] Are not the evils which have befallen us sufficient? [44] Therefore if you forsake us, how much better it would have been for us if we also had been consumed in the burning of Zion! [45] For we are no better than those who died there." And they wept with a loud voice. Then I answered them and said, [46] "Take courage, 0 Israel; and do not be sorrowful, 0 house of Jacob; [47] for the Most High has you in remembrance, and the Mighty One has not forgotten you in your struggle. [48] As for me, I have neither forsaken you nor withdrawn from you; but I have come to this place to pray on account of the desolation of Zion, and to seek mercy on account of the humiliation of our sanctuary. [49] Now go, every one of you to his house, and after these days I will come to you." [50] So the people went into the city, as I told them to do. [51] But I sat in the field seven days, as the angel had commanded me; and I ate only of the flowers of the field, and my food was of plants during those days.

2 ESDRAS. 13

[1] After seven days I dreamed a dream in the night; [2] and behold, a wind arose from the sea and stirred up all its waves. [3] And I looked, and behold, this wind made something like the figure of a man come up out of the heart of the sea. And I looked, and behold, that man flew with the clouds of heaven; and wherever he turned his face to look, everything under his gaze trembled, [4] and whenever his voice issued from his mouth, all who heard his voice melted as wax melts when it feels the fire. [5] After this I looked, and behold, an innumerable multitude of men were gathered together from the four winds of heaven to make war against the man who came up out of the sea. [6] And I looked, and behold, he carved out for himself a great mountain, and flew up upon it. < br> [7] [7] And I tried to see the region or place from which the mountain

was carved, but I could not. [8] After this I looked, and behold, all who had gathered together against him, to wage war with him, were much afraid, yet dared to fight. [9] And behold, when he saw the onrush of the approaching multitude, he neither lifted his hand nor held a spear or any weapon of war; [10] but I saw only how he sent forth from his mouth as it were a stream of fire, and from his lips a flaming breath, and from his tongue he shot forth a storm of sparks. [11] All these were mingled together, the stream of fire and the flaming breath and the great storm, and fell on the onrushing multitude which was prepared to fight, and burned them all up, so that suddenly nothing was seen of the innumerable multitude but only the dust of ashes and the smell of smoke. When I saw it, I was amazed. [12] After this I saw the same man come down from the mountain and call to him another multitude which was peaceable. [13] Then many people came to him, some of whom were joyful and some sorrowful; some of them were bound, and some were bringing others as offerings. Then in great fear I awoke; and I besought the Most High, and said, [14] "From the beginning thou hast shown thy servant these wonders, and hast deemed me worthy to have my prayer heard by thee; [15] now show me also the interpretation of this dream. [16] For as I consider it in my mind, alas for those who will be left in those days! And still more, alas for those who are not left! [17] For those who are not left will be sad, [18] because they understand what is reserved for the last days, but cannot attain it. [19] But alas for those also who are left, and for that very reason! For they shall see great dangers and much distress, as these dreams show. [20] Yet it is better to come into these things, though incurring peril, than to pass from the world like a cloud, and not to see what shall happen in the last days." He answered me and said, [21] "I will tell you the interpretation of the vision, and I will also explain to you the things which you have mentioned. [22] As for what you said about those who are left, this is the interpretation: [23] He who brings the peril at that time will himself protect those who fall into peril, who have works and have faith in the Almighty. [24] Understand therefore that those who are left are more blessed than those who have died. [25] This is the interpretation of the vision: As for your seeing a man come up from the heart of the sea, [26] this is he whom the Most High has been keeping for many ages, who will himself deliver his creation; and he will direct those who are left. [27] And as for your seeing wind and fire and a storm coming out of his mouth, [28] and as for his not holding a spear or weapon of war, yet destroying the onrushing multitude which came to conquer him, this is the interpretation: [29] Behold, the days are coming when the Most High will deliver those who are on the earth. [30] And bewilderment of mind shall come over those who dwell on the earth. [31] And they shall plan to make war against one another, city against city, place against place, people against people, and kingdom against kingdom. [32] And when these things come to pass and the signs occur which I showed you before, then my Son will be revealed, whom you saw as a man coming up from the sea. [33] And when all the nations hear his voice, every man shall leave his own land and the warfare that they have against one another; [34] and an innumerable multitude shall be gathered together, as you saw, desiring to come and conquer him. [35] But he shall stand on the top of Mount Zion. [36] And Zion will come and be made manifest to all people, prepared and built, as you saw the mountain carved out without hands. [37] And he, my Son, will reprove the assembled nations for their ungodliness (this was symbolized by the storm), [38] and will reproach them to their face with their evil thoughts and the torments with which they are to be tortured (which were symbolized by the flames), and will destroy them without effort by the law (which was symbolized by the fire). [39] And as for your seeing him gather to himself another multitude that was peaceable, [40] these are the ten tribes which were led away from their own land into captivity in the days of King Hoshea, whom Shalmaneser the king of the Assyrians led captive; he took them across the river, and they were taken into another land. [41] But they formed this plan for themselves, that they would leave the multitude of the nations and go to a more distant region, where mankind had never lived, [42] that there at least they might keep their statutes which they had not kept in their own land. [43] And they went in by the narrow passages of the Euphrates river. [44] For at that time the Most High performed signs for them, and stopped the channels of the river until they had passed over. [45] Through that region there was a long way to go, a journey of a year and a half; and that country is called Arzareth. [46] "Then they dwelt there until the last times; and now, when they are about to come again, [47] the Most High will stop the channels of the river again, so that they may be able to pass over. Therefore you saw the multitude gathered together in peace. [48] But those who are left of your people, who are found within my holy borders, shall be saved. [49] Therefore when he destroys the multitude of the nations that are gathered together, he will defend the people who remain. [50] And then he will show them very many wonders." [51] I said, "0 sovereign Lord, explain this to me: Why did I see the man coming up from the heart of the sea?" [52] He said to me, "Just as no one can explore or know what is in the depths of the sea, so no one on earth can see my Son or those who are with him, except in the time of his day. [53] This is the interpretation of the dream which you saw. And you alone have been enlightened about this, [54] because you have forsaken your own ways and have applied yourself to mine, and have searched out my law; [55] for you have devoted your life to wisdom, and called understanding your mother. [56] Therefore I have shown you this, for there is a reward laid up with the Most High. And after three more days I will tell you other things, and explain weighty and wondrous matters to you." [57] Then I arose and walked in the field, giving great glory and praise to the Most High because of his wonders, which he did from time to time, [58] and because he governs the times and whatever things come to pass in their seasons. And I stayed there three days.

2 ESDRAS. 14

[1] On the third day, while I was sitting under an oak, behold, a voice came out of a bush opposite me and said, "Ezra, Ezra." [2] And I said, "Here I am, Lord," and I rose to my feet. [3] Then he said to me, "I revealed myself in a bush and spoke to Moses, when my people were in bondage in Egypt; [4] and I sent him and led my people out of Egypt; and I led him up on Mount Sinai, where I kept him with me many days; [5] and I told him many wondrous things, and showed him the secrets of the times and declared to him the end of the times. Then I commanded him, saying, [6] 'These words you shall publish openly, and these you shall keep secret.' [7] And now I say to you; [8] Lay up in your heart the signs that I have shown you, the dreams that you have seen, and the interpretations that you have heard; [9] for you shall be taken up from among men, and henceforth you shall live with my Son and with those who are like you, until the times are ended. [10] For the age has lost its youth, and the times begin to grow old. [11] For the age is divided into twelve parts, and nine of its parts have already passed, [12] as well as half of the tenth part; so two of its parts remain, besides half of the tenth

part. [13] Now therefore, set your house in order, and reprove your people; comfort the lowly among them, and instruct those that are wise. And now renounce the life that is corruptible, [14] and put away from you mortal thoughts; cast away from you the burdens of man, and divest yourself now of your weak nature, [15] and lay to one side the thoughts that are most grievous to you, and hasten to escape from these times. [16] For evils worse than those which you have now seen happen shall be done hereafter. [17] For the weaker the world becomes through old age, the more shall evils be multiplied among its inhabitants. [18] For truth shall go farther away, and falsehood shall come near. For the eagle which you saw in the vision is already hastening to come." [19] Then I answered and said, "Let me speak in thy presence, Lord. [20] For behold, I will go, as thou hast commanded me, and I will reprove the people who are now living; but who will warn those who will be born hereafter? For the world lies in darkness, and its inhabitants are without light. [21] For thy law has been burned, and so no one knows the things which have been done or will be done by thee. [22] If then I have found favor before thee, send the Holy Spirit into me, and I will write everything that has happened in the world from the beginning, the things which were written in thy law, that men may be able to find the path, and that those who wish to live in the last days may live." [23] He answered me and said, "Go and gather the people, and tell them not to seek you for forty days. [24] But prepare for yourself many writing tablets, and take with you Sarea, Dabria, Selemia, Ethanus, and Asiel -- these five, because they are trained to write rapidly; [25] and you shall come here, and I will light in your heart the lamp of understanding, which shall not be put out until what you are about to write is finished. [26] And when you have finished, some things you shall make public, and some you shall deliver in secret to the wise; tomorrow at this hour you shall begin to write." [27] Then I went as he commanded me, and I gathered all the people together, and said, [28] "Hear these words, 0 Israel [29] At first our fathers dwelt as aliens in Egypt, and they were delivered from there, [30] and received the law of life, which they did not keep, which you also have transgressed after them. [31] Then land was given to you for a possession in the land of Zion; but you and your fathers committed iniquity and did not keep the ways which the Most High commanded you. [32] And because he is a righteous judge, in due time he took from you what he had given. [33] And now you are here, and your brethren are farther in the interior. [34] If you, then, will rule over your minds and discipline your hearts, you shall be kept alive, and after death you shall obtain mercy. [35] For after death the judgment will come, when we shall live again; and then the names of the righteous will become manifest, and the deeds of the ungodly will be disclosed. [36] But let no one come to me now, and let no one seek me for forty days." [37] So I took the five men, as he commanded me, and we proceeded to the field, and remained there. [38] And on the next day, behold, a voice called me, saying, "Ezra, open your mouth and drink what I give you to drink." [39] Then I opened my mouth, and behold, a full cup was offered to me; it was full of something like water, but its color was like fire. [40] And I took it and drank; and when I had drunk it, my heart poured forth understanding, and wisdom increased in my breast, for my spirit retained its memory; [41] and my mouth was opened, and was no longer closed. [42] And the Most High gave understanding to the five men, and by turns they wrote what was dictated, in characters which they did not know. They sat forty days, and wrote during the daytime, and ate their bread at night. [43] As for me, I spoke in the daytime and was not silent at night. [44] So during the forty days ninety-four books were written. [45] And when the forty days were ended, the Most High spoke to me, saying, "Make public the twenty-four books that you wrote first and let the worthy and the unworthy read them; [46] but keep the seventy that were written last, in order to give them to the wise among your people. [47] For in them is the spring of understanding, the fountain of wisdom, and the river of knowledge." [48] And I did so.

2 ESDRAS. 15

[1] The Lord says, "Behold, speak in the ears of my people the words of the prophecy which I will put in your mouth, [2] and cause them to be written on paper; for they are trustworthy and true. [3] Do not fear the plots against you, and do not be troubled by the unbelief of those who oppose you. [4] For every unbeliever shall die in his unbelief." [5] "Behold," says the Lord, "I bring evils upon the world, the sword and famine and death and destruction. [6] For iniquity has spread throughout every land, and their harmful deeds have reached their limit. [7] Therefore," says the Lord, [8] "I will be silent no longer concerning their ungodly deeds which they impiously commit, neither will I tolerate their wicked practices. Behold, innocent and righteous blood cries out to me, and the souls of the righteous cry out continually. [9] I will surely avenge them," says the Lord, "and will receive to myself all the innocent blood from among them. [10] Behold, my people is led like a flock to the slaughter; I will not allow them to live any longer in the land of Egypt, [11] but I will bring them out with a mighty hand and with an uplifted arm, and will smite Egypt with plagues, as before, and will destroy all its land." [12] Let Egypt mourn, and its foundations, for the plague of chastisement and punishment that the Lord will bring upon it. [13] Let the farmers that till the ground mourn, because their seed shall fail and their trees shall be ruined by blight and hail and by a terrible tempest. [14] Alas for the world and for those who live in it! [15] For the sword and misery draw near them, and nation shall rise up to fight against nation, with swords in their hands. [16] For there shall be unrest among men; growing strong against one another, they shall in their might have no respect for their king or the chief of their leaders. [17] For a man will desire to go into a city, and shall not be able. [18] For because of their pride the cities shall be in confusion, the houses shall be destroyed, and people shall be afraid. [19] A man shall have no pity upon his neighbors, but shall make an assault upon their houses with the sword, and plunder their goods, because of hunger for bread and because of great tribulation. [20] "Behold," says God, "I call together all the kings of the earth to fear me, from the rising sun and from the south, from the east and from Lebanon; to turn and repay what they have given them. [21] Just as they have done to my elect until this day, so I will do, and will repay into their bosom." Thus says the Lord God: [22] "My right hand will not spare the sinners, and my sword will not cease from those who shed innocent blood on earth." [23] And a fire will go forth from his wrath, and will consume the foundations of the earth, and the sinners, like straw that is kindled. [24] "Woe to those who sin and do not observe my commandments," says the Lord; [25] "I will not spare them. Depart, you faithless children! Do not pollute my sanctuary. " [26] For the Lord knows all who transgress against him; therefore he will hand them over to death and slaughter. [27] For now calamities have come upon the whole earth, and you shall remain in them; for God will not deliver you, because you have sinned against him. [28] Behold, a terrifying sight, appearing from the east! [29] The nations of the dragons of Arabia shall come out with many chariots, and from the day that they set out, their

hissing shall spread over the earth, so that all who hear them fear and tremble. [30] Also the Carmonians, raging in wrath, shall go forth like wild boars of the forest, and with great power they shall come, and engage them in battle, and shall devastate a portion of the land of the Assyrians with their teeth. [31] And then the dragons, remembering their origin, shall become still stronger; and if they combine in great power and turn to pursue them, [32] then these shall be disorganized and silenced by their power, and shall turn and flee. [33] And from the land of the Assyrians an enemy in ambush shall beset them and destroy one of them, and fear and trembling shall come upon their army, and indecision upon their kings. [34] Behold, clouds from the east, and from the north to the south; and their appearance is very threatening, full of wrath and storm. [3S] They shall dash against one another and shall pour out a heavy tempest upon the earth, and their own tempest; and there shall be blood from the sword as high as a horse's belly [36] and a man's thigh and a camel's hock. [37] And there shall be fear and great trembling upon the earth; and those who see that wrath shall be horror-stricken, and they shall be seized with trembling. [38] And, after that, heavy storm clouds shall be stirred up from the south, and from the north, and another part from the west. [39] And the winds from the east shall prevail over the cloud that was raised in wrath, and shall dispel it; and the tempest that was to cause destruction by the east wind shall be driven violently toward the south and west. [40] And great and mighty clouds, full of wrath and tempest, shall rise, to destroy all the earth and its inhabitants, and shall pour out upon every high and lofty place a terrible tempest, [41] fire and hail and flying swords and floods of water, that all the fields and all the streams may be filled with the abundance of those waters. [42] And they shall destroy cities and walls, mountains and hills, trees of the forests, and grass of the meadows, and their grain. [43] And they shall go on steadily to Babylon, and shall destroy her. [44] They shall come to her and surround her; they shall pour out the tempest and all its wrath upon her; then the dust and smoke shall go up to heaven, and all who are about her shall wail over her. [4S] And those who survive shall serve those who have destroyed her. [46] And you, Asia, who share in the glamour of Babylon and the glory of her person -- [47] woe to you, miserable wretch! For you have made yourself like her; you have decked out your daughters in harlotry to please and glory in your lovers, who have always lusted after you. [48] You have imitated that hateful harlot in all her deeds and devices; therefore God says, [49] "I will send evils upon you, widowhood, poverty, famine, sword, and pestilence, to lay waste your houses and bring you to destruction and death. [50] [SO] And the glory of your power shall wither like a flower, when the heat rises that is sent upon you. [Sl] You shall be weakened like a wretched woman who is beaten and wounded, so that you cannot receive your mighty lovers. [S2] Would I have dealt with you so violently," says the Lord, [53] "If you had not always killed my chosen people, exulting and clapping your hands and talking about their death when you were drunk? [54] Trick out the beauty of your face! [55] The reward of a harlot is in your bosom, therefore you shall receive your recompense. [56] As you will do to my chosen people," says the Lord, "so God will do to you, and will hand you over to adversities. [57] Your children shall die of hunger, and you shall fall by the sword, and your cities shall be wiped out, and all your people who are in the open country shall fall by the sword. [58] And those who are in the mountains and highlands shall perish of hunger, and they shall eat their own flesh in hunger for bread and drink their own blood in thirst for water. [59] Unhappy above all others, you shall come and suffer fresh afflictions. [60] And as they pass they shall wreck the hateful city, and shall destroy a part of your land and abolish a portion of your glory, as they return from devastated Babylon. [61] And you shall be broken down by them like stubble, and they shall be like fire to you. [62] And they shall devour you and your cities, your land and your mountains; they shall burn with fire all your forests and your fruitful trees. [63] They shall carry your children away captive, and shall plunder your wealth, and abolish the glory of your countenance."

2 ESDRAS. 16

[1] Woe to you, Babylon and Asia! Woe to you, Egypt and Syria! [2] Gird yourselves with sackcloth and haircloth, and wail for your children, and lament for them; for your destruction is at hand. [3] The sword has been sent upon you, and who is there to turn it back? [4] A fire has been sent upon you, and who is there to quench it? [5] Calamities have been sent upon you, and who is there to drive them away? [6] Can one drive off a hungry lion in the forest, or quench a fire in the stubble, when once it has begun to burn? [7] Can one turn back an arrow shot by a strong archer? [8] The Lord God sends calamities, and who will drive them away? [9] Fire will go forth from his wrath, and who is there to quench it? [10] He will flash lightning, and who will not be afraid? He will thunder, and who will not be terrified? [11] The Lord will threaten, and who will not be utterly shattered at his presence? [12] The earth and its foundations quake, the sea is churned up from the depths, and its waves and the fish also shall be troubled at the presence of the Lord and before the glory of his power. [13] For his right hand that bends the bow is strong, and his arrows that he shoots are sharp and will not miss when they begin to be shot to the ends of the world. [14] Behold, calamities are sent forth and shall not return until they come over the earth. [15] The fire is kindled, and shall not be put out until it consumes the foundations of the earth. [16] Just as an arrow shot by a mighty archer does not return, so the calamities that are sent upon the earth shall not return. [17] Alas for me! Alas for me! Who will deliver me in those days? [18] The beginning of sorrows, when there shall be much lamentation; the beginning of famine, when many shall perish; the beginning of wars, when the powers shall be terrified; the beginning of calamities, when all shall tremble. What shall they do in these circumstances, when the calamities come? [19] Behold, famine and plague, tribulation and anguish are sent as scourges for the correction of men. [20] Yet for all this they will not turn from their iniquities, nor be always mindful of the scourges. [21] Behold, provision will be so cheap upon earth that men will imagine that peace is assured for them, and then the calamities shall spring up on the earth -- the sword, famine, and great confusion. [22] For many of those who live on the earth shall perish by famine; and those who survive the famine shall die by the sword. [23] And the dead shall be cast out like dung, and there shall be no one to console them; for the earth shall be left desolate, and its cities shall be demolished. [24] No one shall be left to cultivate the earth or to sow it. [25] The trees shall bear fruit, and who will gather it? [26] The grapes shall ripen, and who will tread them? For in all places there shall be great solitude; [27] one man will long to see another, or even to hear his voice. [28] For out of a city, ten shall be left; and out of the field, two who have hidden themselves in thick groves and clefts in the rocks. [29] As in an olive orchard three or four olives may be left on every tree, [30] or as when a vineyard is gathered some clusters may be left by those who search carefully through the vineyard, [31] so in those days three or four shall be left by those

who search their houses with the sword. [32] And the earth shall be left desolate, and its fields shall be for briers, and its roads and all its paths shall bring forth thorns, because no sheep will go along them. [33] Virgins shall mourn because they have no bridegrooms; women shall mourn because they have no husbands; their daughters shall mourn, because they have no helpers. [34] Their bridegrooms shall be killed in war, and their husbands shall perish of famine. [35] Listen now to these things, and understand them, 0 servants of the Lord. [36] Behold the word of the Lord, receive it; do not disbelieve what the Lord says. [37] Behold, the calamities draw near, and are not delayed. [38] Just as a woman with child, in the ninth month, when the time of her delivery draws near, has great pains about her womb for two or three hours beforehand, and when the child comes forth from the womb, there will not be a moment's delay, [39] so the calamities will not delay in coming forth upon the earth, and the world will groan, and pains will seize it on every side. [40] "Hear my words, 0 my people; prepare for battle, and in the midst of the calamities be like strangers on the earth. [41] Let him that sells be like one who will flee; let him that buys be like one who will lose; [42] let him that does business be like one who will not make a profit; and let him that builds a house be like one who will not live in it; [43] let him that sows be like one who will not reap; so also him that prunes the vines, like one who will not gather the grapes; [44] them that marry, like those who will have no children; and them that do not marry, like those who are widowed. [45] Because those who labor, labor in vain; [46] for strangers shall gather their fruits, and plunder their goods, and overthrow their houses, and take their children captive; for in captivity and famine they will beget their children. [47] Those who conduct business, do it only to be plundered; the more they adorn their cities, their houses and possessions, and their persons, [48] the more angry I will be with them for their sins," says the Lord. [49] Just as a respectable and virtuous woman abhors a harlot, [50] so righteousness shall abhor iniquity, when she decks herself out, and shall accuse her to her face, when he comes who will defend him who searches out every sin on earth. [51] Therefore do not be like her or her works. [52] For behold, just a little while, and iniquity will be removed from the earth, and righteousness will reign over us. [53] Let no sinner say that he has not sinned; for God will burn coals of fire on the head of him who says, "I have not sinned before God and his glory." [54] Behold, the Lord knows all the works of men, their imaginations and their thoughts and their hearts. [55] He said, "Let the earth be made," and it was made; "Let the heaven be made," and it was made. [56] At his word the stars were fixed, and he knows the number of the stars. [57] It is he who searches the deep and its treasures, who has measured the sea and its contents; [58] who has enclosed the sea in the midst of the waters, and by his word has suspended the earth over the water; [59] who has spread out the heaven like an arch, and founded it upon the waters; [60] who has put springs of water in the desert, and pools on the tops of the mountains, to send rivers from the heights to water the earth; [61] who formed man, and put a heart in the midst of his body, and gave him breath and life and understanding [62] and the spirit of Almighty God; who made all things and searches out hidden things in hidden places. [63] Surely he knows your imaginations and what you think in your hearts! Woe to those who sin and want to hide their sins! [64] Because the Lord will strictly examine all their works, and will make a public spectacle of all of you. [65] And when your sins come out before men, you shall be put to shame; and your own iniquities shall stand as your accusers in that day. [66] What will you do? Or how will you hide your sins before God and his angels? [67] Behold, God is the judge, fear him! Cease from your sins, and forget your iniquities, never to commit them again; so God will lead you forth and deliver you from all tribulation. [68] For behold, the burning wrath of a great multitude is kindled over you, and they shall carry off some of you and shall feed you what was sacrificed to idols. [69] And those who consent to eat shall be held in derision and contempt, and be trodden under foot. [70] For in many places and in neighboring cities there shall be a great insurrection against those who fear the Lord. [71] They shall be like mad men, sparing no one, but plundering and destroying those who continue to fear the Lord. [72] For they shall destroy and plunder their goods, and drive them out of their houses. [73] Then the tested quality of my elect shall be manifest, as gold that is tested by fire. [74] "Hear, my elect," says the Lord. "Behold, the days of tribulation are at hand, and I will deliver you from them. [75] Do not fear or doubt, for God is your guide. [76] You who keep my commandments and precepts," says the Lord God, "do not let your sins pull you down, or your iniquities prevail over you." [77] Woe to those who are choked by their sins and overwhelmed by their iniquities, as a field is choked with underbrush and its path overwhelmed with thorns, so that no one can pass through! [78] It is shut off and given up to be consumed by fire.

THE ADDITIONS TO ESTHER

AddEsth.1

[1] Then Mardocheus said, God hath done these things. [2] For I remember a dream which I saw concerning these matters, and nothing thereof hath failed. [3] A little fountain became a river, and there was light, and the sun, and much water: this river is Esther, whom the king married, and made queen: [4] And the two dragons are I and Aman. [5] And the nations were those that were assembled to destroy the name of the Jews: [6] And my nation is this Israel, which cried to God, and were saved: for the Lord hath saved his people, and the Lord hath delivered us from all those evils, and God hath wrought signs and great wonders, which have not been done among the Gentiles. [7] Therefore hath he made two lots, one for the people of God, and another for all the Gentiles. [8] And these two lots came at the hour, and time, and day of judgment, before God among all nations. [9] So God remembered his people, and justified his inheritance. [10] Therefore those days shall be unto them in the month Adar, the fourteenth and fifteenth day of the same month, with an assembly, and joy, and with gladness before God, according to the generations for ever among his people.

AddEsth.2

[1] In the fourth year of the reign of Ptolemeus and Cleopatra, Dositheus, who said he was a priest and Levite, and Ptolemeus his son, brought this epistle of Phurim, which they said was the same, and that Lysimachus the son of Ptolemeus, that was in Jerusalem, had interpreted it. 2] In the second year of the reign of Artexerxes the great, in the first day of the month Nisan, Mardocheus the son of Jairus, the son of Semei, the son of Cisai, of the tribe of Benjamin, had a dream; [3

] Who was a Jew, and dwelt in the city of Susa, a great man, being a servitor in the king's court. [**4**] He was also one of the captives, which Nabuchodonosor the king of Babylon carried from Jerusalem with Jechonias king of Judea; and this was his dream: [**5**] Behold a noise of a tumult, with thunder, and earthquakes, and uproar in the land: [**6**] And, behold, two great dragons came forth ready to fight, and their cry was great. [**7**] And at their cry all nations were prepared to battle, that they might fight against the righteous people. [**8**] And lo a day of darkness and obscurity, tribulation and anguish, affliction and great uproar, upon earth. [**9**] And the whole righteous nation was troubled, fearing their own evils, and were ready to perish. [**10**] Then they cried unto God, and upon their cry, as it were from a little fountain, was made a great flood, even much water. [**11**] The light and the sun rose up, and the lowly were exalted, and devoured the glorious. [**12**] Now when Mardocheus, who had seen this dream, and what God had determined to do, was awake, he bare this dream in mind, and until night by all means was desirous to know it.

AddEsth.3

[**1**] And Mardocheus took his rest in the court with Gabatha and Tharra, the two eunuchs of the king, and keepers of the palace. [**2**] And he heard their devices, and searched out their purposes, and learned that they were about to lay hands upon Artexerxes the king; and so he certified the king of them. [**3**] Then the king examined the two eunuchs, and after that they had confessed it, they were strangled. [**4**] And the king made a record of these things, and Mardocheus also wrote thereof. [**5**] So the king commanded, Mardocheus to serve in the court, and for this he rewarded him. [**6**] Howbeit Aman the son of Amadathus the Agagite, who was in great honour with the king, sought to molest Mardocheus and his people because of the two eunuchs of the king.

AddEsth.4

[**1**] The copy of the letters was this: The great king Artexerxes writeth these things to the princes and governours that are under him from India unto Ethiopia in an hundred and seven and twenty provinces. [**2**] After that I became lord over many nations and had dominion over the whole world, not lifted up with presumption of my authority, but carrying myself always with equity and mildness, I purposed to settle my subjects continually in a quiet life, and making my kingdom peaceable, and open for passage to the utmost coasts, to renew peace, which is desired of all men. [**3**] Now when I asked my counsellors how this might be brought to pass, Aman, that excelled in wisdom among us, and was approved for his constant good will and steadfast fidelity, and had the honour of the second place in the kingdom, [**4**] Declared unto us, that in all nations throughout the world there was scattered a certain malicious people, that had laws contrary to all nations, and continually despised the commandments of kings, so as the uniting of our kingdoms, honourably intended by us cannot go forward. [**5**] Seeing then we understand that this people alone is continually in opposition unto all men, differing in the strange manner of their laws, and evil affected to our state, working all the mischief they can that our kingdom may not be firmly established: [**6**] Therefore have we commanded, that all they that are signified in writing unto you by Aman, who is ordained over the affairs, and is next unto us, shall all, with their wives and children, be utterly destroyed by the sword of their enemies, without all mercy and pity, the fourteenth day of the twelfth month Adar of this present year: [**7**] That they, who of old and now also are malicious, may in one day with violence go into the grave, and so ever hereafter cause our affairs to be well settled, and without trouble. [**8**] Then Mardocheus thought upon all the works of the Lord, and made his prayer unto him, [**9**] Saying, O Lord, Lord, the King Almighty: for the whole world is in thy power, and if thou hast appointed to save Israel, there is no man that can gainsay thee: [**10**] For thou hast made heaven and earth, and all the wondrous things under the heaven. [**11**] Thou art Lord of all things, and and there is no man that can resist thee, which art the Lord. [**12**] Thou knowest all things, and thou knowest, Lord, that it was neither in contempt nor pride, nor for any desire of glory, that I did not bow down to proud Aman. [**13**] For I could have been content with good will for the salvation of Israel to kiss the soles of his feet. [**14**] But I did this, that I might not prefer the glory of man above the glory of God: neither will I worship any but thee, O God, neither will I do it in pride. [**15**] And now, O Lord God and King, spare thy people: for their eyes are upon us to bring us to nought; yea, they desire to destroy the inheritance, that hath been thine from the beginning. [**16**] Despise not the portion, which thou hast delivered out of Egypt for thine own self. [**17**] Hear my prayer, and be merciful unto thine inheritance: turn our sorrow into joy, that we may live, O Lord, and praise thy name: and destroy not the mouths of them that praise thee, O Lord. [**18**] All Israel in like manner cried most earnestly unto the Lord, because their death was before their eyes.

AddEsth.5

[**1**] Queen Esther also, being in fear of death, resorted unto the Lord: [**2**] And laid away her glorious apparel, and put on the garments of anguish and mourning: and instead of precious ointments, she covered her head with ashes and dung, and she humbled her body greatly, and all the places of her joy she filled with her torn hair. [**3**] And she prayed unto the Lord God of Israel, saying, O my Lord, thou only art our King: help me, desolate woman, which have no helper but thee: [**4**] For my danger is in mine hand. [**5**] From my youth up I have heard in the tribe of my family that thou, O Lord, tookest Israel from among all people, and our fathers from all their predecessors, for a perpetual inheritance, and thou hast performed whatsoever thou didst promise them. [**6**] And now we have sinned before thee: therefore hast thou given us into the hands of our enemies, [**7**] Because we worshipped their gods: O Lord, thou art righteous. [**8**] Nevertheless it satisfieth them not, that we are in bitter captivity: but they have stricken hands with their idols, [**9**] That they will abolish the thing that thou with thy mouth hast ordained, and destroy thine inheritance, and stop the mouth of them that praise thee, and quench the glory of thy house, and of thine altar, [**10**] And open the mouths of the heathen to set forth the praises of the idols, and to magnify a fleshly king for ever. [**11**] O Lord, give not thy sceptre unto them that be nothing, and let them not laugh at our fall; but turn their device upon themselves, and make him an example, that hath begun this against us. [**12**] Remember, O Lord, make thyself known in time of our affliction, and give me boldness, O King of the nations,

and Lord of all power. [13] Give me eloquent speech in my mouth before the lion: turn his heart to hate him that fighteth against us, that there may be an end of him, and of all that are likeminded to him: [14] But deliver us with thine hand, and help me that am desolate, and which have no other help but thee. [15] Thou knowest all things, O Lord; thou knowest that I hate the glory of the unrighteous, and abhor the bed of the uncircumcised, and of all the heathen. [16] Thou knowest my necessity: for I abhor the sign of my high estate, which is upon mine head in the days wherein I shew myself, and that I abhor it as a menstruous rag, and that I wear it not when I am private by myself. [17] And that thine handmaid hath not eaten at Aman's table, and that I have not greatly esteemed the king's feast, nor drunk the wine of the drink offerings. [18] Neither had thine handmaid any joy since the day that I was brought hither to this present, but in thee, O Lord God of Abraham. [19] O thou mighty God above all, hear the voice of the forlorn and deliver us out of the hands of the mischievous, and deliver me out of my fear.

AddEsth.6

[1] And upon the third day, when she had ended her prayers, she laid away her mourning garments, and put on her glorious apparel. [2] And being gloriously adorned, after she had called upon God, who is the beholder and saviour of all things, she took two maids with her: [3] And upon the one she leaned, as carrying herself daintily; [4] And the other followed, bearing up her train. [5] And she was ruddy through the perfection of her beauty, and her countenance was cheerful and very amiable: but her heart was in anguish for fear. [6] Then having passed through all the doors, she stood before the king, who sat upon his royal throne, and was clothed with all his robes of majesty, all glittering with gold and precious stones; and he was very dreadful. [7] Then lifting up his countenance that shone with majesty, he looked very fiercely upon her: and the queen fell down, and was pale, and fainted, and bowed herself upon the head of the maid that went before her. [8] Then God changed the spirit of the king into mildness, who in a fear leaped from his throne, and took her in his arms, till she came to herself again, and comforted her with loving words and said unto her, [9] Esther, what is the matter? I am thy brother, be of good cheer: [10] Thou shalt not die, though our our commandment be general: come near. [11] And so be held up his golden sceptre, and laid it upon her neck, [12] And embraced her, and said, Speak unto me. [13] Then said she unto him, I saw thee, my lord, as an angel of God, and my heart was troubled for fear of thy majesty. [14] For wonderful art thou, lord, and thy countenance is full of grace. [15] And as she was speaking, she fell down for faintness. [16] Then the king was troubled, and ail his servants comforted her.

AddEsth.7

[1] The great king Artexerxes unto the princes and governors of an hundred and seven and twenty provinces from India unto Ethiopia, and unto all our faithful subjects, greeting. [2] Many, the more often they are honoured with the great bounty of their gracious princes, the more proud they are waxen, [3] And endeavour to hurt not our subjects only, but not being able to bear abundance, do take in hand to practise also against those that do them good: [4] And take not only thankfulness away from among men, but also lifted up with the glorious words of lewd persons, that were never good, they think to escape the justice of God, that seeth all things and hateth evil. [5] Oftentimes also fair speech of those, that are put in trust to manage their friends' affairs, hath caused many that are in authority to be partakers of innocent blood, and hath enwrapped them in remediless calamities: [6] Beguiling with the falsehood and deceit of their lewd disposition the innocency and goodness of princes. [7] Now ye may see this, as we have declared, not so much by ancient histories, as ye may, if ye search what hath been wickedly done of late through the pestilent behaviour of them that are unworthily placed in authority. [8] And we must take care for the time to come, that our kingdom may be quiet and peaceable for all men, [9] Both by changing our purposes, and always judging things that are evident with more equal proceeding. [10] For Aman, a Macedonian, the son of Amadatha, being indeed a stranger from the Persian blood, and far distant from our goodness, and as a stranger received of us, [11] Had so far forth obtained the favour that we shew toward every nation, as that he was called our father, and was continually honoured of all the next person unto the king. [12] But he, not bearing his great dignity, went about to deprive us of our kingdom and life: [13] Having by manifold and cunning deceits sought of us the destruction, as well of Mardocheus, who saved our life, and continually procured our good, as also of blameless Esther, partaker of our kingdom, with their whole nation. [14] For by these means he thought, finding us destitute of friends to have translated the kingdom of the Persians to the Macedonians. [15] But we find that the Jews, whom this wicked wretch hath delivered to utter destruction, are no evildoers, but live by most just laws: [16] And that they be children of the most high and most mighty, living God, who hath ordered the kingdom both unto us and to our progenitors in the most excellent manner. [17] Wherefore ye shall do well not to put in execution the letters sent unto you by Aman the son of Amadatha. [18] For he that was the worker of these things, is hanged at the gates of Susa with all his family: God, who ruleth all things, speedily rendering vengeance to him according to his deserts. [19] Therefore ye shall publish the copy of this letter in all places, that the Jews may freely live after their own laws. [20] And ye shall aid them, that even the same day, being the thirteenth day of the twelfth month Adar, they may be avenged on them, who in the time of their affliction shall set upon them. [21] For Almighty God hath turned to joy unto them the day, wherein the chosen people should have perished. [22] Ye shall therefore among your solemn feasts keep it an high day with all feasting: [23] That both now and hereafter there may be safety to us and the well affected Persians; but to those which do conspire against us a memorial of destruction. [24] Therefore every city and country whatsoever, which shall not do according to these things, shall be destroyed without mercy with fire and sword, and shall be made not only unpassable for men, but also most hateful to wild beasts and fowls for ever.

WISDOM APOCRYPHA

THE WISDOM OF SOLOMON

Wis.1

[1] Love righteousness, ye that be judges of the earth: think of the Lord with a good heart, and in simplicity of heart seek him. [2] For he will be found of them that tempt him not; and sheweth himself unto such as do not distrust him. [3] For froward thoughts separate from God: and his power, when it is tried, reproveth the unwise. [4] For into a malicious soul wisdom shall not enter; nor dwell in the body that is subject unto sin. [5] For the holy spirit of discipline will flee deceit, and remove from thoughts that are without understanding, and will not abide when unrighteousness cometh in. [6] For wisdom is a loving spirit; and will not acquit a blasphemer of his words: for God is witness of his reins, and a true beholder of his heart, and a hearer of his tongue. [7] For the Spirit of the Lord filleth the world: and that which containeth all things hath knowledge of the voice. [8] Therefore he that speaketh unrighteous things cannot be hid: neither shall vengeance, when it punisheth, pass by him. [9] For inquisition shall be made into the counsels of the ungodly: and the sound of his words shall come unto the Lord for the manifestation of his wicked deeds. [10] For the ear of jealousy heareth all things: and the noise of murmurings is not hid. [11] Therefore beware of murmuring, which is unprofitable; and refrain your tongue from backbiting: for there is no word so secret, that shall go for nought: and the mouth that belieth slayeth the soul. [12] Seek not death in the error of your life: and pull not upon yourselves destruction with the works of your hands. [13] For God made not death: neither hath he pleasure in the destruction of the living. [14] For he created all things, that they might have their being: and the generations of the world were healthful; and there is no poison of destruction in them, nor the kingdom of death upon the earth: [15] For righteousness is immortal: [16] But ungodly men with their works and words called it to them: for when they thought to have it their friend, they consumed to nought, and made a covenant with it, because they are worthy to take part with it.

Wis.2

[1] For the ungodly said, reasoning with themselves, but not aright, Our life is short and tedious, and in the death of a man there is no remedy: neither was there any man known to have returned from the grave. [2] For we are born at all adventure: and we shall be hereafter as though we had never been: for the breath in our nostrils is as smoke, and a little spark in the moving of our heart: [3] Which being extinguished, our body shall be turned into ashes, and our spirit shall vanish as the soft air, [4] And our name shall be forgotten in time, and no man shall have our works in remembrance, and our life shall pass away as the trace of a cloud, and shall be dispersed as a mist, that is driven away with the beams of the sun, and overcome with the heat thereof. [5] For our time is a very shadow that passeth away; and after our end there is no returning: for it is fast sealed, so that no man cometh again. [6] Come on therefore, let us enjoy the good things that are present: and let us speedily use the creatures like as in youth. [7] Let us fill ourselves with costly wine and ointments: and let no flower of the spring pass by us: [8] Let us crown ourselves with rosebuds, before they be withered: [9] Let none of us go without his part of our voluptuousness: let us leave tokens of our joyfulness in every place: for this is our portion, and our lot is this. [10] Let us oppress the poor righteous man, let us not spare the widow, nor reverence the ancient gray hairs of the aged. [11] Let our strength be the law of justice: for that which is feeble is found to be nothing worth. [12] Therefore let us lie in wait for the righteous; because he is not for our turn, and he is clean contrary to our doings: he upbraideth us with our offending the law, and objecteth to our infamy the transgressings of our education. [13] He professeth to have the knowledge of God: and he calleth himself the child of the Lord. [14] He was made to reprove our thoughts. [15] He is grievous unto us even to behold: for his life is not like other men's, his ways are of another fashion. [16] We are esteemed of him as counterfeits: he abstaineth from our ways as from filthiness: he pronounceth the end of the just to be blessed, and maketh his boast that God is his father. [17] Let us see if his words be true: and let us prove what shall happen in the end of him. [18] For if the just man be the son of God, he will help him, and deliver him from the hand of his enemies. [19] Let us examine him with despitefulness and torture, that we may know his meekness, and prove his patience. [20] Let us condemn him with a shameful death: for by his own saying he shall be respected. [21] Such things they did imagine, and were deceived: for their own wickedness hath blinded them. [22] As for the mysteries of God, they kn ew them not: neither hoped they for the wages of righteousness, nor discerned a reward for blameless souls. [23] For God created man to be immortal, and made him to be an image of his own eternity. [24] Nevertheless through envy of the devil came death into the world: and they that do hold of his side do find it.

Wis.3

[1] But the souls of the righteous are in the hand of God, and there shall no torment touch them. [2] In the sight of the unwise they seemed to die: and their departure is taken for misery, [3] And their going from us to be utter destruction: but they are in peace. [4] For though they be punished in the sight of men, yet is their hope full of immortality. [5] And having been a little chastised, they shall be greatly rewarded: for God proved them, and found them worthy for himself. [6] As gold in the furnace hath he tried them, and received them as a burnt offering. [7] And in the time of their visitation they shall shine, and run to and fro like sparks among the stubble. [8] They shall judge the nations, and have dominion over the people, and their Lord shall reign for ever. [9] They that put their trust in him shall understand the truth: and such as be faithful in love shall abide with him: for grace and mercy is to his saints, and he hath care for his elect. [10] But the ungodly shall be punished according to their own imaginations, which have neglected the righteous, and forsaken the Lord. [11] For whoso despiseth wisdom and nurture, he is miserable, and their hope is vain, their labours unfruitful, and their works unprofitable: [12] Their wives are foolish, and their children wicked: [13] Their offspring is cursed. Wherefore blessed is the barren that is undefiled, which hath not known the sinful bed: she shall have fruit in the visitation

of souls. [14] And blessed is the eunuch, which with his hands hath wrought no iniquity, nor imagined wicked things against God: for unto him shall be given the special gift of faith, and an inheritance in the temple of the Lord more acceptable to his mind. [15] For glorious is the fruit of good labours: and the root of wisdom shall never fall away. [16] As for the children of adulterers, they shall not come to their perfection, and the seed of an unrighteous bed shall be rooted out. [17] For though they live long, yet shall they be nothing regarded: and their last age shall be without honour. [18] Or, if they die quickly, they have no hope, neither comfort in the day of trial. [19] For horrible is the end of the unrighteous generation.

Wis.4

[1] Better it is to have no children, and to have virtue: for the memorial thereof is immortal: because it is known with God, and with men. [2] When it is present, men take example at it; and when it is gone, they desire it: it weareth a crown, and triumpheth for ever, having gotten the victory, striving for undefiled rewards. [3] But the multiplying brood of the ungodly shall not thrive, nor take deep rooting from bastard slips, nor lay any fast foundation. [4] For though they flourish in branches for a time; yet standing not last, they shall be shaken with the wind, and through the force of winds they shall be rooted out. [5] The imperfect branches shall be broken off, their fruit unprofitable, not ripe to eat, yea, meet for nothing. [6] For children begotten of unlawful beds are witnesses of wickedness against their parents in their trial. [7] But though the righteous be prevented with death, yet shall he be in rest. [8] For honourable age is not that which standeth in length of time, nor that is measured by number of years. [9] But wisdom is the gray hair unto men, and an unspotted life is old age. [10] He pleased God, and was beloved of him: so that living among sinners he was translated. [11] Yea speedily was he taken away, lest that wickedness should alter his understanding, or deceit beguile his soul. [12] For the bewitching of naughtiness doth obscure things that are honest; and the wandering of concupiscence doth undermine the simple mind. [13] He, being made perfect in a short time, fulfilled a long time: [14] For his soul pleased the Lord: therefore hasted he to take him away from among the wicked. [15] This the people saw, and understood it not, neither laid they up this in their minds, That his grace and mercy is with his saints, and that he hath respect unto his chosen. [16] Thus the righteous that is dead shall condemn the ungodly which are living; and youth that is soon perfected the many years and old age of the unrighteous. [17] For they shall see the end of the wise, and shall not understand what God in his counsel hath decreed of him, and to what end the Lord hath set him in safety. [18] They shall see him, and despise him; but God shall laugh them to scorn: and they shall hereafter be a vile carcase, and a reproach among the dead for evermore. [19] For he shall rend them, and cast them down headlong, that they shall be speechless; and he shall shake them from the foundation; and they shall be utterly laid waste, and be in sorrow; and their memorial shall perish. [20] And when they cast up the accounts of their sins, they shall come with fear: and their own iniquities shall convince them to their face.

Wis.5

[1] Then shall the righteous man stand in great boldness before the face of such as have afflicted him, and made no account of his labours. [2] When they see it, they shall be troubled with terrible fear, and shall be amazed at the strangeness of his salvation, so far beyond all that they looked for. [3] And they repenting and groaning for anguish of spirit shall say within themselves, This was he, whom we had sometimes in derision, and a proverb of reproach: [4] We fools accounted his life madness, and his end to be without honour: [5] How is he numbered among the children of God, and his lot is among the saints! [6] Therefore have we erred from the way of truth, and the light of righteousness hath not shined unto us, and the sun of righteousness rose not upon us. [7] We wearied ourselves in the way of wickedness and destruction: yea, we have gone through deserts, where there lay no way: but as for the way of the Lord, we have not known it. [8] What hath pride profited us? or what good hath riches with our vaunting brought us? [9] All those things are passed away like a shadow, and as a post that hasted by; [10] And as a ship that passeth over the waves of the water, which when it is gone by, the trace thereof cannot be found, neither the pathway of the keel in the waves; [11] Or as when a bird hath flown through the air, there is no token of her way to be found, but the light air being beaten with the stroke of her wings and parted with the violent noise and motion of them, is passed through, and therein afterwards no sign where she went is to be found; [12] Or like as when an arrow is shot at a mark, it parteth the air, which immediately cometh together again, so that a man cannot know where it went through: [13] Even so we in like manner, as soon as we were born, began to draw to our end, and had no sign of virtue to shew; but were consumed in our own wickedness. [14] For the hope of the Godly is like dust that is blown away with the wind; like a thin froth that is driven away with the storm; like as the smoke which is dispersed here and there with a tempest, and passeth away as the remembrance of a guest that tarrieth but a day. [15] But the righteous live for evermore; their reward also is with the Lord, and the care of them is with the most High. [16] Therefore shall they receive a glorious kingdom, and a beautiful crown from the Lord's hand: for with his right hand shall he cover them, and with his arm shall he protect them. [17] He shall take to him his jealousy for complete armour, and make the creature his weapon for the revenge of his enemies. [18] He shall put on righteousness as a breastplate, and true judgment instead of an helmet. [19] He shall take holiness for an invincible shield. [20] His severe wrath shall he sharpen for a sword, and the world shall fight with him against the unwise. [21] Then shall the right aiming thunderbolts go abroad; and from the clouds, as from a well drawn bow, shall they fly to the mark. [22] And hailstones full of wrath shall be cast as out of a stone bow, and the water of the sea shall rage against them, and the floods shall cruelly drown them. [23] Yea, a mighty wind shall stand up against them, and like a storm shall blow them away: thus iniquity shall lay waste the whole earth, and ill dealing shall overthrow the thrones of the mighty.

Wis.6

[1] Hear therefore, O ye kings, and understand; learn, ye that be judges of the ends of the earth. [2] Give ear, ye that rule the people, and glory in the multitude of nations. [3] For power is given you of the Lord, and sovereignty from the Highest,

who shall try your works, and search out your counsels. [4] Because, being ministers of his kingdom, ye have not judged aright, nor kept the law, nor walked after the counsel of God; [5] Horribly and speedily shall he come upon you: for a sharp judgment shall be to them that be in high places. [6] For mercy will soon pardon the meanest: but mighty men shall be mightily tormented. [7] For he which is Lord over all shall fear no man's person, neither shall he stand in awe of any man's greatness: for he hath made the small and great, and careth for all alike. [8] But a sore trial shall come upon the mighty. [9] Unto you therefore, O kings, do I speak, that ye may learn wisdom, and not fall away. [10] For they that keep holiness holily shall be judged holy: and they that have learned such things shall find what to answer. [11] Wherefore set your affection upon my words; desire them, and ye shall be instructed. [12] Wisdom is glorious, and never fadeth away: yea, she is easily seen of them that love her, and found of such as seek her. [13] She preventeth them that desire her, in making herself first known unto them. [14] Whoso seeketh her early shall have no great travail: for he shall find her sitting at his doors. [15] To think therefore upon her is perfection of wisdom: and whoso watcheth for her shall quickly be without care. [16] For she goeth about seeking such as are worthy of her, sheweth herself favourably unto them in the ways, and meeteth them in every thought. [17] For the very true beginning of her is the desire of discipline; and the care of discipline is love; [18] And love is the keeping of her laws; and the giving heed unto her laws is the assurance of incorruption; [19] And incorruption maketh us near unto God: [20] Therefore the desire of wisdom bringeth to a kingdom. [21] If your delight be then in thrones and sceptres, O ye kings of the people, honour wisdom, that ye may reign for evermore. [22] As for wisdom, what she is, and how she came up, I will tell you, and will not hide mysteries from you: but will seek her out from the beginning of her nativity, and bring the knowledge of her into light, and will not pass over the truth. [23] Neither will I go with consuming envy; for such a man shall have no fellowship with wisdom. [24] But the multitude of the wise is the welfare of the world: and a wise king is the upholding of the people. [25] Receive therefore instruction through my words, and it shall do you good.

Wis. 7

[1] I myself also am a mortal man, like to all, and the offspring of him that was first made of the earth, [2] And in my mother's womb was fashioned to be flesh in the time of ten months, being compacted in blood, of the seed of man, and the pleasure that came with sleep. [3] And when I was born, I drew in the common air, and fell upon the earth, which is of like nature, and the first voice which I uttered was crying, as all others do. [4] I was nursed in swaddling clothes, and that with cares. [5] For there is no king that had any other beginning of birth. [6] For all men have one entrance into life, and the like going out. [7] Wherefore I prayed, and understanding was given me: I called upon God, and the spirit of wisdom came to me [8] I preferred her before sceptres and thrones, and esteemed riches nothing in comparison of her. [9] Neither compared I unto her any precious stone, because all gold in respect of her is as a little sand, and silver shall be counted as clay before her. [10] I loved her above health and beauty, and chose to have her instead of light: for the light that còmeth from her never goeth out. [11] All good things together came to me with her, and innumerable riches in her hands. [12] And I rejoiced in them all, because wisdom goeth before them: and I knew not that she was the mother of them. [13] I learned diligently, and do communicate her liberally: I do not hide her riches. [14] For she is a treasure unto men that never faileth: which they that use become the friends of God, being commended for the gifts that come from learning. [15] God hath granted me to speak as I would, and to conceive as is meet for the things that are given me: because it is he that leadeth unto wisdom, and directeth the wise. [16] For in his hand are both we and our words; all wisdom also, and knowledge of workmanship. [17] For he hath given me certain knowledge of the things that are, namely, to know how the world was made, and the operation of the elements: [18] The beginning, ending, and midst of the times: the alterations of the turning of the sun, and the change of seasons: [19] The circuits of years, and the positions of stars: [20] The natures of living creatures, and the furies of wild beasts: the violence of winds, and the reasonings of men: the diversities of plants and the virtues of roots: [21] And all such things as are either secret or manifest, them I know. [22] For wisdom, which is the worker of all things, taught me: for in her is an understanding spirit holy, one only, manifold, subtil, lively, clear, undefiled, plain, not subject to hurt, loving the thing that is good quick, which cannot be letted, ready to do good, [23] Kind to man, steadfast, sure, free from care, having all power, overseeing all things, and going through all understanding, pure, and most subtil, spirits. [24] For wisdom is more moving than any motion: she passeth and goeth through all things by reason of her pureness. [25] For she is the breath of the power of God, and a pure influence flowing from the glory of the Almighty: therefore can no defiled thing fall into her. [26] For she is the brightness of the everlasting light, the unspotted mirror of the power of God, and the image of his goodness. [27] And being but one, she can do all things: and remaining in herself, she maketh all things new: and in all ages entering into holy souls, she maketh them friends of God, and prophets. [28] For God loveth none but him that dwelleth with wisdom. [29] For she is more beautiful than the sun, and above all the order of stars: being compared with the light, she is found before it. [30] For after this cometh night: but vice shall not prevail against wisdom.

Wis. 8

[1] Wisdom reacheth from one end to another mightily: and sweetly doth she order all things. [2] I loved her, and sought her out from my youth, I desired to make her my spouse, and I was a lover of her beauty. [3] In that she is conversant with God, she magnifieth her nobility: yea, the Lord of all things himself loved her. [4] For she is privy to the mysteries of the knowledge of God, and a lover of his works. [5] If riches be a possession to be desired in this life; what is richer than wisdom, that worketh all things? [6] And if prudence work; who of all that are is a more cunning workman than she? [7] And if a man love righteousness her labours are virtues: for she teacheth temperance and prudence, justice and fortitude: which are such things, as en can have nothing more profitable in their life. [8] If a man desire much experience, she knoweth things of old, and conjectureth aright what is to come: she knoweth the subtilties of speeches, and can expound dark sentences: she foreseeth signs and wonders, and the events of seasons and times. [9] Therefore I purposed to take her to me to live with me, knowing that she would be a counsellor of good things, and a comfort in cares and grief. [10]

For her sake I shall have estimation among the multitude, and honour with the elders, though I be young. [11] I shall be found of a quick conceit in judgment, and shall be admired in the sight of great men. [12] When I hold my tongue, they shall bide my leisure, and when I speak, they shall give good ear unto me: if I talk much, they shall lay their hands upon their mouth. [13] Moreover by the means of her I shall obtain immortality, and leave behind me an everlasting memorial to them that come after me. [14] I shall set the people in order, and the nations shall be subject unto me. [15] Horrible tyrants shall be afraid, when they do but hear of me; I shall be found good among the multitude, and valiant in war. [16] After I am come into mine house, I will repose myself with her: for her conversation hath no bitterness; and to live with her hath no sorrow, but mirth and joy. [17] Now when I considered these things in myself, and pondered them in my heart, how that to be allied unto wisdom is immortality; [18] And great pleasure it is to have her friendship; and in the works of her hands are infinite riches; and in the exercise of conference with her, prudence; and in talking with her, a good report; I went about seeking how to take her to me. [19] For I was a witty child, and had a good spirit. [20] Yea rather, being good, I came into a body undefiled. [21] Nevertheless, when I perceived that I could not otherwise obtain her, except God gave her me; and that was a point of wisdom also to know whose gift she was; I prayed unto the Lord, and besought him, and with my whole heart I said,

Wis.9

[1] O God of my fathers, and Lord of mercy, who hast made all things with thy word, [2] And ordained man through thy wisdom, that he should have dominion over the creatures which thou hast made, [3] And order the world according to equity and righteousness, and execute judgment with an upright heart: [4] Give me wisdom, that sitteth by thy throne; and reject me not from among thy children: [5] For I thy servant and son of thine handmaid am a feeble person, and of a short time, and too young for the understanding of judgment and laws. [6] For though a man be never so perfect among the children of men, yet if thy wisdom be not with him, he shall be nothing regarded. [7] Thou hast chosen me to be a king of thy people, and a judge of thy sons and daughters: [8] Thou hast commanded me to build a temple upon thy holy mount, and an altar in the city wherein thou dwellest, a resemblance of the holy tabernacle, which thou hast prepared from the beginning. [9] And wisdom was with thee: which knoweth thy works, and was present when thou madest the world, and knew what was acceptable in thy sight, and right in thy commandments. [10] O send her out of thy holy heavens, and from the throne of thy glory, that being present she may labour with me, that I may know what is pleasing unto thee. [11] For she knoweth and understandeth all things, and she shall lead me soberly in my doings, and preserve me in her power. [12] So shall my works be acceptable, and then shall I judge thy people righteously, and be worthy to sit in my father's seat. [13] For what man is he that can know the counsel of God? or who can think what the will of the Lord is? [14] For the thoughts of mortal men are miserable, and our devices are but uncertain. [15] For the corruptible body presseth down the soul, and the earthy tabernacle weigheth down the mind that museth upon many things. [16] And hardly do we guess aright at things that are upon earth, and with labour do we find the things that are before us: but the things that are in heaven who hath searched out? [17] And thy counsel who hath known, except thou give wisdom, and send thy Holy Spirit from above? [18] For so the ways of them which lived on the earth were reformed, and men were taught the things that are pleasing unto thee, and were saved through wisdom.

Wis.10

[1] She preserved the first formed father of the world, that was created alone, and brought him out of his fall, [2] And gave him power to rule all things. [3] But when the unrighteous went away from her in his anger, he perished also in the fury wherewith he murdered his brother. [4] For whose cause the earth being drowned with the flood, wisdom again preserved it, and directed the course of the righteous in a piece of wood of small value. [5] Moreover, the nations in their wicked conspiracy being confounded, she found out the righteous, and preserved him blameless unto God, and kept him strong against his tender compassion toward his son. [6] When the ungodly perished, she delivered the righteous man, who fled from the fire which fell down upon the five cities. [7] Of whose wickedness even to this day the waste land that smoketh is a testimony, and plants bearing fruit that never come to ripeness: and a standing pillar of salt is a monument of an unbelieving soul. [8] For regarding not wisdom, they gat not only this hurt, that they knew not the things which were good; but also left behind them to the world a memorial of their foolishness: so that in the things wherein they offended they could not so much as be hid. [9] Rut wisdom delivered from pain those that attended upon her. [10] When the righteous fled from his brother's wrath she guided him in right paths, shewed him the kingdom of God, and gave him knowledge of holy things, made him rich in his travels, and multiplied the fruit of his labours. [11] In the covetousness of such as oppressed him she stood by him, and made him rich. [12] She defended him from his enemies, and kept him safe from those that lay in wait, and in a sore conflict she gave him the victory; that he might know that goodness is stronger than all. [13] When the righteous was sold, she forsook him not, but delivered him from sin: she went down with him into the pit, [14] And left him not in bonds, till she brought him the sceptre of the kingdom, and power against those that oppressed him: as for them that had accused him, she shewed them to be liars, and gave him perpetual glory. [15] She delivered the righteous people and blameless seed from the nation that oppressed them. [16] She entered into the soul of the servant of the Lord, and withstood dreadful kings in wonders and signs; [17] Rendered to the righteous a reward of their labours, guided them in a marvellous way, and was unto them for a cover by day, and a light of stars in the night season; [18] Brought them through the Red sea, and led them through much water: [19] But she drowned their enemies, and cast them up out of the bottom of the deep. [20] Therefore the righteous spoiled the ungodly, and praised thy holy name, O Lord, and magnified with one accord thine hand, that fought for them. [21] For wisdom opened the mouth of the dumb, and made the tongues of them that cannot speak eloquent.

Wis.11

[1] She prospered their works in the hand of the holy prophet. [2] They went through the wilderness that was not inhabited, and pitched tents in places where there lay no way. [3] They stood against their enemies, and were avenged of their adversaries. [4] When they were thirsty, they called upon thee, and water was given them out of the flinty rock, and their thirst was quenched out of the hard stone. [5] For by what things their enemies were punished, by the same they in their need were benefited. [6] For instead of of a perpetual running river troubled with foul blood, [7] For a manifest reproof of that commandment, whereby the infants were slain, thou gavest unto them abundance of water by a means which they hoped not for: [8] Declaring by that thirst then how thou hadst punished their adversaries. [9] For when they were tried albeit but in mercy chastised, they knew how the ungodly were judged in wrath and tormented, thirsting in another manner than the just. [10] For these thou didst admonish and try, as a father: but the other, as a severe king, thou didst condemn and punish. [11] Whether they were absent or present, they were vexed alike. [12] For a double grief came upon them, and a groaning for the remembrance of things past. [13] For when they heard by their own punishments the other to be benefited, they had some feeling of the Lord. [14] For whom they respected with scorn, when he was long before thrown out at the casting forth of the infants, him in the end, when they saw what came to pass, they admired. [15] But for the foolish devices of their wickedness, wherewith being deceived they worshipped serpents void of reason, and vile beasts, thou didst send a multitude of unreasonable beasts upon them for vengeance; [16] That they might know, that wherewithal a man sinneth, by the same also shall he be punished. [17] For thy Almighty hand, that made the world of matter without form, wanted not means to send among them a multitude of bears or fierce lions, [18] Or unknown wild beasts, full of rage, newly created, breathing out either a fiery vapour, or filthy scents of scattered smoke, or shooting horrible sparkles out of their eyes: [19] Whereof not only the harm might dispatch them at once, but also the terrible sight utterly destroy them. [20] Yea, and without these might they have fallen down with one blast, being persecuted of vengeance, and scattered abroad through the breath of thy power: but thou hast ordered all things in measure and number and weight. [21] For thou canst shew thy great strength at all times when thou wilt; and who may withstand the power of thine arm? [22] For the whole world before thee is as a little grain of the balance, yea, as a drop of the morning dew that falleth down upon the earth. [23] But thou hast mercy upon all; for thou canst do all things, and winkest at the sins of men, because they should amend. [24] For thou lovest all the things that are, and abhorrest nothing which thou hast made: for never wouldest thou have made any thing, if thou hadst hated it. [25] And how could any thing have endured, if it had not been thy will? or been preserved, if not called by thee? [26] But thou sparest all: for they are thine, O Lord, thou lover of souls.

Wis.12

[1] For thine incorruptible Spirit is in all things. [2] Therefore chastenest thou them by little and little that offend, and warnest them by putting them in remembrance wherein they have offended, that leaving their wickedness they may believe on thee, O Lord. [3] For it was thy will to destroy by the hands of our fathers both those old inhabitants of thy holy land, [4] Whom thou hatedst for doing most odious works of witchcrafts, and wicked sacrifices; [5] And also those merciless murderers of children, and devourers of man's flesh, and the feasts of blood, [6] With their priests out of the midst of their idolatrous crew, and the parents, that killed with their own hands souls destitute of help: [7] That the land, which thou esteemedst above all other, might receive a worthy colony of God's children. [8] Nevertheless even those thou sparedst as men, and didst send wasps, forerunners of thine host, to destroy them by little and little. [9] Not that thou wast unable to bring the ungodly under the hand of the righteous in battle, or to destroy them at once with cruel beasts, or with one rough word: [10] But executing thy judgments upon them by little and little, thou gavest them place of repentance, not being ignorant that they were a naughty generation, and that their malice was bred in them, and that their cogitation would never be changed. [11] For it was a cursed seed from the beginning; neither didst thou for fear of any man give them pardon for those things wherein they sinned. [12] For who shall say, What hast thou done? or who shall withstand thy judgment? or who shall accuse thee for the nations that perish, whom thou made? or who shall come to stand against thee, to be revenged for the unrighteous men? [13] For neither is there any God but thou that careth for all, to whom thou mightest shew that thy judgment is not unright. [14] Neither shall king or tyrant be able to set his face against thee for any whom thou hast punished. [15] Forsomuch then as thou art righteous thyself, thou orderest all things righteously: thinking it not agreeable with thy power to condemn him that hath not deserved to be punished. [16] For thy power is the beginning of righteousness, and because thou art the Lord of all, it maketh thee to be gracious unto all. [17] For when men will not believe that thou art of a full power, thou shewest thy strength, and among them that know it thou makest their boldness manifest. [18] But thou, mastering thy power, judgest with equity, and orderest us with great favour: for thou mayest use power when thou wilt. [19] But by such works hast thou taught thy people that the just man should be merciful, and hast made thy children to be of a good hope that thou givest repentance for sins. [20] For if thou didst punish the enemies of thy children, and the condemned to death, with such deliberation, giving them time and place, whereby they might be delivered from their malice: [21] With how great circumspection didst thou judge thine own sons, unto whose fathers thou hast sworn, and made covenants of good promises? [22] Therefore, whereas thou dost chasten us, thou scourgest our enemies a thousand times more, to the intent that, when we judge, we should carefully think of thy goodness, and when we ourselves are judged, we should look for mercy. [23] Wherefore, whereas men have lived dissolutely and unrighteously, thou hast tormented them with their own abominations. [24] For they went astray very far in the ways of error, and held them for gods, which even among the beasts of their enemies were despised, being deceived, as children of no understanding. [25] Therefore unto them, as to children without the use of reason, thou didst send a judgment to mock them. [26] But they that would not be reformed by that correction, wherein he dallied with them, shall feel a judgment worthy of God. [27] For, look, for what things they grudged, when they were punished, that is, for them whom they thought to be gods; [now] being punished in them, when they saw it, they acknowledged him to be the true God, whom before they denied to know: and therefore came extreme damnation upon them.

Wis. 13

[1] Surely vain are all men by nature, who are ignorant of God, and could not out of the good things that are seen know him that is: neither by considering the works did they acknowledge the workmaster; [2] But deemed either fire, or wind, or the swift air, or the circle of the stars, or the violent water, or the lights of heaven, to be the gods which govern the world. [3] With whose beauty if they being delighted took them to be gods; let them know how much better the Lord of them is: for the first author of beauty hath created them. [4] But if they were astonished at their power and virtue, let them understand by them, how much mightier he is that made them. [5] For by the greatness and beauty of the creatures proportionably the maker of them is seen. [6] But yet for this they are the less to be blamed: for they peradventure err, seeking God, and desirous to find him. [7] For being conversant in his works they search him diligently, and believe their sight: because the things are beautiful that are seen. [8] Howbeit neither are they to be pardoned. [9] For if they were able to know so much, that they could aim at the world; how did they not sooner find out the Lord thereof? [10] But miserable are they, and in dead things is their hope, who call them gods, which are the works of men's hands, gold and silver, to shew art in, and resemblances of beasts, or a stone good for nothing, the work of an ancient hand. [11] Now a carpenter that felleth timber, after he hath sawn down a tree meet for the purpose, and taken off all the bark skilfully round about, and hath wrought it handsomely, and made a vessel thereof fit for the service of man's life; [12] And after spending the refuse of his work to dress his meat, hath filled himself; [13] And taking the very refuse among those which served to no use, being a crooked piece of wood, and full of knots, hath carved it diligently, when he had nothing else to do, and formed it by the skill of his understanding, and fashioned it to the image of a man; [14] Or made it like some vile beast, laying it over with vermilion, and with paint colouring it red, and covering every spot therein; [15] And when he had made a convenient room for it, set it in a wall, and made it fast with iron: [16] For he provided for it that it might not fall, knowing that it was unable to help itself; for it is an image, and hath need of help: [17] Then maketh he prayer for his goods, for his wife and children, and is not ashamed to speak to that which hath no life. [18] For health he calleth upon that which is weak: for life prayeth to that which is dead; for aid humbly beseecheth that which hath least means to help: and for a good journey he asketh of that which cannot set a foot forward: [19] And for gaining and getting, and for good success of his hands, asketh ability to do of him, that is most unable to do any thing.

Wis. 14

[1] Again, one preparing himself to sail, and about to pass through the raging waves, calleth upon a piece of wood more rotten than the vessel that carrieth him. [2] For verily desire of gain devised that, and the workman built it by his skill. [3] But thy providence, O Father, governeth it: for thou hast made a way in the sea, and a safe path in the waves; [4] Shewing that thou canst save from all danger: yea, though a man went to sea without art. [5] Nevertheless thou wouldest not that the works of thy wisdom should be idle, and therefore do men commit their lives to a small piece of wood, and passing the rough sea in a weak vessel are saved. [6] For in the old time also, when the proud giants perished, the hope of the world governed by thy hand escaped in a weak vessel, and left to all ages a seed of generation. [7] For blessed is the wood whereby righteousness cometh. [8] But that which is made with hands is cursed, as well it, as he that made it: he, because he made it; and it, because, being corruptible, it was called god. [9] For the ungodly and his ungodliness are both alike hateful unto God. [10] For that which is made shall be punished together with him that made it. [11] Therefore even upon the idols of the Gentiles shall there be a visitation: because in the creature of God they are become an abomination, and stumblingblocks to the souls of men, and a snare to the feet of the unwise. [12] For the devising of idols was the beginning of spiritual fornication, and the invention of them the corruption of life. [13] For neither were they from the beginning, neither shall they be for ever. [14] For by the vain glory of men they entered into the world, and therefore shall they come shortly to an end. [15] For a father afflicted with untimely mourning, when he hath made an image of his child soon taken away, now honoured him as a god, which was then a dead man, and delivered to those that were under him ceremonies and sacrifices. [16] Thus in process of time an ungodly custom grown strong was kept as a law, and graven images were worshipped by the commandments of kings. [17] Whom men could not honour in presence, because they dwelt far off, they took the counterfeit of his visage from far, and made an express image of a king whom they honoured, to the end that by this their forwardness they might flatter him that was absent, as if he were present. [18] Also the singular diligence of the artificer did help to set forward the ignorant to more superstition. [19] For he, peradventure willing to please one in authority, forced all his skill to make the resemblance of the best fashion. [20] And so the multitude, allured by the grace of the work, took him now for a god, which a little before was but honoured. [21] And this was an occasion to deceive the world: for men, serving either calamity or tyranny, did ascribe unto stones and stocks the incommunicable name. [22] Moreover this was not enough for them, that they erred in the knowledge of God; but whereas they lived in the great war of ignorance, those so great plagues called they peace. [23] For whilst they slew their children in sacrifices, or used secret ceremonies, or made revellings of strange rites; [24] They kept neither lives nor marriages any longer undefiled: but either one slew another traiterously, or grieved him by adultery. [25] So that there reigned in all men without exception blood, manslaughter, theft, and dissimulation, corruption, unfaithfulness, tumults, perjury, [26] Disquieting of good men, forgetfulness of good turns, defiling of souls, changing of kind, disorder in marriages, adultery, and shameless uncleanness. [27] For the worshipping of idols not to be named is the beginning, the cause, and the end, of all evil. [28] For either they are mad when they be merry, or prophesy lies, or live unjustly, or else lightly forswear themselves. [29] For insomuch as their trust is in idols, which have no life; though they swear falsely, yet they look not to be hurt. [30] Howbeit for both causes shall they be justly punished: both because they thought not well of God, giving heed unto idols, and also unjustly swore in deceit, despising holiness. [31] For it is not the power of them by whom they swear: but it is the just vengeance of sinners, that punisheth always the offence of the ungodly.

Wis.15

[1] But thou, O God, art gracious and true, longsuffering, and in mercy ordering all things, [2] For if we sin, we are thine, knowing thy power: but we will not sin, knowing that we are counted thine. [3] For to know thee is perfect righteousness: yea, to know thy power is the root of immortality. [4] For neither did the mischievous invention of men deceive us, nor an image spotted with divers colours, the painter's fruitless labour; [5] The sight whereof enticeth fools to lust after it, and so they desire the form of a dead image, that hath no breath. [6] Both they that make them, they that desire them, and they that worship them, are lovers of evil things, and are worthy to have such things to trust upon. [7] For the potter, tempering soft earth, fashioneth every vessel with much labour for our service: yea, of the same clay he maketh both the vessels that serve for clean uses, and likewise also all such as serve to the contrary: but what is the use of either sort, the potter himself is the judge. [8] And employing his labours lewdly, he maketh a vain god of the same clay, even he which a little before was made of earth himself, and within a little while after returneth to the same, out when his life which was lent him shall be demanded. [9] Notwithstanding his care is, not that he shall have much labour, nor that his life is short: but striveth to excel goldsmiths and silversmiths, and endeavoureth to do like the workers in brass, and counteth it his glory to make counterfeit things. [10] His heart is ashes, his hope is more vile than earth, and his life of less value than clay: [11] Forasmuch as he knew not his Maker, and him that inspired into him an active soul, and breathed in a living spirit. [12] But they counted our life a pastime, and our time here a market for gain: for, say they, we must be getting every way, though it be by evil means. [13] For this man, that of earthly matter maketh brittle vessels and graven images, knoweth himself to offend above all others. [14] And all the enemies of thy people, that hold them in subjection, are most foolish, and are more miserable than very babes. [15] For they counted all the idols of the heathen to be gods: which neither have the use of eyes to see, nor noses to draw breath, nor ears to hear, nor fingers of hands to handle; and as for their feet, they are slow to go. [16] For man made them, and he that borrowed his own spirit fashioned them: but no man can make a god like unto himself. [17] For being mortal, he worketh a dead thing with wicked hands: for he himself is better than the things which he worshippeth: whereas he lived once, but they never. [18] Yea, they worshipped those beasts also that are most hateful: for being compared together, some are worse than others. [19] Neither are they beautiful, so much as to be desired in respect of beasts: but they went without the praise of God and his blessing.

Wis.16

[1] Therefore by the like were they punished worthily, and by the multitude of beasts tormented. [2] Instead of which punishment, dealing graciously with thine own people, thou preparedst for them meat of a strange taste, even quails to stir up their appetite: [3] To the end that they, desiring food, might for the ugly sight of the beasts sent among them lothe even that, which they must needs desire; but these, suffering penury for a short space, might be made partakers of a strange taste. [4] For it was requisite, that upon them exercising tyranny should come penury, which they could not avoid: but to these it should only be shewed how their enemies were tormented. [5] For when the horrible fierceness of beasts came upon these, and they perished with the stings of crooked serpents, thy wrath endured not for ever: [6] But they were troubled for a small season, that they might be admonished, having a sign of salvation, to put them in remembrance of the commandment of thy law. [7] For he that turned himself toward it was not saved by the thing that he saw, but by thee, that art the Saviour of all. [8] And in this thou madest thine enemies confess, that it is thou who deliverest from all evil: [9] For them the bitings of grasshoppers and flies killed, neither was there found any remedy for their life: for they were worthy to be punished by such. [10] But thy sons not the very teeth of venomous dragons overcame: for thy mercy was ever by them, and healed them. [11] For they were pricked, that they should remember thy words; and were quickly saved, that not falling into deep forgetfulness, they might be continually mindful of thy goodness. [12] For it was neither herb, nor mollifying plaister, that restored them to health: but thy word, O Lord, which healeth all things. [13] For thou hast power of life and death: thou leadest to the gates of hell, and bringest up again. [14] A man indeed killeth through his malice: and the spirit, when it is gone forth, returneth not; neither the soul received up cometh again. [15] But it is not possible to escape thine hand. [16] For the ungodly, that denied to know thee, were scourged by the strength of thine arm: with strange rains, hails, and showers, were they persecuted, that they could not avoid, and through fire were they consumed. [17] For, which is most to be wondered at, the fire had more force in the water, that quencheth all things: for the world fighteth for the righteous. [18] For sometime the flame was mitigated, that it might not burn up the beasts that were sent against the ungodly; but themselves might see and perceive that they were persecuted with the judgment of God. [19] And at another time it burneth even in the midst of water above the power of fire, that it might destroy the fruits of an unjust land. [20] Instead whereof thou feddest thine own people with angels' food, and didst send them from heaven bread prepared without their labour, able to content every man's delight, and agreeing to every taste. [21] For thy sustenance declared thy sweetness unto thy children, and serving to the appetite of the eater, tempered itself to every man's liking. [22] But snow and ice endured the fire, and melted not, that they might know that fire burning in the hail, and sparkling in the rain, did destroy the fruits of the enemies. [23] But this again did even forget his own strength, that the righteous might be nourished. [24] For the creature that serveth thee, who art the Maker increaseth his strength against the unrighteous for their punishment, and abateth his strength for the benefit of such as put their trust in thee. [25] Therefore even then was it altered into all fashions, and was obedient to thy grace, that nourisheth all things, according to the desire of them that had need: [26] That thy children, O Lord, whom thou lovest, might know, that it is not the growing of fruits that nourisheth man: but that it is thy word, which preserveth them that put their trust in thee. [27] For that which was not destroyed of the fire, being warmed with a little sunbeam, soon melted away: [28] That it might be known, that we must prevent the sun to give thee thanks, and at the dayspring pray unto thee. [29] For the hope of the unthankful shall melt away as the winter's hoar frost, and shall run away as unprofitable water.

Wis.17

[1] For great are thy judgments, and cannot be expressed: therefore unnurtured souls have erred. [2] For when unrighteous men thought to oppress the holy nation; they being shut up in their houses, the prisoners of darkness, and fettered with the bonds of a long night, lay there exiled from the eternal providence. [3] For while they supposed to lie hid in their secret sins, they were scattered under a dark veil of forgetfulness, being horribly astonished, and troubled with [strange] apparitions. [4] For neither might the corner that held them keep them from fear: but noises [as of waters] falling down sounded about them, and sad visions appeared unto them with heavy countenances. [5] No power of the fire might give them light: neither could the bright flames of the stars endure to lighten that horrible night. [6] Only there appeared unto them a fire kindled of itself, very dreadful: for being much terrified, they thought the things which they saw to be worse than the sight they saw not. [7] As for the illusions of art magick, they were put down, and their vaunting in wisdom was reproved with disgrace. [8] For they, that promised to drive away terrors and troubles from a sick soul, were sick themselves of fear, worthy to be laughed at. [9] For though no terrible thing did fear them; yet being scared with beasts that passed by, and hissing of serpents, [10] They died for fear, denying that they saw the air, which could of no side be avoided. [11] For wickedness, condemned by her own witness, is very timorous, and being pressed with conscience, always forecasteth grievous things. [12] For fear is nothing else but a betraying of the succours which reason offereth. [13] And the expectation from within, being less, counteth the ignorance more than the cause which bringeth the torment. [14] But they sleeping the same sleep that night, which was indeed intolerable, and which came upon them out of the bottoms of inevitable hell, [15] Were partly vexed with monstrous apparitions, and partly fainted, their heart failing them: for a sudden fear, and not looked for, came upon them. [16] So then whosoever there fell down was straitly kept, shut up in a prison without iron bars, [17] For whether he were husbandman, or shepherd, or a labourer in the field, he was overtaken, and endured that necessity, which could not be avoided: for they were all bound with one chain of darkness. [18] Whether it were a whistling wind, or a melodious noise of birds among the spreading branches, or a pleasing fall of water running violently, [19] Or a terrible sound of stones cast down, or a running that could not be seen of skipping beasts, or a roaring voice of most savage wild beasts, or a rebounding echo from the hollow mountains; these things made them to swoon for fear. [20] For the whole world shined with clear light, and none were hindered in their labour: [21] Over them only was spread an heavy night, an image of that darkness which should afterward receive them: but yet were they unto themselves more grievous than the darkness.

Wis.18

[1] Nevertheless thy saints had a very great light, whose voice they hearing, and not seeing their shape, because they also had not suffered the same things, they counted them happy. [2] But for that they did not hurt them now, of whom they had been wronged before, they thanked them, and besought them pardon for that they had been enemies. [3] Instead whereof thou gavest them a burning pillar of fire, both to be a guide of the unknown journey, and an harmless sun to entertain them honourably. [4] For they were worthy to be deprived of light and imprisoned in darkness, who had kept thy sons shut up, by whom the uncorrupt light of the law was to be given unto the world. [5] And when they had determined to slay the babes of the saints, one child being cast forth, and saved, to reprove them, thou tookest away the multitude of their children, and destroyedst them altogether in a mighty water. [6] Of that night were our fathers certified afore, that assuredly knowing unto what oaths they had given credence, they might afterwards be of good cheer. [7] So of thy people was accepted both the salvation of the righteous, and destruction of the enemies. [8] For wherewith thou didst punish our adversaries, by the same thou didst glorify us, whom thou hadst called. [9] For the righteous children of good men did sacrifice secretly, and with one consent made a holy law, that the saints should be like partakers of the same good and evil, the fathers now singing out the songs of praise. [10] But on the other side there sounded an ill according cry of the enemies, and a lamentable noise was carried abroad for children that were bewailed. [11] The master and the servant were punished after one manner; and like as the king, so suffered the common person. [12] So they all together had innumerable dead with one kind of death; neither were the living sufficient to bury them: for in one moment the noblest offspring of them was destroyed. [13] For whereas they would not believe any thing by reason of the enchantments; upon the destruction of the firstborn, they acknowledged this people to be the sons of God. [14] For while all things were in quiet silence, and that night was in the midst of her swift course, [15] Thine Almighty word leaped down from heaven out of thy royal throne, as a fierce man of war into the midst of a land of destruction, [16] And brought thine unfeigned commandment as a sharp sword, and standing up filled all things with death; and it touched the heaven, but it stood upon the earth. [17] Then suddenly visions of horrible dreams troubled them sore, and terrors came upon them unlooked for [18] And one thrown here, and another there, half dead, shewed the cause of his death. [19] For the dreams that troubled them did foreshew this, lest they should perish, and not know why they were afflicted. [20] Yea, the tasting of death touched the righteous also, and there was a destruction of the multitude in the wilderness: but the wrath endured not long. [21] For then the blameless man made haste, and stood forth to defend them; and bringing the shield of his proper ministry, even prayer, and the propitiation of incense, set himself against the wrath, and so brought the calamity to an end, declaring that he was thy servant. [22] So he overcame the destroyer, not with strength of body, nor force of arms, but with a word subdued him that punished, alleging the oaths and covenants made with the fathers. [23] For when the dead were now fallen down by heaps one upon another, standing between, he stayed the wrath, and parted the way to the living. [24] For in the long garment was the whole world, and in the four rows of the stones was the glory of the fathers graven, and thy Majesty upon the daidem of his head. [25] Unto these the destroyer gave place, and was afraid of them: for it was enough that they only tasted of the wrath.

[1] As for the ungodly, wrath came upon them without mercy unto the end: for he knew before what they would do; [2] How that having given them leave to depart, and sent them hastily away, they would repent and pursue them. [3] For whilst they were yet mourning and making lamentation at the graves of the dead, they added another foolish device, and pursued them as fugitives, whom they had intreated to be gone. [4] For the destiny, whereof they were worthy, drew them unto this end, and made them forget the things that had already happened, that they might fulfil the punishment which was wanting to their torments: [5] And that thy people might pass a wonderful way: but they might find a strange death. [6] For the whole creature in his proper kind was fashioned again anew, serving the peculiar commandments that were given unto them, that thy children might be kept without hurt: [7] As namely, a cloud shadowing the camp; and where water stood before, dry land appeared; and out of the Red sea a way without impediment; and out of the violent stream a green field: [8] Wherethrough all the people went that were defended with thy hand, seeing thy marvellous strange wonders. [9] For they went at large like horses, and leaped like lambs, praising thee, O Lord, who hadst delivered them. [10] For they were yet mindful of the things that were done while they sojourned in the strange land, how the ground brought forth flies instead of cattle, and how the river cast up a multitude of frogs instead of fishes. [11] But afterwards they saw a new generation of fowls, when, being led with their appetite, they asked delicate meats. [12] For quails came up unto them from the sea for their contentment. [13] And punishments came upon the sinners not without former signs by the force of thunders: for they suffered justly according to their own wickedness, insomuch as they used a more hard and hateful behaviour toward strangers. [14] For the Sodomites did not receive those, whom they knew not when they came: but these brought friends into bondage, that had well deserved of them. [15] And not only so, but peradventure some respect shall be had of those, because they used strangers not friendly: [16] But these very grievously afflicted them, whom they had received with feastings, and were already made partakers of the same laws with them. [17] Therefore even with blindness were these stricken, as those were at the doors of the righteous man: when, being compassed about with horrible great darkness, every one sought the passage of his own doors. [18] For the elements were changed in themselves by a kind of harmony, like as in a psaltery notes change the name of the tune, and yet are always sounds; which may well be perceived by the sight of the things that have been done. [19] For earthly things were turned into watery, and the things, that before swam in the water, now went upon the ground. [20] The fire had power in the water, forgetting his own virtue: and the water forgat his own quenching nature. [21] On the other side, the flames wasted not the flesh of the corruptible living things, though they walked therein; neither melted they the icy kind of heavenly meat that was of nature apt to melt. [22] For in all things, O Lord, thou didst magnify thy people, and glorify them, neither didst thou lightly regard them: but didst assist them in every time and place.

THE WISDOM OF SIRACH (ECCLESIASTICUS)

Sir.1

[1] All wisdom cometh from the Lord, and is with him for ever. [2] Who can number the sand of the sea, and the drops of rain, and the days of eternity? [3] Who can find out the height of heaven, and the breadth of the earth, and the deep, and wisdom? [4] Wisdom hath been created before all things, and the understanding of prudence from everlasting. [5] The word of God most high is the fountain of wisdom; and her ways are everlasting commandments. [6] To whom hath the root of wisdom been revealed? or who hath known her wise counsels? [7] Unto whom hath the knowledge of wisdom been made manifest? and who hath understood her great experience? [8] There is one wise and greatly to be feared, the Lord sitting upon his throne. [9] He created her, and saw her, and numbered her, and poured her out upon all his works. [10] She is with all flesh according to his gift, and he hath given her to them that love him. [11] The fear of the Lord is honour, and glory, and gladness, and a crown of rejoicing. [12] The fear of the Lord maketh a merry heart, and giveth joy, and gladness, and a long life. [13] Whoso feareth the Lord, it shall go well with him at the last, and he shall find favour in the day of his death. [14] To fear the Lord is the beginning of wisdom: and it was created with the faithful in the womb. [15] She hath built an everlasting foundation with men, and she shall continue with their seed. [16] To fear the Lord is fulness of wisdom, and filleth men with her fruits. [17] She filleth all their house with things desirable, and the garners with her increase. [18] The fear of the Lord is a crown of wisdom, making peace and perfect health to flourish; both which are the gifts of God: and it enlargeth their rejoicing that love him. [19] Wisdom raineth down skill and knowledge of understanding standing, and exalteth them to honour that hold her fast. [20] The root of wisdom is to fear the Lord, and the branches thereof are long life. [21] The fear of the Lord driveth away sins: and where it is present, it turneth away wrath. [22] A furious man cannot be justified; for the sway of his fury shall be his destruction. [23] A patient man will tear for a time, and afterward joy shall spring up unto him. [24] He will hide his words for a time, and the lips of many shall declare his wisdom. [25] The parables of knowledge are in the treasures of wisdom: but godliness is an abomination to a sinner. [26] If thou desire wisdom, keep the commandments, and the Lord shall give her unto thee. [27] For the fear of the Lord is wisdom and instruction: and faith and meekness are his delight. [28] Distrust not the fear of the Lord when thou art poor: and come not unto him with a double heart. [29] Be not an hypocrite in the sight of men, and take good heed what thou speakest. [30] Exalt not thyself, lest thou fall, and bring dishonour upon thy soul, and so God discover thy secrets, and cast thee down in the midst of the congregation, because thou camest not in truth to the fear of the Lord, but thy heart is full of deceit.

Sir.2

[1] My son, if thou come to serve the Lord, prepare thy soul for temptation. [2] Set thy heart aright, and constantly endure, and make not haste in time of trouble. [3] Cleave unto him, and depart not away, that thou mayest be increased

at thy last end. [**4**] Whatsoever is brought upon thee take cheerfully, and be patient when thou art changed to a low estate. [**5**] For gold is tried in the fire, and acceptable men in the furnace of adversity. [**6**] Believe in him, and he will help thee; order thy way aright, and trust in him. [**7**] Ye that fear the Lord, wait for his mercy; and go not aside, lest ye fall. [**8**] Ye that fear the Lord, believe him; and your reward shall not fail. [**9**] Ye that fear the Lord, hope for good, and for everlasting joy and mercy. [**10**] Look at the generations of old, and see; did ever any trust in the Lord, and was confounded? or did any abide in his fear, and was forsaken? or whom did he ever despise, that called upon him? [**11**] For the Lord is full of compassion and mercy, longsuffering, and very pitiful, and forgiveth sins, and saveth in time of affliction. [**12**] Woe be to fearful hearts, and faint hands, and the sinner that goeth two ways! [**13**] Woe unto him that is fainthearted! for he believeth not; therefore shall he not be defended. [**14**] Woe unto you that have lost patience! and what will ye do when the Lord shall visit you? [**15**] They that fear the Lord will not disobey his Word; and they that love him will keep his ways. [**16**] They that fear the Lord will seek that which is well, pleasing unto him; and they that love him shall be filled with the law. [**17**] They that fear the Lord will prepare their hearts, and humble their souls in his sight, [**18**] Saying, We will fall into the hands of the Lord, and not into the hands of men: for as his majesty is, so is his mercy.

Sir.3

[1] Hear me your father, O children, and do thereafter, that ye may be safe. [**2**] For the Lord hath given the father honour over the children, and hath confirmed the authority of the mother over the sons. [**3**] Whoso honoureth his father maketh an atonement for his sins: [**4**] And he that honoureth his mother is as one that layeth up treasure. [**5**] Whoso honoureth his father shall have joy of his own children; and when he maketh his prayer, he shall be heard. [**6**] He that honoureth his father shall have a long life; and he that is obedient unto the Lord shall be a comfort to his mother. [**7**] He that feareth the Lord will honour his father, and will do service unto his parents, as to his masters. [**8**] Honour thy father and mother both in word and deed, that a blessing may come upon thee from them. [**9**] For the blessing of the father establisheth the houses of children; but the curse of the mother rooteth out foundations. [**10**] Glory not in the dishonour of thy father; for thy father's dishonour is no glory unto thee. [**11**] For the glory of a man is from the honour of his father; and a mother in dishonour is a reproach to the children. [**12**] My son, help thy father in his age, and grieve him not as long as he liveth. [**13**] And if his understanding fail, have patience with him; and despise him not when thou art in thy full strength. [**14**] For the relieving of thy father shall not be forgotten: and instead of sins it shall be added to build thee up. [**15**] In the day of thine affliction it shall be remembered; thy sins also shall melt away, as the ice in the fair warm weather. [**16**] He that forsaketh his father is as a blasphemer; and he that angereth his mother is cursed: of God. [**17**] My son, go on with thy business in meekness; so shalt thou be beloved of him that is approved. [**18**] The greater thou art, the more humble thyself, and thou shalt find favour before the Lord. [**19**] Many are in high place, and of renown: but mysteries are revealed unto the meek. [**20**] For the power of the Lord is great, and he is honoured of the lowly. [**21**] Seek not out things that are too hard for thee, neither search the things that are above thy strength. [**22**] But what is commanded thee, think thereupon with reverence, for it is not needful for thee to see with thine eyes the things that are in secret. [**23**] Be not curious in unnecessary matters: for more things are shewed unto thee than men understand. [**24**] For many are deceived by their own vain opinion; and an evil suspicion hath overthrown their judgment. [**25**] Without eyes thou shalt want light: profess not the knowledge therefore that thou hast not. [**26**] A stubborn heart shall fare evil at the last; and he that loveth danger shall perish therein. [**27**] An obstinate heart shall be laden with sorrows; and the wicked man shall heap sin upon sin. [**28**] In the punishment of the proud there is no remedy; for the plant of wickedness hath taken root in him. [**29**] The heart of the prudent will understand a parable; and an attentive ear is the desire of a wise man. [**30**] Water will quench a flaming fire; and alms maketh an atonement for sins. [**31**] And he that requiteth good turns is mindful of that which may come hereafter; and when he falleth, he shall find a stay.

Sir.4

[1] My son, defraud not the poor of his living, and make not the needy eyes to wait long. [**2**] Make not an hungry soul sorrowful; neither provoke a man in his distress. [**3**] Add not more trouble to an heart that is vexed; and defer not to give to him that is in need. [**4**] Reject not the supplication of the afflicted; neither turn away thy face from a poor man. [**5**] Turn not away thine eye from the needy, and give him none occasion to curse thee: [**6**] For if he curse thee in the bitterness of his soul, his prayer shall be heard of him that made him. [**7**] Get thyself the love of the congregation, and bow thy head to a great man. [**8**] Let it not grieve thee to bow down thine ear to the poor, and give him a friendly answer with meekness. [**9**] Deliver him that suffereth wrong from the hand of the oppressor; and be not fainthearted when thou sittest in judgment. [**10**] Be as a father unto the fatherless, and instead of an husband unto their mother: so shalt thou be as the son of the most High, and he shall love thee more than thy mother doth. [**11**] Wisdom exalteth her children, and layeth hold of them that seek her. [**12**] He that loveth her loveth life; and they that seek to her early shall be filled with joy. [**13**] He that holdeth her fast shall inherit glory; and wheresoever she entereth, the Lord will bless. [**14**] They that serve her shall minister to the Holy One: and them that love her the Lord doth love. [**15**] Whoso giveth ear unto her shall judge the nations: and he that attendeth unto her shall dwell securely. [**16**] If a man commit himself unto her, he shall inherit her; and his generation shall hold her in possession. [**17**] For at the first she will walk with him by crooked ways, and bring fear and dread upon him, and torment him with her discipline, until she may trust his soul, and try him by her laws. [**18**] Then will she return the straight way unto him, and comfort him, and shew him her secrets. [**19•**] But if he go wrong, she will forsake him, and give him over to his own ruin. [**20**] Observe the opportunity, and beware of evil; and be not ashamed when it concerneth thy soul. [**21**] For there is a shame that bringeth sin; and there is a shame which is glory and grace. [**22**] Accept no person against thy soul, and let not the reverence of any man cause thee to fall. [**23**] And refrain not to speak, when there is occasion to do good, and hide not thy wisdom in her beauty. [**24**] For by speech wisdom shall be known: and learning by the word of the tongue. [**25**] In no wise speak against the truth; but be abashed of the error of thine ignorance. [**26**] Be not ashamed to confess thy sins; and force not the course of the river. [**27**] Make not thyself an underling to a foolish

man; neither accept the person of the mighty. [**28**] Strive for the truth unto death, and the Lord shall fight for thee. [**29**] Be not hasty in thy tongue, and in thy deeds slack and remiss. [**30**] Be not as a lion in thy house, nor frantick among thy servants. [**31**] Let not thine hand be stretched out to receive, and shut when thou shouldest repay.

Sir.5

[1] Set thy heart upon thy goods; and say not, I have enough for my life. [**2**] Follow not thine own mind and thy strength, to walk in the ways of thy heart: [**3**] And say not, Who shall controul me for my works? for the Lord will surely revenge thy pride. [**4**] Say not, I have sinned, and what harm hath happened unto me? for the Lord is longsuffering, he will in no wise let thee go. [**5**] Concerning propitiation, be not without fear to add sin unto sin: [**6**] And say not His mercy is great; he will be pacified for the multitude of my sins: for mercy and wrath come from him, and his indignation resteth upon sinners. [**7**] Make no tarrying to turn to the Lord, and put not off from day to day: for suddenly shall the wrath of the Lord come forth, and in thy security thou shalt be destroyed, and perish in the day of vengeance. [**8**] Set not thine heart upon goods unjustly gotten, for they shall not profit thee in the day of calamity. [**9**] Winnow not with every wind, and go not into every way: for so doth the sinner that hath a double tongue. [**10**] Be stedfast in thy understanding; and let thy word be the same. [**11**] Be swift to hear; and let thy life be sincere; and with patience give answer. [**12**] If thou hast understanding, answer thy neighbour; if not, lay thy hand upon thy mouth. [**13**] Honour and shame is in talk: and the tongue of man is his fall. [**14**] Be not called a whisperer, and lie not in wait with thy tongue: for a foul shame is upon the thief, and an evil condemnation upon the double tongue. [**15**] Be not ignorant of any thing in a great matter or a small.

Sir.6

[1] Instead of a friend become not an enemy; for [thereby] thou shalt inherit an ill name, shame, and reproach: even so shall a sinner that hath a double tongue. [**2**] Extol not thyself in the counsel of thine own heart; that thy soul be not torn in pieces as a bull [straying alone.] [**3**] Thou shalt eat up thy leaves, and lose thy fruit, and leave thyself as a dry tree. [**4**] A wicked soul shall destroy him that hath it, and shall make him to be laughed to scorn of his enemies. [**5**] Sweet language will multiply friends: and a fairspeaking tongue will increase kind greetings. [**6**] Be in peace with many: nevertheless have but one counsellor of a thousand. [**7**] If thou wouldest get a friend, prove him first and be not hasty to credit him. [**8**] For some man is a friend for his own occasion, and will not abide in the day of thy trouble. [**9**] And there is a friend, who being turned to enmity, and strife will discover thy reproach. [**10**] Again, some friend is a companion at the table, and will not continue in the day of thy affliction. [**11**] But in thy prosperity he will be as thyself, and will be bold over thy servants. [**12**] If thou be brought low, he will be against thee, and will hide himself from thy face. [**13**] Separate thyself from thine enemies, and take heed of thy friends. [**14**] A faithfull friend is a strong defence: and he that hath found such an one hath found a treasure. [**15**] Nothing doth countervail a faithful friend, and his excellency is invaluable. [**16**] A faithful friend is the medicine of life; and they that fear the Lord shall find him. [**17**] Whoso feareth the Lord shall direct his friendship aright: for as he is, so shall his neighbour be also. [**18**] My son, gather instruction from thy youth up: so shalt thou find wisdom till thine old age. [**19**] Come unto her as one that ploweth and soweth, and wait for her good fruits: for thou shalt not toil much in labouring about her, but thou shalt eat of her fruits right soon. [**20**] She is very unpleasant to the unlearned: he that is without understanding will not remain with her. [**21**] She will lie upon him as a mighty stone of trial; and he will cast her from him ere it be long. [**22**] For wisdom is according to her name, and she is not manifest unto many. [**23**] Give ear, my son, receive my advice, and refuse not my counsel, [**24**] And put thy feet into her fetters, and thy neck into her chain. [**25**] Bow down thy shoulder, and bear her, and be not grieved with her bonds. [**26**] Come unto her with thy whole heart, and keep her ways with all thy power. [**27**] Search, and seek, and she shall be made known unto thee: and when thou hast got hold of her, let her not go. [**28**] For at the last thou shalt find her rest, and that shall be turned to thy joy. [**29**] Then shall her fetters be a strong defence for thee, and her chains a robe of glory. [**30**] For there is a golden ornament upon her, and her bands are purple lace. [**31**] Thou shalt put her on as a robe of honour, and shalt put her about thee as a crown of joy. [**32**] My son, if thou wilt, thou shalt be taught: and if thou wilt apply thy mind, thou shalt be prudent. [**33**] If thou love to hear, thou shalt receive understanding: and if thou bow thine ear, thou shalt be wise, [**34**] Stand in the multitude of the elders; and cleave unto him that is wise. [**35**] Be willing to hear every godly discourse; and let not the parables of understanding escape thee. [**36**] And if thou seest a man of understanding, get thee betimes unto him, and let thy foot wear the steps of his door. [**37**] Let thy mind be upon the ordinances of the Lord and meditate continually in his commandments: he shall establish thine heart, and give thee wisdom at thine owns desire.

Sir.7

[1] Do no evil, so shall no harm come unto thee. [**2**] Depart from the unjust, and iniquity shall turn away from thee. [**3**] My son, sow not upon the furrows of unrighteousness, and thou shalt not reap them sevenfold. [**4**] Seek not of the Lord preeminence, neither of the king the seat of honour. [**5**] justify not thyself before the Lord; and boast not of thy wisdom before the king. [**6**] Seek not to be judge, being not able to take away iniquity; lest at any time thou fear the person of the mighty, an stumblingblock in the way of thy uprightness. [**7**] Offend not against the multitude of a city, and then thou shalt not cast thyself down among the people. [**8**] Bind not one sin upon another; for in one thou shalt not be unpunished. [**9**] Say not, God will look upon the multitude of my oblations, and when I offer to the most high God, he will accept it. [**10**] Be not fainthearted when thou makest thy prayer, and neglect not to give alms. [**11**] Laugh no man to scorn in the bitterness of his soul: for there is one which humbleth and exalteth. [**12**] Devise not a lie against thy brother; neither do the like to thy friend. [**13**] Use not to make any manner of lie: for the custom thereof is not good. [**14**] Use not many words in a multitude of elders, and make not much babbling when thou prayest. [**15**] Hate not laborious work, neither husbandry, which the most High hath ordained. [**16**] Number not thyself among the multitude of sinners, but remember that wrath will not tarry long. [**17**] Humble thyself greatly: for the vengeance of the ungodly is fire and worms. [**18**]

Change not a friend for any good by no means; neither a faithful brother for the gold of Ophir. [19] Forego not a wise and good woman: for her grace is above gold. [20] Whereas thy servant worketh truly, entreat him not evil. nor the hireling that bestoweth himself wholly for thee. [21] Let thy soul love a good servant, and defraud him not of liberty. [22] Hast thou cattle? have an eye to them: and if they be for thy profit, keep them with thee. [23] Hast thou children? instruct them, and bow down their neck from their youth. [24] Hast thou daughters? have a care of their body, and shew not thyself cheerful toward them. [25] Marry thy daughter, and so shalt thou have performed a weighty matter: but give her to a man of understanding. [26] Hast thou a wife after thy mind? forsake her not: but give not thyself over to a light woman. [27] Honour thy father with thy whole heart, and forget not the sorrows of thy mother. [28] Remember that thou wast begotten of them; and how canst thou recompense them the things that they have done for thee? [29] Fear the Lord with all thy soul, and reverence his priests. [30] Love him that made thee with all thy strength, and forsake not his ministers. [31] Fear the Lord, and honor the priest; and give him his portion, as it is commanded thee; the firstfruits, and the trespass offering, and the gift of the shoulders, and the sacrifice of sanctification, and the firstfruits of the holy things. [32] And stretch thine hand unto the poor, that thy blessing may be perfected. [33] A gift hath grace in the sight of every man living; and for the dead detain it not. [34] Fail not to be with them that weep, and mourn with them that mourn. [35] Be not slow to visit the sick: fir that shall make thee to be beloved. [36] Whatsoever thou takest in hand, remember the end, and thou shalt never do amiss.

Sir.8

[1] Strive not with a mighty man' lest thou fall into his hands. [2] Be not at variance with a rich man, lest he overweigh thee: for gold hath destroyed many, and perverted the hearts of kings. [3] Strive not with a man that is full of tongue, and heap not wood upon his fire. [4] Jest not with a rude man, lest thy ancestors be disgraced. [5] Reproach not a man that turneth from sin, but remember that we are all worthy of punishment. [6] Dishonour not a man in his old age: for even some of us wax old. [7] Rejoice not over thy greatest enemy being dead, but remember that we die all. [8] Despise not the discourse of the wise, but acquaint thyself with their proverbs: for of them thou shalt learn instruction, and how to serve great men with ease. [9] Miss not the discourse of the elders: for they also learned of their fathers, and of them thou shalt learn understanding, and to give answer as need requireth. [10] Kindle not the coals of a sinner, lest thou be burnt with the flame of his fire. [11] Rise not up [in anger] at the presence of an injurious person, lest he lie in wait to entrap thee in thy words [12] Lend not unto him that is mightier than thyself; for if thou lendest him, count it but lost. [13] Be not surety above thy power: for if thou be surety, take care to pay it. [14] Go not to law with a judge; for they will judge for him according to his honour. [15] Travel not by the way with a bold fellow, lest he become grievous unto thee: for he will do according to his own will, and thou shalt perish with him through his folly. [16] Strive not with an angry man, and go not with him into a solitary place: for blood is as nothing in his sight, and where there is no help, he will overthrow thee. [17] Consult not with a fool; for he cannot keep counsel. [18] Do no secret thing before a stranger; for thou knowest not what he will bring forth. [19] Open not thine heart to every man, lest he requite thee with a shrewd turn.

Sir.9

[1] Be not jealous over the wife of thy bosom, and teach her not an evil lesson against thyself. [2] Give not thy soul unto a woman to set her foot upon thy substance. [3] Meet not with an harlot, lest thou fall into her snares. [4] Use not much the company of a woman that is a singer, lest thou be taken with her attempts. [5] Gaze not on a maid, that thou fall not by those things that are precious in her. [6] Give not thy soul unto harlots, that thou lose not thine inheritance. [7] Look not round about thee in the streets of the city, neither wander thou in the solitary place thereof. [8] Turn away thine eye from a beautiful woman, and look not upon another's beauty; for many have been deceived by the beauty of a woman; for herewith love is kindled as a fire. [9] Sit not at all with another man's wife, nor sit down with her in thine arms, and spend not thy money with her at the wine; lest thine heart incline unto her, and so through thy desire thou fall into destruction. [10] Forsake not an old friend; for the new is not comparable to him: a new friend is as new wine; when it is old, thou shalt drink it with pleasure. [11] Envy not the glory of a sinner: for thou knowest not what shall be his end. [12] Delight not in the thing that the ungodly have pleasure in; but remember they shall not go unpunished unto their grave. [13] Keep thee far from the man that hath power to kill; so shalt thou not doubt the fear of death: and if thou come unto him, make no fault, lest he take away thy life presently: remember that thou goest in the midst of snares, and that thou walkest upon the battlements of the city. [14] As near as thou canst, guess at thy neighbour, and consult with the wise. [15] Let thy talk be with the wise, and all thy communication in the law of the most High. [16] And let just men eat and drink with thee; and let thy glorying be in the fear of the Lord. [17] For the hand of the artificer the work shall be commended: and the wise ruler of the people for his speech. [18] A man of an ill tongue is dangerous in his city; and he that is rash in his talk shall be hated.

Sir.10

[1] A wise judge will instruct his people; and the government of a prudent man is well ordered. [2] As the judge of the people is himself, so are his officers; and what manner of man the ruler of the city is, such are all they that dwell therein. [3] An unwise king destroyeth his people; but through the prudence of them which are in authority the city shall be inhabited. [4] The power of the earth is in the hand of the Lord, and in due time he will set over it one that is profitable. [5] In the hand of God is the prosperity of man: and upon the person of the scribe shall he lay his honour. [6] Bear not hatred to thy neighbour for every wrong; and do nothing at all by injurious practices. [7] Pride is hateful before God and man: and by both doth one commit iniquity. [8] Because of unrighteous dealings, injuries, and riches got by deceit, the kingdom is translated from one people to another. [9] Why is earth and ashes proud? There is not a more wicked thing than a covetous man: for such an one setteth his own soul to sale; because while he liveth he casteth away his bowels. [10

] The physician cutteth off a long disease; and he that is to day a king to morrow shall die. [**11**] For when a man is dead, he shall inherit creeping things, beasts, and worms. [**12**] The beginning of pride is when one departeth from God, and his heart is turned away from his Maker. [**13**] For pride is the beginning of sin, and he that hath it shall pour out abomination: and therefore the Lord brought upon them strange calamities, and overthrew them utterly. [**14**] The Lord hath cast down the thrones of proud princes, and set up the meek in their stead. [**15**] The Lord hath plucked up the roots of the proud nations, and planted the lowly in their place. [**16**] The Lord overthrew countries of the heathen, and destroyed them to the foundations of the earth. [**17**] He took some of them away, and destroyed them, and hath made their memorial to cease from the earth. [**18**] Pride was not made for men, nor furious anger for them that are born of a woman. [**19**] They that fear the Lord are a sure seed, and they that love him an honourable plant: they that regard not the law are a dishonourable seed; they that transgress the commandments are a deceivable seed. [**20**] Among brethren he that is chief is honorable; so are they that fear the Lord in his eyes. [**21**] The fear of the Lord goeth before the obtaining of authority: but roughness and pride is the losing thereof. [**22**] Whether he be rich, noble, or poor, their glory is the fear of the Lord. [**23**] It is not meet to despise the poor man that hath understanding; neither is it convenient to magnify a sinful man. [**24**] Great men, and judges, and potentates, shall be honoured; yet is there none of them greater than he that feareth the Lord. [**25**] Unto the servant that is wise shall they that are free do service: and he that hath knowledge will not grudge when he is reformed. [**26**] Be not overwise in doing thy business; and boast not thyself in the time of thy distress. [**27**] Better is he that laboureth, and aboundeth in all things, than he that boasteth himself, and wanteth bread. [**28**] My son, glorify thy soul in meekness, and give it honour according to the dignity thereof. [**29**] Who will justify him that sinneth against his own soul? and who will honour him that dishonoureth his own life? [**30**] The poor man is honoured for his skill, and the rich man is honoured for his riches. [**31**] He that is honoured in poverty, how much more in riches? and he that is dishonourable in riches, how much more in poverty?

Sir.11

[1] Wisdom lifteth up the head of him that is of low degree, and maketh him to sit among great men. [**2**] Commend not a man for his beauty; neither abhor a man for his outward appearance. [**3**] The bee is little among such as fly; but her fruit is the chief of sweet things. [**4**] Boast not of thy clothing and raiment, and exalt not thyself in the day of honour: for the works of the Lord are wonderful, and his works among men are hidden. [**5**] Many kings have sat down upon the ground; and one that was never thought of hath worn the crown. [**6**] Many mighty men have been greatly disgraced; and the honourable delivered into other men's hands. [**7**] Blame not before thou hast examined the truth: understand first, and then rebuke. [**8**] Answer not before thou hast heard the cause: neither interrupt men in the midst of their talk. [**9**] Strive not in a matter that concerneth thee not; and sit not in judgment with sinners. [**10**] My son, meddle not with many matters: for if thou meddle much, thou shalt not be innocent; and if thou follow after, thou shalt not obtain, neither shalt thou escape by fleeing. [**11**] There is one that laboureth, and taketh pains, and maketh haste, and is so much the more behind. [**12**] Again, there is another that is slow, and hath need of help, wanting ability, and full of poverty; yet the eye of the Lord looked upon him for good, and set him up from his low estate, [**13**] And lifted up his head from misery; so that many that saw from him is peace over all the [**14**] Prosperity and adversity, life and death, poverty and riches, come of the Lord. [**15**] Wisdom, knowledge, and understanding of the law, are of the Lord: love, and the way of good works, are from him. [**16**] Error and darkness had their beginning together with sinners: and evil shall wax old with them that glory therein. [**17**] The gift of the Lord remaineth with the ungodly, and his favour bringeth prosperity for ever. [**18**] There is that waxeth rich by his wariness and pinching, and this his the portion of his reward: [**19**] Whereas he saith, I have found rest, and now will eat continually of my goods; and yet he knoweth not what time shall come upon him, and that he must leave those things to others, and die. [**20**] Be stedfast in thy covenant, and be conversant therein, and wax old in thy work. [**21**] Marvel not at the works of sinners; but trust in the Lord, and abide in thy labour: for it is an easy thing in the sight of the Lord on the sudden to make a poor man rich. [**22**] The blessing of the Lord is in the reward of the godly, and suddenly he maketh his blessing flourish. [**23**] Say not, What profit is there of my service? and what good things shall I have hereafter? [**24**] Again, say not, I have enough, and possess many things, and what evil shall I have hereafter? [**25**] In the day of prosperity there is a forgetfulness of affliction: and in the day of affliction there is no more remembrance of prosperity. [**26**] For it is an easy thing unto the Lord in the day of death to reward a man according to his ways. [**27**] The affliction of an hour maketh a man forget pleasure: and in his end his deeds shall be discovered. [**28**] Judge none blessed before his death: for a man shall be known in his children. [**29**] Bring not every man into thine house: for the deceitful man hath many trains. [**30**] Like as a partridge taken [and kept] in a cage, so is the heart of the proud; and like as a spy, watcheth he for thy fall: [**31**] For he lieth in wait, and turneth good into evil, and in things worthy praise will lay blame upon thee. [**32**] Of a spark of fire a heap of coals is kindled: and a sinful man layeth wait for blood. [**33**] Take heed of a mischievous man, for he worketh wickedness; lest he bring upon thee a perpetual blot. [**34**] Receive a stranger into thine house, and he will disturb thee, and turn thee out of thine own.

Sir.12

[1] When thou wilt do good know to whom thou doest it; so shalt thou be thanked for thy benefits. [**2**] Do good to the godly man, and thou shalt find a recompence; and if not from him, yet from the most High. [**3**] There can no good come to him that is always occupied in evil, nor to him that giveth no alms. [**4**] Give to the godly man, and help not a sinner. [**5**] Do well unto him that is lowly, but give not to the ungodly: hold back thy bread, and give it not unto him, lest he overmaster thee thereby: for [else] thou shalt receive twice as much evil for all the good thou shalt have done unto him. [**6**] For the most High hateth sinners, and will repay vengeance unto the ungodly, and keepeth them against the mighty day of their punishment. [**7**] Give unto the good, and help not the sinner. [**8**] A friend cannot be known in prosperity: and an enemy cannot be hidden in adversity. [**9**] In the prosperity of a man enemies will be grieved: but in his adversity even a friend will depart. [**10**] Never trust thine enemy: for like as iron rusteth, so is his wickedness. [**11**] Though he humble

himself, and go crouching, yet take good heed and beware of him, and thou shalt be unto him as if thou hadst wiped a lookingglass, and thou shalt know that his rust hath not been altogether wiped away. [12] Set him not by thee, lest, when he hath overthrown thee, he stand up in thy place; neither let him sit at thy right hand, lest he seek to take thy seat, and thou at the last remember my words, and be pricked therewith. [13] Who will pity a charmer that is bitten with a serpent, or any such as come nigh wild beasts? [14] So one that goeth to a sinner, and is defiled with him in his sins, who will pity? [15] For a while he will abide with thee, but if thou begin to fall, he will not tarry. [16] An enemy speaketh sweetly with his lips, but in his heart he imagineth how to throw thee into a pit: he will weep with his eyes, but if he find opportunity, he will not be satisfied with blood. [17] If adversity come upon thee, thou shalt find him there first; and though he pretend to help thee, yet shall he undermine thee. [18] He will shake his head, and clap his hands, and whisper much, and change his countenance.

Sir. 13

[1] He that toucheth pitch shall be defiled therewith; and he that hath fellowship with a proud man shall be like unto him. [2] Burden not thyself above thy power while thou livest; and have no fellowship with one that is mightier and richer than thyself: for how agree the kettle and the earthen pot together? for if the one be smitten against the other, it shall be broken. [3] The rich man hath done wrong, and yet he threateneth withal: the poor is wronged, and he must intreat also. [4] If thou be for his profit, he will use thee: but if thou have nothing, he will forsake thee. [5] If thou have any thing, he will live with thee: yea, he will make thee bare, and will not be sorry for it. [6] If he have need of thee, he will deceive thee, and smile upon thee, and put thee in hope; he will speak thee fair, and say, What wantest thou? [7] And he will shame thee by his meats, until he have drawn thee dry twice or thrice, and at the last he will laugh thee to scorn afterward, when he seeth thee, he will forsake thee, and shake his head at thee. [8] Beware that thou be not deceived and brought down in thy jollity. [9] If thou be invited of a mighty man, withdraw thyself, and so much the more will he invite thee. [10] Press thou not upon him, lest thou be put back; stand not far off, lest thou be forgotten. [11] Affect not to be made equal unto him in talk, and believe not his many words: for with much communication will he tempt thee, and smiling upon thee will get out thy secrets: [12] But cruelly he will lay up thy words, and will not spare to do thee hurt, and to put thee in prison. [13] Observe, and take good heed, for thou walkest in peril of thy overthrowing: when thou hearest these things, awake in thy sleep. [14] Love the Lord all thy life, and call upon him for thy salvation. [15] Every beast loveth his like, and every man loveth his neighbor. [16] All flesh consorteth according to kind, and a man will cleave to his like. [17] What fellowship hath the wolf with the lamb? so the sinner with the godly. [18] What agreement is there between the hyena and a dog? and what peace between the rich and the poor? [19] As the wild ass is the lion's prey in the wilderness: so the rich eat up the poor. [20] As the proud hate humility: so doth the rich abhor the poor. [21] A rich man beginning to fall is held up of his friends: but a poor man being down is thrust away by his friends. [22] When a rich man is fallen, he hath many helpers: he speaketh things not to be spoken, and yet men justify him: the poor man slipped, and yet they rebuked him too; he spake wisely, and could have no place. [23] When a rich man speaketh, every man holdeth his tongue, and, look, what he saith, they extol it to the clouds: but if the poor man speak, they say, What fellow is this? and if he stumble, they will help to overthrow him. [24] Riches are good unto him that hath no sin, and poverty is evil in the mouth of the ungodly. [25] The heart of a man changeth his countenance, whether it be for good or evil: and a merry heart maketh a cheerful countenance. [26] A cheerful countenance is a token of a heart that is in prosperity; and the finding out of parables is a wearisome labour of the mind.

Sir. 14

[1] Blessed is the man that hath not slipped with his mouth, and is not pricked with the multitude of sins. [2] Blessed is he whose conscience hath not condemned him, and who is not fallen from his hope in the Lord. [3] Riches are not comely for a niggard: and what should an envious man do with money? [4] He that gathereth by defrauding his own soul gathereth for others, that shall spend his goods riotously. [5] He that is evil to himself, to whom will he be good? he shall not take pleasure in his goods. [6] There is none worse than he that envieth himself; and this is a recompence of his wickedness. [7] And if he doeth good, he doeth it unwillingly; and at the last he will declare his wickedness. [8] The envious man hath a wicked eye; he turneth away his face, and despiseth men. [9] A covetous man's eye is not satisfied with his portion; and the iniquity of the wicked drieth up his soul. [10] A wicked eye envieth [his] bread, and he is a niggard at his table. [11] My son, according to thy ability do good to thyself, and give the Lord his due offering. [12] Remember that death will not be long in coming, and that the covenant of the grave is not shewed unto thee. [13] Do good unto thy friend before thou die, and according to thy ability stretch out thy hand and give to him. [14] Defraud not thyself of the good day, and let not the part of a good desire overpass thee. [15] Shalt thou not leave thy travails unto another? and thy labours to be divided by lot? [16] Give, and take, and sanctify thy soul; for there is no seeking of dainties in the grave. [17] All flesh waxeth old as a garment: for the covenant from the beginning is, Thou shalt die the death. [18] As of the green leaves on a thick tree, some fall, and some grow; so is the generation of flesh and blood, one cometh to an end, and another is born. [19] Every work rotteth and consumeth away, and the worker thereof shall go withal. [20] Blessed is the man that doth meditate good things in wisdom, and that reasoneth of holy things by his understanding. ing. [21] He that considereth her ways in his heart shall also have understanding in her secrets. [22] Go after her as one that traceth, and lie in wait in her ways. [23] He that prieth in at her windows shall also hearken at her doors. [24] He that doth lodge near her house shall also fasten a pin in her walls. [25] He shall pitch his tent nigh unto her, and shall lodge in a lodging where good things are. [26] He shall set his children under her shelter, and shall lodge under her branches. [27] By her he shall be covered from heat, and in her glory shall he dwell.

Sir.15

[1] He that feareth the Lord will do good, and he that hath the knowledge of the law shall obtain her. [2] And as a mother shall she meet him, and receive him as a wife married of a virgin. [3] With the bread of understanding shall she feed him, and give him the water of wisdom to drink. [4] He shall be stayed upon her, and shall not be moved; and shall rely upon her, and shall not be confounded. [5] She shall exalt him above his neighbours, and in the midst of the congregation shall she open his mouth. [6] He shall find joy and a crown of gladness, and she shall cause him to inherit an everlasting name. [7] But foolish men shall not attain unto her, and sinners shall not see her. [8] For she is far from pride, and men that are liars cannot remember her. [9] Praise is not seemly in the mouth of a sinner, for it was not sent him of the Lord. [10] For praise shall be uttered in wisdom, and the Lord will prosper it. [11] Say not thou, It is through the Lord that I fell away: for thou oughtest not to do the things that he hateth. [12] Say not thou, He hath caused me to err: for he hath no need of the sinful man. [13] The Lord hateth all abomination; and they that fear God love it not. [14] He himself made man from the beginning, and left him in the hand of his counsel; [15] If thou wilt, to keep the commandments, and to perform acceptable faithfulness. [16] He hath set fire and water before thee: stretch forth thy hand unto whether thou wilt. [17] Before man is life and death; and whether him liketh shall be given him. [18] For the wisdom of the Lord is great, and he is mighty in power, and beholdeth all things: [19] And his eyes are upon them that fear him, and he knoweth every work of man. [20] He hath commanded no man to do wickedly, neither hath he given any man licence to sin.

Sir.16

[1] Desire not a multitude of unprofitable children, neither delight in ungodly sons. [2] Though they multiply, rejoice not in them, except the fear of the Lord be with them. [3] Trust not thou in their life, neither respect their multitude: for one that is just is better than a thousand; and better it is to die without children, than to have them that are ungodly. [4] For by one that hath understanding shall the city be replenished: but the kindred of the wicked shall speedily become desolate. [5] Many such things have I seen with mine eyes, and mine ear hath heard greater things than these. [6] In the congregation of the ungodly shall a fire be kindled; and in a rebellious nation wrath is set on fire. [7] He was not pacified toward the old giants, who fell away in the strength of their foolishness. [8] Neither spared he the place where Lot sojourned, but abhorred them for their pride. [9] He pitied not the people of perdition, who were taken away in their sins: [10] Nor the six hundred thousand footmen, who were gathered together in the hardness of their hearts. [11] And if there be one stiffnecked among the people, it is marvel if he escape unpunished: for mercy and wrath are with him; he is mighty to forgive, and to pour out displeasure. [12] As his mercy is great, so is his correction also: he judgeth a man according to his works [13] The sinner shall not escape with his spoils: and the patience of the godly shall not be frustrate. [14] Make way for every work of mercy: for every man shall find according to his works. [15] The Lord hardened Pharaoh, that he should not know him, that his powerful works might be known to the world. [16] His mercy is manifest to every creature; and he hath separated his light from the darkness with an adamant. [17] Say not thou, I will hide myself from the Lord: shall any remember me from above? I shall not be remembered among so many people: for what is my soul among such an infinite number of creatures? [18] Behold, the heaven, and the heaven of heavens, the deep, and the earth, and all that therein is, shall be moved when he shall visit. [19] The mountains also and foundations of the earth be shaken with trembling, when the Lord looketh upon them. [20] No heart can think upon these things worthily: and who is able to conceive his ways? [21] It is a tempest which no man can see: for the most part of his works are hid. [22] Who can declare the works of his justice? or who can endure them? for his covenant is afar off, and the trial of all things is in the end. [23] He that wanteth understanding will think upon vain things: and a foolish man erring imagineth follies. [24] by son, hearken unto me, and learn knowledge, and mark my words with thy heart. [25] I will shew forth doctrine in weight, and declare his knowledge exactly. [26] The works of the Lord are done in judgment from the beginning: and from the time he made them he disposed the parts thereof. [27] He garnished his works for ever, and in his hand are the chief of them unto all generations: they neither labour, nor are weary, nor cease from their works. [28] None of them hindereth another, and they shall never disobey his word. [29] After this the Lord looked upon the earth, and filled it with his blessings. [30] With all manner of living things hath he covered the face thereof; and they shall return into it again.

Sir.17

[1] The Lord created man of the earth, and turned him into it again. [2] He gave them few days, and a short time, and power also over the things therein. [3] He endued them with strength by themselves, and made them according to his image, [4] And put the fear of man upon all flesh, and gave him dominion over beasts and fowls. [5] They received the use of the five operations of the Lord, and in the sixth place he imparted them understanding, and in the seventh speech, an interpreter of the cogitations thereof.] [6] Counsel, and a tongue, and eyes, ears, and a heart, gave he them to understand. [7] Withal he filled them with the knowledge of understanding, and shewed them good and evil. [8] He set his eye upon their hearts, that he might shew them the greatness of his works. [9] He gave them to glory in his marvellous acts for ever, that they might declare his works with understanding. [10] And the elect shall praise his holy name. [11] Beside this he gave them knowledge, and the law of life for an heritage. [12] He made an everlasting covenant with them, and shewed them his judgments. [13] Their eyes saw the majesty of his glory, and their ears heard his glorious voice. [14] And he said unto them, Beware of all unrighteousness; and he gave every man commandment concerning his neighbour. [15] Their ways are ever before him, and shall not be hid from his eyes. [16] Every man from his youth is given to evil; neither could they make to themselves fleshy hearts for stony. [17] For in the division of the nations of the whole earth he set a ruler over every people; but Israel is the Lord's portion: [18] Whom, being his firstborn, he nourisheth with discipline, and giving him the light of his love doth not forsake him. [19] Therefore all their works are as the sun before him, and his eyes are continually upon their ways. [20] None of their unrighteous deeds are hid from him, but all their sins are before the Lord [21] But the Lord being gracious and knowing his workmanship, neither left nor forsook them,

but spared them. [22] The alms of a man is as a signet with him, and he will keep the good deeds of man as the apple of the eye, and give repentance to his sons and daughters. [23] Afterwards he will rise up and reward them, and render their recompence upon their heads. [24] But unto them that repent, he granted them return, and comforted those that failed in patience. [25] Return unto the Lord, and forsake thy sins, make thy prayer before his face, and offend less. [26] Turn again to the most High, and turn away from iniquity: for he will lead thee out of darkness into the light of health, and hate thou abomination vehemently. [27] Who shall praise the most High in the grave, instead of them which live and give thanks? [28] Thanksgiving perisheth from the dead, as from one that is not: the living and sound in heart shall praise the Lord. [29] How great is the lovingkindness of the Lord our God, and his compassion unto such as turn unto him in holiness! [30] For all things cannot be in men, because the son of man is not immortal. [31] What is brighter than the sun? yet the light thereof faileth; and flesh and blood will imagine evil. [32] He vieweth the power of the height of heaven; and all men are but earth and ashes.

Sir. 18

[1] He that liveth for ever Hath created all things in general. [2] The Lord only is righteous, and there is none other but he, [3] Who governeth the world with the palm of his hand, and all things obey his will: for he is the King of all, by his power dividing holy things among them from profane. [4] To whom hath he given power to declare his works? and who shall find out his noble acts? [5] Who shall number the strength of his majesty? and who shall also tell out his mercies? [6] As for the wondrous works of the Lord, there may nothing be taken from them, neither may any thing be put unto them, neither can the ground of them be found out. [7] When a man hath done, then he beginneth; and when he leaveth off, then he shall be doubtful. [8] What is man, and whereto serveth he? what is his good, and what is his evil? [9] The number of a man's days at the most are an hundred years. [10] As a drop of water unto the sea, and a gravelstone in comparison of the sand; so are a thousand years to the days of eternity. [11] Therefore is God patient with them, and poureth forth his mercy upon them. [12] He saw and perceived their end to be evil; therefore he multiplied his compassion. [13] The mercy of man is toward his neighbour; but the mercy of the Lord is upon all flesh: he reproveth, and nurtureth, and teacheth and bringeth again, as a shepherd his flock. [14] He hath mercy on them that receive discipline, and that diligently seek after his judgments. [15] My son, blemish not thy good deeds, neither use uncomfortable words when thou givest any thing. [16] Shall not the dew assuage the heat? so is a word better than a gift. [17] Lo, is not a word better than a gift? but both are with a gracious man. [18] A fool will upbraid churlishly, and a gift of the envious consumeth the eyes. [19] Learn before thou speak, and use physick or ever thou be sick. [20] Before judgment examine thyself, and in the day of visitation thou shalt find mercy. [21] Humble thyself before thou be sick, and in the time of sins shew repentance. [22] Let nothing hinder thee to pay thy vow in due time, and defer not until death to be justified. [23] Before thou prayest, prepare thyself; and be not as one that tempteth the Lord. [24] Think upon the wrath that shall be at the end, and the time of vengeance, when he shall turn away his face. [25] When thou hast enough, remember the time of hunger: and when thou art rich, think upon poverty and need. [26] From the morning until the evening the time is changed, and all things are soon done before the Lord. [27] A wise man will fear in every thing, and in the day of sinning he will beware of offence: but a fool will not observe time. [28] Every man of understanding knoweth wisdom, and will give praise unto him that found her. [29] They that were of understanding in sayings became also wise themselves, and poured forth exquisite parables. [30] Go not after thy lusts, but refrain thyself from thine appetites. [31] If thou givest thy soul the desires that please her, she will make thee a laughingstock to thine enemies that malign thee. [32] Take not pleasure in much good cheer, neither be tied to the expence thereof. [33] Be not made a beggar by banqueting upon borrowing, when thou hast nothing in thy purse: for thou shalt lie in wait for thine own life, and be talked on.

Sir. 19

[1] A labouring man that A is given to drunkenness shall not be rich: and he that contemneth small things shall fall by little and little. [2] Wine and women will make men of understanding to fall away: and he that cleaveth to harlots will become impudent. [3] Moths and worms shall have him to heritage, and a bold man shall be taken away. [4] He that is hasty to give credit is lightminded; and he that sinneth shall offend against his own soul. [5] Whoso taketh pleasure in wickedness shall be condemned: but he that resisteth pleasures crowneth his life. [6] He that can rule his tongue shall live without strife; and he that hateth babbling shall have less evil. [7] Rehearse not unto another that which is told unto thee, and thou shalt fare never the worse. [8] Whether it be to friend or foe, talk not of other men's lives; and if thou canst without offence, reveal them not. [9] For he heard and observed thee, and when time cometh he will hate thee. [10] If thou hast heard a word, let it die with thee; and be bold, it will not burst thee. [11] A fool travaileth with a word, as a woman in labour of a child. [12] As an arrow that sticketh in a man's thigh, so is a word within a fool's belly. [13] Admonish a friend, it may be he hath not done it: and if he have done it, that he do it no more. [14] Admonish thy friend, it may be he hath not said it: and if he have, that he speak it not again. [15] Admonish a friend: for many times it is a slander, and believe not every tale. [16] There is one that slippeth in his speech, but not from his heart; and who is he that hath not offended with his tongue? [17] Admonish thy neighbour before thou threaten him; and not being angry, give place to the law of the most High. [18] The fear of the Lord is the first step to be accepted [of him,] and wisdom obtaineth his love. [19] The knowledge of the commandments of the Lord is the doctrine of life: and they that do things that please him shall receive the fruit of the tree of immortality. [20] The fear of the Lord is all wisdom; and in all wisdom is the performance of the law, and the knowledge of his omnipotency. [21] If a servant say to his master, I will not do as it pleaseth thee; though afterward he do it, he angereth him that nourisheth him. [22] The knowledge of wickedness is not wisdom, neither at any time the counsel of sinners prudence. [23] There is a wickedness, and the same an abomination; and there is a fool wanting in wisdom. [24] He that hath small understanding, and feareth God, is better than one that hath much wisdom, and transgresseth the law of the most High. [25] There is an exquisite subtilty, and the same is unjust; and there is one that turneth aside to make judgment appear; and there is a wise man that justifieth in judgment. [26] There is

a wicked man that hangeth down his head sadly; but inwardly he is full of deceit, [27] Casting down his countenance, and making as if he heard not: where he is not known, he will do thee a mischief before thou be aware. [28] And if for want of power he be hindered from sinning, yet when he findeth opportunity he will do evil. [29] A man may be known by his look, and one that hath understanding by his countenance, when thou meetest him. [30] A man's attire, and excessive laughter, and gait, shew what he is.

Sir.20

[1] There is a reproof that is not comely: again, some man holdeth his tongue, and he is wise. [2] It is much better to reprove, than to be angry secretly: and he that confesseth his fault shall be preserved from hurt. [3] How good is it, when thou art reproved, to shew repentance! for so shalt thou escape wilful sin. [4] As is the lust of an eunuch to deflower a virgin; so is he that executeth judgment with violence. [5] There is one that keepeth silence, and is found wise: and another by much babbling becometh hateful. [6] Some man holdeth his tongue, because he hath not to answer: and some keepeth silence, knowing his time. [7] A wise man will hold his tongue till he see opportunity: but a babbler and a fool will regard no time. [8] He that useth many words shall be abhorred; and he that taketh to himself authority therein shall be hated. [9] There is a sinner that hath good success in evil things; and there is a gain that turneth to loss. [10] There is a gift that shall not profit thee; and there is a gift whose recompence is double. [11] There is an abasement because of glory; and there is that lifteth up his head from a low estate. [12] There is that buyeth much for a little, and repayeth it sevenfold. [13] A wise man by his words maketh him beloved: but the graces of fools shall be poured out. [14] The gift of a fool shall do thee no good when thou hast it; neither yet of the envious for his necessity: for he looketh to receive many things for one. [15] He giveth little, and upbraideth much; he openeth his mouth like a crier; to day he lendeth, and to morrow will he ask it again: such an one is to be hated of God and man. [16] The fool saith, I have no friends, I have no thank for all my good deeds, and they that eat my bread speak evil of me. [17] How oft, and of how many shall he be laughed to scorn! for he knoweth not aright what it is to have; and it is all one unto him as if he had it not. [18] To slip upon a pavement is better than to slip with the tongue: so the fall of the wicked shall come speedily. [19] An unseasonable tale will always be in the mouth of the unwise. [20] A wise sentence shall be rejected when it cometh out of a fool's mouth; for he will not speak it in due season. [21] There is that is hindered from sinning through want: and when he taketh rest, he shall not be troubled. [22] There is that destroyeth his own soul through bashfulness, and by accepting of persons overthroweth himself. [23] There is that for bashfulness promiseth to his friend, and maketh him his enemy for nothing. [24] A lie is a foul blot in a man, yet it is continually in the mouth of the untaught. [25] A thief is better than a man that is accustomed to lie: but they both shall have destruction to heritage. [26] The disposition of a liar is dishonourable, and his shame is ever with him. [27] A wise man shall promote himself to honour with his words: and he that hath understanding will please great men. [28] He that tilleth his land shall increase his heap: and he that pleaseth great men shall get pardon for iniquity. [29] Presents and gifts blind the eyes of the wise, and stop up his mouth that he cannot reprove. [30] Wisdom that is hid, and treasure that is hoarded up, what profit is in them both? [31] Better is he that hideth his folly than a man that hideth his wisdom. [32] Necessary patience in seeking ing the Lord is better than he that leadeth his life without a guide.

Sir.21

[1] My son, hast thou sinned? do so no more, but ask pardon for thy former sins. [2] Flee from sin as from the face of a serpent: for if thou comest too near it, it will bite thee: the teeth thereof are as the teeth of a lion, slaying the souls of men. [3] All iniquity is as a two edged sword, the wounds whereof cannot be healed. [4] To terrify and do wrong will waste riches: thus the house of proud men shall be made desolate. [5] A prayer out of a poor man's mouth reacheth to the ears of God, and his judgment cometh speedily. [6] He that hateth to be reproved is in the way of sinners: but he that feareth the Lord will repent from his heart. [7] An eloquent man is known far and near; but a man of understanding knoweth when he slippeth. [8] He that buildeth his house with other men's money is like one that gathereth himself stones for the tomb of his burial. [9] The congregation of the wicked is like tow wrapped together: and the end of them is a flame of fire to destroy them. [10] The way of sinners is made plain with stones, but at the end thereof is the pit of hell. [11] He that keepeth the law of the Lord getteth the understanding thereof: and the perfection of the fear of the Lord is wisdom. [12] He that is not wise will not be taught: but there is a wisdom which multiplieth bitterness. [13] The knowledge of a wise man shall abound like a flood: and his counsel is like a pure fountain of life. [14] The inner parts of a fool are like a broken vessel, and he will hold no knowledge as long as he liveth. [15] If a skilful man hear a wise word, he will commend it, and add unto it: but as soon as one of no understanding heareth it, it displeaseth him, and he casteth it behind his back. [16] The talking of a fool is like a burden in the way: but grace shall be found in the lips of the wise. [17] They enquire at the mouth of the wise man in the congregation, and they shall ponder his words in their heart. [18] As is a house that is destroyed, so is wisdom to a fool: and the knowledge of the unwise is as talk without sense. [19] Doctrine unto fools is as fetters on the feet, and like manacles on the right hand. [20] A fool lifteth up his voice with laughter; but a wise man doth scarce smile a little. [21] Learning is unto a wise man as an ornament of gold, and like a bracelet upon his right arm. [22] A foolish man's foot is soon in his [neighbour's] house: but a man of experience is ashamed of him. [23] A fool will peep in at the door into the house: but he that is well nurtured will stand without. [24] It is the rudeness of a man to hearken at the door: but a wise man will be grieved with the disgrace. [25] The lips of talkers will be telling such things as pertain not unto them: but the words of such as have understanding are weighed in the balance. [26] The heart of fools is in their mouth: but the mouth of the wise is in their heart. [27] When the ungodly curseth Satan, he curseth his own soul. [28] A whisperer defileth his own soul, and is hated wheresoever he dwelleth.

Sir.22

[1] A slothful man is compared to a filthy stone, and every one will hiss him out to his disgrace. [2] A slothful man is compared to the filth of a dunghill: every man that takes it up will shake his hand. [3] An evilnurtured man is the dishonour of his father that begat him: and a [foolish] daughter is born to his loss. [4] A wise daughter shall bring an inheritance to her husband: but she that liveth dishonestly is her father's heaviness. [5] She that is bold dishonoureth both her father and her husband, but they both shall despise her. [6] A tale out of season [is as] musick in mourning: but stripes and correction of wisdom are never out of time. [7] Whoso teacheth a fool is as one that glueth a potsherd together, and as he that waketh one from a sound sleep. [8] He that telleth a tale to a fool speaketh to one in a slumber: when he hath told his tale, he will say, What is the matter? [9] If children live honestly, and have wherewithal, they shall cover the baseness of their parents. [10] But children, being haughty, through disdain and want of nurture do stain the nobility of their kindred. [11] Weep for the dead, for he hath lost the light: and weep for the fool, for he wanteth understanding: make little weeping for the dead, for he is at rest: but the life of the fool is worse than death. [12] Seven days do men mourn for him that is dead; but for a fool and an ungodly man all the days of his life. [13] Talk not much with a fool, and go not to him that hath no understanding: beware of him, lest thou have trouble, and thou shalt never be defiled with his fooleries: depart from him, and thou shalt find rest, and never be disquieted with madness. [14] What is heavier than lead? and what is the name thereof, but a fool? [15] Sand, and salt, and a mass of iron, is easier to bear, than a man without understanding. [16] As timber girt and bound together in a building cannot be loosed with shaking: so the heart that is stablished by advised counsel shall fear at no time. [17] A heart settled upon a thought of understanding is as a fair plaistering on the wall of a gallery. [18] Pales set on an high place will never stand against the wind: so a fearful heart in the imagination of a fool cannot stand against any fear. [19] He that pricketh the eye will make tears to fall: and he that pricketh the heart maketh it to shew her knowledge. [20] Whoso casteth a stone at the birds frayeth them away: and he that upbraideth his friend breaketh friendship. [21] Though thou drewest a sword at thy friend, yet despair not: for there may be a returning [to favour.] [22] If thou hast opened thy mouth against thy friend, fear not; for there may be a reconciliation: except for upbraiding, or pride, or disclosing of secrets, or a treacherous wound: for for these things every friend will depart. [23] Be faithful to thy neighbour in his poverty, that thou mayest rejoice in his prosperity: abide stedfast unto him in the time of his trouble, that thou mayest be heir with him in his heritage: for a mean estate is not always to be contemned: nor the rich that is foolish to be had in admiration. [24] As the vapour and smoke of a furnace goeth before the fire; so reviling before blood. [25] I will not be ashamed to defend a friend; neither will I hide myself from him. [26] And if any evil happen unto me by him, every one that heareth it will beware of him. [27] Who shall set a watch before my mouth, and a seal of wisdom upon my lips, that I fall not suddenly by them, and that my tongue destroy me not?

Sir.23

[1] O Lord, Father and Governor of all my whole life, leave me not to their counsels, and let me not fall by them. [2] Who will set scourges over my thoughts, and the discipline of wisdom over mine heart? that they spare me not for mine ignorances, and it pass not by my sins: [3] Lest mine ignorances increase, and my sins abound to my destruction, and I fall before mine adversaries, and mine enemy rejoice over me, whose hope is far from thy mercy. [4] O Lord, Father and God of my life, give me not a proud look, but turn away from thy servants always a haughty mind. [5] Turn away from me vain hopes and concupiscence, and thou shalt hold him up that is desirous always to serve thee. [6] Let not the greediness of the belly nor lust of the flesh take hold of me; and give not over me thy servant into an impudent mind. [7] Hear, O ye children, the discipline of the mouth: he that keepeth it shall never be taken in his lips. [8] The sinner shall be left in his foolishness: both the evil speaker and the proud shall fall thereby. [9] Accustom not thy mouth to swearing; neither use thyself to the naming of the Holy One. [10] For as a servant that is continually beaten shall not be without a blue mark: so he that sweareth and nameth God continually shall not be faultless. [11] A man that useth much swearing shall be filled with iniquity, and the plague shall never depart from his house: if he shall offend, his sin shall be upon him: and if he acknowledge not his sin, he maketh a double offence: and if he swear in vain, he shall not be innocent, but his house shall be full of calamities. [12] There is a word that is clothed about with death: God grant that it be not found in the heritage of Jacob; for all such things shall be far from the godly, and they shall not wallow in their sins. [13] Use not thy mouth to intemperate swearing, for therein is the word of sin. [14] Remember thy father and thy mother, when thou sittest among great men. Be not forgetful before them, and so thou by thy custom become a fool, and wish that thou hadst not been born, and curse they day of thy nativity. [15] The man that is accustomed to opprobrious words will never be reformed all the days of his life. [16] Two sorts of men multiply sin, and the third will bring wrath: a hot mind is as a burning fire, it will never be quenched till it be consumed: a fornicator in the body of his flesh will never cease till he hath kindled a fire. [17] All bread is sweet to a whoremonger, he will not leave off till he die. [18] A man that breaketh wedlock, saying thus in his heart, Who seeth me? I am compassed about with darkness, the walls cover me, and no body seeth me; what need I to fear? the most High will not remember my sins: [19] Such a man only feareth the eyes of men, and knoweth not that the eyes of the Lord are ten thousand times brighter than the sun, beholding all the ways of men, and considering the most secret parts. [20] He knew all things ere ever they were created; so also after they were perfected he looked upon them all. [21] This man shall be punished in the streets of the city, and where he suspecteth not he shall be taken. [22] Thus shall it go also with the wife that leaveth her husband, and bringeth in an heir by another. [23] For first, she hath disobeyed the law of the most High; and secondly, she hath trespassed against her own husband; and thirdly, she hath played the whore in adultery, and brought children by another man. [24] She shall be brought out into the congregation, and inquisition shall be made of her children. [25] Her children shall not take root, and her branches shall bring forth no fruit. [26] She shall leave her memory to be cursed, and her reproach shall not be blotted out. [27] And they that remain shall know that there is nothing better than the fear of the Lord, and that there is nothing sweeter than to take heed unto the commandments of the Lord. [28] It is great glory to follow the Lord, and to be received of him is long life.

Sir.24

[1] Wisdom shall praise herself, and shall glory in the midst of her people. [2] In the congregation of the most High shall she open her mouth, and triumph before his power. [3] I came out of the mouth of the most High, and covered the earth as a cloud. [4] I dwelt in high places, and my throne is in a cloudy pillar. [5] I alone compassed the circuit of heaven, and walked in the bottom of the deep. [6] In the waves of the sea and in all the earth, and in every people and nation, I got a possession. [7] With all these I sought rest: and in whose inheritance shall I abide? [8] So the Creator of all things gave me a commandment, and he that made me caused my tabernacle to rest, and said, Let thy dwelling be in Jacob, and thine inheritance in Israel. [9] He created me from the beginning before the world, and I shall never fail. [10] In the holy tabernacle I served before him; and so was I established in Sion. [11] Likewise in the beloved city he gave me rest, and in Jerusalem was my power. [12] And I took root in an honourable people, even in the portion of the Lord's inheritance. [13] I was exalted like a cedar in Libanus, and as a cypress tree upon the mountains of Hermon. [14] I was exalted like a palm tree in En-gaddi, and as a rose plant in Jericho, as a fair olive tree in a pleasant field, and grew up as a plane tree by the water. [15] I gave a sweet smell like cinnamon and aspalathus, and I yielded a pleasant odour like the best myrrh, as galbanum, and onyx, and sweet storax, and as the fume of frankincense in the tabernacle. [16] As the turpentine tree I stretched out my branches, and my branches are the branches of honour and grace. [17] As the vine brought I forth pleasant savour, and my flowers are the fruit of honour and riches. [18] I am the mother of fair love, and fear, and knowledge, and holy hope: I therefore, being eternal, am given to all my children which are named of him. [19] Come unto me, all ye that be desirous of me, and fill yourselves with my fruits. [20] For my memorial is sweeter than honey, and mine inheritance than the honeycomb. [21] They that eat me shall yet be hungry, and they that drink me shall yet be thirsty. [22] He that obeyeth me shall never be confounded, and they that work by me shall not do amiss. [23] All these things are the book of the covenant of the most high God, even the law which Moses commanded for an heritage unto the congregations of Jacob. [24] Faint not to be strong in the Lord; that he may confirm you, cleave unto him: for the Lord Almighty is God alone, and beside him there is no other Saviour. [25] He filleth all things with his wisdom, as Phison and as Tigris in the time of the new fruits. [26] He maketh the understanding to abound like Euphrates, and as Jordan in the time of the harvest. [27] He maketh the doctrine of knowledge appear as the light, and as Geon in the time of vintage. [28] The first man knew her not perfectly: no more shall the last find her out. [29] For her thoughts are more than the sea, and her counsels profounder than the great deep. [30] I also came out as a brook from a river, and as a conduit into a garden. [31] I said, I will water my best garden, and will water abundantly my garden bed: and, lo, my brook became a river, and my river became a sea. [32] I will yet make doctrine to shine as the morning, and will send forth her light afar off. [33] I will yet pour out doctrine as prophecy, and leave it to all ages for ever. [34] Behold that I have not laboured for myself only, but for all them that seek wisdom.

Sir.25

[1] In three things I was beautified, and stood up beautiful both before God and men: the unity of brethren, the love of neighbours, a man and a wife that agree together. [2] Three sorts of men my soul hateth, and I am greatly offended at their life: a poor man that is proud, a rich man that is a liar, and an old adulterer that doateth. [3] If thou hast gathered nothing in thy youth, how canst thou find any thing in thine age? [4] O how comely a thing is judgment for gray hairs, and for ancient men to know counsel! [5] O how comely is the wisdom of old men, and understanding and counsel to men of honour. [6] Much experience is the crown of old men, and the fear of God is their glory. [7] There be nine things which I have judged in mine heart to be happy, and the tenth I will utter with my tongue: A man that hath joy of his children; and he that liveth to see the fall of his enemy: [8] Well is him that dwelleth with a wife of understanding, and that hath not slipped with his tongue, and that hath not served a man more unworthy than himself: [9] Well is him that hath found prudence, and he that speaketh in the ears of them that will hear: [10] O how great is he that findeth wisdom! yet is there none above him that feareth the Lord. [11] But the love of the Lord passeth all things for illumination: he that holdeth it, whereto shall he be likened? [12] The fear of the Lord is the beginning of his love: and faith is the beginning of cleaving unto him. [13] [Give me] any plague, but the plague of the heart: and any wickedness, but the wickedness of a woman: [14] And any affliction, but the affliction from them that hate me: and any revenge, but the revenge of enemies. [15] There is no head above the head of a serpent; and there is no wrath above the wrath of an enemy. [16] I had rather dwell with a lion and a dragon, than to keep house with a wicked woman. [17] The wickedness of a woman changeth her face, and darkeneth her countenance like sackcloth. [18] Her husband shall sit among his neighbours; and when he heareth it shall sigh bitterly. [19] All wickedness is but little to the wickedness of a woman: let the portion of a sinner fall upon her. [20] As the climbing up a sandy way is to the feet of the aged, so is a wife full of words to a quiet man. [21] Stumble not at the beauty of a woman, and desire her not for pleasure. [22] A woman, if she maintain her husband, is full of anger, impudence, and much reproach. [23] A wicked woman abateth the courage, maketh an heavy countenance and a wounded heart: a woman that will not comfort her husband in distress maketh weak hands and feeble knees. [24] Of the woman came the beginning of sin, and through her we all die. [25] Give the water no passage; neither a wicked woman liberty to gad abroad. [26] If she go not as thou wouldest have her, cut her off from thy flesh, and give her a bill of divorce, and let her go.

Sir.26

[1] Blessed is the man that hath a virtuous wife, for the number of his days shall be double. [2] A virtuous woman rejoiceth her husband, and he shall fulfil the years of his life in peace. [3] A good wife is a good portion, which shall be given in the portion of them that fear the Lord. [4] Whether a man be rich or poor, if he have a good heart toward the Lord, he shall at all times rejoice with a cheerful countenance. [5] There be three things that mine heart feareth; and for

the fourth I was sore afraid: the slander of a city, the gathering together of an unruly multitude, and a false accusation: all these are worse than death. [6] But a grief of heart and sorrow is a woman that is jealous over another woman, and a scourge of the tongue which communicateth with all. [7] An evil wife is a yoke shaken to and fro: he that hath hold of her is as though he held a scorpion. [8] A drunken woman and a gadder abroad causeth great anger, and she will not cover her own shame [9] The whoredom of a woman may be known in her haughty looks and eyelids. [10] If thy daughter be shameless, keep her in straitly, lest she abuse herself through overmuch liberty. [11] Watch over an impudent eye: and marvel not if she trespass against thee. [12] She will open her mouth, as a thirsty traveller when he hath found a fountain, and drink of every water near her: by every hedge will she sit down, and open her quiver against every arrow. [13] The grace of a wife delighteth her husband, and her discretion will fatten his bones. [14] A silent and loving woman is a gift of the Lord; and there is nothing so much worth as a mind well instructed. [15] A shamefaced and faithful woman is a double grace, and her continent mind cannot be valued. [16] As the sun when it ariseth in the high heaven; so is the beauty of a good wife in the ordering of her house. [17] As the clear light is upon the holy candlestick; so is the beauty of the face in ripe age. [18] As the golden pillars are upon the sockets of silver; so are the fair feet with a constant heart. [19] My son, keep the flower of thine age sound; and give not thy strength to strangers. [20] When thou hast gotten a fruitful possession through all the field, sow it with thine own seed, trusting in the goodness of thy stock. [21] So thy race which thou leavest shall be magnified, having the confidence of their good descent. [22] An harlot shall be accounted as spittle; but a married woman is a tower against death to her husband. [23] A wicked woman is given as a portion to a wicked man: but a godly woman is given to him that feareth the Lord. [24] A dishonest woman contemneth shame: but an honest woman will reverence her husband. [25] A shameless woman shall be counted as a dog; but she that is shamefaced will fear the Lord. [26] A woman that honoureth her husband shall be judged wise of all; but she that dishonoureth him in her pride shall be counted ungodly of all.[27] A loud crying woman and a scold shall be sought out to drive away the enemies. [28] There be two things that grieve my heart; and the third maketh me angry: a man of war that suffereth poverty; and men of understanding that are not set by; and one that returneth from righteousness to sin; the Lord prepareth such an one for the sword. [29] A merchant shall hardly keep himself from doing wrong; and an huckster shall not be freed from sin.

Sir.27

[1] Many have sinned for a small matter; and he that seeketh for abundance will turn his eyes away. [2] As a nail sticketh fast between the joinings of the stones; so doth sin stick close between buying and selling. [3] Unless a man hold himself diligently in the fear of the Lord, his house shall soon be overthrown. [4] As when one sifteth with a sieve, the refuse remaineth; so the filth of man in his talk. [5] The furnace proveth the potter's vessels; so the trial of man is in his reasoning. [6] The fruit declareth if the tree have been dressed; so is the utterance of a conceit in the heart of man. [7] Praise no man before thou hearest him speak; for this is the trial of men. [8] If thou followest righteousness, thou shalt obtain her, and put her on, as a glorious long robe. [9] The birds will resort unto their like; so will truth return unto them that practise in her. [10] As the lion lieth in wait for the prey; so sin for them that work iniquity. [11] The discourse of a godly man is always with wisdom; but a fool changeth as the moon. [12] If thou be among the indiscreet, observe the time; but be continually among men of understanding. [13] The discourse of fools is irksome, and their sport is the wantonness of sin. [14] The talk of him that sweareth much maketh the hair stand upright; and their brawls make one stop his ears. [15] The strife of the proud is bloodshedding, and their revilings are grievous to the ear. [16] Whoso discovereth secrets loseth his credit; and shall never find friend to his mind. [17] Love thy friend, and be faithful unto him: but if thou betrayest his secrets, follow no more after him. [18] For as a man hath destroyed his enemy; so hast thou lost the love of thy neighbor. [19] As one that letteth a bird go out of his hand, so hast thou let thy neighbour go, and shalt not get him again [20] Follow after him no more, for he is too far off; he is as a roe escaped out of the snare. [21] As for a wound, it may be bound up; and after reviling there may be reconcilement: but he that betrayeth secrets is without hope. [22] He that winketh with the eyes worketh evil: and he that knoweth him will depart from him. [23] When thou art present, he will speak sweetly, and will admire thy words: but at the last he will writhe his mouth, and slander thy sayings. [24] I have hated many things, but nothing like him; for the Lord will hate him. [25] Whoso casteth a stone on high casteth it on his own head; and a deceitful stroke shall make wounds. [26] Whoso diggeth a pit shall fall therein: and he that setteth a trap shall be taken therein. [27] He that worketh mischief, it shall fall upon him, and he shall not know whence it cometh. [28] Mockery and reproach are from the proud; but vengeance, as a lion, shall lie in wait for them. [29] They that rejoice at the fall of the righteous shall be taken in the snare; and anguish shall consume them before they die. [30] Malice and wrath, even these are abominations; and the sinful man shall have them both.

Sir.28

[1] He that revengeth shall find vengeance from the Lord, and he will surely keep his sins [in remembrance.] [2] Forgive thy neighbour the hurt that he hath done unto thee, so shall thy sins also be forgiven when thou prayest. [3] One man beareth hatred against another, and doth he seek pardon from the Lord? [4] He sheweth no mercy to a man, which is like himself: and doth he ask forgiveness of his own sins? [5] If he that is but flesh nourish hatred, who will intreat for pardon of his sins? [6] Remember thy end, and let enmity cease; [remember] corruption and death, and abide in the commandments. [7] Remember the commandments, and bear no malice to thy neighbour: [remember] the covenant of the Highest, and wink at ignorance. [8] Abstain from strife, and thou shalt diminish thy sins: for a furious man will kindle strife, [9] A sinful man disquieteth friends, and maketh debate among them that be at peace. [10] As the matter of the fire is, so it burneth: and as a man's strength is, so is his wrath; and according to his riches his anger riseth; and the stronger they are which contend, the more they will be inflamed. [11] An hasty contention kindleth a fire: and an hasty fighting sheddeth blood. [12] If thou blow the spark, it shall burn: if thou spit upon it, it shall be quenched: and both these come out of thy mouth. [13] Curse the whisperer and doubletongued: for such have destroyed many that were at peace. [14] A backbiting tongue hath disquieted many, and driven them from nation to nation: strong cities hath it pulled down, and

overthrown the houses of great men. [15] A backbiting tongue hath cast out virtuous women, and deprived them of their labours. [16] Whoso hearkeneth unto it shall never find rest, and never dwell quietly. [17] The stroke of the whip maketh marks in the flesh: but the stroke of the tongue breaketh the bones. [18] Many have fallen by the edge of the sword: but not so many as have fallen by the tongue. [19] Well is he that is defended through the venom thereof; who hath not drawn the yoke thereof, nor hath been bound in her bands. [20] For the yoke thereof is a yoke of iron, and the bands thereof are bands of brass. [21] The death thereof is an evil death, the grave were better than it. [22] It shall not have rule over them that fear God, neither shall they be burned with the flame thereof. [23] Such as forsake the Lord shall fall into it; and it shall burn in them, and not be quenched; it shall be sent upon them as a lion, and devour them as a leopard. [24] Look that thou hedge thy possession about with thorns, and bind up thy silver and gold, [25] And weigh thy words in a balance, and make a door and bar for thy mouth. [26] Beware thou slide not by it, lest thou fall before him that lieth in wait.

Sir.29

[1] He that is merciful will lend unto his neighbour; and he that strengtheneth his hand keepeth the commandments. [2] Lend to thy neighbour in time of his need, and pay thou thy neighbour again in due season. [3] Keep thy word, and deal faithfully with him, and thou shalt always find the thing that is necessary for thee. [4] Many, when a thing was lent them, reckoned it to be found, and put them to trouble that helped them. [5] Till he hath received, he will kiss a man's hand; and for his neighbour's money he will speak submissly: but when he should repay, he will prolong the time, and return words of grief, and complain of the time. [6] If he prevail, he shall hardly receive the half, and he will count as if he had found it: if not, he hath deprived him of his money, and he hath gotten him an enemy without cause: he payeth him with cursings and railings; and for honour he will pay him disgrace. [7] Many therefore have refused to lend for other men's ill dealing, fearing to be defrauded. [8] Yet have thou patience with a man in poor estate, and delay not to shew him mercy. [9] Help the poor for the commandment's sake, and turn him not away because of his poverty. [10] Lose thy money for thy brother and thy friend, and let it not rust under a stone to be lost. [11] Lay up thy treasure according to the commandments of the most High, and it shall bring thee more profit than gold. [12] Shut up alms in thy storehouses: and it shall deliver thee from all affliction. [13] It shall fight for thee against thine enemies better than a mighty shield and strong spear. [14] An honest man is surety for his neighbour: but he that is impudent will forsake him. [15] Forget not the friendship of thy surety, for he hath given his life for thee. [16] A sinner will overthrow the good estate of his surety: [17] And he that is of an unthankful mind will leave him [in danger] that delivered him. [18] Suretiship hath undone many of good estate, and shaken them as a wave of the sea: mighty men hath it driven from their houses, so that they wandered among strange nations. [19] A wicked man transgressing the commandments of the Lord shall fall into suretiship: and he that undertaketh and followeth other men's business for gain shall fall into suits. [20] Help thy neighbour according to thy power, and beware that thou thyself fall not into the same. [21] The chief thing for life is water, and bread, and clothing, and an house to cover shame. [22] Better is the life of a poor man in a mean cottage, than delicate fare in another man's house. [23] Be it little or much, hold thee contented, that thou hear not the reproach of thy house. [24] For it is a miserable life to go from house to house: for where thou art a stranger, thou darest not open thy mouth. [25] Thou shalt entertain, and feast, and have no thanks: moreover thou shalt hear bitter words: [26] Come, thou stranger, and furnish a table, and feed me of that thou hast ready. [27] Give place, thou stranger, to an honourable man; my brother cometh to be lodged, and I have need of mine house. [28] These things are grievous to a man of understanding; the upbraiding of houseroom, and reproaching of the lender.

Sir.30

[1] He that loveth his son causeth him oft to feel the rod, that he may have joy of him in the end. [2] He that chastiseth his son shall have joy in him, and shall rejoice of him among his acquaintance. [3] He that teacheth his son grieveth the enemy: and before his friends he shall rejoice of him. [4] Though his father die, yet he is as though he were not dead: for he hath left one behind him that is like himself. [5] While he lived, he saw and rejoiced in him: and when he died, he was not sorrowful. [6] He left behind him an avenger against his enemies, and one that shall requite kindness to his friends. [7] He that maketh too much of his son shall bind up his wounds; and his bowels will be troubled at every cry. [8] An horse not broken becometh headstrong: and a child left to himself will be wilful. [9] Cocker thy child, and he shall make thee afraid: play with him, and he will bring thee to heaviness. [10] Laugh not with him, lest thou have sorrow with him, and lest thou gnash thy teeth in the end. [11] Give him no liberty in his youth, and wink not at his follies. [12] Bow down his neck while he is young, and beat him on the sides while he is a child, lest he wax stubborn, and be disobedient unto thee, and so bring sorrow to thine heart. [13] Chastise thy son, and hold him to labour, lest his lewd behaviour be an offence unto thee. [14] Better is the poor, being sound and strong of constitution, than a rich man that is afflicted in his body. [15] Health and good estate of body are above all gold, and a strong body above infinite wealth. [16] There is no riches above a sound body, and no joy above the joy of the heart. [17] Death is better than a bitter life or continual sickness. [18] Delicates poured upon a mouth shut up are as messes of meat set upon a grave. [19] What good doeth the offering unto an idol? for neither can it eat nor smell: so is he that is persecuted of the Lord. [20] He seeth with his eyes and groaneth, as an eunuch that embraceth a virgin and sigheth. [21] Give not over thy mind to heaviness, and afflict not thyself in thine own counsel. [22] The gladness of the heart is the life of man, and the joyfulness of a man prolongeth his days. [23] Love thine own soul, and comfort thy heart, remove sorrow far from thee: for sorrow hath killed many, and there is no profit therein. [24] Envy and wrath shorten the life, and carefulness bringeth age before the time. [25] A cheerful and good heart will have a care of his meat and diet.

Sir.31

[1] Watching for riches consumeth the flesh, and the care thereof driveth away sleep. [2] Watching care will not let a man slumber, as a sore disease breaketh sleep, [3] The rich hath great labour in gathering riches together; and when he resteth, he is filled with his delicates. [4] The poor laboureth in his poor estate; and when he leaveth off, he is still needy. [5] He that loveth gold shall not be justified, and he that followeth corruption shall have enough thereof. [6] Gold hath been the ruin of many, and their destruction was present. [7] It is a stumblingblock unto them that sacrifice unto it, and every fool shall be taken therewith. [8] Blessed is the rich that is found without blemish, and hath not gone after gold. [9] Who is he? and we will call him blessed: for wonderful things hath he done among his people. [10] Who hath been tried thereby, and found perfect? then let him glory. Who might offend, and hath not offended? or done evil, and hath not done it? [11] His goods shall be established, and the congregation shall declare his alms. [12] If thou sit at a bountiful table, be not greedy upon it, and say not, There is much meat on it. [13] Remember that a wicked eye is an evil thing: and what is created more wicked than an eye? therefore it weepeth upon every occasion. [14] Stretch not thine hand whithersoever it looketh, and thrust it not with him into the dish. [15] Judge not thy neighbour by thyself: and be discreet in every point. [16] Eat as it becometh a man, those things which are set before thee; and devour note, lest thou be hated. [17] Leave off first for manners' sake; and be not unsatiable, lest thou offend. [18] When thou sittest among many, reach not thine hand out first of all. [19] A very little is sufficient for a man well nurtured, and he fetcheth not his wind short upon his bed. [20] Sound sleep cometh of moderate eating: he riseth early, and his wits are with him: but the pain of watching, and choler, and pangs of the belly, are with an unsatiable man. [21] And if thou hast been forced to eat, arise, go forth, vomit, and thou shalt have rest. [22] My son, hear me, and despise me not, and at the last thou shalt find as I told thee: in all thy works be quick, so shall there no sickness come unto thee. [23] Whoso is liberal of his meat, men shall speak well of him; and the report of his good housekeeping will be believed. [24] But against him that is a niggard of his meat the whole city shall murmur; and the testimonies of his niggardness shall not be doubted of. [25] Shew not thy valiantness in wine; for wine hath destroyed many. [26] The furnace proveth the edge by dipping: so doth wine the hearts of the proud by drunkeness. [27] Wine is as good as life to a man, if it be drunk moderately: what life is then to a man that is without wine? for it was made to make men glad. [28] Wine measurably drunk and in season bringeth gladness of the heart, and cheerfulness of the mind: [29] But wine drunken with excess maketh bitterness of the mind, with brawling and quarrelling. [30] Drunkenness increaseth the rage of a fool till he offend: it diminisheth strength, and maketh wounds. [31] Rebuke not thy neighbour at the wine, and despise him not in his mirth: give him no despiteful words, and press not upon him with urging him [to drink.]

Sir.32

[1] If thou be made the master [of a feast,] lift not thyself up, but be among them as one of the rest; take diligent care for them, and so sit down. [2] And when thou hast done all thy office, take thy place, that thou mayest be merry with them, and receive a crown for thy well ordering of the feast. [3] Speak, thou that art the elder, for it becometh thee, but with sound judgment; and hinder not musick. [4] Pour not out words where there is a musician, and shew not forth wisdom out of time. [5] A concert of musick in a banquet of wine is as a signet of carbuncle set in gold. [6] As a signet of an emerald set in a work of gold, so is the melody of musick with pleasant wine. [7] Speak, young man, if there be need of thee: and yet scarcely when thou art twice asked. [8] Let thy speech be short, comprehending much in few words; be as one that knoweth and yet holdeth his tongue. [9] If thou be among great men, make not thyself equal with them; and when ancient men are in place, use not many words. [10] Before the thunder goeth lightning; and before a shamefaced man shall go favour. [11] Rise up betimes, and be not the last; but get thee home without delay. [12] There take thy pastime, and do what thou wilt: but sin not by proud speech. [13] And for these things bless him that made thee, and hath replenished thee with his good things. [14] Whoso feareth the Lord will receive his discipline; and they that seek him early shall find favour. [15] He that seeketh the law shall be filled therewith: but the hypocrite will be offended thereat. [16] They that fear the Lord shall find judgment, and shall kindle justice as a light. [17] A sinful man will not be reproved, but findeth an excuse according to his will. [18] A man of counsel will be considerate; but a strange and proud man is not daunted with fear, even when of himself he hath done without counsel. [19] Do nothing without advice; and when thou hast once done, repent not. [20] Go not in a way wherein thou mayest fall, and stumble not among the stones. [21] Be not confident in a plain way. [22] And beware of thine own children. [23] In every good work trust thy own soul; for this is the keeping of the commandments. [24] He that believeth in the Lord taketh heed to the commandment; and he that trusteth in him shall fare never the worse.

Sir.33

[1] There shall no evil happen unto him that feareth the Lord; but in temptation even again he will deliver him. [2] A wise man hateth not the law; but he that is an hypocrite therein is as a ship in a storm. [3] A man of understanding trusteth in the law; and the law is faithful unto him, as an oracle. [4] Prepare what to say, and so thou shalt be heard: and bind up instruction, and then make answer. [5] The heart of the foolish is like a cartwheel; and his thoughts are like a rolling axletree. [6] A stallion horse is as a mocking friend, he neigheth under every one that sitteth upon him. [7] Why doth one day excel another, when as all the light of every day in the year is of the sun? [8] By the knowledge of the Lord they were distinguished: and he altered seasons and feasts. [9] Some of them hath he made high days, and hallowed them, and some of them hath he made ordinary days. [10] And all men are from the ground, and Adam was created of earth: [11] In much knowledge the Lord hath divided them, and made their ways diverse. [12] Some of them hath he blessed and exalted and some of them he sanctified, and set near himself: but some of them hath he cursed and brought low, and turned out of their places. [13] As the clay is in the potter's hand, to fashion it at his pleasure: so man is in the hand of him that made him, to render to them as liketh him best. [14] Good is set against evil, and life against death: so is the godly against

the sinner, and the sinner against the godly. [15] So look upon all the works of the most High; and there are two and two, one against another. [16] I awaked up last of all, as one that gathereth after the grapegatherers: by the blessing of the Lord I profited, and tred my winepress like a gatherer of grapes. [17] Consider that I laboured not for myself only, but for all them that seek learning. [18] Hear me, O ye great men of the people, and hearken with your ears, ye rulers of the congregation. [19] Give not thy son and wife, thy brother and friend, power over thee while thou livest, and give not thy goods to another: lest it repent thee, and thou intreat for the same again. [20] As long as thou livest and hast breath in thee, give not thyself over to any. [21] For better it is that thy children should seek to thee, than that thou shouldest stand to their courtesy. [22] In all thy works keep to thyself the preeminence; leave not a stain in thine honour. [23] At the time when thou shalt end thy days, and finish thy life, distribute thine inheritance. [24] Fodder, a wand, and burdens, are for the ass; and bread, correction, and work, for a servant. . [25] If thou set thy servant to labour, thou shalt find rest: but if thou let him go idle, he shall seek liberty. [26] A yoke and a collar do bow the neck: so are tortures and torments for an evil servant. [27] Send him to labour, that he be not idle; for idleness teacheth much evil. [28] Set him to work, as is fit for him: if he be not obedient, put on more heavy fetters. [29] But be not excessive toward any; and without discretion do nothing. [30] If thou have a servant, let him be unto thee as thyself, because thou hast bought him with a price. [31] If thou have a servant, entreat him as a brother: for thou hast need of him, as of thine own soul: if thou entreat him evil, and he run from thee, which way wilt thou go to seek him?

Sir.34

[1] The hopes of a man void of understanding are vain and false: and dreams lift up fools. [2] Whoso regardeth dreams is like him that catcheth at a shadow, and followeth after the wind. [3] The vision of dreams is the resemblance of one thing to another, even as the likeness of a face to a face. [4] Of an unclean thing what can be cleansed? and from that thing which is false what truth can come? [5] Divinations, and soothsayings, and dreams, are vain: and the heart fancieth, as a woman's heart in travail. [6] If they be not sent from the most High in thy visitation, set not thy heart upon them. [7] For dreams have deceived many, and they have failed that put their trust in them. [8] The law shall be found perfect without lies: and wisdom is perfection to a faithful mouth. [9] A man that hath travelled knoweth many things; and he that hath much experience will declare wisdom. [10] He that hath no experience knoweth little: but he that hath travelled is full of prudence. [11] When I travelled, I saw many things; and I understand more than I can express. [12] I was ofttimes in danger of death: yet I was delivered because of these things. [13] The spirit of those that fear the Lord shall live; for their hope is in him that saveth them. [14] Whoso feareth the Lord shall not fear nor be afraid; for he is his hope. [15] Blessed is the soul of him that feareth the Lord: to whom doth he look? and who is his strength? [16] For the eyes of the Lord are upon them that love him, he is their mighty protection and strong stay, a defence from heat, and a cover from the sun at noon, a preservation from stumbling, and an help from falling. [17] He raiseth up the soul, and lighteneth the eyes: he giveth health, life, and blessing. [18] He that sacrificeth of a thing wrongfully gotten, his offering is ridiculous; and the gifts of unjust men are not accepted. [19] The most High is not pleased with the offerings of the wicked; neither is he pacified for sin by the multitude of sacrifices. [20] Whoso bringeth an offering of the goods of the poor doeth as one that killeth the son before his father's eyes. [21] The bread of the needy is their life: he that defraudeth him thereof is a man of blood. [22] He that taketh away his neighbour's living slayeth him; and he that defraudeth the labourer of his hire is a bloodshedder. [23] When one buildeth, and another pulleth down, what profit have they then but labour? [24] When one prayeth, and another curseth, whose voice will the Lord hear? [25] He that washeth himself after the touching of a dead body, if he touch it again, what availeth his washing? [26] So is it with a man that fasteth for his sins, and goeth again, and doeth the same: who will hear his prayer? or what doth his humbling profit him?

Sir.35

[1] He that keepeth the law bringeth offerings enough: he that taketh heed to the commandment offereth a peace offering. [2] He that requiteth a goodturn offereth fine flour; and he that giveth alms sacrificeth praise. [3] To depart from wickedness is a thing pleasing to the Lord; and to forsake unrighteousness is a propitiation. [4] Thou shalt not appear empty before the Lord. [5] For all these things [are to be done] because of the commandment. [6] The offering of the righteous maketh the altar fat, and the sweet savour thereof is before the most High. [7] The sacrifice of a just man is acceptable. and the memorial thereof shall never be forgotten. [8] Give the Lord his honour with a good eye, and diminish not the firstfruits of thine hands. [9] In all thy gifts shew a cheerful countenance, and dedicate thy tithes with gladness. [10] Give unto the most High according as he hath enriched thee; and as thou hast gotten, give with a cheerful eye. [11] For the Lord recompenseth, and will give thee seven times as much. [12] Do not think to corrupt with gifts; for such he will not receive: and trust not to unrighteous sacrifices; for the Lord is judge, and with him is no respect of persons. [13] He will not accept any person against a poor man, but will hear the prayer of the oppressed. [14] He will not despise the supplication of the fatherless; nor the widow, when she poureth out her complaint. [15] Do not the tears run down the widow's cheeks? and is not her cry against him that causeth them to fall? [16] He that serveth the Lord shall be accepted with favour, and his prayer shall reach unto the clouds. [17] The prayer of the humble pierceth the clouds: and till it come nigh, he will not be comforted; and will not depart, till the most High shall behold to judge righteously, and execute judgment. [18] For the Lord will not be slack, neither will the Mighty be patient toward them, till he have smitten in sunder the loins of the unmerciful, and repayed vengeance to the heathen; till he have taken away the multitude of the proud, and broken the sceptre of the unrighteous; [19] Till he have rendered to every man according to his deeds, and to the works of men according to their devices; till he have judged the cause of his people, and made them to rejoice in his mercy. [20] Mercy is seasonable in the time of affliction, as clouds of rain in the time of drought.

Sir.36

[1] Have mercy upon us, O Lord God of all, and behold us: [2] And send thy fear upon all the nations that seek not after thee. [3] Lift up thy hand against the strange nations, and let them see thy power [4] As thou wast sanctified in us before them: so be thou magnified among them before us. [5] And let them know thee, as we have known thee, that there is no God but only thou, O God. [6] Shew new signs, and make other strange wonders: glorify thy hand and thy right arm, that they may set forth thy wondrous works. [7] Raise up indignation, and pour out wrath: take away the adversary, and destroy the enemy. [8] Sake the time short, remember the covenant, and let them declare thy wonderful works. [9] Let him that escapeth be consumed by the rage of the fire; and let them perish that oppress the people. [10] Smite in sunder the heads of the rulers of the heathen, that say, There is none other but we. [11] Gather all the tribes of Jacob together, and inherit thou them, as from the beginning. [12] O Lord, have mercy upon the people that is called by thy name, and upon Israel, whom thou hast named thy firstborn. [13] O be merciful unto Jerusalem, thy holy city, the place of thy rest. [14] Fill Sion with thine unspeakable oracles, and thy people with thy glory: [15] Give testimony unto those that thou hast possessed from the beginning, and raise up prophets that have been in thy name. [16] Reward them that wait for thee, and let thy prophets be found faithful. [17] O Lord, hear the prayer of thy servants, according to the blessing of Aaron over thy people, that all they which dwell upon the earth may know that thou art the Lord, the eternal God. [18] The belly devoureth all meats, yet is one meat better than another. [19] As the palate tasteth divers kinds of venison: so doth an heart of understanding false speeches. [20] A froward heart causeth heaviness: but a man of experience will recompense him. [21] A woman will receive every man, yet is one daughter better than another. [22] The beauty of a woman cheereth the countenance, and a man loveth nothing better. [23] If there be kindness, meekness, and comfort, in her tongue, then is not her husband like other men. [24] He that getteth a wife beginneth a possession, a help like unto himself, and a pillar of rest. [25] Where no hedge is, there the possession is spoiled: and he that hath no wife will wander up and down mourning. [26] Who will trust a thief well appointed, that skippeth from city to city? so [who will believe] a man that hath no house, and lodgeth wheresoever the night taketh him?

Sir.37

[1] Every friend saith, I am his friend also: but there is a friend, which is only a friend in name. [2] Is it not a grief unto death, when a companion and friend is turned to an enemy? [3] O wicked imagination, whence camest thou in to cover the earth with deceit? [4] There is a companion, which rejoiceth in the prosperity of a friend, but in the time of trouble will be against him. [5] There is a companion, which helpeth his friend for the belly, and taketh up the buckler against the enemy. [6] Forget not thy friend in thy mind, and be not unmindful of him in thy riches. [7] Every counsellor extolleth counsel; but there is some that counselleth for himself. [8] Beware of a counsellor, and know before what need he hath; for he will counsel for himself; lest he cast the lot upon thee, [9] And say unto thee, Thy way is good: and afterward he stand on the other side, to see what shall befall thee. [10] Consult not with one that suspecteth thee: and hide thy counsel from such as envy thee. [11] Neither consult with a woman touching her of whom she is jealous; neither with a coward in matters of war; nor with a merchant concerning exchange; nor with a buyer of selling; nor with an envious man of thankfulness; nor with an unmerciful man touching kindness; nor with the slothful for any work; nor with an hireling for a year of finishing work; nor with an idle servant of much business: hearken not unto these in any matter of counsel. [12] But be continually with a godly man, whom thou knowest to keep the commandments of the Lord, whose, mind is according to thy mind, and will sorrow with thee, if thou shalt miscarry. [13] And let the counsel of thine own heart stand: for there is no man more faithful unto thee than it. [14] For a man's mind is sometime wont to tell him more than seven watchmen, that sit above in an high tower. [15] And above all this pray to the most High, that he will direct thy way in truth. [16] Let reason go before every enterprize, and counsel before every action. [17] The countenance is a sign of changing of the heart. [18] Four manner of things appear: good and evil, life and death: but the tongue ruleth over them continually. [19] There is one that is wise and teacheth many, and yet is unprofitable to himself. [20] There is one that sheweth wisdom in words, and is hated: he shall be destitute of all food. [21] For grace is not given, him from the Lord, because he is deprived of all wisdom. [22] Another is wise to himself; and the fruits of understanding are commendable in his mouth. [23] A wise man instructeth his people; and the fruits of his understanding fail not. [24] A wise man shall be filled with blessing; and all they that see him shall count him happy. [25] The days of the life of man may be numbered: but the days of Israel are innumerable. [26] A wise man shall inherit glory among his people, and his name shall be perpetual. [27] My son, prove thy soul in thy life, and see what is evil for it, and give not that unto it. [28] For all things are not profitable for all men, neither hath every soul pleasure in every thing. [29] Be not unsatiable in any dainty thing, nor too greedy upon meats: [30] For excess of meats bringeth sickness, and surfeiting will turn into choler. [31] By surfeiting have many perished; but he that taketh heed prolongeth his life.

Sir.38

[1] Honour a physician with the honour due unto him for the uses which ye may have of him: for the Lord hath created him. [2] For of the most High cometh healing, and he shall receive honour of the king. [3] The skill of the physician shall lift up his head: and in the sight of great men he shall be in admiration. [4] The Lord hath created medicines out of the earth; and he that is wise will not abhor them. [5] Was not the water made sweet with wood, that the virtue thereof might be known? [6] And he hath given men skill, that he might be honoured in his marvellous works. [7] With such doth he heal [men,] and taketh away their pains. [8] Of such doth the apothecary make a confection; and of his works there is no end; and from him is peace over all the earth, [9] My son, in thy sickness be not negligent: but pray unto the Lord, and he will make thee whole. [10] Leave off from sin, and order thine hands aright, and cleanse thy heart from all wickedness. [11] Give a sweet savour, and a memorial of fine flour; and make a fat offering, as not being. [12] Then give place to the physician, for the Lord hath created him: let him not go from thee, for thou hast need of him. [13] There

is a time when in their hands there is good success. [**14**] For they shall also pray unto the Lord, that he would prosper that, which they give for ease and remedy to prolong life. [**15**] He that sinneth before his Maker, let him fall into the hand of the physician. [**16**] My son, let tears fall down over the dead, and begin to lament, as if thou hadst suffered great harm thyself; and then cover his body according to the custom, and neglect not his burial. [**17**] Weep bitterly, and make great moan, and use lamentation, as he is worthy, and that a day or two, lest thou be evil spoken of: and then comfort thyself for thy heaviness. [**18**] For of heaviness cometh death, and the heaviness of the heart breaketh strength. [**19**] In affliction also sorrow remaineth: and the life of the poor is the curse of the heart. [**20**] Take no heaviness to heart: drive it away, and member the last end. [**21**] Forget it not, for there is no turning again: thou shalt not do him good, but hurt thyself. [**22**] Remember my judgment: for thine also shall be so; yesterday for me, and to day for thee. [**23**] When the dead is at rest, let his remembrance rest; and be comforted for him, when his Spirit is departed from him. [**24**] The wisdom of a learned man cometh by opportunity of leisure: and he that hath little business shall become wise. [**25**] How can he get wisdom that holdeth the plough, and that glorieth in the goad, that driveth oxen, and is occupied in their labours, and whose talk is of bullocks? [**26**] He giveth his mind to make furrows; and is diligent to give the kine fodder. [**27**] So every carpenter and workmaster, that laboureth night and day: and they that cut and grave seals, and are diligent to make great variety, and give themselves to counterfeit imagery, and watch to finish a work: [**28**] The smith also sitting by the anvil, and considering the iron work, the vapour of the fire wasteth his flesh, and he fighteth with the heat of the furnace: the noise of the hammer and the anvil is ever in his ears, and his eyes look still upon the pattern of the thing that he maketh; he setteth his mind to finish his work, and watcheth to polish it perfectly: [**29**] So doth the potter sitting at his work, and turning the wheel about with his feet, who is alway carefully set at his work, and maketh all his work by number; [**30**] He fashioneth the clay with his arm, and boweth down his strength before his feet; he applieth himself to lead it over; and he is diligent to make clean the furnace: [**31**] All these trust to their hands: and every one is wise in his work. [**32**] Without these cannot a city be inhabited: and they shall not dwell where they will, nor go up and down: [**33**] They shall not be sought for in publick counsel, nor sit high in the congregation: they shall not sit on the judges' seat, nor understand the sentence of judgment: they cannot declare justice and judgment; and they shall not be found where parables are spoken. [**34**] But they will maintain the state of the world, and [all] their desire is in the work of their craft.

Sir.39

[**1**] But he that giveth his mind to the law of the most High, and is occupied in the meditation thereof, will seek out the wisdom of all the ancient, and be occupied in prophecies. [**2**] He will keep the sayings of the renowned men: and where subtil parables are, he will be there also. [**3**] He will seek out the secrets of grave sentences, and be conversant in dark parables. [**4**] He shall serve among great men, and appear before princes: he will travel through strange countries; for he hath tried the good and the evil among men. [**5**] He will give his heart to resort early to the Lord that made him, and will pray before the most High, and will open his mouth in prayer, and make supplication for his sins. [**6**] When the great Lord will, he shall be filled with the spirit of understanding: he shall pour out wise sentences, and give thanks unto the Lord in his prayer. [**7**] He shall direct his counsel and knowledge, and in his secrets shall he meditate. [**8**] He shall shew forth that which he hath learned, and shall glory in the law of the covenant of the Lord. [**9**] Many shall commend his understanding; and so long as the world endureth, it shall not be blotted out; his memorial shall not depart away, and his name shall live from generation to generation. [**10**] Nations shall shew forth his wisdom, and the congregation shall declare his praise. [**11**] If he die, he shall leave a greater name than a thousand: and if he live, he shall increase it. [**12**] Yet have I more to say, which I have thought upon; for I am filled as the moon at the full. [**13**] Hearken unto me, ye holy children, and bud forth as a rose growing by the brook of the field: [**14**] And give ye a sweet savour as frankincense, and flourish as a lily, send forth a smell, and sing a song of praise, bless the Lord in all his works. [**15**] Magnify his name, and shew forth his praise with the songs of your lips, and with harps, and in praising him ye shall say after this manner: [**16**] All the works of the Lord are exceeding good, and whatsoever he commandeth shall be accomplished in due season. [**17**] And none may say, What is this? wherefore is that? for at time convenient they shall all be sought out: at his commandment the waters stood as an heap, and at the words of his mouth the receptacles of waters. [**18**] At his commandment is done whatsoever pleaseth him; and none can hinder, when he will save. [**19**] The works of all flesh are before him, and nothing can be hid from his eyes. [**20**] He seeth from everlasting to everlasting; and there is nothing wonderful before him. [**21**] A man need not to say, What is this? wherefore is that? for he hath made all things for their uses. [**22**] His blessing covered the dry land as a river, and watered it as a flood. [**23**] As he hath turned the waters into saltness: so shall the heathen inherit his wrath. [**24**] As his ways are plain unto the holy; so are they stumblingblocks unto the wicked. [**25**] For the good are good things created from the beginning: so evil things for sinners. [**26**] The principal things for the whole use of man's life are water, fire, iron, and salt, flour of wheat, honey, milk, and the blood of the grape, and oil, and clothing. [**27**] All these things are for good to the godly: so to the sinners they are turned into evil. [**28**] There be spirits that are created for vengeance, which in their fury lay on sore strokes; in the time of destruction they pour out their force, and appease the wrath of him that made them. [**29**] Fire, and hail, and famine, and death, all these were created for vengeance; [**30**] Teeth of wild beasts, and scorpions, serpents, and the sword punishing the wicked to destruction. [**31**] They shall rejoice in his commandment, and they shall be ready upon earth, when need is; and when their time is come, they shall not transgress his word. [**32**] Therefore from the beginning I was resolved, and thought upon these things, and have left them in writing. [**33**] All the works of the Lord are good: and he will give every needful thing in due season. [**34**] So that a man cannot say, This is worse than that: for in time they shall all be well approved. [**35**] And therefore praise ye the Lord with the whole heart and mouth, and bless the name of the Lord.

Sir.40

[**1**] Great travail is created for every man, and an heavy yoke is upon the sons of Adam, from the day that they go out of their mother's womb, till the day that they return to the mother of all things. [**2**] Their imagination of things to come, and

the day of death, [trouble] their thoughts, and [cause] fear of heart; [**3**] From him that sitteth on a throne of glory, unto him that is humbled in earth and ashes; [**4**] From him that weareth purple and a crown, unto him that is clothed with a linen frock. [**5**] Wrath, and envy, trouble, and unquietness, fear of death, and anger, and strife, and in the time of rest upon his bed his night sleep, do change his knowledge. [**6**] A little or nothing is his rest, and afterward he is in his sleep, as in a day of keeping watch, troubled in the vision of his heart, as if he were escaped out of a battle. [**7**] When all is safe, he awaketh, and marvelleth that the fear was nothing. [**8**] [Such things happen] unto all flesh, both man and beast, and that is sevenfold more upon sinners. [**9**] Death, and bloodshed, strife, and sword, calamities, famine, tribulation, and the scourge; [**10**] These things are created for the wicked, and for their sakes came the flood. [**11**] All things that are of the earth shall turn to the earth again: and that which is of the waters doth return into the sea. [**12**] All bribery and injustice shall be blotted out: but true dealing shall endure for ever. [**13**] The goods of the unjust shall be dried up like a river, and shall vanish with noise, like a great thunder in rain. [**14**] While he openeth his hand he shall rejoice: so shall transgressors come to nought. [**15**] The children of the ungodly shall not bring forth many branches: but are as unclean roots upon a hard rock. [**16**] The weed growing upon every water and bank of a river shall be pulled up before all grass. [**17**] Bountifulness is as a most fruitful garden, and mercifulness endureth for ever. [**18**] To labour, and to be content with that a man hath, is a sweet life: but he that findeth a treasure is above them both. [**19**] Children and the building of a city continue a man's name: but a blameless wife is counted above them both. [**20**] Wine and musick rejoice the heart: but the love of wisdom is above them both. [**21**] The pipe and the psaltery make sweet melody: but a pleasant tongue is above them both. [**22**] Thine eye desireth favour and beauty: but more than both corn while it is green. [**23**] A friend and companion never meet amiss: but above both is a wife with her husband. [**24**] Brethren and help are against time of trouble: but alms shall deliver more than them both. [**25**] Gold and silver make the foot stand sure: but counsel is esteemed above them both. [**26**] Riches and strength lift up the heart: but the fear of the Lord is above them both: there is no want in the fear of the Lord, and it needeth not to seek help. [**27**] The fear of the Lord is a fruitful garden, and covereth him above all glory. [**28**] My son, lead not a beggar's life; for better it is to die than to beg. [**29**] The life of him that dependeth on another man's table is not to be counted for a life; for he polluteth himself with other men's meat: but a wise man well nurtured will beware thereof. [**30**] Begging is sweet in the mouth of the shameless: but in his belly there shall burn a fire.

Sir.41

[**1**] O death, how bitter is the remembrance of thee to a man that liveth at rest in his possessions, unto the man that hath nothing to vex him, and that hath prosperity in all things: yea, unto him that is yet able to receive meat! [**2**] O death, acceptable is thy sentence unto the needy, and unto him whose strength faileth, that is now in the last age, and is vexed with all things, and to him that despaireth, and hath lost patience! [**3**] Fear not the sentence of death, remember them that have been before thee, and that come after; for this is the sentence of the Lord over all flesh. [**4**] And why art thou against the pleasure of the most High? there is no inquisition in the grave, whether thou have lived ten, or an hundred, or a thousand years. [**5**] The children of sinners are abominable children, and they that are conversant in the dwelling of the ungodly. [**6**] The inheritance of sinners' children shall perish, and their posterity shall have a perpetual reproach. [**7**] The children will complain of an ungodly father, because they shall be reproached for his sake. [**8**] Woe be unto you, ungodly men, which have forsaken the law of the most high God! for if ye increase, it shall be to your destruction: [**9**] And if ye be born, ye shall be born to a curse: and if ye die, a curse shall be your portion. [**10**] All that are of the earth shall turn to earth again: so the ungodly shall go from a curse to destruction. [**11**] The mourning of men is about their bodies: but an ill name of sinners shall be blotted out. [**12**] Have regard to thy name; for that shall continue with thee above a thousand great treasures of gold. [**13**] A good life hath but few days: but a good name endureth for ever. [**14**] My children, keep discipline in peace: for wisdom that is hid, and a treasure that is not seen, what profit is in them both? [**15**] A man that hideth his foolishness is better than a man that hideth his wisdom. [**16**] Therefore be shamefaced according to my word: for it is not good to retain all shamefacedness; neither is it altogether approved in every thing. [**17**] Be ashamed of whoredom before father and mother: and of a lie before a prince and a mighty man; [**18**] Of an offence before a judge and ruler; of iniquity before a congregation and people; of unjust dealing before thy partner and friend; [**19**] And of theft in regard of the place where thou sojournest, and in regard of the truth of God and his covenant; and to lean with thine elbow upon the meat; and of scorning to give and take; [**20**] And of silence before them that salute thee; and to look upon an harlot; [**21**] And to turn away thy face from thy kinsman; or to take away a portion or a gift; or to gaze upon another man's wife. [**22**] Or to be overbusy with his maid, and come not near her bed; or of upbraiding speeches before friends; and after thou hast given, upbraid not; [**23**] Or of iterating and speaking again that which thou hast heard; and of revealing of secrets. [**24**] So shalt thou be truly shamefaced and find favour before all men.

Sir.42

[**1**] Of these things be not thou ashamed, and accept no person to sin thereby: [**2**] Of the law of the most High, and his covenant; and of judgment to justify the ungodly; [**3**] Of reckoning with thy partners and travellers; or of the gift of the heritage of friends; [**4**] Of exactness of balance and weights; or of getting much or little; [**5**] And of merchants' indifferent selling; of much correction of children; and to make the side of an evil servant to bleed. [**6**] Sure keeping is good, where an evil wife is; and shut up, where many hands are. [**7**] Deliver all things in number and weight; and put all in writing that thou givest out, or receivest in. [**8**] Be not ashamed to inform the unwise and foolish, and the extreme aged that contendeth with those that are young: thus shalt thou be truly learned, and approved of all men living. [**9**] The father waketh for the daughter, when no man knoweth; and the care for her taketh away sleep: when she is young, lest she pass away the flower of her age; and being married, lest she should be hated: [**10**] In her virginity, lest she should be defiled and gotten with child in her father's house; and having an husband, lest she should misbehave herself; and when she is married, lest she should be barren. [**11**] Keep a sure watch over a shameless daughter, lest she make thee a laughingstock to thine enemies, and a byword in the city, and a reproach among the people, and make thee ashamed before the multitude.

[12] Behold not every body's beauty, and sit not in the midst of women. [13] For from garments cometh a moth, and from women wickedness. [14] Better is the churlishness of a man than a courteous woman, a woman, I say, which bringeth shame and reproach. [15] I will now remember the works of the Lord, and declare the things that I have seen: In the words of the Lord are his works. [16] The sun that giveth light looketh upon all things, and the work thereof is full of the glory of the Lord. [17] The Lord hath not given power to the saints to declare all his marvellous works, which the Almighty Lord firmly settled, that whatsoever is might be established for his glory. [18] He seeketh out the deep, and the heart, and considereth their crafty devices: for the Lord knoweth all that may be known, and he beholdeth the signs of the world. [19] He declareth the things that are past, and for to come, and revealeth the steps of hidden things. [20] No thought escapeth him, neither any word is hidden from him. [21] He hath garnished the excellent works of his wisdom, and he is from everlasting to everlasting: unto him may nothing be added, neither can he be diminished, and he hath no need of any counsellor. [22] Oh how desirable are all his works! and that a man may see even to a spark. [23] All these things live and remain for ever for all uses, and they are all obedient. [24] All things are double one against another: and he hath made nothing imperfect. [25] One thing establisheth the good or another: and who shall be filled with beholding his glory?

Sir.43

[1] The pride of the height, the clear firmament, the beauty of heaven, with his glorious shew; [2] The sun when it appeareth, declaring at his rising a marvellous instrument, the work of the most High: [3] At noon it parcheth the country, and who can abide the burning heat thereof? [4] A man blowing a furnace is in works of heat, but the sun burneth the mountains three times more; breathing out fiery vapours, and sending forth bright beams, it dimmeth the eyes. [5] Great is the Lord that made it; and at his commandment runneth hastily. [6] He made the moon also to serve in her season for a declaration of times, and a sign of the world. [7] From the moon is the sign of feasts, a light that decreaseth in her perfection. [8] The month is called after her name, increasing wonderfully in her changing, being an instrument of the armies above, shining in the firmament of heaven; [9] The beauty of heaven, the glory of the stars, an ornament giving light in the highest places of the Lord. [10] At the commandment of the Holy One they will stand in their order, and never faint in their watches. [11] Look upon the rainbow, and praise him that made it; very beautiful it is in the brightness thereof. [12] It compasseth the heaven about with a glorious circle, and the hands of the most High have bended it. [13] By his commandment he maketh the snow to fall aplace, and sendeth swiftly the lightnings of his judgment. [14] Through this the treasures are opened: and clouds fly forth as fowls. [15] By his great power he maketh the clouds firm, and the hailstones are broken small. [16] At his sight the mountains are shaken, and at his will the south wind bloweth. [17] The noise of the thunder maketh the earth to tremble: so doth the northern storm and the whirlwind: as birds flying he scattereth the snow, and the falling down thereof is as the lighting of grasshoppers: [18] The eye marvelleth at the beauty of the whiteness thereof, and the heart is astonished at the raining of it. [19] The hoarfrost also as salt he poureth on the earth, and being congealed, it lieth on the top of sharp stakes. [20] When the cold north wind bloweth, and the water is congealed into ice, it abideth upon every gathering together of water, and clotheth the water as with a breastplate. [21] It devoureth the mountains, and burneth the wilderness, and consumeth the grass as fire. [22] A present remedy of all is a mist coming speedily, a dew coming after heat refresheth. [23] By his counsel he appeaseth the deep, and planteth islands therein. [24] They that sail on the sea tell of the danger thereof; and when we hear it with our ears, we marvel thereat. [25] For therein be strange and wondrous works, variety of all kinds of beasts and whales created. [26] By him the end of them hath prosperous success, and by his word all things consist. [27] We may speak much, and yet come short: wherefore in sum, he is all. [28] How shall we be able to magnify him? for he is great above all his works. [29] The Lord is terrible and very great, and marvellous is his power. [30] When ye glorify the Lord, exalt him as much as ye can; for even yet will he far exceed: and when ye exalt him, put forth all your strength, and be not weary; for ye can never go far enough. [31] Who hath seen him, that he might tell us? and who can magnify him as he is? [32] There are yet hid greater things than these be, for we have seen but a few of his works. [33] For the Lord hath made all things; and to the godly hath he given wisdom.

Sir.44

[1] Let us now praise famous men, and our fathers that begat us. [2] The Lord hath wrought great glory by them through his great power from the beginning. [3] Such as did bear rule in their kingdoms, men renowned for their power, giving counsel by their understanding, and declaring prophecies: [4] Leaders of the people by their counsels, and by their knowledge of learning meet for the people, wise and eloquent are their instructions: [5] Such as found out musical tunes, and recited verses in writing: [6] Rich men furnished with ability, living peaceably in their habitations: [7] All these were honoured in their generations, and were the glory of their times. [8] There be of them, that have left a name behind them, that their praises might be reported. [9] And some there be, which have no memorial; who are perished, as though they had never been; and are become as though they had never been born; and their children after them. [10] But these were merciful men, whose righteousness hath not been forgotten. [11] With their seed shall continually remain a good inheritance, and their children are within the covenant. [12] Their seed standeth fast, and their children for their sakes. [13] Their seed shall remain for ever, and their glory shall not be blotted out. [14] Their bodies are buried in peace; but their name liveth for evermore. [15] The people will tell of their wisdom, and the congregation will shew forth their praise. [16] Enoch pleased the Lord, and was translated, being an example of repentance to all generations. [17] Noah was found perfect and righteous; in the time of wrath he was taken in exchange [for the world;] therefore was he left as a remnant unto the earth, when the flood came. [18] An everlasting covenant was made with him, that all flesh should perish no more by the flood. [19] Abraham was a great father of many people: in glory was there none like unto him; [20] Who kept the law of the most High, and was in covenant with him: he established the covenant in his flesh; and when he was proved, he was found faithful. [21] Therefore he assured him by an oath, that he would bless the nations in his

seed, and that he would multiply him as the dust of the earth, and exalt his seed as the stars, and cause them to inherit from sea to sea, and from the river unto the utmost part of the land. [22] With Isaac did he establish likewise [for Abraham his father's sake] the blessing of all men, and the covenant, And made it rest upon the head of Jacob. He acknowledged him in his blessing, and gave him an heritage, and divided his portions; among the twelve tribes did he part them.

Sir.45

[1] And he brought out of him a merciful man, which found favour in the sight of all flesh, even Moses, beloved of God and men, whose memorial is blessed. [2] He made him like to the glorious saints, and magnified him, so that his enemies stood in fear of him. [3] By his words he caused the wonders to cease, and he made him glorious in the sight of kings, and gave him a commandment for his people, and shewed him part of his glory. [4] He sanctified him in his faithfuless and meekness, and chose him out of all men. [5] He made him to hear his voice, and brought him into the dark cloud, and gave him commandments before his face, even the law of life and knowledge, that he might teach Jacob his covenants, and Israel his judgments. [6] He exalted Aaron, an holy man like unto him, even his brother, of the tribe of Levi. [7] An everlasting covenant he made with him and gave him the priesthood among the people; he beautified him with comely ornaments, and clothed him with a robe of glory. [8] He put upon him perfect glory; and strengthened him with rich garments, with breeches, with a long robe, and the ephod. [9] And he compassed him with pomegranates, and with many golden bells round about, that as he went there might be a sound, and a noise made that might be heard in the temple, for a memorial to the children of his people; [10] With an holy garment, with gold, and blue silk, and purple, the work of the embroidere, with a breastplate of judgment, and with Urim and Thummim; [11] With twisted scarlet, the work of the cunning workman, with precious stones graven like seals, and set in gold, the work of the jeweller, with a writing engraved for a memorial, after the number of the tribes of Israel. [12] He set a crown of gold upon the mitre, wherein was engraved Holiness, an ornament of honour, a costly work, the desires of the eyes, goodly and beautiful. [13] Before him there were none such, neither did ever any stranger put them on, but only his children and his children's children perpetually. [14] Their sacrifices shall be wholly consumed every day twice continually. [15] Moses consecrated him, and anointed him with holy oil: this was appointed unto him by an everlasting covenant, and to his seed, so long as the heavens should remain, that they should minister unto him, and execute the office of the priesthood, and bless the people in his name. [16] He chose him out of all men living to offer sacrifices to the Lord, incense, and a sweet savour, for a memorial, to make reconciliation for his people. [17] He gave unto him his commandments, and authority in the statutes of judgments, that he should teach Jacob the testimonies, and inform Israel in his laws. [18] Strangers conspired together against him, and maligned him in the wilderness, even the men that were of Dathan's and Abiron's side, and the congregation of Core, with fury and wrath. [19] This the Lord saw, and it displeased him, and in his wrathful indignation were they consumed: he did wonders upon them, to consume them with the fiery flame. [20] But he made Aaron more honourable, and gave him an heritage, and divided unto him the firstfruits of the increase; especially he prepared bread in abundance: [21] For they eat of the sacrifices of the Lord, which he gave unto him and his seed. [22] Howbeit in the land of the people he had no inheritance, neither had he any portion among the people: for the Lord himself is his portion and inheritance. [23] The third in glory is Phinees the son of Eleazar, because he had zeal in the fear of the Lord, and stood up with good courage of heart: when the people were turned back, and made reconciliation for Israel. [24] Therefore was there a covenant of peace made with him, that he should be the chief of the sanctuary and of his people, and that he and his posterity should have the dignity of the priesthood for ever: [25] According to the covenant made with David son of Jesse, of the tribe of Juda, that the inheritance of the king should be to his posterity alone: so the inheritance of Aaron should also be unto his seed. [26] God give you wisdom in your heart to judge his people in righteousness, that their good things be not abolished, and that their glory may endure for ever.

Sir.46

[1] Jesus the son a Nave was valiant in the wars, and was the successor of Moses in prophecies, who according to his name was made great for the saving of the elect of God, and taking vengeance of the enemies that rose up against them, that he might set Israel in their inheritance. [2] How great glory gat he, when he did lift up his hands, and stretched out his sword against the cities! [3] Who before him so stood to it? for the Lord himself brought his enemies unto him. [4] Did not the sun go back by his means? and was not one day as long as two? [5] He called upon the most high Lord, when the enemies pressed upon him on every side; and the great Lord heard him. [6] And with hailstones of mighty power he made the battle to fall violently upon the nations, and in the descent [of Beth-horon] he destroyed them that resisted, that the nations might know all their strength, because he fought in the sight of the Lord, and he followed the Mighty One. [7] In the time of Moses also he did a work of mercy, he and Caleb the son of Jephunne, in that they withstood the congregation, and withheld the people from sin, and appeased the wicked murmuring. [8] And of six hundred thousand people on foot, they two were preserved to bring them in to the heritage, even unto the land that floweth with milk and honey. [9] The Lord gave strength also unto Caleb, which remained with him unto his old age: so that he entered upon the high places of the land, and his seed obtained it for an heritage: [10] That all the children of Israel might see that it is good to follow the Lord. [11] And concerning the judges, every one by name, whose heart went not a whoring, nor departed from the Lord, let their memory be blessed. [12] Let their bones flourish out of their place, and let the name of them that were honoured be continued upon their children. [13] Samuel, the prophet of the Lord, beloved of his Lord, established a kingdom, and anointed princes over his people. [14] By the law of the Lord he judged the congregation, and the Lord had respect unto Jacob. [15] By his faithfulness he was found a true prophet, and by his word he was known to be faithful in vision. [16] He called upon the mighty Lord, when his enemies pressed upon him on every side, when he offered the sucking lamb. [17] And the Lord thundered from heaven, and with a great noise made his voice to be heard. [18] And he destroyed the rulers of the Tyrians, and all the princes cf the Philistines. [19] And before his long sleep he made protestations in the sight of the Lord and his anointed, I have not taken any man's goods, so much as a shoe: and no

man did accuse him. [20] And after his death he prophesied, and shewed the king his end, and lifted up his voice from the earth in prophecy, to blot out the wickedness of the people.

Sir.47

[1] And after him rose up Nathan to prophesy in the time of David. [2] As is the fat taken away from the peace offering, so was David chosen out of the children of Israel. [3] He played with lions as with kids, and with bears as with lambs. [4] Slew he not a giant, when he was yet but young? and did he not take away reproach from the people, when he lifted up his hand with the stone in the sling, and beat down the boasting of Goliath? [5] For he called upon the most high Lord; and he gave him strength in his right hand to slay that mighty warrior, and set up the horn of his people. [6] So the people honoured him with ten thousands, and praised him in the blessings of the Lord, in that he gave him a crown of glory. [7] For he destroyed the enemies on every side, and brought to nought the Philistines his adversaries, and brake their horn in sunder unto this day. [8] In all his works he praised the Holy One most high with words of glory; with his whole heart he sung songs, and loved him that made him. [9] He set singers also before the altar, that by their voices they might make sweet melody, and daily sing praises in their songs. [10] He beautified their feasts, and set in order the solemn times until the end, that they might praise his holy name, and that the temple might sound from morning. [11] The Lord took away his sins, and exalted his horn for ever: he gave him a covenant of kings, and a throne of glory in Israel. [12] After him rose up a wise son, and for his sake he dwelt at large. [13] Solomon reigned in a peaceable time, and was honoured; for God made all quiet round about him, that he might build an house in his name, and prepare his sanctuary for ever. [14] How wise wast thou in thy youth and, as a flood, filled with understanding! [15] Thy soul covered the whole earth, and thou filledst it with dark parables. [16] Thy name went far unto the islands; and for thy peace thou wast beloved. [17] The countries marvelled at thee for thy songs, and proverbs, and parables, and interpretations. [18] By the name of the Lord God, which is called the Lord God of Israel, thou didst gather gold as tin and didst multiply silver as lead. [19] Thou didst bow thy loins unto women, and by thy body thou wast brought into subjection. [20] Thou didst stain thy honour, and pollute thy seed: so that thou broughtest wrath upon thy children, and wast grieved for thy folly. [21] So the kingdom was divided, and out of Ephraim ruled a rebellious kingdom. [22] But the Lord will never leave off his mercy, neither shall any of his works perish, neither will he abolish the posterity of his elect, and the seed of him that loveth him he will not take away: wherefore he gave a remnant unto Jacob, and out of him a root unto David. [23] Thus rested Solomon with his fathers, and of his seed he left behind him Roboam, even the foolishness of the people, and one that had no understanding, who turned away the people through his counsel. There was also Jeroboam the son of Nebat, who caused Israel to sin, and shewed Ephraim the way of sin: [24] And their sins were multiplied exceedingly, that they were driven out of the land. [25] For they sought out all wickedness, till the vengeance came upon them.

Sir.48

[1] Then stood up Elias the prophet as fire, and his word burned like a lamp. [2] He brought a sore famine upon them, and by his zeal he diminished their number. [3] By the word of the Lord he shut up the heaven, and also three times brought down fire. [4] O Elias, how wast thou honoured in thy wondrous deeds! and who may glory like unto thee! [5] Who didst raise up a dead man from death, and his soul from the place of the dead, by the word of the most High: [6] Who broughtest kings to destruction, and honorable men from their bed: [7] Who heardest the rebuke of the Lord in Sinai, and in Horeb the judgment of vengeance: [8] Who annointedst kings to take revenge, and prophets to succeed after him: [9] Who was taken up in a whirlwind of fire, and in a chariot of fiery horses: [10] Who wast ordained for reproofs in their times, to pacify the wrath of the Lord's judgment, before it brake forth into fury, and to turn the heart of the father unto the son, and to restore the tribes of Jacob. [11] Blessed are they that saw thee, and slept in love; for we shall surely live. [12] Elias it was, who was covered with a whirlwind: and Eliseus was filled with his spirit: whilst he lived, he was not moved with the presence of any prince, neither could any bring him into subjection. [13] No word could overcome him; and after his death his body prophesied. [14] He did wonders in his life, and at his death were his works marvellous. [15] For all this the people repented not, neither departed they from their sins, till they were spoiled and carried out of their land, and were scattered through all the earth: yet there remained a small people, and a ruler in the house of David: [16] Of whom some did that which was pleasing to God, and some multiplied sins. [17] Ezekias fortified his city, and brought in water into the midst thereof: he digged the hard rock with iron, and made wells for waters. [18] In his time Sennacherib came up, and sent Rabsaces, and lifted up his hand against Sion, and boasted proudly. [19] Then trembled their hearts and hands, and they were in pain, as women in travail. [20] But they called upon the Lord which is merciful, and stretched out their hands toward him: and immediately the Holy One heard them out of heaven, and delivered them by the ministry of Esay. [21] He smote the host of the Assyrians, and his angel destroyed them. [22] For Ezekias had done the thing that pleased the Lord, and was strong in the ways of David his father, as Esay the prophet, who was great and faithful in his vision, had commanded him. [23] In his time the sun went backward, and he lengthened the king's life. [24] He saw by an excellent spirit what should come to pass at the last, and he comforted them that mourned in Sion. [25] He shewed what should come to pass for ever, and secret things or ever they came.

Sir.49

[1] The remembrance of Josias is like the composition of the perfume that is made by the art of the apothecary: it is sweet as honey in all mouths, and as musick at a banquet of wine. [2] He behaved himself uprightly in the conversion of the people, and took away the abominations of iniquity. [3] He directed his heart unto the Lord, and in the time of the ungodly he established the worship of God. [4] All, except David and Ezekias and Josias, were defective: for they forsook the law of the most High, even the kings of Juda failed. [5] Therefore he gave their power unto others, and their glory to a strange nation. [6] They burnt the chosen city of the sanctuary, and made the streets desolate, according to the prophecy of

Jeremias. [7] For they entreated him evil, who nevertheless was a prophet, sanctified in his mother's womb, that he might root out, and afflict, and destroy; and that he might build up also, and plant. [8] It was Ezekiel who saw the glorious vision, which was shewed him upon the chariot of the cherubims. [9] For he made mention of the enemies under the figure of the rain, and directed them that went right. [10] And of the twelve prophets let the memorial be blessed, and let their bones flourish again out of their place: for they comforted Jacob, and delivered them by assured hope. [11] How shall we magnify Zorobabel? even he was as a signet on the right hand: [12] So was Jesus the son of Josedec: who in their time builded the house, and set up an holy temple to the Lord, which was prepared for everlasting glory. [13] And among the elect was Neemias, whose renown is great, who raised up for us the walls that were fallen, and set up the gates and the bars, and raised up our ruins again. [14] But upon the earth was no man created like Enoch; for he was taken from the earth. [15] Neither was there a young man born like Joseph, a governor of his brethren, a stay of the people, whose bones were regarded of the Lord. [16] Sem and Seth were in great honour among men, and so was Adam above every living thing in creation.

Sir.50

[1] Simon the high priest, the son of Onias, who in his life repaired the house again, and in his days fortified the temple: [2] And by him was built from the foundation the double height, the high fortress of the wall about temple: [3] In his days the cistern to receive water, being in compass as the sea, was covered with plates of brass: [4] He took care of the temple that it should not fall, and fortified the city against besieging: [5] How was he honoured in the midst of the people in his coming out of the sanctuary! [6] He was as the morning star in the midst of a cloud, and as the moon at the full: [7] As the sun shining upon the temple of the most High, and as the rainbow giving light in the bright clouds: [8] And as the flower of roses in the spring of the year, as lilies by the rivers of waters, and as the branches of the frankincense tree in the time of summer: [9] As fire and incense in the censer, and as a vessel of beaten gold set with all manner of precious stones: [10] And as a fair olive tree budding forth fruit, and as a cypress tree which groweth up to the clouds. [11] When he put on the robe of honour, and was clothed with the perfection of glory, when he went up to the holy altar, he made the garment of holiness honourable. [12] When he took the portions out of the priests' hands, he himself stood by the hearth of the altar, compassed about, as a young cedar in Libanus; and as palm trees compassed they him round about. [13] So were all the sons of Aaron in their glory, and the oblations of the Lord in their hands, before all the congregation of Israel. [14] And finishing the service at the altar, that he might adorn the offering of the most high Almighty, [15] He stretched out his hand to the cup, and poured of the blood of the grape, he poured out at the foot of the altar a sweetsmelling savour unto the most high King of all. [16] Then shouted the sons of Aaron, and sounded the silver trumpets, and made a great noise to be heard, for a remembrance before the most High. [17] Then all the people together hasted, and fell down to the earth upon their faces to worship their Lord God Almighty, the most High. [18] The singers also sang praises with their voices, with great variety of sounds was there made sweet melody. [19] And the people besought the Lord, the most High, by prayer before him that is merciful, till the solemnity of the Lord was ended, and they had finished his service. [20] Then he went down, and lifted up his hands over the whole congregation of the children of Israel, to give the blessing of the Lord with his lips, and to rejoice in his name. [21] And they bowed themselves down to worship the second time, that they might receive a blessing from the most High. [22] Now therefore bless ye the God of all, which only doeth wondrous things every where, which exalteth our days from the womb, and dealeth with us according to his mercy. [23] He grant us joyfulness of heart, and that peace may be in our days in Israel for ever: [24] That he would confirm his mercy with us, and deliver us at his time! [25] There be two manner of nations which my heart abhorreth, and the third is no nation: [26] They that sit upon the mountain of Samaria, and they that dwell among the Philistines, and that foolish people that dwell in Sichem. [27] Jesus the son of Sirach of Jerusalem hath written in this book the instruction of understanding and knowledge, who out of his heart poured forth wisdom. [28] Blessed is he that shall be exercised in these things; and he that layeth them up in his heart shall become wise. [29] For if he do them, he shall be strong to all things: for the light of the Lord leadeth him, who giveth wisdom to the godly. Blessed be the name of the Lord for ever. Amen, Amen.

Sir.51 [A Prayer of Jesus the son of Sirach.]

[1] I will thank thee, O Lord and King, and praise thee, O God my Saviour: I do give praise unto thy name: [2] For thou art my defender and helper, and has preserved my body from destruction, and from the snare of the slanderous tongue, and from the lips that forge lies, and has been mine helper against mine adversaries: [3] And hast delivered me, according to the multitude of they mercies and greatness of thy name, from the teeth of them that were ready to devour me, and out of the hands of such as sought after my life, and from the manifold afflictions which I had; [4] From the choking of fire on every side, and from the midst of the fire which I kindled not; [5] From the depth of the belly of hell, from an unclean tongue, and from lying words. [6] By an accusation to the king from an unrighteous tongue my soul drew near even unto death, my life was near to the hell beneath. [7] They compassed me on every side, and there was no man to help me: I looked for the succour of men, but there was none. [8] Then thought I upon thy mercy, O Lord, and upon thy acts of old, how thou deliverest such as wait for thee, and savest them out of the hands of the enemies. [9] Then lifted I up my supplications from the earth, and prayed for deliverance from death. [10] I called upon the Lord, the Father of my Lord, that he would not leave me in the days of my trouble, and in the time of the proud, when there was no help. [11] I will praise thy name continually, and will sing praises with thanksgiving; and so my prayer was heard: [12] For thou savedst me from destruction, and deliveredst me from the evil time: therefore will I give thanks, and praise thee, and bless they name, O Lord. [13] When I was yet young, or ever I went abroad, I desired wisdom openly in my prayer. [14] I prayed for her before the temple, and will seek her out even to the end. [15] Even from the flower till the grape was ripe hath my heart delighted in her: my foot went the right way, from my youth up sought I after her. [16] I bowed down mine ear a little, and received her, and gat much learning. [17] I profited therein, therefore will I ascribe glory unto him that giveth

me wisdom. [**18**] For I purposed to do after her, and earnestly I followed that which is good; so shall I not be confounded. [**19**] My soul hath wrestled with her, and in my doings I was exact: I stretched forth my hands to the heaven above, and bewailed my ignorances of her. [**20**] I directed my soul unto her, and I found her in pureness: I have had my heart joined with her from the beginning, therefore shall I not be foresaken. [**21**] My heart was troubled in seeking her: therefore have I gotten a good possession. [**22**] The Lord hath given me a tongue for my reward, and I will praise him therewith. [**23**] Draw near unto me, ye unlearned, and dwell in the house of learning. [**24**] Wherefore are ye slow, and what say ye to these things, seeing your souls are very thirsty? [**25**] I opened my mouth, and said, Buy her for yourselves without money. [**26**] Put your neck under the yoke, and let your soul receive instruction: she is hard at hand to find. [**27**] Behold with your eyes, how that I have but little labour, and have gotten unto me much rest. [**28**] Get learning with a great sum of money, and get much gold by her. [**29**] Let your soul rejoice in his mercy, and be not Aashamed of his praise. [**30**] Work your work betimes, and in his time he will give you your reward

THE PRAYER OF MANASSEH

[1] Lord, Almighty God of our fathers, Abraham, Isaac, and Jacob, and of their righteous seed; [**2**] Who hast made heaven and earth, with all the ornament thereof; [**3**] Who hast bound the sea by the word of thy commandment; [**4**] Whoho hast shut up the deep, and sealed it by thy terrible and glorious name; whom all men fear, and tremble before thy power; [**5**] For the majesty of thy glory cannot be borne, and thine angry threatening toward sinners is importable: but thy merciful promise is unmeasurable and unsearchable; [**6**] For thou art the most high Lord, of great compassion, longsuffering, very merciful, and repentest of the evils of men. [**7**] Thou, O Lord, according to thy great goodness hast promised repentance and forgiveness to them that have sinned against thee: and of thine infinite mercies hast appointed repentance unto sinners, that they may be saved. [**8**] Thou therefore, O Lord, that art the God of the just, hast not appointed repentance to the just, as to [**9**] Abraham, and Isaac, and Jacob, which have not sinned against thee; but thou hast appointed repentance unto me that am a sinner: for I have sinned above the number of the sands of the sea. [**10**] My transgressions, O Lord, are multiplied: my transgressions are multiplied, and I am not worthy to behold and see the height of heaven for the multitude of mine iniquities. [**11**] I am bowed down with many iron bands, that I cannot life up mine head, neither have any release: for I have provoked thy wrath, and done evil before thee: I did not thy will, neither kept I thy commandments: I have set up abominations, and have multiplied offences. [**12**] Now therefore I bow the knee of mine heart, beseeching thee of grace. [**13**] I have sinned, O Lord, I have sinned, and I acknowledge mine iniquities: wherefore, I humbly beseech thee, forgive me, O Lord, forgive me, and destroy me not with mine iniquites. [**14**] Be not angry with me for ever, by reserving evil for me; neither condemn me to the lower parts of the earth. [**15**] For thou art the God, even the God of them that repent; and in me thou wilt shew all thy goodness: for thou wilt save me, that am unworthy, according to thy great mercy. [**16**] Therefore I will praise thee for ever all the days of my life: for all the powers of the heavens do praise thee, and thine is the glory for ever and ever. Amen.

APOCRYPHAL PSALMS

PSALM 151

1 I was the youngest among my brothers, A nd a youth in my father's house. **2** I used to feed my father's flock, A nd I found a lion and a wolf, A nd slew them and tore them. **3** My hands made an organ, A nd my fingers fashioned a harp. **4** Who will show me my Lord? He, my Lord, has become my God. **5** He sent His messenger and took me away from my father's flock, A nd anointed me with the oil of anointing. **6** My brothers, the fair and the tall, I n them the LORD had no pleasure. **7** And I went forth to meet the Philistine, A nd he cursed me by his idols. **8** But I drew his sword and cut off his head, A nd took away the reproach from the sons of Israel.

PSALM 152

1 With a loud voice glorify God; In the assembly of many proclaim His glory. **2** Amid the multitude of the upright glorify His praise; And speak of His glory with the righteous. **3** Join your soul to the good and to the perfect, T o glorify the Most High. **4** Gather yourselves together to make known His strength; And do not be slow in showing forth His deliverance and His glory to all babies. **5** That the honor of the LORD may be known, wisdom has been given; And to tell of His works it has been made known to men: **6** To make known to babies His strength, A nd to make them that lack understanding [[*or* heart]] to comprehend His glory; **7** Who are far from His entrances and distant from His gates: **8** Because the Lord of Jacob is exalted, A nd His glory is on all His works. **9** And a man who glorifies the Most High, in him will He take pleasure; As in one who offers fine meal, A nd as in one who offers male goats and calves; **10** And as in one who makes fat the altar with a multitude of burnt-offerings; And as the smell of incense from the hands of the just. **11** From your upright gates will be heard His voice, A nd from the voice of the upright admonition. **12** And in their eating will be satisfying in truth, A nd in their drinking, when they share together. **13** Their dwelling is in the law of the Most High, A nd their speech is to make known His strength. **14** How far from the wicked is speech of Him, A nd from all transgressors to know Him! **15** Behold, the eye of the LORD takes pity on the good, A nd to them that glorify Him will He multiply mercy, A nd from the time of evil will He deliver their soul. **16** Blessed is the LORD , who has delivered the wretched from the hand of the wicked; Who raises up a horn out of Jacob and a judge of the nations out of Israel; **17** That He may prolong His dwelling in Zion, A nd may adorn our age in Jerusalem.

PSALM 153

1 O LORD , I have cried to You; Listen to me. **2** I have lifted up my hands to Your holy dwelling-place; Incline Your ear to me. **3** And grant me my request; Do not withhold my prayer from me. **4** Build up my soul, and do not destroy it; And do not lay it bare before the wicked. **5** Them that repay evil things—turn [them] away from me, O judge of truth. **6** O LORD , do not judge me according to my sins, B ecause no flesh is innocent before You. **7** Make plain to me, O LORD , Your law, A nd teach me Your judgments; **8** And many will hear of Your works, A nd the nations will praise Your honor. **9** Remember me and do not forget me; And do not lead me into things that are too hard for me. **10** Make the sins of my youth pass from me, A nd my discipline—do not let them remember [it] against me. **11** Cleanse me, O LORD , from the evil leprosy, A nd let it no longer come to me. **12** Dry up its roots from me, A nd do not let its leaves sprout within me. **13** Great are You, O LORD ; Therefore, my request will be fulfilled from before You. **14** To whom will I complain that he may give to me? And what can the strength of men add [to me]? **15** From before You, O LORD , is my confidence; I cried to the LORD and He heard me, and healed the breaking of my heart. **16** I slumbered and slept; I dreamed and was helped, and the LORD sustained me. **17** They severely pained my heart; I will return thanks because the LORD delivered me. **18** Now I will rejoice in their shame; I have hoped in You, and I will not be ashamed. **19** Give You honor for all time— even forever and ever! **20** Deliver Israel, Your chosen one, And them of the house of Jacob Your proved one.

PSALM 154

1 O God, O God, come to my aid; Help me and save me; Deliver my soul from the slayer. **2** Will I go down to Sheol by the mouth of the lion? Or will the wolf confound me? **3** Was it not enough for them that they lay in wait for my father's flock, A nd tore in pieces a sheep of my father's drove, B ut they were also wishing to destroy my soul? **4** Have pity, O LORD , and save Your holy one from destruction; That he may rehearse Your glories in all his times, A nd may praise Your great Name: **5** When You have delivered him from the hands of the destroying lion and of the ravening wolf, A nd when You have rescued my captivity from the hands of the wild beasts. **6** Quickly, O my Lord, send a deliverer from before You, A nd draw me out of the gaping pit, W hich imprisons me in its depths.

PSALM 155

1 Praise the LORD , all you nations; Glorify Him, and bless His Name— **2** Who rescued the soul of His chosen one from the hands of death, A nd delivered His holy one from destruction, **3** And saved me from the nets of Sheol, A nd my soul from the pit that cannot be fathomed. **4** Because, before my deliverance could go forth from before Him, I was well nearly torn in two pieces by two wild beasts. **5** But He sent His messenger, A nd shut up from me the gaping mouths, A nd rescued my life from destruction. **6** My soul will glorify Him and exalt Him, B ecause of all His kindnesses which He has done and will do to me.

ENOCHIAN APOCRYPHA

These books focus on the figure of Enoch and offer insights on angels, creation, and the afterlife

1 ENOCH

The Book Of Watchers

CHAPTER 1

[1] Who will be living in the day of tribulation, when all the wicked and godless are to be removed? [2] And he took up his parable and said -Enoch, a righteous man, whose eyes were opened by God, saw the vision of the Holy One in the heavens, which the angels showed me, and from them I heard everything, and from them I understood as I saw, but not for this generation, but for a remote one which is for to come. [3] Concerning the elect, I said and took up my parable concerning them: The Holy Great One will come forth from His dwelling, [4] And the eternal God will tread upon the earth, even on Mount Sinai, and appear from His camp. And appear in the strength of His might from the heaven of heaaaavens. [5] And all shall be smitten with fear, and the watchers shall quake, and great fear and trembling shall seize them unto the ends of the earth. [6] And the high mountains shall be shaken, and the high hills shall be made low, and shall melt like wax before the flame, [7] And the earth shall be wholly rent in sunder, and all that is upon the earth shall perish, and there shall be a judgement upon all men. [8] But with the righteous, He will make peace, and will protect the elect, and mercy shall be upon them. And they shall all belong to God, and they shall be prospered, and they shall all be blessed. And He will help them all, and light shall appear unto them, and He will make peace with them'. [9] And behold! He cometh with ten thousands of His holy ones to execute judgement upon all, and to destroy all the ungodly: and to convict all flesh of all the works of their ungodliness which they have ungodly committed, and of all the hard things which ungodly sinners have spoken against Him.

CHAPTER 2

[1] Observe ye everything that takes place in the heaven, how they do not change their orbits, and the luminaries which are in the heaven, how they all rise and set in order each in its season, [2] And transgress not against their appointed order. Behold ye the earth, and give heed to the things which take place upon it from first to last, how steadfast they are, how none of the things upon earth change, [3] But all the works of God appear to you. Behold the summer and the winter, how the whole earth is filled with water, and clouds and dew and rain lie upon it.

CHAPTER 3

[1] Observe and see how, in the winter, all the trees seem as though they had withered and shed all their leaves, except fourteen trees, which do not lose their foliage but retain the old foliage from two to three years till the new comes.

CHAPTER 4
[1] And again, observe ye the days of summer how the sun is above the earth over against it. [2] And you seek shade and shelter by reason of the heat of the sun, and the earth also burns with growing heat, and so you cannot tread on the earth, or on a rock by reason of its heat.

CHAPTER 5
[1] Observe ye how the trees cover themselves with green leaves and bear fruit: wherefore give ye heed and know with regard to all His works, and recognize how He that liveth for ever hath made them so. [2] And all His works go on thus from year to year for ever, and all the tasks which they accomplish for Him, and their tasks change not, but according as God hath ordained so is it done. [3] And behold how the sea and the rivers in like manner accomplish and change not their tasks from His commandments'. [4] But ye - ye have not been steadfast, nor done the commandments of the Lord, but ye have turned away and spoken proud and hard words with your impure mouths against His greatness. Oh, ye hard-hearted, ye shall find no peace. [5] Therefore shall ye execrate your days, and the years of your life shall perish, and the years of your destruction shall be multiplied in eternal execration, and ye shall find no mercy. [6] In those days ye shall make your names an eternal execration unto all the righteous, and by you shall all who curse, curse, and all the sinners and godless shall imprecate by you, and for you the godless there shall be a curse. And all shall rejoice, and there shall be forgiveness of sins, and every mercy and peace and forbearance: There shall be salvation unto them, a goodly light. And for all of you sinners there shall be no salvation, but on you all shall abide a curse. [7] But for the elect there shall be light and joy and peace, and they shall inherit the earth. [8] And then there shall be bestowed upon the elect wisdom, and they shall all live and never again sin, either through ungodliness or through pride: but they who are wise shall be humble. [9] And they shall not again transgress, nor shall they sin all the days of their life, nor shall they die of the divine anger or wrath, but they shall complete the number of the days of their life. And their lives shall be increased in peace, and the years of their joy shall be multiplied, in eternal gladness and peace, all the days of their life.

CHAPTER 6
[1] And it came to pass when the children of men had multiplied that in those days were born unto them beautiful and comely daughters. [2] And the angels, the children of the heaven, saw and lusted after them, and said to one another: 'Come, let us choose us wives from among the children of men, [3] And beget us children.' And Semjaza, who was their leader, said unto them: 'I fear ye will not, [4] Indeed agree to do this deed, and I alone shall have to pay the penalty of a great sin.' And they all answered him and said: 'Let us all swear an oath, and all bind ourselves by mutual imprecations, [5] Not to abandon this plan but to do this thing.' Then sware they all together and bound themselves by mutual imprecations upon it. [6] And they were in all two hundred; who descended in the days of Jared on the summit of Mount Hermon, and they called it Mount Hermon, because they had sworn, [7] And bound themselves by mutual imprecations upon it. And these are the names of their leaders: Samlazaz, their leader, Araklba, Rameel, Kokablel, Tamlel, Ramlel, Danel, Ezeqeel, Baraqijal, [8] Asael, Armaros, Batarel, Ananel, Zaq1el, Samsapeel, Satarel, Turel, Jomjael, Sariel. These are their chiefs of tens.

CHAPTER 7
[1] And all the others together with them took unto themselves wives, and each chose for himself one, and they began to go in unto them and to defile themselves with them, and they taught them charms, [2] And enchantments, and the cutting of roots, and made them acquainted with plants. [3] And they became pregnant, and they bare great giants, whose height was three thousand ells: [4] Who consumed all the acquisitions of men. And when men could no longer sustain the m, the giants turned against them, [5] And devoured mankind. And they began to sin against birds, and beasts, and reptiles, [6] And fish, and to devour one another's flesh, and drink the blood. Then the earth laid accusation against the lawless ones.

CHAPTER 8
[1] And Azazel taught men to make swords, and knives, and shields, and breastplates, and made known to them the metals of the earth and the art of working them, and bracelets, and ornaments, and the use of antimony, and the beautifying of the eyelids, and all kinds of costly stones, [2] And all colouring tinctures. And there arose much godlessness, and they committed fornication, [3] And theywere led astray, and became corrupt in all their ways. Semjaza taught enchantments, and root-cuttings, 'Armaros the resolving of enchantments, Baraqijal (taught) astrology, Kokabel the constellations, Ezeqeel the knowledge of the clouds, Araqiel the signs of the earth, Shamsiel the signs of the sun, and Sariel the course of the moon. And as men perished, they cried, and their cry went up to heaven.

CHAPTER 9
[1] And then Michael, Uriel, Raphael, and Gabriel looked down from heaven, [2] And saw much blood being shed upon the earth, and all lawlessness being wrought upon the earth. And they said one to another: 'The earth made without inhabitant cries the voice of their cryingst up to the gates of heaven. [3] And now to you, the holy ones of heaven, the souls of men make their suit, saying, "Bring our cause, [4] Before the Most High."' And they said to the Lord of the ages: 'Lord of lords, God of gods, king of kings, and God of the ages, the throne of Thy glory standeth unto all the generations of the ages, [5] And Thy name holy and glorious and blessed unto all the ages! Thou hast made all things, and power over all things hast Thou: and all things are naked and open in Thy sight, and Thou seest all things, [6] And nothing can hide itself from Thee. Thou seest what Azazel hath done, who hath taught all unrighteousness on earth and revealed the eternal secrets which were preserved in heaven, [7] Which men were striving to learn: And Semjaza, to whom Thou hast given

authority to bear rule over his associates. And they have gone to the daughters of men upon the earth, and have slept with the women, [8] And have defiled themselves, and revealed to them all kinds of sins. And the women have borne giants, [9] And the whole earth has thereby been filled with blood and unrighteousness. [10]And now, behold, the souls of those who have died are crying and making their suit to the gates of heaven, and the ir lamentations have ascended: and cannot cease because of the lawless deeds which are wrought on the earth. [11]And Thou knowest all things before they come to pass, and Thou seest these things and Thou dost suffer them, and Thou dost not say to us what we are to do to them in regard to these.'

CHAPTER 10

[1] Then said the Most High, the Holy and Great One spake, and sent Uriel to the son of Lamech, [2] And said to him: Go to Noah and tell him in my name "Hide thyself!" and reveal to him the end that is approaching: that the whole earth will be destroyed, and a deluge is about to come upon the whole earth, [3] And will destroy all that is on it. And now instruct him that he may escape, [4] And his seed may be preserved for all the generations of the world. And again the Lord said to Raphael: Bind Azazel hand and foot, and cast him into the darkness: and make an opening in the desert, [5] Which is in Dudael, and cast him therein. And place upon him rough and jagged rocks, and cover him with darkness, and let him abide there for ever, and cover his face that he may not see light. [6] And on the day of the great judgement he shall be cast into the fire. [7] And heal the earth which the angels have corrupted, and proclaim the healing of the earth, that they may heal the plague, and that all the children of men may not perish through all the secret things that the Watchers have disclosed and have taught their sons. [8] And the whole earth has been corrupted through the works that were taught by Azazel: to him ascribe all sin. [9] And to Gabriel said the Lord: Proceed against the bastards and the reprobates, and against the children of fornication: and destroy the children of fornication and the children of the Watchers from amongst men and cause them to go forth: send them one against the other that they may destroy each other in [10] battle: for length of days shall they not have. And no request that they make of thee shall be granted unto their fathers on their behalf; for they hope to live an eternal life, [11] And that each one of them will live five hundred years. And the Lord said unto Michael: Go, bind Semjaza and his associates who have united themselves with women so as to have defiled themselves, [12] with them in all their uncleanness. And when their sons have slain one another, and they have seen the destruction of their beloved ones, bind them fast for seventy generations in the valleys of the earth, till the day of their judgement and of their consummation, [13] Till the judgement that is forever and ever is consummated. In those days they shall be led off to the abyss of fire: [14] And to the torment and the prison in which they shall be confined for ever. And whosoever shall be condemned and destroyed will from thenceforth be bound together with them to the end of all generations. [15] And destroy all the spirits of the reprobate and the children of the Watchers, [16] Because they have wronged mankind. Destroy all wrong from the face of the earth and let every evil work come to an end: and let the plant of righteousness and truth appear: and it shall prove a blessing; the works of righteousness and truth shall be planted in truth and joy for evermore. [17] And then shall all the righteous escape, and shall live till they beget thousands of children, and all the days of their youth and their old age shall they complete in peace. [18] And then shall the whole earth be tilled in righteousness, and shall all be planted with trees and be full of blessing. [19] And all desirable trees shall be planted on it, and they sha ll plant vines on it: and the vine which they plant thereon shall yield wine in abundance, and as for all the seed which is sown thereon each measure of it shall bear a thousand, and each measure of olives shall yield ten presses of oil. [20] And cleanse thou the earth from all oppression, and from all unrighteousness, and from all sin, and from all godlessness: and all the uncleanness that is wrought upon the earth destroy from off the earth. And all the children of men shall become righteous, [21] And all nations shall offer adoration and shall praise Me, and all shall worship Me. And the earth shall be cleansed from all defilement, and from all sin, and from all punishment, and from all torment, and I will never again send them upon it from generation to generation and for ever.

CHAPTER 11

[1] And in those days I will open the store chambers of blessing which are in the heaven, [2] So as to send 2 them down upon the earth over the work and labour of the children of men. And truth and peace shall be associated together throughout all the days of the world and throughout all the generations of men.

CHAPTER 12

[3] Before these things Enoch was hidden, and no one of the children of men knew where he was hidden, [4] And where he abode, and what had become of him. And his activities had to do with the Watchers, and his days were with the holy ones. [5] And I Enoch was blessing the Lord of majesty and the King of the ages, and lo! [6] The Watchers called me - Enoch the scribe- and said to me: 'Enoch, thou scribe of righteousness, go, declare to the Watchers of the heaven who have left the high heaven, the holy eternal place, and have defiled themselves with women, and have done as the children of earth do, [7] And have taken unto themselves wives: "Ye have wrought great destruction on the earth: And ye shall have no peace nor forgiveness of sin: [8] And inasmuch as they delight themselves in their children, The murder of their beloved ones shall they see, and over the destruction of their children shall they lament, and shall make supplication unto eternity, but mercy and peace shall ye not attain."

CHAPTER 13

[1] And Enoch went and said: Azazel, thou shalt have no peace: a severe sentence has gone forth, [2] Against thee to put thee in bonds: And thou shalt not have toleration nor request granted to thee, because of the unrighteousness which thou hast taught, and because of all the works of godlessness, [3] And unrighteousness and sin which thou hast shown to men. Then I went and spoke to them all together, [4] And they were all afraid, and fear and trembling seized them. And they besought me to draw up a petition for them that they might find forgiveness, and to read their petition in the presence of the Lord of heaven. [5] For from thenceforward they could not speak with Him nor lift up their eyes to heaven for shame

of their sins for which they had been condemned. Then I wrote out their petition, and the prayer in regard to their spirits and their deeds individually and in regard to their requests that they should have forgiveness and length. [6] And I went off and sat down at the waters of Dan, in the land of Dan, to the south of the west of Hermon: I read their petition till I fell asleep. [7] And behold a dream came to me, and visions fell down upon me, and I saw visions of chastisement, and a voice came bidding me I to tell it to the sons of heaven, and reprimand them. [8] And when I awaked, I came unto them, and they were all sitting gathered together, weeping in Abelsjail, [9] Which is between Lebanon and Seneser, with their faces covered. And I recounted before them all the visions which I had seen in sleep, and I began to speak the words of righteousness, and to reprimand the heavenly Watchers.

CHAPTER 14
[1] The book of the words of righteousness, and of the reprimand of the eternal Watchers, [2] In accordance with the command of the Holy Great One in that vision. I saw in my sleep what I will now say with a tongue of flesh and with the breath of my mouth: which the Great One has given to men to converse therewith and understand with the heart. [3] As He has created and given to man the power of understanding the word of wisdom, so hath He created me also and given me the power of reprimanding the Watchers, [4] The children of heaven. I wrote out your petition, and in my vision it appeared thus, that your petition will not be granted unto you throughout all the days of eternity, [5] And that judgement has been finally passed upon you: yea (your petition) will not be granted unto you. And from henceforth you shall not ascend into heaven unto all eternity, and in bonds of the earth the decree has gone forth to bind you for all the days of the world. [6] And (that) previously you shall have seen the destruction of your beloved sons and ye shall have no pleasure in them, but they shall fall before you by the sword. [7] And your petition on their behalf shall not be granted, nor yet on your own: even though you weep and pray and speak all the words contained in the writing which I have written. [8] And the vision was shown to me thus: Behold, in the vision clouds invited me and a mist summoned me, and the course of the stars and the lightnings sped and hastened me, [9] And the winds in the vision caused me to fly and lifted me upward, and bore me into heaven. And I went in till I drew nigh to a wall which is built of crystals and surrounded by tongues of fire: and it began to affright me. [10] And I went into the tongues of fire and drew nigh to a large house which was built of crystals: and the walls of the house were like a tesselated floor made of crystals, and its groundwork was of crystal. [11] Its ceiling was like the path of the stars and the lightnings, and between them were fiery cherubim, and their heaven was (clear as) water. A flaming fire surrounded the walls, and its portals blazed with fire. [12] And I entered into that house, and it was hot as fire and cold as ice: [13] There were no delights of life therein: fear covered me, and trembling got hold upon me. [14] And as I quaked and trembled, I fell upon my face. [15] And I beheld a vision, And lo! There was a second house, greater than the former, [16] And the entire portal stood open before me, and it was built of flames of fire. And in every respect it so excelled in splendour and magnificence and extent that I cannot describe to you its splendour and its extent. [17] And its floor was of fire, and above it were lightnings and the path of the stars, [18] And its ceiling also was flaming fire. And I looked and saw therein a lofty throne: its appearance was as crystal, and the wheels thereof as the shining sun, and there was the vision of cherubim. [19] And from underneath the throne came streams of flaming fire so that I could not look thereon. [20] And the Great Glory sat thereon, and His raiment shone more brightly than the sun and was whiter than any snow. [21] None of the angels could enter and could behold His face by reason of the magnificence and glory and no flesh could behold Him. [22] The flaming fire was round about Him, and a great fire stood before Him, and none around could draw nigh Him: ten thousand times ten thousand stood before Him, [23] Yet He needed no counselor. And the most holy ones who were nigh to Him did not leave by night nor depart from Him. [24] And until then I had been prostrate on my face, trembling: and the Lord called me with His own mouth, and said to me: 'Come hither, [25] Enoch, and hear my word.' And one of the holy ones came to me and waked me, and He made me rise up and approach the door: and I bowed my face downwards.

CHAPTER 15
[1] And He answered and said to me, and I heard His voice: 'Fear not, Enoch, thou righteous man and scribe of righteousness: [2] Approach hither and hear my voice. And go, say to the Watchers of heaven, who have sent thee to intercede for them: "You should intercede" for men, and not men for you: [3] Wherefore have ye left the high, holy, and eternal heaven, and lain with women, and defiled yourselves with the daughters of men and taken to yourselves wives, and done like the children of earth, [4] And begotten giants as your sons? And though ye were holy, spiritual, living the eternal life, you have defiled yourselves with the blood of women, and have begotten children with the blood of flesh, and, as the children of men, have lusted after flesh and blood as those also do who die and perish. [5] Therefore have I given them wives also that they might impregnate them, and beget children by them, [6] That thus nothing might be wanting to them on earth. But you were formerly spiritual, [7] Living the eternal life, and immortal for all generations of the world. And therefore I have not appointed wives for you; for as for the spiritual ones of the heaven, in heaven is their dwelling. [8] And now, the giants, who are produced from the spirits and flesh, shall be called evil spirits upon the earth, [9] And on the earth shall be their dwelling. Evil spirits have proceeded from their bodies; because they are born from men and from the holy Watchers is their beginning and primal origin; [10] They shall be evil spirits on earth, and evil spirits shall they be called. As for the spirits of heaven, in heaven shall be their dwelling, but as for the spirits of the earth which were born upon the earth, on the earth shall be their dwelling. [11] And the spirits of the giants afflict, oppress, destroy, attack, do battle, and work destruction on the earth, and cause trouble: they take no food, but nevertheless hunger and thirst, [12] And cause offences. And these spirits shall rise up against the children of men and against the women, because they have proceeded from them.

CHAPTER 16
[1] From the days of the slaughter and destruction and death of the giants, from the souls of whose flesh the spirits, having gone forth, shall destroy without incurring judgement –thus shall they destroy until the day of the consummation, the great

judgement in which the age shall be consummated, [2] Over the Watchers and the godless, yea, shall be wholly consummated." And now as to the Watchers who have sent thee to intercede for them, who had been aforetime in heaven, say to them: [3] "You have been in heaven, but all the mysteries had not yet been revealed to you, and you knew worthless ones, and these in the hardness of your hearts you have made known to the women, and through these mysteries women and men work much evil on earth." [4] Say to them therefore: " You have no peace."'

CHAPTER 17

[1] And they took and brought me to a place in which those who were there were like flaming fire, [2] And, when they wished, they appeared as men. And they brought me to the place of darkness, and to a mountain the point of whose summit reached to heaven. [3] And I saw the places of the luminaries and the treasuries of the stars and of the thunder and in the uttermost depths, [4] Where were a fiery bow and arrows and their quiver, and a fiery sword and all the lightnings. And they took me to the living waters, [5] And to the fire of the west, which receives every setting of the sun. And I came to a river of fire in which the fire flows like water and discharges itself into the great sea towards the west. I saw the great rivers and came to the great river and to the great darkness, [6] And went to the place where no flesh walks. I saw the mountains of the darkness of winter and the place, [7] Whence all the waters of the deep flow. I saw the mouths of all the rivers of the earth and the mouth of the deep.

CHAPTER 18

[1] I saw the treasuries of all the winds: I saw how He had furnished with them the whole creation, [2] And the firm foundations of the earth. And I saw the corner-stone of the earth: I saw the four winds, [3] Which bear the earth and the firmament of the heaven. And I saw how the winds stretch out the vaults of heaven, and have their station between heaven and earth: these are the pillars of the heaven. [4] I saw the winds of heaven which turn and bring the circumference of the sun, [5] And all the stars to their setting. I saw the winds on the earth carrying the clouds: I saw the paths of the angels. [6] I saw at the end of the earth the firmament of the heaven above. And I proceeded and saw a place which burns day and night, where there are seven mountains of magnificent stones, [7] Three towards the east, and three towards the south. And as for those towards the east, was of coloured stone, and one of pearl, and one of jacinth, and those towards the south of red stone. [8] But the middle one reached to heaven like the throne of God, of alabaster, and the summit of the throne was of sapphire. [9] And I saw a flaming fire. [10] And beyond these mountains Is a region the end of the great earth: there the heavens were completed. [11] And I saw a deep abyss, with columns of heavenly fire, and among them I saw columns of fire fall, which were beyond measure alike towards [12] the height and towards the depth. And beyond that abyss I saw a place which had no firmament of the heaven above, and no firmly founded earth beneath it: there was no water upon it, [13] And no birds, but it was a waste and horrible place. I saw there seven stars like great burning mountains, [14] And to me, when I inquired regarding them, The angel said: 'This place is the end of heaven and earth: this has become a prison for the stars and the host of heaven. [15] And the stars which roll over the fire are they which have transgressed the commandment of the Lord in the beginning of their rising, [16] Because they did not come forth at their appointed times. And He was wroth with them, and bound them till the time when their guilt should be consummated even for ten thousand years.'

CHAPTER 19

[1] And Uriel said to me: 'Here shall stand the angels who have connected themselves with women, and their spirits assuming many different forms are defiling mankind and shall lead them astray into sacrificing to demons as gods, here shall they stand, till the day of the great judgement in [2] Which they shall be judged till they are made an end of. And the women also of the angels, [3] who went astray shall become sirens.' And I, Enoch, alone saw the vision, the ends of all things: and no man shall see as I have seen.

CHAPTER 20

[1] And these are the names of the holy angels who watch. [2] Uriel, one of the holy angels, [3] Who is over the world and over Tartarus. Raphael, one of the holy angels, who is over the spirits of men. [4] Raguel, one of the holy angels who takes vengeance on the world of the luminaries. [5] Michael, one of the holy angels, to wit, he that is set over the best part of ma nkind and over chaos. [6] Saraqael, one of the holy angels, who is set over the spirits, who sin in the spirit. [7] Gabriel, one of the holy angels, who is over Paradise and the serpents and the Cherubim. [8] Remiel, one of the holy angels, whom God set over those who rise.

CHAPTER 21

[1] And I proceeded to where things were chaotic. [2] And I saw there something horrible: I saw neither [3] Heaven above nor a firmly founded earth, but a place chaotic and horrible. [4] And there I saw seven stars of the heaven bound together in it, like great mountains and burning with fire. [5] Then I said: 'For what sin are they bound, and on what account have they been cast in hither?' Then said Uriel, one of the holy angels, who was with me, and was chief over them, and said: 'Enoch, why dost thou ask, [6] And why art thou eager for the truth? These are of the number of the stars of heaven, which have transgressed the commandment of the Lord, and are bound here till ten thousand years, [7] The time entailed by their sins, are consummated.' And from thence I went to another place, which was still more horrible than the former, and I saw a horrible thing: a great fire there which burnt and blazed, and the place was cleft as far as the abyss, being full of great descending columns of fire: [8] Neither its extent or magnitude could I see, nor could I conjecture. [9] Then I said: 'How fearful is the place and how terrible to look upon!' Then Uriel answered me, one of the holy angels who was with me, and said unto me: 'Enoch, why hast thou such fear and affright?' [10] And I answered: 'Because of this fearful place, and because of the spectacle of the pain.' And he said unto me: 'This place is the prison of the angels, and here they will be imprisoned for ever.'

CHAPTER 22

[1] And thence I went to another place, and he mountain and of hard rock. [2] And there was in it four hollow places, deep and wide and very smooth. How smooth are the hollow places and deep and dark to look at. [3] Then Raphael answered, one of the holy angels who was with me, and said unto me: 'These hollow places have been created for this very purpose, that the spirits of the souls of the dead should assemble therein, [4] Yea that all the souls of the children of men should assemble here. And these places have been made to receive them till the day of their judgement and till their appointed period [till the period appointed], till the great judgement (comes) upon them.' I saw (the spirit of) a dead man making suit, [5] And his voice went forth to heaven and made suit. And I asked Raphael the angel who was with me, [6] And I said unto him: 'This spirit which maketh suit, whose is it, whose voice goeth forth and maketh suit to heaven ?' [7] And he answered me saying: 'This is the spirit which went forth from Abel, whom his brother Cain slew, and he makes his suit against him till his seed is destroyed from the face of the earth, and his seed is annihilated from amongst the seed of men.' [8] The I asked regarding it, and regarding all the hollow places: 'Why is one separated from the other?' [9] And he answered me and said unto me: 'These three have been made that the spirits of the dead might be separated. And such a division has been make for the spirits of the righteous, in which there is the bright spring of water. [10] And such has been made for sinners when they die and are buried in the earth and judgement has not been executed on them in their lifetime. [11] Here their spirits shall be set apart in this great pain till the great day of judgement and punishment and torment of those who curse for ever and retribution for their spirits. [12] There He shall bind them for ever. And such a division has been made for the spirits of those who make their suit, who make disclosures concerning their destruction, when they were slain in the days of the sinners. [13] Such has been made for the spirits of men who were not righteous but sinners, who were complete in transgression, and of the transgressors they shall be companions: but their spirits shall not be slain in the day of judgement nor shall they be raised from thence.' [14] The I blessed the Lord of glory and said: 'Blessed be my Lord, the Lord of righteousness, who ruleth for ever.'

CHAPTER 23

[1] From thence I went to another place to the west of the ends of the earth. [2] And I saw a burning fire which ran without resting, [3] And paused not from its course day or night but ran regularly. [4] And I asked saying: 'What is this which rests not?' Then Raguel, one of the holy angels who was with me, answered me and said unto me: 'This course of fire which thou hast seen is the fire in the west which persecutes all the luminaries of heaven.'

CHAPTER 24

[1] And from thence I went to another place of the earth, and he showed me a mountain range of fire, [2] Which burnt day and night. And I went beyond it and saw seven magnificent mountains all differing each from the other, and the stones thereof were magnificent and beautiful, magnificent as a whole, of glorious appearance and fair exterior: three towards the east, one founded on the other, and three towards the south, one upon the other, and deep rough ravines, no one of which joined with any other. [3] And the seventh mountain was in the midst of these, and it excelled them in height, [4] Resembling the seat of a throne: and fragrant trees encircled the throne. And amongst them was a tree such as I had never yet smelt, neither was any amongst them nor were others like it: it had a fragrance beyond all fragrance, and its leaves and blooms and wood wither not for ever: [5] And its fruit is beautiful, and its fruit n resembles the dates of a palm. Then I said: 'How beautiful is this tree, and fragrant, and its leaves are fair, and its blooms very delightful in appearance.' [6] Then answered Michael, one of the holy and honoured angels who was with me, and was their leader.

CHAPTER 25

[1] And he said unto me: 'Enoch, why dost thou ask me regarding the fragrance of the tree, [2] And why dost thou wish to learn the truth?' Then I answered him saying: 'I wish to know about everything, [3] But especially about this tree.' And he answered saying: 'This high mountain which thou hast seen, whose summit is like the throne of God, is His throne, where the Holy Great One, the Lord of Glory, the Eternal King, will sit, when He shall come down to visit the earth with goodness. [4] And as for this fragrant tree no mortal is permitted to touch it till the great judgement, when He shall take vengeance on all and bring everything to its consummation for ever. [5] It shall then be given to the righteous and holy. Its fruit shall be for food to the elect: it shall be transplanted to the holy place, to the temple of the Lord, the Eternal King. [6] Then shall they rejoice with joy and be glad, and into the holy place shall they enter; And its fragrance shall be in their bones, and they shall live a long life on earth, Such as thy fathers lived: And in their days shall no sorrow or plague or torment or calamity touch them.' [7] Then blessed I the God of Glory, the Eternal King, who hath prepared such things for the righteous, and hath created them and promised to give to them.

CHAPTER 26

[1] And I went from thence to the middle of the earth, and I saw a blessed place, [2] In which there were trees with branches abiding and blooming of a dismembered tree. And there I saw a holy mountain, [3] And underneath the mountain to the east there was a stream and it flowed towards the south. And I saw towards the east another mountain higher than this, and between them a deep and narrow ravine: [4] In it also ran a stream underneath the mountain. And to the west thereof there was another mountain, lower than the former and of small elevation, and a ravine deep and dry between them: and another deep and dry ravine was at the extremities of the three mountains. [5] And all the ravines were deep rand narrow, being formed of hard rock, and trees were not planted upon them. And I marveled at the rocks, and I marveled at the ravine, yea, I marveled very much.

CHAPTER 27

[1] Then said I: 'For what object is this blessed land, which is entirely filled with trees, [2] And this accursed valley between?' Then Uriel, one of the holy angels who was with me, answered and said: 'This accursed valley is for those who are accursed for ever: Here shall all the accursed be gathered together who utter with their lips against the Lord unseemly words and of His glory speak hard things. Here shall they be gathered together, [3] And here shall be their place of judgement. In the last days there shall be upon them the spectacle of righteous judgement in the presence of the righteous for ever: here shall the merciful bless the Lord of glory, the Eternal King. [4] In the days of judgement over the former, they shall bless Him for the mercy in accordance with [5] Which He has assigned them (their lot).' Then I blessed the Lord of Glory and set forth His glory and lauded Him gloriously.

CHAPTER 28

[1] And thence I went towards the east, into the midst of the mountain range of the desert, [2] And I saw a wilderness and it was solitary, full of trees and plants. And water gushed forth from above. [3] Rushing like a copious watercourse which flowed towards the north- west it caused clouds and dew to ascend on every side.

CHAPTER 29

[1] And thence I went to another place in the desert, and approached to the east of this mountain range. [2] And there I saw aromatic trees exhaling the fragrance of frankincense and myrrh, and the trees also were similar to the almond tree.

CHAPTER 30

[1] And beyond these, I went afar to the east, [2] And I saw another place, a valley full of water. [3] And therein there was a tree, the colour of fragrant trees such as the mastic. And on the sides of those valleys I saw fragrant cinnamon. And beyond these I proceeded to the east.

CHAPTER 31

[1] And I saw other mountains, and amongst them were groves of trees, and there flowed forth from them nectar, [2] Which is named sarara and galbanum. And beyond these mountains I saw another mountain to the east of the ends of the earth, whereon were aloe-trees, and all the trees were full of stacte, being like almond-trees. [3] And when one burnt it, it smelt sweeter than any fragrant odour.

CHAPTER 32

[1] And after these fragrant odours, as I looked towards the north over the mountains I saw seven mountains full of choice nard and fragrant trees and cinnamon and pepper. [2] And thence I went over the summits of all these mountains, far towards the east of the earth, and passed above the Erythraean sea and went far from it, and passed over the angel Zotiel. And I came to the Garden of Righteousness, [3] I and from afar off trees more numerous than I these trees and great-two trees there, very great, beautiful, and glorious, and magnificent, and the tree of knowledge, whose holy fruit they eat and know great wisdom. [4] That tree is in height like the fir, and its leaves are like (those of) the Carob tree: [5] And its fruit is like the clusters of the vine, very beautiful: and the fragrance of the tree penetrates afar. [6] Then I said: 'How beautiful is the tree, and how attractive is its look!' Then Raphael the holy angel, who was with me, answered me and said: 'This is the tree of wisdom, of which thy father old (in years) and thy aged mother, who were before thee, have eaten, and they learnt wisdom and their eyes were opened, and they knew that they were naked and they were driven out of the garden.'

CHAPTER 33

[1] And from thence I went to the ends of the earth and saw there great beasts, and each differed from the other; and I saw birds also differing in appearance and beauty and voice, the one differing from the other. And to the east of those beasts I saw the ends of the earth whereon the heaven rests, [2] And the portals of the heaven open. And I saw how the stars of heaven come forth, [3] And I counted the portals out of which they proceed, and wrote down all their outlets, of each individual star by itself, according to their number and their names, their courses and their positions, and their times and their months, [4] As Uriel the holy angel who was with me showed me. He showed all things to me and wrote them down for me: also their names he wrote for me, and their laws and their companies.

CHAPTER 34

[1] And from thence I went towards the north to the ends of the earth, and there I saw a great and glorious device at the ends of the whole earth. And here I saw three portals of heaven open in the heaven: through each of them proceed north winds: when they blow there is cold, hail, frost, snow, dew, and rain. [2] And out of one portal they blow for good: but when they blow through the other two portals, it is with violence and affliction on the earth, and they blow with violence.

CHAPTER 35

[1] And from thence I went towards the west to the ends of the earth, and saw there three portals of the heaven open such as I had seen in the east, the same number of portals, and the same number of outlets.

CHAPTER 36 .

[1] And from thence I went to the south to the ends of the earth, and saw there three open portals of the heaven: [2] And thence there come dew, rain, and wind. And from thence I went to the east to the ends of the heaven, and saw here the three eastern portals of heaven open and small portals above them. [3] Through each of these small portals pass the stars of heaven and run their course to the west on the path which is shown to them. And as often as I saw I blessed always the Lord of Glory, and I continued to bless the Lord of Glory who has wrought great and glorious wonders, to show the

greatness of His work to the angels and to spirits and to men, that they might praise His work and all His creation: that they might see the work of His might and praise the great work of His hands and bless Him for ever.

The Book Of Parables

CHAPTER 37
[1] The second vision which he saw, the vision of wisdom -which Enoch the son of Jared, [2] The son of Mahalalel, the son of Cainan, the son of Enos, the son of Seth, the son of Adam, saw. And this is the beginning of the words of wisdom which I lifted up my voice to speak and say to those which dwell on earth: Hear, ye men of old time, and see, ye that come after, [3] The words of the Holy one which I will speak before the Lord of Spirits. It were better to declare, them only, to the men of old time, but even from those that come after we will not withhold the beginning of wisdom. [4] Till the present day such wisdom has never been given by the Lord of Spirits as I have received according to my insight, according to the good pleasure of the Lord of Spirits by whom the lot of eternal life has been given to me. [5] Now three Parables were imparted to me, and I lifted up my voice and recounted them to those that dwell on the earth.

The First Parable

CHAPTER 38
[1] The first Parable. When the congregation of the righteous shall appear, and sinners shall be judged for their sins, and shall be driven from the face of the earth: [2] And when the Righteous One shall appear before the eyes of the righteous, whose elect works hang upon the Lord of Spirits, and light shall appear to the righteous and the elect who dwell on the earth, where then will be the dwelling of the sinners, and where the resting-place of those who have denied the Lord of Spirits? It had been good for them if they had not been born. [3] When the secrets of the righteous shall be revealed and the sinners judged, and the godless driven from the presence of the righteous and elect, [4] From that time those that possess the earth shall no longer be powerful and exalted: And they shall not be able to behold the face of the holy, For the Lord of Spirits has caused His light to appear on the face of the holy, righteous, and elect. [5] Then shall the kings and the mighty perish and be given into the hands of the righteous and holy. [6] And thenceforward none shall seek for themselves mercy from the Lord of Spirits for their life is at an end.

CHAPTER 39
[1] And it shall come to pass in those days that elect and holy children will descend from the high heaven, [2] And their seed will become one with the children of men. And in those days Enoch received books of zeal and wrath, and books of disquiet and expulsion. And mercy shall not be accorded to them, saith the Lord of Spirits. [3] And in those days a whirlwind carried me off from the earth, and set me down at the end of the heavens. [4] And there I saw another vision, the dwelling-places of the holy, and the resting-places of the righteous. [5] Here mine eyes saw their dwellings with His righteous angels, and their resting-places with the holy. And they petitioned and interceded and prayed for the children of men, and righteousness flowed before them as water, and mercy like dew upon the earth: Thus it is amongst them for ever and ever. [6] And in that place mine eyes saw the Elect One of righteousness and of faith, and I saw his dwelling-place under the wings of the Lord of Spirits. And righteousness shall prevail in his days, and the righteous and elect shall be without number before Him for ever and ever. [7] And all the righteous and elect before Him shall be strong as fiery lights, and their mouth shall be full of blessing, and their lips extol the name of the Lord of Spirits, and righteousness before Him shall never fail, and uprightness shall never fail before Him. [8] There I wished to dwell, and my spirit longed for that dwelling-place: And there heretofore hath been my portion, For so has it been established concerning me before the Lord of Spirits. [9] In those days I praised and extolled the name of the Lord of Spirits with blessings and praises, because He hath destined me for blessing and glory according to the good pleasure of the Lord of Spirits. [10] For a long time my eyes regarded that place, and I blessed Him and praised Him, saying: Blessed is He, and may He be blessed from the beginning and for evermo re. And before Him there is no ceasing. He knows before the world was created what is for ever and what will be from generation unto generation. [11] Those who sleep not bless Thee: they stand before Thy glory and bless, praise, and extol, saying: "Holy, holy, holy, is the Lord of Spirits: [12] He filleth the earth with 12 spirits." And here my eyes saw all those who sleep not: they stand before Him and bless and say: Blessed be Thou, and blessed be the name of the Lord for ever and ever. And my face was changed; for I could no longer behold.

CHAPTER 40
[1] And after that I saw thousands of thousands and ten thousand times ten thousand, I saw a multitude beyond number and reckoning, [2] Who stood before the Lord of Spirits. And on the four sides of the Lord of Spirits I saw four presences, different from those that sleep not, and I learnt their names: for the angel that went with me made known to me their names, and showed me all the hidden things. [3] And I heard the voices of those four presences as they uttered praises before the Lord of glory. [4] The first voice blesses the Lord of Spirits for ever and ever. [5] And the second voice I heard blessing the Elect One, [6] And the elect ones who hang upon the Lord of Spirits. And the third voice I heard pray and intercede for those who dwell on the earth and supplicate in the name of the Lord of Spirits. [7] And I heard the fourth voice fending off the Satans and forbidding them to come before the Lord of Spirits to accuse them who dwell on the earth. [8] After that I asked the angel of peace who went with me, who showed me everything that is hidden: Who are these four presences which I have seen and whose words I have heard and written down? [9] And he said to me: This first is Michael, the merciful and long- suffering: and the second, who is set over all the diseases and all the wounds of the children of men, is Raphael: and the third, who is set over all the powers, is Gabriel: and the fourth, who is set over the repentance unto hope

of those who inherit eternal life, is named Phanuel. [10]   And these are the four angels of the Lord of Spirits and the four voices I heard in those days.

CHAPTER 41

[1] And after that I saw all the secrets of the heavens, and how the kingdom is divided, [2] And how the actions of men are weighed in the balance. And there I saw the mansions of the elect and the mansions of the holy, and mine eyes saw there all the sinners being driven from thence which deny the name of the Lord of Spirits, and being dragged off: and they could not abide because of the punishment which proceeds from the Lord of Spirits. [3] And there mine eyes saw the secrets of the lightning and of the thunder, and the secrets of the winds, how they are divided to blow over the earth, and the secrets of the clouds and dew, [4] And these I saw from whence they proceed in that place and from whence they saturate the dusty earth. And there I saw closed chambers out of which the winds are divided, the chamber of the hail and winds, the chamber of the mist, and of the clouds, and the cloud thereof hovers over the earth from the beginning of the world. [5] And I saw the chambers of the sun and moon, whence they proceed, and whither they come again, and their glorious return, and how one is superior to the other, and their stately orbit, and how they do not leave their orbit, and they add nothing to their orbit, and they take nothing from it, and they keep faith with each other, in accordance with the oath by which they are bound together. [6] And first the sun goes forth and traverses his path according to the commandment of the Lord of Spirits, And mighty is His name for ever and ever. And after that I saw the hidden and the visible path of the moon, and she accomplishes the course of her path in that place by day and by night-the one holding a position opposite to the other before the Lord of Spirits. And they give thanks and praise and rest not; For unto them is their thanksgiving rest. [7] For the sun changes oft for a blessing or a curse, and the course of the path of the moon is light to the righteous. And darkness to the sinners in the name of the Lord, who made a separation between the light and the darkness, and divided the spirits of men, and strengthened the spirits of the righteous, in the name of His righteousness. [8] For no angel hinders and no power is able to hinder; for He appoints a judge for them all and He judges them all before Him.

CHAPTER 42

[1] Wisdom found no place where she might dwell; Then a dwelling-place was assigned her in the heavens. [2] Wisdom went forth to make her dwelling among the children of men, and found no dwelling-place: Wisdom returned to her place, and took her seat among the angels. [3] And unrighteousness went forth from her chambers: Whom she sought not she found, and dwelt with them, as rain in a desert, and dew on a thirsty land.

CHAPTER 43

[1] And I saw other lightnings and the stars of heaven, and I saw how He called them all by their names and they hearkened unto Him. [2] And I saw how they are weighed in a righteous balance according to their proportions of light: I saw the width of their spaces and the day of their appearing, and how their revolution produces lightning: and I saw their revolution according to the number of the angels, [3] And how they keep faith with each other. And I asked the angel who went with me who showed me what was hidden: What are these? And he said to me: The Lord of Spirits hath showed thee their parabolic meaning: these are the names of the holy who dwell on the earth and believe in the name of the Lord of Spirits for ever and ever.

CHAPTER 44

[1] Also another phenomenon I saw in regard to the lightnings: how some of the stars arise and become lightnings and cannot part with their new form.

The Second Parable

CHAPTER 45

[1] And this is the second Parable concerning those who deny the name of the dwelling of the holy ones and the Lord of Spirits. [2] And into the heaven they shall not ascend, and on the earth they shall not come: Such shall be the lot of the sinners who have denied the name of the Lord of Spirits, who are thus preserved for the day of suffering and tribulation. [3] On that day Mine Elect One shall sit on the throne of glory, and shall try their works, and their places of rest shall be innumerable. And their souls shall grow strong within them when they see Mine Elect Ones, and those who have called upon My glorious name: [4] Then will I cause Mine Elect One to dwell among them. And I will transform the heaven and make it an eternal blessing and light, [5] And I will transform the earth and make it a blessing: And I will cause Mine elect ones to dwell upon it: But the sinners and evil-doers shall not set foot thereon. [6] For I have provided and satisfied with peace My righteous ones, and have caused them to dwell before Me: But for the sinners there is judgement impending with Me, so that I shall destroy them from the face of the earth.

CHAPTER 46

[1] And there I saw one who had a head of days, and His head was white like wool, and with Him was another being whose countenance had the appearance of a man, and his face was full of graciousness, like one of the holy angels. [2] And I asked the angel who went with me and showed me all the hidden things, concerning that Son of Man, who he was, and whence he was, and why he went with the Head of Days? And he answered and said unto me: This is the son of Man who hath righteousness, with whom dwelleth righteousness, and who revealeth all the treasures of that which is hidden, because the Lord of Spirits hath chosen him, and whose lot hath the pre-eminence before the Lord of Spirits in uprightness for ever. [3] And this Son of Man whom thou hast seen shall raise up the kings and the mighty from their seats, and the strong from their thrones, and shall loosen the reins of the strong, and break the teeth of the sinners. [4] And he shall put down the

kings from their thrones and kingdoms because they do not extol and praise Him, nor humbly acknowledge whence the kingdom was bestowed upon them. [5] And he shall put down the countenance of the strong, and shall fill them with shame. And darkness shall be their dwelling, and worms shall be their bed, and they shall have no hope of rising from their beds, because they do not extol the name of the Lord of Spirits. [6] And these are they who judge the stars of heaven, and raise their hands against the Most High, and tread upon the earth and dwell upon it. And all their deeds manifest unrighteousness, and their power rests upon their riches, and their faith is in the gods which they have made with their hands, and they deny the name of the Lord of Spirits, [7] And they persecute the houses of His congregations, and the faithful who hang upon the name of the Lord of Spirits.

CHAPTER 47
[1] And in those days shall have ascended the prayer of the righteous, and the blood of the righteous from the earth before the Lord of Spirits. [2] In those days the holy ones who dwell above in the heavens shall unite with one voice and supplicate and pray and praise, and give thanks and bless the name of the Lord of Spirits on behalf of the blood of the righteous which has been shed, and that the prayer of the righteous may not be in vain before the Lord of Spirits, that judgement may be done unto them, and that they may not have to suffer for ever. [3] In those days I saw the Head of Days when He seated himself upon the throne of His glory, and the books of the living were opened before Him: And all His host which is in heaven above and His counselors stood before Him, [4] And the hearts of the holy were filled with joy; Because the number of the righteous had been offered, and the prayer of the righteous had been heard, and the blood of the righteous been required before the Lord of Spirits.

CHAPTER 48
[1] And in that place I saw the fountain of righteousness which was inexhaustible: And around it were many fountains of wisdom: And all the thirsty drank of them, and were filled with wisdom, and their dwellings were with the righteous and holy and elect. [2] And at that hour that Son of Man was named In the presence of the Lord of Spirits, and his name before the Head of Days. [3] Yea, before the sun and the signs were created, before the stars of the heaven were made, his name was named before the Lord of Spirits. [4] He shall be a staff to the righteous whereon to stay themselves and not fall, and he shall be the light of the Gentiles, and the hope of those who are troubled of heart. [5] All who dwell on earth shall fall down and worship before him, and will praise and bless and celebrate with song the Lord of Spirits. [6] And for this reason hath he been chosen and hidden before Him, before the creation of the world and for evermore. [7] And the wisdom of the Lord of Spirits hath revealed him to the holy and righteous; For he hath preserved the lot of the righteous, because they have hated and despised this world of unrighteousness, and have hated all its works and ways in the name of the Lord of Spirits: For in his name they are saved, and according to his good pleasure hath it been in regard to their life. [8] In these days downcast in countenance shall the kings of the earth have become, and the strong who possess the land because of the works of their hands, for on the day of their anguish and affliction they shall not (be able to) save themselves. And I will give them over into the hands of Mine elect: [9] As straw in the fire so shall they burn before the face of the holy: As lead in the water shall they sink before the face of the righteous, and no trace of them shall any more be found. [10] And on the day of their affliction there shall be rest on the earth, and before them they shall fall and not rise again: And there shall be no one to take them with his hands and raise them: For they have denied the Lord of Spirits and His Anointed. The name of the Lord of Spirits be blessed.

CHAPTER 49
[1] For wisdom is poured out like water, and glory faileth not before him for evermore. [2] For he is mighty in all the secrets of righteousness, and unrighteousness shall disappear as a shadow, and have no continuance; Because the Elect One standeth before the Lord of Spirits, and his glory is for ever and ever, and his might unto all generations. [3] And in him dwells the spirit of wisdom, and the spirit which gives insight, and the spirit of understanding and of might, and the spirit of those who have fallen asleep in righteousness. [4] And he shall judge the secret things, and none shall be able to utter a lying word before him; For he is the Elect One before the Lord of Spirits according to His good pleasure.

CHAPTER 50
[1] And in those days a change shall take place for the holy and elect, and the light of days shall abide upon them, and glory and honour shall turn to the holy, [2] On the day of affliction on which evil shall have been treasured up against the sinners. And the righteous shall be victorious in the name of the Lord of Spirits: And He will cause the others to witness this that they may repent, and forgot the works of their hands. [3] They shall have no honour through the name of the Lord of Spirits, yet through His name shall they be saved, and the Lord of Spirits will have compassion on them, for His compassion is great. [4] And He is righteous also in His judgement, and in the presence of His glory unrighteousness also shall not maintain itself: At His judgement the unrepentant shall perish before Him. [5] And from henceforth I will have no mercy on them, saith the Lord of Spirits.

CHAPTER 51
[1] And in those days shall the earth also give back that which has been entrusted to it, and Sheol also shall give back that which it has received, and hell shall give back that which it owes. For in those days the Elect One shall arise, [2] And he shall choose the righteous and holy from among them: For the day has drawn nigh that they should be saved. [3] And the Elect One shall in those days sit on My throne, and his mouth shall pour forth all the secrets of wisdom and counsel: For the Lord of Spirits hath given (them) to him and hath glorified him. [4] And in those days shall the mountains leap like rams, and the hills also shall skip like lambs satisfied with milk, [5] And the faces of all the angels in heaven shall be lighted up with joy. And the earth shall rejoice, and the righteous shall dwell upon it, and the elect shall walk thereon.

CHAPTER 52

[1] And after those days in that place where I had seen all the visions of that which is hidden, [2] For I had been carried off in a whirlwind and they had borne me towards the west-there mine eyes saw all the secret things of heaven that shall be, a mountain of iron, and a mountain of copper, and a mountain of silver, and a mountain of gold, and a mountain of soft metal, and a mountain of lead. [3] And I asked the angel who went with me, saying, What things are these which I have seen in secret? [4] And he said unto me: All these things which thou hast seen shall serve the dominion of His Anointed that he may be potent and mighty on the earth. [5] And that angel of peace answered, saying unto me: Wait a little, and there shall be revealed unto thee all the secret things which surround the Lord of Spirits. [6] And these mountains which thine eyes have seen, the mountain of iron, and the mountain of copper, and the mountain of silver, and the mountain of gold, and the mountain of soft metal, and the mountain of lead, all these shall be in the presence of the Elect One as wax: before the fire, and like the water which streams down from above upon those mountains, and they shall become powerless before his feet. [7] And it shall come to pass in those days that none shall be saved, either by gold or by silver, and none be able to escape. [8] And there shall be no iron for war, nor shall one clothe oneself with a breastplate. Bronze shall be of no service, and tin [shall be of no service and] shall not be esteemed, and lead shall not be desired. [9] And all these things shall be [denied and] destroyed from the surface of the earth, when the Elect One shall appear before the face of the Lord of Spirits.

CHAPTER 53

[1] There mine eyes saw a deep valley with open mouths, and all who dwell on the earth and sea and islands shall bring to him gifts and presents and tokens of homage, but that deep valley shall not become full. [2] And their hands commit lawless deeds, and the sinners devour all whom they lawlessly oppress: Yet the sinners shall be destroyed before the face of the Lord of Spirits, and they shall be banished from off the face of His earth, and they shall perish for ever and ever. [3] For I saw all the angels of punishment abiding there and preparing all the instruments of Satan. [4] And I asked the angel of peace who went with me: For whom are they preparing these instruments? [5] And he said unto me: They prepare these for the kings and the mighty of this earth, that they may thereby be destroyed. [6] And after this the Righteous and Elect One shall cause the house of his congregation to appear: henceforth they shall be no more hindered in the name of the Lord of Spirits. [7] And these mountains shall not stand as the earth before his righteousness, but the hills shall be as a fountain of water, and the righteous shall have rest from the oppression of sinners.

CHAPTER 54

[1] And I looked and turned to another part of the earth, and saw there a deep valley with burning fire. [2] And they brought the kings and the mighty, and began to cast them into this deep valley. [3] And there mine eyes saw how they made these their instruments, iron chains of immeasurable weight. [4] And I asked the angel of peace who went with me, saying: For whom are these chains being prepared? [5] And he said unto me: These are being prepared for the hosts of Azazel, so that they may take them and cast them into the abyss of complete condemnation, and they shall cover their jaws with rough stones as the Lord of Spirits commanded. [6] And Michael, and Gabriel, and Raphael, and Phanuel shall take hold of them on that great day, and cast them on that day into the burning furnace, that the Lord of Spirits may take vengeance on them for their unrighteousness in becoming subject to Satan and leading astray those who dwell on the earth. [7] And in those days shall punishment come from the Lord of Spirits, and he will open all the chambers of waters which are above the heavens, and of the fountains which are beneath the earth. [8] And all the waters shall be joined with the waters: that which is above the heavens is the masculine, [9] And the water which is beneath the earth is the feminine. And they shall destroy all who dwell on the earth, [10] And those who dwell under the ends of the heaven. And when they have recognized their unrighteousness which they have wrought on the earth, then by these shall they perish.

CHAPTER 55

[1] And after that the Head of Days repented and said: In vain have I destroyed all who dwell on the earth. [2] And He sware by His great name: Henceforth I will not do so to all who dwell on the earth, and I will set a sign in the heaven: and this shall be a pledge of good faith between Me and them for ever, so long as heaven is above the earth. And this is in accordance with My command. When I have desired to take hold of them by the hand of the angels on the day of tribulation and pain because of this, I will cause My chastisement and My wrath to abide upon them, saith God, the Lord of Spirits. [3] Ye mighty kings who dwell on the earth, ye shall have to behold Mine Elect One, how he sits on the throne of glory and judges Azazel, and all his associates, and all his hosts in the name of the Lord of Spirits.

CHAPTER 56

[1] And I saw there the hosts of the angels of punishment going, and they held scourges and chains of iron and bronze. And I asked the angel of peace who went with me, saying: [2] To whom are these who hold the scourges going? And he said unto me: [3] To their elect and beloved ones, that they may be cast into the chasm of the abyss of the valley. [4] And then that valley shall be filled with their elect and beloved, And the days of their lives shall be at an end, And the days of their leading astray shall not thenceforward be reckoned. [5] And in those days the angels shall return, and hurl themselves to the east upon the Parthians and Medes: They shall stir up the kings, so that a spirit of unrest shall come upon them, and they shall rouse them from their thrones, that they may break forth as lions from their lairs, and as hungry wolves among their flocks. [6] And they shall go up and tread under foot the land of His elect ones, and the land of His elect ones shall be before the m a threshing-floor and a highway : [7] But the city of my righteous shall be a hindrance to their horses. And they shall begin to fight among themselves, and their right hand shall be strong against themselves, and a man shall not know his brother, nor a son his father or his mother, till there be no number of the corpses through their slaughter, and their punishment be not in vain. [8] In those days Sheol shall open its jaws, and they shall be swallowed up therein, and their destruction shall be at an end; Sheol shall devour the sinners in the presence of the elect.

CHAPTER 57

[1] And it came to pass after this that I saw another host of wagons, and men riding thereon, [2] And coming on the winds from the east, and from the west to the south. And the noise of their wagons was heard, and when this turmoil took place the holy ones from heaven remarked it, and the pillars of the earth were moved from their place, and the sound thereof was heard from the one end of heaven to the other, in one day. [3] And they shall all fall down and worship the Lord of Spirits. And this is the end of the second Parable.

The Third Parable

CHAPTER 58

[1] And I began to speak the third Parable concerning the righteous and elect. [2] Blessed are ye, ye righteous and elect, for glorious shall be your lot. [3] And the righteous shall be in the light of the sun. And the elect in the light of eternal life: The days of their life shall be unending, and the days of the holy without number. [4] And they shall seek the light and find righteousness with the Lord of Spirits: There shall be peace to the righteous in the name of the Eternal Lord. [5] And after this it shall be said to the holy in heaven that they should seek out the secrets of righteousness, the heritage of faith: For it has become bright as the sun upon earth, and the darkness is past. [6] And there shall be a light that never endeth, and to a limit of days they shall not come, for the darkness shall first have been destroyed, and the light established before the Lord of Spirits, and the light of uprightness established for ever before the Lord of Spirits.

CHAPTER 59

[1] In those days mine eyes saw the secrets of the lightnings, and of the lights, and the judgements they execute and they lighten for a blessing or a curse as the Lord of Spirits willeth. [2] And there I saw the secrets of the thunder, and how when it resounds above in the heaven, the sound thereof is heard, and he caused me to see the judgements executed on the earth, whether they be for well-being and blessing, or for a curse according to the word of the Lord of Spirits. [3] And after that all the secrets of the lights and lightnings were shown to me, and they lighten for blessing and for satisfying.

The Book Of Noah

CHAPTER 60

[1] In the year 500, in the seventh month, on the fourteenth day of the month in the life of Enoch. In that Parable I saw how a mighty quaking made the heaven of heavens to quake, and the host of the Most High, and the angels, a thousand thousands and ten thousand times ten thousand, [2] Were disquieted with a great disquiet. And the Head of Days sat on the throne of His glory, and the angels and the righteous stood around Him. [3] And a great trembling seized me, and fear took hold of me, and my loins gave way, and dissolved were my reins, and I fell upon my face. [4] And Michael sent another angel from among the holy ones and he raised me up, and when he had raised me up my spirit returned; for I had not been able to endure the look of this host, [5] And the commotion and the quaking of the heaven. And Michael said unto me: Why art thou disquieted with such a vision ? Until this day lasted the day of His mercy; and He hath been merciful, [6] And long-suffering towards those who dwell on the earth. And when the day, and the power, and the punishment, and the judgement come, which the Lord of Spirits hath prepared for those who worship not the righteous law, and for those who deny the righteous judgement, and for those who take His name in vain- that day is prepared, for the elect a covenant, but for sinners an inquisition. [7] When the punishment of the Lord of Spirits shall rest upon them, it shall rest in order that the punishment of the Lord of Spirits may not come, in vain, and it shall slay the children with their mothers and the children with their fathers. Afterwards the judgement shall take place according to His mercy and His patience. And on that day were two monsters parted, a female monster named Leviathan, [8] To dwell in the abysses of the ocean over the fountains of the waters. But the male is named Behemoth, who occupied with his breast a waste wilderness named Duidain, on the east of the garden where the elect and righteous dwell, where my grandfather was taken up, the seventh from Adam, [9] The first man whom the Lord of Spirits created. And I besought the other angel that he should show me the might of those monsters, how they were parted on one day and cast, the one into the abysses of the sea, [10] And the other unto the dry land of the wilderness. And he said to me: Thou son of man, herein thou dost seek to know what is hidden. [11] And the other angel who went with me and showed me what was hidden told me what is first and last in the heaven in the height, and beneath the earth in the depth, and at the ends of the heaven, [12] And on the foundation of the heaven. And the chambers of the winds, and how the winds are divided, and how they are weighed, and how the portals of the winds are reckoned, each according to the power of the wind, and the power of the lights of the moon, and according to the power that is fitting: and the divisions of the stars according to their names, and how all the divisions are divided. [13] And the thunders according to the places where they fall, and all the divisions that are made among the lightnings that it may lighten, and their host that they may at once obey. [14] For the thunder has places of rest (which) are assigned (to it) while it is waiting for its peal; And the thunder and lightning are inseparable, and although not one and undivided, they both go together through the spirit and separate not. [15] For when the lightning lightens, the thunder utters its voice, and the spirit enforces a pause during the peal, and divides equally between them; for the treasury of their peals is like the sand, and each one of them as it peals is held in with a bridle, and turned back by the power of the spirit, and pushed forward according to the many quarters of the earth. [16] And the spirit of the sea is masculine and strong, and according to the might of his strength he draws it back with a rein, and in like manner it is driven forward and disperses amid all the mountains of the earth. [17] And the spirit of the hoar-frost is his own angel, and the spirit of the hail is a good angel. [18] And the spirit of the snow has forsaken his chambers on account of his strength - There is a special spirit therein, and that which ascends from it is like smoke, and its name is frost. [19] And the spirit of the mist is not united with them in their chambers, but it

has a special chamber; for its course is glorious both in light and in darkness, and in winter and in summer, and in its chamber is an angel. [20] And the spirit of the dew has its dwelling at the ends of the heaven, and is connected with the chambers of the rain, and its course is in winter and summer: and its clouds and the clouds of the mist are connected, [21] And the one gives to the other. And when the spirit of the rain goes forth from its chamber, the angels come and open the chamber and lead it out, and when it is diffused over the whole earth it unites with the water on the earth. And whensoever it unites with the water on the earth. [22] For the waters are for those who dwell on the earth; for they are nourishment for the earthfrom the Most High who is in heaven: therefore there is a measure for the rain, and the angels take it in charge. And these things I saw towards the Garden of the Righteous. [23] And the angel of peace who was with me said to me: These two monsters, prepared conformably to the greatness of God, shall feed.

CHAPTER 61

[1] And I saw in those days how long cords were given to those angels, and they took to themselves wings and flew, and they went towards the north. [2] And I asked the angel, saying unto him: Why have those (angels) taken these cords and gone off? And he said unto me: They have gone to measure. [3] And the angel who went with me said unto me: These shall bring the measures of the righteous, and the ropes of the righteous to the righteous, that they may stay themselves on the name of the Lord of Spirits for ever and ever. [4] The elect shall begin to dwell with the elect, and those are the measures which shall be given to faith, and which shall strengthen righteousness. [5] And these measures shall reveal all the secrets of the depths of the earth, and those who have been destroyed by the desert, and those who have been devoured by the beasts, and those who have been devoured by the fish of the sea, that they may return and stay themselves on the day of the Elect One; For none shall be destroyed before the Lord of Spirits, and none can be destroyed. [6] And all who dwell above in the heaven received a command and power and one voice and one light like unto fire. [7] And that One with their first words they blessed, and extolled and lauded with wisdom, and they were wise in utterance and in the spirit of life. [8] And the Lord of Spirits placed the Elect one on the throne of glory. And he shall judge all the works of the holy above in the heaven, and in the balance shall their deeds be weighed.

CHAPTER 62

[1] And thus the Lord commanded the kings and the mighty and the exalted, and those who dwell on the earth, and said: Open your eyes and lift up your horns if ye are able to recognize the Elect One. [2] And the Lord of Spirits seated him on the throne of His glory, and the spirit of righteousness was poured out upon him, and the word of his mouth slays all the sinners, and all the unrighteous are destroyed from before his face. [3] And there shall stand up in that day all the kings and the mighty, and the exalted and those who hold the earth, and they shall see and recognize How he sits on the throne of his glory, and righteousness is judged before him, and no lying word is spoken before him. [4] Then shall pain come upon them as on a woman in trava il, and she has pain in bringing forth, when her child enters the mouth of the womb, and she has pain in bringing forth. [5] And one portion of them shall look on the other, and they shall be terrified, and they shall be downcast of countenance, and pain shall seize them, when they see that Son of Man Sitting on the throne of his glory. [6] And the kings and the mighty and all who possess the earth shall bless and glorify and extol him who rules over all, who was hidden. [7] For from the beginning the Son of Man was hidden, and the most High preserved him in the presence of His might, and revealed him to the elect.And the congregation of the elect and holy shall be sown, and all the elect shall stand before him on that day. [8] And all the kings and the mighty and the exalted and those who rule the eart. Shall fall down before him on their faces, and worship and set their hope upon that Son of Man, and petition him and supplicate for mercy at his hands. [9] Nevertheless that Lord of Spirits will so press them that they shall hastily go forth from His presence, and their faces shall be filled with shame, and the darkness grow deeper on their faces. [10]And He will deliver them to the angels for punishment, to execute vengeance on them because they have oppressed His children and His elect, [11]And they shall be a spectacle for the righteous and for His elect: They shall rejoice over them, because the wrath of the Lord of Spirits resteth upon them, and His sword is drunk with their blood. [12]And the righteous and elect shall be saved on that day, and they shall never thenceforward see the face of the sinners and unrighteous. [13]And the Lord of Spirits will abide over them, and with that Son of Man shall they eat and lie down and rise up for ever and ever. [14]And the righteous and elect shall have risen from the earth, and ceased to be of downcast countenance. And they shall have been clothed with garments of glory, [15]And these shall be the garments of life from the Lord of Spirits: And your garments shall not grow old, nor your glory pass away before the Lord of Spirits.

CHAPTER 63

[1] In those days shall the mighty and the kings who possess the earth implore Him to grant them a little respite from His angels of punishment to whom they were delivered, [2] That they might fall down and worship before the Lord of Spirits, and confess their sins before Him. And they shall bless and glorify the Lord of Spirits, and say: Blessed is the Lord of Spirits and the Lord of kings, And the Lord of the mighty and the Lord of the rich, And the Lord of glory and the Lord of wisdom, [3] And splendid in every secret thing is Thy power from generation to generation, and Thy glory for ever and ever: Deep are all Thy secrets and innumerable, and Thy righteousness is beyond reckoning. [4] We have now learnt that we should glorify and bless the Lord of kings and Him who is king over all kings. [5] And they shall say: Would that we had rest to glorify and give thanks and confess our faith before His glory ! [6] And now we long for a little rest but find it not: We follow hard upon and obtain (it) not: And light has vanished from before us, and darkness is our dwelling-place for ever and ever: [7] For we have not believed before Him nor glorified the name of the Lord of Spirits, nor glorified our Lord but our hope was in the sceptre of our kingdom, and in our glory. [8] And in the day of our suffering and tribulation He saves us not, and we find no respite for confession that our Lord is true in all His works, and in His judgements and His justice, and His judgements have no respect of persons. [9] And we pass away from before His face on account of our works, and all our sins are reckoned up in righteousness. [10] Now they shall say unto themselves: Our souls are full of unrighteous gain, but it does not prevent us from descending from the midst thereof into the burden of Sheol. [11] And

after that their faces shall be filled with darkness, and shame before that Son of Man, and they shall be driven from his presence, and the sword shall abide before his face in their midst. [12] Thus spake the Lord of Spirits: This is the ordinance and judgement with respect to the mighty and the kings and the exalted and those who possess the earth before the Lord of Spirits.

CHAPTER 64
[1] And other forms I saw hidden in that place. I heard the voice of the angel saying: These are the angels who descended to the earth, [2] And revealed what was hidden to the children of men and seduced the children of men into committing sin.

CHAPTER 65
[1] And in those days Noah saw the earth that it had sunk down and its destruction was nigh. [2] And he arose from thence and went to the ends of the earth, and cried aloud to his grandfather Enoch: [3] And Noah said three times with an embittered voice: Hear me, hear me, hear me. And I said unto him: Tell me what it is that is falling out on the earth that the earth is in such evil plight, [4] And shaken, lest perchance I shall perish with it? And thereupon there was a great commotion , on the earth, and a voice was heard from heaven, and I fell on my face. [5] And Enoch my grandfather came and stood by me, and said unto me: Why hast thou cried unto me with a bitter cry and weeping, [6] And a command has gone forth from the presence of the Lord concerning those who dwell on the earth that their ruin is accomplished because they have learnt all the secrets of the angels, and all the violence of the Satans, and all their powers -the most secret ones-and all the power of those who practice sorcery, and the power of witchcraft, and the power of those who make molten images for the whole earth: [7] And how silver is produced from the dust of the earth, and how soft metal originates in the earth. [8] For lead and tin are not produced from the earth like the first: it is a fountain that produces them, [9] And an angel stands therein, and that angel is pre-eminent. And after that my grandfather Enoch took hold of me by my hand and raised me up, and said unto me: [10]   Go, for I have asked the Lord of Spirits as touching this commotion on the earth. And He said unto me: "Because of their unrighteousness their judgement has been determined upon and shall not be withheld by Me for ever. Because of the sorceries which they have searched out and learnt, the earth, [11]   and those who dwell upon it shall be destroyed." And these-they have no place of repentance forever, because they have shown them what was hidden, and they are the damned: but as for thee, my son, the Lord of Spirits knows that thou art pure, and guiltless of this reproach concerning the secrets. [12]   And He has destined thy name to be among the holy, And will preserve thee amongst those who dwell on the earth, and has destined thy righteous seed both for kingship and for great honours, and from thy seed shall proceed a fountain of the righteous and holy witho ut number forever.

CHAPTER 66
[1] And after that he showed me the angels of punishment who are prepared to come and let loose all the powers of the waters which are beneath in the earth in order to bring judgement and destruction on all who abide and dwell on the earth. [2] And the Lord of Spirits gave commandment to the angels who were going forth, that they should not cause the waters to rise but should hold them in check; [3] For those angels were over the powers of the waters. And I went away from the presence of Enoch.

CHAPTER 67
[1] And in those days the word of God came unto me, and He said unto me: Noah, thy lot has come up before Me, [2] A lot without blame, a lot of love and uprightness. And now the angels are making a wooden building, and when they have completed that task I will place My hand upon it and preserve it, and there shall come forth from it the seed of life, and a change shall set in so that the earth will not remain without inhabitant. [3] And I will make fast thy seed before me for ever and ever, and I will spread abroad those who dwell with thee: it shall not be unfruitful on the face of the earth, but it shall be blessed and multiply on the earth in the name of the Lord. [4] And He will imprison those angels, who have shown unrighteousness, in that burning valley which my grandfather Enoch had formerly shown to me in the west among the mountains of gold and silver and iron and soft metal and tin. [5] And I saw that valley in which there was a great convulsion and a convulsion of the waters. [6] And when all this took place, from that fiery molten metal and from the convulsion thereof in that place, there was produced a smell of sulphur, and it was connected with those waters, and that valley of the angels who had led astray mankind burned beneath that land. [7] And through its valleys proceed streams of fire, where these angels are punished who had led astray those who dwell upon the earth. [8] But those waters shall in those days serve for the kings and the mighty and the exalted, and those who dwell on the earth, for the healing of the body, but for the punishment of the spirit; Now their spirit is full of lust, that they may be punished in their body, for they have denied the Lord of Spirits and see their punishment daily, [9] And yet believe not in His name. And in proportion as the burning of their bodies becomes severe, a corresponding change shall take place in their spirit for ever and ever; [10]   For before the Lord of Spirits none shall utter an idle word. For the judgement shall come upon them, [11]   Because they believe in the lust of their body and deny the Spirit of the Lord. And those same waters will undergo a change in those days; for when those angels are punished in these waters, these water-springs shall change their temperature, and when the angels ascend, this water of the springs shall change and become cold. [12]   And I heard Michael answering and saying: This judgement wherewith the angels are judged is a testimony for the kings and the mighty who possess the earth. [13]   Because these waters of judgement minister to the healing of the body of the kings and the lust of their body; therefore they will not see and will not believe that those waters will change and become a fire which burns for ever.

CHAPTER 68
[1] And after that my grandfather Enoch gave me the teaching of all the secrets in the book in the Parables which had been given to him, and he put them together for me in the words of the book of the Parables. [2] And on that day Michael

answered Raphael and said: The power of the spirit transports and makes me to tremble because of the severity of the judgement of the secrets, the judgement of the angels: who can endure the severe judgement which has been executed, [3] And before which they melt away ? And Michael answered again, and said to Raphael: Who is he whose heart is not softened concerning it, and whose reins are not troubled by this word of judgement that has gone forth upon them because of those who have thus led them out ? [4] And it came to pass when he stood before the Lord of Spirits, Michael said thus to Raphael: I will not take their part under the eye of the Lord; for the Lord of Spirits has been angry with them because they do as if they were the Lord. [5] Therefore all that is hidden shall come upon them forever and ever; for neither angel nor man shall have his portion in it, but alone they have received their judgement for ever and ever.

CHAPTER 69

[1] And after this judgement they shall terrify and make them to tremble because they have shown this to those who dwell on the earth. [2] And behold the names of those angels [and these are their names: the first of them is Samjaza, the second Artaqifa, and the third Armen, the fourth Kokabel, the fifth Turael, the sixth Rumjal, the seventh Danjal, the eighth Neqael, the ninth Baraqel, the tenth Azazel, the eleventh Armaros, the twelfth Batarjal, the thirteenth Busasejal, the fourteenth Hananel, the fifteenth Turel, and the sixteenth Simapesiel, the seventeenth Jetrel, the eighteenth Tumael, the nineteenth Turel, the twentieth Rumael, the twenty- first Azazel. [3] And these are the chiefs of their angels and their names, and their chief ones over hundreds and over fifties and over tens. [4] The name of the first Jeqon: that is, the one who led astray [all] the sons of God, and brought them down to the earth, and led them astray through the daughters of men. [5] And the second was named Asbeel: he imparted to the holy sons of God evil counsel, and led them astray so that they defiled their bodies with the daughters of men. And the third was named Gadreel: he it is who showed the children of men all the blows of death, and he led astray Eve, [6] And showed the weapons of death to the sons of men the shield and the coat of mail, and the sword for battle, and all the weapons of death to the children of men. [7] And from his hand they have proceeded against those who dwell on the earth from that day and for evermore. [8] And the fourth was named Penemue: he taught the children of men the bitter and the sweet, [9] And he taught them all the secrets of their wisdom. And he instructed mankind in writing with ink and paper, and thereby many sinned from eternity to eternity and until this day. [10] For men were not created for such a purpose, to give confirmation to their good faith with pen and ink. [11] For me n were created exactly like the angels, to the intent that they should continue pure and righteous, and death, which destroys everything, could not have taken hold of them, but through this their knowledge they are perishing, and through this power it is consuming me. [12] And the fifth was named Kasdeja: this is he who showed the children of men all the wicked smitings of spirits and demons, and the smitings of the embryo in the womb, that it may pass away, and the smitings of the soul the bites of the serpent, and the smitings, [13] Which befall through the noontide heat, the son of the serpent named Tabaet. And this is the task of Kasbeel, the chief of the oath which he showed to the holy ones when he dwelt high above in glory, and its name is Biqa. [14] This angel requested Michael to show him the hidden name, that he might enunciate it in the oath, so that those might quake before that name and oath who revealed all that was in secret to the children of men. [15] And this is the power of this oath, for it is powerful and strong, and he placed this oath Akae in the hand of Michael. [16] And these are the secrets of this oath , And they are strong through his oath: And the heaven was suspended before the world was created, and forever. [17] And through it the earth was founded upon the water, and from the secret recesses of the mountains come beautiful waters, from the creation of the world and unto eternity. [18] And through that oath the sea was created, and as its foundation He set for it the sand against the time of its anger, and it dare not pass beyond it from the creation of the world unto eternity. [19] And through that oath are the depths made fast, and abide and stir not from their place from eternity to eternity. [20] And through that oath the sun and moon complete their course, and deviate not from their ordinance from eternity to eternity. [21] And through that oath the stars complete their course, and He calls them by their names, and they answer Him from eternity to eternity. [22] And in like manner the spirits of the water, and of the winds, and of all zephyrs, andtheir paths from all the quarters of the winds. [23] And there are preserved the voices of the thunder and the light of the lightnings: and there are preserved the chambers of the hail and the chambers of the hoarfrost, [24] And the chambers of the mist, and the chambers of the rain and the dew. And all these believe and give thanks before the Lord of Spirits, and glorify Him with all their power, and their food is in every act of thanksgiving: they thank and glorify and extol the name of the Lord of Spirits for ever and ever. [25] And this oath is mighty over them and through it they are preserved and their paths are preserved, And their course is not destroyed. [26] And there was great joy amongst them, and they blessed and glorified and extolled because the name of that Son of Man had been revealed unto them. [27] And he sat on the throne of his glory, and the sum of judgement was given unto the Son of Man, and he caused the sinners to pass away and be destroyed from off the face of the earth, and those who have led the world astray. [28] With chains shall they be bound, and in their assemblage-place of destruction shall they be imprisoned, and all their works vanish from the face of the earth. [29] And from henceforth there shall be nothing corruptible; For that Son of Man has appeared, and has seated himself on the throne of his glory, and all evil shall pass away before his face, and the word of that Son of Man shall go forth and be strong before the Lord of Spirits.

CHAPTER 70

[1] And it came to pass after this that his name during his lifetime was raised aloft to that Son of Man, [2] And to the Lord of Spirits from amongst those who dwell on the earth. [3] And he was raised aloft on the chariots of the spirit and his name vanished among them. And from that day I was no longer numbered amongst them: and he set me between the two winds, between the North and the West, [4] Where the angels took the cords to measure for me the place for the elect and righteous. And there I saw the first fathers and the righteous who from the beginning dwell in that place.

CHAPTER 71

[1] And it came to pass after this that my spirit was translated and it ascended into the heavens: And I saw the holy sons of God. They were stepping on flames of fire: Their garments were white and their raiment, and their faces shone like

snow. **[2]** And I saw two streams of fire, and the light of that fire shone like hyacinth, and I fell on my face before the Lord of Spirits. **[3]** And the angel Michael[one of the archangels] seized me by my right hand, and lifted me up and led me forth into all the secrets, and he showed me all the secrets of righteousness. **[4]** And he showed me all the secrets of the ends of the heaven, and all the chambers of all the stars, and all the luminaries, whence they proceed before the face of the holy ones. **[5]** And he translated my spirit into the heaven of heavens, and I saw there as it were a structure built of crystals, and between those crystals tongues of living fire. **[6]** And my spirit saw the girdle which girt that house of fire, and on its four sides were streams full of living fire, and they girt that house. **[7]** And round about were Seraphin, Cherubic, and Ophannin: And these are they who sleep not and guard the throne of His glory. **[8]** And I saw angels who could not be counted, a thousand thousands, and ten thousand times ten thousand, encircling that house. And Michael, and Raphael, and Gabriel, and Phanuel, and the holy angels who are above the heavens, go in and out of that house. **[9]** And they came forth from that house, and Michael and Gabriel, Raphael and Phanuel, and many holy angels without number. **[10]** And with them the Head of Days, His head white and pure as wool, and His raiment indescribable. **[11]** And I fell on my face, and my whole body became relaxed, and my spirit was transfigured; and I cried with a loud voice, with the spirit of power, and blessed and glorified and extolled. **[12]** And these blessings which went forth out of my mouth were well pleasing before that Head of Days. And that Head of Days came with Michael and Gabriel, Raphael and Phanuel, thousands and ten thousands of angels without number. **[13]** Lost passage where in the Son of Man was described as accompanying the Head of Days, and Enoch asked one of the angels concerning the Son of Man as to who he was. **[14]** And he, the angel, came to me and greeted me with His voice, and said unto me this is the Son of Man who is born unto righteousness, and righteousness abides over him, and the righteousness of the Head of Days forsakes him not. **[15]** And he said unto me: He proclaims unto thee peace in the name of the world to come; For from hence has proceeded peace since the creation of the world, and so shall it be unto thee for ever and for ever and ever. **[16]** And all shall walk in his ways since righteousness never forsaketh him: With him will be their dwelling-places, and with him their heritage, and they shall not be separated from him for ever and ever and ever. And so there shall be length of days with that Son of Man, and the righteous shall have peace and an upright way in the name of the Lord of Spirits for ever and ever.

CHAPTER 72

[1] The book of the courses of the luminaries of the heaven, the relations of each, according to their classes, their dominion and their seasons, according to their names and places of origin, and according to their months, which Uriel, the holy angel, who was with me, who is their guide, showed me; and he showed me all their laws exactly as they are, and how it is with regard to all the years of the world and unto eternity, **[2]** Till the new creation is accomplished which dureth till eternity. And this is the first law of the luminaries: the luminary the Sun has its rising in the eastern portals of the heaven, **[3]** And its setting in the western portals of the heaven. And I saw six portals in which the sun rises, and six portals in which the sun sets and the moon rises and sets in these portals, and the leaders of the stars and those whom they lead: six in the east and six in the west, and all following each other in accurately corresponding order: **[4]** also many windows to the right and left of these portals. And first there goes forth the great luminary, named the Sun, and his circumference is like the circumference of the heaven, **[5]** And he is quite filled with illuminating and heating fire. The chariot on which he ascends, the wind drives, and the sun goes down from the heaven and returns through the north in order to reach the east, and is so guided that he comes to the appropriate portal and shines in the face of the heaven. **[6]** In this way he rises in the first month in the great portal, **[7]** Which is the fourth [those six portals in the east]. And in that fourth portal from which the sun rises in the first month are twelve window- openings, from which proceed a flame when they are opened in their season. **[8]** When the sun rises in the heaven, he comes forth through that fourth portal thirty, **[9]** Mornings in succession, and sets accurately in the fourth portal in the west of the heaven. And during this period the day becomes daily longer and the night nightly shorter to the thirtieth morning. **[10]** On that day the day is longer than the night by a ninth part, and the day amounts exactly to ten parts and the night to eight parts. And the sun rises from that fourth portal, and sets in the fourth and returns to the fifth portal of the east thirty mornings, and rises from it and sets in the fifth portal. **[11]** And then the day becomes longer by two parts and amounts to eleven parts, and the night becomes shorter and amounts to seven parts. **[12]** And it returns to the east and enters into the sixth portal, **[13]** And rises and sets in the sixth portal one-and-thirty mornings on account of its sign. **[14]** On that day the day becomes longer than the night, and the day becomes double the night, and the day becomes twelve parts, **[15]** And the night is shortened and becomes six parts. And the sun mounts up to make the day shorter and the night longer, and the sun returns to the east and enters into the sixth portal, **[16]** And rises from it and sets thirty mornings. And when thirty mornings are accomplished, **[17]** The day decreases by exactly one part, and becomes eleven parts, and the night seven. And the sun goes forth from that sixth portal in the west, and goes to the east and rises in the fifth portal for thirty mornings, **[18]** And sets in the west again in the fifth western portal. On that day the day decreases by two parts, and amounts to ten parts and the night to eight parts. **[19]** And the sun goes forth from that fifth portal and sets in the fifth portal of the west, and rises in the fourth portal for one-and-thirty mornings on account of its sign, and sets in the west. **[20]** On that day the day is equalized with the night, and becomes of equal length, and the night amounts to nine parts and the day to nine parts. **[21]** And the sun rises from that portal and sets in the west, and returns to the east and rises thirty mornings in the third portal and sets in the west in the third portal. **[22]** And on that day the night becomes longer than the day, and night becomes longer than day till thhe thirtieth morning, and the night amounts exactly to ten parts and the day to eight parts. **[23]** And the sun rises from that third portal and sets in the third portal in the west and returns to the east, and for thirty mornings rises in the second portal in the east, **[24]** And in like manner sets in the second portal in the west of the heaven. And on that day the night amounts to eleven parts and the day to seven parts. **[25]** And the sun rises on that day from that second portal and sets in the west in the second portal, and returns to the east into the first portal for one and thirty mornings, **[26]** And sets in the first portal in the west of the heaven. And on that day the night becomes longer and amounts to the double of the day: and the night amounts exactly to twelve parts and the day to six. **[27]** And the sun has therewith traversed the divisions of his orbit and turns again on those divisions of his orbit, and enters that portal thirty mornings and sets also in the west opposite to it.

[28] And on that night has the night decreased in length by a ninth part, and the night has become eleven parts and the day seven parts. And the sun has returned and entered into the second portal in the east, and returns on those his divisions of his orbit for thirty mornings, rising and setting. [29] And on that day the night decreases in length, and the night amounts to ten parts and the day to eight. [30] And on that day the sun rises from that portal, and sets in the west, [31] And returns to the east, and rises in the third portal for one-and-thirty mornings, and sets in the west of the heaven. [32] On that day the night decreases and amounts to nine parts, and the day to nine parts, and the night is equal to the day and the year is exactly as to its days three hundred and sixty-four. And the length of the day and of the night, [33] And the shortness of the day and of the night arisethrough the course of the sun these distinctions are made. [34] So it comes that its course becomes daily longer, and its course nightly shorter. [35] And this is the law and the course of the sun, and his return as often as he returns sixty times and rises, i.e. the great luminary which is named the sun, forever and ever. [36] And that which, thus, rises is the great luminary, and is so named according to its appearance, according as the Lord commanded. As he rises, so he sets and decreases not, and rests not, but runs day and night, and his light is sevenfold brighter than that of the moon; but as regards size they are both equal.

CHAPTER 73

[1] And after this law I saw another law dealing with the smaller luminary, which is named the Moon. [2] And her circumference is like the circumference of the heaven, and her chariot in which she rides is driven by the wind, and light is given to her in definite measure. And her rising and setting change every month: [3] And her days are like the days of the sun, and when her light is uniform it amounts to the seventh part of the light of the sun. [4] And thus she rises. And her first phase in the east comes forth on the thirtieth morning: and on that day she becomes visible, and constitutes for you the first phase of the moon on the thirtieth day together with the sun in the portal where the sun rises. [5] And the one half of her goes forth by a seventh part, and her whole circumference is empty, without light, with the exception of one-seventh part of it, and the fourteenth part of her light. [6] And when she receives one-seventh part of the half of her light, her light amounts to one-seventh part and the half thereof. [7] And she sets with the sun, and when the sun rises the moon rises with him and receives the half of one part of light, and in that night in the beginning of her morning in the commencement of the lunar day the moon sets with the sun, [8] And is invisible that night with the fourteen parts and the half of one of them. And she rises on that day with exactly a seventh part, and comes forth and recedes from the rising of the sun, [9] And in her remaining days she becomes bright in the remaining thirteen parts.

CHAPTER 74

[1] And I saw another course, a law for her, (and) how according to that law she performs her monthly revolution. [2] And all these Uriel, the holy angel who is the leader of them all, showed to me, and their positions, and I wrote down their positions as he showed them to me, and I wrote down their months as they were, [3] And the appearance of their lights till fifteen days were accomplished. In single seventh parts she accomplishes all her light in the east, and in single seventh parts accomplishes all her darkness in the west. [4] And in certain months she alters her settings, and in certain months she pursues her own peculiar course. [5] In two months the moon sets with the sun: in those two middle portals the third and the fourth. [6] She goes forth for seven days, and turns about and returns again through the portal where the sun rises, and accomplishes all her light: and she recedes from the sun, and in eight days enters the sixth portal from which the sun goes forth. [7] And when the sun goes forth from the fourth portal she goes forth seven days, until she goes forth from the fifth and turns back again in seven days into the fourth portal and accomplishes all her light: and she recedes and enters into the first portal in eight days. [8] And she returns again in seven days into the fourth portal from which the sun goes forth. [9] Thus I saw their position how the moons rose and the sun set in those days. [10] And if five years are added together the sun has an overplus of thirty days, and all the days which accrue to it for one of those five years, [11] When they are full, amount to 364 days. And the overplus of the sun and of the stars amounts to six days: in 5 years 6 days every year come to 30 days: and the moon falls behind the sun and stars to the number of 30 days. [12] And the sun and the stars bring in all the years exactly, so that they do not advance or delay their position by a single day unto eternity; but complete the years with perfect justice in 364 days. [13] In 3 years there are 1,092 days, and in 5 years 1,820 days, so that in 8 years there are 2,912 days. [14] For the moon alone the days amount in 3 years to 1,062 days, and in 5 years she falls 50 days behind:i.e. to the sum (of 1,770) there is 5 to be added (1,000 and) 62 days. [15] And in 5 years there are 1,770 days, so that for the moon the days 6 in 8 years amount to 21,832 days. [16] For in 8 years she falls behind to the amount of 80 days, all the 17 days she falls behind in 8 years are 80. And the year is accurately completed in conformity with their world stations and the stations of the sun, which rise from the portals through which it the sun rises and sets 30 days.

CHAPTER 75

[1] And the leaders of the heads of the thousands, who are placed over the whole creation and over all the stars, have also to do with the four intercalary days, being inseparable from their office, according to the reckoning of the year, and these render service on the four days which are not reckoned in the reckoning of the year. [2] And owing to them men go wrong therein, for those luminaries truly render service on the world-stations, one in the first portal, one in the third portal of the heaven, one in the fourth portal, and one in the sixth portal, and the exactness of the year is accomplished through its separate three hundred and sixty- four stations. [3] For the signs and the times and the years and the days the angel Uriel showed to me, whom the Lord of glory hath set for ever over all the luminaries of the heaven, in the heaven and in the world, that they should rule on the face of the heaven and be seen on the earth, and be leaders for the day and the night, i.e. the sun, moon, and stars, and all the ministering creatures which make their revolution in all the chariots of the heaven. [4] In like manner twelve doors Uriel showed me, open in the circumference of the suns chariot in the heaven, through which the rays of the sun break forth: and from them is warmth diffused over the earth, when they are opened at their appointed seasons. And for the winds and the spirit of the dew when they are opened, [5] Standing open in the heavens at

the ends. As for the twelve portals in the heaven, at the ends of the earth, out of which go forth the sun, moon, and stars, and all the works of heaven in the east and in the west, [6] There are many windows open to the left and right of them, and one window at its appointed season produces warmth, corresponding as these do to those doors from which the stars come forth according as He has commanded them, and where in they set corresponding to their number. And I saw chariots in the heaven, running in the world, above those portals in which revolve the stars that never set. And one is larger than all the rest, and it is that that makes its course through the entire world.

CHAPTER 76

[1] And at the ends of the earth I saw twelve portals open to all the quarters of the heaven, [2] From which the winds go forth and blow over the earth. Three of them are open on the face of the heavens, and three in the west, and three on the right of the heaven, and three on the left. [3] And the three first are those of the east, and three are of the north, [4] And three after those on the left of the south, and three of the west. Through four of these come winds of blessing and prosperity, and from those eight come hurtful winds: when they are sent, the y bring destruction on all the earth and on the water upon it, and on all who dwell thereon, and on everything which is in the water and on the land. [5] And the first wind from those portals, called the east wind, comes forth through the first portal which is in the east, inclining towards the south: from it come forth desolation, drought, heat, and destruction. [6] And through the second portal in the middle comes what is fitting, and from it there come rain and fruitfulness and prosperity and dew; and through the third portal which lies toward the north come cold and drought. [7] And after these come forth the south winds through three portals: through the first portal of them inclining to the east comes forth a hot wind. [8] And through the middle portal next to it there come forth fragrant smells, [9] And dew and rain, and prosperity and health. And through the third portal lying to the west come forth dew and rain, locusts and desolation. [10] And after these the north winds: from the seventh portal in the east come dew and rain, locusts and desolation. [11] And from the middle portal come in a direct direction health and rain and dew and prosperity; and through the third portal in the west come cloud and hoar-frost, and snow and rain, and dew and locusts. [12] And after thesefour are the west winds: through the first portal adjoining the north come forth dew and hoar- frost, and cold and snow and frost. And from the middle portal come forth dew and rain, and prosperity and blessing; and through the last portal which adjoins the south come forth drought and desolation, and burning and destruction. And the twelve portals of the four quarters of the heaven are therewith completed, and all their laws and all their plagues and all their benefactions have I shown to thee, my son Methuselah.

CHAPTER 77

[1] And the first quarter is called the east, because it is the first: and the second, the south, because the Most High will descend there, yea, there in quite a special sense will He who is blessed for ever descend. [2] And the west quarter is named the diminished, because there all the luminaries of the heaven wane and go down. [3] And the fourth quarter, named the north, is divided into three parts: the first of them is for the dwelling of men: and the second contains seas of water, and the abysses and forests and rivers, and darkness and clouds; and the third part contains the garden of righteousness. [4] I saw seven high mountains, higher than all the mountains which are on the earth: and thence comes forth hoar frost, [5] And days, seasons, and years pass away. I saw seven rivers on the earth larger than all the rivers: one of them coming from the west pours its waters into the Great Sea. [6] And these two come from the north to the sea and pour their waters into the Erythraean Sea in the east. [7] And the remaining, four come forth on the side of the north to their own sea, two of them to the Erythraean Sea, and two into the Great Sea and discharge themselves thereand some say: into the desert. [8] Seven great islands I saw in the sea and in the mainland: two in the mainland and five in the Great Sea.

CHAPTER 78

[1] And the names of the sun are the following: the first Orjares, and the second Tomas. [2] And the moon has four names: the first name is Asonja, the second Ebla, the third Benase, and the fourth Erae. [3] These are the two great luminaries: their circumference is like the circumference of the heaven, and the size of the circumference of both is alike. [4] In the circumference of the sun there are seven portions of light which are added to it more than to the moon, and in definite measures it is s transferred till the seventh portion of the sun is exhausted. [5] And they set and enter the portals of the west, and make their revolution by the north, and come forth through the eastern portals on the face of the heaven. [6] And when the moon rises one- fourteenth part appears in the heaven: [7] The light becomes full in her: on the fourteenth day she accomplishes her light. And fifteen parts of light are transferred to her till the fifteenth day when her light is accomplished, according to the sign of the year, and she becomes fifteen parts, and the moon grows by (the addition of) fourteen parts. [8] And in her waning (the moon) decreases on the first day to fourteen parts of her light, on the second to thirteen parts of light, on the third to twelve, on the fourth to eleven, on the fifth to ten, on the sixth to nine, on the seventh to eight, on the eighth to seven, on the ninth to six, on the tenth to five, on the eleventh to four, on the twelfth to three, on the thirteenth to two, on the fourteenth to the half of a seventh, [9] And all her remaining light disappears wholly on the fifteenth. [10] And in certain months the month has twenty-nine days and once twenty-eight. And Uriel showed me another law: when light is transferred to the moon, and on which side it is transferred to her by the sun. [11] During all the period during which the moon is growing in her light, she is transferring it to herself when opposite to the sun during fourteen daysher light is accomplished in the heaven, [12] And when she is illumined throughout, her light is accomplished full in the heaven. And on the first day she is called the new moon, [13] For on that day the light rises upon her. She becomes full moon exactly on the day when the sun sets in the west, and from the east she rises at night, and the moon shines the whole night through till the sun rises over against her and the moon is seen over against the sun. [14] On the side whence the light of the moon comes forth, there again she wanes till all the light vanishes and all the days of the month are at an end, and her circumference is empty, void of light. [15] And three months she makes of thirty days, and at her time she makes three months of twenty nine days each, in which she accomplishes her waning in the first period of time, [16] And in the first portal for one hundred and seventy-seven days. And in the time of her going out she appears

for three months of thirty days each, and for three months she appears of twentynine each. At night she appears like a man for twenty days each time, and by day she appears like the heaven, and there is nothing else in her save her light.

CHAPTER 79

[1] And now, my son, I have shown thee everything, and the law of all the stars of the heaven is completed. [2] And he showed me all the laws of these for every day, and for every season of bearing rule, and for every year, and for its going forth, and for the order prescribed to it every month and every week: [3] And the waning of the moon which takes place in the sixth portal: for in this sixth portal her light is accomplished, [4] And after that there is the beginning of the waning: And the waning which takes place in the first portal in its season, till one hundred and seventy seven days are accomplished: [5] Reckoned according to weeks, twenty five weeks and two days. She falls behind the sun and the order of the stars exactly five days in the course of one period, [6] And when this place which thou seest has been traversed. Such is the picture and sketch of every luminary which Uriel the archangel, who is their leader, showed unto me.

CHAPTER 80

[1] And in those days the angel Uriel answered and said to me: Behold, I have shown thee everything, Enoch, and I have revealed everything to thee that thou shouldst see this sun and this moon, and the leaders of the stars of the heaven and all those who turn them, their tasks and times and departures. [2] And in the days of the sinners the years shall be shortened, and their seed shall be tardy on their lands and fields, and all things on the earth shall alter, and shall not appear in their time: And the rain shall be kept back and the heaven shall withhold it. [3] And in those times the fruits of the earth shall be backward, and shall not grow in their time, and the fruits of the trees shall be withheld in their time. [4] And the moon shall alter her order, and not appear at her time. [5] And in those days the sun shall be seen and he shall journey in the evening on the extremity of the great chariot in the west and shall shine more brightly than accords with the order of light. [6] And many chiefs of the stars shall transgress the order prescribed. And these shall alter their orbits and tasks, and not appear at the seasons prescribed to them. [7] And the whole order of the stars shall be concealed from the sinners, and the thoughts of those on the earth shall err concerning them, and they shall be altered from all their ways, Yea, they shall err and take them to be gods. [8] And evil shall be multiplied upon them, and punishment shall come upon them So as to destroy all.

CHAPTER 81

[1] And he said unto me: Observe, Enoch, these heavenly tablets, and read what is written thereon, and mark every individual fact. [2] And I observed the heavenly tablets, and read everything whic h was written thereon and understood everything, and read the book of all the deeds of mankind, and of all the children of flesh that shall be upon the earth to the remotest generations. [3] And forthwith I blessed the great Lord the King of glory for ever, in that He has made all the works of the world, and I extolled the Lord because of His patience, and blessed Him because of the children of men. [4] And after that I said: Blessed is the man who dies in righteousness and goodness, Concerning whom there is no book of unrighteousness written, And against whom no day of judgement shall be found. [5] And those seven holy ones brought me and placed me on the earth before the door of my house, and said to me: Declare everything to thy son Methuselah, and show to all thy children that no flesh is righteous in the sight of the Lord, [6] For He is their Creator. One year we will leave thee with thy son, till thou givest thy last commands, that thou mayest teach thy children and record it for them, and testify to all thy children; and in the second year they shall take thee from their midst. [7] Let thy heart be strong, for the good shall announce righteousness to the good; The righteous with the righteous shall rejoice, And shall offer congratulation to one another. [8] But the sinners shall die with the sinners, And the apostate go down with the apostate. [9] And those who practice righteousness shall die on account of the deeds of men, And be taken away on account of the doings of the godless. [10] And in those days they ceased to speak to me, and I came to my people, blessing the Lord of the world.

CHAPTER 82

[1] And now, my son Methuselah, all these things I am recounting to thee and writing down for thee! and I have revealed to thee everything, and given thee books concerning all these: so preserve, my son Methuselah, the books from thy fathers hand, and see that thou deliver them to the generations of the world. [2] I have given Wisdom to thee and to thy children, And thy children that shall be to thee, That they may give it to their children for generations, This wisdom (namely) that passeth their thought. [3] And those who understand it shall not sleep, but shall listen with the ear that they may learn this wisdom, And it shall please those that eat thereof better than good food. [4] Blessed are all the righteous, blessed are all those who walk In the way of righteousness and sin not as the sinners, in the reckoning of all their days in which the sun traverses the heaven, entering into and departing from the portals for thirty days with the heads of thousands of the order of the stars, together with the four which are intercalated which divide the four portions of the year, [5] Which lead them and enter with them four days. Owing to them men shall be at fault and not reckon them in the whole reckoning of the year: yea, men shall be at fault, and not recognize them accurately. [6] For they belong to the reckoning of the year and are truly recorded thereon for ever, one in the first portal and one in the third, and one in the fourth and one in the sixth, and the year is completed in three hundred and sixty-four days. [7] And the account thereof is accurate and the recorded reckoning thereof exact; for the luminaries, and months and festivals, and years and days, has Uriel shown and revealed to me, to whom the Lord of the whole creation of the world hath subjected the host of heaven. [8] And he has power over night and day in the heaven to cause the light to give light to men -sun, moon, and stars, [9] And all the powers of the heaven which revolve in their circular chariots. And these are the orders of the stars, which set in their places, and in their seasons and festivals and months. [10] And these are the names of those who lead them, who watch that they enter at their times, in their orders, in their seasons, in their months, in their periods of dominion, and in their positions. Their four leaders who divide the four parts of the year enter first; and after them the twelve leaders of the orders who divide the

months; [11] And for the three hundred and sixty (days) there are heads over thousands who divide the days; and for the four intercalary days there are the leaders which sunder the four parts of the year. [12] And these heads over thousands are intercalated between leader and leader, each behind a station, but their leaders make the division. [13] And these are the names of the leaders who divide the four parts of the year which are ordained: Milkiel, Helemmelek, and Melejal, and Narel. [14] And the names of those who lead them: Ad narel, and Ijasusael, and Elomeelthese three follow the leaders of the orders, [15] And there is one that follows the three leaders of the orders which follow those leaders of stations that divide the four parts of the year. In the beginning of the year Melkejal rises first and rules, who is named Tamaini and sun, [16] And all the days of his dominion whilst he bears rule are ninety-one days. And these are the signs of the days which are to be seen on earth in the days of his dominion: sweat, and heat, and calms; and all the trees bear fruit, and leaves are produced on all the trees, and the harvest of wheat, and the rose- flowers, and all the flowers which come forth in the field, [17] But the trees of the winter season become withered. And these are the names of the leaders which are under them: Berkael, Zelebsel, and another who is added a head of a thousand, called Hilujaseph: and the days of the dominion of this leader are at an end. [18] The next leader after him is Helemmelek, whom one names the shining sun, and all the days of his light are ninety-one days. [19] And these are the signs of (his) days on the earth: glowing heat and dryness, and the trees ripen their fruits and produce all their fruits ripe and ready, and the sheep pair and become pregnant, and all the fruits of the earth are gathered in, and everything that is in the fields, [20] And the winepress: these things take place in the days of his dominion. These are the names, and the orders, and the leaders of those heads of thousands: Gidaljal, Keel, and Heel, and the name of the head of a thousand which is added to them, Asfael: and the days of his dominion are at an end.

The Book Of Dream And Vision

First Dream and Vision

CHAPTER 83
[1] And now, my son Methuselah, I will show thee all my visions which I have seen, recounting them before thee. [2] Two visions I saw before I took a wife, and the one was quite unlike the other: the first when I was learning to write: the second before I took thy mother, when I saw a terrible vision. [3] And regarding them I prayed to the Lord. I had laid me down in the house of my grandfather Mahalalel, when I saw in a vision how the heaven collapsed and was borne off and fell to the earth. [4] And when it fell to the earth I saw how the earth was swallowed up in a great abyss, and mountains were suspended on mountains, and hills sank down on hills, and high trees were rent from their stems, [5] And hurled down and sunk in the abyss. And thereupon a word fell into my mouth, [6] And I lifted up my voice to cry aloud, and said: The earth is destroyed. And my grandfather Mahalalel waked me as I lay near him, and said unto me: Why dost thou cry so, my son, [7] And why dost thou make such lamentation? And I recounted to him the whole vision which I had seen, and he said unto me: A terrible thing hast thou seen, my son, and of grave moment is thy dream- vision as to the secrets if all the sin of the earth: it must sink into the abyss and be destroyed with a great destruction. [8] And now, my son, arise and make petition to the Lord of glory, since thou art a believer, that a remnant may remain on the earth, and that He may not destroy the whole earth. [9] My son, from heaven all this will come upon the earth, and upon the earth there will be great destruction. [10] After that I arose and prayed and implored and besought, and wrote down my prayer for the generations of the world, and I will show everything to thee, my son Methuselah. And when I had gone forth below and seen the heaven, and the sun rising in the east, and the moon setting in the west, and a few stars, and the whole earth, and everything as He had known it in the beginning, then I blessed the Lord of judgement and extolled Him because He had made the sun to go forth from the windows of the east, and he ascended and rose on the face of the heaven, and set out and kept traversing the path shown unto him.

CHAPTER 84
[1] And I lifted up my hands in righteousness and blessed the Holy and Great One, and spake with the breath of my mouth, and with the tongue of flesh, which God has made for the children of the flesh of men, that they should speak therewith, and He gave them breath and a tongue and a mouth that they should speak therewith: [2] Blessed be Thou, O Lord, King, Great and mighty in Thy greatness, Lord of the whole creation of the heaven, King of kings and God of the whole world. And Thy power and kingship and greatness abide for ever and ever, And throughout all generations Thy dominion; And all the heavens are Thy throne for ever, And the whole earth Thy footstool for ever and ever. [3] For Thou hast made and Thou rule st all things, And nothing is too hard for Thee, Wisdom departs not from the place of Thy throne, Nor turns away from Thy presence. And Thou knowest and seest and hearest everything, And there is nothing hidden from Theefor Thou seest everything. [4] And now the angels of Thy heavens are guilty of trespass, And upon the flesh of men abideth Thy wrath until the great day of judgement. [5] And now, O God and Lord and Great King, I implore and beseech Thee to fulfil my prayer, To leave me a posterity on earth, And not destroy all the flesh of man, And make the earth without inhabitant, So that there should be an eternal destruction. And now, my Lord, destroy from the earth the flesh which has aroused Thy wrath, But the flesh of righteousness and uprightness establish as aplant of the eternal seed, And hide not Thy face from the prayer of Thy servant, O Lord.

The Second Dream and Vision

CHAPTER 85
[1] And after this I saw another dream, and I will show the whole dream to thee, my son. [2] And Enoch lifted up his voice and spake to his son Methuselah: To thee, my son, will I speak: hear my words- incline thine ear to the dream- vision of thy father. [3] Before I took thy mother Edna, I saw in a vision on my bed, and behold a bull came forth from the earth, and that bull was white; and after it came forth a heifer, and along with this latter came forth two bulls, one of them black

and the other red. [4] And that black bull gored the red one and pursued him over the earth, and thereupon I could no longer see that red bull. [5] But that black bull grew and that heifer went with him, and I saw that many oxen proceeded from him which resembled and followed him. [6] And that cow, that first one, went from the presence of that first bull in order to seek that red one, but found him not, [7] And lamented with a great lamentation over him and sought him. And I looked till that first bull came to her and quieted her, [8] And from that time onward she cried no more. And after that she bore another white bull, and after him she bore many bulls and black cows. [9] And I saw in my sleep that white bull likewise grow and become a great white bull, and from Him proceeded many white bulls, and they resembled him. And they began to beget many white bulls, which resembled them, one following the other, even many.

CHAPTER 86

[1] And again I saw with mine eyes as I slept, and I saw the heaven above, and behold a star fell from heaven, and it arose and eat and pastured amongst those oxen. [2] And after that I saw the large and the black oxen, and behold they all changed their stalls and pastures and their cattle, and began to live with each other. [3] And again I saw in the vision, and looked towards the heaven, and behold I saw many stars descend and cast themselves down from heaven to that first star, and they became bulls amongst those cattle and pastured with themamongst them. [4] And I looked at them and saw, and behold they all let out their privy members, like horses, and began to cover the cows of the oxen, and they all became pregnant and bare elephants, camels, and asses. [5] And all the oxen feared them and were affrighted at them, and began to bite with their teeth and to devour, and to gore with their horns. [6] And they began, moreover, to devour those oxen; and behold all the children of the earth began to tremble and quake before them and to flee from them.

CHAPTER 87

[1] And again I saw how they began to gore each other and to devour each other, and the earth began to cry aloud. [2] And I raised mine eyes again to heaven, and I saw in the vision, and behold there came forth from heaven beings who were like white men: and four went forth from that place and three with them. [3] And those three that had last come forth grasped me by my hand and took me up, away from the generations of the earth, and raised me up to a lofty place, and showed me a tower raised high above the earth, and all the hills were lower. [4] And one said unto me: Remain here till thou seest everything that befalls those elephants, camels, and asses, and the stars and the oxen, and all of them.

CHAPTER 88

[1] And I saw one of those four who had come forth first, and he seized that first star which had fallen from the heaven, and bound it hand and foot and cast it into an abyss: now that abyss was narrow and deep, [2] And horrible and dark. And one of them drew a sword, and gave it to those elephants and camels and asses: then they began to smite each other, and the whole earth quaked because of them. [3] And as I was beholding in the vision, lo, one of those four who had come forth stoned (them) from heaven, and gathered and took all the great stars whose privy members were like those of horses, and bound them all hand and foot, and cast them in an abyss of the earth.

CHAPTER 89

[1] And one of those four went to that white bull and instructed him in a secret, without his being terrified: he was born a bull and became a man, and built for himself a great vessel and dwelt thereon; [2] And three bulls dwelt with him in that vessel and they were covered in. And again I raised mine eyes towards heaven and saw a lofty roof, with seven water torrents thereon, and those torrents flowed with much water into an enclosure. [3] And I saw again, and behold fountains were opened on the surface of that great enclosure, and that water began to swell and rise upon the surface, [4] And I saw that enclosure till all its surface was covered with water. And the water, the darkness, and mist increased upon it; and as I looked at the height of that water, that water had risen above the height of that enclosure, and was streaming over that enclosure, and it stood upon the earth. [5] And all the cattle of that enclosure were gathered together until I saw how they sank and were swallowed up and perished in that water. [6] But that vessel floated on the water, while all the oxen and elephants and camels and asses sank to the bottom with all the animals, so that I could no longer see them, [7] And they were not able to escape, but perished and sank into the depths. And again I saw in the vision till those water torrents were removed from that high roof, and the chasms of the earth were leveled up and other abysses were opened. [8] Then the water began to run down into these, till the earth became visible; but that vessel settled on the earth, and the darkness retired and light appeared. [9] But that white bull which had become a man came out of that vessel, and the three bulls with him, and one of those three was white like that bull, and one of them was red as blood, and one black: and that white bull departed from them. [10] And they began to bring forth beasts of the field and birds, so that there arose different genera: lions, tigers, wolves, dogs, hyenas, wild boars, foxes, squirrels, swine, falcons, vultures, kites, eagles, and ravens; [11] And among them was born a white bull. And they began to bite one another; but that white bull which was born amongst them begat a wild ass and a white bull with it, [12] And the wild asses multiplied. But that bull which was born from him begat a black wild boar and a white sheep; [13] And the former begat many boars, but that sheep begat twelve sheep. And when those twelve sheep had grown, they gave up one of them to the asses, and those asses again gave up that sheep to the wolves, [14] And that sheep grew up among the wolves. And the Lord brought the eleven sheep to live with it and to pasture with it among the wolves: and they multiplied and became many flocks of sheep. [15] And the wolves began to fear them, and they oppressed them until they destroyed cry aloud on account of their little ones, [16] And to complain unto their Lord. And a sheep which had been saved from the wolves fled and escaped to the wild asses; and I saw the sheep how they lamented and cried, and besought their Lord with all their might, till that Lord of the sheep descended at the voice of the sheep from a lofty abode, and came to them and pastured them. [17] And He called that sheep which had escaped the wolves, and spake with it concerning the wolves that it should admonish them not to touch the sheep. [18] And the sheep went to the wolves according to the word of the Lord, and another sheep met it and went with it, and the two went and entered together into the assembly of those wolves, and spake with them and admonished

them not to touch the sheep from henceforth. [19]   And thereupon I saw the wolves, and how they oppressed the sheep exceedingly with all their power; and the sheep cried aloud. And the Lord came to the sheep and they began to smite those wolves: [20]   And the wolves began to make lamentation; but the sheep became quiet and forthwith ceased to cry out. [21]   And I saw the sheep till they departed from amongst the wolves; but the eyes of the wolves were blinded, and those wolves departed in pursuit of the sheep with all their power. [22]   And the Lord of the sheep went with them, as their leader, and all His sheep followed Him: [23]   And his face was dazzling and glorious and terrible to behold. But the wolves began to pursue those sheep till they reached a sea of water. [24]   And that sea was divided, and the water stood on this side and on that before their face, and their Lord led them and placed Himself between them and the wolves. [25]   And as those wolves did not yet see the sheep, they proceeded into the midst of that sea, and the wolves followed the sheep, and those wolves ran after them into that sea. [26]   And when they saw the Lord of the sheep, they turned to flee before His face, but that sea gathered itself together, and became as it had been created, and the water swelled and rose till it covered those wolves. [27]   And I saw till all the wolves who pursued those sheep perished and were drowned. [28]   But the sheep escaped from that water and went forth into a wilderness, where there was no water and no grass; and they began to open their eyes and to see; and I saw the Lord of the sheep pasturing them and giving them water and grass, [28]   And that sheep going and leading them. And that sheep ascended to the summit of that lofty rock, and the Lord of the sheep sent it to them. [29]   And after that I saw the Lord of the sheep who stood before them, and His appearance was great and terrible and majestic, [30]   And all those sheep saw Him and were afraid before His face. And they all feared and trembled because of Him, and they cried to that sheep with them which was amongst them: [31]   We are not able to stand before our Lord or to behold Him. And that sheep which led them again ascended to the summit of that rock, but the sheep began to be blinded and to wander from the way which he had showed them, but that sheep wot not thereof. [32]   And the Lord of the sheep was wrathful exceedingly against them, and that sheep discovered it, and went down from the summit of the rock, and came to the sheep, and found the greatest part of them blinded and fallen away. [33]   And when they saw it they feared and trembled at its presence, and desired to return to their folds. [34]   And that sheep took other sheep with it, and came to those sheep which had fallen away, and began to slay them; and the sheep feared its presence, and thus that sheep brought back those sheep that had fallen away, and they returned to their folds. [35]   And I saw in this vision till that sheep became a man and built a house for the Lord of the sheep, and placed all the sheep in that house. And I saw till this sheep which had met that sheep which led them fell asleep: and I saw till all the great sheep perished and little ones arose in their place, and they came to a pasture, and approached a stream of water. [36]   Then that sheep, their leader which had become a man, withdrew from them and fell asleep, [37]   And all the sheep sought it and cried over it with a great crying. [38]   And I saw till they left off crying for that sheep and crossed that stream of water, and there arose the two sheep as leaders in the place of those which had led them and fallen asleep. [39]   And I saw till the sheep came to a goodly place, and a pleasant and glorious land, and I saw till those sheep were satisfied; and that house stood amongst them in the pleasant land. [40]   And sometimes their eyes were opened, and sometimes blinded, till another sheep arose and led them and brought them all back, and their eyes were opened. [41]   And the dogs and the foxes and the wild boars began to devour those sheep till the Lord of the sheep raised up another sheep a ram from their midst, which led them. And that ram began to butt on either side those dogs, foxes, and wild boars till he had destroyed them all. And that sheep whose eyes were opened saw that ram, which was amongst the sheep, till it forsook its glory and began to butt those sheep, and trampled upon the m, and behaved itself unseemly. [42]   And the Lord of the sheep sent the lamb to another lamb and raised it to being a ram and leader of the sheep instead of that ram which had forsaken its glory. [43]   And it went to it and spake to it alone, and raised it to being a ram, [44]   And made it the prince and leader of the sheep; but during all these things those dogs oppressed the sheep. [45]   And the first ram pursued that second ram, and that second ram arose and fled before it; and I saw till those dogs pulled down the first ram. [46]   And that second ram arose and led the little sheep. [47]   And those sheep grew and multiplied; but all the dogs, and foxes, and wild boars feared and fled before it, and that ram butted and killed the wild beasts, and those wild beasts had no longer any power among the sheep and robbed them no more of ought. [48]   And that ram begat many sheep and fell asleep; and a little sheep became ram in its stead, and became prince and leader of those sheep, [49]   And that house became great and broad, and it was built for those sheep: and a tower lofty and great was built on the house for the Lord of the sheep, and that house was low, but the tower was elevated and lofty, and the Lord of the sheep stood on that tower and they offered a full table before Him. [50]   And again I saw those sheep that they again erred and went many ways, and forsook that their house, and the Lord of the sheep called some from amongst the sheep and sent them to the sheep, [51]   But the sheep began to slay them. And one of them was saved and was not slain, and it sped away and cried aloud over the sheep; and they sought to slay it, but the Lord of the sheep saved it from the sheep, and brought it up to me, and caused it to dwell there. [52]   And many other sheep He sent to those sheep to testify unto them and lament over them. [53]   And after that I saw that when they forsook the house of the Lord and His tower they fell away entirely, and their eyes were blinded; and I saw the Lord of the sheep how He wrought much slaughter amongst them in their herds until those sheep invited that slaughter and betrayed His place. [54]   And He gave them over into the hands of the lions and tigers, and wolves and hyenas, and into the hand of the foxes, and to all the wild beasts, [55]   And those wild beasts began to tear in pieces those sheep. And I saw that He forsook that their house and their tower and gave them all into the hand of the lions, to tear and devour them, [56]   Into the hand of all the wild beasts. And I began to cry aloud with all my power, and to appeal to the Lord of the sheep, and to represent to Him in regard to the sheep that they were devoured by all the wild beasts. [57]   But He remained unmoved, though He saw it, and rejoiced that they were devoured and swallowed and robbed, and left them to be devoured in the hand of all the beasts. [58]   And He called seventy shepherds, and cast those sheep to them that they might pasture them, and He spake to the shepherds and their companions: Let each individual of you pasture the sheep henceforward, [59]   And everything that I shall command you that do ye. And I will deliver them over unto you duly numbered, and tell you which of them are to be destroyed-and them destroy ye. [60]   And He gave over unto them those sheep. And He called another and spake unto him: Observe and mark everything that the shepherds will do to those sheep; for they will destroy more of them than I have commanded them. [61]   And every excess and the destruction which will be wrought through the shepherds, record namely how many they destroy according to my command, and how many according to their own caprice: record against every individual shepherd all the destruction he effects. [62] And read out before me by number how many they destroy, and how many they deliver over for destruction, that I may have this as a testimony against them, and know every deed of the shepherds, that I may comprehend and see what they do, whether or not they abide by my command which I have commanded them. [63] But they shall not know it, and thou shalt not declare it to them, [64] Nor admonish them, but only record against each individual all the destruction which the shepherds effect each in his time and lay it all before me. And I saw till those shepherds pastured in their season, and they began to slay and to destroy more than they were bidden, and they delivered those sheep into the hand of the lions. [65] And the lions and tigers eat and devoured the greater part of those sheep, and the wild boars eat along with them; and they burnt that tower and demolished that house. [66] And I became exceedingly sorrowful over that tower because that house of the sheep was demolished, and afterwards I was unable to see if those sheep entered that house. [67] And the shepherds and their associates delivered over those sheep to all the wild beasts, to devour them, and each one of them received in his time a definite number: it was written by the other in a book how many each one of them destroyed of them. [68] And each one slew and destroyed many more than was prescribed; [69] And I began to weep and lament on account of those sheep. And thus in the vision I saw that one who wrote, how he wrote down every one that was destroyed by those shepherds, day by day, and carried up and laid down and showed actually the whole book to the Lord of the sheep-(even) everything that they had done, and all that each one of them had made away with, [70] And all that they had given over to destruction. And the book was read before the Lord of the sheep, and He took the book from his hand and read it and sealed it and laid it down. [71] And forthwith I saw how the shepherds pastured for twelve hours, and behold three of those sheep turned back and came and entered and began to build up all that had fallen down of that house; [72] But the wild boars tried to hinder them, but they were not able. And they began again to build as before, and they reared up that tower, and it was named the high tower; and they began again to place a table before the tower, but all the bread on it was polluted and not pure. [73] And as touching all this the eyes of those sheep were blinded so that they saw not, and the eyes of their shepherds likewise; and they delivered them in large numbers to their shepherds for destruction, [74] And they trampled the sheep with their feet and devoured them. And the Lord of the sheep remained unmoved till all the sheep were dispersed over the field and mingled with them the beasts, [75] And they the shepherds did not save them out of the hand of the beasts. And this one who wrote the book carried it up, and showed it and read it before the Lord of the sheep, and implored Him on their account, and besought Him on their account as he showed Him all the doings of the shepherds, [76] And gave testimony before Him against all the shepherds. And he took the actual book and laid it down beside Him and departed.

CHAPTER 90

[1] And I saw till that in this manner thirty- five shepherds undertook the pasturing of the sheep, and they severally completed their periods as did the first; and others receive them into their hands, [2] To pasture them for their period, each shepherd in his own period. And after that I saw in my vision all the birds of heaven coming, the eagles, the vultures, the kites, the ravens; but the eagles led all the birds; and they began to devour those sheep, and to pick out their eyes and to devour their flesh. [3] And the sheep cried out because their flesh was being devoured by the birds, [4] And as for me I looked and lamented in my sleep over that shepherd who pastured the sheep. And I saw until those sheep were devo ured by the dogs and eagles and kites, and they left neither flesh nor skin nor sinew remaining on them till only their bones stood there: and their bones too fell to the earth and the sheep became few. [5] And I saw until that twenty-three had undertaken the pasturing and completed in their several periods fifty-eight times. [6] But behold lambs were borne by those white sheep, and they began to open their eyes and to see, [7] And to cry to the sheep. Yea, they cried to them, but they did not hearken to what they said to them, [8] But were exceedingly deaf, and their eyes were very exceedingly blinded. And I saw in the vision how the ravens flew upon those lambs and took one of those lambs, and dashed the sheep in pieces and devoured them. [9] And I saw till horns grew upon those lambs, and the ravens cast down their horns; and I saw till there sprouted a great horn of one of those sheep, and their eyes were opened. [10] And it looked at the mand their eyes opened, and it cried to the sheep, [11] And the rams saw it and all ran to it. [12] And notwithstanding all this those eagles and vultures and ravens, [13] And kites still kept tearing the sheep and swooping down upon them and devouring them: [14] Still the sheep remained silent, but the rams lamented and cried out. [15] And those ravens fought and battled with it and sought to lay low its horn, but they had no power over it. [16] All the eagles and vultures and ravens and kites were gathered together, [17] And there came with them all the sheep of the field, [18] Yea, they all came together, and helped each other to break that horn of the ram. [19] And I saw till a great sword was given to the sheep, and the sheep proceeded against all the beasts of the field to slay them, and all the beasts and the birds of the heaven fled before their face. And I saw that man, who wrote the book according to the command of the Lord, till he opened that book concerning the destruction which those twelve last shepherds had wrought, and showed that they had destroyed much more than their predecessors, before the Lord of the sheep. And I saw till the Lord of the sheep came unto them and took in His hand the staff of His wrath, and smote the earth, and the earth clave asunder, and all the beasts and all the birds of the heaven fell from among those sheep, and were swallowed up in the earth and it covered them. [20] And I saw till a throne was erected in the pleasant land, and the Lord of the sheep sat Himself thereon, and the other took the sealed books and opened those books before the Lord of the sheep. [21] And the Lord called those men the seven first white ones, and commanded that they should bring before Him, beginning with the first star which led the way, all the stars whose privy members were like those of horses, [22] And they brought them all before Him. And He said to that man who wrote before Him, being one of those seven white ones, and said unto him: Take those seventy shepherds to whom I delivered the sheep, and who taking them on their own authority slew more than I commanded them. [23] And behold they were all bound, I saw, and they all stood before Him. [24] And the judgement was held first over the stars, and they were judged and found guilty, and went to the place of condemnation, and they were cast into an abyss, full of fire and flaming, and full of pillars of fire. [25] And those seventy shepherds were judged and found guilty, and they were cast into that fiery abyss. [26] And I saw at that time how a like abyss was opened in the midst of the earth, full of fire, and they brought those blinded sheep, and

they were all judged and found guilty, **[27]** And cast into this fiery abyss, and they burned; now this abyss was to the right of that house. And I saw those sheep burning and their bones burning. **[28]** And I stood up to see till they folded up that old house; and carried off all the pillars, and all the beams and ornaments of the house were at the same time folded up with it, and they carried it off and laid it in a place in the south of the land. **[29]** And I saw till the Lord of the sheep brought a new house greater and loftier than that first, and set it up in the place of the first which had been folded up: all its pillars were new, and its ornaments were new and larger than those of the first, the old one which He had taken away, and all the sheep were within it. **[30]** And I saw all the sheep which had been left, and all the beasts on the earth, and all the birds of the heaven, falling down and doing homage to those sheep and making petition to and obeying them in every thing. **[31]** And thereafter those three who were clothed in white and had seized me by my hand who had taken me up before, and the hand of that ram also seizing hold of me, **[32]** They took me up and set me down in the midst of those sheep before the judgement took place. And those sheep were all white, **[33]** And their wool was abundant and clean. And all that had been destroyed and dispersed, and all the beasts of the field, and all the birds of the heaven, assembled in that house, and the Lord of the sheep rejoiced with great joy because they were all good and had returned to His house. **[34]** And I saw till they laid down that sword, which had been given to the sheep, and they brought it back into the house, and it was sealed before the presence of the Lord, and all the sheep were invited into that house, **[35]** But it held them not. And the eyes of them all were opened, and they saw the good, **[36]** And there was not one among them that did not see. And I saw that that house was large and broad and very full. **[37]** And I saw that a white bull was born, with large horns and all the beasts of the field and all the birds of the air feared him and made petition to him all the time of and I saw till all their generations were transformed, **[38]** And they all became white bulls; and the first among them became a lamb, and that lamb became a great animal and had great black horns on its head; and the Lord of the sheep rejoiced over it and over all the oxen. **[39]** And I slept in their midst: and I awoke and saw everything. **[40]** This is the vision which I saw while I slept, and I awoke and blessed the Lord of righteousness and gave Him glory. **[41]** Then I wept with a great weeping and my tears stayed not till I could no longer endure it: when I saw, they flowed on account of what I had seen; for everything shall come and be fulfilled, **[42]** And all the deeds of men in their order were shown to me. On that night I remembered the first dream, and because of it I wept and was troubled-because I had seen that vision.

The Concluding Part of Enoch's Book

CHAPTER 91
[1] And now, my son Methuselah, call to me all thy brothers and gather together to me all the sons of thy mother; For the word calls me, And the spirit is poured out upon me, That I may show you everything that shall befall you for ever. **[2]** And there upon Methuselah went and summoned to him all his brothers and assembled his relatives. **[3]** And he spake unto all the children of righteousness and said: Hear, ye sons of Enoch, all the words of your father, And hearken aright to the voice of my mouth; For I exhort you and say unto you, beloved: **[4]** Love uprightness and walk therein. And draw not nigh to uprightness with a double heart, And associate not with those of a double heart, But walk in righteousness, my sons. And it shall guide you on good paths, And righteousness shall be your companion. **[5]** For I know that violence must increase on the earth, And a great chastisement be executed on the earth, And all unrighteousness come to an end: Yea, it shall be cut off from its roots, And its whole structure be destroyed. **[6]** And unrighteousness shall again be consummated on the earth, And all the deeds of unrighteousness and of violence and transgression shall prevail in a twofold degree. **[7]** And when sin and unrighteousness and blasphemy and violence in all kinds of deeds increase, and apostasy and transgression and uncleanness increase, a great chastisement shall come from heaven upon all these, and the holy Lord will come forth with wrath and chastisement to execute judgement on earth. **[8]** In those days violence shall be cut off from its roots, and the roots of unrighteousness together with deceit, and they shall be destroyed from under heaven. **[9]** And all the idols of the heathen shall be abandoned, and the temples burned with fire, And they shall remove them from the whole earth, And they the heathen shall be cast into the judgement of fire, And shall perish in wrath and in grievous judgement for ever. **[10]** And the righteous shall arise from their sleep, and wisdom shall arise and be given unto them. **[11]** And after that the roots of unrighteousness shall be cut off, and the sinners shall be destroyed by the sword and the blasphemers destroyed in every place, **[12]** And those who plan violence and those who commit blasphemy shall perish by the sword. **[13]** And now I tell you, my sons, and show you the paths of righteousness and the paths of violence. Yea, I will show them to you again that ye may know what will come to pass. **[14]** And now, hearken unto me, my sons, and walk in the paths of righteousness, and walk not in the paths of violence; For all who walk in the paths of unrighteousness shall perish for ever.

CHAPTER 92
[1] The book written by Enoch indeed wrote this complete doctrine of wisdom, which is praised of all men and a judge of all the earth for all my children who shall dwell on the earth. And for the future generations who shall observe uprightness and peace. **[2]** Let not your spirit be troubled on account of the times; For the Holy and Great One has appointed days for all things. **[3]** And the righteous one shall arise from sleep, shall arise and walk in the paths of righteousness, And all his path and conversation shall be in eternal goodness and grace. **[4]** He will be gracious to the righteous and give him eternal uprightness, And He will give him power so that he shall be endowed with goodness and righteousness. And he shall walk in eternal light. **[5]** And sin shall perish in darkness for ever, And shall no more be seen from that day for evermore.

CHAPTER 93
[1] And after that Enoch both gave and began to recount from the books. And Enoch said: Concerning the children of righteousness and concerning the elect of the world, And concerning the plant of uprightness, I will speak these things, Yea, I Enoch will declare (them) unto you, my sons: According to that which appeared to me in the heavenly vision, **[2]**

And which I have known through the word of the holy angels, And have learnt from the heavenly tablets. [3] And Enoch began to recount from the books and said: I was born the seventh in the first week, while judgement and righteousness still endured. [4] And after me there shall arise in the second week great wickedness, And deceit shall have sprung up; And in it there shall be the first end. And in it a man shall be saved; And after it is ended unrighteousness shall grow up, [5] And a law shall be made for the sinners. And after that in the third week at its close a man shall be elected as the plant of righteous judgement, And his posterity shall become the plant of righteousness for evermore. [6] And after that in the fourth week, at its close, Visions of the holy and righteous shall be seen, And a law for all generations and an enclosure shall be made for them. And after that in the fifth week, at its close, The house of glory and dominion shall be built for ever. [7] And after that in the sixth week all who live in it shall be blinded, And the hearts of all of them shall godlessly forsake wisdom. And in it a man shall ascend; [8] And at its close the house of dominion shall be burnt with fire, And the whole race of the chosen root shall be dispersed. [9] And after that in the seventh week shall an apostate generation arise, And many shall be its deeds, And all its deeds shall be apostate. [10] And at its close shall be elected the elect righteous of the eternal plant of righteousness, to receive sevenfold instruction concerning all His creation. [11] For who is there of all the children of men that is able to hear the voice of the Holy One without being troubled? And who can think His thoughts? and who is there that can behold all the works of heaven? [12] And how should there be one who could behold the heaven, and who is there that could understand the things of heaven and see a soul or a spirit and could tell thereof, or ascend and see all their ends and think them or do like them? [13] And who is there of all men that could know what is the breadth and the length of the earth, and to whom has been shown the measure of all of them? Or is there any one who could discern the length of the heaven and how great is its height, [14] and upon what it is founded, and how great is the number of the stars, and where all the luminaries rest?

CHAPTER 94

[1] And now I say unto you, my sons, love righteousness and walk therein; For the paths of righteousness are worthy of acceptation, but the paths of unrighteousness shall suddenly be destroyed and vanish. [2] And to certain men of a generation shall the paths of violence and of death be revealed, And they shall hold themselves afar from them, And shall not follow them. [3] And now I say unto you the righteous: Walk not in the paths of wickedness, nor in the paths of death, And draw not nigh to them, lest ye be destroyed. [4] But seek and choose for yourselves righteousness and an elect life, And walk in the paths of peace, And ye shall live and prosper. [5] And hold fast my words in the thoughts of your hearts, And suffer them not to be effaced from your hearts; For I know that sinners will tempt men to evilly-entreat wisdom, So that no place may be found for her, And no manner of temptation may minish. [6] Woe to those who build unrighteousness and oppression and lay deceit as a foundation; For they shall be suddenly overthrown, And they shall have no peace. [7] Woe to those who build their houses with sin; For from all their foundations shall they be overthrown, And by the sword shall they fall. And those who acquire gold and silver in judgement suddenly shall perish. [8] Woe to you, ye rich, for ye have trusted in your riches, And from your riches shall ye depart, Because ye have not remembered the Most High in the days of your riches. [9] Ye have committed blasphemy and unrighteousness, And have become ready for the day of slaughter, And the day of darkness and the day of the great judgement. [10] Thus I speak and declare unto you: He who hath created you will overthrow you, And for your fall there shall be no compassion, And your Creator will rejoice at your destruction. [11] And your righteous ones in those days shall be a reproach to the sinners and the godless.

CHAPTER 95

[1] Oh that mine eyes were a cloud of waters that I might weep over you, And pour down my tears as a cloud of waters: That so I might rest from my trouble of heart! [2] Who has permitted you to practice reproaches and wickedness? And so judgement shall overtake you, sinners. [3] Fear not the sinners, ye righteous; For again will the Lord deliver them into your hands, that ye may execute judgement upon them according to your desires. [4] Woe to you who fulminate anathemas which cannot be reversed: Healing shall therefore be far from you because of your sins. [5] Woe to you who requite your neighbour with evil; For ye shall be requited according to your works. [6] Woe to you, lying witnesses, And to those who weigh out injustice, For suddenly shall ye perish. [7] Woe to you, sinners, for ye persecute the righteous; For ye shall be delivered up and persecuted because of injustice, And heavy shall its yoke be upon you.

CHAPTER 96

[1] Be hopeful, ye righteous; for suddenly shall the sinners perish before you, And ye shall have lordship over them according to your desires. And in the day of the tribulation of the sinners, Your children shall mount and rise as eagles, And higher than the vultures will be your nest, And ye shall ascend and enter the crevices of the earth, And the clefts of the rock for ever as coneys before the unrighteous, And the sirens shall sigh because of you-and weep wherefore fear not, ye that have suffered; [2] For healing shall be your portion, And a bright light shall enlighten you, And the voice of rest ye shall hear from heaven. [3] Woe unto you, ye sinners, for your riches make you appear like the righteous, But your hearts convict you of being sinners, And this fact shall be a testimony against you for a memorial of (your) evil deeds. [4] Woe to you who devour the finest of the wheat, And drink wine in large bowls, And tread under foot the lowly with your might. [5] Woe to you who drink water from every fountain, For suddenly shall ye be consumed and wither away, Because ye have forsaken the fountain of life. [6] Woe to you who work unrighteousness and deceit and blasphemy: It shall be a memorial against you for evil. [7] Woe to you, ye mighty, Who with might oppress the righteous; For the day of your destruction is coming. In those days many and good days shall come to the righteous- in the day of your judgement.

CHAPTER 97

[1] Believe, ye righteous, that the sinners will become a shame and perish in the day of unrighteousness. [2] Be it known unto you (ye sinners) that the Most High is mindful of your destruction, And the angels of heaven rejoice over your destruction. [3] What will ye do, ye sinners, And whither will ye flee on that day of judgement, when ye hear the voice of

the prayer of the righteous? [4] Yea, ye shall fare like unto them, against whom this word shall be a testimony: " Ye have been companions of sinners." [5] And in those days the prayer of the righteous shall reach unto the Lord, And for you the days of your judgement shall come. [6] And all the words of your unrighteousness shall be read out before the Great Holy One, And your faces shall be covered with shame, And He will reject every work which is grounded on unrighteousness. [7] Woe to you, ye sinners, who live on the mid ocean and on the dry land, Whose remembrance is evil against you. [8] Woe to you who acquire silver and gold in unrighteousness and say: " We have become rich with riches and have possessions; And have acquired everything we have desired. [9] And now let us do what we purposed: For we have gathered silver, And many are the husbandmen in our houses." And our granaries are (brim) full as with water, Yea and like water your lies shall flow away; For your riches shall not abide but speedily ascend from you; For ye have acquired it all in unrighteousness, And ye shall be given over to a great curse.

CHAPTER 98

[1] And now I swear unto you, to the wise and to the foolish, For ye shall have manifold experiences on the earth. [2] For ye men shall put on more adornments than a woman, And coloured garments more than a virgin: In royalty and in grandeur and in power, And in silver and in gold and in purple, And in splendour and in food they shall be poured out as water. [3] Therefore they shall be wanting in doctrine and wisdom, And they shall perish thereby together with their possessions; And with all their glory and their splendour, And in shame and in slaughter and in great destitution, Their spirits shall be cast into the furnace of fire. [4] I have sworn unto you, ye sinners, as a mountain has not become a slave, And a hill does not become the handmaid of a woman, Even so sin has not been sent upon the earth, But man of himself has created it, And under a great curse shall they fall who commit it. [5] And barrenness has not been given to the woman, but on account of the deeds of her own hands she dies without children. [6] I have sworn unto you, ye sinners, by the Holy Great One, that all your evil deeds are revealed in the heavens, And that none of your deeds of oppression are covered and hidden. [7] And do not think in your spirit nor say in your heart that ye do not know and that ye do not see that every sin is every day recorded in heaven in the presence of the Most High. [8] From henceforth ye know that all your oppression wherewith ye oppress is written down every day till the day of your judgement woe to you, ye fools, for through your folly shall ye perish: [9] And ye transgress against the wise, [10] And so good hap shall not be your portion. And now, know ye that ye are prepared for the day of destruction: wherefore do not hope to live, ye sinners, but ye shall depart and die; for ye know no ransom; for ye are prepared for the day of the great judgement, for the day of tribulation and great shame for your spirits. [11] Woe to you, ye obstinate of heart, who work wickedness and eat blood: Whence have ye good things to eat and to drink and to be filled? From all the good things which the Lord the Most High has placed in abundance on the earth; therefore ye shall have no peace. [12] Woe to you who love the deeds of unrighteousness: wherefore do ye hope for good hap unto yourselves? know that ye shall be delivered into the hands of the righteous, and they shall cut off your necks and slay you, [13] And have no mercy upon you. Woe to you who rejoice in the tribulation of the righteous; for no grave shall be dug for you. Woe to you who set at nought the words of the righteous; [14] For ye shall have no hope of life. Woe to you who write down lying and godless words; for they write down their lies that men may hear them and act godlessly towards their neighbour. [15] Therefore they shall have no peace but die a sudden death.

CHAPTER 99

[16] Woe to you who work godlessness, And glory in lying and extol them: Ye shall perish, and no happy life shall be yours. [17] Woe to them who pervert the words of uprightness, And transgress the eternal law, And transform themselves into what they were notinto sinners: They shall be trodden under foot upon the earth. [18] In those days make ready, ye righteous, to raise your prayers as a memorial, And place them as a testimony before the angels, that they may place the sin of the sinners for a memorial before the Most High. [19] In those days the nations shall be stirred up, And the families of the nations shall arise on the day of destruction. [20] And in those days the destitute shall go forth and carry off their children, And they shall abandon them, so that their children shall perish through them: Yea, they shall abandon their children (that are still) sucklings, and not return to them, And shall have no pity on their beloved ones. [21] And again I swear to you, ye sinners, that sin is prepared for a day of unceasing bloodshed. [22] And they who worship stones, and grave images of gold and silver and wood and stone and clay, and those who worship impure spirits and demons, and all kinds of idols not according to knowledge, shall get no manner of help from them. [23] And they shall become godless by reason of the folly of their hearts, And their eyes shall be blinded through the fear of their hearts and through visions in their dreams. [24] Through these they shall become godless and fearful; For they sha ll have wrought all their work in a lie, And shall have worshiped a stone: Therefore in an instant shall they perish. [25] But in those days blessed are all they who accept the words of wisdom, and understand them, And observe the paths of the Most High, and walk in the path of His righteousness, And become not godless with the godless; For they shall be saved. [26] Woe to you who spread evil to your neighbours; For you shall be slain in Sheol. [27] Woe to you who make deceitful and false measures, And who cause bitterness on the earth; For they shall thereby be utterly consumed. [28] Woe to you who build your houses through the grievous toil of others, And all their building materials are the bricks and stones of sin; I tell you ye shall have no peace. [29] Woe to them who reject the measure and eternal heritage of their fathers and whose souls follow after idols; For they shall have no rest. [30] Woe to them who work unrighteousness and help oppression, And slay their neighbours until the day of the great judgement. [31] For He shall cast down your glory, And bring affliction on your hearts, And shall arouse His fierce indignation and destroy you all with the sword; And all the holy and righteous shall remember your sins.

CHAPTER 100

[1] And in those days in one place the fathers together with their sons shall be smitten and brothers one with another shall fall in death till the streams flow with their blood. [2] For a man shall not withhold his hand from slaying his sons and his sons sons, And the sinner shall not withhold his hand from his honoured brother: From dawn till sunset they shall slay one another. [3] And the horse shall walk up to the breast in the blood of sinners, And the chariot shall be submerged to its

height. **[4]** In those days the angels shall descend into the secret places and gather together into one place all those who brought down sin and the Most High will arise on that day of judgement to execute great judgement amongst sinners. **[5]** And over all the righteous and holy He will appoint guardians from amongst the holy angels to guard them as the apple of an eye, until He makes an end of all wickedness and all sin, And though the righteous sleep a long sleep, they have nought to fear. **[6]** And then the children of the earth shall see the wise in security, And shall understand all the words of this book, And recognize that their riches shall not be able to save them in the overthrow of their sins. **[7]** Woe to you, Sinners, on the day of strong anguish, Ye who afflict the righteous and burn them with fire: Ye shall be requited according to your works. **[8]** Woe to you, ye obstinate of heart, who watch in order to devise wickedness: Therefore shall fear come upon you and there shall be none to help you. **[9]** Woe to you, ye sinners, on account of the words of your mouth, And on account of the deeds of your hands which your godlessness as wrought, in blazing flames burning worse than fire shall ye burn. **[10]** And now, know ye that from the angels He will inquire as to your deeds in heaven, from the sun and from the moon and from the stars in reference to your sins because upon the earth ye execute judgement on the righteous. And He will summon to testify against you every cloud and mist and dew and rain; for they shall all be withheld because of you from descending upon you, and they shall be mindful of your sins. And now give presents to the rain that it be not with held from descending upon you, nor yet the dew, when it has received gold and silver from you that it may descend. When the hoar-frost and snow with their chilliness, and all the snowstorms with all their plagues fall upon you, in those days ye shall not be able to stand before them.

CHAPTER 101

[1] Observe the heaven, ye children of heaven, and every work of the Most High, and fear ye Him and work no evil in His presence. **[2]** If He closes the windows of heaven, and withholds the rain and the dew from descending on the earth on your account, what will ye do then? **[3]** And if He sends His anger upon you because of yoour deeds, ye cannot petition Him; for ye spake proud and insolent words against His righteousness: therefore ye shall have no peace. **[4]** And see ye not the sailors of the ships, how their ships are tossed to and fro by the waves, and are shaken by the winds, and are in sore trouble? **[5]** And therefore do they fear because all their goodly possessions go upon the sea with them, and they have evil forebodings of heart that the sea will swallow them and they will perish therein. **[6]** Are not the entire sea and all its waters, and all its movements, the work of the Most High, and has He not set limits to its doings, and confined it throughout by the sand? **[7]** And at His reproof it is afraid and dries up, and all its fish die and all that is in it; But ye sinners that are on the earth fear Him not. **[8]** Has He not made the heaven and the earth, and all that is therein? Who has given understanding and wisdom to everything that moves on the earth and in the sea. **[9]** Do not the sailors of the ships fear the sea ? Yet sinners fear not the Most High.

CHAPTER 102

[1] In those days when He hath brought a grievous fire upon you, Whither will ye flee, and where will ye find deliverance? And when He launches forth His Word against you Will you not be affrighted and fear? **[2]** And all the luminaries shall be affrighted with great fear, And all the earth shall be affrighted and tremble and be alarmed. **[3]** And all the angels shall execute their commandst and shall seek to hide themselves from the presence of the Great Glory, And the children of earth shall tremble and quake; And ye sinners shall be cursed for ever, And ye shall have no peace. **[4]** Fear ye not, ye souls of the righteous, And be hopeful ye that have died in righteousness. **[5]** And grieve not if your soul into Sheol has descended in grief, And that in your life your body fared not according to your goodness, but wait for the day of the judgement of sinners and for the day of cursing and chastisement. **[6]** And yet when ye die the sinners speak over you:" As we die, so die the righteous, And what benefit do they reap for their deeds? Behold, even as we, so do they die in grief and darkness, And what have they more than we? **[7]** From henceforth we are equal. And what will they receive and what will they see for ever? **[8]** Behold, they too have died, And henceforth for ever shall they see no light." **[9]** I tell you, ye sinners, ye are content to eat and drink, and rob and sin, and strip men naked, and acquire wealth and see good days. **[10]** Have ye seen the righteous how their end falls out, that no manner of violence is found in them till their death? "Nevertheless they perished and became as though they had not been, and their spirits descended into Sheol in tribulation."

CHAPTER 103

[1] Now, therefore, I swear to you, the righteous, by the glory of the Great and Honoured and Mighty One in dominion, and by His greatness I swear to you. **[2]** I know a mystery and have read the heavenly tablets, And have seen the holy books, And have found written therein and inscribed regarding them: **[3]** That all goodness and joy and glory are prepared for them, And written down for the spirits of those who have died in righteousness, And that manifold good shall be given to you in recompense for your labours, And that your lot is abundantly beyond the lot of the living. **[4]** And the spirits of you who have died in righteousness shall live and rejoice, And their spirits shall not perish, nor their memorial from before the face of the Great One unto all the generations of the world: wherefore no longer fear their contumely. **[5]** Woe to you, ye sinners, whe n ye have died, If ye die in the wealth of your sins, And those who are like you say regarding you: Blessed are the sinners: they have seen all their days. **[6]** And how they have died in prosperity and in wealth, And have not seen tribulation or murder in their life; And they have died in honour, And judgement has not been executed on them during their life. **[7]** "Know ye, that their souls will be made to descend into Sheol and they shall be wretched in their great tribulation. **[8]** And into darkness and chains and a burning flame where there is grievous judgement shall your spirits enter; And the great judgement shall be for all the generations of the world. Woe to you, for ye shall have no peace. **[9]** Say not in regard to the righteous and good who are in life: "In our troubled days we have toiled laboriously and experienced every trouble, And met with much evil and been consumed, And have become few and our spirit small. **[10]** And we have been destroyed and have not found any to help us even with a word: We have been torturedand destroyed, and not hoped to see life from day to day. **[11]** We hoped to be the head and have become the tail: We have toiled laboriously and had no satisfaction in our toil; And we have become the food of the sinners and the unrighteous, And they have laid their yoke heavily upon us. **[12]** They have had dominion over us that hated us and smote us; And to those that hated us we have bowed our necks But they pitied us not. **[13]** We desired to get away from them that we might escape and be at rest, but found no place whereunto we should flee and be safe from them. **[14]** And are complained to the rulers in our tribulation, And cried out against those who devoured us, but they did not attend to our cries and would not hearken to our voice. **[15]** And they helped those who robbed us and devoured us and those who made us few; and they concealed their oppression, and they did not remove from us the yoke of those that devoured us and dispersed us and murdered us, and they concealed their murder, and remembered not that they had lifted up their hands against us.

CHAPTER 104

[1] I swear unto you, that in heaven the angels remember you for good before the glory of the Great One: and your names are written before the glory of the Great One. **[2]** Be hopeful; for aforetime ye were put to shame through ill and affliction; but now ye shall shine as the lights of heaven, ye shall shine and ye shalll be seen, and the portals of heaven shall be opened to you. **[3]** And in your cry, cry for judgement, and it shall appear to you; for all your tribulation shall be visited on the rulers, and on all who helped those who plundered you. **[4]** Be hopeful, and cast not away your hopes for ye shall have great joy as the angels of heaven. What shall ye be obliged to do? **[5]** Ye shall not have to hide on the day of the great judgement and ye shall not be found as sinners, and the eternal judgement shall be far from you for all the generations of the world. **[6]** And now fear not, ye righteous, when ye see the sinners growing strong and prospering in their ways: be not companions with them, **[7]** But keep afar from their violence; for ye shall become companions of the hosts of heaven. And, although ye sinners say: "All our sins shall not be searched out and be written down", nevertheless they shall write down all your sins every day. **[8]** And now I show unto you that light and darkness, day and night, see all your sins. **[9]** Be not godless in your hearts, and lie not and alter not the words of uprightness, nor charge with lying the words of the Holy Great One, nor take account of your idols; **[10]** For all your lying and all your godlessness issue not in righteousness but in great sin. And now I know this mystery, that sinners will alter and pervert the words of righteousness in many ways, and will speak wicked words, and lie, and practice great deceits, and write books concerning their words. **[11]** But when they write down truthfully all my words in their languages, and do not change or minish ought from my words but write them all down truthfully all that I first testified concerning them. **[12]** Then, I know another mystery, that books will be given to the righteous and the wise to become a cause of joy and uprightness and much wisdom. And to them shall the books be given, and they shall believe in them and rejoice over them, and then shall all the righteous who have learnt therefrom all the paths of uprightness be recompensed.

CHAPTER 105

[1] In those days the Lord bade them to summon and testify to the children of earth concerning their wisdom: Show it unto them; for ye are their guides, and a recompense over the whole earth. **[2]** For I and My son will be united with them for ever in the paths of uprightness in their lives; and ye shall have peace: rejoice, ye children of uprightness. Amen.

CHAPTER 106

[1] And after some days my son Methuselah took a wife for his son Lamech, and she became pregnant by him and bore a son. **[2]** And his body was white as snow and red as the blooming of a rose, and the hair of his head and his long locks were white as wool, and his eyes beautiful. And when he opened his eyes, he lighted up the whole house like the sun, and the whole house was very bright. **[3]** And thereupon he arose in the hands of the midwife, opened his mouth, and conversed with the Lord of righteousness. **[4]** And his father Lamech was afraid of him and fled, and came to his father Methuselah. **[5]** And he said unto him: I have begotten a strange son, diverse from and unlike man, and resembling the sons of the God of heaven; and his nature is different and he is not like us, and his eyes are as the rays of the sun, and his countenance is glorious. **[6]** And it seems to me that he is not sprung from me but from the angels, and I fear that in his days a wonder may be wrought on the earth. **[7]** And now, my father, I am here to petition thee and implore thee that thou mayest go to Enoch, our father, and learn from him the truth, for his dwelling place is amongst the angels. **[8]** And when Methuselah heard the words of his son, he came to me to the ends of the earth; for he had heard that I was there, **[9]** And he cried aloud, and I heard his voice and I came to him. And I said unto him: Behold, here am I, my son, wherefore hast thou come to me? And he answered and said: Because of a great cause of anxiety have I come to thee, and because of a disturbing vision have I approached. **[10]**And now, my father, hear me: unto Lamech my son there hath been born a son, the like of whom there is none, and his nature is not like mans nature, and the colour of his body is whiter than snow and redder than the bloom of a rose, and the hair of his head is whiter than white wool, and his eyes are like the rays of the sun, and he opened his eyes and thereupon lighted up the whole house. **[11]**And he arose in the hands of the midwife, and opened his mouth and blessed the Lord of heaven. **[12]**And his father Lamech became afraid and fled to me, and did not believe that he was sprung from him, but that he was in the likeness of the angels of heaven; and behold I have come to thee that thou mayest make known to me the truth. **[13]**And I, Enoch, answered and said unto him: The Lord will do a new thing on the earth, and this I have already seen in a vision, and make known to thee that in the generation of my father Jared some of the angels of heaven transgressed the word of the Lord. **[14]**And behold they commit sin and transgress the law, and have united themselves with women and commit sin with them, and have married some of them, and have begot children by them. **[15]**And they shall produce on the earth giants not according to the spirit, but according to the flesh, and there shall be a great punishment on the earth, and the earth shall be cleansed from all impurity. Yea, there shall come a great destruction over the whole earth, and there shall be a deluge and a great destruction for one year. **[16]**And this son who has been born unto you shall be left on the earth, and his three children shall be saved with him: when all mankind that are on the earth shall diehe and his sons shall be saved. **[17]**And now make known to thy son Lamech that he who has been born is in truth his son, and call his name Noah; for he shall be left to you, and he and his sons shall be saved from the destruction, which shall come upon the earth on account of all the sin and all the unrighteousness, which shall be consummated on the earth in his days. And after that there shall be still more unrighteousness than that which was first consummated on the earth; for I know the mysteries of the holy ones; for He, the Lord, has showed me and informed me, and I have read them in the heavenly tablets.

CHAPTER 107

[1] And I saw written on them that generation upon generation shall transgress, till a generation of righteousness arises, and transgression is destroyed and sin passes away from the earth, and all manner of good comes upon it. [2] And now, my son, go and make known to thy son Lamech that this son, which has been born, is in truth his son, and that this is no lie. [3] And when Methuselah had heard the words of his father Enoch for he had shown to him everything in secret he returned and showed them to him and called the name of that son Noah; for he will comfort the earth after all the destruction.

CHAPTER 108

[1] Another book which Enoch wrote for his son Methuselah and for those who will come after him, and keep the law in the last days. [2] Ye who have done good shall wait for those days till an end is made of those who work evil; and an end of the might of the transgressors. And wait ye indeed till sin has passed away, [3] For their names shall be blotted out of the book of life and out of the holy books, and their seed shall be destroyed for ever, [4] And their spirits shall be slain, and they shall cry and make lamentation in a place that is a chaotic wilderness, and in the fire shall they burn; for there is no earth there. And I saw there something like an invisible cloud; for by reason of its depth I could not look over, and I saw a flame of fire blazing brightly, and things like shining mountains circling and sweeping to and fro. [5] And I asked one of the holy angels who was with me and said unto him: What is this shining thing? for it is not a heaven but only the flame of a blazing fire, [6] And the voice of weeping and crying and lamentation and strong pain. And he said unto me: This place which thou seest here are cast the spirits of sinners and blasphemers, and of those who work wickedness, and of those who pervert everything that the Lord hath spoken through the mouth of the prophets even the things that shall be. [7] For some of them are written and inscribed above in the heaven, in order tha t the angels may read them and know that which shall befall the sinners, and the spirits of the humble, and of those who have afflicted their bodies, and been recompensed by God; [8] And of those who have been put to shame by wicked men: Who love God and loved neither gold nor silver nor any of the good things which are in the world, but gave over their bodies to torture. [9] Who, since they came into being, longed not after earthly food, but regarded everything as a passing breath, and lived accordingly, and the Lord tried them much, and their spirits were found pure so that they should bless His name. [10] And all the blessings destined for them I have recounted in the books. And he hath assigned them their recompense, because they have been found to be such as loved heaven more than their life in the world, and though they were trodden under foot of wicked men, and experienced abuse and reviling from them and were put to shame, [11] Yet they blessed Me. And now I will summon the spirits of the good who belong to the generation of light, and I will transform those who were born in darkness, who in the flesh were not recompensed with such honour as their faithfulness deserved. [12] And I will bring forth in shining light those who have loved My holy name, and I will seat each on the throne of his honour. [13] And they shall be resplendent for times without number; for righteousness is the judgement of God; for to the faithful He will give faithfulness in the habitation of upright paths. And they shall see those who were, born in darkness led into darkness, while the righteous shall be resplendent. [14] And the sinners shall cry aloud and see them resplendent, and they indeed will go where days and seasons are prescribed for them.

THE BOOK OF GIANTS

CHAPTER 1

[1Q23] 1 . . . they knew the secrets of . . . 2 . . . sin was great in the earth . . . 3 . . . and they killed many . . . 4 . . . [they begot] giants . . .

CHAPTER 2

[4Q531] 1 . . . [everything that the] earth produced . . . 2 . . . the great fish . . . 3 . . . the sky with all that grew . . . 4 . . . [fruit of] the earth and all kinds of grain and all the trees . . . 5 . . . beasts and reptiles . . . all creeping things of the earth, 6 and they observed all . . . 7 . . . every harsh deed and . . . utterance . . . 8 . . . male and female, and among humans . . .

CHAPTER 3

[1Q23] 1 . . . [two hundred] donkeys, two hundred mules, two hundred . . . 2 . . . rams of the flock, two hundred goats, two hundred . . . 3 . . . [beasts of the] field from every animal, 4 from every [bird] . . . 5 . . . for interbreeding . . .

CHAPTER 4

[4Q531] 1 . . . they defiled . . . 2 . . . [they begot] giants and monsters . . . 3 . . . they begot, and behold, all [the earth was corrupted] . . . 4 . . . with its blood and by the hand of . . . 5 . . . which did not suffice for them and . . . 6 . . . and they were seeking to devour many . . . 7 . . . the monsters attacked it.

CHAPTER 5

[4Q532] 1 . . . flesh . . . 2 . . . all . . . monsters . . . will be . . . 3 . . . they would arise . . . lacking in true knowledge . . . because . . . 4 . . . the earth [grew corrupt] . . . mighty . . . 5 . . . they were considering . . . 6 . . . from the messengers on .

. . 7 . . . in the end it will perish and die . . . 8 . . . they caused great corruption in the [earth] . . . 9 . . . [this did not] suffice to . . . 10 "They will be . . ."

CHAPTER 6

[2Q26] 1 . . . they drenched the tablet in the water . . . 2 . . . the waters went up over the [tablet] . . . 3 . . . they lifted the tablet out from the water of . . .

CHAPTER 7

[4Q530] 1 . . . [the vision] is for cursing and sorrow. I am the one who confessed . . . 2 . . . the whole group of the castaways that I will go to . . . 3 . . . the spirits of the slain, complaining about their killers and crying out . . . 4 . . . that we will die together and be made an end of . . . 5 . . . much and I will be sleeping, and bread . . . 6 . . . for my dwelling; 7 the vision and also . . . entered into the gathering of the giants . . . [6Q8] 8 . . . Ohya, and he said to Mahway . . . 9 ". . . without trembling. Who showed you all this vision, brother?" 10 . . . "Barakel, my father, was with me." 11 . . . Before Mahway had finished telling what [he had seen] . . . 12 . . . [said] to him, "Now I have heard wonders! If a barren woman gives birth . . ." [4Q530] 13 Thereon Ohya said to Ha[hya], 14 ". . . [will be destroyed] from on the earth and . . . 15 . . . [the] earth." 16 When . . . 17 . . . they wept before [the giants] . . . 18 ". . . your strength . . ." 19 . . . Thereon Ohya [said] to Hahya, 20 . . . Then he answered, "It is not for us, but for Azaiel, 21 for he did . . . [the offspring of the] messengers are the giants, 22 [and they would not let all their loved ones] be neglected . . . 23 . . . [we have] not been cast down; you have strength . . .

CHAPTER 8

[4Q531] 1 ". . . I am a giant, and by the mighty strength of my arm and my own great strength . . . 2 . . . anyone mortal, and I have made war against them; 3 but I am not . . . able to stand against them, for my opponents . . . 4 . . . reside in Heaven, and they dwell in the holy places. 5 And not . . . [they] are stronger than me. 6 . . . of the wild beast has come, and they call [me] the wild man." 7 . . . Then Ohya said to him, "I have been forced to have a dream . . . the sleep of my eyes [vanished], to let me see a vision. Now I know that on . . ." 8 . . . Gilgamesh . . .

CHAPTER 9

[6Q8] 1 . . . three of its roots . . . 2 . . . [while] I was [watching], there came . . . 3 . . . [the roots were moved into] this garden, all of them, and not . . .

CHAPTER 10

4Q530 1 . . . concerns the death of our souls . . . 2 . . . and all his comrades, [and] Ohya told them what Gilgamesh said to him . . . 3 . . . and it was said . . . ". . . concerning . . . the leader has cursed the potentates." 4 And the giants were glad at his words. Then he turned and left . . .

CHAPTER 11

[4Q530] 1 Thereon two of them had dreams and the sleep of their eye fled from them, 2 and they arose and came to . . . 3 . . . [and recounted] their dreams, and said in the assembly of [the giants and] the monsters, 4 "[In] my dream I was watching this very night, 5 [and within a garden there were] gardeners and they were watering . . . 6 . . . [two hundred trees and] large shoots came out of their root . . . 7 . . . all the water, and the fire burned all [the trees] . . ." 8 . . . They found the giants to tell them [of the dream] . . .

CHAPTER 12

[4Q530] 1 "[Go to Enoch,] the noted scribe, and he will interpret the dream for us." 2 Thereon his companion Ohya declared [this], and said to the giants, "I too had a dream this night, O giants, and behold, the Ruler of Heaven came down to earth . . . 3 . . . and such is the end of the dream." 4 [Then] all the giants [and monsters] grew afraid and called Mahway. 5 He came to them and the giants pleaded with him and sent him to Enoch . . . 6 They said to him, "Go . . . to you that . . . you have heard his voice." 7 And he said to him, "He will . . . interpret the dreams . . . 8 . . . how long the giants have to live."

CHAPTER 13

[4Q530] 1 . . . [he moved through the air] like strong winds, 2 and flew with his hands like eagles . . . [he left] the inhabited world and passed over Desolation, the great desert . . . 3 . . . and Enoch saw him and hailed him, 4 and Mahway said to him . . . 5 . . . here and there a second time to Mahway . . . 6 "The giants await your words, and all the monsters of the earth. 7 If . . . has been carried . . . from the days of . . . their . . . and they will be added . . . 8 . . . we would know from you their meaning . . . 9 . . . [two hundred] trees that [came down] from Heaven . . ."

CHAPTER 14

[4Q530] 1 The scribe [Enoch] . . . 2 . . . a copy of the second tablet that [Enoch] sent . . . 3 . . . in the very handwriting of Enoch the noted scribe . . . 4 "[In the Name of God the great] and Holy One, to Shemihaza and all [his companions] . . . 5 . . . let it be known to you that not . . . 6 and the things you have done, and that your wives . . . 7 . . . they and their sons and the wives of [their sons] . . . 8 . . . by your licentiousness on the earth, and there has been on you . . . 9 . . . [and the earth is crying out] and complaining about you and the deeds of your children, **10** [and] the harm that you have done to it. **11** . . . until Raphael arrives, behold, destruction [is coming, a great flood, and it will destroy all living things] **12** and whatever is in the deserts and the seas. **13** And the meaning of the matter . . . **14** . . . on you for evil. **15** But now, loosen the bonds binding [you to evil] . . . and pray."

CHAPTER 15

[4Q531] **1** . . . [great fear] seized me and I fell on my face; I heard his voice . . . **2** . . . he dwelt among human beings but he did not learn from them . . .

ETHIOPIC BOOK OF MACCABEES

1 MEQABYAN

CHAPTER 1

[1] There were one man whose name are called Tseerutsaydan an who love sin ~ him would boast ina him horses abundance an him troops firmness beneath him authority. **[2]** Him had many priests who serve him idols whom him worship an fe whom him bow an sacrifice sacrifice by night an by daylight. **[3]** But ina him heart dullness it would seem fe him that them give him firmness an Power. **[4]** An ina him heart it would seem fe him that them give him authority ina all him Rule. **[5]** An again ina formation time it would seem fe him that them give him all the desired authority also. **[6]** An him would sacrifice sacrifice fe them day an night. **[7]** Him appointed priests who serve him idols. **[8]** While them ate from that defouled sacrifice - them would tell him pretendin that the idols eat night an day. **[9]** Again them would mek other persons diligent like unto them - that them might sacrifice sacrifice an eat. An again them would mek other persons diligent that them might sacrifice sacrifice - an sacrifice sacrifice like unto them. **[10]** But him would trust ina him idols that don't profit nor benefit. **[11]** By him timeframe bein small - an ina him heart dullness - it would seem fe him that them Irated him - that them feed him an that them crown him ~ it would seem fe him that them Irated him - fe Seythan have deafened him reasonin lest him know him Irator Who Irated him bringin from not livin toward livin - or lest him with him kindreds know him Irator Who Irated him bringin from not livin toward livin - that them might go toward *Gehannem* of Fiyah foriva - it bein judged pon them with him who call them gods without them bein gods. **[12]** As them aren't never well whenever - it are due that him might call them dead ones. **[13]** As Seythan authority that mislead them will lodge ina that idol image - an as him will tell them them reasonin accord - an as him will reveal fe them like unto them loved - him will judge pon the idols wherein them believed an wherein 'Adam childran trust - whose reasonin were like unto ashes. **[14]** An them will marvel pon the time them sight up that him fulfilled what them thought fe them - an them will do him accord fe him reachin up til them sacrifice them dawta childran an them male childran birthed from them nature - up til them spill them dawta childran an male childran blood that were clean. **[15]** Them didn't sadden them - fe Seythan have savoured him sacrifice fe them fe fulfill them evil accord - that him might lower them toward *Gehannem* like unto him - where there are no exits up til Iternity - where him will raceive tribulation. **[16]** But that Tseerutsaydan were arrogant ~ him had fifty idols worked ina males pattern an twenty worked ina dawtaz pattern. **[17]** An him would boast ina those idols that have no benefit ~ him would totally glorify them while him sacrificed sacrifice mornin an evenin. **[18]** An him would command persons that them might sacrifice sacrifice fe the idols - an him would eat from that defouled sacrifice - an him would command other persons that them might eat from the sacrifice ~ him would especially provoke fe evil. **[19]** Him had five houses worked fe him beaten worked idols that were iron an brass an lead. **[20]** An him ornamanted them ina silver an gold ~ him veiled curtains around the houses fe them an planted a tent fe them. **[21]** Him appointed keepers fe them there ~ him would Itinually sacrifice forty fe him idols - ten fattened oxen - ten sterile cows - ten fattened sheep ewes - ten barren goats - with birds that have wings. **[22]** But it would seem fe him that him idols ate ~ him would present fe them fifty *feeqen* of grapes an fifty dishes of wheat kneaded with oil. **[23]** An him told him priests: - "Tek give them ~ mek mi irators eat what mi slaughtered fe them - an mek them drink the grape mi presented fe them ~ as fe if it aren't enough fe them - mi will add fe them." **[24]** An him would command all that them might eat an drink from that defouled sacrifice. **[25]** But ina him evil malice him would send him troops who visit ina all the kingdom - that as it were there were one who neither sacrifice nor bow - them might separate an know an bring him - an might punish him by fiyah an by sword before him - that them might plunder him money an might burn him house ina fiyah - that them might downstroy all him money him had pon him. **[26]** "Fe them are kind an great ones - an fe them have Irated wi ina them charity - an mi will show punishmant an tribulation fe him unless him worshipped mi irators an sacrificed sacrifice fe mi irators. **[27]** An mi will show him punishmant an tribulation - fe them have Irated Earth an Heaven an the sea that were wide an moon an Sun an stars an rains an winds an all that live ina this world fe be food an fe be satiety fe wi." **[28]** But persons who worship them shall be punished ina firm tribulation - an them won't be nice fe them.

CHAPTER 2

[1] There were one man birthed from the tribe of Binyam whose name are called Meqabees; **[2]** him had three childran who were handsome an totally warriors ~ them had bein iloved alongside all persons ina that Midyam an Miedon country that are Tseerutsaydan Rule. **[3]** An like unto the king commanded them pon the time him found them: - "Don't unu bow fe Tseerutsaydan irators? How about don't unu sacrifice sacrifice? **[4]** But if unu refuse - wi will seize an tek unu toward the king - an wi will downstroy all your money like unto the king commanded." **[5]** These youts who were handsome replied fe him sayin - "As fe Him fe Whom InI bow - there are InI Faada Irator Who Irated Earth an Heaven an what are within she - an the sea - moon an Sun an clouds an stars ~ Him are the True Irator Whom InI worship an ina Whom InI believe." **[6]** An these the king youts are four - an them servants who carry shield an spear are a hundred. **[7]** An pon the time them loved that them might seize these hola ones - them escaped from them hands and there are none who touched them ~ as those youts are totally warriors ina Power - them went seizin shields an them spears. [8] An there were from them one who strangle an kill panther - an at that time him would strangle it like unto a chicken. [9] An there were one from them who kill a lion with one rock or strikin at one time with a stick. [10] An there were one from them who kill a hundred persons - strikin ina formation time with one sword - an them name an them hunt were thus ~ it were called ina all Babilon an Mo`ab countries. [11] An them were warriors ina Power - an them had a thing bein iloved an comeliness. [12] An again them features comeliness were wondrous - however becau them worshipped JAH an becau them didn't fear death - it are them reasonin comeliness that surpass all. [13] An pon the time them frightened the troops - there are none who could able fe seize them - but them who were warriors escaped proceedin toward a lofty mountain. [14] An those troops returned toward the city an shut the fortress gate ~ them terrorized the people sayin - "Unless unu brought those warriors the Meqabyans - wi will burn your city ina fiyah - an wi will send toward the king an downstroy your country." [15] An at that time the country persons - rich an poor ones an dawtaz an males - a child whose faada an mother dead pon him an old dawtaz - everyone proceeded an shouted together - an them straightened them necks toward the mountain an shouted toward them sayin - "Don't downstroy InI - an don't downstroy InI country pon InI." [16] At that time them wept together - an them feared - arisin from JAH. [17] Returnin them faces Eastward an streachin forth them hands them begged toward JAH together - "Lord - should InI refuse these men who demolished Thy Command an Thy LAW? [18] Yet him believed ina silver an gold an ina the stone an wood that a person hands worked - but InI don't love that InI might hear that criminal word - who didn't believe Thy LAW" them said. [19] When Thou are the Irator Who save an Who kill - him mek him ras self like unto them Irated him also ~ as fe him - him are who spill a person blood an who eat a person flesh. [20] But InI don't love that InI might sight up that criminal face nor hear him word" them said. [21] "However if Thou commanded InI - InI will go toward him ~ becau InI believe ina Thee-I - InI will pass an give InI bodies fe death - an pon the time him said 'Sacrifice sacrifice fe mi irators' - InI won't hear that criminal word. [22] But InI believed Thee-I - Lord Who examine kidneys an reasonins - InI Faadas Irator - 'Abriham an Yis'haq an Ya`iqob who did Thy Accord an lived firmed up ina Thy LAW. [23] Thou examine a person reasonin an help the sinner an the righteous one - an there be none hidden from Thee-I - an him who took refuge are revealed alongside Thee-I. [24] But InI have no other Irator apart from Thee-I. [25] That InI might give InI bodies fe death becau Thy glorified Name - however be Power an Firmness an a Shelter fe InI ina this Work that InI are ruled fe Thee-I. [26] An pon the time 'Isra'iel entered toward Gibts country Thou heard Ya`iqob plea - an now glorified God - InI beg Thee-I." [27] An pon the time the two men whose features were quite handsome were sight up fe them standin before them - pon the time fiyah swords that frighten like unto lightnin alit an cut them necks an killed them - at that time them arose bein well like unto formerly. [28] Them features comeliness became totally handsome an them shone more than Sun - an them became more handsome than formerly.

CHAPTER 3

[1] Like unto unu sight up before unu these the Most I JAH slaves - 'Abya - Seela - Fentos who dead an arose - unu have that unu might arise likewise after unu dead - an your faces shall shine like unto the Sun ina the Kingdom of Heaven. [2] An them went with those men an raceived martyrdom there. [3] At that time them begged - them praised - an them bowed fe JAH ~ death didn't frighten them an the king punishmant didn't frighten them. [4] An them went toward those youts an became like unto a sheep that have no evil - yet them didn't frighten them - an pon the time them arrived toward them - them seized an beat them an bound an whipped them - an them delivered them toward the king an stood them before him. [5] An the king answered fe them sayin - "How won't unu stubborn ones sacrifice sacrifice an bow fe mi irators?" [6] Those bredren who were cleansed from sin - who were honoured an chosen an Irie - an who shine like unto a jewel whose value were wondrous - Seela an 'Abya an Fentos answered fe him ina one word. [7] Them told that king who were a plague - "As fe InI - InI won't bow nor sacrifice fe defouled idols that have no knowledge nor reasonin." [8] An again them told him - "InI won't bow fe idols that were silver an gold that a person hand worked - that were stone an wood - that have no reasonin nor soul nor knowledge - that don't benefit them friends nor harm them enemies." [9] An the king answered fe them sayin - "Why do unu do thus - an as them know who insult them an who wrong them - why do unu insult the glorified irators?" [10] Them answered fe him sayin - "As them are like unto a trifle alongside InI - as fe InI - InI will insult them an won't glorify them." [11] An the king answered fe them sayin - "Mi will punish unu like unto your Work evil measure ~ mi will downstroy your features comeliness with whippin an firm tribulation an fiyah. [12] An now tell mi whether unu will give or won't give sacrifice fe mi irators - as fe if this didn't happen - mi will punish unu by sword an by whippin." [13] Them answered fe him sayin - "As fe InI - InI won't sacrifice sacrifice nor bow fe defouled idols" - an the king commanded them that them might beat them with a fat stick - an again that them might whip them with a whip - an after it - that them might splinter them up til them inner organs were sight up. [14] An after this them bound an made them while ina jail house up til him counsel by money that punish an kill them. [15] Without niceness them took an bound them a firm imprisonmant ina prison house - an them sat ina prison house three nights an three daylights. [16] An after this third day the king commanded that a Proclamation speaker might turn an that counselors an nobles - country elders an officials - might be gathered. [17] An pon the time the king Tseerutsaydan sat ina square - him commanded that them might bring those honoured ones - Seela an 'Abya an Fentos ~ them stood before him bein wounded an bound. [18] An the king told them - "When unu sat these three days - are there really the returnin that unu returned - or are unu ina your former evil?" [19] An those honoured JAH Souljahs answered fe him sayin - "As fe that InI were cruel - InI won't agree that InI might worship the idols filled of sin an evil that thou check up." [20] An that criminal vexed an commanded that them might stand them up ina lofty place an might renew them wounds ~ them blood flowed pon Earth. [21] An again him commanded that them might burn them with a torch lamp an might char them flesh - an him servants did like unto him commanded them - an those honoured men told him - "Thou who forgot JAH LAW - speak ~ InI reward shall abound ina the measure whereby thou multiply InI punishmant." [22] An again him commanded that them might bring an send pon them bears an tigers an lions that were evil beasts before them eat them food that them might totally eat them flesh with them bones. [23] An him commanded persons who keep the beasts that them might send the beasts pon them - an them did like unto him

commanded them - an them bound those honoured martyrs feet - an again them maliciously beat an bound them with tent-stakes. [24] An those beasts were flung over them while them roared - an pon the time them arrived toward the martyrs them hailed an bowed fe them. [25] Them returned toward them keepers while them roared - an them frightened them keepers ~ them took them toward the square up til them delivered them toward before the king. [26] An them killed seventy five men from the criminals army there. [27] Many persons panicked - the one anguishin pon the one ina fear - up til the king quit him throne an fled - an them seized the beasts with difficulty an took them toward them lodgin. [28] Seela an 'Abya an Fentos two bredren came an released them from the imprisonmant them bound them an told them - "Come mek InI flee lest these skeptics an criminals find InI. [29] An those martyrs answered them bredren sayin - "It aren't procedure that InI might flee after InI set up fe testimony ~ as it were unu had feared - go fleein." [30] An those them likkle bredren said - "InI will stand with unu before the king - an if unu dead InI will dead with unu." [31] An after this the king were pon him lordship hall balcany an sight up that these honoured men were released an that all the five bredren stood together ~ those chiefs who work an punish troops questioned that them were bredren an told the king - an the king vexed an shouted like unto a wilderness boar. [32] An up til the king counseled by money that punish all the five bredren - him commanded that them might seize an add them ina prison house ~ them placed them ina prison house bindin ina firm imprisonmant without niceness with a hollow stalk. [33] An the king Tseerutsaydan said - "These youts who erred wearied mi ~ what should these men reasonin firm up? an them Work evil are like unto them Power firmness ~ if mi say - "Them will return" - them will mek them reasonin evil. [34] An mi will bring the hardship pon them like unto them Work evil measure - an mi will burn them flesh ina fiyah that it might be charred ash - an pon that mi will scattar them flesh ash like unto dust pon mountains." [35] An after him spoke this him waited three days an commanded that them might bring those honoured men - an pon the time those honoured men approached him commanded that them might burn a fiyah within the great pit oven - an that them might add within it a malice Work that flame the fiyah an whereby them boil a yat - the fat an soapberries - sea foam an resin an the sulfur. [36] An pon the time fiyah flamed ina the pit the messengers went toward the king when them said - "Wi did what thou commanded wi - send the men who will be added." [37] An him commanded that them might receive an cast them ina the fiyah pit - an the youts did like unto the king commanded them - an pon the time those honoured men entered toward the fiyah them gave them souls fe JAH. [38] An when the persons who cast them sight up - Angels raceived an took them souls toward the Garden where Yis'haq an 'Abriham an Ya`iqob are - where Irie Ites are found.

CHAPTER 4

[1] An pon the time that criminal sight up that them dead - him commanded that them might burn them flesh ina fiyah up til it are ash an that them might scattar them ina wind - but the fiyah couldn't able fe burn the corpse hair from them corpses side - an them sent them forth from the pit. [2] An again them flamed fiyah over them iginnin from mornin up til evenin ~ it didn't burn them ~ them said - "An now come mek wi cast them corpses seaward." [3] An them did like unto the king commanded them ~ them cast them pon the sea ~ even if them cast them seaward addin great stones an iron hearthstones an a millstone whereby a donkey grind by turnin - there are no sinkin that the sea sank them ~ as JAH Spirit of Support have lodged ina them - them floated pon the sea yet them didn't sink ~ it failed him fe downstroy them by all the malice that were provoked pon them. [4] "As this them death have made weary more than them Life - mek mi cast them corpses fe beasts that them might eat them - yet what will mi do?" him said. [5] An the youts did like unto him commanded them ~ vultures an beasts didn't touch them corpses ~ birds an vultures veiled them with them wings from burnin ina Sun an the five martyrs corpses sat fourteen days. [6] An pon the time them sight them up - them bodies shone up like unto Sun - an Angels incircled them corpses like unto light incircle the Tent. [7] Him counseled counsel ~ him lacked what him do - an after this him dug a grave an buried the five martyrs corpses. [8] An when that king who forgot JAH LAW had reclined pon a bed at night the five martyrs were sight up fe him standin before him at night vexin an seizin swords. [9] As it have seemed fe him that them entered toward him house at night ina crime - pon the time him awoke from him slumber him feared an loved that him might flee from the bedchamber toward the hall - an as it have seemed fe him that them kill him seemin that them committed crime pon him - him feared an him knees trembled. [10] Becaudis thing him said - "Mi lords - what do unu love? as fe mi - what should mi do fe unu?" [11] Them answered fe him sayin - "Aren't InI whom thou killed burnin ina fiyah an InI whom thou commanded that them might cast pon the sea? As JAH have kept InI bodies becau InI believed ina Him - it failed thee fe downstroy InI ~ as a person who believed ina Him won't perish - mek glory an praise due fe JAH - an InI also who believed ina Him didn't shame ina the tribulation. [12] "As mi didn't know that a punishmant like unto this will find mi - what reward should mi give unu becau the stead wherefore mi did a evil thing pon unu? [13] An now separate fe mi the reward mi give unu - lest unu tek mi body ina death an lest unu lower mi body toward See'ol when mi are ina Life. [14] As mi have wronged unu - forgive mi mi sin - becau it were your Faada JAH LAW Niceness" him told them. [15] An those honoured martyrs answered fe him sayin - "Becau the stead wherefore thou did a evil thing pon InI - as fe InI - InI won't pay thee a evil thing ~ as JAH are Who bring hardship pon a soul - as fe Him Who will pay thee hardship - there are JAH [16] However InI were sight up fe thee bein revealed that InI were well fe thy timeframe bein small an becau thy reasonin deafness ~ as fe it seemin fe thee that thou killed InI - thou prepared welfare fe InI. [17] But thy idols priests an thou will downscend toward Gehannem where are no exits foriva. [18] Woe fe thy idols fe whom thou bow havin quit bowin fe JAH Who Irated unu when unu were scorned like unto spit - an fe unu who worship them - an unu don't know JAH Who Irated unu bringin from not livin toward livin ~ aren't unu who are sight up today like unto smoke an tomorrow who perish?" [19] An the king answered fe them sayin - "What will unu command mi that mi might do fe unu all that unu loved?" [20] "It are fe save thy ras self lest thou enter toward the Gehannem of Fiyah - yet it aren't fe save InI ras selves who teach thee. [21] Fe your idols are silver an gold - stone an wood - that have no reasonin nor soul knowledge - that a person hand worked. [22] But them don't kill ~ them don't save ~ them don't benefit them friend [23] ~ them don't harm them enemy ~ them don't downbase ~ them don't honour [24] ~ them don't mek wealthy ~ them don't impoverish ~ them mislead unu by demons authority - who don't love that the one from persons might be saved [25] yet them don't uproot nor plant. [26] Them especially don't love that the persons like unto unu might be saved from death -

unu dull-hearted ones fe whom them seem that them irated unu - when unu are who worked them. [27] As Seythans an demons authority have lodged ina them - them shall return a thing fe unu like unto unu loved - that it might drown unu within the sea of Gehannem [28] But thou - quit this thy error an mek this also be InI reward becau InI dead stead - that InI might benefit InI souls worshippin InI Irator JAH" them told him. [29] But him were alarmed an would totally astony - an as all five have been sight up fe him drawin them swords - him feared - an becaudis thing him bowed fe them. [30] "Hence mi knew that after dead ones who were dust dead them will really arise ~ as fe mi - only a likkle had remained fe mi fe dead." [31] After this them were hidden from before that king face ~ from that day onward that Tseerutsaydan who are totally arrogant quit burnin them corpses. [32] As them have misled them many eras - him would be Irie ina him idols an him reasonin error - an him misled many persons like unto him up til them quit followin ina Worship JAH Who Irated them - yet it aren't only him who erred. [33] An them would sacrifice them dawta childran an them male childran fe demons - yet them work a seducin an downsturbance that are them reasonin accord - that them faada Seythan taught them that him might mek the seducin an downsturbance that JAH don't love. [34] Them marry them mothers - an them abuse them aunts an them sistren ~ them abuse them bodies while them worked all that resemble this filthy Work ~ as Seythan have firmed up those crooked persons reasonin - them said - "Wi won't return." [35] But that Tseerutsaydan - who don't know him Irator - were totally arrogant - an him would boast ina him idols. [36] If them say - "How will JAH give the Kingdom fe the persons who don't know Him ina LAW an ina Worship?" - them will totally return toward Him ina repentance ~ as Him test them thus - it are becaudis. [37] But if them totally return ina repentance Him would love them - an Him would keep them Kingdom - but if them refuse a fiyah will punish them ina Fiyah of *Gehannem* foriva. [38] But it would be due a king fe fear him Irator JAH like unto him lordship fame - an it would be due a judge fe be ruled fe him Irator while him judged goodly judgemant like unto him Rule fame. [39] An it would be due elders an chiefs an envoys an petty kings fe be commanded fe them Irator like unto them lordship abundance measure. [40] As Him are Heaven an Earth Lord Who Irated all the Iration - becau there are no other Irator ina Heavan nor Earth who impoverish an mek rich - Him are Who honour an downbase.

CHAPTER 5

[1] "The one warrior from the sixty warriors were proud ~ JAH made him body Iginnin from him foot up til him head fe swell with one spoon of sulphur ~ him dead ina one plague. [2] An again Keeram who built a iron bed were proud arisin from him powerfulness abundance - an JAH hid him ina death. [3] An again Nabukedenetsor were proud sayin - 'There are no other king without mi - an mi are Irator who mek the Sun rise ina this world' - an him said thus arisin from him arrogance abundance. [4] An JAH separated from persons an sent him toward a wilderness seven years - an him made him fortune with Heaven birds an wilderness beasts up til him knew that JAH were Who Irated him. [5] An pon the time him knew Him ina worship - Him again returned him toward him kingdom ~ who are it who weren't of Earth - bein boldly proud pon JAH Who Irated him? [6] How about who are it demolished HIM LAW an Him Order an whom Earth didn't swallow? [7] An thou Tseerutsaydan love that thou might be proud pon thy Irator - an again thou have that Him might downstroy thee like unto them - an might lower thee toward a grave arisin from thy arrogance. [8] An again after them entered toward *See'ol* where are tooth grindin an mournin - that were darkness fulfillmant - thou have that Him might lower thee toward the deep pit *Gehannem* where are no exits foriva. [9] As fe thou - thou are a man who will dead and be demolished tomorrow like unto arrogant kings who were like unto thee - who quit this world livin. [10] As fe InI - InI say - 'Thou are demolished ruins - but thou aren't JAH - fe JAH are Who Irated Earth an Heaven an thee.' [11] Him downbase arrogant ones ~ Him honour them who were downbased ~ Him give firmness fe persons who wearied. [12] Him kill well ones ~ Him raise up the persons who were Earth - who dead buried ina grave. [13] An Him send slaves forth free ina Life from sin rulership. [14] O king Tseerutsaydan - why do thou boast ina thy defouled idols who have no benefit? [15] But JAH Irated Earth an Heaven an great seas ~ Him Irated moon an Sun - an Him prepared eras. [16] Man graze toward him field - an him while when him plough up til it dusk - an Heaven stars live firmed up by Him Word. [17] An Him call all ina Heaven ~ there are nothing done without JAH knowin it. [18] Him commanded Heaven Angels that them might serve Him an might praise Him glorified Name - an Angels are sent toward all persons who inherit Life. [19] Rufa'iel who were a servant were sent toward Thobeet - an him saved Thobya from death ina Ragu'iel country. [20] Hola Meeka'iel were sent toward Giediewon that him might draw him attention by money that him downstroy 'Iloflee persons; an him were sent toward the prophet Mussie pon the time him made 'Isra'iel cross 'Eritra sea. [21] As only JAH have said him led them - there were no different idol with them. [22] An Him sent them forth toward crops pon Earth. [23] An Him fed them Him plantation grain ~ as Him have totally loved them - Him cherished them feedin the honey that firmed up like unto a rock. [24] An that thou might totally keep Him kindreds by what are due - an that thou might do JAH Accord Who Irated thee - Him crowned thee givin Itority pon the four kingdoms. [25] Fe Him have crowned thee makin loftier than all - an thy Irator totally crowned thee that thou might love JAH. [26] An it are procedure that thou might love thy Irator JAH like unto Him loved thee - like unto Him trusted thee pon all the people - an thou - do JAH Accord that thy era might abound ina this world an that Him might live with thee ina Support. [27] An do JAH Accord that Him might stand fe thee bein a Guardian pon thy enemies - an that Him might seat thee pon thy throne - an that Him might hide thee ina him Wing of Support. [28] As fe if thou don't know - JAH chose an crowned thee pon 'Isra'iel like unto Him chose Sa'ol fron 'Isra'iel childran when him kept him faada donkeys - an Him crowned him pon him kindreds 'Isra'iel - an him sat with 'Isra'iel pon him throne. [29] An Him gave him a lofty fortune separatin from him kindreds ~ JAH crowned thee pon Him kindreds ~ as fe henceforth onward - check - keep Him kindreds. [30] As JAH have Ipointed thee over them that thou might kill an might save - keep them ina evil thing - them who work a goodly thing an them who work a evil thing pon a goodly thing" him told him. [31] "An as JAH have Ipointed thee pon all that thou might do Him Accord be it while thou whipped or while thou saved - pay them evil Work - them who work goodly Work an them who work goodly Work an evil Work. [32] Fe thou are a slave of JAH Who rule all ina Heaven - an thou - do JAH Accord that Him might do thy accord fe thee ina all thou thought an ina all thou begged while thou wheedled before Him. [33] There are none who rule Him - but Him rule all. [34] There are none who Ipoint Him - but Him Ipoint all. [35] There are none who dismiss Him - but Him dismiss all.

[36] There are none who reproach Him - but Him reproach all. [37] There are none who mek Him diligent - but Him mek all diligent ~ as Heaven an Earth rulership are fe Him - there are none who escape from Him Itority; all are revealed alongside Him - yet there are none hidden from Him Face. [38] Him sight up all - but there are none who sight Him up ~ Him hear the person priah who pray toward Him sayin 'Save I' - fe Him have Irated man ina Him Pattern - an Him accept him plea. [39] As Him are a King Who live up til the Iternity - Him feed all from Him unchangin Nature.

CHAPTER 6

[1] As Him crown fe true the kings who do Him Accord - the kings wrote a straight thing becau Him. [2] As them have done JAH Accord - Him shall shine up ina Light that aren't examined Yis'haq an 'Abriham an Ya`iqob - Selomon an Daweet an Hiziqyas lodgins ina the Garden where are all beautiful kings whose lodgin were Light. [3] Heaven Hall are what totally shone - yet Earth halls aren't like unto Heaven Hall ~ it floor - whose features are silver an gold an jewel features - are clean. [4] An it features that totally shine are unexamined by a person reasonin ~ Heaven Hall are what shine like unto jewels. [5] Like unto JAH knew - Who were a Nature Knower - the Heaven Hall that Him Irated are what a person reasonin don't examine an what shine ina total Light ~ it floor - that were worked ina silver an gold - ina jewels - ina white silk an ina blue silk - are clean. [6] It are quite totally beautiful like unto this. [7] Righteous ones who firmed up ina religion an virtue are who shall inherit it ina JAH Charity an fe Pardon. [8] An there are welfare Water that flow from it - an it totally shine like unto Sun - an there are a Light tent within it - an it are incircled by grace perfume. [9] A Garden fruit that were beautiful an Iloved - whose features an taste were different - are around the house - an there are a oil an grape place there - an it are totally beautiful - an it fruit fragrance are sweet. [10] When a fleshly bloodly person enter toward it - him soul would have separated from him flesh from the Irie Ites abundance that are ina it arisin from it fragrance flavour. [11] Beautiful kings who did JAH Accord shall be Irie there ~ them honour an them place are known ina the Kingdom of Heaven that live firmed up foriva - where welfare are found. [12] Him showed that them lordship pon Earth were famed an honoured - an that them lordship ina Heaven were famed an honoured; them shall be honoured an lofty ina Heaven like unto them honour them an bow fe them ina this world ~ if them work goodly Work ina this world them shall be Irie. [13] But kings who were evil ina them Rule an them kingdoms that JAH gave them - them don't judge fe true by what are due ~ as them have ignored the destitute an poor ones cries - them don't judge Truth an save the refugee an the wronged child whose faada an mother dead pon him. [14] Them don't save destitute an poor ones from the wealthy hand that rob them ~ them don't divide an give from them food an satta them who hungered - an them don't divide an give from them drink an give fe drink the persons who thirsted - an them didn't return them ears toward the poor one cry. [15] An Him shall tek them toward *Gehannem* that were a dark endin ~ pon the time that lofty Day arrived pon them when JAH shall come - an pon the time Him wrath were done pon them like unto Daweet spoke ina him Praises 'Lord - don't chastise I ina Thy Judgemant an don't admonish I ina Thy chastisemant' - them problems an them downbasemant shall abound like unto them fame abundance measure. [16] When nobles an kings are who rule this world ina this world - there are persons who didn't keep thy law. [17] But JAH Who rule all are there ina Heaven ~ all persons souls an all persons welfare have been seized by Him Itority ~ Him are Who give honour fe persons who glorify Him - fe Him totally rule all - an Him love the persons who love Him. [18] As Him are Earth an Heaven Lord - Him examine an know what kidneys transported an what a reasonin thought - an fe a person who begged toward Him with a pure reasonin - Him shall give him him plea reward. [19] Him shall downstroy powerful ones arrogance - who work evil Work pon the child whose mother an faada dead pon him - an pon old dawtaz. [20] It aren't by thy Power that thou seized this kingdom ~ it aren't by thy bein able that thou sat pon this throne ~ Him loved fe test thee thus that it be possible fe thee fe rule like unto Sa'ol who ruled him kindreds ina that season - an Him seated thee pon a kingdom throne - yet it aren't by thy Power that thou seized this kingdom ~ it are when Him test thee like unto Sa'ol who ignored the prophet Samu'iel word an JAH Word an didn't serve him army nor 'Amalieq king - yet it aren't by thy bein able that thou seized this kingdom. [21] An JAH told the prophet Samu'iel - Go - an as them have saddened I by demolishin LAW an worshippin the idols an bowin fe the idol an by them mosques an by all them hated Works without benefit - tell Sa'ol - 'Go toward 'Amalieq country an downstroy them hosts an all the kings Iginnin from persons up til livestock.' [22] Pon them who saddened JAH - becaudis thing Him sent Sa'ol that him might downstroy them. [23] But him saved them king from death - an him saved many livestock an beauties an dawtaz an handsome youts from death ~ As him have scorned I thing an as him didn't hear I Command - becaudis thing - JAH told the prophet Samu'iel - Go an divide him kingdom. [24] Becau him stead - Inoint `Issiey child Daweet that him might reign pon 'Isra'iel. [25] But pon him adjourn a demon who will strangle an cast him. [26] As him have refused if I-man gave him a kingdom that him might do I Accord - pon the time him refused I fe do I Accord I-man dismissed him from him kingdom that are due him - but thou - go an tell him sayin - 'Will thou thus ignore JAH Who crowned thee pon Him kindreds 'Isra'iel - Who seated thee pon Him Lordship Throne?' [27] But thou - tell him - 'Thou didn't know JAH Who gave around this much honour an famousness' Him told him. [28] An the prophet Samu'iel went toward the king Sa'ol an entered toward him sittin at a dinnertable - an when 'Amalieq king 'Agag had sat pon him left. [29] 'Why did thou totally ignore JAH Who commanded thee that thou might downstroy the livestock an persons?' him told him. [30] An at that time the king feared an arose from him throne an tellin Samu'iel 'Return fe wi' him seized him clothes - an Samu'iel refused fe return ~ Samu'iel clothes were torn. [31] An Samu'iel told Sa'ol - 'JAH divided thy kingdom.' [32] An again Sa'ol told Samu'iel before the people - 'Honour mi an atone mi sin fe mi before JAH that Him might forgive mi' ~ an as him have feared JAH Word Who Irated him - but as him didn't fear the king who dead - Samu'iel refused fe return ina him word. [33] Becaudis thing him pierced 'Amalieq king 'Agag before him swallowed what him chewed. [34] An a demon seized that Sa'ol who demolished the LAW of JAH - an becau Him were the King of Kings Who rule all - JAH struck pon him head a king who worked sin - fe it don't shame him. [35] Fe Him are all the Iration Lord Who dismiss all the nobles an kings Itority who don't fear Him - but there are none who rule Him. [36] Like unto Him spoke sayin - Daweet kindred shall go while it were famed an honoured - but Sa'ol kindred shall go while it were downbased - Him downstroyed kingdom from him child an from Sa'ol. [37] Becau it saddened Him - an becau Him downstroyed the criminals who saddened Him by them evil Work - JAH revenged an downstroyed Sa'ol kindred childran - fe a person who don't revenge JAH enemy -

him are JAH enemy. [38] When it are possible fe him fe revenge an downstroy - an when him have Itority - a person who don't revenge an downstroy the sinner an don't revenge an downstroy a person who don't keep JAH LAW - as him are JAH enemy - Him downstroyed Sa'ol kindred childran.

CHAPTER 7

[1] An whether thou be a king or a ruler - what important thing are thou? [2] Aren't it JAH Who Irated thee bringin from not livin toward livin - that thou might do Him Accord an might live firmed up by Him Command an might fear Him Judgemant? Like unto thou vex pon thy slaves an governed over them - all likewise there are also JAH Who vex pon thee an govern over thee. [3] Like unto thou beat without niceness persons who worked sin - all likewise there are also JAH Who will strike thee an lower thee toward *Gehannem* where are no exits up til Iternity. [4] Like unto thou whip him who weren't ruled fe thee an didn't bring a tribute fe thee - fe what are it that thou don't introduce a tribute fe JAH? [5] As Him are Who Irated thee in order that thou love that them might fear thee - an Who crowned thee pon all the Iration that thou might keep Him kindreds fe true - fe what are it that thou don't fear thy Irator JAH? [6] Judge by what are due an fe true like unto JAH Ipointed thee - yet don't sight up a face an favour fe small nor great ~ whom will thou fear without Him? keep Him Worship an the Nine Commands. [7] Like unto Mussie commanded 'Isra'iel childran sayin - 'I-man presented Water an fiyah fe thee-I ~ add thy hand toward what thou loved' - don't go neither rightward nor leftward. [8] Hear Him Word that I-man tell thee - that thou might hear Him Word an might do Him Command - lest thou say - 'She are beyond the sea or beyond the deep or beyond the river ~ who will bring fe mi that mi might sight she up an might hear Him Word an might do Him Command?' [9] Lest thou say - 'Who will proceed toward Heaven again an lower that JAH Word fe mi that mi might hear an do she?' - JAH Word are what approached - check - fe thou fe teach she with thy mouth an give alms by she with thy hand. [10] An thou didn't hear thy Irator JAH unless thou heard Him Book - an thou didn't love Him nor keep Him Command unless thou kept Him LAW. [11] An thou have that thou might enter toward *Gehannem* foriva - an unless thou loved Him Command - an unless thou did JAH Accord - Who honoured an famed thee separatin from all thy kindreds that thou might keep them fe true - thou have that thou might enter toward *Gehannem* foriva. [12] Him made thee above all - an Him crowned thee pon all Him kindreds that thou might rule Him kindreds fe true by what are due while thou thought of thy Irator Name Who Irated thee an gave thee a kingdom. [13] There are them whom thou whip from persons who wronged thee - an there are him whom thou pardon while thou thought of JAH Work - an there are him fe whom thou judge by what are due straightenin up thy reasonin. [14] An don't favour havin sight up a face pon the time them argued before thee ~ as Earth physique are thy money - don't accept a bribe that thou might pardon the sinner person an wrong the clean person. [15] If thou did Him Accord - JAH shall multiply thy era ina this world fe thee - but if thou sadden Him - Him will diminish thy era. [16] Think that thou will rise after thou dead - an that thou will be examined standin before Him pon all the Work thou worked whether it be goodly or evil. [17] If thou work goodly Work - thou will live ina Garden ina the Kingdom of Heaven - ina houses where kind kings live an where Light filled. Fe JAH don't shame thy lordship authority - but if thou work evil Work - thou will live ina *See'ol Gehannem* where evil kings live. [18] But pon the time thou sight up thy bein feared famousness - thy warriors award - thy hangin shield an spear - an pon the time thou sight up thy horses an thy troops beneath thy authority an them who beat drum an persons who play pon a harp before thee... [19] But pon the time thou sight up all this - thou mek thy reasonin lofty - an thou firm up thy collar of reasonin - an thou don't think of JAH Who gave thee all this honour - however pon the time Him told thee - Quit all this - thou aren't who quit it. [20] Fe thou have totally neglected the Ipointmant Him Ipointed thee - an Him shall give thy lordship fe another. [21] As death shall suddenly come pon thee - an as Judgemant shall be done ina Resurrection time - an as all man Work shall be examined - Him shall totally investigate an judge pon thee. [22] There are none who will honour this world kings - fe becau Him were Truth Judge - ina Judgemant time poor an wealthy will stand together. This world nobles crowns wherein them boast shall fall. [23] Judgemant are prepared - an a soul shall quake ~ at that time sinners an righteous ones Work shall be examined. [24] An there are none who shall be hidden. Pon the time a dawta arrived fe birthin - an pon the time the fetus ina she belly arrived fe bein birthed - like unto she cyaan prevent she womb - Earth also cyaan prevent she lodgers that are pon she ~ she will return. [25] An like unto clouds cyaan prevent rain lest them tek an rain toward the place JAH commanded them - fe JAH Word have Irated all bringin from not livin toward livin - an fe JAH Word again have introduced all toward a grave; an all likewise - after Resurrection time arrived - it aren't possible fe be that dead persons won't rise. [26] Like unto Mussie spoke sayin - 'It are by Words that proceed from JAH Tongue - yet it aren't only by grain that a person are saved'; an JAH Word again shall arouse all persons from graves. [27] Check - it were known that dead persons shall arise by JAH Word. [28] An again JAH said thus ina Repeatin Law becau persons who were nobles an kings who do Him Accord - As the day have arrived when them are counted fe downstruction - I-man shall revenge an downstroy them pon the day when Judgemant are judged an at the time when them feet stumble Him said. [29] An again JAH told persons who know Him Judgemant - Know know that I-man were your Irator JAH - an that I-man kill an I-man save. [30] I-man chastise ina the tribulation an I-man pardon ~ I-man lower toward *See'ol* an again I-man send forth toward the Garden - an there are none who shall escape from I Itority Him told them. [31] JAH said thus becau nobles an kings who didn't keep Him LAW - As Earthly kingdoms are a passin - an as them pass from mornin up til evenin - keep I Order an I LAW that unu might enter toward the Kingdom of Heaven that live firmed up foriva Him said. [32] Fe JAH callin Righteous ones are fe glory - an sinners fe tribulation ~ Him will mek the sinner wretched but will honour righteous ones. [33] Him will dismiss the person who didn't do Him Accord - but Him will Ipoint the person who did Him Accord.

CHAPTER 8

[1] Hear I - mek I tell thee the thing whereby dead persons shall arise ~ them shall plant a plant an be fertile an grapes shall send forth vines ~ as JAH shall bring the fruit 'imhibe 'albo ~ them shall cast wine from it. [2] Overstand that that plant thou planted were small - but that she sent forth tips fruit an leaves today. [3] JAH give she root fe drink from Earth an Water - from both. [4] But Him feed she wood from fiyah an wind ~ roots give leaves Water fe drink - an Earth give firmness fe woods. [5] But the soul that JAH Irated mek them bear fruit amidst them - an dead persons arisin are likewise.

[6] Pon the time soul were separated from flesh - as each of them ras selves have gone - Him said - Gather souls from the four natures - from Earth an Water - wind an fiyah. [7] But Earth nature lived firmed up ina she nature an became Earth - an Water nature lived firmed up ina she nature an became Water. [8] An wind nature lived firmed up ina she nature an became wind - an fiyah nature lived firmed up ina she nature an became a hot fiyah. [9] But a soul that JAH separated from flesh returned toward she Irator ~ up til Him raise she up inited with flesh pon the time Him loved - Him place she ina Garden ina the place Him loved. [10] Him place righteous souls ina Light house ina Garden - but that Him might send way sinners souls - Him also place them ina darkness house ina *See'ol* up til the time when Him loved. [11] JAH told the prophet Hiziq'iel - Call souls from the four corners - that them might be gathered an be one limb. [12] Pon the time Him spoke ina one Word sayin thus - the souls were gathered from the four corners. [13] An Water nature brought verdure - an again fiyah nature brought fiyah. [14] An again Earth nature brought Earth - an wind nature brought wind. [15] An JAH brought a soul from the Garden place where Him placed it ~ them were gathered by one Word - an a Resurrection were made. [16] An again I-man shall show thee the example that are alongside thee ~ the day dusk ~ thou sleep ~ the night dawn - an thou rise from thy beddin - but pon the time thou slept it are thy death example. [17] An pon the time thou awoke it are thy arisin example - but the night when all persons sleep whose physiques were dark - fe darkness have covered them - are this world example. [18] But the mornin light - when darkness are eliminated an when light are ina all the world an when persons arise an graze toward the field - are dead persons example. [19] An this Kingdom of Heaven where man are renewed are like unto this ~ dead persons Resurrection are like unto this ~ as this world are passin - it are the night example. [20] An like unto Daweet spoke sayin - 'Him placed Him example ina Sun' - as Sun shine pon the time it rose - it are a Kingdom of Heaven example. [21] An like unto Sun shine ina this world today - pon the time Kristos come Him shall shine like unto Sun ina Kingdom of Heaven that are new ~ as Him have said - I-man am a Sun that don't set an a Torch that aren't extinguished - Him JAH are she Light. [22] An Him shall quickly arouse the dead persons again ~ I-man shall bring one example fe thee again from thy food that thou sow an whereby thou are saved - an whether it be a wheat kernel or a barley kernel or a lentil kernel or all man seeds sown pon Earth - there are none that grow unless it were demolished an rotten. [23] An like unto the person flesh thou sight up - pon the time it were demolished an rotten - Earth eat stoutness with the hide. [24] An pon the time Earth ate it stoutness it grow bein around a kernel seventh ~ JAH give a cloud that seized rain like unto Him loved - an roots grow pon Earth an send forth leaves. [25] An if she were demolished an rotten she cyaan grow - but after she grew she send forth many buds. [26] An by JAH Accord fruit are given fe those buds that grew - an Him clothe it stoutness ina straw. [27] Sight up like unto the measure that the seed kernel thou sowed abounded - yet the silver an the leaf - the ear an the straw aren't counted fe thee. [28] Don't be a dull one who don't know - an sight up thy seed that it abounded - an all likewise - think that dead persons shall raceive the arisin that them will arise - an them hardship like unto them Work. [29] Hear I - that if thou sow wheat - it won't grow bein barley - nor bein wheat if thou sow barley - an mek I tell thee again that it won't grow ~ if thou sow wheat will thou gather barley? If thou sow watercress will thou gather linseed? [30] How about from plants kind - if thou plant figs will it really grow fe thee bein nuts? How about if thou plant almonds - will it grow fe thee bein grapes? [31] If thou plant the sweet fruit will it grow fe thee bein bitter? How about if thou plant the bitter fruit - are it possible fe it fe be sweet? [32] How about all likewise - if a sinner dead are it possible fe arise bein righteous ina Resurrection time? How about if a righteous person dead - are it possible fe arise bein a sinner ina Resurrection time? Every one shall raceive him hardship like unto him Work - yet him will raceive him hardship like unto him sin an him hand Work - yet there are none who will be canvicted by him companion sin. [33] A highland tree are planted an it send forth long branches ~ it will totally dry up ~ yet unless Heaven rained rain it leaves won't be verdant. [34] An the cedar will be uprooted from it roots unless summer rain alit pon it. [35] An all likewise - dead persons won't arise unless welfare dew alit fe them bein commanded from JAH.

CHAPTER 9

[1] Unless highland mountains an Gielabuhie regions rained a pardon rain fe them bein commanded from JAH - them won't grow grass fe beasts an animals. [2] An 'Elam mountains an Gele`ad mountains won't give verdant leaves fe sheeps an goats - nor fe oribi an animals ina wilderness - nor fe ibexes an hartebeest. [3] An likewise - pardon an dew bein commanded from JAH didn't alight fe doubters an criminals who made error an crime a money beforehand ~ dead persons won't arise ~ an Deemas an Qophros who worship idols an dig roots an work an instigate a thing... [4] An them who dig roots an practice sorcery an mek persons battle... [5] An them who lust havin departed from LAW - an Miedon an 'Atiena persons who believe ina them idols - an them who play an sing fe them while them beat violins an drums an strummed harps - them won't arise unless pardon dew alit fe them bein commanded from JAH. [6] These are who will be canvicted pon the day when dead persons arise an when Definite Judgemant are done - yet persons who save them ras selves an who lust ina them hands Work - them err by them idols. [7] Thou wasteful of heart dull one - do it seem fe thee that dead persons won't arise? [8] Pon the time a trumpet were blown by the Angels Chief Hola Meeka'iel tongue - that dead ones arise then - as thou won't remain ina grave without arisin - don't think a thing that are thus. [9] Hills an mountains shall be level an shall be a cleared path. [10] An Resurrection shall be done fe all fleshly ones.

CHAPTER 10

[1] However if it weren't thus - it are that former persons might be buried ina them faadas grave Iginnin from 'Adam - Iginnin from Siet an 'Abiel - Siem an Noh - Yis'haq an 'Abriham - Yosief an Ya`iqob - an 'Aron an Mussie - yet fe what are it that them didn't love that them might be buried ina another place? [2] Aren't it fe them fe arise together with them cousins ina Resurrection time? How about aren't it lest them bones be counted with evil ones an pagans bones - them who worship idols? Fe what are it that them didn't love that them might be buried ina another place? [3] But thou - don't mislead thy reasonin while thou said - 'How will dead persons arise after them dead - them who were buried ina one grave bein tens of thousands an whose bodies were demolished an rotten?' [4] An pon the time thou sight up toward a grave - thou speak this ina thy reasonin dullness while thou said - 'A whole fistful of Earth won't be found ~ how will dead persons arise?' [5] Will thou say the seed thou sowed won't grow? Even the seed thou sowed shall grow. [6] An all likewise - the

souls JAH sowed shall quickly arise - as Him have Irated man ina Him Truth bringin from not livin toward livin - Him shall arouse them quickly by Him Word that save ~ Him won't delay Him arousin. [7] An as Him have again returned him from livin - toward a grave ina death - what about aren't it possible fe Him again fe return from death toward Life? [8] Savin an liftin up are possible fe JAH.

CHAPTER 11

[1] 'Armon perished an she fortress were demolished ~ as JAH have brought the hardship pon them like unto them evil an the Work them worked by them hands - persons who worship the idols ina 'Edomyas an Zablon shall be downbased at that time ~ as JAH have approached - Who shall canvict them who worked ina them infancy an didn't quit up til them aged - becau them idols an them evil - Seedona an Theeros shall weep.. [2] Becau them worked sin an seducin fornication an worshipped idols - becaudis thing JAH shall revenge an downstroy them ~ fe them didn't live firmed up ina them Irator JAH Command - an Yihuda dawta childran shall be wretched. [3] She lived firmed up ina killin prophets an ina Irie Ites - yet as she didn't live firmed up ina the Nine Laws an the Worship - pon the time when dead ones arise - 'Iyerusaliem sin shall be revealed. [4] At that time JAH shall examine she ina Him Nature Wisdom ~ Him will revenge an downstroy she pon all she sin that she worked ina she infancy era ~ she didn't quit workin she sin Iginnin from she beauty era up til she age. [5] She entered toward a grave an became dust like unto she former faadas who lived firmed up ina them sin - an ina Resurrection time Him shall revenge an downstroy persons who demolished JAH LAW. [6] It shall be judged pon them - fe Mussie have spoken becau them sayin - 'Them LAW lodgin - them reasonins - became Sedom law lodgin.' [7] An them kindred are Gemorra kindred - an them law are what downstroy - an them Work are evil. [8] An them law are snake poison that downstroy - an viper poison that downstroy from alongside that.

CHAPTER 12

[1] 'Iyerusaliem child - as this thy sin are like unto Gemorra an Sedom sin - 'Iyerusaliem child - this are thy tribulation that were spoken by a prophet. [2] An thy tribulation are like unto Gemorra an Sedom tribulation - an them law lodgin reasonin firmed up ina adultery an arrogance. [3] Aside from adultery an arrogance rain - pardon an humility rain didn't rain from them reasonins by money that them Law reasonin lodgin are fertile - apart from spillin man blood an robbin an forgettin them Irator JAH. [4] An them didn't know them Irator JAH - apart from them evil Work an them idols - an them are Irie ina them hands Work - an them lust pon males an pon livestock. [5] As them eye of reasonin have been blinded lest them sight up secrets - an as them ears have deafened lest them hear or do JAH Accord that Him love - them didn't know JAH ina them Work - an them reasonins are like unto Sedom law lodgin. An them kindred - Gemorra grapes kindred that bear sweet fruit. [6] An if them examine them Work - it are poison that kill - fe it have firmed up ina curse Iginnin from the day when it were worked - an fe it grounation have been ina downstruction era. [7] As them Law lodgin - them reasonins - have firmed up ina sin Work - as them bodies have firmed up ina Seythan burnin Work fe build sin - them Law lodgin - them reasonins - have no goodly Work everytime. [8] An pon the time him shame an were baptise (by one who is led) it were fe chastisemant an downstruction - an him will firm up the persons who drank an them reasonins - an him will mek them who downstroy I - disgustin persons who distanced from JAH. [9] Fe them have lived firmed up ina them Work that were evil - an him will mek them Deeyablos lodgin - an eatin what were sacrificed fe the idols have been begun ina the House of 'Isra'iel - an she proceed toward the mountains an the trees. [10] An she worship the idols that peoples ina she area worship - an she dawta childran an she male childran fe demons who don't know goodly Work separatin from evil. [11] An them spill clean blood ~ them gush an spill grapes from Sedom fe the idols foriva. [12] An she glorify an worship the Dagwon that the 'Iloflans worship - an she sacrifice fe him from she flocks an she fattened cows - that she might be Irie ina demons laziness that them taught she fe sacrifice fe them - an ina them gushin an spillin the grapes - an that she might do them accord. [13] She sacrifice fe him that she might be Irie in demons laziness that them taught she lest she know she Irator JAH Who feed she at each time an Who cherished an raised she Iginnin from she infancy up til she beauty - an again up til she age - an again up til she age day when she dead. [14] An again I-man shall revenge an canvict him ina Resurrection time - an as she didn't return toward I LAW - an as she didn't live firmed up ina I Command - she time when she live ina *Gehannem* shall be up til Iternity. [15] If them were Irators fe true - mek she idols arise with she an downscend toward *Gehannem* an save she pon the time I-man vexed an downstroyed she - an pon the time I-man distanced all the priests of the idols who lust with she. [16] Like unto she made sin an insult pon the Hola Items an pon I Lodgin the Temple - I-man made she wretched by all this. [17] When them told she - 'Check - this are JAH kindred - an she are 'Isra'iel Irator JAH Lodgin' - an the famous King country 'Iyerusaliem who were separate from them who were separate - she are the Most I JAH Name Lodgin' - I-man made she wretched like unto she saddened I Name that were called ina she. [18] She boast ina I that she were I slave an that I-man were she Lord ~ she wink pon I like unto a criminal - yet she aren't who fear I an do I Accord like unto I bein she Lord. [19] Them became a obstacle pon she fe mislead that them might distance she from I - yet she are ruled fe other idols who don't feed she nor clothe she. [20] She sacrifice sacrifice fe them - an she eat the sacrifice - an she spill blood fe them - an she gush an drink from the grapes fe them ~ she smoke up ishence fe them - an she mek the ishence fragrance smell fe them ~ she idols command she - an she are commanded fe them. [21] An again she sacrifice she dawta childran an she male childran fe them - an as she present praises fe them becau them Love - she are Irie ina the thing she spoke by she tongue an ina she hands Work. [22] Woe fe she pon the day when Definite Judgemant are done - an woe fe she idols whom she love an inite; an she shall downscend with them toward *Gehannem* beneath *See'ol* - where the worm don't slumber an the fiyah aren't extinguished. [23] Woe fe thee wretched 'Iyerusaliem child - fe thou have quit I Who Irated thee an have worshipped different idols. [24] An I-man shall bring the hardship pon thee like unto thy Work ~ as thou have saddened I - an as thou have ignored I Word - an as thou didn't work goodly Work - I-man shall canvict thee toward thy pretensions. [25] Fe thou have saddened I Word - an fe thou didn't live firmed up ina I LAW whereby thou swore with I - that thou might keep I LAW an that I- man might live with thee ina Support an might save thee from all who fight thee - an also that thou might keep I Order that I-man commanded thee - an I-man shall ignore thee an won't quickly save thee from the tribulation. [26] Thou didn't keep all this - an I-man ignored thee ~ as I-man have

created thee - an as thou didn't keep I Command nor I Word - I-man shall canvict thee ina Judgemant time - an I-man honoured thee that thou might be I kin. [27] An like unto Gemorra an Sedom were separated from I - thou were separated from I. [28] An I-man judged an downstroyed them - an like unto Sedom an Gemorra were separated from I - thou separated from I - an now like unto I- man vexed an downstroyed them - I-man vexed an downstroyed thee ~ as thou are from Sedom an Gemorra kindred whom I-man downstroyed - I- man downstroyed thee ~ as them whom I-man Irated have saddened I by goin toward a youtmon wife an by lustin without LAW - with animals an males like unto arrivin with dawtaz - I-man downstroyed them name invocation from this world lest them live ina them Irie Ites. [29] There are no fearin JAH ina them faces Iginnin from a infant up til a elder ~ them help him ina all them evil Work - yet Him don't vex pon each one that them might quit workin she ~ as them Work are evil - them are sated of sin an iniquity. [30] All evil Work - robbery an arrogance an greed - are prepared ina them reasonins. [31] An becaudis thing JAH ignored them an downstroyed them countries - an them are there that Him might burn them with fiyah up til them root grounation perish ~ them totally perished up til the Iternity - yet Him didn't mek even one from them remain. [32] As them have firmed up ina sin - them shall wait ina downstruction foriva up til the Day of Advent when Definite Judgemant are done - fe them have saddened I with them evil Work - an I-man won't pardon them nor forgive them. [33] An I-man ignored them ~ fe thou won't find a reason pon the time I- man vexed an seized thee becau all thy Work were robbery an sin - adultery an greed an speakin lies - all error Work an the obstacle that I-man don't love - an thou 'Iyerusaliem child who were wretched - pon the day when Judgemant are done thou will be seized ina Judgemant like unto them. [34] I-man had made thee fe honour - but thou downbased thy ras self ~ I- man had called thee I money - but thou became fe another. [35] I-man had betrothed thee fe honour - but thou became fe Deeyablos - an I-man shall revenge an downstroy thee like unto thy evil Work. [36] Becau thou didn't hear all I Word - an becau thou didn't keep the Command I-man commanded thee pon the time I-man loved thee - I-man shall multiply an bring firm vengeance pon thee - fe I-man am JAH Who Irated thee - an I-man shall judge pon all sinners like unto thee - an pon the day when Judgemant are done I-man shall bring the hardship pon them like unto them evil Work. [37] As thou didn't keep I Word - an as thou have ignored I Judgemant - I- man shall canvict thee with them. [38] Woe fe unu - Gemorra an Sedom - who have no fearin JAH ina your reasonin. [39] All likewise - woe fe thy sista 'Iyerusaliem child pon whom it shall be judged together with thee ina Fiyah of *Gehannem* - fe unu will downscend together toward *Gehannem* that were prepared fe unu - where are no exits foriva - an woe fe all sinners who worked thy sin. [40] As unu didn't keep I Command nor I Word - thou an she who didn't keep I Command nor I Word shall downscend toward *See'ol* together pon the day when Judgemant are judged. [41] But kind persons who kept I Command an I Word shall eat the money that sinner persons accumulated - an like unto JAH commanded - kind persons shall share the loot that evil persons captured - an kind persons shall be totally Irie. [42] But wrongdoers an sinner persons shall weep - an them shall be sad becau all them sin that them wronged havin departed from I Command. [43] Him who keep I Word an live firmed up ina I Command - him are who find I blessin an are honoured alongside I. [44] All person who keep I Word an live firmed up ina I Command shall eat the fatness found from Earth - an shall live havin entered toward the Garden where enter kind kings who have straight reasonins.

CHAPTER 13

[1] As them shall be wretched an perish by I wrath pon the time I-man seized them - woe fe Theeros an Seedona an all Yihuda country regions who mek them ras selves arrogant today. [2] Conquerin JAH said thus ~ Him have said - Deeyablos child who are totally arrogant shall be birthed from them - the False *Messeeh* who fe a Truth thing are she enemy - who firm up him collar of reasonin - who boast an don't know him Irator - an Him said - Woe fe them - an JAH Who rule all said - I-man made him fe I anger pattern that I-man might be revealed ina him Power. [3] An this Qifirnahom Semarya an Geleela an Demasqo an Sorya an 'Akeya an Qophros an all Yordanos region are kindreds who firmed up them collars of reasonin - who live firmed up ina them sin - an whom death shadow an darkness covered - fe Deeyablos have covered them reasonins ina sin - an fe them are commanded fe that arrogant Deeyablos - an them didn't return toward fearin JAH. *[4]* At that time woe fe persons who are commanded fe demons an who sacrifice sacrifice ina them name fe them ~ as them have denied JAH Who Irated them - them resemble animals without minds - fe the False *Messeeh* who forgot JAH LAW an are Deeyablos child shall set up him image ina all the places (fe him have said 'Mi are a god') - an him shall be Irie ina him reasonin accord - ina him hand Work an ina robbery an all the sins an perfidy an iniquity - ina robbery an all the adulteries that a person work. [5] Fe becau it were counted alongside JAH that him work this - the era are known that them work sin. [6] Sun shall darken an moon shall be blood - an stars shall be shaken from Heaven - all the Work shall pass by the miracles that JAH shall bring ina Fulfillmant Era that Him might mek Earth pass - an that Him might mek all pass who live ina sin of persons who live within she. [7] As JAH have been proud pon the Iration Him Irated - an as Him have quickly made all Him loved ina one iwa - the Lord death shall downstroy a small enemy Deeyablos. [8] Fe JAH Who rule all have said - I-man shall judge an downstroy - but after Advent - Deeyablos have no authority. *[9]* An pon the day when him were seized by I anger - him shall downscend toward *Gehannem* - fe which him mek application an where firm tribulation are ~ as him will tek all who are with him toward chastisemant an downstruction an perfidy - becau I-man were Who send forth from *Gehannem* an Who introduce toward *Gehannem* - him will downscend toward *Gehannem.* [10] As Him give firmness an Power fe weak persons - an again as Him give weakness fe powerful an firm persons - mek a powerful one not boast ina him Power. [11] As Him are a Ruler - an as Him judge an save the wronged persons from the persons hands who wrong them - Him will return the grudge of the widows an the child whose faada an mother dead pon him. [12] Woe fe thee who boast an firm up thy collar of reasonin - fe whom it seem that I-man won't rule thee nor judge an downstroy thee - fe ina him boastin an him arrogance him have said - 'Mi will streach mi throne ina stars an Heaven - an mi will be like unto JAH Who are lofty.' [13] An like unto Him spoke sayin - How Deeyablos fell from Heaven - him who shine like unto a mornin star that were Irated precedin all - woe fe thee. [14] An thou dared an spoke this ina thy arrogance - an thou didn't think of JAH Who totally Irated thee by Him Itority ~ why did thou boast thy ras self that thou downscend toward *Gehannem* ina thy reasonin firmness? [15] Thou were downbased separate from all Angels like unto thee - fe them praise them Irator with a humbled reasonin becau them knew that Him were Who Irated

them from fiyah an wind - an fe them don't depart from Him Command - an fe them keep them reasonins from perfidy lest them totally depart from Him Command. [16] But thou did a firm perfidy ina thy reasonin arrogance ~ thou became a wretched man separate from thy companions - fe thou have cherished all the sin an iniquity - robbery an perfidy whereby persons who forgot JAH LAW an sinners like unto thee live firmed up - them who are from thy kindred an commit crime like unto thee - an who live firmed up by thy command an thy accord whereby thou teach sin. [17] Woe fe thee - fe the demons thou misled ina thy malice an thou will downscend toward *Gehannem* together. [18] O unu JAH children who erred by that misleadin criminal Deeyablos - woe fe unu ~ as unu have erred like unto him by the money that him taught unu an that him hosts taught unu - unu will downscend toward *Gehannem* together - where are no exits foriva. [19] An formerly when JAH slave Mussie were there - unu saddened JAH by the Water where argumant were made an pon Korieb - an by 'Amalieq an pon Mount Seena. [20] An moreover pon the time unu sent scouts toward Kene`an - pon the time them told unu this sayin 'The path are far - an them ramparts an them fortresses that reach up til Heaven are firm - an warriors live there' - unu vexed that unu might return towad Gibts country where unu work worrisome Work - an unu saddened JAH Word. [21] Unu didn't think of JAH Who firmed unu up from the tribulation - an Who did great miracles ina Gibts - an Who led unu by Him Angel Itority. Him would veil unu ina cloud by day lest the Sun burn unu an Him would shine a column of fiyah fe unu by night lest your feet stumble ina darkness. [22] An pon the time the army an Fer`on frightened unu - unu totally cried toward Mussie - an Mussie totally cried toward JAH - an Him lodged ina Him Angel an kept unu lest unu meet with Fer`on. [23] But Him introduced them toward 'Eritra ina tribulation ~ JAH led only 'Isra'iel - fe Him have said - An there were no different idol with them - but Him buried them enemies ina sea at one time - an Him didn't preserve none who flee from them. [24] An Him made 'Isra'iel cross amidst the sea by foot ~ there are no tribulation that found them arisin from the Gibtsans ~ Him delivered them toward Mount Seena - an there Him fed them *menna* forty eras. [25] As 'Isra'iel children sadden JAH everytime - Him did all this goodly thing fe them an them neglected fe worship JAH. [26] Them placed evil ina them reasonins Iginnin from them childhood up til them age - fe JAH Mouth have spoken thus ina *'Oreet* where the faadas birth were written ~ as Him have spoken sayin - 'Adam children reasonin are ash - an all them Work are toward robbery an them run toward evil ~ there are none from them who love straight Work - apart from gatherin a person money ina violence an swearin ina lie an wrongin companions an robbin an stealin - them placed evil ina them reasonins. [27] An all go toward evil Work ina the era when them live ina Life ~ 'Isra'iel childran who demolished JAH LAW totally saddened JAH Iginnin from Antiquity up til fufillmant era.

CHAPTER 14

[1] An pon the time JAH downstroyed Qayen children - kindreds who preceded - ina downstruction Water becau them sin - Him baptised Earth ina Water of Downstruction - an Him cleansed she from all Qayel children sin. [2] As Him have said - I-man were sad becau I-man Irated man - Him downstroyed all wrongdoers ~ Him didn't preserve apart from eight persons ~ Him downstroyed all ~ after this Him multiplied them an them filled Earth ~ them shared them faada 'Adam inheritance. [3] But Noh swore with JAH a oath ~ them swore a oath with JAH lest JAH again downstroy Earth ina Downstruction Water - an lest Noh children eat what deceased nor what lodged dead - lest them worship different idols apart from JAH Who Irated them - an that Him might be a Love Faada fe them - an lest Him downstroy them at one time ina them vain sin - an lest Him prevent them the first an the spring rain - an that Him might give fe livestock an persons them food at each time - that Him might give them the grass an the grain fruit an plants - an that them might work goodly Work ina all that JAH love. [4] An after Him gave them this Order - 'Isra'iel children saddened JAH by them sin ~ them didn't live firmed up ina Him LAW like unto them faadas Yis'haq an 'Abriham an Ya`iqob who didn't demolish them Irator JAH LAW. [5] An Iginnin from the small up til the great - those 'Isra'iel children who didn't keep JAH LAW are crooked ina them Work. [6] An whether them be them priests or them chiefs or them scribes - everyone demolish JAH LAW. [7] Them don't live firmed up ina JAH Order an Him LAW that Mussie commanded them ina Repeatin Law sayin - 'Love thy Irator JAH ina thy complete body an thy complete reasonin.' [8] Them don't firm up ina JAH Order an Him LAW that Mussie commanded them ina book where LAW were written sayin - 'Love thy companion like unto thy body - an don't worship him idols that were different - an don't go toward a youtmon wife ~ don't kill a soul ~ don't steal. [9] An don't witness ina lie - an be it him donkey or be it him ox - don't love thy companion money nor all that thy bredda bought.' [10] However after him commanded them all this - 'Isra'iel children who were evil return toward treachery an sin - robbery an iniquity - toward a youtmon wife an toward lies an stealin an worshippin idols. [11] 'Isra'iel children saddened JAH pon Korieb by workin a cow that graze toward grass ~ them bowed sayin - 'Check - these are wi irators who sent wi forth from Gibts.' [12] An them were Irie ina them hand Work ~ if them ate an drank an satta - them arose fe sing. [13] As JAH have told him sayin - Thy kindreds whom thou sent forth from Gibts country where rulership are - them have proceeded from LAW an wronged - an them worked a cow image an bowed fe the idol - becaudis thing Mussie vexed an alit from Seena mountain. [14] While Mussie vexed pon him kindreds - him alit with him canfidante 'Iyasu - an pon the time 'Iyasu heard - him said - 'Check - I-man hear warriors voice ina 'Isra'iel camp.' [15] An Mussie told 'Iyasu - 'It are when 'Isra'iel play havin drunk the unboiled wine - yet as fe a warrior voice - it aren't' - an him alit an broke them image an totally crushed it up til it were like unto dust ~ him mixed it within the Water that 'Isra'iel children drink beside the mountain. [16] An after this him commanded the priests that them might slay one another becau the sin them worked before JAH. [17] Them knew that defyin JAH surpass killin them an killin them faadas - an them did like unto him commanded them. [18] An Mussie told them - 'Becau unu saddened JAH Who fed unu an cherished unu an Who sent unu forth from a rulership house an Who bequeathed fe unu the inheritance that Him swore fe your faadas that Him might give fe them an fe them children after them - becaudis thing unu made JAH Irie.' [19] Fe them go toward sin an a evil thing - an them didn't quit saddenin JAH there. [20] Them aren't like unto them faadas Yis'haq an 'Abriham an Ya`iqob who made JAH Irie with them goodly Work that Him might give them what are pon Earth an what Him prepared fe persons who love Him ina Heaven Iginnin from them infancy up til them youthood an up til them age ~ them aren't like unto 'Abriham an Yis'haq an Ya`iqob who made Him Irie with them Work that Him might give them a Earth of inheritance where Irie Ites are found ina this world - an a garden that mek Irie - prepared fe kind persons ina hereafter world - what

Him prepared fe 'Abriham an Yis'haq an Ya`iqob who made JAH Irie when them were ina Life an who love Him - Whom a eye didn't sight up nor a ear hear an Who aren't thought of ina reasonin. [21] An them childran who denied JAH an were evil an who live firmed up ina them reasonin accord - them didn't hear JAH Command - Him Who fed them an cherished them an kept them Iginnin from them infancy. [22] Them didn't think of JAH - Who sent them forth from Gibts land an saved them from brick Work an a firm rulership. [23] But them totally saddened Him - an Him would arouse peoples ina them area pon them - an them would arise pon them ina enmity an also tax them like unto them loved.

CHAPTER 15

[1] An at that time Midyam persons arose pon them ina enmity - an them aroused them armies pon 'Isra'iel that them might fight them - an them king name are called 'Akrandis ~ him quickly gathered many armies ina Keeliqyas an Sorya an Demasqo. [2] An campin beyond Yordanos him sent messengers sayin - 'An that mi might capture your money - pay tax toward 'Isra'iel fe mi' ~ him told them 'But if unu don't pay tax - mi came that mi might punish unu an might capture your livestocks an tek your mares an capture your childran.' [3] 'Mi will capture an tek unu toward the country unu don't know - an there mi will mek unu Water pourers an wood pickers' him told them. [4] 'Don't boast while unu said - "InI are JAH kindreds an there are nothing able fe InI" - aren't JAH Who sent mi that mi might downstroy unu an plunder your money? an aren't mi whom JAH sent that mi might gather all your kindreds? [5] Are there really a savin that them different idols saved the other kins that mi downstroyed? Mi captured them mares an them horses an mi killed them an captured them childran. [6] An unless unu introduced the tax that mi commanded unu - mi will downstroy unu like unto them' him said - an him crossed Yordanos that him might plunder them livestocks an them money an capture them wives. [7] An after this 'Isra'iel childran wept a firm mournin toward JAH - an them totally cried - however them lacked one who help them. [8] An becaudis thing JAH gave firmness fe the three bredren - an them names are like unto this: - an them are Yihuda an Mebikyas an Meqabees - whose features were handsome an who were warriors ina them Power. [9] An 'Isra'iel childran totally wept there ~ pon the time them heard - it saddened them ina them heart arisin from all 'Isra'iel childran shout ~ the child whose mother an faada dead pon him - an widows - an them officials an them priests - all 'Isra'iel kindred - both dawtaz an males - an all children - would weep sprinklin ash pon them heads - an them nobles had worn sackcloth. [10] But those bredren - who were attractive an comely - went an agreed that them might save them ~ them counseled sayin - 'Mek InI go an give InI bodies fe death becau these persons.' [11] Tellin one another - 'Tek heart - tek heart' - them went girdin them swords pon them waists an seizin them spears ina them hands - an them went prepared that them might incriminate the warrior. [12] An them arrived toward them camp ~ Mebikyus attacked the warrior (the king) when him had sat at a dinnertable ~ him cut him neck ina one blow when food were ina him mouth; an Meqabyus an Yihuda struck him armies pon the king left an right by sword an killed them. [13] An pon the time them king were defeated - them entered toward them spears ina them companions hearts - an them all totally fled an them bows were broken an them were defeated. [14] But those bredren who are attractive an comely were saved from death ~ there are no evil thing that found them - but as JAH have returned chastisemant toward them - them sliced up one another an were depleted. [15] Them were defeated an dead an them crossed Yordanos - an up til them crossed them cast way all them money - an all them money remained - an pom the time 'Isra'iel childran sight up that them enemies fled - them went toward them camp an took both what them plundered an them money fe them ras selves. [16] JAH saved 'Isra'iel doin thus by the bredren an Mebikyu hand. [17] 'Isra'iel sat a few days while them made JAH Irie. [18] But after that them again returned toward them sin ~ 'Isra'iel childran neglected worshippin JAH by what are due. [19] An Him shall again sadden them by kins who don't know them an who will gather them field crops an downstroy them grape places an plunder them flocks an slaughter an feed them livestocks before them... [20] an who will capture them wives an them dawta childran an them male childran ~ becau it were that them sadden JAH everytime; as themare kindreds who demolished the LAW - them will hammer them childran before them pon each of them heads ~ them won't save them.

CHAPTER 16

[1] Them who do this are Theeros an Seedona an them who live beyond Yordanos river an pon the sea edge - Keran an Gele`ad - 'Iyabuseewon an Kenaniewon - 'Edom an Giegiesiewon an 'Amalieq persons. [2] All peoples do thus - who live firmed up ina each of them tribes an countries an regions an ina each of them Works an country languages - an all live firmed up like unto JAH worked them. [3] An there are persons from them who know JAH - an whose Work were beautiful. [4] An there are persons from them whose Work were evil an who don't know JAH Who Irated them - an like unto them worked sin - Him ruled them ina Sorya king Silminasor hand. [5] As him plunder an tek Demasqo money - an as him share Semarya loot that are before Gibts king - Him ruled them ina Silminasor hand. [6] Gielabuhie region an also persons ina Fars an Miedon - Qephedoqya an Sewseegya - who live ina the West mountains - ina Gele`ad fortress an Phasthos that are part of Yihuda land... [7]  an these are who live in them region - an them are kindreds who don't know JAH nor keep Him Command - an whose collar of reasonin were firm. [8]  An Him shall pay them them hardship like unto them Work evil an them hands Work. [9]  Fe Gele`ad kindreds an Qeesarya region an 'Amalieq have become one there - that them might downstroy JAH country that were filled of a Truth thing - an within which 'Isra'iel Irator are praised - Him Who are Most Glorified an Conquerin - an Whom Angels who are many many ina Keerubiel chariots - them who stand before Him - serve fearin an tremblin - an Him shall pay them them hardship like unto them Work evil an them hands Work.

CHAPTER 17

[1] 'Amalieq an 'Edomyas persons don't worship JAH by Whose Itority Earth an Heaven rulership were seized ~ as them are criminals who don't live firmed up ina Truth Work - them don't fear fe demolish Him Lodgin - the Temple. [2] An there are no fearin JAH before them - apart from sheddin blood an adultery an eatin what were beaten an sacrificed fe a idol an all that resemble what lodged dead - an these are scorned sinners. [3] Them have no virtue nor religion ~ as them are who hated goodly Work - an as them don't know JAH - an as them don't know Love Work - apart from robbin a person

money an from sin - an apart from downsturbin a person an all hated Work - apart from games an song like unto them faada Deeyablos taught them - them have no virtue nor religion. [4]   As him have ruled them with him host - demons - him teach them all evil Work that were fe each of them ras selves - all robbery an sin - theft an falsehood - robbin money an eatin what were beaten an what lodged dead - an adultery Work. [5]   An him teach them all that resemble this - an goin toward a youtmon wife - an sheddin blood - eatin what were sacrificed fe idol an what lodged dead - an killin a person soul ina violence - an envy an winkin an greed an all evil Work that JAH don't love ~ Deeyablos who were them enemy teach them this teachin that him might distance them from JAH LAW Who rule all the world. [6]   But JAH Work are innocence an humility - not annoyin a bredren an lovin a companion - harmonisin an lovin with all persons. [7]   Don't be hypocrites fe favour fe a person face - an don't be wrongdoers nor totally robbers nor persons who go toward a youtmon wife - nor persons who work iniquity an evil Work pon them companion - nor who cajole that them might wrong them companion ina violence. [8]   Them wink an shake them heads an provoke fe evil ~ them discourage fe mislead that them might lower them toward Iternity Definite Judgemant.

CHAPTER 18
[1] Think that thou will go ina death toward JAH ina Whose Hand all are - an thou will stand before Him that Him might canvict thee before Him pon all the sin thou Worked. [2] As them who are arrogant an evil - an powerful ones children who aren't strengthenin more than them - were likewise formerly - becau them sight up them stature an them Power an them firm authority - them didn't mek JAH before them - an them didn't know that Him were them Irator Who Irated them bringin from not livin toward livin. [3] An when them faadas bein like unto "Angels" praised pon Mount Hola with Angels - pon the time them accord misled them - them alit toward this world where Definite Judgemant shall be done foriva. [4] As JAH ina the Antiquity have Irated human flesh fe them - that it might mislead them becau them reasonin arrogance an might test them as it were them kept Him LAW an Him Command - them married wives from Qayel children. [5] But them didn't keep Him LAW ~ Him lowered them toward *Gehannem* fiyah with them faada Deeyablos; fe JAH have vexed pon the offspring of Siet who wronged like unto persons - an persons era diminished becau them sin. [6] An them took 'Adam children toward sin with them ~ Him lowered them toward *See'ol* where them shall raceive a verdict. [7] As persons era have been divided becau Siet children erred by Qayel children - when a person eras were nine hundred ina the Antiquity - them returned toward livin a hundred twenty eras. [8] An as them are flesh an blood - JAH said - I Spirit of Support won't live firmed up pon them. [9] An becaudis thing InI era were divided - fe becau InI sin an InI iniquity - InI era have been divided from InI faadas who preceded - an when them are ina them infancy again - them are dyin. [10] But InI faadas era had abounded - becau them kept Him LAW an becau them didn't sadden JAH. [11] But InI faadas era had abounded - becau them vexed pon them dawta children that them might teach them - an becau them vexed pon them male children lest them demolish JAH LAW. [12] Becau them didn't demolish JAH LAW with them dawta children an them male children - becaudis thing them era had abounded fe true.

CHAPTER 19
[1] Pon the time Qayen children abounded them worked drums an harps - *santee* an violins - an them made songs an all the games. [2] Children who are attractive an comely were birthed fe Qayen from the wife of the kind man 'Abiel - whom him killed becau she - fe she were attractive - an after him killed him bredda him took that an she who were him money. [3] An separatin from him faada - him seized them an went toward Qiefaz region that are toward the West - an that attractive one children were attractive like unto them mother. [4] An becaudis thing Siet children downscended toward Qayen children - an after them sight them up them didn't wait one iwa - an them made the dawtaz whom them chose wives fe them ras selves. [5] As them have taken InI toward error together with them becau them error - becaudis thing JAH vexed pon InI an vexed pon them. [6] An Deeyablos havin cajoled sayin - 'Unu will become irators like unto your Irator JAH' - him took InI mother Hiewan an InI faada 'Adam toward him error. [7] But it seemin Truth fe them ina them dullness - them demolished JAH LAW - Him Who Irated them bringin from not-livin toward livin that them might bow an praise Him glorified Name. [8] But Him - them Irator - downbased those 'Adam an Hiewan who made godhood fe them ras selves - an Him downbased him who are arrogant. [9] Like unto Daweet spoke sayin - ' 'Adam perish by the sinner Deeyablos arrogance' - Him abused them - fe InI faada 'Adam have been canvicted pon Deeyablos arrogance by Him true Judgement. [10]   An Siet children who erred by Qayel children took InI toward them sin thus ~ becaudis thing InI era that JAH gave InI were less than InI faadas eras. [11]   But them had worked goodly Work - fe them had firmed up them reasonins ina JAH - fe them had taught them dawta children an them male children lest them depart from JAH LAW that them taught them - an there were no evil enemy who approach them. [12]   But if them worked goodly Work - there are nothing that benefit them if them didn't tell nor teach fe them children. [13]   Like unto Daweet spoke sayin - 'Them didn't hide from them children fe another child - an teach JAH praise - the wondrous miracles Him did - an Him Power' - there are nothing that benefit them if them didn't teach fe them children that them might teach fe them children fe mek heart like unto them knew - an that them might know an do Him Accord - an that them might tell them JAH LAW Trust - an that them might keep Him LAW like unto them faadas who made JAH Irie with them beautiful Work. [14]   An them who told them Trust from them faadas ina them infancy didn't demolish Him Command - like unto them faadas learned JAH Worship an the Nine Laws from them faadas. [15]   Them children learned from them faadas that them might work goodly Work an might present praise fe them Irator - fe them have kept Him LAW - an fe them have loved Him. [16]   An Him shall hear them ina them priah - an Him won't ignore them plea - but Him are a Forgiver. [17]   Havin multiplied Him wrath - Him shall return it fe them - an Him wouldn't downstroy all ina Him chastisemant.

CHAPTER 20
[1] InI bredren - think - don't forget what them told unu formerly - that JAH keep the true Work of persons who work goodly Work. [2] An Him multiply them children ina this world - an them name invocation shall live firmed up fe a goodly thing up til the Iternity - an them children won't be troubled fe grain ina this world. [3] As Him shall dispute fe them becau

them - an as Him won't cast them ina them enemy hand - Him shall save them from them enemies hand who hate them. [4] An fe persons who love Him Name - Him shall be them Helper ina them tribulation time ~ Him shall guard them an pardon them all them sin.

CHAPTER 21

[1] Daweet believed ina JAH - fe Him have believed ina him - an Him saved him bein a Refuge from the king Sa'ol hand. [2] An as him have believed ina Him an kept Him LAW pon the time when him child 'Abiesielom arose - an pon the time when the 'Iloflans arose - an pon the time when the 'Edomyans an the 'Amalieqans arose - pon the time when the one from the four Rafayn arose - JAH saved Daweet from all this tribulation that enemies who disputed him brought pon him. [3] As prevailin are by JAH Accord - them were defeated by them enemies hand - yet but JAH didn't save the evil kings who didn't believe ina Him. [4] An Hiziqyas believed ina JAH ~ Him saved him from Senakriem hand who were arrogant. [5] But him child Minassie were defeated by him enemy hand - fe him didn't mek him trustin ina JAH ~ as him didn't mek him trustin ina JAH an as him didn't fear JAH Who totally honoured an famed him - them bound an took him toward them country - yet but those enemies who defeated Minassie weren't like unto him. [6] At that time Him denied him the kingdom Him gave him - fe him didn't work goodly Work before him Irator JAH - that him era might abound an that Him might dispute him enemy fe him an that him might have Power an firmness behind an in front. [7] Fe it are better fe believe ina JAH than ina many armies - than believin ina horses an bows an shields. [8] Believin ina JAH surpass ~ a person who believed ina Him shall firm up an be honoured an totally lofty. [9] Fe JAH don't favour fe a face - but persons who didn't believe ina JAH - who believed ina them money abundance - became them who departed from the grace an honour that Him gave them. [10] Him shall guard the persons who believe ina Him - but Him shall mek the persons ignorant who call Him ignorant - an as them didn't discipline them reasonins fe follow JAH nor keep Him LAW - Him won't quickly help them ina them tribulation time nor ina the time them enemies disputed with them. [11] But fe a person who were disciplined ina worshippin JAH an fe keep Him LAW - Him shall be a Refuge ina him tribulation time. [12] By downstroyin him enemy - an by plunderin him enemy livestock - an by capturin him enemy country persons - an by rainin eras rain - an by growin sprouts - an by introducin the grain pile - ina the plant fruit... [13] An by rainin the first an the spring rains - an by makin the grass verdant - an by givin the rain that rain at each time that thy kindreds beneath thy Itority might be Irie - Him shall mek him Irie. [14] Him shall mek him Irie - that them might eat the other one money - that them might satta havin eaten the money them plundered from them enemy - that them might plunder animals an sheeps an cows - an that them might eat the other one dinnertable - an that them might tek them enemies childran captive. [15] JAH shall do all this fe the person whom Him love - but Him will mek the person who hate Him fe him enemy ransackery. [16] An Him shall bind him feet an him hands an shall cast him ina him enemy hand - an Him shall mek him fe him enemies derision - an as him have become a blood shedder who demolished JAH LAW - Him won't mek him Irie ina him house seed. [17] An him won't firm up ina Judgemant time - an that Him might bring the hardship fe persons who work sin - Him will also give persons who work evil Work them sin hardship. [18] But it were commanded from alongside JAH fe give persons who work goodly Work them reward - that Him might keep them ina Him Itority. [19] Fe Him are empowered pon all the Iration Him Irated that Him might do goodly Work an might give them Iternal welfare an that them might praise JAH Who Irated them - an Him commanded that him might keep Him LAW ~ apart from only man there are none from all the Irations Him Irated that departed from Him Command. [20] Like unto JAH commanded all who live firmed up ina each of them Works - them all know an are kept ina Him LAW. [21] But man are emboldened pon JAH Who crowned all pon each of them inventions - pon animal an beasts an pon Heaven birds. [22] Be it what are ina sea or all pon land - JAH gave all the Iration Him Irated fe them faada 'Adam ~ JAH gave them that him might do what him loved - an that them might eat them like unto grain that grew pon Earth - an that them might rule an tax them - an that be them beasts or animals them might be commanded fe man - an Him Ipointed them pon all Him Irated that persons who reigned might be commanded fe JAH Who gave them honour an that them might favour Him. [23] But if them depart from Him LAW Him will separate them from the lordship Him gave them ~ as Him are Who rule Earth an Heaven - Him will give it fe him who do Him Accord. [24] Him Ipoint whom Him loved fe Ipoint - but Him dismiss whom Him loved fe dismiss ~ Him kill ~ Him save ~ Him whip ina tribulation ~ Him forgive. [25] There are no other Irator like unto Him ~ as Him are Ruler fe all the Iration Him Irated - as there are no other without Him - the Irator - ina Heaven above Earth nor pon Earth beneath Heaven - there are none who shall criticise Him. [26] Him Ipoint ~ Him dismiss ~ Him kill ~ Him save ~ Him whip ina tribulation ~ Him forgive ~ Him impoverish ~ Him honour. [27] Him hear persons who beg Him ina them plea ~ Him accept a person plea who do Him Accord with a clean reasonin; an Him hear them ina them priah - an Him do them accord fe them ina all that them begged Him. [28] An Him mek the great an the small fe be commanded fe them ~ all this are them money pon hills an mountains an at trees roots an ina caves an Earth wells an all them kindreds pon both dry an sea. [29] An fe persons who do them Irator Accord all this are them money - an Him won't trouble them from them plenty - an Him shall give them them praise reward. [30] An Him shall give them the honour Him prepared ina Heaven fe them faadas Yis'haq an 'Abriham an Ya`iqob ~ Him shall give them what Him prepared fe Hiziqyas an Daweet an Samu'iel who didn't depart from Him LAW an Him Command. [31] That them might be Irie ina Him Lordship - Him shall give them who served Him Iginnin from Antiquity the honour Him prepared fe them faadas Yis'haq an 'Abriham an Ya`iqob - fe whom Him swore fe give them a inheritance.

CHAPTER 22

[1] Please - think of persons name who work goodly Work - an don't forget them Work. [2] Straighten up that thy name be called like unto them name - that thou might be Irie with them ina the Kingdom of Heaven - that were Light Lodgin that Him prepared fe nobles an kings who did JAH Accord an were kind persons. [3] An again - know an be canvinced of evil nobles an kings names - that Him shall canvict them an revile them alongside man after them dead. [4] Fe them didn't line up them Work while them sight up an heard - an know an be canvinced that unless them did JAH Accord - Him shall judge pon them ina the Kingdom of Heaven more than criminals an persons who forgot JAH LAW. [5] Be kindly - innocent

- honest - yet don't thou also go pon persons path who forgot JAH LAW - pon whom JAH vexed becau them evil Work. [6] Judge Truth an save the child whose mother an faada dead pon him - an the widow from sinner persons hand who rob them. [7] Be a guardian like unto him faada fe the child whose mother an faada dead pon him - that thou might save him from the wealthy one hand who rob him - an stand fe him - an be alarmed pon the time the child - whose mother an faada dead pon him - tears flowed before thee-I - lest thou be alarmed ina fiyah sea where sinner persons who didn't enter repentance are punished. [8] An straighten up thy feet toward Love an Inity path ~ as JAH Eyes check up Him friends - an as Him Ears hear them plea - seek Love an follow she. [9] But JAH Face of Him Wrath are toward persons who work evil Work - that Him might downstroy them name invocation from this world - an Him won't preserve a person who near pon ramparts nor mountains. [10] As I-man am JAH Who am jealous pon I Godhood - as I-man am a Irator who revenge an downstroy persons who hate I an don't keep I Word - I-man won't return I Face of Support reachin up til I-man downstroy the person who don't keep I Word. [11] An I-man shall honour persons who honour I an keep I Word.

CHAPTER 23
[1]   Don't live firmed up ina Qayel order - who killed him bredda who followed him ina innocence - it seemin fe him that him bredda love him. [2]   An him killed him bredda envyin pon a dawta ~ persons who mek envy an iniquity an betrayal pon them companion are like unto him. [3]   But as 'Abiel are innocent like unto a sheep - an as him blood are like unto the clean sheep blood that them sacrificed fe JAH by a clean reasonin - them went pon Qayel path that aren't pon 'Abiel path. [4]   Fe becau all the persons who live ina innocence were persons whom JAH love - like unto a kind man 'Abiel - them have been innocent ones like unto 'Abiel - but those persons who live firmed up ina 'Abiel Work love JAH. [5]   But JAH neglect evil ones - an them Definite Judgemant mek application fe them pon them bodies - an it are written pon the record of them reasonins - an pon the time when Judgemant are judged - them shall read she before man an Angels an before all the Iration. [6]   At that time them shall shame ~ wrongdoers an refusers who didn't do JAH Accord shall shame. [7]   An a alarmin Word shall be given them that say - Place them ina *Gehannem* where are no exit up til Iternity.

CHAPTER 24
[1]   But pon the time Giediewon trusted JAH - him defeated uncircumcise peoples armies who were many many ina army of a few tens of thousands an without number like unto locusts. [2]   As there are no Irator without I - o nobles an kings - don't believe ina the different idols. [3]   As I-man am your Irator JAH Who sent unu forth from your mothers wombs an raised unu an fed unu an clothed unu - why do unu pretext? How about why do unu worship other idols without I? [4]   I-man did all this fe unu ~ what did unu give I? It are that unu might live firmed up ina I LAW an I Order an I Command an that I-man might give unu your bodies welfare - yet what will I-man want from unu? [5]   JAH Who rule all said thus ~ Him said - Save your ras selves from worshippin idols an practisin sorcery an discouragin pessimism. [6]   As JAH chastisemant shall come pon these who do this - an pon them who hear them an do them accord an are them friends an who live firmed up ina them command - save your ras selves from worshippin idols. [7]   As peoples - who don't know unu an aren't nice fe unu - shall arise pon unu - unless unu who feared did JAH Accord - them will eat the money wherefor unu wearied ~ like unto Him servants the prophets spoke an like unto Hienok spoke an like unto 'Asaf spoke - unless unu did JAH Accord - them will eat the money wherefor unu wearied. [8]   Evil persons will come havin changed them clothes Him said ~ there are no other law alongside them apart from eatin an drinkin an adornin ina silver an gold - an livin havin firmed up ina sin all the Work JAH don't love. [9]   But them are prepared fe go toward drink an food ~ after them were aroused from them slumber Iginnin from mornin up til evenin them go toward evil Work; there are misery an tribulation ina them path - yet them feet have no Love path. [10]   An them don't know Love an Inity Work - an there are no fearin JAH ina them faces ~ them are crooked evil ones without religion nor virtue ~ them are greedy ones who eat an drink alone ~ them are drunkards - an them sin are without LAW an without measure ~ them are who go toward seducin - sheddin blood - theft an perfidy an violently robbin him money who don't have it. [11]   An them are who criticise without Love an without LAW - fe them don't fear JAH Who Irated them - an there are no fear ina them faces. [12]   Them don't shame ina the person face that them sight up - an them don't shame a grey-hair nor a elder face ~ pon the time them heard when them said - 'An there are money ina this world' - them mek it them ras self money before them sight it up with them eyes - fe there are no fearin JAH ina them faces - an pon the time them sight it up with them eyes it seem fe them that them ate it. [13]   An them nobles eat trust money ~ them are who eat ~ as them are negativists an as there are no straight thing ina them tongues - them don't repeat ina evenin what them spoke ina mornin. [14]   Fe them ignore sufferahs an poor ones cries - an them kings hasten fe evil - them who downsturb a person - him havin saved refugees from wealthy ones hands who rob them. [15]   Mek them save him who were wronged an the refugee - yet mek the kings not be them who begrudge justice becaudis thing. [16]   But them are who exact tribute ~ them are who rob a person money - an them are criminals - an as them Work are evil - them aren't nice when them eat the newborn calf with she mother an a bird with she egg ~ them mek all them sight up an heard them ras self money. [17]   Them love that them might gather fe them ras selves - yet them aren't nice fe sick an poor ones - an them violently rob the money of a person who don't have it - an them gather all them found that them might be fattened an be Irie ina it. [18]   Fe them shall perish quickly like unto a scarab that proceeded from it pit an whose track aren't found an that don't return toward it house - an becau them didn't work goodly Work when them are ina them Life - woe fe them bodies pon the time JAH vexed an seized them. [19]   Pon the time JAH neglected them - them will perish at one time like unto them are ina one chastisemant - fe Him indure them meanin as it were them returned toward repentance - yet Him don't quickly downstroy them - an them shall perish pon the time when them shall perish. [20]   But if them don't return toward repentance - Him will quickly downstroy them like unto former persons who were precedin them - who didn't keep JAH LAW by what are due. [21]   Them are who eat a person flesh an drink a person blood ~ as them gird an work violence fe go toward sin - there are no fearin JAH ina them faces everytime - an after them arose from them beddin them don't rest fe work sin. [22]   An them Work are drink an food - goin toward downstruction an sin - that them might downstroy many persons bodies ina this world.

CHAPTER 25

[1] As them Work are crooked - an as all are who live firmed up ina Seythan Work that mislead - JAH Who rule all said - Woe fe your body pon the time I-man vexed an seized she. [2] But fe them don't know JAH Work - fe them have returned it toward them rear - an fe them have neglected I LAW. [3] An later ina fulfillmant era I-man shall bring the hardship pon them like unto them evil measure ~ like unto them sin were written alongside I - I- man shall revenge an downstroy them pon the day when Judgemant are judged. [4] As I-man JAH am full from horizon up til horizon - an as all the Iration have been seized ina I Itority - there are none who escape from I Itority ina Heaven nor Earth nor depth nor sea. [5] I-man command a snake that are beneath Earth - an I-man command a fish that are within sea - an I-man command birds ina Heaven - an I-man command the desert donkey ina wilderness - fe it are I money Iginnin from horizon up til horizon. [6] As I-man am Who work wondrous Work an do miracles before I - there are none who escape from I Itority pon Earth nor ina Heaven ~ there are none who tell I - 'Where do Thou go? How about what do thou Work?' [7] An I-man command pon Angels chiefs an hosts ~ all Irations whose name are called are I money - an beasts ina wilderness an all birds ina Heaven an livestocks are I moneys. [8] It arise from 'Azieb wind an firm up ina drought ina Mesi` ~ later ina fulfillmant era 'Eritra sea shall perish bein heard - arisin from JAH - Who shall come toward she - bein feared an famousness. [9] Fe Him rule them who dead an persons who are there - an she shall perish bein heard with Saba an Noba an Hindekie an 'Ityopphya limits an all them regions. [10] An Him watch all ina lofty Itority an innocence - fe Him Itority surpass all the itority - an Him keep cangregations ina Him Itority. [11] An fe Him Itority firm up more than all the itority - an fe Him Kingdom surpass all the kingdoms - an fe Him Itority are what rule all the world - fe Him able fe all - an fe there are nothing that fail Him. [12] Him rule all clouds ina Heaven ~ Him grow grass fe livestocks pon Earth - an Him give fruit pon the buds. [13] Him feed fe all ina each of the kinds like unto Him loved ~ Him feed all that Him Irated by each of the fruits an each of the foods - an Him feed ants an locusts beneath Earth an livestocks pon Earth an beasts - an fe a person who prayed Him give him him priah - an Him don't ignore the plea of the child whose mother an faada dead pon him - nor widows. [14] As evil persons rebellion are like unto a swirlin wind an wrongdoers council like unto misty urine - Him shall rather accept the plea of them who beg toward Him at each time an clean ones. [15] An as them body are like unto a flyin bird - an as them features comeliness that are silver an gold are perishable ina this world - examination will benefit persons who forgot JAH LAW yet not them gold - an moths shall eat them clothes. [16] An weevils shall totally eat the wheat an the barley fatness - an all shall pass like unto the day that passed yesterday - an like unto a word that proceeded from a mouth don't return - sinner persons money also are like unto it - an them 'beautiful lifestyle' are like unto a passin shadow ~ sinner persons money before JAH are like unto a lie clothes. [17] But if kind persons are honoured JAH won't ignore them - fe them have been honoured while them were nice fe poor ones - an them hear justice of sufferahs an a child whose mother an faada dead pon him ~ JAH won't ignore them - fe without neglectin them house childran - them honour Him while them clothe the naked from the clothes JAH gave them that them might give fe the refugee sufferah. [18] Them don't favour loyal persons judgemant - an them don't mek a hireling salary lodge ~ as JAH thing are Truth an honoured like unto a sword whose mouths were two - them won't do iniquity ina them seasons number an ina them balance measuremant.

CHAPTER 26

[1] But poor ones will think again pon them beddin - but if wealthy ones don't accept them - them will be like unto dry wood that have no verdure - an a root won't be fertile from alongside where no moisture are - an the leaf won't be fertile if there are no root. [2] As a leaf serve a flower fe be a ornamant fe fruit - unless the leaf were fertile it won't bear fruit ~ as man fulfillmant are religion - a person without religion have no virtue. [3] If him firmed up religion him worked virtue - an JAH are Irie by a person who work Truth an straight Work. [4] An fe the person who begged Him - Him shall give him him plea an him tongue reward - an Him won't wrong the true person becau him true Work that him worked. [5] As JAH are true - an as Him have loved a Truth thing - Him won't justify the sinner person without repentance becau the Work evil him worked - an as all persons souls have been seized ina Him Itority becau Him were Who ruled Earth an Heaven - as Him won't favour for the wealthy more than the poor ina Judgemant time - Him won't justify him without repentance.

CHAPTER 27

[1] Him Irated havin brought all the world from not livin toward livin - an Him totally prepared hills an mountains - an Him firmed up Earth pon Water - an lest sea be shaken Him delineated she by sand - fe ina Him first Word JAH have said Mek Light be Irated. [2] Light were Irated when this world had been covered ina darkness ~ JAH Irated all the Iration - an Him prepared this world - an Him firmed up this world by what are due an by money that are straight ~ Him said - Mek evenin be dark. [3] An again JAH said Mek Light be Irated ~ it dawned an there were Light - an Him Ilivated the upper Water toward Heaven. [4] An Him streached it forth like unto a tent - an Him firmed it up by a wind - an Him placed the lower Water within a pit. [5] An Him shut the sea lock ina sand - an Him firmed them up ina Him Itority lest them drown ina Water - an Him placed animals an beasts within she - an Him placed within she Liewatan an Biehiemot who were great beasts - an Him placed within she the beasts without number - sight up an not sight up. [6] Pon the third day JAH Irated pon Earth plants - all the roots an woods an fruits that bear forth ina each of them kinds - an a welfare wood beautiful fe them fe sight it up.. [7] An Him Irated a welfare wood that were both beautiful fe them fe sight it up an sweet fe them fe eat it - an Him Irated grass - an all plants whose seeds are found from within them - fe be food fe birds an livestocks an beasts. [8] It dusked ~ it dawned - an pon the fourth day Him said - Mek Light be Irated ina Heaven called cosmos ~ JAH havin Irated moon an Sun an stars - Him placed them ina Heaven called cosmos that them might shine ina this world an that them might feed them daylight an night. [9] An after this moon an Sun an stars alternated ina night an daylight. [10] An pon the fifth day JAH Irated all animals an beasts that live within Water an all birds that fly pon Heaven - all that are sight up an not sight up - all this. [11] An pon the sixth day Him Irated livestocks an beasts an others - an havin Irated an prepared all - Him Irated 'Adam ina Him Example an Him Appearance. [12] Him gave him all animals an beasts Him Irated that him might reign pon them - an again - all animals an beasts an all fishes - an Liewatan an Biehiemot that are

ina sea. [13] An Him gave him all cows that live ina this world an sheeps - the animals not sight up an them that are sight up. [14] An Him placed ina Garden 'Adam whom Him Irated ina Him Example an Him Appearance - that him might eat an might cultivate plants an might praise JAH there. [15] An fe lest him demolish Him Command - Him have said - Pon the time when unu ate from this Herb of Fig unu will dead death. [16] An Him commanded him lest him eat from the Herb of Fig that bring death - that draw attention fe evil an good - that bring death. [17] InI mother Hiewan were cajoled by a snake misleadin an she ate from that Herb of Fig an gave it fe InI faada 'Adam. [18] An 'Adam havin eaten from that Herb of Fig brought death pon him childran an pon him ras self. [19] As him have demolished Him Command - an as him have eaten from that Herb of Fig that JAH commanded sayin - Don't eat from she - JAH vexed pon InI faada 'Adam an expelled an sent him way from the Garden - an Him gave him that Earth that grow thistle an thorn - that Him cursed becau him pon the time him demolished Him Command - that him might eat him weariness reward havin toiled an laboured that him might plow she. [20] An pon the time JAH sent him forth toward this land - 'Adam returned toward complete sadness - an havin toiled an laboured that him might plow Earth - him began fe eat ina weariness an also ina struggles.

CHAPTER 28

[1] An after him childran lived havin abounded - there were from them ones who praise an honour JAH an don't demolish Him Command. [2] There were prophets who spoke what were done an what will be done henceforth - an from him childran there were sinners who speak lies an who wrong persons ~ 'Adam firstborn child Qayel became evil an killed him bredda 'Abiel. [3] JAH judged Judgemant pon Qayel becau him killed him bredda 'Abiel - an JAH vexed pon Earth becau she drank him blood. [4] An JAH told Qayel - Where are thy bredda 'Abiel? - an Qayel ina him heart arrogance said - 'Are mi mi bredda 'Abiel keeper?' [5] 'Abiel became a clean man - but Qayel became a sinner man by killin a kind man - him bredda 'Abiel. [6] Again a kind child Siet were birthed ~ 'Adam birthed sixty childran ~ there are kind persons an evil persons from them. [7] An there are kind persons from them ~ an there are persons who were prophets an them who were traitors an sinners. [8] There are blessed persons who were kind persons - who fulfill them faada 'Adam accord an all him told fe him child Siet - Iginnin from 'Adam up til Noh who are a kind man who kept JAH LAW. [9] An him sanctioned JAH LAW fe him childran ~ him told them - 'Guard' - lest them demolish JAH LAW - an that them might tell fe them childran like unto them faada Noh told them - an that them might keep JAH LAW. [10] An them lived while them taught them childran - persons birthed after them. [11] But Seythan lived when him spoke fe them faadas - havin lodged ina idols that reached fe a grave an that have vows pon them - an havin defeated the persons who told him alright - an when them did all that Seythan - who are sin teacher - commanded them. [12] An them lived when them worshipped the idols like unto them order - up til a kind man 'Abriham who fulfill JAH Accord. [13] Fe him have lived firmed up ina the LAW beforehand separate from him cousins - an JAH swore a oath with him - havin lodged ina wind an fiyah. [14] JAH swore fe him that Him might give him a land of inheritance an that Him might give fe him childran up til the Iternity. [15] An Him swore fe Yis'haq like unto him that Him might give him him faada 'Abriham inheritance - an Him swore fe Ya`iqob that Him might give him him faada Yis'haq inheritance ~ Him swore fe him like into Yis'haq. [16] An Him separated them childran - who were birthed after them from Ya`iqob - from the twelve tribes of 'Isra'iel - an made them priests an kings ~ Him blessed them sayin - Abound an totally be many many. [17] An Him gave them them faada inheritance - however while Him fed them an loved them - them didn't quit saddenin JAH ina all. [18] An pon the time Him downstroyed them - at that time them will seek Him ina worship - an them will return from sin an go toward JAH - fe Him love them - an JAH shall pardon them. [19] Fe bein nice fe all Him Irated - Him shall pardon them - an it are becau them faadas Work that Him love them - yet it aren't becau them ras selves Work. [20] An Him streach forth Him Right Hand ina plenty that Him might satta a hungry body - an Him reveal Him Eye fe pardonin that Him might multiply grain fe food. [21] Him give food fe crows chicks an fe beasts that beg Him ~ pon the time them cried toward Him - Him will save 'Isra'iel childran from them enemies hands who delayed from the time. [22] An them will return toward sin again that them might sadden Him - an Him will arouse them enemies peoples ina them area pon them ~ them will downstroy them an kill them an capture them. [23] An again them will shout toward JAH ina mournin an sadness - an there are the time when Him sent help an saved them by prophets hands. [24] An there are the time when Him saved them by princes hands - an pon the time them saddened JAH them enemies taxed them an captured them. [25] An Daweet arose an saved them from the 'Iloflans hands; an again them saddened JAH - an JAH aroused pon them peoples who worry them. [26] An there are the time when Him saved them by Yoftahie hand - an again them forgot JAH Who saved them ina them tribulation time. As JAH have brought the hardship pon them - Him will arouse pon them enemies who were evil who will firm up tribulation pon them an totally capture them. [27] An pon the time them were worried by tribulation them were seized an again cried toward Him - an Him saved them by Giediewon hand - an again them saddened JAH by them hands Work. [28] An again Him aroused pon them peoples who firm up tribulation pon them - an them returned an wept an cried toward JAH. [29] An again Him saved them from peoples by Somson hand - an them rested a likkle from the tribulation. An them arose that them might sadden JAH by them former sin. [30] An again Him aroused pon them other peoples who worry them - an again them cried an wept toward JAH that Him might send help fe them - an Him saved them from peoples by Bariq an Deebora hands. [31] Again them lived a likkle season while them worshipped JAH - an again them forgot JAH ina them former sin an saddened Him. [32] An Him aroused pon them other peoples who worry them - an again Him saved them by Yodeet hand; an havin sat again a likkle season them arose that them might sadden JAH by them sin like unto formerly. [33] An Him aroused pon them peoples who rule them - an them cried an wept toward JAH; fe Him have struck pon him head 'Abiemieliek who were a warrior who came that him might fight Yihuda country. [34] An Him saved them by the childran ina the area an by Matatyu hand - an pon the time that warrior dead him army fled an were scattared - an 'Isra'iel childran followed an fought them up til 'Iyabboq - an them didn't preserve even one person from them. [35] After this them waited a likkle an arose that them might sadden JAH - an Him aroused pon them peoples who rule them - an again them totally cried toward JAH; an JAH ignored them cryin an them mournin - fe them have saddened JAH everytime - an fe them have demolished Him LAW. [36] An them captured an took them with them priests toward Babilon persons country. [37] An then 'Isra'iel childran who were traitors didn't quit saddenin JAH while them worked sin an worshipped idols. [38]

JAH vexed that Him might downstroy them one time ina them sin ~ Hama havin introduced ten thousand gold ina the king box - pon the day when it were known - him lodged anger ina the king 'Arthieksis reasonin - lest him preserve them childran ina Fars country Iginnin from Hindekie an up til 'Ityopphya pon the time him told him that him might downstroy them. [39] Him did thus - an him wrote a letter where a message were written by the king authority - an him gave him a seal ina him hand that him might deliver toward Fars country. [40] Him gave him a seal that him might downstroy them pon one day when him loved them fe downstroy them like unto the king commanded - but him commanded that him might introduce them money - the gold an the silver - toward the king box. [41] An pon the time 'Isra'iel childran heard this thing them totally cried an wept toward JAH - an them told it fe Merdokyos - an Merdokyos told fe 'Astier. [42] An 'Astier said - 'Fast - beg - an all 'Isra'iel childran kindreds - cry toward JAH ina the place where unu are.' [43] An Merdokyos wore sackcloth an sprinkled dust pon him ras self - an 'Isra'iel childran fasted - begged - an entered repentance ina the country where them were. [44] An 'Astier were totally sad - an bein a queen she wore sackcloth ~ she sprinkled dust an shaved she head - an she didn't anoint perfume like unto Fars queens anoint perfume - an ina she deep reasonin she cried an wept toward she faadas Irator JAH. [45] An becaudis thing Him gave she bein loved alongside Fars king 'Arthieksis - an she made a kind lunch fe she faadas Irator. [46] An Hama an the king entered toward the lunch that 'Astier prepared - an like unto him loved that him might do pon Merdokyos - JAH paid the hardship pon that Hama - an them hanged him pon a tall wood. [47] The king letter were commanded that them might quit 'Isra'iel like unto them were ina all them accord - an lest them tax them nor rob them nor wrong them nor tek them money pon them. [48] As JAH shall pardon 'Isra'iel doin thus pon the time them cried enterin repentance - it are that them might love them an honour them ina Fars country where them lived - yet a king letter were commanded lest them downstroy them country nor plunder them livestocks. [49] An pon them time them saddened Him - Him will arouse pon them peoples who worry them ~ at that time them will totally weep an cry that Him might send them help fe them an that Him might save them from peoples hand who firm up tribulation pon them.

CHAPTER 29

[1] An pon the time Gibts persons also made 'Isra'iel childran work by makin them work bricks ina difficulty - an pon the time them worried them all the Work by kickin mud without straw an heatin bricks... [2] An pon the time them made them work havin appointed chiefs pon them who rush workers - them cried toward JAH that Him might save them from workin all Gibts bricks. [3] At that time Him sent fe them 'Aron an Mussie who help them - fe JAH have sent them that them might send forth Him kindreds from Fer`onn rulership house - an Him saved them from brick Work ~ becau ina him arrogance him refused fe adjourn 'Isra'iel lest them be ruled an sacrifice sacrifice fe JAH ina wilderness - JAH have sent them that them might send forth Him kindreds 'Isra'iel from Gibts king Fer`on rulership house - an them saved them. [4] Fe JAH neglect arrogant ones - an Him drowned Fer`on ina 'Eritra sea with him army becau him arrogance. [5] An like unto him - Him shall downstroy them who didn't work goodly Work ina all the kingdoms that Him I-pointed an crowned them - that them who ignore JAH Word when them are nobles an kings might fulfill Him Accord fe Him - an that them might give persons who serve ina goodly thing them wage - an that them might honour Him famous Name. [6] JAH Who rule all said - But if them will straighten up I Kingdom - I- man will straighten up them kingdom fe them. [7] Work goodly Work fe I - an I-man shall work goodly Work fe unu ~ keep I LAW - an I-man shall keep unu your bodies ~ live firmed up ina I LAW - an I-man shall live lodgin honesty ina unu like unto your reasonin. [8] Love I - an I-man shall love your welfare ~ near toward I - an I-man shall heal unu. [9] JAH Who rule all said - Believe ina I - an I-man shall save unu from the tribulation. [10] Don't live side by side ~ as JAH Who rule all love straight Work - Him said - Unu - approach toward I - an I-man shall approach toward unu ~ unu persons who are sinners an traitors - cleanse your hands from sin - an distance your reasonins from evil. [11] An I-man shall distance I anger from unu - an I-man shall return fe unu ina Charity an Forgiveness. [12] I-man shall distance criminals an enemies who work iniquity from unu - like unto I-man saved I slave Daweet from him enemies who met him - from them much malice - an from Gwolyad hand who were a warrior - an also from Sa'ol hand who sought that him might kill him - an from him child 'Abiesielom hand who loved that him might tek him kingdom. [13] I-man shall save persons who keep I LAW an fulfill I Accord like unto him ~ I-man shall bequeath them honour - an them shall be Irie ina the present world an yonder ina the world that shall come ~ I-man shall crown them pon all that them might be Irie. [14] Them shall be one with kings who served JAH an were honoured ina them beautiful way of Life - like unto the prophet Samu'iel served Him ina him beautiful way of Life Iginnin from him infancy - whom JAH - Him bein LAW - chose. [15] Him told him that him might tell 'Elee who were a servant elder - an when him served ina JAH Lodgin the Temple - Samu'iel Work also were merciful an I-loved. [16] An pon the time him grew when him served ina JAH Lodgin the Temple - Him made him fe be Ipointed an Inointed - that him might Ipoint him people an that kings might be Inointed by JAH Accord. As JAH have loved him that the kindred him chose from 'Isra'iel childran might be Ipointed - pon the time him fulfilled JAH Accord Who Irated him - Him gave him the Inointin of the Kingdom ina him hand. [17] An when Sa'ol were ina him kingdom JAH told Him prophet Samu'iel - Go - an as I-man have loved `Issiey child Daweet who were birthed from Yihuda kin - Inoint him.

CHAPTER 30

[1] I-man have hated Sa'ol kin - fe him have saddened I becau him violated I Word. [2] An I-man neglected him - fe him didn't keep I LAW - an I-man won't crown from him kin again. [3] An persons who didn't keep I LAW an I Word an I Order like unto him - I-man shall downstroy I Kingdom an I gift from them childran up til the Iternity. [4] An as them didn't mek I famous pon the time I-man made them famous - I-man shall downstroy them - yet I-man won't again return fe lift them up ~ though I-man honour them - as them didn't honour I - I-man won't mek them famous. [5] Fe them didn't do a goodly thing fe I pon the time I-man did a goodly thing fe them - an fe them didn't forgive I pon the time I-man forgave them. [6] An as them didn't mek I a Ruler pon the time I-man made them rulers pon all - as them didn't honour I pon the time I-man honoured them more than all - I-man won't mek them famous again nor honour them - an fe them didn't keep I LAW. [7] An I-man withheld the gift I-man gave them - an I-man won't return the money I-man withheld from them like unto the measure I-man vexed an swore ~ JAH Who rule all said thus ~ Him said - I-man shall honour them who

honoured I - an love them who loved I. [8] I-man shall separate them who didn't honour I nor keep I LAW from the gift I-man gave them. [9] JAH Who rule all said; I-man love them who loved I - an mek famous him who made I famous - Him said.. [10] As I-man JAH am Who rule all - there are none who escape I Itority ina Earth nor Heaven - fe I-man am JAH Who kill an Who save an Who sadden an Who forgive. [11] As famousness an honour are I money - I-man honour him whom I- man loved - fe I-man am Who judge an Who revenge an downstroy - an I- man mek wretched him whom I-man hated. [12] Fe I-man am Who forgive them who love I an call I Name everytime - fe I-man am Who feed food fe the wealthy an fe the poor. [13] An I-man feed birds an animals - fishes ina sea an beasts an flowers - yet I-man aren't Who feed only man. [14] I-man feed crocodiles an whales - gophers an hippos - an badgers... [15] an all that live within Water - all that fly pon wind - yet I-man aren't Who feed only man ~ all this are I money. [16] I-man am Who feed all that seek I by all that are due an I-loved.

CHAPTER 31
[1] An the kings don't reign without I Accord - an sufferahs are by I Command - yet them aren't poor without I Command - an powerful ones are by I Accord - yet them aren't strong without I Accord. [2] I-man gave bein I-loved fe Daweet an Wisdom fe Selomon - an I-man added eras fe Hiziqyas. [3] I-man diminished Gwolyad era - an I-man gave Power fe Somson - an again I-man weakened him Power. [4] An I-man saved I slave Daweet from Gwolyad hand who were a warrior. [5] An again I-man saved him from the king Sa'ol hand an from the secand warrior who disputed him - an fe him have kept I Command - an I-man saved him from the persons hand who dispute him an fight him. [6] An I-man loved him - an I-man love all the nobles an the kings who keep I LAW ~ as them have made I Irie - I-man shall give them prevailin an Power pon them enemies. [7] An again that them might inherit them faadas land - I-man shall give them the cleansed an shinin land of inheritance that I-man swore fe them faadas.

CHAPTER 32
[1] JAH Who rule all said - An unu the nobles an also the kings - hear I ina I Word - an keep I Command ~ lest unu sadden I an worship like unto 'Isra'iel childran saddened I an worshipped different idols - them whom I- man kept an saved when I-man JAH am them Irator - JAH Who rule all said - Hear I ina I Word; an all whom I-man raised an loved an fed Iginnin that them were birthed from them mother an faada. [2] An whom I-man sent forth toward Earth crops - an whom I-man fed the fatness found from Earth makin like unto are due - an whom I-man gave the grape vine an the oil-tree fruit that them didn't plant an the clear Water well that them didn't dig. [3] Hear I ina I Word lest unu sadden I like unto 'Isra'iel childran saddened I worshippin other idols when I-man JAH am them Irator - Him told them - Who fed them the sheep milk an the honey comb with the hulled wheat - an Who clothed them clothes where ornamant are - an Who gave them all them love. [4] An without it livin that I-man deprived them all them begged I.

CHAPTER 33
[1] Like unto Daweet spoke sayin - "Isra'iel childran were fed the menna that Angels lowered' - an again hear I ina I Word lest unu sadden I like unto 'Isra'iel childran saddened I worshippin the idols when I-man am them Irator JAH Who fed them sweet *menna* ina wilderness - Him said ~ I-man did all this fe them that them might worship I by what are due an fe true. [2] JAH Who rule all said - But them didn't worship I - an I-man neglected them ~ them saddened I an lived firmed up ina law of idols that weren't I LAW. [3] An I-man shall bring the hardship pon them like unto them sin ~ as them have neglected I Worship an as them didn't firm up ina I counsel an I Order - I-man neglected them ina the sin measure that them worked by them hands - an I-man shall lower them toward *Gehannem* ina Definite Judgemant that are done ina Heaven. [4] Fe them didn't keep I LAW - an fe I-man vex pon them - an I-man shall diminish them era ina this world. [5] If thou be a king - aren't thou a man who shall dead an be demolished an tomorrow who shall be worms an dust? [6] But today thou boast an are proud like unto a man who won't dead foriva. [7] JAH Who rule all said - But thou who are sight up bein well today are a man who will dead tomorrow. [8] But if unu keep I Command an I Word - I-man shall bequeath thee-I a honoured country with honoured kings who did I Accord - whose lodgin were Light an whose crowns were beautiful - an whose thrones were silver an gold an whom persons who sit pon them adorned - Him said. [9] An them shall be Irie within Him country that are a place that approached fe persons who worked goodly Work. [10] But fe persons who work sin - as them didn't keep I LAW - said JAH Who rule all... [11] it aren't due them that them might enter toward that country where honoured kings shall enter.

CHAPTER 34
[1] Miedon kingdom shall perish - but Rom kingdom shall totally firm up pon Meqiedonya kingdom - an Nenewie kingdom shall firm up pon Fars kingdom. [2] An 'Ityopphya kingdom shall firm up pon 'Iskindriya kingdom ~ as peoples shall arise - Mo`ab kingdom shall firm up pon 'Amalieq kingdom. [3] An bredda shall arise pon him bredda - an JAH shall revenge an downstroy like unto Him spoke that it might perish. [4] Kingdom shall arise pon kingdom - an the people pon the people an country pon country - Him said. [5] An arguments shall be done an there shall be formations - famine - plague - earthquake - drought ~ as Love have perished from this world JAH chastisemant downscended pon she. [6] Fe the day have arrived suddenly when JAH shall come - Who frighten like unto lightnin that are sight up from East up til West. [7] Pon the day when HIM JAH judge Judgemant - at that time everyone shall raceive him hardship like unto him hand weakness an him sin firmness - fe Him have said I-man shall revenge them pon the day when HIM JAH judge Judgemant an pon the day when them feet are hindered - fe the day when them are counted fe downstruction have arrived. [8] At that time JAH shall downstroy ina *Gehannem* foriva persons who won't live firmed up ina Him LAW - who work sin. [9] An them who live ina the West ilands an Noba an Hindekie - Saba an 'Ityopphya an Gibts persons - all persons who live ina them... [10] at that time shall know I that I-man were JAH Who rule Earth an Heaven - an Who give bein I-loved an honour - an Who save an Who kill. [11] I-man am Who send forth Sun - Who send it toward it settin - Who bring the evil an the good. [12] I-man am Who bring peoples whom unu don't know - who slaughter an eat the money whereby unu wearied -

your sheeps an your cows flocks. [13] An them shall capture your childran while them hammer them before unu - an unu cyaan save them. Becau JAH Spirit of Support didn't lodge ina unu - as unu didn't fear JAH Command that unu heard - Him shall downstroy your lavishmants an your assignmants. [14] But a person ina whom JAH Spirit of Support lodged will know all - like unto Nabukedenetsor told Dan'iel sayin - 'Mi sight up JAH Spirit of Support that lodged ina thee-I.' [15] An a person ina whom JAH Spirit of Support lodged will know all - an what were hidden will be revealed fe him - an him will know all that were revealed an that were hidden - yet there are nothing hidden from a person ina whom JAH Spirit of Support lodged. [16] But as InI are persons who will dead tomorrow - InI sins that InI hid an worked shall be revealed. [17] An like unto them test silver an gold ina fiyah - like unto there are sinners - later pon the Day of Advent them shall be examined - fe them didn't keep JAH Command. [18] At that time all peoples an all 'Isra'iel childran Works shall be examined.

CHAPTER 35

[1] As JAH vex pon unu becau unu didn't judge a Truth Judgemant fe the child whose mother an faada dead pon him - woe fe unu 'Isra'iel nobles. [2] Woe fe unu persons who go toward a drinkin house mornin an evenin an get drunk - who are partial ina judgemant - an who don't hear the widow justice nor the child whose mother an faada dead pon him - who live ina sin an seducin. [3] JAH told 'Isra'iel nobles sayin thus: - Unless unu lived firmed up ina I Command an kept I LAW an loved what I-man love - woe fe unu - Him told them. [4] An I-man shall bring downstruction an chastisemant an tribulation pon unu - an unu will perish like unto what weevils an moths ate - an your tracks an your region won't be found - Him told them. [5] An your country will be a wilderness - an all persons who sight she up formerly shall clap them hands ~ them shall marvel pon she while them said - 'Weren't this country filled of she plenty an all who love it?; JAH made she thus by persons sin who live ina she.' [6] Them shall say - 'As she have made she heart proud - an as she have ilivated she ras self - an as she have firmed up she collar of reasonin up til JAH mek she wretched pon Earth - an as she shall be a desert by persons arrogance who live ina she - an as thorns have grown pon she with thistles - woe fe she.' [7] An she grow weeds an nettles - an she became a wilderness an a desert - an beasts shall live within she. [8] Fe JAH Judgemant have firmed up pon she - an fe she shall raceive JAH Judgemant Chalice becau she reasonin arrogance by persons sin who live ina she - an she became frightenin fe persons who go toward she.

CHAPTER 36

[1] Meqiedon persons - don't boast ~ as JAH are there Who shall downstroy unu - 'Amalieqans - don't firm up your collar of reasonin. [2] Fe unu will be lofty up til Heaven an unu will downscend up til Gehannem. [3] Pon the time 'Isra'iel formerly entered toward Gibts country ina Mo`ab an Miedon kingdom Him said - Don't boast - fe it aren't due fe pretend pon JAH that unu might pretend pon Him. [4] Thou Yisma'iel kindred - slave child - why do thou firm up thy collar of reasonin by what weren't thy money? How about don't thou think that JAH shall judge pon thee pon the time Him arose that it might be judged pon Earth - pon the day when it are judged pon thee? [5] JAH Who rule all said - At that time thou will raceive thy hardship like unto thy hand Work - how about why do thou ilivate thy reasonin? How about why do thou firm up thy collar of reasonin? [6] An I-man shall pretend pon thee like unto thou pretended pon persons who weren't thy kindreds - fe thou do what thou love that thou might work sin - an I-man shall neglect thee ina the place where them sent thee. [7] JAH Who rule all said - An I-man shall do thus pon thee ~ Him said - But if thou worked goodly Work an if thou love what I-man loved - I-man also shall hear thee-I ina all that thou begged. [8] An if thou fulfill I Accord fe I - I-man shall fulfill thy accord fe thee-I - an I-man shall dispute thy enemies fe thee-I - an I-man shall bless thy childran an thy seed fe thee-I. [9] An I-man shall multiply thy sheeps an thy cows flocks fe thee-I - an if thou lived firmed up ina I Command an also if thou did what I-man love - JAH Who rule all said - I-man shall bless fe thee-I all thou seized ina thy hand. [10] But if thou don't do I Accord - if thou don't live firmed up ina I LAW an I Command - all this tribulation that were told formerly shall find thee - fe thou didn't indure tribulation firmed up ina I Command - an fe thou didn't live firmed up ina I LAW - an thou cyaan escape from I anger that will come pon thee everytime. [11] An as thou didn't love what I-man loved - when I-man am Who Irated thee bringin from not livin toward livin... [12] all this were thy money - that thou might kill an heal fe do all that thou loved - that thou might work an demolish - that thou might honour an abuse - that thou might ilivate an downbase - an as thou have neglected I Worship an I praise when I-man am Who gave thee lordship an also honour alongside persons who are beneath thy authority - thou cyaan escape from I anger that will come pon thee. [13] An if thou did JAH Accord an if thou lived frmed up ina Him Command - Him will love thee-I that thou might be Irie with Him ina Him Lordship - an that thou might be a partaker with persons who inherited a honoured country. [14] Fe Him have said - If them indure I - I-man will bequeath them bein I- loved an honour - fe I-man shall mek them Irie ina the Temple where priah are prayed - fe JAH Who rule all have said - An them shall be I-loved an chosen like unto a sacrifice. [15] Don't neglect fe do Work whereby welfare are done an a goodly thing that unu might cross from death toward Life. [16] But persons who work goodly Work - JAH shall keep them ina all Him goodly Work - that them might be Him slaves like unto 'Iyob whom JAH kept from all the tribulation [17] JAH shall keep them ina all goodly Work - that them might be Him slaves fe Him like unto 'Abriham whom Him saved pon the time him killed the kings - an like unto Mussie whom Him saved from Kenaniewon hand an Fer`on hand - ina whom 'Abriham lived - an who were also downsturbin him body evenin an mornin night an day that them might mek him worship idols. [18] But when them took him toward the idols that were them money - him would indure the tribulation while him refused. [19] Fe 'Abriham who believed Him Iginnin from him childhood were fe JAH Him trusted friend - an while him refused him would worship JAH Who Irated him. [20] As him totally love JAH - him didn't quit worshippin JAH up til him dead - an him didn't depart from Him LAW up til when him dead - an him taught him childran that them might keep JAH LAW. [21] An like unto them faada 'Abriham kept Him LAW - them didn't depart from JAH LAW ~ like unto Him told fe Angels sayin - I-man have a friend ina this world called 'Abriham - 'Abriham childran Ya`iqob an Yis'haq - who are Him slaves becau whom JAH spoke - didn't depart from JAH LAW. [22] JAH Who were praised alongside them an Who rule all said - 'Abriham are I friend ~ Yis'haq are I canfidante - an Ya`iqob are I friend whom I Reasonin loved. [23] But when Him totally loved 'Isra'iel childran - them lived when

them Itinually saddened Him - an Him lived when Him indured them an when Him fed them *menna* ina wilderness. [24] Them clothes didn't age - fe them have been fed *menna* that are knowledge *'injera* - an them feet didn't awaken. [25] But them reasonins would distance from JAH everytime ~ as them were who work sin Iginnin from Antiquity - them had no hope fe be saved. [26] Them became like unto a crooked bow - yet them didn't become like unto them faadas Yis'haq an 'Abriham an Ya`iqob who served JAH ina them beautiful way of Life ~ them would sadden Him everytime by them idols pon the mountains an the hills ~ them would eat pon the mountain an at the caves an the trees roots. [27] Them would slaughter a steer ~ them would sacrifice a sacrifice - an them would be Irie ina them hands Work ~ them would eat the rest of the sacrifice ~ them would drink of them sacrifice - an them would play with demons while them sang. [28] An demons would admire all them games an them songs fe them - an them would work them drunkenness an adultery without measure - an them would do the robbery an greed that JAH don't love. [29] Fe Kene`an idols - an fe Midyam idols an fe Be`al - an fe 'Aphlon an Dagon an Seraphyon an 'Arthiemadies who are 'Eloflee idols... [30] an fe all peoples idols ina them area - them would sacrifice sacrifice; an all 'Isra'iel would worship idols like unto peoples worship idols by money that them sight up an heard ~ them would mek them games an them songs an them bluster that peoples mek. [31] All 'Isra'iel kindreds do likewise - who say 'Wi will worship JAH' - without keepin Him Command an Him LAW that Mussie told them ina 'Oreet that them might keep JAH LAW an might distance from worshippin idols. [32] Lest them worship separated idols - apart from them faadas Irator Who fed them the honey found from Maga who fed them the plantation grain an sent them forth toward the Earth crops - an Who fed them the *menna* ... [33] Mussie commanded them sayin 'Don't worship' - fe Him are them Irator - an fe Him feed them who loved Him - an Him won't deprive them who loved Him an desired Him. [34] But them didn't quit saddenin JAH - an them would sadden JAH pon the time Him made them Irie. [35] An pon the time Him saddened them - them would cry toward Him - an Him would save them from the tribulation that found them - an them would again be totally Irie an would live many eras. [36] An at that time them would totally return them heart toward sin that them might sadden JAH like unto formerly - an Him would arouse pon them peoples ina them area that them might downstroy them - an them would worry an tax them. [37] An again them would totally return an cry toward them Irator JAH. [38] An Him would forgive them ~ it are becau them faadas - Noh - Yis'haq an 'Abriham an Ya`iqob - who served JAH ina them beautiful way of Life Iginnnin from Antiquity - fe whom Him firmed up Him Oath - yet it aren't becau them ras selves Work that Him forgive them. [39] An Him loved persons who kept Him LAW lovin that them might multiply them childran like unto Heaven stars an sea sand. [40] But pon the time dead ones arose that them have like unto sea sand - them are sinner persons souls that will separate from 'Isra'iel childran an enter toward Gehannem. [41] As JAH have told 'Abriham - Sight up toward Heaven at night an count Heaven stars as it were thou could count - likewise as Him have told him - Thy childran an righteous ones shall shine ina Heaven like unto Heaven stars - them are like unto stars that shine ina Heaven - but what them have are kind persons souls birthed from 'Isra'iel. [42] An again as Him have told him - Overstand toward the river edge an the sea - an sight up what are amidst the sand ~ count as it were thou could count - an thy sinner childran are likewise - who will downscend toward *Gehannem* pon the time dead ones arose - them are sinner persons souls. [43] An 'Abriham believed ina JAH ~ becaudis thing it were counted fe him bein Truth ~ him found him morale ina this world - an after him wife Sora aged she birthed a child called Yis'haq. [44] Fe him have believed that persons who worked goodly Work shall arise an go toward the Kingdom of Heaven that live firmed up foriva - an again him shall find a Kingdom ina Heaven. [45] But fe him have believed that persons who worked sin shall go toward *Gehannem* that live firmed up foriva pon the time dead ones arose - but that righteous ones who worked goodly Work shall reign with Him foriva. [46] But fe him have believed that it shall be judged foriva fe true without falsehood pon persons who worked sin - fe him shall find Life Kingdom ina Heaven." Mek glory an praise enter fe JAH fe true without falsehood - an the first book that speak the Meqabyans thing were filled an fulfilled.

2 MEQABYAN

CHAPTER 1

[1] This are a book that speak that Meqabees found 'Isra'iel ina Mesphiethomya that are Sorya part an killed them ina them region iginnin from 'Iyabboq up til 'Iyerusaliem square - an that him downstroyed the country. [2] Becau Sorya an 'Edomyas persons an the 'Amalieqans were one with the Mo`ab man Meqabees who downstroyed 'Iyerusaliem country - as them have camped iginnin from Semarya up til 'Iyerusaliem square an up til all she region - them killed ina war without preservin persons who fled apart from a few persons. [3] An pon the time 'Isra'iel childran wronged - Him aroused Mo`ab man Meqabees pon them - an him killed them by a sword. [4] An becaudis thing JAH enemies the peoples bragged pon Him honoured country - an them swore ina them crime. [5] An 'Iloflee an 'Idomyas persons camped - as Him have sent them becau them pretended JAH Word - them began fe revenge an downstroy JAH country. [6] An that Meqabees country are Riemat that are Mo`ab part - an him arose from him country ina Power an them swore also with persons with him. [7] An them camped ina Gielabuhie region that are Mesphiethomya lot up til Sorya that them might downstroy JAH country - an there him begged the 'Amalieqans an 'Iloflans ~ him gave them much silver an gold an chariots an horses that them might be one with him ina crime. [8] Them came together an crushed the fortress ~ persons who lived ina she shed blood like unto Water. [9] An them made 'Iyerusaliem like unto a plant keepin hut - an him made a voice heard within she ~ him worked all the sin Work that JAH don't love - an them also defouled JAH country that were filled of praise an honour. [10] Them made thy friends flesh an thy slaves corpses food fe wilderness beasts an Heaven birds. [11] An them robbed childran whose mother an faada dead pon them an widows - fe without fearin JAH them have done like unto Seythan taught them - an up til JAH Who examine kidneys an reasonins vexed - them took out the fetus ina pregnant dawtaz belly. [12] Them returned toward them country while them were Irie becau them worked evil Work pon JAH kindreds - an them took the plunder that them captured from a honoured country. [13] Pon the time them returned an entered toward them houses them made Ites an song an clappin.

CHAPTER 2

[1] The prophet whom them call Re`ay told him thus: - "Today be Irie a likkle pon the time when Irie Ites were made ~ JAH Whom 'Isra'iel glorified have that Him might revenge an downstroy thee ina the chastisemant thou didn't doubt. [2] Will thou say - 'Mi horses are swift ~ becaudis mi will escape by runnin'? [3] As fe I - I-man tell thee - Persons who will follow thee are swifter than vultures ~ thou won't escape from JAH Judgemant an downstruction that shall come pon thee. [4] Will thou say - 'Mi wear iron clothes - an spear flingin an bow stingin aren't able fe mi'?; JAH Who honour 'Isra'iel said - It aren't by spear flingin that I-man will revenge an downstroy thee" Him told him ~ "I-man shall bring pon thee heart sickness an itch an rheumatism sickness that were worse an firmer than spear flingin an bow stingin - yet it aren't by this that I-man shall revenge an downstroy thee. [5] Thou have aroused I anger ~ I-man shall bring heart sickness pon thee - an thou will lack one who help thee - an thou won't escape from I Itority up til I-man downstroy thy name invocation from this world. [6] As thou have firmed up thy collar of reasonin - an as thou have ilivated thy ras self pon I country - pon the time I-man quickly did this thing like unto a eye wink - thou will know I that I-man were thy Irator ~ as thou are before I like unto grass before the wind that fiyah eat - an as thou are like unto the dust that winds spill an scattar from Earth - thou are like unto them alongside I. [7] Fe thou have aroused I anger - an fe thou didn't know thy Irator - an I- man shall neglect all thy kindred - an neither will I-man preserve him who neared pon thy fortress. [8] An now return from all thy sin that thou worked ~ if thou return from thy sin an totally appease ina mournin an sadness before JAH - an if thou beg toward him ina clean reasonin - JAH will forgive thee all thy sin that thou worked before Him" - him told him. [9] At that time Meqabees wore dust an mourned before JAH becau him sin - fe JAH have vexed pon him. [10] Fe Him eyes are revealed - fe Him don't withhold - an fe Him ears are opened - fe Him don't neglect - an fe Him don't mek the word Him spoke false - an fe Him quickly do she at one time - fe JAH knew lest Him preserve the chastisemant Him spoke by the prophet Word. [11] Him cast him clothes an wore sackcloth an sprinkled dust pon him head an cried an wept before him Irator JAH becau him sin that him worked.

CHAPTER 3

[1] An the prophet came from Riemat an told him - fe Riemat that are Mo`ab part are near fe Sorya. [2] Him dug a pit an entered up til him neck an wept firm tears - an him entered repentance becau him sin that him worked before JAH. [3] An JAH told the prophet thus: - Return from Yihuda country Riemat toward the Mo`ab official Meqabees Him told him. Tell him - "JAH told thee thus" - Tell him - "Him told thee - I-man JAH Who am thy Irator sent thee by I Accord that thou might downstroy I country - lest thou say - 'Mi destroyed the honoured country 'Iyerusaliem by mi Power firmness an mi army abundance' - yet it aren't thou who did this thing. [4] Fe she have saddened I by all she greed an she perfidy an she lustfulness. [5] An I-man neglected an cast she by thy hand - an now JAH forgave thee thy sin becau thy childran whom thou birthed ~ it aren't becau thou who firmed up thy collar of reasonin an say 'Mi incircled the country 'Iyerusaliem by mi authority firmness.' [6] As persons who doubt aren't disciplined fe enter repentance - don't be a doubter - an now enter repentance bein disciplined ina thy complete reasonin." [7] However persons are admired who enter repentance ina them complete reasonins an who don't again return toward thirst an sin by all that entered toward repentance becau them sin. [8] Persons are admired who return toward them Irator JAH bein disciplined ina mournin an sadness - ina bowin an many pleas. Persons are admired who are disciplined an enter repentance - fe Him have told them - Unu are I moneys who entered repentance after unu misled persons who entered repentance. [9] Him told arrogant Meqabees pon the time him returned toward Him ina repentance after him misled - I-man forgive thee thy sin becau thy fright an thy alarm; fe I-man am JAH thy Irator Who bring hardship pon childran by a faada sin up til seven generations if the child work the sin that the faada worked - an Who do Charity up til ten thousand generations fe persons who love I an keep I LAW. [10] An now I-man will firm up I Oath with thee becau these thy childran whom thou birthed - an JAH Who rule all an Who honoured 'Isra'iel said - I-man will accept the repentance thou made becau thy sin that thou worked. [11] At that time him proceeded from the pit an bowed fe the prophet ~ him swore sayin - "As mi have saddened JAH - mek mi what thou loved - yet mek JAH do mi thus thus lest mi separate from thee-I ~ as wi have no Law - mi didn't live firmed up ina Him Command like unto mi faadas ~ thou know that wi faadas taught wi an that wi worship idols. [12] Fe mi are a sinner who lived firmed up ina mi sin - who firmed up ina mi collar of reasonin firmness an mi reasonin arrogance whereby mi saddened JAH Command - but up til now mi hadn't heard JAH servants the prophets Word - an mi didn't live firmed up ina Him LAW an Him Command that Him commanded mi." [13] Him told him sayin - "As there are none from your kindred precedin unu who trusted him sin - mi knew that the prophet raceived repentance today." [14] "But now quit thy worshippin idols an return toward knowin JAH that thou might have true repentance" him told him ~ him fell an bowed at the prophet feet - an the prophet lifted up an commanded him all the goodly Work that are due him. [15] An him returned toward him house doin also like unto JAH commanded him. [16] An that Meqabees returned him body toward worshippin JAH - an him downstroyed from him house the idols an also the sorcery - persons who worship idols an pessimists an magicians. [17] An mornin an evenin like unto them faadas do - him would examine the childran him captured an brought from 'Iyerusaliem ina all JAH Commands an Him Order an Him LAW. [18] An from the childran him captured - him appointed knowin ones pon him house. [19] An again from the infants him appointed knowin childran who keep levelled childran who were small - who enter toward the beddin that them might teach them JAH LAW that 'Isra'iel childran do ~ him would hear from captured 'Isra'iel childran the Order an the LAW an the Nine Laws - that Mo`ab persons order an them mosques that them mek were vain. [20] Him downstroyed them mosques - them idols an them sorcery - an the sacrifice an the grapes sacrificed fe the idols mornin an evenin from the goat kids an fattened sheeps flocks. [21] An him downstroyed him idols whom him worship an beg an believe ina all him Work while him sacrificed sacrifice afternoon an at noon - an fe all priests told him - an him idols fe whom him do them accord. [22] As it would seem fe him that them save him ina all that them told - him wouldn't scorn all the thing them told him. [23] But that Meqabees quit them Work. [24] After him heard the Ra`ay thing - whom them call a prophet - him accomplished him Work ina repentance ~ as 'Isra'iel childran would sadden Him at one time - an pon the time Him chastised them ina the tribulation - as them know an also cry toward JAH - all Him kindreds worked goodly Work more than 'Isra'iel childran ina that season. [25] Pon the time Him heard that them were seized an abused by peoples hand who firm up tribulation pon them an that them cried toward Him - Him

thought of them faadas oath an at that time Him would forgive them becau them faadas Yis'haq - 'Abriham - an Ya`iqob. [26] An pon the time Him saved them - them would forget JAH Who saved them from tribulation - an them would return toward worshippin the idols. [27] An at that time Him would arouse pon them peoples who firm up tribulation pon them - an pon the time them firmed up tribulation pon them an saddened them - them would cry toward JAH ~ as Him love them becau them were Him Itority Iration - at that time Him would be nice an forgive them. [28] An pon the time Him kept them - them again returned toward sin that them might sadden Him by them hands Work that were firm an by worshippin idols ina them councils. [29] But Him would arouse pon them Mo`ab an 'Iloflee - Sorya - Midyam an Gibts persons; an pon the time them enemies defeated them - them would cry an weep ~ pon the time them firmed up pon them an taxed them an ruled them - JAH would arouse princes fe them that Him might save them pon the time Him loved.

CHAPTER 4

[1] An ina 'Iyasu time are a day when Him saved them. [2] An ina Giediewon time are a day when Him saved them. [3] An ina Somson time an ina Deebora an Bariq an Yodeet time are a day when Him saved them - an lodgin whether pon male or pon dawta - Him would arouse princes fe them that them might save them from them enemies hands who firm up tribulation pon them. [4] An like unto JAH loved - Him would save them from persons who firm up tribulation pon them. [5] An them would be totally Irie ina all the Work that Him accomplished fe them ~ them would be Irie ina them land seed an ina multiplyin all them flocks ina wilderness an them livestock. [6] An Him would bless them plants an them livestock fe them - fe Him sight them up ina Eye of Mercy - an fe Him wouldn't diminish them livestock pon them - fe them are kind persons childran an Him would totally love them. [7] But pon the time them were evil ina them Work - Him would cast them ina them enemies hands. [8] An pon the time Him downstroyed them - them would seek Him ina worship - an them would return from sin an march toward JAH ina repentance. [9] An pon the time them returned ina them complete reasonin - Him would atone them sin fe them ~ Him wouldn't think of them former sin pon them - fe Him know them that them were flesh an blood - fe them have this world misleadin thoughts pon them - an fe them have demons ina them. [10] But pon the time that Meqabees heard this Order that JAH worked ina Him worshippin place the Temple - him were slain ina repentance. [11] After him sight up an heard this - him didn't scorn workin goodly Work; him didn't scorn workin all the goodly Work that 'Isra'iel childran work pon the time JAH forgave them - an after them trespassed from Him LAW - them weep an would cry pon the time JAH whipped them - an again Him would forgive them - an them would keep Him LAW. [12] An Meqabees likewise would straighten up him Work - an him would keep Him LAW - an him would live firmed up ina 'Isra'iel Irator JAH Command. [13] At that time after him heard all the Work whereby 'Isra'iel childran boast - Him would boast like unto them ina keepin JAH LAW. [14] Him would urge him kindred an childran that them might live firmed up ina JAH Command an all Him LAW. [15] An him would forbid the order that 'Isra'iel forbid - an him would hear an keep the Law that 'Isra'iel keep - an when him kindred are another Mo`ab man - him would forbid the food that 'Isra'iel forbid. [16] An him would send forth tithes ~ him would give all that were first birthed an that him owned from him cows an him sheeps an him donkeys - an returnin him face toward 'Iyerusaliem him would sacrifice the sacrifice that 'Isra'iel sacrifice. [17] Him would sacrifice sin an vow sacrifices - a sacrifice whereby welfare are done an a accord sacrifice - an the Itinual sacrifice. [18] An him would give him first crops - an him would gush an pour the grapes that 'Isra'iel pour - an him would give this fe him priest whom him I- pointed - an likewise him would do all that 'Isra'iel do - an him would sweeten him ishence. [19] Him built a candlestick an a bowl an a seat an a tent an the four links of rings - an diluted oil fe the Hola of Holas lamps - an the curtain that 'Isra'iel mek ina the Hola of Holas pon the time them served JAH. [20] An like unto them worked goodly Work pon the time them lived firmed up ina Him Order an Him LAW an pon the time JAH didn't neglect an cast them ina them enemies hands - Meqabees also would work goodly Work like unto them. [21] Him would beg toward 'Isra'iel Irator JAH everytime that Him might be him Teacher an lest Him separate him from 'Isra'iel childran whom Him chose an who did Him Accord. [22] An again him would beg Him that Him might give him childran ina Tsiyon an a house ina 'Iyerusaliem - that Him might give them Heavenly Seed of Virtue ina Tsiyon an a Heavenly House of Soul ina 'Iyerusaliem - an that Him might save him from the downstruction spoken by the prophet tongue - that Him might accept him repentance ina all the mournin him wept before JAH bein sad an enterin repentance... [23] an lest Him downstroy childran ina this world pon him - an that Him might keep him ina him proceedin an enterin. [24] Kindreds from Mo`ab peoples beneath Meqabees Itority were Irie that them might believe - fe them chief live firmed up ina straight Work - an them would check up him judgemant an fulfill him accord - an them would scorn them country language an them country justice ~ them would overstand that Meqabees Work surpassed an were straight. [25] An them would come an hear Meqabees charity an Truth judgemants. [26] Him had much money ~ him had dawta slaves an male slaves an camels an donkeys - an him had five hundred horses that wear breastplates ~ him would totally defeat the 'Amalieqans an 'Iloflans an Sorya persons - but formerly when him worshipped idols him lived when them defeated him. [27] Him prevailed - yet but from him worshippin JAH onward - when him went toward battle there are none who defeated him. [28] But them would come ina them idols Power that them might fight him - an them would call them idols names an curse him - however there were none who defeat him - fe him have made him faith pon him Irator JAH. [29] An when him did thus an when him defeated him enemies - him lived when him ruled peoples ina him Itority. [30] Him would revenge an downstroy wronged persons enemy fe them ~ him would judge Truth fe a child whose mother an faada dead pon him. [31] An him would raceive widows ina them trouble time - an him would give from him food an satta them who hungered - an him would clothe the naked from him clothes. [32] An him would be Irie ina him hands Work - an him would give from the money him had without begrudgin - an him would give tithes fe the Temple ~ Meqabees dead havin lived ina Irie Ites when him did this.

CHAPTER 5

[1] An him dead quittin him childran who were small - an them grew up like unto them faada taught them ~ them kept them house Order - an them would keep all them kindred - an them wouldn't mek poor ones cry - nor widows nor a child whose mother an faada dead pon him. [2] Them would fear JAH - an them would give them money alms fe poor ones -

an them would keep all the trust them faada told them - an them would calm the child whose mother an faada dead pon them an widows ina them trouble time - an them would be them mother an faada ~ them would mek them cast from persons hand who wrong them - an calm them from all the downsturbance an sadness that found them. [3] Them lived five years while them did thus. [4] After this the Keledans king Tseerutsaydan came ~ him downstroyed all them country - an him captured Meqabees childran an downstroyed all them villages. [5] An him plundered all them money ~ them lived firmed up ina all evil Work an sin - ina adultery - insult an greed an not thinkin of them Irator - yet persons who don't live firmed up ina JAH LAW an Him Command an who worship idols seized them also an took them toward them country. [6] Them eat what a beast bit an the blood an the carcass - an what a scavenger beat an cast - all that JAH don't love - yet them have no order from all the true Commands written ina 'Oreet . [7] Them don't know JAH them Irator - Who sent them forth from them mothers wombs an fed them by what are due - were them Medicine. [8] Them marry from them aunt an them faada wife - them step mother - an them go toward robbery an evil thing an sin an adultery - yet them have no order ina Judgemant time - an them work all evil Work an them marry them aunts an them sistren an them have no LAW. [9] An all them roads are dark an slippery - an them Work are sin an adultery. [10] But those Meqabees childran would keep ina all them Order ~ them wouldn't eat what a scavenger beat nor what dead an lodged ~ them wouldn't work all the Work that the Keledans childran work - fe them many Works are evil that weren't written ina this book - that sinners work - an doubters an criminals - betrayers totally filled of robbery an sin an pagans childran. [11] All the Work them Irator JAH love aren't there alongside them. [12] An again them would worship a idol called Bi'iel Fiegor ~ them would trust it like unto them Irator JAH when it were deaf an dumb. Fe it are the idol that a person hand worked - fe it are the person hand Work that a smith worked who work silver an gold - that have no breath nor knowledge - an it had nothing that it sight up nor hear. [13] It don't eat nor drink. [14] It don't kill nor save. [15] It don't plant nor uproot. [16] It don't harm it enemy nor benefit it friend. [17] It don't impoverish nor honour. [18] It will be a hindrance fe mislead the Keledans persons who were lazy - yet it don't chastise nor forgive.

CHAPTER 6

[1] JAH enemy Tseerutsaydan who were arrogant appointed them who veil an falsehood priests fe him idols. [2] Him would sacrifice sacrifice fe them an pour the grapes fe them. [3] An it would seem fe him that them eat an drink. [4] An while it dawned him would give them cows an donkeys an heifers - an him would sacrifice sacrifice mornin an evenin - an him would eat from that defouled sacrifice. [5] An again him would downsturb an obligate other persons that them might sacrifice fe him idols - yet it weren't that only them do it. [6] Pon the time them sight up Meqabees childran that them were handsome an that them worship them Irator JAH - the idols priests loved that them might mislead them fe sacrifice sacrifice an fe eat from that hated sacrifice - but these honoured Meqabees childran refused them. [7] As them keep them faada command - an as them have firmed up ina workin goodly Work - an as them totally fear JAH - it failed them fe agree... [8] pon the time them bound them an insulted them an robbed them. [9] Them told fe the king Tseerutsaydan that them refused sacrifice an bowin fe him idols. [10] An becaudis thing the king vexed ~ him were sad an commanded that them might bring them - an them brought an stood them before him - an the king told them fe him idols - "Sacrifice a sacrifice fe mi idols." [11] An them spoke an told him - "An InI won't answer thee ina this thing - an InI won't sacrifice sacrifice fe thy defouled idols." [12] Him frightened them by Works that abounded - yet him couldn't able fe them - fe them have disciplined them reasonins believin ina JAH. [13] Him flamed a fiyah an cast them ina fiyah - an them gave them bodies fe JAH. [14] After them dead them arose an were sight up fe him at night drawin them swords when him had reclined pon him lordship throne - an him totally feared. [15] "Mi sirs - tell mi alright - what should mi do fe unu? Don't tek mi body ina death - that mi might do all thou commanded mi." [16] Them told him all that are due fe him while them said - "Think that JAH were thy Irator - an JAH are there Who shall dismiss from this thy kingdom where thou are arrogant - an Who shall lower thee toward Gehannem of Fiyah with thy faada Deeyablos ~ when InI worshipped InI Irator JAH without a iniquity livin that InI wronged thee - an when InI bowed fe Him ina fearin Him JAH-ness - like unto thou burned InI ina fiyah - thou will finish all thy hardship by that also. [17] Fe Him are Who Irated all - Earth an Heaven an sea an all that are within she. [18] An fe Him are Who Irated moon an Sun an stars - an fe Him Who Irated all the Iration are JAH. [19] Fe there are no other irator withou Him ina Earth nor Heaven - fe Him are Who able fe all - an fe there are nothing that fail Him. As Him are Who kill an Who save - Who whip ina tribulation an Who forgive - when InI bowed fe Him ina fearin JAH - like unto thou burned InI ina fiyah - thou will finish thy hardship by that" them told him. [20] "As Him are Who rule Earth an Heaven - there are none who escape from Him Itority. [21] There are none from the Iration Him Irated who departed from Him Command - apart from thou who are a criminal - an criminals like unto thee whose reasonins thy faada Seythan hid - an thou an those thy priests an thy idols will downscend together toward Gehannem where are no exits up til Iternity. [22] Thy teacher are Seythan who taught thee this evil Work that thou might do a evil thing pon InI - yet as it aren't only thou who do this - unu will downscend toward Gehannem together. [23] Fe thou mek thy ras self like unto thy Irator JAH - yet thou didn't know JAH Who Irated thee. [24] An thou are arrogant ina thy idols an thy hand Work up til JAH mek thee wretched ~ Him shall canvict thee pon all thy sin an iniquity that thou worked ina this world.

CHAPTER 7

[1] Woe fe unu who don't know JAH Who Irated unu - fe thy idols who are like unto thee - an fe thee - an fe unu have that unu might regret a regrets that won't profit pon the time unu were sad bein seized ina See'ol difficulty - an woe fe thee - fe unu who don't keep Him Word an Him LAW. [2] Unu will have no exit from she up til Iternity - thy priests an thou who sacrifice fe them like unto your Irator JAH - fe thy idols who have no breath nor soul - who won't revenge an downstroy him who did a evil thing pon them - nor do a goodly thing fe him who did a goodly thing fe them. [3] Woe fe unu who sacrifice fe them - fe them are a person hands Work where Seythan live - lodgin there fe mislead lazy ones reasonin like unto thee - that him might lower unu toward Gehannem of Fiyah - an the priests who serve demons commanded fe unu an your idols. [4] As unu don't know that there are nothing that will profit unu - unu wrong an err. [5] As fe the animals that

JAH Irated fe be food fe unu - an dogs an beasts - them are better than unu - fe besides one death there are no more candemnation pon them. [6] But as unu will dead an raceive hardship ina *Gehannem* Fiyah where are no exits up til Iternity - animals are better." [7] Havin spoken this - them went an were hidden from him. [8] But that Tseerutsaydan lodged when him trembled - seized by a firm fright - an fright didn't quit him up til it dawned.

CHAPTER 8

[1] An him lived firmed up ina reasonin malice an arrogance. [2] An as iron have been called firm - like unto Dan'iel sight it up pon him kingdom - him turned ina peoples countries ina him area. [3] Him lived firmed up ina evil an all him laziness an ina downsturbin persons. [4] An him totally downstroy what InI spoke formerly - an him eat a person money. [5] Fe him are diligent fe evil like unto him faada Deeyablos who firmed up him collar of reasonin - an him downstroy what remained with him army. [6] Him say - "Mi era became like unto the Sun era" - yet him don't know JAH that Him were him Irator. [7] An ina him reasonin him think that the Sun are found from him. [8] Him arise in Power - him camp ina Tribe of Zablon lot an begin a formation ina Meqiedonya - an him receive him food from Semarya - an them give him presents from Semarya. [9] Him camp ina nomads region - an him reach up til Seedona - an him cast a tax pon 'Akayya - an him elevate him collar of reasonin up til the flowin sea - an him return an send messengers up til Hindekie sea. [10] An likewise him elevate him collar of reasonin up til Heaven. [11] Him live firmed up ina bein arrogant an ina evil - yet him don't have humblin him ras self. [12] An him path are toward darkness an slipperiness - an toward crime an bein arrogant - an toward sheddin blood an tribulation. [13] An all him Work are what JAH hate ~ him do like unto robbery an evil an sin teacher Deeyablos taught him ~ him mek a child cry whose mother an faada dead pon him - an him aren't nice fe a poor one. [14] An him defeated an downstroyed peoples kings by him authority. [15] An him ruled enemies chiefs - an him ruled many peoples - an him taxed them like unto him loved. [16] Even if him downstroyed - him didn't quit ~ there are no person whom him didn't snatch Iginnin from Tersies sea up til 'Iyareeko sea. [17] Him would bow fe idols ~ him would eat what dead an lodged - the blood - what a sword bloated an cut - an what were sacrificed fe idols ~ all him Work are without justice - yet him have no justice ~ as him have been who alarm peoples beneath him authority - him would tax them tax like unto him loved. [18] As him do all that him loved before him - there are no fearin JAH before him - an him live ina malice before JAH Who Irated him. [19] Him didn't do it like unto him Irator - an like unto him did a evil thing pon him companion pon the time him vexed an seized him - JAH shall also pay him him hardship. [20] As JAH have said - I-man shall revenge an downstroy sinner persons who don't live by I Command - that I-man might downstroy them name invocation from this world - like unto Him downstroyed peoples who were precedin him - Him shall revenge an downstroy him pon the time when Him downstroy. [21] An like unto evil persons did evil things - them shall raceive them hardship. [22] But bein commanded from JAH - goodly Work shall follow persons who work goodly Work. [23] Fe like unto 'Iyasu downstroyed the five Kene`an kings ina cave ina one day - an like unto him made Sun stand ina Geba`on by him priah that him might downstroy them armies - Sun have stood amidst Heaven up til him downstroyed 'Ewiewon an Kenaniewon - Fierziewon an Kiethiewon an 'Iyabusiewon armies - an like unto him killed around twenty thousand persons at one time - an like unto him killed them - an like unto him bound them makin foot from neck - an like unto him killed them ina cave by spear - an like unto him fitted a stone pon them... [24] Tribulation like unto this shall find all persons who sadden JAH ina them evil Work.

CHAPTER 9

[1] "O thou weak man who aren't JAH - why are thou proud? thou who are sight up today bein a man are Earth ashes tomorrow - an thou will totally be worms ina thy grave. [2] Fe thy teacher are Deeyablos who return all persons sin hardship toward him ras self becau him misled InI faada 'Adam - an *See'ol* will find thee again - an she will find persons who work thy sin. [3] Fe ina firmin up him collar of reasonin an makin him ras self proud - like unto him refused fe bow fe 'Adam whom the Irator Irated... [4] thou also have refused fe bow fe thy Irator JAH like unto thy teacher Deeyablos did. [5] Like unto thy precedin faadas - who don't know them Irator JAH ina worship - will go toward *Gehannem* - thou also will go toward *Gehannem*. [6] Like unto Him revenged an downstroyed them becau them evil Work that them worked ina this world - an like unto them downscended toward *Gehannem* ... [7] thou also will downscend toward *Gehannem* like unto them. [8] As thou have aroused Him anger - an as thou have neglected fe worship JAH Who gave thee Itority pon the five kingdoms - do it seem fe thee that thou will escape from JAH Itority? [9] Thou don't do thus that thou do Him Accord - thus Him examined thee - but if thou work goodly Work ina this world - JAH will accomplish all thy Work fe thee-I - an Him will accomplish an bless all the Work thou seized ina thy hand fe thee-I - an Him will subject thy Antiquity of enemies an thy day enemies fe thee-I [10] Thou will be Irie ina thy enterins an thy proceedins an ina thy child birthed from thy nature - an ina thy flocks an thy fatnesses - an ina all Work where thou placed thy hand - an ina all that thou thought ina thy heart ~ as Itority have been given thee-I from alongside JAH that thou might do thus an might work an plant an demolish - all will be commanded fe thee-I. [11] However if thou won't hear JAH Word nor live firmed up ina Him LAW - like unto criminals who were precedin thee - an who don't worship JAH by what are due - an who didn't believe firmed up ina HIM straight LAW - there are nothing whereby thou will escape from JAH Itority - fe JAH Judgemant are Truth. [12] All are totally revealed before Him - yet there are nothing hidden from before Him. [13] Him are Who seize the kings Itority an Who overturn powerful ones thrones. [14] Him are Who Ilivate them who were downbased an Who lift up them who fell. [15] Him are Who loose them who were bound an Who arouse them who dead ~ as pardon dew are found from alongside Him - pon the time Him loved Him shall arouse persons whose flesh were demolished an rotten an were like unto dust. [16] An havin aroused an judged persons who worked evil Work - Him will tek them toward *Gehannem* - fe them have saddened Him. [17] Fe them are who demolished JAH Order an Him LAW - an Him will downstroy them child from this world. [18] As kind persons Work are more difficult than sinner persons Work - sinner persons don't love that them might live ina kind persons counsel. [19] Like unto Heavens were distanced from Earth - likewise kind persons Work were distanced from evil persons Work. [20] But sinner persons Work are robbery an sin - adultery an iniquity - greed an perfidy Work ~ it are bein drunk ina iniquity an robbin a person money. [21] It are quickly goin toward sheddin a person

blood - an it are goin toward downstruction that don't benefit - an it are makin a child weep whose mother an faada dead pon him ~ it are eatin blood an what dead an lodged - an it are eatin camel an boar flesh - an it are goin toward a dawta ina she blood before she are cleansed - an toward a dawta ina childbirth. [22] All this are sinner persons Work ~ she are Seythan trap that were a wide an prepared path - an that tek toward *Gehannem* that live firmed up foriva - an toward *See'ol* . [23] But righteous ones path that were totally narrow are what tek toward welfare - an innocence an humbleness - an Inity an Love - an priah an fast - an flesh purity - toward keepin from what don't benefit - from eatin what a sword bloated an cut an what dead an lodged - an from goin toward a youtmon wife an from adultery. [24] Them keep from what weren't commanded by LAW - from eatin disgustin food an from all hated Work - an from all the Work that JAH don't love - fe sinner persons do all this. [25] As fe kind persons - them distance from all the Work that JAH don't love. [26] Him love them an shall keep them from all them tribulation like unto Trust money. [27] Fe them keep Him Order an Him LAW an all that Him love - but Seythan rule sinner persons.

CHAPTER 10

[1] Fear JAH Who Irated unu an kept unu up til today - yet unu the nobles an the kings - don't go pon Seythan path. [2] Live ina the LAW an Command of JAH Who rule all - yet don't go pon Seythan path. [3] As pon the time 'Isra'iel children came toward 'Amalieq that them might inherit Kiethiewon an Kenaniewon an Fierziewon country - Siefor child Balaq an Bele`am... [4] whom thou cursed are cursed - an him whom thou blessed blessed ~ don't go pon Seythan road - fe him have said - "An mi will give thee much silver an gold that honour thee - that thou might curse fe mi an - an havin cursed - that thou might downstroy fe mi." [5] An fe Bele`am have come makin him sorcery reward a morale - an fe Siefor child Balaq have shown him the place where 'Isra'iel children camped. [6] Fe him have done him pessimism - an fe him have sacrificed him sacrifice - an fe him have slaughtered from him fattened cows an sheeps - an fe him have loved that him might curse an downstroy 'Isra'iel children. [7] Him returned a curse toward a bless - yet but as JAH didn't love that him might curse them by Him Word - don't go pon Seythan road. [8] "As thou are the kindred that JAH chose - as thou are JAH Lodgin that shall come from Heaven - mek persons be cursed who curse thee-I - an mek persons who bless thee-I be blessed" him said. [9] Pon the time him blessed them before him - after this Siefor child Balaq were sad - an him totally vexed an commanded that him might curse them. [10] Fe the kindred that JAH blessed have come toward this country - an Bele`am told him - "Mi won't curse 'Isra'iel whom JAH blessed." [11] An Siefor child Balaq told Bele`am - "As fe mi - mi had loved that thou might curse fe mi ~ thou blessed them before mi - yet but thou didn't curse them ~ if thou had cursed fe mi an told mi 'Give mi' - as fe mi - mi would have given thee a house full of silver an gold - but thou totally blessed them - an thou didn't do a goodly thing fe mi - an mi won't do a goodly thing fe thee." [12] Bele`am said - "What JAH told mi Speak with mi tongue - mi will speak it - yet as fe mi - mi cyaan dare fe ignore JAH thing. [13] Lest mi curse a blessed kindred - as JAH shall vex pon mi if mi love money - as fe mi - mi don't love money more than mi soul. [14] As JAH have told them faada Ya`iqob - Mek persons who bless thee-I be blessed an mek persons who curse thee-I be cursed - lest mi curse blessed Ya`iqob - as fe mi - mi don't love money more than mi soul" him said - an as JAH have told him - Him who bless thee-I are blessed... [15] an a person who curse thee-I unjustly are cursed - accomplish thy path an thy Work that JAH might love thee. [16] An don't be like unto former persons who saddened JAH ina them sin an whom Him neglected - an there are them whom Him downstroyed ina Downstruction Water. [17] An there are them whom Him downstroyed by them haters hands ~ there are them whom Him downstroyed by them enemies hands - bringin enemies who were evil persons who firmed up tribulation pon them - an them captured them lords with them priests an them prophets. [18] An them delivered them toward the foreign country them don't know ~ them totally captured them - an them plundered them livestocks pon them an downstroyed them country. [19] Fe them have demolished the honoured country 'Iyerusaliem fences an ramparts - an them made 'Iyerusaliem like unto a field. [20] An the priests were capture - an the LAW were demolished - an warriors fought ina war an fell. [21] An widows were capture ~ as them have been capture - them wept fe them ras selves - yet them didn't weep fe them husbands who dead. [22] An the children wept - an elders shamed - an them weren't nice fe neither a grey haired person nor a elder. [23] Them downstroyed all them found ina the country - yet them weren't nice fe beauties nor fe them ina LAW ~ as JAH have vexed pon Him kindreds pon the time Him loved that Him might beforehand downstroy Him Lodgin the Temple - them captured an took them toward the country them don't know an toward peoples. [24] As them sadden them Irator everytime - becaudis thing pon the time JAH neglected 'Isra'iel children - JAH made 'Iyerusaliem fe be ploughed like unto a field. [25] Fe Him are nice fe them becau them faadas - but Him didn't downstroy them at one time ~ as Him love them faadas Yis'haq an 'Abriham an Ya`iqob who reigned fe true an lived firmed up ina straight LAW before them Irator - it are becau them faadas kindness - yet it aren't becau them ras selves kindness that him forgive them. [26] An Him I-pointed them pon honours that were twofold - an them found two Kingdoms - pon Earth an ina Heaven. [27] An unu the kings an the nobles who live ina this passin world - like unto your faadas who lived firmed up ina Work that are due an who were precedin unu likewise inherited the Kingdom of Heaven - an like unto them names were beautiful fe a child children - think of them. [28] An thou - straighten up thy Work - that Him might straighten up thy Kingdom fe thee - an that thy name might be called ina goodly invocation like unto the kind kings who were precedin thee who served JAH ina them beautiful lifestyle.

CHAPTER 11

[1] Think of JAH slave Mussie who weren't annoyed when him kept around this kindred ina him humbleness an him priah an whom not even one person downstroyed - an him begged toward JAH ina him innocence fe him sista an bredda who backbit him an loved that JAH might downstroy them while him said - "As them have wronged Thee-I - Lord - pardon an don't neglect thy kindreds" - an him atoned them sin fe them - yet Him thought of JAH servant Mussie who weren't annoyed. [2] "Fe I-man have wronged Thee-I - an forgive I Thy slave who am a sinner - fe Thou are Merciful - an fe Thou are a Pardoner - an forgive them them sin." [3] An Mussie likewise atoned them sin fe him sista an bredda who backbit him. [4] An becaudis thing him were called innocent. [5] An JAH totally loved him more than all the priests children who were him bredren - fe Him I-point the priests - an JAH made him like unto Him Ras Self alongside them. [6] But Him also

sank beneath Earth Qorie childran who challenged ~ Him lowered them toward *See'ol* with them livestocks an them tents when them said "Wi are there - wi are there ina flesh an soul" ~ as him Irator JAH have loved him - an as him didn't depart from Him Command - all the word him spoke would be done fe him like unto JAH Word. [7] An unless thou demolished JAH Command likewise - JAH will do thy accord fe thee-I an will love thy thing fe thee-I - an Him will keep thy Kingdom fe thee-I. [8] An 'Asaf an Qorie childran who departed from Mussie command grumbled pon him becau him told them - "Straighten up your reasonins fe be ruled fe JAH." [9] Them grumbled sayin - "How about aren't wi Liewee childran who work priesthood Work ina Tent that were special?" [10] Them went an smoked up ishence seizin them censers that them might smoke up - but JAH didn't accept them plea - an them were burnt by the fiyah ina them censers - an them melted like unto the wax that fiyah melt - an not even one person remained from them ~ as Him have said - Them censers were honoured by them bodies bein burnt - apart from them censers that entered toward JAH Lodgin fe JAH Command - neither them clothes nor them bones remained. [11] Becaudis thing JAH told 'Aron an Mussie - Gather them censers toward the Tent ~ mek it be a instrumant fe I Lodgin wherefor I-man prepared all I-ginnin from outside up til within. [12] An him prepared the honoured Tent instrumants ~ him prepared the rings an the joiners - *Keerubiel* picture sea. [13] Him worked the cups - the curtains - the Tent area grounds fe the mobilisation - the altar an the jugs whereby them sacrifice ina the Tent that were special. [14] Them sacrificed the sacrifice that them sacrifice by them accord - the sacrifice whereby welfare are made - the sacrifice whereby Him atone sin - an the vow sacrifice an the mornin an the evenin sacrifice. [15] All that Him commanded fe Mussie - him commanded them ina the Tent that were special - that them might work Work ina she. [16] Them didn't scorn bein ruled fe them Irator JAH - that Him Name might be praised by them ina the LAW Lodgin Tent of them Irator JAH Who gave them a promise that Him might give them fe give them them faadas inheritance that produce honey an milk that Him swore fe 'Abriham. [17] Them didn't scorn bein ruled fe them Irator JAH - Who swore fe Yis'haq an firmed up Him Worship fe Ya`iqob... [18] an Who firmed up fe 'Aron an Mussie the Tent where Him Worship are kept... [19] an Who firmed up Him Worship fe both 'Elyas an Samu'iel ina the Temple an Tent that Selomon worked up til it became JAH Lodgin ina 'Iyerusaliem - an up til JAH Name Lodgin became JAH Lodgin that honoured 'Isra'iel. [20] Fe she are a supplication - an fe she are a sin atonemant where it are overturned fe them who live ina innocence an fe the priests. [21] An fe she are a place fe persons who do Him Accord where Him will hear them pleas... [22] an JAH LAW Canstruction that honoured 'Isra'iel. [23] Fe she are where sacrifice are sacrificed an where Ishence are smoked up that JAH Who honoured 'Isra'iel be ina goodly Fragrance. [24] An Him would speak bein pon the joiner where Him forgive ina the Tent that were special ~ JAH Light would be revealed fe Ya`iqob childran whom Him chose an fe friends who live firmed up ina Him LAW an Him Command. [25] But persons who ignored JAH LAW will be like unto Qorie children whom Earth sank - an likewise sinner persons have that them might enter toward *Gehannem* that have no exits up til Iternity.

CHAPTER 12

[1] Unu who didn't keep the LAW Him commanded unu ina Tent - woe fe unu 'Isra'iel nobles who also didn't do Him Accord - yet unu did your ras selves accord - an this are bein arrogant an pride - greed an adultery - drink an bein drunk - an swearin ina lie. [2] An becaudis thing I anger - like unto chaff are burnt before a fiyah - an like unto fiyah burn the mountain - an like unto a whirl wind spill the crushed chaff from Earth an scattar it toward Heaven - lest it trace be found ina it place - I anger will downstroy unu like unto that. [3] JAH Who honoured 'Isra'iel said - I-man shall likewise downstroy all persons who work sin - an think of JAH Who rule all an fe Whom nothing fail. [4] Him love persons who love Him - an fe persons who live firmed up ina Him Command - Him will atone them iniquity an them sin fe them ~ don't be dull an stingy of heart by not believin. [5] An mek your reasonins straight fe be ruled fe JAH - an believe ina Him that unu might firm up your bodies - an I-man shall save unu from your enemy hand ina your tribulation day. [6] An ina your plea time I-man tell unu - Check - I-man am there with unu ina Support ~ I-man shall save unu from your enemy hand ~ as unu have believed ina I - an as unu have done I Command - an as unu didn't depart from I LAW - an as unu have loved what I-man love - JAH Who rule all said - I-man won't neglect unu pon your tribulation day. [7] Him love them who love Him - fe Him are a Pardoner - an fe Him are nice - an Him keep persons who keep Him LAW - like unto a trust money. [8] Him return Him anger fe them many times ~ becau Him were who know them that them are flesh an blood - as Him are a Pardoner - Him didn't downstroy all ina Him chastisemant - an pon the time them souls were separated from them flesh - them will return toward them Earthliness. [9] As Him have Irated them bringin from not livin toward livin - them won't know the place where them live up til JAH love that Him might bring them from not livin toward livin ~ again Him separated them souls from them flesh - an Earth nature returned toward it Earthliness. [10] An again Him Accord shall bring them from not livin toward livin." [11] But Tseerutsaydan who denied JAH multiplied bein arrogant before JAH ~ him made him ras self lofty up til the day that him loved pon the time him quit Him. [12] "An mi era became like unto Heaven era - an mi are who send forth Sun - an mi won't dead up til Iternity" him said. [13] An before him finished speakin this thing the Angel of Death whose name are called Thilimyakos alit an struck him heart ~ him dead ina that iwa ~ as him didn't praise him Irator - him were separated from him beautiful lifestyle an him perished arisin from him arrogance abundance an him Work evil. [14] But when the Keledans king army had camped ina the city an the country squares lovin fe fight him - pon the time him dead - them proceeded an downstroyed him country ~ them plundered all him livestock - an them didn't preserve a elder who near an sight up ramparts. [15] Them plundered all him money - an them took him tiny money - an them burned him country ina fiyah an returned toward them country.

CHAPTER 13

[1] But these five Meqabees children who believed gave them bodies fe death refusin fe eat the sacrifice sacrificed fe idols. [2] Fe them have known that pretendin with JAH surpass from pretendin with persons - an JAH anger from the king anger. [3] Havin known that this world will totally pass an that the Irie Ites won't live firmed up foriva - them gave them bodies fe fiyah that them might be saved from fiyah ina Heaven. [4] An as them have known that bein made Irie ina Garden one day are better than livin many eras ina this world - an that findin Thy Pardon one iwa Lord - are better than

many eras - them gave them bodies fe fiyah. [5] What are InI era? Like unto a shadow - like unto passin wax melt an perish pon a fiyah edge - aren't it like unto that? [6] But Thou Lord live foriva - an Thy Era aren't fulfilled - an Thy Name invocation are fe a child childran. [7] An Meqabees childran thought that it seemed all this ~ refusin fe eat a disgustin sacrifice them chose believin ina JAH. [8] Knowin that them will arise with persons who dead - an meanin becau JAH - knowin that Judgemant shall be judged after Resurrection of Council - becaudis thing them gave them bodies fe martyrdom. [9] Unu persons who don't know nor believe persons who dead risin - knowin that the Life them find later will surpass from this them passin Earthly Life - arisin from these five Meqabees childran who gave them bodies together fe the death and whose appearance were handsome - after this them knew Resurrection. [10] Becau them believed ina Him knowin that all shall pass - an becau them didn't bow fe idols - becau them didn't eat a disgustin sacrifice that don't give Support - them gave them bodies fe death that them might find thanks from JAH. [11] Fe becaudis thing knowin that Him will mek them Irie ina flesh an soul ina later era - them didn't know this world flavour an death tribulation a serious thing fe them who have child an wife - an knowin that Resurrection be made ina flesh an soul pon the Day of Advent - them gave them bodies fe death. [12] An knowin that persons who kept JAH LAW - with the nobles an the kings who believed JAH Word an were nice... [13] shall live reignin fe a child childran many eras ina Kingdom of Heaven where are no sadness an tribulation nor death - an knowin ina them reasonins what will be done later - like unto wax melt amidst a fiyah - becaudis thing them gave them bodies fe death. [14] Believin that them faces will shine seven hands more than the Sun - an that them will be Irie ina Him Love pon the time all arose ina flesh an soul - them gave them bodies fe death.

CHAPTER 14

[1] But the Samrans an 'Ayhuds thing - the Seduqans who don't believe persons who dead risin - an the Fereesans thing quite totally sadden I - an it help I fe I reasonin ~ "Wi will dead tomorrow" 'Ayhuds say - "Mek wi eat an drink ~ wi will dead tomorrow ~ there are no Irie Ites wi will sight up ina grave." [2] But the Samrans say - "As wi flesh will be dust - it won't arise. [3] Becau she were invisible like unto wind an like unto iyunder voice - check - she are here - an becau she were what them don't call an invisible - as soul won't arise if flesh dead - pon the time Resurrection are done wi will believe wi souls arisin. [4] But as beasts will eat she an as worms will eat she ina the grave - wi flesh are sight up alongside all ~ she will become dust an ashes. [5] An those beasts who ate she will become dust - fe them have been like unto grass - an fe them have become dust like unto them weren't irated - an fe them trace won't be found - but wi flesh won't arise." [6] An the Fereesans say - "Wi believe as fe persons who dead arisin - however Him will bring an Inite souls with another flesh that are ina Heaven - that aren't pon Earth ~ where will demolished an rotten fleshes be found?" [7] But the Seduqans say - "After wi soul proceeded from wi flesh - wi won't arise with persons who dead - an flesh an soul have no arisin after them dead - an after wi dead wi won't arise." [8] An becaudis thing them totally err - an as them speak insult pon JAH Lordship - them thing sadden I. [9] As them didn't believe JAH Who honour them - them have no hope fe be saved - however them have no hope fe dead an arise an be saved. [10] O 'Ayhudan who are blind of reasonin - when thou are whom Him Irated bringin from not livin toward livin - an scorned like unto spit - will thou mek JAH ignorant - Who made thee a person? Will it fail JAH Who Irated thee ina Him Example an Him Appearance fe arouse Initin thy flesh an thy soul? [11] As thou won't escape from JAH Itority - don't think a thing that are thus ~ thou will arise without thou lovin - fe there are the hardship thou will raceive ina See'ol where thou were seized pon the time thou dead - an it shall be judged pon thee without thou lovin. [12] Fe the sin found from demons that demons place ina thy reasonin are worked alongside thee after thou were birthed from thy mother womb - an fe she are worked abundantly pon the time thou grew up. [13] Them place she ina thy body pon the time thou dead - an she will bring hardship pon them pon the time them worked she. [14] Like unto there are sin ina them collar of reasonin - as there are persons who work sin bein seized by she - she kindreds will present demons. [15] All sinner persons souls shall come from Heaven edge where them are - an thy sin likewise shall introduce thee toward Gehannem pullin an bringin thy soul from where thou are. [16] An after thy flesh lived separate from thy soul - JAH Charity dew shall arouse thee bein seven fold like unto InI faada 'Adam flesh. [17] Thou who live ina grave - thou also err ina thy error - yet mek it not seem fe thee that thou only mislead the others ~ thou say - "The arisin that persons who dead shall arise aren't there" - that them might depart from JAH Command an err. [18] Him shall arouse thee that Him might give thee thy hardship like unto thy Work that thou worked - yet who shall quit thee that thou might remain bein dust? [19] But at that time - whether wind ina wind be thy nature - or if Water ina Water be thy nature - or if Earth ina Earth be thy nature - or if fiyah ina fiyah be thy nature - it shall come. [20] An if a soul that lodged ina thee be what lived ina See'ol - she shall come. [21] An righteous ones souls that live ina Garden ina Ites shall come. [22] But thou 'Ayhudan - Samran - Fereesan - Seduqan - will live ina See'ol up til it are judged pon thee. [23] At that time thou will sight up that JAH shall pay thee the hardship like unto thy sin becau thou misled persons. [24] "Persons who dead won't arise ~ as wi will dead - mek wi eat an drink" - an becau thou sat ina Mussie chair an misled by thy words while thou said - "Persons who dead won't arise" - thou will sight up that Him shall pay thee thy hardship. [25] An without thy knowin 'Oreet Book - an when thou teach the books word - becaudis thing thou erred ~ it would be better had thou remained without learnin from thy misleadin a person. [26] It would have been better if thou didn't know the books word - when thou promulgate JAH kindreds ina thy evil teachin an thy worthless words. [27] Fe JAH don't favour havin sight up a face - an fe Him shall give the grace an glory Him prepared fe Him friends - persons who teach goodly Work - but thou have that thou might raceive thy reward like unto thy Work an the things that thou spoke. [28] But there are nothing whereby thou will escape from JAH Itority Who shall judge pon thee - an Him have that Him might pay thee like unto thy Work - fe them whom thou taught an thou together will raceive a sentance. [29] Know that persons who dead shall arise - an if them are persons who kept Him LAW them shall arise - an like unto Earth send forth grass pon the time rain rained - as Him Command shall send them forth from a grave - it aren't possible fe it fe remain demolished an rotten. [30] Like unto moist wood drink dew an send forth leaves pon the time Him satta she rain fe Earth - like unto wheat bear forth fruit - an like unto grain produce buds - like unto it aren't possible fe she fe withhold that she might prevent she fruit if JAH loved... [31] an like unto it aren't possible fe a dawta who canceived fe close an prevent she womb pon the time labour seized she - like unto it aren't possible fe she fe escape without birthin... [32] as dew have alit toward she bein commanded

from JAH - at that time she shall produce them at one time - yet after she heard JAH Word - a grave also likewise cyaan prevent the persons gathered alongside she from arisin. [33] An fleshes shall be gathered ina the place where them corpses fell - an them places where souls live shall be opened - an souls shall return toward the flesh where them were formerly separated. [34] An pon the time a drum were beaten - persons who dead shall quickly arise like unto a eye wink - an havin arisen them shall stand before JAH - an Him shall give them them reward like unto them hand Work. [35] At that time thou will sight up that thou arise with dead ones - an thou will marvel at all the Work thou worked ina this world - an pon the time thou sight up all thy sins written before thee - at that time thou will regret a useless regret. [36] Thou know that thou will arise with dead ones an that thou will raceive thy hardship like unto the Work that thou worked.

CHAPTER 15

[1] But persons who found them reward by them goodly Work shall be Irie at that time ~ persons who ignored while them said - "Persons who dead won't arise" shall be sad at that time pon the time them sight up that persons who dead arose with them evil Work that don't benefit. [2] That - them Work that them worked shall canvict them - an them ras selves shall know that it canvict them without one livin who will dispute them. [3] Pon the day when Judgemant an mournin are done - pon the day when JAH shall come - pon the day when Definite Judgemant are judged - persons who forgot JAH LAW shall stand ina the place where them stand. [4] Pon the day when there shall be total darkness - an pon the day when mist are pulled - pon the day when flashes are sight up an when lightnin are heard... [5] an pon the day when quakes an fright an heatwave an sleet frost are made... [6] pon the day when a evil person who worked evil Work receive hardship - an pon the day when a clean person raceive him reward like unto him worked clean Work - an pon the day when persons who forgot JAH LAW raceive the hardship like unto a sinner person worked sin - them shall stand ina the place where them stand. [7] Fe pon the day when a master aren't more honoured than him slave - an pon the time when a mistress aren't more honoured than she slave... [8] an pon the time when the king aren't more honoured than a poor one - an pon the time when a elder aren't more honoured than a infant - pon the time when a faada aren't more honoured than him child - an pon the time when a mother aren't more honoured than she child... [9] pon the time when a wealthy one aren't more honoured than a poor one - an pon the time when a arrogant one aren't more honoured than a downbased one - an pon the time when the great aren't more honoured than the small - she are the day when Judgemant are judged - fe she are the day when them raceive sentance an hardship - an fe she are the day when all will raceive hardship like unto them worked sin. [10] An fe she are the day when persons who worked goodly Work raceive them reward - an fe she are the day when persons who worked sin raceive hardship. [11] An as she are the day when persons who found them reward are made Irie - persons who forgot JAH LAW shall stand ina the place where them stand. Persons who mek liars - who digest books while them said - "Persons who dead won't arise" - them shall sight up Resurrection. [12] At that time this world sinners - who didn't work goodly Work ina this world - shall weep pon them sin that them worked - becau sadness found them without calmin. [13] An all likewise - kind persons who worked goodly Work - them Irie Ites won't be fulfilled up til Iternity - fe them have worked goodly Work when them were ina this world. [14] Fe them have known that them will arise after them dead - an them didn't depart from them Irator LAW. [15] Becau them didn't depart from Him LAW - them shall inherit two welfares ~ Him multiplied them seed ina this world - an Him honoured them childran. [16] Him bequeathed them the Kingdom of Heaven where shall be found the welfare him swore fe them faadas pon the time when persons who dead arise - an pon the time when rich ones become poor. [17] Persons shall weep who worked sin - who don't believe persons who dead arisin - who don't keep JAH LAW - an who don't think of Arisin Day. [18] At that time them will sight up the tribulation that shall find them an shall have no endin - an where are no calmin nor welfare - an it have the sadness that have no rest nor calmin ina them reasonin. [19] An a fiyah that don't perish an worms that don't sleep shall find them. [20] An ina the place where are them flesh are fiyah - sulphur - whirl wind - frost - hail - sleet ~ all this shall rain over them. [21] Fe persons who don't believe persons who dead arisin - there are fiyah of *Gehannem* pon them.

CHAPTER 16

[1] Thou - please think of what are pon thy flesh - an thy feet an thy hands nails - an thy head hair - fe them proceed quickly pon the time thou cut them ~ know Resurrection by this - that thou have a reasonin - an that thou have religion an knowledge. [2] Thy feet an thy hands nails an thy head hair - thou say - "Where do these come from?" ~ aren't it JAH Who prepared it that them might proceed - that thou know arisin that shall be done pon thy flesh that aren't pon another flesh - that thou might know that thou will arise after thou dead? [3] Becau thou misled persons while thou said - "There are no Resurrection of the dead ones" - pon the time when dead ones arise thou will raceive thy hardship like unto thou worked sin an iniquity. [4] An as even what thou planted now won't remain refusin that it might grow - whether it be wheat or barley - thou will sight she up pon the time the day arrived when thou raceive thy hardship. [5] An again - the plant thou planted won't say - "I-man won't grow" - an be it a fig wood or a grape vine - it fruit an it leaf won't be changed. [6] If thou plant grapes - it won't be changed that it might be a fig - an if thou plant figs - it won't be changed that it might be grapes - an if thou sow wheat it won't be changed that it might be barley. [7] All - ina each of the seeds - ina each of it kinds - each of the fruits - each of the woods - each of the leaves - each of the roots - send forth fruit havin received Pardon Dew blessin by what are found from JAH - yet if thou sow barley also it won't be changed that it might be wheat. [8] An all likewise - that a grave might produce flesh an soul - she shall produce persons like unto JAH sowed pon she ~ the flesh an soul that JAH sowed shall arise bein Inited - yet persons who worked goodly Work won't be changed ina persons who worked evil Work - an persons who worked evil Work also won't be changed ina persons who worked goodly Work. [9] Pon pon the time the iwa arrived when a drum are beaten - persons who dead shall arise by the Pardon Dew found from JAH ~ persons who worked goodly Work shall arise ina Life Resurrection - an them reward are the Garden where are Irie Ites that JAH prepared fe kind persons - where are no tribulation nor disease - an that are clean ones lodgin where them won't again dead after this. [10] But persons who worked evil Work shall arise a Definite Judgemant arisin - an with Deeyablos who misled them... [11] an with him armies - demons who don't love that even one person might be saved from all 'Adam childran... [12] them shall downscend toward *Gehannem* that were darkness edge - where are tooth grindin an

mournin - where are no charity nor pardon - an where are no exits up til Iternity - that are beneath *See'ol* foriva. Fe them didn't work goodly Work ina them Life ina this world when them were ina them flesh. [13] Becaudis thing it shall be judged pon them pon the time when flesh an soul arise bein Inited. [14] Woe fe persons who don't believe the flesh an soul arisin whereby JAH show Him miracles abundance together. [15] An all an each one shall raceive him reward like unto him Work and him hands weariness.

CHAPTER 17

[1] A wheat kernel won't grow nor bear fruit unless she were demolished. But if a wheat kernel are demolished she will send roots toward Earth ~ she will send forth leaves ~ there will be buds ~ it will bear fruit. [2] Unu know that the one wheat kernel will become many kernels. [3] An all likewise - this kernel grow risin up from Water an wind an Earth dew - fe wheat cyaan bear fruit without Sun - but Sun are becau fiyah stead. [4] An wind are becau a soul stead - an wheat cyaan bear fruit without wind - an the Water give Earth fe drink an satta she. [5] An after Earth that are ashes drank Water - she produce roots - an she tips are lofty upward ~ she bear fruit around what JAH blessed she. [6] But a wheat kernel are 'Adam example - ina whom lodged a resonatin soul that JAH Irated - an likewise a grape wood drink Water an send forth roots - an the thin root kinds drink Water. [7] Fe Pardon Dew found from JAH give fe drink vines tips that were long - an it send the Water upward toward the leaf tips ~ it bud up from the Sun heat - an by JAH Accord it bear fruit. [8] It shall be a goodly fragrance that mek a reasonin Irie - an pon the time them ate it - it shall satta like unto Water that don't mek thirsty an grain that don't mek hungry - an pon the time them immersed it - it will be the cluster blood. [9] An like unto it were told ina Psalm sayin - "Grapes mek a person reasonin Irie" - pon the time them drank it - it mek a person heart Irie - an pon the time a person who came loose opened him mouth an drank it - him are drunk ~ him drink an fill ina him lungs - an the blood flow toward him heart. [10] As grapes drunkenness totally mislead - an as it deprive him him mind - it mek the pit an the cliff like unto a wide meadow - an him don't know obstacles an thorns pon him feet an hands. [11] JAH did thus pon she fruit an grape wood that Him Name might be praised by persons who believe dead persons arisin an who do Him Accord. [12] Ina the Kingdom of Heaven Him shall mek persons Irie who believe persons who dead arisin.

CHAPTER 18

[1] Unu persons who don't believe persons who dead arisin - around what error unu err! An pon the time them took unu toward the place unu don't know - unu will regret a useless regrets - an becau unu didn't believe the arisin that persons who dead shall arise Inited ina soul an flesh - an pon the time persons cast unu toward *Gehannem* ... [2] if unu work whether the good or the evil - unu will raceive your reward like unto your Work - fe unu have misled them companions reasonin while unu said - "Wi know that persons who dead - who were dust an ashes - won't arise." [3] As them death have no exit - an as them have no Power fe them chastisemant that shall come pon them - an as them weren't firm ina them tribulation - becaudis thing them mislead them companions ~ fe them have that them might stand ina JAH Square. [4] Pon the time Him vexed pon them ina Him wrath them will totally fear ~ becau them didn't know that them were Irated bringin from not livin toward livin - as them speak JAH LAW without knowin - it shall be judged pon them all becau them worked evil. [5] Them don't know *Gehannem* where them will go - fe becau them were angry an becau them were crooked ina them Work - them teach fe them companions like unto them reasonin thirst measure - an fe them are evil ones who teach a crooked thing while them said - "There are no Resurrection of dead ones." [6] At that time them shall know that persons who dead shall arise - an them shall know that it shall be judged pon them becau them didn't believe the persons who dead arisin that are fe all 'Adam childran. [7] Fe all InI are 'Adam childran - an fe InI have dead becau 'Adam - an fe death judgemant have found InI all from alongside JAH becau InI faada 'Adam error. [8] InI will again arise there with InI faada 'Adam that InI might raceive InI hardship by InI Work that InI worked - fe the world have been ruled fe death by InI faada 'Adam ignorance. [9] By 'Adam infringin JAH Command - becaudis thing InI raceived hardship ~ InI flesh ina grave melted like unto wax - an InI bodies perished. [10] An Earth drank InI marrow ~ InI perished an InI comeliness perished ina grave - an InI flesh were buried ina grave - an InI beautiful words were buried ina Earth. [11] An worms proceeded from InI shinin eyes - an InI features perished ina grave an became dust. [12] Where are youtmons features comeliness - who were attractive - whose stance were handsome an whose word thing succeeded? How about where are warriors firmness? [13] Where are the kings armies - or how about the nobles lordship? Where are adornin ina horses an adornin ina silver an gold an adornin ina shinin weapons? Didn't it perish? [14] Where are sweet grape drink - an how about food flavour?

CHAPTER 19

[1] O Earth who gathered the nobles an the kings an rich ones an elders an dawtaz who were attractive an beauties who were attractive - woe arisin from thee-I. [2] O Earth who gathered persons who were warriors - them who have comeliness - an them who were fine of leg - an them who have reasonin an knowledge - an them whose words have words that were beautiful like unto a hummin harp an like unto a lyre an a violin beat... [3] an them who have a tune that mek Irie like unto grape drink mek Irie - an them whose eyes shine like unto a mornin star... [4] an them who sketch what were firm like unto them right hands lift up what are given an withheld an like unto them were - an them whose feet were beautiful fe sight up - an them who run like unto rushin wheels - woe arisin from thee-I. [5] O death who separated attractive persons souls from them flesh - woe arisin from thee-I - fe thou have been sent by JAH Accord. [6] As thou have gathered many persons whom JAH produced from thee-I an returned toward thee-I - thou Earth - woe arisin from thee-I ~ InI were found from thee-I ~ InI returned toward thee-I by Accord of JAH ~ InI were Irie over thee-I by JAH Accord. [7] Thou became a carpet fe InI corpses ~ InI recurred over thee-I - an InI were buried within thee-I ~ InI ate thy fruit - an thou ate InI flesh. [8] An InI drank the Water found from thy springs - an thou drank InI blood springs ~ InI ate the fruit found from thy Earthliness - an thou ate InI body flesh. [9] Like unto JAH commanded thee-I fe be InI food - InI ate grain from thy Earthliness that have beautiful dew - an thou raceived InI fleh comeliness an made it dust fe thy food like unto JAH commanded thee-I. [10] O death who gathered the nobles an the kings who were powerful - woe arisin from thee-I ~ thou didn't fear arisin

from them famousness an them frightenin - like unto JAH Who Irated them commanded thee-I ~ o death - woe arisin from thee-I - an thou didn't scorn the sufferah. [11] An thou weren't nice fe persons whose features are beautiful - an thou didn't quit powerful ones an warriors ~ thou didn't quit poor nor rich ones - neither kind nor evil ones - neither childran nor elders - neither dawtaz nor males. [12] Thou didn't quit persons who think a goodly thing an who didn't depart from the LAW - an thou didn't quit them who were like unto animals ina them Work - who think a evil thing - who were totally beautiful ina them features comeliness - ina them thing flavour an ina them words ~ o death - woe arisin from thee-I. [13] Thou didn't quit persons whose words were angry an whose mouths were full of curses ~ thou gathered persons who live in darkness an ina light an them souls ina thy places ~ o death - woe arisin from thee-I. [14] An Earth gathered the persons flesh who live whether ina cave or ina Earth - up til a drum are beaten an persons who dead arise. [15] As persons who dead shall arise quickly like unto a eye wink by JAH Command an pon a drum bein beaten - persons who worked evil Work shall raceive them hardship ina them sin abundance measure that them worked it - an persons who worked goodly Work shall be Irie.

CHAPTER 20
[1] An believe I that all InI Work that InI worked ina this world won't remain nor be hidden pon the time InI stood before Him fearin an tremblin. [2] An pon the time InI didn't seize provisions fe InI path - an pon the time InI won't have clothes fe InI bodies... [3] pon the time InI won't have a staff fe InI hands nor shoes fe InI feet... [4] an pon the time InI won't know the paths where demons tek InI - whether it be slippery or smooth - or be it dark - an whether it be thorns or nettles - or whether it be a Water depth or a pit depth - believe I that InI Work that InI worked ina this world won't remain nor be hidden. [5] InI won't know the demons who tek InI - an InI won't hear them thing. [6] As them are black ones - an as them lead InI toward darkness - InI don't sight up them faces. [7] An like unto the prophet spoke sayin - "Pon the time I soul were separated from I flesh - Lord I Lord - Thou know I path - an them hid a trap pon that path where I-man went - an I-man sight up returnin toward the right ~ I-man lacked one who know I - an I-man have nothing there whereby I-man will escape" - as them tek InI toward darkness - InI won't sight up them faces. [8] As him know that demons ridicule pon him - an as them will lead him toward the path him don't know - him speakin this are becaudis - an if him return leftward an rightward - there are no person who know him. [9] Him are alone amidst demons - an yet there are none who know him. [10] Angels of Light who are subtle are who are sent toward kind persons that them might raceive righteous ones souls - an might tek toward a Light place - toward the Garden - where welfare are found. [11] Demons an Angels of darkness are who are sent that them might raceive them an might tek them toward *Gehannem* that were prepared fe them that them might raceive them hardship by them sin that them worked. [12] Woe fe sinner persons souls who tek them toward downstruction - who have no welfare nor rest - nor escapin from the tribulation that found them - nor proceedin from *Gehannem* up til Iternity. [13] As them have lived firmed up ina Qayel Work - an as them have perished by Bele`am iniquity price - an as them have lacked what them will do - woe fe sinner persons - fe them pretext fe raceive interest an presents that ina downgression them might tek a foreigner money that weren't them money. [14] Them shall raceive them hardship ina *Gehannem* by them sin that them worked.

CHAPTER 21
[1] Where are persons who gather a foreigner money that weren't them hands Work nor them money? [2] Fe them tek a person money for free - an fe them shll be gathered without knowin the day when them dead that shall arrive pon them - however them quit them money for a foreigner. [3] Fe like unto them faadas - them are sinners kindreds who worry an seize sinners like unto them whether it be by theft or by robbery - an them childran won't be Irie by them faadas money. [4] As them have gathered fe them ina downgression - an as it are like unto misty urine an like unto the smoke that wind scattar an like unto wiltin grass - an like unto wax that melt arisin from before a fiyah - as sinners glory shall perish like unto that - there are none whom them faadas money will benefit ~ like unto Daweet spoke sayin - "I-man sight up a sinner man... [5] bein honoured an famed like unto a cordia an like unto a cypress - but pon the time I-man returned I-man lacked him ~ I-man searched an didn't find him place" - there are none whom them faadas money will profit nor benefit. [6] Becau them gathered a person money ina downgression - it seemin fe them that them won't dead - like unto persons who wrong them companions won't boast - sinner persons downstruction are likewise at one time. [7] Unu lazy ones - think that unu will perish an that your money will perish with unu - an if your silver an your gold abound it shall be rusted. [8] An if unu birth many childran them shall be fe many graves - an if unu work many houses them shall be demolished. [9] Fe unu didn't fulfill your Irator JAH Accord - an if unu multiply livestock them shall be for your enemies capture - an all the money unu seized ina your hands won't be found - fe it have been what weren't blessed. [10] Whether it be ina house or ina forest - an be it ina wilderness or a pasture place - an be it ina grape threshinfloor or ina grain threshinfloor - it won't be found. [11] Becau unu didn't keep JAH Command - as JAH won't save unu with all your house hold from the tribulation - there shall be sadness pon unu arisin from all your enemies - yet unu won't be Irie ina your childran birthed from your nature. [12] But from Him plenty - Him won't trouble persons who kept Him Order an Him LAW ~ Him give all who begged Him - yet Him bless them childran birthed from them nature an also them land fruit fe them. [13] An Him mek them rulers pon all peoples ina them area that them might rule lest them be who are ruled - an Him give them all Him plenty ina them pasture place. [14] Him bless fe them all them seized ina them hand - all them field fruit - an all them livestocks places - an Him mek them Irie in them childran birthed from them nature. [15] An Him don't diminish them livestocks pon them ~ Him save them from all them tribulation an from weariness an illness an downstruction - an from them enemy them don't know an from him them know. [16] An Him will dispute fe them ina Judgemant time - an Him shall save them from a evil thing an from tribulation an from all who dispute them ~ ina the first era if a priest lived who work the Tent Work - who keep the LAW an keep the Tent Order an live firmed up ina JAH Accord - by the first Order an all the LAW as them would give him the tithe an what were birthed first Iginnin from man up til livestock - Him would save them from all the tribulation. [17] Like unto Mussie commanded Newie child 'Iyasu - there was a country of sanctuary ina all them country ~ by not knowin an by knowin up til them judged judgemant pon whom them canvicted an

fe whom them acquitted... [18]   if a person lived who killed a soul - him would be measured there that him might be saved. [19]   Him told them - "Examine ina your reasonins that him have a quarrel with him formerly - an be it by axe or be it by a stone or be it by wood - as it have fallen from him hand by not knowin - if him say "That person pon whom it fell dead pon mi" - examine an save him ~ if him did it ina not knowin mek him be saved. [20]   But if him do it knowin - him will raceive him hardship like unto him sin - an there are none who will pardon him; but if him kill him ina not knowin - as him have done it ina not knowin - examine an save him lest him dead. [21]   Him worked fe them that them might distance from all the sin - yet Mussie would work like unto this fe 'Isra'iel childran lest them depart from JAH LAW. [22]   Him commanded them that 'Adam childran - who live firmed up ina JAH Command from worshippin idols an eatin what dead an lodged an what a sword bloated an cut - an who distance from all evil work like unto him worked fe them - that them might work it an might totally distance from all that aren't due. [23]   Him commanded them lest them depart from the Command Him worked fe them ina the Tent example ina Heaven - that them might save them bodies an might find them lodgin with them faadas. [24]   As them have been birthed from Siet an 'Adam who did JAH Accord - persons who believed ina JAH Word an lived firmed up ina Him Command will be called kind persons childran. [25]   As InI are 'Adam childran - as Him have Irated InI ina Him Example an Him Appearance that InI might work all goodly Work that mek JAH Irie - Him won't scorn it. [26]   As Him totally won't separate Him friends - if InI work goodly Work - InI shall inherit the Kingdom of Heaven where are welfare with persons who work goodly Work. [27]   Him totally love persons who beg him cleanly - an Him hear them ina them priah - an Him accept the repentance of persons who are disciplined an enter repentance ~ Him give firmness an Power fe persons who keep Him Order an Him LAW an Him Command. [28]   Persons who did Him Accord shall be Irie with Him ina Him Kingdom foriva - an whether them be persons who preceded or who arose later - them will present praise fe Him Iginnin from today up til Iternity. Mek glory due fe JAH foriva - an the secand Meqabyan arrived an were fulfilled.

3 MEQABYAN

CHAPTER 1

[1] Kristos shall rejoice Gibts persons - becau Him shall come toward them ina later era that Him will revenge an downstroy Deeyablos - who wronged them who were kindly an innocent - an who misled persons - an who hate him Irator Work. [2] Him shall revenge an downstroy him ~ Him shall return him lordship toward wretchedness an bein downbased - fe him have been arrogant ina him reasonin. [3] Him shall return him lordship toward bein downbased - fe him have said - "As mi will enter toward the sea midst - an as mi will proceed toward Heaven - an as mi will sight up depths - an as mi will grasp an seize 'Adam childran like unto bird chicks - who are it who are loftier than mi? [4] Becau mi became by them reason that mi might distance them from the straight LAW of JAH - as mi will strengthen pon persons who live ina this world unless them did JAH Accord - there are none who will depose mi from mi authority" him said. [5] "Fe mi will be a reason fe return them toward a path that were smooth fe go toward *Gehannem* with mi. [6] Persons who loved Him an kept Him LAW hate mi becaudis thing - but persons who departed from them Lord LAW an who erred will come toward mi an love mi an keep mi oath ~ as mi will mek them reasonin evil an change them thoughts lest them return toward them Irator JAH - them will do mi command like unto mi commanded them. [7] An pon the time mi showed them this world money - mi will mislead them reasonin from straight LAW - an pon the time mi showed them beautiful an attractive dawtaz - mi will distance them by these from straight LAW. [8] An pon the time mi showed them shinin Hindekie jewels an silver an gold - mi will distance them by this also from straight LAW that them might return toward mi Work. [9] An pon the time mi showed them thin clothes an red silk an white silk - an linens an white silk - mi will distance them by this also from straight LAW - an mi will return them toward mi thoughts ~ pon the time mi multiplied money an livestocks like unto sand an showed them - by this also mi will return them toward mi Work. [10] An pon the time mi showed them jealousy done in arrogance becau dawtaz an becau anger an quarrels - by all this mi will return them toward mi Work. [11] An pon the time mi showed them signs - mi will lodge ina them companions reasonin - an mi will lodge a sign thing that were fe each of the ras selves ina them reasonin - an mi showed them words signs an misled them. [12] An fe persons ina whom mi lodged mi lodgin - mi will show them signs - an be it ina stars gait - or be it ina cloud proceedin or ina fiyah flickerin - or be it ina beasts an birds cries - as them are mi lodgins - mi will lodge signs ina them reasonin pon them by all this. [13] Them will speak an give signs fe them companions - an like unto those them naysayers told them - mi will precede an be a sign fe them. [14] Mi will do them words signs fe them - that persons who examined them might be misled - an that them might give a wage fe magicians - an that them might tell fe them companions sayin - 'There are no savants like unto so-an-so an so-an-so fe whom it are done like unto them spoke - an who know prophecy - an who separate good an evil - an fe whom all are like unto them spoke - an fe whom it are done like unto them word.' [15] Mi will be Irie pon the time them spoke this - that persons who perish an err by mi might totally abound an that 'Adam childran might perish - fe JAH have downbased mi from mi rank becau them faada 'Adam - pon mi sayin 'Mi won't bow fe 'Adam who are downbased fe mi.' [16] An mi will tek toward downstruction all him childran who live firmed up ina mi command ~ mi have a Oath from JAH Who Irated mi - that all persons whom mi misled might downscend toward *Gehannem* with mi. [17] An pon the time Him multiplied Him anger pon mi - an pon the time Him commanded that them might bind an cast mi toward *Gehannem* - pon the time mi Irator commanded sayin thus - mi interceded with mi Lord ~ mi interceded before Him while mi said - 'As Thou have vexed pon mi - an as Thou have admonished mi by Thy chastisemant - an as Thou have chastised mi by Thy wrath - Lord mi Lord - adjourn mi that mi might speak one thing before Thee-I.' [18] An mi Lord answered fe mi sayin - Speak - I-man will hear thee ~ at that time mi began mi plea toward Him sayin - 'After mi were downbased from mi rank - mek the persons whom mi misled be like unto mi ina *Gehannem* where mi will raceive tribulation. [19] An mek them be fe Thy Lordship who refused mi - who didn't err by mi - who didn't keep mi command - that them might do Thy Command an might fulfill Thy Accord an might keep Thy Word - pon the time them didn't err by mi like unto mi misled them havin refused like unto mi taught them - an pon the time Thou loved mi - mek them tek the

crown Thou gave fe mi. [20] Give them the crown of the authorities called Seythans who were sent with mi ~ seat them pon mi throne pon Thy Right that were a wilderness from mi an mi hosts. [21] An mek them praise Thee-I like unto Thou loved - an mek them be like unto mi hosts an like unto mi ~ becau Thou hated mi an loved them who were Irated from ashes an Earth - as mi authority have perished - an as them authority have been lofty - mek them praise Thee-I like unto Thou loved.' [22] Mi Lord answered fe mi sayin - As thou have misled them while them sight up an while them heard - if thou misled them without them lovin I Order - mek them be fe thee like unto thy accord an like unto thy word. [23] If them quit the Books Word an I Command an came toward thee - an if thou misled them while them downstruction also saddened mi - mek them raceive tribulation ina *Gehannem* like unto thee - Him told mi. [24] Unu will raceive tribulation ina *Gehannem* up til the Iternity - yet unu will have no exits from *Gehannem* up til the Iternity - fe them whom thou misled nor fe thee.

CHAPTER 2

[1] But I-man shall bequeath thy throne ina lordship fe them whom it failed thee fe mislead - like unto I slave 'Iyob ~ JAH Who rule all said - I-man will give the Kingdom of Heaven fe persons whom it failed thee fe mislead. [2] An mi provoke pon 'Adam childran ina all ~ if it were possible fe mi fe mislead them - mi won't quit them that them might firm up ina goodly Work ~ fe mi provoke pon all 'Adam childran - an mi sweeten this world Irie Ites fe them. [3] Be it by lovin drink an food an clothes - or by lovin things - or by withholdin an givin... [4] or be it by lovin fe hear an sight up - or be it by lovin fe caress an go - or be it by multiplyin arrogance an things - or be it by lovin dreams an slumber... [5] or be it by multiplyin drunkenness an drink - or be it by multiplyin insults an anger - be it by speakin games an useless things... [6] or be it by quarrels an by backbitin them companion - or be it by sightin up this world dawtaz who were attractive - be it by smellin perfumes fragrance that mislead them... [7] mi hate them by all this lest them able fe be saved ~ mi distance them from JAH LAW that them might enter with mi toward the downstruction whereby mi were downbased from mi rank." [8] An the prophet told him - "Thou who downstroy persons - perish ~ pon the time thou departed from JAH LAW an committed crime ina thy reasonin firmness an thy arrogance - an by saddenin thy Irator an not worshippin thy Irator ina thy reasonin firmness - will thou thus be arrogant pon JAH Iration? [9] Pon the time thy Irator vexed pon thee - Him downbased thee from thy rank becau thy evil Work ~ why do thou tek 'Adam toward sin - him whom him Irator Irated from Earth - whom Him made like unto Him loved - an whom Him placed fe Him praise?" him told him. [10] "Pon the time thou - who are subtle an were Irated from wind an fiyah - were arrogant ina sayin 'Mi are the Irator'... [11] pon the time thou boasted - as JAH have sight up thy evil Work an thou have denied JAH with thy hosts - Him Irated 'Adam who will praise becau thy stead - that him might praise Him Name without diminishin. [12] As thou have made thy ras self prouder than all Angels hosts who are like unto thee - becau thy arrogance JAH Irated 'Adam with him childran that them might praise JAH Name becau the praise that thou praise with thy hosts whom Him scorned. [13] An becaudis thing JAH downstroyed thee separatin from all Angels chiefs like unto thee - an thy hosts Irated ina one counsel with thee - an thou - unu proceeded an erred from JAH praise becau your useless reasonin arrogance an becau your reasonin firmness - an unu were arrogant pon your Irator - that aren't pon another. [14] Becaudis thing Him Irated 'Adam from Earth that Him might be praised by downbased persons - an Him gave him a Command an Law sayin Don't eat lest him eat from fig fruit. [15] An Him I-pointed him pon all the Iration Him Irated ~ Him notified him sayin - Don't eat from one fig fruit that bring death - lest thou bring death pon thy ras self - yet eat fruit from all the woods amidst the Garden. [16] An pon the time thou heard this Word - thou lodged perfidy ina him arisin from the thing thou spoke ina thy tongue fe Hiewan who were found from 'Adam side bone. [17] Thou misled 'Adam who were clean - ina firm perfidy that thou might mek him a Law demolisher like unto thee. [18] Pon the time thou misled Hiewan - who were Irated bein like unto a innocent dove an who don't know thy malice - thou made she betray by thy thing that succeeded an thy crooked word - an after thou misled that Hiewan who were Irated beforehand - she also went an misled JAH Iration 'Adam who were Irated from Earth beforehand. [19] An thou made him betray a downsturbance that aren't by thy arrogance - an thou made him fe deny that him might deny him Irator Word - an thou downstroyed 'Adam ina thy arrogance. [20] An ina thy malice thou distanced him from him Irator Love - an by thy reason thou sent him way from the Garden where Irie Ites are - an by thy hindrance thou made him quit the Garden food. [21] Fe Iginnin from Antiquity thou have quarreled with the innocent Iration 'Adam that thou might lower him toward *See'ol* where thou will raceive hardship - an that thou might send him way from the Love that brought him an Irated him from not livin toward true livin - an by thy false thing thou made him thirst a drink from the Garden. [22] An when him are Earthly - Him made him a subtle Angel who totally praise him Irator ina him flesh an him soul an him reasonin. [23] An Him Irated many thoughts fe him - like unto harps praise ina each of them styles.

CHAPTER 3

[1] But Him Irated one thought fe thee - that thou might totally praise while thou were sent toward where thy Irator sent thee. [2] But fe 'Adam were given five thoughts that were evil an five thoughts that were goodly - ten thoughts. [3] An again him have many thoughts like unto sea waves - an like unto a whirl wind that scattar dust liftin up from Earth - an like unto the sea waves that shake - an arisin from him unnumbered thoughts abundance ina him heart like unto unnumbered rain drops - 'Adam thoughts are like unto that. [4] But thy thought are one ~ as thou aren't fleshly - thou have no other thought. [5] But thou lodged ina snake reasonin ~ ina evil perfidy thou downstroyed 'Adam who were one limb - an Hiewan heard the snake thing - an havin heard - she did like unto she commanded she. [6] After she ate a fig fruit - she came an misled JAH first Iration 'Adam - an she brought death pon him an pon she childran becau she infringed she Irator Command. [7] Them proceeded from the Garden fe JAH by Him true Judgemant ~ Him calmed them ina the land where them were sent by them childran birthed from them nature an by them crops found from Earth - yet Him didn't distance them from the Garden quarrelin. [8] An pon the time thou expelled them straight from the Garden - that them might plant plants an childran fe be calmed an fe renew them reasonin ina the Earth fruit that Earth prepared from she Earthliness - an that them might be calmed by Earth fruit an the Garden fruit that JAH gave them... [9] JAH gave them woods more verdant than the Garden woods - an Hiewan an 'Adam - whom thou sent way from the Garden pon them eatin it - were totally

calmed from sadness. **[10]** As JAH know fe calm Him Iration - them reasonins are calmed becau them childran an becau the crops found from Earth. **[11]** As them have been sent toward this world that grow nettles an thorns - them firm up them reasonins ina Water an grain.

CHAPTER 4

[1] The Lord have that Him might ransom 'Adam - an Him shall shame thee ~ Him will save a sheep from a wolf mouth ('Adam from Deeyablos).However thou will go toward *Gehannem* seizin with thee the persons whom thou ruled. **[2]** Persons who kept them Irator JAH LAW shall be Irie with them Irator JAH Who hid them from evil Work that Him might mek them Him fortune - an that them might praise Him with honoured Angels who didn't infringe them Irator JAH LAW like unto thee. **[3]** But JAH - Who chose an gave thee more than all Angels like unto thee that thou might praise Him with Him servant Angels - withheld from thee a lofty throne ina thy arrogance. **[4]** But thou became famous an were called one who love godhood - an thy hosts were called demons. **[5]** But persons who loved JAH shall be Him kindreds like unto honoured Angels - an the *Surafiel* an *Keerubiel* who praise Him streach forth them wings an praise without slackness. **[6]** But ina thy arrogance an thy laziness thou downstroyed thy praise that thou might praise Him everytime with thy host an thy kindreds Irated ina thy features. **[7]** Lest the praise of JAH - Who Irated thee makin a tenth tribe - be diminished pon the time thou forgot the praise of JAH Who Irated thee - it havin seemed fe thee that it aren't posssible fe Him fe Irate a Iration like unto thee - an lest the praise of JAH - Who Irated thee - be diminished pon the time thou were separated from thy bredren Inity - Him Irated 'Adam becau thy stead. **[8]** But ina thy reasonin arrogance thou neglected the praise of JAH Who Irated thee - an Him vexed pon thee ~ Him ridiculed thee - an Him bound an banished thee ina *Gehannem* with thy hosts also. **[9]** Him brought Soil from Earth with Him glorified Hands - an addin fiyah an Water an wind - Him Irated 'Adam ina Him Example an Him Features. **[10]** Him I-pointed him pon all the Iration Him Irated ina Him Itority - that Him praise might be filled by the praise thou would praise Him ~ 'Adam praise became one with Angels praise - an them praise were level. **[11]** But ina thy collar of reasonin firmness an thy arrogance thou were downbased from thy rank - an havin departed from JAH Lordship - Who Irated thee - thou downstroyed thy ras self. **[12]** Know that Him praise weren't diminished - fe JAH have Irated 'Adam who praised Him ina him reasonin counsel lest Him JAH-ness praise be diminished. **[13]** Fe Him know all before it are done - an Him knew thee before Him Irated thee that thou will demolish Him Command ~ as there are a counsel hidden alongside Him before Him Irated the world - pon the time thou denied Him - Him Irated Him slave 'Adam ina Him Features an Him Example. **[14]** Like unto Selomon spoke sayin - 'Before hills were Irated an before the world succeeded bein Irated - an before winds that are Earth grounations were Irated... **[15]** an before Him firmed up hills an mountains grounations - an before this world Work firmed up - an before moon an Sun light shone - before eras an stars caretakin were known... **[16]** an before daylight an night alternated - an before the sea were delineated by sand - before all the Irated Iration were Irated... **[17]** an before all sight up today were sight up - before all the names called today were called - Him Irated I Selomon' - Angels like unto unu an thou an Him slave 'Adam were ina JAH Reasonin. **[18]** Him Irated 'Adam that Him glorified Name might be praised pon the time thou mutinied - an that Him might be praised by Him downbased slave 'Adam who were Irated from Earth pon the time thou were arrogant. **[19]** Fe bein ina Heaven JAH hear poor ones plea - an Him love downbased persons praise. **[20]** Him love fe save havin lodged ina persons who fear Him - yet as Him don't love horse Power - an as Him don't step meanin fe the lap of a concubine - JAH shall ignore arrogant ones thing. **[21]** An them shall weep while them cried becau them sin that them worked. **[22]** It failed thee fe plead ina repentance. **[23]** But 'Adam who were Irated from Earth returned ina repentance while him totally wept before JAH becau him sin. **[24]** But ina thy collar of reasonin firmness an thy heart arrogance thou didn't know Love Work an thou didn't know repentance ~ it failed thee fe plead before thy Irator JAH ina repentance an mournin an sadness. **[25]** But that 'Adam who are ashes an Earth returned toward repentance ina mournin an sadness - an him returned toward humbleness an Love Work. **[26]** But thou didn't downbase thy reasonin an thy ras self fe JAH Who Irated thee. **[27]** As fe 'Adam - him downbased him ras self an pleaded pon the iniquity him wronged ~ him weren't proud. **[28]** As thou have totally produced crime - it were found from thee - yet it aren't him who produced that error ~ ina thy arrogance thou took him with thee toward thy downstruction. **[29]** Before him Irated unu both - as Him have known unu that unu were sinners - an as Him have known your Works - Him know that this that were done were ina thy heart arrogance. **[30]** But Him returned that 'Adam - who were without arrogance or malice - ina repentance mournin an sadness. **[31]** Fe a person who wrong an don't plead ina repentance have multiplied him iniquity more than him earlier iniquity - but ina thy heart arrogance it failed thee fe plead ina repentance - but a person who plead an weep enterin repentance before Him Irator JAH... **[32]** him entered repentance fe true - an him found Work whereby him will be saved that him might fear him Lord Heart - an him pleaded before him Irator - fe him have pleaded before Him ina bowin an much repentance - an arisin from the earlier tribulation the Lord shall lighten him sin fe him lest Him vex pon Him slave - an Him will forgive him him former sin. **[33]** If him didn't return toward him former sin an if him did this - this are perfect repentance ~ 'Adam didn't forget fe think of him Irator nor fe implore him Irator JAH ina repentance. **[34]** An thou - plea ina repentance toward thy Irator JAH - an don't wrong them becau them were flesh an blood - fe JAH Who Irated them know them weakness - an don't wrong the persons Him Irated by Him Itority. **[35]** An after them soul were separated from them flesh - them flesh shall be dust up til the day that JAH love.

CHAPTER 5

[1] Know JAH WHo Irated thee-I ~ as JAH have Irated thee-I ina Him Features an Him Example when thou are Earth - don't forget JAH Who firmed thee-I up an saved thee-I an Whom 'Isra'iel glorified ~ Him placed thee-I ina Garden that thou might be Irie an might dig Earth. **[2]** Pon the time thou demolished Him Command - Him sent thee way from the Garden toward this world that Him cursed becau thee - that grow nettles an thorns. **[3]** Fe thou are Earth - an fe she are Earth - fe thou are dust - an fe she are dust - fe thou are Soil - an fe she are Soil - fe thou are fed the grain found from she - an fe thou will return toward she - fe thou will be Soil up til Him love that Him might raise thee - an fe Him shall examine thee the sin thou worked an all the iniquity. **[4]** Know what thou will answer Him at that time ~ think of the good an evil thou worked ina this world ~ examine whether the evil would abound or whether the good would abound ~ try. [5] If thou work a goodly thing - it are a goodly thing fe thee-I that thou might be Irie pon the day when persons who dead will arise. [6] But if thou work evil Work - woe fe thee - fe thou will raceive thy hardship like unto thy hands Work an like unto thy reasonin evil ~ fe if thou work a evil thing pon thy companion an if thou didn't fear JAH - thou will raceive thy hardship. [7] An if thou betray thy companion an if thou call JAH Name an swear ina lie - as thou will raceive thy hardship like unto thy Work - woe fe thee. [8] An thou tell thy false thing fe thy companion simulatin Truth - but thou know that thou spoke a lie. [9] An thou persuade the persons with thee thy false thing simulatin Truth - an thou multiply false things that weren't Truth - an thou will raceive thy hardship like unto thy sin ~ thou deny thy companion while thou tell thy companion 'mi will give thee' what thou won't give him. [10] An pon the time thou said 'Mi will give' ina thy pure reasonin - demons mek application fe thee like unto dogs - an them mek thee forget all - an if thou withhold or if thou love that thou might give - them don't know the person fe whom them gather - yet as Him have said - Them shall fatten - this world money appetise thee that thou might fatten the money that won't benefit thee an that thou won't eat. [11] An again - as Him have said - 'Adam liar children mek a balance false ~ as fe them - them go from robbery toward robbery - this world money appetise thee. [12] O persons - don't mek hope ina distortin scales an balances - an ina stealin a person money - an ina makin a person money one ina downgression - an ina infringin your companions money - an ina stealin him field - ina all the lies unu do fe your ras selves profit that aren't fe your companions. [13] If unu do this unu will raceive your hardship like unto your Work. [14] O persons - be fed by your hands Work that were straight - yet don't desire robbery ~ don't love that unu might totally rob an eat a person money without justice by what aren't due. [15] An if unu eat it - it won't satta unu ~ pon the time unu dead unu will quit it fe another - yet even if unu fatten - it won't benefit unu. [16] An if your money abound - don't distort your reasonins ~ as sinner persons money are like unto the smoke that proceed from a griddle an the wind tek it - better than sinner persons money are the likkle money them accumulated ina Truth.

CHAPTER 6
[1] Think of the day when unu will dead ~ pon the time your souls were separated from your flesh - an pon the time unu quit your money fe another - an pon the time unu went pon the path unu don't know - think of the tribulation that shall come pon unu. [2] An the demons that will raceive unu are evil - an them features are ugly - an them are frightenin ina them splendour - an them won't hear your words. [3] An becau unu didn't do your Irator JAH Accord - them won't hear unu ina your plea pon the time unu begged them ~ becaudis thing them will totally frighten unu. [4] But persons who fulfilled JAH Accord have no fear - fe demons fear them. But demons shall ridicule sinner persons souls pon them. [5] But kind persons souls shall be Irie pon Angels ina Irie Ites - fe them shall totally mek them Irie becau them scorned this world - but angels who are evil shall raceive sinner persons souls. [6] Pardon Angels shall raceive kind persons an righteous ones souls - fe them are sent from JAH that them might calm righteous ones souls ~ as Angels that were evil are sent from Deeyablos that them might ridicule pon sinner persons souls - demons shall raceive sinner persons souls. [7] Sinner persons - woe fe unu ~ weep fe your ras selves before the day when unu dead arrive pon unu ~ pon the time unu reach toward JAH... [8] enter repentance ina your era that are there before your era pass - that unu might live ina Irieness an Ites without tribulation nor disease - yet as after unu dead your era won't return that passed - weep. [9] Lest it be pon unu toward a vain accord that distance from JAH - ina your firm criticism mek lovin fe be lavished an food an Irie Ites not be found ina unu ~ as a body that are sated without measure won't think of JAH Name - Deeyablos wealth shall lodge pon it - yet as the Hola Spirit won't lodge ina it - mek lovin the Irie Ites not be found ina unu. [10] Like unto Mussie spoke - Mussie havin said - "Ya`iqob ate an were sated an fattened an tall an wide - an JAH Who Irated him were separated from him. [11] An him lifestyle distanced from JAH" - as a body that were sated without measure nor moderation won't think of JAH Name - mek lovin Irie Ites not be found alongside unu ~ as belly satiety without measure are bein like unto a boar an like unto a wanderin horse - mek drinkin an eatin without measure an adultery not be found ina unu. [12] But a person who eat ina measure shall live firmed up ina JAH Support - an him shall live firmed up like unto the horizon an like unto a tower that have a stone fence; a person who forgot JAH LAW shall flee without one livin who chase him. [13] A kind person shall live ina bein raspected like unto a lion. [14] But persons who don't love JAH won't keep Him LAW - an them reasonins aren't straight. [15] An JAH shall bring sadness an alarm pon them when them are ina this world - an bein seized ina tremblin an fright - an bein seized ina the tribulations without number by them money bein snatched - bein bound by them hands ina chains from them masters hands... [16] lest them be who rested from the tribulation - an lest them lifestyle be ina Irie Ites - lest them rest when them are ina alarmin tribulations that are pon each of them ras selves - Him shall bring sadness an alarm pon them.

CHAPTER 7
[1] But like unto Daweet spoke sayin - "I-man believed ina JAH ~ I-man won't fear havin said - 'What would a person mek I?'" - there are no fright an alarm pon persons who believed ina JAH. [2] An again like unto him spoke sayin - "If warriors surround I - I-man believed ina Him ~ I-man begged JAH one thing ~ I-man seek that" - persons who believed ina Him have no fright pon them ~ a person who believed ina Him shall live ina Life foriva - an him won't fear arisin from a evil thing. [3] Who are a person who shamed believin in JAH? how about who ignored Him fe a desire? [4] As Him have said - I-man love him who loved I - an I-man shall honour him who glorified I ~ I-man shall keep him who returned toward I ina repentance - who are a person who shamed believin ina Him? [5] Judge Truth an save the widow body ~ save them that JAH might save unu from all that oppose unu ina evil thing ~ keep them ~ as kind persons childran are honoured - them are given makin a profit - an yet Him shall save your childran after unu - fe them won't be troubled fe grain.

CHAPTER 8
[1] 'Iyob believed ina JAH ~ as him didn't neglect fe praise him Irator JAH - JAH saved him from all the tribulation that 'Adam children enemy Deeyablos brought pon him ~ him said - "JAH gave ~ JAH withheld ~ it happened like unto JAH loved pon I - an mek JAH Name be praised by all pon Earth an ina Heaven" - yet as him didn't sadden him reasonin - JAH

saved him. [2] An pon the time JAH sight up 'Iyob that him heart were cleansed from sin - Him raceived him ina much honour. [3] An Him gave him money that abounded more than him money that preceded ~ fe him have totally indured him tribulation - an Him cured him from him wounds becau him indurin all the tribulation that arrived pon him. [4] An if unu like unto him indure the tribulation arisin from demons sent toward unu - unu will be admired. [5] Indure the tribulation ~ that JAH might be fe unu a fortress Refuge from persons who hate unu - an that Him might be a fortress Refuge fe your childran childran an fe your childran after unu - don't sadden your reasonins arisin from the tribulation that came pon unu ~ believe ina Him - an Him shall be a fortress Refuge fe unu. [6] Beg Him ~ Him will hear unu ~ mek hope - an Him will forgive unu ~ beg Him - an Him will be a Faada fe unu; [7] Think of Merdokyos an 'Astier - Yodeet an Giediewon an Deebora an Bariq an Yoftahie an Somson... an other persons like unto them who were disciplined fe believe ina JAH an whose enemies didn't defeat them. [8] Fe JAH are True - an fe Him don't favour havin sight up a face - but persons raceived hardship who love that them might work sin pon them ras selves ~ all persons who fear Him an keep Him LAW shall keep bodies - an Him shall give them bein I-loved an honour. [9] Him shall mek them Irie ina them proceedin an them enterin - ina them Life an them death - an ina them arisin an sittin ~ Fe Him save - an Him seclude. [10] Fe Him sadden - an Him pardon. [11] Fe Him mek poor - an Him honour ~ Him mek wretched - an as Him honour - Him mek them Irie.

CHAPTER 9

[1] An whether it be what are ina Heaven - or whether it be what are pon Earth - an be it either subtle or stout - everything n all Him money live bein firmed up ina Him Order. [2] There are nothing that departed from JAH LAW an Him Order - Who Irated all the world ~ be it a vulture track that fly ina Heaven - Him command toward it destination where Him loved. [3] An Him command a Earth snake path that live ina cave toward where Him loved - an a boat path that go pon sea - apart from only JAH there are none who know it path. [4] An apart from only JAH - there are none who know the path where a soul go pon the time it were separated from it flesh - be it a righteous or a sinner soul. [5] Who know where it will turn - that it would turn ina wilderness or pon a mountain? or that it would fly like unto a bird - that it would be like unto Heaven dew that alight pon a mountain... [6] or that it would be like unto deep wind - or that it would be like unto lightnin that straighten up it path... [7] or that it would be like unto stars that shine amidst the deep - or that it would be like unto sand pon a sea shore that are piled amidst the deep... [8] or that it would be like unto a horizon stone that firmed up pon the sea deep edge - or like unto a wood that give she beautiful fruit that grew by a Water spout... [9] or that it would be that I likened unto the reed that heat of the Sun burnt - an that wind lift an tek toward another place where it didn't grow - an whose trace aren't found... [10] or that it would be like unto misty urine whose trace aren't found - who know JAH Work? who are Him counsellors? how about with whom did Him counsel? [11] As JAH Thoughts are hidden from persons - who will examine an know Him Work? [12] As Him have Irated Earth pon Water - an as Him have firmed she up without stakes - there are none who examine an know JAH Counsel or Him Wisdom - an Him Irated Heaven ina Him perfect Wisdom an firmed it up ina winds - an Him streached forth a lofty cosmos like unto a tent. [13] Him commanded clouds that them might rain rain pon Earth - an Him grow grass - an Him grow fruits without number fe be food fe persons - that InI might believe ina JAH an be Irie ina Inity. [14] JAH are Who give 'Adam childran the Irie Ites an all the fatness an all the satiety ~ JAH are Who give that them might satta an praise JAH Who gave them fruit from Earth... [15] an Who dressed them ina beautiful robes - Who gave them all the I- loved plenty - the Irieness an the Ites that are given fe persons who fulfill JAH Accord. [16] Him give bein I-loved an honour ina the house Him prepared an ina the Kingdom of Heaven fe them faadas who keep JAH LAW. [17] Him give bein I-loved an honour ina the place Him prepared an ina the Kingdom of Heaven fe them faadas who lived firmed up ina Him Worship an Him LAW - an who didn't depart from Him LAW - whom Him famed an raised that them might keep Him Order an Him LAW - an I-man sight up what JAH do fe Him friends ina this world by weakenin them enemies an by keepin them bodies. [18] I-man sight up that Him give them all them begged Him an that Him fulfill them accord fe them ~ don't depart from JAH - an fulfill JAH Accord. [19] Don't depart from Him Command an Him LAW - lest Him vex pon unu an lest Him downstroy unu at one time - an lest Him vex an whip unu ina the tribulation from where unu lived formerly - lest unu depart from your faadas Order where unu were formerly - an lest uour lodgin be ina Gehannem where are no exits up til the Iternity. [20] Keep your Irator JAH LAW when your soul are separated from your flesh that Him might do goodly Work fe unu pon the time unu stood before JAH. [21] Fe Earth an Heaven Kingdoms are fe Him - an fe Kingdom an capability are fe Him - an fe bein nice an pardonin are only fe Him. [22] As Him mek rich an Him mek poor - as Him mek wretched an Him honour - keep JAH LAW. [23] An Daweet spoke becau Him while him said - "Man seem vain - an him era pass like unto a shadow." [24] Him spoke becau Him sayin - "But Lord - Thou live foriva - an Thy Name Invocation are fe a child childran." [25] An again him said - "Thy Kingdom are all the world Kingdom - an Thy Rulership are fe a child childran" ~ Thou returned a kingdom fe Daweet bringin from Sa'ol. [26] But there are none who will I-point Thee-I ~ there are none who can dismiss ~ Thou sight up all - yet there are none who can sight up Thee-I. [27] An Thy kingdom won't perish foriva fe a child childran ~ there are none who will rule Him - but Him rule all ~ Him sight up all - but there are none who sight Him up. [28] As Him have Irated man ina Him Features an ina Him example that them might praise Him an might know Him Worship ina straight reasonin without doubt - Him examine an know what kidneys smoked up an what a reasonin transported. [29] Yet them bow fe stone - fe wood - an fe silver an gold that a person hand worked. [30] An them sacrifice sacrifice fe them up til them sacrifice smoke proceed toward Heaven - that them sin might live firmed up before JAH - but yet them refused fe worship JAH Who Irated them ~ Him shall downcuse them becau all them sin that them worked ina worshippin them idols. [31] Them learned bowin fe idols an all stained Work that aren't due - naysayin by stars - sorcery - worshippin idols - evil accord - an all the Work that JAH don't love - yet them didn't keep JAH Command that them learned. [32] As them didn't love fe worship JAH that them might save them bodies from sin an iniquity by Him servants the Angels an by money that them praise before JAH - them work all this ina lackin goodly Work. [33] An pon the time them all arose together from the graves where them were buried an where them bodies perished - them souls shall stand empty before JAH - an them souls lived ina the Kingdom of Heaven prepared fe kind persons. [34] But sinner persons souls shall live ina *Gehannem* - an pon the time graves were opened - persons who dead shall arise - an souls shall return toward the flesh that them were separated formerly. [35] Like

unto them were bithed ina them nakedness from them mother belly - them shall stand ina them nakedness before JAH - an them sins that them worked Iginnin from them infancy up til that time shall be revealed. [36] Them shall raceive them sin hardship pon them bodies - an whether them likkle or much sin - them shall raceive them hardship like unto them sin.

CHAPTER 10

[1] Fe the blood of soul found from JAH shall lodge ina them like unto it lodged ina them formerly - an if unu didn't believe persons who dead arisin - hear that Irations shall arise ina rainy season without bein birthed from them mother nor faada. [2] An Him command them formerly by Him Word that them dead. [3] An them flesh bein demolished an rotten an again renewed - them shall arise like unto Him loved. [4] An again pon the time rain alit an pon the time it sated Earth - them shall live havin arisin like unto them were Irated formerly. [5] As them who are everlivin ina bloodly soul an who live ina this world an them whom Water produce have been Irated - Him havin said Mek them be Irated - an as JAH Itority lodge pon the Water - she give them a bloodly soul by Him Itority an by Him Word. [6] As them are Irated by Him Itority an by Him Word without a faada nor mother - thou blind of reasonin who say "Persons who dead won't arise" - if thou have knowledge or Wisdom - how will thou say persons who dead won't arise by them Irator JAH Word? [7] As persons who dead - who were ashes an dust ina grave - shall arise by JAH Word - as fe thou - enter repentance an return toward thy religion. [8] Like unto Him Word spoke formerly - them shall arise by the Pardon Dew found from JAH - an that Word shall turn all the world an arouse the persons who dead like unto Him loved. [9] An know that thou will arise an stand before Him - an mek it not seem fe thee ina thy reasonin dullness that thou will remain ina grave. [10] It aren't thus ~ thou will arise an raceive thy hardship like unto the Work measure that thou worked - whether it be goodly or evil - yet mek it not seem fe thee that thou will remain - fe this Day are the day when them will raceive hardship. [11] An ina Resurrection time thou will raceive thy hardship by all thy sin that thou worked ~ thou will finish thy sin hardship that were written Iginnin from thy infancy up til that time - an thou have no reason that thou will pretext pon thy sin like unto this world Work that thou might deny thy sin. [12] Like unto thou mek thy false word truth before thee - an like unto thou mek the lie thing that thou spoke truth - thou have no reason that thou will pretext like unto this world Work. [13] Becau it were that she know pon thee all thy evil Work thou worked - an becau it were that she will reveal pon thee before she Irator JAH - as JAH Word shall lodge pon thee an speak pon thee - thou have no reason pon what thou pretext. [14] Thou will shame there becau thy sin that thou worked ~ it are that thou might be thanked with persons who are thanke pon them beautiful Work - yet lest thou shame before man an Angels pon the day when Judgemant are judged - quickly enter repentance ina this world before thou arrive toward there. [15] Persons who praise JAH with Angels shall raceive them reward from them Irator without shamin - an them shall be Irie ina the Kingdom of Heaven - however unless thou worked goodly Work when thou are ina thy flesh ina Life - thou have no fortune with righteous ones. [16] As thou weren't prepared when thou have knowledge an when thou have this world where thou enter repentance - there shall be a useless regret pon thee - an fe thou didn't give a morsel fe the hungry when thou have money. [17] An fe thou didn't clothe the naked when thou have clothes - an fe thou didn't save the wronged when thou have Itority. [18] Fe thou didn't teach the sinner person when thou have knowledge - that him might return an enter repentance - an that JAH might forgive him him sin that him formerly worked ina ignorance - an fe thou didn't fight with demons who quarrel with thee when thou have Power that thou able fe prevail. [19] An fe thou didn't fast nor pray when thou have firmness that thou might weaken thy infancy Power that are pon flesh - an that thou might subject thy ras self fe Rightness that aren't favorin pon flesh... [20] that aren't favorin Irie Ites when it are ina this world ina beautiful drink an sweet food - an that aren't adornin ina thin clothes an silver an gold... [21] an as thou didn't fast nor pray when thou have firmness that thou might subject thy ras self fe Rightness that aren't adornin ina honoured Hindekie jewels called emerald an phazyon - there shall be a useless regret pon thee ~ this aren't a person ornamant that are due. [22] As fe a person ornamant - it are purity - Wisdom - knowledge - lovin one another by what are due without envyin nor jealousy nor doubtin nor quarrels ~ while thou loved thy companion like unto thy ras self... [23] an without thy doin a evil thing pon a person who did a evil thing pon thee-I - it are lovin one another by what are due - that thou might enter toward the Kingdom of Heaven that are given fe person who indured the tribulation - that Him might give thee the honoured Kingdom of Heaven an thy reward pon makin hope ina the Kingdom of Heaven ina Resurrection time with honoured persons ina knowledge an Wisdom. [24] An don't say "After wi dead wi won't arise" - fe Deeyablos cut off hope of persons who speak an think this lest them be saved in Resurrection time ~ them will know that them have hardship pon them pon the time Advent arrived pon them ~ ina Resurrection time persons will be totally sad who worked sin ina not knowin that Him might think of them sin pon them - fe them didn't believe ina Him that them will arise pon that Day. [25] Becaudis thing them shall be reproached like unto them Work evil measure that them worked ina this world - an them shall sight up the Resurrection that them denied whereby them will arise together ina flesh. *[26]* Them shall weep at that time becau them didn't work goodly Work ~ it would have been better fe them if them wept ina this world if it are possible fe them lest them be who weep ina *Gehannem*. [27] If InI didn't weep ina this world by InI accord - demons will mek InI weep without InI accord ina *Gehannem* ~ if InI didn't enter repentance ina this world - InI prepare worthless an useless cries an mournin ina *Gehannem*. [28] Prepare goodly Work - that unu might cross from death toward Life - an that unu might go from this passin world toward the Kingdom of Heaven - an that unu might sight up the Kingdom of Heaven Light that surpass light ina this world. [29] Refuse Irie Ites that are ina this world - that thou might be Irie without measure ina the Kingdom of Heaven ina Irie Ites that aren't fulfilled Iginnin from today up til the Iternity with persons who believe persons who dead arisin. Mek Glory an praise due JAH foriva - an the third book that speak the Meqabyans thing were fulfilled. .

PROPHETIC APOCRYPHA

This book offers a prayer of deliverance attributed to figures in the book of Daniel

THE PRAYER OF AZARIAH

[1] And they walked in the midst of the fire, praising God, and blessing the Lord. [2] Then Azarias stood up, and prayed on this manner; and opening his mouth in the midst of the fire said, [3] Blessed art thou, O Lord God of our fathers: thy name is worthy to be praised and glorified for evermore: [4] For thou art righteous in all the things that thou hast done to us: yea, true are all thy works, thy ways are right, and all thy judgments truth. [5] In all the things that thou hast brought upon us, and upon the holy city of our fathers, even Jerusalem, thou hast executed true judgment: for according to truth and judgment didst thou bring all these things upon us because of our sins. [6] For we have sinned and committed iniquity, departing from thee. [7] In all things have we trespassed, and not obeyed thy commandments, nor kept them, neither done as thou hast commanded us, that it might go well with us. [8] Wherefore all that thou hast brought upon us, and every thing that thou hast done to us, thou hast done in true judgment. [9] And thou didst deliver us into the hands of lawless enemies, most hateful forsakers of God, and to an unjust king, and the most wicked in all the world. [10] And now we cannot open our mouths, we are become a shame and reproach to thy servants; and to them that worship thee. [11] Yet deliver us not up wholly, for thy name's sake, neither disannul thou thy covenant: [12] And cause not thy mercy to depart from us, for thy beloved Abraham's sake, for thy servant Issac's sake, and for thy holy Israel's sake; [13] To whom thou hast spoken and promised, that thou wouldest multiply their seed as the stars of heaven, and as the sand that lieth upon the seashore. [14] For we, O Lord, are become less than any nation, and be kept under this day in all the world because of our sins. [15] Neither is there at this time prince, or prophet, or leader, or burnt offering, or sacrifice, or oblation, or incense, or place to sacrifice before thee, and to find mercy. [16] Nevertheless in a contrite heart and an humble spirit let us be accepted. [17] Like as in the burnt offerings of rams and bullocks, and like as in ten thousands of fat lambs: so let our sacrifice be in thy sight this day, and grant that we may wholly go after thee: for they shall not be confounded that put their trust in thee. [18] And now we follow thee with all our heart, we fear thee, and seek thy face. [19] Put us not to shame: but deal with us after thy lovingkindness, and according to the multitude of thy mercies. [20] Deliver us also according to thy marvellous works, and give glory to thy name, O Lord: and let all them that do thy servants hurt be ashamed; [21] And let them be confounded in all their power and might, and let their strength be broken; [22] And let them know that thou art God, the only God, and glorious over the whole world. [23] And the king's servants, that put them in, ceased not to make the oven hot with rosin, pitch, tow, and small wood; [24] So that the flame streamed forth above the furnace forty and nine cubits. [25] And it passed through, and burned those Chaldeans it found about the furnace. [26] But the angel of the Lord came down into the oven together with Azarias and his fellows, and smote the flame of the fire out of the oven; [27] And made the midst of the furnace as it had been a moist whistling wind, so that the fire touched them not at all, neither hurt nor troubled them. [28] Then the three, as out of one mouth, praised, glorified, and blessed, God in the furnace, saying, [29] Blessed art thou, O Lord God of our fathers: and to be praised and exalted above all for ever. [30] And blessed is thy glorious and holy name: and to be praised and exalted above all for ever. [31] Blessed art thou in the temple of thine holy glory: and to be praised and glorified above all for ever. [32] Blessed art thou that beholdest the depths, and sittest upon the cherubims: and to be praised and exalted above all for ever. [33] Blessed art thou on the glorious throne of thy kingdom: and to be praised and glorified above all for ever. [34] Blessed art thou in the firmament of heaven: and above ail to be praised and glorified for ever. [35] O all ye works of the Lord, bless ye the Lord : praise and exalt him above all for ever, [36] O ye heavens, bless ye the Lord : praise and exalt him above all for ever. [37] O ye angels of the Lord, bless ye the Lord: praise and exalt him above all for ever. [38] O all ye waters that be above the heaven, bless ye the Lord: praise and exalt him above all for ever. [39] O all ye powers of the Lord, bless ye the Lord: praise and exalt him above all for ever. [40] O ye sun and moon, bless ye the Lord: praise and exalt him above all for ever. [41] O ye stars of heaven, bless ye the Lord: praise and exalt him above all for ever. [42] O every shower and dew, bless ye the Lord: praise and exalt him above all for ever. [43] O all ye winds, bless ye the Lord: praise and exalt him above all for ever, [44] O ye fire and heat, bless ye the Lord: praise and exalt him above all for ever. [45] O ye winter and summer, bless ye the Lord: praise and exalt him above all for ever. [46] 0 ye dews and storms of snow, bless ye the Lord: praise and exalt him above all for ever. [47] O ye nights and days, bless ye the Lord: bless and exalt him above all for ever. [48] O ye light and darkness, bless ye the Lord: praise and exalt him above all for ever. [49] O ye ice and cold, bless ye the Lord: praise and exalt him above all for ever. [50] O ye frost and snow, bless ye the Lord: praise and exalt him above all for ever. [51] O ye lightnings and clouds, bless ye the Lord: praise and exalt him above all for ever. [52] O let the earth bless the Lord: praise and exalt him above all for ever. [53] O ye mountains and little hills, bless ye the Lord: praise and exalt him above all for ever. [54] O all ye things that grow in the earth, bless ye the Lord: praise and exalt him above all for ever. [55] O ye mountains, bless ye the Lord: Praise and exalt him above all for ever. [56] O ye seas and rivers, bless ye the Lord: praise and exalt him above all for ever. [57] O ye whales, and all that move in the waters, bless ye the Lord: praise and exalt him above all for ever. [58] O all ye fowls of the air, bless ye the Lord: praise and exalt him above all for ever. [59] O all ye beasts and cattle, bless ye the Lord: praise and exalt him above all for ever. [60] O ye children of men, bless ye the Lord: praise and exalt him above all for ever. [61] O Israel, bless ye the Lord: praise and exalt him above all for ever. [62] O ye priests of the Lord, bless ye the Lord: praise and exalt him above all for ever. [63] O ye servants of the Lord, bless ye the Lord: praise and exalt him above all for ever. [64] O ye spirits and souls of the righteous, bless ye the Lord: praise and exalt him above all for ever. [65] O ye holy and humble men of heart, bless ye the Lord: praise and exalt him above all for ever. [66] O Ananias, Azarias, and Misael, bless ye the Lord: praise and exalt him above all for ever: far he hath delivered us from hell, and saved us from the hand of death, and delivered us out of the midst of the furnace and burning flame: even out of the midst of the fire hath he delivered us. [67] O give thanks unto the Lord, because he is gracious: for his mercy endureth for ever. [68] O all ye that worship the Lord, bless the God of gods, praise him, and give him thanks: for his mercy endureth for ever.

ADDITIONAL TEXTS

1 BARUCH

CHAPTER 1

1 These are the words of the scroll, which Baruch the son of Neriah, the son of Mahseiah, the son of Zedekiah, the son of Hasadiah, the son of Hilkiah, wrote in Babylon, **2** in the fifth year, [and] in the seventh day of the month, at the time the Chaldeans took Jerusalem, and burned it with fire. **3** And Baruch read the words of this scroll in the hearing of Jehoiachin the son of Jehoiakim king of Judah, and in the hearing of all the people that came to [hear] the scroll, **4** and in the hearing of the mighty men, and of the kings' sons, and in the hearing of the elders, and in the hearing of all the people, from the least to the greatest, even of all those who lived at Babylon by the River Sud. **5** And they wept, and fasted, and prayed before the LORD ; **6** they also made a collection of money according to every man's power: **7** and they sent [it] to Jerusalem to Jehoiakim the [high] priest, the son of Hilkiah, the son of Salom, and to the priests, and to all the people which were found with him at Jerusalem, **8** at the same time when he took the vessels of the house of the LORD , that had been carried out of the temple, to return [them] into the land of Judah, the tenth day of the [month] Sivan, [namely,] silver vessels, which Zedekiah the son of Josiah king of Judah had made, **9** after Nebuchadnezzar king of Babylon had carried away Jehoiachin, and the princes, and the captives, and the mighty men, and the people of the land, from Jerusalem, and brought them to Babylon. **10** And they said: "Behold, we have sent you money; therefore buy with the money burnt-offerings, and sin offerings, and incense, and prepare an oblation, and offer on the altar of the LORD our God; **11** and pray for the life of Nebuchadnezzar king of Babylon, and for the life of his son Belshazzar, that their days may be as the days of Heaven above the earth: **12** and the LORD will give us strength, and lighten our eyes, and we will live under the shadow of Nebuchadnezzar king of Babylon, and under the shadow of his son Belshazzar, and we will serve them many days, and find favor in their sight. **13** Pray for us also to the LORD our God, for we have sinned against the LORD our God; and to this day the wrath of the LORD and His indignation is not turned from us. **14** And you will read this scroll which we have sent to you, to make confession in the house of the LORD , on the day of the feast and on the days of the solemn assembly." **15** And you will say: To the LORD our God [belongs] righteousness, but to us confusion of face, as at this day, to the men of Judah, and to the inhabitants of Jerusalem, **16** and to our kings, and to our princes, and to our priests, and to our prophets, and to our fathers: **17** for that we have sinned before the LORD , **18** and disobeyed Him, and have not listened to the voice of the LORD our God, to walk in the commands of the LORD that He has set before us: **19** since the day that the LORD brought our fathers out of the land of Egypt, to this present day, we have been disobedient to the LORD our God, and we have dealt unadvisedly in not listening to His voice. **20** Why the plagues cleaved to us, and the curse, which the LORD commanded Moses His servant [to pronounce] in the day that He brought our fathers out of the land of Egypt, to give us a land that flows with milk and honey, as at this day. **21** Nevertheless, we did not listen to the voice of the LORD our God, according to all the words of the prophets, whom He sent to us, **22** but we walked—every man—in the imagination of his own wicked heart, to serve strange gods, and to do that which is evil in the sight of the LORD our God.

CHAPTER 2

1 Therefore the LORD has made good His word, which He pronounced against us, and against our judges that judged Israel, and against our kings, and against our princes, and against the men of Israel and Judah, **2** to bring on us great plagues, such as never happened under the whole Heaven, as it came to pass in Jerusalem, according to the things that are written in the Law of Moses; **3** That we should eat—every man—the flesh of his own son, and every man the flesh of his own daughter. **4** Moreover, He has given them to be in subjection to all the kingdoms that are around us, to be a reproach and a desolation among all the surrounding people, where the LORD has scattered them. **5** So were they cast down, and not exalted, because we sinned against the LORD our God, in not listening to His voice. **6** To the LORD our God [belongs] righteousness, but to us and to our fathers confusion of face, as at this day. **7** [For] all these plagues have come on us, which the LORD has pronounced against us. **8** Yet we have not entreated the favor of the LORD , in turning everyone from the thoughts of his wicked heart. **9** Therefore the LORD has kept watch over the plagues, and the LORD has brought [them] on us; for the LORD is righteous in all His works which He has commanded us. **10** Yet we have not listened to His voice, to walk in the commands of the LORD that He has set before us. **11** And now, O LORD , You God of Israel, that have brought Your people out of the land of Egypt with a mighty hand, and with signs, and with wonders, and with great power, and with a high arm, and have gotten Yourself a Name, as at this day: **12** O LORD our God, we have sinned, we have been ungodly, we have dealt unrighteously in all Your ordinances. **13** Let Your wrath turn from us, for we are but a few left among the heathen, where You have scattered us. Hear our prayer, O LORD , and our petition, and deliver us for Your own sake, and give us favor in the sight of them which have led us away captive, that all the earth may know that You are the LORD our God, because Israel and his posterity is called by Your Name. **16** O LORD , look down from Your holy house, and consider us: incline Your ear, O LORD , and hear: **17** open Your eyes, and behold, for the dead that are in the grave, whose breath is taken from their bodies, will give to the LORD neither glory nor righteousness: **18** but the soul that is greatly vexed, which goes stooping and feeble, and the eyes that fail, and the hungry soul, will give You glory and righteousness, O LORD . **19** For we do not present our supplication before You, O LORD our God, for the righteousness of our fathers, and of our kings. **20** For You have sent Your wrath and Your indignation on us, as You have spoken by Your servants the prophets, [saying,] **21** "The LORD says, Bow your shoulders to serve the king of Babylon, and remain in the land that I gave to your fathers. **22** But if you will not hear the voice of the LORD , to serve the king of Babylon, **23** I will cause to cease out of the cities of Judah, and from the region near Jerusalem, the voice of mirth, and the voice of gladness, the voice of the bridegroom, and the voice of the bride: and the whole land will be desolate without inhabitant." **24** But we would not listen to Your voice, to serve the king of Babylon: therefore You have made good Your words that You spoke by Your servants the prophets, [namely,] that the bones of our kings, and the bones of our fathers, should be taken out of their places. **25** And behold, they are cast out to the heat by day, and to the frost by night, and they died in great miseries by famine, by sword, and by pestilence. **26** And the house which is called by Your Name have You laid [waste], as at this day, for the wickedness of the house of Israel and the house of Judah. **27** Yet, O LORD our God, You have dealt with us after all Your kindness, and according to all Your great mercy, **28** as You spoke by Your servant Moses in the day when You commanded him to write Your law before the sons of Israel, saying, **29** "If you will not hear My voice, surely this very great multitude will be turned into a small [number] among the nations, where I will scatter them. **30** For I know that they will not hear Me, because it is a stiff-necked people, but in the land of their captivity they will take it to heart, **31** and will know that I am the LORD their God: and I will give them a heart, and ears to hear: **32** and they will praise Me in the land of their captivity, and think on My Name, **33** and will return from their stiff neck, and from their wicked deeds, for they will remember the way of their fathers, which sinned before the LORD . **34** And I will bring them again into the land which I swore to their fathers, to Abraham, to Isaac, and to Jacob, and they will be lords of it: and I will increase them, and they will not be diminished. **35** And I will make a perpetual covenant with them to be their God, and they will be My people: and I will no longer remove My people Israel out of the land that I have given them."

CHAPTER 3

1 O LORD Almighty, You God of Israel, the soul in anguish, the troubled spirit, cries to You. **2** Hear, O LORD , and have mercy; for You are a merciful God: yes, have mercy on us, because we have sinned before You. **3** For You sit [as king] forever, and we perish forevermore. **4** O LORD Almighty, You God of Israel, hear now the prayer of the dead Israelites, and of the children of them which were sinners before You, that did not listen to the voice of You their God, for this reason these plagues cleaved to us. **5** Do not remember the iniquities of our fathers, but remember Your power and Your Name [now] at this time. **6** For You are the LORD our God, and You, O LORD , will we praise. **7** For this reason You have put Your fear in our hearts, to the intent that we should call on Your Name, and we will praise You in our captivity, for we have called to mind all the iniquity of our fathers, that sinned before You. **8** Behold, we are yet this day in our captivity, where You have scattered us, for a reproach and a curse, and to be subject to penalty, according to all the iniquities of our fathers, which departed from the LORD our God. **9** Hear, O Israel, the commands of life: give ear to understand wisdom. **10** How is it, O Israel, that you are in your enemies' land, that you have become old in a strange country, that you are defiled with the dead, **11** that you are counted with those who [go down] into the grave? **12** You have forsaken the fountain of wisdom. **13** [For] if you had walked in the way of God, you should have dwelled in peace forever. **14** Learn where is wisdom, where is strength, where is understanding; that you may also know where is length of days, and life, where is the light of the eyes, and peace. **15** Who has found out her place ? A nd who has come into her treasuries? **16** Where are the princes of the heathen, and such as ruled the beasts that are on the earth; **17** those who had their pastime with the birds of the air, and those who hoarded up silver and gold, wherein men trust; and of whose getting there is no end? **18** For those who made in silver, and were so careful, and whose works are past finding out, **19** they are vanished and gone down to the grave, and others have come up in their steads. **20** Younger men have seen the light and lived on the earth, but the way of knowledge they have not known, **21** neither did they understand the paths thereof, neither have their children embraced it: they are far off from their way. **22** It has not been heard of in Canaan, neither has it been seen in Teman. **23** The sons also of Agar that seek understanding, which are in the land, the merchants of Merran and Teman, and the authors of fables, and the searchers out of understanding; none of these have known the way of wisdom or remembered her paths. **24** O Israel, how great is the house of God ! A nd how large is the place of His possession! **25** [It is] great, and has no end; high, and unmeasurable. **26** There were the giants born that were famous of old, great of stature, [and] expert in war. **27** God did not choose these, nor did He give the way of knowledge to them; **28** so they perished, because they had no wisdom, they perished through their own foolishness. **29** Who has gone up into Heaven, and taken her, and brought her down from the clouds? **30** Who has gone over the sea, and found her, and will bring her for choice gold? **31** There is none that knows her way, nor any that comprehends her path. **32** But He that knows all things knows her, He found her out with His understanding: He that prepared the earth forevermore has filled it with four-footed beasts: **33** He that sends out the light, and it goes; He called it, and it obeyed Him with fear: **34** and the stars shone in their watches, and were glad when He called them, they said, "Here we are." They shone with gladness to Him that made them. **35** This is our God, [and] there will none other be accounted of in comparison of Him. **36** He has found out all the way of knowledge, and has given it to His servant Jacob, and to Israel that is beloved of Him. **37** Afterward she appeared on earth and was conversant with men.

CHAPTER 4

1 This is the scroll of the commands of God, and the law that endures forever: All those who hold it fast [are appointed] to life; but such as leave it will die. **2** Turn, O Jacob, and take hold of it: walk toward her shining in the presence of the light thereof. **3** Do not give your glory to another, nor the things that are profitable to you to a strange nation. **4** O Israel, happy are we, for the things that are pleasing to God are made known to us. **5** Be of good cheer, my people, the memorial of Israel. **6** You were sold to the nations, [but] not for destruction: because you moved God to wrath, you were delivered to your adversaries. **7** For you provoked Him that made you by sacrificing to demons, and not to God. **8** You forgot the perpetual God that brought you up; you also grieved Jerusalem that nursed you. **9** For she saw the wrath that has come on you from God, and said, "Listen, you [women] that dwell about Zion, for God has brought on me great mourning; **10** for I have seen the captivity of my sons and daughters, which the Perpetual has brought on them. **11** For with joy I nourished them, but sent them away with weeping and mourning. **12** Let no man rejoice over me, a widow, and forsaken of many, for the sins of my children I am left desolate, because they turned away from the law of God, **13** and had no regard to His statutes, neither did they walk in the ways of God's commands, nor trod in the paths of discipline in His righteousness. **14** Let those who dwell about Zion come, and remember the captivity of my sons and daughters, which the Perpetual has brought on them. **15** For He has brought a nation on them from far, a shameless nation, and of a strange language, who neither gave reverence to old man, nor pitied child. **16** And they have carried away the dear beloved sons of the widow and left her that was alone desolate of her daughters. **17** But I—how can I help you? **18** For He that brought these plagues on you will deliver you from the hand of your enemies. **19** Go your way, O my children, go your way, for I am left desolate. **20** I have put off the garment of peace and put on myself the sackcloth of my petition: I will cry to the Perpetual as long as I live. **21** Be of good cheer, O my children, cry to God, and He will deliver you from the power and hand of the enemies. **22** For I have trusted in the Perpetual, that He will save you; and joy has come to me from the Holy One, because of the mercy which will soon come to you from your continuous Savior. **23** For I sent you out with mourning and weeping, but God will give you to me again with joy and gladness forever. **24** For like as now those who dwell about Zion have seen your captivity, so they will shortly see your salvation from our God, which will come on you with great glory, and brightness of the Perpetual. **25** My children, suffer patiently the wrath that has come on you from God, for your enemy has persecuted you; but shortly you will see his destruction, and will tread on their necks. **26** My delicate ones have gone rough ways; they were taken away as a flock carried off by the enemies. **27** Be of good cheer, O my children, and cry to God, for you will be remembered of Him that has brought [these things] on you. **28** For as it was your mind to go astray from God, return and seek Him ten times more. **29** For He that brought these plagues on you will bring you continuous joy again with your salvation." **30** Be of good cheer, O Jerusalem, for He that called you by name will comfort you. **31** Miserable are those who afflicted you and rejoiced at your fall. **32** Miserable are the cities which your children served; miserable is she that received your sons. **33** For as she rejoiced at your fall, and was glad of your ruin, so she will be grieved for her own desolation. **34** And I will take away her exultation in her great multitude, and her boasting will be turned into mourning. **35** For fire will come on her from the Perpetual, long to endure; and she will be inhabited of devils for a great time. **36** O Jerusalem look around you toward the east and behold the joy that comes to you from God. **37** Behold, your sons come, whom you sent away, they come gathered together from the east to the west at the word of the Holy One, rejoicing in the glory of God.

CHAPTER 5

1 Put off, O Jerusalem, the garment of your mourning and affliction, and put on the beauty of the glory that [comes] from God forever. **2** Cast about you the robe of the righteousness which [comes] from God; set a diadem on your head of the glory of the Perpetual. **3** For God will show your brightness to every [region] under Heaven. **4** For your name will be called of God forever, THE PEACE OF RIGHTEOUSNESS , and, THE GLORY OF GODLINESS . **5** Arise, O Jerusalem, and stand on the height, and look around you toward the east, and behold your children gathered from the going down of the sun to the rising thereof at the word of the Holy One, rejoicing that God has remembered them. **6** For they went from you on foot, being led away of their enemies, but God brings them in to you, borne on high with glory, as [on] a royal throne. **7** For God has appointed that every high mountain, and the perpetual hills, should be made low, and the valleys filled up, to make plain the ground, that Israel may go safely in the glory of God. **8** Moreover the woods and every sweet-smelling tree have overshadowed Israel by the command of God. **9** For God will lead Israel with joy in the light of His glory with the mercy and righteousness that comes from Him.

CHAPTER 6

1 A COPY OF A LETTER, WHICH JEREMIAH SENT TO THEM WHICH WERE TO BE LED CAPTIVES INTO BABYLON BY THE KING OF THE BABYLONIANS, TO CERTIFY THEM, AS IT WAS COMMANDED HIM OF GOD . **2** Because of the sins which you have committed before God, you will be led away captives to Babylon by Nebuchadnezzar king of the Babylonians. **3** So when you come to Babylon, you will remain there many years, and for a long season, even for seven generations: and after that I will bring you out peaceably from there. **4** But now you will see in Babylon gods of silver, and of gold, and of wood, borne on shoulders, which cause the nations to fear. **5** Beware, therefore, that you in no way become like to the strangers, neither let fear take hold on you because of them, when you see the multitude before them and behind them, worshiping them. **6** But say in your hearts, "O LORD , we must worship You." **7** For My messenger is with you, and I Myself care for your souls. **8** For their tongue is polished by the workman, and they themselves are overlaid with gold and with silver; yet they are but false and cannot speak. **9** And taking gold, as it were for a virgin that loves to be happy, they make crowns for the heads of their gods: **10** and sometimes also the priests carry from their gods gold and silver and bestow it on themselves; **11** and will even give thereof to the common prostitutes: and they deck them as men with garments, [even] the gods of silver, and gods of gold, and of wood. **12** Yet these gods cannot save themselves from rust and moths, though they are covered with purple raiment. **13** They wipe their faces because of the dust of the temple, which is thick on them. **14** And he that cannot put to death one that offends against him holds a scepter, as though he were judge of a country. **15** He also has a dagger in his right hand, and an axe, but cannot deliver himself from war and robbers. **16** Whereby they are not known to be gods: therefore, do not fear them. **17** For like as a vessel that a man uses is worth nothing when it is broken, even so it is with their gods: when they are set up in the temples their eyes are full of dust through the feet of those who come in. **18** And as the courts are made sure on every side on him that offends the king, as being committed to suffer death, [even so] the priests make fast their temples with doors, with locks, and bars, lest they are carried off by robbers. **19** They light the candles, yes, more than for themselves, of which they cannot see one. **20** They are as one of the beams of the temple; and men say their hearts are eaten out, when things creeping out of the earth devour both them and their raiment: **21** they do not feel it when their faces are blackened through the smoke that comes out of the temple: **22** bats, swallows, and birds land on their bodies and heads; and in like manner the cats also. **23** Whereby you may know that they are no gods: therefore, do not fear them. **24** Notwithstanding the gold with which they are beset to make them beautiful, except one wipe off the rust, they will not shine, for not even when they were molten did they feel it. **25** Things wherein there is no breath are bought at any cost. **26** Having no feet, they are borne on shoulders, whereby they declare to men that they are worth nothing. **27** They also that serve them are ashamed, for if they fall to the ground at any time, they cannot rise up again of themselves; neither, if they are bowed down, can they make themselves straight, but the offerings are set before them, as if they were dead men. **28** And the things that are

sacrificed to them, their priests sell and spend; and in like manner their wives also lay up part thereof in salt; but to the poor and to the impotent they will give nothing thereof. **29** The menstruous woman and the woman in childbirth touch their sacrifices, knowing, therefore, by these things, that they are not gods, [and so] do not fear them. **30** For how can they be called gods ? B ecause women set meat before the gods of silver, gold, and wood. **31** And in their temples the priests sit on seats, having their clothes torn, and their heads and beards shaven, and nothing on their heads. **32** They roar and cry before their gods, as men do at the feast when one is dead. **33** The priests also take off garments from them and clothe their wives and children in addition. **34** Whether it be evil that one does to them, or good, they are not able to repay it: they can neither set up a king, nor put him down. **35** In like manner, they can neither give riches nor money; though a man makes a vow to them, and does not keep it, they will never exact it. **36** They can save no man from death, neither deliver the weak from the mighty. **37** They cannot restore a blind man to his sight, nor deliver any that is in distress. **38** They can show no mercy to the widow, nor do good to the fatherless. **39** They are like the stones that are [hewn] out of the mountain, [these gods] of wood, and that are overlaid with gold and with silver. Those who minister to them will be confounded. **40** How should a man then think or say that they are gods, when even the Chaldeans themselves dishonor them? **41** Who if they will see one mute that cannot speak, they bring him, and entreat him to call on Bel, as though he were able to understand. **42** Yet they cannot perceive this themselves and forsake them, for they have no understanding. **43** The women also with cords around them sit in the ways, burning bran for incense, but if any of them, drawn by some that passes by, lies with him, she reproaches her fellow, that she was not thought as worthy as herself, nor her cord broken. **44** Whatever is done among them is false. How should a man then think or say that they are gods? **45** They are fashioned by carpenters and goldsmiths—they can be nothing else than the workmen will have them to be. **46** And they themselves that fashioned them can never continue long; how then should the things that are fashioned by them? **47** For they have left lies and reproaches to those who come after. **48** For when there comes any war or plague on them, the priests consult with themselves, where they may be hidden with them. **49** How then can men not understand that they are not gods, which can neither save themselves from war, nor from plague? **50** For seeing they are but of wood, and overlaid with gold and with silver, it will be known hereafter that they are false; **51** and it will be manifest to all nations and kings that they are no gods, but the works of men's hands, and that there is no work of God in them. **52** Who then may not know that they are no gods? **53** For neither can they set up a king in a land, nor give rain to men. **54** Neither can they judge their own cause, nor redress a wrong, being unable, for they are as crows between the heavens and earth. **55** For even when fire falls on the house of gods of wood, or overlaid with gold or with silver, their priests will flee away, and escape, but they themselves will be burned apart like beams. **56** Moreover they cannot withstand any king or enemies. How should a man then allow or think that they are gods? **57** Neither are those gods of wood, and overlaid with silver or with gold, able to escape either from thieves or robbers. **58** Whose gold, and silver, and garments with which they are clothed, they that are strong will take from them, and go away with [them]; neither will they be able to help themselves. **59** Therefore it is better to be a king that shows his manhood, or else a vessel in a house profitable for that of which the owner will have need, than such false gods; or even a door in a house, to keep the things safe that are therein, than such false gods; or a pillar of wood in a palace, than such false gods. **60** For sun, and moon, and stars, being bright and sent to do their offices, are obedient. **61** Likewise also, the lightning when it glitters is fair to see; and after the same manner the wind also blows in every country. **62** And when God commands the clouds to go over the whole world, they do as they are told. **63** And the fire sent from above to consume mountains and woods does as it is commanded, but these are to be likened to them neither in show nor power. **64** Why a man should neither think nor say that they are gods, seeing they are neither able to judge causes, nor to do good to men. **65** Knowing, therefore, that they are not gods, do not fear them. **66** For they can neither curse nor bless kings; **67** neither can they show signs in the heavens among the nations, nor shine as the sun, nor give light as the moon. **68** The beasts are better than they, for they can get under a covert and help themselves. **69** In no way then is it manifest to us that they are gods. Therefore, do not fear them. **70** For as a scarecrow in a garden of cucumbers that keeps nothing, so are their gods of wood, and overlaid with gold and with silver. **71** Likewise also, their gods of wood, and overlaid with gold and with silver, are like to a white thorn in an orchard, that every bird sits on; as also to a dead body that is cast out into the dark. **72** And you will know them to be no gods by the bright purple that rots on them: And they themselves afterward will be consumed and will be a reproach in the country. **73** Better therefore is the just man that has no idols, for he will be far from reproach.

2 BARUCH

CHAPTER 1

1 And it came to pass in the twenty-fifth year of Jehoiachin, king of Judah, that the word of the LORD came to Baruch, the son of Neriah, and said to him: **2** "Have you seen all that this people are doing to Me, that the evils which these two tribes which remained have done are greater than [those of] the ten tribes which were carried away captive? **3** For the former tribes were forced by their kings to commit sin, but these two of themselves have been forcing and compelling their kings to commit sin. **4** For this reason, behold, I bring calamity on this city and on its inhabitants, and it will be removed from before Me for a time, and I will scatter this people among the nations that they may do good to the nations. And My people will be disciplined, and the time will come when they will seek for the prosperity of their times."

CHAPTER 2

1 "For I have said these things to you that you may bid Jeremiah, and all those that are like you, to retire from this city. **2** For your works are to this city as a firm pillar, And your prayers as a strong wall."

CHAPTER 3

1 And I said, "O LORD , my Lord, have I come into the world for this purpose that I might see the calamities of my mother? No, my Lord. **2** If I have found grace in Your sight, first take my spirit that I may go to my fathers and not behold the destruction of my mother. For two things vehemently constrain me: for I cannot resist You, and my soul, moreover, cannot behold the calamities of my mother. **4** But one thing I will say in Your presence, O LORD . **5** What, therefore, will there be after these things ? F or if You destroy Your city, and deliver up Your land to those that hate us, how will the name of Israel be remembered again? **6** Or how will one speak of Your praises ? O r to whom will that which is in Your law be explained? Or will the world return to its nature of former times, and the age revert to primeval silence? And will the multitude of souls be taken away, and the nature of man not again be named? And where is all that which You said regarding us?"

CHAPTER 4

1 And the LORD said to me: "This city will be delivered up for a time, And the people will be disciplined during a time, And the world will not be given over to oblivion." [[**2** "Do you think that this is that city of which I said, On the palms of My hands I have graven you? **3** This building now built in your midst is not that which is revealed with Me, that which [was] prepared beforehand here from the time when I took counsel to make Paradise, and showed Adam before he sinned, but when he transgressed the commandment it was removed from him, as also Paradise. **4** And after these things I showed it to My servant Abraham by night among the portions of the victims. **5** And again I also showed it to Moses on Mount Sinai when I showed to the likeness of the Dwelling Place and all its vessels. **6** And now, behold, it is preserved with Me, as Paradise. **7** Go, therefore, and do as I command you."]]

CHAPTER 5

1 And I answered and said, "So then I am destined to grieve for Zion, For Your enemies will come to this place and pollute Your sanctuary, And lead Your inheritance into captivity, And make themselves masters of those whom You have loved, And they will depart again to the place of their idols, And will boast before them: And what will You do for Your great Name?" **2** And the LORD said to me: "My Name and My glory are to all eternity; And My judgment will maintain its right in its own time. **3** And you will see with your eyes That the enemy will not overthrow Zion, Nor will they burn Jerusalem, But be the ministers of the Judge for the time. **4** But you go and do whatever I have said to you." **5** And I went and took Jeremiah, and Adu, and Seriah, and Jabish, and Gedaliah, and all the honorable men of the people, and I led them to the Valley of Kidron, and I narrated to them all that had been said to me. **6** And they lifted up their voice, and they all wept. **7** And we sat there and fasted until the evening.

CHAPTER 6

1 And it came to pass on the next day that, behold, the army of the Chaldees surrounded the city, and at the time of the evening, I, Baruch, left the people, and I went forth and stood by the oak. **2** And I was grieving over Zion and lamenting over the captivity which had come on the people. **3** And behold, suddenly a strong spirit raised me, and bore me aloft over the wall of Jerusalem. **4** And I beheld, and behold, four messengers standing at the four corners of the city, each of them holding a torch of fire in his hands. **5** And another messenger began to descend from Heaven, and said to them, "Hold your lamps, and do not light them until I tell you. **6** For I am first sent to speak a word to the earth, and to place in it what the LORD the Most High has commanded me." **7** And I saw him descend into the Holy of Holies, and take from there the veil, and holy Ark, and the propitiatory covering, and the two tablets, and the holy raiment of the priests, and the altar of incense, and the forty-eight precious stones with which the priest was adorned, and all the holy vessels of the Dwelling Place. **8** And he spoke to the earth with a loud voice: "Earth, earth, earth! Hear the word of the mighty God, And receive what I commit to you, And guard them until the last times, So that, when you are ordered, you may restore them, So that strangers may not get possession of them. **9** For the time comes when Jerusalem will also be delivered for a time, Until it is said that it is again restored forever." **10** And the earth opened its mouth and swallowed them up.

CHAPTER 7

1 And after these things I heard that messenger saying to those messengers who held the lamps: "Destroy, therefore, and overthrow its wall to its foundations, lest the enemy should boast and say, We have overthrown the wall of Zion, And we have burned the place of the mighty God." **2** And they have seized the place where I had been standing before.

CHAPTER 8

1 Now the messengers did as he had commanded them, and when they had broken up the corners of the walls, a voice was heard from the interior of the temple, after the wall had fallen, saying, **2** "Enter, you enemies, And come, you adversaries; For He who kept the house has forsaken [it]." **3** And I, Baruch, departed. **4** And it came to pass after these things that the army of the Chaldees entered and seized the house, and all that was around it. And they led the people away captive and slew some of them, and bound Zedekiah the king, and sent him to the king of Babylon.

CHAPTER 9

1 And I, Baruch, came, and Jeremiah, whose heart was found pure from sins, who had not been captured in the seizure of the city. **2** And we tore our garments, we wept, and mourned, and fasted seven days.

CHAPTER 10

1 And it came to pass after seven days, that the word of God came to me, and said to me: **2** "Tell Jeremiah to go and support the captivity of the people to Babylon. **3** But remain here amid the desolation of Zion, and I will show to you after these days what will befall at the end of days." **4** And I spoke to Jeremiah as the LORD commanded me. **5** And he, indeed, departed with the people, but I, Baruch, returned and sat before the gates of the temple, and I lamented with the following lamentation over Zion and said, **6** "Blessed is he who was not born, Or he, who having been born, has died. **7** But as for us who live, woe to us, Because we see the afflictions of Zion, And what has befallen Jerusalem. **8** I will call the Sirens from the sea, And you Lilin, come from the desert, And you Shedim and dragons from the forests: Awake and gird up your loins to mourning, And take up the dirges with me, And make lamentation with me. **9** You farmers, do not sow again; And, O earth, why do you give your harvest fruits? Keep within you the sweets of your sustenance. **10** And you, vine, why further do you give your wine? For an offering will not be made again from there in Zion, Nor will first-fruits be offered again. **11** And you, O heavens, withhold your dew, And do not open the treasuries of rain; **12** And you, O sun, withhold the light of your rays; And you, O moon, extinguish the multitude of your light. For why should light rise again Where the light of Zion is darkened? **13** And you—you bridegrooms—do not enter in, And do not let the brides adorn themselves with garlands; And, you women, do not pray that you may bear. **14** For the barren will above all rejoice, And those who have no sons will be glad, And those who have sons will have anguish. **15** For why should they bear in pain, Only to bury in grief? **16** Or why, again, should mankind have sons? Or why should the seed of their kind be named again, Where this mother is desolate, And her sons are led into captivity? **17** From this time forward, do not speak of beauty, And do not discourse of gracefulness. **18** Moreover, you priests, take the keys of the sanctuary, And cast them into the height of Heaven, And give them to the LORD and say, Guard Your house Yourself, For behold, we are found false stewards. **19** And you— you virgins who weave fine linen And silk with gold of Ophir—Take all [these] things with haste And cast [them] into the fire, That it may bear them to Him who made them, And the flame send them to Him who created them, Lest the enemy get possession of them."

CHAPTER 11

1 Moreover, I, Baruch, say this against you, Babylon: "If you had prospered, And Zion had dwelt in her glory, Yet the grief to us had been great That you should be equal to Zion. **2** But now, behold, the grief is infinite, And the lamentation measureless, For behold, you are prospered And Zion desolate. **3** Who will be judge regarding these things? Or to whom will we complain regarding that which has befallen us? O LORD , how have You borne [it]? **4** Our fathers went to rest without grief, And behold, the righteous sleep in the earth in tranquility; **5** For they did not know this anguish, Nor yet had they heard of that which had befallen us. **6** Would that you had ears, O earth, And that you had a heart, O dust, That you might go and announce in Sheol, And say to the dead: **7** Blessed are you more than we who live."

CHAPTER 12

1 "But I will say this as I think, And speak against you—the land that is prospering. **2** The noonday does not always burn, Nor do the rays of the sun constantly give light. **3** And do not expect to rejoice, Nor condemn greatly. **4** For assuredly in its season the [divine] wrath will be awakened against you, Which is now restrained by long-suffering as it were by a rein." **5** And when I had said these things, I fasted seven days.

CHAPTER 13

1 And it came to pass after these things that I, Baruch, was standing on Mount Zion, and behold, a voice came forth from the height and said to me: **2** "Stand on your feet, Baruch, and hear the word of the mighty God. **3** Because you have been astonished at what has befallen Zion, you will therefore be assuredly preserved to the consummation of the times, that you may be for a testimony. **4** So that, if ever those prosperous cities say: **5** Why has the mighty God brought this retribution on us? Say to them, You and those like you will have seen this evil and retribution which is coming on you and on your people in its [appointed] time that the nations may be thoroughly smitten. **6** And then they will be in anguish. **7** And if they say at that time: **8** For how long ? Y ou will say to them: You who have drunk the strained wine, Drink also of its dregs— The judgment of the Lofty One Who has no respect of persons; **9** On this account He formerly had no mercy on His own sons, But afflicted them as His enemies, because they sinned, **10** Then, therefore, they were disciplined That they might be sanctified. **11** But now, you peoples and nations, you are guilty Because you have always trodden down the earth, And used the creation unrighteously. **12** For I have always benefited you. And you have always been ungrateful for the beneficence."

CHAPTER 14

1 And I answered and said, "Behold, You have shown me the methods of the times, and that which will be. And You have said to me that the retribution which was spoken of by You will be endured by the nations. **2** And now I know that those who have sinned are many, and they have lived . . . and departed from the world, but that few nations will be left in those times to whom . . . the words [which] You said. **3** And what advantage [is there] in this or what worse than [these?] **4** But I will again speak in Your presence: **5** What have they profited who had knowledge before You and have not walked in vanity as the rest of the nations, and have not said to the dead, Give us life, but always feared You, and have not left Your ways? **6** And behold, they have been carried off, nor on their account have You had mercy on Zion. **7** And if others did evil, it was due to Zion that on account of the works of those who worked good works she should be forgiven and should not be overwhelmed on account of the works of those who worked unrighteousness. **8** But who, O LORD , my Lord, will comprehend Your judgment, Or who will search out the profoundness of Your way? Or who will think out the weight of Your path? **9** Or who will be able to think out Your incomprehensible counsel? Or who of those that are born has ever found The beginning or end of Your wisdom? **10** For we have all been made like a breath. **11** For as the breath ascends involuntarily, and again dies, so it is with the nature of men, who do not depart according to their own will, and do not know what will befall them in the end. 12 For the righteous justly hope for the end, and without fear depart from this habitation, because they have with You a store of works preserved in treasuries. 13 On this account also, these without fear leave this world, and trusting with joy they hope to receive the world which You have promised them. 14 But as for us—woe to us, who are also now shamefully entreated, and at that time look forward [only] to calamities. 15 But You know accurately what You have done by means of Your servants; for we are not able to understand that which is good as You are, our Creator. 16 But again I will speak in Your presence, O LORD , my Lord. 17 When of old there was no world with its inhabitants, You devised and spoke with a word, and immediately the works of creation stood before You. 18 And You said that You would make for Your world man as the administrator of Your works, that it might be known that he was by no means made on account of the world, but the world on account of him. 19 And now I see that as for the world which was made on account of us, behold, it abides; but we, on account of whom it was made, depart."

CHAPTER 15

1 And the LORD answered and said to me: "You are rightly astonished regarding the departure of man, but you have not judged well regarding the calamities which befall those who sin. 2 And as regards what you have said, that the righteous are carried off and the impious are prospered, 3 and as regards what you have said, Man does not know Your judgment— on this account hear, and I will speak to you, and listen, and I will cause you to hear My words. 5 Man would not rightly have understood My judgment, unless he had accepted the law, and I had instructed him in understanding. 6 But now, because he transgressed willfully, yes, just on this ground that he knows, he will be tormented. 7 And as regards what you said touching the righteous, that on account of them this world has come, so also again, that which is to come will come on their account. 8 For this world is to them a strife and a labor with much trouble; and that accordingly which is to come —a crown with great glory."

CHAPTER 16

1 And I answered and said, 2 " LORD , my Lord, behold, the years of this time are few and evil, and who is able in his short time to acquire that which is measureless?"

CHAPTER 17

1 And the LORD answered and said to me: "With the Most High account is not taken of time nor of a few years. 2 For what did it profit Adam that he lived nine hundred and thirty years and transgressed that which he was commanded? Therefore, the multitude of time that he lived did not profit him, but brought death and cut off the years of those who were born from him, wherein Moses suffered loss in that he lived only one hundred and twenty years, and inasmuch he was subject to Him who formed him, brought the law to the seed of Jacob, and lighted a lamp for the nation of Israel?"

CHAPTER 18

1 And I answered and said, "He that lighted has taken from the light, and there are but few that have imitated him. 2 But those many whom he has lighted have taken from the darkness of Adam and have not rejoiced in the light of the lamp."

CHAPTER 19

1 And He answered and said to me: "For what reason at that time he appointed for them a covenant and said, Behold, I have placed before you life and death, And he called the heavens and earth to witness against them. 2 For he knew that his time was but short, But that the heavens and earth always endure. 3 But after his death they sinned and transgressed, Though they knew that they had the law reproving [them], And the light in which nothing could err, Also the spheres which testify, and Me. 4 Now regarding everything that is, it is I that judge, but do not take counsel in your soul regarding these things, nor afflict yourself because of those which have been. 5 For now it is the consummation of time that should be considered, whether of business, or of prosperity, or of shame, and not the beginning thereof. 6 Because if a man is prospered in his beginnings and shamefully entreated in his old age, he forgets all the prosperity that he had. 7 And again, if a man is shamefully entreated in his beginnings, and at his end is prospered, he does not remember again his evil entreatment. 8 And again listen: though each one were prospered all that time—all the time from the day on which death was decreed against those who transgress— and in his end was destroyed, everything would have been in vain."

CHAPTER 20

1 "Therefore, behold ! T he days come, And the times will hasten more than the former, And the seasons will speed by more than those that are past, And the years will pass more quickly than the present [years]. 2 Therefore I have now taken Zion away, That I may the more speedily visit the world in its season. 3 Now therefore, hold fast in your heart everything that I command you, And seal it in the recesses of your mind. 4 And then I will show you the judgment of My might, And My ways which are unsearchable. 5 Go therefore and sanctify yourself seven days, and eat no bread, nor drink water, nor speak to anyone. 6 And afterward come to that place and I will reveal Myself to you, and speak true things with you, and I will give you commandment regarding the method of the times; for they are coming and do not tarry."

CHAPTER 21

1 And I went there and sat in the Valley of Kidron in a cave of the earth, and I sanctified my soul there, and I ate no bread, yet I was not hungry, and I drank no water, yet I did not thirst, and I was there until the seventh day, as He had commanded me. 2 And afterward I came to that place where He had spoken with me. 3   And it came to pass at sunset that my soul

took much thought, and I began to speak in the presence of the Mighty One, and said, **4** "O You that have made the earth, hear me, that have fixed the expanse by the word, and have made firm the height of the Heaven by the Spirit, that have called from the beginning of the world that which did not yet exist, and they obey You. **5** You that have commanded the air by Your nod and have seen those things which are to be as those things which You are doing. **6** You that rule with great thought the hosts that stand before You; also the countless holy beings, which You made from the beginning, of flame and fire, which stand around Your throne, You rule with indignation. **7** To You only does this belong that You should immediately do whatever You wish. **8** [You] who cause the drops of rain to rain by number on the earth, and alone knows the consummation of the times before they come, have respect to my prayer. **9** For You alone are able to sustain all who are, and those who have passed away, and those who are to be, those who sin, and those who are righteous (as living and being past finding out). **10** For You alone live [as] immortal and past finding out, and know the number of mankind. **11** And if in time many have sinned, yet others—not a few— have been righteous. **12** You know where You preserve the end of those who have sinned, or the consummation of those who have been righteous. **13** For if there were this life only, which belongs to all men, nothing could be more bitter than this. **14** For of what profit is strength that turns to sickness, Or fullness of food that turns to famine, Or beauty that turns to ugliness. **15** For the nature of man is always changeable. **16** For what we were formerly now we no longer are and what we now are we will not afterward remain. **16** For if a consummation had not been prepared for all, in vain would have been their beginning. But regarding everything that comes from You, You inform me, and regarding everything about which I ask You, You enlighten me. **19** How long will that which is corruptible remain, and how long will the time of mortals be prospered, and until what time will those who transgress in the world be polluted with much wickedness? **20** Therefore command in mercy and accomplish all that You said You would bring, that Your might may be made known to those who think that Your long- suffering is weakness. **21** And show to those who do not know, that everything that has befallen us and our city until now has been according to the long-suffering of Your power, because on account of Your Name You have called us a beloved people. **22** Therefore, henceforth, bring mortality to an end. **23** And reprove the messenger of death accordingly, and let Your glory appear, and let the might of Your beauty be known, and let Sheol be sealed so that from this time forward it may not receive the dead, and let the treasuries of souls restore those which are enclosed in them. **24** For there have been many years like those that are desolate from the days of Abraham, and Isaac, and Jacob, and of all those who are like them, who sleep in the earth, on whose account You said that You had created the world. **25** And now quickly show Your glory, and do not defer what has been promised by You." **26** And [when] I had completed the words of this prayer I was greatly weakened.

CHAPTER 22

1 And it came to pass after these things that, behold, the heavens were opened, and I saw, and power was given to me, and a voice was heard from on high, and it said to me: **2** "Baruch, Baruch, why are you troubled? **3** He who travels by a road but does not complete it, or who departs by sea but does not arrive at the port, can he be comforted? **4** Or he who promises to give a present to another, but does not fulfill it, is it not robbery? **5** Or he who sows the earth, but does not reap its fruit in its season, does he not lose everything? **6** Or he who plants a plant unless it grows until the time suitable to it, does he who planted it expect to receive fruit from it? **7** Or a woman who has conceived, if she brings forth untimely, does she not assuredly slay her infant? **8** Or he who builds a house, if he does not roof it and complete it, can it be called a house? Tell Me that first."

CHAPTER 23

1 And I answered and said, "Not so, O LORD , my Lord." **2** And He answered and said to me, "Why are you therefore troubled about that which you do not know, and why are you ill at ease about things in which you are ignorant? **3** For as you have not forgotten the people who now are and those who have passed away, so I remember those who are appointed to come. **4** Because when Adam sinned and death was decreed against those who should be born, then the multitude of those who should be born was numbered, and for that number a place was prepared where the living might dwell and the dead might be guarded. Therefore, before the number previously mentioned is fulfilled, the creature will not live again [[for My Spirit is the creator of life]] , and Sheol will receive the dead. **6** And again it is given to you to hear what things are to come after these times. **7** For My redemption has truly drawn near and is not far distant as before."

CHAPTER 24

1 "For behold ! T he days come and the scrolls will be opened in which are written the sins of all those who have sinned, and again also the treasuries in which the righteousness of all those who have been righteous in creation is gathered. **2** For it will come to pass at that time that you will see—and the many that are with you—the long-suffering of the Most High, which has been throughout all generations, who has been long-suffering toward all who are born, [both] those who sin and [those who] are righteous." **3** And I answered and said, "But, behold! O LORD , no one knows the number of those things which have passed nor yet of those things which are to come. **4** For I indeed know that which has befallen us, but I do not know what will happen to our enemies, and when You will visit Your works."

CHAPTER 25

1 And He answered and said to me: "You, too, will be preserved until that time until that sign which the Most High will work for the inhabitants of the earth in the end of days. **2** This will therefore be the sign: **3** when a stupor will seize the inhabitants of the earth, and they will fall into many tribulations, and again when they will fall into great torments. And it will come to pass when they say in their thoughts by reason of their much tribulation: The Mighty One no longer remembers the earth—yes, it will come to pass when they abandon hope, that the time will then awake."

CHAPTER 26

1 And I answered and said, "Will that tribulation which is to come continue [for] a long time, and will that necessarily comprise many years?"

CHAPTER 27

1 And He answered and said to me: "That time is divided into twelve parts, and each one of them is reserved for that which is appointed for it. **2** In the first part there will be the beginning of commotions. **3** And in the second part [there will be] slayings of the great ones. **4** And in the third part the fall of many by death. **5** And in the fourth part the sending of the sword. **6** And in the fifth part famine and the withholding of rain. **7** And in the sixth part earthquakes and terrors. **8** [And in the seventh part] . . . **9** And in the eighth part a multitude of specters and attacks of the Shedim. **10** And in the ninth part the fall of fire. **11** And in the tenth part plunder and much oppression. **12** And in the eleventh part wickedness and unchastity. **13** And in the twelfth part confusion from the mingling together of all those things previously mentioned. **14** For these parts of that time are reserved and will be mingled with one another and minister to one another. **15** For some will leave out some of their own, and receive [in its stead] from others, and some complete their own and that of others, so that those may not understand who are on the earth in those days that this is the consummation of the times."

CHAPTER 28

1 "Nevertheless, whoever understands will then be wise. **2** For the measure and reckoning of that time are two parts a week of seven weeks." **3** And I answered and said, "It is good for a man to come and behold, but it is better that he should not come lest he fall. **4** [[But I will say this also: **5** Will He who is incorruptible despise those things which are corruptible, and whatever befalls in the case of those things which are corruptible, so that He might look only to those things which are not corruptible?]] **6** But if, O LORD , those things will assuredly come to pass which You have foretold to me, so also show this to me if indeed I have found grace in Your sight. **7** Is it in one place or in one of the parts of the earth that those things have come to pass, or will the whole earth experience [them]?"

CHAPTER 29

1 And He answered and said to me: "Whatever will then befall [will befall] the whole earth; therefore, all who live will experience [them]. **2** For at that time I will only protect those who are found in those same days in this land. **3** And it will come to pass when all is accomplished that was to come to pass in those parts, that the Messiah will then begin to be revealed. **4** And Behemoth will be revealed from his place and Leviathan will ascend from the sea—those two great monsters which I created on the fifth day of creation, and will have kept until that time; and then they will be for food for all that are left. **5** The earth will also yield its fruit ten-thousandfold, and on each vine there will be one thousand branches, and each branch will produce one thousand clusters, and each cluster produce one thousand grapes, and each grape produce a cor of wine. **6** And those who have hungered will rejoice: moreover also, they will behold marvels every day. **7** For winds will go forth from before Me to bring every morning the fragrance of aromatic fruits, and at the close of the day clouds distilling the dew of health. **8** And it will come to pass at that same time that the treasury of manna will again descend from on high, and they will eat of it in those years, because these are they who have come to the consummation of time."

CHAPTER 30

1 "And it will come to pass after these things, when the time of the advent of the Messiah is fulfilled, that He will return in glory. **2** Then all who have fallen asleep in hope of Him will rise again. And it will come to pass at that time that the treasuries will be opened in which is preserved the number of the souls of the righteous, and they will come forth, and a multitude of souls will be seen together in one assemblage of one thought, and the first will rejoice and the last will not be grieved. **3** For they know that the time has come of which it is said that it is the consummation of the times. **4** But the souls of the wicked, when they behold all these things, will then waste away more. **5** For they will know that their torment has come, and their perdition has arrived."

CHAPTER 31

1 And it came to pass after these things that I went to the people and said to them: "Assemble to me all your elders and I will speak words to them." **2** And they all assembled in the Valley of the Kidron. **3** And I answered and said to them: "Hear, O Israel, and I will speak to you, And give ear, O seed of Jacob, and I will instruct you. **4** Do not forget Zion, But hold in remembrance the anguish of Jerusalem. **5** For behold, the days come When everything that is will become the prey of corruption And be as though it had not been."

CHAPTER 32

1 "But as for you, if you prepare your hearts so as to sow in them the fruits of the law, it will protect you in that time in which the Mighty One is to shake the whole creation. **2** [[Because after a short time the building of Zion will be shaken in order that it may be built again. But that building will not remain, but will again after a time be rooted out, and will remain desolate until the time. **4** And afterward it must be renewed in glory and perfected forevermore.]] **5** Therefore we should not be distressed so much over the calamity which has now come as over that which is still to be. **6** For there will be a greater trial than these two tribulations when the Mighty One will renew His creation. **7** And now do not draw near to me for a few days, nor seek me until I come to you." **8** And it came to pass when I had spoken all these words to them, that I, Baruch, went my way, and when the people saw me setting out, they lifted up their voice and lamented and said, **9**

"To where are you departing from us, Baruch, and are you forsaking us as a father who forsakes his orphan children, and departs from them?"

CHAPTER 33

1 "Are these the commands which your companion, Jeremiah the prophet, commanded you, and said to you: Look to this people until I go and make ready the rest of the brothers in Babylon against whom has gone forth the sentence that they should be led into captivity? And now if you also forsake us, it were good for us all to die before you, then that you should withdraw from us."

CHAPTER 34

1 And I answered and said to the people: "Far be it from me to forsake you or to withdraw from you, **2** but I will only go to the Holy of Holies to inquire of the Mighty One concerning you and concerning Zion, if in some respect I should receive more illumination: and after these things I will return to you."

CHAPTER 35

1 And I, Baruch, went to the holy place, and sat down on the ruins and wept, and said, **2** "O that my eyes were springs, And my eyelids a fount of tears. **3** For how will I lament for Zion, And how will I mourn for Jerusalem? **4** Because in that place where I am now prostrate, Of old the high priest offered holy sacrifices, And placed an incense of fragrant odors thereon. **5** But now our glorying has been made into dust, And the desire of our soul into sand."

CHAPTER 36

1 And when I had said these things, I fell asleep there, and I saw a vision in the night. **2** And behold, a forest of trees planted on the plain, and lofty and rugged rocky mountains surrounded it, and that forest occupied much space. **3** And behold, over against it arose a vine, and from under it there went forth a fountain peacefully. **4** Now that fountain came to the forest and was [stirred] into great waves, and those waves submerged that forest, and suddenly they rooted out the greater part of that forest and overthrew all the mountains which were around it. **5** And the height of the forest began to be made low, and the top of the mountains was made low, and that fountain prevailed greatly, so that it left nothing of that great forest save one cedar only. **6** Also, when it had cast it down and had destroyed and rooted out the greater part of that forest, so that nothing was left of it, nor could its place be recognized, then that vine began to come with the fountain in peace and great tranquility, and it came to a place which was not far from that cedar, and they brought the cedar which had been cast down to it. **7** And I beheld, and behold, that vine opened its mouth and spoke and said to that cedar: "Are you not that cedar which was left of the forest of wickedness, and by whose means wickedness persisted, and was worked all those years, and never for good? **8** And you kept conquering that which was not yours, and to that which was yours you never showed compassion, and you kept extending your power over those who were far from you, and those who drew near you, you held fast in the toils of your wickedness, and you always uplifted yourself as one that could not be rooted out! **9** But now your time has sped, and your hour has come. **10** Do you also therefore depart, O cedar, after the forest, which departed before you, and become dust with it, and let your ashes be mingled together? **11** And now recline in anguish and rest in torment until your last time comes, in which you will come again, and be tormented still more."

CHAPTER 37

1 And after these things I saw that cedar burning, and the vine growing, itself and all around it, the plain full of unfading flowers. **2** And I indeed awoke and arose.

CHAPTER 38

1 And I prayed and said, "O LORD , my Lord, You always enlighten those who are led by understanding. **2** Your law is life, and Your wisdom is right guidance. **3** Therefore make known to me the interpretation of this vision. **4** For You know that my soul has always walked in Your law, and from my [earliest] days I did not depart from Your wisdom."

CHAPTER 39

1 And He answered and said to me: "Baruch, this is the interpretation of the vision which you have seen. **2** As you have seen the great forest, which lofty and rugged mountains surrounded, this is the word. **3** Behold ! T he days come, and this kingdom will be destroyed which once destroyed Zion, and it will be subjected to that which comes after it. **4** Moreover, that also again after a time will be destroyed, and another, a third, will arise, and that also will have dominion for its time, and will be destroyed. **5** And after these things a fourth kingdom will arise, whose power will be harsh and evil far beyond those which were before it, and it will rule many times as the forests on the plain, and it will hold fast for times, and will exalt itself more than the cedars of Lebanon. **6** And by it the truth will be hidden, and all those who are polluted with iniquity will flee to it, as evil beasts flee and creep into the forest. **7** And it will come to pass when the time of its consummation—that it should fall—has approached, then the principate of My Messiah will be revealed, which is like the fountain and the vine, and when it is revealed it will root out the multitude of its host. **8** And as touching that which you have seen, the lofty cedar, which was left of that forest, and the fact that the vine spoke those words with it which you heard, this is the word."

CHAPTER 40

1 "The last leader of that time will be left alive, when the multitude of his hosts will be put to the sword, and he will be bound, and they will take him up to Mount Zion, and My Messiah will convict him of all his impieties, and will gather and set before him all the works of his hosts. **2** And afterward he will put him to death, and protect the rest of My people which will be found in the place which I have chosen. **3** And His principate will stand forever, until the world of corruption is at an end, and until the times previously mentioned are fulfilled. **4** This is your vision, and this is its interpretation."

CHAPTER 41

1 And I answered and said, "For whom and for how many will these things be ? O r who will be worthy to live at that time? **2** For I will speak before You everything that I think, and I will ask of You regarding those things which I meditate. **3** For behold, I see many of Your people who have withdrawn from Your covenant, and cast from themselves the yoke of Your law. **4** But others again I have seen who have forsaken their vanity and fled for refuge beneath Your wings. **5** What therefore will be to them ? O r how will the last time receive them? **6** Or perhaps the time of these will assuredly be weighed, and as the beam inclines will they be judged accordingly?"

CHAPTER 42

1 And He answered and said to me: "I will also show these things to you. **2** As for what you said—To whom will these things be, and how many [will they be]? To those who have believed there will be the good which was spoken of formerly, and to those who despise there will be the contrary of these things. **3** And as for what you said regarding those who have drawn near and those who have withdrawn this in the word. **4** As for those who were before subject, and afterward withdrew and mingled themselves with the seed of mingled peoples, the time of these was the former, and was accounted as something exalted. **5** And as for those who before did not know but afterward knew life, and mingled [only] with the seed of the people which had separated itself, the time of these [is] the latter, and is accounted as something exalted. **6** And time will succeed to time and season to season, and one will receive from another, and then with a view to the consummation, everything will be compared according to the measure of the times and the hours of the seasons. **7** For corruption will take those that belong to it, and life those that belong to it. **8** And the dust will be called, and there will be said to it: Give back that which is not yours and raise up all that you have kept until its time."

CHAPTER 43

1 "But you, Baruch, direct your heart to that which has been said to you, And understand those things which have been shown to you; For there are many continuous consolations for you. **2** For you will depart from this place, And you will pass from the regions which are now seen by you, And you will forget whatever is corruptible, And will not again recall those things which happen among mortals. **3** Therefore go and command your people, and come to this place, and afterward fast seven days, and then I will come to you and speak with you."

CHAPTER 44

1 And I, Baruch, went from there, and came to my people, and I called my firstborn son and [the Gedaliahs] my friends, and seven of the elders of the people, and I said to them: "Behold, I go to my fathers According to the way of all the earth. **3** But do not withdraw from the way of the law, But guard and admonish the people which remain, Lest they withdraw from the commandments of the Mighty One. **4** For you see that He whom we serve is just, And our Creator is no respecter of persons. **5** And see what has befallen Zion, And what has happened to Jerusalem. **6** For the judgment of the Mighty One will [thereby] be made known, And His ways, which, though past finding out, are right. **7** For if you endure and persevere in His fear, And do not forget His law, The times will change over you for good, And you will see the consolation of Zion. **8** Because whatever is now is nothing, But that which will be is very great. **9** For everything that is corruptible will pass away, And everything that dies will depart, And all the present time will be forgotten, Nor will there be any remembrance of the present time, which is defiled with evils. **10** For that which runs now runs to vanity, And that which prospers will quickly fall and be humiliated. **11** For that which is to be will be the object of desire, And for that which comes afterward will we hope; For it is a time that does not pass away, **12** And the hour comes which abides forever. And the new world [comes] which does not turn to corruption those who depart to its blessedness, And has no mercy on those who depart to torment, And does not lead to perdition those who live in it. **13** For these are they who will inherit that time which has been spoken of, And theirs is the inheritance of the promised time. **14** These are they who have acquired for themselves treasures of wisdom, And with them are found stores of understanding, And they have not withdrawn from mercy, And they have preserved the truth of the law. **15** For the world to come will be given to them, But the dwelling of the rest, who are many, will be in the fire."

CHAPTER 45

1 "Therefore, so far as you are able, instruct the people, for that labor is ours. **2** For if you teach them, you will restore them."

CHAPTER 46

1 And my son and the elders of the people answered and said to me: "Has the Mighty One humiliated us to such a degree As to take you from us quickly? **2** And we will truly be in darkness, And there will be no light to the people who are left, **3** For where again will we seek the law, Or who will distinguish between death and life for us?" **4** And I said to them, "I cannot resist the throne of the Mighty One; Nevertheless, there will not be wanting to Israel a wise man Nor a son of the law to the race of Jacob. **5** But only prepare your hearts, that you may obey the law, And be subject to those who in fear are wise and understanding; And prepare your souls that you may not depart from them. **6** For if you do these things, Good tidings will come to you, **||** Which I before told you of; Nor will you fall into the torment, of which I testified to you before." **7** (But with regard to the word that I was to have taken, I did not make [it] known to them or to my son.) **||**

CHAPTER 47

1 And when I had gone forth and dismissed them, I went there and said to them: "Behold! I go to Hebron; for the Mighty One has sent me there." **2** And I came to that place where the word had been spoken to me, and I sat there, and fasted seven days.

CHAPTER 48

1 And it came to pass after the seventh day, that I prayed before the Mighty One and said, **2** "O my Lord, You summon the advent of the times, And they stand before You; You cause the power of the ages to pass away, And they do not resist You; You arrange the method of the seasons, And they obey You. **3** You alone know the duration of the generations, And You do not reveal Your mysteries to many. **4** You make known the multitude of the fire, And You weigh the lightness of the wind. **5** You explore the limit of the heights, And You scrutinize the depths of the darkness. **6** You care for the number which pass away that they may be preserved, And You prepare an abode for those that are to be. **7** You remember the beginning which You have made, And the destruction that is to be, You do not forget. **8** With nods of fear and indignation You command the flames, And they change into spirits, And with a word You give life to that which was not, And with mighty power You hold that which has not yet come. **9** You instruct created things in Your understanding, And You make wise the spheres so as to minister in their orders. **10** Innumerable armies stand before You And minister in their orders quietly at Your nod. **11** Hear Your servant And give ear to my petition. **12** For in a short time are we born, And in a short time we return. **13** But with You hours are as an age, And days as generations. **14** Therefore, do not be angry with man, for he is nothing; **15** And do not take account of our works; For what are we? For behold, by Your gift we come into the world, And we do not depart of our own will. **16** For we did not say to our parents, Beget us, Nor did we send to Sheol and say, Receive us. **17** What therefore is our strength that we should bear Your wrath, Or what are we that we should endure Your judgment? **18** Protect us in Your compassions, And help us in Your mercy. **19** Behold the little ones that are subject to You, And save all that draw near to You: And do not destroy the hope of our people, And do not cut short the times of our aid. **20** For this is the nation which You have chosen, And these are the people to whom You find no equal. **21** But now I will speak before You, And I will say as my heart thinks. **22** We trust in You, for behold, Your law is with us, And we know that we will not fall so long as we keep Your statutes. **23 ||** We are blessed for all time at all events in this—That we have not mingled with the nations. **|| 24** For we are all one celebrated people, Who have received one law from One: And the law which is among us will aid us, And the surpassing wisdom which is in us will help us." **25** And when I had prayed and said these things, I was greatly weakened. **26** And He answered and said to me: "You have prayed simply, O Baruch, And all your words have been heard. **27** But My judgment exacts its own And My law exacts its rights. **28** For from your words I will answer you, And from your prayer I will speak to you. **29** For this is as follows: he that is corrupted is not at all; he has both worked iniquity so far as deceit could do anything, and has not remembered My goodness, nor accepted My long-suffering. **30** Therefore, you will surely be taken up, as I before told you. **31** For that time will arise which brings affliction; for it will come and pass by with quick vehemence, and it will be turbulent, coming in the heat of indignation. **32** And it will come to pass in those days that all the inhabitants of the earth will be moved against one another, because they do not know that My judgment has drawn near. **33** For there will not be found many wise at that time, And the intelligent will be but a few: Moreover, even those who know will most of all be silent. **34** And there will be many rumors and tidings—not a few, And the doing of illusions will be manifest, And promises—not a few—will be recounted, Some of them [will prove] idle, And some of them will be confirmed. **35** And honor will be turned into shame, And strength humiliated into contempt, And integrity destroyed, And beauty will become ugliness. **36** And many will say to many at that time: Where has the multitude of intelligence hidden itself, And to where has the multitude of wisdom removed itself? **37** And while they are meditating on these things, Then envy will arise in those who had not thought anything of themselves And passion will seize him that is peaceful, And many will be stirred up in anger to injure many, And they will rouse up armies in order to shed blood, And in the end they will perish together with them. **38** And it will come to pass at the same time, That a change of times will manifestly appeal to every man, Because in all those times they polluted themselves And they practiced oppression, And every man walked in his own works, And did not remember the Law of the Mighty One. **39** Therefore a fire will consume their thoughts, And in flame the meditations of their reins will be tried; For the Judge will come and will not tarry. **40** Because each of the inhabitants of the earth knew when he was transgressing. But they did not know My Law by reason of their pride. **41** But many will then assuredly weep, Yes, over the living more than over the dead." **42** And I answered and said, "O Adam, what have you done to all those who are born from you? And what will be said to the first Eve who listened to the serpent? **43** For all this multitude are going to corruption, Nor is there any numbering of those whom the fire devours. **44** But again I will speak in Your presence. **45** You, O LORD, my Lord, know what is in Your creature. **46** For You commanded the ancient dust to produce Adam, and You know the number of those who are born from him, and how far they have sinned before You, who have existed and not confessed You as their Creator. **47** And as regards all these their end will convict them, and Your law which they have transgressed will repay them on Your day." **48 ||** "But now let us dismiss the wicked and inquire about the righteous. **49** And I will recount their blessedness and not be silent in celebrating their glory, which is reserved for them. **50** For assuredly as in a short time in this transitory world in which you live you have endured much labor, so in that world to which there is no end, you will receive great light."

CHAPTER 49

1 "Nevertheless, I will again ask from You, O Mighty One, yes, I will ask You who made all things. **2** In what shape will those live who live in Your day? Or how will the splendor of those who [are] after that time continue? **3** Will they then resume this form of the present, And put on these entangling members, Which are now involved in evils, And in which evils are consummated, Or will You perhaps change these things which have been in the world As also the world?"

CHAPTER 50

1 And He answered and said to me: "Hear, Baruch, this word, and write in the remembrance of your heart all that you will learn. **2** For the earth will then assuredly restore the dead, [[which it now receives, in order to preserve them.]] It will make no change in their form, but as it has received, so will it restore them, and as I delivered them to it, so also will it raise them. **3** For then it will be necessary to show the living that the dead have come to life again, and that those who had departed have returned [again]. **4** And it will come to pass, when they have individually recognized those whom they now know, then judgment will grow strong, and those things which before were spoken of will come."

CHAPTER 51

1 "And it will come to pass, when that appointed day has gone by, that then will the aspect of those who are condemned be afterward changed, and the glory of those who are justified. **2** For the aspect of those who now act wickedly will become worse than it is, as they will suffer torment. **3** Also, the glory of those who have now been justified in My law, who have had understanding in their life, and who have planted in their heart the root of wisdom, then their splendor will be glorified in changes, and the form of their face will be turned into the light of their beauty, that they may be able to acquire and receive the world which does not die, which is then promised to them. **4** For over this, above all, those who come will then lament that they rejected My law and stopped their ears that they might not hear wisdom or receive understanding. **5** When, therefore, they see those over whom they are now exalted, [but] who will then be exalted and glorified more than they, they will respectively be transformed, the latter into the splendor of messengers, and the former will yet more waste away in wonder at the visions and in the beholding of the forms. **6** For they will first behold and afterward depart to be tormented. **7** But those who have been saved by their works, And to whom the law has now been a hope, And understanding an expectation, And wisdom a confidence, Will wondrously appear in their time. **8** For they will behold the world which is now invisible to them, And they will behold the time which is now hidden from them: **9** And time will no longer age them. **10** For they will dwell in the heights of that world, And they will be made like to the messengers, And be made equal to the stars, And they will be changed into every form they desire, From beauty into loveliness, And from light into the splendor of glory. **11** For there will be spread before them the extents of Paradise, And there will be shown to them the beauty of the majesty of the living creatures which are beneath the throne, And all the armies of the messengers, who are now held fast by My word, Lest they should appear, and are held fast by a command, that they may stand in their places until their advent comes. **12** Moreover, there will then be excellency in the righteous surpassing that in the messengers. **13** For the first will receive the last, those whom they were expecting, And the last, those of whom they used to hear that they had passed away. **14** For they have been delivered from this world of tribulation, And laid down the burden of anguish. **15** For what then have men lost their life, And for what have those who were on the earth exchanged their soul? **16** For then they did not choose for themselves this time, Which, beyond the reach of anguish, could not pass away, But they chose for themselves that time, Whose issues are full of lamentations and evils, And they denied the world which does not age those who come to it, And they rejected the time of glory, So that they will not come to the honor of which I told you before."

CHAPTER 52

1 And I answered and said, "How can we forget those for whom woe is then reserved? **2** And why therefore do we again mourn for those who die? Or why do we weep for those who depart to Sheol? **3** Let lamentations be reserved for the beginning of that coming torment, And let tears be laid up for the advent of the destruction of that time. **4** [[But even in the face of these things I will speak. **5** And as for the righteous, what will they do now? **6** Rejoice in the suffering which you now suffer; For why do you look for the decline of your enemies? **7** Make ready your soul for that which is reserved for you, And prepare your souls for the reward which is laid up for you."]]

CHAPTER 53

1 And when I had said these things, I fell asleep there, and I saw a vision, and behold, a cloud was ascending from a very great sea, and I kept gazing on it, and behold, it was full of white and black waters, and there were many colors in those same waters, and as it were the likeness of great lightning was seen at its summit. **2** And I saw the cloud passing swiftly in quick courses, and it covered all the earth. **3** And it came to pass after these things that that cloud began to pour on the earth the waters that were in it. **4** And I saw that there was not one and the same likeness in the waters which descended from it. **5** For in the first beginning they were black and many, and afterward I saw that the waters became bright, but they were not many, and after these things again I saw black [waters], and after these things again bright, and again black and again bright. **6** Now this was done twelve times, but the black were always more numerous than the bright. **7** And it came to pass at the end of the cloud, that behold, it rained black waters, and they were darker than had been all those waters that were before, and fire was mingled with them, and where those waters descended, they worked devastation and destruction. **8** And after these things I saw how that lightning which I had seen on the summit of the cloud, seized hold of it and hurled it to the earth. **9** Now that lightning shone exceedingly, so as to illuminate the whole earth, and it healed those regions where the last waters had descended and worked devastation. **10** And it took hold of the whole earth and had dominion over it. **11** And I saw after these things, and behold, twelve rivers were ascending from the sea, and they began to surround that lightning and to become subject to it. **12** And by reason of my fear I awoke.

CHAPTER 54

1 And I implored the Mighty One, and said, "You alone, O LORD , know of the former times—the deep things of the world, And the things which befall in their times You bring about by Your word, And against the works of the inhabitants of the earth You hasten the beginnings of the times, And You alone know the end of the seasons. **2** [You] for whom nothing is too hard, But who does everything easily by a nod: **3** [You] to whom the depths come as the heights, And whose word the beginnings of the ages serve: **4** [You] who reveal to those who fear You what is prepared for them, That from then on they may be comforted. **5** You show great acts to those who do not know; You break up the enclosure of those who are ignorant, And light up what is dark, And reveal what is hidden to the pure, || Who in faith have submitted themselves to You and Your law. || **6** You have shown this vision to Your servant; Also reveal its interpretation to me. **7** For I know that as regards those things wherein I implored You, I have received a response, And as regards what I implored, You revealed to me with what voice I should praise You, And from what members I should cause praises and hallelujahs to ascend to You. **8** For if my members were mouths, And the hairs of my head voices, Even so I could not give You the reward of praise, Nor laud You as is befitting, Nor could I recount Your praise, Nor tell the glory of Your beauty. **9** For what am I among men, Or why am I reckoned among those who are more excellent than I, That I have heard all these marvelous things from the Most High, And numberless promises from Him who created me? **10** Blessed is my mother among those that bear, And praised among women is she that bore me. **11** For I will not be silent in praising the Mighty One, And with the voice of praise I will recount His marvelous deeds. **12** For who does like to Your marvelous deeds, O God, Or who comprehends Your deep thought of life? **13** For with Your counsel You govern all the creatures which Your right hand has created, And You have established every fountain of light beside You, And You have prepared the treasures of wisdom beneath Your throne. **14** And justly do they perish who have not loved Your law, And the torment of judgment will await those who have not submitted themselves to Your power. **15** For though Adam first sinned And brought untimely death on all, Yet of those who were born from him Each one of them has prepared for his own soul torment to come, And again each one of them has chosen for himself glories to come. **16** [[For assuredly he who believes will receive reward. **17** But now, as for you, you wicked that now are, Turn to destruction, because you will be speedily visited, in that formerly you rejected the understanding of the Most High. **18** For His works have not taught you, Nor has the skill of His creation—which is at all times—persuaded you.]] **19** Adam is therefore not the cause, save only of his own soul, But each of us has been the Adam of his own soul. **20** But You, O LORD , expound to me regarding those things which You have revealed to me, And inform me regarding that which I implored You. **21** For at the consummation of the world vengeance will be taken on those who have done wickedness according to their wickedness, And You will glorify the faithful according to their faithfulness. **22** For those who are among Your own You rule, And those who sin You blot out from among Your own."

CHAPTER 55

1 And it came to pass when I had finished speaking the words of this prayer, that I sat there under a tree, that I might rest in the shade of the branches. **2** And I wondered and was astonished, and pondered in my thoughts regarding the multitude of goodness which sinners who are on the earth have rejected, and regarding the great torment which they have despised, though they knew that they should be tormented because of the sin they had committed. And when I was pondering on these things and the like, behold, the messenger Ramiel who presides over true visions was sent to me, and he said to me: **4** "Why does your heart trouble you, Baruch, And why does your thought disturb you? **5** For if owing to the report which you have only heard of judgment you are so moved, What [will you be] when you will see it manifestly with your eyes? **6** And if with the expectation with which you do expect the day of the Mighty One you are so overcome, What [will you be] when you will come to its advent? **7** And, if at the word of the announcement of the torment of those who have done foolishly you are so wholly distraught, How much more when the event will reveal marvelous things? **8** And if you have heard tidings of the good and evil things which are then coming and are grieved, What—when you will behold what the majesty will reveal, Which will convict these and cause those to rejoice?"

CHAPTER 56

1 "Nevertheless, because you have implored the Most High to reveal to you the interpretation of the vision which you have seen, I have been sent to tell you. **2** And the Mighty One has assuredly made known to you the methods of the times that have passed, and of those that are destined to pass in His world from the beginning of its creation even to its consummation, of those things which [are] deceit and of those which [are] in truth. **3** For as you saw a great cloud which ascended from the sea, and went and covered the earth, this is the duration of the age which the Mighty One made when he took counsel to make the world. **4** And it came to pass when the word had gone forth from His presence, that the duration of the world had come into being in a small degree, and was established according to the multitude of the intelligence of Him who sent it. **5** And as you previously saw on the summit of the cloud black waters which descended previously on the earth, this is the transgression with which Adam the first man transgressed. **6** For [since] when he transgressed Untimely death came into being, Grief was named And anguish was prepared, And pain was created, And trouble consummated, And disease began to be established, And Sheol kept demanding that it should be renewed in blood, And the begetting of children was brought about, And the passion of parents produced, And the greatness of humanity was humiliated, And goodness languished. **7** What therefore can be blacker or darker than these things? **8** This is the beginning of the black waters which you have seen. **9** And from these black [waters] again were black derived, and the darkness of darkness was produced. **10** For he became a danger to his own soul: even to the messengers. **11** For moreover, at that time when he was created, they enjoyed liberty. **12** And he became a danger; some of them descended and mingled with the women. **13** And then those who did so were tormented in chains. **14** But the rest of the multitude of the messengers, of which there is [no] number, restrained themselves. **15** And those who dwelt on the earth perished together [with them] through the waters of the deluge. **16** These are the black first waters."

CHAPTER 57

1 "And after these [waters] you saw bright waters: this is the fount of Abraham, also his generations and advent of his son, and of his son's son, and of those like them. **2** Because at that time the unwritten law was named among them, And the works of the commandments were then fulfilled, And belief in the coming judgment was then generated, And hope of the world that was to be renewed was then built up, And the promise of the life that should come hereafter was implanted. **3** These are the bright waters, which you have seen."

CHAPTER 58

1 "And the black third waters which you have seen, these are the mingling of all sins, which the nations afterward worked after the death of those righteous men, and the wickedness of the land of Egypt, wherein they did wickedly in the service with which they made their sons to serve. **2** Nevertheless, these also perished at last."

CHAPTER 59

1 "And the bright fourth waters which you have seen are the advent of Moses, and Aaron, and Miriam, and Joshua the son of Nun, and Caleb, and of all those like them. **2** For at that time the lamp of the perpetual law shone on all those who sat in darkness, which announced to them that believe the promise of their reward, and to them that deny, the torment of fire which is reserved for them. **3** But also the heavens at that time were shaken from their place, and those who were under the throne of the Mighty One were perturbed, when He was taking Moses to Himself. **4** For He showed him many admonitions together with the principles of the law and the consummation of the times, as also to you, and likewise the pattern of Zion and its measures, in the pattern of which the sanctuary of the present time was to be made. **5** But then He also showed to him the measures of the fire, also the depths of the abyss, and the weight of the winds, and the number of the drops of rain; **6** and the suppression of anger, and the multitude of long- suffering, and the truth of judgment; **7** and the root of wisdom, and the riches of understanding, and the fount of knowledge; **8** and the height of the air, and the greatness of Paradise, and the consummation of the ages, and the beginning of the Day of Judgment; **9** and the number of the offerings, and the earths which have not yet come; **10** and the mouth of Gehenna, and the station of vengeance, and the place of faith, and the region of hope; **11** and the likeness of future torment, and the multitude of innumerable messengers, and the flaming hosts, and the splendor of the lightnings, and the voice of the thunders, and the orders of the chiefs of the messengers, and the treasuries of light, and the changes of the times, and the investigations of the law. **12** These are the bright fourth waters which you have seen."

CHAPTER 60

1 "And the black fifth waters which you have seen raining are the works which the Amorites worked, and the spells of their incantations which they worked, and the wickedness of their mysteries, and the mingling of their pollution. **2** But even Israel was then polluted by sins in the days of the judges, though they saw many signs which were from Him who made them."

CHAPTER 61

1 "And the bright sixth waters which you saw, this is the time in which David and Solomon were born. **2** And there was at that time the building of Zion, And the dedication of the sanctuary, And the shedding of much blood of the nations that sinned then, And many offerings which were offered then in the dedication of the sanctuary. **3** And peace and tranquility existed at that time, **4** And wisdom was heard in the assembly; And the riches of understanding were magnified in the congregations, **5** And the holy festivals were fulfilled in blessedness and in much joy. **6** And the judgment of the rulers was then seen to be without guile, And the righteousness of the precepts of the Mighty One was accomplished with truth. **7** And the land [which] was then beloved by the LORD , And because its inhabitants did not sin, it was glorified beyond all lands, And the city Zion ruled then over all lands and regions. **8** These are the bright waters which you have seen."

CHAPTER 62

1 "And the black seventh waters which you have seen, this is the perversion [brought about] by the counsel of Jeroboam, who took counsel to make two calves of gold; **2** and all the iniquities which kings who were after him iniquitously worked. **3** And the curse of Jezebel and the worship of idols which Israel practiced at that time. **4** And the withholding of rain, and the famines which occurred until women ate the fruit of their wombs. **5** And the time of their captivity which came on the nine and a half tribes, because they were in many sins. **6** And Shalmanezzar king of Assyria came and led them away captive. **7** But regarding the nations, it is tedious to tell how they always worked impiety and wickedness, and never worked righteousness. **8** These are the black seventh waters which you have seen."

CHAPTER 63

1 "And the bright eighth waters which you have seen, this is the rectitude and uprightness of Hezekiah king of Judah, and the grace [of God] which came on him **2** when Sennacherib was stirred up in order that he might perish, and his wrath troubled him in order that he might thereby perish, for the multitude also of the nations which were with him. **3** When, moreover, Hezekiah the king heard those things which the king of Assyria was devising, to come and seize him and destroy his people—the two and a half tribes which remained—moreover, that he wished to overthrow Zion also, Hezekiah then trusted in his works, and had hope in his righteousness, and spoke with the Mighty One and said, **4** For behold, Sennacherib is prepared to destroy us, and he will be boastful and uplifted when he has destroyed Zion." **5** And the Mighty One heard him, for Hezekiah was wise, and He had respect to his prayer, because he was righteous. **6** And thereon the Mighty One commanded His messenger Ramiel who speaks with you. **7** And I went forth and destroyed their multitude, the number of whose chiefs alone was one hundred and eighty-five thousand, and each one of them had an equal number [at his command]. **8** And at that time I burned their bodies within, but their raiment and arms I preserved outwardly, in order that the still more wonderful deeds of the Mighty One might appear, and that His Name might thereby be spoken of throughout the whole earth. **9** And Zion was saved and Jerusalem delivered: Israel was also freed from tribulation. **10** And all those who were in the holy land rejoiced, and the Name of the Mighty One was glorified so that it was spoken of. **11** These are the bright waters which you have seen."

CHAPTER 64

1 "And the black ninth waters which you have seen, this is all the wickedness which was in the days of Manasseh the son of Hezekiah. **2** For he worked much impiety, and he slew the righteous, and he wrested judgment, and he shed the blood of the innocent, and he violently polluted wedded women, and he overturned the altars, and destroyed their offerings, and drove forth their priests lest they should minister in the sanctuary. **3** And he made an image with five faces: four of them looked to the four winds, and the fifth on the summit of the image as an adversary of the zeal of the Mighty One. **4** And then wrath went forth from the presence of the Mighty One to the intent that Zion should be rooted out, as also it befell in your days. But also, against the two and a half tribes went forth a decree that they should also be led away captive, as you have now seen. **5** And the impiety of Manasseh increased to such a degree that it removed the praise of the Most High from the sanctuary. **7** On this account Manasseh was at that time named the impious, and finally his abode was in the fire. **8** For though his prayer was heard with the Most High, finally, when he was cast into the brazen horse and the brazen horse was melted, it served as a sign to him for the hour. **9** For he had not lived perfectly, for he was not worthy— but that from then on he might know by whom finally he should be tormented. **10** For he who is able to benefit is also able to torment."

CHAPTER 65

1 "Thus, moreover, Manasseh acted impiously, and thought that in his time the Mighty One would not inquire into these things. **2** These are the black ninth waters which you have seen."

CHAPTER 66

1 "And the bright tenth waters which you have seen: this is the purity of the generations of Josiah king of Judah, who was the only one at the time who submitted himself to the Mighty One with all his heart and with all his soul. **2** And he cleansed the land from idols, and hallowed all the vessels which had been polluted, and restored the offerings to the altar, and raised the horn of the holy, and exalted the righteous, and honored all that were wise in understanding, and brought back the priests to their ministry, and destroyed and removed the magicians, and enchanters, and necromancers from the land. **3** And not only did he slay the impious that were living, but they also took from the graves the bones of the dead and burned them with fire. **4** [[And the festivals and the Sabbaths he established in their sanctity]] , and their polluted ones he burned in the fire, and the lying prophets which deceived the people, these he also burned in the fire, and the people who listened to them when they were living, he cast them into the Brook of Kidron, and heaped stones on them. **5** And he was zealous with zeal for the Mighty One with all his soul, and he alone was firm in the law at that time, so that he left none that was uncircumcised, or that worked impiety in all the land, all the days of his life. **6** Therefore he will receive a continuous reward, and he will be glorified with the Mighty One beyond many at a later time. **7** For on his account and on account of those who are like him were the honorable glories, of which you were told before, created and prepared. These are the bright waters which you have seen."

CHAPTER 67

1 "And the black eleventh waters which you have seen: this is the calamity which is now befalling Zion. **2** Do you think that there is no anguish to the messengers in the presence of the Mighty One, that Zion was so delivered up, and that, behold, the nations boast in their hearts, and assemble before their idols and say, She is trodden down who oftentimes trod down, and she has been reduced to servitude who reduced [other nations to servitude]? **3** Do you think that in these things the Most High rejoices, or that His Name is glorified? **4** [[But how will it serve toward His righteous judgment?]] **5** Yet after these things the dispersed among the nations will be taken hold of by tribulation, and in shame they will dwell in every place. **6** Because so far as Zion is delivered up and Jerusalem laid waste, idols will prosper in the cities of the nations, and the vapor of the smoke of the incense of the righteousness which is by the law is extinguished in Zion; and in the region of Zion in every place, behold, there is the smoke of impiety. **7** But the king of Babylon will arise who has now destroyed Zion, and he will boast over the people, and he will speak great things in his heart in the presence of the Most High. **8** But he will also fall at last. These are the black waters."

CHAPTER 68

1 "And the bright twelfth waters which you have seen: this is the word. For after these things, a time will come when your people will fall into distress, so that they will all run the risk of perishing together. **3** Nevertheless, they will be saved, and their enemies will fall in their presence. **4** And they will have in [due] time much joy. **5** And at that time, after a short interval, Zion will again be rebuilt, and its offerings will again be restored, and the priests will return to their ministry, and also the nations will come to glorify it. **6** Nevertheless, not fully as in the beginning. **7** But it will come to pass after these things that there will be the fall of many nations. **8** These are the bright waters which you have seen."

CHAPTER 69

1 "For the last waters which you have seen which were darker than all that were before them, those which were after the twelfth number, which were collected together, belong to the whole world. **2** For the Most High made division from the beginning, because He alone knows what will befall. **3** For as to the enormities and the impieties which should be worked before Him, He foresaw six kinds of them. **4** And of the good works of the righteous which should be accomplished before Him, He foresaw six kinds of them, beyond those which He should work at the consummation of the age. **5** On his account there were not black waters with black, nor bright with bright; for it is the consummation."

CHAPTER 70

1 "Therefore hear the interpretation of the last black waters which are to come: this [is] the word. **2** Behold ! The days come, and it will be when the time of the age has ripened, And the harvest of its evil and good seeds has come, That the Mighty One will bring on the earth and its inhabitants and on its rulers Perturbation of spirit and stupor of heart. **3** And they will hate one another, And provoke one another to fight, And the mean will rule over the honorable, And those of low degree will be extolled above the famous. **4** And the many will be delivered into the hands of the few, And those who were nothing will rule over the strong, And the poor will have abundance beyond the rich, And the impious will exalt themselves above the heroic. **5** And the wise will be silent, And the foolish will speak, Neither will the thought of men be then confirmed, Nor the counsel of the mighty, Nor will the hope of those who hope be confirmed. **6** And when those things which were predicted have come to pass, Then confusion will fall on all men, And some of them will fall in battle, And some of them will perish in anguish, **7** And some of them will be destroyed by their own. Then the peoples of the Most High, whom He has prepared before, Will come and make war with the leaders that will then be left. **8** And it will come to pass that whoever gets safe out of the war will die in the earthquake, And whoever gets safe out of the earthquake will be burned by the fire, And whoever gets safe out of the fire will be destroyed by famine. **9** [[And it will come to pass that whoever of the victors and the vanquished gets safe out of and escapes all these things previously mentioned will be delivered into the hands of My servant Messiah.]] **10** For all the earth will devour its inhabitants."

CHAPTER 71

1 "And the holy land will have mercy on its own, and it will protect its inhabitants at that time. **2** This is the vision which you have seen, and this is the interpretation. **3** For I have come to tell you these things, because your prayer has been heard with the Most High."

CHAPTER 72

1 "Now also hear regarding the bright lightning which is to come at the consummation after these black [waters]: this is the word. **2** After the signs have come of which you were told before, when the nations become turbulent, and the time of My Messiah is come, He will both summon all the nations, and some of them He will spare, and some of them He will slay. **3** Therefore these things will come on the nations which are to be spared by Him. **4** Every nation which does not know Israel and has not trodden down the seed of Jacob, will indeed be spared. **5** And this because some out of every nation will be subjected to your people. **6** But all those who have ruled over you, or have known you, will be given up to the sword."

CHAPTER 73

1 "And it will come to pass, when He has brought low everything that is in the world, And has sat down in peace for the age on the throne of His kingdom, That joy will then be revealed, And rest will appear. **2** And then healing will descend in dew, And disease will withdraw, And anxiety, and anguish, and lamentation will pass from among men, And gladness will proceed through the whole earth. **3** And no one will die untimely again, Nor will any adversity suddenly befall. **4** And judgments, and abusive talk, and contentions, and revenges, And blood, and passions, and envy, and hatred, And whatever things are like these will go into condemnation when they are removed. **5** For it is these very things which have filled this world with evils, And on account of these the life of man has been greatly troubled. **6** And wild beasts will come from the forest and minister to men And asps and dragons will come forth from their holes to submit themselves to a little child. **7** And women will no longer then have pain when they bear, Nor will they suffer torment when they yield the fruit of the womb."

CHAPTER 74

1 "And it will come to pass in those days that the reapers will not grow weary, Nor those that build be toil-worn; For the works will of themselves speedily advance Together with those who do them in much tranquility. **2** For that time is the consummation of that which is corruptible, And the beginning of that which is not corruptible. **3** Therefore those things which were predicted will belong to it: Therefore, it is far away from evils, and near to those things which do not die. **4** This is the bright lightning which came after the last dark waters."

CHAPTER 75

1 And I answered and said, "Who can understand, O LORD , Your goodness? For it is incomprehensible. **2** Or who can search into Your compassions, Which are infinite? **3** Or who can comprehend Your intelligence? **4** Or who is able to recount the thoughts of Your mind? **5** Or who of those who are born can hope to come to those things, Unless he is one to whom You are merciful and gracious? **6** Because, assuredly, if You did not have compassion on man, Those who are under Your right hand, They could not come to those things, But those who are in the numbers named can be called. **7**

But if, indeed, we who exist know why we have come, And submit ourselves to Him who brought us out of Egypt, We will come again and remember those things which have passed, And will rejoice regarding that which has been. **8** But if now we do not know why we have come, And do not recognize the principate of Him who brought us up out of Egypt, We will come again and seek after those things which have been now, And be grieved with pain because of those things which have befallen."

CHAPTER 76

1 And He answered and said to me: " ‖ Inasmuch as the revelation of this vision has been interpreted to you as you requested ‖ , hear the word of the Most High that you may know what is to befall you after these things. **2** For you will surely depart from this earth, nevertheless not to death, but you will be preserved to the consummation of the times. **3** Therefore go up to the top of that mountain, and there will pass before you all the regions of that land, and the figure of the inhabited world, and the top of the mountains, and the depth of the valleys, and the depths of the seas, and the number of the rivers, that you may see what you are leaving, and to where you are going. **4** Now this will befall after forty days. Therefore, go now during these days and instruct the people so far as you are able, that they may learn so as not to die at the last time, but may learn in order that they may live at the last times."

CHAPTER 77

1 And I, Baruch, went there and came to the people, and assembled them together from the greatest to the least, and said to them: **2** "Hear, you sons of Israel, behold how many you are who remain of the twelve tribes of Israel. **3** For to you and to your fathers the LORD gave a law more excellent than to all peoples. **4** And because your brothers transgressed the commandments of the Most High, He brought vengeance on you and on them, And He did not spare the former, And the latter He also gave into captivity: And He did not leave a residue of them, **5** But behold ! Y ou are here with me. **6** If, therefore, you direct your ways correctly, You also will not depart as your brothers departed, But they will come to you. **7** For He is merciful whom you worship, And He is gracious in whom you hope, And He is true, so that He will do good and not evil. **8** Have you not seen here what has befallen Zion? **9** Or do you perhaps think that the place had sinned, And that on this account it was overthrown? Or that the land had worked foolishness, And that therefore it was delivered up? **10** And do you not know that on account of you who sinned, That which did not sin was overthrown, And, on account of those who worked wickedly, That which did not work foolishness was delivered up to enemies?" **11** And the whole people answered and said to me: "So far as we can recall the good things which the Mighty One has done to us, we do recall them; and those things which we do not remember He in His mercy knows. **12** Nevertheless, do this for us your people: also write to our brothers in Babylon a letter of doctrine and a scroll of hope, that you may confirm them also before you depart from us. **13** For the shepherds of Israel have perished, And the lamps which gave light are extinguished, And the fountains have withheld their stream from which we used to drink. **14** And we are left in the darkness, And amid the trees of the forest, And the thirst of the wilderness." **15** And I answered and said to them: "Shepherds, and lamps, and fountains come from the law: And though we depart, yet the law abides. **16** If, therefore, you have respect to the law, And are intent on wisdom, A lamp will not be wanting, And a shepherd will not fail, And a fountain will not dry up. **17** Nevertheless, as you said to me, I will also write to your brothers in Babylon, and I will send by means of men, and I will write in like manner to the nine and a half tribes, and send by means of a bird." **18** And it came to pass on the twenty-first day in the eighth month that I, Baruch, came and sat down under the oak under the shadow of the branches, and no man was with me, but I was alone. **19** And I wrote these two letters: one I sent by an eagle to the nine and a half tribes; and the other I sent to those that were at Babylon by means of three men. **20** And I called the eagle and spoke these words to it: **21** "The Most High has made you that you should be higher than all birds. **22** And now go and do not tarry in [any] place, nor enter a nest, nor settle on any tree, until you have passed over the breadth of the many waters of the Euphrates River, and have gone to the people that dwell there, and cast down this letter to them. **23** Remember, moreover, that, at the time of the deluge, Noah received from a dove the fruit of the olive, when he sent it forth from the Ark. **24** Yes, also the ravens ministered to Elijah, bearing him food, as they had been commanded. **25** Solomon also, in the time of his kingdom, wherever he wished to send or seek for anything, commanded a bird, and it obeyed him as he commanded it. **26** And now, do not let it weary you, and do not turn to the right hand nor the left, but fly and go by a direct way, that you may preserve the command of the Mighty One, according as I spoke to you."

THE EPISTLE OF BARUCH, THE SON OF NERIAH, WHICH HE WROTE TO THE NINE AND A HALF TRIBES

CHAPTER 78

1 These are the words of that letter which Baruch the son of Neriah sent to the nine and a half tribes, which were across the River Euphrates, in which these things were written. **2** Thus says Baruch the son of Neriah to the brothers carried into captivity: "Mercy and peace." I bear in mind, my brothers, the love of Him who created us, who loved us from of old, and never hated us, but above all educated us. **3** And truly I know, that behold, all of us—the twelve tribes—are bound by one bond, inasmuch as we are born from one father. **4** For what reason I have been more careful to leave you the words of this letter before I die, that you may be comforted regarding the calamities which have come on you, and that you may also be grieved regarding the evil that has befallen your brothers; and again, also, that you may justify His judgment which **5** He has decreed against you that you should be carried away captive—for what you have suffered is disproportioned to what you have done—in order that, at the last times, you may be found worthy of your fathers. **6** Therefore, if you consider that you have now suffered those things for your good, that you may not finally be condemned and tormented, then you will receive continuous hope; if above all you destroy from your heart vain error, on account of which you departed hence. **7** For if you so do these things, He will continually remember you, He who always promised on our behalf to those who were more excellent than we, that He will never forget or forsake us, but with much mercy will again gather together those who were dispersed.

CHAPTER 79

1 Now, my brothers, first learn what befell Zion: how that Nebuchadnezzar king of Babylon came up against us. **2** For we have sinned against Him who made us, and we have not kept the commandments which He commanded us, yet He has not disciplined us as we deserved. **3** For what befell you we also suffer in a preeminent degree, for it befell us also.

CHAPTER 80

1 And now, my brothers, I make known to you that when the enemy had surrounded the city, the messengers of the Most High were sent, and they overthrew the fortifications of the strong wall, and they destroyed the firm iron corners, which could not be rooted out. **2** Nevertheless, they hid all the vessels of the sanctuary, lest the enemy should get possession of them. **3** And when they had done these things, they delivered thereon to the enemy the overthrown wall, and the plundered house, and the burnt temple, and the people who were overcome because they were delivered up, lest the enemy should boast and say: "Thus by force we have been able to lay waste even the house of the Most High in war." They have also bound your brothers and led [them] away to Babylon, and have caused them to dwell there. **5** But we have been left here, being very few. **6** This is the tribulation about which I wrote to you. **7** For assuredly I know that [the consolation of] the inhabitants of Zion consoles you; so far as you knew that it was prospered, [your consolation] was greater than the tribulation which you endured in having to depart from it.

CHAPTER 81

1 But regarding consolation, hear the word. **2** For I was mourning regarding Zion, and I prayed for mercy from the Most High, and I said, **3** "How long will these things endure for us? And will these calamities always come on us?" **4** And the Mighty One did according to the multitude of His mercies, And the Most High according to the greatness of His compassion, And He revealed to me the word, that I might receive consolation, And He showed me visions that I should not again endure anguish, And He made known to me the mystery of the times, And He showed me the advent of the hours.

CHAPTER 82

1 Therefore, my brothers, I have written to you that you may comfort yourselves regarding the multitude of your tribulations. **2** For know that our Maker will assuredly avenge us on all our enemies, according to all that they have done to us, also that the consummation which the Most High will make is very near, and His mercy that is coming, and the consummation of His judgment, is by no means far off. **3** For behold, we see now the multitude of the prosperity of the nations, Though they act impiously, But they will be like a vapor: **4** And we behold the multitude of their power, Though they do wickedly, But they will be made like to a drop: **5** And we see the firmness of their might, Though they resist the Mighty One every hour, But they will be accounted as spittle. **6** And we consider the glory of their greatness, Though they do not keep the statutes of the Most High, But they will pass away as smoke. **7** And we meditate on the beauty of their gracefulness, Though they have to do with pollutions, But as grass that withers, they will fade away. **8** And we consider the strength of their cruelty, Though they do not remember the end, But as a wave that passes, they will be broken. **9** And we remark [regarding] the boastfulness of their might, Though they deny the beneficence of God, who gave [it] to them, But they will pass away as a passing cloud.

CHAPTER 83

1 For the Most High will assuredly hasten His times, And He will assuredly bring on His hours. **2** And He will assuredly judge those who are in His world, And will visit in truth all things by means of all their hidden works. **3** And He will assuredly examine the secret thoughts, And that which is laid up in the secret chambers of all the members of mail, And will make manifest in the presence of all with reproof. **4** Let none therefore of these present things ascend into your hearts, but above all let us be expectant, because that which is promised to us will come. **5** And let us not now look to the delights of the nations in the present, but let us remember what has been promised to us in the end. **6** For the ends of the times, and of the seasons, and whatever is with them will assuredly pass by together. **7** Moreover, the consummation of the age will then show the great might of its ruler, when all things come to judgment. **8** Therefore, prepare your hearts for that which before you believed, lest you come to be in bondage in both worlds, so that you be led away captive here and be tormented there. **9** For that which exists now, or which has passed away, or which is to come, in all these things, neither is the evil fully evil, nor again the good fully good. **10** For all healthinesses of this time are turning into diseases, **11** And all might of this time is turning into weakness, And all the force of this time is turning into impotence, **12** And every energy of youth is turning into old age and consummation. And every beauty of gracefulness of this time is turning faded and hateful, **13** And every proud dominion of the present is turning into humiliation and shame, **14** And every praise of the glory of this time is turning into the shame of silence, And every vain splendor and insolence of this time is turning into voiceless ruin. **15** And every delight and joy of this time is turning to worms and corruption, **16** And every clamor of the pride of this time is turning into dust and stillness. **17** And every possession of riches of this time is being turned into Sheol alone, **18** And all the plunder of passion of this time is turning into involuntary death, And every passion of the lusts of this time is turning into a judgment of torment. **19** And every artifice and craftiness of this time is turning into a proof of the truth, **20** And every sweetness of ointments of this time is turning into judgment and condemnation, **21** And every love of lying is turning to insult through truth. [[**22** Since therefore all these things are done now, does anyone think that they will not be avenged? But the consummation of all things will come to the truth.]]

CHAPTER 84

1 Behold! I have therefore made known to you [these things] while I live, for I have said [it] that you should learn the things that are excellent; for the Mighty One has commanded me to instruct you: and I will set before you some of the commandments of His judgment before I die. **2** Remember that formerly Moses assuredly called the heavens and earth to witness against you and said, "If you transgress the law you will be dispersed, but if you keep it you will be kept." **3** And other things he also used to say to you when you, the twelve tribes, were together in the desert. **4** And after his death you cast them away from you. On this account there came on you what had been predicted. **5** And now Moses used to tell you before they befell you, and behold, they have befallen you, for you have forsaken the law. **6** Behold, I also say to you after you have suffered, that if you obey those things which have been said to you, you will receive from the Mighty One whatever has been laid up and reserved for you. **7** Moreover, let this letter be for a testimony between me and you, that you may remember the commandments of the Mighty One, and that there may also be a defense for me in the presence of Him who sent me. **8** And remember the law and Zion, and the holy land and your brothers, and the covenant of your fathers, and do not forget the festivals and the Sabbaths. And deliver this letter and the traditions of the law to your sons after you, as your fathers also delivered [them] to you. **10** And at all times make request perseveringly and pray diligently with your whole heart that the Mighty One may be reconciled to you, and that He may not reckon the multitude of your sins, but remember the rectitude of your fathers. **11** For if He does not judge us according to the multitude of His mercies, woe to all of us who are born.

CHAPTER 85

1 Know, moreover, that in former times and in the generations of old our fathers had helpers, righteous men and holy prophets, [but] no longer. **2** We were in our own land, [[and they helped us when we sinned]] , and they prayed for us to Him who made us, because they trusted in their works, and the Mighty One heard their prayer and was gracious to us. **3** But now the righteous have been gathered and the prophets have fallen asleep, and we have also gone forth from the land, and Zion has been taken from us, and we have nothing now except the Mighty One and His law. **4** If, therefore, we direct and dispose our hearts, we will receive everything that we lost, and much better things than we lost by many times. **5** For what we have lost was to corruption, and what we will receive will not be corruptible. [[**6** Moreover, I also have written thus to our brothers to Babylon, that I also may attest to them those very things.]] **7** And let all those things previously mentioned always be before your eyes, because we are still in the spirit and the power of our liberty. **8** Again, moreover, the Most High is also long- suffering toward us here, and He has shown to us that which is to be, and has not concealed from us what will befall in the end. **9** Therefore, before judgment exacts its own, and truth that which is its due, let us prepare our soul that we may enter into possession of, and not be taken possession of, and that we may hope and not be put to shame, and that we may rest with our fathers and not be tormented with our enemies. **10** And the strength of the creation is already exhausted, and the advent of the times is very short, yes, they have passed by; and the pitcher is near to the cistern, and the ship to the port, and the course of the journey to the city, and life to consummation. **11** And again prepare your souls, so that when you sail and ascend from the ship you may have rest and not be condemned when you depart. **12** For behold, when the Most High will bring to pass all these things, there will not again be there an opportunity for returning, nor a limit to the times, nor adjournment to the hours, nor change of ways, nor place for prayer, nor sending of petitions, nor receiving of knowledge, nor giving of love, nor place of conversion, nor supplication for offenses, nor intercession of the fathers, nor prayer of the prophets, nor help of the righteous. **13** There, there, is the sentence of corruption, the way of fire, and the path which brings to Gehenna. **14** On this account there is one law by one, one age and an end for all who are in it. **15** Then He will preserve those to whom He finds He may be gracious, and at the same time destroy those who are polluted with sins.

CHAPTER 86

1 When you therefore receive this—my letter—read it in your congregations with care. **2** And meditate thereon, above all on the days of your fasts. **3** And bear me in mind by means of this letter, as I also bear you in mind in it, and always farewell.

CHAPTER 87

1 And it came to pass when I had ended all the words of this letter, and had written it sedulously to its close, **2** that I folded it, and sealed it carefully, and bound it to the neck of the eagle, and dismissed and sent it. Here ends the Scroll of Baruch, the son of Neriah.

3 BARUCH

CHAPTER 1

1 Truly I, Baruch, was weeping in my mind and sorrowing on account of the people, and that Nebuchadnezzar the king was permitted by God to destroy His city, saying, **2** "Lord, why did You set Your vineyard on fire, and lay it waste? Why did You do this? And why, Lord, did You not repay us with another discipline, but delivered us to nations such as these, so that they reproach us and say, Where is their God?" **3** And behold, as I was weeping and saying such things, I saw a messenger of the LORD coming and saying to me, "Understand, O man, greatly beloved, and do not trouble yourself so greatly concerning the salvation of Jerusalem, for thus says the LORD God, the Almighty. **4** For He sent me before you, to make known and to show to you all [the things] of God. **5** For your prayer was heard before Him, and entered into the ears of the LORD God." **6** And when he had said these things to me, I was silent. **7** And the messenger said to me, "Cease to provoke God, and I will show you other mysteries, greater than these." And I Baruch said, "As the LORD God lives, if you will show me, and I hear a word of yours, I will not continue to speak any longer. 8 God will add to my judgment in the Day of Judgment, if I speak hereafter." And the messenger of the powers said to me, "Come, and I will show you the mysteries of God."

CHAPTER 2

1 And he took me and led me where the expanse has been set fast, and where there was a river which no one can cross, nor any strange breeze of all those which God created. 2 And he took me and led me to the first heaven and showed me a door of great size. 3 And he said to me, "Let us enter through it," and we entered as though borne on wings, a distance of about thirty days' journey. And he showed me a plain within the heaven; and there were men dwelling thereon, with the faces of oxen, and the horns of stags, and the feet of goats, and the haunches of lambs. 4 And I, Baruch, asked the messenger, "Make known to me, please, what is the thickness of the heaven in which we journeyed, or what is its extent, or what is the plain, in order that I may also tell the sons of men?" 5 And the messenger whose name is Phamael said to me, "This door which you see is the door of Heaven, and as great as is the distance from earth to Heaven, so great also is its thickness; and again as great as is the distance || from north to south, so great || is the length of the plain which you saw." 6 And again the messenger of the powers said to me, "Come, and I will show you greater mysteries." 7 But I said, "Please show me what these men are." And he said to me, "These are they who built the tower of strife against God, and the LORD banished them."

CHAPTER 3

1 And the messenger of the LORD took me and led me to [the] second heaven. 2 And he also showed me a door there like the first and said, "Let us enter through it." 3 And we entered, being borne on wings a distance of about sixty days' journey. 4 And he also showed me a plain there, and it was full of men, whose appearance was like that of dogs, and whose feet were like those of stags. 5 And I asked the messenger: "Please, Lord, tell me who these are." 6 And he said, "These are they who gave counsel to build the tower, for they whom you see drove forth multitudes of both men and women to make bricks; among whom, a woman making bricks was not allowed to be released in the hour of child-birth, but brought forth while she was making bricks, and carried her child in her apron, and continued to make bricks. 7 And the LORD appeared to them and confused their speech, when they had built the tower to the height of four hundred and sixty-three cubits. 8 And they took a gimlet, and sought to pierce the heaven, saying, Let us see [whether] the heaven is made of clay, or of brass, or of iron. 9 When God saw this, He did not permit them, but struck them with blindness and confusion of speech, and rendered them as you see."

CHAPTER 4

1 And I, Baruch, said, "Behold, Lord, you showed me great and wonderful things; and now show me all things for the sake of the LORD ." 2 And the messenger said to me, "Come, let us proceed." 3 [And I proceeded] with the messenger from that place about one hundred and eighty-five days' journey. 4 And he showed me a plain and a serpent, which appeared to be two hundred plethra in length. And he showed me Hades, and its appearance was dark and abominable. 5 And I said, "Who is this dragon, and who is this monster around him?" 6 And the messenger said, "The dragon is he who eats the bodies of those who spend their life wickedly, and he is nourished by them. And this is Hades, which itself also closely resembles him, in that it also drinks about a cubit from the sea, which does not sink at all." 7 Baruch said, "And how?" And the messenger said, "Listen, the LORD God made three hundred and sixty rivers, of which the chief of all are Alphias, Abyrus, and the Gericus; and because of these the sea does not sink." 8 And I said, "Please show me which is the tree which led Adam astray." And the messenger said to me, "It is the vine, which the messenger Sammael planted, at which the LORD God was angry, and He cursed him and his plant, while also on this account He did not permit Adam to touch it, and therefore the Devil being envious deceived him through his vine." || 9 And I, Baruch, said, "Since also the vine has been the cause of such great evil, and is under judgment of the curse of God, and was the destruction of the first created, how is it now so useful?" And the messenger said, "You ask correctly. 10 When God caused the deluge on earth, and destroyed all flesh, and four hundred and nine thousand giants, and the water rose fifteen cubits above the highest mountains, then the water entered into Paradise and destroyed every flower; but it wholly removed the shoot of the vine outside the bounds and cast it outside. 11 And when the earth appeared out of the water, and Noah came out of the Ark, he began to plant of the plants which he found. But he also found the shoot of the vine; and he took it, and was reasoning in himself, What then is it? 12 And I came and spoke to him the things concerning it. And he said, Will I plant it, or what will I do? 13 Since Adam was destroyed because of it, let me not also meet with the anger of God because of it. 14 And saying these things he prayed that God would reveal to him what he should do concerning it. 15 And when he had completed the prayer which lasted forty days, and having implored many things and wept, he said, Lord, I entreat You to reveal to me what I will do concerning this plant. But God sent His messenger Sarasael, and said to him, Arise, Noah, and plant the shoot of the vine, for thus says the LORD : Its bitterness will be changed into sweetness, and its curse will become a blessing, and that which is produced from it will become the blood of God; and as through it the human race obtained condemnation, so again through Jesus Christ, the Immanuel, they will receive in Him the upward calling, and the entry into Paradise. || 16 Know therefore, O Baruch, that as Adam through this very tree obtained condemnation, and was divested of the glory of God, so also the men who now drink insatiably the wine which is begotten of it, transgress worse than Adam, and are far from the glory of God, and are surrendering themselves to the continuous fire. 17 For [no] good comes through it. For those who drink it to excess do these things: neither does a brother pity his brother, nor a father his son, nor children their parents, but from the drinking of wine come all evils, such as murders, adulteries, fornications, perjuries, thefts, and such like. And nothing good is established by it."

CHAPTER 5

1 And I, Baruch, said to the messenger, "Let me ask you one thing, Lord. **2** Since you said to me that the dragon drinks one cubit out of the sea, say to me also, how great is his belly?" **3** And the messenger said, "His belly is Hades; and as far as a plummet is thrown [by] three hundred men, so great is his belly. Come, then, that I may show you also greater works than these."

CHAPTER 6

1 And he took me and led me where the sun goes forth; **2** and he showed me a chariot and four, under which burned a fire, and in the chariot was sitting a man, wearing a crown of fire, [and] the chariot [was] drawn by forty messengers. **3** And behold, a bird circling before the sun, about nine cubits away. **4** And I said to the messenger, "What is this bird?" And he said to me, "This is the guardian of the earth." **5** And I said, "Lord, how is he the guardian of the earth? Teach me." **6** And the messenger said to me, "This bird flies alongside of the sun, and expanding his wings, receives its fiery rays. For if he were not receiving them, the human race would not be preserved, nor any other living creature. **7** But God appointed this bird to that." And he expanded his wings, and I saw on his right wing very large letters, as large as the space of a threshing-floor, the size of about four thousand modii; and the letters were of gold. **8** And the messenger said to me, "Read them." **9** And I read, and they ran thus: NEITHER EARTH NOR HEAVEN BRING ME FORTH, BUT WINGS OF FIRE BRING ME FORTH . **10** And I said, "Lord, what is this bird, and what is his name?" **11** And the messenger said to me, "His name is called Phoenix." [And I said,] "And what does he eat?" And he said to me, "The manna of Heaven and the dew of earth." **12** And I said, "Does the bird excrete?" And he said to me, "He excretes a worm, and the excrement of the worm is cinnamon, which kings and princes use. **13** But wait and you will see the glory of God." And while he was conversing with me, there was as a thunderclap, and the place was shaken on which we were standing. **14** And I asked the messenger, "My Lord, what is this sound?" And the messenger said to me, "Even now the messengers are opening the three hundred and sixty-five gates of Heaven, and the light is being separated from the darkness." **15** And a voice came which said, "Light giver, give to the world radiance." **16** And when I heard the noise of the bird, I said, "Lord, what is this noise?" **17** And he said, "This is the bird who awakens from slumber the cocks on earth. For as men do through the mouth, so also does the cock signify to those in the world, in his own speech. For the sun is made ready by the messengers, and the cock crows."

CHAPTER 7

1 And I said, "And where does the sun begin its labors, after the cock crows?" **2** And the messenger said to me, "Listen, Baruch: all things, whatever I showed you, are in the first and second heaven, and in the third heaven the sun passes through and gives light to the world. But wait, and you will see the glory of God." **3** And while I was conversing with him, I saw the bird, and he appeared in front, and grew less and less, and at length returned to his full size. **4** And behind him I saw the shining sun, and the messengers which draw it, and a crown on its head, the sight of which we were not able to gaze on and behold. **5** And as soon as the sun shone, the phoenix also stretched out his wings. **6** But I, when I beheld such great glory, was brought low with great fear, and I fled and hid in the wings of the messenger. **7** And the messenger said to me, "Do not fear, Baruch, but wait and you will also see their setting."

CHAPTER 8

1 And he took me and led me toward the west; and when the time of the setting came, I again saw the bird coming before it, and as soon as it came, I saw the messengers, and they lifted the crown from its head. **2** But the bird stood exhausted and with wings contracted. **3** And beholding these things, I said, "Lord, why did they lift the crown from the head of the sun, and why is the bird so exhausted?" **4** And the messenger said to me, "The crown of the sun, when it has run through the day, four messengers take it, and bear it up to Heaven, and renew it, because it and its rays have been defiled on earth; moreover, it is so renewed each day." **5** And I Baruch said, "Lord, and why are its beams defiled on earth?" **6** And the messenger said to me, "Because it beholds the lawlessness and unrighteousness of men, namely fornications, adulteries, thefts, extortions, idolatries, drunkenness, murders, strife, jealousies, evil-speakings, murmurings, whisperings, divinations, and such like [these], which are not well-pleasing to God. On account of these things is it defiled, and therefore is it renewed. **7** But you ask concerning the bird, how it is exhausted: because by restraining the rays of the sun through the fire and burning heat of the whole day, it is exhausted thereby. **8** For, as we said before, unless his wings were screening the rays of the sun, no living creature would be preserved."

CHAPTER 9

1 And they having retired, the night also fell, and at the same time the chariot of the moon came, along with the stars. **2** And I, Baruch, said, "Lord, show me it also, I implore of you, how it goes forth, where it departs, and in what form it moves along." **3** And the messenger said, "Wait and you will also see it shortly." And on the next day I also saw it in the form of a woman, and [she was] sitting on a wheeled chariot. And before it there were oxen and lambs in the chariot, and a multitude of messengers in like manner. **4** And I said, "Lord, what are the oxen and the lambs?" **5** And he said to me, "They are also messengers." And again I asked, "Why is it that it at one time increases, but at another time decreases?" **6** And [he said to me], "Listen, O Baruch: this which you see had been written by God beautiful as no other. **7** And at the transgression of the first Adam, it was near to Sammael when he took the serpent as a garment. **8** And it did not hide itself but increased, and God was angry with it, and afflicted it, and shortened its days." **9** And I said, "And how does it not also shine always, but only in the night?" **10** And the messenger said, "Listen: as in the presence of a king, the courtiers cannot speak freely, so the moon and the stars cannot shine in the presence of the sun; for the stars are always suspended, but they are screened by the sun, and the moon, although it is uninjured, is consumed by the heat of the sun."

CHAPTER 10

1 And when I had learned all these things from the chief-messenger, he took [me] and led me into [the] fourth heaven. **2** And I saw a monotonous plain, and in the middle of it a pool of water. **3** And there were multitudes of birds in it of all kinds, but not like those here on earth. **4** But I saw a crane as great as great oxen; and all the birds were great beyond those in the world. **5** And I asked the messenger, "What is the plain, and what the pool, and what the multitudes of birds around it?" **6** And the messenger said, "Listen, Baruch: the plain which contains the pool in it and other wonders is the place where the souls of the righteous come, when they hold converse, living together in choirs. **7** But the water is that which the clouds receive, and rain on the earth, and the fruits increase." **8** And I said again to the messenger of the LORD , "But [what] are these birds?" And he said to me, "They are those which continually sing praise to the LORD ." **9** And I said, "Lord, and how do men say that the water which descends in rain is from the sea?" **10** And the messenger said, "The water which descends in rain— this is also from the sea, and from the waters on earth; but that which stimulates the fruits is [only] from the latter source. **11** Know therefore, henceforth, that from this source is what is called the dew of Heaven."

CHAPTER 11

1 And the messenger took me and led me from there to [the] fifth heaven. And the gate was closed. **2** And I said, "Lord, is this gateway not open that we may enter?" And the messenger said to me, "We cannot enter until Michael comes, who holds the keys of the Kingdom of Heaven; but wait and you will see the glory of God." **3** And there was a great sound, as thunder. And I said, "Lord, what is this sound?" **4** And he said to me, "Even now Michael, the commander of the messengers, comes down to receive the prayers of men." **5** And behold a voice came, "Let the gates be opened." **6** And they opened them, and there was a roar as of thunder. **7** And Michael came, and the messenger who was with me came face to face with him and said, "Greetings, my commander, and that of all our order." **8** And the commander Michael said, "Greetings you also, our brother, and the interpreter of the revelations to those who pass through life virtuously." And having saluted one another thus, they stood still. **9** And I saw the commander Michael say, "Greetings you also, our brother, and the interpreter of the revelations to those who pass through life virtuously." **10** And having saluted one another thus, they stood still. And I saw the commander Michael, holding an exceedingly great vessel; its depth was as great as the distance from Heaven to earth, and its breadth as great as the distance from north to south. **11** And I said, "Lord, what is that which Michael the chief-messenger is holding?" **12** And he said to me, "This is where the merits of the righteous enter, and such good works as they do, which are escorted before the heavenly God."

CHAPTER 12

1 And as I was conversing with them, behold, messengers came bearing baskets full of flowers. **2** And they gave them to Michael. And I asked the messenger, "Lord, who are these, and what are the things brought here from beside them?" **3** And he said to me, "These are messengers [who] are over the righteous." **4** And the chief-messenger took the baskets and cast them into the vessel. **5** And the messenger said to me, "These flowers are the merits of the righteous." **6** And I saw other messengers bearing baskets which were [neither] empty nor full. **7** And they began to lament, and did not venture to draw near, because they did not have the prizes complete. **8** And Michael cried and said, "Come here, also, you messengers; bring what you have brought." And Michael was exceedingly grieved, and the messenger who was with me, because they did not fill the vessel.

CHAPTER 13

1 And then other messengers came in like manner, weeping and lamenting, and saying with fear, "Behold, how we are over-clouded, O Lord, for we were delivered to evil men, and we wish to depart from them." **2** And Michael said, "You cannot depart from them, in order that the enemy may not prevail to the end; but say to me what you ask." **3** And they said, "Please, Michael our commander, transfer us from them, for we cannot abide with wicked and foolish men, for there is nothing good in them, but every kind of unrighteousness and greed. **4** For we do not behold them entering [[into [the] assembly at all, nor among spiritual fathers, nor]] into any good work. **5** But where there is murder, there also are they in the midst, and where are fornications, adulteries, thefts, slanders, perjuries, jealousies, drunkenness, strife, envy, murmurings, whispering, idolatry, divination, and such like [these], then are they workers of such works, and of others worse. **6** For what reason we entreat that we may depart from them." **7** And Michael said to the messengers, "Wait until I learn from the LORD what will come to pass."

CHAPTER 14

1 And in that very hour Michael departed, and the doors were closed. **2** And there was a sound like thunder. And I asked the messenger, "What is the sound?" **3** And he said to me, "Michael is even now presenting the merits of men to God."

CHAPTER 15

1 And in that very hour Michael descended, and the gate was opened; and he brought oil. **2** And as for the messengers which brought the baskets which were full, he filled them with oil, saying, "Take it away, reward our friends a hundredfold, and those who have laboriously worked good works. For those who sowed virtuously, also reap virtuously." **3** And he also said to those bringing the half-empty baskets, "Come here you also; take away the reward according as you brought, and deliver it to the sons of men." [[**4** Then he also said to those who brought the full and to those who brought the half-empty baskets: "Go and bless our friends, and say to them that thus says the LORD , You are faithful over a few things, I will set you over many things; enter into the joy of your Lord."]]

CHAPTER 16

1 And turning, he also said to those who brought nothing: "Thus says the LORD , Do not be sad of countenance, and do not weep, nor leave the sons of men alone. **2** But since they angered Me in their works, go and make them envious and angry and provoked against a people that is no people, a people that has no understanding. **3** Further, besides these, send forth the caterpillar and the unwinged locust, and the mildew, and the common locust, [and] hail with lightnings and anger, and punish them severely with the sword and with death, and their children with demons. **4** For they did not listen to My voice, nor did they observe My commandments, nor do them, but were despisers of My commandments, and insolent toward the priests who proclaimed My words to them."

CHAPTER 17

1 And while he yet spoke, the door was closed, and we withdrew. **2** And the messenger took me and restored me to the place where I was at the beginning. **3** And having come to myself, I gave glory to God, who counted me worthy of such honor. **4** For what reason you also, brothers, who obtained such a revelation, yourselves also glorify God, so that He also may glorify you, now and ever, and to all eternity. Amen.

SUSANNA

Sus.1

[1] There dwelt a man in Babylon, called Joacim: [2] And he took a wife, whose name was Susanna, the daughter of Chelcias, a very fair woman, and one that feared the Lord. [3] Her parents also were righteous, and taught their daughter according to the law of Moses. [4] Now Joacim was a great rich man, and had a fair garden joining unto his house: and to him resorted the Jews; because he was more honourable than all others. [5] The same year were appointed two of the ancients of the people to be judges, such as the Lord spake of, that wickedness came from Babylon from ancient judges, who seemed to govern the people. [6] These kept much at Joacim's house: and all that had any suits in law came unto them. [7] Now when the people departed away at noon, Susanna went into her husband's garden to walk. [8] And the two elders saw her going in every day, and walking; so that their lust was inflamed toward her. [9] And they perverted their own mind, and turned away their eyes, that they might not look unto heaven, nor remember just judgments. [10] And albeit they both were wounded with her love, yet durst not one shew another his grief. [11] For they were ashamed to declare their lust, that they desired to have to do with her. [12] Yet they watched diligently from day to day to see her. [13] And the one said to the other, Let us now go home: for it is dinner time. [14] So when they were gone out, they parted the one from the other, and turning back again they came to the same place; and after that they had asked one another the cause, they acknowledged their lust: then appointed they a time both together, when they might find her alone. [15] And it fell out, as they watched a fit time, she went in as before with two maids only, and she was desirous to wash herself in the garden: for it was hot. [16] And there was no body there save the two elders, that had hid themselves, and watched her. [17] Then she said to her maids, Bring me oil and washing balls, and shut the garden doors, that I may wash me. [18] And they did as she bade them, and shut the garden doors, and went out themselves at privy doors to fetch the things that she had commanded them: but they saw not the elders, because they were hid. [19] Now when the maids were gone forth, the two elders rose up, and ran unto her, saying, [20] Behold, the garden doors are shut, that no man can see us, and we are in love with thee; therefore consent unto us, and lie with us. [21] If thou wilt not, we will bear witness against thee, that a young man was with thee: and therefore thou didst send away thy maids from thee. [22] Then Susanna sighed, and said, I am straitened on every side: for if I do this thing, it is death unto me: and if I do it not I cannot escape your hands. [23] It is better for me to fall into your hands, and not do it, than to sin in the sight of the Lord. [24] With that Susanna cried with a loud voice: and the two elders cried out against her. [25] Then ran the one, and opened the garden door. [26] So when the servants of the house heard the cry in the garden, they rushed in at the privy door, to see what was done unto her. [27] But when the elders had declared their matter, the servants were greatly ashamed: for there was never such a report made of Susanna. [28] And it came to pass the next day, when the people were assembled to her husband Joacim, the two elders came also full of mischievous imagination against Susanna to put her to death; [29] And said before the people, Send for Susanna, the daughter of Chelcias, Joacim's wife. And so they sent. [30] So she came with her father and mother, her children, and all her kindred. [31] Now Susanna was a very delicate woman, and beauteous to behold. [32] And these wicked men commanded to uncover her face, (for she was covered) that they might be filled with her beauty. [33] Therefore her friends and all that saw her wept. [34] Then the two elders stood up in the midst of the people, and laid their hands upon her head. [35] And she weeping looked up toward heaven: for her heart trusted in the Lord. [36] And the elders said, As we walked in the garden alone, this woman came in with two maids, and shut the garden doors, and sent the maids away. [37] Then a young man, who there was hid, came unto her, and lay with her. [38] Then we that stood in a corner of the garden, seeing this wickedness, ran unto them. [39] And when we saw them together, the man we could not hold: for he was stronger than we, and opened the door, and leaped out. [40] But having taken this woman, we asked who the young man was, but she would not tell us: these things do we testify. [41] Then the assembly believed them as those that were the elders and judges of the people: so they condemned her to death. [42] Then Susanna cried out with a loud voice, and said, O everlasting God, that knowest the secrets, and knowest all things before they be: [43] Thou knowest that they have borne false witness against me, and, behold, I must die; whereas I never did such things as these men have maliciously invented against me. [44] And the Lord heard her voice. [45] Therefore when she was led to be put to death, the Lord raised up the holy spirit of a young youth whose name was Daniel: [46] Who cried with a loud voice, I am clear from the blood of this woman. [47] Then all the people turned them toward him, and said, What mean these words that thou hast spoken? [48] So he standing in the midst of them said, Are ye such fools, ye

sons of Israel, that without examination or knowledge of the truth ye have condemned a daughter of Israel? [**49**] Return again to the place of judgment: for they have borne false witness against her. [**50**] Wherefore all the people turned again in haste, and the elders said unto him, Come, sit down among us, and shew it us, seeing God hath given thee the honour of an elder. [**51**] Then said Daniel unto them, Put these two aside one far from another, and I will examine them. [**52**] So when they were put asunder one from another, he called one of them, and said unto him, O thou that art waxen old in wickedness, now thy sins which thou hast committed aforetime are come to light. [**53**] For thou hast pronounced false judgment and hast condemned the innocent and hast let the guilty go free; albeit the Lord saith, The innocent and righteous shalt thou not slay. [**54**] Now then, if thou hast seen her, tell me, Under what tree sawest thou them companying together? Who answered, Under a mastick tree. [**55**] And Daniel said, Very well; thou hast lied against thine own head; for even now the angel of God hath received the sentence of God to cut thee in two. [**56**] So he put him aside, and commanded to bring the other, and said unto him, O thou seed of Chanaan, and not of Juda, beauty hath deceived thee, and lust hath perverted thine heart. [**57**] Thus have ye dealt with the daughters of Israel, and they for fear companied with you: but the daughter of Juda would not abide your wickedness. [**58**] Now therefore tell me, Under what tree didst thou take them companying together? Who answered, Under an holm tree. [**59**] Then said Daniel unto him, Well; thou hast also lied against thine own head: for the angel of God waiteth with the sword to cut thee in two, that he may destroy you. [**60**] With that all the assembly cried out with a loud voice, and praised God, who saveth them that trust in him. [**61**] And they arose against the two elders, for Daniel had convicted them of false witness by their own mouth: [**62**] And according to the law of Moses they did unto them in such sort as they maliciously intended to do to their neighbour: and they put them to death. Thus the innocent blood was saved the same day. [**63**] Therefore Chelcias and his wife praised God for their daughter Susanna, with Joacim her husband, and all the kindred, because there was no dishonesty found in her. [**64**] From that day forth was Daniel had in great reputation in the sight of the people.

THE LETTER OF JEREMIAH

Letter of Jer.1

[1] Because of the sins which ye have committed before God, ye shall be led away captives into Babylon by Nabuchodonosor king of the Babylonians. [2] So when ye be come unto Babylon, ye shall remain there many years, and for a long season, namely, seven generations: and after that I will bring you away peaceably from thence. [3] Now shall ye see in Babylon gods of silver, and of gold, and of wood, borne upon shoulders, which cause the nations to fear. [4] Beware therefore that ye in no wise be like to strangers, neither be ye and of them, when ye see the multitude before them and behind them, worshipping them. [5] But say ye in your hearts, O Lord, we must worship thee. [6] For mine angel is with you, and I myself caring for your souls. [7] As for their tongue, it is polished by the workman, and they themselves are gilded and laid over with silver; yet are they but false, and cannot speak. [8] And taking gold, as it were for a virgin that loveth to go gay, they make crowns for the heads of their gods. [9] Sometimes also the priests convey from their gods gold and silver, and bestow it upon themselves. [10] Yea, they will give thereof to the common harlots, and deck them as men with garments, [being] gods of silver, and gods of gold, and wood. [11] Yet cannot these gods save themselves from rust and moth, though they be covered with purple raiment. [12] They wipe their faces because of the dust of the temple, when there is much upon them. [13] And he that cannot put to death one that offendeth him holdeth a sceptre, as though he were a judge of the country. [14] He hath also in his right hand a dagger and an ax: but cannot deliver himself from war and thieves. [15] Whereby they are known not to be gods: therefore fear them not. [16] For like as a vessel that a man useth is nothing worth when it is broken; even so it is with their gods: when they be set up in the temple, their eyes be full of dust through the feet of them that come in. [17] And as the doors are made sure on every side upon him that offendeth the king, as being committed to suffer death: even so the priests make fast their temples with doors, with locks, and bars, lest their gods be spoiled with robbers. [18] They light them candles, yea, more than for themselves, whereof they cannot see one. [19] They are as one of the beams of the temple, yet they say their hearts are gnawed upon by things creeping out of the earth; and when they eat them and their clothes, they feel it not. [20] Their faces are blacked through the smoke that cometh out of the temple. [21] Upon their bodies and heads sit bats, swallows, and birds, and the cats also. [22] By this ye may know that they are no gods: therefore fear them not. [23] Notwithstanding the gold that is about them to make them beautiful, except they wipe off the rust, they will not shine: for neither when they were molten did they feel it. [24] The things wherein there is no breath are bought for a most high price. [25] They are borne upon shoulders, having no feet whereby they declare unto men that they be nothing worth. [26] They also that serve them are ashamed: for if they fall to the ground at any time, they cannot rise up again of themselves: neither, if one set them upright, can they move of themselves: neither, if they be bowed down, can they make themselves straight: but they set gifts before them as unto dead men. [27] As for the things that are sacrificed unto them, their priests sell and abuse; in like manner their wives lay up part thereof in salt; but unto the poor and impotent they give nothing of it. [28] Menstruous women and women in childbed eat their sacrifices: by these things ye may know that they are no gods: fear them not. [29] For how can they be called gods? because women set meat before the gods of silver, gold, and wood. [30] And the priests sit in their temples, having their clothes rent, and their heads and beards shaven, and nothing upon their heads. [31] They roar and cry before their gods, as men do at the feast when one is dead. [32] The priests also take off their garments, and clothe their wives and children. [33] Whether it be evil that one doeth unto them, or good, they are not able to recompense it: they can neither set up a king, nor put him down. [34] In like manner, they can neither give riches nor money: though a man make

a vow unto them, and keep it not, they will not require it. [35] They can save no man from death, neither deliver the weak from the mighty. [36] They cannot restore a blind man to his sight, nor help any man in his distress. [37] They can shew no mercy to the widow, nor do good to the fatherless. [38] Their gods of wood, and which are overlaid with gold and silver, are like the stones that be hewn out of the mountain: they that worship them shall be confounded. [39] How should a man then think and say that they are gods, when even the Chaldeans themselves dishonour them? [40] Who if they shall see one dumb that cannot speak, they bring him, and intreat Bel that he may speak, as though he were able to understand. [41] Yet they cannot understand this themselves, and leave them: for they have no knowledge. [42] The women also with cords about them, sitting in the ways, burn bran for perfume: but if any of them, drawn by some that passeth by, lie with him, she reproacheth her fellow, that she was not thought as worthy as herself, nor her cord broken. [43] Whatsoever is done among them is false: how may it then be thought or said that they are gods? [44] They are made of carpenters and goldsmiths: they can be nothing else than the workmen will have them to be. [45] And they themselves that made them can never continue long; how should then the things that are made of them be gods? [46] For they left lies and reproaches to them that come after. [47] For when there cometh any war or plague upon them, the priests consult with themselves, where they may be hidden with them. [48] How then cannot men perceive that they be no gods, which can neither save themselves from war, nor from plague? [49] For seeing they be but of wood, and overlaid with silver and gold, it shall be known hereafter that they are false: [50] And it shall manifestly appear to all nations and kings that they are no gods, but the works of men's hands, and that there is no work of God in them. [51] Who then may not know that they are no gods? [52] For neither can they set up a king in the land, nor give rain unto men. [53] Neither can they judge their own cause, nor redress a wrong, being unable: for they are as crows between heaven and earth. [54] Whereupon when fire falleth upon the house of gods of wood, or laid over with gold or silver, their priests will flee away, and escape; but they themselves shall be burned asunder like beams. [55] Moreover they cannot withstand any king or enemies: how can it then be thought or said that they be gods? [56] Neither are those gods of wood, and laid over with silver or gold, able to escape either from thieves or robbers. [57] Whose gold, and silver, and garments wherewith they are clothed, they that are strong take, and go away withal: neither are they able to help themselves. [58] Therefore it is better to be a king that sheweth his power, or else a profitable vessel in an house, which the owner shall have use of, than such false gods; or to be a door in an house, to keep such things therein, than such false gods. or a pillar of wood in a a palace, than such false gods. [59] For sun, moon, and stars, being bright and sent to do their offices, are obedient. [60] In like manner the lightning when it breaketh forth is easy to be seen; and after the same manner the wind bloweth in every country. [61] And when God commandeth the clouds to go over the whole world, they do as they are bidden. [62] And the fire sent from above to consume hills and woods doeth as it is commanded: but these are like unto them neither in shew nor power. [63] Wherefore it is neither to be supposed nor said that they are gods, seeing, they are able neither to judge causes, nor to do good unto men. [64] Knowing therefore that they are no gods, fear them not, [65] For they can neither curse nor bless kings: [66] Neither can they shew signs in the heavens among the heathen, nor shine as the sun, nor give light as the moon. [67] The beasts are better than they: for they can get under a cover and help themselves. [68] It is then by no means manifest unto us that they are gods: therefore fear them not. [69] For as a scarecrow in a garden of cucumbers keepeth nothing: so are their gods of wood, and laid over with silver and gold. [70] And likewise their gods of wood, and laid over with silver and gold, are like to a white thorn in an orchard, that every bird sitteth upon; as also to a dead body, that is east into the dark. [71] And ye shall know them to be no gods by the bright purple that rotteth upon then: and they themselves afterward shall be eaten, and shall be a reproach in the country. [72] Better therefore is the just man that hath none idols: for he shall be far from reproach.

NEW TESTAMENT

THE GOSPELS

These books tell the life, teachings, death, and resurrection of Jesus Christ

MATTHEW

CHAPTER 1

1 The book of the generation of Jesus Christ, son of Dauid, son of Abraham. 2 Abraham begat Isaac. Isaac begat Jacob. Iacob begat Iudas and his brothers. 3 Iudas begat Phares and Zara of Thamar. Phares begat Esrom. Esrom begat Aram. 4 Aram begat Aminad- ab. Aminadab begat Naasson. Naasson begat Salmon. 5 Salmon begat Booz from Rachab. Booz begat Obed from Ruth, and Obed begat Jesse. 6 Jesse begat Dauid the king. Dauid the king begat Solomon from Vrias' wife. 7 Solo- mon begat Rehoboam. Rehoboam begat Abia. Abia begat Asa. 8 Asa begat Jehoshaphat. Je-hoshaphat begat Ioram. Ioram begat Hozi- as. 9 Hozias begat Ioatham. Ioatham begat Achaz. Achaz begat Hezekiah. 10 Hezekiah begat Manasses. Manasses begat Amon. Amon begat Iosiah. 11 Iosiah begat Iakim. Iakim begat Jeconiah and his brothers about the time they were transported to Babylon. 12 After they left for Babylon, Jeconiah begat Salathiel. And Salathiel begat Zerubbabel. 13 Zerubbabel begat Abiud. And Abiud begat Eliachim. Eliachim begat Azor. 14 Azor be- gat Sadoc. Sadoc begat Achim. Achim begat Eliud. 15 Eliud begat Eleazar. Eleazar begat Matthan. Matthan begat Iacob. 16 Iacob begat Ioseph, husband of Mary, from whom was born Jesus, who is called Christ. 17 So all the generations from Abraham to Dauid are four generations. And from Dauid until the depor- tation to Babylon, four generations; and after the deportation to Babylon until Christ, four generations. 18 The birth of Jesus Christ came about thus: when his mother Mary, betrothed to Ioseph, before they were united, was found with child by the Holy Spirit. 19 Then Ioseph, her husband, being a righteous man and not wishing to make an example of her in public- ity, had intended to turn her away secretly. 20 But while he was thinking about these things, behold, the angel of the Lord appeared to him in a dream, saying, "Ioseph, son of Dauid, do not be afraid to take Mary your wife, for what is conceived in her comes from the Holy Spirit. 21 She will bear a son, and you shall call his name JESUS, for he will save his peo- ple from their sins." 22 All this was done so that what the LORD said through his prophet might be fulfilled, 23 Behold, a virgin shall be with child, and shall bring forth a son, and they shall call his name Emmanuel, which means, by interpretation, God with vs. 24 Then Ioseph arose from sleep, and did as the angel of the LORD had commanded him, and took his wife. 25 But he did not know her until she had borne his first son, and he called his name JESUS.

CHAPTER 2

1 When Jesus was born in Bethlehem of Ju- dea, in the days of King Herod, behold, wise men came to Jerusalem from the East, 2 say- ing, "Where is the King of the peoples who was delivered? For we have seen his star in the East and have come to worship him." 3 When King Herod heard this, he was troubled, and with him all Jerusalem. 4 And gathering all the chief priests and scribes of the people, he asked them where the Christ should be taken. 5 They answered him, "To Beth-leem in Judea, for so it is written in the Prophet, 6 Thou, Beth-leem, in the land of Judah, art not the least of the princes of Judah: for out of thee shall come forth the nourishment that shall feed my people of Israel." 7 Then Herod hasti- ly called the wise men and inquired diligently about the hour when the star had appeared, 8 and sent them to Bet-leem, saying, "Go and search diligently for the child; and when you have found him, bring me news again, that I may come also and worship him." 9 So having heard the king, they departed; and behold, the star which they had seen in the east went before them, until it came and stood in the place where the child was. 10 And when they saw the star, they recovered with exceeding great joy, 11 And they entered into the house, and found the child with Mary his mother, and bowed down, and worshipped him, and opened their treasures, and presented him gifts: gold, frankincense, and myrrh. 12 And after being warned by God at a time of respite, so that they would not go to Herod again, they returned to their county by another road. 13 After their departure, behold, the angel of the Lord appeared to Ioseph in a dream, saying, "Get up, take the child and his mother, flee to Egypt, and stay there until I give you news, for Herod wants to see the child in order to destroy him." 14 Then he arose, took the child and his mother by night, and departed for Egypt, 15 and remained there until Herod's death, that it might be fulfilled what the Lord had said through the Prophet, "Out of Egypt I have called my son." 16 Then Herod, seeing that he had been mocked by the Knowledg- es, was exceedingly angry, and sent to kill all the male children who were in Bethlehem and in all its coasts, from the age of two years old downward, according to the time that he had diligently sought from the Knowledges. 17 Then was fulfilled what was spoken by the prophet Jeremiah, 18 A voice was heard in Rhama, a mourning, weeping, and a great howling: Rachel mourned for her children, and would not be comforted because they were not there. 19 While Herod was dead, be- hold, an angel of the Lord appeared in a dream to Ioseph in Egypt, 20 saying, "Arise, take the child and his mother and go into the land of Israel, for those who sought the life of the child are dead." 21 So he arose, and took the child and his mother, and came into the land of Israel. 22 But when he heard that Archelaus reigned in Judea in place of his father Herod, he did not want to go there; nevertheless, af- ter being warned by God in a quiet hour, he departed from the parts of Galilee, 23 and went and dwelt in a city called Nazareth, that what had been said by the prophets might be fulfilled, that he should be called a Nazarite.

CHAPTER 3

1 In those days, John the Baptist came to preach in the wilderness of Iudea, :2 and said, "Repent, for the kingdom of Heauen is at hand." 3 For this is he of whom the prophet Esaias speaks, saying, "The voice of him who cries in the wilderness, 'Prepare the way of the Lord, straighten his paths.'" 4 This Iohn had a camel's wool robe and a leather belt around his loins; his food was locusts and wild bone. 5 Then Jerusalem and all Judea and all the region around Iordan came to him. 6 And they were baptized by him in Jordan, confessing their sins. 7 When he saw many Pharisees and Sadites coming to his baptism, he said to them, "O generations of vipers, who warned you to flee from the wrath to come? 8 Make your lives fruitful therefore in a worthy way. 9 And do not think to say among

your-selves, "We have Abraham for a father," for I say to you that God is able to beget children to Abraham even from these stones. 10 Now the axe has also been laid on the roots of the trees; therefore every tree that does not bear good fruit is cut down and thrown into the fire. 11 I baptize you with water to amend life, but he who comes after me is stronger than I, and I am not worthy to wear shoes; he will baptize you with the Holy Spirit and with fire. 12 Who has his fan in his hand, he will cleanse his plain and gather his wheat into his barn, but he will bury the darnel with unquench- able fire. 13 Then Jesus came from Galilee to Jordan to John, to be baptized by him. 14 But John strongly rejected him, saying, "I need to be baptized by you, and you come to me? 15 Then Iesus, answering, said to him, "Let it be, for thus all righteousness is fulfilled." And so he suffered it. 16 When he was baptized, Jesus immediately came out of the water. And be- hold, the doors were opened to him, and Iohn saw the Spirit of God descending like thunder and enlightening him. 17 And behold, there came a voice from Eauen saying, "This is my beautiful Son, in whom I am well pleased."

CHAPTER 4

1 Then Jesus was led by the Spirit into the wilderness to be tempted by the devil. 2 And after he had fasted fourteen days and four- teen nights, he was hungry. 3 Then the tempt- er came to him and said, "If you are the Son of God, command these stones to become bread." 4 But he answered and said, "It is written that man does not live by bread alone, but by every word that comes from the mouth of God." 5 Then the dean led him into the holy city and set him on a pillar of the temple, 6 and said to him, "If you are the Son of God, cast yourself down, for it is written that he will give his angels charge over you, and with their hands they will lift you up, lest at any time you should dash your foot against a stone." 7 Jesus said to him, "It is written again, 'You shall not tempt the Lord your God.'" 8 Then the Lord led him to a very high mountain and showed him all the kingdoms of the world and their glory, 9 and said to him, "All these things I will give you, if you will fall down and worship me." 10 Then Jesus said to him, "Abandon Satan, for it is written, 'You shall worship the Lord your God, and him only you shall serve.'" 11 Then the devil left him; and behold, the Angels came and assisted him. 12 When Iesus had heard that John had been put in prison, he re- turned to Galilee. 13 And having left Nazareth, he went and dwelt in Capernaum, which is by the sea, on the borders of Zebulun and Neph- thalim, 14 that what had been spoken by Esa- ias the prophet might be fulfilled, 15 The land of Zebulun and the land of Naphtalim, by the way of the sea, beyond Iordan, Galilee of the Gentiles: 16 The people who were in darkness saw a great light; and for those who were in the region and in the shadow of death, light came forth. 17 From that time Jesus began to preach and to say, "Take up your lives, for the kingdom of Heauen is at hand." 18 And Jesus, as he was walking along the Sea of Galilee, saw two brothers, Simon, whose name was Peter, and Andrew his brother, casting a net into the sea (for they were fishermen). 19 And he said to them, "Follow me, and I will make you fish- ers of men." 20 And they immediately, having cast their nets, followed him. 21 And when he was gone from there, he saw two other broth- ers, Iames the son of Zebedee, and Iohn his brother, in a ship with Zebedee their father, mending nets, and he called them. 22 And they, not caring, left the ship and their father and followed him.

23 So Jesus went about all Galilee, teaching in their synagogues, preach- ing the gospel of the kingdom and healing ev- ery sickness and every infirmity of the people. 24 And his fame spread throughout all Syria, and they brought to him all who were sick, those who were afflicted with various diseas- es and torments, those who were possessed with sicknesses, those who were moody, and those who had paralysis; and he healed them. 25 Great crowds followed him from Galilee, from Decapolis, from Jerusalem, from Judea, and from beyond Iordan.

CHAPTER 5

1 After greeting the crowd, he went to a mountain; and when he was in position, his disciples came to him. 2 And opening his mouth, he taught them, saying, "Blessed are the poor in spirit, for theirs is the task of teaching." 3 Blessed are the poor in spirit, for theirs is the kingdom of God. 4 Blessed are those who mourn, for they will be comforted. 5 Blessed are the weak, for they shall inherit the earth. 6 Blessed are those who hunger and thirst for righteousness, for they will be satis- fied. 7 Blessed are the merciful, for they shall have mercy. 8 Blessed are the pure in heart, for they shall see God. 9 Blessed are the peace- makers, for they will be called children of God. 10 Blessed are those who suffer persecution for righteousness' sake, for to them belongs the kingdom of God. 11 You will be blessed when men persecute you and say all kinds of evil against you falsely on my account. 12 Re- joice and be glad, for great is your reward in heaven, for so persecuted the prophets who were before you. 13 You are the salt of the earth; but if salt has lost its savor, with what will it be salted? It will be of no use except to be cast out and to be trodden down by men. 14 You are the light of the world. A city set on a hill cannot be hidden. 15 Nor do you light a candle and put it under a bushel, but on a candelabra, and it gives light to all who are in the house. 16 Let your light shine before men, that they may see your good works and glorify your Father who is in heaven. 17 Do not think that I have come to destroy the Law or the Prophets. I have not come to destroy them, but to fulfill them. 18 For verily I say unto you, until eauen and the earth perish, not one word or one title of the Law shall disappear, until all things are fulfilled. 19 Whosoever therefore shall break one of these least precepts, and shall teach it unto men, shall be called least in the kingdom of Heauen; but whosoever shall keep and teach them, shall be called great in the kingdom of Heauen. 20 For I say to you, unless your righteousness exceeds that of the Scribes and Pharisees, you will not enter the kingdom of God. 21 You have heard that an- ciently it was said to them, "You shall not kill, for he who kills will be liable to judgment." 22 But I say to you, whoever is angry with his brother in a vnaduistic manner will be guilty of iudicio. And he who shall say to his brother, "Raca," shall be worthy of punishment by the council. And he who shall say, "Foole," shall be punished with hellfire. 23 If you then bring your gift to the altar and remember that your brother has done evil against you, 24 leave your offering there before the altar and go your way; first reconcile with your brother and then come and offer your gift. 25 Agree quickly with your aduersary, while you are on your way with him, lest your aduersary hand you over to the judge, and the judge hand you over to the sergeant, and you be cast into prison. 26 Verily I say unto thee, thou shalt not go out from thence until thou hast paid the utmost. 27 You have heard that anciently it was said to them, "Do not commit adultery." 28

But I tell you that anyone who looks at a woman to concupt her has already commit- ted adultery with her in his heart. 29 There- fore, if your right eye causes you to commit an offense, pluck it out and cast it from you, for it is better for you that one of your mem- bers should perish than that your whole body should be cast into hell. 30 If your right hand also causes you to commit an offense, cut it off and cast it from you, for it is better for you that one of your members should perish than that your whole body should be cast into hell. 31 It was also said, "Whoever wants to remove his wife, let him make a declaration of divorce to her." 32 But I say to you that whoever puts away his own wife (except for fornication) makes her commit adultery; and whoever marries a diuorced woman commits adultery. 33 Moreover, you have heard that anciently it was said to them, "You must not forsake your- self, but you must do homage to the Lord." 34 But I say to you that you need not fear at all for heaven, for it is the throne of God: 35 Nor for the earth, for it is his foot, nor for Jerusalem, for it is the city of the great King. 36 Neither will you swear by your head, for you cannot make one head white or one head black. 37 But let your communication be Yes, yes: No, no. For that which is more than these is from afar. 38 You have heard that it was said, "An eye for an eye and a tooth for a tooth." 39 But I say to you, Do not resist unrighteousness; whoever strikes you on your right hand, turn him the other also. 40 And if anyone sues you and takes away your cloak, let him also have your cloak. 41 And whoever forces you to go a mile, go with him for two. 42 Accept those who ask you, and do not turn away from those who want to lend you. 43 You have heard that it was said, "You shall love your neighbor and hate your enemy." 44 But I say to you, "Love your enemies, bless those who curse you, do good to those who hate you, and pray for those who hurt and persecute you, 45 that you may be children of your father who is in heaven, for he makes his sun to rise on the honest and the good, and sends rain on the unjust and the vniust. 46 For if you love those who love you, what reward will you have? Is it not the same for the public? 47 And if you are friendly only to your brothers, what sin- gular thing do you do? Do not the publicans also do the same? 48 Ye shall therefore be per- fect, even as your Father which is in heaven is perfect.

CHAPTER 6

1 Take care that you do not give your alms before men to be seen by them, otherwise you will not have the reward of your Father who is in heaven. 2 Therefore, when you deliver up your alms, you shall not blow a trumpet before you, as the hypocrites do in the syna- gogues and in the streets, to be prayed for by men. Verily I say unto you, they have their re- ward. 3 But when you do your chores, do not let your left hand know what your right hand is doing, 4 That your prayers may be secret, and your Father, who sees in secret, will re- ward you openly. 5 And when you pray, do not be like the hypocrites, for they love to stand and pray in synagogues and on street corners, because they want to be seen by men. Verily I tell you, they have their reward. 6 But when you pray, go into your chamber and, after you have shut your door, pray to your Father who is in secret, and your Father who sees in secret will reward you openly. 7 Moreover, when you pray, do not repeat too much like the heathen, for they think they will be heard because of their great babbling. 8 Therefore do not be like them, for your Father knows what you need before you ask him. 9 In this way therefore pray, "Our Father who art in heaven, hallowed be thy name." 10 Thy king- dom come. Thy will be done on earth as it is in heaven. 11 Give us this day our daily bread. 12 And forgive our sayings, as we also forgive our sayings. 13 And do not give yourselves over to temptation, but give yourselves over to joy, for yours is the kingdom and the pow- er and the glory forever. Amen. 14 For if you forgive men their trespasses, your eternal Father will also forgive you. 15 But if you do not forgive men their trespasses, your Father will not forgive you any more. 16 Moreover, when you fast, do not have the appearance of hypocrites, for they disfigure their faces to appear to men who fast. Verily I tell you, they have their reward. 17 But when you fast, anoint your head and wash your face, 18 That you may not appear to fast to men, but to your Father who is in secret; and your Father who sees in secret will reward you openly. 19 Do not store up treasures for yourselves on the earth, where mold and decay corrupt, and where rogues dig and steal. 20 But store up your treasures in the earth, where neither mold nor decay corrupts, and where nei- ther digging nor stealing takes place. 21 For where your treasure is, there your heart will be also. 22 The light of the body is the eye; if therefore your eye is single, your whole body will be bright. 23 But if your eye is evil, your whole body will be dark. Therefore if the light that is in you is darkened, how great is this darkness? 24 No one can serve two masters, for either he will hate the one and love the other, or he will become attached to the one and despise the other. You cannot serve God and riches. 25 Therefore I tell you not to wor- ry about your life, what you will eat or drink, nor about your body, what you will wear. Is not life worth more than food and the body more than clothing? 26 Look at the creatures of the earth, for they do not sow or reap or bring produce to the barns; yet your heaven- ly Father feeds them. Are not you better than they? 27 Which of you, being careful, is able to add a cubit to his stature? 28 And why are you concerned about clothing? Learn how the lilies of the field grow: they do not grow weary and spin: 29 But I tell you that already Solomon, in all his splendor, was not down- cast like one of these. 30 Therefore, if God so clothes the grass of the field that is cast into the ocean today, will he not do much more with you, O people of little faith? 31 Therefore do not think to say, "What shall we eat, what shall we drink, what shall we clothe ourselves with? 32 (for of all these things the Gentiles are concerned) for your Father knows that you have need of all these things. 33 But seek first the kingdom of God and his righteousness, and all these things will be communicated to you. 34 Therefore do not worry about death, for death will take care of itself; the day has enough to do with its own sufferings.

CHAPTER 7

1 Do not judge, lest you be judged. 2 Or with what judgment you judge, you will be judged, and with what measure you measure, you will be measured again. 3 And why do you see the speck that is in your brother's eye and do not perceive the speck that is in your own eye? 4 Or how do you say to your brother, "Let me drive the louse out of your eye," and behold, the louse is in your eye? 5 Hypocrite, first cast out the pupil from your own eye, and then you will see clearly how to cast out the pupil from your brother's eye. 6 Do not feed what is holy to the dogs, nor cast your pearls before swine, lest they swipe them under their feet and turn all against you. 7 Ask, and it shall be given you; look, and you shall find; knock, and it shall be

opened to you. 8 For he who asks, receives; he who seeks, finds; and to him who knocks, it will be opened. 9 For what man is there among you who, if his son asked him for bread, would give him a stone? 10 Or if he asks him for fish, will he give him a snake? 11 If therefore you, who are good, can give your children good gifts, how much more will your Father in heaven give good things to those who ask him? 12 Therefore, what you want men to do to you, do you also to them, for this is the Law and the Prophets. 13 Enter by the straight gate, for it is the wide gate and the middle way that leads to destruction, and many are those who enter it, 14 For the gate is straight and the narrow way that leads to life, and few are those who find it. 15 Beware of false prophets who come to you dressed as sheep, but who in reality are ravening wolves. 16 You will know them by their fruit. Do men gather grapes from thorns or figs from thistles? 17 So every good tree produces good fruit, while a corrupt tree produces mediocre fruit. 18 A good tree cannot produce good fruit, nor can a corrupt tree produce good fruit. 19 Every tree that does not produce good fruit is cut down and thrown into the fire. 20 Therefore you will know them by their fruit. 21 Not ev- eryone who says to me, Lord, Lord, will enter the kingdom of God, but those who do the will of my Father who is in heaven. 22 In that day many will say to me, Lord, Lord, have we not prophesied through your name? And through your name have we driven out diseases? And through your name have we done many great works?" 23 Then I will prophesy to them, "I did not know you; depart from me, you who work iniquity." 24 Whoever therefore hears these words and puts them into practice, I will lik- en him to a wise man who built his house on the rock." 25 But the rain fell, the floods came, and the wind blew on that house, but it did not fall, for it was founded on a rock. 26 But whoever hears these words of mine and does not put them into practice will be like a fool- ish man who built his house on sand: 27 Then the rain fell, and the floods came, and the wind blew upon that house, and it fell, and its fall was great. 28 When Jesus had finished these words, the people were amazed at his doctrine. 29 For he taught them as one having authority and not as the scribes.

CHAPTER 8

1 Now when he had come down from the mountain, great crowds followed him. 2 And behold, there came a leper and worshipped him, saying, "Master, if you will, you can make me well." 3 Jesus, putting forth his hand, touched him, saying, "I will, be cleansed"; and immediately his leprosy was removed. 4 Then Jesus said to him, "Tell no one, but go, present yourself to the priest, and offer the gift that Moses commanded, as a testimony for them." 5 When Jesus had entered Capernaum, there came to him a centurion beseeching him, 6 and said to him, "Teacher, my servant lies sick at home with paralysis and is grievous- ly suffering." 7 Jesus said to him, "I will come and heal him." 8 But the centurion answered, "Master, I am not worthy that you should come under my roof; but just say the word, and my servant will be healed. 9 For I also am a man under the authority of another, and I have helpers under me; I say to one, 'Go,' and he goes; and to another, 'Come,' and he comes; and to my servant, 'Do this,' and he does it." 10 When Jesus heard this, he marveled and said to those who followed him, "Truly, I say to you, I have not found such great faith, even in Israel. 11 But I tell you that many will come from the East and the West and will sit with Abraham, Isaac and Jacob in the kingdom of Heauen. 12 The children

of the kingdom will be cast out into the deepest darkness, and there will be weeping and gnashing of teeth." 13 Then Jesus said to the centurion, "Go your way, and as you have asked, so be it for you." 14 When Iesus came to Peter's house, he saw his mother lying on the ground and sick with fever. 15 He touched her hand and the fe- ver left her; then she got up and ministered to them. 16 When Europe had come, they brought to him many who were possessed with diseases; and he cast out the spirits by his word and healed all who were sick, 17 so that what had been said by the prophet Esaias might be fulfilled, "He took upon himself our infirmities and bore our diseases." 18 When Jesus saw a great multitude of people around him, he commanded them to come out of the water. 19 Then a scribe came and said to him, "Teacher, I will follow you wherever you go." 20 But Jesus said to him, "The foxes have holes and the birds of the air have nests, but the Son of Man has nowhere to lay his head." 21 Another of his disciples said to him, "Mas- ter, let me go first to bury my father." 22 But Jesus said to him, "Follow me, and let the dead bury their dead." 23 When he had en- tered the ship, his disciples followed him. 24 And behold, a great storm arose in the sea, so that the ship was struck by the waves, but he slept. 25 Then his disciples came and woke him, saying, "Master, say something: we are going to die." 26 And he said to them, "Why are you afraid, O people of little faith? Then he arose and rebuked the winds and the sea; and so there was a great calm. 27 And the men marveled, saying, "What a man is this, that the winds and the sea obey him! 28 And when he was come to the other side, into the county of Gergesenes, there came to him two deuil invaders, which came out of the graves very fierce, so that no man could pass that way. 29 And behold, they cried out, saying, "Jesus, the Son of God, what shall we do with you? Have you come here to torment before the time? 30 Now there was, far from them, a great number of swine feeding. 31 The watch- men pleaded with him, saying, "If you drive them out, allow them to go into the hearing of the swine." 32 And he said to them, "Go." Then they went out and went to the hearing of the swine; and behold, all the hearing of the swine threw themselves headlong into the sea and died in the water. 33 Then the hearers fled; and when they had come to the city, they told everything and what had happened to those who had been possessed by demons. 34 And behold, the whole city went out to meet Jesus; and when they saw him, they begged him to depart from their shores.

CHAPTER 9

1 Then he entered a ship, went out of it and came to his own city. 2 They brought to Him a man sick with paralysis, who was lying on a bed. And Jesus, seeing their faith, said to the sick man with palsy, "Son, take comfort: your sins are forgiven you." 3 And behold, some of the scribes said among themselves, "This man blasphemes." 4 But when Jesus saw their thoughts, he said, "Why do you think these things in your hearts? 5 For if it is easier to say, 'Your sins forgive you,' or to say, 'Get up and walk?' 6 So that you may know that the Son of Man has authority on earth to forgive sins, he said to the sick man with palsy, "Get up, take your bed and go to your home." 7 He got up and went to his house. 8 When the crowd heard this, they marveled and glorified God, who had given such authority to men. 9 As Iesus passed by, he saw a man sitting at the chair, named Matthewe, and said to him, "Follow me." And he arose and followed him. 10 And while Jesus was at table in his house,

behold, many publicans and sinners came there and sat down at table with Jesus and his disciples. 11 When the Pharisees saw this, they said to his disciples, "Why does your master eat with publicans and sinners? 12 When Jesus heard this, he said to them, "Not everyone needs care, but only those who are sick. 13 But go and learn what this is: I want to have mercy and not sacrifices, for I have not come to call the righteous but sinners to repentance." 14 Then John's disciples came to him, saying, "Why do we and the Pharisees fast often, and your disciples do not fast?" 15 Jesus said to them, "Can the children of the bridal chamber fast while the bride is with them? But the day will come when the bride- groom will be taken from them, and then they will fast. 16 Moreover, no one shall sew up an old robe with a piece of new cloth, for that which would fill it takes it away from the robe, and the rupture is worse. 17 Nor shall anyone put new wine into old vessels, for then the vessels would break, and the wine would spill out, and the vessels would die; but new wine shall be put into new vessels, and so both shall be preserved. 18 While he was speaking to them in this way, behold, a certain ruler came and worshipped him, saying, "My daughter is now dead, but come and lay your hand on her and she will live." 19 Then Iesus arose and fol- lowed him with his disciples. 20 And behold, a woman, who had been sick for two years with a discharge of blood, came behind him and touched the hem of his garment. 21 For she said within herself, "If I could only touch his garment, I would be healed." 22 Then Je- sus turned and, seeing her, said, "Daughter, take comfort: your faith has healed you." And the woman was healed at that same time). 23 Now when Jesus entered the house of the rulers and saw the minstrels and the crowd making noise, 24 He said to them, "Go away, for the maiden is not dead, but asleep." And they mocked him. 25 And when the crowd had departed, he went in and took her by the hand, and the mother stood up. 26 And this bruising spread through all that land. 27 As Jesus was leaving, two blind men followed him, crying out and saying, "O son of Dauid, have mercy on you." 28 When he had entered the house, the blind men came up to him, and Jesus said to them, "Do you think that I am able to do this? And they answered him, "Yes, Lord." 29 Then he touched their eyes, saying, "According to your faith, let it be done to you." 30 And their eyes were opened, and Jesus gave them a great charge, saying, "See that no one knows." 31 But when they had de- parted, they spread his fame throughout the whole land. 32 As they were leaving, behold, they brought to him a domme man possessed by a deuill. 33 When the deuill was cast out, the domme spoke; then the crowd marveled, saying, "Nothing like this had ever been seen in Israel." 34 But the Pharisees said, "He cast out wickedness through the prince of wick- edness." 35 And Jesus went about all the cit- ies and towns, teaching in their synagogues, preaching the gospel of the kingdom and healing every sickness and every infirmity of the people. 36 But when he saw the mul- titude, he had compassion on them, for they were scattered and scattered everywhere, like sheep that have no shepherd. 37 Then he said to his disciples, "Certainly the harvest is great, but the laborers are few. 38 Therefore pray to the Lord of the land, that he will send workers into his land.

CHAPTER 10

1 He called his two disciples to himself and gave them power against the living spirits, to cast them out and heal every disease and every infirmity. 2 The names of the two apostles are these. The first is Simon, called Peter, and An- drew his brother: Iames the son of Zebedee, and Iohn his brother. 3 Philippe and Bartle- mewe: Thomas and Matthewe, the publican: Iames the son of Alpheus, and Lebbeus, whose surname was Thaddaeus: 4 Simon the Ca- naanite and Iudas Iscariot, who had betrayed him. 5 These two sent Jesus and commanded them, "Do not go by the way of the Gentiles or enter the cities of the Samaritans: 6 But go rather to the lost sheep of the house of Israel. 7 And as you go, preach, saying, 'The kingdom of God is at hand.' 8 Heal the sick, cleanse the lepers, raise the dead, cast out the sick. Free- ly you have received, freely give. 9 You do not possess gold, nor silver, nor money in your belts, 10 Nor a scrip for the journey, nor two cloaks, nor shoes, nor a staff, for the laborer is worthy of his meal. 11 And in whatever city or town you arrive, ask who is worthy, and stay there until you have departed. 12 When you enter a house, greet it. 13 If the house is worthy, let your peace come upon it; but if it is not worthy, let your peace return to you. 14 And whosoever will not receive you and hear your words, when you leave that house or that city, shake off the dust of your feet. 15 Truly I tell you, it will be easier for those in the land of Sodom and Gomorrah in the day of judg- ment than for that city. 16 Behold, I send you as sheep in the midst of wolves; be ye there- fore wise as serpents, and innocent as dogs. 17 But beware of men, for they will hand you over to the councils and scourge you in their synagogues. 18 And you shall be brought be- fore governors and kings for my sake, to tes- tify to them and to the Gentiles. 19 But when they deliver you up, pay no attention to how or what you will speak, for in that hour it will be given you to know what you will say. 20 For it is not you who speak, but the spirit of your father speaking in you. 21 Brother shall betray brother to death, father to son, and children shall rise up against their parents and cause them to die. 22 You will be hated by all men because of my Name; but he who endures to the end will be saved. 23 And when they persecute you in this city, flee to another: for verily I say unto you, ye shall not go out from all the cities of Israel until the Son of Man cometh. 24 The disciple does not deal with his master, nor the servant with his Lord. 25 It is enough for the disciple to be like his master and the servant like his Lord. If they called the master of the house Beelzebub, how much more those of his house? 26 Therefore do not fear them, for there is nothing hidden that is not revealed, nor hidden that is not known. 27 What I say to you in the darkness, I say to you in the light; and what you hear in the night, I preach to you in the houses. 28 Do not fear those who kill the body, but are not able to kill the soul; rather fear him who is able to destroy the soul and the body in hell. 29 Do you not sell two sparrows for a penny, and one of them will not fall to the ground with- out your Father? 30 Yea, and all the shears of your head are appointed.31 Fear not there-fore, ye are more precious than many spar- rows. 32 Whosoever therefore shall confess me before men, I will also confess him before my Father which is in heaven. 33 But whoev- er denies me before me, I will also deny him before my Father who is in heaven. 34 Do not think that I have come to send peace on earth; I have not come to send peace, but the sword. 35 For I have come to set the man against his father, the daughter against her mother, and the daughter-in-law against her mother. 36 A man's enemies will be those of his own house. 37 Whoever loves father or mother more than me is not worthy of me. And whoever loves his son or daughter more than me, he is not wor- thy of me. 38 Whoever does not take up his cross and follow me, is not worthy of me. 39 Whoever wants to find his life will lose it; and whoever

loses his life for my sake will find it. 40 He who receives you, receives me; and he who receives me, receives him who sent me. 41 Whoever receives a prophet in the name of a prophet, shall receive the prophet's reward; and whoever receives a righteous man, in the name of a righteous man, shall receive a righteous man's reward. 42 And whosoever shall give one of these little ones to drink a cup of cold water in the name of a disciple, verily I say unto you, he shall not lose his reward.

CHAPTER 11

1 And it came to pass that after Iesus had finished gathering his two disciples, he departed from there to teach and preach in their cities. 2 When Iohn heard in the prison the works of Christ, he sent two of his disciples to say to him, "Are you the one who has done his part? 3 Are you the one who is to come, or should we look for another? 4 And Jesus, answering, said to them, "Go and tell John what you hear and see." 5 The blind receive sight and the still walk; lepers are sterilized and the deaf hear; the dead are raised and the poor receive the gospel. 6 And blessed is he who will not be offended in me. 7 As they were leaving, Jesus began to speak to Iohn's crowd, "What have you gone out into the wilderness to see? A reed shaken by the wind? 8 But what did you go out to see? A man clothed in soft garments? Behold, those who wear soft garments are in the houses of kings. 9 But what have you gone out to see? A prophet? Yes, I tell you, he is much more than a prophet. 10 For this is he of whom it is written, "Behold, I send my messenger before your face, who will prepare your way before you." 11 Verily I say unto you, that among those begotten of women there hath not arisen another greater than John the Baptist; nay, he that is the least in the kingdom of Heauen is greater than he. 12 From the time of John the Baptist onward, the kingdom of Heauen suffers violence, and the violent take it by force. 13 For all the prophets and laymen have prophesied about John. 14 And if you will accept it, this is that Elijah who was to come. 15 He who has ears to hear, let him hear. 16 But to what shall I compare this generation? It is like the little children who sit in the markets and call their companions, 17 And they say, "We wept for you and you did not weep; we wept for you and you did not weep." 18 For Iohn came neither to eat nor to drink, and they say, "He has a sickness." 19 The son of man came eating and drinking, and they say, "Behold, a glutton and a drinker of wine, a friend of publicans and sinners; but wisdom is justified by his sons." 20 Then he began to vpbrace the cities where most of his great works had been done, because they had not repented. 21 Woe to you, Chorazin; woe to you, Bethsaida, for if the great works that were done in you had been done in Tyre and Sidon, they would long ago have repented in sackcloth and ashes. 22 But I tell you that it will be easier for Tyre and Sidon on the day of judgment than for you. 23 And you, Capernaum, who are lifted upward, shall be brought down to hell; for if the great works that were done in you had been done among those of Sodom, they would have remained to this day. 24 But I tell you, it will be easier for those in the land of Sodom on the day of judgment than for you. 25 Then Jesus answered and said, "I thank you, O Father, Lord of heaven and earth, because you have hidden these things from the wise and intelligent men and opened them to children. 26 It is so, O Father, for so it has been your good pleasure. 27 Everything has been given to me by my Father; and no one knows the Son, except the Father; and no one knows

the Father, except the Son, and the one to whom the Son wishes to deliver him. 28 Come unto me, all ye that labor and are heavy laden, and I will lighten you. 29 Take my yoke upon you and learn from me that I am meek and lowly in heart, and you will find rest for your souls. 30 For my yoke is easy and my burden light.

CHAPTER 12

1 At that time, Jesus went on the Sabbath day for corneas; his disciples were hungry and began to pluck corneas and eat. 2 And when the Pharisees saw him, they said to him, "Behold, your disciples are doing what is not lawful to do on the Sabbath." 3 But he said to them, "Have you not read what Dauid did when he was a hungry man and those who were with him? 4 How he entered the house of God and ate the sheep's bread, which it was not lawful for him to eat, nor for those who were with him, but only for the priests? 5 Or have you not read in the Bible that on the Sabbath days the priests in the Temple violate the Sabbath and are blasphemous? 6 But I tell you that here is one greater than the Temple. 7 Therefore, if you had known what this is, I want mercy and not sacrifice, you would not have condemned the innocent. 8 For the son of man is Lord, even of the Sabbath." 9 Then he departed from there and entered their synagogue: 10 And behold a man whose hand was withered. And they asked him, "Is it lawful to eat on the Sabbath day?" to accuse him. 11 And he said to them, "What man will there be among you who has a sheep and, if it falls on a Sabbath day into a pit, does not take it and bring it out? 12 How much better is a man than a sheep? Therefore it is lawful to act well on the Sabbath day." 13 Then he said to the man, "Stretch out your hand." And he stretched it out, and it was as complete as the other. 14 Then the Pharisees went out and consulted against him to destroy him. 15 But when Jesus heard this, he went out, and great crowds followed him, and he healed them all, 16 and charged them in a threatening way not to make him known, 17 so that what had been said by the prophet Esaias might be fulfilled, "Behold my servant." 18 Behold my servant whom I have chosen, my protégé to whom my soul is committed: I will put my Spirit upon him, and he shall give judgment to the Gentiles. 19 He will not strip and shout, and no one will hear his voice in the streets. 20 He will not break the bruised reed or quench the smoking flax, until he has brought judgment to victory. 21 And in his Name shall the nations trust. 22 Then there was brought to him one who was possessed of a deformity, blind and dumb, and he healed him, so that he who was blind and dumb spoke and saw. 23 All the people rejoiced and said, "Is not this the son of Dauid?" 24 But when the Pharisees heard this, they said, "This man does not cast out curses otherwise than through Beelzebub, the prince of curses." 25 But Jesus, knowing their thoughts, said to them, "Every kingdom that opposes itself is destroyed, and every city or house that opposes itself will not stand." 26 So if Satan casts out Satan, he is opposed to himself; how then shall his kingdom endure? 27 And if I, through Beelzebub, cast out witches, by whom do your children cast them out? Therefore they shall be your judges. 28 But if I cast out sins by the Spirit of God, then the kingdom of God has come to you. 29 How can a man enter a strong man's house and strip his possessions, unless he first binds the strong man and then ruins his house? 30 Whoever is not with me is against me; and whoever does not gather with me scatters. 31 Therefore I tell you that every sin and every blasphemy will be forgiven

to men, but blas- phemy against the Holy Spirit will not be for- given to men. 32 Whoever shall speak a word against the Son of Man, it shall be forgiven; but whoever shall speak a word against the Holy Spirit, it shall not be forgiven either in this world or in the world to come. 33 O make good the tree and good its fruit, or make evil the tree and evil its fruit, for the tree is known by its fruit. 34 O generation of vipers, how can you say good things, if you are sick? For out of the abundance of the heart the mouth speaks. 35 A good man, from the good trea- sure of his heart, produces good things; and a weak man, from a weak treasure, produces weak things. 36 But I say to you, of every vain word that men shall speak, they shall give ac- count in the day of judgment. 37 For by your words you will be justified, and by your words you will be condemned." 38 Then some of the scribes and Pharisees answered, "Master, we want to see a sign from you." 39 But he an- swered them, "An evil and adulterous gener- ation seeks a sign, but no sign will be given to it, like the sign of the prophet Ionas. 40 For as Ionas was three days and three nights in the belly of the whales, so the Son of Man will be three days and three nights in the heart of the earth. 41 And the men of Niniue shall stand in judgment with this generation, and condemn it, because they repented at the preaching of Ionas; and behold, another greater than Ionas is here. 42 The queen of the south will stand in judgment with this generation and condemn it, because she came from the farthest parts of the earth to hear the wisdom of Solomon; and behold, one greater than Solomon is here. 43 Now when the vnclean spirit departs from a man, he walks many places, seeking rest, but does not find it. 44 Then he says, "I will return to my house whence I came"; and when he ar- rives, he finds it empty, swept and tidied up. 45 Then he goes away and takes with him two other spirits worse than himself, who come in and dwell there; and the end of that man is worse than the beginning. So shall it be also with this wicked generation." 46 While he was still speaking to the crowd, behold, his moth- er and his brothers stood by and desired to speak with him. 47 Then one said to him, "Be- hold, your mother and your brothers stand outside and desire to speak with you." 48 But he answered the one who had said to him, "Who is my mother and who are my broth- ers?" 49 He stretched out his hand toward his disciples and said, "Here are my mother and my brothers. 50 For whoever will do the will of my Father who is in heaven is also my brother and my sister and my mother.

CHAPTER 13

1 That same day Jesus went out of the house and stood on the seashore. 2 And great crowds resorted to him, so that he went into a ship and sat down on the shore; and the whole crowd stood on the shore. 3 Then he spoke to them of many things in parables, saying, "Behold, a sower goes out to sow. 4 While he was sowing, some fell by the wayside, and the birds came and made them fall. 5 And some fell on stony ground, where there was not much soil, and immediately they sprout- ed, because they had no depth of soil. 6 But when the sun was high, they withered and, for lack of roots, withered away. 7 Some fell among the thorns, and the thorns sprouted and choked them. 8 Some, on the other hand, felted in good soil and produced fruit, one horn for a hundred leaves, another for sixty leaves, and yet another for thirty leaves. 9 He who has ears to hear, let him hear. 10 Then the disciples came and said to him, "Why do you speak to them in parables?" 11 He answered them,

"Because it is granted to you to know the secrets of the kingdom of Heauen, but it is not granted to them. 12 For whoever has, to him shall be given and have abundance; but whoever does not have, from him shall be taken away what he has. 13 Therefore I speak to them in parables, because, seeing, they do not see; and hearing, they do not hear or un- derstand. 14 Thus the prophecy of Esaias was fulfilled in them, which says, "Hearing, you will hear and not understand; and seeing, you will see and not perceive." 15 For the heart of this people is fattened, their ears are dull, and their eyes have winked, lest they see with their eyes, hear with their ears, understand with their hearts, and turn back, that I may heal them. 16 But blessed are your eyes, for they see, and your ears, for they hear. 17 For verily I say unto you, that many prophets and righteous men have desired to see the things which ye see, and have not seen them, and to hear the things which ye hear, and have not heard them. 18 Therefore listen to the para- ble of the sower. 19 When someone hears the word of that kingdom and does not under- stand it, another comes and takes away what he has sown in his heart; and this is the one who received the seed along the way. 20 The one who has gathered the seed in the stony ground is the one who hears the word and re- ceives it unwillingly, 21 but has not yet a root in himself, and lasts only a season; for when tribulation or persecution comes because of the Word, he is always reviled. 22 He who has received the seed among thorns is he who hears the Word; but the care of this world and the deceitfulness of riches choke the Word, and he is made unfruitful. 23 But he who has received the seed in good soil is he who hears the word and understands it, who also bears fruit and brings home, who a hundred sheets and who a hundred sheets and who a hundred sheets. 24 Another parable he expounded to them, saying, "The kingdom of Heauen is like a man who has sown good seed in his field. 25 But while the men slept, his enemy came, sowed weeds in the midst of the wheat, and departed. 26 When the wheat sprouted and bore fruit, the tares also appeared. 27 Then the servants of the master of the house came and said to him, "Master, have you not sown good seed in your field? Whence then comes the tares?" 28 And he answered them, "An en- vious man has done this." Then the servants said to him, "Do you therefore want us to go and gather them?" 29 But he said, "No, lest, as you go to gather the darnel, you also cause the wheat to fall with it. 30 Let the one and the other grow together until the time of the plague, and in the time of the plague I will say to the harvesters, 'Gather the darnel first and put it in the fences to bury it; but gather the wheat into my barn. 31 Then he expounded to them another parable, saying, "The king- dom of Heauen is like a mustard seed that a man takes and sows in his field: 32 which in the beginning is the smallest of all seeds; but when it grows, it is the greatest among the grasses, and is a tree, so that the birds of Heauen come and build on its branches." 33 Another parable said to them, "The kingdom of Heauen is like the ryegrass, which a wom- an takes and hides in three honeycombs, until it is all ryegrass." 34 All these things Jesus told the crowd in parables, and without parables he did not speak to them, 35 so that what had been said by the prophet might be fulfilled, "I will open my mouth in parables and reveal the things that have been kept secret since the foundation of the world." 36 Then Jesus sent the crowd away and went into the house. And his disciples joined him, saying, "Tell me the parable of the tares of the field." 37 Then he answered and said to them, "He who sows the good seed is the Son of Man. 38 The field is the world, the good seed is the children of the kingdom, and the darnel is the children of the wicked. 39 The enemy that sows them is the devil, and the worst is the end of the world, and the reapers are the angels. 40 As the dar- nel is gathered and burned in the fire, so it will be at the end of this world. 41 The Son of Man will send his Angels, and they will gather out of his kingdom all things that offend and those that commit iniquity, 42 And they will cast them into a furnace of fire. There will be wailing and gnashing of teeth. 43 Then righ- teous men will shine like the sun in their Fa- ther's kingdom. He who has ears to hear, let him hear. 44 The kingdom of Heauen is like a treasure hidden in a field, which a man, when he finds it, hides, and therefore he goes away and sells all that he has, and goes away into that field. 45 The kingdom of Heauen is like a merchant who seeks good pearls, 46 who, hav- ing found a pearl of great price, sold all that he had and bought it. 47 Moreover, the king- dom of Heauen is similar to a net cast into the sea that gathers all kinds of things. 48 When it is full, the men pull it ashore, and sit down and gather the good things into vessels, and throw away the bad. 49 So it will be at the end of the world. The angels will go and take the bad from among the righteous, 50 and they will throw them into a furnace of fire, where there will be weeping and gnashing of teeth. 51 Jesus said to them, Do you understand all these things? They answered him, "Yes, Lord." 52 Then he said to them, "Therefore ev- ery scribe who is instructed for the kingdom of Heauen is like a householder who brings out of his treasure things new and old." 53 And when Jesus had finished these parables, he departed, 54 and came to his county and taught them in their synagogue, so that they were astonished and said, "Whence came this wisdom and these great works to this man? 55 Is not this man the son of carpenters? Is not his mother named Mary, and his brothers Ia- mes and Ioses, and Simon and Iudas? 56 Are not all his sisters with him? Whence then do all these things come to him? 57 They were offended with him. Then Jesus said to them, "A prophet is not without honor, both in his own country and in his own house." 58 And he did not do many great works there, because of their unbelief.

CHAPTER 14

1 At that time Herod the Tetrarch heard of the fame of Jesus, 2 and said to his servants, "This is John the Baptist; he has risen from the dead, and for this reason great works are be- ing done by him." 3 For Herod had taken Iohn, bound him, and put him in prison because of Herodias, the wife of his brother Philips. 4 Iohn said to him, "It is not lawful for you to have her." 5 And when he wanted to put him to death, he feared the crowd, because they considered him a prophet. 6 But when the day of Herod's birth was celebrated, Herodi- as' daughter prostrated herself before them and pleased Herod. 7 Therefore he promised another that he would give her whatever she asked for. 8 And she, instructed by her moth- er, said, "Give me here the head of John the Baptist in a dish." 9 And the king was sorry; nevertheless, because of the other and those who sat with him at the table, he command- ed that it be given her, 10 And he sent Iohn to be beheaded in the prison. 11 His head was brought in a dish and given to his mother, who took it to her mother. 12 And his disciples came, and took the body, and buried it, and went and talked with Jesus. 13 And when Iesus heard of it, he departed from there in a ship to a deserted and isolated place. And when the crowd had heard him, they followed him on foot out of the cities. 14 And Iesus went toward them and saw a great multitude and was moved with compassion toward them and healed their diseases. 15 When the time had come, his disciples came to him, saying, "This is a deserted place, and the hour is al- ready past; let the crowd leave, to go into the cities and give them life." 16 But Jesus said to them, "They need not go away; give them food." 17 Then they said to him, "We have here but a few loaves and two fish." 18 And he said, "Bring them here to me." 19 He commanded the crowd to sit on the gridiron, took the five loaves and two fish, looked up and blessed, and stood and gave the loaves to his disciples and the disciples to the crowd. 20 They all ate and were filled, and they took two baskets full of the remaining fragments. 21 Those who had eaten were about five thousand men, besides women and small children. 22 Imme- diately afterward, Jesus compelled his disci- ples to get into a ship and depart before him, while he sent the crowd away. 23 And when he had sent the crowd away, he retired into a room alone to pray; and when it was evening, he stood there alone. 24 The ship was now in the middle of the sea and was tossed about by the waves, for the wind was against it. 25 At the fourth hour of the night, Jesus went to them, walking on the sea. 26 And when his disciples saw him walking on the sea, they were troubled, saying, "It is a spirit," and they cried out in fear. 27 But immediately Jesus spoke to them, saying, "Take comfort, it is I; do not be afraid." 28 Then Peter answered him and said, "Master, if it is so, let me come to you on the waters." 29 And he said, "Come." And when Peter was off the ship, he walked on the waters to go to Jesus. 30 But when he saw a strong wind, he was frightened; and as he began to sin, he cried out, "Master, save me." 31 Then Jesus immediately stretched out his hand, took him, and said to him, "O you who have little faith, why did you doubt? 32 And as they had entered the ship, the wind ceased. 33 Then those who were in the ship came up and worshiped him, saying, "It is true that you are the Son of God." 34 And when they had gone out, they came to the land of Gennezaret. 35 And when the men of that place knew him, they sent into all the surrounding county and brought to him all who were sick, 36 And they begged him to touch the hem of his garment; and as many as touched it were healed.

CHAPTER 15

1 Then came to Jesus the Scribes and Phar- isees, who were from Jerusalem, saying, 2 "Why do your disciples transgress the tradi- tion of the elders? Because they do not wash their hands when they eat bread." 3 But he answered them, "Why do you also transgress the commandment of God by your tradition? 4 For God has commanded, 'Honor your fa- ther and your mother; and whoever curses father or mother, let him die by death.' 5 But you say, "Whoever shall say to his father or mother, 'With the gift that is offered to me, you will ever profit, 6 even if he does not hon- or his father or mother, he shall be free; thus you have made God's commandment worth- less by your tradition. 7 O hypocrites, Esaias prophesied well of you, saying, 8 This peo- ple draw near to me with their mouths and honor me with their lips, but their hearts are far from me. 9 But in vein they worship me, teaching for doctrines the precepts of men." 10 Then he called the crowd to him and said to them, "Listen and understand. 11 What goes into the mouth does not defile the man, but what comes out of the mouth defiles the man. 12 Then his disciples came and said to him, "Do you not understand that the Pharisees were offended at hearing this saying?" 13 But he answered, "Every plant that

my Eternal Fa- ther has not planted can never take root." 14 Leave them alone; it is the blind who lead the blind; and if the blind make you blind, both of you will fall into the pit." 15 Then Peter an- swered and said to him, "Tell me this parable." 16 Then Jesus said, "Are you still without un- derstanding? 17 Do you still not understand that what goes into the mouth goes into the belly and is thrown into the stream? 18 But the things that come out of the mouth come from the heart and defile the man. 19 For out of the heart come evil thoughts, murders, adulter- ies, fornications, thefts, false witness, mur- ders. 20 These are the things that defile man; but eating with washed hands does not defile man. 21 Then Iesus departed and went to the coasts of Tyre and Sidon. 22 And behold, a Canaanite woman came out of those shores and cried out to him, saying, "Have mercy on me, O Lord, son of Dauid; my daughter is miserably afflicted with a disease." 23 But he did not answer her a word. Then his disciples came to him and begged him, saying, "Send her away, for she cries out behind herself." 24 But he answered, "I was not sent except to the lost sheep of the house of Israel." 25 But she drew near and worshipped him, saying, "Lord, help me." 26 He answered, "It is not good to take the children's bread and throw it to the kids." 27 But she answered, "True, Lord, but actually the little ones eat the grain that falls from their masters' table." 28 Then Jesus answered and said to her, "O woman, great is your faith; may it be for you as you wish." And the daughter was healed at that instant. 29 Then Jesus departed from there and came near the Sea of Galilee and went up to a mountain and sat down there. 30 And great crowds came to him, having with them the sick, the blind, the dumb, the maimed, and many others, and they threw them at the feet of Jesus, who healed them. 31 So much so that the crowd marveled to see the dumb speak, the maimed be whole, the hindered go, and the blind see; and they glorified the God of Israel. 32 Then Jesus called his disci- ples to him and said, "I have compassion on this crowd, for they have been with me three days already and have nothing to eat; and I do not want them to go away fasting, lest they faint on the way." 33 His disciples said to him, "Where will we get enough bread in the wil- derness to suffice for such a great multitude?" 34 Jesus said to them, "How many loaves do you have?" And they answered, "Ten and a few small fish." 35 Then he commanded the crowd to sit down on the ground, 36 and he took the two loaves and fishes, gave thanks, broke them, and gave them to his disciples, and the disciples to the crowd. 37 They all ate and were filled; then they took from the fragments that remained, ten full baskets. 38 Those who had eaten were four thousand men, besides wom- en and small children. 39 Then Iesus sent the crowd away, took the ship, and came to the parts of Magdala.

CHAPTER 16

1 Then the Pharisees and Sadducees came and tempted him, wanting him to show them a sign from above. 2 But he answered and said to them, "When evening comes, you say, 'Faire wether,' for your skin is red. 3 And in the morning you say, 'The day will be a storm, for the sky is red and low.' O hypocrites, do you know how to discern the face of the sky and cannot discern the signs of the times? 4 The wicked and adulterous generation seeks a sign, but no other sign will be given them than that of the prophet Ionas; so he left them and departed. 5 When his disciples had come to the other shore, they had forgotten to take bread with them.

6 Then Jesus said to them, "Take heed and beware of the law of the Pharisees and Sadducees." 7 They reasoned among themselves, saying, "It is because we did not bring bread." 8 But Jesus, knowing this, said to them, "O you of little faith, why do you reason so among yourselves, because you have not brought bread? 9 Do you not yet realize and remember the first times there were five thousand men and how many bas- kets you brought? 10 Nor of the ten loaves of bread, when there were four thousand men, and how many baskets did you gather? 11 Why do you not see that I said nothing to you concerning bread, that you might beware of the law of the Pharisees and Sadducees? 12 Then they understood that He had not said to beware of bread, but of the doctrine of the Pharisees and Sadducees. 13 Now when Jesus came to the shores of Caesarea Philippi, he asked his disciples, "Who do men say that I am the son of man? 14 They answered, "Some say John the Baptist, others Elijah, still others Jeremiah or one of the Prophets." 15 He said to them, "But who do you say that I am?" 16 Simon Peter answered and said, "You are that Christ, the Son of the laughing God." 17 Then Jesus answered and said to him, "Blessed are you, Simon, son of Ionas, for flesh and blood has not revealed him to you, but my Father who is in heaven. 18 And I also tell you that you are Peter, and on this cross I will build my Church, and the gates of hell will not be able to prevent it. 19 I will give you the keys of the kingdom of Heauen, and what you bind on earth shall be bound in Heauen, and what you loose on earth shall be loosed in Heauen." 20 Then he instructed his disciples not to tell anyone that he was Jesus, the Christ. 21 From that time on, Jesus began to make it clear to his disciples that he was to go to Jerusa- lem and suffer many things from the elders, priests and scribes, be killed and rise again on the thirteenth day. 22 Then Peter took him aside and began to rebuke him, saying, "Master, have mercy on yourself; this will not happen to you." 23 Then he turned and said to Peter, "Get away from me, Satan; you are an offense to me, for you do not understand the things of God, but those of men." 24 Then Je- sus said to his disciples, "If anyone wants to follow me, let him abandon himself and take up his cross and follow me. 25 For whoever wants to save his life will lose it; and whoev- er loses his life for my sake will find it. 26 For what does it profit a man to win the whole world, if he then loses his own soul? Or what will a man give as the reward of his own soul? 27 For the Son of man will come in the glory of his Father with his Angels, and then he will render to each man according to his deeds. 28 Verily I tell you that there are some of those who stand here who will not taste death until they see the Son of Man coming in His king- dom.

CHAPTER 17

1 After six days, Jesus took Peter, Iames and Iohn, his brother, and led them to an isolated mountain, 2 And he was transfigured before them; his face shone like the sun, and his gar- ments were white as the light. 3 And behold, Moses and Elijah appeared to them, speak- ing with him. 4 Then Peter answered Jesus, "Master, it is good that you are here; if you will, let us make three tabernacles here, one for you, one for Moses and one for Elijah." 5 While he was still speaking, behold, a bright cloud overshadowed them; and out of the cloud came a voice saying, "This is my beau- tiful Son, in whom I am well pleased: listen to him." 6 On hearing this, the disciples fell on their faces and were frightened. 7 Then Jesus touched them and said, "Get up

and do not be afraid." 8 And when they lifted up their eyes, they saw no one but Jesus. 9 And as they came down from the mountain, Jesus instructed them to say, "Do not reveal the vision to any- one until the Son of Man rises from the dead." 10 His disciples questioned him, saying, "Why then do the scribes say that Elijah must come first?" 11 Jesus answered them, "Certainly Eli- jah must come first and restore all things. 12 But I tell you that Elijah has already come, and they did not know him, but did to him what they wanted; so also the Son of Man will suf- fer of them." 13 Then the disciples noticed that he was speaking to them about John the Bap- tist. 14 When they had approached the crowd, a certain man came up to him and fell at his feet, 15 and said, "Master, have mercy on my son, for he is moody and very irritated, for he often falls into fire and often into water. 16 I took him to your disciples, but they could not heal him. 17 Then Iesus answered and said, "O faithless and crooked generation, how much longer shall I be with you, how much longer shall I make you suffer, bring him here to me." 18 Jesus rebuked the curse, and it went out from him; and the child was healed in that hour. 19 Then the disciples came to Jesus and said, "Why were we not able to drive him out?" 20 Jesus answered them, "Because of your un- belief, for verily I say to you, if you have faith as much as a grain of mustard seed, you will say to this mountain, 'Move to that place,' and it will stand again, and nothing will be impos- sible for you." 21 Yet this kind does not go out except by prayer and fasting." 22 And because they were in Galilee, Jesus said to them, "The Son of Man will be delivered into the hands of men, 23 and they will kill him, but on the thirteenth day he will rise again; and they were greatly grieved. 24 And when they had come to Capernaum, they that received the money for the fowl came to Peter and said to him, "Does not your Master pay the money for the fowl?" 25 He answered, "Yes." And when he had entered the house, Jesus forestalled him, saying, "What do you think, Simon? From whom do the kings of the earth take tribute or money for the fowl? From their children or from foreigners? 26 Peter answered him, "From foreigners." Then Jesus said to him, "Then the children are free." 27 Lest you of- fend them, go into the sea, cast a corner and catch the first fish that comes along, and when you have opened your mouth, you will find a twenty-five-pence piece; take it and give it to them for me and for you.

CHAPTER 18

1 At the same time the disciples came to Je- sus and asked Him, "Who is the greatest in the kingdom of God? 2 Jesus called to Himself a little child and placed Him in their midst, 3 and said, "Truly I tell you, unless you are conquered and become like little children, you will not enter the kingdom of Heauen. 4 Whosoever therefore shall humble himself as this little child, he shall be the greatest in the kingdom of Heauen. 5 Whoever shall re- ceive one of these little children in my name shall receive me. 6 But whoever offends one of these little ones who grow in me, it would be better for him if a millstone were hung around his neck and he were drowned in the depths of the sea. 7 Cursed be the world because of offenses, for it is necessary for offenses to come, but cursed be the man from whom the offense comes. 8 Therefore, if thy hand or thy foot cause thee offense, cut them off and cast them from thee; it is better for thee to enter into life, crippled or maimed, than to have two hands or two feet and be cast into eternal fire. 9 And if your eye hurts, pluck it out and cast it from you; it is better for you to enter life with one eye, and with two eyes to be cast into hellfire. 10 See that you do not despise one of these little ones, for I tell you that in heaven their angels always look upon the face of my Father who is in heaven. 11 For the Son of Man came to save what was lost. 12 How do you think that if a man has a hundred sheep and one of them goes astray, does he not leave ninety-nine of them and go to the mountains to see the one that went astray? 13 And if he finds it, verily I say to you that he cares more for that sheep than for the ninety-nine and nine that have not gone astray: 14 Therefore it is not the will of your Father which is in heav- en that one of these little ones should perish. 15 Moreover, if your brother commits an of- fense against you, go and tell him his fault be- tween you and him alone; if he hears you, you have overcome your brother. 16 But if he does not listen to you, take still one or two with you, that the mouth of two or three witnesses may confirm every word. 17 And if he refus- es to listen to them, refer him to the Church; and if he refuses to listen to the Church also, let him be to you as a heathen and a pub- lican. 18 Verily, I say to you, what you bind on earth shall be bound in heaven; and what you loose on earth shall be loosed in heaven. 19 Moreover, verily I say unto you, that if two of you agree on earth concerning any thing, that which they desire shall be granted unto them of my Father which is in heaven. 20 For where two or three are gathered together in my Name, there am I in the midst of them." 21 Then Peter approached him and said, "Teacher, how many times shall my brother sin against me, and I will forgive him? Up to ten times?" 22 Jesus answered him, "I do not say to you, 'Up to ten times,' but 'Up to seventy times.' 23 Therefore the kingdom of Heauen is compared to a certain king who wants to give an account of his servants. 24 When he began to reckon, one was brought to him who owed him ten thousand talents. 25 Since he had nothing to pay, his lord commanded that he be liquidated, together with his wife, his children, and everything he owned, and that the sum be paid. 26 So the servant fell to the ground and worshiped him, saying, "Lord, turn away your wrath from me, and I will pay you everything." 27 Then the Lord of the ser- vant had compassion, and loosed him, and condemned his imprisonment. 28 But when the servant was gone, he found one of his servants who owed him a hundred pence; he laid his hands on him and shook him, saying, "Pay me what you owe." 29 Then his servant fell at his feet and pleaded with him, saying, "Calm your anger toward me, and I will pay you everything." 30 But he would not, rather he threw him into prison until he had paid the deduction. 31 When his other feline ser- vants heard what had been done, they were very sorry, and came and reported to their lord all that had been done. 32 Then his lord called him to himself and said, "O euile ser- vant, I forgive you all that you have done, be- cause you have prayed to me. 33 Should not you also have mercy on your fellow servant, just as I have had mercy on you? 34 Then his lord was angry and delivered him to torment until he paid all that was due him. 35 So will my Eternal Father also do to you, if you do not heartily forgive, each one to his own brother, his debts.

CHAPTER 19

1 When Jesus had finished these discours- es, he departed from Galilee and came to the shores of Judea, beyond Iordan. 2 Large crowds followed him, and he healed them. 3 Then came to him the Pharisees tempting him and saying, "Is it lawful for a man to leave his wife on any occasion?"

4 He answered and said to them, "Have you not read that He who created them in the beginning made them male and female? 5 And He said, "Therefore a man shall leave his father and his mother and separate from his wife, and the two shall be one flesh. 6 Therefore they are no longer two, but one flesh. Let no man therefore separate what God has joined together." 7 They said to him, "Why then did Moses command to do an act of divorce and to remove the woman? 8 He said to them, "Moses, because of the hardness of your hearts, permitted you to separate your wives; but from the beginning it was not so. 9 Therefore I say to you, whoever renounces his wife, except for prostitution, and mar- ries another, commits adultery; and whoever marries her who has been divorced, commits adultery." 10 Then his disciples said to him, "If the thing is so between man and wife, it is not good to marry." 11 But he said to them, "All men cannot receive this thing, only those to whom it has been granted. 12 For there are eunuchs who were delivered thus from their mothers' wombs, and there are eunuchs who were castrated by men, and there are eunuchs who castrated themselves for the kingdom of Heauen. Whoever is able to receive this, let him receive it." 13 Then little children were brought to Him, that He might lay His hands on them and pray; and the disciples rebuked them. 14 But Jesus said, "Leave the little chil- dren alone and forbid them to come to me, for of such is the kingdom of God." 15 And hav- ing laid his hands on them, he departed. 16 And behold, one came and said to him, "Good Teacher, what good thing must I do to have eternal life?" 17 And he answered him, "Why do you call me good? There is none good but one, that is God; but if you want to enter life, observe your commands." 18 He said to him, "Which ones?" And Jesus said, "These: Thou shalt not kill: Thou shalt not commit adultery: Thou shalt not steal; Thou shalt not bear false witness. 19 Honor thy father and thy moth- er, and love thy neighbor as thyself. 20 The young man said to him, "I have observed all these things from my youth; what am I still lacking? 21 Jesus said to him, "If you want to be perfect, go, sell what you have and give to the poor, and you will have treasure in heav- en; then come and follow me." 22 When the young man heard these words, he went away sorrowful, for he had many possessions. 23 Then Jesus said to his disciples, "Truly I tell you, a rich man will hardly enter the king- dom of God. 24 And again I tell you that it is easier for a camel to go through the eye of a needle than for a rich man to enter the king- dom of God. 25 And when his disciples heard this, they were exceedingly amazed and said, Who then can be killed? 26 Jesus looked at them and said, "With men this is impossible, but with God all things are possible." 27 Then Peter answered and said to them, "Behold, we have forsaken all things and followed you; what shall we have therefore?" 28 And Jesus said to them, "Truly I tell you, when the Son of Man sits on the throne of his kingdom, you who have followed me in regeneration will also sit on two thrones and will judge the two tribes of Israel. 29 And whosoever shall for- sake houses, brothers, sisters, father, mother, wife, children, or lands for my names' sake, he shall receive a hundredfold and inherit eter- nal life. 30 But many of those who are first will be last, and the last will be first.

CHAPTER 20

1 For the kingdom of Heauen is like a certain landlord who went out at daybreak to hire la- borers in his vineyard. 2 He agreed with the laborers for a penny a day and sent them to his vineyard. 3 About the third hour he went out and saw others idling in the marketplace, 4 And he said to them, "Go you also into my vineyard, and I will give you what is right"; and they went out. 5 Then he went out about the sixth and ninth hour and did the same. 6 About the eleventh hour he found others idling, and said to them, "Why do you stand idle here all day long? 7 They answered him, "Because no one has hired anyone." He said to them, "You also go into my vineyard and receive what is right." 8 When the time had come, the master of the vineyard said to his steward, "Call the laborers and give them their wages, beginning with the last, until you come to the first." 9 Those who had been hired about the eleventh hour came and each received a pen. 10 And when the first came, they thought to receive more, but they also received each man a coin. 11 And when they had received them, they murmured against the master of the house, 12 saying, "These last have labored but an hour, and you have equat- ed them with those who have borne the bur- den and toil of the day." 13 He answered one of them, saying, "Friend, I do you no wrong; did you not agree with me for a pen? 14 Take what is yours and go your way: I will give the latter as much to you. 15 Is it not lawful for me to do what I will with my possessions? Is not your eye weak because I am good? 16 So the last shall be first, and the first the last; for many are the called, but few the elect. 17 Then Jesus went to Jerusalem and took the two disciples on the road and said to them, 18 Behold, we are going to Jerusalem, and the Son of Man will be handed over to the chief priests and the scribes, and they will con- demn him to death, 19 and they will hand him over to the Gentiles to mock, scourge and crucify him, but on the third day he will rise again." 20 Then came to him the mother of the sons of Zebedee with her sons, who wor- shipped him and desired a certain thing from him. 21 He said to her, "What do you desire?" She answered him, "Desire these two sons of mine to sit, one at your right hand and the other at your left, in your kingdom." 22 Jesus answered, "You do not know what you ask. Are you able to drink the cup that I will drink and be baptized with the baptism that I will baptize? They answered him, "We are able." 23 And he said to them, "You shall drink of my cup as a gift and be baptized with the baptism with which I will be baptized, but to sit at my right hand and at my left is not for me, but it will be given to those for whom it has been prepared by my Father." 24 When the other ten heard this, they became indignant with the two brothers. 25 Then Jesus called them to himself and said, "We know that the lords of the Gentiles have dominion over them and that those who are great exercise authority over them. 26 But among you it shall not be so; but whoever wishes to be great among you shall be your servant. 27 And whoever will be chief among you shall be your servant. 28 As the Son of Man came not to be served, but to serve and to give his life for the ransom of many. 29 As they departed from Jericho, a great crowd followed him. 30 And behold, two blind men sitting by the road, when they heard that Jesus was passing by, cried out, "O Lord, Son of Dauid, have mercy on them." 31 The crowd rebuked them, so that they did not rest; but they cried out even more, saying, "O Lord, Son of Dauid, have mercy on me." 32 Then Jesus stopped, called them, and said, "What do you want me to do to you?" 33 They said to Him, "Lord, let our eyes be opened." 34 Jesus, moved with compassion, touched their eyes, and immediately their eyes received sight and followed him.

CHAPTER 21

1 When they had come to Jerusalem and Bethphage on the Mount of Olives, Jesus sent two disciples, 2 saying to them, "Go into the city that is opposite you, and immediately you will find a horse tied and a colt with her; untie them and bring them to me. 3 And if anyone says no to you, answer that the Lord has need of them, and immediately he will let them go. 4 All this was done so that what was spoken by the prophet might be fulfilled, 5 Say to the daughter of Zion, "Behold, your king comes to you, clothed and seated on a plank and on a blanket, the foot of a plank tied to a yoke." 6 Then the disciples went and did as Jesus had commanded them, 7 And they brought the horse and the colt, and clothed them, and brought him up. 8 And a great multitude stripped along the road; others cut branches from the trees and straw them along the road. 9 What is more, the people that went before and the people that followed cried out, say- ing, "Hosanna to the Son of Dauid, blessed be he who comes in the Name of the Lord, hosanna to you who are in the highest heav- ens." 10 And when he had come to Jerusalem, the whole city was in an uproar, saying, "Who is this man?" 11 And the people said, "This is Jesus, the prophet from Nazareth in Galilee." 12 And Jesus went into the Temple of God and cast out all those who were selling and buy- ing in the Temple, and overthrew the tables of the moneychangers and the counters of those who were selling gifts, 13 and said to them, "It is written, 'My house shall be called a house of prayer,' but you have made it a den of theo- logians." 14 Then the blind and the sick came to him in the Temple, and he healed them. 15 But when the chief priests and scribes saw the wonders he did and the children weeping in the Temple and saying, "Hosanna to the Son of Dauid," they were outraged, 16 and said to him, "Do you realize what these are saying?" And Jesus answered them, "Yes; do you not read that by the mouths of babes and infants you have made praise perfect?" 17 Then he left them and went out of the city to Betha- ny and settled there. 18 In the morning, as he was returning to the city, he was seized with hunger, 19 and, seeing a fig tree by the road, he approached it and found nothing there but leaves, and said to it, "From now on no more fruit will grow on you." And immediately the fig tree withered. 20 And when his disciples saw it, they marveled, saying, "How the fig tree has withered! 21 Then Jesus answered and said to them, "Truly I tell you, if you have faith and do not doubt, not only will you do what I did to the fig tree, but also if you say to this mountain, 'Take it away and throw it into the sea,' it will be done. 22 And whatev- er you ask in prayer, if you are heard, you will receive." 23 When he had entered the Temple, the chief priests and the elders of the people came to him as he was teaching and said, "By what authority do you do these things? And who gave you this authority?" 24 Then Jesus answered and said to them, "I also will ask you a certain thing; if you will tell me, I also will tell you by what authority I do these things." 25 The baptism of John, where did it come from? From him or from men? Then they reasoned among themselves, saying, "If we say, From him, he will say to us, Why did you not baptize him? 26 But if we say, From men, we fear the crowd, for they all consider John a prophet." 27 Then they answered Ie- sus and said, "We cannot say." And he said to them, "I do not even tell you by what authority I do these things. 28 But what do you think? A certain man had two sons, and he came to the eldest and said to him, "Son, go work to- day in my vineyard." 29 But he answered, "I will not"; but then he repented and went. 30 Then he approached the second and said the same to him. And he answered and said, "I will, Syr," but he did not go. 31 Which of the two of them did their father's will? They said to him, "The first." Jesus said to them, "Tru- ly I tell you, publicans and harlots go before you in the kingdom of God." 32 For John came to you in the way of righteousness, and you did not hear him; but the publicans and the harlots heard him, and you, though you said so, did not repent afterward that you might hear him." 33 Listen to another parable: there was a certain landlord who planted a vine- yard, fenced it all around, made a vineyard there, built a tower, leased it to the peasants, and went to a foreign country. 34 When the time of the fruit approached, he sent his ser- vants to the vinedressers to receive the fruit. 35 His servants were clubbed by one of them, killed another, and stoned another. 36 Then he sent other servants, more numerous than the first, and they did the same to them. 37 But last of all he sent them his own son, say- ing, "They will take care of my son." 38 But when the householders saw the son, they said among themselves, "This is the heir; come, kill him and take his inheritance." 39 So they took him and drove him out of the vineyard and killed him. 40 When therefore the Lord of the vineyards comes, what will he do to those vinedressers? 41 They said to him, "He will cruelly destroy those wicked men and en- trust his vineyard to other vinedressers, who will deliver the fruit to him in their seasons." 42 Jesus said to them, "Do you not read in the Scriptures that the stone which the builders rejected has become the head of the corner? This the Lord has done, and it is marvelous in our eyes. 43 Therefore I say to you that the kingdom of God will be taken away from you and given to a nation that will bear its fruit. 44 Whoever falls on this stone will break it; but whoever falls on it will break it to pieces. 45 And when the chief priests and Pharisees had heard his parables, they saw that he was speaking of them. 46 And seeking to lay hands on him, they feared the people, because they regarded him as a prophet.

CHAPTER 22

1 Then Iesus answered and spoke to them again in parables, saying 2 The kingdom of Heauen is like a certain king who married his son, 3 and sent his servants to call those who had been invited to the wedding, but they would not come. 4 Then he sent for other servants, saying. Say to those who were invit- ed, "Behold, I have prepared my supper: my oxen and my fat ones have been killed, and everything is ready; come to the wedding." 5 But they played dumb and went their way, the one to his house and the other to his wares. 6 The remaining ones took his servants, ques- tioned them sharply, and killed them. 7 But when the king heard this, he was angry and sent his warriors and destroyed those mur- derers and burned down their city. 8 Then he said to his servants, "Truly the wedding was prepared, but those who were invited were not worthy. 9 Go therefore through the main streets, and as many as you find, invite them to the wedding." 10 And the servants went out into the main streets and gathered all those whom they found, both good and bad; so the wedding was prepared lavishly. 11 Then the king went in to see the garments and saw a man who had no wedding garment. 12 And he said to him, Friend, how did you come here and have no wedding garment? And he began to speak. 13 Then the king said to the servants, "Take him by the hand and carry him away and cast him into darkness, where there will be weeping and gnashing of teeth. 14 For many are the called, but few the elect. 15 Then

the Pharisees began to study how to hinder him with talk. 16 They sent their dis- ciples to him with the Herodians, saying, "Teacher, we know that you are truthful and teach the way of God truthfully, and you care for no one, for you do not consider the person of men. 17 Tell me, then, how do you think? Is it lawful or not to give tribute to Caesar? 18 But Jesus, perceiving their wickedness, said, "Why do you tempt me, you hypocrites? 19 Give me tribute money." And they brought him a coin. 20 And he said to them, "Whose image and inscription is this? 21 They an- swered him, "Caesars." Then he said to them, "Give therefore to Caesar the things that are Caesar's, and give to God the things that are God's." 22 On hearing this, they marveled and left him and went their way. 23 On the same day the Sadducees (who say there is no res- urrection) came to him and questioned him, 24 saying, "Teacher, Moses said, 'If a man dies and has no children, his brother shall marry his wife by right of covenant and shall be- get offspring for his brother.'" 25 Now there were two brothers with them; the first mar- ried a wife and died; and having no children, he left his wife to his brother. 26 So also the second and the third until the tenth. 27 And last also the woman died. 28 So in the resur- rection, whose wife will the two be? For they all had her." 29 Then Jesus answered and said to them, "You deceive yourselves, not know- ing the Scriptures nor the power of God. 30 For in the resurrection they neither marry wives nor receive wives in marriage, but are like the angels of God in heaven. 31 Concern- ing the resurrection of the dead, have you not read what has been told you by God? 32 Am I the God of Abraham, the God of Isaac, and the God of Jacob? God is not the God of the dead, but of the living." 33 On hearing this, the crowd was amazed at his doctrine. 34 But when the Pharisees had heard that he had si- lenced the Sadducees, they gathered togeth- er. 35 And one of them, who was an exegete of the Lawe, put a question to him, tempting him and saying, "Teacher, what is your name? 36 Master, what is your great commandment in the Lawe? 37 Jesus said to him, "You must love the Lord your God with all your heart, with all your soul and with all your mind." 38 This is the first and great commandment. 39 The second is similar to this, "You shall love your neighbor as yourself." 40 On these two commandments depend all the Law and the Prophets. 41 While the Pharisees were gathered, Jesus questioned them, 42 saying, "What do you think of Christ? Whose son is he?" They answered him, "Dauids." 43 He said to them, "How is it that Dauidi in spirit calls him Lord." 44 Has the Lord said to my Lord, 'Sit at my right hand until I make your enemies your feet'?" 45 So if Dauid calls him Lord, how is he his son? 46 No one could an- swer him a word, and from that day on no one asked him any more questions.

CHAPTER 23

1 Then Jesus spoke to the crowd and to his disciples, 2 saying, "The scribes and Pharisees sit in the seat of Moses. 3 Whatever they tell you to observe, observe and do; but do not follow their works, for they say and do not do. 4 For they bear burdens heavy and heavy to bear, and lay them on men's shoulders, but they themselves do not crush them with a finger. 5 All their works they do to be seen of men, for they make their phylacteries broad, and make the bangs of their garments long, 6 And they win the first places in feasts and the first places in assemblies, 7 greeting in the markets and being called by men, "Rabbi, Rabbi." 8 But do not be called "Rabbi," for one is your doctor, that is Christ,

and all of you are brothers. 9 And do not call anyone your father on earth, for there is only one, your father who is in heaven. 10 Do not be called doctors, for there is only one who is your doctor, that is Christ. 11 But he who is the greatest among you, let him be your servant. 12 For whoever wishes to exalt himself will be brought low; and whoever wishes to humble himself will be exalted. 13 Woe therefore to you, Scribes and Pharisees, hypocrites, because you close the kingdom of Heauen before men; for you yourselves do not enter in, and do not allow those who want to enter in. 14 Woe to you, Scribes and Pharisees, hypocrites, for you de- stroy the houses of widows, under the color of long prayers; for this you shall receive greater damnation. 15 Woe to you, Scribes and Phar- isees, hypocrites, because you toil on the sea and on the land to do one of your trades; and when you have done it, you make it twice as much a child of hell as yourselves. 16 Woe to you blind guides, who say, "He who swears by the Temple, he is nothing; but he who swears by the coin of the Temple, he offends." 17 Fools and blind men, who is greater, the coin or the Temple that sanctifies the coin? 18 He who swears by the altar, is nothing; but he who swears by the offering on it, offends. 19 Fools and blind men, who is greater, the offering or the altar that sanctifies the offering? 20 Who- ever therefore swears by the altar, swears by it and by all that is on it. 21 Whoever swears by the Temple, swears by it and by those who dwell therein. 22 He who swears by heaven, swears by the throne of God and by him who sits there. 23 Woe to you, Scribes and Phari- sees, hypocrites, because you decry my mon- ey, orange and heap, and neglect the more important matters of the law, such as judg- ment, mercy and faithfulness. These things you should have done and not left the others behind. 24 You blind guides, who pluck out a gnat and swallow a camel. 25 Woe to you, Scribes and Pharisees, hypocrites, because you make transparent the back side of the cup and dish, but inside they are full of cor- ruption and excess. 26 Blind Pharisee, cleanse first the inside of the cup and dish, that the outside may also be clean. 27 Woe to you, Scribes and Pharisees, hypocrites, for you are like whitened sepulchers, looking beautiful on the outside, but inside they are full of dead men's bones and every filth. 28 So are you also, for on the outside you appear righteous in the eyes of men, but inside you are full of hypocrisy and iniquity. 29 Woe to you, Scribes and Pharisees, hypocrites, because you build the tombs of the Prophets and line the sepul- chres of the righteous, 30 and say, "If we had been in the days of our fathers, we would not have associated with them in the blood of the Prophets." 31 Thus you shall be witnesses for yourselves that you are children of those who killed the Prophets. 32 Fulfill also the measure of your fathers. 33 O serpents, gen- eration of vipers, how could you escape the damnation of hell? 34 Therefore, behold, I send you prophets and wise men and scribes, whom you shall kill and crucify; you shall scourge them in your synagogues and perse- cute them from town to town, 35 that on you may fall all the righteous blood that has been shed on the earth, from the blood of Abel the righteous, even to the blood of Zechariah the son of Barachiah, whom you killed between the Temple and the altar. 36 Truly I tell you, all these things will come upon this genera- tion. 37 Jerusalem, Jerusalem, you who kill the Prophets and stone those who are sent to you, how often I wanted to gather your children together, as the hen gathers her chicks un- der her wings, and you would not! 38 Behold, your dwelling place shall be desolate to you, 39 For I say to you that you shall see me no more until you say, "Blessed is he who comes in the Name of the Lord."

CHAPTER 24

1 Then Jesus went out and departed from the Temple, and his disciples came to him to show him the building of the Temple. 2 And Jesus said to them, "Do you not see all these things? Verily I say unto you, there shall not remain here a stone upon a stone that shall not be cast." 3 While he was on the Mount of Olives, his disciples joined him on the sidelines, saying, "Tell me when these things will take place and what will be the sign of your coming and of the end of the world." 4 Jesus answered them, "See that no one deceives you. 5 For many will come in my name, say- ing, 'I am the Christ,' and will deceive many. 6 And you will hear of wars and rumors of wars; see that you are not troubled, for all these things must take place, but the end has not yet come. 7 For nation shall rise up against nation, and reality against reality, and there shall be famine and pestilence and earth- quakes in many places. 8 All these things are but the beginning of sorrows. 9 Then they will deliver you up to be afflicted, and they will kill you, and you will be hated by all nations for My names' sake. 10 Then many will offend and betray one another and hate one another. 11 Many false prophets will arise and deceive many. 12 And because iniquity will increase, the joy of many will be extinguished. 13 But he who endures to the end will be saved. 14 This gospel of the kingdom will be preached in all the world to witness to all nations, and then the end will come. 15 When therefore you see the abomination of desolation spoken of by Daniel the prophet, set in the holy place (let those who read consider it). 16 then let those who are in Iudea flee to the mountains. 17 He who is on the top of the house let him not go down to take anything from his house. 18 And whoever is in the fields, let him not go back to get his clothes. 19 Woe to those who are preg- nant and to those who are deceived in those days. 20 But see to it that your escape does not take place in winter or on the Sabbath day. 21 For then there will be great tribulation, such as there has not been from the beginning of the world until now, nor will there ever be. 22 And if those days were not shortened, no flesh would be killed; but for the elect those days shall be shortened. 23 If then anyone shall say to you, "Behold the Christ, or there," do not do it. 24 For false Christs and false prophets shall arise, and they shall do great signs and wonders, so that, if it were possible, they would deceive the very elect. 25 Behold, I have already told you. 26 Therefore if they shall say unto you, Behold, it is in the wilderness, go not away: Beholde, it is in the secret places, go not away. 27 For as the thunderbolt comes out of the east and is seen in the west, so shall also the coming of the Son of Man be. 28 For where there is a dead car, there the Egles will gather. 29 And immediately after the tribula- tion of those days, the sun will be darkened, the moon will not give its light, the stars will recede from above, and the powers of heaven will be shaken. 30 Then the sign of the Son of Man will appear in heaven; and then all the peoples of the earth will be converted and will see the Son of Man coming in the clouds of heaven with power and great glory. 31 And he will send his angels with a great sound of a trumpet, and they will gather his elect from the four winds and from one end of the heav- ens to the other. 32 Now learn the parable of the fig tree: when its branch is still tender and producing leaves, you know that the morn- ing is near. 33 So you also, when you see all these things, will know that the kingdom of God is near, and that it is at the gates. 34 Truly I tell you, this generation will not pass away until all these things are fulfilled. 35 Heaven and earth will pass away, but my words will not pass away. 36 But of that day and hour no one knows anything, not even the angels of Heauen, but only my father. 37 But as the days of Noe were, so shall also the coming of the Son of Man be. 38 For as in the days before the flood they ate and drank, and married and gave themselves in marriage, until the day that Noe entered the Ark, 39 And they knew nothing, until the flood came and took them all away; so shall also the coming of the Son of Man be. 40 Then two will be in the fields, the one will be accepted and the other will be re- jected. 41 Two women shall be grinding at the mill: the one shall be accepted and the other rejected. 42 Watch therefore, for you do not know at what hour your master will come. 43 Of this be sure: if the good man of the house knew what hour the thief would come, he would surely watch and not allow his house to be dug up. 44 Therefore you also be ready, for in the hour when you do not think, the Son of Man will come. 45 Who then is a faithful and wise servant, whom his master has appointed head of his house, to give them food in due season? 46 Blessed is that servant whom his master, when he comes, will find doing so. 47 Verily I say unto you, that he shall make him master of all his goods. 48 But if that eu- ile servant shall say in his heart, "My master postpones his coming." 49 and begins to beat his companions, and to eat and drink with the drunkards, 50 that the servant's master will come in a day when he does not seek him and in an hour when he does not notice, 51 he will cut him off and give him his portion with the hypocrites; there will be weeping and gnash- ing of teeth.

CHAPTER 25

1 Then the kingdom of Heauen will be com- pared to ten virgins who, after lighting their lamps, went to meet the bridegroom. 2 Five of them were wise and others foolish. 3 The fool- ish ones lit their lamps, but took no oil with them. 4 The wise, on the other hand, made oil in their vessels with their lamps. 5 While the bridegroom lingered, they all fell asleep and slept. 6 At midnight a cry was heard, "Be- hold, the bridegroom comes; go out to meet him." 7 Then all the virgins arose and lit their lamps. 8 The foolish said to the wise, "Come out of your lamps, for ours have gone out." 9 But the wise answered, "Not so, for there is not enough for you and for you; but go rath- er to those who sell and make your own." 10 While they were bidding farewell, the bride- groom came; and those who were ready went in with him to the wedding, and the door was shut. 11 Then the other virgins also came and said, "Lord, Lord, open to me! 12 But he an- swered, "Truly I say to you, I do not know you. 13 Watch therefore, for you know neither the day nor the hour when the son of man will come. 14 For the kingdom of Heauen is like a man who, going into a foreign country, calls his servants and delivers his goods to them. 15 To one he gave five talents, to another two, to yet another one, to each according to his ability, and immediately he left home. 16 The one who had received the five talents went and took care of them and gained another five talents. 17 Likewise, he who had received two talents earned two more. 18 But he who had received that one went and dug in the ground and hid his masters' money. 19 After a long time, the master of those servants came to reckon with them. 20 Then he who had re- ceived five talents came and brought another

five talents, saying, "Master, you delivered me five talents; behold, I have gained with them another five talents." 21 Then his master said to him, "It is well done, thou good and faithful servant: thou hast been faithful in the little, I will make thee ruler over the much; enter in thy master." 22 He also who had received two talents came and said, "Master, thou de- liveredst unto me two talents; behold, I have gained two more talents." 23 His master said to him, "It is well done, good and faithful ser- vant: you have been faithful in the little, I will make you master of the much; enter into your master." 24 Then he who had received the one talent approached and said, "Master, I knew that you were a hard man, reaping where you did not sow and gathering where you did not straw: 25 Therefore I was afraid, and went and hid thy talent in the earth; behold, thou hast thine own. 26 And his master answered and said unto him, Thou unhappy and sloth- ful servant, thou knewest that I reap where I sowed not, and that I gather where I sowed not. 27 You should therefore have made my money available to the money-changers, and then, when I came, I should have received my money with advantage. 28 Therefore take away his talent, and give it to him who has ten talents. 29 For to him who has, it will be given and he will have abundance, and to him who does not have, what he has will be tak- en away. 30 Cast therefore that vnprofitable servant into the deepest darkness; there shall be weeping and gnashing of teeth there. 31 When the Son of Man comes in his glory, and all the holy angels with him, he will sit on the throne of his glory, 32 and before him all the nations will be gathered, and he will separate them one from another, as a shepherd sepa- rates the sheep from the goats. 33 He will put the sheep on his right hand and the goats on his left. 34 Then the king will say to those on his right, "Come, you blessed of my father, take the inheritance of the kingdom prepared for you from the foundation of the world. 35 For I was hungry, and you gave me food: I was thirsty, and you gave me drink: I was a strang- er, and you welcomed me into your house. 36 I was naked, and ye clothed me: I was sick, and ye visited me: I was in prison, and ye came unto me. 37 Then the righteous shall answer him, saying, Lord, when did we tell you that you were hungry and gave you food, or that you were thirsty and gave you drink? 38 When did we see you a stranger and welcome you in? Or naked and we clothed you? 39 Or when we saw you sick or in prison and came to you? 40 The king will answer and say to them, "Tru- ly I tell you, inasmuch as you did it to one of the least of these brothers of mine, you did it to me." 41 Then he will say to those on the left, "Depart from me, ye cursed, into everlast- ing fire, which is prepared for the devil and his angels. 42 For I was hungry, and ye gave me no food: I was thirsty, and ye gave me no drink: 43 I was a stranger, and ye took me not in: I was naked, and ye clothed me not: I was sick, and in prison, and ye visited me not. 44 Then shall they also answer him, Lord, when did we tell you that you were hungry, thirsty, a stranger, naked, sick, or in prison, and did not visit you? 45 Then he will answer them and say, "Truly I tell you, if you did not do it to one of the least of these, you did not do it to me."

CHAPTER 26

1 When Jesus had finished all this talk, he said to his disciples, 2 You know that after two days is the Passover, and that the Son of Man will be delivered up to be crucified." 3 Then the chief priests, scribes and elders of the people gathered together in the hall of the high priest called Caiaphas: 4 And they con- sulted together about taking Jesus by decep- tion and killing him. 5 But they said, "Not on the feast day, at least let there be no vprore among the people." 6 When Jesus was in Beth- any, in the house of Simon the leper, 7 there came to him a woman who had a box of very costly things and placed it on his head, while he sat at the table. 8 When his disciples saw this, they were indignant, saying, "What need was there for this waste? 9 For that wineskin could have been sold for much and given to the poor. 10 And Jesus, knowing this, said to them, "Why do you grieve over the woman? Because she has done me a good deed. 11 For you always have the poor with you, but I will never have them. 12 For she has made this touching up of my body to bury me. 13 Verily I say unto you, when this gospel shall be preached in all the world, it shall also be spo- ken of this that she hath done, to remember her." 14 Then one of the two, named Iudas Is- cariot, went to the chief priest, 15 and said, "What will you give me, and I will deliver it to you?" And they assigned him three pieces of silver. 16 And from that time he looked for an opportunity to betray him. 17 Now on the first day of the feast of vnleauened bread, the dis- ciples came to Iesus and said to him, "Where do you want us to prepare you to eat the Past?" 18 He said, "Go into the city to such a one and say to him, 'The master says, "My hour is near: I want to celebrate the Pastime at your house with my disciples.'" 19 The disciples did as Ie- sus had instructed them and set about pre- paring the Passover. 20 When summer had come, he sat down with the two disciples. 21 As they were eating, he said, "Truly I tell you, one of you will betray me." 22 They were great- ly grieved and began to say to him, "Is it I, master?" 23 He answered, "Whoever dips his hand with me in the dish, this one will betray me." 24 Certainly the Son of Man goes his way, as it is written of him; but woe to that man by whom the Son of Man is betrayed; it would have been good for that man, if he had never been endured. 25 Then Iudas, who betrayed him, answered and said, "Is it I, master?" He answered him, "You said so." 26 While they were eating, Jesus took the bread, and having blessed it, he broke it, gave it to the disciples, and said, "Take, eat: this is my body." 27 And he also took the cup, and after giving thanks, he gave it to them, saying, "Drink of it, all of you." 28 For this is my blood of the New Testa- ment, shed for many, for the remission of sins. 29 I tell you that I will drink no more of this fruit of the vine until that day when I will drink it again with you in the kingdom of my fathers." 30 When they had sung a psalm, they went out to the mount of Olius. 31 Then Jesus said to them, "All of you will be offended by me this night, for it is written, 'I will strike the shepherd, and the sheep of the flock will be scattered. 32 But after I am risen, I will go be- fore you into Galilee." 33 But Peter answered and said to him, "Even if all men were offend- ed by you, I will never be offended." 34 Jesus said to him, "Truly I tell you, this night, before the rooster crows, you will deny me three times." 35 Peter said to him, "Even if I should die with you, I will by no means deny you." So also said all the disciples. 36 Then Jesus went with them to a place called Gethsemane and said to his disciples, "Sit here while I go, and pray there." 37 He took Peter and the two sons of Zebedee with him and began to grieve and to be grievously troubled. 38 Then Iesus said to them, "My soul is in great pain, even unto death; stay here and watch with me." 39 Then he went a little farther, and fell on his face, and praised, saying, "O my Father, if it be pos- sible, let this cup pass from me; not as I will, but as you will." 40 Then he came to the disci- ples, found them asleep, and said to Peter,

"What is it? Could you not watch with me one hour? 41 Watch and be careful not to enter into temptation; the spirit in faith is ready, but the flesh is weak. 42 Then he left a second time and prayed, saying, "O my Father, if this cup cannot pass away from me, but I must drink it, may your will be done."43 Then he came and found them asleep again, for their eyes were dull. 44 Then he left them and went away again, and praised for the third time, saying the same words. 45 Then he ap- proached his disciples and said to them, "Sleep from now on and rest; behold, the hour is near, and the Son of Man is given into the hands of sinners. 46 Arise, let go; behold, he who betrays me is at hand. 47 While he was still speaking, Iudas, one of the two, came, and with him a great multitude with swords and staffs, from the chief priests and elders of the people. 48 He who had betrayed him had given them a sign, saying, "Whom I will kill, it is he, and do not let him out of your sight." 49 He approached Jesus and said, "God bless you, Master," and kissed him. 50 Then Iesus said to him, "Friend, why have you come?" Then they came and laid their hands on Jesus and took him. 51 And behold, one of those who were with Jesus stretched out his hand, drew his sword, and struck a servant of the high priest and cut off his ear. 52 Then Jesus said to him, "Put your sword back in its place, for everyone who takes the sword will perish by the sword." 53 Do you think that I cannot pray to my Father and that he will give me more than two legions of angels? 54 How then should the Scriptures that say it must be so be fulfilled? 55 In that same hour Jesus said to the crowd, "You came out as against a thief, with swords and clubs to take me; I was teaching every day in the temple among you, and you did not take me." 56 But all this was done that the Scriptures of the Prophets might be fulfilled. Then all the disciples left him and fled. 57 Then they took Jesus and led him to Caiaphas the priest, where the scribes and elders were gathered. 58 Peter followed him far away to the hall of the priests, went in and sat down with the servants to see the end. 59 Now the chief priests, the elders and the whole council were looking for a false testi- mony against Jesus to put him to death. 60 But they found none, and though many false witnesses came, they found none; but at last two false witnesses came, 61 and said, "This man says, 'I can destroy the temple of God and rebuild it in three days.'" 62 Then the chief priest stood up and said to them, "Do you an- swer nothing? What is it that these men testi- fy against you? 63 But Jesus kept silent. Then the chief priest answered and said to him, "I command you to swear before God, who is pleased, to tell him whether you are the Christ, the Son of God, or not." 64 Jesus said to him, "You have said it; nevertheless I tell you that afterward you will see the Son of Man sitting at the right hand of the power of God and coming in the clouds of heaven." 65 Then the priest tore his clothes, saying, "He has blasphemed; what more need have we of witnesses? Behold, now you have heard his blasphemy. 66 What do you think of it? They answered, "He is guilty of death." 67 Then they spit in his face and beat him, and others struck him with rods, 68 saying, "Prophesy, O Christ, who is the one who struck you?" 69 Pe- ter stood apart in the hall, and a teacher came to him and said, "You also have been with Je- sus of Galilee. 70 But he denied before all, say- ing, "I did not understand what you said." 71 When he went out into the porch, another teacher saw him and said to those who were there, "This man also was with Jesus of Naza- reth." 72 And he denied again with another, saying, "I do not know that man." 73 Then, af- ter a while, they came to him who were stand- ing by and said to Peter, "Surely you also are one of them, for your speech makes you un- derstand." 74 Then he began to curse and swear, saying, "I do not know that man." And immediately the rooster grew up. 75 Then Pe- ter remembered the words of Jesus who had said to him, "Before the rooster croaks, you will deny me three times." So he went out and wept bitterly.

CHAPTER 27

1 When it was morning, all the chief priests and the elders of the people agreed against Jesus to put him to death, 2 and they led him away in chains and handed him over to Pon- tius Pilate, the warrior. 3 When Iudas, who had betrayed him, heard that he had been condemned, he repented and again brought the three pieces of silver to the chief priests and elders, 4 saying, "I have sinned, betray- ing innocent blood." But they said, "What is wrong with that? You provide." 5 And when he had thrown the pieces of silk into the Temple, he went away and hanged himself. 6 The chief priests took the pieces of silver and said, "It is not lawful for vs to put them in the treasury, for they are the price of blood." 7 They took counsel and bought a potter's field to bury the strangers. 8 That is why that field is called "The field of the bloud," to this day.9 Then was fulfilled what had been spoken by the proph- et Jeremiah: "They took thirty pieces of silver, the price of him who had been valued and whom the children of Israel had valued. 10 And they gave them for the potters' field, as the Lord had commanded me.) 11 Then Jesus stood before an innkeeper, and the innkeep- er questioned him, saying, "Are you the king of the Iewes? Jesus answered him, "You say so." 12 And when he was accused by the chief priests and elders, he answered nothing. 13 Then Pilate said to him, "Do you not know how many things they have brought against you? 14 But he answered him not a word, so that the speaker was greatly astonished. 15 During the feast, the governor used to give the peo- ple a prisoner to whomever they wished. 16 They then had an important prisoner, named Barabbas. 17 When they were assembled, Pi- late said to them, "Do you want Barabbas or Jesus, who is called Christ, to be released to you? 18 For he knew well that they had deliv- ered him up for enuity. 19 Even when he was laid on the judgment seat, his wife sent word to him, "Have nothing to do with that righ- teous man, for today I have suffered many things in a gloom because of him.") 20 But the chief priests and elders had persuaded the people to demand Barabbas and destroy Je- sus. 21 Then the governor answered and said to them, "Which of the two do you want me to release to you?" And they answered, "Barab- bas." 22 Pilate said to them, "What shall I do with Jesus, who is called Christ? They all an- swered him, "Let him be crucified." 23 Then the judge said, "But what has he done? Then they cried out even more, saying, "Let him be crucified." 24 Pilate, seeing that he was get- ting nowhere, but that an uproar was break- ing out, took water and washed his hands before the crowd, saying, "I am innocent of the blood of this righteous man; look you." 25 Then all the people answered, "His guilt be upon you and upon our children." 26 So Barabbas let them go free, scourged Iesus and handed him over to be crucified. 27 Then the prison warders brought Jesus into the common room and gathered the whole band around him, 28 they stripped him and put a leather tunic on him, 29 they put a crown of thorns on his head, and put a reed in his right hand, and they knelt down before him and mocked him, saying, "God has declared you king of the peoples." 30 they spit on him, took a reed and struck him on the head. 31 So after

they had mocked him, they took off his robe, put his own food on him, and led him away to crucify him. 32 And when they had gone out, they found a man of Cyrene, named Simon, and forced him to carry his cross. 33 And when they came to the place called Gol- gotha (that is, the place of the skulls of the dead) 34 And they gave him wine to drink, mixed with gall; but when he had tasted of it, he would not drink. 35 And when they had crucified him, they divided his garments and made lotteries, that it might be fulfilled what had been said by the Prophet, "They divided my garments among them, and over my gar- ment they made lotteries." 36 They sat down and looked at him there. 37 They also placed on his head the inscription, "This is IESVS, the king of the Ievites." 38 And there were two theologians crucified with him, one on the right and the other on the left. 39 Those who passed by rebuked him, shaking their heads, 40 and said, "You who destroy the Temple and build it in three days, speak your mind; if you are the Son of God, come down from your cross."41 Even the priests, who mocked him, with the scribes, elders and Pharisees, were saying, 42 He has saved others, but he cannot save himself; if he is the king of Israel, let him now come down from his cross, and we will join him." 43 He trusted in God, let him de- liver him now if he will, for he said, "I am the Son of God." 44 You also, who had been cruci- fied with him, cast him in your teeth. 45 Now from the sixth hour it became dark over all the land until the ninth hour. 46 About the ninth hour Jesus cried out with a loud voice, saying, "Eli, Eli, lamasabachthani?" that is, "My God, my God, why have you forsaken me? 47 And some of those who stood there, when they heard him, said, "This man's name is Elijah." 48 Immediately one of them ran and took a sponge and filled it with wine and put it on a reed and made him drink it. 49 The other said, "Let it be, let us see if Elijah will come and greet him." 50 Then Iesus cried out again with a loud voice and released the ghost. 51 And behold, the vault of the Temple was torn in two, from top to bottom, and the earth trembled and the stones clouded over. 52 And the graves were opened, and many bodies of the saints who slept arose, 53 and came out of the graves after his resurrection, and entered into the holy city, and appeared to many. 54 When the centurion and those who were with him to see Jesus saw the earthquake and the things that had been done, they were greatly afraid, saying, "This is truly the Son of God." 55 There were also many women who saw him from afar and who had followed Jesus from Galilee and attended him. 56 Among them was Mary Magdalene, Mary the mother of Iames, Ioses, and the mother of the sons of Zebedee. 57 When it was day, there came a rich man from Arimathea named Ioseph, who had also been a disciple of Jesus. 58 He went to Pilate and asked for the body of Jesus. Then Pilate ordered the body to be handed over. 59 Then Ioseph took the body and wrapped it in a clean linen cloth, 60 and placed it in his new tomb, which he had had built in a rock, then he rolled a large stone to the end of the tomb and departed. 61 And behold, Mary Magda- lene and the other Mary sat in front of the tomb. 62 And on the day following the prepa- ration of the Sabbath, the priests and Phar- isees came together to Pilate, 63 and said, "Siri, we remember that that deceiver said while he was still alive, 'Within three days I will rise again.' 64 Order therefore that the tomb be made safe until the third day, lest his disciples come by night and take him away, saying to the people, 'He has risen from the dead'; so the last error will be worse than the first." 65 Then Pilate said to them, "You have a watch; go and make it as sure as you

know." 66 They went and secured the tomb with the watch and sealed the stone.

CHAPTER 28

1 At the end of the Sabbath, when the first day of the week was beginning to rise, Mary Magdalene and the other Mary came to see the tomb, 2 and behold, a great earthquake, for the angel of the Lord came down from on high and rolled away the stone from the tomb and stood upon it. 3 His face was like light- ning, and his garments white as snow. 4 For fear of him, the watchmen were stunned and became as dead. 5 But the angel answered and said to the women, "Do not fear, for I know that you see Jesus who has been cruci- fied: 6 He is not here, for He is risen, as He said; come and see the place where the Lord was laid, 7 And go quickly and tell his disci- ples that he is risen from the dead; and be- hold, he goes before you into Galilee; there you shall see him; behold, I have told you." 8 So they hurried away from the tomb with fear and great joy, and ran to bring news to his disciples. 9 And as they were about to warn his disciples, behold, Jesus also met them, saying, "God greets you." And they came and took him by the feet and worshiped him. 10 Then Jesus said to them, "Do not be afraid. Go and tell my brothers that they should go to Galilee, and there they will see me." 11 As they were leaving, behold, some of the guard entered the city and showed the priests all that had been done. 12 They gathered them together with the elders, took counsel, and gave a large sum of money to the priests, 13 saying, "His disciples came by night and took him away while we slept." 14 If the matter is discussed before the judge, we will convince him and settle the matter so that you need not worry." 15 So they took the money and did as they had been taught; and this saying is still known among the young people. 16 Then you disciples went to Galilee, to a mountain, where Jesus had appointed to go. 17 When they saw him, they worshiped him, but some refused. 18 Then Jesus came and spoke to them, saying, "To me has been given all power in heaven and on earth. 19 Go therefore and teach all nations, baptizing them in the Name of the Father and of the Son and of the Holy Spirit, 20 teaching them to observe all things that I have commanded you; and behold, I am with you always, even to the end of the world, Amen.

MARK

CHAPTER 1

1 Beginning of the Gospel of Jesus Christ, Son of God: 2 As it is written in the Proph- ets, "Behold, I send my messenger before your face, who will prepare your way before you. 3 The word of him who cries out in the wilderness is, "Prepare the way of the LORD, straighten his paths." 4 Iohn baptized in the wilderness and preached the baptism of amendment of life, for the remission of sins. 5 All the people of Judea and Jerusalem came to him and were all baptized by him in the Jordan River, confessing their sins. 6 Now Iohn was clothed in camel's skins and a leath- er belt around his loins, and he ate locusts and wild bone, 7 And he preached, saying, "There comes after me a man mightier than I, than whom I am not worthy to put down the hook of his shoes and unloose him." 8 It is true that I have baptized you with water, but he will baptize you with the Holy Spirit." 9 In those days, Jesus came from Nazareth, a town in Galilee, and was baptized by John in

Jordan. 10 As he came out of the water, Iohn saw the heavens veil in two and the Holy Spirit descend on him as a gift. 11 Then there was a voice from above, saying, "You are my beautiful Son, in whom I am well pleased." 12 And immediately the Spirit led him into the wilderness. 13 He stayed in the wilderness for four days and was tempted by Satan; he was also with the wild beasts, and the angels attended him. 14 Now after Iohn was put in prison, Jesus came to Galilee, preaching the gospel of the kingdom of God, 15 saying, "The time is fulfilled, and the kingdom of God is at hand: be converted, and hear the gospel." 16 As he was walking along the Sea of Galilee, he saw Simon and Andrew, his brother, casting a net into the sea (for they were fishermen). 17 Then Jesus said to them, "Follow me, and I will make you fishers of men." 18 Immediately they left their nets and followed him. 19 Whenhe had gone a little farther, he saw Iames, son of Zebedee, and Iohn, his brother, as they were in the ship repairing their nets. 20 He called them, and they left their father Zebe- dee in the ship with his servants and set out after him. 21 They then entered Capernaum, and immediately, on the Sabbath day, he en- tered the synagogue and taught. 22 They were amazed at his doctrine, for he taught them as one having authority and not as the scribes. 23 There was a man in their synagogue who had a vncleane spirit and cried out, 24 say- ing, "Ah, what have we to do with you, O Je- sus of Nazareth? Have you come to destroy? I know you for what you are, that is, the Holy One of God." 25 Then Iesus rebuked him, say- ing, "Be still and come out of him." 26 Then the vnclean spirit tare him, cried out with a loud voice, and went out from him. 27 And they were all shocked, so that they asked one another, "What is this? What new doctrine is this? For he always commands the harmful spirits with authority, and they obey him." 28 And immediately his fame spread throughout the whole region bordering Galilee. 29 As they were leaving the synagogue, they entered the house of Simon and Andrew, with Iames and Iohn. 30 Simon's mother lay sick with fever, and immediately they told him about it. 31 He came and took her by the hand and lift- ed her up, and the fever took hold of her and she attended them. 32 When it was the hour of sunset, they brought to him all the sick and the possessed. 33 The whole city gathered be- fore him. 34 He healed many who were sick of various diseases, cast out many sick people, and did not allow the sick people to say that they knew him. 35 Very early in the morning, before daylight, Jesus got up and went out to a lonely place and began to pray. 36 Simon and those who were with him followed him closely. 37 And when they had found him, they said to him, "All men are looking for you." 38 Then he said to them, "Go into the neigh- boring towns, that I may preach there also; for I have gone out for this purpose." 39 And he preached in their synagogues through- out Galilee, and cast out executions. 40 Then there came to him a leper who pleaded with him, knelt down before him, and said, "If you will, you can make me well." 41 And Jesus had compassion on him, and stretched out his hand, and touched him, and said, "I will: be healed." 42 And as he had spoken, immediate- ly the leprosy departed from him, and he was cleansed. 43 And having given him a definite command, he sent him away immediately, 44 and said to him, "See that you say nothing to anyone, but go, present yourself to the priest, and offer for your imposition those things which Moses commanded, as a testimony for them." 45 But when he was gone, he began to tell many things and to divulge the fact, so that Jesus could no longer enter openly into the city, but stood outside in deserted places; and they came to him from all sides.

CHAPTER 2

1 After a few days, he entered Capernaum again and was noticed to be in the house. 2 Soon many gathered together, so that the places around the house could no longer re- ceive, and he preached the word to them. 3 And there came to him one bearing one sick of the palsy, carried by four men. 4 And be- cause they could not come near him because of the crowd, they went through the roof of the house where he was, and when they had opened it, they brought down the bed where the sick of palsy was lying. 5 Now when Iesus saw their faith, he said to the sick of palsy, "Son, your sins are forgiven you." 6 And some scribes were sitting there and reasoning in their hearts, 7 Why does this man speak such blasphemies? Who can forgive sins but God alone? 8 And immediately, when Jesus noticed in his spirit that they were thus reasoning among themselves, he said to them, "Why do you reason about these things in your hearts? 9 Whether it is easier to say to the sick person with paralysis, "Your sins forgive you," or to say, "Get up, take up your bed, and walk?" 10 But that you may know that the Son of Man has authority on earth to forgive sins (he said to the sick man with palsy). 11 I say to you, "Get up, take up your bed, and go to your house." 12 Then he got up, took his bed, and left before everyone, so that everyone rejoiced and glorified God, saying, "We had never seen such a thing." 13 Then he resumed his journey to the sea, and all the people resorted to him, and he taught them. 14 As Iesus was passing by, he saw Levi, the son of Alphaeus, sitting at the pew of the guests and said to him, "Follow me." And he got up and followed him. 15 While Jesus was at table in his house, many publi- cans and sinners were at table with him and his disciples, for there were many who fol- lowed him. 16 When the scribes and Pharisees saw him eating with publicans and sinners, they said to his disciples, "How is it that he eats and drinks with publicans and sinners? 17 When Jesus heard this, he said to them, "Not the whole need care, but the sick. I have not come to call the righteous, but sinners to repentance." 18 The disciples of John and the Pharisees fasted and came and said to him, "Why do the disciples of John and the Phar- isees fast and your disciples do not? 19 And Jesus said to them, "Can the sons of the bridal chamber fast while the bride is with them? As long as they have the bride with them, they cannot fast." 20 But the days will come when the bridegroom will be taken from them, and then they will fast in those days. 21 Moreover, no one shall sow a piece of new cloth in an old garment, because the new piece that filled it takes something away from the old, and the breakage is worse. 22 Likewise, no one shall put new wine into old jars, for otherwise the new wine breaks the jars, the wine goes out, and the jars are lost; but the new wine must be put into new jars. 23 As he passed through the horn on the Sabbath day, his disciples, as they went their way, began to pluck out horn ears. 24 And the Pharisees said to him, "Well, why do they do on the Sabbath day what is not lawful?" 25 And he said to them, "Have you never read what Dauid did when he was in need and hungry, both he and those who were with him? 26 How he entered the house of God in the days of Abiathar the priest, and ate the loaves that were not lawful to eat ex- cept for the priests, and gave them also to those who were with him? 27 He said to them, "The Sabbath was made for man, and not man for the Sabbath." 28 Therefore the Son of Man is Lord, even of the Sabbath.

CHAPTER 3

1 Entering the synagogue again, there was a man there whose hands were withered. 2 They looked at him to know if he would heal him on the Sabbath day, so that they could accuse him. 3 Then he said to the man whose hand was withered, "Get up, stand in the midst." 4 And he said to them, "Is it lawful to do a good deed on the Sabbath day or to do an evil deed? To save life or to kill?" But they kept silent. 5 Then he looked around them in anger, pity- ing also the hardness of their hearts, and said to the man, "Stretch out your hand." And he stretched it out; and his hand was restored, as whole as the other. 6 Then the Pharisees de- parted, and immediately gathered a council with the Herodians against him, to destroy him. 7 But Jesus set out with his disciples to- ward the sea, and a great crowd followed him from Galilee and Judea, 8 from Jerusalem, from Idumea, and from beyond Jordane; and those who dwelt around Tyre and Sidon, hav- ing heard the great things he was doing, came to him in great numbers. 9 And he command- ed his disciples that a small ship should wait for him, because of the crowd, lest they should assail him. 10 For he had healed many, so that they flocked to him to touch him, as many as had sores. 11 And when the vnclean spirits saw him, they prostrated themselves before him and cried out, saying, "You are the Son of God." 12 And he rebuked them sharply, to the point that they should not betray him. 13 Then he went to a mountain and called whom he would, and they came to him. 14 He asked two of them to stay with him and to send them to preach, 15 and that they should have power to heal diseases and to cast out sicknesses. 16 The first was Simon, whom he called Peter, 17 then Iames the son of Zebedee, and Iohn the brother of Iames (and he called them Boan- erges, that is, sons of thunder). 18 Andrew, Philip, Bartholomew, Matthewe, Thomas, Iames the son of Alphaeus, Thaddeus, and Simon the Canaanite, 19 and Iudas Iscariot, who had betrayed him, and they returned home. 20 The crowd gathered again, so that they could not eat even a little bread. 21 When his relatives heard about it, they went out to seize him, for they said he was beside himself. 22 The scribes who came down from Jerusa- lem said, "He has Beelzebub, and through the prince of the deuils he drives out the deuils." 23 But he called them to himself and said to them in parables, "How can Satan cast out Sa- tan? 24 For if a kingdom is set against itself, that kingdom cannot stand. 25 Or if a house is set against itself, that house cannot continue. 26 So if Satan makes an insurrection against himself and is diverted, he cannot stand, but is at the end. 27 No one can enter the house of a strong man and take away his possessions, unless he has first become a strong man and then stripped his house. 28 Truly I tell you, all sins will be forgiven to the sons of men, and the blasphemies with which they blaspheme: 29 But he that blasphemeth against the Holy Ghost shall never have forgiveness, but shall be guilty of eternal damnation. 30 For they said, "He had a vncleane spirit." 31 Then his brothers and his mother came and stood out- side and sent for him. 32 And the people sat around him and said to him, "Behold, your mother and your brothers are looking for you outside." 33 But he answered them, saying, "Who are my mother and my brothers?" 34 He looked around them, who sat compactly around him, and said, "Behold, my mother and my brothers." 35 For he who does the will of God is my brother and my sister and my mother.

CHAPTER 4

1 He resumed teaching on the seashore, and a great crowd gathered to him, so that he en- tered a ship and stood on the sea, while all the people were on the seashore on land. 2 Then he taught them many things in parables and told them his doctrine, 3 Listen: behold, there went out a sower to sow. 4 While he was sow- ing, some of them fell by the wayside, and the birds of the earth came and made them fall. 5 And some fell on stony ground, where there was not much soil, and at any moment they sprang up, because they had no depth of soil. 6 But when the sun was high, it was scorched, and because it had no roots, it withered away. 7 Some fell among the thorns, and the thorns grew fat and choked it, so that it bore no fruit. 8 Others fell into good soil and produced fruit that sprouted and grew and bore fruit, some of thirty sheets, some of sixty, and some of a hundred. 9 Then he said to them, "He who has ears to hear, let him hear." 10 While he was alone, those around him with the twins questioned him about the parable. 11 And he said to them, "To you it is granted to know the mysteries of the kingdom of God; but to those outside, everything is done in parables, 12 that, seeing, they may see and not discern; and hearing, they may hear and not under- stand, lest at any time they should turn away and their sins be forgiven." 13 Then he said to them, "Do you not understand this parable? How then could you understand all the other parables? 14 The sower sows the word. 15 And these are those who receive the seed by the way, in whom the word has been sown; but when they have heard it, Satan comes imme- diately and takes away the word that had been sown in their hearts. 16 Likewise, those who receive the seed in stony ground are those who, after hearing the word, immediately re- ceive it with joy. 17 However, they have no root in themselves and endure only for a while; for when trouble and persecution arise for the word, they immediately take offense. 18 Even those who receive the seed among the thorns are those who hear the word: 19 But the cares of this world, and the deceitfulness of riches, and the covetousness of other things, enter in, and choke the word, that it has no more fruit. 20 But those who have received the seed in good soil are those who hear the word, and receive it, and bear fruit: one horn has thirty, another six, and some a hundred. 21 Moreover he said to them, "Is the candle to be put under a shell or under the bed, and not to be put on a candlestick? 22 For there is nothing hidden that is not opened; nor is there a secret that does not come to light. 23 If anyone has ears to hear, let him hear." 24 And he said to them, "Take heed to what you hear. By what mea- sure you measure, it will be measured to you; and to you who listen, more will be given. 25 For to him who has will be given, and to him who does not have will be taken away what he has. 26 He also said, "The kingdom of God is like a man casting seed into the ground, 27 and sleeps and rises by night and day, and the seed springs up and grows, not knowing how. 28 For the earth produces its fruit by itself: first the berries, then the ears, then the horn in the ears. 29 When the fruit shows itself, he immediately puts his hand to the sickle, for the hardest season has come. 30 He said again, "To what shall we compare the king- dom of God? Or to what should we compare it? 31 It is like a grain of mustard seed, which, when it is sown in the earth, is the smallest of all the seeds that are on the earth: 32 but af- ter it is sown, it grows and is the largest of all grasses, and bears great branches, so that the clouds of Heauen can build under its shadow. 33 And with many parables he preached the word to them, as they were able to hear it. 34 Without parables he spoke to them nothing, but expounded everything to his disciples. 35 Now on the same day, when the day of arrival had come, he said

to them, "Pass over, to the other shore." 36 They left the crowd and took him as he was in the ship, and with him were also other small ships. 37 A great windstorm arose, and the waves swept into the ship, so that it was now full. 38 He was in the sternum, asleep on a pillow; but they woke him up and said, "Master, do you not care that we die?" 39 He arose, rebuked the wind, and said to the sea, "Peace and quiet." Then the wind ceased and there was a great calm. 40 Then he said to them, "Why are you so fearful? How is it that you have no faith? 41 They feared greatly and said to one another, "Who is this man, that the wind and the sea obey him?

CHAPTER 5

1 And they came to the other side of the sea, to the land of the Gadarenes. 2 And when he was gone out of the ship, there came to him, incontinent, among the graves, a man hav- ing a vnclean spirit: 3 who dwelt among the graves, and no one could bind him, not even with chains: 4 For when he was often bound with chains and fetters, he tore the chains and broke the fetters, and no one could tame him. 5 And always, night and day, he wept on the mountains and in the graves, and struck himself with stones. 6 When he saw Jesus far away, he ran and worshipped him, 7 and crying with a loud voice said, "What shall I do with you, Jesus, Son of the most high God? I want you to swear to me by God that you will not torment me." 8 (For he said to him, "Come out of that man, vnclean spirit.") 9 Then she asked him, "What is your name?" And he answered, "My name is Legion, for we are many." 10 And he immediately begged him not to send them out of the county. 11 Now on the mountains there were a great number of swine feeding. 12 All of you begged him, say- ing, "Send us to the swine, that we may enter them." 13 And incontinently Iesus let them in. Then the vnclean spirits went out and entered the swine, who threw themselves headlong from the top of the quay into the sea (there were about two thousand swine) and were smothered in the sea. 14 And the swine fled and told it in the city and in the country, and went out to see what had been done. 15 And they came to Iesus and saw him who had been possessed with the curse and had the legion, sitting, clothed and in his right mind; and they were astonished. 16 Those who saw him told what had been done to him who was pos- sessed with the curse and to the swineherds. 17 Then they began to beg him to depart from their shores. 18 When he had entered the ship, the one who had been possessed by the curse begged him to stay with him. 19 But Jesus would not let him and said to him, "Go home to your friends and tell them about the great things the Lord has done to you and how he had compassion on you." 20 So he departed and began to publish in the Decapolis the great things that Jesus had done to him; and all men marveled. 21 When Iesus had come again by ship to the other shore, a great crowd gathered near him, and he was by the sea. 22 And behold, there came one of the leaders of the synagogue, whose name was Iairus; and when he saw him, he fell at his feet, 23 and prayed to him instantly, saying, "My daughter lies at the point of death: I pray thee to come and lay thy hands upon her, that she may be healed and live." 24 Then he went with him, and a great crowd followed him and thronged him. 25 There was a certain woman who had been sick with hemorrhage for two years, 26 and had undergone many physical cures and had spent all she had, but it had done her no good; on the contrary, she had grown worse. 27 When she had heard about Jesus, she came up behind him and touched his robe. 28 For she said, "If I can touch his garments, I will heal." 29 And immediately the course of her blood dried up, and she felt in her body that she was healed of that sore. 30 And imme- diately afterward, when Jesus knew in him- self the virtue that came forth from him, he turned in prey and said, "Who has touched my garments?" 31 And his disciples said to him, "You see the crowd assailing you and saying, Who touched me?" 32 He looked around to see the one who had done this. 33 The woman was afraid and trembled, for she knew what had been done in her; and she came and fell down before him and told him the whole truth. 34 He said to her, "Daughter, your faith has healed you; go in peace and be healed of your plague.") 35 While he was still speaking, there came from the same house as the leader of the synagogues a certain person who said, "Your daughter is dead; why do you further trouble the Master? 36 When Iesus heard that word, he said to the leader of the synagogue, "Do not be frightened, but only turn away." 37 And he did not allow anyone to follow him ex- cept Peter and Iames and Iohn, Iames' broth- er. 38 So he came to the house of the leader of the synagogue and saw the tumult and those who were weeping and lamenting greatly. 39 He went in and said to them, "Why do you fret and weep? The child is not dead, but asleep." 40 They rebuked him for being discouraged, but he drove them all away, took the child's father and mother and those who were with him, and went in where the child lay, 41 and took the child by the hand and said to her, "Ta- litha cumi," which means, "Mayden, I tell you to get up."42 Immediately the little girl got up and walked, for she was two years old, and they were amazed beyond measure. 43 He in- structed them to make sure that no one knew and ordered them to give her food.

CHAPTER 6

1 Then he departed from there and came to his county, and his disciples followed him. 2 When the Sabbath was past, he began to teach in the synagogue, and many of those who heard him were amazed and said, "Where do these things come to this man? And what wis- dom is it that is imparted to him, that so great works are done with his hands every time? 3 Is not this man the carpenter the son of Mary, the brother of James and Joses, of Judah and Simon? And are not his sisters here with him? And they were offended in him. 4 Then Jesus said to them, "A prophet is not without honor, except in his own country, among his relatives and in his own house." 5 He could do no great works, but only laid hands on some sick peo- ple and healed them, 6 He marveled at their unbelief and went around the cities on all sides to teach. 7 Then he called the twins to himself and began to send them two by two, giving them power against evil spirits, 8 and commanded them to take nothing for their journey but a staff for their work: neither scrip, nor bread, nor money in their belts: 9 but that they should be shod with sandals, and that they should not wear two cloaks. 10 Then he said to them, "Wherever you enter a house, stay there until you leave. 11 And who- ever will not receive you and will not listen to you, when you leave, shake off the dust under your feet, as a testimony to them. Truly I tell you, it will be easier for Sodom or Gomorrah on the day of judgment than for that city." 12 Then they went out and preached for men to correct themselves. 13 They cast out many sick people and anointed with oil many sick people and healed them. 14 Then King Herod, having heard of him (for his name had been made manifest), said, "John the

Baptist has risen from the dead, and therefore he does great works." 15 Others said, "He is Elijah," and still others, "He is a prophet or one of those prophets." 16 When Herod heard this, he said, "It is Iohn, whom I beheaded: he is risen from the dead." 17 For Herod himself had sent for Iohn and had locked him up in prison because of Herodias, the wife of his brother Philip, because he had married her. 18 Iohn said to Herod, "It is not lawful for you to have your brother's wife." 19 Therefore Hero- dias stood waiting against him and would have liked to kill him, but she could not: 20 For Herod feared John, knowing that he was a righteous and holy man, and esteemed him; and when he heard him, he did many things and listened to him gladly. 21 But the time being favorable, Herod, on the day of his delivery, made a banquet to his princes and captains and to the principal estates of Gal- ilee: 22 And Herodias' daughter came in and prostrated herself and pleased Herod and all who sat at table together, and the king said to the Mayde, "Ask me what you want, and I will give it to you." 23 And he swore to her, "What- ever you ask of me, I will give it to you, even for half my kingdom." 24 So she went out and said to her mother, "What shall I ask?" And she answered, "The head of John the Baptist." 25 Then she went at once in haste to the king and asked him, "I would like you to give me at once the head of John the Baptist in a cloak." 26 The king was greatly displeased, but for her sake and for the sake of those who sat at table with him, he would not refuse her. 27 Immediately the king sent the executioner and gave orders to bring his head. So he went and beheaded him in the prison, 28 And he brought his head in a chariot and delivered it to his mother, and his mother delivered it to his mother. 29 When his disciples heard this, they came and took his body and put it in a tomb. 30 And the apostles gathered them- selves to Jesus and told him all that they had done and all that they had taught. 31 And he said to them, "Come aside into the thicket and rest a while, for there were many who came and went and had no pleasure in eat- ing." 32 So they went away by ship from the road to a deserted place. 33 And when they went away, the people saw them, and many knew him, and they ran in that direction from all the cities, and went before them, and gathered themselves together to him. 34 Then Jesus went out and saw a great crowd and had compassion on them, for they were like sheep without a shepherd; and he began to teach them many things. 35 When the day was now long past, his disciples came to him, saying, "This is a deserted place, and now the day is long past. 36 Let them depart to go into the surrounding countryside and towns to buy bread, for they have nothing to eat." 37 But he answered them, "Give them food." And they said to him, "Shall we go and buy two hun- dred pence of bread and give them food?" 38 Then he said to them, "How many loaves do you have? Go and see." And they, knowing this, said, "Two and two fish." 39 Then he com- manded them to sit them all by company on the green grill. 40 Then they sat down by rows, by hundreds and by fifties. 41 Then he took the five loaves and the two fish, looked upward, gave thanks, broke the loaves and gave them to his disciples to place before them, while the two fish he distributed to all. 42 So they all ate and were filled. 43 Then they took two baskets full of fragments and fish. 44 Those who had eaten were about five thousand men. 45 And immediately he got his disciples into the ship and set them off for the other shore toward Bethsaida, while he sent the people away. 46 Then when he had sent them away, he went away to a mountain to pray. 47 When the time had come, the ship was in the middle of the sea and he was alone on dry land. 48 He saw them struggling to row (because the wind was against them), and about the fourth watch of the night he came up to them, walk- ing on the sea, and wanted to pass by them. 49 When they saw him walking on the sea, they thought he was a spirit and cried out. 50 Because they all saw him, they were deeply afraid; but immediately he spoke to them and said, "Take comfort: it is I; do not be afraid." 51 Then he went in with them into the ship, and the wind ceased, and they were much more pleased with themselves, and they felt guilty. 52 For they had not considered the matter of the loaves, because their hearts were hard- ened. 53 Then they went out and entered the land of Gennesaret and came. 54 When they had come out of the ship, immediately they recognized him, 55 And they ran through all the surrounding region, and began to carry hither and thither, on beds, all who were sick, where they had heard that he was. 56 And when he came into cities, towns or villages, they lay down in the street with their sick and begged him that they might at least touch the hem of his garment. And as many as touched him were healed.

CHAPTER 7

1 Then the Pharisees and some scribes who had come from Jerusalem gathered with him. 2 When they saw that some of his disciples were eating food with common hands, they complained. 3 For the Pharisees and all the Jews, if they did not wash their hands often, they did not eat, according to the tradition of the elders. 4 And when they returned from the marketplace, if they did not wash, they did not eat; and there were many other things which they took into account to observe, such as the washing of cups, pots, bronze vessels, and beds). 5 Then the Pharisees and scribes asked him, "Why do your disciples not walk according to the tradition of the elders, but eat food with unclean hands?" 6 He answered them, "Surely Esay has prophesied well of you hypocrites, as it is written, This people hon- ors me with their lips, but their hearts are far from me. 7 But they worship me in vein, teaching for doctrines the commands of men. 8 For you set aside the commands of God and observe the tradition of men, such as the washing of vessels and bowls and many oth- er such things that you do." 9 And he said to them, "Well, you neglect the commandment of God to observe your tradition. 10 For Moses had said, 'Honor your father and your moth- er; and whoever speaks evil of father or moth- er, let him die by death.' 11 But you say, "If any- one says to his father or mother, 'Corban,' that is, 'With the gift I offer you you may profit,' he shall be free." 12 So you will no longer allow him to do any thing for his father or mother, 13 making the word of God void of authori- ty, because of your tradition which you have imposed upon yourselves; and do many such things. 14 Then he called the whole crowd to him and said to them, "Listen to me all and understand." 15 There is nothing without man that can defile him, when it enters into him; but the things that come out of him are those that defile man. 16 If anyone has ears to hear, let him hear. 17 When he had entered a house, away from the people, his disciples questioned him about the parable. 18 And he said to them, "What, are you also without understanding? Do you not know that what enters a man from without cannot defile him? 19 Why does it not enter into his heart, but into his belly, and go out into the stream that is the cleansing of all flesh?" 20 Then he said, "What comes out of the man defiles the man." 21 For from within, that is, from the heart of man, come forth evil thoughts, adulteries, fornications,

murders, 22 theft, couetousnes, wickedness, deceit, vncleannes, evil eye, backbiting, pride, foolishness. 23 All these things come from within and defile the man. 24 From there he arose and went to the borders of Tyre and Sidon, entered a house, and wanted no one to know, but he could not be hidden. 25 For a certain woman, whose lit- tle daughter had a violent spirit, heard him, came and fell at his feet, 26 (the woman was Greek and Syrophoenician) and begged him to cast the spirit out of her daughter. 27 But Jesus said to her, "Let the children be fed first, for it is not good to take the children's bread and throw it to the little ones." 28 She an- swered and said to him, "True, Lord, but in- deed the little ones eat under the table of the children." 29 Then he said to her, "Therefore go your way: sin is gone from your daughter." 30 When she had returned to her house, she found death gone and her daughter lying on the bed. 31 And he departed again from the coasts of Tyre and Sidon, and came to the sea of Galilee, through the coasts of Decapo- lis. 32 They brought to him one who was deaf and lame in speech and begged him to lay his hand on him. 33 Then he took him aside from the crowd, put his fingers in his ears, spit, and touched his tongue. 34 Then, looking up, he sighed and said to him, "Ephatha," that is, "Open up." 35 Immediately his ears were opened, the thread of his tongue loosened, and he spoke clearly. 36 Then he command- ed them not to tell anyone; but the more he forbade them, the more they published it in great numbers, 37 and they were exceedingly amazed, saying, "He has done all things well; he makes both the deaf and the domme to hear and speak."

CHAPTER 8

1 In those days, when the crowd was very large and had nothing to eat, Jesus called his disciples to him and said to them 2 I have compassion on the crowd, for now they have been with me three days and have nothing to eat. 3 And if I sent them away fasting to their homes, they would faint on the road, for some of them have come from afar." 4 Then his dis- ciples answered him, "Whence can these be satisfied with bread here in the wilderness?" 5 And he asked them, "How many loaves do you have?" And they answered, "Seuen." 6 Then he commanded the crowd to sit on the ground; then he took the ten loaves, gave thanks, broke them, and gave them to his disciples to put before them, and they put them before the people. 7 They also had some little fishes, and after giving thanks, he commanded them to put those also before them. 8 They ate and were filled, and they took from the stale meat that was left, ten full baskets. 9 (Those who had eaten were about four thousand) and he sent them away. 10 Then he got into a ship with his disciples and came to the parts of Dalmanut- ha. 11 The Pharisees approached and began to argue with him, seeking a sign from God and tempting him. 12 Then he sighed deeply in his spirit and said, "Why does this genera- tion seek a sign? Truly I tell you, a sign will not be given to this generation." 13 Then he left them, entered the ship again, and departed for the other shore. 14 They had forgotten to take bread, and they had only one pound with them in the ship. 15 And he charged them, saying, "Take heed and beware of the law of the Pharisees and the law of Herod." 16 They reasoned among themselves, saying, "It is be- cause we have no bread." 17 And when Jesus heard this, he said to them, "Why do you rea- son thus, because you have no bread? Do you not yet perceive it, nor do you understand it? Is your heart still hardened? 18 Have you

eyes and do not see? Have ye ears and hear not? And do ye not remember? 19 When I broke the five loaves among five thousand people, how many baskets full of broken meat did you take? They answered him, "Two." 20 And when I broke ten among four thousand, how many baskets full of rotten meat did you take from them? And they answered, "Seuen." 21 Then he said to them, "How is it that you do not understand?" 22 When he had come to Bethsaida, they brought him a blind man and wanted him to touch him. 23 Then he took the blind man by the hand, led him out of the city, spit in his eyes, laid his hands on him, and asked him if he knew anything. 24 He looked and said, "I see men, for I see them walking like trees." 25 Then she put her hands over his eyes again and made him look again. And he regained his sight and saw clearly every man afar off. 26 Then he sent him back to his house, saying, "Do not go into the city or tell anyone in the city." 27 Then Jesus went out with his disciples to the city of Caesarea Philippi. And on the way he asked his disciples, "Who do men say that I am?" 28 They answered, "Some say John the Baptist, some say Elijah, and some say one of the Prophets." 29 And he said to them, "But who do you say that I am?" Then Peter answered and said to him, "You are that Christ." 30 And he sternly charged them not to say anything about him to anyone. 31 Then he began to teach them that the Son of Man was to suffer many things, to be rebuked by the elders, priests and scribes, to be killed and to rise again within three days. 32 And he said these things boldly. Then Peter took him aside and began to rebuke him. 33 Then he turned back and looked at his disciples and rebuked Peter, saying, "Get away from me, Satan, for you do not understand the things of God but those of men." 34 Then he called the people to him with his disciples and said to them, "Whoever wants to follow me, let him aban- don himself and take up his cross and follow me. 35 Whoever wants to save his life will lose it; but whoever loses his life because of me and the Gospels will lose it. 36 For what does it profit a man, even if he should win the whole world, if he loses his soul? 37 Or what recom- pense will a man give for his soul? 38 For who- ever will be ashamed of me and my words in this adulterous and sinful generation, of him will the Son of Man also be ashamed, when he comes in the glory of his Father with the holy Angels.

CHAPTER 9

1 And he said to them, "Truly I tell you, there are some of those who are here who will not taste death until they see the kingdom of God coming with power." 2 Six days later, Jesus took Peter, Iames and Iohn with him and led them to an isolated mountain off the road, and his appearance changed before them. 3 His robe shone and was very white, like snow, so white that no fuller can make on earth. 4 Then Elijah appeared to them with Moses, who were talking with Jesus. 5 Then Peter answered and said to Jesus, "Master, it is good that you are here; let us also make three tabernacles, one for you, one for Moses, and one for Elijah." 6 But he did not know what he said, for they were afraid. 7 Then a cloud overshadowed them, and out of the cloud came a voice saying, "This is my beautiful Son: listen to him." 8 Suddenly they looked around and saw no one who spoke of Jesus alone with them. 9 As they came down from the moun- tain, he instructed them not to tell anyone about what they had seen, except when the Son of Man had risen from the dead. 10 So they kept it to themselves and asked each other what the rising again from the dead meant. 11 They

also asked him, "Why do the scribes say that Elijah must come first?" 12 And he, answering, said to them, "First Elijah himself will come and restore all things; and as it is written of the Son of Man, he will have to suffer many things and be put in danger. 13 But I say to you that Elijah came (and they did to him what they wanted) as it is written of him. 14 When he came to his disciples, he saw a large crowd around them and the scribes disputing with them. 15 Immediately all the people, seeing him, rejoiced and ran to him and greeted him. 16 Then he asked the scribes, "What do you have to dispute among yourselves?" 17 One of the company answered and said, "Teacher, I have brought you my son who has a mute spirit: 18 And where he brings him, he teases him, and frets, and gnashes his teeth, and pushes away; and I spoke to your disciples that they might cast him out, but they could not." 19 Then he answered and said to them, "O faithless generation, as long as I am with you, as long as I suffer you! Bring him to me." 20 So they led him to him; and, as the spirit saw him, it clutched him, and he fell to the ground walking and choking. 21 Then he asked his father, "How long has it been since he has been like this?" And he an- swered, "Since a child." 22 Often he throws him into fire and water to destroy him; but if you can do anything, help the son and have compassion on him. 23 And Jesus said to him, "If you can do it, all things are possible to him who wants to do it." 24 And immediately the child's father, weeping in anguish, said, "Lord, I am in distress; help my unbelief." 25 And when Jesus saw that the people flocked, he rebuked the vncleane spirit, saying to him, "You dominating and deaf spirit, I command you to come out of him and enter him no more." 26 Then the spirit cried out, cut him open, and went out, and he was as if dead, so that many said, "He is dead." 27 But Jesus took his hand and lifted him up, and he arose. 28 When he had entered the house, his disci- ples asked him in secret, "Why could we not cast him out?" 29 And he said to them, "This kind cannot go out by any other means than by prayer and fasting." 30 And they departed from there and went together through Gali- lee, and he did not want anyone to know. 31 For he taught his disciples and said to them, "The Son of Man will be delivered into the hands of men, and they will kill him; but af- ter he has been killed, he will rise again on the third day." 32 But they did not understand this saying and did not want to ask him. 33 Then he came to Capernaum; and when he was in the house, he asked them, "What is it that you disputed among yourselves on the way?" 34 They held their peace, for on the way they reasoned among themselves as to who should be most important. 35 He sat down and called the two and said to them, "If anyone wants to be first, he shall be last of all and servant of all." 36 Then he took a little child, placed him in their midst, took him in his arms, and said to them, "Whoever will be first, he will be last and servant of all." 37 Whosoever shall receive one of these little ones in my Name shall re- ceive me; and whosoever shall receive me shall receive not me, but him that sent me." 38 Then Iohn answered him, saying, "Master, we saw one who was driving out disease by your Name and not following the law, and we for- bade him because he did not follow the law. 39 But Jesus said, "Do not forbid him, for there is no one who can perform a miracle through my Name, who can speak lightly of me. 40 For he who is not against us is on our side. 41 And whoever shall give you a cup of water to drink by my Name, because you are Christ's, verily I say unto you, he shall not lose his reward. 42 And whoever offends one of these little ones who live in me, it would be better for him if a millstone were hung around his neck and

he were cast into the sea. 43 Therefore, if your hand causes you to commit an offense, cut it off; it is better for you to enter life, maimed, than to have two hands and go to hell, into the fire that never dies out, 44 where their flesh does not die and the fire is never quenched. 45 In the same way, if your foot causes you to commit an offense, cut it off; it is better for you to go on in life and then, having two feet, to be cast into hell, into the fire that never goes out, 46 where their flesh does not die and the fire is never quenched. 47 And if your eye hurts, pluck it out; it is better for you to enter the kingdom of God with one eye, than with two eyes to be cast into the fire of hell, 48 where their flesh does not die and the fire is never quenched. 49 For every man shall be salted with fire, and every sacrifice shall be salted with salt. 50 Salt is good; but if salt is bad, with what shall it be seasoned? Have salt in yourselves and have peace with one anoth- er.

CHAPTER 10

1 Then he got up from there and went to the coasts of Iudea, to the end of the Iordane, and the people again resorted to him, and, as he was wont to do, he instructed them again. 2 Then the Pharisees came and asked him whether it was lawful for a man to renounce his wife, and they tempted him. 3 He an- swered and said to them, "What did Moses command you?" 4 They answered, "Moses permitted to write a deed of divorce and to remove his wife." 5 Then Jesus answered and said to them, "Because of the hardness of your hearts he has written this precept to you." 6 But at the beginning of creation God made them male and female: 7 Therefore a man shall leave his father and his mother, and shall separate himself from his wife. 8 And the two shall be one flesh, so that they shall no longer be two, but one flesh. 9 Therefore what God has joined together, let not man separate. 10 And in the house his disciples questioned him again about that matter. 11 And he said to them, "Whoever abandons his wife and mar- ries another commits adultery against her. 12 And if a woman abandons her husband and marries another, she commits adultery." 13 Then they brought him little children for him to touch, and his disciples rebuked those who had brought them. 14 But when Jesus heard this, he was sorry and said to them, "Let the little children come to me and do not forbid them, for of such is the kingdom of God. 15 Truly I tell you, whoever will not receive the kingdom of God as a little child will not enter it." 16 Then he took them under his arms and laid his hands on them and blessed them. 17 As he was going on his way, there came one running, knelt down to him and asked him, "Good Teacher, what must I do to have eter- nal life?" 18 Jesus said to him, "Why do you call me good? There is no one good but one, that is God. 19 You know the commandments, 'You shall not commit adultery. You shall not kill. Thou shall not steal. You shall not bear false witness. You shall not harm anyone. Hon- or your father and your mother." 20 Then he answered and said to him, "Master, all these things I have observed from my youth." 21 Then Iesus looked at him and looked at him and said, "You lack one thing. Go, sell all that you have and give it to the poor, and you will have treasure in heaven; and come, follow me and take up your cross." 22 But he was sad- dened at that word and went away sorrowful, for he had great possessions. 23 Then Jesus looked around and said to his disciples, "How hardly do those who have riches enter the kingdom of God! 24 His disciples were bewil- dered by his words. But Jesus answered again and said to them, "My

children, how difficult it is for those who trust in riches to enter the kingdom of God! 25 It is easier for a camel to go through the eye of a needle than for a rich man to enter the kingdom of God." 26 And they were much more amazed, saying among themselves, "Who then can be saved?" 27 But Jesus, looking on them, said, "With men it is impossible, but not with God, for with God all things are possible." 28 Then Peter began to say to him, "Lord, we have forsaken every- thing and followed you." 29 Jesus answered and said, "Truly I tell you, there is no one who has forsaken house, brothers, sisters, father, mother, wife, children or lands because of me and the Gospels, 30 but he will receive a hundred times, now as now, houses, broth- ers, sisters, mothers, children and lands with persecution, and in the world to come eternal life. 31 But many of those who are first will be last, and the last will be first. 32 As they were on their way to Jerusalem, Jesus went ahead of them, and they were troubled; as they fol- lowed, they were astounded; then Jesus took up the two and began to tell them what things should happen, 33 saying, "Behold, we are go- ing to Jerusalem, and the Son of Man will be handed over to the priests and scribes, who will condemn him to death and hand him over to the Gentiles. 34 They will mock him, scourge him, spit on him, and kill him; but on the third day he will rise again. 35 Then Iames and Iohn, the sons of Zebedee, came to him, saying, "Master, we would have you do what we desire." 36 And he said to them, "What do you want me to do for you?" 37 And they answered him, "Take your place, that we may sit, one on your right hand and the other on your left, in your glory." 38 But Jesus said to them, "You do not know what you ask. Can you drink of the cup that I shall drink, and be baptized with the baptism with which I shall be baptized? 39 They answered him, "We can." But Jesus said to them, "You shall drink of the cup that I shall drink as a gift, and be baptized with the baptism with which I shall be bap- tized: 40 But to sit at my right hand and at my left is not for me, but it will be given to those for whom it has been prepared." 41 When the ten heard this, they began to despise Iames and Iohn. 42 But Jesus called them to him- self and said to them, "You know that those who are princes among the Gentiles have do- minion over them, and those who are great among them exercise authority over them. 43 But among you it shall not be so; whoever is great among you shall be your servant. 44 And whoever will be chief among you will be servant of all. 45 For the Son of Man did not come to be served, but to serve and to give his life for the sake of many. 46 Then they came to Jericho; and while he was going out from Jericho with his disciples and a large crowd, Bartimaeus the son of Timaeus, a blind man, went begging along the road. 47 When he heard that it was Jesus of Nazareth, he began to weep and to say, "Jesus, son of David, have mercy on me." 48 Many rebuked him, so that he did not give himself peace; but he cried out even more, "Son of Dauid, have mercy on me." 49 Then Jesus stopped and commanded them to call him; and they called the blind man, saying to him, "Take comfort, arise, he is call- ing you." 50 Then he took off his cloak, stood up, and came to Jesus. 51 Jesus answered and said to him, "What do you want me to do with you?" And the blind man said to him, "Lord, may I receive my sight." 52 Then Jesus said to him, "Go your way; your destiny has forsaken you." And he received his sight and followed Jesus on the road.

CHAPTER 11

1 When they came to Jerusalem, to Bethphage and Bethany, toward the Mount of Olives, he sent two of his disciples, 2 and said to them, "Go to that city which is opposite you, and as soon as you have entered it, you will find a bound colt, where there was no one; untie it and take it with you. 3 And if anyone says to you, "Why are you doing this? Say that the Lord has need of him, and immediately he will send him here." 4 Then they set out and found a colt tied to the shore, in a place where two roads met, and they untied it. 5 Then some of them who were there said to them, "Why do you untie the colt? 6 And they answered them, As Iesus commanded: so they let them go. 7 Then they brought the colt to Jesus, and cast their garments upon him, and he sat on him. 8 Many scattered their garments along the road; others cut branches from the trees and scattered them along the road. 9 Those who went before and those who followed shout- ed, "Hosanna! Blessed is he who comes in the name of the Lord." 10 Blessed be the kingdom that comes in the Name of the Lord of our fa- ther Dauid: hosanna, O thou who art in the highest." 11 Then Jesus entered Jerusalem and the Temple, and having observed all things, and after it was daylight, he went away to Bethany with the twins. 12 The next day, when they had come out of Bethany, he was hungry. 13 And seeing a fig tree afar off, which had leaves, he went to see if he could find anything there; but when he came to it, he found noth- ing but leaves, for it was not yet the time for figs. 14 Then Iesus answered and said, "No one shall eat your fruit in the future, as long as the world stands"; and his disciples heard him. 15 When they had come to Jerusalem, Jesus en- tered the Temple and began to drive out those who sold and bought in the Temple and to up- root the tables of the moneychangers and the chairs of those who sold gifts. 16 Nor did he want any one to bring a vessel for the Temple. 17 And he taught, saying to them, "Is it not written that my house shall be called a house of prayer for all nations? But you have made it a den of theologians." 18 The scribes and priests heard him and sought to destroy him, for they feared him, since the whole crowd was amazed at his doctrine. 19 But when the day had come, Jesus went out of the city. 20 In the morning, as they were walking together, they saw the fig tree withering away from the roots. 21 Then Peter remembered and said to him, "Teacher, behold, the fig tree you cursed has withered away." 22 Jesus answered and said to them, "Have the faith of God. 23 For verily I say unto you, that whosoever shall say unto this mountain, Be taken away, and cast into the sea, and shall not be troubled in his heart, but shall find that the things which he saith shall come to pass; what he saith shall be done unto him. 24 Therefore I say to you, what you desire when you pray, see that you get it, and it will be done to you. 25 But when you stand and pray, forgive, if you have any- thing against anyone, so that your Father in heaven may also forgive you your debts. 26 For if you do not forgive, your Father who is in heaven will not forgive you your debts." 27 Then they came again to Jerusalem, and as he was walking in the Temple, the priests and the scribes and the elders came to meet him, 28 and said to him, "By what authority do you do these things? And who gave you this authori- ty, that you should do these things?" 29 Then Jesus answered and said to them, "I also will ask you a certain thing; answer me and I will tell you by what authority I do these things." 30 The baptism of John, was it done by him or by men? Answer me. 31 They thought among themselves, saying, "If we say, 'By God,' he will say, 'Why did you not baptize him?' 32 But if we say, "From men," we fear the people, for all men regarded John as a prophet in faith." 33 Then they answered and said to

Iesus, "We cannot say." And Jesus, answering, said to them, "Nor will I tell you by what authority I do these things."

CHAPTER 12

1 Then he began to speak to them in parables, "A man planted a vineyard, fenced it with a hedge, dug a pit for the vineyard, built a tower on it, leased it to the vinedressers, and went to a foreign country. 2 At that time he sent to the vinedressers a servant, that he might receive from the vinedressers the fruit of the vineyard. 3 But they took him, beat him, and sent him away emptied. 4 And again he sent them another servant, against whom they threw stones, broke his head, and sent him away empty-handed. 5 Then he sent another, whom they killed, and many others, beating some and killing others. 6 He still had a son, his beloved, and to him also he sent the last, saying, "They will return my son to me." 7 But the masters said among themselves, "This is the heir; come, kill him, and the inheritance shall be ours." 8 So they took him, killed him, and drove him out of the vineyard. 9 What then will the owner of the vineyard do? He will come and destroy these vinedressers and give the vineyard to others. 10 Have you not read this Scripture? The stone that the builders re- jected has become the head of the corner. 11 This has been done by the LORD and is mar- velous in our eyes." 12 So they set out to get him, but they feared the people, for they saw that he had spoken that parable against them; so they left him and went their way. 13 Then they sent to him some Pharisees and some Herodians to take him in his speech. 14 When they came, they said to him, "Teacher, we know that you are sincere and that you care for no one, for you do not concern yourself with the person of men, but truly teach the way of God: is it lawful or not to give tribute to Caesar? 15 Shall we give it or not give it? But he, knowing their hypocrisy, said to them, "Why do you tempt me? Bring me a pen, that I may see it." 16 They brought it to him, and he said to them, "Whose image and inscription is this?" And they answered him, "Caesar's." 17 Then Jesus answered and said to them, "Give to Caesar the things that are Caesar's, and to God the things that are God's." 18 Then came to him the Sadducees (who say there is no resurrection) and questioned him, saying, 19 Master, Moses wrote against him, "If a broth- er dies and leaves his wife and leaves no chil- dren, let the brother take his wife and beget children for his brother." 20 There were two brothers; the first took a wife and, when she died, left no children. 21 The second took her to wife and died, leaving no children, and so did the third: 22 So the two had a wife and left no children; the last of all his wife also died. 23 In the resurrection, therefore, when they rise again, whose wife will the wife of these men be? For others have had her to wife." 24 Then Jesus answered and said to them, "Are you therefore not deceived, because you do not know the Scriptures and the power of God? 25 For when they rise from the dead, men will not marry and women will not marry, but they will be like the angels who are in heaven. 26 And as for the dead, who shall rise, have you not read in the book of Moses, how in the bush God spoke to him, saying, "I am the God of Abraham, the God of Isaac, and the God of Jacob"? 27 God is not the God of the dead, but the God of the living. You are therefore great- ly deceived." 28 Then came one of the scribes who had heard them arguing together and, seeing that he had answered them well, asked him, "What is the first commandment of all?" 29 Jesus answered him, "The first of all com- mands

is, 'Listen, Israel, the Lord our God is the only Lord. 30 Therefore you shall love the Lord your God with all your heart, with all your soul, with all your mind, and with all your strength; this is the first commandment. 31 And the second is similar, namely, "You shall love your neighbor as yourself." There is no other commandment greater than these. 32 Then the scribe said to him, "Well, teacher, you have spoken the truth, that there is only one God and that there is none other than he, 33 and to love him with all your heart, with all your understanding, with all your soul, and with all your strength, and to love your neigh- bor as yourself, is more than all burnt offer- ings and sacrifices." 34 Then Iesus, seeing that he answered with discretion, said to him, "You are not far from the kingdom of God." And no one, after this, ventured to question him. 35 Jesus answered and said, teaching in the Temple, "How do the scribes say that Christ is the son of Dauid? 36 For Dauid him- self said by the Holy Spirit, "The Lord said to my Lord, 'Sit at my right hand, until I have made your enemies your feet.'" 37 Then Dauid himself called him Lord: by what means then is he his son? and many people heard him with joy. 38 Moreover he said to them in his doctrine, "Beware of the scribes who love to go in long robes and greet in the markets, 39 and the leading places in the synagogues and the first places in the feasts, 40 who occupy the houses of widows, even under a color of long prayers. These will receive the greatest damnation. 41 As Iesus was sitting in front of the treasury, he saw how people were throw- ing money into the treasury, and many rich people were throwing a lot. 42 There came a certain poor widow who threw in two pen- nies, which make a square. 43 Then he called his disciples to him and said to them, "Truly I tell you, this poor widow threw more than all those who threw into the treasury. 44 For they all poured out their surplus, but she poured out all that she had, that is, all her money.

CHAPTER 13

1 As he was leaving the Temple, one of his disciples said to him, "Teacher, look at the stones and buildings here." 2 Then Jesus an- swered and said to him, "Do you see these great buildings? There will not be a stone left on a stone that will not be thrown down." 3 While he was on the Mount of Olives, facing the Temple, Peter, Iames, Iohn and Andrew questioned him in secret, 4 "Tell me, when will these things take place and what will be the sign in which all these things will be fulfilled?" 5 Jesus answered them and began to say, "Be careful that no one deceives you. 6 For many will come in my Name, saying, 'I am the Christ,' and they will deceive many. 7 Moreover, when you hear of wars and rumors of wars, do not be troubled, for it is necessary for these things to take place, but the end has not yet come. 8 For nation shall rise up against nation, and kingdom against kingdom, and there shall be earthquakes in many quarters, and there shall be famines and troubles; these are the beginnings of sorrows. 9 But take heed to yourselves, for they will hand you over to the councils and synagogues; you will be beaten and brought before rulers and kings for my sake, as a testimony for them. 10 And the gospel must first be published among all the nations. 11 But when they let you go and deliver you, do not be prudent first, nor study what you are to say; but speak what is given you at the same time, for it is not you who speak, but the Holy Spirit. 12 Yea, and brother shall deliver up brother to death, and father to son, and children shall rise up against their parents and cause them to die. 13 You will be hated by

all men because of my names, but he who endures to the end will be saved. 14 Moreover, when you see the abomination of desolation (spoken of by Daniel the prophet) placed where it should not (let those who read consider it), then let those who are in Iudea flee to the mountains, 15 and those who are above the house let them not go down into the house or enter it to take anything from their house. 16 And he who is in the fields shall not turn back to take his clothes. 17 Then there will be trouble for pregnant women and for those who give birth in those days. 18 Pray therefore that your flight will not take place in winter. 19 For in those days there will be such tribulation as there has not been since the beginning of the creation that God made until now, nor will there be. 20 If the LORD had not shortened those days, no flesh would have been affected; but for the elect, whom he has chosen, he has shortened those days. 21 Therefore if anyone says to you, "Here is the Christ," or "Behold, he is there," do not believe it. 22 For false Christs and false prophets will arise, and they will do signs and wonders to deceive, if possible, the very elect. 23 But take heed: behold, I have shown you all things before. 24 Moreover, in those days, after the tribulation, the sun will be darkened and the moon will not give its light, 25 And the stars of Heauen shall fall, and the powers that are in Heauen shall tremble. 26 And then they will see the Son of Man coming in the midst of the clouds, with great power and glory. 27 And he will send his angels and gather his elect from the four winds and from the greatest part of the earth to the greatest part of Heauen. 28 Now learn the parable of the fig tree. When its branch is still tender and producing leaves, you know that the morning is near. 29 So like- wise, when you see these things happening, know that the kingdom of God is near, that is, at the gates. 30 Truly I tell you, this genera- tion will not pass away until all these things are fulfilled. 31 Heaven and earth will pass away, but my words will not pass away. 32 But of that day and hour no one knows anything, not the angels who are in heaven, nor the Son Himself, but the Father. 33 Take heed: watch and pray, for you do not know when the time will be. 34 For the Son of man is like a man who goes into a foreign country, and leaves his house, and gives authority to his servants, and to each his table, and commands the doorkeeper to keep watch. 35 Watch therefore (for you do not know whether the master of the house will come, at dawn or at midnight, at cockcrow or at sunrise). 36 Lest, if he come suddenly, he find you asleep. 37 And the things that I say to you, I say to everyone: watch.

CHAPTER 14

1 Two days later the feast of the Passer and the soggy Bread was celebrated; the priests and scribes tried to catch him by deception and put him to death. 2 But they said, "Not on a feast day, otherwise there would be an up- roar among the people." 3 While he was in Bethany, in the house of Simon the leper, as he was sitting at table, there came a woman carrying a box of ears of corn, very costly; she broke the box and placed it on his head. 4 Therefore some were indignant among them- selves and said, "What is the use of this waste of oil? 5 Since it could have been sold for more than three hundred pence and given to the poor, they murmured against her. 6 But Jesus said, "Let her alone; why do you trouble her? She has done a good work with me. 7 For you always have the poor with you, and when you wish you can do good to them, but to me you will do none. 8 She did what she could; she came before me to announce my body at the burial. 9 Truly I tell you, when this gospel is preached in all the world, she will be spoken of in remembrance also of what she has done." 10 Then Iudas Iscariot, one of the two, went away to the priests to betray him. 11 When they heard this, they rejoiced and promised that they would give him money; so he looked for a way to betray him convincingly. 12 Now on the first day of the vnleauened bread, when the Passover was being sacrificed, his disciples said to him, "Where do you want us to go to prepare, so that you may eat the Pass- over?" 13 Then he sent two of his disciples and said to them, "Go into the city and a man will come to meet you with a pitcher of water; fol- low him. 14 When he enters, he will say to the master of the house, "The Master said, 'Where is the lodging where I will eat on Passover Day with my disciples?' 15 He will point out to you a large room, furnished and prepared, and make it available for the meal. 16 So his disci- ples departed, came to the city, found as he had told them, and prepared supper. 17 At that time he came with the two. 18 As they sat at the table and ate, Jesus said, "Truly I tell you, one of you will betray me and eat with me." 19 Then they began to be grieved and to say to him one by one, "Is it I?" and another, "Is it I?" 20 He answered them, "It is one of the two who dips with me in the dish." 21 Verily the Son of Man goes his way, as it is written of him; but woe to that man, by whom the Son of Man was betrayed; it would have been good for that man, if he had never been brought. 22 While they were eating, Jesus took the bread, and having given thanks, he broke it and gave it to them, saying, "Take, eat; this is my body." 23 He also took the cup and, after giving thanks, gave it to them; and they all drank from it. 24 Then he said to them, "This is my blood of the New Testament, shed for many." 25 Truly I tell you, I will drink no more of the fruit of your vine until that day when I drink it new in the kingdom of God." 26 After singing a psalm, they went out to the Mount of Olives. 27 Then Jesus said to them, "This night you will be offended by me, for it is written that I will strike the shepherd and the sheep will be scattered. 28 But after I am risen, I will go into Galilee before you." 29 Peter said to him, "Even if all men were offended at you, I would not." 30 Then Jesus said to him, "Truly I tell you, today, and in this night, before the cock crows twice, you will deny me three times." 31 But he said more seriously. If I should die with you, I will not deny you; and so said they all. 32 Then they came to a place called Geth- semane; then he said to his disciples, "Sit here, until I praise you." 33 And he took with him Peter, Iames, and Iohn, and began to be troubled and in great anxiety, 34 and said to them, "My soul is greatly tried, even unto death; stay here and watch." 35 Then he ad- vanced a little, and fell down, and prayed, if it were possible, that that hour might pass from him. 36 And he said, "Abba, Father, all things are possible to you; take this cup away from me; I do not want my will to be done, but yours." 37 Then he came and found them sleeping and said to Peter, "Simon, are you asleep? Could you not keep watch for an hour? 38 Watch and pray, that you may not enter into temptation; the spirit in faith is ready, but the flesh is weak. 39 Then he went away and praised and said the same words. 40 Then he returned and found them asleep again, for their eyes were dull and they did not know what to answer him. 41 Then he returned for the third time and said to them, "Sleep and rest; it is already enough; the hour has come; behold, the Son of Man is delivered into the hands of sinners. 42 Arise, let yourselves go; behold, he who betrays me is near." 43 And immediately, while he was speaking, came Iudas, who was one of the two, and with him a great multitude with swords

and staffs of the priests and scribes and elders. 44 He who had betrayed him had given them a sign, say- ing, "Whom I will kill, it is he; take him and carry him away safely." 45 And when he had come, he went straight to him and said, "Mas- ter Haile," and kissed him. 46 Then they laid their hands on him and took him. 47 One of them, who stood by, took out a sword and struck a servant of the priest, cutting off his ear. 48 Then Jesus answered and said to them, "You came out as against a thief with swords and clubs to take me. 49 I was daily with you teaching in the temple, and you did not take me; but this was done that the Scriptures might be fulfilled." 50 Then they all left him and fled. 51 A certain young man followed him, clothed in linen on his naked body, and the young men took him. 52 But he left his linen garment and fled from them naked. 53 Then they led Jesus to the priest, and all the priests, elders and scribes were gathered to him. 54 Peter followed him far away to the priest's hall and sat down with the servants and warmed himself by the fire. 55 The priests and all the counselors sought witnesses against Jesus to put him to death, but they found none. 56 For many brought false testi- monies against him, but their testimonies did not agree. 57 Then some rose up and brought false testimony against him, saying, "We heard him say that he was dead, 58 We heard him say, "I will destroy this Temple made with hands, and within three days I will build another Temple, made without hands." 59 But their testimonies still did not agree. 60 Then the priest stood in their midst and asked Jesus, "Do you answer nothing? What is the reason why these testify against you? 61 But he kept silent and answered nothing. Then the priest questioned him and said, "Are you that Christ, the Son of the Blessed One?" 62 And Jesus answered, "I am he, and you will see the Son of Man sitting at the right hand of the power of God and coming on the clouds of heaven." 63 Then the priest tore his clothes and said, "What more need have we of wit- nesses? 64 You have heard the blasphemies; what do you think of them? And they all con- demned him to be worthy of death. 65 And some began to spit at him, and to strike him in the face, and to beat him with fists, and to say to him, "Prophecy." And the sergeants struck him with their staffs. 66 And while Pe- ter was below in the chapel, there came one of the priest's women. 67 When she saw Peter warming himself, she looked at him and said, "You were also with Jesus of Nazareth." 68 But he denied it, saying, "I do not know him and do not know what you say." Then he went out into the porch, and the rooster grew. 69 Then a servant girl saw him again and began to say to those standing there, "This is one of them." 70 But he denied it again; and immediately afterward those who stood by said to Peter again, "Surely you are one of them, for you are from Galilee, and your speech is similar." 71 He began to curse and swear, saying, "I do not know this man of whom you speak." 72 Then the second time the rooster croaked, and Pe- ter remembered the speech Jesus had given him, "Before the rooster croaks twice, you will deny me three times."

CHAPTER 15

1 At daybreak, the priests held a council with the elders, scribes and the whole council, bound Jesus, led him away and handed him over to Pilate. 2 Then Pilate asked him, "Are you the king of the Jews?" And he, answering, said to him, "You say so." 3 The priests accused him of many things. 4 Therefore Pilate ques- tioned him again, saying, "Do you answer nothing? This is how many things they

testify against you." 5 But Iesus answered nothing more, so that Pilate was amazed. 6 Now at the feast Pilate delivered to them a prisoner, whom they desired. 7 There was one named Barabbas, bound with his companions, who had made an insurrection and in the insur- rection had committed murder. 8 The people cried out and began to desire him to do as he had done before with them. 9 Then Pilate answered them and said, "Do you want me to let you free king of yourselves? 10 For he knew that the high priests had delivered him from the enuie. 11 But the high priests had led the people to wish that he would rather deliver Barabbas to them. 12 Pilate answered and said to them, "What then do you want me to do with him whom you call the king of the Jews? 13 And they cried out again, "Crucify him." 14 Then Pilate said to them, "But what has he done wrong?" And they cried out even more fiercely, "Crucify him." 15 Then Pilate, wanting to please the people, untied Barab- bas and handed Jesus over, having scourged him, to be crucified. 16 Then the armigers led him into the hall, which is the common hall, and called together the whole band, 17 and clothed him with purple, and put a crown of thorns upon his head, 18 and they began to greet him, saying, "Haile, king of the Iewes." 19 They struck him on the head with a reed, spit on him, knelt down and saluted him. 20 After they had mocked him, they took off his purple, put his clothes on him, and led him out to crucify him. 21 And they forced one who was passing by, named Simon of Cyrene (who came from the county and was the father of Alexander and Rufus) to carry his cross. 22 And they led him to a place called Golgotha, which by interpretation is the place of the skulls of the dead. 23 And they made him drink wine mixed with myrrh, but he did not receive it. 24 And when they had crucified him, they divided his garments, drawing lots for what each one was to have. 25 It was the third hour when they crucified him. 26 And on his cause was written, "THE KING OF THE JEWS." 27 With him they also crucified two theologians, one on his right and the other on his left. 28 Thus was fulfilled the Scripture that says, "And he was numbered among the ungodly." 29 Those who were passing by railed at him, shaking their heads and saying, "Hey, you who destroy the Temple and rebuild it in three days! 30 Save yourself and come down from the cross." 31 Likewise also the priests, mocking, were saying among themselves and with the scribes, "He has spoken of other men; he himself cannot speak." 32 Let Christ, the king of Israel, now come down from the crucifixion, that we may see and know. Even those who had been crucified with him re-ed- ucated him. 33 When it was the sixth hour, it became dark over all the land until the ninth hour. 34 And at the ninth hour Jesus cried out with a loud voice, saying, "Eloi, Eloi, lam- ma- sabachthani," which means, by inter- pretation, "My God, my God, why have you forsaken me? 35 Some of those who stood by, on hearing this, said, "Behold, he calls Elijah." 6 And one ran and filled a sponge with wine, and put it on a reed, and made him drink, saying, "Let him alone; let us see if Elijah comes and brings him down." 37 Then Iesus cried out with a loud voice and brought out the ghost. 38 The vault of the Temple was torn in two parts, from top to bottom. 39 When the centurion who stood before him saw that he, by shouting, had released the ghost, he said, "Truly this man was the Son of God." 40 There were also women who saw from a distance, including Mary Magdalene, Mary (mother of Iames the younger and of Ioses) and Salome, 41 who, when he was in Galilee, followed and attended him, and many other women who came with him to Jerusalem. 42 When it was now night (for it was the day of preparation preceding the Sabbath) 43 came Ioseph of Ari- mathea, an honorable counselor who desired the kingdom of God, and went boldly to Pilate to ask for the body of Iesus. 44 Pilate asked if he was already dead, called the centurion, and asked him if he was already dead. 45 When he heard the centurion's truth, he handed the body over to Ioseph: 46 who bought a linen cloth, brought it down, wrapped it in the lin- en cloth, and laid it in a tomb made out of a log, and rolled a stone to the bottom of the tomb: 47 Mary Magdalene and Mary Ioses mother looked where he was to be laid.

CHAPTER 16

1 When the Sabbath was past, Mary Magda- lene, Mary the mother of James and Salome bought sweetmeats to come and hear him. 2 Therefore early in the morning, on the first day of the week, they went to the tomb, when the sun had now risen. 3 And they said one to another, "Who will remove the stone from the bottom of the tomb?" 4 And when they looked, they saw that the stone had been rolled away (for it was very large). 5 Then they went into the tomb and saw a young man sitting on the right side, clothed in a long white robe; and they were greatly troubled. 6 But he said to them, "Do not be so troubled: you see Jesus of Nazareth, who was crucified; he is risen, he is not here; look at the place where they have placed him. 7 But go your way, and tell his disciples and Peter that he will go before you into Galilee; there you will see him, as he told you." 8 And they left in haste and fled from the tomb, for they were trembling and sick; and they said nothing to anyone, for they were afraid. 9 And when Jesus was risen again, at the beginning of the first day of the week, he appeared first to Mary Magdalene, from whom he had cast out ten decorations: 10 And she went and reported to those who had been with him, who wept and despaired. 11 And when they heard that he was an alien and had appeared to her, they did not believe him. 12 Then he appeared to two of them in another form, as they were walking and go- ing toward the countryside. 13 They went and told the remaining ones about it, but they did not notice. 14 Finally, he appeared to the eleu- omini as they sat together and rebuked them for their unbelief and hardness of heart, be- cause they had not believed those who had seen him, having risen again. 15 And he said to them, "Go into all the world and preach the gospel to every creature. 16 Whosoever shall be baptized and be baptized shall be saved; but whosoever shall not be baptized shall be damned. 17 And these signs will follow those who are baptized: in my Name they will drive out diseases and speak with new tongues, 18 they shall remove serpents, and if they drink any deadly thing, it shall not hurt them; they shall lay hands on the sick, and they shall be healed." 19 So after the Lord had spoken to them, he was received up into heàven and sat down at the right hand of God. 20 And they departed and preached in every place. And the Lord worked with them and confirmed the word with signs that followed. Amen.

LUKE

CHAPTER 1

1 For many have taken hold of the history of these things, of which we are fully convinced, 2 as they have delivered them to those who from the beginning have seen them for them- selves and have been ministers of the word, 3 it seemed good to me also (most noble The- ophilus), as I have sought all things perfectly from the beginning, to write of them from point to point, 4 that you might acknowledge the certainty of those things of which you have been instructed. 5 In the days of Herod, king of Judea, there was a certain priest named Zechariah, from the region of Abia, and his wife was one of the daughters of Aar- on, and her name was Elizabeth. 6 Both of them were righteous before God and walked in all the commands and provisions of the Lord, without reproach. 7 They had no chil- dren, for Elizabeth was barren, and both were in old age. 8 While he exercised the priestly office before God, his walk was conducted in a regular manner, 9 according to the rules of the priestly office, it fell to his lot to burn in- cense when he entered the temple of the LORD. 10 While the incense was burning, all the multitude of the people were praying. 11 Then an angel of the Lord appeared to him, standing at the right hand of the altar of in- cense. 12 When Zechariah saw him, he was troubled and frightened. 13 But the angel said to him, "Do not be afraid, Zechariah, for your prayer has been answered, and your wise Elizabeth will bear you a son, whom you shall call Iohn. 14 You shall have joy and gladness, and many shall rejoice at his birth. 15 For he shall be great in the sight of the LORD, he shall not drink wine or strong drink, and he shall be full of the Holy Spirit, from his moth- er's womb. 16 Many of the children of Israel will be converted to their Lord God. 17 For he shall go before him with the spirit and power of Elijah, to convert the hearts of fathers to sons, and the disobedient to the wisdom of righteous men, to prepare a people ready for the LORD." 18 Then Zechariah said to the an- gel, "How can I know this? For I am old and my wife is very old." 19 The angel answered and said to him, "I am Gabriel, who stand in the presence of God and have been sent to speak to you and to tell you this good news. 20 And behold, you will be tamed and will not be able to speak until the day when these things are fulfilled, because you have not believed my words, which will be fulfilled in due time." 21 Now the people waited for Zechariah and marveled that he stayed so long in the Tem- ple. 22 When he came out, he could not speak to them; then they understood that he had had a vision in the Temple: For he made signs to them, and remained asleep. 23 When the days of his commission were fulfilled, he went out to his house. 24 After those days his wife Elisabeth conceived and hid five money, saying, 25 Thus hath the LORD done with me, in the days that he looked upon me, to take away my reproach among men. 26 In the sixth month, the angel Gabriel was sent by God to a town in Galilee called Nazareth, 27 to a virgin betrothed to a man named Ioseph, of the house of Dauid, and the virgin's name was Mary. 28 The angel came in to her and said, "Hail, thou who art freely born, the Lord is with thee; blessed art thou among women." 29 When she saw him, she was troubled by his words and thought about what way to greet him. 30 Then the angel said to her, "Do not be afraid, Marie, for you have found favor with God. 31 For, behold, you will conceive in your womb and bear a son, and you will call his name Jesus. 32 He shall be great and shall be called the Son of the Most High, and the Lord God shall give him the throne of his father Dauid. 33 He shall reign over the house of Ja- cob forever, and his kingdom shall have no end." 34 Then Marie said to the angel, "How will this take place, since I do not know the man?" 35 And the angel answered and said to her, "The Holy Spirit will come upon you, and the power of the Most High will overshadow you; therefore also the holy thing that will be born of you will be called the Son of God. 36 And behold, your cousin Elizabeth also

has conceived a son in her old age; and this is her sixtieth month, which was called barren. 37 For with God nothing is impossible. 38 Then Mary said, "Behold the servant of the Lord: let it come to pass for me what you desire." The angel departed from her. 39 In those days Mary arose and went to the county of Hil, to a city of Judah, 40 she entered the house of Zechariah and greeted Elizabeth. 41 When Elizabeth heard Mary's greeting, the baby sprang up in her womb and Elizabeth was filled with the Holy Spirit. 42 She cried out with a loud voice and said, "You are blessed among women, for the fruit of your womb is blessed. 43 And whence is this to me, that the mother of my Lord should come to me? 44 For as the voice of your greeting has sounded in my ears, the child has arisen in my womb for me, 45 Blessed is she who believed, for the things spoken to her by the Lord will be ful- filled." 46 Then Marie said, "My soul magnifies the Lord, 47 and my spirit rejoices in God my Savior. 48 For he has looked upon the degree of his servant's poverty; for behold, from now on all ages shall call me blessed, 49 For he who is mighty has done great things for me, and holy is his Name. 50 His mercy is from gener- ation to generation upon those who fear him. 51 He has proved strength by his armor; he has scattered pride in the imagination of their hearts. 52 He has deposed the mighty from their places and exalted those of low rank. 53 He has filled the poor with goods, and sent away the rich with nothing. 54 He has made Israel, his servant, to be aware of his mercy. 55 As he said to our fathers, that is, to Abraham and his descendants, forever. 56 Marie stayed with her for about three months and then returned to her home. 57 Now the time had come when Elizabeth was to be de- livered, and she gave birth to a son. 58 Her neighbors and cousins heard how the Lord had manifested his great mercy toward her and were reconciled to her. 59 And so it was that on the eighth day they came to circum- cise the child and named him Zechariah, after his father. 60 But his mother answered, "Not so, but he shall be called Iohn." 61 They said to her, "There is no one of your lineage named by this name." 62 Then they made a sign to their father to call him by this name. 63 He asked for writing tablets and wrote, "His name is Iohn," and they all married him. 64 Immedi- ately his mouth and his tongue opened, and he spoke and praised God. 65 Then all who lived nearby were afraid, and all these words were spread throughout the whole hill coun- try of Judea. 66 All who heard them put them into their hearts, saying, "What kind of a son shall this be?" 67 Then her father Zechariah was filled with the Holy Spirit and prophe- sied, saying, 68 Blessed be the LORD, the God of Israel, for he has visited and redeemed his people, 69 and has raised the horn of salva- tion in the house of his servant Dauid." 70 as he said by the mouth of his holy Prophets, who have existed from the beginning of the world, saying that he would send his people to another city, 71 that he would send vs. delight from our enemies and from the hands of all who hate her, 72 to have mercy on our fathers and to remember his holy countryman, 73 and the other oath sworn to Abraham our fa- ther. 74 namely, that he would pledge himself to us, that we would be delivered out of the hand of our enemies and serve him without fear, 75 all the days of our life, in holiness and righteousness before him. 76 You, little one, shall be called a Prophet of the Most High, be- cause you shall go before the face of the Lord to prepare his expectations, 77 and to give knowledge of salvation to his people through the remission of their sins, 78 by the tender mercy of our God, who has visited the spring of the day from an hour, 79 to give light to those who sit in darkness and in the shadow of death, and to guide

our feet into the way of peace. 80 The child grew, grew stronger in spirit, and remained in the wilderness until the day came when he should reveal himself to Israel.

CHAPTER 2

1 In those days a decree was issued by Au- gustus Caesar that the whole world should be taxed. 2 (This first taxation was done when Cyrenius was governor of Syria). 3 So they all went to be taxed, each to his own city. 4 Ioseph also departed from Galilee, from a city called Nazareth, into Judea, to the city of Dauid, called Beth-leem (because he was of the house and lineage of Dauid). 5 to be taxed with Mary, who had been given to him as his wife and was with child. 6 And it was so that while they were there, the days were fulfilled in which she was to be delivered, 7 And she brought her firstborn with her, and wrapped him in swaddling clothes, and put him in a basket, because there was no room for them in the year. 8 There were also shepherds in the same county who stood in the fields and guarded their flocks at night. 9 Well, the an- gel of the Lord came upon them, and the glory of the Lord shone upon them, and they were greatly afraid. 10 Then the angel said to them, "Do not be afraid, for behold, I bring you glad tidings of great joy, which shall be to all the people, 11 namely, that there is born to you this day in the city of Dauid a Savior, who is Christ the Lord. 12 And this shall be a sign to you: you shall find the child swaddled and laid in a cradle." 13 And immediately there was with the angel a multitude of entertainers of great worth, praising God and saying, 14 Glory to God in the highest, peace on earth, and good- will toward men. 15 As the angels departed from them on high, the watchmen said to one another, "Let us therefore go to Bethlehem and see how the thing the Lord has shown them has happened." 16 So they came quickly and found Mary and Iosef and the baby laid in the cradle. 17 When they had seen it, they pub- lished the fact that they had been told about that child. 18 And all who heard it marveled at the things that had been told them by the shepherds. 19 But Mary kept all those words and pondered them in her heart. 20 The shep- herds returned to glorify and praise God for all that they had heard and seen, as they had been told. 21 When the eight days necessary to circumcise the child had elapsed, the name of Iesus was imposed on him, which had been so named by Angell before he was conceived in the woman. 22 When the days of his pu- rification according to the law of Moses were completed, they brought him to Jerusalem to present him to the Lord, 23 (as it is written in the Law of the Lord, "Every male child who first opens his womb shall be called holy by the Lord"). 24 and to offer an oblation, as it is written in the Law of the Lord: a pair of turtle doves or two young pigeons. 25 There was a man in Jerusalem whose name was Simeon; this man was righteous and feared God and waited for the consolation of Israel, and the Holy Spirit was upon him. 26 It was declared to him by God through the Holy Spirit that he would not see death before he saw the Lord's Anointed One. 27 By a motion of the Spirit, he entered the Temple, and when the parents brought the child Jesus, he set about doing for him according to the rules of the law, 28 he took him under his arms, praised God, and said 29 Lord, let your servant go in peace, ac- cording to your will, 30 for my eyes have seen your salvation, 31 which you have prepared before all peoples, 32 a light for the nations and the glory of your people Israel. 33 Ioseph and his mother marveled at these things that had been said about him. 34

Simeon blessed them and said to Mary his mother, "Behold, this child has been appointed for the fall and revival of many in Israel and for a sign that will be spoken of." 35 (Yes, and a sword shall pierce your soul) that the thoughts of many hearts may be opened." 36 There was a prophetess, Anna, daughter of Phanuel, of the tribe of Asher, who was of a great age, having lain with a husband for ten years since her virgin- ity: 37 She had been a widow for about four and a half years and did not leave the Tem- ple, but served God with fasts and prayers, night and day. 38 At that same time, coming to them, she confessed the Lord and spoke of him to all who sought redemption in Jerusa- lem. 39 When they had fulfilled all things ac- cording to the word of the Lord, they returned to Galilee, to their city, Nazareth. 40 The child grew and was strengthened in spirit, and was full of wisdom, and the grace of God was with him. 41 His parents went to Jerusalem every year on the Feast of the Passer. 42 When he was two years old, they came to Jerusalem after the feast, 43 and when the days of the feast were over, as they returned, the child Ie- sus remained in Jerusalem, without Ioseph's knowledge or his mother's knowledge, 44 but they, supposing that he had been in company, made a day's journey and searched for him among their relatives and acquaintances. 45 Not having found him, they returned to Je- rusalem and searched for him. 46 Three days later, they found him in the Temple, sitting among the doctors, listening to them and questioning them: 47 All who heard him were amazed at his understanding and his an- swers. 48 When they saw him, they felt admi- ration, and his mother said to him, "Son, why have you behaved so? Behold, your father and I have sought you with very sensitive hearts." 49 Then he said to them, "How is it that you sought me? Did you not know that I had to go for my father's buses? 50 But they did not understand the word that he spoke to them. 51 So he went down with them and came to Nazareth and was subject to them; and his mother kept all these words in her heart. 52 And Jesus grew in wisdom, in stature, and in reputation with God and men.

CHAPTER 3

1 Now in the fifteenth year of the regency of Tiberius Caesar, Pontius Pilate was gov- ernor of Judea, Herod was tetrarch of Gali- lee, his brother Philip was tetrarch of Iturea and the county of Trachonite, and Lysanias was tetrarch of Abilene, 2 (when Annas and Caiaphas were priests) the word of God came to John the son of Zechariah in the wilder- ness. 3 He came to all the coasts of Iordane, preaching the baptism of repentance for the remission of sins, 4 as it is written in the book of the sayings of Esaias the prophet, who says, "The word of him who cries out in the wilderness is, 'Prepare the way of the Lord, straighten his paths. 5 Every valley shall be filled, every mountain and hill shall be low- ered, crooked things shall be made straight, and rough paths shall be made smooth. 6 And all flesh shall see the salvation of God." 7 Then he said to the people going out to be bap- tized by him, "O generations of vipers, who warned you to flee from the wrath to come? 8 Bear therefore fruit worthy of life, and do not begin to say among yourselves, 'We have Abraham for a father,' for I tell you that God is able to bring forth from these stones chil- dren for Abraham. 9 Now the axe has also been laid on the roots of the trees; therefore all the trees that do not bear good fruit will be cut down and thrown into the fire." 10 Then the people questioned him, saying, "What shall we do then?" 11 He answered and said to them, "Whoever has two spoils, let him divide them with him who has none; and whoever has mate, let him do likewise." 12 Then came also some Publicans to be baptized, and they said to him, "Master, what shall we do?" 13 He said to them, "Ask nothing but what you have been commanded." 14 The souls also came to him, saying, "What shall we do? And he said to them, "Do violence to no one, accuse no one unjustly, and be content with your wag- es." 15 While the people were waiting and all the men were wondering in their hearts about John, whether he was not that Christ, 16 Iohn answered and said to all, "I baptize you with water, but there comes one mightier than I, whose knot of shoes I am not worthy to untie; he will baptize you with the Holy Spirit and with fire. 17 Whose fan is in his hand, and he shall make clean his plain, and gather wheat into his barn, but the darnel he shall bury with a fire that shall never be quenched." 18 Thus, exhorting with many other things, he preached to the people. 19 But when Herod, the tetrarch, was rebuked by him for Herodi- as, the wife of Philip, his brother, and for all the crimes Herod had committed, 20 yet he added this to all this: he locked Iohn in pris- on. 21 Now while all the people were being baptized and Iohn was being baptized and praying, the church was opened: 22 and the Holy Spirit descended upon him in bodily form, like a flute, and there was a voice from above, saying, "You are my beloved Son; in you I am well pleased." 23 Jesus himself began to be about thirty years old, being, as men sup- posed, the son of Ioseph, who was the son of Eli, 24 the son of Matthat, the son of Leui, the son of Melchi, the son of Ianna, the son of Ioseph, 25 son of Mattathias, son of Amos, son of Naum, son of Esli, son of Nagge, 26 son of Maath, son of Mattathias, son of Semei, son of Ioseph, son of Judah, 27 son of Ioanna, son of Rhesa, son of Zerubbabel, son of Salathiel, son of Neri, 28 son of Melchi, son of Addi, son of Cosam, son of Elmodam, son of Er, 29 son of Joses, son of Eliezer, son of Iorim, son of Matthat, son of Leui, 30 the son of Sime- on, the son of Judah, the son of Ioseph, the son of Ionan, the son of Eliachim, 31 son of Melea, son of Mainan, son of Mattatha, son of Nathan, son of Dauid, 32 son of Jesse, son of Obed, son of Booz, son of Salmon, son of Naasson, 33 son of Aminadab, son of Aram, son of Esrom, son of Phares, son of Judah, 34 son of Jacob, son of Isaac, son of Abraham, son of Thara, son of Nachor, 35 son of Saruch, son of Ragau, son of Phalec, son of Eber, son of Sala, 36 son of Cainan, son of Arphaxad, son of Shem, son of Noah, son of Lamech, 37 son of Mathusala, son of Enoch, son of Iared, son of Maleleel, son of Cainan, 38 son of Enos, son of Seth, son of Adam, son of God.

CHAPTER 4

1 Jesus, full of the Holy Spirit, returned from Iordan and was led by that Spirit into the wil- derness, 2 and remained there for four days, tempted by the flood, and in those days he ate nothing; but when they were finished, after- ward he was hungry. 3 Then the devil said to him, "If you are the Son of God, command this stone to become bread." 4 But Jesus an- swered him, "It is written that man does not live by bread alone, but by every word of God." 5 Then the Lord led him to a high mountain and showed him all the kingdoms of the world in the twinkling of an eye. 6 And the Lord said to him, "I will give you all this power and the glory of those kingdoms, for this has been given to me, and I will give it to whom I will. 7 If therefore you will worship

Me, they shall all be yours." 8 But Jesus answered him and said, "Get away from me, Satan, for it is written, 'You shall worship the Lord your God, and him alone you shall serve.'" 9 Then he led him to Jerusalem and set him on a pinnacle of the Temple and said to him, "If you are the Son of God, throw yourself down from here, 10 for it is written that he will entrust his an- gels to guard you: 11 and with their hands they will lift you up, if ever you should strike your foot against a stone." 12 Jesus answered and said to him, "It is said, 'You shall not tempt the Lord your God.'" 13 And when the Lord had finished all the temptation, he departed from him for a while. 14 Then Jesus returned to Gal- ilee by the power of the Spirit, and his fame spread throughout the surrounding region. 15 For he taught in their synagogues and was honored by all men. 16 When he had come to Nazareth, where he had been led, he entered the synagogue on the Sabbath and stopped to speak. 17 The book of the prophet Esaias was handed to him; and when he had opened the book, he found the place where it was written, 18 The Spirit of the Lord is upon me, because he has appointed me to preach the gospel to the poor; he has sent me to succor the bro- kenhearted, to preach deliverance to the cap- tives and recovery of sight to the blind, to set at liberty the wounded: 19 And that I should preach the acceptable year of the Lord." 20 He closed the book, gave it again to the minister, and sat down; and the eyes of all who were in the synagogue were fixed on him. 21 Then he began to say to them, "Today the Scripture has been fulfilled in your ears." 22 They all bore witness to him and marveled at the gra- cious words that came out of his mouth and said, "Is not this the son of Jeoseph?" 23 Then he said to them, "You will surely say to me this proverb, 'Physician, heal yourself; what we heard done in Capernaum, do also here in your own country.'" 24 And he said, "Truly I tell you, no prophet is welcome in his own country. 25 But I tell you a truth: there were many widows in Israel in the days of Elijah, when the Heauen had been closed for three years and six months, when there was a great famine throughout the land: 26 But to none of them was Elijah sent, except to Sarepta, a city of Sidon, to a certain widow. 27 At the time of Elisha the prophet there were many lep- ers in Israel, but none of them were healed, except Naaman the Syrian. 28 Then all who were in the synagogue, on hearing this, were filled with wrath, 29 and rose up, and drove him out of the city, and led him to the brink of the hill, where their city was built, to cast him down headlong. 30 But he passed through the midst of them and went his way, 31 and went down to Capernaum, a city in Galilee, and there he taught them on the Sabbath days. 32 They were amazed at his doctrine, for his word was authoritative. 33 There was a man in the synagogue who had a spirit of deuill vncleane, crying out with a loud voice, 34 saying, "Oh, what shall we do with you, you, Jesus of Nazareth, have you come to destroy people? I know who you are, that is, the Holy One of God." 35 Jesus rebuked him, saying, "Be at peace and come out of him." Then the devil, throwing him into their midst, came out of him and did him no harm. 36 Then they were all afraid and spoke among themselves, saying, "What is this, because with author- ity and power he commands unclean spirits and they come out? 37 And his fame spread through all the places of the land around. 38 And he arose and went out of the synagogue and entered Simon's house. Simon's mother had been seized with a great fever, and they required him for her. 39 Then he stood before her, rebuked her fever, and she left her; im- mediately he arose and ministered to them. 40 At the setting of the sun, all those who had people sick of various diseases brought them to him, and he laid his hands on each of them and healed them. 41 Out of many also came cries and said, "You are the Christ, the Son of God"; but he rebuked them and would not allow them to say that they knew that he was that Christ. 42 Then, when it was daylight, he went away and withdrew to a deserted place; and the people sought him, and came near him, and held him that he might not depart from them. 43 But he said to them, "Surely I must preach the kingdom of God in other cities also, for for this I was sent." 44 And he preached in the synagogues of Galilee.

CHAPTER 5

1 Then as the people came to him to hear the word of God, he stopped by the lake of Gen- nesaret, 2 and he saw two ships standing on the shore of the lake, but the fishermen had come out of them and were washing their nets. 3 He went into one of the ships, which was Simoni's, and asked him to move a little way from the shore; then he sat down and taught the people outside the ship. 4 When he had left the ship, he said to Simon, "Go out to sea and let down your nets to fish." 5 Then Simon answered and said to him, "Master, we have walked all night and caught nothing; nevertheless, at your beckoning, I will lower my net." 6 And when they had done so, they caught a great quantity of fish, so that the net broke. 7 Then they beckoned to their compan- ions, who were in the other ship, to come and help them, who came and filled both ships, which sinned. 8 When Simon Peter noticed this, he prostrated himself at Jesus' knees, saying, "Lord, depart from me, for I am a sinful man." 9 For he and all who were with him were greatly amazed at the fish they had caught. 10 And so were Iames and Iohn, sons of Zebedee, who were Simon's companions. Then Jesus said to Simon, "Do not be afraid; from now on you will catch men." 11 And when they had brought the ships ashore, they left them all and followed him. 12 Now while he was in a certain city, behold, there was a man full of leprosy, who, at the sight of Jesus, fell on his face and prayed to him, saying, "Lord, if you are willing, you can make me well." 13 Then he stretched out his hand and touched him, saying, "I will, be cleansed." And imme- diately the leprosy departed from him. 14 And he commanded him not to tell anyone; but to go, he said, and to present himself to the priest, and to offer for your clensure, as Moses commanded, a testimony for them. 15 But the fame of him spread more and more, and great crowds gathered to hear him and to be healed by him of their infirmities. 16 But he secluded himself in the wilderness and prayed. 17 One certain day while he was teaching, Pharisees and doctors of the Law who had come from all the cities of Galilee and Judea and Jerusa- lem passed by, and the power of the Lord was in him to heal them. 18 Then men brought a man lying in a bed, suffering from paral- ysis, and sought a way to bring him in and lay him down before them. 19 And not being able to find a way to bring him in, because of the dangerous situation, they went toward the house and brought him down through the curtain, bed and all, in the middle, be- fore Jesus. 20 And seeing their faith, he said to them, "Man, your sins have forgiven you." 21 Then the scribes and Pharisees began to reason, saying, "Who is this man who speaks blasphemy? Who can forgive sins but God alone?" 22 But Jesus, seeing their reasoning, answered them, "What are you reasoning about in your hearts? 23 Whether it is easier to say, Your sins forgive you, or to say, Get up and walk? 24 But that

you may know that the Son of Man has authority to forgive sins on earth, (he said to the sick man with palsy) I say to you, Arise, take up your bed, and go to your house." 25 And immediately he got up before them, took up the bed on which he was lying, and went to his house, praying to God. 26 And they were all troubled, praying to God and full of fear, saying, "No doubt we have seen strange things today." 27 After this, he went and saw a publican named Leui sitting at the customer's counter and said to him, "Follow me." 28 He left everything, got up and followed him.29 Then Leui made him a great banquet in his house, where there was a large company of publicans and others sitting at ta- ble with them. 30 But those who were scribes and Pharisees among them murmured against his disciples, saying, "Why do you eat and drink with publicans and sinners?" 31 Then Jesus answered and said to them, "He who is healthy does not need a physician, but he who is sick. 32 I have not come to call the righteous, but sinners to repentance." 33 Then they said to him, "Why do John's disciples of- ten fast and pray, and also the disciples of the Pharisees, but yours eat and drink?" 34 And he answered them, "Can you perhaps cause the children of the bridal chamber to fast while the bride is with them? 35 But the days will come when the bridegroom will be taken from them; then they will fast in those days." 36 Then he spoke to them a parable, "No one puts a piece of a new robe into an old robe, for then the new one is torn, and the piece taken out of the new one does not agree with the old one. 37 Also, no one shall put new wine into old vessels, for the new wine breaks the ves- sels and runs out and the vessels die: 38 but new wine must be poured into new vessels; so both are preserved. 39 Moreover, those who drink old wine do not immediately desire new wine, because they say, "The old is better."

CHAPTER 6

1 On a second solemn Sabbath, he passed through the wheat fields, and his disci- ples plucked the ears of corn, ate them and rubbed them in their hands. 2 Some Phar- isees said to them, "Why do you do what is not lawful to do on the Sabbath? 3 Then Jesus answered them and said, "Have you not read what Dauid did while he was still a hanged man and those who were with him? 4 How he went into the house of God, and took and ate bread, and gave it also to those who were with him, which it was not lawful to eat, but only for the priests? 5 And he said to them, "The Son of Man is lord even of the Sabbath day." 6 On another Sabbath he went into the synagogue and taught, and there was a man whose right hand was withered. 7 The Scribes and Pharisees watched him to know whether he would speak on the Sabbath, to find an ac- cusation against him. 8 But he, knowing their thoughts, said to the man whose hand was withered, "Get up and stand in the midst." And he arose and stood. 9 Then Jesus said to them, "I ask you a question, whether it is lawful on the Sabbath days to do good or to do evil; whether it is lawful to save life or to destroy? 10 He looked at them all together and said to the man, "Stretch out your hand." And he did so, and his hand became whole again like the other. 11 Then they were filled with

madness and argued with one another about what they might do to Jesus. 12 In those days he went to a mountain to pray and spent the night praying to God. 13 When it was daylight, he called his disciples and chose two whom he called apostles. 14 Simon, whom he also called Peter, and Andrew his brother, Iames and Iohn, Philip and Bartlemewe: 15 Matthew and Thomas; Iames the son of Alpheus, and Simon, called Zelous, 16 Iudas, brother of Iames, and Iudas Iscariot, who was also the traitor). 17 Then he went down with them and stood in a plain place, with the company of his disciples and a great multitude of people from all Judea, from Jerusalem and the sea coast of Tyre and Sidon, who came to hear him and to be healed of their diseases: 18 And those who were afflicted with harmful spirits were healed. 19 And all the crowd sought to touch him, because virtue came forth from him and healed them all. 20 Then he lifted up his eyes to his disciples and said, "Blessed are you who are poor, for yours is the king- dom of God. 21 Blessed are you who hunger now, for you will be filled; blessed are you who weep now, for you will laugh. 22 Blessed are you when men hate you, when they separate you and reject you and blot out your name as evil, for the Son of Man's sake. 23 Rejoice in that day and be glad, for your reward is great in heaven, for their fathers did so with the prophets. 24 But woe to you who are rich, for you have received your consolation. 25 Woe to you who are full, for you shall hunger. Woe to you who now laugh, for you will be sad- dened and weep. 26 Woe to you when all men speak well of you, for so did their fathers with false prophets. 27 But I say to you who listen, "Watch your enemies; do good to those who hate you. 28 Bless those who curse you and pray for those who hurt you. 29 And to those who beat you on one bite, offer the other also; and to those who take away your cloak, do not forbid them to take your cloak also. 30 Give to anyone who asks you anything, and from anyone who takes away things that are yours, do not ask him again. 31 And as you want men to do to you, so do you also to them. 32 For if you love those who love you, what will you have in return? For already sinners love those who love them. 33 And if you do good to those who do good to you, what reward will you have? For already sinners do the same. 34 And if you lend to those from whom you hope to receive, what reward will you have? For when sinners lend to sinners, they receive the same. 35 Therefore, look to your enemies, do good and lend, seeking nothing, and your reward will be great, and you will be the children of the Most High, for he is kind to the needy and to the weak. 36 Be ye therefore merciful, as your Father also is merciful. 37 Judge not, and ye shall not be judged: condemn not, and ye shall not be condemned; forgive, and ye shall be forgiven. 38 Give yourselves up, and it shall be given you; a good measure, pressed down, shaken, and dripping out, shall be given you in your bosom: for by what measure you mea- sure yourselves, by the same measure shall you be measured again." 39 And he spoke to them in a parable, "Can the blind lead the blind? Will they not both fall into the pit? 40 The disciple is not above his master; but he who wants to be a perfect disciple will be like his master. 41 Why do you see the speck in your brother's eye and do not consider the speck that is in your own eye? 42 How can you say to your brother, "Brother, let me remove the louse in your eye," if you do not see the light in your own eye? Hypocrite, first cast out the light from your own eye, and then you will see, perfectly able to pluck out the speck that is in your brother's eye. 43 For it is not a good tree that bears good fruit, nor an ill tree that bears good fruit. 44 Every tree is known by its fruit, for neither from thorns do you gather figs, nor from bushes do you gather grapes. 45 A good man, from the good treasure of his heart, brings home good, and an evil man, from the evil treasure of his heart, brings home evil; for out of the abundance of the heart his mouth speaks. 46 But why do you call me Lord,

Lord, and do not do the things that I say? 47 Whoever comes to me and hears my words and puts them into practice, I will show you to whom he is like: :48 He is like a man who built a house and dug deep and laid the foundation on a pole; and when the wa- ters rose up, the flood came upon that house and failed to shake it, because it was resting on a pole. 49 But he who hears and does not do, is like a man who built a house on the earth without a foundation, against which the flood came down, and it fell continually; and the fall of that house was great.

CHAPTER 7

1 When he had finished all his speeches among the people, he entered Capernaum. 2 A certain servant of Ceturion was sick and ready to die, and his affections had been tak- en away. 3 When he heard about Iesus, he sent the elders of the village to him, begging him to come and cure his servant. 4 So they came to Iesus and instantly pleaded with him, say- ing that it was worthy that he should do this for him: 5 For, they said, he is the spokesman of our nation and has built a synagogue. 6 So Iesus went with them; but when he was now not far from the house, the Centurion sent friends to him, saying, "Lord, do not trouble yourself, for I am not worthy that you should enter under my roof: 7 Therefore I have not thought myself worthy to come to you; but say the word, and my servant shall be whole: 8 For I also am a man placed under authority, and have helpers under me; I say to one, Go, and he goes; and to another, Come, and he comes; and to my servant, Do this, and he does it." 9 And when Jesus heard these things, he mar- veled at him, and turned him around, and said to the people who followed him, "I say to you, I have not found such great faith, not in Israel." 10 And when those who had been sent turned back to the house, they found the ser- vant who was sick, whole. 11 The next day he went to a town called Nain, and many of his disciples went with him and a large crowd. 12 When he reached the gates of the city, behold, a dead man was taken away, the only son of his mother, who was a widow, and many people of the city were with her. 13 When the LORD saw her, he had compassion on her and said, "Do not weep." 14 Then he went and touched the coffin (and those who carried it stood still) and said, "Young man, I say to you, get up." 15 And he who had died arose and began to speak and handed him over to his mother. 16 Then all were afraid and glori- fied God, saying, "A great prophet has arisen among you, and God has visited his people." 17 And the news of him spread throughout Ju- dea and all the surrounding region. 18 Iohn's disciples explained all these things to him. 19 Then Iohn called to himself two certain men of his disciples and sent them to Iesus, say- ing, "Are you the one who is to come, or must we wait for another?" 20 When the men had come, they said, "Did John the Baptist send you to say, 'Are you the one who is to come or must we wait for another?' 21 At that time he healed many of their diseases, sores and weak spirits, and to many who were blind he freely gave sight. 22 Then Jesus answered and said to them, "Go your way and tell John what you have seen and heard: that the blind see, the sick go, the lepers are cleansed, the deaf hear, the dead are raised, and the poor receive the gospel. 23 And blessed is he that shall not be offended in me. 24 When John's messengers had departed, he began to speak to John's people, "What have you gone out into the wil- derness to see? A reed shaken by the wind? 25 But what did you go out to see? A man clothed in soft garments? Behold, those

who are gor- geously attired and who live with delicacy are in the courts of kings. 26 But what did you go out to see? A prophet? Yes, I tell you, and more than one prophet. 27 This is he of whom it is written, "Behold, I send my messenger before your face, who will prepare your way before you." 28 For I say to you that there is no greater prophet than John, among those begotten of women; and there is none who is the least in the kingdom of God, greater than he." 29 Then all the people who had heard and the publicans justified God by being baptized with John's baptism. 30 But the Pharisees and the doctors of the Law despised God's coun- sel against them and did not let him bap- tize them. 31 The Lord said, "To what shall I compare the men of this generation, and to what are they like? 32 They are similar to little children who sit in the marketplace and weep with one another, saying, "We have wept for you and you have not grown weary; we have wept for you and you have not wept." 33 For John the Baptist came without eating bread or drinking wine, and you say, "He has the devil." 34 The Son of Man came, eating and drinking, and you say, "Behold, a man gluttonous and a drinker of wine, a friend of publicans and sinners." 35 But wisdom is justified by all his sons. 36 And one of the Pharisees asked him to eat with him; and he went into the Phari- see's house, and sat down to eat. 37 And be- hold, a woman of the city, who was a sinner, when she heard that Jesus was at table in the Pharisees' house, brought a box of wine. 38 And she stood at his feet behind him weep- ing, and began to wash his feet with herbal teas, and dried them with the lashes of her head, and kissed his feet, and anointed them with oyntment. 39 Now when the Pharisee who had commanded him saw this, he spoke within himself, saying, "If this man were a prophet, he would surely have known who and what kind of woman this is who touch- es him, for she is a sinner." 40 Then Jesus an- swered and said to him, "Simon, I have some- thing to tell you." And he answered, "Master, say it." 41 There was a certain money lender who had two banks: one had five hundred pence and the other had fifty: 42 When they had nothing to pay, he condoned them both: which of them, then, tell me, will appreciate it more? 43 Simon answered, I suppose it is he to whom he gave the most money. And he said to him, "You have judged well." 44 Then he turned to the woman and said to Simon, "Do you see this woman? I entered your house, and you did not give me water for my feet; but she washed my feet with herbal teas and dried them with her lashes. 45 Thou givest me no drink, but she hath not ceased to wash my feet since I came in. 46 You have not anoint- ed my head with oil, but she has anointed my feet with oil. 47 Therefore I tell you that she has been forgiven many sins, because she has drunk much. To those who are forgiven a lit- tle, they make a little noise." 48 He said to her, "Your sins have been forgiven you." 49 Those who sat at table with him began to say among themselves, "Who is this one who forgives sins? 50 And he said to the woman, "Your faith has saved you; go in peace."

CHAPTER 8

1 Afterward he himself went throughout all the cities and towns preaching and making known the kingdom of God, and the two were with him, 2 and some women, who had been healed of sick spirits and infirmities, such as Mary, called Magdalene, out of whom came forth various discourses, 3 Ioanna, wife of Chuza, Herod's steward, Susanna, and many others who assisted him with their

substance. 4 Now when many people had gathered and had come to him from all the cities, he spoke in a parable. 5 A sower went out to sow his seed, and as he sowed, some fell by the way- side and were trodden down by his feet, and the wicked of Heauen consumed them. 6 Some fell on the stones, and when it sprout- ed, it withered, because it lacked moisture. 7 Some fell among the thorns, and the thorns sprouted with it and smothered it. 8 Some fell on good ground and sprouted and bore fruit for a hundred sheets. And while he was say- ing these things, he cried out, "He who has ears to hear, let him hear." 9 Then his disciples questioned him, asking him what the parable was. 10 And he said, "To you it is given to know the secrets of the house of God, but to others by parables, so that when they see, they may not see, and when they hear, they may not understand." 11 The parable is this, "The seed is the word of God." 12 Those who are on the other side of the road are the ones who hear; then the curse comes and takes the word out of their hearts, so that they do not wake up and are not affected. 13 But those who are on the stones are those who, when they have heard, receive the word with joy; but they have no roots; for a little while they stand, but in the time of temptation they go away. 14 Those who have fallen among the thorns are those who have heard and who, after their departure, are choked with cares, riches, and voluptuous pleasures and do not produce fruit. 15 But those who have fallen into good soil are those who with an honest and good heart hear the word, keep it and produce fruit with patience. 16 No one, when he has lighted a candle, shall put it under a jar, nor shall he place it under his bed, but he shall place it on a candlestick, that those who come in may see the light. 17 For there is nothing secret that is not made known, nor any hidden thing that is not known and comes to light. 18 Take heed therefore how you hear, for he who has, will be given to him; and he who does not have, what he seems to have will be taken away from him. 19 Then came to him his mother and his brothers, and they could not come to him for prey. 20 And some said to him, "Your mother and your brothers are out here, and they want to see you." 21 But he answered and said to them, "My mother and my brothers are those who hear the word of God and put it into practice." 22 One certain day he went up in a ship with his disciples and said to them, "Go to the other side of the lake." And they de- parted. 23 As they were saying, he fell asleep, and a windstorm came upon the lake, and they were filled with water and were in de- spair. 24 Then they went to him and woke him up, saying, "Master, master, we perish." And he arose and rebuked the wind and the noise of the water; and they ceased, and it subsid- ed. 25 Then he said to them, "Where is your destiny?" And they feared and asked one an- other, "Who is this who commands the winds and the waters and they obey him! 26 So they sailed to the region of the Gadarenes, which is opposite Galilee. 27 And as he was about to land, there came to him a certain man out of the city, who had been in the wilderness for a long time, and had not put on raiment, nor dwelt in houses, but in tombs. 28 And when he saw Iesus, he cried out and fell down be- fore him, and with a loud voice said, "What shall I do with you, Iesus, the Son of God the Most High? Please do not torment me." 29 For he commanded the evil spirit to come out of the man (for many times he had caught him; therefore he had been bound with chains and kept in fetters; but he broke the chains and was carried from death into the wilder- ness). 30 Then Iesus questioned him, saying, "What is your name?" And he answered, "Le- gion," for many scourges had crept into him. 31 And they begged him not to let them out into the depths. 32 There was near there a

hostelry of many swine feeding on a hill; and the devils begged him to let them in them. And he granted them. 33 Then the keepers went out of the man and entered the swine; and the keepers were dragged violently from a steep place to the lake and were choked. 34 When the hearers saw what had been done, they fled; and when they had departed, they told it in the city and in the country. 35 Then they went out to see what had been done, and when they had come before Iesus, they found the man, from whom the precepts had been taken away, sitting at the feet of Iesus, clothed and with his mind right; and they were afraid. 36 Those who saw him also told by what means the one who was possessed with the disease had been healed. 37 Then all the crowd in the county of the Gadarenes begged him to depart from them, for they were seized with great fear; and he went into the ship and re- turned. 38 Then the man from whom the dis- ciples had departed begged him to stay with him, but Jesus sent him away, saying, 39 Go back to your house and tell of the great things God has done to you." So he went on his way and preached throughout the city the great things that Iesus had done to him. 40 When Jesus was here again, the people welcomed him, for they were all waiting for him. 41 And behold, there came a man named Iairus, lead- er of the synagogue, who prostrated himself at Jesus' feet and begged him to come into his house. 42 For he had only a daughter about two years old, who was lying dying (and as he went away, people were crowding around him). 43 And a woman who had a hemorrhage of two years, who had spent all her posses- sions on physicians and could not be healed by anyone: 44 And when she was behind him, she touched the hem of his garment, and im- mediately her bleeding ceased. 45 Then Jesus said, "Who is it that touched me?" When they all denied it, Peter and those with him said, "Master, the crowd is pushing and trampling you, and you say, 'Who touched me?'" 46 And Jesus said, "Someone has touched me, for I feel that virtue has gone out from me." 47 And when the woman saw that she had not been hidden, she drew near trembling, fell down before him, and told him before all the people for what reason she had touched him and how she had been healed immediately. 48 He said to her, "Daughter, take comfort, your faith has saved you; go in peace.") 49 While he was still speaking, there came one from the house of the synagogue leader who said to him, "Your daughter is dead; do not make the Master ill." 50 When Jesus heard this, he answered him, saying, "Do not be afraid; be careful, and she will be healed." 51 When he entered the house, he allowed no one to go in with him except Peter, Iames and Iohn, and the mother's father and mother. 52 They all wept and grieved for her, but he said, "Do not weep, for she is not dead but asleep." 53 They mocked him, knowing that she was dead. 54 Then he drove them all away, took her by the hand, and cried, "Maide, get up." 55 And her spirit awoke, and she arose at once; and he commanded to feed her. 56 The parents were astonished, but he commanded them not to tell anyone what had been done.

CHAPTER 9

1 Then he called together his two disciples and gave them power and authority over all diseases and the cure of diseases. 2 He sent them out to preach the kingdom of God and to cure diseases. 3 And he said to them, "Take nothing for your journey, neither banknotes, nor paper money, nor bread, nor silk, nor have two chests each. 4 And whatever houses you enter, stay there and then depart. 5 And as many

as will not receive you, when you go out of that city, shake the dust from your feet as a testimony against them." 6 Then they went out and went through all the cities preaching the gospel and healing everywhere. 7 Now Herod, the tetrarch, learned of all that had been done by him; and he was dismayed, because some said that John had risen from the dead: 8 And by some that Elijah had ap- peared, and by others that one of the ancient prophets had risen. 9 Then Herod said, "I have had John beheaded; who then is this man of whom I hear?" and he desired to see him. 10 When the apostles returned, they told him of the great things they had done. Then he took them with him and went away to a lonely place near the town called Bethsaida. 11 And the people followed him; and he received them, and spoke to them about the kingdom of God, and healed those who needed heal- ing. 12 And when the day began to fade, the two young men came and said to him, "Send the people away, that they may go to the sur- rounding towns and villages, lodge and take food, for we are here in a deserted place." 13 But he said to them, "Take them to eat." And they answered, "We have no more than five loaves and two fish, unless we go and buy food for all these people." 14 For they were about five thousand men. Then he said to his disciples, "Let them sit in company for fifty."15 They did so and made everyone sit down. 16 Then he took the five loaves and the two fish, looked up, blessed them, broke them, and gave them to the disciples to put before the people. 17 So they all ate and were filled; and out of what was left to them were taken two baskets full of spoiled food. 18 While he was praying alone, his disciples were with him; and he asked them, "Who do people say that I am? 19 They answered, "John the Baptist"; others said, "Elijah"; still others, "One of the ancient prophets is risen." 20 And he said to them, "But who do you say that I am?" Peter answered, "That Christ of God." 21 And he ad- monished them and commanded them not to tell anyone, 22 saying, "The Son of Man must suffer many things and be rebuked by the el- ders and the priests and the scribes, and be killed, and on the third day rise again." 23 And he said to them all, "If anyone wants to come after me, let him deny himself and take up his cross daily and follow me. 24 For whoever wishes to save his life will lose it; and who- ever loses his life for my sake will save it. 25 For what does it profit a man, if he overcomes the whole world and destroys himself or loses himself? 26 For whoever will be ashamed of me, and my words, of him will the Son of Man be ashamed, when he comes in his glory, in the glory of the Father and of the holy angels. 27 And I tell you with certainty that there are some standing here who will not taste death until they have seen the kingdom of God." 28 About a day after these words, he took Peter, John and James and went to a mountain to pray. 29 As he prayed, the features of his face changed, and his robe became white and glis- tening. 30 And behold, two men were talking with him, who were Moses and Elijah: 31 Who appeared in glory, and told of his departure, which he would accomplish in Jerusalem. 32 But Peter and those who were with him were exhausted with sleep, and when they awoke, they saw his glory and the two men who were with him. 33 As they walked away from him, Peter said to Jesus, "Master, it is good that you are here; let us therefore make three tabernacles, one for you, one for Mo- ses and one for Elijah." 34 While he was thus speaking, a cloud came and darkened them, and they feared to enter the cloud. 35 And out of the cloud came a voice saying, "This is my beautiful Son; listen to him." 36 And when the journey was finished, Jesus was found alone; and they shrank from it, and told no one in those days anything of what they had seen. 37 The next day, as they were coming down from the mountain, many people came to him. 38 And behold, a man of the company cried out, saying, "Master, please look upon my son, for he is all that I have." 39 And behold, a spirit seized him, and suddenly made him cry out, and stunned him, and went away from him with difficulty, when he had struck him. 40 Now I begged your disciples to cast him out, but they could not." 41 Then Iesus answered and said, "O faithless and crooked genera- tion, how long will I be with you and let you be? Bring your son here." 42 While he was still coming, the devil ripped him open and tared him; then Jesus rebuked the vncleane spirit, healed the child and delivered him to his fa- ther. 43 And they all marveled at the power of God; and while they all marveled at all the things Jesus did, he said to his disciples, 44 Follow these words carefully, for it will come to pass that the Son of Man will be delivered into the hands of men." 45 But they did not understand that word, for it was hidden from them, so that they could not perceive it; and they feared to ask him about it. 46 Then a dis- pute arose among them as to which of them should be the greatest. 47 And when Iesus had understood the thoughts of their hearts, he took a little child and put it beside him, 48 and said to them, "Whoever receives this little child in my Name, receives me; and whoever receives me, receives him who sent me; for he who is the least among you all shall be great." 49 Then Iohn answered and said, "Master, we saw one driving out disease in your Name, and we forbade him, because he does not follow you closely." 50 Then Jesus said to him, "Do not forbid him, for he who is not against is with." 51 When the days were fulfilled in which he was to be received, he set his mind to go to Jerusalem, 52 and sent messengers ahead of him; and they went into a village of Samaritans to prepare lodging for him. 53 But they would not receive him, for his behavior was as if he wanted to go to Jerusalem. 54 And when his disciples, Iames and Iohn, heard of this, they said, "Lord, do you want us to bring down fire from above and consume them, as Elijah did?" 55 But Jesus turned and rebuked them and said, "You do not know what spir- it you are of." 56 For the Son of Man did not come to destroy the lie of men, but to save them." Then they went to another city. 57 And it came to pass, as they went on their way, that a certain man said to him, "I will follow you, Lord, wherever you go." 58 And Jesus said to him, "The foxes have dens and the birds of the air nests, but the Son of Man has nowhere to lay his head." 59 But he said to another, "Fol- low me." And that one said, "Lord, let me go first to bury my father." 60 Jesus said to him, "Let the dead bury their dead, but you go and preach the kingdom of God." 61 Then another said, "I will follow you, Lord, but first let me go and greet those who are in my house." 62 And Jesus said to him, "No one who puts his hand to the plow and looks back is fit for the kingdom of God.

CHAPTER 10

1 After these things, the LORD also appoint- ed other seuentsand sent them two by two before him to every city and place, where he himself would come. 2 And he said to them, "The harvest is great, but the laborers are few; therefore pray the Lord of the harvest to send more laborers into his harvest. 3 Go your way; behold, I am sending you as lambs in the midst of wolves. 4 Carry no bags, nor cas- kets, nor shoes, and greet no one on the way. 5 And whatever house you enter, say first, "Peace to this house."

6 If the son of peace is there, your peace shall rest upon him; if he is not there, peace shall come upon you. 7 And in that house abide still, eating and drinking the things that shall be offered you, for the workman is worthy of his wages. Do not go from house to house. 8 But in whatever city you enter, if they receive you, eat the things that will be offered to you, 9 And heal the sick who are there, saying to them, "The kingdom of God has come to you." 10 But in whatever city you enter, if they will not receive you, go out into the streets of the same and say, 11 The same dust that settles on your city, we wipe it out against you; but know that the kingdom of God has come to you. 12 For I tell you that in that day it will be easier for those of Sodom than for that city. 13 Woe to you, Chorazin, woe to you, Beth-Saida, for if the miracles were done to Tyre and Sidon that were done to you, they would have long ago repented, sitting in sackcloth and ashes. 14 Therefore it will be easier for Tyre and Sidon at the judg- ment than for you. 15 And you, Capernaum, who were exalted in heaven, will be thrust into hell. 16 He who hears you, hears me; and he who despises you, despises me; and he who despises me, despises him who sent me. 17 And the seuenties turned with joy, saying, Lord, the lands are subdued through your name. 18 And he said to them, "I saw Satan, like lightning, falling from above. 19 Behold, I give you power to deal with serpents and scorpions and to defeat all the power of the enemy, and nothing will harm you. 20 In this do not believe that the spirits are subject to you, but rather believe that your names are written in heaven. 21 In that same hour, Jesus reemerged in spirit and said, "I confess to you, Father, Lord of heaven and earth, that you have hidden these things from the wise and the intelligent and revealed them to babes; and so, Father, because it pleased you. 22 Ev- erything has been given to me by my Father; and no one knows who the Son is, except the Father; and who the Father is, the Son says, and he to whom the Son wishes to deliver him. 23 Then he turned to his disciples and said in secret, "Blessed are the eyes that see what you see. 24 For I tell you that many prophets and kings have desired to see the things that you see and have not seen them, and to hear the things that you hear and have not heard them. 25 Then a certain lawyer stopped and tempted him, saying, "Master, what must I do to inherit eternal life? 26 And he said to him, "What is written in the Law? How do you read?" 27 He answered, "You must love your Lord God with all your heart, with all your soul, with all your strength and with all your thoughts, and your neighbor as yourself." 28 Then he said to him, "You have answered well; do this and you will die." 29 But he, wanting to justify himself, said to Iesus, "Who then is my neighbor?" 30 Jesus answered, "A certain man came down from Jerusalem to Jericho and fell among them; they robbed him of his clothes, wounded him, and went away, leaving him half dead." 31 Now it came to pass that a cer- tain priest went down that same road, and having seen him, he passed by on the other side. 32 And a Leuite also, having come near the place, went and looked at him and passed by on the other side. 33 Then a certain Samar- itan, as he was walking, came up to him, and seeing him, he had compassion on him, 34 and went to him, and bound up his wounds, and gave him oil and wine, and put him on his beast, and brought him into a cell, where he made a cure for him. 35 The next morning when he departed, he took two pennies and gave them to the innkeeper, saying, "Take care of him, and if you spend more, when I return, I will reward you." 36 Which of these three do you think was close to the one who had fall- en among the theologians? 37 He answered, "The one who showed him mercy." Then Jesus said to him, "Go and do the same." 38 As they were going, he entered a certain town, and a woman named Martha received him into her house. 39 She had a sister named Mary, who had also sat at Jesus' feet and listened to his preaching. 40 But Martha, who was busy with many matters, approached him and said, "Master, do you not care that my sister has left me to serve alone? Therefore ask her to help me." 41 Jesus answered and said to her, "Mar- tha, Martha, you worry and fret about many things: 42 but one thing is necessary: Mary has chosen the good part, which shall not be taken away from her.

CHAPTER 11

1 And so it was that while he was praying in a certain place, when he ceased, one of his dis- ciples said to him, "Lord, teach us to pray, as John also taught his disciples." 2 And he said to them, "When you pray, say, Our Father, which art in heaven, praised be thy name: thy kingdom come: thy will be done, on earth as it is in heaven: 3 Our daily bread be given for the day: 4 And forgive us our sins, that we also may forgive every man that is stained with sin: and let us not go into temptation, but deliver us from error. 5 Moreover he said to them, "Which of you has a friend and goes to him at midnight and says, Friend, lend me three pennies? 6 For a friend of mine has come astray from me, and I have nothing to put before him: 7 And he that is within should answer and say, Do not trouble me; the door is now shut, and my children are with me in bed: I cannot get up and give it to you. 8 And I say unto you, that even if he would not get up and give them to him, because he is his friend, yet, doubtless, because of his importity, he would get up and give him as many as he needs. 9 And I say unto you, Ask, and it shall be given you; look, and ye shall find; knock, and it shall be opened unto you. 10 For who- ever asks, receives; and whoever seeks, finds; and to him who knocks, it will be opened. 11 If a son asks one of you who is a father for bread, will he give him a stone? Or if he asks for a fish, will you give him a snake for a fish? 12 Or if he asks for a fish, will you give him a scorpi- on? 13 If therefore you who are good can give good gifts to your children, how much more will your heavenly Father give the Holy Spirit to those who desire Him? 14 Then he cast out a demon that was domme; and when the de- mon was gone out, the domme spoke, and the people marveled. 15 But some of them said, "He cast out diseases by means of Beelzebub, the chief of diseases." 16 Others tempted him, seeking in him a sign from God. 17 But he, knowing their thoughts, said to them, "Ev- ery kingdom that has set itself against itself will be desolate, and a house that has set it- self against a house will fall." 18 If therefore Satan also has been set against himself, how will his kingdom stand, because you say that I cast out failures through Beelzebub? 19 If I, through Beelzebub, cast out sins, by whom do your children cast them out? Therefore they shall be your judges. 20 But if I, through the finger of God, drive out disorders, then the kingdom of God has come to you. 21 When a strong and armed man guards his palace, the things he owns are at peace. 22 But when a stronger man than he swoops down on him and defeats him, he takes away all his armor in which he trusted and steals his spoils. 23 Whoever is not with me is against me; and whoever does not gather with me scatters. 24 And when the spirit of vncleane is gone out of a man, he walketh in different places, seek- ing rest; and when he findeth none, he saith, I will return to my house whence I went out. 25 And when he comes, he finds it swept

and tidied up. 26 Then he goes and takes with him two other spirits worse than himself; they enter in and dwell there; so the last state of that man is worse than the first. 27 While he was saying these things, a certain woman of the company lifted up her head and said to him, "Blessed is the woman who gave birth to you and the gruel you sucked." 28 But he said, "Yea, indeed, blessed are those who hear the word of God and keep it." 29 And when the people were gathered together, he began to say, "This is an evil generation; they see a sign, and no sign will be given them, except the sign of Ionas the prophet." 30 For as Ionas was a sign to the Nineites, so will the Son of Man be a sign to this generation. 31 The queen of the South will stand in judgment with the men of this generation and condemn them, because she has come from the farthest parts of the earth to hear the wisdom of Solomon, and behold, one greater than Solomon has come. 32 The men of Niniue shall stand in judgment with this generation and condemn it, because they repented at the preaching of Ionas; and behold, another greater than Ion- as is here. 33 No one, when he has lighted a candle, shall put it in a reserved place, nor under a shell, but on a candlestick, that those who come in may see the light. 34 The light of the body is the eye; therefore, when your eye is clear, your whole body is clear; but if your eye is dim, your body is dark. 35 See therefore that the light that is in you is not darkened. 36 If therefore your whole body be clear, without any dark part, then all will be clear, as when a candle lights you with splendor. 37 While he was speaking, a certain Pharisee begged him to dine with him; he went in and sat down to table. 38 When the Pharisee saw him, he marveled that he had not washed before he dined. 39 The LORD said to him, "Indeed, you Pharisees make the outside of the cup and dish clean, but the inside is full of din and wickedness. 40 You fools, is it not true that he who has done what is outside has also done what is inside? 41 Therefore, give your- selves peace of what you have, and behold, all things will be clear to you. 42 But woe to you, Pharisees, because you tithe the blueberry and the reed, and all the herbs, and pass over the judgment and praise of God; these things you should do, and not leave the other vn- done. 43 Woe to you, Pharisees, because you hoard the high places in the synagogues and the salutations in the marketplaces. 44 Woe to you, Scribes and Pharisees, hypocrites, for you are like the dead who do not appear and the men who walk outside them do not notice." 45 Then one of the Lawyers answered and said to him, "Master, with these words you question even yourself." 46 And he said, "Let it be for you also, you lawyers, because you load men with burdensome burdens to bear and do not touch the burdens with a finger. 47 Woe to you, because you build the sepulchres of the Prophets, and your fathers killed them. 48 Verily you witness and permit the deeds of your fathers, for they killed them and you build their sepulchres." 49 Therefore the wisdom of God has said, "I will send them prophets and apostles, and they will slaugh- ter them and persecute them, 50 so that the blood of all the Prophets, shed since the foun- dation of the world, may be required of this generation, 51 from the blood of Abel unto the blood of Zechariah, who was slain between the altar and the Temple; verily I say unto you, it shall be required of this generation. 52 Woe to you, lawyers, for you have taken away the key of knowledge; you have not entered in yourselves, and those who have entered you have forbidden." 53 While he was telling them these things, the Scribes and Pharisees began to harass and provoke him to speak of many things, 54 they waited for him and tried to catch something from his mouth so that they could accuse him.

CHAPTER 12

1 At that time an innumerable multitude of people gathered, so that they trampled one another; and he began to say to his disciples, "Beware of the law of the Pharisees, which is hypocrisy. 2 For there is nothing hidden that is not revealed, nor hidden that is not known. 3 Therefore what you have spoken in darkness will be heard in the light; and what you have spoken in darkness, in secret places, will be preached in homes. 4 And I say to you, my friends, do not be afraid of those who kill the body and then are no longer able to do it. 5 But I foretell you who you should fear: fear him who, after he has killed, has power to cast into hell; yes, I say to you, fear him. 6 Do you not buy five sparrowhawks for two pennies and forget not even one of them before God? 7 Yea, and all the heads of your heads are ap- pointed; therefore fear not: you are more pre- cious than many sparrowhawks. 8 Moreover I tell you, whoever confesses me before men, the Son of Man will also confess him before the angels of God. 9 But whoever denies me before men will be denied before the angels of God. 10 Whosoever shall utter blasphemy against the Son of man, he shall be forgiv- en; but whosoever shall blaspheme the Holy Spirit, he shall not be forgiven. 11 And when they lead you into the synagogues, before the leaders and princes, do not mind how or what you answer or what you speak. 12 For the Holy Spirit will teach you in that same hour what you are to say. 13 And one of the company said to him, "Teacher, tell my brother to lay down his inheritance with me." 14 And he answered him, "Man, who has made me a judge, O deuider, apart from you? 15 Therefore he said to them, "Take heed, and beware of twists and turns; for though a man has abundance, his life is not in his riches." 16 Then he expounded to them a parable, saying, "The land of a cer- tain rich man bore abundant fruit." 17 There- fore he thought to himself, saying, "What shall I do, because I have no land where I can lay my fruit?" 18 And he said, "I will do this: I will throw down my barns and build larger ones, and I will gather all my fruit and goods there. 19 And I will say to my soul, 'Soul, you have many goods accumulated for many years; make yourself comfortable, eat, drink, and take your diversions. 20 But God said to him, "O imp, this night they will take away your soul; and then whose will be the things you have boasted of? 21 So is he who accumu- lates riches for himself and is not rich in God." 22 And he said to his disciples, "Therefore I say to you, do not think about your life, what you will eat, nor about your body, what you will wear. 23 Life is more than food and the body more than clothing. 24 Consider the rauens, who neither sow nor reap, who have neither storehouse nor shack, yet God feeds them: how much better are you than the foules? 25 And which of you, on reflection, can increase his stature by one cubit? 26 If therefore you are not able to do the least thing, why are you concerned about the rest? 27 Consider the lil- ies how they grow: they do not toil and spin; yet I tell you that Solomon himself, in all his kingship, was not clothed like one of these. 28 If therefore God so clothes the grass that is in the field today and then is cast into the wilderness, how much more will He clothe you, O ye of little faith? 29 Therefore do not ask what you will eat or what you will drink, and do not keep yourselves in suspense. 30 For all these things the people of the world deal with, while your Father knows that you have need of these things. 31 But seek rather the kingdom of God, and all these things will be thrown upon you. 32 Fear not, little

flakes, for it is your Father's pleasure to give you the kingdom. 33 Sell what you have and give away the coins; make for yourselves purses that do not grow old, a treasure that can never fail in heaven, where neither plague comes nor your mother is corrupted. 34 For where your trea- sure is, there shall your heart be also. 35 Gird up your bonds and kindle your lights, 36 And be like men who wait for their master when he returns from the wedding, so that when he comes and knocks, they may open to him at once. 37 Blessed are the servants whom the Lord, when he comes, will find awake; ver- ily I say unto you, that he will gird himself, and seat them at table, and go out, and serve them. 38 And if he shall come in the second or third watch and find them so, blessed are those servants. 39 Now understand that if the good man of the house had known what time the enemy would come, he would have watched and not allowed his house to be dug in. 40 Therefore you also be ready, for the Son of Man will come at a time when you do not think." 41 Then Peter said to him, "Teacher, do you tell this parable only to yourself or also to everyone?" 42 The Lord said, "Who is the faithful and wise steward whom the master will make to rule his house, to give them the portion of food in due season? 43 Blessed is that servant whom his master, on his arrival, will find doing so. 44 Verily I say unto you, that he shall make him master of all that he hath. 45 But if that servant says in his heart, "My master postpones his coming, and goes about beating the servants, and eating, and drinking, and getting drunk, 46 the master of that servant will come in a day he does not think of and in an hour he does not know, and he will cut him off and give him his portion with the vnbeleu men. 47 The servant who knows the will of his master and has not pre- pared himself and has not done according to his will will be beaten with many blows. 48 But he who did not know it, yet committed things worthy of punishment, shall be beaten with few strokes; for to him who has been given much, from him shall be required much, and to him whom men commit much, more than him shall they require. 49 I have come to set fire to the earth, and what do I desire but that it be already kindled? 50 Nevertheless I must be baptized with a baptism, and how can I be kept, until it is finished? 51 Do you think that I have come to give peace on earth? I say to you no, but rather discuss. 52 For from now on there will be a dispute in a house between three against two and two against three. 53 The father shall be set against the son, and the son against the father; the mother against the daughter, and the daughter against the moth- er; the mother in lawe against the daughter in lawe, and the daughter in lawe against the mother in lawe." 54 Then he said to the people, "When you see a cloud rising from the west, immediately say, 'A storm is coming'; and so it is. 55 And when you see the south wind blow- ing, you say it will be a storm; and so it is. 56 Hypocrites, you know how to discern the face of the earth and the sky, but why do you not do so this time? 57 And why do you not judge yourselves what is right? 58 As you go with your aduersary to the ruler, while you are in the street, be careful, so that you may get away from him, otherwise he will drag you to the judge, and the judge will hand you over to the jester, and the jester will put you in pris- on. 59 I tell you that you shall not leave there until you have paid the full amount of alms.

CHAPTER 13

1 At that time there were some men pres- ent who told Him about the Galileans whose blood Pilate had mixed with their sacrifices. 2 Jesus answered and said to them, "Do you suppose that these Galileans are more sinful than all the other Galileans, because they have suffered these things? 3 I say to you, no; but unless you amend, you will all perish in the same way. 4 Or do you think that those octo- genarians, on whom the tower of Siloam fell and killed them, were sinners compared to all the men who lived in Jerusalem? 5 I say to you, no; but if you do not amend your lives, you will all perish in the same way." 6 He also told this parable, "A certain man had a fig tree planted in his vineyard; he came looking for its fruit, but found none. 7 Then he said to the tenant of his vineyard, "Behold, I have been coming for three years seeking the fruit of this fig tree, and I find none; cut it down; why does it also keep the ground barren?" 8 He answered and said to him, "Lord, let it stand again this year, until I dig around it and cut it down. 9 And if it bears fruit, good; if not, af- terward you shall cut it down." 10 On the Sab- bath day he taught in one of the synagogues. 11 And behold, there was a woman who had a spirit of infirmity for eighty years, and she was prostrate and could not rise in any way. 12 When Jesus saw her, He called her to Him- self and said to her, "Woman, you are loosed from your sickness." 13 He laid his hands on her, and immediately she recovered and glo- rified God. 14 The leader of the synagogue was indignant that Jesus was healing on the Sabbath, and he said to the people, "There are six days when men must work; on these days come and be healed, and not on the Sabbath." 15 Then the LORD answered him, "Hypocrite, on the Sabbath day does not one of you untie his ox or his horse from the stable and take it to the water? 16 And this daughter of Abra- ham, whom Satan had bound for many years, should she not be loosed from this bond on the Sabbath day? 17 When he said these things, all his helpers were ashamed; but all the people rejoiced at all the excellent things that had been done by him. 18 Then he said, "To what does the kingdom of God resemble or to what shall I compare it? 19 It is like a mustard seed, which a man took and sowed in his garden, and it grew and became a great tree, and the birds of the air made nests in its branches. 20 And again he said, "To what can I compare the kingdom of God? 21 It is like the ryegrass which a woman took and hid in three bundles of flour, until it was all smoothed. 22 And he went through all the cities and towns, teaching and traveling to Jerusalem. 23 Then one said to him, "Lord, are there few who are to be saved?" And he answered them, 24 Try to enter through the narrow gate, for many, I tell you, will try to enter and will not succeed." 25 When the master of the house has risen and closed the door, and you will begin to stand outside and knock at the door, saying, "Lord, Lord, open to us," and he will answer, "I do not know where you are." 26 Then you will begin to say, "We have eaten and drunk in your pres- ence, and you have taught in our streets." 27 But he will say, "I say to you, I do not know where you are; depart from me, all you work- ers of iniquity." 28 There will be weeping and gnashing of teeth when you see Abraham, Isaac, Jacob, and all the prophets in the king- dom of God, and your own people will be driv- en away with sticks. 29 Then shall come many from the East, and from the West, and from the North, and from the South, and shall sit at table in the kingdom of God. 30 And be- hold, there are the last who will be first, and there are the first who will be last. 31 In that same day there came some Pharisees and said to him, "Go away, go away, for Herod will kill you." 32 Then he said to them, "Go and say to that fox, 'Behold, I cast out the tithes, and I will heal again by day and by night, and on the third day I shall be perfected. 33 I must walk until today,

until tomorrow and the next day, for it is not possible for a prophet to perish from Jerusalem. 34 O Jerusalem, Jerusalem, you who kill the Prophets and stone those who are sent to you, how often I wanted to gather your children together, as the hen gathers her brood under her wings, and you would not! 35 Behold, your house is left desolate; and tru- ly I say to you, you shall not see me until the time comes when you say, "Blessed is he who comes in the Name of the Lord."

CHAPTER 14

1 And it came to pass that as he went into the house of one of the leaders of the Pharisees on the Sabbath day to eat bread, they looked at him. 2 And behold, there stood before him a certain man who had drops. 3 Then Jesus an- swered and spoke to the jurists and Pharisees, saying, "Is it lawful to eat on the Sabbath?" 4 They kept silent. Then he took him, healed him, and let him go, 5 Then he answered them, saying, "Which one of you has a plank or an ox that has fallen into a pit and does not immediately take it out on the Sabbath day?" 6 And they could not answer him again to these things. 7 He also told a parable to the ghestes, when he marked the way in which they chose the principal rooms, and said to them 8 When you are invited by someone to a wedding, do not put yourself in the highest place, lest a man more honorable than you be invited by him." 9 and he who invited both him and you come and say, "Give this man a roof," and you begin to be ashamed to take the lowest roof. 10 But when you are commanded, go and sit in the lowest room, so that he who command- ed you may come and say to you, "Friend, sit here"; then you will have worship in the presence of those who sit at table with you. 11 For he who exalts himself will be brought low, and he who humbles himself will be ex- alted." 12 Then he also said to the one who had commanded him, "When you prepare a supper or a meal, do not call your friends, nor your brothers, nor your relatives, nor your rich neighbors, lest they also offer you another time and a reward be made to you. 13 But when you make a feast, call the poor, the maimed, the lame and the blind, 14 And thou shalt be blessed, for they cannot reward thee; for thou shalt be rewarded at the resurrection of the righteous.15 Now when one of those who sat at the table heard these things, he said to him, "Blessed is he who eats bread in the kingdom of God." 16 Then he said to him, "A certain man made a great supper and in- vited many, 17 and at suppertime he sent his servant to say to those who had been invited, 'Come, for everything is ready.' 18 But they all together began to make excuses: the first said to him, "I have bought an automobile, and I must go and see it: please let me excuse my- self." 19 Another said, "I have bought five yoke of oxen and must go and try them: Please ex-

cuse me." 20 Another said, "I have married a wife, so I cannot come." 21 Then that servant returned and told these things to his master. Then the good man of the house became an- gry and said to his servant, "Go out at once into the streets and alleys of the city and bring in the poor, the maimed, the halting and the blind." 22 The servant said, "Lord, it has been done as you commanded, yet there is still bread." 23 Then the master said to the ser- vant, "Go out through the streets and hedg- es and force them in, so that my house may be filled. 24 For I tell you that none of those who were invited will taste my supper." 25 Now as a great crowd came to him, he turned and said to them, 26 If anyone comes to me and does not hate his father, his mother, his wife, his children, his brothers and sisters, and even his own life, he cannot be my disci- ple. 27 And whoever does not bear his cross and come after me, cannot be my disciple. 28 For which of you, wanting to build a tower, does not sit down first and count the cost, to know whether he has enough to complete it? 29 lest, having laid the foundation and not be- ing able to complete it, all who see it should begin to mock him, 30 saying, "This man be- gan to build and was unable to finish"? 31 Or what king, going to make war against another king, does not first sit down and take counsel whether he is able, with ten thousand men, to face him who comes against him with twenty thousand? 32 Or, while he is still far away, he sends an embassy and desires peace. 33 Like- wise, whoever among you does not give up all that he has cannot be my disciple. 34 Salt is good; but if salt has lost its savor, with what shall it be salted? 35 It is not good for the earth nor for the dunghill, but men throw it away. He who has ears to hear, let him hear.

CHAPTER 15

1 Then all publicans and sinners resorted to him to hear him. 2 Therefore the Pharisees and Scribes murmured, saying, "He receives sinners and eats with them." 3 Then he spoke to them about this parable, saying, 4 Which of you, having a hundred sheep, if he loses one, does not leave ninety-nine in the wilder- ness and go after the lost one until he finds it? 5 And when he has found it, he puts it on his shoulders with joy. 6 And when he returns home, he calls together his friends and neigh- bors, saying to them, "Receive me, for I have found my sheep that was lost." 7 I tell you that the same joy will be in heaven over one sin- ner who gathers, more than over ninety-nine righteous men, who need no change of life. 8 And what woman who has ten groatas, if she loses one, does not light a candle, sweep her house, and diligently seek to find it?9 And when she has found it, she calls her friends and her neighbors, saying, "Come with me, for I have found the croup that I had lost." 10 In the same way I tell you that there is joy in the presence of the angels of God over a sinner who is gathered together. 11 He said again, "A certain man had two sons. 12 The first of the two said to their father, 'Father, give me my due share of goods.' So he gave them his share of goods. 13 So, not many days later, when the younger son had gathered everyone together, he set out on his journey to a distant county, and there he squandered his possessions with unbridled amusement. 14 When he had spent everything, a great famine occurred through- out the whole country, and he began to be in need. 15 So he went and asked a citizen of that country for help, and he sent him to his farm to feed swine. 16 He would have liked to fill his belly with the husks that the swine ate, but no one would give them to him. 17 Then he returned to himself and said, "How many servants of my fathers have bread enough and I am starving? 18 I will get up and go to my father and say to him, 'Father, I have sinned against him and against you, 19 and I am no longer worthy to be called your son; make me as one of your hired servants." 20 Then he arose and came to his father; and when he was yet far off, his father saw him, and had compassion on him, and ran and fell on his neck and kissed him. 21 And the son said to him, "Father, I have sinned against him and against you, and I am no longer worthy to be called your son." 22 Then the father said to his servants, "Bring the best robe and put it on, and put a ring on his hand and shoes on his feet, 23 bring the fatted calf, kill it and make it eat, and be happy: 24 For this my son was

dead and has returned; he was lost, but has been found." And they began to be merry. 25 Now the elder brother was in the field, and when he came and approached the house, he heard melodies and pangs, 26 he called one of his servants and asked him what those things meant. 27 He said to him, "Your brother has come, and your father has killed his son, for he received him safe and sound." 28 Then he was angry and would not go in; therefore his father went out and begged him. 29 But he answered his father, "Loe, all these years I have done you service and never restrained your efforts, yet you never gave me a kid so that I could feast with my friends. 30 But when this son of yours came, who spoiled your good with prostitutes, you killed the fatted calf because of him." 31 He said to him, "Son, you are still with me and all that I have is yours. It was right that we should celebrate and rejoice, for this brother of yours was dead and has returned; he was lost, but has been found."

CHAPTER 16

1 And he also said to his disciples, "There was a certain rich man, who had a steward, and he was accused by him of wasting his goods." 2 He called him and said, "How is it that I hear this from you? Give me an account of your stewardship, for never again will you be a steward." 3 Then the steward said within him- self, "What shall I do, for my master has taken away my stewardship. I cannot dig, and I am ashamed to beg. 4 I know what I shall do, so that when I am taken out of the administra- tion, they may receive me into their houses." 5 Then he called to himself each of his mas- ters and said to the first, "How much do you desire from my master?" 6 And he answered, "A hectoliter of oil." And he said to him, "Take your writing and sit down at once and write fifty." 7 Then he said to another, "How much do you want?" And he answered, "A hundred measures of grain." Then he said to him, "Take your writing and write four scores." 8 The LORD praised the vniust stewarde, for he had acted wisely. Therefore the sons of this world are in their generation wiser than the sons of light. 9 And I say to you, "Make friends for yourselves out of the riches of iniquity, that when you need them they may receive you into everlasting dwellings." 10 He that is faithful in the little, is faithful also in the much; and he that is vnient in the little, is vnient also in the much. 11 If therefore you have not been faithful in evil riches, who will give you confidence in true treasure? 12 And if you have not been faithful in the goods of oth- ers, who will give you what is yours? 13 No ser- vant can serve two masters, for either he will hate the one and love the other, or he will trust in the one and despise the other. You cannot serve God and riches. 14 All these things the Pharisees also heard, and they were in a pan- ic and mocked him. 15 Then he said to them, "You are those who justify yourselves before men, but God knows your hearts, for what is esteemed by men is abominable in the sight of God." 16 Lawe and the Prophets lasted un- til John; since then the kingdom of God is preached and every man enters it. 17 Now it is easier for wrath and land to pass away than for a title of the Law to fall. 18 Whoever aban- dons his wife and marries another, commits adultery; and whoever marries her who has been estranged from her husband, commits adultery. 19 There was a certain rich man, clothed in purple and fine linen, who behaved himself well and with gentleness every day. 20 There was also a certain beggar, named Lazarus, who lay at his door full of sores, 21 And he longed to be refreshed with the grains that fell from the rich man's table; and dogs came and licked his sores. 22 And so it was that the beggar died and was carried by angels into Abraham's bosom. The rich man also died and was buried. 23 Being in hell in torment, he looked up and saw Abraham far away and Lazarus in his womb. 24 Then he cried out and said, "Father Abraham, have mercy on me and send Lazarus so that he may dip the tip of his finger in the water and be my tongue, for I am tormented in this flame." 25 But Abraham said, "Son, remember that in your life you re-

ceived your pleasures, and Lazarus also suf- fers; now therefore he is comforted, while you are tormented." 26 Besides all this, between you and Vs. there is a great ravine, so that those who want to go from here to you can- not; nor can they come from there to Vs. 27 Then he said, "Please, father, send him to my fathers' house." 28 (for I have five brothers) that I may testify to them, lest they also en- ter this place of torment. 29 Abraham said to him, "They have Moses and the Prophets; let them hear them." 30 He answered, "No, father Abraham, but if one came to them from the dead, they would be changed." 31 Then he said to him, "If they do not listen to Moses and the Prophets, they will not be persuaded, even if one were to rise again from the dead."

CHAPTER 17

1 Then he said to his disciples, "They cannot be prevented from being offended, but woe to him from whom they come. 2 It is better for him that a great millstone be hung around his neck and that he be cast into the sea than that he offend one of these little ones. 3 Take heed to yourselves; if your brother commits an offense against you, rebuke him; and if he repents, forgive him. 4 Even if he sins against you ten times in one day and ten times in one day turns again to you, saying, "He repents of me," you will forgive him. 5 The apostles said to the Lord, "Increase our faith." 6 The LORD answered, "If you had faith as much as a mustard seed and said to this mulberry tree, 'Push beyond the roots and plant your- self in the sea,' it would obey you. 7 Which of you, moreover, having a servant who plows or feeds cattle, would say to him from time to time, when he comes from the field, "Go and sit down at the table"? 8 And would he not rather say to him, "Get you a garment in which I may dine, and make yourself com- fortable, and serve me until I have eaten and drunk, and then you eat and drink?" 9 Does he mock that servant because he did what he was commanded? I do not. 10 So you also, when you have done all the things you have been commanded, will say, "We are good servants; we have done what was our duty to do." 11 So as he went to Jerusalem, he passed through the middle of Samaria and Galilee. 12 When he entered a certain city, ten lep- rous men who were standing far away came to meet him. 13 They raised their voices and said, "Jesus, Master, have mercy on them." 14 And when he saw them, he said to them, "Go, present yourselves to the priests." And it came to pass that as they went, they were cloned. 15 And one of them, seeing that he had been healed, turned back and with a ringing voice praised God, 16 and fell with his face at his feet and thanked him; he was a Samaritan. 17 Then Jesus answered and said, "Are there not ten clents? But where are the nine? 18 Not one can be found who has returned to give praise to God, as this stranger says." 19 And he said to him, "Get up, go your way; your faith has saved you." 20 When he was asked by the Pharisees when

the kingdom of God would come, he answered them, "The kingdom of God does not come with observation. 21 Nor will men say, 'Here it is or there it is,' for be- hold, the kingdom of God is within you." 22 And he said to the disciples, "There will come days when you will want to see one of the days of the Son of Man, and you will not see him. 23 Then they will say to you, 'Look here or look there'; but do not go there and follow them. 24 For as the lightning that shines on one side under the sky shines on the other side under the sky, so will the Son of Man be in his day. 25 But first he will have to suffer many things and be rebuked by this generation. 26 As it was in the days of Noah, so shall it be in the days of the Son of Man. 27 They ate, drank, married wives and gave themselves in mar- riage until the day that Noah entered the Ark; then the flood came and destroyed them all. 28 As also in the days of Lot: they ate, they drank, they bought, they sold, they planted, they built. 29 But on the day Lot came out of Sodom, fire and brimstone rained down from above and destroyed them all. 30 It will be like these examples on the day when the Son of Man will be delivered. 31 On that day, he who is in the house and his things in the house, let him not go down to get them; and he who is in the field, let him not go back to what he left behind. 32 Remember your wife. 33 Whoso- ever will save his soul shall lose it; and who- soever shall lose it shall have life. 34 I tell you that in that night there shall be two in one bed: the one shall be received, and the other shall be left. 35 Two women shall mill togeth- er: the one shall be taken, and the other left. 36 Two are in the field: one shall be taken and the other left. 37 They answered and said to him, "Where, Lord?" And he answered them, "Where the body is, there shall the eagles also be gathered."

CHAPTER 18

1 And he also told them about a parable, con- cerning the fact that they should always pray and not toil, 2 saying, "There was a judge in a certain city, who did not fear God and did not care for men. 3 There was a widow in that city who came to him and said, 'Do me jus- tice against my adversary." 4 He would not, but afterward he said, "Although I do not fear God and do not trust in man, :5 nevertheless, since this widow troubles me, I will do her good, lest at the last she come and weary me." 6 The LORD said, "Listen to what the righ- teous judge says." 7 Now will not God hear his elect, who cry out to him day and night, even though he suffers long for them? 8 I tell you that he will hear them quickly; but when the Son of Man comes, will he find faith on earth? 9 He also spoke this parable to certain men who trusted in themselves that they were righteous and despised others. 10 Two men entered the Temple to pray: one was a Phar- isee and the other a publican. 11 The Phari- see stopped and prayed thus with himself, "O God, I ask you not to be like other men, extortioners, vniusti, adulterers, or like this publican. 12 I fast twice a week; I tithe every- thing I own. 13 But the publican, standing afar off, would not lift up his eyes, but beat his breast, saying, "O God, be merciful to me, a sinner." 14 I tell you that this man went away to his house, more than the other; for who- ever exalts himself will be brought low, and whoever humbles himself will be exalted. 15 They also brought him children that he might touch them. And when his disciples saw it, they rebuked them. 16 But Jesus called them to himself and said, "Let the children come to me and do not forbid them, for of such is the

kingdom of God. 17 Truly I tell you, whoever does not receive the kingdom of God like a child will not enter it. 18 Then a certain ruler asked him, "Teacher, what must I do to inher- it eternal life? 19 Jesus answered him, "Why do you call me good? No one is good except God. 20 Thou knowest the commandments, Thou shalt not commit adultery: Thou shalt not kill: Thou shalt not steal; Thou shalt not bear false witness: Thou shalt honor thy father and thy mother." 21 And he said, "All these things I have observed from my youth. 22 When Iesus heard this, he said to him, "You still lack one thing. Sell all that you have and distribute it to the poor, and you will have treasure in heav- en, and come with me." 23 But when he heard these things, he felt very bad, because he was very rich. 24 And when Iesus saw him great- ly grieved, he said, "With what difficulty will those who have riches enter the kingdom of God! 25 It is easier for a camel to pass through a needle's eye than for a rich man to enter the kingdom of God." 26 Then those who heard him said, "And who then can be saved?" 27 And he answered, "The things that are im- possible to men are possible to God." 28 Then Peter said, "Behold, we have left everything and followed you." 29 And he said to them, "Truly I tell you, there is no one who has left home, parents, brothers, wife or children for the kingdom of God, 30 who will not receive much more in this world and in the world to come eternal life. 31 Then Jesus turned to the two of you and said to them, "Behold, we are going to Jerusalem, and all things written by the prophets will be fulfilled for the Son of Man. 32 For he will be handed over to the Gentiles, he will be mocked, he will be an ob- ject of scorn and spitting. 33 When they have scourged him, they will put him to death; but on the thirteenth day he will rise again. 34 But they understood nothing of these things, and this saying was hidden from them, and they did not understand the things spoken. 35 As he was approaching Jericho, a certain blind man stopped along the road to ask alms. 36 When he heard people passing by, he asked what it meant. 37 They told him that Jesus of Nazareth was passing by. 38 Then he cried out, saying, "Jesus, the Son of David, have mercy on me." 39 Those before him rebuked him that he might be at peace, but he cried out even more, "O Son of Dauid, have mercy on me." 40 Then Jesus stopped and command- ed that he should be led to him. And when he was near, he questioned him, 41 saying, "What do you want me to do to you?" And he answered, "Lord, that I may receive sight." 42 And Jesus said to him, "Receive sight; your faith has saved you." 43 Then he immediately received sight and followed him, praying to God; and all the people, when they heard this, gave praise to God.

CHAPTER 19

1 When Iesus came in and passed through Jericho, 2 there was a man named Zacchaeus, who was the chief collector of the tribute and was rich. 3 He tried to see Iesus, who must have been him, but he could not because he was short in stature. 4 So he ran ahead of him and climbed a wild fig tree so that he could see him, for he would come from there. 5 When Iesus came to the place, he looked and saw him and said to him, "Zacchaeus, come down at once, for I must stop at your house today." 6 So he came down quickly and re- ceived him with joy. 7 And when they all saw him, they murmured, saying that he had gone to lodge with a sinful man. 8 And Zacchaeus stood up and said to the Lord, "Lord, half of my goods I give to the poor; and if I have tak- en away from anyone by fraud, I will give him back four

pennies." 9 Then Jesus said to him, "Today salvation has come to this house, be- cause he too has become a son of Abraham. 10 For the Son of Man has come to see and to save what was lost. 11 While they were listen- ing to these things, he continued to speak in parables, because he was near Jerusalem and because they too thought that the kingdom of God would soon appear. 12 So he said, "A cer- tain noble man went to a distant county to re- ceive a kingdom for himself and then return. 13 He called his ten servants, handed them ten pieces of money, and said to them, 'Occupy until I come.' 14 Now his citizens hated him and sent an embassy after him, saying, "We will not allow this man to rule outside us." 15 When he was here again and received his kingdom, he ordered the servants to whom he gave his money to be called to him, to know what each had earned. 16 Then came the first, saying, "Sir, your piece is increased by ten pieces." 17 And he said to him, "Well, good servant, because you have been faithful in a little thing, take charge of ten cities." 18 And the second came, saying, "Sir, your piece is increased by five pieces." 19 And to the second he said, "Be you also the ruler of five cities." 20 Then the other came and said, "Lord, look at your piece, which I have put in a napkin: 21 For I feared thee, because thou art a righteous man; thou takest what thou hast not laid down, and reap what thou hast not sown." 22 Then he said to him, "From your own mouth I will judge you, O faithful servant. You knew that I am a righteous man, who takes what he has not laid down and reaps what he has not sown. 23 Why therefore do you not put my money in the bank, that when I come I may claim it with advantage? 24 And he said to those who stood by, "Take from him that piece, and give it to him who has ten pieces." 25 (And they said to him, "Sir, he has ten piec- es"). 26 For I say to you that to everyone who has, it will be given; and to the one who does not have, what he has will be taken away. 27 Moreover, my enemies, who do not want me to rule over them, let them bring them here and kill them before me." 28 Having spoken thus, he set out before him, going up toward Jerusalem. 29 When he had come near Beth- phage and Bethany, besides the mountain called the Mount of Olives, he sent two of his disciples, 30 saying, "Go to the city opposite, where, as soon as you have arrived, you will find a bound blanket, on which no one had ever been; untie it and bring it here. 31 And if anyone asks you why you untie it, answer him, 'Because the LORD has need of him. 32 So those who had been sent set out and found as he had told them. 33 As they were loosen- ing the covering, the owners said to them, "Why do you loosen the covering? 34 And they said, "The Lord has need of him." 35 So they led him to Jesus, threw their garments on the pall, and laid Jesus on it. 36 As he went, they spread their garments on the street. 37 And when he was now near the descent of the Mount of Olives, the whole crowd of disciples began to gather together and to pray to God with a loud voice for all the great works they had seen, 38 saying, "Blessed be the king who comes in the name of the Lord; peace in heav- en and glory in the highest places." 39 Then some of the Pharisees of the company said to him, "Teacher, rebuke your disciples." 40 But he answered and said to them, "I say to you, if these would put themselves at peace, the stones would weep." 41 When he was near, he saw the city and wept over it, 42 saying, "If you had known at least in this your day the things that belong to your peace, but now they are hidden from your eyes. 43 For the day will come when your enemies will put you in the trenches and surround you and keep you closed on every side, 44 And they shall reduce thee to a fray with the earth and with thy chil- dren that are

in thee, and shall not leave in thee stone upon stone, because thou knew- est not the time of thy visitation. 45 He also entered the Temple and began to drive out those who were selling there and those who were buying, 46 saying to them, "It is written, 'My house is the house of prayer, but you have made it a den of theologians.'" 47 And every day he taught in the Temple. And the priests and the scribes and the leaders of the people were trying to destroy him. 48 But they could not find what to do to him, for all the people would hang themselves on him when they heard him.

CHAPTER 20

1 And it came to pass in one of those days, while he was teaching the people in the Tem- ple and preaching the gospel, the priests and the scribes came to him with the elders, 2 and they spoke to him, saying, "Tell me by what authority do you do these things, or who is it that gave you this authority?" 3 He answered and said to them, "I also ask you one thing: tell me therefore." 4 Was John's baptism done by him or by men? 5 They reasoned among themselves, saying, If we shall say, by God, he will say, Why did you not baptize him? 6 But if we say, By men, all the people will stone him, because they are convinced that John was a prophet." 7 Therefore they answered that they could not tell from whence he came. 8 Then Jesus said to them, "I will not even tell you by what authority I do these things." 9 Then he began to tell the people this parable, "A cer- tain man planted a vineyard and gave it into the hands of the farmers; then he went to a foreign country for a long time. 10 When the time came, he sent a servant to the vinedress- ers so that they would give him the fruit of the vineyard; but the vinedressers beat him and sent him away with nothing. 11 Then he sent another servant, but they mistreated him and sent him away empty-handed. 12 Then he sent the third, who was wounded and cast out. 13 Then the master of the vineyard said, "What shall I do? I will send my beloved son; it may be that, when they see him, they will behave themselves." 14 But when the masters of the vineyard saw him, they reasoned among themselves, saying, "This is the heir; come, let us kill him, that the inheritance may be ours." 15 So they drove him out of the vineyard and killed him. What then will the lord of the vineyard do with them? 16 He will come and destroy these vinedressers and give his vine- yard to others. But they, hearing this, said, "God forbid." 17 He looked at them and said, "What then is the meaning of what is written, 'The stone which the builders rejected has be- come the head of the corner'?" 18 Whosoever shall fall on that stone, he shall be broken; and on whom he shall fall, he shall make him fall. 19 Then the priests and scribes laid hands on him, but they feared the people, for they saw that he had spoken this parable against them. 20 They kept an eye on him and sent spies, who were to pass themselves off as righteous men, to take him at his word and turn him over to the power and authority of the government. 21 They questioned him, saying, "Teacher, we know that you speak and teach well; you do not accept the person of men, but you teach the true way of God. 22 Is it lawful or not for the people to give tribute to Caesar? 23 But he, noticing their wiles, said to them, "Why do you tempt me? 24 Show me a pen. Whose image and writing is it? They answered, "Ce- sar." 25 Then he said to them, "Give therefore to Caesar the things that are Caesar's, and to God the things that are God's." 26 They could not repeat his words before the people, but they marveled at his answer and kept silent. 27 Then came to

him some of the Sadducees (who deny the existence of a resurrection) and questioned him,28 saying, "Teacher, Moses wrote against him, 'If a brother dies having a wife and dies childless, let the brother take his wife and generate offspring for his brother.'" 29 There were two brothers; the first took a wife and died childless. 30 The second took a wife and died childless. 31 The third took her to wife, and so the two brothers also died and left no children. 32 And last of all the woman also died. 33 Therefore, at the resurrection, whose wife will be the wife of these men? For two had taken her to wife." 34 Then Jesus an- swered them, "The sons of this world marry wives and are married. 35 But those who will be deemed worthy to enjoy that world and the resurrection from the dead do not mar- ry wives and are not married. 36 For they can no longer die, in that they are equal to the angels and are the children of God, for they are children of the resurrection. 37 And that the dead shall rise again, Moses proved it by the bush, when he said, "The LORD is the God of Abraham, the God of Isaac, and the God of Jacob." 38 For he is not the God of the dead, but of those who live, for all live in him. 39 Then some of the scribes answered and said, "Teacher, you have spoken well." 40 Then they asked him no more. 41 Then he said to them, "How can they say that Christ is the son of Dauid?" 42 Dauid himself says in the book of Psalms, "The Lord said to my Lord, Sit at my right hand, 43 until I have made your enemies your feet. 44 For Dauid called him Lord, how then is he his son? 45 Then, in the midst of all the people, he said to his disciples, 46 Beware of the scribes, who go willingly in long robes and are saluted in the marketplaces, and oc- cupy the highest places in assemblies and the most important rooms at banquets: 47 Who occupy widows' houses, and make long prayers in them: these shall receive greater damnation.

CHAPTER 21

1 And as he watched, he saw the rich men throwing their gifts into the treasury. 2 And he also saw a certain poor widow who threw two pennies into it: 3 And he said, "Truly I tell you, this poor widow has poured out more than all of them. 4 For they all threw their surplus into God's offerings, but she, for her penance, threw in all the money she had. 5 Now as some spoke of the Temple, how it was adorned with beautiful stones and consecrat- ed things, he said, 6 Are these the things you look upon? The days will come when you will not leave a stone upon a stone and throw it down." 7 Then they asked him, saying, "Mas- ter, but when will these things be? And what sign will there be when these things shall come to pass?" 8 And he said, "Take heed lest ye be deceived, for many shall come in my Name, saying, I am the Christ, and the time draws near; therefore follow them not. 9 And when ye hear of wars and sedition, fear not: for these things must first come, but the end shall not follow from one moment to another." 10 Then he said to them, "Nation shall rise up against nation, and kingdom against king- dom, 11 And there shall be great earthquakes in many places, and famine, and pestilence, and fearful things, and there shall be great signs from Heauen. 12 But before all this, they will lay their hands on you and persecute you, delivering you to the assemblies and to the prisons, and they 'will bring you before kings and rulers for my names' sake. 13 And this shall be a testimony to you. 14 Therefore put it into your hearts that you do not throw into your heads what you will have to answer. 15 For I will give you such a mouth and wis- dom that all your adversaries will not be able to speak or resist. 16 You will also be betrayed by your parents, your brothers, your relatives, and your friends, and some of you will be put to death. 17 And you will be hated by all men for My names' sake. 18 Yet not a single head of yours shall perish. 19 By your patience you shall possess your souls. 20 When you see Je- rusalem besieged by soldiers, you will under- stand that its desolation is near. 21 Then let those who are in Judea flee to the mountains, and those who are in the midst of it leave, and those who are in the county do not enter it. 22 For these are the days of vengeance, for the fulfillment of all things written. 23 But woe to them that bring forth, and to them that bring forth in those days, for there shall be great distress in this land, and wrath upon this people. 24 And they shall fall by the edge of the sword, and shall be led into captivity in all nations, and Jerusalem shall be subject to the dominion of the Gentiles, until the time of the Gentiles is fulfilled. 25 Then there will be signs in the sun, moon and stars, and on earth there will be trouble among the nations with perplexity; the sea and the waters will be troubled. 26 And the hearts of men shall be troubled with fear and examination of what shall take place in the world, for the powers of Eauen shall be shaken. 27 And then they will see the Son of Man coming in a cloud, with power and great glory. 28 When these things begin to be fulfilled, watch and lift up your heads, for your redemption draws near." 29 Then he spoke to them a parable, "Behold the fig tree and all the trees." 30 When they take flight, you, seeing them, know for yourselves that the morning is now near. 31 So you also, when you see these things happening, will know that the kingdom of God is near. 32 Tru- ly I tell you, this age will not pass away until all these things are fulfilled: 33 Heaven and earth shall pass away, but my words shall not pass away. 34 Take heed to yourselves, lest at any time your hearts be oppressed by surfing, drunkenness, and the cares of this life, and lest vnwares come upon you that day. 35 For as a snare shall come upon all who dwell on the face of all the earth. 36 Watch therefore and pray continually, that you may be count- ed worthy to escape all these things that will happen, and that you may stand before the Son of Man. 37 By day he taught in the tem- ple, and by night he went out and stood on the mountain called the Mount of Olives. 38 In the morning all the people came to him to hear him in the Temple.

CHAPTER 22

1 The feast of vnleauened bread, which is called Passer, was now near. 2 The priests and scribes were trying to kill him, because they feared the people. 3 Then Satan entered Iudas, who was called Iscariot and was of the name of the two. 4 Then he went on his way and ar- gued with the priests and captains about how to betray him. 5 They rejoiced and agreed to give him money. 6 He agreed and looked for an opportunity to betray him when the peo- ple were far away. 7 Then came the day of vn- leauened bread, when the Passer was to be sacrificed. 8 He sent Peter and John, saying, "Go and prepare the Passover, that we may eat it." 9 They said to him, "Where do you want us to prepare him?" 10 Then he said to them, "Be- hold, when you have entered the city, a man will come to meet you with a pitcher of water; follow him into the house into which he will enter, 11 and say to the good man of the house, 'The Master said to you, "Where is the lodging where I will eat my meal with my disciples?"' 12 Then he will show you a large bedroom, fur- nished and ready." 13 So they went and found as he had told them, and

they prepared the Pastime. 14 When it was time, he sat down, and the two apostles with him. 15 Then he said to them, "I have longed to eat this supper with you, before I suffered. 16 For I tell you that from now on I will eat no more of it, until it is fulfilled in the kingdom of God." 17 Then he took the cup, gave thanks, and said, "Take and distribute among yourselves, 18 for I tell you that I will not drink of the fruit of the vine until the kingdom of God has come." 19 Then he took the bread and, after giving thanks, broke it and gave it into their hands, saying, "This is my body, which was given for you; do this in remembrance of me." 20 Likewise, af- ter the supper, he took the cup, saying, "This cup is the New Testament in my blood, which was poured out for you." 21 But behold, the hand of him who betrayed me is with me at the table. 22 And verily the Son of Man goes as it was appointed; but woe to that man by whom he was betrayed." 23 Then they began to wonder which of them should do this. 24 And there arose also a dispute among them, as to which of them should seem the great- er.25 But he said to them, "The kings of the Gentiles rule over them, and those who rule over them are called rich. 26 But you shall not be so; the greatest among you shall be as the least, and the chief as the one who serves. 27 For who is greater, the one who sits at the table or the one who serves? Is it not he who sits at the table? And I am among you as the one who serves. 28 And you are those who have continued with me in my temptations. 29 Therefore I appoint you a kingdom, as my Father has done to me, 30 That you may eat and drink at my table in my kingdom, and sit on the seats, and judge the two tribes of Isra- el." 31 The Lord said, "Simon, Simon, behold, Satan has lusted after you to win you like a roe. 32 But I have prayed for you, that your faith may not fail; therefore, when you are convinced, strengthen your brothers." 33 He said to him, "Lord, I am ready to go with you to prison and to die." 34 But he answered, "I tell you, Peter, that the rooster will not croak today before you have thrice denied knowing me." 35 And he said to them, "When I sent you without bag, without paper, and with- out shoes, were you lacking anything? And they answered, "Nothing." 36 Then he said to them, "Whoever has a bag, let him take it, and also a coin; and whoever has none, let him sell his cloak and buy a sword. 37 For I say to you that what is written must also be fulfilled in me, for he was appointed with the wicked; for doubtless the things that are written about me have an end." 38 They said, "Lord, here are two swords." And he said to them, "It is suffi- cient." 39 Then he went out and set out (as he was wont to do) to the Mount of Olives; and his disciples also followed him. 40 When he had come to the place, he said to them, "Pray, lest you enter into temptation." 41 He depart- ed from them about a stone, knelt down and prayed, 42 saying, "Father, if you are willing, turn this cup away from me; not my will but yours be done." 43 And there appeared to him an angel from above, who comforted him. 44 But being in agony, he prayed more earnestly; and his sweat was like drops of blood running down to the ground. 45 Then he arose from prayer and came to his disciples and found them asleep from exhaustion. 46 He said to them, "Why are you asleep? Get up and pray, otherwise you will enter into temptation." 47 While he was still speaking, behold, a com- pany, and he whose name was Iudas, one of them, came before them and approached Jesus to kill him. 48 And Jesus said to him, "Iudas, do you betray the Son of Man with a stroke of your hand? 49 When those around him saw what was to happen, they said to him, "Lord, shall we strike with the sword?" 50 One of them struck one of the priest's ser- vants and took

off his right ear. 51 Then Iesus answered and said, "Bear them up to this point"; and he touched his ear and healed it. 52 Then Jesus said to the priests, and to the captains of the Temple, and to the elders who had come to him, "Did you perhaps come out as if from a feast with swords and clubs? 53 When I was daily with you in the Temple, you did not stretch out your hands against me; but this is your own hour and the power of darkness." 54 So they took him and led him and brought him to the house of the priests. And Peter followed him at a distance. 55 And when they had lighted the fire in the middle of the hall and were seated together, Peter also sat down among them. 56 A certain elder saw him as he was sitting by the fire, and af- ter he had a good look at him, he said, "This man was also with him." 57 But he denied it, saying, "Woman, I do not know him." 58 After a while, another man saw him and said, "You are also of those." But Peter said, "Man, I am not." 59 And about an hour later another man affirmed, "Verily, this man was killed and is not one of them. Verily also this man was with him, for he also is a Galilean." 60 Peter said, "Man, I do not know what you say." And immediately, while he was still speaking, the rooster croaked. 61 Then the Lord turned back and looked at Peter; and Peter remembered the word of the Lord, who had said to him, "Before the rooster croaks, you shall deny me three times." 62 Peter went out and wept bit- terly. 63 The men who held Jesus taunted him and stabbed him. 64 When they had blind- folded him, they struck him on the face and asked him, "Prophesy who it was that struck you." 65 And many other blasphemous things they said against him. 66 And because it was day, the elders of the people, the priests, and the scribes gathered together and led him into their council, 67 saying, "Are you that Christ? say it." And he answered them, "If I tell you, you will not accept him." 68 And even if I ask you, you will not answer me or let me go. 69 Afterward the Son of Man will sit at the right hand of the power of God." 70 Then they all said, "Are you then Son of God?" And he said to them, "You say that I am." 71 Then they said, "What need is there for further testimony, for we ourselves have heard it from his mouth."

CHAPTER 23

1 Then the whole crowd arose and brought him before Pilate. 2 And they began to ac- cuse him, saying, "We have found this man disrupting the nation and forbidding to pay tribute to Caesar, saying that he is Christ the king." 3 Pilate questioned him, saying, "Are you the king of the nations?" And he an- swered him, "You say so." 4 Then Pilate said to the priests and the people, "I find no fault in this man." 5 But they became even more heated, saying, "This man mistreats the peo- ple, teaching throughout all Judea, beginning from Galilee and ending here." 6 When Pilate heard about Galilee, he asked if the man was a Galilean. 7 When he heard that he was from Herod's jurisdiction, he sent him to Herod, who was in Jerusalem in those days. 8 When Herod saw Iesus, he rejoiced greatly, for he had longed to see him, for he had heard of him and trusted that he had seen some sign done by him. 9 Then she questioned him about many things, but he answered him nothing. 10 The priests and scribes also came forward and accused him vehemently. 11 Herod, with his men of war, despised him, mocked him, dressed him in white, and sent him again to Pilate. 12 The same day Pilate and Herod be- came friends, for before they had been ene- mies of each other. 13 Then Pilate summoned the priests and the leaders and the people, 14 and said to them, "You have brought this man to me as

one who perturbs the people; and behold, I have examined him before you, and have found in this man no guilt for the things of which you accuse him: 15 No, neither did Herod: for I sent you to him, and verily he did nothing worthy of death. 16 Therefore I will chastise him and set him free. 17 (For by ne- cessity he had to let one of them go free during the feast). 18 Then all the crowd cried out, say- ing, "Away with him and deliver up Barabbas." 19 who, for a certain insurrection made in the city and for murder, had been put in prison. 20 Then Pilate spoke with them again, willing to release Jesus. 21 But they cried out, "Cruci- fy him, crucify him." 22 And he said to them for the third time, "But what has he done wrong? I find no cause of death in him: There- fore I will chastise him and set him free." 23 But they went forth with loud voices and de- manded that he be crucified; and the voices of them and of the priests were heard. 24 Then Pilate pronounced sentence, so that what was demanded might take place. 25 Then he released for them the one who had been put in prison for insurrection and murder, whom they desired, and handed him over to Jesus to do with him as they wished. 26 While they were leading him away, they took one Simon of Cyrene, who was coming out of the camp, and laid the cross on him, that he might car- ry it after Jesus. 27 And a great multitude of people and women followed him, weeping and lamenting him. 28 But Jesus turned to them and said, "Daughters of Jerusalem, do not weep for me, but weep for yourselves and for your children. 29 For behold, the days will come when men will say, 'Blessed are the bar- ren, and the wombs that never bore, and the sons that never bore.' 30 Then they will be- gin to say to the mountains, "Fall on vs," and to the hills, "Yield vs."31 For if they do these things to a green tree, what will be done to a dry tree? 32 And two others, who were very skillful in the deed, were led with him to be killed. 33 When they came to the place called Caluarie, they crucified him with the others, one on the right and the other on the left. 34 Then Jesus said, "Father, forgive them, for they do not know what they are doing." And they divided his garments and cast praises. 35 The people stood and watched; and the lead- ers mocked him with them, saying, "He has judged others; let him judge himself, if he is that Christ, God's chosen one." 36 The soldiers also mocked him and came and offered him wine, 37 And they said, "If you are the king of the peoples, say it to yourself." 38 And it was also written about him in Greek, Latin and Hebrew letters, "THIS IS THE KING OF THE JEWS." 39 And one of the torturers, who were hanged, railed against him, saying, "If you are that Christ, say it to yourself and against him." 40 But the other answered and rebuked him, saying, "Are not you God, since you are in the same condemnation? 41 We here are in judgment with righteousness, for we receive things worthy of what we have done; but this man has done nothing good." 42 He said to Jesus, "Lord, remember me when you enter your kingdom." 43 Then Jesus said to him, "Truly I tell you, today you will be with me in Paradise." 44 It was about 6:00 a.m. and it be- came dark over the whole country until 9:00 a.m. 45 The sun went dark, and the vault of the temple was ripped open in the middle. 46 Then Jesus cried out with a loud voice and said, "Father, into your hands I commend my spirit." And when he had said so, he left the ghost. 47 Now when the centurion saw what had been done, he glorified God, say- ing, "Surely this man was righteous." 48 And all the people who had gathered at that sight, seeing the things that had been done, shook their crests and turned back. 49 And all his acquaintances stood afar off, and the women who followed him from Galilee, seeing these things. 50 There was a man

named Ioseph, who was a counselor, a good and righteous man. 51 He did not consent to the advice and decisions of these men, who were from Ari- mathea, a city of the Iewes; he too was wait- ing for the kingdom of God. 52 He went to Pilate and asked for the body of Jesus, 53 and brought him down, and wrapped him in linen cloth, and laid him in a tomb hewn out of a rock, where there was no one yet. 54 That day was the preparation, and the Sabbath passed away. 55 The women who followed him, who had come with him from Galilee, also saw the tomb and how his body had been laid. 56 Then they returned, prepared odors and oint- ments, and rested on the Sabbath according to the commandment.

CHAPTER 24

1 Now on the first day of the week, early in the morning, they came to the tomb and brought the odors they had prepared and some wom- en with them. 2 They found the stone rolled away from the tomb, 3 And they went in, but they did not find the body of the Lord Jesus. 4 And it came to pass that while they were admiring this, behold, suddenly there came to them two men in shining garments. 5 And while they were astonished and bowed their faces to the ground, they said to them, "Why do you see Him who lives among the dead? 6 He is not here, but is risen; remember how He spoke to you when He was still in Galilee, 7 saying that the Son of Man was to be deliv- ered into the hands of sinful men, to be cruci- fied, and on the third day to rise again." 8 And they remembered his words, 9 And when they returned from the tomb, they told all these things to the eleous and all the rest 10 It was Mary Magdalene, Ioanna, Mary the moth- er of James, and other women with them who told these things to the apostles. 11 But their words seemed to them as a vain thing, and they did not believe them. 12 Then Peter arose, ran to the tomb, looked in, and saw the linen garments spread out by themselves, and went away marveling at what had happened. 13 On that same day, two of them went to a town that was about sixty kilometers from Je- rusalem, called Emmaus. 14 And they talked together about all these things that had been done. 15 While they were discussing together and reasoning, it happened that Jesus himself departed and went with them. 16 But their eyes were closed, and they could not recog- nize him. 17 And he said to them, "What kind of communications are these that you have with one another as you walk and are sad?" 18 And the one (named Cleopas) answered and said to him, "Are you only a stranger in Jeru- salem, and do you not know the things that have taken place there in these days?" 19 And he said to them, "What things?" And they an- swered him, "Of Jesus of Nazareth, who was a prophet, mighty in deed and word before God and all peoples, 20 and how the priests and our rulers condemned him to death and crucified him. 21 But we trusted that it was he who delivered Israel, and as for all these things, today is the third day that they were done. 22 Yea, and some women among them were astonished, coming early to the tomb. 23 When they did not find his body, they came and said that they had also had a vision of an- gels saying that he was an alien. 24 Therefore some of those who were with them went to the tomb and found that it was as the wom- en had said, but they did not see him. 25 Then he said to them, "Fools and slow of heart to listen to all that the prophets have said! 26 Should not Christ have suffered these things and entered into his glory? 27 He began with Moses and all the Prophets and interpreted to them in all the Scriptures the things that had been written

about him. 28 And they ap- proached a city toward which they went, but he made as if he would go over. 29 But they constrained him, saying, "Stay with us, for it is getting dark and the day is already past." So he went in to stay with them. 30 While he was at table with them, he took bread, bless- ed it, broke it, and gave it to them. 31 Then their eyes were opened, and they recognized him; and they saw him no more. 32 And they said among themselves, "Did not our hearts burst within us, while he talked with you on the way, and when he opened the Scriptures to you?" 33 And they arose at that same hour, and returned to Jerusalem, and found the Eleo-men gathered together, and those who were with them, 34 who said, "The Lord is ris- en in death and has appeared to Simon." 35 Then they related what things had been done on the way and how he was known to them in the breaking of the bread. 36 While they were saying these things, Jesus himself stood in their midst and said to them, "Peace be with you." 37 But they were bewildered and afraid, thinking that they had seen a spirit. 38 Then he said to them, "Why are you troubled and why do doubts arise in your hearts? 39 Look at my hands and my feet, for I am myself; handle me and see, for a spirit has no flesh and bones, as you see that I have." 40 When he had spoken thus, he showed them his hands and his feet. 41 And while they still did not marvel, he said to them, "Do you have any food here?" 42 They gave him a piece of brothy fish and a piece of fine bread, 43 he took it and ate before them. 44 Then he said to them, "These are the words that I spoke to you while I was still with you, so that all that is written about me in the Word of Moses, in the Prophets and in the Psalms might be fulfilled." 45 Then he opened their understanding, that they might understand the Scriptures, 46 and said to them, "Thus it is written, and thus it came to pass that Christ suffered and rose from the dead on the third day, 47 and that in His Name repentance and remission of sins should be preached among all nations, beginning at Jerusalem. 48 You are witnesses of these things. 49 And behold, I convey the promise of My Father concerning you; but remain in the city of Jerusalem, until you are clothed with power from heaven. 50 Then he led them to Bethany, and lifted up his hands, and blessed them. 51 And as he bless- ed them, he departed from them and was led to Heauen. 52 And they worshiped him and returned to Jerusalem with great joy, 53 And they stood continually in the Temple, praying and praising God, Amen.

JOHN

CHAPTER 1

1 In the beginning was the Word, and the Word was with God, and the Word was God. 2 This same was in the beginning with God. 3 Through it all things were made, and with- out it nothing was made that was made. 4 In it was life, and this life was the light of men. 5 The light shone in the darkness, and the darkness did not understand it. 6 There was a man sent from God, whose name was John. 7 This one came as a witness, to bear witness to that light, so that all men through him might come to know it. 8 He was not that light, but he was sent to bear witness of that light. 9 He was the true light, who enlightens every man who comes into the world. 10 He was in the world, and the world was made by him, but the world did not know him. 11 He came to his own, but his own did not receive him. 12 But to those who received him, he gave the prerogative of being children of God, that is, to those who fought in his Name. 13 Who were born not of blood, nor of the will of flesh, nor

of the will of man, but of God. 14 The Word became flesh and dwelt among us (and we know its glory, as the glory of the only begotten Son of the Father) full of grace and truth. 15 Iohn bore witness and cried out, "This is he of whom I said, 'He who comes af- ter me was before me,' for he was better than I." 16 And of his fullness we have received ev- erything, grace for grace. 17 For the law came from Moses, but grace and truth came from Jesus Christ. 18 No one has ever seen God; the only begotten Son, who is in the bosom of the Father, has declared him. 19 This is the account of Iohn, when the kings sent out from Jerusalem priests and leuites to ask him, "Who are you? 20 He confessed and did not deny, and said plainly, "I am not that Christ." 1 Then they asked him, "What then? Are you Elijah?" and he answered, "I am not. Are you that Prophet? And he answered, "No." 22 Then they said to him, "Who are you, that we may give an answer to those who sent you? What do you say about yourself? 23 He answered, "I am the voice of him who cries out in the wil- derness, 'Straighten up the way of the Lord,' as the prophet Esaias said." 24 Those who had been sent were Pharisees. 25 They asked him and said, "Why then do you baptize, if you are not that Christ, nor Elijah, nor that prophet?" 26 Iohn answered and said to them, "I bap- tize with water; but there is one among you whom you do not know. 27 It is he who comes after me, who was before me, whose shoelace I am not worthy to untie. 28 These things were done at Bethabara, beyond Iordan, where John was baptizing. 29 The next day John saw Jesus joining him and said, "Here is the Lamb of God who takes away the sin of the world. 30 This is he of whom I said, "After me comes a man who was before me, for he was better than I." 31 I did not know him; but because he was to be declared to Israel, I came and bap- tized with water. 32 Then John related, "I saw the Spirit descending from above, like thun- der, and abiding on him, 33 and I did not know him; but he who had sent me to baptize with water said to me, "He whom you will see the Spirit descending and abiding on him, it is he who baptizes with the Holy Spirit." 34 I said, and bore witness, that this one is the Son of God. 35 The next day John stopped again with two of his disciples. 36 He saw Jesus passing by and said, "Behold, the Son of God." 37 The two disciples heard him speak and followed Jesus. 38 Then Jesus turned and saw them fol- lowing, and said to them, "What do you see?" And they said to him, "Rabbi (that is, by in- terpretation, Master), where do you dwell?" 39 He said to them, "Come and see." And they came and saw where he dwelt and stayed with him that day, for it was about the tenth hour. 40 Andrew, Simon Peter's brother, was one of the two who had heard about John and followed him. 41 The latter found his brother Simon first and said to him, "We have found that Messias, who, by interpretation, is the Christ." 42 And he led him to Jesus. Jesus saw him and said, "You are Simon, son of Iona; you shall be called Cephas, that is, by inter- pretation, stone." 43 The next day Jesus went to Galilee and found Philip and said to him, "Follow me." 44 Philip was from Bethsaida, the town of Andrew and Peter. 45 Philip found Nathanael and said to him, "We have found him of whom Moses in the Bible and the Prophets wrote, Jesus the son of Jeoseph, who was from Nazareth." 46 Then Nathanael said to him, "Is there any good thing that comes from Nazareth? Philip said to him, "Come and see." 47 Jesus saw Nathanael approaching him and said to him, "Here is to you an Israelite in whom there is no malice." 48 Nathanael said to him, "How is it that you have come to know me? Jesus answered and said to him, "Before Philip called you, when you were under the fig tree, I knew you." 49 Nathanael answered and said to him, "Rabbi, you are the Son of God, you are the king of Israel." 50 Jesus answered and said to him, "Because I told you that I saw you under the fig tree, do you not worry? You will see greater things than these." 51 And he said to him, "Truly, truly, I say to you, from now on you will see heaven opened and the angels of God ascending and descending on the Son of Man."

CHAPTER 2

1 On the thirteenth day there was a wedding in Cana, a town in Galilee, and Jesus' moth- er was present. 2 Jesus and his disciples were also called to the wedding. 3 When the wine ran out, Jesus' mother said to him, "They have no wine." 4 Jesus said to her, "Woman, what shall I do with you? My hour has not yet come." 5 His mother said to the servants, "Do what- ever he tells you." 6 Six stone water jars were placed, according to the method of purify- ing souls, containing two or three wineskins each. 7 And Jesus said to them, "Fill the ves- sels with water." And they filled them to the brim. 8 Then he said to them, "Take out now and bring the food for the banquet." And they brought it. 9 When the master of the feast had tasted the water that had become wine (for he did not know where it came from, but the servants who drank the water knew), the master of the feast called the bridegroom, 10 and said to him, "All men at first prepare good wine, and when they have drunk well, worse; but you have withheld good wine until now." 11 This beginning of miracles Jesus did at Cana, a town in Galilee, and showed his glory; and his disciples fell in love with him. 12 Then he went down to Capernaum, he, his mother, his brothers and his disciples, but they did not stay there many days. 13 For the Old Man's Passage was at hand. Therefore Je- sus went to Jerusalem. 14 And in the Temple he found sitting those who sold oxen, sheep and dogs, and the moneychangers. 15 Then he made a scourge of cords and dragged them all out of the Temple, together with the sheep and oxen, and took away the money of the moneychangers and uprooted the tables, 16 and said to those who sold dice, "Take these things away; do not make the house of my fa- thers a house of merchants." 17 His disciples remembered that it was written, "The zeal of your house has devoured me." 18 Then the disciples answered and said to him, "What sign have you done, that you should do these things?" 19 Jesus answered and said to them, "Destroy this temple, and in three days I will raise it up." 20 Then the witnesses said, "For forty-six years this Temple has been built, and you will raise it up in three days? 21 But he spoke of the temple of his body. 22 When he was raised from the dead, his disciples re- membered that he had told them so; and they believed the Scriptures and the words that Iesus had spoken. 23 Now when he was in Je- rusalem during the Feast of the Passer, many were fighting for his name, when the miracles he performed were told. 24 But Jesus did not engage with them, for he knew them all, 25 and he did not need anyone to testify from man, for he knew what was in man.

CHAPTER 3

1 There was now a man among the Pharisees, named Nicodemus, a leader of the Jews. 2 This man came to Jesus by night and said to him, "Rabbi, we know that you are a teacher who has come from God, for no one could do these miracles that you do if God were not with him." 3 Jesus answered and said to him, "Truly, truly, I say to you, unless a man is brought to life, he cannot see the kingdom of God." 4 Nicodemus said to him, "How can a man who is old be borne? Can he enter his mother's womb again and be borne?" 5 Jesus answered, "Truly, truly, I say to you, unless a man is begotten of water and the Spirit, he cannot enter the kingdom of God." 6 What is borne of the flesh is flesh, and what is borne of the Spirit is Spirit. 7 Do not believe that I said to you, "You must be endured again." 8 The wind blows where it wills, and you hear its sound, but you cannot tell where it comes from and where it goes; so is every man who is carried by the Spirit." 9 Nicodemus answered and said to him, "How can these things be?" 10 Jesus answered and said to him, "Are you a teacher of Israel and do not know these things? 11 Verily, verily, I say to you, we speak that we know and testify that we have seen, but you do not receive our testimony. 12 If when I speak to you about earthly things, you are not comfortable, how should you be comfortable if I speak to you about eternal things? 13 For no one goes up to heaven except he who came down from heaven, the Son of Man who is in heaven. 14 And as Moses lifted up the serpent in the thicket, so must the Son of man be lifted up, 15 so that whoever be- lieves in him shall not perish but have eternal life. 16 For God so desired the world that he gave his only Son, that whoever struggles in him should not perish but have eternal life. 17 For God did not send his Son into the world to condemn the world, but that the world might be saved through him. 18 Whoever be- lieves in him is not condemned; but whoever does not believe is already condemned, be- cause he has not believed in the name of the only begotten Son of God. 19 And this is the condemnation: that light has come into the world, and men have preferred darkness to light, because their deeds have been evil. 20 For he who does lawlessness hates the light and does not come near the light, if he does not want his deeds to be rebuked. 21 But he who does lawlessness comes to the light, that his deeds may be made manifest, which are done according to God. 22 After these things, Jesus and his disciples came to the land of Ju- dea, stood with them, and baptized. 23 Iohn also baptized in Enon, as well as in Salim, for there was much water there; and they came and were baptized. 24 For Iohn had not yet been put in prison. 25 Then a question arose between Iohn's disciples and the young men, concerning purification. 26 They came to John and said to him, "Rabbi, he who was with you beyond Iorden, to whom you bore witness, behold, he baptizes, and all men come to him." 27 Iohn answered and said, "A man can receive nothing unless it is given to him from the LORD. 28 You yourselves are witnesses to me that I said that I am not that Christ, but that I was sent before him. 29 He who has the bride is the bridegroom; but the friend of the bridegroom, who stands and listens to him, rejoices greatly because of the bridegroom's journey. This thought of mine is therefore fulfilled. 30 He must increase, but I must de- crease. 31 He that cometh from an island, he is all; he that is of the earth, is of the earth, and speaketh of the earth; he that cometh from heaven, he is all. 32 What he has seen and heard, he testifies; but no one receives his testimony. 33 He who has received his tes- timony has sealed that God is true. 34 For he whom God has sent speaks the words of God; for God does not give him the Spirit by mea- sure. 35 The Father gave voice to the Son and gave all things into his hands. 36 Whoever believes in the Son has eternal life; whoever does not obey the Son will not see life, but the wrath of God remains on him.

CHAPTER 4

1 When the Lord heard that the Pharisees had heard that Jesus had made and baptized more disciples than John, 2 (even though it was not Jesus himself who was baptizing, but his disciples) 3 He left Judea and set out again for Galilee. 4 And he had to pass through Samaria. 5 So he came to a town in Samaria called Sychar, near the possession that Iacob had given to his son Ioseph. 6 There was Jacob's well there. Jesus, tired from the journey, thus sat down at the well: it was about six hours. 7 There came a woman from Samaria to draw water. Jesus said to her, "Give me a drink." 8 For his disciples had gone into the city to buy food. 9 Then the woman of Samaria said to him, "How is it that you, who are a woman, ask me, who am a woman of Samaria, for a drink? Because the Iewes do not meddle with the Samaritans. 10 Jesus answered and said to her, "If you knew the gift of God and who it is who says to you, Give me a drink, you would have asked him and he would have given you the water of life." 11 The woman said to him, "Lord, you have nothing with which to draw, and the well is deep; whence then have you the water of life? 12 Are you greater than our father Jacob, who gave the well and drew from it himself and his sons and his cattle? 13 Jesus answered and said to her, "Whoever drinks of this water will thirst again: 14 but whoso- ever drinketh of the water that I shall give him, he shall thirst no more: but the water that I shall give him shall be in him a well of water, springing up into everlasting life." 15 The woman said to him, "Syr, give me of that water, that I may thirst no more and come no more to drink." 16 Jesus said to her, "Go, call your husband and come here." 17 The woman answered, "I have no husband." Jesus said to her, "You said well, I have no husband. 18 For you have had five husbands, and the one you have now is not your husband; this is true." 19 The woman said to him, "Lord, I see that you are a prophet. 20 Our fathers worshiped on this mountain, and you say that the place of men's worship is Jerusalem." 21 Jesus said to her, "Woman, depart from me; the hour is coming when you will not worship the Father either on this mountain or in Jerusalem. 22 You worship what you do not know; we wor- ship what we know, for salvation comes from the light. 23 But the hour will come, and is al- ready now, when true worshipers will worship the Father in spirit and truth, for the Father requires that they be such to worship him. 24 God is a Spirit, and those who worship him must worship him in spirit and truth. 25 The woman said to him, "I know well that the Messiah will come, who is called Christ; when he has come, he will tell you everything." 26 Jesus said to her, "I am the one who speaks to you." 27 Then his disciples came and noticed that he was talking to a woman; but no one said to him, "What do you ask?" or "Why are you talking to her?" 28 The woman then left her water jar, went toward the city, and said to the men, 29 Come and see a man who has told me all the things I have done in the past; is he not that Christ?" 30 Then they went out of the city and came to him. 31 Meanwhile, the disci- ples begged him, saying, "Master, eat." 32 But he answered them, "I have a dish to eat that you do not know." 33 Then the disciples said among themselves, "Has anyone brought him any food?" 34 Jesus said to them, "My food is to do the will of him who sent me and to finish his work." 35 Do you not say, "There are still four months, and then the harangue will come"? Behold, I say to you, lift up your eyes and look at the regions, for they are already white from the plague. 36 He who reaps, re- ceives reward and gathers fruit for eternal life, so that both he who sows and he who reaps may receive together. 37 For the saying is true that one sows and the other reaps. 38 I have sent you to reap that for which you did not labor; other men have labored, and you have entered into their labors. 39 Now many of the Samaritans in that city believed in him, for the woman who had testified had said, "He has told me all the things I have done." 40 Then when the Samaritans had come to him, they begged him to stay with them; and he stayed there two days. 41 And many others felt sick because of his word. 42 And they said to the woman, "Now we feel bad, not because of your word, for we have heard it ourselves and know that this is indeed Christ the Savior of the world." 43 So two days later he departed from there and went to Galilee. 44 For Jesus himself had testified that a prophet has no honor in his own country. 45 When he had come to Galilee, the Galileans who had seen all the things he had done in Jerusalem at the feast welcomed him; for they too were go- ing to the feast. 46 Then Jesus came again to Cana, a town in Galilee, where he had made water into wine. And there was a certain gen- tleman there, whose son was sick in Caper- naum. 47 When he heard that Jesus had left Judea to go to Galilee, he went to him and begged him to come down and take care of his son, for he was now ready to die. 48 Then Iesus said to him, "Unless you see signs and wonders, you will not be converted." 49 The ruler said to him, "Sirius, come down before my son dies." 50 Jesus said to him, "Go your way, your son dies"; and the man realized the words Jesus had spoken to him and went his way. 51 As he went down, his servants came to him, saying, "Your son is dying." 52 Then he asked them the hour when he had begun to be sick. And they answered him, "Yester- day, at the seventh hour, the fever left him." 53 Then the father understood that it was the same hour when Jesus had said to him, "Your son lives." And he felt guilty, along with all his family. 54 This second miracle Jesus did again, after he had left Judea to go to Galilee.

CHAPTER 5

1 After this, a feast of the Kinsmen was cel- ebrated, and Jesus went to Jerusalem. 2 In Jerusalem, by the place of the sheep, there is a well called in Hebrew Bethesda, with five porches: 3 In which lay a great multitude of sick, blind, diseased and withered peo- ple, who went to drink the water. 4 For an angel at a certain time came down into the well and stirred up the water; and whosoev- er first, after stirring up the water, went in, was healed of what he had. 5 There was a man there who had been sick for eight years and thirty years. :6 When Jesus saw him lying and learned that he had been sick for a long time, he said to him, "Do you want to be healed? 7 The sick man answered him, "Lord, when the water is troubled, I have no one to put me in the pool; but as I am coming, another comes down before me." 8 Jesus said to him, "Get up, take up your bed, and walk." 9 And immedi- ately the man was restored, and took up his bed, and walked; and that same day was the Sabbath. 10 So the witnesses said to the man who had been healed, "It is the Sabbath day; it is not lawful for you to carry your bed." 11 He answered them, "He who healed me said to me, 'Take up your bed and walk.'" 12 Then they asked him, "Which is the man who said to you, 'Take up your bed and walk'?" 13 The one who had been healed did not know who it was, because Jesus had departed from the crowd there. 14 After that, Jesus found him in the Temple and said to him, "Behold, you are healed; sin no more, or something worse will happen to you." 15 The man went away and told the

witnesses that it was Jesus who had healed him. 16 Therefore the Israelites perse- cuted Jesus and tried to kill him, because he had done these things on the Sabbath. 17 But Jesus answered them, "My Father works so far, and I work." 18 Therefore the Jews sought to kill him even more, not only because he had transgressed the Sabbath, but also because he said that God was his Father and made him- self equal with God. 19 Then Jesus answered and said to them, "Verily, verily, I say unto you, the Son can do nothing by himself, ex- cept what he sees the Father doing; for what- ever he does, the Son does likewise. 20 For the Father calls the Son and shows him all the things that he does, and will show him great- er works than these, that you may husband. 21 For as the Father raises the dead and makes them alive, so the Son makes alive whom he will. 22 For the Father judges no one, but has entrusted all judgment to the Son, 23 that all men may honor the Son as they honor the Fa- ther; whoever does not honor the Son, does not honor even the Father who sent him. 24 Verily, verily, I say unto you, he that heareth my word, and believeth on him that sent me, hath everlasting life, and shall not be con- demned, but is passed from death unto life. 25 Verily, verily, I say unto you, the hour shall come, and is already now, when the dead shall hear the word of the Son of God; and they that have heard it shall live. 26 For as the Father has life in Himself, so He has given the Son life in Himself, 27 and has also given him power to execute judgment, in that he is the Son of man. 28 Fear not, for the hour will come when all who are in the graves will hear his voice. 29 And those who have done good will come to the resurrection of life, but those who have done evil to the resurrection of condemna- tion. 30 I can do nothing by myself; as I hear, I judge; and my judgment is right, because I do not see my own will, but the will of the Father who sent me. 31 If I testify of myself, my tes- timony would not be true. 32 There is another who bears testimony of Me, and I know that the testimony he bears of Me is true. 33 You have sent to Iohn, and he has borne witness to the truth.34 But I do not receive the testimo- ny of man; nevertheless, these things I say so that you may be warned. 35 He was a burning and shining candle, and you would for a time enjoy his light. 36 But I have a greater testi- mony than John, for the works that the Father has given me to do, the very works that I do, testify of me that the Father has sent me. 37 And the Father himself, who sent me, bears witness of me. You have never heard his voice, nor have you seen his form. 38 And his word has no abode in you; for he whom he sent, you have not believed him. 39 Seek ye the Scrip- tures, for in them ye think that ye have eternal life; and they are they which testify of me. 40 But you do not want to come to me to have life. 41 I do not receive the prayers of men. 42 But I know that you do not have the will of God in you. 43 I have come in my Father's name, and you do not receive me; if another comes in his name, you will receive him. 44 How can you be quiet, you who receive honor from another and do not see the honor that comes from God alone? 45 Do not think that I accuse you to my Father; there is one who accuses you, and that is Moses, in whom you trust. 46 For if you had believed Moses, you would have believed me, for he wrote of me. 47 But if you do not believe his writings, how can you believe my words?

CHAPTER 6

1 After these things, Jesus took the way to the Sea of Galilee, which is Tiberias. 2 And a great crowd followed him, because they saw his miracles, which he did on those who were sick. 3 Then Jesus went to a mountain and stood there with his disciples. 4 It was the day of Passover, a feast of the dead. 5 Then Jesus lifted up his eyes and, seeing that a great multitude was coming to him, said to Philip, "From where shall we buy bread that these may eat?" 6 (And this he said to convince him, for he himself knew what he would do). 7 Philip answered him, "Two hundred cents' worth of bread is not enough for them, so that each of them may take some." 8 Then one of his disciples, Andrew, Simon Peter's brother, told him, 9 There is a child here who has five loaves and two fish; but what are they among so many? 10 And Jesus said, "Let the people sit down." (Then the men sat down in num- bers of about five thousand. 11 And Jesus took bread, and gave thanks, and gave it to the dis- ciples, and to the disciples, and to them that were sitting down; and likewise of the fish, as much as they desired. 12 And when they were full, he said to his disciples, "Gather up the broken meat that remains, that nothing may be lost." 13 Then they gathered them up and filled two baskets with the broken flesh of the five fish, which was left for those who had eat- en. 14 Then the men, having seen the miracle that Iesus had done, said, "It is true that there is a prophet who is to come into the world." 15 So when Jesus saw that they were coming to take him to make him a king, he went away again to a mountain, alone. 16 When the time had come, his disciples went down to the sea, 17 they got into a ship and headed out to sea, in the direction of Capernaum; but by now it was dark and Jesus had not come to them. 18 And the sea arose with a great wind, and it melted away. 19 And when they had rowed about fifty-two or thirty miles, they saw Je- sus walking on the sea and approaching the ship. 20 But he said to them, "It is I; do not be afraid." 21 So they willingly welcomed him into the ship, and the ship was nearer and nearer to the land, toward which they went. 22 The next day the people on the other side of the sea saw that there was no other ship like the one his disciples had entered, and that Jesus had not entered with his disciples into the ship, but that his disciples had gone alone, 23 and that other ships came from Tiberias to the place where they ate bread, after the Lord had given thanks. 24 Now when the people saw that Jesus was not there, nor his disciples, they also embarked and came to Capernaum, looking for Jesus. 25 And when they found him on the other side of the sea, they said to him, "Rabbi, when did you come so far?" 26 And Jesus answered them and said, "Verily, verily, I say unto you, ye see me, not because ye do miracles, but because ye have eaten of your loaves, and been satisfied. 27 Do not work for the flesh that perishes, but for the flesh that endures to eternal life, which the Son of Man will give you; for he has sealed God the Father." 28 Then they said to him, "What must we do to do the works of God?" 29 Jesus an- swered and said to them, "This is the work of God, that you should be in him, whom he has sent." 30 They said to him, "What sign have you done, that we might see him and follow you? What do you want to do? 31 Our fathers ate manna in the wilderness, as it is written, "He gave them bread from above to eat." 32 Then Jesus said to them, "Truly, truly, I say to you, Moses did not give you that bread from Eauen, but my Father gives you the true bread from Eauen. 33 For the bread of God is that which comes down from the Eauen and gives life to the world. 34 Then they said to him, "Lord, give me this bread again." 35 And Jesus said to them, "I am the bread of life; whoev- er comes to me will no longer hunger, and whoever lives in me will no longer thirst. 36 But I have told you that you also have seen me and have not turned away. 37 Whatever the Father

grants me, will come to me; and who- ever comes to me, I will not cast out. 38 For I came down from Eauen not to do my will, but the will of him who sent me. 39 And this is the will of the Father who sent me: that of all that he has given me I should lose nothing, but raise it up at the last day. 40 And this is the will of him who sent me: that every man who sees the Son and believes in him should have eternal life; and I will raise him up at the last day. 41 Then the witnesses murmured against him because he said, "I am that bread which is from the LORD." 42 They said, "Is not this Jesus the son of Jeoseph, whose father and mother we know? How is it then that he says, 'I am come down from Eauen'?" 43 Then Jesus answered and said to them, "Do not mur- mur among yourselves. 44 No one can come to me unless the Father who sent me draws him; and I will raise him up at the last day. 45 It is written in the Prophets, "They shall all be taught by God. Every man therefore who has heard and learned from the Father comes to me: 46 Not that anyone has seen the Father, but he who is from God has seen the Father. 47 Verily, verily, I say unto you, he that belie- veth on me hath everlasting life. 48 I am that bread of life. 49 Your fathers ate manna in the wilderness and died. 50 This is the bread that comes down from the LORD, so that whoever eats of it will not perish. 51 I am that bread which is nourished, which came down from Eauen; if any man eat of this bread, he shall die forever; and the bread which I will give is my flesh, which I will give for the life of the world." 52 Then the witnesses argued among themselves, saying, "How can this man give to eat his flesh? 53 Then Jesus said to them, "Truly, truly, I say to you, unless you eat the flesh of the Son of Man and drink his blood, you do not have life in you. 54 Whoever eats my flesh and drinks my blood has eternal life, and I will raise him up on the last day. 55 For my flesh is meat in death, and my blood is drink in death. 56 He who eats my flesh and drinks my blood abides in me and I in him. 57 As the Father who loves has sent me, so I live by the Father, and he who eats me lives by me. 58 This is the bread that came down from Heauen; not like your fathers who ate manna and died. Whoever eats of this bread will live forever." 59 These things he said in the Syna- gogue as he taught in Capernaum. 60 There- fore many of his disciples, hearing this, said, "This is a hard saying; who can hear it? 61 But Jesus, knowing that his disciples murmured, said to them, "Does this offend you? 62 What would happen if you saw the Son of Man come up where He was before? 63 It is the spirit that vivifies; the flesh is of no use; the words that I say to you are spirit and life. 64 But there are some of you who are not deceived; for I knew from the beginning which ones were not de- ceived, and who would betray him. 65 And he said, "Therefore I say to you, no one can come to me unless he is granted by my Father." 66 From that time, many of his disciples left and no longer walked with him. 67 Then Iesus said to the two, "Will you also go away?" 68 Simon Peter answered him, "Master, to whom shall we go? You have words of eternal life." 69 and we know that you are the Christ, the Son of the living God." 70 Jesus answered them, "Have I not chosen you two, and one of you is a devil? 71 He spoke of Iudas Iscariot, son of Simon, for it was he who was to betray him, though he was one of the two.

CHAPTER 7

1 After these things, Jesus walked in Galilee and would not walk in Judea, because the Jews were trying to kill him. 2 Now the Feast of Tabernacles was near. 3 His brothers there- fore said to him, "Depart and go into Iudea, that your disciples may see the trouble you are doing. 4 For there is no man who does any- thing secretly and seeks to be famous. If you do these things, show yourself to the world. 5 For his brothers did not yet believe in him. 6 Then Jesus said to them, "My hour has not yet come, but your hour is always ready." 7 The world cannot hate you, but it hates me, for I testify of it that its works are useless. 8 Go ye to this feast: I will not yet go to this feast, for my time is not yet fulfilled." 9 These things he said to them, and he still remained in Galilee. 10 But when his brothers had gone away, he also went to the feast, not openly, but as if in secret. 11 Then his relatives sought him at the feast and said, "Where is he?" 12 The people murmured much about him. Some said, "He is a good man"; others said, "No, but he de- ceives the people." 13 Yet no one spoke openly about him for fear of the people. 14 When half the feast was over, Jesus entered the temple and taught. 15 The witnesses marveled, say- ing, "How can this man know the Scriptures, since he never learned! 16 Jesus answered them and said, "My doctrine is not mine but the one who sent me. 17 If anyone wants to do his will, he will know the doctrine, whether it comes from God or whether I speak from myself. 18 He who speaks of himself seeks his own glory; but he who seeks the glory of him who sent him is truthful, and there is no boastfulness in him. 19 Did not Moses give you a Law, yet none of you observe it? Why are you about to kill me? 20 The people answered, "You have a Law; who is about to kill you?" 21 Jesus answered and said to them, "I have done one work, and you all marvel at it. 22 Moses therefore enjoined upon you circumcision (not because it is Moses', but the fathers'), and you on the Sabbath day shall circumcise a man. 23 If a man receives circumcision on the Sabbath day, so that the law of Moses is not broken, are you angry with me because I have made a man whole on the Sabbath day? 24 I do not judge according to appearance, but I judge righteously." 25 Then some of Jerusalem said, "Is not this the one they are about to kill? 26 And behold, he speaks openly, and they say nothing to him; do the rulers know that this is indeed that Christ? 27 Yet we know where this man is from; but when the Christ comes, no one will know where he is from." 28 Then, as he was teaching, Jesus cried out in the Temple, "You know me, and you know where I am; nevertheless I have not come of myself, but he who sent me, it is true, whom you do not know. 29 But I know him, for I am from him, and he has sent me." 30 Then they tried to take him, but no one laid hands on him, for his hour had not yet come. 31 Now many of the people believed in him and said, "When the Christ comes, will he do more miracles than this man has done? 32 The Pharisees heard that the people were murmuring these things about him, and the Pharisees and the high priests sent officers to take him. 33 Then Jesus said to them, "I will stay with you a little longer, and then I will go away to the one who sent me. 34 You will see me and not find me, and where I am you cannot come." 35 Then the young men said among themselves, "Where will he go, that we shall not find him? Will he go to those who are scattered among the Greeks and teach the Greeks? 36 What does it mean that he said, 'You will see me and not find me?' And where I am, you cannot come"? 37 Now on the last and great day of the feast, Jesus stood still and cried out, saying, "If any- one thirsts, let him come to me and drink. 38 Whoever believes in me, as the Scripture says, out of his belly shall flow the water of life." 39 (This spoke of the Spirit that those who be- lieved in him would receive; for the Holy Spir- it had not yet been

granted, for Iesus had not yet been glorified). 40 So many of the people, hearing this saying, said, "It is true that this is that prophet." 41 Others said, "This is the Christ"; still others said, "But will the Christ come out of Galilee? 42 Does not the Scripture say that that Christ will come from the de- scendants of Dauid and from the city of Beth- leem, where Dauid was? 43 So there was dis- sension among the people over him. 44 Some of them would have liked to take him, but no one laid hands on him. 45 Then the officers came to the priests and Pharisees and said to them, "Why did you not take him with you?" 46 The officers answered, "No one has spo- ken like this man." 47 Then the Pharisees an- swered, "Are you also deceived? 48 Is there any of the leaders or Pharisees who have rested on him? 49 But this people, who do not know the Law, are accursed." 50 Nicodemus said to them, "He who came to Jesus by night is one of them." 51 Does our Law judge a man before we hear him and know what he has done? 52 They answered and said to him, "Are you also from Galilee? Search and see, for from Galilee no prophet has arisen." 53 Everyone bathed in his own house.

CHAPTER 8

1 Jesus went to the Mount of Olives, 2 And early in the morning he entered the Temple again, and all the people came to him, and he sat down and taught them. 3 Then the scribes and Pharisees brought to him a woman tak- en in adultery and put her in the middle of the road, 4 And they said to him, "Teacher, we found this woman committing adultery, in the very act of doing it." 5 Now Moses, in our Law, had commanded that these people should be stoned to death; what then say- est thou? 6 And this they said to tempt him, to have a reason to accuse him. But Jesus stooped down and with his finger wrote on the carpet. 7 While they continued to ques- tion him, he rose up and said to them, "Who- ever of you is without sin, let him cast the first stone against her." 8 Then he stooped down and wrote on the ground. 9 And when they heard him, charged by their conscience, they went away one by one, beginning with the eldest to the last; so Jesus was left alone and the woman in the midst. 10 When Jesus got up again and saw no one but the woman, he said to her, "Woman, where are your accus- ers? Has no one condemned you?" 11 She an- swered, "No one, Lord." And Jesus said, "Nei- ther do I condemn you; go and sin no more." 12 Then Jesus spoke to them again, saying, "I am the light of the world; whoever follows me will not walk in darkness, but will have the light of life." 13 The Pharisees therefore said to him, "You bear a testimony of yourself; your testimony is not true." 14 Jesus answered and said to them, "Though I bear testimony of myself, yet my testimony is true, for I know whence I came and whither I am going; but you cannot tell whence I came and whither I am going. 15 You judge according to the flesh; I judge no one. 16 And if I also judge, my judg- ment is true, for it is not I alone, but I and the Father who sent me. 17 It is also written in your Bible that the testimony of two men is true. 18 I am one who testifies of himself, and the Father who sent me testifies of me." 19 Then they said to him, "Where is this Father of yours?" Jesus answered, "You know neither me nor that Father of mine. If you had known me, you would also have known that Father of mine." 20 These words Jesus said in the trea- sury, while he was teaching in the Temple, and no one laid hands on him, for his hour had not yet come. 21 Then Jesus said to them again, "I go my way; you will see me and die in your sins." 22 Then the

Israelites said, "Will he kill himself, because he says, Where I go, you cannot come?" 23 And he said to them, "You are from below, I am from without; you are of this world, I am not of this world. 24 Therefore I have told you that you will die in your sins; for if you do not believe that I am he, you will die in your sins." 25 Then they said to him, "Who are you?" And Jesus said to them, "It is the same thing that I have told you from the beginning. 26 I have many things to say and to judge about you; but he who sent me is true, and the things I have heard from him I say to the world. 27 They did not un- derstand that he was speaking to them about the Father. 28 Then Jesus said to them, "When you have raised up the Son of Man, then you will know that I am he, and that I do nothing of myself, but as my Father has taught me, so I say these things. 29 For he who sent me is with me; the Father has not left me alone, because I always do the things that please him. 30 While he was speaking these things, many dwelled in him. 31 Then Jesus said to those who had believed in him, "If you con- tinue in my word, you are truly my disciples, 32 you will know the truth, and the truth will make you free." 33 They answered him, "We are descendants of Abraham and have never been faithful to anyone; why then do you say, 'You will be set free'?" 34 Jesus answered them, "Truly, truly, I say to you, he who commits sin is a servant of sin. 35 The servant does not remain in the house forever, but the Son re- mains forever. 36 If therefore the Son makes you free, you will be free even in death. 37 I know that you are descendants of Abraham, but you seek to kill me, because my word has no place in you. 38 I say what I have seen with my Father, and you do what you have seen with your father." 39 They answered and said to him, "Abraham is our father." Jesus said to them, "If you were children of Abraham, you would do the works of Abraham. 40 But now you are about to kill me, a man who told you the truth, which I have heard from God; this Abraham did not do. 41 You do the works of your father." Then they said to him, "We are not born of fornication; we have one Father, who is God." 42 Therefore Jesus said to them, "If God were your Father, then you would love me; for I came from afar, from God, and I did not come of myself, but it is he who sent me." 43 Why do you not understand my speeches? Because you cannot hear my words. 44 You are of your father, the deuill, and the lusts of your father you will do; he has been a murder- er from the beginning and has not remained in the truth, because there is no truth in him. When he speaks a lie, he speaks of himself, for he is a liar, and he is the father of it. 45 And because I tell you the truth, you do not listen to me. 46 Which of you can reproach me with sin? And if I speak the truth, why do you not listen to me? 47 He who is from God hears the words of God; you therefore do not hear them, for you are not from God." 48 Then the witnesses answered and said to him, "Is it not true that you are a Samaritan and have a dis- ease?" 49 Jesus answered, "I have no fault, but I honor my Father, and you have dishonored me. 50 I do not see my praise, but there is one who seeks it and judges it. 51 Verily, verily, I say unto you, if any man keep my word, he shall never see death." 52 Then the witness- es said to him, "Now we know that you have a will. Abraham died, and the Prophets; and you say, If any man keep my word, he shall never taste death." 53 Are you greater than our father Abraham, who died? And the Prophets are dead; who do you think you are? 54 Jesus answered, "If I honor myself, my honor is worth nothing; it is my Father who honors me, whom you say is your God. 55 You have not known him, but I know him, and if I said

I did not know him, I would be a liar like you; but I know him and keep his word. 56 And Abraham your father saw my day, and saw it, and rejoiced. 57 Then they said to him, "Are you not yet fifty years old and have you seen Abraham?" 58 Jesus said to them, "Truly, tru- ly, I say to you, before Abraham was, I am." 59 Then they took stones to hurl at him, but Jesus hid himself and came out of the Temple: He passed among them and went his way.

CHAPTER 9

1 As he was passing by, he saw a man who was blind from birth. 2 His disciples questioned him, saying, "Teacher, who sinned, this man or his parents, that he was born blind?" 3 Jesus answered, "Neither this man nor his parents sinned, but that the works of God might be manifested on him. 4 I must do the works of him who sent me, while it is day; night comes, when no one can work. 5 As long as I am in the world, I am the light of the world. 6 As soon as he had spoken, he spat on the ground, and made clay, and anointed the eyes of the blind with clay, 7 and said to him, "Go and wash in the well of Siloam" (which, by interpretation, means "Sent"). 8 The neighbors and those who had seen him before, when he was blind, said, "Is not this the one who sat and asked alms?" 9 Some said, "It is he"; others said, "It is like him"; but he himself said, "It is I." 10 There- fore they said to him, "How were your eyes opened?" 11 He answered, "He who is called Jesus made clay and anointed my eyes and said to me, 'Go to the well of Siloam and wash yourself.' So I went and washed and received sight. 12 Then they said to him, "Where is it?" He answered, "I cannot say." 13 They brought to the Pharisees the one who was once blind. 14 It was the Sabbath day when Jesus made clay and opened his eyes. 15 Then the Phar- isees also asked him how he had obtained sight. And he said to them, "He laid clay on my eyes, and I washed and see." 16 Then some of the Pharisees said, "This man is not from God, for he does not keep the Sabbath." Oth- ers said, "How can a man who is a sinner do such miracles?" And there was dissension among them. 17 Then they said again to the blind man, "What do you say of him, because he has opened your eyes?" And he said, "He is a prophet." 18 Then the witnesses did not notice him (who had been blind and had re- ceived sight) until they had called the parents of the one who had received sight. 19 They questioned them, saying, "Is this your son, whom you say was born blind? How does he now see? 20 His parents answered them and said, "We know that this is our son and that he was born blind: 21 But we do not know by what means he sees now, nor who opened his eyes, we cannot tell; he is already old; ask him: he will answer for himself." 22 His parents said these words, because they feared the badgers; for the badgers had already determined that if anyone confessed that he was the Christ, he would be excommunicated from the Syn- agogue. 23 Therefore his parents said, "He is old enough; ask him." 24 Then they called again the man who had been blinded and said to him, "Give glory to God; we know that this man is a sinner." 25 He answered and said, "I do not know whether he is a sinner or not; one thing I do know: that I was blind and now I see." 26 Then they said to him again, "What has he done to you? How did he open your eyes?" 27 He answered them, "I have already told you and you have not heard; why do you want to hear it again? Do you also want to be his disciples? 28 Then they called him back and said, "Be you his disciple; we are disciples of Moses." 29 We know that God spoke to Mo- ses, but this man we do not know where he came from." 30 The man answered and said to them, "No doubt it is a wonderful thing that you do not know where he is from, yet he has opened my eyes." 31 Now we know that God does not listen to sinners; but if one is a wor- shipper of God and does his will, he listens to him. 32 Since the world began, it has never been heard of anyone opening the eyes of one who had been blinded. 33 If this man had not been from God, he could have done nothing. 34 They answered and said to him, "Are you utterly prone to sin and teaching others?" And they cast him out. 35 Jesus heard that they had driven him out, and finding him, said to him, "Do you believe in the Son of God?" 36 He answered and said, "Who is he, Lord, that I may believe in him?" 37 And Jesus said to him, "You have seen him, and it is he who speaks to you." 38 Then the man said, "Lord, I drew near to him and worshipped him." 39 And Jesus said, "I have come to judge in this world, that those who do not see may see, and that those who see may be made blind." 40 Some of the Pharisees who were with him heard these things and said to him, "Are we also blind?" 41 Jesus said to them, "If you were blind, you would not have sinned; but now you say, 'We see'; therefore your sin remains."

CHAPTER 10

1 Verily, verily, I say unto you, he that enter- eth not in by the gate into the flock, but goeth up by another way, he is a thief and a robber. 2 But he who enters by the door is the keeper of the flock. 3 To him the gatekeeper opens, and the sheep listen for his passage; he calls his sheep by name and leads them out. 4 When he has brought his sheep out, he goes before them, and the sheep follow him, for they know his journey. 5 They do not follow the stranger, but flee from him, because they do not know the stranger's journey. 6 This parable Jesus told them, but they did not un- derstand what the things were that he had told them. 7 Then Jesus said to them again, "Truly, truly, I say to you, I am the owner of the sheep. 8 All those who came before me are thieves and robbers, but the sheep did not listen to them. 9 I am that door; if one en- ters by me, he will be saved; he will go in and come out and find pasture. 10 The LORD does not come except to steal, kill, and destroy; I have come that they may have life and have it abundantly. 11 I am that good shepherd who lays down his life for his flock. 12 But a hireling, who is not a shepherd and does not own his sheep, if he sees the wolf coming, abandons the sheep and flees, and the wolf catches them and tears them to pieces.13 So the hireling flees, because he is a hireling and does not care for the sheep. 14 I am the good shepherd; I know my own and am acquainted with mine. 15 As the Father knows me, I also know the Father; and I lay down my life for my sheep. 16 I also have other flocks, which are not of this flock; these also I will take with me, and they shall hear my journey; and there shall be one flock and one shepherd. 17 There- fore my Father loves me, because I gave my life to take it again. 18 No one takes it from me, but I lay it down from myself; I have pow- er to lay it down, and I have power to take it up again; this command I have received from my Father." 19 Then again there was dissen- sion among the young men over these words, 20 Many of them said, "He has a sickness and is mad; why do you listen to him? 21 Others said, "These are not the words of him who has a mind; can the mind open the eyes of a blind man?" 22 It was in Jerusalem the Feast of Dedication, and it was winter. 23 Jesus was walking in the Temple, in Solomon's

porch. 24 Then they came around him and said, "How long are you playing dead? If you are that Christ, say it plainly." 25 Jesus answered them, "I have told you, and you have not heard me: the works I do in my Father's name testify of me. 26 But you do not, because you are not of my sheep, as I have told you. 27 My sheep hear my voice; I know them, and they follow me, 28 And I give them eternal life, and they shall never perish, nor shall any man pluck them out of my hand. 29 My Father who gave them to me is greater than all, and no one can take them out of my Father's hand. 30 My Father and I are one. 31 Then you again took stones to stone him. 32 Jesus answered them, "I have shown you many good works from my Father; for which of these works do you stone me?" 33 They answered him, "We do not stone you for good works, but for blasphemy: you, who are a man, make yourself God." 34 Jesus answered them, "Is it not written in your Bi- ble that I said, 'You are gods'?" 35 If you have called them gods, to whom the word of God has been given, and the Scripture cannot be broken, 36 do you say of him whom the Father sanctified and sent into the world, "You blas- pheme because I said, 'I am the Son of God'"? 37 If I do not do the works of my Father, do not turn away from me. 38 But if I do, even if you do not acknowledge Me, acknowledge the works, that you may know and know that the Father is in Me and I in Him." 39 Then they set out to take him, but he escaped their hands, 40 and went again beyond Iordan, to the place where Iohn had first baptized, and there he remained. 41 And many resorted to him and said, "Iohn has done no miracle; but all the things that Iohn said of this man were true." 42 And many believed in him.

CHAPTER 11

1 A man was sick, named Lazarus, from Bethany, Mary's city, and his sister Martha. 2 (And it was Mary who anointed the Lord with oil and dried his feet with her robe, whose brother Lazarus was sick.) 3 Therefore his sisters sent to him saying, "Lord, behold, he whom you love is sick." 4 When Iesus heard this, he said, "This sick man is not dead, but for the glory of God, that the Son of God may be glorified. 5 Now Jesus heard Martha and her sister and Lazarus. 6 And after he heard that he was sick, he stayed two more days in the same place where he was. 7 Then, after this, he said to his disciples, "Let us go again to Judea." 8 The disciples said to him, "Mas- ter, lately witnesses have been trying to stone you, and you are going there again?" 9 Jesus answered, "Are there not two hours in the day? If a man walks by day, he does not stum- ble, for he sees the light of this world. 10 But if a man walks by night, he stumbles, because there is no light in him." 11 After saying these things, he said to them, "Our friend Lazarus is asleep, but I am going to wake him up." 12 Then his disciples said, "Lord, if he sleeps, he will be saved." 13 However, Jesus spoke of his death, but they thought he had spoken of natural sleep. 14 Then Jesus told them plainly, "Lazarus is dead. 15 I am glad for you that I was not there, that you may be received; but let them go to him." 16 Then Thomas (who is called Didymus) said to his disciples, "Go you also, that we may die with him." 17 Then Iesus came and found that he had already been ly- ing in the tomb for four days. 18 (Bethany was near Jerusalem, about fifty kilometers away). 19 Many of you came to Martha and Mary to console them about their brother. 20 When Martha heard that Iesus was coming, she went to fetch him; but Mary still remained in the house. 21 Martha said to Jesus,

"Lord, if you had been here, my brother would not have died. 22 But now I also know that what you ask of God, God will give you." 23 Jesus said to her, "Your brother will rise again." 24 Mar- tha said to him, "I know that he will rise again in the resurrection on the last day." 25 Jesus said to her, "I am the resurrection and the life; whoever believes in me, even if he were dead, he will live. 26 Whoever lives and believes in me will never die. 27 She answered him, "Yes, Lord, I believe that you are the Christ, the Son of God who is to come into the world." 28 And having said this, he went his way and secretly called Mary, his sister, saying, "The Master has come and is calling you." 29 When she heard this, she got up quickly and went to him. 30 For Jesus had not yet entered the city, but was in the place where Martha had met him. 31 The sisters who were with her in the house and comforting her, when they saw Mary get- ting up quickly and going out, followed her, saying, "Go to the tomb and weep." 32 When Mary came to where Jesus was and saw him, she fell at his feet and said to him, "Lord, if you had been here, my brother would not have died." 33 When therefore Iesus saw her weep- ing and the weeping also of the women who came with her, he was saddened in spirit and troubled in himself, 34 and said, "Where have you laid him?" They answered him, "Lord, come and see." 35 And Jesus wept. 36 Then the watchmen said, "Behold, how he made him weep." 37 Some of them said, "Could not he, who opened the eyes of the blind, see to it that this man did not die? 38 Then Jesus resumed walking in himself and approached the tomb. It was a chest and a stone was laid on it. 39 Jesus said, "Remove the stone." Martha, the sister of the one who had died, said to him, "Lord, it stinks already, for he has been dead for four days." 40 Jesus said to her, "Did I not tell you that if you woke up, you would see the glory of God?" 41 Then they removed the stone from the place where the dead man lay. Jesus looked up and said, "Father, I thank you that you have heard me. 42 I know that you always listen to me, but because of the people stand- ing nearby, I have said this so that they may see that you have sent me." 43 After saying these things, he cried out in a loud voice, "Lazarus, come here." 44 Then he who had died came out, bound hand and foot with bandages, and his face was bound with a napkin. Jesus said to them, "Unbind him and let him go." 45 Then many of those present, who had come from Mary and had seen the things Jesus had done, believed in him. 46 But some of them went to the Pharisees and told them the things Jesus had done. 47 Then the priests and Pharisees gathered in council and said, "What shall we do? For this man does many miracles. 48 If we leave him alone, all men will fall in love with him, and the Romans will come and take away our place and nation." 49 Then one of them named Caiaphas, who was the priest in that same year, said to them, "You do not perceive anything at all, 50 and yet you do not consider that it is fitting for the people that one man should die for the people and that the whole nation should not perish." 51 This he did not say himself, but being a priest in that same year, he prophesied that Jesus would die for that nation: 52 and not for that nation only, but to gather into one the children of God who were scattered. 53 From that day forward they consulted to put him to death. 54 There- fore Jesus no longer walked openly among the Gentiles, but went away to a county closer to the wilderness, to a town called Ephraim, and there he stayed with his disciples. 55 The Passing of the Youngest was near, and many went out of the county to Jerusalem before the Passing, to purify themselves. 56 So they sought Jesus and talked among themselves as they stood in the Temple, "What do you think, that he does not come to the Feast? 57 The high priests and Pharisees had given orders that if anyone knew where he was, to show him, that they might take him.

CHAPTER 12

1 Then Jesus, six days before the Passer, came to Bethany, where Lazarus was, who had died and whom he had raised from the dead. 2 There they prepared a supper for him, and Martha served; but Lazarus was one of those who sat at table with him. 3 Then Mary took a pound of very costly oil of ears of corn, and anointed Jesus' feet and dried his feet with her hands, and the house was filled with the smell of the oil. 4 Then one of his disciples said, "Iu- das Iscariot, son of Simon, who would betray him." 5 Why was not this oyntment sold for three hundred pence and given to the poor? 6 He said this not because he cared for the poor, but because he was a theologian and had the purse and took away what was given to him. 7 Then Iesus said, "Let it be; against the day of my burial he kept it." 8 For the poor are al- ways with you, but I am not always with you." 9 Then many people of the village noticed that he was there; and they came not only for Jesus, but also to see Lazarus, whom he had raised from the dead. 10 The priests there- fore consulted to put Lazarus to death also, 11 for because of him many of the faithful went away and believed in Jesus. 12 The next day a great multitude of people who had come to the banquet when they heard that Jesus was coming to Jerusalem, 13 took palm branches and went out to meet him, crying, "Hosan- na, blessed is the king of Israel who comes in the name of the Lord." 14 Jesus found a long plank and sat down on it, as it is written, 15 Fear not, daughter of Zion: behold, your King comes sitting on a pack ass. 16 But his disci- ples at first did not understand these things; but when Jesus was glorified, they remem- bered that these things were written about him and that they had done these things for him. 17 The people who were with him testi- fied that he had called Lazarus from the grave and raised him from the dead. 18 Therefore the people also came to him, because they had heard that he had done this miracle. 19 The Pharisees said among themselves, "How can you do nothing? Behold, the world goes after him." 20 Now there were some Greeks among them who had come to worship at the feast. 21 They came to Philip, who was from Bethsaida in Galilee, and sought him, saying, "Lord, we want to see that Jesus." 22 Philip came and talked with Andrew; and again Andrew and Philip talked with Jesus. 23 Jesus answered them, saying, "The hour has come for the Son of Man to be glorified. 24 Verily, verily, I say to you, unless the grain of wheat falls into the earth and dies, it remains alone; but if it dies, it bears much fruit. 25 Whoever loves his life will lose it, and whoever hates his life in this world will keep it for eternal life. 26 If anyone serves me, let him follow me; for where I am, there will my servant be also; and if anyone serves me, my Father will honor him. 27 Now my soul is troubled; and what shall I say? Fa- ther, save me from this hour; but for this I have come to this hour. 28 Father, glorify Your Name." Then came a message from Heauen saying, "I have glorified Him and will glori- fy Him again." 29 Then the people who were standing nearby and had heard said it was thunder; others said, "An angel spoke to him." 30 Jesus answered and said, "This journey did not take place because of me, but because of you." 31 Now is the judgment of this world; now the prince of this world shall be cast out. 32 And I, if I were lifted up from the earth, would drag all men to me. 33 Now he said this, indicating what death he was to suffer. 34 And the people answered him, "We have heard from the Law that that Christ offers himself for eternity; and how say you that the Son of Man must be lifted up? Who is this Son of Man? 35 Then Jesus said to them, "Yet a lit- tle while the light is with you; walk while you have this light, lest darkness come upon you; for he who walks in darkness does not know where he is going. 36 As long as you have the light, be in it, that you may be children of the light." These things Jesus said, then He went away and hid Himself from them. 37 And though he had done many miracles before them, they did not trust him, 38 that the say- ing of Esaias the prophet might be fulfilled, saying, "Lord, who has betrayed our testimo- ny? And to whom is the weapon of the Lord entrusted? 39 Therefore they could not blind themselves, for Esaias says again, 40 He has blinded their eyes and hardened their hearts, that they may not see with their eyes and un- derstand with their hearts, and that they may be convinced and I may heal them. 41 These things Esaias said when he saw his glory and spoke of him. 42 Many believed in him, even among the rulers, but because of the Phari- sees they did not confess him, lest they should be cast out of the synagogue. 43 For they gave more heed to the prayers of men than to the prayers of God. 44 Jesus cried out and said, "He who believes in me does not believe in me, but in him who sent me." 45 Whoever sees me sees the one who sent me. 46 I have come as a light into the world, so that those who rise up in me may not remain in darkness. 47 And if anyone hears my words and does not follow them, I will not judge him; for I have not come to judge the world, but to save the world. 48 Anyone who rejects me and does not receive my words has one who judges him; the word I have spoken will judge him on the last day. 49 For I have not spoken from myself, but the Father who sent me gave me commandment to speak and to speak. 50 And I know that his command is eternal life; therefore the things that I say, I say as the Father has told me.

CHAPTER 13

1 Now before the Feast of the Passover, when Jesus knew that his hour had come to depart from this world to the Father, because he had loved his own who were in the world, to the end he had loved them. 2 And when the sup- per was finished (and which wickedness had now put into the heart of Iudas Iscariot, son of Simon, to betray him) 3 Jesus, knowing that the Father had given all things into his hands and that he had gone out from God and was going to God, 4 He rose from the supper, laid down his garments, took a towel and girded himself. 5 Then he put water in a basin and began to wash the disciples' feet and dry them with the towel with which he was girded. 6 Then he approached Simon Peter, who said to him, "Lord, will you wash my feet?" 7 Jesus answered and said to him, "What I do, you do not know now, but you will know later." 8 Peter said to him, "You will never wash my feet." Jesus answered him, "If I do not wash you, you will have no part with me." 9 Simon Peter said to him, "Lord, not only my feet, but also my hands and my head." 10 Jesus said to him, "He who has been washed does not need to wash his feet, but is clean in every part; and you are clean, but not all." 11 Because he knew who would betray him, he said, "You are not all clean." 12 So after he had washed their feet, taken his garments and sat down again, he said to them, "Do you know what I have done to you? 13 You call me Master and Lord, and you say well, for so I am. 14 If therefore I, your

Lord and Master, have washed your feet, you also must wash one another's feet. 15 For I have given you an example, that you may do as I have done to you. 16 Verily, verily, I say unto you, the servant is not greater than his master, nor the ambassador greater than he that sent him. 17 If you know these things, blessed are you if you do them. 18 I do not speak of all of you; I know whom I have chosen, but it is so that the Scripture may be ful- filled, "Whoever eats bread with me shall lift up his head against me." 19 From now on I will tell you before he comes, so that when it has happened you may understand that I am he. 20 Verily, verily, I say unto you, if I send any man, he that receiveth him receiveth me, and he that receiveth me receiveth him that sent me. 21 And when Jesus had said these things, he was troubled in the Spirit, and testified, and said, Verily, verily, I say unto you, one of you shall betray me. 22 Then the disciples looked at one another, doubting whom he was talking about. 23 Now there was one of his disciples, leaning on Jesus' chest, whom Jesus had heard. 24 Simon Peter turned to him so that he might ask who it was of whom he was speaking. 25 He then, as he leaned on Jesus' breast, said to him, "Lord, who is he?" 26 Jesus answered, "It is he to whom I will give a nap, when I have dipped it"; and he dipped a nap and gave it to Iudas Iscariot, son of Simon. 27 And after the nap, Satan entered him. Then Jesus said to him, "What you do, do it quick- ly." 28 But none of those at the table knew for what reason he had spoken to him. 29 For some thought that because Iudas had the purse, Iesus had said to him, "Buy the things we need for the banquet," or that he should give something to the poor. 30 As soon as he had received the bag, he went out immedi- ately, as night was breaking. 31 When he had gone out, Jesus said, "Now the Son of Man is glorified, and God is glorified in him. 32 If God has been glorified in him, God will also glorify him in himself and glorify him im- mediately. 33 Little children, for a little while longer I am with you; you will see me, but as I said to the babes, "Where I go, you cannot come," even to you I say now, 34 I give you a new command: that you love one another; as I have loved you, you also love one another. 35 By this everyone will know that you are my disciples, if you have love for one another." 36 Simon Peter said to him, "Lord, where are you going?" Jesus answered him, "Where I go, you cannot follow me now; but you will follow me later." 37 Peter said to him, "Lord, why can't I follow you now? I will lay down my life for your sake." 38 Jesus answered him, "Will you lay down your life for my sake? Verily, verily, I say to you, the rooster will not croak until you deny me three times.

CHAPTER 14

1 Let not your heart be troubled: ye are in God, and ye are also in me. 2 In the house of my fathers are many mansions; if it were not so, I would have told you, I go to prepare a place for you. 3 And if I go to prepare a place for you, I will come again and receive you into myself, so that where I am, you may be also. 4 You know where I am going, and you also know the way." 5 Thomas said to him, "Lord, we do not know where you are going; how then can we know your way?" 6 Jesus said to him, "I am that way, that truth and that life. No one comes to the Father except through me. 7 If you had known me, you would have known my Father also; and from now on you know him and have seen him. 8 Philip said to him, "Lord, speak to your Father, and it will be enough for you." 9 Jesus said to him, "Have I been so long with you, and have you not known me, Philip? He who

has seen me has also seen my Father; how then can you say, 'Speak against your Father'?" 10 Do you not believe that I am in the Father and the Father is in me? The words I say to you I do not speak from myself, but it is the Father who dwells in me who does the works. 11 Grant me that I am in the Father and the Father is in me; at least, grant me for the works themselves. 12 Verily, verily, I say unto you, that whosoever believeth in me, the works that I do he shall do also, and he shall do greater works, because I go unto my Father. 13 And whatever you ask in my Name, I will do, that the Father may be glorified in the Son. 14 If you ask anything in my Name, I will do it. 15 If you love me, keep my commands, 16 I will pray to the Father, and he will give you another Comforter, that he may abide with you forever, 17 the Spirit of truth, whom the world cannot receive, for it neither sees him nor knows him; but you know him, for he dwells with you and will abide in you. 18 I will not leave you fathers, but will come to you. 19 A little while longer, and the world will not see me, but you will see me; for I live, you also will live. 20 In that day you shall know that I am in my Father, and you in me, and I in you. 21 He that hath my com- mands, and keepeth them, is he that loveth me: and he that loveth me shall be loved of my Father: and I will love him, and do him hom- age. 22 Iudas said to him (not Iscariot), "Lord, what is the reason why you want to give your face to him and not to the world?" 23 Jesus answered and said to him, "If anyone loves me, he will keep my word, and my Father will love him, and we will come to him and dwell with him. 24 Whoever does not hear me, does not keep my words; and the word you hear is not mine, but the Father's who sent me. 25 These things I have told you, being present with you. 26 But the Comforter, who is the Holy Spirit, whom the Father will send in my Name, will teach you all things, and bring to your remembrance all the things that I have spoken to you. 27 I leave you peace; my peace I give you; not as the world does, I give it to you. Let not your heart be troubled or afraid. 28 You have heard how I said to you, "I leave and will come to you." If you appreciated me, you would reconsider, for I said, "I am going to the Father," for the Father is greater than I am. 29 And now I have spoken to you, before he comes, so that when he is past, you may be received. 30 Thereafter I will speak to you no more of many things, because the prince of this world comes and has nothing in me. 31 But it is so that the world may know that I love my Father; and as the Father has commanded me, so I do. Arise, let us depart.

CHAPTER 15

1 I am the true vine, and my Father is the hus- bandman. 2 Every branch that does not bear fruit in me, he takes away; and every branch that bears fruit, he purifies so that it bears more fruit. 3 Now you are pure because of the word that I have spoken to you. 4 Abide in me, and I in you; just as the branch cannot bear fruit of itself, unless it abides in the vine, nei- ther can you, unless you abide in me. 5 I am the vine, you are the branches; he who abides in me and I in him produces much fruit, for without me you can do nothing. 6 If one does not abide in me, he is cast away like a branch and withers; men gather them, throw them into the fire, and they are burned. 7 If you abide in me and my words abide in you, ask what you will and it will be done to you. 8 In this my Father is glorified, who makes you fruitful greatly and makes you my disciples. 9 As the Father has welcomed me, so I have wel- comed you; continue in this my welcome. 10 If you keep my commands, you will remain in

my grace, just as I have kept my Father's com- mands and remained in his grace. 11 These things I have said to you, that my I may abide in you and that your I may be full. 12 This is my command: that you love one another, as I have loved you. 13 No one has greater love than this, when one lays down his life for his friends. 14 You are my friends, if you do what I have commanded you. 15 From now on I will no longer call you servants, because the servant does not know what his master does; but I have called you friends, because all the things I have heard from my Father I have made known to you. 16 You have not chosen me, but I have chosen you, and I have com- manded you to go and bear fruit, and let your fruit remain, so that whatever you ask of the Father in my Name, he will grant you. 17 These things I have told you, that you may love one another. 18 If the world hates you, you know that before you it hated me. 19 If you were of the world, the world would love its own; but because you are not of the world, but I have chosen you out of the world, the world hates you. 20 Remember the word I told you, "The servant is not greater than his master." If they have persecuted me, they will also persecute you; if they have kept my word, they will also keep yours. 21 But all these things they will do because of my names, because they have not known him who sent me. 22 If I had not come and spoken to them, they would not have sin; but now they have no cloak for their sin. 23 Whoever hates me hates my Father also. 24 If I had not done among them works that no other man did, they would not have had sin; but now they have seen both, and they have hated both me and my Father. 25 But it is so that the word written in their Bible would be fulfilled, "They hated Me without cause." 26 But when the Comforter comes whom I will send to you from the Father, that is, the Spirit of truth who proceeds from the Father, he will testify of me. 27 And you also will testify, for you have been with me from the beginning.

CHAPTER 16

1 I told you these things so that you would not be offended. 2 They will excommunicate you; yes, the time will come when those who kill you will think that they are doing God a service. 3 And these things they will do to you, because they have known neither the Father nor me. 4 But these things I have said to you so that when the hour comes, you may remem- ber that I have said them to you. And these things I did not tell you from the beginning, for I was with you. 5 But now I go my way to him who sent me, and not one of you asks me, "Where are you going?" 6 But because I have told you these things, your hearts are filled with sadness. 7 But I tell you the truth: it is expedient for you that I go away; for if I do not go away, the Comforter will not come to you; but if I go away, I will send him to you. 8 And when he is come, he will take back the world from sin and from righteousness and from judgment. 9 Of sin, because they have not believed in me: 10 Of righteousness, because I go to my Father, and you shall not see me again: 11 Of righteousness, because the prince of this world has been judged. 12 I still have many things to say to you, but you cannot bear them now. 13 Nevertheless, when he who is the Spirit of truth comes, he will guide you into all truth, for he will not speak of himself, but will speak of what he hears, and will show you things to come. 14 He will glorify me, for he will receive my information and report it to you. 15 All that the Father has is mine; there- fore I said that he will take of mine and pass it on to you. 16 A little longer, and you will not see me; a little longer, and you will see me,

for I am going to the Father." 17 Then some of his disciples said among themselves, "What is this that says to you, 'Yet a little while and you will not see me'; and yet a little while and you will see me, for I go to the Father." 18 They said therefore, "What is this that says, 'Yet a little while'? We do not know what it says." 19 Now Jesus, knowing that they would question him, said to them, "Ask among yourselves whether I said, 'A little while longer and you will not see me'; and again, 'A little while longer and you will see me'?" 20 Verily, verily, I say unto you, ye shall weep and lament, and the world shall weep again; and ye shall afflict yourselves, but your affliction shall be turned into joy. 21 And the woman, when she is in travail, is afflicted, because her hour is come; but when her son is delivered to her, she remembers no more her anguish, for it is a man that is brought into the world. 22 Now therefore you are in sor- row; but I will see you again, and your hearts will be revived, and your joy will not be taken away from you by anyone. 23 In that day you shall not ask me for anything. Verily, verily, I say unto you, whatsoever ye shall ask of the Father in My Name, He will give it you. 24 Hitherto you have asked nothing in my Name; ask and you shall receive, that your joy may be full. 25 These things I have spoken to you in parables; but the time will come when I will no longer speak to you in parables, but will speak to you plainly of the Father. 26 In that day you will ask in My Name, and I will not tell you that I will pray to the Father for you: 27 For the Father Himself loves you, because you loved Me and believed that I came forth from God. 28 I went out from the Father and came into the world; again I leave the world and go to the Father." 29 His disciples said to him, "Behold, now you speak plainly and do not make parables. 30 Now we know that you know everything and do not need any- one to ask you. From this we conclude that you have come forth from God." 31 Jesus an- swered them, "Do you now realize? 32 Behold, the hour cometh, and is already come, when every one shall scatter for himself and leave me alone; but I am not alone, for the Father is with me. 33 These things have I spoken unto you, that in me ye may have peace: in the world ye shall have afflictions, but ye shall be of good comfort: I am gone out of the world.

CHAPTER 17

1 These things Jesus said, and lifted up his eyes and said, "Father, the hour is come: glo- rify your Son, that your Son also may glorify you, 2 For thou hast given him power over all flesh, that he may give eternal life to all whom thou hast given him. 3 And this is eternal life: that they may know that you are the only God and that you sent Jesus Christ. 4 I have glori- fied you on earth; I have completed the work you gave me to do. 5 And now glorify me, you Father, with yourself, with the glory that I had with you before the world was. 6 I declared thy name to the men whom thou didst bring me out of the world: they were thine, and thou didst make them to be me, and they kept thy word. 7 Now they know that all things which thou hast given me are from thee. 8 For I have given them the words which thou hast given me, and they have received them, and have known with certainty that I came forth from thee, and have believed that thou hast sent me. 9 I pray for them: I pray not for the world, but for those whom thou hast given me, for they are thine. 10 All mine are thine, and thine are mine, and I am glorified in them. 11 And now I am no longer in the world, but these are in the world and I come to you. Holy Fa- ther, keep them in your Name, even those whom

you have given me, that they may be one, as we are one. 12 While I was with them in the world, I kept them in your Name; those whom you entrusted to me I kept, and not one of them was lost except the son of perdi- tion, that the Scripture might be fulfilled. 13 Now I come to you, and these things I have spoken to the world, that my will might be fulfilled in them. 14 I gave them your word, and the world hated them, because they are not of the world, as I am not of the world. 15 I do not beg you to take them out of the world, but to preserve them from death. 16 They are not of the world, as I am not of the world. 17 Sanctify them with your truth: your word is true. 18 As thou hast sent me into the world, even so have I sent them into the world. 19 And for them I sanctify myself, that they also may be sanctified through the truth. 20 I pray not only for these, but also for those who will be covenanted in me, through their work, 21 That they may all be one, as you, O Father, are in me, and I in you; and that they also may be one in you, that the world may see that you have sent me. 22 And the glory that you have given me, I have given to them, that they may be one, as we are one, 23 I in them and you in me, that they may be perfected into one, and that the world may know that you sent me and received them as you received me. 24 Father, I want those you have given me to be with me where I am, to see my glory that you have giv- en me, for you gave me before the foundation of the world. 25 O righteous Father, even the world has not known you, but I have known you, and these have known that you have sent me. 26 And I have declared and will declare your name, that the grace with which you loved me may be in them and I in them.

CHAPTER 18

1 When Iesus had said these things, he went with his disciples beyond the Cedron brook, where there was a garden, into which he entered with his disciples. 2 Iudas, who ac- companied him, also knew the place, for Iesus often went there with his disciples. 3 Then Iudas, having received a group of men and officers from the high priests and Phar- isees, came there with lanterns, flashlights and weapons. 4 Then Jesus, knowing all that was to happen, approached and said to them, "Who do you see?" 5 They answered him, "Je- sus of Nazareth." Jesus said to them, "I am he." Now Iudas, who had betrayed him, was also with them. 6 When he said to them, "I am he," they went backward and fell to the ground. 7 Then he asked them again, "Who sees you?" And they said, "Jesus of Nazareth." 8 Jesus an- swered, "I have told you that I am he; there- fore, if you see me, let these go their way." 9 This was so that the word he said might be fulfilled, "Of those you have entrusted to me, I have lost none." 10 Then Simon Peter took a sword and drew it and struck the servant of the priests, cutting off his right ear. The ser- vant's name was Malchus. 11 Then Jesus said to Peter, "Put your sword back in its sheath; must I not drink of the cup that my Father has given me?" 12 Then the band and the captain and the officers of the Indies took Jesus and bound him, 13 and they led him first to Annas (who was the father of Caiaphas, who was the priest in that same year). 14 And Caiaphas was the one who gave counsel to the leaders that it was fitting for a man to die for the people. 15 Now Simon Peter followed Jesus and anoth- er disciple, who knew the priest; therefore he entered with Jesus into the priest's hall: 16 But Peter stood by. Then the other disciple, who was known to the priest, went out and spoke to the one who guarded the hall

and brought Peter in. 17 Then the woman who kept the house said to Peter, "Are you not also one of this man's disciples? He answered, "I am not." 18 Then the servants and officers stood there, who had kindled a fire of coles; because it was cold, they warmed themselves. Peter also stood among them and warmed himself. 19 The priest asked Jesus about his disciples and his doctrine. 20 Jesus answered him, "I have spoken openly to the world: I have always taught in the Synagogue and in the Temple, where visitors continually recur, and in secret I have said nothing. 21 Why do you ask me? Ask those who have heard me what I have said to them; behold, they know what I have said." 22 When he had said these things, one of the officers standing nearby struck Jesus with his rod, saying, "Do you answer the priest this way? 23 Jesus answered him, "If I have spoken evil, bear witness to the truth; but if I have spoken good, why do you strike me? 24 Now Annas had sent him to Caiaphas the priest and told him to do nothing).25 Simon Peter stood still and warmed himself, and they said to him, "Are not you also one of his disciples? He denied and said, "I am not." 26 One of the priest's servants, his cousin, whose head Pe- ter had cut off, said, "Did I not see you in the garden with him? 27 Peter then denied again, and immediately the cock grew. 28 Then they led Jesus to Caiaphas in the common room. It was now morning, and they themselves did not enter the common room, lest they defile themselves, but to eat the Past. 29 Then Pi- late came out to them and said, "What charge do you bring against this man? 30 Those an- swered and said to him, "If he had not been an evildoer, we would not have handed him over to you." 31 Then Pilate said to them, "Take him and judge him according to your law." Then the witnesses said to him, "It is not lawful for you to put a man to death." 32 It was desired that the word of Jesus that he had spoken, in- dicating what death he should suffer, should be fulfilled. 33 Pilate again entered the com- mon room, called Jesus, and said to him, "Are you the king of the Jews? 34 Jesus answered him, "Do you know this for yourself, or have others told you from me?" 35 Pilate answered, "Am I a Jew? Your nation and the priests have handed you over to me. What have you done? 36 Jesus answered, "My kingdom is not of this world; if my kingdom were of this world, my servants would fight not to hand me over to the Jews; but now my kingdom is not from here." 37 Pilate then said to him, "Are you then a king?" Jesus answered, "You say that I am a king; for this I was born, and for this I came into the world, to bear witness to the truth; everyone who is of the truth hears my word." 38 Pilate said to him, "What is truth?" And when he had said this, he went out again to the witnesses and said to them, "I find no cause in him." 39 But you have an obligation that I should deliver you one loose at the pas- sage; do you therefore want me to loose the king of yourselves? 40 Then they all cried out again, saying, "Not he, but Barabbas; now this Barabbas was a murderer."

CHAPTER 19

1 Then Pilate took Jesus and had him scourged. 2 And the soldiers put a crown of thorns on his head, and put a robe of pur- ple on him, 3 And they said, "Haile, king of the Themis." And they struck him with their sticks. 4 Then Pilate went away again and said to them, "Behold, I present him to you so that you may know that I find no fault in him." 5 Then Jesus came with a crown of thorns and a robe of purple. And Pilate said to them, "Be- hold the man." 6 When the priests and offi- cers saw him, they cried out,

"Crucify him, crucify him." Pilate said to them, "Take him and crucify him, for I find no fault in him." 7 The witnesses answered him, "We have a law, and by our law he must die, because he called himself the Son of God." 8 When Pilate heard these words, he was even more frightened, 9 and entering the common room again, he said to Jesus, "Where are you? But Jesus gave him no answer. 10 Then Pilate said to him, "Do you not speak to me? Do you not know that I have power to crucify you and have power to set you free? 11 Jesus answered, "You could have no power against me, unless it were given to you from without; therefore he who delivered me to you has the greater sin." 12 From that time Pilate tried to release him, but the wit- nesses cried out, "If you hand him over, you will not be Caesar's friend; for he who makes himself king speaks against Caesar." 13 When Pilate heard these words, he led Jesus home and sat in the judgment seat in a place called Pauement and, in Hebrew, Gabbatha 19:14 It was the preparation of the Passover, about six o'clock, and he said to the Jews, "Here is your king." 15 But they cried out, "Away with him, away with him, crucify him." Pilate said to them, "Shall I crucify your king?" The high priests answered, "We have no king but Cae- sar." 16 Then he handed him over to them to be crucified. And they took Jesus and led him away. 17 And he astride them and came to a place called "of the skulls of the dead," which in Hebrew is called Golgotha: 18 where they crucified him, and two others with him, on ei- ther side, and Jesus in between. 19 Pilate also wrote a title and placed it on the cross, "JESUS OF NAZARETH, KING OF THE JEWS." 20 This title was read by many Jews, because the place where Jesus was crucified was near the city, and it was written in Hebrew, Greek and Lat- in. 21 Then the priests of the Iewes said to Pi- late, "Do not write, The king of the Iewes, but that he said, I am the king of the Iewes." 22 Pilate answered, "What I have written, I have written." 23 Then the armigers, after they had crucified Jesus, took his garments (and they made four parts of them, to each armigers one part) and his cloak; and the cloak was seamless from top to bottom. 24 Therefore they said to one another, "Do not decide, but cast lots, whose it shall be." This was so that the Scripture would be fulfilled which says, "They divided my garments among them and cast lots for my cloak." So the souls did these things in surrender. 25 Then they stood by the cross of Jesus his mother and his mother's sis- ter, Mary the wife of Cleopas, and Mary Mag- dalene. 26 When Jesus saw his mother and the disciple standing, whom he valued, he said to his mother, "Woman, look at your son." 27 Then he said to the disciple, "Here is your mother"; and from that time the disciple took her to his house. 28 When he had ascertained that all things had been fulfilled, so that the Scripture might be fulfilled, Iesus said, "I am thirsty." 29 Then a vessel full of wine was placed; they filled a sponge with wine, put it around a stall of hyssop, and put it in his mouth. 30 When Iesus had received the wine, he said, "It is finished," bowed his head, and left the ghost. 31 Then the witnesses (for it had been decreed that the dead bodies should not remain on the cross on the Sabbath day, for the Sabbath was a feast day) asked Pilate that their legs be broken and that they be brought down. 32 Then the soldiers came and broke the legs of the first and the other, who had been crucified with Jesus. 33 But when they came to Jesus and saw that he was already dead, they did not break his legs. 34 But one of the soldiers pierced his side with a spear, and immediately blood and water came out. 35 He who related it has given an account of it, and his account is true; and he knows that he speaks the truth, so that you may know. 36 For these things were done that the Scripture might be fulfilled, "Not a bone of him shall be broken." 37 And another Scripture says, "They shall see him whom they have pierced." 38 After these things, Joseph of Arimathea (who was a disciple of Jesus, but in secret for fear of witnesses) asked Pilate if he could take Je- sus' body away. And Pilate gave him permis- sion. So he came and took the body of Jesus. 39 Nicodemus (who had first come to Jesus by night) also came and brought myrrh and al- oes mixed together about a hundred pounds. 40 Then they took Jesus' body and wrapped it in linen cloths with odors, as is customary for Jews to bury. 41 In that place where Jesus had been crucified there was a garden, and in the garden a new tomb, where no man had yet been laid. 42 There therefore they laided Ie- sus, because of the day of preparation of the Gospels, for the sepulcher was new.

CHAPTER 20

1 On the first day of the week Mary Magda- lene went early, when it was still dark, to the tomb and saw the stone removed from the tomb. :2 Then she ran and came to Simon Peter and the other disciple whom Iesus had called, and said to them, "They have taken the Lord away from the tomb, and we do not know where they have laid him. 20:3 Peter, therefore, and the other disciple went out and came to the tomb. 4 So they ran togeth- er, but the other disciple overtook Peter and came to the tomb first. 5 He lowered himself and saw the linen garments spread out, but he did not enter. 6 Then Simon Peter followed him and entered the tomb and saw the linen garments lying there, 7 and the handkerchief that was on his head did not lie with the linen cloths, but was wrapped together in a place apart. 8 Then the other disciple also came in, who came first to the tomb, and he saw it and was astonished. 9 For they did not yet know the Scripture, that he was to rise from the dead. 10 The disciples went away again to their house. 11 But Mary stood outside the tomb weeping; and as she wept, she prostrat- ed herself in the tomb, 12 and saw two Angels clothed in white, sitting, one at the head and the other at the feet, where the body of Jesus lay. 13 They said to her, "Woman, why are you weeping?" She answered them, "They have taken my Lord away, and I do not know where they have laid him 14 After saying this, she turned back and saw Jesus standing there, not knowing that it was Jesus. 15 Jesus said to her, "Woman, why are you weeping, whom do you seek? She, supposing it was the garden- er, said to him, "Lord, if you have taken him away, tell me where you have laid him, and I will take him away." 16 Jesus said to her, "Ma- rie." She turned and said to him, "Rabboni," that is, "Master." 17 Jesus said to her, "Do not touch me, for I have not yet ascended to my Father; but go to my brothers and tell them, I am ascending to my Father and your Father, to my God and your God." 18 Mary Magda- lene came and told the disciples that she had seen the Lord and that he had told her these things. 19 The same day, by night, which was the first day of the week, and when the doors were shut, where the disciples were gathered together for fear of witnesses, Jesus came and stood in the midst and said to them, "Peace be with you." 20 And having said this, he showed them his hands and his side. Then the disci- ples rejoiced when they saw the Lord. 21 Then he said to them again, "Peace be with you; as my Father has sent me, so I am sending you." 22 And after he had said this, he breathed on them and said to them, "Receive the Holy Spirit. 23 To whom you forgive sins, they shall be forgiven; and to whom

you forgive sins, they shall be forgiven. 24 But Thomas, one of them, called Didymus, was not with them when Jesus came. the Lord"; but he answered them, "Unless I see in his hands the imprint of the nails, unless I put my finger in the im- print of the nails and put my hand in his side, I will not leave him." 26 Eight days later, his disciples were again in the house and Thomas with them. Then when the doors were shut, Jesus came and stood in the midst and said, "Peace be with you." 27 Then he said to Thom- as, "Put your finger here and see my hands; stretch out your hand and put it in my side and do not be unfaithful but faithful." 28 Then Thomas answered and said to him, "You are my Lord and my God." 29 Jesus said to him, "Thomas, because you have seen me, you are faithful; blessed are those who have not seen and are faithful." 30 And many other signs did Jesus do in the presence of his disciples, which are not written in this book. 31 But these things are written that you may under- stand that Jesus is the Christ, the Son of God, and that you may have life in his name.

CHAPTER 21

1 After these things, Jesus presented himself again to his disciples by the Sea of Tiberias; and so he presented himself: 2 There were together Simon Peter, Thomas, called Didy- mus, Nathanael of Cana of Galilee, the sons of Zebedee, and two others of his disciples. 3 Si- mon Peter said to them, "I am going fishing." They answered him, "We will also go with you." They went their way and immediately entered a ship, and that night they took nothing. 4 But when it was now morning, Jesus stood on the shore; yet the disciples did not notice that it was Jesus. 5 Then Jesus said to them, "Sisters, do you have any food? They answered him, "No." 6 Then He said to them, "Cast the net from the right side of the ship and you will find." So they cast the net and could not pull it at all, because of the multitude of fish. 7 Therefore the disciple whom Jesus had called said to Peter, "It is the Lord." When Simon Pe- ter heard that it was the Lord, he girded his cloak (for he was naked) and threw himself into the sea. 8 But the other disciples came with the ship (for they were not far from land but about two hundred cubits) and took out the net with the fish. 9 When they had come ashore, they saw wooden boxes, with fish and bread. 10 Jesus said to them, "Bring the fish you have caught." 11 Simon Peter went out and cast the net ashore, full of large fish, a hundred, fifty and three; and though there were so many, the net did not break. 12 Jesus said to them, "Come and dine." And none of the disciples dared to ask him, "Who are you?" for they knew that he was the Lord. 13 Then Je- sus came and took bread and gave it to them, and also the fish. 14 This was the third time that Jesus showed himself to his disciples, af- ter he had risen from the dead. 15 When they had dined, Jesus said to Simon Peter, "Simon, son of Iona, do you hear me more than these? He answered him, "Yes, Lord, you know that I love you." He said to him, "Feed my lambs."16 He said to him again, "Simon, son of Iona, do you love me?" He said to him, "Yes, Lord, you know that I love you." He said to him, "Feed my sheep." 17 He said to him a third time, "Simon, son of Iona, do you love me?" Peter was sorry because he had said to him for the third time, "Do you love me?" and said to him, "Lord, you know everything; you know that I love you." Jesus said to him, "Shepherd my sheep." 18 Verily, verily, I say unto thee, when thou wast young, thou girdedst thyself, and walked whither thou wouldst; but when thou art old, thou shalt stretch forth thy hands, and another shall gird thee, and lead thee whither thou wilt not." 19 Thus he spoke, indicating by what death he should glorify God. And having said this, he said to him, "Follow me." 20 Then Peter turned around and saw that he was fol- lowing the disciple whom JESUS had heard, who had leaned on his breast at supper and said, "Lord, who is the one who betrayed you? 21 When therefore Peter saw him, he said to Jesus, "Lord, what is this man to do?" 22 Je- sus said to him, "If I want him to stay until I come, what do you care? Follow me." 23 Then this word spread among the brothers, so that this disciple would not die. But Jesus did not say to him, "He will not die"; but if I want him to stay until I come, what do you care? 24 This is the disciple who testifies of these things and has written these things, and we know that his testimony is true. 25 There are also many other things that Iesus did, and if they were to be written all of them, I suppose the world could not count the books that should be written, Amen.

ACTS OF THE APOSTLES

This book narrates the early spread of Christianity by the disciples

ACTS

CHAPTER 1

1 I have already spoken, O Theophilus, of all that Jesus began to do and teach, 2 until the day He was raptured, after He had given or- ders through the Holy Spirit to the apostles whom He had chosen: 3 To these he presented himself even after suffering, with many infal- lible signs, being seen by them for the space of forty days, and speaking those things which relate to the kingdom of God. 4 And when he had gathered them together, he command- ed them not to depart from Jerusalem, but to wait for the promise of the Father, who said, "You have heard of me." 5 For Iohn inede baptized with water, but you will be baptized with the Holy Spirit within these few days. 6 When they were therefore gathered together, they questioned him, saying, "Lord, will you at this time restore the kingdom to Israel?" 7 He said to them, "It is not for you to know the times and seasons that the Father has placed in his power, 8 but you shall receive the power of the Holy Spirit when he comes upon you; and you shall be witnesses to me in Jerusa- lem, and in all Judea, and in Samaria, and to the uttermost part of the earth." 9 When he had said these things, while they were look- ing, he was raptured, for a cloud took him out of their sight. 10 And while they were looking intently toward him, as he went away, be- hold, two men stood beside them, clothed in white, 11 who said, "You men of Galilee, why are you entering heaven? This Iesus who was taken away from you in Eauen will come just as you saw him go into Eauen." 12 Then they returned to Jerusalem from the mountain called the Mount of Olives, which is near Jeru- salem and from which they set out on a Sab- bath journey. 13 When they had arrived, they entered an upper chamber, where were Peter and Iames, Iohn, Andrew, Philip, Thomas, Bartlemew, Matthewe, Iames son of Alpheus, Simon Zelotes, and Iudas brother of Iames. 14 All of them continued to pray and supplicate together with the women, Mary the mother of Jesus, and his brothers. 15 In those days Peter stood in the midst of the disciples and said (now the

names that were in the same place were about a hundred and twenty). 16 Men and brethren, it is necessary for this Scripture to have been fulfilled, which the Holy Spirit, by the mouth of Dauid, spoke before Iudas, who was a guide for those who took Jesus. 17 For he had been baptized with Yourself and had obtained to participate in this ministry. 18 Therefore he purchased a field with the re- ward of iniquity; and when he threw himself headlong, he broke in the middle, and all his bowels gushed out. 19 This fact is known to all the inhabitants of Jerusalem, so that that field is called in their language Aceldama, that is, the field of blood. 20 For in the book of Psalms it is written, "Let his dwelling be empty, and let no one dwell therein"; and again, "Let an- other take care of him." 21 Therefore of these men who attended vv, for as long as the Lord Iesus attended vv, 22 beginning from the bap- tism of John until the day he was taken away from you, one of them must be made a wit- ness with you of his resurrection. 23 They pre- sented two of them, Ioseph, called Barsabas, whose surname was Iustus, and Matthias. 24 They praised, saying, "Lord, who knows the hearts of all men, tell me whether you have chosen these two, 25 that I may take the wit- ness of this ministry and apostleship, from which Iudas has departed, to go in his place. 26 Then the lot was cast; the lot fell on Matthi- as, who was by common consent numbered among the other apostles.

CHAPTER 2

1 When the day of Pentecost came, they were all together in the same place. 2 Suddenly a sound was heard from above, as of a rushing mighty wind, which filled the whole house where they were. 3 And there appeared to them cloudy tongues, as of fire, and they rest- ed on each of them. 4 And they were all filled with the Holy Spirit and began to speak with other tongues, as the Spirit gave them power to speak. 5 There lived in Jerusalem men who feared God, from every nation and from every country. 6 When this was heard, the crowds gathered and were amazed, for each one heard them speaking in his own language. 7 They marveled and wondered, saying among themselves, "But are not these who speak all from Galilee? 8 How then can we each know our own language, in which we were born? 9 Parthians, Medes, Elamites, and inhabitants of Mesopotamia, Iudea, Cappadocia, Pontus, and Asia, 10 of Phrygia, Pamphylia, Egypt, the parts of Libya that are next to Cyrene, the foreigners of Rome, the Iewes and pros- elytes, 11 Cretans and Arabs; we heard them speaking in our own languages of the won- derful works of God. 12 All then were amazed and dismayed, saying to one another, "What shall it be? 13 Others mocked and said, "They are full of new wine." 14 But Peter, standing with you, lifted up his voice and said to them, "Men of Judea and inhabitants of Jerusalem, know this and listen to my words. 15 For these are not drunk, as you think, since it is only the third hour of the day. 16 But this is what was spoken by the prophet Joel, 17 In the last days, says God, I will pour out my Spirit on all flesh, and your sons and your daughters will prophesy, your young men will see visions, and your old men will fall asleep. 18 And upon my servants and upon my handmaidens I will send forth my Spirit in those days, and they shall prophesy. 19 I will perform miracles in heaven and signs on the earth below, blood, fire and vapor of smoke. 20 The sun will turn to darkness and the moon to blood, be- fore that great and notable day of the LORD comes. 21 Whoever shall call upon the name of the LORD shall be saved. 22 You, men of Israel, hear these words, JESUS of Nazareth, a man acknowledged by God in your midst with great works, wonders and signs, which God did through him in your midst, as you yourselves know: 23 He, I say, who was deliv- ered according to the determined counsel and foreknowledge of God, after you took him, with wicked hands crucified and killed him. 24 Whom God raised up and loosed from the pain of death, because it was impossible for him to be restrained by it. 25 For Dauid says of him, "I always saw the Lord before me, for he is at my right hand, that I may not be shak- en. 26 Therefore my heart has rejoiced and my tongue has rejoiced, and more still shall my flesh rest in hope, 27 For thou wilt not leave my soul in the grave, nor allow thy Holy One to see corruption. 28 Thou hast shown me the ways of life, and thou wilt make me full of joy by thy sight. 29 Men and brethren, may I speak to you boldly of the patriarch Dauid, who died and was buried, and his sepulcher has remained with us to this day. 30 There- fore, for he was a prophet and knew that God had sworn to him by another person that, for the fruit of his faithfulness, he would raise up Christ in the flesh, to set him on his throne, 31 And he, knowing this, spoke of the res- urrection of Christ, that his soul might not remain in the grave, and his flesh might not see corruption. 32 This Jesus was raised from the dead by God, and we are all witnesses of this. 33 For then he, by the right hand of God, was exalted and received from the Father the promise of the Holy Spirit, he poured out this which you now see and hear. 34 For Dauid did not ascend into heaven, but says, "The Lord said to my Lord, 'Sit at my right hand, 35 Until I have made your enemies your feet. 36 Therefore let all the house of Israel know with certainty that God has made him Lord and Christ, this Jesus, I say, whom you cru- cified." 37 Now on hearing this, they felt their hearts pricked and said to Peter and the other apostles, "Men and brothers, what shall we do?" 38 Then Peter said to them, "Change your ways and be baptized all of you in the name of Jesus Christ for the remission of sins, and you will receive the gift of the Holy Spirit." 39 For the promise is made to you and to your children and to all who are far off, that is, to everyone whom the Lord our God will call." 40 And with many other words he beseeched and exhorted them, saying, "Save yourselves from this adverse generation." 41 Then those who gladly accepted his word were baptized; and on that same day about three thousand souls were added to the Church. 42 And they con- tinued to follow the apostles' doctrine, fellow- ship, breaking of bread, and prayers. 43 Every soul was seized with fear, and the apostles performed many wonders and signs. 44 Ev- eryone who was present gathered in one place and had everything in common. 45 They sold their goods and possessions and distributed them to all, according to each one's need. 46 Every day they continued to be together in the Temple and at home, breaking bread, they ate together with joy and simplicity of heart, 47 they prayed to God and were on good terms with all the people; and the Lord added from day to day to the Church those who needed to be fed.

CHAPTER 3

1 Now Peter and John went together to the Temple at the ninth hour of prayer. 2 A cer- tain man was charged, who was a creeper who had come out of his mother's wife, and who stood every day at the door of the Tem- ple called Beautiful, to inquire of those who entered the Temple. 3 Peter and John, seeing that they wanted to enter the Temple,

desired to receive an offering. 4 Peter, seeing him in earnest with Iohn, said, "Look, look." 5 And he went to them, trusting to receive something from them. 6 Then Peter said, "I have nei- ther silver nor gold, but what I have I give to you: in the name of Jesus Christ of Nazareth, arise and walk." 7 He took him by the right hand and lifted him up, and immediately his feet and the bones of his ankles received strength. 8 Then he stood up and walked and entered the Temple with them, walking and jumping and praying to God. 9 All the peo- ple saw him walking and praying to God. 10 They recognized him that he was the one who sat by the alms at the Beautiful Gate of the Temple; and they marveled and were greatly astonished at what had happened to him. 11 And because the creeper who had been healed held Peter and John, all the people flocked in admiration toward them to the porch which is called Solomon. 12 When Peter noticed this, he answered the people, "You people of Israel, why do you marvel at this? Or why do you look so insistently, as if by our own power or means we had made this man go? 13 The God of Abraham, Isaac and Jacob, the God of our fathers, glorified his Son Iesus, whom you betrayed and denied in the presence of Pilate, when he had judged him to be deliv- ered up. 14 But you denied the Holy One and the Righteous One and wanted a murderer to be given to you, 15 and you killed the Lord of life, whom God raised from the dead and of whom we are witnesses. 16 His Name has made this man healthy, whom you see and know, by faith in His Name; and the faith that is in him has brought him this perfect health of the whole body in the presence of you all. 17 Now, brethren, I know that you did it in igno- rance, as your masters also did it. 18 But those things which God had already foretold by the mouth of all his prophets, namely, that Christ should suffer, he has thus fulfilled. 19 There- fore change your lives and be converted, that your sins may be done away with, when the time of refreshment from the presence of the Lord comes. 20 He will send Jesus Christ, who was preached to you before, 21 whom man- kind must keep until the time when all that God has spoken by the mouth of all his holy prophets from the beginning of the world shall be restored. 22 For Moses said to the fathers, "The Lord your God will raise up for you a Prophet, one of your brothers, similar to me; you shall listen to him in everything he says to you. 23 For whoever does not listen to that Prophet will be eliminated from the peo- ple. 24 Also all the prophets from Samuel on- ward, and all who spoke, foretold these days. 25 You are the children of the prophets and of the covenant that God made to our fathers, saying to Abraham, "In your descendants all the seed of the earth shall be blessed."26 First of all to you God made known his Son Jesus, and sent him to bless you and to make each one of you recant from your iniquities.

CHAPTER 4

1 While they were speaking to the people, the priests, the temple leader and the Sadducees approached them ,2 deeming it serious that they were teaching the people and preaching in the name of Jesus about the resurrection from the dead. 3 And they put them in prison until the next day, for it was now summer. 4 Nevertheless many of those who had heard the word stood up, and the number of the men was about five thousand. 5 The next day the leaders, elders and scribes gathered in Jerusalem, 6 Annas, the chief of the priests, Caiaphas, Iohn, Alexander, and all who be- longed to the family of the priests. 7 When they had set them before

them, they asked, "By what power or in what name have you done this?" 8 Then Peter, filled with the Holy Spirit, said to them, "You, leaders of the peo- ple and elders of Israel, 9 for today we have been examined concerning the good done to the powerless man, that is, by what means he has been made whole, 10 let it be known to all of you and to all the people of Israel that by the name of Jesus Christ of Nazareth, whom you crucified and whom God raised from the dead, and through him this man stands here before you whole. 11 This is the stone discard- ed by you builders that has become the head of the corner. 12 And there is salvation in no one else, for among men there is no other Name under man, whereby we must be saved. 13 Now when they saw the boldness of Peter and John and understood that they were ignorant and unlearned men, they marveled and knew that they had been with Jesus: 14 And seeing also the healed man standing with them, they had no objection. 15 Then they commanded them to depart from the council and to con- fer with one another, 16 saying, "What shall we do to these men? For surely an evident sign has been done by them, and it is openly known to all who dwell in Jerusalem; and we cannot deny it." 17 But so that the thing may no longer be denied by the people, threaten them and charge them that from now on they may not speak to anyone in this Name." 18 So they called them and commanded them not to speak or teach in any way in the Name of Jesus. 19 But Peter and John answered them and said, "Whether it is right in the sight of God to obey you rather than God, you judge. 20 For we cannot but speak the things which we have seen and heard." 21 So they threat- ened them, and let them go, and found noth- ing to punish them, because of the people; for all men praised God for what had been done. 22 For the man was about forty years old, and this miracle of healing had been performed on him. 23 Then, as they were let go, they pre- sented themselves to their companions and related all that the priests and elders had told them. 24 When they had heard it, they raised their voices in agreement to God and said, "O LORD, you are the God who made heaven, earth, the sea and all things that are in them, 25 whom by the mouth of your servant Dauid you said, "Why have the nations raged and the peoples imagined vain things? 26 The kings of the earth have gathered together and the rulers have gathered against the LORD and against his Christ. 27 For absurdly, against your holy Son Iesus, whom you had anoin- ished, Herod and Pontius Pilate and the Gen- tiles and the people of Israel have gathered to- gether, 28 to do what thy hand and thy counsel had determined to do .29 Now, O LORD, ob- serve their threats, and give your servants all the boldness they need to speak your word, 30 that thou mayest stretch forth thy hand, that healings and signs and wonders may be done in the Name of thy holy Son Iesus." 31 As they prayed, the place where they were gathered was shaken, and all were filled with the Holy Spirit and spoke the word of God with power. 32 The multitude of those gathered were of one heart and mind; none of them said that anything they owned was theirs, but they had all things in common. 33 With great power the apostles testified to the resurrection of the Lord Jesus, and great grace was granted to all of them. 34 And there was not one among them who lacked, for as many as owned land or houses, they sold them and brought the price of the things sold, 35 and they laid it at the feet of the Apostles, and it was distributed to each one according to his need. 36 Ioses, who was called by the Apostles Barnabas (that is, by interpretation, the son of consolation), was also a Leuite and came from the county of Cyprus, 37 where he had land, sold it, brought the money, and laid it at the Apostles' feet.

CHAPTER 5

1 But a certain man named Ananias, with Sapphira his wife, sold property, 2 and kept aside a portion of the price; his wife also, be- ing advised, brought a certain portion and laid it at the Apostles' feet. 3 Then Peter said, "Ananias, why has Satan filled your heart, that you should disdain the Holy Spirit and keep aside part of the price of this property? 4 While it remained, did it not belong to you? And after it had been sold, was it not in your power? How is it that you conceived this thing in your heart? You have not lied to men, but to God." 5 When Ananias had heard these words, he fell to the ground and expired. Then all who heard these things were greatly afraid. 6 The young men arose, took him away, and buried him. 7 About three hours later his wife came in, unaware of what had been done. 8 And Peter said to her, "Tell me, did you sell the land for so much?" And she answered, "Yes, for so much." 9 Then Peter said to her, "Why did you agree to tempt the Spirit of the Lord? Behold, the feet of those who bur- ied your husband are on the shore, and they will carry you away." 10 Then she fell at once at his feet and expired; and the young men came in, found her dead, took her away, and buried her beside her husband. 11 And great was the fear of all the church and of those who heard these things. 12 So, by the hands of the apostles, many signs and wonders were per- formed among the people (and all agreed in Solomon's porch). 13 And no one could help but notice the other things; nevertheless the people magnified them. 14 The number of those who believed in the Lord, both men and women, was increasing more and more). 15 so much so that they brought the sick into the streets and laid them on beds and cots, so that when Peter's shadow passed by, it would overshadow some of them. 16 Also from the surrounding towns there came to Jerusalem a crowd bringing people who were sick and af- flicted with vicious spirits, all of whom were healed. 17 Then the chief priest arose, and all those who were with him (that is, the sect of Sadducees), and they were filled with indig- nation, 18 And they laid hands on the Apos- tles and put them in the common prison. 19 But the angel of the Lord by night opened the prison doors and brought them out and said to them 20 Go your way, stand in the Temple, and speak to the people all the words of this life." 21 So when they heard this, they entered the Temple early in the morning and taught. The chief priest and those who were with him came and summoned the counselors and all the elders of the children of Israel and sent to the prison to be led. 22 But when the officers came and did not find them in the prison, they went back and reported it, 23 saying, "Surely we found the prison locked as secure- ly as we could, and the keepers standing out- side before the doors; but when we opened it, we found no one inside." 24 When the chief priest, the head of the temple and the oth- er priests heard these things, they doubted them, to see where this would occur. 25 Then one came and informed them, saying, "Be- hold, the men whom you have put in prison stand in the Temple and teach the people." 26 Then the captain went with the officers and brought them in without violence (because they feared the people, lest they should be stoned). 27 When they had brought them, they put them before the council, and the chief priest questioned them, 28 saying, "Did we not advise you not to teach in this name? And behold, you have filled Jerusalem with your doctrine and

want to bring blood upon this man." 29 Then Peter and the apostles answered, "We must rather obey God than men." 30 The God of our fathers raised up Je- sus, whom you killed and hanged on a tree. 31 He was raised up by God with his right hand, to be a prince and a savior, to give repentance to Israel and to forgive sins. 32 And we are his witnesses of these things which we say, and of the Holy Spirit which God has given to those who obey him. 33 When they heard this, they were enraged with anger and consulted to kill them. 34 Then there stood in the council a cer- tain Pharisee named Gamaliel, a doctor of the Law, honored by all the people, and he ordered the Apostles to go out for a while, 35 and said to them, "Men of Israel, be careful what you intend to do with these men. 36 For before these times there arose Theudas, who boast- ed that he was a man of about four hundred, and he was slain; and all those who obeyed him were scattered and reduced to nothing. 37 After this man, Iudas of Galilee arose in the days of the tribute, and dragged away many people behind him; and he also died, and all who obeyed him were scattered. 38 Now I say to you, turn away from these men and leave them alone, for if this counsel or this work is of men, it will accomplish nothing: 39 but if it is from God, you cannot destroy it, lest you be found to be fighting against God." 40 Then they agreed with him and called the apostles; and after they had beaten them, they com- manded that they should not speak in the name of Jesus and let them go. 41 So they de- parted from the council, remembering that they had been found worthy to be rebuked for his Name. 42 And every day, in the Temple and from house to house, they did not cease teaching and preaching Jesus Christ.

CHAPTER 6

1 In those days, as the name of the disciples grew, there arose a murmuring of the Greeks against the Jews, because their widows were neglected in the daily service. 2 Then the two called together the multitude of the disciples and said, "It is not fitting that we should leave the word of God to serve tables." 3 Therefore, brothers, seek out from among you some honest men, full of the Holy Spirit and wis- dom, whom we can appoint for these tasks. 4 And we will devote ourselves continually to prayer and to teaching the word." 5 This pleased the whole crowd, and they chose Steuen, a man full of wisdom and the Holy Spirit, Philippe, Prochorus, Nicanor, Timon, Parmenas, and Nicolas, a proselyte from An- tioch, 6 whom they set before the Apostles, who, after praying, laid their hands on them. 7 The word of God increased, and the name of the disciples multiplied greatly in Jerusalem, and a great host of priests were converted to the faith. 8 Now Steuen, full of faith and pow- er, did great wonders and miracles among the people. 9 Then there arose some of the syna- gogue, who are called Libertines, Cyrenians, from Alexandria, Cilicia, and Asia, and they argued with Steuen. 10 But they could not resist the wisdom and the Spirit with which he spoke. 11 Then they baited men who said, "We heard him speaking blasphemous words against Moses and against God." 12 So they brought in the people, and the elders, and the scribes; and, rushing upon him, they seized him and brought him before the council, 13 and presented false witnesses who said, "This man does not cease to speak blasphemous words against this holy place and against the Law. 14 For we have heard him say that this Jesus of Nazareth will destroy this place and change the regulations that Moses had given. 15

And as all who sat in the Council looked at him intently, they saw his face as if it had been that of an angel.

CHAPTER 7

1 Then the chief priest said, "Are these things?" 2 And he said, "Men, brothers and fathers, lis- ten. The God of glory appeared to our father Abraham while he was in Mesopotamia, be- fore he dwelt in Charran, 3 and said to him, "Come out of your country and your lineage and come to the land that I will show you." 4 Then he went out of the land of the Chaldeans and dwelt in Charran. And after his father was dead, God led him from there to this land, where you now dwell, 5 And he gave him no inheritance in it, not the seed of a foote; yet he promised him that he would give it to him as his property and to his descendants af- ter him, when he was yet childless.6 But God said that his descendants would be guests in a foreign land and that he would keep them in bondage for four hundred years. 7 But the na- tion to which they shall be in bondage, I will judge, says God; and after that they shall go out and serve me in this place. 8 He also gave him consent to circumcision; so Abraham be- gat Isaac and circumcised him on the eighth day; Isaac begat Jacob and Jacob the two pa- triarchs. 9 The patriarchs went down on their knees and abandoned Ioseph in Egypt, but God was with him, 10 and delivered him from all his afflictions and gave him strength and wisdom in the eyes of Pharaoh king of Egypt, who made him master of Egypt and of all his house. 11 Then there was a famine throughout all the land of Egypt and Chanaan and great affliction, so that our fathers could not find enough to feed themselves. 12 But when Jacob heard that there was horn in Egypt, he sent our fathers first: 13 At a later time Ioseph was known to his brothers, and his lineage was made known to Pharaoh. 14 Then Iacob sent for his father and all his relatives, about six- ty-five persons. 15 Iacob went down to Egypt and died, as did our fathers, 16 they were transferred to Shechem and were put in the tomb that Abraham had bought for money from the sons of Emor the son of Shechem. 17 But when the time of the promise, which God had sworn to Abraham, departed, the people grew and multiplied in Egypt, 18 until another king arose who did not know Ioseph. 19 He dealt underhandedly with our kinsmen, and with great insistence caused our fathers to drive out their young sons, lest they should remain strangers. 20 At the same time Mo- ses was born, who was pleasing to God and was nurtured in the house of his fathers for three months. 21 When he was cast out, Pha- raoh's daughter took him and fed him as her own son. 22 Moses was instructed in all the knowledge of the Egyptians and was mighty in word and deed. 23 When he had complet- ed his fourteenth year, it came into his mind to visit his brothers, the children of Israel. 24 When he saw that one of them was suffering injustice, he defended him, stood up for his companion who had harmed him, and struck down the Egyptian. 25 For he thought that his brothers would understand that God, with his hand, would grant them deliverance; but they did not understand him. 26 The next day he showed himself to them how they behaved, and he would have liked to put them in agree- ment, saying, "Gentlemen, you are brothers; why do you harm one another? 27 But whoev- er wronged his neighbor, he cast him out, say- ing, "Who made you prince and judge outside us? 28 Will you kill me, as you did the Egyp- tian yesterday? 29 At these words Moses fled and remained a stranger in the land of Midi- an, where he begat two sons.

30 When he was forty years old, there appeared to him in the thicket of Mout Sina an angel of the LORD in a flame of fire in a bush. 31 When Moses saw it, he marveled at the sight; and as he drew near to consider it, the voice of the LORD came to him, saying, "I am the God of the LORD, 32 I am the God of your fathers, the God of Abra- ham, the God of Isaac, and the God of Jacob. Then Moses trembled and could not see him. 33 Then the LORD said to him, "Take off your shoes from your feet, for the place where you stand is holy ground. 34 I have seen, I have seen the affliction of my people who are in Egypt, I have heard their lamentation, and I have come down to deliver them; now come and I will send you to Egypt." 35 This Moses, whom they rebuked, saying, "Who made you a prince and a judge?" God himself sent for a prince and a deliverer by the hand of the angel who had appeared to him in the bush. 36 He led them out, performing wonders and mir- acles in the land of Egypt, in the Red Sea and in the wilderness for forty years. 37 This is the one Moses who said to the children of Israel, "The LORD your God will raise up for you a prophet, one of your brothers, similar to me; to him you will give heed." 38 This is he who was in the congregation, in the wilderness, with the angel who spoke to him on Mount Sinah, and with our fathers, who received the oracles of lies to give to them. 39 Whom our fathers would not obey, but refused, and in their hearts returned back to Egypt: 40 And they said to Aaron, "Build you gods that you may go before you, for we know not what has become of this Moses who brought us out of the land of Egypt." 41 In those days they made a calfe, offered sacrifices to the idol, and de- voted themselves to the works of their hands. 42 Then God turned away and gave them to serve the army of Heauen, as it is written in the book of the Prophets, "O house of Israel, have you offered me beasts of slaughter and sacrifices for the space of forty years in the wilderness? 43 You have built the tabernacle of Moloch and the star of your god Remphan, figures you made to worship them; therefore I will lead you beyond Babylon. 44 Our fathers had the tabernacle of the witches, in the wil- derness, as he had appointed, speaking to Moses, that he should make it according to the pattern which he had seen. 45 This tab- ernacle also our fathers received and carried with Jesus into the possession of the Gentiles, whom God had brought forth before our fa- thers, until the days of Dauid: 46 Who, being in trouble before God, desired to find a tab- ernacle for the God of Jacob. 47 But Solomon built him a house. 48 But the Most High does not dwell in temples made with hands, as the Prophet says, 49 Heaven is my throne, and the earth is my foot; what house will you build for me, says the LORD, or what will be the place where I will rest? 50 Has not my hand made all these things? 51 You stiff-necked and vn- circumcised hearts and ears have always re- sisted the Holy Spirit; as your fathers did, so do you. 52 What prophets did not persecute your fathers? They killed them and foretold the coming of that righteousness of which you are now the traitors and murderers, 53 who received the law at the command of an- gels and did not keep it. 54 On hearing these things, their hearts were inflamed with wrath and they gnashed their teeth at him. 55 But he, filled with the Holy Spirit, looked fixedly into heaven and saw the glory of God and Je- sus standing at the right hand of God, 56 and said, "Behold, I see the heavens opened and the Son of Man standing at the right hand of God." 57 Then they gave a cry with a loud voice, stopped their ears, and came upon him violently, all at once, 58 they drove him out of the city and stoned him; and the witnesses spread their garments at the feet of a young man named Saul. 59 Then they stoned

Steuen, who had called on God, saying, "Lord Jesus, receive my spirit." 60 He knelt down and cried with a loud voice, "Lord, do not impute this sin to them." And having spoken thus, he fell asleep.

CHAPTER 8

1 Saul consented to his death, and at that time there was great persecution against the Church that was in Jerusalem, and all were scattered throughout the regions of Judea and Samaria except the Apostles. 2 Then some God-fearing men brought Steuèn among them, to bury him, and they made great mourning for him. 3 But Saul made havoc of the Church, and went into all the houses, and brought men and women out of them, and put them in prison. 4 Therefore those who were scattered abroad went hither and thither preaching the word. 5 Then Philip en- tered the city of Samaria and preached Christ to them. 6 The people paid attention to the things Philip said, with one accord, hearing and seeing the miracles he performed. 7 For the living spirits, which cried out with a loud voice, came out of many of those who were possessed by them; and many of those who were afflicted with paralysis and who had stood still were healed. 8 And there was great joy in that city. 9 Earlier in the city there was a man named Simon, who practiced witchcraft and beguiled the people of Samaria, saying that he was a great man. 10 To these people they gave heed from the least to the greatest, saying, "This man is the great power of God." 11 And they listened to him, for he had long since bewitched them with spells. 12 But as they had listened to Philip, who preached the things concerning the kingdom of God and the name of Jesus Christ, both men and wom- en were baptized. 13 Simon also was baptized and continued to be with Philip and marveled when he saw the signs and great miracles that were being performed. 14 Now when the apostles who were in Jerusalem heard that Sa- maria had received the word of God, they sent Peter and John to them. 15 Who, when they had come down, prayed for them, that they might receive the Holy Spirit. 16 (For he had not yet descended on any of them, but they had been baptized only in the name of the Lord Jesus). 17 Then they laid their hands on them and received the Holy Spirit. 18 When Simon heard that by the laying on of the apos- tles' hands the Holy Spirit had been received, he offered them money, 19 saying, "Give me also this power, that those who lay hands may receive the Holy Spirit." 20 Then Peter said to him, "Your money perishes with you, because you think that the gift of God can be obeyed with money. 21 You have no part or fellowship in this business, because your heart is not up- right in the sight of God. 22 Repent therefore of this wickedness of yours, and pray to God that, if it is possible, the thought of your heart may be forgiven you. 23 For I see that you are in the gall of bitterness and in the blood of in- iquity." 24 Then Simon answered, "Pray to the Lord for me, that none of these things which you have spoken may come upon me." 25 So they, having witnessed and preached the word of the Lord, returned to Jerusalem and preached the gospel in many towns of the Sa- maritans. 26 Then the angel of the Lord spoke to Philip, saying, "Get up and go south, on the road that goes down from Jerusalem to Gaza, which is deserted." 27 And he arose and went on; and behold, a certain Eunuche of Ethio- pia, Candaces, the queen of the Ethiopians, chief of Governour, who had control of all its treasures, came to Jerusalem to worship: 28 As he returned, sitting in his charet, he read the prophet Esaias. 29 Then the Spirit said to Philip, "Go thence, and go to thy charet." 30 Philip hastened, and heard him reading the prophet Esaias, and said, "But do you under- stand what you read? 31 And he said, "How could I, if I had no guide?" And he wanted Philip to come and sit with him. 32 Now the Scripture that he read said, "He was led like a sheep to the slaughter, and, like a tame sheep before its shearer, he did not open his mouth." 33 In his humility his judgment was exalted, but who shall declare his generation, for his life was taken from the earth." 34 Then the Eunuch answered Philip and said, "Please, of whom does the prophet speak? Of himself or of some other man?" 35 Then Philip opened his mouth and began to speak the same Scripture and to preach Jesus to him. 36 As they went on their way, they came to a certain water, and the Eunuch said, "See, here is water; what enables me to be baptized?" 37 Philip said to him, "If you want to be baptized with all your heart, you may do so." Then he answered, "I believe that Jesus Christ is the Son of God." 38 Then he commanded the chariot to stand still; and they both went down into the water, both Philip and the Eunuch, and he baptized him. 39 As they came out of the water, the Spirit of the Lord ravished Philip, and the Eunuch saw him no more; so he resumed his journey. 40 But Philip was found in Azotus, and he went back and forth preaching in all the cities, until he came to Caesarea.

CHAPTER 9

1 Saul, who was threatening and slaugh- tering the disciples of the Lord, went to the priest, 2 and asked him for letters for Da- mascus and for the synagogues, so that if he found anyone who was from there (men or women), he might take him to Jerusalem. 3 As he was traveling, it happened that as he approached Damascus, suddenly a light from above shone around him. 4 He fell to the ground and heard a voice saying to him, "Saul, Saul, why do you persecute me?" 5 And he said, "Who are you, Lord?" And the Lord answered, "I am Jesus whom you persecute; it is hard for you to strike goads." 6 He then, trembling and amazed, said, "Lord, what do you want me to do? And the Lord said to him, "Arise and go into the city, and you will be told what you are to do." 7 The men who were traveling with him were also dumbfounded, hearing his speech but seeing no one. 8 Saul got up from the ground and opened his eyes, but he saw no one. So they took him by the hand and led him to Damascus, 9 where he remained three days without sight, without eating or drinking. 10 In Damascus there was a certain disciple named Ananias, to whom the Lord said in a vision, "Ananias." And he said, "Behold, I am here, Lord." 11 Then the Lord said to him, "Arise, go into the street that is called Straight and look into the house of Iudas, to one named Saul of Tarsus, for be- hold, he prays." 12 (And in a vision he saw a man named Ananias coming to him and lay- ing his hands on him that he might receive the sight). 13 Then Ananias answered, "Lord, I have heard from many about this man, about how much evil he has done to your saints in Jerusalem. 14 Moreover here he has the au- thority of the priests to kill everyone who calls on your name." 15 Then the LORD said to him, "Go your way, for he is a chosen vassal for me, to bear my Name before the Gentiles, the kings and the children of Israel. 16 For I will explain to him how many things he must suffer for My Names' sake." 17 Then Ananias went his way, entered that house, laid his hands on him, and said, "Brother Saul, the Lord has sent me (that is, Jesus who appeared to you on the road as you were coming) that you may receive sight and be filled with the

Holy Spirit." 18 And immediately there fell from his eyes like scales, and suddenly he re- ceived sight, and stood up and was baptized, 19 he received food and was strengthened. So was Saul some days with the disciples who were in Damascus. 20 And immediately he preached Christ in the synagogues, who was the Son of God, 21 so that all who heard him were admired and said, "Is not this he who slaughtered those who called on this name in Jerusalem and came here for this purpose, to bring them to prison to the priests? 22 But Saul grew stronger and stronger and con- fused the people who lived in Damascus, con- firming that this was the Christ. 23 And after many days had passed, the witnesses agreed to kill him, 24 but their departure was known to Saul; now they guarded the gates day and night to kill him. 25 Then the disciples took him by night, put him through the wall, and brought him down with a rope in a basket. 26 When Saul came to Jerusalem, he tried to join the disciples, but they turned away from him and did not believe that he was a disciple. 27 But Barnabas took him and led him to the apostles and told them how he had seen the Lord on the way, how he had spoken to him and how he had spoken boldly in Damascus in the name of Jesus. 28 And he lingered with them in Jerusalem, 29 he spoke boldly in the name of the Lord Jesus, and talked and ar- gued with the Greeks, but they wanted to kill him. 30 But when the brothers heard of it, they took him to Caesarea and sent him to Tarsus. 31 Then the churches rested through- out all Judea, Galilee and Samaria, and were built up and walked in the fear of the Lord and multiplied by the comfort of the Holy Spirit. 32 And as Peter walked through all the quarters, he also came to the saints who lived in Lydda. 33 There he found a certain man named Aeneas, who had kept his bed for eight years and was sick with paralysis. 34 Then Pe- ter said to him, "Aeneas, Jesus Christ heals you; get up and make up your bed." And he immediately got up. 35 All those who lived in Lydda and Saron saw him and were converted to the Lord. 36 There was also in Ioppa a cer- tain woman, a disciple named Tabitha (who by interpretation is called Dorcas), who was full of good works and almes that she did. 37 And it came to pass in those days that she fell sick and was dyed; and when they had washed her, they deposited her in a safe room. 38 Now because Lydda was near Ioppa and the disci- ples had heard that Peter was there, they sent two men to him, wishing that he would not delay in coming to them. 39 Then Peter got up and came with them; and when he had ar- rived, they led him into the VIP room, where all the widows stood beside him weeping and showing the cloaks and robes that Dorcas had made while he was with them. 40 But Peter brought them all out, knelt down, prayed, turned him to the body and said, "Tabitha, get up." And she opened her eyes and, seeing Peter, stood up. 41 Then he gave her his hand and lifted her up, and called the saints and the widows, and restored her wings. 42 And the thing was known throughout all the Joppa, and many were converted to the Lord. 43 And it came to pass that he stayed many days in Ioppa with a certain Simon, a tanner.

CHAPTER 10

1 Also in Caesarea there was a certain man named Cornelius, captain of the band called the Italians, 2 a prudent man, who feared God with all his strength, who gave much counsel to the people and prayed to God continually. :3 In a vision he saw (about the ninth hour of the day) an angel of God coming to him and saying, "Cornelius." 4 But when he looked at him, he was bewildered and said, "What is it, Lord?" And he said to him, "Your prayers and prayers have been remembered before God. 5 Therefore send men to Ioppa and call Simon, whose name is Peter. 6 He is staying with one Simon, a tanner, whose house is on the seashore; he will tell you what you are to do." 7 When the angel who had spoken to Cor- nelius was gone, he called two of his servants and a God- fearing soul, one of those waiting for him, 8 and told them everything and sent them to Ioppa. 9 The next day, as they contin- ued their journey and approached the city, Peter went into the house to pray, about six o'clock. 10 Then he felt hungry and wanted to eat; but as they prepared something, he fell into a trance. 11 He saw the heavens open and a certain vessel descending toward him, as if it had been a large cloth, joined at the four corners and brought down to the earth. 12 In it was every kind of four-legged cattle of the earth, wild cattle, creeping things, and animals of the earth. 13 A voice came to him, "Rise, Peter, kill and eat." 14 But Peter said, "It is not so, Lord, for I have never eaten anything defiled or vandalous." 15 Then the seer said to him again, for the second time, "The things that God has cleansed, do not pollute them." 16 This was done three times, and the vessel was taken up to heaven again. 17 While Peter was pondering what the vision he had seen meant, behold, the men sent by Cornelius had searched Simon's house and stopped at the door, 18 and calling, they asked if Simon, whose name was Peter, was staying there. 19 While Peter was reflecting on the vision, the Spirit said to him, "Behold, three men see you. 20 Get up therefore, go down and go with them, doubting nothing, for I have sent them." 21 Then Peter went to the men who had been sent to him by Cornelius and said, "Behold, I am he whom you see; what is the reason why you have come?" 22 Those answered, "Cor- nelius, the captain, a righteous, God-fearing man of good repute among all the nation of the Israelites, was warned from above by a holy angel to send for you to his house to hear your words." 23 So he called and lodged them; the next day Peter went with them, and some of Ioppa's brothers accompanied him. 24 The next day they entered Caesarea. Cornelius was waiting for them and had called togeth- er his relatives and special friends. 25 As Peter entered, Cornelius went to meet him, prostrated himself at his feet and worshiped him. 26 But Peter made him stand up, saying, "Stand up, for I myself am a man." 27 While he was talking with him, he went in and found many who had gathered together. 28 And he said to them, "You know that it is an unlaw- ful thing for a man who is a Jew to associate with or approach one of another nation; but God has taught me that I must not call anyone defiled or vnclean. 29 Therefore I came to you without saying no, when they sent for me. I ask therefore, for what reason did you send for me? 30 Then Cornelius said, "Four days ago, about this hour, I fasted, and at the ninth hour I prayed in my house, and behold, a man dressed in shining garments stood before me." 31 and said, "Cornelius, your prayer has been answered, and your prayers have been remembered in the sight of God." 32 There- fore send to Ioppa and call Simon, whose name is Peter (he is staying in the house of Simon, a tanner, on the seashore), who, when he has come, will speak to you. 33 So I im- mediately sent for you, and you did well to come. Now therefore we are all present here before God, to hear all the things that have been commanded you by God." 34 Then Peter opened his mouth and said, "It is true that I understood that God does not accept people. 35 But in every nation those who fear him

and work righteousness are accepted with him. 36 You know the word that God sent to the chil- dren of Israel, preaching peace through Jesus Christ, who is Lord of all: 37 And the word which passed through all Judea, beginning from Galilee, after the baptism which Iohn preached. 38 And that is, how God anointed with the Holy Spirit and with power Jesus of Nazareth, who went about doing good and healing all who were oppressed with wicked- ness, because God was with him. 39 And we are witnesses of all the things which he did both in the land of the Israelites and in Jeru- salem, and whom they killed, hanging him on a tree. 40 And God raised him up on the third day, and caused him to be openly displayed: 41 not to all the people, but to God's chosen witnesses, that is, to those who had eaten and drunk with him, after he had risen from the dead. 42 And he commanded the witnesses to preach to the people and to testify that he is the judge of the dead and the dead ordained by God. 43 To him also is due the testimony of all the prophets that through his name all who believe in him will receive remission of sins. 44 As Peter spoke these words, the Holy Spirit descended on all who heard them. 45 So those of the circumcision who were attending were amazed, as many as had come with Peter, be- cause even on the Gentiles the gift of the Holy Spirit had been poured out. 46 For they heard them speaking with tongues and magnifying God. Then Peter answered, 47 Can anyone forbid water, lest these should be baptized, who have received the Holy Spirit as we have? 48 So he commanded them to be baptized in the Name of the Lord. Then he begged him to set some days.

CHAPTER 11

1 Now the apostles and brethren who were in Judea came to know that the Gentiles also had received the word of God. 2 And when Peter had come to Jerusalem, those of the circum- cision challenged him, 3 saying, "You went in to circumcised men and ate with them." 4 Then Peter began to expound it to them in an orderly manner, saying, 5 I was in the city of Ioppa praying, and in a trance-like state I had this vision: a certain vessel descending as if it had been a great sheet, brought down from Heauen by the four corners, and came to me. 6 And when I had fixed mine eyes, I saw four-footed beasts of the earth, wild beasts, creeping things, and wastes of the earth. 7 I also heard a voice saying to me, "Get up, Pe- ter, kill and eat." 8 I answered, "God forbid, Lord, for nothing defiled or vnclean has ever entered my mouth." 9 But the seer answered me the second time from above, "The things God has cleansed, do not pollute them." 10 This was done three times, and all were taken up to heaven again. 11 Then behold, immedi- ately three men came to the house where I was, sent from Caesarea for me. 12 The Spir- it told me that I should go with them, not doubting; moreover these six brothers came with me and we entered the man's house. 13 He related how he had seen an angel in his house, who stopped and said to him, "Send men to Ioppa and call Simon, whose name is Peter. 14 He will speak words to you that will save you and all your house." 15 As I be- gan to speak, the Holy Spirit fell on them, as at the beginning. 16 Then I remembered the word of the Lord that said, "I have baptized with water, but you shall be baptized with the Holy Spirit." 17 For if God granted them a gift similar to that which he granted to us when we were baptized into the Lord Jesus Christ, who was I that I should allow God to do so? 18 On hearing these things, they held their peace and glorified God, saying, "Then God has also given the Gentiles repentance to life." 19 Those who had been scattered be- cause of the affliction that had arisen around Steuen went everywhere as far as Phoenix, Cyprus and Antioch, preaching the word to no one but only to the Gentiles. 20 Some of them were men from Cyprus and Cyrene who came to Antioch and spoke to the Greeks and preached the Lord Jesus. 21 The hand of the Lord was with them, so that a great number of people were converted to the Lord. 22 Then the news of these things reached the ears of the church that was in Jerusalem, and they sent for Barnabas to go to Antioch. 23 Who, when he had come and saw the grace of God, rejoiced and exhorted everyone to go on with a firm mind in the Lord. 24 For he was a good man, full of the Holy Spirit and faith, and many people had been converted to the Lord. 25 Then Barnabas set out for Tarsus to see Saul: 26 And when he had found him, he led him to Antioch; and it came to pass that all the year they were in contact with the church and taught many people, so that the disciples were called Christians for the first time in Antioch. 27 In those days prophets also came from Jerusalem to Antioch.28 One of them, named Agabus, stopped and announced by the Spirit that there would be a great famine throughout the world, which also happened under Claudius Caesar. 29 Then the disciples, each according to his ability, set out to send help to the brothers who lived in Iudea. 30 And so they also did and sent it to the elders, by the hand of Barnabas and Saul.

CHAPTER 12

1 At that time, King Herod stretched out his hands to kill some members of the Church, 2 And he slew Iames the brother of Iohn by the sword. 3 And when he heard that this pleased the kings, he proceeded further, to take Peter also (then were the days of bread vnleauened). 4 And when he had caught him, he put him in prison, and gave him over to four quater- nions of soldiers to guard him, intending to take him to the people after the passage. 5 So Peter was kept in prison, but the church earnestly prayed to God for him. 6 And when Herod would have liked to take him out to the people, the same night Peter fell asleep be- tween two soldiers, bound with two chains, and the watchmen before the door guarded the prison. 7 And behold, the angel of the Lord came upon them, and a light shone in the house, and he struck Peter on the side and made him stand up, saying, "Get up at once." And the chains fell from his hands. 8 And the angel said to him, "Turn around and put on your sandals." And he did so. Then he said to him, "Throw on your garments and follow me." 9 Then Peter went out and followed him, not knowing that it was true what the angel had done, but believing that he had seen a vision. 10 Now when the first and the second guard had passed, they came to the yron gate, which leads into the city, which opened to them of its own accord; and they went out, and passed through a street, and the angel departed from him. 11 And when Peter had come to himself, he said, "Now I know for certain that the Lord has sent his angel and delivered me out of the hand of Herod and out of all the ways of the people of the Jews." 12 As he considered the matter, he came to the house of Mary, the mother of Iohn, whose surname was Marke, where many were gath- ered, and prayed. 13 When Peter knocked at the front door, a woman named Rhode came to hear him, 14 But when she heard of Peter's journey, she did not open the front door to re- joice, but came running in and told how Peter stood before the entrance. 15 But they said to her, "You are mad." But she always

affirmed that she was. Then they said, "It is her angel." 16 But Peter kept knocking, and when they opened and saw him, they were astonished. 17 He beckoned to them with his hand to be silent and told how the Lord had brought him out of prison. And he said, "Go and tell these things to Iames and the brothers"; then he departed and went to another place. 18 By this time it was daylight, and there was no little trouble among the people of the city as to what had become of Peter. 19 When Herod had searched for him and could not find him, he examined the keepers and ordered them to be led to punishment. Then he went down from Judea to Caesarea and stopped there. 20 Then Herod was angry with those of Tyre and Sidon, but they all came to him together and persuaded Blasto, the king's chamberlain, and desired peace, for their county was nour- ished by the king's land. 21 On the appoint- ed day, Herod came in royal robes, sat on the judgment seat, and gave a prayer before them. 22 The people cried out, saying, "The word is of God and not of man." 23 But imme- diately the angel of the Lord struck him, be- cause he did not give glory to God, so that he was devoured by worms and left the ghost. 24 The word of God grew and multiplied. 25 So Barnabas and Saul returned from Jerusalem, having fulfilled their commission, and took with them Iohn, whose name was Marke.

CHAPTER 13

1 There were also some prophets and teachers in the Church at Antioch, such as Barnabas, Simeon called Niger, Lucius of Cyrene, Mana- hen (who had been brought with Herod the Tetrarch) and Saul. 2 While they were wor- shiping the Lord and fasting, the Holy Spirit said, "Separate me Barnabas and Saul for the work to which I have called them." 3 Then they fasted and prayed, laid their hands on them, and let them go. 4 After they had been sent by the Holy Spirit, they went down to Seleucia, and from there they went to Cyprus. 5 When they were in Salamis, they preached the word of God in the synagogues of the Jews; and they also had John as a minister. 6 When they had gone all the way through the yle to Paphus, they found a certain sorcerer, a false prophet, who was a Iewe, named Bariesus, 7 who was with the deputy Sergius Paulus, a prudent man. He called Barnabas and Saul to himself and wanted to hear the word of God. 8 But Elima, a sorcerer (so his name was interpret- ed), hindered them and tried to turn the dep- uty away from the faith. 9 Then Saul (who is also called Paul), full of the Holy Spirit, set his eyes on him, 10 and said, "O full of all guile and all malice, a son of wickedness and an enemy of all righteousness, will you not cease to disturb the righteous ways of the Lord? 11 Now therefore, behold, the hand of the LORD is upon thee, and thou shalt be blinded, and shalt not see the sun for a season." And im- mediately there came upon him a mist and a darkness; and he set out to find someone to hold his hand. 12 Then the deputy, when he heard what had been done, was bewildered and astonished at the doctrine of the Lord. 13 Now when Paul and those who were with him departed by ship from Paphus, they came to Perga, a city in Pamphylia; then John departed from them and returned to Jeru- salem. 14 And they departed from Perga and came to Antioch, a city of Pisidia, and entered the synagogue on the Sabbath day and sat down. 15 After the reading of the Law and the Prophets, the leaders of the synagogue joined them, saying, "Men and brothers, if you have any words of exhortation for the people, say them." 16 Then Paul stopped, beckoned with his hand and said, "Men of Israel and you who fear God,

listen." 17 The God of this people of Israel chose our fathers, and exalted the people when they dwelt in the land of Egypt, and with high arms brought them out of it. 18 About forty years of age, he suffered their forsaking in the wilderness. 19 Then he de- stroyed some nations in the land of Chanaan and gave them their children as their lot. 20 Then he gave them rights for about four hun- dred and fifty years, until the time of Samuel the prophet. 21 Then they wanted a king, and God gave them Saul the son of Cis, a man of the tribe of Benjamin, for a period of forty years. 22 After taking him away, he raised up Dauid as their king, of whom he testified, saying, "I have found Dauid the son of Jesse, a man after my own heart, who will do all that I want." 23 Of this seed God, according to his promise, has raised up to Israel your Jesus: 24 When John, before his coming, had preached the baptism of repentance to all the people of Israel. 25 When Iohn had fulfilled his course, he said, "Whom ye think that I am, I am not he; but behold, there cometh after me one whom I am not worthy to unloose his feet." 26 Men and brethren, children of Abraham's generation, and everyone among you who fears God, to you has been sent the message of this salvation. 27 For the inhabitants of Jerusalem and their rulers, not knowing him nor the words of the Prophets that are read every Sabbath, complied with them by con- demning him. 28 And though they found no cause of death in him, yet Pilate wanted to kill him. 29 And when they had fulfilled all the things written about him, they took him off the tree and put him in a tomb. 30 But God raised him from the dead. 31 And he was seen many days by those who had come with him from Galilee to Jerusalem, who are his wit- nesses to the people. 32 We declare to you concerning the promise made to the fathers, 33 God fulfilled it in regard to their children, in that he begat Jesus, as it is written in the second Psalm, "You are my Son, today I have begotten you." 34 Now concerning the fact that he raised him from the dead, so that he would never again return to corruption, he said thus, "I will give you the holy things of Dauid, which are faithful." 35 Therefore he also says in another place, "You shall not al- low your Holy One to see corruption." 36 Nev- ertheless, Dauid, having observed his time according to the counsel of God, fell asleep and was laid down with his fathers and saw corruption. 37 But he whom God raised up did not suffer corruption. 38 Know therefore, men and brethren, that through this man was preached to you the forgiveness of sins. 39 And from all things, from which you could not be justified by the Law of Moses, through him was justified everyone who was convert- ed. 40 Beware, therefore, lest that which is spoken of in the Prophets come upon you, 41 Behold, ye scorners, be astonished, and be gone: for I have wrought a work in your days, a work which ye shall not see, though a man should declare it unto you." 42 When they had come out of the synagogue of the Gentiles, the Gentiles begged them to preach these words to them on the following Sabbath. 43 Now when the assembly broke up, many of the Jews and proselytes who feared God fol- lowed Paul and Barnabas, who spoke to them and urged them to continue in the grace of God. 44 On the following Sabbath almost the whole city gathered to hear the word of God. 45 But when the witnesses saw the people, they were filled with envy and spoke against those things that had been spoken by Paul, contradicting them and railing against them. 46 Then Paul and Barnabas spoke boldly and said, "It was necessary that the word of God should first be proclaimed to you; but because you have turned it away from you and judge yourselves worthy of eternal life, behold, we turn to the Gentiles. 47 For thus hath the Lord commanded, saying, I have made you a light unto the Gentiles, that you may be salvation unto the end of the world. 48 When the Gen- tiles heard this, they rejoiced and glorified the work of the Lord; and as many as were destined for eternal life were accepted. 49 So the word of the LORD was spread throughout the whole land. 50 But the witnesses stirred up some good and honorable women, and the leading men of the city, and raised a persecu- tion against Paul and Barnabas, and expelled them from their shores. 51 But they shook off the dust of their feet and came to Iconium. 52 The disciples were filled with joy and the Holy Spirit.

CHAPTER 14

1 At Iconium, the two of them went into the synagogue of the Jews together and spoke in such a way that a great multitude of Jews and Greeks became heated. 2 And the vnbelee became agitated and corrupted the minds of the Gentiles against the brothers. 3 There- fore they stood there a long time and spoke boldly in the Lord, testifying the word of his grace and doing signs and wonders with their hands. 4 But the crowd in the city was in dis- agreement, and some were with the witness- es and others with the apostles. 5 When there was an assault by the Gentiles and Israelites with their leaders, to do violence to them and to stone them, 6 they became aware of it and fled to Lystra and Derbe, cities of Ly- caonia, and the surrounding region, 7 and there they preached the gospel. 8 At Lystra there was a certain man, impotent in his feet, who had been born of his mother and had never walked. 9 This man heard Paul speak, who, seeing him and seeing that he had faith, healed him, 10 and said to him in a loud voice, "Stand on your feet." And he sprang to his feet and walked. 11 Then when the people heard what Paul had done, they raised their voices, saying in the Lycaonic language, "The gods have come down to heaven in the like- ness of men." 12 And they called Barnabas, Iupiter, and Paul, Mercurius, because he was the chief speaker. 13 Then Iupiters the priest, who stood in front of their city, brought to the gates bullets with garlands, and wanted to sacrifice with the people. 14 But when the apostles, Barnabas and Paul, heard of it, they tore their garments and ran among the peo- ple, crying out, 15 and said, "O men, why do you do these things? We too are men subject to the same passions as you, and we preach to you to forsake these vain things and turn your eyes to the living God, who made the ocean, the earth, the sea and all things that are in them: 16 Who in the past enabled all the Gentiles to walk in their own lives. 17 He has not left Himself without witnesses, in that He has done good and granted the Heauen raine and fruitful seasons, filling our hearts with food and joy. 18 Speaking of these things, the crowd was hardly quiet, for they had not sacrificed to them. 19 Then came some people from Antioch and Iconium, who, after per- suading the people, stoned Paul and dragged him out of the city, believing him to be dead. 20 However, while the disciples stood around him, he got up, entered the city, and the next day left with Barnabas for Derbe. 21 And after preaching the glad tidings of the gospel in that city and teaching many, they returned to Ly- stra, Iconium and Antioch, 22 confirming the hearts of the disciples and exhorting them to continue in the faith, affirming that we must enter the kingdom of God through many af- flictions. 23 And after appointing them elders by election in each church, having prayed and fasted, they commended them to the Lord in whom they were believers. 24 So they went through Pisidia and came to Pamphylia. 25 After preaching the Word in Perga, they went down to Attaliah, 26 and from there they set sail to Antioch, from where they had been admitted to the grace of God, because of the program they had completed. 27 When they had arrived and gathered the church togeth- er, they related all the things that God had done through them and how he had opened the door of faith to the Gentiles. 28 So they stayed a long time with the disciples.

CHAPTER 15

1 Then some came down from Judea and taught the brothers, saying, "Unless you are circumcised according to the method of Mo- ses, you cannot be saved." 2 And when there was a great dissension and dispute from Paul and Barnabas against them, they ordered that Paul and Barnabas, and some others of them, should go to Jerusalem to the apos- tles and elders about this matter. 3 So, led by the church, they passed through Phoenix and Samaria, declaring the conquest of the Gentiles, and procured great joy for all the brethren. 4 When they reached Jerusalem, they were received by the Church, the apos- tles and the elders, and declared what God had done through them. 5 But they said that some of the sect of the Pharisees, who were in the business of election, stood up, saying that it was necessary to circumcise them and command them to keep the law of Moses. 6 Then the apostles and elders gathered to con- sider the matter. 7 After much discussion, Peter stood up and said to them, "Men and brethren, you know that long ago God chose me from among others, that the Gentiles might hear by my mouth the word of the gos- pel and be converted. 8 And God, who knows hearts, bore witness to them, giving them the Holy Spirit, just as He did to Yours. 9 And He placed no difference between the former and the latter, after He had purified their hearts by faith. 10 Why, then, do you tempt God to put on the necks of the disciples a yoke that neither our fathers nor we were able to bear? 11 But we are able, by the grace of the Lord Je- sus Christ, to be saved, just as they were." 12 Then the whole crowd fell silent and listened to Barnabas and Paul telling of the signs and wonders God had done among the Gentiles through them. 13 When they had quieted down, Iames answered and said, "Men and brothers, listen to me. 14 Simeon declared how God first visited the Gentiles to draw out of them a people to be dedicated to His Name. 15 And on this agree the words of the Prophets, as it is written, 16 After this, I will return and I will rebuild the tent of Dauid, which has fallen, and its ruins I will rebuild and set up, 17 That the remnant of men may seek the LORD, and all the nations over whom my Name is invoked, says the LORD who does all these things. 18 From the beginning of the world God knows all his works. 19 Therefore my judgment is not to trouble the Gentiles who have turned to God, 20 but that we send word to them that they should abstain from the filthiness of idols, from fornication, from that which is strangled and from blood. 21 For Moses has always had in every city those who preach it, since it is read in the synagogues every Sabbath. 22 Then it seemed good to the apostles and elders, with the whole church, to send to Antioch, with Paul and Barnabas, some chosen men of their company, Iudas, whose surname was Barsabas, and Silas, who were prominent men among the brethren, 23 and they wrote letters to them in this way, "The apostles, elders and brethren greet the brethren who are among the Gentiles in An- tioch, Syria and Cilicia." 24 For we have heard that

some of those who left here have troubled you with words and recoiled your minds, say- ing, "You must be circumcised and keep the law," and we have given no commandment to that effect, 25 Therefore it seemed good to us, when we came together by common consent, to send to you chosen men, with our broth- ers Barnabas and Paul, 26 men who have giv- en their lives for the name of our Lord Jesus Christ. 27 Therefore we sent Iudas and Silas, who will tell you the same things by word of mouth. 28 For it has seemed good to the Holy Spirit and to you to lay upon you no other bur- den than these necessary things, 29 that is, that you abstain from things offered to idols, from blood, from that which is strangled, and from fornication; from which, if you keep yourselves away, you will do well. Farewell. 30 Now having departed, they came to Antioch, and having assembled the crowd, they deliv- ered the epistle. 31 After reading it, they gath- ered together for consolation. 32 Iudas and Silas, being prophets, exhorted the brothers in many words and strengthened them. 33 Af- ter they stood there for a while, they were let go in peace by the brothers to the apostles. 34 However, Silas thought good to remain there still.35 Paul and Barnabas also continued to stay in Antioch, teaching and preaching with many others the word of the Lord. 36 But af- ter a few days, Paul said to Barnabas, "Let us go back and visit our brethren in every city where we have preached the word of the Lord, and see how they conduct themselves." 37 Barnabas advised taking Iohn, called Marke, with him. 38 But Paul did not see fit to take him with him, because he had departed from them from Pamphylia and had not gone with them to work. 39 Then they became so agitat- ed that they separated from one another, so that Barnabas took Marke and set sail for Cy- prus. 40 Paul chose Silas and departed, hav- ing been commended by his brothers for the grace of God. 41 Then he went through Syria and Cilicia, establishing the churches.

CHAPTER 16

1 Then he came to Derbe and Lystra; and behold, there was a certain disciple named Timothy, the son of a woman, who was Jew- ish and unmarried, but his father was Greek, 2 of whom the brethren who were at Lystra and Iconium reported well. 3 Therefore Paul desired him to go with him, and took him and circumcised him, because of you Jews who were in those quarters; for they all knew that his father was a Greek. 4 And as they went through the cities, they delivered to them the decrees to be observed, laid down by the apostles and elders who were in Jerusalem. 5 Thus the churches were established in the faith and increased in number every day. 6 Now after they had passed through Phrygia and the region of Galatia, the Holy Spirit for- bade them to preach the word in Asia. 7 So they came to Mysia and tried to go to Bithyn- ia, but the Spirit would not let them. 8 So they passed through Mysia and went down to Troas,9 where, at night, a vision appeared to Paul. There stood a man from Macedonia and begged him, saying, "Come to Macedonia and help us." 10 After he had had the vision, we immediately prepared to enter Mace- donia, certain that the Lord had called us to preach the gospel to them. 11 So we set out from Troas and by a straight course arrived in Samothrace and the next day in Neapolis, 12 and from there to Philippi, which is the most important city in Macedonia and whose inhabitants have come from Rome to dwell there; we remained in that city for several days. 13 On the Sabbath day we went out of the city and went to a river where they used to pray; and we sat down and spoke to the women who had gathered together. 14 A cer- tain woman named Lydia, a seller of purple, from the city of Thyatira, who worshipped God, listened; and the Lord opened her heart, that she might hear the things that Paul said. 15 When she was baptized and her house, she prayed vs. saying, "If you have persuaded me to be faithful to the Lord, come into my house and stay there. 16 And it came to pass, as we were going to pray, that a certain teacher, who had a spirit of diuination, came in contact with her, and brought her masters into a spir- it of diuination. 17 She followed Paul and his people, and cried out, saying, "These men are the servants of the most high God, who teach you the way of salvation." 18 And this she did for many days; but Paul, seized with fear, turned and said to the spirit, "I command you in the name of Jesus Christ to go out from her." And he went out in that same hour. 19 Now when his masters saw that the hope of their salvation was gone, they took Paul and Silas and led them into the marketplace be- fore the magistrates, 20 and they led them to the magistrates, saying, "These men, who are badgers, disturb our city, 21 and they preach rules which it is not lawful for us to receive or to observe, since we are Romans." 22 The peo- ple also rose up against them, and the gover- nours tore their garments and commanded them to be beaten with rods. 23 And after they had beaten them severely, they threw them into prison, instructing the governor to keep them safe. 24 Who, having received such an order, threw them into the inner prison and fastened their feet in the stocks. 25 At mid- night Paul and Silas prayed and sang psalms to God, and the prisoners listened to them. 26 Suddenly there was a great earthquake, so that the foundations of the prison were shak- en; and presently all the doors were opened, and all the men were loosed. 27 Then the keeper of the prison awoke from sleep and, seeing the prison doors open, drew his sword and would have killed himself, thinking that the prisoners had escaped. 28 But Paul cried out with a loud voice, saying, "Do not hurt yourself, for we are all here." 29 Then he called a light, leaped in, came trembling, and fell down before Paul and Silas, 30 and brought them out, and said, "Sisters, what must I do to be saved?" 31 And they answered, "Covenant in the Lord Jesus Christ, and you and your house will be healed." 32 They preached to him the word of the Lord and to all who were in the house. 33 Then he took them, in that same hour of the night, and washed them, and was baptized with all that belonged to him, in a straight manner. 34 And when he had brought them into his house, he set food before them and pointed out that he and all his household were believers in God. 35 When it was day, the governors sent the sergeants to say, "Let those men go." 36 Then the prison warden report- ed these words to Paul, saying, "The warders have sent to set you free; now therefore leave and go in peace." 37 Then Paul said to them, "Having openly beaten the vncodemons, who are Romans, they have thrown them into pris- on, and now would they like to let them out confidentially? No, of course not, but let them come and let them out." 38 The sergeants re- ported these words to the soldiers, who feared to know that they were Romans. 39 Then they came and praised them and brought them out and asked them to leave the city. 40 And they went out of the prison and entered the house of Lydia; and when they saw the brothers, they comforted them and departed.

CHAPTER 17

1 Now, passing through Amphipolis and Apollonia, they came to Thessalonica, where there was a synagogue of Jews. 2 Paul, as was his wont, went in to them and for three Sab- baths discussed the Scriptures with them, 3 affirming that Christ had suffered and had risen from the dead; and this is Jesus Christ, whom I preach to you, he said. 4 And some of them were converted and joined Paul and Silas; also among the Greeks who feared God there was a great multitude, and among the leading women not a few. 5 But the people who had not acceded to the call, they moved with enuie, and took with them some wan- derers and wicked companions; and having gathered the crowd together, they made a tumult in the city, and stormed the house of Iason, and sought to bring them out among the people. 6 But not having found them, they drew Iason and some brothers to the leaders of the city, crying, "These are they who have subdued the state of the world, and here they are, 7 whom Iason received, and all of them oppose the decrees of Caesar, saying that there is another king, one Iesus." 8 Then, on hearing these things, they troubled the people and the leaders of the city. 9 However, having received sufficient assurance about Iason and the other, they let them go. 10 The brothers immediately sent Paul and Silas by night to Berea, and when they arrived there they en- tered the synagogue of the Jews. 11 These were also more noble men than those who were in Thessalonica, who received the word with all readiness and searched the Scriptures every day whether those things were true. 12 There- fore many of them withdrew, and of honest women, who were Greeks, and of men not a few. 13 But when the witnesses from Thessa- lonica heard that the word of God had been preached by Paul also in Berea, they came there also and asked the people questions. 14 But then the brothers sent Paul away to go, as it were, to the sea; but Silas and Timothy still remained there. 15 Those who were leading Paul led him to Athens, and having received orders from Silas and Timothy to go to him at once, they departed. 16 Now while Paul was waiting for them in Athens, his spirit was stirred in him when he saw the city subject to idolatry. 17 Therefore he disputed in the syna- gogue with Jews and religious men, and every day in the marketplace with anyone he met. 18 Some philosophers, among the Epicure- ans and Stoics, argued with him, and some said, "What will this chatterer say? Others said, "It seems that he is an impostor of se- vere gods (because he preached Jesus and the resurrection to them)." 19 They took him and brought him to Mars Street, saying, "Can we not know what is this new doctrine of which you speak?20 For you bring to our ears certain strange things; therefore we want to know what these things mean. 21 For all the Athe- nians and the strangers who live there do not devote themselves to anything else but telling or listening to some new thing. 22 Then Paul stopped in the middle of Mars Street and said, "Men of Athens, I notice that in everything you are too superstitious. 23 For as I passed by and observed your deviations, I found an altar on which was written, 'VNTO THE UN- KNOWN GOD. To him whom you worship in ignorance, I told you to worship him. 24 The God who made the world and all things in it, being the Lord of earth and heaven, does not dwell in temples made with hands, 25 nor is he worshipped with the hands of men, as if he needed anything, for he gives to all life and breath and all things, 26 and has made of one blood all men, to dwell on all the face of the earth, and has assigned to them the seasons that were set beforehand and the boundaries of their dwelling place, 27 So that they may see the Lord, if it is true that they have sought him, and have found him, though doubtless he is not far from every one of you. 28 For in him we live and move and are, as some of your poets also have said, for we are also his gener- ation. 29 Since, therefore, we are God's gen- eration, we must not think that your deity is like gold or silk or stone worked by the art and ingenuity of man. 30 God did not take into ac- count the time of this ignorance, but now he admonishes all men everywhere to repent, 31 for he has fixed the day when he will judge the world with righteousness, by that man whom he has fixed, and of whom he has assured all men that he raised him from the dead. 32 Now when they heard of the resurrection from the dead, some mocked and others said, "We will hear you again on this thing." 33 So Paul went out from among them. 34 But some men came to Paul and felt betrayed; among them were Denys Areopagite, a woman named Damaris, and others with them.

CHAPTER 18

1 After these things Paul departed from Ath- ens and came to Corinth, 2 and he found a certain Iewe named Aquila, born in Pontus, who had recently come from Italy, and his wife Priscilla (for Claudius had command- ed all the Iewes to depart from Rome), and he approached them. 3 And because he was of the same stock, he stayed with them and worked (for their art was to make tents). 4 Ev- ery Sabbath he disputed in the synagogue and exhorted the Jews and the Greeks. 5 When Si- las and Timothy came from Macedonia, Paul, compelled by the spirit, testified to the Greeks that Jesus was the Christ. 6 When they resist- ed and blasphemed, he shook off his garments and said to them, "Let your blood be on your head: I am clean; henceforth I will go among the Gentiles." 7 So he departed from there and entered the house of a certain man named Iustus, a worshipper of God, whose house was near the synagogue. 8 Crispus, the leader of the synagogue, baptized himself into the Lord with all his household; and many of the Corinthians, hearing this, were baptized. 9 Then the Lord said to Paul in a vision by night, "Fear not, speak and be not at peace. 10 For I am with you, and no one will lay hands on you to harm you, for I have many people in this city." 11 So he stayed there for a year and six months and taught the word of God among them.12 When Gallio was deputy of Achaia, the Jews rose up with one accord against Paul and brought him before the judicial tribunal, 13 saying, "This man persuades me to worship God in a way different from that established by the Law." 14 And as Paul was about to open his mouth, Gallio said to the witnesses, "If it were a matter of error or injustice, O witness- es, I would keep you according to reason. 15 But if it were a matter of words and names and your faith, mind yourselves, for I will not be a judge of these things." 16 And he dragged them away from the judgment seat. 17 Then all the Greeks seized Sosthenes, the leader of the Synagogue, and beat him before the tri- bunal; but Gallio cared not for these things. 18 But when Paul had stood there for quite a while, he broke away from the brethren and departed for Syria (and with him Priscilla and Aquila), having shaken his head at Cenchrea, for he had made a vow. 19 Then he came to Ephesus and left them there; but he entered the synagogue and disputed with the Jews. 20 Who wanted him to stay longer with them, but he would not consent, 21 but took his leave, saying, "I must necessarily celebrate the feast that is about to begin in Jerusalem, but I will return to you again, God willing." So he departed from Ephesus. 22 When he reached Caesarea, he went to Jerusalem and, after greeting

the Church, went down to An- tioch. 23 After stopping there for a while, he departed and went through Galatia and Phry- gia, strengthening all the disciples. 24 There came to Ephesus a certain Apollos, born in Alexandria, a man of eloquence and much versed in the Scriptures. 25 This man had been instructed in the way of the Lord, spoke with power in the Spirit, taught diligently the things of the Lord, and knew nothing but the baptism of John. 26 And he began to speak boldly in the synagogue. When Aquila and Priscilla had heard him, they took him with them and expounded to him more perfectly the way of God. 27 And when he determined to depart for Achaia, the brethren, exhorting him, wrote to the disciples that they might receive him; and after he was come thither, he saluted them much, which he had received by grace. 28 For he strongly and with great vehe- mence refuted the witnesses, proving by the Scriptures that Jesus was that Christ.

CHAPTER 19

1 While Apollos was in Corinth, Paul, passing through the southern coasts, came to Ephe- sus and found some disciples, 2 and said to them, "Have you received the Holy Spirit since you were baptized?" And they answered him, "We have not even heard whether there is a Holy Spirit." 3 And he said to them, "In what were you baptized then?" And they said, "In the baptism of John." 4 Then Paul said, "Iohn truly baptized with the baptism of re- pentance, telling the people that they should be baptized into him, who was to come after him, that is, into Christ Iesus." 5 And when they heard this, they were baptized in the Name of the Lord Iesus. 6 Then Paul stretched out his hands over them, and the Holy Spirit came upon them, and they spoke tongues and prophesied. 7 And all the men were about two. 8 Then he went into the synagogue and spoke boldly for three months, discussing and ex- horting the things concerning the kingdom of God. 9 But when some hardened and dis- obeyed, speaking evil of the way of God before the crowd, he departed from them, separated the disciples, and disputed every day in the school of a certain Tyrant. 10 This took place for the space of two years, so that all who dwelt in Asia heard the word of the Lord Iesus, both the Jevians and the Greeks. 11 God worked no small miracles at the hands of Paul, 12 so that from his body were brought to the sick, chéfs or handkerchefs, and the diseases departed from them and the sick spirits went out from them. 13 Then some of the handkerchefs, ex- orcists, took up the name of the Lord Jesus to name those who had sick spirits, saying, "We adore you for Jesus, whom Paul preaches." 14 (And there were some sons of Sheua in Iewe, the priest, about ten doing this). 15 The euilic spirit answered and said, "Jesus I know, and Paul I know; but who are you? 16 Then the man in whom the evil spirit was came upon them, and smote them, and hurled himself at them, so that they fled out of that house, naked and wounded. 17 And this was known also to all the Iewes and Greeks who dwelt in Ephesus, and all were afraid, and the name of the Lord Iesus was magnified, 18 and many of those who were believers came to confess and to show their works. 19 Also many of those who engaged in curious arts brought their books and burned them before all; then they counted the price of them and found it to be fifty thousand pieces of silver. 20 Thus the word of God spread with power and went forth. 21 Now when these things were accom- plished, Paul determined by the Spirit to pass through Macedonia and Achaia and to go to Jerusalem, saying, "After I have been there, I must see Rome also." 22 So he sent two of those who assisted him, Timothy and Eras- tus, to Macedonia, but he remained in Asia for some time. 23 And at the same time not a little trouble arose on that side. 24 For a certain Demetrius, a maker of the temples of Diana, brought great gains to the craftsmen, 25 and having assembled the craftsmen who worked in like manner, he said, "Gentlemen, you know that by this craft we have obtained our goods." 26 Moreover you see and hear that not only in Ephesus but almost all over Asia this Paul convinced and turned away many people, saying, "They are not gods who are made with hands." 27 Therefore not only is this thing dangerous for us, that this part of us should be repudiated, but also that the temple of the great goddess Diana should not be esteemed, and that it should come to de- stroy her magnificence, which all Asia and the world worship. 28 On hearing this, they were filled with wrath and cried, "Great is Diana of the Ephesians." 29 And the whole city was in confusion, and they rushed into the common place with one assent, and seized Gaius and Aristarchus, men of Macedonia and Paul's fel- low travelers. 30 And when Paul wanted to go in among the people, the disciples would not allow him. 31 Also some of the leaders of Asia, who were his friends, sent word to him that he would not come into the common place. 32 Some were shouting one thing and others another, for the assembly was disorderly and most did not know why they had gathered. 33 Some of the company drew Alexander in, pushing him forward. Alexander then beck- oned with his hand and wanted to apologize to the people. 34 But when they found that he was a Iewe, there was a shout almost for two hours, of all the men crying out, "Great is Diana of the Ephesians." 35 Then the sheriff of the city, having stopped the people, said, "Men of Ephesus, who is it that does not know that the city of the Ephesians is a worshipper of the great goddess Diana and the image that came down from Jupiter? 36 Since therefore no one can speak against these things, you must be quiet and do nothing rash. 37 For you have brought these men here who have not committed sacrilege nor blasphemed your goddess. 38 Therefore, if Demetrius and the cunning men who are with him have anything to say about anyone, the law is open and there are deputies; let them accuse one another. 39 But if you ask anything about other matters, it can be decided in a lawful assembly. 40 For we are in a situation of ieopardia to be ac- cused of today's sedition, for there is no cause to justify this gathering of people." 41 Having spoken thus, he let the assembly leave.

CHAPTER 20

1 Now when the tumult had subsided, Paul called the disciples to himself, embraced them, and set out for Macedonia. 2 After pass- ing through those parts and exhorting them with many words, he came to Greece. 3 After stopping there for three months, because the Israelites were waiting for him, as he was about to enter Syria, he decided to return through Macedonia. 4 Accompanying him in Asia were Sopater of Berea, Aristarchus, Secundus, Gaius of Derbe, Timotheus, Ty- chicus and Trophimus. 5 These preceded and stopped at Troas. 6 We set sail from Philippi, after the days of vnleauened bread, and came to them to Troas in five days, where we stayed seven days. 7 On the first day of the week, while the disciples were gathering to prepare bread, Paul preached to them, ready to leave the next day, and continued preaching until midnight.8 There were many lamps in an up- per room

where they were gathered. 9 At the window stood a certain young man named Eutychius, who had fallen into a deadly sleep; and while Paul was preaching at length, he, overcome by sleep, fell down from the thir- teenth floor and was carried away dead. 10 But Paul came down and lay on him and em- braced him, saying, "Do not be troubled, for his life is in him." 11 Then Paul returned home and broke bread and ate, and after speak- ing at length until daybreak, he departed. 12 They brought the child and were not a little comforted. 13 Then we embarked and sailed to the city of Assos, to receive Paul there, for so he had determined and wanted to depart himself. 14 When he had come to Assos and we had received him, we arrived at Mytilene. 15 From there we sailed, and the next day we arrived at Chios; the next day we came to Sa- mos and stopped at Trogyllium; the next day we arrived at Miletus. 16 For Paul had decided to pass through Ephesus, because he did not want to spend time in Asia, for he wished to be, if possible, in Jerusalem on the day of Pen- tecost. 17 Therefore from Miletus he sent to Ephesus and called the elders of the church. 18 When they had come to him, he said to them, "You know that from the first day that I came to Asia I have been with you at all times, 19 serving the Lord with all modesty and with many conferences and temptations, which have been made to me through the waiting plans of the seers, 20 and how I withheld nothing useful, but showed and taught you openly and in all houses, 21 testifying unto you both to Jews and to Greeks repentance toward God and faith toward our Lord Jesus Christ. 22 And now behold, I go bound in the Spirit to Jerusalem, and I do not know what things will happen to me there, 23 But you, Holy Spirit, are witnesses in every city, say- ing that bonds and afflictions have been laid upon me. 24 But I do not pass away at all, and my life is no longer in danger to myself, that I may fulfill with joy my course and ministry which I have received from the Lord Iesus, to witness the gospel of the grace of God. 25 And now, behold, I know that from now on you all, through whom I have gone to preach the kingdom of God, will no longer see my face. 26 Therefore I point out to you today that I am pure from the blood of all men. 27 For I have withheld nothing, but have set forth to you all the counsels of God. 28 Take heed therefore to yourselves and to all the flock, of which the Holy Spirit has made you overser, to feed the Church of God, which he purchased with his own blood. 29 For I know that after my departure cruel wolves will enter in among you, who will not spare the flock. 30 More- over there will arise among you men who will speak perverse things, to draw disciples after them. 31 Therefore be careful and remember that for three years I have not ceased to make war on each of you, both by night and by day, with teas. 32 Now, brothers, I commend you to God and to the word of his grace, which is able to edify you further and to give you an inheritance among all who are sanctified. 33 I have borrowed neither silk nor gold nor men's clothing. 34 You know that these hands assisted my needs and the needs of those who were with me. 35 I have explained everything to you, how, in working, you should support those who are weak and remember the words of the Lord Jesus, who says, "It is a blessed thing to give rather than to receive." 36 After speaking thus, he knelt down and prayed with all of them. 37 Then they all wept abundantly and fell on Paul's neck and kissed him, 38 es- pecially because they were sorry for the words he had spoken; they would never see his face again. And they accompanied him to the ship.

CHAPTER 21

1 When we left and departed from them, we came by a straight course to Coos and the next day to Rhodes and from there to Patara. 2 We found a ship going toward Phoenix, boarded it and departed. 3 And when we had discovered Cyprus, we left it on our left, and sailed to Syria, and came to Tyre, for there the ship carried the cargo there. 4 And when we had found disciples, we stayed there for a few days. And they told Paul by the Spirit that he should not go to Jerusalem. 5 And when the days were ended, we departed, and took our way, and they accompanied us all with their wives and children, going out of the city; and we, kneeling on the shore, prayed. 6 Then, after we had embraced one another, we took ship again, and they returned home. 7 Having finished our course from Tyre, we arrived at Ptolemais, said goodbye to the brothers and stayed with them one day. 8 The next day Paul and we who were with him left and arrived at Caesarea; we entered the house of Philip the Evangelist, who was one of the ten deacons, and stayed with him. 9 He had four virgin daughters who prophesied. 10 While we were staying there for many days, there came a certain prophet from Judea, named Agabus. 11 When he came in sight, he took Paul's belt, bound his hands and feet, and said, "Thus says the Holy Spirit, 'The judges in Jerusalem will take the man who has this belt and deliver him into the hands of the Gentiles.'" 12 When we heard these things, we and others of the same place begged him not to go to Jerusa- lem. 13 Then Paul answered and said, "Why do you weep and break my heart? For I am ready not only to be bound, but also to die in Jerusalem for the name of the Lord Jesus." 14 Then, because he would not be persuaded, we ceased, saying, "The will of the Lord be done." 15 After those days, we prepared our burdens and went to Jerusalem. 16 Some disciples from Caesarea also went with them, and they brought a certain Mnasone of Cyprus, an old disciple, with whom we were to lodge. 17 When we had arrived in Jerusalem, the brothers welcomed us with joy. 18 The next day Paul went with them to Iames, where all the elders were gathered. 19 When he had re- ceived them, he related in full detail all that God had worked among the Gentiles through his ministry. 20 So when they heard this, they glorified God and said to him, "See, brother, how many thousands of Jews are present and are all zealous for the Law." 21 Now they were informed of you, that you teach all the people who are among the Gentiles to forsake Moses and say that they must not circumcise their children or follow the customs. 22 What is to be done then? It is necessary for the multi- tude to gather together, for they will hear that you have come. 23 Do therefore what we say to you. We have four men who have taken a vow, 24 take them, purify yourself with them, and help with them to shave their heads; and they shall all know that the things which they have been told about you are nothing, but that you also walk and keep the Law. 25 For as for the Gentiles, who are on the run, we have written and decreed that they should observe nothing like this, but that they should keep themselves from things offended by idols, from blood, from that which is strangled, and from forni- cation." 26 Then Paul took the men, and the next day he purified himself with them and entered the Temple, declaring the fulfillment of the days of purification, until an offering was offered for each of them. 27 And when the ten days were almost finished, the witnesses from Asia, when they saw him in the Temple, called all the people together and laid their hands on him, 28 crying, "Men of Israel, come to the rescue! This is the man who teaches all men

everywhere against the people, against the law, and against this place; moreover, he has brought Greeks into the Temple and pol- luted this holy place." 29 For they had seen before Trophimus, an Ephesian who was with him in the city and whom they thought Paul had brought into the Temple. 30 Then the whole city moved and the people rushed in; and they took Paul and brought him out of the Temple, and the doors were shut. 31 But as they were about to kill him, news came to the ringleader that all Jerusalem was on the alert. 32 And the latter immediately took soldiers and centurions and ran to them; and when they saw the chief of the band and the soldiers, they departed from Paul. 33 Then the chief of the captains came and seized him, and commanded him to be bound with two chains, and asked him who he was and what he had done. 34 One cried out this, another that, among the people. And not being able to know what was the cause of the tumult, he or- dered him to be brought into the fortress. 35 And when he came to the walls, he was taken away by the soldiers, because of the violence of the people. 36 For the multitude of the peo- ple followed him, crying, "Away with him." 37 And as Paul was to be led to his cell, he said to the leader of the prison, "May I speak to you?" Who answered, "Can you speak in Greek? 38 Are you not the Egyptian who before these days raised up a sedition and led into the wil- derness four thousand men who were making slaughter? 39 Then Paul answered, "Doubtful, I am a man, a Jew, a citizen of Tarsus, a fa- mous city of Cilicia, and I beg you to allow me to speak to the people." 40 Having given him leave, Paul stood on the handles and beck- oned with his hand to the people; and when there was a great silence, he spoke to them in the Hebrew language, saying

CHAPTER 22

1 You men, brothers and fathers, listen to my defense to you. 2 (And when they heard that he spoke to them in the Hebrew language, they were still more silent, and he said) 3 I am only a man, who is a Jew, born in Tarsus in Cilicia, but brought up in this city at the feet of Gamaliel and instructed according to the perfect manner of the word of the fathers, and I was zealous for God, as you all are to- day. 4 I pursued this way to the death, binding and imprisoning men and women. 5 As also the chief of the priests and all the company of the elders testify to me, of whom I received letters to the brethren, and went to Damas- cus to bring to Jerusalem those who were there bound, that they might be punished. 6 And so as I was on my way and was com- ing to Damascus, without anyone seeing me, suddenly there appeared from above a great light around me. 7 Then I fell to the ground and heard a voice saying to me, "Saul, Saul, why are you persecuting me?" 8 Then I an- swered, "Who are you, Lord?" And he said to me, "I am Jesus of Nazareth, whom you per- secute." 9 Moreover those who were with me saw a light and stood speechless, but they did not hear the voice of him who spoke to me. 10 Then I said, "What shall I do, Lord?" And the Lord said to me, "Arise and go to Damascus; and there all that is appointed for you to do shall be explained to you." 11 So when I could no longer see for the glory of that light, I was led by the hand by those who were with me and came to Damascus. 12 A certain Ananias, a godly man, who was going to Lawe and who had good news of all the people of Damascus, came to Damascus, 13 and came to me and stood and said, "Brother Saul, receive your sight"; and at that same hour I looked at him. 14 And he said, "The God of our fathers has ap- pointed you that you may know his will, and see that righteous man, and hear the voice of his mouth. 15 For you shall be his witness to all men of the things that you have seen and heard. 16 Why then will you not stand? Get up, be baptized, and wash away your sins by calling on the Name of the Lord." 17 When I was again in Jerusalem and went to pray in the Temple, I was in a panic, 18 and I saw him saying to me, "Hurry and get out of Jerusalem quickly, for they do not want to hear your tes- timonies about me." 19 Then I said, "Lord, they know that I have imprisoned and beaten in every synagogue those who believed in you." 20 And when the blood of your martyr Steuen was shed, I also stood by and consented to his death and kept the garments of those who killed him." 21 Then he said, "Depart, for I will send you far away, to the Gentiles." 22 They listened to him to these words, but then they raised their voices and said, "Away with such a one from the land, for it is not right that he should remain." 23 And as they cried out, they stripped off their garments and threw dust into the air, 24 and the chief of the chiefs or- dered him to be led into the castle and com- manded to be scourged and examined to know why they were shouting so about him. 25 While they were binding him with laces, Paul said to the centurion standing nearby, "Is it lawful for you to scourge one who is a Roman and has not been condemned? 26 Now when the centurion heard this, he went and reported to the chieftain, "Be careful what you do, for this man is a Roman." 27 Then the chieftain approached him and said, "Tell me, are you a Roman?" And he answered, "Yes." 28 And the chieftain answered, "With a great sum I obtained this freedom." Then Paul said, "But I have been borne thus." 29 Then imme- diately those who should have examined him departed from him; and the chieftain also de- parted, having learned that he was a Roman and that he had bound him. 30 And the next day, because he wanted to know for certain why he was accused of crimes, he loosed him from his bonds and ordered the priests and all their councils to assemble; and he brought Paul in and set him before them.

CHAPTER 23

1 Paul looked earnestly at the council and said, "Men and brethren, I have served God in all conscience until this day." 2 Then Ana- nias the priest ordered those standing nearby to strike him on the mouth. 3 Then Paul said to him, "God shall smite thee, white wall, be- cause thou sittest down to judge me accord- ing to the law, and, transgressing the law, hast condemned me to be smitten? 4 Those who stood nearby said, "Are you the priest of the gods?" 5 Then Paul said, "I did not know, brothers, that he was the priest, for it is writ- ten, 'You shall not speak evil of the ruler of your people.'" 6 But when Paul saw that the one was a Sadducee and the other a Pharisee, he cried out in council, "Men and brethren, I am a Pharisee, the son of Pharisees; I am charged with the hope and resurrection of the dead." 7 And when he had said this, there was dissension between the Pharisees and the Sadducees, so that the multitude was de- fiant. 8 For the Sadducees say that there is no resurrection, either of angels or of spirits, but the Pharisees confess both. 9 Then there was a great cry; and the scribes of the Pharisees stood up and marched out, saying, "We find nothing good in this man; but if a spirit or an Angel has spoken to him, do not fight against God." 10 And when there was a great discord, the chief of the leaders, fearing that Paul had been torn in pieces by them, commanded the

soldiers to go down, and to take him among them, and to bring him into the cell. 11 The next night, the Lord stood beside him and said to him, "Take courage, Paul, for as you testified of me in Jerusalem, so you must also testify in Rome." 12 When it was day, some of them gathered together and bound them- selves with a curse, saying that they would not eat or drink until they had killed Paul. 13 There were more than forty who had made this conspiracy. 14 They presented themselves to the chief priests and elders and said, "We have bound ourselves with a solemn curse: we will eat nothing until we have killed Paul." 15 Now, therefore, you and the council make a sign to the chieftain to bring him here to you to die, as if you wanted to know something more definite about him, and we, or whoev- er comes again, will be ready to kill him." 16 But when Paul's sisters' son heard that they were waiting, he went and entered the castle and informed Paul. 17 Paul called one of the centurions and said to him, "Take this young man to the chief of the leaders, for he has something important to tell him." 18 He took him and led him to the chief of the chiefs and said to him, "Paul, the prisoner, called me and begged me to bring you this young man who has something to tell you." 19 Then the chief of the leaders took him by the hand, went off with him alone, and asked him, "What do you have to say to me?" 20 He said, "The witness- es have conspired to want you to bring Paul into the council, as if they wanted to know something more definite about him: 21 But do not be persuaded, for more than forty men are waiting for him, who have pledged themselves by a curse not to eat or drink until they have killed him; and now they are ready and waiting for your promise. 22 The head of state then let the young man depart, having instructed him not to reveal to anyone that he had shown him these things. 23 Then he called to himself two certain centurions, say- ing, "Prepare two hundred soldiers, that they may go to Cæsarea, and horsemen three doz- en and two hundred in number with darts, at thirteen o'clock at night. 24 And let them prepare a horse, that Paul, when he has gone up, may be brought safely to Felix the gover- nor. 25 He wrote an epistle in this manner: 26 Claudius Lysias greets the most noble warrior Felix. 27 Since this man was captured by for- eigners and should have been killed by them, I intervened on them with the garrison and rescued him, having understood that he was a Roman. 28 When I wanted to know why they were accusing him, I led him into their council. 29 There I found that he had been ac- cused of matters relating to their law, but that he had committed no crime worthy of death or of being put in prison. 30 And when it was shown to me how the witnesses were waiting for that man, I sent him straightway to you and commanded his accusers to say before you the things they had against him. Fare- well. 31 Then the soldiers, as they had been ordered, took Paul and brought him by night to Antipatris. 32 The next day, leaving the horsemen to accompany him, they returned to the castle. 33 When they reached Cæsarea, they delivered the epistle to the Governour and also presented Paul to him. 34 When the governor had read it, he asked him what province he was from; and when he found that he was from Cilicia, 35 I will hear you, he said, when your accusers also have arrived, and he ordered him to be detained in Herod's judgment hall.

CHAPTER 24

1 After five days, Ananias the priest went down with the elders and with Tertullus, a certain speaker, who came to the tribunal against Paul. 2 When he was called, Tertullus began to accuse him, saying, "Seeing that we have obtained a great peace of mind because of you, and that many noteworthy things have been done to this nation because of your se- curity, 3 we acknowledge it in all things, most noble Felix, with all thanks, 4 but, so as not to be tedious to you, I beg you for your cour- tesy to hear a few words. 5 Certainly we have found this man a pestiferous companion and a promoter of sedition among all the peoples of the world, as well as one of the chief sup- porters of the sect of the Nazarenes: 6 and he went out of his way to pollute the Tem- ple; therefore we took him and would judge him according to our law: 7 but the chief Ly- sias came upon him, and with great violence snatched him out of our hand, 8 ordering his accusers to come to you, from whom you may know, if you will, all the things of which we accuse him. 9 The witnesses also affirmed that this was so. 10 Then Paul, after the pas- tor had beckoned him to speak, answered, "I answer more willingly for myself, for I know that for many years you have been a judge of this nation, 11 for you know that only two days have passed since I came to worship in Jerusalem. 12 And they have not found me in the Temple arguing with anyone, nor vitu- perating among the people, nor in the Syna- gogues, nor in the city. 13 Nor can they prove the things of which they now accuse me. 14 But I confess to you that, according to the way (which they call "heresies"), I worship the God of my fathers, abiding in all things written in the Bible and the Prophets, 15 And I hope in God that the resurrection of the dead, which they themselves await, will be just and real. 16 And here I pledge myself to always have a clear conscience toward God and toward men. 17 After many years, I came to bring almes to my nation and offerings. 18 At that time, some of the countries of Asia found me purified in the Temple, without a crowd and without turmoil. 19 Who should have been present before you and accused me, if they had anything against me. 20 Or let these say, if they found anything vniust in me, while I stood in the Council, 21 Except for this one thing, that I cried out standing among them, "Of the resurrection of the dead I am accused by you this day." 22 Now when Felix heard these things, he put them off and said, "When I know more perfectly the things concerning this way of proceeding, thanks to the coming of Lysias, the chief of the leaders, I will decide your matter." 23 Then he ordered a centurion to guard Paul, to keep him quiet, and to for- bid any of his acquaintances to serve him or to come to him. 24 After a few days, Felix ar- rived with his wife Drusilla, who was a wom- an, and called Paul and listened to him about faith in Christ. 25 While he was discussing righteousness and temperance and the judg- ment to come, Felix trembled and answered, "Go your way this time, and when I have the proper time I will call you." 26 He also hoped that he had been given money by Paul, so that he could set him free; therefore he sent for him several times and got in touch with him. 27 When two years had elapsed, Porcius Fes- tus entered the kingdom of Felix; and Felix, wanting to be pardoned by the authorities, left Paul bound.

CHAPTER 25

1 When Festus was on the scene, after three days he went from Caesarea to Jerusalem. 2 Then the high priest and the heads of the courts came before him against Paul and pleaded with him, 3 and demanded to make him pay, that he should send for him to Jeru- salem; and they prepared to kill him on the way. 4 But Festus answered that Paul was to

be detained in Caesarea, and that he him- self would shortly depart. 5 Let those among you, therefore, who are able, go down with them; and if there is any wickedness in the man, let them accuse him. 6 After he had tar- ried among them not more than ten days, he went down to Caesarea, and the next day he sat down at the judgment seat and ordered Paul to be brought. 7 When he arrived, the witnesses who had come from Jerusalem stood around him and made many and seri- ous complaints against Paul, for which they could adduce no clear evidence, 8 for he an- swered that he had given no offense either to the law of the Greeks or to the temple or to Caesar. 9 Nevertheless Festus, desiring to be forgiven by the witnesses, answered Paul and said, "Will you go to Jerusalem and there be judged of these things before me?" 10 Then Paul said, "I stand before the tribu- nal of Caesar, where I should be judged; to the witnesses I have done nothing wrong, as you well know. 11 For if I have done any evil or committed any thing deserving of death, I do not refuse to die; but if there is none of these things of which they accuse me, no one, to please them, can deliver me up to them: I appeal to Caesar." 12 Then Festus, having spoken to the council, answered, "You have appealed to Caesar? To Caesar you shall go." 13 After a few days, King Agrippa and Bernice went down to Caesarea to greet Festus. 14 And when they had been there for many days, Fes- tus declared Paul's cause to the king, saying, "There is a certain man left in prison by Felix, 15 of whom, when I came to Jerusalem, I was informed by the chief priests and elders of the people, who desired to have judgment on him. 16 To these I answered that it is not the business of the Romans to consign a man to death before the one who is accused has his accusers before him and can defend himself concerning the crime. 17 Therefore, when they had come here, on the following day I sat down without delay on the judgment seat and ordered the man to be brought in. :18 When the accusers appeared, they brought no crime as I had supposed: 19 but they challenged him on some matters related to their superstition and a dead Jesus, which Paul claimed was false. 20 And because I doubted these kinds of questions, I asked him if he would go to Je- rusalem and there be judged on these things. 21 But because he appealed to be examined by Augustus, I ordered him to be detained until I sent him to Caesar. 22 Then Agrippa said to Festus, "I would like to hear that man also." He replied, "You will hear him the next day." 23 The next day, while Agrippa and Bernice, with great pomp, had entered the common room with the principal captains and men of the city, at Festus' order Paul was brought out. 24 Festus said, "King Agrippa and all the men who are present with you, see this man, con- cerning whom all the multitude of the Jews have called upon me, both in Jerusalem and here, crying out that he must lie no more. 25 Nevertheless I found nothing worthy of death that he had committed; nevertheless, seeing that he appealed to Augustus, I determined to send him. 26 Of him I have nothing certain to write to my lord; therefore I have brought him to you, and particularly to you, King Agrippa, so that after examining him I might have something to write. 27 For I hold that it is rea- sonable to send a prisoner and not to reveal the causes that have been brought against him.

CHAPTER 26

1 Then Agrippa said to Paul, "You are permit- ted to speak for yourself." Then Paul stretched out his hand and answered for himself. 2 I think myself happy, King Agrippa, because today I will answer before you for all the things of which I am accused by the Jews. 3 Especially because you are acquainted with all the customs and all the matters among the Jews; therefore I beg you to listen to me patiently. 4 Concerning my life since child- hood and what has been from the beginning among my nation in Jerusalem, let all the Jews know, 5 who knew me from before, even from my elders (if they would testify) that, accord- ing to the strictest sect of our religion, I was a Pharisee. 6 Now I am charged for the hope of God's promise to our fathers. 7 For which our two tribes, who devote themselves to God day and night, hope to come; for this hope, O King Agrippa, I am accused by the judicial author- ities. 8 Why should it seem to you an incred- ible thing that God raises the dead? 9 I also thought very well in myself to do many things contrary to the name of Jesus of Nazareth. 10 Which I also did in Jerusalem, for many saints I shut them up in prison, having received per- mission from the priests, and when they were put to death, I passed my sentence. 11 I pun- ished them in all the synagogues, forced them to blaspheme, and being most furious against them, I persecuted them, even in unknown cities. 12 Then I went to Damascus with the permission and charge of the priests, 13 at noon, O king, I saw on the road a light from Heauen, exceeding the splendor of the sun, shining around me and those who came with me. 14 When we had all fallen to the ground, I heard a voice speaking to me and saying in the Hebrew language, "Saul, Saul, why do you persecute me? It is hard for you to strike the stingers." 15 Then I said, "Who are you, Lord?" And he answered, "I am Jesus whom you per- secute." 16 But get up and stand, for I have ap- peared to you for this purpose, to appoint you a minister and witness of the things you have seen and those in which I will appear to you, 17 to turn you away from this people and from the Gentiles, to whom I am now sending you, 18 to open their eyes, that they may turn from darkness to light and from the power of Satan to God, that they may receive forgiveness of sins and inheritance among them, who are sanctified by faith in me. 19 Therefore, King Agrippa, I was not disobedient to your vision, 20 but I spoke first to those of Damascus, and of Jerusalem, and of all the coasts of Judea, and then to the Gentiles, that they might re- pent and be converted to God, and do works worthy of the amendment of life. 21 For this reason the Jews captured me in the Temple and set out to kill me. 22 But I, as a neophyte, obtained God's help and continue to this day to testify to the small and the great, saying no other things than what the prophets and Mo- ses said would come, 23 namely, that Christ would suffer and be the first to rise from the dead and give light to this people and to the nations." 24 While he was thus answer- ing for himself, Festus said in a loud voice, "Paul, you are beside yourself; many notions make you mad." 25 But he answered, "I am not mad, O noble Festus, but I speak true and sober words. 26 Because the king is aware of these things, even before him I speak boldly, for I am convinced that none of these things are hidden from him, for this thing was not made in a corner. 27 O King Agrippa, do you believe the prophets? I know that you ignore them." 28 Then Agrippa said to Paul, "You al- most persuade me to become a Christian." 29 Then Paul said, "I wish that not only you, but also everyone who listens to me today, were almost and completely like me, except for these bonds." 30 When he had spoken thus, the king stood up, the governor, Bernice and those who sat with them. 31 When they had departed, they spoke among themselves, say- ing, "This man does nothing worthy of

death or bonds." 32 Then Agrippa said to Festus, "This man might have been loosed, if he had not appealed to Caesar.

CHAPTER 27

1 When it was decided that we should go to Italy, they handed Paul and some other prisoners over to a centurion named Iulius, of Augustus' band. 2 Then, having boarded a ship from Adramyttium with the inten- tion of passing through the coast of Asia, we embarked and had with us Aristarchus of Macedonia, a Thessalonian. 3 The next day we arrived at Sidon, and Iulius courteously ad- dressed Paul and gave him liberty to go to his friends to refresh him. 4 From there we de- parted and stopped at Cyprus, for the winds were contrary. 5 Then, after passing over the sea to Cilicia and Pamphylia, we came to Myra, a city in Lycia. 6 There the centurion found a ship from Alexandria, which was go- ing toward Italy, and he brought it up. 7 After we had sailed slowly for many days, and after we had hardly arrived at Gnidum, because the wind gave us no respite, we sailed for Candia, near Salmone, 8 and, with much effort, we pushed on and came to a certain place called "Faire hauens," near which was the city of La- sea. 9 When much time had elapsed, and the speeches were now ieoparded, for the fasting was also past, Paul exhorted them, 10 and said to them, "Yessir, I see that this journey will be of great harm, not only to the cargo and the ship, but also to our goods." 11 But the centurion Neuchâtel, instead of annoy- ing the sailor and the captain of the ship, said the things that had been said to Paul. 12 And because the island was not convenient for wintering, many advised that he should de- part from there, and somehow get to Phoenix and winter there, which is an island of Candia and is to the southwest and west and north- west and west. 13 When the south wind blew gently, they thought that they had achieved their purpose, and they let loose and sailed to Candia. 14 But soon afterward a stormy wind called Euroclydon arose. 15 When the ship was caught and could not withstand the wind, we let her go and were carried away. 16 We came upon a small island named Clauda, and we had to struggle hard to catch the boat. 17 They got up and helped us with all their help, girding the boat, in fear of falling into a syrinx, but they embarked into the sea and so were taken away. 18 The next day, when we were tossed about by a very strong storm, they lightened the ship. 19 On the third day, with our own hands, we made the ship's broadside. 20 When for many days neither the sun nor the stars appeared, and the storm came upon us, all hope of being saved was removed. 21 But after a long abstinence, Paul came among them and said, "Gentlemen, you should have listened to me and not disbanded from Can- dia; then you would have obtained this dam- age and this defeat. 22 But now I urge you to be brave, for there will be no loss of life for anyone among you, only for the ship. 23 For this night the angel of God, whose servant I am, stood by me, 24 saying, "Fear not, Paul, for you must be brought before Caesar; and be- hold, God has freely granted you all those who say with you." 25 Therefore, gentlemen, take courage, for I believe God that it shall be so as I have been told. 26 However, we must be cast into a certain island. 27 When the fourteenth night came, as we were going to and fro from the Adriatic Sea about midnight, the sailors thought that some county was approaching them, 28 And having sounded, they found twenty fathoms; and when they had gone a little farther, they sounded again and found fifty fathoms. 29 Then, fearing that they had fallen into some rough place, they cast four anchors out of the sternum and wished for the day to come. 30 As the sailors were about to flee from the ship and had lowered the boat into the sea with a color as if they were go- ing to throw the ankers out of the bow, Paul said, 31 Paul said to the centurion and the armigers, "If these do not remain in the ship, you cannot be safe." 32 Then the armigers cut the ropes of the boat and let it fall. 33 When it began to get light, Paul urged them all to take their meal, saying, "This is the fourteenth day that you have stayed fasting without receiving anything: 34 Therefore I urge you to take the food, for this is for your safety, lest an ear fall from the head of any of you." 35 After he had spoken thus, he took bread and gave thanks to God in the presence of them all, broke it, and began to eat. 36 Then they all took courage and ate also. 37 Now in the ship there were in all two hundred, three hundred and six hun- dred of us. 38 When they had eaten enough, they lightened the ship and threw the grain into the sea. 39 When it was daylight, they did not know the county, but they caught sight of a certain inlet with a dock, into which they wanted (if it were possible) to push the ship. 40 So having taken the hooks, they sailed the ship out to sea, loosed the bonds of the rud- der, hoisted the ship to the wind, and headed for the shore. 41 When they came to a point where two seas met, they pushed the ship; the front part stuck and could not move, but the back part broke by the violence of the waves. 42 Then the soldiers advised that they would kill the prisoners if none of them, after swim- ming, escaped. 43 But the centurion, wanting to save Paul, restrained them from this ad- vice and ordered that those who could swim should first throw themselves into the sea and then go ashore: 44 and the others, some on board and others on some pieces of the ship; and so it came to pass that they all reached land safely.

CHAPTER 28

1 When they had reached safety, they under- stood that the island was called Melita. 2 The barbarians proved to be not unkind: they lit a fire and welcomed everyone, because of the spectacle and the cold. 3 When Paul had gath- ered a number of sticks and put them on the fire, a viper came out of the fire and jumped on his hand. 4 When the barbarians saw the viper hanging on his hand, they said among themselves, "This man is certainly a murder- er who, though he escaped the sea, has not suffered vengeance. 5 But he threw the meat into the fire and experienced no suffering. 6 However, they wondered whether he had fallen into the sea or died suddenly; but after looking for quite a while and seeing that no misfortune had befallen him, they changed their minds and said that he was a God. 7 In the same quarters, the chief of the Yle (whose name was Publius) had possessions; these received him and graciously lodged him for three days. 8 So it was that Publius' father lay sick with a fever and a bloody fever; whereup- on Paul went in and, praying, laid his hands on him and healed him. 9 Having done this, others also in the Yle, who had diseases, came to him and were healed, 10 And they also did him great honor; and when we left, they filled us with necessary things. 11 Now after three months, we departed in a ship from Alexan- dria, which had called at the Yle, whose badge was Castor and Pollux. 12 When we arrived at Syracuse, we stopped there three days. 13 From there we set out and arrived at Rhegium; after one day the south wind ceased, and on the second day we arrived at Putioli: 14 where we found brethren, whom we asked to stay with them for ten days, and then we set out for Rome.

15 From there, when the brethren heard of us, they came to meet us at the mar- ketplace of Appius and at the three tauernes, and when Paul heard of it, he thanked God and rejoiced. 16 When we arrived in Rome, the centurion handed the prisoners over to the captain general, but Paul was left to live alone with a soul to guard him. 17 On the third day afterward, Paul summoned the leaders of the Jews; and when they had arrived, he said to them, "Men and brethren, although I have committed nothing against the people or the laws of the fathers, yet I have been delivered captive from Jerusalem into the hands of the Romans." 18 Who, after examining me, would let me go, for there was no cause of death in me. 19 But when the witnesses said other- wise, I was compelled to appeal to Caesar, not because I should accuse my nation. 20 For this reason I summoned you to see you and to speak with you; for the hope of Israel's good, I am bound with this chain." 21 Then they said to him, "We have received no letters from Ju- dea about you, nor has any of the brothers come and spoken of you. 22 But we want to know from you what you think; for as far as this sect is concerned, we know that in every place evil is spoken of it." 23 And when they had appointed him a day, there came to him many to his lodging, to whom he expounded the testimony of the kingdom of God from morning till evening, and persuaded them of the things concerning Jesus, both from the word of Moses and from the Prophets. 24 Some were persuaded of the things spo- ken, but others were not. 25 And because they disagreed among themselves, they went away, after Paul had spoken a word, "The Holy Spirit has spoken through the prophet Esaias to our fathers." 26 saying, "Go to this peo- ple and say, With hearing you will hear and not understand, with sight you will see and not perceive." 27 For the heart of this people has grown faint, and their ears are dull, and their eyes have winked, while they would not see with their eyes, nor hear with their ears, nor understand with their hearts, nor turn back to be healed by me. 28 Know therefore that this greeting of God has been sent to the Gentiles, and they will hear it." 29 And when he had said these things, those present went away and discussed much among themselves. 30 Paul stayed two full years in a house rent- ed for himself and received all who came to him, 31 preaching the kingdom of God and teaching the things concerning the Lord Jesus Christ, with all boldness of speech, not letting anything slip out.

PAULINE EPISTLES

These letters written by Paul offer theological teachings and instructions for Christian communities

ROMANS

CHAPTER 1

1 Paul, servant of Jesus Christ, called to be an apostle and commissioned to preach the gospel of God, 2 (which he had already prom- ised through his prophets in the sacred Scrip- tures). 3 concerning his Son Jesus Christ, our Lord, who was made from the descendants of Dauid according to the flesh, 4 and declared emphatically to be the Son of God, touching the Spirit of sanctification through the res- urrection from the dead) 5 through whom we have received grace and apostleship (so that obedience may be made possible to your faith) for his Name among all the Gentiles, 6 among whom you are also the called of Jesus Christ: 7 To all of you who are in Rome, promoted by God and called to be saints: grace to you and peace from God our Father and the Lord Jesus Christ. 8 First of all I thank my God through Jesus Christ for all of you, because your faith is published throughout the world. 9 For God is my witness (that I serve in my spirit in the gospel of his Son) that without ceasing I make mention of you. 10 always in my prayers, be- seeching that by some means, sometime or other, I may have a prosperous journey, by God's will, to come to you. 11 For I desire to see you, that I may bestow among you some spiritual gift, that you may be strengthened: 12 That is, that I may be comforted together with you, because of our mutual faith, yours and mine. 13 Now, my brethren, I wish you not to be ignorant of the fact that I have often proposed to come to you (but so far have not done so) in order to have some fruit among you also, as among other Gentiles. 14 I am a deterrent both to the Greeks and to the Bar- barians, both to the wise and to the unwise. 15 Therefore, as far as it is in me, I am ready to preach the gospel also to you who are in Rome. 16 For I am not ashamed of the gospel of Christ, for it is the power of God for the sal- vation of everyone who believes, first of all of foreigners and also of Greeks. 17 For through it the righteousness of God is transmitted from faith to faith, as it is written, "The righ- teous shall live by faith." 18 For the wrath of God has been unleashed from above against all the vices and righteousness of men who deny the truth in righteousness. 19 Inasmuch as that which can be known by God is man- ifest in them, for God has shown it to them. 20 For the inaudible things of him, that is, his eternal power and divinity, are visible from the creation of the world, being considered in his works, so that they have no excuse: 21 For although they knew God, they did not glorify him as God and were not thankful, but became vain in their thoughts, and their foolish heart was full of darkness. 22 When they professed themselves wise, they became foolish. 23 For they turned the glory of the incorruptible God into an image of corruptible man, birds, four-legged beasts and creeping things. 24 Therefore God also left them free to indulge the lusts of their hearts and to defile their bodies among themselves: 25 who turned the truth of God into a lie and worshiped and served the creature, forsaking the Creator, who is blessed forever, Amen. 26 Therefore God gave them up to vile affections, because their women changed nature into that which is against nature. 27 In the same way, men also forsook the nature of woman and burned in their lust toward one another, and man with man committed filthiness, and received in themselves the just reward for their error. 28 For as they did not acknowledge God, so God gave them over to a reprobate mind, to do those things which are not fitting, 29 being full of all iniquity, of fornication, of wicked- ness, of couetousnes, of evil, full of envy, of murders, of arguments, of deceptions, taking all things at face value, murmurers, 30 back- biters, haters of God, doers of evil, proud, boasters, envious of all things, disobedient to parents, lacking in understanding, violators of couples, deprived of natural affection, such that they can never be appeased, hirelings. 31 Which men, although they know the word of God, that those who commit such things are deserving of death, not only do the same, but also vituperate those who commit them.

CHAPTER 2

1 Therefore you are inexcusable, O man, who- ever you are that you condemn; for inasmuch as you condemn another, you condemn your- self; for you who condemn, you do the same things. 2 But we know that God's judgment is according to truth, against those who com- mit such things. 3 And do you think this, O man, that you condemn those who do such things and do the same, to escape the judg- ment of God? 4 Or do you despise the riches of His bounty, patience and long-suffering, not knowing that God's bounty leads you to repentance? 5 But you, with your hardness and your heart that cannot repent, accumu- late as a treasure for yourself wrath against the day of wrath and the declaration of God's righteous judgment, 6 who will reward every man according to his works: 7 that is, to those who, through patience in doing right, shall see glory, honor, and immortality, eternal life: 8 But to those who are quarrelsome and disobey the truth and obey justice, shall be indignation and wrath. 9 Tribulation and dis- tress shall come upon the soul of every man that doeth iniquity, first of all of foreigners, and also of Greeks. 10 But to every man that doeth good shall belong glory and honor and peace: to the first and also to the Greek. 11 For with God there is no respect for people. 12 For as many as have sinned without the Law, shall also perish without the Law; and as many as have sinned in the Law, shall be judged by the Law, 13 For he who hears the Law is not righteous before God, but he who does it will be justified. 14 For when the Gentiles who do not have the Law do by nature the things con- tained in the Law, they who do not have the Law are a Law unto themselves, 15 who show the effect of the Lawe written in their hearts, their conscience also witnesses it, and their thoughts accuse or exonerate each other). 16 In the day when God will judge the secrets of men through Jesus Christ, according to my gospel. 17 Behold, you are called "Iewe," you rest in the Lawe and glory in God, 18 You know his will and discuss things that do not comply with it, because you are instructed in the Law: 19 and you are convinced that you are a guide for the blind, a light for those who are in darkness, 20 an instructor of those who lack discretion, a teacher of those who learn, who have the form of the knowledge and truth of the Law. 21 You therefore who teach another, do you not teach yourself? You who preach, "Man shall not steal," do you also do so? 22 You who say, "Man shall not commit adultery," do you commit adultery? You who abhor idols, do you commit sacrilege? 23 You who glory in the Law, by violating the Law do you dishonor God? 24 For the Name of God is blasphemed among the Gentiles through you, as it is written. 25 For circumcision is in- deed useful if you do the Lawe; but if you are a transgressor of the Lawe, your circumcision has become vncircumcision. 26 Therefore, if the vncircumcision observes the orders of the Lawe, will not his vncircumcision be re- garded as circumcision? 27 And will not vncir- cumcision, which is by nature (if it observes the Lawe), condemn you who by letter and circumcision are a transgressor of the Lawe? 28 For he is not a Lawe, which is an outward thing; nor is he a circumcision, which is out- ward in the flesh: 29 but he is an inward Iewe, and circumcision is of the heart, in the spirit, and not in the letter, whose praise is not of men, but of God.

CHAPTER 3

1 What then is the preference of faith or what is the advantage of circumcision? 2 In every way, especially because the oracles of God have been entrusted to them. 3

Why, if some are not converted, will their unbelief make the faith of God of no effect? 4 Let not God allow it; nay, let God be truthful, and let every man be a liar, as it is written, "That thou mayest be justified in thy words and in thy conduct, when thou shalt be judged." 5 Now if our righteousness is God's righteousness, what shall we say? Is God just who punishes? (I speak as a man). 6 God will not; otherwise how will God judge the world? 7 For if God's truth is increased through my loss for his glo- ry, why am I still condemned as a sinner? 8 And (as we are reproached and as some say), why do we not strive, that good may come of it? Whose damnation is just. 9 What then, are we more excellent? No, by no means; for we have already shown that all, both Jews and Gentiles, are under sin, 10 as it is written, "There is none righteous, no one." 11 There is no one who understands, there is no one who seeks God. 12 They have all gone out of the way, they have become utterly vnprofitable; there is no one who does good, no one. 13 Their throat is an open tomb; they have used their tongue to deceive; the pit of aspi is un- der their lips. 14 Their mouth is full of curses and bitterness. 15 Their feet are quick in shed- ding blood. 16 Destruction and calamity are in their lives, 17 And they do not know the way of peace. 18 The fear of God is not before their eyes. 19 Now we know that what the Law says, it says to those who are under the Law, so that every mouth may be shut and the whole world may be subject to the judgment of God. 20 Therefore, through the works of the Law, no flesh will be justified in his sight, because from the Law comes the knowledge of sin. 21 But now the righteousness of God has been manifested without the plague, through the testimonies of the plague and the prophets, 22 that is, the righteousness of God through the faith of Jesus Christ, toward all and upon all who are raised. 23 There is no difference, for all have sinned and are deprived of the glory of God, 24 and are justified freely by his grace, through the redemption that is in Christ Iesus, 25 whom God has set as recon- ciliation, through faith in his blood, to declare his righteousness, through the forgiveness of sins committed, 26 through the patience of God, to show his righteousness at this time, that he might be just and the justifier of those who have faith in Jesus. 27 Where, then, is the revival? It is excluded. By what law? The one of works? No, but by faith. 28 Therefore we con- clude that a man is justified by faith, without the works of faith. 29 God, is he the God of the Gentiles only and not also of the Gentiles? Yes, also of the Gentiles. 30 For it is one God who justifies the circumcision of faith and the cir- cumcision through faith. 31 Do we therefore make the Lawe through faith irrelevant? God forbid; yea, we establish the Law.

CHAPTER 4

1 What then shall we say that Abraham our father found concerning the flesh? 2 For if Abraham had been justified by works, he would have been reconciled, but not with God. 3 For what does Scripture say? Abraham believed God and this was acknowledged to him as righteousness. 4 Now for those who work, wages are not calculated according to value, but according to merit: 5 But to him who does not work, but believes in him who justifies the righteous, his faith is counted for righteousness. 6 Just as Dauid declares the blessedness of him to whom God im- putes righteousness without works, saying, 7 Blessed are those whose iniquities are for- given and whose sins are removed. 8 Blessed is the man to whom the Lord does not im- pute

sin. 9 Is this blessedness then due only to circumcision or also to circumcision? For we say that faith was imputed to Abraham as righteousness. 10 How was it imputed to him, when he was circumcised or vncircumcised? Not when he was circumcised, but when he was vncircumcised. 11 Having received the sign of circumcision, as a seal of the righ- teousness of the faith which he had, when he was circumcised, to be the father of all those who are born, not being circumcised, that righteousness may be imputed to them also, 12 and the father of circumcision, not only for those who are circumcised, but also for those who walk in the steps of the faith of our father Abraham, which he had when he was circumcised. 13 For the promise to be the heir of the world was not given to Abra- ham or to his descendants by faith, but by the righteousness of faith. 14 For if those who are of the Law are heirs, faith is nullified and the promise is without effect. 15 For plague caus- es wrath; for where there is no plague, there is no transgression. 16 Therefore it is by faith, that it may come to pass by grace, and the promise be sure for all descendants, not only for those who come from the Law, but also for those who come from the faith of Abraham, who is the father of all, 17 (as it is written, "I have made you the father of many nations") even before God, whom he believed, who vivi- fies the dead and calls the things that are not, as if they were. 18 Abraham, who hoped to be a father of many nations, had earned the hope of being a father of many nations, according to what he had been told, "So shall your de- scendants be." 19 He was not weak in faith and did not consider his own body, which was now dead, being nearly a hundred years old, nor the death of Sarah's wife. 20 Nor did he doubt the promise of God because of unbe- lief, but he strengthened himself in faith and gave glory to God, 21 being fully assured that he whom he had promised was also able to do it. 22 Therefore righteousness was imputed to him. 23 Now it is not only written for him that it was imputed to him for righteousness, 24 but also for those to whom it will be imput- ed for righteousness that which took place in him who raised Jesus our Lord from the dead, 25 who was delivered up to death for our sins and rose again for our justification.

CHAPTER 5

1 Being therefore justified by faith, we have peace toward God through our Lord Jesus Christ. 2 Through whom, by faith, we have had access to this grace, in which we stand, and are looking forward to the hope of the glory of God. 3 And not only that, but also in tribulation, knowing that tribulation begets patience, 4 and patience brings about experi- ence, and experience brings about hope, 5 and hope does not make one ashamed, because the joy of God is spread in our hearts through the Holy Spirit, who has been given to us. 6 For Christ, when we still had no strength, in his time died for the ungodly. 7 We hardly die for the righteous, but for a good man we are likely to die. 8 But God has set his love toward you, seeing that while we were still sinners, Christ died for you. 9 Much more therefore, being now justified by his blood, we shall be saved from wrath through him. 10 For if, when we were enemies, we were reconciled to God through the death of his Son, much more shall we be reconciled through his life, 11 and not only so, but we also live again in God through our Lord Jesus Christ, through whom we have received the atonement. 12 Therefore, as by one man sin entered into the world, and death by sin, so death passed to all men: in them

all men have sinned. 13 For until the time of the Law there was sin in the world, but sin is not imputed, until there is lying. 14 But death reigned from Adam until Moses, even for those who did not sin, as the transgression of Adam, who was the image of him who was to come. 15 But the gift is not so like the offense, for if by the offense of one many have died, much more the grace of God and the gift by grace, which is through one man, Jesus Christ, have abounded to many. 16 Nor is the gift like that which came in through one who sinned; for guilt came by one offense unto condemnation, but the gift is by many offenses unto justification. 17 For if by the offense of one alone death reigned through one alone, much more those who receive the abundance of grace and the gift of righteous- ness will reign in life through one alone, that is, Jesus Christ. 18 Therefore as by the offense of one alone guilt has come upon all men to condemn them, so by the justification of one alone benefit has overflowed toward all men for the justification of life. 19 For as by the disobedience of one man many were made sinners, so by the obedience of that one many will be made righteous. 20 Moreover, the Law was introduced so that offense abounded; yet where sin abounded, grace abounded much more: 21 That as sin had reigned unto death, so also grace might reign with righteousness unto eternal life, through Jesus Christ our Lord.

CHAPTER 6

1 What shall we say then? Will we continue to sin so that grace may abound? God forbid. 2 How shall we who are dead to sin still abide in it? 3 Do you not know that all of us who were baptized into Jesus Christ were baptized into his death? 4 We are therefore buried with him through baptism into his death, so that as Christ was raised from the dead to the glory of the Father, so we also walk in newness of life. 5 For if we have been baptized with him in the likeness of his death, we shall also be baptized in the likeness of his resurrection, 6 knowing that our old man has been crucified with him, so that the body of sin may be destroyed, so that from now on we no longer serve sin. 7 For he who is dead is freed from sin. 8 Therefore, if we have died with Christ, we believe that we shall also live with him, 9 knowing that Christ, raised from the dead, no longer dies; death no longer has dominion over him. 10 For in that he died, he died once to sin, but in that he lives, he lives to God. 11 In the same way think ye also that ye are dead to sin, but are alive to God in Jesus Christ our Lord. 12 Therefore do not let sin reign in your mortal body, to obey it in your lusts: 13 And do not give your mem- bers as weapons of righteousness against sin, but give your selves to God, as those who are dead, and give your members as weapons of righteousness against God. 14 For sin shall not have dominion over you, because you are not under the law but under grace. 15 What shall we do, then, if we sin because we are not under the Law but under grace? God for- bid. 16 Do you not know that to whom you give yourselves as servants to obey, you are his servants to whom you obey, whether it is sin unto death or obedience unto righteous- ness? 17 But God be thanked that you were servants of sin, but obeyed heartily the form of doctrine, for which you were delivered. 18 Being therefore delivered from sin, you have become servants of righteousness. 19 I speak in the manner of man, because of the infirmi- ty of your flesh; for as you gave your members as servants of vices and iniquity, to commit iniquity, so now you give your members as servants of

righteousness in holiness. 20 For when you were servants of sin, you were de- livered from righteousness. 21 What fruit did you have then in those things of which you are now ashamed? For the end of those things is death. 22 But now, freed from sin and made servants of God, you have your fruit in holi- ness and the end, eternal life. 23 For the wag- es of sin is death, but the gift of God is eternal life, through Jesus Christ our Lord.

CHAPTER 7

1 Do you not know, brothers, (for I speak to those who know the Law) that the Law has do- minion over the man as long as he lives? 2 For the woman who is subject to a man is bound by the Law to the man as long as he lives; but if the man is dead, she is freed from the Law of the man. 3 If therefore, while the man lives, she takes another man, she shall be called an adulteress; but if the man is dead, she is freed from the Law, so that she is not an adulteress, even if she takes another man. 4 So you also, my brethren, are dead to the Law through the body of Christ, that you may be conformed to another, that is, to him who rose from the dead, to bear fruit unto God. 5 For when we were in the flesh, the afflictions of sins, which were due to the Law, had power in our mem- bers, to bear fruit at death. 6 But now we have been delivered from the plague, the one in whom we were kept having died, that we might serve in the newness of the Spirit and not in the oldness of the letter. 7 What shall we say then? Is Lawe a sin? God forbid. No, I did not know sin except through the Law; for I did not know lust, unless the Law said, "Thou shalt not lust." 8 But sin took occasion from your command and worked in me all kinds of concupiscence; for without the Lawe sin is dead. 9 For I was once alien, without the Law; but when the commandment came, sin took over again, 10 but I am dead; and the same commandment that was intended for life, proved to be for me a commandment of death. 11 For sin took occasion from the com- mandment, deceived me, and so killed me. 12 Therefore the law is holy and the command is holy, just and good. 13 Is it therefore what is good that has caused me to die? God for- bid it not; but sin, that it might appear to be sin, hath wrought death in me through that which is good, that sin might be exceedingly through the commandment. 14 For we know that the Law is spiritual, but I am carnal, solid under sin. 15 For I do not permit what I do; for what I would, I do not do; but what I hate, I do. 16 If therefore I do that which I would not, I consent to the Lawe, which is good. 17 Now, therefore, it is no longer I who do it, but it is sin that dwells in me. 18 For I know that no good thing dwells in me, that is, in my flesh, because the intention to desire is already present in me, but I do not find the means to accomplish what is good. 19 For I do not do the good thing that I would, but the evil thing, which I would not, that I do. 20 Now if I do what I would not, it is no longer I who do it, but sin that dwells in me. 21 Then I find that when I would like to do good, I am so busy, that euillia is present with me. 22 For I delight in the Law of God, which concerns the inner man: 23 But I see another law in my members, which rebels against the law of my mind, and makes me a prisoner of the law of sin, which is in my members. 24 O wretched man that I am, who shall deliver me from the body of this death? 25 I give thanks to God through Jesus Christ our Lord. Then I myself, in my mind, serve the weakness of God, but in my flesh the weakness of sin.

CHAPTER 8

1 There is therefore no condemnation for those who are in Christ Iesus, who do not walk according to the flesh but according to the Spirit. 2 For the power of the Spirit of life, which is in Christ Iesus, has delivered me from the power of sin and death. 3 For (what was impossible to the Law, in that it was false, because of the flesh) God sent his own Son, in a flesh like unto sin and for sin, condemn- ing sin in the flesh, 4 that the righteousness of the Law might be fulfilled in those who do not walk according to the flesh but according to the Spirit. 5 For those who are according to the flesh, feed on the things of the flesh; but those who are according to the Spirit, on the things of the Spirit. 6 For the wisdom of the flesh is death, but the wisdom of the Spirit is life and peace, 7 For the wisdom of the flesh is enmity against God, because it is not sub- ject to the law of God, nor can be. 8 Therefore those who are in the flesh cannot please God. 9 Now you are not in the flesh, but in the Spir- it, for the Spirit of God dwells in you; but if anyone does not have the Spirit of Christ, he is not his own. 10 If Christ is in you, the body is dead because of sin, but the Spirit is life through righteousness. 11 But if the Spirit of him who raised Jesus from the dead dwells in you, he who raised Christ from the dead will also vivify your mortal bodies, through his Spirit who dwells in you. 12 Therefore, breth- ren, we are not bound to follow the flesh, to live according to the flesh: 13 For if you live according to the flesh, you will die; but if you mortify the deeds of the body by the Spirit, you will live. 14 For as many as are led by the Spirit of God, they are children of God. 15 For you have not received the Spirit of the body to fear death, but you have received the Spirit of adoption by which we cry Abba, Father. 16 The same Spirit testifies with our spirit that we are children of God. 17 If we are children, we are also heirs, that is, heirs of God, and heirs annexed to Christ; if it is true that we suffer with him, we shall also be glorified with him. 18 For I believe that the afflictions of this time are not worthy of the glory that will be shown to us. 19 For the fervent desire of the creature waits for the children of God to be delivered, 20 because the creature is subject to vanity, not because of its own will, but because of him who has subjected it to hope, 21 because the creature also will be delivered from the bondage of corruption to the glorious free- dom of the sons of God. 22 For we know that every creature suffers together with us, and until now has suffered together. 23 And not only the creature, but we also, who have the first fruits of the Spirit, sigh within ourselves, waiting for the adoption, that is, the redemp- tion of our body. 24 For we are animated by hope; but the hope that is seen is not hope, for how can a man hope in what he sees? 25 But if we hope in what we do not see, with patience we stand waiting for it. 26 The Spirit also helps our infirmities, for we do not know how to pray as we ought, but the Spirit him- self asks to be heard with sighs that cannot be expressed. 27 But he who scrutinizes hearts knows what the meaning of the Spirit is, for he asks for you saints, according to the will of God. 28 We also know that everything con- curs for the best for those who love God, that is, for those who are called by his purpose. 29 For those whom he knew before, he also pre- destined them to be made like unto the im- age of his Son, that he might be the first born among many brethren. 30 Moreover, those whom he predestined, he also called; and those whom he called, he also justified; and those whom he justified, he also

glorified. 31 What then shall we say of these things? If God is on our side, who can be against us? 32 He who did not spare his own Son, but gave him up to death for all, how will he not also give all things with him? 33 Who can impute anything to God's elect? It is God who justi- fies, 34 Who will condemn? It is Christ who died, indeed who rose again, who is also at the right hand of God and who also asks for them. 35 Who will be able to separate Yours from the joy of Christ? Tribulation, distress, persecution, famine, nakedness, perdition or the sword? 36 As it is written, "For Your sake we are killed all day long; we are counted as sheep for slaughter." 37 Nevertheless, in all these things we are more than conquerors be- cause of him who overcame. 38 For I am con- vinced that neither death, nor life, nor angels, nor principalities, nor powers, nor things present, nor things to come, 39 nor height, nor depth, nor any other creature will be able to separate us from the joy of God, which is in Christ Jesus our Lord.

CHAPTER 9

1 I speak the truth in Christ, I have not slum- bered, my conscience testifies to me in the Holy Spirit, 2 that I have great suffering and continual sorrow in my heart. 3 For I would be separated from Christ, for my brethren who are my kinsmen according to the flesh, 4 Who are the Israelites, to whom belong the adoption, the glory, the privileges, the grant of peace, the service of God, and the promis- es. 5 Of whom are the fathers, and of whom, as to the flesh, came Christ, who is God over all, blessed forever, Amen. 6 Nevertheless it cannot be that the word of God has no effect, for all who are of Israel are not Israel: 7 nei- ther are they all sons, for they are Abraham's seed, but, "In Isaac shall your seed be called." 8 That is, those who are children of the flesh are not children of God, but the children of the promise are counted as descendants. 9 For this is a word of promise: "At this very time I will come, and Sarah shall have a son." 10 And this he heard not only, but Rebecca also, when she conceived by one, that is, by our father Isaac. 11 For while the children were being borne, they had done neither good nor evil (so that God's purpose might remain according to election, not by works, but by him who calls). 12 It was said to her, "The elder shall serve the younger." 13 As it is written, "I loved Jacob and hated Esau." 14 What shall we say then? Is there any justice with God? God will not. 15 For he says to Moses, "I will have mercy on him on whom I will show mercy, and I will have compassion on him on whom I will have compassion." 16 Therefore it is not in him who wills, nor in him who runs, but it is God who gives mercy. 17 For the Scripture says to Pharaoh, "For this very purpose have I raised you up, to manifest my power in you, and that my Name may be declared in all the earth." 18 Therefore he has mercy on whom he wills, and whom he wills he hardens. 19 Then you will say, "Why does he still com- plain? Who has resisted his will?" 20 But, O man, who are you that opposes God? Shall the thing formed say to him who formed it, "Why have you made me thus?" 21 Has not the pot- ter power to make of the same clay one vessel to honor and another to dishonor? 22 What if God, in order to show his wrath and make known his power, would suffer with long pa- tience the vessels of wrath, prepared for de- struction? 23 And to make known the riches of his glory on the vessels of mercy which he has prepared for glory? 24 And those whom he has called, not only among the young, but also among the Gentiles, 25 as he also says in Osee, "I will call them, my people, who were not my people, and she, Beloved, who was not Beloved." 26 In the place where it was said to them, "You are not my people," they shall be called "Children of the God who loves." 27 Es- aiah also cries out concerning Israel, "Even if the number of the children of Israel were as the sand of the sea, there will be nothing left of them but a remnant. 28 For he will make his reckoning and gather it into a short sum with justice; for the LORD will make a short reckoning on the earth. 29 As Esaias said be- fore, "If the LORD of hosts had not left us an offspring, we would have become like Sodom and like Gomorrah." 30 What shall we say then? That the Gentiles, who did not follow righteousness, attained righteousness, that of faith. 31 But Israel, who followed the Law of righteousness, failed to keep the Law of justice. 32 Why? Because they did not seek it by faith, but by the works of the Law, for they stumbled over the stumbling block, 33 As it is written, "Behold, I lay in Zion a stumbling stone and a staff for men to fall; and whosoev- er believes in him shall not be shamed."

CHAPTER 10

1 Brethren, the desire of my heart and my prayer to God for Israel is that they be healed. 2 For I put them on record that they have the zeal of God, but not according to knowledge. 3 For they, ignoring the righteousness of God and seeking to establish their own righteous- ness, have not submitted themselves to the righteousness of God. 4 For Christ is the end of the Law for the righteousness of all who keep it. 5 For Moses describes the righteous- ness of the Law in this way, "Whoever does these things will benefit." 6 But the righteous- ness of faith says thus, "Say not in your heart, Who shall ascend into heaven?" (i.e., to bring Christ from above). 7 Nor, "Who will descend into the depths?" (i.e., who will bring Christ again from the dead). 8 But what does it say? The word is in you, in your mouth and in your heart. This is the word of faith that we preach. 9 For if you confess with your mouth the Lord Jesus and believe in your heart that God raised him from the dead, you will be saved: 10 For with the heart a man rises to righteousness, and with the mouth he confesses to salvation. 11 For the Scripture says, "He that believeth on him shall not be shamed." 12 For there is no difference between the Italian and the Greek, for he who is Lord of all is rich for all who call upon him. 13 For whosoever shall call upon the Name of the Lord shall be saved. 14 But how shall they call upon him in whom they have not believed? And how shall they believe in him of whom they have not heard? And how will they be able to listen without a preacher? 15 And how shall they preach if they are not sent? As it is written, "How beautiful are the feet of those who bring glad tidings of peace and bring glad tidings of good things! 16 But not all have obeyed your gospel, for Esaias says, "Lord, who has believed our testimony?" 17 Then faith comes by hearing, and hearing by the word of God. 18 But I ask, "Have they not heard? No doubt their sound has spread over all the earth and their words to the ends of the world. 19 But I ask, Has not Israel come to know God? First Moses says, "I will expose you from a nation that is not my nation, and from a foolish nation I will make you angry." 20 Esaiah is bold and says, "I have been found by those who did not seek me, and I have been made manifest to those who did not seek me." 21 And to Israel he says, "All day long I have stretched out my hand against a disobedient and stingy people.

CHAPTER 11

1 Then I ask, "Has God forsaken his peo- ple? God forbid, for I too am an Israelite, of the descendants of Abraham, of the tribe of Benjamin. 2 God has not forsaken his people whom he knew before. Don't you know what the Scripture says about Elijah, how he com- muned with God against Israel, saying, "Lord, they have done a work of mass destruction, 3 Lord, have they killed your prophets and dug up your altars; I am left alone and they seek my life? 4 But what does God answer them? I have reserved for myself six thousand men who have not bowed the knee to Baal. 5 Even at this time there is a remnant according to the election of grace. 6 And if it is of grace, it is no longer of works, or if it was grace, it is no longer grace; but if it is of works, it is no longer grace, or if it was works, it is no lon- ger works. 7 What then? Israel did not obtain what he sought; but election he obtained, while others were hardened, 8 as it is written, "God gave them the spirit of sleep: eyes not to see and ears not to hear until now." 9 And Dauid says, "Let their table become a snare, a net and a stumbling block, as a reward for them. 10 Let their eyes be darkened, that they may not see, and always stoop down upon their backs. 11 Then I ask, Have they stum- bled to fall? God forbid; but through their fall, salvation comes to the Gentiles, to persuade them to follow. 12 Therefore, if their fall is the riches of the world and their decrease the riches of the Gentiles, how much more will their abundance be? 13 For in speaking to you Gentiles, inasmuch as I am the apos- tle of you Gentiles, I magnify my office, 14 to try to persuade them by some means to fol- low my flesh and save some. 15 For if their casting out is the reconciliation of the world, what will their reception be but life from the dead? 16 For if the first fruits are holy, so is the whole lamp; and if the root is holy, so are the branches. 17 Though some of the branches have been broken off, and you, who are a wild olive tree, have been grafted in for them and made partakers of the root and fatness of the olive tree. 18 Do not boast against the branch- es; and if you boast of yourself, it is not you who have the root, but the root of yourself. 19 Then you will say, "The branches have been broken off that I may be grafted in." 20 Well, they have been broken off because of unbelief, and you stand by faith; do not be afraid, but fear. 21 For if God has not spared the natural branches, see that he does not spare you also. 22 Observe therefore the abundance and the severity of God: toward those who have fall- en, severity; but toward you, abundance, if you continue in his abundance, otherwise you will be cut off. 23 And they also, if they do not stand firm in the faith, will be transferred, for God is able to transfer them back. 24 For if you were cut off from the olive tree, which was wild by nature, and were made to grow, contrary to nature, into a righteous olive tree, how much more shall those who are by nature be made to grow into their own olive tree? 25 For I do not want you, brethren, to be ignorant of this secret (or to be arrogant in yourselves), that in part obstinacy has come to Israel, until the fullness of the Gentiles has come. 26 And so all Israel shall be saved, as it is written, "The Deliverer shall go out from Zion, and shall wrest away strength from Jacob." 27 And this is my counsel for them, when I take away their sins. 28 As for the gos- pel, they are enemies for your sake; but as for the election, they are unwelcome for the sake of the fathers. 29 For the gifts and calling of God are without repentance. 30 For if in the past you did not believe God, now you have obtained grace through your faith: 31 so also now they have not realized the mercy that has been shown to you, that they too may obtain mercy. 32 For God has shut up all in unbelief, that he might have mercy on all. 33 How deep are the riches of God's wisdom and knowl- edge! How clear are His judgments and ways to be discovered! 34 Who has known the mind of the Lord or who has been his counselor? 35 Or who has given him precedence and will be rewarded? 36 For of him, through him, and in view of him are all things; to him be glory forever. Amen.

CHAPTER 12

1 I beseech you therefore, brethren, by the mercies of God, to make of your bodies a glad, holy, acceptable sacrifice to God, which is your reasonable service to God. 2 And be not like unto this world, but be changed through the renewing of your minds, that you may prove what is the good, acceptable and per- fect will of God. 3 For by the grace that has been given me, I say to everyone among you that no one presume to understand what is right to understand, but let him do it accord- ing to sobriety, as God has distributed to each one the measure of faith. 4 For just as we have many members in one body, and all the mem- bers do not have one office, 5 so we, being many, are one body in Christ, and each one is a member of the other. 6 Since therefore we have different gifts, according to the grace given us, if we have a prophecy, we prophesy according to the part of faith: 7 or of an office, be ready for the office; or he who teaches, for teaching: 8 or he who exhorts, on exhortation; he who distributes, do it with simplicity; he who governs, with diligence; he who shows mercy, with cheerfulness. 9 Let joy be without dissimulation. Abhor what is evil, and cherish what is good. 10 Be fond of loving one another with brotherly love. In giving honor, go before one another, 11 be not slothful in doing ser- vice, but serene in spirit in serving the Lord, 12 reviving hope, pacifying tribulation, con- tinuing to pray, 13 distributing the needs of the saints and devoting yourselves to hospi- talization. 14 Bless those who persecute you; bless, I say, and do not curse. 15 Recover with those who recover and mourn with those who mourn. 16 Be affectionate toward one anoth- er; do not be timid, but make yourselves equal with those who are inferior; do not be wise in yourselves. 17 Reward no one euillity for euil- lity; procure things honest in the sight of all men. 18 If it be possible, so far as it is in you, have peace with all men. 19 Fear not, do not do justice to yourselves, but give place to wrath: for it is written, Vengeance is mine: I will re- pay, saith the LORD. 20 Therefore, if your en- emy is hungry, feed him; if he is thirsty, give him drink; for in so doing, you will cast scales of fire on his head. 21 Do not be a guest of ill will, but a guest of kindness.

CHAPTER 13

1 Let every soul be subject to the higher pow- ers, for there is no power except from God; and the powers that be are ordained of God. 2 Whoever therefore resists the power, re- sists the order of God; and whoever resists will receive his own condemnation. 3 For the magistrates are not to be feared for good works, but for wickedness. Will you therefore not fear power? Do well, so you will have the praise of the same. 4 For he is God's minister for your riches, but if you do evil, fear him; for he does not bear the sword for anything, for he is God's minister to take vengeance on those who do evil. 5 For this reason you must be submissive, not only for wrath, but also for conscience.

6 For this reason also pay tribute, for they are ministers of God and apply them- selves for the same thing. 7 Therefore give all men their tribute: tribute, to whom you owe tribute; custome, to whom you owe custome; pheare, to whom you owe pheare; honor, to whom you owe honor. 8 You owe nothing to anyone but to love one another, for he who loves another has fulfilled the Law. 9 Where- fore thou shalt not commit adultery, thou shalt not kill, thou shalt not steal, thou shalt not bear false witness, thou shalt not do brib- ery; and if there be any other commandment, it is briefly included in this saying, namely, "Thou shalt love thy neighbor as thyself." 10 He who does not harm his neighbor is the fulfillment of the Law. 11 Considering the sea- son, it is time for us to rise from sleep, for our salvation is nearer now than when we ignored it. 12 The night is past and the day is near; let us therefore cast off the works of darkness and put on the armor of light, 13 so that we may walk honestly, as by day: not in the grip of gluttony and drunkenness, nor in the grip of horns and lusts, nor in the grip of strife and enmity. 14 but clothe yourselves with the Lord JESUS CHRIST and do not think of the flesh to satisfy its desires.

CHAPTER 14

1 He who is sound in faith, let him receive you, but not for controversy or dispute. 2 One eats to eat of everything, and another, who is awake, eats herbs. 3 Let him who eats not de- spise him who does not eat, and let him who does not eat not condemn him who eats, for God has received him. 4 Who are you who condemns another's servant? He shall stand or fall according to his master; yea, he shall be established, for God is able to make him stand. 5 This man regards one day as different from another day, and another man regards every day as the same; let every man be fully persuaded in his own mind. 6 Whoever ob- serves the day, observes it for the LORD; and whoever does not observe the day, does not observe it for the LORD. Whoever eats, eats to the Lord, for he gives thanks to God; and whoever does not eat, does not eat to the Lord and give thanks to God. 7 For none of you lives for himself, and no one dies for himself. 8 For whether we lie, we lie to the Lord, or whether we die, we die to the Lord; whether we lie, or whether we die, we are the Lords. 9 Therefore Christ died, rose again, and was restored, to be the Lord of the dead and dying. 10 But why do you condemn your brother or why do you despise your brother? For we shall all ap- pear before the tribunal of Christ. 11 For it is written, "I am, says the Lord, and every knee shall bow to me, and all tongues shall confess to God." 12 Thus each one of you will give an account of himself to God. 13 Therefore do not judge one another any longer, but rather consider this: that no one lay a falling occa- sion or a stumbling block for his brother. 14 I know, and am persuaded of it through the Lord Iesus, that there is nothing vncleane in itself; but he who judges a vncleane thing, to him it is vncleane. 15 But if your brother is afflicted for food, now you are not charitable; do not destroy him with your food, for which Christ died. 16 Do not cause your possessions to be spoken ill of. 17 For the kingdom of God is neither food nor drink, but righteousness and peace and joy in the Holy Spirit. 18 For he who serves Christ in these things is accept- able to God and is esteemed by men. 19 Let us therefore follow the things that pertain to peace and by which one may edify the other. 20 Destroy not the work of God for God's sake; all things in God are pure, but it is evil for man to eat with offense. 21 It is not good either to eat meat, or to drink wine, or to do any thing that makes your brother stumble, or that of- fends him, or that makes him sad. 22 Do you have faith? Have faith in yourself before God; blessed is he who does not condemn himself in what He grants. 23 For he who doubts is condemned if he eats, because he does not eat by faith; and what is not by faith is sin.

CHAPTER 15

1 We who are strong must bear the infirmi- ties of the weak and not please ourselves. 2 Therefore let each one please his neighbor in what is good for edification. 3 For Christ also did not wish to please himself, but as it is written, "The reproaches of those who reproach you have fallen on me." 4 For the things that were written before were written for our instruction, that through patience and the comfort of the Scriptures we might have hope. 5 Now may the God of patience and comfort grant you that you may be like one another, according to Christ Iesus, 6 that with one mind and with one mouth you may pray to God, that is, to the Father of our Lord Jesus Christ. 7 Therefore receive from one an- other, as Christ also received, to the glory of God. 8 Now I say that Jesus Christ was a min- ister of circumcision, for the truth of God, to confirm the promises made to the fathers. 9 And let the Gentiles pray to God for his mercy, as it is written, "Therefore I will confess you among the Gentiles and sing your Name." 10 And again he says, "Gather yourselves togeth- er, Gentiles, with his people." 11 And again, "Pray to the Lord, all you Gentiles, and praise him, all peoples together." 12 And again Esa- iah says, "There shall be a chief of Jesse, and he who shall arise to reign over the Gentiles; in him shall the Gentiles trust." 13 Now may the God of hope fill you with all joy and peace in faith, that you may abound in hope through the power of the Holy Spirit. 14 And I also am persuaded of you, my brethren, that you also are full of goodness and full of all knowledge, and are able to admonish one another. 15 Nev- ertheless, brethren, I have written to you with a certain boldness, as one who reminds you, because of the grace that has been granted to me by God, 16 that I may be the minister of Jesus Christ to the Gentiles, ministering the gospel of God, that the offering of the Gen- tiles may be acceptable, being sanctified by the Holy Spirit. 17 I have therefore to rejoice in Christ Iesus in the things that relate to God. 18 For I dare not speak of anything that Christ has not worked through me, to make the Gentiles obedient in word and deed, 19 by the power of signs and wonders, by the Spirit of God, so that from Jerusalem and from all around as far as Illyricum, I caused the gos- pel of Christ to spread. 20 Yea, I set myself to preach the gospel not where Christ was ap- pointed, lest I should build on another foun- dation. 21 But as it is written, "Those to whom he has not been spoken of will see him, and those who have not heard will understand him." 22 Therefore I also let me come to you often: 23 but now, seeing I have no more place in these quarters, I have desired already for many years to come to you, 24 when I take my journey to Spain, I will come to you, for I trust to see you on my journey and to be led by you on my way, after I have filled myself a little with your company. 25 But now I am go- ing to Jerusalem to minister to the saints. 26 For it pleased those of Macedonia and Achaia to make some distribution to the poor saints who are in Jerusalem. 27 For it has pleased them, and they are their possessors, for if the Gentiles have been made partakers of their spiritual things, their duet is also to serve them in

carnal things. 28 Therefore when I have accomplished this and sealed this fruit to them, I will pass over to you in Spain. 29 And I know that when I come, I will come to you with an abundance of the blessing of the gospel of Christ. 30 Moreover, brethren, I beseech you, for the sake of our Lord Jesus Christ and for the joy of the spirit, to wrestle with me by praying to God for me, 31 that I may be delivered from those who are disobe- dient in Judea, and that my service which I am to perform in Jerusalem may be accepted by the saints, 32 that I may come to you with joy, by the will of God, and may with you be refreshed. 33 So may the God of peace be with you all. Amen.

CHAPTER 16

1 I commend to you Phebe, our sister, who is a servant of the Church of Cenchrea: 2 That you may receive her in the Lord, as is fitting for the saints, and assist her in all the affairs in which she needs your help, for she has given hospi- tality to many and also to me. 3 Greet Priscilla and Aquila, my fellow helpers in Christ Iesus, 4 Who for my life have had their own necks killed. To whom not only I give thanks, but also all the Churches of the Gentiles). 5 Salute also the Church that is in their house. Greet my beloved Epenetus, who is the first fruit of Achaia in Christ. 6 Greet Marie, who has worked hard in this field. 7 Salute Andronicus and Iunia, my cousins and fellow prisoners, who are prominent among the apostles and were in Christ before me. 8 Greet Amplias, my companion in the Lord. 9 Greet Vrba- nus, our companion in Christ, and Stachys, my companion. 10 Greet Apelles, who is my companion in Christ. Greet those who are friends of Aristobulus. 11 Greet Herodion, my kinsman. Greet the friends of Narcissus who are in the Lord. 12 Greet Triphena and Trifo- sa, women who labor in the Lord. Greet the beautiful Persides, who has labored much in the Lord. 13 Salute Rufus, chosen in the Lord, his mother and mine. 14 Salute Asyncritus, Phlegon, Hermas, Patroba, Mercury, and the brothers who are with them. 15 Greet Philolo- gus and Julia, Nerea and her sister, Olympia and all the saints who are with them. 16 Greet one another with a holy kisse. The churches of Christ greet you. 17 Now, brethren, I urge you to consider those who cause divisions and offenses, contrary to the doctrine you have learned, and to remove them. 18 For they that are such serve not the Lord Jesus Christ, but their own belly, and by false and flattering speech deceive the hearts of the simple. 19 Be- cause your obedience has spread among all, I rejoice in you, but I wish you to be wise in what is good and simple in what is right. 20 The God of peace will soon bring Satan down under your feet. The grace of our Lord Jesus Christ be with you. 21 Timothy, my helper, Lu- cius, Iason and Sosipater, my relatives, greet you. 22 I, Tertius, who wrote this letter, greet you in the Lord. 23 Guadagno, my guest and of the whole church, greets you. Erastus, ad- ministrator of the city, and Quartus, a broth- er, greet you. 24 The grace of our Lord Jesus Christ be with you all. Amen. 25 To him who has power to establish you according to my gospel and the preaching of Jesus Christ, by the revelation of the mystery that has been kept secret from the beginning of the world: 26 (but now has been opened and published among all nations through the Scriptures of the Prophets, at the command of the eternal God by the obedience of faith). 27 To God, I say, the only knower, be praise through Jesus Christ for eternity. Amen.

I CORINTHIANS

CHAPTER 1

1 Paul, called to be an apostle of Jesus Christ by the will of God, and our brother Sosthenes, 2 to the Church of God which is at Corinth, to those who are sanctified in Iesus Christ, holy by vocation, and to all who call on the name of our Lord Iesus Christ, theirs and our Lord, in every place: 3 Grace to you and peace from God our Father and the Lord Jesus Christ. 4 I always thank my God for the grace of God given to you in Jesus Christ, 5 that in every- thing you may be enriched in him, in every kind of speech and in all knowledge: 6 as the testimony of Jesus Christ has been confirmed in you: 7 That ye may not be destitute of any gift, waiting for the appearing of our Lord Jesus Christ. 8 Who shall also confirm you in the end, that ye may be blameless in the day of our Lord Jesus Christ. 9 God is faithful, through whom you were called to the fellow- ship of his Son, Jesus Christ our Lord. 10 Now I beseech you, brethren, by the name of our Lord Jesus Christ, that you all speak alike, and that there be no dissension among you, but that you be united in one mind and in one judgment. 11 For it has been declared to me, my brethren, by those of the house of Cloe, that there are contentions among you. 12 Now I say that each one of you says, "I am Paul, I am Apollos, I am Cephas, and I am Christ." 13 Did Christ die? Was Paul crucified for you? Or have you been baptized in Paul's name? 14 I thank God that I have not baptized any of you except Crispus and Gaius, 15 lest anyone should say that I baptized in my own name. 16 I also baptized the house of Stephanas; also I do not know whether I baptized anyone else. 17 For CHRIST did not send me to baptize, but to preach the gospel, not with wisdom of words, lest the cross of Christ should be made vain. 18 For the preaching of the cross is for those who perish foolishness, but for those who are saved it is the power of God. 19 For it is written, "I will destroy the wisdom of the wise and throw out the understanding of the prudent." 20 Where is the wise, where is the scribe, where is the dispenser of this world? Has not God made the wise man of this world foolish? 21 Since the world, through wisdom, has not known God in the wisdom of GOD, it has pleased God, through the foolishness of preaching, to save those who are alive: 22 seeing also that the Irish peoples need a sign and the Greeks seek wisdom. 23 But we preach Christ crucified, who to the Turks is a stumbling block and to the Greeks fool- ishness: 24 But to those who are called, both among the Greeks and among the Irish, we preach Christ, the power of God and the wis- dom of God. 25 For the foolishness of God is wiser than men, and the weakness of God is stronger than men. 26 For, brethren, see your calling: not many wise according to the flesh were called, nor many mighty, nor many no- ble. 27 But God chose the foolish things of the world to confound the wise, and God chose the weak things of the world to confound the things mighty, 28 and has chosen the vile things of the world, and the things that are despised, and the things that are not, to re- duce to nothing the things that are, 29 so that no flesh may be recognized in his presence. 30 But you are of him in Christ Iesus, who by God was made wise and righteous and sancti- fied and redeemed, 31 so that, as it is written, "Whoever withdraws, withdraw himself into the Lord."

CHAPTER 2

1 And I, brethren, when I came to you, did not come with excellence of words or wisdom, illustrating to you the

testimony of God. 2 For I did not think that I knew any thing among you except Jesus Christ and him crucified. 3 I was among you in weakness and fear and great trembling. 4 Neither my word nor my preaching was based on the enticing speeches of human wisdom, but on the efficacy of the Spirit and power, 5 so that your faith may not be in the wisdom of men, but in the power of God. 6 We speak of the wisdom of those who are perfect; not of the wisdom of this world, nor of the princes of this world, who are of no use. 7 But we speak of the wisdom of God in a mystery, that is, of the hidden wisdom which God had established before the world, to our glory. 8 Which none of the princes of this world knew; for if they had known it, they would not have crucified the Lord of glory. 9 But as it is written, "The things which eye has not seen, nor ear heard, nor the heart of man, are those which God has prepared for those who love him." 10 But God has revealed them by his Spirit, for the Spirit searches all things, even the deep things of God. 11 For who knows the things of a man but the spirit of a man that is in him? So also the things of God no one knows except the spirit of God. 12 Now we have not received the spirit of the world, but the Spirit that is of God, to know the things that have been given us by God. 13 Of these things we also speak, not with the words which the wisdom of men teaches, but with those which the Holy Spirit teach- es, comparing spiritual things with spiritual things. 14 But the natural man does not per- ceive the things of the Spirit of God, because they are foolish to him; he cannot know them, because they are spiritually discussed. 15 But he who is spiritually discerns all things; nev- ertheless he is not judged by anyone. 16 Who has known the mind of the Lord to instruct him? But we have the mind of Christ.

CHAPTER 3

1 I could not speak to you, brothers, as to spiritual men, but as to carnal men, that is, as to babes in Christ. 2 I gave you milk to drink and not meat, because you were not yet able to bear it, nor are you now. 3 For you are still carnal; for while there is strife, quarreling and division among you, are you not carnal and walking as men? 4 For if one says, "I am Paul," and another, "I am Apollos," are you not carnal? 5 Who then is Paul and who is Apollos, if not the ministers by whom you were raised, as the Lord has given to each? 6 I planted, Apollos watered, but God gave the harvest. 7 So then it is not he who plants, nor he who waters, but it is God who gives the harvest. 8 He who plants and he who waters are one, and each will receive his wages, according to his work. 9 For we all together are God's work- ers; you are God's factory and God's building. 10 According to the grace of God that has been given to me, like a skillful master builder, I have laid the foundation, and another builds on it; but let each one mind how he builds on it. 11 For no other foundation can be laid but the one that has been laid, that is, Jesus Christ. 12 And if anyone builds on this foun- dation, gold, silver, precious stones, timber, hay or stubble, 13 every man's work shall be made manifest, for the day shall declare it, for it shall be reworked by fire; and the fire shall judge the quality of every man's work. 14 If a man's work, on which he has built, re- mains, he shall receive wages. 15 If a man's work burns, he shall lose, but he shall be saved by himself; nevertheless, as if he were in the fire. 16 Know ye not that ye are the Temple of God, and that the Spirit of God dwelleth in you? 17 If anyone destroys the Temple of God, God will destroy him, for the Temple of God is holy, as you are. 18 Let no one be

deceived; if anyone among you seems to be wise in this world, let him be foolish to become wise. 19 For the wisdom of this world is foolishness with God, for it is written, "He catches the wise in their own craftiness." 20 And again, "The Lord knows that the thoughts of the wise are vain." 21 Therefore let no one have illu- sions about men, for everything is yours. 22 Whether it is Paul, Apollos or Cephas, wheth- er it is the world, life or death, whether it is present things or future things, all are yours, 23 and you are Christ, and Christ God.

CHAPTER 4

1 I have not spoken to you, brethren, as to spiritual men, but as to carnal men, that is, as to babes in Christ. 2 I gave you milk to drink and not meat, because you were not yet able to bear it, nor are you now. 3 For you are still carnal, for if there are quarrels and disputes and divisions among you, are you not carnal and walking as men? 4 For if one says, "I am Paul," and another, "I am Apollos," are you not carnal? 5 Who then is Paul and who is Apollos, if not the ministers by whom you were taught, as the Lord has given to each? 6 I sowed, Apol- lo watered, but God gave the harvest. 7 There- fore it is not he who plants, nor he who wa- ters, but it is God who gives the harvest. 8 He who plants and he who waters are one, and each will receive his wages, according to his work. 9 For all of us together are God's work- ers; you are God's factory and God's building. 10 According to the grace of God that has been given to me, like a skillful master builder, I have laid the foundation, and another builds on it; but let each one mind how he builds. 11 For no other foundation can be laid than that which has been laid, that is, Jesus Christ. 12 And if anyone builds on this foundation, gold, silver, precious stones, timber, hay or stubble, 13 the work of every one shall be made man- ifest, for the day shall declare it, for it shall be reworked by fire; and the fire shall judge the quality of every one's work. 14 If a man's work, on which he has built, remains, he shall receive wages. 15 If a man's work burns, he shall lose, but he shall save himself, as if he were in the fire. 16 Do you not know that you are the Temple of God and that the Spirit of God dwells in you? 17 If anyone destroys the Temple of God, God will destroy him, for the Temple of God is holy, as you are. 18 Let no one be deceived; if anyone among you seems to be wise in this world, let him be foolish to become wise. 19 For the wisdom of this world is foolishness with God, for it is written, "He catches the wise in their craftiness." 20 And again, "The Lord knows that the thoughts of the wise are vain." 21 Therefore let no one be deceived about men, for everything is yours. 22 Whether it is Paul or Apollos or Cephas, whether it is the world, life or death, things present or things to come, everything is yours, 23 and you are Christ, and Christ God.

CHAPTER 4

1 Let the ministers of Christ and the dis- pensers of God's secrets be thought of: 2 As for the rest, it is required of those who dis- pose, that every man be found faithful. 3 As for me, I spend very little to be judged by you or by the judgment of men; no, I do not judge myself. 4 Since I know nothing by myself, I am not justified for it; but the one who judg- es me is the Lord. 5 Therefore judge nothing before the time, until the Lord comes, who will illuminate the things hidden in darkness and make manifest the counsels

of hearts; and then every man shall have praise of God. 6 Now, brethren, these things I have applied figuratively to myself and Apollos, for your sakes, that you may learn through them that no one presumes on what is written, that one does not puff himself up against another for any cause whatsoever. 7 For who separates you, and what do you have that you have not received? If you have received it, why do you take it back as if you had not received it? 8 Now you are satiated, now you have become rich; you reign as kings without any disadvan- tage, and I would that God would make you to reign, that we also might reign with you. 9 For I believe that God appointed the last apostles as men destined for death, because we have become a provision for the world, for angels and for men. 10 We are foolish for Christ's sake, and you are wise in Christ; we are weak, and you are strong; you are honorable, and we are despised. 11 To this day we hunger and thirst, we are naked, we are beset, and we have no certain dwelling place, 12 And we toil, working with our hands; we are oppressed, yet we are blessed; we are persecuted, and we suffer it. 13 We are always spoken of, and we pray; we are made like the filth of the world, the offence of all things, until now. 14 I do not write these things to shame you, but as My beloved children I admonish you. 15 For though you have ten thousand instructors in Christ, yet you do not have many fathers, for in Christ Iesus I have begotten you through the gospel. 16 Therefore, I pray you, be my followers. 17 For this reason I have sent you Timothy, who is my beloved and faithful son in the Lord, who will make you remember my ways in Christ, as I teach in every place in ev- ery church. 18 Some puff themselves up as if I would not come to you. 19 But I will come to you soon, if the Lord wills, and you will know not the words of those who puff themselves up, but power. 20 For the kingdom of God is not in words, but in power. 21 What do you want? Shall I come to you with a rod or with grace and a spirit of meekness?

CHAPTER 5

1 It has been known with certainty that there is fornication among you; and such forni- cation as has never been named among the Gentiles, namely, that one should have his father's wife. 2 And you puff yourselves up and do not grieve rather that he who has done this misdeed should be removed from you. 3 For I, absent in body but present in spirit, have already decided, as if I were present, that he who did this thing should be removed from you, 4 when you are gathered together, and my spirit, in the Name of our Lord Jesus Christ, that such a one, I say, by the power of our Lord Jesus Christ, 5 be delivered to Satan, for the destruction of the flesh, that the spirit may be saved in the day of the Lord Jesus. 6 Your way of doing things is not good; do you not know that a little smoke makes the whole slug go away? 7 Purge away therefore the old losses, that you may be a new light, just as you have been delivered, for Christ, our pastor, has been sacrificed for you. 8 Therefore do not keep the feast with old bread, nor with the bread of malice and wickedness, but with the leavened bread of sincerity and truth. 9 I wrote to you in an epistle that you should not be with fornicators, 10 and not with the for- nicators of this world, nor with the corrupt, nor with extortioners, nor with idolaters, for then you must go out of the world. 11 But now I have written to you not to be together: if one who is called a brother is a fornicator, or a coke addict, or an idolater, or a libertine, or a drunkard, or an extortioner, with him you shall not eat. 12 For what must

I do, to judge even those who are outside? Do ye not judge those who are within? 13 But God judges those outside. Therefore turn away from you that wicked man.

CHAPTER 6

1 Or can any of you who have business against another be judged by the judge and not by the saints? 2 Do you not know that the saints will judge the world? If the world will be judged by you, are you worthy to judge the smallest things? 3 Do you not know that we will judge the angels? And all the more the things that pertain to this life? 4 If therefore you have judgments about the things pertain- ing to this life, consider those things that are least esteemed in the Church. 5 I say this to your shame. Is there not a wise man among you, not one who can judge among his broth- ers? 6 But a brother goes into judgment with a brother, and this under unbelievers. 7 Now, therefore, there is total infirmity in you, in that you go and quarrel with one another; why do you not suffer wrong? Why do you not hurt yourselves? 8 Nay, you yourselves do evil and harm your brethren. 9 Know ye not that the righteous shall not inherit the kingdom of God? Do not be deceived: neither fornicators, nor idolaters, nor adulterers, nor philander- ers, nor cheaters, 10 nor theoids, nor couet- ous, nor drunkards, nor libertines, nor ex- tortioners shall inherit the kingdom of God." 11 Some of you were like that, but you were washed, you were sanctified, you were justi- fied in the name of the Lord Jesus and by the Spirit of our God. 12 Everything is lawful for me, but everything is not profitable for me. I can do everything, but I do not want to be brought under the power of anything. 13 The flesh is intended for the belly and the belly for the flesh, but God will destroy both the bel- ly and the flesh. The body is not intended for fornication, but for the LORD, and the LORD for the body. 14 God also raised up the Lord and will raise him up by his power. 15 Do you not know that your bodies are the members of Christ? Should I take the members of Christ and make them the members of a harlot? God forbid. 16 Do you not know that he who mates with a harlot is one body? For two, it says, shall be one flesh. 17 But he who is faithful to the LORD is one spirit. 18 Flee fornication: every sin that a man does is out of the body; but he who commits fornication sins against his own body. 19 Do you not know that your body is the temple of the Holy Spirit who is in you and whom you have from God? And you are not your own. 20 Because you have been bought dearly, glorify God in your body and in your spirit, for they are gods.

CHAPTER 7

1 Now concerning the things of which you have written to me, it is good that the man should not touch the woman. 2 To avoid for- nication, let every man have his own wife, and let every woman have her own husband. 3 Let the husband give his wife due kindness, and so also let the wife give her husband. 4 The wife has no power over her own body, but the husband; and the husband also has no power over his own body, but the wife. 5 Do not defraud one another, except by mu- tual agreement and for a time, that you may devote yourselves to fasting and prayer, and come together again so that Satan may not tempt you by your incontinence. 6 But this I say by permission, not by command. 7 For I wish that all men were like me; but each man has his own gift from God, one according to this way

and another according to that. 8 Therefore I say to the betrothed and widows, "It is good for them if they remain like me." 9 But if they cannot abstain, let them marry, for it is better to marry than to bury. 10 And to you who are married I command, not I, but the Lord, "Do not let your wife depart from her husband." 11 But if she depart, let her remain married or be reconciled to her hus- band, and let her husband not put away his wife. 12 But I speak to you, and not to you, Lord, "If a brother has a wife, do not forsake her; if she is content to dwell with him, do not forsake her." 13 And the woman who has a husband who is not deceived, if he is content to dwell with her, do not forsake him. 14 For the vnbeleeant husband is sanctified to his wife, and the vnbeleeant wife is sanctified to her husband; formerly your children were vn- clean, but now they are holy. 15 But if the vn- beleeant depart, let him depart; a brother or a sister is not in subjection in these things; but God hath called in peace. 16 For what know- est thou, O wife, whether thou wilt bid fare- well to thy husband? Or what do you know, O man, if you will greet your wife? 17 But as God has distributed to each one, as the Lord has called each one, so let him walk; and so have I ordained, in all the churches. 18 If anyone is called to be circumcised, let not his circum- cision be gathered; if anyone is called to be circumcised, let him not be circumcised. 19 Circumcision is nothing, and uncircumcision is nothing but keeping God's commands. 20 Let each one remain in the same calling in which he was called. 21 Are you called to be a servant? Do not worry about that; but if you want to be free, do so rather. 22 For he who is called in the Lord, being a servant, is the Lord free; and also he who is called, being free, is Christ's servant. 23 Ye have been bought dearly; be not servants of men. 24 Brethren, let every man, where he is called, abide with God. 25 As for virgins, I have received no com- mand from the Lord, but I give my consent, as one who has obtained from the Lord grace to be faithful. 26 I suppose therefore that this is good for present needs; I believe that it is good for a man to be so. 27 Are you bound to a wife? You do not want to be loosed; are you loosed from a wife? You do not want a wife. 28 But if you take a wife, you do not sin; and if a virgin marry, she does not sin; nevertheless, they shall have trouble in the flesh; but I spare you. 29 And this I say unto you, brethren, because the time is short; afterward he that hath health shall be as if he had it not: 30 And they that mourn, as if they did not mourn; and they that rejoice, as if they did not rejoice; and they that depart, as if they did not pos- sess: 31 And they that see this world, as if they did not see it; for the fashion of this world departeth. 32 Would that ye were without worry. The sane man worries about the things of the Lord, as he may please the Lord. 33 But he who is married worries about the things of the world, to please his wife. 34 There is also a difference between a virgin and a wife: the married woman worries about the things of the Lord, to be holy, both in body and spirit; but the married one worries about the things of the world, to please her husband. 35 And this I say for your sakes, not to entangle you in a snare, but that you may follow that which is honest, and that you may make yourselves clear in the Lord without separating. 36 But if anyone thinks it expedient for his virgin, if he passes the flower of his age and needs it, let him do as he pleases, he is not sinning; let them marry. 37 He who is convinced in his heart that he needs nothing, but has power over his own will, and has decided in his heart to keep his virgin, does well. 38 He who gives her to wife does well, but he who does not give her to wife does better. 39 The wife is bound by the Law as long as her husband lives; but if her husband is dead, she is free to marry whomever she pleases, only in the Lord. 40 But she is more blessed, if she remains so, ac- cording to my judgment; and I believe that I also have the Spirit of God.

CHAPTER 8

1 Concerning things sacrificed to idols, we know that we all have knowledge; knowledge puffs up, but goodness edifies. 2 Now if one thinks he knows something, he still knows nothing that he ought to know. 3 But if one loves God, he also knows. 4 Concerning eat- ing things sacrificed to idols, we know that an idol is nothing in the world and that there is no God but one. 5 For although there are gods who are called gods, both in heaven and on earth (for there are many gods and many lords) 6 Yet there is one God, who is that Fa- ther from whom all things come, and we in him; and one Lord, Jesus Christ, from whom all things come, and we from him. 7 But ev- ery man hath not this knowledge, because many, being conscious of the idol, even unto this hour eat as a thing sacrificed to the idol, and so their conscience, being diseased, is de- filed. :8 But food is not acceptable to God, for if we eat, we have not more; if we do not eat, we have less. 9 But take care that this power of yours is not, in some way, an occasion of falling for those who are melancholy. 10 For if anyone sees you, who have knowledge, sit- ting at table in the temple of idols, will not the conscience of the one who is sick be moved to eat those things that are sacrificed to idols? 11 And by your knowledge shall the weak brother perish, for whom Christ died. 12 Now when you sin thus against the brethren and wound their weak conscience, you sin against Christ. 13 Therefore, if flesh offends my brother, I will not eat flesh as long as the world stands, lest I offend my brother.

CHAPTER 9

1 Am I not an apostle? Am I not free? Have I not seen Jesus Christ our Lord? Are you not my work in the Lord? 2 If I am not an apostle to others, I am undoubtedly an apostle to you, for you are the sign of my apostolicity in the Lord. 3 My defense to those who examine me is this, 4 Do we not have the power to eat and drink? 5 Have we not the power to lead a wife who is a sister, like the other apostles, like the brothers of the Lord and Cephas? 6 Or do not Barnabas and I alone have power not to work? 7 Who goes to war at his own expense? Who plants a vineyard and does not eat of its fruit? Or who feeds a flock and does not eat of its milk? 8 Do I say these things according to man? Does not the Lawe also say the same? 9 For in the Law of Moses it is written, "Do not muzzle the mouth of the ox that treads on the horn"; does God care for oxen? 10 Or does He not do so for our good? For our good, no doubt, it is written, "He who eats must hope, and he who threshes in hope must be partak- er of his hope." 11 If we have sown spiritual things to you, is it a great thing if we reap your carnal things? 12 If others, along with you, are partakers of this power, are we not rather? Nevertheless, we have not overcome this power, but suffer all things not to hinder the gospel of Christ. 13 Do you not know that those who exercise the ministry of holy things eat of the things of the temple, and that those who wait at the altar are partakers of the al- tar? 14 So also the Lord has determined that those who preach the gospel should eat of the gospel. 15 But I never said any of these things, nor wrote these things so that it might be done so

with me; for it is better that I should die than that someone should be my witness. 16 For though I preach the gospel, I have nothing to rejoice in; for necessity is laid upon me, and woe to me if I do not preach the gospel. 17 For if I do it willingly, I have a reward; but if I do it against my will, notwith- standing the dispensation has been entrusted to me. 18 What then is my reward? Only that when I preach the gospel, I make the gospel of Christ free, and do not abuse my author- ity in the gospel. 19 For though I was free from all men, yet I made myself the servant of all men to win more. 20 And for children, I became like a child, to conquer children; for those who are under the law, as if I were under the law, to conquer those who are un- der the law: 21 to those who are without lawe, as if I were without lawe, (whereas I am not without lawe as far as God is concerned, but I am in the lawe through Christ) that I may conquer those who are without lawe: 22 For the weak I have become like a weakling, that I may conquer the weak; I have become all things to all men, that I may conquer some by all means. 23 And this I do for the sake of the gospel, that I may be partaker of it with you. 24 Do you not know that those who run in a race all run, but one receives the prize? Run therefore to obtain. 25 He who boasts that he is a master, abstains from all things; and they do so to obtain a corruptible crown, but we for a vncorruptible one. 26 Therefore I run, not as a vncertain, and I fight, not as one who beats the threshing floor. 27 But I lower my body, and put it under restraint, lest, after preach- ing to others, I myself should be taken back.

CHAPTER 10

1 Moreover, brethren, I would not have you ignorant that all our fathers were under that cloud and passed through that sea, 2 and they were all baptized with Moses in that cloud and in that sea, 3 and they all ate the same spiritual meat, 4 and they all drank the same spiritual drink (for they drank of the spiritu- al rock that followed them, and the rock was Christ). 5 But with many of them God was not pleased, for they were cast into the wil- derness. 6 Now these things are our example, so that we may not be caught up in covetous- ness for illicit things, as they were caught up in covetousness. 7 Do not be idolaters as some of them were, as it is written, "The peo- ple sat down to eat and drink and got up to play." :8 Do not commit fornication, as some of them committed fornication and fell in one day three thousand and twenty thousand. 9 Nor let them tempt Christ, as also some of them tempted Him and were destroyed by serpents. 10 Do not murmur, as some of them murmured and were destroyed by the destroyer. 11 Now all these things came to them as an example and were written to warn those about whom the end of the world is ap- proaching. 12 Therefore, let those who think they are standing beware lest they fall. 13 No temptation has been taken from you, except those that come to man; and God is faithful, who does not want you to be tempted above your ability, but will give you the solution with the temptation, so that you may be able to endure it. 14 Therefore, beloved, flee from idolatry. 15 I speak as to those who have un- derstanding; listen to what I say 16 Is not the cup of blessing that we bless the communion of Christ's blood? The bread that we break, is it not the communion of the body of Christ? 17 For we, who are many, are one bread and one body, for we are all partakers of one bread. 18 Behold Israel, which is according to the flesh: are not those who eat of the sacrifices partak- ers of the altar? 19 What say I, then, that the idol is any thing, or that what is sacrificed to idols is any thing? 20 No, but that these things which the Gentiles sacrifice, they sacrifice to the deuiles and not to God; and I do not want you to have fellowship with the deuiles. 21 You cannot drink the cup of the Lord and the cup of the disciples. You cannot be partakers of the Lord's table and the table of the disciples. 22 Do we anger the Lord? Are we stronger than him? 23 Everything is lawful for me, but everything is not convenient; everything is lawful for me, but everything is not edifying. 24 Let no one see his own, but let everyone see the wealth of others. 25 What is lonely in the shanties, eat of it, and ask not for the sake of conscience. 26 For the land is the Lords', and all that is in it. 27 If anyone of those who are not at home calls you to a banquet, and if you want to go, eat what is set before you, and do not ask questions for the sake of conscience. 28 But if anyone says to you, "This is sacrificed to idols," do not eat it, because of the one who showed it to you and because of conscience (for the land is the Lords' and everything in it). 29 And conscience, I say, not yours, but that other's; why should my freedom be con- demned by another's conscience? 30 For if I, because of the benefit of God, am a partak- er of it, why is it ever spoken of me on that account? 31 Whether you eat or drink or do anything, do everything to the glory of God. 32 Offend no one, neither the badgers, nor the Greeks, nor the Church of God: 33 just as I please all men in all things, not seeking my own profit, but the profit of many, that they may be saved.

CHAPTER 11

1 Be followers of me, as I am of Christ. 2 Now, brothers, I commend you to remember all my things and keep the ordinances as I have giv- en them to you. 3 But I want you to know that Christ is the head of every man, and man is the head of woman, and God is the head of Christ. 4 Whoever prays or prophesies having anything on his head dishonors his own head. 5 But every woman who prays or prophesies having something on her head dishonors her head, for she is one, as if she were a woman. 6 Therefore, if the woman is not stamped, let her be stamped; and if it is shameful for a woman to be stamped or stamped, let her be stamped. 7 For man must not shave his head, for he is the image and glory of God; but woman is the glory of man. 8 For the man is not from the woman, but the woman from the man. 9 For the man was not created for the woman, but the woman for the man.10 Therefore the woman must have power over his head, because of the Angels. 11 Neuerthe- les, the man is not without the woman, nor the woman without the man in the Lord. 12 For as the woman is from the man, so also the man is from the woman; but everything comes from God. 13 Judge for yourselves, "Is it fitting for a woman to pray to God without being heard? 14 Does not nature itself teach you that if a man has long ears it is a disgrace to him? 15 But if a woman has a long ear, it is a prayer for her, because the ear was given to her to be used. 16 But if anyone wishes to be contentious, we have no such claim, nor do the Churches of God. 17 Now in this statement of mine, I beseech you not to come together, not to profit, but to do evil. 18 For first of all, when you come together in the Church, I feel that there are disagreements among you; and I believe that this is partly true. 19 For it is necessary that there be heresies among you also, that those who are approved among you may be known. 20 When therefore you gather yourselves together in one place, it is not to eat the Lord's Supper. 21 For each one, when he must eat, takes

his supper first, and one is hungry and the other is drunk. 22 Have ye no houses in which to eat and drink? Do you de- spise the Church of God and shame those who do not have it? What shall I say to you? Shall I pray to you for this? I do not pray to you. 23 For I received from the Lord what I delivered also to you: that the Lord Jesus, on the night when he was betrayed, took bread: 24 And when he had given thanks, he broke it and said, "Take, eat; this is my body, which was broken for you; this do in remembrance of me." 25 In the same way he also took the cup, after he had eaten dinner, saying, "This cup is the New Testament in my blood; do this every time you drink it, in remembrance of me." 26 For as often as you eat this bread and drink this cup, you will witness the Lord's death until he comes. 27 Therefore whoever eats this bread and drinks the cup of the Lord unworthily will be guilty of the body and blood of the Lord. 28 Let each one therefore examine himself and eat of this bread and drink of this cup. 29 For whoever eats and drinks unworthily eats and drinks his own damnation, because he does not recognize the body of the Lord. 30 For this reason many are weary and sick among you, and many sleep. 31 For if we would judge ourselves, we would not be judged. 32 But when we are judged, we are chastened by the Lord, lest we be condemned with the world. 33 Therefore, my brothers, when you come together to eat, take care of one another. 34 And if anyone is hungry, let him eat at home, lest you be condemned together. Other things I will put in order when I come.

CHAPTER 12

1 Now concerning spiritual gifts, brethren, I would not have you ignorant. 2 You know that you were Gentiles and that you were led away by the idiocies, as you were led. 3 Therefore I declare to you that no one who speaks by the Spirit of God calls Jesus execrable; and no one can say that Jesus is Lord except by the Holy Spirit. 4 Now the gifts are different, but the Spirit is the same. 5 There is diversity of ad- ministrations, but the same Lord, 6 and there is diversity of operations, but God is the same who works all things in all. 7 But the manifes- tation of the Spirit is granted to every man, to profit by it. 8 For to one is given by the Spir- it the word of wisdom, and to another the word of knowledge, by the same Spirit: :9 to another is given faith by the same Spirit, and to another gifts of healing by the same Spirit: 10 to another the operations of great works, to another prophecy, to another discernment of spirits, to another godliness of tongues, to another interpretation of tongues. 11 All these things are worked by one and the same Spirit, who distributes to each one as he wills. 12 For as the body is one and has many members, and all the members of the body, which is one, though many, are but one body, so also is Christ. 13 For by one Spirit we have all been baptized into one body, whether we are Iew- es, or Greeks, or bondi, or free, and we have all been made to drink in one Spirit. 14 For even the body is not composed of one mem- ber, but of many. 15 If the foot said, "For I am not the hand, I am not of the body," would it not then be of the body? 16 And if the eye said, "Since I am not the eye, I am not of the body," is it not therefore of the body? 17 If the whole body were an eye, where is the hearing? If the whole body were a hearing, where would be the smells? 18 But now God has arranged the members in the body as He pleases. 19 For if they were all one member, where would the body be? 20 But now the members are many, but the body is one. 21 The eye cannot say to the hand, "I do not need you," nor the head to the feet, "I do not need you." 22 On the con- trary, the members of the body, which seem weaker, are needed. 23 And on those mem- bers of the body which we deem most honest, we put on more honesty; and our better parts have more comfort. 24 For our better parts have no need of them; but God has hardened the body and given more honor to that part which was without, 25 That there might be no division in the body, but the members might have equal care for one another. 26 Therefore if one member suffers, all suffer with him; if one member is in honor, all the members re- joice with him. 27 You are the body of Christ and are members for your part. 28 God has ordained some in the church: first the apos- tles, second the prophets, third the teachers, then those who do miracles; after that, the gifts of healing, the helpers, the warriors, the diuersity of tongues. 29 Are they all apostles? Are they all prophets? Are they all teachers? 30 Are they all miracle workers? Do they all have the gifts of healing? Do they all speak with tongues? Do they all interpret? 31 But you de- sire the better gifts, and I will still show you a more excellent way.

CHAPTER 13

1 Though I speak with the tongues of men and of angels and have no voice, I am like a sounding reed or a tinkling cymbal. 2 Even if I had the gift of prophecy and knew all se- crets and all knowledge, if I had all faith, so that I could climb mountains, and had no voice, I would be nothing. 3 Even if I fed the poor with all my goods and gave my body to be burned, and had not wealth, it would profit me nothing. 4 Wealth suffers long, it is gener- ous, it does not gorge itself, it does not boast itself, it does not puff itself up: 5 It does not do pleasant things, it does not seek its own things, it is not provoked to anger, it does not think of happiness: 6 She does not indulge in iniquity, but is guided by the truth: 7 It en- dures all things, it is faithful to all things, it hopes in all things, it endures all things. 8 It never falls, though prophecies are abolished, tongues cease, or knowledge fade away. :9 For in part we know and in part we prophesy. 10 But when that which is perfect comes, that which is in part will be abolished. 11 When I was a child, I spoke like a child, saw like a child, thought like a child; but when I be- came a man, I did away with childish things. 12 For now we see through a glass darkly, but then we shall see face to face. Now I know in part, but then I shall know as I am known. 13 Now faith, hope and joy remain, that is, these three, but the most important of them is joy.

CHAPTER 14

1 Follow love and obtain spiritual gifts and rather that you may prophesy. 2 For he who speaks in an unknown tongue does not speak to men, but to God, for no one hears him; but in the spirit he speaks of secret things. 3 But he who prophesies speaks to me for edification, exhortation and comfort. 4 He who speaks strange language, edifies himself; but he who prophesies, edifies the Church. 5 I would that all of you should speak strange tongues, but rather that you should prophesy; for greater is he that prophesies, than he that speaks sev- eral tongues, if he does not expound it, that the Church may receive edification. 6 And now, brethren, if I come to you speaking in several tongues, what does it profit you if I do not speak to you by revelation, by knowledge, by prophecy, or by doctrine? 7 Moreover, the lifeless things that make a sound, be it a pipe

or a harp, if they do not make a distinction in sounds, how can you know what is played or sounded? 8 And if the trumpet makes a vi- olent sound, who will prepare to fight? 9 So you also, by means of the tongue, if you do not use words that have meaning, how will people understand what is said? For you will speak in the air. 10 There are many kinds of voices in the world, and none of them is stupid. 11 If I did not know the power of this magic, I would be a barbarian to the speaker, and the speak- er would be a barbarian to me. 12 So as much as you may have spiritual gifts, see to it that you excel for the edification of the Church. 13 Therefore, whoever speaks a foreign tongue, let him pray, that he may interpret. 14 For if I pray in a foreign tongue, my spirit prays, but my interpretation is fruitless. 15 What is it then? I will pray with the spirit, but also with the understanding: I will sing with the spirit, but I will also sing with the understanding. 16 Otherwise, when you bless with the spirit, how shall he who occupies the house of the ig- norant say "Amen" to your thanksgiving, since he does not know what you say? 17 For you give thanks well, but the other is not edified. 18 I give thanks to my God, I speak tongues more than all of you. 19 But I would rather, in the Church, have spoken five words with my understanding, to instruct others also, than ten thousand words in an unknown tongue. 20 Brethren, be not children in understand- ing, but in malice be children, but in under- standing be of mature age. 21 In the Bible it is written, "Through men of other tongues and other languages will I speak to this people; yet they will not hear me, says the Lord." 22 Therefore foreign languages are a sign, not for those who know each other, but for those who do not know each other; but prophecy is not for those who do not know each other, but for those who do know each other. 23 If therefore, when the whole Church is gathered into one, and all speak strange tongues, those who are ignorant come in, or those who are not, will they not say that you are out of your senses? 24 But if all prophesy, and one comes who has not been studied, or one who has not learned, he shall be rebuked by all men and shall be judged by all, 25 and so the secrets of his heart are made manifest, and he falls on his face and worships God, and plainly says that God is in you in faith. 26 What then is to be done, brethren? When you come together, according as each of you has a psalm, or has a doctrine, or has a language, or has a rework- ing, or has an interpretation, let everything be done for edification. 27 If anyone speaks in a foreign tongue, let him do it with two, or at most with three, and so on, and let one inter- pret. 28 But if there is no interpreter, let those who speak tongues be silent in the Church, and let them speak to themselves and to God. 29 Let the prophets speak in two or three, and let others judge. 30 And if a thing is report- ed to another who sits, let the first one rest. 31 For all of you may prophesy one by one, that all may learn and all may have comfort. 32 The spirits of the prophets are subject to the prophets. 33 For God is not the author of confusion, but of peace, as we see in all the Churches of the Saints. 34 Let your women be silent in the Churches, for they are not per- mitted to speak, but must be submissive, as Lawe also says. 35 If they want to learn any- thing, let them ask their husbands at home, for it is shameful for women to speak in the Church." 36 Did the word of God go out from you? Or has it come to you on its own? 37 If anyone thinks he is a prophet or a spirit, let him acknowledge that the things I write to you are the Lord's commands. 38 And if any- one is ignorant, let him also be ignorant. 39 Therefore, brethren, do not allow prophesy- ing and do not forbid speaking tongues. 40 Let everything be done honestly and in order.

CHAPTER 15

1 Moreover, brothers, I declare to you the gospel which I preached to you, which you also received and continue to receive, 2 and by which you are saved, if you remember in what manner I preached it to you, unless you have been betrayed in life. 3 For first of all I expounded to you what I received: that Christ died for our sins, according to the Scriptures, 4 that he was buried and that he rose again on the third day, according to the Scriptures, 5 and that he was seen by Cephas, then by the two. 6 After that he was seen by more than five brethren at once; and of these many re- main to this time, and some are also asleep. 7 Then he was seen by Iames and then by all the apostles. 8 And finally he saw me also, as one brought out of the utmost time. 9 For I am the least of the apostles, and I am not fit to be called an apostle, because I have perse- cuted the church of God. 10 But by the grace of God, I am what I am; and his grace that is in me has not been in vain; but I have labored more abundantly than all of them; neverthe- less not I, but the grace of God that is with me. 11 Therefore, whether it is me or them, so we preach, and so you have been received. 12 Now if you preach that Christ is risen from the dead, how do some among you say that there is no resurrection of the dead? 13 For if there is no resurrection of the dead, Christ is not risen: 14 and if Christ is not risen, then our preaching is in vain, and your faith is also in vain. 15 And we were also found false witnesses of God, because we testified of God that He raised Christ, who did not raise, if the dead are not raised. 16 For if the dead are not raised, Christ is not raised. :17 And if Christ has not risen, your faith is in vain; you are still in your sins. 18 So those who sleep in Christ have perished. 19 If in this life we have only hope in Christ, we are the most miserable of all men. 20 But now Christ has risen from the dead and has been made the first fruit of those who slept. 21 For from man came death, from man came also the resurrection of the dead. 22 For as in Adam all die, so in Christ all will be made alive, 23 but each according to his own order: the first fruit is Christ, then, those who are Christ's, at his coming shall rise again. 24 Then shall be the end, when he shall have delivered up the kingdom to God, that is, to the Father, when he shall have laid down all government and all authority and all power. 25 For he must reign until he has put all his enemies under his feet. 26 The last en- emy that will be destroyed is death. 27 For he has put all things under his feet. (And when he says that all things are subject to him, it is evident that it is excluding him, who has put all things under him.) 28 When all things are subdued to him, the Son also will be subdued to him, who has subdued all things under himself, so that God may be all in all. 29 What will those who have been baptized do for the dead? If the dead do not rise at all, why were they baptized for the dead? 30 Why are we also in ieopardies every hour? 31 Because of your faith that I have in Christ Jesus our Lord, I die daily. 32 If at Ephesus I fought with the beast- men according to your way, what good is it to me, if the dead do not rise? Eat and drink, for hereafter we shall die. 33 Do not be deceived: idle talk corrupts good manners. 34 Wake up to live righteously and not to sin; for some have not the knowledge of God, I say this to your shame. 35 But some will say, "How do the dead rise? And with what body do they come home?" 36 O leprechaun, what you sow is not resurrected unless it dies. 37 And what you sow, it is not the body that will come, but the naked horn that falls, of grain or otherwise. 38 But God

gives him a body at his pleasure, and to each seed his own body, 39 The flesh is not all alike, but there is one flesh of men, another of cattle, another of fish, and another of birds. 40 There are also etheric bodies and earthly bodies; but the glory of the etheric is one, and the glory of the earthly is another. 41 There is another glory of the sun, another glory of the moon, and another glory of the stars, for one star differs from another star in glory. 42 So also is the resurrection of the dead. The body is sown in corruption and is radiated in incorruption. 43 It is sown in dishonor and is radiated in glory; it is sown in weakness and is radiated in power. 44 A natural body is sown and a spiritual body is radiated; there is a natural body and there is a spiritual body. 45 As it is also written, "The first man, Adam, was made as a living soul, and the last Adam was made as a life-giving Spirit." 46 However, it was not first that which is spiritual, but that which is natural and then that which is spir- itual. 47 The first man is of the earth, earthly; the second man is the Lord from above. 48 As the earthly are, so are the earthly; and as the earthly are, so are the earthly. 49 And as we have borne the image of the earthly, so shall we bear the image of the eternal. 50 This I say, brethren, that flesh and blood cannot inherit the kingdom of God, nor corruption inherit incorruption. 51 Behold, I reveal a secret to you: we shall not all sleep, but we shall all be changed, 52 in a moment, in the twinkling of an eye, at the last trumpet; for the trum- pet shall sound, and the dead shall be vivified incorruptible, and we shall be changed. 53 For this corruptible must put on incorruption, and this mortal must put on immortality. 54 Therefore when the corruptible shall have put on incorruption and the mortal shall put on immortality, the saying that is written shall be fulfilled, "Death is swallowed up in victory." 55 O death, where is thy sting? O death, where is your victory? 56 The sting of death is sin, and the power of sin is the plague. 57 But thanks be to God, who has given the victory through our Lord Jesus Christ. 58 Therefore, my breth- ren, be steadfast, persevering, abounding in the work of the Lord, for you know that your labor is not in vain in the Lord.

CHAPTER 16

1 As for the gathering for the saints, as I have ordained in the churches of Galatia, so do you also. 2 Every first day of the week let ev- ery one of you set aside himself and lay down as God has favored him, that there may be no gathering when I come. 3 And when I come, to whom you will give your consent by letter, I will send to bring your liberality to Jerusa- lem. 4 And if it is expedient for me to go, they will come with me. 5 Now I will come to you, having passed through Macedonia (for I will pass through Macedonia). 6 It may be that I will stay, yea, or that I will winter with you, that you may take me on my way, wherever I go. 7 For I will not see you now during my passage, but I trust that I will stay some time with you, if the Lord permits. 8 I will remain in Ephesus until Pentecost. 9 For a great work and a great effect has been opened to me, and there are many companions. 10 Now if Timo- thy comes, see that he is not afraid of you, for he works at the work of the Lord, just as I do. 11 Let no one therefore despise him, but lead him in peace that he may come to me, for I seek him among the brethren. 12 As for our brother Apollos, I longed for him to come to you with the brethren, but he was not at all intending to come at this time; nevertheless he will come when he has the proper time. 13 Watch, stand firm in the faith, be like men and strong. 14

Do all your things righteously. 15 Now, brethren, I beseech you (you know the house of Stephanas, who are the first fruits of Achaia, and who have labored to serve the saints) 16 that you also be obedient to them and to all who help them with their work. 17 I rejoice at the coming of Stephanas, Fortu- natus and Achaicus, for they have provided for your lack. 18 For they have comforted my spirit and your spirit; therefore acknowledge these men. 19 The churches of Asia greet you; Aquila and Priscilla, with the church that is in their house, greet you greatly in the Lord. 20 All the brethren greet you. Greet one another with a holy kisse. 21 The greeting of me Paul with my hand. 22 If anyone does not love the Lord Jesus Christ, let him be put in execration maran-atha. 23 The grace of our Lord Jesus Christ be with you. 24 My greeting be with you all in Christ Iesus, Amen.

II CORINTHIANS

CHAPTER 1

1 Pavl, an apostle of Christ, by the will of God, and Timothy, our brother, to the church of God that is at Corinth and to all the saints that are in all Achaia: 2 Grace to you and peace from God our Father and the Lord Je- sus Christ. 3 Blessed be God, that is, the Fa- ther of our Lord Jesus Christ, the Father of mercies and the God of all comfort, 4 who comforts us in all our tribulation, that we may comfort those who are in any affliction with the comfort with which we ourselves are comforted by God. 5 For as the sufferings of Christ abound, so our consolation through Christ abounds. 6 And if we are afflicted, it is for your consolation and salvation, which is accomplished in the continuance of the same sufferings that we also suffer; or if we are comforted, it is for your consolation and salvation. 7 Our hope is steadfast toward you, for we know that as you are partakers of the sufferings, so you will also be partakers of the consolation. 8 For, brethren, we do not want you to be ignorant of our affliction that has befallen us in Asia, as we have been pressed to excess by the passing forces, so much so that we have doubted life altogether. 9 We received the sentence of death in ourselves, because we did not trust in ourselves, but in God, who makes the dead shine. 10 Who has delivered us from so great a death and will deliver us, and in whom we trust that he will also deliver us hereafter, 11 That you may toil together in prayer for Vs, that for the gift given to Vs for many, many people may be thanked for Vs. 12 Our acknowledgment is this, the testimony of our conscience, that in simplicity and godly purity, and not in the wisdom of the flesh, but by the grace of God, we have had our conu- ersation in the world, and especially to you. 3 For we do not write other things to you than what you do or others that you acknowledge, and I trust that you will acknowledge to the end. 14 As you have acknowledged, in part, that we are your support, even as you are ours, in the day of our Lord Jesus. 15 And with this confidence I thought to come to you first, that you might have a double grace, 16 That I might pass from you into Macedonia, and that I might go out again from Macedonia to you, and that I might be led into Judea by you. 17 When therefore I was in this state of mind, did I see levity or think those things which I think, according to the flesh, which with me should be, "Yes, yes, and no, no"? 18 Yes, God is faithful: our word toward you has not been "yes" and "no." 19 For the Son of God, Jesus Christ, who was preached among you through me and Siluaneus and Timothy, was not yea and nay, but in him was yea. 20 For all the promises of God in

him are yea, and are in him amen, to the glory of God through vs. 21 It is God who upholds you in Christ and has anointed you. 22 Who has also sealed vs and put the outpouring of the Spirit in our hearts. 23 Now I ask God to remind my soul that, to spare you, I have not yet come to Corinth. 24 Not that we have dominion over your faith, but we are helpers of your joy, because by faith you stand.

CHAPTER 2

1 But I have decided not to come to you any more in sorrow. 2 For if I make you sorry, who is it that should make me sorry, but you yourselves who have been made sorry by me? 3 And I wrote this same thing to you, lest, as I came, I should take notice of them; this con- fidence I have in you all, that my joy is the joy of you all. 4 For in great affliction and anguish of heart I have written to you with many mes- sages, not that you may be sorry, but that you may perceive the joy I have for you. 5 And if anyone has caused sorrow, he has not caused sorrow to me, but in part (so that he may not charge more) to all of you. 6 It is sufficient that the man was rebuked by many. 7 So now, on the contrary, you should rather forgive him and comfort him, lest he be overwhelmed with undue gravity. 8 Therefore I beg you to confirm your love toward him. 9 For this rea- son also I have written to you, to know your trial, if you will be obedient in everything. 10 To whom you forgive anything, I also forgive; for if I forgive anything, to whom I forgive it, for your sakes I forgive it before Christ, 11 lest Satan surround you, lest we ignore his deeds. 12 Moreover, when I came to Troas to preach the gospel of Christ, a door was opened to me by the Lord, 13 I had no peace in my spirit, for I did not find Titus my brother, but left them and went away to Macedonia. 14 Now thanks be to God, who always causes Christ to tri- umph and manifests the value of his knowl- edge in every place. 15 For we are to God the sweet savor of Christ, both in those who are saved and in those who perish. 16 To some we are the savor of death, unto death, and to others the savor of life, unto life; and who is sufficient for these things? 17 For we are not as many that mock the work of God, but as sincere, but as of God, in the sight of God, we speak in Christ.

CHAPTER 3

1 Do we need to begin praising ourselves again, or do we, like others, need letters of recommendation for you or letters of recom- mendation from you? 2 You are our epistle, written in our hearts, which is understood and read by all men, 3 in that you show your- selves as the epistle of Christ, proclaimed through God and written not with ink but with the Spirit of the living God, not on tables of stone but on tables of flesh of the heart. 4 And such confidence have we through Christ toward God: 5 Not that we are sufficient on our own to think of anything, as if we were ourselves; but our sufficiency comes from God, 6 Who has also enabled us to be minis- ters of the New Testament, not of the letter, but of the Spirit; for the letter kills, but the Spirit gives life. 7 If, therefore, the ministry of death, written in letters and engraved on stones, was glorious, so that the children of Israel could not see the face of Moses, for the glory of his face (glory that is gone). 8 How will not the ministry of the Spirit be more glorious? 9 For if the ministry of condemna- tion was glorious, much more is the ministry of righteousness. 10 For that which has been glorified, has not been glorified in this point, that is, in regard to the excess of glory. 11 For if that which is to be abolished was glorious, much more will that which remains be glo- rious. 12 Since therefore we have this confi- dence, we have great assurance of speech. 13 We are not like Moses, who put a veil over his face so that the children of Israel would not look at the end of what was to be abolished. 14 Therefore their minds are hardened, because to this day the same corruption, taken away in the Old Testament reading, has remained in Christ. 15 But to this day, when Moses is read, the vile is laid up in their hearts. 16 When their hearts are turned to the Lord, the vile will be taken away. 17 The Lord is the Spirit, and where the Spirit of the Lord is, there is freedom. 18 But we look as in a mirror at the glory of the Lord with an open face and are changed into the same image, from glory to glory, as by the Spirit of the Lord.

CHAPTER 4

1 Therefore, since we have this ministry, as we have received mercy, let us not waver: 2 but we have cast off from you the cloaks of shame, and we do not walk craftily, nor han- dle the word of God deceitfully; but declaring the truth, we stand before the conscience of every man before God. 3 If our gospel is hid- den, it is hidden from those who are lost. 4 The God of this world has blinded the minds, that is, the unbelievers, so that the light of the glorious Gospel of Christ, who is the image of God, does not shine to them. 5 For we do not preach ourselves, but Christ Iesus, the Lord, and ourselves your servants for Iesus' sake. 6 For God, who caused light to shine out of darkness, is the one who has shone in our hearts to give the light of the knowledge of the glory of God in the face of Jesus Christ. 7 But we have this treasure in earthen vessels, that the excellency of this power may be of God and not of God. 8 We are afflicted on ev- ery side, but we are not distressed; we are in doubt, but we do not despair. 9 We are per- secuted, but not forsaken; we are cast down, but we do not perish. 10 Whenever we carry in our bodies the death of the Lord Iesus, that the life of Iesus may also be manifested in our bodies. 11 For we who live are always delivered over to death for Jesus' sake, that the life of Jesus may be manifested even in our mortal flesh. 12 Thus therefore death works in you and life in you. 13 And because we have the same spirit of faith, as it is written, "I be- lieved and therefore I spoke," we also believe and therefore we speak, 14 knowing that he who raised up the Lord Iesus will also raise up through Iesus and settle with you. 15 For all things are for your good, that more abundant grace through the thanksgiving of many may contribute to the praise of God. 16 Therefore we do not fail, but though our outward man perishes, yet the inward man is renewed dai- ly. 17 For our light affliction, which is but a moment, procures for us a far more excellent and eternal expectation of glory: 18 while we look not to the things that are seen, but to the things that are not seen; for the things that are seen are temporal, but the things that are not seen are eternal.

CHAPTER 5

1 For we know that if our earthly house, this tabernacle, is destroyed, we have a building created by God, that is, a house not made with hands, but eternal in heaven. 2 Therefore we sigh, desiring to be clothed with our house,

which is in heaven. 3 For if we are clothed, we shall not be found naked. 4 For we who are in this tabernacle sigh and grieve because we do not want to be clothed, but we want to be clothed, so that mortality may be over- whelmed by life. 5 And the one who created us for this is God, who also gave us the effect of the Spirit. 6 Therefore we are always strong, even though we know that while we are at home in the body, we are absent from the Lord. 7 (For we walk by faith and not by sight). 8 Nevertheless, we are courageous and desire rather to go out of the body and dwell with the Lord. 9 Therefore we hope that whether we dwell in the house or depart from the house, we may be pleasing to him. 10 For we must all appear before the judgment seat of Christ, that each one may receive the things done in his body, according to what he has done, both for good and evil. 11 Knowing therefore the terror of the Lord, we persuade men and are made manifest to God, and I trust also that we are made manifest in your consciences. 12 For we do not pray for you ourselves, but we give occasion to speak to you, that you may answer against those who speak in the face and not in the heart. 13 For whether we are out of our minds, we are for God; whether we are in our reason, we are for you. 14 Because the will of Christ compels us to do so, 15 for we hold that if one died for all, then all were dead and he died for all, so that those who live should no longer live for themselves, but for him who died for them and rose again. 16 Therefore, henceforth we know no man according to the flesh; yea, though we had known Christ according to the flesh, hence- forth we know him no more. 17 If therefore anyone is in Christ, let him be a new crea- ture. Old things have passed away; behold, all things have become new. 18 All things come from God, who reconciled to himself through Jesus Christ and gave him the minister of reconciliation. 19 For God was in Christ and reconciled the world to himself, not imputing sins to them, and entrusted to him the word of reconciliation. 20 Now, therefore, we are ambassadors for Christ; as if God were ask- ing through you, we pray you in the steps of Christ, that you may be reconciled to God. 21 For he caused him to be sin for you, who knew no sin, that we might be made the righteous- ness of God in him.

CHAPTER 6

1 Therefore we, as laborers together, beseech you not to receive God's grace in vain. 2 For he says, "I have heard you in an acceptable time, and in the day of salvation I have suc- cored you; behold the acceptable time, behold the day of salvation." 3 We give no occasion for offense in any thing, that our minister may not be rebuked. 4 But in everything we acknowledge ourselves as ministers of God, with much patience, in afflictions, in neces- sities, in distresses, 5 in labors, in prisons, in tumults, in labors, 6 in vigils, in fastings, in purity, in knowledge, in long- suffering, in kindness, in the Holy Spirit, in joy won, 7 in the word of truth, in the power of God, in the armor of righteousness on the right hand and on the left, 8 with honor and dishonor, with evil and good fame, as deceivers, yet true: 9 as known, yet known; as dying, and behold, we live; as chastened, yet not slain: 10 as afflicted, yet ever redeemed; as poor, yet rich in many; as having nothing, yet possessing everything. 11 O Corinthians, our mouth is open to you, our heart has become great. 12 You are not held fast in vs, but are held fast in your bowels. 13 Now for the same reward, I say to my sons, "Be ye also enlarged." 14 Do not be even with the unbelievers, for what fellowship is there

between righteousness and justice, and what fellowship is there between light and dark- ness? 15 And what fellowship has Christ with Belial? Or what part has the beleeuer with the unbeliever? 16 What concord is there between the Temple of God and idols? For you are the Temple of the living God, as God has said, "I will dwell among them and walk therein; I will be their God and they shall be my people." 17 Therefore come out from among them and separate, says the LORD, and touch nothing vnclean, and I will receive you. 18 I will be a Father to you, and you shall be my sons and daughters, says the Lord Almighty.

CHAPTER 7

1 Since we therefore have these promises, accurately believed, let us cleanse ourselves from all filthiness of the flesh and spirit and complete our sanctification in the fear of God. 2 Receive: we have harmed no one, we have corrupted no one, we have defrauded no one. 3 I do not say this to condemn you, for I have already said that you are in our hearts to die and live together. 4 I have great boldness of speech toward you: I have great confidence in you: I am full of comfort, and am very glad in all our tribulation. 5 For when we entered Macedonia, our flesh had no peace, but we were tormented on every side, with strife on the outside and terrors within. 6 But God, who comforts the abject, comforted us at the coming of Titus: 7 And not only by his com- ing, but also by the consolation with which he was comforted by you, when he told of your great longing, your mourning, your fervent spirit of war, so that I rejoiced much more. 8 For though I made you sorry with a letter, I do not regret it, even though I repented; for I realized that the same letter made you sor- ry, even if only for a time. 9 Now I realize that you were not sorry, but that you were sorry to the point of repentance, because you were divinely sorry, so that no harm was done to you. 10 For godly sorrow causes repentance to salvation, not to be repudiated; but worldly sorrow causes death. 11 For, behold, this thing of which you have been divinely afflicted, what great care it has produced in you, what cleansing of yourselves, what indignation, what fear, what great desire, what joy, what redemption, in all things you have proved to yourselves that you are pure in this matter. 12 Therefore, even as I wrote to you, I did not do it for the cause of him who did the wrong, nor for the cause of him who committed iniury, but that our care for you might appear to you before God. 13 Therefore we were comforted, because you were comforted; but indeed we rejoiced much more for the joy of Titus, be- cause his spirit was refreshed by all of you. 14 For if I boasted anything to him about you, I was not ashamed; but as I told you all things in truth, so also our boasting to Titus was true. 15 His inward affection is greater toward you, when he remembers the obedience of you all and how you received him with fear and trembling. 16 I hope therefore that I can put my trust in you in all things.

CHAPTER 8

1 We also give you an account, brethren, of the grace of God given to the churches of Macedonia, 2 For in the great trial of afflic- tion their joy is increased, and their extreme fullness is increased unto their rich liberality. 3 For as for their power (I bear witness), yea, and beyond their power, they were willing, 4 And they praised with great effort that we might receive the grace and fellowship of the ministry

toward the saints. 5 And this they did, not as we expected, but making their contribution first to the Lord and then to you by the will of God, 6 that we might exhort Ti- tus to see to it that, as he had begun, so the same grace might do among you. 7 There- fore, as you abound in all things, in faith, and in strength, and in knowledge, and in all diligence, and in your love toward Your- self, so make sure that you also abound in this grace. 8 This I say not by command, but because of the diligence of others; therefore I show you the naturalness of your joy. 9 For you know the grace of our Lord Jesus Christ: for he, being rich, became poor for you, that you might be enriched through his help. 10 And I explain my thought to you, for this is expedient for you, who for a year have be- gun not only to do but also to want. 11 Now therefore perform this also, that as there has been a readiness in willing, so you may per- form it with what you have. 12 For if there is a willing mind first, it is accepted according to what a man has and not according to what he does not have. 13 Nor is it right that other men should be lightened and you afflicted: But all things being equal, at this time your abundance makes up for their lack: 14 That their abundance also may be for your lack, so that there may be equality: 15 As it is written, "He that gathered much, had nothing more, and he that gathered little, had not less." 16 And thanks be to God, who put in Titus' heart the same care for you. 17 For he accepted the exhortation; indeed, he was so careful that of his own accord he went to you. 18 With him we also sent the brother who was praised in the gospel to all the churches. 19 (And not only that, but he was also chosen by the Churches to be a companion in our journey, concern- ing this grace which is ministration for the glory of the same Lord, and the declaration of your ready mind). 20 making sure that no one can be blamed in this superabundance of grace that is distributed by Vs, 21 seeking to be honest, not only before the Lord, but also before men. 22 And we have sent with them our brother, to whom we have often recommended to be diligent in many things, but now much more diligent, because of the great confidence I have in you. 23 If anyone inquires about Titus, he is my companion and helper to you; or about our brothers, they are messengers of the Churches and of the glory of Christ. 24 So show them and the Churches the evidence of your joy and the recognition we have of you.

CHAPTER 9

1 As for the ministry of the saints, it is su- perfluous for me to write to you. 2 For I know your readiness of spirit, of which I boast to- ward the Macedonians, and I say that Achaia has been prepared already for a year, and your zeal has caused many to waver. 3 Now I have sent the brethren, lest our visit outside you should be in danger in this respect, lest you (as I said) should be ready: 4 lest, if the Macedonians should come with me and find you prepared, we (and we do not say you) should be ashamed of this constant boasting of mine. 5 Therefore I have found it necessary to exhort the brethren to come before you and finish your work of benevolence, that it may be ready and come as a benevolence and not as a neglect. 6 Remember, however, that he who sows sparingly will also reap sparingly, and he who sows liberally will also reap liber- ally. 7 As each one desires in his heart, so let him give, not grudgingly or out of necessity, for God loves a happy gift. 8 And God is able to cause all grace to abound toward you, so that you may always be sufficient in everything and abound in every good work, 9 (as it is written, "He did the

spending and gave to the poor; his kindness abides forever"). 10 He also who finds seed to the sower, and gives him bread for food, will multiply your seed and in- crease the fruits of your kindness.") 11 That on all sides you may be enriched with all liberal- ity, which causes thanksgiving to God. 12 For the ministry of this service not only provides for the needs of the saints, but also causes many to give thanks to God, 13 (who, through experiencing this service, praise God for your voluntary submission to the gospel of Christ and for your free distribution to them and to all men). 14 And in their praise toward you, to seek you much, because of the abundance of God's grace in you. 15 Therefore thanks be to God for his tremendous gift.

CHAPTER 10

1 Now I myself, Paul, plead with you with the meekness and kindness of Christ, that when I am present among you I am weak, but I am courageous toward you when I am absent: 2 And this I ask of you, that I need not be brave when I am present, with that same confi- dence with which I think I am brave against some, who esteem us as walking according to the flesh. 3 However, although we walk in the flesh, we do not wage war according to the flesh. 4 (For the weapons of our warfare are not carnal, but mighty through God, to break down the sockets). 5 casting down imagina- tions and every high thing that exalts itself against the knowledge of God, and bringing into captivity every thought to the obedience of Christ, 6 and holding ready vengeance against all disobedience, when your obedi- ence is fulfilled. 7 Will you look at things after appearance? If anyone trusts in himself to be Christ, let him also consider this: that as he is Christ, so we also are Christ. 8 For even if I were to boast a little more of our authority, which the Lord has granted for edification and not for your destruction, I should not be ashamed. 9 This I say so that I do not seem to frighten you with letters. 10 For the letters, he says, are grave and strong, but his bodily presence is weak, and his word is worthless. 11 Let it be thought of this, that as we are in trouble with letters, when we are absent, so we shall also be in trouble with faith, when we are present. 12 For we dare not make a name for ourselves, nor compare ourselves with those who praise themselves; but they do not understand that they measure themselves by themselves and compare themselves with themselves. 13 But we do not occupy ourselves with things that are not within our reach, but according to the measure of the line, whose measure God has distributed to deliver also to you. 14 For we do not stretch our strength beyond our measure, as if we had not come as far as you, for to you also we have come to preach the gospel of Christ, 15 not boast- ing of things that are not within our reach, that is, of other men's labors; and we hope, when your faith shall increase, to be magni- fied by you according to our line abundantly, 16 and to preach the gospel in those regions which are beyond you; not to continue to do the work of another, that is, to do the things which have already been prepared. 17 But he who commits himself, commits himself to the Lord. 18 For he is not admitted who prais- es himself, but he whom the Lord praises.

CHAPTER 11

1 You would, to God, bear a little of my fool- ishness, and verily you bear me. 2 For I am anxious for you, with godly

jealousy, because I have prepared you for a bridegroom, to present you as a pure virgin to Christ: 3 But I fear that, as the serpent deceived Eue by his deviousness, so your minds are corrupted from the simplicity that is in Christ. 4 For if he who comes, preaches another Jesus that we have not preached, or if you receive an- other spirit that you have not received, or an- other gospel that you have not received, you could have suffered him. 5 Verily I hold that I am not inferior to the leading apostles. 6 Though I am rough in speech, I am not rough in knowledge, but among you we have been made manifest to the uttermost in all things. 7 Have I committed an offense because I have stooped to exalt you and because I have free- ly preached to you the gospel of God? 8 Have I robbed other churches and taken wages from them to render service to you. 9 When I was present with you and had need, I was not slothful for anyone's hindrance; for what I lacked, the brethren who came from Mace- donia provided, and in everything I have kept and will keep myself, so as not to be a hindrance to you. 10 The truth of Christ is in me, lest this refuge be shut against me in the regions of Achaia. 11 Why? Why do I not love you? God knows. 12 But what I do, I will do: to take away the occasion from those who desire it, that they may be found similar to them in what they do. 13 For these false apos- tles are workers of deception, and they turn themselves into apostles of Christ. 14 And no wonder, for Satan himself is transformed into an angel of light. 15 Therefore it is no great thing if his ministers are transformed, as if they were ministers of righteousness, whose end shall be according to their works. 16 I say again, Let no one think that I am foolish, nor take me for a fool, that I too may boast a little of myself. 17 What I say, I say not according to the LORD, but as if I were foolish, in this my great boasting. 18 Because many boast ac- cording to the flesh, I also boast. 19 For you gladly suffer fools, because you are wise. 20 For you suffer, even if a man brings you into bondage, if a man robs you, if a man takes your property, if a man exalts himself, if a man beats you on the face. 21 I speak as if it were a rebuke, as if we had been awake; but if one is bold (I speak foolishly) so am I. 22 They are Jews, so am I; they are Israelites, so am I; they are the descendants of Abraham, so am I: 23 They are the ministers of Christ (I speak as a fowl) I am more: in labors more abundantly, in stripes more abundantly, in prison more abundantly, in death more often. 24 Of the five times I received the badgers, I received the stripes four times, once only. 25 Three times have I been beaten with rods: once was I stoned: three times have I suffered ship- wreck; night and day have I been in the deep sea. 26 In traveling I have often been in dan- ger of waters, in danger of robbers, in danger of my nation, in danger among the Gentiles, in danger in the city, in danger in the wilder- ness, in danger in the sea, in danger among false brethren, 27 in labors and sorrows, in watching often, in hunger and thirst, in fast- ing often, in cold and nakedness. 28 Besides external things, I am combed daily and have the care of all the churches. 29 Who is weary and I am not? Who is offended and I am not? 30 If I need to be healed, I will do so with my infirmities. 31 The God, that is, the Father of our Lord Jesus Christ, who is blessed forever, knows that I do not lie. 32 In Damascus, the people of King Aretas were watching in the city of the Damascenes and wanted to capture me. 33 But at a window I was brought down in a basket through the wall and escaped his hands.

CHAPTER 12

1 No doubt it is not appropriate for me to re- sume, for I will have visions and revelations from the Lord. 2 I know such a man in Christ about fourteen years (whether he was in the body, I cannot tell, or out of the body, I cannot tell: God knows) who was brought in the thir- teenth century. 3 I know such a man (whether he was in the body or out of the body, I can- not say: God knows). 4 Who was brought into heaven and heard words that cannot be spo- ken and that are not possible for man to hear. 5 Of such a man I will take care; of myself I will not take care, except for my infirmities. 6 For even if I would speak of myself, I would not be an impostor, for I would speak the truth; but I refuse, lest anyone should think of me what he sees in me or hears from me. 7 And lest I should exalt myself exceedingly through the abundance of publications, a goad was given me in the flesh, the messenger of Satan, to torment me, lest I should exalt myself exceed- ingly. 8 For this thing I prayed three times to the Lord that he would depart from me. 9 And he said to me, "My grace is sufficient for you, for my power is perfected in weakness. Very gladly, therefore, I will rather rejoice in my infirmities, that the power of Christ may dwell in me. 10 Therefore I rejoice in infir- mities, in reproaches, in necessities, in per- secutions, in distresses for Christ's sake, for when I am weak, then I am strong. 11 I was a fanatic to boast of myself, but you compelled me, for I should have been praised by you, for in nothing was I inferior to the greatest apos- tles, though I was nothing. 12 The signs of an apostle were performed among you with all patience, with signs and wonders and great works. 13 What is it that made you inferior to the other churches, except that I was sloth- ful through your hindrance? Forgive me this wrong. 14 Behold, the thirteenth time I am ready to come to you, yet I will not be slothful in your hindrance, for I do not see your own, but you; for children must not reckon with fathers, but fathers with children. 15 And I will be well pleased to give and to be given for your souls, though the more I appreciate you, the less they appreciate me. 16 But be aware that I have not charged you; nevertheless, cunning though I was, I have taken you by deception. 17 Did I deceive you through any of those whom I sent you? 18 I wanted Titus, and with him I sent a brother; did Titus cheat you of anything? Have we not walked in the same spirit? Have we not walked in the same steps? 19 Do you think we apologize to you? We speak before God in Christ. But we do all things, with fear, for your edification. 20 For I fear that when I come, I shall not find you as I would wish; and that I shall find you as you would not, and that at least there shall be strife, enmity, wrath, contention, mur- muring, swelling, and discord. 21 I am afraid that when I come again, my God will bring me down among you, and that I will make the acquaintance of many of them who have already sinned and have not repented of the violence, fornication, and lust that they have committed.

CHAPTER 13

1 Here is the third time I am coming to you. In the mouths of two or three witnesses ev- ery word will remain. 2 I have told you before and I will tell you again: as I was present the second time, so I write now that I am absent to those who have sinned hitherto and to all others, that if I come again, I will not spare, 3 seeing that you see the experience of Christ, who speaks in me, who toward you is not weak,

but is mighty in you. 4 For though he was crucified because of his infirmity, yet he lives by the power of God. And we, no doubt, are weak in him, but we shall be with him in life, by the power of God toward you. 5 Test yourselves whether you are in the faith; ex-amine yourselves: do you not know yourselves that Jesus Christ is in you, if you are not reprobate? 6 But I trust that you will know that we are not reprobates. 7 Now I pray God that you do nothing wrong, not that we may seem approved, but that you may do that which is honest, even though we are reprobates. 8 For we cannot do anything against the truth, but for the truth. 9 For we rejoice when we are awake and that you are strong; this also we desire, that is, your perfection. 10 There-fore I write these things when I am absent, lest, when I am present, I may see sharply, according to the power which the Lord has given me, edification and not destruction. 11 Finally, brethren, be well: be perfect, be of good comfort, be of one mind, live in peace, and the God of joy and peace will be with you. 12 Greet one another with a holy kisse. 13 All the saints greet you. 14 The grace of our Lord Jesus Christ, the joy of God and the fellowship of the Holy Spirit be with you all, Amen.

GALATIANS

CHAPTER 1

1 Pavl is an apostle (not from men, nor from men, but from Jesus Christ and God the Fa-ther who raised him from the dead). 2 And all the brethren who are with me in the churches of Galatia: 3 Grace to you and peace from God the Father and our Lord Jesus Christ, 4 who gave himself for our sins, to deliver us from this present world, according to the will of God our Father, 5 to whom be glory forever, amen. 6 I marvel that you have turned away so soon from another gospel, from him who had called you into the grace of Christ, 7 which is not another gospel, because there are some who disturb you and intend to disrupt the gospel of Christ. 8 But if we or an angel from Eauen should preach to you anything other than what we have preached to you, let him be accursed. 9 As we said before, so I say now again: if anyone preaches to you otherwise than what you have received, let him be ac-cursed. 10 For I now preach human doctrine or divine doctrine, or go about pleasing men, for if I should still please men, I would not be the servant of Christ. 1 Now I certify you, brethren, that the gospel which was preached by me was not made by men. 12 For I did not receive it from man nor was it taught to me, but by revelation from Jesus Christ. 13 For you have heard of my frequentations in time past in the Jewish religion, how I persecuted the Church of God in the extreme, and wasted it, 14 and that I profited in the Jewish religion from many companions of my nation, and that I was much more zealous of the tradi-tions of my fathers. 15 But when it pleased God (who had separated me from my moth-er's womb and called me by his grace) 16 to raise up his Son in me, that I might preach him among the Gentiles, immediately I did not communicate with flesh and blood: 17 I came no more to Jerusalem to those who were apostles before me, but went to Arabia and re-turned to Damascus. 18 Then after three years I came again to Jerusalem to visit Peter and stayed with him fifteen days. 19 And none of the apostles said, "Iames, the brother of the Lord." 20 Now the things that I write to you, behold, I testify before God that I do not lie. 21 Then I went to the coasts of Syria and Cilicia: 22 For I was known by face by the churches of Judea which were in Christ. 23 But they had heard some say: "He who formerly persecut-ed, now preaches the faith which he formerly destroyed." 24 And they glorified God for me.

CHAPTER 2

1 Then, four years later, I went again to Je-rusalem with Barnabas and took Titus with me also. 2 And I went to Jerusalem for a re-working and declared to them the gospel that I preached among the Gentiles, but particu-larly to those who were the most important, lest they should run, or run, for any reason: 3 But not even Titus, who was with me, though he was a Greek, was compelled to be cir-cumcised, 4 for the false brethren who were brought in by guile and crept in premeditat-edly to spy out our freedom, which we have in Christ Iesus, to bring us into bondage. 5 To whom we left no subsection for an hour, that the truth of the gospel might continue with you. 6 But from those who seemed great, I was not instructed (however they were in time past, I am nothing better: God accepts no person) because those who are the greatest added nothing to me about what I had. 7 But on the contrary, when they saw that the gospel of circumcision had been entrusted to me, as the gospel of circumcision had been entrust-ed to Peter: 8 (for he who was mighty from Peter in the apostleship of circumcision was also mighty from me toward the Gentiles). 9 And when Iames, Cephas, and Iohn came to know of the grace that had been given to me, and are counted as pillars, they gave me and Barnabas the right hand of fellowship, that we might preach to the Gentiles and they to the Circumcision, 10 warning us only to re-member the poor; which I also undertook to do. 11 When Peter came to Antioch, I opposed him to his face, for he was to be condemned. 12 For before that fellow came from Iames, he ate with the Gentiles; but when they were come, he withdrew and separated himself, fearing those of the Circumcision. 13 And the other Imeans also were being hypocrites with him, so that Barnabas was dragged away with them by their hypocrisy. 14 But when I saw that they were not following the straight path of the truth of the gospel, I said to Peter in front of everyone, "If you, who are a Jew, live like the Gentiles and not like the Jews, why do you force the Gentiles to do like the Jews? 15 We, who are Jews by nature, are not sinners like the Gentiles, 16 we know that man is not justified by the works of the Law, but by the faith of Jesus Christ, and we, I say, have be-lieved in Jesus Christ, to be justified by the faith of Christ and not by the works of the Law, for by the works of the Law no flesh is justified. 17 If therefore, while we see that we are made righteous by Christ, we ourselves are found to be sinners, is Christ then the minister of sin? God forbid. 18 For if I rebuild the things that I have destroyed, I make my-self a transgressor. 19 For I, through the Law, died to the Law, that I might live in God. 20 I was crucified with Christ, but I live, no longer I, but Christ lives in me; and in what I now live in the flesh, I live by faith in the Son of God, who received me and gave himself for me. 21 I do not abrogate the grace of God, for if righteousness is by faith, Christ died with-out cause.

CHAPTER 3

1 O foolish Galatians, who has bewitched you that you should not obey the truth, to which Jesus Christ was first described in your eyes and crucified among you? 2 Only this I would like to know from you, "Have you received the Spirit through the works of Lawe or through hearing the

faith preached?" 3 Are you so foolish that, having begun in the Spirit, you now want to be made perfect by the flesh? 4 Have you suffered many things in vein? If so, it is always in vein. 5 Does He who therefore teaches you the Spirit and works miracles among you do so through the works of the Law or through hearing the faith preached? 6 Like Abraham who believed God and was imputed to him for righteousness. 7 Know then that those who have faith are children of Abraham. 8 For the Scripture, foreseeing that God would justify the Gentiles by faith, preached before the gospel to Abraham, say- ing, "In you shall all the Gentiles be blessed." 9 So those who have faith are blessed with faithful Abraham. 10 For all who belong to the works of the Law are under the curse, for it is written, "Cursed is every man who does not continue to do all the things that are written in the book of the Law." 11 That no one is jus- tified by the Law in God's sight is evident, for the righteous man lives by faith. 12 The Law does not come by faith, but the man who does these things lives in them. 13 Christ redeemed Yours from the curse of the Law, He became a curse for You (for it is written, "Cursed is everyone who hangs on a tree"). 14 That the blessing of Abraham might come upon the Gentiles through Christ Iesus, that we might receive the promise of the Spirit by faith. 15 Brethren, I speak as men do; although it is but human advice, when it is confirmed, yet no one abrogates it or adds to it. 16 The promises were made to Abraham and his descendants. He does not say, "And to the descendants," as if he were speaking of many, but, "And to your descendants," as if he were speaking of one, who is Christ. 17 And this I say, that the covenant which was confirmed beforehand by God concerning Christ, the Law which was four hundred and thirty years afterward, can- not be annulled, to make the promise void. 18 For if the inheritance is of the Lawe, it is no longer because of the promise, but God freely gave it to Abraham by promise. 19 Why then is the Law needed? It was added because of transgressions, until the seed to whom the promise was made came; and it was ordained by angels into the hands of a mediator. 20 Now a mediator is not a mediator of one, but God is one. 21 Is Lawe then contrary to the promises of God? God forbid, for if there had been a Law that could have given life, surely justice should have been guaranteed by the Law. 22 But the Scripture concluded every- thing under sin, so that the promise, through the faith of Jesus Christ, might be granted to those who were born. 23 But before faith came, we were kept under the Law, as under a garter, and closed to that faith which was later to be regained. 24 Therefore the Law was our schoolmaster to lead us to Christ, that we might be made righteous by faith. 25 But after faith has come, we are no longer under a schoolmaster. 26 For you are all children of God by faith, in Christ Iesus. 27 For all of you who have been baptized into Christ have put on Christ. 28 There is neither Greek nor Ital- ian, there is neither blond nor free, there is neither male nor female, for all of you are one in Christ Jesus. 29 And if you are Christ, you are children of Abraham and heirs by prom- ise.

CHAPTER 4

1 Then I say that the heir, as long as he is a child, does not differ at all from a servant, even though he is Lord of all 2 But he is un- der guardians and tutors until the time ap- pointed by the Father. 3 We also, when we were children, were in bondage under the rudiments of the world. 4 But when the full- ness of time had come, God sent His Son made of a woman and made under the Lawe, 5 that He might redeem those who were un- der the Law, to receive the adoption of sons. 6 And because you are sons, God has sent the Spirit of his Son into your hearts, crying, Abba, Father. 7 Therefore you are no longer servants, but sons; now, if you are sons, you are also heirs of God through Christ. 8 But even then, when you did not know God, you served them, who by nature are not gods: 9 But now that you know God, indeed are known by God, how can you return to help- less and beggarly rudiments, for which, from the beginning, you will still be in bondage? 10 You observe the days, the months, the times and the years. 11 I am afraid of you, because I have not made you work in haste. 12 Be like me (for I also am like you) brothers, I pray you; you have done me no harm. 13 And you know that at first I preached the gospel to you through infirmity of the flesh. 14 And the trial which I suffered in my flesh you neither despised nor abhorred, but received me as an angel of God, yea, as Christ Jesus. 15 What then has been your happiness? For I remind you that, had it been possible, you would have plucked out your eyes and given them to me. 16 Have I therefore become your enemy because I tell you the truth? 17 They are jealous of you, friend; indeed, they would like to exclude you, because you value them com- pletely. 18 But it is good for you always to like a good thing, and not only when I am pres- ent with you, 19 My children, of whom I bring you forth again, until Christ is formed in you. 20 I wish I were with you now, that I might change my journey, for I am in doubt about you. 21 Tell me, you who want to be under the Law, do you not listen to the Law? 22 For it is written that Abraham had two sons, one by a maidservant and one by a free woman. 23 The one he had by the maidservant was begotten according to the flesh, while the one he had by the free woman was begotten by promise. 24 By these things is meant another thing, for these mothers are the two wills, that of Hagar of Mount Sinah, which leads to bondage. 25 (Hagar, or Sinah, is a mountain of Arabia and answers to Jerusalem) and she is in bondage with her children. 26 But Jerusalem, which is outside, is free: she is the mother of all. 27 For it is written, "Take again, barren, thou that hast no children; arise and cry, thou that hast no children: for the desolate hath many more children than she that hath a husband." 28 Therefore, brethren, we are like Isaac, chil- dren of the promise. 29 But as then he who was born according to the flesh persecuted him who was born according to the Spirit, so it is also now. 30 But what does the Scripture say? Cast out the maidservant and her son, for the son of the maidservant shall not be hereditary with the son of the free woman. 31 Then, brethren, we are not the sons of the handmaid, but of the free woman.

CHAPTER 5

1 Stand firm, therefore, in the freedom with which Christ has made you free, and do not let the yoke of slavery entangle you again. 2 Be- hold, I Paul say to you that if you are circum- cised, Christ will profit you nothing. 3 For I testify again to every man who is circumcised that he is bound to keep the whole law. 4 You have been abolished by Christ; whoever is jus- tified by the Law is fallen from grace. 5 For we through the Spirit wait for the hope of righ- teousness by faith. 6 For in Jesus Christ there is no longer circumcision, nor vncircumci- sion, but faith working through the Law. 7 You have run righteous; who has allowed you not to obey the truth? 8 It is not the persua-

sion of him who calls you. 9 A little loss causes all light to be lost. 10 I have confidence in you through the Lord, that you may not have a dif- ferent mindset; but he who troubles you will suffer his condemnation, whoever he may be. 11 And brethren, if I still preach circum- cision, why do I still suffer persecution? Then the bondage of circumcision is abolished. 12 I wish that those who disturb you were also cut off. 13 Since, brothers, you have been called to freedom, do not make your freedom an occasion for the flesh, but serve one another. 14 For the whole Law is fulfilled in one word, "You must love your neighbor as yourself." 15 If you bite and hurt one another, be careful not to consume one another. 16 Then I say, "Walk in the Spirit and do not fulfill the de- sires of the flesh." 17 For the flesh is contrary to the Spirit, and the Spirit is contrary to the flesh; and these are contrary to each other, so that you cannot do the same things that you would. 18 And if you are led by the Spirit, you are not under the Law. 19 Moreover the works of the flesh are manifested, which are adul- tery, fornication, vncleannes, wantonnes, 20 idolatries, sorceries, hatreds, arguments, emulations, wrath, contentions, seditions, heresies, 21 enmities, murders, drunkenness, gluttony, and the like, of which I told you be- fore, as I also told you before, that those who do these things will not inherit the kingdom of God. 22 But the fruit of the Spirit is joy, gladness, peace, patience, kindness, good- ness, cheerfulness, 23 meekness, temperance; against them there is no weakness. 24 For they who are Christ have crucified the flesh with the affections and passions. 25 If we live in the Spirit, let us also walk in the Spirit. 26 Do not be eager for vain glory, provoking one another, envying one another.

CHAPTER 6

1 Brethren, if a man is suddenly seized with an offense, you who are spiritual, restore him with a spirit of meekness, thinking of your- selves, if you do not wish to be tempted also. 2 Bear one another's burdens and thus fulfill the word of Christ. 3 For if anyone seems to himself to be something, while he is noth- ing, he deceives himself in his imagination. 4 But let every man do his own work, and then he will be able to rely on himself and not on another. 5 For every man shall bear his own burden. 6 Whoever is instructed in the word, let him who instructed him par- take of all his goods. 7 Do not be deceived; God is not mocked, for what a man sows, he will also reap. 8 For he who sows for his flesh, from the flesh he will draw corruption; but he who sows for the spirit, from the spirit he will draw eternal life. 9 Therefore do not grow weary in doing good, for in due season we shall reap, if we do not toil. 10 While we have time, let us do good to all men, but especial- ly to those who have faith. 11 See how great is the letter I have written to you from my own hand. 12 As many as desire to make a good impression in the flesh, they force you to be circumcised, just because they do not want to suffer persecution for the cause of Christ. 13 For they themselves, who are circumcised, do not keep the law, but desire to make you cir- cumcised, that they may act in your flesh. 14 But God forbid that I should live again, except in the cross of our Lord Jesus Christ, where- by the world was crucified to me and I to the world. 15 For in Christ Iesus there is no more circumcision nor vncircumcision, but a new creature. 16 And as many as walk according to this rule, peace and mercy shall be to them and to the Israel of God. 17 Henceforth let no one put me in the midst of the buses, for

I bear in my body the marks of the Lord Iesus. 18 Brethren, the grace of our Lord Jesus Christ be with your spirit, amen.

EPHESIANS

CHAPTER1

1 Pavl, an apostle of Jesus Christ by the will of God, to the saints who are at Ephesus and to you who are faithful in Christ Iesus: 2 Grace to you and peace from God our Father and the Lord Jesus Christ. 3 Blessed be God and the Father of our Lord Jesus Christ, who has blessed you with every spiritual blessing in things eternal in Christ, 4 as he chose us in him before the foundation of the world, that we should be holy and blameless before him in righteousness: 5 Who predestinated his own kind to be adopted through Jesus Christ in himself, according to the good pleasure of his will, 6 for the joy of the glory of his grace, by which he caused you to be freely accepted into his bosom, 7 through whom we have re- demption through his blood, that is, the for- giveness of sins, according to his rich grace: 8 wherewith he hath abounded toward you in all wisdom and understanding, 9 And hath opened unto you the mysteries of his will, according to his good pleasure, which he had established in him, 10 that, in the dispensa- tion of the fullness of times, he might gather into one all things, both those things which are in heaven and those things which are on earth, that is, in Christ: 11 in whom also we were chosen, when we were predestinated, according to the purpose of him, who works all things according to the plan of his will, 12 that we, who first trusted in Christ, might be to the praise of his glory: 13 in whom also you have trusted, after you have heard the word of truth, that is, the gospel of your salvation, and where also after you have believed, you have been sealed with the holy Spirit of promise, 14 which is the attestation of our inheritance, for the redemption of that freedom purchased unto the prayer of his glory. 15 Therefore, having heard of the faith you have in the Lord Iesus and the charity toward all the saints, 16 I have not ceased to give thanks for you, making mention of you in my prayers, 7 that the God of our Lord Jesus Christ, the Father of glory, may give you the Spirit of wisdom and reworking through recognition of him, 18 that the eyes of your understanding may be enlightened, so that you may know the hope of his calling and the riches of his glorious inheritance in the saints, 19 and what is the immense greatness of his power in regard to those who are alive, according to the work of his mighty power, 20 which he wrought in Christ, when he raised him from the dead and set him at his right hand in the lofty places, 21 and who made all principalities, powers, dominions, and every other name that can be named, disappear, not only in this world, but also in that which is to come, 22 and placed all things under his feet and appointed him above all things to be the head of the Church, 23 which is his body, that is, the fullness of him who fills all things.

CHAPTER 2

1 He has awakened you who were dead in sins and trespasses, 2 where you formerly walked according to the course of this world and ac- cording to the prince that rules in the air, that is, the spirit that now works in the children of disobedience, 3 among whom also we in the past had our cohabitation in the lusts of our flesh, in fulfilling the will of the flesh and of the mind, and were by nature children of

wrath, like others. 4 But God, who is rich in mercy, because of his great joy with which he received our children, made it so that we were not more than two years old, 5 when we were dead because of our sins, he vivified them in Christ, by whose grace you were saved, 6 has vivified you together and made you sit togeth- er in the lofty places in Christ Iesus, 7 that he might show in the ages to come the exceeding riches of his grace, through his kindness to you in Christ Iesus. 8 For by grace you have been saved through faith, and not of your- selves; it is a gift from God, 9 not of works, so that no one may boast. 10 For we are his workmanship created in Christ Iesus by good works, which God established that we should walk in them. 11 Therefore remember that you were formerly Gentiles in the flesh and were called circumcision by those who are called circumcision in the flesh, made with hands, 12 at that time you were, I say, without Christ, you were strangers to the common heritage of Israel, you were strangers to the promis- es, you had no hope, and you were without God in the world. 13 But now, in Christ Iesus, you who once were estranged have become new through the blood of Christ. 14 For he is our peace, who has made us both one and broken down the wall of separation,15 abro- gating, by his flesh, hatred, that is, the law of commandments which is in the ordinances, to make the two a new man in himself, thus making peace, 16 and to reconcile both to God in one body by his cross, thus killing hatred, 17 and he came to preach peace to you who were far off and to those who were afar off. 18 For through him we both have an entrance to the Father by one Spirit. 19 Now therefore you are no longer strangers and foreigners, but citizens of the saints and of the house of God, 20 and you are built on the foundation of the Apostles and Prophets, Jesus Christ himself being the cornerstone, 21 in whom the whole building, joined together, becomes a holy temple in the Lord. 22 In whom also you are built together to be the dwelling place of God through the Spirit.

CHAPTER 3

1 For this reason, I Paul am the captive of Jesus Christ for you Gentiles, 2 if you have heard of the dispensation of God's grace, which has been granted to me to you for war, 3 that is, that God, by revelation, has revealed this mystery to me (as I wrote in a few words), 4 whereby, when you read, you may know my understanding of the mystery of Christ). 5 which in other times had not been opened to the sons of men, as now it has been revealed to his holy Apostles and Prophets by the Spir- it, 6 that the Gentiles also might be inheritors and of the same body and partakers of his promise in Christ through the gospel, 7 of which I have been made a minister by the gift of God's grace given to me through the effica- cious work of his power. 8 To me, who am the least of the saints, this grace has been granted to preach among the Gentiles the inestima- ble riches of Christ, 9 and to make clear to all men the fellowship of the mystery which, from 10 so that the Church may now know through principalities and powers in ecclesi- astical places the manifold wisdom of God, 11 according to the eternal purpose which he has fulfilled in Christ Iesus our Lord: 12 through whom we have boldness and entrance with confidence, through faith in him. 13 Therefore I desire you not to toil in my tribulations for your own sake, which is your glory. 14 For this reason I bend my knees to the Father of our Lord Jesus Christ, 15 (whose whole family in heaven and on earth is called). 16 That he may please you

according to the riches of his glo- ry, that you may be strengthened by his Spirit in the inner man, 17 that Christ may dwell in your hearts through faith: 18 That, being root- ed and grounded in God, you may understand with all the saints what is the breadth and length and depth and height: 19 and to know the greatness of Christ, which surpasses all knowledge, that you may be filled with all the fullness of God. 20 To him therefore who is able to do superabundantly all that we ask or think, according to the power that works in us, 21 Be praised in the Church by Christ Iesus, for all generations and forever, Amen.

CHAPTER 4

1 I therefore, a prisoner in the Lord, praise you that you may walk worthily in the calling to which you have been called 2 with humility of mind and meekness, with long-suffering, supporting one another in righteousness, 3 striving to maintain the life of the Spirit in the bond of peace. 4 There is one body and one Spirit, just as you are called in one hope of your calling. 5 There is one Lord, one faith, one baptism, 6 one God and Father of all, who is over all, through all and in all of you. 7 But to each of you is granted grace, according to the measure of the gift of Christ. 8 Therefore he says, "When he went up, he led captives into captivity and gave gifts to men." 9 Now since he ascended, what is it but that he first descended even into the lowest parts of the earth? 10 He who descended is the same who ascended, far from all the heavens, to fill all things). 11 Therefore he destined some to be Apostles, others Prophets, others Euange- lists, others Pastors and Teachers, 12 for the repair of the saints, for the strengthening of the ministry, and for the edification of the body of Christ, 13 until we all come together (in faith and in recognition of the Son of God) to become a perfect man and to reach the measure of the age of the fullness of Christ, 14 that henceforth we may not be children, lost and carried away with all manner of doctrine, with the deceitfulness of men, and with the wiles by which they prepare to deceive. 15 But let us follow the truth in all things and grow up in him who is the head, that is, Christ. 16 By whom the whole body, which is joined and bound together by every single element, so far as the furniture is concerned, according to the actual power that is in the measure of each part, receives the increase of the body, for the building up of itself in the light. 17 Therefore I say and testify in the Lord that henceforth you shall not walk as the other Gentiles do, in the vanity of their mind, 18 having their understanding darkened and being strangers to the life of God through the ignorance that is in them, because of the hardness of their hearts: 19 and having lost their sense of feeling, they gave themselves over to debauchery and began to do all kinds of violence, especially with the gray. 20 But you have not so learned Christ, 21 if, on the contrary, you have heard him and been in- structed by him, as the truth is in Jesus, 22 that is, that you have forsaken, so far as your living together in time past is concerned, the old man, corrupted by deceitful lusts, 23 and be born again in the spirit of your mind, 24 and clothe yourselves with the new man, who according to God was created for righteous- ness and true holiness. 25 Therefore forsake falsehood and tell each one the truth to his neighbor, for we are members one of anoth- er. 26 Be angry, but do not sin; do not let the sun go down on your wrath, 27 And give no room for deceit. 28 Let those who steal steal no more, but rather get busy and

work with your hands at what is good, so that you may give to those who need it. 29 Let no corrupt

communications come out of your mouth, but good ones, that they may be edifying, that they may give grace to those who hear them. 30 And do not deprive yourselves of the holy Spirit of God, by whom you have been sealed until the day of redemption. 31 Turn away from you all bitterness, anger, wrath, shout- ing and evil speech, and all malignity. 32 Be courteous to one another and tenderhearted, freely forgiving one another, as God, through Christ, has freely forgiven you.

CHAPTER 5

1 Therefore be followers of God, as beloved children, 2 and walk in goodness, as Christ did with goodness and gave himself for good- ness, to be an offering and a sacrifice of a fragrant savor to God. 3 But fornication and every vncleannesse or couetousnesse be not once named among you, as befits the saints, 4 Nor filthiness, nor foolish talk, nor jesting, which are not pleasant things, but rather thanksgiving. 5 For this you know, that no whoremonger, nor vnclean person, nor cou- etous person, who is an idolater, has any in- heritance in the kingdom of Christ and God. 6 Let no one deceive you with vain words, for for such things the wrath of God comes upon the children of disobedience. 7 Therefore do not be companions with them. 8 For you were once darkness, now you are light in the Lord; walk as sons of light, 9 (for the fruit of the Spirit consists in all good, righteousness and truth). 10 Doing what is pleasing to the Lord. 11 And do not have fellowship with the vnfruitful works of darkness, but rather re- produce them. 12 For it is shameful to speak of the things that are done in secret. 13 But all things, when they are reproduced by light, are manifest; for it is light that makes all things manifest. 14 Therefore he says, "Wake up, you who sleep, and get out of bed, and Christ will give you light." 15 Take heed therefore to walk circumspectly, not as fools, but as wise, 16 paying attention to the season, for the days are long. 17 Therefore do not be wise, but un- derstand what the will of the Lord is. 18 Do not be drunk with wine, which is an excess, but be filled with the Spirit, 19 speaking to yourselves in psalms, hymns and spiritual songs, singing and making melodies to the Lord in your hearts, 20 giving thanks always for everything to God and the Father, in the name of our Lord Jesus Christ, 21 submit- ting yourselves to one another in the fear of God. 22 Women, submit yourselves to your husbands as to the Lord. 23 For the husband is the head of the wife, as Christ is the head of the Church, and the same is the savior of his body. 24 Therefore, as the Church is sub- missive to Christ, so let wives be in all things submissive to their husbands. 25 Husbands, love your wives as Christ loved the Church and was committed to it, 26 that he might sanctify and protect it by the washing of wa- ter through the word, 27 to make it a glorious Church, that it may not have spot or wrinkle or anything else, but may be holy and blame- less. 28 So men must love their wives as their bodies: whoever loves his wife, loves himself. 29 For no man ever hated his own flesh, but nourishes and cherishes it, as the Lord does the Church. 30 For we are members of his body, of his flesh and bones. 31 Therefore a man shall leave his father and his mother and be joined to his wife, and the two shall be one flesh. 32 This is a great secret, but I speak of Christ and the Church. 33 Therefore let each one of you do this: let each one love

his wife as himself, and let his wife see that she fears her husband.

CHAPTER 6

1 Children, obey your parents in the Lord, for this is right. 2 Honor your father and your mother (which is the first command- ment with the promise) 3 That it may go well with you, and that you may live long on the earth. 4 And you, fathers, do not provoke your children to anger, but educate them in the instruction and knowledge of the Lord. 5 Servants, be obedient to those who are your masters, according to the flesh, with fear and trembling in one heart as toward Christ, 6 not as servants of the eye, as men who please, but as servants of Christ, doing from the heart the will of God, 7 with good will, serving the Lord and not men. 8 And know that every good thing that anyone does, he will receive from the Lord, whether he is bound or free. 9 And you, masters, do the same with them, turning away threats; and know that your master also is in health, and there is no respect of person with him. 10 Finally, my brethren, be strong in the Lord and in the power of his might. 11 Clothe yourselves with the whole armor of God, that you may be able to withstand the assaults of the devil. 12 For we do not wrestle against flesh and blood, but against princi- palities, against powers, against worldlings, against the princes of the darkness of this world, against the spiritual wickednesses that are in these places. 13 For this reason, take the whole armor of God with you, that you may be able to stand firm in the last day and, having finished all things, stand firm. 14 Stand there- fore, with your bonds girded with truth and with the belt of righteousness, 15 and let your feet be clothed with the preparation of the gospel of peace. 16 Take all of you the shield of faith, with which you may quench all the fierce darts of the wicked, 17 take the helmet of salvation and the sword of the Spirit, which is the word of God. 18 And pray always with all prayer and supplication in the Spirit, and watch with all perseverance and supplication for all the saints, 19 and for me, that I may be given grace to open my mouth boldly to pub- lish the secret of the gospel, 20 of which I am the ambassador in chains, that I may speak boldly, as I ought to speak. 21 But that you may also know my business and what I do, Tychicus, my dear brother and faithful minis- ter in the Lord, will inform you of everything, 22 whom I have sent to you for the same pur- pose, that you may know my affairs and that he may comfort your hearts. 23 Peace to the brethren and health to the faith from God the Father and the Lord Jesus Christ. 24 Grace be with all who love our Lord Jesus Christ, even to their immortality, Amen.

PHILIPPIANS

CHAPTER 1

1 Paul and Timothy, servants of IESVS CHRIST, to all the saints in Christ Iesus who are in Philippi, with the bishops and deacons: 2 Grace to you and peace from God our Fa- ther and the Lord Jesus Christ. 3 I thank my God, having you in perfect remembrance, 4 (always in all my prayers for you all, praying with joy). 5 For the fellowship you have in the gospel, from the first day until now.6 And I am convinced of this same thing: that he who began this good work in you will bring it to completion until the day of Jesus Christ, 7 as it suits me to judge of you all, for I remind you that both in my bands and in my defense and in the

confirmation of the gospel you have all been partakers of my grace. 8 For God is my remembrance, as I heartily desire you all in Jesus Christ. 9 And this I pray: that your joy may increase more and more in knowledge and in all judgment, 10 that you may rely on what is best, to be pure and without offense until the day of Christ, 11 filled with the fruits of righteousness, which are through Jesus Christ, to the glory and praise of God. 12 I would like you to understand, brethren, that the things that have happened to me are di- rected rather to the promotion of the gospel, 13 so that my groups in Christ are famous throughout the judgment hall and in all other places, 14 so that many brethren in the Lord have taken courage because of my groups and dare to speak the word more frankly. 15 Some preach. Christ even by enmity and strife, and some also of good will. 16 One party preaches Christ with contention and not with loyalty, thinking to add more affliction to my bands. 17 Others, however, of good will, knowing that I have been appointed for the defense of the gospel. 18 So what? Christ is preached in all ways, whether in pretense or in earnest, and I do, yea and will. 19 For I know that this will result in my salvation through your prayers and the help of the Spirit of Jesus Christ, 20 as I earnestly seek and hope that in nothing I may be ashamed, but that with all confidence, as always, so now Christ may be magnified in my body, both by life and death. 21 For Christ is precious to me both in life and in death. 22 Whether living in the flesh has been worthwhile for me, and what to choose I do not know. 23 For I am distressed between the one and the other, desiring to be loosed and to be with Christ, which is the best thing of all. 24 But abiding in the flesh is more nec- essary for you. 25 Of this I am certain: that I will remain and continue to be with all of you, for your deepening and for your faith, 26 that you may live again more abundantly in IESVS CHRIST for me, because of my return to you. 27 In particular, see to it that your living to- gether is as befits the gospel of Christ, so that whether I visit you or am absent, I may know of your affairs that you continue in one Spirit and one mind, striving together for the faith of the gospel. 28 And by no means fear your adversaries, who to them are signs of perdi- tion, while to you they are signs of salvation and of God. 29 For it has been granted to you through Christ, not only to grow up in him, but also to suffer for his sake, 30 having the same combat that you have seen in me and now feel to be in me.

CHAPTER 2

1 If therefore there is any consolation in Christ, if there is any comfort of joy, if there is any fellowship of the Spirit, if there is any compassion and mercy, 2 do as I do: be like- minded, that you have the same will, that you agree, and that you have one judgment, 3 that nothing may be done for contention or for vain glory, but that in meekness of mind each may esteem the other better than him- self. 4 Look not each one to his own things, but also to the things of other men. 5 Let the same mind be in you that was in Christ Ie- sus, 6 Who, being in the form of God, did not think it robbery to be equal with God: 7 But made himself without reputation, and took the form of a servant, and was made like unto men, and was found in the form of a man. 8 He humbled himself and became obedient unto death, that is, the death of the cross. 9 Therefore God also highly exalted him and gave him a name that surpasses every other name, 10 that at the name of Jesus all knees should bow, both of things in heaven, and of things on earth, and of things under

the earth, 11 and that every tongue confess that Jesus Christ is Lord, to the glory of God the Father. 12 Therefore, beloved, as you have al- ways obeyed me, not only in my presence, but now much more in my absence, so let your own salvation be done with fear and trem- bling. 13 For it is God who works in you, both will and deed, and this by his good will. 14 Do all things without murmuring and rea- soning, 15 that you may be blasphemous and pure, children of God without reproach in the midst of an evil and crooked nation, in whose midst you shine as lights in the world, 16 keeping alive the word of life, that I may say again in the day of Christ, I have not run in toil, nor toiled in toil. 17 Yea, and though I have been offered for the sacrifice and service of your faith, I am glad and rejoin you all. 18 Therefore you also be glad and be with me. 19 I trust in the Lord Jesus to send Timothy to you soon, that I too may be of good comfort when I know your situation. 20 For I have no one who is like-minded and who faithfully attends to your affairs. 21 For everyone sees his own, and not the one who is Jesus Christ. 22 But you know his trial: as a son with his father, he served with me in the gospel. 23 Therefore I hope to send an asoon, for I know how it will go with me, 24 and I trust in the Lord that I too will come soon. 25 But I found it necessary to send to you my brother Epa- phroditus, my companion in labor and work, and your messenger, and the one who min- istered to me about the things I desired. 26 For he desired all of you and was full of de- sire, for you had heard that he was sick. 27 No doubt he was sick, very near death; but God had mercy on him, and not only on him, but also on me, so that I should not have sorrow upon sorrow. 28 Therefore I have sent him more diligently, that when you see him again, you may recover, and I may be less grieved. 29 Receive him therefore in the Lord with all joy, and treasure him: 30 For for the sake of Christ's desire he went to his death and was not concerned about his life, to perform that service which has been lacking on your part toward me.

CHAPTER 3

1 Once again, my brethren, believe in the Lord. It does not grieve me to write the same things to you, and for you it is a sure thing. 2 Beware of dogs, beware of evil workers, be- ware of concision. 3 For we are the circum- cised, who worship God in the spirit and be- lieve in Christ Iesus, and have no confidence in the flesh: 4 though I also trust in the flesh. If another man thinks he trusts in the flesh, so much the more I, 5 circumcised the eighth day, of the seed of Israel, of the tribe of Ben- jamin, a Jew of the Jews, a Pharisee of Lawe. 6 As for zeal, I persecuted the Church; as for the righteousness that is in the Law, I was vn- rebukeable. 7 But the things that were useful to me, I considered lost for Christ's sake. 8 Indeed, without doubt, I consider all things to be lost for the excellent knowledge of Christ Iesus, my Lord, for whose sake I con- sidered all things to be lost and judged them as tongues, that I might win Christ, 9 and to be found in him, that is, not to have my own righteousness, which is that of the Law, but that which is through the faith of Christ, that is, the righteousness which is of God through faith, 10 that I may know him, the virtue of his resurrection and the fellowship of his afflic- tions, and be made conformable to his death, 11 if, in any way, I could be made conformable to the resurrection of the dead: 12 not as if I had already attained it, or were already per- fect; but I follow it, if I would understand that by which I also am understood in Christ Ie- sus. 13 Brethren, I do not

hold that I have at- tained perfection, but one thing I do: I forget what is behind and devote myself to what is ahead, 14 and I follow the goal earnestly, for the pursuit of God's calling in Christ Iesus. 15 Therefore, as many as are perfect, let them have this mindset; and if you have a different mindset, God will restore you the same. 16 In any case, in what we have come to do, let us proceed according to one rule, so that we may keep one thing in mind. 17 Brethren, be my followers and look to those who walk thus, as you have done for example. 18 For there walk many, of whom I have often spoken to you, and now I tell you weeping, who are enemies of the cross of Christ: 19 Whose end is damnation, whose God is their belly, and whose glory is to their shame, who mind earthly things. 20 But our habitation is in heaven, from whence we seek the Savior, that is, the Lord Jesus Christ, 21 who will change our vile body to make it like his glorious body, accord- ing to the work by which he is able to subdue all things to himself.

CHAPTER 4

1 Therefore, my brethren, beloved and de- sired, my joy and my crown, continue in the Lord, you beloved. 2 I pray Euodias and be- seech Syntheca to be concordant in the Lord, 3 Yea, and I beseech thee, faithful yoke-mate, help those women who have worked with me in the gospel, with Clement and with others of my fellow workers, whose names are in the book of life. 4 Take back always in the Lord, once more, I say, take back. 5 Let your patient mind be known to all men. The Lord is near. 6 Do not be prudent, but in everything turn your requests to God with praise and sup- plication and thanksgiving. 7 And the peace of God, which surpasses all understanding, will preserve your hearts and minds in Christ Iesus. 8 Moreover, brethren, what things are true, what things are honest, what things are right, what things are pure, what things are worthy of esteem, what things are of good re- pute, whether there is any virtue or whether there is any praise, think about these things, 9 which you have learned and received, heard and seen in me; do these things, and the God of peace will be with you. 10 Now I also greatly rejoice in the Lord, because now, at the last, your care for me is rekindled, where- as, although you have been careful, you have missed the opportunity. 11 I do not speak because of lack, for I have learned to be glad in whatever state I find myself. 12 I can be downcast and I can abound; in any case, in all things I am instructed, whether to be full, or to be hungry, or to abound, or to have no need. 13 I am able to do all things through the help of Christ, who strengthens me. 14 Never- theless, you have done well to communicate to my affliction. 15 And you Philippians also know that at the beginning of the gospel, when I departed from Macedonia, no church communicated with me, as far as the matter of giving and receiving was concerned, but you alone. 16 For when I was in Thessaloni- ca, you sent me once and then again for my needs, 17 not that I desire a gift, but I desire the fruit that may further your accounts. 18 Now I have received everything, and I have an abundance of it; I was filled after receiv- ing from Epaphroditus what came from you, an odor that smells sweet, a sacrifice pleasing to God. 19 My God will supply all your needs through His riches with glory in Jesus Christ. 20 To God, our Father, be praise forever, Amen. 21 Greet all the saints in Christ Iesus. The brothers who are with me greet you. 22 Greet you all the saints and especially those in the house of Caesar. 23 The grace of our Lord Jesus Christ be with you all, Amen.

COLOSSIANS

CHAPTER 1

1 Paul, an apostle of Jesus Christ, by the will of God, and Timothy, our brother, 2 To those who are at Colosse, holy and faithful breth- ren in Christ: grace to you and peace from God our Father and the Lord Jesus Christ. 3 We thank God, the Father of our Lord Jesus Christ, praying always for you: 4 since we have heard of your faith in Christ Iesus and of your love for all the saints, 5 for the hope that has been offered to you in heaven, of which you have already heard through the word of truth, which is the gospel, 6 which has come to you, as to all the world, and is fruitful, as it is also to you, from the day that you heard and truly knew the grace of God, 7 as you also learned from Epaphras, our dear fellow servant, who is for you a faithful minister of Christ: :8 who also declared to you your grace in the Spirit. 9 For this reason we also, from the day we heard of it, have not ceased to pray for you and to desire that you may be fulfilled with the knowledge of his will in all wisdom and spiritual understanding, 10 that you may walk worthy of the Lord and please him in all things, being fruitful in every good work and growing in the knowledge of God, 11 strengthened with all might through his glorious power, unto patience and long-suf- fering with joy, 12 thanking the Father, who has made us partakers of the inheritance of the saints in light, 13 who has delivered vs from the power of darkness and translated vs into the kingdom of his dear Son, 14 in whom we have redemption through his blood, that is, the forgiveness of sins, 15 who is the im- age of the inuisible God, the firstborn of every creature. 16 For by him were all things creat- ed, those that are in heaven and those that are on earth, things visible and things inuisible; whether thrones or dominions, principali- ties or powers, all things were created by him and for him, 17 He is before all things, and in him all things consist. 18 He is the head of the body of the Church; he is the beginning and firstborn of the dead, that in all things he may have preeminence. 19 For it pleased the Father that in him all fullness should dwell, 20 and through the peace made by the blood of his cross, to reconcile to himself, through him, I say, all things, both they that are on earth, and they that are in heaven. 21 And you, who formerly were strangers and ene- mies, because your mind was devoted to un- lawful works, now he has also reconciled you, 22 in the body of his flesh, through death, to make you holy, blameless and blameless in his sight, 23 if you continue, grounded and steadfast in the faith, and do not turn away from the hope of the gospel, which you have heard of and which has been preached to ev- ery creature under heaven, of which I Paul am a minister. 24 Now I continue to suffer for you and to fulfill the rest of Christ's afflictions in my flesh for the sake of his bodies, which are the Church, 25 Of whom I am a minister, according to the dispensation of God, which was given me for you, to fulfill the word of God, 26 which is the mystery hidden from the beginning of the world and from all ages, but now made manifest to his saints, 27 to whom God wishes to make known the riches of his glorious mystery among the Gentiles, which riches is Christ in you, the hope of glory, 28 whom we preach, admonishing every man and instructing him in all wisdom, to pres- ent every man perfect in Christ Iesus, 29 for whom also I also toil and strive, according to his working in me with power.

CHAPTER 2

1 For I would have you know the great strug- gle I have for you and for those in Laodicea and for all those who have not seen my person in the flesh, 2 that their hearts may be com- forted and united in joy and in all the riches of the full assurance of understanding, to know the mysteries of God, that is, of the Father and of Christ: 3 In whom are hid all the trea- sures of wisdom and knowledge. 4 And this I say lest any should deceive you with enticing words: 5 For though I am absent in the flesh, yet am I with you in the spirit, remembering and observing your order and your steadfast faith in Christ. 6 As therefore you have re- ceived Christ Iesus, the Lord, so walk in him, 7 rooted and built up in him, and established in the faith, as you have been taught, adher- ing to him with gratitude. 8 Beware of those who spoil you by philosophy and deceit, by the traditions of men, according to the ru- diments of the world and not according to Christ. 9 For in him dwells all the fullness of the Godhead. 10 And you are complete in him, who is the head of all princes and all powers. 11 In him also you have been circumcised with a circumcision made without hands, remov- ing the sinful body of the flesh, by the circum- cision of Christ, 12 in that you were buried with him through baptism, in which you were also raised together through faith in the oper- ation of God who raised him from the dead. 13 And you who were dead in sins and in the cir- cumcision of your flesh, he raised you up to- gether with him, forgiving you all your debts, 14 and, taking out of the way the writing of ordinances which was against you and which was contrary to you, he took it out of the way and fixed it on the cross, 15 and defeated the principalities and the Powers, and made an open trial of them, and triumphed over them in the cross itself. 16 Let no one therefore condemn you in eating and drinking, nor in regard to the holy day, the new moon or the Sabbath, 17 which are but a shadow of things to come; but the body is in Christ. 18 Let no one, as he pleases, rule over you with humility of mind and the worship of angels, endeav- oring in things which he does not know, and which he has imposed upon himself with his carnal mind, 19 and does not keep his head, while the whole body, supplied and united by bonds and ties, increases with the increase of God. 20 Therefore, if you are dead with Christ from the ordinances of the world, why, as if you lived in the world, are you burdened with traditions? 21 Such as, "Touch not, taste not, handle not." 22 Which with death perish and go after the teachings and doctrines of men. 23 Which things have wisdom in them, in vol- untary religion and humility of mind, and in not sparing the body, which are things of no value, inasmuch as they pertain to the filling of the flesh.

CHAPTER 3

1 If therefore you have risen with Christ, look at the things that are outside, where Christ sits at the right hand of God. 2 Focus on the things that are outside and not on those things that are on earth. 3 For you are dead and your life is hidden with Christ in God. 4 When Christ, who is our life, appears, you also will appear with him in glory. 5 Mortify therefore your members that are on earth, fornication, vi- olence, inordinate affection, concupiscence, and couetousnes, which is idolatry. 6 For these things the wrath of God comes upon the children of disobedience. 7 In which you also once walked, when you lived in them. 8 But now take all these things out of your mouth: wrath, anger, malice, cursed speech, filthy speech. 9 Do not lie to one another, since you have gotten rid of the old man and his works, 10 and have put on the new man, who is re- newed in knowledge according to the image of him who created him, 11 where there is neither Greek nor Irish, neither circumcision nor vncircumcision, neither barbarian nor Scythian, neither slave nor free: but Christ is all and in all things. 12 Therefore, as God's elect, holy and blessed, clothe yourselves with bowels of mercy, kindness, humility of mind, meekness, long-suffering: 13 forbearing and forgiving one another, if anyone has a quarrel with another; as Christ forgave, so do ye also. 14 And on all these things put joy, which is the bond of perfection. 15 And let the peace of God reign in your hearts, to which you are called in one body, and be thankful. 16 Let the word of Christ abide in you abundantly in all wisdom, teaching and admonishing yourselves, in psalms and hymns and spiritual songs, sing- ing with grace in your hearts to the Lord. 17 And whatever you do, in word or deed, do it in the name of the Lord Jesus, giving thanks to God and the Father through him. 18 Women, submit yourselves to your husbands, as is fit- ting in the Lord. 19 Husbands, love your wives and do not be bitter toward them. 20 Sons, obey your parents in everything, for this is well-pleasing to the Lord. 21 Fathers, do not provoke your children to anger, lest they be discouraged. 22 Servants, be obedient to those who are your masters according to the flesh in all things, not with eyes as serene as men's, but with a sincere heart, fearing God. 23 And whatever you do, do it from the heart, as to the Lord and not to men, 24 knowing that from the Lord you will receive the reward of the inheritance, because you serve the Lord Christ. 25 But he who does evil will receive the evil he has done; and there is no respect for people.

CHAPTER 4

1 You masters, do to your servants what is right and just, knowing that you also have a master in heaven. 2 Continue to pray and watch in fame with gratitude, 3 praying also for you, that God may open to you the door of power, to speak the mysteries of Christ; for this I also am in prison, 4 that I may speak of them, as is fitting. 5 Walk in wisdom to those who are outside, and redeem the season. 6 Let your speeches be always kind and full of salt, that you may know how to answer every man. 7 Tychicus, our esteemed brother and faithful minister and fellow-servant in the Lord, will declare to you my whole state: 8 whom I have sent to you for the same purpose, that he may know your situation and comfort your hearts, 9 with Onesimus, a faithful and well-liked brother, who is one of you. They will explain to you all the things that are going on here. 10 Aristarchus, my fellow prisoner, greets you, and Mark, a cousin of Barnabas (whose orders you have received; if he comes to you, receive him). 11 And Iesus, called Iustus, who is of the circumcision. These alone are my companions in the kingdom of God, who have contributed to my consolation. 12 Epaphras, a servant of Christ, who is one of you, greets you and always works for you in prayers, that you may be perfect and complete in all the will of God. 13 For I point out to him that he has great zeal for you, for those of Laodicea and for those of Hierapolis. 14 Luke, the well-known physician, greets you and Demas. 15 Greet the brethren of Laodicea, Nymph, and the church that is in her house. 16 When this letter is read to you, see that it is also read in the Church of the Laodiceans and that you also read again the epistle written from Laodicea. 17 And say to

Archippus, "Keep ac- count of the ministry you have received in the Lord, that you may fulfill it." 18 Greet him by the hand of me Paul. Remember my bundles. Grace be with you, Amen.

I THESSALONIANS

CHAPTER 1

1 Pavl, Siluano and Timothy to the Church of the Thessalonians, which is in God the Father and the Lord Jesus Christ: grace to you and peace from God our Father and the Lord Jesus Christ. 2 We always thank God for all of you, mentioning you in our prayers. 3 Remember- ing always your effectual faith, your diligence, and the patience of your hope in our Lord Je- sus Christ, in the sight of God our Father, 4 knowing, brethren, that you are God's elect. 5 For our gospel has not only been given to you in words, but also in power, and in the Holy Spirit, and in many certainties, as you know how we have been among you for your sake. 6 You became followers of Vs. and of the Lord and received the word in many afflictions, with the help of the Holy Spirit, 7 so that you were an example to all who lived in Macedo- nia and Achaia. 8 For by you resounded the word of the Lord, not only in Macedonia and Achaia, but also your faith, which is toward God, spread throughout all the quarters, so that we had no need to speak of anything. 9 For they themselves show what our way was to enter you and how you turned to God from idolatries to serve the true and upright God, 10 and to seek his son from hell, whom he raised from the dead, that is, Jesus who deliv- ers you from future wrath.

CHAPTER 2

1 For you yourselves know, brethren, that our entrance among you was not accidental, 2 but, having previously suffered and been humbled in Philippi, (as you know) we have been strong in our God, to speak to you the gospel of God with much effort. 3 For our exhortation was not made by vncleannes, nor by deceit. 4 But as it was granted to us by God that the gos- pel should be entrusted to you, so we spoke not as those who please men, but as God, who approves our hearts. 5 Nor have we used flat- tering words, as you know, nor colored couet- ousnes, God is recorde. 6 We have not sought to pray men, neither you nor others, when we might have been accused, as Christ's apostles were. 7 But we have been meek among you, as a mother cares for her children. 8 Being so fond of you, our good will was to have passed on to you, not only the gospel of God, but also our own souls, because you were dear to you. 9 For remember, brethren, our toil and travail; we toiled day and night not to be chargeable to any of you, and we preached to you the gospel of God. 10 You are witnesses, and so is God, of how we behaved holy, righteous and blamelessly among you who were present. 11 As you know that we exhorted, comforted and pleaded with each of you (as a father his children) 12 that you may walk in a manner worthy of God, who has called you to his king- dom and glory. 13 Therefore we also ask God that when you received the word of God that you heard, you did not receive it as the word of men, but as the word of God, which also works in you who believe. 14 For, brethren, you have become followers of the Churches of God which in Iudea are in Christ Iesus, be- cause you also have suffered the same things from your countrymen, just as they have suf- fered

those of the witnesses, 15 who killed the Lord Jesus and their own prophets and perse- cuted them, while God is not pleasing to them and they are contrary to all men, 16 and have forbidden them to preach to the Gentiles, that they may be led astray, to fulfill their sins always; for the wrath of God is come upon them, even to the uttermost. 17 For, brethren, since we have been kept away from you for some time, so far as our sight is concerned, but not so far as our heart is concerned, we desire all the more to see your face with great longing. 18 Therefore we would have come to you (I Paul, at least once or twice), but Satan has prevented us. 19 For what is our hope, our joy, our crown of victory? Are you not in the presence of our Lord Jesus Christ at his com- ing? 20 You are our glory and our joy.

CHAPTER 3

1 Therefore, since we could force no more, we thought it well to remain in Athens alone, 2 and we sent Timothy, our brother and minis- ter of God and our companion in the gospel of Christ, to support and comfort you con- cerning your faith, 3 so that no one may feel oppressed by these afflictions, for you your- selves know that we have been appointed for this purpose. 4 For verily, when we were with you, we had already told you that we would suffer tribulation, as then it came to pass, and you yourselves know it. 5 For this reason, when I could no longer prevent you, I sent him to know your faith, lest the tempter had tempted you in some way and our labor had been in vain. 6 But lately Timothy has come to you and brought you good news of your faith and joy, and of the fact that you always remember you well, desiring to see you, as we also do you, 7 Therefore, brethren, we have had comfort in you, in all our afflictions and needs, because of your faith. 8 For now are we ourselves, if you stand firm in the Lord. 9 What thanks can we give to God once again for you, for all the joy we enjoy because of you before our God? 10 Night and day, praying much to see your face and to accomplish what is lacking in your faith? 11 Now God himself, that is, our Father, and our Lord Jesus Christ, guide our journey to you, 12 and may the Lord increase you and make you abound in love to- ward one another and toward all people, just as we do toward you: 13 to make your hearts stable and blameless in holiness before God and our Father, at the coming of our Lord Je- sus Christ with all his saints.

CHAPTER 4

1 Moreover we beseech you, brethren, and exhort you in the Lord Jesus, to increase more and more, as you have received from you, the way of walking and pleasing God. 2 For you know what commands we give you from the Lord Jesus. 3 For this is the will of God con- cerning your sanctification and abstention from fornication, 4 so that each one of you may know how to own his own ship in holi- ness and honor, 5 and not in concupiscence, like the Gentiles who do not know God: 6 let no one oppress or defraud his brother in any way, for the Lord is the arbiter of all these things, as we also have told you before the time and testified to you. 7 For God has not called the brothers to vncleannesse, but to holiness. 8 Whoever therefore despises these things does not despise man, but God, who has given you his Holy Spirit. 9 But as for brotherly charity, you do not need me to write to you, for God has taught you to love one an- other. 10 Yea, and this thing ye do indeed

with all the brethren that are in all Macedonia; but we beseech you, brethren, to increase more and more, 11 and that you endeavor to be qui- et, minding your own business and working with your own hands, as we have commanded you, 12 that you may be honest to those out- side and lack nothing. 13 I would not have you, brethren, to be ignorant concerning those who are asleep, lest you grieve as oth- ers who have no hope. 14 For if we believe that Jesus died and rose again, those who sleep in Jesus will also be brought by God with him. 15 Therefore we say to you by the mouth of the Lord that we who are alive and who are wait- ing for the coming of the Lord will not prevail over those who sleep.16 For the Lord himself will come down from Eauen with a shout, with the voice of the archangel and with the trumpet of God; and the dead in Christ will rise first: 17 then we also who live and remain shall be rapt with them in the clouds, to meet the Lord in the air; and so shall we always be with the Lord. 18 Therefore comfort one an- other with these words.

CHAPTER 5

1 As for the times and seasons, brothers, you do not need me to write to you. 2 For you your- selves know perfectly well that the day of the Lord will come like a thief in the night. 3 For when they say, "Peace and safety," sudden de- struction will come upon them, like the snare upon a pregnant woman, and they will not escape, 4 But you, brethren, are not in dark- ness that that day should come upon you like a thief. 5 You are all children of the light and children of the day; we are not of the night nor of darkness. 6 Therefore do not sleep like others, but watch and be sober. 7 For those who sleep, sleep by night, and those who are drunk, are drunk by night. 8 But let those who are by day be sober, wearing the breastplate of faith and joy and the hope of salvation as a helmet. 9 For God has not destined men to wrath, but to obtain salvation through our Lord Jesus Christ, 10 who died for you, so that whether we wake or sleep, we may live togeth- er with him. 11 Therefore exhort one another and edify one another, as you do. :12 Now we beseech you, brethren, to acknowledge those who labor among you, who are outside you in the Lord, and who admonish you, 13 that you may appreciate them individually for their works. Be at peace among yourselves. 14 We ask you, brethren, to admonish those who are out of order; to comfort the feeble-minded; to bear with the weak; to be at peace with all men. 15 See that no one rewards injustice for injustice to anyone, but follow what is good, both toward yourselves and toward all men. 16 Seek more and more. 17 Pray continually. 18 In everything give thanks, for this is the will of God in Christ Iesus toward you. 19 Do not quench the Spirit. 20 Do not despise prophe- cy. 21 Test everything and keep what is good. 22 Refrain from every appearance of wicked- ness. 23 Now may the God of peace sanctify you in all things; and I pray God that your whole spirit, soul and body may be preserved blameless until the coming of our Lord Jesus Christ. 24 Faithful is he who calls you, and he will do so also. 25 Brothers, pray for you. 26 Greet all the brethren with a holy kisse. 27 I command you in the Lord that this letter be read to all the holy brethren. 28 The grace of our Lord Jesus Christ be with you, amen.

II THESSALONIANS

CHAPTER 1

1 Paul and Siluano and Timothy to the Church of the Thessalonians, which is in God our Father and the Lord Jesus Christ: 2 Grace to you and peace from God our Father and the Lord Jesus Christ. 3 We must always give thanks to God for you, brothers, as is fitting, because your faith grows more and more and the charity of each of you toward one another increases, 4 so that we ourselves rejoice in you in the Churches of God, for your patience and faith in all the persecutions and tribulations you endure, 5 which is a manifest sign of the righteous judgment of God, that you may be counted worthy of the kingdom of God, for which you also suffer. 6 For it is a just thing with God to reward tribulation to those who afflict you, 7 and to you who are afflicted, rest, when the Lord Jesus will manifest Him- self from on high with His mighty angels, 8 in flaming fire, avenging those who do not know God and who do not obey the gospel of our Lord Jesus Christ, 9 who shall be punished with everlasting perdition, from the presence of the Lord and from the glory of his power, 10 when he will come to be glorified in his saints and to be made marvelous in all who will be present (for our testimony concern- ing you has been made known) in that day. 11 Therefore we also always pray for you, that our God may make you worthy of this calling and may fulfill with power all the pleasures of his goodness and the work of faith, 12 that the name of our Lord Jesus Christ may be glori- fied in you and you in him, according to the grace of our God and the Lord Jesus Christ.

CHAPTER 2

1 Now we exhort you, brethren, for the com- ing of our Lord Jesus Christ and for our gath- ering together with him, 2 that you may not be suddenly astray from your minds and be troubled either by spirit or words or letters, as though the day of Christ were near. 3 Let no one deceive you in any way, for that day will not come unless first there is a turning away and the man of sin, that is, the son of perdi- tion, is manifested, 4 who is an aduersary and exalts himself against all that is called God or that is worshiped; so much so that he sits as God in the temple of God, making himself be- lieve that he is God. 5 Do you not remember that when I was still with you I told you these things? 6 Now you know what he holds back to be released in his own time. 7 For the mys- tery of iniquity is already in place; only he who now withholds will leave until he is taken out of the way. 8 Then shall be removed that un- godly one whom the Lord shall consume with the Spirit of his mouth and abolish with the splendor of his coming, 9 and he whose com- ing is by the effectual working of Satan, with all power, signs and lying wonders, 10 and in all deceptions of righteousness among those who perish, because they have not received the voice of truth to be saved. 11 Therefore God will send them strong delusion, that they may feed on lies, 12 that they may be damned all who did not believe the truth, but were pleased with righteousness. 13 But we should always thank God for you, brothers blessed by the Lord, because God has chosen you from the beginning for salvation, through sanctifi- cation of the Spirit and faith in the truth, 14 to whom he has called you through our gospel, to obtain the glory of our Lord Jesus Christ. 15 Therefore, brethren, stand firm and observe the instructions that have been given to you, whether by word or by our letter. 16 Now the same Jesus Christ, our Lord, and our God, the Father, who has received you and given you eternal consolation and good hope through grace, 17 comforts your hearts and comforts you in every word and good work.

CHAPTER 3

1 Moreover, brethren, pray for you, that the word of the Lord may have free course and be glorified, just as it is for you, 2 and that we may be delivered from vnreasonable and wicked men, for all men have no faith. 3 But the Lord is faithful and will strengthen you and preserve you from evil. 4 We are persuad- ed of you through the Lord that you do and will do the things of which we have spoken to you. 5 May the Lord guide your hearts to the joy of God and the expectation of Christ. 6 We urge you, brethren, in the Name of our Lord Jesus Christ, to withdraw yourselves from every brother who walks immoderate- ly and not according to the instruction you have previously received. 7 For you yourselves know how you ought to follow the gospel, for we have not behaved immoderately among you, 8 we have not taken bread from anyone for anything, but have labored with toil and toil night and day, not to be imputed to any of you. 9 Not because we had no authority, but to make ourselves an example for you to follow. 10 For when we were with you, we warned you that if there was anyone who did not want to work, he should not eat. 11 For we have heard that there are some who walk among you in- ordinately and do not work at all, but are busy bodies. 12 Therefore, through our Lord Jesus Christ, we admonish and exhort them to work quietly and to eat their own bread. 13 And you, brothers, do not grow weary in doing right. 14 If anyone does not obey what we have said in this letter, warn him and do not associate with him, that he may be ashamed: 15 but do not regard him as an enemy, but warn him as a brother. 16 May the Lord of peace himself al- ways give you peace by all means. The Lord be with you all. 17 The greeting of me Paul, with my hand, which is the sign of every epistle; so I write, 18 The grace of our Lord Jesus Christ be with you all, amen.

I TIMOTHY

CHAPTER 1

1 Pavl, an apostle of Christ, by the command- ment of God our Savior and the Lord Jesus Christ our hope, 2 To Timothy, my natural son in the faith: Grace, mercy and peace from God our Father and Christ Jesus our Lord. 3 As I begged you to remain still in Ephesus when I left for Macedonia, so do, that you may warn some, lest they teach other doctrines, 4 and that they may not give heed to fables and ge- nealogies which are ends, which ask questions rather than to the divine edification which is by faith. 5 For the end of the commandment is the joy of a pure heart, a good conscience and an established faith. 6 By these things some have erred and have given themselves over to confusion. 7 They would like to be doctors of the Law, but they do not understand what they say or what they affirm. 8 We know that the Law is good, if man lawfully observes it, 9 knowing that the Law was not given to the righteous man, but to the transgressors and disobedient, to the ungodly and sinful, to the ungodly and profane, to the murderers of fa- thers and mothers, to the murderers of men, 10 to whoremongers, to cheaters, to thieves, to swindlers, to perverts, and if there is any other thing that is contrary to sound doctrine, 11 which is in accordance with the glorious gospel of the blessed God, which has been en- trusted to me. 12 Therefore I thank him who has made me strong, that is, Christ Iesus our Lord, because he has held me faithful and put me in his service: 13 whereas before I was a blasphemer, a persecutor, and an oppressor, yet I was received with mercy, because I did it through ignorance and unbelief. 14 But the grace of the Lord was very abundant with the faith and joy that is in Christ Jesus. 15 This is a true saying and in every way worthy to be re- ceived, that Christ Iesus came into the world to save sinners, among whom I am first. 16 However, for this reason I have been credit- ed with making Jesus Christ first to show me all his long-suffering as an example for those who in due time will join him for eternal life. 17 Now to the King eternal, immortal, inuis- ible, to God only wise, be honor and glory, forever and ever, Amen. 18 This command I entrust to you, son Timothy, according to the prophecies before you, that you may fight a good fight, 19 preserving faith and a good conscience, which some have forsaken, and which, as far as faith is concerned, they have made a work of art. 20 Among them are Hy- menaeus and Alexander, whom I handed over to Satan that they might learn not to blas- pheme.

CHAPTER 2

1 I therefore exhort us first of all to make sup- plications, prayers, intercessions and thanks- giving for all men, 2 for kings and for all in authority, that we may lead a quiet and peace- ful life, in all godliness and honesty. 3 For this is good and acceptable in the sight of God our Savior, 4 Who wants all men to be sanctified and to come to acknowledge the truth. 5 For there is one God and one Mediator between God and men, who is the man Christ Iesus, 6 Who became a ransom for all men, to be in due time the testimony, 7 for whom I have been appointed as preacher and apostle (I speak the truth in Christ and do not lie) and as teacher of the Gentiles in faith and truth. 8 Therefore I want men to pray, lifting up pure hands everywhere, without wrath and with- out shouting. 9 And so also let the women dress themselves in fine clothing, with mod- esty and modesty, not with brothy garments, nor with gold, nor with pearls, nor with costly garments, 10 but (as befits women who pro- fess the fear of God) with good works. 11 Let the woman learn in silence with all submis- sion. 12 I will not permit a woman to teach, nor to oppose the authority of man, but to be silent. 13 For first Adam was formed and then Eue. 14 Adam was not deceived, but the wom- an was deceived and was in transgression. 15 However, the birth of her children will save her, if they continue to have faith, joy and ho- liness with modesty.

CHAPTER 3

1 This is a true saying, "If one desires the office of bishop, he desires a worthy job." 2 A bishop must therefore be respectable, the husband of one wife, vigilant, temperate, modest, arrogant, suitable for teaching, 3 not given to wine, not quarrelsome, not giv- en to profit, but meek, not quarrelsome, not crotchety, 4 one who knows how to rule his house honestly, and who has children to obey with all honesty. :5 For if one does not know how to rule his own house, how will he be able to take care of the Church of God? 6 He must not be a long scholar, lest, swelling up, he fall into the condemnation of death. 7 He must also be well regarded, even by those who are not, lest he fall into reproach and the snare of deception. 8 Similarly, deacons must be gen- tle, not duplicitous, not given to wine and not given to gain, 9 having the mysteries of faith in pure conscience. 10 Let them first be pro- terbs, then exercise

their ministry, if they are found blasphemous. 11 Likewise, their wives should be honest, not talking in vain, but so- ber and faithful in all things. 12 Let the dea- cons be husbands of one wife and know how to govern their children and their houses well. 13 For those who have exercised their ministry well have obtained a good degree and great freedom in the faith, which is in Christ Iesus. 14 These things I write to you, trusting that I will come to you very soon. 15 But if I tarry long, that you may yet know how you should conduct yourself in the house of God, which is the Church of the living God, the pillar and foundation of the truth. 16 Undoubted- ly, great is the mystery of the Godhead: God was manifested in the flesh, was justified in the Spirit, was seen by angels, was preached to the Gentiles, was seen in the world, and re- ceived glory.

CHAPTER 4

1 Now the Spirit says with certainty that in the last times some will depart from the faith and give heed to spirits of wandering and doc- trines of disorder, 2 who speak lies with hy- pocrisy and make their consciences burn with fireworks, 3 forbid to marry and command to abstain from the foods that God created to be received with gratitude by those who know the truth. 4 For every creature of God is good, and nothing is to be refused if it is gratefully received. 5 For it is sanctified by God's word and prayer. 6 If you remember these things to the brethren, you will be a good minister of Jesus Christ, whom you have nurtured in the words of faith and good doctrine, which you have always followed. 7 But cast away prophecies and old fables and train yourself in godliness. 8 For bodily exercise is of little value, but godliness is useful for everything, because it promises present and future life. 9 This is a true saying, and by all means worthy to be received. 10 For this reason we toil and are reproached, because we trust in a God who lies and is the savior of all men, especially of those who are saved. 11 These things are to be taught and to be understood. 12 Let no one despise your youth, but be for those who be- have as an example, in speech, conversation, language, spirit, faith and purity. 13 Until I come, give place to reading, exhortation and doctrine. 14 Do not despise the gift that is in you, which has been granted to you through prophecy by the laying on of hands by the community of elders. 15 Practice these things, and make your contribution to them, that it may be seen how useful you are to all men. 16 Pay attention to yourself and to learning; keep on doing this, for in so doing you will save yourself and those who listen to you.

CHAPTER 5

1 Do not rebuke an elder, but exhort him as a father, and the young men as brothers, 2 the elderly women as mothers, the young as sis- ters, with all possible purity. 3 Honor widows, who are widows by right. 4 But if a widow has children or grandchildren, let her learn first to be charitable to her own household and to reward her relatives, for this is an honest thing and pleasing to God. 5 She who is wid- owed and forsaken, trust in God and continue to supplicate and pray night and day. 6 But she who lives in pleasure is dead while she lives. 7 Of these things, therefore, we warn them, that they may be blasphemous. 8 If there is anyone who does not care for his own children and those of his family, he denies the faith and is worse than an infidel. 9 Consider not

a widow under three and a half years of age, who has been the wife of one husband, 10 and who is well known for her good deeds: whether she has fed her children, whether she has housed strangers, whether she has washed the feet of the saints, whether she has assisted those who were in distress, whether she has been continually engaged in every good deed. 11 But reject the younger widows, for when they have begun to become wan- ton against Christ, they marry, 12 and damn themselves, because they have broken the first faith. 13 Moreover, being idle, they learn to go from house to house; they are not only idle, but also talkative and busy, saying things that are not pleasant. 14 Therefore I want the younger women to marry and bear children and take care of the house, and not to give occasion to the aduersary to talk idly. 15 For some have already turned back after Satan. 16 If a faithful man or a faithful woman have widows, let them assist them, and let them not charge the church, that it may be suffi- cient for widows in distress. 17 Let the elders who rule well be held in double honor, espe- cially those who labor in word and doctrine, 18 For the Scripture says, "Do not bite the mouth of the ox that treads the grain," and, "The laborer is worthy of his wages." 19 Do not accuse an elder except with two or three witnesses. 20 Those who sin, rebuke them openly, so that others also may be afraid. 21 I command you before God, the Lord Jesus Christ and the elect angels, to observe these things without preferring one over the other and to do nothing in a partial way. 22 Lay not your hands suddenly on anyone, and be not a partaker of the sins of other men; keep your- self pure. 23 Drink no more water, but drink a little wine for your stomach and for your frequent infirmities. 24 Some of men's sins are open first and go on until judgment, but others follow after them. 25 In the same way, good deeds are also overt, and those that are not cannot be hidden.

CHAPTER 6

1 Let the servants who are under the yoke consider their masters worthy of all hon- or, lest the name of God and his doctrine be spoken ill of. 2 And those who have allied masters, let them not despise them because they are brothers, but rather let them serve because they are faithful, believing and par- takers of the benefit. These things teach and exhort. 3 If anyone teaches otherwise and does not abide in the sound words of our Lord Jesus Christ and the doctrine that is accord- ing to God, 4 such a one knows nothing, but dwells in matters and disputes of words, out of which arise enmities, quarrels, railing, suppositions, 5 the unpleasant disputes of men of corrupt minds and devoid of truth, who think that gaiety is godliness; from such as these separate yourselves. 6 But godliness is great wealth, if a man be content with what he has. 7 For we have brought nothing into the world, and it is certain that we can take nothing away. 8 Therefore, when we have food and clothing, let us be content with what we have. 9 For those who want to be rich fall into temptations and snares, and into many fool- ish and pleasant desires, which sink men into perdition and destruction. 10 For the desire for money is the root of all evil, and some of them, while desiring it, have erred from the faith and have been pierced with many sor- rows. 11 But you, O man of God, flee these things and follow righteousness, godliness, faith, joy, patience and meekness. 12 Fight the good fight of faith, and take hold of eter- nal life, to which also thou hast been called, and hast made a good profession before many witnesses. 13 I

command you to do this before God, who vivifies all things, and before Jesus Christ, who under Pontius Pilate witnessed a good confession, 14 that you keep this com- mandment without blemish and blameless, until the appearing of our Lord Jesus Christ, 15 who, in due time, will reveal to you that he is the only blessed one and prince, the King of kings and Lord of lords, 16 who is the only one who is immortal and dwells in a light that no one can reach, that no one knows and no one can see, and to whom is due eternal hon- or and power, Amen. 17 Urge those who are rich in this world not to be haughty and not to trust in vncertaine riches, but in the God who lives (who gives in abundance all that is needed for prosperity). 18 let them do good and be rich in good works, ready to distrib- ute and communicate, 19 creating for them a good foundation for the times to come, that they may obtain eternal life. 20 O Timothy, guard that which has been entrusted to you, and turn away profane and vain vain cares and oppositions to falsely named science, 21 who, though professing, have erred on faith. Grace be with you, Amen.

II TIMOTHY

CHAPTER 1

1 Paul, an apostle of Jesus Christ, by the will of God, according to the promise of life that is in Christ Jesus, 2 To Timothy, my beloved son: grace, mercy and peace from God the Father and Jesus Christ our Lord. 3 I thank God, whom I serve from my elders with a pure conscience, that without ceasing I re- member you in my prayers night and day, 4 desiring to see you, mindful of your teas, to be full of joy: 5 when I call to remembrance the inveterate faith that is in you, which dwelt first in your grandmother Lois and in your mother Eunice, and I am sure that it dwells in you also. 6 Therefore I remind you that you have strengthened the gift of God that is in you through the laying on of my hands. 7 For God has not given you the Spirit of fear, but of power and joy and a sound mind. 8 Therefore do not be ashamed of the testimony of the Lord, nor of me his prisoner, but share in the afflictions of the gospel, according to the pow- er of God, 9 Who hath chosen and called with a holy calling, not according to our works, but according to his purpose and grace, which was given us through Christ Iesus before the world was, 10 but which has now been mani- fested by the appearance of our Savior Jesus Christ, who abolished death and brought forth life and immortality through the gospel. 11 For this reason I was appointed preacher, apostle and teacher to the Gentiles. 12 For this reason I also suffer these things, but I am not ashamed, for I know whom I have entrusted and I am convinced that he is able to guard what I have entrusted to him until that day. 13 Keep the true authorship of the sound words you have heard from me in the faith and praise that is in Christ Iesus. 14 The precious thing that has been entrusted to you, keep it through the Holy Spirit who dwells in you. 15 This you know, that all who are in Asia have departed from me; of the same kind are Phy- gellus and Hermogenes. 16 May the Lord give credit to the house of Onesiphorus, because he often refreshed me and was not ashamed of my captivity, 17 but when he was in Rome, he sought me very diligently and found me. 18 The Lord gave him grace, that in that day he might find mercy with the Lord; and in how many things he assisted me at Ephesus, you know it well.

CHAPTER 2

1 You therefore, my son, be strong in the grace that is in Christ Iesus. 2 And what you have heard from me through many witnesses, deliver it also to faithful men, who will be able to teach others also. 3 Suffer therefore afflic- tions as a good entertainer of Jesus Christ. 4 Let no one who makes war meddle in the af- fairs of this life, because he wants to please him who chose him as his soul. 5 And if any man strip himself even for a master, he is not crowned, unless he strip himself as he ought. 6 The cultivator must toil before he receives fruit. 7 Consider what I say, and may the Lord give you understanding in all things: 8 Re- member that Jesus Christ, made of the seed of Dauid, was raised from the dead according to my gospel, 9 Therefore I suffer trouble as one who does wrong, even as to bonds; but the word of God has no bounds. 10 Therefore I suffer all things for the elect, that they too may obtain the salvation that is in Christ Ie- sus, with everlasting glory. 1 It is true that if we have died with him, we shall live with him. 12 If we suffer, we will also reign together with him; if we deny him, he will also deny him against us. 13 If we are not faithful, he remains faithful; he cannot deny himself. 14 Of these things remember and protest be- fore the LORD, lest they argue about words, which are of no use, but to perturb those who hear them. 15 Study to be recognized by God, to be a man who has no need to be ashamed and who knows how to use the word of truth well. 16 Avoid profanities and vain talk, for they will increase until they become more vngodlinesse. 17 And their word will flare up like a cavity; of the same kind are Hymenaeus and Philetus, 18 Who, as for you, have erred from the truth, saying that the resurrection is already past, and destroy the faith of some. 19 But God's foundation remains sure, and it has this meaning, "The Lord knows who his own are," and "Whoever calls on the name of Christ turns away from iniquity." 20 However, in a great house there are not only vessels of gold and silver, but also of wood and earth, some for honor and some for dishonor. 21 If therefore one purifies himself from these, he will be a vessel of honor, sanctified and fit for the Lord, and prepared for every good work. 22 Flee also from youthful concupiscences and follow righteousness, faith, joy and peace, with those who call on the Lord with a pure heart, 23 and leave aside foolish and vain questions, knowing that they fuel discord. 24 The servant of the Lord, on the other hand, must not make war, but must be meek to all men, ready to teach and to suffer injustice, 25 instructing with meekness those who are of the opposite mind, hoping that God will grant them repentance at any time, that they may recognize the truth, 26 and to come out of the snare of the devil, whose captive they are, to do his will.

CHAPTER 3

1 Know also that in the last days perilous times will come. 2 For men will be self-righ- teous, cultured, boastful, proud, cursed, dis- obedient to parents, vnthankefull, vnholy, 3 devoid of natural affections, violators of the truce, false accusers, intemperate, fierce, who do not mock at all those who are good, 4 treacherous, stubborn, haughty, lovers of pleasures more than of God, 5 have a sem- blance of godliness, but have denied the pow- er thereof; therefore turn away from them. 6 For they are of this kind who creep into hous- es and take simple women captive, laden with sins and driven by excessive lust, 7 who never learn and are

unable to recognize the truth. 8 And as Iannes and Iambres opposed Moses, so these also oppose the truth, men of corrupt minds, reprobate concerning the faith. 9 But they shall prevail no more, for their folly shall be common to all men, as theirs also was. 10 But you have thoroughly known my doctrine, way of life, purpose, faith, long-suffering, joy, patience, 11 the persecutions and afflictions that were inflicted on me in Antioch, at Iconi- um and Lystra, persecutions which I suffered, but from which the Lord delivered me. 12 Yes, and all who live piously in Christ Iesus will suffer persecution. 13 But wicked men and deceivers will grow worse and worse, deceiv- ing and being deceived. 14 But you continue in the things that you have learned and that have been entrusted to you, knowing from whom you learned them: 15 and that thou hast known as a child the holy Scriptures, which are able to make thee wise unto salva- tion, through the faith that is in Christ Iesus. 6 For all Scripture was issued by inspiration of God and is useful for teaching, persuading, correcting, and instructing in righteousness, 17 that the man of God may be absolute, being made perfect for every good work.

CHAPTER 4

1 I commend you therefore to God and to the Lord Jesus Christ, who will judge the dead and the dying at his appearing and in his king- dom, 2 preach the word; be timely, in good time and out of good time; learn, rebuke, ex- hort with every affliction and doctrine. 3 For the time will come when they will not endure sound doctrine, but, having itching ears, will procure, according to their own lusts, a heap of teachers, 4 And they will turn away their ears from the truth and indulge in fables. 5 But thou shalt watch in all things, suffer adu- ersity, do the work of an evangelist, make thy minister to be esteemed in all things. :6 For I am now ready to be offered, and the time of my departure is at hand. 7 I have fought a good battle and finished my course: I have kept the faith. 8 Therefore from now on the crown of righteousness is ready for me, which the Lord, the righteous judge, will give me in that day; and not to me alone, but also to all who love his appearing. 9 Make haste to come to me at once: 10 For Demas has forsaken me, has embraced this present world, and has de- parted for Thessalonica. Crescens has gone to Galatia, Titus to Dalmatia. 11 Only Luke is with me. Take Mark and bring him with you, for he is useful to me for ministry. 12 And Tychicus I sent to Ephesus. 13 The cloak I left in Troas with Carpus, when you come, take it with you and the books, but especially the scrolls. 14 Alexander the coppersmith has done me much good; the LORD rewards him according to his works. 15 Take account of him also, for he hindered our preaching much. 16 At my first answer no one attended me, but all forsook me: I pray God that it may not be imputed to them. 17 Nevertheless the LORD assisted me, and strengthened me, that the preaching might be fully satisfied, and all the Gentiles might hear; and I was delivered out of the lion's mouth. 18 The LORD will deliver me from all toil and preserve me unto his ev- erlasting kingdom; to him be praise forever, Amen. 9 Greet Prisca and Aquila and the fam- ily of Onesiphorus. 20 Erastus was in Corinth: Trophimus I left in Miletus, in sickness. 21 Make haste to come before winter. Eubulus greets you, Pudens, Linus, Claudia, and all the brethren. 22 The Lord Jesus Christ be with your spirit. Grace be with you, Amen.

TITUS

CHAPTER 1

1 Paul, a servant of God and an apostle of Jesus Christ, according to the faith of God's elect and the acknowledgment of the truth, which is according to divine lines, 2 for the hope of eternal life, which God, who cannot lie, promised before the world began: 3 But hath in due time manifested his word by the preaching committed to me, according to the commandment of God our Saviour: 4 To Ti- tus my natural son, according to the common faith, grace, mercy and peace from God the Father and the Lord Jesus Christ our Savior. 5 Wherefore I have left you in Crete, that you may continue to draw up the things that re- main, and to appoint elders in every city, as I have appointed you, 6 if anyone is respect- able, husband of one wife, who has faithful children, who are not slandered by disorder and are not disobedient. 7 A bishop must be blameless, like a steward of God, not averse, not angry, not given to wine, not quarrel- some, not given to reproach, 8 but arbores- cent, one who loves goodness, wise, righ- teous, holy, temperate, 9 who holds fast the faithful word according to doctrine, that he may exhort with sound doctrine and convince those who say otherwise. 10 For there are many disobedient, vain talkers and deceivers of minds, especially among the circumcised, 11 whose mouths must be stopped, who sub- jugate whole houses, teaching things they ought not, for the sake of mockery. 12 And one of them, one of their prophets, said, "The Cre- tans are always liars, spaghetti-eaters, bel- ly-laughers." 13 This testimony is true; that is why you sternly counsel them, that they may be sound in your faith, 14 Not giving heed to the fables and teachings of men, which lead away from the truth. 15 To the pure all things are pure, but to those who are defiled and vnbeleeuing there is nothing pure, but their minds and consciences are defiled. 16 They profess to know God, but by works they deny Him, and are abominable and disobedient and reprobate toward every good work.

CHAPTER 2

1 Speak what is sound for doctrine, 2 that the older men be watchful, earnest, perse- vering, firm in faith, goodness and patience: 3 The older women also, that they may have conduct befitting holiness, that they may not be false accusers, that they may not in- dulge in wine, but may teach honest things, 4 that they may instruct young women to be sober, to love their husbands and their chil- dren, 5 that they may be temperate, chaste, attentive to the home, good and submissive to their husbands, that the word of God may not be impaired. 6 Urge other men also to be sober. 7 In everything, be an example of good works, of corrupt doctrine, of integrity and grace, 8 and with a sound soul, which cannot be condemned, that he who resists may be ashamed, having nothing of you to speak ill of. 9 Let the servants be submissive to their masters and please them in all things, not an- swering back, 10 and let them not be snitch- es, but give evidence of good faithfulness, so that in everything they uphold the doctrine of God our savior. 11 For the grace of God has ap- peared, which brings salvation to all men, 12 and teaches us to deny corruption and world- ly lusts and to live soberly, righteously and godly in this present world, 13 awaiting the blessed hope and the appearing of the glory of the mighty God and our Savior Jesus Christ, 14 who gave himself for you, to redeem you from all unrighteousness and purify you to be a peculiar people, zealous of good works. 15 Speak these things,

exhort and conclude with all authority. See that no one despises you.

CHAPTER 3

1 Remind them to be submissive to the prin- cipalities and powers, to be obedient and to be ready for every good deed, 2 that they speak evil of no one, that they be not quarrelsome, but be meek, showing themselves meek to all men. 3 For we also in the past were wise, disobedient, deceived, indulging in the lusts and pleasures of life, living in malice and envy, hating one another: 4 but when the generosity and joy of God our Savior toward men appeared, 5 not by works of righteous- ness, which we had done, but according to his mercy, he healed man, by the washing of the new birth and the renewing of the Holy Spirit, 6 whom he shed on you abundantly, through Jesus Christ our Savior, 7 that we, justified by his grace, might be made heirs according to the hope of eternal life. 8 This is a truthful saying, and these things I want you to affirm, so that those who have believed in God may be careful to do good works. These things are good and useful to men. 9 But avoid foolish questions, genealogies, con- tentions and quarrels about the Law, for they are vnprofitable and vain. 10 Withdraw those who are heretics, after admonishing them once or twice, 11 knowing that he who is such is perverted and sinful, being damned of his own accord. 12 When I send you Artemas or Tychicus, take care to come to me to Nicop- olis, for I have determined to winter there. 13 Lead Zenas, the Bible exegete, and Apollo on their journey with diligence, that they may not omit anything. 14 And let our people also learn to prepare good works for necessary things, that they may not be vnfruitful. 15 Everyone who is with me salutes you. Greet those who watch you in faith. Grace be with you all, Amen.

PHILEMON

1 Paul, a prisoner of Jesus Christ, and our brother Timothy, to Philemon, our dear friend and helper, 2 to our dear sister Ap- phia, to Archippus, our soulmate, and to the church that is in your house: 3 Grace to you and peace from God our Father and the Lord Jesus Christ. 4 I give thanks to my God, al- ways making mention of you in my prayers, :5 when I hear of your love and faith toward the Lord Jesus and toward all the saints. 6 That the fellowship of your faith may be made effectual and that what is good in you may be known through Christ Iesus. 7 For we have great joy and consolation in your honor, for by you, brother, the bowels of the saints are comforted. 8 Therefore, although I am very bold in Christ in communicating to you what is convenient, 9 nevertheless, for God's sake, I beg you rather to be as I am, Paul aged and now a prisoner for Jesus Christ. 10 I beseech you for my son Onesimus, whom I begat among my bonds, 11 who was formerly very advantageous to you, but now is advanta- geous both to you and to me, 12 whom I have sent again; you therefore receive him, who is my bowels, 13 whom I would have gathered to me, that in your stead he might assist me in the bonds of the gospel. 14 But without your thought I would do nothing, that your benefit might not be as of necessity, but voluntarily. 15 It may be that he has departed for a time, that you may receive him forever, 16 no lon- ger as a servant, but as a servant, that is, as a brother who is especially dear to me; how much more than you, both in the flesh and in the Lord? 17 If therefore you regard our com- mon things, receive him as myself. 18

If he has harmed you or owes you money, put it on my account. 19 I Paul wrote this with my own hand: I will repay him, though I do not tell you that you have done more toward me than you have done yourself. 20 Yea, brother, let me obey this thy pleasure in the Lord; comfort my bowels in the Lord. 21 Trusting in your obe- dience, I have written to you, knowing that you will do more than I have told you. 22 Also prepare me lodging, for I trust that through your prayers it will be freely granted to me. 23 I greet you Epaphras, my prisoner in Christ Jesus, 24 Mark, Aristarchus, Demas and Luke, my fellow prisoners. 25 The grace of our Lord Jesus Christ be with your spirit, Amen.

GENERAL EPISTLES

These letters offer encouragement, guidance, and warnings to early Christian believers

HEBREWS

CHAPTER 1

1 At different times and in different manners God spoke anciently to our fathers through the prophets; in these last days he has spoken to his Son, 2 whom he made heir of all things, through whom also he made the world, 3 Who, being the radiance of glory and the in- gratiating form of his person, and upholding all things by his mighty word, has cleansed from himself our sins and sits at the right hand of the Majesty in the highest places, 4 and has been made far more excellent than the angels, in that he has obtained a more excellent name than they. 5 For to what angel has he ever said, "You are my son, today I have begotten you"? And then, "I will be his father and he shall be my son"? 6 And again, when He introduces His firstborn Son into the world, He says, "And let all the angels of God worship Him." 7 And of the angels he says, "He makes the spirits his messengers and his ministers a flame of fire." 8 But of the Son he says, "O God, your throne is forever; the scepter of your kingdom is a scepter of righteousness. 9 You have valued righteousness and hated in- iquity. Therefore God, your God, has anointed you with the oil of joy toward your fellow men. 10 You, O Lord, in the beginning founded the earth, and the heavens are the work of your hands. 11 They shall perish, but you remain; and all shall grow old like a garment. 12 Like a garment, you will wrap them, and they will change; but you are the same, and your years will not fade away. 13 To what angel did he say, "Sit at my right hand until I make your ene- mies your feet"? 14 Are they not all minister- ing spirits, sent out to minister, for the sake of those who will be recipients of salvation?

CHAPTER 2

1 Therefore we must pay diligent attention to the things we have heard, lest at any time they fail us. 2 For if the word spoken by the angels has been firm, and every transgression and disobedience has received a just reward, 3 how shall we escape if we neglect so great a salvation, which was preached by the Lord in the beginning and then was confirmed by those who heard him? 4 Has God borne wit- ness to it by signs and wonders and numerous miracles and gifts of the Holy Spirit, accord- ing to his will? 5 For he did not subject to the angels the world to come, of which we speak. 6 But one in a specific place testified, saying, "What

is man, that you should care for him? Or the son of man, for you to consider him? 7 You have made him somewhat inferior to the angels; you have crowned him with glory and honor and placed him above the works of your hands. 8 You have placed all things under his feet. And because he has put all things under himself, he has left nothing that is not subject to him. But we do not yet see all things sub- dued to him, 9 but we see Jesus crowned with glory and honor, who was made a little low- er than the angels, through the suffering of death, that by the grace of God he might taste death for all men. 10 For to him, for whom are all these things, and for whom are all these things, seeing he brought many sons to glo- ry, it fell to him to anoint the Prince of their salvation through afflictions. 1 For he who sanctifies and those who are sanctified are all of one race; therefore he is not ashamed to call them brothers, 12 saying, "I will declare your name to my brothers; in the midst of the Church I will sing your praises." 13 And again, "I will put my trust in him." And again, "Here I am with the sons whom God has given me." 14 Since therefore the sons are partakers of flesh and blood, he also partook of them, to destroy by death him who had the power of death, that is, the devil, 15 and to set free all those who, for fear of death, had remained all their lives in bondage. 16 For he did not take upon himself the nature of angels, but he took upon himself the seed of Abraham. 17 Therefore in all things he was to be made like his brethren, that he might be merciful and a faithful priest in things pertaining to God, to reconcile the sins of the people. 18 Because he suffered and was tempted, he is able to help those who are tempted.

CHAPTER 3

1 Therefore, brothers and sisters, partakers of the priestly vocation, consider the apostle and high priest of our profession, Christ Ie- sus: 2 who was faithful to him who appointed him, just as Moses was in all his house. 3 For this man is counted worthy of greater glory than Moses, in that he who built the house has more honor than the house itself. 4 For every house is built by a man, and the one who built it all is God. 5 Moses was very faith- ful throughout his house, like a servant, to testify to the things that were to be said later. 6 But Christ is like the Son, outside his house, whose house we are, if we keep trust and hope to the end. 7 Therefore, as the Holy Spirit says, "Today, if you will listen to his voice, 8 hard- en not your hearts as in the prouocation, as in the day of temptation in the wilderness, 9 where your fathers tempted me and test- ed me and saw my works for four years. 10 Therefore I was vexed with that generation and said, "They err in their hearts and do not know my ways." 11 Therefore I swore in my wrath, "If they will enter into my rest." 12 Take heed, brethren, if there is ever in any of you an evil and vain heart that turns away from the God he loves. 13 But exhort one another daily while it is day, lest any of you be hard- ened by the deceitfulness of sin. 14 For we are made partakers of Christ, if we hold fast that principle, by which we were promoted, 15 As long as it is said, "Today, if you hear his word, do not harden your hearts as in the prouoca- tion." 16 For some, on hearing it, provoked him to anger; but not all who came out of Egypt through Moses. 17 But with whom was he displeased for four hundred years? Was he not displeased with those who sinned, whose cars fell in the wilderness? 18 And to whom did he swear that they would not enter his rest, except to those who did not obey? 19 So we see that they could not enter because of unbelief.

CHAPTER 4

1 Fear therefore that at any time, forsaking the promise of entering his rest, any of you may seem to be deprived. 2 For to you also the gospel was preached, as to them; but the word which they heard did not profit them, because it was not mingled with faith in those who heard it. 3 For we, who have been deliv- ered, enter into rest, as he said to the other, "As I have sworn in my wrath, if they will enter into my rest," though the works were finished from the foundation of the world. 4 For in a certain place he spoke of the tenth day in this way, "God rested on the tenth day from all his works." 5 And again in this place, "If they shall enter into my rest." 6 For therefore it is necessary for some to enter it, and those to whom it was first preached did not enter it on account of faith: 7 Then, after a long time, he fixed in Dauid a specific day, the day of Pass- over, saying, as it is said, "Today, if you hear his message, do not harden your hearts." 8 For if Jesus had granted them rest, he would not have spoken of another day. 9 There remains therefore a rest for God's people. 10 For he who has entered into his rest has also ceased from his works, just as God has ceased from his. 11 Let us therefore study to enter that rest, lest any should fall into the same exam- ple of disobedience. 12 For the word of God is mighty and powerful in action, sharper than any two-edged sword, and penetrates even to the separation of soul and spirit, of the hyotes and the sea, and is able to discern the thoughts and intents of the heart. 13 There is no creature that is not manifest before him, but all things are naked and open to his eyes, with which we must reckon. 14 Since there- fore we have a great priest, who has entered heaven, namely, Jesus, the Son of God, let us hold fast our profession. 15 For we have not a priest who cannot be touched in feeling our infirmities, but who has been tempted in all things as we are, though without sinning. 16 Let us therefore go boldly to the throne of grace, that we may receive mercy and find grace to help in time of need.

CHAPTER 5

1 For every priest is taken from among men and is destined for men, in things pertaining to God, to offer gifts and sacrifices for sins, 2 that he is able to have compassion on those who are ignorant and out of the way, because he too is afflicted with infirmities, 3 and for the same reason he is obliged to offer for sins, both for his part and for you peoples. 4 And no one takes this honor alone, except he who is called of God, like Aaron. 5 So also Christ did not take this honor of being appointed priest on his own, but it was given him by the one who said to him, "You are my son, today I have begotten you." 6 As also in another place he says, "You are a priest forever, according to the order of Melchi-sedec." 7 Who, in the days of his flesh, offered prayers and suppli- cations, with loud cries and invocations to him who could save him from death, and was also heard in what he feared. 8 Though he was Son, he learned obedience through the things he suffered. 9 And being anointed, he was constituted the author of eternal salvation for all who obey him: 10 And he is called of God a priest according to the order of Melchi-sedec. 11 Of him we have many things to say, which are hard to hear, because you are dull of hear- ing. 12 For while in regard to time you ought to be teachers, you still need us to teach you what the first principles of God's word are; and you have become like

those who need milk, and not a strong meal. 13 For he who does not drink milk is inexperienced in the word of righteousness, because he is a child. 14 But strong milk belongs to those who are of advanced age and who, through long practice, have exercised their wits to discern good and evil.

CHAPTER 6

1 Therefore, leaving the doctrine of the be- ginning of Christ, let yourselves be led toward perfection, not laying again the foundation of the repetition of dead works and faith in God, 2 of the doctrine of baptisms and the laying on of hands, of the resurrection from the dead and eternal judgment. 3 And this we will do, if God permits. 4 For it is impossible that those who have been enlightened once, and have tasted the eternal gift, should have been made partakers of the Holy Spirit, 5 and who have tasted the good word of God and the powers of the world to come, 6 if they turn away, they must be denied again through repentance, for they crucify again for themselves the Son of God and mock him. 7 For the earth that drinks the rain that falls upon it and produces herbs fit for those by whom it is clothed re- ceives God's blessing. 8 But that which bears thorns and briers is taken up and is destined for the curse, the end of which is to be burned. 9 But, believe us, we have convinced ourselves of better things than you and of things that accompany salvation, though we speak thus. 10 For God is not right that he should forget your labor and toil that you have done for his name's sake, inasmuch as you have served and are serving the saints. 11 And we desire that each of you show the same diligence, in the full assurance of hope to the end, 12 that you may not be slothful, but followers of those who, through faith and patience, inherit the promises. 13 For when God made the promise to Abraham, because he had no one else with whom to swear, he swore by himself, 14 say- ing, "Surely I will bless you abundantly and multiply you exceedingly." 15 So after waiting patiently, he obtained the promise. 16 For men swear much by him who is greater than they, and another for confirmation is among them an end of all strife. 17 So God, wishing to show more widely to the heirs of the promise the stability of his counsels, bound himself with another, 18 That by two immutable things, for which it is impossible that God should tarry, we might have strong consolation, that we might take refuge in the hope set before us, 19 The hope which we have, as an anchor of the soul, sure and steadfast, and which enters into that which is within the heart, 20 where the forerunner entered, that is, Jesus who was made a priest forever according to the order of Melchi-sedec.

CHAPTER 7

1 This Melchi-sedec was the king of Salem, the priest of the most high God, who met Abraham on his return from the slaughter of the kings and blessed him: 2 to whom Abra- ham also gave the tithe of all things; who is first of all, by interpretation, king of righ- teousness; then he is also king of Salem, that is, king of peace, 3 without father, without mother, without relatives, without beginning of his days and without end of his life, but he is compared to the Son of God and contin- ues to be Priest forever. 4 Now consider how great this man was, to whom the patriarch Abraham gave the tithe of the sponges. 5 For only the sons of Leui,

who receive the office of priest, are commanded to take, according to the Law, the tithe of the people (i.e., of their lands), even if they come from the lineage of Abraham. 6 But he whose kinship has not been mentioned among them receives the tithe from Abraham and blesses him who had the promises. 7 Without any contradiction, the least is blessed by the greatest. 8 Here the men who die receive tithes, but there he of whom it is testified that he lives receives them. 9 And to tell how it is, even Leui, who receives tithes, paid tithes to Abraham. 10 For he was still in the bonds of his father Abra- ham, when Melchi-sedec met him. 11 If there- fore the priesthood of the Leuites had been perfected (for under it the Lawe had been es- tablished for the people), what need was there for another priest to arise according to the or- der of Melchi-sedec and not be called accord- ing to the order of Aaron? 12 For if the priest- hood is changed, the law must necessarily change as well. 13 For he of whom it is spo- ken belongs to another tribe, of which none served at the altar. 14 For it is evident that our Lord was born of Judah, of whose tribe Moses said nothing about the priesthood. 15 And it is still more evident that, along the lines of Melchi-sedec, another priest arose, 16 who was not constituted a priest according to the law of carnal command, but according to the power of eternal life. 17 For he testifies thus, "You are a Priest forever, according to the or- der of Melchi-sedec." 18 For the former order has been annulled, because of its weaknesses and advantages. 19 For the Law made nothing perfect, but it made perfect the introduction of a better hope, by which we draw near to God. 20 And though it is not without another (for these are made priests without another): 21 but this one was made with another by him who said to him, "The Lord has sworn and will not repent: you are a priest forever, ac- cording to the order of Melchi-sedec.") 22 In this way Jesus became a guarantee of a better Testament. 23 Many of them were appointed priests because they could not endure death. 24 But this man, because he endures long, has a priesthood that cannot pass from one to another. 25 Therefore he is also able perfectly to vouch for those who turn to God through him, for he still lives, to intercede for them. 26 For such a Priest has become an added val- ue, holy, harmless, undefiled, separate from sinners, and who has made a difference with the heavens: 27 Who does not need, like those priests, to offer sacrifices every day, first for his own sins and then for the peoples, for this he did once, when he offered himself. 28 For the Law makes men Priests, who have infir- mities; but the word of the other who was after the Law, makes the Son, who is conse- crated forever.

CHAPTER 8

1 Now of the things that we have said, this is the sum, that we have such a priest, who sits at the right hand of the throne of the Mai- estie in heaven, :2 And he is a minister of the Sanctuary and of that true Tabernacle which the Lord built, and not man. 3 For every high priest is destined to offer both gifts and sac- rifices; therefore it was necessary that this man also should have something to offer. 4 For he would not have been a priest if he had been on earth, since there are priests who, according to the law, offer gifts, 5 who serve in the paternal and shadow of eternal things, as Moses was warned by God when he was about to finish the Tabernacle. See, he said, that you do all things according to the pattern that was shown you on the mount. 6 But now our priest has obtained a more excellent com- mission, in that he is the mediator of a better Testament, founded on

better promises. 7 For if the first Testament had been blameless, no place should have been sought for the second. 8 In fact, rebuking them, he says, "Behold, the day will come, says the Lord, when I will make with the house of Israel and with the house of Judah a new Testament." 9 Not like the Testament that I made with their fathers, in the day that I took them by the hand to bring them out of the land of Egypt; for they have not continued to follow my Testament, and I have not regarded them, says the LORD. 10 For this is the testament that I will make with the house of Israel, after those days, says the LORD, I will put my laws in their minds, and in their hearts I will write them, and I will be their God, and they shall be my people, 11 And they shall not teach each one his neighbor and each one his brother, saying, "Know the LORD," for they shall all know me, from the least of them to the greatest of them. 12 For I will be merciful to their righteous ones, and will remember their sins and their iniquities no more. 13 In speaking a new Testament, he has abrogated the old; now that which has been blotted out and has become old is ready to disappear.

CHAPTER 9

1 Also in the First Testament there were reli- gious ordinances and a worldly sanctuary. 2 The first Tabernacle was made, where there was the candlestick, the table and the bread; this Tabernacle is called the holy places. 3 After the second Tabernacle was made, the Tabernacle which is called the holiest of all, 4 which had the censer of gold and the ark of the Testament surrounded with gold, where was the golden vessel with the manna, the rod of Aaron that was sprouted, and the tables of the Testament. 5 And beyond the ark were the glorious Cherubim, shading the Lord's seat; of these things we will not now speak partic- ularly 6 When these things were thus defined, the priests always entered the first Tabernacle and performed the service. 7 But into the sec- ond only the priest entered, once every year, not without the blood which he offered for himself and for the ignorance of the people. 8 By this the Holy Spirit meant that the way into the Most Holy had not yet been opened, while the first tabernacle was still standing, 9 which was a figure for that present time, in which gifts and sacrifices were offered that could not make holy, as far as conscience was con- cerned, the one who performed the service, 10 which were based only on food and drink, various washings and carnal rites, which had been inhibited until the time of the reforma- tion. 11 But Christ, having come as high priest of the good things to come, with a greater and more perfect tabernacle, not made with hands, that is, not of this building, 12 nor with the blood of goats and calves, but with his own blood he entered the holy place once and obtained eternal redemption. 13 For if the blood of bullets and of goats and the ashes of a heifer, sprinkling those who are vnclean, sanctifies as the cleansing of the flesh, 14 how much more will the blood of Christ, who through the eternal Spirit offered himself blamelessly to God, cleanse your conscience from dead works, to serve the living God? 15 And for this reason he is the mediator of the New Testament, so that through death for the redemption of the transgressions of the for- mer Testament, those who are called may re- ceive the promise of the eternal inheritance. 16 For where there is a Testament, there must be the death of him who made the Testament. 17 For the Testament is confirmed when men are dead, for it is not yet of value until the one who made it is dead. 18 Therefore even the first Testament was not made without blood. 19 For when

Moses had told the people every precept, according to the Law, he took the blood of calves and goats, with water, purple wool and isoppo, and sprinkled the book and all the people, 20 saying, "This is the blood of the Testament that God has established for you." 21 He also sprinkled the tabernacle and all the utensils of the ministry with blood. 22 Almost all things were cleansed by the Law with blood, and without the sprinkling of blood there is no remission. 23 It was there- fore necessary that the similitudes of eternal things should be cleansed with such things; but eternal things are cleansed with better sacrifices than these. 24 For Christ did not en- ter those holy places made with hands, which are simulacra of the true sanctuary, but en- tered into the sanctuary itself, to appear now before God, 25 not that he offered himself of- ten, as the priest entered the holy place every year with other blood, 26 (for then he would have had to suffer often from the foundation of the world), but now, at the end of the world, he has manifested himself, once only, to do away with sin by the sacrifice of himself. 27 And since it is appointed for men to die once, after that comes judgment: 28 so Christ was offered once to take away the sins of many, and for those who seek him, he will appear a second time sinless for salvation.

CHAPTER 10

1 For the Law, being the shadow of good things to come, and not the very image of things, certainly cannot by those sacrifices, which they offer from year to year continual- ly, sanctify those who partake of them. 2 For would they not then have ceased to be offered, because the offerers, once purified, would no longer be conscious of sins? 3 But in those sacrifices there is every year a remembrance of sins. 4 For it is impossible for the blood of bullets and goats to take away sins. 5 That is why, when he came into the world, he said, "You did not want sacrifices and offerings, but you destined a body for me." 6 You did not want sacrifices and offerings for sin. 7 Then I said, "Behold, I come (at the beginning of the book it is written of me) to do your will, O God." 8 When he said, "Sacrifices and burnt offerings and sinful sacrifices you did not want them and did not like them (which are offered by the Law)." 9 Then he said, "Behold, I come to do your will, O God, which takes away the former to establish the latter." 10 By whose will we are sanctified, that is, by the offering of the body of Jesus Christ once made. 11 Every priest engages in a ministry every day and of- ten offers a type of offense that can never take away sins: 12 But this man, having offered a sacrifice for sins, sits forever at the right hand of God, 13 and henceforth he abides until his enemies have become his feet. 14 For by one offering he has consecrated forever those who are sanctified. 15 For the Holy Spirit also bears witness to this, having said before, 16 This is the testament I will make to them after those days, says the Lord: I will put my laws in their hearts and write them in their minds. 17 I will remember their sins and their iniquities no more. 18 Now where there is remission of these things, A is no more offering for sin. 19 Seeing therefore, brethren, that through the blood of Iesus we may be bold to enter the holy place, 20 by the new and beautiful way which he has prepared for us, through the rampart, that is, his flesh: 21 and since we have a priest, who is outside the house of God, 22 we prepare ourselves with a sincere heart in the certainty of faith, our hearts be- ing pure in conscience, 23 and washed in our bodies with pure water, let us hold fast the profession of our hope, without wavering (for he is faithful who

promised). 24 And let us consider one another, to promote love and good works, 25 not forsaking the fellowship we have with one another, as some do; but ex- horting one another, all the more as you see the day approaching. 26 For if we sin willfully after we have received and acknowledged the truth, there remains no more sacrifice for sins, 27 But a fearful waiting for judgment and a violent fire that will destroy adulterers. 28 Whoever despises the Law of Moses shall die without mercy under two or three wit- nesses: 29 Of what more severe punishment do you think worthy of him who treacherously tramples underfoot the Son of God, and con- siders the blood of the Testament with which he was sanctified a vain thing, and mocks the Spirit of grace? 30 For we know him who said, "Vengeance belongs to me; I will reward it, says the Lord." And again, "The LORD will judge his people." 31 It is a fearful thing to fall into the hands of a lying God. 32 Now remem- ber the days that passed, in which, after you received the light, you endured a great strug- gle in afflictions, 33 partly while you were made the object of observation because of re- proaches and afflictions, and partly while you became the companions of those who were thus tossed to and fro. 34 For you have grieved with me for my bonds and suffered with me for the loss of your possessions, knowing in yourselves that you have in inheritance a bet- ter and lasting substance. 35 Therefore do not forsake your confidence, which has a great reward. 36 For you need patience, that after you have done the will of God you may receive the promise. 37 For very little is yet to come, and he who will come, will come and will not delay. 38 Now the righteous will live by faith; but if anyone withdraws, my soul will have no pleasure in him. 39 But we are not those who retreat to perdition, but we follow faith for the preservation of the soul.

CHAPTER 11

1 Faith is the basis of things hoped for and the certainty of things not seen. 2 Indeed, through it our elders received good news. 3 By faith we understand that the world was created by the word of God, so that the things we see are not made of things that have ap- peared. 4 By faith Abel offered to God a great- er sacrifice than Cain, whereby he obtained the testimony that he was righteous, God tes- tifying to his gifts; by the same faith he also, though dead, speaks. 5 By faith Enoch was translated, that he might not see death; and he was not found, because God had translat- ed him; for before he was translated, it was said that it pleased God. 6 But without faith it is impossible to please him, for those who turn to God must know that God is and that he rewards those who seek him. 7 By faith Noe, having been warned by God of things not yet seen, moved with reverence, prepar- ing the ark for the slaying of his dwelling place; by which ark he condemned the world and was made heir of righteousness, which is by faith. 8 By faith Abraham, when he was called, obeyed God to go to a place that he would later receive as an inheritance; and he departed, not knowing where he was going. 9 By faith he remained in the land of prom- ise, as in a foreign country, as one dwelling in tents with Isaac and Jacob, heirs with him of the same promise. 10 For he sought a city that had a foundation, whose builder and maker is God. 11 Sarah also, by faith, received strength to conceive offspring, and was given a son when she was past her years, because she had believed in the faithfulness of him whom she had promised. 12 Therefore from one, though dead, were born as many sons as the stars of heaven and as the land of the sea, which

is innumerable. 13 All these died in faith and did not receive the promises, but saw them afar off and blessed them and received them with gratitude and confessed that they were strangers and pilgrims on earth. 14 For those who say these things clearly declare that they see a country. 15 And if they had been mindful of that county, from which they had gone out, they would have been pleased to return. 16 But now they desire a better thing, namely, a city, and for this reason God is not ashamed to be called their God, for he has prepared for them a city. 17 By faith Abraham offered Isaac when he was tested, and he who had received the promises offered his only begotten son. 18 (to whom it was said, "In Isaac shall thy seed be called."). 19 For he believed that God was able to raise him from the dead, and therefore he received him in like manner. 20 By faith Isaac blessed Jacob and Esau, concerning things to come. 21 By faith Iacob, dying, blessed the two sons of Ioseph and, leaning on his staff, worshipped God. 22 By faith Ioseph, when he died, made mention of the departure of the sons of Israel and set his bones in order. 23 By faith Moses, when he was delivered, was hidden for three months from his parents, because they knew that he was a true son and did not fear the king's orders. 24 By faith Moses, when he came of age, refused to be called the son of Pharaoh's daughter, 25 and chose rather to suffer aduersity with God's people and to indulge in the pleasures of sin for a time, 26 believing that the reproach of Christ was richer than the treasures of Egypt, because he had respect for the reward of the prize. 27 By faith he departed from Egypt and did not fear the king's wounds, for he endured as one who knows that he is harmless. 28 By faith he ordered the passage and the outpour- ing of blood, lest he who had destroyed the firstborn should touch them. 29 By faith they passed through the Red Sea as through a dry land; when the Egyptians had tried to do so, they were swallowed up. 30 By faith the walls of Jericho fell down after they had been tra- versed for several days. 31 By faith the harlot Rahab did not perish with those who did not obey, when she received the spies in peace. 32 And what more shall I say, for the time would be too short to tell of Gideon, Barac, Sampson, Jephthah, Dauid, Samuel, and the Prophets: 33 who by faith subdued kingdoms, worked righteousness, kept promises, stopped the mouths of lions, 34 they quenched the vio- lence of fire, they escaped the blade of the sword, they were made strong by weakness, they became valiant in battle, they put the armies of foreigners to flight. 35 Women re- ceived their resurrected dead; others were tormented and did not want to be set free in order to receive a better resurrection. 36 Still others were tried with taunts and scourging, and still more with binding and imprison- ment. 37 They were stoned, they were torn, they were tempted, they were killed with the sword, they wandered up and down in sheep- skins and in goatskins, being destitute, af- flicted and tormented: 38 Of whom the world was not worthy; they wandered in deserts, on mountains, in dens and caves of the earth. 39 And all these, by faith, obeyed the good report, but they did not receive the promise, 40 God had provided a better thing for them, that they might not be made perfect without it.

CHAPTER 12

1 Therefore, we also, seeing that we are sur- rounded by such a great cloud of witnesses, let us cast off everything that oppresses us and the sin that is so upon us; let us run with pa- tience the race that is set before us, 2 looking to

Jesus, the author and perfecter of our faith, who, for the love set before him, endured the cross, despised the shame, and sits at the right hand of the throne of God. 3 Therefore consider him who endured such talk against sinners, lest you become weary and weaken your minds. 4 You have not yet endured the blood, struggling against sin. 5 You have for- gotten the consolation that speaks to you as to children, "My son, do not despise the chas- tening of the Lord, and do not be discouraged when you are rebuked by him." 6 For the Lord chastens those who desire it, and scourges every son whom he receives: 7 If you endure chastisement, God offers you himself as to sons; for what is the son whom the father does not chasten? 8 If therefore you are with- out correction, in which we are all partakers, you are bastards and not sons. 9 Moreover, we had the fathers of our bodies who corrected us and gave them confidence; should we not rather be subject to the father of spirits, that we may live? 10 For they chastened for a few days according to their pleasure, but he chas- tens for our good, that we may be partakers of his holiness. 11 Now no chastisement for the moment seems to be pleasant, but pain- ful; but afterward, it brings the quiet fruit of righteousness to those who are exercised in this way. 12 Lift up therefore your hands that hang down and your weak knees, 13 And make straight steps for your feet, lest the one who is stuck be moved from the way, but rather be healed.14 Follow peace with all men and holiness, without which no one can see the Lord. 15 Take heed that no one depart from the grace of God; let there arise no roots of bitterness to trouble you, lest many defile themselves. 16 Let there be no fornicators or profaners like Esau, who for a portion of meat gave up his birthright. 17 For you know that even afterward, when he wanted to inher- it the blessing, he was rejected, because he found no room for repentance, though he had sought the blessing with his ears.18 For you have not come to the mountain that can be touched, nor to burning fire, nor to darkness and storms, 19 nor at the sound of a trum- pet, nor at the sound of words, that those who heard them excused themselves so that the word was no longer spoken to them, 20 for they were not able to bear what had been commanded, "If a beast touches the moun- tain, it must be stoned or pierced with a dart." 21 And so terrible was the sight that appeared, that Moses said, "I am afraid and trembling.") 22 But you have come to Mount Zion, to the city of the living God, the heavenly Jerusalem, and to the company of countless angels, 23 and to the assembly and congregation of the firstborn, which are written in heaven, and to God, the judge of all, and to the spirits of righteous and perfect men, 24 and to Jesus, the Mediator of the New Testament, and to the blood of sprinkling, which speaks better than that of Abel. 25 See that you do not de- spise him who speaks; for if those who reject- ed him who spoke on earth did not escape, all the more will we not escape if we turn away from him who speaks from the LORD. 26 Who shook the earth and now has declared, "Once more I will shake, not only the earth, but also Eauen." 27 This word, "once more," indicates the removal of the things that have been shaken, as of things made with hands, so that the things that have not been shaken remain. 28 Therefore, since we receive a king- dom that cannot be shaken, we want to have the grace to serve God in a way that pleases him with care and fear. 29 For our God is a consuming fire.

CHAPTER 13

1 Continue to have brotherly love. 2 Do not forget to entertain strangers, for thus some have welcomed angels into their homes. 3 Re- member those who are bound, as if you were bound to them; and those who are in afflic- tion, as if you also were afflicted in body. 4 Marriage is honorable among all, and the bed undefiled; but whoremongers and adulterers God will judge them. 5 Let your cohabitation be without confusion, and be content with the things that you have, for he has said, 6 "I will not forsake you nor leave you." 7 That we may boldly say, "The Lord is my help, and I will not fear what man can do to me." 8 Remem- ber those who went before you and revealed the word of God to you; follow their faith, considering what was the purpose of their meeting. Jesus Christ, yesterday and today, is also forever. 9 Do not be mocked by different and strange doctrines, for it is good for the heart to be established by grace and not by talk, which has not benefited those who have dealt with it. 10 We have an altar, on which they have no right to eat, serving in the tab- ernacle. 11 For the bodies of those beastmen whose blood is brought into the holy place by the high priest for sin, are burned without the campeus. 12 Therefore Jesus also, to sanctify the people with his blood, suffered outside the gate. 13 Let us therefore go to him out- side the campeus, bearing his reproach. 14 For here we do not have a city that continues, but we see one that is to come. 15 Therefore through him always offer to God the sacrifice of prayer, that is, the fruit of lips that confess his name. 16 Do not forget to do good and to distribute, for God is pleased with such sacri- fices. 17 Obey those who watch over you and submit yourselves, for they watch over your souls as those who must give an account, that they may do it with joy and not with sorrow, for this is profitable for you. 18 Pray for you, that we may be assured of a good conscience in all things, desiring to live honestly. 19 And I desire that you do so, more heartily, that I may be restored to you more quickly. 20 May the God of peace who raised from the dead our Lord Jesus, the great shepherd of the sheep, by the blood of the eternal Courage, 21 make you perfect in every good work, to do his will, working in you what is pleasing in his sight, through Jesus Christ, to whom be praise for- ever, Amen. 22 I beseech you also, brethren, to suffer the words of exhortation, for I have written to you in a few words. 23 Know that our brother Timothy has been disappointed, with whom (if he comes soon) I will see you. 24 Greet all who see you and all the saints. The Italians also greet you. 25 Grace be with you all, amen.

JAMES

CHAPTER 1

1 The servant of God and the Lord Jesus Christ greets the two tribes that are scattered abroad. 2 My brethren, consider it very im- portant when you fall into different temp- tations, 3 knowing that the testing of your faith breeds patience, 4 and let patience do its perfect work, that you may be perfect and complete, lacking nothing. 5 If any of you lack wisdom, let him ask of God, who grants to all men liberally and reproaches no one, and it will be granted to him. 6 But let him ask in faith and not wriggle, for he who wriggles is like a wave of the sea, which is carried away by the wind. 7 Nor let him who thinks he will receive anything from the LORD. 8 A dou- ble-minded man is unstable in all his actions. 9 Let the brother of low degree acknowledge himself in the one who has been exalted: 10 He who is rich is brought low, for, like the flower of the weed, he fades

away. 11 For as, when the sun rises with heat, the weed with- ers, its flower falls off, and its beautiful form perishes, so also the rich man shall wither in all his expectations. 12 Blessed is the man who endures the trial, for when he is tried he will receive the crown of life, which the LORD has promised to those who love him. 13 Let no one, when he is tempted, say, "I am tempted of God," for God cannot be tempted by force and tempts no one. 14 But every man is tempted when he is carried away by his own concupiscence and is tempted. 15 Then, when concupiscence has conceived, it brings with it sin, and sin, when it is finished, brings

with it death. 16 Do not err, my brethren. 17 Every good gift and every perfect gift comes from without and descends from the Father of lights, with whom there is no variableness nor shadow of change. 18 By his will he begat us with the web of truth, that we might be as the first fruits of his creatures. 19 Therefore, my brethren, let each one be quick in hear- ing, slow in speaking, and slow in wrath. 20 For the wrath of man does not fulfill the righteousness of God. 21 Therefore lay aside all filthiness and all superfluity of malice and receive with meekness the word that is grav- en in you, which is able to save your souls. 22 And be doers of the word and not solitary hearers, deceiving yourselves. 23 For if one hears the word and does not do it, he is like a man who sees his natural face in a mirror. 24 For after considering himself, he goes his own way and immediately forgets what kind of person he was. 25 But he who looks into the perfect Lawe of libertie and continues there, not being a forgetful hearer but a worker of the work, will be blessed in his destiny. 26 If anyone among you seems religious and does not hold his tongue, but deceives his heart, this religion is vain. 27 Pure and vndefiled re- ligion before God, that is, the Father, is this: to visit the paternal family and the girls in their condition and to keep away from the world.

CHAPTER 2

1 My brethren, do not have the faith of our glorious Lord Jesus Christ with respect to people. 2 For if there comes into your compa- ny a man with a gold ring and in fine clothing, and there comes also a poor man in vile cloth- ing, 3 you have respect for him who wears the good clothing, and you say to him, "Sit here in a good place," and you say to the poor man, "Stand there or sit here under my feet." :4 Are you not part of yourselves, and have you be- come judges of evil thoughts? 5 Listen, my dear brethren: has not God chosen the poor of this world to be rich in faith and heirs of the kingdom he has promised to those who love him? 6 But you have despised the poor. Do not the rich oppress you with tyranny and drag you before judgment? 7 Do they not blaspheme the worthy Name by which you were called? 8 But if you fulfill the Royal Law according to the Scripture, which says, "You shall love your neighbor as yourself," you do well. 9 But if you watch people, you commit sin and are rebuked by the Law as transgres- sors. 10 For he who keeps the whole Law and yet sins in one point is guilty of the whole. 11 For he who says, Do not commit adultery, also says: Thou shalt not kill. Now even if you do not commit adultery, if you kill, you are a transgressor of the Law. 12 Thus you speak and thus you do, as those who will be judged by the Law of Liberty. 13 For he will be con- demned who does not show mercy, and mer- cy is opposed to condemnation. 14 What does it mean, my brethren, that

a man says he has faith when he has no works? Can this faith save him? 15 For if a brother or sister is na- ked and without daily food, 16 and one of you says to them, "Go away in peace; make war on yourselves and fill your bellies, without giving them the things necessary for the body, what good can it do? 17 So also faith, if it has no is- sue, is dead in itself. 18 But someone might say, "You have faith and I have labors; give me your faith from your labors and I will give you my faith from my labors." 19 You believe that there is one God; you do well; even the deuiles believe it and tremble. 20 But do you understand, O vague man, that faith that is without works is dead? 21 Was not Abraham, our father, justified through works, when he offered Isaac his son on the altar? 22 Do you not see that faith worked through his works? And through works faith was made perfect. 23 Thus was fulfilled the Scripture that says, "Abraham believed God and was imputed to him as righteousness; and he was called the friend of God." 24 So you see how man is justified by works and not by faith alone. 25 Likewise was not Rahab, the harlot, justified by works, when she received the messengers and sent them by another way? 26 For just as the body without the spirit is dead, so also faith without works is dead.

CHAPTER 3

1 My brethren, do not be many teachers, knowing that we will receive greater condem- nation. 2 For in many things we all sin. If one does not sin in speech, he is a perfect man and able to bridle the whole body. 3 Behold, we put bites in the mouths of horses, that they may obey, and turn their whole bodies. 4 Observe also the ships, which, though they are so large and moved by raging winds, are turned with a very small rudder, where the sailor wants to go. 5 So also the tongue is a small member, and boasts of great things; be- hold, how it kindles a great fire a small fire. 6 The tongue is a fire, yea, a world of wick- edness; the tongue is so inserted among our members, that it defiles the whole body and sets on fire the course of nature, and is set on fire by hell. 7 For all the nature of the beasts, and of the birds, and of the reptiles, and of the things of the sea, is tamed, and has been tamed by the nature of man. 8 But the tongue cannot be tamed. It is a vituperative tongue, full of deadly poisons. 9 With this we bless God and the Father, and with this we curse men, who are made in the likeness of God. 10 Out of one mouth come blessing and cursing; my brethren, these things should not be so. 11 Does a fountain put out sweet water and bit- ter water in the same place? 12 Can a fig tree, my brethren, produce olives, or a vine figs? So no fountain can produce both salt water and sweet water. 13 Whoever is among you a wise man and endowed with wisdom, let him show with a good combination his works in the meekness of wisdom. 14 But if there is bitterness and strife in your hearts, do not scruple and do not be liars in regard to the truth. 15 This wisdom does not descend from above, but is earthly, sensual and deformed. 16 For where there is enmity and strife, there is sedition and all manner of unlawful works. 17 But the wisdom that comes from outside is first of all pure, then peaceable, mild, easy to deal with, full of mercy and good fruit, with- out judgment and without hypocrisy. 18 The fruit of justice is sown in peace, by those who make peace.

CHAPTER 4

1 Whence come the wars and contentions among you? Are not your pleasures fighting in your members? 2 You covet and do not have; you seek and desire inordinately and cannot obtain; you fight and make war and obtain nothing, because you do not ask. 3 You ask and do not receive, because you ask for amenities, that you may spend them in your pleasures. 4 Do not you adulterers and adul- teresses know that the friendship of the world is the friendship of God? Whoever therefore wants to be a friend of the world makes him- self an enemy of God. 5 Do you think that the Scripture says in vaticinium, "The spirit that dwells in the world, lusts after the enuie"? 6 But Scripture offers more grace, and there- fore it says, "God resists the proud and gives grace to the humble." 7 Submit yourselves to God; resist unrighteousness, and he will flee from you. 8 Attract God's attention, and he will draw attention to you. Clasp your hands, O sinners, and purify your hearts, O dou- ble-minded. 9 Suffer afflictions, grieve and weep; turn your laughter into mourning and your joy into melancholy. 10 Lay down your self before the LORD, and he will lift you up. 11 Do not speak evil of one another, brothers. He who speaks evil of his brother or he who condemns his brother, speaks evil of the Law and condemns the Law; and if you condemn the Law, you are not an observer of the Law, but a judge. 12 There is only one Lawgiver, who is able to say and to destroy. Who are you that you judge another man? 13 Go away, you who say, "Today or tomorrow we will go to such a city and stay there for a year, and then we will go and sell and make money." 14 (yet you cannot say what will happen in the future. For what is your life? It is a vapor that appears for a short time and then vanishes). 15 For you should say, "If the Lord wills, and if it pleases us, we will do this or that." 16 But now you bask in your boasting: all such boast- ing is useless. 17 Therefore he who knows how to do right and does not do it, to him it is sin.

CHAPTER 5

1 Go now, you rich, weep and howl for your miseries that will befall you. 2 Your riches are corrupted, and your garments are eaten by moths. 3 Your gold and your silver have become corrupt, and their rust shall be a wit- ness against you and shall devour your flesh as if it were fire. You have accumulated trea- sure for the last days. 4 Behold, the wages of you laborers who have reaped your fields (which is that of you held back by fraud) cry out, and the cries of those who have reaped have entered the ears of the LORD of hosts. 5 You have given yourselves up to the pleasures of the land and to the lusts. You have fed your hearts as on a day of slaughter. 6 You have condemned and killed the righteous, and he has not resisted you. 7 Therefore be patient, brethren, until the coming of the Lord. Be- hold, the cultivator seeks the precious fruits of the earth and has long patience with them, until he receives the first and the last ray. 8 Therefore you also be patient and calm your hearts, for the coming of the Lord is drawing near. 9 Do not grudge one another, brethren, lest you be condemned; behold, the judge stands before the judge. 10 Take, my brethren, the prophets as an example of suffering and longsuffering, who spoke in the name of the Lord. 11 We count blessed those who endure. You have heard of Iob's patience and have known what end the Lord has made of it. For the Lord is very merciful and gracious. 12 But before all things, my brethren, do not swear by heaven, or by earth, or by anything else; but let your yes be yes, and your no be no, lest you fall into condemnation. 13 Is there anyone among you who is afflicted? Let him pray. Is there anyone who is happy? Let him sing. 14 Is there anyone among you who is sick? Let him call the elders of the Church, and let them pray for him and assist him with prayer in the name of the Lord. 15 The prayer of faith will save the sick person, and the Lord will raise him up; and if he has committed sins, they will be forgiven him. 16 Acknowledge your faults to one another, and pray for one anoth- er, that you may be healed; for the prayer of a righteous man profiteth much, if it be fer- vent. 17 Elijah was a man subject to the same passions as we are, and he prayed earnestly that it might not rain, and it did not rain on the earth for three years and six months. 18 Then he prayed again, and the sky brightened and the earth bore fruit. 19 Brothers, if any of you have erred from the truth and anyone has persuaded him, 20 know that he who has persuaded the sinner not to go astray from his way will save a soul from death and hide a multitude of sins.

I PETER

CHAPTER 1

1 Peter, apostle of Christ, to the foreigners dwelling here and there in Pontus, Galatia, Cappadocia, Asia, and Bithynia, 2 elect ac- cording to the foreknowledge of God the Father by the sanctification of the Spirit, through obedience and sprinkling of the blood of Jesus Christ: grace and peace be mul- tiplied to you. 3 Blessed be God, that is, the Father of our Lord Jesus Christ, who accord- ing to his superabundant mercy has caused a joyful hope to be revived in us through the resurrection of Jesus Christ from the dead, 4 for an immortal and vndefiled inheritance, which does not wither, preserved for the future, 5 who are kept by the power of God through faith unto salvation, which is pre- pared to be displayed in the last times. 6 In this way, though for a time (if necessary), you are waiting, through multiple temptations, 7 so that the proof of your faith, which is far more precious than gold that perishes (even if it is tried by fire), may be revealed to your praise, honor and glory at the appearing of Jesus Christ: 8 whom you have never seen, yet you love him, and in whom now, though you do not see him, you rejoice and be glad with extraordinary and glorious joy, 9 receiv- ing the end of your faith, that is, the salvation of your souls. 10 Of this salvation you have inquired and searched the Prophets, who prophesied of the grace that was to come to you, 11 seeking when or at what time the Spirit who formerly testified of Christ, who was in them, would declare the sufferings that were to come to Christ and the glory that was to follow. 12 They were entrusted with the task of proclaiming, not to themselves, but to themselves, the things which are now being shown to you by those who preached the gos- pel to you, through the Holy Spirit sent from Heauen, and which the angels desire to see. 13 Therefore, strengthen your minds, be sober, and trust perfectly in the grace that has been brought to you, in the revival of Jesus Christ, 14 as obedient children, not conforming your- selves to the lusts of your ignorance: 15 but as he who called you is holy, so be holy in every way of living together; 16 for it is written, "Be ye holy, for I am holy." 17 And if you call Father the one who, without respect for the person, judges according to each one's desires, spend the time of your stay here in fear, 18 knowing that you were not redeemed with corruptible things, such as silver and coin, by your vain conuration, received from the traditions of the fathers, 19 but with the precious blood of Christ, as of a lamb vndefiled and without blemish. 20

Which was established before the foundation of the world, but was declared in the last times for your sakes, 21 who through him you trusted in God, who raised him from the dead, and gave him glory, that your faith and hope might be in God, 22 having puri- fied your souls in obedience to the truth by the spirit, to love brotherly without striving, loving one another with a pure and fervent heart, 23 having been begotten again, not of mortal seed but immortal, by the work of God, who lives and endures forever. 24 For all flesh is like the fat one, and all the glory of man is like the flower of the fat one. The fat one withers and the flower falls. 25 But the word of the Lord endures forever; and this is the word that is preached among you.

CHAPTER 2

1 Therefore, laying aside all malice, all de- ceit, all dissimulation, all enuie and all false speech, 2 like newborn children, desire the sincere milk of the earth, that you may grow, 3 for you have tasted that the Lord is boun- tiful. 4 To those who come as to a chewing stone not accepted by men, but chosen by God and precious, 5 you also, like fine stones, have become a spiritual house, a holy priest- hood to offer spiritual sacrifices acceptable to God through Jesus Christ. 6 Therefore also the Scripture says, "Behold, I have set in Zion a cornerstone, elect and precious, and he who sits therein shall not be shamed." 7 To you, therefore, who are faithful, it is precious; but to the disobedient, the stone which the build- ers disowned has become the head of the corner, 8 a stone of stumbling and a stone of offense, for those who stumble in the way, be- ing disobedient, for which they were already appointed. 9 But you are a chosen generation, a royal priesthood, a holy nation, a freed peo- ple, that you may show forth the virtues of him who called you out of darkness into his marvelous light, 10 who formerly were not a people, but now are the people of God; who formerly were not under mercy, but now have obtained mercy. 11 Please, as strangers and pilgrims, refrain from carnal lusts, which fight against the soul, 12 and make yourselves known honestly to the Gentiles, so that those who speak ill of you as people who do good may glorify God on the day of visitation be- cause of your good works, which they will see. 13 Therefore submit yourselves to every order of man for the Lord's sake, whether to the king or to the ruler, 14 or toward the rulers, as toward those who are sent by him, to punish the wicked and praise those who act well. 15 For this is the will of God, that by good deeds you should put to silence the ignorance of fools, 16 as free, and not as if you had freedom as a cloak of malice, but as servants of God. 17 Honor all men, love fellowship, fear God, honor the King. 18 Servants, be submissive to your masters with all fear, not only to the good and courteous, but also to the adverse. 19 For this is more than worthy, if a man out of conscience toward God endures pain, suf- fering unjustly. 20 For what praise is there if, when you are stricken for your faults, you take them with serenity? But if, when you do well, you suffer wrong and take it with seren- ity, this is pleasing to God. 21 To this you are called, for Christ also suffered for you, leaving you an example so that you may follow in his steps. 22 Who committed no sin and there was no malice in his mouth. 23 Who, when he was put to trouble, did not rebel; when he suffered, he did not threaten, but trusted in him who judges righteously. 24 Who, in Him- self, bore our sins in His body on the tree, that we, dead to sin, might live in righteousness. 25 For you were like sheep that went astray, but now you have returned to the keeper and bishop of your souls.

CHAPTER 3

1 Likewise let the wives be submissive to their husbands, so that those who do not obey the word may be conquered without the word by the cohabitation of their wives, 2 While they observe your pure cohabitation, but with fear. 3 Whose apparel shall not be the outward ap- parel, with shoulders covered with swill and gold, nor that which you wear: 4 But let it be the hidden man of the heart, which consists in the incorruption of a meek and quiet spirit, which is before God a very great thing. 5 For in the past holy women who trusted in God grew weary and were subject to their hus- bands. 6 As Sarah obeyed Abraham and called him lord, you are the daughters of those who do well and are not afraid of any terror. 7 Likewise, you husbands, live with them as men of science, giving honor to the woman as to the weaker member, and as those who are heirs together of the grace of life, so that your prayers may not be interrupted. 8 Finally, be all of one mind: suffer one another, look upon one another as brothers, be merciful, be cour- teous, 9 render not euil for euill, nor reproach for reproach, but on the contrary bless, know- ing that you were called for this purpose, to be heirs of blessing. 10 For if one desires life and to see happy days, let him refrain from speaking evil and from speaking evil. 11 Let him abstain from wickedness and do good; let him seek peace and follow it. 12 For the eyes of the LORD are on the righteous and his ears are open to their prayers, while the face of the LORD is against those who do evil. 13 Who will persecute you if you follow the good? 14 Nevertheless, you are blessed if you suffer for righteousness' sake. Do not fear them, and do not be troubled. 15 But sanctify the Lord God in your hearts and always be ready to answer anyone who asks you for a reason for the hope that is in you, with meekness and respect, 16 having a good conscience, so that when peo- ple speak evil of you as people who do evil, let those who slander your good fellowship in Christ be ashamed. 17 For it is better (if this is God's will) that you suffer for good deeds than for bad deeds. 18 For Christ also suffered once for sins, the righteous for the vniust, to bring to God, and was put to death as to the flesh, but was made alive by the spirit. 19 There- fore he went and preached to the spirits who were in prison. 20 Who, in his time, had been disobedient, when once the long-suffering of God went on in the days of Noe, while the ark was being prepared, in which few, that is, eight souls, were immersed in the water. 21 The baptism there is now, responding to that figure, (which is not a removal of the filthi- ness of the flesh, but a demonstration of trust that a good conscience makes to God) is salt- ed also by the resurrection of Jesus Christ, 22 who is at the right hand of God, gone to heav- en, to whom the angels, powers and might are subject.

CHAPTER 4

1 Since therefore Christ suffered by contrast in the flesh, prepare yourselves also with the same mind, namely, that he who suffered in the flesh has ceased from sin, 2 that he hence- forth may live (for as long as he remains in the flesh) not according to the desires of men, but according to the will of God. 3 For it is suffi- cient that we have spent the past time of your life according to the concupiscence of the

Gentiles, walking in lusts, lusts, drunkenness, gluttony, drinking, and abominable idola- tries. 4 And it seems strange to them that you do not run with them to the same level of dis- order; therefore they speak evil of you, 5 And this will give account to those who are ready to judge quickly and to die. 6 For for this pur- pose the gospel was also preached to the dead, that they might be condemned according to men in the flesh, but might live according to God in the spirit. 7 Now the end of all things is near. Therefore be sober and watch in prayer. 8 But about all things have fervent calmness in your midst, for calmness will be the cause of the multitude of sins. 9 Be severe toward one another, without rancor. 10 Let each one, as he has received the gift, distribute it to an- other, as good dispensers of God's manifold grace. 11 If anyone speaks, let him speak as the word of God. If anyone ministers, let him do so with the ability God gives him, that God may be glorified in all things through Jesus Christ, to whom go the prayer and dominion for all and forever, Amen. 12 Do not think that the trial that is going on among you to test you is strange, as if some strange thing had happened to you: 13 but be glad, inasmuch as you are partakers of Christ's afflictions, that when his glory appears, you may rejoice and be glad. 14 If ye be reviled for Christ's name's sake, blessed are ye, for upon you rests the spirit of glory and of God, which on his part is disputed, but on your part is glorified. 15 But let none of you suffer as a murderer, or as a thief, or as an evildoer, or as a trafficker in other human affairs. 16 But if anyone suf- fers as a Christian, let him not be ashamed, but let him glorify God in this way. 17 For the time has come when judgment must begin from the house of God. If it begins from here, what will be the end of those who do not obey the gospel of God? 18 And if the righteous are hardly ever judged, where will the vngodium and the sinner appear? 19 Therefore, let those who suffer according to God's will entrust their souls to him in goodness, as to a faithful creator.

CHAPTER 5

1 Elders who are among you, I pray you, I too am an elder, a witness of Christ's sufferings and a partaker of the glory to come, 2 feed the flock of God that depends on you, dealing with it not by compulsion, but willingly; not for profit, but with a ready mind: 3 not as if you were lords of God's inheritance, but to be an example to the flock. 4 And when the chief of the shepherds shall appear, ye shall receive a crown of incorruptible glory. 5 You also, young men, submit yourselves to the el- ders, and submit your bodies, one to another, and be guided inwardly by a humble mind, for God resists the proud and gives grace to the humble. 6 Humble yourselves therefore under the mighty hand of God, that he may exalt you in his time. 7 Entrust all your con- cerns to him, for he cares for you. 8 Be sober and watch, for your adversary, the devil, like a roaring lyre, prowls around seeking whom he will strike: 9 And stand firm in the faith, knowing that the same afflictions are fulfilled in your brethren that are in the world. 10 And may the God of all grace, whom he has called to his eternal glory through Christ Iesus, af- ter you have suffered a little, make you per- fect, and confirm you, and strengthen you. 11 To him be glory and dominion forever, amen. 12 From Syluanus, a faithful brother to you, as I suppose, I wrote briefly, exhorting and testifying how this is the true grace of God, in which you are. 13 The Church that is in Baby- lon, elected together with you, greets you and Mark, my son. 14 Greet one another with the kiss of joy. Peace be with you all who are in Christ Iesus, amen.

II PETER

CHAPTER 1

1 Simon Peter, servant and apostle of Jesus Christ, to you who have obtained precious faith like yours for the righteousness of our God and Savior Jesus Christ: 2 Grace and peace be multiplied to you, through the ac- knowledgment of God and Jesus our Lord, 3 as his divine power has granted to you all things that lead to life and godliness, through the ac- knowledgment of him who called you to glo- ry and perfection. 4 Therefore very great and precious promises have been made to you, that you may be partakers of the divine nature, fleeing the corruption that is in the world be- cause of concupiscence.5 Therefore, make ev- ery effort to achieve the goal; strengthen your faith, and with faith, knowledge: 6 and with knowledge, temperance; and with temper- ance, patience; and with patience, godly lines: 7 and with godliness, brotherly friendship; and with brotherly friendship, joy. 8 For if these things are among you and abound, they will cause you to be neither idle nor unfruit- ful in acknowledging our Lord Jesus Christ: 9 For he who does not have these things is blind, and does not see far, and has forgotten that he has been cleansed from his old sins. 10 Wherefore, brethren, work to make your calling and election sure; for if ye do these things, ye shall never fall. 11 For by this means you will be ministered an abundant entrance into the eternal kingdom of our Lord and Sav- ior Jesus Christ. 12 Therefore I will not neglect to remind you always of these things, even though you have knowledge of them and are established in the present truth. 13 For I deem it fitting, as long as I remain in this tent, to stimulate you by reminding you, 14 for I know that the time has come to lay down this tab- ernacle of mine, as our Lord Jesus Christ has shown me. 15 For this reason, I want you al- ways to remember these things even after my departure. 16 For we did not follow deceitful fables when we revealed to you the power and coming of our Lord Jesus Christ, but we saw with our own eyes his majesty: 17 For he re- ceived from God the Father honor and glory, when the word came to him from that exalted glory, "This is my beautiful Son, in whom I am well pleased." 18 This word we heard when it came from Heauen, standing with him on the Holy Mountain. 19 We also have a very sure word from the Prophets, to which you do well to pay attention, as to a light shining in a dark place, until the day dawns and the day star rises in your hearts. 20 So that you may know first of all that no prophecy of Scripture is of privileged interpretation. 21 For prophecies did not happen anciently by the will of man, but holy men of God spoke as they were led by the Holy Spirit.

CHAPTER 2

1 There were also false prophets among the people, just as there will be false teachers among you, who, in the first place, will in- troduce harmful heresies, denying the Lord who bought them, and will procure quick damnation for themselves. 2 And many will follow their destructions, by which the way of truth will always be questioned, 3 And with false words they will make of you a com- modity, whose condemnation has not ceased and whose destruction has not diminished. 4 For if God did not spare the angels

who had sinned, but cast them into hell and de- livered them into chains of darkness, to be kept alive unto damnation: 5 neither spared the old world, but spared Noah, the eighth, as a preacher of righteousness, and brought the flood upon the world of the wicked, 6 re- duced the cities of Sodom and Gomorrah to ashes, condemned and exterminated them, making them an example to those who would live ungodly, 7 and delighted in righteous Loth, annoyed by the vncleanly coexistence of the wicked: 8 (for he, being righteous and dwelling among them, seeing and hearing, from day to day grieved his righteous soul by their unlawful deeds). 9 The Lord knows how to deliver the saints from temptation and how to reserve the vniusti for the day of judgment with punishment. 10 Especially those who walk according to the flesh, in the concupis- cence of violence, and who despise prudence, who are bold, who stand in their own conceit, and who are not afraid to speak evil of those who are in dignity. 11 Whereas the angels, who are greater both in power and in might, do not make angry judgments against them before the Lord. 12 But these, like natural brute beasts, driven by sensuality and made to be taken and destroyed, speak in idle talk of things they do not know, and will perish by their own corruption, 13 and they shall re- ceive the wages of unrighteousness, like those who consider it a daily pleasure to enjoy a de- lightful life. They are stained and tainted, de- lighting in their deceptions, in feasting with you, 14 they have eyes full of adultery, who do not cease from sin, who beguile unstable souls; they have hearts wearied with wicked- ness, they are children of the curse: 15 Who, forsaking the straight way, have gone astray, following the way of Balaam the son of Bosor, who lured the wages of righteousness. 16 But he was rebuked for his iniquity, for the foolish beast, speaking with a human voice, forbade the foolishness of the prophet. 17 These are wells without water, and storm-laden clouds, for whom black darkness is reserved forever. 18 For, uttering words puffed up with vanity, they deceive with the lust of the flesh those who were clean, fleeing from those who are wrapped up in error, 19 promising them free- dom, and instead they themselves are ser- vants of corruption; for from whom a man came forth, he is always in bondage. 20 For if, having escaped the filthiness of the world, through the recognition of the Lord and Sav- ior Jesus Christ, they are still entangled in it and have come out, the end of the latter is worse than the beginning. 21 For it was bet- ter for them not to have recognized the way of righteousness, and then, having recognized it, to turn away from the holy commandment given to them. 22 But the time has come for them, according to the true Proverb, for the dog to return to his vomit, and for the sow that has been washed to wallow in myrrh.

CHAPTER 3

1 This second Epistle I write to you now, be- lievers, with which I stimulate and watch your pure minds, 2 to recall the words that were spoken beforehand by the holy proph- ets and also the commands of the apostles of the Lord and Savior. 3 First, it is understood that in the last days scoffers will come, who will walk according to their lusts, 4 And they will say, "Where is the promise of his coming? For since the fathers have died, all things have remained the same since the beginning of creation." 5 For this they do not want to know, that the heavens were ancient and the earth that was from water and out of water, by the word of God. 6 Therefore the world that was then is gone,

overflowing from the water. 7 But the heavens and the earth that are now are preserved by the same word and kept in fire for the day of condemnation and destruc- tion of ungodly men. 8 Do not ignore that one day is to the LORD as a thousand years and a thousand years as one day. 9 The LORD of promise is not slow (as some consider slow- ness), but is peaceable toward others and does not want anyone to perish, but wants all men to repent. 10 But the day of the LORD will come like a thief in the night, in which the heavens will pass away with a noise, and the elements will melt away with burning, and the earth with the works that are in it will be burned up. 11 Since therefore all these things must be dissolved, what people must you be in holy coexistence and in God? 12 waiting and looking forward to the coming of that day of God, when the heavens, being on fire, will be dissolved and the elements will melt with heat? 13 But we wait for new heavens and a new earth, according to his promise, where- in dwells righteousness. 14 Therefore, believ- ers, since you are waiting for these things, be diligent to be found by him in peace, with- out spot or blemish. 15 And suppose that the long-suffering of the Lord is a salvation, as our dear brother Paul wrote to you according to the wisdom given him, 16 as one who in all his epistles speaks of these things, among which some are hard to understand, and which those who are ignorant and stable tear away, as they do also with other Scriptures, to their destruction. 17 You therefore, who al- ready know these things, be careful, lest you be carried away by the error of the ungodly and fall from your own steadfastness. 18 But grow in the grace and knowledge of our Lord and Savior Jesus Christ; to him be the glory now and forever. Amen.

I JOHN

CHAPTER 1

1 That which was from the beginning, which we have heard, which we have seen with these our eyes, which we have looked upon, and which these our hands have handled of that Word of life, 2 (for that life has been manifest- ed, and we have seen it and are witnesses to it, and present to you that eternal life which was with the Father and has been manifested to you). 3 This, I say, which we have seen and heard, we declare to you, that you also may have fellowship with you, and that our fellow- ship also may be with the Father and with his Son Iesvs Christ. 4 And these things we write to you, that your joy may be full. 5 This then is the message which we have heard from him and declare to you: God is light, and in him there is no darkness. 6 If we say that we have fellowship with him and walk in darkness, we lie and do not do the truth: 7 But if we walk in the light, as he is in the light, we have fellow- ship with one another, and the blood of Jesus Christ, his Son, delivers us from all sin. 8 If we say that we have no sin, we deceive our- selves and the truth is not in us. 9 If we ac- knowledge our sins, he is faithful and just in forgiving our sins and delivering us from all sin. 10 If we say that we have not sinned, we make him a liar, and his word is not in him.

CHAPTER 2

1 My children, these things I write to you so that you may not sin; and if anyone sins, we have an interlocutor with the Father, Jesus Christ, the righteous one. 2 He is reconcilia- tion for our sins, and not for ours alone, but also for the sins

of the whole world. 3 There- fore we are certain that we know him, if we keep his commands. 4 He who says, "I know him and does not keep his commands," is a liar, and the truth is not in him. 5 But who- ever keeps his word, in him the joy of God is perfect; so we know that you are in him. 6 Whoever says he abides in him, he must also walk as he walked. 7 Brethren, I do not write to you a new commandment, but an old com- mandment that you have had from the be- ginning; this old commandment is that word which you have heard from the beginning. 8 Then I write to you a new commandment, that which is true in him and also in you, be- cause the darkness has passed away and the true light now shines. 9 Whoever says he is in that light and hates his own brother is in darkness until now. 10 Whoever hates his own brother, he remains in that light, and there is no occasion of sickness in him. 11 But he who hates his own brother is in darkness, he walks in darkness and does not know where he is going, because darkness has blinded his eyes. 12 Little children, I write to you because your sins are forgiven you for His names' sake. 13 I write to you, fathers, because you have known him who is from the beginning. I write to you, young men, because you have known the wicked one. I write to you, little children, be- cause you have known the Father. 14 I write to you, fathers, because you have known him from the beginning. I write to you, young men, because you are strong and the word of God abides in you and you have overcome the wicked. 15 Do not love this world or the things that are in this world. If anyone loves this world, the love of the Father is not in him. 16 For whatever is in this world (such as the con- cupiscence of the flesh, the concupiscence of the eyes, and the pride of life) is not from the Father, but is of this world. 17 This world pass- es away and its concupiscence; but he who does the will of God abides forever. 18 My chil- dren, it is the last time, and as you have heard that the Antichrist will come, so now there are many Antichrists; therefore we know that it is the last time. 19 They came out of the Vs. but they were not of the Vs. for if they had been of the Vs. they would have had to continue with the Vs. But this is so that it may appear that they are not all of the Vs. 20 But you have an ointment from that Holy One, and you know all things. 21 I have not written to you that you may not know the truth, but that you may know it and know that no lie belongs to the truth. 22 Who is a liar but he who denies that Jesus is the Christ? The same is the Anti- christ who denies the Father and the Son. 23 He who denies the Son has not the Father. 24 Let it therefore remain in you what you have heard from the beginning. If what you have heard from the beginning remains in you, you also will continue in the Son and the Father. 25 And this is the promise that he has made to you, that is, eternal life. 26 These things I have written to you concerning those who deceive you. 27 But the anointing which you have received from him dwells in you; and you do not need anyone to teach you; but as the same anointing teaches you all things, and is true and untruthful, and as he has taught you, you will abide in him. 28 And now, little children, abide in him, that when he shall appear, we may be bold and not ashamed before him at his coming. 29 If you know that he is righ- teous, know that those who act righteously are upheld by him.

CHAPTER 3

1 This is what the Father has done for us, that we are called children of God; therefore the world does not know you, because it does not know him. 2 Alas, now we are children of God, but it is not yet manifest what we shall be; and we know that when he is manifested, we shall be like him, for we shall see him as he is. 3 He who has this hope in himself purifies himself as he is pure. 4 Whoever commits a sin also transgresses the Law, for sin is the transgres- sion of the Law. 5 And you know that he was manifested to take away our sins, and that in him there is no sin. 6 He who abides in him does not sin; he who sins has not seen him or known him. 7 Little children, let no one de- ceive you: he who does righteousness is righ- teous, as he is righteous. 8 He who commits sin is of the evil-doer, for the evil-doer sins from the beginning; for this purpose the Son of God was manifested, that he might melt away the works of evil- doing. 9 He who is be- gotten of God does not sin, because his seed remains in him, and he cannot sin, because he is begotten of God. 10 In this are known the sons of God and the sons of the devil: whoever does not do righteousness is not of God, and whoever does not love his brother. 11 For this is the message you have heard from the be- ginning: that we love one another, 12 not like Cain, who was of that wickedness and killed his brother; and why did he kill him? Because his works were good and his brothers good. 13 Do not be downcast, my brothers, even though the world hates you. 14 We know that we have passed from death to life because we love our brothers; whoever does not love his brother remains in death. 15 Whoever hates his brother is a murderer; and you know that no murderer has eternal life in himself. 16 In this way we perceived the Lord who laid down his life for others; therefore we also should lay down our lives for our brothers. 17 Who- ever has this good of the world and sees his brother in need and closes his compassion to him, how does the joy of God dwell in him? 18 My children, do not love only words and tongues, but also faith and truth. 19 For thus we know that we are from the truth, and be- fore him we will reassure our hearts. 20 For if our heart condemns us, God is greater than our heart and knows all things. 21 But if our heart does not condemn him, then we have confidence in God. 22 And what we ask we receive from him, because we keep his com- mands and do the things that are pleasing in his sight. 23 This then is his commandment: that we gather together in the name of his Son Jesus Christ and love one another as he has commanded us. 24 For whoever keeps his commands abides in him and he in him; and so we know that he abides in you, through the Spirit he has given you.

CHAPTER 4

1 Believe no spirit, but examine the spirits if they are from God, for many false prophets have gone out into this world. 2 In this way you will know the Spirit of God: every spirit that confesses that Jesus Christ has come in the flesh is from God. 3 And every spirit that does not confess that Jesus Christ has come in the flesh is not from God; but this is the spir- it of the Antichrist, of whom you have heard that he would come and who is now already in this world. 4 Little children, you are from God and have overcome them, for greater is he who is in you than he who is in this world. 5 They are of this world, therefore they speak of this world, and this world hears them. 6 We are from God: whoever knows God, hears him; whoever is not from God, does not hear him. We know the spirit of truth and the spir- it of wandering. 7 Believe, let one another hear, for the voice is from God, and whoever hears the voice is from God and knows God. 8 Whoever does not cry out does not know God, for God is crying out. 9 Behold, the great- ness of God

has been manifested among us, for God sent his only begotten Son into this world, that we might live through him. 10 This is where God's greatness is manifested: not that we have injured it, but that he has injured it and sent his Son to be a reconcili- ation for our sins. 11 If God has praised God, we should also praise one another. 12 No one has ever seen God. If we love one another, God dwells in you and his love is perfect in you. 13 In this way we know that we dwell in him and he in vs, because he has given vs his Spirit. 14 We have seen, and we testify, that the Father sent the Son to be the Savior of the world. 15 Whoever confesses that Jesus is the Son of God, in him dwells God and he in God. 16 We have known and come to know the joy that God has in him. God is joy, and he who dwells in joy dwells in God and God in him. 17 It is here that greatness is perfected in God, that we may be secure in the day of judgment, for as he is, so are we in this world. 18 There is no fear in joy, but perfect joy casts out fear, for fear is painful, and he who is afraid is not perfect in joy. 19 We praise him, for he praised first. 20 If anyone says, "I love God and hate his brother," he is a liar; for how can anyone who does not love his brother whom he has seen, love God whom he has not seen? 21 And this command we have from him: whoever loves God, let him also love his brother.

CHAPTER 5

1 Whoever believes that Jesus is the Christ is begotten of God; and whoever loves him whom he begat, loves also him who was begot- ten of him. 2 In this we know that we are chil- dren of God when we love God and keep his commands. 3 For this is God's pleasure, that we keep his commands; and his commands are not burdensome. 4 For all that is upheld by God is the fruit of this world; and this is the victory that has overcome this world, that is, our faith. 5 Who is it that causes this world to be overcome but he who believes that Jesus is the Son of God? 6 This is that Jesus Christ who came by water and blood; not by water only, but by water and blood; and it is that Spirit who bears witness, for that Spirit is true. 7 For there are three who testify in heaven: the Father, the Word, and the Holy Spirit; and these three are one. 8 And there are three that record in the earth, the Spirit, the water, and the blood; and these three agree in one. 9 If we receive the testimony of men, the testimo- ny of God is greater; for this is the testimony of God, who testified of his Son. 10 Whoever believes in the Son of God has the testimony in himself; whoever does not believe in God has made him a liar, because he did not be- lieve the testimony God gave of his Son. 11 And this is the testimony: that God has given eternal life, and this life is in his Son. 12 Who- ever has that Son, has that life; and whoever does not have that Son of God, does not have that life. 13 These things I have written to you, who raise you up in the Name of the Son of God, that you may know that you have eternal life, and that you may covenant in the Name of the Son of God. 14 And this is the assurance we have in him: if we ask anything according to his will, he hears us. 15 And if we know that he hears what we ask, we know that we have obtained the requests we have desired from him. 16 If anyone sees his brother committing a sin that does not go to death, let him ques- tion him, and he will give him life for those who do not sin unto death. There is a sin that leads to death: I do not say that you should pray for it. 17 All sin is sin, but there is a sin that does not lead to death. 18 We know that he who is begotten of God does not sin; but he who is begotten of God is preserved, and the

wicked does not touch him. 19 We know that we are from God and that the whole world lies in wickedness. 20 But we know that the Son of God has come and given us to know him, who is the truth; and we are in him who is the truth, that is, in his Son Jesus Christ, who is the true God and eternal life. 21 Children, keep yourselves from idols, amen.

II JOHN

1 The anciant to the elect Lady and her chil- dren, whom I love in truth, and not only I, but also all who have known the truth, 2 for the truth that dwells in you and will abide with you forever: 3 Grace to you, mercy and peace from God the Father and the Lord Je- sus Christ, Son of the Father, with truth and praise. 4 I rejoiced greatly that I found your children walking in the truth, as we have re- ceived from the Father. 5 And now I ask you, madam, (not as if I were writing you a new command, but the same as we had from the beginning) that we love one another. 6 And this is this love, that we walk according to his commands. This command is that, as you have heard from the beginning, walk in it. 7 For many deceivers have come into this world and do not confess that Jesus Christ has come in the flesh. Those who are like this are deceivers and antichrists. 8 Take heed to yourselves, that we may not lose the things we have done, but may receive the full reward. 9 Whoever transgresses and does not remain in the doctrine of Christ has no God. But who- ever remains in the doctrine of Christ has the Father and the Son. 10 If anyone comes to you and does not carry this doctrine, do not receive him into your house and say to him, "God help you." 11 For whoever says to him, "God help you," is a partaker of his evil deeds. 12 Although I had many things to write to you, I will not write with pen and paper, but I trust to come to you and to speak from mouth to mouth, that our joy may be full. 13 The chil- dren of your chosen sister greet you, Amen.

III JOHN

1 The elder to the beautiful Gaius, whom I love in truth. 2 Beloved, I wish above all things that you may prosper and be well as your soul prospers. 3 For I rejoiced greatly when the brothers came and testified to the truth that is in you, how you walk in the truth. 4 I have no greater pleasure than these, which is to hear that my children walk in the truth. 5 You do faithfully what you do to the brethren and to the strangers, 6 Who have borne witness of your love before the churches. And if you take them on a journey as is fitting for God, you will do well, 7 For for the sake of his names they have departed and have taken nothing from the Gentiles. 8 We therefore must re- ceive them, to be a help to the truth. 9 I have written to the Church, but Diotrephes, who wants to have preeminence among them, does not receive it. 10 Therefore, if I come, I will remind you of his deeds which he does, waving evil words against you, not content- ing himself, and not receiving the brethren himself, but forbidding those who desire it and driving them out of the Church. 11 Be- lieve, do not follow what is useless, but what is good; he who does good, is from God; but he who does evil, has not seen God. 12 Deme- trius has a good reputation from all men and the truth itself; yes, and we ourselves have a record, and you know that our record is true. 13 I have many things to write, but I do not want to write to you with pen and quill: 14 for I trust that in a little while I shall see you and we shall speak mouth to mouth. Peace be with you. Friends greet you. Greet friends by name.

JUDE

1 IVde, servant of Iesus Christ and brother of Iames, to those who are called and sanctified by God the Father and who have returned to Iesus Christ: 2 I thank you, and peace and joy be multiplied. 3 Believe, when I took the time to write to you about the common salvation, it was necessary for me to write to exhort you to strive earnestly for the maintenance of your faith, which was once granted to the saints. 4 For there are some men who have crept in and who were already destined for this con- demnation before; they are ungodly men who turn the grace of our God into avarice and deny God, the only Lord, and our Lord Jesus Christ. 5 I will therefore bring to your remembrance, for you once knew it, that the Lord, having brought the people out of Egypt, later destroyed those who were not convert- ed. 6 Even the angels who did not keep their first estate but left their own dwelling place, he reserved them in eternal chains under darkness until the judgment of the great day. 7 Just as Sodom and Gomorrah and the cities around them, which like them committed fornication and followed foreign flesh, have been pointed out as an example and will suf- fer the vengeance of eternal fire. 8 Likewise, these sleepers also defiled the flesh, despised the government and spoke evil of those in au- thority. 9 Yet Michael the archangel, when he clashed with the disciples and disputed over the body of Moses, did not rebuke him with curse words, but said, "The Lord rebukes you." 10 But these speak in vain of things they know not; and what things they know naturally, like beasts without reason, in these things they corrupt themselves. 11 Woe to them, for they have followed the way of Cain, have been forsaken by the deceit of Balaam's wages, and perish in the deceit of Korah. 12 They are rocks in your charitable feasts, when they feast with you, without fear, feeding on themselves; they are waterless clouds, carried away by the winds, corrupt and fruitless trees, twice dead and torn from you. 13 They are the rushing waves of the sea, lashing out with their own shame; they are wandering stars, for whom the darkness of darkness is reserved forev- er. 14 Enoch, the penultimate of Adam, also prophesied about them, saying, "Behold, the Lord is coming with thousands of his saints, 15 to judge all men, and to rebuke all the wick- ed among them of all their evil deeds which they have ungodly committed, and of all their cruel speeches which wicked sinners have spoken against him. 16 These are murmurers, complainers, walking after their own lusts: whose mouths speak proud things, making people admire the persons of men, because of their aversion. 17 But ye believers, remem- ber the words that were spoken before by the apostles of our Lord Jesus Christ, 18 How they told you that in the last times there would be mockers, who would walk according to their vngole passions. 19 These are those who sep- arate themselves from others by nature, not having the Spirit. 20 But you, believers, edify yourselves in your most holy faith, praying in the Holy Spirit, 21 and keep yourselves in the joy of God, seeking the grace of our Lord Jesus Christ for eternal life. 22 And have com- passion on some, setting aside differences: 23 But others fear being taken out of the fire, and hate garments stained by the flesh. 24 Now to him who is able to guard you, that you may not fall, and to present you without blemish in the presence of his glory with joy, 25 that is, to God, the only wise, our Savior, be glory, majesty, dominion and power, now and forever, Amen.

THE BOOK OF VISION

This book presents a symbolic vision of the future and God's ultimate triumph.

REVELATION

CHAPTER 1

1 The Revelation of Jesus Christ, which God gave him to show his servants the things that were to be done shortly; and which he sent and showed by his angel to his servant John, 2 who brought back the word of God, the testi- mony of Jesus Christ, and all the things which he saw. 3 Blessed is he who reads and hears the words of this prophecy and observes the things written therein, for the time is at hand. 4 To the churches that are in Asia, Grace to you and peace from Him who is, who was, and who is to come, and from the ten Spirits who are before His throne, 5 and from Jesus Christ, who is the faithful witness, the first- born of the dead and the prince of the kings of the earth, to him who has given luster to us and washed us from our sins by his blood, 6 and made them kings and priests with God his Father, to him I say, to him be glory and dominion forever, amen. 7 Behold, he comes with clouds, and all eyes shall see him, even those who have seen him before; and all the peoples of the earth shall bow down before him, and so on, Amen. 8 I am Alpha and Ome- ga, the beginning and the end, says the LORD, who is, who was, and who is to come, that is, the Almighty. 9 Iohn, your brother and com- panion in tribulation, in the kingdom and patience of Jesus Christ, I was in the island called Patmos, for the word of God and for the testimony of Jesus Christ. 10 On the Lord's day I was rapt in spirit and heard behind me a great voice, as of a trumpet, 11 saying, "I am the Alpha and the Omega, the first and the last; and what you see, write it in a book and send it to the other churches that are in Asia, to Ephesus, to Smyrna, to Pergamum, to Thyatira, to Sardis, to Philadelphia and to La- odicea." 12 Then I turned back to see the seer speaking to me; and when I had turned back, I saw ten golden candlesticks, 13 and in the center of these candlesticks, one resembling the Son of Man, clothed in a robe down to his feet and girded about his shoulders with a golden girdle. 14 His head and his hair were white as white wool and as snow, and his eyes were like a flame of fire, 15 his feet were like fine brasse, burning as in a furnace, and his voice was like the sound of many waters. 16 He had in his right hand ten stars, and out of his mouth came a sharp two-edged sword; his face shone as the sun shines in its strength. 17 When I saw him, I fell at his feet as if dead; then he laid his right hand upon me, saying, "Fear not: I am the first and the last, 18 And I am alive, but was dead; and behold, I am alive forever, amen, and have the keys of hell and death. 19 Write down the things that you have seen, the things that are and the things that are to come hereafter. 20 The mystery of the ten stars you saw in my right hand and the ten golden candlesticks is this: the ten stars are the angels of the ten Churches, and the ten candlesticks you saw are the ten Churches.

CHAPTER 2

1 To the angel of the church at Ephesus write, "These things says he who holds the ten stars in his right hand and walks in the midst of the ten golden candlesticks. 2 I know your

works and your toil and your patience, and I know that you cannot bear those who are sick, and you have examined those who say they are apostles and are not, and you have found liars. 3 You have been oppressed and have been patient, and for My names sake you have toiled and not fainted. 4 Neuertheles, I have something against you, because you have forsaken your first love. 5 Remember therefore whence thou hast fallen, and re- pent, and do the first works; otherwise I will soon come against thee, and remove thy can- dlestick from its place, unless thou amend. 6 But you have this: that you hate the works of the Nicolaitans, which I also hate. 7 He who has ears to hear, let him hear what the Spirit says to the churches, "To him who commits himself, I will give to eat of the tree of life that is in the midst of the Paradise of God." 8 And to the angel of the Church at Smyrna write, "These things says he who is the first and the last, who was dead and is dead. 9 I know your works, your tribulation and your despair (but you are rich), and I know the blasphemies of those who say they are Jews and are not, but are the synagogue of Satan. 10 Do not be afraid of the things that you will have to suf- fer; behold, it shall come to pass that the will of God shall cast some of you into prison, that you may be tried, and you shall have tribula- tion for ten days; be faithful unto death, and I will give you the horn of life. 11 He who has an ear, let him hear what the Spirit says to the churches. He who commits himself will not be smitten by the second death." 12 To the angel of the Church who is at Pergamum write, "This says he who has the sharp two- edged sword. 13 I know your works and the place where you dwell, that is, where Satan's throne is, and you guard my Name and have not denied my faith, as in the days when An- tipas, my faithful martyr, was slain among you, where Satan dwells. 14 But I have some things against you, because you have there those who keep the doctrine of Balaam, who taught Balak to set a stumbling block before the children of Israel, that they should eat of things sacrificed to idols and commit forni- cation. 15 So also you have done with those who maintain the doctrine of the Nicolaitans, which I detest. 16 Repent, or else I will soon come to you and fight against them with the sword of my mouth. 17 He who has an ear, let him hear what the Spirit says to the churches. To the one who presents himself, I will feed him of the hidden Manna, and I will give him a white stone, and in the stone will be writ- ten a new name, which no one knows except the one who receives it. 18 And to the angel of the Church who is at Thyatira write, "These things says the Son of God, whose eyes are like a flame of fire and whose feet are like thin britches. 19 I know your works, your love, your service, your faith, your patience and your works, and I know that they are more to the last than to the first. 20 However, I have some things against you: that you allow the woman Jezebel, who calls herself a prophet- ess, to teach and to deceive my servants into committing fornication and eating food sac- rificed to idols. 21 I gave her room to repent of her fornication, but she did not repent. 22 Behold, I will cast her into a bed, and those who commit fornication with her, into great affliction, unless they repent of their works. 23 And I will kill her children with death; and all the churches shall know that I am he who searches minds and hearts; and I will give to every one of you according to his works. 24 And to you others of Thyatira I say, "To those who do not have this culture and do not know the depths of Satan (as they speak) I will not impose any other burden. 25 But what you al- ready have, hold fast to it until I come. 26 For he who strives and observes my works to the end, to him will I give power over the nations, 27 And he shall rule them with a rod of iron; and like vessels of a potter, they shall be bro- ken. 28 As I have received from my Father, so will I give him the morning star. 29 He who has ears, let him hear what the Spirit says to the churches.

CHAPTER 3

1 And write to the angel of the Church that is in Sardis, "These things saith he that hath the seven Spirits of God and the ten stars, I know thy works, for thou hast a name that thou bearest, but thou art dead. 2 Awake and strengthen the things that remain and are ready to die, for I have not found your works perfect before God. 3 Remember therefore what you have received and heard, hold fast and repent. If therefore you will not watch, I will come upon you like a thief, and you will not know at what hour I will come upon you. 4 Nevertheless thou hast still some names in Sardis, who have not stained their garments; they shall walk with me clothed in white, for they are worthy. 5 He who commends us shall be clothed in white araye, and I will not blot out his name from the book of life, but I will confess his name before my Father and his angels. 6 He who has an ear, let him hear what the Spirit says to the churches. 7 And write to your angel of the Church in Philadel- phia, "These things says he who is Holy and True, who has the key of Dauid, who opens and no one closes, and closes and no one opens, 8 I know thy works; behold, I have set before thee an open door, and none can shut it, because thou hast little strength, and hast kept my word, and hast not denied my Name. 9 Behold, I will cause those of the Synagogue of Satan, who call themselves "saints" and are not, to stand by and watch; behold, I say that I will cause them to come and worship before your feet and know that I have heard you. 10 Because you have observed the plot of my patience, I will deliver you from the hour of temptation that will come upon the whole world to smite the inhabitants of the earth. 11 Behold, I am coming shortly; keep what you have, that no one may take your crown. 12 Of him that shall be commended unto thee I will make a pillar in the Temple of my God, and he shall come no more out of it; and I will write upon him the Name of my God, and the name of the city of my God, which is the new Jerusalem, which cometh down from above from my God, and I will write upon him my new Name. 13 He who has an ear, let him hear what the Spirit says to the churches. 14 And to the angel of the Church of Laodicea write, "These things says Amen, the faithful and true witness, who is the beginning of the creatures of God. 15 I know your trouble, for you are neither cold nor hot; I wish you were cold or hot. 16 Therefore, because you are lukewarm and neither cold nor hot, it will happen that I will spit you out of my mouth. 17 For you say, "I am rich and wealthy and have need of nothing," and you do not know how misera- ble, poor, blind and naked you are. 18 I advise you to take fire-tested gold from me, that you may become rich, and white garments, that you may be clothed and your filthy naked- ness not appear; and to cover your eyes with salt, that you may see. 19 As many as please me, I rebuke and chastise them; therefore be zealous and amend. 20 Behold, I stand at the door and knock. If anyone hears my voice and opens the door, I will come in to him and dine with him and he with me. 21 To him who comes, I will make him sit with me in my throne, just as I came and sit with my Father in his throne. 22 He who has ears to hear let him hear what the Spirit says to the churches.

CHAPTER 4

1 After this I looked, and behold, a door was opened in heaven, and the first voice I heard was like that of a trumpet speaking to me, saying, "Come here, and I will show you the things that are to be done hereafter." 2 And immediately I was ravished by the spirit, and behold, a throne was set in heaven, and one sat on the throne. 3 He who was seated was to look up, like a jasper stone and a sar- dine, and around the throne was a rainbow, resembling a surfacing. 4 Around the throne were four and twenty seats, and on the seats I saw sitting four and twenty elders, clothed in white robes and with golden crowns on their heads. 5 Out of the throne came lightning and thunder and visions, and before the throne burned ten lamps of fire, which are the seven spirits of God. 6 In front of the throne was a sea of ice resembling crystal, and in the midst of the throne and around the throne were four beasts full of eyes in front and behind. 7 The first beast was like a lion, the second like a calf, the third had the face of a man, and the fourth was like a flying eagle. 8 The four beasts each had six wings around them, and they were full of eyes within, and they did not cease day or night to say, "Holy, holy, holy the Lord God Almighty, who was, who is, and who is to come." 9 And when those beasts gave glory and honor and thanksgiving to him who sat on the throne, who lives forever, 10 the four and twenty elders prostrated themselves before him who sat on the throne and wor- shipped him who lives for eternity and cast their crowns before the throne, saying 1 You are worthy, O LORD, to receive glory and hon- or and power, for you created all things, and by your will they are and were created.

CHAPTER 5

1 And I saw in the right hand of him who sat on the throne a book written on the in- side and on the back, sealed with ten seals. 2 And I saw a strong angel preaching with a loud voice, "Who is worthy to open the book and undo its seals? 3 And no one in heaven or on earth or under the earth was able to open the book and look at it. 4 Then I wept great-ly, for no one was worthy to open and reread the Book and look at it. 5 But one of the elders said to me, "Do not weep; behold, that Lion of the tribe of Judah, who is a native of Dauid, has decided to open the Book and undo its seven seals." 6 Then I saw and beheld, in the midst of the throne, the four beasts, and in the midst of the elders, a Labe as if he had been slain, who had ten horns and ten eyes, which are the ten spirits of God, sent into all the world. 7 He came and took the Book from the right hand of him who sat on the throne. 8 And when he had taken the Book, the four beasts and the four hundred and twenty el- ders fell down before the Lambe, each car- rying harps and golden vials full of odors, which are the prayers of the saints, 9 and they intoned a new song, saying, "You are worthy to take the Book and to open its seals, because you were slain and have redeemed to God by your blood every race, tongue, people and nation, 10 and you have constituted for our God kings and priests, and we will reign on the earth. 11 Then I saw and heard the voice of many angels round about the throne, the bea- vers and elders, and they were ten thousand times ten thousand and thousands, 12 saying with a loud voice, "Worthy is the lamb that was slain to receive power, wealth,

wisdom, strength, honor, glory and praise." 13 And all the creatures that are in heaven, on the earth, under the earth and in the sea, and all that are in them, heard that I said, "Praise, honor, glo- ry and power to him who sits on the throne and to the Lambe forever." 14 The four beasts said, "Amen," and the four hundred and twen- ty elders fell to the ground and worshiped him who lives for eternity.

CHAPTER 6

1 Afterward, I saw that the Lambe had opened one of the seals, and I heard one of the four behemoths say, as if it were a noise of thunder, "Come and see." 2 Then I saw that there was a white horse, and he who was sit- ting on him had a bow, and he had been given a horn, and he was going to the conquest that he might come. 3 And when he had opened the second seal, I heard the second beast say, "Come and see." 4 Then there came forth an- other horse, red, and he who sat on it was giv- en power to take peace from the earth and to kill one another, and a great sword was given to him. 5 And when he had opened the third seal, I heard the thirteenth beast say, "Come and see:" Then I saw and beheld a black horse, and he that sat upon it had scales in his hand. 6 And I heard a voice in the midst of the four beasts saying, "A measure of wheat for a pen- ny, and three measures of barrel for a penny, and oil and wine do you no harm." 7 When he had opened the fourth seal, I heard the voice of the fourth beast saying, "Come and see." 8 And I looked, and behold, a pale horse, whose name was Death, and Hell followed him, and to whom was given power to kill with the sword, with hunger, with death, and with the beasts of the earth from the fourth part of the earth. 9 When he opened the fifth seal, I saw under the altar the souls of those who had been slain for the word of God and for the tes- timony they had kept. 10 And they cried out with a loud voice, saying, "Until when, O Lord, who art holy and true, wilt thou not judge and charge our blood to those who dwell on the earth? 11 Long white robes were given to each one, and they were told that they should rest for a while, until their fellow servants and their brothers who were to be slain like them were killed. 12 When he opened the sixth seal, I saw a great earthquake, and the sun became black as sackcloth and the moon was like blood. 13 The stars of Heauen fell to the earth, as a fig tree throws out its green figs when it is shaken by a strong wind. 14 Heauen fell away like a sow when it is rolled up, and all the mountains and hills were swept from their places. 15 And the kings of the earth, and the great, and the rich, and the chief, and the mighty, and all the servants, and all the free, hid themselves in the dens and among the rocks of the mountains, 16 And they said to the mountains and the rocks, "Come forward and hide yourselves from the presence of him who sits on the throne and from the wrath of Lambe." 17 For the great day of his wrath has come, and who can stand?

CHAPTER 7

1 Then I saw four angels standing at the four corners of the earth and holding the four winds of the earth, so that the winds would not blow on the earth, nor on the sea, nor on any tree. 2 Then I saw another angel coming from the east, who had the seal of the laugh- ing God, and cried with a loud voice to the four angels to whom power had been given to injure the earth and the sea, saying 3 Wound not the earth, nor the sea, nor the trees, un- til we have sealed the servants

of our God in their foreheads." 4 Then I heard the number of those who had been sealed, and a hundred and forty thousand of all the tribes of the children of Israel were sealed. 5 Of the tribe of Judah two thousand were sealed. Of the tribe of Reuben two thousand were sealed. Of the tribe of Gad two thousand people were sealed. 6 Of the tribe of Aser two thousand people were sealed. Of the tribe of Nephth- ali two thousand people were sealed. Of the tribe of Manasses two thousand people were sealed 7 Of the tribe of Simeon two thousand people were sealed. Of the tribe of Leui two thousand people were sealed. Of the tribe of Issachar two thousand people were sealed. Of the tribe of Zabulon two thousand peo- ple were sealed. 8 Of the tribe of Ioseph two thousand people were sealed. Of the tribe of Benjamin two thousand people were sealed. 9 After these things I saw a great multitude, which no one could count, of all nations and lineages, peoples and languages, standing before the throne and the Lambs, clothed in long white robes and with palms in their hands. 10 And they cried with a loud voice, saying, "Salvation comes from our God, who sits on the throne, and from the Lambe." 11 And all the angels stood round about the throne, and the elders, and the four beasts, and fell down before the throne on their fac- es, and worshipped God, 12 saying, "Amen. Praise, glory, wisdom, graces, honor, power and strength be to our God forever, Amen." 13 One of the elders spoke and said to me, "What are these who are clothed in white garments and from whence did they come? 14 I said to him, "Lord, you know." And he answered me, "These are those who have come out of the great tribulation and have washed their long robes and made them white in the blood of Lambe. 15 They are therefore in the presence of the throne of God and attend him day and night in his Temple, and he who sits on the throne will dwell among them. 16 They shall hunger no more, nor thirst, nor shall the sun shine upon them, nor the heat. 17 For the Lambe, who is at the center of the throne, will guide them and lead them to the springs of clear waters, and God will wipe out all sorrow from their eyes.

CHAPTER 8

1 When he opened the seventh seal, there was silence in heaven for about half an hour. 2 Then I saw the seven angels standing be- fore God, and to them were given as many trumpets. 3 Then another angel came and stood before the altar with a golden censer, and he was given many odors that he might offer with the prayers of all the saints on the golden altar, which is before the throne. 4 The smoke of the odors and prayers of the saints went up before God from the hand of the angel. 5 The angel took the censer, filled it with the fire from the altar, and threw it on the earth, and there were voices, thunder, lightning, and earthquakes. 6 Then the ten angels who had the ten trumpets prepared to blow the trumpets. 7 And the first angel blew the trumpet, and there was hail and fire, mingled with blood, and they were cast upon the earth, and the third part of the trees was burned, and all the vegetation was burned. 8 And the second Angel blew the trumpet, and as a great mountain, burning with fire, was thrown into the sea, and the third part of the sea became blood. 9 The third part of the crea- tures that were in the sea and had life died, and the third part of the ships was destroyed. 10 Then the third angel blew the trumpet, and from the Eauen fell a great star, which burned like a flashlight, and fell into the third part of the rivers and into the springs of the waters. 11 The name of the star is called vermilion; therefore the third part of the waters

became vermilion, and many men died because of the waters, because they had become bitter. 12 And the fourth angel sounded the trumpet, and the third part of the sun was smitten, and the third part of the moon, and the third part of the stars, so that the third part of them was darkened; and the day was smitten, so that the third part of it could not shine, and so also the night. 13 Then I saw and heard an Angel flying over the hills of Heauen and saying in a loud voice, "Woe, woe, woe to the inhabitants of the earth, because of the sounds that would be made with the trumpets of the three An- gels who were yet to blow the trumpets."

CHAPTER 9

1 The fifth angel blew the trumpet, and I saw a star falling from above to the earth, and to him was given the key to the bottomless pit. 2 He opened the bottomless pit, and the smoke of the pit rose up, like the smoke of a great furnace, and the sun and the sky were darkened by the smoke of the pit. 3 Out of the smoke came locusts upon the earth, and power was given them that the scorpions of the earth have. 4 And they were commanded not to injure the earth, nor any green thing, nor any tree, but only men who have not the seal of God on their foreheads. 5 And they were commanded not to kill them, but to torment them for five months, and that their pain should be like that of a scorpion sting- ing a man. 6 Therefore in those days men shall see death, and shall not find it; they shall want to die, and death shall flee from them. 7 The shape of the locusts was like horses prepared for battle, and on their heads were like crowns, as of gold, and their faces were like the faces of men. 8 They had hearing like that of women, and their teeth were like the teeth of lions. 9 They had habbergions like the habbergions of yron, and the sound of their wings was like the sound of chariots when many horses are running to battle. 10 They had tails like scorpions, with stingers in their tails, and their power was to wound men five times. 11 And they have a king outside them, who is the angel of the bottomless pit, whose name in Hebrew is Abaddon, and in Greek is called Apollyon, that is, destroyer. 12 One woe has passed away, and behold, after this two more will follow. 13 Then the sixth angel blew the trumpet, and I heard a sound from the four trumpets of the golden altar, which is before God, 14 saying to the sixth angel, who had the trumpet, "Untie the four angels who are bound in the great river Euphra- tes." 15 And the four angels were loosed, who were ready at an hour, and at a day, and at a month, and at a year, to kill the third part of the men. 16 And the number of the horsemen of war was twenty thousand by ten thou- sand, for I heard the name of them. 17 So I saw in vision the horses and those who sat on them, emitting firi habbergion, hyacinth, and sulfur, and the heads of the horses were like lion heads; and from their mouths came forth fire, smoke, and brimstone. 18 Of these three the thirteenth part of the men was slain, that is, by fire, smoke, and brimstone coming out of their mouths. 19 For their power is in their mouths and in their tails, for their tails were like serpents and they had heads with which they wounded. 20 The rest of the men who were not slain by these plagues did not repent of the works of their hands, lest they worship devils and idols of gold and silk, of brasse, stone, and wood, which are not seen, nor heard, nor go. 21 Moreover they did not repent of their murders, their sorceries, their fornications, and their thefts.

CHAPTER 10

1 And I saw another mighty Angel coming down from Heauen, clothed in a cloud and with his head covered with rain; his face was like the sun and his feet like pillars of fire. 2 He had a small open book in his hand, and he placed his right foot on the sea and his left foot on the earth, 3 And he cried out with a loud voice, as when a livid roars; and when he had cried out, ten thunders uttered their voices. 4 And when the thunders had uttered their utterances, I was about to write; but I heard a voice from above saying to me, "Keep the things that the thunders had uttered, and do not write them down." :5 And the an- gel whom I saw standing on the sea and on the earth lifted up his hand toward Eauen, 6 and swore by him who lives for eternity, who had created the Eauen and the things that are therein, the earth and the things that are therein, the sea and the things that are there- in, that time would be no more. 7 But in the days of the journey of the tenth angel, when he shall begin to sound the trumpet, then shall the mystery of God be finished, as he declared to his servants, the prophets. 8 The seer whom I had heard from Heauen spoke to me again and said, "Go and take the little book that is open in the hand of the Angel who is on the sea and on the land." 9 So I went to the angel and said to him, "Give me the little book." And he said to me, "Take it and eat it; it will make your belly bitter, but it will be in your mouth sweet as gold." 10 Then I took the little book from the hand of the angels, and ate it, and it was in my mouth sweet as gold, but after I had eaten it my belly was bitter. 11 And he said to me, "You must prophesy again among peoples, nations and tongues and to many kings."

CHAPTER 11

1 Then I was given a staff, like a rod, and the angel stood and said, "Arise and beat the tem- ple of God and the altar and those who wor- ship there. 2 But the court that is outside the temple drive it out and do not beat it, for it is given to the Gentiles, and the holy city shall be taken from them two and four times half. 3 But I will give power to my two witnesses, and they shall prophesy for a thousand and two hundred and sixty days, clothed in sack- cloth. 4 These are two olive trees and two candlesticks that stand before the God of the earth. 5 If anyone wants to harm them, fire comes out of their mouths and annihilates their enemies; for if anyone wants to harm them, he must be killed. 6 These have power to shut up the heavens, that it may not rain in the days of their prophecy, and they have power to turn the waters into blood, and to smite the earth with all the plagues, as often as they will. 7 And when they have finished their testimony, the beast that comes out of the bottomless pit shall make war against them, and shall smite and kill them. 8 And their dead bodies shall lie in the streets of the great city, which spiritually is called Sodom and Egypt, where also our Lord was crucified. 9 And the peoples, races, tongues and nations shall see their dead bodies for three and a half days, and they shall not allow their dead bodies to be placed in the graves. 10 And those who dwell on the earth shall rejoice over them and be glad and send gifts to one another, because these two Prophets have vexed those who dwell on the earth. 11 But after three and a half days, the spirit of life that comes from God will enter them, and they will stand on their feet; and great fear will come upon those who hear them. 12 And they shall hear a great voice from Heauen saying to them, "Come here." And they shall go up to the Heauen in a cloud, and their enemies shall see them. 13 In that same hour there shall be a great earth- quake, and the tenth part of the city shall fall, and in the earthquake six thousand shall be slain; and the remnant shall be frightened, and shall give glory to the God of Heauen. 14 The second woe has passed, and behold, the third woe will soon come. 15 And the seventh angel blew the trumpet, and there were great voices in heaven, saying, "The kingdoms of this world are our Lord's and his Christ's, and he shall reign forever." 16 Then the four and twenty elders, who sat before God on their seats, fell on their faces and worshiped God, 17 saying, "We give thanks to you, Lord God Almighty, who are, who were, and who will come, for you have received your great power and have won your kingdom." 18 The nations were distressed, and your wrath is come, and the time of the dead, that they may be judged, and that you may give reward to your ser- vants, the prophets, the saints, and those who fear your Name, small and great, and destroy those who destroy the earth. 19 Then the Tem- ple of God was opened in heaven, and the Ark of his covenant was seen in his Temple; and there was heard lightning, and voices, and thunder, and earthquakes, and much com- motion.

CHAPTER 12

1 And there appeared a great wonder in heaven: A woman clothed with the sun, with the moon under her feet and on her head a crown of two stars. 2 She was with child, weeping for childbirth and suffering to be delivered. 3 Then another wonder appeared: behold, a great red dragon had ten heads, ten horns, and ten crowns on his heads: 4 And his tail drew the thirteenth part of the stars of Heauen, and cast them upon the earth. And the dragon stood before the woman, who was ready to be disappointed, to destroy her child, when she had brought it home. 5 So she brought forth a male child, who would rule all nations with a rod of yron; and that child was brought to God and to his throne. 6 And the woman fled into the wilderness, where she had a place prepared by God, that they might feed her there a thousand, two hundred and three hundred days. 7 And there was a bat- tle in heaven; Michael and his angels fought against the dragon, and the dragon fought with his angels. 8 But they did not give up, and found no more place in heaven. 9 And the great dragon was cast out, that old serpent, called the devil and Satan, who deceives the whole world; he was then cast down to the earth, and his angels were cast out with him. 10 Then I heard a loud voice in heaven, say- ing, "Now there is salvation, and strength, and the kingdom of our God, and the power of his Christ; for the accuser of our brethren has been cast down, who accused them before our God day and night." 11 But they overcame him by the blood of that lamb and by the word of their testimony, and they did not lie until death. 12 Therefore remember, you heavens, and you who dwell in them. Woe to the inhab- itants of the earth and the sea, for the drag- on has descended upon you, who has great wrath, knowing that he has little time. 13 When the dragon heard that he had been cast upon the earth, he pursued the woman who had borne the male child. 14 But the woman was given two wings of a great eagle, that she might fly into the wilderness, to her place where she fed for a time, a time and a half, from the presence of the serpent. 15 And the serpent cast water out of his mouth like a rag- ing river behind the woman, that she might be carried away by the river. 16 But the earth seized the woman, and the earth opened its mouth and swallowed up the flood that the dragon had cast from its

mouth. 17 Then the dragon was angry with the woman and went to make war with the rest of her descendants, who keep the commandments of God and have the testimony of Jesus Christ. 18 And I stood on the sand of the sea.

CHAPTER 13

1 And I saw a beast arise out of the sea, hav- ing ten heads and ten horns; on his horns were ten crowns, and on his heads the name of blasphemy. 2 And the beast which I saw was like a leopard, and his feet were like the feet of a lion, and his mouth was like the mouth of a lion; and the dragon gave him his power, and his throne, and great authority. 3 And I saw one of his heads as wounded to death, but his deadly wound was healed, and all the world marveled and followed the beast. 4 And they worshipped the dragon that gave power to the beast, and they worshipped the beast, say- ing, "Who is like unto the beast? Who is able to fight with him?" 5 And there was opened to him a mouth speaking great things and blasphemies, and power was given to him to make two and four money. 6 And he opened his mouth to blaspheme against God, to blas- pheme his Name, and his tabernacle, and those who dwell in the Eauen. 7 It was grant- ed to him to make war against the saints and to defeat them, and power was given him over every race, tongue and nation. 8 Therefore all the inhabitants of the earth shall worship him, whose names are not written in the book of the life of that Lambe who was slain from the beginning of the world. 9 If anyone has an ear, let him hear. 10 If anyone goes into captivity, he shall go into captivity; if anyone kills by the sword, he shall be killed by the sword; behold the patience and faith of the saints. 11 Then I saw another beast coming out of the earth, having two horns like the Lambe, but speak- ing like the dragon. 12 And he did all that the first beast could do before him, and made the earth and those who dwell therein to worship the first beast, whose deadly wound had been healed. 13 And he did great wonders, so that he sent down fire from above upon the earth before the eyes of men, 14 And he deceived the inhabitants of the earth with the signs which he was permitted to do in sight of the beast, telling those who dwelt on the earth to make the image of the beast, which had a wound of the sword and died. 15 He was permitted to give a spirit to the image of the beast, so that the image of the beast would speak and cause those who would not worship the image of the beast to be killed. 16 And he caused every- one, small and great, rich and poor, free and obligated, to receive a mark in his right hand or forehead, 17 and that no one could buy or sell except he who had the mark, the name of the beast or the number of his name. 18 Here is wisdom. He who has wisdom shall count the number of the beast, for it is the number of a man, and his number is six hundred and sixty-five.

CHAPTER 14

1 Then I looked, and behold, a Lamb stood on Mount Zion, and with him a hundred thou- sand, four thousand and four hundred thou- sand, who had the Name of his Father writ- ten on their foreheads. 2 And I heard a sound coming from Eauen, like the sound of many waters and like the sound of great thunder; and I heard the sound of harpers playing their harps. 3 And they sang as a new song before the throne, and before the four beasts, and before the elders; and no one could learn that song but the hundred, and the forty, and the

forty thousand that were bought from the earth. 4 These are the ones who do not defile themselves with women, because they are virgins; these follow the Lambe wherever he goes; these were bought from men, being the first fruits for God and for the Lambe. 5 And in their mouths was found no guile, for they are without blemish before the throne of God. 6 Then I saw another angel flying in the midst of heaven, with an everlasting gospel to preach to all who dwell on the earth, to every nation, kindred, tongue, and people, 7 saying with a loud voice, "Fear God and give him glo- ry, for the hour of his satisfaction has come; and worship him who made the earth and the land, the sea and the springs of waters." 8 An- other Angel followed and said, "Babylon, the great city, is fallen, is fallen, because she has made all nations drink the wine of the wrath of her fornication." 9 The third Angel followed them, saying in a loud voice, "If anyone wor- ships the beast and his image and receives his mark on his forehead or on his hand, 10 he shall drink of the wine of the wrath of God, yea, of the pure wine that is poured into the cup of his wrath, and he shall be tormented in fire and brimstone before the holy angels and before the Lambes. 11 The smoke of their tor- ment shall go up again, and they shall have no rest day or night who worship the beast and his image, and those who receive the imprint of his name. 12 Behold the patience of the saints, behold those who keep the commands of God and the rules of Jesus. 13 Then I heard a voice from Heauen saying, "Write, The dead who die in the Lord are fully blessed. Thus says the Spirit, for they rest from their labors and their works follow them. 14 Then I looked, and behold, a white cloud, and on the cloud one sitting like the Son of Man, who had on his head a golden crown and in his hand a sharp sickle. 15 And another angel came out of the temple and cried with a loud voice to him who was sitting on the cloud, "Thrust in your sickle and reap, for the hour of reaping has come, for the hardest earth is ripe." 16 He who was sitting on the cloud thrust his scythe into the earth, and the earth was reaped. 17 Then another Angel came out of the Temple, which is in heaven, with a sharp sickle. 18 Another Angel went out from the altar, which had power over the fire, and cried with a loud voice to the one who had the sharp scythe, saying, "Thrust in your sharp scythe and gath- er the clusters from the vineyard of the earth, for the grapes are ripe." 19 The angel thrust his sharp sickle into the earth, cut off the clusters of the vineyard of the earth, and threw them into the great wine cellar of the wrath of God. 20 And the wine cellar was carried outside the city, and the blood came out of the cellar to the reins of the horses, for a space of a thou- sand and six hundred furlongs.

CHAPTER 15

1 And I saw another sign in heaven, great and marvelous, seven Angels, bearing the last plagues, for with them the wrath of God is fulfilled. 2 And I saw as a sea of glass, mingled with fire, and those who had obtained the victory of the beast, his image, his mark, and the number of his name, standing in the sea of glass, playing the harps of God, 3 And they sang the song of Moses, God's servant, and the song of Lambe, saying, "Great and mar- velous are your works, Lord God Almighty; righteous and true are your ways, King of the Saints. 4 Who does not fear you, O Lord, and glorify your Name, for you alone are holy, and all nations will come to worship you, for your decrees have been made manifest." 5 Then I looked, and behold, the temple of the tent of testimony was open in heaven. 6 And

the seven angels came out of the temple, which had the seven plagues, clothed in pure and bright linen, and with their breasts girded with sheaths of gold. 7 One of the four beasts gave the ten angels ten golden vials filled with the wrath of God, which endures long. 8 The Temple was filled with the smoke of God's glory and power, and no one could enter the Temple until the seven plagues of the ten an- gels were fulfilled.

CHAPTER 16

1 And I heard a great voice from the Temple, saying to the ten angels, "Go your way and sprinkle the seven vials of the wrath of God on the earth." 2 The first went and sprinkled his vial on the earth; and a sore plague came upon the men who had the mark of the beast and upon those who worshipped his image. 3 The second angel issued his power over the sea, which became like the blood of a dead man, and every living thing was dyed in the sea. 4 And the third angel emitted his beam of power upon the rivers and springs of wa- ter, which became blood. 5 And I heard the angel of the waters say, "Lord, you are righ- teous, which you are and were, and holy, for you have judged these things. 6 For they have shed the blood of the saints and prophets, you have given them blood to drink, for they are worthy. 7 And I heard another from the sanc- tuary saying, "Thus it is, Lord God Almighty, true and righteous are your judgments." 8 And the fourth angel poured out his viall upon the sun, and it was granted to him to torment men with the ardor of fire, 9 And men cow- ered with great fury, and blasphemed the Name of God, which hath power over these plagues, and repented not to give him glory. 10 And the fifth angel poured out his power upon the throne of the beast, and his king- dom was darkened, and they bit their tongues in sorrow, 11 And they blasphemed the God of Heauen for their sorrows and their plagues, not repenting of their works. 12 Then the sixth angel poured out his power upon the great river Euphrates, and its waters dried up, that the way of the kings of the east might be pre- pared. 13 And I saw three vnclean spirits like frogs coming out of the mouth of the dragon, out of the mouth of the beast, and out of the mouth of the false prophet. 14 For they are spirits of disciples, working miracles to go to the kings of the earth and of all the world, to gather them to the battle of that great day of Almighty God. 15 (Behold, I come as a priest. Blessed is he who keeps watch and guards his garments, if he does not walk naked and men do not see his filthiness). 16 And they gathered them together to a place called in Hebrew Ar- ma-gedon. 17 And the seventh angel brought forth his viall in the ayre; and out of the tem- ple of Heauen came a loud voice from the throne, saying, "It is done." 18 And there were voices, and thunder, and lightning, and there was a great earthquake, such as there had not been since men were on the earth, such a great earthquake. 19 And the great city was divided into three parts, and the cities of the nations fell; and great Babylon was remem- bered before God, to give her the cup of the wine of the fierceness of his wrath. 20 Every place fled, and the mountains were found no more. :21 Then there fell a great hail, like tal- ents, from the island upon the men, and the men blasphemed God because of the plague of the hail, for its plague was very great.

CHAPTER 17

1 Then came one of the ten angels who had the ten vials and spoke to me, saying, "Come, I will show you the damnation of the great harlot who sits on many waters, 2 with whom the kings of the earth have committed for- nication, and the inhabitants of the earth are drunk with the wine of her fornication." 3 Then he brought me into the wilderness with the Spirit, and I saw a woman sitting on a beast of skin, full of blasphemous names, which had ten heads and ten horns. 4 And the woman was clothed with purple and with skins, gilded with gold and with precious stones and with pearls, and she had in her hand a golden cup full of abominations and filthiness of her fornication. 5 And on her forehead was written the name, "Mystery, the great Babylon, the mother of harlots and abominations of the earth." 6 And I saw that woman drunk with the blood of the saints and with the blood of the martyrs of IESVS; and when I saw her, I marveled with great wonder. 7 Then the angel said to me, "Why do you marvel? I will show you the mystery of that woman and the beast that gives birth to her, which has ten heads and ten horns. 8 The beast which thou sawest was and is not, and she shall come up out of the black pit and go into perdition, and they that dwell on the earth shall marvel (whose names are not writ- ten in the book of life from the foundation of the world) when they see the beast that was and is not, and yet is. 9 Behold the mind that has wisdom. The seven heads are as many mountains on which the woman sits; they are also as many kings. 10 Five have fallen, and one is, and another has not yet come; and when he comes, he must remain for a short time. 11 The beast that was and is no more, is the eighth, is one of the ten, and shall go down. 12 The ten horns that you saw are ten kings, who have not yet received a kingdom, but will receive power, as kings at an hour from the beast. 13 These have one mind and will give their power and authority to the beast. 14 These shall fight with the Lambe, and the Lambe shall overcome them, for he is Lord of Lords and King of Kings, and those who are on his side are called, chosen and faithful." 15 Then he said to me, "The waters you have seen, here the harlot sits, are peoples, multitudes, nations and languages. 16 The ten horns you saw on the beast are those who will hate the harlot, make her desolate and naked, eat her flesh, and bury her with fire. 17 For God has put it in their hearts to do his will and to agree unanimously to yield their kingdom to the beast, until the words of God are fulfilled. 18 The woman whom you saw is the great city that reigns over the kings of the earth.

CHAPTER 18

1 After these things, I saw another angel de- scending from on high, with great power, so that the earth was illuminated by his splen- dor, 2 and cried with power and with a loud voice, "It is fallen, it is fallen, Babylon, that great city, which has become the habitation of devils, the refuge of all evil spirits, and the cage of all vile and hateful birds. 3 For all the nations have drunk of the wine of the wrath of her fornication, and the kings of the earth have committed fornication with her, and the marchers of the earth have enriched them- selves with the abundance of her pleasures. 4 And I heard another voice from Heauen say- ing, "Come out of her, my people, lest you be partakers of her sins and receive her plagues. 5 For her sins have come to heaven, and God has remembered her iniquities. 6 Reward her, as she has rewarded you, and give her double according to her works; and in the cup that she has filled you, fill her double. 7 As much as she has glorified herself and pleased herself

with pleasure, give her double for her torment and sorrow, for she says in her heart, "I sit as a queen, I am not a widow, and I shall not see mourning." 8 Therefore her plagues shall come in one day, death, sorrow and famine, and she shall be burned with fire, for the God who condemns her is a strong Lord. 9 And the kings of the earth shall rebuke her, and they shall complain for her, who committed fornication, and took pleasure in her, when they see the smoke of her burning, 10 And they will turn away for fear of her torment, saying, "Alas, alas, great city, Babylon, mighty city, for in one hour your judgment has come." 11 The marchers of the earth shall mourn and com- plain about her, for no one shall take care of their goods anymore. 12 Articles of gold, of silk, of precious stones, of pearls, of fine lin- en, of purple, of silk, of leather, of all kinds of wood of Thyne, of all vessels of yuorie, of all vessels of fine wood, of brasse, of yron, and of marble, 13 of cinamom, of odors, of oint- ments, of frankincense, of wine, of oil, of flour, of wheat, of cattle, of sheep, of horses, of chariots, of servants, and of the souls of men. 14 (The apples that your soul longed for have departed from you, and all things that were beautiful and excellent have departed from you, and you will find them no more). 15 The marchers of these things that had become rich shall depart from you, for fear of your torment, weeping and wandering, 16 saying, "Alas, alas, that great city which was clothed with linen, with purple and with skins, gild- ed with gold, with precious stones and with pearls. 17 For in a single moment so many great riches were ruined. And all the captains of ships, all the people who occupy ships, the sailors and all those who traffic on the sea will be found far away, 18 And they shall cry out, when they see the smoke of its fire, saying, "What city was like this great city? 19 They shall throw dust on their heads, and weep, and lament, and say, Alas, alas, that great city, which enriched all those who had ships on the sea with its expenses, for in an hour it became desolate. 20 O Heir, recover from her and from you, holy Apostles and Prophets, for God has punished her with reinstatement for your sake." 21 Then a mighty angel took a stone like a great milestone and threw it into the sea, saying, "With such violence shall the great city of Babylon be thrown down, and it shall be found no more. 22 The voice of harp- ists, musicians, bagpipers, and trumpeters shall be heard no more in you, and no crafts- man, of whatever trade, shall be found in you, and the sound of a milestone shall be heard no more in you. 23 The light of a candle shall no longer shine in you, and the voice of the bridegroom and of the bride shall no lon- ger be heard in you, because your marchers were the great ones of the earth, and by your spells all the nations were deceived. 24 In her was found the blood of the prophets and the saints and all who were slain on earth.

CHAPTER 19

1 And after these things I heard a great shouting of a great multitude in heaven, say- ing, "Hallelujah, salvation, glory, honor and power to the Lord our God. 2 For true and righteous are his judgments, for he has con- demned that great harlot who has corrupted the earth with her fornication, and has made void the blood of her servants shed at her hands. 3 And again they said, "Hallelujah!" and his smoke rose again forever. 4 The four and twenty elders and the four beasts fell to the ground and worshiped God who sat on the throne, saying, "Amen, Alleluia." 5 Then a voice came out from the throne, saying, "Pray to our God, all you his servants and you who fear him, small and great."

6 And I heard as the sound of a great multitude, as the sound of many waters, and as the sound of loud thunder, saying, "Hallelujah, for the LORD, that almighty God, has reigned." 7 Rejoice and be glad and give glory to him, for the wedding of that Lambe has come, and his wife has made herself ready. 8 She was granted to be clothed in pure fine linen and shining, for fine linen is the righteousness of the saints. 9 Then he said to me, "Write, 'Blessed are those who are called to the supper of the Lamb.'" And he said to me, "These words of God are true." 10 I fell down before his feet to worship him, but he said to me, "See that you do not: I am your servant and one of your brothers who have the testimony of Jesus. Worship God, for the testimony of Jesus is the Spirit of prophecy." 11 Then I saw the heavens open, and behold, a white horse, and he who sat on it was called, "Faithful and true, who judges and fights righteously." 12 His eyes were like a flame of fire, and on his head were many crowns; he had a name written that no one knew but him. 13 He was clothed in a robe soaked in blood, and his name was called the WORD OF GOD. 14 And the armies that were in heaven followed him on white horses, clothed in fine and pure linen. 15 Out of his mouth came a sharp sword, with which he was to smite the heathen; he shall rule them with a rod of iron, for it is he that treadeth down the wine of the fierceness and wrath of Almighty God. 16 On his garments and on his thigh is writ- ten, "THE KING OF KINGS AND THE LORD OF LORDS." 17 And I saw an angel standing in the sun, crying with a loud voice, saying to all the birds that fluttered through the streets of Heauen, "Come and gather yourselves to- gether for the supper of your great God, 18 that you may eat the flesh of kings, the flesh of captains, the flesh of mighty men, the flesh of horses and those who sit on them, the flesh of all the free and servants, small and great." 19 I saw the beast and the kings of the earth and their hosts gathered together to give battle to him who sat on the horse and his army. 20 But the beast was taken and with her the false prophet who performed miracles before him, deceiving those who received his mark and those who worshipped his image. Both were cast into a lake of fire, burning with sulfur. 21 The remaining ones were killed with the sword of him who sits on the horse, coming out of his mouth, and all the marshes were filled with their flesh.

CHAPTER 20

1 And I saw an Angel coming down from above, with the key of the bottom pit and a great chain in his hand. 2 And he took the dragon, the old serpent, which is the devil and Satan, and bound him for a thousand years: 3 And cast him into the bottom pit, and shut him up, and sealed the door upon him, that he should deceive the people no more, until the thousand years were expired; for then he should be loosed for a short time. 4 Then I saw seats; they sat on them, and judgment was given to them; I saw the souls of those who had been beheaded because of the testimo- nies of Jesus and because of the word of God, and who had not worshipped the beast, nor his image, nor taken his mark on their fore- heads or hands; they lived and reigned with Christ for a thousand years. 5 But the rest of the dead cannot live again until the thousand years have passed; this is the first resurrec- tion. 6 Blessed and holy is he who partakes of the first resurrection, for on him the sec- ond death has no power, but he shall be the priest of God and of Christ and reign with him a thousand years. 7 And when the thou- sand years are expired, Satan shall be loosed from his

prison, 8 and he will go and deceive the peoples who are in the four corners of the earth, that is, Gog and Magog, to gather them to fight, whose number is like the sand of the sea. 9 And they went forth into the plain of the earth and surrounded the tents of the saints and the bounded city; but fire came down from God from above and struck them. 10 And the deceiver who deceived them was cast into a lake of fire and brimstone, where the beast and the false prophet are, and he shall be tormented day and night all his life. 11 Then I saw a great white throne and one sitting on it, from whose face the earth and the heavens fled, and their place was not found. 12 And I saw the dead, both great and small, standing before God; and the books were opened, and another book was opened, which is the book of life, and the dead were judged of those things which were written in the books, ac- cording to their sorrows. 13 And the sea released its dead, which were in it, and death and hell released the dead, which were in them; and they were judged each according to their pains. 14 And death and hell were cast into the lake of fire; this is the second death. 15 And he who was not found written in the book of life was cast into the lake of fire.

man, that is, of the angel. 18 The surrounding wall was of jasper, and the city was of pure gold, like clear glass. 19 And the foundations of the wall of the city were adorned with all manner of precious stones: the first founda- tion was of jasper, the second of sapphire, the third of chalcedony, the fourth of emeraude: 20 the fifth of a Sardonix, the sixth of a Sar- dius, the seventh of a Chrysolite, the eighth of a Beryl, the ninth of a Topaze, the tenth of a Chrysoprasus, the eleventh of a Iacynth, the twelfth of an Amethyst. 21 The two gates were two pearls, and each gate was of a pearl, and the streets of the city were of pure gold, like a shining glaze. 22 I saw no temple there, for the LORD God Almighty and the Lambe are his temple. 23 This city does not need the sun or the moon to shine in it, for the glory of God has illuminated it and the Lambe is its light. 24 The peoplea who have been saved will walk in its light, and the kings of the earth will bring their glory and honor to it. 25 Its gates shall not be shut by day, for there shall be no night there. 26 The glory and honor of the Gentiles shall be brought into it. 27 And no vnclean thing shall enter into it, nor that which worketh abomination or falsehood, but those which are written in the book of the Lamb's life.

CHAPTER 21

1 And I saw a new heaven and a new earth, for the first heaven and the first earth had passed away, and there was no more sea. 2 And I saw the holy city, the new Jerusalem, coming down from God from on high, pre- pared as a bride clothed for her husband. 3 And I heard a great voice from above, saying, Behold, the Tabernacle of God is with men, and he will dwell with them; and they shall be his people, and God himself shall be their God with them. 4 God will wipe away all sadness from their eyes, and there will be no more death, nor sorrow, nor crying, nor will there be any more fear, for the former things have passed away. 5 He who sat on the throne said, "Behold, I make all things new," and he said to me, "Write, for these words are faithful and true." 6 And he said to me, "It is done: I am the Alpha and the Omega, the beginning and the end. To him who is thirsty I will freely give the water of life. 7 He who commits himself shall inherit all things; I will be his God, and he shall be my son. 8 But the fearful and the vnbeleeing, the abominable and the murder- ous, the whoremongers, the sorcerers, the idolaters and all liars shall have their part in the lake that burns with fire and brimstone, which is the second death. 9 Then came to me one of the ten angels who had the ten vials full of the last plagues and spoke to me, saying, "Come, I present to you the bride, the Lamb's wife." 10 He took me in spirit to a great moun- tain and showed me the great city, the holy Jerusalem, which descended from God from above, 11 which housed the glory of God; and its splendor was like that of a most precious stone, like a jasper stone as clear as crystal, 12 It had a great wall and a gate, with two gates and two angels at the gates, with the names of the two tribes of the children of Israel written on it. 13 To the east were three gates, to the north three gates, to the south three gates, and to the west three gates. 14 The wall of the city had two foundations, and in them were the names of the two apostles of Lambes. 15 The one who spoke to me had a golden reed to measure the city, its gates and its wall. 16 The city has four squares, and its length is as great as its height; he measured the city with the golden rod by two thousand furlongs; the length, height and length are equal. 17 He measured its walls by a hundred and for- ty-five cubits, according to the measure of

CHAPTER 22

1 He showed me a pure river of water of life, clear as crystal, flowing out of the throne of God and the Lamb. 2 In the middle of his way, and on both sides of the river, was the tree of life, which bore two kinds of fruit and bore fruit every month; and the leaves of the tree were for warming the nations. 3 And there shall be no more curse, but there shall be the throne of God and of Lambe, and his servants shall serve him. 4 They shall see his face, and his Name shall be on their foreheads. 5 There will be no night there, and they will not need candles or sunlight, for the Lord God gives them light, and they will reign forever." 6 He said to me, "These words are faithful and true; and the Lord God of the holy prophets has sent his angel to show his servants the things that are shortly to be fulfilled. 7 Behold, I am coming soon. Blessed is he who observes the words of the prophecies of this book. 8 I am Iohn, who heard and heard these things; and when I heard and saw, I prostrated my- self to worship before the feet of the angel who showed me these things. 9 But he said to me, "See that you do not do this, for I am your fellow servant, of your brother prophets and of those who keep the words of this book; worship God." 10 He said to me, "Do not seal the words of the prophecy of this book, for the time is near." 11 He who is vniust, let him be vniust still, and he who is filthy, let him be filthy still; he who is righteous, let him be righteous still, and he who is holy, let him be holy still. 12 Behold, I am coming soon, and my reward is with me, to give to each one ac- cording to his work. 13 I am the Alpha and the Omega, the beginning and the end, the first and the last. 14 Blessed are those who do his bidding, that they may have right to the tree of life and may enter through the gates into the city. 15 For outside there will be dogs and inchanters, whoremongers, murderers, idol- aters, and those who shout or do lies. 16 I have sent my angel to testify these things to you in the churches: I am the root and generation of Dauid, and the bright morning star. 17 The Spirit and the bride say, "Come." And he who hears say, "Come"; and he who is thirsty, let him who is thirsty come; and he who wants take the water of life freely. 18 For I protest to everyone who hears the words of the proph- ecy of this book, If anyone

shall add to these things, God will add to him the plagues that are written in this book: 19 And if anyone shall diminish the words of the book of this proph- ecy, God shall take away his portion from the book of life, and from the holy city, and from the things written in this book. 20 He who bears witness to these things says, "Surely, I am coming soon." Amen. And so, come Lord Jesus. 21 The grace of our Lord Jesus Christ be with you all, Amen.